AMERICAN WRITERS

AMERICAN WRITERS

JAY PARINI
Editor

SUPPLEMENT XXV

CHARLES SCRIBNER'S SONS
A part of Gale, Cengage Learning

GALE
CENGAGE Learning®

Farmington Hills, Mich • San Francisco • New York • Waterville, Maine
Meriden, Conn • Mason, Ohio • Chicago

GALE
CENGAGE Learning®

American Writers Supplement XXV

Editor in Chief: Jay Parini

Project Editor: Lisa Kumar

Permissions: Moriam Aigoro

Composition and Electronic Capture: Gary Leach

Manufacturing: Cynde Lentz

For product information and technology assistance, contact us at
Gale Customer Support, 1-800-877-4253.
For permission to use material from this text or product,
submit all requests online at **www.cengage.com/permissions**
Further permissions questions can be emailed to
permissionrequest@cengage.com

While every effort has been made to ensure the reliability of the information presented in this publication, Gale, a part of Cengage Learning, does not guarantee the accuracy of the data contained herein. Gale accepts no payment for listing; and inclusion in the publication of any organization, agency, institution, publication, service, or individual does not imply endorsement of the editors or publisher. Errors brought to the attention of the publisher and verified to the satisfaction of the publisher will be corrected in future editions.

EDITORIAL DATA PRIVACY POLICY. Does this publication contain information about you as an individual? If so, for more information about our editorial data privacy policies, please see our Privacy Statement at www.gale.cengage.com

LIBRARY OF CONGRESS CATALOGING-IN-PUBLICATION DATA

American writers: a collection of literary biographies / Leonard Unger, editor in chief.
   p. cm.
   The 4-vol. main set consists of 97 of the pamphlets originally published as the University of Minnesota pamphlets on American writers; some have been rev. and updated. The supplements cover writers not included in the original series.
   Supplement 2, has editor in chief, A. Walton Litz; Retrospective suppl. 1, c. 1998, was edited by A. Walton Litz & Molly Weigel; Suppl. 5–7 have as editor-in-chief, Jay Parini.
   Includes bibliographies and index.
   Contents: v. 1. Henry Adams to T.S. Eliot — v. 2. Ralph Waldo Emerson to Carson McCullers — v. 3. Archibald MacLeish to George Santayana — v. 4. Isaac Bashevis Singer to Richard Wright — Supplement\[s\]: 1, pt. 1. Jane Addams to Sidney Lanier. 1, pt. 2. Vachel Lindsay to Elinor Wylie. 2, pt. 1. W.H. Auden to O. Henry. 2, pt. 2. Robinson Jeffers to Yvor Winters. — 4, pt. 1. Maya Angelou to Linda Hogan. 4, pt. 2. Susan Howe to Gore Vidal — Suppl. 5. Russell Banks to Charles Wright — Suppl. 6. Don DeLillo to W. D. Snodgrass — Suppl. 7. Julia Alvarez to Tobias Wolff — Suppl. 8. T.C. Boyle to August Wilson. — Suppl. 11 Toni Cade Bambara to Richard Yates.
   ISBN 978-1-4144-9609-2
   1. American literature—History and criticism. 2. American literature—Bio-bibliography. 3. Authors, American—Biography. I. Unger, Leonard. II. Litz, A. Walton. III. Weigel, Molly. IV. Parini, Jay. V. University of Minnesota pamphlets on American writers.

PS129 .A55
810'.9
\[B\]   73-001759

ISBN-13: 978-0-684-32498-2

Charles Scribner's Sons an imprint of Gale, Cengage Learning
27500 Drake Rd.
Farmington Hills, MI 48331-3535

Printed in Mexico
1 2 3 4 5 6 7 18 17 16 15 14

Acknowledgments

The editors wish to thank the copyright holders of the excerpted criticism included in this volume and the permissions managers of many book and magazine publishing companies for assisting us in securing reproduction rights. Following is a list of the copyright holders who have granted us permission to reproduce material in this volume of *American Writers*. Every effort has been made to trace copyright, but if omissions have been made, please let us know.

COPYRIGHTED EXCERPTS IN *AMERICAN WRITERS*, VOLUME 25, WERE REPRODUCED FROM THE FOLLOWING SOURCES:

BECHDEL, ALISON. Donahue, Dierdre, "Alison Bechdel Shines in Graphic Memoir 'Are You My Mother?'" *USA Today,* May 2, 2012. Copyright © 2012 by USA Today, a division of Gannett Satellite Information Network, Inc. / Gangemi, Merry, "Alison Bechdel's Fun Home," *Off Our Backs,* October 1, 2007. Copyright © 2013 by ProQuest LLC. / Garner, Dwight, "Artist, Draw Thyself (and Your Mother and Therapist)," *New York Times,* May 2, 2012. Copyright © 2012 by The New York Times Company. / Miller, Laura, "Are You My Mother? By Alison Bechdel review," *Guardian,* May 24, 2012. Copyright © 2012 by The Guardian News and Media Limited. / Thomas, June, "Drawing on the Lesbian Community: An Interview with Alison Bechdel," *Off Our Backs,* September 20, 1988. Copyright © 1988 by Off Our Backs. / Wilsey Sean, "The Things They Buried," *New York Times Sunday Book Review,* June 18, 2006. Copyright © 2006 by The New York Times Company.

BODENHEIM, MAXWELL. Spector, Herman, from *Bastard in the Ragged Suit,* Bud Johns and Judith S. Clancy, eds., Synergistic Press, 1977. Copyright © 1977 by Synergistic Press. /

Bodenheim, Maxwell, from the dust jacket of *Duke Herring,* Horace Liveright, 1931. Copyright © 1931 by Horace Liveright. / Bodenheim, Maxwell, "To a Revolutionary Girl," *The New Masses,* April 3, 1934.

GOLDMAN, FRANCISCO. Brownrigg, Sylvia, "Book review: 'Say Her Name' by Francisco Goldman," *Los Angeles Times,* May 15, 2011. Copyright © 2011 by Los Angeles Times. / Goldman, Francisco, "In Guatemala, All Is Forgotten," *New York Times,* December 23, 1996. Copyright © 1996 by The New York Times Company. / Jaggi, Maya, "A Path in the Darkness," *Guardian,* February 1, 2008. Copyright © 2008 by the Guardian News and Media Limited.

GROSSMAN, LEV. DuChateau, Christian, "'Magician King' helps Potter fans," *CNN.com,* August 7, 2011. Copyright © 2011 by Cable News Network Turner Broadcasting System, Inc. / Grossman, Lev, "Benedictus: Thoughts on Being a Writer and Having Children," *Lev-Grossman.com,* September 15, 2012. / Grossman, Lev. Personal Interview with Scott Earle.

ACKNOWLEDGEMENTS

22, 26 August 2013. Copyright © 2012 by Lev Grossman.

LOVECRAFT, H. P. Lovecraft, H. P., "Nemesis", "Pacifist War Song 1917", "The Conscript", "The Poe-et's Nightmare", "To Edward John Moreton Drax Plunkett Eighteenth Baron Dunsany", *The Ancient Track: The Complete Poetical Works of H. P. Lovecraft,* S. T. Joshi, ed., Hippocampus Press, 2013. Copyright © 2013 by Estate of H.P. Lovecraft. / Lovecraft, H. P., "Fungi From Yuggoth", *Beyond the Wall of Sleep,* Arkham House, 1943. Copyright © 1943 by Estate of H.P. Lovecraft.

MUÑOZ, MANUEL. Fields, Amanda, unpublished interview with Manuel Muñoz, August 8, 2013. Copyright © 2013 by Amanda Fields. Reproduced by permission of the author. / Porter Brown, Nell, "Echoes of the Central Valley," *Harvard Magazine,* May 1, 2011. Copyright © 2011 by Harvard Magazine.

O'NAN, STEWART. Bryant, Edward, from *Something Wicked,* Wormhole Books, 2003. Copyright © 2003 by Edward Bryant. / Freudenberger, Nell, "The Good Wife: Spouse Arrest," *New York Times,* May 8, 2005. Copyright © 2005 by The New York Times Company. / O'Nan, Stewart, from *Emily, Alone,* Viking Press, 2011. Copyright © 2007 by Stewart O'Nan. / O'Nan, Stewart, from *Last Night at the Lobster,* Viking Press, 2007. Copyright © 2007 by Stewart O'Nan. / O'Nan, Stewart, from *Snow Angels,* Picador, 1994. Copyright © 1994 by Stewart O'Nan. / O'Nan, Stewart, from *Something Wicked,* Wormhole Books, 2003. Copyright © 2003 by Stewart O'Nan. / O'Nan, Stewart, "Timeline," *Stewart-ONan.com,* copyright © 2014 by Stewart-ONan.com.

ORLEAN, SUSAN. Orlean, Susan, "About Me," *SusanOrlean.com.* Copyright © 2014 by Susan Orlean. / Mock, Kristin, personal interview with Susan Orlean, August 16, 2013. Copyright © 2013 by Kristin Mock. Quotes reproduced by permission of Susan Orlean.

RINEHART, MARY ROBERTS. Butcher, Fanny, "Alluring Novel by Mrs. Rinehart: Story of Rich Experience in the Publishing Business," *Chicago Daily Tribune,* January 11, 1948. Copyright © 1948 by Chicago Tribune. / Roberts Rinehart, Mary, "Author Tells Why Readers Prefer Crime: Mary Roberts Rinehart Confesses!", *Chicago Daily Tribune,* December 6, 1930. Copyright © 1930 by Chicago Daily Tribune.

STALLINGS, A. E. Lucretius, "Book II: The Dance of Atoms", "Book IV: The Senses", "Book V: Cosmos and Civilization", *The Nature of Things,* A. E. Stallings, trans., Penguin Books, 2007. Copyright © 2007 by A. E. Stallings. / Stallings, A. E., "A Postcard from Greece", "Ariadne and the Rest", "Elegy for Lost Umbrella", "Eurydice Reveals Her Strength", "Eurydice's Footnote", "Hades Welcomes His Bride", "Moving Sale", "RepRoach", "Words of Prey", *Archaic Smile,* The University of Evansville Press, 1999. Copyright © 1999 by A. E. Stallings. / Stallings, A. E., "Actaeon", "Aftershocks", "An Ancient Dog Grave, Unearthed During Construction of the Athens Metro", "Arrowhead Hunting", "Explaining an Affinity for Bats", "Hapax", "Implements for the 'Tomb of the Poet'", "Sine Qua Non", "The Dollhouse", "Thyme", "Ubi Sunt Lament for the Eccentric Museums of My Childhood", *Hapax,* TriQuarterly Books/ Northwestern University Press, 2006. Copyright © 2006 by A. E. Stallings. / Stallings, A. E., "Alice in the Looking Glass", "Burned", "Country Song", "Extinction of Silence", "Fairy-tale Logic", "Olives", "On Visiting a Borrowed Country House in Arcadia", "The Boatman to Psyche, on the River Styx", "The Dress of One Occasion", *Olives, TriQuarterly Books/ Northwestern University Press,* 2012. Copyright © 2012 by A. E. Stallings. / Stallings, A. E., "Presto Manifesto!", *Poetry Magazine,* February 2009. Copyright © 2009 by Poetry Foundation. / Stallings, A. E., from *TEDxTalks,* October 4, 2012. Copyright © 2012 by A. E. Stallings. / Stallings, A. E., from *The Nature of Things,* Penguin Books, 2007. Copyright © 2007 by A. E. Stallings. / Browning, Robert. "My Last Duchess," *The Oxford Authors: Robert Browning,* Adam Roberts, ed., Oxford University

ACKNOWLEDGEMENTS

Press, 1997. Copyright © 1997 by Estate of Robert Browning.

VERY, JONES. Very, Jones, "A Whithered Leaf—seen on a Poet's Table", "Ehu! Fugaces, Posthume, Posthume, Labuntur anni", "I Am the Way", "Enoch", "no title", "Pleasure", "Poem No. 160", "Poem No .175", "The Columbine", "The Fossil Flower", "The Garden", "The Kingdom of God is Within You", "The Latter Rain", "The New Birth", "The New World", "The Prophet", "The Resurrection", "The Sabbatia", "The Voice of God", "Time", "To The Pure All Things Are Pure", *Jones Very: The Complete Poems,* Helen R. Dees, ed., University of Georgia Press, 1993. Copyright © 1993 by University of Georgia Press.

ZITKALA-ŠA. Zitkala-Ša, from *American Indian Stories, Legends, and Other Writings,* Cathy N. Davidson and Ada Norris, eds., Penguin Books, 2003. Copyright © 2003 by Zitkala-Ša.

List of Subjects

Introduction   xi

List of Contributors   xiii

ALISON BECHDEL   1
Deborah Kay Ferrell

MAXWELL BODENHEIM   17
Robert Niemi

HANNAH WEBSTER FOSTER   35
Sarah L. Peters

FRANCISCO GOLDMAN   49
Carolyn Alessio

LEV GROSSMAN   63
Scott Earle

MARK HELPRIN   79
Josh Crain

WILLIAM INGE   93
John M. Clum

H. P. LOVECRAFT   109
Jonas Prida

MANUEL MUÑOZ   127
Amanda Fields

STEWART O'NAN   141
John A. McDermott

SUSAN ORLEAN   157
Kristin Winet

SARA PARETSKY   169
James Lewin

MARY ROBERTS RINEHART   189
Windy Counsell Petrie

JOSHUA SLOCUM   205
Dan Brayton

A. E. STALLINGS   221
Emily Setina

JONES VERY   237
Edward Sugden

HERMAN WOUK   253
Jack Fischel

ZITKALA-ŠA   271
Kelly Clasen

Cumulative Index   289

Introduction

I've always loved a line from W. H. Auden: "A real book is not one that's read, but one that reads us." That is, books that fall into the category of literature, whether in the form of poetry or fiction, nonfiction or drama, are "real" if they dig into our skin, empty us out, make us see ourselves for what we are, and for what we are not. In the pursuit of this special kind of self-knowledge, we read, and our reading is a major part of our lives. My hope is that, in this volume of essays on a range of American writers from the eighteenth century to the present, we deal with work that will read us, the mirrors our needs, that explains something about the nature of living in a complex world that we can't do easily without.

In this twenty-fifth volume of *American Writers,* we put forward articles on authors from a variety of genres; they are well-known figures who have aspired to write books that read us— serious work, that is; yet none has yet been discussed in this series. The reasons for this are many, but American literature is a vast trove of writing, and important new work is not only produced at an amazing rate, we seem also to discover terrific examples of good writing from the past that have been overlooked until recently.

This series itself has its origins in a series of critical and biographical monographs that appeared between 1959 and 1972. The *Minnesota Pamphlets on American Writers* achieved fame in their time; they were incisively written and informative, treating ninety-seven American writers in a format and style that attracted a devoted following of readers. The series proved invaluable to a generation of students and teachers, who could depend on these reliable and interesting critiques of major figures. The idea of reprinting these essays occurred to Charles Scribner, Jr. (1921-1995). The series appeared in four volumes titled *American Writers: A Collection of Literary Biographies* (1974).

Since then, twenty-five supplements (including this one) have appeared, treating hundreds of poets, novelists, playwrights, screenwriters, essayists, and memoirists, even a handful of literary critics who have managed to create texts that somebody might want to read in future years. The idea has been consistent throughout the series: to present well-informed essays for students and that somewhat elusive audience, the so-called general reader. This critical writing often rises to a reasonably high level of craft, but the essays are designed carefully to introduce a body of important work, and to offer a sense of the scope and quality of the unfolding career at hand. Context is taken very seriously in this series: historical as well as biographical context. Due weight is given to each of these.

Supplement twenty-five examines the work of authors going back to Hannah Webster Foster, an important writer of fiction born in the late eighteenth century. Another older writer is Joshua Slocum, born in 1844, an adventurer and travel writer. A number of our subjects here were born in the nineteenth century, including the Native American writer Zitkala-Ša, who has only in recent years been given her due. Jones Very was among the early Transcendental writers, born in 1813. And novelists Mary Roberts Rinehart, Maxwell Bodenheim, and H. P. Lovecraft— all masters of popular fiction—were born near the end of the nineteenth century. (Bodenheim was also, of course, a gifted poet as well as novelist.)

Most of the writers included here are from the twentieth and twenty-first centuries, including fiction writers Francisco Goldman, Lev Grossman, Mark Helprin, Manuel Muñoz, Stew-

INTRODUCTION

art O'Nan, and Sara Paretsky. A. E. Stallings is still a relatively young poet, one of unusual gifts, while Susan Orlean is a brilliant essayist and writer of nonfiction, often seen in the pages of the *New Yorker*. We also devote an essay to William Inge, one of the most popular of modern American playwrights. Alison Bechdel, a writer of illustrated memoirs, remains difficult to classify, but she has attracted a great deal of attention in recent years, and it's time we looked at her closely.

While each of these writers has been written about in journals and newspapers, none of them has had the kind of sustained critical attention he or she deserves, and we hope to make a beginning here, as the work certainly merits close reading. It's also worth noting that we reach beyond the confines of classic fiction and literature, looking at some genre writers, from the horror fiction of Lovecraft to the mysteries

of Rinehart and Paretsky. Herman Wouk, in some ways, stands out on his own, as one of the most popular novelists of the past century, a man still writing as he reaches nearly the age of one hundred.

We have tried to ensure that each of these critical and biographical essays is accessible to the non-specialist reader or student; that is, we discourage the use of critical jargon—so prevalent in literary criticism in our time. Our goal has been simply to present, as clearly as possible, biographical and critical readings of authors who—going back to the quotation from Auden above—write books that read us, that open us to ourselves, to each other. We focus on a range of authors here, but each of them, in his or her own way, has created work on this high level that Auden writes about.

—*JAY PARINI*

Contributors

Carolyn Alessio. Carolyn Alessio is the editor of a bilingual anthology of Guatemalan children's writing. Her fiction and nonfiction have appeared in the *Pushcart Prize,* the *Chicago Tribune,* the *Chronicle of Higher Education,* and elsewhere. She is the recipient of a fellowship in creative writing from the National Endowment for the Arts. FRANCISCO GOLD-MAN

Dan Brayton. Dan Brayton is Associate Professor of English and American Literatures at Middlebury College, where he also teaches in the Environmental Studies Program. A lifelong sailor, he has held visiting appointments at Sea Semester on Cape Cod and in the Pacific, Atlantic, and Caribbean. He has also taught for the Williams-Mystic Program in Maritime Studies. His book, *Shakespeare's Ocean: An Eco-critical Exploration* (UVA Press, 2012) won the Northeast Modern Language Association Book Award. JOSHUA SLOCUM

Kelly Clasen. Kelly Clasen is an Assistant Professor of English and Director of the Academic Resource Center at Newman University, a private liberal arts university in Wichita, Kansas. A native of rural Kansas, she received her doctorate in English in 2011 from the University of North Texas. Her research focuses on questions of race, gender, and the environment in American regional writing by women. ZITKALA-SA

John M. Clum. John M. Clum is Professor Emeritus of Theater Studies and English at Duke University. His books include *Still Acting Gay: Male Homosexuality in Modern Drama, Something for the Boys: Musical Theatre and Gay Culture,* both from St. Martin's Press; *He's All Man: Learning Masculinity, Homosexuality and Love from American Movies* and, most recently, *The Drama of Marriage: Gay Playwrights/Straight Unions from Oscar Wilde to the Present,* both from Palgrave Macmillan. He is the author of numerous essays on modern and contemporary British and American drama and musical theatre and has edited a number of anthologies of gay drama, most recently *Gay Drama Now,* published by Cambria Press. He is General Editor for the Cambria Contemporary Global Performing Arts Series. His plays have been produced by a number of theatres around the United States and he has directed over seventy-five theatrical and operatic productions. His theatre blog can be found at *http://clumtheater.blogspot.com* WILLIAM INGE

Josh Crain. Josh Crain received his B.A. in English and Classics from Hillsdale College and his MA in English Literature from Baylor University. His master's thesis focused on Ben Jonson's attitudes toward censorship in his late dramatic comedies. Besides Renaissance Drama, Crain also takes a lively interest in contemporary fiction and has written about Mark Helprin, Clyde Edgerton, Barry Hannah, and Cormac McCarthy. He is a soldier in the US Army and is currently a student at the Defense Language Institute in Monterey, California, where he lives with his wife and two children. MARK HELPRIN

Scott Earle. After two years of teaching English in a Japanese fishing village, Scott Earle earned a doctorate from the University of Arkansas. He now teaches at Tacoma Community College and is raising a family by the waters of Puget Sound. LEV GROSSMAN

CONTRIBUTORS

Deborah Kay Ferrell. Deborah Kay Ferrell is an award winning short story writer whose work concentrates on what it was like growing up as a lesbian in the South as a fundamental Christian. She teaches at SUNY-Finger Lakes Community College and is currently working on her memoir. ALISON BECHDEL

Amanda Fields. Amanda Fields is a Ph.D. candidate in Rhetoric and Composition at the University of Arizona, where she is a Scholar on the Ford Foundation-funded Crossroads Collaborative: Youth, Sexuality, Health, Rights. Her research emphases are youth activism, slam poetry, and third space consciousness. She received an M.F.A. from the University of Minnesota and has published creative writing in journals such as *Indiana Review* and *Brevity*. MANUEL MUÑOZ

Jack Fischel. Jack Fischel is Emeritus Professor of History at Millersville University and presently Visiting Professor of the Humanities at Messiah College. He is the author of a number books on the Holocaust and his essay on Sholem Asch appeared in Supplement XXIII of *American Writers*. HERMAN WOUK

James Lewin. James Lewin received a B.A. (1967)from Oberlin College, as well as an M.A. (1985) and a Ph.D. (1994) from the University of Illinois at Chicago. Since 1995, he has served as a full-time member of the faculty at Shepherd University in West Virginia, where he teaches Shakespeare and advises the student newspaper. He has previously written articles for the *American Writers* series on Nelson Algren, Isaac Bashevis Singer, and Willard Motley. His appreciation for the creative fiction of Sara Paretsky is based, in part, on a close study of Chicago streets and neighborhoods that he made as an all-night Chicago taxi-cab driver in the early 1970s. SARA PARETSKY

John A. McDermott. John A. McDermott is an associate professor of English at Stephen F. Austin State University in Nacogdoches, Texas, where he teaches American literature and

creative writing. His criticism and reviews have appeared in *American Book Review, Journal of Popular Culture,* and the *Raymond Carver Review*. His fiction and poetry have appeared in a variety of journals, including *Alaska Quarterly Review, Florida Review, Southern Humanities Review,* and *Valparaiso Poetry Review*. STEWART O'NAN

Robert Niemi. Robert Niemi is Professor of English and American Studies at St. Michael's College, Colchester, Vermont. He has published extensively on topics in American literature, film, and cultural studies, including books on novelist Russell Banks, poet Weldon Kees, film and history, and the Beat writers. MAXWELL BODENHEIM

Sarah L. Peters. Sarah L. Peters is Assistant Professor of English at East Central University in Ada, Oklahoma. She specializes in American literature and women's studies, and her work has been published in *South Central Review* and the *Eudora Welty Review*. HANNAH WEBSTER FOSTER

Windy Counsell Petrie. Windy Counsell Petrie received her Ph.D. from the University of Delaware in 2001 and is currently an associate professor of English at Colorado Christian University, specializing in the interstices between autobiography and fiction in nineteenth- and twentieth-century female kunstlerroman. In 2006, she served as a Fulbright Scholar to Lithuania, where she lectured on representations of exile in literature, as well as the role of female and African-American authors in American literary history. Recently, she has published work examining the role of expatriatism in turn-of-the-century American literature, and the careers of early twentieth-century women writers of genre and mystery fiction. MARY ROBERTS RINEHART

Jonas Prida. Jonas Prida is an Associate Professor of English at the College of St. Joseph, where he teaches courses in literature and a variety of popular culture topics. He has a Ph.D.

CONTRIBUTORS

in English from Tulane University, with a specialization in antebellum American Literature. In addition to his work on H. P. Lovecraft, he has written on the character of Conan the Barbarian and the antebellum American popular writer, George Lippard. H. P. LOVECRAFT

Emily Setina. Emily Setina is Assistant Professor of English at Baylor University in Waco, Texas, where she teaches courses in twentieth-century poetry and American literature. She is co-editor with Susannah Hollister of *Gertrude Stein's Stanzas in Meditation: The Corrected Edition* (2012), which received the MLA's Committee on Scholarly Editions Seal. Her essays and reviews have appeared or are forthcoming in *Modernism/modernity, Genre, English Language Notes, Woolf Studies Annual,* and *Literature Compass.* A. E. STALLINGS

Edward Sugden. Edward Sugden is a Lecturer in American Literature 1770-1900 at King's College, London. He completed his doctorate at the University of Oxford and is currently in the process of revising his dissertation into a book. His work concentrates on the various ways in which literature of the antebellum period creates its own sustainable histories and geographies and how these, in turn, work to revise the historical moment of which they are ostensibly a part. He is also the founding editor of *Wave Composition* and has also previously served as editor-in-chief of the *Oxonian Review.* JONES VERY

Kristin Winet. Kristin Winet received her M.F.A. in Creative Writing from the University of Arizona and is now working toward her Ph.D. in Rhetoric, Composition, and the Teaching of English (also at Arizona). She is currently writing her dissertation on transnational feminism and digital travel writing practices. Kristin also works as a freelance travel writer (hence her adoration for Susan Orlean) and she frequently contributes to a number of magazines and blogs. SUSAN ORLEAN

AMERICAN WRITERS

ALISON BECHDEL

(1960—)

Deborah Kay Ferrell

SELF-PROCLAIMED AUTEUR, darling of the literati, Alison Bechdel has evolved from a cartoonist to a graphic novelist to an author. Bechdel's fame was initially limited to her long-standing cult cartoon strip, *Dykes to Watch Out For*, which was published in about sixty gay, lesbian, and alternative newspapers. While still inking her strip, Bechdel began to work on her groundbreaking graphic memoir *Fun Home: A Family Tragicomic* (2006), which won the Will Eisner Comic Industry Award in 2007 for Best Reality-Based Work.

Not only did Bechdel achieve success in the world of cartoons, a genre dominated by males, but the memoir went on to widespread critical acclaim. Sean Wilsey wrote in the *New York Times*: "It is a pioneering work, pushing two genres (comics and memoir) in multiple new directions, with panels that combine the detail and technical proficiency of R. Crumb with a seriousness, emotional complexity and innovation completely its own." Bechdel, a private person who lives in the woods of Vermont, took her increasing fame in stride. While being interviewed at Comic Con, she pointed out that *Fun Home* had not just earned critical praise as a graphic novel, but it was named *Time* magazine's Book of the Year. Of course praise of her work was not new to Bechdel. She had spent years giving lectures about her earlier work to members of the intelligentsia, even presenting slide shows and discussing her work in the hallowed halls of the University of Pennsylvania and Yale.

Following the success of her first graphic memoir, Bechdel was given a contract to produce another book. Grappling with her new subject matter, her relationship with her mother, Bechdel's memoir ran behind schedule. She was often frustrated with the writing process and

scrapped what she had been working on for four years upon the advice of her editor. Meticulous in her creative techniques, Bechdel used a corkboard with different colored sticky notes to track the development of her characters and story arcs. She also took more than four thousand photographs to be used as references for her drawings. Opening each chapter with a dream, Bechdel began to create a complex, nonlinear graphic memoir that incorporated her therapy sessions and the works of the psychotherapist Donald Winnicott, the psychologist Alice Miller, and the writer Virginia Woolf, all of whom have had a great impact on Bechdel. The result was *Are You My Mother? A Comic Drama* (2012). The title is taken from the book by P. D. Eastman that tells the story of a baby bird's search for its mother as she is hunting for food. In the end, both are reunited and elated that they have found one another as they affectionately embrace. Bechdel's memoir's ending is not so easy. It seems hard won and open-ended, perhaps because Bechdel's mother was alive at the time of the writing and initial reception of the memoir.

EARLY LIFE

Alison Bechdel was born on September 10, 1960, in Lock Haven, Pennsylvania, to Bruce Allen Bechdel and Helen Fontana Bechdel. The couple met in a college production of *The Taming of the Shrew*. Bechdel's mother, a gifted actress, was the star of the play while her father had a bit part. Helen later took a year off college to apprentice at the Cleveland Playhouse. She returned to State College, Pennsylvania, and after she graduated she worked in New York City for two years as a secretary. The couple married, and eleven months later, Alison was born. Before Ali-

son's birth, Bruce, who was a soldier stationed in Germany, and Helen, then a stay-at- home wife, had dreams of living and traveling in Europe. That hope was abruptly ended when Bruce's father had a heart attack, and Bruce returned to Beech Creek, Pennsylvania, to run the family's funeral home, which the Bechdel children later nicknamed, macabrely, Fun Home.

After the couple returned to the United States, Alison was born. While she was an infant, the family moved temporarily into the family funeral home, a time that was especially stressful for Helen. A year after her birth Alison's brother Christian was born, followed by the birth of the youngest child, John. Bruce Bechdel became a high school English teacher, a part-time mortician, and an antiques collector. Helen eventually went back to work, teaching high school English for twenty years. Despite the responsibilities of three children, Helen still managed to act and even sometimes star in summer stock theater productions. The arts were revered in the Bechdel household, and Alison was encouraged in her creative pursuits. In an interview with Trixi Simply, Alison said, "They were really great about giving me stacks of paper and pens and telling me I was really good at what I did. I'll say that for them" (p. 1). Alison began to draw at the same age as other children with a crayon, but she never stopped. She has been an archivist of her work, saving her drawings and writings. As a child, Alison was obsessed with drawing pictures of musclemen much like those in the Charles Atlas ads found in the back of the comic books she read as a child. In a 1988 interview with June Thomas of *Off Our Backs*, she states, "As a kid I drew all the time, but I never drew women, I only drew pictures of men" (p. 1).

Life in the Bechdel household could be volatile at times. Alison writes in *Are You My Mother?*: "At three months, I had seen enough of my father's rage to be wary of him" (p. 33). Judith Thurman notes that "he had noble qualities, but a violent temper and isolating secrets" (p. 48). Alison's parents pursued their individual differences as refuges. Bruce's true devotion was the authentic restoration of a four-thousand-square-foot Gothic Revival mansion, complete with period replica wallpaper. The Bechdels' home was a carefully constructed museum. In a panel from *Fun Home,* Alison draws a younger version of herself dusting an ornate piece of furniture. She questions her father about why the house has to have such elaborate furnishings that need such tender care. Bruce replies simply, "it's beautiful" (p. 15). At times, Alison was at odds with her father. She preferred to dress like a boy, wore her hair short, and participated in activities that were considered "boylike." Her father's response was to put barrettes in her hair, choose the style of a shirt she wore under a jumper, and drape pearls around her neck. "My father was as uncomfortable with the gayness that he intuited in me as he was with it himself.... He wanted me to conform" (Thurman, p. 48).

As a high school student, Bechdel emulated what is deemed traditional beauty for women. She did her hair and wore makeup and earrings. When she returned home from school, she released all of her pent-up frustration with the pen.

Seeking help from a high school guidance counselor as to a future career, Bechdel was told that she would be good at dentistry, but in the cartoonist's introduction to *The Essential Dykes to Watch Out For* she informs the reader that as early as 1972, she had hopes of being a cartoonist. In a high school that was filled with conformity, when given the opportunity to go to college early, she left home and attended Bard College at Simon's Rock, an elite early college for students seeking an alternative to traditional high school. Students begin taking college classes early and come from all over the world to experience the unique challenges and offerings that Simon's Rock presents. Bechdel earned her A.A. degree from the institution in 1979, and then she transferred to Oberlin College, where she received her B.A. in 1981.

Bechdel has joked that she "unofficially double-majored in art and coming out" (Rhoads, p. 13). It was during her first year at Oberlin that she wrote her parents a letter and told them she was a lesbian. "My father called after receiving it," she writes in *Fun Home.* Her mother would not come to the phone. "Helen was silent at first,

then disapproving, but several weeks later she breached a lifetime of reticence to confide in Alison that Bruce was gay too" (Thurman, p. 48). Throughout the marriage, he had had affairs with men and boys, even the children's babysitter, a young man who went on trips with the family. The marriage had been problematic in other ways. Bruce was arrested for buying beer for minors, and he was mandated by a court order to go to a psychiatrist for six months. Alison's mother began divorce proceedings, and four months after receiving Alison's letter, Bruce Bechdel was killed by a Sunbeam bread truck as he crossed the road to another old house he was restoring. Alison waited over twenty years before she began to tell the story of her father and her complicated relationship with him. There was always the unanswered question of whether Bruce's death was an accident or a suicide. After her graduation, Alison, who was living with her girlfriend's family at that time, writes, "I was adrift that summer. Aimless, lost, at sixes and sevens. In short, bewildered" (*The Essential Dykes to Watch Out For,* p. xi).

Bechdel was rejected from the graduate art schools that she applied to, and like her mother before her, she moved to New York City and worked at various office jobs. There she continued drawing and submitting her literary endeavors for publication. In her interview with June Thomas, she discusses her transition from drawing men to women:

> I came out when I was 19, and I was still just drawing men and it really started to bug me. I stopped drawing altogether for a while since I didn't want to draw men and I couldn't draw women. Then one day I just said, well why don't you try drawing a lesbian? I don't know why it hadn't occurred to me before, but I tried it and I could do it. They still looked like men at first, but I got over it. For some reason if I thought of the woman I was drawing as a lesbian I could do it. I was starting to meet lesbians, and all these women with really positive identities and this whole other way of being a woman, and I could draw women that weren't men in drag.

This revelation forever changed Bechdel and the trajectory she would follow as her career began to unfold. She submitted her literary work to

feminist lesbian journals, but she was also rejected. In July 1982 she received a letter from Adrienne Rich, one of her most prized possessions to this day. Rich wrote, "We're sorry to be returning this, but we feel that it's the kind of writing that may be important for the writer, but it is not sufficiently dense or rich for us to consider publishing" (*The Essential Dykes to Watch Out For,* p. xiii). Bechdel eventually concluded that she was neither a writer nor an artist, but that she was both, and soon her career as a cartoonist began.

DYKES TO WATCH OUT FOR

In 1982 Bechdel began drawing comics as marginalia in letters to a friend. First there were only pictures, and then she began to add words. Encouraged in her work, she began *Dykes to Watch Out For* as a single panel drawing, panel number 27: "Marianne dissatisfied with the breakfast brew." The figure is clearly a woman, naked and lightly muscled, holding a coffeepot with steam coming out of it. In 1983 Bechdel first published her comics as one-panel gags in the feminist newspaper *WomanNews.* She joined the collective that published the strips and began to write film and book reviews. The comic strip eventually became bimonthly, and she began to learn to do layout designs. At first the panels were unrelated, just snippets and observations by Bechdel about the gay and lesbian community. However, as she became more confident in her ability to draw these women characters, she began to develop story lines. In her interview with June Thomas, Bechdel refers to how intimidating it was to develop "real" characters.

> I first started doing these single panel cartoons, ... a one shot thing with a punch line like the sort they have in *The New Yorker.* Eventually I got up the nerve to do full strips with several panels. That was really scary for me because I was intimidated about drawing the same character more than once. I tried it and figured that as long as they looked recognizable from panel to panel that was okay.

What grew out of this was a community—not a family of origin, as Bechdel notes in one of her strips, but a family of choice. The early cartoons

are rather flat in their design. The backdrop is almost blank, and the panels appear to be roughly sketched. As for her character Mo, sometimes called Bechdel's alter ego or cartoon avatar, Bechdel writes in *The Indelible Alison Bechdel:* "Mo is the nucleus of the strip for me. She embodies all the values that I assumed were part of being a lesbian when I came out. She's basically an antiracist, anticlassist, anti-big business, anticonsumerist feminist socialist" (p. 65).

Mo (short for Monica) lives in a multicultural world. She works at MadwimminBooks owned by the feisty Jezanna, an African American woman. A great deal of the action in the cartoons revolves around the bookstore, and dates usually occur at the Café Topaz, a vegan restaurant. The standard cast of characters includes Clarice, Mo's first lover, who is African American, and Toni, Clarice's longtime partner, who is Puerto Rican. Sparrow, who is Asian American, is a "bisexual, lesbian" who ends up partnered with Stuart, who becomes the stay-at-home dad of their child. Lois is the group's womanizer, the foil to Mo's nerdy self. She lives with Ginger, a graduate student, and they are roommates with Sparrow and Stuart. Rather than creating characters who are all politically, environmentally, and socially aware, Bechdel later added Sydney, who eventually becomes Mo's partner. She is an insufferable, arrogant professor of women's studies. Sydney yields a credit card freely, much to Mo's horror, and she seemingly has no boundaries with her father, who is equally materialistic.

The *Dykes to Watch Out For* characters live their everyday lives against the backdrop of world events. They march for LGBT rights, protest against the Bush administrations' wars, and attend the Michigan Womyn's Music Festival. Clarice and Toni become mothers while dealing with the homophobia of Toni's parents. Lois becomes depressed and starts taking Prozac, and after ten years, Ginger finishes her Ph.D. and finally gets a job as an English professor in a very competitive job market. Sparrow and Stuart face the challenges of bringing up a child in a very corrupt world, and Sydney conquers breast cancer.

Bechdel continually refined her skills over the twenty-five-year life span of *Dykes to Watch out For.* She became an artist who is assiduously attentive to her craft. Her characters became fully fleshed out, and each panel is a scene rich with content and imagery. Kathleen DeBold, writing for the *Lambda Book Report*, remarks of Bechdel's strip: "The realistic drawing, sharp lettering, and tight layout enhance the storylines, and the details in the artwork often reveal as much about the characters as does the text."

FUN HOME: A FAMILY TRAGICOMIC

A self-described workaholic, Bechdel has claimed that if she did not have such a disciplined approach to her work, she would not know what to do with herself. The very idea of an unscheduled life would immobilize her with its unlimited freedoms. "I could never have six months clear for a graphic novel. It's taken me this long to have a grip just on using my time well," Bechdel said in a 1998 interview with Sarah Van Arsdale (p. 6). Yet sometime afterward, Bechdel began a graphic memoir, telling no one about it until she had worked on it for a year. It took seven years to write *Fun Home* while she continued to work on other projects, including her strip *Dykes to Watch Out For.* When it finally emerged in 2006, *Fun Home* took the literary world by storm. Lev Grossman and Richard Lacayo of *Time* selected it as the Book of the Year, writing that *Fun Home* was "the unlikeliest literary success of 2006 ... a stunning memoir about a girl growing up in a small town with her cryptic, perfectionist dad and slowly realizing that a) she is gay and b) he is too."

Fun Home was something that Bechdel pondered writing since she had been twenty. The genesis was her father Bruce Bechdel's untimely death at age forty-four, hit by a Sunbeam truck as he was crossing a highway to throw away brush from a house he had recently decided to renovate. She wonders about the causes of a probable suicide. Her mother had asked Bruce for a divorce two weeks before his death, and four months prior, Alison had written a letter to her parents declaring her lesbianism. In *Fun*

Home, she writes that perhaps her declaration of her lesbianism was the impetus to his suicide. "If I had not felt compelled to share my little sexual discovery, perhaps the semi would have passed without incident four months later" (p. 59). The driver of the truck recalled Bruce crossing the street successfully and then jumping back as if he had seen a snake. Alison and her mother both believe that he had killed himself; in a panel where Alison and Helen are discussing Bruce's death over dinner, Helen says, "I think it (suicide) was something he always meant to do" (p. 29). But no one can be sure, and the mystery of his death haunted Alison and inspired her to explore her relationship with her father, endeavoring to define it, him, and his influence on her life.

The graphic memoir opens with Alison, as a child, prevailing upon her father for a game of airplane. In the circus, when one acrobat balances on top of another this is called Icarian Games. Bechdel uses the theme of Icarus and Daedalus throughout *Fun Home.* She writes, "In our particular reenactment of this mythic relationship, it was not me but my father who was to plummet from the sky" (p. 4), setting up her quest to reveal the truth concerning not only their individual realities but how their lives affected one another. Literary themes run throughout the text as Bechdel refers to the works of Albert Camus, Henry James, James Joyce, F. Scott Fitzgerald, Adrienne Rich, and Colette, among others. In fact, writers and their works are used as a framework for *Fun Home.* While her father pushed books on Alison to the point where she almost rebelled (in college she was glad to be done with her last English course), some of her happiest moments growing up were with her mother as they ran lines for plays together. Alison was mesmerized when she saw her mother on stage. In a family where dysfunction was the norm—Bruce threw fits, slapped his children, and used them as extensions of himself to do work around the house, while her mother played the piano and acted in plays as an escape from the uneasy relationship between herself and her husband—each person in the household retreated to his or her individual interests. Alison writes, "It was a vicious circle, though. The more

gratification we found in our own geniuses, the more isolated we grew" (p. 134).

Bechdel's memoir has been called "autographic" (Julia Watson) and the narrator ironically detached and discursive. The plot is recursive and not linear. There will be a page with a panel of her as a child, and on the same page, a panel where she is a college student. Her writing is erudite with its references to literature and her likening of her families' experiences, particularly those of her father, to the aforementioned authors. F. Scott Fitzgerald was especially a favorite of Bruce's, influencing his own letters to Helen when he was away in the army. After he read a biography of Fitzgerald, Bruce was fascinated by Scott and Zelda's drunken revelries. He tore through the couple's biography and then voraciously read the writer's other works. Alison believes that her father saw himself as various characters in Fitzgerald's works, and she likens his handsomeness to Robert Redford's in one of the film versions of *The Great Gatsby.* She writes that the camera could not capture how handsome he [her father] was, and that "Zelda Fitzgerald also had a fluid charm, it was said, which eluded the still camera" (p. 64).

If her father saw himself in Fitzgerald's characters, her mother came straight out of a Henry James novel. Like Isabel Archer in *Portrait of a Lady,* Helen is an idealistic and naive young woman who falls prey to more sophisticated influences while in Europe. In Helen's case this happened when she moved to Germany to marry Bruce. Helen, as a young woman, was an innocent adrift in the early years of her marriage. Although Isabel turns away many fine suitors, it is Gilbert Osmond, a penniless art collector she marries after being introduced to him by his lover, Madame Merle. Bruce and Helen travel to France to meet an old army buddy who is later discovered to have been Bruce's lover. In her earlier passport photograph Helen is drawn as luminous with hope, but eight years later, when a family passport is taken, all of her youthful dreams seem to be gone, and her face is dull. Alison writes, "I employ these allusions to James and Fitzgerald not only as descriptive devices,

but because my parents are most real to me in fictional terms" (p. 67).

In her memoir, Alison writes that much of her identity was shaped by books. At thirteen she began to suspect she was a lesbian when she came across the definition in a dictionary. At nineteen, she called this knowledge "a revelation not of the flesh, but of the mind" (p. 74). She stumbled upon a series of books, *Word Is Out,* in the library and learned about gay people living authentic lives despite the existence of homophobia, and one volume led to another. She finally summoned the courage to buy Jill Johnston's *Lesbian Nation: The Feminist Solution* (1973), which led her to even more books. She found a section of the library that was devoted to lesbianism, and she used the card catalog to find additional information on the topic. After assiduously reading, she began to realize that she needed to move from her solitary existence of books to seeking out others like herself. She eventually stumbled upon the Gay Union, which she warily attended at first, remaining anonymous, until other lesbians befriended her. Bechdel then mustered the courage to tell her parents about her sexual identity, which she did via a letter. For the Bechdel family, not only was their identity formed by books, but their primary means of communication was through the written word, "a remote medium, but as I have explained, we were that sort of family," she writes (p. 77).

At the core of *Fun Home* is Alison's relationship with her father, a man she loves but whose return of that love she sometimes questions. Her graphic memoir is in quest of that love, especially her father's love for her. As Merry Gangemi of *Off Our Backs* wrote of the book: "*Fun Home* not only explores the subtlety through which an influential role-model parent informs the child, but also how that parent and child become enmeshed in a parallel world of secrets and shame.... *Fun Home* shows the erotic honesty of the child as redeeming the erotic dishonesty of her father" (p. 70).

Alison marvels at how her father could make something out of nothing. He rebuilt the family's Gothic home, found items for the house from trash heaps, rearranged furniture with the small-est of flourishes, and decorated a room's entire interior from a paint chip. He also transformed the grounds of the house into lush gardens, incorporating dogwood trees from the surrounding areas. She writes, "He was an alchemist of appearance, a savant of surface, a Daedalus of décor" (p. 6). Allison believes he enjoyed having a family if for nothing else than having a still life that was at times perfect.

Through hindsight, Alison delves into the question of this perfection created by her father. She draws panels of herself dusting furniture and the glass prisms of a chandelier, catching her father using a bronzing stick before mass, and presenting himself to the world as an ideal husband and father. But, she questions, "Would an ideal husband and father have sex with teenage boys?" (p. 17). And while her family was not an affectionate one, Alison yearned to be close to her father. When she was a child, she bussed his hand and then fled from the room in embarrassment, and while she acknowledges that her mother must have bathed her countless times, it was her father giving her a bath that she remembers most. As an older child, she remembers Bruce showing her her first dead body. She is taken aback not so much by seeing the dead man's genitals as by seeing the gaping hole in his chest. She begins to question Bruce as a father, especially his motivation for showing her something so macabre. Was this act one of careless disregard? Or was he so inured to death that he wanted to see a more traditional reaction to it? Alison walks away nonplussed, a reaction to later things she would respond to in life.

As a teenager she begins to question her father's relationship with his high school students, boys he brings to his house and to whom he recommends books. Alison writes, "The promise was very likely sexual in some cases" (p. 61). As the memoir progresses, a young man is depicted sitting in Bruce's library, and he questions what is in a cut-glass liquor bottle. It is sherry, and Bruce asks him if would he like some. The panel shows the young man drinking while Helen comes into the library and informs her husband that he is a half-hour late for picking up his younger son from a Cub Scout meeting. Bechdel

likens her father to Proust, who often fell in love with young, straight men—in Bruce's case, male students, babysitters, and yard workers. She writes, "He would cultivate these young men like orchids" (p. 95).

As Alison comes to understand and accept her sexuality, her story is one of triumph; however, after Bruce is killed, and she begins to construct her memoir, she writes of moments in time when she should have realized his sexuality was questionable. While Alison's trajectory is one of growth, her father's is one of death—literally, if it is a suicide, as she believes. Writing of his death, she ponders the possibility that it was an accident. "But that would only confirm that his death was not my fault. That, in fact, it had nothing to do with me at all. And I'm reluctant to let go of that last, tenuous bond" (p. 86).

Constructing her memoir from memory and the details she took from her assiduously saved journals and drawings, she found that the realities of her existence were more compelling than she actually remembered them to be. That is why she chooses not to write fiction. Throughout the graphic memoir, the reader is introduced to moments in time that represent her father's sexuality. Since the memoir is not linear, it is as if she is assembling the pieces of a puzzle. Alison remarks that, when asking her parents how they met, she encountered mumbled answers. She notes that her father does not even call her mother by her name. Instead he uses the vague second-person pronoun to refer to her. In fact, Alison can recall her mother and father exchanging signs of affection only twice in her life. She writes, "On both occasions I was astonished and discomfited" (p. 68).

What seems more genuine are the interactions her father had with various men and boys throughout his married life. The centerfold of *Fun Home* is literal, right in the middle of the memoir. Bechdel draws a replica of a photograph that her father took of Roy, the family babysitter, in the early morning light. The captions make it clear that it is a moment in time that she discovered when she was leafing through family photographs after her father had died. Roy, who has gone to the Jersey Shore with Bruce and the children, is lying supine, his youthful beauty aglow in the early morning sunshine. Alison's hand that is holding the photograph is life-size, although the picture itself is larger than a normal photograph taken at that time. It is literally larger than life. She writes, "The blurriness of the photo gives it an ethereal, painterly quality. Roy is gilded with morning seaside light. His hair is an aureole" (p. 100). Another notable point about the photograph is that Bruce tried to obscure identifying information on the photo with a black marker. All that is left untouched is the year, although the blotted out information can still be discerned. Alison writes, "In an act of prestidigitation typical of the way my father juggled his public appearance and private reality, the evidence is simultaneously hidden and revealed" (p. 101).

Alison continues to piece together her father's sexuality. There is a scene where she is thirteen, and her father reveals to her that he has to go see a psychiatrist. She writes about how she almost found out his secret then. Another time, Bruce is summoned to court for picking up a teenaged boy and buying him a beer. He is sentenced to six months of counseling. There are questions that perhaps he had an affair with his psychiatrist. When Alison turns fifteen, her father takes his children to New York City to celebrate the Bicentennial. Alison realizes that she is in a gay neighborhood: "It was like the moment the manicurist in the Palmolive commercial informs her client, 'You're soaking in it'" (p. 190). Alison is exposed to her first gay couple, she sees the ballet and *A Chorus Line*, and her father goes out one night alone. As an adult, she is reminiscing about what his life would have been like had he had the chance to be an openly homosexual man; she muses, "If my father had 'come out' in his youth, if he had not met and married my mother … where would that leave me?" (p. 197). She calls this moment a "literary cul-de-sac" (p. 197).

Later on, when Alison is a sophomore at college and writes her parents to inform them that she is a lesbian, her father is more accepting but does not believe she should label herself. A few weeks later, Helen confesses her desire to divorce

Bruce. She is sick of the lying, the affairs, and the cooking and cleaning. The family has fallen apart. She is sick of her husband's lying and his affairs, and she is sick of cooking and cleaning for the family. Alison writes, "Some crucial part of the structure seemed to be missing, like in dreams I would have later where termites had eaten through the floor joists" (p. 216). Still she remains close to her father, seeking an ally in her sexuality. On one occasion, while she and Bruce are on the way to the movies, that alliance almost occurs. In the memoir she renders that occasion with a two-page spread of twenty-four panels, which "is the only time that Bechdel uses the square box style of the traditional comic book, and she employs it for a tightly framed sequence of headshots depicting the dialogue between Alison and Bruce" (Watson, 2011, p. 140). The result is tangibly painful as Alison and her father ride in an awkward silence punctuated by brief bits of conversation. He tells her that he wanted to dress in girl's clothes when he was little, and Alison reminds him that she wanted to dress as a boy. She seems to be hoping for an epiphany, an acknowledgment. But before she can receive it, they have arrived at the movie theater. Afterward her father tries to take her to a gay bar, but they are thwarted in their attempt because the bartender demands to see her identification card. Alison writes, "As it was, we drove home in mortified silence" (p. 223).

At the end of the memoir, Bechdel returns to the story of Icarus and Daedalus, wondering what would have happened if the myth had turned out differently. The narrative comes full circle as Bechdel returns once again to a significant interaction between her and Bruce. They are in a swimming pool together. Alison, probably eight or nine, is poised on top of a diving board, and then she is drawn leaping, in midair. Her father's arms are stretched out to catch her. The narrative voice reflects on the myth of Icarus and Daedalus. "He did hurtle into the sea, of course. But in the tricky reverse narration that impels our entwined stories, he was there to catch me when I leapt" (p. 232). Julia Watson writes in "Autographic Disclosures and Genealogies of Desire in Alison Bechdel's *Fun Home*" that the ending

captures Alison's quest to come of age, come out, and come to truth about the mysteries of her father's life.... The frame also recalls and reverses the Icarus-Daedalus myth, because Bechdel's retelling of the story of her father's life, for all its duplicities and shame, as intertwined with her own, enables her to "fly" as an artist and woman.

(2011, p. 147)

Fun Home earned many literary accolades and was on the *New York Times* best-seller list for two weeks. Writing for the *Sunday Book Review*, Sean Wilsey pronounced *Fun Home: A Family Tragicomic* as "the most ingeniously compact, hyper-verbose example of autobiography to have been produced." While the graphic memoir won almost universal acclaim, Carrellin Brooks wrote that "parts of *Fun Home* feel forced, namely the narrator's insistence on linking her story to those of various Greek myths, American novels and classic plays."

In regard to her creative process for her two memoirs, Bechdel is as compulsive as her father with his restorations or her mother with her acting. She began the memoir by writing the script. She has said that for every line she wrote, she erased two. Sean Wilsey calls the memoir a "comic book for lovers of words" and writes that "Bechdel's rich language and precise images combine to create a lush piece of work—a memoir where concision and detail are melded for maximum, obsessive density." *Fun Home* consists of more than a thousand panels meticulously drawn from family photographs as well as those Bechdel took of herself posing as everyone in the image, so that she could draw them. She relies heavily on Google Images for historical accuracy and has noted that she would never have remembered such a minor detail as people wearing tube socks in the seventies on her own. Her drawing process is laborious. First she writes the script in Adobe Illustrator and creates a storyboard. She then prints out her script on typing paper and layers sketching paper on top of it until she is satisfied. Bechdel is so exacting that she will copy even the most minute of details, such as the print of a newspaper, by hand. Although she began to avoid color in her drawings at an early age (most likely after the time her father took

over her coloring of the canary-colored caravan from *The Wind in the Willows*), *Fun Home: A Family Tragicomic* is washed in two shades of green ink, giving it a contemplative effect.

ARE YOU MY MOTHER? A COMIC DRAMA

If *Fun Home* is a memoir with a nonlinear plot, then Bechdel's companion memoir, *Are You My Mother? A Comic Drama,* is a downright labyrinth. Highly erudite in its construction, the reader has to be able to follow Alison's relationships with her mother, girlfriends, and therapists while incorporating and understanding the works of the psychotherapist Donald Winnicott, the psychologist Alice Miller, and the writer Virginia Woolf. During all of this, *Are You My Mother?* becomes ultimately an exploration of Alison's self. In lesser hands, the memoir could be a study in solipsism, but, as Dierdre Donahue of *USA Today* writes, "the book is a page turner, thanks in part to Bechdel's lovely and subtle illustrations. Bechdel's examination of her relationship with her mother also touches on the universal push and pull between mothers and children." Other reviewers were not so generous. Dwight Garner of the *New York Times* sums up many critics' opinions: "Ms. Bechdel returns now with a second memoir, this one about her mother, and it is—sometimes you need to come right out and say these things—not nearly so good. In fact, *Are You My Mother?* flirts with being, front to back, somewhat actively dismal."

Are You My Mother? is a memoir about Alison trying to figure out who her mother really is, especially in relation to herself, the only daughter in the family. Bechdel points out that her mother stopped kissing her good night when she was seven. This action hurts her—she writes that "When Mom abruptly stopped kissing me good night, I felt almost as if she had slapped me" (p. 137)—and makes the reader extremely empathic with her. It is a pivotal moment in Alison's life, and it is mentioned in almost every review about the memoir. More than anything, *Are You My Mother?* seems to be about this one moment in time as Alison endeavors to understand the bonds

and conflicts between mother and daughter, between Helen and herself.

There are seven chapters to the memoir, each beginning with a dream that is later illustrated with a theory of Donald Winnicott's regarding infant development. The first chapter is entitled "The Ordinary Devoted Mother." Alison dreams that she is stuck in a cellar, and the only way out is through a small window where a spider has built its web. One panel is devoted to showing this inaccessible window. The gray cellar seems to be closing in upon itself as two additional spiderwebs dominate the scene. Clearly the spiders function as a hindrance to her escape, an interesting point because later in the memoir it is revealed that Helen suffered severe arachnophobia, so much so that no one could even say the word "spider" around her. In the dream there magically appears a door, and when Alison opens it there is a brook. She jumps into it, hesitant at first, but once immersed has "a sublime feeling of surrender" (*Are You My Mother?*, p. 3). The chapter then begins when Alison is contemplating telling her mother about writing the Dad book. While dreams provide the scaffolding for the memoir, a recurrent theme is Bechdel's own creative process, one she frets about continuously. Time moves forward as she writes, "I see that perhaps the real problem with this memoir about my mother is that it has no beginning" (p. 6).

Much of the memoir is constructed as an archive of Alison's interactions with her mother. A particularly relevant scene in this first chapter is a two-page photo montage of Helen playing with her daughter as an infant. In the memoir, Alison has arranged the pictures "according to her own narrative" (p. 32). In the five photographs, Helen is cooing at Alison, and Alison is mimicking the look on her mother's face. Alison cites Donald Winnicott: "ordinarily the woman enters into a phase, a phase from which she ordinarily recovers in the weeks and months after the baby's birth, in which to a large extent she is the baby and the baby is her" (p. 32). In this scene, Helen and the three-month-old Alison look blissfully happy. The chapter ends with Alison returning to the present, her hands on the keyboard of her computer. She and Helen are separated now, and

her chief means of communication is via the telephone. As Alison listens to her mother, Helen's voice is drawn larger and larger as Alison transcribes her words.

The second chapter of the book is called "Transitional Objects," and it refers to Winnicott's theory that for an infant, the first transitional object is the mother's breast. According to Winnicott, "The mother, at the beginning, by an almost 100 percent adaptation affords the infant the opportunity for the illusion that her breast is part of the infant" (p. 57). The baby assumes that the breast is not separate from her, that she and the mother are still one. When a baby starts to realize that she and her mother are separate beings, the child may pick up a transitional object, such as a teddy bear, and use that as a substitute. The chapter begins with Alison in a therapy session that introduces the reader to Carol, Alison's second therapist, and Jocelyn, her first therapist, but they are not introduced in chronological order. As Katie Roiphe describes it, "Things happen at the same time. Associations are made. The past is superimposed on the present. Thought bubbles and squares complicate and illuminate unobtrusively." The topics of loss of innocence and self-doubt dominate this chapter. Helen insisted on breastfeeding Alison, much to everyone's objections. She persists for a month but is unsuccessful. Alison writes, "I don't think it's going too far to claim that our 'failure' must have been deeply frustrating for both of us. Or even that a pattern of mutual, preemptive rejection could have been set in motion, each of us withholding in order to foreclose future rejection" (p. 60). Here Alison ponders the cause for her initial hurt, a wound she carries throughout the memoir. She is plagued by self-doubt. The nonfulfillment between Alison and her mother of not being able to nurse is devastating. In the memoir, Helen is drawn in dejection as she puts baby bottles into a pot on the stove to sterilize them. At the end of the chapter, Jocelyn asks Alison if she is angry at her father for killing himself, and "eventually and repeatedly, Jocelyn would suggest that I was angry at my mother too, but that emotion would prove much more elusive" (pp. 74–75).

Chapter 3, titled "True and False Self," is perhaps one of the more complicated and circuitous of the memoir as Bechdel explores Winnicott's theory, the subject of the title. There is the true self, the one that only the individual knows, and there is the false self that in its most simplistic terms can be explained as the self we present to the outer world. Of course there is a natural degree of false self in almost every human. Actions such as social niceties are considered those of the false self, but they are ones that we need to incorporate in order to successfully function in society. The dream in this chapter begins with Alison's therapist Carol. Alison opens the door in her underwear, clearly denoting partial nakedness and vulnerability. Carol gives Alison a massage and then notices a pair of pants that need mending. The therapist takes the pants with her, and the narrator writes, "As she leaves with my pants, I feel as secure and happy as I ever have" (p. 79). There is then a segue back in time when Alison was a child and her mother patched a pair of pants for her. Things that are broken and need mending become a predominant theme throughout this chapter. Meghan O'Rourke, writing for *Slate,* notes: "What Winnicott—and Bechdel—was interested in was what happened when this crucial mother-child mirroring broke down, and the child became precociously attuned to the mother's needs instead of her own." An adult Alison finds a dress she wore as a child that was mended by her mother. In a conversation with Helen, her mother tells her she is mending some period costumes for a fashion show to demonstrate the evolution of style throughout the decades. Alison's childhood bear, Mr. Beezum, has a tear in it that needs to be mended. Alison's sins are mended through the act of confession and the taking of communion. Eloise, Alison's girlfriend, has an affair, and the two try to mend their relationship by having sex. Alison kicks a hole in the wall that is never mended. Most importantly, Alison explores how she has tried to mend her mother. In a pivotal therapy session, Alison is asked, "Do you think you're trying to heal your mother with the book about your father?" (p. 82).

Chapter 4 is framed by scenes of a telephone that serves as an adult Alison's main form of

communicating with her mother. In the dream sequence at the beginning, Alison is trying to reach Helen but is unable to because she cannot dial the correct numbers. The cord that dangles from the telephone is not too subtly reminiscent of an umbilical cord. "Mmm. The phone is literally a lifeline," one of her therapists tells her (p. 123). Alison draws pictures of herself in her mother's womb, writing that "the womb is an environment that adapts absolutely, nothing impinges because there's no outside or inside. No separation" (p. 138). These panels of the womb are reinforced by the dominant two-page spread that Alison has drawn from *Dr. Seuss's Sleep Book*. The image looks like a pregnant uterus. In her rendering, Alison points out the similarities between this drawing and her own life, citing Donald Winnicott and his theory about the good-enough mother: "As a more common result of the lesser degrees of tantalizing infant-care in the earliest stages we find mental functioning becoming a thing in itself, practically replacing the good mother and making her unnecessary" (p. 134). In this chapter the scene of Alison's mother telling her that she is too old to kiss goodnight is tangibly painful. It is at this moment that Alison realizes her mother will not nurture her in the way that she desires—the subject of many therapy sessions. The chapter ends with Helen reaching Alison on the phone after she has tried for days to do so. On this page, in a series of panels, the phone and its cord are the only things shaded in red, the latter looping its way to Alison's ear as Helen tells her that she has asked Bruce for a divorce. Alison comments, "I wasn't there when she needed me" (p. 158), a reversal of the traditional mother-daughter paradigm and an indication of how Alison sees her relationship with her mother.

At first the dream sequence in chapter 5 is terrifying. Alison is depicted climbing up an icy cliff. There is water below her. Then suddenly she is safely on top of the cliff, only to realize that she is really on the roof of her childhood home. Alison tries to show her neighbor and then her father her dire predicament, "but in this thawed, mild climate, it's impossible to convey the extremity of my situation" (p. 164). This chapter focuses on Alison's relationship with her mother in regard to what should be stated and what should be kept silent. The ideas of Donald Winnicott and of Alice Miller's book *The Drama of the Gifted Child* are also expounded upon. Not only does Alison write this memoir about her mother, she sends her drafts to review for her opinion. Her mother's response to the book is telling, as Alison, lying on the floor despondent, tells her girlfriend of Helen's reaction to the chapters: "She said my brother was there knocking out a wall of her garage with a concrete cutter, and she felt like Christian is wrecking my garage, Alison is wrecking my life" (p. 165). That night, Alison is reading from *The Drama of the Gifted Child*: "Narcissistic cathexis of her child by the mother does not exclude emotional devotion. On the contrary, she loves the child, as her self-object, excessively, though not in the manner that he needs, and always on the condition that he presents his false self" (p. 167). Alison's attempts to show her mother her true self are rejected throughout the memoir, and Helen makes it clear that she is not comfortable with Alison's lesbianism. Panels are drawn of a phone conversation Alison has with her mother about her comic strips being gathered into a book that is going to be published. She breaks the news to her mother that her cartoons are about lesbians. Helen responds, "I would love to see your name on a book, but not on a book of lesbian cartoons" (p. 182). The chapter then goes back in time to when Alison is a young writer is just starting out. She sends her mother a short memoir piece. Five months later, Helen responds to her writing with red ink scribbled all over it, correcting it for style. Alison comments: "I would not attempt to write about my own life again until I began to write the book about my father seventeen years later" (p. 193). In this chapter, there are several scenes in which Helen speaks of things that are too personal to write about. In an attempt to appease her mother, Alison reads a selection from Donald Winnicott to her: "At the center of each person is an incommunicado element, and this is sacred and most worthy of preservation." Helen approves: "That's good. Some things are private" (p. 198). Helen and Alison discuss the nature of

writing about the personal. Their opinions differ as Helen notes that her favorite poet, Wallace Stevens, wrote about the transcendent without using the "I." She does not hold the genre of the memoir in high esteem. Alison returns again to Donald Winnicott in an attempt to explain this conflict with her mother: "The child must be able to move away from the mother and come back to her—again and again—in order to complete this process of separation" (p. 200), a relationship that Alison seems unable to create with Helen, especially since Alison is so eager for her mother's approval. As Peter Terzian of the *Paris Review* wrote of this aspect of the memoir, "thrillingly discursive, it's framed by the artist's struggle to create *Fun Home* and broker her mother's acceptance of its public unearthing of family secrets."

Chapter 6 is titled "Mirrors"—objects that are both literally and symbolically focused on throughout this section of the memoir. Alison sees her mother in a mirror; Alison, as a toddler, is almost killed when she climbs up on a mirror; and, according to Winnicott, the mother functions as a mirror to her child. Winnicott has his own twist on Descartes' famous idea "I think, therefore I am." He writes instead that "When I look I am seen, so I exist" (p. 233). The self must be reflected in order to verify one's own identity. In this chapter's dream, Helen is rehearsing for a play, and she is wearing period undergarments. Instead of rehearsing her lines in front of Alison, she does so in front of "the grand pier mirror" (p. 207). Much of the chapter is focused on Helen's roles as an actor. Although no one can go backstage before the play, Alison imagines her mother putting on her makeup in front of the mirror, much as she does at home when she "puts on her face" (p. 213). Alison cites information from one of Donald Winnicott's papers: "the precursor of the mirror is the mother's face" (p. 213). In a reversal of roles, Helen is the one who seeks approval as she looks in the mirror and declares herself hideous. It is her daughter who tells her she is not. Scenes are drawn where Alison attempts to seek approval from her mother, but she is not reflected as she desperately needs to be. In fact, as a child, Alison is an observer as

she draws panels where her mother plucks her eyebrows in front of a mirror for relaxation and her father stands before a mirror applying bronzer. These actions create an illusion, not an accurate mirroring, but a false self. Alison, once again, seeks her mother's approval of her lesbianism and tells her that she has signed a contract to do a book of cartoons. She and her mother are at odds as Helen asks if these are about her lesbian cartoons. "But what if someone sees your name?" she asks in a phone conversation. Alison responds, "Well that's kind of the idea. This is what I'm doing, it's who I am" (p. 228). Alison, who hangs up the phone on Helen, is now able to cry freely. She realizes that her mother resolutely refuses to mirror her daughter's success. At the end of the chapter, Alison notes that in the foyer of her house two mirrors faced one another. Laura Miller of the *Guardian* observes, "The key image of *Are You My Mother?* comes toward the end of the book.... Two mirrors faced each other in the foyer, creating an infinite regression of images of whoever happened to be standing in the little room." Bechdel writes, "In one way, what I saw in those mirrors was the self trapped inside the self, forever. But in another way, the self in the mirror was opening out, in an infinite unfurling" (p. 244).

In chapter 7, "The Use of an Object," Alison dreams that she has a large pimple on her face, and as she squeezes it out she realizes it is a tumor. She calls to her mother who has her back to her, "but she won't even turn around. She's still mad at me about the book" (p. 249). Time moves in and out, backward and forward, as Alison nears her conclusion. She writes, "The story has no end, but now it's five years later, and I must manufacture one" (p. 284). Alison believes that she, like Virginia Woolf, must write about her mother to get her out of her head. At the beginning of the chapter, Alison is full of doubt. She has sent *Fun Home* to her mother and waited anxiously for her mother's response. To Alison's relief, Helen has very few changes that she wants done to the manuscript. Although she is not happy, she is resigned. Helen tells Alison that she is not close to her story about her relationship with her husband, but she allows Alison her

freedom to be an artist. Alison continues to read books on psychotherapy and she feels a lucidity: "I see now that my heightened state was the conception, the very first stirrings, of this book about my mother" (p. 253). Referring back to the pimple dream, she "uproot[s] [her] mother's encampment" (p. 255). Alison compares her family's own narrative in the context of *To the Lighthouse* to Lily Briscoe's struggles with discerning the truth about the relationship between her parents. The narrative corresponds with panels from Alison's own life. The first two consist of her holding cut-out photographs of her parents and leaning them together, one at arm's length and the other focusing in so that they are drawn to scale. Below the narrative she writes of Lily, "She's trying to work out the relation of shapes in her painting, but she's also trying to understand the relations between Mr. and Mrs. Ramsey" (p. 256), the former a man who is difficult and prone to throwing fits, just like her own father. Alison attempts to figure out the relationship with her and her mother through the family structures that have spanned generations. An older Alison asks her mother, "What's the main thing you learned from your mother?" (p. 263), and without skipping a beat, Helen responds, "That boys are more important than girls" (p. 264). Alison has had difficulty accepting this notion throughout her life, and in her therapy sessions, she has been asked if she is mad at her mother, a theme that has resounded throughout the memoir as Alison strives to understand her relationship with Helen in the works of Virginia Woolf, Alice Miller, Sigmund Freud, and Donald Winnicott. She summarizes, "Here's the vital core of Winnicott's theory: the subject must destroy the object. And the object must survive this destruction" (p. 267). Through Alison's very act of writing the memoir, she has destroyed the object of her mother, but at the end we see that Helen has survived. After receiving four chapters from Alison, Helen comments, "There are clear themes.... It's ... a metabook" (p. 285). Bechdel writes, "At last, I have destroyed my mother, and she has survived my destruction" (p. 285). The memoir then ends with a young Alison and Helen as they play the crippled child game together, a game where Alison has always had her mother's undivided attention. Alison is lying on the floor and her mother asks if she needs braces—"and special shoes," she tells Helen (p. 287). Although she and her mother have often been at odds, Alison remembers this game more than any other. Drawn as if taking the shot from above, Helen is standing as she watches her daughter struggling to her feet. Alison recalls that "there was a certain thing I did not get from my mother.... But she has given me the way out" (pp. 288–289). Helen has enabled Alison to be who she is, which has provided her the chance to be an artist.

Are You My Mother? is a challenging book to read. Laura Miller writes, "The concepts Winnicott contributed to object relations theory ... provide themes for each of the book's seven chapters, but its swirling, circular structure derives from Woolf." Calling *Are You My Mother?* a furiously literary memoir from the lesbian Woody Allen, Miller also writes, "The cartoon version of Bechdel is boyish and fretful, ... equally prone to seizure by doubt or by the giddy, centrifugal force of some idea. She is comical and, as a therapist ... tells her, adorable, a quality that allows her to carry readers where they might not otherwise be keen to go." The astute reader must follow a labyrinth through time and space, with no continuum, to understand Bechdel's relationship to her mother, but it is a well-spent investment. With regard to the shading of the memoir, Bechdel told Peter Terzian, "the red is a spot color, and there's a gray ink-washed layer of shading that interacts with it in different ways, so there's actually a wide range of tones. I think that more nuanced coloring is part of this more complicated story."

Bechdel's second memoir was highly anticipated. It immediately landed on the *New York Times* best-seller list, and she went on a whirlwind tour of speaking engagements and book signings until her mother became ill in March of 2013. Alison went home to take care of Helen, who passed away in May. Alison calls this time spent with her mother a tremendous gift. In September she began her speaking engagements again. When asked what her next project will be, she has responded by saying she

is going to write about exploring relationships or the family as it functions together.

Bechdel tries to do something creative every day. She has a studio in her home, in West Bolton, Vermont, where she spends most of her time. In order to keep her legion of fans satisfied, she keeps a blog, a Twitter account, and a Facebook page where she periodically posts information that is relevant to her life. She remains a private figure despite her touring and multimedia communications. Bechdel's significance cannot be overrated. She has been a pioneer in her cartoons, breaking through as a lesbian and as a woman in a male-dominated field, and she has achieved popular and critical acclaim through a body of work that has spanned more than thirty years.

Selected Bibliography

WORKS OF ALISON BECHDEL

GRAPHIC MEMOIRS

Fun Home: A Family Tragicomic. Boston: Houghton Mifflin, 2006.

Are You My Mother? A Comic Drama. Boston: Houghton Mifflin Harcourt, 2012.

CARTOON STRIP COLLECTIONS

Dykes to Watch Out For. Ithaca, N.Y.: Firebrand Books, 1986.

More Dykes to Watch Out For. Ithaca, N.Y.: Firebrand Books, 1988.

New Improved! Dykes to Watch Out For. Ithaca, N.Y.: Firebrand Books, 1990.

Dykes to Watch Out For: The Sequel. Ithaca, N.Y.: Firebrand Books, 1992.

Spawn of Dykes to Watch Out For. Ithaca, N.Y.: Firebrand Books. 1993.

Unnatural Dykes to Watch Out For. Ithaca, N.Y.: Firebrand Books, 1995.

Hot, Throbbing Dykes to Watch Out For. Ithaca, N.Y.: Firebrand Books, 1997.

The Indelible Alison Bechdel: Confessions, Comix, and Miscellaneous Dykes to Watch Out For. Ithaca, N.Y.: Firebrand Books, 1998.

Split-Level Dykes to Watch Out For. Ithaca, N.Y.: Firebrand Books, 1998.

Post-Dykes to Watch Out For. Ithaca, N.Y.: Firebrand Books, 2000.

Dykes and Sundry Other Carbon-Based Life-Forms to Watch Out For. Los Angeles: Alyson Books, 2003.

Invasion of the Dykes to Watch Out For. New York: Alyson Books, 2005; Boston: Houghton Mifflin, 2008.

The Essential Dykes to Watch Out For. Boston: Houghton Mifflin Harcourt, 2008.

CRITICAL AND BIOGRAPHICAL STUDIES

REVIEWS

Brooks, Carrellin. "A Dyke to Watch Out For." *Tyee* (British Columbia), August 23, 2006. http://thetyee.ca/Books/2006/08/23/FunHome/

DeBold, Kathleen. "The Women We Know: Alison Bechdel Hits the G Spot." *Lambda Book Report* 3, no. 4:33 (May 1992).

Donahue, Deirdre. "Alison Bechdel Shines in Graphic Memoir *Are You My Mother?*" *USA Today*, May 2, 2012. http://books.usatoday.com/book/alison-bechdel-shines-in-graphic-memoir-are-you-my-mother/r686506

Gangemi, Merry. "Alison Bechdel's *Fun Home.*" *Off Our Backs*, October 1, 2007.

Garner, Dwight. "Artist, Draw Thyself (and Your Mother and Therapist)." *New York Times*, May 2, 2012. http://www.nytimes.com/2012/05/03/books/are-you-my-mother-by-alison-bechdel.html

Grossman, Lev, and Richard Lacayo. "10 Best Books." *Time*, December 17, 2006. http://content.time.com/time/magazine/article/0,9171,1570801,00.html

Miller, Laura. "*Are You My Mother?* by Alison Bechdel—Review." *Guardian*, May 24, 2012. http://www.theguardian.com/books/2012/may/24/are-you-my-mother-alison-bechdel-review

O'Rourke, Meghan. "A Mother Is a Story with Neither Beginning nor End." *Slate*, May 5, 2012. http://www.slate.com/articles/arts/books/2012/05/fun_home_sequel_alison_bechdel_s_are_you_my_mother_reviewed_by_meghan_o_rourke_.html

Roiphe, Katie. "Drawn Together." *New York Times*, April 27, 2012. http://www.nytimes.com/2012/04/29/books/review/are-you-my-mother-by-alison-bechdel.html

Watson, Julia. "Autographic Disclosures and Genealogies of Desire in Alison Bechdel's *Fun Home.*" *Biography* 31, no. 1:27–58 (winter 2008). Reprinted in *Graphic Subjects: Critical Essays on Autobiography and Graphic Novels.* Edited by Michael A. Chaney, 123–156. Madison: University of Wisconsin Press, 2011.

Wilsey, Sean. "The Things They Buried." *New York Times*

Sunday Book Review, June 18, 2006. http://www.nytimes .com/2006/06/18/books/review/18wilsey.html?page wanted=all&_r=0

INTERVIEWS

Rhoads, Heather. "Cartoonist to Watch Out For." *Progressive* 56, no. 4:13 (April 1992).

Simply, Trixi. "An Interview with Alison Bechdel." *Gay Community News*, October 19, 1991, pp. 1, 8, 10.

Terzian, Peter. "Family Matters: Alison Bechdel on *Are You My Mother?*" *Paris Review*, May 9, 2012. http://www.the parisreview.org/blog/2012/05/09/alison-bechdel-on-%E2 %80%98are-you-my-mother%E2%80%99/

Thomas, June. "Drawing on the Lesbian Community: An Interview with Alison Bechdel." *Off Our Backs*, September 30, 1988, p. 1.

Thurman, Judith. "Drawn from Life." *New Yorker*, April 23, 2012, pp. 48–55.

Van Arsdale, Sarah. "Drawing on Life: Alison Bechdel Shows and Tells." *Lambda Book Report* 6, no. 12:1, 6–7 (July 1998).

PLAY BASED ON THE WORK OF ALISON BECHDEL

Fun Home. Music by Jeanine Tesori, book and lyrics by Lisa Kron. Directed by Sam Gold. Off-Broadway premiere, September 30, 2013, at the Public Theater, New York City.

MAXWELL BODENHEIM

(1892—1954)

Robert Niemi

OF ALL THE colorful artistic characters associated with Greenwich Village bohemia in the early decades of the twentieth century, none was more colorful, notorious, or controversial than Maxwell "Bogie" Bodenheim: poet, critic, novelist, gadabout, rake, rebel, radical, drunkard, vagabond, and ultimately murder victim. Once considered one of the best poets of his generation, in the early days of high modernism, Bodenheim's reputation later plummeted as scandal, alcoholism, and dissipation turned him into a sad and sodden caricature of his former self. Largely forgotten now or remembered only as a grotesque oddity, Maxwell Bodenheim's ignominy, though admittedly self-inflicted, is not entirely deserved; he lived a fascinating, tumultuous life and produced two dozen books of verse and fiction, a number of which are of estimable quality. In sum, Bodenheim epitomized the bohemian revolt against the soul-crushing imperatives of American business civilization—and paid a heavy price for doing so.

YOUTH

Maxwell Bodenheim was born in Hermanville, Mississippi—a Claiborne County hamlet situated about twenty miles south of Vicksburg—on May 26, 1892. Bodenheim's maternal uncle, Maxwell B. Herman (1853–1930), a successful dry goods merchant who later attended medical school and became a distinguished surgeon in Memphis, Tennessee, founded Hermanville in the 1880s. Bodenheim's father, Solomon Bodenheimer (Max later dropped the "er"), emigrated from Alsace-Lorraine in 1890 and opened his own store in Hermanville. Unfortunately, Solomon possessed none of his brother-in-law's ambition or business acumen. He dispensed credit too easily and the store failed, ultimately forcing him to resort to the arduous life of a traveling salesman. Solomon's wife, Caroline (Carrie), a strong-willed, acerbic woman, was unstinting when it came to voicing her disappointments in her hapless husband, her cramped circumstances, and life in general. In his autobiographical first novel, *Blackguard* (1923), Bodenheim described his parents as "middle-aged Jews with starved imaginations and an anger at the respectable poverty of their lives" (p. 3). Brought up in a contentious, angst-ridden household, young Bodenheim instinctively absorbed his mother's aggrieved sense of victimhood and embraced glum misanthropy and nihilism as his métier. Later, after gaining some fame as a poet, Bodenheim assumed the flamboyantly haughty manner of a literary dandy: an obnoxious persona that brought him unending trouble.

Some time around 1900 the Bodenheimer family left Mississippi for Chicago. Solomon took a job as a clothing salesman and installed his family in a row house apartment at East Fifty-Fifth Place in the Washington Park neighborhood on the city's South Side. By the time he entered Hyde Park High School in 1906 at the age of fourteen, Max Bodenheim, isolated and friendless, was obsessively writing poetry—and submitting it for publication but without luck. In 1908 Bodenheim's formal schooling came to an end when he was expelled from Hyde Park High for some undisclosed infraction, most likely sexual in nature. In 1910 Bodenheim stole fifteen dollars from his father, took a train out of Chicago, and joined the U.S. Army in some distant city under an assumed name.

Stationed at an army base in Texas, Bodenheim eventually buckled under the boredom, harsh discipline, and oppressive routines of army

life. In *Blackguard* he describes "the army as an excellent prison for men to whom life holds a fixed horizon—men whose hearts and minds have reduced curiosity to an ashen foothold" (p. 38). In 1912 Bodenheim went absent without leave and was subsequently located and arrested by military police. In the throes of despair, he tried to commit suicide by swallowing lye but only succeeded in permanently damaging his taste buds and teeth. After a six-month stint in a military jail, Bodenheim was dishonorably discharged and proceeded to drift around the country for a year, working at farm and factory jobs, sometimes resorting to petty theft, and occasionally being arrested for vagrancy before returning to Chicago in 1913.

POET, EDITOR, ACTOR, AND PLAYWRIGHT

Bodenheim's return to Chicago in May 1913 was, to him, an admission of shamefaced defeat but also happened to be fortuitously timed; the city was in the midst of an upsurge in literary creativity that would become renowned as the Chicago Literary Renaissance. Floyd Dell, the editor of the *Chicago Evening Post*'s "Friday Literary Review" supplement, would soon decamp to New York City to help edit the radical journal *The Masses,* with Max Eastman, but Harriet Monroe's *Poetry* magazine (started in 1912) was flourishing and Margaret Anderson would begin publishing the *Little Review* in March 1914. First published in *Poetry* in 1913, the "Prairie Troubadour" Vachel Lindsay would bring out his first collection, *The Congo and Other Poems,* in 1914. Theodore Dreiser's *The Titan,* the second book of his "Trilogy of Desire," was published that same year; Edgar Lee Masters would publish *Spoon River Anthology* in 1915; Sherwood Anderson was working on his first novel, *Windy McPherson's Son* (published in 1916); Carl Sandburg's *Chicago Poems* would also appear in 1916. For an aspiring young man of letters, Chicago in the 1910s was rife with energy and promise.

At first Bodenheim lived with his parents and found work at a succession of menial jobs—telephone lineman's helper, plumber's helper,

tobacco store clerk. In his off hours he continued to write poetry and immersed himself in Chicago's literary milieu and night life to counter the tedium and exhaustion of his day job. After eight years of nothing but rejection slips, Bodenheim finally broke into print: Harriet Monroe published five short Bodenheim poems in the August 1914 issue of *Poetry* and Margaret Anderson published six Bodenheim poems in the November 1914 issue of the *Little Review.* From then on, Bodenheim had little trouble placing his work in a wide array of modernist literary journals.

Bodenheim's social life was equally earnest but more complicated. Soon after returning to Chicago he met a young writer named Ben Hecht. The son of Russian-Jewish garment workers from New York's Lower East Side, Hecht had immigrated to Chicago in 1910 and was working as a reporter for the *Chicago Daily News.* The two young men had much in common: both were transplanted Jews, highly intelligent, verbal, rebellious, and cynical beyond their years. They were soon close friends and quarrelsome artistic collaborators and rivals and would remain so until a final falling out some fourteen years later. Toward the end of 1914 Bodenheim began to cultivate an epistolary friendship with Alfred Kreymborg—imagist poet, chess enthusiast, and editor (with Man Ray) of the modernist journal *The Glebe* (1913–1914). Bodenheim also met Ellen "Fedya" Ramsay at a candlelit soiree at Sherwood Anderson's rooming house at 735 Cass Street on Chicago's West Side. Tall, beautiful, blond, and blue-eyed, Fedya Ramsay, twenty-eight in 1913, came to Chicago from an Aurora, Illinois, farm family and was a dancer with the Chicago Opera Ballet and a member of Chicago's little theater groups when she wasn't waitressing to make ends meet. Convinced that Ramsay understood and empathized with him as no one else ever had or would, Bodenheim fell deeply in love. On June 21, 1915, just before he was to reunite with her out West while she was on a theater tour, Bodenheim glanced at a newspaper and learned that Ramsay had been killed in a fall from a horse in Laguna Beach, California, and was being buried that day in a Santa Barbara

Cemetery. Stricken to his soul, Bodenheim blacked out and later woke up in a ditch. He would go on to dedicate ten of his books to her memory and would even claim to have conversations with her spectral presence. Whatever Fedya was to Max Bodenheim in life, she became an enduring Platonic ideal of love and goodness to him in death.

In 1915, after a trip down South to visit his wealthy uncle, Max Herman, Bodenheim took the train to New York to meet Alfred "Krimmie" Kreymborg and his wife, Christine, at their home, 29 Bank Street, in the West Village. Kreymborg installed Bodenheim in a room above his apartment and made him an assistant editor of his new literary journal, *Others: A Magazine of the New Verse*. Over the four years of its existence (July 1915 to July 1919) *Others* would publish poems by such modernist luminaries as T. S. Eliot, Ezra Pound, Marianne Moore, William Carlos Williams, Wallace Stevens, Amy Lowell, Mina Loy, H.D., and Marsden Hartley. Editorial meetings were held at a rented shack in Grantwood, New Jersey, just across the Hudson River from Manhattan and, later, in Greenwich Village. As aspiring poet, editor, all-around gadfly and self-promoter, Bodenheim constantly shuttled between Chicago, New York, and Boston, meeting and mingling with the cream of the American literati. He immersed himself in the experimental theater scene in New York and Chicago, "discovered" Hart Crane, befriended Conrad Aiken, helped fur thief John Coffey (the model for John Carley in Bodenheim's 1924 novel, *Crazy Man*) escape from Blackwell's Island Prison, became a regular drinking companion of Eugene O'Neill and Dorothy Day at the Golden Swan at West Fourth Street and Sixth Avenue in the Village (known as the "Hell Hole," the inspiration for Harry Hope's Saloon in *The Iceman Cometh*), and continued to publish his own poems at a furious rate.

Back in Chicago in the summer of 1915 Bodenheim, Ben Hecht, the playwright and painter William Saphier, and the Polish-born painter and sculptor Stanislaus Szukalski formed the Vagabonds, an informal debating society and lecture forum put together to raise money for the

Little Review. The Vagabonds met at Szukalski's top-floor studio at the George F. Kimball Building on East Congress Parkway in Chicago's Loop and featured lectures, readings, and debates by such notables as the Industrial Workers of the World leader Big Bill Haywood, the imagist poet Max Michelson, Chicago's Little Theatre founder Maurice Browne, Sherwood Anderson, and Clarence Darrow. Out of the Vagabonds sprang the Questioners, an experimental theater and intellectual forum that met in a studio at 1544 East Fifty-Seventh Street near Jackson Park. In May 1916 the indefatigable Bodenheim and Hecht formed the Players Workshop with the sculptor-dancer Lou Wall Moore (whom Bodenheim called "Princess Lou") and Elizabeth Bingham, who became the group's artistic director. In the year the workshop was in operation it put on some two dozen short avant-garde plays (two per month) at East Fifty-Seventh Street, including *Brown* by Bodenheim and William Saphier, *Poet's Heart* by Bodenheim, and *Mrs. Margaret Calhoun* by Bodenheim and Hecht. Bodenheim also furthered his reputation for making waves by calling Harriet Monroe "an intangible coward"—an insult that William Carlos Williams tried to smooth over by writing Monroe that "being the artist he is [Bodenheim] should be forgiven much" (Mariani, p. 127). In September 1916 Bodenheim nearly torpedoed Ben Hecht's *Dregs* on opening night. Playing a drunken bum, Bodenheim was supposed to cling to a lamppost, sing only the line "Every morning I bring her violets!" and then stagger off stage. Instead Bodenheim sang, a capella, the entire three-minute song from which the line was derived—twice—to the mortification of Hecht and the entire company.

Bodenheim's growing notoriety was further enhanced the following summer after he published "Army Recruiting Methods," an essay critical of the military, in Alexander Berkman's anarchist journal *The Blast* (June 1917). Returning to Chicago shortly thereafter, Bodenheim told a reporter for the *Chicago Dispatch* that he had taken to living in a cellar in Chicago's Loop district, was translating thirty-two volumes of Chinese poetry, and had sequestered himself in disillusionment: "I have a malady of the soul.

The world interests me not at all. I believe neither in war nor peace, and do not think the war of sufficient importance to think about.... I am not exactly a fugitive from justice. More might you say I am in pursuit of beauty" (*Washington Post*, June 30, 1917, p. 6). He told his friends and associates a different tale: that he had fled New York because he was being investigated by government authorities for his antiwar activities, a story that he soon parlayed into a luxury apartment and free food, supplied by sympathetic admirers on the West Side—until it was discovered that he was, in fact, a faker; Bodenheim had registered for the draft but was safe from induction anyway, given his earlier dishonorable discharge.

Embarrassed in Chicago, Bodenheim was back in New York by the fall to pursue his theatrical activities. From November 30 to December 5, 1917, the Provincetown Players staged *Knot-Holes*, a *fantasy* by Bodenheim and William Saphier and Bodenheim's *The Gentle Furniture-Shop* at a small theater at 139 Macdougal Street, just off Washington Square Park. On the same program: *Funiculi-Funicula* by Rita Wellman and *Ile* by Eugene O'Neill: grittier, more realistic fare that was more in keeping with the Players' usual offerings.

A plea for a renewed sense of wonder and rekindled imagination over commercial requisites, *Knot-Holes* features an opportunistic "Jaunty Bricklayer" (played by publisher Horace "Otto" Liveright) trying to convince his "Sleepy Mayor" (played by Bodenheim) that the knothole-filled wooden fence surrounding the town cemetery should be replaced by a sturdier brick wall. Two Ghosts (played by Alice MacDougal and Dorothy Upjohn) appear; according to Jeffery Kennedy in his 2007 assessment for Provincetownplayhouse.com, they represent "'the romance of the past' [who] object to the brick wall because the knotholes in the wooden fence are 'tiny windows of our moon-walled house, through which they can sip a second life and watch mothers with children, young lovers and men like the Bricklayer, who are like walking coffins carrying dead children.'" Kennedy goes on: "They grab the Bricklayer and, by making him dance and spin,

they 'shake to life the dead child within him.'" Spiritually transformed, the Bricklayer opts to leave the old fence alone, and, per Kennedy, "the play ends with the Mayor and Bricklayer looking up at the moon, arms around each other like little children."

The Gentle Furniture-Shop is a short allegorical play about making conscious, sometimes unconventional, life choices rather than accepting the finality of one's circumstances. For the play's setting, Bodenheim posits three stores on a street, standing for the three broad phases of life: for youth there is the Dancing Robe shop, for middle-aged people there is the Fortune-Telling Booth, and for old people there is the Gentle Furniture shop. The play unfolds inside the furniture shop, a store where customers can never buy the chairs they want but "must take whatever they are given or get nothing at all" (Kennedy, 2007). As a salesman tells a customer, "Life rules this shop and we must obey him." As Kennedy recounts, when an Old Man (Otto Liveright) and Old Woman (Dorothy Upjohn) enter the store, they are told that

they cannot have the chairs they desire … they stand dejected. This causes the Proprietor [(W. S. Matthews)—allegorically, Life—] to encourage them to take what they've been given because "life's choices can only narrow down to a graceful unconcern—there is nothing else." Suddenly a "Young Girl" [played by Edith Unger, sculptor and Village tea room owner] "dances into the shop," and she asks for a "slender black chair" so that her "favorite mood" will find its "refuge." When the Proprietor tells her she's in the wrong store, she replies that she isn't interested in dancing robes that day, sees the chair she wants, takes it, and skips away saying "Good-bye, amazed merchants." One of the salesmen breaks their astonishment by exclaiming, "Why, she didn't even pay for the chair she took away!" As the Old Man turns to question the Proprietor about the chair he has been given, finding newfound courage from the Young Girl, the Proprietor doesn't even let him finish, ending the play with: "Take what you like, old man. This Gentle Furniture-Shop is a fraud.... Shops of all kinds exist, I suppose, to unknowingly deceive their customers." The last image before the curtain is the Proprietor—Life—standing and looking "downcast."

Neither *Knot-Holes* nor *The Gentle Furniture-Shop* made any lasting impression on their audience. In her book on the Provincetown Players (edited by Travis Bogard and Jackson R. Bryer), Edna Kenton only notes that, with these two plays, "fancy and stage mechanics lapsed" (p. 74).

POET, CRITIC, AND NOVELIST

Sometime in 1918, at a Greenwich Village tearoom, Bodenheim, age twenty-six, met Minna Schein, a petite, pretty, but pragmatic nineteen-year-old writer's secretary from an East Village Austrian-Jewish garment-worker family. Schein was dazzled by Bodenheim's verbal and emotional extravagances, and he recognized and appreciated her steadfast ways. They married on November 22, 1918. Bodenheim immortalized their union with *Minna and Myself,* his first book of verse, published in 1918 by Joseph Kling, editor and publisher of *The Pagan,* a Greenwich Village literary journal. Typically destitute, Bodenheim prevailed upon his friend John Coffey to subsidize publication. Five hundred copies were printed but few were sold.

Following a politely adulatory foreword by the poet and critic Louis Untermeyer, *Minna and Myself* presents twenty-seven short, numbered free-verse poems addressed to Minna; twenty-six short, titled poems on various subjects; and the texts of two plays: "The Master Poisoner," by Bodenheim and Ben Hecht, and "Poet's Heart" by Bodenheim. The poems to Minna follow well-established romantic conventions but also display Bodenheim's characteristically superheated and florid diction. Often addressing himself directly to his beloved, the poet describes her cheeks as "spent diminuendos / Sheering into the rose-veiled silence of your lips" (p. 12); her eyes as "gossamer coquettes" (p. 12) and "Chinese mirrors" (p. 20); her breast as "the bridal couch of our stillness" (p. 29); her body as "a closed fan / Holding long brush-strokes of glowing repose" (p. 31). Wild metaphors ("The gown you wear is curiously like sound," p. 32), maudlin utterances ("Griefs, phosphorescent with unborn tears," p. 33), and a general breathlessness of swooning

emotional intensity date the Minna poems as coincident with the dawning age of Rudolph Valentino; studied bombast and melodrama drown out sincerity. Fortunately, Bodenheim reached firmer ground with the poems of the second section (titled "Myself"). Freed from romantic requisites, the poems in this section depict working-class folk ("Cotton Picker," "Factory Girl," "Soldiers"), nature settings ("Hillside Tree") and cityscapes ("Rear Porches of an Apartment Building"). They also deal quite bluntly with real-life concerns: change, aging, infirmity, and especially mortality. In a review of *Minna and Myself* the poet Babette Deutsch noted that "Bodenheim's subtlety is apt to become a labyrinth of crowding images [yet] retains, however, a rare and exciting savor; the intriguing strength of those content to be solitary, the beauty of those in whom the passions of the body are no more imperative than the passions of the mind" (p. 68).

By 1919 Bodenheim—prone to imagining and amplifying friends' slights and betrayals—had finally exhausted his five-year friendship with Alfred Kreymborg. (Another factor contributing to the break was that Bodenheim had become infatuated with Kreymborg's wife, Dorothy.) In a bid to become financially independent Max and Minna Bodenheim opened a coffee shop at the corner of West Eighth and Macdougal Streets in the West Village, but Bodenheim's boorish manners and sketchy work ethic caused it to fail after a few months. Minna worked secretarial jobs, and Max brought in a few dollars for paid poetry readings at such bohemian venues as Jack Jones's Dill Pickle Club in Chicago and at Goody's Bar in Manhattan's West Village, but lack of money was a constant headache. Despite their poverty and Minna being pregnant, the Bodenheims managed a transatlantic voyage to London in the summer of 1920. On June 26, just after disembarkation in Liverpool, Minna gave birth to a son they named Solbert. In England the Bodenheims met T. S. Eliot, Wyndham Lewis, the Belgian poet and book illustrator Jean de Bosschère (and his lover Vera Anne Hamilton), and stayed with Osbert Sitwell, brother of Edith and a writer of some note. Hard up as always, Bodenheim had to bor-

row money from Blanche Knopf and Conrad Aiken to get his family home.

The early 1920s saw Bodenheim at the peak of his creative powers. In the space of just five years he published four volumes of poetry and two novels: *Advice* (1920), *Introducing Irony* (1922), *Against This Age* (1923), *The Sardonic Arm* (1923), *Blackguard* (1923), and *Crazy Man* (1924). As if all that were not enough, Bodenheim also founded and coedited the *Chicago Literary Times* with Ben Hecht in 1924–1925. In the process he cemented his growing reputation as the enfant terrible of Jazz Age American letters.

Published by Alfred A. Knopf in the fall of 1920, *Advice* contains forty-one mostly short poems. Of that number, ten poems employ the coy trope of jauntily proffering "advice" to all sorts of things, animate and inanimate, for example, "Advice to a Street-Pavement," "Advice to a Butter-Cup," "Advice to a River Steamboat," and "Advice to a Hornèd Toad." While the advice poems display rhetorical inventiveness and are often amusing, they are of no great moment. The strongest poems in the collection mostly fall into two other categories: a short series of nature poems set at Rattle-Snake Mountain (presumably the one located in southern New Hampshire, not far from the MacDowell Colony, where Bodenheim stayed and wrote in the summers of 1921, 1922, 1923, and 1925) and visually vivid portraits of working-class folk. Bodenheim's working-class poems often focus on marks of physical decrepitude as signs of dehumanization and the adamantine hardness of life in industrial America. For example, "Foundry Workers" delineates the exhausting rigors of factory life as manifest in workers' faces: "Brown faces twisted back / Into an ecstasy of tight resistance; / Eyes that are huge sweat drops ..." (p. 16). "East-Side: New York" features a Jewish pushcart peddler munching an apple "With conquering immersion / All the thwarted longings of his life / Urge on his determined teeth" (p. 32). In "Track-Workers" the poet describes a railroad crew as "the living cuspidors of day. / Dirt, its teasing ghost, dust, / And passionless kicks of steel, fill you" (p. 53). Their sweated grime mirrors a dulling of the soul—except for "a meek and burly Pole" who

peers for a moment at a "strutting blackbird / With a fleeting shade of dull resentment.... / There is always one among you / Who recoils from glimpsing corpses" (p. 54). "Negroes" depicts a black boy as having a "sluggish innocence" and "the loose eyes of an old man" (p. 56). He sings a hymn "caught from his elders" and his life finds "a refuge in his voice" though "the rest of him" is "sickly flesh / Ignorant of life and death" (p. 56). "Vaudeville Moment" charts the lined, "hard" face of a "Middle aged Vaudeville conductor" who belies his profession as a purveyor of light entertainment (p. 70). The book closes with its longest and most ambitious poems: "Steel Mills: South Chicago" (four sections; 166 lines) and "South State Street: Chicago" (three sections; 110 lines). In the first of these poems the poet observes "an endless stream of men" leaving the mills at the end of a night shift and "scatter[ing] out / Into the cool bewilderment of morning" (p. 80). Among them, by the steel-mill gate are "Three bent women and a child" (p. 79): perhaps the three fates and a living symbol of an equally bleak future. "South State Street: Chicago" deliberately echoes T. S. Eliot's "The Love Song of J. Alfred Prufrock" (1915). Like Eliot, Bodenheim invites the reader on a nocturnal tour of the modern metropolis: "Wander with me down this street / Where the spectral night is caught / Like moon-paint on a colorless lane ..." (p. 82). But Bodenheim's poem is markedly different. Eliot uses London's proletarian precincts as an objective correlative for the degraded state of Prufrock's soul; Bodenheim presents Chicago's "tawdrily resplendent street" as a cityscape unto itself that says more about oppressive social and class arrangements than about the consciousness of the alienated poet (p. 84).

Bodenheim's third volume of verse, *Introducing Irony: A Book of Poetic Short Stories and Poems* (1922), is dedicated to Fedya Ramsay and contains twenty-two lyric poems and ten prose poems (i.e., "poetic short stories"), the latter exploring in symbolic terms such diverse topics as "Insanity," "Poetry," "Religion," "Scientific Philosophy," "Art," "Music," "Ethics," "History," "Psychic Phenomena," and "Love." The collection proper is also varied and ambitious. There

are autobiographical poems ("Simple Account of a Poet's Life"), satiric poems ("Manners," "Seaweed from Mars," "Uneasy Reflections"), love poems ("Two Sonnets to My Wife"), Edgar Lee Masters–style character studies ("Jack Rose," "Turmoil in a Morgue," "The Scrub-Woman"), city poems ("Summer Evening: New York Subway Station"), poems about death ("Meditations in a Cemetery"), and the usual, linguistically extravagant exercises in imagistic experimentation and mood conjuring. Hanging over all these poems is Bodenheim's obsessive quest for originality of expression and his characteristic contempt for "pretentious praise and blame," the "harlots' wine that men call fame" (p. 47) and an America where literature and art "present … a mildewed but decorous mien" (p. 34). Reviewing *Introducing Irony* for the *Bookman,* the always perceptive and fair-minded Louis Untermeyer found Bodenheim's poetic agility fascinating: "He is sometimes garrulous, grotesque, narcistic, verbally dandified, frequently irritating, seldom unintelligible. He may be—and, at times, is—precious and perverse, but, he is none the less (possibly all the more) provocative" (p. 635).

Bodenheim's fourth book of verse, *The Sardonic Arm,* published in 1923 by Covici-McGee in an edition of 575 copies, contains thirty-one poems, two rather grotesque illustrations by Bodenheim's friend Stanislaus Szukalski, and a "Reluctant Foreword" by the author in which he once again blasts his contemporaries as philistines:

> The poetic situation in America is, indeed, a blustering and verbose invitation to boredom and a slight, reviling headache. When not engaged in scrubbing the window pane ten times over, lest it prove opaque to an astigmatic public, American poets are discovering, with great glee, the perspiring habits and routines of sex, or naively deifying the local mannerisms of a blithely juvenile country.… You must leave the theater unless you desire the thankless experience of vomiting.

As Edward Thomas De Voe notes, Bodenheim advocates "an amalgamation of Intellect, Delicate Fantasy, and Irony as the components of an original poetic style, with subtlety as its handmaiden" (p. 95). Critical reaction to *The Sardonic Arm* was less than enthusiastic. An anonymous reviewer writing in the *Bookman* (September 1923, p. 83) accused Bodenheim of "self-deceit" and "flamboyant egotism." Virgil Geddes in *Poetry* found fault with Bodenheim's linguistic excesses: "Too fantastic in its artistry for fine irony embodying ideas, this one achieves a burlesque of irony" (p. 281).

Also in 1923, on the heels of *The Sardonic Arm,* came *Against This Age,* Bodenheim's fifth book of verse: twenty-seven poems in full-throated indictment of modern society and, moreover, life itself. Standing against the cruel quotidian, rife with degradation, disappointment, and death is "Only fantasy and irony / Incongruous brothers / [that] Can lift themselves above / The harassed interval that Death permits" ("Nightmare and Something Delicate," p. 21). De Voe writes: "Since this earthly paradise is a travesty of life as it should be, the poet's only recourse is to withdraw into his hardened shell and regard the world with asperity. Everything is an ironic jest perpetrated by man to satisfy his greed [and only] the poet stands aloof in supreme isolation from the tinsel lies and petty deceptions" (p. 103).

Bodenheim's autobiographical first novel, *Blackguard* (1923), is cast in the form of an urban-centered bildungsroman that fictionalizes his life circa 1914–1915. In part 1, "The Struggle," Bodenheim's alter ego Carl Felman returns to his parents' home in Chicago after a stint in the army and a period of wandering. Constantly "harassed by a feeling of inarticulate insignificance" (p. 12), Felman has "frozen his emotions in self-defense" (p. 18) but is determined to "sing his juvenile ballade within his contorted heart" (p. 88) and express himself through his poetry. Hounded by his conventional, poverty-stricken parents to get a job, Felman finds work as a telephone lineman's helper and his life falls "into a regular stride—days of wrenching labor and nights of rebellious weariness" (p. 84). Soon discharged, Felman constantly argues with his disapproving parents, piles up publishers' rejection slips, and is jilted by his girlfriend, Luce. Then, almost miraculously, Felman places poems with an "aristocratic little magazine of the muse" (p. 105), and his vocation

as a poet begins to flower. In part 2, "The Knife," Felman begins to discover "another world nestled between the dull apartment houses, raucous markets, and underworld saloons," a world of "'poets,' painters, sculptors, novelists, critics, Little Theater actors, art patrons, students of the arts ..." (p. 121). He meets Olga Ramely (i.e., Fedya Ramsay), falls deeply in love, and subsequently experiences unfathomable anguish when he learns of her death. In part 3, "Instigation," Felman, half-crazed with grief and frustration, assaults his father, is arrested and jailed—and has a strange epiphany: "He began to see that physical blows and silence were crude and ineffective weapons in his attack upon the insulting commotion of life and that, if he desired to injure human beings so that both he and they might become real for a moment, he must use more indirect and ingenious methods" (p. 191). Felman talks his way out of jail and takes a train down South to visit his uncle, Dr. Max Edleman (i.e., Maxwell B. Herman). The novel ends with Felman meeting Crazy Georgie May, "an ascetic prostitute," with whom he proposes "a unique monastery of thought and emotion" (p. 215).

Like *Blackguard, Crazy Man* (1924), Bodenheim's second novel, is divided into three parts. The first part—somewhat reminiscent of Stephen Crane's *Maggie, a Girl of the Streets*—delineates the sad and tawdry life of Selma Thallinger, a dance-hall girl from urban poverty who harbors vague aspirations for something better. The novel's second part focuses on John Carley, the "crazy man" of the title who is based on Bodenheim's friend John Coffey, fur-thief, autodidact, writer, and amateur philosopher. Like Coffey, Carley is a nonviolent nonconformist. Though a thief by profession, he is paradoxically an altruistic soul who embraces the true spirit of Christian brotherhood. Carley's symbolic martyrdom occurs when he is savagely beaten while trying to enter Selma's dance hall. The third part of the novel explores Carley's salutary moral and spiritual influence on Selma. Though more tightly plotted than *Blackguard, Crazy Man* exhibits Bodenheim's penchant for philosophical digression. Jack B. Moore calls the book's "urban investigation of the viciousness of contemporary

life ... sharp, and its revelation of city behavior patterns, especially sexual ... significant and in greater part valid" (1970, p. 86). *Crazy Man* sold a modest 2,380 copies.

In the summer of 1925 Bodenheim's reputation as a libertine was notably amplified when Boni & Liveright published his third novel, *Replenishing Jessica.* On June 30, at the instigation of John S. Sumner, head of the New York Society for the Suppression of Vice, a grand jury indicted Horace B. Liveright and Thomas R. Smith (Liveright's editor) for publishing *Replenishing Jessica,* an allegedly "obscene book." On July 7 Bodenheim had to interrupt his fourth stay at the MacDowell Colony in New Hampshire to make an arraignment appearance before Judge John F. McIntyre of the Court of General Sessions in New York City for writing "an indecent novel." Released on bond and later acquitted, Bodenheim may have been innocent of obscenity but he was certainly guilty of writing a superficial, trashy exploitation novel that does nothing more than recount the sexual exploits of his nymphomaniac heroine, Jessica Maringold, and the numerous lovers who are all too happy to oblige her scandalously outsized libido. At a time when America was just emerging from the pall of repressive Victorian mores, the reading public found *Replenishing Jessica* titillating fare—especially inasmuch as Jessica was the sexual aggressor, not the usual passive recipient of male lust. The novel went on to sell 38,700 copies—Bodenheim's most commercially successful book.

With his fourth novel, *Ninth Avenue* (1926), Bodenheim turned to a more realistic and gritty approach to more serious subject matter with his depiction of the life of Blanche Palmer, yet another example of a young woman from humble circumstances struggling to find self-realization and sexual fulfillment in the degraded, hostile purview of the modern city, this time epitomized by Hell's Kitchen on Manhattan's West Side. Ultimately venturing into Greenwich Village literary circles, Blanche falls in love with Eric Starling, a genteel black poet who is so light-skinned he is able to pass for white. By novel's end the couple is preparing to escape the abrasive confines of New York for Chicago. As usual,

Bodenheim excelled in his depiction of urban squalor but was less convincing in dramatizing relationships. Reviews were harsh. An anonymous reviewer for the *New York Times* judged *Ninth Avenue* "feeble and jejune"; *Bookman* deemed the novel "an unconvincing and rather silly story"; and Herbert Gorman in the *Saturday Review of Literature* found Bodenheim's characters "moving automatons" and the book's philosophical significance "nil." *Ninth Avenue* sold 7,600 copies.

A BIZARRE YEAR

Separated from Minna in 1927 after nine years of marriage, Bodenheim played the field with reckless abandon and dire consequences. On February 14, 1928, Amelia Klein, a.k.a. Aimee Cortez, a nineteen-year-old artist's model and Sheridan Square café dancer—playfully dubbed the "Mayoress" of the Village—was found dead in a bare, gas-filled room at 22 University Place in Greenwich Village. A framed photograph of Max Bodenheim, her lover, was found among her effects. Though Bodenheim's connection to Miss Cortez's demise was the subject of intense gossip in the Village, he avoided full-blown public scandal because most newspapers failed to mention his name. Bodenheim got lucky again a month later (March 19, 1928) when, after a delay of almost three years, the *Replenishing Jessica* obscenity case finally came to trial before General Sessions Judge Charles C. Nott in New York. Nott dropped Bodenheim's name from the indictment after Bodenheim's lawyer argued that his client had sold the book to Boni & Liveright outright for a flat fee of $1,000, had received no royalties, and therefore could not be held accountable for its manufacture or sale.

Three months later Bodenheim once again skirted the precincts of scandal when his fifth novel, *Georgie May*—a hard-boiled, naturalistic character study of an oft-homeless Memphis prostitute—was published by Boni & Liveright. Introduced toward the end of his first novel, *Blackguard,* Georgie May is based on a streetwalker Bodenheim had met on a Memphis park bench while visiting his uncle, Max Herman, in 1915. In *Blackguard, Georgie May,* and the poem "To Georgie May," Bodenheim depicts Georgie May as both "sensitive and corrupt" (Moore 1970, p. 112), with a face both "ruined" and "twined with youth" ("To Georgie May," in *Minna and Myself,* p. 43). A despoiled innocent unable to fully adapt to the physical and moral squalor of her surroundings—not unlike Stephen Crane's Maggie—Georgie can only resolve her dilemma through suicide. Castigated by critics as lurid and bleak, *Georgie May* nonetheless sold a very respectable 33,400 copies.

Persistent rumors that Bodenheim was an amoral, sex-obsessed roué finally boiled over into the realm of public scandal in the summer of 1928. In early June another lovelorn Bodenheim protégé named Gladys Loeb, eighteen years old, tried to emulate Aimee Cortez by gassing herself in her garret room next to Bodenheim's temporary residence at 144 Macdougal. Fortunately, she was discovered in time, revived, and taken home to her parents. Six weeks later yet another Bodenheim lover and protégé named Virginia Drew, age twenty-four, came to a sadder end. On Sunday night, July 15, Drew went to visit Bodenheim at his twenty-five-dollar-a-week room at 119 West Forty-Fifth Street. Having already told her that her work was "hopeless" and "sentimental slush," Bodenheim reiterated his judgment, driving Drew to a fit of suicidal hysteria. The next day she went missing. That night Drew's father and young brother called on Bodenheim to try to ascertain Virginia's whereabouts. Bodenheim avoided them and—suspecting the worst about Drew's fate—fled New York by train on Tuesday morning for Boston. Two days later he ended up at a rented seaside shack dubbed "Peggy" at 602 Commercial Street, Provincetown, on Cape Cod. On Thursday afternoon, July 19, Virginia Drew's corpse was fished out of the Hudson River. Then Gladys Loeb suddenly went missing, setting off a frantic and well-publicized search for her and/or Bodenheim by her father, Dr. Martin J. Loeb, a prominent Bronx urologist. Somehow, on Saturday, July 21, Dr. Loeb managed to locate Bodenheim at his rented shack in Provincetown and the two men had a tête-à-tête that calmed Loeb's concerns—at least

temporarily. Shortly thereafter Gladys showed up and was intercepted by her father. Adamant that she would not return to New York City without her beloved Max, Gladys convinced her father to take Bodenheim with them in a hired car back down the Cape. On the road to Hyannis, where the three actually stayed the night, the good doctor and the poet argued heatedly while Gladys chain-smoked cigarettes. Reluctant to return to New York to face a cyclone of bad publicity, Bodenheim easily convinced Dr. Loeb to let him out of the car before it crossed the Cape Cod Canal. Evidently tired of the whole affair, Gladys did not object. After a few days in Boston, Bodenheim quietly returned to Manhattan—until detectives located him at a dance hall on Seventh Avenue and 125th Street, where he was visiting another lady friend. No charges were pending; the police simply wanted to know what Bodenheim knew about Virginia Drew's death. Five weeks later (on August 24) a subway derailment at Times Square and Forty-Second Street killed sixteen passengers and injured another ninety-seven. Among the dead was a young woman eventually identified as Dorothy Dear. In her purse the police found a sheaf of love letters from Max Bodenheim.

TWILIGHT OF THE JAZZ AGE

Despite its impressively ambitious title poem, Bodenheim's *The King of Spain* (his seventh book of verse, published by Liveright in 1928), "reveal[ed] a general decline," as Jack B. Moore aptly puts it (1970, p. 106). Herman Spector's assessment of *The King of Spain*—and of Bodenheim's strengths and weaknesses as a poet—is especially astute: "The verse of Maxwell Bodenheim is competent, brilliant and pleasing to the ear [yet] it rarely attains intensity because the words are tricky and often carelessly used, and tend to become meaningless. For this reason, a good deal of the imagery falls flat.... His affectation and nervously self-conscious sneers affects unfavorably the intrinsic qualities of particular poems. The bourgeois reviewers accuse him of being disgruntled and overly-sentimental, and they are right" (p. 28).

With his sixth novel, *Sixty Seconds* (1929), Bodenheim employed a *roman noir* narrative structure that recounts the life of his protagonist, the convicted killer John Musselman, in a series of flashbacks that occur in the last minute before his death by execution: a scheme perhaps based upon Ambrose Bierce's famous 1890 short story "An Occurrence at Owl Creek Bridge" and one that would soon be approximated by Horace Mc-Coy in his crime novella *They Shoot Horses, Don't They?* (1935). Where Bodenheim differs from Bierce and McCoy is in his insistent avoidance of realism. Embedded within *Sixty Seconds* is an extended scene written in the form of a play (complete with stage directions), a free-verse poem, the case history of Chicago dance hall girl, impressionistic, stream-of-consciousness passages, and philosophical digressions.

Literary experimentation aside, *Sixty Seconds* centers on John Musselman's travails as a young man adrift in a hostile, bigoted, uncaring society—a journey of gradual disillusionment and moral degeneration that culminates in his murdering Frances Hemmingway (a.k.a. Helen Proctor), a bored society widow who uses Musselman for sex and then rejects him. Tellingly, Bodenheim clearly bases Musselman's travels in the South and his struggles in northern cities on his own life. Gradually driven under by the warping pressures of his upbringing, his neighborhood, the road, the modern city, ultimately society itself, Musselman *is* Bodenheim as he masochistically imagined himself: the tragic victim of an indifferent world populated by uncomprehending philistines and brutes.

Given its hybrid form and unrelieved grimness, *Sixty Seconds* had sales that were modest and reviews were ambivalent at best. An anonymous reviewer in the *Outlook* found the novel "done with such technical slovenliness, and with so little artistic discretion, that the idea becomes no more than a blind to veil an otherwise mediocre treatise on the opinions of Maxwell Bodenheim. The lies and the half-lies that most of us take for granted in the relationships between men and women give Mr. Bodenheim convulsive fits of intellectual colic. And with sex as his

trump card, he writes viciously beautiful prose, astounding and disgusting by turns" (p. 514).

In the early 1930s, as the Great Depression began to grip the economy and Bodenheim's always shaky personal fortunes grew ever more tenuous, he made a couple of last-ditch attempts to establish himself as a popular novelist. The first of these was *A Virtuous Girl* (1930): yet another Bodenheim character study of a rebellious young woman—in this case, Emmy Lou Wilkins, a friend of Georgie May—who seeks personal liberation through healthy sexual gratification. As Jack B. Moore notes, "Emmy does not, like Jessica Maringold, become jaded or corrupted by her erotic adventures. She remains throughout the novel untainted, 'a virtuous girl' " (1970, p. 121). The novel sold 12,400 copies. On the heels of *A Virtuous Girl* came the sensationally titled *Naked on Roller Skates* (1930). Bodenheim's eighth novel and last one to make a profit with sales of about 10,000 copies, *Naked on Roller Skates* is a breezy comic romp recounting the adventures of Terry Barberlit, a roving, virile, and pugnacious snake-oil salesman who meets up with Ruth Riatt, a naive but restless young woman, in a small town in Connecticut. The couple proceeds on to Harlem in New York City, where they carry on a tumultuous affair while immersing themselves in Harlem's vibrant nightlife.

In 1926 Bodenheim's friend, Ben Hecht, had satirized him at length in a novel entitled *Count Bruga*. Five years later Bodenheim finally got his revenge with *Duke Herring* (1931), a savage satiric portrait of Hecht as the fiendishly egomaniacal Arturo "Duke" Herring. The book's dustjacket blurb conveys its flavor: "Duke Herring's religion is a constant effort to disembowel other people while he shields his own skin with every variety of posturing, insolence, condescension, and falsehood. Rejected by almost all women, he concocts a fable in which they are slaves whom he disdains to patronize." Though undoubtedly gratifying for Bodenheim, *Duke Herring* pleased no one but himself. In *Saturday Review*, Basil Davenport aptly described the book as "a violent loss of temper sustained through two hundred and forty-two pages" (p. 105). Another critic called *Duke Herring* "structurally unsound, inordinately verbose, and totally lacking in wit ... might better have been left unwritten were it not for the insight it adds to the Hecht-Bodenheim feud" (*Book Review Digest*, 1931, pp. 110–101).

STRUGGLING PROLETARIAN WRITER

After a second trip to Europe in 1931, where he visited with Ezra Pound, Bodenheim came home to an America now fully engulfed and transformed by the Great Depression. The bohemian world he had known—the one animated by literary salons, little magazines, experimental theater, aesthetic squabbles, sexual escapades, and all the rest—was now submerged in a grim and squalid universe of mass unemployment, breadlines, labor strife, evictions, and poverty. Bodenheim attempted another sensationalistic potboiler—a novel titled *6 A.M.* (1932)—before shelving his otherworldly aestheticism in poetry and commercial forays in popular fiction to write a genuine proletarian novel: *Run, Sheep, Run* (1932). As is typical for Bodenheim he presents a wandering, marginalized protagonist. This time his hero is George Romaine, an avowed Communist in search of the best means to help bring about the downfall of capitalist America. At first Romaine's perambulations take him through the world of leftist New York intellectuals, fellow travelers, and "parlor pinks." His lover, Ann Rubens, epitomizes the elitist art-for-art's-sake aesthete who cannot relate to the plight of the working masses. George's friend, Myron Cohen, is a radical editor who espouses solidarity with the working class but, as an educated intellectual, has little contact with or understanding of the real people he purports to champion. After a not wholly successful organizing stint in the South, George returns to New York and rejects Ann for Kathleen, his new proletarian lover. As Moore notes, "*Run, Sheep, Run* was too corrosive in its depiction of America to please those who wanted reassurances of the nation's greatness and emphasized too greatly individual action isolated from support of the masses to be trustworthy as a Marxist critique of capitalism" (1981, p. 75).

After a final, failed attempt at another sensationalistic potboiler (*New York Madness*, 1933), Bodenheim published a second proletarian novel, his thirteenth overall, titled *Slow Vision* (1934). As the Great Depression worsens, Bodenheim's two young protagonist-lovers, Ray Bailey and Allene Baum, sink from borderline middle-class respectability into the lower depths of the social order—and become increasingly radicalized in the process. The novel's somewhat cryptic title refers to that slow process of realization, driven by intense personal suffering and disillusionment, which ultimately results in a true vision of the nature of capitalist society in all its crushing injustice, brutality, and human degradation: an insight hard to refute during the darkest days the Depression. Edwin Seaver in *New Masses* pronounced "*Slow Vision* ... easily Maxwell Bodenheim's best novel, perhaps because he has now found something worth writing about" (p. 25).

FEDERAL WRITERS' PROJECT INTERLUDE

If it was not already obvious from *Slow Vision* that Bodenheim was somewhat ambiguously advocating for the revolutionary overthrow of capitalism, his poem "To a Revolutionary Girl" (*New Masses,* April 3, 1934) expressed both his disdain for "the ruling swine" and his belief that tough-minded revolutionary ardor must ultimately be tempered with a romantic sensibility: "the hope / Of less impeded tenderness / In a freedom yet to come." In his own struggle to survive, Bodenheim had little time for either stance. In May he ventured to Los Angeles to try to find work as a Hollywood screenwriter but was not hired. He returned to New York City after a few weeks—but not before visiting Fedya Ramsay's grave. On January 15, 1935, Bodenheim applied for welfare relief, but investigators could not find him at his listed address at 70 Seventh Avenue in the West Village because he had been evicted and was living with a friend. On March 4, near starvation and homeless, Bodenheim lobbied for public relief by picketing the Department of Welfare office with five other unemployed writers. Welfare granted him $15 a month for room rent and $5.10 every two weeks for food. On August 3 the *Chicago Daily Tribune* reported that Bodenheim was "broke and in an alcoholic ward" at Bellevue after having been found lying in the street outside a friend's apartment building.

Bodenheim's downward spiral was inadvertently arrested by presidential decree when Franklin Roosevelt created, as part of the Works Progress Administration, the Federal Writers' Project in July 1935 to aid the nation's unemployed writers. The FWP was no make-work boondoggle; dozens of state and city guides, oral history archives, and countless other books were produced during its eight-year existence. The New York City office where Bodenheim worked—first as a writer and later as a supervisor making $115 a month—produced more than its fair share: for example, *Almanac for New Yorkers* (1938 and 1939 editions); *New York Panorama* (1938); *New York City Guide* (1939); and *New York: A Guide to the Empire State* (1940).

The Federal Writers' Project historian Jerre Mangione notes that at first Bodenheim took his "new [supervisory] responsibilities seriously," but

> his career as a steady and fairly sober employee came to an abrupt end when he ... was unofficially permitted to do his own work at home. The only strings attached to this arrangement were that he report to the Project office once a week and show what writing he had done. For Bodenheim, who until then had managed to report to work punctually every day, the once-a-week trip to the office became a prodigious ordeal. He would arrive in front of the office building [at 110 King Street] in a semi-inebriated state; then, unable to summon enough will power to enter, would go to a bar across the street to continue his drinking. Eventually, it would take two of his Project friends to escort him, protesting and staggering, from the bar to the office.
>
> (p. 160)

Bodenheim's stint with the FWP came to an abrupt end on August 2, 1940, when he was caught in an anti-Red purge. Suspended for fraudulently signing an affidavit denying membership in the Communist Party, Bodenheim was quietly fired from the Bibliographies and Indices Project a short time later.

MAXWELL BODENHEIM

FINAL YEARS

Estranged from Minna Schein since 1927, Bodenheim made their separation official with a divorce in 1938, a move that permanently estranged him from his eighteen-year-old son, Solbert. Bodenheim remarried in 1939. His second wife, Grace Fawcett Finan, the forty-one-year-old widow of an FWP coworker, was a diabetic who soon developed cancer. A devoted husband, Bodenheim struggled mightily to take care of his ailing wife—even to the point of selling the republication rights to his books, which came out in twenty-five-cent paperback editions. For a few hundred dollars to pay for food and Grace's medicines and doctor bills (and later her burial), Bodenheim lost all his book royalties, modest as they were. Caring for an invalid also took an enormous emotional toll. In his memoir, *A Child of the Century,* Ben Hecht reports that Bodenheim confessed that he was suicidal but stayed alive to care for his loving wife: "I'd commit suicide tonight except that I am in love with my wife. She is very sick and full of suffering. And she needs me. Yes, Ben … that poor little Grace needs me. And she loves me. I can't imagine why—can you? A scarecrow body and a dead soul!" (p. 218).

Somehow, despite his mounting private woes, Bodenheim managed to publish *Lights in the Valley,* his ninth and last original book of verse in March 1942. Bodenheim was briefly back in public notice in the summer of 1942 when William Saroyan cast him in *Across the Board on Tomorrow Morning,* a one-act play that opened at the Belasco Theatre on August 17. Bedraggled and corpselike, Bodenheim recited his own poem, "Jazz Music," to the extreme discomfort of the audience. The actress Carol Matthau told Saroyan's biographers Lawrence Lee and Barry Gifford that "he was like a derelict you thought you'd see in some gutter" (p. 91). After only eight performances in the sweltering August heat, the play mercifully closed. In 1945–1946 Bodenheim brought formal closure to his career as a writer by reading his poetry for a Library of Congress recording and by publishing his *Selected Poems.*

In 1950 Bodenheim's second wife, Grace, finally succumbed to cancer. On December 21 of that year the gossip columnist Walter Winchell reported that Bodenheim was living in a fleabag hotel on Washington Square, broke, depressed, and contemplating suicide. Very near the end of his tether, Bodenheim was given the proverbial new lease on life outside the Waldorf Cafeteria at Fiftieth Street and Sixth Avenue on a stormy night in April 1951. An attractive, vivacious farmer's daughter from Minden Township, Michigan, named Ruth Fagan had just purchased one of Bodenheim's poems for a quarter. When he left, she followed him out into the rain and asked to share the shelter of Bodenheim's umbrella—and soon came to share his desultory life. Fagan, age thirty-two, had a history of mental illness, but exactly why she latched onto Bodenheim—a toothless, scrawny, probably impotent fifty-nine-year-old alcoholic—remains something of a mystery. De Voe reports that a "few of Bodenheim's friends think she was [mistakenly] interested in royalties due her husband for republication rights. Others believe she sought notoriety by attaching herself to a man whose name had once commanded attention, if not respect. Still others contend her maternal instincts were aroused and that she needed someone 'to mother' " (p. 39). Whatever her motives were, Ruth Fagan would remain with Bodenheim until the very end.

Bodenheim had another encounter of note on September 24, 1951. That night he made the acquaintance of Jack Kerouac, age twenty-nine, and Allen Ginsberg, age twenty-five, at the San Remo Bar on Bleecker Street, and the torch was figuratively passed to a new generation of literary bohemians more than willing to carry on Bodenheim's raucous and reckless ways on the fringes of society. After a night of serious drinking, Kerouac and Ginsberg escorted Bodenheim back to his room on Macdougal Street but were unceremoniously kicked out by the landlady for making too much noise.

Bodenheim's decline proceeded apace. On February 3, 1952, he was arrested in Brooklyn for sleeping in a subway car and had to spend

MAXWELL BODENHEIM

several hours in jail before Ruth Fagan could scrape together twenty-five dollars from friends to post bail. That fall the poet Karl Shapiro (editor of *Poetry* magazine) and Ellen Borden Stevenson (Adlai Stevenson's former wife and *Poetry*'s chief benefactor) invited Bodenheim and Fagan to a Chicago Renaissance reunion at the 1020 Art Center, formerly the Borden ancestral mansion at 1020 Lake Shore Drive. Bodenheim was sober when he attended *Poetry*'s fortieth birthday party on October 18 at the Newberry Library and sober again, a few days later, at a luncheon of the Society of Midland Authors. After that, things rapidly went downhill as he and Ruth Fagan began to frequent North Side bars, get drunk, and quarrel loudly. One evening Bodenheim was seen slapping Ruth's face, "evidently his usual way of quieting her" (De Voe, p. 44). Slovenly, odiferous, loud, and often inebriated, both Bodenheim and Fagan panhandled everyone they met and were soon ostracized by the other literati. To make the Chicago trip a consummate fiasco, Bodenheim somehow broke his leg.

Upon returning to New York, Ruth tried to right her common-law husband and bring in desperately needed cash by arranging a poetry reading for Bodenheim at the Jabberwocky Café in the Village. The event was widely publicized and a good crowd gathered, but Bodenheim, still in a leg cast and blind drunk, half-heartedly stammered through a few poems before departing the stage, claiming the room was too stuffy—an unsurprising outcome as formal readings had long ceased to be Bodenheim's métier. For more than a decade he had been selling copies of his poems for twenty-five cents apiece (autographed copies for fifty cents) on the street or at Village watering holes like the San Remo or the Minetta Tavern, where he would immediately convert his meager takings into a drink of whiskey at the bar.

Destitute and homeless again in February 1953, Bodenheim and Fagan trudged over to St. Joseph's House, 223 Chrystie Street in New York's Bowery neighborhood, to call upon Bodenheim's old friend Dorothy Day, the cofounder (with Peter Maurin) of the Catholic Worker Movement. They asked Day if they could stay at one of her organization's farms (communes also accommodating the homeless). She obliged and they stayed at the Maryfarm Retreat House in Newburgh, New York, for five or six weeks—until a Russian "guest" grew enamored of Ruth. According to Day, he "kissed her hand and flirted outrageously with her while he crudely insulted her husband." Unable to tolerate an all-too-familiar situation, Bodenheim got himself and Fagan transferred to the Peter Maurin Farm on Staten Island until after Easter (mid-April that year). Day recounts: "When spring came and the warm weather and his leg was better, Max and Ruth disappeared. Ruth came back later to get some things he left in a seaman's duffle bag and she and her companion, a young lad rather somber and silent, walked down the road to the train about eleven." The young man's name was Harold "Charlie" Weinberg, and just ten months later he would figure prominently in the fate of Maxwell Bodenheim.

During this period Bodenheim reconnected with an old acquaintance named Sam Roth (1893–1974), a roguish Village bookstore proprietor, onetime poet, editor, and convicted pornographer. Roth soon contracted with Bodenheim to pay him ten dollars a week for a few months to tell his life's story, which Roth—or possibly his assistant, David George Kin—transformed into a ghostwritten "memoir" under Bodenheim's name: *My Life and Loves in Greenwich Village* (Bridgehead Books, 1954). Roth's description of his association with Bodenheim captures his overall state:

> Max would arrive at our office for his daily stint somewhere between eleven in the morning and noon. As the elevator opened for him it seemed to spew out the staleness of a thousand nights. He was bent forward and his eyes, gray almost to whiteness, were half closed. His hands continually twitched as if trying to recapture something they had held the previous night, which had been lost in the fog of drink. Settled at his typewriter, he would sometimes rest his head on it before starting to pound away on the white sheet placed there for him. Often he would take the sheet out of the machine and fill it with his tiny penciled scrawl

before handing it over to my assistant, the novelist, David George Kin, who laboriously copied and edited the material.

(p. 254)

Even in the depths of degradation and decrepitude, Bodenheim remained proud, bitter, and defiant. A young British poet named David Watmough met him in a Tenth Avenue bar in May 1953. The poets W. H. Auden and Dylan Thomas were also present. Watmough recalls the encounter: "[Bodenheim's] own bloodshot [eyes] steadily regarded me before he essayed a friendly conversation. 'Who the fuck are you, kid? And what you starin' at me for?' " Bodenheim went on to denounce everyone and everything north of Forty-Second Street: "They tell me it's full of the fucking rich. So there's another reason to stay here—even if you have to share the Village with more and more assholes" (Watmough, pp. 68–69).

Bodenheim's blustery arrogance could not shield him from fate. For more than a year Ruth Fagan had been keeping company with Harold Weinberg, the sullen young man Dorothy Day had observed at the Peter Maurin Farm. Weinberg, age twenty-five, a dishwasher at a Village restaurant—also a former mental patient with a long criminal record—had designs on Ruth. On several occasions Bodenheim threatened Weinberg with physical harm if he did not leave Ruth alone. Sexual tensions notwithstanding, the Bodenheims were staying with Weinberg in his rented room on the fifth floor of a flophouse at 97 Third Avenue (near East Thirteenth Street) on Saturday night, February 6, 1954. When Weinberg renewed his amorous advances on Ruth, Bodenheim tried to intervene. In a fit of frustrated rage, Weinberg fatally shot Max once in the chest with a .22-caliber rifle and then beat and stabbed Ruth to death. He then padlocked his room and fled the city. The bodies, fully clothed, were discovered by a landlord the following afternoon. Harold Weinberg was arrested in Baltimore on Wednesday morning, February 11, 1954. As he was led away by detectives, Weinberg shouted, "I killed two communists.... I ought to get a medal from Washington, D.C. Don't forget to get that in the paper!" (*Tuscaloosa News*, February 11,

1954) (Two months later Harold Weinberg was adjudged insane and indefinitely committed to Matteawan State Hospital for the Criminally Insane in Fishkill, New York.)

On February 10, 1954, before his burial at Cedar Park Cemetery near Oradell, New Jersey, a memorial service was held for Bodenheim at Riverside Memorial Chapel on the Upper West Side, presided over by Rabbi Edward Klein of Stephen Wise Free Synagogue. The event attracted an overflow crowd of over five hundred mourners, some of them Bogie's old Village friends and acquaintances, many of them just curiosity seekers. Bodenheim, who had always felt underappreciated, would have found the impressive turnout grimly amusing.

Selected Bibliography

WORKS OF MAXWELL BODENHEIM

POETRY COLLECTIONS
Minna and Myself. New York: Pagan Publishing, 1918.
Advice: A Book of Poems. New York: Knopf, 1920.
Introducing Irony: A Book of Poetic Short Stories and Poems. New York: Boni & Liveright, 1922.
The Sardonic Arm. Chicago: Covici-McGee, 1923.
Against This Age. New York: Boni & Liveright, 1923.
Returning to Emotion. New York: Boni & Liveright, 1927.
The King of Spain: A Book of Poems. New York: Boni & Liveright, 1928.
Bringing Jazz! New York: Liveright, 1930.
Lights in the Valley. New York: Harbinger House, 1942.
Selected Poems of Maxwell Bodenheim, 1914–1944. New York: Beechhurst Press/Bernard Ackerman, 1946.

NOVELS
Blackguard. Chicago: Covici-McGee, 1923.
Crazy Man. New York: Harcourt, Brace, 1924.
Replenishing Jessica. New York: Boni & Liveright, 1925.
Ninth Avenue. New York: Boni & Liveright, 1926.
Georgie May. New York: Boni & Liveright, 1928.
Sixty Seconds. New York: Liveright, 1929.
A Virtuous Girl. New York: Liveright, 1930.
Naked on Roller Skates. New York: Liveright, 1931.

Duke Herring. New York: Liveright, 1931.

6 A.M. New York: Liveright, 1932.

Run, Sheep, Run. New York: Liveright, 1932.

New York Madness. New York: Macaulay, 1933.

Slow Vision. New York: Macaulay, 1934.

OTHER WORKS

The Gentle Furniture-Shop. Drama 10:132–133 (January 1920).

Cutie, a Warm Mama. With Ben Hecht. Chicago: Hecht-shaw, 1924.

"To a Revolutionary Girl." *New Masses,* April 3, 1934, p. 38.

Seven Poets in Search of an Answer: Maxwell Bodenheim, Joy Davidman, Langston Hughes, Aaron Kramer, Alfred Kreymborg, Martha Millet, Norman Rosten. A poetic symposium edited by Thomas Yoseloff. New York: Bernard Ackerman, 1944.

"Recordings of Poets Reading Their Own Poems: Maxwell Bodenheim." Library of Congress Recording Laboratory PL 24. June 1, 1945. (Eleven poems.)

My Life and Loves in Greenwich Village. New York: Bridgehead Books, 1954. (Memoir attributed to Bodenheim but ghostwritten by Sam Roth and/or David George Kin.)

The Left Bank Revisited: Selections from the Paris Tribune, 1917–1934. Edited by Hugh Ford. University Park: Pennsylvania State University Press, 1972. (Includes articles by Bodenheim.)

The Provincetown Players: A Choice of the Shorter Works. Edited by Barbara Ozieblo Rajkowska. Sheffield, U.K.: Sheffield Academic Press, 1994.

PAPERS

Maxwell Bodenheim Papers, 1917–1981 [bulk dates: 1917–1938]. Rare Book and Manuscript Library Collections, Columbia University.

CRITICAL AND BIOGRAPHICAL STUDIES

Anonymous. "Poetical License: Bard Seeks Shelter in Cellar to Translate Chinese Poetry." *Washington Post,* June 30, 1917, p. 6.

Charney, Maurice. "Maxwell Bodenheim and the Theater." *Journal of the Rutgers University Library* 21, no. 1:42–47 (1957).

Day, Dorothy. "Max Bodenheim." *Catholic Worker,* March 1954. http://www.catholicworker.org/dorothyday/reprint2.cfm?TextID=663

De Voe, Edward T. "'A Soul in Gaudy Tatters': A Critical Biography of Maxwell Bodenheim." D.Ed. thesis, Pennsylvania State University, 1957.

Hecht, Ben. *A Child of the Century.* New York: Simon & Schuster, 1954.

———. *Letters from Bohemia.* New York: Doubleday, 1964.

———. "Mr. Winkelberg." In his *A Thousand and One Afternoons in Chicago.* 1922. Chicago: University of Chicago Press, 1992. Pp. 39-43.

Kennedy, Jeffery. "The Artistic Legacy of the Provincetown Playhouse, 1918–1922." Ph,D. dissertation, New York University, 2007.

———. "The Gentle Furniture-Shop." 2007. http://www.provincetownplayhouse.com/gentlefurnitureshop.html

———. *Knot-Holes,* 2007. http://www.provincetownplayhouse.com/knotholes.html

Kenton, Edna. *The Provincetown Players and the Playwrights' Theatre, 1915–1922.* Edited by Travis Bogard and Jackson R. Bryer. Jefferson, N.C.: McFarland, 2004.

Kotynek, Roy, and John Cohasse. *American Cultural Rebels: Avant-Garde and Bohemian Artists, Writers, and Musicians from the 1850s Through the 1960s.* Jefferson, N.C.: MacFarland, 2008. Pp. 65–67.

Lee, Lawrence, and Barry Gifford. *Saroyan: A Biography.* Berkeley: University of California Press, 1998. Pp. 90–91.

Maeder, Jay, ed. "Matters Unannounced: The Poet, 1954." Chap. 120 in *Big Town, Big Time: A New York Epic, 1898–1998.* New York: Sports Publishing, 1998. P. 126.

Mangione, Jerre. *The Dream and the Deal: The Federal Writers' Project, 1935–1943.* Syracuse, N.Y.: Syracuse University Press, 1996.

Mariani, Paul. *William Carlos Williams: A New World Naked.* New York: W. W. Norton, 1990.

Monroe, Harriet. "Maxwell Bodenheim." *Poetry,* March 1925, pp. 320–327.

Moore, Jack B. *Maxwell Bodenheim.* New York: Twayne, 1970.

———. "Maxwell Bodenheim." In *American Novelists, 1910–1945.* Edited by James J. Martine. *Dictionary of Literary Biography.* Vol. 9. Detroit: Gale Research, 1981. Pp. 69–77.

Murphy, Brenda. *The Provincetown Players and the Culture of Modernity.* Cambridge, U.K., and New York: Cambridge University Press, 2006.

Murphy, Russell. "Maxwell Bodenheim." In *American Poets, 1880–1945: First Series.* Edited by Peter Quartermain. *Dictionary of Literary Biography.* Vol. 45. Detroit: Gale, 1986. Pp. 46–52.

Parry, Albert. "Young Giants in Chicago." Chap. 16 in his *Garrets and Pretenders: Bohemian Life in America from Poe to Kerouac.* New York: Dover, 2012. Pp. 187–199.

Phillips, Louis. "Maxwell Bodenheim's Harlem Slang." *Verbatim* 15, no. 2:16 (autumn 1988).

Ravitz, Abe C. "Assault with Deadly Typewriter: The Hecht-

Bodenheim Vendetta." *Cabellian* 4:104–111 (spring 1972).

———. "Maxwell Bodenheim." In *Lives of Mississippi Authors, 1817–1967.* Edited by James B. Lloyd. Jackson: University Press of Mississippi, 1981. Pp. 42–45.

Sacks, Arthur Bruce. "The Necessity of Rebellion: The Novels of Maxwell Bodenheim." Ph.D. dissertation, University of Wisconsin, Madison, 1975.

Untermeyer, Louis. "Maxwell Bodenheim." *Modern American Poetry.* New York: Harcourt, Brace, 1919.

Van Doren, Mark. "Bodenheim." *Nation,* June 6, 1923, p. 668.

Watmough, David. *Myself Through Others: Memoirs.* Tonawanda, N.Y.: Dundurn Press, 2008. Pp. 68–69.

Wetzsteon, Ross. "Maxwell Bodenheim: Poems Twenty-Five Cents Each." Chapt. 9 in his *Republic of Dreams: Greenwich Village, the American Bohemia, 1910–1960.* New York: Simon & Schuster, 2002. Pp. 380–390.

Yagoda, Ben. "Maxwell Bodenheim: Catastrophe and Corrective." *Boulevard* 10, nos. 1–2:199–209 (spring 1995).

REVIEWS

Davenport, Basil. "A Violent Blast." *Saturday Review of Literature,* September 5, 1931, p. 105. (Review of *Duke Herring.*)

Deutsch, Babette. "Two First Books." *Little Review* 6:65–68 (May 1919). (Review of *Minna and Myself.*)

"Duke Herring." Book Review Digest, 1931, pp. 110–101.

Geddes, Virgil. "A Lyrical Travesty." *Poetry,* February 1924, p. 281. (Review of *The Sardonic Arm.*)

Gorman, Herbert. "Sui Generis." *Saturday Review of Literature,* June 18, 1927, p. 912. (Review of *Ninth Avenue.*)

Hansen, Harry. "Incurable Intelligence." *Nation,* April 16, 1924, pp. 441–442. (Review of *Crazy Man.*)

"Hell's Kitchen." *New York Times,* December 12, 1926. (Review of *Ninth Avenue.*)

"Ninth Avenue." Bookman 64:735 (February 1927).

"The Sardonic Arm." Bookman 58:83 (September 1923).

Seaver, Edwin. "Not So Slow." *New Masses,* September 25, 1934, p. 25. (Review of *Slow Vision.*)

"Sixty Seconds." Outlook, March 27, 1929, p. 514.

Spector, Herman. "Beautiful but Dumb." In *Bastard in the Ragged Suit: Writings of, with Drawings by, Herman Spector.* P. 28. (Review of *The King of Spain,* from *New Masses,* July 1928.)

Untermeyer, Louis. "The Impulse of Irony." *Bookman* 55:635–636 (August 1922). (Review of *Introducing Irony.*)

HANNAH WEBSTER FOSTER

(1758—1840)

Sarah L. Peters

HANNAH WEBSTER FOSTER is best known as author of one of the most popular early American novels, *The Coquette*. In fact, only two best-selling novels were published in the United States before the nineteenth century—including Susanna Rowson's *Charlotte Temple*—both written by women and both telling stories of virtuous women seduced, ruined, and abandoned by immoral and disreputable men. In a period when people expressed skepticism of the merits of fiction, some even condemning novel reading as sinful, the print culture worked to meet great demand for these stories. Foster walked a thin line between appealing to the unsavory and prurient interests of the public and promoting moral, Christian behavior among young women. In *The Coquette* as well as in her second novel, *The Boarding School*, Foster offers a portrait of women's lives in postrevolutionary America as they worked to define their roles in the new republic and find ways to make their voices heard.

LIFE

Foster's parents were Grant Webster, a Harvard-educated and financially successful merchant, and Hannah Wainwright, the daughter of Captain John Wainwright of Haverhill, Massachusetts. The two were married in Haverhill in May 1739, and (despite a conviction of premarital fornication, for which they paid a fine of ten shillings each) they were well known and respected in their communities of Haverhill and then Salisbury, where Hannah Webster was born September 10, 1758, the sixth of seven children. When young Hannah was only six years old, her mother died, and many scholars speculate that she was sent to boarding school for care and instruction. While little is known about Foster's childhood,

her second book, *The Boarding School*, demonstrates a deep understanding of the educational system of late-eighteenth-century America likely gained through direct experience. What is known for certain is that Foster was educated and well read, as indicated by the historical and literary allusions in her two novels, and that she was known in the educated circles of Boston, where her family moved in the early 1760s. Family documents suggest that Foster wrote political articles for local periodicals, but the common practice of anonymous publication, especially of women's writing, makes that claim difficult to confirm.

On February 15, 1785, Hannah Webster married the Reverend John Foster, a Dartmouth graduate and pastor of the First Parish Church in Brighton. A newspaper account of the marriage described an enthusiastic welcoming of the young couple and admiration of the new Mrs. Foster. The couple made their first home at 15-17 Peaceable Street, where Foster began her duties as a minister's wife overseeing the construction of the First Church Parsonage at 10 Academy Road, where they moved in 1790. Foster gave birth to six children between 1786 and 1796; her first child died soon after birth. As leaders of the only church in Brighton and members of some of the oldest families in Massachusetts, the Fosters were at the center of Brighton's social life. A visit from the Fosters would have been an important event in the lives of community members. One local resident, Mary Ann Kingsley Merwin, wrote that her parents spent a week preparing for a visit from the couple, an occasion that provoked as much anxiety as celebration. Always under the eye of the congregation, Foster would have been subject to scrutiny and criticism, and she gave voice to the pressures and rewards of the clerical

lifestyle in her first novel. While she was admired by many, some saw her as distant, snobbish, or pretentious for her visible spending—on large houses, for example—and patronage of arts and education as well as her apparent preference for associating with the gentry. While her husband's career promised a modest income, they had a substantial fortune, likely from her family inheritance.

While maintaining the many responsibilities of a minister's wife and mother to young children, Foster published two novels in a short span of time, one in 1797, titled *The Coquette; or, The History of Eliza Wharton; A Novel: Founded on Fact*; the other in 1798, titled *The Boarding School; or, Lessons of a Preceptress to Her Pupils*. Both books were written in epistolary form, ideal for writing short, distinct pieces over a long period and combining them later. References to current events, however, indicate that she was actively composing and revising her manuscript for *The Boarding School* just a few months before its publication. If she used material written earlier in her life, she added to it substantially after marriage and motherhood. The reason she published only two books is unknown, but it is possible that she turned her time and attention to the education of her children and preferred to publish small pieces in local periodicals.

Foster's literary interests were well known, but her books were published anonymously, attributed to "A Lady of Massachusetts." Although the 1791 novel *Charlotte Temple* carried Susanna Rowson's name on its title page, many other American and British women of the late eighteenth and early nineteenth century published under pseudonyms, "A Lady" the most common choice. Anonymous publication offered some protection of an author's reputation, an especially appealing option for a prominent minister's wife already open to public scrutiny. The active controversy over women's novel reading, thought by many to waste time and hinder the good judgment and virtue of young women, along with the scandalous subject matter of *The Coquette,* certainly opened Foster to accusations of impropriety, and a few such opinions were published

in New England periodicals that reviewed the popular book. As Blevin Shelnutt points out, however, variations in the marketing of *The Coquette* suggest that Foster's authorship was not entirely anonymous. The book's title page identifies her as "A Lady of Massachusetts," a moniker that reveals some identifying information even as it withholds her name. Later advertisements for the book, appearing in a variety of newspapers and magazines, added small details, including her proximity to Boston and her marriage to a clergyman. Many famous female writers have chosen to write under a masculine pen name in an effort to compete and be taken seriously in a male-dominated print market. Emphasizing female authorship, rather than disguising gender, employed femininity and social standing as a marketing device, especially in the case of Foster, whose identity as the author of *The Coquette* was widely known in her lifetime. Novel writers and readers alike had to be cautious about their reading material as romances were believed to inspire unrealistic expectations in young women, influence poor decisions in the marriage market, and make them vulnerable to the devices of a well-spoken seducer. Identifying the author as a "Lady" implied respectability and status, assuaging some of those negative associations while at the same time claiming the authority of the female sensibility, more attuned to the emotions that drove such stories. The inclusion of the author's state of residence enhanced the marketability as well. Readers were drawn to the works of a local author and enticed to speculate on her true identity. Because Foster's novel was based on a true story that had piqued the interest of readers across the country, identifying her as a lady of Massachusetts, where the actual events had taken place, had the added appeal of suggesting access to privileged information related to the case. Even after she published her second book and her authorship of both was widely known, Hannah Foster's name did not appear on her novels. Editions of *The Coquette* published in 1855, 1866, and 1874, long after the author's death, identify Foster in a "Historical Preface" but retain her pseudonym on the title page. The first edition to list Foster's name under the title

HANNAH WEBSTER FOSTER

of *The Coquette* was published by Herbert Ross Brown in 1939.

Although she published no other books after 1798, Foster continued her extensive reading and intellectual activities, keeping abreast of current events, encouraging local writers, and promoting education of young men and women. She appears to have inherited a substantial fortune from her father, who died August 30, 1797, and she oversaw the building of an impressive mansion on Seaver Lane, which later became Foster Street. Foster also used her wealth to support local schools and maintain an impressive library, from which she would lend books to her young neighbors. From *The Boarding School*'s idealized portrait of a female intellectual community, of mutual affection and support among the students and loving guidance from the preceptress, the reader can draw conclusions about Foster's own commitment to education. Her three daughters became writers themselves, and several of her granddaughters pursued literary endeavors, suggesting that her sons carried a commitment to female education into their own families. Foster financed the Harvard education of Phineas Adams, a young man from Boston who, after his graduation, founded the *Monthly Anthology; or, Magazine of Polite Literature*, later called the *North American Review*. The fact that Hannah Foster, not her husband, was known as Adams' patron suggests that Foster had control of her own money and possibly that she participated in Adams' literary projects herself, contributing to the periodical, still under anonymous authorship.

John Foster retired from his clerical position on October 31, 1827, after long tensions led to a division of his congregation, but Hannah Foster continued to be visible and active in the community. In April of 1829, Hannah Foster was noted as an attendant at the founding meeting of the Brighton Ladies Club, the first Massachusetts women's club. On September 16 of that year John Foster died and was buried in Brighton. After her husband's death, Foster made a bequest to the Massachusetts Historical Society and then left Brighton, destroying her personal papers at some point, perhaps concerned with family privacy. She moved to Montreal, Canada, to live with her

daughters Eliza Lanesford Cushing and Harriet Vaughan Cheney, who were authors, editors, and Unitarian activists. She was also near the surviving family of her deceased daughter, Hannah White Barrett. Hannah Foster died on April 17, 1840, and was buried in Montreal at Saint Andrew's Presbyterian Church.

ELIZABETH WHITMAN: INSPIRATION FOR THE COQUETTE

Claims to truth were a common convention of novels in Foster's time, but in the case of *The Coquette*, the subtitle, *Founded on Fact*, was famously accurate. Foster was the second author to write a fictionalized account of the life of Elizabeth Whitman, a woman whose mysterious death became a newspaper sensation in the summer of 1788. Whitman was born into a pastor's family in Hartford, Connecticut, in 1752. Her well-connected family included associations with politicians, ministers, and educators throughout New England. Whitman herself was a poet whose work was published in newspapers alongside accounts of her death. Her remaining correspondence and her friends' recollections portray her as a witty, well-read, and charming young lady. She saw plenty of young suitors before becoming engaged to Joseph Howe, a young minister who fell ill and died in 1775, with Elizabeth caring for him in her parents' home for weeks. It is rumored that she was also engaged to Joseph Buckminster, another clergyman, in 1778 but did not marry him.

In the early summer of 1788, more than ten years after the death of her father, Elnathan Whitman, the thirty-six-year-old Elizabeth left her family's home to travel to Boston. She changed carriages along the way and traveled, instead, twenty miles north to Danvers, Massachusetts, where she checked into the Bell Tavern under the name of Mrs. E. Walker. She told the people she met at the inn that she was waiting for her husband, but a husband never came. Those who met her recalled her as a cheerful, educated lady of a respectable family who spent her time in reading and needlework, but she told them little else about herself. A few weeks after arriving in

Danvers, Whitman gave birth to a stillborn child. Locals who had attended her childbirth and cared for her tried to send for her family, but Whitman would give them no information and destroyed all personal papers that might reveal her true identity. She died two weeks later, on July 25.

Whitman was buried in Danvers, and on July 29, 1788, an article about her death was printed in the Salem newspaper, asking for help in identifying the unfortunate woman. Other papers throughout New England picked up the story, and the effort to identify the stranger became an opportunity to spin her tale into a moral lesson for other young women. When the public learned that the stranger was Miss Whitman from a respected family in Connecticut, curiosity only intensified as readers sought an explanation for her tragic fate. Most famously, the Revered Jeremy Belknap in Boston wrote to the physician Benjamin Rush in Philadelphia a letter that was published in at least nine newspapers describing Elizabeth Whitman as a sensible and genteel woman who had, through the dangerous habit of reading romances, fallen into the fatal sins of vanity and coquetry, turning down advantageous offers of marriage until she had become an old maid. Once past her prime, she sacrificed her virtue and made the fateful errors that left her pregnant, alone, and finally, dead. Others read Whitman's story with much more sympathy, remembering her as a beautiful, intelligent, and lively woman who was dear to her friends and ever faithful to her lover, protecting his name and reputation even when he did not come to her in the end. She became something of a romantic heroine; young women wept over her story, and lovers visited her grave to pledge their undying commitment to each other.

Whitman's remarkable story, already well known across the country, appeared in the first American novel, William Hill Brown's *The Power of Sympathy*, published in 1789. Eight years later—after the death of Whitman's mother in November of 1797—Hannah Foster's fictionalized account of the story was published in Boston. Foster drew on speculation about the various characters in Whitman's life, especially the father of her child, whom Foster based on the

poet Joel Barlow. Whitman and Barlow had been acquainted and exchanged correspondence for years, and Whitman dedicated a New Year's Day poem to him in 1783, two years after Barlow married Ruth Baldwin. Foster's book was incredibly popular, and many readers assumed that Foster was related to Whitman and had privileged information that had not been released in the newspapers. Many people even took the letters printed in the novel to be the authentic correspondence of Elizabeth Whitman. In an introduction to the 1855 edition of *The Coquette*, Jane Ermine Locke connected Foster and Whitman explicitly, claiming that Foster's position as Whitman's relative and a clergyman's wife placed her, by necessity, in the company of the actual people involved in the story. In fact, Foster was only distantly related to Whitman, and her elaboration on the details of Whitman's life were from Foster's own imagination. *The Coquette* intensified public interest in Whitman and inspired stage adaptations as well as a sequel titled *Clara Wharton,* written by William R. Hayden in 1851, which imagines the life of Eliza Wharton's daughter, this time surviving her lost mother. The public fascination with Elizabeth Whitman continues; a celebration of her life and the unveiling of a new tombstone was held in Peabody (formerly Danvers), Massachusetts, in 2004.

THE COQUETTE

Foster's first novel tells Whitman's story in the letters of the fictional protagonist, Eliza Wharton, and her associates. Because public opinion about romance novels was controversial—the books sold well, but were criticized for promoting unrealistic and immoral ideas about heterosexual relationships—Foster's appropriation of a true story allowed her to claim a moral value for the book. Didactic books, intended to teach lessons about appropriate behavior to young men and women, were common in eighteenth-century America and England. Elizabeth Whitman's life story had, as explained above, already been used in that context, reproduced in periodicals and books as a cautionary tale about the dangers of

delaying marriage, trusting a well-spoken charmer, surrendering virtue, and, of course, reading novels. Foster's book anticipates and resists criticism not only by presenting itself as a true story intended for the improvement of readers, but also by adding to the rhetoric denouncing dangerous literature. When Eliza loses her suitor and bemoans the direction her life has turned, her friend Lucy chastises her for her dramatic and impractical response. "Your truly romantic letter came safe to hand," Lucy writes in Letter XLIX. "Indeed, my dear, it would make a very pretty figure in a novel. A bleeding heart, slighted love, and all the *et ceteras* of romance enter into the composition!" (p. 84). If Eliza's behavior is inappropriate within the context of *The Coquette*, then Foster's readers have a chance to see Eliza's error and avoid that corrupting influence themselves.

Eliza is a young woman whose fiancé has just died from a long illness, freeing her from an engagement that she entered under the wishes of her parents, not out of love or personal choice. Newly emancipated, Eliza wishes to enjoy her youth without further demands that she find a husband, but her friends and family have other plans. As her friends conspire to match her with the respectable Reverend Boyer, whose occupation and temperament match closely those of Eliza's deceased fiancé, Eliza herself becomes infatuated with Peter Sanford, a handsome and sociable charmer but a known rake, a man whose word cannot be trusted, especially when given to a lady. Sanford's reputation raises concerns, but his personality seems more compatible with that of Eliza, who enjoys parties, dancing, and flattery a bit more than her friends believe is prudent. Recognizing that he has a rival in the contest for Eliza's affection, Sanford sets out to seduce the young woman with no plans to actually marry her. When Boyer discovers them in intimate conversation, his confidence in Eliza's virtue (but not her chastity) is shaken irredeemably, and he withdraws his affections and offers of marriage. As readers familiar with Whitman's story will expect, Eliza's fate is sealed when she succumbs to the advances of Sanford, by then a married man. Eliza dies, abandoned and ashamed, soon after her stillborn child. While this novel fits squarely within a tradition of sentimental literature in which the surrender of virtue leads to the heroine's death, Foster's retelling of the tale gives readers opportunities to understand the heroine's feelings and motivations. While Eliza's fate remains the same as Whitman's, Foster's story offers a complexity that challenges oversimplified versions of the Whitman story that circulated in the years before *The Coquette*'s debut.

EPISTOLARY FORM AND FEMALE FRIENDSHIP

The subject matter and epistolary form locates *The Coquette* in a literary tradition already active in Europe. *The Coquette* is often compared to Samuel Richardson's *Clarissa Harlow; or, The History of a Young Lady*, an English novel published in 1748. Foster invites such comparison in Letter XIX when Lucy refers to the popular seduction novel and calls Sanford "a second Lovelace" (p. 30), after the fiendish and devious man who preys on the innocent Clarissa. The conventional seduction novel centers on a young, naive female who breaks from her family under the influence of a deceitful male. These books present the value of virtue and the wages of sin, as the seduced heroine, or fallen woman, almost always conceives a child and dies in childbirth, the evidence of her seduction connected inexorably to her demise. Foster's novel stands out among other novels that feature purely innocent female victims, however, as Eliza's flaws and weaknesses, revealed candidly in her letters, are at least partially to blame for her downfall.

In addition to participating in the conventions of epistolary novels, telling the story in letters enhances the verisimilitude of the story; readers can imagine that they are reading the genuine correspondence of Eliza (or even Elizabeth Whitman) and gaining insight into her true feelings as she seeks guidance from her closest friends. This revelation allows the reader to develop sympathy for Eliza, who is presented not as an irresponsible flirt who throws away marriage proposals but as a young woman who struggles to balance her personal desires with her social and familial obligations. When Eliza

expresses her feelings openly and describes her actions honestly, she opens her choices up to scrutiny by her friends and her mother, who might keep her within the bounds of appropriate behavior. Likewise, a lack of communication indicates a break with the social network. When the prolific and enthusiastic letter writer stops writing to her friends and to her mother, her decline is imminent. When her friend Julia Granby begins describing Eliza's action rather than Eliza speaking for herself, it is a sign that Eliza has given up working toward the right choice and has made herself vulnerable to corruption.

A marked difference between her competing suitors is their own willingness to submit to such review. The respectable Boyer remains consistent in his expectations and intentions toward Eliza as he expresses them first to his friend Mr. Selby, and then to Eliza herself. Boyer seeks the approval of General and Mrs. Richman, the close friends with whom Eliza resides for most of the novel, and asks their permission and assistance in courting her. The communication between Boyer and Selby is reciprocal, and Boyer and Eliza exchange several letters as well. Through the act of writing, Boyer submits to a system of social examination that takes for granted an audience broader than the addressee. Several times throughout the novel, letters are shared among friends, specifically for the purpose of soliciting advice and approval, and Boyer's willing participation in this practice ensures his respectability and protects his reputation. Sanford, on the other hand, seeks no one's approval and is reluctant to commit words to paper in his pursuit of Eliza. Sanford's letters to his friend Charles Deighton describe intentions to deceive Eliza and exact revenge on behalf of all men who have fallen under the spell of a coquette, or flirt. Deighton never returns a letter, leaving the reader to wonder if Sanford's plots are approved or merely ignored by his confidant. The open reproach and warnings that come from Eliza's friends are never leveled directly at Sanford, and he actively avoids the presence of the Richmans once he realizes that they discourage Eliza's association with him. Knowing that he is acting outside of acceptable boundaries, courting a woman whom he swears he will never marry, Sanford works to evade the forces that would regulate and censor his behavior. Speech is the medium of seduction; an artful speaker may shape his words in response to his mark, adapting his approach to manipulate her, but leaving no evidence to incriminate himself. Sanford's only letter to Eliza (which she immediately shows to her mother) comes in a moment of desperation, and it is quoted within a letter Eliza writes to Lucy (Letter XLI). Full of pleading questions and dramatic exclamations, the content of Sanford's letter does not make his case for him. Rather, he begs Eliza to meet him in secret so that he may persuade her to reject Boyer. When she meets him, he weeps on his knees to inspire her pity, a sharp contrast to the highly controlled reaction of Boyer, who merely turns and leaves when he finds Eliza with another man. Sanford's resistance to putting his seduction to paper emphasizes his refusal to submit to social and moral order.

In addition to representing a broader social order, the epistolary form highlights the importance of a network of female friends in the life of a young, single woman. The bulk of the novel's letters are between Eliza and Lucy, and once Eliza begins her decline, Julia takes up the correspondence. Within the letters, the close friendship between Eliza and Mrs. Richman is also described. This network of female friends provides support, guidance, and regulation of behavior for Eliza, who is at a crucial moment of transition in her life. As Claire C. Pettengill explains, eighteenth-century American women relied on a complex sisterhood network to navigate the move from daughter to wife and mother. Women were expected to operate within a domestic sphere separate from the public sphere of men. During the premarital stage of life, when a woman begins to develop an identity independent of parental authority, social rituals like dances, dinner parties, and personal visits provided opportunities for women to solidify relationships with other women and to encounter a variety of people who moved within approved social circles, including potential mates who

might meet with the approval of a young woman's watchful friends.

The novel begins as Eliza confesses to Lucy her pleasure at leaving her mother's home to stay with her friends, the Richmans, indicating a break from the parental authority that governed her childhood and obligated her to Mr. Haly. Mrs. Richman is happily established as a wife, and her stable home promises an ideal model of proper living and a setting for Eliza's social development. Lucy, Eliza's constant confidant, is engaged and happy in her match, placing her also in a position to guide Eliza toward accepting adult responsibilities. As the novel progresses, both Lucy and Mrs. Richman advance through significant stages in their lives, Lucy getting married and Mrs. Richman giving birth to, but sadly losing, her first child. Julia, who appears late in the novel, remains unmarried but witnesses Eliza's tragic errors in time to learn from them and avoid them herself. The relationships among these women dramatize the uses as well as the limits of friendship, as those networks are most important and most active in that temporary state between childhood and marriage.

Eliza's stage in life and her uncertainty about entering the next phase of womanhood makes her the character who most needs the direction of her sisters. She reveals her feelings openly even when they might reflect poorly on her, as when she admits in the first letter that she felt admiration but not real love for her deceased fiancé. Honesty in these revelations is necessary, as Eliza says in Letter III: "I must write to you the impulses of my mind or I must not write at all" (p. 6). Knowing her friends will not to abuse her trust but rather advise her lovingly, Eliza opens herself to criticism and takes Lucy's admonishments seriously. Although Eliza is resistant to marriage, after Boyer declares his affection for her, Eliza immediately writes to Lucy, "without a single observation on the subject, until I know your opinion" (Letter XII, p. 21). She also admits her attraction to Sanford even when she knows her good friends are unlikely to approve. In Letter XXVI, Eliza pleads, "Pray write me impartially; let me know your real sentiments, for I rely greatly on your opinion" (p. 42). Advice

from her female friends is a crucial part of Eliza's decision-making process, and her respect for their judgment keeps her for a time out of Sanford's traps.

For their part, Lucy and Mrs. Richmond, and later Julia, criticize Eliza frankly and sometimes harshly, framing their reproaches as the obligations of true friends. Eliza mentions in Letter II that she receives Lucy's response, her "moral lecture rather" (p. 6), and promises to heed her advice; Eliza also gently defends herself against the label of "coquette" that the title of the book and, apparently, her closest friends have applied to her. Advising Eliza to consider Boyer's proposal, Lucy adds that "it is the task of friendship, sometimes to tell disagreeable truths" (Letter XIII, p. 22). But Lucy and Mrs. Richmond do not reciprocate Eliza's openness to sharing her life and receiving criticism; they do not share details of their own lives and Eliza does not attempt to sway their choices. In the social and historical context of the novel, the married women are situated in their appropriate spheres and no longer require the support of the sisterhood network to review and endorse their decisions. Eliza comments on this shift in the function of friendship in conversation with Mrs. Richmond:

> Marriage is the tomb of friendship. It appears to me a very selfish state. Why do people, in general, as soon as they are married, centre all their cares, their concerns, and pleasures in their own families? Former acquaintances are neglected or forgotten. The tenderest ties between friends are weakened or dissolved; and benevolence itself moves in a very limited sphere.
>
> (Letter XII, pp. 20–21)

Eliza's reluctance to graduate from her reliance on female friends to commitment to husband and children is an indication of her immaturity, consistent with her earlier expressed desires to embrace playfulness and youth for a while longer before resigning to become a matron.

As the reader has access to Sanford's candid accounts of his schemes and motives, Foster presents the friends' advice as Eliza's best hope. The centrality of this network is underscored by its consistent effectiveness. Because Lucy has

warned her of his game, Eliza is able to recognize Sanford's rhetorical tricks, as she describes in Letter XIX, and Mrs. Richman's persistent persuasion leads Eliza to cut off contact with Sanford and declare Boyer as her choice. It is only when Eliza begins to hide her behavior from this sisterhood that she falls prey to the seducer. The protective circle of trust is broken and Eliza steps fatally outside the boundaries of socially sanctioned relationships.

MARRIAGE AND INDIVIDUAL LIBERTY

The commitment of the characters in *The Coquette* to their roles within society reflects the larger political philosophy of the new American republic. As one of the earliest works in the newly founded United States, Foster's novel draws not only on British literary traditions with which Americans were most familiar but also on distinctly American notions of personal and social responsibility and, more powerfully, individual liberty. The Declaration of Independence appeals to a belief in natural law and natural rights, including "life, liberty, and the pursuit of happiness," the exercise of which may require a break with established authority. In this spirit, Eliza's first letter claims that she possesses natural inclinations that align her with her parents' wishes, but against their choice of a mate for her. "Both nature and education has instilled into my mind an implicit obedience to the will and desires of my parents," she tells Lucy. "I sacrificed my fancy in this affair; determined that my reason should concur with theirs; and on that to risk my future happiness" (Letter I, p. 4). In this explanation of her consent to marry Mr. Haly, Eliza reveals herself to be a good daughter who submits to parental authority under expected social conventions. At the same time, she claims a natural desire to be matched to someone who is compatible with her personality and temperament. A combined commitment to personal freedom and social responsibility in the new republic, influenced by the social philosophy of John Locke, supported the idea that one should be free to choose a marriage partner, and popular literature of the time, including famous seduction novels, dramatized the negative consequences of a daughter forced to marry an undesired partner. Eliza's letter also reveals a strategy underlying her "risk"; Mr. Haly's poor health allows her to comply more confidently with her parents' wishes knowing that her suitor is unlikely to make it to the altar. Eliza presents this as a kind of trade— she has fulfilled her filial obligations and has been set free by circumstances, specifically the deaths of the two men who had claim on her future: her father and her fiancé.

Before the reader meets Eliza, she is labeled a coquette by the novel's title and by the reputation of Elizabeth Whitman. This first letter, however, complicates this character by presenting her resistance to marriage not in terms of lust or vanity but as a desire for freedom. Foster foregrounds the dominating voices that limit women's freedom, including social, economic, and familial expectations and responsibilities, and she also depicts her title character working within those constraints, balancing compliance and resistance, in an effort to pursue happiness as she defines it. Eliza assures the reader that she has learned valuable lessons about Christian virtue and the fleeting pleasures of mortal life from her clerical mate. She wishes to nurture his influence on her mind and live her life "thoughtful of my duty, and benevolent to all around me." Significantly, she also wishes "for no other connection than that of friendship" (Letter I, p. 5).

Almost married to a man she does not love, Eliza sees marriage only as a confining institution that she is happy to have evaded for a time, and she must actively resist her friends' efforts to match her again quickly. When Mrs. Richman asks Eliza if her heart "is now free" to consider a new suitor, Eliza tells her frankly that she hopes "my friends will never again interpose in my concerns of that nature" (Letter V, p. 10). Like her parents, Eliza's friends are encroaching on her freedom to choose her marriage partner while Eliza hopes to avoid the "shackles" from which she has so recently been extricated. Their warnings against coquetry are employed to exert control over Eliza's behavior and direct her toward a "suitabl[e] and agreeabl[e]" connection

of their choosing, deliberately distancing her from Sanford, the man who promises Eliza the amusement and pleasures of youth (Letter V, 10).

Foster intensifies the threat to Eliza's freedom by emphasizing the added social pressures of a minister's wife, a role that Foster understood well. Boyer is almost a reincarnation of Haly; both men are ministers who profess a great love that Eliza does not reciprocate. The sober personalities of these men are incompatible with Eliza's own vivacity and passion, and their occupations carry with them the scrutiny of the entire community. Her description of this "scene of constraint and confinement" presents not merely a frivolous inclination to pleasure but deep anxiety about the direction of her life, which she expresses directly to Boyer:

> I recoil at the thought of immediately forming a connection, which must confine me to the duties of domestic life, and make me dependent for happiness, perhaps too, for subsistence, upon a class of people, who will claim the right of scrutinising every part of my conduct; and by censuring those foibles, which I am conscious of not having prudence to avoid, may render me completely miserable.
>
> (Letter XIV, p. 23)

The solicited advice from the close female circle, which occasionally includes Eliza's mother, is accepted even when it conflicts with Eliza's own ideas. The judgment of strangers, however, expands the controlling forces in her life farther than Eliza can stand. Her loss of freedom is repeatedly presented not as the desire to deviate from appropriate behavior (she assures Boyer that she wishes to enjoy "the charms of youth and freedom, regulated by virtue and innocence") but as a threat to her sense of self and individual identity (Letter XIV, p. 23). Readers familiar with the republican rhetoric of liberty and natural rights can sympathize with the heroine for whom the marriage market provides no desirable options. Boyer is rigid and bland and no match for Eliza, as her friends refuse to acknowledge.

Foster elicits sympathy for Eliza's view of marriage, but through her artful use of the epistolary form she provides multiple perspectives on the same events, complicating the narrative and its implied values. While the reader may identify with Eliza's desire for freedom, her characterization of marriage as an instrument of confinement is aligned disturbingly with Sanford's stance. In a frank confession to Deighton, Sanford says that Eliza "would make an excellent wife" but he hopes to "keep out of the noose" as long as possible. "Whenever I do submit to be shackled, it must be from a necessity of mending my fortune" (Letter XI, p. 19). The repeated language of constraints and imprisonment, this time in a much more sinister context, foreshadows the danger that awaits Eliza if she continues her acquaintance with Sanford. His perspective on marriage is further aligned with Eliza's by his admission of economic hardship. Despite his great attraction to her, Sanford cannot marry Eliza because she is not wealthy enough to support him. As a middle-class woman and daughter of a widow, Eliza also needs an economically beneficial match. Women in the eighteenth century had little opportunity to support themselves financially, so just as social convention and familial obligations coerced her to marry, so did economic necessity. The very reason that Eliza must marry is the reason that Sanford cannot marry her—she has no money or means of earning it.

If Boyer represents a bad match for Eliza, Sanford is worse. Sanford has more emotional depth than conventional villains of seduction novels, and he expresses earnest regret and shame at his behavior after he knows that Eliza is dead, writing to Deighton, "I am undone! Misery irremediable is my future lot!" (Letter LXXII, p. 129). However, before he reaches this degree of self-awareness, he admits to deliberate deception aimed at keeping Eliza single. Sanford cites Eliza's reputation for coquetry as justification for his games, which he calls vengeance. As he gains more access to her, he determines to have revenge on the friends who deter his designs and on his rival, Boyer. Eliza has employed strategies to maintain a degree of freedom allowed by her social circumstances, but she is always honest, more so than the label "coquette" suggests. Sanford's strategies to remain free are based on

lies and deception, and he intentionally victimizes women to serve his needs. Standing as the emblem of immoral behavior that threatens virtue, he also provides an example of the worst kind of marriage. After he succeeds in ruining Eliza's relationship with Boyer, Sanford submits to the "noose" and marries another woman for her money. He feels no love for his wife and expresses no grief or sympathy when she gives birth to a stillborn son. His marriage dissolves after he loses his wife's fortune and commits adultery with Eliza. Foster's development of the two men in Eliza's life contributes significantly to the complex and sympathetic portrait of the heroine/victim. Eliza's choice is not between obedience and defiance, nor is it between coquetry and marriage. If her choice is between Boyer, with whom she feels incompatible, and Sanford, who only wants to manipulate and use her, she is in a bind, indeed.

Foster balances these negative depictions of marriage with some positive examples, most prominently the Richmans, whose marriage embodies the political values of the new republic. The seduction novel's popularity in early America was due in part to a sense that the young nation was vulnerable to corrupt influences that might threaten the union. The nuclear family was understood as a crucial institution, a microcosm of the country, that strengthened, supported, and perpetuated republican values. Scholars often use the term "republican motherhood," coined by the historian Linda K. Kerber in her essay "The Republican Mother: Women and the Enlightenment—An American Perspective," to describe the role of women in the early American social structure. Contrary to earlier Puritan beliefs that women were inherently lustful and corruptible, late-eighteenth-century American Christianity, influenced by Enlightenment values, understood women as good and virtuous, ideal for raising young children with moral principles and a sense of civic duty. Marriage and motherhood were patriotic missions, carried out in the domestic sphere, ensuring the future of the nation by raising boys to be community leaders and girls to be a new generation of republican mothers. Appealing to these principles, education for females was significantly expanded based on the belief that a good wife and mother needed a broad foundation in the liberal arts to support a well-informed democracy.

Although Mrs. Richman is not yet a mother, she and General Richman embody the ideal marital relationship. Eliza observes their compatibility and companionship right away and admits to some envy and hope on watching them together: "Happy pair, said I. Should it ever be my fate to wear the hymenial chain, may I be thus united! The purest and most ardent affection, the greatest consonance of taste and disposition, and the most congenial virtue and wishes distinguish this lovely couple.... They have no satisfaction to look for beyond each other" (Letter VI, p. 12). Eliza's appreciation for the happy union of her friends indicates to the reader that she is not opposed to marriage and that she can imagine herself in a marriage based on friendship and love. The stability of the Richmans' marriage is enhanced by Mrs. Richman's own knowledge of literature and politics, which she demonstrates "judiciously, yet modestly" in the company of her guests (Letter XXIII, p. 35). When one of the female guests suggests that women should remain silent on the subject, Mrs. Richman argues persuasively that because women are affected by politics, they should share their observations and opinions, within the appropriate context:

> We shall not be called to the senate or the field to assert its privileges, and defend its rights, but we should feel for the honor and safety of our friends and connections who are thus employed. If the community flourish and enjoy health and freedom, shall we not share in the happy effects? If it be oppressed and disturbed, shall we not endure our proportion of the evil? Why then should the love of our country be a masculine passion only?
>
> (Letter XXIII, p. 35)

Through the character of Mrs. Richman, Foster develops an image of a virtuous, education, civically active woman, working within the bounds of her role. Eliza's participation in the conversation (impressive to Boyer but worrisome to Sanford, who cannot hold his own in such intellectual

discussion) indicates her own potential to mature into the role of the republican wife, a contrast to the foolish Mrs. Laurence, who casually dismisses political discussion.

This important scene illustrates an underlying theme of the novel, that of freedom enjoyed within prescribed limits. As Eliza repeatedly connects marriage to loss of freedom, her friends remind her that appropriate freedoms can exist within marriage. Mrs. Richman states frankly that Eliza has "wrong ideas of freedom, and matrimony" (Letter XIV, p. 24), and Lucy encourages Eliza's connection with Boyer, echoing his own defense of himself: "A man of Boyer's honor and good sense will never abridge any privileges which virtue can claim" (Letter XV, p. 24). More specifically, when Eliza writes to her mother about her concern that she cannot live up to the expectations of a minister's wife (those fears increased by Sanford's suggestions of the same), Mrs. Wharton draws on her own experience as well as republicanism to assuage her daughter's fears. "No class of society has domestic enjoyment more at command than clergymen.... With regard to its being a dependent situation, which one is not so? Are we not all links in the great chain of society, some more, some less important; but each upheld by others, throughout the confederated whole?" (Letter XXI, p. 33). Through Lucy, Mrs. Richman, and Mrs. Whitman, Foster depicts marriage as a potentially positive institution, when entered wisely, and connects marital union to broader social responsibilities. In this context, the appeal to liberty and pursuit of happiness must be tempered by prudence. Sanford is associated repeatedly with pleasure and diversion, a self-centered and irresponsible definition of liberty. His behavior costs him economically, socially, and personally, and this seductive version of freedom persuades Eliza, against the advice of her friends and her own better judgment. Foster's story is a warning against liberty without restraint, a lesson relevant not only to impressionable young women but also to the young nation. True sustainable freedom must be exercised responsibly with the needs of others and the good of the community in mind.

THE BOARDING SCHOOL

Foster's second book, *The Boarding School*, also published anonymously, was not a best seller and has received much less critical attention than *The Coquette*. It does not include the engaging plot and real-life scandal that has continued to draw readers to the first novel, but it does provide a fascinating picture of women's education in the eighteenth century and develop some of the themes introduced in *The Coquette*, like the dangers of seduction, the importance of female friendship, and the uses of fiction. *The Boarding School* has no coherent plot. It is composed of a series of farewell lectures from a preceptress to her students, followed by letters exchanged among the graduates after they leave the school. It is part epistolary fiction and part conduct book, an explicitly didactic genre consisting of instructions in virtuous behavior. The opening setting of the novel is Harmony Grove, a boarding school opened by Mrs. Williams, the widow of a clergyman who wishes to provide financial security and good company for her two daughters. To her seven students, Mrs. Williams intends to impart lessons on the virtues of "piety, morality, benevolence, prudence and economy" (p. 138). She focuses her attention on the improvement of their private, domestic lives and to teach them to avoid the pitfalls of vanity and frivolity.

The Boarding School was published at a time when boarding schools were criticized for distancing girls from their domestic duties and education. The moral precepts and the letters exchanged among the girls defend these educational institutions for discouraging coquetry and superficiality and preparing well-informed women for domestic responsibilities. The instructor's lectures offer lessons in categories conventional for conduct books—reading, manners, dress, and filial and fraternal affections—but the letters that follow present a dialogue among the students as they question and negotiate the application of their lessons to their own experiences in the premarital stage of life that makes female friendships so valuable to character development. While the centrality of friendship is similar to that represented in *The Coquette*, there is comparatively little concern with marriage. The girls

of Harmony Grove are more concerned with finding reading material to improve their minds than with finding a husband. Harriot Henley, in a letter to her classmate Cleora Partridge, expresses quite serious concerns about marriage and speculates that the revelry of a wedding celebration works to distract the party from the seriousness of the commitment and the risk the couple undertakes, considering the number of unhappy marriages unforeseen in the midst of romantic optimism., Harriot answers that the two girls might commit to each other to remain single and together "retrieve *old-maidism* from the imputation of ill nature, oddity, and many other mortifying charges" and as a result "save many a good girl from an unequal and unhappy marriage" (p. 202). This exchange, while not endorsed by the teacher, indicates that the idealized environment of the girls' school has provided students with the tools to imagine their lives beyond the limited domestic sphere and to see single life as opportunity rather than failure or tragedy.

In addition to proposing expanded acceptance of single women, *The Boarding School* teaches sympathy for and obligation toward their sisters who are led astray by seducers. In a lecture on love, Mrs. Williams criticizes coquettes for their improper conduct, and in her lesson on music and dancing, she warns that excessive indulgence in superficial diversions makes young women vulnerable to seducers. She balances these admonitions with appeals to her pupils to have compassion for those who have surrendered their virtue. Responsibility to female friends is held as one of their highest obligations, and while the girls are taught to guard themselves against romantic ideas and deceptive men, they are encouraged to reach out to comfort troubled friends and restore fallen women to the watchful care of their loved ones. While the teacher does offer multiple stories warning against seduction, her lessons impress upon the girls a responsibility beyond protecting their own virtues, suggesting a far-reaching influence that well-raised and well-educated young women may have.

One of the most thorough lessons in the book addresses appropriate reading, through which Foster creates an opportunity to defend her own work as a novelist. Effective reading requires the reader to "enter into the spirit of the subject" in order to benefit from the activity, but that endeavor makes the reader susceptible to the influence of the material. Romance is dismissed immediately as outdated and unappealing. Novel reading—"the most dangerous kind of reading"—is a more complicated concern (p. 143). The captivating style excites the imagination and creates irrational fantasies that distort the reader's view of reality. A "sober, rational courtship" would pale in comparison to the dramatic pronouncements of a fictional hero, making a girl vulnerable to the insincere suitor who can put on a good show (p. 144). The only acceptable novels, then, are those that relate tales of virtue rewarded and vice punished, providing models for prudent girls to imitate or avoid. Reading must not only be for amusement but for moral and intellectual improvement. In this pursuit, girls must incorporate poetry, essays, history, and the Bible alongside their fiction reading, providing a useful context to interpret the wisdom and value of a novel's message.

The emphasis on diverse and methodical reading, as well as education in other subjects, is compatible with the increased emphasis on women's roles in the home and the relationship between the domestic sphere and national values. But the letters that make up the second half of the book expand the possibility of their influence by calling for women's voices to be heard in the world. Laura Guilford, in a letter to Matilda Fielding, acknowledges the stereotype of women as talkative, but insists on the value of her own voice in refusing to let politeness silence her. "Our sex are often rallied on their volubility: and for myself, I frankly confess, that I am so averse to taciturnity, and so highly prize the advantages of society and friendship, that I had rather plead guilty to the charge than relinquish them" (p. 220). Matilda answers with a description of a ladies' party during which a member suggests that they can speak more freely without fear of judgment or criticism because no men are present. Rather than agree, Matilda writes that the highest benefit comes from "mutual interchange of sentiment and knowledge" (p. 221).

Not quite asserting gender equality, Matilda's call for active discussion among men and women rejects the notion that a woman's opinion is less worthy of serious consideration than that of a man. A more powerful assertion of the importance of women's activities and women's voices comes in Sophia Manchester's review of Jeremy Belknap's *History of New Hampshire, and American Biography*, along with the works of Jonathon Swift and Laurence Sterne. Sophia is bold and confident as she engages the voices of these male writers, and she highlights the significant female roles in famous stories of male heroes of American history. She celebrates the generosity and intelligence of Isabella, who made possible Columbus's journey, as well as the compassion and bravery of Pocahontas, who saved the life of John Smith. Though Sophia ends her letter on a note of modesty, "astonished at my own presumption in undertaking to play the critic," her enthusiastic and intelligent engagement of celebrated male authors and masculine historical narratives belies her polite humility (p. 236). The very inclusion of the girls' letters challenges the primacy of the teacher's lectures, defining the most beneficial education as that which empowers the students to apply their own intellect and ethics to develop their own worldview, informed but not confined by the stories and instruction of parental and social authority figures.

Foster's work does not radically challenge eighteenth-century gender roles, but her depiction of the ideal goals and results of female education argues for expanded opportunities for women's ideas and engagement with the world. Any subversive messages attributable to her books are woven subtly into generic forms that privilege a multiplicity of voices rather than a singular, authoritative stance. Foster depicts her characters as engaged in the kind of negotiations she herself had to carry out. Her economic privilege provided tremendous opportunities for her to pursue creative and intellectual endeavors, but she worked within the limits of her social role as a mother and a minister's wife. As author of one of the most significant literary works of the early United States, Foster provides us with stories that ground liberal republican philosophy and revolutionary values in the daily lives of American women. Her imaginative contributions to the genres of the seduction novel and the conduct book give voice to often silenced or marginalized perspectives within a culture that called for liberty but limited women's freedom.

Selected Bibliography

WORKS OF HANNAH FOSTER

The Coquette; or, The History of Eliza Wharton; A Novel: Founded on Fact. Boston: Printed by Samuel Etheridge for E. Larkin, 1797.

The Boarding School; or, Lessons of a Preceptress to Her Pupils. Boston: Printed by I. Thomas & E. T. Andrews, 1798.

The Coquette and The Boarding School. Norton Critical Edition. Edited by Jennifer Harris and Bryan Waterman. New York: Norton, 2013.

CRITICAL AND BIOGRAPHICAL STUDIES

Brown, Gillian. "Consent, Coquetry, and Consequences." *American Literary History* 9, no. 4.625–652 (winter 1997).

Dill, Elizabeth. "A Mob of Lusty Villagers: Operations of Domestic Desires in Hannah Webster Foster's *The Coquette.*" *Eighteenth-Century Fiction* 15, no. 2:255–279 (2003).

Harris, Jennifer. "Writing Vice: Hannah Webster Foster and *The Coquette.*" *Canadian Review of American Studies* 39, no. 4:363–382 (2009).

Hessinger, Rodney. *Seduced, Abandoned, and Reborn: Visions of Youth in Middle-Class America, 1780–1850.* Philadelphia: University of Pennsylvania Press, 2005.

Hewitt, Elizabeth. *Correspondence and American Literature, 1770–1865.* New York: Cambridge University Press, 2004.

Jarenski, Shelly. "The Voice of the Preceptress: Female Education in and as the Seduction Novel." *Journal of the Midwest Modern Language Association* 37, no. 1:59–68 (2004).

Kerber, Linda K.. "The Republican Mother: Women and the Enlightenment—An American Perspective." *American Quarterly* 28, no. 2:187–205 (1976).

Korobkin, Laura H. "'Can Your Volatile Daughter Ever

Acquire Your Wisdom?' Luxury and False Ideals in *The Coquette*." *Early American Literature* 41, no. 1:79–107 (2006).

Pettengill, Claire C. "Sisterhood in a Separate Sphere: Female Friendship in Hannah Webster Foster's *The Coquette* and *The Boarding School*." *Early American Literature* 27, no. 3:185–203 (1992).

Robbins, Sarah. "'The Future Good and Great of Our Land': Republican Mothers, Female Authors, and Domesticated Literacy in Antebellum New England." *New England Quarterly* 75, no. 4:562–591 (2002).

Shelnutt, Blevin. "*The Coquette* and Pseudonymous Attribution." In *The Coquette and The Boarding School*. Norton Critical Edition. Edited by Jennifer Harris and Bryan Waterman. New York: Norton, 2013. Pp. 419–427.

Smith-Rosenberg, Carroll. "Domesticating 'Virtue': Coquettes and Revolutionaries in Young America." In *Literature and the Body: Essays on Populations and Persons*. Edited by Elaine Scarry. Baltimore: Johns Hopkins University Press, 1988. Pp. 169–178.

FRANCISCO GOLDMAN

(1954—)

Carolyn Alessio

W. H. AUDEN WROTE that "mad" Ireland "hurt" William Butler Yeats into writing poetry. The same might be said of the effect of Guatemala's long, gruesome civil war on the prose writer Francisco Goldman.

In both his fiction and nonfiction, Goldman pays vivid tribute to Latin Americans who did not have the opportunity or time to properly shape their own stories. A bicultural writer of Jewish American and Catholic Guatemalan lineage, Goldman explores the rich, freighted relationship between the United States and its Latin American neighbors. In fiction and investigative journalism, the author frequently sifts through accounts of grisly war, premature death, political corruption, and stark class divisions. The alternate narrative that Goldman ultimately portrays is more accurate and wrenching, but at times, also lively and even optimistic. As the author himself admits, he focuses on documenting historical violence and tragedy but remains constantly mindful of the artistic obligation to "balance light and darkness" (Messer). In mining Latin America's (and his own) past, Goldman resurrects troubling but also entertaining *fantasmas*, or ghosts.

Born on May 12, 1954, Goldman is the author of three novels, one book of investigative nonfiction, numerous articles, and a "fictionalized memoir." Also a professor of writing, Goldman is the winner of many literary prizes including a Guggenheim Fellowship. The author best sums up his sprawling, narrative approach in his own description of his first novel, *The Long Night of White Chickens* (1992): "An interrogation through storytelling of all the ways we try to figure out and express the truth, about nation, family, self, identify, love, politics" (Wachtel).

Goldman's artistic goal is decidedly ambitious, but his terrain demands it. As with the work of his literary influences, such as William Faulkner and Gabriel García Márquez, and that of his contemporaries Roberto Bolaño and Junot Díaz, Goldman's writings depict the vivid, daily life of communities as well as the confounding forces that sometimes threaten them. He finds few details too small or absurd to eliminate, such as the kennel-incarceration of a priest's dog that was initially thought to have played a role in the 1998 assassination of Archbishop Juan José Gerardi Conedera—about which Goldman writes in *The Art of Political Murder* (2007). A forensics expert makes the link, but as Goldman reports, the theory is quickly debunked. For a brief time, however, the aging rectory German shepherd is considered a potential accomplice in the murder of the Roman Catholic human rights activist. Goldman likely includes the short, strange episode to demonstrate the general confusion and corruption of authorities. In the process, he underscores the turns in the true-crime case that seem as fantastic as if they came from a folktale.

As with *The Art of Political Murder* and many of Goldman's investigative articles about Latin America, his fiction is also deeply rooted in reality. *The Long Night of White Chickens* is based in part on a shattering event in Goldman's own life and includes characters obviously based upon high-profile Guatemalan intellectuals and businessmen. It also includes an informative primer on Guatemalan history and its pertinent texts. *The Ordinary Seaman* (1997), Goldman's second novel, arose directly from a 1982 incident in an abandoned Brooklyn dockyard that Goldman first read about in the *New York Daily News*. *The Divine Husband* (2004), Goldman's third novel, incorporates the life of José Martí, the

celebrated Cuban intellectual and crusader for independence from Spain. And *Say Her Name* (2011) is Goldman's autobiographical novel/memoir about the tragic, early death of Aura Estrada, his talented thirty-year-old wife.

Goldman, who calls Spanish his "emotional language" (Ortiz), regularly mixes his mother's native language, its sayings and rhythms, into his English prose. He does not limit himself to Guatemalan-specific Spanish, though; he shows an impressive knowledge of myriad Latin American dialects. In *The Ordinary Seaman*, for instance, single conversations among the crew members include phrases and slang from a panorama of countries: Nicaragua, Honduras, Mexico, and Guatemala.

Critics do not have to look far for potent metaphor in Goldman's work. In fact, a *Los Angeles Times* review of Goldman's first novel bore the title "A Metaphor for Guatemala: The Long Night of White Chickens." In the review, the Guatemalan author Victor Perera wrote that Goldman's "candescent material plumbs the lower depths of Guatemala, and Goldman pulls together the threads of the story brilliantly, moving back and forth in time like a nimble Mayan weaver creating an elaborate huipil."

Guatemala may only be roughly the size of Tennessee, but it is a disproportionately large political minefield, according to Goldman. As he points out, the United States, and "gringos" in general, have exerted much more influence on Central America than have other nearby countries like Mexico. As a result of its relative isolation and the opportunism of more dominant countries, Guatemala has suffered at the hands of U.S.-backed armies and remains a "violent, primitive" society, in Goldman's view (Ortiz).

Despite the author's background, he says he did not understand the true duality of his heritage until his early twenties. Growing up outside Boston in an Irish-Italian suburb, Goldman says he was mostly a "naive, suburban American kid" (Jaggi, 2008). His father, descended from a family of Ukrainian immigrants, was inclined toward medical school, but quotas and his Jewish background discouraged it. Instead, he worked as a chemical engineer for a dental products

company. He met Goldman's mother, who was eighteen years younger, at work, where she was employed as a bilingual secretary (*Say Her Name*, p. 133). Their differences in age and culture added to their largely contentious relationship.

Goldman, who was the couple's only son, grew up making frequent trips to his mother's Guatemala. He says that he nearly ended up being raised there, but came down with tuberculosis and had to recover in the United States. Not unlike Oscar Hijuelos, the late Cuban American author, Goldman ended up being rooted in the English-speaking, North American culture because of a chance medical convalescence.

Goldman began to write fiction as an undergraduate, both at Hobart College and at the University of Michigan, where he graduated with a B.A. degree in 1977. While at Michigan, he heard a lecture by the great Argentinean writer Jorge Luis Borges, in which Borges said, "you never end up writing like the writer you imagine yourself to be." Goldman recalled Borges telling the audience that he had always imagined himself writing "like Conrad, Kipling or James" (Allen). Coincidentally, Goldman's future wife, Aura, would be a Borges scholar.

The observations took root in Goldman's memory, but he did not locate his own style and subject until 1979, when a friend sneaked him in to visit a Guatemalan morgue during a particularly savage period in the country's civil war. Previously unaware of the conflicts and carnage between the government and Ladino landowners against the indigenous population, Goldman says he looked around with horror: "There were bodies piled up like firewood," he recalled in a 2008 interview with Maya Jaggi of the *Guardian*. "Some were horribly mutilated, burned with cigarettes, or with their genitals cut off. It was like falling into a bottomless hole I've never completely crawled out of."

Nearly thirty years later, Goldman would experience a similar, shattering moment in his personal life, when his young wife died suddenly in a bizarre body-surfing accident in Mexico. As a result, Goldman would later connect his own experience with post-traumatic stress disorder to

those suffered by many of the war survivors he chronicled (Ortiz).

Goldman's 1979 encounter in the Guatemalan morgue moved him into confronting the ghastly history of the Central American country and reconciling that with its vexed relationship with the United States. He published a short story in *Esquire* that was set in Guatemala. Soon afterward Goldman received assignments to report on the wars in Guatemala and Nicaragua.

"MORO LIKE ME"

For six years Goldman immersed himself in grim reporting, before relocating to Spain in 1985 to begin work on his first novel (he was also recovering from the breakup of his first marriage). Rather than offering a serene refuge from the previous, draining years, Goldman's experience in Madrid unexpectedly ended up demonstrating to him the profound alienation of racial prejudice. His treatment in Madrid prompted him to further consider both his own ethnic profile and his metaphoric place in the world. In his essay "Moro Like Me," collected in *Half and Half: Writers on Growing Up Biracial and Bicultural* (1998), Goldman discusses how Spaniards in Madrid quickly labeled him with disdain as a *moro*, or Moor, a person from Morocco, Algeria, or some other nearby Muslim country.

Despite Goldman's excellent Spanish (and English), he found himself the victim of frequent prejudice. Shopkeepers ignored him or waved him away, taxi drivers drove quickly past his signaling arm, and owners of nightclubs claimed to have "quotas" for the number of *moros* in their establishment. Coming on the heels of covering wars in Central America that involved ethnicity and social class, the experience in Spain prompted Goldman to meditate on the searing and lasting ways that prejudice erodes an individual: "While bigotry is certainly a part of too many people's lives, it feels like the opposite of life … this was all about denying a person's humanity, his very existence, of humiliating and even castrating him every day" (*Half and Half*, p. 57).

Not only is it unnerving to be mistaken for someone else, Goldman writes, but it can be equally complicated to be taken for one's own self. In "Moro Like Me," whose title is likely an allusion to *Black Like Me* (1961), John Howard Griffin's daring autobiography of passing as a black man in pre-civil-rights America, Goldman jumps ahead a few years to an encounter in his hometown near Boston. While promoting his second novel, he is featured in a local newspaper. Goldman is astonished when a classmate from his high school days, a white cheerleader of Irish background, writes to the newspaper to protest that Frank Goldman, as he was then called, could not have been Guatemalan American, because he was "a Jewish kid." It was inconceivable to Goldman's former classmate, and likely others that he had grown up with, that he could have had a more nuanced heritage—and worldview— than they had assumed.

THE LONG NIGHT OF WHITE CHICKENS

In his first novel, *The Long Night of White Chickens* (1992), the author revisits his past by creating the narrator, Roger Graetz. A young man of Jewish American and Catholic Guatemalan heritage like Goldman's, Roger finds himself called upon to investigate the brutal murder of his adopted older "sister." Flor de Mayo Puac is an indigenous Guatemalan teen plucked from an orphanage by Roger's wealthy grandmother to serve as a maid to the family in Boston. Flor's character is based on a former maid for the Goldman family who was murdered in Guatemala (Bach).

Beautiful and resilient, Flor is part Victorian heroine and part poster child for U.S. immigration and education. Her résumé as a character, which Goldman provides quickly at the beginning of the novel, leans toward the fantastic. When Flor arrives in Massachusetts as a teen, Roger's police officer father insists the girl attend school (as she also continues to work part-time for the family). After several years of struggling with English—and suffering the humiliation of having considerably younger classmates—Flor triumphs academically and even wins a full scholarship to nearby Wellesley College. Her

observations of American culture, and of her well-heeled classmates, are engaging and humorous.

After graduating from the prestigious institution, Flor surprises her family and friends by returning to Guatemala, where she becomes the director of a private orphanage and malnutrition center, Los Quetzalitos. Despite the fact that she is literally returning to her roots, nobody else in Flor's circle is completely sure why she chooses this career path. The orphanage is renowned for its many ties to wealthy foreign benefactors. Flor apparently values the children and takes great measures to place them with appropriate families. But four years later, in 1983, she meets a violent demise; she is found murdered in the orphanage, her throat cut. The story generates publicity, and horrible allegations soon follow, contending that the orphanage was actually a "fattening house" (p. 4) for illegally purchased and foreign babies.

In choosing his topics for his first novel, Goldman proved to be savvy and even prescient. In 2012 he would return in his nonfiction to the volatile subject of Latin American orphans and war. In "Children of the Dirty War," an investigative essay published in the *New Yorker*, Goldman examines the lasting effects of the Argentinean military junta during the late 1970s and early 1980s. Approximately five hundred babies and young children lost their parents to military violence and were illegally adopted, sometimes even by their parents' military assassins.

Such narratives of murder and illegal adoptions in Latin America are better known today, but in 1992 Goldman was one of only a few writers working in English to bring such matters to the literary public. With Flor, his first major heroine, he takes on potentially moralistic themes but manages to balance them with Flor's perceptive, energetic, and even caustically witty character. As a young, new immigrant in Boston, she finds her way around by sheer pluck, even in a major blizzard. In college she provides sage commentary about her Wellesley classmates. And when strangers hear about her unusual background, Flor has no time for admiration and especially not pity. "Not exactly the Helen Keller story, you know what I mean?" she quips (p. 132).

Flor's unusual background and innate understanding of dual cultures makes her privy to a unique, complicated worldview. She also inhabits different social classes, and this rarified position sometimes makes both Flor and the others around her uncomfortable. In fact, when she is still in school in the United States and accompanies Roger and his mother back on a short visit to Guatemala, Flor eats her meals in the kitchen with the maid. Everyone reacts with discomfort, and the irony is not lost on either Flor or Roger. In one particularly vivid memory, Roger recalls Flor calling out a brutal critique of Guatemalan society—all from the kitchen.

Later, as an adult living in Guatemala, Flor contemplates her two countries' cultures in an equally astute but more measured way. In her letters to Roger, which he scours for clues after her death, Flor comments on the disparities between the two countries, and the way that history and past sorrows weigh differently on them: "You would not ever sum up your understanding of the United States over a cup of coffee or two and then find yourself weeping over it.... *Triste*—that is much too flea sized a word to ever apply to the United States. Guatemala is bottomless grief in a demitasse" (p. 177).

Like Flor, Roger is a cultural interlocutor. As he later learns, his sister has been involved with two significant Guatemalan men, one likely modeled on an actual Guatemalan entrepreneur/ newspaper publisher and the other on an up-and-coming intellectual and journalist with ties to a revolutionary group. As Victor Perera points out, the latter is likely Julio Godoy, whom Goldman knew and thanks as "Julio" in the introduction, bemoaning his exile from his native country.

While Flor claims the center of the novel, Roger is the indispensable narrator-detective. The novel becomes a bildungsroman in terms of his development and maturation, but it is also a shrewd introduction to Guatemalan history. Flor's murder propels Roger into a full-scale investigation of both her life and the country's roiling political climate. Just as Roger discovers the inconsistencies in his sister's life, he also begins to grasp his own convoluted cultural legacy:

Origins such as mine—Catholic, Jewish, Guatemala, USA—can't always exist comfortably inside just one person ... the easiest thing is to just ignore it.... But what if you're not the ignoring type? Then you've been born into a kind of labyrinth, you have to pick and choose your way through it and there's no getting back to the beginning because there isn't any one true point of origin. Flor used to tell me to think of it as a great opportunity.

(p. 185)

The Long Night of White Chickens won the 1993 Sue Kaufman Prize for First Fiction from the American Academy of Arts and Letters and also was named a finalist for the PEN/Faulkner Award. Reviewers in the United States and Europe largely praised the book for its depth and fearless confrontation of basic, moral questions. For Goldman, the book did more than establish his career as a fiction writer; it offered catharsis and a foundation for his future work. As he told Caleb Bach of *Americas* magazine in 2005, "As a young writer I had an ambition to grow more, to know more, to bring my two worlds together. I went to Central America to immerse myself in a war, and that war was such an overwhelming experience that for almost six years I didn't write fiction. I tried, but *Long Night* was my way to see if fiction could bring me out of this horrible morass of politics."

THE ORDINARY SEAMAN

Goldman's second novel, published in 1994, also concentrates on characters who straddle boundaries, both physically and culturally. A 1982 article in the *New York Daily News* sparked the idea for Goldman. Seventeen Central American sailors had been abandoned for months on a decrepit ship on the Brooklyn waterfront, without plumbing, electricity, or sufficient food. The scurrilous owners who lured the mostly young sailors there with promises of good pay had only a minimal, shady registry for the ship. They also reneged on pay, and as a result, the Nicaraguan and Costa Rican sailors were essentially marooned. The only way to escape and cross over to terra firma took them through a neighborhood with a history of violence, and a few feckless sailors who attempted this route were physically attacked.

The story of the displaced, immigrant sailors and the doomed, ghostly ship attracted Goldman. He researched the story thoroughly, first by visiting the infamous ship and later conducting long interviews with the actual crew. He even named one character, an older sailor, "Bernardo," after an especially informative crew member, who in the book meets with a more macabre end. In his research, Goldman traveled for a month aboard a ship for Mexican Maritime Transportation. As Goldman demonstrated in *The Long Night of White Chickens*, he understands his responsibility to create convincing, detailed settings and characters for his readers.

The ship, named the *Urus*, is a conscious metaphor for Goldman. He describes it as the "perfect literary vessel: *Heart of Darkness* backwards, with brown men coming to the big white jungle. An urban Robinson Crusoe, a modernist Beckett, like the Odyssey, but the ship doesn't go anywhere" (Jaggi, 2008).

The sailors in *The Ordinary Seaman* come to their assignment with high hopes as well as painful personal stories. Esteban Gaitán, the main third-person narrator, is nineteen years old but has the brutal memories of a much older man. A veteran of a Sandinista antiguerrilla group in Nicaragua, he carries with him the arresting image of his comrade and former lover, Marta, who perished in gunfire. Esteban also secretly carries her watch. Other crew members, hailing from Honduras and Guatemala, are initially united in their optimism about their anticipated job and journey but soon find despair rather than dignity.

As in Latin American literature and the larger culture, the men soon have picaresque nicknames. Canario, or "Canary," has a high, twittering voice and ends up sniffing paint solvent with other crew members. Caratumba, or "Tomb Face," is Guatemalan, and gets his nickname both from his reserved demeanor and, as Goldman writes grimly, a "well-known joke all over Central America that Guatemaltecos are only born to give their army more people to murder" (p. 17). The purser, Panzón, or "Big-Belly," tries to conduct

himself as though the ship was an actual, working concern. He is bedeviled, however, by the fact that the ship's only clock no longer works because a rat made it into a nest, breaking off the hour hand.

Rats continue to appear on the vulnerable ship, in literal and human forms, until they make a striking exodus late in the novel. Early on, a dead rat is discovered in the ship's heavily used water supply. The ship's owners, Elías and Mark, the few part-"yanqui" characters, are pampered and woefully ignorant about nautical matters. They become increasingly callous about the situation and sometimes even take on a sneering tone. To Goldman's credit, however, he sketches them a bit more fully by showing them away from the wharf and interacting with their lovers and offspring. Elías, it turns out, has surprising experience as a homeopath, and attempts to use herbs to cure the men of maladies ranging from sickness derived from drinking rat-tainted water to more serious wounds.

The multinational marooned crew is a paradigm of the plight of illegal immigrants. Onboard, the owners tell them, they are "Panamanians." Ashore, they have only expired visas and the prospect of braving rough, struggling neighborhoods. Jobless and nationless, the men increasingly turn toward escape, however risky. Early on, a group of the men foray onto land for the night and end up badly beaten in the nearby housing projects, which the shipowners have haughtily warned them to avoid because of "los blacks."

Some of the men end up addicted to sniffing paint solvent. Esteban, however, manages to figure out a circuitous route to alternative (and respectable) employment in Brooklyn, as well as Latino friends and a steady lover. Throughout, the men continue to surprise each other and even themselves.

"From details like cats that perform tricks (and sometimes return as ghosts) to grand thematic matters like the pathos and stupidity of death, from the kindness of strangers in Brooklyn to the vapidity of artsy yuppies in Manhattan, from jungle war to ghetto hope, *The Ordinary Seaman* contains multitudes," wrote Robert

Houston in a review in the *New York Times.* "Sharp satire, warm humor and tenderness are all comfortably within Mr. Goldman's ken."

Goldman cuts the sheer desperation of the situation with vivid, sensual memories as well as humor, which consists of the men's endless ribbing of each other. Their moments of unity and conflict flesh out the story of the modern-day Ancient Mariner's "skeleton" crew. The men banter in an appealing way, filled with idiom, endearments, and merciless teasing. Goldman, who has said he strives to write "English sentences that sound like Spanish" (Jaggi, 2008), dazzles with his easy use of country-specific phrases and idioms.

The Ordinary Seaman, with its extraordinary story, captured several international distinctions, including the Los Angeles Times Book Prize in Fiction, and the novel was named a finalist for the International IMPAC-Dublin Literary Award. Like *The Long Night of White Chickens*, Goldman's second novel was also a finalist for the PEN/Faulkner Award.

"THE AUTUMN OF THE REVOLUTIONARY"

Despite Goldman's focus on fiction, he managed to find time to continue writing journalism about timely, often controversial, subjects and people. In 1998 he published a profile in the *New York Times Magazine* of Daniel Ortega, the founder of the 1980s Sandinista Liberation Front and the elected president of Nicaragua from 1984 to 1990 and again beginning in 2007. Called "The Autumn of the Revolutionary," in a play on the title of García Márquez's novel *The Autumn of the Patriarch*, Goldman's piece considers the long, sometimes celebrated career of the Nicaraguan leader as well as his presidential defeat in 1990 and the accusations of sexual abuse from his daughter.

The article is more subdued in tone than much of Goldman's political writing (and fiction, to an extent), perhaps owing to Ortega's uncomfortable political situation and the overall predicament of Nicaragua, a country which then suffered from 60 percent unemployment, diminished

literacy rates, and the disappearance of free health care. Setting the scene, Goldman notes the faded, past-tense glory of Ortega's former empire. He describes the comandante as fit, however, and potentially looking for renewed causes. Ortega, however, is quoted minimally, possibly due to agreements with his press agent about limited responses to inquiries about the controversial charges.

Another, behind-the-scenes fact may have influenced the overall muted tone of Goldman's piece: his tape recorder malfunctioned, and his interview with Ortega failed to be recorded. As Goldman admitted in 2007 to Silvana Paternostro of *BOMB*, it was fortunate he had a good memory. And the other interviews he conducted for the piece were not only successfully taped but provided him with important, moving material.

THE DIVINE HUSBAND

In Goldman's third novel, *The Divine Husband* (2004), he moves back more than a century to take on 1870s Central America and New York. Mixing historical figures and events with imagined ones, Goldman takes readers through the lives of two women closely involved in events in turn-of-the century Latin America—with its plantations, religious and military upheaval, and artistic and intellectual salons—as well as in entrepreneurial New York.

The scope of the four-hundred-plus-page novel is vast and even epic, but the overall tone is a bit more jocular than in Goldman's first two novels. The narrator even jokes around a bit with readers, and challenges them as well: "What if we read history the way we do love poems, or even the life stories of sainted Sacred Virgins?" the researcher-narrator asks in the opening.

María de las Nieves ("of the snows") Moran is the inimitable and determined protagonist. Part Mam Indian and part New York Irish, María is discovered as a child living a nearly feral existence in the remote mountains of an unnamed Central American country. Physically she bespeaks a mixture of backgrounds and ideologies:

she has rust-colored hair and cinnamon-colored skin.

The novel follows the wildly adventurous life of María, who is "rescued" from her remote mountain life and brought to live at the home of the Aparicio family. Prominent, Liberal criollos, the family owns a successful coffee plantation, or finca. They represent the growing entrepreneurial class of turn-of-the-century Central America (here, likely Guatemala). Young María conveniently becomes close to young Paquita Aparicio, who will also turn out to have a memorable role in history. Only, even members of the entrepreneurial class, who stake their fortune on coffee and cochineal (a beetle that produces dye), are not immune to pressure from the taciturn government.

When a much-older revolutionary named Justo Rufino (a reference to the historical Guatemalan president Justo Rufino Barrios) shows interest in eleven-year-old Paquita, the Aparicio family sends their daughter and María away to a cloistered convent school. Still, in a sign of the vulnerability of the Church to political climate, the revolutionary eventually manages to begin a secret correspondence with Paquita, who teasingly refers to her formidable admirer as "El Anticristo," or "the Antichrist." Soon after María attempts to end the secret correspondence between her bosom buddy and the Antichrist (as well as a pledge of virginity), the convents are closed suddenly (and the Jesuits driven from the country), and the military suitor has the opportunity to propose.

The historically modeled revolutionary becomes president (and cruel dictator), marries Paquita, and the two have seven children. Of course, given the cycles of overthrow in the country, it is not a complete shock when he is executed. Eventually Paquita and the children (along with María and her daughter) move to New York, which is experiencing its own fin-de-siècle restlessness and growth.

Through the lives of María and Paquita, readers experience the surge and suppression of revolution (and religion) in late-1800s Central America. As women, they are under pressure to align themselves with a partner—whether it be

the nun's theoretical husband, Jesus, or the all-too-real swashbuckling Antichrist. However, not only the women are pressured into making loaded alliances. The novel's title literally refers to the nickname of José Martí as the "husband of Cuba" (Jaggi, 2005).

Exiles and those in danger of exile dominate the novel, adding tension and a heightened desperation to the plot. The most dashing exile is Martí himself, a founding poet of Hispanic American modernism and revolutionary for Cuban independence. In 1877–1878 he spent eighteen months in Guatemala. In including him in the novel, Goldman picked up on Guatemala's long-standing veneration of the author-revolutionary. As recently as spring 2013, the country erected a statue of Martí with fanfare in the capital city. Another statue of Martí stands in New York's Central Park, where he lived for approximately sixteen years not long after his time in Guatemala. "La Niña de Guatemala," one of Martí's most famous poems, alludes to an enamored young woman who dies of a broken heart because her *enamorado* (likely Martí) has another lover. The source of the passionate poem is said to be the daughter of a famous revolutionary. As Goldman has remarked in interviews, the poem remains a part of common culture in Guatemala.

While Goldman includes many elements of Martí's actual life, he also uses him as a conduit in a fictional story. In the novel, he is both inspiration and a potential source of danger (with his very own undercover—and antic—Pinkerton detective following him around New York). As a teacher of night lessons in composition for women, he meets María in a salon-like atmosphere. She has been working as a translator for the British embassy and quickly becomes bewitched by the poet.

Eventually María becomes the mother of Mathilde, a daughter, though she coyly keeps secret the identity of the child's father. She loses her job at the embassy and stoically endures ridicule as a fallen woman, à la Hester Prynne. Martí is held up as a definite possibility for paternity; in one scene, María's childhood friend and benefactress asks her outright about an afternoon spent with the dashing figure, but a shaken María remains mum.

As with *The Ordinary Seaman*, characters constantly escape situations as well as identities in *The Divine Husband*. One of the more compelling figures, Don José, is a sage umbrella mender and "Polish-English-Hebrew immigrant from Manchester who now went by the perverse-sounding surname of Pryzpyz instead of his birth one of Ginsburg" (p. 134). Wise about matters as disparate as world history, politics, and the manufacture and uses of India rubber, Don José also becomes the confidant of restless, promising young people, including María de la Nieves. Don José also befriends Mack Chinchilla—a.k.a. Marco Aureliano Chinchilla, Mack Caleph, Cohen, or Nahón—an enterprising young (and half-Indian) man from New York who is obsessed with María, attracted by her reputation and past. Mack follows María and Mathilde back to New York, where he becomes a leader in the rubber trade.

Some critics argued that the multiple story lines and intricate language clutter the novel unnecessarily. "Goldman weaves airborne imagery through almost Dantean permutations into the narrative, but all this poetry crushes the characters' psychology," wrote the reviewer Lee Siegel in the *New York Times*. Other critics, like Maya Jaggi of the *Guardian*, argued that "Goldman's lyricism saves this lengthy book from its sometimes meandering and obsessive detail."

As with Goldman's previous novels, *The Divine Husband* is brimming with factual information, on topics ranging from the process of growing cochineal beetles for ink to the writings of the mystic Sor María de Ágreda, an actual nun from the seventeenth century known for her ability to pray for heathens in far-flung places. Faith is strength too for María de la Nieves, at least during the first portion of the book, as well as a potential way to prevent her best friend from continuing her marriage with "the Antichrist." When the thirteen-year-old María officially enters the convent, she even takes the name Sor San Jorge, "Slayer of Dragons, Defender of Virgins" (p. 1).

Goldman focuses much more on religion in *The Divine Husband* than in his previous novels, particularly in the first section, but the shift is not too surprising considering the time period he was chronicling. In addition, while Goldman worked on the novel he was simultaneously writing the nonfiction book *The Art of Political Murder: Who Killed the Bishop?* As he remarked to Maya Jaggi, in contrast to the weighty, nonfiction account, writing *The Divine Husband* felt "almost girly and sweet, an antidote to the darkness of the case."

THE ART OF POLITICAL MURDER: WHO KILLED THE BISHOP?

Goldman spent nine years covering the notorious 1998 murder of the Guatemalan bishop and prominent human rights activist Juan José Gerardi Conedera. Published in 2007, his detailed detective story, linked to the genocide of the war, is told in a compelling narrative that nevertheless includes moments of hope and even humor. In fact, the book opens by establishing the bishop as a well-known raconteur, a teller of funny stories. *Chistes*, or jokes, Goldman informs us in the opening paragraph, are admired in the ordinarily reserved society of Guatemala as a "defense against fear, despair, and the loneliness of not daring to speak your mind" (*The Art of Political Murder*, p. 3).

Four days before Bishop Gerardi was attacked and beaten to death in his home, he presided over the momentous release of a long-awaited report on the two hundred thousand victims of the thirty-six-year civil war. *Guatemala: Never Again!* was four volumes and produced by the Recovery of Historical Memory Project, which Gerardi had overseen as founding director of the Guatemalan Archdiocese's Office of Human Rights. The unprecedented project had been compiled over two years, with some eight hundred people interviewing and collecting testimony in fifteen Mayan languages and Spanish (p. 6).

Goldman writes that the seventy-five-year-old bishop firmly believed that the report was "crucial for repairing the country's shredded social fabric and for ensuring that human rights abuses would no longer be protected by an official culture of silence and lies or by a legal system that effectively gave certain institutions and sectors of society carte blanche to commit crimes" (p. 7). At the formal presentation of the report, which had sections on "The Impact of the Violence" and "The Mechanisms of Horror," the Metropolitan Cathedral was filled with a formidable audience. Diplomats, politicians, members of nongovernmental organizations, former guerrillas, journalists, human activists, and others sat in the audience. The only seeming absence, Goldman notes, was the government of the then-president of Guatemala, Álvaro Árzu Irigoyen.

The audience, as well as its absent members, set the stage effectively for Goldman's engrossing—and haunting—story of a man whose bold, cold-blooded murder is inextricably linked to the violent deaths of two hundred thousand others. The bishop, a liberation theologian who had already survived one assassination attempt, was particularly beloved by Guatemalans. The day before his funeral, a crowd of twenty thousand marched through the streets as a protest against the murder.

The tense, vivid book is as much a detective story or police procedural as it is a tour of the leading agencies of power in Guatemala, including law enforcement, the military, the government, and human-rights and truth commissions like the United Nations Verification Mission, the Recovery of Historical Memory Project, and the Guatemalan Archdiocese's Office of Human Rights.

The Art of Political Murder began with Goldman's 1999 article in the *New Yorker*, "Murder Comes for the Bishop," which he originally was assigned without assured publication, or "on spec" (p. 66). Critics have compared *The Art of Political Murder* to Truman Capote's *In Cold Blood* (1966) and to García Márquez's *News of a Kidnapping* (1996), an investigation of the 1990s kidnappings of prominent Colombians by the drug lord Pablo Escobar's Medellín cartel. (Goldman has also taught at the school founded by García Márquez, the Institute of New Journalism in Colombia.)

Guatemala's civil war officially ended with the 1996 peace accords. The military largely received amnesty, a fact that was widely questioned. In Goldman's 1996 *New York Times* editorial about the amnesty, "In Guatemala, All Is Forgotten," he wrote with passionate indignation:

> Guatemala's commission will be allowed to report on who died or disappeared and perhaps under what circumstances, but it will not be allowed to investigate who committed this violence. The Guatemalan Armed Forces and the guerrillas have negotiated a law forgiving themselves for 36 years of crimes that sear the heart and stupefy the mind, and are asking their fellow citizens to believe that this is the gateway to the rule of law in a new democratic society.... The amnesty, passed last week by the rightist-dominated National Assembly, is essentially a political act sealed by a few individuals concerned with their own reputations and perquisites, not to mention their possible legal vulnerability.

Bishop Gerardi and his team created their report in a valiant attempt to find a fact-based way around the limitations of the accords. Scrupulously researched and translated, "Guatemala: Never Again!" alleged that 80 percent of the brutal assassinations of the primarily indigenous victims could be traced to the military and not to guerrilla insurgents supported by ethnic Mayans and peasant Ladinos. Yet the publication of "Never Again!" held out the possibility of finding ways around the amnesty in order to prosecute specific individuals.

Organizations associated with the Roman Catholic Church, Goldman tells us, were uniquely qualified in eliciting honest narratives from the survivors of the war and widespread carnage. To offer a sense of the atrocities, Goldman includes excerpts from eyewitnesses that echo the horrors of the Holocaust. "The two-year-olds were all pressed into a tight ball, and they were set on fire all pressed together, into a ball, all the children were burned" said a survivor of an army massacre in Huehuetenango (p. 24).

Gerardi, generally known for his good humor, had expressed a desire that the grisly accounts would "enter readers through their pores" (p. 23). Similarly, Goldman enables readers to experience Gerardi's bludgeoning death in his own home, and its prolonged, chaotic aftermath.

Early in the writing process of *The Art of Political Murder*, Goldman decided that he could not take on the immense task of tracing the endemic violence of Guatemala's civil war. "Once you start with that in Guatemala, you end up in a labyrinth of arguments about how responsible were the Guerrillas for the violence that occurred in the '80s, whether it really was a genocide, what's in the peace accords ... all these kinds of tangential questions that people who cover Guatemala and write about Guatemala can argue about forever," he told Silvana Paternostro in 2007. "I decided I would stay away from all that, and just make this case and the unfolding of what is essentially, after all, a detective story—who killed the bishop?—metaphorically speak for everything."

Goldman simultaneously builds tension for the reader and interprets enormous amounts of background information on the military, government, and overall bureaucracy of the country. Though the murder-related events take place in a relatively confined physical space in the heart of Guatemala City, Goldman defines several distinct arenas for the investigation. He acknowledges the large "cast" at the back of the book by including a helpful listing of characters under the heading "Dramatis Personae" (p. 359).

Despite Goldman's diligent reporting on numerous leads, large and small, he does not employ the more circuitous storytelling techniques of *The Divine Husband*. He does, however, manage to include the palpable physical descriptions and poetic language that animate his fiction. Noting the looming (and usually inactive) volcanoes in the distance, Goldman vividly portrays the murder scene of downtown Guatemala City, a "uniquely ugly place" that resembles a "vast, grimy old cemetery" at night (p. 6). The book provides us with a physical map at the beginning of the book as well as a portrait of the usually busy Plaza Nacional.

Goldman's own investigation relies equally on clues and character. As if assembling a police lineup, Goldman trots out the colorful and formidable array of suspects and informants, including a priest-roommate of Gerardi, Colonel Byron Disrael Lima Estrada (and Colonel Lima's

son, a captain), Sergeant Major Obdulio Villanueva, and members of the Presidential Guard who had once helped foil a supposed assassination attempt on Arzú and his wife. Villanueva was imprisoned as a result of gunning down the would-be assassin but was inexplicably let out of prison for a few hours the night of the bishop's murder.

Other suspects include a group of a group of indigents, the *bolitos*, who regularly slept outside the palace at night. To some of the investigators, the *bolitos* as well as members of local street gangs served as convenient fall guys. But Goldman made a point of getting to know them and, ultimately, extracting key information. Goldman even takes the reader through a list of their picaresque nicknames, reminiscent of both the Turks in *Don Quixote* and the crew members aboard the *Urus* in *The Ordinary Seaman*. The author becomes quite familiar with them, especially Rubén Chanax, or "Curly," a likely military informant.

In covering the 2001 trial that lasted several months, Goldman shows us even more action offscreen than on. He follows suspects, members of the military and law enforcement, and individuals associated with other important cases.

Goldman also fleshes out some members of the media as well the investigators, especially a memorable group of four young professionals referred to as the Untouchables or "Los Intocables." The idealists, men in their twenties, devote endless hours to the investigation. Their work is somewhat vindicated in the trial and the sentencing of the two Limas and Villanueva, but the young investigators also meet with retribution. After the trial, the younger brother of one of the Untouchables (the only litigation lawyer working for the Office of Human Rights) is tortured and killed. The murder method mimics crimes perpetuated against the Indian victims of the war— the young man's limbs are torn from his body before he is shot.

More than ten people associated with the case were killed, according to Goldman. He himself lived with the possibility of danger, and he says that he is "glad" that the book scares people because "the danger was relentless for the people who were working on the case and living with it" (Paternostro).

Widely admired by critics across the world, *The Art of Political Murder* made lists for best books of the year in the *New York Times, Washington Post Book World, Chicago Tribune, Economist*, and others. It was praised by acclaimed writers such as Eduardo Galeano, Richard Ford, and Junot Díaz. Some even theorized that Goldman's book may have helped discredit President Árzu, who was not reelected.

SAY HER NAME

Say Her Name (2011) is also a wrenching meditation on memory and pain, but of a specific, deeply personal kind. In 2001 Goldman's wife of nearly two years, Aura Estrada, died suddenly in a bizarre body-surfing accident in Oaxaca. Aura, who had recently turned thirty, was a brilliant and energetic scholar and artist. She held unusual dual posts: as a graduate student and teaching assistant in the doctoral program of Latin and Spanish literature at Columbia University and as a fellow in the M.F.A. creative writing program at Hunter College. Though young, she had published her scholarship as well as some pieces in academic and popular periodicals—in both Spanish and English. In addition, at the time of her death, Aura had begun writing an ambitious novel set largely in France. Goldman, of course, was biased in his effusive description of her, but Aura's myriad, empirical accomplishments and promise backed up his claims. In fact, he helped to publish two short stories of hers posthumously in prestigious magazines including *Harper's* and *Zoetrope*.

Even though Goldman uses many actual names and events in *Say My Name*, he calls it a "nonfiction novel", and emphatically denies that it is a memoir. In fact, in an interview with CBC Radio, he said that he had never "considered writing a memoir" (Wachtel).

Some critics praised the book but also questioned his intentional melding of fact and fiction. The novelist and reviewer Sylvia Brownrigg wrote in the *Los Angeles Times*: "He keeps

his own and his wife's name the same, and has said that the gripping account of her accident, which appears in the book's harrowing later pages, was just as it happened—leaving a reader to wonder uneasily which of the book's details are real and which invented."

The novelist and reviewer Roxana Robinson of the *Washington Post* echoed Brownrigg's points, describing the powerful book as more memoir than novel and likening it to Joan Didion's *The Year of Magical Thinking* (2005) and Joyce Carol Oates's *A Widow's Story* (2011). "Regardless of form," she writes, "Goldman shares their dark territory."

Another, more practical possibility for Goldman's unusual labeling of the book could be legal protection: as he says early on, Aura's mother threatened to sue him for failing to sufficiently protect her daughter. In fact, on the first page of the book, Goldman informs the reader that Aura's mother and uncle accused him of being responsible for her death. If he were Aura's mother, he says, he would have wanted to put himself in prison, too: "Though not for the reasons she and her brother gave."

Just as Aura struggled with reconciling her analytical and theoretical skills with her artistic aims, Goldman tries repeatedly to make some sense out of the sudden, quick demise of his larger-than-life bride. Memories, clear, fractured, and perhaps even manufactured, float through this haunting book. *Say Her Name* shows the couple's contented past together, down to the names of music stores and delis they used to visit together. The book also portrays Aura's girlhood in Mexico City as the only child of a single mother who had ambitions for her daughter as a renowned academic in French. As Juanita, her mother, had hoped, Aura excelled academically (even if her chosen area was Latin and Spanish literature). By the time she was thirty, she had studied at the respected National Autonomous University of Mexico, the University of Texas, and Brown University before she even came to New York. In between her stints in Mexico and the United States, she also studied in France, where she would set her future novel.

Goldman traverses the literal landscape of Aura's past, but takes his investigation a step further by including scenes he has conjured for the novel she had to leave unfinished after just two chapters. Aura had chosen as a setting a famous, experimental utopian asylum in France, and by the end of the book, Goldman goes there in a moving effort to finally deliver his wife's memory to her planned site of research.

In *Say Her Name*, Aura's voice bursts through the text in a variety of ways, from snippets of her quirky, insightful prose to her lively comments and philosophies. One mock-scolding refrain that Goldman often heard regarded her assertion that she did not get married to eat lunch by herself, or to spend time by herself. The saying becomes especially painful as Goldman thinks ruefully of the times that he could not break away from his work on projects such as *The Art of Political Murder*. Perhaps ironically, *Say Her Name* is his chance to spend an entire book with her.

Not surprisingly, Aura and Goldman's life together centered on narratives. As with many newly enamored couples, especially those devoted to literature, Goldman and Aura delighted in telling each other their stories. Goldman takes this somewhat routine habit of couples, and combines it with an imagined future together, in which they even have the child they had planned—a girl, named Natalia.

Goldman, who has spent part of every year since 1995 in Mexico, actually met Aura, a native of Mexico, in the United States at the book release of a mutual acquaintance who had published a book in Spanish. In describing his instant smittenness—and later, its continuation—Goldman admits that his enthusiasm was almost puppylike, or childlike. Despite his years of covering long, macabre wars, and having a first marriage fail (not to mention the vivid memories of his own parents' contentious marriage), Goldman realized that he was still essentially a romantic: "I really was the kind of person who believed that this was the way it happened: at the most unexpected moment you met somebody, there was a magical connection, and your life changed" (p. 44).

Named after the title character of Carlos Fuentes' magical realist ghost story, Aura (and her memory) hovers over *Say Her Name*. In one scene, Goldman even thinks he senses her spirit in a tree, smiling down on him. Also hovering over the book is Aura's promise, her likely future as a successful artist and critic, as well as her fears she would never truly succeed.

In many ways, the book is a battle between Goldman's instinctive, forensic reporting and his desire to sketch a detailed alternate world. The two competing forces animate the narrative, but sometimes also pull it in distracting directions. With this method, Goldman likely wants the reader to feel his disorientation after Aura's death, and his somewhat scattered attempts to seek solace, or achieve a sense of understanding, or both.

In reflecting on *Say Her Name* in a conversation with fellow author Junot Díaz, Goldman said that the essential conflict he faced in writing concerned "the traumatic reality versus the dream of another reality. I think that's a fundamental conflict for me. The reality of death versus the dream of life … I'm probably pretty happy by nature, yet, as for so many others, the reality has often been cruel, incomprehensible, sad, overwhelming, whatever. I'd always dreamed of loving and being loved and had rarely experienced it, and when I finally truly did, it was taken away in an instant" (Messer).

Despite the heartrending sadness of the book, Goldman manages to stay true to his personal writing dictum of providing at least some sources of levity and light. He includes humorous anecdotes about Aura, such as the time her mother sent her, as a thirteen-year-old, to a summer camp in Cuba. Her mother had hoped to stamp out Aura's youthful communist tendencies, but instead young Aura reported having entertained herself by making out with boys from Denmark.

In addition to writing *Say Her Name*, Goldman created a lasting tribute to his young wife and her unrealized promise. In 2009 he established the Aura Estrada Writing Prize, for a woman aged thirty-five or younger from Mexico or the United States and writing in Spanish. The *Boston Review*, where Aura had published shortly before her death, also holds the annual Aura Estrada Short Story Contest. Finally, in 2009, a collection of Aura's writings was published in Spanish. Called *Mis días en Shanghai /* (My Days in Shanghai), the book includes both fiction and essays, and quickly garnered praise.

As Goldman shows with *Say Her Name*, as well as *The Art of Political Murder* and his more autobiographical fiction, he is sadly adept at memorializing people who depart in abrupt and seemingly unfair ways. His prose serves as a permanent requiem that gathers unrealized life stories and promise, sets them loose in readers' imaginations, and gives them life again.

Selected Bibliography

WORKS OF FRANCISCO GOLDMAN

BOOKS

The Long Night of White Chickens. New York: Atlantic Monthly Press, 1992.

The Ordinary Seaman. New York: Atlantic Monthly Press, 1997.

The Divine Husband: A Novel. New York: Atlantic Monthly Press, 2004.

The Art of Political Murder: Who Killed the Bishop? New York: Grove Press, 2007. (Nonfiction.)

Say Her Name. New York: Grove Press, 2011.

ARTICLES AND ESSAYS

"In Guatemala, All Is Forgotten." *New York Times*, December 23, 1996. http://www.nytimes.com/1996/12/23/opinion/in-guatemala-all-is-forgotten.html

"The Autumn of the Revolutionary." *New York Times Magazine*, August 23, 1998. http://www.nytimes.com/1998/08/23/magazine/the-autumn-of-the-revolutionary.html?pagewanted=all&src=pm

"Murder Comes for the Bishop." *New Yorker*, March 15, 1999, p. 60.

"The Wave." *New Yorker*, February 7, 2011, p. 54.

"Children of the Dirty War." *New Yorker*, March 19, 2012, p. 54.

"Moro Like Me." In *Half and Half: Writers on Growing Up Biracial and Bicultural*. Edited by Claudine C. Hearn.

New York: Pantheon, 1998. Kindle Edition, 2013.

REVIEWS

Brownrigg, Sylvia. "*Say Her Name* by Francisco Goldman." *Los Angeles Times*, May 15, 2011. http://articles.latimes.com/2011/may/15/entertainment/la-ca-francisco-goldman-20110515

Curiel, Carolyn. "Murder in Guatemala." *New York Times Sunday Book Review*, September 30, 2013. http://www.nytimes.com/2007/09/30/books/review/Curiel-t.html

Houston, Robert. "Barely Afloat." *New York Times*, March 16, 1997. http://www.nytimes.com/books/97/03/16/reviews/970316.16houstot.html (Review of *The Ordinary Seaman*.)

Jaggi, Maya. "Mongrel River." *Guardian*, May 6, 2005. http://www.theguardian.com/books/2005/may/07/featuresreviews.guardianreview17 (Review of *The Divine Husband*.)

Mullan, John. "Zone of Anecdotes." *London Review of Books*, February 17, 2005. http://www.lrb.co.uk/v27/n04/john-mullan/zone-of-anecdotes

Perera, Victor. "A Metaphor for Guatemala: *The Long Night of White Chickens* by Francisco Goldman." *Los Angeles Times*, July 19, 1992. http://articles.latimes.com/1992-07-19/books/bk-4382_1_long-night-of-white-chickens

Robinson, Roxana. "Book Review: Francisco Goldman's *Say Her Name*." *Washington Post*, April 14, 2011. http://www.washingtonpost.com/entertainment/books/book-review-francisco-goldmans-say-her-name/2011/03/22/AFGTz5eD_story.html

Siegel, Lee. "*The Divine Husband*: Grand Illusions." *New York Times*, September 26, 2004. http://www.nytimes.com/2004/09/26/books/review/26SIEGELL.html?pagewanted=1

INTERVIEWS

Allen, Esther. "Francisco Goldman." *BOMB*, summer 2004. http://bombsite.com/issues/88/articles/2665

Bach, Caleb. "Francisco Goldman: Writing Astride Two Worlds." *Americas* 57, no. 4 (July 2005). http://www.thefreelibrary.com/Francisco+Goldman%3A+writing+astride+two+worlds%3A+raised+between...-a0133946767

Jaggi, Maya. "A Path in the Darkness: Francisco Goldman." *Guardian*, February 1, 2008. http://www.theguardian.com/books/2008/feb/02/featuresreviews.guardianreview12

Messer, Miwa. "Back into the Abyss: Junot Díaz and Francisco Goldman." *Barnes and Noble Review*, September 11, 2012. http://bnreview.barnesandnoble.com/t5/Interview/Back-into-the-Abyss-Junot-D%C3%ADaz-and-Francisco-Goldman/ba-p/8849

Ortiz, Sara. "Francisco Goldman." *Bodega* 11 (July 2013). http://bodegamag.com/articles/70-francisco-goldman-an-interview-conducted-by-sara-ortiz

Paternostro, Silvana. "Francisco Goldman." *BOMB*, December 2007. http://bombsite.com/issues/999/articles/3068

Wachtel, Eleanor. "*Say Her Name* and Writer Francisco Goldman." Writers and Company, CBC Radio, November 27, 2011. http://www.cbc.ca/player/Radio/Writers+and+Company/2013/ID/2397452456/

LEV GROSSMAN

(1969—)

Scott Earle

IN THE DARK days of the Blitz, many Londoners sent their children to the relative safety of the British countryside. But the gap between urban and rural cultures was wide, and, incredibly, "naughty" children were sometimes sent back— back to London and Hitler's buzz bombs. Such was the fate of a young girl named Judith Spink, who fortunately survived her return. Much later, her son Lev Grossman would describe a scene much like those she might have experienced: "It looked like [Quentin] remembered pictures from the London Blitz looking. There was no roof, and most of what had been the second floor had fallen in and lay in ruins on top of the first. The floor was awash with paper, stirred in slow circles by the wind" (*The Magician King*, p. 295). Though born into a poor part of London, Spink would go on to attend Oxford, where, at the famous Eagle and Child (or "Bird and Baby") pub, she met C. S. Lewis. Finding that she was about to sit for her oral exams, he told her, "Well, you better have a drink before you go." One brandy became two, but she passed her exams anyway (personal interview with Lev Grossman).

Spink's intelligence and drive had taken her to Oxford on scholarship, but many there did not consider her their peer, while to her family she seemed overeducated. Egalitarian America offered an alternative. She chose graduate studies at Brandeis in Waltham, Massachusetts, simply because "it was first on her list alphabetically" (personal interview). At Brandeis she met her intellectual equal in her dissertation adviser, the poet and critic Allen Grossman. Over time a relationship developed and they started a family, settling in nearby Lexington. In addition to boys Jon and Adam from Grossman's previous marriage, they raised three children of their own: a girl named Bathsheba and, later, identical twins Austin and Lev, born ten minutes apart on June 26, 1969, in Concord.

All three children proved to be precociously bright, high achievers in a high-achieving family. Bathsheba became an artist whose sculptures embodied mathematical models; Austin went into video game design before turning his hand to writing novels. Lev Grossman has earned a name in American letters not only for novels like *The Magicians* (2010) but also for his work as a journalist and critic. One of America's foremost bibliophiles, he has done a very great deal to nurture our love of books—real, physical books with ink on paper—while never losing sight of technology's power; and he has championed genre fiction to the extent that a latter-day Boston Brahmin could proclaim herself a Potterhead, a Twi-hard, or a similar geek with neither irony nor shame.

EARLY LIFE

Lev Grossman describes the family home as "white and brown and designed in the Gropius tradition … long and boxy and vaguely modernist.… Being a terrace, our street was especially quiet and pleasant—there was no traffic, and all the kids from the neighborhood came there to play" (personal interview). Books dominated life indoors. Once Judith earned her Ph.D. she joined her husband in teaching—at Brandeis and at other places—as well as writing, penning the family's first novel. She had studied Chaucer while Allen studied Dante, Wordsworth, and Yeats; the children grew up reading books and hearing them discussed by professionals who happened to be their parents. Allen was not to be crossed in matters canonical, and indeed, says Lev, "we weren't meant to have our own opinions

about [literature]," though he does remember his father reading *The Hobbit* and *The Once and Future King* to him. Comic books and genre fiction were safe in the sense that the adults in the house did not care to argue their merits; and so Lev's literary interests were both proscribed by his parents' interests and curiously free of them.

As a twin, Lev sometimes felt his individuality threatened. He and Austin never played games whereby one would take another's test in school or fool a friend; the idea paled in comparison to the deadly serious business of establishing separate identities "both to ourselves and to other people" (personal interview). Even today Lev shares drafts with his brother but finds him almost too simpatico an audience, all too ready to understand the message being conveyed. For clarity of prose, he says, it is better to imagine one's reader as a stranger, picking the book up at a random page.

Lev stood out in school, wedding a vigorous mind to the study habits of a machine. He equated much of his self-worth with success as a student—and, later, with the prestige of the university that would accept him as an undergraduate. An outstanding student can rightly take pride in academics, and *The Magicians'* Quentin Coldwater is, in this, autobiographical:

> The room filled with a collective rustling of paper, like a flock of birds taking off. Heads bowed in unison. Quentin recognized this motion. It was the motion of a bunch of high-powered type-A test killers getting down to their bloody work.
>
> That was all right. He was one of them.
>
> (p. 22)

Lev was accepted into Harvard, where he majored in literature and graduated magna cum laude with a B.A. degree (1991); after a two-year hiatus he went on to study comparative literature at Yale, completing course work for the Ph.D. and passing his orals but deciding not to write a dissertation, having finally come to terms with the idea that his identity might lie outside the bounds of a classroom.

STRUGGLES

The time between Harvard and Yale proved problematic on several levels. Graduation meant a loss of focus—"I didn't have any more classes to get an A in," Grossman admits—which left him struggling to fill that gap. He knew he wanted to be a writer but not how to go about it; what would he do without the discipline of formal study? The answer, at first, was "virtually nothing" (personal interview). With a desire to write but no fixed subject, he sought inspiration in the country, arriving circuitously in rural Maine. "Conventional wisdom has it that solitude is good for a writer. But I quickly discovered that you can only Write for so many hours a day, especially if you don't have anything to say" ("How Not to Become a Writer," 2010). After six months he moved to New York and cycled through job searches and temp agencies, fighting his own demons all the while: undiagnosed depression, a tendency to drink, a tendency to self-sabotage. "I remember once getting a call about a promising temp assignment, and just as they were about to give me the details and close the deal, my left hand grew a life of its own and spontaneously ripped the phone line out of the wall" ("Why I Went to Yale," 2010). The struggles left him broke, forcing him to shift from one substandard apartment to another and contemplating suicide. A writer mines his pain the way a comic mines his life for material, and so it is not terribly surprising that Grossman's twenties inform a great deal of his work. In the *Magicians* series, Quentin and Julia bear the scars of these lost years; the successful Edward Wozny from *Codex* (2004) flirts with dissolution over the course of the plot; and most directly, Hollis Kessler (from *Warp*, Grossman's first novel) reflects a life lived sans direction. Every novel has the imprint of this struggle.

Grossman recounts that he wrote the first draft of *Warp* in 1993 before going off to Yale, returned to the project after his time there ended in 1996, and saw it published in 1997. While at Yale he met Heather O'Donnell, a fellow student of literature; their brief marriage produced daughter Lily O'Donnell. He was "very depressed during this period" and managed to arrange a diagnostic session with a Yale psychiatrist. Bitterly, he notes that no one followed through on the session, and he did not seek another (personal

interview). Mirroring his author, Quentin feels puzzlement at the absence of happiness: "He had painstakingly assembled all the ingredients of happiness. He had performed all the necessary rituals, spoken the words, lit the candles, made the sacrifices. But happiness, like a disobedient spirit, refused to come" (*The Magicians*, p. 5). Eventually Grossman found the therapy he needed, but things really began to turn with a hire at Time, Inc., where he was tasked with deleting offensive posts from message boards. "Over the course of five years ... I parlayed this into a job writing for *Time*" (personal interview). He would go on to become *Time*'s book critic, its senior technology writer, and a freelancer for magazines and newspapers like *Salon*, the *Village Voice*, *Wired*, and the *Wall Street Journal*. In addition, he can be found answering questions for an online audience on Reddit, blogging, or granting interviews to webzines.

Grossman's second wife, Sophie Gee, is an Australian novelist who teaches "the long eighteenth century" at Princeton; their children are Halcyon and Benedict (called "Baz"). And it is living with them in a house in Brooklyn which has grounded Grossman and enabled him to produce his best fiction. Having felt an emotional distance from his father, he dotes on his own family (personal interview). This connection is both a blessing and a curse in the sense that family time cannot also be writing time. In his blog Grossman considers both sides of the dynamic and concludes that family wins even from the narrow perspective of the writer peeking out from within the man:

> I never wrote a book I was proud of till I had children. I started *The Magicians* two months after Lily was born, and that's not a coincidence. Before that happened I never wrote anything worth a damn. Maybe I would write more if I didn't have kids, but I'm not at all convinced that anything I wrote would be worth reading.
>
> ("Benedictus," 2012)

Allusions and sly humor abound in Grossman's work. He leavens it with pop culture references and more erudite nods to literature, philosophy, technology, and even physics. This is especially true of his first novel, *Warp*. Based on *Ulysses*—

or, rather, *Ulysses* as filtered through Flann O'Brien's 1939 novel *At Swim-Two-Birds*—the story is bathed in mid-1990s pop culture, with sensibilities perhaps best described as one part *Star Trek* and one part *Less Than Zero*. The novel's plot involves little more than a group of debauched youths attempting to become temporary squatters. Its autobiographical protagonist is a Harvard graduate in his twenties who finds himself existentially adrift. Like Hamlet, he thinks too much and acts too little; but unlike Hamlet he makes no attempt to rise to the level of a tragic hero. Indeed, there is no overt tragedy to be found, though the tone of the novel might be described as bleak. Glimmers of hope persist in that Hollis has a sense of humor and a vital inner life of dreaming; it is the latter which best simulates Joyce's stream of consciousness, transfigured here into quotes from sci-fi television and film, children's literature, and every genre imaginable. It is almost as if Hollis cannot express himself or even think except by cultural regurgitation.

For Grossman, there really is no distinction between so-called high culture and low culture. At one point, Hollis reacts to a friend's suggestion that he commit suicide by saying, "I cannot self-terminate" (p. 23), an obvious reference to *Terminator II*; in the span of a few pages Grossman reaches back to Sir Thomas Malory to describe Hollis' inner alter ego having his hands examined by peasants, the leader of whom says, "I wote well ye're of an higher blood than we wend ye were" (p. 27). This is almost exactly the language Arthur's adoptive father Sir Ector uses to describe the young king: "but I wote wel ye are of an hyher blood than I wende ye were" (*The Works of Sir Thomas Malory*, edited by Eugène Vinaver, Oxford UP, 1954, p. 9). These allusions—to a blockbuster movie and a book so old its English has been translated into English—seem dissimilar, but they may have more in common than first appears. In interviews, Grossman consistently points out how literature used to include magic, the strange, and the supernatural as a matter of course. It is only since the rise of the Realists that Romantic ideas about the supernatural, which of course reflected much of

mainstream public opinion reaching back centuries, finally fell into scorn and disrepute. ("Show me an angel and I'll paint one," Gustave Courbet's defiant insistence on the empirical, encapsulates this idea well.) Finally, Grossman argues with more than a little brio that genre fiction can showcase writing that is just as good as can be found in typical mainstream work ("Literary Revolution in the Supermarket Aisle," 2012).

To some readers, the characters of *Warp* encapsulated much of what felt wrong about late-twentieth-century America, and as a result the novel's customer reviews included more than a little vitriol. Grossman could not resist rising to the defense of his work, writing his own reviews praising it to form a sort of counterbalance. But we only know that because he himself wrote about the experience in "Terrors of the Amazon," his first published article (*Salon*, 1999). What are we to feel about this admission? Grossman's honesty surely deserves some praise; on the other hand, the subterfuge in passing oneself off as a reader (or readers) is hardly praiseworthy—even if he was not the first writer to pursue that strategy. The literary community has said its piece with a collective shrug: Grossman will be remembered, but not for this.

CODEX

His second novel, *Codex*, came out in 2004 to rave reviews. A bibliophile's delight in the tradition of Umberto Eco's *Name of the Rose* and Arturo Pérez-Reverte's *Club Dumas* (the former referenced explicitly on page 191), it is also a page-turner; and while *Codex* does much to illumine a reader's passion for books, it makes the case that computer games will prove just as addictive, just as worthy of our collective obsession. Edward Wozny is an interesting and likable protagonist. Flexible enough to go from English studies to investment banking, canny enough to stand out in the field—for example, suggesting that certain securities be moved to a French haven because he knows French insurance companies aren't exposed to drought—he is also capable of

going off the rails, of being browbeaten and fooled. His weaknesses make him human, three-dimensional. As a child, he found a gift for chess that took him to national recognition, but the gift vanished as quickly as it had appeared, leaving him philosophical rather than devastated. This is one of many examples of foreshadowing in the novel: Edward will lose something valuable, he may or may not learn from the loss, but he will survive it.

The novel's twin plot threads involve a life lived through a powerful new computer game and Edward's real life as lived in New York. Once the game is introduced, time begins to speed up there, and the Edward character playing the game quickly falls behind; as a result, the professional, successful Edward tastes digital failure before setbacks begin to mount in his life. Grossman weaves the threads with a deft hand, and the foreshadowing is not so overt as to spoil the reader's suspense in guessing what will happen. Early on Edward meets the Duke and Duchess of Bowmry, guessing rightly at their wealth but not their peerage nor how greatly they will unsettle his life: "Edward watched [their car] go with a sense of mild relief. But he felt a trace of belated disappointment, too—the way Alice might have felt if she had decided, sensibly and prudently but boringly, not to follow the White Rabbit down the rabbit hole" (p. 6). (Grossman likes the character of Alice; she will also serve as inspiration for the name of Quentin's girlfriend in *The Magicians* [personal interview].) That same morning Edward meets Laura Crowlyk, a haughty Brit who also works for the couple. Observing the social niceties, she offers him tea or wine, but he refuses: "He never ate or drank in front of clients if he could help it" (p. 9). This telling detail shows how professional, how careful, he is. The events of the novel completely break down this persona.

Edward is asked to do something for which he is incredibly overqualified: catalog the Duke's personal library, which on the whole now sits in crates, not only uncataloged but unpacked. In particular he is asked to look for a fourteenth-century book by one Gervase of Langford, *A Viage to the Contree of the Cimmerians*. Soon he

finds that it is the Duchess rather than the Duke who has made the strange request: "'This project is her idea,' [Laura] went on, 'in case you hadn't gathered that. You're her idea, too' " (p. 63). But rather than turn the project down, Edward accepts. Strangely, the vast room with its crates full of books—some of them quite old—has a calming, hypnotic effect. His life as an investment banker has not allowed for reflection, and he begins to remember why he became an English major, long ago. The books themselves are almost irresistible in their history and variety:

> He started quickly transferring the rest of the smaller packages to the table and shucking off the wrapping paper. He uncovered triple-decker novels, chunky dictionaries, vast, sprawling atlases, nineteenth-century textbooks scribbled on by schoolboys who had long since grown up and died, crumbling religious tracts, a miniature set of Shakespeare's tragedies, three inches high and equipped with its own magnifying glass.
>
> (p. 25)

Later, as the time demands of the job become apparent to the reader, Grossman adds seductive sensory detail to help us understand why Edward persists: "A moist and pungent smell billowed softly out from each volume as he opened it. The catalogue in the computer lengthened, entry by entry, and he lost track of time" (p. 58). *Codex*, like Garth Nix's *Lirael*, is must reading for the aspiring librarian.

The fact that Grossman's twin worked in video game design helps to explain how the novel arrives at its completely believable insights into gaming culture. One of Edward's old college friends, a hulking gamer named Zeph, gives Edward a disk with a game on it called MOMUS. While relaxing at Zeph's apartment, Edward also meets a tiny "man-child" dubbed the Artiste, who expounds on the marvel of e-mail:

> Consider the example of packet data. The moment you click SEND on an e-mail, your message splits up into a hundred separate pieces—we call them "packets." It's like mailing a letter by ripping up a sheet of paper and tossing the pieces out the window. They wend their separate ways over the Internet, moving independently, wandering from server to server, but they all arrive at the same destination at the same time, where they spontaneously self-assemble again into a coherent message: your e-mail. Chaos becomes order. What is scattered is made whole.
>
> (p. 33)

This may seem merely a fascinating aside, but it is more than that: it reminds us that computer games are products of modern technology, just as printed books from long ago represented the cutting edge of technology in their day. And technophiles like the Artiste control the technology precisely because they understand it. Edward will find that the Artiste is intimately familiar with the game he is about to play, or rather with both games: one virtual, one real.

At one point Edward stays up all night playing a massively multiplayer online game with Zeph and others, an event that dazzles him with its immediacy. His banker's mind immediately understands the game's financial potential:

> Edward's thoughts drifted to buying into one of these computer games companies. Something this addictive must be disgustingly profitable. The initial hostility he'd sensed around him when he arrived had dissipated, and an ad hoc esprit de corps had settled over the room, embracing even him.... They were all in it together, a Local Area Network of brothers in arms, bound by the electric bond of virtual combat. Could a book do this?
>
> (p. 139)

The book by Gervase, which may or may not exist, is the codex of the title and the key to the novel's plot. The Duchess seeks it to undo her husband's seat of power: his lineage itself. Somehow she has discovered that this book, if found and verified, would prove that he had a commoner's blood in his veins. Edward cannot find it, at least not alone. He meets a graduate student named Margaret Napier at the Chenowith Rare Book and Manuscript Repository and enlists her aid. Along the way he develops feelings for Margaret, and when they find the codex and she gives it to the Duke (reciprocating Edward's feelings, she is trying to protect him), he feels betrayed. The Duchess reels off into exile after showing Edward the depths of her contempt, and he returns to investment banking, albeit in

London rather than New York, bemused, hurt, and perhaps a bit wiser.

Codex is filled with clever ideas, from the "Easter egg" that the Artiste develops to the physical puzzle that is the codex itself (it's been hidden in pieces within the other books of the Duke's library). Edward has a strong cast of supporting characters as well—the Artiste, for example, also worked for the Duchess and fell much more deeply under her spell, while Margaret is a smart, independent, and tightly wound cipher whose heart requires patience to crack. The thoughtful reader is rewarded for reading and even rereading this novel.

THE MAGICIANS

Grossman's third novel, *The Magicians* (2004), cemented his critical and commercial success and, like *Codex*, represents another step forward in his evolution as a writer. Often referred to as "Harry Potter for grown-ups," it tells the story of Quentin Coldwater, named after Faulkner's Quentin Compson (personal interview); his education at the Brakebills College for Magical Pedagogy; and the fulfillment of his lifelong dream to find Fillory (Grossman's own creation and an homage to Narnia). For most of the novel, the action takes place in a world recognizably our own in its language, its books, its geography, and its feel. The only addition is the presence of magic. The tone of the novel is key: smart, arch, adult rather than juvenile, it allows the reader to enjoy a satisfying fantasy while casting other books in the genre as puerile. The novel's protagonist is young enough—and grows enough over the course of his adventures—that we might term this a bildungsroman. Still in high school, "Quentin was thin and tall, though he habitually hunched his shoulders in a vain attempt to brace himself against whatever blow was coming from the heavens, and which would logically hit the tall people first" (p. 4). A genius of a student and a gifted magician (of the mundane sleight-of-hand variety), Quentin nevertheless lacks confidence and experience. Frustrated in love,

insecure about college, cynical about his parents, he has more than a little of Holden Caulfield about him.

Quentin and his friends Julia and James have all been invited to take an entrance exam at Brakebills, though they don't know that yet. The three have been friends since elementary school because they are the brightest students in Brooklyn, the "nerdiest of the nerds" (p. 4), and hence have always been thrown together. Quentin and James are rivals for Julia's affection—or rather Quentin apprehends, very clearly, how firmly James has already bested him, so his longing goes unspoken. Julia is walking her men to what they believe will be a college interview at someone's home, intending to drop them off and study at the library. The corpse of the supposed interviewer is the first sign of something wrong. A striking and cheeky paramedic jokes about the death, then intimates that Quentin and James had better not leave before picking up their interview packets:

> The pretty paramedic's dark hair was in two heavy ropes of braid. She wore a shiny yellow enamel ring and some kind of fancy silver antique wristwatch. Her nose and chin were tiny and pointy. She was a pale, skinny, pretty angel of death, and she held two manila envelopes with their names on them in block Magic Marker letters. Probably transcripts, confidential recommendations. For some reason, maybe just because he knew James wouldn't, Quentin took the one with his name on it.
>
> (p. 13)

Quentin's move has great significance; James blows his chance by failing to act. He's too concerned with propriety, the dead body being nearby. One might draw two lessons here: magic requires an instinctive response to its invitation, and it requires irreverence, even subversion. (The woman, who isn't really a paramedic, plays an important if hidden role in the events to come.) Quentin now has his invitation; meanwhile Julia's invitation takes place in the library, though her story will wait for the next book.

Opening his packet alone on the sidewalk, Quentin finds what appears to be an apocryphal book about Fillory called *The Magicians*, but no sooner does this information register than a slip

of notebook paper flies away on the wind, and as he chases it, he finds himself transitioning from the mundane. It has flown into a dense community garden, which in November is mostly dead: "Quentin waded into [the plants] hip-deep, dry stems catching on his pants, his leather shoes crunching brown broken glass. It crossed his mind that the note might just possibly contain the hot paramedic's phone number. The garden was narrow, but it went surprisingly far back" (p. 15). And so, like the Pevensie children finding no back to the wardrobe in *The Lion, the Witch, and the Wardrobe*—or, since C. S. Lewis' novel is notably absent in Quentin's world—like the Chatwin children finding Fillory, Quentin passes through the garden into somewhere else entirely.

That somewhere else, as it turns out, is only upstate New York. But the grounds of Brakebills are astounding nevertheless, not least because they observe a different schedule regarding the seasons (the heat of summer instantly replacing fall's chill). Sweating, dizzy from the loss of his equilibrium, Quentin feels at a loss. A young man smoking a cigarette tells him it's New York rather than Fillory and introduces himself, rather disinterestedly, as Eliot. With a fairly hideous jaw he "looked like a child who had been slightly misdelivered, with some subpar forceps handling by the attending. But despite his odd appearance Eliot had an air of effortless self-possession that made Quentin urgently want to be his friend, or maybe just be him period" (p. 19). Eliot is matriculating at Brakebills, which is exactly what Quentin wants (though his conscious mind hasn't quite caught up to this yet). Appropriately enough, then, Eliot becomes Quentin's guide through the extensive grounds to the college proper:

> It was a good five minutes before they stepped out of the maze, through an opening flanked by two towering topiary bears reared up on their hind legs, onto a stone terrace in the shadow of the large house Quentin had seen from a distance. A breeze made one of the tall, leafy bears seem to turn its head slightly in his direction.
>
> (p. 19)

Grossman layers the magic carefully onto our world, much like a craftsman applying coats of veneer to carved wood. The result is something that feels organic, familiar, and yet startlingly fresh. More a fan of modernism than postmodernism, Grossman nevertheless has read and appreciated writers like Jorge Luis Borges and Gabriel García Márquez (personal interview), and their influence might be seen in the delicate interweaving of magic and reality, the touch of magic realism.

For more direct influence, we don't have to go very far: only to Lev's twin, Austin. Answering a question about inspiration, Lev says,

> There are always a few different sparks, but the one I'd point to is reading an early manuscript of my brother's book *Soon I Will Be Invincible*. Austin and I are twins, and I understood immediately what he was doing. He was taking the mythologies that we'd loved as children and using them as raw material.
>
> It was just so primal and so right. I didn't realize it was possible, but when I saw him do it, I knew I had to do something along those lines too. He worked with superhero stories. I drew more on the fantasy novels.
>
> (DuChateau interview)

So the novel will explore the "primal" nature of magic and show how magic exists not just in Fillory but right here, in America and everywhere else, another layer of the laws of physics ready to be discovered by the population at large.

Quentin has only been invited to the college admissions exam; if he fails that, he must go home. The exam is one part SAT, one part orals, and other parts largely unrecognizable. Other students taking the exam seem to be vanishing, their desks emptying as the first stage of the exam winnows them out; but a fellow test-taker "must have finished, or given up, because he was dicking around by ordering more and more glasses of water" (p. 24). Penny (his adopted name) later tells Quentin, "I love finding shit like that, where the system screws itself with its own rules" (p. 24). He and Quentin are the only students to pass the first stage.

To be accepted, Quentin must pass the final stage: performing magic on demand. No sleight of hand, no brilliance in math or logic or other

conventional test-taking skill, can help him. And it is in his moment of doubt that he realizes how much failure would cost: his one best chance at breaking through to magic, of realizing his fullest potential and seeing reality transformed. The Brakebills dean comes to his rescue, albeit in the harshest way possible:

> "Stop fucking with us, Quentin!" Fogg barked. He snapped his fingers. "Come on. Wake up!"

> He reached across the table and grabbed Quentin's hands roughly. The contact was a shock. His fingers were strong and strangely dry and hot. He was moving Quentin's fingers, physically forcing them into positions they didn't want to be in.

> "Like this," he was saying. "Like *this*. Like *this*."
> (p. 32)

Quentin breaks through to magic on a wave of anger and intuition. He makes magic effortlessly, gloriously, ending with a flourish reminiscent of the Arthurian legend, particularly the T. H. White treatment of the legend: "He picked up the stack of nickels in his fist, only it was no longer a stack of coins, it was the hilt of a bright, burning sword that he drew easily out of the tabletop, as if it had been left there buried up to the hilt" (p. 33). Like Arthur, he is about to be initiated into a new, a higher, state of being.

The realization of magic is like a drink of the most potent spirits. And it lifts the veil of depression for the first time in Quentin's young life: "Sometimes he burst out laughing out of nowhere, for no reason. He was experimenting cautiously with the idea of being happy, dipping an uncertain toe into those intoxicatingly carbonated waters. It wasn't something he'd had much practice at" (pp. 41–42). Magic more than compensates for the world he has left behind: his family, Julia and James, the promise of the Ivy League and a prestigious career in the city. It seems to fill the void he had always known. But human nature being what it is, he falls into a routine and discovers that even here his life falls short of the ideal: "He recognized the irritable, unpleasant, unhappy person he was becoming: he looked strangely like the Quentin he thought he'd left behind in Brooklyn" (p. 64).

The obvious comparison to Quentin's world is the world of Harry Potter, with Brakebills forming the analogue, then, to Hogwarts. And certainly this is true to some degree. Not only has Grossman interviewed J. K. Rowling (recounted rather apologetically in his blog entry "The Post About the Time I Met J. K. Rowling [Part 2]," 2010) and written fan fiction based on her work ("Buckbeak and the Three Potions," written for Lily), but at various points in the novel Grossman makes unmistakable references to the Potter-verse. Welters is a game that stands in for quidditch, and when Quentin is introduced to it he asks a fellow student, "Where's the broomsticks?" (p. 79). Joining a team, he helps his teammate and friend Josh (who's gotten smashed) find his way to the course, as Josh says things like "Send me an owl" and "Gotta get my quidditch costume" (p. 129). Also there is a version of the hat that chooses the student's path in the way that Brakebills faculty interview students to classify them into Disciplines. People with the same discipline tend to hang out together, like the Physical Kids, which is how Quentin becomes close with Josh. Just as the hat struggles to identify a place for Harry, Quentin doesn't fall neatly into any one discipline ("I'll put you down as Undetermined," Professor Sunderland tells him [p. 93]) and is lumped with the Physical Kids seemingly by virtue of rarity.

But despite the occasional homage to Harry, this is a different kind of book. Dean Fogg does not fall like Dumbledore into the fantasy trope of the wise and nurturing mage-mentor; his relationship with Quentin is more complicated and fractious than that. Responding to a question about what type of wizard influenced his own, Grossman began his answer this way: "A lot of the point of *The Magicians* was tearing down archetypes, rather than exploring them. So I didn't want wise, mysterious wizards full of fatherly wisdom. No Gandalf, no Dumbledore" (Carroll interview). And Grossman, being the child of English professors, borrowed not just from fantasy but from canonical literature for the book, admitting to stealing his "narrative structure" from Evelyn Waugh: "[*Brideshead Revisited* is] built around this innocence and experience

structure: People go to Oxford, and then terrible things ... happen to them in their later lives. I substituted Brakebills for Oxford" (Canavan interview). Any doubts that his book departs from the Rowling template are dispelled when Quentin stumbles upon a private scene involving Eliot.

> "Careful," Eric warned. There wasn't much affection in his playacting, if that's what it was. "Little bitch. You know the rules."
>
> Quentin couldn't have said why he waited an extra minute before he ducked back down the ladder, back into his staid, predictable home universe, but he couldn't stop watching. He was looking directly at the exposed wiring of Eliot's emotional machinery....
>
> The desperate hunger with which Eliot regarded the object on which he would perform his chores was unlike anything Quentin had ever seen. He was right in Eliot's line of sight, but he never once glanced over at him.
>
> (pp. 65–66)

The scene was inspired by Proust's *In Search of Lost Time,* when a glimpse into a lesbian sexual encounter catapults the narrator into the realization that his world is much larger than he had thought (personal interview). Grossman's wide range, his omnivorous reading habits, and the way he blurs high and low culture allow him to craft scenes like this.

Quentin is not the only new member of the Physical Kids, as a gifted magician named Alice joins him; but to enter the house, they first must get through the door (the Physical Kids have their own cottage on the school grounds). Since the Physical Kids specialize in things like kinetics and the manipulation of matter, it makes sense that the test involve a physical barrier. He persuades Alice to burn through it, and within they find acceptance rather than disapproval. "'It used to be you could say "friend" in Elvish and it would let you in,' Josh said. 'Now too many people have read Tolkien' " (p. 101). Eliot and a girl named Janet are the other members, and with them and Alice, Quentin finally begins to feel at home.

Alice has emotional problems of her own. Rarely does a Grossman character appear well-balanced: each carries a personal pain of some type or another, whether grief, addiction, or emotional distance from parents who don't know how to parent. This realization comes as a surprise to Quentin:

> It occurred to him, long after it should have, that he wasn't the only person here who had problems and felt like an outsider. Alice wasn't just the competition, someone whose only purpose in life was to succeed and by doing so subtract from his happiness. She was a person with her own hopes and feelings and history and nightmares. In her own way she was as lost as he was.
>
> (p. 69)

In his case, the feelings of alienation stem mainly from an obsession with Fillory and the sense that he does not belong in this reality; in her case, it is grief from her brother's death (which foreshadows her own) and resentment at never receiving an invitation to Brakebills. She was the girl who crashed the party.

Grossman is influenced by games as well as fiction, and the premiere game of the 1970s, when he was absorbing so much genre fiction and the like, was Dungeons and Dragons. For those who have read the D&D *Players Handbook*, the many spells attributed to the Greyhawk wizard Bigby may spring to mind, almost all of them having to do with oversized helping hands; in Grossman's hands Bigby becomes an exiled member of our own Earth (rather than Oerth) and a member of the faculty at Brakebills. He is also a pixie. In a 2011 interview with Bart Carroll, Grossman says of Bigby's spells, "Those crushing, grasping hands ... they haunt me." Later, Penny creates a battle spell with Alice's help: "One of [the missiles] snapped the bottle's neck off cleanly, leaving the base standing headlessly upright.... 'We call it "Magic Missile,"' [Penny] said" (p. 272), acknowledging that this spell and the fireball which he likewise demonstrates were both inspired by the old D & D games.

Fillory begins to loom large not only in Quentin's mind but in the events of the novel, reaching an early crisis point with an unexpected visitor to Brakebills. After the visitor eats one of the students in Quentin's class, he is labeled the Beast, but his real identity is Martin Chatwin, the

first of the children to find Fillory and the only one who became lost there. Or at least he used to be Martin before he abandoned his humanity, gaining an immense reserve of power and a cruel sense of humor in the process. If *The Magicians* has a single antagonist, he is it. Enigmatic, fast, dislocating his jaw like a snake, caught up with Quentin in a metaphysical orbit that leaves them circling each other, he brings horror and dread to the novel. The resolution of his story has much to do with the resolution of every other character's story. But at the time of this early attack, Dean Fogg knows only that he came from outside our own world; no one at Brakebills knows he came from Fillory or even that this literary fiction exists at all—not even Quentin, for whom it remains a dream.

Christopher Plover, an American Anglophile and the stand-in here for C. S. Lewis, wrote the Fillory series of children's books but always claimed that "the Chatwin children would come over and tell him stories about Fillory, and … he just wrote them down." He died mysteriously in his fifties, a death that the Beast later takes credit for: "He earned that. That and more. I wish I had him to kill again" (p. 356). More than most authors, Plover learned the hard way how deadly the criticism of one's work can be.

The nasty episode with the Beast behind them, the students at Brakebills are ready to embark upon their most vivid course of study: a flight to Antarctica to receive personal instruction at the so-called Brakebills South. Grossman's debt to T. H. White is obvious as Quentin and his classmates are turned into geese and start thinking like geese as they fly, the body having a tremendous impact in its feedback-loop with the mind (see Arthur's training as an owl, and his finding that the skin of a mouse was much like the skin of a peach). While at Brakebills South they meet the exiled Professor Mayakovsky and begin to learn how to internalize magic, to learn it so thoroughly that it can be called up at will, no matter the circumstances. This is to their instruction at Brakebills what senior-level experiments are to a college freshman halfway through his first chemistry text. The lessons are rigorous, occasionally eye-opening, and often tedious, but

they advance everyone's knowledge immensely. When Quentin and Alice decide to reach the South Pole itself, racing there as a kind of extra-credit assignment, the reader feels that a corner has been turned, that their training is nearing its end. Utterly drained after the ordeal of the Pole, Quentin arrives back in New York:

> It was late May, and the air was full of pollen. After the rarefied atmosphere of Antarctica it tasted hot and thick as soup. It was a lot like that first day he'd come to Brakebills, straight through from that frigid Brooklyn afternoon. The sun beat down. He sneezed....
>
> Quentin knew he had only a minute or two before he burst into tears and passed out. He still had Mayakovsky's scratchy wool blanket wrapped around him. He looked down at his pale, frozen feet. Nothing looked frostbitten, anyway, though one of his toes was sticking out at an angle. It didn't hurt yet.
>
> (p. 164)

He would learn from his friends that Alice had beaten him by days and that they were the only two students daring enough—or stupid enough—to have made the attempt.

Graduation now seeming like a foregone conclusion—Quentin and his friends really will become magicians now—he meets Julia again and sees how badly she has been damaged by her brush with magic; in a halfhearted way he offers to help, thinking it would be best if she forgot everything instead. After disentangling himself from this very personal reminder of his old life, Quentin takes the initiative in moving forward with Alice and becoming her lover, his childlike belief in the transformative power of magic melting the final barrier between them. Sex is a revelation, a bridge between the two loners, and a liberating act that rivals magic itself.

It is Penny of all people who discovers that Fillory is real. Mirroring Grossman's own pilgrimage to Maine, he meets a traveling salesman there who had often appeared at Brakebills and who had found an object of inestimably greater value than his usual wares: a magic button. That button teleports one to the Neitherlands, an in-between intersection of world portals, and from there one can go to Fillory. Grossman's

interest in Roger Zelazny's Amber books can be seen with names (Fiona, Benedict, Eric) and here in the Neitherlands description Penny gives. Although Grossman has acknowledged that the most direct antecedent to the Neitherlands is Lewis' Wood Between the Worlds in the Narnia series (Raets interview), Penny describes this artifact-city in a way that immediately recalls Zelazny's Amber: "The thing is, the more I study it, the more I think it's exactly the opposite—that our world has much less substance than the City, and what we experience as reality is really just a footnote to what goes on there. An epi-phenomenon" (p. 250). Grossman has acknowledged that the Amber series is never very far from his mind (personal interview).

Eight young magicians make the leap to the Nietherlands and thence to Fillory. "They had been scattered by the transition, like a freshly deployed stick of paratroopers, but they were still in sight of one another" (p. 286). They promptly begin freezing, having been fooled into thinking it was summer by Fillory's ragingly fast time stream. "Fine light snow sifted down from the white sky. The ground was hard under the fallen leaves" (p. 286). Returning with coats, they find that now it's autumn. Soon they see a deer: "looking back over its shoulder with an air of genuinely exceptional intelligence, they all agreed, but if it could speak it declined to address them" (p. 295). Other animals will, echoing the world of Narnia.

The expedition mood sours because Quentin and Alice have broken up in the most juvenile way possible, entangling other members of the group in their sexual imbroglio. And so when the quest finally comes, it cuts through their narcissism. The stakes are high: four of them can become kings and queens of Fillory if they are successful, and indeed Fillory needs their rule. Grossman's sly humor can be seen in Quentin's meditation on his boyhood obsession: "They must keep Fillory in its pre-industrial, agrarian state on purpose, by choice. Like the Amish" (p. 317). Once in the ominously labeled Ember's Tomb, the magicians encounter a red giant who further embodies this sense of humor: "He was bald, and his expression was blank. His huge, hairless, glowing-red cock and balls swung loose between his thighs like the clapper of a bell" (p. 340). Josh takes him out with a black hole spell and remarks, "Did you check out his dick though? That guy was hung!" (p. 345).

While in the tomb they encounter Ember himself (one of the gods of Fillory) and then, more problematically, the Beast. The former Martin Chatwin has become strong enough to vanquish Ember and proceeds to bite off Penny's hands to forestall one of those battle spells.

> Then the Beast dropped him, chewing busily, and Penny fell back on the sand. Arterial blood sprayed crazily from the stumps, then he rolled over and they were underneath him. His legs thrashed like he was being electrocuted. He didn't scream, but frantic snuffling noises came from where his face was pushed into the sandy floor.
>
> (p. 355)

Alice sacrifices herself in the only way that she or anyone there could defeat Martin: she becomes a niffin, a creature of pure magic, by deliberately flubbing a powerful Renaissance-era spell. And as a niffin she is able to end the Beast's life. This long set piece of a battle is one of the most exhilarating and grief-inducing to be found in fantasy literature.

Quentin suffers at the Beast's hands, his physical injuries taking months to heal. He will emerge transformed in ways both obvious and subtle. The emotional damage he suffers is more interesting; with some little justification, he sees himself as responsible for Alice's death. And he longs to be with her again:

> If he was feeling daring, he thought about the time he'd spent as a goose flying south, wingtip to wingtip with Alice, buoyed up by pillowy masses of empty air, gazing coolly down at looping, squiggly, switchbacked rivers. If he did it now, he thought, he would remember to look out for the Nazca Lines in Peru. He wondered if he could go back to Professor Van der Weghe and have her change him back, and he would just stay that way, live and die as a stupid goose and forget that he'd ever been a human.
>
> (p. 372)

He finds an outlet for both guilt and anger when the mysterious paramedic appears and reveals

herself to be the Watcherwoman, one of the Chatwins. She explains that Quentin and his friends had actually fought Martin before. So had many, many others. But they had always lost. She has been pulling the strings from afar, replaying their fight through her ability to manipulate time. A gamer might think of it this way: the Beast was a difficult boss fight, requiring multiple lives lost and tremendous persistence from the player playing the game; but the boss only has to be beaten once. The Watcherwoman was the player, Quentin one of her characters. Though she is Martin's sister, she recognizes the monster he became and she is going to take this outcome as "by far the best … I've ever achieved," Alice be damned.

THE MAGICIAN KING

Quentin still bears the marks of his loss in *The Magician King* (2011), sequel to *The Magicians*, but he has also grown up. Now, along with Eliot, Janet, and Julia, he rules Fillory. Julia's presence among the four is of course the most surprising, and her story easily proves the equal of Quentin's. Grossman says that Julia was originally based on his sister Bathsheba (personal interview), but that her role grew as the author came to identify with her more and more; despite her gender, she channels him more effectively than even Quentin. Eliot tells Quentin how he and Janet reacted to Julia at first sight: "She was disgustingly bright and rather sad and slightly askew. To tell you the truth I think one of the things we liked about her was that she reminded us of you" (p. 32). Once the central quest of the story is established—based loosely on Lewis' *Voyage of the Dawn Treader* (Canavan interview)—the novel alternates between present-day scenes and those that tell the story of Julia's past. The two threads come together powerfully in the novel's climax, a remarkably effective example of plot texturing.

The quest is both simple and profoundly grand: something is ailing Fillory and perhaps magic itself, something that may very well bring about their destruction. The rulers of Fillory must find out what this something is and stop it if they can. Quentin responds to the call of the quest, though in its first iteration he does not understand it and ultimately turns it down. One is reminded of the second step in the "hero's journey," that archetype identified by Joseph Campbell, and indeed Grossman has said, "I'm interested in the quest now, the hero's journey" (Severson interview). The quest manifests again in humble form—as a journey to collect taxes from an outer island claimed by Fillory. Quentin accepts the task and feels he is on the right path: "He was feeling good. He was full of energy and a determination that he hadn't felt for a long time. This is what he'd been waiting for" (p. 35).

He saves the life of a sentient ship of the Lorian Deer Class, or rather he has it lifted off a sandbar and repaired in dry dock; his instincts prove correct when the ship (rechristened the *Muntjac*) saves the quest. Not only is it faster than any ship of Fillory, but it is capable of jettisoning its mass to navigate the shallow waters that prevail near the outer edge of reality. *The Muntjac* proves essential in ways no one could have foreseen, though to their credit both Julia and Eliot support Quentin even in the face of the time and expense required for the ship's repair.

In the meantime Quentin sponsors a tournament to find Fillory's greatest warrior for the expedition. Grossman, as he proved with the scenes in Ember's Tomb, has a real eye for combat. In the tradition of great writers of combat like Joe Abercrombie (whose work he has touted in venues like Reddit), Grossman creates a stirring tournament. Its winner, a man named Bingle, recalls both Bruce Lee and the Amber general Benedict (this novel's Benedict, a mapmaker, will become Bingle's apprentice). His philosophy of combat resembles Bruce Lee's no-style:

"What do you call this style?" Quentin asked.

"The mistake people make," Bingle said, "is thinking that there are different styles."

"All right."

"Force, balance, leverage, momentum—these principles never change. They are your style."

(p. 97)

This echoes Bruce Lee saying to an interviewer, "Be water, my friend," an apt metaphor for his Jeet Kune Do method. "Jeet Kune Do is not limited in any way and draws from many cultures, which is actually a very American way of doing things," the philosophy's website asserts (*The Jeet Kune Do Philosophy*). It is interesting to consider Grossman's nationality, for it really is a quintessentially American activity to borrow extensively, to fuse disparate concepts and philosophies, and to emphasize freedom from cant.

The trip to the Outer Island seems a bust: no obvious antagonist awaits them, and the locals, though few in number, readily acknowledge Quentin and Julia as their sovereigns. So why did Quentin feel the call of this quest? Once again, as so often happens in a Grossman novel, the answer lies in a book. In this case, it is a Fillorian children's story concerning a key that winds up the world, one of seven magical keys, and the people of Outer believe that After Island has one.

After Island, like all the islands beyond the bounds of Fillory proper, illustrates Heisenberg's uncertainty principle. Benedict explains that "they didn't stay still once they caught on that they'd been mapped. They didn't like it, and through some kind of tectonic magic they wandered around to make sure the maps didn't stay too accurate. More chaos" (p. 85). As with the Artiste in *Codex,* as with the Watcherwoman playing a kind of computer game, as with Bingle's reference to the laws of physics, Grossman never quite abandons science; his fantasies rest upon its bedrock.

Unfortunately for Quentin and Julia, they find the key and it works. The problem is that it opens a door to a place they never wanted to go: home. Rather than embrace the chance to see their parents or revisit old haunts, they sit on a Massachusetts sidewalk and despair. The contrast between Fillory and the Eastern seaboard gives Grossman opportunity to comment on the ugly, artificial nature of human civilization. Inside a stolen car, this feeling crystallizes: "The car smelled of its owner's cigarette smoke. Everything was toxic and chemical and unnatural: the plastic walnut trim, the electric lights, the burning gasoline that was shoving them forward. This whole world was a processed petroleum product. Julia kept the radio on classic rock the whole way" (p. 111). Thus even the music comes via amplified electric guitar.

At Quentin's behest they visit Brakebills, Julia less than eager to seek help from the place that shunned her; but Dean Fogg and the faculty there cannot help them. Fogg does offer apropos advice while Quentin is leaving: "Magic knows better, not you. Do you remember what I told you the night before you graduated? Magic isn't ours. I don't know whose it is, but we've got it on loan, on loan at best" (p. 118). The events of the novel will bear out his words.

When they switch to Julia's network of friends, the quest to return to Fillory gains traction. Quentin is astounded to find an entire counterculture centered on magic: the anti-Brakebills. Grossman never liked how neatly the Potter-verse split into wizard and Muggles; there had to be a gray area somewhere (personal interview). Even with spells of forgetting, some people remember their exam at Brakebills, while others who were never invited persevere in their studies based on instinct alone. Julia's friends operate a series of safe houses—some of this the reader learns in the present, and some in the "Julia chapters" set in the past—that offer a crude form of teleportation, so in multiple hops the erstwhile rulers travel to Venice. "The one factoid Quentin remembered about the Grand Canal was that after Byron was done screwing his mistresses he used to like to swim home along it, carrying a lighted torch in one hand so that boats wouldn't run him over" (p. 149). The canal matters because they need to talk to the dragon inside it.

In Grossman's world, dragons live in Earth's greatest rivers and in major waterways. They are as old and intelligent as the dragons most often found in Eastern folklore. Josh, Quentin's old friend from Brakebills, had left Fillory, adventured in the Neitherlands, and eventually sold the magic button to this dragon and bought himself a palazzo whose "comforts were many. You could spend the morning in bed, reading and watching

the Venetian light track slowly over an oriental carpet that was so fractally ornate it practically scintillated right there on the floor in front of you" (p. 172). Despite Josh's hospitality, Venice has little effect on Julia, but Quentin can almost forget Fillory here. The luxury, the history both magical and mundane, very much suit him. Josh arranges for them to meet the dragon, which tells Quentin, "The first door is still open" to Fillory (p. 180). And so Quentin and Julia travel to England, to the Chatwin home and environs, to find that door; Josh and an Australian named Poppy join them. (Of the latter, Grossman told Todd VanDerWerff in 2011:, "I knew there must be magicians out there who are, to use a glib expression, well-adjusted.... I felt it was important that they met somebody like that and be challenged by that worldview.") All four find their way to Fillory and to rescue aboard the *Muntjac*.

Julia was hardly affected by Venice because her backstory is even more soul-crushing than Quentin believes. Failing her Brakebills exam, she becomes obsessed with getting back in; failing that, she determines to study magic on her own. This leads to a series of dead ends. The following months bring depression, a trip to an asylum, the depression drug Lexapro (which the author has also taken), and an online support group of fellow geniuses named Free Trader Beowulf. But a mathematical series extrapolated onto houses and storefronts draws her to a magic safe house in her own town. She reacts with a welter of pent-up emotion to the revelation that magic can be hers after all, Grossman adding an apropos allusion to *The Tempest*:

> Julia squatted down on her haunches on the sidewalk, like a toddler, and put her head in her hands and laughed and cried at the same time. She felt like she was going to pass out or throw up or go insane. She had tried to walk away from the disaster, to run away from it, she really, truly had. She'd broken her staff and drowned her book and sworn off magic forever.
>
> (pp. 189–190)

Julia comes to dominate this safe house and others like it owing to her immense appetite for learning; while others sip magic, she gulps it. Later, she finds that the other members of Free

Trader Beowulf were waiting for her to find magic on her own, and when they feel she is ready they invite her to the ultimate safe house, set just for the pleasure of it in the French countryside. There they finish her education and allow her to join their unsupervised postdoc experiment. This experiment, as it turns out, will be the genesis of Fillory's problem and Quentin's quest.

Meanwhile Quentin finds that Eliot has been leading the expedition without him for over a year. Most of the keys have been found. The old children's book and its characters are important for the next key, as the book's protagonist (in undead form) guards it. At Ember's urging, Quentin assaults his keep without knowing whose it is, deciding to take a very wizardly aerial approach:

> Up he rose through the twilight air. The ancient brick rushed by his face in the dimness. There was no noise. He felt his chest empty out a little with the effort. It wasn't so much a feeling of being weightless as one of being supported, touchlessly, somewhere around your shoulders. You were a baby being lifted up by a giant parent.
>
> (p. 259)

The assault proves successful and Quentin comes back down the tower expecting a triumphant welcome—the hero's return. At the ship, however, he finds that Benedict has been slain.

The hero's journey requires a trip to the underworld, one which Quentin makes to visit Benedict. While there, Julia joins him, showing her support once again. They find Benedict in a kind of endless gymnasium, but they also find that the dead won't let them go. Enter the goddess Our Lady Underground. She, it seems, was the divine being the Free Traders had been attempting to summon, the being who would introduce them to the radically greater energies they craved. Instead they had summoned Reynard the Fox, who slew half the Traders and raped Julia, extracting her humanity when he withdrew his penis. Instead they alerted all the gods, not just the kindly ones, that humanity sought more magic, and convinced the oldest gods to cut humans off at the source; Fillory, being pure magic, cannot survive without it. But now, finally, Our Lady Underground signals a

turning of the tide, and she helps Julia complete her transformation into something more than human, turning her into a dryad. Julia and Quentin leave with the goddess and take a bonus back to the others: the final missing key. Once Quentin makes it to the edge of the world and uses the keys, he prevents Fillory's destruction and saves magic in the human sphere. For his troubles, he is banished by Ember, but it is a testament to the character's growth that he survives the disappointment. It helps that he is able to square his debt to Julia by helping her reach her special tree. So the quest ends, but like so many in literature and myth, the ending is bittersweet.

CONCLUSION

Transformations are a standard trope in fantasy, but Grossman's work is unusually packed with them. After the battle with the Beast, for example, Quentin finds himself with hair "like … an Andy Warhol wig" (*The Magicians,* p. 374) and living wood replacing certain bones; Alice becomes a niffin and Julia a dryad; the Brakebills students become geese to fly to Brakebills South; and while there, Quentin's first lovemaking session with Alice happens while they are both foxes (p. 155). If fantasy is really about how people deal with problems in this world, then these transformations, taken figuratively, can be linked to the life stages we all traverse—for example, the pivotal transition from adolescence to adulthood. The Magicians series (the last of the trilogy, *The Magician's Land,* was scheduled for release in August 2014) centers on the transformative power of love and belonging as much as it does magic. And that is the central problem of the adolescent's journey: how to make a new life of one's own and find love and belonging in it. Lev Grossman, novelist, reminds us of this truth.

As a thinker, Grossman has had ample opportunity to reflect on the future; as a journalist, he has had opportunity to interview those who shape it. And he has found that they have not thought very deeply about the consequences of innovation (personal interview). We are going to be transformed by technology in multiple ways, as individuals and as a society, a prospect he

contemplates with ambivalence. When it comes to books, at least, he regards "progress" as illusory: "I'm a luddite on e-books. I've used them, but I'm with Maurice Sendak on this: 'I hate them. It's like making believe there's another kind of sex. There isn't another kind of sex. There isn't another kind of book! A book is a book is a book' " (*Reddit* interview). Elaborating later, he says,

> I've never seen any story, any written story, enhanced by technology—not as an ebook, an enhanced book, a vook, a hypertext novel. Storytelling is our way of organizing reality, it's how we organize the chaos of experience. In many ways technology performs the same function. But storytelling is older and bigger than technology. It supersedes it.

Whatever innovations are coming, Lev Grossman is particularly well placed to help us understand them and to navigate the changes they will bring.

Selected Bibliography

WORKS OF LEV GROSSMAN

NOVELS

Warp. New York: St. Martin's Griffin, 1997.

Codex. Orlando, Fla.: Harcourt Books, 2004; Harvest, 2005.

The Magicians. New York: Viking, 2009; Plume, 2010.

The Magician King. New York: Viking, 2011; Plume, 2012.

The Magician's Land. New York: Viking, 2014.

SHORT STORIES

"Endgame." In *The Way of the Wizard.* Edited by John Joseph Adams. Rockville, Md.: Prime Books, 2010.

"Sir Ranulph Wykeham-Rackham, GBE, a.k.a. Roboticus the All-Knowing." In *The Thackery T. Lambshead Cabinet of Curiosities: Exhibits, Oddities, Images, and Stories from Top Authors and Artists.* Edited by Ann VanderMeer and Jeff VanderMeer. New York: Harper Voyager, 2011. (Also published in *Steampunk III: Steampunk Revolution.* Edited by Ann VanderMeer. San Francisco: Tachyon Publications, 2012.)

"The Duel." In *Unfettered: Tales by Masters of Fantasy.* Edited by Shawn Speakman. Seattle: Grim Oak Press, 2013.

Fan Fiction

"Buckbeak and the Three Potions." http://levgrossman.com/?s=buckbeak+and+the+three+potions

"Toothless and the Missing Nightmare." http://levgrossman.com/?s=toothless+and+the+missing+nightmare

Articles

"Terrors of the Amazon." *Salon*, March 2, 1999. http://www.salon.com/1999/03/02/feature_222/

"How Apple Does It." *Time*, October 16, 2005. http://content.time.com/time/magazine/article/0,9171,1118384,00.html

"Bill Gates Goes Back to School." *Time*, June 7 2007. http://content.time.com/time/magazine/article/0,9171,1630564,00.html

"Writing *The Magician King*." *Fantasy Matters*, August 9, 2011. http://base.fantasy-matters.com/node/158

"The Mechanic Muse: From Scroll to Screen." *New York Times Book Review*, September 2, 2011. http://www.nytimes.com/2011/09/04/books/review/the-mechanic-muse-from-scroll-to-screen.html

"Literary Revolution in the Supermarket Aisle." *Time*, May 23, 2012. http://entertainment.time.com/2012/05/23/genre-fiction-is-disruptive-technology/

Blog Entries

"The Post About the Time I Met J. K. Rowling (Part 2)." May 27, 2010. http://levgrossman.com/2010/05/the-post-about-the-time-i-met-j-k-rowling-part-2/

"How Not to Become a Writer." Levgrossman.com, August 2, 2010. http://levgrossman.com/2010/08/how-not-to-become-a-writer-or-why-i-have-not-been-to-maine-for-20-years/

"Why I Went to Yale." Levgrossman.com, October 13, 2010. http://levgrossman.com/2010/10/why-i-went-to-yale-or-the-other-worst-year-of-my-life/

"Benedictus: Thoughts on Being a Writer and Having Children." Levgrossman.com. September 15, 2012. http://levgrossman.com/2012/09/benedict/

INTERVIEWS

Canavan, Gerry. "Adult Fantasy Author Lev Grossman on His Work, Harry Potter, and Evelyn Waugh." *IndyWeek*, Aug. 24, 2011. http://www.indyweek.com/indyweek/adult-fantasy-author-lev-grossman-on-his-work-harry-potter-and-evelyn-waugh/Content?oid=2640669

Carroll, Bart. "Lev Grossman Interview." *Wizards of the Coast*, January 13, 2011. http://www.wizards.com/DnD/Article.aspx?x=dnd%2F4spot%2F20110113

Chai, Barbara. "Lev Grossman on Exploring Magic, Moment by Moment." *Speakeasy* (blog at WallStreetJournal.com), August 9, 2011. http://blogs.wsj.com/speakeasy/2011/08/09/lev-grossman-on-exploring-magic-moment-by-moment/

DuChateau, Christian. "*Magician King* Helps Potter Fans." CNN, August 7, 2011. http://www.cnn.com/2011/LIVING/08/07/lev.grossman.interview/

Personal interview, August 22 and 26, 2013.

Raets, Steven. "Author Interview: Lev Grossman." *Far Beyond Reality*, April 8, 2013. http://farbeyondreality.com/2012/05/08/author-interview-lev-grossman/

Reddit. Interview with Lev Grossman. May 30–31, 2012. http://www.reddit.com/r/books/comments/1aqlik/im_new_york_times_bestselling_author_journalist/

Severson, Jessica, et al. Author Q&A with Lev Grossman. *Don't Mind the Mess* (blog), August 10, 2010. http://theseversons.net/reading-list/author-qa-lev-grossman/

VanDerWerff, Todd. "Interview: Lev Grossman." A.V. Club, August 8, 2011. http://www.avclub.com/articles/lev-grossman,60027/

MARK HELPRIN

(1947—)

Josh Crain

MARK HELPRIN IS one of America's most lauded contemporary fiction writers. He has lived a life so varied and full of astonishing exploits that a 1992 book tour served the dual purpose of promoting his latest novel and, in the face of a challenge from the *New York Times*, exhibiting documentation to prove some of the facts of his existence. He has been a soldier, sailor, dishwasher, mountain climber, police officer, and political speechwriter, among other things, and the breadth of his experience has contributed to the wide range of his fiction. He writes with familiarity and ease of places as diverse as Jamaica, British Columbia, Italy, Israel, and the American West, and he vividly evokes historical settings, such as the First and Second World Wars, belle époque New York City, and the Civil War era.

At the core of Helprin's fiction is a search for beauty, truth, and strength—a search both animated and circumscribed by mortality. We often first encounter his characters in their old age as the nearness of death prompts a reminiscence of the struggles they endured in their prime. Love, war, exercise, education in the liberal arts, and the piercing beauty of nature form a crucible in which his protagonists hone their bodies and refine their minds, so that the dissolution of mind and body may be faced with dignity and fearless acceptance. Helprin directs his readers to very traditional sources of hope and inspiration: marriage, family, honor, and courage.

Withdrawn and independent, Helprin insists that he adheres to no school of writing and steadfastly refuses the society of the literary establishment. His methods and opinions are his own. When asked about his influences, he rarely mentions contemporaries or early twentieth-century writers. Instead, he usually invokes Dante, Shakespeare, and the Bible. It is essential to his art, he feels, to make his own way as much as possible and to accept guidance only, or at least primarily, from what has endured.

Helprin's principled lack of involvement in literary public life began in 1975 when he asked John Cheever to write a review of his first collection of short stories, *A Dove of the East*, of which Cheever had spoken admiringly in private. Cheever refused to write the review, however, explaining that he had made a pact with Saul Bellow that the two of them would review only each other's work that year. Repelled by this and ashamed of his own efforts to ingratiate himself, Helprin swore that he would never write a fiction review, provide a blurb for fiction, serve on a prize jury, or in any other way trade favors with other writers—a resolution he has never violated.

Indicative of his determination to forge his own path, Helprin's prose, for which he is often praised, neatly avoids the struggle of so many writers of the late twentieth century to escape the influence of Ernest Hemingway's terse, vigorous sentences and William Faulkner's swelling, rolling periodicity. Helprin's writing conforms syntactically to the complex and heavily subordinated periods of Latinate Ciceronian style, but in his vocabulary short, stark words of Anglo-Saxon origin predominate. Thus, while his sentences resemble in structure the early American prose style of *The Federalist Papers* or Nathaniel Hawthorne, most of the individual words, which are clean, bright, and often monosyllabic, would be more at home in a speech by Lincoln or a poem by William Blake. A passage from his most widely known novel, *Winter's Tale*, will illustrate:

> Outside, the wind picked up in a sudden clear gale
> that had come unflinchingly from the north, de-

scending quite easily from the pole, because all the ground between it and New York was white and windblown. On nights of arch cold and blazing stars, when the moon was in league with the snow, Beverly sometimes wondered why white bears did not arrive on the river ice, prowling silently in the silver light. The trees bent despite their winter stiffness, and some, in desperation, knocked and scratched against the windows. If a channel had been kept open in the frozen Hudson, any little bravely lighted boats would now be flying south, nearly airborne with sudden winter speed.

(p. 98)

Because his work often depicts miraculous occurrences intersecting seamlessly with the natural world, some critics have compared Helprin to writers of the South American magical realist tradition, such as Gabriel García Márquez. The comparison is in some sense appropriate, as both Helprin and the magical realists stress the ordinariness (though not the triviality) of the supernatural. But the origins of these common characteristics are very different: the magical realists glean inspiration from the hybridization of American Indian animism and European rationalism, whereas Helprin's magical elements are drawn from his Jewish background. His writing is often concerned with Jewish issues and demonstrates the diversity of Jewish experience, involving characters both Orthodox and nonpracticing in such places as Eastern Europe, Israel, and New York City. Like the animism of the magical realists, Jewish mysticism and folklore treat the supernatural not as an invasive force that occasionally penetrates into the natural, but as an essential quality of reality coexistent with the natural world. The influence of this view is readily apparent in Helprin's fiction. Consider, for instance, the short story "A Jew of Persia" (collected in *A Dove of the East*), where the devil shoots with a rifle at a Jewish traveler and is slain with a barber's razor. Where Helprin's supernatural fiction differs from that of the magical realists is in the implied, or sometimes openly stated, theism of his underlying Jewish perspective. Both the natural and the supernatural elements of the world function as signs of an inscrutable, wise, and provident deity.

Helprin's characters are, for the most part, written so as to be morally and physically exemplary. Rather than focus on the problem of evil or the nature of depravity, he holds up for his readers a picture of what people can do, and become, when they live in harmony with their surroundings, govern their lives with discipline, and allow love to move them. To be sure, there are wicked and corrupt characters in Helprin's writing, but they receive far less attention than the exemplary protagonists. Vice and crudity are sometimes satirized, but not nearly as often as sharp thinking and athletic daring are valorized. Helprin has on several occasions mentioned his contempt for fiction that strives to portray realistically the mundaneness and squalor of the everyday lives of the vicious and small-minded. Instead, he creates characters that defy such realism in their tremendous and exceptional drive to improve their lives and to achieve the classical ideal of excellence. They are intended to be models of adventurousness, learning, hard work, and good judgment; yet, it is a tribute to Helprin's talent that characters of such goodness (and greatness) still retain a vivid humanity, full of nuance and eccentricity.

The desire to improve one's life dramatized in Helprin's fiction is, however, subject to important qualifications. First, the search for excellence does not imply a search for perfection. The humble acknowledgment of human limitations is as necessary to excellence as the fervor of determined striving. Two edifices from *Winter's Tale*, a "golden room" and a "bridge of light," seem to represent modern towers of Babel, and the failed attempts to build them cast aspersions on the notion of human perfectibility. Even in the short story called "Perfection" (from *The Pacific and Other Stories*, 2004), when a young Hasidic boy gifted with supernatural baseball abilities makes it his mission to get the Yankees to the pennant, he insists that they must win the pennant on their own, and the story becomes in the end an exploration of why God, who could create a perfect world as easily as he could a perfect baseball player, allowed the Holocaust to happen. A rightly ordered life, then, as depicted in Helprin's fiction, accepts with humility the limitations placed upon it, even as it celebrates human potential.

For Helprin, it is also important that the pursuit of greatness is an individual, not a collective, endeavor. In his narratives of war, for instance, it is the bravery and cunning of particular soldiers, rather than the schemes of generals, that turn the tide of battle. Though the individual life benefits from strict self-discipline, it withers under control imposed from the outside. In the Swan Lake Trilogy, Helprin portrays the repressiveness of totalitarian government that seeks to centralize and regulate all social and economic activity. Such pressures against the freedoms of the individual may come not only from the forces of the state but from the social urge to conform and the allure of technology, as Helprin illustrates in the short story "Jacob Bayer and the Telephone" (in *The Pacific*), in which a Jewish village loses its sense of identity and community in its enthusiasm for the newly invented telephone. The ways in which the pressures of conformity, the collective impulse, and the denigration of individual merit can accompany scientific and technological progress is a central theme in Helprin's one nonfiction book, *Digital Barbarism* (2009). Thus, despite his emphasis on human improvement, in Helprin's view people ought not be organized, but inspired; not treated as components of societal progress, but allowed to flourish individually.

One of the driving forces behind Helprin's narratives of the pursuit of excellence is the question of how those who become rich can retain the virtues associated with poverty. The problem with wealth is that money begets the sort of decadence that diminishes whatever meritorious conduct earned the wealth in the first place. In "The End of the Line" (from *A Dove of the East*) the father is honest, intelligent, and hardworking; the son spoiled, profligate, and effeminate. *Freddy and Fredericka* (2005) treats the burdens of royalty. No fewer than three Helprin novels ponder the anxieties of a man who falls in love with an heiress. In all these cases, the overabundance of money is an impediment to excellence, though an impediment that can be overcome. Helprin's prescription for this dilemma is to live the kind of life that is not dependent upon money—to go about one's life as if not wealthy.

Freddy and Fredericka, Prince and Princess of Wales, whose idiosyncrasies are an embarrassment to the royal family, must parachute naked into America to earn a living among the poor, so that they might come to understand that the nature of true royalty is service, not entitlement. In Helprin's 2012 novel *In Sunlight and in Shadow*, Harry Copeland marries an heiress but considers it a point of honor to save his deceased father's dying leather goods business without the assistance of his father-in-law's vast reserves of wealth. In these situations money seems not an intrinsic evil, but nevertheless a powerful temptation away from true self-improvement, and the difficulties of the rich should not be discounted, however more obvious the trials of poverty may be.

The foregoing emphases—the importance of the individual, the denial of utopian notions of human perfectibility, the avoidance of collective conceptions of progress, and concern for the right use of wealth—point to Helprin's conservative politics. In 1983 he provoked controversy by writing an article in the *New York Times Magazine* recommending that the United States deploy missiles in Europe. This was the first time his political views had been expressed to a large public audience. He has written speeches for a number of Republican politicians, most notably for Robert Dole's 1996 presidential campaign. From 1985 to 2006 Helprin served as contributing editor to the *Wall Street Journal* and is a senior fellow at the Claremont Institute for the Study of Statesmanship and Political Philosophy. He is also a former fellow of the Hudson Institute. Despite his relationship to these conservative institutions, Helprin's political opinions have never been rigidly partisan. Informed by his experience in manual labor, he has long supported a high minimum wage, and he spoke out vigorously against the George W. Bush administration's handling of the war in Iraq. Like the fictional newspaper *The Sun* in *Winter's Tale*, whose editorial positions seem to be modeled on Helprin's own politics, Helprin himself has from time to time challenged the opinions of the Right as well as the Left.

Literary critics have spoken of Helprin's writing with extraordinary praise. He has been compared variously with Leo Tolstoy, James Joyce, Vladimir Nabokov, Franz Kafka, Ernest Hemingway, and Boris Pasternak, among others. Unlike many novelists, whose short fiction is generally regarded as early exercises, Helprin has continued to treat the genre of short story as a craft equal to the novel in literary value. In fact, a number of critics have argued that, however meritorious his longer works, Helprin's lasting reputation will be based on his short fiction.

Helprin has been the recipient of numerous honors and awards. For his second short-story collection, *Ellis Island* (1981), Helprin won the National Jewish Book Award, was a finalist for the PEN/Faulkner Award and the National Book Award, and was awarded the Prix de Rome in 1982. He received a Guggenheim Fellowship in 1984 and the Peggy V. Helmrich Distinguished Author Award by the Tulsa Library Trust in 2006. In May 2006 the *New York Times Book Review* asked a select group of authors and eminent literary critics for nominations of the best works of fiction from the past twenty-five years. *Winter's Tale* was one of a very few books that received multiple votes. His books have been translated into twenty foreign languages. Helprin has also produced more than four hundred pieces of journalism in his career. He has been noted in particular for his prescient military analysis. In 2001 he received the Mightier Pen Award from the Center for Security Policy, and in 2010 the Claremont Institute presented him with the Salvatori Prize in the American Founding. He has written for the *Washington Post, Los Angeles Times, Atlantic Monthly, New Criterion, National Review, Commentary*, and *Claremont Review of Books*, among many others in the United States and abroad.

LIFE

Mark Helprin was born in Manhattan on June 28, 1947, to Morris and Eleanor Lynn Helprin. His father was a film executive who later became the president of London Films. His mother was a respected stage actress. His birth was two months premature, and he was not expected to survive. In his early life he was beset with numerous illnesses and conditions, including rickets and spina bifida. Though his mother cared for him devotedly while he was unwell, both of his parents were dedicated to their careers, and Helprin reports that he spent much time alone in their Central Park West apartment watching clouds float by.

In 1953 his family moved to the suburb of Ossining, New York. Here he began to cultivate an enjoyment of the outdoors, tramping through the woods and swimming in the Hudson River. He was especially drawn to the New York Central tracks running by the Hudson. Hopping trains would later become a favorite pastime, and it occurs often in his fiction. On one trek through the forest he met an old man collecting railroad spikes who claimed to have known Walt Whitman. The nearby Hudson River also inspired Helprin's imagination. Rowing and sailing are common themes in a number of his works.

Helprin's storytelling talents were apparent from an early age. He enthralled his friends and acquaintances by extemporaneously concocting and narrating stories of surprising depth, and his third-grade teacher took down from dictation a number of his childhood tales. He received his first offer of a book deal when he was seven years old: Golden Books asked him to write a biography of Lincoln, whom the young Helprin idolized. Morris Helprin would not allow his son to accept the offer, since he felt that Eleanor Helprin's early stardom on the stage had debilitated her childhood, and he did not want his son to experience the same kind of trauma.

Helprin's family next lived in the British West Indies, where he encountered British culture and the wilds of the jungle, both of which fascinated him. Recklessly adventurous, Helprin nearly lost his life several times during his adolescence. After a life-threatening attack by a Pakistani immigrant on the island of Jamaica, he had to be sewn up without anesthetic. Traveling on his own in Europe at age seventeen, he wrecked a rented motorcycle and recuperated in a hotel room where, incidentally, he shared a balcony with Vladimir Nabokov.

He matriculated in 1965 at Harvard, where he majored in English and received his A.B. degree in 1969. While still a student there, in 1967, he made his first trip to Israel. Helprin was struck, especially in hindsight, with the informality of Israel during that time: to enter the country, he simply got off the boat and began to hitchhike. He also spent part of a summer sailing with the British Merchant Navy on the M.V. *Stonepool,* where he was impressed with British tidiness and order. During his senior year at Harvard, he had his first stories accepted for publication at the *New Yorker*, one of which was published the same year. At this time in his life, Helprin strongly opposed the Vietnam War, and he dodged the draft with 4-F status—a decision for which he later expressed regret.

After graduation, Helprin enrolled in the comparative literature Ph.D. program at Stanford, but he evidently was not happy there and left after a short time to go to Israel. He returned to Harvard in 1970 and began work on a master's degree in Middle Eastern studies, which he completed in 1972. He went back to Israel, where he became an Israeli citizen and enlisted in the Israeli army. Later, he was reassigned to a combat infantry position in the Israeli Air Force. Though he enjoyed living the life of a soldier, he experienced constant frustration with the disorganized and chaotic way in which the Israeli military was run. In 1973 he warned of the impending Yom Kippur War, but Golda Meir and Moshe Dayan (to whom he had access through his mentor and Harvard graduate school adviser) and the Israeli chief of staff (whose plane he guarded) refused to listen to the strategic assessments of an enlisted man. He returned to the United States that same year.

Helprin's first volume of short stories, *A Dove of the East*, appeared in 1975 and received generous praise from critics. Though it sold only a few thousand copies in its first printing, these numbers were considered impressive for a collection of short stories. At this time, Helprin began to take an interest in mountain climbing. Between 1976 and 1987 he climbed in the Hudson Highlands, the Sierra Nevada, the Cascades, the Alps, and other ranges. He also did postgraduate work at Princeton, Columbia, and Oxford. In 1977 Knopf published Helprin's first novel, *Refiner's Fire*. It was this novel that, indirectly, introduced Helprin to his future wife, Lisa Kennedy, a tax attorney and banker. Seeing on the will-call shelf at the Scribner Book Store a copy of *Refiner's Fire* next to a book on petroleum geology he had ordered, he inquired as to its purchaser and discovered that she lived in the apartment building next to his own. When he called on her sometime later, she happened to be reading the book, and when he told her his name over the intercom, she supposed that someone must have been spying in her window, and she met him downstairs with a knife in her hand. They were married on June 28, 1980, and would have two daughters, Alexandra and Olivia.

Helprin's next book, *Ellis Island and Other Stories*, was published in 1981 and received several major honors and awards. Troubled by the unwillingness of Democrats to confront the USSR, he began to be more outspoken about political issues. His 1983 piece for the *New York Times Magazine* recommending that the United States deploy missiles in Europe generated irate criticism from many on the Left who had previously spoken highly of Helprin's fiction. *Winter's Tale*, published in the same year, was widely admired by many critics and stayed on the best-seller list for four months, but was passed over for prize nominations. Helprin has expressed his suspicion that the outing of his conservative leanings may have played a role in his conspicuous exclusion by prize committees ever since. His political journalism did, however, draw favorable attention from the *Wall Street Journal*, for which Helprin began writing in 1985. The following year, the Helprins moved to Seattle.

At the advice of his father, Helprin eschewed the more fantastical elements of *Winter's Tale* in writing his next novel, *A Soldier of the Great War*, published in 1991. While he was still working on *A Soldier of the Great War*, he published *Swan Lake* (1989), a children's novella and a retelling of the ballet, which he dedicated to his young daughters. The story, illustrated by Chris Van Allsburg, would eventually grow into a trilogy.

As part of the publicity campaign for *A Soldier of the Great War*, Helprin agreed to an interview with Paul Alexander of the *New York Times Magazine*. Alexander's subsequently published article expressed doubts about Helprin's honesty, questioning whether the stories told in that interview and others were really true. In addition to his account of sailing with the British Merchant Navy and being a soldier in the Israeli Army, Helprin had related some extraordinary anecdotes about his family: the acclaimed photographer Robert Capa was his godfather; his father had traveled in the Soviet Union as a purchasing agent for the family's food processing business and did intelligence work; his mother was a Communist until Ayn Rand personally persuaded her to leave the party. Alexander's magazine report dismissed Helprin's accounts as falsehoods designed to drum up publicity. To answer Alexander's insinuation, Helprin undertook extensive research to prove his own honesty. There were many impediments—the M.V. *Stonepool* had by this time been retired and scrapped. But Helprin was able to produce a selection of convincing evidence, including crew records from the British Merchant Navy and a signed letter from the doctor who operated on him in Jamaica. This documentation became a part of his 1991 promotional book tour. He traveled with his family in a Volkswagen Westphalia, delivering speeches, signing books, and exhibiting his portfolio of documents. (It is a peculiarity of Helprin's that he never gives readings on tour, but rather always delivers a speech, and in early years insisted on never giving the same speech twice, though he eventually abandoned that practice, if only from exhaustion.)

Helprin's next novel, *Memoir from Antproof Case*, and two sequels to *Swan Lake* (*A City in Winter* and *The Veil of Snows*) were published in 1995, 1996, and 1997, respectively. During this time, Helprin was also involved in Bob Dole's presidential campaign as both a speechwriter and foreign policy adviser—an experience that left him disillusioned with the machinations of American politics. He was also among the first to call for the impeachment of President Bill Clinton, long before the Monica Lewinski scandal,

for his acceptance of campaign contributions from Chinese foreign nationals. In 1997 Helprin and his family moved to Virginia.

Writing articles for the *Wall Street Journal*, raising two children, and renovating two homes kept Helprin from publishing again until 2004, when *The Pacific and Other Stories* debuted. It was quickly followed by another novel, *Freddy and Fredericka*, published in 2005. In 2006, as a result of differences of opinion concerning the Iraq War, Helprin resigned his post at the *Wall Street Journal*. The following year, the editors at the *New York Times*, seeing that Helprin no longer had a connection to another paper, asked him to write a piece for their op-ed page. His inaptly headlined article, "A Great Idea Lives Forever: Shouldn't Its Copyright?" (he was arguing for extended, not perpetual copyright protection, and was well aware that ideas cannot be copyrighted), drew such enraged and virulent criticism from online commenters that he wrote a book-length response, *Digital Barbarism* (2009), not only defending the principle of copyright but also exploring the cultural hazards of the digital age.

Today, their daughters grown, Helprin and his wife live on their farm near Charlottesville, Virginia, where they grow millet and hay. Though some of the work is contracted out to locals, Helprin mends fences, maintains machinery, uses a brush hog, and does many other chores himself. The study where he writes is an immense room, almost as wide as and slightly longer than a basketball court. One wall is taken up entirely with a huge two-story bookshelf. Rooms of exaggerated size have long been a recurring feature in his fiction (as a young man he dreamed of buying Grand Central Station and turning it into the world's largest studio apartment), and his study actualizes, on a more realistic scale, that preoccupation of his imagination.

SHORT STORY COLLECTIONS

The short stories in Helprin's first collection, *A Dove of the East* (1975), many of which had previously been published in the *New Yorker* and some in the Jewish magazine *Moment*, impressed critics with their powerful images and range of

subject matter. They are, as a rule, quite short, some taking only four pages to tell. The author's emphasis on character and setting rather than plot is already apparent in these early stories. They are primarily character sketches, evoking with nuance a vast spectrum of human feeling: combat, rebellion, anticipation, unrequited love, the death of a spouse, satisfaction in one's own death. Rather than following a narrative arc, most of these stories isolate and capture a vivid moment in time, so that the effect is sometimes more like that of painting than of narrative. "Because of the Waters of the Flood" is perhaps the best-known story from this collection. The first of Helprin's stories to be published, it tells of Henry and Agnes, who have married despite the protestations of their families and have set out to make a life for themselves as sheep ranchers in Nevada. Their dreams are put in peril by the draft for the Vietnam War, and Agnes meditates on their life together as she waits for Henry to return from the draft office. The story "A Jew of Persia" is one of Helprin's most fascinating explorations of the Jewish folklore tradition.

The stories in Helprin's second collection, *Ellis Island* (1981), are generally longer and more plotted than their predecessors and are thematically linked by the examination of the (often blurry) division between the imagination and reality. In "A Vermont Tale," a young child gradually comes to understand that his grandfather's tale about two loons is an allegory for his parents' disintegrating marriage. In "Letters from the *Samantha*," a story with many interesting echoes of Samuel Taylor Coleridge's *Rime of the Ancient Mariner*, a strange ape that refuses to come down from the mast of a ship of the British Merchant Navy begins to erode the crew's sense of the distinction between ape and man, nature and magic. The title novella, "Ellis Island," blends a realistic picture of the American immigrant experience with whimsical supernatural strangeness. "The Schreuderspitze," perhaps Helprin's best-known short story, tells of a German commercial photographer who decides that climbing a certain mountain—the Schreuderspitze—is the only way to come to terms with the death of his family in a car crash. After

months of intense training, his dreams and the real world begin to lose distinction, with striking implications for the power of the imagination.

Helprin's next collection of short stories, *The Pacific* (2004), demonstrates a mature range of even greater depth and fullness. Helprin deals familiarly with the details of renovation and construction projects, of World War II–era factory work, of the career trajectory of an Italian opera singer, and of mending fences in the Pacific Northwest. The time in which the stories are set alternates between the present and past, as if each story set in the present must have the past for context. Of those stories with a historical setting, most are about World War II. The extraordinary sacrifices of American GIs, their wives, and the European Jews who suffered in the Holocaust are a reference point to which Helprin's post–World War II narratives continually return. Another prominent preoccupation of *The Pacific* is the consideration of morally exceptional circumstances. Several of the stories here contemplate whether there might be situations in which actions normally considered immoral or unwise (adultery, suicide, allowing one's own house to burn down) might be excusable. This same question is also treated in some of Helprin's novels.

NOVELS

Helprin's first full-length novel, *Refiner's Fire: The Life and Adventures of Marshall Pearl, a Foundling* (1977), is plotted as a traditional bildungsroman, a novel of maturation into adulthood. It traces the life of its protagonist from his birth on a ship full of illegal immigrants bound for Israel to his participation in the 1973 Yom Kippur War. Though beginning and ending in Israel, most of Marshall's adventures take place in the Western Hemisphere, for his mother dies in childbirth and he is adopted by a wealthy American couple. He hops trains running through his hometown of Ossining, falls in love at a summer camp in Colorado, raids Rastafarian guerrilla camps in Jamaica, attends Harvard, works in a slaughterhouse in the Midwest, and discovers his origins with the help of an admiral in Norfolk, Virginia. Many of the incidents in the book are

drawn from Helprin's life, and in a later interview he expressed dissatisfaction with the amount of autobiographical material in the novel.

Refiner's Fire not only conforms to the genre of bildungsroman, but also, as Joyce Carol Oates noted in her glowing review, contains many picaresque elements. Throughout his career, Helprin has been quite unashamed of closely adhering to the structures of traditional genres, from Jewish folktale to memoir, romance, and fantasy. Though, in the picaresque style, Marshall's adventures are discrete and episodic, the novel is united by his commitment to his Jewish identity, to the nation state of Israel, and (paradoxically) to the British Empire that prevented him from being born in Israel in the first place. Just as the nation of Israel draws Marshall to itself, Marshall's salient virtue is his natural leadership, by which he magnetically draws others into adventure and heroism.

Helprin's second novel, *Winter's Tale* (1983), provoked sharply divided reactions from critics. The front page of the *New York Times Book Review* carried Benjamin DeMott's extraordinary compliment, "I find myself nervous, to a degree I don't recall in my past as a reviewer, about failing the work, inadequately displaying its brilliance." But reviewers who prize plot and organization found the book's structure unintelligible. For Robert Towers, writing in the *Atlantic Monthly*, the book seemed to be no more than a collection of "set-piece[s], dazzling or otherwise." Though *Winter's Tale* defies summary, the plot runs something like this: In New York City near the turn of the twentieth century an Irish picklock, Peter Lake, who has a close rapport with a magical flying horse, Athansor, stumbles upon the beautiful Beverly Penn while burgling her father's mansion. They enjoy a passionate love affair that is cut short by Beverly's untimely death. Chased by a rival street gang, Peter disappears into a mysterious wall of cloud. In the present time, an eccentric scientist leads the construction of a light bridge that will reach to the heavens, and *The Sun*, the spirited newspaper begun by Beverly's father, has brought together an admirable set of writers and employees. Two of the newspaper's employees,

Hardesty and Virginia Maratta, have a young daughter who is dying of a mysterious illness. The wall of cloud returns to Manhattan, and Peter Lake, still pursued by gangsters, emerges and gradually discovers the unconscious power of his past life.

While its episodic plotline, its complex chains of seemingly unrelated characters, and its strange evocations of the supernatural are indeed difficult to understand, it is precisely this resistance to easy interpretation that has made *Winter's Tale* Helprin's most celebrated work. Though the title comes from the name of a Shakespeare play, the theme of Helprin's novel is winter itself—ice, snow, wind, and stars. Lush and striking descriptions of wintry scenery, both urban and rural, appear throughout the novel. *Winter's Tale* is also a tribute to New York City, Helprin's birthplace. In fact, in one interview, he described the novel as a "love letter" to the city. A film version of *Winter's Tale*, directed by Akiva Goldsman and starring Colin Farrell as Peter Lake, was released in 2014.

In Helprin's longest work, *A Soldier of the Great War* (1991), Alessandro Giuliani, an elderly Italian professor of aesthetics, undertakes a walking journey with Nicolò, an illiterate factory worker. Over the course of the seventy kilometers from Rome to Monte Prato, Alessandro tells the story of his life—his idyllic early childhood, his studies at the university, and finally his exploits in World War I. During the war, he loses his family but finds the love that enables him to build a new home and a new life.

Despite the title, *A Soldier of the Great War* is not a typical war narrative. Instead of giving a realistic description of the service of a typical soldier, Helprin places Alessandro at the most exotic corners of the Italian conflict. He guards a citadel on the banks of the Isonzo River, tracks deserters in Sicily and then deserts himself, languishes in a military prison, and spies out German positions from a cave cut into the top of a mountain. Though the setting of the Great War predominates, the deeper conflict of the novel takes place within Alessandro's heart and mind: how he deals with his loneliness and isolation when everyone he knows has died or disappeared. Often his response is to hurl himself deeper into

the fighting, which, though it steels his courage and refines his wits, leads to yet more heartbreak. Thus the "Great War" of the title has a double meaning—the physical war, but also the universal human struggle to come to terms with the death of those we love and to find love again in the midst of death.

In *A Soldier of the Great War*, Helprin also began to explore the questions of exceptionalism that are so prevalent in his later collection, *The Pacific*. Throughout Alessandro's trials, Helprin often raises the possibility of exceptions to moral norms in extreme circumstances. For instance, in addition to his brave service as a soldier, Alessandro is also a deserter and later a murderer. Yet the circumstances under which these actions take place seem to justify them to some extent.

The books of the Swan Lake Trilogy—*Swan Lake* (1989), *A City in Winter* (1996), and *The Veil of Snows* (1997)—follow the struggles of a young queen to reclaim her kingdom from the clutches of a tyrannical usurper, Von Rothbart. Illustrated by Chris Van Allsburg, known for his previous works *Jumanji* and *The Polar Express,* the books are intended for children but are uncompromising in their vocabulary and prose style. Helprin felt that most young adult fiction expected too little of its readers, and he did not scruple to include words like "inviolable," "brocade," "reprisal," and "meted" (all of which are found within the first six pages). The first novella is essentially a retelling of the eponymous ballet, but told through the guardian of a young girl born to the Prince and Odette. The second novella, narrated by the same girl, now in her later years, tells how she took back her kingdom from Von Rothbart. In the third volume, Von Rothbart's power looms again and threatens to retake the kingdom a second time.

These stories are Helprin's most overtly political fiction. Von Rothbart's penchant for heavy taxation and oppressive regulation stands against the freedom and tolerance of the rightful regime. The setting, a mythical Eurasian kingdom, evokes parallels to the experience of Eastern Europe during and after Communism. Von Rothbart is also Helprin's fullest exploration of villainy and evil. While most of his protagonists struggle against their own limitations, circumstances, or the faceless enemies of modern warfare, the heroes of the Swan Lake Trilogy fight an embodied evil that through ruthlessness is almost purified of goodness.

In 2011 the three novellas and their illustrations were brought together in one volume under the title *A Kingdom Far and Clear: The Complete Swan Lake Trilogy*. Helprin has said that the works of Jonathan Swift and Lewis Carroll were models for these books.

Like *Ellis Island*, the novel *Memoir from Antproof Case* (1995) is full of quirky humor, but not without tragic pathos. It is Helprin's only full-length novel written in the first person. The narrator calls himself Oscar Progresso (not his real name, we are told). Neurotic, eccentric, at times prudish, and always ready to fall in love, Oscar has a single-minded, self-appointed quest in life to rid the world of its enslavement to coffee. In one of the few postmodern touches in Helprin's fiction, the reader cannot always be sure that Oscar is a reliable narrator, as his obsessions often color his account. Yet for all his peculiarities, he is still admirable and endearing. *Memoir from Antproof Case* is also Helprin's most intricately plotted work. Oscar tells his story with an almost total disregard for chronology, but the elements of his narrative come together in the end to give a richly completed picture of his life. An epigraph from *Hamlet* at the beginning of the book gives the reader a method for reading the narrative: "by indirections find directions out." In other words, Oscar's unreliable nonchronological account through its very circuitousness provides a fuller understanding of his life and personality than a straightforward narration would.

Like Alessandro from *A Soldier of the Great War*, Oscar encounters a number of situations that seem to call for an exception to moral norms. He commits murder twice and orchestrates the largest bank heist of the twentieth century, yet in light of his circumstances it is hard not to consider these actions both justifiable and even morally praiseworthy.

In *Freddy and Fredericka* (2005), Helprin's most humorous novel, the two title characters, the Prince and Princess of Wales, are an embar-

rassment to the royal family for opposite reasons. Freddy, though strong and intelligent, is reclusive and prone to public mishaps. Fredericka's beautiful and fabulous appearance endears her to the public, but her vapidity and profligacy make her unfit for her royal position. As a kind of purgatory to burn away their failings, they are sent without clothes or provisions into the United States to reclaim it for the crown.

The humor of *Freddy and Fredericka* ranges from lofty verbal acrobatics to slapstick physical comedy: reworkings of Shakespearean soliloquies in contemporary slang, a nutritionist who dies of malnutrition, a hilarious scene in which Freddy appears in front of Buckingham Palace tarred and feathered with an empty bucket of chicken on his head. Helprin's love of language is in evidence here, as he creates elaborate puns and ridiculous names of mythical kings of England. Freddy and Fredericka's journey across the United States is a kind of Twainesque travel narrative, and it provides Helprin with the opportunity to describe eloquently the diverse beauties of the American landscape. Yet, for all its picaresque hijinks, *Freddy and Fredericka* in its structure follows a very specific paradigm: the genre of medieval romance. There is a frame story, which introduces the knights errant (Freddy and Fredericka), who go on a heroic quest, and the brave warrior (Freddy) wins the favor of a great lady (Fredericka). The presence of Merlin and a silver chalice, representing the Holy Grail, are also carefully concealed within the story.

Helprin's next novel, *In Sunlight and in Shadow* (2012), returns to New York City, where in 1947 Harry Copeland comes back from World War II hoping to revive his family's dying leather goods business. He falls in love with Catherine Thomas Hale, a beautiful heiress with aspirations of becoming a famous stage actress. Her ex-fiancé, Victor, the powerful and ruthless son of a billionaire banker, uses his money and influence to try to destroy both Catherine's stage career and Harry's business. Harry must balance love and courtship with the difficulties of Copeland Leather. Beset by gangsters and the prospect of financial ruin on the one hand and the temptation to surrender to the ease and security that would come from his wife's money on the other, he turns to his military training for the strength to act decisively.

The narrative voice of *In Sunlight and in Shadow* is a more mature and authoritative voice than in Helprin's previous fiction. The tone is imbued with reflective wisdom and the lessons of time. Concern for moral order pervades the book, as well as nostalgia for an era in which courage, perhaps because it was more necessary, could more easily be found. The central paradox of the book is that wartime experience can be among the finest catalysts for encouraging peacetime virtue. Many reviewers found fault with the novel's length—it takes a long time to tell a relatively simple story. An important part of the reason for this, however, is that every moral question in the book is carefully considered. What kind of loyalty does a son owe his father? Can a Christian and a Jew have a harmonious marriage? When is vigilantism permissible? The novel takes a slow, meditative approach to these questions.

NONFICTION

In 2007 the *New York Times* asked Helprin to write something for its op-ed page on a topic of his choice. Wishing to avoid a dispute, he decided to write about an issue he thought could not possibly arouse controversy: copyright law. Acknowledging the U.S. Constitution's stipulation that copyrights be issued "for limited times," Helprin argued for an extension of copyright protection beyond the current term of seventy years after the author's death, on the grounds that intellectual property deserves the same respect and protection as physical property. When the article appeared online, it elicited a hailstorm of negative responses; by the end of the week, there were more than 750,000 comments, virtually all of them opposed. To Helprin it seemed that the Internet had cultivated an anarchic and insatiable class of users who felt entitled to any and all digitally replicable content. In response to his angry critics in the Creative Commons movement, Helprin wrote *Digital Barbarism: A Writer's Manifesto* (2009).

Not intended to be a didactic or strictly legal defense of his position, *Digital Barbarism* instead probes the question of how humans ought to live in relation to their technology and maintains that advances in technology can never obviate the necessity of certain principles, such as property rights, to flourishing human civilization. Helprin recasts the debate as the conflict of two very different views of the world—one that imagines humanity and machines will someday converge in total symbiosis and another that believes that human beings, as infinitely complex creatures with inalienable spiritual dignity, should neither expect nor desire such a union. Those who hold the former view accept change uncritically, while those of the latter frame of mind, in which Helprin would number himself, call for caution and prudence in accepting new developments, lest valuable and transcendent human qualities be trampled in the process.

CONCLUSION

Helprin has compared his writing to woodworking and other manual arts, as he, like any other craftsman, combines knowledge and expertise with physical practice (his first two drafts are always longhand). By thinking of writing not just as an intellectual exercise but as craft, he attempts to preserve a sense of the tradition and nobility of the art. Intensely admiring of his literary forebears, but intent on forging his own way, Helprin is a model of the conservative tension between reverence for the past and respect for the individual. Believing that the artist does not create, but merely discovers the splendors of creation, he is a tireless explorer of the beauties of language and the intricacies of human feeling. The predominant themes of his work are love, bravery, hope, humor, and wisdom. To evoke such traditional categories without irony is rare in contemporary fiction, for it carries the risk of being treacly or sentimental, as Helprin has indeed sometimes been accused of being. He seems to regard the risk as worthwhile, perhaps because he holds with utter seriousness the belief, now out of fashion and seemingly excessively optimistic, that art can enable transcendence.

Selected Bibliography

WORKS OF MARK HELPRIN

NOVELS

Refiner's Fire: The Life and Adventures of Marshall Pearl, a Foundling. New York: Knopf, 1977.

Winter's Tale. San Diego: Harcourt Brace Jovanovich, 1983.

Swan Lake. Boston: Houghton Mifflin, 1989.

A Soldier of the Great War. San Diego: Harcourt Brace Jovanovich, 1991.

Memoir from Antproof Case. San Diego: Harcourt Brace, 1995.

A City in Winter. New York: Viking, 1996.

The Veil of Snows. New York: Viking, 1997.

Freddy and Fredericka. New York: Penguin, 2005.

A Kingdom Far and Clear: The Complete Swan Lake Trilogy. New York: Dover, 2011.

In Sunlight and in Shadow. New York: Houghton Mifflin Harcourt, 2012.

SHORT STORIES

A Dove of the East and Other Stories. New York: Knopf, 1975.

Ellis Island and Other Stories. New York: Delacorte/Seymour Lawrence, 1981.

The Pacific and Other Stories. New York: Penguin, 2004.

NONFICTION

Digital Barbarism: A Writer's Manifesto. New York: HarperCollins, 2009.

INTRODUCTIONS, PREFACES, AND BOOK CHAPTERS

"The Canon Under Siege." Introduction to *The Best American Short Stories, 1988*. Edited by Mark Helprin and Shannon Ravenel. Boston: Houghton Mifflin, 1988.

"City of Sunlight and Shadow." Introduction to *Manhattan Lightscape*. Photographs by Nathaniel Lieberman. New York: Abbeville, 1990.

"Melville: The Uses of Oblivion." Preface to *Moby Dick*. New York: Barnes and Noble, 1994.

"Helprin and I." In *Who's Writing This? Notations on the Authorial I, with Self-Portraits*. Edited by Daniel Halpern. Hopewell, N.J.: Ecco, 1995.

"Lucas." Foreword to *Only Spring: On Mourning the Death of My Son*, by Gordon Livingston. San Francisco: Harper, 1995.

"The Rivers of Babylon, and Gulnare of the Sea." Introduction to *The Arabian Nights*. Edited by Kate Douglas Wig-

gin and Nora A. Smith. New York: Book-of-the-Month Club, 1996.

"God Is … Like the Linnet.…" In *How Can I Find God?* Edited by James Martin. Liguori, Mo.: Triumph Books. 1997.

ARTICLES

"American Jews and Israel: Seizing a New Opportunity." *New York Times Magazine,* November 7, 1982.

"Drawing the Line in Europe: The Case for Missile Deployment." *New York Times Magazine.* December 4, 1983.

"Saddam in the Shadow of His Undoing." *Wall Street Journal,* August 6, 1990.

"I Dodged the Draft, and I Was Wrong." *Wall Street Journal,* October 16, 1992.

"At Rest Between the Wars." *Congressional Record* 139, pt. 10 (January 28, 1993). (Transcript of a speech given at the United States Military Academy, West Point, on October 15, 1992.)

"Against the Dehumanization of Art." *New Criterion* 13, no. 1:91–94 (1994).

"Diversity Is Not a Virtue." *Wall Street Journal,* November 25, 1994.

"Let Dole Lead." *Wall Street Journal,* February 2, 1996.

"The Acceleration of Tranquility." *Forbes ASAP,* December 2, 1996.

"Impeach." *Wall Street Journal,* October 10, 1997.

"What Israel Must Now Do to Survive." *Commentary,* November 2001, pp. 25–29.

"Defend Civilization Itself." *Imprimis,* July 2002.

"No Way to Run a War." *Wall Street Journal,* May 17, 2004.

"Our Blindness." *Wall Street Journal,* January 24, 2005.

"After Diplomacy Fails." *Washington Post,* April 13, 2006.

"The Literary Tenor of the Times." *Claremont Review of Books* 7, no. 1:78 (2006).

"A Great Idea Lives Forever: Shouldn't Its Copyright?" *New York Times,* May 20, 2007.

"In Defense of the Book." *National Review,* September 21, 2009, pp. 43–45.

"Obama and the Politics of Concession." *Wall Street Journal,* September 23, 2009.

"Farewell to America's China Station." *Wall Street Journal,* May 17, 2010.

"America's Dangerous Rush to Shrink Its Military Power." *Wall Street Journal,* December 27, 2010.

"Iran's Mortal Threat." *Claremont Review of Books* 12, no. 1:90 (2011).

"Bumping into the Characters." *New York Times,* October 3, 2012.

FEATURES, ARTICLES, AND INTERVIEWS

Alexander, Paul. "Big Books, Tall Tales." *New York Times Magazine,* April 28, 1991, pp. 32–36.

Bodine, Paul. "Mark Helprin." In *Operative Words: Essays and Reviews on Literature and Culture.* New York: Writer's Club Press, 2002. Pp. 154–56.

Butterfield, Isabel. "A Metaphysical Scamp? On Mark Helprin." *Encounter* 37: 48–52 (January 1989).

Fadiman, Anne. "A Dreamer Who Writes on Every Place and Time." *Life* 4: 29–30 (May 1981).

Field, Leslie. "Mark Helprin and Postmodern Jewish-American Fiction and Fantasy." *Yiddish* 7, no. 1:57–65 (1987).

Green, David B. "An Intimate Look at a Superb Storyteller." *Vogue* 172: 430–431 (March 1982).

Hiltbrand, David. "With Helprin, There's Always a Backstory." *Philadelphia Inquirer,* July 28, 2005. http://articles.philly.com/2005-07-28/news/25432547_1_mark-helprin-freddy-and-fredericka-anatole-broyard

Johnson, Mark. "A Conversation with Mark Helprin." *Image: A Journal of the Arts and Religion* 17: 48–49 (fall 1997).

Kakutani, Michiko. "The Making of a Writer: Tell a Yarn or No Dinner." *New York Times,* March 5, 1981, p. C17.

Lambert, Craig. "Literary Warrior: Mark Helprin's Fictional Marvels and Political Heterodoxies." *Harvard Magazine,* May–June 2005, pp. 38–43.

Linville, James. "The Art of Fiction No. 132: Mark Helprin." Interview. *Paris Review* 35: 160–199 (1993).

Royal, Derek Parker. "Unfinalized Moments in Jewish American Narrative." *Shofar: An Interdisciplinary Journal of Jewish Studies* 22, no. 3:1–11 (2004).

Torrance, Kelly Jane. "Interview: Mark Helprin." *AFF Doublethink,* July 26, 2006. http://americasfuture.org/doublethink/2006/07/interview-mark-helprin/

REVIEWS

Birkerts, Sven. "Pursued by a Bean." *New York Times Book Review,* April 9, 1995, p. 3. (Review of *Memoir from Antproof Case.*)

De Mott, Benjamin. "A Vision of the Just City." *New York Times Book Review,* September 4, 1983, pp. 1, 21–22. (Review of *Winter's Tale.*)

Epstein, Joseph. "©Inequality." *Claremont Review of Books* 10:8–10 (2009). (Review of *Digital Barbarism.*)

Junod, Tom. "The Last Epic Novelist." *Esquire* 158, no. 3:54 (October 2012). (Review of *In Sunlight and in Shadow.*)

Kakutani, Michiko. "A Royal Odd Couple on a Bizarre Quest." *New York Times,* July 14, 2005, p. E1. (Review of *Freddy and Fredericka.*)

———. "Boy Meets Girl, and All Goes Downhill." *New York Times,* October 5, 2012, p. C31. (Review of *In Sunlight and in Shadow.*)

Keneally, Thomas. "War and Memory." *New York Times Book Review*, May 5, 1991, pp. 1–2. (Review of *A Soldier of the Great War*.)

Oates, Joyce Carol. "Picaresque Tale: *Refiner's Fire*." *New York Times Book Review,* January 1, 1978, p. 2.

Oppenheim, Noah. "Big Important Book of the Month." *Esquire* 142, no. 6:58 (December 2004). (Review of *The Pacific and Other Stories*.)

Towers, Robert. "Assaulting Realism." *Atlantic Monthly* 252, no. 3:122 (1983). (Review of *Winter's Tale*.)

WILLIAM INGE

(1913—1973)

John M. Clum

FOR A BRIEF period of time (1949–1957), William Inge was Broadway's most critically and commercially successful playwright. While *Picnic*, *Bus Stop*, and *The Dark at the Top of the Stairs* all had healthy runs of more than 400 performances, Tennessee Williams had only one hit play, *Cat on a Hot Tin Roof* (1955, 694 performances). Though Arthur Miller's *The Crucible* (1953) is now considered a classic, it ran for only 197 performances; *A View from the Bridge* (1955) for 149 performances. The four plays by William Inge that were produced during that period (*Come Back, Little Sheba; Picnic; Bus Stop;* and *The Dark at the Top of the Stairs*) were adapted into successful Hollywood productions, and *Picnic* and *Bus Stop* have received numerous revivals on Broadway and elsewhere. A few years later (1961), Inge's screenplay for *Splendor in the Grass* won the Academy Award for Best Screenplay. At his best, Inge was a chronicler of the clash between the libido and midwestern sexual morality. Like his friend and sometime rival, Tennessee Williams, he was fascinated with outsiders, men and women who could not live by the social and sexual codes of their time and place.

LIFE

William Motter Inge was born on May 3, 1913, in Independence, Kansas, a small town not far from the Oklahoma border. He was the fifth and last child of Luther Clayton and Maude Sarah Gibson Inge. Inge's father was a traveling salesman for a dry-goods company who spent most weekdays on the road and was known to find female companionship outside of his marriage. Maude, somewhat high strung, was quite protective of her children and was especially fond of her shy youngest son.

With an absent father and a brother fourteen years older, "Billy" Inge had little in the way of masculine influence in his life. At home he had his mother, three sisters, and frequent visits from his aunt. In addition, during Inge's high school years, after the death of his older brother in 1920, Maude started to take in unmarried schoolteachers as boarders to supplement the household income. Billy found an outlet in performing. From third grade, he became adept at comic and dramatic "recitations," which gained him the approval of Maude and his teachers, though it didn't help gain the friendship of his peers, who taunted him for being a "mama's boy" and a sissy. His biographer Ralph E. Voss notes that "Inge developed a special talent for satiric comedy involving female impersonation" (p. 22). At Independence High School, he became active in dramatic activities. After graduating in 1930, Inge went to the University of Kansas. He had to take a year off after his freshman year because of family finances, but returned in 1932 and completed his degree in 1935. Since the University of Kansas did not have a drama major, Inge majored in English, but he took part in many campus productions. At the time, his goal was to become an actor.

No one knows when Inge became aware of his homosexuality. In his 1971 autobiographical novel *My Son Is a Splendid Driver*, Joey, Inge's alter ego, remembers sharing a bed with a college friend who made sexual advances. Joey spurned the advances, but later comments, "I never asked myself if I was rejecting a love that I might need or enjoy.... I only feared that to have surrendered to Bob's awkward attempts at lovemaking would have made me feel weak and womanly. But maybe I feared the same personal degradation in any love affair" (pp. 140–141).

What we do know from friends of Inge over the years is that he never reconciled himself to his homosexuality, "a signal cause for unhappiness in a life that was predominantly unhappy" (Voss, p. 24).

While acting was Inge's goal, it seemed a remote one in the midst of Depression-era Kansas. After graduating from the University of Kansas, he chose the more practical route of training to be a teacher at George Peabody College in Nashville, Tennessee. Unfortunately, surrendering his dreams of a career in theater and training for a job he didn't really want placed Inge on the emotional roller coaster he would ride for the rest of his life. Sleeplessness led to depression, which led to a full-blown emotional breakdown. Inge had to return home to Independence to recover. To regain his physical health and mental stability, and to make some money, Inge worked for a while on a road gang. In the fall of 1936 he took a job as an announcer at a Wichita radio station, but decided after a few months to go back to teaching. After a year of teaching English and dramatics at a high school in Columbus, Kansas, Inge finished his master's thesis for George Peabody College on "David Belasco and the Age of Photographic Realism in American Theatre."

From 1938 to 1943 Inge taught English composition and drama at Stephens College, a two-year women's college in Columbia, Missouri. He also participated in community theater productions until the stage fright set in that would finally put an end to his dream of becoming an actor. While at Stephens, Inge continued to experience bouts of sleeplessness and depression. A local doctor suggested that a drink before dinner and before bed might help, a prescription that began Inge's slide into alcoholism. Another doctor suggested that he find a psychiatrist, so Inge began commuting to regular sessions with a doctor in Kansas City.

In 1943 Reed Hynds, the arts writer for the *St. Louis Star-Times,* was drafted. Exempt from the draft, Inge was able to take the job, which he maintained until Hynds's return in 1946. Finally he was in a big city with a cultural life and the opportunity to write about the things he loved.

The most important event of his time with the *Star-Times* was his meeting with Tennessee Williams, who was in St. Louis visiting his mother before going to Chicago for the tryout of his first triumph, *The Glass Menagerie.* Inge interviewed Williams for the paper and the two men became friends and probably, for a brief time, lovers. Williams invited Inge to see his play in Chicago, an event that would change Inge's life. If Williams could make a play out of his family and the claustrophobic environment of his youth, so could Inge. He became determined to be a playwright. Rather quickly he began an autobiographical play, *Farther off from Heaven* (later heavily revised to become *The Dark at the Top of the Stairs*). Williams sent the play to his agent, Audrey Wood, who was not impressed, and to Margo Jones, who was beginning a theater in Dallas. Jones added the play to her inaugural season in Dallas.

When Reed Hynds returned from his military service, Inge lost his temporary position on the newspaper and began another teaching job, this time at Washington University in St. Louis. It would be a few years before playwriting would sustain him financially. Unfortunately it never sustained him emotionally. Problems with drinking and depression become more acute, and occasionally Inge had to be hospitalized at the Menninger Clinic in Topeka, Kansas. Throughout the rest of his life, during periods of great success and periods of failure, Inge's drinking and psychological problems would repeatedly get out of control. He joined Alcoholics Anonymous in 1948 but would often relapse.

Farther off from Heaven was well received at its premiere in Dallas in 1947. Shortly after that, another play, *Front Porch* (later revised as *Picnic*), was produced by the Morse Players in St. Louis. The agent Audrey Wood was impressed enough with Inge's third full-length play, *Come Back, Little Sheba,* to take the budding playwright as a client. After a successful one-week tryout at the Westport Country Playhouse in early September 1949, the Theatre Guild decided to bring the play to Broadway with the veteran comic actress Shirley Booth. To keep him away from alcohol and ensure his participation in the process, the

producers put Inge in a sanatorium in Westport, Connecticut. During the tryout period in Wilmington, Delaware, Inge's clothes were sent to the hotel laundry until curtain time and no orders from room service were allowed. Although some critics had reservations about the play, all loved Shirley Booth, and the play had a respectable run of 190 performances, publication, and a lucrative film sale. The film version of *Come Back, Little Sheba* (screenplay by Ketti Frings) won the award for Best Picture at the Cannes Film Festival and a Best Actress Oscar for Shirley Booth. Though Inge had nothing to do with the film, it added to his celebrity and marketability. He was now in a position to live in style and to indulge in his passion for collecting modern art. Success brought money and fame, but not happiness. In his foreword to the published edition of his collected plays, Inge lamented his inability to be happy at the success of *Come Back, Little Sheba* or his subsequent hits: "None of them has brought me the kind of joy, the hilarity, I had craved as a boy, as a young man, living in Kansas and Missouri back in the thirties and forties" (p. vi). Inge was never to know real happiness.

His next play, *Picnic* (1953), a revision of the earlier *Front Porch*, was staged by Joshua Logan, who had directed a number of Broadway hits including *Mr. Roberts* and *South Pacific*. Relations were strained between Inge and Logan as the director insisted on a number of revisions, including a happy ending for the two leading characters. Logan knew what audiences and critics wanted in 1953, however, and *Picnic* ran for more than four hundred performances and won a number of awards including the Pulitzer Prize for Drama. The film version (screenplay by Daniel Taradash) was an immense hit. *Bus Stop*, which Inge called "the closest thing to a fantasy that I ever wrote" (Voss, p. 154), opened in 1955 and was an even bigger hit than *Picnic*. A film version (screenplay by George Axelrod), was a vehicle for Marilyn Monroe. Two years later, *The Dark at the Top of the Stairs* (a revision of Inge's first play, *Farther off from Heaven*), under the direction of Elia Kazan, opened at the Music Box Theatre, where *Picnic* and *Bus Stop* had played.

It too ran for more than four hundred performances and was sold to Hollywood. During the 1950s Inge also wrote a number of one-act plays. Some, like "Bus Riley's Back in Town," were drafts for longer works. Others were written as part of Inge's psychoanalysis. Eleven of the plays were licensed for production and published. Others remained in manuscript form.

During the period of Inge's success, he also had the closest thing to a real relationship that he ever experienced, though it had its problems. Inge and Barbara Baxley, an attractive blond actress with a distinctive voice, became close friends in 1953. Though there was an occasional sexual moment, Baxley knew Inge was homosexual. She saw that he was unhappy with his sexual orientation, but she didn't try to change what could not be changed. They remained the closest of friends until Inge approved of her being fired from the cast of *A Loss of Roses* in 1960. Though their relationship was never as close after that, Baxley remained concerned about Inge's well-being throughout the rest of his life.

The Dark at the Top of the Stairs was Inge's last successful play. After that, his Broadway career consisted of a series of critical and commercial failures. Though *A Loss of Roses* (1959) was sold to Hollywood and released under the sensational title *The Stripper*, it lasted only twenty-one performances. *Natural Affection* (1963) and *Where's Daddy?* (1966) fared as poorly. Emotionally delicate in the best of times, Inge was battered by the reviews. He now was dependent on barbiturates as well as alcohol. After the success of his screenplay for *Splendor in the Grass* in 1961, Inge decided to make Hollywood his base, but he had little success there. His adaptation of James Leo Herlihy's novel *All Fall Down* was produced, but his screenplay for *Bus Riley's Back in Town*, which began as a one-act play in the 1950s, was so mangled by the studio that he took his name off the project. He did publish two novels, *Good Luck, Miss Wyckoff* (1970) and the autobiographical *My Son Is a Splendid Driver* (1971). Neither sold well.

Inge remained in Hollywood, but his last years were a continual cycle of alcohol, drugs, and depression. His sister Helene came to Los

Angeles to take care of him. According to R. Baird Shuman, the journalist Lloyd Steele went to interview Inge in 1973 and found "a broken man struggling for survival but not really wanting to survive" (Shuman, n.p.). Old friends Tennessee Williams and Barbara Baxley urged Helene to have the playwright institutionalized, but she had promised her brother that she wouldn't do that. On June 10, 1973, he went into his closed garage, got into his car, and turned on the engine, ending a life that could find neither joy in success nor the strength to weather failure.

The work Inge left behind can be divided into four categories: the hits (*Come Back, Little Sheba*, *Picnic*, *Bus Stop*, and *The Dark at the Top of the Stairs*); the melodramas of troubled youth (*Splendor in the Grass*, *A Loss of Roses*, and *Natural Affection*); the plays in which Inge's homosexuality was overtly expressed (*Where's Daddy?* and the one-act plays); and the two novels he published in the 1970s.

THE HITS

Come Back, Little Sheba, Inge's first Broadway play, is a lament for lost youth and compromised marriages. Like Tennessee Williams' *The Glass Menagerie*, the work that inspired Inge to become a playwright, *Come Back, Little Sheba* takes place in St. Louis. The setting is the kitchen and living room of the home of Doc Delaney, a chiropractor, and his wife, Lola, both in their forties. Doc's nickname is a badge of his failure. While he was a premedical student, Doc, a pampered only child, got his beauty queen girlfriend, Lola, pregnant. Doc did "the right thing" according to the morality of the late 1920s by dropping out of college and marrying Lola. His dream of becoming a doctor diminished into a career as a chiropractor. When Lola's pregnancy developed complications, Doc didn't want her to go to a doctor because of the scandal that might ensue when it was uncovered that she was pregnant before she was married. The baby died and Lola was not able to have another child. While her mother has been in contact with her, Lola's father has never forgiven her for her teenage mistakes. Like Inge, Doc sporadically drank

himself into a state that demanded hospitalization. He drank away the inheritance from his parents, but he won't allow Lola to work because that would diminish his position as breadwinner. In other words, Doc and Lola's marriage has been crippled by their surrender over the years to the prevailing social mores. When the curtain rises on *Come Back, Little Sheba*, Doc and Lola have been married twenty years. He is an alcoholic trying to stay sober and she is clearly depressed. The house is messy and the former beauty queen has become fat and sloppy. Even their dog, Sheba, has abandoned this sad domicile. When Lola appears in the kitchen, she tells Doc that she dreamed of Sheba.

> LOLA: She was such a cute little puppy. I hated to see her grow old, didn't you, Doc?
>
> DOC: Yah. Little Sheba should have stayed young forever. Some things should never grow old. That's what it amounts to, I guess.
>
> (*Four Plays*, p. 8)

This exchange establishes a crucial theme in *Come Back, Little Sheba* and all of Inge's later plays: the tragedy of aging, which seems inevitably to involve disillusionment. Lola is only happy when she remembers her youthful courtship with Doc: "We had awful good times—for a while, didn't we?" (*Four Plays*, p. 31). If the past is an escape for Lola, it only reminds Doc of his failures: "I gotta keep goin', and not let things upset me, or … or …" (p. 34).

In Inge plays, the catalyst for the action is often the arrival of a sexually vibrant outsider. Here it is Marie, a lovely college girl who becomes a boarder in Doc and Lola's house. Lola comes to see Marie as the child she never had; Doc wants to see her as an icon of female purity, a girl who wouldn't sully herself the way Lola did. Marie, however, is a modern girl, even for 1950, who takes what she wants from life. She plans to marry Bruce, a solid young man from a wealthy family who has a good job, but in the meantime is happy to have fun with Turk, a handsome young athlete, the first of the young studs who inhabit many of Inge's plays. Turk, who has no problem displaying his body, makes extra money modeling for university art classes.

Like Tennessee Williams, William Inge liked to reverse the usual gender order and place a beautiful young man as the object of the spectator's gaze rather than a woman.

Lola, who is deeply lonely—she tries to have long conversations with the milkman, the mailman, and anyone else who comes to the door as a way of relieving her sadness and boredom—becomes deeply involved in Marie's love life. She enjoys furtively watching Marie and Turk "make out" in the living room and does all she can to encourage their sexual encounters. She also plans a dinner for Marie and Bruce when he comes to visit. Doc, who wants to protect Marie's purity, particularly from Turk, whom he sees as a threat, dislikes Lola's interference: "If anything happens to that girl, I'll never forgive you" (p. 27). Inge writes that Doc's *"spiritual ideal of Ave Maria is shattered"* (p. 44) when he discovers that Turk has spent the night. The sound of Turk's laugh from Marie's room, like *"the laugh of a sated Bacchus"* (p. 44), is too much for Doc, and drives him back to the bottle. Youth and a powerful, healthy sexuality go together in Inge's plays. For its time, *Come Back, Little Sheba* is quite daring in its portrayal of Marie's enjoyment of sex. She understands that Turk is a man she can have fun with, but not the man she should marry. Doc is trapped in a more conventional morality. When he returns home drunk the next morning all his resentment pours out. "You and Marie are both a couple of sluts" (p. 56), he yells, before attacking Lola verbally and physically.

After a week in the hospital, Doc returns home. Lola has cleaned house and has fixed herself up for his arrival. Doc is off the bottle again and frightened that Lola might leave him: "If you do, they'd have to keep me down at that place all the time" (p. 67). Inge's description of Lola's response is telling: *"There is surprise on her face and new contentment. She becomes almost angelic in demeanor"* (p. 67). Lola is clearly more content when her husband is weaker, more dependent on her. In the final moments of the play, she is making Doc's breakfast and describing another dream. In this one, she and Marie are watching a track meet. Turk is the center of attention as he throws the javelin, but

Lola's father is in charge and disqualifies Turk—the stern father eliminates the representative of masculine sexuality. Turk is replaced on the field by Doc, who throws the javelin so high that it never returns to earth. If the javelin is a phallic symbol, Doc has both displayed his prowess and eliminated the phallus, the symbol of male sexual power. Finally she sees Little Sheba dead in the middle of the field, but Doc won't let her go pick up the dog: "We can't stay here, honey; we gotta go on" (p. 69). As she is throughout the play, Sheba is a symbol of Lola's and Doc's lost youth and dreams of a rosy future. There is a tentative resolution at the end of the play. Doc and Lola might find qualified happiness if they can once and for all lose their memories and dreams of past youth; Doc's of a long-lost sexual purity, his ideal of the Ave Maria, and Lola's of a youthful passion she will never feel again. Doc and Lola may call each other "Daddy" and "Baby," but at the end of the play they are more doting mother and dependent son.

We can see aspects of Inge's own experience in the play, such as his alcoholism and experience with Alcoholics Anonymous and institutionalization. We also see evidence of his psychoanalysis in Lola's dreams. Moreover, we see signs in Doc of Inge's own ambivalence about sex. Turk's masculine beauty and open sexuality are presented as both attractive and threatening to Doc, who must also deal with the horrifying (to him) fact that women have sexual appetites. Like his friend Tennessee Williams, Inge presented sex as a primary force in the lives of his characters and, like Williams, his plays end with marriages that are compromises, in great part to attempt to stave off the deep loneliness his characters feel. In or out of marriage, they are never totally happy.

In *Come Back, Little Sheba,* the catalyst for crisis is the discovery of the sexual pleasure being experienced by a handsome young stud and a beautiful young woman. The same is true of *Picnic* (1953), in which the sexual heat generated by a handsome young drifter upsets a community of women. The setting of *Picnic* is the locale Inge knew best, the midwestern small town. The action takes place within twenty-four hours.

When the curtain rises on *Picnic*, we see two adjoining houses. The center of the stage is occupied by the front porch of the home of Flo Owens, a widow, and her two daughters, Madge and Millie. Flo's husband was a feckless man more interested in drinking with his buddies and enjoying other women than staying home. Madge, eighteen, works at the local five-and-dime. She is beautiful, but not very bright. Fortunately, her looks have attracted the wealthiest young man in town, Alan Seymour, though Madge doesn't feel comfortable around Alan and his family, nor does Alan arouse much sexual desire. Madge's younger sister, Millie, is much smarter, but envies her sister's beauty. Millie understands that in her world, power comes from appearance rather than substance. Like Inge's mother, Flo also rents a room to a middle-aged schoolteacher, Rosemary.

Next door to the Owens household is the home of another middle-aged woman, Helen Potts, and her invalid mother. Helen was once briefly married, but her mother had the wedding annulled because the young man was not deemed worthy. Out of loneliness and kindness, Helen has a habit of feeding and caring for young vagrants who pass through town. On this Labor Day morning, she has found another vagrant and has put him to work doing odd jobs in exchange for a hearty breakfast. The sexual heat generated by this handsome young man, Hal Carter, will upset this little community of women.

Hal's character demonstrates the ways in which Inge subverts the gender order. He comes from a working-class version of the classic Inge household—an irresponsible, drunken father and a bitter, powerful mother who had had the father declared insane so she could take over what was left of his business, and wouldn't pay for a decent funeral when he died. There was no legacy for Hal but a pair of boots. Hal isn't bright, but he had enough athletic prowess to get a football scholarship to the university and such sexual attraction that the girls were swarming over him. Hal's body is his only asset. He went to Hollywood, where, in exchange for sexual favors, he got a screen test that didn't lead to work. Later, Hal was picked up by two women who took him to a motel for a ménage à trois, then robbed him

of everything he owned. Hal is constantly the object of the female gaze, but it doesn't give him power over women. Rather it puts him in the traditional feminine position of weakness and subservience. As Jeff Johnson observes in his book *William Inge and the Subversion of Gender*: "For all his masculine guise of control, Hal finds himself most often the casualty, not the perpetrator, a guilty hedonist prey to his libido" (p. 63).

Hal's only male friend in college was Madge's boyfriend, Alan Seymour. Other male peers didn't approve of Hal because he came from the wrong side of the tracks and because they couldn't compete with him physically or sexually. Alan's first act on seeing Hal is to jump onto his shoulders and ride piggyback, an impulsive gesture for a seemingly controlled young man. Alan, like the women in the play, desires to connect physically with his old friend, but he has to do so in the socially approved manner of male horseplay. Alan offers Hal the use of his car and clothes.

On the afternoon before the annual Labor Day picnic, Hal's often shirtless presence leads to bacchic chaos. When a local dance band begins practicing nearby, everyone, fueled by the bootleg liquor provided by Rosemary's boyfriend, Howard, starts to dance. Hal tries to teach young Millie how to dance, but when Madge arrives, her dance with Hal is a display of their immediate sexual magnetism. Mrs. Potts observes, "It's like they were *made* to dance together, isn't it?" (*Four Plays*, p. 120). Millie gets drunk when she sees she doesn't stand a chance with him. When Hal spurns Rosemary's advances, she viciously lashes out at him: "But you won't stay young forever, didja ever thinka that? What'll become of you then? You'll end your life in the gutter and it'll serve you right, 'cause the gutter's where you came from and the gutter's where you belong" (p. 124). Hal is devastated by Rosemary's remarks: "She saw though me like a goddamn X-ray machine" (p. 126). When everyone else has left for the picnic, he and Madge are left alone. Madge kisses Hal and he quickly responds. At the end of the second act, he carries her off in his arms. Both Madge and Hal feel like outsiders, uncomfortable in the conventional small-

town world. Their common insecurity and their powerful sexual attraction lead to expulsion for Hal and a tainted reputation for Madge.

Act 3 gives us the aftermath of Hal and Madge's night together. Local boys spotted them having sex in the car Alan loaned Hal, thus giving Madge the reputation of an "easy" girl. Alan is so furious at Hal's behavior that he has told the police that Hal stole his car. To avoid arrest, Hal hops a freight train across the state line to Tulsa, where he will try to get a job as a hotel bellhop. Rosemary's loneliness and desperation, which came to a head when Hal spurned her, have led to a desperate plea for her boyfriend, Howard, to marry her: "Then what's the next thing in store for me? To be nice to the next man, then the next—till there's no one left to care whether I'm nice to him or not. Till I'm ready for the grave and don't have anyone to take me there.... You can't let that happen to me, Howard" (p. 129). Howard reluctantly drives Rosemary off for a speedy wedding. His reason for acquiescing to Rosemary's pleading is anything but romantic: "Folks'd rather do business with a married man" (p. 139). Alan announces that he won't be back to see Madge again, and Madge decides to take a bus to Tulsa to live with Hal, despite her mother's protestations: "He's no good. He'll never be able to support you. When he does have a job, he'll spend all his money on booze. After a while, there'll be other women" (p. 147). Flo sees that her daughter is going to repeat her own unhappy history. Madge's attraction is not only to Hal: it is also to getting away from her small town where she now hears the hungry, mocking voices of the local boys. Throughout the play, the train whistle is the siren call away to some place freer.

The ending of *Picnic* as it was originally produced on Broadway is at best bittersweet. Madge's mother is not just projecting her own unhappy marriage when she warns her daughter about Hal. He is a man with no goals or discipline, but it may be just that sense of chaos and danger that attracts Madge. At eighteen, love in a basement room in a Tulsa hotel may seem more enticing than staying in her small town. Madge and Hal are two beautiful losers who will, for a while, have a passionate romance. What follows

is likely to be the same disillusionment we see in other marriages in Inge's plays. In *Picnic*, as in Tennessee Williams' plays, love may simply be sexual desire, the attraction Madge and Hal feel for each other. Madge doesn't say anything about marriage. Perhaps she's realistic enough not to plan on a lifetime commitment with Hal.

Despite *Picnic*'s success, Inge was never convinced that Madge would follow Hal to Tulsa. In his preferred version, *Summer Brave*, published in 1962 and produced unsuccessfully in 1975, Madge's mother, Flo, is far more eloquent in her warnings to her daughter of the dangers of a life with a drifter like Hal:

> There's true love in this life ... and there's something else, excitement and heart throbs and thrills. All of them vanish after a few years, maybe after a few days. Then you hate yourself for having been such a fool, to let yourself be tricked, to have given up your entire life and all the years that lie ahead ... because one night ... something happened that made blood trickle up your spine ... that made your heart beat like a gong inside a cavern ... that made you feel all of a sudden ... like you'd found the whole reason for being born.
>
> (*Summer Brave*, p. 90)

Madge decides to stay and, at the final curtain, leaves for work as we hear the taunts and propositions of the boys who now see her as "easy." Madge is now spoiled goods in the eyes of Alan and the other boys in town, but at least she won't trap herself in a relationship that is bound to sour. Young love—youthful desire—in Inge's work seems to lead either to nowhere or to an unhappy marriage.

For Madge in *Picnic*, her first sexual experience is powerful enough to make her follow Hal, even though she knows that he is not likely to be the kind of person who can settle down. Sexual magnetism is enough, for her at least. Cherie, in Inge's romantic comedy *Bus Stop*, is only a year older than Madge, but she has been sexually active since she was fourteen. She knows sex isn't enough for a real relationship: "I just gotta feel that ... whoever I marry ... has some real regard for me, apart from all the lovin' and sex. Know what I mean?" (*Four Plays*, p. 186). Cherie, a Kansas City "chantoosie," has a problem. After one night with her, Bo, a Montana rancher, has

decided that she is the perfect wife for him and has carried her onto a bus to start the journey back home. On paper, Bo looks like a good catch. He's young, handsome, rich, and a rodeo champion. He's also totally uncivilized and clueless regarding polite behavior around women. Bo assumes that because Cherie, the first woman he has ever had sex with, was "familiar" with him, she is obligated to marry him. Cherie would like to get away from him, but circumstances make that difficult.

The setting of *Bus Stop* is a café in a small Kansas town that serves as a rest and refreshment stop for buses passing through. It is early March, and a snowstorm has closed the roads to the west, so the bus carrying Bo and Cherie will have to stay a while. During the four-hour stay, Bo has to learn some humility. As his sidekick Virgil tells him: "Ya *got* a tender side, Bo, but ya don't know how to *show* it" (p. 192). Virgil has been Bo's surrogate father and best friend since Bo was ten. He is coming to realize that he should have found a mate and settled down: "A fella can't live his whole life dependin' on buddies" (p. 185). Spurned by Cherie, Bo gets increasingly frustrated and violent, finally picking a fight with the sheriff who is trying to protect Cherie. To his chagrin, he loses the fight.

One theme of *Bus Stop* is the relationship of loneliness to love. Bo is in love with Cherie, but he is also desperately lonely. He tells Virgil that his ranch is "the lonesomest damn place I ever did see" (p. 208). Grace, the forty-year-old owner of the café, tells her young waitress, Elma, about her marriage: "I got just as lonesome when he was here. He wasn't much company 'cept when we were makin' love. But makin' love is *one* thing and bein' lonesome is another" (p. 155). She's content now with an occasional one-night stand with Carl, the bus driver: "I'm a restless sort of woman, and every once in a while, I gotta have me a man, just to keep m'self from gettin' grouchy" (p. 218). Cherie too is frightened that marriage to a man she doesn't love can be worse than being alone. Fortunately Bo, beaten down physically and emotionally, learns something about respecting a woman. He apologizes to Cherie for his rude behavior and tells her how much

he loves her: "I couldn't be *familiar* ... with a gal I din love" (p. 211). After a "long and tender" kiss, Cherie relents and the two head off to Montana without sidekick Virgil, who decides that it's time to head out on his own: his place as the central person in Bo's life is now taken by someone else.

There is another major character in *Bus Stop* who will appear in different guises in Inge's later plays: the drunken, disillusioned professor, who is to some extent a projection of the playwright. Dr. Lyman is a former English professor with a love of Shakespeare. He has had three failed marriages, and his attraction to teenage girls has forced him across the state line. Throughout the play, between drinks, Lyman tries to court Elma, the young waitress. Despite these rather major flaws, it is Lyman who can articulate what love is and should be: "It takes strong men and women to *love*.... People strong enough inside themselves to love ... without humiliation.... People brave enough to bear the responsibility of *being* loved and not fear it as a burden" (p. 200). In many of Inge's plays, it is the outsider to marriage and to social convention who most understands love and marriage even though they are impossible for him: "I never had the generosity to love, to give my own most private self to another, for I was weak" (p. 200). Lyman's drunkenness is a function of his self-hatred. At the end, he considers going to the Menninger Clinic in Topeka, where Inge occasionally went to dry out and receive psychotherapy.

The women win Pyrrhic victories in *Bus Stop*. Cherie consents to marry Bo when he shows the tenderness and vulnerability she wants in a man, but she also will face life on a remote Montana ranch. Grace gets occasional sex and companionship but keeps her independence—and her loneliness. Like Hal in *Picnic*, Bo needs a woman to civilize him, though he will never be totally tamed.

Inge's next play, the semiautobiographical *Dark at the Top of the Stairs* (1957), a revision of his first play *Farther off from Heaven*, shows us the stresses and strains in a seventeen-year marriage between a wild man and a civilized woman. Cora met Rubin Flood when she was

seventeen years old. As her sister Lottie describes it, they were coming out of the five-and-ten when "Here comes Rubin, like a picture of Sin, riding down the street on a shiny black horse. My God, he was handsome" (*Four Plays*, p. 254). Within a few weeks, Cora was pregnant and Rubin had to marry her. Now it is the early 1920s and Rubin's job as a traveling harness salesman is in jeopardy thanks to the automobile. Like Inge's father, Rubin Flood spends the better part of the week on the road, where he has his work, his comradeship with other men, and his visits to women. Cora, lonely at home, has become an overly doting mother to her teenage daughter and ten-year-old son. The daughter, Reenie, like Laura in Tennessee Williams' *The Glass Menagerie*, has become almost pathologically shy. Nonetheless, Cora pushes her to go to fancy parties where she will meet "nice boys." The son, Sonny, is taunted by the other boys for being a mama's boy and a sissy as Inge was, and, like the young Inge, Sonny impresses adults with his dramatic recitations. Sonny, who lives for the movies and his pictures of movie stars, is so spoiled that he throws tantrums if he doesn't get his way.

Cora hates the fact that Rubin is away so much, but they don't get along when he is home. She has the values of the midwestern middle class, but Rubin is a vestige of the frontier past. Cora tells Sonny, "He and his family were pioneers. They fought Indians and buffalo, and they settled this country when it was just a wilderness" (p. 233). Yet Cora keeps trying to tame Rubin, who tells her: "We been married seventeen years now. It seems t'me, you'd be ready t'accept me the way I am, or start lookin' for a new man" (p. 229). Their argument throughout the first act gets increasingly heated as Cora voices her resentment at Rubin's travels and his women and Rubin expresses his anger at Cora's nagging and her overprotection of their children. Finally, Cora goads Rubin into hitting her, which he does before slamming out of the house. Yet by the end of the play Rubin, like Bo, becomes more sensitive. Having lost his job—no one needs harnesses anymore—he expresses his fear of adapting to the machine age:

> Sometimes I wonder if it's not a lot easier to pioneer a country than it is to settle down in it. I look at the town now and don't recognize anything in it. I come home here, and I still have to get used to the piano, and the telephone, and the gas stove, and the lace curtains at the windows, the carpets on the floor. All these things are still *new* to me. I don't know what to make of them. How can *I* feel I've got anything to give to my children when the world's as strange to me as it is to them?

> (p. 298)

Many of those alien elements are the touches of domesticity Cora has brought into their lives. Rubin has become more open emotionally, willing to express his fears, but he still wants some freedom and will still work away from home. Cora will be less protective of their children. She comes to realize that her relationship with Sonny is much too close and that he can no longer sleep in her bed when Rubin is away: "Oh, God, I've kept you too close to me, Sonny. Too close" (p. 290). Reenie, too, has to learn that her self-consciousness has consequences. At a country club dance she leaves her blind date, a handsome Jewish boy, convinced that he doesn't care for her. After her departure, he is deeply hurt by the public humiliation he receives from one of the society matrons who makes clear to him that Jews aren't welcome in the country club. Having been rejected by his own mother, a Hollywood actress who doesn't want anyone to know that she has a teenage son, and abandoned by Reenie, he commits suicide. As Cora tells her, "It's a fine thing when we have so little confidence in ourselves, we can't stop to think of the other person" (p. 294).

We see at the end that there is still a strong physical attraction between Cora and Rubin. At the final curtain, Cora is going upstairs to have sex with her husband. There has also been a reconciliation between Sonny and Reenie, who have squabbled throughout most of the play. They go off to the movies together so that Cora and Rubin can be alone. The resolution of the problems in the Flood family come a bit too easily, but Inge and his director Elia Kazan understood that Broadway audiences want a play's problems solved at the final curtain.

There's another troubled couple in *The Dark at the Top of the Stairs*. Cora's sister Lottie is in a sexless marriage to her dentist husband, Morris, who has become psychologically distant: "Did you notice the way Morris got up out of his chair suddenly and just walked away with no explanation at all? Well, something inside Morris did the same thing several years ago. Something inside him just got up and went for a walk, and never came back" (p. 278). Morris' sadness and remoteness resembles the depression Inge described in his foreword to the plays, his "persisting solemnity" (*Four Plays*, p. vii). Sexually and emotionally frustrated, Lottie cannot understand why Cora is not happy with Rubin: "I wish to God someone loved me enough to hit me.... Anything'd be better than this *nothing* (p. 279). Lottie may be frustrated by Morris' remoteness, but she admits to Cora that she never got any pleasure out of sex. Ironically, Morris and Lottie call each other "Momma" and "Daddy," as if they had a family other than a house full of cats. During their final reconciliation scene, Rubin says to Cora:

> RUBIN: It's hard for a man t'admit his fears, even to hisself.
>
> CORA: Why? Why?
>
> RUBIN: He's always afraid of endin' up like ... like your brother-in-law, Morris.
>
> (p. 299)

Morris has been emasculated and, above all, Rubin wants to remain a man, according to his view of masculinity. Throughout this play, and Inge's earlier plays, there is a focus on conventional gender roles. In *Picnic*, *Bus Stop*, and *The Dark at the Top of the Stairs*, we are presented with hyper-masculine men trying to forge relationships with women who represent different ideas of conventional femininity—the beautiful girl, the chanteuse, versus the housewife and too-doting mother—without losing the wildness Inge associates with masculinity and male sexuality. On the other side are the emasculated men—Doc and Morris—who are overly domesticated. Morris even runs his dentistry practice in his home. The attraction of the beautiful wild man is the core of Inge's successful plays. Failed masculinity is a dreaded prospect. What will become of Sonny? Since we know he is to a great extent a depiction of Inge as a young man, he will grow up to think of himself as a failed man. At the end of the film version (screenplay by Irving Ravetch and Harriet Frank, Jr.), Sonny proudly tells his father that he has beaten up the boy who bullied him. He will grow up to be a "real man." The play doesn't offer such a facile conversion. Inge wrote of *The Dark at the Top of the Stairs*, "I suppose it represents my belated attempt to come to terms with the past, to rearrange its parts and make them balance, to bring a mature understanding to everyday phenomena that mystified me as a boy" (*Four Plays*, p. xi). In Rubin, as with Hal and Bo, he created a masculine ideal he could never live up to.

In *The Dark at the Top of the Stairs*, as in all of Inge's successful plays, we are presented with characters who do not feel that they fully fit into conventional societal roles. The marriages we see certainly do not fit the ideal of marriage, and all the children—Reenie, Sonny, and Sammy, the Jewish boy who briefly befriends Sonny and Reenie—are outside of conventional social and gender roles. No one in Inge's work "fits in."

TROUBLED YOUTH

In the 1960s Inge's work focused on the relationship between troubled young people and their parents or parent surrogates. The work became more emotional, even overwrought at times. The only commercially successful work he created in this decade was the film *Splendor in the Grass*, for which he wrote the screenplay and in which he plays a small role as the ineffectual preacher. The film was directed by Elia Kazan, who had directed *The Dark at the Top of the Stairs* as well as another highly successful coming-of-age film, *East of Eden*, in 1955.

Splendor in the Grass, set in a small Kansas town in 1928, centers on the turbulent relationship of two adolescents, Deanie Loomis and Bud Stamper, who are facing the conflict between their intense sexual desire and the prevailing morality. At the opening of the film they are

necking by a large waterfall, which rather obviously represents the force of nature and natural sexual urges. Deanie stops Bud from going beyond kissing, which frustrates him. When Deanie asks her mother, "Is it terrible to have those feelings about a boy?" her mother responds, "No nice girl does." (Quotations from *Splendor in the Grass* are transcribed from the DVD of the film.) Mrs. Loomis has a Victorian view of sex within marriage—"A woman doesn't enjoy those things the way a man does. She just lets her husband near her in order to have children"—yet she knows that Bud would be "the catch of a lifetime." Bud's father has a more pragmatic approach—he doesn't want Bud to get trapped: "You're watching yourself with her, son? If anything was to happen, you'd have to marry her." Bud's dream is to marry Deanie and run a ranch the family owns, but Mr. Stamper, who has made a fortune in oil, wants Bud to go to Yale and take over the business. He sees Deanie as a distraction keeping Bud from his grand plan.

The marriages of both sets of parents are the sort of passionless compromises we have seen in other Inge plays. Deanie's parents converse with one another, but there obviously has been no physical intimacy for years. Mr. Loomis is a quiet, withdrawn husband, one of Inge's emasculated men. The boisterous Mr. Stamper loves carousing with his employees, but barely talks to his timid wife. Their daughter, Ginnie, has become an extreme version of a "fast woman," drinking too much and sleeping with bootleggers and married men.

Deanie is crippled emotionally by her mother's sexual morality, and Bud is crippled by his overbearing father's insistence that Bud follow his plan. The only cure for Bud's sexual frustration is to give up Deanie and take up with the "fast girl" in his class. Without Bud, Deanie literally goes mad and has to be institutionalized. Bud spends most of his short Yale career drunk until he meets and marries Angelina, a kind waitress at a local Italian restaurant but hardly a girl his father would have chosen for him.

The final scenes in the film take place two and a half years later. Deanie has left the sanatorium, where she met and became engaged to a young doctor. Bud's father committed suicide when the stock market crashed, and Bud is fulfilling his dream of running the small ranch that is all that is left of the family fortune. Angelina is expecting a second child, and Bud is working hard to make the farm a success. On the advice of her psychiatrist, Deanie has a final meeting with Bud. When she asks Bud if he is happy, he responds, "I guess so. I don't ask myself that question much any more." He is doing the job he always wanted to do and has a loving, if not passionate, relationship with his wife. Deanie doesn't "think too much about happiness either." She will marry a man she loves less than she loved Bud. At the end of the film, we hear Deanie's voice reciting lines from William Wordsworth's "Ode on Intimations of Immortality":

Though nothing can bring back the hour
Of splendor in the grass, of glory in the flower;
We will grieve not, rather find
Strength in what remains behind.

The film wants to be a lament for lost youth, for lost passion, but the relationship of Bud and Deanie is so overwrought, so dysfunctional, that it is difficult to see it as ideal youthful romance. What Bud and Deanie had, particularly as played by Natalie Wood and Warren Beatty, is youthful beauty and a powerful sexual desire. That, for Inge, seems to be the glory of youth. There is a telling edit three quarters of the way through the film: an image of Deanie hand in hand with John, her husband to be, cuts to an image of the feet of her parents as they sit in their rockers on their front porch. The juxtaposition tells us that this is what Deanie's marriage will be. "Ya gotta take what comes," Bud tells Deanie, and what comes will never meet one's ideals.

Inge's unsuccessful plays of the period, *A Loss of Roses* (1959) and *Natural Affection* (1963), offer equally melodramatic pictures of troubled young men in fraught relationships with their mothers. *A Loss of Roses* takes place in a small Kansas town. Helen, a woman in her forties, shares her home with her twenty-year-old son, Kenny. Kenny's father died saving him from drowning. Since that time, Kenny has been overly

attached to his mother. He remains jealous of her love for his father and of her independence:

KENNY: Dad was the only man in this family you ever loved. Oh sure, *he* was the hero of this family. Not me.

HELEN: I've loved you as much as I dared, Son.

KENNY: Oh, sure!

HELEN: If I'd loved you any more, I'd have destroyed you.

(*A Loss of Roses*, p. 71)

Helen has felt guilty for harboring too much love for her son. Despite his devotion to Helen, Kenny drinks, steals, and, as Helen puts it, "goes out with the trashiest girls in town" (p. 37), his way of spiting Helen for not allowing him to replace his father. Nonetheless, he has no desire to leave home and the mother to whom he is too devoted. Enter Helen's old friend Lila, an entertainer in a traveling show. If Helen is disciplined, Lila has no control over her impulses. She has a history of failed affairs and has spent years as an itinerant performer. Like Deanie in *Splendor in the Grass*, Lila was institutionalized after a suicide attempt. Lila's troupe of eccentric traveling actors is out of work, so Helen offers her a place to stay. For Kenny, Lila is a boyhood memory. He recalls that while Helen was always strict with him, Lila used to indulge him. Now, years later, she repeats her role of indulgent mother surrogate. When Helen refuses an expensive gift from Kenny, he gets furious and, later that evening, goes to bed with Lila. At the end, Lila, after another failed suicide attempt, goes off to get the only job she can find, as a stripper and performer in pornographic movies. Lila's lack of self-discipline makes her the pawn of men: of Kenny, who has sex with her but doesn't want a relationship; and of her erstwhile boyfriend Ricky, who wants to exploit her. For all the unhappiness "good women" may feel in Inge's work, the "bad girls" always come to an unhappy end. Ginny in *Splendor in the Grass* dies in an automobile accident, and Lila becomes a sex worker. There is no decent life outside of the economy of marriage.

If *A Loss of Roses* demonstrates the dangers of a young man being too close to his mother, *Natural Affection* shows the price of neglect of one's son. Sue Barker gave up her son Donnie after his father ran off. He spent his youth in orphanages and, later, in reform school after beating up a young woman, clearly acting out his bitterness at being abandoned by his mother. He is now returning home to his mother and her boyfriend, Bernie. Sue has a good job and is supporting her lazy, unfaithful boyfriend. Inge doesn't ask why an able, successful woman would feel the need to support such a parasite. Bernie is also having sex with the married woman in the apartment across the hall and sending other men to her when he isn't interested. When Donnie arrives, Sue begins overcompensating for her past neglect. Bernie and Donnie vie for Sue's affection. After Bernie leaves, partly out of jealousy and partly to be with the woman next door, Sue must choose between Bernie and Donnie, whose love for his mother contains more than normal maternal affection. Frightened of Donnie's obvious sexual advances and afraid of losing Bernie, Sue lashes out, "I'm not going to give up the rest of my life to keep a worthless kid I never wanted in the first place" (*Natural Affection*, p. 114). When a drunken woman wanders in from a party across the hall and makes sexual advances toward Donnie using the unfortunate phrase "Be nice to mama," Donnie stabs her to death, an ending critics rightfully found gratuitous and illogical.

Both plays offer a bizarre group of subordinate characters who define a chaotic world of sexual freedom. Lila's fellow performers include Ronny, a flamboyant homosexual who has been playing juvenile parts for twenty years (Inge's view of homosexuality as arrested development), a grotesque aging actress (shades of what Lila could become), and Ricky, the handsome actor who plays villains onstage and wants to serve as Lila's pimp offstage. In *Natural Affection*, both husband and wife across the hall are attracted to Bernie. Claire is having sex with Bernie and his friends, and her husband, Vince, keeps giving Bernie presents, a sign of his attraction to Bernie. Their drunken parties are a contrast to Sue's ideal

of domestic order. Sue, too, lives a compromised life with Bernie. He won't marry her because she violates his sense of the gender order: "I'm not gonna marry a broad who can brag she makes more money'n I do" (p. 15). The violence at the end of the play is a consequence of the violations of appropriate gender roles. For all her success in the business world, Sue is, in Inge's eyes, a domestic failure. While Donnie is the primary victim of her failure, his violent action at the end of the play robs him of any sympathy. Indeed, the problem with *Natural Affection* is that no character commands our sympathy. As the critic John Chapman put it: "In such greatly superior plays as *Come Back, Little Sheba* and *Picnic*, Inge has shown a natural affection for many of his characters, and touching insight into them. He just doesn't seem to like anybody, or understand anybody, in his newest play" (p. 384). Moreover, Inge has moved from his usual midwestern small town locale to an urban setting where his idea of urban slang doesn't ring true.

INGE'S UNHAPPY HOMOSEXUALS

In *Where's Daddy?* (1966), his final Broadway play, Inge satirizes psychoanalysis and once again valorizes the conventional gender order and nuclear family. Tom is a feckless young actor. He can't do stage work because his issues with authority make it impossible for him to take direction, so he depends on income from commercials. He has been in analysis for years and uses it to rationalize his irresponsibility toward his pregnant wife. He sees the coming child as a threat to his career and to his freedom. Tom had virtually no parental guidance in his own life. He was a street kid until he was picked up by Pinky, a homosexual professor who became both lover and father figure, but Pinky was too indulgent with Tom, paying off his debts and protecting him when he got into trouble. Tom's wife, Teena, comes from an upper-middle-class background, but she never felt any love from her parents. She has been psychoanalyzed into a state of passivity and dependence on her husband. The culprits, then, are poor or nonexistent parenting and psychoanalysis.

Pinky may seem an odd choice for the voice of conventional morality given his relationship with an underage partner. Nonetheless, it is he who is the most vociferous advocate for marriage and family: "I'm a very old-fashioned man.... I still believe in God, and love, and the sanctity of the home, and all those comforting mores that everyone today considers terribly reactionary. To tell the truth, I seldom witness these phenomena, but I believe in them devoutly" (*Where's Daddy?*, p. 62). When Pinky excoriates Tom, when even Tom's psychiatrist calls him a bastard and hangs up, Tom finally chooses wife and child over freedom.

Pinky is the last in a line of homosexual characters in Inge's plays (one is loath to call them gay). Before the longtime juvenile actor in *A Loss of Roses* (the homosexual as arrested development), and the seemingly homosexual Vince in *Natural Affection*, who can neither satisfy his wife nor admit his longing for Bernie, there were deeply unhappy homosexual characters in the one-act plays Inge wrote in the 1950s and early 1960s. Among the eleven one-act plays Inge published were two written in the early 1950s, "The Tiny Closet" and "The Boy in the Basement." Both dramatize the agony of living a hidden life.

In "The Tiny Closet," Mrs. Crosby, a nosy landlady, and her friend gossip about Mr. Newbold, a middle-aged tenant, who insists that no one open his locked closet. This is the era of Senator Joseph McCarthy and the House Un-American Activities Committee, and Mrs. Crosby thinks secrets are unpatriotic: "I'm a real American, and I say, if anyone's got any secrets he wants to keep hid, let 'em come out in the open and declare himself" (*Eleven Short Plays*, p. 61). This good American and her friend open Mr. Newbold's closet and find it full of ladies' hats that he has made. Mrs. Newbold is horrified at this inversion of the gender order: "I'd rather be harboring a communist than a man who makes hats" (p. 64). When Mr. Newbold discovers that his secret has been exposed, he loses all his self-possession and becomes "a shy and frightened young girl" (p. 65). While it is the fear of exposure and punishment that causes one to lead

a closeted life, Inge equates homosexuality with effeminacy and immaturity. Masculine authority is a role for Mr. Newbold that he surrenders the minute his secret is revealed.

In the more elaborate "The Boy in the Basement," Spencer Scranton is an undertaker who lives with his mean-spirited mother and his father, who is crippled and speechless because of a stroke. His brother is in an asylum because of "whiskey and women" (p. 41), and Spencer is excoriated by his mother for being caught in a police raid in a gay bar, "a meeting place for degenerates" (p. 38). In fury at his mother's attack, Spencer rushes out of the house, but returns the next morning to embrace his mother: "Their need, their desperate dependence on each other, their deep love bring them together like lovers" (p. 50). Here we find another version of the intense Oedipal attachment that Inge expresses in *A Loss of Roses* and *Natural Affection*, but in "The Boy in the Basement" it is offered as a cause for Spencer's homosexuality. Spencer's only real moments of joy are the minutes he spends in innocent banter with the grocery delivery boy, Joker. They behave like real pals, partly because Joker understands that "in some ways you never grew up, Spence" (p. 46). When Spencer returns home after his angry exit and brief attempt at independence from his mother, he finds that he has a new corpse to prepare for burial—that of Joker, who has accidentally drowned. At the end, he is standing over the naked body of the young man he loves, preparing to drain his blood. Sex can only be furtive and sad for a "degenerate" like Spencer, trapped in a codependence with his nagging mother. With this view of homosexuality, it is no wonder that Inge could never make peace with his own sexual orientation.

More than a decade after these two one-act plays, Pinky in *Where's Daddy?* sees himself as another case of arrested development, another old boy who never grows into a man, one of the men who "go to [their] graves without dignity or bearing" (p. 31). In his spare time, Pinky knits sweaters for his poodle, hardly a conventionally masculine pastime. Inge could be candid about presenting homosexuals in his plays in the 1960s, but he couldn't conceive of a proud, strong gay man. If he had, he might have been able to live a happier life. He is very much a product of his time and place.

Inge and his colleagues Tennessee Williams and Edward Albee were attacked by critics, particularly Howard Taubman of the *New York Times*, for writing plays in which the female characters were really gay men in disguise in plays that presented an insidious homosexual message. Taubman's 1963 article "Modern Primer: Helpful Hints to Tell Appearances from Truth," occasioned in part by the opening of *Natural Affection*, was really a primer in unveiling "the intimations and symbols of homosexuality in our theater." The covert homosexuality had always been there, particularly in the loving presentation of the male body and the magnetic attractiveness of the beautiful young man in *Come Back, Little Sheba* and *Picnic*.

THE NOVELS

By 1970 Inge had lost his confidence in playwriting and Hollywood was no longer seeking his services. In order to keep writing and to keep his name before the public, he wrote two novels, neither of which was a critical nor a commercial success, though both offer insights into the author's psyche. Both novels are set in Freedom, Kansas, a fictional small town similar to the one in which Inge grew up.

Evelyn Wyckoff, the title character of *Good Luck, Miss Wyckoff*, published in 1970, is what used to be called an "old maid schoolteacher." She teaches Latin in the local high school and has a room in a boardinghouse. Evelyn seems to be a model citizen: a fine teacher and an active advocate for good local education. She is in her late thirties and is still a virgin. After years of following a strict routine, Evelyn finds herself in the throes of a major depression: "After the few hours of sleep she would get at night, she would awaken early in the morning with a despair so overpowering she couldn't fight it" (p. 64). The depression Evelyn experiences is one Inge knew well and, as the playwright did when he taught in Kansas, Evelyn goes to the city (Wichita) to see

a psychiatrist. Her local doctor had suggested that what she needed was a discreet sexual affair. Unfortunately, Evelyn has an affair that is anything but discreet—sex in her classroom after hours with a young black man who is working as the janitor. The affair is discovered, Evelyn loses her job and her place in the boardinghouse, and she must leave town.

Inge chronicles the stages of Evelyn's affair. "Desire and repulsion were so fused in her, she could not distinguish one from the other" (p. 153), but desire for more of "the rapture she had never dared to hope that her body would ever feel" (p. 159) drove her to continue until she and Rafe, her sexual partner, are caught in flagrante delicto. Her expulsion from the community leads her to realize "how a human being is totally alone in the universe" (p. 174). Leaving Freedom for an uncertain future, "She felt no shame for having let Rafe Collins use her as he did, for she saw that what happened was inevitable. And she wouldn't now want to be without the experience he had given her" (p. 45).

While the novel suggests that sex was the proper cure for Evelyn Wyckoff's depression, it also reflects Inge's own fear of expressing his forbidden sexual desire. Here miscegenation stands in for homosexuality, and sex outside of the norms of marriage and the barriers of race and class lead to guilt, shame, and expulsion, as Inge seemed to fear expression of his homosexuality would.

The major weakness of the novel is its treatment of Rafe, who emerges as a racist's cartoon vision of the priapic black man: sexually aggressive and sadistic. Inge describes him as having the "physical ease and grace and pride of a jungle lord" (p. 36). At first, Rafe seems to be an African American version of the Inge ideal; beautiful, virile, athletic, and sexually magnetic. The girls at the junior college Rafe attends "avoided being around him because it was difficult to be within his physical radius without feeling the animal attraction of his body" (p. 50). Yet Rafe sees sex as domination and humiliation. He makes Evelyn crawl across the floor to him and, later, inflicts physical pain. Evelyn was aware that "the sexual act was a release of Rafe's contempt for her

rather than his lust" (p. 159), but that didn't diminish her need for what he offered her. Of course, sex with a twenty-two-year-old white man would not have been as scandalous, but Inge makes Rafe such a caricature that the novel loses all credibility.

My Son Is a Splendid Driver (1971) is, for the most part, autobiography disguised as fiction. Much of the novel is a family memoir, and one can see the basis for several Inge characters in the portraits presented here. Inge also presents his alter ego's earlier sexual experiences. Joey, the narrator and Inge's alter ego, describes the sad fate of the shopkeeper Mr. Ogden, whose proclivity for sex with homeless or poor boys led to his divorce, his loss of his property, and his expulsion from town: "No one ever heard where he went. No one ever inquired" (p. 99). When in college a friend, Bob, makes sexual advances, Joey, Inge's alter ego, remembers: "I of course still retained dark memories of the social fate of Mr. Ogden years before" (p. 140). Joey describes his repulsion toward effeminate men and his equation of effeminacy with homosexuality: "I avoided them in all my classes on campus, fearing an effeminate element in myself that might classify me as one of them" (p. 140). Later Joey has a brief affair with a rather Bohemian young woman, Betsy, that gives him more confidence in his masculinity: "I accepted my maleness. Betsy had given it to me, easily and without fuss, and it was the greatest gift that I ever received" (p. 185). In Inge's view of sexuality, heterosexual coitus reinforces one's sense of "maleness," while homosexuality would involve a loss of masculinity. Unfortunately, Betsy had too stained a reputation even to be allowed as Joey's companion at fraternity parties, and she leaves for New York. Years later, Joey is reunited with Betsy, now married and devoted to Alcoholics Anonymous. The novel ends with the death of Joey's parents.

My Son Is a Splendid Driver holds interest for devotees of Inge's work, but this thinly veiled memoir doesn't offer the vivid characterizations of his best work. Joey doesn't emerge as a very interesting guide to a lost, past Midwest.

Inge's work always had a homosexual slant, but its main themes were broader than that. His work is a celebration of youth and beauty and a lament for its transience. It offers heterosexual marriage as a necessary human relationship, but also one that diminishes as one's youth and sexual potency diminishes. Heterosexual relationships are also compromised by the basic differences between men and women who are attracted to the men least likely to want to settle down. Above all, there is the conflict between powerful sexual desire and the strict social mores of a midwestern small town. There is a prevailing melancholy in Inge's work, but at its best, in the plays that were hits in the 1950s, there is a depth of characterization and authenticity of language that has led to many revivals and serious critical analysis.

Selected Bibliography

WORKS OF WILLIAM INGE

PLAYS

Four Plays. New York: Grove Press, 1958. (Contains *Come Back, Little Sheba; Picnic; Bus Stop;* and *The Dark at the Top of the Stairs.*)

Splendor in the Grass. Screenplay for Warner Bros., film directed by Elia Kazan, 1961.) Warner Home Video, 2009.

Eleven Short Plays. New York: Dramatists Play Service, 1962. (Contains *To Bobolink for Her Spirit, People in the Wind* [an earlier version of *Bus Stop*], *A Social Event, The Boy in the Basement, The Tiny Closet, Memory of Summer, Bus Riley's Back in Town, The Rainy Afternoon, The Mall, An Incident at Standish Arms,* and *The Strains of Triumph.*)

Summer Brave and Eleven Short Plays. New York: Random House, 1962.

A Loss of Roses. New York: Dramatists Play Service, 1963.

Natural Affection. New York: Random House, 1963.

Where's Daddy?. New York: Dramatists Play Service, 1966.

NOVELS

Good Luck, Miss Wyckoff. New York: Atlantic Monthly Press, 1970.

My Son Is a Splendid Driver. New York: Atlantic Monthly Press, 1971.

PAPERS

William Inge Collection, Independence Community College, Independence, Kansas.

CRITICAL AND BIOGRAPHICAL STUDIES

Brustein, Robert. "The Men-Taming Women of William Inge." *Harper's,* November 1958, pp. 52–57.

Chapman, John. Review of *Natural Affection.* In *New York Theatre Critics' Reviews.* Vol. 24. New York: Critics' Theatre Reviews, 1963. P. 384.

Clum, John M. *Still Acting Gay: Male Homosexuality in Modern Drama.* New York: St. Martins, 2000. Pp. 135–141.

———. *The Drama of Marriage.* New York: Palgrave, 2012. Pp. 143–144, 156–172.

Johnson, Jeff. *William Inge and the Subversion of Gender: Rewriting Stereotypes in the Plays, Novels, and Screenplays.* Jefferson, N.C.: McFarland, 2005.

McClure, Arthur F. *Memories of Splendor: The Midwestern World of William Inge.* Topeka: Kansas State Historical Society, 1989.

Shuman, R. Baird. *William Inge.* Rev. ed. Boston: Twayne, 1989.

Taubman, Howard. "Modern Primer: Helpful Hints to Tell Appearances from Truth." *New York Times,* April 28, 1963, sec. 2, p. 1.

Voss, Ralph F. *William Inge: The Strains of Triumph.* Lawrence: University of Kansas Press, 1989.

Wertheim, Albert. "Dorothy's Friends in Kansas: The Gay Inflections of William Inge." In *Staging Desire: Queer Readings of American Theatre History.* Edited by Kim Marra and Robert Schanke. Ann Arbor: University of Michigan Press, 2002. Pp. 194–217.

FILMS BASED ON THE WORKS OF WILLIAM INGE

Come Back, Little Sheba. Screenplay by Ketti Frings. Directed by Daniel Mann. Paramount, 1952.

Picnic. Screenplay by Daniel Taradash. Directed by Joshua Logan. Columbia Pictures, 1955.

Bus Stop. Screenplay by George Axelrod. Directed by Joshua Logan. 20th Century Fox, 1956.

The Dark at the Top of the Stairs. Screenplay by Harriet Frank, Jr., and Irving Ravetch. Directed by Delbert Mann. Warner Bros., 1960.

The Stripper. Screenplay by Meade Roberts (based on *A Loss of Roses*). Directed by Franklin J. Schaffner. 20th Century Fox, 1963.

Bus Riley's Back in Town. Screenplay by "Walter Cage" (pseudonym for Inge after studio massively revised his screenplay). Directed by Harvey Hart. Universal Pictures, 1965.

H. P. LOVECRAFT

(1890—1937)

Jonas Prida

BORN INTO GENTEEL wealth and dying in poverty, Howard Phillips Lovecraft changed American supernatural writing, updating its themes and adding the element of cosmic horror. His early reading in his grandfather's library of classical literature, mixed with his own interest in Edgar Allan Poe, Sherlock Holmes, and the *Arabian Nights*, acted as fertile soil for Lovecraft's imagination. This imagination led to what was arguably America's first modern science fiction story, "The Colour out of Space" (1927); the creation of the fictional city of Arkham, home of Miskatonic University and its library's notorious *Necronomicon*; and his most famous story, "The Call of Cthulhu" (1928), which continues to be appropriated, rewritten, and parodied. Despite publishing almost exclusively in amateur periodicals and pulp magazines such as *Weird Tales*, Lovecraft's influence on twentieth- and twenty-first-century horror continues to be felt in the work of writers like Stephen King and filmmakers like Guillermo del Toro.

Separating Lovecraft from early-twentieth-century writers, especially those writing for pulps and other popular magazines, is the paranoid state of his first-person narrators and the cosmic scope of his dramas, ideas brought about by advances in physics, astronomy, evolutionary biology, and other sciences. The usual sources of certainty—religion, science, human interaction—were stripped away by Albert Einstein's new theory of relativity and the developing fields of anthropology and comparative religions. Lovecraft's narrators move from a state of security in their knowledge to a state of radical doubt, confronting nameless cults whose aim is recalling other dimensional beings bent on destroying the Earth. However, these entities hold no direct ill will toward humanity; instead, these cosmic forces

are indifferent to humankind, and for Lovecraft, this lack of feeling—the absence of even a feeling of hate—makes for cosmic horror.

But as much as Lovecraft's narratives explore lost cities in Antarctica, as in his *At the Mountains of Madness* (1936), or hereditary castles, as in "The Rats in the Walls" (1924), he always saw himself as a citizen of Providence, Rhode Island. Born there in 1897 and dying in Providence's Jane Brown Memorial Hospital at age forty-seven, Lovecraft spent all but two years of his adult life in Providence. He used family connections to gain access to Brown University's telescope and wrote extensively of the city's architecture. Chronically looking into the past for stability and order, Lovecraft imagined eighteenth-century Providence to be the epitome of New England values. But changes in Providence brought about by immigration and industrialization also gave rise to Lovecraft's undeniable nativism and racism. Much like his writings, Lovecraft's life straddles the certainties of the late nineteenth century with the confusing dynamism of the early twentieth.

BIOGRAPHY

Born in his family's Providence home on August 20, 1890, to Winfield Scott Lovecraft, a commercial salesman, and Sarah Susan Phillips, the daughter of a wealthy family, Lovecraft's early life was marred by his father's mental illness. By 1893 Winfield Lovecraft was unable to care for himself and remained in Providence's Butler Hospital until his death in 1898. Surviving medical records state the cause of death as "general paresis," most likely caused by tertiary syphilis. There is no documented evidence that Lovecraft ever visited his father during his time in Butler,

but the lack of a father from age three would lead to Lovecraft's tight-knit and claustrophobic relationship with his mother and her sisters, and his equally influential relationship with his grandfather, Whipple Van Buren Phillips.

Lovecraft's maternal grandfather, whom Lovecraft called "the centre of my entire universe," gave a young Lovecraft access to culture and learning that sustained Lovecraft throughout his life (Joshi, 2010, p. 28). A moderately successful business person, Phillips brought Lovecraft art from Europe, allowed access to his well-stocked library, and inculcated a sense of wonder in the young Lovecraft. At the same time, Lovecraft's mother and aunts provided Lovecraft with the comforts of a spoiled child: Lovecraft was given almost anything within reason: "my array of toys, books, and other youthful pleasures was virtually unlimited" (p. 65). But this array came with a price: Lovecraft's mother and sisters protected the young Lovecraft, walking him to school, isolating him from the neighborhood's undesirable elements, and, on one occasion, trying to enroll him in dancing lessons. This combination of literary imagination and domestic enclosure, a strain of the outward and the inward, underpins much of Lovecraft's later fiction.

The 1904 death of Lovecraft's grandfather changed the Lovecraft family for the worse. The family's finances collapsed, forcing Lovecraft and his mother to move from their large home into a shared duplex. Lovecraft's nervousness, already manifested in an 1898 breakdown, contributed to his spotty academic record at Hope Street English and Classical High School. A second breakdown in 1908, right before his hoped-for acceptance into Brown University, forced Lovecraft to largely withdraw from school, leading to one of the ironies in Lovecraft's life: this erudite and scientifically minded twentieth-century writer failed to graduate high school. Complicating matters was his mother's complex love-hate relationship with her son: Lovecraft was both a brilliant mind and an economic liability. Additionally, Lovecraft's appearance so disturbed his mother that she claimed he was "hideous" and "did not like to walk upon the street where people could gaze at him" (p. 131).

Despite his mother's antipathy for his looks and his inability to get a job, Lovecraft continued to live with her for the next decade, spending his time reading voluminously in the classics and early pulp magazines, as well as writing prose and poetry for a variety of amateur journals. He became directly involved in the internal politics of the amateur publishing field, serving as the interim president of the United Amateur Press Association in 1917, in addition to editing his own journal, *The Conservative*. Although writing for these magazines was not financially rewarding, it brought Lovecraft into a community of writers around America, forging literary friendships that would last a lifetime, in addition to providing a venue to explore his craft.

In a strange way, the 1919 institutionalization of his mother and her death in 1921 was one of the best things that happened to Lovecraft. His own health improved; he traveled to Boston and New Hampshire to visit literary friends and see one of his literary idols, Lord Dunsany; and he began to submit stories, letters, and collaborations to the new magazine *Weird Tales*. Between 1923 and 1924 the pulp magazine published five of Lovecraft's stories, giving him his first professional writing paychecks and introducing his work to a wider audience. Additionally, Lovecraft started to do revisions and ghostwriting projects for figures as diverse as Harry Houdini and the pop psychologist David Van Bush. It was also during this period that Lovecraft was wooed by Sonia Greene; the two were married on March 3, 1924.

Lovecraft's marriage to Greene, while largely an unhappy one, did provide Lovecraft an opportunity to live outside of Providence. He and Greene moved to Brooklyn, where Greene owned a business, and where Lovecraft would have an opportunity to commercialize his writing. However, Greene's business failed, Lovecraft published only sporadically, and the couple lived apart as Greene traveled in an effort to stay solvent. Additionally, Lovecraft hated New York City and its polyglot nature; his writings from the period, such as "The Horror at Red Hook" (1927) and "Cool Air" (1928), are filled with invectives about swarthy visages and uncontrolled

immigrants. The two maintained their marriage of convenience until early 1929, when divorce proceedings were filed by Lovecraft. In a sad end to an already sad affair, the divorce papers were never officially processed, and Greene, who remarried in 1936, became an accidental bigamist.

Back in Providence, Lovecraft continued his correspondence with other supernatural writers, who began to take parts of Lovecraft's "The Call of Cthulhu" and rework them. Frank Belknap Long, Clark Ashton Smith, Robert Bloch (the author of *Psycho* [1959]), and August Derleth, who later formed Arkham House Publishing in an effort to keep Lovecraft's work in circulation, began publishing stories in what would come to be called "The Cthulhu Mythos" (a term invented by Derleth). Additionally, Lovecraft published two pieces that cemented his place as a worthy descendant to Poe: the modern science fiction masterpiece "The Colour out of Space" and "The Dunwich Horror" (1929), a tale of interdimensional sorcery set in rural Massachusetts. Lovecraft also traveled extensively between 1928 and 1930, visiting Vermont, South Carolina, and Quebec. Despite the popular conception of Lovecraft as a recluse, his travels and voluminous letter writing (the Lovecraft scholar S. T. Joshi estimates that Lovecraft wrote more than 100,000 letters in his life) show a socially active Lovecraft with interests in architecture and history.

As it did for many other Americans, the Great Depression corresponded to Lovecraft's most crushing poverty, with Lovecraft claiming that he could live on $15 a week. But it was also the period in which Lovecraft wrote his "non-supernatural cosmic" novel *At the Mountains of Madness* and his masterful novella *The Shadow over Innsmouth*. Although *Mountains* was never published as a novel in Lovecraft's lifetime, being rejected by *Weird Tales* and later appearing in an edited form in *Astounding Stories*(1936), it yokes science fiction with cosmic horror in ways only equaled by his own "Colour out of Space." *Shadow*, submitted to and rejected by *Weird Tales* in 1933, was published in a limited edition of 200 copies in 1936; it takes the reader through the decaying seaport of Innsmouth, Massachusetts, mixing Lovecraft's own anxieties about

race and immigration and melding them into a paranoid amalgam.

The last years of Lovecraft's life, spent living in Providence, entertaining friends who visited, and traveling when he could afford it, were marred by his ever-declining financial state and worsening health. His later stories, such as "The Dreams in the Witch House" (1933) and "The Shadow out of Time" (1936) are complex explorations of extradimensional space and mind exchange, but it became difficult for Lovecraft to maintain the output needed to support himself. By early 1937 he knew that he was ill, and by March he was no longer able to feed himself. On March 15, 1937, America's foremost horror writer, and the man who is largely responsible for bringing the supernatural into the twentieth century, died in his beloved Providence.

EARLY WRITINGS

A young Lovecraft wrote traditional horror stories influenced by one of his literary idols, Edgar Allan Poe. Poe visited Providence in the 1840s, and the stories of his infatuation with Providence native Sarah Whitman, along with Poe's appealing aesthetic, made for an unsurprising period in which Lovecraft constructed short pieces in the vein of Poe.

Lovecraft's "Dagon" (1919), for example, uses Poe's trope of an unreliable first-person narrator. Told as a flashback, the unnamed protagonist, the survivor of a German submarine attack, is adrift in the Pacific. Going in and out of consciousness, the narrator awakens to find himself in "a slimy expanse of hellish black mire" (*Dagon*, p. 15); engulfed by the smell of rotting fish, the narrator makes his way to a monolith and a series of bas-reliefs. While investigating the statues, he glimpses something "vast, Polyphemus-like, and loathsome" (p. 18). In a bit of literary deflation that would do his literary idol justice, the next sentence is simply, "I think I went mad then" (p. 18). The story ends with the narrator hearing sloshing sounds outside of his door as he prepares to kill himself by jumping out of the window.

Roughly three years later, Lovecraft published the serial "Herbert West—Reanimator" (1922). Told again by an unnamed first-person narrator, this six-part story, set largely in Lovecraft's recurring fictional town of Arkham and its Miskatonic University, uses Poe's mixture of horror and black comedy from works like "Hop Frog" (1849) to follow the grave-robbing, corpse-reanimating exploits of Herbert West. A brilliant but eccentric student, West is known for spouting "wild theories" that hinge on "the essentially mechanistic nature of life" and concern "means for operating the organic machinery of mankind by calculated chemical action" (*Dagon* , p. 134). To prove his theories, West and the narrator-assistant begin to disinter bodies from the local potter's field, where the dead are too poor to have been embalmed. To both men's surprise, the first experiment works, but the newly animated corpse escapes. The rest of the serial follows West's reanimation efforts during a typhoid epidemic, a boxing match, and World War I, where he is successful in animating a Canadian pilot's headless body. The story ends with the pilot, now sporting a wax head, leading the other corpses on a raid on West's Boston home, where they rip him to pieces, taking his head as a trophy.

"Herbert West" combines comedic touches—the headless pilot carries his decapitated head in a bag, and a pitiful underground boxing match provides another fresh corpse for West—with horrific scenes of violence and gore. Dr. Halsey, a Miskatonic professor who dies while tending typhoid patients only to be reanimated by West, kills seventeen people before being placed in an asylum. West's lab in Flanders is filled "with blood and lesser human debris almost ankle-deep on the slimy floor, and with hideous reptilian abnormalities sprouting, bubbling, and baking over a winking bluish-green spectre of dim flame in a far corner of black shadows" (p. 157). In the tradition of Poe, Lovecraft's text oscillates between the poles of laughing and screaming.

In 1924 *Weird Tales* published Lovecraft's "The Rats in the Walls." The first-person narrator, an American by the name of Delapore, inherits the long-abandoned Exham Priory in England. During the refurbishing of the Priory and his discussions with the locals, Delapore uncovers his family's sinister past: described as a "race of hereditary daemons" (*Annotated Lovecraft*, p. 32), several of his ancestors were suspected of kidnapping, murder, and witchcraft. After moving into the house, Delapore begins to have terrible dreams, which, along with the continual unease of his house cats and the furtive skittering of paws behind the newly repaired walls, lead Delapore to discover a vault in the subbasement. Delapore engages scientists and archaeologists to explore beneath the vault. What they discover is terrifying: "an insane tangle of human bones, or bones at least as human as those on the steps" (p. 49). The final pages chart Delapore's linguistic retrogression into primitive grunts mirroring his return to his ancestral cannibalism: "they … found me crouching in the blackness over the plump, half-eaten body of Capt. Norrys, with my own cat leaping and tearing at my throat" (p. 54). Delapore is institutionalized, but he can hear "the daemon rats that race behind the padding in this room and beckon me down to greater horrors than I have ever known; the rats they can never hear; the rats, the rats in the walls" (p. 55).

As much as any Lovecraft text, "Rats" displays indebtedness to Poe. Before the family's flight to America, the last name was de la Pore, a less-than-subtle allusion to Poe. The doubling that occurs between the physical house and the decaying familial lineage mimics Poe's "Fall of the House of Usher." Walter de la Pore, the ancestor who leaves for America, flees to Virginia, boyhood home of Poe. The unreliable narrator who slides into madness at some point in the narrative is a standard Poe device, used in such classic stories as "The Tell-Tale Heart" (1843) and "The Black Cat" (1843). Delapore's black cat is the key for finding the vault beneath the subbasement. The titular cat in "The Black Cat" is the key for the police finding the narrator's murdered wife; but instead of discovering the tomb, Poe's cat is walled up within one.

If Lovecraft had done nothing more than imitate Poe, he would have joined the host of writers from the 1920s and 1930s who have

largely vanished from public, and in many cases scholarly, view. But a second influence from Ireland would present Lovecraft with another set of aesthetics, and, with it, grounding for his most famous pieces.

THE DUNSANIAN PERIOD

Poe gave birth to Lovecraft's consistent use of unreliable narrators and unifying aesthetic principles; the Irish writer and fantasist Edward Plunkett, better known in literary circles as Lord Dunsany, introduced the fantastical, otherworldly element. The publication of Dunsany's *The Gods of Pegāna* (1905), a collection of stories centered on an invented world, captured Lovecraft's imagination, as did Dunsany's *Book of Wonder* (1912), which Lovecraft wrote a poem about in 1920. In addition to reading Dunsany's material, Lovecraft heard him speak during a 1920 American tour. It was soon after this lecture that Lovecraft began his "Dunsany" period, creating some of the most densely imaginative writings of the 1920s.

Lovecraft's first Dunsanian fiction is his short story "The White Ship" (1919), where an unnamed narrator is taken aboard a dream ship, travels through various realities, and when awakening, causes the ship to crash. In this otherwise slight story, several themes that Lovecraft would return to are evident: a narrator wishing to escape reality, the importance of dreaming and a dream world, and an embellished, almost rococo writing style. Also in 1919, before Dunsany's visit, Lovecraft wrote "To Edward John Moreton Drax Plunkett, Eighteenth Baron Dunsany," an extended paean to Dunsany. Lines such as "Monarch of Fancy! whose ethereal mind, / Mounts fairy peaks, and leaves the throng behind" (*Ancient Track*, p. 66) are indicative of Lovecraft's infatuation with the Irish writer.

Lovecraft's most extended Dunsanian writing is his novel *The Dream-Quest of Unknown Kadath*, which was written in 1926–1927 but never published during Lovecraft's lifetime, only appearing in the 1943 collection *Beyond the Wall of Sleep*. Lovecraft never expected the novel to be published; he saw it merely as "useful practice for later and more authentic attempts in the novel form" (Joshi, 2010, vol. 2, p. 659). It is not surprising that Lovecraft made no effort to publish the novel, given the text's complex narrative and baroque writing style. Roughly broken into five narrative sections, *Dream-Quest* centers on Lovecraft's oft-used narrator Randolph Carter, who dreams of a majestic sunset city, only to have the dream end before he can see the city closely. Undaunted, Carter dreams his way into the various landscapes, looking for Kadath, home of the gods, in hopes that he can learn of the dream city's location.

While in the dream universe, Carter encounters assorted bizarre creatures: the Zoogs, predatory rodents who rule the Enchanted Forest; the cats of Ulthar, who provide him with information about Kadath's location and later save him from the Moon-Beasts and the god Nyarlathotep; the night-gaunts, who kidnap Carter and leave him in the underworld; and a race of sentient ghouls led by Richard Pickman, a character from the earlier Lovecraft story "Pickman's Model" (1927). After successfully escaping from the underworld, Carter visits the onyx city of Inganok, believing it to be near to Kadath. What Carter finds instead is captivity at the hands of a priest of Leng, another mysterious place in a continent of mysterious places. Carter escapes into the monastery's mazelike architecture, reconnecting with a group of Pickman's ghouls who have also been taken captive. The combined force of the ghouls and Carter defeat the Lengians, and the ghouls summon night-gaunts to finally take Carter to Kadath.

Finding Kadath initially empty, Carter is rewarded for his patience: a procession arrives, led by "a tall, slim figure with the young face of an antique Pharaoh, gay with prismatic robes and crowned with a golden pshent that glowed with inherent light" (*Dream Quest*, pp. 127–128). The figure explains that Kadath's gods have left, renouncing their godhood. Only by returning the gods to Kadath, the figure explains, can the natural order of the universe be restored. After giving a skeptical Carter this information, the figure reveals itself as Nyarlathotep. Summoning

a giant bird that can fly through space, Nyarlathotep sends Carter "toward those inconceivable, unlighted chambers beyond time" (p. 138). At first reconciled to his doom, Carter realizes that he is dreaming and all he needs to do to escape is wake up. Falling through space, his thoughts return to New England and he awakens in his room in Boston. Nyarlathotep is left brooding over the cold waste of Kadath and taunting the gods he has recalled from the sunset city.

This summary of *The Dream-Quest of Unknown Kadath* does not do justice to the novel's outré complexity. After the battle between the cats of Ulthar and the Zoogs, Carter shakes the paw of the cat elder; the night-gaunts have "bat wings whose beating made no sound, ugly prehensile paws, and barbed tails that lashed needlessly and disquietingly" (p. 41); the landscape Carter dreams his way through is filled with basalt pillars, onyx mines, Cyclopean towers, and endless mazes. Carter's captivity on the moon is at the hands, or rather tentacles, of "great greyish-white slippery things which could expand and contract at will … whose principal shape … was that of a sort of toad without any eyes, but with a curious vibrating mass of short pink tentacles on the end of its blunt, vague snout" (pp. 20–21). Lovecraft spills out exotic name after exotic name: Snireth-Ko, the great dreamer; as well as the "templed terraces of Zar," "the spires of infamous Thalarion," "the charnel gardens of Zura," and "Sona-Nyl, blessed land of fancy," the latter four in one sentence (p. 17).

Dream-Quest plays an important role in both the creation of Lovecraft's mythology and the interconnected nature of his stories. Nyarlathotep, the Crawling Chaos, and Azathoth, the blind idiot god, become developed deities in *Dream-Quest*, and these gods appear in other, more famous, Lovecraft texts. Through these gods Lovecraft begins to explore the cosmic nature of his mythology; Carter's flight at the novel's end finds him "leaving behind the stars and the realms of matter, and darting meteor-like through stark formlessness" (p. 138). Lovecraft will continue to explore deep time and space in stories such as "The Call of Cthulhu," "The Whisperer in Darkness" (1931), and his other novel, *At the Mountains of Madness*. Lovecraft incorporates characters from his other works in *Dream-Quest*: Pickman is from "Pickman's Model"; the priest Atal is a character in two earlier Dunsanian-influenced stories, "The Cats of Ulthar" (1920) and "The Other Gods" (1921); and Randolph Carter himself is a character in the 1919 short story "The Statement of Randolph Carter" as well as other dream-cycle texts, including "The Silver Key" (1929) and a later collaboration with E. Hoffman Price, "Through the Gates of the Silver Key" (first published in 1934). Although Lovecraft moved away from Dunsany's influence as he became more confident in his own writing, the fantasy and mythology building that he gleaned from Dunsany were never far from the surface.

What propelled Lovecraft to his place as the most important supernatural writer of the middle twentieth century was his ability to synthesize Dunsany's skills of world building and myth creation with Poe's focused aesthetic and grounding of texts in the real. By mixing the fantastic with the mundane, the horrifying with the banal, Lovecraft altered the trajectory of weird fiction, beginning with two of his masterworks, "The Call of Cthulhu" and the first modern science fiction story, "The Colour out of Space."

MAJOR WORKS

Although written after Lovecraft began work on "The Call of Cthulhu," "The Colour out of Space" was the first of the major works to be published, appearing the September 1927 issue of *Amazing Stories*. Lovecraft considered it one of his best works, especially the extraterrestrial entity at the story's center. In one of his letters, he writes, "Most of my monsters fail altogether to satisfy my sense of the cosmic—the abnormally chromatic entity in 'The Colour out of Space' being the only one of the lot which I take any pride in" (*Annotated Lovecraft*, p. 57). However, there is much more to take pride in: "Colour" does a masterful job of mixing contemporary science, already a passion of Lovecraft's, with a rural Massachusetts setting. The dynamic

of the new with the old, along with the collision of the interstellar with the domestic, propels the narrative.

Much like his Poe-influenced material of the early 1920s, "Colour" uses a first-person narrator, a surveyor measuring the countryside in preparation for a new reservoir for Boston's drinking water, based on the Quabbin Reservoir construction project, which began in 1926. But "Colour" diverges from Lovecraft's early material in the narrator's distance: instead of being a participant, as in "Rats in the Walls," for example, the narrator of "Colour" hears about the "strange days" from older residents and then from Ammi Pierce, the family's next-door neighbor. By shifting the narrative perspective, the accumulation of stories, details, scientific testing, and, finally, the alien's destructive capability, becomes the focus of the action.

"Colour" revolves around a meteorite landing near the well at Nahum Gardner's farm. News of the meteorite brings out professors and scientists from Lovecraft's Miskatonic University, who are amazed at the rock's properties. Testing reveals it to be unlike anything of this world; to make matters even more confusing, the sample fragment disappears overnight. The scientists return to the crash site and pry off the meteorite's outside layers, exposing the core, which, says the narrator, "resembled some of the bands in the meteor's strange spectrum, was almost impossible to describe; and it was only by analogy that they called it colour at all" (*Annotated Lovecraft*, p. 69). After lightning strikes destroy what is left of the meteorite, the true horror begins. The fall's harvest grows to incredible size, but all the fruit is rotten and the trees move when no wind is blowing; animal footprints in the snow look unnatural; the local vegetation seems to glow in the dark.

The Gardner family begins to show similar effects. Nahum's wife, Nabby, has periodic fits of screaming: "Something was taken away—she was being drained of something—something was fastening itself on her that ought not to be" (p. 77). Thaddeus follows his mother into madness, driven insane by "the moving colours down there" in the well (p. 79). Two brothers, Merwin

and Zenas Gardner, simply disappear on trips to the well. Ammi pays a visit to the Gardner house and finds the now-crumbling figure of Mrs. Gardner locked in the attic. After performing a mercy killing on the "blasphemous monstrosity," Ammi finds the disintegrating body of Nahum; as Nahum dies, he gives Ammi an extended explanation of what has happened, ending with "an' it burns an' sucks … it come from some place whar things ain't as they is here" (p. 86).

The rest of the narrative follows Ammi and six other men who investigate the deaths. After discovering the skeletons of Merwin and Zenas, the group watches as colors begin swarming around the well: "a monstrous constellation of unnatural light, like a glutted swarm of corpse-fed fireflies dancing hellish sarabands over an accursed marsh" (p. 92). The constellation is met by a shaft of phosphorescent light pouring out of the well. Ammi and the men realize that the farmhouse is about to be engulfed and flee; looking back from a safe distance, they see the "hideous thing [shoot] vertically up toward the sky like a rocket or meteor, leaving behind no trail and disappearing through a round and curiously regular hole in the clouds before any man could gasp or cry out" (p. 95). Ammi, however, notices that one of the lights drops back to earth. The story ends with the narrator hoping for the creation of the reservoir and resolving never to drink from it.

"The Colour out of Space" uses a variety of scientific technologies to explain what the color is, or more accurately, what the color is not. Miskatonic scientists subject the meteorite to heating with a blowpipe, beating with a hammer, examining it under a spectroscope, and dropping hydrochloric acid on it. For all their testing, the scientists only discover that the rock is magnetic and has colors with no correspondence with the normal color spectrum. Lovecraft takes great pains to describe the various reagents and instruments used to examine "a piece of the great outside" (pp. 69–70). It is this grounding of the text in early-twentieth-century science that makes the transformation of the Gardners horrific. Since not even the best minds can figure out what the globes are, humanity is largely helpless in the

face of the "frightful messenger from unformed realms of infinity" (p. 99). The alien forms are not motivated by human desires or fears; they land, they feed, and they leave without explanation. This indifference and pure alienness are central to "The Colour out of Space" operating as the first modern science fiction story.

This same indifference is expanded and coalesced in Lovecraft's masterwork, "The Call of Cthulhu." Written in the summer of 1926 and published in the February 1928 *Weird Tales,* it is arguably Lovecraft's most influential piece. The sleeping god Cthulhu, the murderous cult that wants to wake him, the cosmic forces at work, and the tantalizing clues that are put together have spawned pastiches, reworkings, comic books, movies, role-playing games, television episodes, and music. Without dismissing other important Lovecraft material like "The Colour out of Space" or "The Dunwich Horror," if Lovecraft would have only penned "Call of Cthulhu" his cultural influence would still be measurable.

The three-part narrative follows Lovecraft's typical first-person narrator. While going through the papers of his recently deceased granduncle, Professor Angell, he finds a disturbing idol and a packet with the words "Cthulhu Cult" written on it. Reading the packet, the narrator learns of the strange dreams of an artist, Wilcox, who dreams about "great Cyclopean cities of titan blocks and sky-flung monoliths, all dripping with green ooze and sinister with latent horror" (*Dunwich Horror* p. 133). Through a scattered collection of news clippings, the narrator also discovers that these unsettling dreams are affecting artists and sensitive people around the globe.

The second part of a manuscript he finds revolves around a 1908 meeting of the American Archaeological Society. The meeting is interrupted by John Raymond Legrasse, a police inspector from New Orleans, who brings a small idol and a disturbing story. The idol, a "monster of vaguely anthropoid outline, but with an octopus-like head whose face was a mass of feelers, a scaly, rubbery-looking body, prodigious claws on hind and fore feet, and long, narrow wings behind" (p. 138), was captured during a raid on a group of degenerates living in the

Louisiana swamp. During the interrogation of the surviving cultists, Legrasse learns two important facts: the phrase and meaning of *Ph'nglui mglw'nafh Cthulhu R'lyeh wgah'nagl fhtagn* and a disorienting but potentially earth-shattering story of the Great Old Ones. The incomprehensible phrase translates into "In his house at R'lyeh dead Cthulhu waits dreaming," and it is from this brief phrase that the horror of the Great Old Ones comes into disturbing focus.

The story's third part follows the narrator's journey to Oslo, Norway, in hopes of talking to the one surviving member of a derelict ship briefly mentioned in a newspaper clipping. When the narrator arrives in Norway, Johansen, the survivor, is dead, leaving behind another journal to examine. The journal recounts the *Alert*'s landing on a heretofore unknown island in the Pacific, an island with "surfaces too great to belong to any thing right or proper for this earth, and impious with horrible images and hieroglyphs" (p. 155). During the crew's exploration, they accidentally release the giant, gelatinous entity that is Cthulhu. Several of the crew die of fright or are eaten, and it is only Johansen's quick thinking of driving the ship through the membranous Cthulhu that he survives. The text ends with the narrator putting the statue of Cthulhu, Professor Angell's papers, and his own story back into a box, knowing that Cthulhu's forces still wait, patiently dreaming.

"The Call of Cthulhu" begins with Lovecraft's memorable lines: "The most merciful thing in the world, I think, is the inability of the human mind to correlate all its contents. We live on a placid island of ignorance in the midst of black seas of infinity, and it was not meant that we should voyage far" (p. 130). Throughout "Call," the characters who correlate the contents—the narrator, Professor Angell, Johansen— are the ones facing the most psychic and physical danger, and the latter two men are killed because of their ability to correlate. The narrator's gathering of the clues is replicated in the reader; as he knows more, we know more, and this knowledge is terrifying.

"Call" also introduces Lovecraft's "Great Old Ones," entities from the deepest recesses of space

and time, who came to Earth long before there were humans. Trapped because of the incorrect alignment of the stars, the Old Ones wait in suspended animation, a suspension that will be broken when the stars are right and Cthulhu, acting as a gatekeeper for vigintillions of years, awakens them. The couplet "That is not dead which can eternal lie, / And with strange aeons even death may die" (p. 146), found in the story's fictional *Necronomicon* (penned by the equally fictional Mad Arab Abdul Alhazred) and repeated by the cultists, describes the Old Ones' state. Dead but not dead, anticipating the celestial conjunction that will result in their freedom, the Old Ones will teach humanity to be "free and wild and beyond good and evil, with laws and morals thrown aside and all men shouting and killing and revelling in joy.... and all the earth would flame with a holocaust of ecstasy and freedom" (p. 145). Much like the aliens in "Colour," the Old Ones have no specific agenda, no love or hate for humans, only cosmic desires beyond comprehension.

The cultists who work to wake dreaming Cthulhu are the third element in "Call" that gives it cultural resonance. Made up of various castoffs, sailors, degenerates, and others from society's fringes, the cult's members, like the dreamers, are scattered around the world. During the Archaeological Society meeting where Legrasse displays the statue of Cthulhu, another member recounts finding a similar idol among Arctic devil worshippers. Johansen fights off a group of cultists in the South Pacific, who are looking for R'yleh; he is killed in Oslo under mysterious circumstances, and Professor Angell suddenly dies after a trip to Providence's wharves. The cult "had always existed and always would exist, hidden in distant wastes and dark places all over the world" (p. 144). Playing on anxieties over immigration and a more heterogeneous America, the Cthulhu cult ties the deep past with the modernizing present. These cults and their hidden webs of violence and power act as shadowy arbiters of human events, challenging overt structures with their sub rosa ones.

Lovecraft's other short story that influenced a wide range of other artists is *The Shadow over Innsmouth*, which Lovecraft wrote late in 1931. Interestingly, the story, now considered one of Lovecraft's best, was not well known in his lifetime: it was first published as a limited-run hardback in 1936 and did not come out in paperback until 1971. However, the late publication in no way diminishes its importance in the Lovecraft canon.

Like the majority of Lovecraft's work, *Shadow* revolves around a first-person narrator who learns things that no human should know, knowledge dangerous to life and sanity. To celebrate his coming-of-age, the narrator is touring New England and, in order to save money, travels by bus through the decaying fishing village of Innsmouth, despite the warning of the ticket agent. On the bus, the narrator encounters the "Innsmouth look": "a narrow head, bulging, watery blue eyes that seemed never to wink, a flat nose, a receding forehead and chin, and singularly undeveloped ears," combined with flipper-like hands and a shuffling walk (*Dunwich Horror*, p. 318).

A walking tour of the town increases his nervousness. The decay is visible, along with an overpowering smell of fish, and furtive sounds emanate from the abandoned buildings. Through a conversation with a store clerk who is not from Innsmouth and another with the town drunk, Zadok Allen, the dark story of Innsmouth is pieced together. Fishing had dried up, and extreme measures were taken to keep the town alive. Obed Marsh, a ship's captain with extensive knowledge of the South Pacific, brought back rituals ensuring a full catch and gold to smelt. Of course, this bounty came with a cost: the town was purged of traditional religion and the Esoteric Order of Dagon replaced it. Young people were taken to the reef outside of the town and either sacrificed to, or crossbred with, an aquatic race. Modern-day Innsmouth is populated by the results of this interbreeding, its citizens growing increasingly piscine as they age.

The story then traces the narrator's frantic flight from Innsmouth. His discussion with Zadok has been seen; the bus suddenly is no longer in service, forcing the narrator to check into the

aptly named Gilman House, where the narrator is attacked by the townsfolk of Innsmouth. The narrator escapes the search parties but cannot escape the call of Innsmouth. The story ends with the narrator realizing that he is a descendent of Innsmouth blood and, after deciding not to commit suicide, he plans a return to Innsmouth, where "We shall swim out to that brooding reef in the sea and dive down through black abysses to Cyclopean and many-columned Y'ha-nthlei, and in that lair of the Deep Ones we shall dwell amidst wonder and glory for ever" (p. 369).

The Shadow over Innsmouth engages a wide range of cultural and social anxieties, in addition to continuing Lovecraft's engagement with alien gods. For example, the crossbreeding between the Deep Ones and the humans resulting in the Innsmouth look has been read as Lovecraft's commentary on miscegenation and the watering down of Anglo-Saxon bloodlines. The results of these unions do not die, but return to live under the sea, indicating Lovecraft's wish that immigrants would return to their respective countries, leaving New England to its traditional inhabitants. The economic distress of coastal towns underlies much of the narrative: if not for the loss of fishing, Captain Marsh would never have had a reason to join with the Deep Ones. Lovecraft's own fastidiousness is also displayed in *Shadow*: everything associated with the town is dingy, dirty, or in a state of disrepair. The Gilman House, where the narrator spends a few sleepless hours before escaping, has a "lethal mustiness blended hideously with the town's general fishy odour and persistently focussed one's fancy on death and decay" (p. 346).

The paranoia permeating *The Shadow over Innsmouth* makes it an apt successor to "The Call of Cthulhu." Innsmouth is almost a microcosm of what the Cthulhu cult strives for: a place where the distinction between Deep One and human has been erased, where the institutional power of church and state have been co-opted to work for the cultists. Innsmouth is filled with furtive glances, with creatures hiding just out of sight. Starting with the ticketing agent who tells the narrator, "You can bet that prying strangers ain't welcome around Innsmouth" (p. 314), to the narrator's long talk with Zadok that ends with "*Git aout o' here!* Git aout o' here! *They seen us*—git aout fer your life!" (p. 343), secrecy and menace are endemic to rotting Innsmouth.

The Shadow over Innsmouth is also an appropriate site to discuss Lovecraft's racism, which, although no greater than that of many other thinkers in the early part of the century, must be addressed. As mentioned previously, Lovecraft's stay in New York City was disastrous, leading Sonia Greene to recount a stroll on Broadway where Lovecraft became "livid with anger and rage" at the "workers of minority races" (Joshi, 2010, vol. 2, p. 593). His entire marriage with Greene, a Jewish woman, was clouded by Lovecraft's anti-Semitic beliefs, exacerbated by New York City's large Jewish population. Lovecraft consistently argued for cultural homogeneity and against miscegenation, starting with his early works in amateur journals and continuing until *The Shadow over Innsmouth*. There are even pro-Hitler letters written in the early 1930s, one of which ends with "I know he's a clown, but by God, I like the boy" (Joshi, 2010, vol. 2, p. 940). As his biographer, S. T. Joshi, observes, despite Lovecraft's ability to incorporate new scientific and intellectual ideas into his own thought, racism and racial hierarchies remained one of his blind spots.

However, Lovecraft's racism and cultural nativism should not completely cloud the imaginative skills he brought to bear in texts like *The Shadow over Innsmouth* and "The Call of Cthulhu." These two stories stand as some of the best weird writing in America since Edgar Allan Poe's, shifting the terrain from haunted houses and lost continents into a horror that was both more intimate and more profound. "The Colour out of Space" helped tie advances in the physical sciences to an increasing anxiety about humanity's place in the universe. While Lovecraft's literary production during the roughly ten-year period between the publication of "Colour" to the end of his life are not numerous, his writings made much of modern horror and science fiction possible.

H. P. LOVECRAFT

POETRY

Although Lovecraft is best known for his fiction, he originally saw himself as a poet. This interest in poetry can be traced to two factors: his love of Poe and the influence of Neoclassical poets such as John Dryden and Alexander Pope. As an eleven-year-old, Lovecraft wrote a volume of poetry in eighteenth-century style titled *Poemata Minora* (collected in *The Ancient Track*), which begins with an invocation to Gods and Ancients. Lovecraft's poetic output past his adolescent years did not expand much beyond these themes, with many of his poems using traditional forms and classical mythology. However, despite these limitations, certain poems are worth attention.

The first set is his militaristic pieces, produced during World War I. Lovecraft's Anglophile leanings led to several poems that pushed for American involvement in the Great War. For example, "Pacifist War Song" (1917) begins:

We are the valiant Knights of Peace
Who prattle for the Right:
Our banner is of snowy fleece,
Inscribed: "TOO PROUD TO FIGHT!"

(Ancient Track p. 401)

The poem has a stanza implicating Germany in fomenting the Mexican Revolution and also displays Lovecraft's casual racism:

What tho' their hireling Greaser bands
Invade our southern plains?
We well can spare those boist'rous lands,
Content with what remains!

(p. 401)

However, by 1918, Lovecraft's war poetry shifted, perhaps reflecting increasing American casualties. In "The Conscript," a working man is drafted into the military, despite the fact that

I hate no man, and yet they say
That I must fight and kill;
That I must suffer day by day
To please a master's will.

(p. 417)

The piece ends with the soldier suffering from a breakdown caused by combat; Lovecraft's final lines, "Things seem so odd, I can do naught / But laugh, and laugh, and laugh!" (p. 418), are a fitting coda to his changing views of war's cost.

A second, more familiar, subject matter for Lovecraft's poetry is the horrific. Even before he started writing prose that included forbidden books or nameless terrors from beyond time and space, Lovecraft explored these themes in his poetry. Written in 1916, and published in 1919, "The Poe-et's Nightmare" contains seeds of what became Lovecraft's cosmic pessimism. After a grocery clerk falls asleep to Poe's poetry, he dreams of a guide taking him around the universe, where he sees "That crude experiment; that cosmic sport / Which holds our proud, aspiring race of mites / And moral vermin" (p. 43) and realizes that humanity is "That misbegotten accident of space; / That globe of insignificance" (p. 43), an entity in a vast universe that has no conception of its own unimportance. In 1918 Lovecraft published "Nemesis," arguably his first exploration into his trademark horror beyond human comprehension. It opens:

Thro' the ghoul-guarded gateways of slumber,
Past the wan-moon'd abysses of night,
I have liv'd o'er my lives without number,
I have sounded all things with my sight.

(Ancient Track, p. 46)

The nemesis has existed for as long as the Earth itself, spreading sin and pestilence. Although neither poem is particularly sophisticated in its meter or style, both are useful access points for exploring Lovecraft's horrific poetry.

No study of Lovecraft's verse is complete without discussing his sonnet cycle *Fungi from Yuggoth*. Appearing periodically in *Weird Tales*, these sonnets, a mixture of Shakespearean and Petrarchan styles, are a series of thirty-six vignettes. Although not all of the poems are directly connected with the poems that precede and follow them, a rough outline can be constructed. An unnamed narrator finds a tome filled with "curious words" that provides him the key to the "undimensioned worlds" that exist beyond human understanding (p. 81). But, as is a common theme for Lovecraft, knowledge comes at a price, and the narrator travels to various

places on both Earth and the cosmos (Yuggoth itself is "past the starry voids"), learning of forces that threaten to destroy his sanity. Familiar settings such as Arkham and Innsmouth mix with Lovecraftian gods such as Nyarlathotep and Azathoth, but the cycle itself does not inform other Lovecraft works, and the events within the cycle are linked more by association and indirection than by any central plot. However, the lack of formal unity does not keep *Fungi from Yuggoth* from being a sophisticated poetic experiment. The cycle drew the attention of the Los Angeles Institute of Musical Art's director, who, in 1932, received Lovecraft's permission to put two of the sonnets to music.

As should be evident, Lovecraft's poetry was never his strongest writing field. Most of his poems were written in his early period, with the exception of the occasional poems that he wrote for friends throughout his career. His early poetry's devotion to classical and neoclassical influences makes it stilted and excessively formal to the modern reader, but those interested in seeing Lovecraft's development as a writer will find a wide range of material to explore. The publication of his collected poems, *The Ancient Track* (2001; rev. ed. 2013) is a tremendous resource for students and scholars devoted to this phase of Lovecraft.

ESSAYS AND CRITICISM

Much like the essay by his literary hero Poe, "The Philosophy of Composition," Lovecraft's essay "Supernatural Horror in Literature" (1927) remains a landmark in its field of weird tales. It is not the only piece of criticism that Lovecraft wrote, but it is inarguably the best. Starting with his early work in amateur journals and continuing throughout his life, Lovecraft explored topics from the plague of free verse in "The Vers Libre Epidemic" (1917) to his underappreciated "Notes on Writing Weird Fiction" (1937). In these various pieces, Lovecraft displays his wide reading in the classics and also his prejudice against many modern forms, an irony given Lovecraft's influence on creating the modern science fiction and horror story.

Lovecraft's first published critical piece, "Metrical Regularity" (1915), is indicative of both trends. He opens the essay by stating, "Of the various forms of decadence manifest in the poetical art of the present age, none strikes more harshly on our sensibilities than the alarming decline in that harmonious regularity of metre which adorned the poetry of our immediate ancestors," and he invokes Dionysius and Hegel in his call for an end to the modern emphasis on emotion (*Collected Essays, Volume 2*, p. 11). He claims that modern poets have lost the ability to subsume content into form and are thereby in danger of becoming "a race of churlish, cacophonous hybrids, whose amorphous outcries will waver uncertainly betwixt prose and verse" (p. 12). Lovecraft's anxiety over hybridity, on display in better-known pieces such as *The Shadow over Innsmouth* or "The Dunwich Horror," is manifest here, more than a decade before either short story.

Of more interest to students of the weird tale are "The Supernatural Horror in Literature" and "Notes on Writing Weird Fiction." "Supernatural Horror," although now almost eighty years old, remains one of the genre's most effective discussions. The essay begins with one of Lovecraft's most famous statements: "The oldest and strongest emotion of mankind is fear, and the oldest and strongest kind of fear is fear of the unknown" (*Collected Essays, Volume 2*, p. 82). From this proposition, Lovecraft proceeds to catalog literature exploring this fear. Starting with the ancient Egyptians and continuing through the twentieth century, Lovecraft includes analyses of the gothic tale and the "spectral literature" of the European continent; a section on his literary mentor Edgar Allan Poe, to whom "we owe the modern horror-story in its final and perfected state" (p. 100); an exploration of horror's flowering in America after Poe; and a discussion of modern writers, highlighted by Arthur Machen and Lord Dunsany. Any modern reader interested in the historical development of supernatural writing will find this essay insightful.

Lovecraft's less-known later essay "Notes on Writing Weird Fiction" is also an excellent discussion of his own writing. Written well into

his fiction writing career, it parallels Poe's "Philosophy of Composition" with its specific breakdown of the writer's process. The essay begins with Lovecraft's admission, "I choose weird stories because they suit my inclination best—one of my strongest and most persistent wishes being to achieve, momentarily, the illusion of some strange suspension or violation of the galling limitations of time, space, and natural law" (*Collected Essays, Volume 2*, pp. 175–176). After outlining his usual steps in constructing a story, he goes on to categorize four distinct types of weird stories—stories with a "mood or feeling," a "pictorial conception," a "general situation, condition, legend, or intellectual conception," and a "definite tableau or specific dramatic situation or climax" (p. 177).

The essay concludes with two dicta informing almost all of Lovecraft's fiction. The first is his admonition that "inconceivable events and conditions have a special handicap to overcome, and this can be accomplished only through the maintenance of a careful realism in every phase of the story *except* that touching on the one given marvel" (p. 177). As seen in "The Colour out of Space" or *The Shadow over Innsmouth*, Lovecraft goes to great lengths to make the narratives real in all ways except for a singular marvelous event. The second dictum is that "atmosphere, not action, is the great desideratum of weird fiction" (p. 177). The rotting wharves of Innsmouth or the vaguely Cyclopean statues in "Dagon" privilege atmosphere above action. In fact, much of the criticism aimed at Lovecraft's writing is based on too much atmosphere and not enough action, where Lovecraft's love of "subtle suggestion" gets in the way of understanding exactly what, if anything, is going on. Regardless of these critiques, Lovecraft's aesthetic principles, developed in these essays, continue to influence supernatural writing.

Much like his poetry, Lovecraft's critical essays are of varying quality and interest, with many of the early pieces reading like jeremiads against the encroaching experimental form in poetry. However, these essays also display modernism's uneven acceptance in the United States, especially given Lovecraft's own modern-ist tendencies. His later essays on the weird tale continue to provide an excellent background on both the genesis of supernatural fiction and the literary techniques that would sustain it in the future. The 2004 publication of Lovecraft's *Collected Essays, Volume 2: Literary Criticism* provides an indispensable resource for those interested in Lovecraft's critical output.

OTHER WRITINGS

In addition to his creative work, Lovecraft wrote extensively as a ghost writer and collaborator. These collaborations took two forms: working with a better-known but less talented writer to polish a manuscript; or working informally with other supernatural writers who sought out Lovecraft for his specific skill set. While the first group produced little in the way of quality texts, the second arrangement led to several interesting narratives.

Lovecraft ghostwrote for one reason: money. Since payment from pulp magazines was erratic, especially for writers who were not famous, economic necessity forced Lovecraft to edit texts in which he otherwise had no interest. However, this unwanted career did lead Lovecraft into a relationship with another famous figure in American popular culture: the magician Harry Houdini. To gain readership, *Weird Tales* hired Houdini to tell of his various adventures around the world. The May 1924 issue, headlined "Imprisoned with the Pharaohs," was a Houdini-Lovecraft collaboration. Featuring a largely, if not completely, manufactured narrative of Houdini's capture and escape from beneath one of the Egyptian pyramids, "Imprisoned" displays a variety of Lovecraftian touches. There are half-human, half-animal mummies, a tentacled beast, and an allusion to deeper mysteries lost in time. Houdini reportedly enjoyed the relationship with Lovecraft and hired him on at least one other occasion.

Lovecraft's other collaborative work ranged in quality from the merely competent to the outrageous. Many of his earlier works are passable fictions, notable largely because of the

biographical connections; for example, "The Horror at Martin's Beach" (1923), a tale of a vengeful giant sea monster eating the denizens of "the fashionable Wavecrest Inn," a New England coastal resort, was written with Lovecraft's future wife, Sonia Greene. His later collaborations are more interesting. "The Curse of Yig" (1929), which Lovecraft wrote with Zealia Bishop, is set in Oklahoma and follows an ethnographer's pursuit of serpent legends. What the ethnographer uncovers is more than legend; he learns that the curse of Yig is real, and its results are ghastly. Lovecraft and Bishop would collaborate again in 1929–1930 with the long piece "The Mound," not published until 1940. Once again set in Oklahoma with an adventurous ethnologist, "The Mound" concerns a lost kingdom of spacefaring humans who exist underground, using their advanced mental powers to teleport, resist aging, and remain hidden from human sight. Filled with Lovecraftian "Cyclopean ruins" and a cult of Tsathoggua, "The Mound" is an effective take on the lost-world genre.

Two other collaborations are of use to both Lovecraft scholars and those interested more generally in pulp fiction. "The Battle That Ended the Century" (1934), a collaboration with Lovecraft's friend and literary executor R. H. Barlow, recounts a futuristic fight between Lovecraft's correspondent and Conan creator Robert E. Howard and weird fiction fan Bernard Austin Dwyer. What makes "Battle" notable are its references to almost all of the major contributors of the 1930s supernatural writing scene: Clark Ashton Smith, E. Hoffman Price, Seabury Quinn, and the illustrator Margaret Brundage, to name a few. Another late collaboration is "The Challenge from Beyond" (1935), which combines the writing of Lovecraft, Howard, Frank Belknap Long, A. Merritt, and C. L. Moore. Starting with Moore, the text was passed from writer to writer, each adding to the narrative. Lovecraft's section is obviously his own: when describing the Eltdown Shards, he writes, "They came, clearly, from a time when no human beings could exist on the globe—but their contours and figurings were damnably puzzling" (*Miscellaneous Writings*, p. 75). Much like "Battle," "Challenge from Beyond" uses many allusions and in-jokes, making it fertile ground for investigation.

As previously mentioned, Lovecraft maintained a voluminous correspondence with his friends, editors, collaborators, and, toward the end of his life, fans. The range of Lovecraft's letters is equally impressive: art, culture, civilization, and barbarism vie for space along with diagrams of his various apartments and listings of what he ate in a given week. Through his letters, Lovecraft explored his own ideas and philosophies, sharpening his own thinking. For example, in a 1923 letter to James F. Morton, he writes, "All the cosmos is a jest, and fit be treated only as a jest, and one thing is as true as another" (Joshi, 2010, p. 485). This cosmic skepticism will come to literary fruition four years later in "The Call of Cthulhu." Additionally, in these letters, Lovecraft takes on more human qualities: his love for antiquarian architecture, his chronic self-doubt, his quest for a three-button suit. The publication of Lovecraft's letters to Robert Howard (2009), as well as other collections of his correspondence, are useful avenues for continued Lovecraft exploration.

CRITICAL TRADITION

After Lovecraft's death, his literary estate became a source of contention. Former colleagues R. H. Barlow and August Derleth each claimed to represent Lovecraft's wishes: Barlow's claim was based on a nonbinding legal document and Derleth's on a conversation with Lovecraft. Each man did his part in continuing Lovecraft studies. Barlow gave Brown University's John Hay Library the bulk of his correspondence with Lovecraft, the Lovecraft papers he had access to, and Lovecraft's copies of *Weird Tales*. Derleth started his Arkham House publishing company, releasing Lovecraft's stories along with his own elaborations and reworkings of Lovecraft fragments. However, Derleth is also responsible for some erroneous interpretations, including his attribution of a Lovecraft letter purported to say that the cosmic battles are between good and evil, instead of uncaring forces. Derleth was never able to produce this letter; later scholarship by

S. T. Joshi traced the material to another Lovecraft colleague who had mistakenly extrapolated a dualistic universe out of a brief exchange. Despite this figment, and Derleth's consistent use of Lovecraft's name as a way to sell his own revisions, he did produce and circulate Lovecraft's works and letters for three decades.

A central figure in Lovecraft scholarship has been S. T. Joshi, whose work on collecting and editing Lovecraft has been tireless and illuminating. Starting at the end of the 1970s, Joshi has released editions of Lovecraft's letters, collected essays, annotated versions of Lovecraft's major tales, and the definitive two-volume biography *I Am Providence: The Life and Times of H. P. Lovecraft* (2010). As importantly, Joshi has consistently argued for Lovecraft's place in the American literary canon as something more than a supernatural writer, seeing Lovecraft as a writer who used the supernatural to explore sophisticated philosophical constructs. Joshi continues to be active, revising previous collections as more Lovecraft information comes to light. Another valuable figure in maintaining Lovecraft's literary importance is the author Joyce Carol Oates, who edited and wrote the introduction to *Tales of H. P. Lovecraft* (2007) and has long campaigned for his importance in imaginative fiction. Stephen King, America's best-known horror writer, also discusses Lovecraft's importance in American literature in general, and his influence on King's writing in particular, in *Danse Macabre* (1981).

Contemporary Lovecraft scholarship draws writers and thinkers from a wide variety of disciplines. There are many collections tracing the influences on Lovecraft's writing and later writers' debt to him, and the volume *Lovecraft and Influence* (2013), edited by Robert H. Waugh, tackles both these questions. In addition to traditional literary readings such as *H. P. Lovecraft* (by Peter Canan) from the Twayne author series or Joshi's various annotated volumes, the influential poststructuralist critics Gilles Deleuze and Félix Guattari, in *A Thousand Plateaus* (1980), use Lovecraft's "Through the Gates of the Silver Key" in exploring the multiplicity of self brought about by modernity. In the last decade, popular culture and cultural studies have investigated Lovecraft's importance in coalescing specific anxieties and desires. Monographs such as Jason Calavito's *The Cult of Alien Gods: H. P. Lovecraft and Extraterrestrial Pop Culture* (2005), which looks at how Lovecraft's science fiction became appropriated as science fact, and the volume *New Critical Essays on H. P. Lovecraft* (2013), edited by David Simmons, use a variety of methodologies to analyze the enduring quality of Lovecraft's creations. Bennett Lovett-Graff's "Shadows over Lovecraft: Reactionary Fantasy and Immigrant Eugenics" (1997) is a representative example of using cultural history to investigate Lovecraft's racial, and in some cases, racist, modernism. The intersection of science, mathematics, and Lovecraft also is a site of recent scholarship: Paul Halpern's article on Lovecraft's use of the fourth dimension, Thomas Hull's reading of mathematical horror in Lovecraft, and Dan Look's analysis of the sophisticated math behind "The Statement of Randolph Carter" and "The Dreams in the Witch House" display interesting new takes on Lovecraftian scholarship.

CONCLUSION

Lovecraft's position as an American writer of note is no longer in doubt, as seen by the degree of contemporary scholarly and popular interest. With his creations showing up in texts as diverse as the television show *South Park* and the *Call of Cthulhu* role-playing game, Lovecraft is better known now than at any point in his literary career. His name has been attached to many horror films, and the adjective "Lovecraftian" has become a standard term for forbidden knowledge that leads to disaster. Lovecraft fans and scholars have a strong Internet presence, and in 2013 Providence hosted its first Necronomicon, a conference celebrating the life and works of Lovecraft. For a writer who spent much of his adult life struggling to get material into print, the proliferation of his material in various editions, along with the accessibility of his writings in the public domain, is an irony that takes on—unsurprisingly given Lovecraft's love of the interstellar—almost cosmic import.

It is this use of the cosmic that is Lovecraft's greatest contribution to American letters. He helped bring supernatural and weird fiction out of abandoned houses inhabited by chain-wielding ghosts and into a world where questions of reality, sanity, and the fine line between the two became paramount. Despite his traditionalist beliefs in aesthetics and cultural politics, his paranoid narrators stumbling upon forbidden lore, often aided by modern scientific advancements and technologies, are Lovecraft's radical innovations to a genre that continues to resonate with a wide reading public. Although Lovecraft's gravestone in the beloved city of his birth bears the inscription "I am Providence," his influence on later writers, filmmakers, and other artists demonstrates that his world was much larger than that.

Selected Bibliography

WORKS OF H. P. LOVECRAFT

FICTION

"Dagon." *Vagrant* no. 11:23–29 (November 1919). (Republished in the October 1923 issue of *Weird Tales,* making it the first Lovecraft story to be published in *Weird Tales.*) Reprinted in *Dagon and Other Macabre Tales.* Edited by S. T. Joshi. Sauk City, Wis.: Arkham House, 1987 (rev. ed.). Pp. 14–19.

"The White Ship." *United Amateur* 19, no. 2:30–33 (November 1919).

"The Statement of Randolph Carter." *Vagrant* no. 13:41–48 (May 1920).

"The Cats of Ulthar." *Tryout* 6, no. 11:3–9 (November 1920).

"Herbert West—Reanimator." *Home Brew*, 1922. (The serial ran in six parts from February 1922 to July 1922.) Reprinted in *Dagon and Other Macabre Tales.* Edited by S. T. Joshi. Sauk City, Wis.: Arkham House, 1987 (rev. ed.). Pp. 133–163.

"The Rats in the Walls." *Weird Tales* 3, no. 3:25–31 (March 1924). In *The Annotated Lovecraft,* Edited by S. T. Joshi. New York: Dell, 1997.

"The Horror at Red Hook." *Weird Tales* 9, no. 1:59–73 (January 1927).

"The Colour out of Space." *Amazing Stories* 2, no. 6:557–567 (September 1927). (An excellent resource for the scientific equipment used in the text is *The Annotated H. P. Lovecraft,* Edited by S. T. Joshi. New York: Dell, 1997. Pp. 58–100.)

"Pickman's Model." *Weird Tales* 10, no. 4:505–514 (October 1927).

"The Call of Cthulhu." *Weird Tales* 11, no. 2:159–178, 287 (February 1928). In *The Dunwich Horror and Others.* Edited by August Derleth. Sauk City, Wis.: Arkham House, 1963. Pp. 130–159.

"Cool Air." *Tales of Magic and Mystery* 1, no. 4:29–34 (March 1928).

"The Silver Key." *Weird Tales* 13, no. 1:41–49, 144 (January 1929).

"The Dunwich Horror." *Weird Tales* 13, no. 4:481–508 (April 1929).

"The Whisperer in Darkness." *Weird Tales* 18, no. 1:32–73 (August 1931).

"The Dreams in the Witch House." *Weird Tales* 22, no. 1:86–111 (July 1933).

"The Other Gods." *Fantasy Fan* 1, no. 3:35–38 (November 1933). (Lovecraft wrote this story in 1921.)

At the Mountains of Madness. Astounding Stories 16, no. 6:8–32 (February 1936); 17, no. 1:125–155 (March 1936); 17, no. 2:132–150 (April 1936). (This version is a vastly edited one. The complete text was first published in *At the Mountains of Madness and Other Tales of Terror,* New York: Ballantine Books, 1971, pp. 1–110.)

"The Shadow out of Time." *Astounding Stories* 17, no. 4:110–154 (June 1936).

The Shadow over Innsmouth. Everett, Pa.: Visionary Publishing, 1936. Pp. 13–158. (This version is an extremely limited print run of 200 copies.) In *The Dunwich Horror and Others.* Edited by August Derleth. Sauk City, Wis.: Arkham House, 1963. Pp. 308–369.

The Dream-Quest of Unknown Kadath. The first printing of this novel, written in 1926–1927, is in *Beyond the Wall of Sleep,* Sauk City, Wis.: Arkham House, 1943, pp. 76–134.) In *The Dream-Quest of Unknown Kadath.* New York: Ballantine Books, 1970.

FICTION COLLECTIONS

Tales of H. P. Lovecraft. Edited by Joyce Carol Oates. New York: Harper Perennial, 2007.

POETRY

"Pacifist War Song." *Tryout* 3, no. 4:10 (March 1917). *The Ancient Track: The Complete Poetical Works of H. P. Lovecraft.* Edited by S. T. Joshi. New York; Hippocampus Press, 2013. Pp. 401.

"Nemesis." *Vagrant*, no. 7:41–43 (June 1918). In *The Ancient Track: The Complete Poetical Works of H. P. Lovecraft.* Edited by S. T. Joshi. New York: Hippocampus Press, 2013. Pp. 46–48.

"The Poe-et's Nightmare." *Vagrant*, no. 8:13–23 (July 1918). In *The Ancient Track: The Complete Poetical Works of H. P. Lovecraft*. Edited by S. T. Joshi. New York; Hippocampus Press, 2013. Pp. 38–45.

"To Edward John Moreton Drax Plunkett, Eighteenth Baron Dunsany." *Tryout* 5, no. 11:11–12 (November 1919). In *The Ancient Track: The Complete Poetical Works of H. P. Lovecraft*. Edited by S. T. Joshi. New York; Hippocampus Press, 2013. Pp. 66–67.

"Fungi from Yuggoth." In *Beyond the Wall of Sleep*. Sauk City, Wis.: Arkham House, 1943. Pp. 395–407. (Specific sonnets from this cycle appeared in various issues of *Weird Tales* before being collected here.) In *The Ancient Track: The Complete Poetical Works of H. P. Lovecraft*. Edited by S. T. Joshi. New York: Hippocampus Press, 2013. Pp. 80–95.

"The Conscript." In *The Ancient Track: The Complete Poetical Works of H. P. Lovecraft*. Edited by S. T. Joshi. New York: Hippocampus Press, 2013. Pp. 421–423. (This poem was not published in Lovecraft's lifetime and was not available in any form until the 1970s.)

The Ancient Track: The Complete Poetical Works of H. P. Lovecraft. San Francisco, Calif.: Night Shade Books, 2001. Rev. ed., New York: Hippocampus Press, 2013. (An invaluable resource for those interested in Lovecraft's poetics.)

CRITICAL ESSAYS

"Metrical Regularity." *Conservative* 1, no. 2:2–4 (July 1915). Reprinted with editorial notes in *Collected Essays, Volume 2: Literary Criticism*. Edited by S. T. Joshi. New York: Hippocampus Press, 2004. Pp. 11–13.

"The Supernatural Horror in Literature." *Recluse*, no. 1:23–59 (1927). Reprinted with editorial notes in *Collected Essays, Volume 2: Literary Criticism*. Edited by S. T. Joshi. New York: Hippocampus Press, 2004. Pp. 82–135.

"Notes on Writing Weird Fiction." *Amateur Correspondent* 2, no. 1:7–10 (May–June 1937). Reprinted with editorial notes in *Collected Essays, Volume 2: Literary Criticism*. Edited by S. T. Joshi. New York: Hippocampus Press, 2004. Pp. 175–178.

COLLABORATIONS

With Sonia Greene. "The Horror at Martin's Beach." *Weird Tales* 2, no. 4:75–76, 83 (November 1923).

With Harry Houdini. "Imprisoned with the Pharaohs." *Weird Tales* 4, no. 2:3–12 (May–June–July 1924). (Later reprinted with the title "Under the Pyramid.")

With Zealia Bishop. "The Curse of Yig." *Weird Tales* 14, no. 5:625–636 (November 1929).

With R. H. Barlow. "The Battle That Ended the Century." Mimeographed flyer published June 1934. Reprinted in *Miscellaneous Writings*. Edited by S. T. Joshi. Sauk City, Wis.: Arkham House, 1995. Pp. 66–71.

With E. Hoffman Price. "Through the Gates of the Silver Key." *Weird Tales* 24, no. 1:60–85 (July 1934).

With Robert Howard, Frank Belknap Long, A. Merrit, and C. L. Moore. "The Challenge from Beyond." *Fantasy Magazine* 5, no. 4:221–229 (September 1935). In *Miscellaneous Writings*. Edited by S. T. Joshi. Sauk City, Wis.: Arkham House, 1995. Pp. 74–79.

With Zealia Bishop. "The Mound." *Weird Tales* 35, no. 6:98–120 (November 1940).

CORRESPONDENCE

Selected Letters. 5 vols. Edited by August Derleth, Donald Wandrei, and James Turner. Sauk City, Wis.: Arkham House, 1965–1976. (It is estimated Lovecraft wrote more than 100,000 letters, of which an estimated 20,000 survive.)

A Means to Freedom: The Letters of H. P. Lovecraft and Robert E. Howard. Edited by S. T. Joshi, David E. Schultz, and Rusty Burke. New York: Hippocampus Press, 2009.

CRITICAL AND BIOGRAPHICAL STUDIES

Canon, Peter. *H. P. Lovecraft*. Boston: Twayne, 1989.

Calavito, Jason. *The Cult of Alien Gods: H. P. Lovecraft and Extraterrestrial Pop Culture*. Amherst, N.Y.: Prometheus Books, 2005.

Deleuze, Gilles, and Félix Guattari. *A Thousand Plateaus: Capitalism and Schizophrenia*. 1980. Translated by Brian Massumi. Minneapolis: University of Minnesota Press, 1987.

Halpern, Paul, and Michael C. LaBossiere. "'Mind out of Time': Identity, Perception, and the Fourth Dimension in H. P. Lovecraft's 'The Shadow out of Time' and 'The Dreams in the Witch House.'" *Extrapolation* 50, no. 3:512–533 (2009).

Hull, Thomas. "H. P. Lovecraft: A Horror in Higher Dimensions." *Math Horizons* 13, no. 3:10–12 (February 2006).

Joshi, S. T. *H. P. Lovecraft: A Life*. West Warwick, R.I.: Necronomicon Press, 1996.

———. *I Am Providence: The Life and Times of H. P. Lovecraft*. New York: Hippocampus Press, 2010. (This is a two-volume set that expands on the earlier Joshi biography.)

King, Stephen. *Danse Macabre*. New York: Everest House, 1981.

Look, Dan. "The Cosmic Angle of Regarding: Mathematics and the Fiction of H. P. Lovecraft." In *Journeys into Fear 1*. Edited by S. R. Bissette. Hertford, N.C.: Crossroad Press/SpiderBaby Grafix, 2014.

Lovett-Graff, Bennett. "Shadows over Lovecraft: Reactionary Fantasy and Immigrant Eugenics." *Extrapolation* 38.

no. 3:175–192 (1997).

Simmons, David, ed. *New Critical Essays on H. P. Lovecraft.* Basingstoke, U.K.: Palgrave Macmillan, 2013.

Waugh, Robert H., ed. *Lovecraft and Influence: His Predecessors and Successors.* Lanham, Md.: Scarecrow Press, 2013.

MANUEL MUÑOZ

(1972—)

Amanda Fields

On March 4, 1972, the writer Manuel Muñoz was born in Dinuba, California, a town of around 15,000 near Fresno in the Central Valley, where he was raised by his mother, stepfather, and maternal grandmother. He is the author of two short-story collections, *Zigzagger* (2003) and *The Faith Healer of Olive Avenue* (2007), and a novel, *What You See in the Dark* (2011). He received his B.A. degree from Harvard University in 1994 and an M.F.A. from Cornell University in 1998 and is an associate professor at the University of Arizona's creative writing program, where he has been teaching since 2008. He lives in Tucson, Arizona.

Muñoz has published his writing in numerous venues, such as the *New York Times, Glimmer Train, Epoch, Eleven Eleven,* and *Boston Review*. His work has been read on National Public Radio's *Selected Shorts*. He has received numerous accolades, including a 2008 Whiting Writers' Award as well as fellowships from the National Endowment for the Arts in 2006 and the New York Foundation for the Arts in 2008. The critical success of his writing has led to service for the literary community as a juror for the 2011 PEN/O. Henry Awards and as a judge for the 2014 PEN/Faulkner Awards.

Most of Muñoz's work is set in the Central Valley region of California. On his website, he describes the complexities of his relationship with this region, where there is an abundance of crops to be tended yet people are often in need of work. About his fiction, he says, "I cut very close to the bone when it comes to the things I choose to write about" (personal interview). Any analysis of his work must take into account the significance of the Central Valley as the basis for his writing. As Muñoz writes on his website, "the presence of that living geography has always been the key to how I create characters, how I know their lives, and, most important, how I empathize with their choices, no matter what they are."

FAMILY BACKGROUND

Muñoz is the youngest of five children, with two brothers and two sisters. He grew up in a family of farmworkers who were very poor, working in the California fields picking and harvesting crops such as oranges, plums, cotton, and tomatoes. As a child, starting in fourth grade, he too worked in the fields, but, as he describes it, he and his younger sister "were the ones who got off easy." He says, "I didn't bear the brunt of it. I did some of it, but it was just enough. My parents really did not want us out there" (personal interview). While other family members worked on "heavy stuff," Muñoz and his sister worked in the vineyards, picking grapes, removing leaves and twigs, and then laying out the grapes flat on thick paper so that they would dry into raisins. They were then responsible for rolling up the paper, and they were paid by the tray. In the winter, they tied up the vines.

While his sister claims she enjoyed this work, comparing the tying of the vines to braiding hair, Muñoz says, "I hated it." On one occasion when he was complaining about this work, his mother, Esmeralda, ripped a hole in his jeans and told him that was how he would know what hard work was, and that she wanted him to know so that he would not want to grow up doing this work. As he puts it, it was drilled into him that "if you want to moan and groan because we're yanking you out of bed at five in the morning because we've gotta get out there by six before it gets really, really hot, then you better stay in school

because otherwise this is your life. This is your life. And, man, I learned that lesson quick" (personal interview). He and his sister were excellent students in school, and Muñoz learned English in kindergarten. On his website, Muñoz says he was "a very resourceful student, muy obediente, and a shy bookworm to boot." He attributes his parents' motivation to encourage him and his sister in school to their frustration at seeing his older siblings take school less seriously. He says, "I just don't think they wanted that sort of destiny for us." His family also expected all members to work and provide for themselves. On his website, Muñoz writes that, at the age of fourteen, he supported his early education by working at a warehouse where he made enough money to buy school supplies and clothing.

Muñoz sees a cyclical effect for most of his family members who have remained in the Central Valley: "the cycle of poverty has kept going. And it's not fieldwork anymore. But it's other kinds of very low wage service employment" (personal interview). He sees people in their mid-thirties not knowing what to do with their lives or how to provide for their children, people with frustrations about finances, a lack of opportunities, people who feel they have made the wrong choice or didn't even get a chance to make a choice. People who go to work because it seems easier than to go to school. These are the kinds of people who populate his fiction.

Muñoz's stepfather, Antonio ("Tony"), would often say that he wished he had stayed in school but that it had been easier to work. The kind of regret he expressed was "so palpable," and Muñoz sees such regret with other family members. He tells the story of a cousin who bought land and built a house on a vineyard that used to belong to a family she worked for when she was growing up. She keeps an acre behind the house for her children to work. It is not much, and she does not make much money from it, but its purpose is to help them understand where their house came from. It also means that her children "get a taste of what it's like to be out there in the middle of July, or in December in the cold and mud and all of that, having to wrap the goddamned vines all around, all the way down, and

your fingers are frozen" (personal interview). Like Muñoz's mother, she wants her children to know that this is not a life they should desire.

His mother, Esmeralda, also made it clear to him that if she had made it in school, things would have been different. She didn't make it in school past the third grade, so she never learned basic things such as how to spell or add. Muñoz recalls a story his mother told him that encapsulates her regret at not being able to complete her schooling. When her first husband, Muñoz's father, ran away from the family to Mexico and she found herself raising five children on her own, she became an Avon lady, selling cosmetics and skin products door-to-door. One of the things she had to do was itemize her sales in a little book. She had problems calculating the orders and couldn't make her lengthy name fit in the sales book. Muñoz finds significance in this story because it says something about what kind of day-to-day knowledge people are assumed to have and how difficult it is to make even a small amount of money without the ability to perform these basic tasks. All of these experiences contributed to Muñoz's desire for higher education and to his future writing.

EDUCATION

Muñoz didn't travel beyond the Central Valley until 1990, when he went to college at age eighteen. He attended Harvard University on a nearly full scholarship and graduated in 1994. He was the first person in his family to graduate from college, and he says that he applied to Harvard not because he knew much about it but simply because he had heard of it. In fact, in high school he had been discouraged from applying by a Harvard recruiter who suggested he consider a state university instead. His sister attended the University of California at Santa Barbara but did not finish. They were the only two from the family to try to go to college. Muñoz completed the Undergraduate Teacher Education Program at Harvard.

Muñoz says he has always been "a book reader and a dabbler" (personal interview). On

his website, he writes that his favorite books growing up were L. Frank Baum's *The Wonderful Wizard of Oz* and Theodore Dreiser's *Sister Carrie*. Muñoz attributes his love of these books to the fact that they both "opened with departures." His life when he went to Harvard was marked by a significant departure from his experiences up to that point.

Of Harvard, Muñoz says on his website: "It was not my world." Yet his time at Harvard greatly contributed to his writing career. In his sophomore year he was admitted to creative writing classes, which were competitive; these classes required an application and consisted of twelve to fifteen students in workshops where they critiqued each other's work.

In his first creative writing class, Muñoz did not have a pleasant experience being workshopped by other students. However, he admired his instructor, Susan Dodd, the author of several critically acclaimed books who has taught creative writing at both Harvard and the acclaimed Iowa Writers' Workshop. Dodd helped him in a pivotal way when he had a workshop in which he got "skewered" by his peers (personal interview). She called him shortly after the workshop took place and told him that all writers need to go through the experience of hearing criticism but that she wanted to let him know that she thought he was very talented. She offered to help him embark on a novel if he agreed not to drop the workshop, since he needed to participate and get a thick skin. Of this experience, he says, "So I did [stay in the workshop]. It was tough. It was really tough because I was just really shy, and I had a terrible time speaking in class. I was just a real wallflower."

Dodd's encouragement was crucial to Muñoz's future career. Both Dodd and Jill McCorkle, another prolific fiction writer who was a Briggs-Copeland Lecturer in Fiction at Harvard for five years and the chair of the creative writing program, encouraged him to consider applying for an M.F.A. in creative writing, though he did not yet know what that degree was. Muñoz attended Cornell University for his M.F.A., which he earned in 1998.

Hearkening back to that first creative writing workshop at Harvard University, he contrasts his background experiences with the background of his peers. The majority of the students at Harvard were "accustomed to rigor at a much earlier age," having come from higher-income families and attended prep schools. He did not have these opportunities and so came into the workshop "essentially cold," "with a lot of eagerness" but little experience (personal interview). He says another problem was that he wasn't reading as much as a writer should. Dodd was one of the first people to tell him that if he never read he would never become a better writer. Muñoz believes that writers are responsible for appealing to a variety of readers, an opinion that other literary writers might contest, since one could argue that the readers of literary writing are more often than not of a particular race and class, and writing to please these readers does not allow the writer to reflect the realities and complexities of marginalized experiences. But Muñoz does not subscribe to this line of argument.

Muñoz's experiences with McCorkle were also formative. He believes she is the definition of a "compassionate teacher." Both McCorkle and Dodd "had a capacity to not tell me what to do. They really trusted me as a talented young writer who needed to find himself" (personal interview). For instance, he had a "really bad, terrible" novel he was working on for his thesis at Harvard. There was a chapter in which the mother at the center of the novel was grappling with a conflict, and he was not sure where to go with this chapter. McCorkle suggested giving the mother a physical change. She asked him how long the mother's hair was and suggested that she get a haircut. McCorkle's point was to get Muñoz to think more deeply about what his characters looked like and to consider what happens to characters when their physical details change.

So, in the next chapter, Muñoz decided to write in a visit from a friend who was going to give the mother a home permanent. He remembers McCorkle's praise for this decision because he had taken her advice yet written from his own experiences. He says, "Jill didn't tell me to do a

home perm, but it made sense for this character who had no money and who would never walk into a beauty salon, and here you have this opportunity for these two women to talk" (personal interview). The kind of respect afforded to him by McCorkle in this instance is evidence, for Muñoz, of her compassion and strengths as a creative writing teacher. And in a profile of Muñoz by Nell Porter Brown in *Harvard Magazine*, McCorkle says about Muñoz that he "didn't know how superior he was, coming into the class, in terms of what he was able to do on the page. He was so fully formed already."

Much of Muñoz's time as an M.F.A. student was spent in discovering how to write about the kinds of people he grew up with, and the lack of privileges that go hand in hand with the socioeconomic status of his upbringing. He says that he sometimes has to "check people" now in discussions about class and privilege when they make assumptions about his academic background at Harvard and Cornell (personal interview). In his work, it is important to take note of the intersections between race, class, and education, as his fiction captures so aptly the realities he knew growing up.

In the Cornell M.F.A. program he also met his mentor, Helena María Viramontes, author of *Under the Feet of Jesus* and *Their Dogs Came with Them*. On his website, Muñoz describes her as his "literary godmother." When Muñoz expressed doubt about attending the program because of his familial obligations, Viramontes called his mother, speaking to her in Spanish and reassuring her that he would be fine at Cornell. Viramontes also pushed Muñoz to learn about Chicano/a literature and to be confident in his place as a writer.

FIRST PUBLICATIONS

After graduating from Cornell, Muñoz taught for two years as a lecturer. He then worked at Houghton Mifflin in Boston. Muñoz moved to New York City in 2001. His first story publication was in the *Mid-American Review* in the fall of 1998. That same year, five stories collected as

Greetings from Ice Country appeared as part of the Chicano Chapbook Series published by the poet Gary Soto, which gave several Chicano/a writers a stepping-stone into publication before they published their first full books. However, Muñoz's first actual acceptance for publication was for the highly regarded literary journal *Glimmer Train*. The story, "Campo," was accepted in 1997 but did not come out until 1999.

He had worked on "Campo" at a time after he had graduated from Cornell. He was very tired of the workshop environment of the M.F.A. program and looking forward to writing something that he would not have to show anybody. He decided to submit the story to *Glimmer Train* and was surprised that it was accepted. He says that this acceptance gave him a false sense of confidence. He thought, "If it's that easy, just let me write some more and send them out to other places and I'll just wait for them to roll in. Of course, that didn't happen. I got humbled very quickly" (personal interview). He still has the answering machine that took the message of acceptance from *Glimmer Train*.

THE COMPLEXITIES OF WRITING ABOUT PLACE

Muñoz is an associate professor at the University of Arizona in Tucson, where he teaches in the prestigious M.F.A. program with acclaimed writers such as Ander Monson and Fenton Johnson. He makes use of his past workshop experience when he teaches workshops now.

About his negative workshop experience at Harvard, Muñoz says: "I didn't have the language, I didn't have the questions, I didn't have the depth of reading knowledge, either, to think about why the people I was writing about ... were not connecting to the people in the room. To me, it's fairly obvious now, but back then it wasn't" (personal interview). He applies these issues when he helps emerging writers now.

When asked how he deals as a teacher with writing that, like his writing at Harvard, doesn't come from a place and perspective that most of the students will understand, he says,

I always bring it back to the work. The thing that I didn't know when I was an undergraduate was feel-

ing that any time my pieces were critiqued I was being critiqued, or my world was being critiqued, or what I knew was being critiqued. Whereas [when] Susan [Dodd] and Jill [McCorkle] gave me those critiques, they always brought it back to what I put on the page. What's missing? What is it about this character that isn't allowing a certain kind of reader to understand that this is what they have the capacity of doing? Always bring it back to the page....

I guess that becomes the craft discussion. That's a discussion that, I know, with some of my peers, we have a pretty fierce disagreement about. Because it becomes a question of elitism. Which I just completely disagree with because to me it's the challenge of how do you render a world. No matter what the world is, you still have to render it, and you have to do it through language.... I never feel it's about a failing of the reader to understand this particular world. It has to be both. Yeah, there's change that can be effected in a reader, but that's their own work. I can't affect that as a writer. But as a writer I can affect the paragraph. And I can go over the lines and maybe be too explicit, or I can make too many assumptions about people being able to read the lines. I'd like to think that I keep gestures ambiguous sometimes, like you don't really know why particular people act in particular ways.

(personal interview)

Muñoz speaks here to a debate among literary writers concerning whether the story can be critiqued solely on "craft," meaning the elements that create story, such as sentence structure, characterization, plot, and word choice. One might argue, however (and Muñoz hints at this argument in his comment about elitism), that particular craft preferences are established through a dominant order that does not take into account marginalized experiences or ways of writing or being.

If reaching out to readers who do not know the place Muñoz writes about presents one kind of challenge, reaching out to readers who know it quite intimately presents another. Muñoz calls up two examples of this type of reader. First, a man he went to school with in the Central Valley came to one of his readings in New York City. The man told Muñoz that he really enjoyed his work and recognized the streets and places. He could recall the town and everything in the books;

he related to the community, and this meant a great deal to Muñoz because it verified that he was able to depict the place he came from in a way that speaks to an insider. Second, Nuala Ní Chonchúir, a judge for the 2007 Frank O'Connor International Short Story Award, for which *The Faith Healer of Olive Avenue* earned a nomination, mentioned that one of the reasons she was such an advocate for Muñoz's book in 2007 was that the world in the book was so like Ireland in terms of the deeply embedded Catholicism and the depiction of poverty and its ramifications. It was the first time Muñoz realized that similarities of religion and class could be so instantly recognizable across such seemingly disparate cultures (personal interview).

In his interview with Nell Porter Brown, Muñoz says that his family, on the other hand, does not talk much about his writing. He has given his siblings his books but is not sure if they have read them. When members of his family attended a reading for *The Faith Healer of Olive Avenue* at California State University, they looked as if they felt out of place. Yet the reading offered a way for him to be out about being gay in front of his family because they do not discuss it, though they are aware of it.

Muñoz's writing often focuses on places that are changing or breaking down in some way. He is fascinated by the kind of incremental changes that are occurring in the Central Valley and the ways in which the place is being "left behind" in terms of social and cultural progression and ideas (personal interview). When he was growing up, he was not really aware of how politically and socially conservative the area was, a cultural stance he chalks up to a resistance to change.

Many of Muñoz's stories take place at some point in the past. He does not tend to identify specific years in his stories but uses, instead, historical references. For instance, "The Happiest Girl in the Whole U.S.A.," a story published in *Glimmer Train* (winter 2014), makes a reference to Jessica Savitch, an NBC newscaster who died in a car crash in 1983. Through small references such as this, he paints a portrait of a particular time and place without specifying these logistical

details. He marks time by cultural references. Almost every story he writes takes on this aspect.

Movies and theaters are also a significant part of Muñoz's depiction of place. He claims that he is not sure why they figure so prominently in his stories, but he likens them to the bars that function as a backdrop in so many books. And some of the most interesting of his family stories are associated with movies or going to the movies. For instance, back when his mother, Esmeralda, was a little girl, one of her sisters had eloped on a day when the family was visiting the cinema. She went to the bathroom and didn't come back. Her fiancé was waiting outside for her so they could run away to get married. Esmeralda was scared and thought her sister had been kidnapped. Stories such as this from his family inspire his writing and cause him to consider technical questions about how to depict a narrative, such as whose point of view he might choose if he were writing this particular story of his aunt and uncle's elopement as well as what film the family was watching (personal interview).

Movies also figure so prominently in his writing and thoughts because they were such a rarity when he was a child; he says they felt like "a refuge from our lives." His house was small and crowded, "falling apart," and so it was a huge treat to get out to the movies when, most of the time, there was little money to do anything. He still remembers seeing *Jaws* on a third or fourth run around the time he was five years old. He was sitting on his sister's lap during a scene where a skeleton surfaces in the water, and he peed from fright (personal interview).

Family stories such as this also relate to how Muñoz calls up key moments and people from his past about which to write and imagine. Sometimes his search for a subject is about nostalgia because of a focus on the way "things change so slowly, and to me it's like the same dynamic [as nostalgia]." But this recognition is also about the capacity to recognize the emotional home of certain experiences: "I might not have known my parents, what they were like in their twenties and thirties, but I can recognize what their frustrations were about finances, opportunity,

lack, feeling that you made the wrong choice, feeling that you didn't get a chance." Capturing such feelings and experiences is a complex part of depicting the place Muñoz is from.

As of this writing, Muñoz is working on a new short-story collection and has been thinking about what it means to write, particularly in terms of who it is written for and how it is received.

IDENTIFICATION MATTERS: THE ROLES OF ETHNICITY AND SEXUALITY IN MUÑOZ'S WRITING

In many of his discussions about his work, Muñoz identifies his stories as Chicano/a literature but rarely as queer literature, though he is an openly gay man whose characters are often gay. He struggles with expectations from particular identity groups in terms of what he should be writing and why. For instance, "The Happiest Girl in the Whole U.S.A." is about a straight woman. Two other stories he is currently working on are also about straight women. Of this situation, he says, "I haven't had a queer character demand—it's like, Hey, where am I? It hasn't happened in a while. I worry about that a little bit. Because it's so fraught" (personal interview). He recalls that, when he was trying to publish *Zigzagger* in the late nineties, the book was turned down by editors at some presses because they did not think the Chicano/a community was ready for the depictions of Chicano gay men. He says, "They couldn't have been more wrong. The book's still in print ten years later. I think it becomes a question of what does the work start to do over the course of time." Yet he also worries about being repetitive in the subjects he chooses to write about. In the case of different stories: "Do they start to sound the same if they're stacked up against each other? If I had to make a list of the men in [*Zigzagger*] and the men in [*The*] *Faith Healer* [*of Olive Avenue*], I'd be really interested to see how are they different or close to each other."

Muñoz's *Zigzagger* has also been part of a controversy in Arizona, which began in 2010 when the state legislature passed HB 2281, a bill that banned "ethnic studies" in Arizona public

schools. The bill targeted a specific Mexican American studies course being taught in the Tucson Unified School District. As a result of the bill, that particular course was no longer taught, but also several books were pulled from the shelves of the school, including Arturo Rosales' *Chicano! The History of the Mexican American Civil Rights Movement*, Paolo Freire's *Pedagogy of the Oppressed*, and Sandra Cisneros' much-beloved *House on Mango Street*. Muñoz's *Zigzagger* was also banned.

In response to the book banning in Arizona high schools, Muñoz and other members of the University of Arizona faculty, including Associate Professor Adela C. Licona, organized a public reading on October 5, 2012, during Banned Books Week. The reading featured Muñoz as well as two other writers whose work had made Arizona's banned books list: Sandra Cisneros and Helena María Viramontes. Muñoz says it was "humbling" to have these women come to Tucson to read from their work and speak about HB 2281, because it was a reminder that everything they and other Chicano/a writers fought so long and hard to achieve—access to publishing venues, being considered part of a literature, having books in the curriculum—"could easily be snatched away. And it was. And it has been. And it continues to be." Cisneros and Viramontes, he says, "have the authority of experience and age and elder status to let us know: This is not new. This is *not* new. And as angry and as hurt as we [were] in the audience, they have seen this before, and they have seen far worse. So it was incredibly humbling to have that" (personal interview).

The experience of having one of his books banned and organizing a public reading for awareness also brought home to Muñoz how important his visibility as a writer and professor can be in terms of his potential influence on young people: "You're standing as a person of color to young students, to impressionable students, students who need to see that this is a possible achievement" (personal interview). The context of HB 2281 also caused Muñoz to rethink his concept of "what to write and how to write and who gets it—meaning, like, who has access to it now, who's reading me at a certain level."

He realized how often *Zigzagger* is used at the high school level, which surprised him because some of the stories are "pretty graphic" in terms of sex. He thinks that a conversation about sex and sexuality is healthy and brings up an interesting question for a high school curriculum: "What do you do with a book that may feel objectionable because of sexual content yet at the same time is vital to a particular population, at an age when they're impressionable, vulnerable, and sometimes in desperate need of just seeing themselves somehow, and saying, OK, at least literature can show me, not just show me, present me. I exist."

As a result of this developing understanding of audience, Muñoz has a new concern— understanding and reaching out to younger readers. He was surprised that his book was on the banned list because the list focused on Chicano/a issues. He says, "that's how I know no one in Phoenix [i.e., state government officials] had read it, because if they had read it, they would probably have other objections to it. And I'd rather have *that* conversation" (personal interview). In other words, Muñoz would rather be talking about the representation of queer characters as a way of reaching out to queer youth. Such reflections have also prompted Muñoz to consider the question of reading comprehension. "We think about content first and foremost, but rarely do we think about comprehension, and I think that's the thing for me that is so damaging about what happened here [in Arizona]," he says. "We have students who are struggling with comprehension, and when we take away the [key] we need to get into literature, which is, 'You can see yourself'—when you take that away, you're guaranteeing that they're not going to get the skill. And that's what's so enraging about what happened here."

Muñoz saw himself in Cisneros' work, particularly *The House on Mango Street*, but he also thinks that the more one reads, the more one is able to see oneself in different kinds of characters and situations. The first step in reading, he says, is that the character or situation is very much like the reader's. "You take that first rung out of the ladder, and you're robbing

people" (personal interview). Muñoz feels that he can pick up almost any book and learn something from it and that the opportunity to become a wide-ranging reader started very early for him "because no one ever took books from me." He received encouragement from his professors to read widely and read whatever he could find, and "that kind of encouragement is the exact opposite of what we find here in Arizona."

Arizona has been a troubling place for Muñoz for many reasons. Tucson itself is not as accommodating to gay people as New York City, and he says, "it felt like I was going back into the closet" (Brown). Restrictive immigration laws encouraging racial profiling, such as SB 1070, have also given Muñoz pause. He has considered leaving his job as a professor but also believes in "maintaining my visibility as a Chicano professor.... The need for such role models in higher education is pressing" (Brown).

ZIGZAGGER

Like Manuel Muñoz's other books, his first short-story collection, *Zigzagger* (2003), is set in California's Central Valley, a place of agricultural work that houses many poor Chicano/a farm laborers. This setting is key since the place descriptions themselves are often like characters. The collection is full of juxtaposed stories; it spins back and forth between stories of a more conventional length and vignettes or flash fiction. These juxtapositions have the effect of creating a sense of the collective and the feeling that we cannot exactly know the nature of the many individuals that make up a community. And, as the title suggests, readers zigzag across the community, almost as if they are encountering the space in a dream, where doors may be entered or merely opened for a quick glance before moving to the next sequence. This collection also focuses on young gay Latino men. The stories present these men in a complex, realistic light, as individuals with deep familial concerns who are anything but a stereotype.

Many of the characters in *Zigzagger* do not have names but are referred to with common nouns such as "the mother" or "the boy." Of

some of the writing produced for *Zigzagger*, Muñoz says he was working on how to convey the people he was writing about to his readers. He went through a period in which he wrote his characters in these general terms (e.g., he, she, the mother, the girl) as a way to explore identity without using particular names. This also served as a way to think about the roles people play or are placed into when they have certain situational markers, like "older brother" or "younger sister." He began to conceptualize his characters through these identifications, and he feels that such an exercise was necessary for him to understand how to appeal to a variety of readers (personal interview).

In the title story, which opens the collection, an adolescent boy is recovering at his home, his parents concerned about him and a group of neighborhood kids hovering outside and wondering what has happened to their friend. We learn that the boy was attracted to a man, an out-of-towner, at a dance, and that the man had sexually assaulted him. In another story, "The Third Myth," two adolescent boys are romantically involved but keep it a secret. In "Good As Yesterday," a young woman accompanies her younger brother to a prison where he meets with a man with whom he has been romantically involved, and the sister attempts to protect him from calling too much attention to the romance in an environment that will not deal kindly with it. In "By the Time You Get There, by the Time You Get Back," a father asks his gay son for money to travel to Mexico, where the father routinely lies to their relatives, saying that his son is married to a white woman.

The characters of *Zigzagger* are often isolated in their small, rural communities, or they have emerged elsewhere from this isolation. They have strong and conflicted family ties, and they come from poverty and hard labor. These stories provide a multiplicity of identities for young gay Chicano men in a rural community and, thus, shatter some of the stereotypes of stories about homosexuality, while simultaneously emphasizing gay issues that are recognizable across many contexts.

THE FAITH HEALER OF OLIVE AVENUE

Short-listed for the Frank O'Connor International Short Story Award, *The Faith Healer of Olive Avenue* (2007) is composed of stories that are all set in the same Mexican American neighborhood south of Fresno in the Central Valley. Before being published in this collection, some of these stories appeared in *Glimmer Train, Epoch, Rush Hour*, and *Swink*.

Muñoz began writing *The Faith Healer of Olive Avenue* when he was unable to publish *Zigzagger*. He had tried an agent, contests, small presses, and university presses but was having no luck. Many of his peers were publishing their books, and he had published several of the stories from *Zigzagger* in literary journals, but he could not find a home for the entire collection. He began to wonder what about the collection was not working for publication: whether it was the arrangement of the stories, the tonal shifts, or the various styles. His puzzlement inspired him to start a new book (personal interview).

One of the last stories he had written for Zigzagger was "Good As Yesterday," which, in terms of its continuity, is more like the stories from *The Faith Healer of Olive Avenue* than the other stories in *Zigzagger*. The structure of *The Faith Healer of Olive Avenue* is more linear and less anecdotal than *Zigzagger*. This capacity to write in a linear fashion was something Muñoz had been afraid to do, so he "started with a very simple premise" (personal interview). He was thinking about the triplets living on Gold Street who were mentioned early on in *Zigzagger*, and he considered that these characters provided the potential for three stories about three people. As he thought about their stories, he suddenly found that he was populating an entire neighborhood. He says, "It became intensely fun to do it, and the stories came at a really terrific clip." He completed the book in two years and says, "It was the best time of my life." The stories in this collection are evidence that, for the first time, Muñoz felt that the place he came from really mattered and that he could honor it through his writing.

The ten stories in this collection are brief but tend to cling to the reader like memory fragments.

These stories are told from various perspectives. For example, there is a mother whose gay son dies in a motorcycle accident, a man who returns to San Francisco to encounter his estranged sister after his partner dies, and a woman trying to protect a male cousin who is being pursued by an abusive boyfriend. These characters' stories dovetail and intersect to reveal a neighborhood etched by persistent myths and misunderstandings but also by love and connection. The stories underscore the significance of history in a close-knit yet judgmental community. The community remains unnamed, but there are specific place names within and outside of the town, such as Gold Street. The stories follow people from the town at various points over the years but not in chronological fashion. The keen eyes and ears of the community figure into the stories, where all the residents know (or think they know) the lives of those they see across the street.

Many of the stories in *The Faith Healer of Olive Avenue* are about death, grief, desire, and coming to terms with the reality of loss. The collection opens and closes with the triplets, Carlos, Chris, and Claudio. In the opening story, "Lindo y Querido," the main character, Connie, a Latina housekeeper for a white woman, is dealing with the tragedy of her son, Isidro, being mortally wounded in a motorcycle accident. Isidro's boyfriend died immediately, while Connie must care for Isidro as he dies at home. The boyfriend is Carlos, one of the triplets. Like other stories in this collection, "Lindo y Querido" waits until the end to reveal the circumstances of the death. "Señor X," which appears in the middle of the collection, is about the triplet Chris, who is starting over at home after being released from prison. And "Good Brother," which appears toward the end of the collection, follows the protagonist Sebastían's sexual encounters during his teenage years with another one of the triplets, who remains unnamed.

Returning home to this place is a common theme in the collection. In "Bring Brang Brung," for instance, Martín has been living in San Francisco and taking care of Adán, a child whom he and his partner had adopted. His partner Adrian, who is deceased, is the one who really

had wanted to adopt a child, not Martín. The story follows his return with Adán and his attempts to reconcile with his estranged sister. As with other stories, the ending provides a flashback description of what happened shortly before Martín's partner died.

Muñoz's stories in this collection have powerful conclusions that are often worded simply. "Bring Brang Brung" contains an example of the power of Muñoz's concluding lines. In this part of the story, readers are anticipating an explanation of Adrian's death, but Muñoz flashes back to just before the death, or so readers can assume. It is a rainy day in San Francisco, and Adán has a fever. Adrian has gone on a trip to Denver, so Martín is alone in taking care of Adán, and he is experiencing some doubt about his relationship with Adrian. The story ends with the following: "All day it rained. Nothing changed. It rained all day" (*Faith Healer*, p. 46). The sentences here focus on the seemingly mundane—rain in San Francisco. But the emotional weight of the lines is tethered to the previous paragraphs in which Martín is bored with his relationship, his adopted son is sick, and his partner is gone, while readers know that there is an impending death. Muñoz's stories often have repeated words or lines at the end, and this adds to the emotional impact. For instance, in "When You Come into Your Kingdom," a father, Santiago, is grieving the loss of his family upon the death of his son. As with other stories, readers do not know what happened to the son until the end, when the father returns to the site of the son's death, a hotel room where his son leaped from a balcony. The word "love" is repeated at the end of the story, and in this repetition readers may get a sense of resolution for Santiago, who feels that it is his fault that his son jumped from the balcony, as he had given him a hard time for being overweight and not acting in a stereotypical male fashion.

Muñoz's stories also tend to focus on physical changes to places that evoke strong memories in his characters, as well as a sense of nostalgia. For example, "The Heart Finds Its Own Conclusion" is told from the point of view of Cecilia, whose cousin Sergio needs her to pick him up because he is afraid of his boyfriend. She is supposed to pick him up at a bus station downtown near a cinema, a place that used to be vibrant and that she remembers going to as a little girl. Downtown has become an isolated place, dark and lifeless at night. Cecilia remembers the place being active and filled with a little more hope. Sergio's boyfriend shows up, and he takes Sergio away when his bus comes in. The boyfriend is sinister in a way that is comparable with Cecilia's impression of the current downtown. Such a juxtaposition connects the story of her cousin, outcast by his father because he is gay, to the feeling of loss experienced by Cecilia when she returns to this part of town and sees the cinema.

"Tell Him About Brother John" also follows the motif of home and departure. The story is about the cultural differences between those who leave home and those who still live in those homes, in a world both myopic and emotionally rich, where gossip coexists with respect and caretaking of others. The setting reveals the community's obligation to care for those who are in their midst even as they may be politely shunned, as in the case of Brother John, who is gay. An analysis of this story would focus on the ways that community and individual silences figure into the actions and insights of the characters. This story, like others in the collection, explores what it means to be gay and to leave home, only to find oneself returning and being out about one's relationships.

Indeed, the complexity of relationships among gay and straight cultures is a significant overall theme in the book. The writing is most effective when it captures the capacity to both love and judge, or even love and hate. "Tell Him About Brother John" captures this through the narrator's father. In another story, "Ida y Vuelta," Roberto lets his former lover Joaquín and Joaquín's boyfriend stay with him when they return to town to see Joaquín's father, who is dying from cancer. While Roberto is not without malice, Joaquín's family is kind to him even though they disapprove of homosexuality. Their kindness is a veil over their intolerance, which is an example of the ways Muñoz is able to capture the tensions between gay and straight cultures.

Overall, *The Faith Healer of Olive Avenue* captures the nuances of a community that struggles economically and suffers from racial injustice. Muñoz integrates gay characters who are negotiating identities that are not always welcomed in this suffering community, and he does all of this while describing lived experience in a way that is believable and does not lend itself to tidy resolutions. Muñoz's writing is effective in capturing these issues without naming them; his stories provide implicit connections, which adds to the sense of complex reality in the collection.

WHAT YOU SEE IN THE DARK

Muñoz's novel *What You See in the Dark* (2011) is set in Bakersfield, California, in the late 1950s. Like his other books, this one takes place in the Central Valley. The story is told through four viewpoints. First is Teresa, who works at a shoe store and dreams of being a singer, and, as a Chicana, she is an anomaly in this town where most of the visible people are white. Next is Arlene Watson, the mother of a man who ends up murdering Teresa and fleeing town. Arlene is a waitress and owns a small hotel that is losing business as a highway is built that will cause the town itself to change. The third major character is known as the Actress, a woman who visits Bakersfield with the director of an upcoming movie, who is scouting out hotels, including Arlene's. It should be clear to readers that "the Actress" is a fictionalized version of Janet Leigh, who played Marion Crane in Alfred Hitchcock's *Psycho*, part of which was filmed in Bakersfield, and that the director who accompanies her is Alfred Hitchcock. The Actress has achieved things that Teresa and other young women in the town dream about, but she herself is plagued with a lack of self-confidence, particularly as she ages out of acting roles that she would have been chosen for earlier in her career. The fourth major character is never named but opens and closes the book and is referred to in the second person. This character is a young woman who works at the shoe store with Teresa. She is obsessed with and jealous of Teresa, who dates Dan Watson, a popular and good-looking man.

The novel is narrated as if through the lens of a movie camera. And indeed, readers are at times made to feel as if they are in a movie theater—that feeling of entering a darkened place and being open to whatever the film will show and tell. Darkness and visibility are motifs through the novel. In a theater, one is immersed in darkness in order to see, while in the daylight our capacity to see is dependent on our biases and perspectives. In many ways, this novel is about visibility—who becomes visible and why, whose lives the camera is trained on while it neglects others. As with *The Faith Healer of Olive Avenue*, people make assumptions about the lives they see, and those lives are the subject of gossip and speculation. For instance, Teresa, whose racial and class status normally render her invisible in this place, becomes visible when she falls in love with a white man who is established and popular in town. We are reminded most of her invisibility as she walks to work in the mornings; on her way, she passes a backdrop of Chicano men waiting to see if they can get work for the day. One of them quietly pursues Teresa before she becomes involved with Dan Watson. This significant motif encourages hard questions: What do people see? How do our perceptions affect the stories we tell about each other and ourselves? This is why it is important that the book opens and closes with a character who keenly watches others.

The visibility and sight motif is so important that the book closes with a line about sight. In this passage, the second-person character is telling the story of Teresa's murder. We can assume that this account is speculation, but in the context of not having any "true" story, readers will hunger for this detailed description. This narrative of the murder is also told as if through a movie camera lens. The final line of the novel: "You wanted that girl to see something, and there was no going back once she did" (*What You See in the Dark*, p. 251). Once certain characters are exposed to realities they had not seen before, there is "no going back." The shoe saleswoman, who readers will likely assume to be

white, heavily characterizes Teresa, perhaps because she yearns so much to be like her. Yet she also exoticizes Teresa, revealing her limitations as a narrator.

The novel is a departure from Muñoz's short-story collections. Muñoz says that "the novel answered something in me, my preoccupations, and the questions I'm most fascinated by," such as the frequent appearance of movies in his writing and the theater as a site (personal interview). He thinks that "there's still something to be said about living in a place and longing to escape it, and you can't. And one of the ways to do that is fantasy." The movies offer such an escape but are compromised by "a world that's lily white"—it is rare to see title characters who are not white, and characters of a minority status are often sidekicks or stereotypes. Nonetheless, Muñoz says, "that experience of walking into a theater and asking for immersion into a story—we do it anyway. I mean, I do it anyway. If anything, I should be more critical of movies for not representing lives." He remains fascinated by movies and the cinema as a site, and continues to reflect upon this fascination.

It does seem that in *What You See in the Dark* the movie and the filming of the movie are about a set of privileges. And outside of the context of the movie is a setting where characters think that they lack accomplishment, where they feel compelled to succeed in something more exciting than what is in front of their faces and have a longing to escape. Teresa experiences this when she begins to sing with Dan Watson at a nightclub; she begins to achieve something beyond being a shoe saleswoman being courted by a quiet, ordinary man who waits to find work each morning. The characters' desires and capacities to achieve those desires are limited by factors of class and race privilege that are implicit in the descriptive prose of the novel.

What You See in the Dark received good reviews, but it was not as widely reviewed or acclaimed as Muñoz's short-story collections. Muñoz suggests that the book was more difficult than his other work and that "a difficult book is not the best way to get people talking" (personal interview). He cites two examples: Helena María Viramontes' *Their Dogs Came with Them* and Dagoberto Gilb's *The Flowers*. Viramontes' book had been published for several years before people began to take note of it critically, and Gilb's book is stylistically challenging. He places this conversation in the context of how Chicano/a literature is received, in that those books that are not part of a norm for that type of literature are not paid as much attention. *What You See in the Dark* is a more experimental book for Muñoz, and it was met with some silence from critics in comparison with his other works.

One of the major differences between the novel and the short-story collections is that the novel's social, cultural, and political undercurrents are not as explicit. These issues are still there, "but you can't quite put your finger on them because the apparatus of movies is what dominates everything" (personal interview). Overall, the main issues of the novel, according to Muñoz, are the question of seeing versus looking and how people construct a story out of the visual alone. He is also interested in the origin of gossip, and storytelling when one doesn't have all the facts.

Muñoz is also interested in moving away from having to focus on literature that only reflects an identity he is comfortable expressing. He says, "I was fascinated by [the main issues in the novel] for some reason, but that might not be the first thing you think of when you think of Chicano lit" (personal interview). In his interview with Nell Porter Brown, he says that "having three women form the core [of the novel], two white women and a Mexican-American girl, was not what I had planned, nor what people might expect from me as a Chicano writer." But, he points out, "The best art always breaks that pattern of what we think is our experience. That's the great, humanizing effect of literature. Chicano writers are capable of all sorts of things, not just writing about immigration or poverty or working-class lives or geography. I want to start new discussions. Here we have a Chicano writer writing about Hitchcock—what do we do with that?" He brings up interesting questions worth pursuit in any analysis of an author's life as related to his or her work: to what extent are we

obligated to write about what we know, and how do readers' understandings of a writer's life influence how they perceive his or her writing? As he put it later, the novel

> has a higher level of difficulty than questions of representation, seeing yourself. That's not to say there are two camps. But it's just, as an artist, what kind of range you will be granted. Will you be granted the range to do whatever you need to do to satisfy yourself? Because at the end of the day you have to sit at the desk by yourself, you have to give up your hours, to be alone, you have to give up time with other people.... To do all that has to satisfy something; it doesn't always just have to satisfy other people, it's gotta satisfy what questions roll around in your head. I feel as if I've moved to a place where it's OK that I can ask these strange questions. I didn't have the capacity to do it when I was in college, I was afraid to do it when I was in college and graduate school.... Sometimes the pushback you get for your choices can be really painful and unfair. But none of those people are with me at the desk by myself.
>
> (personal interview)

These words might serve as a précis of the major theme of the novel, and indeed of much of Muñoz's work: characters cross paths in ways that emphasize their loneliness in small places.

Selected Bibliography

WORKS OF MANUEL MUÑOZ

BOOKS
Zigzagger: Stories. Evanston, Ill.: Northwestern University Press, 2003.

The Faith Healer of Olive Avenue: Stories. Chapel Hill, N.C.: Algonquin Books, 2007.

What You See in the Dark: A Novel. Chapel Hill, N.C.: Algonquin Books, 2011.

OTHER SHORT FICTION
Greetings from Ice Country. Berkeley, Calif.: Chicano Chapbook Series, 1998.

"The Happiest Girl in the Whole U.S.A." *Glimmer Train* 89 (winter 2014).

CRITICAL STUDIES AND REVIEWS

Aceves, Andres. "Review of *What You See in the Dark: A Novel.*" *Southwestern American Literature* 37, no. 2:94–95 (spring 2012).

Martínez, Ernesto Javier. "Shifting the Site of Queer Enunciation: Manuel Muñoz and the Politics of Form." In *Gay Latino Studies: A Critical Reader.* Edited by Michael Hames-García and Ernesto Javier Martínez. Durham, N.C.: Duke University Press, 2011. Pp. 226–249.

Rodriguez, Miguel. "Book Review: *What You See in the Dark.*" *Cinema Junkie*, KPBS, May 3, 2011. http://www.ifc.com/fix/2011/05/peering-into-munozs-hitchcocki

Taylor, Charles. "Peering into Munoz's Hitchcockian Thriller, *What You See in the Dark.*" IFC.com, May 4, 2011. http://www.ifc.com/fix/2011/05/peering-into-munozs-hitchcocki

INTERVIEWS AND WEBSITE

Brown, Nell Porter. "Echoes of the Central Valley." *Harvard Magazine,* May 2011. http://harvardmagazine.com/2011/05/echoes-of-the-central-valley?page=all

Manuel Muñoz website. http://www.manuel-munoz.com

Personal interview with the author. August 8, 2013.

STEWART O'NAN

(1961—)

John A. McDermott

SINCE 1993 STEWART O'Nan has published a prize-winning short-story collection, fourteen novels, a novella, two books of nonfiction, and a screenplay. He also has edited a posthumous anthology of essays by John Gardner and a mammoth anthology of Vietnam War literature. Along the way, he has published critical reviews, essays, and uncollected short stories in a range of magazines and newspapers, toured the United States and Europe with readings too numerous to count, held workshops and panels at the most prestigious conferences, and chatted with dozens of interviewers. He has done all of this while in a successful marriage, raising two children, and indulging in a passion for baseball and reading, always reading.

His fiction is varied, with broad shifts in locales, eras, and communities. While some of his work is classified as horror and other books seem aimed at a more literary crowd, his themes recur like a symphony: moods shift and return, replayed in slightly different keys but highlighting the same notes, notes of grief and redemption, celebrating the capacity for humans to endure great pain and still reach out to one another. He is a realist in both form and matter, because his primary goal is the creation of characters—humans behaving well, humans behaving badly. "I want the form, the structure, and the language all to be in service to the characters' emotional world," O'Nan states (Longino, p. 78). It's this devotion to character that is a tenet of his creative philosophy, that and generosity. Generosity is at the core of O'Nan's character development, whether he's dealing with mourning parents or serial killers: no one is off the hook and no one is thoroughly condemned. We are privy to every emotional landscape, for good or ill, and we are asked to judge—and forgive—accordingly.

BIOGRAPHY: FROM READER TO WRITER

Born on February 4, 1961, Stewart O'Nan is a native of Pittsburgh, Pennsylvania, a city he left at eighteen to pursue an education and work in varied fields, but to which he returned after thirty years and again calls home.

O'Nan supplies one of the most useful explanations of his youth in Pittsburgh with a time line on the page of his website titled "How I Became a Writer," where he lists his influences during his childhood, with his age on one side and the art he was ingesting on the other:

5 Cartoons
9 Horror comics
10 TV
11 Edgar Rice Burroughs—the Tarzan series
12 Horror movies—George Romero
13 Genesis with Gabriel
14 Bradbury, Ellison, Matheson; World War II flying
  stories
16 Stephen King
17 Garage punk, Iggy and the Stooges, Syd Barrett

It's not difficult to see the influence of pulp stories in his work—there would be no *The Night Country* (2003) if there were no Ray Bradbury, no *A Prayer for the Dying* (1999) without Richard Matheson's *I Am Legend* (1954). The World War II stories are clearly seen in his historical novel *A World Away* (1998), and of course the sixteen-year-old O'Nan reading King could never have imagined he would later collaborate with the most popular author in America someday, not once but twice. O'Nan gives us another time line for his early adulthood and first job, in Boston and then Long Island, to his graduate school years in Ithaca, New York:

18 Aerospace engineering
19 The Velvet Underground, William S. Burroughs, beats
20 Camus, Breton, Peret
21 The nouveau roman, Robert Coover, William H. Gass
22 Foreign film, blues, baroque, Coltrane
24 Structural test engineering
25 Flannery O'Connor, Sylvia Plath, John Cheever
26 Terrence Malick, Antonioni
27 Chekhov, Tolstoy, Toni Morrison, Virginia Woolf
28 Quit engineering to write
29 James Salter, Jayne Anne Phillips, Tim O'Brien, Denis Johnson

Again, it isn't difficult to see the effect of Flannery O'Connor's use of regionalism and social mores, her "mystery and manners" on O'Nan, as it isn't difficult to see Cheever's domestic turmoil, Morrison's sense of race and history, or Tolstoy's interest in the dysfunctional family saga. Certainly living American authors have had an effect on O'Nan as well, such as the influence of Tim O'Brien on his Vietnam War novel *The Names of the Dead* (1996) and his anthology of literature addressing the war. It's possible to draw direct lines from any of these influences to moments or even whole works of O'Nan's. This is nearly a recipe card for his literature. Reviewers consistently remark on the protean nature of his books, and his passionate reading across the board is a sure clue to the variety of his novels.

O'Nan's father, John Lee O'Nan, was an engineer and his mother, Mary Ann, a schoolteacher. O'Nan followed in his father's path and studied engineering at Boston University, graduating in 1983. He married his high school sweetheart, Trudy, in 1984 and then took a job as a test engineer with Grumman Aerospace Corporation in Long Island. He worked there for four years through his mid-twenties and, at the urging of his wife, left engineering in 1989 to pursue a master of fine arts degree in creative writing at Cornell University in Ithaca, New York (a city that plays a prominent role in his early novel *The Names of the Dead*). There he was fortunate to study with the writers Lorrie Moore and Stephanie Vaughn; one of his classmates was the novelist and short-story writer A. Manette Ansay. His story collection, *In the Walled City*,

was published by the University of Pittsburgh Press in 1993 as the winner of the prestigious Drue Heinz Literature Prize, and his novel *Snow Angels* appeared the following year. He taught at the University of Central Oklahoma and the University of New Mexico before moving to Avon, Connecticut, in 1995 to teach at Trinity College in Hartford. In 1996 *Granta*, the prominent British literary magazine, named him one of America's Best Young Novelists along with such peers as Sherman Alexie, Jeffrey Eugenides, Jonathan Franzen, and Lorrie Moore. He was a professor at Trinity until 1998, when he quit teaching to write full time. He has used his time fruitfully, producing almost a book a year.

EARLY WORKS, 1993–2001

In the Walled City, reissued by Grove Press in 2001, contains a dozen stories that set the tone for much of O'Nan's later work. Addressing the deep sadness that can pervade the average human's life, he gives us detailed portraits of middle- and working-class Americans as they confront issues of divorce and custody, illness and aging, poverty and ethics. The stories also reflect where O'Nan began his publishing career while still a graduate student, in literary journals such as *Ascent, Columbia, South Dakota Review*, and *Threepenny Review*. He had won a few contests with those stories, and Tobias Wolff, the senior judge for the Heinz prize that year, praised O'Nan's gift for "shifting perspectives" and his "feel for the weight of the histories" that burden his characters. Shifting perspectives is one of the elements that keeps O'Nan's work so diverse. He has used multiple first-person narrators and close third-person narrators within the same novel, as in later works such as *Everyday People* (2001) or *Wish You Were Here* (2002); more aggressive perspectives like the use of second person, not just in a short story but for the duration of a novel, as in *A Prayer for the Dying*; and direct address to listeners who give the narrator an occasion for the tale, as in the tape-recorded confession of *The Speed Queen*'s title character. All these allow O'Nan to demonstrate prominently his painstaking ventriloquism. He is equally adept

at portraying the concerns of an elderly upper-middle-class white woman and those of an inner-city black teenage paraplegic, as adept at speaking for men caught in the wildness of the Vietnam War as he is for teenagers caught in the restlessness of American youth culture.

His first novel, *Snow Angels*, won the Pirate's Alley Faulkner Prize as a manuscript in 1993 and was published by Doubleday in 1994. The novel sprang from one of the short stories of *In the Walled City*, "Finding Amy." While the short story addresses the troubled marriage between Annie and Glenn Marchand, Annie's affair with Glenn's friend, Brock, and the disappearance of the Marchands' five-year-old daughter, Amy, it isn't until the last paragraph of the story that the protagonist of *Snow Angels* is mentioned. Arthur Parkinson, the teenage boy who finds Amy's corpse, becomes the first voice of the novel. "Finding Amy" is crucial to the development of O'Nan's fiction because it contains the first use of a motif in his novels: the search party, the volunteers who enlist to scour the woods and fields of wooded America in hopes of finding the body of a child or teen who has gone missing. This scene repeats itself most prominently in a much later novel, *Songs for the Missing* (2008).

Snow Angels begins with the adult Arthur looking back on fall of his freshman year in high school, the year his father left the family, the season his old babysitter, Annie Marchand, was murdered by her estranged husband, Glenn. Their daughter—the Amy of the story, now revised to Tara—dies after she has wandered off from home, supposedly under the care of her mother, a frazzled waitress bedeviled by her increasingly erratic husband, by her lover (a man she steals from her best friend and fellow waitress), and by her own mother, who looks down on her daughter's troubled life. But Annie, for all her troubles, is a sympathetic victim, just as Glenn, her murderer, isn't portrayed as thoroughly evil. Glenn's slide into psychosis and religious mania is painted as O'Nan always does, with generosity. Following Anton Chekhov's advice to treat characters with cool empathy, O'Nan never hides the flaws of his characters, whether they are heroes or villains, but he never lets us forget their humanity either.

His second novel, *The Names of the Dead* (1996), set in Ithaca, New York, in the 1980s, focuses on Vietnam vet Larry Markham, as he deals with his dissolving marriage, his dying father, and his brain-damaged son—perhaps a victim of Agent Orange—and his job as a baked-goods delivery driver. The novel counters Larry's current troubles with graphic flashbacks of his stint in Vietnam as an army medic. On top of Larry's domestic woes, O'Nan weaves a thriller plot: the return of a potentially homicidal covert-op vet who first infiltrates Larry's recovery group at the local VA hospital and then disappears into the New York countryside to stalk Larry and his family. O'Nan's plots often focus on real-life tragedy turned into obsessive guilt, as in the case of Larry's survivor guilt over being the last man alive from his core group of comrades in the war. The action follows Larry through his memories in Vietnam, culminating in a particularly graphic recounting of the Battle of Hamburger Hill, a bloody confrontation in May 1969. As Larry negotiates his failing marriage—his wife is exhausted from dealing with Larry's remorse and has entered into an affair with a married man—he begins a brief but potent liaison with a troubled neighbor woman, a recovering addict and mental patient, a woman whose ex-husband was once a friend of Larry and his wife. The novel ends with Larry alone, his marriage done, his father dead, his lover off to reunite with her estranged husband, and the terrorizing vet a victim of suicide.

While the book could be classified a mystery, its real strength lies in O'Nan's faithful research in the history of the Vietnam War and its effects on the young men who fought it. In the tradition of Tim O'Brien, it is best when it paints the gruesome realities of war and the love that such hardship engenders in the men who live the trials day by day. The novel also shows O'Nan's early preoccupation with Halloween and "ghost" stories that aren't really supernatural. The real terror of war is used to counter the fun of our spooky traditions (just as it is years later in *The Night Country*). Larry's job as delivery man also

allows O'Nan to use one of his favorite means of establishing place: the character in the car (or bus or truck) who tours the town. The integral part automobiles and travel play in American life, along with O'Nan's use of holidays (especially Halloween) to both underscore and undermine our need for continuity and ritual, are two patterns that repeat again and again in his works.

His third novel, *The Speed Queen* (1997)—titled "Dear Stephen King" in manuscript—is his first "literary" genre novel, this one an homage to pulp novels, B movies with violent women on the loose, and buddy road movies, a sort of madcap version of the Charles Starkweather story, this time with a female lead. The idea came to him while he was researching *The Names of the Dead,* listening to oral histories of veterans who served hard time. As he recalled in an interview, "This guy was telling how he and a friend kidnapped and killed this other guy—and he was like laughing and getting off on it until he realized he was supposed to be sorry and then his tone changed completely, he was sorry, he was a different man now.... I was like whoa, that's so sickly evil and human, so uncaring, I've gotta get that" (Bryant, pp. 34–35).

Marjorie Standiford, the title character and narrator, is just "that." Hers is a first-person confession/defense as she waits on death row. Her monologue is aimed at a celebrated author who has bought the rights to her story (it's King, but not directly named in the text, though there are allusions to his books). The author, as O'Nan has noted, is a sort of father-confessor for Marjorie. Ironically, the original title was the basis for a legal fight—O'Nan was prevented from using King's name—but was also the beginning of the friendship between O'Nan and King, which later led to their collaborations. *The Speed Queen*, like the later novel *A Prayer for the Dying*, is a fan favorite. Unlike the narrators in most of his novels, Marjorie is decidedly unreliable. From the beginning she announces she never killed anyone, and then we progress through a bloody crime spree along the old Route 66, filled with diner stops, meth taking, and mayhem. O'Nan gets to indulge in two of his favorite sto-rytelling techniques: the road as locale and American's pop culture, especially fast food. Marjorie, of course, attributes all the violence to Lamont, her dead husband, and their lover, Natalie, who is defending herself in an alternate book, one that blames Marjorie. Marjorie is the sole voice of the novel, and she is busy impressing the famous novelist and denying her complicity. She records the tapes on the eve of her scheduled execution, and her monologue is interrupted by details of protestors and a (failed) last-minute stay.

The story is told in 114 tiny chapters, and Marjorie's voice is the driving force of the narrative. O'Nan calls her "a sort of comic figure ... there's an ironic distance there with an unreliable narrator" (Longino, p. 88), and it's just her unreliability that makes her either comic or hateful, or mostly likely both, to the average reader. By the end of the novel, Marjorie has revealed every bloody detail, yet continues to express her innocence: "Just remember, everything I've told you is true. I'm completely innocent. Try to be nice to me, okay? Just tell a good story" (p. 212). Even Marjorie deserves a voice—a crass and compelling one, yes—and as she is off to the electric chair it's up to the reader, and that "novelist," to decide how much of her version of the story is true.

O'Nan's next novel, *A World Away* (1998), is another historical war novel, this time set in World War II. He likes research:

> My wife Trudy says I only write the books so I can do the research and that's partly true. It's a great excuse to dig into subjects I've always been vaguely interested in—Vietnam, photography, speed, prison, whatever. I interview people with first-hand experience, read tons of articles and books and watch any associated films, stocking up on the subcultures traditions and lingo, then pare it all down so it seems the characters know what they're talking about. Then I give it to people who really know what they're talking about and they generously beat the crap out of it.
>
> (Bryant, p. 39)

Here O'Nan's research spanned the homefront side of the war as well as the Pacific front, the women working in factories and life on both coasts. The plot focuses on an ensemble: James

and Annie Langer, with their younger son, Jay, move to the Hamptons to care for James's aging father while their elder son, Rennie, once a conscientious objector, is shipped to the Pacific front to work as a medic. Rennie's wife, Dorothy, is pregnant and living in San Diego, working in a factory and waiting for the birth of the child and for Rennie to return. Calamitous events predate the opening of the novel: James's affair with a teenage girl—one of his high school students— enrages Annie, and the marriage seems frozen. Rennie and Dorothy had suffered public humiliation in her hometown of Galesburg, the locals angry over his CO status, and Jay is confused about the death of his maternal grandfather and then the deterioration of his paternal grandfather. While James takes a factory job, Annie goes to work as a nurse and begins an affair with a married man, Martin. Her infidelity is perhaps driven by a desire to settle scores, to even it up, but in the end, the novel has a carefully hopeful ending. Rennie returns, damaged physically and emotionally but alive, and marriage and fatherhood, after an initial postwar adjustment, seem to suit him; James and Annie's marriage is on the mend. The grandfather dies, yet that suits the natural course of life. Unlike in his previous novels, here O'Nan works toward a sense of healing for his major characters.

As with *The Names of the Dead*, *A World Away* has at its thematic core issues of grief and guilt and redemption. It also has the domestic concerns—marital strife, infidelity, parenthood— that continually play out in O'Nan's work. Deep echoes between the two books seem deliberate; Rennie Langer, like Larry Markham in the earlier novel, is a military medic; the Battle of Attu, a bloody confrontation between American forces and the Japanese off the coast of Alaska, seems an echo of the Battle of Hamburger Hill, so prominent in *Names*; and the father-son angst played out here between Rennie and Jay and their disgraced father summons up that between Larry and his doctor father in the earlier work. Dorothy, the isolated, pregnant young wife, acts as a precursor to Patty, the titular character of *The Good Wife* (2005), and even of Emily Maxwell, the geriatric widow of *Emily, Alone* (2011). *A World Away* has literary precursors as well, in the World War II novels of Norman Mailer, James Jones, and Anton Myrer.

A Prayer for the Dying (1999) is a historical horror novel, set in Wisconsin in the 1870s. Many readers consider this his breakout "horror" novel, and it consistently turns up on horror top ten lists, rated alongside the works of Robert Bloch, Joe R. Lansdale, and Peter Straub. The protagonist is Jacob Hansen, a Civil War veteran with a trio of jobs in the small town of Friendship; Jacob is the undertaker, constable, and preacher. When his town is beset with an outbreak of diphtheria, it is Jacob's job to bury the dead and contain the contagious, but a forest fire threatens the town and he must choose to break the quarantine and let the townspeople go or know he is killing everyone left in his hometown. This is complicated by the deaths of Jacob's beloved wife, Marta; his daughter, Amelia; and their new baby. Jacob's slow descent into grief-instigated insanity is poignant and chilling. O'Nan goes into dark territory: graphic portraits of disease, suicide, and necrophilia—Jacob refuses to admit Marta is dead—and eventually Jacob's admission of cannibalism. The grief and guilt that haunt Jacob are the most brutal sort of curse; we learn late in the novel that the only way he survived the war was by eating a fellow soldier and friend:

> You remember tending to the little Norwegian, taking great care with him. They all thought he was your friend, that the two of you were inseparable, the way you looked at him, so devoted. You wouldn't let anyone touch him. You buttoned his sleeves so they didn't see the marks on his arms where you stripped the meat off when they were asleep. You said a prayer after you buried him, made another promise to God, instantly became a different man. But did you really change? You thought you had. Now you don't know.
>
> (p. 194)

For this novel O'Nan chose that aggressive point of view, the second person, so the events are told by Jacob, but a Jacob who is so uncomfortable with his choices that he must distance himself from them by use of the "you" rather than "I." It becomes a masked first-person narrator—readers

know it is Jacob, but the connection is so direct, we become "you" even as his mind slips into deep grief.

O'Nan thanks the sociologist Michael Lesy, who in 1973 published *Wisconsin Death Trip*, a book-length collection of newspaper clippings and photographs that highlight the grim nature of life in the midwestern frontier. This was no *Little House on the Prairie*, and readers of Lesy's work are confronted with arson, madness, suicide, murder, and more on every page. O'Nan recognized the horrific potential of *Wisconsin Death Trip* and made the most of it. The real horror of the novel is Lesy's bleak research coupled with Jacob's burning internal guilt. "All of this is your fault" (p. 173) he tells himself, as if he alone were in control of disease and infernos and war— but how does that differ so from Larry Markham? Marjorie Standiford stands alone: she works busily to avoid a sentiment like that. This may be the primal battle of O'Nan's characters: those who embrace guilt in a destructive self-flagellation and those who spend their time running far from responsibility.

In 1999 O'Nan also made a sly departure from his own name and published a thriller titled *A Good Day to Die* under the pen name James Coltrane (the last name a nod to one of his favorite musicians, John Coltrane). The novel is a swift tale featuring Jorge Ortega, a "Company" operative who is sent into Cuba after the death of Fidel Castro. Ortega has mixed feelings about the mission: his grandfather had died in the Bay of Pigs disaster, his missions in El Salvador have left him scarred, and he remembers both his father's suicide and the death of Catalina, a woman he loved for whose murder he feels responsible. The book is a tribute to Ernest Hemingway's *For Whom the Bell Tolls* (1940), and O'Nan has stated that he wasn't entirely happy with its execution, which was one reason he went with a pseudonym. The writing is elegant for a suspense novel and its sparse lyricism does owe a debt to Hemingway. While currently out of print, the book did garner fans and the reviews were solid. The *Publishers Weekly* review sums up the problems of the novel as a genre dispute: "Coltrane's narrative style—more literary than

Tom Clancy's, less so than Robert Stone's—achieves its limited objectives. Ultimately, however, his attempt to transcend the military thriller genre with a literary interiority traps this narrative in a formidable category crisis." While this "category crisis" may have doomed Coltrane's career, the aggressive blending of categories—literary, horror, historical, domestic, all of the labels reviewers and critics want to pin on novels—is central to O'Nan's fiction. Rather than a "crisis," in most cases, it is a cause for celebration.

Everyday People (2001) is dedicated to John Edgar Wideman, the well-known African American novelist who has spent much of his career documenting Homewood, a black area of Pittsburgh. O'Nan's book is truly an ode to Wideman's world. *Everyday People* is set in East Liberty, another black area of Pittsburgh, and follows an ensemble cast from the crisis of two teenaged boys, one who dies, the other who becomes paralyzed, as they try to tag a construction area. This is the first long work set in O'Nan's hometown, and it's a brave choice. Contemporary white American writers don't often set entire novels in communities outside their own— perhaps O'Nan was testing the waters when he published a chapter of the novel as a short story in *Glimmer Train*, a respected literary journal. The voices are a profound departure from his typically white characters, and O'Nan takes pains to get the lives of East Liberty down truthfully. O'Nan sent the manuscript to Wideman for his approval, prepublication, knowing how important it was to get it right. As much as these are fictional characters, *Everyday People* feels like a love letter to the people of East Liberty.

The plot centers on the building of an expressway that is going to cut off the neighborhoods of East Liberty from the rest of Pittsburgh and further the economic decline of the area. Chris "Crest" Tolbert is the paralyzed teenaged father who is at the center of this swirling novel. While he grapples with the death of his best friend, Bean, his love for his girlfriend, Vanessa, and their young son, Rashaan, his father, Harold, struggles with his own ghost, that of his ex-lover, a young gay man with whom he has recently

broken off. Jackie, Crest's mother, is overworked and overwhelmed, convinced that Harold is seeing some young woman from his work at the Nabisco plant (she's only partially right) and Crest's brother, U, has recently returned from prison a changed man. Now using his given name, Eugene, he has found Christ and wants to spread the Gospel. Crest spends his time holed up in his room, watching television and dreaming of a mural he could paint across the expressway, a painting to honor the dead of East Liberty, with Bean at its heart. Each chapter shifts the narrative point of view, from Crest to Vanessa to Harold, even to side characters such as Sister Marita Payne and Tony, the Italian ice cream truck vendor who has kept his route through East Liberty for years, despite his daughter's warnings. The theft of Tony's ice cream truck and subsequent death of the young man who was responsible—a young man whom Eugene felt morally bound to try to save—brings to a peak the emotions of the novel. It ends with the dedication of the expressway, both a blessing and a curse for these characters, and the final image of the book is of Crest's mural, now called simply "The Wall"—so reminiscent of the Vietnam War Memorial's wall, a focal point in *The Names of the Dead*.

O'Nan is fully aware of the cultural risks he is taking with the novel. When Vanessa attends her first college class, a course on African American history, and the professor turns out to be white, the students are alarmed. "'Excuse me,' one big guy right behind [Vanessa] said, 'Do you think this is appropriate?'" When the white female professor answers, "Actually, I don't" (p. 43), it's a surprise, but a compelling move. O'Nan is compelled to tell the story, but even he senses it's only temporary. The voice of black Pittsburgh is John Edgar Wideman's, but this novel seems a reaching out over the walls between the neighborhoods, a recognition that O'Nan is fully aware of the other Pittsburgh.

LATER WORKS: THE NEXT SIX NOVELS, 2002–2011

O'Nan's 2002 novel, *Wish You Were Here*, is again an ensemble work, this time focusing on the Maxwells: the recently widowed matriarch, Emily, and her two adult children and their children, as they spend a last week in their old summer place in Chautauqua, New York. It's one of O'Nan's longer books and is a deep character study of the entire family: Emily; her sister-in-law, Irene; Emily's son, Jeffrey; Jeffrey's wife, Lisa, and their two children; Emily's daughter, Margaret, and her two children; and even Margaret's ex-husband. As with *Everyday People*, everybody gets coverage, even the younger grandchildren who have troubles of their own. The chapters within the eight sections (the novel is laid out in the days of the week, from the arrival Saturday to the departure Saturday) switch close third-person position, with each character getting time.

The themes are issues O'Nan has surveyed before, but not in such a thoroughly Tolstoy-inspired way. This is family saga writ large, or as large as a weeklong vacation at a modest lakefront property can get. Emily is suffering survivor's guilt and more than a little grief over the death of her husband, Henry, and her decision to sell the summerhouse. The trip to the cabin inspires many moments of nostalgia in Emily, a nostalgia she is fully aware of and conflicted about. Jeffrey is a struggling photographer with a wife who barely tolerates his mother. Margaret is a divorced recovering alcoholic with money problems. The grandchildren are bored; the boys play too many video games (one is also acting out his angst with kleptomania) and the girls are dealing with sexuality: the older of the teen girls is suffering a long-distance breakup and the younger is tormented by her budding homosexuality and unrequited attraction to her cousin. As with *Everyday People,* this novel reads like a love letter: to a vacation spot O'Nan's own family knows well, to a generation of older Americans who are dying off every day, to a family—no Norman Rockwell painting, but one of real love and real struggle.

Two smaller but notable aspects of *Wish You Were Here* are the sister-in-law, Arlene—who comes back to play such an important role in the sequel novel, *Emily, Alone*—and a subplot involving a missing convenience store clerk that

sparks Jeffrey's curiosity. It is Arlene's sudden illness that is the catalyst for the later novel's action, and Arlene and Emily's relationship that serves the first novel so well. These women didn't choose each other—Arlene's friendship with Emily is simply a byproduct of her marriage to Arlene's brother, Henry—but now they are stuck with each other and know each other probably better than anyone else in their lives. It's a compelling relationship and not one of the more typical family dynamics—father-son/husband wife/child-parent—that O'Nan has confronted in earlier works. The missing-clerk plot of *Wish You Were Here* is a foreshadowing of O'Nan's much later novel, *Songs for the Missing*, which centers on the family dynamics after the teenage daughter is abducted from her job as a store clerk. It's as if O'Nan wrote the earlier novel and was then devoted to exploring that side note more fully in *Songs*. While readers of both novels will understand that it can't possibly be the same crime (the later novel is set in Ohio), it feels like a moment from William Faulkner or Honoré de Balzac: the world of O'Nan's novels, while not locally grounded in a single place like Yoknapatawpha County or Paris, feels connected. The family of the missing girl in New York will surely go through much the same struggle as the family of the missing girl in Ohio, a family we come to know very well, as well as we know the Maxwells in this earlier work. O'Nan circles in on himself in becoming ways. He's no broken record; it's more like a round, with one novel singing a refrain and the next novel picking it up in a different spot. It makes for a rich song across books.

The Night Country (2003) is a lyrical ghost story set in Avon, Connecticut (where O'Nan lived while teaching at nearby Trinity College). The action takes place at Halloween and the book is dedicated to Ray Bradbury, one of his earliest influences; more than the movie allusions of the section titles ("Dawn of the Dead," "Night of the Living"), more than the epigraph from Kurt Cobain ("I hate myself and want to die"), *The Night Country* has the autumnal lyricism of *Something Wicked This Way Comes*. O'Nan published a portion of the work as a stand-alone excerpt titled "Something Wicked" with a small art publisher,

Wormhole Books, and that section, the first chapter of the book, begins with a call to the reader:

> Come, do you hear it? The wind—murmuring in the eaves, scouring the bare trees. How it howls, almost musical, a harmony of old moans. The house seems to breathe, an invalid. Leave your scary movie marathon, this is better than TV. Leave the lights out. The blue glow follows you down the hall. Go to the window in the unused room, the cold seeping through the glass. The moon is risen, caught in nodding branches. The image holds you, black trunks backlit, one silver ray fallen across the deck, beckoning. It's a romance, this invitation to lunacy (lycanthropy, a dance with the vampire), elemental yet forbidden, tempting, something remembered in the blood.
>
> (p. 3)

Though it seems like the voice of *A Prayer for the Dying*—which could serve as a title to the novel as well—the narrator is not in second person, but first, the voice of a dead teenager named Marco who speaks for his group of ghosts, kids killed in a car accident the previous Halloween. Marco and his friends, Danielle and Toe, are condemned to haunt their small town on this day and must flit from spot to spot whenever someone thinks of them. Two teens survived the wreck, Tim—the guilt-ridden boyfriend of Danielle—and Kyle, who has lived, but with a price: his mental capacity has been reduced to that of a child and his once Goth, independent personality has vanished. Brooks is the police officer who was chasing the teens that fateful night, and he too feels responsible for the tragedy, so much so that it has ruined his marriage. Readers also get to know Kyle's parents—particularly his mother—who must now care for him and are torn between gratitude their son lived and despair over the rest of his life.

The fatal auto accident is, sadly, a staple of American high school life and O'Nan treats it with respect, at the same time reminding readers that this is ghost story. He gives us a litany of Halloween traditions: carving pumpkins, the name-brand candy, the stories we tell around campfires. But this too is a category crisis: a horror novel or a paean to teen life? A B movie with dead kids who can torment the local cop, or a

literary ode to parental grief over dead children? Rather than an either/or, O'Nan gives us the both/and novel; *The Night Country* is both a horror story and a reflection on teen life in small-town America.

Yet the real horror of the novel is not the ghosts—they're just kids—but the sorrow the parents and surviving friends feel, the wreaths we pass on the highway every time we drive the roads but don't really see unless it's our kids who died on that spot. In many ways, *The Night Country* feels like *The Names of the Dead* retold: the grief-burdened soldier transformed into a local cop suffering guilt over the death of a group of local teens, the vets at the VA transformed into teens at the high school. Here, too, are allusions to Charles Dickens' *A Christmas Carol*. These are the Ghosts of Halloweens Past, and their mission is not so dissimilar: remember us and change your ways. Even the finale of the novel—Tim's mission to kill himself and perhaps Kyle in a mimicry of the original accident—feels like the climax to the thriller plot in *The Names of the Dead*. Whether or not Tim is successful is arguable—is suicide ever a success?—but the urge to change is also complicated: the ghosts themselves are condemned to travel the night country like sailors on the *Flying Dutchman*, but it isn't all bad. The book ends with as much unpretentious lyricism as it began: "And it's all right, right here. We're happy in this present past, just driving, all of us in the car together like a tribe, a band of outlaws on the lam. There's no future, only now, this minute.... We're just a bunch of dumb kids having fun. We want the night to last forever" (p. 229).

The Good Wife (2005) features O'Nan's second solo female protagonist. This time the woman is not a criminal à la Marjorie Standiford. Here is his isolated female voice, more akin to Dorothy, the pregnant wife in *A World Away*, but also a precursor to Emily Maxwell's solo flight in *Emily, Alone*. And as with Dorothy and Emily, Patty Dickerson, the titular character, isn't given a direct first-person opportunity to speak. Told in a close third-person perspective, readers follow Patty as she deals with her husband's imprisonment for the murder of an old woman during a botched burglary. Unlike *The Night Country*, the novel carries no hint of genre categories, yet it is as terrifying as any "horror" novel. Nell Freudenberger, reviewing for the *New York Times*, identified a clear risk for O'Nan in his creation of Patty: "The writer who speaks in the voice of a character less powerful than himself risks either canonizing her or condescending to her. Patty is impressively good, as the novel's title suggests: when she learns how long Tommy's going to be in jail, she barely hesitates before promising to wait for him. And yet she never seems saccharine." Freudenberger also called it "one of the most authentic contemporary political novels ... by an American," and it is, in the way O'Nan quietly takes us through Patty's grappling with an uncaring justice system and the harrowing economic threats to single mothers. This is the domestic as the political, yet O'Nan never falls into tract writing. The trials of a single parent navigating the vagaries of the American prison system and a host of low-paying, low-esteem jobs is a frightening journey. The ghosts of Patty's youth haunt her as clearly as the literal teen ghosts from the earlier book, and the terrors are also institutional.

Last Night at the Lobster (2007) is a rarity—a low-key, literary novella that garnered impressive reviews and sold well. Manny DeLeon is the manager of a doomed Red Lobster in suburban Connecticut. The corporation has decided to shut down his location and has offered him a job at the Olive Garden. Manny has the opportunity to take some staff with him, while he has to let the rest go. O'Nan takes us through Manny's last day at a place he has tended for many years with people he has gotten to know, flaws and all. Manny himself is no saint; living with his pregnant girlfriend, he has been carrying on an affair with one of the waitresses and is torn between the responsibilities on the horizon and his heart's pull to the waitress. The novel begins midmorning as Manny and his crew ready for the lunch rush, and takes us to the moments Manny leaves the now-dark restaurant to its ignominious fate.

O'Nan writes this book with care and authenticity. No one who has ever worked in a

restaurant can help but notice the duties O'Nan describes and the research that went getting it right. Again, this is O'Nan's mode: make sure the facts are right so that authenticity of place or occupation never gets in the way of the higher aim of the fiction, which is too a sort of truth. The dedication of the novel reads, "for my brother John and everyone who works the shifts nobody wants." Yes, Manny is a dog at times, a man thinking with his hormones when he should be using his head, but he's also a solid leader, a decent boss. As with all of O'Nan's books, this novel becomes an ode, as the dedication clearly states. It is also notable for its economy; though O'Nan has published only one story collection, the tightness of his shorter books, such as *Last Night at the Lobster*, and in 2012, *The Odds*, show he is adept at nearly novella-length brevity as well as multilayered longer novels. His agility with the compressed form is further displayed in *A Face in the Crowd* (2012), his novella written with Stephen King.

Songs for the Missing (2008) is a return to the missing-girl scene of "Finding Amy" and *Snow Angels*. O'Nan, in interviews, has mentioned a moment in his youth when he was part of a search party, and clearly that activity haunts him. The Larsens are a middle-class, middle-American family whose daily lives are turned upside down when the elder daughter, a high school senior named Kim, goes missing, possibly abducted from her job at a local Conoco. The novel plays out the responses to her disappearance from the mother and father, the younger sister, the boyfriend, the best friends. Everyone is given a rich voice—except for Kim, who only appears in the novel in the first scenes. The book works on two levels. First, it is a suspense novel: the mystery of Kim's disappearance is investigated as a crime, and readers are left in the dark for most of the novel; it seems even deep into the novel that readers may never discover the facts around her vanishing. Second, it is a study in grief and its attendant, guilt.

In some ways, this is the archetype of O'Nan's novels, or the culmination of years of writing and ruminating on sorrow. *Songs for the Missing* contains thematic notes from every prior

O'Nan novel. If there is one book that represents all of O'Nan's concerns and many of his stylistic tics, this is it. Survivor guilt? Check. Parental clashes? Check. Teen life? Check. Community responsibility versus estrangement in a community? Check. Mundane jobs? Check. At times, O'Nan's fiction feels like a combination of a pair of Raymonds, Carver and Chandler, but that is too reductive. O'Nan is nothing if not the product of a lifetime of reading everything from pulp mysteries to highbrow literature, listening to everything from classical to punk, and his characters reflect that. His prose style is frequently spare but always lyrical, sometimes reaching the lyricism of poetry; he has said that *The Night Country* really wanted to be a poem, but even his longer works aim for that sort of attention to syllabic detail. O'Nan admits to writing with word-by-word care early in the process, an approach like that of a poet, and though he claims this is actually a mistake as far as technique goes, it works for his style.

O'Nan's next novel, *Emily, Alone* (2011), centers on the matriarch of the Maxwell family from *Wish You Were Here*, which makes the book his first sequel. Unlike, for example, his peer Dennis Lehane, O'Nan has never ventured into the realm of series books, so it is the first time he has revisited characters. It is eight years after the summer of *Wish You Were Here*, and Emily is now an experienced widow, though even more isolated since the death of her best friend the previous year. Now she must come to grips with the deterioration of her husband's only sibling, Arlene, her closest companion save for her equally aged dog, Rufus. This is the other side of Pittsburgh from *Everyday People*, and together they make of Pittsburgh what Dublin was to James Joyce—a locale-as-character as important to the progression of the novel as any human character. Emily Maxwell is a product of her rural Pennsylvania upbringing, a product of her long-married life in upper-class Pittsburgh, just as Sister Marita Payne, an old woman living alone with her beloved old dog in *Everyday People*, is a product of her side of the city. Marita and Emily are unlikely to meet, as close as their homes may be, but they share a common fate—isolation, both

physical and emotional. In the book club notes for *Emily, Alone* (O'Nan's works often come with book club questions and interviews—an indication of his mainstream audience), he states, "what I'd like readers to understand is that the worlds of *Everyday People* and *Emily, Alone* exist side by side, within blocks of each other, and that the world of *Snow Angels* exists maybe twenty minutes away." This is also an ode to widows, to the millions of women across the United States who live alone and face the days after the energy of professions and child rearing and marriage has quieted. In an interview with J. Robert Lennon at Cornell University for the Writers at Cornell series, O'Nan spoke of the women he wanted Emily to speak for in the novel and his belief that his work could be summed up in the word "endurance." Emily endures. This is her struggle. It feels like the struggle of so many O'Nan protagonists. Endurance, in the end, made both common and heroic.

Though it lacks the conceit of a traditional horror novel, *Emily, Alone* grapples with the mundane horror of aging: the mutiny of the body as it is bent with illness; the limits the old endure, which can become as horrific as enemy combatants. Ghosts appear as liberally in *Emily, Alone* as in *The Night Country*, but not as literally. The ghosts of her youth in Chautauqua, New York, played out so bittersweetly in *Wish You Were Here*, are echoed in the ghosts of Pittsburgh: the Pittsburgh of her courtship and young marriage, the Pittsburgh of her mothering her two children, Margaret and Kenneth, now the Pittsburgh of rust-belt economies and once-grand traditions. Pittsburgh, like Emily, is no longer at its peak, but the ghosts of its beauty remain, quiet and elegant, if a little angry and more than a little contrite. The other horror of old age, aside from the physical terror, is the isolation. Emily spends her days largely alone, filling up the hours with classical music and books and gardening. O'Nan loves to set his stories at holiday times, to underscore our need for traditions in a chaotic world, and here Emily is trying to gather her family for Thanksgiving, then Christmas. A recurrent concern of older women of a certain class in O'Nan's work is the choice of music for their

funerals: Larry Markham's mother, in *The Names of the Dead,* and Emily, here, both have firm desires for their funeral music. It seems like a slight motif, but it gets to a central character question: whether the end is marked by inferno and madness, as Jacob Hansen finds, or by the quiet demise in store for Emily. How we face the end is, for O'Nan, one of the most revealing notions of character.

MORE RECENT WORK: 2012 AND LATER

The Odds (2012) marks a return to the short form O'Nan used so successfully in *Last Night at the Lobster*. Art and Marion Fowler are a middle-aged couple with two adult children, two failed careers, and a beautiful home they can't sell. Unemployment and foreclosure are killing their finances and the marriage has sputtered along for decades, so they decide to take what savings they have and head to the casinos by the Niagara Falls and have a second honeymoon/predivorce/prebankruptcy vacation while they gamble what's left of their liquid assets on a roulette wheel in a last-ditch effort to confront their debts. The compact nature of the book hides its layers, the swift unpacking of Art and Marion's history of infidelities and the daily slights and small coldnesses of a soured marriage as we literally unpack their luggage and venture off through the tourist attractions, restaurants, and casinos. Like *Last Night at the Lobster*, the novel tracks in specific detail the events of a brief period. We follow the Fowlers for just a weekend, and not even the full extent of their trip from Cleveland to Canada, yet readers feel fully acquainted with Art and Marion by the time we reach the climactic scene of risk in the last chapter.

The novel is laid out in twenty-six short chapters, some only a page long, others as long as a dozen pages, each titled with the odds of a certain event: "Odds of a married couple reaching their 25th anniversary: 1 in 6," "Odds of getting sick on vacation: 1 in 9," "Odds of a U.S. citizen filing for bankruptcy: 1 in 17," and, the last, "Odds of a divorced couple remarrying: 1 in 20,480." The narration is a close third-person perspective on both Marion and Art; we are privy,

sometimes in the space of few paragraphs, to the inner desires of both. Marion sees the trip as a last hurrah, a way to lead into an amicable divorce and the freedom of a single life that is both enticing and terrifying. She has played the victim for so long in the marriage—the wronged spouse, still angry over Art's long-ago affair with a woman named Wendy Daigle, but also carrying the secret of her more recent affair with her colleague, Karen—Marion is exhausted and ready to let go. Her tone with Art flips between snappish and intimate, and she has promised herself not to give Art any hope of a reconciliation, despite the romantic nature of the trip. Art, however, is still in love with Marion. Conciliatory, agreeable to a fault, he has bought an expensive second wedding ring and plans to surprise her with a proposal—he will always love her despite what may come after this trip.

O'Nan is typically generous to these flawed characters. Marion can seem brittle, Art immature, yet, as we follow their sightseeing—to the falls (in a scene that directly echoes a trip to the same spot in *Wish You Were Here*), to the Ripley's Believe It or Not Museum, to a Heart concert ("Odds of Heart playing 'Crazy on You' in concert: 1 in 1"), through food poisoning, miserable long lines of tourists, too much alcohol, and ultimately, a careful, if grueling and potentially devastating, scheme to double their money by betting all their chips on the final night of their journey—we can't help hoping that somehow things will work out for them. And indeed, O'Nan ends the book hopefully—a victory in Niagara suggests that the Fowlers' marriage may overcome the odds that their amalgam of disasters seems destined to destroy. For all the casual spitefulness and tawdry commercialism of the weekend, O'Nan lets readers go with the idea that the Fowlers have "won."

A Face in the Crowd (2012), his second joint work with Stephen King (the first being a book about their beloved Red Sox), was published solely as an e-book or audio book. A horror novella, it is based on a story idea King pitched during a speech at a writer's conference, telling the audience that the core of the story—a man who sees a dead friend in the stands of a televised baseball game—was theirs for the taking. O'Nan was in the audience and shortly afterward the two collaborated on the project. With its swift pace, its close third-person narration, and its preoccupation with grief and regret at its heart, it is the perfect love child of the two authors. Its high concept is horrifying. The narrator sees long-dead friends and family in the crowd and then is led to the stadium as it fills with all of the people he has wronged in the course of his life. He then learns that he too is dead, his body back in his condo, after an accidental overdose of tranquilizers and Scotch. Once again O'Nan prods readers to remember Scrooge in Dickens' *Christmas Carol*, here with a widower retiree haunted by the apparitions of his past: a child he helped torment in his own youth; his late business partner (a man he blackmailed with sexual secrets during a tense moment in their partnership); and his recently dead wife, a woman who knew of his affair with his longtime secretary. While the story hangs on a grand scene, that stadium filled with the dead, it is the more mundane moments, the easy ethical lapses in the business world and the casual unfaithfulness in marriage, that are truly terrifying.

NONFICTION: FROM BIG TOP TO BIG LEAGUE

O'Nan has written a pair of book-length nonfiction works and edited two anthologies, even though he has declared that "I try my best not to write nonfiction. I try my best to avoid it," (Longino, p. 79).

The first work of nonfiction O'Nan edited was an anthology of essays by John Gardner, the famed author and teacher of creative writing and literature. Titled *On Writers and Writing* and published in 1994, the volume includes an introduction by the National Book Award–winning novelist and professor Charles Johnson. The Gardner essays were culled from a variety of sources, mostly the *New York Times Book Review* but also journals such as the *Southern Review* and *Antaeus* and Gardner's own *MSS*. The topics range from Italo Calvino and John Cheever to Joyce Carol Oates and Philip Roth. It's an expansive collection, true to Gardner's ambitious

work, and though O'Nan includes no editor's note, it's clear how much labor went into the project.

His second editorial project was *The Vietnam Reader: The Definitive Collection of Fiction and Nonfiction on the War* (1998), which grew out of his research for *The Names of the Dead* and from a course on the literature that O'Nan was teaching at Trinity College. As impossible as the task seems, O'Nan does an impressive job of narrowing down the material to a hefty eight hundred pages. The anthology includes works by Philip Caputo, Bobbie Ann Mason, Tim O'Brien, David Rabe, and many others. He includes selections of fiction, screenplays, memoir, and poetry. The back matter includes a bibliography and filmography. It is structured for classroom use, but the general reader wouldn't find it too scholarly, and the richness of the material, while daunting, reveals our continuing engagement with and varied creative impulses toward the controversial era. According to *Publishers Weekly*, O'Nan used $45,000 of his own money to secure permissions, so it is clearly a labor of love, a tribute to the artists chosen and, ultimately, the men and women affected by the war.

His next nonfiction project was a research-based book on the Ringling Circus fire in Hartford, Connecticut, in 1944. *The Circus Fire* (2000) charts the causes and aftermath of a big-top fire that killed 167 people and injured hundreds more. O'Nan interviewed dozens of survivors to get the full picture and uses the book to paint the events as clearly as scenes in his novels. The book also covers similar thematic ground. It has an ensemble cast—circus people, spectators, cops, and reporters—and is filled with stories of people behaving bravely and people behaving cowardly in the terrifying moments of the fire. The canvas used for big tops in that era was rainproofed with paraffin and gasoline, and it didn't take much for the fire to spread quickly across the top of the entire tent. Amid burning embers and collapsing poles, people pushed in a panic to escape the blaze. Some folks in the low bleacher seats were crushed in the stampede, others held back and assisted the elderly and young, despite the danger. The history is told chronologi-

cally, with the first half of the book leading up to the tragedy on July 6 as a moment-by-moment suspense tale; the second half of the book covers the reporting and subsequent trials resulting from the negligence. O'Nan also covers the would-be suspects and, most poignantly, the unclaimed body of a little girl, Little Miss 1565, whose identity was long shrouded and whose family remained a mystery. The book closes with her identity still unclear. "I did the circus book because I thought there was really interesting subject matter and no one had done it. It was a book I wanted to read," he explains plainly (Longino, p. 79), and though O'Nan claims not to have succeeded, it's a chilling and bittersweet story that fits well into his canon.

His second book of nonfiction was written in conjunction with Stephen King. *Faithful: Two Diehard Boston Red Sox Fans Chronicle the Historic 2004 Season* (2004) is what O'Nan has called an "occasional" book, in the sense that it was written to document a moment and how the moment changed in a dramatic way. King and O'Nan went into the project with a question: why do Red Sox fans stay faithful despite the history of the team collapsing in the postseason and never winning the championship? Unexpectedly, the 2004 season turned out to be the year the Red Sox won the World Series, and, as O'Nan says, "that Red Sox fan [accustomed to loss] is no longer in existence" (p. 80). Told in a friendly exchange between King and O'Nan, the book is an ode to those resilient fans who remain fans despite the odds. Considering works such as *The Good Wife* and *Last Night at the Lobster*, novels focused on questions of loyalty in the face of dire circumstances, *Faithful* makes sense despite its genre and form. Regardless of surface differences in his works, O'Nan's thematic concerns remain the same.

SCREENPLAYS: HOLLYWOOD AND ITHACA

Surprisingly, only one of O'Nan's novels has been adapted for cinema: *Snow Angels*, in 2007, with a screenplay written by the director David Gordon Green and starring Kate Beckinsale and Sam Rockwell. It's a faithful depiction of the novel and did well critically, though the box of-

fice was only fair. In the Picador paperback's author interview, O'Nan states, "I read an early screenplay by David Gordon Green, but had no contact with him or anyone in the production thereafter. While it may share some dramatic elements, the movie has to stand on its own as a separate work of art operating by its own internal logic. I'm grateful, though, that the film may win Arthur and Annie some new readers" (p. 319).

O'Nan has published one screenplay, *Poe*, published by Lonely Books in 2008. He had written it years earlier, right after he finished *The Speed Queen*—he admits to writing screenplays frequently after he finishes a novel, to clear his mind—and though it remains unproduced, it's a notable achievement partially for the art book production of it (the screenplay was published in a limited run of 200 numbered copies) but also because of its foreword by Roger Corman, the famed horror director, and because the gothic nature fits with O'Nan's other works. *Poe* is a biopic of the life of Edgar Allan Poe, father of the modern mystery and favorite of horror readers and writers since the mid-1800s.

There are other unproduced screenplays mentioned in the collection of O'Nan papers housed at Cornell University, including "Ghost Ship" (a project that predates *Wish You Were Here* and ultimately has nothing to do with the final outcome of that novel); another biographical portrait, this time of Clara Schumann; and three adaptations of other notable authors' works: John Edgar Wideman's *The Lynchers,* Denis Johnson's *Ghosts,* and Tim O'Brien's *Going After Cacciato.* He admits to writing them for fun, without the intent of selling them, though it wouldn't be surprising to see O'Nan write more screenplays, including ones that are eventually on the big screen.

CONCLUSION

In 1999 O'Nan wrote an essay for the *Boston Review* that served as a call to reignite interest in the career of the novelist and short story writer Richard Yates. At the time, nearly a decade prior to the acclaimed film version of *Revolutionary Road*, Yates was an undersung American novel-

ist, largely out of print, beloved only by other writers. Perhaps O'Nan spoke subconsciously about his own fears of someday becoming a "writer's writer," the well-respected but obscure artist who, like Yates, developed a narrative style far more accessible than most "writer's writers." O'Nan's fourteen novels over the course of twenty years have had good sales, and some even have grown into cult favorites, yet he has had no blockbuster success; perhaps this fear still confounds him. Unlike his friend and sometime collaborator King, he isn't a household name. It's not difficult to replace Yates with O'Nan in O'Nan's assessment of Yates:

> The surface of his prose is so clear, in fact, and the people and events he writes about so average and identifiable, so much like the world we know, that it seems his books would merit a larger general audience than those of his more difficult literary peers. But that has not been the case.

As with Yates's interest in the "mundane sadness of domestic life," at the core of O'Nan's work is a preoccupation with grief and its handmaiden, guilt. The parental grief over a dead child—the most recurrent emotional preoccupation in his work—is accompanied by a spectrum of other griefs in his books: the sour marriage, the dead-end job, the betrayed spouse, the bloody choices of war, the remorse of the elderly. Yet the fear of ending up a well-respected but largely unread writer is one that needn't haunt Stewart O'Nan. If his last twenty years are any indication of the next twenty years, this is an author whose batting average will remain stellar. O'Nan suffers no curse, like his beloved Boston Red Sox, and if the Red Sox can win the World Series three times in a decade, O'Nan seems bound for year after year of exemplary novels.

Selected Bibliography

WORKS OF STEWART O'NAN

NOVELS

Snow Angels. New York: Doubleday, 1994.
The Names of the Dead. New York: Doubleday, 1996.
The Speed Queen. New York: Doubleday, 1997.

A World Away. New York: Henry Holt, 1998.

A Prayer for the Dying. New York: Henry Holt, 1999.

A Good Day to Die. (As James Coltrane.) New York: Norton, 1999.

Everyday People. New York: Grove Press, 2001.

Wish You Were Here. New York: Grove Press, 2002.

The Night Country. New York: Farrar, Straus and Giroux, 2003.

The Good Wife. New York: Farrar, Straus and Giroux, 2005.

Last Night at the Lobster. New York: Viking, 2007.

Songs for the Missing. New York: Viking, 2008.

Emily, Alone. New York: Viking, 2011.

The Odds. New York: Viking, 2012.

SHORT FICTION

In the Walled City. Pittsburgh, Pa.: University of Pittsburgh Press, 1993. New York: Grove Press, 2001. (Short-story collection.)

A Face in the Crowd. Simon & Schuster Digital, 2012. (Novella, with Stephen King.)

UNCOLLECTED STORIES

"Please Help Find." *Ploughshares* 25, nos. 2–3:142–149 (fall 1999).

"Good Morning, Heartache." *Glimmer Train* 33 (winter 2000).

"The Reward." In *Boston Noir.* Edited by Dennis Lehane. New York: Akashic Books, 2009. Pp. 137–146.

"Land of the Lost." In *Stories: All-New Tales.* Edited by Neil Gaiman and Al Sarrantonio. New York: William Morrow, 2010. Pp. 216–220.

"Monsters: A Halloween Story." Cemetery Dance Publications e-book, 2012.

NONFICTION

"The Lost World of Richard Yates." *Boston Review,* October 1, 1999. http://bostonreview.net/stewart-onan-the-lost-world-of-richard-yates

The Circus Fire. New York: Doubleday, 2000.

Faithful: Two Diehard Boston Red Sox Fans Chronicle the Historic 2004 Season. With Stephen King. New York: Scribner, 2004.

OTHER

Poe. Baltimore, Md.: Lonely Road Books, 2008. (Screenplay.)

Stewart O'Nan website. http://stewart-onan.com/

AS EDITOR

On Writers and Writing, by John Gardner. Reading, Mass.: Addison-Wesley, 1994.

The Vietnam Reader: The Definitive Collection of Fiction and Nonfiction on the War. New York: Anchor Books, 1998.

PAPERS

The Stewart O'Nan Papers, 1987–2009. Division of Rare and Manuscript Collections, Cornell University Library, Ithaca, New York.

REVIEWS

Corrigan, Maureen. "The Joy of the Mundance in *Emily, Alone.*" NPR, March 22, 2011. http://www.npr.org/2011/06/23/137084790/nancy-pearl-presents-10-terrific-summer-reads

Freudenberger, Nell. "*The Good Wife*': Spouse Arrest." *New York Times,* May 8, 2005. http://www.nytimes.com/2005/05/08/books/review/08FREUDEN.html?pagewanted=print

McAlpin, Heller. "The Odds Stacked Against a Struggling Couple." NPR, January 19, 2012. http://www.npr.org/2012/01/19/145345253/the-odds-stacked-against-a-struggling-couple

Publishers Weekly. "*A Good Day to Die.*" May 3, 1999. http://www.publishersweekly.com/978-0-393-04766-0

INTERVIEWS

Bryant, Edward. "Wormhold Books Holds a Conversation with the Highly Conversational Stewart O'Nan." In *Something Wicked,* by O'Nan. (Chapbook.) Fort Wayne, Ind., and Denver: Wormhole Books, 2003.

"A Conversation with Stewart O'Nan." *Reading Guide to "Emily, Alone."* Penguin.com. http://www.us.penguingroup.com/static/rguides/us/emily_alone.html

Gross, Terry. "What It's Like to Be an Elderly Widow, All 'Alone.'" NPR, April 18, 2011. http://www.npr.org/2011/05/05/135514997/what-its-like-to-be-an-elderly-widow-all-alone

"An Interview with Stewart O'Nan." In *Snow Angels.* New York: Picador, 2008.

Lennon, J. Robert. "Interview: Stewart O'Nan." Writers at Cornell, interview podcast, February 17, 2011. http://writersatcornell.blogspot.com/2011/02/interview-stewart-onan.html

Longino, Billy. "Exhuming America: An Interview with Stewart O'Nan." *REAL: Regarding Arts & Letters* 36, no. 2 (fall–winter 2012). http://regardingartsandletters.wordpress.com/2013/04/16/onan/

McLaughlin, Mark. "Interview with Stewart O'Nan." ChiZine.com, 2010. http://www.chizine.com/stewart_onan_interview.htm

FILM BASED ON THE WORK OF STEWART O'NAN

Snow Angels. Screenplay and direction by David Gordon Green. Warner Independent Pictures, 2006.

SUSAN ORLEAN

(1955—)

Kristin Winet

SUSAN ORLEAN IS not a writer of the fantastic, the phenomenal, the unusual, or the out-of-the-ordinary. She is a writer fascinated by the world as it is: watching a donkey meander down the road in Morocco, talking to a ten-year-old boy who has nothing too extraordinary to say, riding around in a New York taxi with an unexpected driver, wandering through swamps in Florida looking for flowers, imagining what a dog could say if he could dictate his favorite mouth-watering recipes to his owner. With sharp humor, a careful rendering of detail, and the rare ability to see the unusual in the everyday, Orlean has become a central figure not just in contemporary journalism circles but also in the literary nonfiction world. Straddling the line between reportage and literature, a line that she declares is nothing more than an arbitrary border, Orlean's work (while her topics might suggest otherwise) is anything but ordinary—she is a storyteller whose journalism has brought to light the magnificent search for meaning in the lives of the people we pass by every day, often without notice.

Orlean's wry sense of humor and colloquial yet sophisticated style resonate with the publications that have made her famous: *GQ, Esquire,* the *Boston Globe*, and, of course, the *New Yorker*, where her name has become synonymous with literary reportage and where she makes a living as a full-time staff writer. With side projects that include writing a cookbook with the sage advice of her canine companion Cooper, coauthoring a children's book, and curating the winning essays for popular anthologies such as *The Best American Travel Writing 2007,* Orlean is an excellent example of a writer whose success lies in equal parts literary dexterity, a superb ability to multi-task, and a prolific desire to tell stories. She is strong-willed, fearless, and has no qualms whatsoever about asking strangers to allow her to follow them through their daily lives. At the same time, she is the kind of reporter who doesn't get frustrated when people say no, when a story doesn't turn out as she imagined it would, or when the research doesn't necessarily cooperate with the time line she is working with. A dedicated journalist who never wanted to be a journalist, Orlean is a prime example of a writer who believes that true storytelling should be completely informed by the facts. As she says, if a nonfiction writer is going to write a story and has to embellish the setting, the dialogue, or the plot, she believes that person hasn't thought enough about her or his story. The world, she says, is brimming with people with stories worth telling.

Though she is well known within journalism and literature circles, her contributions to American letters have received little scholarly attention, perhaps because she writes in a genre little explored by literary critics. However, as a writer who has made (and continues to make) such an indelible impact on literary journalism—and creative nonfiction in general—Orlean deserves her place among the best contemporary American authors. In attempting to remedy this fissure, then, this essay offers insight into Orlean's life and works through a retelling of her biography and a short synopsis and analysis of each of her major works. It also considers the ways in which contemporary critics might reimagine the slippery world of literary journalism, a form that resists definition in its unusual approach to reporting the complexities of the contemporary world—and of the distinct individuals who make up that world.

BIOGRAPHY

Susan Orlean, born on October 31, 1955, in Cleveland, Ohio, lived the kind of childhood she

decided was unextraordinary at the time but which later convinced her that the best stories lie in finding the humor and the exceptional in what most people perceive to be ordinary. In a section on her personal website, for instance, she introduces herself by saying that she is "the product of a happy and relatively uneventful childhood in Cleveland, Ohio," which was shortly followed by "a happy and relatively squandered college career at the University of Michigan in Ann Arbor." While her tone is certainly meant to be humorous and mildly self-deprecating, it reveals her personal connection to stories of people and cultures that tend to go unnoticed—stories that are both beautifully and archetypically, as she has put it, "heroic and plain." Orlean has recounted the joy she found in reading *Life* magazine's "slice of life" stories during her childhood reading days, features that unveiled what it was like to be a policeman, a bartender, or a doctor. In an interview with Robert S. Boynton, Orlean revealed that "there was this notion in *Life* that subjects like these were genuine 'stories.' The idea of writing about something real was enormously appealing to me" (p. 271). This is not entirely surprising, as Orlean's own upbringing—in the suburbs, the child of a father who was a real estate developer and a mother who worked in a bank—keenly reflects the kind of American life and lifestyle she would commit herself to as a writer and a journalist. However, though she was a regular librarygoer (at least a couple times a week, she recalls) and read voraciously (splitting her reading time among the local newspaper, youth fiction, and *Life* magazine), it wasn't until she discovered the genre of literary journalism in college that she knew exactly the kind of writer she aspired to be and which publication she desperately wanted to write for.

At the University of Michigan, Orlean studied literature and history, writing poetry in her spare time and wondering what life would be like as an artist. Though she recalls being inspired by her many poetry classes and remembers them fondly, she never considered being a poet professionally; she also knew she didn't want to be a newspaper reporter. Though she once signed up for a journalism class, initially believing it would speak to her inclination for telling true stories, she quickly realized that it wasn't what she was looking for and did not complete the class. In her leisure time, she turned to what she calls "great fiction" and also discovered some of the quintessential literary journalism prototypes of the 1960s like Truman Capote's *In Cold Blood* and Tom Wolfe's *Electric Kool-Aid Acid Test* (texts, she remembers, that completely blew her mind). As she read these books, she knew that what she wanted was to be "the first person to learn about something," to devour archives, conduct interviews, spend time getting to know her subjects, and share those stories through the literary devices she had learned about and come to love (personal interview). At a friend's suggestion, she subscribed to the *New Yorker*, immediately fell in love with the style of the publication, and realized that she could combine her poetic voice with her love for reportage within the genre that she was coming to know as literary journalism, a kind of creative nonfiction that wasn't limited to a particular genre. Because she wasn't able to study this form in school, she focused on finding her inspiration from the writers themselves, studying their craft and thinking about which stories she might like to tell. Asked what advice she gives to young writers who desire to follow in her footsteps, she says that she always tells them the same thing: read great writing, learn about topics that seem curious, and never, ever stop studying the world.

After her self-proclaimed "relatively squandered college career," she followed her sister and then-boyfriend to Portland, Oregon, to pursue the bohemian life of the artist she had yearned for so deeply. Her first writing job—writing music reviews and feature pieces for the now-defunct alternative newsweekly magazine *Paper Rose*—was both painful and exhilarating. While it paid her less than she made as a waitress in college, she was surrounded by young, exuberant writers who, like her, had no formal training in journalism but wanted to become journalists and were excited about learning the ropes of the profession. In an interview with *The Days of Yore*, a website that features interviews with writers on their lives

before fame, she says that she shared an apartment with her boyfriend and sister and primarily subsisted on Kraft Macaroni & Cheese, with household items and clothing scavenged from the Goodwill store. With a certain sense of pride, nostalgia, and incredulity, she even remembers her first coffee table, a discarded telephone wire spool, and the moment she saw her bank account at zero for the first time in her life. However, in what would seem to many to be a dire situation, Orlean never failed to enjoy her budget-friendly artist's life, exploring Portland on the weekends, roaming around the unique neighborhoods, camping in the wilderness, and hanging out at bowling alleys and pie shops. These first few years, while financially impractical, did not dampen or exhaust her passion for writing; instead, her simultaneously tenuous and whimsical situation—and her dedication to keep up with her craft—proved to her that she wanted nothing in the world but to become a writer. She just didn't quite know how to do it and actually make the rent.

After freelancing for four years in Portland and building up her repertoire of clips, Orlean moved to Boston with her then-husband, a law school student, to take a job writing for the *Boston Phoenix* and *Boston Globe*. In her characteristically frank way, Orlean remembers feeling like she was "sort of done with living in Portland" by that time and felt she had run the course of what she could do there personally and artistically. As she says, making the move was not actually that difficult for her: "It was a very simple thing. No big mystery. I got in touch with the *Boston Phoenix* and told them I was moving to Boston and would they meet with me and take a look at my clips. And that is the whole story.... it's not really a story where there are a lot of twists and turns" (personal interview). Her first collection of essays, *Red Sox and Bluefish: And Other Things That Make New England New England* (1987), is composed primarily of essays and features she wrote during her tenure at the *Globe*. Around this same time, she also started working on *Saturday Night* (published in 1990), a book focused entirely on exploring the ways in which people across the United States spend their Saturday nights. Then, in 1986, four years after

moving to Boston, Orlean finally made the writer's pilgrimage to New York City, where she began writing for *Rolling Stone* and *Vogue*. Soon after she moved there, she learned that the *New Yorker* was interviewing writers to contribute to their "Talk of the Town" series, and, having long idealized the publication as the ultimate triumph in the journalism world, she applied.

After declining an offer from *Esquire* to write a profile on the child star Macauley Culkin in the early 1990s, Orlean decided to pitch an alternative idea to her editor: she would do the piece on a ten-year-old American boy if she could personally choose that American boy. Her editor agreed, and she wrote her first profile on Colin Duffy, a ten-year-old boy from the New Jersey suburbs who was afraid of girls and loved Nintendo. Soon after the success of this piece, she published her first *New Yorker* feature, a profile of Nana Kwabena Oppong, the Ashanti king who moonlighted as a New York City cabdriver. What differed most between Duffy and Oppong, of course, was the unusual circumstances of Oppong's double life. As Orlean writes, here is a man with a humdrum life as cabdriver busing people around, a father who prods his kids to do their homework, a man who seems always to be looking for a new apartment. And at the same time, here is a man who faces royal predicaments on a daily basis: Who would officiate the next Ashanti ceremony? How should his tribe return its deceased to the motherland in Ghana to be properly buried? As she states in the introduction to her 2001 collection of essays, *The Bullfighter Checks Her Makeup: My Encounters with Extraordinary People*, after spending months working on the Ashanti story, Orlean realized why she felt so drawn to ordinary people: "An ordinary life examined closely reveals itself to be exquisite and complicated and exceptional, somehow managing to be both heroic and plain" (p. xii). This statement would become the mantra for her career.

Once Orlean had written features for the *New Yorker* on a freelance basis for a few years and defined her niche, she became a regular contributor and then full-time staff writer in 1992. In 1994 she read a newspaper article about a man

named John Laroche who stole two hundred extremely rare orchids from a state park in Florida. The article she wrote about him, "Orchid Fever," turned into her first full-length study, *The Orchid Thief: A True Story of Beauty and Obsession*, which was published in 1998 and then translated into the film *Adaptation* (2002). In addition to her work at the *New Yorker*, writing features and keeping a blog, she has continued to produce books (*My Kind of Place: Travel Stories from a Woman Who's Been Everywhere* was published in 2004 and *Rin Tin Tin: The Life and the Legend* in 2011). Orlean lives with her husband, David Gillespie; her son, Austin; and their Welsh springer spaniel, Cooper, in Columbia County, New York, enjoying the life of the writer she always knew she could have if she only gave herself the time to get there.

ON CRAFT AND WRITING

Orlean's beliefs about writing nonfiction both dovetail with and depart from conventional wisdom about the role of journalism: in her opinion, the writer should tell a good story and stick to the facts. To her, the literary journalist should approach her subject in much the same way as a student learning a new subject, spending time with the subject in as unbiased a way as possible in order to learn what the crux of the story might actually be and refraining from putting pen to paper until the writer is ready to teach that subject to someone else. Not all creative writers work this methodically, but it is the process that works for her, even though waiting to put words on the page can be difficult for her simply because it often takes so long: she comes up with an idea, begins to research it, lets the research change and alter the course of the story, and only then starts to write. In some cases the process can take many years, as it did with her 2011 book, *Rin Tin Tin,* which took her nearly a decade to complete.

Because of this self-imposed meticulousness in her writing process, Orlean is disappointed with recent debates concerning creative liberties in telling a good nonfiction story. To her, there is no blurred line between facts and embellishments

of any kind: As she claims, "there are no creative liberties [in literary journalism] and I object strenuously to the idea that anyone perceives it that way. Nonfiction is nonfiction.... there is absolutely no gray area" (personal interview). Though some nonfiction writers believe that embellishment can actually aid in the stitching together of a story (conflating time, reconstructing dialogue from memory, altering the setting), Orlean believes this is nothing short of lying. If she does not know something or must speculate, she is always careful to tell her readers that she is wondering about something, not stating it as verifiable fact. This is the only way to properly and effectively deal with the fallibility of memory, she says. A work of nonfiction should be nothing short of a factual representation of what actually happened.

She believes the major themes in her work center around questions of life, community, family bonds, and mastering a particular universe. She is curious about people who are like her as well as those who are unlike her, and has always been drawn to the idea of helping them share their stories with broader audiences. How, for instance, do people form communities, whether those communities are based on bloodlines, shared hobbies, communal interests, or serendipity? Why do people form the bonds they do? And how do these bonds translate into communities? These questions have preoccupied her since her childhood, when she began reading the newspaper and *Life* magazine, and they are the questions that have propelled her into the world of literary journalism in often unexpected ways. As Orlean admits, she thinks of much of her work as being a kind of "human tourism":

> I think the theme of mastering a universe, whether it's a universe of something very small or very large, interests me a lot. I think the extraordinariness that exists within something that appears ordinary is maybe the best way of putting it. I like the idea that you can look into a very simple world and find in it all the complexity and drama and emotion that you would not expect, whether it's a neighborhood supermarket or a ten-year-old boy or you name it.... I'm just interested in people and I'm curious about what they do and what makes them tick and why they do what they do.
>
> (personal interview)

SATURDAY NIGHT

Orlean's essay collection *Saturday Night* (1990), marked her entrance into the literary market because of its simple elegance and its intriguing premise: how do people in the United States spend their Saturday nights, and why do they spend them that way? Throughout the book's fifteen chapters, Orlean attempts to discover the reasons why people across the country spend their leisure time in different ways and how these differences reflect personal, regional, and national identity.

In the introduction, Orlean admits that she toyed with the idea of exploring this topic for about a year before actually devoting herself to researching and composing this unusual study. The real impetus, she says, came from two independent sources that surfaced at around the same time: an article from the *Chicago Tribune* wire service indicating that free time had shrunk by nearly 32 percent since the 1970s; and a statistic from a national survey revealing that 54 percent of those in the survey ranked sex and free time below gardening and visiting relatives as regular activities. While she did not at first make the connection between the two pieces of data, she decided to cut out the articles and taped the clippings over her desk as visual reminders that in a country with less and less free time, quality over quantity is what matters—and Saturday night, Orlean speculated, was where that quality was still happening.

Interestingly, while the text reveals much about the demographic differences between populations across the United States, its inadvertent emphasis on the AIDS crisis places *Saturday Night* in an important anthropological context. While Orlean certainly does not consider herself an anthropologist of any kind, the book, which moves from Phoenix, Arizona, to Miami Beach, Florida, offers compelling insight into a world in the aftermath of an epidemic and a general fear of promiscuity and sexual freedom. The chapters, each highlighting a specific verb that people "do" in that place on Saturday nights, cover everyone from young Mayor Perron in rural Indiana, who is bent on outlawing car cruising in one of the most popular Saturday night cruising strips in the

country, to freshman girls at Wellesley College, who take a chaperoned bus into Harvard Square every Saturday night to drink beer, go to parties, and generally fraternize with the local boys. Another chapter is devoted to Frank Peacock, a reverend from a "poor church in a scruffy South Phoenix neighborhood" (p. 40) who does the majority of the city's *quinceañeras,* a tradition brought from Mexico in which a fifteen-year-old Latina girl celebrates her transition into womanhood by wearing a white dress and throwing a party not unlike a wedding.

Underneath these stories, which on the surface seem like simple retellings of others' lives, there is a distinct echo of concern over sexuality and Saturdays, themes that Orlean unexpectedly realized as she worked on weaving the stories together. As she says in one chapter, "According to the latest wisdom about contemporary behavior … fear of AIDS has tempered intemperate social appetites and post-sexual-revolution habits have run their course, replaced by the ceremony, custom, and restraint that characterized social life of the past. In such an atmosphere, Saturday night naturally emerges as the signal event" (p. 24). By weaving her research on sexuality and sexual habits into the stories she tells, she moves her work from being mere storytelling to a frank and literary journalistic account of life in the United States in the aftermath of a devastating sexual disease. Moving through the stories of the people she has highlighted, it becomes clear that the Saturday night she was so focused on exploring is really no more than a microcosm of the ceremonial routines and rituals that we have traditionally participated in to make sense of our lives and our communities.

THE ORCHID THIEF: A TRUE STORY OF BEAUTY AND OBSESSION

The Orchid Thief (1998), Orlean's first book-length character study, chronicles the life of John Laroche, a man she became interested in while writing a feature piece on him for the *New Yorker.* As she says in an interview with Tim McHenry published as an appendix to the 2000 paperback

printing of *The Orchid Thief*, she felt that writing the feature was much like "peeling an onion" because "every aspect of the story seemed richer than [she] imagined" (p. 287). As she began researching Laroche's life and the underworld of flower selling, she realized that she "loved the idea of taking a single event, something very specific and examining it thoroughly and deeply, rather than a big, sprawling event," and turning that very specific event into a book (p. 287). As in much of her literary journalism, Orlean uses Laroche's story to explore a subculture little studied in American letters. From Florida's humid swamplands to the Seminole Indian tribes' homes to city courtrooms, *The Orchid Thief* tells the story of a man possessed of both a passionate love for nature and a dogged determination to find a rare and highly endangered ghost orchid in order to harvest it, clone it, and "get rich quick" off of the plant's offspring (p. 289).

Throughout the text, Orlean's close relationship with place and its people is apparent, illustrating her signature way of using her setting to reveal the nature of the people she is investigating. The eerie beauty of the book grows out of her initial description of the dichotomy that is Florida:

> It is a collision of things you would never expect to find together in one place—condominiums and panthers and raw woods and hypermarkets and Monkey Jungles and strip malls and superhighways and groves of carnivorous plants and theme parks and royal palms and hibiscus trees and those hot swamps with acres and acres that no has ever even seen—all toasting together under the same sunny vault of Florida sky.
>
> (p. 11)

By characterizing the setting in this way—as an inconsistent but beautiful place "swamped by incongruity and paradox" (p. 11)—Orlean has indirectly introduced Laroche before actually introducing him at all. By the time readers eventually learn about Laroche, a man who is just as dichotomous as the place in which he lives, Florida has already spoken on his behalf and set up his character in a way that reflects Orlean's ability to weave together people and place in delicate and profound ways.

Like many of her other works, *The Orchid Thief* speaks to much more than just one man or the underworld of illegal flower selling; instead, it illuminates the power of passion and determination and explores how the disenfranchised (in this case, Laroche and the Seminole Indian tribes) work against the grain in ways that the U.S. justice system doesn't tolerate. When we first meet Laroche, we learn that he and a number of Seminole Indian assistants have been caught exiting the Fakahatchee Strand State Preserve with four pillowcases stuffed with 200 of the rare orchids. In his defense, he claims that he planned to clone them by the millions and make them available to flower collectors around the world, democratizing the flower and its ghostly beauty. Orlean travels to Florida to spend time with Laroche as he awaits trial and to learn about his illegal pursuits from his perspective, hoping to find out exactly what kind of person could become so passionate about collecting something and sharing it with the world that he was willing to go to jail over it. However, as often happens in her work, Orlean discovers that the person she thought she was going to profile is a lot more complicated than she had expected. What she finds—and what makes the story such a realistic and heartbreaking one—is that Laroche is not the underground hero she had hoped for; instead, he slowly emerges as a man whose passions are short-lived and full of whimsy. As she learns, Laroche's earlier fascinations (including his ex-wife) have all been intensely passionate and short-term: from ice-age fossils to live snapping turtles to antique mirrors, he loves and leaves, often abandoning one passion for another without so much as a backward glance. After he is minimally convicted for his orchid crimes, he almost immediately renounces orchids and turns to his new passion: web design and pornography, both of which he decides will be much more lucrative businesses anyway. This quick change of heart, which Orlean does not reveal until the end of the book, has a profound effect on the subject matter of her story, revealing the difficult and often troubling aspects of writing about people whose lives and decisions the writer cannot control.

THE BULLFIGHTER CHECKS HER MAKEUP:
MY ENCOUNTERS WITH EXTRAORDINARY
PEOPLE

Published eleven years after *Saturday Night*, the collection *The Bullfighter Checks Her Makeup* (2001) is Orlean's return to the form for which she is so well known: the short essay highlighting a particular person or small community of interest. In contrast to *Saturday Night*, this volume focuses less on what people do with their free time and more with the people themselves. Many of the pieces in the collection were previously published in venues including *Esquire,* the *New Yorker, Outside*, and *Rolling Stone*. Some of them came out of Orlean's first few years at the *New Yorker*, when she was writing small character studies for the popular "Talk of the Town" series. The result is a surprising collection of intimate peeks into the lives of others, some of whom are very much like the author and some with whom she finds surprising connections. Essays range from a study of a short-lived 1960s sister band, the Shaggs, to the title piece about Cristina Sánchez, the first woman to professionally fight bulls in Spain. The subjects even span species: one piece chronicles her connections with canines ("Show Dog"), a subject that would later find expression in her work on the famous show dog Rin Tin Tin.

In her characteristic style, Orlean is both present and not present in each of the pieces, briefly mentioning herself for purposes of moving the narrative forward but keeping the lens focused on the person being highlighted. For instance, in a piece on a group of Maui surfer girls, she mentions her hair in the opening paragraph, telling her readers that the Maui surfer girls love the wild, knotty, un-straight, un-sleek, un-ordinary kind of hair she had—and hated— when she was fourteen (p. 37). In another, she lets readers know the context of her arrival at the home of a woman named Heather, a news reporter who has been single-handedly covering the entirety of the news in Millerton, New York, by saying that when she went to spend a week with her, she "though it might be a week of dog days, but Heather told [her] that all sorts of things were going on" (p. 169). Though in each of these examples Orlean portrays herself slightly differently (in one as a nervous teenager who never quite came to grips with her frizzy hair, in the other as an investigative news journalist on the hunt for a good story in a seemingly boring town), their effect is the same: Orlean is able to keep the focus of her pieces on her encounters with the people she interviews and studies, rather than try to turn each piece into a memoirist's account of her reactions and feelings about meeting them. This brief mention of herself as a narrator is common in her work and helps to juxtapose her characters with herself as the writer.

More than just simple snapshots of lives, however, the pieces in this collection reveal a delicate and interconnected meditation on the complications of family, love, race, and gender relations; femininity and masculinity; childhood, youth, and self-fulfillment. While her studies do not consciously interact with each other, each of them offers a slightly different angle on similar issues, illuminating both the complications of defining one "American experience" and bringing to light more global issues of feminism, fame, and the ways in which people find meaning in their lives. For instance, in a brief piece on Mark Wahlberg when he was still the Calvin Klein underwear model Marky Mark, Orlean indirectly explores the male fixation with upper-body workouts by excusing her interviewee for being late to their meeting due to getting caught up at the gym: "If photographs of you nearly naked were plastered everywhere—this happens to be Marky's current situation—then upper-body work is exactly the sort of thing you would be wise not to neglect" (p. 126). While this side comment is certainly meant to be humorous, it also highlights the privileging of preserving and sculpting the male upper body over other commitments. This illustration is placed alongside a piece in which Orlean attends a press conference unveiling Jaleel White's nerdy, skinny, nasal-congested Steve Urkel doll and matching products. Both pieces mention boxer shorts (one pair on a Calvin Klein model, one on an infamous TV nerd), dream dates, and whether good looks or intelligence matters more in terms of attractiveness. Simply by juxtaposing the two,

SUSAN ORLEAN

Orlean manages to say quite a lot about the state of masculinity and desirability in the United States in the mid-1990s.

MY KIND OF PLACE: TRAVEL STORIES FROM A WOMAN WHO'S BEEN EVERYWHERE

Almost all of the pieces in *My Kind of Place* (2004) were previously published in the *New Yorker*, along with a few pieces from the *Atlantic, Outside,* and *Conde Nast Traveler.* Similar to her other collections but distinctly more travel-focused, this grouping of essays continues to reflect her fascination with the everyday and her commitment to profiling the people and places often overlooked by mainstream media and feature journalism. It also introduces readers to Orlean's love of travel. As she says, journeys are the only constant in a person's life: "Journeys are the essential text of the human experience—the journey from birth to death, from innocence to wisdom, from ignorance to knowledge, from where we start to where we end" (p. xiv). In her characteristic way of only briefly mentioning herself and instead focusing primarily on a particular person, place, or event she has traveled to write about, *My Kind of Place* offers homage to these journeys, providing narrative glimpses into everything from fertility pilgrimages in Bhutan to the annual World Taxidermy Championship in Illinois to the Olympics in Sydney. The book, in three parts, is organized geographically to move the reader through her global wanderings.

Though no real narrative thread connects these pieces other than their general theme of profiling people and containing some element of travel (though many of the stories in the first section go no farther than her backyard), Orlean weaves them together through her love of setting: "When I wrote these pieces," she writes in the introduction, "the sense of where I was—of where the stories were unfolding—seemed to saturate every element of the experience, to inform it and shape it, and to be what made the story whole" (p. xiv). She offers an example of this, retelling the story of how, when she set out to profile a New Jersey woman who had corralled

twenty-seven tigers into her suburban backyard, she had naturally thought the subject would be "tiger." However, as she went deeper into her research, she discovered that it was, in fact, "New Jersey," a tale of how a rural and almost wild neighborhood (one in which a woman could actually raise and feed more than two dozen tigers) rapidly and unexpectedly became a mapped urban center where everything was now monitored and planned.

Other stories, too, expose the intertwined nature of subject and setting, such as Orlean's treatment of budget backpackers in Khao San, Thailand ("The Place to Disappear"), or her piece about women who religiously visit Héviz, Hungary, to dip in the thermal pools rumored to restore youth in natural ways. In all of these instances, the subjects are desperately seeking something, either a return to a rural lifestyle, an escape from an unfulfilling lifestyle, or a restoration of their appearance before life happened. These pieces explore the motivations behind people's decisions to give up their urban lifestyles, globetrot to Thailand with a backpack, or dip into sulfuric waters. (Amid her description of the magic thermal waters, for instance, she suddenly wonders exactly how many years the lake was rumored to "take off your age," because she realizes she isn't that old and doesn't want to return to her not-so-enjoyable teenage years.) Without ever being explicitly moralistic at the end of her pieces, what she discovers is that tigers can't live in a suburban backyard forever, most of the travelers eventually go home, and that her mother still looks like her mother even after a few weeks at a magical lake.

Almost all of the stories in this collection follow a similar trajectory, revealing something complicated about the places in which the tales take place, lamenting the many realities of globalization and industrialization and also celebrating the fact that "the world is an endlessly surprising and amazing place" (p. 277). The tales are hopeful and yet realistic, evoking the idea that even when life doesn't work out exactly as planned, there will always be another day to climb Mount Fuji, attend another Olympics, find another hot spring. A hiker can climb Mount Fuji

164

on a cloudy day and see nothing at all; a woman can travel to Bhutan to attend a fertility retreat and then miscarry just weeks later. These are the realities that connect us, through unmediated desire, through the excitement and promise of travel, and through the perseverance of the audacious human spirit.

RIN TIN TIN: THE LIFE AND THE LEGEND

Rin Tin Tin (2011) demonstrates Orlean's view that canines too deserve biographical accounts. (She has even coauthored a cookbook with her dog, Cooper, titled *Throw Me a Bone*.) By the end of *Rin Tin Tin*, even the most dubious skeptic will likely be convinced that the lovable German shepherd who initially won an Oscar for Best Actor in 1929 (it was soon after revoked by the Academy of Motion Picture Arts and Sciences and given to a human being instead) should have been able to keep the coveted golden award. While the book is not necessarily a defense in favor of reopening the Academy Awards to additional species, it sparkles with a different—and yet related—sort of defense: that the all-too-familiar American bootstraps narrative is by no means limited to human beings, and that dogs are just as capable as people of emigrating to the United States and remaking their lives into something better. This is the story of a dog who was born on a World War I battlefield, came to the United States, became a movie star, and helped inspire a resurgence of love for the German shepherd breed, a breed that many people had become wary of after so many had been bred for the war.

It took Orlean more than ten years to write *Rin Tin Tin* (her initial deadline was hampered both by an enormous pile of research that kept getting bigger and by the birth of her son). The book traces the famous show dog's rise from orphaned puppy to globally recognized movie star and face of the largest—and most lucrative—dog franchise in the world. Perhaps somewhat ironically, her profile of Rin Tin Tin also demonstrates a move into celebrity profiling, something she never aspired to do in her early days of

journalism. However, the dog's fame—and the fact that she cannot physically interview him—does not alter her treatment of the beloved subject, who appeared in twenty-seven Hollywood films. Instead, the limitations actually turn into the book's strengths, as the impetus for the text sprang from her own childhood fascination with a plastic replica of Rin Tin Tin owned by her grandfather. In true form, Orlean treats the subject as any other, rummaging through archives, sifting through hundreds of news clips, interviewing unusual people she has tracked down, finding stories from those who knew him and those who didn't, watching his entire repertoire of films, analyzing his photographs (there were plenty), and unearthing public rumors about the canine star. The result is a book not so much about biography as about the idea that, no matter the evidence to the contrary, steadfast belief and the stories we tell are often more true than any set of verifiable facts. It is also a kind of retelling of World War I from a very different perspective.

As in her treatment of John Laroche's character in *The Orchid Thief*, not all she discovers about Rin Tin Tin supports the idea that he was the perfect German shepherd. In fact, this is one of the ways that Orlean allows her characters to shine in such a multifaceted way: she discovers, for instance, that Rin Tin Tin was actually rather unfriendly and that many of his descendants have been unintelligent and lazy. While such realities might dissuade some writers from memorializing their subjects, this complexity only serves to increase Orlean's ethos as a passionate dog lover who is willing to find out the not-so-happy details about this iconic dog's life and impact. Rin Tin Tin's owner, Leland Duncan, fondly remembers the powerfully nimble canine as "lustrous and dark, nearly black, with gold marbling on his legs and chin and chest" with a tail "as bushy as a squirrel's," but simultaneously, as a dog with a "hot temper" who snapped and barked and "was nearly unmanageable" at times (p. 47). While Duncan attributes Rin Tin Tin's beauty and fierceness to the fact that the dog had seen so much and was so full of life, Orlean's treatment is a little more cautious, ensuring that "Rinty" (as he was affectionately called by Duncan) is rendered in his natural complexity without neces-

sarily trying to explain the motivations behind those traits.

Through her investigations and interviews, Orlean begins to understand that Rin Tin Tin was not merely a symbol of the war and its aftermath, but rather an iconic representation of what it meant to be an American in the early part of the twentieth century. Firstly, Rin Tin Tin wasn't born in the United States (neither were his parents). He was an immigrant: brave, enterprising, bold, fierce, unique, and hardened by history. Like so many of the people Orlean meets on her journey to reconstruct Rin Tin Tin's identity, she realizes that what she is really reconstructing is the notion of the United States resident in a time "where identities were exploded and recombined" in an effort to reconcile ambition with private desires and the demands of disparate communities (p. 89). Secondly, Rin Tin Tin is clearly an archetypal success story: he found his path to stardom, ate out of silver bowls, listened to classical music during dinnertime, wore a diamond-studded collar, made more money per hour than most of his human cohort, and even had a personal phone number placed in the Los Angeles phonebook. Photographers would pose him standing up at ticket counters, operating movie cameras, working as a clerk, receiving a pedicure, playing golf, laying in a hammock, and sitting in director's chairs on movie sets. He was also a dog who liked to chase squirrels, hunt skunks, run around the yard, sleep in the sun, and enjoy a hearty meal of dog food. These are the complexities that make Orlean's subject so lovable and curious, and that make Rin Tin Tin another memorable addition to the elegant tapestry of characters Orlean has woven over more than twenty years.

Selected Bibliography

WORKS OF SUSAN ORLEAN

NONFICTION BOOKS

Red Sox and Bluefish: And Other Things That Make New England New England. Faber & Faber, 1987.

Saturday Night. New York: Knopf, 1990.

The Orchid Thief: A True Story of Beauty and Obsession. New York: Random House, 1998.

The Bullfighter Checks Her Makeup: My Encounters with Extraordinary People. New York: Random House, 2001.

My Kind of Place: Travel Stories from a Woman Who's Been Everywhere. New York: Random House, 2004.

Rin Tin Tin: The Life and the Legend. New York: Simon & Schuster, 2011.

EDITED COLLECTIONS

The Best American Essays 2005. New York: Mariner, 2005.

The Best American Travel Writing 2007. New York: Mariner, 2007.

OTHER WORKS

Throw Me a Bone: 50 Healthy, Canine Taste-Tested Recipes for Snacks, Meals, and Treats. With Cooper Gillespie and Sally Sampson. New York: Simon & Schuster, 2003.

Lazy Little Loafers. With G. Brian Karas. New York: Abrams Books for Young Readers, 2008.

Animalish. Kindle Single. Amazon Digital Services, 2011.

REVIEWS

Banville, John. "*Rin Tin Tin: The Life and the Legend* by Susan Orlean—Review." *Guardian*, February 2, 2012. http://www.guardian.co.uk/books/2012/feb/02/rin-tin-tin-life-susan-orlean-review

Kakutani, Michiko. "An Action Hero Who Needed No Words." *New York Times*, November 3, 2011. http://www.nytimes.com/2011/11/04/books/rin-tin-tin-by-susan-orlean-review.html?pagewanted=all&_r=0

Shakespeare, Nicholas. "*Rin Tin Tin* by Susan Orlean: Review." *Telegraph*, January 23, 2012. http://www.telegraph.co.uk/culture/books/bookreviews/9025258/Rin-Tin-Tin-by-Susan-Orlean-review.html

INTERVIEWS

Allan, Nicole. "Susan Orlean: What I Read." *Atlantic Wire*, March 8, 2010. http://www.theatlanticwire.com/entertainment/2010/03/susan-orlean-what-i-read/20095/

Arbin Ahlander, Astri von. "Susan Orlean." *The Days of Yore*, March 26, 2012. http://www.thedaysofyore.com/susan-orlean/

Boynton, Robert S. "Susan Orlean." In *The New New Journalism.* New York: Random House, 2007. Pp. 271–292. http://www.newnewjournalism.com/bio.php?last_name=orlean

Bramucci, Steve. "How I Travel: Susan Orlean." *Bootsnall*, September 14, 2010. http://www.bootsnall.com/articles/

10-09/how-i-travel-susan-orlean.html

Colin, Chris. "Susan Orlean." *Salon*, February 26, 2001. http://www.salon.com/2001/02/26/orlean/

Garber, Megan. "Twitter Queen Susan Orlean on the Mini-Medium, the Interactive Narrative, and the Writing Persona." *Nieman Journalism Lab,* September 14, 2010. http://www.niemanlab.org/2010/09/twitter-queen-susan-orlean-on-the-mini-medium-the-interactive-narrative-and-the-writing-persona/

McHenry, Tim. "A Conversation with Susan Orlean, Author of *The Orchid Thief*." In *The Orchid Thief: A True Story of Beauty and Obsession*. Ballantine Reader's Circle Edition. New York: Ballantine Books, 2000.

Sagal, Peter. "Writer Susan Orlean Plays 'Not My Job.' " NPR, December 2, 2011. http://www.npr.org/2011/12/03/143066848/writer-susan-orlean-plays-not-my-job

Vukotic, Kristin. "Susan Orlean on Organic Writing." *Columbia: A Journal of Literature and Art* no 46:43–54 (2009).

Winet, Kristin. Telephone interview with Susan Orlean. August 16, 2013.

"Yale Literary Magazine Interview with Susan Orlean." *Yale Literary Magazine.* http://www.susanorlean.com/news/yaleinterview.html

FILMS BASED ON THE WORKS OF SUSAN ORLEAN

Adaptation. Screenplay by Charlie Kaufman and Donald Kaufman. Directly by Spike Jonze. Good Machine Intermedia, Propaganda Films, Saturn Films, 2002.

SARA PARETSKY

(1947—)

James Lewin

As a writer of private-eye narratives, Sara Paretsky has expanded the genre beyond its prejudices and conventions. With her first-person protagonist, V. I. Warshawski, the author turns Everywoman's everyday struggles into a multivolume epic. Smart, tough, and compassionate, Warshawski belongs to Chicago as surely as Raymond Chandler's Philip Marlowe does to Los Angeles. On the mean streets of her ethnic working-class neighborhood, Warshawski develops a gut-level devotion to social justice, combining the traditions of King Arthur and radical feminism. Yet, in many ways, Sara Paretsky and V. I. Warshawski are mirror opposites, sharing similar perspectives while coming from very different backgrounds.

AUTHOR AND HEROINE

Born on June 8, 1947, in Ames, Iowa, and raised in Lawrence, Kansas, Paretsky describes growing up in a family that was brilliant and accomplished but unhappy. In her autobiographical *Writing in an Age of Silence* (2007), Paretsky writes that, as the only daughter in a family of six, she was expected to provide full-service cooking, cleaning, and care of the younger children. Her father, a professor of bacteriology at the University of Kansas, had a gift for languages as well as a successful career in scientific research. A domestic tyrant, he sometimes would refuse to speak to any of the family for days; meanwhile, his presence "filled with a ferocious anger" intimidated everyone (*Silence*, p. 22). His idea of a joke was to sport a lapel button opposing a woman's right to vote. The author's mother was also highly educated, with a wide knowledge of both literature and history. In 1941 she had been accepted to medical school, a rare achievement for a woman at that time. But "she chose not to take the bus from her home town to the University of Illinois on the day she needed to report to class" (*Silence*, p. 3). Subsequently, she became "bitter over opportunities lost or denied and took a savage delight in the failures of other women" (p. 3). Finally, in later years, the author's mother found work in the local library where "her dedication to books and children's literacy led the library to name the children's reading room for her" (*Silence*, p. xix, n. 2).

Unlike the author, who grew up in a farmhouse outside of Lawrence, the fictional heroine V. I. Warshawski recalls her childhood years in a bungalow in South Chicago supported by the loving care of both her parents, a Polish cop and an Italian opera singer, who devoted themselves to her well-being. After her parents die, Warshawski defines herself, in her grief and rage at the injustice of life, as a female street-fighter, instinctual and independent to a fault. Sara Paretsky, on the other hand, admits that she allowed her father to choose all of her undergraduate courses for her when she attended the University of Kansas (B.A., 1967) and confesses to being haunted by her parents' verbal abuse well into adulthood. Her father's parting shot was to warn Paretsky, when she started graduate study at the University of Chicago, that her "second-rate mind" would be unlikely to measure up at a "first-rate school" (*Silence*, p. 11). Evidently the first-rate school disagreed, for she went on to earn both an M.B.A. and a doctorate in history at Chicago (1977), with a dissertation titled "The Breakdown of Moral Philosophy in New England Before the Civil War."

Warshawski also attends the University of Chicago—on a basketball scholarship. At their shared alma mater, both author and heroine

discover themselves in the context of the 1970s feminist movement. "It was feminism," Paretsky writes, "that triggered my wish to write a private eye novel, and it shaped the character of my detective, V. I. Warshawski" (*Silence,* p. xvi). Defying stereotypes, Paretsky decided that her heroine could not be a helpless virgin just because she was considered "good" as opposed to the "evil" femme fatale of noir tradition. Determined to "turn the tables on the dominant views of women in fiction and society," Paretsky wanted her detective to be "a sexual being and a moral person at the same time" (*Silence,* pp. 60, 62).

Paretsky writes about feeling isolated, introverted, and intimidated by her father, "a mercurial man, charming, nervous, but subject to rages that were all the more bewildering because we never knew what might trigger them" (*Silence,* p. xv). Meanwhile, Paretsky's mother, prone to undermining her daughter at every occasion, withdrew into an alcoholic "private hell" of her own (p. xiii). Perhaps, Paretsky muses, "my father and mother both wanted a mother so desperately that they tried to make me assume that role in their lives" (p. 12). Both parents were socially progressive, supporting the rights of African Americans in a time and place of deeply rooted racism. They gave their children a "great love for books and language" as well as a sense of the "importance of service for the public good." Paretsky notes that her father's parents "met walking a picket line for the International Ladies Garment Workers Union" hoping to "improve the loathsome conditions in New York's sweatshops." Her mother's father was a small-town doctor in Illinois who "refused a job offer from the Mayo Clinic at the height of the Great Depression" out of loyalty to patients in his community (p. 13).

The roots of the family's internalized violence may go back to the fact that the author's parents were children of immigrants who came to America on the heels of persecution and pogroms. Her grandmothers, Paretsky notes, "were essentially orphans" from heartbroken homes: "My mother's mother died giving birth to her, my father's was sent to New York from eastern

Europe after her own father was murdered in a pogrom when she was twelve. She became a mother at fifteen and ... never saw her own mother or most of her siblings again; they perished in the Holocaust" (*Silence,* p. 12).

Belonging to one of the few Jewish families in Lawrence, Kansas, added to the author's alienation: "We were like giraffes, an oddity that invited staring. I knew that if I revealed any of the ugliness of our home life to the larger world ... I would be bringing shame to the Jews, who were beleaguered enough" (*Silence,* p. 40). V. I. Warshawski also has a Jewish heritage. Her father, Tony, is a Polish cop, but her mother, Gabriella, daughter of Italian Jews, first comes to America to escape from World War II. The shadow of the Holocaust haunts Warshawski, through the prism of Dr. Lotty Herschel, a survivor of prewar Germany.

Yet for Paretsky, neither her parents' neuroses nor her Jewish identity were the source of her isolation. Rather, she blames the "unnatural vision" of the "self-abnegating nature" of women, perpetuated through a long-cherished and mostly unacknowledged stereotype described as the "Angel in the House" (p. 14):

> The angel kept me from a sense of a writer's vocation, or, indeed, any vocation when I was a child, and she still comes flying around my head, telling me not to be selfish, to give myself over to domestic or public duties first, that my writing, like Jo March's, can wait.
>
> (pp. 16–17)

Although her parents subsidized her brothers to go away to college, they insisted that she pay her own way at the University of Kansas "if I was going to go to university at all" (p. xv). To establish her independence, she "made a private vow that I would spend my summers away from home" (p. xv). As a consequence, she came to Chicago in June 1966 as a volunteer community activist.

Her experience that summer "changed my life forever" (*Silence,* p. 35). The nineteen-year-old Paretsky had been assigned to work in the Gage Park area of the white ethnic Southwest Side, along with two fellow idealists. The

volunteers felt disappointed not to be in the black neighborhood where a Presbyterian minister was trying to convert street gangs into social action organizations. Nevertheless, they found themselves in the center of the protest against segregated housing in Chicago. When Martin Luther King led a march on August 5 in the nearby neighborhood of Marquette Park, Paretsky felt a reality shock.

> Everyone in the city knew that King's march would lead to violence in Marquette Park. I don't think anyone knew how ugly it would be: white mobs torching cars, throwing rocks and Molotov cocktails, hitting out with motorcycle chains, while the police and fire departments, all-white forces who had grown up on the south side—and who knew many of the mob members by name—would absorb physical and verbal abuse for protecting Dr. King.
>
> (p. 31)

The segregation of Chicago neighborhoods had become so entrenched that, for defenders of the status quo, the call for open housing seemed like an incitement to race war. In a counterprotest, local residents sang racist lyrics to the tunes of familiar television commercials and hurled rocks, bottles, and knives, including a rock that hit King in the head. Kept away from the confrontation by their program supervisors, the three volunteers still had the opportunity to extinguish a fire started by parishioners in their neighborhood church. Far from discouraged, Paretsky decided that her "destiny lay in Chicago" (p. 36). Her impressions of that summer also led to the conception of a female protagonist who grew up in a neighborhood of racial, ethnic, and religious divisions. Most of all, she writes, "the summer of 1966 made me aware of the issues of voice and voicelessness" at the center of both her work and her life (p. 38). It is out of the spirit of the 1960s that Paretsky draws her inspiration for social justice.

Paretsky is married to Courtney Wright, a University of Chicago professor of physics, with whom she raised three children—Kimball, Timothy, and Philip. Before becoming a full-time novelist, among other jobs, she worked for a large insurance company, providing background in financial investigations that became the area of expertise for her fictional investigator, V. I. Warshawski.

PARETSKY'S "OTHER" CHICAGO

Knowledge of Chicago streets is not required for an appreciation of Paretsky's fiction. But the "other" Chicago that outsiders rarely visit permeates her work and enhances her authenticity. Paretsky's detective novels traverse the length and breadth of the city, forcing to awareness the repressed truths of a violent, exploitative, materialistic, class-conscious free-for-all covered with a shimmering veneer of civilized pretense and well-hyped culture.

"The eye with which I see Chicago," Paretsky writes in her introduction to the story collection *Windy City Blues* (1995), is always looking for the signs of "alienation and despair" lurking "just below the surface" (p. 2). She describes her first impressions of driving into town at two in the morning in June 1966:

> The vastness of the city at night was overwhelming. Red flares glowed against a yellow sky, followed by mile on mile of unbending lights: street lamps, neon signs, traffic lights, flashing police blues— lights that didn't illuminate but threw shadows, and made the city seem a monster, ready to devour the unwary.
>
> (p. 2)

Anyone who has glimpsed the city from the top of Sears Tower knows that the West Side of Chicago seems endless. It merely fades over the horizon. The North Shore stretches from the former Great Lakes Naval Base down through the wealthy suburbs, along Lakeshore Drive, past high-rise apartment buildings facing Lake Michigan, into the Loop, a walled castle of world-famous skyscrapers to which armies of workers trudge day in and day out.

At the other end of the Loop, the Outer Drive continues south, taking a curve at Seventy-Ninth Street to become Route 41 South—heading through the ruins of USX South Works and Wisconsin Steel, which shut down abruptly in the 1980s, leaving thousands of mill workers unemployed. This is the area of South Chicago,

which includes an enclave known as the East Side (because it is east of the Calumet River), separated within its own geography, sociology, and psychological attitude. Visitors to Chicago rarely wander these streets. The hotels along Michigan Avenue near the Chicago River, the Water Tower Place, and the McCormick Place convention center along the lakefront all seem to exist on a different planet from that of the bungalows of the East Side.

V. I. Warshawski describes the neighborhood where she grew up as a place where fists count for more than money and your ethnic identity is who you are:

> Five bridges form the neighborhood's only link to the rest of the city. Its members live in a stubborn isolation, trying to recreate the Eastern European villages of their grandparents. They don't like people from across the river, and anyone north of Seventy-first Street might as well have rolled in on a Soviet tank for the reception they get.
>
> (*Blood Shot*, p. 30)

She recalls her neighborhood as a refuge for Croatians, Serbs, Poles, and other ethnic groups that "stored grudges as carefully as if they were food in a bomb shelter" (*Fire Sale*, 2005, p. 173). Warshawski's Chicago is a place of unpredictable, often fatal violence. Death can come through car crashes, slips of the foot or the tongue, firebomb explosions, drowning and asphyxiation, gunshots and poison. Usually, the dirty work of intentional homicide occurs in the gritty streets and alleys of the lower-class neighborhoods where the small-time criminals live and thrive. But these seemingly random incidents of mayhem connect directly to the higher echelons of true evil, ensconced in the skyscraper offices of corporate power and, to the north of the city, among the wealthy executives and their overprivileged families and familiars.

The Chicago of Sara Paretsky's heroine is a battleground where the evil forces of corporate profiteers trump the petty hoodlums of street crime. Along with her radical feminism, Paretsky's awareness of the unconscionable division between the haves and the have-nots establish the basis for her central theme of the blatant inequality before the law in the business-as-usual

world of everyday Chicago crime and punishment. Class consciousness is a key to Paretsky's driving moral purpose, often designated by definite boundaries between sections of the city.

In her first novel, *Indemnity Only*, published in 1982, the narrative begins in a "July in Chicago" during the summer of 1979. The protagonist drives to her office in an unglamorous part of the South Loop—Wabash and Monroe—in the fictitious Pulteney Building "next to the Monroe Street Tobacco Store," the kind of neglected rental property where the elevator is ordinarily out of order (p. 1). When she turns up the air conditioner, a fuse blows and the lights go out. She meets her first client in a dark sweltering office that both seem to take for granted as being not untypical of life in the big city.

Paretsky's Chicago is a metropolis of neglected neighborhoods and downtrodden underdogs. The elites, who own and control the city, reside behind an elegant and respectable facade:

> By two I was on the Edens Expressway heading toward the North Shore.... For some reason the Edens ceases to be a beautiful expressway as it nears the homes of the rich. Close to Chicago it's lined with greensward and neat bungalows, but as you go farther out, shopping centers crop up and industrial parks and drive-ins take over. Once I turned right on Willow Road, though, and headed toward the lake, the view became more impressive—large stately homes set well back on giant, carefully manicured lawns.
>
> (*Indemnity Only*, p. 74)

In a howler that signals a double entendre, the author invents a "ten-story building" with a "white Italian marble" facade like the Standard Oil building in downtown Chicago "on Sheridan Road just south of Evanston" as the site of the union headquarters for the International Brotherhood of Knifegrinders, Shear Edgers, and Blade Sharpeners (*Indemnity Only*, p. 31). The location is correctly identified in *Total Recall* (2001) as the upscale "Calvary Cemetery, whose mausoleums separate Evanston from Chicago" (p. 415). But neither corrupt unions nor the thugs who do their dirty work are the source of evil in *Indemnity Only*. The real villain turns out to be a

"Claims Department vice-president" who operates out of an "office big enough for the Bears to work out in, with a magnificent view of the lake" in the Ajax Insurance building, another fictional edifice supposedly occupying "all sixty floors of a modern glass-and-steel skyscraper" in the Chicago Loop (pp. 15–16). Mr. Masters is a two-dimensional corporate executive whose smiling respectability barely masks his ruthless criminal greed. Although he remains obscure through most of the narrative, Masters pulls the strings on his unwitting junior colleagues, who only partly understand that they are being compromised, while relying on cruder thugs to do his dirty work by proxy. The thrill of the plot is not merely the suspense of exposing the scoundrel, but an exposé of the consequences of unbridled materialism.

In her second novel, *Deadlock*, published in 1984, Paretsky introduces readers to the Port of Chicago. Developed to take advantage of the St. Lawrence Seaway, the Illinois International Port covers fifteen hundred acres of land on Lake Calumet and moves about 19 million tons of cargo each year. The author gives the reader a sense of Chicago's context as a midwestern capital on a lake that could be considered one of the world's oceans. The Great Lakes that connect the Port of Chicago to the world of international commerce extend up to the northern Thunder Bay, formerly Port Arthur, "Canada's westernmost port on Lake Superior" (p. 145).

The focus of the narrative, set in 1982, is the death of V. I.'s cousin, a former hockey star known as Boom-Boom Warshawski. V. I.'s sense of guilt impels her to take on the investigation of his death, especially since neither the police nor anyone else seems to find anything worth investigating. "We'd always counted on the other being around to help us out. And I hadn't helped him out" (p. 10). After a long day, capped by a dinner at a fancy restaurant, Warshawski finds herself driving from 130th Street onto I-94 heading toward the Loop:

> At 103rd Street the highway merged with the Dan Ryan. I was back in the city now, the Dan Ryan el on my left and a steep grassy bank on my right. Perched on top were tiny bungalows and liquor stores. A peaceful urban sight, but not a place to stop in the middle of the night. A lot of unwary tourists had been mugged close to the Dan Ryan.
>
> (*Deadlock*, pp. 100–101)

The sense of a city divided within itself, concealing menace behind the facade of a quiet nightscape, comes to a crashing climax when Warshawski discovers that her brake fluid has been drained and her steering lines cut, leaving her adrift in seventy-mile-per-hour traffic. She wakes up in the hospital, lucky to be alive. Others involved in the multivehicle crash did not survive.

Eventually she tracks the killers of Boom-Boom (and would-be killers of herself) to Lake Bluff, a "tiny pocket of wealth" (p. 124). Using a combination of deception and sheer chutzpah, Warshawski worms her way into the living rooms of the mansions where the villains reign over society. Nothing about the lifestyles of the Phillips and Grafalk families seems worth the superficial perks of their fancy automobiles, cavernous living rooms, and private yachts. In fact, they are miserable wretches of their own making. Yet that existential despair does not excuse the suffering and injustice they wreak on others. At the conclusion of *Deadlock*, Paretsky's heroine looks out on Lake Michigan from the perspective of a stone terrace under a green canvas awning, sharing champagne and petits fours with the widow of the dead tycoon who instigated Boom-Boom's death. As the "water, pale blue under a soft summer sky lapped gently at the sand," Warshawski feels knots in her stomach. "It looked so peaceful now under the May sun, but it is not a tame lake" (pp. 307, 310).

Like the lake, which embraces the city with an aura of natural splendor that conceals its tragic potential, Chicago rests on a labyrinth of underground tunnels that bring the dangerous waters once again to the surface of Paretsky's narrative flow in *Tunnel Vision*, published in 1994, a decade after *Deadlock*. If it were not based on an actual event, the novel would seem like a surrealistic departure from hard-boiled realism. Most Chicagoans had never heard of the sixty-mile network of interlocking railroad tunnels built forty miles beneath the surface of the Loop until

April 1992, when 250 million gallons of water from the Chicago River came rushing through a breach in a tunnel wall, causing widespread flooding in the business district.

Paretsky uses this actual event as a metaphor representing the twisted subconscious of a metropolis haunted by its own monumental hypocrisy. Returning to Warshawski's office in the aging Pulteney Building, even a reader who does not know Chicago well can almost smell the musty odors of the interior with "its usual fetid smell of moldy tile and stale urine" and share the frustration associated with the "twice-weekly occurrence" of an out-of order elevator described in *Bitter Medicine* (1987, p. 39).

In this now-condemned structure, Warshawski inadvertently discovers a homeless mother and her three children dwelling furtively in the basement. Tamar Hawkings and her brood play a secondary role in the epic narrative of the novel, but they symbolize the forgotten victims of a winner-take-all society in which "people seem to take more pleasure in money than in justice," as Warshawski's old law professor from the University of Chicago notes in a particularly uncomfortable reunion of his former students (*Tunnel Vision*, p. 63). These colleagues and former friends of Warshawski, including her own circle of feminist activists, provide the bulk of the plot, involving murder, money laundering, political chicanery, and incestuous child abuse. Nobody emerges untainted from the conclusion, which leaves intact a legal system rotten to its core.

Cynicism in Chicago seems to be justified because that is the way the City-That-Works works. As Paretsky notes: "One thing all Chicagoans understand is loyalty, especially loyalty to someone who has bribed you. For years the definition of an honest Chicago politician has been one who stays bought" (*Windy City Blues*, p. 4). But although Warshawski gets older and sadder as the series of novels develops, she never loses her fierce commitment to idealism.

For instance, in her sixth Warshawski novel, *Burn Marks* (1990), the author tackles the accepted but not acceptable attitude of Chicago politics to the incorrigible corruption in everything from the machinery of local elections to the awarding of city contracts to the inner workings of the police department. In *Burn Marks* the author indicts urban society from top to bottom for its lax resignation to injustice. By the end, little if anything changes for the better. After a series of confrontations involving multiple deaths to cover up criminal collusion, V. I. concludes that the presumed scandal makes no sense: "Turns out it was just business as usual in this town" (p. 333). Yet V. I. Warshawski never succumbs to the apathy of business as usual.

As often happens in Paretsky's books, her protagonist gets involved in a complicated narrative through a personal relationship or seemingly chance encounter. *Burn Marks* begins with Warshawski waking from disturbing dreams at 3 a.m. The doorbell is ringing and Aunt Elena, her father's younger sister, is at her door. Aunt Elena is an inveterate drunk who has been living in a single-room-occupancy (SRO) hotel at Cermak and Indiana on the Near South Side. When the Indiana Arms burns down, Aunt Elena has no one to turn to except her niece, who feels obligated to take her in.

Because of the construction of Presidential Towers in the former skid row area of the city, there are few options for Elena. But Warshawski has enough old-fashioned Chicago clout to find her a place in another marginal neighborhood, on the North Side of the city at Kenmore Avenue between Wilson and Lawrence. This political favor comes courtesy of Warshawski's old friend and feminist ally Roz Fuentes, the first Hispanic woman with a chance to be elected to a county-wide office. Guilt-tripped into donating $250 to the campaign, Warshawski uses her resulting status to extort a promise from the campaign manager, Marissa Duncan, to find a cheap room for Aunt Elena.

Warshawski describes the Near South Side, a district that had slid from an area for the mansions of millionaires to a wasteland of industrial sites and public housing, as resembling "postwar Berlin": "The lifeless shells of warehouses and factories were surrounded by mountains of brick-filled rubble" (p. 174). The Uptown neighborhood on the North Side is almost equally depressed. The Windsor Arms "had gone up when

the Duke was in his heyday.... If the facade had been washed since George VI's ascension, it didn't show. Not much more attention had been paid to basic repairs—a number of windows had pieces of cardboard filling in for missing panes" (p. 31).

Between the slums of the North and South Side, however, there is an implied racial division. Aunt Elena would be a rare white face at the Indiana Arms, while none of the residents at the Windsor Arms would be black. Presumably, in both places, Elena would have been one of the few women in a kind of facility known as a refuge for down-and-out male tramps (transients) and bums (permanent residents). But the author makes it clear that Chicago is a place of stark contrasts, divided by class and race. In the North Lawndale area, where wholesale destruction still remains decades after the 1968 riots, the block at 1600 South Christiana is a dangerous wasteland, especially for a white woman alone after dark: "Vacant lots interspersed with gray stone three-flats ... [with] broken or boarded windows ... looked like Beirut.... The only businesses seemed to be the taverns sprinkled liberally on every corner" (p. 165). In contrast, on the North West Side, Norwood Park, home to police officers, contractors, and city officials, is "a place of tidy tiny bungalows on miniscule well-tended lots." This neighborhood, where her father Tony and Aunt Elena as well as the main villains of *Burn Marks* grew up, "seems to have nothing to do with the sprawling, graffiti-laden, garbage-ridden city to the southeast" (p. 336).

In *Fire Sale*, published in 2005, Warshawski has been able to keep herself well enough in shape to fit into her old basketball uniform for a reunion of the championship high school team that propelled her to a University of Chicago scholarship and the escape route from her dead-end South Chicago neighborhood. Yet the old ties still bind. When her former basketball coach, in a terminal battle with cancer, asks Warshawski to fill in as her substitute, how can she say no?

Of course, no good deed goes unpunished in Paretsky's Chicago. Once involved with the team of Bertha Palmer High School, Warshawski becomes immersed in the lives of her players,

despite the warnings, threats, and underhanded assaults of almost everyone involved. She cannot help herself: "I hadn't wanted to be sucked back into South Chicago, but as soon as someone told me to stay away my hackles went up and I dug in my heels" (p. 181). The source of the problem is a self-righteous billionaire who himself graduated from Bertha Palmer High and now owns the all-purpose superstore that employs many of the residents of his old neighborhood. Along with a remnant of the Eastern European families, most of the neighborhood is now Latino, complicated by an undercurrent of street gangs and illegal immigration as well as an insurgent Christian activism. But the bottom line remains the same. With no other jobs available, the employees of Buffalo Bill Bysen's By-Smart enterprises must endure his systematic exploitation for the survival of their families in an economic food chain stretching from suburban Barrington Hills—forty miles northwest of the city where the Bysen family lives in baronial splendor—back to the sweatshops where undocumented immigrants work in virtual slavery, to the gangsters who have brought them from their native countries to make the plastic flags and other patriotic knickknacks for a mass market of post-9/11 American consumers. This novel also introduces the reader to the former landfill at 122nd Street, where Warshawski is left for dead amid "ten thousand tons of garbage" produced by the city on a daily basis (Introduction, p. x).

Paretsky's protagonist notes the details that still thrill her about her city, such as the "orange legs of the three-story Calder" mobile designed for the Federal Building at Dearborn and Adams: "We pride ourselves in Chicago on our outdoors sculptures by famous artists. My favorite is the bronze wind chimes in front of the Standard Oil Building, but I have a secret fondness for the Chagall mosaics in front of the First National Bank. My artist friends tell me they are banal" (*Killing Orders*, 1985, p. 49).

At the same time, she is unsparing in her disgust for the city's crude materialism, embodied in the concrete spirals of the Dan Ryan Expressway:

I hate the Ryan, not just because of the traffic, although there isn't an hour of the night or day when all fourteen lanes aren't heavy with trucks and cars. I hate the way it was built and everything about how it got built. The road is dug deep into the earth. All you see as you drive are high concrete walls. They're full of cracks with ragweed and crabgrass poking through. If you look up, you get a glimpse of scraggly trees and the occasional run-down tire warehouse or apartment building. Since money for the expressway came from the cronyism in the Democratic machine, they called it Dan Ryan, after the chairman of the Cook County Board who anted up the bucks for it in 1960.

(*Body Work*, 2010, pp. 60–61)

From the perspective of the John Hancock building at the top of the Chicago socioeconomic pyramid, Warshawski can glimpse the city through a "field of gray-white clouds … so that the city, with all its art and music and corruption and gang wars, seemed as silent and distant as if it existed only in a child's pop-up book" (*Body Work*, p. 463). Meanwhile, at the base of the hierarchical pyramid, three miles southwest of the Loop in the Pilsen neighborhood known as the "Heart of Chicago," the immigrant Guaman family suffers in a daily struggle for survival, for dignity, for the future that is constantly receding into a distant chimera of lost hopes. The father, Lazar, works as a baggage handler at O'Hare airport. His wife, Cristina, is a cashier in a neighborhood store. In their bungalow on Twenty-First Place, the Guamans raise three daughters and one son, all seemingly marked by tragic fate. But it is not mere misfortune that plagues the Guamans. Rather, they have become unwitting victims of an elaborate corporate cover-up engineered by the Tintrey Company when their second daughter, Alexandra, turns up dead on a work assignment in Iraq.

WARSHAWSKI AS EVERYWOMAN

Q: "Why did you become a detective?"

A: "I can be my own boss."

(*Burn Marks*, pp. 95–96)

V. I. Warshawski is a virtual superheroine with an ability to rise to almost any challenge. Yet her swashbuckling derring-do is not her most fascinating characteristic. Instead, she engages the reader's empathy because of how she copes with the baffling challenges that confront everyone. Clearly, Ms. Warshawski is anything but ordinary. Yet we identify with her because of her awareness, within the morality tradition, of the inner struggle between body and soul.

Typically American, she identifies with whatever automobile she happens to be driving. Her ride reflects not only her socioeconomic status, but also her personal style and panache. In *Indemnity Only*, Warshawski zooms around the city in a Chevy Monza, a four-passenger subcompact phased out of production after 1980. In *Deadlock*, she drives a Mercury Lynx, another modest compact car, while Paige Carrington wheels a sleek, silver Audi 5000, known for reported problems with unintended acceleration. In *Killing Orders*, Warshawski owns a "little Omega," more recommended for its Greek name than its reliability. In 1988, at age thirty-seven, she buys her first new car, a Pontiac Trans Am: "I didn't know what I was going to do for money to pay for it, but when it moved up to fifty with just a whisper of gas it seemed like the car I'd been waiting for all my life" (*Burn Marks*, p. 335). At the beginning of *Hard Time* (1999), the Trans Am that she was so proud of ten years earlier is totaled in an accident, so she buys a rusting Skylark for twelve hundred dollars from a recent college graduate. Allowing herself to imagine the benefits of a bonus she is offered (but turns down) to work for the corporate moguls, Warshawski muses about a "red Jaguar XJ-12" that she has seen in an advertisement (p. 141). But, finally, she decides a Jaguar convertible would be "a fantasy, not a car for a working detective who has to use her wheels in the grime of Chicago," and she is pleased to settle for a "late-model green Mustang" with enough pizzazz to represent her style yet without seeming ostentatious (*Hard Time*, p. 493).

One of the mysteries of the series is how Warshawski pays her bills. She often pursues investigations for personal reasons, letting paying clients wait for her to return their calls. With poetic justice, Warshwaski frequently receives an

unexpected check, cut for her as a gratuity by a figure on the periphery after a long and complicated adventure. At the end of *Killing Orders*, an unmarked envelope arrives containing twenty-five new thousand-dollar bills. The payoff is from the Mafia boss Don Pasquale, but she uses the cash to make a down payment on a co-op apartment. Her new flat is a step up from her apartment on Halsted and Belmont, which had been burned down during her investigation, but it still requires a monthly payment of seven hundred dollars (*Guardian Angel*, 1992, p. 307). At the end of *Tunnel Vision*, her most upscale regular client, Darraugh Graham, gifts her with ten thousand dollars, mainly for finding Ken a job that can keep Darraugh's son out of jail. Warshawski uses this windfall to move into a new office in a "converted warehouse near North and Damen, on Leavitt" in the trendy Chicago neighborhood of Bucktown, which she shares with the sculptor Tessa Reynolds (*Hard Time*, p. 46). Similarly, she is able to pay for her new-used Mustang ("with only six thousand miles on it") thanks to a forty-thousand-dollar bonus she receives from movie star Lacy Dowell, whose endorsements led to the murder and exploitation *Hard Time* exposes. Pondering whether she is compromising her integrity by accepting the profits that came "from T-shirts sewn by women in prisons here or abroad," V. I. admits: "I could have turned it down, but I didn't" (*Hard Time*, pp. 493–494). And at the conclusion of *Hardball* (2009), V. I. is offered a twenty-five-thousand-dollar check from her aunt to assuage the guilt for a criminal conspiracy involving Warshawski's uncle. Wondering whether to accept tainted money, she turns to her closest friend and adviser, Dr. Lotty Herschel, who tells her, "Victoria, all money is tainted.... Especially reparations money. Take it. Pay your bills" (p. 518).

Having escaped from the neighborhood of her childhood via a basketball scholarship to the University of Chicago, where she earned a degree to practice law, Warshawski worked first for the Public Defender's office before becoming a self-employed private investigator. After being forced out of her apartment at Halsted Avenue north of Belmont she moves to the third floor of a build-ing on nearby Racine Avenue near Belmont. Located in the area of Wrigleyville, she becomes an avid Cubs fan, even though her South Side origins would have mandated a devotion to the White Sox. Warshawski lives in the Chicago of Chicagoans: gritty but human, tough yet engaged, not totally indifferent to humanity but unapologetically concerned with self-interest. Siding with the working-class survivors of her neighborhood against the young urban professionals who have gained the upper hand, Warshawski bucks the trends of both suburban flight and gentrification.

While not motivated primarily by money, Warshawski does enjoy certain things money can buy. Her drink of choice is Johnny Walker Black Label Scotch, and she turns up her nose at cheaper brands. She also likes stylish clothes and the pleasures of travel. In *Body Work*, Warshawski spends Christmas in Mexico City "for a week of art, music, and warmth" (p. 26). There, she enhances her wardrobe with the purchase of "a burgundy Carolina Herrera pantsuit" (p. 435). Still, her most precious possessions are the print of the Uffizi gallery in her office and the red Venetian glasses her mother brought as an immigrant from Italy. When fire breaks out, the wine glasses are what she thinks of saving first.

The other object that Warshawski locks up is her Smith & Wesson thirty-eight. Because Chicago has prohibited the sale of handguns she drives to the suburb of Hazel Crest and uses her private investigator's license and state security certificate to legally buy and register her firearm. She fires it only in extreme emergencies, and when she kills a sadistic gangster who has been torturing her Aunt Elena, she seems shocked by her own violence: "I had never killed a man before.... I couldn't bring myself to walk close enough to check" (*Burn Marks*, p. 323).

Eschewing the classical investigative logic of a Sherlock Holmes, Warshawski's "theory of detection resembles Julia Child's approach to cooking: Grab a lot of ingredients from the shelves, put them in a pot and stir, and see what happens" (*Killing Orders*, p. 58). Her housekeeping is sporadic, but she refuses to feel guilty about it: "I'm messy but not a slob" (*Indemnity Only*, p. 10). She casually throws out her mail

unopened, except envelopes that could contain a check. Chronically sleep deprived, she rises early and retires late, driving from the distant northern suburbs to the far southern dumping grounds, then out to the western reaches of the city and back to the lakefront. Her hyperactivity prompts the comment: "You bounce around Chicago like a pinball in the hands of a demented wizard" (*Total Recall*, p. 109).

Although she appreciates the cuisine of upscale restaurants, she often takes her meals at the Belmont Diner. Although she strives to eat nutritious fare, under stress she fuels up on fast food, such as "a double hamburger, a chocolate shake and fries" (*Bitter Medicine*, p. 252). In lieu of a strict diet, she runs five miles a day to burn up the calories and keep in shape. But one of the endearing aspects of her character is how she can make a mess of the mundane details of the everywoman's day. In a paradigmatic Warshawski slice of life:

> It was almost three: I hadn't eaten since my yogurt at eight this morning. Maybe the situation would seem less depressing if I had some food. I passed a strip mall on my way to the expressway and bought a slice of cheese pizza. The crust was gooey, the surface glistened with oil, but I ate every bite with gusto. When I got out of my car at the office I realized I'd dripped oil down the front of my rose silk sweater.
>
> (*Total Recall*, p. 73)

Like many other baby boomers, she tries to resist the technological new millennium. In *Deadlock*, she has to go searching for a pay phone. To receive messages, she relies on a professional answering service through *Guardian Angel* (the seventh V. I. Warshawski book), published in 1992, and well into *Tunnel Vision*, published two years later. Belatedly, in *Tunnel Vision*, she decides to "invest in my own portable phone" (p. 94). She seems even more reluctant about buying her own computer, ignoring the sarcasm of her trusted lawyer Freeman Carter in *Burn Marks:* "You still don't have a computer? Christ, Vic, when are you going to join the eighties?" (p. 261). In *Guardian Angel*, she is still shrugging off Freeman Carter's advice—"It's time you got your own computer, Warshawski"—and stub-

bornly using her "mother's old Olivetti" portable typewriter not only because it got her through "six years at the University of Chicago" but also because "using it keeps my gun wrist strong" (*Guardian Angel*, pp. 103, 175). When she finally installs a desktop computer, it simplifies background checks to a few clicks on the keyboard rather than quests through archives and back alleys. Yet in *Body Work*, published in 2010, the brave new era of communication has evolved into the "Age of Paranoia" as cell phones become tracking devices and laptop computers store evidence for either good or evil purposes (p. 451).

Warshawski takes lovers where she finds them. Occasionally these relationships with handsome male partners stretch over more than one novel, but generally they are physically gratifying and emotionally superficial. Beginning with *Indemnity Only*, her relationship to Ralph Devereux establishes the fact that Warshawski is sexually active. Like the male hard-boiled detectives who preceded her, she never pretends to be a plastic saint. She likes men and enjoys physical intimacy. But, like Sam Spade and Philip Marlowe, she has an undefined hang-up about too much emotional intimacy with the opposite sex.

Her affair with Devereux is the first in a series of mostly monogamous but temporary love interests that Warshawski takes seriously only as long as they do not compromise her independence. She and Devereux are clearly unsuited. He is a corporate clone: in other words, an *enemy*. When she admits to being "an ardent Cub fan," Devereux expresses his preference for the Yankees, which she likens to "rooting for the Cosa Nostra" (p. 63). Even more crucially, Devereux cannot accept a woman as the equal of a man. Devereux minimizes Warshawski's investigation of his boss, Masters, and pays a nearly fatal price for his misplaced loyalty. "I guess deep down I didn't take your detecting seriously" (p. 208). Yet, Devereux proves himself gallant in the end, and earns a return appearance in *Fire Sale*. Other lovers, such as Roger Ferrant, move in and out of her life without making a major impact. After beginning an affair with Ferrant in *Deadlock*, Warshawski sets the limits in the subsequent novel: "No one protects me, Roger. I

don't live in that kind of universe" (*Killing Orders*, p. 255). Occasionally she has a one-night stand (Martin Bledsoe, Murray Ryerson). But wild promiscuity is not Warshawski's style.

Her relationship with Conrad Rawlings has a more profound impact on her life. She meets Detective Rawlings while accompanying Lotty to a murder investigation. The issue of Rawlings being black is dealt with in a sensitive and good-natured way. The author is adept at portraying black characters as belonging to a distinctive subculture of Chicago society. But Conrad being a cop creates greater conflict than the difference of their races. They do not become lovers until they have known each other for years. Warshawski soon realizes her error: "I should have known better than to get in bed with a policeman" (*Guardian Angel*, p. 294).

In *Hard Time*, Warshawski meets Morrell, a freelance journalist of Cuban descent, who becomes her ally in the cause of social justice as well as her lover. The author of a book on the Disappeared in Chile and Argentina, Morrell shares Warshawski's passion for the rights of the underdog. He is also a better listener and less self-centered than her previous lovers. But his devotion to his own work makes him perhaps too much like Warshawski herself in his stubborn independence. In *Body Work*, she hooks up with a bass player named Jake Thibault, who is sufficiently involved in his music to make too many demands. Because of their conflicting schedules, she and Jake share only occasional moments of intimacy. Their relationship seems unlikely to lead to marriage, but perhaps Warshawski feels that one marriage, in her youth, was one too many.

Her "short, unhappy marriage" is already ancient history when she describes to Ralph Devereux how she met Richard Yarborough: "Dick thought he'd fallen in love with me because I'm so independent; afterwards it seemed to me that it was because he saw my independence as a challenge, and when he couldn't break it down, he got angry" (*Indemnity Only*, p. 141).

In *Bitter Medicine*, her former husband turns up on the side of the bad guys, hired at a rate of $200 an hour. In *Guardian Angel*, a plot twist involves the testing of Dick Yarborough's level of venality. Could Warshawksi have been married to a monster of evil, or is Dick a humanly self-serving but basically law-abiding citizen? The answer is not surprising, but reassuring in terms of Warshawski's tolerance and judgment.

In *Killing Orders*, the reader learns that Warshawski is not a "girl" and not a Catholic, as she makes clear to anyone who presumes to patronize her (p. 28). Her mother was "half Jewish" from "a family of scholars in Pitigliano" (p. 38). Warshawski's own faith is a radical feminism forged in the protest movement at the University of Chicago in the 1960s. But when her friend Agnes became a lesbian it "was a small miracle" that they could remain close (*Killing Orders*, p. 107).

Agnes Paciorek is a "short, compact dynamo" in an eight-hundred-dollar "brown-plaid suit" and earning twice that much per day (p. 60). Agnes and V. I. share a zeal of competition for success in a man's world. In terms of their sexuality, however, while Warshawski goes through a series of heterosexual affairs, often with men who are not able to allow her the independence she requires, Agnes enjoys a stable lesbian relationship with Phyllis Lording, a professor of English from the University of Illinois at Chicago, who shares her apartment "on Chestnut and the Drive, a very posh neighborhood just north of the loop overlooking Lake Michigan" (*Killing Orders*, p. 121).

In almost every novel, Warshawski confronts Lieutenant (later Captain) Bobby Mallory, her deceased father's best friend on the police force and grudging conduit between Warshawski and the by-the-book world of officialdom. For his part, Mallory cannot believe that Warshawski's involvement in police business can have any purpose other than showing up the cops as less-than-perfect protectors of the social order. He eschews profanity in his diatribes against her interference in police affairs. "Oh, nuts, Vicki. Why can't you stay home and raise a family and just stay the heck out of this kind of mess?" is Mallory's response to Warshawski's crusade for equality before the law (*Deadlock*, p. 105). But when Bobby Mallory accuses her of being a

lesbian, based on allegations by Agnes' mother, he vents his fury: "When Tony was dying you were up at the University of Chicago screwing around like a pervert, weren't you?" (*Killing Orders*, p. 104). Reacting coolly, Warshawski recalls: "When our rap group followed the national trend and split between radical lesbians and, well, straights, she became a lesbian and I didn't. But we remained very good friends—an achievement for that era, when politics divided marriages and friends alike" (*Killing Orders*, p. 107). The definition of lesbianism as a political choice rather than a gender identity may seem reductive. But Warshawski makes her proclivities plain when she tells Agnes' sister Catherine that she and Agnes were never lovers. "And while I love many women dearly, I've never had women lovers" (*Killing Orders*, p. 169).

Bobby Mallory is the only person Warshawski allows to call her by her childhood nickname of Vicki. To her friends, she is Vic; to all others the initials "V. I." indicate a defense against sexist stereotypes. Although Mallory rarely acknowledges her contribution to solving a crime, at the end of *Burn Marks*, when he has been proven consistently wrong and Warshawski presciently correct, he finally has to admit his bias:

> I never could understand the way Tony and Gabriella brought you up, not making you mind the way my girls did.... But you're the daughter of the two people I loved best, next to Eileen, and you can't do things different than you do, shouldn't do them different, not with Gabriella and Tony bringing you up. Do you understand?
>
> (pp. 339–340)

V. I. Warshawski is a self-made woman, in the great tradition of American individualism. Yet, she is not a loner. Although she fights corruption without compromising, she is not too proud to call on the help of her friends. Raymond Chandler's Philip Marlowe spends his time between cases "alone, brooding with his bottle of rye, his chess board and his records" (*Silence*, p. 101). For her part, Warshawski is more likely to have dinner with Dr. Lotty Herschel.

A perinatal specialist at Beth Israel hospital, Lotty also runs her own storefront clinic for people who could not otherwise afford health care. A Jewish survivor of World War II, Lotty is approximately twenty years older than Warshawski. In *Total Recall*, Warshawski recalls how, as "an undergraduate at the University of Chicago," she began her friendship with Lotty:

> I was a blue-collar girl on an upscale campus, feeling rawly out of place when I met her—she was providing medical advice to an abortion underground where I volunteered. She took me under her wing, giving me the kind of social skills I'd lost when I lost my mother, keeping me from losing my way in those days of drugs and violent protest, taking time from a dense-packed schedule to cheer my successes and condole over failures. She'd even gone to some college basketball games to see me play—true friendship since sports of all kind bore her.
>
> (*Total Recall*, p. 135)

Almost every Warshawski novel includes a significant involvement with Lotty, who can be sharply critical, even furious, or worried sick about Warshawski's flouting of danger and protocol. Nevertheless, Warshawski turns instinctively to the older woman for advice: "I know myself better when I talk to Lotty" (*Killing Orders*, p. 67).

Another key ally is Mr. Contreras, a retired machinist living on the first floor of Warshawski's co-op (*Bitter Medicine*, p. 24). His favorite weapon in a ruckus turns out to be his pipe wrench. But, despite his bluster and overprotective hovering, pointedly confronting any younger man she brings home, Contreras saves Warshawski's life more than once. He also shares ownership of a golden retriever, Peppy, and her canine offspring, Mitch, born when a neighbor's black Labrador jumps over the fence. The four of them become a kind of unconventional extended family.

Other members of Warshawski's crew include Murray Ryerson, a crime reporter for the fictional *Herald-Star*, who appears in every Warshawski novel as a sometime lover, professional rival, and often useful journalistic ally to her investigations. Freeman Carter, her lawyer, must also be available, night or day, when Warshawski runs into the wrong end of the legal apparatus. In almost every book, she is guilty of illegal entry through misrepresentation, or straightforward breaking

and entering with her trusty set of picklocks. Over the years, she builds up a backlog of legal fees. In *Total Recall*, she is paying Freeman Carter monthly installments on her tab of $13,000. In *Body Work*, her "outstanding balance" is up to $60,000 and each phone call for legal advice "added a hundred dollars to my bill" (p. 74).

Gradually, Warshawski's network expands, adding Father Lou of St. Remegio's parish in Humboldt Park, a former boxer turned Catholic priest, with street smarts and a canny gift for tough love; Mary Louise Neely, who leaves the police force to work for Warshawski; V. I.'s terminally naive niece Petra (who follows a series of adolescent assistants in previous books); and others. Warshawski's favorite watering-hole, the Golden Glow, is a "tiny saloon dating back to the last century" owned by Sal Barthele, "a magnificent black woman, close to six feet tall" who rules the "mahogany horseshoe-shaped bar" with sovereign authority (*Indemnity Only*, p. 19). Warshawski describes the Golden Glow as "the closest place I have to a club" (*Bitter Medicine*, p. 174).

Warshawski and her friends hold out the possibility of authenticity within a phony world. But it may be overstated to claim that she belongs to a coherent inner-city community. Her friends often have little in common except their allegiance to her. Almost all are stubborn individualists like Warshawski herself. Dr. Herschel and Mr. Contreras are rarely in the same room, except in the hospital after Contreras is injured defending Lotty's clinic from fanatics. Warshawski's one upper-class client, Darraugh Graham, moves in an economic strata far removed from her cohort. Still, Warshawski has an advantage over Sam Spade and Philip Marlowe. She belongs to somebody other than herself.

At the end of *Tunnel Vision*, Warshawski's friends throw her a surprise fortieth birthday party. The date is July 27, 1992, "a blisteringly hot day" (p. 463). For once, Lotty Herschel and Mr. Contreras share the same space, along with Bobby Mallory and his wife, Eileen. Other guests include Sal Barthele "with her current love, a young actress"; Murray Ryerson, with a woman

he has met during the investigation; Darraugh Graham and his son; Mary Louise Neely; and other allies including her old basketball squad. Camilla Rawlings is there, but not her brother Conrad or any other of Warshawski's former lovers. Despite all the unresolved criminal networks continuing to operate both above and beneath the surface, the book ends on an upbeat if melancholy note. In a mood of bittersweet gratitude, Warshawski notes: "What else can I say, except that good friends are a balm for a bruised spirit?... And that champagne flowed like water, and we danced until the pale moon sank" (*Tunnel Vision*, p. 464).

WARSHAWSKI'S TRAGIC AWARENESS

If Warshawski were simply an idealist, she would be a less compelling protagonist. Not just a naive do-gooder, she bases her sense of self on the inherent despair of the human condition and a hard-wired reaction against allowing herself to be defined as a victim. Her street-fighting skills do not derive from any esoteric teachings of the martial arts. As she explains to Ralph Devereux, she went to a high school ruled by the law of the jungle: "If you couldn't swing a mean toe or fist, you might as well forget it" (*Indemnity Only*, p. 70).

In her memoir, *Writing in an Age of Silence*, Paretsky writes about meeting a young woman who could have been a prototype of her protagonist: "She liked to go into bars, get guys to buy her drinks, and beat them up if they asked for sexual favors in return. She had learned fighting in the toughest streets in the city. When I created my detective in 1982, I wanted her to be a street-fighter ... so it was natural to turn to South Chicago for her roots" (p. 43).

Although she does not flirt with young men in order to beat them up, Warshawski never backs down from a trial-by-battle, whether to stomp or be stomped. Not that she prefers physical combat to legal defense. But she would rather risk a beating than to accept defeat. Street-fighting is not merely a quirk of her character. It is who she is: a female warrior. In a letter to Lotty from the prison for women, where she has gone under-

ground as an inmate, she apologizes for the pain she causes those who love her. Yet, she disavows "masculine swagger" or devotion to "honor." Instead: "Something more restless drives me, a kind of terror that if I don't take care of things myself I will be left with a terrible helplessness" (*Hard Time*, pp. 404–405). As much as social justice means to her, individual empowerment is the fire that forces her forward.

In *Hard Time*, published in 1999, her stubborn idealism contrasts with women like Alex Fisher, the public relations flack for Global Media. Warshawski remembers Alex as Sandy Fishbein, a firebrand protestor at the University of Chicago when they were law students together. The irony of Warshawski still defending the downtrodden while Alex-Sandy has moved up to serving the rich and powerful is not lost on either woman. As mirror images of divergent career choices, they are rivals in values and begrudging allies in professional pursuit of self-actualization.

Her defiance in the face of vulnerability seems to have begun following the death of her parents. The work of grieving is, for Warshawski, an unending labor of the soul. Tony and Gabriella remain palpable influences on her, in poignant memories and sometimes terrifying dreams. Challenged by the murderous Renee Bayard in *Blacklist* (2003) to defend her own family values, Warshawski recalls her parents: "I thought of my mother's fierce love for me, and my father's more level affection; the price they demanded in return was not adoration, nor achievement, but integrity. I could not lie or cheat to avoid trouble" (p. 434). Her mother seems to haunt her continually, challenging her to resist mediocrity and moral corruption. Her father is, if anything, even closer to her heart. In *Hardball*, she dreams of a church burning in the midst of a snow blizzard and the priest preventing her father from saving it from the flames: "'Papa!' I tried to shout, but dreamlike, I had no voice. I sat up sweating and weeping. I'm a grown woman, and there are still nights when I need my father so badly that the pain of losing him cuts through and takes my breath away" (*Hardball*, p. 146).

In *Killing Orders*, Warshawski relates how, on her deathbed, Gabriella "made me promise to help Rosa if my aunt ever needed me. I had tried to argue with Gabriella: Rosa hated her, hated me—we had no obligation. But my mother insisted and I could not refuse" (p. 10). Warshawski has heard from her childhood how Rosa threw the eighteen-year-old Gabriella, "an immigrant with minimal English," out on the street. When Gabriella tried to earn a living by singing in bars on Milwaukee Avenue, Warshawski's police officer father fortuitously appeared in order to rescue her "from a group of men who were trying to force her to strip" (*Killing Orders*, p. 11). But the secret of why Gabriella felt obligated to Rosa remains a skeleton in the family closet until, in a final fit of madness and revenge, Rosa spews forth her version of events:

> Sweet Gabriella. Beautiful Gabriella. Talented Gabriella.... She came to me. I took her in from the goodness of my heart. How did she thank me? While I worked my fingers to the bone for her, she seduced my husband.... So I threw her into the street. Who would not have? I made her promise to disappear and leave no word. Yes, she had that much shame. And what did Carl do? He shot himself. Shot himself because of a whore from the streets.
>
> (*Killing Orders*, p. 330)

Even more disturbing is the doubt that her father may have been implicated in a police cover-up. She has always idealized him as an intelligent man who "never had a lot of ambition, certainly not enough to buck the prejudice against Polish cops in an all-Irish world" (*Killing Orders*, p. 102). It seems impossible that her honest cop image of Tony could be an illusion, yet she finds his name on the warrant for the arrest of a black gang member who is subsequently tortured into a confession for a crime he never committed. As the truth behind the case unravels, the horrors of the back room in a Chicago precinct station cross with the bonds of family loyalty. It turns out that Tony concealed evidence to protect his brother, Peter. At the same time, she discovers, thanks to Bobby Mallory, that her father wrote a letter of protest, contained in the file of the case. That formal protest did not stop the torture of suspects by Chicago cops, continuing into the nineties. But it may have prevented Tony from being considered for promotion. Still, she cannot accept her father's acquiescence to peer pressure, even

to save his own brother. After all the truth comes out, Bobby Mallory's wife, Eileen, consoles her: "Tony did the best he could under very painful circumstances. He spoke up. Do you know how much courage that took?" (p. 514).

In *Hard Time*, Warshawski compares herself to a female Don Quixote, tilting at giant windmills. At the conclusion of the Warshawski novels, the high-flying evildoers rarely pay as severe a price as she and the reader hope for. So, what *does* drive her to risk life and limb for what is almost always a qualified triumph in the name of social justice? The question of why the innocent suffer is posed in the Book of Job, which Warshawski begins to study, prompted by an invitation from Father Lou to read a lesson for Mass "about how God desires humans to see the light" (*Hard Time,* p. 446). Struggling to recover from her traumatic incarceration, Warshawski begins to attend St. Remegio's on a daily basis: "As I made my way through the biblical book of Job. I thought about the women at Coolis. If there was a God, had he delivered the women into the hands of Satan for a wager? And would he finally appear in the whirlwind and rescue them?" (*Hard Time*, p. 485).

Finally, perhaps, the only antidote to Warshawski's sense of despair is that she never gives up. In *Bitter Medicine* she compares herself with derisive irony to her mentor Lotty: "Sometimes when Lotty gets me angry I goad her by accusing her of thinking she can save the world.... I don't have such grand ideals as a detective. Not only do I not think I can save the world, I suspect most people are past redemption. I'm just the garbage collector" (*Bitter Medicine,* p. 225). Yet, even as she grows older and more resigned to her limitations, Warshawski raises the ante of her idealism. Refusing to surrender becomes an axiom—with a corollary sense of purpose that cannot be compromised by failure or disappointment. Again, Lotty Herschel conveys the message through a recollection of her Orthodox Jewish grandfather in the Vienna ghetto in the winter of 1938:

He gathered all his grandchildren together and told us that the rabbis say when you die and present yourself before the Divine Justice, you will be asked four questions: Were you fair and honest in your business dealings? Did you spend loving time with your family? Did you study Torah? And, last but most important, did you live in hope for the coming of the Messiah? We were living then without food, let alone hope, but he refused to live hopelessly....

(*Fire Sale*, p. 530)

Even an atheist, Lotty tells her, "must live in hope, the hope that your work can make a difference in the world.... If a Messiah ever does come, it will only be because of people like you, doing these small, hard jobs, making changes in this hard world" (p. 531).

CRUSADING IN AN AGE OF PARANOIA

Over a span of more than three decades, Sara Paretsky has continued to evolve. Building upon her generic plot structure, her later works involve complex narratives and deal with issues usually beyond the normal scope of detective fiction. In two non-Warshawski novels, each of them important in their own terms, Paretsky clarifies the underlying ideology that informs the author's point of view. In *Ghost Country* (1998), Paretsky brings together a disparate cast of characters in a Chicago not unlike Warshawski's, with an emphasis on a mystical heterodoxy, embodied in a preternatural figure representing the eternal feminine. In *Bleeding Kansas* (2008), the author extrapolates from the America of the Civil War era and reinterprets the conflict of the national soul in terms of the cultural wars of the present day. Using these excursions to explore her own ideas, the author returns, in each case, to V. I. Warshawski with a renewed sense of purpose. In her more recent works, it has been increasingly clear that the author is not satisfied with being limited to the conventions of a single genre. More than a crime writer, Paretsky has devoted herself to becoming a voice for the voiceless in the post-9/11 new millennium.

In *Total Recall*, published on the cusp of the 9/11 attacks, the author tackles the subconscious traces of the Nazi Holocaust. For those who have not experienced it themselves, Lotty Herschel notes, the suffering of the Jews during World War II is easy to "romanticize or kitschify or use

for titillation" (p. 83). In this novel, the reader learns how Lotty survived as a child born in Austria in the 1930s. The narrative is framed by Lotty's story, told in her own voice. The gradual self-revelation goes through layers of cover stories and authentic feelings. Weaving the nightmares of history with the individual retrieval of repressed memory, Rhea Weill appears as an alleged expert in recovering events buried in the subconscious. Her prize client, with a name connected to Lotty's past, claims that he has recalled from oblivion his childhood in a concentration camp. At the end, readers learn that Dr. Lotty Herschel, savior of pregnant mothers, herself had an unwanted pregnancy in the aftermath of World War II.

The central plot is a tale of two ghettos, one in Austria in 1939 and the other in the present day. The connection is made by Ulrich Hoffman, a model for the banality of evil. During the thirties, Hoffman sold burial policies to poor Jews. Four decades later, he sold similar policies to African Americans on the South Side of Chicago. Meanwhile, he has been cashing in on counterfeit death certificates for Jews who died during the war. But a forged death certificate for Aaron Sommers, a Jew in Austria, winds up in the file of Aaron Summers, an African American man in Chicago. When the Summers family is told that their uncle's insurance will not cover his funeral costs, they turn to Warshawski. That an international insurance company cheated a Jew and an African American with the same name seems plausible. But the morality tradition of good versus evil, in which Paretsky customarily works, could be more effective if her vice figures were more nuanced. The world of Chicago should also afford a place for more charismatic criminals than a phony European power-couple who shrink into two-dimensional stereotypes.

Evidently aware of this weakness, the author found a way to make her evil characters fascinating, even attractive, in *Blacklist*, published in 2003, with a gothic plot of secret sexual alliances mixed with the politics of relentless paranoia. The author was just beginning to work on this novel when the 9/11 terrorist attacks intervened. "For some weeks," she notes, "I was so frozen

with shock that I couldn't write at all" (*Silence*, p. 132). Attempting to escape from the facts of 2001 into a fictional version of the 1950s, the author found the web of history and her own imagination connecting the War on Terror with the Communist Menace.

Beginning with this novel, the sense of American society losing its grip on reality becomes Paretsky's central focus. When the FBI agent Derek Hatfield accuses Warshawski of treating the attacks on the Twin Towers in New York City and the subsequent U.S. military incursions in Afghanistan and Iraq as a joke, she replies:

> I think this is the most serious thing that has happened in my lifetime. Not just the Trade Center, but the fear we've unleashed on ourselves since, so we can say that the Bill of Rights doesn't matter anymore. My lover is in Afghanistan. I don't know if he's dead or alive.... If he's dead, my heart will break, but if the Bill of Rights is dead my life, my faith in America, will break.
>
> (*Blacklist*, p. 275)

In *Hardball*, published in 2009, Warshawski ponders the price she must pay for her independence. The parting of ways between her and Morrell invokes a fear that she will never be able to maintain a long-term romantic relationship. On a deeper level, she questions her own effect on those who love her most. "Did I bring destruction to everyone around me?" (p. 270). The title refers to a symbolic Major League baseball autographed by the Hall of Fame second baseman Nelson ("Nellie") Fox. Linking fictional crimes to historical facts, the plot moves through an extended narrative flashback into a profound investigation of past traumas that still haunt Chicago. Returning to her own first impressions of the city, Paretsky focuses on the 1966 riot in Marquette Park as a Rorschach test for the collective psyche of Chicago.

In *Body Work*, published in 2010, the author diagnoses the symptoms of the Age of Paranoia: "You know people can trace you, given the resources, but you don't know if they are actually doing so" (p. 451). The title has multiple levels of meaning. On the most basic level it refers to "the Body Artist," a performer featured

at the Club Gouge, "the hippest scene on the strip" (p. 10) of abandoned warehouses under the Lake Street El. This mystery lady emerges from a staged blackout perched on a stool like a mannequin, "naked except for an electron-sized thong" (p. 11). The raucous and raunchy bar crowd become participants as she challenges the audience to step up and paint images of their own creation on her bare flesh. As an anonymous woman without identifying characteristics or personal history, she represents a detached alter ego in contrast to the compassion and commitment of V. I. Warshawski. Her view of "art" is a distorted reflection or, perhaps, a rebuttal of Paretsky's challenge to the individual social conscience: "Art is in the hands of the maker. It's in the eyes of the beholder." At ease with herself, the Body Artist dares members of the audience to confront their own repressed fantasies: "Draw your heart's desire on my body" (p. 13). On another level, the title refers to the defective body armor that a local company has been supplying to American troops in Iraq. A third strand of significance connects to the body work of a Ukrainian gangster named Anton Kystarnik, who uses the bare buttocks of the Body Artist as a message board for his money-laundering operations. Far from running out of fresh material, the writer seems driven to create an epic tale of unlimited degradation with only partial hope of redemption in the end. Finally, Warshawski must impersonate the Body Artist to unmask the evil done in the name of family and country.

In *Breakdown*, published in 2012, corruption has spread like a disease in the body politic. Noticing how Murray Ryerson's freckles and blue eyes contrast with the gray streaks in his red hair, Warshawski muses: "So much time had passed since he and I worked on our first story together.... We not only hadn't cleaned up the city. We hadn't even made a dent. Instead, fraud had spread along every corridor of American life" (*Breakdown*, pp. 193–194). Evil forces in this novel have taken on monstrous proportions, embodied in a self-promoting television personality who thrives on smearing the reputations of others in the name of an ideology of hate. The title refers to Warshawski's brilliant but unstable friend who

uncovers clues to crimes of the past in the mental hospital where she is confined. Incorporating both teenage girls in a vampire-book reading group and the untold horrors of a Holocaust survivor who has become one of the richest men in the world, the thrust of the novel is to indict a contemporary culture based on fear and lies.

In her 2013 novel, *Critical Mass*, the author proves that she has lost none of her verve and even extends the range of her subject matter to include the research and development of the first atomic bomb. Paretsky adapts the history of the Austrian physicist Marietta Blau, a female scientist who "did groundbreaking research in cosmic ray physics in the 1930s" (*Critical Mass* p. 463). Warshwaski is still charging a standard rate of "a hundred dollars an hour" (p. 39). Her Mustang has "rolled over the hundred-thousand-mile marker" (p. 109). The plot is purely fictional, but the author deftly continues her championing of feminist issues past and present, and develops her concern about the expanding role of Homeland Security in threatening the privacy of American citizens in the here-and-now.

Named by her mother for King Victor Emanuel of Italy and the heroine of the opera in which Gabriella once performed, Victoria Iphigenia Warshawski maintains her dignity and devotion to the pursuit of justice. Her anger at the status quo continues undiminished. Being interrogated by the Chicago cops, the FBI, and Homeland Security does not faze her. When their questions make her realize that a meeting she had with an activist nun was taped, Warshawski is not surprised. But one of the local detectives demands to know why that particular room was being bugged, only to be told: "National security... I can't say more." Warshawski picks up the theme: "'Beautiful umbrella,' I murmured. 'From now on, whenever I do anything particularly embarrassing, I'll just cry "National security!" and refuse to say anything else' " (*Hardball*, p. 301).

Like V. I. Warshawski, the author is ready to challenge the legal power structure in the name of her own conscience and for the sake of humanity. In her work, she tips her hat to the influence of Nelson Algren (*Body Work*, p. 198). She also notes, wryly, that Warshawski was a pen

name of Isaac Bashevis Singer "when he wrote for the *Daily Forward* in the thirties" (*Hardball*, p. 107). Throughout her texts, she drops allusions to predecessors and contemporaries in the detective genre. But, clearly, she has created her own perspective, in terms of both style and substance. The mission of her writing, and of her principle protagonist, is to speak out "against those forces which seek to silence us, to rob us of our voices and our precious freedoms" (*Silence*, p. 138).

That is her story. And Sara Paretsky is sticking to it.

Selected Bibliography

WORKS OF SARA PARETSKY

NOVELS

Indemnity Only. New York: Dial, 1982. New York: Ballantine, 1983.

Deadlock. New York: Dial, 1984. New York: Ballantine, 1992.

Killing Orders. New York: Morrow, 1985. New York: Dell, 1993.

Bitter Medicine. New York: Morrow, 1987; New York: Ballantine, 1988.

Blood Shot. New York: Delacorte, 1988. New York: Dell, 1989.

Burn Marks. New York: Delacorte, 1990. New York: Dell, 1991.

Guardian Angel. New York: Delacorte, 1992. New York: Dell, 1993.

Tunnel Vision. New York: Delacorte, 1994. New York: Dell, 1995.

Ghost Country. New York: Delacorte, 1998. New York: Dell, 1999.

Hard Time. New York: Delacorte, 1999. New York: Dell, 2000.

Total Recall. New York: Delacorte, 2001. New York: Dell, 2002.

V. I. Times Two: Photo Finish and *Publicity Stunts.* Chicago: Women and Children, 2002.

Blacklist. New York: Putnam, 2003. New York: Signet, 2004.

Fire Sale. New York: Putnam, 2005. New York: Signet, 2006.

Bleeding Kansas. New York: Putnam, 2008. New York: Signet, 2008.

Hardball. New York: Putnam, 2009. New York: Signet, 2010.

Body Work. New York: Putnam, 2010. New York: Signet, 2011.

Breakdown. New York: Putnam, 2012. New York: Signet, 2012.

Critical Mass. New York: Putnam, 2013.

OTHER WORKS

Windy City Blues: V. I. Warshawski Stories. New York: Delacorte, 1995. New York: Dell, 1996.

Writing in an Age of Silence. New York: Verso, 2007, 2009. (Memoir.)

AS EDITOR

Beastly Tales: The Mystery Writers of America Anthology. New York: Wynwood Press, 1989.

A Woman's Eye. New York: Delacorte, 1991. (Collection of mystery stories.)

Women on the Case: Twenty-Six Original Stories by the Best Women Crime Writers of Our Time. New York: Delacorte, 1996.

Sisters on the Case: Celebrating Twenty Years of Sisters in Crime. New York: New American Library, 2007.

PAPERS

Sara Paretsky Papers, 1966–1993. Newberry Library, Chicago, Illinois.

CRITICAL AND BIOGRAPHICAL STUDIES

Bakerman, Jane S. "Living 'Openly and with Dignity': Sara Paretsky's New-Boiled Feminist Fiction." In *MidAmerica XII: The Yearbook of the Society for the Study of Midwestern Literature.* Edited by David D. Anderson. East Lansing, Mich.: Midwestern Press, 1985. Pp. 120–135.

Décuré, Nicole. "From Chicago to Hollywood: The Metamorphosis of V. I. Warshawski." In *Crime Fictions: Subverted Codes and New Structures.* Edited by François Gallix and Vanessa Guignery. Paris: PU de Paris-Sorbonne, 2004. Pp. 177–183.

Dempsey, Peter. "Sara Paretsky." In *American Mystery and Detective Writers.* Edited by George Parker Anderson. *Dictionary of Literary Biography.* Vol. 306. Detroit: Gale, 2005. Pp. 306–320.

Goodkin, Richard E. "Killing Order(s): Iphigenia and the Detection of Tragic Intertextuality." *Yale French Studies*, no. 76:81–10 (1989).

Jansson, Siv. "The Difference of Viewing: Female Detectives in Fiction and on Film." In *Sisterhoods: Across the Literature/Media Divide.* Edited by Deborah Cartmell, I. Q. Hunter, Heidi Kaye, and Imelda Whelehan. London:

Pluto, 1998. Pp. 149–166.

Jones, Manina. "Shot/Reverse Shot: Dis-Solving the Feminist Detective Story in Kanew's Film *V. I. Warshawski.*" *Diversity and Detective Fiction.* Edited by Kathleen Gregory Klein. Bowling Green, Ohio: Bowling Green State Popular University Press, 1999. Pp. 22–37.

Kinsman, Margaret. "Sara Paretsky." *Mystery and Suspense Writers: The Literature of Crime, Detection, and Espionage, I–II.* Edited by Robin W. Winks and Maureen Corrigan. New York: Scribners, 1998. Pp. 699–713.

Klein, Kathleen Gregory. "Watching Warshawski." In *It's a Print! Detective Fiction from Page to Screen.* Edited by William Reynolds and Elizabeth Trembley. Bowling Green, Ohio: Bowling Green State University Popular Press, 1994. Pp. 145–156.

Paradis, Kenneth. "Warshawski's Situation: Beauvoirean Feminism and the Hard-Boiled Detective." *South Central Review* 18, nos. 3–4:86–101 (fall–winter 2001).

Pepper, Andrew. "Policing the Globe: State Sovereignty and the International in the Post-9/11 Crime Novel." *MFS: Modern Fiction Studies* 57, no. 3:401–424 (fall 2011).

Pope, Rebecca A. "'Friends Is a Weak Word for It': Female Friendship and the Spectre of Lesbianism in Sara Paretsky." In *Feminism in Women's Detective Fiction.* Edited by Glenwood Irons. Toronto: University of Toronto Press, 1995. Pp. 156–169.

Shuker-Haines, Timothy, and Martha M. Umphrey. "Gender (De)Mystified: Resistance and Recuperation in Hard-Boiled Female Detective Fiction." In *The Detective in American Fiction, Film, and Television.* Edited by Jerome H. Delamater and Ruth Prigozy. Westport, Conn.: Greenwood, 1998. Pp. 71–82.

Six, Beverly G. "Breaking the Silence: Sara Paretsky's Seizure of Ideology and Discourse in Blacklist." *South Central Review* 27, nos. 1–2:144–158 (spring–summer 2010).

Szuberla, Guy. "Paretsky, Turow, and the Importance of Symbolic Ethnicity." In *MidAmerica XVIII: The Yearbook of the Society for the Study of Midwestern Literature.* Edited by David D. Anderson. East Lansing, Mich.: Midwestern Press, 1991. Pp. 124–135.

———. "The Ties That Bind: V. I. Warshawski and the Burdens of Family." In *Armchair Detective: A Quarterly Journal Devoted to the Appreciation of Mystery, Detective, and Suspense Fiction* 27, no. 2:146–153 (spring 1994).

Walton, Priscilla L. "Paretsky's V. I. as P.I.: Revising the Script and Recasting the Dick." *Lit: Literature Interpretation Theory* 4, no. 3:203–213 (1993).

Wells, Linda S. "Popular Literature and Postmodernism: Sara Paretsky's Hard-Boiled Feminist." *Proteus* 6, no. 1:51–56 (spring 1989).

FILM AND MULTIMEDIA BASED ON THE WORK OF SARA PARETSKY

V. I. Warshawski. Film with screenplay by Edward Taylor, David Aaron Cohen, and Nick Thiel. Directed by Jeff Kanew. With Kathleen Turner as V. I. Warshawski. Hollywood Pictures/Chestnut Hill Productions, 1991. (Adaptation of *Indemnity Only* and *Deadlock.*)

"V. I. Warshawski's Chicago." *Community Walk.* http://www.communitywalk.com/vi_warshawskis_chicago 2008. (Interactive map with landmarks from the texts.)

MARY ROBERTS RINEHART

(1876—1958)

Windy Counsell Petrie

WHEN MARY ROBERTS Rinehart published her first mystery novel, *The Circular Staircase* (1908), a book hailed by critics for its newness of technique, she surely could not have foreseen all that would lie between that book and the positive reviews of her final full-length novel, *The Swimming Pool* (1952), written just six years before her death. After writing the first mystery ever to become a best seller in the United States, she would go on to publish more than a dozen additional mysteries, as well as sentimental romances, adventure novels, comic sketches, travel narratives, plays, works of serious fiction, and more than a hundred short stories, interspersed with articles encompassing everything from household tips to political, economic, and intellectual commentary. In addition to her voluminous literary output, Mary Roberts Rinehart worked as a trained nurse, raised three sons, reported from the Belgian and French fronts in World War I, met royalty and dignitaries from around the world, explored the national park system on horseback, became a member of the Native American Blackfoot tribe, volunteered as a World War II air-raid warden while in her mid-sixties, and became the first American woman to bring breast cancer into the national spotlight. The fullness of her life and the enduring appeal of her work made her an American celebrity for almost fifty years, the American equivalent of Britain's Dame Agatha Christie. Amid the chaos of the first half of the twentieth century, Rinehart's unflagging work ethic, deep concern for injustice, instinctual need to find and present a balanced perspective on life, and marvelous ability to laugh at her own foibles all contributed to a long career that was not a whit less exciting than her most suspenseful fictions.

CHILDHOOD AMBITIONS

Mary Roberts was born on August 12, 1876, in Allegheny City, Pennsylvania (now part of Pittsburgh), and as a little girl lived in her grandmother's house with not only her parents but her uncle and his wife and aunts. The neighborhood was a fascinating place for a little girl with a big imagination, and its eclectic mixture of people and businesses would populate her imagination for decades to come. For one thing, there were the seasonal floods that were a fact of life there. Years later, Rinehart recalled her father rowing them to his office one day during flood season. The boat trip was a treat, but she also recalled seeing the death and devastation the waters brought to the families who were already on the edge of poverty in the neighboring areas. For an inquisitive mind, scenes like these created a deep sense of tragedy, and she witnessed acts of both selfishness and kindness. She heard stories of piracy; if a neighbor's belongings floated into your home, or yours into the neighbor's, then nature had redistributed the wealth, and that was all there was to it. But Mary also saw the little man who rowed about feeding and rescuing stranded pets. There were many other interesting people in her neighborhood: the "deaf and dumb" insurance salesman who carried on jovial conversations with everyone on an endless supply of notepaper; the woman without a husband—but with a child—whom her mother avoided; the butcher's wife who wasn't in the shop one morning because her stepdaughter had hacked her to death with an ax the night before; and, most of all, the lady doctor who rented a house and hung her own shingle in front. All of these folk would live again in various guises in Rinehart's fictional oeuvre in the years to come.

It was the lady doctor in whose footsteps young Mary decided she wanted to follow, once she realized that her mother probably would not approve of her going on the stage (although she remained fascinated by drama her whole life, and as a result saw some success—and some failures—as a playwright in future years). Cornelia Roberts was an unstinting perfectionist as a housekeeper, an excellent needlewoman, and a mother with primarily social ambitions for her two daughters, Mary and Olive. It was Cornelia who insisted that the family move to their own little brick house and reupholstered the family's heirloom rosewood parlor set to create a bright new living room, Cornelia who fashioned a chic little cycling outfit for Mary when the bicycle came to town, Cornelia who made sure the silver was heated before dinner on cold days, even when she no longer had servants to perform the task.

Cornelia Roberts also taught her daughter to politely deny her to the bill collectors who came because Mary's father, Tom Roberts, was an inventor with big dreams and very little practical capacity for making them come true. In an era rife with inventors and inventions, Tom Roberts had numerous ideas in the same vein as many other hopeful inventors, but he had one idea—a rotary bobbin for sewing machines, which he sold for a living—that was a winner and did eventually become the industry standard. Unfortunately, he turned down a ten-thousand-dollar offer for his patent, which was a huge sum for its time, and then, lacking the money to renew it, lost the patent that eventually made other people rich. Thus, when Mary was a teenager, she had already learned of both the potential and the difficulties of earning money by selling one's ideas; she may have also concluded that a chance to succeed, once lost, might never come again, which would help explain the pace at which she later wrote and sold her fiction. At that time, the growing magazine culture of the 1880s and 1890s, documented so well in the work of Ellen Gruber Garvey, was already known as a source for work females could do from their own homes, and through it Mary was able to earn one dollar per poem to help the family.

Despite this experience, Mary Roberts did not consider writing as a possible career, even though she had realized by the middle of high school that her dreams of going to college and becoming a doctor were not financially possible. Instead, she opted for a more cost-effective career option: becoming a nurse. At that time, one studied nursing by becoming a probationer in a hospital, learning nursing through a sort of baptism of fire, assisting at all shifts, alternating between day and night in the wards, the operating room, and the morgue. The small wages of the probationer's labor would largely be spent on the elaborate uniforms required for the work, but room and board were provided, so it would cost her family nothing. Cornelia was horrified by her daughter's desire to pursue work in which she would be exposed to things most Victorian women would not know of until after marriage, if they ever knew of them at all. But seventeen-year-old Mary wanted self-sufficiency: she had no thought then of service to humanity, a concept that became sacred to her through the process, after she had been on the wards for months watching the older, more experienced nurses.

So Mary marched down to her family doctor's office to ask for a reference and an introduction to the local hospital. The younger brother of her family doctor, who was also a doctor and was handling his brother's practice that day, smiled amusedly at the frilled, filmy white dress of the delicate teenager in front of him, but he took her on a tour of the hospital anyway. Perhaps he did so just to scare her back into her senses. Dr. Stanley Rinehart could not have foreseen that the mental and physical toughness of this girl (who had just lied to him about her age) would allow her to survive and succeed despite the shocks, traumas, and exhaustion of hospital work, any more than he could have foreseen that in a couple of years he would find himself shouting at the hospital's board of trustees that he was going to marry her despite its nonfraternization policy.

After weeks of backbreaking, grueling, and often grisly work in the hospital, Mary Roberts had proven the skeptics wrong. When they gave her a bucket to carry her first day in the operat-

ing room and she looked down to find a foot in it, she kept walking. When she cleaned thirty-plus knife wounds on the face, torso, and arms of a prostitute, she learned something about human frailties. When she saw an intern slice off his own skin to graft onto a burn victim, she learned something about human nobility. Decades later in her autobiography (1931), she recalled these memories as formative moments that refined her beliefs about good and evil, and about "the injustices and the kindnesses and the violence" of life (*My Story,* p. 64). During that time, she also learned to "resent ... death by violence ... with a bitterness it is hard to put into words" (p. 67). Perhaps these experiences were the seeds of her work as a writer of crime stories, where the truth is always discovered and the guilty always punished (although not necessarily in conventional ways). In her fictions, she may have been righting the injustices she could not heal as a nurse.

ESCAPE FICTIONS

Though she had learned to endure the fatigue of sitting with a dying child for days without sleep, to manage her anger at witnessing the slow death of a woman shunned by her neighbors and attended only by the illegitimate daughter who was the cause of her shunning, and to laugh at the momentary terror of having a recently deceased body fling her backward onto the floor when the onset of rigor mortis caused it to fall off of its bed, Mary Roberts was not destined for a career in nursing after all. Once she was engaged to Stanley Rinehart, she was seemingly headed for the role her mother had always envisioned for her: respectable matron. The Rineharts were an influential, well-known family in Pittsburgh, full of successful businessmen, politicians, and doctors, and it was considered a very good match indeed. Tom Roberts' successful brother, Mary's Uncle John, was to buy her a wedding dress fit for the society girls whom she knew but whose lavish hospitality she could never return (and whose parties she had stopped attending when she realized that, for a nurse probationer, a night of sleep was worth more than a soiree). As the

wedding plans proceeded, however, tragedy intervened: Tom Roberts, who had been fired from his job as a traveling salesman, committed suicide, shooting himself in a Boston hotel room with a gun his family did not know he had. The newspaper coverage of her father's death would cause a note of bitterness whenever Mary wrote of the popular press in years to come. But life had to go on, and on April 21, 1896, Mary and Stanley were successfully wed. After a honeymoon of Stanley's planning in Bermuda (the bride previously had not even known where or what Bermuda was), the couple settled down to build a married life and a family and Stanley's private practice.

These were all good things, important things to the new Mrs. Rinehart, but they came with their own difficulties, and her autobiography indicates that the early years of her marriage taught her that every gift life can give brings with it its own demand for compromise. Helping to build Stanley's career as a doctor required much additional responsibility beyond housekeeping, such as bookkeeping and not a little unpaid nursing, and also meant that the two could never plan an evening together, for in those days general practitioners made house calls at all hours of the day and night. She had three sons in five years and was determined that they would have neither nurse nor governess, which meant that her shift as a mother did not end, either when they were sick or when they were well. She took pride in her home and sought to uphold her mother's stringent standards of housekeeping by making her own jams, jellies, curtains, and clothes, which, when added to her roles as her husband's assistant and her children's mother, left her little leisure. And life was expensive. Like her mother before her, Mary Roberts Rinehart had more debts than she could pay. Forced to stay in bed after she had caught diphtheria nursing her youngest son, she turned again to writing for the magazines, this time earning twenty-two dollars for poems written during her convalescence in 1903. After that, her creativity became a consistent source of extra money. Though her other responsibilities did not allow her the time for a writing "routine," she earned

one hundred dollars in 1904 by selling poems, short stories, and housekeeping articles. At the time, she recalled, she wrote to "escape" from the pressures of life, from the memories of hospital horrors, from fears that her children would succumb to childhood diseases or to the curse of violence she felt was on her family. (Not only had her father committed suicide, but her grandmother had died suddenly by falling down stairs, an aunt had been permanently injured by a collapsing balcony, and her little niece would die suddenly from drinking a household poison.) In times of worry, she "turned to [writing] romance, to crime, to farce … to anything but reality" (*My Story,* p. 90). And as she wrote, she also escaped from debt. Looking back, Rinehart estimated that in her first year as a real writer she made $1,842 from sheer "hard work," completing an astounding forty-five short stories (*My Story,* p. 86).

Her biographers Charlotte MacLeod and Jan Cohn, along with the critics Martha Dubose and Catherine Nickerson, wonder if Rinehart's continual insistence that her family was her top priority, that her writing was solely a means to earn for the household, was simply a sop to the domestic ideologies of the time. But it cannot be denied that she used the money to keep building the family's future, to send the children to school, to pay the butcher bill, to buy a bigger house. These economic bonuses also bought her more time and leisure to write: they paid for servants to help around the house and no doubt partially paid for the summer the family spent at a rented country house in 1907—a highly significant summer, during which Rinehart wrote the two early novels that would make her famous, *The Circular Staircase* and *The Man in Lower Ten.* She wrote these longer pieces in order to serialize them in magazines, which would earn more money than her short fiction, and indeed, *The Circular Staircase* earned her five hundred dollars for its serial publication in *All-Story* magazine. But she also sent the *Circular Staircase* manuscript to Hewitt Howland, an editor for the book publisher Bobbs-Merrill, who immediately decided to publish it along with the two other novels she had completed thus far. Howland brought them out strategically, one per year. *The Circular Stair-*

case, which he judged to be the best, came first in 1908, then in 1909 the entertaining and complex *The Man in Lower Ten* (first published serially in 1906) to solidify Rinehart's reputation, and in 1910 *The Window at the White Cat* (first serialized in 1908), which took its plot from the rampant political corruption of the era. All three books exhibit what would become the Rinehart formula: the world can be an ugly place, with liars and cheaters and violence everywhere, but when a person of integrity, however weak or imperfect they might be, comes in contact with corruption, he or she can, with perseverance, track it down and expose the truth. In the first book, a middle-aged lady, whose curiosity just barely triumphs over her desire for creature comforts, untangles the web woven by a corrupt bank president, and in the other two books, young male lawyers are injured—mostly in their pride—not just for the sake of law and order but because young women to whom they are attracted have been innocently implicated in legal and political scandal. Rinehart's fictional mix of light humor and the serious pursuit of truth made the books all the more palatable to a reading public accustomed to getting only one or the other in their literature, and all three novels were more successful than Rinehart or Bobbs-Merrill could have hoped.

A PROFESSION AND A PROBLEM

After she had become not only a best-selling novelist but had also been hailed for originating the "new technique" of adding comic relief to a crime story, Rinehart remarked, "I [now] found myself with a profession; a profession and a problem" (*My Story,* p. 111). The problem lay in the conventional wisdom that an artist "must be free," and Rinehart was not and did not wish to be: her confidence was in compromise and balance between her work and her family (p. 111). In fact, decades later, invited to a panel interview on marriage and the professional woman, Rinehart referred to family and domestic responsibilities as "chains," declaring that "I wouldn't give up my chains for anything in the world, but I would never fail to recognize that they are

chains" (quoted in Cohn, p. 201). In her autobiography and in numerous interviews, she explained that she would write all day while her family was at work or school but that the writing ceased as soon as the front door slammed every afternoon. This is not to say that all the household and child-care responsibilities devolved upon her. Dr. Rinehart was a devoted and active father and husband, and one of Mary's most vivid memories of her early marriage in her autobiography is of Stanley heating milk over a burner in the nursery with one hand and holding their youngest son in the other. When a gossipy newspaper article was published in Pittsburgh suggesting that her husband's crippling arthritis was a convenient fiction, invented as an excuse for him to live off his now-famous wife, Rinehart learned that there was indeed more than one problem that had come with her profession. Although, in articles and interviews, she always claimed to have become the family breadwinner "by accident" (Freier, p. 129), her biographers point out that there was a prolonged tension about money—about who earned it, and who decided how to spend it—in her marriage from that time forward. Though her autobiography acknowledges that there were long-standing marital difficulties and tensions stemming from her celebrity, she continued to pursue compromise. If the balance failed, then she claimed, "I would forfeit every particle of success that has come to me rather than lose any part, even the smallest, of my family life" (Overton, p. 55).

The couple decided that Dr. Rinehart would take a specialty course in Europe that would allow him to continue to practice medicine in a way that would spare his arthritic hands. It was to be a family venture, so the Rineharts all moved to Vienna, where Dr. Rinehart pursued his specialty in tuberculosis. During their time abroad, the boys enjoyed drinking the daily Viennese hot chocolate and teasing their German governess, while their mother gathered material for *The Street of Seven Stars* (1914). The book was a change for Rinehart: the story is a sentimental romance in which a pair of young lovers—she living in Vienna to study violin, he to take a medical specialization—are thwarted by

both the corruption of Viennese society and the prejudices of American conventionality but come together in the end. The trip also resulted in the novel *Where There's a Will* (1912), a comedy with a little romance and suspense thrown in, which is set at an American health sanatorium but inspired by an entanglement Rinehart watched develop at a popular spa in Europe. In the book, a society girl and a female servant work together to save a family business and to discover what sort of man makes a good husband.

Upon the family's return to America in the spring of 1911, both Dr. and Mrs. Rinehart were celebrities: he was put in charge of the Pennsylvania tuberculosis dispensary, and they purchased a large home in the posh Sewickley area outside Pittsburgh. This home had a large and lovely study in which Mary could write her books, which was very important since the house was extremely expensive and the renovations cost much more than they had imagined. Once again, Rinehart drove herself at quite a pace to pay for the beautiful place, the stuff of her mother's dreams, a dream Mary shared and was determined to realize for herself. The house, in fact, was such an endeavor that Dr. Rinehart nicknamed it "The Bluff," since, in his opinion, bluffing was what they were doing by owning such a place (MacLeod, pp. 156–157). Rinehart overworked herself for two years, including writing the best seller *The Case of Jennie Brice* (1913), a mystery set in and based upon the floods in less desirable neighborhoods of her childhood, and *The After House* (1914), a reenactment of a murder on a private yacht that Rinehart had read about in the papers. Following the trial for this murder, she had privately determined that the convicted man in the case was innocent and wrote the novel as an alternative scenario to the one that had sent him to prison. Later, it was determined that her theory was correct, and the wrongly imprisoned man was released. She also published *K* (1915), a serious novel that her husband considered her best work, and one that also reflects and explores many of the characters and themes of her youth. The story follows a young nurse trainee's coming-of-age, exploring the interconnectedness of people from all walks of life, the intimate world

of the American hospital at the turn of the century, and the far-reaching effects of human selfishness and prejudice.

As time went on, and her profession grew into a much bigger and more serious part of her life, Rinehart began to need an office outside the house, free from interruptions. Her mother was living with them by then, recovering from a stroke that had permanently disabled her speech, and she had a habit of quietly appearing behind her daughter in her home study to tell her something, which often resulted in hours of guessing what her frustrated mother wanted. Although Rinehart was a dutiful daughter who agonized over trying to help her mother recover, and who painstakingly investigated ways to help her mother comfortably fill her days, she felt that she could not afford to be startled out of her concentration and thus lose entire workdays in this way. Dr. Rinehart suggested that his wife could work in his offices, offering her a black-painted room he had been planning to use for an X-ray machine. She took him up on the offer, but eventually the tiny office in Stanley's practice was abandoned for her own office elsewhere downtown, which later included a secretary.

During this period, a family camping trip to Canada inspired one of her funniest stories about "Tish," the heroine of a comic series that Rinehart began publishing in the *Saturday Evening Post* in 1910. Tish, an indomitable middle-aged New England spinster, and her faithful (and sarcastic) companions, Lizzie and Aggie, were often found in the *Post* roughing it, camping, or taking walking and riding tours in the same wilderness areas in which the Rineharts camped. When, on one such trip, Mary had to sit naked in cold water in a bathing cove for hours waiting for a strange young man fishing in a rowboat to go away, Aggie suffered the same fate in "Tish's Spy." The Tish stories would periodically be collected into anthologies, and the five collections, *The Amazing Adventures of Leticia Carberry* (1911), *Tish* (1916), *More Tish* (1921), *Tish Plays the Game* (1926), and *Tish Marches On* (1937) are among the Rinehart works still being reprinted today.

AMAZING INTERLUDES

In 1914, World War I brought dramatic changes to the Rinehart family, as it did for many around the globe. Rinehart was hired by the *Post* to go to the Belgian front to report on atrocities there, and when her sixteen-year-old eldest son wired from his boarding school demanding that he be allowed to escort her, she may have known that in a couple of years he would enlist, and that she would be demanding to go to France to watch over him, as Tish does for her nephew in "My Country Tish of Thee" and "Salvage." In reality, both requests were denied. Rinehart's adventures getting to the front were every bit as extraordinary as what her character Sara Lee Kennedy goes through in *The Amazing Interlude* (1918), which fictionalizes Mary's successful stowaway crossing to Calais, where war reporters were not allowed at the time; her meeting with the king of Belgium; and both the horrors of the front lines and the kindnesses she saw in the makeshift soup kitchens and hospitals. She and her biographers have all noted that the ships upon which she crossed both ways were torpedoed and sunk later in the war. The dangers were real throughout her journey, but she sublimated her fear to her purpose for the trip, just as she had sublimated her horror at some of her hospital experiences to perform her work as a nurse.

Safely back home, depressed by America's inaction and by the war profiteering she saw going on in Pittsburgh, Rinehart jumped at the chance to go on a horseback trip through Glacier National Park, part of the new National Parks System. The entrepreneur and rancher Howard Eaton wanted her to go on the expedition for publicity, as he had also started what would become a hugely successful dude ranch in Wyoming (one where the Rineharts would have a vacation cabin for many years after). On that trip, riding all day and tenting at night, Rinehart was introduced to local Blackfoot Indians, was accorded the honor of becoming a member of the tribe, and pledged to fight for better treatment of Native Americans. She kept her promise: after the expedition was finished she headed straight to the office of the U.S. secretary of the interior to demand change on their behalf. She then wrote

Through Glacier Park in 1915 (1916), one of several travel books she would eventually produce, including *Tenting Tonight* (1918) and *Nomad's Land* (1926), covering her 1925 trip to Egypt, adding travel and nature writing to her growing repertoire, which by now included suspense, crime, comedy, romance, adventure, war reporting, and serious literary fiction. She also wrote *Dangerous Days* (1919), a work of romantic suspense, during this anxious period, for by 1918 not only was her eldest son in France, but her husband was serving at an army training camp, her middle son had enlisted in the U.S. Marine Corps, and her youngest had joined the National Guard. At that point she found a way to get to France, to report for the U.S. secretary of war's office, and found herself in Paris on the day of the Armistice—though it was no armistice to her, she recalled later, until she found her son alive. Once she knew he was safe, she did her job of visiting battlegrounds and graveyards and touring devastated Germany.

EMINENT AUTHOR

Upon her return to America, Rinehart was so well known that she was offered the editorship of the *Ladies' Home Journal*, a position she turned down despite its opportunities to influence American life and thought, because it would not have left her enough time for the other things she wanted to do. She did, however, join Samuel Goldwyn's "eminent authors" project in 1919, and was horribly disappointed to find it was all a "publicity feature for the studio" (*My Story,* p. 295). The studio wanted to film her being met by a baby blimp (a tiny one-man dirigible) and to pay her a large salary, but they did not want her to generate screenplays. Unable to get any writing done for Goldwyn, Rinehart instead wrote another hilarious Tish story featuring a blustering movie producer, a teenaged elephant, and a baby blimp. She also published a two-mystery volume in 1921, *Sight Unseen and The Confession,* which explores the dark secrets underlying civilized communities. In the first story, a neighborhood is disrupted by inexplicable violence and, as every move anyone makes becomes suspicious, they

question whether what is acting among them is even human, only to find that the causes of these events lie in a secret past the protagonist's sister will do anything to keep hidden. In the second book, one spinster discovers the truth about a murder another one has committed, but protects the dying woman from the public consequences of her crime. A number of silent films were made of her works over those years as well, but Rinehart was never very happy with the changes that occurred between the page and the screen. She was especially irked when the film of *K* (1915) was retitled *The Doctor and the Woman,* commenting that she wished she had Edith Wharton's ability to maintain creative control of her titles.

For Rinehart, the greatest success of these "eminent" years was that she had finally written a successful play, *The Bat* (1920), with the well-known playwright Avery Hopwood, who had been her collaborator off and on for years. In the play, entirely set in an elegant country house, an elderly spinster pits her wits against a legendary master criminal, and with the help of her maid, the Japanese butler, and her young niece, she exposes his identity and crimes. Still balancing her profession and her family, Rinehart had rushed off to the hospital the moment the last word of *The Bat* was on the page to attend the birth of her first granddaughter, who was christened for the Rinehart short-story character "Bab, the Sub-Deb" (a phrase Dr. Rinehart had coined, indicating a girl almost old enough to make her debut into society). Bab's naive, turgid, and horribly misspelled journals, chronicling the hilariously disastrous results of her teenaged romances and delusions, appeared in the *Post* from 1916 to 1919. Rinehart then left New York before *The Bat* even opened to visit her middle son, Alan, who had dropped out of Harvard to become a cowboy on Eaton's ranch (although he eventually became a writer like his mother). Thus, after feeling the sting of previous theatrical failures, Rinehart heard of the play's wild success by telegram while camping in New Mexico with her family. By 1921 she had four successful plays running: *The Bat,* adaptations of the *Tish* and *Bab, a Sub-Deb* (1917) stories, and a play called *Spanish Love.* So eminent an author and American voice

had she become by that time that she was called upon to cover the presidential elections and the disarmament conference in Washington, D.C. While she and her husband were there, Dr. Rinehart was offered a job in the Veteran's Affairs Administration, so the couple moved to the city and soon found themselves dining at the White House.

SIDELINED BY "A CULT OF UGLINESS"

As postwar America evolved into the Jazz Age, and high modernists and Progressive Era naturalists started to garner more and more literary influence and vogue, Rinehart found that being eminent and popular was now considered old-fashioned and frivolous, and that her conventionally resolved endings now barred her from "serious" consideration as a writer. Rinehart didn't like modernism any more than it liked her, and she criticized it in articles written then and reflections written later. However, facing the implication that her fictional formulas were not art, and perhaps also influenced by the changing literary atmosphere, Rinehart began to explore new territory, and the 1920s became her "decade of serious fiction" (Cohn, p. 188). In an era that produced *The Waste Land, The Great Gatsby,* and *Main Street,* Rinehart wrote *The Breaking Point* (1921), an exploration of the dangers and possibilities of repressed traumatic memories, and *Lost Ecstasy* (1927), a romance that examines the issue of class and regional divides in America through the depiction of the physical and psychological obstacles in a hasty and tense marriage between a western cattleman and an eastern society girl. She also published two short-story collections, titled *Temperamental People* (1924) and *The Romantics* (1929), examining the physical and psychological minutiae that lie behind our everyday activities and relationships.

Though she poked fun at certain romantic illusions in these stories, she nevertheless declared that modernism was "a cult of ugliness" and that the newly popular 1920s sex novel "stress[ed] only the ugly" and thus was "as false as that other school which ignored it" (*My Story,* pp. 329, 370–371). During this period she began to feel that,

notwithstanding the critical community's embrace of modernism, she too had a place in American literary history. She received a letter from a college professor who said he often used her stories to teach his students about plot structure and characterization, and in a short *Chicago Daily Tribune* piece by Genevieve Forbes, it was noted that "no less than twenty-seven classes of embryo fictionalists ha[d] made their pilgrimages to study the technique of her chill mystery manner" when *The Bat* came to town (p. 7). Thus, Rinehart was being studied as a model of commercial success, and copied as a master craftsman of mystery, while simultaneously endeavoring to expand her literary repertoire and redefine her scope. Her focus on more serious, less formulaic work in this decade may have also stemmed from the fact that she was not facing any financial pressures at the time: after all, throughout the Roaring Twenties, stocks were going up, up, up, and money was abundant—on paper, anyway.

NEW VENTURES, OLD FORMULAS

Just before the stock market crash of 1929, Rinehart's eldest son, Stan Jr., informed her that he wished to start his own publishing company with his youngest brother, Ted. Rinehart gave each of her boys a "stake" to start the business, but never asked for any creative control in return. Her only contribution was to give them the exclusive rights to any novel she wrote from then on. When the crash was in full swing, leaving the Rineharts as stupefied and scared as the rest of the country, Mary put the long-standing work ethic she learned from her mother back into action and wrote at a furious pace, as she had in 1903 when she and Stanley were in debt, and in 1911, when she had bought and was remodeling The Bluff. Facing financial losses and worried about her sons' fledgling business, Rinehart dismissed the notion of waiting for inspiration as an amateur's excuse. "Inspiration," she was to say later in an interview, only ever follows from "a long exercise in effort" (Van Gelder, p. 147). Once again, her determined labors paid off. She had pledged a best seller to help get her sons off to a good start, and she delivered with the scintil-

lating mystery *The Door* in 1930. The book uses some of her familiar techniques—the wry spinster narrator, the young-love plot woven in, the "had I but known" development of plot and suspense—but also something new, a murderer thought to be the origin of the now-old joke "the butler did it." She completed that novel while also penning her charming and well-reviewed autobiography, which appeared in 1931, and then *Miss Pinkerton* in 1932, which revived the narrator-character of nurse Hilda Adams, who had been successful in a 1914 novella, *The Buckled Bag*. Mary Freier observes that the reprise of the Miss Pinkerton character, Hilda Adams, is a bit more fatigued and cynical than the 1914 version, and wonders if the seasoned professional Miss Adams was a medium through which Rinehart could express her own fatigue and professional tensions. All the while, Rinehart was also doing monthly op-ed work on culture, society, and the economic crisis for the *Ladies' Home Journal* at a whopping twenty-five hundred dollars per page. However, all this activity ground to a halt, and the *LHJ* column was canceled, when doctors confirmed that her husband was gravely ill. They took him to Florida, then Baden-Baden, then the Adirondacks seeking rest, medical advice, and rejuvenation for him, but their efforts failed, and he died on October 28, 1932.

After losing her husband of thirty-six years, Rinehart went to the Eaton ranch to rest, but she couldn't stand being there without Stan and ended up writing at a pace more frenetic than ever back in their D.C. home (another one of her lavish but lovely renovation projects, complete with a billiard room for family, friends, and Washington bigwigs). This writing frenzy resulted in two novels in 1933, *The Album* and *The State Versus Elinor Norton*, both with elements of her usual mystery and suspense but with some serious psychological explorations of repression and desire. *The Album* was inspired by the infamous ax murders of Lizzie Borden, who had remained in the American popular imagination in poetry, song, drama, and the sensational press for decades after the case was closed. There are no fewer than four thwarted spinster daughters in this novel, and they all react to their plight in

very different ways: surreptitious outings, small rebellions, secret identities, suppression of personality, and, in one case, committing three murders. *Elinor Norton* meticulously traces the long trail a woman's life takes before she picks up a gun and kills her lover, pressing the question of who is really guilty in a case such as hers. Both books received praise in highbrow periodicals like the *Saturday Review of Books* and the *New York Times*, which headlined the page: "Mrs. Rinehart Writes a Realistic Novel" (Cohn, p. 203). In 1934, after recovering from a heart attack, she was invited to go on a trip to Communist Russia and was upset and unhappy with what she saw. Officials there were putting on a show for her, she thought, perhaps hoping she would report favorably on the still relatively new state, but she perceived that the ordinary people there were suffering, and wrote that instead.

A LIGHT IN THE WINDOW

Not long after her return to America, Rinehart moved to New York to be close to her children and grandchildren now that Stan was gone. While summering in Bar Harbor, Maine, she fell in love with one last grand home that needed renovation, bought it in 1935, and set to work restoring it. In 1936 she found a lump in her breast that turned out to be cancerous. She underwent a radical mastectomy, which she later wrote about publicly at a time when the words "breast cancer" almost never appeared in print. As always, in a reaction to any loss or setback, she turned her worry into work (often she had whiled away the time in a hospital or sickbed by writing, to avoid thinking about what was happening to her or might be about to happen). During her cancer treatment she wrote four more comical "Tish" stories. But by this time, George Lorimer, longtime editor at the *Saturday Evening Post,* had retired and the new editor actually rejected one of the stories, to Rinehart's annoyance, especially since she felt that the hit play and film *Arsenic and Old Lace* had been inspired by them, "elderberry wine and all" (Cohn, p. 219). This minor shock did not slow down her literary output, however, for in 1938 the classic Rinehart mystery *The Wall* was

serialized for the huge sum of sixty-five thousand dollars; apparently the *Post* had not outgrown her works of suspense.

The following year, the *Post* published what was perhaps Rinehart's longest manifesto on her craft: "Writing Is Work," in which she outlines the changes in working conditions for writers over the years of her long career. The key points that emerge from this dense six-page article represent the sum of her motivation, method, and mores as an author. First, she explains, "Writers who began before [World War I] were trained in a hard school. We sent in our material, complete to the last semicolon, got it back or had it accepted at any price an editor chose to pay, and that was that. But it made troupers of those who survived ... [for] not only is life always about, pressing on [the writer] with its problems and incessant demands. It is frequently necessary to work against extremely adverse conditions" (p. 11). One of the pen-and-ink illustrations shows a humorous scene from the article, set in the family room where she first started writing, with three toddlers on the floor dismembering a doll with their father's scalpels, a pile of unfolded sheets lying nearby, and a drawing of their young mother scolding them with a pen in her hand. It is an even more humorous and striking picture when one contrasts it to the writing habits of other successful women writers of her day: Edith Wharton writing in bed on her breakfast tray each day from 9 a.m. to noon, or Gertrude Atherton and Charlotte Perkins Gilman handing over their children to friends and relatives and leaving home permanently to pursue their careers. It is perhaps no wonder that Rinehart calls writing "the blessed relief of work" from the demands of everyday life (p. 11).

The article goes on to develop a contrast between the average professional writer—that worker bee who must revise and throw failed stories in the trash, burn bad novels in the furnace, and keep on writing—and the "people with such utter self-confidence that every word they write is precious," ending with the zinger, "it is usually the dilettante who has the superiority complex" (p. 82). If any readers might be tempted to think writing crime fiction is not hard

work and is an easy road to publishing, she invites them to picture "a haggard, wild-eyed woman despairingly searching through mounds of yellow paper for the caliber of a bullet" (p. 84). In a more hopeful tone, she also notes that "it is no longer considered fatal to all literary craftsmanship to sell a lot of books" (p. 83). The Depression had perhaps helped with that: anyone who could successfully make a living at that time was to be admired and emulated. The very existence of the Isabella Taves's 1943 book *Successful Women*, with its chapter on Rinehart as a model of literary success, demonstrates how salability and survival were new virtues after the Depression.

Between 1940 and 1950 Rinehart published *The Great Mistake* (1940), *The Haunted Lady* (1942), *The Episode of the Wandering Knife* (1950), and *The Yellow Room* (1945), making a total of fifty-six books, seven plays, and numerous short stories and articles (Van Gelder, p. 146). By then, she was nearly seventy years old, and those works were generally as well reviewed as ever. Recurring heart problems had prevented her desired trip to London in 1946 to report on the effects of World War II, much to the relief of her family, who stopped her from leaving for England with a telegram that read, "What are you doing? You are scaring the pants off us!" (Cohn, p. 225). They later joked that they were "sure she [would] be magnificent going down into a dugout, but how would [she] get up again?" (p. 225), since her doctor had forbidden her to climb stairs, much less ladders, after she had had the first in what would become a series of heart attacks from 1934 until her death twenty-four years later.

The Bar Harbor home she had enjoyed so much burned down in 1947, and the indefatigable Rinehart kept working, often in bed in her New York apartment, where her family was always welcome to drop in and where her grandchildren later remembered doing puzzles with her. By her standards, she was slowing down, publishing *A Light in the Window* in 1948, *The Swimming Pool* in 1952, and a novella, *The Frightened Wife*, in 1953. The last two were classic Rinehart fictions, showing how men and women of integrity and courage can survive the messes life hands them

and rebuild on their own terms. *A Light in the Window* is a family saga, where the crimes are not illegal and the suspense is all psychological. The novel tells the story of three generations of one fictional family, from before World War I to after World War II, and is equally about the mysteries of marriage, sex and infidelity, and the future of humanity in an atomic age, with a fascinating retrospective of fifty years of American publishing thrown in, since that is the business the Waynes hand down through all three generations. Fanny Butcher of the *Chicago Daily Tribune* praised its "rich record" and "deep understanding," while also commenting that Rinehart showed "deeper tenderness for human frailties than most modern writers allow themselves" (p. F3). During that time, Rinehart also threw a small luncheon for the reigning British queen of mystery, Agatha Christie, which served as the only meeting for those two grande dames of suspense. She continued to be interviewed and written up in the newspapers, including an appearance on Edward R. Murrow's *Person to Person* in 1956. After that, she used her writing time to pen a private autobiography for her children, and was still reminiscing over what it had all meant when a final heart attack ended her life on September 22, 1958. She was eighty-three, and those who knew her declared she still exuded a sense of the energy, power, and charm that made her a "tycoon" in literature—and in life—to the day she died.

MISTRESS OF MYSTERY

Though the reprints of her books published in the 1990s bear the emblem "America's Mistress of Mystery" under her name, Rinehart had perhaps envisioned more than that as her legacy. In her foreword to the 1933 *The Mary Roberts Rinehart Crime Book*, Rinehart wrote: "I shall probably always be known as a writer of detective books, which I emphatically am not" (p. vi). The statement in its context may sound ironic until one remembers that this compendium of multiple novels, re-released in one volume, was only one of the three such volumes (the others being the *Mary Roberts Rinehart Mystery Book* and *Ro-*

mance Book) that she agreed to allow her sons' new firm to publish during the Depression. The collection format would appeal to a newly thrifty book-buying public, and her name would help bolster the sales of the otherwise quite highbrow booklist her sons were publishing, which included biographies of statesmen and a new edition of the seventeenth-century tome *Anatomy of Melancholy*. Her wry prediction, to this point, has largely come true. In *Women of Mystery: The Lives and Works of Notable Women Crime Novelists* (2000), Martha Hailey DuBose calls her one of the mothers of detection in American literature, along with the nineteenth-century author Anna Katherine Green, observing that in 1941 Rinehart's contemporary Howard Haycroft had declared her the dean of crime writing for and by women (p. 24). Nevertheless, Rinehart always had a complicated response to the success of her mysteries, and she begins a 1930 article by pointing out, "Of the 38 books which I have published, only 10 have been crime stories; yet I find that these ten continue to have a surprising vitality" ("Author Tells Why Readers Prefer Crime," p. 19). The duality of the statement—pointing out that her mysteries form only about a quarter of her output but have always been the most enduringly popular of the bunch—illustrates how the reading public had cemented her position in the literary world more than she herself had. The article goes on to illustrate how crime fiction is read by men more often than by women and to give a few amusing examples of the "addictions" of presidents Theodore Roosevelt and Herbert Hoover to her mysteries (pp. 19–20). This piece, written the same year that *The Maltese Falcon* was published, reflects one possible reason for Rinehart's astounding longevity as a best-selling author: she was one of very few women who wrote books that broadly appealed to both male and female audiences. Hers were not "hard-boiled" mysteries, such as the ones coming into vogue by Dashiell Hammett, or both hard-boiled and comical, like the Nero Wolfe books by Rex Stout (whose use of humor surely shows his indebtedness to Rinehart's innovations), but were simultaneously serious about crime and injustice and lightly mocking of human foibles.

Perhaps becoming resigned to the twin labels of "mystery writer" and "literary mother" over time, it became Rinehart's consistent claim that writing crime and suspense fiction was as legitimate, and harder to do well, than standard realistic fiction, romance, or novels of manners. A crime story, Rinehart claimed, is really "two stories," with the double structure of a submerged narrative and a surface narrative ("Writing Is Work," p. 84). Most of Rinehart's submerged narratives offer proof of the old maxim "old sins cast long shadows." Some old sins are hasty, ill-advised marriages, as in *The Case of Jennie Brice, The State Versus Elinor Norton, Episode of the Wandering Knife, The Great Mistake, The Wall, The Yellow Room, The Haunted Lady, The Frightened Wife,* and *The Swimming Pool.* Others are guilty secrets, as in *The Confession, The Circular Staircase, The Man in Lower Ten, K, Sight Unseen, The Album,* and *The Door.* Often, Rinehart's narrator-detectives (none of whom are police or private detectives) are spinsters, who vary in age from their mid-twenties to their sixties. In her study of early American detective fiction by women, *The Web of Iniquity* (1998), Catherine Ross Nickerson makes an in-depth exploration of three of Rinehart's spinster narrators and characters, explaining that genteel women must learn to be suspicious, since suspicion "is the precise opposite of gentility" (p. 118). Nickerson further observes that, no matter their ages, Rinehart's spinsters are "witty, ethical, and difficult to deceive" (p. 120). Scholars of the detective story have found that this double structure can also contain both "conservative" and "subversive" elements (Nickerson, p. 128). In this way, those ladylike spinsters can transgress the bounds of propriety and femininity in the name of detection, participating in exhumations, like Rachel Innes in *The Circular Staircase*; nocturnal wanderings, like Elizabeth Bell in *The Door*; hiding evidence, like Agnes Blakiston in *The Confession*; and toting a gun, like Miss Cornelia Van Gorder in *The Bat*, scaring her personal maid of thirty-five years nearly to death. Often enough, they are acting to undo the deleterious effects of "male behaviors [like] greed and dissipation" that threaten the home (Nickerson, p.

146). Their responsibility to sustain the moral order by righting injustice gives them new authority in a world where they could so easily be considered unimportant. For instance, in *The Album*, Louisa Hall's insistence upon collecting evidence and solving the series of murders in her staid, closed, upper-class circle is the catalyst for her defying her mother for the first time. It is this defiance, the novel suggests, that gives Louisa a chance to live her own life, which will now include marriage to a man she loves but who is not one of the family's closed inner circle. She is not the only narrator who finds herself engaged (on her own terms and for her own reasons) after solving the local crime; nor is that plot twist reserved for the young spinsters. *Jennie Brice*'s middle-aged narrator finds herself, on the last page of the book, engaged to the nice man who rows around saving stranded animals in her neighborhood, because she is "tired of watching the gas meter" and wants a man in the house because her dog has just died (p. 192).

STORYTELLER OR CRITIC?

Interviewed in 1918 by Grant Overton for his book *The Women Who Make Our Novels*, Rinehart claimed, "I have never had any illusions about the work I do. I am, frankly, a story teller. Some day I may be a novelist" (p. 54). Overton, however, in describing her earliest serious effort, *K*, responds, "if [that] is not novelizing, then we do not know what novelizing is," and goes on to declare that "the tenth chapter of *K* will not be easily be overmatched in American fiction" (pp. 64–65). Four years earlier, in a *New York Times* article, Rinehart had proclaimed: "This writing of short stories is a game, and a game in which a woman has just as good a chance as a man, but she must stand in back of her work" ("The Short Story," p. 156). Cohn and Dubose both agree that, like many successful people of her time, Rinehart was essentially a social Darwinist at heart, believing that success was a tribute to superior strength, survival skills, and hard work, and that failure was a sign of weakness.

Perhaps the criticism that recurred most during Rinehart's long career was her refusal (some

would say inability) to join the widespread and long-standing movement of literary realism. American realism has its roots in the nineteenth-century in the work of William Dean Howells and Mark Twain, and continued well into the middle of the twentieth century, often within the subgenre of literary naturalism, at which writers like Stephen Crane and Theodore Dreiser succeeded so well. The highbrow female novelists of Rinehart's generation, including Edith Wharton, Willa Cather, and Ellen Glasgow, were some of the finest writers of realistic fiction America has ever produced. Rinehart could quite possibly have joined their elite, critically acclaimed ranks had she eschewed the neat, happy endings her long fictions always provide, and had she slowed down her literary output, as Cather once advised her to do (*My Story*, p. 87). At the time, Rinehart asserted, her ideas came so quickly that she was in a continual sprint to keep up with them, not to mention the fact that she snatched her writing time out of an already full schedule of responsibilities. But her full personal life (the women in the realist coterie had neither husbands nor children to care for) cannot be the only reason, and the implication that she lacked the fineness of perception to rise to their ranks does not withstand scrutiny. Literary critics in her own time speculated that Rinehart could have had a more highbrow career and reputation had she chosen to do so. In 1941 Steven Vincent and Rosemary Benét of the *New York Herald Tribune*, speaking of her work in short fiction, said her stories in *Married People* (1937) demonstrated "what her gifts might have been, under other stars, as a realist" (quoted in Cohn, p. 210). Why, then, did she choose a divergent path, one that has led to relative obscurity now, except in anthologies of detective fiction? Nickerson asserts that it may have been her husband's violent disapproval of the new realism that kept her from fully joining the movement. This is possible, given that she praised, to a limited degree, the work of its young male practitioners, like Sinclair Lewis and F. Scott Fitzgerald, and its older female originators, such as Wharton and Cather.

Perhaps her 1922 *Bookman* article "The Unreality of Modern Realism" can help resolve this conundrum. It seems she felt she was a true realist, and the modernist writers who laid claim to the title were, in fact, not. The article has a complex argument, focusing on the need for human ideals, and the soullessness of purely materialist fiction. "Just what is the province of creative literature?" she asks. "To lead men on and up? To depict them as they are? Or to drag them down?" (p. 462). She declares that the "ruthless iconoclast" modernist writer only spreads a false sense of cynicism among readers. She credits the "mainly young, frankly cynical and disillusioned " writers of the 1920s as "honest in their convictions," but finds them misguided nonetheless. "If realism be truth, then let us have truth," she demands, "and neither a portion of it nor a distortion of it.... For life is a fluid thing. It has its high moments and its low.... From the standpoint of reality one is as incorrect as the other" (p. 463). Let the "Gloomy Clever Ones … [mellow] with experience" and discover "that they cannot live without ideals, nor help others to live," she expounded, and "then we shall have a school of great realists" (p. 464).

The goal of "helping others to live" through her fiction elucidates the controversially paternalistic stance that Rinehart took toward her audience throughout her career. In the 1920 article, "My Public," Rinehart speaks of her "responsibility to her public," which includes "keep[ing] faith with my readers, to give them my best, to spread such happiness as I could, never to preach an evil thing.... For the printed word has tremendous influence" (pp. 290–291). In her autobiography, she reflects that she wished never to write a word she would not want her children to read, perhaps explaining why she largely opted out of realism, naturalism, and modernism, instead keeping true to happy endings and clean reading. To the end of her career, she felt that virtue must conquer injustice when we have the power to imagine it that way ("The Repute of the Crime Story").

Rinehart's insider/outsider status in the early to mid-twentieth century raises the question of where she stands in American literary history. With Wharton and Cather? Or with Hammett and Stout, with whom she served on the advisory council of the Writers' War Board in the 1940s?

By 1946 she had been practically discarded from serious critical consideration, and was accused of writing only for "maiden aunts" (Nickerson, p. 119). Did it perhaps take some courage to retain her voice as an elderly woman with a commitment to middle-class morality, marriage, and motherhood in the era of Sam Spade and Nero Wolfe? She may have felt that remaking her work in the image of the new "hard-boiled," cynical style of writing would have been as grotesque and graceless as the face-lift her character Mrs. Matthew Wayne gets in *The Light in the Window* in order to keep up with the times. Just as Mr. Wayne feels he has lost his wife, his sense of stability, so might Rinehart's readers have felt had she suddenly silenced her spinsters, stopped laughing at herself, and started chewing on cigars in public.

Since the late twentieth century, a bit more critical attention has been paid to Rinehart in the expanding fields of detective fiction and the middlebrow. Through this attention, Rinehart's reputation has been reclaimed to an extent. Nickerson points out that she was read by Dorothy Parker and Gertrude Stein, who was known to have admired Rinehart's style. Nickerson also points out that her portrayal of the American upper classes "rivals, in its vividness and specificity, the one created by Edith Wharton" (p. 120). Rinehart herself was aware of her middlebrow status and made mention that her sons discovered at college that her books were not considered literature (*My Story*, p. 383). In her critically and popularly acclaimed last full-length work, *The Swimming Pool*, Rinehart's narrator, Lois Maynard, is also a middlebrow toiler in the world of letters. Lois is the tough, practical young relict of an old society family that has been decimated by the Depression and by the poor choices of her mother and older sister. Lois writes crime fiction to pay the bills for the family's old summer country home, which she and her brother now share. If her brother is sick of Jell-O, she states, he can try to pick up his earnings a bit as a lawyer—if not, she has shown that her work can carry them along. Like Rinehart herself, Lois writes in snatched time, praying for enough silence to finish and sell some stories. Unlike

Lois, Rinehart was also besieged by fans who sailed by on tour boats in Bar Harbor, where she would hear the tour guide point out her house and would later find the bolder fans on her doorstep. Always gracious, always grateful to her readers, she would politely escort them on a tour through the house. Secure, at least, about her place in her public's esteem, at the end of her life she was still wondering if she would ever be accorded a place in the American canon. "It is just possible," she mused, in her typically wry fashion. "I still believe in miracles" (*My Story*, p. 407).

Selected Bibliography

WORKS OF MARY ROBERTS RINEHART

NOVELS

The Circular Staircase. Indianapolis: Bobbs-Merrill, 1908.

The Man in Lower Ten. Indianapolis: Bobbs-Merrill, 1909.

The Window at the White Cat. Indianapolis: Bobbs-Merrill, 1910.

Where There's a Will. Indianapolis: Bobbs-Merrill, 1912.

The Case of Jennie Brice. Indianapolis: Bobbs-Merrill, 1913.

The After House. Boston: Houghton Mifflin, 1914.

The Street of Seven Stars. Boston: Houghton Mifflin, 1914.

K. Boston: Houghton Mifflin, 1915.

The Amazing Interlude. New York: Doran, 1918.

Dangerous Days. New York: Doran, 1919.

Sight Unseen and The Confession. New York: Doran, 1921.

The Breaking Point. Doylestown, Pa.: Wildside Press, 1921.

The Red Lamp. New York: Doran, 1925.

The Bat: A Novel from the Play. New York: Doran, 1926.

Lost Ecstasy. New York: Doran, 1927.

The Door. New York: Farrar & Rinehart, 1930.

Miss Pinkerton. New York: Farrar & Rinehart, 1932.

The Album. New York: Farrar & Rinehart, 1933.

The State Versus Elinor Norton. New York: Farrar & Rinehart, 1934.

The Wall. New York: Farrar & Rinehart, 1938.

The Great Mistake. New York: Farrar & Rinehart, 1940.

The Haunted Lady. New York: Farrar & Rinehart, 1942.

The Yellow Room. New York: Farrar & Rinehart, 1945.

A Light in the Window. New York: Farrar & Rinehart, 1948.

The Swimming Pool. New York: Rinehart, 1952.

Short Fiction

The Amazing Adventures of Letitia Carberry. Indianapolis: Bobbs-Merrill, 1911.

Tish. Boston: Houghton Mifflin, 1916.

Bab, a Sub-Deb. New York: Doran, 1917.

More Tish. New York: Doran, 1921.

Temperamental People. New York: Doran, 1924.

Mary Roberts Rinehart's Crime Book. New York: Farrar & Rinehart, 1925. Reprint, 1933. (Contains *The After House, The Buckled Bag, Locked Doors, The Red Lamp,* and *The Window at the White Cat.*)

Tish Plays the Game. New York: Doran, 1926.

The Romantics. New York: Farrar & Rinehart, 1929.

Married People. New York: Farrar & Rinehart, 1937.

Tish Marches On. New York: Farrar & Rinehart, 1937.

Episode of the Wandering Knife: Three Mystery Tales. New York: Rinehart, 1950.

The Frightened Wife, and Other Murder Stories. New York: Rinehart, 1953.

Nonfiction and Memoir

Through Glacier Park in 1915: Seeing America First with Howard Eaton. Boston: Houghton Mifflin, 1916.

Tenting Tonight: A Chronicle of Sport and Adventure in Glacier Park and the Cascade Mountains. Boston: Houghton Mifflin, 1918.

Nomad's Land. New York: Doran, 1926.

My Story. New York: Farrar & Rinehart, 1931.

Articles

"The Short Story: Mrs. Rinehart Describes Her Methods in Writing Fiction." *New York Times,* April 5, 1914.

"My Public." *Bookman* 54, no. 4:289–291 (December 1920).

"The Unreality of Modern Realism." *Bookman* 56: 462–463 (December 1922).

"The Repute of the Crime Story." *Publishers Weekly,* February 1, 1930.

"Author Tells Why Readers Prefer Crime: Mary Roberts Rinehart Confesses!" *Chicago Daily Tribune,* December 6, 1930.

"Writing Is Work." *Saturday Evening Post,* March 11, 1939.

Papers

Mary Roberts Rinehart Papers. University Library Systems Special Collections, University of Pittsburgh.

CRITICAL AND BIOGRAPHICAL STUDIES

Butcher, Fanny. "Alluring Novel by Mrs. Rinehart: Story of Rich Experience in the Publishing Business." *Chicago Daily Tribune,* January 11, 1948, p. F3.

Cohn, Jan. *Improbable Fiction: The Life of Mary Roberts Rinehart.* Pittsburgh, Pa.: University of Pittsburgh Press, 1980.

DuBose, Martha Hailey. *Women of Mystery: The Lives and Works of Notable Women Crime Novelists.* New York: St. Martin's Minotaur, 2000.

Forbes, Genevieve. "Informally." *Chicago Daily Tribune,* May 14, 1921, p. 7.

Freier, Mary. "The Decline of Hilda Adams." In *Women Times Three: Writers, Detectives, Readers.* Edited by Katherine Gregory Klein. Bowling Green, Ohio: Bowling Green State University Popular Press, 1995.

Garvey, Ellen Gruber. *The Adman in the Parlor: Magazines and the Gendering of Consumer Culture, 1880s to 1910s.* New York: Oxford University Press, 1996.

Kungl, Carla T. *Creating the Fictional Female Detective: The Sleuth Heroines of British Women Writers, 1890–1940.* Jefferson, N.C.: McFarland, 2006.

MacLeod, Charlotte. *Had She but Known: A Biography of Mary Roberts Rinehart.* New York: Warner Books, 1994.

Nickerson, Catherine Ross. *The Web of Iniquity: Early Detective Fiction by American Women.* Durham, N.C.: Duke University Press, 1998.

Overton, Grant M. *The Women Who Make Our Novels.* New York: Moffat, Yard, 1918.

Taves, Isabella. *Successful Women, and How They Attained Success.* New York: Dutton, 1943.

Van Gelder, Robert. *Writers and Writings.* New York: Charles Scribner's Sons, 1946.

JOSHUA SLOCUM

(1844—1909)

Dan Brayton

IN NOVEMBER 1908 an old oyster sloop called *Spray* set out from Martha's Vineyard, Massachusetts, for the northern coast of South America. The *Spray* never made landfall, disappearing somewhere in the North Atlantic. The boat's lone occupant, a sixty-five-year-old man named Joshua Slocum, was a professional mariner, a best-selling author, and the acquaintance of such noteworthy figures as Theodore Roosevelt and Mark Twain. At the time of his disappearance Slocum was an internationally celebrated writer making a living by telling the story, in print and lectures, of his adventures at sea. Joshua Slocum's fame derives almost entirely from the success of his book *Sailing Alone Around the World,* a masterpiece of nautical travel writing first published serially in 1899–1900 by the *Century Illustrated Monthly Magazine* and as a book on March 3, 1900.

Written at the end of Slocum's topsy-turvy career as a sea captain in the waning days of the great clipper ships, *Sailing Alone Around the World* tells the story of the first solo circumnavigation in history. Although others had circumnavigated the Earth centuries earlier, no human being had ever completed such a voyage alone. *Sailing Alone,* thus, is the record of an unprecedented feat of seamanship—a nautical stunt of staggering proportions. But the book is much more than just the record of an unlikely voyage: it is a classic of travel writing, a midlife memoir, and a major contribution to the literature of solitude that has been read as a manifesto for independent living—not unlike Henry David Thoreau's *Walden* (1854)—by generations.

The popularity of *Sailing Alone* can scarcely be overstated. From the first book reviews, some of which sang its praises to the skies, to recent books by emulators and admirers, Slocum's account of his journey has been profoundly influential. It has remained in print for the better part of the last century. Written at the moment when the United States was emerging as a global naval power, when Alfred Thayer Mahan's argument for the importance of sea power was becoming the cornerstone of U.S. international policy, Slocum's sea voyage narrative struck a chord with American readers as well as with Anglophone readers and audiences around the world. In 1947 the British writer Arthur Ransome wrote, "A school library without this book is incomplete. It should be part of the education of every English or American boy" (p. 17). Admired for its elegant descriptive prose, lively narrative voice, and unforgettable vignettes of solitary life at sea, the book became an international best seller and has, in the century-plus since its publication, inspired countless readers, sailors, and solitary adventurers.

LIFE

It seems unlikely that the masterful narrative voice of *Sailing Alone Around the World* could belong to a man whose formal schooling ended in childhood, but such is the case. Joshua Slocum's origins could hardly have been less auspicious for a future writer; they are far more typical of professional seamen. Like the great eighteenth-century mariner Captain James Cook, Slocum came from humble origins and rose through the nautical ranks by dint of natural talent—mental and physical toughness combined with a prodigious intellect. Like Cook, too, he was destined to make some of the most fabled voyages in history.

The Joshua Slocum known to generations of readers around the world was a famous American

citizen in an era of U.S. expansionism, and the note of Yankee patriotism that runs through *Sailing Alone* at times borders on jingoism. Yet Slocum began his life in Nova Scotia—and not even as "Joshua Slocum." He was born on February 20, 1844, in Mount Hanley, a small town in Annapolis County, near the Bay of Fundy, the fifth of eleven children of John and Sarah Jane (née Southern) Slocombe. John was descended from immigrants who had been Quaker Loyalists opposed to the American War of Independence. Like many other Loyalists from the original thirteen colonies, the Slocombes emigrated to Nova Scotia in the 1780s and were granted land by the British Crown. As the autobiographical opening lines of *Sailing Alone* relate, "In the fair land of Nova Scotia, a maritime province, there is a ridge called North Mountain, overlooking the Bay of Fundy on one side and the fertile Annapolis Valley on the other.... I was born in a cold spot, on coldest North Mountain, on a cold February 20, though I am a citizen of the United States—a naturalized Yankee, if it may be said that Nova Scotians are not Yankees in the truest sense of the word" (pp. 1–2). Thus begins Slocum's famous narrative.

At the age of eight young Joshua moved with his family to the village of Westport, on Brier Island, farther south along the Nova Scotia coast. There in the turbulent tide-ridden waters off the southern tip of Digby Neck his maternal grandfather had been a lighthouse keeper. His father opened a boot-making shop for local fishermen, and at age ten Joshua was taken out of school to help around the shop pegging boots and doing chores. With the sea on his doorstep, however, Joshua was naturally drawn to a life on the water. At fourteen he tried to escape his strict father by running away to sea, hiring on aboard a coastal fishing schooner as cabin boy and cook, but his lack of skill as a "culinary artist," he later recalled, soon forced his return home. After the death of his mother in February 1860, when he turned sixteen, he managed to leave home for good, hiring on as an ordinary seaman on a ship bound for Dublin. From there he sailed to Liverpool, where he joined the crew of the British ship *Tanjore,* bound for China. For two years

Slocum sailed extensively in Indonesian waters and the South China Sea, stopping in the Moluccas, Manila, Hong Kong, Batavia (Jakarta), and Saigon. He also crossed the Pacific to San Francisco, where he would live, off and on, for many years. In 1865 Slocum became a naturalized U.S. citizen and began a series of passages between San Francisco and the Oregon Territory engaged in the salmon fishery and fur trade at a time when sea otter pelts were highly lucrative. He achieved his first command aboard the bark *Washington* in 1869, which he then sailed around most of the Pacific Rim—to Australia, Alaska, and California.

Just before Christmas in 1870, in Sydney, Australia, Slocum met a young American woman, Virginia Albertina Walker. She came from a gold-prospecting family that originally hailed from New York. The two were married on January 31, 1871, and would sail together for the next thirteen years, during which time Virginia bore seven children, four of whom survived to adulthood (sons Victor, Benjamin Aymar, and Garfield, and daughter Jessie). Virginia was Joshua Slocum's one great love (besides the sea), and their relatively brief marriage is the haunting truth behind the lonesome voice of *Sailing Alone*.

Slocum's adventures at sea as a ship's officer were so numerous and genuinely perilous that they could easily fill volumes. On his first voyage with Virginia aboard the *Washington* they were wrecked in a storm on the Alaskan coast. Slocum found himself a castaway with his new wife, his crew, and a load of salmon caught in the cold waters of "Seward's Icebox" (recently purchased from tsarist Russia) and proceeded to demonstrate his extraordinary resourcefulness. With the *Washington* smashed to a pile of wreckage on the beach, Slocum brought his wife and crew, along with a good deal of the ship's cargo, safely back to Seattle and then San Francisco in the ship's boats, selling the salmon for a profit. This would not be the last time Slocum found himself in such a predicament. Indeed, disaster, rescue, salvage, and return would become the pattern for Slocum's greatest adventures and his first two books. At one point, in the Philippines, Slocum built a 150-ton steamship with a crew of

local shipyard workers. In payment he received the 90-ton schooner *Pato,* owning his own vessel for the first time. He then sailed the *Pato* between San Francisco and Hawaii carrying freight, and his new command gave him the time and authority to take up writing. For a brief period he became a shipboard correspondent for the *San Franciso Bee.*

Slocum referred to his time aboard the *Northern Light 2,* a clipper of 233 feet length on deck, 44 feet beam (width), and 28 feet depth of hold, as "my best command." It was aboard the *Northern Light* that Slocum would rescue five Gilbert Islanders adrift in a twenty-foot open boat and bring them to Japan, where he arranged to have them returned to their native island aboard a mission ship. Shortly after leaving Japan the Slocums found themselves in the Sunda Strait, between Java and Sumatra, near the island of Krakatoa. The island was then erupting, and the ash covered the decks of the *Northern Light.* Huge waves caused by the massive amount of material thrown into the sea from the exploding island broke over the ship's decks. The Slocums were fortunate. Had they sailed in those waters just a few days later they would likely have been suffocated by the volcanic gases in the air.

Yet his command of the *Northern Light* was also something of a plague to Slocum, involving him in numerous mechanical difficulties, an abortive mutiny, and a lawsuit with a mutineer. Slocum was an irascible and at times violent ship's officer trained in an era when violence was a customary instrument of command, and more than once his willingness to impose ship's discipline by any means available to him—his ever-ready fists, weapons lying at hand, or imprisonment—led him into legal trouble. After a fifty-three-day passage from South Africa to New York, Slocum was arrested, convicted, and fined for having imprisoned the second mate, Henry A. Slater, for allegedly inciting mutiny. Slocum was forced in 1884 to releaase his share of the ownership of the *Northern Light.* Slater later apologized to Slocum for his part in the mutiny and subsequent legal case.

Slocum was not ready to give up the sea. After losing his command and share of the ownership of the *Northern Light* he purchased the *Aquidneck,* a bark—much smaller than a full-rigged ship—that had been built in Mystic, Connecticut, in 1865. The *Aquidneck* would prove a fateful vessel in many ways and the end of Slocum's life as a sea captain. Aboard the new vessel the Slocums engaged in business in South America, carrying various cargoes—hay, yerba mate, lumber—between Brazil, Uruguay, and Argentina. On July 25, 1884, Virginia Walker Slocum died aboard the vessel off Buenos Aires. Her husband and children knew her health was in decline, but they did not know why. In all likelihood Virginia had a serious heart condition. When she died she was not yet thirty-five. Joshua Slocum was forty.

Bereft of his life companion and deeply lonely, Slocum commenced a new series of voyages between Baltimore and Pernambuco, Brazil, with cargoes of cordwood, pianos, and whatever freight he could get. On February 22, 1886, he married his cousin Henrietta "Hettie" Elliott, a woman scarcely more than half his own age (she was twenty-four). Hettie was not the sailor Virginia had been, and her life at sea proved unhappy. On the new couple's first voyage together the *Aquidneck* was damaged in a hurricane, and subsequently the crew contracted cholera and was quarantined for half a year. Captain Slocum at one point fended off pirates, shooting and killing one, and he again found himself in court (he was acquitted). The woes of the *Aquidneck* continued: those aboard contracted smallpox, and shortly thereafter, in 1887, the ship was wrecked on the coast of Brazil.

The wreck of the *Aquidneck* spelled the end of Slocum's career as a professional merchant officer. Losing a ship stigmatized a sea captain, in the world of shipping, as a risky prospect. Moreover, by the last two decades of the nineteenth century sailing ships were rapidly being replaced by steamships, and many lifelong sailors found themselves out of date and out of a job. In middle age, then, shortly after he reached the zenith of his career, Slocum hit rock bottom. Yet it was this nadir that gave birth to Slocum's new career as a writer.

In the nineteenth century, nautical nonfiction had been popular since the publication of Richard Henry Dana, Jr.'s *Two Years Before the Mast* (1840). A vogue of books about voyages alone in small boats held wide appeal on both sides of the Atlantic. As the writer Jonathan Raban points out, "by the time that Slocum wrote *Sailing Alone Around the World* ... the small-boat voyage was a well-established genre in Britain, with a set of rigid formal conventions" (p. 25). Slocum breathed new life into the genre. *Sailing Alone* is a gripping sea story that reads like a first-person novel.

Like his near contemporary Joseph Conrad, who also made the transition from life in the merchant navy (as a professional sea captain and ship's officer) to that of a highly successful author, Slocum drew directly on his own experiences in his writing. Unlike Conrad, however, Slocum did not write fiction. His three books, of which *Sailing Alone* is by far the most famous (and most worth reading), belong to the category of creative nonfiction in which factual events are recounted in narrative form using the rhetorical tools of the novelist and short story writer. Since its publication the American reading public has become accustomed to such nonfiction, examples of which include Edward Abbey's *Desert Solitaire: A Season in the Wilderness* (1968), Tobias Wolff's *This Boy's Life* (1989), and Joan Didion's *The Year of Magical Thinking* (2005). These books remind us of the sheer literary power that some creative nonfiction achieves. Slocum's *Sailing Alone* compares well with any of them.

Although Slocum was not strictly speaking a one-hit wonder, his first two books, *The Voyage of the* Liberdade (1890) and *The Voyage of the* Destroyer (1894) met with only fraction of the success of *Sailing Alone*. It is squarely on his third and final book that Joshua Slocum's legacy and reputation rest. *Sailing Alone Around the World* ranks with Herman Melville's *Moby-Dick* (1851) as one of the great works of nautical literature in English. Its popularity owes as much to the author's narrative gifts as to the thrilling adventure it recounts. It would be a mistake to assume that the book's appeal derives merely from good timing and sensationalism. For Slocum

was a masterful storyteller whose prose is an elegantly spare mix of lyrical description, reportage, and sparkling vignettes delivered in a droll, devil-may-care tone.

Slocum's first book tells the story of his return from Brazil, after the *Aquidneck* was wrecked, to the United States aboard a small boat he built himself with salvaged materials. He named the boat *Liberdade,* in honor of the liberation of the Brazilian slaves on the day he launched the vessel, May 13, 1888. By this time Slocum had considerable experience with boatbuilding and small-boat handling, and he was no stranger to unconventional voyages. With his second wife, Hettie, aboard; his sixteen-year-old son, Victor, as mate; and the seven-year-old Garfield for crew, Slocum soon set sail for the States, arriving on the South Carolina coast after a lengthy fifty-five days and over 5,500 miles at sea. From there they continued to Washington, D.C., and eventually to Boston, where in 1889 he settled in to write his chronicle of their voyage, publishing it the following year. While *The Voyage of the* Liberdade did little to solve his financial problems, it set the stage for his transition from professional mariner to mariner-writer for good.

In the winter of 1892 Slocum found himself still ashore in Boston, without a job and with little hope of continuing to ply his trade. He was a middle-aged relic from the age of sail become a beachcomber in the age of steam. Intent on making his living from the sea any way he could, either as a mariner, boatbuilder, shipyard worker, or fisherman, Slocum kept his eyes open for opportunities on the coast. He even looked into finding work on steamships, but he just could not stomach the transition. At about this time a fellow sea captain named Eben Pierce, who had been a whaler out of New Bedford, mentioned that he had an old fishing smack lying "on the hard" (as sailors speak of boats on shore) and available for the right price—free. The boat was the *Spray,* then a derelict craft of uncertain origin, destined to become the most celebrated sailboat in modern history.

The *Spray* was an unlikely vessel for ocean voyaging. Built for shallow coastal waters where

oyster beds abounded on the East Coast, she was a broad, almost tubby boat with a large gaff mainsail that could be difficult for one man to handle. The boat was also extraordinarily heavy, or "burdensome," in nautical parlance, which made it significantly different in performance from a lighter, nimbler craft such as the *Liberdade*. On the one hand, the *Spray* was more like a small ship; on the other, she was a coastal boat not designed for sailing the open ocean. The seaworthiness of the *Spray* has been the subject of an ongoing debate among sailors, yacht designers, and maritime historians since the boat was lost, with expert opinions on both sides of the matter. The debate seems pointless, however, since the *Spray*'s achievement speaks for itself.

When Slocum first saw her the *Spray* was in very poor shape, and he commenced a thoroughgoing reconstruction with local materials, including a "pasture oak" (a white oak, *Quercus alba,* growing in a pasture) that provided the new keel, floors, and frames. Slocum enjoyed "gamming" (chatting) with the salty locals in the region. Famously, some locals predicted that his reconstruction of the boat would fail—particularly the way he recaulked the seams of the planking. "It'll crawl," one old mariner predicted, meaning the caulking would spill from between the planks and sink the boat (p. 8). That Slocum's reconstruction of the *Spray* was entirely successful is attested to, of course, by the spectacular success of the unprecedented voyage he would soon accomplish. His initial plan for the boat was not to embark on any grand voyages, however; it was to go fishing. He had a plan to run a charter-fishing business for paying customers, but the fish did not bite.

His plans were soon interrupted. Not long after he commenced rebuilding the *Spray,* Slocum was offered an unusual opportunity to deliver a gunboat called *Destroyer* from the United States to the government of Brazil, for the purpose of quelling a regional rebellion. Slocum could not resist the sum of money offered to lead the journey, and he found himself returning by sea to the shores of Brazil. The irony of the situation is exquisite, for here was a man who lost his career arguably because of his inability to gain restitu-

tion for the loss of the *Aquidneck* in Brazil choosing to return to the very region where he was shipwrecked. The grotesque and occasionally hilarious misadventures that transpired on the subsequent voyage, which Slocum successfully completed, are the subject of his second book, the self-published *Voyage of the* Destroyer *from New York to Brazil.* Only a few hundred copies were printed, not all of which were sold.

What followed this unlikely interlude is the subject of Slocum's masterpiece, *Sailing Alone Around the World,* a voyage that took him across the North Atlantic for Gibraltar, where he intended to continue sailing the length of the Mediterranean and through the newly created Suez Canal, down the length of the Red Sea and then into the Arabian Sea. Upon encountering an unfriendly craft off the coast of North Africa, however, he decided instead to turn around and make for the South American coast he knew so well, and thence around Cape Horn, going "west about" instead of "east about." In doing so he chose to follow roughly the same route as Sir Francis Drake more than three centuries earlier.

The circumnavigation was a successful—indeed a triumphant—adventure. On June 27, 1898, after three years at sea, Slocum sailed carefully into the harbor at Newport, Rhode Island, which was mined because of the Spanish-American War. The *Spray* had covered over 46,000 miles, a distance nearly twice the circumference of the Earth (necessitated in part by the need to go around South America and Africa). It was not until the war's end that many major American newspapers published articles on Slocum's voyage. Finding his reception at Newport somewhat lacking in the kind of nautical comradery from fellow mariners he had come to expect from the rest of his voyage, Slocum continued to the old *Spray*'s point of origin: Fairhaven, Massachusetts.

After his circumnavigation Slocum's life became that of a literary celebrity. His subsequent income from book sales and lectures allowed him in 1901 to buy a farm named Fag End, in West Tisbury, a village on the island of Martha's Vineyard, Massachusetts. The aging mariner was simply unable to find life ashore to his taste, and

he began to sail the *Spray* along the East Coast during summer and in the West Indies in winter. He earned a steady income giving public lectures and selling copies of *Sailing Alone*; his celebrity meant that he had audiences everywhere he went. His wife, Hettie, remained for the most part at Fag End while he enjoyed a more migratory existence sailing between ports, giving talks, and making the acquaintance of the luminaries and celebrities of his day.

One of the darkest chapters in a life replete with danger, hardship, and tragedy occurred near its end, after Slocum's fame had spread nationwide. In May 1906 in Riverton, New Jersey, Slocum experienced a new kind of shipwreck, not a real one but a metaphorical one. He was arrested and charged with raping a twelve-year-old girl, an accusation soon changed to indecent exposure. Pleading no contest, Slocum insisted he remembered nothing of the incident—it must have taken place during one of the mental lapses he was experiencing with increasing frequency. After waiting forty-two days in jail for his trial, Slocum was released for time served, the judge stating that the accuser's family wished for leniency. By the start of his final voyage, then, Slocum was—to use a twenty-first-century phrase—a sex offender.

The Riverton episode did not prevent Theodore Roosevelt, one of Slocum's most influential admirers, from allowing his own son, Archie, to sail with Slocum from the Roosevelts' summer home on the north shore of Long Island to Newport, Rhode Island (accompanied by a guardian the while). This trip seems to have gone well, and the next time Slocum encountered Roosevelt was at the White House in May 1907. In an exchange related by Slocum's son Victor the president said to the master mariner, "Captain, our adventures have been a little different," to which Slocum replied, "That is true, Mr. President; but you got here first" (V. Slocum, p. 18). This episode comes as no surprise to anyone who has read *Sailing Alone*, which amply demonstrates Joshua Slocum's ready wit, cool head, and presence of mind.

The last several years of Slocum's life were not entirely happy ones. The old sea captain suf-

fered, by his own admission, from mental lapses such as the one that precipitated his arrest and trial at Riverton. Many of his admirers believe he suffered from depression after the death of his beloved first wife, Virginia. Certain aspects of his writings suggest he may have had bipolar disorder. In any case, his relationship with his second wife, Hettie, was by all accounts less than perfectly happy. Moreover, by the last year of his life Slocum's financial situation had deteriorated as book sales began to taper off. Always more comfortable at sea than ashore and never acclimated to life at the farm in West Tisbury, at sixty-five the aging master mariner plotted a new voyage, this time hoping to return to the northern coast of South America where he had been wrecked so many years before.

In the years immediately after his circumnavigation Slocum made the Caribbean his home during the winter months, so his final voyage was in familiar waters. We can only imagine it was a hopeful one. Maybe he could write another best seller. Maybe he could salvage his fortunes one more time. So he determined to make another long passage once more aboard the *Spray,* now an aged craft indeed, in waters he knew from many a voyage. He had the sloop fitted out at the famous Herreshoff boatbuilding works in Bristol, Rhode Island, under the supervision of Nathanael Greene Herreshoff, America's great boat designer. He then set sail for warmer waters. The last time he was seen alive was on November 14, 1908. Joshua Slocum was not declared legally dead until 1924.

THE VOYAGE OF THE *LIBERDADE*

In 1890 Slocum self-published a narrative describing his misfortunes aboard the *Aquidneck* and his subsequent return to the United States in the homemade sailboat *Liberdade* with his second wife and two sons. The narrative foreshadows *Sailing Alone* in its lively descriptions of adversity and triumph, boat-building, and life at sea in a small craft. Favorably reviewed but largely unnoticed at the time of its first publication, this story of hardship and adventure belongs today in the canon of nautical nonfiction. It recounts an

altogether remarkable story of shipwreck, survival, small-boat construction, and open-ocean sailing.

On February 28, 1886, Slocum set sail on the *Aquidneck* from New York for Montevideo, Uruguay, with his second wife, Hettie (they had recently been married); his son Victor along as chief mate; his son Garfield, then just shy of his fifth birthday; and six deckhands. The narrative begins with a well-turned metaphor: "This literary craft of mine, in its native model and rig, goes out laden with the facts of the strange happenings on a home afloat" (p. 39). Here Slocum exploits the age-old metaphor of story-as-voyage. The first half of the narrative concerns the fate of the *Aquidneck*; it is a tragedy of illness and shipwreck shot through with extraordinary firsthand accounts of the specifics of commanding a tall ship in the last days of sail. Slocum moves rapidly through the events that would lead to the wreck of the *Aquidneck*.

Near the mouth of the Paraná River, in Brazil, the crew loaded hay and, along with it, cholera. Men soon began to die. The ship was quarantined, unable to conduct business for an excruciatingly long time, and eventually fumigated. Working with a tiny skeleton crew in shallow waters, Slocum soon found himself in the worst situation any mariner can face: the loss of his craft. The *Aquidneck* ran aground on a sandbar near the mouth of Paranaguá Bay, and large swells washed over the vessel, eventually breaking its backbone (keel, keelson, stem, and sternpost). Slocum survived the wreck, and he and his family were even offered passage back to the United States by the U.S. consulate in Brazil. Slocum refused and instead attempted to recoup some of his losses by way of the Brazilian court system. His plan failed, but at some point in this series of misadventures—and this is when the narrative becomes altogether extraordinary—Joshua, Hettie, Victor, and Garfield decided to build a small boat and make the voyage home on their own.

The result was the *Liberdade,* a hybrid sailboat consisting of design features from various regions of the world with which Slocum was familiar. Only thirty-five feet on deck, the boat had a Chinese-inspired junk rig (three masts with fully battened sails and no staysails) and a hull shape described by Slocum himself as "half Cape Ann dory, half Japanese sampan" (*The Voyages of Joshua Slocum*, p. 35). In the narrative the boat is often referred to as a canoe, and indeed her long, narrow, shallow hull resembles a large dugout. Slocum had made good use of his time abroad, observing the dimensions of various craft; he was also a very capable boatbuilder, making good use of local lumber and salvaged material from the *Aquidneck* in the construction of their new boat.

Venturing on a sea voyage of many thousands of miles with a young family aboard a home-built boat might seem imprudent for some, but Slocum had spent over three decades at sea and knew the waters between Brazil and the United States East Coast intimately. He also knew a large number of mariners who plied the waters on which he had embarked. Early in the voyage, he accepted a tow from the captain of a steamer, which greatly accelerated the first part of their voyage. Even with assistance from other vessels, the progress of the *Liberdade* around Brazil and, eventually, across the Caribbean to the United States makes for gripping reading.

Having spent his entire adult life—and much of the latter part of his childhood—at sea, Slocum belonged to a sort of international fraternity of ships' officers. When Slocum and his young family arrived at Barbados nineteen days out of Pernambuco, they were greeted by familiar faces, the captains and officers of the merchant shipping on parallel courses to the *Liberdade*—the *Palmer,* the *Condor,* and the *Finance.* "Meeting so many of this class of old friends of vast and varied experiences, gave contentment to our visit and we concluded to remain over at this port till the hurricane season should pass" (p. 107). In such passages Slocum's professional familiarity with the ports of the world lend an air of the casual to the narrative. One becomes aware that the sailor-narrator has plied these waters before, and what most people would consider an adventure of a high order is all in a few months' work to him.

It also becomes clear in the course of the narrative that Slocum was not at all averse to

publicity and the admiration of mariner-colleagues and journalists alike. At some point in the narrative Slocum finds his voice as a writer, striking the perfect balance between self-promotion, understatement, and graceful log-book entry that he would employ to such spectacular effect again in *Sailing Alone*. Somewhere in his passage aboard *Liberdade,* Joshua Slocum the best-selling author and sailing guru is born.

The *Liberdade* arrived at Beaufort, North Carolina, on November 28, 1888, with a healthy, grateful crew and, after some interactions with locals on the coast, proceeded to the Chesapeake, where the happy crew spent Christmas. Two days later they arrived at Washington, D.C., where the *Liberdade* was docked and the unprecedented voyage was over.

Stories of shipwreck—fictional and otherwise—abound, and writers of all kinds have exploited the metaphorical potential of shipwreck to comment on politics, mortality, transience, providence, and much more. But what makes *The Voyage of the* Liberdade unusual is the voice that emerges in the course of the narrative, a voice at once dashing and personal, devil-may-care and yet still inviting. Slocum established a literary paradigm for future blue-water sailor-writers in which observations of the sea's natural history (birds, flying fish) mingle with detailed accounts of ingenious solutions to quotidian challenges. The distinctive voice that generations of readers have noted in *Sailing Alone* begins, in *The Voyage of the* Liberdade, to emerge and to strengthen as the narrative rounds to a close.

THE VOYAGE OF THE *DESTROYER* FROM NEW YORK TO BRAZIL

Slocum's second book—really a brief narrative pamphlet, and self-published—not surprisingly recounts the story of an unlikely voyage taken at great risk to the author. This, of course, was the main theme of Slocum's life, and he seems at this point to have achieved enough self-reflexivity to realize it. This time the eponymous vessel was not a sailboat but a massive warship sold to Brazil by the United States government.

The *Destroyer* was a 130-foot "ironclad" designed by John Ericsson, the same naval architect who had designed the *Monitor* of Civil War fame. As Slocum puts it in his inimitable style, "Great quantities of water goes [sic] over the ship. She washes heavily, still, going often under the seas, like a great duck, fond of diving. Everything is wet.... The good Swede, Ericsson, whom we all know, conceived the *Destroyer,* a ship to turn navies topsy turvy" (p. 176). This was an ungainly steam-powered gunboat designed for modern warfare, armed with a pneumatic cannon (which fired cannonballs full of dynamite); it was also an abomination in the eyes of a lifelong sailor. The U.S. government sold the *Destroyer* to Brazil for the sake of quelling a rebellion, but it would never see live action.

Slocum's position aboard *Destroyer* was "navigator in command," his responsibility the delivery of the gunboat to the Brazilians who had purchased it. "Being a man of a peaceful turn of mind, however, no fighting was expected of me, except in the battle with the elements, which should begin at Sandy Hook" (p. 173). While this sentence explains Slocum's role on a naval vessel, one cannot help wondering at the irony of the claim. Few who know the details of his life would accuse Slocum of having had "a peaceful turn of mind," for this was a man who had twice gone to trial for acts of violence on the high seas, including murder, and although he was acquitted both times it is quite clear that he could be a violent and ruthless commander. One suspects that his willingness to return to Brazil, where he had suffered a good deal upon losing the *Aquidneck,* was motivated as much by a taste for revenge as by the financial rewards of the trip.

There is a good bit of vaudeville in *The Voyage of the* Destroyer; it is a sort of nautical Keystone Cops narrative replete with racially charged set pieces, slapstick humor, social and mechanical dysfunction of numerous kinds, and even a description of the wanton shooting of a shark. It is not, in short, great literature. But it is a story that details the hazards of transporting a high-tech war machine thousands of miles across the sea with a motley crew and a tough yet determined navigator in command. The story is

also unusual in the annals of nautical narratives because it is humorous to the point of farce. One can read it as a warm-up act to *Sailing Alone* only in this sense: the author gets some of his least appealing descriptions of a sea voyage out of his system.

SAILING ALONE AROUND THE WORLD

The circumnavigation that would make Slocum famous could only have been achieved by a mariner of supreme skill and immense experience. As a living relic of the Age of Sail, Slocum shared the fate of many a master mariner at the turn of the twentieth century, stuck on shore with no command to be had. Even ashore, Slocum kept his eye on boats and the sea, for they were all he knew. Frequently in *Sailing Alone* the reader is reminded how little of his adult life the author had spent on land: "Thus the voyage which I am now to narrate was a natural outcome not only of my love of adventure, but of my lifelong experience" (p. 4). Thus Slocum's masterpiece begins with autobiographical vignettes describing a thoroughly aquatic life.

The actual sailing voyage does not commence until the second chapter. The narrative introduces the *Spray* and describes Slocum's thorough reconstruction of the dilapidated old sloop. The manner in which Slocum procured a decrepit thirty-seven-foot oyster smack, which he intended to use for fishing charters, is worth quoting:

> One midwinter day of 1892, in Boston, where I had been cast up from old ocean, so to speak, a year or two before, I was cogitating whether I should apply for a command, and again eat my bread and butter on the sea, or go to work at the shipyard, when I met an old acquaintance, a whaling-captain, who said: "Come to Fairhaven and I'll give you a ship. But," he added, "she wants some repairs."
>
> (p. 4)

Here we see Slocum's habitual rhetorical strategy, understatement, put in the voice of a fellow mariner. The *Spray* did indeed "want some repairs"; in fact, the boat needed to be almost entirely rebuilt. Lying like a shipwreck on land, the *Spray* was as much a relic as her new master.

As he had so often done before, Slocum rose to the occasion.

The "ship" offered by his "old acquaintance," the retired whalerman Eban Pierce, was miniscule in the eyes of a clipper ship captain. The boat lay in a pasture on the shores of Buzzards Bay, Massachusetts, at a place appropriately called Poverty Point in Fairhaven, Massachusetts, the same small town (near New Bedford) from which Herman Melville had shipped out aboard the whaling bark *Acushnet* in 1841. Slocum spent considerable time rebuilding his new command.

Slocum had something of the venture capitalist in him, raising support for his grand scheme to circumnavigate the globe in various ways. From the publisher Adam Willis Wagnalls, of Funk & Wagnalls, he acquired a library, including books by Charles Darwin, Mark Twain, and H. Rider Haggard. He brought James Boswell's *Life of Johnson* and poetry by Alfred, Lord Tennyson, Robert Burns, and Henry Wadsworth Longfellow. He brought the essays of Charles Lamb. Not surprisingly he also carried a copy of *Don Quixote,* and he planned to visit Robert Louis Stevenson in the South Pacific. This was to be a thoroughly literary voyage. He also acquired an agent, Roberts Brothers of Boston, to help him sell his dispatches to newspapers around the country.

The *Spray* left Boston on April 24, 1895, without escaping the notice of the press, as the departure is described in the following evocative passage from *Sailing Alone:*

> I had resolved on a voyage around the world, and as the wind on the morning of April 24, 1895, was fair, at noon I weighed anchor, set sail, and filled away from Boston, where the *Spray* had been moored snugly all winter. The twelve o'clock whistles were blowing just as the sloop shot ahead under full sail. A short board was made up the harbor on the port tack, then coming about she stood seaward, with her boom well off to port, and swung past the ferries with lively heels. A photographer on the outer pier of East Boston got a picture of her as she swept by, her flag at the peak throwing its folds clear. A thrilling pulse beat high in me. My step was light on deck in the crisp air. I felt that there could be no turning back, and that I was engaging

in an adventure the meaning of which I thoroughly understood.

(p. 11)

Slocum first steered for Gloucester, Massachusetts, at the time one of the leading East Coast fishing ports, where he describes entering a seaport alone for the first time in his seagoing life. From Gloucester the *Spray* crossed the Gulf of Maine to the mouth of the Bay of Fundy, touching at his native Brier Island, Nova Scotia, where he stayed for a few days. He then set off across St. Mary's Bay, rounded the southern tip of Nova Scotia, and finally left the North American coast for good near Halifax on July 3, 1895. The next land Slocum would see, after nearly three weeks alone on the open ocean, was Flores Island, in the Azores, where he benefited from the global community of mariners (especially whalers) that connected the Portuguese-speaking denizens of those islands with the port towns of New Bedford and Fairhaven that he knew so well. Thus, he writes of the hospitable treatment he received at Horta with a familiar tone that makes his stop there more like a neighborly chat than an exotic sojourn.

Solitude is relative, and the kind Slocum experienced at sea was certainly not absolute. One of the most entertaining features of the narrative is his penchant for humorously describing his numerous encounters with the captains, mates, and crews of other ships and with locals in port. In the North Atlantic he encounters ships and "speaks them," trading news with their astonished captains and officers, who were not entirely accustomed to meeting solitary mariners on small boats in mid-ocean. A friendly rivalry of mariners animates these conversations, and the dialogue is nearly always crisp and jocular. Instead of dwelling on his own misfortunes as a down-at-heels former sea captain tramping around the world like a wind-driven hobo, Slocum makes light of himself, poking fun at his boat's diminutive size and describing his own adventures in slapstick fashion. At other moments the narrative lyrically describes the glories of a fast twenty-four hours' run or relates the admirable seakeeping qualities of the *Spray*.

After leaving the Azores, Slocum had an entertaining encounter with a ghost. Incapacitated by severe indigestion brought on by eating too many Azorean plums and "white cheese," Slocum lay moaning on the floor of his cabin while the Spray careened through a gale, when, "to my surprise I saw a tall man at the helm." This apparition addresses Slocum, saying "I have come to do you no harm.... I am the pilot of the *Pinta* come to aid you" (p. 39). This providential visit from a ghost of Columbus' voyages, one imagines, was caused by the hallucinogenic nature of Slocum's intestinal suffering; or it may also be an effect of the author's poetic license. In any case, the episode demonstrates what is meant when we call *Sailing Alone* a work of creative nonfiction. Never was a minor character more deftly called to life than Slocum's ghostly pilot.

The *Spray*'s next landfall was Gibraltar, where Slocum enjoyed the hospitality of the British officers, their wives, and their supplies. Slocum tells of his time there with a certain glee, for he was extremely well treated by the British naval officers of the port—in part, no doubt, out of admiration for the feat of having crossed the North Atlantic alone in a small boat in a mere twenty-nine days. After a happy stay at Gibraltar, Slocum found himself beset by Barbary pirates off the north coast of Africa and wisely chose to turn around and head west-southwest for Rio de Janeiro, and thence around Cape Horn.

At this point in the narrative Slocum redraws the map of his adventure, setting his course in the wake of the great early modern navigators— Ferdinand Magellan, Sir Francis Drake, and Willem Schouten. There is something breathtaking about Slocum's temerity in recrossing the Atlantic at this point, and, at the same time, something poignant about the aging mariner in his aged vessel steering for the Brazilian coast where he had already endured so much hardship and heartbreak. But Slocum knew very well what he was doing: staying in latitudes where the trade winds prevail, winds that blow steady and strong from east to west.

Slocum never dwells on his long passages at sea. Instead he focuses on his encounters with ships and strangers on far shores. *Sailing Alone*

Around the World was published when the young United States was expanding as an imperial power. The American reading public's interest in far-flung lands and peoples was high. It is no surprise, then, that Slocum serves up vivid descriptions of his encounters with locals in various ports and islands. In Patagonia, where the *Spray* traversed the Strait of Magellan, Slocum tells of his encounters with indigenous people of the region, Fuegians who were apparently intent on robbing him. Like the Barbary pirates who chased him out of the Mediterranean, the Fuegians add an element of drama to Slocum's narrative of navigation and seamanship.

The narrative of *Sailing Alone* never fails to delight experienced sailors because of its author's thorough mastery of the arts of the sailor. From boatbuilding to boat handling, blue-water navigation to sail tending, Slocum is entirely the master of his nautical situation. Thus, while the entire narrative amounts to one enormously protracted boast, it is also endearingly self-effacing in tone, frequently understating the dangers faced and obstacles overcome by its narrator-protagonist. In his spare, nonchalant way Slocum boasts of his skill at sea by recounting his adventures as a series of minor follies.

For example, on setting out he recounts the purchase of a cheap tin clock, not the usual expensive chronometer of navigators, which he used to navigate by dead reckoning—calculating his mileage by dividing distance by time (characteristically, the tin clock had a broken face). By this method he calculated his longitude; for his latitude he used celestial navigation, "shooting the sun" with a sextant at local apparent noon of each day. While on the Pacific he also performed a lunar distance observation, a rare feat that allowed him to double-check his longitude. Only a very skilled navigator could accomplish this, but Slocum characteristically downplays his own feats while, nonetheless, describing them in careful, apparently offhand detail.

The skills of the solitary small-boat sailor overlap considerably with those of the clipper ship captain, but they are not entirely the same. Circumnavigation required that Slocum develop special skills. One of Slocum's nautical feats was his mastery of the art of self-steering, a requisite technique for any solitary sailor today, but not standard practice at the turn of the twentieth century. Famously, the *Spray's* captain rarely touched the helm while sailing long distances at sea; instead, he lashed the helm and set the sails so as to keep the boat on course. To do this he had to be sure the sailing rig of the *Spray* was well balanced to begin with. This has been one of the most celebrated and debated aspects of the voyage, among mariners, for Slocum claimed to have sailed immense—almost absurd—distances without steering the boat.

He did, however, make modifications to the rig, just as he had modified the hull when rebuilding it. In South America he added a mizzenmast near the stern of the boat to add windward helm, changing the rig from sloop to yawl, which helped it point up into the wind more readily. With this arrangement and a long, straight keel the boat tracked exceptionally well. "For one whole month," claims Slocum, "my vessel held her course true; I had not, the while, so much as a light in the binnacle" (p. 145). There is no reason to doubt him.

In the Pacific, Slocum stuck to the pattern that had served him well in the Atlantic, in sailor's parlance "running down the trades," or keeping his course within the belt of latitude where the easterly trade winds prevailed. Doing so brought him first to Juan Fernández Island (now called Robinson Crusoe Island), well to the west of Chile, and then across many thousands of miles to Samoa, where he met Robert Louis Stevenson's widow, Fanny. From Samoa he continued on to Australia, where he had met his first wife, Virginia, many years before.

In between his encounters with local people, celebrities, naval officers, and port dwellers, Slocum spent most of his time alone. The word "alone" jumps out from the title of the narrative, and it animates nearly every section of the book. But his solitude led Slocum to seek company in unlikely companions—in spiders at Tierra del Fuego, in the dancing wave tops of mid-ocean, and in the *Spray*. At times he apostrophizes the boat, addressing it directly like an old friend (or

like Don Quixote's horse Rozinante). At other times the old sailor speaks to himself, sings songs, and speaks with ghosts. But never is he truly solitary—or, at least, never ineluctably so.

At every port, too, Slocum was welcomed by people who could, and did, appreciate the magnitude of the feat he was in the act of accomplishing. In Australia, a nation of sailors, he was treated like an old friend. In the Azores, at Gibraltar, Juan Ferná ndez, and Samoa, too, he was welcomed with great hospitality. In part this welcome owes, no doubt, to Slocum's growing celebrity. For his dispatches home, published serially in the *Century Illustrated Monthly Magazine,* the *Louisville Courier-Journal,* the *New York World,* and the *Boston Globe,* were reaching a broad readership.

Slocum was already a celebrity when he reached Australia, with the Sydney, Melbourne, and Hobart newspapers trumpeting his arrival. He arrived in Newcastle, New South Wales, in the fall of 1896 and subsequently lingered on the Australian coast, visiting his first wife Virginia's family, giving newspaper interviews, and sailing to multiple ports and across the Tasman Sea to Tasmania. His next task was to cross the Indian Ocean, which brought him to the Keeling (Cocos) Islands, Mauritius, Réunion, and round the southern tip of Africa to Cape Town. There the *Spray* underwent a refit while Slocum took an inland sojourn to the Transvaal, traveling for free on the new rail system with a complimentary rail pass. In Pretoria he met the Transvaal president, Paul Kruger, who, after learning Slocum was on a voyage "around the world," refused to speak to him any further because his eminence believed the world to be flat.

Typically, however, he was warmly welcomed wherever he went—in the Keeling Islands by throngs of children, in Mauritius by the governor of the island, and in mid-ocean by American naval ships, including the battleship *Oregon,* which he met twice on his voyage. After setting sail from South Africa, Slocum next made port at the island of Saint Helena, in the mid–South Atlantic, anchoring in the harbor and spending a night in the room where Napoleon Bonaparte lived out his final days. He did not forget to toast his old friend and sailing companion, the ghostly pilot of the *Pinta* who first joined him off the Azores, a delightfully internationalist touch on Slocum's part, especially considering the fact that the United States was then at war with Spain.

The remainder of the voyage brought Slocum and the *Spray* through the familiar waters he had traversed so many times before aboard the *Aquidneck* and the *Liberdade.* His voyage had lasted almost exactly three years. Only the fact of war could have prevented Slocum from receiving a hero's welcome on his return to the United States. It did, but not for long. The tepid reception Slocum received in the Newport, Rhode Island, was atypical, and soon Slocum would be sailing to port towns where an eager public thronged to hear him recount his adventures. Shortly after completing his circumnavigation Slocum saw his narrative published in book form, and sales were brisk from the start. Unlike Odysseus, Slocum never felt the need to bid farewell to the sea, walking inland and "swallowing the anchor." His last years were spent promoting book sales, giving lectures, sailing the *Spray* to familiar ports, and plotting another voyage.

LEGACY AND REPUTATION

Slocum has been celebrated and memorialized in a surprising variety of ways and places. In this age of modern literary pilgrimages Slocum's life offers quite a treasure hunt for tourists. The Slocum River in southeastern Massachusetts, where he initially rebuilt the *Spray,* was renamed in his honor. Just a few miles away a museum exhibit honors him at the New Bedford Whaling Museum of New Bedford, Massachusetts, and in Boston, the sculptor Daniel Chester French built a memorial to Joshua Slocum in Forest Hill Cemetery. In Nova Scotia tourists can visit the Mount Hanley Schoolhouse Museum, where he learned to read and write as a child. Farther south, there is a stone monument to him on Brier Island, and two local ferryboats have been named the *Joshua Slocum* and the *Spray.* Another exhibit honors him at the Maritime Museum of the Atlantic in Halifax. Several biographies about Slocum have been published, and books continue

to be written about his life and accomplishments; among these is Geoffrey Wolff's *The Hard Way Around: The Passages of Joshua Slocum,* published in 2010.

Slocum's admirers include many writers of note. Wolff has called *Sailing Alone* "a tour de force of descriptive and narrative power" (p. 3). In a similar vein, the scholar Robert Foulke has called Slocum an "extremely effective writer, who developed a laconic, self-deprecating style laced with subtle humor and well-turned anecdotes" (1997, p. 161). Jonathan Raban remarks that "his reading and his temperament inclined Slocum to a keen appreciation of the physical beauty of water under the influence of wind and tide," noting how "at regular intervals throughout the book, his customarily gruff manner suddenly breaks, to make way for a paragraph-long prose poem" (p. 28). These admiring statements attest to the ongoing appeal of Slocum's literary masterpiece.

Slocum and the *Spray* have not evaded criticism. Throughout the twentieth century mariners and writers have criticized Slocum's foolhardiness in voyaging solo, and the design of the *Spray* has been blamed for Slocum's eventual loss, the keel allegedly too shallow and the stability of the hull in question. The maritime historian Howard I. Chappelle, known for his compendious writings on traditional American boats and curator at the Smithsonian Institution, argued that the *Spray* was intrinsically susceptible to capsizing because of her low stability beyond a shallow angle. Slocum's writing style has been called childish, his letters used as evidence, and the charge of moral turpitude has been leveled at the man convicted of indecently exposing himself to a twelve-year-old girl. Others have argued that his writing style simply fails to live up to its reputation. None of these charges can diminish the nautical and literary achievement of *Sailing Alone Around the World*.

Slocum is easily the most influential figure in modern sailing history, having inspired generations of deep-water sailors and solo circumnavigators of numerous national identities. For most of the twentieth century the *Spray* was the single most frequently replicated sailboat on the planet. To this day *Spray* replicas can be found, although it is scarcely imaginable that their owners would choose such spartan accommodations as Slocum had. Countless twentieth-century readers of *Sailing Alone* have attempted to sail in Slocum's wake, retracing his circumnavigation and, in some cases, attempting to re-create his nautical feats.

Some of Slocum's emulators have become celebrities themselves. The first of these was the Canadian J. C. Voss, who in 1901 embarked aboard his homemade thirty-eight-foot log canoe *Tilikum* from Victoria, British Columbia, on a Slocum-like solo voyage. In 1913 *The Venturesome Voyages of Captain Voss* was published, shortly after Jack London's book *The Cruise of the Snark* (1911) first saw print. These books contributed to a boom of nautical literature produced in the early decades of the twentieth century, when the great age of sail had given way to a new era of steam-powered iron ships, with engineers replacing seamen. Joseph Conrad, for example, wrote about sail-powered sea voyages in works of fiction such as *The Shadow-Line* (1917) and "The Secret Sharer" (1910). The popularity of sea fiction on both sides of the English-speaking Atlantic undoubtedly created an audience for *Sailing Alone*.

Slocum, in turn, exercised an immense influence on all subsequent nautical literature in English. Nautical narratives both fictional and nonfictional continued to be popular long into the twentieth century, as did the idea of solo navigation. The French long-distance sailor Bernard Moitessier named his thirty-nine-foot sailboat, built for circumnavigation, *Joshua* in honor of Slocum. Francis Chichester, who completed a series of celebrated solo voyages across oceans, was knighted in 1967. Not surprisingly, his books recounting those voyages sold well.

Joshua Slocum casts a long shadow, but his fame and influence are undoubtedly in decline. While *Sailing Alone* was required reading in many grade schools for much of the twentieth century, today it is a book known mainly to weekend mariners and literary aficionados. Countless other single-handed sailors continue to read and admire it, and almost any weekend

sailor knows Slocum's name. In the twenty-first century, however, Slocum's literary achievement has become less interesting to a reading public for which high-tech globalization in all aspects of life diminishes the sensationalism of a solitary circumnavigation and threatens to render sailboats and three-year voyages quaint relics of a bygone age.

As a master mariner and the captain of sailing ships whose career declined with the waning days of sail, Slocum was in a sense on the wrong side of history. In the last decades of the nineteenth century sailing ships grew fewer and crews smaller. The international labor market for sailors was shrinking, while steamship mariners increased in number and began to monopolize world trade. *Sailing Alone Around the World* can, thus, be read as the swan song of a dying breed of master mariners, an ode to seafaring under sail in an increasingly mechanized and crowded world. A tone of jaunty rivalry between sail and steam runs *Sailing Alone,* and many of Slocum's admirers themselves have been critical of modern mechanized life, finding in the pages of that book a manifesto for their own desire for independence, self-reliance, and freedom. It is not uncommon to see *Sailing Alone* on a bookshelf next to *Walden,* which may indeed be its rightful place.

Selected Bibliography

WORKS OF JOSHUA SLOCUM

Nonfiction

The Voyage of the Liberdade*: Description of a Voyage "Down to the Sea."* Boston: Robinson & Stephenson, 1890.

The Voyage of the Destroyer *from New York to Brazil.* Boston: Robinson Printing Company, 1894.

Sailing Alone Around the World. Illustrated by Thomas Fogarty and George Varian. New York: Century, 1900.

Sailing Alone Around the World. Mariners' Library Series. London: Butler and Tanner, 1948.

Sailing Alone Around the World. Introduction by Walter Magnes Teller. New York: Sheridan House, 1954. (Page references in the text refer to this edition.)

Sailing Alone Around the World. New York: Dover, 1956.

"The Voyage of the *Aquidneck*." In *Five Sea Captains: Amasa Delano, Edmund Fanning, Richard Cleveland, George Coggeshall, Joshua Slocum; Their Own Accounts of Voyages Under Sail.* Edited by Walter Magnes Teller. New York: Atheneum, 1960.

The Voyages of Joshua Slocum. Special anniversary edition. Edited by Walter Magnes Teller. Dobbs Ferry, N.Y.: Sheridan House, 1995. (Page references in the text for *The Voyage of the* Liberdade and *The Voyage of the* Destroyer refer to this edition.)

Sailing Alone Around the World and The Voyage of the Liberdade. Introduction by Anthony Brandt. Washington, D.C.: National Geographic Society, 2003.

The Annotated "Sailing Alone Around the World." Annotated by Rod Scher. Dobbs Ferry, N.Y.: Sheridan House, 2009.

Papers

A limited collection of Slocum's papers is held by the Phillips Library at the Peabody Essex Museum, Salem, Massachusetts.

CRITICAL AND BIOGRAPHICAL STUDIES

Bender, Bert. "Joshua Slocum and the Reality of Solitude." *American Transcendental Quarterly* 6, no. 1:59–71 (March 1992).

Foulke, Robert D. "Life in the Dying World of Sail, 1870–1910." *Journal of British Studies* 3, no. 1:105–136 (1963).

———. *The Sea Voyage Narrative.* New York: Twayne, 1997.

Holm, Donald. *The Circumnavigators: Small Boat Voyagers of Modern Times.* Englewood Cliffs, N.J.: Prentice-Hall, 1974.

Joyce, Jessie Slocum, and Beth Day. *Joshua Slocum, Sailor.* Boston: Houghton Mifflin, 1953.

Lopes, Myra A. *Captain Joshua Slocum: A Centennial Tribute.* Chehalis, Wash.: RPI, 1994.

———. "Captain Slocum's Life Before and After the *Spray*." Chehalis, Wash.: RPI, 1997.

Ransome, Arthur. Introduction to *Sailing Alone Around the World.* Mariners Library No. 1. London: Rupert Hart-Davis, 1948.

Slack, Kenneth E. *In the Wake of the* Spray. New Brunswick, N.J.: Rutgers University Press, 1966.

Slocum, Charles Elihu. *A Short History of the Slocums, Slocumbs, and Slocombs of America.* Vol. 1, 1637–1881. Vol. 2, 1882–1908. Syracuse, N.Y., and Defiance, Ohio: The author, 1882, 1908.

Slocum, Victor. *Capt. Joshua Slocum: The Life and Voyages of America's Best-Known Sailor.* New York: Sheridan House, 1993.

Spencer, Ann. *Alone at Sea: The Adventures of Joshua*

Slocum. Richmond Hill, Ont.: Firefly Books, 1999.

Teller, Walter Magnes. "Any Word of Captain Slocum?" *Vineyard Gazette,* June 19, 1953, sec. 2, pp. 1, 4–5.

———. *The Search for Captain Slocum: A Biography.* New York: Scribners, 1956.

———. "Postscripts to *The Search for Captain Slocum.*" *American Neptune,* July 1958, pp. 189–200.

Wilson, Derek. *The Circumnavigators: A History.* New York: Carroll & Graf, 2004.

Wolff, Geoffrey. *The Hard Way Around: The Passages of Joshua Slocum.* New York: Knopf, 2010.

OTHER SOURCES

Bernardin, Guy. *Sailing Around the World: A Family Retraces Joshua Slocum's Voyage.* Translated by Jeremy McGeary. Dobbs Ferry, N.Y.: Sheridan House, 2002.

Blondin, Robert, and Hedley King. *The Solitary Slocum.* Halifax, N.S.: Nimbus, 1993.

Day, Thomas Fleming. "On Capt. Joshua Slocum." In *The Rudder Treasury.* Edited by Tom Davin. New York: Sheridan, 1953. Pp. 153–155.

Hugo, David T. "Nova Scotia to Martha's Vineyard: Notes on Captain Joshua Slocum." *Dukes County Intelligencer* August 1969, p. 3.

Johnson, Clifton. "Captain Joshua Slocum: The Man Who Sailed Alone Around the World in a Thirty-Seven-Foot Boat." In *Tales of Old New England.* Edited by Frank Oppel. Secaucus, N.J.: Castle, 1986.

Raban, Jonathan. *The Oxford Book of the Sea.* Oxford and New York: Oxford University Press, 1992.

Roberts-Goodson, R. Bruce. Spray*, the Ultimate Cruising Boat.* Dobbs Ferry, N.Y.: Sheridan House, 1995.

A. E. STALLINGS

(1968—)

Emily Setina

A. E. (ALICIA Elsbeth) Stallings is an American-born poet, critic, and translator. One of contemporary poetry's foremost practitioners of formal verse and winner of the prestigious MacArthur Fellowship, Stallings has a biography that reads as though it was scripted by a fairy godmother with a poet's fondness for echoes and symmetries. Raised outside Atlanta, Stallings studied classics in Athens, Georgia, and has lived, since 1999, in Athens, Greece. She shares her first two initials, A. E., with a great predecessor, the Edwardian writer A. E. Housman, whom she has called her favorite poet. She shares with Housman too her dual calling, as both poet and classicist.

Stallings has published poems, translations, and prose. Her first book, titled *Archaic Smile,* won the 1999 Richard Wilbur Award. Her second book, titled *Hapax* and published in 2006, won the Poets' Prize. Her third book, *Olives,* appeared in 2012. In her original poems, Stallings brings a deep knowledge of Greek and Roman literature and culture to personal and contemporary themes including memory, family, mortality, marriage, and motherhood. In these poems, mythic and personal voices blend. Ancient mythology provides a resource for continuing invention, and the personae of Mount Olympus, classical history, and modern life reappear in multiple guises. The Greek goddess Persephone, for example, speaks in each of Stallings' three full-length collections of poems, each time in a different voice. In Stallings' first collection, Persephone speaks as a homesick girl penning notes her mother will never receive ("Persephone Writes a Letter to Her Mother"). In *Olives,* she speaks as a disillusioned woman drinking bitters at the bar who dispenses straight talk to the pregnant wife of Eros and goddess of the soul, Psyche ("Persephone to Psyche"). In *Hapax,*

Persephone's voice takes another form, as the alternately besotted and haunted first-person subject of "First Love: A Quiz." With its multiple-choice format and knowing tone the poem recalls the pop quizzes that Stallings might have found in *Seventeen,* the fashion and advice magazine for young women that published one of her earliest poems, just as it had once published the work of a young Sylvia Plath.

While tackling texts more often associated with dons than teens, Stallings' translations also evince flair and vigor, a relish for the pleasures of rhyme, precision of imagery, and quirks of found form that can render long classical poems startlingly fresh. In 2007 she published her largest and perhaps most audacious project to date: a translation of Lucretius' long philosophical poem *De Rerum Natura,* or *The Nature of Things* as Stallings translates it. For her rendering, Stallings received the Willis Barnstone Translation Prize in 2010. Her Lucretius has become a touchstone for contemporary classical translation: Peter Stothard described it in the *Times Literary Supplement* as "One of the most extraordinary classical translations of recent times." Stallings has begun work on a second volume of translations, *Works and Days (Erga Kai Hēmerai)* by the eighth-century B.C. Greek poet Hesiod. In addition to her book-length translations of Lucretius and Hesiod, she has also translated poems from modern Greek and Old English. Living in Athens in the first decades of the twenty-first century, Stallings has been firsthand witness to a painful epoch in modern Greek history, which she has also written about in both verse and prose ("Austerity Measures," "Austerity Measures: A Letter from Greece").

In his review of *Hapax,* Mark Jarman wrote, "A. E. Stallings is the most gifted formalist of

her generation and writes with a grace and ease of older generations, which included Richard Wilbur and, before him, Edna St. Vincent Millay" (p. 325). For her talent for precise description and her engagement with and reinvention of traditional forms, Stallings has also been likened to Elizabeth Bishop. Like Bishop in Brazil, too, Stallings, Erica McAlpine writes, is "an emigrant poet engaged in living history, not a tourist" (p. 396). Adam Kirsch finds that Stallings shares with Bishop a rare "worldly" sensibility, a "coolly ironic sense of the way things fall, not dramatically apart, but unsettlingly askew." Stallings herself invites the comparison to Bishop when she echoes a rhyme familiar from the villanelle "One Art" ("disaster" / "master") in "Aftershocks," a sonnet about a relationship that seems suddenly precarious, and when she titles a poem "For the Losers of Things." Bishop's "One Art" is, after all, the "art of losing" (Bishop, p. 178). Other predecessors mentioned as influences and in comparison with Stallings include Robert Frost, for deft use of forms; W. H. Auden, for comic grace and moral seriousness; Sylvia Plath, and even Sappho, for darker treatment of feminist themes; and James Merrill, for love of both ornament and Athens. Among contemporaries, Stallings has been compared to her fellow MacArthur recipient Kay Ryan and, for her use of Greek and Latin myth, to Louise Glück and Stallings' fellow classicists, poets, and translators Anne Carson and David Ferry.

Though living at a geographical distance from the American poetry scene, Stallings has gained increasing recognition within it. She received the 1997 Eunice Tietjens Memorial Prize from *Poetry* magazine and the 1999 James Dickey Prize from *Five Points.* Her first collection, *Archaic Smile,* won the 1999 Richard Wilbur Award, judged by Dana Gioia. Stallings received the 2004 Howard Nemerov Sonnet Award for "Country Song," originally published in *The Formalist* as "Long Gone Lonesome Blues." For *Hapax,* she won the 2008 Poets' Prize, and in the same year she was awarded the Benjamin H. Danks prize from the American Academy of Arts and Letters. In 2011 she received both a Guggenheim Fellowship and the

MacArthur Fellowship. Award of the MacArthur Fellowship especially, known popularly as the "genius grant," has made her an increasingly public figure.

Stallings is in the unlikely, perhaps unique, position for her varied accomplishments of being cited in poetry journals for statements on poetry and knitting and, alternately, interviewed by *Forbes* magazine on "Power, Ambition, Glory." She is a frequent contributor to *Poetry* magazine and the Poetry Foundation's "Harriet" blog site. Her poems have also appeared in *Best American Poetry,* on the online sites *Poetry Daily* (www. poems.com) and *Verse Daily* (www.versedaily. com), and in a host of other literary venues, from the *Hudson Review, Southern Review,* and *Iron Horse Literary Review* to the *New Yorker, Atlantic Monthly,* and *New Criterion.* Poems included in *Hapax* also appeared in a limited-edition letterpress chapbook, *Aftershocks,* printed by Michael Peich at the Aralia Press in 2003. In her mid-forties and living a continent away, she has established herself as a major American poet.

LIFE

Alicia Elsbeth Stallings was born in Decatur, Georgia, a suburb of Atlanta, on July 2, 1968. Her mother, Alice Stallings, was a school librarian, which contributed to Alicia's wanting "from the get-go, really," to be a writer (Byrne interview). Her father, William M. Stallings, was a professor in the Department of Educational Policy Studies at Georgia State University, where he specialized in applied statistics and evaluations. One can imagine that the author of academic articles such as "Return to Our Roots: Raising Radishes to Teach Experimental Design" and "Mind Your p's and Alphas" (referring to two Greek letters used as variables in statistical reporting) might have taken a creative and independent approach to parenting as well. Stallings affirmed in a 1999 interview with Ginger Murchison that she had "an unusual childhood," thanks, in part, to her parents' approach to raising daughters, their disregard of boundaries and gender conventions that would have been more

strictly enforced in less progressive households, perhaps especially in a city famous for its belles and debutantes. William Stallings was "intellectual and outdoorsy; so he could discuss Proust or skinning deer, and we, my sister Jocelyn and I, grew up, not exactly tomboys, but I did know how to gut a fish when I was four. I think my parents had a theory that children should be treated as if they had no gender. We had a workbench for carpentry, and we played with dolls" (Murchison).

In "Ariadne and the Rest," a poem in Stallings' first collection *Archaic Smile*, she imagines Ariadne, princess of Thebes, as too polite and too good a student of the myths "concocted / To beguile the little girls indoors" while the boys, out sword-fighting, sing "hero-tales" (pp. 37, 39). Ariadne's feminine education dooms her: taught to paint her lips, cinch her waist, and keep an "eye peeled for princes," she ends up "another princess / Jilted" (pp. 37, 39). Stallings seems to sympathize with Ariadne's position, but her very different girlhood and broad-minded parents spared her some of the pains of the late twentieth century's versions of these beauty myths. Most of the women who populate Stallings' poems, likewise, have disregarded or learned to disregard the lesson to coo "yes, yes, at every pause" (p. 38).

The Stallings sisters, in their reading, were not confined to those tales "concocted / To beguile the little girls indoors." Alice Stallings' job meant that there was always something to read in the house. The girls brought home from the library laundry baskets filled with books and were read to by their parents. "Fairy-Tale Logic," Stallings titles a poem and section of *Olives,* and she has claimed that her love for fairy tales, especially sad ones like Hans Christian Anderson's *Little Mermaid*, began early. She told Ginger Murchison that she always liked "the original, uncut versions, the ones with violent, horrible endings," for these tales are "a lot more cathartic." Her early exposure to books went far beyond fairy tales and sparked her interest in writing and in becoming a writer. Both of her parents encouraged her interest. Her father took her out of school to hear visiting writers speak at nearby universities. She heard Eudora Welty read at Agnes Scott, Stephen Spender, James Dickey, "all kinds of writers" (Murchison). Through this exposure, she realized very early "that books were written by people and that one could be a writer, and I wanted to write books" (Murchison). She also credits her high school education, at Atlanta's small, soon-to-be-defunct Briarcliff High School, as unusually suited to the needs of a bookish, intellectually-bent Georgia teenager. Classes were filled with children of other professors, from Emory University, Georgia Tech, and Georgia State. It was a school that "had an excellent English teacher, but a terrible football team" (Murchison).

After high school, Stallings moved to Athens, Georgia, to attend the University of Georgia. She tried English as a major, but "it didn't take" (Gylys interview). Instead she majored in music (she plays the violin) and in Latin, a major she chose, she has said, because she thought that that was what poets did, and several poets she admired most had taken that path, including Housman, E. E. Cummings, and T. S. Eliot. At Georgia, she studied Virgil under Robert Harris, who also gave her a taste of Lucretius' "beauty and strangeness ... quoting the lines about flocks of stars grazing their way across the night sky" (*The Nature of Things,* p. xxx). She tried her hand at verse translation, too, beginning with Catullus, in a graduate workshop she was recruited into as a freshman by the classicist Richard A. LaFleur. After earning her bachelor's degree in 1990, she moved to England to pursue a master's degree in classics at Oxford University, writing on Virgil under the direction of Richard Jenkyns. Jenkyns also suggested, both to Stallings and a publisher, the project of her translating all of Lucretius. Lucretius' translator paid the bills by working as a "tea girl," a job whose exhaustions are commemorated in the poem "Menielle" in *Archaic Smile* (Murchison). If the work, at a shop in London, was less than glorious, she met her future husband, John Psaropoulos, then doing his graduate work in the city. After completing their studies, the couple moved to Atlanta for a time and lived in an apartment in an old house in the

Clarkston neighborhood of the city, the house remembered in "Lovejoy Street" (*Hapax*).

When Stallings first began trying to publish poems, "there was still a lot of active antipathy to formal verse," and, less committed to rhyme and meter than she was to become, she wrote poems that she thought might get accepted in that climate—that is, mostly, poems in free verse (Gylys interview). She describes a "turning point" that came when she submitted a group of poems to the *Beloit Poetry Journal,* and "the lone rhyming one" was the one accepted; the experience "gave me the confidence to … write the poems I really wanted to be writing" (Gylys). More votes of confidence followed: publications and, in 1997, the Eunice Tietjens Memorial Prize from *Poetry* magazine, a venue where she continues to appear regularly. During this period, she was also repeatedly shortlisted for awards that bring first-book publication, including the prestigious Yale Younger Poets Prize and the Walt Whitman Award. The near-wins were exciting but also, for hopes raised and disappointed, wearing.

In 1999 Stallings topped the short list to win the Richard Wilbur Award and publish her first book, *Archaic Smile.* That same year she and Psaropoulos moved to Greece. Stallings got the job she continues to hold, as poetry program director at the Athens Centre. Personal loss and change from her early years in Greece make their way into the poems of *Hapax:* the death of her father in 2000, her pregnancy with her son Jason. Her "decade-old" project of translating Lucretius came to an end with the book's publication in 2007 ("Numbers Trouble"). Beginning that same year, Stallings also became a regular and popular contributor to the Poetry Foundation's *Harriet* poetry blog. There she began exploring in essay form some of the ideas—about motherhood, about poetry and contemporary culture, about language—that she returns to in poetry in *Olives.*

She has also used the blog forum, as befits a site that carries the name of *Poetry* magazine's founder, Harriet Monroe, to discuss issues of poetry and gender, in practice (advocating, for instance, that fellowships be given to support time off from child care as they are for time away from prestigious teaching jobs) and theory (analyzing and debunking assumptions about the gendered essence of poetic forms and gendered politics of formalism). "What was exhilarating" about a panel on "Afro-Formalism" that she attended at the 2010 Association of Writers and Poets conference, she wrote in one post, was that "what came out of this was that the tradition and form were not about exclusion or elitism or who owns or is allowed to do what. It was about inclusion and access and taking all things human as belonging to everybody, about the ongoing conversation, dialogue really, of the dead and the living" ("Afro-formalism").

Her feminism also takes the shape, like Virginia Woolf's, of appreciation for the lives and works of women predecessors—for instance, Lucy Hutchinson, the first English writer to translate Lucretius in full. In her introductory note to her own translation, Stallings cites Hutchinson's description of the room in which she worked, with her children practicing tutors' lessons as Hutchinson counted syllables by her embroidery threads "and sett them downe with a pen and inke that stood by me" (quoted in *The Nature of Things,* p. xxviii). As she finished the project juggling her own baby son, Stallings writes, "it was encouraging to think that the person who had first blazed this trail was a busy mother" (*The Nature of Things,* p. xxviii).

Stallings and Psaropoulos initially thought their 1999 move to Greece would be temporary. "The one thing people will ask you here if you are, as I am, clearly a foreigner, is: Are you here permanently?" ("Austerity Measures: A Letter from Greece"). Stallings says she always thought the answer was no. She and her husband have considered returning to the United States, particularly in the economic downturn, and then disaster, that followed the worldwide financial recession of 2008 and the subsequent Greek government debt crisis beginning in 2010. Drastic tax increases, massive spending cuts, and restrictive labor and pension reforms—the so-called "austerity measures" implemented by the Greek government in response to demands of European Union and International Monetary Fund creditors—sparked widespread anger amid worsening recession. Protests, strikes, and riots followed in

Athens, where Stallings and Psaropoulos live, and elsewhere in Greece.

The crisis has kept Greek journalists busy; Psaropoulos has reported from Athens for a number of media outlets including Al Jazeera, National Public Radio, and the *Daily Beast.* For a while, however, even his income—which, despite Stallings' successes, the family had depended upon—seemed threatened by the wider financial devastation. The couple went so far as to apply for jobs in the United States. Asked by one academic interviewer whether she was prepared to "give up [her] idyllic life" in Greece "to 'do battle' at the office," Stallings reported that she found herself "at a loss … since my actual life in Athens involves negotiating a baby stroller through street protests while dodging billows of tear gas" ("Austerity Measures: A Letter from Greece"). A "deus ex machina in the form of generous grants," including the 2011 Guggenheim and MacArthur Fellowships, enabled the family to stay in Greece ("Austerity Measures: A Letter from Greece"). Even with relief from personal financial anxieties, Stallings describes the strain that comes with living amid the country's widespread poverty and distress, despite her realization, too, of the gulf that separates her family from those that do not have the option to leave ("Austerity Measures: A Letter from Greece").

Nevertheless, the crisis has also reminded her that her "forebears" among modern Greek poets have "seen worse" ("Austerity Measures: A Letter from Greece"). In an essay about life in Athens during the crisis, Stallings writes about making a trip with fellow poet Fani Papageorgiou and a class of poetry students, mostly visiting Americans, to the First Cemetery of Athens—the site of the earlier sonnet, "Mornings, I Walk Past the First Cemetery of Athens," and her poem "Cenotaph"—to look for the graves of modern Greek poets: Angelos Sikelianos (1884–1951), Kostis Palamas (1859–1943), Odysseus Elytis (1911–1996), and George Seferis (1900–1971). The search for their graves is also a chance to remember the events that marked the poets' lives and the country's previous century: the occupation and famine of World War II, civil war, military dictatorship, exile. This turbulent recent history, Stallings has said, makes Greek poets less vexed than their American counterparts about the value of beauty and pleasure for their own sake.

Indeed, in modern-day austerity-era Greece, Stallings finds verse "everywhere": in graffiti scrawled on buildings, in the meters of protest chants and Greek rap, and in carefully quoted or loosely paraphrased lines of Seferis and C. P. Cavafy that come from the mouths of government officials. "Even I," she writes, "find myself working at a feverish pace … reading intensely, translating furiously" ("Austerity Measures: A Letter from Greece"). She finds herself, too, contemplating something she had previously rejected, the possibility of staying put. She quotes a Greek proverb that she also uses as the refrain of a recent poem: "Nothing is more permanent than the temporary" ("Austerity Measures: A Letter from Greece," "After a Greek Proverb"). One day, she writes, you find yourself looking "at the cemeteries, and at the graves of poets, in a different way. The way a young girl, perhaps, shyly glances at wedding dresses," as though anticipating that one day she might have one of her own ("Austerity Measures: A Letter from Greece").

The fellowship "deus ex machina" not only allowed Stallings to remain in Greece with her family; it also gave her means to obtain something she had long been desiring: an office. "You Don't Need Time to Write. You Need Space," she titled a blog post, affirming and reiterating Virginia Woolf's dictum that to write one needs "a room of one's own." Hers, as she describes it, is in the apartment next door to the one she shares with her family, close enough for her to see her two children at play in the yard as she writes. Motherhood as a theme also has made its way into her poetry, beginning with the eerie images of "Ultrasound," the final poem in *Hapax,* and continuing in the poems of *Olives,* particularly its final section, "Fairy Tale Logic." Asked how motherhood has changed her, she told an interviewer that it has changed how she views her own mortality: since having children, she said, it "no longer concerns me much.… I fear for lives other than my own, but with that same primal

terror. More so" (Gylys). Asked how motherhood has affected her poetry, she says, "my traditional line is that there is less of it," but being a mother also "brings you into this grey space … when you're not trying to control your thoughts" and up with colicky baby ("The Courage of Poetry"). Sometimes, she says, that's when a poem comes.

ANCIENTS AND MODERNS: TRANSLATION, FORM, AND THE FUTURE OF POETRY

"The ancients," Stallings has said in speaking of the paradoxical cross-pollination between her writing and translation projects, "taught me how to sound modern" (Perlroth interview). Stallings learned a kind of license in her use of classical myths from classical writers themselves; in Greek and Latin poetry, different tellers often give the same stories different forms. She has spoken of the usefulness of myth as a way of telling the personal, as Emily Dickinson wrote, at a "slant," or useful remove. Stallings told Murchison, "Sometimes when I want to write something personal, I'll write through a persona; then it's neither personal nor mythical, and it sort of becomes a combination of the two things, and if I'm trying to write about the myth, I'll deliberately search for a wholly different point of view because the traditional one doesn't make for a very interesting poem." On the other hand, whereas Greek myths have often in contemporary poetry been recast in a contemporary setting, Stallings, Steffen Horstmann notes, "resists … these kinds of departures." Her figures from classical mythology remain recognizable. Her expertise in classical languages, however, has also found more unusual venues, as when she composed the opening Latin lyrics for the soundtrack of the 2002 film *The Sum of All Fears*.

Stallings joked to Edward Byrne in 2011 about her seeming "affinity for curmudgeonly didactic male poets in dead languages." Written in the first century B.C.E., Lucretius' *Nature of Things* meditates on the order of man and the cosmos, from the indivisible atom through civilization and the planets. Stallings' translation is especially impressive not just for its learning and lively rendering of Lucretius' imagery but also for its formal virtuosity. The poem's translators have often put aside its metrical features— the patterns of sound in the Latin verse—in an attempt to hold on to the poem's content, which encompasses both philosophy and physics. For Stallings, though, the form of the translation mattered, as it does in her own writing. To capture the effect of the Latin original, she renders its 1,286 lines in rhyming fourteeners, or couplets made of paired fourteen-syllable lines. Rarely used, the verse form nevertheless has some notable precedents: Arthur Golding in his translation of Ovid's *Metamorphoses* (1567) and George Chapman in his rendition of the *Iliad* (1611). It was Chapman's rhyming fourteeners, "loud and bold," that astonished John Keats, another of Stallings' favorite poets, a reading he memorialized in "On First Looking into Chapman's Homer" (*Complete Poems,* p. 34).

Stallings has described Lucretius as a great teacher by analogy, for instance in his description of the movement of atoms. To illustrate their invisible dance, he points, in Stallings' translation, to "A paradigm of this that's dancing right before your eyes": dust motes in sunlight

> all moving many ways
> Throughout the void and intermingling in the golden
>   rays
> As if in everlasting struggle, battling in troops,
> Ceaselessly separating and regathering in groups.
> (*The Nature of Things,* book 2, lines 113, 116–119; p. 39)

Later in the poem, Lucretius compares writing natural philosophy in verse, his method of cloaking "so darkling a subject in a poetry so bright," to that of a doctor who coats the lip of a goblet that will hold bitter medicine with "honey's sweet blond stickiness" (book 4, lines 8, 13; p. 106). "Since those who've never tasted of it think / This philosophy's a bitter pill to swallow, and the throng / Recoils from it, I want to coat this physic in rich song" (Book IV, lines 18–20; p. 106). By preserving Lucretius' rhymes, Stallings carried forward this music, keeping the "honey" of the verse. She is also unafraid to grasp images "ready to hand" and echo lines that remind us we are reading a contemporary translation, by a passionate reader of English as well as Latin poetry

(book 4, line 798; p. 131). When she translates Lucretius on the crumbling of monuments, she emblazons hers with a legend from Percy Bysshe Shelley's "Ozymandias" (1818): "'Look upon my works ye mighty, and despair!'" (book 5, line 312; p. 157). A corruption in the source text at this line, Stallings notes, allowed her leeway, and as tone and context suggested the famous line, "the translator found appropriating it irresistible" (p. 253, n. 13).

If mythology provides one way of complicating a poem, of making it more "interesting" and more difficult, verse provides another. Stallings has distinguished herself by her craft. In an age of free verse, her poetry celebrates and reinvigorates traditional forms. In an era where poems written without fixed form or meter are the norm, Stallings is a master practitioner of the sonnet. She also writes masterful villanelles, pantoums, triolets, Sapphics, and even limericks. Her book-length translation of Lucretius in rhyming hendecasyllabics is another display and gift of her technical expertise and invention. She has written of the pleasure she takes in rhyme and meter, and in part these are also the pleasures of her often formally playful and precise poems. She calls rhyme and meter "a physical thing—they work differently upon the brain, I'm sure of it" (Murchison). As a reader, she has commented, "I am just not one of those people who think that rhymes, like obedient Victorian children, should be seen but not heard" ("Sonnetude"). Her "Presto Manifesto," published in *Poetry*, begins, "The freedom to not-rhyme must include the freedom to rhyme. Then verse will be free," and writes that the tag "rhyme-driven" should no longer be considered "pejorative."

She has felt the need to defend her preference and has taken criticism for it, perhaps most publicly and controversially in Peter Campion's review of *Hapax* for *Poetry* magazine, which includes the judgment that, in some lines of the collection, "meter and rhyme unfold elegantly, but at the expense of idiom." Campion expanded his criticism from Stallings to "the so-called 'New Formalists,'" a shorthand term for the loosely collected group of contemporary poets dedicated to traditional techniques (a group that has been variously configured to include poets such as Mark Jarman, David Mason, Elizabeth Alexander, Rafael Campo, Dana Gioia, Marilyn Hacker, Rachel Hadas, Andrew Hudgins, Brad Leithauser, Phillis Levin, Charles Martin, Wyatt Prunty, and Rachel Wetzsteon). Criticizing much dedication to technique as rote "display," Campion found that in Stallings' work adherence to convention could get in the way of her finding poems' "actual, essential forms."

Perhaps in part because her work has been taken as occasion to debate the viability of rhyme-driven poetry, Stallings has become one of rhyme's most ardent defenders. The idea of "pleasure" recurs in her claims on its behalf. Rhyme, she says, "really gets people worked up, perhaps because of its irrational pleasures" (Gylys). She has called rhyme and meter "some of the most powerful tools in the poet's kit" (Murchison). Rhyme is "a method of composition," she told Edward Byrne, one whose "dream-logic connections … lead the poem forward, perhaps into territory the poet herself had not intuited." She has spoken repeatedly about form as a means of intellectual and emotional discovery for the writer: "A meter may help you to tap into a forgotten emotion. With form, certain decisions have already been, arbitrarily, made for you—a certain number of lines, a designated meter with a particular pattern of rhymes. That frees you up to think about other, more interesting choices in the poem" (Murchison). Like mythology, that is, form provides a way of focusing elsewhere, getting outside of oneself. "I'm not really for self-expression, I guess," Stallings has said. "I don't really think I'm that interesting. I'm interested in expressing the poem and finding out what the poem has to say to me and learning something from the poem" ("The Courage of Poetry"). What might seem controlling, she views as "a giving up of control." In the ars poetica "Explaining an Affinity for Bats," Stallings describes being drawn to a creatures that "find their way by calling into darkness / To hear their voice bounce off the shape of things" (*Hapax*, p. 61).

Another American poet who lived in Greece, James Merrill, described seeing moving vans on

the streets of Athens "blazoned" with the word "*METAPHOROS*" (*Collected Prose,* p. 15). Merrill was amazed: in modern-day Athens even traffic could produce metaphors for metaphor, reminding him that the English word "metaphor" was descended from the Greek word for transport. Stallings' poems suggest a poet practiced in the art of transport, whether between languages, times, or continents. Her poems are often also about the feeling of being displaced, whether that feeling is due to jet lag or, as in "Persephone Writes a Letter to Her Mother," a new husband. Stallings describes rhyme and meter, those traditional measuring and shaping tools of the poet, as themselves sources of productive instability: "I do need some sort of difficulty," she has said, "to catch myself off balance, to make me keep my wits about me" (Gylys).

In Stallings' poems not only people but things get displaced. Indeed, here we meet the varied artifacts of the past. They come in the form of muddled wax tablets, disintegrated dog collars, classical myths, arrowheads, drowned houses, and great works of painting, and even more personal remnants—a childhood dollhouse, a favorite umbrella mislaid on a train. Some are available for further inspection at a museum, some are themselves both inventions and occasions for further invention, like the obsolete technologies that speak in "The Machines Mourn the Passing of People." "How came we by this quantity of junk?" asks the speaker in "Moving Sale" (*Archaic Smile,* p. 62). For all their engagement with loss, Stallings' poems are also, often, very funny. But then, as she has said, "Humor and rhyme are related—they work much the same way technically, that is in terms of setting up an expectation and then undermining it or else fulfilling it in a surprising way" (Byrne).

Stallings has been outspoken in a number of venues about her sense, too, that there is no need to worry about poetry's own ability to survive—that it does not need the cheery "boosterism" or anxious discussion that sometimes gets lavished upon it in the American poetry circles ("Biting the Hand"). It will, she has said, be here long after we are no longer here to debate its demise. Her husband's profession, journalism, she has said, needs support and advocacy; poetry, on the other hand, "has always been around, and will always be around, in one way or another" ("Biting the Hand"). Stallings' own career has borne witness to poetry's ability to speak in new venues. She is an active and engaging reader of her own work. In 2012 this classicist and inventor within traditional restrictive forms posted a piece in a distinctly contemporary one, an eighteen-minute TEDx talk titled "The Courage of Poetry."

ARCHAIC SMILE

Archaic Smile (1999) announces in its title an interest in the past, with a twist. If "archaic" suggests something out-of-date and long since cold, "smile" suggests warmth, humor, recognition. "Smile" undermines the seriousness of the classicism, while "archaic" troubles the ease of the "smile." The photograph on the book's cover, reproduced from the National Archaeological Museum in Athens, Greece, shows a sculpture of a woman's head and bust, with stylized waves of hair trailing down each shoulder and still-painted lips. The figure's expression is no more transparent, no more legible, than the Mona Lisa's. The image looks ahead, too, to the book that follows, giving a visual emblem of the women from Greek poetry and myth who speak or are the subjects of the book's dramatic monologues: Persephone, Eurydice, Penelope, Arachne, Daphne.

Enacting the collection's interest in memory and the reappearance of objects from the past, individual lines and images reappear, creating echoes between poems. "No dog is so loyal as the dead," Persephone writes in the middle of her letter to her mother (p. 7); the line generates a further poem, recurring as the first line and governing image of "The Dogdom of the Dead" (p. 13). In "Consolation for Tamar," Stallings imagines that the ancient vessel that shattered in her friend's hands "forgot / That it was not a rosebud, but a pot, / And, trying to unfold for you, was brittle" (p. 32). If the pot breaks like a bloom causing Stallings' friend (the poem's addressee and muse) distress, on the facing page, in

"Apollo Takes Charge of His Muses," one of the Muses addressed by Apollo, in her distress, "let[s] fall a mangled flower from her hands" (p. 33). In "Tour of the Labyrinth," we hear a rumbling from "Ariadne and the Rest": "The cellar" in Ariadne's palace in Thebes "where they kept deformity / Hungry in the dark beneath the stair" (p. 37) becomes the tour guide's "And this is where they kept it, though their own, / Hungry in the dark beneath the stair" (p. 40). Voices echo, too, through the poem's dramatic monologues, especially those of Persephone and Eurydice, queen and cursed subject of the Underworld.

"Underworld" is the title of the book's first section. Most of its poems are set in Hades' kingdom; the first poem, however, "Postcard from Greece," is about not quite making it there. The speaker recounts a drive that nearly ends with a quick turn off a wet curve of cliff-edged road. The repeating sibilants catch the slickness of the road in the opening line's "Hatched from sleep, as we slipped out of orbit" (p. 3). The speaker sees "the sea, the sky, as bright as pain" (p. 3). When the car hits an olive tree instead of continuing its course into the sea, everything stops: "We clung together, shade to pagan shade, / Surprised by sunlight, air, this afterlife" (p. 3). The speaker and her companion have come close enough to glimpse themselves as characters from the underworld, and their near end knits them together, "shade to pagan shade," makes them privileged foreigners to the sunlit world of the living. Sonic patterning—the assonance of long *i*'s and long and short *a*'s, the chime of "bright" and "light"—connects the searing "sky, as bright as pain" in line 3 to the gentler "sunlight, air, this afterlife" of the last line. The final line has its own music, though, and, after the rush of earlier lines, the caesura, or pause, created by the commas on either side of "air" bring air, a reprieve, into the poem, a sign of the suspension of death and continuing (though perhaps more ethereal) life. If panic causes the speaker to be "Hatched from sleep," she has by the poem's end been awakened into the wonder of "this afterlife."

Why is this poem a "Postcard" from Greece? It contains iconic elements of the Greek landscape, the kind that might sell on a picture postcard: "the sea, the sky," "antique" shrines, an olive tree. Hurtling violently through and into elements of this landscape, though, the speaker gets much more than a picture-postcard view. "Postcard" may also indicate the dimensions of the poem, a sonnet, about the right length and size to fill a one-sided card. The title might also suggest a modern, updated version of another epistolary poem in the section, "Persephone Writes a Letter to Her Mother." Though the speaker of "Postcard from Greece" lives to write "this afterlife," Persephone writes letters that, as her husband reminds her, will never get to their addressee.

The poem is the collection's second dramatic monologue, following "Hades Welcomes His Bride," an address spoken to Persephone by her new husband. Stallings' Hades bears a family resemblance to Robert Browning's dramatic speakers. The remarried husband of Browning's "My Last Duchess" complains of his last wife that "She had / A heart—how shall I say?—too soon made glad" (*Robert Browning,* p. 102). "No smile?" asks Stallings' Hades of Persephone, "Well, some solemnity befits a queen" (p. 4). Whereas Browning suggests his Duke has done away with the previous wife, however, as King of the Dead, Hades has no need to resort to murder. And, indeed, the comparison to Browning's Duke is unfair to the King of the Dead. Stallings' Hades is better intentioned than Browning's Duke, sinister only unintentionally, because of differences of taste and culture. To make his bride "feel at home," he paints the ceiling like the night sky, but, assuming she shares his preferences, he omits the heavenly bodies that would make a night sky familiar, the "garish stars and lurid moon" (p. 4). He chooses for Persephone three servants, "friends and loyal maids" (p. 4). She need not fear their gossip, he tells her, for "They have / Not mouth nor eyes and cannot thus speak ill / Of you" (p. 4). His reassurance about her protection against idle chatter summons graver fears: a terror of suffocation, physical and metaphorical, both loss of the senses and a loss of identity, voice, human connection, easy (or any) conversation. And of course the terror that Persephone feels, since Persephone (though

Hades speaks) is at the heart of this poem, is not only a fear of death, but of marriage and sex, a loss of childhood, innocence, freedom. "Come now, child," Hades begins his address, and ends by following Persephone's eyes: "That stark shape crouching in the corner? / Sweet, that is to be our bed" (p. 4, pp. 4–5). The poem rewrites the Persephone myth as a species of "female gothic."

If the Persephone poems explore homesickness and displacement, loss of the familiar and familiar distinctions, perhaps the highest drama of the collection comes in its Eurydice poems, a series of dramatic monologues, all spoken by Orpheus' dead wife: "Eurydice Reveals Her Strength," "Eurydice's Footnote," and "Vale." In Ovid's rendition of the myth, Orpheus descends to the Underworld to retrieve Eurydice, dead by a viper bite, and nearly succeeds. Charmed by Orpheus' music, Hades and Persephone agree to let him take Eurydice on the condition that he walk ahead of her and not look back until they reach the upper world. At the last moment, however, he forgets and looks back, losing her forever.

In Stallings' "Eurydice Reveals Her Strength," spoken to Orpheus, Eurydice is not in need of saving. She asks, "my dear, why did you come?" (p. 9). Sensory life and his song in her ear is now just remembered mechanics, "A quiver in the membrane of the ear, / And love, a complicated lust" (p. 9). She remembers their lovemaking as violence "against, this death," for "we feared this calm of being dead" (p. 9). He will disagree with a "shiver," she says (p. 9). The poem's lyrical and grotesque final image, a hypothetical severed head floating down the river singing to itself "not looking back" (though it is unclear from the syntax whether the head is Eurydice's or Orpheus') looks forward to Orpheus' eventual, legendary demise—his body rent by spurned women, his head and lyre washed upon Lesbos' shore (p. 10).

"Eurydice's Footnote" is even more damning of Orpheus. The poem takes as epigraph a footnote on Hellenistic poetic history from a 1952 scholarly article. In early versions of the myth, Eurydice was recovered; a single version of the

poem revised this story to make the recovery instead a tragic loss. In Stallings' poem, Eurydice responds to that revision, as though it were Orpheus' own—a sacrifice for art, for "Disappointment in the end was more aesthetic" (p. 11). The poem raises the uncomfortable and serious question for any artist of the ethics of using loss (or, perhaps more pointedly, marriage) as material for art. Here Orpheus sacrifices his wife for a better song, a better poem. "Vale," the longest poem in the collection, included in the third section, returns to the Eurydice myth, with another dramatic monologue spoken by Eurydice, though in a different style. Here we encounter a dream version of the legend, sewn with surreal contemporary imagery (the viper that bites Eurydice's ankle becomes the vise of a green snakeskin shoe, the gods' deafness to appeals becomes a humming bureaucratic office. The poem shows Stallings' ability to translate myth into more familiar registers without losing its strangeness.

The poems of "A Bestiary," the book's second section, shift the scene and subject to Georgia, with poems about love and death in the animal world and poems of early marriage. In the sonnet "Words of Prey," a speaker and a companion look on as an eagle eviscerates a squirrel, pulling out intestine "long as magic handkerchieves" (p. 19). Another squirrel looks on, too, "perhaps in grief, / But likelier in safety, heart-beat blunt" (p. 19). The heartbeat's moral message, too, is blunt, about relief at being spared even in the face of another's loss. Humans and surviving squirrel are united by a cold common sense: "How we all look on disaster, with relief, / Thinking, while it feeds it does not hunt" (p. 19). The turn of the sonnet, between the two initial quartets and a final, divided sestet, enacts the turn from visual to moral observation. The poems in this section continue to look at what might disgust, rendering it with vividness and dark comedy. "Watching the Vulture at the Road Kill," one poem is titled, and Stallings looks long enough to render his "slow, hot-air-balloon descent" and "moon-walk bounce" (p. 20). In "RepRoach," she reproaches herself for loathing the roach, an insect whose "elegance appalls" (p. 24). The poem's quick end-rhymes and hard *t*'s

and *c*'s suggest the sound of their furtive retreat, "Tapping away into the bruise / Of dark like patent leather shoes" (p. 24).

Archaic Smile returns to mythological themes in its third section, with poems on Penelope and Odysseus, Medea, Ariadne, the Minotaur, Daphne, Apollo's Muses, and the third Eurydice poem, "Vale." The final section, "For the Losers of Things," however, closes the book in a more familiar world, with poems about moving, marriage and domestic tasks, insomnia, childhood remembered, and a tragicomic "Elegy for the Lost Umbrella." The poems' technical virtuosity, their graceful use of forms (particularly sonnets, villanelles, quatrains), their precise observations, and their bridging of ancient and contemporary, mythic and personal, marked *Archaic Smile* as the debut of an impressive and distinctive new talent.

HAPAX

While the image on its cover shows the Second Coming (a Byzantine *Harrowing of Hell,* from Athens' Benaki Museum), Stallings' second collection, *Hapax* (2006), takes its title from a lexicographer's term, *hapax legomenon,* meaning a word or form that appears only once in its context. The term, Stallings indicates at the head of the book, is derived from the Greek word meaning "once, once only, once for all" and is first cited in book 12 of the *Odyssey,* when Odysseus chastises his men for having gone to Hades alive "when other mean die only once" (*Odyssey,* 12:21–22). As in *Archaic Smile,* the title tells us, we are again in a collection interested in the ancient as well as the fleeting.

Like *Archaic Smile,* too, *Hapax* begins with a sonnet, "Aftershocks." Whereas in "A Postcard from Greece," a disaster barely averted ended with a couple clasped together in shock and relief, the "disaster" of "Aftershocks" is shocking because it reveals a rift. The opening announces separation: "We are not in the same place after all" (p. 5). The subjects of the poem are displaced, reading in the "fissur[ed]" walls "A new cartography for us to master" (p. 5). But was the disaster natural or personal? Are they estranged from each other, safety, or both? A Spenserian sonnet, three interlocking quatrains and a couplet, the poem describes the aftermath of the "disaster" without ever making explicit its nature, suggesting both an earthquake and a fight, holding both meanings in sway. Like "A Postcard from Greece," "Aftershocks" ends in suspension:

> We fall mute, as when two lovers come
> To the brink of the apology, and halt,
> Each standing on the wrong side of the fault.
>
> (p. 5)

Discord in love and the consequences of words said in anger or carelessness are a continuing theme in the book, words said "once, only once" but "once for all," that follow their speaker and do not go away. The speaker in "The Dollhouse," a thirty-line poem in rhyming couplets, remembers the incidents and alarms of play with dolls,

> If we made something happen every day,
> Or night, it was the game we knew to play,
> Not realizing then how lives accrue,
> With interest, the smallest things we do.
>
> (p. 7)

Diminutive, homey make-believe—bottle cap pie tins, tinfoil mirrors, "little beds"—suddenly turns creepily consequential (p. 6). If "play" suggests actions without costs, the last lines suggest that there is no such thing. Just as the speaker and her sister concocted mishaps and mayhem in the doll world to stave off boredom, here "lives" might be read as not only collecting but, more oddly, taking "interest" in the deeds and misdeeds of the living.

The idea that lives could be given shape early on, that futures could be set in play by words spoken early, seems suited to a poet who speaks about ceding control in poems, too, to the patterns set in motion by words. She follows this idea to its darkest, most vivid and violent conclusion in her rewriting of the myth of Actaeon. In Ovid's legend, the hounds that Actaeon raises turn against him, tearing him to pieces after he is metamorphosed into a stag by the goddess Diana, for spying on her at her bath. "The hounds, you knew them all by name," Stallings' poem begins (p. 25), and ends by telling us that words too

come back to bite. If dramatic monologue is the primary mode for the classical poems of *Archaic Smile*, "Actaeon," like other poems in *Hapax*, addresses a "you," creating an intimate tone and putting the reader in the position of her mythological addressee. From the start, "Actaeon" takes naming, and with it language, as a sign of intimacy, affection, perhaps even control.

But though Actaeon raised them, though he can catalog and call their names and temperaments—"High-strung Anthee," "bluetick-coated Philomel, / And freckled Chloë"—his hounds are hunters,

> All fleet of foot, and swift to scent,
> Inexorable once on the track,
> Like angry words you might have meant,
> But do not mean, and can't take back.
>
> (p. 25)

The quatrain's chasing rhymes and, after the smooth four-syllable "Inexorable," the beat of simple, mostly one-syllable (except for "angry") words and hard consonants, particularly in "can't take back," suggests aggressive pursuit. Compared to the more formal, even archaic vocabulary and syntax elsewhere in the poem ("purblind whelps," "hopeless belling," "the foundered hart," "nursed of a winter night"), the lines also suggest the simplicity of their truth. Like "Aftershocks," the poem maintains a delicate balance, speaking at once on two registers, here the mythological and the personal, holding two worlds in tow, each amplified by the other. The theme of words spoken indelibly also suggests the appeal of art that permits revision, where words can be scraped out. When Stallings addresses the ancient poet whose tools of the trade are cataloged in "Implements from the 'Tomb of the Poet,'" she addresses him as a fellow reviser, who wrote on beeswax and "fled still weighing one word with another, / Since wax forgives and warms beneath revision" (p. 19).

Hapax includes two elegies for Stallings' father: "Last Will" and the sonnet "Sine Qua Non," a phrase meaning "without which not." "Sine Qua Non," another poem of address, sets itself the difficult task of precisely describing absence and uses the form of the sonnet to give that absence a shape. "Your absence, father, is nothing. It is naught—," the poem's octave begins, a line echoed and revised in the first line of the sestet: "Your absence, father, is nothing— for it is" (p. 11). The poem proceeds through numerical, domestic, and cosmic analogies for his absence. It is a nullifying "factor," a "fraction of impossible division," "a dropped stitch, the needle's eye," "the interstice of lace," a pause in the refrigerator's hum, the crickets' silence in winter, the "void" of night sky, "Omega's long last O," and, in the final line, "The zero that still holds the sum in place" (p. 11). It is the nothing on which everything else depends and by which everything else is measured. If the speaker of the earlier "Elegy for the Lost Umbrella" rued a lovely lost piece of rain gear—"As if it were that hook that was holding you steady"—through the years (*Archaic Smile*, p. 67), the speaker of "Sine Qua Non" describes a more shaking loss with moving equanimity.

Consciousness of mortality comes through elsewhere in the collection—even watching a late-night black-and-white movie in "Noir." Relics of the past, domestic and archeological, abound: in "The Dollhouse" (rediscovered "in the attic of forgotten shapes"), in "Arrowhead Hunting" ("You cannot help but think how they were lost"), in "*Ubi Sunt* Lament for the Eccentric Museums of My Childhood" ("Why, we used to muse, // did this thing, not that, / survive its gone moment") (pp. 6, 13, 15). What "stops" the speaker in "An Ancient Dog Grave, Unearthed During Construction of the Athens Metro" is not "the curled-up bones," but a blue bead placed by a "careful master" on a collar long since disintegrated (p. 24). The poem imagines the dog's journey into the afterlife, "the loyal companion, bereaved of her master, / Trotting the long, dark way that slopes to the river … In the press for the ferry, who will lift her into the boat?" (p. 24). If the poems of *Hapax* think about separation, about what is passing and what remains, the poet also asserts her place among the living. The poem "Thyme," playing on the herb's homophone, begins, "I have some of it still" (p. 16). Picked when she and a companion stopped to buy honey,

it teaches a paradoxical lesson about the relationship between sweetness, pain, and passing: "the sting, / A swiftness on the wing, / Things that sweetness cannot be without" (p. 16).

Stallings returns to Greek and Roman poetry and culture as a resource in this collection, but rather than taking the voices of the ancients, the poems of *Hapax* often address them (as in "Actaeon") or access the past through artifacts (graves, artwork, continuing cultural practices) found in modern Greece. The collection includes several ekphrastic poems, poems that take visual images as their basis: "The Charioteer," "Amateur Iconography: Resurrection," "Empty Icon Frame," "The Song Rehearsal." Other poems unearth images and distinctions buried in language itself: "The Modern Greek for 'Nightmare' Is *Ephialtes,*" "Dead Language Lesson," "Cassandra." There are poems of exile, including "The City" after C. P. Cavafy, which makes up the fourth and final poem of the series "Exile: Picture Postcards." And there is playfulness, as in the inventive form of "First Love: A Quiz" and the punning limericks of "Klassikal Lymnaeryx."

While Peter Campion found the formalism of *Hapax* stiff, the collection won wide admiration: "Stallings hits her technical stride in *Hapax,*" Erica McAlpine wrote in *Parnassus* (p. 402). Adam Kirsch faulted Stallings' Greek puns for "donnishness," but he found her fluency with and "precise imagination" of ancient Greece capable of conveying its "real foreignness." To his judgment, however, "the most intriguing direction that *Hapax* opens up for the future of Stallings' poetry lies in more personal subjects." The final poem in the collection, "Ultrasound," a poem about pregnancy (or is it too an *ars poetica*?), points in this direction. The title recalls Stallings' professed "Affinity for Bats," and the poem depicts pregnancy as inhabitation by a creature mysterious as anything on wings.

OLIVES

"O lives!" Stallings has said that she hoped the title of her third collection of poetry (2012) would be read both as the salty fruit and the odic exclamation compressed into its name. The book includes two title poems: the anagrammatic one inscribed on its back, and the longer poem that comes first in the collection. That poem declares an affinity for olives, Greece's dark and salty fruit:

Sometimes a craving comes for salt, not sweet,
For fruits that you can eat
Only if pickled in a vat of tears—
A rich and dark and indehiscent meat
Clinging tightly to the pit....

(p. 5)

Brined in "tears," "Washed down with swigs of barrel wine that stab // The palate with pine-sharpness," product of hard labor and "summers that decline," but "Full of the golden past," the olives possess a richness and complexity that the speaker claims as her own: "These fruits are mine— / Small bitter drupes" (p. 5). The poem's language too is full of richness: the precision of "indehiscent" (a botanical term naming fruits that hold their seeds when ripe), the plosive consonants of "pickled," "pit," "barrel," "palate," "pine," "past," "bitter."

The first section of *Olives* is titled "The Argument" and most of it centers on a married couple, once they are far enough from new love for a wedding gown to seem both the "Most innocent and decadent of frocks" (p. 12). In "The Dress of One Occasion," she revises an old saw, writing, "you thought the blue / Above your heads was yours to keep and new, // When really it was something old, to borrow" (p. 12). As *Archaic Smile* demythologized the stories of romance told to Ariadne and her kin, so too the poems in *Olives* suggest that the fruits of love and marriage are sometimes bitter, while tackling the subject in a much more personal register. The theme of angry words and deeds that cannot be unsaid or undone comes back in these poems, perhaps most powerfully in the villanelle "Burned," which concludes with the lesson that "what is burned is burned is burned" (p. 16). In "On Visiting a Borrowed Country House in Arcadia," an argument that erupts getting out of the city disperses on the drive to the countryside, the "out-of-doors that

wins us our release" does so "Not because it is pristine or pretty / But because it has no pity or self-pity" (p. 19). The peace brokered by nature's indifference is only "temporary," or perhaps cyclical, as the poem tells us by rhyming its final lines with the ones in the first stanza that started the fight (p. 19).

The poems of part 2, "The Extinction of Silence," include both personal and public elegies, many of which foreground sound and song. The eleven-line poem "The Sabbatical" describes in compact but glorious detail the rebirth of cicadas, who like her father have been gone seven years; the signs of their return and departure—a swell of voices followed by abrupt silence—again mark his absence. The speaker of "The Cenotaph" sets off for the First Cemetery of Athens in search of tombs of the famous, but she finds herself wandering "the lesser alleys of the dead" (p. 35). Her attention is caught by the traffic of the living and by monuments that seem to live—by priests, florists, old women tending graves to repair the damage of acid rain, and a stone statue of a little girl. In the sonnet "Country Song," the speaker remembers listening to Hank Williams on the radio in her father's pickup truck when she herself was a small girl, back when "Death was something that hadn't happened yet" (p. 26). In the closing couplet the speaker measures her own age and response against her childhood self and the sound of the voice, "twice" as sad now that she is older than the country singer ever lived to be (p. 26). The sonnet from which part 2 takes its title, "The Extinction of Silence," is also a kind of elegy, at once playful and mournful, for a lost singer, a "once common bird" whose "song is lost" to us (p. 31).

Part 3 is made up of three dramatic monologues, each addressed to a pregnant Psyche, Greek goddess of the Soul and wife of Eros. The first poem, voiced by Psyche's Eldest Sister, is a mirror poem, with its first sixteen lines reversed across the single stanza break to form its second half, so that doubts about the father of Psyche's child turn into doubts about the nature of the child. If the sister's nightmarish imagining recalls the doubts of the pregnant speaker in "Ultra-sound," the second poem of the series, spoken by Charon, boatman on the River Styx, and written in terza rima, echoes that earlier poem more explicitly. Charon imagines Psyche's child as a bomb "ticking and ticking" and tells her that, despite their blindness, "My eyes are ultrasound" (p. 43). In "Persephone to Psyche," the Queen of the Underworld, drinking at the bar, admits that when lonely she "rock[s] the stillborns in [her] arms" (p. 45). In contrast to her earlier refashioning of myth, Stallings' mythological poems in *Olives*, Erica McAlpine writes, are "deeply personal, almost psychoanalytic" (p. 409).

Motherhood provides a new set of mythologies in the poems in the final section. The octave of the first sonnet, "Fairy-Tale Logic," seems whimsical enough, cataloging the fantastic "impossible tasks" that fairy-tale heroes have to perform; the sestet advises conquering these tasks by ascribing "impossible" powers to yourself. Its final lines, though, turn deadly serious: "Marry a monster. Hand over your firstborn son" (p. 49). These demands echo Psyche's predicament, but they're also universal: What spouse won't at some moment seem a stranger? What mother won't say goodbye to her son? In "Alice in the Looking Glass," the poet looks back at her own childhood self as though in a mirror, and the childhood self, like the stone girl in the cemetery in "Cenotaph," looks back at her. Like "The Eldest Sister to Psyche," this poem works a formal reversal. Here, though, the poem is a single stanza and its form hinges on the final word of each line, answered or reversed, rather than repeated, across the divide (so that, for instance, the last word of the seventh line, "why," is answered by the last word of the eighth line, "because" [p. 58]). The only end word that repeats is the first line's, for, as the poem tells us in its last line, "everything reverses save for time" (p. 58). If *Olives* declares its preference for bitter fruits, though, these poems about change and passing are hardly grim. A child's mispronunciation "enchant[s]" language, tulips age exuberantly, and Stallings' poetry promises rich harvests to come (p. 61).

Selected Bibliography

WORKS OF A. E. STALLINGS

COLLECTED POETRY

Archaic Smile. Evansville, Ind.: University of Evansville Press, 1999.

Aftershocks. West Chester, Pa.: Aralia Press, 2003. (Chapbook.)

Hapax. Evanston, Ill.: Triquarterly/Northwestern University Press, 2006.

Olives. Evanston, Ill.: Triquarterly/Northwestern University Press, 2012.

OTHER POEMS

"The Man Who Wouldn't Plant Willow Trees" and "A Lament for the Dead Pets of Our Childhood." In *Starting Rumors: America's Next Generation of Writers.* Edited by Allen Learst and Randy Phyllis. Grand Junction, Colo.: Pinyon Press, 1999. Pp. 15–16.

"The Tantrum." In *The Penguin Anthology of Twentieth-Century American Poetry.* Edited by Rita Dove. New York: Penguin, 2011.

"After a Greek Proverb." *Poetry Magazine*, January 2012. http://www.poetryfoundation.org/poetrymagazine/poem/243216

TRANSLATIONS

The Nature of Things, by Lucretius. Introduction by Richard Jenkyns. London and New York: Penguin, 2007.

"The Riming Poem." (Translation from the Old English.) In *The Word Exchange: Anglo-Saxon Poems in Translation.* Edited by Greg Delanty and Michael Matto. New York: Norton, 2011. Pp. 199–206.

PROSE AND LECTURES

"Missing the Vernacular." *Harriet: A Poetry Blog.* Poetry Foundation, September 15, 2007. http://www.poetryfoundation.org/harriet/2007/09/missing-the-vernacular/

"I'm with Wendy Cope When She Says ..." *Harriet: A Poetry Blog.* Poetry Foundation, October 5, 2007. http://www.poetryfoundation.org/harriet/2007/10/im-with-wendy-cope-when-she-says/

"Numbers Trouble." *Harriet: A Poetry Blog.* Poetry Foundation, November 3, 2007. http://www.poetryfoundation.org/harriet/2007/11/numbers-trouble/ 2007

"Why No One Wants to Be a New Formalist." *Harriet: A Poetry Blog.* Poetry Foundation, November 29, 2007. http://www.poetryfoundation.org/harriet/2007/11/why-no-one-wants-to-be-a-new-formalist/

"Sonnetude." *Harriet: A Poetry Blog.* Poetry Foundation, December 8, 2007. http://www.poetryfoundation.org/harriet/2007/12/sonnetude/

"Interview with the Sonnet." *Harriet: A Poetry Blog.* Poetry Foundation, December 14, 2007. http://www.poetryfoundation.org/harriet/2007/12/interview-with-the-sonnet/

"Rhyme Driven." *Harriet: A Poetry Blog.* Poetry Foundation, January 13, 2008. http://www.poetryfoundation.org/harriet/2008/01/rhyme-driven/

"Translation: Rhyme & Reason." *Harriet: A Poetry Blog.* Poetry Foundation, January 20, 2008. http://www.poetryfoundation.org/harriet/2008/01/translation-rhyme-reason/

"Alice." *Harriet: A Poetry Blog.* Poetry Foundation, January 28, 2008. http://www.poetryfoundation.org/harriet/2008/01/alice/

"Presto Manifesto!" *Poetry Magazine,* February 2009. http://www.poetryfoundation.org/poetrymagazine/article/182841

"Biting the Hand." *Harriet: A Poetry Blog.* Poetry Foundation, April 1, 2010. http://www.poetryfoundation.org/harriet/2010/04/biting-the-hand/

"We're All Praxillas Now ..." *Harriet: A Poetry Blog.* Poetry Foundation, April 16, 2010. http://www.poetryfoundation.org/harriet/2010/04/were-all-praxillas-now/

"Eyjafjallajökull." *Harriet: A Poetry Blog.* Poetry Foundation, April 18, 2010. http://www.poetryfoundation.org/harriet/2010/04/eyjafjallajokull/

"Afro-Formalism." *Harriet: A Poetry Blog.* Poetry Foundation, April 21, 2010. http://www.poetryfoundation.org/harriet/2010/04/afro-formalism/

"Knitting for Poets: Elizabeth Zimmermann." *Harriet: A Poetry Blog.* Poetry Foundation, April 25, 2010. http://www.poetryfoundation.org/harriet/2010/04/knitting-for-poets-elizabeth-zimmermann/

"You Don't Need Time to Write. You Need Space." *Harriet: A Poetry Blog.* Poetry Foundation, April 27, 2010. http://www.poetryfoundation.org/harriet/2010/04/you-dont-need-time-to-write-you-need-space/

"Finish/Line." *Harriet: A Poetry Blog.* Poetry Foundation, April 30, 2010. http://www.poetryfoundation.org/harriet/2010/04/finishline/

"Pleasures of the Didactic." *Harriet: A Poetry Blog.* Poetry Foundation, April 1, 2011. http://www.poetryfoundation.org/harriet/2011/04/pleasures-of-the-didactic/

"Lucy Pevensie and the Magic Facebook." *Harriet: A Poetry Blog.* Poetry Foundation, April 4, 2011. http://www.poetryfoundation.org/harriet/2011/04/lucy-pevensie-and-the-magic-facebook/

"We'd Rather Have the Iceberg than the Ship." *Harriet: A Poetry Blog.* Poetry Foundation, April 10, 2011. http://www.poetryfoundation.org/harriet/2011/04/wed-rather-have-the-iceberg-than-the-ship/

"The Wife of Pontius Pilate." *Harriet: A Poetry Blog.* Poetry Foundation, April 17, 2011. http://www.poetryfoundation. org/harriet/2011/04/the-wife-of-pontius-pilate/

"Austerity Measures: A Letter from Greece." *Poetry Magazine,* September 2012. www.poetryfoundation.org/ poetrymagazine/article/244460

"The Courage of Poetry: Alicia Stallings at TEDxThessaloniki." TEDxTalks, October 4, 2012. http:// tedxtalks.ted.com/video/The-Courage-of-Poetry-Alicia-St

"Brass Tacks." *Parnassus: Poetry in Review* 33, nos. 1–2:181–198 (May 2013).

CRITICAL AND BIOGRAPHICAL ARTICLES

Campion, Peter. "Eight Takes: Fenton, Strand, Hopler, Zukofsky, Stallings, Voigt, Kinnell, Wohahn." *Poetry Magazine,* January 2007. www.poetryfoundation.org/ poetrymagazine/article/178921. (Review of *Hapax.*)

Deutsch, Abigail. "In the Penile Colony: Michael Robbins's *Alien vs. Predator* and A. E. Stallings's *Olives.*" *Poetry Magazine,* October 2012. www.poetryfoundation.org/ poetrymagazine/article/244610

Hammes, Mary Jessica. "Poetic Genius." *Georgia Magazine,* December 2011. www.uga.edu/gm/ee/index.php?/single/ 2011/12/1319/

Horstmann, Steffen. Review of *Hapax,* by A. E. Stallings. *Contemporary Rhyme* 4, no. 1 (winter 2007). http://www. contemporaryrhyme.com/hapax_review_horstmann.PDF

Jarman, Mark. "Good Company: Six Voices." *Hudson Review* 59, no. 2:317–326 (summer 2006). (Review of *Hapax.*)

Kirsch, Adam. "Young Poets Calling: Part 2." *Contemporary Poetry Review,* August 9, 2006. http://www.cprw.com/ Kirsch/youngpoets2.htm). (Review of *Hapax* and *The Optimist,* by Joshua Mehigan.)

Mason, David. "The Limits of the Literary Movement." In *Two Minds of a Western Poet.* Ann Arbor: University of Michigan Press, 2011. Pp. 133–140.

McAlpine, Erica. "'To Catch the Last Applause': The Poetry of A. E. Stallings." *Parnassus: Poetry in Review* 33, nos. 1–2:393–413 (May 2013).

Stothard, Peter. "In This Week's *TLS.*" *Times Literary Supplement,* September 4, 2013. www.the-tls.co.uk/tls/ public/article1308916.ece

Taraskiewicz, Angela. "String Theory: The Poetry of A. E. Stallings." *Valaparaiso Poetry Review* 12, no. 1 (fall– winter 2010–2011). www.valpo.edu/vpr/v12n1/ v12n1prose/stallingsessay.php

Welch, Milton L. Review of *Hapax,* by A. E. Stallings. *The Believer,* June–July 2006. http://www.believermag.com/

issues/200606/?read=review_stallings

Yezzi, David. Review of *Archaic Smile,* by A. E. Stallings. *Poetry Magazine,* May 2001, pp. 109–110. http://www. poetryfoundation.org/poetrymagazine/browse/178/2#!/ 20605

INTERVIEWS

Brown, Jeffrey. "Conversation: A. E. Stallings, Poet and Translator, Inspired by the Classics." *PBS NewsHour,* September 30, 2011. http://www.pbs.org/newshour/art/ blog/2011/09/conversation-ae-stallings-poet-and-translator-inspired-by-the-classics.html (Includes readings of her poems "Austerity Measures" and "The Mother's Loathing of Balloons.")

Byrne, Edward. "A. E. Stallings Interviewed by Edward Byrne*." Valparaiso Poetry Review* 12, no. 1 (fall–winter 2010–2011). www.valpo.edu/vpr/v12n1/v12n1prose/ stallingsinterview.php

Gylys, Beth. "An Interview with A. E. Stallings." *Five Points: A Journal of Literature and Art* 14, no. 3:32–41 (2012). http://poems.com/special_features/prose/ essay_stallings2.php

Murchison, Ginger. "The Interview with A. E. Stallings." *Cortland Review* 19, February 2002. www.cortlandreview. com/issue/19/stallings19.html

Perlroth, Nicole. "A. E. Stallings on Power Ambition Glory." *Forbes,* June 18, 2009. www.Forbes.com/2009/06/18/ae-stallings/classics-leadership-stallings.html

Pousner, Howard. "Decatur-Reared Poet Wins MacArthur 'Genius' Prize." *Atlanta Journal-Constitution,* September 20, 2011. http://www.ajc.com/news/news/local/decatur-reared-poet-wins-macarthur-genius-prize/nQLy8/

OTHER SOURCES

Browning, Robert. *Robert Browning.* Edited by Adam Roberts. Oxford: Oxford University Press, 1997.

Bishop, Elizabeth. *The Complete Poems, 1927–1979.* New York: Farrar Straus and Giroux, 1983.

Keats, John. *Complete Poems.* Edited by Jack Stillinger. Cambridge, Mass.: Belknap Press, 1982.

Merrill, James. *Collected Prose.* Edited by J. D. McClatchy and Stephen Yenser. New York: Knopf, 2004.

Stallings, William. "Mind Your *p*'s and Alphas." *Educational Researcher* 14, no. 9:19–20 (November 1985).

———. "Return to Our Roots: Raising Radishes to Teach Experimental Design." *Teaching of Psychology* 20, no. 3:165–167 (October 1993).

JONES VERY

(1813—1880)

Edward Sugden

ALTHOUGH JONES VERY is certainly a marginal figure in American literary history, one senses that he would have been absolutely content with his position on the peripheries. In his life he stood on the edges of various religious, social, and cultural movements, remaining an outsider in spite of, or perhaps because of, the intensity of his written oeuvre. In the years subsequent to his death, this pattern has repeated, with Very entering and exiting the canon, anthologies printing then dropping him, and the various interpretative modes that have shaped literary study failing to provide an enduring motif for rendering his work popularly accessible.

All of which is to say that his life and works pose a problem of historical and critical positioning. He was loosely affiliated with the already baggy philosophical cadre known as the transcendentalists, but was nonetheless as much shunned by them as he was welcomed. These arbiters of the nineteenth-century New England intellectual scene often steered clear of him because of the religious excesses of his poetry and his frequent lack of social graces. He was a prophet, or at least claimed to be one for a while, but nonetheless struggled to align his ecstatic visions with any of the major churches of the day, be they Calvinist or Unitarian. The obstinate battles that he fought against religious orthodoxy proved disastrous for his reputation and social standing. He was a poet, too, but one whose work somehow manages to be both frustratingly narrow in focus while also quite radically uneven in tone, voice, and form.

Moreover, such an unevenness permeates the entirety of his life. Any critical claims of Very's enduring interest essentially rest on a period of eighteen months between the fall of 1838 and the spring of 1840 during which he produced a third, and the very best, of his almost nine hundred poems. Fired by a belief of an impending apocalypse of which he was the sole prophet, Very poured out reams and reams of verse. To those few who listened to him, he claimed that they were not the product of his own mind but rather the direct and unmediated voice of the Holy Spirit speaking to him, which it was his duty to transcribe.

During these seemingly terrifying months Very lost his job, was institutionalized, and alienated himself from many of his friends as well as the townsfolk of Salem, Massachusetts, where he lived. Outside of this sudden pulse of divine frenzy, he lived an ostensibly quiet and reclusive life with his sisters in a middle-class house in Salem, only surfacing sporadically to preach. He spent much time in his garden, writing occasional verse on various subjects, from politics to the wonders of technology.

We can nonetheless find one adhesive rubric for reading Very in W. H. Auden's introduction to *Nineteenth-Century Minor Poets* (1967). In this book Auden seeks to rediscover, and account for his enthusiasm for, a number of British writers passed over by the canon. For Auden "major" poets have five features: they must produce a lot of work; they must have a wide range of subject matter; they must be original in style as well as insight; they must be technically adept; and, finally, they must continue developing throughout their lifetime so that a reader can always distinguish when a poem was written.

Very lacks many, if not all, of these attributes. Even though he certainly was a voluminous writer, his enduring and often sententious piety meant that he orbited around themes of salvation and purgation throughout his career. Glib images recur and cliché sometimes predominates. Far

from being original in style, or formally imperious, his poems tend to bear the imprint of a somewhat overwrought Romanticism and biblical high-handedness. His rhythm is clunky and his rhymes almost comically bathetic at times. And though it is reasonably easy to distinguish between the poems of Very's inspired phase and everything else, within these biographical folds it is famously difficult to order or periodize the work.

Yet, just as Auden found himself weirdly attracted to "minor" poets like William Barnes, there is something ineluctably compelling about Jones Very's life and work, a yawing gravitational field made up of a mix of vatic insight, frenzied religious intensity, wondrous egotism, and febrile, half-realized, spiritual and sexual desperation. Vladimir Nabokov once remarked that there was only a thin linguistic dividing line separating the cosmic from the comic, and much of the energy of Very's work comes from him not so much walking that line as grabbing it by the neck and throttling it to within an inch of its life. And so, in this way, it is precisely all the attributes that have condemned Very to a life on the margins, this constant toying with aesthetic and doctrinal disaster, that comprise his greatest strength. There is a gripping sense in his work that, at any moment, the wheels could fall off and, indeed, that they might have flown off somewhere into the far distance already anyhow.

If we read Very's marginality as representing something positive, something we can use to empower his work, he appears, all of a sudden, to cast a fractured and oblique, if intense, light on some of the repeated tropes of American literary history. We can see in his reclusiveness, for instance, a pattern of behavior that many American writers, from Henry David Thoreau to Annie Dillard to Thomas Pynchon, would repeat. Nor is Very alone in the American canon in his reliance on extraphenomenal conversations to create his finest work: think of James Merrill at his Ouija board, or Philip K. Dick's terrifying dreams and visions that would lead to his prophetic late style. Indeed, even a figure as cryptic and seemingly alone as Emily Dickinson makes considerably more cultural sense when placed in relation to Very's own religious ecstasies and visceral isolationism.

What this means is that when we analyze Very, we have to cast certain critical judgments to one side by accepting his excesses and letting his faults slide. This way we can start to see what story they might tell us. There is certainly much verbiage in his work, but this linguistic detritus grants his poetry an unalloyed and almost confessional intensity, while also blessing those many fragmented moments of brilliance scattered throughout his career with an eerie, quivering radiance.

THE MAJOR PHASES

The consensus among critics is that there are four major phases of Jones Very's life. First is the period between his birth in 1813 and his departure to Harvard in 1833. In these years he lived in Salem and grappled with an unconventional family life replete with loss. Second is the period up to 1838, when he was a respectable and precocious Harvard student, then tutor, studying and teaching classical subjects. Then follow the eighteen months after the fall of 1838, when the fabric of everyday reality seemed to sunder for him, granting him a privileged view into the heavenly realms that told him of an imminent apocalypse. This was a period of struggle and ostracization for him, as he was cast out of Harvard in shame and returned home to a town equally unwilling to listen to his dogma. Edwin Gittleman, Very's second biographer, referred to these years between 1833 and 1840 when Very was an eccentric mainstay of the New England academic community as the "effective years." And, finally, comes the rest of his life, the forty years between 1840 and 1880 where, ostensibly, little of note occurred. In this period Very continued to write verse, though much of it was conventional in manner and message, while also acting as a supply preacher to various churches in New England.

THE EARLY YEARS

On Saturday, August 28, 1813, Jones Very was born in the seaport town of Salem, Massachusetts.

His father, Captain Jones Very, was a man of the sea and a Mason, with a reputation for being kind to his men in this era of flogging and maritime autocracy. During the War of 1812 he had been captured by the British. While in captivity he developed consumption, a condition he would never fully shake off. Upon his release in 1813, he married his first cousin Lydia in a strange "noncontractual" ceremony that continues to be covered in mystery to this day. Lydia was a strong-willed and intellectually nonconformist woman, who feuded with her close family. She later gained a reputation as a disciple of the radical atheist thinker Fanny Wright. Jones was their first child but was swiftly followed by Washington, Franklin, Horace, Frances Eliza, and Lydia Louisa Ann. Franklin, who was born blind, died at the age of four, and Horace passed at the age of only one month. This set the tenor for a childhood beset by loss.

Very grew up in the houses of his grandfather and granduncle and was often left with his mother as Captain Very embarked on long sea cruises. His father desired that his firstborn should go into the family business and become a sailor. Meanwhile his mother cultivated his interest in poetry and art. Nonetheless, in spite of their divergent views, Jones went on his first sea voyage with his father at the age of nine on board the *Aurelia*. Together they visited the icy wastes of Kronstadt, Russia—which worsened Captain Very's health—as well as Hamlet's mythical home, Elsinore. Afterward they headed to the American South together, docking at New Orleans for supplies. While in New Orleans, as they waited for the cargo to load, Jones was sent to school and picked up his first formal education.

On their return to Salem in August 1824, it was clear that Captain Very was unwell, as the tuberculosis took control of his lungs once more. After a brief struggle of a few months, he died on December 22, 1824, leaving behind a tangled estate. His father, Isaac Very, was initially appointed as his executor but was soon replaced, leading to a lawsuit in which he accused Lydia of stealing $1,250. Although the courts found in her favor, the case did nothing to improve her already tarnished reputation in Salem.

Had Captain Very survived, it is quite possible that Jones Very the poet would never have come into existence. As it was, the death catalyzed Very's education and led to a burgeoning interest in the classics and literature. His mother sent him to a local grammar school, where he got his first sustained education and by all accounts thrived. In a school competition, he won a copy of *Biographia Americana*, the first of many such prizes he would win over the course of his student days.

It was while working a summer job in an auction room that the formative moment of his early years occurred. As he sorted his way through the books that were to be sold, the young Very found a rare copy of Shakespeare. Seizing the opportunity, Very purchased it for a low price and in so doing gained an item that would provide both intellectual nourishment and economic gain. In the coming years, he subsequently exchanged it for the textbooks that he needed to attend Harvard.

During this period he became acquainted with Henry Kemble Oliver, a tutor who enabled him to enter a local private Latin school. Seeing Very's obvious talent, Oliver encouraged him to keep commonplace books of his reading. These reveal a serious young man, grappling with religious books that warned of the perils of materialism and the arrogance of rationalism. It was, perhaps, in reading these books that he first began to develop the notion that all inspiration comes directly from God.

As he emerged from his teens he began to publish poetry. His first three poems, "O heaven born muse! inspire my humble lay," "The earth is parched with heat," and "Lines, Written on Reading Stuart's Account of the Treatment of Slaves in Charleston," appeared in the *Salem Observer* between May and August of 1833. These works immediately established some of the themes he would return to over the next decade, including the dependence of created matter on divine will and the fragility of earthly existence. They display the first flickerings of an aggressive piety that remained with him throughout the rest of his life. His poem on slavery marked a rare foray, in these early years at least,

into political polemic, deploying several abolitionist tropes common to the antebellum era.

HARVARD, 1833–1838

Having published these poems and completed his elementary education, Very decided that it was time for him to head to Harvard. At the age of twenty, he was considerably older than many of his classmates. He was a serious student and gained a reputation for aloofness. Although his contemporaries respected his intellect, Very found himself desperately short of friends and cultivated, instead, intense relationships with the faculty.

Foremost among these intellectual guides was Edward Tyrrel Channing, his tutor in rhetoric. Very would eventually dedicate the only volume of his poems published during his lifetime to Channing. Against a Harvard backdrop that emphasized memorization and staid recitation above all else, Channing encouraged Very to write in a formally well-executed but simple, plain Greek style. With this in mind, perhaps, Very joined the Harvard debating club, the Institute of 1770, becoming its only ever official "maker of Rhymes." This role resulted in some atypical poems that reveled in a rare (for Very) spirit of levity, mirth, and community.

In 1834 Very found his studies interrupted by the "Dunkin Rebellion," where students refused to work and trashed classrooms in response to the appointment of the conservative Christopher Dunkin as tutor of Greek and Latin. Even though the obedient Very was one of the few students not to get involved in this minor uprising, he was nonetheless rusticated, and only readmitted in August of the same year. This enforced return to Salem proved fruitful for Very's poetry, with several more pieces appearing in the *Salem Observer*. He also found plentiful time to read, becoming interested in the Scottish poet Robert Pollok and the work of Lord Byron in particular.

On his return, Very continued to saturate himself with the Romantics. His discovery of the prose work of Samuel Taylor Coleridge was particularly important for him. This engagement with Romantic praxis led to his poetry becoming increasingly complex. "The New Year," written in early January 1835, marks a key moment in Very's development. This poem, the first he had composed for many months, gave early voice to the prevailing narrative motifs of all of his written output. Formed upon a binary between inner goodness and exterior corruption, "The New Year" meditates on a snowstorm that rages in the (presumably) New England wilds. The narrator feels the cold of the ice, wonders at the purity of its whiteness, before concluding, in a cyclical structure that Very often repeats, that all this privation is worthwhile as "'twill melt as soon into / The tide of warm and ever-flowing love" (*Complete Poems,* p. 19; unless otherwise indicated, all poetic quotations in the text refer to this volume).

"The New Year," with its motif of rebirth, was certainly an appropriate way to begin 1835. It would prove to be the most important year of the young Very's life, up until that point at least. His wide reading meant that he was now ready to formulate his own distinctive program of aesthetics. He directed his intellectual energies toward one essay in particular, "The Practical Application in This Life, by Men as Social and Intellectual Beings, of the Certainty of a Future State," which won him the Bowdoin Prize at Harvard. In this piece, he contrasted the classical tradition with a Christian one, arguing that the journey man had taken toward a purely inward religion evidenced an increasing proximity to the Godhead. The knowledge of the afterlife they thus gained could be used, he suggested, as the fountainhead of a newly virtuous ethics.

But alongside this energizing intellectual foment, Very also underwent a religious crisis that set the prevalent tone for the subsequent years. Although the precise details are unclear, it appears that Very had a sudden and devastating realization of his own worthlessness in relation to the might of God. This is how he remembered it in a letter he later wrote to a friend:

> In my senior year in college I experienced what is commonly called a *change of heart*, which tells us that all we have belongs to God and that we ought to have no *will* of our own. It was a great happiness

to me to find this change yet I could not rest in it. The temptation I always felt to be in thought and as long as I had a thought of what I ought to banish I felt that some of my will remained.

(Deese, Introduction, p. lvi)

With its emphasis on self-abnegation and purgation, as well as its lexicon of temptation and banishment, it is reasonable to assume that this epiphany was in part sexual in nature. Among the gossipy undergraduate circle at Harvard, Very had gained a reputation for certain strange proclivities in his personal life. After this "change in heart," he not only refused to talk to women but also attempted to avoid looking at them at all. Having decided to submit his will absolutely to God, it was natural that Very soon decided to enroll in the Divinity School to train as a minister.

Very continued to excel at his undergraduate studies in spite of these spiritual perturbations. In July 1836 he again won the Bowdoin Prize, this time for a dissertation on epic poetry. This essay would eventually become one of the three published alongside his selected poems in 1839. In its final form, printed as "Epic Poetry," it gives one of the most cogent statements of Very's thinking, as well as providing an insight into his wide reading of classical literature, religious theory, and modern literature. It also provides a useful marker of Very's piety at this phase of his life, outlining the strength of his belief in Christian dogma.

The essay builds upon his previous work on the Greeks by creating a dichotomy between the classical and modern traditions. For Very, the heroic age of Homer was entirely based on observing the external world. Heroism came from visible actions, which then were judged according to their merit. This relentless materialism allowed Homer to describe all that he saw before him in an epic mode.

As the modern era rolled into view, however, the situation had changed. The coming of Christianity catalyzed a shift in the location of true heroism. Where the Greeks could rest easy in the phenomenal world, the heroic in this age of progress could only be found through the depiction of internal struggles. Hence there occurred a shift away from the classical epic form toward the dramatic, whether in the work of John Milton or William Shakespeare. However, given that these inward narratives took place on a higher plane, grappling with eternity, the epic became impossible. So Very concludes that, now, in the nineteenth century, there is simply no way to represent heroic action in direct language. But for him this is a good thing. From it he gathers evidence of the gradual movement of man toward a divine goal:

> By removing the bounds of time, Christianity has, I think, rendered every finite subject unsuited for an epic poem. The Christian creed, in opening the vista of eternity before the poet's view, and leaving him unrestrained by prescriptive forms, while it freed him from the bounds of history, by giving him a place beyond its limits where he might transfer the heroic spirit of his age, and surround his heroes with supernatural agents, capable of raising for his action the highest admiration, subjected him to a far greater difficulty than any yet experienced by former poets; that of finding a subject, an action to fill those boundless realms of space, and call forth the energies of the spirits that people it.
>
> (*Essays and Poems,* pp. 21–22)

Very ended up graduating second in his class and was soon appointed as a tutor in Greek while continuing his theological studies. By all accounts, he made a considerable impact on his students, a group that included the future transcendentalist Samuel Johnson, Jr., and the much-overlooked poet Frederick Goddard Tuckerman. In his first years as a teacher, Very was renowned for openness as well as the intensity of the relationship he demanded with his students. As much as he encouraged his students to live the Greek language, he also frequently digressed into unorthodox religious terrains. These verbal peregrinations would, in time, come to enrage the staidly Unitarian faculty of Harvard.

It was no coincidence that as Very grew frustrated with the deadening orthodoxy of Unitarian teaching he found himself drawn to another alienated nonconformist rejected by the Harvard establishment: Ralph Waldo Emerson. In Emerson's *Nature* (1836), Very found a manual for how God ought to relate to man, drawing on that essay's demand for a direct, self-willed experience of divinity. An experience on a train,

where this new technology had seemed to Very a fitting metaphor for Providence, convinced him more than ever of a divinely saturated Earth in which man has perpetually to search for divinity.

Circumstance soon threw Emerson and Very into direct contact. While back home in Salem, Very became acquainted with Elizabeth Palmer Peabody, fresh from her own experience of unorthodox teaching at Bronson Alcott's Temple School. She was already close to several other members of the burgeoning transcendentalist movement and, after seeing Very lecture on epic poetry at the Salem Lyceum, talked extensively with him. In the period that followed, Very was a frequent caller at her home. Here he met other luminaries of the cultural scene, such as the rising writer of gothic tales Nathaniel Hawthorne. After getting to know Very, Peabody decided to write to Emerson to try to set up a meeting between the two. Although she admired Very's intellect, she worried that his intensity would unnerve the aloof and often withdrawn sage of Concord.

She need not have worried. Emerson invited Very to deliver his epic poetry lecture at the Concord Lyceum and to stay at his house afterward. So began a friendship that was intellectually profitable to both men, but wracked with ambivalences, disagreements, jealousies, and equivocations. At this early point, however, Emerson was pleased to meet a young American who fitted, at least in part, the transcendentalist mold. At dinner, he guided the discussion toward Very's favorite subjects, namely religious vision and self-abnegation. Upon Very's departure he wrote an approving letter to Peabody, in which he thanked her for introducing him to so intriguing and refreshing a character.

Even though Very was ever more devout and difficult to be around, he was invited to a meeting of the Transcendental Club in May 1838. Appropriately enough, given what would soon follow, the theme they discussed that day was "Is Mysticism an Element of Christianity?" It is reasonably easy to guess Very's own position on this subject. Even though there is no direct evidence, it is likely that Very in part inspired Emerson's Divinity School address, which he

was formulating in these months. The influence went both ways. Very's was the first name on a subscription list for the most recent collection of Thomas Carlyle's essays, released that year. Moreover, his poems of this time, "A Sonnet", "The Columbine," "Nature," "The Song," "To the pure all things are pure," and "The Stranger's Gift," show the distinct impress of Emersonian thought.

POEMS, 1833–1838: JONES VERY AND THE SENSES

Throughout this period Very never stopped writing poetry though he did not publish widely. Most of his work appeared in either the *Salem Observer* or the *Harvardiana*. Nonetheless he was still fairly prolific and gained a reputation as a writer who might have a significant future. For the most part, these poems show a young poet clearly in thrall to British Romanticism, both in terms of language and message. They tend to tell the story of a solitary wanderer, walking around an etherealized natural zone, searching for a meaning and moral that exceeds the real. The style is precocious, forced, full of zephyrs, azures, thees, and thous. The imagery gravitates around various emblems of alienated Romantic heroism, be these oceans, mountains, lightning storms, stars, or children. Though the potential of a disastrous perceptual collapse lurks in many of these works, the threat is rarely realized, and instead is often resolved with a sententious lesson, usually laid out in the last few lines. This quote, from the poem "Pleasure," which laments human sensuality, is representative of a pretty but directionless lyricism: the speaker asks, "Goddess of pleasure, where thy golden car? / Rides it on zephyrs through the unclouded sky?" (p. 15).

This early period is best regarded as one of purgation for Very. In these five years he attempted to burn off the impurities of his style while he also simultaneously developed a moral universe that was analogously austere and stripped of sensuality. He was a writer in search of a mode of his own and, very gradually, he started to find a simplicity of expression that overrode the grandiloquence of his first poems.

In these years he searched for an idiom that combined his Romantic heritage with the particularities of his own youth in New England, while also attempting to align Coleridgean aesthetics with his eccentric religious promptings.

In terms of his moral universe, Very was always on firmer ground. Right from the start, his poems evinced a squeamishness at the body and a dislike of strong sensations. Ever one to emphasize the vanity of human wishes, the predominant message of these juvenile works is that beauty will fade, possessions will disappear, and man will die and be cast into oblivion. As he puts it in "Ehue! fugaces, Posthume, Posthume, Labuntur anni,"

Fleeting years are ever bearing
In their silent course away,
All that in our pleasures sharing,
Lent to life a cheering ray.

(p. 26)

That Very titled one poem, very simply, "Death Decay and Change" demonstrates the extent of his morbid obsession with the transience of human endeavor. But for him, hope always sprang eternal. His poems usually conclude with the message that the cataclysmic obliteration of mind can be avoided through an absolute faith in the goodness of God. If one lives well, a truer life awaits. Usually underpinning this fairly standard dogmatic move are images and narratives of cyclicity, winter emerging into spring, seeds growing into flowers, and the like. As such, Very sacrificed the sensory world of mankind upon the altar of higher, purer, eternal truths.

Nonetheless, it is by looking through the prism of the senses that we can gain the most traction on these poems, particularly if we think about sound, voice, touch, and vision. In terms of voice, Very's ideal for the poetic speaker over the course of this five-year period is less a being of flesh and blood than a disembodied, abstract ether. This pure heavenly emissary does not use words, or anything that impacts on the debased organs of man, and instead communicates directly to the mind in the form of thoughts. In "A Withered Leaf—Seen on a Poet's Table," Very

gives a succinct statement of what a poet should be:

Far above these realms he soars
Realms of Death and pale Decay;
And above God's throne adores,
Mid the spirit's native day.

(p. 30)

This is a characteristic gesture. The true poet leaves mankind behind and instead converses with spirits. It is not difficult to see why Very would soon embark on a mystical program—he was already an open receptacle for the divine. As he put it in "The Voice of God," "God dwells no more afar from me, / His voice in all that lives is heard" (p. 59).

This perpetual ethereality bestows a certain iciness upon his work. Even though the imagery is lush, images of snow, ice, and the cold recur. As such, Very's religiosity contributes to a frigid, deadening aura that enshrouds most of his poems. These outpourings are full of stilled, frozen life, natural specimens on the point of absolute decay, and scenes in which beauty transitions to its final end. In this sense, the sailors frozen in ice in "The Frozen Ship," sailing in a landscape perhaps remembered from his early trip to Kronstadt, offer another, less resplendent paradigm for the poetic speaker. In a moment that verges on self-address, the speaker intones,

Speak, ye cold lips! say what ye lock
Within that marble breast;
Though deep *our* souls the tale should shock,
It cannot break *your* rest.

(p. 37)

The most arresting lines occur when this obsession with a pellucid, suddenly ceased beauty inflects the conventional Romantic palette of Very's imagination. Scattered across these works are Romantic tropes self-consciously sucked of life, be this the form of a butterfly lying on a tomb or a fossil flower.

Indeed, to read Very's thoughts on the fossil flower is to realize another tenet of his early phase. That is, not only did he desire a vatic mode of speaking, one purged of the impurities

of everyday human earthliness, but also an equivalent mode of seeing. As he generated his poetic aesthetic, Very attempted to call into being a way of viewing the world that would pierce through the false surfaces of reality into the true, eternal realms of the divine. The way in which he looks upon the titular fossil flower in the poem of 1837 is paradigmatic:

Flower of the past!
Now as I look on thee, life's echoing tread
Falls noiseless on my ear; the present dies;
And o'er my soul the thoughts of distant time,
In silent waves, like billows from the sea,
Come rolling on and on, with ceaseless flow,
Innumerable.

(p. 54)

Very's eye sees through the flower in front of him, deep into the past, and onward to a heavenly realm where "the mind's mysterious touch" might "recall / The bloom and fragrance of thy early prime" (p. 55). In "The Columbine," another reflection on a flower, Very goes even further, imagining absolute self-negation, a complete incorporation into nature, in the face of poetic ecstasy. Starting with his predominant urge toward frozen life, he writes,

Still, still my eye will gaze long-fixed on thee,
Till I forget that I am called a man,
And at thy side fast-rooted seem to be,
And the breeze comes my cheek with thine to fan.

(p. 61)

These lines enact a transition that would obsess Very, using intense visual observation to move from the phenomenal world into the realm of the spirit.

Such a movement had a direct impact on his conceptualizations of poetic setting. Very was drawn to these isolated semidivine regions of nature throughout the course of these five years. These places were not just spatially removed from the tread of man but also separate in time. Indeed, it is quite remarkable how few people or living bodies are described in his work. What this movement away from society allowed him to do was to focus absolutely on the mind, which was the only organ that he could bear to be

touched by sensory impression. Just as he wanted the "mind's mysterious touch" to recall to him the fossil flower, in "Pleasure" he writes, in a moment that eerily anticipates the work of Wallace Stevens, that "It is the mind, communing with itself, / That cast a sunshine on the paths of life" (p. 16). When he was confronted by a sensory overload, his solution was always to direct his sensations toward the heavens: in "The Sabbatia" he addresses a plant, saying, "To me thou art a pure, ideal flower, / So delicate that mortal touch might mar" (p. 60). The result is that a claustrophobic egotism, one that perpetually verges on devastating loneliness, mixes with a desperate urge to enforce a sense of newness and wonder. "What more delightful than to wander forth" focuses on a dawn scene where "Nature seems / As young, as when the morning light first broke / On Eden" (p. 9). This is transcendent poetry, but one that lacks the warmth of human company.

The exception to this rule is Very's obsession with scenes of domestic life. As if trying to make up for the loss of his father and brothers in his own childhood, Very consistently drew on sentimental depictions of middle-class family life. "The New Year," for instance, presents a loving family surrounding a glowing hearth, warm and protected from the snow, in an image plucked from thousands of picture postcards. Other depictions of an idealized family occur in poems like "My Mother's Voice" and "The Boy's Dream Ballad." His home in Salem seemingly exerted a gravitational pull on his mind, drawing him back from his scholarly pursuits. In another poem he intones, "Home of my youth would that a worthy lay / Might tell my love for thee to distant time" (p. 50). Similarly, in a valedictory poem, perhaps written as he left for Harvard, he again looks back on his youth, lamenting, "Haunts of my youth farewell! A while I leave / You in your loveliness! A while I go / To visit other scenes, more fair, perhaps, but none / I love so well" (p. 51). Two mutually reinforcing versions of "home" exist in his work in this period then. One is the heavenly sphere that redeems the earthly, the spiritual place of rest where the saved shall go. The other is the private sphere, the rooms in

which he grew up, which render meaningful the loneliness and isolation of Very's scholarly wanderings.

The poems show Jones Very in a transitional state then. He was not yet a prophet, but the need to see through the veil of reality shows that he was not far off. His poems exist in a divine hinterland, a purgatory, poised between the heavenly world he came to so suddenly in 1838 and the earthly one in which he felt so isolated. The promptings of the spirit that these poems half-articulately record would soon effloresce into the prophetic mode that would dominate his life from mid-1838 to 1840. And, in this enchanted period, the dramas of the senses that these works bear witness to would appear to him as part of a larger, ontological plan. In this narrative, Jones Very, prophet and preparer of the way, having suffered through the iniquities of the body and purged himself of will and desire, could start his mission to bring his sinful countrymen into a renewed fellowship with their cryptic, forgotten maker.

SPIRITUAL CRISIS, 1838–1840

At some point in early September 1838, Jones Very experienced an overwhelming, transformative religious experience that changed his life. Although he had long desired to enter into an unmediated communion with his maker, the shift in his personality that subsequently occurred was profound. In a letter, he described how it seemed to him that he developed a dual consciousness, in which his human mind coexisted with that of God. He wrote:

> I felt within me a new will something which came some time in the week but I could not tell what day exactly. It seemed like my old will only it was to the good—it was not a feeling of my own but a sensible will that was not my own.
>
> (Deese, Introduction, p. xvi)

Opinion has been split as to the cause of this sudden, but not entirely unexpected, religious cataclysm. His contemporaries veered between believing that his experience was legitimately noumenal and dismissing him as utterly cracked.

Literary critics have given various explanations for this fissure in his self, from seeing it as part of a psychosexual drama involving his atheistic mother, to bipolar disorder, to temporal lobe epilepsy.

It would also be true to say that Very was far from alone in undergoing a religious awakening in this period. The antebellum era saw many visionaries augur apocalypse and other prophets claim direct converse with God. For numerous people—from Joseph Smith and the Mormons, who thought of America as the land of the Bible, through to the followers of William Miller, who believed that the world would end in 1844—the everyday world was suffused with the immanent presence of the Godhead.

No matter the historical or psychological reasons for Very's own particular brand of religious enthusiasm, the results of it were immediate and extremely visible. Whatever the Holy Spirit had told him meant that he became convinced that an apocalypse was immediately impending and that he occupied a special role in leading his contemporaries to repent. Although he was inconsistent in saying who it was he identified with, at various points he claimed either to be Jesus, or at least an equivalent figure, to fill the role of an ignored Old Testament prophet, or to possess similarities to John the Baptist, preparing the way for a new world of grace.

Harvard felt the full force of his visions. On one occasion he interrupted the class of a fellow professor, Henry Ware, because he disagreed with his teachings of the Gospels. Although Very said that he wanted to stop his vitriolic words to Ware, he argued that he could not as it was the Holy Spirit speaking through him. On another, he told his own students to "flee to the mountains, for the end of all things is at hand" (Deese, Introduction, p. xvi). Even though he had long been regarded as an eccentric teacher, this was too much for his students and the Harvard authorities. On September 14 he was temporarily relieved of his duties as a Greek tutor, with the administration citing worries over his mental health.

To understand the actions of Harvard with regard to Very, it is worth bearing two things in mind. The first is the fallout from Emerson's

deeply controversial Divinity School address, in which he excoriated the graduating class for failing to regard the sacredness of their own souls. This speech had shocked the Harvard authorities, and they were not ready to keep another religiously unorthodox thinker, clearly influenced by Emerson, on their payroll. The second is a wider social context in which debates raged about what could legitimately be said about religion under the provisions of the U.S. Constitution. The trial of the blasphemer Abner Kneeland was roughly contemporaneous and it demonstrates the anxiety that many felt about the clash between free expression and religious order. Those at Harvard, quite clearly, took the side of those in favor of sustaining religious orthodoxy.

Very's brother Washington came to Harvard to pick him up and take him back to Salem. Before he left Very took the time to send Emerson a letter containing an essay, "Shakespeare," that he had worked on in bouts of feverish inspiration over the previous weeks. This essay, which also would appear in his volume of poems, is tough to follow and full of apocalyptic digressions. The core argument is that Shakespeare's genius involved a sacrifice of the will, a self-forgetfulness that allowed him to move through nature and many different strata of life with ease. The negative of this malleability, for Very, is that it made Shakespeare incapable of distinguishing between good and bad, virtue and moral turpitude. Nonetheless, he argues, a true model for genius still depends on a similar act of self-sacrifice, but to God rather than nature.

On his return to Salem, Very was in a rancorous mood. He turned up unannounced at Elizabeth Peabody's house, where he carried out some eccentric scriptural exegesis on his clearly frightened friend before baptizing her. Having already confronted several ministers who he believed were false shepherds, he visited the Reverend Samuel Upham, preached to him at length, and then left. Upham, an upstanding member of the community, moved to have him forcefully institutionalized for posing a danger to public order. As the disciplinary cogs were turning, Very managed to visit Peabody again, presenting to her reams and reams of sonnets that

he said were divinely inspired. However, on September 17 the machinations of Upham prevailed and Very was admitted to the McLean Hospital in Charlestown as a madman.

By all accounts, Very was a model inmate here, exercising regularly and appearing reasonably pliable. He was released exactly a month after he was taken in and proceeded immediately to Harvard where he asked to be reinstated. Although the authorities there were sympathetic to his plight, they turned down his request, as they would do a few more times in the future. During this febrile month, Very also finished off an essay on *Hamlet*, the final one of the triptych that would open his selected poems.

Stories concerning Very's breakdown had spread throughout transcendentalist circles, mainly through Peabody's reports. They had reached Emerson, who somewhat noncommittally invited him to stay, an invitation Very took up a mere week after his release. He stayed in Concord for five days and was fairly well behaved. However, on the last day of his stay, Very was in a foul mood and denounced a local preacher who had dared enter into converse with him at Emerson's house. Nonetheless, even if Emerson thought him mad, it was a socially useful madness, one that condemned the strictures, pieties, and manners of the New England intelligentsia.

In this state of religious exaltation, Very wrote sonnet after sonnet after sonnet giving voice to his view of the changed world, producing poems that include the vitally important "The New Birth." Indeed, between leaving McLean and the eventual publication of his book in 1839, Very published eighty-nine poems in the *Salem Observer*. Believing that he was proselytizing the world anew, Very sent "In him we live, & move, & have our being" and "Enoch" to Emerson, who was duly impressed. In spite of Very's many publications, Emerson had apparently been unaware of his talent as poet up until this point. After reading the poems, Emerson volunteered to oversee the creation of a volume of Very's verse, an offer that Very accepted with evident relish.

Given Very's excitable mental state, bringing this book together was always likely to be a frac-

tious process and so it proved. The two men quarreled over both the general composition of the book and more minor editorial issues. Very wanted the book to be an equivalent to the Gospels, a set of sonnets that would tell his countrymen about the Second Coming of Jesus. Emerson, on the other hand, was, in spite of his ostensible nonconformism, a pragmatist when it came to issues of the literary marketplace. Emerson wanted Very's work to reach as wide an audience as possible, with the book emphasizing his more tranquil thoughts on nature and mind.

Further problems arose from the fact that Very no longer considered himself to be the author of his work. Instead he insisted that he had merely transcribed the voice of the Holy Spirit, which spoke to him. This, of course, made it extremely difficult for Emerson to carry out even the most minor syntactical or grammatical correction. Very considered every edit to be an act of sacrilege that undermined the pervasive wisdom of the God with whom he communed. These differences led to some terse exchanges between the men, with Emerson caustically wondering why it was that the Holy Spirit struggled with spelling.

When *Essays and Poems* finally emerged in 1839, the contents of the volume made it clear that Emerson had won these arguments. The book opened with three essays, which perhaps indicates that Emerson felt Very's talents lay mainly in exposition rather than creation. The selections that Emerson made from the poems themselves softened Very's rougher evangelical edges, with many coming from his earlier, less-inspired phase. Indeed, of the sixty-five poems that appeared, only seven of them were being published for the first time. So although works like "Enoch" and "The New Birth" appear, they sit uneasily next to more sentimental efforts such as "Ehue! fugaces, Posthume, Posthume, Labuntur anni." The result was that the edition of five hundred poems did not fare particularly well, garnering only a few, lukewarm reviews.

Very seemed curiously resigned to the diminished fate of his volume. Whatever it was that had so inspired him over the course of the previous twelve months was slowly relenting, releasing its grip on his mind. The visions came with less frequency. Nonetheless, the published and unpublished work that he produced in these eighteen months bear witness to the intensity of his fervor.

POEMS, 1838–1840

Very's poems from this eighteen-month period pulse with the urgency of unrelenting divine vision. Although they are uneven, aggressive, and scattershot, they are propelled by an intoxicatingly errant energy and a ferocious doctrinal commitment rarely matched in American poetry. They capture all the messy detritus of religious frenzy, its extreme emotions, its ecstasies, to create a wild fantasia of the last days. In contrast to his early work, which he revised regularly, these poems were left almost untouched by him, remaining in the unedited form in which they emerged. We get a window directly into Very's mind as he sought to grapple with ontological dramas that exceeded the ken of man. Although there are traces of his old sententiousness, as well as a tendency toward Romantic turgidity, these poems mark the birth of a writer transformed. The change is not just one of style and tone. These works reveal that, for Very, the fundamental purpose of poetry had irrevocably shifted. Where previously he wrote to a pious, middle-class audience, at ease with sentiment and pretty pictures of nature, he now preached to a world in need of immediate conversion.

The poems contain motifs similar to those found in his earlier work, but they are all directed toward a new, visionary end: namely, that the apocalypse is at hand. Cyclical patterns in nature start to suggest the inevitability of resurrection. The mutability of earthly things indicates the dependence of human will on that of God. If his early poems saw him living in a purgatory of the senses, these later ones record a world in which the gates to paradise are terrifyingly open, with the heaven within flowing out. On numerous occasions, it appears as though Very were certain that the Day of Judgment was imminent. There are visions of the dead rising like this one in "The Resurrection":

The dead! the dead! they throw their grave clothes
  by,
And burst the prisons where they long have lain;
I hear them send their shouts of triumph high,
For he the king of terrors now is slain; ...

(p. 83)

Images like these combine with sonorous admonitions of divine wrath for all those who refuse to pay heed. This, from "I Am the Way," is representative:

And thou shalt flee the approaching day of wrath
Whose dawn e'en now the horizon's border shows
And with its kindling fires prophetic glows.

(p. 129)

This is an unmediated, resurrected voice, one that has passed through sin into a new vision, haranguing a cursed and soon-to-be destroyed land.

"The New Birth" is the crucial document in this regard. This poem tells the story of Very's own awakening, his resurrection from the death of sin to the life of redemption. It provides a unique insight into his fevered mind. Here we learn of how he has found

a new life—thoughts move not as they did
With slow uncertain steps across my mind,
In thronging haste fast pressing on they bid
The portals open to the viewless wind; ...

(p. 64)

The effect of this newly perspicacious and frenzied thought process is that the speaker feels as though he possesses a new sight, one that allows him to see into "The heavens and earth" whose "walls are falling now" (p. 64). Some of Very's best writing emerges when he gives sustained attention to exactly what this visionary world where the heavenly and human mix looks like. Taking a tone that recalls William Blake at his most urgent, Very presents in "The New World" a man who

beholds around the earth and sky
That ever real stands; the rolling spheres,
And heaving billows of the boundless main,
That show though time is past no trace of years,

And earth restored he sees as his again;
That earth fades not, and the heavens that stand;
Their strong foundations laid by God's right hand.

(p. 171)

As he composed these verses, Very walked in a world that was ineluctably changed, charged with a luminous divine presence.

In this new world, Very's relation to the senses has changed. Outlining his differing treatment of voice, touch, and vision provides a marker of the shifts that had occurred in how he conceived of the work of poetry in the wake of his religious crisis. The universe of these later poems is almost unutterably etherealized while simultaneously remaining a realm of pure sensation. It is just that these sensations are directed toward an acutely sensitive and open mind, rather than a debased body. In "The Garden," for instance, he presents his body as though it were more like a ray of light or a chunk of diamond than a living, breathing thing: following his revelation,

My eye seemed but a part of every sight,
My ear heard music in each sound that rose,
Each sense forever found a new delight,
Such as the spirit's vision only knows; ...

(p. 69)

Just as Emerson's transparent eyeball hovered within and without the world, with all things flowing through it, this synesthetic form views everything in a drenched state of utter purity— where "every sight and sound new pleasure yields" (p. 135), as he puts it in "To the pure all things are pure.") The eye, then, is clarified, purified, and so can see into the heavenly world.

Very's voice too has changed, transitioning from that of an alienated Romantic to a thunderous prophetic tenor. This is a way of speaking straight out of the Old Testament, full of thees and thous, and angry denunciations of sin. These poems meditate on what exactly a prophetic voice ought to do and the change it ought to bring about. In the appropriately named "The Prophet," he intones that

The Prophet speaks, the world attentive stands!
The voice that stirs the people's countless host,

Issues again the Living God's commands;
And who before the King of Kings can boast?

(p. 98)

In "Time," he suggests that his age is in need of a prophet by comparing himself to "some sweet bird [who] must sing / To tell the story of the passing hour … [which] waits the utterance of some nobler tongue / Like that which spoke in prophet tones of old" (p. 74). Occasionally this desire to speak like a prophet of old means that he, well, does just that, taking biblical lines and paraphrasing them, adding little of his own. Take this from "The Kingdom of God Is Within You": "For I am life and they who seek me find / The keys of heaven I hold to loose and bind" (p. 129). The irony is that some of his most notable verse in these eighteen months displays less a prophetic voice than one almost naked in its direct simplicity. In "The Latter Rain," he comes across as an American John Clare, simply describing how "The rain falls still—the fruit all ripened drops, / It pierces chestnut burr and walnut shell, / The furrowed fields disclose the yellowed crops" (p. 72).

As these lines would imply, Very, the poetic speaker, was still an isolated figure in these works. Again, these are depopulated poems, taking place in a visionary nature, or a postapocalyptic world purged of sinners. Such is the fate of all prophets, for as he puts it in his reflection on Enoch, "God walked alone unhonored through the earth; / For him no heart-built temple open stood" (p. 65). In contrast to his earlier phase, however, the reason for this loneliness is less Very's squeamishness at a sensual, decaying human form than a more generalized sense of terror at an unredeemed and vicious human crowd. In "The Graveyard," he writes, "My heart grows sick before the wide-spread death, / That walks and speaks in seeming life around" (p. 103). Similarly, in "The Dead," he says, "I see them crowd on crowd they walk the earth / Dry, leafless trees no Autumn laid bare" (p. 77). Very here communicates his utter distaste for the mass and communicates what he feels to be his own uniquely privileged position.

In this way, even though these are theological poems, they are also deeply autobiographical, communicating Very's loneliness in his desperate, and isolated, search for transcendence. There is a sense, as Nathaniel Hawthorne would note, that Very was no longer of this earth, living in a world utterly alien to those around him. "Jones Very," as Hawthorne put it, "stood alone, within a circle which no other of mortal race could enter, nor himself escape from" (Deese, Introduction, p. xxvii). Very orients these poems around an apocalyptic event, with many of the poems taking place in the moments directly prior to the event or in its immediate aftermath. This is a visionary world where the boundary between the spiritual and the real, the living and the dead, the earthly and the heavenly, is terrifyingly permeable.

But as the months went on and the apocalypse failed to materialize, Very began to qualify his pronouncements. The eschaton started to appear to him as an absolutely personal occurrence, unique to every individual. As the intensity of his religious fervor began to fade, his utterances became increasingly defeated, their tone hollow. As 1840 came into view, Very had to grapple with the fact that he still lived in a world that, to all intents and purposes, had ended for him, professionally, personally, and spiritually, long ago. His response was to withdraw from the world, living with his mother and his sisters in Salem, writing occasional verse. What was left was a diminished poetic talent, a mind singed by the fires of revelation, and a simple, rocklike faith in the precepts of Christianity. As he reflects in the valedictory poem "'Tis Finished," a title that appears to refer to his poetic talent, his visionary state, and his engagement with the world, "Tis done the world has vanished Christ remains / The only sure the only lasting trust" (p. 134).

CRITICAL RECEPTION AND LATER LIFE

Essays and Poems received scant attention on its release. The reviews it garnered were generally approving, though most came with some qualifications. Nonetheless, he did gain several fans in the small transcendentalist world of New England, among whom Margaret Fuller was the

most influential and James Freeman Clarke the most voluble. In spite of Emerson overseeing and editing the collection, he did not throw his weight behind the publication, only reviewing it after several years had elapsed. By this point in time, Very had all but renounced the intellectual world of which he was once a part.

It was Very's life rather than his work that interested the transcendentalists. His personal eccentricities, his extraphenomenal insights, and his theology were the subjects of much speculation. Among the many who gave thought to Very in letters, essays, or, one suspects, in gossipy discussion, were Amos Bronson Alcott, Elizabeth Palmer Peabody, William Ellery Channing, Richard Henry Dana, Sr., William Cullen Bryant, and Samuel Johnson, Jr. The most enduring tribute to Very, however, occurs in Emerson's essay "Friendship." Here he holds up Very as an icon of truth in a false world:

> I knew a man who, under a certain religious frenzy, cast off this drapery, and, omitting all compliment and commonplace, spoke to the conscience of every person he encountered, and that with great insight and beauty. At first he was resisted, and all men agreed he was mad. But persisting, as indeed he could not help doing, for some time in this course, he attained the advantage of bringing every man of his acquaintance into true relations with him. No man would think of speaking falsely with him, or of putting him off with any chat of markets or reading-rooms.... To stand in true relations with men in a false age is worth a fit of insanity, is it not?
>
> (*Essays and Lectures*, p. 347)

Even though Very receded from public view, he still continued to write poetry. Over the 1850s and 1860s his by-now occasional verse appeared with reasonable regularity in the *Christian Register* and the *Salem Gazette*. These poems took on a number of subjects, from slavery, to new technology, to religion. Among the most interesting is a reflection he wrote on visiting Thoreau's and Hawthorne's tombs.

His reputation as a poet was maintained through the anthologization of his earlier poems, not these later works. Even though they only appeared in small numbers, Very's poems feature in the *Cyclopedia of American Literature* (1855), by the brothers Evert Augustus Duyckinck and

George Long Duyckinck, and in Rufus Griswold's *Poets and Poetry of America* (1842). This pattern continued throughout the 1870s, with his work appearing in a number of collections, variously dedicated to the sonnet form, the American voice, and religious poetry.

Upon Very's death on May 8, 1880, there was renewed interest in his work. Obituaries published in the *New York Times* and the *Boston Transcript* demanded a new edition of his poems. These calls were heeded in 1883 when a collection edited by William P. Andrews appeared. A number of reviews heralded Very's reappearance as a poet, casting him as an exemplum of faith in an ever more secular and utilitarian age. Very's sisters, however, disagreed with Andrews' editing job, thinking that it presented an incomplete picture of their saintly brother. So within three years, under their auspices, another, more complete collection of 676 of Very's poems appeared, this one edited by James Freeman Clarke.

This Very revival did not last long. Between 1900 and 1918 Very all but disappeared from view. Even though there was a centenary celebration of his birth at the North Church in Salem in 1913, he did not feature in any anthologies in this period and was not included in any scholarly studies. An intellectual climate dedicated to aggressively skeptical and fragmented modernist aesthetics meant that the pious, formally constrained rhymes of Very naturally fell out of favor. One unpublished doctoral dissertation emerged in 1918 and another article in 1922.

It was not until the 1930s that people started reading Very again. In keeping with a general mania for rescuing forgotten American writers, a number of scholars were drawn toward this strange mystical companion of the transcendentalists. Most notably, Yvor Winters made the claim that Very was the equal of Herman Melville and Emily Dickinson and that he was a figure capable of supplanting Emerson as the leader of American aesthetics. The first biography, written by William Irving Bartlett, duly appeared in 1942. This introductory study cast Very as a New England saint, an otherworldly presence crushed by an orthodox reli-

gious establishment and an uncaring and debased society.

These scholarly studies contributed to Very's inclusion in anthologies edited by F. O. Matthiessen and Perry Miller in the 1950s. The most sustained critical attention given to Very, however, occurred in the late 1960s, with the publication of a volume of selected poems with a critical introduction written by Nathan Lyons, a new, considerably more in-depth biography by Edwin Gittleman, and a dissertation by Harry L. Jones concerning Very's use of religious symbolism. These materials provided the basis for a comparatively large number of articles, book chapters, and books on Very in the 1970s and 1980s. This varied critical corpus examined Very's religion, newly discovered archival material from his later life, and his use of rhetoric.

But all of these studies suffered from the lack of a scholarly edition. This lacuna was remedied by the publication of Helen Deese's volume of Very's complete poems in 1993, which finally gathered all his writing from his entire career in a single place. In the thorough introduction Deese concluded by hoping that the book would allow for a rediscovery and reevaluation of Very's work. However, even though Very surfaced once again in anthologies, including Jay Parini's *Columbia Anthology of American Poetry* (1995), and was granted a place in Harold Bloom's *Western Canon* (1994), there has not been any sustained renaissance in his work. In 1999 Sarah Turner Clayton published her study of Very's critical reception, but he remains condemned to the literary margins to this day.

CONCLUSION

Jones Very is a curious figure. Even though his life and works have enjoyed sustained critical attention, he has rarely troubled the literary mainstream. His reputation depends on the unexplainable raptures of his inspired phase. Yet is precisely the hermetic, isolated obscurity of these verses that preclude any wide readership. But there is a way in which Very wrote and anticipated this marginality in his work. These are poems that are not meant for the masses of unredeemed, but rather the cleansed vision of the saved. And even if this radically reduces the potential size of his poetic constituency, it does not strip his work of any of the compelling, religious intensity that makes it so rewarding.

Selected Bibliography

WORKS OF JONES VERY

Essays and Poems. Edited by Ralph Waldo Emerson. Boston: Little and Brown, 1839.

Poems. Edited by William P. Andrews. Boston: Houghton Mifflin, 1883.

Poems and Essays: Complete and Revised Edition. Edited by James Freeman Clarke. Boston: Houghton Mifflin, 1886.

Jones Very: Selected Poems. Edited by Nathan Lyons. New Brunswick, N.J.: Rutgers University Press, 1966.

Jones Very: The Complete Poems. Edited by Helen R. Deese. Athens and London: University of Georgia Press, 1993.

CRITICAL AND BIOGRAPHICAL STUDIES

Andrews, William P. "Memoir." In *Poems*, by Jones Very. Boston: Houghton Mifflin, 1883.

Arner, Robert D. "Hawthorne and Jones Very: Two Dimensions of Satire in 'Egotism; or, The Bosom Serpent.'" *New England Quarterly* 42: 267–275 (June 1969).

Baker, Carlos. "Emerson and Jones Very." *New England Quarterly* 7: 90–99 (March 1934).

———. *Emerson Among the Eccentrics: A Group Portrait.* New York: Viking, 1996.

Bartlett, William Irving. *Jones Very: Emerson's "Brave Saint."* Durham, N.C.: Duke University Press, 1942.

Berthoff, Warner B. "Jones Very: New England Mystic." *Boston Public Library Quarterly* 2: 63–76 (January 1950).

Boswell, Jeanetta. *Spokesman for the Minority: A Bibliography of Sidney Lanier, William Vaughn Moody, Henry Timrod, Frederick Goddard Tuckerman, and Jones Very.* Metuchen, N.J.: Scarecrow, 1987.

Brooks, Van Wyke. *The Flowering of New England, 1815–1865.* New York: Dutton, 1936.

Buell, Lawrence. *Literary Transcendentalism: Style and Vision in the American Renaissance.* Ithaca, N.Y.: Cornell University Press, 1973. Pp. 312–330.

Burns, Percy Pratt. "Jones Very." *Howard College Bulletin* 80: 42–66 (June 1922).

Cameron, Kenneth Walter. "Jones Very's Academic Standing at Harvard." *Emerson Society Quarterly*, no. 7, quarter 2:39–40 (1957).

———. "Jones Very and Emerson's Friends in College Church Records." *Emerson Society Quarterly*, no. 14, quarter 1:18 (1959).

Clarke, James Freeman. "Biographical Notice of Jones Very." In *Poems and Essays,* by Jones Very. Boston and New York: Houghton Mifflin, 1886.

Clayton, Sarah Turner. *The Angelic Sins of Jones Very.* New York: Peter Lang, 1999.

Deese, Helen R. "Selected Sermons of Jones Very." In *Studies in the American Renaissance, 1984.* Edited by Joel Myerson. Charlottesville: University Press of Virginia, 1984. Pp. 1–78.

———. "Unpublished and Uncollected Poems of Jones Very." *ESQ* 30, no. 3:154–162 (1984).

———. "A Calendar of the Poems of Jones Very." In *Studies in the American Renaissance 1986.* Edited by Joel Myerson. Charlottesville: University Press of Virginia, 1986. Pp. 305–372.

———. "The Peabody Family and the Jones Very 'Insanity': Two Letters of Mary Peabody." *Harvard Library Bulletin* 35, no. 2:218–229 (1987).

———. "The Presumptuous Task of Editing the 'Holy Spirit': The Jones Very Edition." *Documentary Editing* 11: 5–9 (March 1989).

———. Introduction to *Jones Very: The Complete Poems.* Athens: University of Georgia Press, 1993.

Dennis, Carl. "Correspondence in Very's Nature Poetry." *New England Quarterly* 43: 250–273 (June 1970).

Deringer, Ludwig. *Die Rhetorik in der Sonettkunst von Jones Very.* Frankfurt: Lang, 1983.

Emerson, Ralph Waldo, *Essays and Lectures.* Edited by Joel Porte. New York: Library of America, 1983).

Fleck, Richard. "Jones Very—Another White Indian." *Concord Saunterer* 9: 6–12 (September 1974).

Gittleman, Edwin. *Jones Very: The Effective Years, 1833–40.* New York and London: Columbia University Press, 1967.

Herbold, Anthony. "Nature as Concept and Technique in the Poetry of Jones Very." *New England Quarterly* 40: 244–259 (June 1967).

Jones, Harry L. "Symbolism in the Mystical Poetry of Jones Very." Ph.D. dissertation, Catholic University of America, 1967.

Levernier, James A. "Calvinism and Transcendentalism in the Poetry of Jones Very." *ESQ* 24, no. 1:30–41 (1978).

Lyons, Nathan. Introduction to *Jones Very: Selected Poems.* New Brunswick, N.J.: Rutgers University Press, 1966. Pp. 3–34.

Proudfoot, Bessie Whitmore. "Jones Very: A Biographical Study." Ph.D. dissertation, University of Chicago, 1918.

Reeves, Paschal. "The Making of a Mystic: A Reconstruction of the Life of Jones Very." *Essex Institute Historical Collections* 103: 3–30 (January 1967).

———. "Jones Very as Preacher: The Extant Sermons." *Emerson Society Quarterly*, no. 57, quarter 4:16–22 (1969).

Robinson, David. "Jones Very: An Essay in Bibliography." *Resources for American Literary Study* 5: 131–146 (autumn 1975).

———."Jones Very, the Transcendentalists, and the Unitarian Tradition." *Harvard Theological Review* 68, no. 2:103–124 (1975).

———. "The Exemplary Self and the Transcendent Self in the Poetry of Jones Very." *ESQ* 24, no. 4:207–214 (1978).

———. "Jones Very." In *The American Renaissance in New England, First Series.* Edited by Joel Myerson. *Dictionary of Literary Biography.* Vol. 1. Detroit: Gale Research, 1978. Pp. 184–185.

———. "Four Early Poems of Jones Very." *Harvard Library Bulletin* 28: 146–151 (April 1980).

Seed, David. "Alone with God and Nature: The Poetry of Jones Very and Frederick Goddard Tuckerman." In *Nineteenth-Century American Poetry.* Edited by A. Robert Lee. Totowa, N.J.: Barnes & Noble, 1987. Pp. 166–193.

Williams, David R. *Wilderness Lost: The Religious Origins of the American Mind.* Selinsgrove, Pa.: Susquehanna University Press, 1987. Pp. 180–212.

Winters, Yvor. *Maule's Curse: Seven Studies in the History of American Obscurantism.* Norfolk, Conn.: New Directions, 1938.

HERMAN WOUK

(1915—)

Jack Fischel

IN 2012 PHILIP Roth, at age seventy-nine, announced that he would no longer continue to write the novels that made him one of the most critically acclaimed novelists of his generation. At about the same time, the ninety-seven-year-old Herman Wouk's new novel, *The Lawgiver*, was published, along with his announcement that he planned to write two additional works of fiction. Between 1951, when Wouk published *The Caine Mutiny*, and the publication of *War and Remembrance* in 1978, he was possibly the most celebrated living American Jewish writer of his time. During this period he produced eight novels, the hit play *The Caine Mutiny Court-Martial*, and a work of nonfiction, *This Is My God: The Jewish Way of Life*. All told, Wouk has authored fifteen novels, three works of nonfiction, and three plays, including the unsuccessful *Nature's Way*.

Although a number of Wouk's books made the best-seller list, his fiction was especially popular among American Jews. Before Leon Uris' *Exodus* (1959) became essential reading for American Jews, Wouk's *Marjorie Morningstar* (1955), a novel about an assimilated American Jewish family whose daughter, Marjorie, had aspirations to become an actress, was widely read within the Jewish community. Given the diverse themes that characterized his work, Wouk, although considered an excellent storyteller, was, like Uris, not generally included by critics among the top tier of American Jewish writers, such as Saul Bellow, Albert Kazin, Philip Roth, and Bernard Malamud.

Indeed, more recent critics have written about the negative comments Wouk's works garnered from reviewers at the time the novels were published, chief among them the highbrow literary critic Norman Podhoretz, longtime editor of *Commentary*. In a 2013 *Commentary* article titled "How This Magazine Wronged Herman Wouk," Michael J. Lewis characterizes Podhoretz's 1956 review of *Marjorie Morningstar* this way: "While it may have been 'the first novel to treat American Jews intimately as Jews without making them seem exotic,' everything else about it was wrong, [Podhoretz] wrote, from its 'indigestible prose' to its simplistic moral analysis" (Lewis, p. 40). Adam Kirsch, writing in the *Tablet* in 2012, points out that Podhoretz once compared Wouk's blundering prose style to "a blind man trying to locate an unfamiliar room." Edward S. Shapiro, discussing the critical reception of *War and Remembrance*, found that its literary qualities fared little better with reviewers of the 1970s. Shapiro notes that the literary critic Pearl K. Bell "described *War and Remembrance* as a 'good-bad book,' bereft of 'any daunting complexities of thought, craft, or human behavior,' [whose] 'major characters are preposterous and irritating' " (Shapiro, p. 50). And although the historian Paul K. Fussell had a more "balanced" view, writes Shapiro, and praised Wouk's skill as a historian by comparing him to Samuel Eliot Morison and B H. Liddell Hart, he nevertheless considered the book a "literary disaster" written by an author "who was in reality a historian who had been attracted to fiction " (p. 51).

Laurence W. Mazzeno, in his critical study of Wouk's work, summarizes best the venomous attacks toward his subject by quoting Stanley Heyman's review of Wouk's *Youngblood Hawke* (1962):

> Wouk is now a phenomenal merchandising success, sold as a detergent is sold. He can compete with the worst of television because he *is* the worst of television, without the commercials.... His readers really are ... boobs ... "so starved for an interesting story"

that they will ignore the reviews to read him. They are yahoos who hate culture and the mind.

(quoted in Mazzeno, *Herman Wouk*, p. ix)

Despite this type of devastating criticism, Wouk continued to write best sellers and attained a place among the nation's most widely read novelists.

The range of subjects that mark Wouk's oeuvre include subjects gleaned from his own experiences: his years at Columbia University, where he studied philosophy and literature; working as a sketch and gag writer for the *Fred Allen Show*; his tenure as a naval officer during World War II; and above all his family experience, especially learning to study the Talmud from his Russian-born grandfather. Wouk's Orthodox Judaism was not only important to him but found its way—sometimes subtly and at times directly—into his writings. His respect for Jewish tradition led to his disdain for writers and artists such as Woody Allen and Philip Roth, who lampooned the angst of American Jews. In *Inside, Outside* (1985), for example, he includes a Roth-like character named Peter Quat, who becomes controversial when he writes an offensive novel about Jews titled *Onan's Way*—a novel that mirrors Roth's *Portnoy's Complaint* (1969). In contrast, Wouk's protagonist in the novel is an Orthodox Jew, who is an advisor to President Richard Nixon, studies the Talmud, and wears a skullcap at work.

Additional influences on Wouk's writings include World War II, the Holocaust, and the creation of the state of Israel. For *The Winds of War* (1971) and *War and Remembrance* (1978), his monumental fictional history of both the war and the Holocaust, Wouk and his family moved to Washington, D.C., where he spent years researching both subjects. This research resulted in as accurate a picture of World War II and the extermination of the European Jews as can be found in academic studies on the subject.

Wouk spent time in Israel researching its historical archives and meeting many of the founding fathers of the Jewish state. The result was an epic account of Israel's history, *The Hope* (1993). This novel tells the story of the early years of Israel—from the 1948 war for independence through the Suez War to the 1967 Six-Day War—through the lives of three families, mixing his fictional characters with real-life figures such as David Ben-Gurion, Moshe Dayan, and Golda Meir. *The Glory* (1994) continues the story from the late 1960s to the bombing of Iraq's nuclear reactor in 1981.

Wouk's novels were predicated on reaching large audiences. Consequently he was, on principle, opposed to the techniques of literary modernism. Rather, eighteenth- and nineteenth-century novelists were his writing models: Henry Fielding (he loved *Tom Jones*), Charles Dickens, and Mark Twain, among others, plus Cervantes' *Don Quixote*, which he read at age thirty and which moved him in the direction of writing fiction. Wouk's writings include virtuous characters, intricate plots, and moralistic resolutions. As Arnold Beichman has written of Wouk:

> For him, man's fate is meaningful, not a random, capricious happening.... The Freudian-Marxist age which sits heavily on our literary culture holds no attraction for Wouk. Final answers are hard to come by even with prayer and devotion. And surely final answers are not to be found lying on a couch or peering over a barricade.
>
> (p. 127)

EARLY LIFE AND CAREER

Herman Wouk was born on May 27, 1915, in the Bronx, New York, the child of Abraham Isaac and Esther Levine Wouk, Jewish immigrants from Minsk, Russia (now Belarus). Wouk's father rose from poverty to become a successful businessman. In this Orthodox Jewish household, Herman Wouk was the middle of three siblings born to the Wouks. His younger brother, Victor, would go on to win renown as an American scientist who pioneered in the development of the hybrid car; and a sister, Irene, eight years older than Herman, was the model for the character of Marjorie in *Marjorie Morningstar* (Boroson, p. 2).

Wouk's commitment to Orthodox Judaism was strengthened in 1928 when, at age thirteen, his *zaideh* (grandfather), Rabbi Mendel Leib Levin, arrived from Russia. A Lubavitcher Hasid,

HERMAN WOUK

"Reb" Mendel took over Herman's religious education. A picture of this relationship is told in *Inside, Outside*, Wouk's autobiographical novel: "Little did I grasp what I was letting myself in for! Ten hours of English and Hebrew subjects, two hours of study with my grandfather... that was the daily schedule. I could hold my own in Talmud only if Zaideh drilled me.... Once I told Pop in no uncertain terms how tired I was of this interminable Talmudic brain-twisting over laws two-thousand years old" (pp. 244–245). His father replied with words that Wouk would later repeat in life: "If I were on my deathbed, and I had breath enough to say one more thing to you, I would say 'Study the Talmud' " (p. 245).

Eventually Wouk took his father's advice, and Judaism would become integral to both his personal life and professional career. Wouk would write that "for a long time I thought of Zaideh as the one who shaped me the most. Wrong. It was Pop, always Pop. All my life long, I have only been trying to be like my father" (*Inside, Outside*, p. 245).

After graduating from Townsend Harris High School, then in Manhattan, Wouk attended Columbia University as a philosophy and comparative literature major, graduating in 1934 with a B.A. degree. At Columbia he studied under the noted philosopher Irwin Edman, chairman of the philosophy department and a man Wouk called a "naturalistic skeptic of the deepest die—quite a contrast with my Old Orthodox grandfather" (Beichman, p. 16). As he later summarized the influences on his future career, Wouk wrote, "The two teachers who most influenced my life were a man without a trace of Western culture and a man who is its embodiment" (Beichman, p. 16).

During his years at Columbia he also edited the college humor magazine, the *Jester*, and wrote several variety shows. At the same time, Wouk's commitment to Judaism lapsed, and he informed his family that he wanted to become a comic writer. By 1936 he had been hired by the comedian Fred Allen to write sketches as well as gags. This association with Allen lasted until 1941. He also did gag writing for Henry Morgan, another popular radio comedian, as well as for the comic writer David Freedman. Although he

was paid well, he became disenchanted with show business culture and missed the depth of his studies in Judaism (much of Wouk's experience in writing gags and sketches is caricatured in *Inside, Outside*).

With the outbreak of World War II, Wouk left Allen to work as a scriptwriter for the U.S. Treasury Department's Defense Bond Campaign. Following the attack on Pearl Harbor, Wouk enlisted in the U.S. Navy, where he was commissioned an officer after completing Officer Candidate School, and then attended Communication School at the U.S. Naval Academy in Annapolis, Maryland. Between 1943 and 1945 Wouk was assigned to a destroyer-minesweeper, the U.S.S. *Zane*, and later the U.S.S. *Southard*, and served for three years in the South Pacific, where he took part in eight naval actions, winning four campaign stars and a unit citation. When the war ended, Wouk was the *Southard*'s executive officer and was intended to be its new captain, but the ship was wrecked in a typhoon off Okinawa before he could assume command. Wouk drew on these experiences in writing *The Caine Mutiny*. During his service in the navy, Wouk, in order to relieve hours and days of boredom, began work on his first novel, a satire of Madison Avenue radio advertising titled *Aurora Dawn*. Thanks to Irwin Edman, who had connections with Simon & Schuster, the novel impressed its editor, who recommend the work for publication. *Aurora Dawn* was published in 1947 and became a Book-of-the-Month Club selection.

Wouk's navy experience, like his Judaism, meant much to him. (Wouk observed the Jewish dietary laws and dutifully prayed each day while carrying out his naval responsibilities.) In *This Is My God* (1959) he wrote:

> I have always thought that the Jewish place among mankind somewhat resembles the position of navy men among other Americans.... They have special commitments and disciplines, odd ways of dress, sharp limits on their freedom. They have, at least in their own minds, compensations of glory, or vital service performed.... I remember being looked up to as a naval officer in wartime; then when peace came and I travelled to take my Reserve cruises, people in trains and planes tended to regard me as an unfortunate misfit. One or two actually said, "How

come you're still in?" I think that is essentially the question agnostics address to observant Jews.

(p. 33)

The navy also marked an important turning point in his life. In 1944 Wouk met Betty Carol Brown in California. A Protestant, Betty was a navy personnel specialist. They fell in love and subsequently Betty Brown converted to Judaism in order to marry him. They were wed in 1946 in a traditional Jewish wedding, after which she became Betty Sarah Wouk. The couple went on to have three sons: Abraham (who died in a tragic accident in Mexico shortly before his fifth birthday), Nathaniel, and Isaac.

Although Wouk often portrayed people in his own life as fictional characters in his novels, he almost never created a fictional surrogate for Sarah—that is, until *The Lawgiver* (2012), where she figures prominently in the novel. Betty Sarah Wouk died on March 17, 2011, of a massive stroke. In the epilogue to the novel, Wouk notes that they had been married for sixty-three years and says that "before we met I wrote nothing that mattered. Whoever reads a book by Herman Wouk will be reading art deeply infused with her self-effacing and incisive brilliance, books composed during a long literary career managed by her common sense, with which I am sparsely endowed" (p. 234). Insight into the contributions Betty Sarah Wouk made to Wouk's literary career can be gleaned in a passage in *Youngblood Hawke*, a novel about a novelist. Wouk writes: "Beyond technical editing … and help as some author's wives do … often the wife of a writer serves him as copyist, sounding board, research assistant, day-to-day critic, encourager of his strong points and suppressor of his failings; all this in addition to her household labors" (p. 474).

Following his discharge from the navy and the success of *Aurora Dawn*, Wouk decided to pursue a full-time literary career as a writer. At the time, Wouk was working on a play, *The Traitor*, which would make it to the Broadway stage in 1949. This was followed by a second novel, *The City Boy* (1948), which was better received by critics than *Aurora Dawn*, but it was not a commercial success. In 1951, Wouk published *The Caine Mutiny*, the novel that made him one of America's most popular writers and was awarded the Pulitzer Prize for fiction in 1952. The novel was also made into a film starring Humphrey Bogart as Captain Queeg. As Laurence Mazzeno notes, "Captain Queeg joined Huckleberry Finn and Captain Ahab in the pantheon of memorable figures in American fiction" (p. 6). Wouk's novel was also turned into a play, *The Caine Mutiny Court-Martial*, which opened on Broadway on January 20, 1954, in a production directed by Charles Laughton. A huge success, the play had a long-running Broadway life, and has had several notable stage and television revivals since.

Between 1953 and 1959 Wouk became a public figure. He delivered the commencement address at Yeshiva University and received an honorary L.H.D degree from the institution in 1955. In the following year he was invited to be part of an American delegation to the seventh-anniversary celebration of Israel's independence. In Israel, Wouk and his wife visited Prime Minister David Ben-Gurion at his Negev retreat. The visit was notable for the story that emerged from the meeting. According to Wouk, "'Toward the end of our visit, Ben-Gurion said he would like to have us stay for dinner, but we couldn't. You see'—with a chuckle—'he doesn't keep a kosher home' " (quoted in Beichman, p. 30).

It was also during this period that Wouk wrote *Marjorie Morningstar* (1955), a novel that became a best seller and later a major film. The novel disproved the conventional wisdom that novels on Jewish themes could not be successful. This novel was followed by *The Lomokome Papers* (1956), Wouk's only effort at writing science fiction, and his first nonfiction book, *This Is My God* (1959), which was Wouk's effort to educate the public about the traditions of his faith. The royalties from *The Caine Mutiny* and *Marjorie Morningstar* assured him that he could write unimpeded, thus liberating Wouk from financial concerns and enabling him to observe Judaism in the style that his grandfather had taught him. In 1958 the family moved to St. Thomas in the U.S. Virgin Islands. The experiences in St. Thomas provided him with the mate-

rial that resulted in *Don't Stop the Carnival* (1965), one of Wouk's least successful novels. During this period, Wouk also spent time in Hollywood writing the screen treatment for *Slattery's Hurricane* for 20th Century Fox. The unusual aspect of this project was that Wouk's research was first turned into a magazine article, then a screenplay. The film was released in 1949 and featured Richard Widmark, Linda Darnell, and Veronica Lake. Wouk then lengthened the magazine article into a full-length novel, which was published in 1956.

In 1962 Wouk published *Youngblood Hawke.* The novel, about a young writer from Kentucky who comes to New York to find fame and fortune in the publishing world, quickly became a best seller. Following its success, Wouk's interests turned elsewhere. In 1964 the family moved to Washington, D.C., so that he could conduct research for his novels about World War II and the Holocaust. In addition to perusing the historical archives in D.C., he made several trips to Europe, Russia, Israel, and Iran. In all, the project took Wouk five years of research to write *The Winds of War* (1971), and another seven to complete *War and Remembrance* (1978). Both books became best sellers and were subsequently adapted as television miniseries for Paramount/ABC that aired in 1983 and 1988 respectively. *War and Remembrance* went on to win the 1989 Emmy Award for Outstanding Miniseries. Both productions received very high ratings and, more importantly, contributed to educating the American public about the genocidal Holocaust.

Following the publication of both novels, Wouk's energies turned to Israel and Zionism. In 1980 he wrote the introduction to the letters of Jonathan Netanyahu, who was killed in Israel's raid on Entebbe in 1976. Wouk, states Shapiro, believed "that the same values and ideals that had animated Americans during World War II were now inspiring Netanyahu and other Israelis" (p. 61). Wouk described the Entebbe raid as a beacon in the defense of the struggle between civilization and terrorism, further stating that Netanyahu died not merely for Jews but for free men everywhere.

Inside, Outside, published in 1985, includes a series of autobiographical vignettes, from growing up in an Orthodox Jewish household to his emergence as one of the most widely read novelists in America. The title derives from Wouk's inside life as an Orthodox Jew and the lure of the outside world to adapt to "the lax moral code of twentieth-century America" (Mazzeno, p. 102). The novel received mixed reviews from critics.

In 1990 Wouk received an honorary Ph.D. from Bar-Ilan University in Israel. The award was given at the time he was researching his two novels about Israel, *The Hope* (1993) and *The Glory* (1994). Wouk, at the peak of his literary career, was honored by the Library of Congress in 1995 with a symposium, "The Historical Novel: A Celebration of the Achievements of Herman Wouk," in honor of his eightieth birthday.

During the first decade of the twenty-first century, Wouk continued to be a prolific writer. Marking the new century, he published *The Will to Live On: This Is Our Heritage* (2000), a book concerned with the future survival of the American Jewish community, wherein Wouk urges cultural survival through the promotion of Jewish cultural literacy. Wouk was always interested in science, and his next book, *A Hole in Texas* (2004), is a satirical novel whose story line concerns U.S.–China relations over the Higgs boson, a scientific discovery that could lead to a weapon that would give nuclear supremacy to the country that develops it first. This novel was followed by a nonfiction work, *The Language God Talks: On Science and Religion* (2010), where, in conversations he had shared with the theoretical physicist Richard Feynman (1918–1988), Wouk attempts to reconcile the sparring ideas of science and religion. *The Lawgiver* (2012) is about a project to write a screenplay for a projected film about Moses, whose life Wouk also hoped to write about and found too difficult.

WOUK'S STORYTELLING STYLE

Wouk's fiction falls into a number of categories linked by his personal experiences and his

convictions based on his commitment to Judaism. And both his life experiences and his religious convictions are brought to bear on the way he chooses to tell those stories. Wouk's novels, such as *The Caine Mutiny*, do not contain profanity, nor examples of the obscenity or blasphemy that one would expect of shipboard talk. Nor does Wouk describe protracted descriptions of sexual union. This is not meant to imply that his novels are void of sexual engagement; quite the contrary. But in *Youngblood Hawke* and *Marjorie Morningstar*, or in describing the infidelities of Rhoda Henry in *Winds of War* and *War and Remembrance*, Wouk is careful not to tantalize his reading audience with scenes of gratuitous sex. This possibly can be attributed to his observance of Judaism, which teaches modesty in all aspects of life and frowns on infidelity as well as vulgarity in the use of language. There is also the influence of the eighteenth- and nineteenth-century novel, wherein Wouk was more interested in telling a story in the manner of a Dickens or Fielding than attracting an audience interested in prurient literature. In writing his novels, Wouk borrowed the advice of his mentor Irwin Edman, who wrote: "As for the respectable bourgeois rabble whom our sophisticated despise, these comfortable bumpkins cannot get enough of the traditional simple virtues.... Write them a story ... and you will have hundreds of thousands at your feet and at your publisher's" (Mazzeno, pp. 14–15). It would appear that from *Aurora Dawn* to *The Lawgiver*, Wouk never forgot that advice.

AURORA DAWN

The full title of Wouk's first novel (1947) is *Aurora Dawn; or, The True History of Andrew Reale: Containing a Faithful Account of the Great Riot, Together with the Complete Texts of Michael Wilde's Oration and Father Stanfield's Sermon*. Wouk deliberately set his story within the framework of the eighteenth-century novel, wherein novelists introduced each chapter with expanded titles that provided a brief summation of the action. *Aurora Dawn* was influenced by Henry Fielding, who, like Tobias Smollett and Victorian novelists such as Charles Dickens, was a literary inspiration for Wouk.

The publication of *Aurora Dawn* coincided with the publication of another novel about the advertising industry, *The Hucksters* (1946) by Frederic Wakeman. According to Arnold Beichman, Wouk was aware of the slightly earlier novel and it did have an influence on his own work. Wouk, in his introduction to *Aurora Dawn*, refers to the "points of similarities" between his novel and others "intended to expose the inner workings of the advertising industry" (Beichman, p. 45).

Aurora Dawn is a humorous satire of radio advertising and advertising in general. Wouk wrote much of the novel while in the navy and completed it after his release from active service in 1946. Relying on his insider knowledge of radio program production, Wouk created a story about an ambitious advertising executive, Andrew Reale, who is involved with two women, one of whom, Honey Beaton, he is in love with; the other, Carol Marquis, is the daughter of a business mogul, Talmadge Marquis. Each of the women represents different values. Will Reale marry the woman he is in love with? Or the one who will mean upward mobility by his becoming the boss's son-in-law? The plot unfolds when Reale is asked to conduct an advertising campaign to promote Marquis' product, Aurora Dawn soap. Several subplots follow; Reale is sent to convince a popular backwoods evangelist to bring his brand of Christianity to radio with the understanding that the sponsor will advertise Aurora Dawn soap. Reale subsequently comes to realize that the preacher's spirituality is an alternative to the commercialism of Talmadge and his daughter. Yet another character, Mike Wilde, an artist, is Wouk's representation of the decadence of modern art. The novel concludes when Reale marries Honey Beaton, resigns his position in advertising, and moves to the West to restart his life. Mazzeno suggests that Wouk attempted to make Andrew Reale a young Everyman similar to eighteenth-century figures such as Joseph Andrews and Tom Jones. The novel sold thousands of copies and was a selection of the Book-of-the-Month Club.

THE CITY BOY: THE ADVENTURES OF HERBIE BOOKBINDER

The City Boy (1948), subtitled *The Adventures of Herbie Bookbinder and His Cousin, Cliff*, is based on Wouk's childhood growing up in the Bronx. It is the often humorous story of Herbie, a chubby and bright eleven-year-old. After the success of *The Caine Mutiny*, the novel was republished without the subtitle.

The novel follows Hymie Bookbinder, from his public school days in New York, where he is smitten with the unobtainable Lucy Glass, a pretty red-haired classmate. Much of the novel describes how Hymie, an excellent student but a poor athlete, learns that Lucy will be enrolled in Camp Manitou, a summer camp in upstate New York, and prevails on his parents to send him to the camp.

What follows is a series of escapades wherein Hymie tries to win Lucy only to find her attracted to the son of his father's business partner, Lennie Krieger, who is dense but an excellent athlete. Unable to compete with Lenny's superior athletic ability, Hymie attempts to use wit and guile to win Lucy—but to no avail.

A secondary plot describes a series of humorous misadventures, which cause a desperate Hymie to leave camp and return to the Bronx to ask his father for money. While sneaking into his father's laundry, however, he uncovers a plot by his father's business associates to ruin the family business. Hymie reveals the plot to his father and saves the family's enterprise. The quest for Lucy, however, proves elusive.

Wouk's second novel was not as successful as *Aurora Dawn*, perhaps because the story of early adolescence in the aftermath of the Second World War lacked appeal to a large reading audience. Mazzeno writes that a majority of the critics judged the novel a "complete failure" (p. 21), but it's worth noting that the book has been reissued a number of times over the years, including in 2009 as an e-book.

THE TRAITOR

Following *The City Boy*, Wouk turned to the theater, where his play *The Traitor* was produced on Broadway in 1949 and ran for sixty-seven performances. The play was written during the cold war, prior to the disclosures surrounding Klaus Fuchs, a German physicist, who in 1950 was convicted of supplying information about the Manhattan Project to the Soviet Union. Wouk's drama concerns an idealistic scientist who, fearful that the American ownership of the bomb would lead to the destruction of the world, decides to betray the secrets of the atomic bomb to the Soviet Union, believing that if both sides had the weapon, war would become too terrible to contemplate. He is convinced to undertake this action by a liberal professor of philosophy who, among other things, espouses opposition, on principal, to signing a loyalty questionnaire.

The scientist, however, soon has a change of heart and turns his Communist contact over to the FBI. And even the professor of philosophy decides to sign a loyalty questionnaire. Interestingly, in *Youngblood Hawke,* the conservative-minded Wouk has one of his characters, Karl Fry, an editor at a prestigious publishing house, refuse on principal to reveal the names of fellow members of the Communist cell. Having refused to name names, Fry then proceeds to do so, thus standing on his constitutional rights under the Fifth Amendment in the first instance, and then performing what he believes to be his patriotic duty in the other.

THE CAINE MUTINY

Herman Wouk's third novel, *The Caine Mutiny* (1951), made him a best-selling author. Wouk's tale of a mutiny on an American ship during World War II climbed to the top of the *New York Times* best-seller list in August 1951 and remained there off and on until mid-1952. Much of the story is drawn from Wouk's recollections of navy life during the war, where he had held various posts of increasing responsibility, rising to the position of executive officer aboard the U.S.S. *Southard*. In the novel's prefatory note, Wouk is careful to point out that the novel is "a work of fiction," and that no mutiny like the one described in his novel has ever happened in the U.S. Navy. Mazzeno states that in writing *The Caine Mutiny*,

Wouk was "deeply concerned with a problem that he saw during the war: the tension between regular navy men, who had chosen a service career long before the outbreak of hostilities, and reservists who joined the navy ... when the country needed them in a time of crisis" (p. 24).

The novel centers around Willie Keith, a raw, easygoing young midshipman through whose eyes unfold the events that lead to the mutiny. These events begin when Keith's captain, William De Vriess, is relieved of command of the U.S.S. *Caine* and replaced by Captain Philip Francis Queeg, an officer who commands by the book. Queeg enlists Keith's loyalty because Willie believes the new captain has the qualities to bring about the discipline of the often rowdy crew. It becomes apparent, however, that Captain Queeg had never before handled a ship such as the *Caine*, and he quickly loses the respect of his crew through his inability to admit error and his obsessive behavior, such as his elevation of a petty theft of a quart of strawberries into a major search of the ship to discover the thief who stole it from a locker. As tensions rise, Queeg increasingly withdraws to his cabin and isolates himself from both the crew and his officers, who find him unfit to command the *Caine* and view him as a coward.

At this point Wouk, who eschewed modernist writer such as T. S. Eliot and Virginia Woolf, assigns the role of the villain to communication officer (and aspiring novelist) Lieutenant Thomas Keefer. It is the highbrow Keefer, with a penchant for modernist novelists such as James Joyce, who spreads the seeds of the later mutiny by suggesting to the *Caine*'s executive officer, Lieutenant Stephen Maryk, that Queeg may be a mentally ill paranoid. Keefer also alerts Maryk to "Section 184" of the navy regulations, which states that in time of extraordinary circumstances, a commanding officer can be relieved of command by a subordinate officer. Maryk thereafter keeps a secret log of Queeg's behavior.

The mutiny that follows is the result of the *Caine* being caught in the middle of a typhoon that causes great damage to the ship. At the height of the typhoon, Queeg freezes and becomes incapable of command, refusing to even listen to Maryk's advice to turn the ship into the wind. Queeg's inability to act leads Maryk to relieve Queeg on the grounds of mental illness. Willie Keith, who by now hates Queeg, supports the decision as officer of the deck. Maryk proceeds to turn the ship into the wind and sail out of the storm, rescuing the survivors of a capsized destroyer along the way. Marek and Keith are subsequently court-martialed for "conduct to the prejudice of good order and discipline," instead of directly for mutiny, and Queeg is found to be sane by navy psychiatrists. Lieutenant Barney Greenwald, an attorney in civilian life, accepts the task of defending Maryk after concluding that Keefer encouraged the mutiny. In fact, when the court-martial commences, Keefer, Wouk's literary nemesis, evades any responsibility for the role he played in the ship takeover. During the trial, Greenwald's relentless cross-examination of Queeg (for those who viewed the film, it is hard to forget the memorable scene where Humphrey Bogart, who played the role of Queeg, continually rolls the steel balls in the palm of his hand) results in Maryk's acquittal, and charges against Keith are dropped.

All of the parties involved in the trial get together for a celebration of the acquittals, but the gathering takes an unexpected turn when an intoxicated Greenwald confronts Keefer and calls him a coward. Greenwald accuses Keefer of forcing him to destroy Queeg on the stand, and by extension all the Queegs of the nation who did their duty guarding America in the peacetime navy, a job people like Keefer deem beneath them. Greenwald asserts that men like Queeg kept Greenwald's Jewish mother from being "melted down into a bar of soap" by the Nazis. After accusing Keefer as the true author of the mutiny, Greenwald throws a glass of "yellow" wine in Keefer's face and leaves the party (pp. 446–448).

In the closing days of the war, Willie Keith returns to the *Caine* as its executive officer. Keefer is now the ship's captain. Ironically, during a kamikaze attack, Keefer reverts to behavior reminiscent of Queeg's during the typhoon. During the attack, Keith discovers that he has

matured as a naval officer, whereas Keefer panics and orders the ship abandoned. Keith, however, remains on board, and rescues the situation. As the novel concludes, Keefer returns home at war's end, ashamed of his cowardly behavior during the kamikaze attack. Willie Keith, on the other hand, receives a Bronze Star Medal for his action during the kamikaze attack, and subsequently becomes the last captain of the *Caine*. He eventually comes to the realization that relieving Queeg was unjustified and probably unnecessary.

Although *The Caine Mutiny* was a best seller, awarded the Pulitzer Prize, and made into a highly successful film, the book had its critics, both at the time of publication and in the years since. Perhaps the most blistering criticism has come from Joel Brodkin, who wrote in *New Politics* in 2005:

> The crime of the Holocaust demonstrated the need for individuals to respond to their consciences and not merely obey superiors. In 1945 and for sometime afterwards the idea of an authoritarian moral lesson—the importance of "following orders" as the lesson of the Holocaust—seemed unimaginable. Only Wouk's story-telling ability makes this assertion seem plausible.

> Fifty years later it appears that the about face in *Caine*, while not logical, was hardly irrelevant. It foreshadows the neoconservative reverential stance towards state authority and the institutions of society. Ironically, Wouk's theme of obedience to authority does come strikingly close to the World War II slogan, "Obey, believe, fight" that covered the walls of fascist Italy ... Ironically,... Wouk set the groundwork for a specifically Jewish-referenced conservatism—a set of values and attitudes that privileged the existing institutions of society, particularly the military ones, and demonized the voices of critical opposition. The character of Keefer would figure greatly in the neoconservative ideology of the 1970s–1990s with its enemy being a new class of intellectuals who allegedly hated their country and its culture.

MARJORIE MORNINGSTAR

With the success of *The Caine Mutiny*, Wouk turned to the conflict between tradition and assimilation within the American Jewish community. *Marjorie Morningstar* (1955) centers on the daughter of a prosperous middle-class Jewish family who aspires to become an actress. Toward this end, Marjorie Morgenstern adopts a stage name, Marjorie Morningstar, and is persuaded by her friend Marsha to become a drama counselor at a summer camp where Marjorie is assigned to teach arts and crafts. Subsequently Marsha urges Marjorie to surreptitiously visit South Wind, an exclusive adult resort that features a staff of entertainers. Violating her camp's rule that staff is prohibited from visiting the resort, Marjorie joins Marsha for the trip to South Wind, where she meets Noel Airman (a literal translation of the Yiddish word *luftmensch,* someone more concerned with airy intellectual pursuits than practical matters like earning an income), an agnostic Jewish wannabe composer of musicals. She falls in love with Noel, who is well known for breaking the hearts of pretty young girls like Marjorie but is nevertheless attracted to her. The 565-page novel proceeds to trace the on-again, off-again relationship between the two until eventually the relationship is consummated in a sexual affair. Soon after Marjorie loses her virginity she sees through Noel's superficiality and the liaison comes to an end.

During the course of the relationship, Noel Airman chides Marjorie for her adherence to Jewish tradition, such as her reluctance to eat bacon, her unwillingness to engage in premarital sex, and her general adherence to Jewish ritual. Noel, angered by Marjorie's refusal to compromise her feelings about her Jewishness, accuses her of being a "Shirley," that is, a typical middle-class Jewish girl who will emulate the lifestyle of her parents: marriage to a successful middle-class Jewish person, raising children within the traditions of Judaism, and embracing a lifestyle in which the stability of family life is paramount. In short, she will become someone like her mother.

The novel concludes with Marjorie's return to Jewish tradition, becoming what Noel Airman had predicted, a "Shirley." As Mrs. Milton Schwartz, Marjorie has children, lights the Sabbath candles, lives in the suburbs, has separate milk and meat dishes, and is active in her temple and community.

It is apparent that Wouk approves of Marjorie's return to Judaism and middle-class conformity. Wouk, however, is condemning of Marjorie's loss of her virginity, and critics have noted the following passage at the close of his novel: "He [Milton Schwartz] took her as she was, with her deformity: a deformity that could no longer be helped; a permanent crippling, like a crooked arm" (p. 553). One can imagine the reaction of feminists to Wouk's condemnation of Marjorie's loss of virginity prior to her marriage.

Marjorie Morningstar was the best-selling novel of 1955 and put Wouk on the cover of *Time* magazine (September 5, 1955). The novel was also made into a film in 1958 starring Natalie Wood as Marjorie and Gene Kelly as Noel Airman. The film is notable for its inclusion of Jewish religious scenes—including a Passover seder, a bar mitzvah scene in a synagogue, and Jewish artifacts in the Morgenstern home. These depictions were among the first instances in which Jews and Judaism were portrayed overtly in film since *The Jazz Singer* in 1927.

According to Adam Kirsch, despite the film perpetuating the stereotype of the "Jewish American princess," the novel still commands a large following, especially among women readers.

THE LOMOKOME PAPERS

Written in 1949 but not published until 1956, *The Lomokome Papers* was Wouk's first and only attempt at writing science fiction. Although he wrote it in the late 1940s, Wouk meant for the novella to be a satire on nuclear confrontation. The story follows the aftermath of the U.S. Navy's successful mission to send two piloted extra-gravitational projectiles to the moon. The first projectile crashes on the satellite's surface with its pilot reported missing and presumed dead. The second projectile returns to Earth, containing the missing pilot's notes.

The contents of 107 sheets of notes in the pilot's handwriting describes his encounter with the inhabitants of the moon and his experiences with them in their homeland under the surface of the satellite. The notes reveal a people, the Lomokome (the Hebrew for "utopia" or "nowhere"), constantly at war with their enemy the Lomadine (which in Hebrew can mean "no country"). After long decades of war, both sides conclude that the only way to control conflict is to follow the "Law of Reasonable War." Under this system, a College of Judges, with equal representation from both combatants, will declare victory in time of war to the side that was most proficient in battle.

As Wouk imagines it, without large number of deaths in battle, war might become too popular, so the judges will calculate the number of people to die on each side in proportion to its population. Each government will thereupon kill the required number of the population on each side in what will be observed as "Death Day."

Arnold Beichman's comment on the novella is that Wouk had offered a Hobbesian world whose survival depended not on an optimistic view of human nature, but rather "on making the unreasonable appear reasonable" (p. 104).

SLATTERY'S HURRICANE

The 1956 novel *Slattery's Hurricane* is not one of Wouk's better efforts. It originated as a short story in the magazine *American*, and subsequently was turned into a film in 1949, with Wouk writing the screenplay. The novel, based on Wouk's navy experience, tells the story of Will Slattery, a naval pilot, who is passed over for a medal he earned for sinking a Japanese ship that his squadron leader has taken credit for. Following his discharge from the navy, Will goes to work for a mysterious millionaire as a private pilot. What follows is a series of meaningless love affairs, and Will, ignoring the obvious, also fails to notice that his employer is a shady character. Will's best friend and fellow pilot, "Hobby," remains in the navy and becomes a hurricane chaser, helping to track storms that develop in the Atlantic off the coast of Florida. Hobby also has a beautiful wife, and when Slattery meets her, they are attracted to one another.

The novel follows a predictable trajectory, from the romantic triangle to Slattery's discovery

that his millionaire boss runs a drug-smuggling ring. Toward the climax of the novel, Slattery attempts to redeem himself during a violent hurricane bearing down on Miami.

THIS IS MY GOD: THE JEWISH WAY OF LIFE

Written from the perspective of a modern Orthodox Jew, Wouk wrote *This Is My God* (1959; rev. ed., 1973) at the height of his popularity as a novelist, thus assuring him a wide reading audience. According to Mazzeno, Wouk did not intend *This Is My God* as a religious text but sought to address a larger non-Jewish audience, not to convert them but simply to make them understand why Orthodox Jews behave and believe the way they do (p. 71). Wouk's first nonfiction work includes his reasons for strictly observing *halacha* (Jewish law) and an explanation of customs, the importance of the Torah and the Talmud, the relationship of Jews to Israel, and other areas of Jewish life, making the book an important introduction to Jewish life and beliefs. The book also contains fragments of autobiography, which include his recollections of his Jewish upbringing and his *zaideh*'s role in his religious education. (Wouk dedicated the book to his grandfather, Mendel Leib Levine.) Wouk also reveals the turn in his life that led him to become an observant Jew: "When I worked for Fred Allen, I dreamed of higher success as a playwright or novelist—like Noel Airman in *Marjorie Morningstar*, all I wanted was a succession of hits—but even as I lived this conventional existence ... and dreamed the conventional dreams, it all seemed thin.... I was gambling my whole existence on one hunch: that being a Jew was not a trivial and somewhat inconvenient accident, but the best thing in my life" (p. 228).

The book was well received by the public, but there was also criticism within the Jewish community. The nature of the criticism is best summarized by Jill Krementz who, in reviewing the book for *Kirkus Reviews,* wrote, "nonpractising Jews will feel resentful at the clear call to acceptance and understanding of their faith; Conservative and Reform Jews will resent the rejection of any path other than orthodoxy; assimilationists will resent the presumption that they are betraying themselves in attempting to wipe out their heritage."

YOUNGBLOOD HAWKE

Youngblood Hawke, a lengthy 1962 novel (878 pages in the paperback edition), featuring a Thomas Wolfe–like novelist from the Kentucky hills, was yet another best seller. Like Wouk, Arthur Youngblood Hawke is a former navy man who comes to New York to publish his novel and win fame and fortune. The novel draws on Wouk's experiences in the world of publishing and with literary agents. During the course of the novel, Youngblood is hailed as a rising star in New York literary circles, has an affair with a married woman, and, because of this illicit relationship, loses his one true love, Jeanne Green, his literary editor. Youngblood goes on to write five novels, win the Pulitzer Prize (as did Wouk), and, because he is obsessed with acquiring wealth, gets involved in schemes that lead him to bankruptcy. In the end, he works himself to death because of the money he owes and the loss of Jeanne, who marries a colleague to spite Youngblood. There is also a subplot involving Youngblood's mother and a lawsuit against a coal company that is attempting to defraud his family.

The novel was made into a fairly popular film in 1964. The Warner Bros. version of the novel featured James Franciscus as Youngblood and Suzanne Pleshette as Jeanne Green. Wouk and Delmer Daves wrote the screenplay.

DON'T STOP THE CARNIVAL

Having lived with his family in St. Thomas, Virgin Islands, Wouk decided to draw on his experiences in the Caribbean to write a comedy about a New York theater agent, Norman Paperman, who decides to leave the pressure of Manhattan for a life as a hotel owner on the island of Amerigo (a fictitious island in the Caribbean Sea). *Don't Stop the Carnival* (1965) is loosely based on Wouk's own experience in managing an actual hotel, the Royal Mail, in the

early 1960s, and is a marked departure from his earlier works. The former sketch and gag writer for Fred Allen invites his readers into a world filled with bizarre characters, hilarious situations, and an illicit sexual encounter, wherein, to recapture his youth, the middle-aged Paperman enters into a love affair with a film actress he once idolized. After enduring one absurdity and calamity after another in running the hotel, Paperman decides he has had enough and returns to Manhattan to his wife and daughter.

A subplot has to do with the relationship of Paperman's daughter, Hazel, who is sleeping with Sheldon Klug, her married English professor. Arnold Beichman points out that, for Paperman, "Klug is endowed with most of the characteristics Wouk least likes, reminiscent of Churchill's line, 'He has all the virtues I dislike and none of the vices I admire.' Klug is a Jew who has abandoned religion for what he calls 'paganism.' He is vain, pompous, trendy and a great Freud quoter" (p. 5). Klug's antithesis is Bob Cohn, a brave and intelligent Israeli frogman. Hazel, whose emotions begin to shift from Klug to Cohn, eventually chooses the Israeli—thus the happy ending to this very funny novel. The novel was a Book-of-the Month Club selection and a best seller.

A musical version of *Don't Stop the Carnival*, scripted by Wouk with music and lyrics by Jimmy Buffet, opened at the Coconut Grove Theatre in Miami in 1997. It had a brief run.

THE WORLD WAR II NOVELS: THE WINDS OF WAR *AND* WAR AND REMEMBRANCE

In *War and Remembrance* (1978), Wouk tells the history of America's involvement in the war through two fictional families, the Henrys and the Jastrows. Wouk's protagonist is Victor "Pug" Henry, a navy captain who, as a personal emissary for President Franklin Delano Roosevelt, meets many of the political and military personalities of World War II. Through Henry, Wouk provides us with vivid portraits of Churchill, Stalin, Eisenhower, Admiral Halsey and, prior to the outbreak of war, Hitler and Goering, among others. Wouk also creates a fictional character,

General Armin von Roon, who, in prison awaiting trial as a war criminal, authors *World Empire Lost*, which is his critique of Nazi strategy during the war. Von Roon's analysis of why Germany lost the war is based on actual postwar writings of German officers. In regard to both World War II novels, Henry Kissinger wrote that Wouk's "treatment of history is brilliant.... he has ... supplied enormous insight into the larger forces and ideas that were at work" (quoted in Beichman, p. 124), and the political scientist Michael Mandelbaum stated that the events in both volumes "are described in scrupulous detail with impressive fidelity to the historical record" (p. 516).

Pug Henry is a Methodist, is married to Rhoda, and has three children, each of whom has his or her own story line. His older son, Warren, a carrier pilot, loses his life on a mission at the Battle of Midway. His daughter, Madeline, has a job in radio and is involved in a relationship without her family's approval.

The sibling most prominent in the story, however, is the younger son, Byron, a submariner during the war in the Pacific. In 1939 he accepts a job as a research assistant to an expatriate Jewish author and agnostic, Aaron Jastrow, who is best known for his book *A Jew's Jesus* and lives in Siena, Italy. Jastrow's character is modeled after Bernard Berenson (Mandelbaum, p. 519). Byron also meets Jastrow's niece, Natalie, and her soon-to-be fiancé, Leslie Slote, who works for the State Department. As the soap-opera aspects of the book unfold, Byron and Natalie fall in love and subsequently will marry. During Byron's courtship of Natalie, the Henrys disapprove of her because she is Jewish. One theme in both novels is the prevalence of anti-Semitism within American life, including the State Department, which contributed to the prejudice that prevented the Roosevelt administration from circumventing the immigration law, so as to help Jewish victims of the Nazis gain admission to the United States.

With the outbreak of war in 1939, Natalie refuses to leave her uncle Aaron, who is adamant about not leaving Italy. Eventually they flee the Nazis only to be apprehended, sent to Theresienstadt, and then to Auschwitz. Wouk based his

research on the studies of historians such as Raul Hilberg, and he provides a detailed account of the evolution of the Holocaust through the travails of Natalie and Aaron Jastrow. Natalie survives the war, but Aaron is murdered by gas in Auschwitz. Jastrow, who migrated from Poland at an early age and subsequently became an American citizen, attended Harvard, and, because of his alienation from Judaism, converted to Catholicism. While in Theresienstadt he is overcome with guilt about his apostasy, and in a manuscript, "A Jew's Journey," Jastrow writes: "I dropped my Jewishness outside and inside, and strove only to be like other people, and to be accepted by them.... here under the Germans I resumed my Jewishness because they forced me to" (*War and Remembrance*, p. 1027). Moments before his murder in the gas chamber, Aaron, in "breath-stopping pain," says the Shema Yisrael, the centerpiece of the Jewish prayer service ("Hear O Israel, the Lord our God. Blessed be His name for ever and ever. God is One God") and "falls to the cement" (p. 1070).

Liberated from Auschwitz, Natalie is reunited with Byron, and both agree to settle in Jewish Palestine. Wouk's novel includes the efforts of Palestinian Jews to smuggle European Jews to the future Jewish state.

In their adaptations as television miniseries, both *The Winds of War* (1983) and *War and Remembrance* (1988–1989) were blockbuster hits with millions of viewers. *War and Remembrance* won an Emmy (1989) for Outstanding Miniseries. The two novels and the miniseries, along with Gerald Green's 1978 miniseries *Holocaust*, contributed to America's awareness of the Holocaust, wherein death camps such as Auschwitz increasingly became familiar to the American public.

INSIDE, OUTSIDE

Although I. David Goodkind, the protagonist of *Inside, Outside* (1985), denies that the story which follows is autobiographical, it is evident that much of the novel is indeed based on Wouk's memories, ranging from family history, to his work as a sketch and gag writer, to his descrip-

tion of his deeply Orthodox Jewish life. The novel's title derives from Wouk's insight about the two lives of Orthodox Jews: "Every Jew who has ever stepped into a synagogue or temple knows that we have two names: the outside name with which we go through life, and the inside name, the Jewish name, used in blessings and Torah call-ups, marriage and divorce ceremonies, and on tombstones" (p. 36). Goodkind is a devout Orthodox Jew on the inside, and Nixon's trusted advisor on cultural and Jewish affairs on the outside, attempting to balance both worlds.

The novel alternates between fact and fiction and is centered on Goodkind, who writes President Nixon's Watergate speech and is entrusted by the president with a secret mission to Israel during the Yom Kippur War. Although Goodkind believes that Nixon has engaged in covering up criminal activity, he nevertheless believes that Nixon is the best friend of Israel since Harry Truman (this view of Nixon and Israel will be fleshed out in Wouk's later novel, *The Glory*).

The novel goes on to detail Goodkind's first love affair, which is rekindled after forty years; his ribald adventures in show business; and the debt he owes to his *zaideh* for providing his love of Judaism. The novel offers some hearty laughs and valuable information about Judaism, and, in the section on Goodkind's early years, provides a nostalgic picture of the 1930s.

ISRAEL: THE HOPE *AND* THE GLORY

Published in 1993 and 1994, respectively, *The Hope* and *The Glory* use the same format as Wouk's World War II novels to present a history of Israel's conflicts, from its war for independence in 1948 to the bombing of the Iraqi nuclear reactor in 1981. As in *The Winds of War* and *War and Remembrance*, Wouk's Israeli novels tell its history through a fictional character, General Zev Barak, who, like Pug Henry, describes the events that shape the novel. Barak, as Israel's attaché in Washington, and then the military assistant to Golda Meir, Yitzhak Rabin, and Menachem Begin, provides us with the behind-the-scenes decision-making process that enabled Israel to

defeat its Arab enemies. From the Six-Day War to the Yom Kippur War, the fictional Barak engages with not only Israel's prime ministers but also, among others, the charismatic Moshe Dayan, Ariel Sharon, and the tragic David Elazar (the commander in chief of the Israel army, who shouldered the blame for Israel's lack of preparedness during the Yom Kippur War, which led to his forced resignation).

Wouk also describes Israel's relationship with the United States during the Yom Kippur War, weighing in on the controversy over the airlift that supplied Israel with needed supplies to defeat the Egyptian army. Wouk credits President Nixon, rather than Henry Kissinger, for ordering the airlift. Kissinger, a State Department diplomat tells Barak, argued that there was "No need to rush material to Israel and anger the Arabs. This war is our opportunity to break the political stalemate. Our aim is to play honest broker" (*The Glory*, pp. 405–406).

Both novels present Israeli history through the personal lives of its fictional characters. The married Zev Barak, for example, is involved in a longtime affair with Emily Cunningham Halliday, whose husband is an American general and an advisor on Israeli affairs. Other characters who move the story line forward are an air force general, Benny Luria, and his two sons, both fighter pilots; Yossi Nitzan, known as "Don Kishote" (Hebrew for Don Quixote) for his bravery; and many others.

In his conclusion to *The Glory*, Wouk adds an appendix in which he describes the nature of his research, which included interviews with Israeli military and political figures and entailed delving into the primary and secondary source material. The result is a work comparable in scope and authenticity to his World War II novels.

THE WILL TO LIVE ON: THIS IS OUR HERITAGE

In *The Will to Live On*, a nonfiction work published in 2000, Wouk is concerned about the future of the Jewish heritage. He notes that mankind may have adopted "Holocaust" as a catchword for ultimate evil, but "it cannot adopt or handle our tragedy" (p. 33). Wouk refers to the Holocaust as the Third Destruction, alluding to the destruction of Judaism's first two Temples. He notes that the twentieth century has brought traumatic changes to the Jewish people: the Holocaust, the birth of Israel, and the precarious future of the Jewish people through assimilation and the deepening religious divide within the Jewish community, as well as the growing challenge of secularism. Toward an answer to the crisis faced by the Jewish people, Wouk turns to the Bible as the key to Jewish survival, noting that every Jewish child in eastern Europe was taught it as his or her natural heritage. Thus Wouk's raison d'être for his work is to ask, To what extent is that heritage retrievable?

The Will to Live On is peppered with stories of Wouk's conversations with Yitzhak Rabin, Saul Bellow, Richard Feynman, and others, in his search for answers. Wouk concludes that Jewish survival will depend on cultural literacy: the Hebrew Bible, the Talmud, the Kabbalah, and Yiddish culture. In short, he sees learning and living by Judaism's classics as Jewry's only hope for survival in the diaspora. Wouk ruefully concludes that the hope for a Jewish revival may have to be qualitative rather than quantitative.

A HOLE IN TEXAS

Wouk's 2004 novel *A Hole in Texas* is a witty and satiric work that brings together politics, the media, and science. The story centers around Guy Carpenter, an astrophysicist who spent five years on the superconducting collider for the Department of Energy and found himself unemployed when President Bill Clinton cut the budget for the project. Among the many results that the collider was expected to uncover was the Higgs boson, an elementary particle that allows atoms to attain mass and thus produce the substance of the material universe, a discovery that might create a boson bomb, a weapon that would surpass the power of the hydrogen bomb—in other words, the ultimate weapon. When Chinese physicists announce that they have uncovered the boson,

Congress gets nervous and holds hearings, questioning how it was that the Chinese beat the United States to the bomb. Enter Wen Mei Li, a physicist and head of the Chinese boson project; she is scheduled to attend a conference in the United States. It turns out, however, that Guy once had a torrid relationship with Wen Mei Li when they were both graduate students. Meanwhile Guy, who has been hired as a consultant for a Hollywood film about the boson, is called before the congressional hearings. But when the movie company finds out he has been called to the hearings, he is fired. Adding to the plot is that Guy's wife, Penny, is jealous of her husband's long ago relationship with Wen Mei Li. Matters become even worse when a *Washington Post* reporter labels Guy the "Deep Throat Physicist" who passed secrets to the Chinese. All is ultimately resolved: there is no boson bomb, Guy is exonerated of any wrongdoing, he is rehired by the movie studio, and his wife realizes that Wen Me Li is no threat to her marriage. This novel shows Wouk at his comical best as well as displaying his knowledge of science.

THE LANGUAGE GOD TALKS: ON SCIENCE AND RELIGION

Wouk's third nonfiction work, *The Language God Talks*, published in 2010, is really two books in one. The first is Wouk's engagement with the Nobel laureate Richard Feynman in a dialogue on science and religion. In their first meeting, Feynman asked Wouk, "Do you know calculus?" and after Wouk admitted that he didn't, the physicist responded, "You had better learn it,... It's the language God talks" (p. 5). So begins Wouk's quest to address the questions of why we are here, what purpose faith serves, and how scientific fact fits into the picture. Along this journey Wouk concludes that Feynman was closing himself off to the possibility that God also speaks in the language of the Bible.

The other book deals with aspects of Wouk's life. He cites a conversation with S. Y. Agnon, the Nobel laureate in literature (1966), who cautions him: "Remember, Herman Wouk, we are storytellers. Stories, pictures, people! No

thoughts." Wouk goes on to write that Agnon pointed the way " for me to meet the challenge; too much thought already in these pages" (p. 119). In taking Agnon's advice, Wouk turns to sharing his memories of significant moments in his life, as well as insight into the body of his literary work. A few examples would include his disclosure that the model for the gag writer "Harry Goldhandler," in *Inside, Outside*, is the comic writer David Freedman. He reveals that "Pug Henry," in the World War II novels, was based on his friendship with Admiral Dan Gallery. Wouk writes a great deal about the characters and battles in both *The Winds of War* and *War and Remembrance*, and informs us that both Tom Keefer and Barney Greenwald in *The Caine Mutiny* "are aspects of myself, before and after four years of naval service" (pp. 82–83).

Ultimately, however, even speaking with great physicists—not only Feynman but also Murray Gell-Mann, Freeman Dyson, and Steven Weinberg—is not enough to satisfactorily reconcile the impact of science on religion.

THE LAWGIVER

Herman Wouk's novel *The Lawgiver* (2012) will not be ranked among the best of his fiction, but it is an enjoyable read despite the unorthodoxy of the style used by the author. Drawing on the epistolary novel of the eighteenth century, wherein a story was told in the form of letters, journal entries, diaries, and newspapers, *The Lawgiver* consists of a mixture of memos, faxes, letters, e-mails, biography, and some narrative, as well as Wouk's appearance as a character in his own work. The story tells of an Australian Jewish multibillionaire, Louis Gluck, who is solicited to finance a motion picture about Moses. Wouk reveals that when he was writing *The Caine Mutiny*, it occurred to him that there was no greater theme for a novel than the life of Moses, without whom Christianity and Islam becomes meaningless. However, he states that for years he never found a way to overcome the difficulties in

writing such a novel, and he became increasingly frustrated with the endeavor until "a bolt of lightning struck: Write a lighthearted novel about the impossibility of writing a novel about Moses" (*The Will to Live On*, p. 143).

Determined to create a realistic depiction of Moses that was absent from Cecil B. DeMille's kitschy epic *The Ten Commandments* (both the 1923 and 1956 versions), the novel describes the search for a screenwriter-director who could create a believable Moses screenplay. The novel's conceit, however, is that Gluck demands that once the script is written, Wouk (and his wife, Betty Sarah Wouk) would have the final say in approving the project. Enter Margolit Solovei. Margo, the center of *The Lawgiver*, is a Bais Yaakov (girls' yeshiva) graduate whose father is a Bobover Rebbe (the Bobover is one of the many sects within the Hasidic movement). Margo, however, broke with her strict Jewish upbringing and went on to become a brilliant young film director, who is subsequently commissioned to direct the film.

The novel deals with the machinations involved in making the film, including finding an actor to play Moses, who turns out to be an Australian gentile—the only non-Jew in the novel. In addition, there are secondary themes involving Margo and her reunion with her first love, a restored relationship with a Columbia University professor who is also a Bais Yaakov graduate, and a "fade to black," wherein the novel ends abruptly with Margot's apparent reconciliation with her father and a double Orthodox Jewish wedding.

Also running through *The Lawgiver* are many biographical details about Wouk, including his relationship with his wife Betty Sarah (referred to as "BSW" in the novel), who died in March 2011 of a massive stroke. Along with his tribute in the book's epilogue to her contributions to his long literary career, he makes her role is evident in the novel, wherein BSW advises and sometimes scolds her husband as the script goes through its many rewrites. A convert to Judaism, BSW was her husband's literary agent as well as instrumental in advising him on all aspects of his writing career.

CONCLUSION

Throughout his literary career, Herman Wouk has been attacked by the doyens of the American literary establishment, who included Leslie Fiedler, Dwight MacDonald, and Norman Podhoretz, to name a few. Among the reasons for this criticism was that, to Wouk, the story was all-important, and the form (and prose) it took was secondary. Wouk rejected the influence of T. S. Eliot, James Joyce, and other modernists in favor of writing realistic novels that reflected the influence of Dickens and other nineteenth-century novelists. As an Orthodox Jew, Wouk was also influenced by the religious traditions of Judaism, manifesting itself with his concern with virtue and morality, a recurrent theme in his novels. The Freudian-Marxist influence that sits heavily on twentieth-century literary culture has no attraction for Wouk.

Although Wouk's books have often made the best-seller list, and he is one of the more prolific writers of the twentieth century, it is also true that a number of his works address the condition of the Jewish people in contemporary times. In his World War II novels, as well as in his historical novels about the state of Israel, Wouk, more than any other writer of fiction, can lay claim as the literary chronicler of the Jewish people. In his works *Marjorie Morningstar* and *This Is My God,* Wouk also advances a vision of Jewish life in the United States wherein the key to happiness can be attained through chastity, conformity, and Jewish cultural literacy. As Adam Kirsch writes in the *Tablet:*

> Wouk, for one, recognized ... that Philip Roth, in his fiction and his comic vision of Jewishness, effectively superseded Wouk's pious one.... That Roth's novels are likely to keep on being read when Wouk's are forgotten is certain; that American Jews still want to see themselves in Rothian or Woody Allen–esque terms, as hyperarticulate, sex-obsessed, neurotic intellectuals, is doubtful.

Kirsch may not be entirely right. Wouk's novels may yet find a wide reading audience as a new generation of more pious and tradition-minded Jewish writers, such as Jonathan Safran Foer and Nathan Englander, have appeared on the literary

landscape and found their fiction warmly received by the general public.

Selected Bibliography

WORKS OF HERMAN WOUK

NOVELS
Aurora Dawn. New York: Simon & Schuster, 1947.

The City Boy. New York: Simon & Schuster, 1948.

The Caine Mutiny. Garden City, N.Y.: Doubleday, 1951.

Marjorie Morningstar. Garden City, N.Y.: Doubleday, 1955.

The Lomokome Papers. New York: Pocket Books, 1956.

Slattery's Hurricane. New York: Permabooks, 1956.

Youngblood Hawke. Garden City, N.Y.: Doubleday, 1962.

Don't Stop the Carnival. Garden City, N.Y.: Doubleday, 1965.

The Winds of War. Boston: Little, Brown, 1971.

War and Remembrance. Boston: Little, Brown, 1978.

Inside, Outside. Boston: Little, Brown, 1985.

The Hope. Boston: Little, Brown, 1993.

The Glory. Boston: Little, Brown, 1994.

A Hole in Texas. Boston: Little, Brown, 2004.

The Lawgiver. New York: Simon & Schuster, 2012.

NONFICTION
This Is My God: The Jewish Way of Life. Garden City, N.Y.: Doubleday, 1959. Rev. ed. 1973.

Introduction to *Self-Portrait of a Hero: From the Letters of Jonathan Netanyahu, 1963–1976.* New York: Random House, 1980.

The Will to Live On: This Is Our Heritage. New York: HarperCollins, 2000.

The Language God Talks: On Science and Religion. Boston: Little, Brown, 2010.

PLAYS
The Traitor. New York: Samuel French, 1949.

The Caine Mutiny Court-Martial. Garden City, N.Y.: Doubleday, 1954.

Nature's Way. Garden City, N.Y.: Doubleday, 1958.

FILMS AND TV MINISERIES BASED ON THE WORK OF HERMAN WOUK
Slattery's Hurricane. Screenplay by Richard Murphy and Herman Wouk. Film directed by André de Toth. 20th Century Fox, 1949.

The Caine Mutiny. Screenplay by Stanley Roberts. Film directed by Edward Dmytryk. Columbia Pictures, 1954.

Marjorie Morningstar. Screenplay by Everett Freeman. Film directed by Irving Rapper. Warner Bros., 1958.

Youngblood Hawke. Screenplay by Delmer Daves and Herman Wouk. Film directed by Delmer Daves. Warner Bros., 1964.

The Winds of War. Screenplay by Herman Wouk. TV miniseries directed by Dan Curtis. Paramount/ABC, 1983.

War and Remembrance. Screenplay by Dan Curtis, Earl W. Wallace, and Herman Wouk. TV miniseries directed by Dan Curtis. Paramount/ABC, 1988.

PAPERS
Herman Wouk Papers, 1915–2003. Rare Book and Manuscript Collections, Columbia University Libraries, New York City.

CRITICAL STUDIES
Beichman, Arnold. *Herman Wouk: The Novelist as Social Historian.* New Brunswick, N.J.: Transaction, 1984.

Guttmann, Allen. *The Jewish Writer in America: Assimilation and the Crisis in Identity.* New York: Oxford University Press, 1971.

Heyman, Stanley Edgar. *Standards: A Chronicle of Books for Our Time.* New York: Horizon, 1966.

Fiedler, Leslie. *Love and Death in the American Novel.* New York: Criterion, 1960.

Jones, Peter G. *War and the Novelist: Appraising the American War Novel.* Ann Arbor: University of Michigan Press, 1976.

Mazzeno, Laurence W. *Herman Wouk.* New York: Twayne, 1994.

Paulson, Barbara A., ed. *The Historical Novel: A Celebration of the Achievements of Herman Wouk.* Washington, D.C.: Library of Congress, 1999.

ARTICLES AND ESSAYS
Bell, Pearl K. "Good-Bad and Bad-Bad," *Commentary,* December 1978, pp. 70–72.

Bolton, Richard R. "*The Winds of War* and Wouk's Wish for the World." *Midwest Quarterly* 16: 389–408 (1975).

Boroson, Warren. "The Fathers of the Hybrid Car." *New Jersey Jewish Standard,* July 30, 2010. http://jstandard .com/index.php/content/item/14315/

Brodkin, Joel. "The First Neoconservative: Herman Wouk, the Americanization of the Holocaust, and the Rise of Neoconservatism." *New Politics* 10, no. 3 (summer 2005). http://newpol.org/content/first-neoconservative-herman -wouk-americanization-holocaust-and-rise-

neoconservatism

Brown, Kathleen A. "Vestments of Civil Life in *Caine Mutiny* and *Attack*." *Film & History* 36, no. 2:38–57 (spring 2006).

Browne, James R. "Distortion in *The Caine Mutiny*." *College English* 17, no. 4:216–218 (January 1956).

Carpenter, Frederick I. "Herman Wouk." *College English* 17, no. 4:211–215 (January 1956).

Cohen, Joseph. "Wouk's *Morningstar* and Hemingway's *Sun*." *South Atlantic Quarterly* 58: 213–224 (spring 1959).

Fitch, Robert E. "The Bourgeois and the Bohemian." *Antioch Review* 16, no. 2:131–145 (June 1956).

Gordon, Jeff. "*Slattery's Hurricane*." *Films of the Golden Age*. http://www.filmsofthegoldenage.com/articles/2003/12/17/current_issue/hurricane.txt

Kirsch, Adam. "Herman Wouk's Last Shot." *Tablet*, November 20, 2012. http://www.tabletmag.com/jewish-arts-and-culture/books/117174/herman-wouk-last-shot/2

Lewis, Michael J. "How This Magazine Wronged Herman Wouk," *Commentary*, February 2013, pp. 35–40.

Mandelbaum, Michael. "The Political Lessons of Two World War II Novels: A Review Essay." *Political Science Quarterly* 94, no. 3:515–522 (autumn 1979).

McElderry, B. R. "The Conservative as Novelist: Herman Wouk." *Arizona Quarterly* 15: 128–136 (summer 1959).

Podhoretz, Norman. "Jew as Bourgeois." *Commentary*, February 1956, pp. 186–188.

Shapiro, Edward S. "The Jew as Patriot: Herman Wouk and American Jewish Identity." In his *We Are Many: Reflections on American Jewish History and Identity*. Syracuse, N.Y.: Syracuse University Press, 2005. Pp. 50–67.

Swados, Harvey. "Popular Taste and *The Caine Mutiny*." *Partisan Review* 20: 248–256 (March–April 1953).

Vogel, Dan. "Remembering *Marjorie Morningstar*." *Studies in American Jewish Literature* 13: 21–26 (1994).

Zhang, Yidong. "Two Panoramas About the Great Wars." *Journal of Popular Culture* 19, no. 1:57–63 (September 1985).

REVIEWS

Baldwin, Hanson W. "The *Caine Mutiny* Issue." *New York Times*, March 21, 1954.

Fussell, Paul. "Review of *War and Remembrance*." *New Republic*, October 14, 1978, pp. 32–33.

Gordis, Robert. "Religion in One Dimension: The Judaism of Herman Wouk." *Midstream* 6 no. 1:82–90 (winter 1960).

Herberg, Will. "Confession of Faith." *New York Times Book Review*, September 27, 1959, p. 50.

Krementz, Jill. "This Is My God." *Kirkus Reviews*, September 16, 1959. https://www.kirkusreviews.com/book-reviews/herman-wouk/this-is-my-god/

Review of *Aurora Dawn. Kirkus Reviews*, April 21, 1947. https://www.kirkusreviews.com/book-reviews/herman-wouk/aurora-dawn/

Review of *The Will to Live On: This Is Our Heritage. Kirkus Reviews*, January 1, 2000. https://www.kirkusreviews.com/book-reviews/herman-wouk/the-will-to-live-on/

ZITKALA-ŠA (GERTRUDE SIMMONS BONNIN)

(1876—1938)

Kelly Clasen

LESS THAN A decade after the second Treaty of Fort Laramie was signed in 1868, establishing the "Great Sioux Reservation" and outlining measures for its protection, Gertrude Simmons, later known as Zitkala-Ša, was born on the Yankton Sioux Reservation in South Dakota. By the time of her birth on February 22, 1876, however, reservation lands were already being threatened by European American prospectors who had discovered gold in the Black Hills. These miners were in violation of the treaty that had granted the Sioux rights to the region, as were the Native Americans who retaliated against the intruders. Resulting skirmishes escalated into the Great Sioux War of 1876 (also known as the Black Hills War), which included such violent battles as General George Armstrong Custer's defeat with the Seventh Cavalry Regiment at the hands of the Lakota, Northern Cheyenne, and Arapaho in the Battle of Little Big Horn. Although the warriors were famously victorious in this Montana Territory conflict, their triumph would do little to forestall the continued military pressure from the U.S. government, which resulted in the tribes' surrender and the government's seizure of the Black Hills in 1877. The years following the end of the Great Sioux War were characterized by the widespread forced and voluntary assimilation of tribal citizens into Anglo America and, paradoxically, a growing public interest in indigenous people and customs of the sort exemplified by the popularity of Buffalo Bill's Wild West shows. The tensions between such movements created a dynamic period in the history of cultural relations in the United States and were essential to Zitkala-Ša's development as a literary and political innovator.

As one of only a handful of Native American writers publishing during this transitional era, Zitkala-Ša confronted the monumental task of trying to protect and honor her cultural past in a way that appealed to a predominantly white readership. The push and pull of bicultural expectations would pose challenges for Zitkala-Ša throughout her lifetime, but an exceptional combination of on- and off-reservation experiences, ranging in locale from America's great cities to its Great Plains, made her increasingly savvy to the finicky nature of the public eye. She had a keen sense of how alterations to her carefully crafted public persona, which at times emphasized her indigenous heritage and at other times her conformation to Euro-American societal expectations, could widen her audience. With rhetorical deftness, she utilized numerous public platforms and modes of artistic expression to fulfill her humanitarian objectives, which included the preservation of Native American history, the protection of indigenous peoples, and the unsettling of cultural stereotypes, among other goals.

AUTOBIOGRAPHICAL STORIES

The writer, orator, teacher, musician, and activist Zitkala-Ša was given the name Gertrude Simmons by her mother, Ellen Simmons, whose Yankton name was Taté I Yóhin Win, or "Reaches for the Wind." Ellen's first marriage was to Pierre St. Pierre, with whom she had two sons before his death in 1853. She married another white man, named John Simmons, whose surname was given to her daughter, although Gertrude's father is believed to have been a French American man

ZITKALA-ŠA (GERTRUDE SIMMONS BONNIN)

named Felker who left her mother before Gertrude was born. Zitkala-Ša, or "Red Bird," is a name she chose for herself in young adulthood and under which she published most of her literary work; she would later use her married name, Gertrude Simmons Bonnin, when signing business documents and some magazine articles.

Gertrude (or "Gertie") resided with her mother and her older brother David on the Yankton Reservation until she was eight years old, and her early, largely autobiographical writings reveal the nostalgia with which she would look back upon these relatively carefree days. They also document the "first turning away from the easy, natural flow of [her] life," which occurred with the arrival in 1884 of Quaker missionaries from White's Manual Labor Institute in Wabash, Indiana, to the Yankton Reservation ("Impressions of an Indian Childhood," collected in *American Indian Stories, Legends, and Other Writings*, p. 83). Leaving her mother and the comfort of tribal customs behind to receive a boarding school education had traumatic repercussions, but these experiences inspired some of her most widely read work, which called attention to the suffering and resilience of indigenous schoolchildren. Zitkala-Ša chronicled this formative period, as well as her stint as a boarding school instructor, in three autobiographical stories published over three months in 1900 in the *Atlantic Monthly*: "Impressions of an Indian Childhood," "The School Days of an Indian Girl," and "An Indian Teacher Among Indians," first collected in *American Indian Stories* (1921).

These stories are notable as some of the first by a Native American woman to be published in popular magazines, an industry dominated by white men at the turn of the century. "Impressions of an Indian Childhood" is composed of seven vignettes that offered the reading public a firsthand account of Yankton Reservation customs such as the frequent sharing of oral legends, the beading of buckskin clothing, and the preservation of food in autumn. Zitkala-Ša painted a childhood rich in close-knit bonds among family and community members who were frequent visitors to one another's wigwams in times of celebration, work, and need. Zitkala-Ša's first

Atlantic Monthly piece also provided insight into the author's complicated relationship with her mother, a frequently sad woman whom Zitkala-Ša recalls as being resentful toward the "heartless paleface" who had driven her family to the reservation. Her mother also, paradoxically, grew increasingly accustomed to Euro-American modes of living under the influence of her son (referred to as "Dawée" in the tales), who had received schooling in the East.

In what is one of the most complex depictions of emotion in Zitkala-Ša's early writings, she records a mother's agony when deciding whether to keep her youngest child on the reservation or let her daughter follow in her brother's footsteps and seek an education in the East. The Dakota mother in the narrative is well aware of the challenges that will confront her daughter if she takes the "iron horse" to the land of the "big red apples," but she is also wise to the potential benefits of an Anglo education because she foresees an imminent decline in the number of "real Dakotas" and their way of life ("Impressions," *American Indian Stories, Legends, and Other Writings*, p. 85). Thus, she chooses to send her child away with Quaker missionaries. This careful consideration of the benefits and pitfalls of boarding school contrasts sharply with the young narrator's naive eagerness, which is easily dismantled in "The School Days of an Indian Girl."

The rude scrutiny of white passengers during the train ride east, an experience that begins "The School Days of an Indian Girl," quickly shakes the confidence of the young narrator and the seven other Native American children who accompany her. Other distressing experiences follow, including the onslaught of homesickness, the cutting of her long braids, an inability to understand the strict English-speaking missionaries, and a nightmare featuring a book illustration of the Christian devil. The excerpt from "School Days" that perhaps best illuminates the cultural shock experienced by the Native American boarding school student is "Iron Routine," in which the author explains the difficult transition from "unlassoed freedom" on the reservation to her forced adherence to the unwavering schedule kept

by the "civilizing machine" of the school (*American Indian Stories, Legends, and Other Writings*, p. 96). The structure of each day, coupled with the depersonalizing nature of the school culture, leaves the author feeling "heavy-footed, like a dumb sick brute" (p. 96). Moreover, she blames the teachers' standardized medical care for children with widely varying degrees of illnesses for the death of a beloved classmate. Such negative experiences contribute to a rebellious streak that builds quietly and underscores her tenure at the boarding school. As an adult, she recalls "the melancholy of those black days" over the "smoothly grinding school days" (p. 97).

Despite such hardships, Zitkala-Ša developed an appreciation for education during her years at school. Her academic interests, however, would contribute to her liminal position on the reservation when she returned after a three-year term. Not yet as fully assimilated as the older students (including her older brother, who embraced Anglo attire and spoke fluent English), she donned moccasins again upon returning but nonetheless she felt lonely and disconnected from her mother, which contributed to her decision to return to school. She briefly attended the Santee Technical School in Nebraska before reentering White's Manual Labor Institute in 1891. There, she received her first diploma and decided, against her mother's wishes, to continue her education at Earlham College in Richmond, Indiana, where she garnered admiration through her talent as a competitive orator. In 1896 she took second place in the Indiana State Oratorical Contest, achieving a small victory against the raucous students from a competing school who brandished a white flag upon which they had scrawled "Squaw." In its March 16, 1896, edition, the school newspaper, the *Earlhamite*, published the speech, which was called "Side by Side" and which argued for improved relationships between the Indian and white races. The *Earlhamite* also published some of her early poems as well as articles noting her various accomplishments and involvement in school activities. As her academic successes mounted, Zitkala-Ša would increasingly be pulled between two forces: "a hunger in [her] heart" to please her mother and her yearning to make a

way for herself off the reservation ("School Days," *American Indian Stories, Legends, and Other Writings*, p. 103).

An unspecified illness in the spring of 1897 kept her from graduating from college, and, fearful of returning home to criticism from her mother, she accepted a teaching position at the Carlisle Indian Industrial School in Pennsylvania, the first off-reservation boarding school for Native Americans in the nation. The school was founded in 1879 by Richard Henry Pratt, a retired army officer, whom Zitkala-Ša described as a "stately gray-haired man" with an "imposing figure" ("An Indian Teacher Among Indians," *American Indian Stories, Legends, and Other Writings*, p. 105), who upheld a rigid agenda of forced cultural assimilation. During her tenure at Carlisle, Zitkala-Ša was active in the music program, overseeing the glee club and playing piano during church services. She was also briefly engaged to Thomas Marshall, a Lakota Sioux from the Pine Ridge Agency who had attended classes with her at White's Manual Labor Institute and who later studied at Carlisle and Dickinson College. Marshall died suddenly from measles in 1899.

In addition to teaching music, Zitkala-Ša was expected to aid in Carlisle recruitment efforts. Early in her career, Pratt ordered her to travel west to identify potential pupils, an experience she would later chronicle in "An Indian Teacher Among Indians" (1900). Seeking a restorative break from her work at Carlisle, she looked forward to returning to the Yankton Reservation and to seeing her mother. When she arrived, however, she was dismayed to find her mother's cabin in disrepair and empty of food due to her brother's recent unemployment. One night during her visit, as she and her mother looked out upon the many twinkling lights of the "poverty-stricken white settlers" who defied law and homesteaded ever closer to the Yankton village, her mother warned her of the hypocritical actions of the "white rascal" who espoused Christian beliefs while indulging in "firewater" and "gloat[ing] upon the sufferings of the Indian race" (p. 110). This trip resonated with the young teacher, and upon returning to Carlisle, she began to reexam-

ine the white missionaries' motives, concluding during the following months that many of their actions were self-serving. She also began to regret the lapse in her relationship with the "Great Spirit," as well as her denunciation of other influences informed by her Dakota childhood: "Like a slender tree, I had been uprooted from my mother, nature, and God," she recalled (p. 112).

STORIES AND LEGENDS

At the end of 1898, Zitkala-Ša resigned from Carlisle and moved to Boston, where she entered the New England Conservatory of Music and studied violin for the next couple of years. An accomplished musician, she was invited to travel to Europe to perform with the Carlisle School at the Paris Exposition of 1900. During this period, Zitkala-Ša also saw her first stories and essays printed in the era's most prestigious publications and was welcomed into literary society. In addition to the three autobiographical narratives of her educational experiences published by the *Atlantic Monthly* in 1900, two stories, "The Soft-Hearted Sioux" (which was illustrated by Frederic Remington) and "The Trial Path," appeared in *Harper's Monthly Magazine* in 1901. In 1902 *Everybody's Magazine* printed "A Warrior's Daughter." With these early stories (all later collected in *American Indian Stories*), Zitkala-Ša made her presence in the early twentieth-century literary scene known by being published alongside some of the most noted fiction writers of the day. She flexed her narrative voice, writing from both the male and female perspective; exposed her mostly white audience to the trauma of forced assimilation; and introduced readers to the allure of Native American storytelling.

In "The Soft-Hearted Sioux," Zitkala-Ša depicts with stark clarity the alienation experienced by an assimilated student who returns to his reservation after ten years of boarding school to "preach Christianity" to its people (*American Indian Stories, Legends, and Other Writings*, p. 120). The cultural and ideological gulf separating the Bible-carrying son and the tribal elders, including his dying father and a medicine man, becomes sharply apparent when they curse him

for his "soft heart" and apparent inability to help provide for his starving family by hunting. Desperate for meat and to stop such ridicule, he ventures out into a barren, snowy plain, where he at last spies a herd of cattle belonging to a white man. He stabs and kills a steer and then the cattle owner himself when the owner tries to stop the young man from stealing. The Sioux man returns home to find that his father has perished, that he faces execution, and that his soul's fate is unknowable. The story relies heavily on irony, as the white Christians who dissuaded the young man from killing living creatures to survive will be his executioners. It forces readers to acknowledge contrasts between the ideological expectations of the missionaries and the practical necessities of life on the reservation.

With "The Trial Path" and "A Warrior's Daughter," the author employs female heroines and imbues the stories with romantic elements that mark them as less interested in religious criticism than "The Soft-Hearted Sioux" and more clearly bent on honoring indigenous women's strength and storytelling. Indeed, these stories and others suggest that Zitkala-Ša was increasingly appreciative of the traditional roles upheld by Native American women and the ways in which the influence they exerted over their tribes defied models of European femininity and domesticity. "The Trial Path," for example, highlights a Sioux matriarch's obligation to protect her family's oral history by passing it on to her granddaughter. "Listen!" the Dakota grandmother asserts as she begins to tell her granddaughter the story of how her young lover (the girl's grandfather) decades ago redeemed himself to his tribe after killing "his most intimate friend" and his competitor for her hand in love (*American Indian Stories, Legends, and Other Writings*, pp. 127–128). In the story, the slain man's father decides that the "man-killer" must either ride a wild pony to a tepee in the center of the village and be pardoned, or fall from the pony and face execution (p. 129). The rider tames the "ranting beast" and is pardoned. The pony becomes a valued pet and years later is killed on the rider's grave so that the pony, "already bound on the spirit-trail," might ac-

company him "on the journey along the ghost-path" (p. 131). Although male characters figure at the center of this story, they are notably absent from the present-day frame narrative. This absence emphasizes the women's role in ensuring that an important lesson about moral decrepitude and the possibility of tribal and spiritual redemption survives through storytelling. The women who preserve such lessons are stewards of an entire tribe's oral history and values.

Zitkala-Ša's story "A Warrior's Daughter" is an even more overtly feminist text, although it privileges physical strength and cleverness over women's roles as storytellers. With this tale Zitkala-Ša builds on the theme of impassioned young romance with her depiction of Tusee, a woman who embarks upon a daring rescue mission when her lover is captured by an enemy camp. After appealing to the Great Spirit for "swift cunning for a weapon," Tusee lures her lover's captor out of a celebration dance with her suggestive behavior and then slays him with her knife (*American Indian Stories, Legends, and Other Writings*, p. 137). She disguises herself as an old woman and picks her way back to the camp to release her grateful lover and carry him to safety. As she does in "The Trial Path," Zitkala-Ša appeals to a reading public's appetite for drama by sanctioning the protection of passionate love with bloodshed. She also establishes a distinctly feminist image of a young woman who draws upon her physical, spiritual, and intellectual strengths to rescue her partner—exhibiting all of the skills her "warrior" father would presumably possess.

Around this time, the first of two books Zitkala-Ša would write, *Old Indian Legends* (1901), was published by Ginn & Co. Many of the collection's stories feature an immortal, shape-shifting trickster figure called Iktomi who is common among the oral legends of various Sioux bands. Although *Old Indian Legends* was intended to help preserve Sioux oral mythologies, some of the stories' morality lessons are undoubtedly applicable to the trials of Native Americans around the turn of the century. In the book's preface, Zitkala-Ša intertwines such motives by issuing a direct plea for the continued study of "Indian folklore, a study which so strongly suggests our near kinship with the rest of humanity and points a steady finger toward the great brotherhood of mankind" (reprinted in *American Indian Stories, Legends, and Other Writings*, p. 5). The tales themselves impart similar messages about the need for members of a diverse society to respect one another, honing virtues such as self-restraint, generosity, and understanding.

Indeed, animals are "people" too in the world of Sioux mythology, and humans communicate with all of the creatures of the earth, as well as with some creatures with ties to the spirit realm. The intimacy of these relationships is exemplified in *Old Indian Legends* in "The Badger and the Bear," the first in a three-story cycle in which a father badger offers the Great Spirit a small clot of buffalo blood, and from this gift springs forth a human brave—a "man-son" to the badger ("The Tree Bound," *American Indian Stories, Legends, and Other Writings*, p. 35). The Dakota brave and badger work together to cast out a cruel bear who has taken over the badger lair. Later, in "Shooting of the Red Eagle," the same brave helps a Sioux tribe defeat both a murderous eagle and the shape-shifter Iktomi. Such stories emphasize looking well beyond physical appearances—for they are often misleading in this mythological world—to forge personal alliances based on a shared desire for peace and a general communal well-being.

The trickster Iktomi, a spider spirit, features prominently in these stories, for he enacts alternatingly crafty and foolish behaviors that allow morality lessons to surface through a series of humorous misfortunes. In the opening tale of the 1901 volume, "Iktomi and the Ducks," a hungry Iktomi coerces a flock of ducks into entering his home and tricks many of them into dancing blindly to their deaths at his hands. As he cooks his gluttonous meal, a nearby tree calls upon him for help buffering the wind and then ensnares him after he dismisses its cries. Stuck in the tree, Iktomi foolishly alerts a passing pack of wolves to his roasting meat by warning them to stay away from his food. Thus, the tale cautions against overconsumption of resources, for the

half-flock is a more suitably sized meal for an entire pack of wolves, and urges paying close attention to the well-being of natural elements like the tree. In other stories, Iktomi continues to suffer consequences such as hunger and humiliation as a result of his vices, which are multitudinous and include selfishness, greed, a lack of gratitude, and a perverse yearning to "be like other people"—more specifically, a handsome peacock, a high-flying arrow, and a brown-spotted fawn, among others ("Iktomi and the Fawn," *American Indian Stories, Legends, and Other Writings*, p. 25).

Further legends in the collection center on other "people" such as the muskrat and the rabbit, as well as the spirit-creature "Iya, the Camp-Eater," a far more ominous trickster than Iktomi. Zitkala-Ša's version of the Iya story—a dark tale in which the camp-swallowing trickster takes the guise of a baby—was also printed in 1902 in *Twin Territories: The Indian Magazine*, a periodical devoted to publishing Native American authors. In the story, some hunters discover a crying, abandoned baby, and he is welcomed into camp by a chieftain who wishes for his daughter to raise the infant as her own, despite a general tribal awareness (expressed by one huntsman) that "bad spirits come as little children into a camp which they mean to destroy" (*American Indian Stories, Legends, and Other Writings*, p. 52). Later, the young mother hears the sounds of an entire Indian camp rushing from the mouth of the sleeping babe and realizes that he is, in fact, an "evil spirit" with cruel designs. She alerts her father, and the camp flees under the cover of night. When Iya chases them down the next day, he assumes "his own ugly shape," his too-thin legs not strong enough to support his cumbersome body (p. 54). Mirthful warriors kill the writhing, sweating spirit-beast and, in doing so, release an entire tribe that he had devoured before coming to their camp. The grotesqueness of the Iya figure in this story helps exemplify the admirable qualities exhibited by the story's human characters, who are quick to open their arms and their homes to an orphan child, but who also band together unquestioningly when threatened by an outsider. Once again, a female character is almost wholly responsible for the preservation of her tribe, sacrificing her immediate hopes of motherhood and rousing her community to action.

Cumulatively, the stories in *Old Indian Legends* offer an entrance into the diverse world of Sioux mythology and a pleasing sense of variety, despite the repeated trope of the mischief-making protagonist who is punished for his immoral acts. While stories that feature Iktomi and Iya generally issue serious warnings about one's tribal and ethical responsibilities, others, like "Dance in a Buffalo Skull"—a charming tale about a mouse party that is disrupted by a cat—bring levity to the collection. The result is a narrative equilibrium that allows the book's lessons in morality to sit easily alongside its more amusing components. Some stories in the collection were included in textbooks for schoolchildren in the East during the 1920s. Today, although they are recognized for their preservation of Sioux legends, they are less well known than the autobiographical works and essays that would be included in the 1921 collection *American Indian Stories*.

In addition to publishing autobiographical narratives, short stories, and legends embedded in the oral storytelling tradition, Zitkala-Ša also experimented successfully with the essay form around the turn of the century. Most notably, in December 1902, the *Atlantic Monthly* published "Why I Am a Pagan," which was reprinted in the 1921 collection *American Indian Stories* under the title "The Great Spirit." In this controversial essay, which remains one of Zitkala-Ša's most widely anthologized and studied, she announces her rejection of Christianity and expresses her faith in a natural world that is embodied by the Great Spirit. She justifies her beliefs while maintaining a tone that is redolent with bliss and void of defiance, making the essay all the more compelling. She describes a day of reflection on the banks of the Missouri River and a bucolic walk back to the Indian village where her mother is living that leaves her "buoyant with good nature" (*Atlantic Monthly*, p. 802). The natural elements around her and the greeting of her beloved dog Chän when she returns inspire her to feel a kinship with her "fellow creatures," a

group in which she includes people of all races (p. 802). The presence of a converted Native American preacher on her doorstep and the interaction that follows his expression of a "bigoted creed" leaves her unruffled (p. 803). She listens placidly as he describes the "after-doom of hell fire" she will experience should she fail to join his congregation, and she offers him lunch before he heads off to his sermon (p. 803).

The essay's conclusion is noteworthy, for Zitkala-Ša later excised the final sentence, renamed the piece, and added a brief paragraph honoring the Great Spirit. In the original version, the final sentences read:

> Still I would not forget that the pale-faced missionary and the hoodooed aborigine are both God's creatures, though small indeed their own conceptions of Infinite Love. A wee child toddling in a wonder world, I prefer to their dogma my excursions into the natural gardens where the voice of the Great Spirit is heard in the twittering of birds, the rippling of mighty waters, and the sweet breathing of flowers. If this is Paganism, then at present, at least, I am a Pagan.
>
> (p. 803)

The qualifying phrase "at present, at least" in the final sentence is fitting for a writer who embarked upon numerous spiritual journeys during her lifetime. Her changes to the conclusion and to the essay's title for *American Indian Stories* suggest an eventual reluctance to cast a negative pallor over indigenous faiths by associating one's belief in the Great Spirit with the potentially offensive term "paganism."

Thus, the period from 1900 to 1902 was a time of great artistic growth and productivity for Zitkala-Ša. Noted for her musical skill as well as her writing, she became a sort of society darling during her time at the New England Conservatory of Music in Boston. Her poise and attractiveness contributed to this reputation, as did white society's yearning for examples of successfully "Americanized" products of boarding-school educations. In March 1900 she traveled with the Carlisle band to Washington, D.C., where she recited "The Famine" from Henry Wadsworth Longfellow's epic 1855 poem *The Song of Hiawatha* and met the poet's daughter. She also visited the White House during the trip and was presented with a gift of violets from First Lady Ida McKinley. In addition to such public appearances and her work's inclusion in popular periodicals, articles noting her achievements contributed to her celebrity.

In its April 14, 1900, issue, *Harper's Bazaar* featured her in a segment titled "Persons Who Interest Us" and printed a photo of her alongside a one-paragraph celebration of her "beauty and many talents" in the worlds of music and literature (p. 330). On May 5, 1900, the weekly magazine the *Outlook* mentioned her briefly in an article titled "The Representative Indian" that lauded her musical skills and noted her recent publications in the *Atlantic Monthly,* as well as the accomplishments of other assimilated people—among them her future fiancé, Dr. Carlos Montezuma "of the dreaded Apaches" (Cook, p. 81). One of the photos that accompany "The Representative Indian" captures Zitkala-Ša holding her violin and wearing an all-white dress in the Euro-American style. Her dark hair falls well past her waist as she gazes directly but demurely at the camera—an alluring mixture of exoticism and the dominant society's feminine ideal.

The rumor (disseminated in part by Zitkala-Ša herself) that she was directly descended from the legendary Hunkpapa Lakota Sioux chief Sitting Bull circulated in the popular press and added to her notoriety. Whether Zitkala-Ša believed she was related to Sitting Bull or knowingly made a false claim to manipulate ignorant readers—or, perhaps more likely, referred to herself on occasion as his "granddaughter" in a wider cultural sense only—remains unclear. Regardless of its veracity, such a story, coupled with her diverse talents and beauty, appealed to the American public's growing fascination with the country's declining indigenous population.

Although her stories and essays were generally well received, not everyone embraced them, and some critical commentary includes thinly veiled cultural biases of the era. Even as the *Harper's* writer praises Zitkala-Ša, he or she disparages the former "veritable little savage" by noting that her autobiographical writings "display

a rare command for English and much artistic feeling" ("Persons Who Interest Us," p. 330). This sort of unrepressed surprise at her accomplishments surfaces in the *Outlook* piece as well when the author, Jessie W. Cook, acknowledges her "unusual musical genius" in an article that urges white readers to recognize Native Americans' educational and professional accomplishments and exhorts Native Americans to "live *with* the people whose ways they must adopt" ("The Representative Indian," pp. 82–83). Moreover (and perhaps unsurprisingly), her former employer Pratt responded harshly to her autobiographical stories and "The Soft-Hearted Sioux," printing derisive articles about the pieces in Carlisle's weekly publication the *Red Man.* For example, one article characterized Zitkala-Ša's boarding-school narratives as misleading in their generalizations and declared the author ungrateful for the advantages she had experienced because of her education. Despite her literary success, Zitkala-Ša was clearly affected by the critiques, for she wrote about them with vitriol in letters to her then-fiancé, Carlos Montezuma.

This animosity toward Pratt likely strained her relationship with Montezuma, a Yavapai (Mohave-Apache) man whose activist ideologies were more closely aligned with Pratt's than with his fiancée's. Montezuma was born with the name Wassaja (which means "Signaling"), kidnapped as a child by Pima Indians, and sold to an itinerant Italian photographer named Carlo Gentile. Gentile adopted the boy and gave him the name Carlos Montezuma. Montezuma, who was more than a decade Zitkala-Ša's senior, earned his medical license in 1889 from Chicago Medical College and from 1893 to 1896 worked at the Carlisle Indian Industrial School before eventually returning to Chicago to open a private practice. Although Montezuma and Zitkala-Ša did not work together at Carlisle, they both traveled with the Carlisle Indian School Band in 1900. They wrote to each other extensively during Zitkala-Ša's time in Boston and later North Dakota, and Montezuma's letters, which provide valuable insight into the evolution of her political ideologies and rhetorical dexterity, have been archived by the State Historical Society of Wisconsin at the University of Wisconsin–Madison.

The two were scheduled to be married in November 1901, but divergent career goals and perspectives on Eurocentric gender roles created irreconcilable conflict. While Montezuma wanted to continue practicing medicine in Chicago, Zitkala-Ša already had her sights set on returning to the Yankton Reservation to conduct research for *Old Indian Legends* and spend time with her aging mother. Moreover, unlike Zitkala-Ša, Montezuma was an ardent supporter of Pratt's mission at Carlisle, including the separation of Indian children from their parents and the stripping away of native languages and customs. The Carlisle program also emphasized female students' education in the domestic tasks traditionally performed by Euro-American women, and, as Ruth Spack has demonstrated, although Zitkala-Ša's public persona suggested the refining influence of an off-reservation boarding-school education, she had little personal interest in fulfilling the "government's goal of turning Native females into paragons of domestic virtue" ("Dis/engagement: Zitkala-Ša's Letters to Carlos Montezuma, 1901–1902," p. 181). After a series of confrontational letters exchanged during 1901 and 1902, Zitkala-Ša broke off her relationship with Montezuma by declaring her affections for another man. The two rekindled their correspondence as friends and comembers of the Society of American Indians (SAI) about a decade later.

In 1902, while working as a clerk at Standing Rock Reservation, she married the man to whom she had referred in her letters, Raymond Talesfase Bonnin, who was also of mixed Anglo and Yankton Sioux heritage and who supported more fully Zitkala-Ša's aspirations of helping fellow Native Americans through active participation in reservation life. They moved to the Uintah and Ouray Indian Reservation at Fort Duchesne, Utah, where he had a job working among the Utes. In 1903 Zitkala-Ša gave birth to the couple's only child, Raymond Ohiya ("Winner") Bonnin, who was placed in a Catholic boarding school in 1913.

ZITKALA-ŠA (GERTRUDE SIMMONS BONNIN)

During her residency in Utah, Zitkala-Ša stepped quietly out of the literary limelight, no longer writing for major eastern publications. She continued to experiment with discursive forms, however, and had an active role in reservation undertakings. She helped educate Ute schoolchildren in a manner that defied the strict assimilationist practices of Richard Henry Pratt. She also helped found a community center where women learned to sew, visitors living miles away could receive a weekly hot lunch, and neighbors met to discuss community news—all part of a Society for American Indians program devoted to "laboring for the uplift of our kinsmen" (Zitkala-Ša, "A Year's Experience in Community Service Work Among the Ute Tribe of Indians," p. 310). Additionally, she composed a number of stories, essays, and poems, and she collaborated with a young Mormon musician, William F. Hanson, on the first Native American opera to be produced in the country.

THE SUN DANCE OPERA

Zitkala-Ša was able to draw on her diverse talents as a musician, writer, activist, and cultural historian in the development of *The Sun Dance Opera*, which featured Native American performers, Plains Indian rituals and dances, and traditional Sioux melodies. She wrote the libretto and used her violin to re-create traditionally sung melodies for Hanson, who produced the musical score. True to its medium, *The Sun Dance Opera* includes a melodramatic romance; its plot features the young lovers Winona and Ohiya (also the name of Zitkala-Ša and Raymond Bonnin's son) and a man who threatens their union. The opera debuted in February 1913 at Orpheus Hall in Vernal, Utah, and was well received, filling the hall for its three-night run. It was performed several times around Utah the following year as well. It then remained unstaged for two decades but was revived in 1935 by Brigham Young University, where Hanson was a music professor. In 1938, just months after Zitkala-Ša's death, the opera was staged in New York by the New York Opera Guild but received lackluster reviews. Although a number of Euro-American composers of the early twentieth century also centered operas on Native American themes, *The Sun Dance Opera* was and remains notable for featuring an indigenous composer-librettist and cast members.

The opera was inspired by an important and controversial religious ceremony practiced by many Plains Indians tribes. The Sun Dance spanned several days and required fasting and, at times, self-mortification such as skin piercing. Although various tribal members assisted in preparations for the ceremony and performed dances, only a select few would go through the grueling Sun Dance ritual itself. These particular dancers endured such physical trials in an effort to ascend spiritually by honoring the sun, one of the controlling forces of their universe. The events of *The Sun Dance Opera* revolve around its three main characters' involvement in the ceremony.

Winona and Ohiya are young Sioux sweethearts whose relationship has yet to be sanctioned by Winona's father, the Chieftain. Ohiya hopes to earn his approval through his display of endurance during five days and nights of dancing. Sweet Singer, a Shoshone man who has grown weary of his own lover's affections—amplified by his administration of "sacred love leaves" to her (p. 131)—arrives in their camp full of nefarious plans. He also hopes to capture Winona's hand through songs performed during the Sun Dance and gifts bestowed upon the Chieftain. The first three acts feature declarations of love from Ohiya and Winona and expressions of their religious fidelity. The Gossips and Hebo, a Heyoka trickster, also emerge in these early acts as characters who offer some comic relief as they tease and banter with Sweet Singer. During act 4, the Shoshone Maid comes to fetch Sweet Singer and implores him not to desert her again, but Sweet Singer is agitated by her presence and refuses to leave with her. He vows to Winona that he will sing until Ohiya falls from exhaustion during the Sun Dance, Ohiya's weaknesses exposed for all to see. However, Winona has prayed extensively to the "fairy Indian people—People of the night world" (p. 139) for Ohiya's protection during the dance, and these spirits heed

her call. In the final acts, the opera's focus shifts to the Sun Dance itself, which Ohiya survives, presumably to be united with Winona.

This simplistic love triangle plot barely hints at what a production of *The Sun Dance Opera* would have entailed on stage. Vague textual breaks are common throughout the libretto and indicate unwritten scenes with phrases such as "Dialogue Insert" and "#1 Sun Dance No Orchestra." The libretto does not include stage directions, but it seems clear that during these breaks the indigenous cast members would have conversed in their native language and performed certain aspects of the Sun Dance for the audience without the accompaniment of the orchestra. Such a fusion of Native American and Western cultural traditions would have been quite innovative for the era, catering to a white audience's primitivism as well as to their appreciation for Europe's classical music tradition. At the same time, the production would have offered indigenous participants a platform for the expression of their religious beliefs, although some aspects of the Sun Dance were considered too sacred to be performed publicly.

P. Jane Hafen is one of only a few people to have written at length on *The Sun Dance Opera* and has addressed the paradoxes associated with transforming traditional indigenous music and ideas into a quintessentially Western art form. Hafen suggests that Zitkala-Ša may have seen the exhibition of forbidden rituals in a Western context as means of challenging an oppressive hierarchy ("A Cultural Duet," p. 105). Certainly, the opera makes a bold political statement by encouraging Native Americans (mostly local Utes, who had adopted the Sun Dance) to perform in a public sphere dances that had been banned on reservations by the U.S. secretary of the interior at the recommendation of the Bureau of Indian Affairs, purportedly in the name of public safety. This agenda sits uneasily with the colonialist impulses that may have inspired Hanson's interest in indigenous customs, however. Unfortunately, Zitkala-Ša did not leave behind writings that comment on her involvement in the opera or her sentiments about the production. Her name is also conspicuously absent from its title page, although Hanson acknowledged Zitkala-Ša as coauthor in his 1967 memoir, *Sun Dance Land*. The predominantly Sioux characters, including the Heyoka trickster figure, as well as the opera's setting near Yankton, South Dakota, also bespeak Zitkala-Ša's influence upon the project.

POLITICAL WRITINGS

The overwhelming majority of Zitkala-Ša's publications during the latter half of her career were linked to her fervent activism. In October 1916 she was elected secretary of the Society of American Indians, an organization founded in 1911 in Ohio by a group of influential Native Americans that included Carlos Montezuma and the Santee Dakota author and physician Charles Eastman, among others. She and her husband left Utah a few months later for Washington, D.C., where Raymond studied law and enlisted in the U.S. Army. The SAI was opposed to the paternalistic programs of the federal government's Bureau of Indian Affairs, such as the land-grant system established by the Dawes General Allotment Act of 1887, and promoted societal advancement through autonomous efforts. Zitkala-Ša often acted as a liaison between the organizations. While the SAI advocated Native American self-sufficiency, many of its goals were assimilationist in nature and compromised its relationship with reservations. Political discord among members further weakened the organization, which broke up in 1919.

Before its end, Zitkala-Ša was a regular contributor to the society's quarterly journal, the *American Indian Magazine* (known in its early years as the *Quarterly Journal of the Society of American Indians*), and she became its editor in the fall of 1918. The magazine featured mostly Native American contributors and printed a wide variety of content, including essays, poetry, columns, letters, stories, illustrations, and photographs. The poetry of Zitkala-Ša appeared in its pages, as did many editorials and articles written by the now-seasoned journalist. Her poems revisit many of the themes that surfaced in her earliest work, including spirituality, the

mistreatment of tribal peoples, and the influence of matriarchs. The 1916 poem "The Indian's Awakening," for example, chronicles her spiritual wandering from her school days to adulthood, which is punctuated by a trip to the "Spirit-world" upon a lightning-fast steed that renews her faith in "God and the land" (reprinted in *American Indian Stories, Legends, and Other Writings*, pp. 166–167). In 1917 she adapted the lyrics to Samuel Francis Smith's anthem "America" (or "My Country, 'Tis of Thee") to reflect the injustices experienced by indigenous people on their native soil:

Land where OUR fathers died,
Whose offspring are denied
The Franchise given wide,
Hark, while I sing.

("The Red Man's America," p. 64)

The 1917 poem "A Sioux Woman's Love for Her Grandchild" also condemns the government, although the work resonates with sadness rather than defiance. It describes a grandmother's tender relationship with "little Bright eyes," a child she has cared for since her own daughter's death and who one day does not return from going out to play (p. 230). The grandmother receives warning that a "dust-cloud of an army" is headed her way and that she must flee, yet she stays on the prairie alone: "A soul in torture / Sacrificing life than leave behind her lost one" (p. 231). The missing girl in the story seems to represent all of the children who have been extracted from their traditional upbringings under steady pressure from the government, while the grandmother's anguish reflects a widespread cultural phenomenon—the grief of not knowing what lies ahead for an entire race.

Like her poems, Zitkala-Ša's *American Indian Magazine* editorials and articles address a range of topics but return frequently to the dominant theme of Native American uplift, which she believed could be achieved by people who learned English, sought a higher education, and refused to sell their inherited lands. The pieces also reflect her increasing devotion to lobbying for the extension of U.S. citizenship to all indigenous people. In an editorial comment from the July–September 1918 issue of the *American Indian Magazine*, she uses World War I and the European battlefields upon which Native American soldiers died, "having intermingled their blood with that of every other race in the supreme sacrifice for an ideal" (p. 113), as a backdrop for an argument that pinpoints the hypocrisy of fighting for democracy abroad when such ideals are not comprehensively upheld at home. Both "Indian Gifts to Civilized Man" (1918) and "America, Home of the Red Man" (1919) build on this argument by delving into the specific contributions made by Native Americans, both on and off the battlefields, during World War I. Ultimately, her diverse contributions to the *American Indian Magazine* reinforce her modern-day image as a dedicated reformist who wielded her rhetorical talents in the battle for a more egalitarian future.

The suppression of peyote eating was a cause to which Zitkala-Ša devoted a good deal of time and energy during this era, for she had witnessed and been disturbed by the debilitating effects the drug had upon the Utes. Although her outspoken criticism of Native Americans' use of the cactus for its psychoactive properties has at times been called hypocritical based on her opposition to the governmental regulation of other indigenous religious customs such as the Sun Dance, her writings indicate a genuine concern for the physical and spiritual health of the increasing numbers of people who were reportedly using peyote recreationally. In "The Menace of Peyote" (c. 1916), Zitkala-Ša challenges the representation of peyote as a religious sacrament under indigenous traditions and links its ceremonial use to Christian rituals. The article "Chipeta, Widow of Chief Ouray with a Word About a Deal in Blankets" from the July–September 1917 edition of the *American Indian Magazine* reveals that Zitkala-Ša traveled to Utah to visit the widow of the influential Ute leader and discuss the drug. After warning her listeners of the "inevitable degeneration that follows the habitual and indiscriminate use of narcotics," Zitkala-Ša is dismayed by Chipeta's frank admission to using peyote to relieve symptoms of rheumatism and also by Chipeta's brother's declaration that he

will continue its use until the "Great White Father" in Washington instructs him otherwise (p. 169). As it was, the U.S. Congress had begun hearings on peyote use in 1916, and the narcotic was banned in Colorado, Nevada, and Utah in 1917.

Although Zitkala-Ša continued to lobby for Native American interests into the 1920s, with a particular devotion to citizenship, her literary talents garnered attention again in 1921 with the publication of her second collection, *American Indian Stories*.

AMERICAN INDIAN STORIES

Published by Hayworth Publishing House, *American Indian Stories* (1921) is a multifaceted work that reprints the three acclaimed autobiographical boarding-school stories of her burgeoning career; the early stories "The Soft-Hearted Sioux," "The Trial Path," and "A Warrior's Daughter"; and two previously unpublished stories, "A Dream of Her Grandfather" and "The Widespread Enigma Concerning Blue-Star Woman." In addition, the collection includes the essays "The Great Spirit" (a slightly longer version of 1902's "Why I Am a Pagan") and "America's Indian Problem," in which she calls for Native Americans to be granted citizenship and for Bureau of Indian Affairs activities to be placed under closer scrutiny. This essay was also published in 1921 in the Illinois Federation of Women's Clubs magazine, *Edict*. The diverse selections in *American Indian Stories* seem to have been chosen to showcase Zitkala-Ša's ideological development over the course of her career, as well as her discursive range. They also complement one another in their overlapping efforts to dispel erroneous notions about Native American customs and beliefs by capitalizing on white readers' widespread interest in the "savage." Common themes throughout the collection help to link the various autobiographical, fiction, and nonfiction pieces.

The previously unpublished story "A Dream of Her Grandfather" contributes to the thematic consistency of the work because it helps relate the theme of the youthful quest for identity, so prominent in her early stories, to the questions about Native American rights and responsibilities that arise in her essays. The succinct tale describes a young woman's recollections of her grandfather, a revered Dakota medicine man, who died in Washington, D.C., after a long journey by horseback as a delegate of a peacemaking mission. The granddaughter, an Indian rights activist visiting Washington, dreams that her grandfather brings her a cedar chest containing "dream-stuff"—an image—rather than the coveted medicine bags she had hoped for (*American Indian Stories, Legends, and Other Writings*, p. 142). As the "vision" takes shape in her mind, she glimpses a Dakota village far removed from her in space. Its village crier is resplendent with a "head-dress of eagle plumes," and he rides a "prancing white pony" as he urges listeners to "Be glad! Rejoice! Look up, and see the new day dawning! Help is near! Hear me, every one!" (p. 142). The scene lifts her heart, leaving the granddaughter "thrilled with new hope for her people" (p. 142). Even though the activist has assimilated to white culture, the vision reinvigorates her sense of cultural identity. The story's outcome reinforces the importance of her efforts in Washington and reminds her that there are still places where Native American people and customs might be protected and preserved through such work.

The plot of "The Widespread Enigma Concerning Blue-Star Woman" also centers on an Indian character's receipt of a fortifying "vision." Set some time after the passage of the Dawes General Allotment Act in 1887, the story calls attention to the bureaucratic barriers plaguing the allotment process, which kept some people from receiving land that was to be issued to them by the government. The act, which allowed the government to break up reservations by issuing tracts to individuals, was hugely detrimental to the general health of indigenous communities and was fiercely opposed by the SAI. "The Widespread Enigma Concerning Blue-Star Woman" calls attention to this system and condemns educated Native Americans who during this period used their knowledge of convo-

luted governmental processes to swindle older people out of their land and money. The story relies heavily on pathos and features two impoverished elderly Native Americans, Blue-Star Woman and Chief High Flier, who are victimized by these human "tricksters" (*American Indian Stories, Legends, and Other Writings*, p. 149).

The story opens with Blue-Star Woman sitting alone in her log cabin on the plains, puzzling over the "white man's law" that keeps her from owning a "piece of earth," which she considers to be her "birthright" (pp. 143–144). Two Indian men in western attire appear and promise to resolve the issue in return for half of her land and money. Weeks later and miles away, the Sioux chief High Flier receives governmental notice that he must hand over part of his land to someone he does not know named "Blue-Star Woman." The chief travels by pony to the nearest the post office with a letter to an American woman, a friend, explaining the mix-up and soliciting help, but once he arrives, he decides it would be pointless to ask her to go to Washington on his behalf and sets the letter on fire. Indian police thereupon arrest him, charging him with attempting to burn down a government building.

The concluding events point to the rapidly increasing political power of American women at the beginning of the 1920s. As he sits in his cell, Chief High Flier struggles to retain his faith in humankind and is strengthened in his plight when a "luminous light" appears to him. It is his American friend, and she has with her a "legion" of women with "earnest" faces looking upon a "huge stone image": the Statue of Liberty. The chief witnesses the statue's "light of liberty" sweeping across the nation to touch even the corners of the reservations (p. 153). Like the activist in "A Dream of Her Grandfather," the chief's spirit is bolstered by his vision, and he is able to survive his sentence. However, this story's conclusion is less hopeful than that of "A Dream," for readers learn that the two young men who cheated Blue-Star Woman are also responsible for organizing Chief High Flier's release—a task they took on in exchange for half of his land.

The vision narrative in this story calls attention to what Zitkala-Ša perceived to be women's humanitarian responsibilities, particularly to Native Americans who were without land and equal opportunities. Female American citizens had been given the right to vote a year earlier, and the story draws upon this history by suggesting that by banding together within a society founded upon democratic ideals women could enact great change. The appeal parallels Zitkala-Ša's involvement beginning in the 1920s with the General Federation of Women's Clubs (GFWC), a mostly white organization established in 1890 that sought to enhance the lives of others through community service. "The Widespread Enigma Concerning Blue-Star Woman" urges white female readers to do what Zitkala-Ša argued for explicitly in the pamphlet *Americanize the First American*, also published in 1921, in which she appeals to the "womanhood of America" to "revoke the tyrannical powers of Government superintendents over a voiceless people and extend American opportunities to the first American—the Red Man" (*American Indian Stories, Legends, and Other Writings*, p. 244). This belief in women's roles as cultural stewards inspired her to encourage the GFWC to start an Indian Welfare Committee, an influential organization in which she would play an active part.

As a representative of the GFWC, she went to Oklahoma to investigate reports of corruption involving oil and reservation land for a study commissioned by the Indian Rights Association. As a result, she coauthored the pamphlet *Oklahoma's Poor Rich Indians: An Orgy of Graft and Exploitation of the Five Civilized Tribes— Legalized Robbery* (1924) with Matthew Sniffen of the Indian Rights Association and Charles Fabens of the American Indian Defense Association. The report called for governmental intervention and redress, and it contributed to the formation of the Meriam Commission, an organization that visited reservations across the nation to evaluate and record living conditions. The Meriam group issued a lengthy report commissioned by the Institute for Government Research called *The Problem of Indian Administration*, which exposed deplorable circumstances on reservations, cri-

tiqued the Dawes Act of 1887, and made recommendations for improving indigenous life. Its release in 1928 marked the beginning of major governmental changes to Indian policy.

In the early 1920s Zitkala-Ša also accepted invitations to visit California Native Americans and wrote four articles about these people of the "forests of pines and big trees" that were published serially in 1922 in the *San Francisco Bulletin* and then in the *California Indian Herald*. She channels (and directly acknowledges) the ideas of the transcendentalist Henry David Thoreau in the first article, "California Indian Trails and Prayer Trees," which paints a portrait of Indian spirituality that is deeply rooted in respect for the natural world and the history of a people. The following two articles focus on threats to the indigenous population in California and trace its decline, beginning with the signing of treaties in the early 1850s and the subsequent infusion of "lawless gold seekers" ("Lost Treaties of the California Indians," *American Indian Stories, Legends, and Other Writings*, p. 256). Zitkala-Ša urges readers to acknowledge such hardships and to extend "public welfare work" to the California Indians struggling because of insufficient educations, jobs, and medical care ("The California Indians of Today," *American Indian Stories, Legends, and Other Writings*, p. 260). In the final California piece, titled "Heart to Heart," she appeals directly to the indigenous people of the state to remain strong in their faith in the Great Spirit and organized in their self-improvement efforts. In these four articles, Zitkala-Ša brings into unique creative cohesion her spiritual connection to nature, interest in cultural history, and humanitarian objectives.

In addition to visiting Oklahoma and California during the early 1920s, Zitkala-Ša toured cities across the United States, speaking to various community organizations about the need for comprehensive Native American citizenship and voting rights. At last, in 1924, President Calvin Coolidge signed the Indian Citizenship Act, which naturalized all indigenous people born in the United States. The legislation marked a significant victory for Zitkala-Ša and other activists, but it did not quell her desire to improve conditions for Native Americans. Two years later, in 1926, she founded and became president of the nonprofit National Council of American Indians (NCAI), an influential group that encouraged Native American self-sufficiency in the protection of rights and property, and in which she would remain active until her death. Her husband served as secretary. Over the following years, Zitkala-Ša lobbied relentlessly in Washington for governmental policy reform and redresses for the exploitation of many different indigenous populations, at times visiting reservations across the United States to garner firsthand accounts of life there and consult with their residents. Many of Zitkala-Ša's and Raymond Bonnin's letters and business documents chronicle their involvement from 1926 to 1938 in the National Council of American Indians and are preserved among the L. Tom Perry Special Collections at the Harold B. Lee Library at Brigham Young University.

On January 26, 1938, Zitkala-Ša died at age sixty-one of cardiac dilation and kidney disease after falling into a coma the previous day. Like the Dakota medicine man in "A Dream of Her Grandfather," who perished after an arduous journey to Washington, D.C., "in behalf of peace among men" (p. 141), Zitkala-Ša would have the American capital as her final resting place. Her tombstone bears both the name "Gertrude Simmons Bonnin" and the name "Zitkala-Ša" and acknowledges her Sioux heritage. She had a Mormon funeral and was buried at Arlington National Cemetery because of her husband's service in the U.S. Army. Captain Raymond Bonnin died in 1942 and is also buried there.

Although Zitkala-Ša's writing fell in popularity after her death, there was a resurgence of interest in her work in the 1970s and 1980s that coincided with a general upswing in attention to multicultural American literature. Both of her collections were brought back into print in 1985 by the University of Nebraska Press. In the twenty-first century, Zitkala-Ša's stories, articles, and essays are considered essential to both the Native American and American literary canons. The pieces collected in *American Indian Stories*, particularly her autobiographical narratives and

early short stories, are widely anthologized and studied for their articulation of turn-of-the-century cultural alienation from a female indigenous perspective. Though less well known, the stories preserved in *Old Indian Legends* serve as a historical bridge between oral and written storytelling eras, as Zitkala-Ša was one of the first authors to recount Sioux legends in written English. By introducing the early-twentieth-century reading public to indigenous writing, she set the stage for the publication of Native American novels, such as *Cogewea the Half-Blood: A Depiction of the Great Montana Cattle Range* (1927), by Mourning Dove (Christal Quintasket). Her fiction was also a forerunner of the so-called Native American Renaissance that occurred during the late 1960s and 1970s and that catapulted fiction by authors such as N. Scott Momaday and Leslie Marmon Silko into the literary mainstream.

Early literary scholarship on Zitkala-Ša focuses primarily on questions of cultural identity and history, encouraging readers to confront the marginalization of indigenous people—particularly in a government-controlled educational system—and to consider how such experiences have shaped a country's literature and its national identity. Attempts to recover a Native American intellectual tradition and to make room for indigenous writers' works in American literary movements such as regionalism and realism are also prominent in such studies, as their originators sought to complicate and expand conceptualizations about American literature and canonicity. As a result, since the 1990s, Zitkala-Ša's writing has figured prominently in studies of turn-of-the-century regionalism because it reinforces the extent to which the movement was driven by widespread concerns over issues of race, gender, and nationalism. Judith Fetterly and Marjorie Pryse, for example, characterize Zitkala-Ša as regionalist in part because of her childhood on the reservation, a place that had literally been "marked off," or regionalized, as well as the extent to which her autobiographical stories document the "patriarchal imperialism" of the era (*Writing out of Place*, pp. 375–376).

Feminist scholars have been drawn to Zitkala-Ša's fiction for its frequent images of resilient indigenous women who are intrinsic to the well-being of their communities. Such depictions are particularly noteworthy because most were imagined in an era before women's suffrage, when many female Americans succumbed to the frustrating pressure of socially prescribed gender roles. Gynocentric tribal social structures contrast sharply with the patriarchal Euro-American model that many women rallied against during Zitkala-Ša's lifetime, offering clues about the ways in which gendered expectations are a product of one's culture. The many mothers and grandmothers of Zitkala-Ša's fiction and nonfiction who assume collective responsibility for a tribe's children, in addition to its legacy, traditions, and moral code—frequently under the threat of duress—grant insight into the limitations historically placed upon women of other cultures. With the emergence of ecofeminist scholarship in the last decades of the twentieth century, more writers have also begun to examine how a society's commonly held attitudes about nature might influence or mirror its subjugation of women and racial minorities. Such inquiries only increase the present-day critical relevance of the various works by Zitkala-Ša that examine the spiritual and cultural connection to the natural world from the perspective of a female minority.

Despite the many professional hats Zitkala-Ša wore during her lifetime and the variety in her publication mediums, a handful of interwoven aspirations undergirded the majority of her literary output and included the preservation of Native American stories and traditions, the protection of basic human rights, and the dismantling of a dominant society's misconceptions, especially those about Native American women. She achieved such goals to astonishing degrees during her lifetime and continues to influence critical discussions about oppressive social hierarchies. Although her activist ideologies were dynamic, shifting alongside other public attitudes as the nation entered the modern era, her devotion to improving the welfare of others was unwavering.

Selected Bibliography

WORKS OF ZITKALA-ŠA

COLLECTIONS

Old Indian Legends. Boston: Ginn & Co., 1901. Reprinted with an introduction by Agnes M. Picotte. Lincoln: University of Nebraska Press, 1985 and 2013.

American Indian Stories. Washington, D.C.: Hayworth, 1921. Reprinted with an introduction by Susan Rose Dominguez. Lincoln: University of Nebraska Press, 1985. New ed. 2003.

ARTICLES, ESSAYS, AND PAMPHLETS

"Side by Side." *Earlhamite* 2, no. 12:177–179 (March 16, 1896).

"Why I Am a Pagan." *Atlantic Monthly*, December 1902, pp. 801–803.

"A Year's Experience in Community Service Work Among the Ute Tribe of Indians." *American Indian Magazine* 4:307–310 (October–December 1916).

"The Menace of Peyote" (c. 1916). Reprinted in *American Indian Stories, Legends, and Other Writings.* Edited by Cathy N. Davidson and Ada Norris. London: Penguin, 2003.

"Chipeta, Widow of Chief Ouray with a Word About a Deal in Blankets." *American Indian Magazine* 5, no. 3:168–170 (July–September 1917).

"Editorial Comment." *American Indian Magazine* 6, no. 3:113–114 (July–September 1918).

"Indian Gifts to Civilized Man." *American Indian Magazine* 6, no. 3:115–116 (July–September 1918).

"America, Home of the Red Man." *American Indian Magazine* 6, no. 4:165–167 (winter 1919).

"The Coronation of Chief Powhatan Retold." *American Indian Magazine* 6, no. 4:180–181 (winter 1919).

"Letter to the Chiefs and Headmen of Tribes." *American Indian Magazine* 6, no. 4:196–197 (winter 1919).

Americanize the First American: A Plan of Regeneration. Indian Rights Association, 1921. Reprinted in *American Indian Stories, Legends, and Other Writings.*

Bureaucracy Versus Democracy. Indian Rights Association, 1921. Reprinted in *American Indian Stories, Legends, and Other Writings.*

"California Indian Trails and Prayer Trees." *California Indian Herald* 1:6 (1923). Reprinted from the *Bulletin* (San Francisco), 1922, and in *American Indian Stories, Legends, and Other Writings.*

"Lost Treaties of the California Indians." *California Indian Herald* 1:7 (1923). Reprinted from the *Bulletin* (San Francisco), 1922, and in *American Indian Stories, Legends, and Other Writings.*

"The California Indians of Today." *California Indian Herald* 1:10 (1923). Reprinted from the *Bulletin* (San Francisco), 1922, and in *American Indian Stories, Legends, and Other Writings.*

"Heart to Heart Talk." *California Indian Herald* 2:2–3 (1924). Reprinted from the *Bulletin* (San Francisco), 1922, and in *American Indian Stories, Legends, and Other Writings.*

POETRY

"A Ballad." *Earlhamite* 3, no. 7:97–98 (January 9, 1897).

"Iris of Life." *Earlhamite* 5:31 (November 1, 1898).

"The Indian's Awakening." *American Indian Magazine* 4: 57–59 (January–March 1916).

"The Red Man's America." *American Indian Magazine* 5, no. 1:64 (January–March 1917).

"A Sioux Woman's Love for Her Grandchild." *American Indian Magazine* 5, no. 4:230–231 (October–December 1917).

OTHER WORKS

The Sun Dance Opera. With William Hanson. Orpheus Hall, Vernal, Utah, 1913. Libretto reprinted in *Dreams and Thunder: Stories, Poems, and* The Sun Dance Opera, with an introduction by P. Jane Hafen. Lincoln: University of Nebraska Press, 2001.

Oklahoma's Poor Rich Indians: An Orgy of Graft and Exploitation of the Five Civilized Tribes—Legalized Robbery. With Charles H. Fabens and Matthew K. Sniffen. Philadelphia: Office of the Indian Rights Association, 1924.

COLLECTED WORKS

Dreams and Thunder: Stories, Poems, and The Sun Dance Opera. Edited by P. Jane Hafen. Lincoln: University of Nebraska Press, 2001.

American Indian Stories, Legends, and Other Writings. Edited by Cathy N. Davidson and Ada Norris. London: Penguin, 2003. (Includes the full text of *Old Indian Legends* and *American Indian Stories*, as well as additional poems, essays, and articles. Page references in the text are for this volume.)

MANUSCRIPTS AND LETTERS

Carlos Montezuma Papers. State Historical Society of Wisconsin, University of Wisconsin–Madison.

Gertrude and Raymond Bonnin Collection, 1926–1938. L. Tom Perry Special Collections, Harold B. Lee Library, Brigham Young University, Provo, Utah.

National Council of American Indians Records, 1926–1938. L. Tom Perry Special Collections, Harold B. Lee Library, Brigham Young University, Provo, Utah.

ZITKALA-ŠA (GERTRUDE SIMMONS BONNIN)

William F. Hanson Collection, 1913–1962. L. Tom Perry Special Collections, Harold B. Lee Library, Brigham Young University, Provo, Utah.

CRITICAL AND BIOGRAPHICAL STUDIES

Bernardin, Susan. "The Lessons of a Sentimental Education: Zitkala-Ša's Autobiographical Narratives." *Western American Literature* 32, no. 3:212–238 (November 1997).

Carpenter, Cari. "Detecting Indianness: Gertrude Bonnin's Investigation of Native American Identity." *Wicazo Sa Review* 20, no. 1:139–159 (2005).

Cook, Jessie W. "The Representative Indian." *Outlook*, May 5, 1900, pp. 80–83.

Cutter, Martha J. "Zitkala-Ša's Autobiographical Writings: The Problems of a Canonical Search for Language and Identity." *MELUS* 19, no. 1:31–45 (spring 1994).

Dominguez, Susan Rose. "Zitkala-Ša: The Representative Indian." Introduction to *American Indian Stories by Zitkala-Ša*. Lincoln: University. of Nebraska Press, 2003. Pp. v–xxv.

Enoch, Jessica. "Resisting the Script of an Indian Education: Zitkala-Ša and the Carlisle Indian School." *College English* 65, no. 2:114–141 (November 2002).

Fetterly, Judith, and Marjorie Pryse. *Writing Out of Place: Regionalism, Women, and American Literary Culture*. Urbana: University of Illinois Press, 2003.

Fisher, Dexter. "Zitkala-Ša: The Evolution of a Writer." *American Indian Quarterly* 5, no. 3:229–238 (1978).

———. "The Transformation of Tradition: A Study of Zitkala-Ša and Mourning Dove, Two Transitional American Indian Writers." In *Critical Essays on Native American Literature*. Edited by Andrew Wiget. Boston: Hall, 1985. Pp. 202–211.

Hafen, P. Jane. "Zitkala-Ša: Sentimentality and Sovereignty." *Wicazo Sa Review* 12, no. 2:31–41 (1997).

———. "A Cultural Duet: Zitkala-Ša and *The Sun Dance Opera*." *Great Plains Quarterly* 18, no. 2:102–111 (spring 1998).

Lukens, Margaret A. "The American Story of Zitkala-Ša." In *In Her Own Voice: Nineteenth-Century American Women Essayists*. Edited by Sherry Lee Linkon. New York: Garland, 1997. Pp. 141–155.

Meisenheimer, D. K., Jr. "Regionalist Bodies/Embodied Regions: Sarah Orne Jewett and Zitkala-Ša." In *Breaking Boundaries: New Perspectives on Women's Regional Writing*. Edited by Sherrie A. Inness and Diana Royer. Iowa City: University of Iowa Press, 1997. Pp. 109–123.

Newmark, Julianne. "Writing (and Speaking) in Tongues: Zitkala-Ša's American Indian Stories." *Western American Literature* 37, no. 3:335–358 (fall 2002).

———. "Pluralism, Place, and Gertrude Bonnin's Counter-nativism from Utah to Washington, D.C." *American Indian Quarterly* 36, no. 3:318–347 (summer 2012).

Okker, Patricia. "Native American Literatures and the Canon: The Case of Zitkala-Ša." In *American Realism and the Canon*. Edited by Tom Quirk and Gary Scharnhorst. Newark: University of Delaware Press, 1994. Pp. 87–101.

"Persons Who Interest Us." *Harper's Bazaar*, April 14, 1900, p. 330.

Rappaport, Doreen. *The Flight of Red Bird: The Life of Zitkala-Ša*. New York: Puffin, 1999.

Ruoff, A. LaVonne Brown. "Early Native American Women Authors: Jane Johnston Schoolcraft, Sarah Winnemucca, S. Alice Callahan, E. Pauline Johnson, and Zitkala-Ša." In *Nineteenth-Century American Women Writers: A Critical Reader*. Edited by Karen L. Kilcup. Malden, Mass.: Blackwell, 1998. Pp. 81–111.

Six, Beverly G. "Zitkala-Ša (Gertrude Simmons Bonnin)." In *American Women Writers, 1900–1945: A Bio-Bibliographical Critical Sourcebook*. Edited by Laurie Champion. Westport, Conn.: Greenwood Press, 2000. Pp. 383–387.

Smith, Jeanne. "'A Second Tongue': The Trickster's Voice in the Works of Zitkala-Ša." In *Tricksterism in Turn-of-the-Century American Literature: A Multicultural Perspective*. Edited by Elizabeth Ammons and Annette White-Parks. Hanover, N.H.: University Press of New England, 1994. Pp. 46–60.

Spack, Ruth. "Re-Visioning American Indian Women: Zitkala-Ša's Revolutionary *American Indian Stories*." *Legacy* 14, no. 1:25–43 (1997).

———. "Dis/Engagement: Zitkala-Ša's Letters to Carlos Montezuma, 1901–1902." *MELUS* 26, no. 1:173–204 (spring 2001).

Susag, Dorothea M. "Zitkala-Ša (Gertrude Simmons Bonnin): A Power(full) Literary Voice." *Studies in American Indian Literatures* 5, no. 4:3–24 (1993).

Totten, Gary. "Zitkala-Ša and the Problem of Regionalism: Nations, Narratives, and Critical Traditions." *American Indian Quarterly* 29, nos. 1–2:84–123 (winter–spring 2005).

Warrior, Robert Allen. *Tribal Secrets: Recovering American Indian Intellectual Traditions*. Minneapolis: University of Minnesota Press, 1995.

Welch, Deborah. "Gertrude Simmons Bonnin (Zitkala-Ša)." In *The New Warriors: Native American Leaders Since 1900*. Edited by R. David Edmunds. Lincoln: University of Nebraska Press, 2001. Pp. 35–53.

Wexler, Laura. "Tender Violence: Literary Eavesdropping, Domestic Fiction, and Educational Reform." In *The Culture of Sentiment: Race, Gender, Sentimentality in Nineteenth-Century America*. Edited by Shirley Samuels. New York: Oxford University Press, 1992. Pp. 9–38.

Cumulative Index

All references include volume numbers in boldface roman numerals followed by page numbers within that volume. Subjects of articles are indicated by boldface type.

A

"A" (Zukofsky), **Supp. III Part 2:** 611, 612, 614, 617, 619, 620, 621, 622, 623, 624, 626, 627, 628, 629, 630, 631; **Supp. IV Part 1:** 154; **Supp. XVI:** 287, 287

Aal, Katharyn Machan, **Supp. IV Part 1:** 332; **Supp. XXIII:** 54

Aaron, Daniel, **IV:** 429; **Supp. I Part 2:** 647, 650

Aaron's Rod (Lawrence), **Supp. I Part 1:** 255

Abacus (Karr), **Supp. XI:** 240–242, 248, 254

Abádi-Nagy, Zoltán, **Supp. IV Part 1:** 280, 289, 291

"Abandoned Farmhouse" (Kooser), **Supp. XIX:** 117, 119

"Abandoned House, The" (L. Michaels), **Supp. XVI:** 214

"Abandoned Newborn, The" (Olds), **Supp. X:** 207

"Abandoned Stone Schoolhouse in the Nebraska Sandhills, An" (Kooser), **Supp. XIX:** 124–125

"Abba Jacob" (Nelson), **Supp. XVIII:** 177

"Abbé François Picquet"(Kenny), **Supp. XXIII:** 153

Abbey, Edward, **Supp. VIII:** 42; **Supp. X:** 24, 29, 30, 31, 36; **Supp. XIII:** 1–18; **Supp. XIV:** 179; **Supp. XXV:** 208

Abbey's Road (Abbey), **Supp. XIII:** 12

Abbott, Carl, **Supp. XVIII:** 142

Abbott, Edith, **Supp. I Part 1:** 5

Abbott, Grace, **Supp. I Part 1:** 5

Abbott, Jack Henry, **Retro. Supp. II:** 210

Abbott, Jacob, **Supp. I Part 1:** 38, 39

Abbott, Lyman, **III:** 293

Abbott, Sean, **Retro. Supp. II:** 213

ABC of Color, An: Selections from Over a Half Century of Writings (Du Bois), **Supp. II Part 1:** 186

ABC of Reading (Pound), **III:** 468, 474–475

"Abdication, An" (Merrill), **Supp. III Part 1:** 326

'Abdu'l-Bahá, **Supp. XX: 117, 122**

Abel, Lionel, **Supp. XIII:** 98

Abel, Sam, **Supp. XIII:** 199

Abelard, Peter, **I:** 14, 22

Abeles, Sigmund, **Supp. VIII:** 272

Abeng (Cliff), **Supp. XXII:** 66, 69–71

Abercrombie, Joe, **Supp. XXV:** 74

Abercrombie, Lascelles, **III:** 471; **Retro. Supp. I:** 127, 128

Abernathy, Milton, **Supp. III Part 2:** 616

Abernon, Edgar Vincent, Viscount d', **Supp. XVI:** 191

Aberration of Starlight (Sorrentino), **Supp. XXI:** 234–235

Abhau, Anna. *See* Mencken, Mrs. August (Anna Abhau)

"Abide with Me" (Hoffman), **Supp. XVIII:** 86

Abide with Me (Strout), **Supp. XXIII:** 273, 275, **278–280,** 285

"Ability" (Emerson), **II:** 6

Abingdon, Alexander, **Supp. XVI:** 99

Abish, Walter, **Supp. V:** 44

"Abishag" (Glück), **Supp. V:** 82

"Abnegation, The" (Bronk), **Supp. XXI:** 32

Abney, Lisa, **Supp. XXII:** 9

Abood, Maureen, **Supp. XXII:** 90

"Abortion, The" (Sexton), **Supp. II Part 2:** 682

"Abortions" (Dixon), **Supp. XII:** 153

"About C. D. Wright" (Colburn), **Supp. XV:** 341

"About Effie" (Findley), **Supp. XX: 50**

"About Hospitality" (Jewett), **Retro. Supp. II:** 131

"About Kathryn" (Dubus), **Supp. VII:** 91

"About Language" (Wrigley), **Supp. XVIII:** 300–301

"About Looking Alone at a Place: Arles" (M. F. K. Fisher), **Supp. XVII:** 89, 91

About the House (Auden), **Supp. II Part 1:** 24

About Town: "The New Yorker" and the World It Made (Yagoda), **Supp. VIII:** 151

"About Zhivago and His Poems"(O'Hara), **Supp. XXIII:** 214

"Above Pate Valley" (Snyder), **Supp. VIII:** 293

Above the River (Wright), **Supp. III Part 2:** 589, 606

"Abraham" (Schwartz), **Supp. II Part 2:** 663

Abraham, Nelson Algren. *See* Algren, Nelson

Abraham, Pearl, **Supp. XVII:** 49; **Supp. XX: 177; Supp. XXIV: 1–15**

"Abraham Davenport" (Whittier), **Supp. I Part 2:** 699

"Abraham Lincoln" (Emerson), **II:** 13

Abraham Lincoln: The Prairie Years (Sandburg), **III:** 580, 587–589, 590

Abraham Lincoln: The Prairie Years and the War Years (Sandburg), **III:** 588, 590

Abraham Lincoln: The War Years (Sandburg), **III:** 588, 589–590; **Supp. XVII:** 105

"Abraham Lincoln Walks at Midnight" (Lindsay), **Supp. I Part 2:** 390–391

"Abram Morrison" (Whittier), **Supp. I Part 2:** 699

Abramovich, Alex, **Supp. X:** 302, 309

Abrams, David, **Supp. XXII:** 61

Abrams, M. H., **Supp. XVI:** 19; **Supp. XXIII:** 42

Abridgment of Universal Geography, An: Together with Sketches of History (Rowson), **Supp. XV:** 243

"Absalom" (Rukeyser), **Supp. VI:** 278–279

Absalom, Absalom! (Faulkner), **II:** 64, 65–67, 72, 223; **IV:** 207; **Retro. Supp. I:** 75, 81, 82, 84, 85, 86, 87, 88, 89, 90, 92, 382; **Supp. V:** 261; **Supp. X:** 51; **Supp. XIV:** 12–13

"Absence"(J. Schoolcraft), **Supp. XXIII:** 228, 231

"Absence of Mercy" (Stone), **Supp. V:** 295

"Absentee, The" (Levertov), **Supp. III Part 1:** 284

Absentee Ownership (Veblen), **Supp. I Part 2:** 642

"Absent-Minded Bartender" (X. J. Kennedy), **Supp. XV:** 159

"Absent Thee from Felicity Awhile" (Wylie), **Supp. I Part 2:** 727, 729

"Absolution" (Fitzgerald), **Retro. Supp. I:** 108

"Absolution" (Sobin), **Supp. XVI:** 289

"Abuelita's Ache" (Mora), **Supp. XIII:** 218

Abysmal Brute, The (London), **II:** 467

Abyssinia and the Imperialists (C. L. R. James), **Supp. XXI:** 166

Abyss of Human Illusion, The (Sorrentino), **Supp. XXI:** 225, 227, 237–238

"Academic Story, An" (Simpson), **Supp. IX:** 279–280

"Academic Zoo, The: Theory—in Practice" (Epstein), **Supp. XIV:** 107–108, 109

"A Capella" (Wrigley), **Supp. XVIII:** 300

"Accident" (Minot), **Supp. VI: 208–209**

"Accident, The" (Southern), **Supp. XI:** 295

"Accident, The" (Strand), **Supp. IV Part 2:** 624

Accident/A Day's News (Wolf), **Supp. IV Part 1:** 310

Accidental Tourist, The (Tyler), **Supp. IV Part 2:** 657, 668–669; **Supp. V:** 227

Accordion Crimes (Proulx), **Supp. VII:** 259–261

"Accountability" (Dunbar), **Supp. II Part 1:** 197, 204

"Account of the Method of Drawing Birds" (Audubon), **Supp. XVI:** 12

"Accusation, The" (Wright), **Supp. III Part 2:** 595

"Accusation of the Inward Man, The" (Taylor), **IV:** 156

"Accusing Message from Dead Father" (Karr), **Supp. XI:** 244

Ace, Goodman, **Supp. IV Part 2:** 574

Ache of Appetite, The (Hadas), **Supp. XXIII: 120–121**

Achievement in American Poetry (Bogan), **Supp. III Part 1:** 63–64

Acker, Kathy, **Supp. XII:1–20; Supp. XXI:** 236

Ackerley, J. R., **Supp. XX: 237**

Ackerman, Diane, **Supp. XIII:** 154

"Acknowledgment" (Lanier), **Supp. I Part 1:** 364

Ackroyd, Peter, **Supp. V:** 233; **Supp. XVII:** 180

"Acquaintance in the Heavens, An" (Dillard), **Supp. VI:** 34

"Acquainted with the Night" (Frost), **II:** 155; **Retro. Supp. I:** 137; **Supp. XXI:** 26

Across Spoon River (Masters), **Supp. I Part 2:** 455, 457, 459, 460, 466, 474–475, 476

Across the Layers: Poems Old and New (Goldbarth), **Supp. XII:** 181, **187–189**

Across the River and into the Trees (Hemingway), **I:** 491; **II:** 255–256, 261; **Retro. Supp. I:** 172, **184–185; Supp. XIX:** 248

"Acteon" (Stallings), **Supp. XXV:** 231–232

"Actfive" (MacLeish), **III:** 18–19, 22

Actfive and Other Poems (MacLeish), **III:** 3, 17–19, 21

Action (Shepard), **Supp. III Part 2:** 446

Active Anthology (Pound), **Supp. III Part 2:** 617

Active Service (Crane), **I:** 409

"Act of Creation and Its Artifact, The" (Sorrentino), **Supp. XXI:** 229, 235

Act of Love, An (Wolfert), **Supp. XXI:** 270, **275–277**

Act of Love, An: A Completely Retold Version of the Novel (Wolfert), **Supp. XXI:** 276

Acton, Patricia Nassif, **Supp. X:** 233

Actor's Nightmare, The (Durang), **Supp. XXIV:** 116, 119

Acts and Monuments of These Latter and Perilous Days (Fox), **Supp. XXII:** 36

Acts of Faith (Caputo), **Supp. XIX: 29–30**

"Acts of the Apostles, The" (Bronk), **Supp. XXI:** 28

Actual, The (Bellow), **Retro. Supp. II:** 33

"Actual Experience, Preferred Narratives" (Julier), **Supp. IV Part 1:** 211

Acuff, Roy, **Supp. V:** 335

Ada (Nabokov), **Retro. Supp. I:** 265, 266, 270, 276–277, 278, 279

"Ada" (Stein), **IV:** 43

"Adagia" (Stevens), **IV:** 78, 80, 88, 92

"Adagio" (Hull), **Supp. XXI:** 136–137

"Adam" (Hecht), **Supp. X:** 62

"Adam" (W. C. Williams), **Retro. Supp. I:** 422, 423

"Adam and Eve" (Eugene), **Supp. X:** 204

"Adam and Eve" (Shapiro), **Supp. II Part 2:** 708, 712

"Adamantine Practice of Poetry, The" (Wright), **Supp. XV:** 341–342, 343–344

Adam Bede (G. Eliot), **II:** 181

Adamé, Leonard, **Supp. XIII:** 316

Adam & Eve & the City (W. C. Williams), **Retro. Supp. I:** 423

Adamic, Louis, **Supp. XXIII:** 166

"Adamic Purity as Double Agent" (Whalen-Bridge), **Retro. Supp. II:** 211–212

"Adam Robinson Acquires Grandparents and a Little Sister" (P. E. Jones), **Supp. XXII:** 151

"Adams" (Saunders), **Supp. XIX:** 232

Adams, Althea. *See* Thurber, Mrs. James (Althea Adams)

Adams, Annie. *See* Fields, Annie Adams

Adams, Brooks, **Supp. I Part 2:** 484

Adams, Charles, **Supp. I Part 2:** 644

Adams, Charles Francis, **I:** 1, 4; **Supp. I Part 2:** 484

Adams, Franklin P., **Supp. I Part 2:** 653; **Supp. IX:** 190; **Supp. XV:** 294, 297

Adams, Henry, **I: 1–24,** 111, 243, 258; **II:** 278, 542; **III:** 396, 504; **IV:** 191, 349; **Retro. Supp. I:** 53, 59; **Retro. Supp. II:** 207; **Supp. I Part 1:** 299–300, 301, 314; **Supp. I Part 2:** 417, 492, 543, 644; **Supp. II Part 1:** 93–94, 105; **Supp. III Part 2:** 613; **Supp. IV Part 1:** 31, 208; **Supp. XXIV:** 224

Adams, Mrs. Henry (Marian Hooper), **I:** 1, 5, 10, 17–18

Adams, Henry B., **Supp. I Part 1:** 369

Adams, James Truslow, **Supp. I Part 2:** 481, 484, 486

Adams, J. Donald, **IV:** 438

Adams, John, **I:** 1; **II:** 103, 301; **III:** 17, 473; **Supp. I Part 2:** 483, 506, 507, 509, 510, 511, 517, 518, 520, 524

Adams, John Luther, **Supp. XII:** 209

Adams, John Quincy, **I:** 1, 3, 16–17; **Supp. I Part 2:** 685, 686

Adams, Léonie, **Supp. I Part 2:** 707; **Supp. V:** 79; **Supp. IX:** 229; **Supp. XVII:** 75

Adams, Luella, **Supp. I Part 2:** 652

Adams, Noah, **Supp. XVII:** 218

Adams, Phineas, **Supp. XXV:** 37

Adams, Phoebe, **Supp. IV Part 1:** 203; **Supp. VIII:** 124

Adams, Samuel, **Supp. I Part 2:** 516, 525

Adams, Timothy Dow, **Supp. XVI:** 67, 69

Ada; or Ardor (Nabokov), **III:** 247

Adaptation (film), **Supp. XXV:** 160

"Ad Castitatem" (Bogan), **Supp. III Part 1:** 50

Adcock, Betty, **Supp. XVIII:** 181–182, 182

Addams, Jane, **Supp. I Part 1: 1–26; Supp. XI:** 200, 202

Addams, John Huy, **Supp. I Part 1:** 2

"Addendum" (Wright), **Supp. V:** 339

Addiego, John, **Supp. XII:** 182

Adding Machine, The (Rice), **I:** 479

Adding Machine, The: Selected Essays (Burroughs), **Supp. III Part 1:** 93, 97

"Adding to the Unhappiness: Those Poems You Are Writing" (Gallagher), **Supp. XXIV:** 172

Addison, Joseph, **I:** 8, 105, 106–107, 108, 114, 131, 300, 304; **III:** 430

"Address Delivered at Lenox, An" (Channing), **Supp. XXIV: 79–80**

"Addressed to a Political Shrimp, or, Fly upon the Wheel" (Freneau), **Supp. II Part 1:** 267

"Address to My Soul" (Wylie), **Supp. I Part 2:** 729

"Address to the Deist, An" (Wheatley), **Supp. XX: 287**

"Address to the Devil" (Jarman), **Supp. XVII:** 114

Address to the Government of the United States on the Cession of Louisiana to the French, An (Brown), **Supp. I Part 1:** 146

"Address to the Scholars of New England" (Ransom), **III:** 491

"Address with Exclamation Points, A" (Simic), **Supp. VIII:** 283

"Adieu to Norman, Bon Jour to Joan and Jean-Paul"(O'Hara), **Supp. XXIII:** 219

Adisa, Opal Palmer, **Supp. XXII:** 66, 74, 78

"Adjutant Bird, The" (Banks), **Supp. V:** 5

Adkins, Nelson F., **II:** 20

Adler, Alfred, **I:** 248

Adler, Betty, **III:** 103

Adler, George J., **III:** 81

Adler, Renata, **Supp. X:** 171

Admiral of the Ocean Sea: A Life of Christopher Columbus (Morison), **Supp. I Part 2:** 486–488

"Admirals" (Chabon), **Supp. XI:** 72

"Admonition, An" (Brodsky), **Supp. VIII:** 33

"Adolescence" (Bidart), **Supp. XV:** 32

"Adolescence" (Dove), **Supp. IV Part 1:** 245

"Adolescence" (Olds), **Supp. X:** 211

"Adolescence II" (Dove), **Supp. IV Part 1:** 242, 244–245

Adolescent's Christmas, An: 1944 (C. Bly), **Supp. XVI:** 31–32

"Adolf Eichmann" (Carruth), **Supp. XVI:** 47

"Adonais" (Shelley), **II:** 516, 540

Adonai: The Pilgrim of Eternity (Lippard), **Supp. XXIII:** 180, 189, 190

Adorno, Theodor, **Supp. I Part 2:** 645, 650; **Supp. IV Part 1:** 301

"Adrienne Rich: The Poetics of Change" (Gelpi), **Supp. I Part 2:** 554

Adrift in Macao (Durang), **Supp. XXIV:** 125

"Adultery" (Banks), **Supp. V:** 15

"Adultery" (Dubus), **Supp. VII:** 85

Adultery and Other Choices (Dubus), **Supp. VII:** 83–85

Adulthood Rites (O. Butler), **Supp. XIII:** 63, **64–65**

Adult Life of Toulouse Lautrec by Henri Toulouse Lautrec, The (Acker), **Supp. XII:** 5, 6, **8–9**

Adventure (London), **II:** 466

Adventures in Ancient Egypt (Goldbarth), **Supp. XII:** 191

Adventures in Value (Cummings), **I:** 430

"Adventures of a Book Reviewer" (Cowley), **Supp. II Part 1:** 137, 142

Adventures of a Novelist (Atherton), **Supp. XXIV:** 17–18, 19–20, 21

Adventures of Augie March, The (Bellow), **I:** 144, 147, 149, 150, 151, 152–153, 154, 155, 157, 158–159, 164; **Retro. Supp. II:** 19, 20, **22–23**, 24, 30; **Supp. VIII:** 234, 236–237; **Supp. XXIV:** 220

Adventures of a Young Man (Dos Passos), **I:** 488, 489, 492

Adventures of Captain Bonneville (Irving), **II:** 312

Adventures of Harry Franco, The: A Tale of the Great Panic (Briggs), **Supp. XVIII:** 1, 2, 5–8

Adventures of Harry Richmond, The (Meredith), **Supp. XX: 234**

Adventures of Huckleberry Finn, The (Twain), **I:** 307, 506; **II:** 26, 72, 262, 266–268, 290, 418, 430; **III:** 101, 112–113, 357, 554, 558, 577; **IV:** 198, 201–204, 207; **Retro. Supp. I:** 188; **Retro. Supp. II:** 121; **Supp. I Part 1:** 247; **Supp. IV Part 1:** 247, 257; **Supp. IV Part 2:** 502; **Supp. V:** 131; **Supp. VIII:** 198; **Supp. X:** 230; **Supp. XII:** 16; **Supp. XVI:** 222; **Supp. XX: 171; Supp. XXII:** 81

Adventures of Jimmy (Broughton), **Supp. XV:** 146

Adventures of Roderick Random, The (Smollett), **I:** 134

Adventures of the Letter I (Simpson), **Supp. IX:** 266, **273–274**

Adventures of Tom Sawyer, The (Twain), **II:** 26; **III:** 223, 572, 577; **IV:** 199–200, 203, 204; **Supp. I Part 2:** 456, 470; **Supp. XVI:** 66

Adventures While Preaching the Gospel of Beauty (Lindsay), **Supp. I Part 2:** 374, 376, 381, 382–384, 389, 399

Adventures with Ed (Loeffler), **Supp. XIII:** 1

Advertisements for Myself (Mailer), **III:** 27, 35–38, 41–42, 45, 46; **Retro. Supp. II:** 196, 199, 200, 202, 203,

212; **Supp. IV Part 1:** 90, 284; **Supp. XIV:** 157; **Supp. XXIV:** 281

"Advertisements for Myself on the Way Out" (Mailer), **III:** 37

Advice (Bodenheim), **Supp. XXV:** 22

"Advice to a Prophet" (Wilbur), **Supp. III Part 2:** 555–557

Advice to a Prophet and Other Poems (Wilbur), **Supp. III Part 2:** 554–558

"Advice to a Raven in Russia" (Barlow), **Supp. II Part 1:** 65, 74, 80, 83

"Advice to Players" (Bidart), **Supp. XV:** 35

Advice to the Lovelorn (film), **Retro. Supp. II:** 328

Advice to the Privileged Orders, Part I (Barlow), **Supp. II Part 1:** 80

Aegerter, Lindsay Pentolfe, **Supp. XXII:** 69

"Aeneas and Dido" (Brodsky), **Supp. VIII:** 24–25

"Aeneas at Washington" (Tate), **IV:** 129

Aeneid (Virgil), **I:** 396; **II:** 542; **III:** 124; **Supp. XV:** 23; **Supp. XXIV:** 162–163

Aeneus Tacticus, **I:** 136

Aerial View (Barabtarlo), **Retro. Supp. I:** 278

"Aeria the Evanescent" (Sobin), **Supp. XVI:** 292

Aeschylus, **I:** 274, 433; **III:** 398; **IV:** 358, 368, 370; **Retro. Supp. I:** 65; **Supp. I Part 2:** 458, 494

Aesop, **I:** 387; **II:** 154, 169, 302; **III:** 587

Aesthetic (Croce), **III:** 610

"Aesthetics" (Mumford), **Supp. II Part 2:** 476

"Aesthetics of Silence, The" (Sontag), **Supp. III Part 2:** 459

"Aesthetics of the Shah" (Olds), **Supp. X:** 205

"Affair at Coulter's Notch, The" (Bierce), **I:** 202

Affaire de viol, Une (C. Himes). *See Case of Rape, A* (C. Himes)

"Affair of Outposts, An" (Bierce), **I:** 202

Affliction (Banks), **Supp. V:** 15, 16

Affluent Society, The (Galbraith), **Supp. I Part 2:** 648

Afghanistan Picture Show, An: or, How I Saved the World (Vollmann), **Supp. XVII:** 226, **228–229**, 233

"Aficionados, The" (Carver), **Supp. III Part 1:** 137

"Afloat" (Beattie), **Supp. V:** 29

Afloat and Ashore (Cooper), **I:** 351, 355

"Afoot" (P. N. Warren as Kilina), **Supp. XX: 261–262**

Africa, Its Geography, People, and Products (Du Bois), **Supp. II Part 1:** 179

Africa, Its Place in Modern History (Du Bois), **Supp. II Part 1:** 179

"Africa, to My Mother" (D. Diop), **Supp. IV Part 1:** 16

Africana (H. L. Gates, ed.), **Supp. XX: 99**

African American Century, The : How Black Americans Have Shaped Our Country (H. L. Gates), **Supp. XX: 102**

African American Lives (television production), **Supp. XX: 99**

African American Lives 2 (television production), **Supp. XX: 99**

African American National Biography (H. L. Gates, ed.), **Supp. XX: 99**

African American Writers (Smith, ed.), **Supp. XIII:** 115, 127

"African Book" (Hemingway), **II:** 259

"African Chief, The" (Bryant), **Supp. I Part 1:** 168

"African Fragment" (Brooks), **Supp. III Part 1:** 85

African Queen, The (film), **Supp. XI:** 17

"African Roots of War, The" (Du Bois), **Supp. II Part 1:** 174

African Silences (Matthiessen), **Supp. V:** 203

African Treasury, An (Hughes, ed.), **Supp. I Part 1:** 344

"Afrika Revolution" (Baraka), **Supp. II Part 1:** 53

"AFRO-AMERICAN LYRIC" (Baraka), **Supp. II Part 1:** 59

After (Bukiet), **Supp. XVII:** 43, **44–45**

After (Hirshfield), **Supp. XXIII:** 133–135, 139

"After a Greek Proverb" (Stallings), **Supp. XXV:** 225

After All: Last Poems (Matthews), **Supp. IX:** 155, **167–169**

After and Before the Lightning (Ortiz), **Supp. IV Part 2:** 513

"After a Party" (Salinas), **Supp. XIII:** 327

"After Apple-Picking" (Frost), **Retro. Supp. I:** 126, 128

"After Arguing against the Contention That Art Must Come from Discontent" (Stafford), **Supp. XI:** 327

After Confession: Poetry as Autobiography (Harris), **Supp. XIV:** 269

After Confession: Poetry as Autobiography (K. Sontag and D. Graham), **Supp. XV:** 104

"After Cowboy Chicken Came to Town" (Jin), **Supp. XVIII:** 97–98

"After Disappointment" (Jarman), **Supp. XVII:** 118–119

After Disillusion: Poems (Wolf), **Supp. XXII:** 275

"After Edward Hopper: Somebody in a Bar" (Ferry), **Supp. XXIV:** 162

After Experience (Snodgrass), **Supp. VI:** 314–316, 317

"After great pain, a formal feeling comes" (Dickinson), **Retro. Supp. I:** 37

"After Hearing a Waltz by Bartók" (Lowell), **II:** 522

After Henry (Didion), **Supp. IV Part 1:** 195, 196, 199, 207, 208, 211

"After Henry" (Didion), **Supp. IV Part 1:** 211

"After Holbein" (Wharton), **IV:** 325; **Retro. Supp. I:** 382

After House, The (Rinehart), **Supp. XXV:** 193

After Ikkyu and Other Poems (Harrison), **Supp. VIII:** 42

"After-Image" (Bierds), **Supp. XVII:** 31–32

"After-Image" (Caldwell), **I:** 309

After-Images: Autobiographical Sketches (Snodgrass), **Supp. VI:** 314, **319**, **323**, 324, 326–327

After I's (Zukofsky), **Supp. III Part 2:** 628, 629

Afterlife (Monette), **Supp. X:** 153

Afterlife (Updike), **Retro. Supp. I:** 322

Afterlife, The (Levis), **Supp. XI:** 259, **260–264**

"After Magritte" (McClatchy), **Supp. XII:** 264

"After Making Love" (Dunn), **Supp. XI:** 153

Aftermath (Longfellow), **II:** 490

"Aftermath" (Longfellow), **II:** 498

After New Formalism (A. Finch, ed.), **Supp. XVII:** 74

"Afternoon" (Ellison), **Supp. II Part 1:** 238

"Afternoon at MacDowell" (Kenyon), **Supp. VII:** 159

"Afternoon Miracle, An" (O. Henry), **Supp. II Part 1:** 390

Afternoon of a Faun (Hearon), **Supp. VIII: 63–64**

Afternoon of an Author: A Selection of Uncollected Stories and Essays (Fitzgerald), **II:** 94

"Afternoon of a Playwright" (Thurber), **Supp. I Part 2:** 620

Afternoon of the Unreal (Salinas), **Supp. XIII:** 311, **316–318**

"Afternoon with the Old Man, An" (Dubus), **Supp. VII:** 84

"After Punishment Was Done with Me" (Olds), **Supp. X:** 213

"After Reading *Barely and Widely*," (Zukofsky), **Supp. III Part 2:** 625, 631

"After Reading 'In the Clearing' for the Author, Robert Frost" (Corso), **Supp. XII:** 130

"After Reading *Mickey in the Night Kitchen* for the Third Time before Bed" (Dove), **Supp. IV Part 1:** 249

"After Reading the Greek Poet"(Kenny), **Supp. XXIII:** 150

"After Reading Tu Fu, I Go Outside to the Dwarf Orchard" (Wright), **Supp. V:** 343

"After Reading Wang Wei, I Go Outside to the Full Moon" (Wright), **Supp. V:** 343

Aftershocks (Stallings), **Supp. XXV:** 222

"Aftershocks" (Stallings), **Supp. XXV:** 222, 231

After Shocks, Near Escapes (Dobyns), **Supp. XIII: 80–82**

"After Song, An" (W. C. Williams), **Retro. Supp. I:** 413

After Strange Gods (T. S. Eliot), **I:** 588

After Such Knowledge: Memory, History, and the Legacy of the Holocaust (E. Hoffman), **Supp. XVI:** 152–153, **158– 161**

"After the Alphabets" (Merwin), **Supp. III Part 1:** 356

"After the Argument" (Dunn), **Supp. XI:** 149

"After the Baptism" (C. Bly), **Supp. XVI:** 40

"After the Burial" (Lowell), **Supp. I Part 2:** 409

"After the Curfew" (Holmes), **Supp. I Part 1:** 308

"After the Death of John Brown" (Thoreau), **IV:** 185

"After the Denim" (Carver), **Supp. III Part 1:** 144

"After the Dentist" (Swenson), **Supp. IV Part 2:** 645

After the Fall (A. Miller), **III:** 148, 149, 156, 161, 162, 163–165, 166

"After the Fire" (Merrill), **Supp. III Part 1:** 328

"After the Flood" (Sanders), **Supp. XVI:** 274–275

After the Fox (film), **Supp. IV Part 2:** 575

After the Genteel Tradition (Cowley), **Supp. II Part 1:** 143

"After the Heart's Interrogation" (Komunyakaa), **Supp. XIII:** 120

After the Lost Generation: A Critical Study of the Writers of Two Wars (Aldridge), **Supp. IV Part 2:** 680; **Supp. XIX:** 250

"After the Night Office—Gethsemani Abbey" (Merton), **Supp. VIII:** 195–196

After the Others (Weigl), **Supp. XIX:** 282, 283–284

"After the Persian" (Bogan), **Supp. III Part 1:** 64

After the Plague (Boyle), **Supp. XX: 20**

"After the Plague" (Boyle), **Supp. XX: 20**

"After the Pleasure Party" (Melville), **III:** 93

"After the Rain" (Halliday), **Supp. XIX:** 91

"After the Resolution" (Dunn), **Supp. XI:** 151

After the Stroke (Sarton), **Supp. VIII:** 264

"After the Surprising Conversions" (Lowell), **I:** 544, 545; **II:** 550; **Retro. Supp. II:** 187

"After 37 Years My Mother Apologizes for My Childhood" (Olds), **Supp. X:** 208

After This (McDermott), **Supp. XVIII:** 155, **166–167**

Afterthoughts (L. P. Smith), **Supp. XIV:** 339, 345

"Afterthoughts on the Rosenbergs" (Fiedler), **Supp. XIII:** 99

"After Twenty Years" (Rich), **Supp. I Part 2:** 559–560

"Afterwake, The" (Rich), **Supp. I Part 2:** 553

"Afterward" (Wharton), **Retro. Supp. I:** 372

"Afterword"(Hadas), **Supp. XXIII:** 113

"After Working Long" (Kenyon), **Supp. VII:** 170

"After Yitzl" (Goldbarth), **Supp. XII:** 186

"After You, My Dear Alphonse" (Jackson), **Supp. IX:** 119

"After Your Death" (Trethewey), **Supp. XXI:** 255

"After Your Nap" (B. Kelly), **Supp. XVII:** 124

"Again" (Dixon), **Supp. XII:** 157

"Again, Kapowsin" (Hugo), **Supp. VI:** 141

"Again Just Now" (Budbill), **Supp. XIX:** 11

"Against" (Goldbarth), **Supp. XII:** 193

"Against Decoration" (Karr), **Supp. XI:** 248

"Against Epiphanies" (C. Baxter), **Supp. XVII:** 20

Against Interpretation (Sontag), **Supp. III Part 2:** 451, 455; **Supp. XIV:** 15

"Against Interpretation" (Sontag), **Supp. III Part 2:** 456–458, 463

"Against Modernity" (Ozick), **Supp. V:** 272

"Against Nature" (Karr), **Supp. XI:** 243

Against Nature (Updike), **Retro. Supp. I:** 323

Against Our Vanishing: Winter Conversations with Allen Grossman on the Theory and Practice of Poetry (Halliday), **Supp. XIX: 82–84,** 88

"Against Realism" (Halliday), **Supp. XIX:** 93

Against the Cold (Bynner), **Supp. XV:** 51

"Against the Crusades" (Stern), **Supp. IX:** 300

Against the Current: As I Remember F. Scott Fitzgerald (Kroll Ring), **Supp. IX:** 63

Agamben, Giorgio, **Supp. XVI:** 289

Agapida, Fray Antonio (pseudonym). *See* Irving, Washington

"Agassiz" (Lowell), **Supp. I Part 2:** 414, 416

Agassiz, Louis, **II:** 343; **Supp. I Part 1:** 312; **Supp. IX:** 180

Âge cassant, L' (Char; Sobin, trans.), **Supp. XVI:** 282

"Aged Wino's Counsel to a Young Man on the Brink of Marriage, The" (X. J. Kennedy), **Supp. XV:** 156

Agee, Emma, **I:** 26

Agee, James, **I: 25–47,** 293; **IV:** 215; **Supp. IX:** 109; **Supp. XIV:** 92; **Supp. XV:** 143

"Agent, The" (Wilbur), **Supp. III Part 2:** 557–561

Age of Anxiety, The (Auden), **Supp. II Part 1:** 2, 19, 21

"Age of Conformity, The" (Howe), **Supp. VI:** 117

Age of Grief, The: A Novella and Stories (Smiley), **Supp. VI:** 292, **299–301**

Age of Innocence, The (Wharton), **IV:** 320–322, 327–328; **Retro. Supp. I:** 372, 374, **380–381**; **Supp. IV Part 1:** 23

Age of Longing, The (Koestler), **I:** 258

Age of Reason, The (Paine), **Supp. I Part 2:** 503, 515–517, 520

"Age of Strolling, The" (Stern), **Supp. IX:** 297

"Ages, The" (Bryant), **Supp. I Part 1:** 152, 155, 166, 167

"Ages of the Women, The" (Gibran), **Supp. XX: 115**

"Aggrandizement, The" (Bronk), **Supp. XXI:** 32

"Aging" (Jarrell), **II:** 388

Aging and Gender in Literature (George), **Supp. IV Part 2:** 450

"Agio Neró" (Mora), **Supp. XIII:** 224

"Agitato ma non Troppo" (Ransom), **III:** 493

"Agnes of Iowa" (Moore), **Supp. X:** 165, 178

Agnes of Sorrento (Stowe), **Supp. I Part 2:** 592, 595–596

Agnon, S. Y., **Supp. V:** 266; **Supp. XXV:** 267

Agony & the Agony, The (Silver), **Supp. XXIV:** 265, **274–275**

"Agosta the Winged Man and Rasha the Black Dove" (Dove), **Supp. IV Part 1:** 246–247

Agrarian Justice (Paine), **Supp. I Part 2:** 517–518

"Agricultural Show, The" (McKay), **Supp. X:** 139

Agrippa: A Book of the Dead (W. Gibson), **Supp. XVI:** 125

Agua de dos ríos/Water from Two Rivers (Espaillat), **Supp. XXI:** 104, 112–113

Agua Fresca: An Anthology of Raza Poetry (Rodríguez, ed.), **Supp. IV Part 2:** 540

Agua Santa/Holy Water (Mora), **Supp. XIII: 222–225**

Agüero Sisters, The (García), **Supp. XI: 185–190**

Aguiar, Marian, **Supp. XXII:** 68

Aguiar, Sarah Appleton, **Supp. XIII:** 30

Aguilar, Carmen, **Supp. XXIII:** 200

Ah, Wilderness! (O'Neill), **III:** 400–401; **Supp. IV Part 2:** 587

Ah, Wilderness!: The Frontier in American Literature (Humphrey), **Supp. IX:** 104

Ahearn, Barry, **Retro. Supp. I:** 415

Ahearn, Frederick L., Jr., **Supp. XI:** 184

Ahearn, Kerry, **Supp. IV Part 2:** 604

Ahmed Arabi Pasha, **I:** 453

Ahnebrink, Lars, **III:** 328

Ahrens, Sylvia, **Supp. XX: 162**

Ah Sin (Harte), **Supp. II Part 1:** 354–355

"Ah! Sun-flower" (Blake), **III:** 19

Aida (rock musical), **Supp. XXI:** 148

Aidoo, Ama Ato, **Supp. XXII:** 68

AIDS and Its Metaphors (Sontag), **Supp. III Part 2:** 452, 466–468

Aids to Reflection (Coleridge), **II:** 10

Aiieeeee! An Anthology of Asian-American Writers (The Combined Asian Resources Project), **Supp. X:** 292

Aiken, Conrad, **I: 48–70,** 190, 211, 243; **II:** 55, 530, 542; **III:** 458, 460; **Retro. Supp. I:** 55, 56, 57, 58, 60, 62; **Supp. X:** 50, 115; **Supp. XV:** 144, 297, 298,

302, 306, 309; **Supp. XVII:** 135; **Supp. XXIV:** 36; **Supp. XXV:** 19

"Aimless Love" (Collins), **Supp. XXI:** 61

"Aim Was Song, The" (Frost), **Retro. Supp. I:** 133

Ainger, Arthur Campbell, **Supp. XX: 230**

Ainsworth, Linda, **Supp. IV Part 1:** 274

Ainsworth, William, **III:** 423

Air-Conditioned Nightmare, The (H. Miller), **III:** 186

Airing Dirty Laundry (Reed), **Supp. X:** 241

"Air Is Full of Little Holes, The" (Brockmeier), **Supp. XXII:** 60

"Airmail from Mother" (Kooser), **Supp. XIX:** 120

"Air Plant, The" (Crane), **I:** 401

Air Raid: A Verse Play for Radio (MacLeish), **III:** 21

"Airs above the Ground" (Sarton), **Supp. VIII:** 261

Air Tight: A Novel of Red Russia. See We the Living (Rand)

Air Up There, The (film, Glaser), **Supp. XVII:** 9

"Airwaves" (Mason), **Supp. VIII:** 146

Airways, Inc. (Dos Passos), **I:** 482

A Is for Anne: Mistress Hutchinson Disturbs the Commonwealth (Schott), **Supp. XXIII:** 240, **246–247**

"A is for Dining Alone" (M. F. K. Fisher), **Supp. XVII:** 86

Aitken, Robert, **Supp. I Part 2:** 504

Aizenberg, Susan, **Supp. XXI:** 131

Akhmadulina, Bella, **Supp. III Part 1:** 268

Akhmatova, Anna, **Supp. III Part 1:** 268, 269; **Supp. VIII:** 20, 21, 25, 27, 30; **Supp. XXI:** 132

Akhmatova Translations, The (Kenyon), **Supp. VII:** 160

"Akhnilo" (Salter), **Supp. IX:** 260

Akins, Zoë, **Supp. XVI:** 187

Aksenev, Vasily P., **Retro. Supp. I:** 278

"Al Aaraaf" (Poe), **III:** 426–427

Al Aaraaf, Tamerlane, and Minor Poems (Poe), **III:** 410

"Alabama Jones" (Mosher), **Supp. XXII:** 204, 211

"Alain Locke and Cultural Pluralism" (Kallen), **Supp. XIV:** 197

"Alain Locke: Bahá'í Philosopher" (Buck), **Supp. XIV:** 199

Alain Locke: Faith and Philosophy (Buck), **Supp. XIV:** 200

Alarçon, **Supp. XVII:** 74

Alarcón, Justo, **Supp. IV Part 2:** 538, 539, 540

Alarcón, Norma, **Supp. XXIII:** 194, 204–205

À la Recherche du Temps Perdu (Proust), **IV:** 428

"Alarm" (X. J. Kennedy), **Supp. XV:** 163

"Alastor" (Shelley), **Supp. I Part 2:** 728

"Alatus" (Wilbur), **Supp. III Part 2:** 563

Alaya (Hirshfield), **Supp. XXIII:** 131

"Alba" (Creeley), **Supp. IV Part 1:** 150

Alba, Richard D., **Supp. XX: 43**

Albee, Edward, **I: 71–96,** 113; **II:** 558, 591; **III:** 281, 387; **IV:** 4, 230; **Retro. Supp. II:** 104; **Supp. VIII:** 331; **Supp. XIII:** 196, 197; **Supp. XXIV:** 113, 263, 270

Albers, Joseph, **Supp. IV Part 2:** 621

Alberti, Rafael, **Supp. XV:** 75

Albright, Margery, **Supp. I Part 2:** 613

"Album, The" (Morris), **III:** 220

Album, The (Rinehart), **Supp. XXV:** 197, 200

Alcestiad, The (Wilder), **IV:** 357, 374

"Alchemist, The" (Bogan), **Supp. III Part 1:** 50

"Alchemist in the City, The" (Hopkins), **Supp. IV Part 2:** 639

Alchymist's Journal, The (Connell), **Supp. XIV:** 80

"Alcmena" (Winters), **Supp. II Part 2:** 801

Alcott, Abba. See Alcott, Mrs. Amos Bronson (Abigail May)

Alcott, Amos Bronson, **II:** 7, 225; **IV:** 172, 173, 184; **Retro. Supp. I:** 217; **Supp. I Part 1:** 28, 29–32, 35, 39, 41, 45; **Supp. II Part 1:** 290; **Supp. XVI:** 84, 89; **Supp. XXV:** 250

Alcott, Mrs. Amos Bronson (Abigail May), **IV:** 184; **Supp. I Part 1:** 29, 30, 31, 32, 35

Alcott, Anna. See Pratt, Anna

Alcott, Louisa May, **IV:** 172; **Supp. I Part 1: 28–46; Supp. IX:** 128; **Supp. XV:** 338; **Supp. XVI:** 84

Alcott, May, **Supp. I Part 1:** 41

Alcuin: A Dialogue (Brown), **Supp. I Part 1:** 126–127, 133

Alden, Hortense. See Farrell, Mrs. James T. (Hortense Alden)

Alden, John, **I:** 471; **II:** 502–503

"Alder Fork, The" (Leopold), **Supp. XIV:** 186

Aldington, Perdita, **Supp. I Part 1:** 258

Aldington, Richard, **II:** 517; **III:** 458, 459, 465, 472; **Retro. Supp. I:** 63, 127; **Supp. I Part 1:** 257–262, 270

Aldington, Mrs. Richard. See Doolittle, Hilda

Aldo Leopold: His Life and Work (Meine), **Supp. XIV:** 179

"Aldo Leopold's Intellectual Heritage" (Nash), **Supp. XIV:** 191–192

Aldon, Raymond, **Supp. XV:** 297

Aldrich, Thomas Bailey, **II:** 400; **Supp. II Part 1:** 192; **Supp. XIV:** 45; **Supp. XVIII:** 4

Aldrich, Tom, **Supp. I Part 2:** 415

Aldridge, John W., **Supp. I Part 1:** 196; **Supp. IV Part 1:** 286; **Supp. IV Part 2:** 680, 681; **Supp. VIII:** 189; **Supp. XI:** 228; **Supp. XIX:** 250

Aleck Maury Sportsman (Gordon), **II:** 197, 200, 203–204

Alegría, Claribel, **Supp. IV Part 1:** 208

Aleichem, Sholem, **Supp. XXIII:** 4, 7

Aleichem, Sholom, **IV:** 3, 10; **Supp. IV Part 2:** 585

"Alert Lovers, Hidden Sides, and Ice Travelers: Notes on Poetic Form and Energy" (Dunn), **Supp. XI:** 153

"Alesă; Debeljak" (Simic), **Supp. VIII:** 279

"Alex" (Oliver), **Supp. VII:** 232

Alexander, Doris, **Supp. XVII:** 99

Alexander, Elizabeth, **Supp. XVIII:** 171, 185, 186; **Supp. XXI:** 246, 257

Alexander, George, **II:** 331

Alexander, Michael, **Retro. Supp. I:** 293

Alexander, Paul, **Supp. XXV:** 84

"Alexander Crummell Dead" (Dunbar), **Supp. II Part 1:** 207, 208–209

Alexander's Bridge (Cather), **I:** 313, 314, 316–317, 326; **Retro. Supp. I:** 1, 6, 7, 8

Alexander the Great, **IV:** 322

"Alexandra" (Cather), **Retro. Supp. I:** 7, 9, 17

Alexandrov, V. E., **Retro. Supp. I:** 270

Alexie, Sherman, **Supp. XVIII:** 58

Algic Researches (H. Schoolcraft), **Supp. XXIII:** 227

Algonquin Round Table, **Supp. IX:** 190, 191, 197

Algren, Nelson, **I:** 211; **Supp. V:** 4; **Supp. IX: 1–18; Supp. XII:** 126; **Supp. XIII:** 173; **Supp. XIV:** 3; **Supp. XVII:** 161; **Supp. XXI:** 264; **Supp. XXIII:** 165; **Supp. XXV:** 185

Alhambra, The (Irving), **II:** 310–311

Ali, Agha Shahid, **Supp. XVII:** 74

Ali, Ayaan Hirsi, **Supp. XXIV:** 15

Alias Grace (Atwood), **Supp. XIII:** 20, 31–32

Alice (film; Allen), **Supp. XV:** 2, 11

"Alice Doane's Appeal" (Hawthorne), **II:** 227

"Alice Drops Her Cigarette on the Floor ... " (Findley), **Supp. XX: 50–51**

"Alice in the Looking Glass" (Stallings), **Supp. XXV:** 234

Alice in Wonderland (Carroll), **Supp. I Part 2:** 622

Alice Ordered Me to Be Made (Notley), **Supp. XXII:** 224, 227, 228

"Alice Ordered Me to Be Made" (Notley), **Supp. XXII:** 227

Alice's Adventures in Wonderland (Carroll), **Supp. XVI:** 261

"Alicia and I Talking on Edna's Steps" (Cisneros), **Supp. VII:** 64

"Alicia Who Sees Mice" (Cisneros), **Supp. VII:** 60

Alien 3 (screenplay, W. Gibson), **Supp. XVI:** 120, 124

"Ali in Havana" (Talese), **Supp. XVII:** 207, 208

Alison, Archibald, **Supp. I Part 1:** 151, 159

Alison's House (Glaspell), **Supp. III Part 1:** 182, 188, 189

Alive (screenplay, Shanley), **Supp. XIV:** 316

Alive and Writing: Interviews with American Authors of the 1980s (McCaffery and Gregory), **Supp. X:** 260

"Alki Beach" (Hugo), **Supp. VI:** 135

Alla Breve Loving (Wright), **Supp. XV:** 339, 340

"Alla Breve Loving" (Wright), **Supp. XV:** 340

"All Around the Town" (Benét), **Supp. XI:** 48, 58

All at Sea (Lardner), **II:** 427

All Aunt Hagar's Children (E. P. Jones), **Supp. XXII:** 140, 143, **150–153**

"All Aunt Hagar's Children" (E. P. Jones), **Supp. XXII:** 151

"All Boy" (Rawlings), **Supp. X:** 222

Allegiances (Stafford), **Supp. XI: 322–323,** 329

"Allegory of the Cave" (Dunn), **Supp. XI:** 150

"Allegory Unlimited" (Cassill), **Supp. XIX:** 266

Allegro, Johnny (film, Tetzloff), **Supp. XVII:** 62

"Allegro, L' " (Milton), **Supp. XIV:** 8

Allen, Brooke, **Supp. VIII:** 153

Allen, Bruce, **Supp. XXII:** 205, 212; **Supp. XXIII:** 106, 300

Allen, Claudia, **Supp. XXIII:** 79

Allen, Dick, **Supp. IX:** 279

Allen, Donald, **Supp. VIII:** 291; **Supp. XIII:** 112; **Supp. XXIII:** 215, 220

Allen, Frank, **Supp. XI:** 126; **Supp. XII:** 186

Allen, Fred, **Supp. XXV:** 255

Allen, Frederick Lewis, **Supp. I Part 2:** 655

Allen, Gay Wilson, **IV:** 352; **Supp. I Part 2:** 418

Allen, Ivan, **Supp. XXII:** 245

Allen, Paula Gunn. *See* Gunn Allen, Paula

Allen, Robert Moore, **Supp. XX:** 164

Allen, Walter, **I:** 505; **III:** 352; **Supp. IV Part 2:** 685; **Supp. IX:** 231

Allen, Woody, **Supp. I Part 2:** 607, 623; **Supp. IV Part 1:** 205; **Supp. X:** 164; **Supp. XI:** 307; **Supp. XV: 1–18; Supp. XVII:** 48

"Aller et Retour" (Barnes), **Supp. III Part 1:** 36

Aller Retour New York (H. Miller), **III:** 178, 182, 183

Allerton, Isaac, **Supp. XXII:** 44

Allessandrini, Goffredo, **Supp. IV Part 2:** 520

Alleys of Eden, The (R. O. Butler), **Supp. XII:** 62, **62–64,** 68

All God's Children Need Traveling Shoes (Angelou), **Supp. IV Part 1:** 2, 9–10, 12–13, 17

All God's Chillun Got Wings (O'Neill), **III:** 387, 391, 393–394

All Gone (Dixon), **Supp. XII:** 148, 149

"All Hallows" (Glück), **Supp. V:** 82

"All I Can Remember" (Jackson), **Supp. IX:** 115

"Alligators, The" (Updike), **IV:** 219

Allingham, John Till, **Supp. XV:** 243

All in the Family (Boyce), **Supp. XXI:** 8

"ALL IN THE STREET" (Baraka), **Supp. II Part 1:** 53

Allison, Dorothy, **Supp. XVIII:** 195

"All I Want" (Tapahonso), **Supp. IV Part 2:** 508

"All Little Colored Children Should Play the Harmonica" (Patchett), **Supp. XII:** 309

"All Mountains" (Doolittle), **Supp. I Part 1:** 271

All My Friends Are Going to Be Strangers (McMurtry), **Supp. V:** 224, 228, 229

"All My Pretty Ones" (Sexton), **Supp. II Part 2:** 678, 679–683

"All My Pretty Ones" (Sexton), **Supp. II Part 2:** 681–682

"All My Sad Captains" (Jewett), **Retro. Supp. II:** 134

All My Sons (A. Miller), **III:** 148, 149, 150, 151–153, 154, 155, 156, 158, 159, 160, 164, 166

All New People (Lamott), **Supp. XX: 135–136**

"All Night, All Night" (Schwartz), **Supp. II Part 2:** 665

All Night Long (Caldwell), **I:** 297

"All-Night Melodies" (Nelson), **Supp. XVIII:** 185

All-Night Visitors (Major), **Supp. XXII: 173–174**

"All of Us" (Major), **Supp. XXII:** 185

All of Us: The Collected Poems (Carver), **Supp. XXIV:** 167

All of What We Loved (Bronk), **Supp. XXI:** 32

"All Our Lost Children: Trauma and Testimony in the Performance of Childhood" (Pace), **Supp. XI:** 245

All Our Yesterdays (Parker), **Supp. XIX: 187–188**

"All Out" (Hecht), **Supp. X:** 72

All Over (Albee), **I:** 91–94

"Allowance" (Minot), **Supp. VI:** 206, 207–208

"Alloy" (Rukeyser), **Supp. VI:** 279

"All Parrots Speak" (Bowles), **Supp. IV Part 1:** 89

Allport, Gordon, **II:** 363–364

All Quiet on the Western Front (Remarque), **Supp. IV Part 1:** 380, 381

"ALL REACTION IS DOOMED-!-!-!" (Baraka), **Supp. II Part 1:** 59

"All Revelation" (Frost), **II:** 160–162

Allsburg, Christ Van, **Supp. XXV:** 83, 87

"All Shall Love Me and Despair"(Thompson), **Supp. XXIII:** 295

All Shot Up (C. Himes), **Supp. XVI:** 143, 144

"All Souls" (Gioia), **Supp. XV:** 117

"All Souls" (Wharton), **IV:** 315–316; **Retro. Supp. I:** 382

"All Souls' Night" (Yeats), **Supp. X:** 69

All Souls' Rising (Bell), **Supp. X:** 12, **13–16, 17**

"All-Star Literary Vaudeville" (Wilson), **IV:** 434–435

Allston, Washington, **II:** 298

All Stories Are True (Wideman), **Supp. X:** 320

"All That Is" (Wilbur), **Supp. III Part 2:** 563

All That Was Possible (Sturgis), **Supp. XX: 227, 232, 235–237**

"All the Bearded Irises of Life: Confessions of a Homospiritual" (Walker),

Supp. III Part 2: 527

"All the Beautiful Are Blameless" (Wright), **Supp. III Part 2:** 597

ALL: The Collected Poems, 1956–1964 (Zukofsky), **Supp. III Part 2:** 630

ALL: The Collected Short Poems, 1923–1958 (Zukofsky), **Supp. III Part 2:** 629

All the Conspirators (Isherwood), **Supp. XIV:** 156, 159, 160

All the Dark and Beautiful Warriors (Hansberry), **Supp. IV Part 1:** 360, 374

All the Days and Nights: The Collected Stories (Maxwell), **Supp. VIII:** 151, 158, 169

"All the Dead Dears" (Plath), **Retro. Supp. II:** 246; **Supp. I Part 2:** 537

"All the Dead"(P. Benedict), **Supp. XXIII:** 37

All the Good People I've Left Behind (Oates), **Supp. II Part 2:** 510, 522, 523

"All the Hippos Were Boiled in Their Tanks" (Burroughs and Kerouac), **Supp. III Part 1:** 94

All the King's Men (Warren), **I:** 489; **IV:** 243, 248–249, 252; **Supp. V:** 261; **Supp. VIII:** 126; **Supp. X:** 1; **Supp. XVIII:** 77, 79; **Supp. XXIV:** 226

All the Little Live Things (Stegner), **Supp. IV Part 2:** 599, 604, 605, 606, 609–610, 611, 613

All the Pretty Horses (film), **Supp. VIII:** 175

All the Pretty Horses (McCarthy), **Supp. VIII:** 175, **182–183,** 188

All the Sad Young Men (Fitzgerald), **II:** 94; **Retro. Supp. I:** 108

"All the Time in the World" (Dubus), **Supp. VII:** 91

"All the Way to Flagstaff, Arizona" (Bausch), **Supp. VII:** 47, 49

"All This and More" (Karr), **Supp. XI:** 243

All Tomorrow's Parties (W. Gibson), **Supp. XVI:** 119, 121, 123, 124, **130**

"All Too Real" (Vendler), **Supp. V:** 189

All Trivia: Triva, More Trivia, Afterthoughts, Last Words (L. P. Smith), **Supp. XIV:** 339

All-True Travels and Adventures of Lidie Newton (Smiley), **Supp. VI:** 292, **305–307**

All We Need of Hell (Crews), **Supp. XI:** **114**

Almack, Edward, **Supp. IV Part 2:** 435

al-Maghut, Muhammad, **Supp. XIII:** 278

"Almanac" (Swenson), **Supp. IV Part 2:** 641

Almanac of the Dead (Silko), **Supp. IV Part 2:** 558–559, 560, 561, 570–571

Alma: or, The Dead Women (Notley), **Supp. XXII:** 223, 224, 231, 236

Almon, Bert, **Supp. IX:** 93

"Almost" (Untermeyer), **Supp. XV:** 304

Almost Learning to Live in This World (Schott), **Supp. XXIII:** **247–248**

Almost Revolution, The (Priaulx and Ungar), **Supp. XI:** 228

Alnilam (Dickey), **Supp. IV Part 1:** 176, 186, 188–189

"Alone" (Caputo), **Supp. XIX:** 29

"Alone" (Levine), **Supp. V:** 184, 185, 186

"Alone" (Pickering), **Supp. XXI:** 204

"Alone" (Poe), **Retro. Supp. II:** 266

"Alone" (Singer), **IV:** 15

"Alone" (Winters), **Supp. II Part 2:** 786, 811

"Alone and Lonely" (Budbill), **Supp. XIX:** 10

Aloneness (Brooks), **Supp. III Part 1:** 85, 86

Alone with America (Corso), **Supp. XII:** 131

Alone with America (Howard), **Supp. IX:** 326

"Along America's Edges" (Sobin), **Supp. XVI:** 288

"Along the Color Line" (Du Bois), **Supp. II Part 1:** 173

Along the Illinois (Masters), **Supp. I Part 2:** 472

Alouette, L' (Anouilh), *Supp. I Part 1:* 286–288

"Alphabet" (Nye), **Supp. XIII:** 283

Alphabet, An (Doty), **Supp. XI:** 120

Alphabet for Gourmets, An (M. F. K. Fisher), **Supp. XVII:** 86, 87, 92

Alphabet of Grace, The (Buechner), **Supp. XII:** 52

"Alphabet of My Dead, An" (Pinsky), **Supp. VI:** 235, 250

"Alphabet of Subjects, An" (Zukofsky), **Supp. III Part 2:** 624

"Alpine Christ, The" (Jeffers), **Supp. II Part 2:** 415, 419

Alpine Christ and Other Poems, The (Jeffers), **Supp. II Part 2:** 419

"Alpine Idyll, An" (Hemingway), **II:** 249; **Retro. Supp. I:** 176

Al Que Quiere! (W. C. Williams), **Retro. Supp. I:** 414, 416, **417,** 428

Alraune (Ewers; Endore, trans.), **Supp. XVII:** 54

Alsop, Joseph, **II:** 579

"Altar, The" (Herbert), **Supp. IV Part 2:** 646

"Altar, The" (MacLeish), **III:** 4

"Altar Boy" (Fante), **Supp. XI:** 160, 164

"Altar of the Dead, The" (James), **Retro. Supp. I:** 229

"Altars in the Street, The" (Levertov), **Supp. III Part 1:** 280

Alter, Robert, **Supp. XII:** 167

Altgeld, John Peter, **Supp. I Part 2:** 382, 455

Althea (Masters), **Supp. I Part 2:** 455, 459

Altick, Richard, **Supp. I Part 2:** 423

Altieri, Charles, **Supp. VIII:** 297, 303; **Supp. XXIII:** 220

Altman, Robert, **Supp. IX:** 143; **Supp. XXIV:** 166, 172

"Alto" (C. Frost), **Supp. XV:** 101

"Altra Ego" (Brodsky), **Supp. VIII:** 31–32

Altruists, The (Silver), **Supp. XXIV:** **273**

A Lume Spento (Pound), **Retro. Supp. I:** 283, 285

"Aluminum House" (F. Barthelme), **Supp. XI:** 26

Alvares, Mosseh, **Supp. V:** 11

Alvarez, A., **Supp. I Part 2:** 526, 527; **Supp. II Part 1:** 99; **Supp. IX:** 248

Alvarez, Joseph A., **Supp. XXII:** 13–14

Alvarez, Julia, **Supp. VII:** **1–21;** **Supp. XI:** 177; **Supp. XVII:** 71, 112; **Supp. XXIV:** 86, 89

"Always a Rose" (L.-Y. Lee), **Supp. XV:** 215, 216

"Always in Good Humor" (Adams), **Supp. XV:** 294

Always Outnumbered, Always Outgunned (Mosley), **Supp. XIII:** 242

"Always the Stories" (Ortiz), **Supp. IV Part 2:** 499, 500, 502, 504, 512

Always the Young Strangers (Sandburg), **III:** 577–578, 579

Always Young and Fair (Richter), **Supp. XVIII:** **215–216**

Amadeus (Shaffer), **Supp. XIV:** 330

"Amahl and the Night Visitors: A Guide to the Tenor of Love" (Moore), **Supp. X:** 167

"Am and Am Not" (Olds), **Supp. X:** 212

"Amanita, The" (Francis), **Supp. IX:** 81

Amaranth (Robinson), **III:** 509, 510, 512, 513, 522, 523

"Amateur Iconography: Resurrection" (Stallings), **Supp. XXV:** 233

"Amateurs, The" (Swados), **Supp. XIX:** 256

Amazing Adele, The (Barillet and Grédy; Loos, trans.), **Supp. XVI:** 194

Amazing Adventures of Kavalier and Clay, The (Chabon), **Supp. XI:** 68, 76, **77–80; Supp. XXII:** 49

Amazing Adventures of Leticia Carberry (Rinehart), **Supp. XXV:** 194

Amazing Adventures of the Escapist, The (Chabon, ed.), **Supp. XIX:** 174

Amazing Interlude, The (Rinehart), **Supp. XXV:** 194

Amazing Science Fiction Stories, **Supp. XVI:** 121

Amazons: An Intimate Memoir by the First Woman to Play in the National Hockey League (DeLillo), **Supp. VI:** 2

Ambassador Morgenthau's Story (Morgenthau), **Supp. XXIII:** 21, 22

Ambassador of Peace, An (Abernon), **Supp. XVI:** 191

Ambassadors, The (H. James), **II:** 320, 333–334, 600; **III:** 517; **IV:** 322; **Retro. Supp. I:** 215, 218, 219, 220, 221, **232–233**

Ambelain, Robert, **Supp. I Part 1:** 260, 273, 274

"Ambition Bird, The" (Sexton), **Supp. II Part 2:** 693

Ambition: The Secret Passion (Epstein), **Supp. XIV:** 113–114

Ambler, Eric, **III:** 57

Ambrose Holt and Family (Glaspell), **Supp. III Part 1:** 175, 181, 184, 187, 188

"Ambrose Seyffert" (Masters), **Supp. I Part 2:** 464

"Ambush" (Komunyakaa), **Supp. XIII:** 122

Amen Corner, The (Baldwin), **Retro. Supp. II:** 5, 7; **Supp. I Part 1:** 48, 51, 54, 55, 56

America (Benét), **Supp. XI:** 46, 47, 51

"America" (Ginsberg), **Supp. II Part 1:** 58–59, 317

"America" (song), **IV:** 410

"America, America!" (poem) (Schwartz), **Supp. II Part 2:** 665

"America, Commerce, and Freedom" (Rowson and Reinagle), **Supp. XV:** 240

"America, Home of the Red Man" (Zitkala-Ša), **Supp. XXV:** 281

"America, Seen Through Photographs, Darkly" (Sontag), **Supp. III Part 2:** 464

"America! America!" (story) (Schwartz), **Supp. II Part 2:** 640, 658–659, 660

America and Americans (Steinbeck), **IV:** 52

"America and the Vidal Chronicles" (Pease), **Supp. IV Part 2:** 687

America as a Civilization (Lerner), **III:** 60

America Behind the Color Line (H. L. Gates), **Supp. XX:** 102, 105

America Beyond the Color Line (television program), **Supp. XX:** 99

America Hispana: A Portrait and a Prospect (W. Frank), **Supp. XX:** 76

"America Independent" (Freneau), **Supp. II Part 1:** 261

America Is Worth Saving (Dreiser), **Retro. Supp. II:** 96

American, The (James), **I:** 226; **II:** 326–327, 328, 331, 334; **IV:** 318; **Retro. Supp. I:** 220, **221**, 228, 376, 381

Americana (DeLillo), **Supp. VI:** 2, **3**, 5, 6, 8, 13, 14

American Adam, The (R. W. B. Lewis), **II:** 457–458; **Supp. XIII:** 93

American Almanac (Leeds), **II:** 110

American Anthem (Doctorow and Suares), **Supp. IV Part 1:** 234

"American Apocalypse" (Gunn Allen), **Supp. IV Part 1:** 325

American Aristocracy (film), **Supp. XVI:** 185–186

American Blood, (Nichols), **Supp. XIII:** 268

American Blues (T. Williams), **IV:** 381, 383

American Buffalo (Mamet), **Supp. XIV:** 239, 241, 242, 244–245, 246, 254, 255

American Caravan: A Yearbook of American Literature (Mumford, ed.), **Supp. II Part 2:** 482

American Cause, The (MacLeish), **III:** 3

American Childhood, An (Dillard), **Supp. VI:** **19–21**, 23, 24, 25, 26, 30, 31

"American Childhood in the Dominican Republic, An" (Alvarez), **Supp. VII:** 2, 5

American Child Supreme, An: The Education of a Liberation Ecologist

(Nichols), **Supp. XIII:** 256, 257, 258, 264, 265, 266, 267, 268, 269

American Civilization (C. L. R. James), **Supp. XXI:** 169

American Claimant, The (Twain), **IV:** 194, 198–199

American Crisis I (Paine), **Supp. I Part 2:** 508

American Crisis II (Paine), **Supp. I Part 2:** 508

American Crisis XIII (Paine), **Supp. I Part 2:** 509

"American Critic, The" (J. Spingarn), **I:** 266

American Culture, Canons, and the Case of Elizabeth Stoddard (Smith and Weinauer), **Supp. XV:** 270

American Daughter, An (Wasserstein), **Supp. XV:** **330–332**, 333

American Democrat, The (Cooper), **I:** 343, 346, 347, 353

American Desert (Everett), **Supp. XVIII:** **62–63**

American Diary (Webb), **Supp. I Part 1:** 5

American Drama since World War II (Weales), **IV:** 385

American Dream, An (Mailer), **III:** 27, 33–34, 35, 39, 41, 43, 44; **Retro. Supp. II:** 203, **204–205**

American Dream, The (Albee), **I:** 74–76, 77, 89, 94; **Supp. XXIV:** 113

"American Dreams" (Simpson), **Supp. IX:** 274

American Earth (Caldwell), **I:** 290, 308

"American Emperors" (Poirier), **Supp. IV Part 2:** 690

American English (Marckwardt), **Supp. XXIV:** 255

American Exodus, An (Lange and Taylor), **I:** 293

American Experience, The (Parkes), **Supp. I Part 2:** 617–618

American Express (Corso), **Supp. XII:** 129

"American Express" (Salter), **Supp. IX:** 260–261

"American Fear of Literature, The" (Lewis), **II:** 451

American Female Patriotism (S. Warner as Wetherell), **Supp. XVIII:** **260–261**, 262, 263

American Fictions (Hardwick), **Supp. X:** 171

American Fictions, 1940–1980 (Karl), **Supp. IV Part 1:** 384; **Supp. XXI:** 234

"American Financier, The" (Dreiser), **II:** 428

American Folkways (book series), **I:** 290

American Guerilla in the Philippines (Wolfert), **Supp. XXI:** 267

"American Heart of Darkness: The Moral Vision of Five Novels of the Vietnam War" (Palm), **Supp. XXII:** 103

American Heroine: The Life and Legend of Jane Addams (A. F. Davis), **Supp. I Part 1:** 1

American Historical Novel, The (Leisy), **Supp. II Part 1:** 125

"American Horse" (Erdrich), **Supp. IV Part 1:** 333

American Humor: A Study of the National Character (Rourke), **IV:** 339, 352; **Supp. XIX:** 147

American Hunger (Wright), **Supp. IV Part 1:** 11

"American Husband, The" (Atherton), **Supp. XXIV:** 24

American Indian Anthology, An (Tvedten, ed.), **Supp. IV Part 2:** 505

American Indian Stories (Zitkala-Ša), **Supp. XXV:** 272–273, 282–283, 284–285

"American Indian Women: At the Center of Indigenous Resistance in Contemporary North America" (Jaimes and Halsey), **Supp. IV Part 1:** 331

"American in England, An" (Wylie), **Supp. I Part 2:** 707

Americanize the First American (Zitkala-Ša), **Supp. XXV:** 283

American Jitters, The: A Year of the Slump (Wilson), **IV:** 427, 428

American Journal (Hayden), **Supp. II Part 1:** 367

American Journey: The Times of Robert F. Kennedy (Plimpton, ed.), **Supp. XVI:** 245

"American Land Ethic, An" (Momaday), **Supp. IV Part 2:** 488

American Landscape, The, **Supp. I Part 1:** 157

American Language, The (Mencken), **II:** 289, 430; **III:** 100, 104, 105, 108, 111, 119–120

American Language, The: Supplement One (Mencken), **III:** 111

American Language, The: Supplement Two (Mencken), **III:** 111

"American Letter" (MacLeish), **III:** 13

"American Liberty" (Freneau), **Supp. II Part 1:** 257

"American Life in Poetry" (column, Kooser), **Supp. XIX:** 116, 127

American Literary History (Harrison), **Supp. VIII:** 37

American Mercury, **Supp. XI:** 163, 164

American Mind, The (Commager), **Supp. I Part 2:** 650

American Moderns: Bohemian New York and the Creation of a New Century (Stansell), **Supp. XVII:** 106

American Moderns: From Rebellion to Conformity (Geismar), **Supp. IX:** 15; **Supp. XI:** 223

"American Names" (Benét), **Supp. XI:** 47

American Nature Writers (Elder, ed.), **Supp. IX:** 25

American Nature Writers (Winter), **Supp. X:** 104

American Negro, The (W. H. Thomas), **Supp. II Part 1:** 168

American Notebooks, The (Hawthorne), **II:** 226

American Novel Since World War II, The (Klein, ed.), **Supp. XI:** 233

Americano, The (film), **Supp. XVI:** 185

"American Original, An: Learning from a Literary Master" (Wilkinson), **Supp. VIII:** 164, 165, 168

American Ornithology (Wilson), **Supp. XVI:** 4, 6

American Pastoral (P. Roth), **Retro. Supp. II:** 279, 289, **292–293; Supp. XI:** 68

American Places (Porter, Stegner and Stegner), **Supp. IV Part 2:** 599

"American Poet" (Shapiro), **Supp. II Part 2:** 701

"American Poetry" (Simpson), **Supp. IX:** 272

American Poetry, 1922: A Miscellany (Untermeyer, ed.), **Supp. XV:** 306

"American Poetry and American Life" (Pinsky), **Supp. VI:** 239–240

American Poetry from the Beginning to Whitman (Untermeyer, ed.), **Supp. XV:** 310

American Poetry since 1900 (Untermeyer, ed.), **Supp. XV:** 306

American Poetry since 1945: A Critical Survey (Stepanchev), **Supp. XI:** 312

American Poetry since 1960 (Mesic), **Supp. IV Part 1:** 175

American Poets since World War II Dictionary of Literary Biography (Gwynn, ed.), **Supp. XV:** 343

American Primer, An (Boorstin), **I:** 253

American Primer, An (Whitman), **IV:** 348

"American Primitive" (W. J. Smith), **Supp. XIII:** 333

American Primitive: Poems (Oliver), **Supp. VII:** 234–237, 238

American Procession, An: The Major American Writers from 1830–1930—the Crucial Century (Kazin), **Supp. VIII:** 105–106, 108

"American Prose Writers" articles (Briggs), **Supp. XVIII:** 11

American Radio Company, The (radio show, Keillor), **Supp. XVI:** 176–177

"American Realist Playwrights, The" (McCarthy), **II:** 562

American Register, or General Repository of History, Politics, and Science, The (Brown, ed.), **Supp. I Part 1:** 146

American Renaissance (Matthiessen), **I:** 259–260; **III:** 310; **Supp. XIII:** 93

"American Rendezvous, An" (Beauvoir), **Supp. IX:** 4

American Scene, The (James), **II:** 336; **III:** 460; **Retro. Supp. I:** 232, 235

American Scenes (Kozlenko, ed.), **IV:** 378

"American Scholar, The" (Emerson), **I:** 239; **II:** 8, 12–13; **Retro. Supp. I:** 62, 74–75, 149, 298; **Retro. Supp. II:** 155; **Supp. I Part 2:** 420; **Supp. IX:** 227, 271; **Supp. XIV:** 104

"American Scholar, The" (Pickering), **Supp. XXI:** 196

Americans in England; or, Lessons for Daughters (Rowson), **Supp. XV:** 240

"American Soldier, The" (Freneau), **Supp. II Part 1:** 269

American Songbag, The (Sandburg), **III:** 583

"American Student in Paris, An" (Farrell), **II:** 45

"American Sublime, The" (Stevens), **IV:** 74

American Taliban (Abraham), **Supp. XXIV:** 2, **12–14**

"American Tar, The; or, The Press Gang Defeated" (Rowson and Taylor), **Supp. XV:** 238

"American Temperament, The" (Locke), **Supp. XIV:** 211

American Tragedy, An (Dreiser), **I:** 497, 498, 499, 501, 502, 503, 511–515, 517, 518, 519; **III:** 251; **IV:** 35, 484; **Retro. Supp. II:** 93, 95, **104–108; Supp. XVII:** 155

"American Triptych" (Kenyon), **Supp. VII:** 165

"American Use for German Ideals" (Bourne), **I:** 228

American Village, The (Freneau), **Supp. II Part 1:** 256, 257

"American Village, The" (Freneau), **Supp. II Part 1:** 256

American Wives and English Husbands (Atherton), **Supp. XXIV:** 18, 22

America's Coming-of-Age (Brooks), **I:** 228, 230, 240, 245, 258; **IV:** 427

America's Humor: From Poor Richard to Doonesbury (Blair and Hill), **Retro. Supp. II:** 286

"America's Indian Problem" (Zitkala-Ša), **Supp. XXV:** 282

"America's Part in World Peace" (Locke), **Supp. XIV:** 208

America's Rome (Vance), **Supp. IV Part 2:** 684

America: The Story of a Free People (Commager and Nevins), **I:** 253

America Was Promises (MacLeish), **III:** 16, 17

"Amerika" (Snyder), **Supp. VIII:** 301

Ames, Christopher, **Supp. XVIII:** 242–243

Ames, Fisher, **Supp. I Part 2:** 486

Ames, Lois, **Supp. I Part 2:** 541, 547

Ames, William, **IV:** 158

Ames Stewart, Beatrice, **Supp. IX:** 200

Amichai, Yehuda, **Supp. XI:** 267

Amick, Steve, **Supp. XXII:** 205, 216

Amidon, Stephen, **Supp. XI:** 333

Amiel, Henri F., **I:** 241, 243, 250

Amis, Kingsley, **IV:** 430; **Supp. IV Part 2:** 688; **Supp. VIII:** 167; **Supp. XIII:** 93; **Supp. XV:** 117

Amis, Martin, **Retro. Supp. I:** 278

"Amish, The"(Thompson), **Supp. XXIII:** 295–296

"Amity Hills" (Skloot), **Supp. XX: 204**

Ammons, A. R., **Supp. III Part 2:** 541; **Supp. VII: 23–38; Supp. IX:** 41, 42, 46; **Supp. XII:** 121; **Supp. XV:** 115; **Supp. XVII:** 242; **Supp. XIX:** 83

Ammons, Elizabeth, **Retro. Supp. I:** 364, 369; **Retro. Supp. II:** 140

Amnesia Moon (Lethem), **Supp. XVIII:** 136, **138–139**

"Among Children" (Levine), **Supp. V:** 192

Among Friends (M. F. K. Fisher), **Supp. XVII:** 89, 90–91, 92

Among My Books (Lowell), **Supp. I Part 2:** 407

"Among School Children" (Yeats), **III:** 249; **Supp. IX:** 52; **Supp. XIV:** 8

"Among the Hills" (Whittier), **Supp. I Part 2:** 703

Among the Isles of Shoals (Thaxter), **Supp. XIII:** 152

"Among Those Present" (Benét), **Supp. XI:** 53

"Amoral Moralist" (White), **Supp. I Part 2:** 648

Amory, Cleveland, **Supp. I Part 1:** 316

Amory, Fred, **Supp. III Part 1:** 2

Amos (biblical book), **II:** 166

Amos and Andy (television program), **Supp. XX: 103**

Amplitude (Gallagher), **Supp. XXIV:** 166, 170

Amran, David, **Supp. XIV:** 150

"Am Strand von Tanger" (Salter), **Supp. IX:** 257

"AMTRAK" (Baraka), **Supp. II Part 1:** 60

"Amulet, The" (Antin), **Supp. XX: 10**

"Amulets" (Hull), **Supp. XXI:** 139

Amy and Isabelle (film), **Supp. XXIII:** 275–276

Amy and Isabelle (Strout), **Supp. X:** 86; **Supp. XXIII:** 273, 274–275, **276–278,** 285

"Amy Lowell of Brookline, Mass." (Scott), **II:** 512

Amy Lowell: Portrait of the Poet in Her Time (Gregory), **II:** 512

"Amy Wentworth" (Whittier), **Supp. I Part 2:** 694, 696

Anabase (Perse), **III:** 12

"Anabasis (I)" (Merwin), **Supp. III Part 1:** 342, 346

"Anabasis (II)" (Merwin), **Supp. III Part 1:** 342, 346

Anagrams: A Novel (Moore), **Supp. X:** 163, 164, 167, **169–171,** 172

Analects (Confucius), **Supp. IV Part 1:** 14

Analects, The (Pound, trans.), **III:** 472

Analogy (J. Butler), **II:** 8

"Analysis of a Theme" (Stevens), **IV:** 81

Anarchiad, The, A Poem on the Restoration of Chaos and Substantial Night, in Twenty Four Books (Barlow), **Supp. II Part 1:** 70

Anarchist Woman, An (Hapgood), **Supp. XVII:** 102–103; **Supp. XXI:** 5

Anatomy Lesson, and Other Stories, The (Connell), **Supp. XIV:** 84, 87, 89

"Anatomy Lesson, The" (Connell), **Supp. XIV:** 84, 86, 87

Anatomy Lesson, The (P. Roth), **Retro. Supp. II:** 286, 290; **Supp. III Part 2:** 422–423, 425

"Anatomy Lesson of Dr. Nicholaas Tulp, Amsterdam, 1632, The" (Bierds), **Supp. XVII:** 27–28

Anatomy of Criticism (Frye), **Supp. XIII:** 19; **Supp. XIV:** 15

Anatomy of Melancholy (Burton), **III:** 78; **Supp. XVII:** 229

Anatomy of Nonsense, The (Winters), **Supp. II Part 2:** 811, 812

Anaya, Rudolfo A., **Supp. IV Part 2:** 502; **Supp. XIII:** 213, 220; **Supp. XIX:** 97

"Ancestor" (A. Finch), **Supp. XVII:** 72

Ancestors (Atherton), **Supp. XXIV:** 23, 25

Ancestors (Maxwell), **Supp. VIII:** 152, 168

"Ancestors, The" (Tate), **IV:** 128

Ancestral Voice: Conversations with N. Scott Momaday (Woodard), **Supp. IV Part 2:** 484, 485, 486, 489, 493

"Anchorage" (Harjo), **Supp. XII:** 220–221

Ancient Child, The: A Novel (Momaday), **Supp. IV Part 2:** 488, 489–491, 492, 493

"Ancient Dog Grave, Unearthed During Construction of the Athens Metro, An" (Stallings), **Supp. XXV:** 232

"Ancient Egypt/Fannie Goldbarth" (Goldbarth), **Supp. XII:** 191–192

Ancient Evenings (Mailer), **Retro. Supp. II:** 206, 210, 213

Ancient Law, The (Glasgow), **II:** 179–180, 192

Ancient Musics (Goldbarth), **Supp. XII:** 191–192

"Ancient Semitic Rituals for the Dead" (Goldbarth), **Supp. XII:** 191–192

Ancient Track, The (Lovecraft), **Supp. XXV:** 120

"Ancient World, The" (Doty), **Supp. XI:** 122

& (And) (Cummings), **I:** 429, 431, 432, 437, 445, 446, 448

Andersen, Hans Christian, **I:** 441; **Supp. I Part 2:** 622

Andersen, Hendrik Christian, **Supp. XX:** 232

Anderson, Charles R., **Supp. I Part 1:** 356, 360, 368, 371, 372

Anderson, Frances, **I:** 231

Anderson, Guy, **Supp. X:** 264, 265

Anderson, Henry J., **Supp. I Part 1:** 156

Anderson, Irwin M., **I:** 98–99

Anderson, Mrs. Irwin M., **I:** 98–99

Anderson, Jon, **Supp. V:** 338

Anderson, Judith, **III:** 399

Anderson, Karl, **I:** 99, 103

Anderson, Lorraine, **Supp. XVIII:** 189

Anderson, Margaret, **I:** 103; **III:** 471; **Supp. XXV:** 18

Anderson, Margaret Bartlett, **III:** 171

Anderson, Marian, **Supp. XXII:** 283

Anderson, Mary Jane. *See* Lanier, Mrs. Robert Sampson (Mary Jane Anderson)

Anderson, Maxwell, **III:** 159

Anderson, Quentin, **Retro. Supp. I:** 392

Anderson, Robert, **Supp. I Part 1:** 277; **Supp. V:** 108

Anderson, Sally, **Supp. XIII:** 95

Anderson, Sherwood, **I: 97–120,** 211, 374, 375, 384, 405, 423, 445, 480, 487, 495, 506, 518; **II:** 27, 38, 44, 55, 56, 68, 250–251, 263, 271, 289, 451, 456–457; **III:** 220, 224, 382–383, 453, 483, 545, 576, 579; **IV:** 27, 40, 46, 190, 207, 433, 451, 482; **Retro. Supp. I:** 79, 80, 177; **Supp. I Part 2:** 378, 430, 459, 472, 613; **Supp. IV Part 2:** 502; **Supp. V:** 12, 250; **Supp. VIII:** 39, 152; **Supp. IX:** 14, 309; **Supp. XI:** 159, 164; **Supp. XII:** 343; **Supp. XV:** 298; **Supp. XVI:** 17, 20; **Supp. XVII:** 105; **Supp. XX: 69, 75; Supp. XXIII:** 68, 162, 164; **Supp. XXIV:** 136; **Supp. XXV:** 18

Anderson, Mrs. Sherwood (Tennessee Mitchell), **I:** 100; **Supp. I Part 2:** 459, 460

Anderson, T. J., **Supp. XIII:** 132

Anderson, Wendy, **Supp. XXI:** 255

Anderssen, A., **III:** 252

"And Hickman Arrives" (Ellison), **Retro. Supp. II:** 118, 126; **Supp. II Part 1:** 248

And in the Hanging Gardens (Aiken), **I:** 63

"And It Came to Pass" (Wright), **Supp. XV:** 348

And I Worked at the Writer's Trade (Cowley), **Supp. II Part 1:** 137, 139, 141, 143, 147, 148

"...And Ladies of the Club" (J. W. Miller), **Supp. XX: 161**

And Live Apart (Peacock), **Supp. XIX: 196–197**

Andorra (Cameron), **Supp. XII:** 79, 81, **88–91**

"—and Other Poets" (column; Untermeyer), **Supp. XV:** 294

"—and Other Poets" (Untermeyer), *Supp. XV:* 297

Andral, Gabriel, **Supp. I Part 1:** 302

Andre, Michael, **Supp. XII:** 117–118, 129, 132, 133–134

"Andrea Is Changing Her Name" (Brockmeier), **Supp. XXII:** 61

Andre's Mother (McNally), **Supp. XIII:** 206

Andress, Ursula, **Supp. XI:** 307

"Andrew Jackson" (Masters), **Supp. I Part 2:** 472

Andrews, Bruce, **Supp. IV Part 2:** 426

Andrews, Peter, **Supp. XX: 87**

Andrews, Roy Chapman, **Supp. X:** 172

Andrews, Tom, **Supp. XI:** 317

Andrews, Wayne, **IV:** 310

Andrews, William L., **Supp. IV Part 1:** 13; **Supp. XIX:** 72; **Supp. XX: 105**

Andrews, William P., **Supp. XXV:** 250

Andreyev, Leonid Nikolaevich, **I:** 53; **II:** 425

Andria (Terence), **IV:** 363

"Androgynous Kiss" (Gallagher), **Supp. XXIV:** 170

"Andromache" (Dubus), **Supp. VII:** 84

"And Summer Will Not Come Again" (Plath), **Retro. Supp. II:** 242

"And That Night Clifford Died" (Levine), **Supp. V:** 195

And the Band Played On (Shilts), **Supp. X:** 145

"And the Moon Be Still as Bright" (Bradbury), **Supp. IV Part 1:** 106

"And the Sea Shall Give up Its Dead" (Wilder), **IV:** 358

And Things That Go Bump in the Night (McNally), **Supp. XIII: 196–197,** 205, 208

And to Think That I Saw It on Mulberry Street (Geisel), **Supp. XVI:** 100, 101, 104

"And *Ut Pictura Poesis* Is Her Name" (Ashbery), **Supp. III Part 1:** 19

And We Are Millions (Ryan), **Supp. XVIII:** 225

"And Winter" (Boyle), **Supp. XXIV:** 63

"Anecdote and Storyteller" (Howe), **Supp. VI:** 127

"Anecdote of the Jar" (Stevens), **IV:** 83–84

"Anemone" (Rukeyser), **Supp. VI:** 281, 285

"Angel, The" (Buck), **Supp. II Part 1:** 127

"Angel and Unicorn and Butterfly" (Everwine), **Supp. XV:** 76

Angela's Ashes (McCourt), **Supp. XII: 271–279,** 283, 285; **Supp. XXII:** 94

"Angel at the Grave, The" (Wharton), **IV:** 310; **Retro. Supp. I:** 365

"Angel Butcher" (Levine), **Supp. V:** 181

Angel City (Shepard), **Supp. III Part 2:** 432, 445

Angelica (Holding), **Supp. XXII: 120–121**

"Angel Is My Watermark!, The" (H. Miller), **III:** 180

Angell, Carol, **Supp. I Part 2:** 655

Angell, Katharine Sergeant. *See* White, Katharine

Angell, Roger, **Supp. I Part 2:** 655; **Supp. V:** 22; **Supp. VIII:** 139

Angel Landing (Hoffman), **Supp. X: 82–83**

"Angel Levine" (Malamud), **Supp. I Part 2:** 431, 432, 433–434, 437

Angel of Bethesda, The (Mather), **Supp. II Part 2:** 464

"Angel of the Bridge, The" (Cheever), **Supp. I Part 1:** 186–187

"Angel of the Odd, The" (Poe), **III:** 425

Angelo Herndon Jones (Hughes), **Retro. Supp. I:** 203

"Angel on the Porch, An" (Wolfe), **IV:** 451

Angelou, Maya, **Supp. IV Part 1: 1–19; Supp. XI:** 20, 245; **Supp. XIII:** 185; **Supp. XVI:** 259; **Supp. XXI:** 172

"Angel Poem, The" (Stern), **Supp. IX:** 292

Angels and Earthly Creatures (Wylie), **Supp. I Part 2:** 709, 713, 724–730

Angels Flight (Connelly), **Supp. XXI:** 72, **72–73,** 75, 80

"Angels for Djuna Barnes" (Boyle), **Supp. XXIV:** 63

Angels in America: A Gay Fantasia on National Themes (Kushner), **Supp. IX:** 131, 134, **141–146; Supp. XXIV:** 272

"Angels of the Love Affair" (Sexton), **Supp. II Part 2:** 692
"Angel's Trumpet, The"(P. Benedict), **Supp. XXIII:** 48
"Angel Surrounded by Paysans" (Stevens), **IV:** 93
Angel That Troubled the Waters, The (Wilder), **IV:** 356, 357–358
"Anger" (Creeley), **Supp. IV Part 1:** 150–152
Anger (Sarton), **Supp. VIII: 256**
"Anger against Children" (R. Bly), **Supp. IV Part 1:** 73
Angle of Ascent (Hayden), **Supp. II Part 1:** 363, 367, 370
"Angle of Geese" (Momaday), **Supp. IV Part 2:** 485
Angle of Geese and Other Poems (Momaday), **Supp. IV Part 2:** 487, 491
Angle of Repose (Stegner), **Supp. IV Part 2:** 599, 605, 606, 610–611
"*Angle of Repose* and the Writings of Mary Hallock Foote: A Source Study" (Williams-Walsh), **Supp. IV Part 2:** 611
"Anglo-Mongrels and the Rose" (Loy), **Supp. XXII:** 156, 159, 166–167
Anglo-Saxon Century, The (Dos Passos), **I:** 474–475, 483
Angoff, Charles, **III:** 107
"Angola Question Mark" (Hughes), **Supp. I Part 1:** 344
Angry Hills, The (Uris), **Supp. XX: 246, 250**
Angry Wife, The (Sedges), **Supp. II Part 1:** 125
"Angry Women Are Building: Issues and Struggles Facing American Indian Women Today" (Gunn Allen), **Supp. IV Part 1:** 324
"Animal, Vegetable, and Mineral" (Bogan), **Supp. III Part 1:** 66
"Animal Acts" (Simic), **Supp. VIII:** 278
Animal and Vegetable Physiology Considered with Reference to Natural Theology (Roget), **Supp. I Part 1:** 312
"Animal Bodies: Corporeality, Class, and Subject Formation in *The Wide, Wide World*" (Mason), **Supp. XVIII:** 263
Animal Dreams (Kingsolver), **Supp. VII:** 199, 204–207
Animal Magnetism (Prose), **Supp. XVI:** 251, 260
"Animals, The" (Merwin), **Supp. III Part 1:** 348
"Animals Are Passing from Our Lives" (Levine), **Supp. V:** 181, 182
Animals in That Country, The (Atwood), **Supp. XIII:** 20, 33
Animals of the Soul: Sacred Animals of the Oglala Sioux (Brown), **Supp. IV Part 2:** 487
"Animals You Eat, The" (X. J. Kennedy), **Supp. XV:** 169
"Animula" (Eliot), **Retro. Supp. I:** 64
Anita Loos Rediscovered (M. A. Loos), **Supp. XVI:** 196
Ankor Wat (Ginsberg), **Supp. II Part 1:** 323

Ann, Leslee, **Supp. XXIV:** 264
"Annabelle" (Komunyakaa), **Supp. XIII:** 117
"Annabel Lee" (Poe), **Retro. Supp. I:** 273; **Retro. Supp. II:** 266
Anna Christie (O'Neill), **III:** 386, 389, 390; **Supp. XXII:** 24
"Anna Grasa" (Weigl), **Supp. XIX:** 278
"Anna in Mourning" (Weigl), **Supp. XIX:** 288
Anna Karenina (Tolstoy), **I:** 10; **II:** 290; **Retro. Supp. I:** 225; **Supp. V:** 323
"*Anna Karenina*" (Trilling), *Supp. III Part 2:* 508
Annan, Noel, **Supp. XX: 240**
"Anna's Grace" (Weigl), **Supp. XIX:** 282–283
"Anna Who Was Mad" (Sexton), **Supp. II Part 2:** 692
"Ann Burlak" (Rukeyser), **Supp. VI:** 280
"Anne" (Oliver), **Supp. VII:** 232
"Anne" (R. H. Davis), **Supp. XVI:** 91, 92
"Anne at the Symphony" (Shields), **Supp. VII:** 310
"Anne Bradstreet's Poetic Voices" (Requa), **Supp. I Part 1:** 107
Anne of Geierstein: or, The Maiden of the Mist (Scott), **Supp. XX: 234**
Anne Sexton: The Artist and Her Critics (McClatchy), **Supp. XII:** 253
"Ann from the Street" (Dixon), **Supp. XII:** 146–147
"Ann Garner" (Agee), **I:** 27
"Anniad, The" (Brooks), **Supp. III Part 1:** 77, 78
Annie (musical), **Supp. IV Part 2:** 577
Annie Allen (Brooks), **Supp. III Part 1:** 76–79
Annie Dillard Reader, The (Dillard), **Supp. VI:** 23
Annie Hall (film; Allen), **Supp. IV Part 1:** 205; **Supp. XV:** 1, 2, 4, 5, **6–7,** 14
Annie John (Kincaid), **Supp. VII:** 184–186, 193
Annie Kilburn, a Novel (Howells), **II:** 275, 286, 287
"Annihilation" (X. J. Kennedy), **Supp. XV:** 168
"Annihilation of Matter, The" (Bronk), **Supp. XXI:** 30
Anniversary (Shields), **Supp. VII:** 320, 322, 323, 324
"Annunciation" (Nelson), **Supp. XVIII:** 174
"Annunciation, The" (Le Sueur), **Supp. V:** 130
Ann Vickers (Lewis), **II:** 453
"A No-Account Creole, A" (Chopin), **Retro. Supp. II:** 64
"Anodyne" (Komunyakaa), **Supp. XIII:** 130
Another America/Otra America (Kingsolver), **Supp. VII:** 207–209
"Another Animal" (Swenson), **Supp. IV Part 2:** 639
Another Animal: Poems (Swenson), **Supp. IV Part 2:** 639–641, 649
Another Antigone (Gurney), **Supp. V:** 97, 98, 100, 101, 102, 105

"Another August" (Merrill), **Supp. III Part 1:** 326
"Another Beer" (Matthews), **Supp. IX:** 158
Another Country (Baldwin), **Retro. Supp. II: 9–11,** 14; **Supp. I Part 1:** 51, 52, 56–58, 63, 67, 337; **Supp. II Part 1:** 40; **Supp. VIII:** 349
"Another Language" (Jong), **Supp. V:** 131
Another Mother Tongue: Gay Words, Gay Worlds (Grahn), **Supp. IV Part 1:** 330
"Another Night in the Ruins" (Kinnell), **Supp. III Part 1:** 239, 251
"Another Night with Snow" (W. V. Davis), **Supp. XXI:** 90, 91
"Another Old Woman" (W. C. Williams), **Retro. Supp. I:** 423
Another Part of the Forest (Hellman), **Supp. I Part 1:** 282–283, 297
Another Republic: 17 European and South American Writers (Strand, trans.), **Supp. IV Part 2:** 630
Another Roadside Attraction (Robbins), **Supp. X:** 259, 261, 262, 263, 264, 265–266, **267–269,** 274, 275, 277, 284
Another Side of Bob Dylan (album, Dylan), **Supp. XVIII:** 25
"Another Spring Uncovered" (Swenson), **Supp. IV Part 2:** 644
Another Thin Man (film), **Supp. IV Part 1:** 355
Another Time (Auden), **Supp. II Part 1:** 15
Another Turn of the Crank (Berry), **Supp. X:** 25, 35
"Another upon the Same" (Taylor), **IV:** 161
"Another Voice" (Wilbur), **Supp. III Part 2:** 557
"Another Wife" (Anderson), **I:** 114
"Another Winter Night" (Budbill), **Supp. XIX:** 10
Another Woman (film; Allen), **Supp. XV:** 11
Another You (Beattie), **Supp. V:** 29, 31, 33–34
Anouilh, Jean, **Supp. I Part 1:** 286–288, 297
Ansa, Tina McElroy, **Supp. XVIII:** 195
Ansay, A. Manette, **Supp. XXV:** 142
"Anselm" (Berrigan), **Supp. XXIV:** 43
Ansen, Alan, **Supp. XXIII:** 112, 122, 123
Ansky, S., **IV:** 6
Ansky, Shloime, **Supp. IX:** 131, 138
"Answer, The" (Jeffers), **Supp. III Part 2:** 423
Answered Prayers: The Unfinished Novel (Capote), **Supp. III Part 1:** 113, 125, 131–132; **Supp. XVI:** 245
"Answering the Deer: Genocide and Continuance in the Poetry of American Indian Women" (Gunn Allen), **Supp. IV Part 1:** 322, 325
"Answer of Minerva, The: Pacifism and Resistance in Simone Weil" (Merton), **Supp. VIII:** 204
Antaeus (Wolfe), **IV:** 461
"Ante-Bellum Sermon, An" (Dunbar), **Supp. II Part 1:** 203–204

Antheil, George, **III:** 471, 472; **IV:** 404
Anthem (Rand), **Supp. IV Part 2:** 523
Anthology of Holocaust Literature (Glatstein, Knox, and Margoshes, eds.), **Supp. X:** 70
Anthology of Modern American Poetry (Nelson, ed.), **Supp. XXII:** 271
Anthology of Twentieth-Century Brazilian Poetry, An (Bishop and Brasil, eds.), **Retro. Supp. II:** 50; **Supp. I Part 1:** 94
Anthon, Kate, **I:** 452
Anthony, Adelina, **Supp. XXIII:** 197
Anthony, Andrew, **Supp. XVI:** 235, 245, 246
Anthony, Saint, **III:** 395
Anthony, Susan B., **Supp. XI:** 200
"Anthropologist as Hero, The" (Sontag), **Supp. III Part 2:** 451
"Anthropology of Water, The" (Carson), **Supp. XII:** 102–103
Anthropos: The Future of Art (Cummings), **I:** 430
Antichrist (Nietzsche), **III:** 176
"Anti-Father" (Dove), **Supp. IV Part 1:** 246
"Anti-Feminist Woman, The" (Rich), **Supp. I Part 2:** 550
Antigone (Sophocles), **Supp. I Part 1:** 284; **Supp. X:** 249
"Anti-Memoir"(Dybek), **Supp. XXIII:** 78
Antin, David, **Supp. VIII:** 292; **Supp. XII:** 2, 8
Antin, Mary, **Supp. IX:** 227; **Supp. XVI:** 148, 149; **Supp. XX: 1–16**
Anti-Oedipus: Capitalism and Schizophrenia (Deleuze and Guattari), **Supp. XII:** 4
Antiphon, The (Barnes), **Supp. III Part 1:** 43–44
"Antiquities" (Mather), **Supp. II Part 2:** 452
"Antiquity of Freedom, The" (Bryant), **Supp. I Part 1:** 168
"Antislavery Tocsin, An" (Douglass), **Supp. III Part 1:** 171
Antoine, Andre, **III:** 387
Antonioni, Michelangelo, **Supp. IV Part 1:** 46, 47, 48
Antony and Cleopatra (Shakespeare), **I:** 285
"Antony on Behalf of the Play" (Burke), **I:** 284
"An trentiesme de mon Eage, L'" (MacLeish), **III:** 9
Antrim, Donald, **Supp. XX:** 90
"Ants" (R. Bly), **Supp. IV Part 1:** 71
Anxiety of Influence, The (Bloom), **Supp. XIII:** 46
"Any City" (Untermeyer), **Supp. XV:** 296
"Any Object" (Swenson), **Supp. IV Part 2:** 640
Anyplace but Here (Bontemps and Conroy), **Supp. XXII:** 11
"Any Porch" (Parker), **Supp. IX:** 194
Anything Else (film; Allen), **Supp. XV:** 2, 11

"Anywhere Out of This World" (Baudelaire), **II:** 552
Any Woman Can't (Wasserstein), **Supp. XV:** 322
Any Woman's Blues (Jong), **Supp. V:** 115, 123, 126
Anzaldúa, Gloria, **Supp. IV Part 1:** 330; **Supp. XIII:** 223; **Supp. XXIII:** 193, 194, 205
"Apache Tears" (Cliff), **Supp. XXII:** 76
"Aphorisms on Futurism" (Loy), **Supp. XXII:** 159
"Aphorisms on Society" (Stevens), **Retro. Supp. I:** 303
"Apiary IX" (C. Frost), **Supp. XV:** 106
"Apisculptures" (Bierds), **Supp. XVII:** 29
"Apocalypse: What Disaster Reveals" (Díaz), **Supp. XXIV:** 94–95
Apollinaire, Guillaume, **I:** 432; **II:** 529; **III:** 196; **IV:** 80; **Retro. Supp. II:** 326; **Supp. XV:** 182; **Supp. XXIII:** 208
"Apollo Takes Charge of His Muses" (Stallings), **Supp. XXV:** 229
Apologies to the Iroquois (Wilson), **IV:** 429
"Apology" (C. Frost), **Supp. XV:** 103
"Apology, An" (Malamud), **Supp. I Part 2:** 435, 437
"Apology for Bad Dreams" (Jeffers), **Supp. II Part 2:** 427, 438; **Supp. XVII:** 112
"Apology for Crudity, An" (Anderson), **I:** 109
Apology for Poetry (Sidney), **Supp. II Part 1:** 105
Apostle, The (Asch), **Supp. XXIII:** 2, 4, 9, **13–14**
"Apostle of the Tules, An" (Harte), **Supp. II Part 1:** 356
"Apostrophe to a Dead Friend" (Kumin), **Supp. IV Part 2:** 442, 451, 452
"Apostrophe to a Pram Rider" (White), **Supp. I Part 2:** 678
"Apostrophe to Man (on reflecting that the world is ready to go to war again)" (Millay), **III:** 127
"Apostrophe to Vincentine, The" (Stevens), **IV:** 90
"Apotheosis" (Kingsolver), **Supp. VII:** 208
"Apotheosis of Martin Luther King, The" (Hardwick), **Supp. III Part 1:** 203–204
Appalachia (Wright), **Supp. V:** 333, 345
Appalachia Inside Out (Miller, Higgs, and Manning, eds.), **Supp. XX: 166**
"Appalachian Book of the Dead III" (Wright), **Supp. V:** 345
"Appalachian Education: A Critique and Suggestions for Reform" (J. W. Miller), **Supp. XX: 165**
"Appalachian Literature: At Home in This World" (J. W. Miller), **Supp. XX: 165**
"Appalachian Values/American Values" (J. W. Miller), **Supp. XX: 165**
Appaloosa (Parker), **Supp. XIX:** 187
"Appeal to H. G. Wells" (Sturgis), **Supp. XX: 233, 240**

"Appeal to Progressives, An" (Wilson), **IV:** 429
Appeal to Reason (Paine), **I:** 490
Appeal to the World, An (Du Bois), **Supp. II Part 1:** 184
Appearance and Reality (Bradley), **I:** 572
"Appendix to 'The Anniad' " (Brooks), **Supp. III Part 1:** 77
"Applause, Applause"(Thompson), **Supp. XXIII:** 289, 291, 301
Apple, Max, **Supp. VIII:** 14; **Supp. XVII: 1–11,** 49–50
Apple, Sam, **Supp. XVII:** 8
"Apple, The" (Kinnell), **Supp. III Part 1:** 250
Applebaum, Anne, **Supp. XVI:** 153
Applebome, Peter, **Supp. XXI:** 38
Applegarth, Mabel, **II:** 465, 478
"Apple-Maggot Fly, The" (Major), **Supp. XXII:** 182
"Apple of Discord, The" (Humphrey), **Supp. IX:** 109
"Apple Peeler" (Francis), **Supp. IX:** 82
"Apple Rind" (C. Frost), **Supp. XV:** 102
"Apples" (Brockmeier), **Supp. XXII:** 51, 53
"Apples, The" (Di Piero), **Supp. XIX:** 46
Appleseed, Johnny (pseudonym). *See* Chapman, John (Johnny Appleseed)
Apple That Astonished Paris, The (Collins), **Supp. XXI:** 53, 57
Appleton, Nathan, **II:** 488
Appleton, Thomas Gold, **Supp. I Part 1:** 306; **Supp. I Part 2:** 415
"Apple Tree, The" (McCarriston), **Supp. XIV:** 263, 268
"Applicant, The" (Plath), **Retro. Supp. II:** 252; **Supp. I Part 2:** 535, 544, 545
"Application, The" (Neugeboren), **Supp. XVI:** 219, 220, 225
"Applications of the Doctrine" (Hass), **Supp. VI: 100–101**
Appointment, The (film), **Supp. IX:** 253
Appointment in Samarra (O'Hara), **III:** 361, 363–364, 365–367, 371, 374, 375, 383
Appreciation of Sarah Orne Jewett (Cary), **Retro. Supp. II:** 132
"Apprentice, The"(Dybek), **Supp. XXIII:** 71
"Approaches, The" (Merwin), **Supp. III Part 1:** 350
"Approaching Artaud" (Sontag), **Supp. III Part 2:** 470–471
"Approaching Prayer" (Dickey), **Supp. IV Part 1:** 175
"Approaching the Mohawk Village: Jogues' Journal"(Kenny), **Supp. XXIII:** 152
Approach to Literature, An: A Collection of Prose and Verse with Analyses and Discussions (Brooks, Warren, and Purser), **Su pp. XIV:**4
"Approach to Thebes, The" (Kunitz), **Supp. III Part 1:** 265–267
Approach to Vedanta, An (Isherwood), **Supp. XIV:** 157, 163, 164
"Appropriation of Cultures, The" (Everett), **Supp. XVIII:** 66

Approximately Paradise (Skloot), **Supp. XX: 196, 202, 203–204**

"Après-midi d'un faune, L' " (Mallarmé), **III:** 8

"April" (Bierds), **Supp. XVII:** 29

"April" (W. C. Williams), **Retro. Supp. I:** 422

"April" (Winters), **Supp. II Part 2:** 788

April, Steve. *See* Lacy, Ed

April Galleons (Ashbery), **Supp. III Part 1:** 26

"April Galleons" (Ashbery), **Supp. III Part 1:** 26

April Hopes (Howells), **II:** 285, 289

"April Lovers" (Ransom), **III:** 489–490

"April Showers" (Wharton), **Retro. Supp. I:** 361

"April Today Main Street" (Olson), **Supp. II Part 2:** 581

April Twilights (Cather), **I:** 313; **Retro. Supp. I:** 5

"Apt Pupil" (King), **Supp. V:** 152

Arabian Nights, **I:** 204; **II:** 8; **Supp. I Part 2:** 584, 599; **Supp. IV Part 1:** 1

"Arabic Coffee" (Nye), **Supp. XIII:** 276

"Araby" (Joyce), **I:** 174; **Supp. VIII:** 15

Aragon, Louis, **I:** 429; **III:** 471; **Retro. Supp. II:** 85, 321

Arana-Ward, Marie, **Supp. VIII:** 84

Ararat (Glück), **Supp. V:** 79, 86–87

Aratani, Mariko, **Supp. XXIII:** 136

Arbre du voyageur, L' (W. J. Smith; Haussmann, trans.), Supp. XIII: 347

Arbus, Diane, **Supp. XII:** 188

Arbuthnott, John (pseudonym). *See* Henry, O.

"Arc, The" (Bidart), **Supp. XV:** 25–26, 27

Archaeologist of Morning (Olson), **Supp. II Part 2:** 557

Archaeology of the Circle: New and Selected Poems (Weigl), **Supp. XIX:** 282

"Archaic Maker, The" (Merwin), **Supp. III Part 1:** 357

Archaic Smile (Stallings), **Supp. XXV:** 221, 222, 223, 224, 228–231, 233

"Archaic Torso of Apollo" (Rilke), **Supp. XV:** 148

"Archaischer Torso Apollos" (Rilke), **Supp. XVII:** 244

"Archbishop, The" (Gioia), **Supp. XV:** 126, 127

Archer (television show), **Supp. IV Part 2:** 474

Archer, William, **IV:** 131; **Retro. Supp. I:** 228

Archer at Large (Macdonald), **Supp. IV Part 2:** 473

Archer in Hollywood (Macdonald), **Supp. IV Part 2:** 474

"Archetype and Signature: The Relationship of Poet and Poem" (Fiedler), **Supp. XIII:** 101

"Archibald Higbie" (Masters), **Supp. I Part 2:** 461

"Architect, The" (Bourne), **I:** 223

Architect, The (Briggs and Ranlett), **Supp. XVIII:** 3

Arctic Dreams (Lopez), **Supp. V:** 211

Arctic Refuge: A Circle of Testimony (Haines), **Supp. XII:** 205

"Arcturus" (Connell), **Supp. XIV:** 88

À rebours (Huysmans), **Supp. XX:** 239

Arendt, Hannah, **II:** 544; **Retro. Supp. I:** 87; **Retro. Supp. II:** 28, 117; **Supp. I Part 2:** 570; **Supp. IV Part 1:** 386; **Supp. VIII:** 98, 99, 100, 243; **Supp. XII:** 166–167

Arensberg, Louise, **Supp. XXII:** 162

Arensberg, Walter, **IV:** 408; **Retro. Supp. I:** 416; **Supp. XXII:** 162

Aren't You Happy for Me? (Bausch), **Supp. VII:** 42, 51, 54

Areopagitica (Milton), **Supp. I Part 2:** 422

"Are You a Doctor?" (Carver), **Supp. III Part 1:** 139–141

"Are You Mr. William Stafford? (Stafford), **Supp. XI:** 317

Are You My Mother? A Comic Drama (Bechdel), **Supp. XXV:** 1, 2, 9–14

Argall: The True Story of Pocahontas and Captain John Smith (Vollmann), **Supp. XVII:** 225, 226, 231, 232, 233

"Argonauts of 49, California's Golden Age" (Harte), **Supp. II Part 1:** 353, 355

"Arguantando" (Díaz), **Supp. XXIV:** 88–89

"Arguments of Everlasting" (B. Kelly), **Supp. XVII:** 129

"Arguments with the Gestapo Continued: II" (Wright), **Supp. XV:** 344

"Arguments with the Gestapo Continued: Literary Resistance" (Wright), **Supp. XV:** 344

Ari (musical, Uris), **Supp. XX:** 247

Aria da Capo (Millay), **III:** 137–138

"Ariadne and the Rest" (Stallings), **Supp. XXV:** 223, 229

Ariadne's Thread: A Collection of Contemporary Women's Journals (Lifshin, ed.), **Supp. XVI:** 37–38

"Arias, 1971" (Hull), **Supp. XXI:** 135

Ariel (Plath), **Retro. Supp. II: 250–255; Supp. I Part 2:** 526, 539, 541; **Supp. V:** 79; **Supp. XXI:** 58; **Supp. XXII:** 93

"Ariel" (Plath), **Supp. I Part 2:** 542, 546

"Ariel Poems" (Eliot), **I:** 579

Ariosto, Ludovico, **Supp. XV:** 175

"Ariosto: Critical Notice of His Life and Genius" (Hunt), **Supp. XV:** 175

Arise, Arise (Zukofsky), **Supp. III Part 2:** 619, 629

Aristides. *See* Epstein, Joseph

"Aristocracy" (Emerson), **II:** 6

Aristocracy and Justice (More), **I:** 223

Aristocrat, The (Richter), **Supp. XVIII:** 220

Aristophanes, **I:** 436; **II:** 577; **Supp. I Part 2:** 406

Aristotle, **I:** 58, 265, 280, 527; **II:** 9, 12, 198, 536; **III:** 20, 115, 145, 157, 362, 422, 423; **IV:** 10, 18, 74–75, 89; **Supp. I Part 1:** 104, 296; **Supp. I Part 2:** 423; **Supp. IV Part 1:** 391; **Supp. IV Part 2:** 526, 530; **Supp. X:** 78; **Supp. XI:** 249; **Supp. XII:** 106; **Supp. XIV: 242–243**

Aristotle Contemplating the Bust of Homer (Rembrandt), **Supp. IV Part 1:** 390, 391

"Arkansas Traveller" (Wright), **Supp. V:** 334

Arlen, Harold, **Supp. XXII:** 6

"Arm, The" (X. J. Kennedy), **Supp. XV:** 169

"Armadillo, The" (Bishop), **Supp. I Part 1:** 93

Armadillo in the Grass (Hearon), **Supp. VIII: 58–59**

"Armageddon" (Ransom), **III:** 489, 492

Armageddon (Uris), **Supp. XX: 243, 247, 248, 252–253**

Armah, Aiy Kwei, **Supp. IV Part 1:** 373

Armenian Golgotha: A Memoir of the Armenian Genocide, 1915– 1918 (Grigoris Balakian; trans. Peter Balakian and Sevag), **Supp. XXIII:** 28, **29–32**

Armies of the Night, The (Mailer), **III:** 39–40, 41, 42, 44, 45, 46; **Retro. Supp. II:** 205, 206–207, 208; **Supp. IV Part 1:** 207; **Supp. XIV:** 49, 162

"Arm in Arm" (Simpson), **Supp. IX:** 267–268

Arminius, Jacobus, **I:** 557

Armitage, Shelley, **Supp. IV Part 2:** 439

Arm of Flesh, The (Salter), **Supp. IX:** 251

"Armor" (Dickey), **Supp. IV Part 1:** 179

Armored Attack (film), **Supp. I Part 1:** 281

Arms, George W., **Supp. I Part 2:** 416–417

Armstrong, George, **Supp. I Part 2:** 386

Armstrong, Louis, **Retro. Supp. II:** 114

"'Arm the Paper Arm': Kenneth Koch's Postmodern Comedy" (Chinitz), **Supp. XV:** 180, 185

"Army" (Corso), **Supp. XII:** 117, 127

Army Brat (W. J. Smith), **Supp. XIII:** 331, 347

"Army Recruiting Methods" (Bodenheim), **Supp. XXV:** 19

Arna Bontemps Langston Hughes: Letters 1925–1967 (Nichols), **Retro. Supp. I:** 194

"Arna Bontemps Talks About the Renaissance" (Collins), **Supp. XXII:** 7

Arner, Robert D., **Retro. Supp. II:** 62

"Arnie" (Budbill), **Supp. XIX:** 6

Arnold, Edwin T., **Supp. VIII:** 189

Arnold, George W., **Supp. I Part 2:** 411

Arnold, Marilyn, **Supp. IV Part 1:** 220

Arnold, Matthew, **I:** 222, 228, 275; **II:** 20, 110, 338, 541; **III:** 604; **IV:** 349; **Retro. Supp. I:** 56, 325; **Supp. I Part 2:** 416, 417, 419, 529, 552, 602; **Supp. IX:** 298; **Supp. XIV:** 11, 335; **Supp. XIX:** 41; **Supp. XXI:** 90

Arnold, Thurman, **Supp. I Part 2:** 645

Aronson, Steven M. L., **Supp. V:** 4

Around about America (Caldwell), **I:** 290

"Arrangement in Black and White" (Parker), **Supp. IX:** 198

"Arrival at Santos" (Bishop), **Retro. Supp. II:** 46; **Supp. IX:** 45–46

"Arrival of the Bee Box, The" (Plath), **Retro. Supp. II:** 255

Arrivistes, The: Poem 1940–1949 (Simpson), **Supp. IX:** 265, **267–268**

Arrogance (J. Scott), **Supp. XVII: 186–188,** 189, 191, 192, 194

"Arrow" (Dove), **Supp. IV Part 1:** 250

"Arrowhead Hunting" (Stallings), **Supp. XXV:** 232

Arrowsmith (Lewis), **I:** 362; **II:** 445–446, 449

"Arsenal at Springfield, The" (Longfellow), **Retro. Supp. II:** 168

"Arson at Midnight" (Nelson), **Supp. XVIII:** 186

"Arson Plus" (Hammett), **Supp. IV Part 1:** 343; **Supp. XXI:** 68

"Ars Poetica" (Dove), **Supp. IV Part 1:** 250

"Ars Poetica" (Dunn), **Supp. XI:** 154

"Ars Poetica" (MacLeish), **III:** 9–10

"Ars Poetica" (X. J. Kennedy), **Supp. XV:** 154

"Ars Poetica: A Found Poem" (Kumin), **Supp. IV Part 2:** 455

"Ars Poetica; or, Who Lives in the Ivory Tower" (McGrath), **Supp. X:** 117

"Ars Poetica: Some Recent Criticism" (Wright), **Supp. III Part 2:** 603

"Art" (Emerson), **II:** 13

Art (Reza), **Supp. XXI:** 148

"Art and Architecture of the Double Ending, The"(Painter), **Supp. XXIII:** 295

"Art and Neurosis" (Trilling), **Supp. III Part 2:** 502

Art and Technics (Mumford), **Supp. II Part 2:** 483

Art & Ardor: Essays (Ozick), **Supp. V:** 258, 272

Art as Experience (Dewey), **I:** 266

Art by Subtraction (Reid), **IV:** 41

Art Chronicles 1954–1966 (O'Hara), **Supp. XXIII:** 220

Art de toucher le clavecin, L' (Couperin), III: 464

Artemis to Actaeon and Other Verse (Wharton), **Retro. Supp. I:** 372

Arte of English Poesie (Puttenham), **Supp. I Part 1:** 113

"Art"(Hadas), **Supp. XXIII:** 115–116

"Art History" (Cliff), **Supp. XXII:** 75–76

Arthur, Anthony, **Supp. IV Part 2:** 606

Arthur Mervyn; or, Memoirs of the Year 1793 (Brown), **Supp. I Part 1:** 137–140, 144

"Article of Faith" (Sobin), **Supp. XVI:** 291

Articles of Light & Elation (Sobin), **Supp. XVI:** 291

Articulation of Sound Forms in Time (Howe), **Supp. IV Part 2:** 419, 431–433

"Artificer" (X. J. Kennedy), **Supp. XV:** 160

"Artificial Nigger, The" (O'Connor), **III:** 343, 351, 356, 358; **Retro. Supp. II:** 229, 232

Artist, The: A Drama without Words (Mencken), **III:** 104

Artist as Revolutionary, The (Buhle), **Supp. XXI:** 172

"Artist of the Beautiful, The" (Hawthorne), **Retro. Supp. I:** 149

Artistry of Grief (Torsney), **Retro. Supp. I:** 224

Artists and Concubines (Silver), **Supp. XXIV:** 265

"Artists' and Models' Ball, The" (Brooks), **Supp. III Part 1:** 72

Art of Detective Fiction, The (Swales), **Supp. XIX:** 183

"Art of Disappearing, The" (Nye), **Supp. XIII:** 287

Art of Drowning, The (Collins), **Supp. XXI:** 54, 60, 64

Art of Eating, The (M. F. K. Fisher), **Supp. XVII:** 87, 90, 91

Art of Fiction, The (Gardner), **Supp. VI:** 73

Art of Fiction, The (H. James), **Retro. Supp. I:** 226; **Retro. Supp. II:** 223

Art of Hunger, The (Auster), **Supp. XII:** 22

"Art of Keeping Your Mouth Shut, The" (Heller), **Supp. IV Part 1:** 383

"Art of Literature and Commonsense, The" (Nabokov), **Retro. Supp. I:** 271

Art of Living and Other Stories, The (Gardner), **Supp. VI:** 72

Art of Love, The (Koch), **Supp. XV:** 182

"Art of Love, The" (Koch), **Supp. XV:** 182

Art of Poetry, The (Koch), **Supp. XV:** 175–176, 178, 188

"Art of Poetry, The" (Koch), **Supp. XV:** 182

"Art of Poetry, The" (McClatchy), **Supp. XII:** 262

Art of Political Murder, The (Goldman), **Supp. XXV:** 49, 57–59

"Art of Romare Bearden, The" (Ellison), **Retro. Supp. II:** 123

"Art of Storytelling, The" (Simpson), **Supp. IX:** 277

Art of Sylvia Plath, The (Newman), **Supp. I Part 2:** 527

Art of the Moving Picture, The (Lindsay), **Supp. I Part 2:** 376, 391–392, 394; **Supp. XVI:** 185

Art of the Novel (H. James), **Retro. Supp. I:** 227

"Art of Theodore Dreiser, The" (Bourne), **I:** 235

Art of the Personal Essay, The (Lopate, comp.), **Supp. XIII:** 280–281; **Supp. XVI:** 266

Art of the Self, The: Essays a Propos "Steps" (Kosinski), Supp. VII: 222

Art of the Wasted Day, The (Hampl), **Supp. XXII:** 85

Arts and Sciences (Goldbarth), **Supp. XII: 184–186**

Arts and Sciences: A Seventies Seduction (Mallon), **Supp. XIX:** 132, 135

"Art's Bread and Butter" (Benét), **Retro. Supp. I:** 108

Artsybashev, Mikhail, **Supp. XXIII:** 1

Arvin, Newton, **I:** 259; **II:** 508; **Retro. Supp. I:** 19, 137

Asali, Muna, **Supp. XIII:** 121, 126

"As a Little Child" (Taggard), **Supp. XXII:** 272

Asbury, Herbert, **Supp. IV Part 1:** 353

Ascent of F6, The (Auden), **Supp. II Part 1:** 11, 13

Ascent to Truth, The (Merton), **Supp. VIII:** 208

Asch, Nathan, **Supp. XV:** 133, 134; **Supp. XXIII:** 4

Asch, Sholem, **IV:** 1, 9, 11, 14; **Retro. Supp. II:** 299; **Supp. XXIII: 1–18**

Ascherson, Neal, **Supp. XII:** 167

Ascher-Walsh, Rebecca, **Supp. XIX:** 54

"As Close as Breathing" (Jarman), **Supp. XVII:** 120

As David Danced (Bronk), **Supp. XXI:** 24

"As David Danced" (Bronk), **Supp. XXI:** 26

As Does New Hampshire and Other Poems (Sarton), **Supp. VIII:** 259

"As Evening Lays Dying" (Salinas), **Supp. XIII:** 319

"As Flowers Are" (Kunitz), **Supp. III Part 1:** 265

"Ash" (Sobin), **Supp. XVI:** 284–285

Ash, Nathan, **Supp. XXII:** 277

Ashbery, John, **Retro. Supp. I:** 313; **Supp. I Part 1:** 96; **Supp. III Part 1: 1–29; Supp. III Part 2:** 541; **Supp. IV Part 2:** 620; **Supp. VIII:** 272; **Supp. IX:** 52; **Supp. XI:** 139; **Supp. XIII:** 85; **Supp. XV:** 176, 177, 178, 188, 250; **Supp. XIX:** 40, 83; **Supp. XXI:** 227; **Supp. XXIII:** 207, 209, 210, 211, 215, 217, 220; **Supp. XXIV:** 33, 37, 44

"Ashes" (Lamott), **Supp. XX:** 141

"Ashes" (Levine), **Supp. V:** 188

"Ashes of the Beacon" (Bierce), **I:** 209

Ashes: Poems Old and New (Levine), **Supp. V:** 178, 188–189

Ashford, Margaret Mary (Daisy), **II:** 426

Ashman, Angela, **Supp. XXIV:** 200

"Ash Wednesday" (Garrett), **Supp. VII:** 109–110

"Ash Wednesday" (Merton), **Supp. VIII:** 199

Ash Wednesday (T. S. Eliot), **I:** 570, 574–575, 578–579, 580, 582, 584, 585; **Retro. Supp. I:** 64

"Ash Wednesday" (T. S. Eliot), **Supp. IV Part 2:** 436

Asian American Authors (Hsu and Palubinskas, eds.), **Supp. X:** 292

Asian American Heritage: An Anthology of Prose and Poetry (Wand), **Supp. X:** 292

Asian Figures (Mervin), **Supp. III Part 1:** 341

Asian Journal of Thomas Merton, The (Merton), **Supp. VIII:** 196, 206, 208

"Asian Peace Offers Rejected without Publication" (R. Bly), **Supp. IV Part 1:** 61

"Asides on the Oboe" (Stevens), **Retro. Supp. I:** 305

"As I Ebb'd with the Ocean of Life" (Whitman), **IV:** 342, 345–346; **Retro. Supp. I:** 404, 405

As I Lay Dying (Faulkner), **II:** 60–61, 69, 73, 74; **IV:** 100; **Retro. Supp. I:** 75, 82, 84, 85, 86, 88, 89, 91, 92; **Supp. IV Part 1:** 47; **Supp. VIII:** 37, 178; **Supp. IX:** 99, 103, 251; **Supp. XIV:** 24

"As I Lay with My Head in Your Lap, Camerado" (Whitman), **IV:** 347

Asimov, Isaac, **Supp. IV Part 1:** 116; **Supp. XVI:** 122

Asinof, Eliot, **II:** 424

As I Remember It (PBS documentary), **Supp. XVIII:** 277

Asirvatham, Sandy, **Supp. XVI:** 249

"As Is the Daughter, So Is Her Mother" (Patchett), **Supp. XII:** 310

"As It Was in the Beginning" (Benét), **Supp. XI:** 56

"As I Walked Out One Evening" (Auden), **Supp. II Part 1:** 13; **Supp. XV:** 126; **Supp. XX: 138**

"As I Went Down by Havre de Grace" (Wylie), **Supp. I Part 2:** 723

Ask a Policeman (Hinojosa), **Supp. XIX: 110–111**

"Ask Me" (Stafford), **Supp. XI:** 326–327

Ask Me Tomorrow (Cozzens), **I:** 365–367, 379

Ask the Dust (Fante), **Supp. XI:** 159, 160, 166, **167–169,** 172, 173, 174

"Ask the Optimist!" (Saunders), **Supp. XIX:** 235

Ask Your Mama (Hughes), **Supp. I Part 1:** 339, 341–342

Ask Your Mama: 12 Moods for Jazz (Hughes), **Retro. Supp. I:** 210, 211

As Little Children (R. P. Smith), **Supp. XIV:** 333

"As One Put Drunk into the Packet Boat" (Ashbery), **Supp. III Part 1:** 18

"Asparagus" (Nelson), **Supp. XVIII:** 178

"Aspects of Robinson" (Kees), **Supp. XV:** 134

Aspects of the Novel (Forster), **Retro. Supp. I:** 232; **Supp. VIII:** 155; **Supp. XXI:** 233

"Aspen and the Stream, The" (Wilbur), **Supp. III Part 2:** 555, 556

Aspern Papers, The (James), **Supp. V:** 101, 102

"Aspern Papers, The" (James), **Retro. Supp. I:** 219, 227, 228

Asphalt Georgics (Carruth), **Supp. XVI:** 54

Asphalt Jungle (film, Huston), **Supp. XIII:** 174

"Asphodel" (Welty), **IV:** 265, 271

"Asphodel, That Greeny Flower" (W. C. Williams), **Retro. Supp. I:** 429

"Aspic and Buttermilk" (Olds), **Supp. X:** 213

Asquith, Herbert Henry, **Retro. Supp. I:** 59

"Ass" (Cisneros), **Supp. VII:** 67

Assante, Armand, **Supp. VIII:** 74

Assassin, The: A Play in Three Acts (Shaw), **Supp. XIX:** 248

Assassins, The (Oates), **Supp. II Part 2:** 512, 517–519

"Assault" (Millay), **III:** 130–131

"Assemblage of Husbands and Wives, An" (Lewis), **II:** 455–456

"Assembloir" (Monson), **Supp. XXIV:** 237

Assembly (O'Hara), **III:** 361

As She Climbed Across the Table (Lethem), **Supp. XVIII: 140–141,** 148

Assignment, Wildlife (LaBastille), **Supp. X:** 99, 104

"Assimiliation in Recent American Jewish Autobiographies" (Krupnick), **Supp. XVI:** 153

Assistant, The (Malamud), **Supp. I Part 2:** 427, 428, 429, 431, 435, 441–445, 451; **Supp. XVI:** 220

Assommoir, L' (Zola), *II:* 291; *III:* 318

Assorted Prose (Updike), **IV:** 215–216, 218; **Retro. Supp. I:** 317, 319, 327

Astaire, Adele, **Supp. XVI:** 187

As They Were (M. F. K. Fisher), **Supp. XVII:** 88, 89, 91

Astor, Mary, **Supp. IV Part 1:** 356; **Supp. XII:** 173

Astoria, or, Anecdotes of an Enterprise beyond the Rocky Mountains (Irving), **II:** 312

"Astounding News by Electric Express via Norfolk! The Atlantic Crossed in Three Days Signal Triumph of Mr. Monck's Flying-Machine . . ." (Poe), **III:** 413, 420

Astraea (Holmes), **III:** 82

Astro, Richard, **Supp. I Part 2:** 429, 445

"Astrological Fricassee" (H. Miller), **III:** 187

"Astronomer's Wife" (Boyle), **Supp. XXIV:** 58

Astrophil and Stella (Sidney), **Supp. XIV:** 128

Asturias, Miguel Ángel, **Supp. XXIV:** 89

"As Weary Pilgrim" (Bradstreet), **Supp. I Part 1:** 103, 109, 122

As We Know (Ashbery), **Supp. III Part 1:** 9, 21–25

"As We Know" (Ashbery), **Supp. III Part 1:** 21–22

Aswell, Edward C., **IV:** 458, 459, 461

"Asylum, The" (Carruth), **Supp. XVI:** 48–49

"As You Like It" (Chopin), **Supp. I Part 1:** 217

As You Like It (Shakespeare), **Supp. I Part 1:** 308

"At a Bar" (Ferry), **Supp. XXIV:** 162

"At a Bar in Charlotte Amalie" (Updike), **IV:** 214

"At a Lecture" (Brodsky), **Supp. VIII:** 33

"At a Low Bar" (Ferry), **Supp. XXIV:** 149

"At a March against the Vietnam War" (R. Bly), **Supp. IV Part 1:** 61

"At a Reading" (McClatchy), **Supp. XII:** 256–257

"Atavism of John Tom Little Bear, The" (O. Henry), **Supp. II Part 1:** 410

"At Chênière Caminada" (Chopin), **Supp. I Part 1:** 220

"At Chinese Checkers" (Berryman), **I:** 182

Atchity, Kenneth John, **Supp. XI:** 227

"At Death's Window" (Lamott), **Supp. XX: 144**

At Eighty-Two (Sarton), **Supp. VIII:** 264

"At Every Gas Station There Are Mechanics" (Dunn), **Supp. XI:** 144

At Fault (Chopin), **Retro. Supp. II:** 57, 60, **62–63; Supp. I Part 1:** 207, 209–211, 220

"At Fifty" (Bronk), **Supp. XXI:** 31

At Heaven's Gate (Warren), **IV:** 243, 247–248, 251

Atheism Refuted: in a Discourse to Prove the Existence of God (Paine), **Supp. I Part 2:** 517

"Athénaïse" (Chopin), **Retro. Supp. II:** 66, 67; **Supp. I Part 1:** 219–220

Atherton, Gertrude, **I:** 199, 207–208; **Supp. XXIV: 17–32**

Athey, Jean L., **Supp. XI:** 184

At Home: Essays, 1982–1988 (Vidal), **Supp. IV Part 2:** 682, 687, 688

"At Home With" (column; Leland), **Supp. XV:** 69

"At Kino Viejo, Mexico" (Ríos), **Supp. IV Part 2:** 541

Atkinson, Brooks, **IV:** 288; **Supp. IV Part 2:** 683; **Supp. XIX:** 244

Atlanta (film, July), **Supp. XXIV:** 201, 209–210

Atlantis (Doty), **Supp. XI:** 121, **126–129**

"Atlantis" (Doty), **Supp. XI:** 127–128

Atlas, James, **Supp. V:** 233; **Supp. XV:** 25; **Supp. XXIV:** 172

Atlas, The (Vollmann), **Supp. XVII:** 226, 227

Atlas Shrugged (Rand), **Supp. IV Part 2:** 517, 521, 523, 524–526, 528, 531

At Liberty (T. Williams), **IV:** 378

"At Melville's Tomb" (H. Crane), **I:** 393; **Retro. Supp. II:** 76, 78, 80, 82

"At Mother Teresa's" (Nye), **Supp. XIII:** 276

"At Nightfall" (Kooser), **Supp. XIX:** 122–123

At Night the Salmon Move (Carver), **Supp. III Part 1:** 142

At Night the States (Notley), **Supp. XXII:** 224, 231–232

"At night the states" (Notley), **Supp. XXII:** 232

"At North Farm" (Ashbery), **Supp. III Part 1:** 1–2

At Paradise Gate (Smiley), **Supp. VI:** 292, **293–294**

"At Paso Rojo" (Bowles), **Supp. IV Part 1:** 87

At Play in the Fields of the Lord (Matthiessen), **Supp. V:** 199, 202, 204–206, 212

"At Play in the Paradise of Bombs" (Sanders), **Supp. XVI:** 272–273, 274, 277

"At Pleasure By" (Pinsky), **Supp. VI:** 245

"A-Train / Ziggurat / Elegy"(Balakian), **Supp. XXIII:** 32

At Risk (Hoffman), **Supp. X:** 87

"At Sea" (Hemingway), **II:** 258

"At Shaft 11" (Dunbar), **Supp. II Part 1:** 212

"At Slim's River" (Haines), **Supp. XII:** 208–209

"At St. Croix" (Dubus), **Supp. VII:** 83, 87

At Sundown (Whittier), **Supp. I Part 2:** 704

"At Sunset" (Simic), **Supp. VIII:** 282

At Swim-Two-Birds (O'Brien), **Supp. XXV:** 65

Attaway, William, **Supp. XXI:** 264

Attebery, Brian, **Supp. IV Part 1:** 101

Attendant, The (Bronk), **Supp. XXI:** 24

"Attendant, The" (Bronk), **Supp. XXI:** 26

"Attention"(Hadas), **Supp. XXIII:** 121

"At That Time, or The History of a Joke" (Paley), **Supp. VI:** 229–230

"At the Alhambra"(P. Benedict), **Supp. XXIII:** 40

At the Back of the North Wind (Macdonald), **Supp. XIII:** 75

"At the Birth of an Age" (Jeffers), **Supp. II Part 2:** 432

"At the Bomb Testing Site" (Stafford), **Supp. XI:** 317–318, 321, 323

At the Bottom of the River (Kincaid), **Supp. VII:** 182–184, 185

"At the 'Cadian Ball" (Chopin), **Retro. Supp. II:** 64, 65, 68

"At the Cancer Clinic" (Kooser), **Supp. XIX:** 127

"At the Chelton-Pulver Game" (Auchincloss), **Supp. IV Part 1:** 27

"At the Drugstore" (Taylor), **Supp. V:** 323

At the Edge of the Body (Jong), **Supp. V:** 115, 130

"At the End of the Curse, a Blessing" (Verducci), **Supp. XXII:** 209

At the End of the Open Road (Simpson), **Supp. IX:** 265, 269, **271–273,** 277

At the End of This Summer: Poems 1948–1954, **Supp. XII:** 211

"At the End of War" (Eberhart), **I:** 522–523

"At the Executed Murderer's Grave" (Wright), **Supp. III Part 2:** 595, 597

"At the Fishhouses" (Bishop), **Retro. Supp. II:** 45; **Supp. I Part 1:** 90, 92

At the Gates of the Animal Kingdom (Hempel), **Supp. XXI:** 115, **122–124**

"At the Grave of My Guardian Angel: St. Louis Cemetery, New Orleans" (Levis), **Supp. XI:** 268–269

"At the Gym" (Doty), **Supp. XI:** 135

"At the Indian Store" (McCarriston), **Supp. XIV:** 271

"At the Lake" (Oliver), **Supp. VII:** 244

"At the Landing" (Welty), **IV:** 265–266; **Retro. Supp. I:** 348

"At the Last" (Bynner), **Supp. XV:** 44

"At the Last Rites for Two Hot Rodders" (X. J. Kennedy), **Supp. XV:** 166

At the Mountains of Madness (Lovecraft), **Supp. XXII:** 58; **Supp. XXV:** 109, 111, 114

"At the Owl Club, North Gulfport, Mississippi, 1950" (Trethewey), **Supp. XXI:** 249

At the Owl Woman Saloon (Gallagher), **Supp. XXIV:** 166, 172, 173, 174, 175–177

"At the Premiere" (Keillor), **Supp. XVI:** 167

At the Rendezvous of Victory (C. L. R. James), **Supp. XXI:** 172

At the Root of Stars (Barnes), **Supp. III Part 1:** 34

"At the Slackening of the Tide" (Wright), **Supp. III Part 2:** 597

"At the Street Corner" (Ferry), **Supp. XXIV:** 162

"At the Tomb of Walt Whitman" (Kunitz), **Supp. III Part 1:** 262

"At the Tourist Centre in Boston" (Atwood), **Supp. XIII:** 33

"At the Town Dump" (Kenyon), **Supp. VII:** 167

"At the Worcester Museum" (Pinsky), **Supp. VI:** 251

"At the Zoo in Spain" (Major), **Supp. XXII:** 182

"Atticus Finch and the Mad Dog: Harper Lee's *To Kill a Mockingbird*" (Jones), **Supp. VIII:** 128

"Atticus Finch—Right and Wrong" (Freedman), **Supp. VIII:** 127–128

"Attic Which Is Desire, The" (W. C. Williams), **Retro. Supp. I:** 422

"At Tikal" (Bronk), **Supp. XXI:** **28–29**

"At Times in Flight: A Parable" (H. Roth), **Supp. IX:** 234

Attitudes toward History (Burke), **I:** 274

Atwan, Robert, **Supp. XVI:** 273, 277

At Weddings and Wakes (McDermott), **Supp. XVIII:** 155, **160–162,** 166

"At White River" (Haines), **Supp. XII:** 208–209

Atwood, Margaret, **Supp. IV Part 1:** 252; **Supp. V:** 119; **Supp. XI:** 317; **Supp. XIII:** **19–39,** 291, 306; **Supp. XXI:** 39, 42

"Atwood's Gorgon Touch" (Davey), **Supp. XIII:** 33

"Aubade" (McCarriston), **Supp. XIV:** 271

"Aubade: November" (McCarriston), **Supp. XIV:** 261–262

"Aubade of an Early Homo Sapiens" (C. Frost), **Supp. XV:** 97–98

"Aubade: Opal and Silver" (Doty), **Supp. XI:** 129

"Au Bal Musette" (Van Vechten), **Supp. II Part 2:** 735

Auchincloss, Hugh D., **Supp. IV Part 2:** 679

Auchincloss, Louis, **I:** 375; **III:** 66; **Retro. Supp. I:** 370, 373; **Supp. IV Part 1: 21–38**

"Auction" (Simic), **Supp. VIII:** 278

"Auction, The" (Crane), **I:** 411

"Auction Model 1934" (Z. Fitzgerald), **Supp. IX:** 61

Auden, W. H., **I:** 71, 381, 539; **II:** 367, 368, 371, 376, 586; **III:** 17, 134, 269, 271, 292, 476–477, 504, 527, 530, 542, 615; **IV:** 136, 138, 240, 430; **Retro. Supp. I:** 430; **Retro. Supp. II:** 183, 242, 244, 323; **Supp. I Part 1:** 270; **Supp. I Part 2:** 552, 610; **Supp. II Part 1: 1–28; Supp. III Part 1:** 2, 3, 14, 26, 60, 61, 64, 341; **Supp. III Part 2:** 591, 595; **Supp. IV Part 1:** 79, 84, 136, 225, 302, 313; **Supp. IV Part 2:** 440, 465; **Supp. V:** 337; **Supp. VIII:** 19, 21, 22, 23, 30, 32, 155, 190; **Supp. IX:** 94, 287, 288; **Supp. X:** 35, 57, 59, 115–116, 117, 118–119; **Supp. XI:** 243, 244; **Supp. XII:** 253, 264–265, 266, 269–270; **Supp. XIV:** 156, 158, 160, 162, 163; **Supp. XV:** 74, 117–118, 139, 144, 186; **Supp. XIX:** 147, 151; **Supp. XX: 138; Supp. XXI:** 60, 98; **Supp. XXIII:** 117, 207

"Auden's OED" (McClatchy), **Supp. XII:** 264–265

"Audition" (Alvarez), **Supp. VII:** 10

Audubon, John James, **III:** 210; **IV:** 265; **Supp. IX:** 171; **Supp. XVI: 1–14**

Audubon, John Woodhouse, **Supp. XVI:** 10

Audubon, Maria Rebecca, **Supp. XVI:** 11

Audubon, Victor Gifford, **Supp. XVI:** 10

Audubon and His Journals (M. Audubon, ed.), **Supp. XVI:** 11, 12

Audubon Reader, The: The Best Writings of John James Audubon (Sanders, ed.), **Supp. XVI:** 269

Auer, Jane. *See* Bowles, Jane

Auerbach, Eric, **III:** 453

Auerbach, Nina, **Supp. I Part 1:** 40

"August" (Oliver), **Supp. VII:** 235

"August" (Rich), **Supp. I Part 2:** 564

"August 1968" (Auden), **Supp. II Part 1:** 25

"August Darks, The" (Clampitt), **Supp. IX:** 43, **50–51,** 52

Augustine, Saint, **I:** 279, 290; **II:** 537; **III:** 259, 270, 292, 300; **IV:** 69, 126; **Retro. Supp. I:** 247; **Supp. VIII:** 203; **Supp. XI:** 245; **Supp. XIII:** 89; **Supp. XXI:** 83; **Supp. XXII:** 92–93

August Snow (Price), **Supp. VI:** 264

"Au Jardin" (Pound), **III:** 465–466

Aunt Carmen's Book of Practical Saints (Mora), **Supp. XIII: 227–229**

"Aunt Cynthy Dallett" (Jewett), **II:** 393

"Aunt Gladys" (Karr), **Supp. XI:** 241

"Aunt Granny Lith" (Offutt), **Supp. XIX:** 165, 166

"Aunties, The" (Lamott), **Supp. XX: 141**

"Aunt Imogen" (Robinson), **III:** 521

"Aunt Jemima of the Ocean Waves" (Hayden), **Supp. II Part 1:** 368, 379

"Aunt Jennifer's Tigers" (Rich), **Supp. XV:** 252

Aunt Jo's Scrapbooks (Alcott), **Supp. I Part 1:** 43

"Aunt Mary" (Oliver), **Supp. VII:** 232

"Aunt Mary" (Stowe), **Supp. I Part 2:** 587

"Aunt Moon's Young Man" (Hogan), **Supp. IV Part 1:** 400

"Aunt Rectita's Good Friday" (X. J. Kennedy), **Supp. XV:** 166

"Aunt Sarah" (Lowell), **II:** 554

"Aunt Sue's Stories" (Hughes), **Retro. Supp. I:** 197, 199

"Aunt Violet's Canadian Honeymoon/ 1932" (Shields), **Supp. VII:** 311

"Aunt Violet's Things" (Shields), **Supp. VII:** 311–312

"Aurelia: Moon Jellies" (Mora), **Supp. XIII:** 224

"Aurelio" (Di Piero), **Supp. XIX:** 38

Au revoir les enfants (film, Malle), **Supp. XXIII:** 122

Aurora 7 (Mallon), **Supp. XIX:** 132, **135–136**

Aurora Dawn (Wouk), **Supp. XXV:** 255, 258

Aurora Leigh (E. Browning), **Retro. Supp. I:** 33; **Supp. XI:** 197

Aurora Means Dawn (Sanders), **Supp. XVI:** 268

Auroras of Autumn, The (Stevens), **Retro. Supp. I:** 297, 300, **309–312**

"Auroras of Autumn, The" (Stevens), **Retro. Supp. I:** 311, 312; **Supp. III Part 1:** 12

Auschwitz: the Nazis and the "Final Solution" (television documentary), Supp. XVII: 40

Auslander, Joseph, **Supp. XIV:** 120

"Auspex" (Frost), **Retro. Supp. I:** 122

"Auspex" (Lowell), **Supp. I Part 2:** 424

Austen, Jane, **I:** 130, 339, 375, 378; **II:** 272, 278, 287, 568–569, 577; **IV:** 8; **Retro. Supp. I:** 354; **Supp. I Part 1:** 267; **Supp. I Part 2:** 656, 715; **Supp. IV Part 1:** 300; **Supp. VIII:** 125, 167; **Supp. IX:** 128; **Supp. XII:** 310; **Supp. XV:** 338; **Supp. XX:** 108; **Supp. XXII:** 206

Austenfeld, Thomas, **Supp. XXIV:** 64

Auster, Paul, **Supp. XII:** **21–39; Supp. XIV:** 292; **Supp. XXI:** 20

Austerities (Simic), **Supp. VIII: 276– 278,** 283

"Austerities" (Simic), **Supp. VIII:** 277

"Austerity Measures" (Stallings), **Supp. XXV:** 221

"Austerity Measures: A Letter from Greece" (Stallings), **Supp. XXV:** 221, 224, 225

Austin, Mary Hunter, **Retro. Supp. I:** 7; **Supp. IV Part 2:** 503; **Supp. X:** 29; **Supp. XIII:** 154

"Authentic Unconscious, The" (Trilling), **Supp. III Part 2:** 512

Author and Agent: Eudora Welty and Diarmuid Russell (Kreyling), **Retro. Supp. I:** 342, 345, 347, 349–350

"Author at Sixty, The" (Wilson), **IV:** 426

"Author of 'Beltraffio,' The" (James), **Retro. Supp. I:** 227

"Author's Explanation, The" (Larsen), **Supp. XVIII:** 131

"Author's House" (Fitzgerald), **Retro. Supp. I:** 98

"Author's Reflections, An: Willie Loman, Walter Younger, and He Who Must Live" (Hansberry), **Supp. IV Part 1:** 370

"Author to Her Book, The" (Bradstreet), **Supp. I Part 1:** 119; **Supp. V:** 117– 118; **Supp. XV:** 125–126

"Autism Poem #20: The Knot Garden"(Crooker), **Supp. XXIII:** 56–57

"Autobiographical Note" (H. Miller), **III:** 174–175

"Autobiographical Notes" (Baldwin), **Supp. I Part 1:** 54

"Autobiographical Notes" (Holmes), **Supp. I Part 1:** 301

"Autobiographic Chapter, An" (Bourne), **I:** 236

Autobiography (Franklin), **II:** 102, 103, 108, 121–122, 302

Autobiography (James), **I:** 462

"Autobiography" (MacLeish), **III:** 20

Autobiography (Van Buren), **III:** 473

Autobiography (W. C. Williams), **Supp. I Part 1:** 254

Autobiography (Zukofsky), **Supp. III Part 2:** 627

Autobiography by Jesus of Nazareth (Pettis), **Supp. XXIII:** 189

"Autobiography"(Dybek), **Supp. XXIII:** 78

"Autobiography in the Shape of a Book Review" (Bynner), **Supp. XV:** 40

"Autobiography of a Confluence, The" (Gunn Allen), **Supp. IV Part 1:** 321

Autobiography of Alice B. Toklas, The (Stein), **IV:** 26, 30, 35, 43; **Supp. IV Part 1:** 11, 81

Autobiography of an Ex-Colored Man, The (Johnson), **Supp. II Part 1:** 33, 194; **Supp. XVIII:** 127; **Supp. XXII:** 7

Autobiography of a Schizophrenic Girl (Renée), **Supp. XVI:** 64, 66

Autobiography of a Thief, The (Hapgood), **Supp. XVII:** 96, 101–102

Autobiography of Benjamin Franklin (Franklin), **Supp. IV Part 1:** 5

Autobiography of LeRoi Jones, The (Baraka), **Retro. Supp. I:** 411

Autobiography of Malcolm X (Little), **Supp. I Part 1:** 66; **Supp. X:** 27; **Supp. XIII:** 264; **Supp. XXII:** 95

Autobiography of Mark Twain, The (Twain), **IV:** 209

Autobiography of My Mother, The (Kincaid), **Supp. VII:** 182, 188–190, 191, 192, 193

Autobiography of Red: A Novel in Verse (Carson), **Supp. XII:** 97, **106–110**

Autobiography of Upton Sinclair, The (Sinclair), **Supp. V:** 276, 282

Autobiography of W. E. B. Du Bois, The (Du Bois), **Supp. II Part 1:** 159, 186

Autobiography of William Carlos Williams, The (W. C. Williams), **Retro. Supp. I:** 51, 428

Autocrat of the Breakfast-Table, The (Holmes), **Supp. I Part 1:** 306–307

"Autographic Disclosures and Genealogies of Desire in Alison Bechdel's *Fun Home*" (Watson), **Supp. XXV:** 8

"Automatic Gate, The" (Southern), **Supp. XI:** 294

"Automotive Passacaglia" (H. Miller), **III:** 186

"Autopsy Room, The" (Carver), **Supp. III Part 1:** 137

"Auto Wreck" (Shapiro), **Supp. II Part 2:** 706

"Autre Temps" (Wharton), **IV:** 320, 324

"Autumn" (Berrigan), **Supp. XXIV:** 37

"Autumn, Mist" (Hull), **Supp. XXI:** 133

"Autumn Afternoon" (Farrell), **II:** 45

"Autumnal" (Eberhart), **I:** 540–541

"Autumn Begins in Martins Ferry, Ohio" (Wright), **Supp. III Part 2:** 599

"Autumn Courtship, An" (Caldwell), **I:** 309

"Autumn Equinox" (Skloot), **Supp. XX: 202**

Autumn Garden, The (Hellman), **Supp. I Part 1:** 285–286, 290

"Autumn Garden, The: Mechanics and Dialectics" (Felheim), **Supp. I Part 1:** 297

"Autumn Holiday, An" (Jewett), **II:** 391; **Retro. Supp. II:** 140–141

"Autumn Musings" (Harte), **Supp. II Part 1:** 336

"Autumn of the Revolutionary, The" (Goldman), **Supp. XXV:** 54–55

"Autumn's Day" (Rilke; Berrigan, trans.), **Supp. XXIV:** 37

Autumn Spring (Pickering), **Supp. XXI:** 204–205, 206

"Autumn Within" (Longfellow), **II:** 499

"Autumn Woods" (Bryant), **Supp. I Part 1:** 164

Autum of the Patriarch, The (García Márquez), **Supp. XXIV:** 89

"Au Vieux Jardin" (Aldington), **Supp. I Part 1:** 257

"Aux Imagistes" (W. C. Williams), **Supp. I Part 1:** 266

Available World, The (Monson), **Supp. XXIV:** 230, **239–240,** 241

Avakian, Aram, **Supp. XI:** 294, 295, 309

Avalanche (Boyle), **Supp. XXIV:** 62

Avalanche, The (Atherton), **Supp. XXIV:** 24–25

"Ave Atque Vale" (Bynner), Supp. XV: 49

Avedon, Richard, **Supp. I Part 1:** 58; **Supp. V:** 194; **Supp. X:** 15

Aveling, Edward, **Supp. XVI:** 85

"Avenue" (Pinsky), **Supp. VI:** 248

Avenue Bearing the Initial of Christ into the New World: Poems 1946–1964 (Kinnell), **Supp. III Part 1:** 235, 239– 241

"Avenue of the Americas" (Simic), **Supp. VIII:** 278

"Average Torture" (Karr), **Supp. XI:** 243

Avery, George C., **Supp. XX: 84**

Avery, John, **Supp. I Part 1:** 153

"Avey" (Toomer), **Supp. IX:** 317

Avon's Harvest (Robinson), **III:** 510

Awake and Sing! (Odets), **Supp. II Part 2:** 530, 531, 536–538, 550; **Supp. IV**

Part 2: 587
"Awake at Midnight"(Schott), **Supp. XXIII**: 246
Awake in Spain (O'Hara), **Supp. XXIII**: 216
Awakening, The (Chopin), **Retro. Supp. I**: 10; **Retro. Supp. II**: 57, 59, 60, 67, **68–71**, 73; **Supp. I Part 1**: 200, 201, 202, 211, 220–225; **Supp. V**: 304; **Supp. VIII**: 198; **Supp. XII**: 170
Awakening Land, The (Richter), **Supp. XVIII**: 207, 215
Awful Rowing Toward God, The (Sexton), **Supp. II Part 2**: 694–696
Awiakta, Marilou, **Supp. IV Part 1**: 319, 335
Awkward Age, The (James), **II**: 332; **Retro. Supp. I**: 229, **230–231**
Axe Handles (Snyder), **Supp. VIII: 303–305**
Axel's Castle: A Study in the Imaginative Literature of 1870 to 1930 (Wilson), **I**: 185; **II**: 577; **IV**: 428, 431, 438, 439, 443; **Supp. VIII**: 101
"Ax-Helve, The" (Frost), **Retro. Supp. I**: 133
Azikewe, Nnamdi, **Supp. IV Part 1**: 361
"Aztec Angel" (Salinas), **Supp. XIII**: 314
Aztec Treasure House, The: New and Selected Essays (Connell), **Supp. XIV**: 80, 97

B

"Bab, the Sub-Deb" (Rinehart), **Supp. XXV**: 195
Babbitt (Lewis), **II**: 442, 443–445, 446, 447, 449; **III**: 63–64, 394; **IV**: 326
Babbitt, Irving, **I**: 247; **II**: 456; **III**: 315, 461, 613; **IV**: 439; **Retro. Supp. I**: 55; **Supp. I Part 2**: 423
Babcock, Elisha, **Supp. II Part 1**: 69
Babel, Isaac, **IV**: 1; **Supp. IX**: 260; **Supp. XII**: 308–309; **Supp. XVII**: 41; **Supp. XXIII**: 68
Babel, Isaak, **Supp. XIV**: 83, 84
Babel to Byzantium (Dickey), **Supp. IV Part 1**: 177, 185
Baber, Asa, **Supp. XXIII**: 52
Baber, Bob Henry, **Supp. XXIII**: 39
Babeuf, François, **Supp. I Part 2**: 518
"Babies, The" (Strand), **Supp. IV Part 2**: 625
Babouk (Endore), **Supp. XVII: 56–57,** 61, 64
Baby, Come on Inside (Wagoner), **Supp. IX**: 335
"Baby, The" (Barthelme), **Supp. IV Part 1**: 49
Baby Doll (T. Williams), **IV**: 383, 386, 387, 389, 395
"Baby Face" (Sandburg), **III**: 584
"Babylon Revisited" (Fitzgerald), **II**: 95; **Retro. Supp. I**: 109
"Baby or the Botticelli, The" (Gass), **Supp. VI**: 92
"Baby Pictures of Famous Dictators" (Simic), **Supp. VIII**: 276
"Baby's Breath" (Bambara), **Supp. XI**: 15, 16

"Babysitter, The" (Coover), **Supp. V**: 43–44
"Baby Villon" (Levine), **Supp. V**: 182
Baby with the Bathwater (Durang), **Supp. XXIV: 121–122**
Bacall, Lauren, **Supp. IV Part 1**: 130
"Baccalaureate" (MacLeish), **III**: 4
Bacchae, The (Euripides), **Supp. VIII**: 182
Bach, Caleb, **Supp. XXV**: 53
Bach, Johann Sebastian, **Supp. I Part 1**: 363; **Supp. III Part 2**: 611, 612, 619
Bachardy, Don, **Supp. XIV**: 166, 170, 172, 173
Bache, Richard, **Supp. I Part 2**: 504
Bachelard, Gaston, **Supp. XIII**: 225; **Supp. XVI**: 292
"Bachelor Girl, The" (Boyce), **Supp. XXI**: 3
Bachelor Girls (Wasserstein), **Supp. XV: 327–328**, 332
Bachman, John, **Supp. XVI**: 10, 11
Bachmann, Ingeborg, **Supp. IV Part 1**: 310; **Supp. VIII**: 272
Bachofen, J. J., **Supp. I Part 2**: 560, 567
Back Bog Beast Bait (Shepard), **Supp. III Part 2**: 437, 438
Backbone (C. Bly), **Supp. XVI: 34–36,** 37, 40, 41
Back Country, The (Snyder), **Supp. VIII: 296–299**
"Back from the Argentine" (Leopold), **Supp. XIV**: 186
"Background with Revolutionaries" (MacLeish), **III**: 14–15
"Back in the Saddle Again" (Swados), **Supp. XIX**: 259
Back in the World (Wolff), **Supp. VII**: 344, 345
Backis, Charles, **Supp. XXI**: 195
"Backlash Blues, The" (Hughes), **Supp. I Part 1**: 343
"Backlash of Kindness, A" (Nye), **Supp. XIII**: 285, 286
"Backslider, The" (R. Fisher), **Supp. XIX**: 70, 71
"Back Street Guy" (Halliday), **Supp. XIX**: 88
Back to China (Fiedler), **Supp. XIII: 102–103**
Back to Methuselah (Shaw), **IV**: 64
"Backwacking: A Plea to the Senator" (Ellison), **Retro. Supp. II**: 126; **Supp. II Part 1**: 248
Backward Glance, A (Wharton), **Retro. Supp. I**: 360, 363, 366, 378, 380, 382; **Supp. XX**: 229
"Backward Glance o'er Travel'd Roads, A" (Whitman), **IV**: 348
Bacon, Francis, **II**: 1, 8, 11, 15–16, 111; **III**: 284; **Retro. Supp. I**: 247; **Supp. I Part 1**: 310; **Supp. I Part 2**: 388; **Supp. IX**: 104; **Supp. XIV**: 22, 210
Bacon, Helen, **Supp. X**: 57
Bacon, Katie, **Supp. XXII**: 207; **Supp. XXIII**: 275
Bacon, Leonard, **II**: 530; **Supp. XXII**: 273
Bacon, Roger, **IV**: 69
"Bacterial War, The" (Nemerov), **III**: 272

Bad and the Beautiful, The (film), **Supp. XVIII**: 250
Bad Boy Brawly Brown (Mosley), **Supp. XIII**: 237, 239, 240–241
Bad Boys (Cisneros), **Supp. VII**: 58
"Bad Company" (Gallagher), **Supp. XXIV**: 174, 176
"Bad Dream" (Taylor), **Supp. V**: 320
Badè, William Frederic, **Supp. IX**: 178
"Bad Fisherman, The" (Wagoner), **Supp. IX**: 328
Bad for Each Other (film), **Supp. XIII**: 174
"Badger" (Clare), **II**: 387
Badger, A. G., **Supp. I Part 1**: 356
"Badger and the Bear, The" (Zitkala-Ša), **Supp. XXV**: 275
Bad Government and Silly Literature (C. Bly), **Supp. XVI**: 37, 38, 40
Badlands (film; Malick), **Supp. XV**: 351
"Bad Lay" (McCarriston), **Supp. XIV**: 267
Badley, Linda, **Supp. V**: 148
Bad Man, A (Elkin), **Supp. VI: 47**
Bad Man Ballad (Sanders), **Supp. XVI**: 268
Bad Man Blues: A Portable George Garrett (Garrett), **Supp. VII**: 111
"Bad Music, The" (Jarrell), **II**: 369
"Bad People" (Halliday), **Supp. XIX**: 90, 91
"Bad Summer on K2, A" (Krakauer and Child), **Supp. XVIII**: 107, 108
"Bad Woman, A" (Fante), **Supp. XI**: 165
Baeck, Leo, **Supp. V**: 260
Baecker, Diann L., **Supp. VIII**: 128
Baer, William, **Supp. XIII**: 112, 118, 129; **Supp. XXIII**: 124
Baez, Joan, **Supp. IV Part 1**: 200; **Supp. VIII**: 200, 202; **Supp. XVIII**: 24, 25–26, 27
Bag of Bones (King), **Supp. V**: 139, 148, 151
"Bagpipe Music" (MacNeice), **Supp. X**: 117
"Bahá'í Faith: Only Church in World That Does Not Discriminate" (Locke), **Supp. XIV**: 200
Bahá'u'lláh, **Supp. XX: 117, 121, 122**
"Bahá'u'lláh in the Garden of Ridwan" (Hayden), **Supp. II Part 1**: 370, 378
Bahr, David, **Supp. XV**: 66
Bahr, Thomas, **Supp. XXII**: 206, 214
"Bailbondsman, The" (Elkin), **Supp. VI**: 49, **50,** 54
Bailey, Gamaliel, **Supp. I Part 2**: 587, 590
Bailey, Peter, **Supp. XVI**: 69
Bailey, William, **Supp. IV Part 2**: 631, 634
Bailey's Café (Naylor), **Supp. VIII: 226–228**
Bailyn, Bernard, **Supp. I Part 2**: 484, 506
Bair, Deirdre, **Supp. X**: 181, 186, 187, 188, 192, 194, 195, 196, 197
Baird, Linnett, **Supp. XII**: 299
Baird, Peggy, **I**: 385, 401
Baiting the Void (Schott), **Supp. XXIII: 247–248**

Bakan, David, **I:** 59

Baker, Carlos, **II:** 259

Baker, Chet, **Supp. XXI:** 131

Baker, David, **Supp. IX:** 298; **Supp. XI:** 121, 142, 153; **Supp. XII:** 175, 191–192; **Supp. XIX:** 115

Baker, George Pierce, **III:** 387; **IV:** 453, 455

Baker, Gladys, **Supp. XIV:** 121

Baker, Houston, **Supp. XXII:** 6

Baker, Houston A., Jr., **Retro. Supp. II:** 121; **Supp. IV Part 1:** 365; **Supp. X:** 324

Baker, Jeff, **Supp. XXIV:** 166, 178

Baker, Katherine, **Supp. XX: 69**

Baker, Kevin, **Supp. XIV:** 96

Baker, Mabel, **Supp. XVIII:** 259, 263, 266–267, 269

Baker, Nicholson, **Supp. XIII: 41–57**

Baker, Robert, **Supp. XVI:** 288, 290

Bakerman, Jane S., **Supp. IV Part 2:** 468

Bakhtin, Mikhail, **Retro. Supp. II:** 273; **Supp. IV Part 1:** 301; **Supp. X:** 120, 239; **Supp. XXII:** 259

Bakst, Léon, **Supp. IX:** 66

Bakunin, Mikhail Aleksandrovich, **IV:** 429

Balaban, John, **Supp. XIX:** 281

Balakian, Anna, **Supp. XXIII:** 20

Balakian, Diran, **Supp. XXIII:** 28

Balakian, Grigoris, **Supp. XXIII:** 28, 29–32

Balakian, Jan, **Supp. XV:** 327

Balakian, Nona, **Supp. XXIII:** 20

Balakian, Peter, **Supp. XXIII: 19–34**

"Balance" (Bierds), **Supp. XVII:** 31

"Balance" (Nelson), **Supp. XVIII:** 174–175

Balbo, Ned, **Supp. XVII:** 120; **Supp. XIX:** 161

Balbuena, Bernado de, **Supp. V:** 11

Balch, Emily Greene, **Supp. I Part 1:** 25

Balcony, The (Genet), **I:** 84

Bald Soprano, The (Ionesco), **I:** 74

Baldwin, David, **Supp. I Part 1:** 47, 48, 49, 50, 51, 54, 65, 66

Baldwin, James, **Retro. Supp. II: 1–17;** **Supp. I Part 1: 47–71,** 337, 341; **Supp. II Part 1:** 40; **Supp. III Part 1:** 125; **Supp. IV Part 1:** 1, 10, 11, 163, 369; **Supp. V:** 201; **Supp. VIII:** 88, 198, 235, 349; **Supp. X:** 136, 324; **Supp. XI:** 288, 294; **Supp. XIII:** 46, 111, 181, 186, 294; **Supp. XIV:** 54, 71, 73, 306; **Supp. XVI:** 135, 141, 143; **Supp. XVIII:** 25; **Supp. XX: 147; Supp. XXI:** 245; **Supp. XXIV:** 185

Baldwin, Samuel, **Supp. I Part 1:** 48

Balitas, Vincent D., **Supp. XVI:** 222

Balkian, Nona, **Supp. XI:** 230

Balkun, Mary McAleer, **Supp. XX: 281**

Ball, Gordon, **Supp. XIV:** 148

Ball, John, **Supp. XV:** 202

"Ballad: Between the Box Cars" (Warren), **IV:** 245

"Ballade" (MacLeish), **III:** 4

"Ballade at Thirty-Five" (Parker), **Supp. IX:** 192

"Ballade for the Duke of Orléans" (Wilbur), **Supp. III Part 2:** 556

"Ballade of Broken Flutes, The" (Robinson), **III:** 505

"Ballade of Meaty Inversions" (White), **Supp. I Part 2:** 676

"Ballad of a Thin Man" (song, Dylan), **Supp. XVIII:** 30, 31

"Ballad of Aunt Geneva, The" (Nelson), **Supp. XVIII:** 175

"Ballad of Billie Potts, The" (Warren), **IV:** 241–242, 243, 253

"Ballad of Carmilhan, The" (Longfellow), **II:** 505

"ballad of chocolate Mabbie, the" (Brooks), **Supp. IV Part 1:** 15

"Ballad of Dead Ladies, The" (Villon), **Retro. Supp. I:** 286

Ballad of Dingus Magee, The (Markson), **Supp. XVII:** 139, 141

"Ballad of East and West, The" (Kipling), **Supp. IX:** 246; **Supp. XX:** 23

"Ballad of Jesse Neighbours, The" (Humphrey), **Supp. IX:** 100

"Ballad of Jesus of Nazareth, A" (Masters), **Supp. I Part 2:** 459

"Ballad of John Cable and Three Gentlemen" (Merwin), **Supp. III Part 1:** 342

"Ballad of Larry and Club" (Jarman), **Supp. XVII:** 115

"Ballad of Nat Turner, The" (Hayden), **Supp. II Part 1:** 378

"Ballad of Pearl May Lee, The" (Brooks), **Supp. III Part 1:** 74, 75

Ballad of Remembrance, A (Hayden), **Supp. II Part 1:** 367

"Ballad of Remembrance, A" (Hayden), **Supp. II Part 1:** 368, 372, 373

"Ballad of Ruby, The" (Sarton), **Supp. VIII:** 259–260

"Ballad of San Isidro, The" (Espaillat), **Supp. XXI:** 108

"Ballad of Sue Ellen Westerfield, The" (Hayden), **Supp. II Part 1:** 364

Ballad of the Brown Girl, The (Cullen), **Supp. IV Part 1:** 167, 168, 169–170, 173

"Ballad of the Brown Girl, The" (Cullen), **Supp. IV Part 1:** 168

"Ballad of the Children of the Czar, The" (Schwartz), **Supp. II Part 2:** 649

"Ballad of the Girl Whose Name Is Mud" (Hughes), **Retro. Supp. I:** 205

"Ballad of the Goodly Fere", **III:** 458

"Ballad of the Harp-Weaver" (Millay), **III:** 135

"Ballad of the Sad Cafe, The" (McCullers), **II:** 586, 587, 588, 592, 595, 596–600, 604, 605, 606

"Ballad of the Sixties" (Sarton), **Supp. VIII:** 259

"Ballad of Trees and the Master, A" (Lanier), **Supp. I Part 1:** 370

"Ballad of Typical Lovers" (Taggard), **Supp. XXII:** 277

"Ballad of William Sycamore, The" (Benét), **Supp. XI:** 44, 47

Ballads and Other Poems (Longfellow), **II:** 489; **III:** 412, 422; **Retro. Supp. II:** 157, 168

Ballads for Sale (Lowell), **II:** 527

"Ballads of Lenin" (Hughes), **Supp. I Part 1:** 331

Ballantyne, Sheila, **Supp. V:** 70

Ballard, J. G., **Supp. XVI:** 123, 124; **Supp. XVIII:** 136

Ballard, Josephine. *See* McMurtry, Josephine

"Ballena" (Mora), **Supp. XIII:** 224

"Ballet in Numbers for Mary Ellen, A" (Karr), **Supp. XI:** 241

"Ballet of a Buffoon, The" (Sexton), **Supp. II Part 2:** 693

"Ballet of Central Park, The" (Boyle), **Supp. XXIV:** 59

"Ballet of the Fifth Year, The" (Schwartz), **Supp. II Part 2:** 650

Ball Four (Bouton), **Supp. XX: 274**

"Ball Game, The" (Creeley), **Supp. IV Part 1:** 140

Ballistics (Collins), **Supp. XXI:** 57, 65

"Ballistics" (Collins), **Supp. XXI:** 65

"Balloon Hoax, The" (Poe), **III:** 413, 420

"Balm of Recognition, The: Rectifying Wrongs through Generations" (E. Hoffman, lecture), **Supp. XVI:** 155

Balo (Toomer), **Supp. III Part 2:** 484

Balsan, Consuelo, **IV:** 313–314

Balthus, **Supp. IV Part 2:** 623

Balthus Poems, The (Dobyns), **Supp. XIII:** 87

Baltimore, Lord, **I:** 132

Balzac, Honoré de, **I:** 103, 123, 339, 376, 474, 485, 499, 509, 518; **II:** 307, 322, 324, 328, 336, 337; **III:** 61, 174, 184, 320, 382; **IV:** 192; **Retro. Supp. I:** 91, 217, 218, 235; **Retro. Supp. II:** 93; **Supp. I Part 2:** 647; **Supp. XVI:** 72

Bambara, Toni Cade, **Supp. XI: 1–23**

Bam opgrunt (At the abyss) (Asch), **Supp. XXIII:** 6

Banana Bottom (McKay), **Supp. X:** 132, **139–140**

Bananas (film; Allen), **Supp. XV:** 3, 4

Bancal, Jean, **Supp. I Part 2:** 514

Bancroft, George, **I:** 544; **Supp. I Part 2:** 479; **Supp. XXII:** 33

Band, Millen, **Supp. XVIII:** 238

Bandaged Nude, The (Ryan as Finnegan), **Supp. XVIII:** 233, **235–236**

Bandbox (Mallon), **Supp. XIX:** 132, 143

Band of Angels (Warren), **IV:** 245, 254–255

Bandung Files (television series), **Supp. XXI:** 170

Bang the Drum Slowly (Harris), **II:** 424–425

Banjo: A Story without a Plot (McKay), **Supp. X:** 132, **138–139**

"Banjo Song, A" (Dunbar), **Supp. II Part 1:** 197

Bank Director's Son, The: A Real and Intensely Interesting Revelation of City Life (Lippard), **Supp. XXIII:** 184

Bankhead, Tallulah, **IV:** 357; **Supp. IV Part 2:** 574

"Banking Potatoes" (Komunyakaa), **Supp. XIII:** 126

"Bank of England Restriction, The" (Adams), **I:** 4

Banks, Joanne Trautmann, **Supp. XIII:** 297

Banks, Russell, **Supp. V:** 1–19, 227; **Supp. IX:** 153; **Supp. X:** 85; **Supp. XI:** 178; **Supp. XII:** 295, 309, 343; **Supp. XX: 90; Supp. XXIV:** 97

"Banned Poem" (Nye), **Supp. XIII:** 282

Bannon, Barbara, **Supp. XI:** 228

"Banyan" (Swenson), **Supp. IV Part 2:** 651, 652

"Baptism" (Olsen). *See* "O Yes" (Olsen)

"Baptism" (Trethewey), **Supp. XXI:** 246

Baptism, The (Baraka), **Supp. II Part 1:** 40, 41–42, 43

Baptism of Desire (Erdrich), **Supp. IV Part 1:** 259

Barabtarlo, Gennady, **Retro. Supp. I:** 278

Baraka, Imamu Amiri (LeRoi Jones), **Retro. Supp. I:** 411; **Retro. Supp. II:** 280; **Supp. I Part 1:** 63; **Supp. II Part 1: 29–63,** 247, 250; **Supp. III Part 1:** 83; **Supp. IV Part 1:** 169, 244, 369; **Supp. VIII:** 295, 329, 330, 332; **Supp. X:** 324, 328; **Supp. XIII:** 94; **Supp. XIV:** 125, 144; **Supp. XXI:** 172, 227, 228; **Supp. XXIII:** 215; **Supp. XXIV:** 34, 183

"Bar at the Andover Inn, The" (Matthews), **Supp. IX:** 168

"Barbados" (Marshall), **Supp. XI:** 281

"Barbara Frietchie" (Whittier), **Supp. I Part 2:** 695–696

Barbarella (film), **Supp. XI:** 293, **307–308**

"Barbarian Status of Women, The" (Veblen), **Supp. I Part 2:** 636–637

Barbarous Coast, The (Macdonald), **Supp. IV Part 2:** 472, 474

Barbary Shore (Mailer), **III:** 27, 28, 30–31, 33, 35, 36, 40, 44; **Retro. Supp. II: 199–200,** 207; **Supp. XIV:** 162

Barber, Charles, **Supp. XXIII:** 125

Barber, David, **Supp. IV Part 2:** 550; **Supp. XII:** 188–189

Barber, Rowland, **Supp. IV Part 2:** 581

Barber, Samuel, **Supp. IV Part 1:** 84

"Barber's Unhappiness, The" (Saunders), **Supp. XIX:** 229

"Barclay of Ury" (Whittier), **Supp. I Part 2:** 693

Barcott, Bruce, **Supp. XVII:** 32

Bard of Savagery, The: Thorstein Veblen and Modern Social Theory (Diggins), **Supp. I Part 2:** 650

"Barefoot Boy, The" (Whittier), **Supp. I Part 2:** 691, 699–700

Barefoot in the Park (Simon), **Supp. IV Part 2:** 575, 578–579, 586, 590

Bare Hills, The (Winters), **Supp. II Part 2:** 786, 788

"Bare Hills, The" (Winters), **Supp. II Part 2:** 790

Barely and Widely (Zukofsky), **Supp. III Part 2:** 627, 628, 635

Barenblat, Rachel, **Supp. XIII:** 274

Barfield, Owen, **III:** 274, 279

"Bargain Lost, The" (Poe), **III:** 411

Barillas, William, **Supp. XIV:** 177

Barillet, Pierre, **Supp. XVI:** 194

Barker, Arthur, **Supp. XIII:** 167

Barker, Clive, **Supp. V:** 142

Barking Dog (Budbill), **Supp. XIX:** 1, 5

"Barking Man" (Bell), **Supp. X:** 9

Barking Man and Other Stories (Bell), **Supp. X:** 9

Barksdale, Richard, **Retro. Supp. I:** 202, 205; **Supp. I Part 1:** 341, 346

Barlow, Joel, **Supp. I Part 1:** 124; **Supp. I Part 2:** 511, 515, 521; **Supp. II Part 1: 65–86,** 268

Barlow, Judith, **Supp. XXI:** 6

Barlow, R. H., **Supp. XXV:** 122

Barlow, Ruth Baldwin (Mrs. Joel Barlow), **Supp. II Part 1:** 69

"B.A.R. Man, The" (Yates), **Supp. XI:** 341

Barnaby Rudge (Dickens), **III:** 421

Barnacle Soup and Other Stories of the West of Ireland (Gallagher and Gray), **Supp. XXIV:** 166, 172, 178

Barnard, Frederick, **Supp. I Part 2:** 684

Barnard, Rita, **Retro. Supp. II:** 324

Barn Blind (Smiley), **Supp. VI: 292–293**

"Barn Burning" (Faulkner), **II:** 72, 73; **Supp. IV Part 2:** 682; **Supp. XX: 174**

Barnes, Djuna, **Supp. III Part 1: 31–46; Supp. IV Part 1:** 79, 80; **Supp. XVI:** 282; **Supp. XXII:** 165, 167

Barnes, Kim, **Supp. XVIII:** 293

Barnet, Andrea, **Supp. XXII:** 159, 164

Barnett, Claudia, **Supp. XV:** 323, 330, 334

Barnett, Samuel, **Supp. I Part 1:** 2

Barnhardt, Wilton, **Supp. XXII:** 266

"Barn Owl" (Kooser), **Supp. XIX:** 123

Barnstone, Tony, **Supp. XIII:** 115, 126

Barnstone, Willis, **Supp. I Part 2:** 458

Barnum, P. T., **Supp. I Part 2:** 703

Baroja, Pío, **I:** 478

Baron, Zach, **Supp. XVIII:** 150

"Baroque Comment" (Bogan), **Supp. III Part 1:** 56, 58

"Baroque Sunburst, A" (Clampitt), **Supp. IX:** 49

"Baroque Wall-Fountain in the Villa Sciarra, A" (Wilbur), **Supp. III Part 2:** 553

Barr, Robert, **I:** 409, 424

Barracks Thief, The (Wolff), **Supp. VII:** 344–345

"Barred Owl" (Offutt), **Supp. XIX:** 170

Barren Ground (Glasgow), **II:** 174, 175, 178, 179, 184–185, 186, 187, 188, 189, 191, 192, 193, 194; **Supp. X:** 228

Barrés, Auguste M., **I:** 228

Barresi, Dorothy, **Supp. XV:** 100, 102

Barrett, Amy, **Supp. XVIII:** 136

Barrett, E. B., **Supp. XV:** 309

Barrett, Elizabeth, **Supp. IV Part 2:** 430

Barrett, George, **Supp. IX:** 250

Barrett, Ralph, **Supp. I Part 2:** 462

Barrie, J. M., **Supp. XX: 234**

"Barrie Cooke Painting" (Gallagher), **Supp. XXIV:** 171

Barrier, Rober G., **Supp. XXI:** 48–49

Barrier of a Common Language: An American Looks at Contemporary

British Poetry (Gioia), **Supp. XV:** 112, **116–117**

"Barroco: An Essay" (Sobin), **Supp. XVI:** 291

Barron, Jonathan, **Supp. IX:** 299

Barrow, John, **II:** 18

Barrus, Clara, **I:** 220

Barry, Iris, **Supp. XIII:** 170

Barry, Philip, **Retro. Supp. I:** 104; **Supp. IV Part 1:** 83; **Supp. V:** 95

Barstow, Elizabeth Drew. *See* Stoddard, Elizabeth

Bartas, Seigneur du, **IV:** 157

Barth, John, **I:** 121–143; **Supp. I Part 1:** 100; **Supp. III Part 1:** 217; **Supp. IV Part 1:** 48, 379; **Supp. V:** 39, 40; **Supp. IX:** 208; **Supp. X:** 263, 301, 302, 307; **Supp. XI:** 309; **Supp. XII:** 29, 289, 316; **Supp. XIII:** 41, 101, 104; **Supp. XVII:** 183; **Supp. XVIII:** 136, 140, 141; **Supp. XX: 21; Supp. XXII:** 259, 261; **Supp. XXIII:** 42

Barth, Karl, **III:** 40, 258, 291, 303, 309; **IV:** 225; **Retro. Supp. I:** 325, 326, 327

Barth, Robert C., **Supp. XV:** 169

Barthé, Richmond, **Retro. Supp. II:** 115

Barthelme, Donald, **Supp. IV Part 1: 39–58,** 227; **Supp. V:** 2, 39, 44; **Supp. VIII:** 75, 138; **Supp. X:** 263; **Supp. XI:** 25; **Supp. XII:** 29; **Supp. XIII:** 41, 46; **Supp. XVI:** 206; **Supp. XIX:** 235

Barthelme, Frederick, **Supp. XI: 25–41; Supp. XXI:** 38

Barthelme, Peter, **Supp. XI:** 25

Barthelme, Steven, **Supp. XI:** 25, 27, 37

Barthes, Roland, **Supp. IV Part 1:** 39, 119, 126; **Supp. XIII:** 83; **Supp. XVI:** 285, 294; **Supp. XVII:** 244

Bartholomew and the Oobleck (Geisel), **Supp. XVI:** 104

"Bar Time" (B. Collins), **Supp. XVII:** 245

"Bartleby, the Scrivener; A Story of Wall-Street" (Melville), **III:** 88–89; **Retro. Supp. I:** 255

Bartleby in Manhattan and Other Essays (Hardwick), **Supp. III Part 1:** 204, 210

"Bartleby the Scrivener" (Melville), **Supp. XVIII:** 4

Bartlet, Phebe, **I:** 562

Bartlett, Lee, **Supp. VIII:** 291

Bartlett, Mary Dougherty, **Supp. IV Part 1:** 335

Bartlett, William Irving, **Supp. XXV:** 250–251

Barton, Bruce, **III:** 14; **Retro. Supp. I:** 179

Barton, Priscilla. *See* Morison, Mrs. Samuel Eliot (Priscilla Barton)

Barton, Ralph, **Supp. XVI:** 195

Barton, Rev. William E., **Retro. Supp. I:** 179

Bartov, Omer, **Supp. XVI:** 153–154

Bartram, John, **Supp. I Part 1:** 244

Bartram, William, **II:** 313; **Supp. IX:** 171; **Supp. X:** 223

Barzun, Jacques, **Supp. XIV:** 54

"Basement" (Bambara), **Supp. XI:** 5

Basement Tapes, The (album, Dylan), **Supp. XVIII:** 27, 30, 32

"Base of All Metaphysics, The" (Whitman), **IV:** 348

"Base Stealer, The" (Francis), **Supp. IX:** 82

Bashevis, Isaac. *See* Singer, Isaac Bashevis

Bashir, Antonious, **Supp. XX: 116, 120**

Basil Stories, The (Fitzgerald), **Retro. Supp. I:** 109

Basin and Range (McPhee), **Supp. III Part 1:** 309

"Basin of Eggs, A" (Swenson), **Supp. IV Part 2:** 645

"Basket, The" (Lowell), **II:** 522

"Basketball and Beefeaters" (McPhee), **Supp. III Part 1:** 296

"Basketball and Poetry: The Two Richies" (Dunn), **Supp. XI:** 140

"Basketball Player" (L. Michaels), **Supp. XVI:** 209

"Basket of Trips"(Strout), **Supp. XXIII:** 283, 285

Baskin, Leonard, **Supp. X:** 58, 71; **Supp. XV:** 348

Bass, George, **Supp. XXII:** 6

Bass, Rick, **Supp. XIV:** 227; **Supp. XVI: 15–29; Supp. XXI:** 40, 45

Bassard, Katherine Clay, **Supp. XXII:** 148

Basso, Hamilton, **Retro. Supp. I:** 80

Bastard, The (Caldwell), **I:** 291, 292, 308

"Bastille Day" (Lamott), **Supp. XX: 143**

"Bat, The" (Kenyon), **Supp. VII:** 168

Bat, The (Rinehart and Hopwood), **Supp. XXV:** 195, 200

Bataille, Georges, **Supp. VIII:** 4; **Supp. XII:** 1

"Batard" (London), **II:** 468–469

Batchelor, John Calvin, **Supp. XIX:** 142

Bate, W. J., **II:** 531

"Bateau ivre, Le" (Rimbaud; Berrigan, trans.), **Supp. XXIV:** 40

Bates, Arlo, **Retro. Supp. I:** 35

Bates, Blanche, **Supp. XVI:** 182

Bates, Kathy, **Supp. XIII:** 207

Bates, Lee, **Retro. Supp. II:** 46

Bates, Milton J., **Supp. XII:** 62

Bates, Sylvia Chatfield, **II:** 586

Bateson, Gregory, **Supp. XV:** 146

"Bath, The" (Carver), **Supp. III Part 1:** 144, 145

"Bath, The" (Snyder), **Supp. VIII:** 302

Bathwater Wine (Coleman), **Supp. XI:** 83, 90, **91**

"Batter my heart, three person'd God" (Donne), **Supp. I Part 2:** 726; **Supp. XVII:** 119

"Battle, The" (Simpson), **Supp. IX:** 268–269

Battle Cry (film), **Supp. XX: 246**

Battle Cry (Uris), **Supp. XX: 243, 246, 248–250, 255, 256**

Battlefield Where the Moon Says I Love You, The (Stanford), **Supp. XV:** 345

Battle for the Solomons (Wolfert), **Supp. XXI:** 267

Battle-Ground, The (Glasgow), **II:** 175, 176, 177, 178, 193

"Battle Hymn of the Republic" (Sandburg), **III:** 585

"Battle Hymn of the Republic, The" (Howe), **III:** 505

"Battle Hymn of the Republic, The" (Updike), **Retro. Supp. I:** 324

Battle of Angels (T. Williams), **IV:** 380, 381, 383, 385, 386, 387

"Battle of Aspen, The" (Thompson), **Supp. XXIV:** 286–287

"Battle of Lovell's Pond, The" (Longfellow), **II:** 493

Battle of the Atlantic, The (Morison), **Supp. I Part 2:** 490

"Battle of the Baltic, The" (Campbell), **Supp. I Part 1:** 309

"Battle of the Bunker, The" (Snodgrass), **Supp. VI:** 319–320

"***Battle of the Century!!!, The***" (Goldbarth), **Supp. XII:** 193

Battle of the Little Big Horn, The (Sandoz), **Supp. XXIII:** 146

Battle-Pieces and Aspects of the War (Melville), **II:** 538–539; **III:** 92; **IV:** 350; **Retro. Supp. I:** 257

"Battler, The" (Hemingway), **II:** 248; **Retro. Supp. I:** 175

"Battle That Ended the Century, The" (Lovecraft and Barlow), **Supp. XXV:** 122

"Baubles after Bombs" (Peacock), **Supp. XIX:** 200

"Baudelaire" (Schwartz), **Supp. II Part 2:** 663

Baudelaire, Charles, **I:** 58, 63, 384, 389, 420, 569; **II:** 543, 544–545, 552; **III:** 137, 141–142, 143, 409, 417, 418, 421, 428, 448, 466, 474; **IV:** 74, 79, 80, 87, 211, 286; **Retro. Supp. I:** 56, 90; **Retro. Supp. II:** 261, 262, 322, 326; **Supp. I Part 1:** 271; **Supp. III Part 1:** 4, 6, 105; **Supp. XIII:** 77, 284; **Supp. XV:** 165; **Supp. XXI:** 228; **Supp. XXIV:** 152

Baudrillard, Jean, **Supp. IV Part 1:** 45

Bauer, Dale, **Retro. Supp. I:** 381

Bauer, Douglas, **Supp. XII:** 290

Baum, L. Frank, **Supp. I Part 2:** 621; **Supp. IV Part 1:** 101, 113; **Supp. XII:** 42

Baumann, Walter, **III:** 478

Bausch, Richard, **Supp. VII: 39–56; Supp. XVII:** 21

Bawer, Bruce, **Supp. VIII:** 153; **Supp. IX:** 135; **Supp. X:** 187

Baxter, Charles, **Supp. XII:** 22; **Supp. XIV:** 89, 92; **Supp. XVII: 13–24; Supp. XXIII:** 289

Baxter, John, **Supp. XI:** 302

Baxter, Richard, **III:** 199; **IV:** 151, 153; **Supp. I Part 2:** 683

"Baxter's Procrustes" (Chesnutt), **Supp. XIV:** 76

"Bay City Blues" (Chandler), **Supp. IV Part 1:** 129

Baylies, William, **Supp. I Part 1:** 153

Baym, Nina, **Supp. IV Part 2:** 463; **Supp. X:** 229; **Supp. XVI:** 92; **Supp.**

XVIII: 258, 259; **Supp. XXIV:** 28

"Bayou" (Di Piero), **Supp. XIX:** 37

Bayou Folk (Chopin), **Retro. Supp. II: 64–65,** 73; **Supp. I Part 1:** 200, 216, 218

Baziotes, William, **Supp. XV:** 144

"B.C." (Taggard), **Supp. XXII:** 278

Beach, Anna Hampstead, **Supp. XVII:** 75

Beach, Joseph Warren, **I:** 309, 500; **II:** 27; **III:** 319

Beach, Sylvia, **IV:** 404; **Retro. Supp. I:** 109, 422; **Supp. XXII:** 165

"Beaches in Winter" (Kriegel), **Supp. XXIV:** 220, 225

"Beach Women, The" (Pinsky), **Supp. VI:** 241

"Beaded Pear, The" (Simpson), **Supp. IX:** 276

Beagle, Peter, **Supp. X:** 24

Beam, Jeffrey, **Supp. XII:** 98

Beaman, E. O., **Supp. IV Part 2:** 604

Bean, Michael, **Supp. V:** 203

Bean, Robert Bennett, **Supp. II Part 1:** 170

Bean Eaters, The (Brooks), **Supp. III Part 1:** 79–81

Be Angry at the Sun (Jeffers), **Supp. II Part 2:** 434

Bean Spasms (Berrigan, Padgett, and Brainard), **Supp. XXIV:** 41–42

"Beanstalk Country, The" (T. Williams), **IV:** 383

Bean Trees, The (Kingsolver), **Supp. VII:** 197, 199–201, 202, 207, 209

"Bear" (Hogan), **Supp. IV Part 1:** 412

Bear, The (Faulkner), **Supp. VIII:** 184

"Bear, The" (Faulkner), **II:** 71–72, 73, 228; **IV:** 203; **Supp. IV Part 2:** 434; **Supp. IX:** 95; **Supp. X:** 30; **Supp. XIV:** 32; **Supp. XXI:** 37

"Bear, The" (Kinnell), **Supp. III Part 1:** 244

"Bear, The" (Momaday), **Supp. IV Part 2:** 480, 487

Bear and His Daughter: Stories (Stone), **Supp. V:** 295, 308

Beard, Charles, **I:** 214; **IV:** 429; **Supp. I Part 2:** 481, 490, 492, 632, 640, 643, 647

Beard, James, **I:** 341; **Supp. XVII:** 89, 90

Beard, Mary, **Supp. I Part 2:** 481

"Bearded Oaks" (Warren), **IV:** 240

Bearden, Romare, **Retro. Supp. I:** 209; **Supp. VIII:** 337, 342; **Supp. XXI:** 249

"Beard of Bees, A" (X. J. Kennedy), **Supp. XV:** 171

Beardon, Romare, **Supp. XV:** 144

"Beards, The" (Lethem), **Supp. XVIII:** 148

Beardsley, Aubrey, **II:** 56; **IV:** 77

Beaser, Robert, **Supp. XV:** 259

"Beast" (Swenson), **Supp. IV Part 2:** 639

"Beast & Burden, The: Seven Improvisations" (Komunyakaa), **Supp. XIII:** 120, 121

Beast God Forgot to Invent, The (Harrison), **Supp. VIII:** 37, 46, **51–52**

Beast in Me, The (Thurber), **Supp. I Part 2:** 615

"Beast in the Jungle, The" (James), **I:** 570; **II:** 335; **Retro. Supp. I:** 235; **Supp. V:** 103–104

Beast in View (Rukeyser), **Supp. VI:** 272, 273, 279, 280

Beasts of Bethlehem, The (X. J. Kennedy), **Supp. XV:** 163

"Beat! Beat! Drums!" (Whitman), **III:** 585

Beat Down to Your Soul: What Was the Beat Generation? (Charters, ed.), **Supp. XIV:** 152

"Beatific Effigies" (Bronk), **Supp. XXI:** 31

Beaton, Cecil, **Supp. XVI:** 191

"Beatrice Palmato" (Wharton), **Retro. Supp. I:** 379

Beats, The (Krim, ed.), **Supp. XV:** 338

Beattie, Ann, **Supp. V:** 21–37; **Supp. XI:** 26; **Supp. XII:** 80, 139, 294; **Supp. XXI:** 118; **Supp. XXIII:** 289

Beattie, L. Elisabeth, **Supp. XX:** 164, 165

Beatty, General Sam, **I:** 193

Beaty, Jerome, **Supp. IV Part 1:** 331

"Beau Monde of Mrs. Bridge, The" (Connell), **Supp. XIV:** 88, 89

Beaumont, Francis, **Supp. I Part 2:** 422

"Beauties of Santa Cruz, The" (Freneau), **Supp. II Part 1:** 260

Beautiful and Damned, The (Fitzgerald), **II:** 88, 89–91, 93, 263; **Retro. Supp. I:** 103–105, 105, 106, 110; **Supp. IX:** 56, 57

Beautiful Changes, The (Wilbur), **Supp. III Part 2:** 544–550

"Beautiful Changes, The" (Wilbur), **Supp. III Part 2:** 549, 550

Beautiful Child (Silver), **Supp. XXIV:** 273–274

"Beautiful Child, A" (Capote), **Supp. III Part 1:** 113, 125

"Beautiful & Cruel" (Cisneros), **Supp. VII:** 63, 67

"Beautiful Wall, Machu Picchu, The" (Bronk), **Supp. XXI:** 31, 32

"Beautiful Woman Who Sings, The" (Gunn Allen), **Supp. IV Part 1:** 326

"Beauty" (Emerson), **II:** 2, 5

"Beauty" (Sanders), **Supp. XVI:** 277

"Beauty" (Wylie), **Supp. I Part 2:** 710

"Beauty and the Beast" (Dove), **Supp. IV Part 1:** 245

"Beauty and the Beast" (fairy tale), **IV:** 266; **Supp. X:** 88

"Beauty and the Shoe Sluts" (Karr), **Supp. XI:** 250

Beauty of the Husband, The: A Fictional Essay in Twenty-Nine Tangos (Carson), **Supp. XII:** 113–114

Beauty Queen, The (P. N. Warren), **Supp. XX:** 268–269

Beauty's Punishment (Rice), **Supp. VII:** 301

Beauty's Release: The Continued Erotic Adventures of Sleeping Beauty (Rice), **Supp. VII:** 301

Beauvoir, Simone de, **IV:** 477; **Supp. I Part 1:** 51; **Supp. III Part 1:** 200–201, 208; **Supp. IV Part 1:** 360; **Supp. IX:** 4

Beaver Men: Spearheads of Empire (Sandoz), **Supp. XXIV:** 244, **246–247**

"Be Careful" (Zach; Everwine, trans.), **Supp. XV:** 86

Be Careful How You Live (Lacy), **Supp. XV:** 203–204

"Because I could not stop for Death—" (Dickinson), **Retro. Supp. I:** 38–40, 41, 43, 44

"Because It Happened" (Goldbarth), **Supp. XII:** 192

"Because of Libraries We Can Say These Things" (Nye), **Supp. XIII:** 283

"Because of the Waters of the Flood" (Helprin), **Supp. XXV:** 85

"Because the Body Is a Flower"(Crooker), **Supp. XXIII:** 55

"Because You Mentioned the Spiritual Life" (Dunn), **Supp. XI:** 154

Bech: A Book (Updike), **IV:** 214; **Retro. Supp. I:** 329, 335

Bechdel, Alison, **Supp. XXV:** 1–15

Beck, Dave, **I:** 493

Beck, Ervin, **Supp. XXIII:** 94, 95

Beck, Jack, **Supp. IV Part 2:** 560

Beck, Nicholas, **Supp. XVIII:** 252

Beck, Stefan, **Supp. XXII:** 268

Becker, Carl, **Supp. I Part 2:** 492, 493

Becker, Paula. *See* Modersohn, Mrs. Otto (Paula Becker)

Beckett, Samuel, **I:** 71, 91, 142, 298, 461; **III:** 387; **IV:** 95; **Retro. Supp. I:** 206; **Supp. IV Part 1:** 297, 368–369; **Supp. IV Part 2:** 424; **Supp. V:** 23, 53; **Supp. XI:** 104; **Supp. XII:** 21, 150–151; **Supp. XIII:** 74; **Supp. XIV:** 239; **Supp. XVII:** 185; **Supp. XX:** 17; **Supp. XXI:** 18; **Supp. XXII:** 263

Beckett, Tom, **Supp. IV Part 2:** 419

Beckford, William, **I:** 204

Beckonings (Brooks), **Supp. III Part 1:** 85

"Becky" (Toomer), **Supp. III Part 2:** 481, 483; **Supp. IX:** 312

Becky and Her Friends (Hinojosa), **Supp. XIX:** 108–109

Becoming a Man: Half a Life Story (Monette), **Supp. X:** 146, 147, 149, 151, 152, **155–157**

"Becoming a Meadow" (Doty), **Supp. XI:** 124–125

"Becoming and Breaking: Poet and Poem" (Ríos), **Supp. IV Part 2:** 539

Becoming Canonical in American Poetry (Morris), **Retro. Supp. I:** 40

Becoming Light: New and Selected Poems (Jong), **Supp. V:** 115

Bécquer, Gustavo Adolfo, **Supp. XIII:** 312

"Bed, The" (Dixon), **Supp. XII:** 154

Beddoes, Thomas Lovell, **III:** 469; **Retro. Supp. I:** 285

Bedichek, Roy, **Supp. V:** 225

Bedient, Calvin, **Supp. IX:** 298; **Supp. XII:** 98

"Bed in the Sky, The" (Snyder), **Supp. VIII:** 300

Bednarik, Joseph, **Supp. VIII:** 39

"Bedrock" (Proulx), **Supp. VII:** 253

"Bee, The" (Lanier), **Supp. I Part 1:** 364

Beecher, Catharine, **Supp. I Part 2:** 581, 582–583, 584, 586, 588, 589, 591, 599; **Supp. X:** 103; **Supp. XI:** 193

Beecher, Charles, **Supp. I Part 2:** 588, 589

Beecher, Edward, **Supp. I Part 2:** 581, 582, 583, 584, 588, 591

Beecher, Harriet. *See* Stowe, Harriet Beecher

Beecher, Henry Ward, **II:** 275; **Supp. I Part 2:** 581; **Supp. XI:** 193; **Supp. XVIII:** 4

Beecher, Lyman, **Supp. I Part 2:** 580–581, 582, 583, 587, 588, 599; **Supp. XI:** 193

Beecher, Mrs. Lyman (Roxanna Foote), **Supp. I Part 2:** 580–581, 582, 588, 599

Beeching, Jack, **Supp. X:** 114, 117, 118, 123, 125, 126

"Beehive" (Toomer), **Supp. IX:** 317

"Bee Hunt, The" (Irving), **II:** 313

"Beekeeper's Daughter, The" (Plath), **Retro. Supp. II:** 246–247

"Bee Meeting, The" (Plath), **Retro. Supp. II:** 254–255

Bee Poems (Plath), **Retro. Supp. II:** 254–255

Beer, John, **Supp. XVII:** 239

Beer, Thomas, **I:** 405

Beerbohm, Max, **III:** 472; **IV:** 436; **Supp. I Part 2:** 714

"Beer Bottle" (Kooser), **Supp. XIX:** 117

"Beer in the Sergeant Major's Hat, or The Sun Also Sneezes" (Chandler), **Supp. IV Part 1:** 121

Beers, Henry A., **Supp. XX:** 68

"Bees Bees Bees" (J. Scott), **Supp. XVII:** 188, 190

Beethoven, Ludwig van, **II:** 536; **III:** 118; **IV:** 274, 358; **Supp. I Part 1:** 363; **Supp. VIII:** 103

Beet Queen, The (Erdrich), **Supp. IV Part 1:** 259, 260, 264–265, 266, 273, 274, 275

Befo' de War: Echoes in Negro Dialect (Gordon), **Supp. II Part 1:** 201

"Before" (Goldbarth), **Supp. XII:** 175

"Before" (Snyder), **Supp. VIII:** 301

Before Adam (London), **II:** 466

Before Breakfast (O'Neill), **Supp. XXII:** 22

Before Disaster (Winters), **Supp. II Part 2:** 786, 800

"Before Disaster" (Winters), **Supp. II Part 2:** 801, 815

"Before I Knocked" (D. Thomas), **III:** 534

Beforelife, The (F. Wright), **Supp. XVII:** 240, 245–246

"Before March" (MacLeish), **III:** 15

Before My Life Began (Neugeboren), **Supp. XVI:** 224–225

"Before the Altar" (Lowell), **II:** 516

"Before the Birth of one of her children" (Bradstreet), **Supp. I Part 1:** 118

Before the Gringo Came (Atherton), **Supp. XXIV:** 22

"Before the Sky Darkens" (Dunn), **Supp. XI:** 155

"Begat" (Sexton), **Supp. II Part 2: 693**

Beget, Philippe, **Supp. XXIII:** 74

Beggarman, Thief (Shaw), **Supp. XIX:** 251–252

Beggar on Horseback (Kaufman and Connelly), **III:** 394

"Beggar Said So, The" (Singer), **IV:** 12

Beggars in the House of Plenty (Shanley), **Supp. XIV:** 316, **327–328**

Beggar's Opera, The (Gay), **Supp. I Part 2:** 523

Begiebing, Robert, **Retro. Supp. II:** 210

Begin Again (Paley), **Supp. VI:** 221

Beginners (Carver), **Supp. XXIV:** 177

"Beginning and the End, The" (Jeffers), **Supp. II Part 2:** 420–421, 424

"Beginning of Decadence, The" (Jeffers), **Supp. II Part 2:** 420

"Beginning of Enthusiasm, The" (Salinas), **Supp. XIII:** 327–328

Beginning of Wisdom, The (Benét), **I:** 358; **Supp. XI:** 44

"Beginnings of Sorrow, The" (P. Benedict), **Supp. XXIII:** 48

Be Glad You're Neurotic (Bisch), **Supp. I Part 2:** 608

"Begotten of the Spleen" (Simic), **Supp. VIII:** 277

"Behaving Like a Jew" (Stern), **Supp. IX: 290–291,** 294

"Behavior" (Emerson), **II:** 2, 4

Behavior of Titans, The (Merton), **Supp. VIII:** 201

Behind a Mask (Alcott), **Supp. I Part 1:** 36–37, 43–44

"Behind a Wall" (Lowell), **II:** 516

Behind the Movie Camera (radio show), **Supp. XV:** 147

"Behold the Key" (Malamud), **Supp. I Part 2:** 437

Behrendt, Stephen, **Supp. X:** 204

Behrman, S. N., **Supp. V:** 95

Beichman, Arnold, **Supp. XXV:** 254, 258, 264

Beidler, Peter G., **Supp. IV Part 2:** 557

Beidler, Philip D., **Supp. XII:** 69

Beige Dolorosa (Harrison), **Supp. VIII:** 40, 51

Beiles, Sinclair, **Supp. XII:** 129

Beiliss, Mendel, **Supp. I Part 2:** 427, 446, 447, 448

"Being a Constellation" (A. Finch), **Supp. XVII:** 72

"Being a Lutheran Boy-God in Minnesota" (R. Bly), **Supp. IV Part 1:** 59, 67

Being and Race (Johnson), **Supp. VI:** 193, 199

Being and Time (Heidegger), **Supp. VIII:** 9

Being Busted (Fiedler), **Supp. XIII:** 95, 102, 104

Being Geniuses Together: 1920–1930 (Boyle), **Supp. XXIV:** 63, 64

Being John Malkovich (Kaufman), **Supp. XV:** 16

Being Perfect (Quindlen), **Supp. XVII:** 167, 179

Being There (Kosinski), **Supp. VII:** 215, 216, 222–223

Beiswanger, George, **Retro. Supp. II:** 220

Beka Lamb (Edgell), **Supp. XXIII:** 83, 85, **86–88,** 93–94, 95

Belasco, David, **Supp. XVI:** 182; **Supp. XXI:** 151

Bel Canto (Patchett), **Supp. XII:** 307, 310, **320–322**

Belchamber (Sturgis), **Supp. XX: 227, 233, 238–240**

"Beleaguered City, The" (Longfellow), **II:** 498

Belfry of Bruges, The, and Other Poems (Longfellow), **II:** 489; **Retro. Supp. II:** 157, 168

"Belief" (Levine), **Supp. V:** 186, 190

"Belief in the Self Abandoned, The" (Bronk), **Supp. XXI:** 30

"Beliefs of Writers, The" (Doctorow), **Supp. IV Part 1:** 235–236

Believeniks! (Lethem and Sorrentino), **Supp. XVIII:** 148–149

Believers (C. Baxter), **Supp. XVII:** 20–21, 22

"Believers" (C. Baxter), **Supp. XVII:** 21

"Believers, The/Los Creyentes" (Kingsolver), **Supp. VII:** 208

Belinda (Rice), **Supp. VII:** 301–302

"Belinda's Petition" (Dove), **Supp. IV Part 1:** 245

"Belita" (Ríos), **Supp. IV Part 2:** 541

Belitt, Ben, **Supp. XII:** 260

Bell, Archibald, **Supp. XX: 284, 285**

Bell, Bernard, **Supp. XXII:** 182

Bell, Clive, **IV:** 87

Bell, Daniel, **Supp. I Part 2:** 648

Bell, George Kennedy Allen, **Retro. Supp. I:** 65

Bell, Madison Smartt, **Supp. X: 1–20; Supp. XVII:** 236; **Supp. XIX:** 58–59, 60–61; **Supp. XXI:** 48; **Supp. XXIII:** 43

Bell, Marvin, **Supp. V:** 337, 339; **Supp. IX:** 152; **Supp. XI:** 316; **Supp. XXIV:** 165

Bell, Michael, **Retro. Supp. II:** 139

Bell, Pearl K., **Supp. XI:** 233; **Supp. XXV:** 253

Bell, Quentin, **Supp. I Part 2:** 636

Bell, Whitfield J., Jr., **II:** 123

Bellafante, Gina, **Supp. VIII:** 85

Bellamy, Edward, **II:** 276; **Supp. I Part 2:** 641; **Supp. XI:** 200, 203

Bellarosa Connection, The (Bellow), **Retro. Supp. II:** 31, 32

"Belle Dollinger" (Masters), **Supp. I Part 2:** 463

Belleforest, François de, **IV:** 370

"Belle Zoraïde, La" (Chopin), **Supp. I Part 1:** 215–216

Bell in the Fog and Other Stories, The (Atherton), **Supp. XXIV:** 23

Bell Jar, The (Plath), **Retro. Supp. II:** 242, **249–250;** **Supp. I Part 2:** 526, 527, 529, 531–536, 539, 540, 541, 542, 544

Belloc, Hilary, **III:** 176; **IV:** 432

"Bellocq" (Trethewey), **Supp. XXI:** 253

Bellocq, E. J., **Supp. XXI:** 246, 251

Bellocq's Ophelia (Trethewey), **Supp. XXI:** 243, 246, **251–254**

"Bellocq's Ophelia" (Trethewey), **Supp. XXI:** 254

Bellow, Saul, **I:** 113, 138–139, **144–166,** 375, 517; **II:** 579; **III:** 40; **IV:** 3, 19, 217, 340; **Retro. Supp. II: 19–36,** 118, 279, 307, 324; **Supp. I Part 2:** 428, 451; **Supp. II Part 1:** 109; **Supp. IV Part 1:** 30; **Supp. V:** 258; **Supp. VIII:** 98, 176, 234, 236–237, 245; **Supp. IX:** 212, 227; **Supp. XI:** 64, 233; **Supp. XII:** 159, 165, 170, 310; **Supp. XIII:** 106; **Supp. XV:** 143; **Supp. XVI:** 208; **Supp. XVIII:** 90; **Supp. XIX:** 157, 158, 261; **Supp. XX: 244; Supp. XXII:** 268; **Supp. XXIII:** 166; **Supp. XXV:** 79

Bellows, George, **Supp. XV:** 295

"Bells, The" (Poe), **III:** 593; **Retro. Supp. II:** 266; **Supp. I Part 2:** 388

"Bells, The" (Sexton), **Supp. II Part 2:** 673

"Bells for John Whiteside's Daughter" (Ransom), **III:** 490

"Bells of Lynn, The" (Longfellow), **II:** 498

"Bells of San Blas, The" (Longfellow), **II:** 490–491, 493, 498

"Bell Tower, The" (Melville), **III:** 91

"Belly, The" (Dobyns), **Supp. XIII:** 87

'Bel of Prairie Eden (Lippard), **Supp. XXIII:** 178, 186

"Belonging" (Pickering), **Supp. XXI:** 202

"Belonging Kind, The" (W. Gibson and J. Shirley), **Supp. XVI:** 123

Beloved (Morrison), **Supp. III Part 1:** 364, 372–379; **Supp. IV Part 1:** 13–14; **Supp. V:** 259; **Supp. VIII:** 343; **Supp. XIII:** 60; **Supp. XXII:** 78, 109; **Supp. XXIV:** 186

Beloved, The (Gibran), **Supp. XX: 125**

"Beloved, The" (Halliday), **Supp. XIX:** 92

Beloved Lady: A History of Jane Addams' Ideas on Reform and Peace (Farrell), **Supp. I Part 1:** 24

Beloved Stranger, The (Bynner), **Supp. XV:** 44, 50

Bemorse, John, **Supp. XX: 62**

Benchley, Robert, **I:** 48, 482; **II:** 435; **III:** 53; **Supp. IX:** 190, 195, 204

Benda, W. T., **Retro. Supp. I:** 13

Bender, Aimee, **Supp. XXII:** 49

Bending of a Twig, The (Coke), **Supp. XX: 235**

Bend Sinister (Nabokov), **III:** 253–254; **Retro. Supp. I:** 265, 266, 270

"Beneath the Sidewalk" (Dunn), **Supp. XI:** 145

"Beneath the Smooth Skin of America" (Sanders), **Supp. XVI:** 275

Benedict, Elizabeth, **Supp. XVIII:** 289

Benedict, Laura, **Supp. XXIII:** 35, 36, 49

Benedict, Pinckney, **Supp. XXIII: 35–50**

Benedict, Ruth, **Supp. IX:** 229

Benefactor, The (Sontag), **Supp. III Part 2:** 451, 455, 468, 469

"Benefit Performance" (Malamud), **Supp. I Part 2:** 431

Benét, Laura, **Supp. XI:** 44

Benét, Rosemary, **Supp. XI:** 44, 51; **Supp. XXV:** 201

Benét, Stephen Vincent, **I:** 358; **II:** 177; **III:** 22; **IV:** 129; **Supp. XI: 43–61**

Benét, William Rose, **II:** 530; **Retro. Supp. I:** 108; **Supp. I Part 2:** 709; **Supp. XI:** 43, 44; **Supp. XIV:** 119, 122, 129

Ben Franklin's Wit and Wisdom (Franklin), **II:** 111

Ben-Gurion, David, **Supp. XX: 243**

Ben-Hur (film), **Supp. IV Part 2:** 683

Benigna Machiavelli (Gilman), **Supp. XI:** 201, 208

Benitez, R. Michael, **Retro. Supp. II:** 264

Benito Cereno (Lowell), **II:** 546; **Retro. Supp. II:** 181

"Benito Cereno" (Melville), **III:** 91; **Retro. Supp. I:** 255; **Retro. Supp. II:** 188; **Supp. XVII:** 185

Benito's Dream Bottle (Nye), **Supp. XIII:** 278

"Bênitou's Slave, The" (Chopin), **Retro. Supp. II:** 64

Benjamin, Walter, **Supp. IX:** 133; **Supp. XVI:** 290, 291; **Supp. XXIII:** 28, 29, 30, 31

Benjamin Franklin (Van Doren), **Supp. I Part 2:** 486

"Benjamin Pantier" (Masters), **Supp. I Part 2:** 461

Bennett, Anne Virginia, **II:** 184

Bennett, Arnold, **I:** 103; **II:** 337; **Supp. XVI:** 190

Bennett, Elizabeth, **Supp. VIII:** 58

Bennett, Patrick, **Supp. V:** 225

Bennett, Paula, **Retro. Supp. I:** 29, 33, 42; **Supp. XX: 286**

Bennett, Reginald, **Supp. XXII:** 218

Bennett, William, **Supp. VIII:** 245

Benson, A. C., **Supp. XX: 238**

Benson, Arthur, **Supp. XX: 233**

Benson, E. F., **Supp. XX:** 229

Benson, Heidi, **Supp. XVIII:** 136

Benson, Jackson J., **Supp. IV Part 2:** 613

Benson, Martin, **Supp. XVIII:** 38

Benstock, Shari, **Retro. Supp. I:** 361, 368, 371, 382; **Supp. XX: 240**

Bentham, Jeremy, **I:** 279; **Supp. I Part 2:** 635

Bentley, Anna, **Supp. XXI:** 5

Bentley, Arthur, **Supp. XXI:** 4, 5

Bentley, Eric R., **IV:** 396

Bentley, Nelson, **Supp. IX:** 324

Bentley, Richard, **III:** 79, 86

Benton, Robert, **Supp. IV Part 1:** 236

"Bent Tones" (Wright), **Supp. XV:** 346

Benveniste, Emile, **Supp. XVI:** 292

Benzel, Jan, **Supp. XVI:** 112

Beowulf, **Supp. II Part 1:** 6; **Supp. XVII:** 70, 73

Beran, Carol, **Supp. XIII:** 25

"Berck-Plage" (Plath), **Retro. Supp. II:** 253–254

Bercovitch, Sacvan, **Retro. Supp. I:** 408; **Retro. Supp. II:** 325, 330; **Supp. I Part 1:** 99; **Supp. I Part 2:** 659

Berdyaev, Nikolai, **I:** 494; **III:** 292

"Bereaved Apartments" (Kingsolver), **Supp. VII:** 203

"Bereavement in their death to feel" (Dickinson), **Retro. Supp. I:** 43, 44

"Berenice" (Poe), **III:** 415, 416, 425; **Retro. Supp. II:** 270

Bérénice (Racine), **II:** 573

Berenson, Bernard, **Retro. Supp. I:** 381; **Supp. IV Part 1:** 314; **Supp. XIV:** 335, 336, 337; **Supp. XVII:** 99; **Supp. XXI:** 5

Berenson, Mary Smith, **Supp. XXI:** 4, 5, 6

Berg, James, **Supp. XIV:** 157, 159

Berg, Stephen, **Supp. IV Part 1:** 60

Berger, Alan, **Supp. XVII:** 39

Berger, Charles, **Retro. Supp. I:** 311

Berger, John, **Supp. XVI:** 284; **Supp. XXIII:** 167, 168–169; **Supp. XXIV:** 94

Berger, Roger, **Supp. XIII:** 237

Berger, Thomas, **III:** 258; **Supp. XII:** 171

Berghash, Rachel, **Supp. XXIV:** 172

Bergman, Ingmar, **I:** 291; **Supp. XV:** 7, 8, 12

Bergson, Henri, **I:** 224; **II:** 163, 165, 166, 359; **III:** 8, 9, 488, 619; **IV:** 86, 122, 466, 467; **Retro. Supp. I:** 55, 57, 80; **Supp. IV Part 1:** 42; **Supp. XXII:** 158

Berkeley, Anthony, **Supp. IV Part 1:** 341

Berkeley, George, **II:** 10, 349, 357, 480, 554

Berkman, Alexander, **Supp. XXIII:** 161; **Supp. XXV:** 19

Berkman, Leonard, **Supp. XV:** 321

Berkowitz, Gerald, **Supp. IV Part 2:** 590

Berkson, Bill, **Supp. XXIII:** 217, 218

Berlin, Isaiah, **Supp. XXII:** 258

Berlin Alexanderplatz (Döblin), **Supp. XV:** 137

Berlin Stories (Isherwood), **Supp. IV Part 1:** 82; **Supp. XIV:** 155, 156, 161, 162, 164, 165

Berlioz, Hector, **Supp. XV:** 33

Berlyne, Daniel E., **Supp. I Part 2:** 672

Berman, Alexander, **Supp. XVII:** 103

Berman, Carolyn Vellenga, **Supp. XXII:** 147

Bernard Clare (Farrell), **II:** 38, 39

Bernard of Clairvaux, Saint, **I:** 22; **II:** 538

Bernays, Thekla, **Retro. Supp. II:** 65

Berne, Suzanne, **Supp. XII:** 320

Berne, Victoria (pseudonym). *See* Fisher, M. F. K.

Berneis, Peter, **IV:** 383

Bernhard, Brendan, **Supp. XIV:** 163

Bernhard, Thomas, **Supp. XX:** 91

Bernhardt, Sarah, **I:** 484; **Retro. Supp. I:** 377

Bernice (Glaspell), **Supp. III Part 1:** 179

"Bernice Bobs Her Hair" (Fitzgerald), **II:** 88; **Retro. Supp. I:** 103

Bernstein, Aline, **IV:** 455, 456

Bernstein, Andrea, **Supp. IX:** 146

Bernstein, Carl, **Supp. XXIV:** 293

Bernstein, Charles, **Supp. IV Part 2:** 421, 426; **Supp. XXIV:** 40, 41, 45–46

Bernstein, Elizabeth, **Supp. XII:** 318

Bernstein, Leonard, **I:** 28; **Supp. I Part 1:** 288, 289; **Supp. IV Part 1:** 83, 84

Bernstein, Melvin, **Supp. XIV:** 41, 46

Bernstein, Michael André, **Retro. Supp. I:** 427

Bernstein, Richard, **Supp. IX:** 253, 262; **Supp. XII:** 113; **Supp. XIV:** 33; **Supp. XXII:** 261

Berrett, Jesse, **Supp. XIII:** 241, 242

Berrigan, Ted, **Supp. XIV:** 150; **Supp. XXII:** 224, 225, 228, 231; **Supp. XXIII:** 218, 221; **Supp. XXIV: 33–47**

Berroa y Canelo, Quiterio, **Supp. XXI:** 104

"Berry" (Hughes), **Supp. I Part 1:** 329, 330

Berry, Eleanor, **Supp. XXIII:** 246

Berry, Faith, **Retro. Supp. I:** 194, 201

Berry, Walter, **IV:** 313–314, 326

Berry, Wendell, **Supp. VIII:** 304; **Supp. X: 21–39; Supp. XII:** 202; **Supp. XIII: 1–2; Supp. XIV:** 179; **Supp. XVI:** 39, 56; **Supp. XVIII:** 192; **Supp. XXI:** 90

"Berry Feast, A" (Snyder), **Supp. VIII:** 289, 297

Berryman, John, **I: 167–189,** 405, 441–442, 521; **II:** 554; **III:** 273; **IV:** 138, 430; **Retro. Supp. I:** 430; **Retro. Supp. II:** 175, 178; **Supp. I Part 2:** 546; **Supp. II Part 1:** 109; **Supp. III Part 2:** 541, 561, 595, 596, 603; **Supp. IV Part 2:** 620, 639; **Supp. V:** 179–180, 337; **Supp. IX:** 152; **Supp. XI:** 240; **Supp. XV:** 93; **Supp. XVII:** 111; **Supp. XXII:** 83

Berryman, Mrs. John, **I:** 168–169

Berryman's Sonnets (Berryman), **I:** 168, 175–178

"Berry Territory" (Snyder), **Supp. VIII:** 304

Berthoff, Warner, **Supp. I Part 1:** 133

Bertolucci, Bernardo, **Supp. IV Part 1:** 94

"Bertrand Hume" (Masters), **Supp. I Part 2:** 463–464

Besco, Glenn, **Supp. XXIII:** 125

"Best, the Most, The" (Carruth), **Supp. XVI:** 59

Best American Essays 1987, The (G. Talese and R. Atwan, eds.), **Supp. XVI:** 273

Best American Essays 1988, The (Dillard, ed.), **Supp. VIII:** 272

Best American Essays 1989, The (Wolff, ed.), **Supp. XVII:** 208

Best American Essays 1993, The (J. Epstein, ed.), **Supp. XVI:** 275

Best American Essays 1997, The (Frazier, ed.), **Supp. VIII:** 272; **Supp. XVII:** 207

Best American Essays 1999, The (E. Hoagland and R. Atwan, eds.), **Supp. XVI:** 277

Best American Essays 2008, The, **Supp. XXIV:** 230

Best American Essays 2009, The, **Supp. XXIV:** 230

Best American Essays for College Students, The (R. Atwan, ed.), **Supp. XVI:** 273

Best American Fantasy, 2010 (Brockmeier, ed.), **Supp. XXII:** 49–50

Best American New Voices 2001 (C. Baxter, ed.), **Supp. XVII:** 22

Best American Poetry, The: 1988 (Ashbery, ed.), **Supp. III Part 1:** 26

Best American Poetry 2000, The (Dove and Lehman, eds.), **Supp. XXI:** 246

Best American Poetry 2006, The (Collins, ed.), **Supp. XXI:** 54

Best American Short Stories, **I:**174; **II:** 587; **III:** 443; **Supp. IV Part 1:** 102, 315; **Supp. IX:** 114; **Supp. X:** 301

Best American Short Stories, 1915–1050, The, **Supp. IX:** 4

Best American Short Stories 1965, The (Foley, ed.), **Supp. XVI:** 225

Best American Short Stories 1979, The, **Supp. XXIII:** 290

Best American Short Stories 1982, The (Gardner, ed.), **Supp. XVII:** 16

Best American Short Stories 1983, The (A. Tyler, ed.), **Supp. XVI:** 37

Best American Short Stories 1986, The (Carver, ed.), **Supp. XVII:** 17

Best American Short Stories 1988, The (Helprin, ed.), **Supp. XVI:** 16

Best American Short Stories 1989, The (Atwood, ed.), **Supp. XVII:** 18; **Supp. XXI:** 39, 42

Best American Short Stories 1991, The (Adams and Kenison, eds.), **Supp. XVI:** 256

Best American Short Stories 1996, The, **Supp. XXIII:** 295

Best American Short Stories 1997, **Supp. XXII:** 75

Best American Short Stories 2001, The (Kenison and Kingsover, eds.), **Supp. XVI:** 24

Best American Short Stories 2007, The, **Supp. XXIII:** 290

Best American Short Stories of 1942, The, **Supp. V:** 316

Best American Short Stories of 1944, The, **Supp. IX:** 119

Best American Short Stories of the Century (Updike, ed.), **Supp. X:** 163

Best American Short Stories of the Eighties, The (Ravenal, ed.), **Supp. IV Part 1:** 93

Best American Sports Writing of the Century, The (Halberstam, ed.), **Supp. XVII:** 204

"Best China Saucer, The" (Jewett), **Retro. Supp. II:** 145–146

Best Creative Nonfiction Volume 2, The, **Supp. XXIV:** 230

Bester, Alfred, **Supp. XVI:** 123

Best Hour of the Night, The (Simpson), **Supp. IX: 277–279**

Bestiaire, Le (Apollinaire), **IV:** 80

Bestiary, A (Wilbur), **Supp. III Part 2:** 552

"Bestiary for the Fingers of My Right Hand" (Simic), **Supp. VIII:** 274, 275

Best Man, The: A Play About Politics (Vidal), **Supp. IV Part 2:** 683

"Best of Everything, The" (Yates), **Supp. XI:** 341

Best of Pickering, The (Pickering), **Supp. XXI:** 192, 198

Best of Plimpton (Plimpton), **Supp. XVI:** 238, 239, 240

Best Short Plays, The (Mayorga), **IV:** 381

Best Short Stories, The (O'Brien, ed.), **I:** 289

Best Short Stories by Negro Writers, The (Hughes, ed.), **Supp. I Part 1:** 345

Best Short Stories of 1926, The (O'Brien, ed.), **Supp. XVIII:** 279

Best Short Stories of 1934 (O'Brien, ed.), **Supp. XVIII:** 227

Best Short Stories of 1938 (O'Brien, ed.), **Supp. XIX:** 256; **Supp. XX:** 34

Best That Ever Did It, The (Lacy), **Supp. XV:** 201–202

Best Times, The: An Informal Memoir (Dos Passos), **I:** 475, 482

Best Words, Best Order: Essays on Poetry (Dobyns), **Supp. XIII:** 74, **76–78,** 87

Best Years of Our Lives, The (film; Wyler), **Supp. XV:** 195

"BETANCOURT" (Baraka), **Supp. II Part 1:** 33, 34

Bête humaine, La (Zola), **III:** 316, 318

"Bethe" (Hellman), **Supp. I Part 1:** 293

Bethea, David, **Supp. VIII:** 27

Bethel Merriday (Lewis), **II:** 455

Bethke, Bruce, **Supp. XVI:** 121

Bethlehem in Broad Daylight (Doty), **Supp. XI:** 121, **122–123**

Bethune, Mary McLeod, **Retro. Supp. I:** 197; **Supp. I Part 1:** 333

Bethurum, Dorothy, **IV:** 121

"Betrayal" (Lanier), **Supp. I Part 1:** 364

"Betrothed" (Bogan), **Supp. III Part 1:** 49–51

Bettelheim, Bruno, **Supp. I Part 2:** 622; **Supp. X:** 77, 84; **Supp. XIV:** 126; **Supp. XVI:** 33

Better Days (Price), **Supp. VI:** 264

Better Sort, The (James), **II:** 335

Better Than Sex (Thompson), **Supp. XXIV:** 283

"Better Things in Life, The" (Loos), **Supp. XVI:** 194

Betty Leicester (Jewett), **II:** 406

Betty Leicester's Christmas (Jewett), **II:** 406; **Retro. Supp. II:** 145

Betty's Summer Vacation (Durang), **Supp. XXIV: 125–126**

Between Angels (Dunn), **Supp. XI: 149–159**

"Between Angels" (Dunn), **Supp. XI:** 150

Between Fantoine and Agapa (Pinget), **Supp. V:** 39

"Between Memory and History: A Writer's Voice" (Kreisler), **Supp. XVI:** 155

Between Silences: A Voice from China (Jin), **Supp. XVIII:** 91, 92, 93

"Between the Porch and the Altar" (Lowell), **II:** 540–541

"Between the World and Me" (Wright), **Supp. II Part 1:** 228

Between Time and Timbuktu (Vonnegut), **Supp. II Part 2:** 753, 759

Between Two Rivers (Kenny), **Supp. XXIII:** 143

Beuka, Robert A., **Supp. XIX:** 263; **Supp. XXI:** 47

"Be Very Afraid—Of Loss of Liberty at Home" (P. N. Warren), **Supp. XX: 272–273**

Bevis, Howard L., **Supp. I Part 2:** 611

Bevis, John, **Supp. I Part 2:** 503

Bewilderment: New Poems and Translations (Ferry), **Supp. XXIV: 160–161**

"Bewitched" (Wharton), **IV:** 316

Bewley, Marius, **I:** 336

Beyer, Werner, **Supp. XXIII:** 145

Beyle, Marie Henri. *See* Stendhal

Beyond (Goldbarth), **Supp. XII:** 192

Beyond a Boundary (C. L. R. James), **Supp. XXI:** 159, 170–171

Beyond Black Bear Lake (LaBastille), **Supp. X:** 95, **99–102,** 108

"Beyond Charles River to the Acheron" (Lowell), **II:** 541

Beyond Criticism (Shapiro), **Supp. II Part 2:** 703, 711

Beyond Culture (Trilling), **Supp. III Part 2:** 508–512

Beyond Desire (Anderson), **I:** 111

Beyond Document: The Art of Nonfiction Film (Warren, ed.), **Supp. IV Part 2:** 434

Beyond Forgetting (Hughes, ed.; foreword by Gallagher), **Supp. XXIV:** 167, 171

Beyond Good and Evil (Nietzsche), **Supp. IV Part 2:** 519

"Beyond Harm" (Olds), **Supp. X:** 210

Beyond Katrina: A Meditation on the Mississippi Gulf Coast (Trethewey), **Supp. XXI:** 248

"Beyond My Solitude" (Gibran), **Supp. XX:** 119

"Beyond the Alps" (Lowell), **II:** 547, 550

"Beyond the Bayou" (Chopin), **Supp. I Part 1:** 215

Beyond the Boom: New Voices on American Life, Culture and Politics (Teachout), **Supp. XIX:** 137

Beyond the Horizon (O'Neill), **III:** 389; **Supp. XXI:** 13; **Supp. XXII:** 22

Beyond the Hundredth Meridian: John Wesley Powell and the Second Opening of the West (Stegner), **Supp. IV Part 2:** 599, 603–604, 611

"Beyond the Kittery Bridge" (Hatlen), **Supp. V:** 138

Beyond the Law (film) (Mailer), **Retro. Supp. II:** 205

Beyond Therapy (Durang), **Supp. XXIV:** **119–120**

"Beyond the Sea (at the sanatorium)" (Salinas), **Supp. XIII:** 325

Beyond the Wall: Essays from the Outside (Abbey), **Supp. XIII:** 13

Beyond the Wall of Sleep (Lovecraft), **Supp. XXV:** 113

Beyond the Writers' Workshop: New Ways to Write Creative Nonfiction (C. Bly), **Supp. XVI:** 41

Beyond Tragedy (Niebuhr), **III:** 300–303

Bezner, Kevin, **Supp. XII:** 202

B. F.'s Daughter (Marquand), **III:** 59, 65, 68, 69

Bhagavad Gita, **III:** 566; **IV:** 183

"Biafra: A People Betrayed" (Vonnegut), **Supp. II Part 2:** 760

Bianchi, Martha Dickinson, **I:** 470; **Retro. Supp. I:** 35, 37, 38

Bible, **I:** 191, 280, 414, 421, 490, 506; **II:** 6, 12, 15, 17, 108, 231, 237, 238, 252, 267, 302; **III:** 28, 199, 308–309, 341, 343, 350, 356, 402, 492, 519, 565, 577; **IV:** 11, 13, 42, 57, 60, 67, 152, 153, 154, 155, 164, 165, 296, 337, 341, 367, 369, 370, 371, 438; **Retro. Supp. I:** 91; **Supp. I Part 1:** 4, 6, 63, 101, 104, 105, 113, 193, 369; **Supp. I Part 2:** 388, 433, 494, 515, 516, 517, 583, 584, 587, 589, 653, 689, 690, 691; **Supp. IV Part 1:** 284; **Supp. VIII:** 20; **Supp. IX:** 246; **Supp. XIV:** 225. *See also* names of biblical books; New Testament; Old Testament

Biblia Americana (Mather), **Supp. II Part 2:** 442

Biblical Dialogues between a Father and His Family (Rowson), **Supp. XV:** 245–246

"Bibliography of the King's Book, A, or, Eikon Basilike" (Howe), **Supp. IV Part 2:** 435

Bibliography of the King's Book, A; or, Eikon Basilike (Almack), **Supp. IV Part 2:** 435

Bickel, Freddy. *See* March, Fredric

Bidart, Frank, **Retro. Supp. II:** 48, 50, 52, 182, 183, 184; **Supp. XV:** **19–37;** **Supp. XVIII:** 91,92; **Supp. XIX:** 82

Bid Me to Live (Doolittle), **Supp. I Part 1:** 258, 260, 268, 269, 270

"*Bien Pretty*" (Cisneros), **Supp. VII:** 70

"Bienvenidos" (Mora), **Supp. XIII:** 220

Bierce, Albert, **I:** 191, 209

Bierce, Ambrose, **I:** **190–213,** 419; **II:** 74, 264, 271; **IV:** 350; **Retro. Supp. II:** 72; **Supp. XXV:** 26

Bierce, Mrs. Ambrose, **I:** 194–195, 199

Bierce, Day, **I:** 195, 199

Bierce, Helen, **I:** 210

Bierce, Leigh, **I:** 195, 198, 208

Bierce, General Lucius Verus, **I:** 191

Bierce, Marcus, **I:** 190, 191

Bierce, Mrs. Marcus, **I:** 190, 191

Bierds, Linda, **Supp. XVII:** **25–37**

Biffle, Kent, **Supp. V:** 225

"Bi-Focal" (Stafford), **Supp. XI:** 318, 321

Bigamist's Daughter, A (McDermott), **Supp. XVIII:** 155, **156–158,** 160, 166

Big as Life (Doctorow), **Supp. IV Part 1:** 231, 234

Big Bad Love (film, Howard), **Supp. XXI:** 39

Big Bad Love (L. Brown), **Supp. XXI:** 40, 42, **44–45**

"Big Bite" (Mailer), **Retro. Supp. II:** 204

"Big Blonde" (Parker), **Supp. IX:** 189, 192, 193, 195, 196, 203

Big Bozo, The (Glaspell), **Supp. III Part 1:** 182

Bigelow, Gordon, **Supp. X:** 222, 227, 229

Bigelow, Jacob, **Supp. I Part 1:** 302

Bigelow Papers, Second Series, The (Lowell), **Supp. I Part 2:** 406, 415–416

Bigelow Papers, The (Lowell), **Supp. I Part 2:** 406, 407, 408, 410, 411–412, 415, 417, 424

"Big Fiddle" (Boyle), **Supp. XXIV:** 54

Big Fix, The (Lacy), **Supp. XV:** 204–205

Bigfoot Dreams (Prose), **Supp. XVI:** 253–254

Big Funk, The: A Casual Play (Shanley), **Supp. XIV:** 316, **327**

"Big Game" (Boyle), **Supp. XX:** 20

Big Game, The (film), **Supp. XIX:** 244

Big Gold Dream, The (C. Himes), **Supp. XVI:** 143, 144

"Bight, The" (Bishop), **Retro. Supp. II:** 38, 45

Big Hunger: Stories 1932–1959 (Fante), **Supp. XI:** 160

Big Knife, The (Odets), **Supp. II Part 2:** 546, 547, 548

Big Knockover, The (Hammett), **Supp. I Part 1:** 292; **Supp. IV Part 1:** 344, 345, 356

Big Laugh, The (O'Hara), **III:** 362, 373–375

Big Man (Neugeboren), **Supp. XVI:** 219, **220,** 221, 225

Big Money, The (Dos Passos), **I:** 482, 483, 486–487, 489; **Supp. I Part 2:** 646, 647

Big Picture (Everett), **Supp. XVIII:** 54, 66

"Big Picture" (Everett), **Supp. XVIII:** 66

"Big Picture" (Halliday), **Supp. XIX:** 93

"Big Rock Candy Figgy Pudding Pitfall, The" (Didion), **Supp. IV Part 1:** 195

Big Rock Candy Mountain, The (Stegner), **Supp. IV Part 2:** 596, 597, 598, 599, 600, 603, 604, 605, 606–607, 608, 610–611

Bigsby, C. W. E. (Christopher), **Supp. IX:** 137, 140; **Supp. XV:** 332

Big Sea, The (Hughes), **Retro. Supp. I:** 195, 197, 199, 201, 204; **Supp. I Part 1:** 322, 332, 333; **Supp. II Part 1:** 233–234; **Supp. XIX:** 77; **Supp. XXII:** 3

Big Sky, The (Mora), **Supp. XIII:** 221

Big Sleep, The (Chandler), **Supp. IV Part 1:** 122–125, 127, 128, 134

Big Sleep, The (film), **Supp. IV Part 1:** 130; **Supp. XVIII:** 148

Big Strike, The (Ryan as Quin), **Supp. XVIII:** 226,**232–233**

Big Sur (Kerouac), **Supp. III Part 1:** 230

Big Sur and the Oranges of Hieronymous Bosch (H. Miller), **III:** 189–190

Big Town, The (Lardner), **II:** 426, 429

"Big Two-Hearted River" (Hemingway), **II:** 249; **Retro. Supp. I:** 170–171; **Supp. IX:** 106; **Supp. XIV:** 227, 235

"Big Wind" (Roethke), **III:** 531

"Big Winner Rises Late, The" (Dunn), **Supp. XI:** 146

"Bilingual/*Bilingüe*" (essay; Espaillat), **Supp. XXI:** 103

"Bilingual/*Bilingüe*" (poem; Espaillat), **Supp. XXI:** 104

"Bilingual Christmas" (Mora), **Supp. XIII:** 216–217

"Bilingual Sestina" (Alvarez), **Supp. VII:** 10

"Bill" (Winters), **Supp. II Part 2:** 792

"Bill, The" (Malamud), **Supp. I Part 2:** 427, 430, 434

"Bill Collector's Vacation, The" (Hampl), **Supp. XXII:** 83

"Billie Holiday" (Carruth), **Supp. XVI:** 50

Billings, Gladys. *See* Brooks, Mrs. Van Wyck

Billings, Josh, **Supp. XVIII:** 1, 4

Bill of Rites, a Bill of Wrongs, a Bill of Goods, A (Morris), **III:** 237

"Bill's Beans" (Nye), **Supp. XIII:** 283

"Billy" (Gordon), **Supp. IV Part 1:** 306

"Billy" (McCarriston), **Supp. XIV:** 265

Billy Bathgate (Doctorow), **Supp. IV Part 1:** 217, 219, 222, 224, 227, 229–231, 231, 232, 233, 238

Billy Bathgate (film), **Supp. IV Part 1:** 236

Billy Budd, Sailor (Melville), **III:** 40, 93–95; **IV:** 105; **Retro. Supp. I:** 249, **258–260**

Billy Collins Live: A Performance at the Peter Norton Symphony Space April 20, 2005 (CD, Collins), **Supp. XXI:** 51

"Billy Gardner's Ground Out" (Skloot), **Supp. XX:** 205, 207

Billy Phelan's Greatest Game (W. Kennedy), **Supp. VII:** 131, 132, 134, 135, 142–147, 149, 151, 153, 155

Billy Ray's Farm: Essays from a Place Called Tula (L. Brown), **Supp. XXI:** 48, 49

Billy's Boy (P. N. Warren), **Supp. XX:** **261, 265–267**

Billy the Kid, **Supp. IV Part 2:** 489, 490, 492

Biloxi Blues (Simon), **Supp. IV Part 2:** 576, 577, 584, 586–587, 590

"Bimini" (Hemingway), **II:** 258

Bingham, Anne, **Supp. XV:** 239

Bingham, Millicent Todd, **I:** 470; **Retro. Supp. I:** 36

Bingham, Remica L., **Supp. XXI:** 256

Bingo Palace, The (Erdrich), **Supp. IV Part 1:** 259, 260, 261, 263–264, 265, 266–267, 268–269, 270, 271–273, 274, 275

"Binsey Poplars" (Hopkins), **Supp. I Part 1:** 94; **Supp. IV Part 2:** 639
Binswanger, Ludwig, **Supp. XV:** 26
Biographia Literaria (Coleridge), **II:** 10; **Retro. Supp. I:** 308
"Biography" (Francis), **Supp. IX:** 77
"Biography" (Pinsky), **Supp. VI:** 235, 236, 239, 241, **243,** 249, 250
Biography and Poetical Remains of the Late Margaret Miller Davidson (Irving), **II:** 314
"Biography in the First Person" (Dunn), **Supp. XI:** 144
"Biography of an Armenian Schoolgirl" (Nye), **Supp. XIII:** 275, 280
"Biography of a Story" (Jackson), **Supp. IX:** 113
Biondi, Joann, **Supp. XI:** 103
"Biopoetics Sketch for *Greenfield Review*" (Harjo), **Supp. XII:** 216
"Biotherm"(O'Hara), **Supp. XXIII:** 208, 218–219
"Birchbrook Mill" (Whittier), **Supp. I Part 2:** 699
"Birches" (Frost), **II:** 154; **Retro. Supp. I:** 132; **Supp. XIII:** 147
Bird, Alan, **Supp. I Part 1:** 260
Bird, Gloria, **Supp. XII:** 216
Bird, Isabella, **Supp. X:** 103
Bird, Robert M., **III:** 423
"Bird, The" (Simpson), **Supp. IX:** 269–270
"Bird, the Bird, the Bird, The" (Creeley), **Supp. IV Part 1:** 149
"Bird, The"(Le Sueur), **Supp. XXIII:** 167
"Bird Banding with the Biologists" (Ray), **Supp. XVIII:** 194
Bird by Bird: Some Instructions on Writing and Life (Lamott), **Supp. XX: 132,** 137–138
"Bird came down the Walk, A" (Dickinson), **Retro. Supp. I:** 37
"Bird Frau, The" (Dove), **Supp. IV Part 1:** 245
"Bird in Hand" (screen story) (West and Ingster), **Retro. Supp. II:** 330
Bird Kingdom of the Mayas (LaBastille), **Supp. X:** 96
Birds and Beasts (W. J. Smith), **Supp. XIII:** 346
"Birds for Christmas, The" (Richard), **Supp. XIX:** 221
Bird's Nest, The (Jackson), **Supp. IX:** 124–125
Birds of America (McCarthy), **II:** 579–583; **Supp. X:** 177
Birds of America (Moore), **Supp. X:** 163, 165, 167, 168, 171, **177–179**
Birds of America, The (Audubon), **Supp. XVI:** 5–6, 7, 9, 10, 12, 13
"Birds of Killingsworth, The" (Longfellow), **Retro. Supp. II:** 164
Birds of North America (Audubon Society), **Supp. X:** 177
"Birds of Vietnam, The" (Carruth), **Supp. XVI:** 55
"Bird-Window-Flying" (Gallagher), **Supp. XXIV:** 169
"Bird-Witted" (Moore), **III:** 214

Birkelo, Cheryl, **Supp. XX:** 220–221
Birkerts, Sven, **Supp. IV Part 2:** 650; **Supp. V:** 212; **Supp. VIII:** 85; **Supp. X:** 311; **Supp. XX: 92**
Birkhead, L. M., **III:** 116
"Birmingham Sunday" (Hughes), **Supp. I Part 1:** 343
Birnbaum, Henry, **Supp. XII:** 128
Birnbaum, Robert, **Supp. X:** 13; **Supp. XVI:** 75; **Supp. XXIII:** 73, 75, 275
Birney, James G., **Supp. I Part 2:** 587, 588
Birstein, Ann, **Supp. VIII:** 100
"Birthday, A" (Untermeyer), **Supp. XV:** 296
Birthday Basket for Tía, A (Mora), **Supp. XIII:** 221
"Birthday Cake" (Carruth), **Supp. XVI:** 59
"Birthday Cake for Lionel, A" (Wylie), **Supp. I Part 2:** 721
"Birthday Girl: 1950" (McCarriston), **Supp. XIV:** 261
"Birthday of Mrs. Pineda, The" (Ríos), **Supp. IV Part 2:** 542, 546
"Birthday Poem, A" (Hecht), **Supp. X:** 64
"Birthday Present, A" (Plath), **Supp. I Part 2:** 531
"Birthmark" (July), **Supp. XXIV:** 206
"Birthmark, The" (Ellison), **Retro. Supp. II:** 116; **Supp. II Part 1:** 237–238
"Birth-mark, The" (Hawthorne), **Retro. Supp. I:** 152
Birth-mark, The: Unsettling the Wilderness in American Literary History (Howe), **Supp. IV Part 2:** 422, 431, 434
Birth of a Nation, The (film), **Supp. I Part 1:** 66
Birth of a World: Bolívar in Terms of His Peoples (W. Frank), **Supp. XX:** 80
Birth of the Poet, The (Gordon), **Supp. XII:** 7
Birth of Tragedy, The (Nietzsche), **Supp. IV Part 1:** 105, 110; **Supp. IV Part 2:** 519; **Supp. VIII:** 182
"Birth of Venus, The" (Botticelli), **IV:** 410
"Birth of Venus, The" (Rukeyser), **Supp. VI:** 281
"Birthplace Revisited" (Corso), **Supp. XII:** 123
"Birthright" (McKay), **Supp. X:** 136
Bisch, Louis E., **Supp. I Part 2:** 608
Bisco, John, **Supp. XVIII:** 11
"B is for Bachelors" (M. F. K. Fisher), **Supp. XVII:** 86
Bishop, Elizabeth, **Retro. Supp. I:** 140, 296, 303; **Retro. Supp. II: 37–56,** 175, 178, 189, 233, 234, 235; **Supp. I Part 1: 72–97,** 239, 320, 326; **Supp. III Part 1:** 6, 7, 10, 18, 64, 239, 320, 326; **Supp. III Part 2:** 541, 561; **Supp. IV Part 1:** 249, 257; **Supp. IV Part 2:** 439, 626, 639, 641, 644, 647, 651, 653; **Supp. V:** 337; **Supp. IX:** 40, 41, 45, 47, 48; **Supp. X:** 58; **Supp. XI:** 123, 136; **Supp. XIII:** 115, 348; **Supp. XV:** 20–21, 100, 101, 112, 119,

249, 251; **Supp. XVII:** 36, 76; **Supp. XXI:** 58, 84, 131; **Supp. XXIII:** 117; **Supp. XXV:** 222
Bishop, James, Jr., **Supp. XIII:** 1, 5, 6, 7, 9, 11, 15
Bishop, John Peale, **I:** 432, 440; **II:** 81, 85, 86–87, 91, 209; **IV:** 35, 140, 427; **Retro. Supp. I:** 109; **Supp. I Part 2:** 709
Bishop, John W., **Supp. I Part 1:** 83
Bishop, Judith, **Supp. XVI:** 295
Bishop, Morris, **Supp. I Part 2:** 676
Bishop, William Thomas, **Supp. I Part 1:** 83
"Bishop Orders His Tomb at St. Praxed's Church, The" (R. Browning), **Supp. XV:** 127
"Bishop's Beggar, The" (Benét), **Supp. XI:** 56
"Bismarck" (Chapman), **Supp. XIV:** 52, 53
Bismark, Otto von, **Supp. I Part 2:** 643
"Bistro Styx, The" (Dove), **Supp. IV Part 1:** 250–251
Bitov, Andrei, **Retro. Supp. I:** 278
Bits of Gossip (R. H. Davis), **Supp. XVI:** 82–83, 84, 85, 89
"Bitte Nehmen Sie Die Blumen" (Boyle), **Supp. XXIV:** 57
"Bitter Drink, The" (Dos Passos), **Supp. I Part 2:** 647
"Bitter Farce, A" (Schwartz), **Supp. II Part 2:** 640, 657–658
Bitter Medicine (Paretsky), **Supp. XXV:** 174, 179, 183
"Bitter Pills for the Dark Ladies" (Jong), **Supp. V:** 118
Bitterroot (Burke), **Supp. XIV:** 34, 35
"Bittersweet Nightshade" (Skloot), **Supp. XX:** 202
Bitter Victory (Hardy; Kinnell, trans.), **Supp. III Part 1:** 235
Bittner, William, **Supp. XX: 74,Supp. XX: 77, 76, 78, 80**
Bitzer, G. W. "Billy", **Supp. XVI:** 183
Bixby, Horace, **IV:** 194
Bjerre, Thomas Aervold, **Supp. XXI:** 41, 47
Bjorkman, Frances Maule, **Supp. V:** 285
Bjorkman, Stig, **Supp. XV:** 6
Björnson, Björnstjerne, **II:** 275
Black, Cheryl, **Supp. XXI:** 6
Black 100, The (Salley), **Supp. XIV:** 195
Blackamerican Literature, 1760-Present (R. Miller), **Supp. X:** 324
Black American Literature Forum, **Supp. XI:** 86, 92, 93
Black and Blue (Quindlen), **Supp. XVII:** 166, **176–178**
"Black and Tan" (Bell), **Supp. X:** 9
Black and White (Sorrentino), **Supp. XXI:** 228
Black Armour (Wylie), **Supp. I Part 2:** 708, 709, 712–714, 729
"Black Art" (Baraka), **Supp. II Part 1:** 49, 50–51, 59, 60
"Black Art, The" (Sexton), **Supp. II Part 2:** 682
"Black Ball, The" (Ellison), **Retro. Supp. II:** 124

Black Bart and the Sacred Hills (Wilson), **Supp. VIII:** 330, 331

Black Beetles in Amber (Bierce), **I:** 204, 209

"Blackberries" (Komunyakaa), **Supp. XIII:** 126

"Blackberry Eating" (Kinnell), **Supp. III Part 1:** 250

"Blackberrying" (D. West), **Supp. XVIII:** 283

Blackberry Winter (Warren), **IV:** 243, 251, 252

Black Betty (Mosley), **Supp. XIII:** 237, **Supp. XIII:** 240, 243

"Black Birch in Winter, A" (Wilbur), **Supp. III Part 2:** 561

"Black Boy" (Boyle), **Supp. XXIV:** 59

Black Boy (Wright), **IV:** 477, 478, 479, 480–482, 488, 489, 494; **Retro. Supp. II:** 117; **Supp. II Part 1:** 235–236; **Supp. IV Part 1:** 11; **Supp. XVIII:** 286

"Black Boys and Native Sons" (Howe), **Retro. Supp. II:** 112

Blackburn, Alex, **Supp. XIII:** 112

Blackburn, Paul, **Supp. XXII:** 164, 169; **Supp. XXIV:** 34, 37

Blackburn, William, **IV:** 100

"Black Buttercups" (Clampitt), **Supp. IX:** 42

Black Cargo, The (Marquand), **III:** 55, 60

Black Cargoes: A History of the Atlantic Slave Trade (Cowley), **Supp. II Part 1:** 140

"Black Cat, The" (Poe), **III:** 413, 414, 415; **Retro. Supp. II:** 264, 267, 269, 270; **Supp. XXV:** 112

Black Cherry Blues (Burke), **Supp. XIV:** 30

"Black Christ, The" (Cullen), **Supp. IV Part 1:** 170, 171–172

Black Christ and Other Poems, The (Cullen), **Supp. IV Part 1:** 166, 170

"Black Clay Fish from Oaxaca, A" (Bronk), **Supp. XXI:** 31

"Black Cottage, The" (Frost), **Retro. Supp. I:** 128

"BLACK DADA NIHILISMUS" (Baraka), **Supp. II Part 1:** 39, 41

"Black Death" (Hurston), **Supp. VI:** 153

Black Dog, Red Dog (Dobyns), **Supp. XIII:** 87, **88–89**

"Black Dog, Red Dog" (Dobyns), **Supp. XIII:** 89

Black Dog of Fate: A Memoir (Balakian), **Supp. XXIII:** 19, **20–24**, 24, 25

"Black Earth" (Moore), **III:** 197, 212

Black Echo, The (Connelly), **Supp. XXI:** 67, 68, 75, 80

Black Fire (Jones and Neal, eds.), **Supp. X:** 324, 328

Black Fire: An Anthology of Afro American Writing (Baraka, ed.), **Supp. II Part 1:** 53

Black Flame, The (Du Bois), **Supp. II Part 1:** 159, 185–186

Black Folk, Then and Now: An Essay in the History and Sociology of the Negro Race (Du Bois), **Supp. II Part 1:** 159,

178, 183, 185

Blackford, Holly, **Supp. XXII:** 300

"Black Fox, The" (Whittier), **Supp. I Part 2:** 692

Black Freckles (Levis), **Supp. XI:** 257, 271

"Black Gang", **IV:** 406, 407

Black Genius (Mosley, ed.), **Supp. XIII:** 246

Blackguard (Bodenheim), **Supp. XXV:** 17, 18, 22, 23–24

"Black Hood, The" (Francis), **Supp. IX:** 83, 91

Black House, The (Theroux), **Supp. VIII:** 319

Black Humor (Johnson), **Supp. VI:** 187, 199

Black Ice, The (Connelly), **Supp. XXI:** **70,** 75

Black Image in the White Mind, The (Fredrickson), **Supp. I Part 2:** 589

"Black Is My Favorite Color" (Malamud), **Supp. I Part 2:** 437

Black Jacobins, The (C. L. R. James), **Supp. XXI:** 159, 166–167

"Black Jewel, The" (Merwin), **Supp. III Part 1:** 355

Black Lamb and Grey Falcon (R. West), **Supp. XVI:** 152

"Black Laughter" (Taggard), **Supp. XXII:** 274

"Blacklegs" (B. Kelly), **Supp. XVII:** 131

Black Light (Kinnell), **Supp. III Part 1:** 235, 243

Black Like Me (Griffin), **Supp. XXV:** 51

Blacklist (Paretsky), **Supp. XXV:** 182, 184

"Blacklist and the Cold War, The" (Kramer), **Supp. I Part 1:** 295

Black Literature in America (Baker), **Supp. X:** 324

Black Magic, A Pictorial History of the Negro in American Entertainment (Hughes), **Supp. I Part 1:** 345

Black Magic: Collected Poetry 1961–1967 (Baraka), **Supp. II Part 1:** 45, 49–50

"Blackmailers Don't Shoot" (Chandler), **Supp. IV Part 1:** 121–122

Black Manhattan (Johnson), **Supp. IV Part 1:** 169

Black Mass, A (Baraka), **Supp. II Part 1:** 46, 48–49, 56, 57

"Black Mesa, The" (Merrill), **Supp. III Part 1:** 328

Black Metropolis (Cayton and Drake), **IV:** 475, 486, 488

Black Misery (Hughes), **Supp. I Part 1:** 336

Blackmur, Helen Dickson (Mrs. R. P. Blackmur), **Supp. II Part 1:** 90

Blackmur, Richard P., **I:** 50, 63, 67, 280, 282, 386, 455, 472; **II:** 320, 537; **III:** 194, 208, 462, 478, 497; **Supp. II Part 1: 87–112,** 136; **Supp. II Part 2:** 543, 643; **Supp. XII:** 45

Black Music (Baraka), **Supp. II Part 1:** 47, 51

Black Nativity (Hughes), **Retro. Supp. I:** 196

Black No More (Schuyler), **Supp. XVI:** 142; **Supp. XIX:** 73

Black on Black: "Baby Sister" and Selected Writings (C. Himes), **Supp. XVI:** 145

"Black or White" (Major), **Supp. XXII:** 185

"Blackout" (Hay), **Supp. XIV:** 121

Black Oxen (Atherton), **Supp. XXIV:** 25–26

Black Oxen (Atherton, Dawson, ed.), **Supp. XXIV:** 31

"Black Panther" (Hughes), **Retro. Supp. I:** 211

"Black Petal" (L.-Y. Lee), **Supp. XV:** 224–225

Black Power (Wright), **IV:** 478, 488, 494

"Black Rainbow, A: Modern Afro-American Poetry" (Dove and Waniek), **Supp. IV Part 1:** 244

Black Reconstruction (Du Bois), **Supp. II Part 1:** 159, 162, 171, 182

Black Riders and Other Lines, The (Crane), **I:** 406, 419

Black Riviera, The (Jarman), **Supp. XVII:** 109, 110, **115–116**

Blackrobe: Isaac Jogues (Kenny), **Supp. XXIII:** 143, 147, **151–152,** 153, 154

"Black Rook in Rainy Weather" (Plath), **Supp. I Part 2:** 543, 544; **Supp. XXIII:** 63

Blacks (Brooks), **Supp. III Part 1:** 69, 72, 86, 87

Blacks, The (Genet), **Supp. IV Part 1:** 8

Black Skin, White Masks (Fanon), **Retro. Supp. II:** 118

Black Sleuth, The (J. Bruce), **Supp. XVI:** 143

Black Spear, The (Hayden), **Supp. II Part 1:** 375

Black Spring (H. Miller), **III:** 170, 175, 178, 180–182, 183, 184; **Supp. X:** 187

"Black Stone Lying on a White Stone" (Vallejo), **Supp. XIII:** 324

Black Sun (Abbey), **Supp. XIII:** 4, **8–9,** 17

"Black Swan" (B. Kelly), **Supp. XVII:** 130–131

"Black Swan, The" (Jarrell), **II:** 382

Black Swan, The (Merrill), **Supp. III Part 1:** 319, 320

"Black Tambourine" (Crane), **I:** 387–388; **II:** 371

Black Thunder (Bontemps), **Supp. XXII:** 4, 9

"Black Tuesday" (Swenson), **Supp. IV Part 2:** 646

Black Virgin Mountain (Heinemann), **Supp. XXII:** 103, **114–116**

Black Voices (Chapman), **IV:** 485

"Blackwater Mountain" (Wright), **Supp. V:** 335, 340

"Black Wedding, The" (Singer), **IV:** 12–13

Blackwell, Alice Stone, **Supp. XI:** 195, 197

Blackwell, Elizabeth, **Retro. Supp. II:** 146

Black Woman, The (Bambara, ed.), **Supp. XI:** 1

"Black Workers" (Hughes), **Retro. Supp. I:** 202

"Black Writer and the Southern Experience, The" (Walker), **Supp. III Part 2:** 521

Black Zodiac (Wright), **Supp. V:** 333, 344, 345

Blade Runner (film), **Supp. XI:** 84

Blades, John, **Supp. XX: 87**

"Blades of Steel" (R. Fisher), **Supp. XIX:** 72

Blaine, Anita McCormick, **Supp. I Part 1:** 5

Blaine, Nell, **Supp. XV:** 179; **Supp. XXIII:** 217

Blair, Hugh, **II:** 8, 17; **Supp. I Part 2:** 422

Blair, Robert, **Supp. I Part 1:** 150

Blair, Walter, **II:** 20; **Retro. Supp. II:** 286

Blaisdell, Gus, **Supp. XIV:** 87

Blake, Casey Nelson, **Supp. XX: 69, 70, 78**

Blake, William, **I:** 381, 383, 389, 390, 398, 447, 476, 525, 526, 533; **II:** 321; **III:** 5, 19, 22, 195, 196, 197, 205, 485, 528, 540, 544–545, 567, 572; **IV:** 129; **Retro. Supp. II:** 76, 300; **Supp. I Part 1:** 80; **Supp. I Part 2:** 385, 514, 517, 539, 552, 708; **Supp. V:** 208, 257, 258; **Supp. VIII:** 26, 99, 103; **Supp. X:** 120; **Supp. XII:** 45; **Supp. XIV:** 344; **Supp. XVI:** 282; **Supp. XVII:** 119; **Supp. XX: 115, 116; Supp. XXII:** 225, 257; **Supp. XXIV:** 159; **Supp. XXV:** 248

Blakely, Barbara, **Supp. XIII:** 32

Blanc, Marie Thérèse, **Retro. Supp. II:** 135

Blanc-Bentzon, Mme. Thérèse, **II:** 405

Blanchard, Paula, **Retro. Supp. II:** 131, 133–134, 135

Blanche, Jacques-Émile, **Supp. XX: 232**

Blanche of Brandywine (Lippard), **Supp. XXIII:** 178, 185

Blanchot, Maurice, **Supp. XVI:** 288; **Supp. XXIV:** 40

Blancs, Les (Hansberry), **Supp. IV Part 1:** 359, 364, 365, 369, 372–374

Blancs, Les: The Collected Last Plays of Lorraine Hansberry (Nemiroff, ed.), **Supp. IV Part 1:** 365, 368, 374

"'Blandula, Tenulla, Vagula'" (Pound), **III:** 463; **Supp. V:** 336, 337, 345

Blankenship, Tom, **IV:** 193

"Blank Paper" (Peacock), **Supp. XIX:** 198–199

Blank Wall, The (Holding), **Supp. XXII:** 119, 120, 121, 130, **131–133,** 134

Blanshard, Rufus A., **I:** 67

Blassingame, John, **Supp. XX: 106**

Blauvelt, William Satake, **Supp. V:** 171, 173

Blavatsky, Elena Petrovna, **III:** 176

"Blazing in Gold and Quenching in Purple" (Dickinson), **Retro. Supp. I:** 30

Bleak House (Dickens), **II:** 291; **Supp. IV Part 1:** 293

Blechman, Burt, **Supp. I Part 1:** 290

"Bleeder" (Dobyns), **Supp. XIII:** 88

"Bleeding" (Swenson), **Supp. IV Part 2:** 646–647

Bleeding Kansas (Paretsky), **Supp. XXV:** 183

"Blessed Is the Man" (Moore), **III:** 215

"Blessed Man of Boston, My Grandmother's Thimble, and Fanning Island, The" (Updike), **IV:** 219

"Blessing, A" (Wright), **Supp. III Part 2:** 600, 606

Blessing on the Moon, A (Skibell), **Supp. XVII:** 48

Blessings (Quindlen), **Supp. XVII:** 167, **178–179**

"Blessing the Animals" (Komunyakaa), **Supp. XIII:** 129–130

"Blessing the Children" (Hogan), **Supp. IV Part 1:** 401

Bless Me, Ultima (Anya), **Supp. XIII:** 220

Blew, Mary Clearman, **Supp. XIV:** 227

Bligh, S. M., **I:** 226

"Blight"(Dybek), **Supp. XXIII:** 72

Blind Alleys (film), **Supp. XXI:** 146

Blind Assassin, The (Atwood), **Supp. XIII:** 20, **32**

Blind Bow-Boy, The (Van Vechten), **Supp. II Part 2:** 737, 740–742

"Blind Date" (Halliday), **Supp. XIX:** 85

Blind Date (Kosinski), **Supp. VII:** 215, 224–225

"Blinded by the Light" (Boyle), **Supp. XX: 20**

Blind Lion, The (Gunn Allen), **Supp. IV Part 1:** 324

"Blind Man's Holiday" (O. Henry), **Supp. II Part 1:** 401

Blind Man with a Pistol (C. Himes), **Supp. XVI:** 143, 144

Blindness and Insight (de Man), **Retro. Supp. I:** 67

"Blind Poet, The: Sidney Lanier" (Warren), **Supp. I Part 1:** 371, 373

"Blindsided" (E. P. Jones), **Supp. XXII:** 151–152

"Blind Tom" (R. H. Davis), **Supp. XVI:** 89, 90

Blithedale Romance, The (Hawthorne), **II:** 225, 231, 239, 241–242, 271, 282, 290; **IV:** 194; **Retro. Supp. I:** 63, 149, 152, 156–157, **162–163; Supp. I Part 2:** 579; **Supp. II Part 1:** 280; **Supp. VIII:** 153, 201

Blitzstein, Marc, **Supp. I Part 1:** 277

Blix (Norris), **III:** 314, 322, 327, 328, 333

Blixen, Karen Denisen Baroness. *See* Dinesen, Isak

"Blizzard in Cambridge" (Lowell), **II:** 554

Blizzard Voices, The (Kooser), **Supp. XIX:** 123

Bloch, Ernest, **Supp. XX: 75**

Bloch, Robert, **Supp. XXV:** 111, 145

Block, Lawrence, **Supp. XXI:** 67

"Blocks"(O'Hara), **Supp. XXIII:** 214

Blok, Aleksandr Aleksandrovich, **IV:** 443

"Blond" (Trethewey), **Supp. XXI:** 244

Blonde Bait (Lacy), **Supp. XV:** 204

Blonde on Blonde (album, Dylan), **Supp. XVIII:** 20, 27, 30

Blondin, Antoine, **Supp. XVI:** 230

"Blood" (Hoffman), **Supp. XVIII:** 86

"Blood" (Singer), **IV:** 15, 19

Blood, Tin, Straw (Olds), **Supp. X: 212–215**

Blood and Guile (Hoffman), **Supp. XVIII: 83–84**

Blood and Guts in High School (Acker), **Supp. XII:** 5, 6, **11–12**

"Blood Bay, The" (Proulx), **Supp. VII:** 262–263

"Blood-Burning Moon" (Toomer), **Supp. III Part 2:** 483; **Supp. IX:** 314–315

"Bloodchild" (O. Butler), **Supp. XIII:** 61, **69–70**

Bloodchild and Other Stories (O. Butler), **Supp. XIII:** 69

"Blood Donor" (Hay), **Supp. XIV:** 121

Blood for a Stranger (Jarrell), **II:** 367, 368–369, 370–371, 375, 377

Blood Issue (Crews), **Supp. XI:** 103

Bloodlines (Wright), **Supp. V:** 332, 335, 340

Blood Meridian (McCarthy), **Supp. XXIII:** 42

Blood Meridian; or, The Evening Redness in the West (McCarthy), **Supp. VIII:** 175, 177, **180–182,** 188, 190

Blood of My Blood (Gambino), **Supp. XX: 35**

"Blood of the Conquistadores, The" (Alvarez), **Supp. VII:** 7

"Blood of the Lamb, The" (hymn), **Supp. I Part 2:** 385

Blood of the Martyr (Crane), **I:** 422

"Blood of the Martyrs, The" (Benét), **Supp. XI:** 56, 58

Blood of the Prophets, The (Masters), **Supp. I Part 2:** 458, 459, 461

Blood on the Forge (Attaway), **Supp. II Part 1:** 234–235

Blood on the Tracks (album, Dylan), **Supp. XVIII:** 20, 27, 30

"Blood Relatives" (Apple), **Supp. XVII:** 6

"Blood Returns, The" (Kingsolver), **Supp. VII:** 209

"Bloodshed" (C. Ozick), **Supp. XVII:** 43

Bloodshed and Three Novellas (Ozick), **Supp. V:** 259–260, 261, 266–268

"Blood Soup"(Dybek), **Supp. XXIII:** 71

"Blood Stains" (Francis), **Supp. IX:** 86

Blood Work (Connelly), **Supp. XXI:** 72

Blood Work (film, Eastwood), **Supp. XXI:** 74

Bloody Crossroads, The: Where Literature and Politics Meet (Podhoretz), **Supp. VIII: 241–242**

Bloody News from My Friend (Samianto, trans. Balakian), **Supp. XXIII:** 28

Bloom, Alice, **Supp. IV Part 1:** 308

Bloom, Allan, **Retro. Supp. II:** 19, 30, 31, 33–34

Bloom, Claire, **Retro. Supp. II:** 281; **Supp. IX:** 125

Bloom, Harold, **Retro. Supp. I:** 67, 193, 299; **Retro. Supp. II:** 81, 210, 262; **Supp. IV Part 2:** 620, 689; **Supp. V:**

178, 272; **Supp. VIII:** 180; **Supp. IX:** 146, 259; **Supp. XII:** 261; **Supp. XIII:** 46, 47; **Supp. XIV:** 14; **Supp. XV:** 134; **Supp. XVII:** 70, 141; **Supp. XXIII:** 42; **Supp. XXV:** 251

Bloom, Larry, **Supp. XIII:** 133

Bloom, Leopold, **I:** 27, 150; **III:** 10

Bloom, Lynn Z., **Supp. IV Part 1:** 6

Bloomfield, Leonard, **I:** 64

Bloomingdale Papers, The (Carruth), **Supp. XVI:** 48–50

"Blossom and Fruit" (Benét), **Supp. XI:** 52–53

Blotner, Joseph, **Retro. Supp. I:** 88

Blouin, Lenora, **Supp. VIII:** 266

"Blouse, The"(Rudman), **Supp. XXIII:** 124

"Blowing Soap Bubbles"(Crooker), **Supp. XXIII:** 56

"Blowin' in the Wind" (song, Dylan), **Supp. XVIII:** 24, 25, 26, 29

Bluckled Bag, The (Rinehart), **Supp. XXV:** 197

Blue Angel (Prose), **Supp. XVI:** 249, 259–260

Blue Angel, The (film), **Supp. XVIII:** 243

Blue Arabesque: A Search for the Sublime (Hampl), **Supp. XXII:** 86, 98–99

"Blue Battalions, The" (Crane), **I:** 419–420

"Blue Bead, The"(Hadas), **Supp. XXIII:** 118, 119

"Bluebeard" (Barthelme), **Supp. IV Part 1:** 47

"Bluebeard" (Millay), **III:** 130

"Blueberries" (Frost), **Retro. Supp. I:** 121, 128

"Blue Boy"(Dybek), **Supp. XXIII:** 76

Blue Calhoun (Price), **Supp. VI:** 265–266

Blue Caterpillar, The (Pickering), **Supp. XXI:** 202–203

Blue City (Macdonald, as Millar), **Supp. IV Part 2:** 466–467

Blue Devils of Nada, The: A Contemporary American Approach to Aesthetics (Murray), **Supp. XIX:** 159–160

Blue Estuaries, The: Poems, 1923–1968 (Bogan), **Supp. III Part 1:** 48, 57, 66

Blue Hammer, The (Macdonald), **Supp. IV Part 2:** 462

"Blue Hotel, The" (Crane), **I:** 34, 415–416, 423

"Blue Hour, The" (Komunyakaa), **Supp. XIII:** 130

Blue in the Face (Auster), **Supp. XII:** 21

Blue Jay's Dance, The: A Birth Year (Erdrich), **Supp. IV Part 1:** 259–260, 265, 270, 272

"Blue Juniata" (Cowley), **Supp. II Part 1:** 144

Blue Juniata: Collected Poems (Cowley), **Supp. II Part 1:** 140

"Blue Lick" (Offutt), **Supp. XIX:** 164, 165

Blue Light (Mosley), **Supp. XIII:** 245–247, 248, 249

"Blue Light Lounge Sutra for the Performance Poets at Harold Park Hotel" (Komunyakaa), **Supp. XIII:** 125

"Blue Meridian" (Toomer), **Supp. III Part 2:** 476, 487; **Supp. IX:** 320

"Blue Moles" (Plath), **Supp. I Part 2:** 539

Blue Mountain Ballads (music) (Bowles), **Supp. IV Part 1:** 84

Blue Movie (Southern), **Supp. XI:** 309

"Blue Notes" (Matthews), **Supp. IX:** 169

Blue Pastoral (Sorrentino), **Supp. XXI:** 226, 235–236

Blue Pastures (Oliver), **Supp. VII:** 229–230, 245

"Blueprint for Negro Writing" (Wright), **Supp. XVIII:** 282–283

"Blueprints" (Kingsolver), **Supp. VII:** 203

Blue Religion, The (Connelly, ed.), **Supp. XXI:** 74–75, 79

Blue Rhine, Black Forest (Untermeyer), **Supp. XV:** 310

"Blue Ribbon at Amesbury, A" (Frost), **Retro. Supp. I:** 138

"Blues Ain't No Mockin Bird" (Bambara), **Supp. XI:** 3

"Blues and the Fable in the Flesh, The" (lecture, Murray), **Supp. XIX:** 153

"Blues Chant Hoodoo Rival" (Komunyakaa), **Supp. XIII:** 117, 118

Blue Screen (Parker), **Supp. XIX:** 186

"Blues for Another Time" (Dunn), **Supp. XI:** 148

"Blues for Jimmy" (McGrath), **Supp. X:** 116

"Blues for John Coltraine, Dead at 41" (Matthews), **Supp. IX:** 157

Blues for Mister Charlie (Baldwin), **Retro. Supp. II:** 8; **Supp. I Part 1:** 48, 61–62, 63

"Blues for Warren" (McGrath), **Supp. X:** 116

Blue Shoe (Lamott), **Supp. XX: 138–140**

Blues If You Want (Matthews), **Supp. IX:** 155, **163–165**

"Blues I'm Playing, The" (Hughes), **Retro. Supp. I:** 204; **Supp. XIX:** 75

"Blue Sky, The" (Snyder), **Supp. VIII:** 306

Bluesman (Dubus III), **Supp. XXIV: 102–104**

"Blues on a Box" (Hughes), **Retro. Supp. I:** 208

"Blues People" (Ellison), **Retro. Supp. II:** 124

Blues People: Negro Music in White America (Baraka), **Retro. Supp. II:** 124; **Supp. II Part 1:** 30, 31, 33–35, 37, 41, 42, 53

"Blue Spruces in Pairs, a Bird Bath Between": (Bronk), **Supp. XXI:** 30

Bluest Eye, The (Morrison), **Supp. III Part 1:** 362, 363–367, 379; **Supp. IV Part 1:** 2, 253; **Supp. VIII:** 213, 214, 227; **Supp. XI:** 4, 91

Bluestone, George, **Supp. IX:** 7, 15

Blue Swallows, The (Nemerov), **III:** 269, 270, 271, 274–275, 278, 284, 286–288

"Blue Tattoo" (Nelson and Espeland), **Supp. XVIII:** 181

Blue Voyage (Aiken), **I:** 53, 56

Bluhm, Norman, **Supp. XXIII:** 217

Blum, Gustav, **Supp. XV:** 194

Blum, Morgan, **I:** 169

Blum, W. C (pseudonym). *See* Watson, James Sibley, Jr.

Blumenthal, Nathaniel. *See* Branden, Nathaniel

Blumenthal, Sidney, **Supp. VIII:** 241

Blunden, Edmund, **Supp. XIX:** 133

Blunt, Wilfrid Scawen, **III:** 459

Bly, Carol, **Supp. XVI: 31–43**

Bly, Robert, **I:** 291; **Supp. III Part 2:** 599; **Supp. IV Part 1: 59–77,** 177; **Supp. IV Part 2:** 623; **Supp. V:** 332; **Supp. VIII:** 279; **Supp. IX:** 152, 155, 265, 271, 290; **Supp. X:** 127; **Supp. XI:** 142; **Supp. XIII:** 284; **Supp. XV:** 74, 176; **Supp. XVI:** 32, 36, 39, 177, 212, 230; **Supp. XVII:** 243, 244; **Supp. XXI:** 83, 84–86, 87, 91, 93, 94, 95; **Supp. XXII:** 83; **Supp. XXIII:** 136; **Supp. XXIV:** 219

"B Negative" (X. J. Kennedy), **Supp. XV: 156–157**

"Boarder, The" (Simpson), **Supp. IX:** 269

Boarding House Blues (Farrell), **II:** 30, 43, 45

Boarding School, The (Foster), **Supp. XXV:** 35, 36, 37, 45–47

Boas, Franz, **I:** 214; **Supp. I Part 2:** 641; **Supp. VIII:** 295; **Supp. IX:** 329; **Supp. XIV:** 199, 209, 210

"Boat, The" (Oliver), **Supp. VII:** 247

"Boat, The" (Sexton), **Supp. II Part 2:** 692

Boating Party, The (Renoir), **Supp. XII:** 188

Boat of Quiet Hours, The (Kenyon), **Supp. VII:** 167–169, 171

"Boat of Quiet Hours, The" (Kenyon), **Supp. VII:** 168

"Boat Ride" (Gallagher), **Supp. XXIV:** 169

"Bob and Spike" (Wolfe), **Supp. III Part 2:** 580

"Bobby Shafter's Gone to Sea" (Swados), **Supp. XIX:** 267

"Bob Dylan's 115th Dream" (song, Dylan), **Supp. XVIII:** 25

Bobrowski, Johannes, **Supp. XV:** 78

Bob the Gambler (F. Barthelme), **Supp. XI:** 30, 31, 32, 34–35, 36–37

Boccaccio, Giovanni, **III:** 283, 411; **IV:** 230

Bocock, Maclin, **Supp. X:** 79

Boddy, Kasia, **Supp. XXII:** 261

Bodelson, Anders, **Supp. XVI:** 33

Bodenheim, Maxwell, **II:** 42, 530; **Retro. Supp. I:** 417; **Supp. I Part 1:** 257; **Supp. XXV: 17–33**

"Bodies" (Oates), **Supp. II Part 2:** 520

"Bodies and Souls: The Haitian Revolution and Madison Smartt Bell's *All Souls' Rising*" (Trouillot), **Supp. X:** 14

Bodies of Water (Cliff), **Supp. XXII:** 66–67, 74–75

Bodies of Work: Essays (Acker), **Supp. XII:** 7

Bodily Harm (Atwood), **Supp. XIII:** 25–27

Bodley Head Jack London (London), **II:** 483

Body (Crews), **Supp. XI: 108–109**

"Body, The" (Heldreth), **Supp. V:** 151

Body and Soul (Conroy), **Supp. XVI:** 63, **72–74,** 77

"Body and Soul: A Meditation" (Kumin), **Supp. IV Part 2:** 442, 452

Body and Soul: Essays on Poetry (Jarman), **Supp. XVII:** 110, **111–112**

"Body and Soul: Parts of a Life" (Jarman), **Supp. XVII:** 112, 113

Body and the Song, The (Bishop), **Retro. Supp. II:** 40

"Body Bright" (Sanders), **Supp. XVI:** 276

Body of Martin Aquilera, The (Everett), **Supp. XVIII:** 57

Body of Poetry, The: Essays on Women, Form, and the Poetic Self (A. Finch), **Supp. XVII: 69–70, 77–78**

Body of This Death: Poems (Bogan), **Supp. III Part 1:** 47, 49–52, 58

Body of Waking (Rukeyser), **Supp. VI:** 274, 281

"Body of Waking" (Rukeyser), **Supp. VI:** 279

"Body on Fire, the Soul in Flight, The" (Jarman), **Supp. XVII:** 111, 112

Body Rags (Kinnell), **Supp. III Part 1:** 235, 236, 243–245, 250, 253, 254

"Body's Curse, The" (Dobyns), **Supp. XIII:** 87

"Body's Weight" (Espaillat), **Supp. XXI:** 111

"Body's Weight, The" (Dobyns), **Supp. XIII:** 89

Body Traffic (Dobyns), **Supp. XIII:** 87, 89

"'Body with the Lamp Lit Inside, The' " (Mills), **Supp. IV Part 1:** 64

Body Work (Paretsky), **Supp. XXV:** 177, 178, 179, 181, 184–185

Boehm, David, **Supp. XVII:** 58

Boehme, Jakob, **I:** 10

Bogan, Louise, **I:** 169, 185; **Retro. Supp. I:** 36; **Supp. I Part 2:** 707, 726; **Supp. III Part 1: 47–68; Supp. VIII:** 171, 265; **Supp. IX:** 229; **Supp. X:** 58, 102; **Supp. XIII:** 347; **Supp. XIV:** 129; **Supp. XVII:** 75; **Supp. XXIII:** 145

Bogan, Major Benjamin Lewis, **IV:** 120

Bogart, Humphrey, **Supp. I Part 2:** 623; **Supp. IV Part 1:** 130, 356

Bogdanovich, Peter, **Supp. V:** 226

Bogey Man, The (Plimpton), **Supp. XVI:** 241

Boggs, Francis W., **Supp. XVI:** 182

"Bogs" (Pickering), **Supp. XXI:** 198

"Bohemian, The" (Hapgood), **Supp. XVII:** 103

"Bohemian, The" (Harte), **Supp. II Part 1:** 339

"Bohemian Girl, The" (Cather), **Retro. Supp. I:** 7

"Bohemian Hymn, The" (Emerson), **II:** 19

"Bohemians" (Saunders), **Supp. XIX:** 234

"Boids and Beasties" (Geisel), **Supp. XVI:** 100

Boissevain, Eugen, **III:** 124

Boissière, Ralph de, **Supp. XXI:** 160

Boit, Edward, **Retro. Supp. I:** 366

Bojorquez, Jennifer, **Supp. XII:** 318

"Boke, A" (Berrigan), **Supp. XXIV:** 42

Boker, George, **Supp. XV:** 269

Bolaño, Roberto, **Supp. XXV:** 49

"Bold Words at the Bridge" (Jewett), **II:** 394

Boleslavsky, Richard, **Supp. XIV:** 240, 243

Boleyn, Anne, **Supp. I Part 2:** 461

Bolick, Katie, **Supp. XVI:** 167; **Supp. XXIII:** 135, 137, 138; **Supp. XXIV:** 167, 173, 177

Bolivar, Simon, **Supp. I Part 1:** 283, 284, 285

Bolonik, Kera, **Supp. XVIII:** 60

Bolton, Guy, **Supp. I Part 1:** 281

Bolts of Melody: New Poems of Emily Dickinson (Todd and Bingham, eds.), **I:** 470; **Retro. Supp. I:** 36

"Bomb" (Corso), **Supp. XII:** 117, 124, 125–126, 127

Bombeck, Erma, **Supp. XVII:** 168

Bombs Away (Steinbeck), **IV:** 51–52

"Bona and Paul" (Toomer), **Supp. IX:** 307, 318–319

Bonaparte, Marie, **III:** 418; **Retro. Supp. II:** 264, 266

"Bon-Bon" (Poe), **III:** 425

Bond, The (Boyce), **Supp. XXI:** 5, **11–12**

Bond, The (N. Boyce), **Supp. XVII:** 99, 100

Bondage (Hwang), **Supp. XXI:** 147

Bondsman, The (Massinger), **Supp. XV:** 238

Bondwoman's Narrative, by Hannah Crafts, a Fugitive Slave, Recently Escaped from North Carolina, The, **Supp. XX: 105**

Bone, Martyn, **Supp. XXII:** 247

Bone, Robert, **Supp. IX:** 318–319; **Supp. XI:** 283; **Supp. XVIII:** 285

Bone by Bone (Matthiessen), **Supp. V:** 199, 212, 213, 214

"Bone Deposit" (Ray), **Supp. XVIII:** 194

Boners (Abingdon). *See Schoolboy Howlers* (Abingdon)

"Bones" (Goldbarth), **Supp. XII: 173–174**

"Bones and Jewels" (Monette), **Supp. X:** 159

"Bones and Shells" (Sanders), **Supp. XVI:** 271–272

"Bones of a House" (Cowley). *See* "Blue Juniata"

Bones on Black Spruce Mountain, The (Budbill), **Supp. XIX:** 11–12

Bonetti, Kay, **Supp. VIII:** 47, 152, 159, 160, 165, 168, 170, 223; **Supp. XII:** 61; **Supp. XIV:** 232, 234; **Supp. XXI:** 36

"Bonfire" (Gallagher), **Supp. XXIV:** 170

Bonfire of the Vanities, The (Wolfe), **Supp. III Part 2:** 584–586

Bonheur, Rosa, **Supp. XV:** 276

Bonhoeffer, Dietrich, **Supp. VIII:** 198

Boni, Charles, **Supp. XIV:** 288

Boni and Liveright, **Retro. Supp. I:** 59, 80, 178

Bonicelli, Vittorio, **Supp. XI:** 307

Bonifacius (Mather), **Supp. II Part 2:** 461, 464

Bonnefoy, Yves, **Supp. III Part 1:** 235, 243

Bonner, Robert, **Retro. Supp. I:** 246

Bonneville, Mme. Marguerite, **Supp. I Part 2:** 520, 521

Bonneville, Nicolas de, **Supp. I Part 2:** 511, 518, 519

Bonney, William. *See* Billy the Kid

Bontemps, Arna, **Retro. Supp. I:** 194, 196, 203; **Supp. I Part 1:** 325; **Supp. IV Part 1:** 170; **Supp. IX:** 306, 309; **Supp. XVIII:** 282; **Supp. XXII: 1–16**

Book, A (Barnes), **Supp. III Part 1:** 36, 39, 44

Book about Myself, A (Dreiser), **I:** 515; **Retro. Supp. II:** 104

"Book as a Container of Consciousness, The" (Gass), **Supp. VI:** 92

Booker, Keith, **Supp. XV:** 197

"Bookies, Beware!" (Heller), **Supp. IV Part 1:** 383

"Book Notes and News" (column, Boyce), **Supp. XXI:** 2

Book of American Negro Poetry, The (Johnson), **Supp. IV Part 1:** 165, 166; **Supp. XXII:** 11

Book of Americans, A (Benét), **Supp. XI:** 46, 47, 51

Book of Beb, The (Buechner), **Supp. XII:** 53

Book of Breeething, The (Burroughs), **Supp. III Part 1:** 97, 103

Book of Burlesques, A (Mencken), **III:** 104

Book of Common Prayer, A (Didion), **Supp. IV Part 1:** 196, 198, 203–205, 207, 208

Book of Daniel, The (Doctorow), **Supp. IV Part 1:** 218, 219, 220–222, 227, 231, 237–238, 238; **Supp. V:** 45

Book of Dreams (Kerouac), **Supp. III Part 1:** 225

"Book of Ephraim, The" (Merrill), **Supp. III Part 1:** 330–334

Book of Folly, The (Sexton), **Supp. II Part 2:** 691, 692–694

Book of Gods and Devils, The (Simic), **Supp. VIII: 281**

Book of Guys, The (Keillor), **Supp. XVI:** 177

"Book of Hours of Sister Clotilde, The" (Lowell), **II:** 522

Book of Jamaica, The (Banks), **Supp. V:** 11, 12, 16

"Book of Life" (Bidart), **Supp. XV:** 23

Book of Living Verse, The; English and American Poetry from the Thirteenth Century to the Present Day (Untermeyer, ed.), **Supp. XV:** 310

Book of Love, A (Vildrac; Bynner, trans.), **Supp. XV:** 50

Book of Lyrics (Bynner), **Supp. XV:** 51

Book of Martyrs (Fox). *See Acts and Monuments of These Latter and Perilous Days* (Fox)

Book of Medicines, The (Hogan), **Supp. IV Part 1:** 397, 410, 411–414

"Book of Medicines, The" (Hogan), **Supp. IV Part 1:** 412, 413

"Book of Memory, The" (Auster), **Supp. XII:** 21–22

Book of My Nights (L.-Y. Lee), **Supp. XV:** 215, **223–226**

Book of Negro Folklore, The (Hughes, ed.), **Supp. I Part 1:** 345; **Supp. XXII:** 11–12

Book of Nightmares, The (Kinnell), **Supp. III Part 1:** 235, 236, 243, 244, 246–254

Book of One's Own, A: People and Their Diaries (Mallon), **Supp. XIX:** 134

Book of Prefaces, A (Mencken), **III:** 99–100, 105

Book of Repulsive Women, The (Barnes), **Supp. III Part 1:** 33

Book of Revelation, **Supp. XXIII:** 44

Book of Roses, The (Parkman), **Supp. II Part 2:** 597, 598

Book of the Body, The (Bidart), **Supp. XV:** 21, **25–27**

"Book of the Dead, The" (Rukeyser), **Supp. VI:** 272, 278, 279; **Supp. XV:** 349

"Book of the Grotesque, The" (Anderson), **I:** 106

Book of the Homeless, The (Wharton), **Retro. Supp. I:** 377

Book of the Hopi (Waters), **Supp. X:** 124

Book of Tobit (Bible), **Supp. XII:** 54

Book of Verses, A (Masters), **Supp. I Part 2:** 458

Book of Wonder (Dunsany), **Supp. XXV:** 113

Book of Yaak, The (Bass), **Supp. XVI: 18–19**

"Book of Yolek, The" (Hecht), **Supp. X:** 69, **70–71**

"Books" (Collins), **Supp. XXI:** 55

"Books Considered" (Bloom), **Supp. I Part 1:** 96

"Books I Left Behind, The" (Pickering), **Supp. XXI:** 196

Books in My Life, The (H. Miller), **II:** 176, 189

"Books/P,L,E, The" (Goldbarth), **Supp. XII:** 190

Bookviews, **Supp. XI:** 216

"Book World Live", **Supp. XVIII:** 143–144

"Boolean Algebra: X2=X" (Bronk), **Supp. XXI:** 30

"Boom" (Nemerov), **III:** 278

Boom! (T. Williams), **IV:** 383

Boomer Girls: Poems by Women of the Baby Boom Generation (Gemin and Sergi, eds.), **Supp. XXI:** 246

Boom Town (Wolfe), **IV:** 456

"Boom Town" (Wolfe), **IV:** 469

Boone, Daniel, **II:** 207; **III:** 444; **IV:** 192, 193

Boorstin, Daniel, **I:** 253

Booth, Charles, **Supp. I Part 1:** 13

Booth, John Wilkes, **III:** 588

Booth, Philip, **I:** 522; **Supp. IX:** 269; **Supp. XI:** 141; **Supp. XIII:** 277; **Supp. XV:** 92

Booth, General William, **Supp. I Part 2:** 384, 386

"Booze"(P. Benedict), **Supp. XXIII:** 36

Borah, William, **III:** 475

Borden, Lizzie, **II:** 5

Border and the Buffalo, The (J. Cook), **Supp. XXIV:** 248

Borderlands/La Frontera: The New Mestiza (Anzaldúa), **Supp. XIII:** 223

Border Matters (Saldívar), **Supp. XIX:** 112–113

Borders (Mora), **Supp. XIII:** 213, **215–217**

Border Trilogy (McCarthy), **Supp. VIII:** 175, 182

"Border View, Hot Springs, Texas" (W. V. Davis), **Supp. XXI:** 95

Borel, Pétrus, **III:** 320

Borges, Jorge Luis, **I:** 123, 135, 138, 140, 142; **Supp. III Part 2:** 560; **Supp. IV Part 2:** 623, 626, 630; **Supp. V:** 238; **Supp. VIII:** 15, 348, 349; **Supp. XII:** 21, 147; **Supp. XV:** 34; **Supp. XVI:** 201, 206; **Supp. XVII:** 47; **Supp. XIX:** 131; **Supp. XXIII:** 68; **Supp. XXV:** 50, 69

"Borges and I" (Bidart), **Supp. XV:** 34, 35

"Borinken Blues" (Komunyakaa), **Supp. XIII:** 117

"Born, The" (Lamott), **Supp. XX: 143–144**

"Born a Square: The Westerner's Dilemma" (Stegner), **Supp. IV Part 2:** 595; **Supp. V:** 224

"Born Bad" (Cisneros), **Supp. VII:** 62

Born on the Fourth of July (Kovic), **Supp. XIX:** 17

"Borough of Cemeteries" (Shaw), **Supp. XIX:** 246

Borrowed Time: An AIDS Memoir (Monette), **Supp. X:** 145, 146, 147, 152, 154, 155

Bose, Sudip, **Supp. XXII:** 205, 206, 214

Bosmajian, Hamida, **Supp. XXII:** 290

"Bosque del Apache Wildlife Refuge" (Mora), **Supp. XIII:** 218

Boss Dog, The: A Story of Provence (M. F. K. Fisher), **Supp. XVII:** 91

Bost, Suzanne, **Supp. XXII:** 66, 70, 75, 78

"Boston" (Hardwick), **Supp. III Part 1:** 201

Boston (Sinclair), **Supp. V:** 282, 288–289

Boston, B. H., **Supp. XIII:** 312

Boston Adventure (Stafford), **Retro. Supp. II:** 177, 178

"Boston Common" (Berryman), **I:** 172

"Boston Hymn" (Emerson), **II:** 13, 19

Bostonians, The (H. James), **I:** 9; **II:** 282; **IV:** 202; **Retro. Supp. I:** 216, 225

Boston Marriage (Mamet), **Supp. XIV:** 247

"Boston Nativity, The" (Lowell), **II:** 538

Boswell, James, **IV:** 431; **Supp. I Part 2:** 656

Boswell: A Modern Comedy (Elkin), **Supp. VI:** 42, **44–45,** 57

Bosworth, Patricia, **Supp. IV Part 2:** 573, 591

"Bothersome Sex and O'Brien, The" (Ryan as Quin), **Supp. XVIII:** 238

Botticelli (McNally), **Supp. XIII:** 197

Botticelli, Sandro, **IV:** 410; **Retro. Supp. I:** 422

"Botticellian Trees, The" (W. C. Williams), **Retro. Supp. I:** 422

"Bottle of Milk for Mother, A" (Algren), **Supp. IX:** 3

"Bottle of Perrier, A" (Wharton), **IV:** 316

"Bottles" (Kenyon), **Supp. VII:** 171

"Bottom Line, The" (Elkin), **Supp. VI:** 52, **53**

Bottom: On Shakespeare (Zukofsky), **Supp. III Part 2:** 622, 624, 625, 626, 627, 629

Boublil, Alain, **Supp. XXI:** 155

Boucher, Anthony, **Supp. IV Part 2:** 473; **Supp. XV:** 203, 205

Boucicault, Dion, **Supp. XXII:** 70

Boughton, Henrietta Breckenridge. *See* Young, Barbara

Boukreev, Anatoli, **Supp. XVIII:** 112

Boulanger, Nadia, **Supp. IV Part 1:** 81

"Boulot and Boulette" (Chopin), **Supp. I Part 1:** 211

Boulton, Agnes, **III:** 403; **Supp. XXII: 17–31**

Bound East for Cardiff (O'Neill), **III:** 388

Bound for Glory (Guthrie), **Supp. XVIII:** 23

"Bounty" (Saunders), **Supp. XIX:** 226, 227

"Bounty"(P. Benedict), **Supp. XXIII:** 41

"Bouquet, The" (Stevens), **IV:** 90

"Bouquet of Dark Red Mums, The" (Notley), **Supp. XXII:** 230

"Bouquet of Roses in Sunlight" (Stevens), **IV:** 93

Bourdin, Henri L., **Supp. I Part 1:** 251

Bourgeois, Monique, **Supp. XXII:** 99–100

Bourgeois Poet, The (Shapiro), **Supp. II Part 2:** 701, 703, 704, 713, 714–716

Bourget, James, **IV:** 319

Bourget, Paul, **II:** 325, 338; **IV:** 311, 315; **Retro. Supp. I:** 224, 359, 373; **Supp. XX: 232;** **Supp. XXIV:** 23

Bourjaily, Vance, **III:** 43; **Supp. IX:** 260; **Supp. XXIV:** 225

Bourke-White, Margaret, **I:** 290, 293, 295, 297

Bourne, Charles Rogers, **I:** 215

Bourne, Mrs. Charles Rogers, **I:** 215

Bourne, Randolph, **I: 214–238,** 243, 245, 246–247, 251, 259; **Supp. I Part 2:** 524; **Supp. XV:** 141, 298, 301

Boursicot, Bernard, **Supp. XXI:** 152, 153, 154

Bouton, Jim "Bulldog", **Supp. XX: 274**

Bouton, John Bell, **Supp. XXIII:** 188, 189

Bowden, Charles, **Supp. XIII:** 17

Bowditch, Nathaniel, **Supp. I Part 2:** 482

Bowen, Barbara, **Supp. IX:** 311

Bowen, Elizabeth, **Retro. Supp. I:** 351;
Supp. IV Part 1: 299; **Supp. VIII:**
65, 165, 251, 265; **Supp. IX:** 128
Bowen, Francis, **Supp. I Part 2:** 413
Bowen, Henry, **Supp. XVIII:** 4
Bowen, Louise de Koven, **Supp. I Part
1:** 5
Bowen, Michael, **Supp. VIII:** 73
Bowers, John, **Supp. XI:** 217–218
"Bowlers Anonymous" (Dobyns), **Supp.
XIII:** 86
Bowles, Emily, **Supp. XVIII:** 200, 202
Bowles, Jane (Jane Auer), **II:** 586; **Supp.
IV Part 1:** 89, 92
Bowles, Paul, **I:** 211; **II:** 586; **Supp. II
Part 1:** 17; **Supp. IV Part 1: 79–99**
Bowles, Samuel, **I:** 454, 457; **Retro.
Supp. I:** 30, 32, 33
"Bowl of Blood, The" (Jeffers), **Supp. II
Part 2:** 434
"Bowls" (Moore), **III:** 196
Bowman, James, **I:** 193
"Bows to Drouth" (Snyder), **Supp. VIII:**
303
Box, Edgar (pseudonym). *See* Vidal, Gore
*Box and Quotations from Chairman Mao
Tse-tung* (Albee), **I:** 89–91, 94
Boxer and the Spy, The (Parker), **Supp.
XIX:** 190
Box Garden, The (Shields), **Supp. VII:**
314–315, 320
"Box of Pastels, A" (Kooser), **Supp.
XIX:** 128
"Box of Rocks, A" (Gallagher), **Supp.
XXIV:** 175
"Box Seat" (Toomer), **Supp. III Part 2:**
484; **Supp. IX:** 316, 318
Boy, A (Ashbery), **Supp. III Part 1:** 5
"Boy and Dog" (L. Brown), **Supp. XXI:**
38, 42, **43–44**
Boyce, Horace, **II:** 136
Boyce, Neith, **Supp. XVII:** 96, 97, 98–
99, 100, 106; **Supp. XXI: 1–16**
Boyd, Brian, **Retro. Supp. I:** 270, 275
Boyd, Janet L., **Supp. X:** 229
Boyd, Kristen, **Supp. XXIII:** 246
Boyd, Nancy (pseudonym). *See* Millay,
Edna St. Vincent
Boyd, Thomas, **I:** 99; **IV:** 427
Boyesen, H. H., **II:** 289
"Boy from Lam Kien, The" (July), **Supp.
XXIV:** 200, 204
"Boyhood" (Collins), **Supp. XXI:** 64
"Boyhood" (Farrell), **II:** 28
"Boy in France, A" (Salinger), **III:** 552–
553
"Boy in the Basement, The" (Inge), **Supp.
XXV:** 105, 106
Boy in the Water (Dobyns), **Supp. XIII:**
75, **84**
Boyle, Kay, **IV:** 404; **Supp. XXIV: 49–66**
Boyle, T. Coraghessan, **Supp. VIII:**
1–17; Supp. XX: 17–32; Supp. XXI:
226; **Supp. XXII:** 262
Boyle, Thomas John. *See* Boyle, T. C.
Boynton, H. W., **Supp. IX:** 7
Boynton, Percy Holmes, **Supp. I Part 2:**
415
Boynton, Robert, **Supp. XVII:** 209;
Supp. XVIII: 105, 107, 116

Boynton, Robert S., **Supp. XXV:** 158
"Boy on a Train" (Ellison), **Retro. Supp.
II:** 124
"Boy Riding Forward Backward"
(Francis), **Supp. IX:** 82
"Boys and Girls" (Cisneros), **Supp. VII:**
59–60
"Boy's Dream Ballad, The" (Very), **Supp.
XXV:** 244
Boy's Froissart, The (Lanier), **Supp. I
Part 1:** 361
"Boys"(Kenny), **Supp. XXIII:** 149
Boy's King Arthur, The (Lanier), **Supp. I
Part 1:** 361
Boy's Mabinogion, The (Lanier), **Supp. I
Part 1:** 361
"Boys of '29, The" (Holmes), **Supp. I
Part 1:** 308
Boys of '76, The (Coffin), **III:** 577
Boy's Percy, The (Lanier), **Supp. I Part
1:** 361
Boy's Town (Howells), **I:** 418
Boy's Will, A (Frost), **II:** 152, 153, 155–
156, 159, 164, 166; **Retro. Supp. I:**
124, 127, 128, 131; **Retro. Supp. II:**
168
"Boy Up a Tree" (Hoffman), **Supp.
XVIII:** 86
"Boy Who Wrestled with Angels, The"
(Hoffman), **Supp. X:** 90
"Boy with One Shoe, The" (Jewett),
Retro. Supp. II: 132
"Brace, The" (Bausch), **Supp. VII:** 48
Bracebridge Hall, or, The Humorists
(Irving), **I:** 339, 341; **II:** 308–309, 313
Bracher, Frederick, **I:** 378, 380; **Supp. I
Part 1:** 185
Brackenridge, Hugh Henry, **Supp. I Part
1:** 124, 127, 145; **Supp. II Part 1:** 65
Brackett, Leigh, **Supp. IV Part 1:** 130
Bradbury, John M., **I:** 288–289; **IV:** 130,
135
Bradbury, Malcolm, **Supp. VIII:** 124;
Supp. XVIII: 140
Bradbury, Ray, **Supp. I Part 2:** 621–622;
**Supp. IV Part 1: 101–118; Supp.
XVI:** 122; **Supp. XVII:** 41; **Supp.
XXIII:** 290; **Supp. XXV:** 141
"Brad Carrigan, American" (Saunders),
Supp. XIX: 233
Braddon, Mary E., **Supp. I Part 1:** 35,
36
Bradfield, Scott, **Supp. VIII:** 88
Bradford, Gamaliel, **I:** 248, 250
Bradford, Roark, **Retro. Supp. I:** 80
Bradford, William, **Retro. Supp. II:** 161,
162; **Supp. I Part 1:** 110, 112; **Supp.
I Part 2:** 486, 494; **Supp. XXII:**
33–47
Bradlee, Ben, **Supp. V:** 201
Bradley, Bill, **Supp. VIII:** 47
Bradley, F. H., **Retro. Supp. I:** 57, 58
Bradley, Francis Herbert, **I:** 59, 567–568,
572, 573
Bradshaw, Barbara, **Supp. XIII:** 313
Bradstreet, Anne, **I:** 178–179, 180, 181,
182, 184; **III:** 505; **Retro. Supp. I:**
40; **Supp. I Part 1: 98–123,** 300;
Supp. I Part 2: 484, 485, 496, 546,
705; **Supp. V:** 113, 117–118; **Supp.**

XIII: 152; **Supp. XIV:** 128; **Supp.
XVIII:** 304; **Supp. XXII:** 46
Bradstreet, Elizabeth, **Supp. I Part 1:**
108, 122
Bradstreet, Simon, **I:** 178; **Supp. I Part
1:** 103, 110, 116
Bradstreet, Mrs. Simon. *See* Bradstreet,
Anne
Brady, Alice, **III:** 399
Brady, Catherine, **Supp. XXIII:** 301
Brady, Matthew, **Supp. XVIII:** 4
Bragdon, Claude, **Supp. XX:** 117
"Bragdowdy and the Busybody, The"
(Thurber), **Supp. I Part 2:** 617
Bragg, Rick, **Supp. XVIII:** 195
"Brahma" (Emerson), **II:** 19, 20
Brahms, Johannes, **III:** 118, 448
"Brahms in Delirium" (Skloot), **Supp.
XX:** 203
Braided Creek (Kooser and Harrison),
Supp. XIX: 126
"Braiding" (L.-Y. Lee), **Supp. XV:** 214
"Brain and the Mind, The" (James), **II:**
346
Brainard, Joe, **Supp. XV:** 33; **Supp.
XXIII:** 217; **Supp. XXIV:** 33, 34, 35,
39, 41, 42, 43
"Brain Damage" (Barthelme), **Supp. IV
Part 1:** 44
"Braindead Megaphone, The" (Saunders),
Supp. XIX: 235
Braindead Megaphone, The: Essays
(Saunders), **Supp. XIX:** 234–236
"Brain Scan" (Skloot), **Supp. XX:** 200
"Brain to the Heart, The" (Komunyakaa),
Supp. XIII: 120
Braithwaite, Chris, **Supp. XXII:** 212
Braithwaite, William Stanley, **Retro.
Supp. I:** 131; **Supp. IX:** 309; **Supp.
XV:** 296–297, 301–302, 305, 306
Brakhage, Stan, **Supp. XII:** 2
Braly, Malcolm, **Supp. XVIII:** 147
"Bramble, The" (Wrigley), **Supp. XVIII:**
301
Brame, Gloria, **Supp. XV:** 113; **Supp.
XXIII:** 122
Bramen, Carrie Tirado, **Supp. XXIV:** 192
Bramer, Monte, **Supp. X:** 152
Branch Will Not Break, The (Wright),
Supp. III Part 2: 596, 598–601;
Supp. IV Part 1: 60; **Supp. IX:** 159
Brancusi, Constantin, **III:** 201; **Retro.
Supp. I:** 292
Brande, Dorothea, **Supp. I Part 2:** 608
Brandel, Marc, **Supp. XXI:** 276
Branden, Nathaniel, **Supp. IV Part 2:**
526, 528
"Branding Cities" (Greenberg), **Supp.
XXII:** 244
"Brand-Name Blues" (Kaufmann), **Supp.
XI:** 39
Brand New Life, A (Farrell), **II:** 46, 48
Brando, Marlon, **II:** 588; **Supp. IV Part
2:** 560; **Supp. XVIII:** 251
Brandon, Henry, **Supp. I Part 2:** 604,
612, 618
Brandt, Alice, **Supp. I Part 1:** 92
Brandt, Carl, **Supp. XI:** 45
Brant, Sebastian, **III:** 447, 448

Brantley, Ben, **Supp. XXIV:** 268, 269–270, 271, 272, 274

Braque, Georges, **III:** 197; **Supp. IX:** 66

Brashford, Jake, **Supp. X:** 252

Brasil, Emanuel, **Supp. I Part 1:** 94

"Brasília" (Plath), **Supp. I Part 2:** 544, 545

"Brass Buttons" (McCoy), **Supp. XIII:** 161

"Brass Candlestick, The" (Francis), **Supp. IX:** 89

Brass Check, The (Sinclair), **Supp. V:** 276, 281, 282, 284–285

Brass Knuckles (Dybek), **Supp. XXIII:** **68–69**

"Brass Ring, The" (Carver), **Supp. III Part 1:** 137

"Brass Spittoons" (Hughes), **Supp. I Part 1:** 326–327

Brass Verdict, The (Connelly), **Supp. XXI:** **78–79**

Brats (X. J. Kennedy), **Supp. XV:** 163

Brautigan, Richard, **III:** 174; **Supp. VIII:** 42, 43; **Supp. XII:** 139; **Supp. XVI:** 172; **Supp. XXI:** 53

Brave Cowboy, The (Abbey), **Supp. XIII:** 4–5

Brave Men (Pyle), **Supp. XVII:** 61

Brave New World (Huxley), **II:** 454; **Supp. XIII:** 29; **Supp. XVIII:** 137

"Brave New World" (MacLeish), **III:** 18

Bravery of Earth, A (Eberhart), **I:** 522, 524, 525, 526, 530

"Brave Tailors of Maida, The" (Talese), **Supp. XVII:** 208

"Brave Words for a Startling Occasion" (Ellison), **Retro. Supp. II:** 118

Braving the Elements (Merrill), **Supp. III Part 1:** 320, 323, 325–327, 329

Bravo, The (Cooper), **I:** 345–346, 348

"Bravura" (Francis), **Supp. IX:** 90

Brawley, Benjamin, **Supp. I Part 1:** 327, 332

Brawl in a Tavern, A (Shaw), **Supp. XIX:** 241

Brawne, Fanny, **I:** 284; **II:** 531

Braxton, Joanne, **Supp. IV Part 1:** 12, 15

Brazil (Bishop), **Retro. Supp. II:** 45; **Supp. I Part 1:** 92

"Brazil" (Marshall), **Supp. XI:** 281

Brazil (Updike), **Retro. Supp. I:** 329, 330, 334

"Brazil, January 1, 1502" (Bishop), **Retro. Supp. II:** 47

Braziller, George, **Supp. X:** 24; **Supp. XXIII:** 214

Brazzi, Rossano, **Supp. IV Part 2:** 520

"Bread" (Dickey), **Supp. IV Part 1:** 182

"Bread" (Olds), **Supp. X:** 206

"Bread Alone" (Wylie), **Supp. I Part 2:** 727

Bread in the Wilderness (Merton), **Supp. VIII:** 197, 208

"Bread of Desire, The" (Nelson), **Supp. XVIII:** 177

Bread of Idleness, The (Masters), **Supp. I Part 2:** 460

"Bread of This World, The" (McGrath), **Supp. X:** 119, 127

Bread of Time, The (Levine), **Supp. V:** 180

Bread without Sugar (Stern), **Supp. IX:** **297–298**

"Break, The" (Sexton), **Supp. II Part 2:** 689

"Breakaways, The" (Siddons), **Supp. XXII:** 244

Breakdown (Paretsky), **Supp. XXV:** 185

Breakfast at Tiffany's (Capote), **Supp. III Part 1:** 113, 117, 119–121, 124, 126

Breakfast of Champions (Vonnegut), **Supp. II Part 2:** 755, 759, 769, 770, 777–778

Breaking and a Death, A (Kees), **Supp. XV:** 145

Breaking and Entering (X. J. Kennedy), **Supp. XV:** 153, **160–162**

Breaking Hard Ground (D. Hunter), **Supp. XVI:** 38

Breaking Ice (McMillan, ed.), **Supp. XIII:** 182–183

Breaking Open (Rukeyser), **Supp. VI:** 274, 281

"Breaking Open" (Rukeyser), **Supp. VI:** 286

Breaking Point, The (Rinehart), **Supp. XXV:** 196

Breaking Ranks: A Political Memoir (Podhoretz), **Supp. VIII:** **239–241,** 245

"Breaking the Code of Silence: Ideology and Women's Confessional Poetry" (Harris), **Supp. XIV:** 269

"Breaking Up of the Winships, The" (Thurber), **Supp. I Part 2:** 616

Brearton, Fran, **Supp. XXIV:** 167

Breast, The (P. Roth), **Retro. Supp. II:** 287–288; **Supp. III Part 2:** 416, 418

"Breast, The" (Sexton), **Supp. II Part 2:** 687

"Breasts" (Gallagher), **Supp. XXIV:** 168, 174

"Breasts" (Simic), **Supp. VIII:** 275

"Breasts"(Dybek), **Supp. XXIII:** 77

"Breath" (Espaillat), **Supp. XXI:** 109

"Breath" (Levine), **Supp. V:** 185

Breathe No More, My Lady (Lacy), **Supp. XV:** 203

Breathing Lessons (Tyler), **Supp. IV Part 2:** 669–670

Breathing the Water (Levertov), **Supp. III Part 1:** 274, 283, 284

"Breath of Life, The" (C. Baxter), **Supp. XVII:** 23

Breath's Burials (Sobin), **Supp. XVI:** **288–289**

Breaux, Zelia, **Retro. Supp. II:** 114

Brecht, Bertolt, **I:** 60, 301; **III:** 161, 162; **IV:** 394; **Supp. I Part 1:** 292; **Supp. II Part 1:** 10, 26, 56; **Supp. IV Part 1:** 359; **Supp. IX:** 131, 133, 140; **Supp. X:** 112; **Supp. XIII:** 206, 286; **Supp. XIV:** 162; **Supp. XVIII:** 33; **Supp. XXIV:** 267

Breen, Joseph I., **IV:** 390

Breines, Ron, **Supp. XVIII:** 97

Breit, Harvey, **I:** 433; **III:** 575; **Retro. Supp. II:** 230; **Supp. XVIII:** 254; **Supp. XXI:** 277

Breman, Paul, **Supp. XXII:** 8

Bremer, Anne, **Supp. XXII:** 277

Bremer, Fredrika, **Supp. I Part 1:** 407

Bremer, Richard, **Supp. XXIII:** 236

Brendan: A Novel (Buechner), **Supp. XII:** 53

Brennan, Matthew C., **Supp. XV:** 113, 125; **Supp. XIX:** 121

Brent, David, **Supp. XXII:** 259

Brent, Linda, **Supp. IV Part 1:** 12, 13

Brentano, Franz, **II:** 350; **Supp. XIV:** 198, 199

Brer Rabbit (tales), **Supp. IV Part 1:** 11, 13; **Supp. XIV:** 88

Breslin, James E. B., **Retro. Supp. I:** 430

Breslin, John B., **Supp. IV Part 1:** 308

Breslin, Paul, **Supp. VIII:** 283

Bresson, Robert, **Supp. IV Part 1:** 156

"Bresson's Movies" (Creeley), **Supp. IV Part 1:** 156–157

Breton, André, **III:** 425; **Supp. XIII:** 114; **Supp. XVII:** 244

Brett, George, **II:** 466; **Supp. V:** 286

Brett, Reginald Baliol, **Supp. XX: 230**

Brevoort, Henry, **II:** 298

Brew, Kwesi, **Supp. IV Part 1:** 10, 16

Brewer, Gaylord, **Supp. XV:** 330

"Brewing of Soma, The" (Whittier), **Supp. I Part 2:** 704

Brewsie and Willie (Stein), **IV:** 27

Brewster, Martha, **Supp. I Part 1:** 114

"Brewsterville Croesus, A" (Briggs), **Supp. XVIII:** 16

Brewsterville letters (Briggs), **Supp. XVIII:** 1, 5, **15–16**

"Brian Age 7" (Doty), **Supp. XI:** 136

Briand, Paul, **Supp. XVIII:** 155

"Briar Patch, The" (Warren), **IV:** 237

Briar Rose (Coover), **Supp. V:** 52

"Briar Rose (Sleeping Beauty)" (Sexton), **Supp. II Part 2:** 690

Brice, Fanny, **II:** 427

"Brick, The" (Nye), **Supp. XIII:** 276

"Bricklayer in the Snow" (Fante), **Supp. XI:** 164–165

"Brick Layer's Lunch Hour, The" (Ginsberg), **Supp. II Part 1:** 318

Brickman, Marshall, **Supp. XV:** 5

"Bricks, The" (Hogan), **Supp. IV Part 1:** 413

"Bridal Ballad, The" (Poe), **III:** 428

"Bridal Bed, The" (Gibran), **Supp. XX: 124**

Bridal Dinner, The (Gurney), **Supp. V:** 109, 110

Bridal Hunt (Silver), **Supp. XXIV:** 264

"Bride Comes to Yellow Sky, The" (Crane), **I:** 34, 415, 416, 423

Bridegroom, The (Jin), **Supp. XVIII:** **97–98**

"Bridegroom, The" (Jin), **Supp. XVIII:** 98

Bridegroom Cometh, The (W. Frank), **Supp. XX: 77**

"Bridegroom's Body, The" (Boyle), **Supp. XXIV:** 54, **55–56**

"Bride in the 30's, A" (Auden), **Supp. II Part 1:** 9

Bride of Lammermoor (Scott), **II:** 291

Bride of Samoa (film), **Supp. IV Part 1:** 82

"Bride of the Innisfallen, The" (Welty), **IV:** 278–279; **Retro. Supp. I:** 353

Bride of the Innisfallen, The, and Other Stories (Welty), **IV:** 261, 275–279; **Retro. Supp. I:** 352–353, 355

Brides of the South Wind: Poems 1917–1922 (Jeffers), **Supp. II Part 2:** 419

Bridge, Horatio, **II:** 226

"BRIDGE, THE" (Baraka), **Supp. II Part 1:** 32, 36

Bridge, The (Crane), **Supp. XXIII:** 146

Bridge, The (H. Crane), **I:** 62, 109, 266, 385, 386, 387, 395–399, 400, 402; **IV:** 123, 341, 418, 419, 420; **Retro. Supp. I:** 427; **Retro. Supp. II:** 76, 77, 81, 83, **84–87; Supp. V:** 342; **Supp. IX:** 306

Bridge, The (Talese), **Supp. XVII:** 202, 203, 208

Bridge at Remagen, The (film), **Supp. XI:** 343

"Bridge Burners, The" (Van Vechten), **Supp. II Part 2:** 733

Bridgehead: The Drama of Israel (W. Frank), **Supp. XX:** 80

Bridge of San Luis Rey, The (Wilder), **I:** 360; **IV:** 356, 357, 360–363, 365, 366

"Bridge of Sighs"(P. Benedict), **Supp. XXIII:** 47–48

Bridge of Years, The (Sarton), **Supp. VIII:** 253

"Bridges" (Kingsolver), **Supp. VII:** 208

Bridges, Harry, **I:** 493; **Supp. XVIII:** 238; **Supp. XIX:** 264

Bridges, Lloyd, **Supp. XV:** 202

Bridges, Robert, **II:** 537; **III:** 527; **Supp. I Part 2:** 721; **Supp. II Part 1:** 21; **Supp. XIV:** 336, 341, 342, 343

"Bridging" (Apple), **Supp. XVII:** 5

Bridgman, P. W., **I:** 278

"Bridle, The" (Carver), **Supp. III Part 1:** 138

"Brief and Blameless Outline of the Ontogeny of Crow, A" (Wright), **Supp. XV:** 347

Brief and Frightening Reign of Phil, The (Saunders), **Supp. XIX: 230–231,** 233

"Brief Début of Tildy, The" (O. Henry), **Supp. II Part 1:** 408

"Brief Encounters on the Inland Waterway" (Vonnegut), **Supp. II Part 2:** 760

Brief History of the Dead, The (Brockmeier), **Supp. XXII: 57–59,** 61

Briefings (Ammons), **Supp. VII:** 29

Brief Interviews with Hideous Men (Wallace), **Supp. X: 308–310**

"Brief Interviews with Hideous Men" (Wallace), **Supp. X:** 309

"Briefly It Enters, and Briefly Speaks" (Kenyon), **Supp. VII:** 174

"Brief Study of the British, A" (Saunders), **Supp. XIX:** 235

Brief Wondrous Life of Oscar Wao, The (Díaz), **Supp. XXIV:** 83, 84, 85, 87, **89–92,** 93

Brier, His Book (J. W. Miller), **Supp. XX: 165, 168, 170**

"Brier Grows Wild, The" (J. W. Miller), **Supp. XX:** 170

"Brier Losing Touch with His Traditions, The" (J. W. Miller), **Supp. XX: 165, 169**

Brier Poems, The (J. W. Miller), **Supp. XX:** 168

"Brier Sermon, The—You Must Be Born Again" (J. W. Miller), **Supp. XX: 165, 169–170**

Briffault, Robert, **Supp. I Part 2:** 560, 567

"Brigade de Cuisine" (McPhee), **Supp. III Part 1:** 307–308

Brigadier and the Golf Widow, The (Cheever), **Supp. I Part 1:** 184–185, 192

Briggs, Charles Frederick, **Supp. I Part 2:** 411; **Supp. XVIII: 1–18**

brigham, besmilr, **Supp. XV:** 349

"Bright and Morning Star" (Wright), **IV:** 488

Bright Book of Life: American Novelists and Storytellers from Hemingway to Mailer (Kazin), **Supp. VIII:** 102, 104

Bright Center of Heaven (Maxwell), **Supp. VIII: 153–155,** 164

"Brightness from the North" (B. Kelly), **Supp. XVII:** 131

Brighton Beach Memoirs (Simon), **Supp. IV Part 2:** 576, 577, 584, 586–587, 590

Bright Procession (Sedges), **Supp. II Part 1:** 125

Bright Room Called Day, A (Kushner), **Supp. IX:** 133, **138–141,** 142

Brillat-Savarin, Jean Anthelme, **Supp. XVII:** 82, 86, 87

"Brilliance" (Doty), **Supp. XI:** 124, 128

"Brilliant California Novelist, A" (Forman), **Supp. XXIV:** 30

"Brilliant Leaves" (Gordon), **II:** 199

"Brilliant Sad Sun" (W. C. Williams), **Retro. Supp. I:** 422

"Bring Brang Brung" (Muñoz), **Supp. XXV:** 135–136

"Bringing Back the Trumpeter Swan" (Kumin), **Supp. IV Part 2:** 454

Bringing It All Back Home (album, Dylan), **Supp. XVIII:** 20, 25, 26, 30

Bringing It All Back Home (McNally), **Supp. XIII:** 197–198

Bringing the Devil to His Knees (C. Baxter), **Supp. XVII:** 22

"Bringing the Strange Home" (Dunn), **Supp. XI:** 141

"Bring the Day!" (Roethke), **III:** 536

Brinkley, Douglas, **Supp. XIII:** 9; **Supp. XXIV:** 281, 293

Brinkmeyer, Robert H., Jr., **Supp. XI:** 38

Brinnin, John Malcolm, **IV:** 26, 27, 28, 42, 46; **Supp. XV:** 139

Brissot, Jacques Pierre, **Supp. I Part 2:** 511

"Britain's Negro Problem in Sierra Leone" (Du Bois), **Supp. I Part 1:** 176

"British Guiana" (Marshall), **Supp. XI:** 281–282

"British Poets, The" (Holmes), **Supp. I Part 1:** 306

"British Prison Ship, The" (Freneau), **Supp. II Part 1:** 261

Brittan, Gordon G., Jr., **Supp. XIV:** 234

Britten, Benjamin, **II:** 586; **Supp. II Part 1:** 17; **Supp. IV Part 1:** 84

Broadwater, Bowden, **II:** 562

Broadway, Broadway (McNally). *See It's Only a Play* (McNally)

Broadway, J. William, **Supp. V:** 316

Broadway Bound (Simon), **Supp. IV Part 2:** 576, 577, 584, 586–587, 590

Broadway Danny Rose (film; Allen), **Supp. XV:** 9

"Broadway Sights" (Whitman), **IV:** 350

Broccoli, Albert R. "Cubby", **Supp. XI:** 307

Brock

Bröck, Sabine, **Supp. XI:** 275, 277, 278

Brockmeier, Kevin, **Supp. XXII: 49–63**

Brodhead, Richard, **Retro. Supp. II:** 139; **Supp. XIV:** 61

Brodkey, Harold, **Supp. VIII:** 151; **Supp. X:** 160

Brodkin, Joel, **Supp. XXV:** 261

Brodskii, Iosif Alexsandrovich. *See* Brodsky, Joseph

Brodsky, Joseph, **Supp. VIII: 19–35; Supp. X:** 65, 73; **Supp. XV:** 134, 135, 256; **Supp. XXIII:** 122

Brody, Alter, **Supp. XV:** 302, 307

Brodyar, Anatole, **Supp. XIV:** 106

Brokeback Mountain (film), **Supp. XX: 273**

"Brokeback Mountain" (Proulx), **Supp. VII:** 264–265

"Broken Balance, The" (Jeffers), **Supp. II Part 2:** 426

"Broken Field Running" (Bambara), **Supp. XI:** 10, 11

Broken Frieze, The (Everwine), **Supp. XV:** 74, 75, 89

Broken Ground, The (Berry), **Supp. X:** 30

"Broken Home, The" (Merrill), **Supp. III Part 1:** 319, 325

"Broken Oar, The" (Longfellow), **Retro. Supp. II:** 169

"Broken Promise" (MacLeish), **III:** 15

Broken Span, The (W. C. Williams), **IV:** 419; **Retro. Supp. I:** 424

"Broken Tower, The" (H. Crane), **I:** 385, 386, 400, 401–402; **Retro. Supp. II:** 89, 90

Broken Vessels (Dubus), **Supp. VII:** 90–91; **Supp. XI:** 347

"Broken Vessels" (Dubus), **Supp. VII:** 90

Broken Wings, The (al-Ajni&hudot;a al-Mutakassirah) (Gibran), **Supp. XX: 115, 124, 125**

"Broker" (H. Roth), **Supp. IX:** 234

Bromfield, Louis, **IV:** 380

"Brompton Cocktail" (Mamet), **Supp. XIV:** 252

Bromwich, David, **Retro. Supp. I:** 305; **Supp. XII:** 162

"Broncho That Would Not Be Broken, The" (Lindsay), **Supp. I Part 2:** 383

Bronk, William, **Supp. XV:** 115; **Supp. XXI: 17–34**

Brontë, Anne, **Supp. IV Part 2:** 430
Brontë, Branwell, **I:** 462
Brontë, Charlotte, **I:** 458; **II:** 175; **Supp. IV Part 2:** 430; **Supp. IX:** 128; **Supp. XII:** 104, 303; **Supp. XV:** 338; **Supp. XVI:** 158; **Supp. XX: 108**
Brontë, Emily, **I:** 458; **Retro. Supp. I:** 43; **Supp. IV Part 2:** 430; **Supp. IX:** 128; **Supp. X:** 78, 89; **Supp. XV:** 338
"Bronze" (Francis), **Supp. IX:** 76
"Bronze" (Merrill), **Supp. III Part 1:** 336
Bronze Booklets on the History, Problems, and Cultural Contributions of the Negro series, **Supp. XIV:** 202
"Bronze Buckaroo, The" (Baraka), **Supp. II Part 1:** 49
"Bronze Horses, The" (Lowell), **II:** 524
"Bronze Tablets" (Lowell), **II:** 523
Bronzeville Boys and Girls (Brooks), **Supp. III Part 1:** 79
"Bronzeville Mother Loiters in Mississippi, A. Meanwhile, a Mississippi Mother Burns Bacon" (Brooks), **Supp. III Part 1:** 80
"Brooch, The" (Singer), **IV:** 20
Brook, Peter, **Retro. Supp. II:** 182
Brooke, Rupert, **II:** 82; **III:** 3
Brook Evans (Glaspell), **Supp. III Part 1:** 182–185
"Brooking Likeness" (Glück), **Supp. V:** 85
"Brooklyn" (Marshall), **Supp. XI:** 281, 282
"Brooklyn" (Shaw), **Supp. XIX:** 239, 240
Brooklyn Noir (McLoughlin, ed.), **Supp. XXIV:** 14
Brooks, Albert (Al Pew), **Supp. XXI:** 22
Brooks, Carrellin, **Supp. XXV:** 8
Brooks, Cleanth, **I:** 280, 282; **III:** 517; **IV:** 236, 279; **Retro. Supp. I:** 40, 41, 90; **Retro. Supp. II:** 235; **Supp. I Part 2:** 423; **Supp. III Part 2:** 542; **Supp. V:** 316; **Supp. IX:** 153, 155; **Supp. X:** 115, 123; **Supp. XIV: 1–20; Supp. XIX:** 246
Brooks, David, **Supp. IV Part 2:** 623, 626, 630; **Supp. VIII:** 232
Brooks, Gwendolyn, **Retro. Supp. I:** 208; **Supp. III Part 1: 69–90; Supp. IV Part 1:** 2, 15, 244, 251, 257; **Supp. XI:** 1, 278; **Supp. XIII:** 111, 112, 296; **Supp. XIV:** 73; **Supp. XVIII:** 175, 181, 185; **Supp. XXI:** 230
Brooks, Mel, **Supp. IV Part 1:** 390; **Supp. IV Part 2:** 591
Brooks, Paul, **Supp. IX:** 26, 31, 32
Brooks, Phillips, **II:** 542; **Retro. Supp. II:** 134; **Supp. XIII:** 142
Brooks, Van Wyck, **I:** 106, 117, 215, 222, 228, 230, 231, 233, 236, **239–263,** 266, 480; **II:** 30, 271, 285, 309, 337, 482; **III:** 394, 606; **IV:** 171, 312, 427, 433; **Retro. Supp. II:** 46, 137; **Supp. I Part 2:** 423, 424, 650; **Supp. II Part 1:** 137; **Supp. VIII:** 98, 101; **Supp. XIV:** 11; **Supp. XV:** 298, 301; **Supp. XX: 68**
Brooks, Mrs. Van Wyck (Eleanor Kenyon Stimson), **I:** 240, 245, 250, 252

Brooks, Mrs. Van Wyck (Gladys Billings), **I:** 258
Broom of the System, The (Wallace), **Supp. X:** 301, **302–305,** 310
"Brooms" (Simic), **Supp. VIII:** 275
Brosi, George, **Supp. XX: 166; Supp. XXIII:** 39
Brosnan, Jim, **II:** 424–425; **Supp. XX: 195**
Brossard, Chandler, **Supp. XXII:** 258
Brother Carl (Sontag), **Supp. III Part 2:** 452
"Brother Death" (Anderson), **I:** 114
Brother Fire (Di Piero), **Supp. XIX:** 35, 38, 45–47
Brotherhood of the Grape, The (Fante), **Supp. XI:** 160, **171–172**
Brother in Elysium, The: Ideas of Friendship and Society in the United States (Bronk), **Supp. XXI:** 21, 22, 25, 31
"Brothers" (Anderson), **I:** 114
Brothers, The (F. Barthelme), **Supp. XI:** 25, 28, 29, 30, 32–33
Brothers and Keepers (Wideman), **Supp. X:** 320, 321–322, 323, **325–327,** 328, 329–330, 331, 332
Brothers Ashkenazi, The (Singer), **IV:** 2
Brothers Karamazov, The (Dostoevsky), **II:** 60; **III:** 146, 150, 283; **Supp. IX:** 102, 106; **Supp. XI:** 172; **Supp. XII:** 322
Brothers of No Kin (Richter), **Supp. XVIII:** 209
"Brothers of No Kin" (Richter), **Supp. XVIII:** 208
Brother to Dragons: A Tale in Verse and Voices (Warren), **IV:** 243–244, 245, 246, 251, 252, 254, 257
Broughton, James, **Supp. XV:** 146
Broughton, Rhoda, **II:** 174; **IV:** 309, 310; **Supp. XX: 232**
Broun, Heywood, **I:** 478; **II:** 417; **IV:** 432; **Supp. IX:** 190; **Supp. XXII:** 277
Broussais, François, **Supp. I Part 1:** 302
Brouwer, Joel, **Supp. XXII:** 223, 237
Browder, Earl, **I:** 515; **Supp. XX: 76, 77**
Brower, David, **Supp. X:** 29
Brower, Reuben, **Supp. XV:** 20
Brown, Alice, **II:** 523; **Retro. Supp. II:** 136
Brown, Andrew, **Supp. XVI:** 150
Brown, Ashley, **Retro. Supp. II:** 48; **Supp. I Part 1:** 79, 80, 82, 84, 92
Brown, Charles Brockden, **I:** 54, 211, 335; **II:** 74, 267, 298; **III:** 415; **Supp. I Part 1: 124–149; Supp. II Part 1:** 65, 292; **Supp. XXIII:** 178
Brown, Mrs. Charles Brockden (Elizabeth Linn), **Supp. I Part 1:** 145, 146
Brown, Clifford, **Supp. V:** 195
Brown, Deborah, **Supp. XVII:** 75
Brown, Dee, **Supp. IV Part 2:** 504
Brown, Elijah, **Supp. I Part 1:** 125
Brown, Fleda, **Supp. XXIII:** 59
Brown, George Douglas, **III:** 473
Brown, Harry, **Supp. IV Part 2:** 560
Brown, Harvey, **Supp. XIV:** 148
Brown, Himan, **Supp. XIX:** 241, 242
Brown, H. Rap, **Supp. XXI:** 171

Brown, John, **II:** 13; **IV:** 125, 126, 172, 237, 249, 254; **Supp. I Part 1:** 345; **Supp. VIII:** 204
Brown, Joseph Epes, **Supp. IV Part 2:** 487
Brown, Larry, **Supp. XVIII:** 195; **Supp. XXI: 35–50**
Brown, Leonard, **Supp. IX:** 117
Brown, Mary Armitt, **Supp. I Part 1:** 125
Brown, Nell Porter, **Supp. XXV:** 130, 131, 138
Brown, Percy, **II:** 20
Brown, Robert E., **Supp. X:** 12
Brown, Scott, **Supp. XI:** 178
Brown, Slater, **IV:** 123; **Retro. Supp. II:** 79
Brown, Solyman, **Supp. I Part 1:** 156
Brown, Sterling, **Retro. Supp. I:** 198; **Supp. IV Part 1:** 169; **Supp. XIV:** 202; **Supp. XXII:** 1, 8, 12
Brown, Tina, **Supp. XVI:** 176–177
Brown, Wesley, **Supp. V:** 6
Brown, William Hill, **Supp. XXV:** 38
Brown, William Wells, **Supp. XXIII:** 184
Brown Decades, The (Mumford), **Supp. II Part 2:** 475, 478, 491–492
Brown Dog (Harrison), **Supp. VIII:** 51
Brown Dog of the Yaak: Essays on Art and Activism (Bass), **Supp. XVI:** 22
"Brown Dwarf of Rügen, The" (Whittier), **Supp. I Part 2:** 696
Browne, Charles Farrar, **II:** 289; **IV:** 193, 196; **Supp. XVIII:** 1, 4
Browne, Roscoe Lee, **Supp. VIII:** 345
Browne, Thomas, **II:** 15–16, 304; **III:** 77, 78, 198, 487; **IV:** 147; **Supp. IX:** 136; **Supp. XII:** 45; **Supp. XVI:** 292
Browne, William, **Supp. I Part 1:** 98
Brownell, W. C., **II:** 14
Brownell, William Crary, **Retro. Supp. I:** 365, 366
Browner, Stephanie P., **Supp. XVIII:** 17
Brown Girl, Brownstones (Marshall), **Supp. XI:** 275, 276, **278–280,** 282
Brownies' Book, The (Hughes), **Supp. I Part 1:** 321
Browning, Elizabeth Barrett, **I:** 458, 459; **Retro. Supp. I:** 33, 43; **Supp. XVIII:** 175–176; **Supp. XX: 108**
Browning, Oscar, **Supp. XX: 231**
Browning, Robert, **I:** 50, 66, 103, 458, 460, 468; **II:** 338, 478, 522; **III:** 5, 8, 467, 469, 484, 511, 521, 524, 606, 609; **IV:** 135, 245, 366, 416; **Retro. Supp. I:** 43, 55, 217; **Retro. Supp. II:** 188, 190; **Supp. I Part 1:** 2, 6, 79, 311; **Supp. I Part 2:** 416, 468, 622; **Supp. III Part 1:** 5, 6; **Supp. IV Part 2:** 430; **Supp. X:** 65; **Supp. XV:** 92, 250, 275
Brownmiller, Susan, **Supp. X:** 252
Brownrigg, Sylvia, **Supp. XXV:** 59–60
"Brown River, Smile" (Toomer), **Supp. IV Part 1:** 16
Brownstone Eclogues and Other Poems (Aiken), **I:** 65, 67
Brown: The Last Discovery of America (Rodriguez), **Supp. XIV:** 297, 298, 300, **305–309,** 310, 311–312

Broyard, Anatole, **Supp. IV Part 1:** 39; **Supp. VIII:** 140; **Supp. X:** 186; **Supp. XI:** 348; **Supp. XVI:** 213

Broyles, Yolanda Julia, **Supp. XIX:** 112

Bruccoli, Matthew, **Retro. Supp. I:** 98, 102, 105, 114, 115, 359; **Supp. IV Part 2:** 468, 470

Bruce, John Edward, **Supp. XVI:** 143

Bruce, Lenny, **Supp. VIII:** 198

Bruce, Virginia, **Supp. XII:** 173

Bruce-Novoa, Juan, **Supp. VIII:** 73, 74

Bruchac, Joseph, **Supp. IV Part 1:** 261, 319, 320, 321, 322, 323, 325, 328, 398, 399, 403, 408, 414; **Supp. IV Part 2:** 502, 506

Brueghel, Pieter, **I:** 174; **Supp. I Part 2:** 475

Brueghel, Pieter, the Elder, **Retro. Supp. I:** 430

Bruell, Edwin, **Supp. VIII:** 126

Brugh, Spangler Arlington. *See* Taylor, Robert

"Bruja: Witch" (Mora), **Supp. XIII:** 214, 220, 221, **Supp. XIII:** 222

Brulé, Claude, **Supp. XI:** 307

Brumer, Andy, **Supp. XIII:** 88

Brummels, J. V., **Supp. XIX:** 119

Brunner, Emil, **III:** 291, 303

"Brush Fire" (J. Wright), **Supp. XVII:** 241

Brustein, Robert, **Supp. VIII:** 331; **Supp. XXIV:** 116

Brutus, **IV:** 373, 374; **Supp. I Part 2:** 471

"Brutus and Antony" (Masters), **Supp. I Part 2:** 472

"Bryan, Bryan, Bryan, Bryan" (Lindsay), **Supp. I Part 2:** 394, 395, 398

Bryan, George, **Retro. Supp. II:** 76

Bryan, Sharon, **Supp. IX:** 154

Bryan, William Jennings, **I:** 483; **IV:** 124; **Supp. I Part 2:** 385, 395–396, 455, 456

Bryant, Austin, **Supp. I Part 1:** 152, 153

Bryant, Frances, **Supp. I Part 1:** 153

Bryant, Louise, **Supp. X:** 136

Bryant, Peter, **Supp. I Part 1:** 150, 151, 152, 153. *See also* George, Peter

Bryant, William Cullen, **I:** 335, 458; **II:** 311; **III:** 81; **IV:** 309; **Retro. Supp. I:** 217; **Retro. Supp. II:** 155; **Supp. I Part 1: 150–173,** 312, 362; **Supp. I Part 2:** 413, 416, 420; **Supp. IV Part 1:** 165; **Supp. XIII:** 145; **Supp. XIX:** 4; **Supp. XXV:** 250

Bryant, Mrs. William Cullen (Frances Fairchild), **Supp. I Part 1:** 153, 169

Bryer, Jackson R., **Supp. IV Part 2:** 575, 583, 585, 586, 589, 591; **Supp. XIII:** 200, **Supp. XIII:** 205

Bryher, Jackson R. (pseudonym). *See* Ellerman, Winifred

Brynner, Witter, **Supp. XXII:** 273

Bubber Goes to Heaven (Bontemps), **Supp. XXII:** 4

"Bubbs Creek Haircut" (Snyder), **Supp. VIII:** 306

Buber, Martin, **II:** 228; **III:** 45, 308, 528; **IV:** 11; **Supp. I Part 1:** 83, 88; **Supp. XVI:** 291

Buccaneers, The (Wharton), **IV:** 327; **Retro. Supp. I:** 382

Buchanan Dying (Updike), **Retro. Supp. I:** 331, 335

Buchbinder, David, **Supp. XIII:** 32

Buchwald, Art, **Supp. XII:** 124–125; **Supp. XVI:** 110–111

Buchwald, Emilie, **Supp. XVI:** 35, 36

Buck, Dudley, **Supp. I Part 1:** 362

Buck, Gene, **II:** 427

Buck, Pearl S., **Supp. II Part 1: 113–134; Supp. XIV:** 274

Buckdancer's Choice (Dickey), **Supp. IV Part 1:** 176, 177, 178, 180

"Buckdancer's Choice" (Dickey), **Supp. IV Part 1:** 191

Bucke, Richard Maurice, **Retro. Supp. I:** 407

"Buckeyes"(P. Benedict), **Supp. XXIII:** 46

"Buck Fever" (Humphrey), **Supp. IX:** 109

"Buck in the Snow, The" (Millay), **III:** 135

Buckley, Christopher, **Supp. IX:** 169; **Supp. XI:** 257, 329; **Supp. XV:** 76–77, 86

Buckley, James, Jr., **Supp. XVII:** 220

Buckminster, Joseph, **Supp. II Part 1:** 66–67, 69

Bucknell, Katherine, **Supp. XIV:** 170

Bucolics (Auden), **Supp. II Part 1:** 21, 24

Budbill, David, **Supp. XIX:** 1–16

Budd, Louis J., **IV:** 210

Buddha, **I:** 136; **II:** 1; **III:** 173, 179, 239, 567; **Supp. I Part 1:** 363; **Supp. I Part 2:** 397

Buddha, The: The Story of Siddhartha (film, Grubin), **Supp. XXIII:** 138, 140

"Buddha Boy" (Saunders), **Supp. XIX:** 235

"Buddha's Last Instruction, The" (Oliver), **Supp. VII:** 239

"Buddies"(Kenny), **Supp. XXIII:** 150

Budding Prospects (Boyle), **Supp. VIII: 8–9; Supp. XX: 27–28**

Buechner, Frederick, **III:** 310; **Supp. XII: 41–59**

Buell, Lawrence, **Supp. V:** 209; **Supp. IX:** 29; **Supp. XV:** 269, 282

"Buffalo" (Peacock), **Supp. XIX:** 198

"Buffalo, The" (Moore), **III:** 215

"Buffalo Bill". *See* Cody, William

Buffalo Girls (screenplay) (McMurtry), **Supp. V:** 232

Buffalo Girls (McMurtry), **Supp. V:** 229

Buffalo Hunters, The: The Story of the Hide Men (Sandoz), **Supp. XXIV:** 244, **247–249,** 256

Buffett, Jimmy, **Supp. VIII:** 42

Buffon, Comte de, **II:** 101

Buford, Fanny McConnell, **Retro. Supp. II:** 117

Bugeja, Michael, **Supp. X:** 201

Bugged for Murder (Lacy), **Supp. XV:** 205

"Buglesong" (Stegner), **Supp. IV Part 2:** 606

Buhle, Paul, **Supp. XXI:** 172

"Buick" (Shapiro), **Supp. II Part 2:** 705

"Builders" (Yates), **Supp. XI:** 342–343

Builders, The (Glasgow), **II:** 183–184, 193

"Builders, The" (Hay), **Supp. XIV:** 125

Builders in Sand (W. Frank), **Supp. XX:** 68

Builders of the Bay Colony (Morison), **Supp. I Part 2:** 484–485

"Builders of the Bridge, The" (Mumford), **Supp. II Part 2:** 475

"Building" (Snyder), **Supp. VIII:** 305

"Building, Dwelling, Thinking" (Heidegger), **Retro. Supp. II:** 87

Building a Character (Stanislavsky), **Supp. XIV:** 243

" 'Building' Larry Brown(s) at Algonquin Books of Chapel Hill" (Perry), **Supp. XXI:** 42

"Building of the Ship, The" (Longfellow), **II:** 498; **Retro. Supp. II:** 159, 167, 168

"Build Soil" (Frost), **Retro. Supp. I:** 138, 139

"Build Soil" (Snyder), **Supp. VIII:** 304

Build-Up, The (W. C. Williams), **Retro. Supp. I:** 423

Bukiet, Melvin Jules, **Supp. XVII: 39–51**

Bukowski, Charles, **Supp. III Part 1:** 147; **Supp. XI:** 159, 161, 172, 173; **Supp. XVII:** 245

Bulgakov, Mikhail, **Supp. XIV:** 97

"Bulgarian Poetess, The" (Updike), **IV:** 215, 227; **Retro. Supp. I:** 329

Bull, Ole, **II:** 504

"Bulldozer, The" (Francis), **Supp. IX:** 87

"Bullet in the Brain" (Wolff), **Supp. VII:** 342–343

Bullet Park (Cheever), **Supp. I Part 1:** 185, 187–193, 194, 195

Bullets over Broadway (film; Allen), **Supp. XV:** 12, **12–13**

Bullfight, The (Mailer), **Retro. Supp. II:** 205

Bullfighter Checks Her Makeup, The: My Encounters with Extraordinary People (Orlean), **Supp. XXV:** 159, 163–164

Bullins, Ed, **Supp. II Part 1:** 34, 42

Bullock, Sandra, **Supp. X:** 80

"Bull-Roarer, The" (Stern), **Supp. IX:** 297

"Bully, The" (Dubus), **Supp. VII:** 84

"Bulsh" (X. J. Kennedy), **Supp. XV:** 161

Bultmann, Rudolf, **III:** 309

Bulwark, The (Dreiser), **I:** 497, 506, 516–517; **Retro. Supp. II:** 95, 96, 105, 108

Bulwer-Lytton, Edward George, **IV:** 350

"Bums in the Attic" (Cisneros), **Supp. VII:** 62

Bunche, Ralph, **Supp. I Part 1:** 343; **Supp. XIV:** 202; **Supp. XXII:** 12

"Bunchgrass Edge of the World, The" (Proulx), **Supp. VII:** 263

Bunge, Nancy, **Supp. XVII:** 218; **Supp. XXII:** 175, 177, 178, 180, 183

"Bunner Sisters, The" (Wharton), **IV:** 317

Bunting, Basil, **Retro. Supp. I:** 422; **Supp. III Part 2:** 616, 620, 624; **Supp. XIV:** 286

Buntline, Ned, **Supp. XXIII:** 182

Buñuel, Luis, **III:** 184; **Retro. Supp. II:** 337

Bunyan, John, **I:** 445; **II:** 15, 104, 228; **IV:** 80, 84, 156, 437; **Supp. I Part 1:** 32

Bunyan, Paul, **Supp. XXII:** 203

Burana, Lily, **Supp. XI:** 253

Burbank, Luther, **I:** 483

Burbank, Rex, **IV:** 363

Burch, Michael, **Supp. XXI:** 99

Burchfield, Alice, **Supp. I Part 2:** 652, 660

Burden of Proof, The (Turow), **Supp. XVII:** 216–217, 218

Burden of Southern History, The (Woodward), **Retro. Supp. I:** 75

Burdens of Formality, The (Lea, ed.), **Supp. X:** 58

Burger, Gottfried August, **II:** 306

Burgess, Anthony, **Supp. IV Part 1:** 227; **Supp. IV Part 2:** 685; **Supp. V:** 128; **Supp. XXIII:** 42

Burgh, James, **Supp. I Part 2:** 522

"Burglar of Babylon, The" (Bishop), **Retro. Supp. II:** 47; **Supp. I Part 1:** 93

Burgum, E. B., **IV:** 469, 470

Burham, Philip, **Supp. XX:** 44

"Burial of Jonathan Brown, The" (Hadas), **Supp. XXIII:** 115

Buried Child (Shepard), **Supp. III Part 2:** 433, 447, 448; **Supp. XIV:** 327

"Buried Lake, The" (Tate), **IV:** 136

Burkard, Michael, **Supp. XXIV:** 165

Burke, Carolyn, **Supp. XXII:** 156, 158, 162, 165, 167, 168

Burke, Edmund, **I:** 9; **III:** 310; **Supp. I Part 2:** 496, 511, 512, 513, 523; **Supp. II Part 1:** 80; **Supp. XVII:** 236

Burke, James Lee, **Supp. XIV:** 21–38; **Supp. XXI:** 67, 72, 80

Burke, Kenneth, **I:** 264–287, 291; **III:** 497, 499, 546; **IV:** 123, 408; **Retro. Supp. I:** 297; **Retro. Supp. II:** 117, 120; **Supp. I Part 2:** 630; **Supp. II Part 1:** 136; **Supp. VIII:** 105; **Supp. IX:** 229; **Supp. XIV:** 3; **Supp. XXI:** 89

Burke, William, **Supp. XXI:** 215

"Burl" (Mosher), **Supp. XXII:** 204, 211

Burley, Justin, **Supp. XVI:** 158

"Burly Fading One, The" (Hayden), **Supp. II Part 1:** 366

Burn, Stephen J., **Supp. XX:** 85; **Supp. XXII:** 266, 268

"Burned" (Levine), **Supp. V:** 186, 192

"Burned" (Stallings), **Supp. XXV:** 233

"Burned Diary, The" (Olds), **Supp. X:** 215

Burne-Jones, Edward, **Supp. XXII:** 156

Burnett, Allison, **Supp. XVII:** 22

Burnett, David, **Supp. XI:** 299

Burnett, Frances Hodgson, **Supp. I Part 1:** 44

Burnett, Whit, **III:** 551; **Supp. XI:** 294

Burney, Fanny, **Supp. XV:** 232; **Supp. XX:** 108

Burnham, James, **Supp. I Part 2:** 648

Burnham, John Chynoweth, **I:** 59

"Burning, The" (Welty), **IV:** 277–278; **Retro. Supp. I:** 353

Burning Angel (Burke), **Supp. XIV:** 30, 32

Burning Bright (Steinbeck), **IV:** 51, 61–62

Burning Bright: An Anthology of Sacred Poetry (Hampl, ed.), **Supp. XXII:** 87

"Burning Bush" (Cliff), **Supp. XXII:** 75

Burning Bush (Untermeyer), **Supp. XV:** 309

"Burning Bush" (Untermeyer), **Supp. XV:** 309

Burning Bush, The (Asch), **Supp. XXIII:** 7

Burning Bush, The (H. and G. Herczeg), **Supp. XVII:** 62

Burning Chrome (W. Gibson), **Supp. XVI:** 118, 122, **128**

"Burning Chrome" (W. Gibson), **Supp. XVI:** 117, 120, 123, 124, 128

Burning City (Benét), **Supp. XI:** 46, 58

Burning Daylight (London), **II:** 474, 481

Burning Down the House: Essays on Fiction (C. Baxter), **Supp. XVII:** 13, 20, 21

Burning House, The (Beattie), **Supp. V:** 29

"Burning Ladder, The" (Gioia), **Supp. XV:** 118

Burning Mystery of Anna in 1951, The (Koch), **Supp. XV:** 182–183

"Burning of Paper Instead of Children, The" (Rich), **Supp. I Part 2:** 558

"Burning Shit at An Khe" (Weigl), **Supp. XIX:** 279–280

Burning the Days (Salter), **Supp. XIX:** 252

Burning the Days: Recollections (Salter), **Supp. IX:** 245, 246, 248, 260, **261–262**

"Burning the Small Dead" (Snyder), **Supp. VIII:** 298

Burning Tigris, The: The Armenian Genocide and America's Response (Balakian), **Supp. XXIII:** 19, 21, 22, **25–28,** 30

"Burning Tobacco Beds" (J. W. Miller), **Supp. XX: 167**

Burn Marks (Paretsky), **Supp. XXV:** 174–175, 178, 180

Burns, Carol, **Supp. XVIII:** 162

Burns, David, **III:** 165–166

Burns, Ken, **Supp. XIV:** 14

Burns, Michael, **Supp. XV:** 339

Burns, Robert, **II:** 150, 306; **III:** 592; **IV:** 453; **Supp. I Part 1:** 158; **Supp. I Part 2:** 410, 455, 683, 685, 691, 692; **Supp. IX:** 173; **Supp. XII:** 171; **Supp. XIII:** 3; **Supp. XVIII:** 82

Burnshaw, Stanley, **Retro. Supp. I:** 298, 303; **Supp. III Part 2:** 615

"Burn the Cities" (West), **Retro. Supp. II:** 338

Burnt Mountain (Siddons), **Supp. XXII:** 253

Burnt Norton (T. S. Eliot), **I:** 575, 580–581, 582, 584, 585; **III:** 10

"Burnt Norton" (T. S. Eliot), **Retro. Supp. I:** 66; **Supp. XV:** 216

Burnt-Out Case, A (Greene), **Supp. VIII:** 4

"Burnt-out Spa, The" (Plath), **Retro. Supp. II:** 246

Burn Witch Burn (A. Merritt), **Supp. XVII:** 58

Burr, Aaron, **I:** 7, 549, 550; **II:** 300; **IV:** 264; **Supp. I Part 2:** 461, 483

Burr: A Novel (Vidal), **Supp. IV Part 2:** 677, 682, 684, 685, 687, 688, 689, 691

Burr Oaks (Eberhart), **I:** 533, 535

Burroughs, Edgar Rice, **Supp. IV Part 1:** 101

Burroughs, John, **I:** 220, 236, 506; **IV:** 346; **Supp. IX:** 171

Burroughs, William S., **III:** 45, 174, 258; **Supp. II Part 1:** 320, 328; **Supp. III Part 1:** 91–110, 217, 226; **Supp. IV Part 1:** 79, 87, 90; **Supp. XI:** 297, 308; **Supp. XII:** 1, 3, 118, 121, 124, 129, 131, 136; **Supp. XIV:** 137, 140–141, 143–144, 150; **Supp. XVI:** 123, 135; **Supp. XVII:** 225; **Supp. XVIII:** 137; **Supp. XXIII:** 213; **Supp. XXIV:** 42

Burrow, Trigant, **Supp. II Part 1:** 6

Burrows, Ken, **Supp. V:** 115

Bursey, Jeff, **Supp. XXII:** 257

Burson, Claudia, **Supp. XV:** 343

Burstein, Janet, **Supp. XVII:** 41, 44, 48

"Bursts of Light" (Bronk), **Supp. XXI:** 33

Burt, Stephen, **Supp. XV:** 341, 342, 345, 347, 351; **Supp. XVII:** 18, 246

Burt, Steve, **Supp. V:** 83

Burtis, Thomson, **Supp. XIII:** 163

Burton, Robert, **II:** 535; **III:** 77, 78; **Supp. I Part 1:** 349

Burton, Sue D., **Supp. XIX:** 90

Burton, William Evans, **III:** 412

"Burying Ground by the Ties" (MacLeish), **III:** 14

Bury My Heart at Wounded Knee (Brown), **Supp. IV Part 2:** 504

Bury the Dead (Shaw), **IV:** 381; **Supp. XIX:** 242–244, 249, 252

"Bus Along St. Clair: December, A" (Atwood), **Supp. XIII:** 33

Busch, Frederick, **Supp. X:** 78; **Supp. XII:** 343; **Supp. XVII:** 175

Bush, Barney, **Supp. XII:** 218, 222

Bush, Douglas, **Supp. I Part 1:** 268; **Supp. XIV:** 10

"Busher Comes Back, The" (Lardner), **II:** 422

"Busher's Letters Home, A" (Lardner), **II:** 418–419, 421

Bushrui, Suheil, **Supp. XX: 113, 117, 120, 122, 126–127**

"Business and Poetry" (Gioia), **Supp. XV:** 113, 115

"Business Deal" (West), **IV:** 287

"Business Man, A" (Jewett), **Retro. Supp. II:** 132

Business of Memory, The: The Art of Remembering in an Age of Forgetting (C. Baxter, ed.), **Supp. XVII:** 21

"Business Trip" (Hoffman), **Supp. XVIII:** 86

"Bus Riley's Back in Town" (Inge), **Supp. XXV:** 95

Buss, Helen M., **Supp. IV Part 1:** 12

Bus Stop (Inge), **Supp. XXV:** 93, 99–100

Butcher, Fanny, **Supp. XXV:** 199

Butcher, Margaret Just, **Supp. XIV:** 203

"Butcher, The" (Southern), **Supp. XI:** 294

"Butcher Cock, The"(P. Benedict), **Supp. XXIII:** 46–47

"Butcher Shop" (Simic), **Supp. VIII:** 273

But Gentlemen Marry Brunettes (Loos), **Supp. XVI:** 190–191

"But He Says I Misunderstood" (Notley), **Supp. XXII:** 227

Butler, Benjamin, **I:** 457

Butler, Dorothy. *See* Farrell, Mrs. James T. (Dorothy Butler)

Butler, Elizabeth, **Supp. I Part 1:** 260

Butler, Ethel, **Supp. XIV:** 125

Butler, Hugo, **Supp. XVII:** 63

Butler, James D., **Supp. IX:** 175

Butler, Joseph, **II:** 8, 9

Butler, Judith, **Supp. XII:** 6

Butler, Maud. *See* Falkner, Mrs. Murray C. (Maud Butler)

Butler, Nicholas Murray, **I:** 223; **Supp. I Part 1:** 23; **Supp. III Part 2:** 499

Butler, Octavia, **Supp. XIII:** 59–72

Butler, Robert Olen, **Supp. XII:** 61–78, 319

Butler, Samuel, **II:** 82, 86; **IV:** 121, 440; **Supp. VIII:** 171

Butler-Evans, Elliot, **Retro. Supp. II:** 121

"But Only Mine" (Wright), **Supp. III Part 2:** 595

Butscher, Edward, **Supp. I Part 2:** 526

Butter Battle Book, The (Geisel), **Supp. XVI:** 110

"Buttercups" (Lowell), **Retro. Supp. II:** 187

Butterfield, R. W., **I:** 386

Butterfield, Stephen, **Supp. IV Part 1:** 3, 11

Butterfield 8 (O'Hara), **III:** 361

"Butterflies Under Persimmon" (Jarman), **Supp. XVII:** 120

Butterfly (Harvey), **Supp. XIII:** 184

"Butterfly, The" (Brodksy), **Supp. VIII:** 26

"Butterfly and the Traffic Light, The" (Ozick), **Supp. V:** 263, 265

Butterfly Plague, The (Findley), **Supp. XX:** 50, 52, 53

Butterfly Stories (Vollmann), **Supp. XVII:** 226

"Butterfly-toed Shoes" (Komunyakaa), **Supp. XIII:** 126

Butter Hill and Other Poems (Francis), **Supp. IX:** 88, 89

"Button-Down Builders, The" (Siddons), **Supp. XXII:** 243–244

Buttons, Red, **Supp. IV Part 2:** 574

Buttrick, George, **III:** 301; **Supp. XII:** 47–48

"But What Is the Reader to Make of This?" (Ashbery), **Supp. III Part 1:** 25

Butz, Earl, **Supp. X:** 35

"Buz" (Alcott), **Supp. I Part 1:** 43

Buzinski, Jim, **Supp. XX:** 273

"By an *Objibwa Female* Pen: Invitation to sisters to a walk in the Garden, after a shower"(J. Schoolcraft), **Supp. XXIII:** 230

Byatt, A. S., **Supp. XXI:** 147

By Avon River (Doolittle), **Supp. I Part 1:** 272

"By Blue Ontario's Shore" (Whitman), **Retro. Supp. I:** 399, 400

"By Candlelight" (Major), **Supp. XXII:** 185

"By Disposition of Angels" (Moore), **III:** 214

"By Earth" (Olds), **Supp. X:** 214

"Bye for Now, Broadway, My New Friend" (Silver), **Supp. XXIV:** 276

"By Fire" (Olds), **Supp. X:** 214

Bygones (Untermeyer), **Supp. XV:** 304, 308–309, 312, 313

By Land, By Sea (Hoffman), **Supp. XVIII:** 86

By Land and by Sea (Morison), **Supp. I Part 2:** 492

Byles, Mather, **Supp. XX:** 279, 282

By-Line: Ernest Hemingway (Hemingway), **II:** 257–258

By Love Possessed (Cozens), **I:** 358, 365, 372–374, 375, 376, 377, 378, 379

"By Morning" (Swenson), **Supp. IV Part 2:** 642

"By Night" (Francis), **Supp. IX:** 76

Bynner, Witter, **II:** 513, 527; **Supp. XIII:** 347; **Supp. XV:** 39–54

Byrd, William, **Supp. IV Part 2:** 425; **Supp. XXI:** 35; **Supp. XXII:** 193

Byrne, Donn, **IV:** 67

Byrne, Edward, **Supp. XXV:** 226, 227

Byron, George Gordon, Lord, **I:** 343, 568, 577; **II:** 135, 193, 296, 301, 303, 310, 315, 331, 566; **III:** 82, 137, 170, 409, 410, 412, 469; **IV:** 245, 435; **Supp. I Part 1:** 150, 312, 349; **Supp. I Part 2:** 580, 591, 683, 685, 719; **Supp. XIII:** 139; **Supp. XVI:** 188, 203, 206, 210

"Byron's Cain" (L. Michaels), **Supp. XVI:** 203

"Bystanders" (Matthews), **Supp. IX:** 160

By the Bias of Sound (Sobin), **Supp. XVI:** 281

By the North Gate (Oates), **Supp. II Part 2:** 504

"By the People" (Stratton-Porter), **Supp. XX:** 221

By the Shores of Silver Lake (L. I. Wilder), **Supp. XXII:** 294, 295, 299

"By the Time You Get There, by the Time You Get Back" (Muñoz), **Supp. XXV:** 134

"By the Waters of Babylon" (Benét), **Supp. XI:** 56, 58

By the Waters of Manhattan (Reznikoff), **Supp. XIV:** 288, 293, 294

By the Waters of Manhattan: An Annual (Reznikoff), **Supp. XIV:** 277, 280, 289

By the Waters of Manhattan: Selected Verse (Reznikoff), **Supp. XIV:** 281, 291

By the Well of Living and Seeing and the Fifth Book of the Maccabees (Reznikoff), **Supp. XIV:** 281

By the Well of Living and Seeing: New and Selected Poems 1918–1973 (Reznikoff), **Supp. XIV:** 281, 287–288, 295

By Way of Orbit (O'Neill), **III:** 405

Byzantine Parables (Notley), **Supp. XXII:** 235, 237

C

"C 33" (H. Crane), **I:** 384; **Retro. Supp. II:** 76

Cabala, The (Wilder), **IV:** 356, 358–360, 369, 374

"Cabaret" (Boyle), **Supp. XXIV:** 61

Cabaret (film), **Supp. XIV:** 155, 162

Cabaret (play), **Supp. XIV:** 162; **Supp. XVII:** 45

Cabbages and Kings (O. Henry), **Supp. II Part 1:** 394, 409

Cabell, James Branch, **II:** 42; **III:** 394; **IV:** 67, 359, 360; **Retro. Supp. I:** 80; **Supp. I Part 2:** 613, 714, 718, 721; **Supp. X:** 223

"Cabin, The" (Carver), **Supp. III Part 1:** 137, 146

Cabin, The: Reminiscence and Diversions (Mamet), **Supp. XIV:** 240

Cabinet of Dr. Caligari, The (film), **Retro. Supp. I:** 268

Cable, George Washington, **II:** 289; **Retro. Supp. II:** 65; **Supp. I Part 1:** 200; **Supp. II Part 1:** 198; **Supp. XIV:** 63

Cables to the Ace; or, Familiar Liturgies of Misunderstanding (Merton), **Supp. VIII:** 208

Cabot, James, **II:** 14; **IV:** 173

Cabot, John, **Supp. I Part 2:** 496, 497

Cachoeira Tales and Other Poems, The (Nelson), **Supp. XVIII:** 178–179

"Cachoiera Tales, The" (Nelson), **Supp. XVIII:** 179

Cactus Flower (Barillet and Grédy), **Supp. XVI:** 194

"Caddy's Diary, A" (Lardner), **II:** 421–422

"Cadence" (Dubus), **Supp. VII:** 84–85

Cadieux, Isabelle, **Supp. XIII:** 127

"Cadillac Flambé" (Ellison), **Retro. Supp. II:** 119, 126; **Supp. II Part 1:** 248

Cadillac Jack (McMurtry), **Supp. V:** 225

Cadillac Jukebox (Burke), **Supp. XIV:** 32

Cadle, Dean, **Supp. I Part 2:** 429

Cady, Edwin H., **II:** 272

"Caedmon" (Garrett), **Supp. VII:** 96–97

Caesar, Julius, **II:** 12, 502, 561–562; **IV:** 372, 373

Caesar, Sid, **Supp. IV Part 2:** 574, 591

"Cafeteria, The" (Singer), **Retro. Supp. II:** 316

Cage, John, **Supp. IV Part 1:** 84; **Supp. V:** 337, 341; **Supp. XXIII:** 211

"Cage and the Prairie: Two Notes on Symbolism, The" (Bewley), **Supp. I**

Part 1: 251
Cage Keeper, The (Dubus III), Supp. XXIV: 99–102
"Cage Keeper, The" (Dubus III), Supp. XXIV: 101–102, 104
Cage of Age, The (Bronk), Supp. XXI: 32
Cage of Spines, A (Swenson), Supp. IV Part 2: 641–642, 647
"Cage of the Body, The"(Schott), Supp. XXIII: 243–244
Cagney, James, Supp. IV Part 1: 236; Supp. XIII: 174
Cagney, William, Supp. XIII: 174
Cahalan, James, Supp. XIII: 1, 2, 3, 4, 12
Cahan, Abraham, Supp. IX: 227; Supp. XIII: 106; Supp. XXI: 3, 14; Supp. XXIII: 1, 2, 9, 16
Cahill, Tim, Supp. XIII: 13
Cain, James M., III: 99; Supp. IV Part 1: 130; Supp. XI: 160; Supp. XIII: 159, 165
Cain, Kathleen Shine, Supp. XX: 247, 248
Caine Mutiny, The (film), Supp. XXV: 260, 261
Caine Mutiny, The (Wouk), Supp. XXV: 253, 255, 256, 259–261
Caine Mutiny Court-Martial, The (Wouk), Supp. XXV: 253, 256
Caird, G. B., Supp. XXI: 91–92
Cairns, Huntington, III: 103, 108, 114, 119
Cairo! Shanghai! Bombay! (Williams and Shapiro), IV: 380
Cake (Bynner), Supp. XV: 50
Cakes and Ale (Maugham), III: 64
Calabria, Frank, Supp. XIII: 164
Calamity Jane (Martha Jane Canary), Supp. V: 229–230; Supp. X: 103
"Calamus" (Whitman), IV: 342–343; Retro. Supp. I: 52, 403, 404, 407
Calasso, Roberto, Supp. IV Part 1: 301
Calavito, Jason, Supp. XXV: 123
Calder, William M., III, Supp. XXIII: 112
Calderón, Hector, Supp. IV Part 2: 544
Caldwell, Christopher, Supp. IV Part 1: 211
Caldwell, Erskine, I: 97, 211, 288–311; IV: 286; Supp. IV Part 2: 601; Supp. XXI: 35; Supp. XXII: 196
Caldwell, Mrs. Erskine (Helen Lannegan), I: 289
Caldwell, Mrs. Erskine (Margaret Bourke-White), I: 290, 293–295, 297
Caldwell, Mrs. Erskine (Virginia Fletcher), I: 290
Caldwell, Reverend Ira Sylvester, I: 289, 305
Caldwell, Zoe, Supp. XIII: 207
Caleb Williams (Godwin), III: 415
"Calendar" (Creeley), Supp. IV Part 1: 158
Calendar of Saints for Unbelievers, A (Wescott), Supp. XIV: 342
Calendars (A. Finch), Supp. XVII: 76–77
Calhoun, John C., I: 8; III: 309

"Caliban in the Coal Mines" (Untermeyer), Supp. XV: 296
"California" (Carruth), Supp. XVI: 56
"California" (Didion), Supp. IV Part 1: 195
"California, This Is Minnesota Speaking" (Dunn), Supp. XI: 146
California and Oregon Trail, The (Parkman), Supp. I Part 2: 486
California: An Intimate History (Atherton), Supp. XXIV: 27
California Daughter (Leider), Supp. XXIV: 30
"California Hills in August" (Gioia), Supp. XV: 118–119
"California Indians of Today, The" (Zitkala-Ša), Supp. XXV: 284
"California Indian Trails and Prayer Trees" (Zitkala-Ša), Supp. XXV: 284
Californians (Jeffers), Supp. II Part 2: 415, 418, 420
Californians, The (Atherton), Supp. XXIV: 18, 21, 22
"California Oaks, The" (Winters), Supp. II Part 2: 798
"California Plush" (Bidart), Supp. XV: 23
"California Republic" (Didion), Supp. IV Part 1: 205
"California Requiem, A" (Gioia), Supp. XV: 126
California Suite (film), Supp. IV Part 2: 589
California Suite (Simon), Supp. IV Part 2: 581, 582
"Caligula" (Lowell), II: 554
Callahan, John F., Retro. Supp. II: 119, 126, 127
"Call at Corazón" (Bowles), Supp. IV Part 1: 82, 87
Calle, Sophia, Supp. XII: 22
"Called Back" (Kazin), Supp. VIII: 104
Calley, Captain William, II: 579
Calley, John, Supp. XI: 305
Callicott, J. Baird, Supp. XIV: 184
Calligrammes (Apollinaire), I: 432
"Calling Jesus" (Toomer), Supp. III Part 2: 484
Calling Myself Home (Hogan), Supp. IV Part 1: 397, 399, 400, 401, 413
Calling the Wind: Twentieth Century African-American Short Stories (Major, ed.), Supp. XXII: 172
Calling Western Union (Taggard), Supp. XXII: 271–272, 281–283
Call It Experience (Caldwell), I: 290–291, 297
"Call It Fear" (Harjo), Supp. XII: 220
Call It Sleep (H. Roth), Supp. VIII: 233; Supp. IX: 227, 228, 229–231; Supp. XIII: 106
"Call Letters: Mrs. V. B." (Angelou), Supp. IV Part 1: 15
Call Me Ishmael (Olson), Supp. II Part 2: 556; Supp. XXI: 21
Call Me Shakespeare (Endore), Supp. XVII: 65
"Call of Cthulhu, The" (Lovecraft), Supp. XXV: 109, 114, 116–117, 118

Call of the Gospel, The (Mather), Supp. II Part 2: 448
Call of the Wild, The (London), II: 466, 470–471, 472, 481
"Call of the Wild, The" (Snyder), Supp. VIII: 301
"Calloway's Code" (O. Henry), Supp. II Part 1: 404
"Call to Arms" (Mumford), Supp. II Part 2: 479
Call to Arms, The (film), Retro. Supp. I: 325
Calmer, Ned, Supp. XI: 219
Calvert, George H., Supp. I Part 1: 361
Calverton, V. F., Supp. VIII: 96
Calvin, John, II: 342; IV: 160, 490
Calvino, Italo, Supp. IV Part 2: 623, 678; Supp. XIX: 34; Supp. XXI: 225; Supp. XXII: 263
Cambridge Companion to Native American Literature, The (Porter and Roemer, eds.), Supp. XX: 270
Cambridge Edition of the Works of F. Scott Fitzgerald, The (Bruccoli, ed.), Retro. Supp. I: 115
Cambridge Film Handbook for On the Waterfront (Rapf), Supp. XVIII: 251
"Cambridge"(O'Hara), Supp. XXIII: 219
"Cambridge Thirty Years Ago" (Lowell), Supp. I Part 2: 419
Cambridge University Press, Retro. Supp. I: 115
"Camellia Sabina" (Moore), III: 208, 215
"Cameo" (Trethewey), Supp. XXI: 250
"Cameo Appearance" (Simic), Supp. VIII: 283
"Camera Notes" (column, Stratton-Porter), Supp. XX: 217
Camera Obscura (Nabokov), III: 255
Cameron, Angus, Supp. XXI: 268, 269, 275, 278
Cameron, Elizabeth, I: 10, 17
Cameron, Kenneth W., II: 16
Cameron, Peter, Supp. XII: 79–95
Cameron, Sharon, Retro. Supp. I: 43; Retro. Supp. II: 40
Camerson, Don, I: 10, 17
Camino, Léon Felipe, Retro. Supp. II: 89
Camino Real (T. Williams), IV: 382, 385, 386, 387, 388, 391, 392, 395, 398
Camões, Luiz Vaz de, II: 133; Supp. I Part 1: 94
"Camouflaging the Chimera" (Komunyakaa), Supp. XIII: 122–123
Camp, James, Supp. XV: 165
Camp, Walter, II: 423
Campana, Dino, Supp. V: 337
Campbell, Alan, Supp. IV Part 1: 353; Supp. IX: 196, 198, 201
Campbell, Alexander, Supp. I Part 2: 381, 395
Campbell, Donna, Retro. Supp. II: 139
Campbell, E. Simms, Supp. XXII: 12
Campbell, Helen, Supp. XI: 200, 206
Campbell, James, Supp. XII: 127
Campbell, James Edwin, Supp. II Part 1: 202
Campbell, Joanna (pseudonym). See Bly, Carol

Campbell, Joseph, **I:** 135; **IV:** 369, 370; **Supp. IX:** 245; **Supp. XXV:** 74

Campbell, Lewis, **III:** 476

Campbell, Thomas, **II:** 8, 303, 314; **III:** 410; **Supp. I Part 1:** 309, 310

Campbell, Virginia, **Supp. XIII:** 114

Campbell, Will D., **Supp. XXI:** 247

Campbell (Hale), Janet, **Supp. IV Part 2:** 503

"Campers Leaving: Summer 1981" (Kenyon), **Supp. VII:** 169

"Camp Evergreen" (Kenyon), **Supp. VII:** 168

"Camping in Madera Canyon" (Swenson), **Supp. IV Part 2:** 649

Campion, Jane, **Supp. XXIV:** 172

Campion, Peter, **Supp. XXV:** 227, 233

Campion, Thomas, **I:** 439; **Supp. VIII:** 272

"Campo" (Muñoz), **Supp. XXV:** 130

Campo, Rafael, **Supp. XVII:** 112

Camus, Albert, **I:** 53, 61, 292, 294, 494; **II:** 57, 244; **III:** 292, 306, 453; **IV:** 6, 211, 236, 442, 487; **Retro. Supp. I:** 73; **Retro. Supp. II:** 20; **Supp. I Part 2:** 621; **Supp. VIII:** 11, 195, 241; **Supp. XI:** 96; **Supp. XIII:** 74, 165, 233, 247; **Supp. XVII:** 137

Camuto, Christopher, **Supp. V:** 212–213

"Canada" (Di Piero), **Supp. XIX:** 39

Canada Fragrant with Resin, **Supp. XVI:** 149

Canadé, Eugene, **Supp. XXI:** 22, 23

"Canadian Mosaic, The" (Beran), **Supp. XIII:** 25

"Canadians and Pottawatomies" (Sandburg), **III:** 592–593

"Can a Good Wife Be a Good Sport?" (T. Williams), **IV:** 380

"Canal, The: A Poem on the Application of Physical Science to Political Economy" (Barlow), **Supp. II Part 1:** 73

Canan, Peter, **Supp. XXV:** 123

Canary, Martha Jane. *See* Calamity Jane (Martha Jane Canary)

"Canary for One, A" (Hemingway), **Retro. Supp. I:** 170, 189

Canary in a Cat House (Vonnegut), **Supp. II Part 2:** 758

"Canary in Bloom" (Dove), **Supp. IV Part 1:** 248

Canby, Henry Seidel, **IV:** 65, 363

"Cancer" (McClatchy), **Supp. XII:** 266

"Cancer Match, The" (Dickey), **Supp. IV Part 1:** 182

"Canción y Glosa" (Merwin), **Supp. III Part 1:** 342

Candide (Hellman), **I:** 28; **Supp. I Part 1:** 288–289, 292

Candide (Voltaire), **Supp. I Part 1:** 288–289; **Supp. XI:** 297; **Supp. XVI:** 189

Candide (Voltaire; Wilbur, trans.), **Supp. III Part 2:** 560

"Candle Hat" (Collins), **Supp. XXI:** 60

Candle in the Cabin, The (Lindsay), **Supp. I Part 2:** 398, 400

"Candles" (Plath), **Retro. Supp. II:** 248, 257

Candles in Babylon (Levertov), **Supp. III Part 1:** 283

Candles in the Sun (T. Williams), **IV:** 381

Candles of Your Eyes, The (Purdy), **Supp. VII:** 278

Candy (Southern), **Supp. XI:** 297, **298–299,** 305

"Candy-Man Beechum" (Caldwell), **I:** 309

Cane (Toomer), **Supp. III Part 2:** 475, 481–486, 488; **Supp. IV Part 1:** 164, 168; **Supp. IX:** 305, 306, 307, **308–320; Supp. XIX:** 73; **Supp. XX:** 73

"Cane in the Corridor, The" (Thurber), **Supp. I Part 2:** 616

Canfield, Cass, **Supp. I Part 2:** 668

Canfield, Dorothy, **Retro. Supp. I:** 4, 11, 14, 18; **Supp. XX:** 39. *See also* Fisher, Dorothy Canfield

Can Grande's Castle (Lowell), **II:** 518, 524

"Canicula di Anna" (Carson), **Supp. XII:** **101–102**

"Can I Get You Anything?" (Carver and Gallagher), **Supp. XXIV:** 178

"Canis Major" (Frost), **Retro. Supp. I:** 137

"Canned Stuff" (Pickering), **Supp. XXI:** 198

Cannery Row (Steinbeck), **IV:** 50, 51, 64–65, 66, 68

Cannibal Galaxy, The (Ozick), **Supp. V:** 270

Cannibals and Christians (Mailer), **III:** 38–39, 40, 42; **Retro. Supp. II:** 203, 204, 205; **Supp. XXIV:** 281

Canning, George, **I:** 7, 8

Canning, Richard, **Supp. X:** 147

Cannon, Jimmy, **II:** 424

Cannon, Steve, **Retro. Supp. II:** 111

Cannon between My Knees, A (Gunn Allen), **Supp. IV Part 1:** 324

Canolle, Jean, **Supp. XVI:** 194

"Canonization, The" (Donne), **Supp. XIV:** 8

"Can Poetry Matter?" (Gioia), **Supp. XV:** 113, 114

Can Poetry Matter?: Essays on Poetry and American Culture (Gioia), **Supp. XV:** 112, **113–115**

"Canso" (Merwin), **Supp. III Part 1:** 344

Can Such Things Be? (Bierce), **I:** 203, 204, 205, 209

Canterbury Tales (Chaucer), **II:** 504; **III:** 411; **IV:** 65

Canterbury Tales, The (Chaucer), **Supp. XIX:** 4

"Canticle of Her Coming and Going" (Espaillat), **Supp. XXI:** 106

"Canto Amor" (Berryman), **I:** 173

Canto I (Pound), **III:** 469, 470; **Retro. Supp. I:** 286

Canto II (Pound), **III:** 470

Canto III (Pound), **III:** 470

Canto IV (Pound), **III:** 470

Canto VIII (Pound), **III:** 472

Canto IX (Pound), **III:** 472

Canto X (Pound), **III:** 472

Canto XIII (Pound), **III:** 472

Canto XXXIX (Pound), **III:** 468

Canto LXV (Pound), **Retro. Supp. I:** 292

Canto LXXXI (Pound), **III:** 459; **Retro. Supp. I:** 293

Cantor, Lois, **Supp. IV Part 1:** 285

Cantos (Pound), **I:** 482; **III:** 13–14, 17, 457, 462, 463, 466, 467, 469–470, 472–473, 474, 475, 476, 492; **Retro. Supp. I:** 284, 292, **292–293,** 293, 427; **Supp. I Part 1:** 272; **Supp. II Part 1:** 5; **Supp. II Part 2:** 420, 557, 564, 644; **Supp. IV Part 1:** 153; **Supp. V:** 343, 345; **Supp. VIII:** 305; **Supp. XIV:** 55, 96; **Supp. XV:** 349

"Cantus Planis" (Pound), **III:** 466

Cantwell, Robert, **Retro. Supp. I:** 85; **Supp. VIII:** 96; **Supp. XIII:** 292

Can Women Be Gentlemen? (Atherton), **Supp. XXIV:** 20–21, 30

"Canyon de Chelly, Return, 1978"(Kenny), **Supp. XXIII:** 155

"Can You Carry Me" (O'Hara), **III:** 369

Can You See Me Yet? (Findley), **Supp. XX:** **52–53**

Canzoneri, Robert, **IV:** 114, 116

Canzoni (Pound), **Retro. Supp. I:** 286, 288, 413

"Cap" (Shaw), **Supp. IV Part 1:** 345

"Cape Breton" (Bishop), **Supp. I Part 1:** 92; **Supp. IX:** 45

Cape Cod (Thoreau), **II:** 540

"Cape Cod, Rome, and Jerusalem" (Chapman), **Supp. XIV:** 55

Capital City (Sandoz), **Supp. XXIV:** 244, **252–253,** 255

Capitalism: The Unknown Ideal (Rand), **Supp. IV Part 2:** 518, 527, 531, 532

Caponi, Gena Dagel, **Supp. IV Part 1:** 95

Capote, Truman, **Supp. I Part 1:** 291, 292; **Supp. III Part 1:** **111–133; Supp. III Part 2:** 574; **Supp. IV Part 1:** 198, 220; **Supp. VIII:** 105; **Supp. XII:** 43, 249; **Supp. XV:** 146; **Supp. XVI:** 245–246; **Supp. XVII:** 236

Capouya, Emile, **Supp. I Part 1:** 50

Cappetti, Carla, **Supp. IX:** 4, 8

Capra, Frank, **Supp. XVI:** 102

Capra, Fritjof, **Supp. X:** 261

"Capricious Gardens" (Eugenides), **Supp. XXIV:** 133–134

Capron, Marion, **Supp. IX:** 193

"Capsule History of Conservation, A" (Stegner), **Supp. IV Part 2:** 600

"Captain Carpenter" (Ransom), **III:** 491

Captain Craig (Robinson), **III:** 508, 523; **Supp. II Part 1:** 192

"Captain Jim's Friend" (Harte), **Supp. II Part 1:** 337

"Captain Jones's Invitation" (Freneau), **Supp. II Part 1:** 261

"Captain's Son, The" (Taylor), **Supp. V:** 314, 325, 327

"Captain's Wife, The" (Salter), **Supp. IX:** 261

"Capt Christopher Levett (of York)" (Olson), **Supp. II Part 2:** 576, 577

Captive Israel (Reznikoff), **Supp. XIV:** 283

"Captivity and Restoration of Mrs. Mary Rowlandson, The" (Howe), **Supp. IV**

Part 2: 419, 431, 434
"Captivity of the Fly" (MacLeish), **III:** 19
"Captured Goddess, The" (Lowell), **II:** 520
Caputi, Jane, **Supp. IV Part 1:** 334, 335
Caputo, Philip, **Supp. XI:** 234; **Supp. XIX: 17–31; Supp. XXII:** 104; **Supp. XXV:** 153
Capuzzo, Michael, **Supp. XIII:** 254
Car (Crews), **Supp. XI: 110–111**
Carabi, Angels, **Supp. VIII:** 223; **Supp. XII:** 215
"Caramels" (Zinberg), **Supp. XV:** 195
"Caravaggio: Swirl & Vortex" (Levis), **Supp. XI:** 258, 269
Caravan (Bynner), **Supp. XV:** 50
Carby, Hazel B., **Supp. IV Part 1:** 13; **Supp. XXI:** 171
"Carcassonne" (Faulkner), **Retro. Supp. I:** 81
Card, Antha E., **Supp. I Part 2:** 496
Cárdenas, Lupe, **Supp. IV Part 2:** 538, 539, 540
Cardinale, Anthony, **Supp. XVII:** 239
Cardinale, Ernesto, **Supp. XII:** 225
"Cardinal Ideograms" (Swenson), **Supp. IV Part 2:** 645
"Cards" (Beattie), **Supp. V:** 31
"Career Woman" (Hay), **Supp. XIV:** 131
Carefree (film, Sandrich), **Supp. XVII:** 59
"Careful" (Carver), **Supp. III Part 1:** 138
Careful and Strict Enquiry into the Modern Prevailing Notions of That Freedom of Will, Which Is Supposed to be Essential to Moral Agency, Vertue and Vice, Reward and Punishment, Praise and Blame, A (Edwards), **I:** 549, 557, 558, 562
Carel: A Poem and Pilgrimage in the Holy Land (Melville), **III:** 92–93
Careless Love and Its Apostrophes (Bronk), **Supp. XXI:** 32
"Carentan O Carentan" (Simpson), **Supp. IX:** 267
Carew, Thomas, **IV:** 453
Carey, Gary, **Supp. XVI:** 186
Carey, Lynn, **Supp. XXIII:** 273
Carey, Mathew, **Supp. XV:** 238
"Car Games" (Conroy), **Supp. XVI:** 72
Cargill, Oscar, **Supp. II Part 1:** 117
Caribbean as Columbus Saw It (Morison and Obregon), **Supp. I Part 2:** 488
"Caribou Kitchen" (A. Finch), **Supp. XVII:** 76–77
Caribou Rising: Defending the Porcupine Herd, Gwich-'in Culture, and the Arctic National Wildlife Refuge (Bass), **Supp. XVI:** 27–28, 28
"Caring for the World"(Schott), **Supp. XXIII:** 249–250
Carl, K. A., **III:** 475
Carleton, George W., **Supp. XVIII:** 4
Carlin, George, **Supp. XXI:** 51
Carlin, Terry, **Supp. XXI:** 4, 5, 14
Carlisle, Harry, **Supp. XVIII:** 223, 233
Carl Krinken: His Christmas Stocking (S. and A. Warner), **Supp. XVIII:** 264

"Carlos Who Died, and Left Only This, The" (Ríos), **Supp. IV Part 2:** 547
Carlotta (empress of Mexico), **Supp. I Part 2:** 457
Carl Sandburg (Golden), **III:** 579
Carlson, Susan L., **Supp. XV:** 323
Carlyle, Thomas, **I:** 103, 279; **II:** 5, 7, 11, 15–16, 17, 20, 145, 315; **III:** 82, 84, 85, 87; **IV:** 169, 182, 338, 350; **Retro. Supp. I:** 360, 408; **Supp. I Part 1:** 2, 349; **Supp. I Part 2:** 410, 422, 482, 485, 552; **Supp. XXV:** 242
"Carma" (Toomer), **Supp. III Part 2:** 481–483; **Supp. IX:** 312–313
"Carmen de Boheme" (Crane), **I:** 384
Carmen Jones (film), **Supp. I Part 1:** 66
Carmina Burana, **Supp. X:** 63
Carmon, Walt, **Supp. XXII:** 277
Carnegie, Andrew, **I:** 483; **IV:** 192; **Supp. I Part 2:** 639, 644; **Supp. V:** 285
Carnegie, Dale, **Supp. I Part 2:** 608
"Carnegie Hall: Rescued" (Moore), **III:** 215
Carne-Ross, Donald S., **Supp. I Part 1:** 268, 269; **Supp. XXIV:** 153
Carnes, Mark C., **Supp. X:** 14
"Carnets" poems (Sobin), **Supp. XVI:** 286–287
Carnovsky, Morris, **III:** 154
"Carol for Carolyn, A" (A. Finch), **Supp. XVII:** 74, 75
Caroling Dusk: An Anthology of Verse by Negro Poets (Cullen), **Supp. IV Part 1:** 166, 169
"Carol of Occupations" (Whitman), **I:** 486
"Carolyn Kizer and the Chain of Women" (A. Finch), **Supp. XVII:** 74–75
Carolyn Kizer: Perspectives on Her Life and Work (A. Finch), **Supp. XVII: 74–75**
"Carpe Diem" (Frost), **Supp. XII:** 303
"Carpe Noctem, if You Can" (Thurber), **Supp. I Part 2:** 620
Carpenter, Dan, **Supp. V:** 250
Carpenter, David, **Supp. VIII:** 297
Carpenter, Edward, **Supp. XX: 230**
Carpenter, Frederic I., **II:** 20
"Carpenter Bee" (Trethewey), **Supp. XXI:** 250
Carpentered Hen and Other Tame Creatures, The (Updike), **IV:** 214; **Retro. Supp. I:** 320
Carpenter's Gothic (Gaddis), **Supp. IV Part 1:** 288, 289–291, 293, 294
Carr, Dennis W., **Supp. IV Part 2:** 560
Carr, Elias, **Supp. XIV:** 57
Carr, Rosemary. *See* Benét, Rosemary
Carrall, Aaron, **Supp. IV Part 2:** 499
Carrel, Alexis, **IV:** 240
"Carrell/Klee/and Cosmos's Groom" (Goldbarth), **Supp. XII:** 183
"Carriage from Sweden, A" (Moore), **III:** 212
Carrie (King), **Supp. V:** 137
Carried Away (Harrison), **Supp. VIII:** 39
Carrier of Ladders (Merwin), **Supp. III Part 1:** 339, 346, 350–352, 356, 357
"Carriers of the Dream Wheel" (Momaday), **Supp. IV Part 2:** 481

Carriers of the Dream Wheel: Contemporary Native American Poetry (Niatum, ed.), **Supp. IV Part 2:** 484, 505
Carrington, Carroll, **I:** 199
"Carrion Spring" (Stegner), **Supp. IV Part 2:** 604
Carroll, Bart, **Supp. XXV:** 71
Carroll, Charles, **Supp. I Part 2:** 525
Carroll, Lewis, **I:** 432; **II:** 431; **III:** 181; **Supp. I Part 1:** 44; **Supp. I Part 2:** 622, 656; **Supp. XVI:** 103; **Supp. XXV:** 87
Carroll, Maureen P., **Supp. XXIV:** 177
"Carrots, Noses, Snow, Rose, Roses" (Gass), **Supp. VI:** 87
Carrouges, Michel, **Supp. IV Part 1:** 104
"Carrousel, The" (Rilke), **III:** 558
Carruth, Hayden, **Supp. IV Part 1:** 66; **Supp. VIII:** 39; **Supp. IX:** 291; **Supp. XIII:** 112; **Supp. XIV:** 273–274; **Supp. XVI: 45–61; Supp. XIX:** 1; **Supp. XXI:** 31; **Supp. XXIV:** 167
Carruth, Joe-Anne McLaughlin, **Supp. XVI:** 47
"Carry" (Hogan), **Supp. IV Part 1:** 412
"Carrying On" (Dunn), **Supp. XI:** 145
Cars of Cuba (García), **Supp. XI:** 190
Carson, Anne, **Supp. XII: 97–116; Supp. XV:** 252; **Supp. XXV:** 222
Carson, Johnny, **Supp. IV Part 2:** 526
Carson, Rachel, **Supp. V:** 202; **Supp. IX: 19–36; Supp. X:** 99; **Supp. XVI:** 36
Carson, Tom, **Supp. XI:** 227
Cart, Michael, **Supp. X:** 12
Carter, Elliott, **Supp. III Part 1:** 21
Carter, Hodding, **Supp. XIV:** 2
Carter, Jared, **Supp. XVII:** 110
Carter, Jimmy, **Supp. I Part 2:** 638; **Supp. XIV:** 107
Carter, Marcia, **Supp. V:** 223
Carter, Mary, **Supp. IV Part 2:** 444
Carter, Paul, **Supp. XX: 77, 78**
Carter, Peter, **Supp. XVIII:** 267
Carter, Stephen, **Supp. XI:** 220
Cartesian Sonata and Other Novellas (Gass), **Supp. VI:** 92–93
Cartier, Jacques, **Supp. I Part 2:** 496, 497
Cartier-Bresson, Henri, **Supp. VIII:** 98
"Cartographies of Silence" (Rich), **Supp. I Part 2:** 571–572
"Cartography" (Espaillat), **Supp. XXI:** 107
Cartwright, Louis, **Supp. XIV:** 147, 149, 151
Carver, Raymond, **Supp. III Part 1: 135–151; Supp. IV Part 1:** 342; **Supp. V:** 22, 23, 220, 326; **Supp. VIII:** 15; **Supp. X:** 85, 167; **Supp. XI:** 26, 65, 116, 153; **Supp. XII:** 79, 139, 289, 294; **Supp. XIX:** 209; **Supp. XXI:** 36, 115, 116, 118, 119; **Supp. XXIII:** 289, 296; **Supp. XXIV:** 97, 166, 167, 173, 177–178
Carver: A Life in Poems (Nelson), **Supp. XVIII:** 171, 172, **181–182,** 183
Carville, James, **Supp. XXIV:** 282
Carving Hawk (Kenny), **Supp. XXIII:** 143, 150

Cary, Alice, **Retro. Supp. II:** 145; **Supp. XV:** 273; **Supp. XXII:** 206
Cary, Phoebe, **Supp. XV:** 273
Cary, Richard, **Retro. Supp. II:** 132, 137
"Casabianca" (Bishop), **Retro. Supp. II:** 42; **Supp. I Part 1:** 86
Casablanca (film), **Supp. VIII:** 61; **Supp. XV:** 14
Casanova: His Known and Unknown Life (Endore), **Supp. XVII:** 54
"Casa solariega, La" ("The Family Mansion") (Espaillat), **Supp. XXI:** 107
"Case Against Mist, The" (Halliday), **Supp. XIX:** 91
Case for West-Indian Self-Government, The (C. L. R. James), **Supp. XXI:** 159, 161
Case of Jennie Brice, The (Rinehart), **Supp. XXV:** 193, 200
Case of Rape, A (C. Himes), **Supp. XVI:** 143
Case of the Crushed Petunias, The (T. Williams), **IV:** 381
Case of the Officers of Excise (Paine), **Supp. I Part 2:** 503–504
Casey, Helen Marie, **Supp. XXIII:** 246
Casey, John, **Supp. X:** 164
Cash, Arthur, **Supp. IV Part 1:** 299
Cashman, Nellie, **Supp. X:** 103
Casiero, Robert, **Supp. XIV:** 167
Casino Royale (film), **Supp. XI: 306–307**
Caskey, William, **Supp. XIV:** 166
"Cask of Amontillado, The" (Poe), **II:** 475; **III:** 413; **Retro. Supp. II:** 268, 269, 270, 273
Caso, Frank, **Supp. XVIII:** 95
Caspary, Vera, **Supp. XIX:** 78
Casper, Robert N., **Supp. XV:** 339, 347
Casper and His Friends (S. and A. Warner), **Supp. XVIII:** 264
Cassada (Salter), **Supp. IX: 251–252**
Cassada, Jackie, **Supp. XXIII:** 291
Cassady, Carolyn, **Supp. XIV:** 150
Cassady, Neal, **Supp. II Part 1:** 309, 311; **Supp. XIV:** 137, 144
"Cassandra" (Stallings), **Supp. XXV:** 233
"Cassandra Southwick" (Whittier), **Supp. I Part 2:** 693
Cassell, Verlin, **Supp. XI:** 315
Cassill, Ronald Verlin, **Supp. V:** 323; **Supp. XVIII:** 72; **Supp. XIX:** 266
Cassirer, Ernst, **I:** 265; **IV:** 87, 89
Cass Timberlane (Lewis), **II:** 455–456
Cast a Cold Eye (McCarthy), **II:** 566
Castaway (Cozzens), **I:** 363, 370, 374, 375, 379
"Caste in America" (Du Bois), **Supp. II Part 1:** 169
Castiglione, Baldassare, **I:** 279; **III:** 282
"Castilian" (Wylie), **Supp. I Part 2:** 714
Castillo, Ana, **Supp. XI:** 177; **Supp. XXIII:** 194
"Castle in Lynn, A" (McCarriston), **Supp. XIV:** 265, 268
"Castles and Distances" (Wilbur), **Supp. III Part 2:** 550
Castle Sinister (Marquand), **III:** 58

Cast of Thousands (Loos), **Supp. XVI:** 192, 193, 195
Castro, Fidel, **II:** 261, 434; **Supp. XX: 80**
Cast the First Stone (C. Himes), **Supp. XVI:** 135, 137–138
"Casual Incident, A" (Hemingway), **II:** 44
"Casualty Report" (Halliday), **Supp. XIX:** 85
Caswell, Michelle, **Supp. XXII:** 262
"Cat, The" (Matthews), **Supp. IX: 157–158**
Cat, You Better Come Home (Keillor), **Supp. XVI:** 177
"Catbird Seat, The" (Thurber), **Supp. I Part 2:** 623
"Catch" (Francis), **Supp. IX:** 82
Catch-22 (Heller), **III:** 558; **Supp. IV Part 1:** 379, 380, 381–382, 383, 384–386, 387, 390, 391, 392, 393, 394; **Supp. V:** 244, 248; **Supp. XII:** 167–168; **Supp. XXIII:** 100
Catcher in the Rye, The (Salinger), **I:** 493; **III:** 551, 552, 553–558, 567, 571; **Retro. Supp. I:** 102; **Retro. Supp. II:** 222, 249; **Supp. I Part 2:** 535; **Supp. V:** 119; **Supp. VIII:** 242; **Supp. XI:** 65; **Supp. XVII:** 2; **Supp. XXIII:** 100; **Supp. XXIV:** 133
"Catching Frogs" (Kenyon), **Supp. VII:** 170
Catching the Mermother (A. Finch), **Supp. XVII:** 72
catechism of d neoamerican hoodoo church (Reed), **Supp. X:** 240, 241
Catered Affair, The (film), **Supp. IV Part 2:** 683
"Cathay" (Goldbarth), **Supp. XII:** 185, 186
Cathay (Pound), **II:** 527; **Retro. Supp. I:** 289
Cathedral (Carver), **Supp. III Part 1:** 144–146; **Supp. XII:** 139
"Cathedral" (Carver), **Supp. III Part 1:** 144–145; **Supp. XXIV:** 177
Cathedral, The (Lowell), **Supp. I Part 2:** 407, 416–417
Cather, Willa, **I: 312–334**, 405; **II:** 51, 96, 177, 404, 412; **III:** 453; **IV:** 190; **Retro. Supp. I: 1–23**, 355, 382; **Retro. Supp. II:** 71, 136; **Supp. I Part 2:** 609, 719; **Supp. IV Part 1:** 31; **Supp. VIII:** 101, 102, 263; **Supp. X:** 103; **Supp. XIII:** 253; **Supp. XIV:** 112; **Supp. XV:** 40, 51; **Supp. XVI:** 226; **Supp. XVIII:** 207; **Supp. XIX:** 131; **Supp. XXIII:** 290; **Supp. XXIV:** 29, 30, 244; **Supp. XXV:** 201
Catherine, Saint, **II:** 211
Catherine II, **Supp. I Part 2:** 433
Catholic Art and Culture (Watkin), **Retro. Supp. II:** 187
"Catholic Novelist in the Protestant South, The" (O'Connor), **Retro. Supp. II:** 223, 224
"Cathy Queen of Cats" (Cisneros), **Supp. VII:** 59
Cat Inside, The (Burroughs), **Supp. III Part 1:** 105

Cat in the Hat, The (Geisel), **Supp. XVI:** 106–107, 112
Cat in the Hat Come Back, The (Geisel), **Supp. XVI:** 107
"Cat in the Hat for President, The" (Coover), **Supp. V:** 44, 46–47
Cat in The Hat Songbook, The (Geisel), **Supp. XVI:** 104
Cato, **II:** 114, 117
Cat on a Hot Tin Roof (T. Williams), **II:** 190; **IV:** 380, 382, 383, 386, 387, 389, 390, 391, 394, 395, 397–398; **Supp. XXV:** 93
"Cat People: What Dr. Seuss Really Taught Us" (Menand), **Supp. XVI:** 106
Cats and Dogs (Silver), **Supp. XXIV:** 265, 274
Cat's Cradle (Vonnegut), **Supp. II Part 2:** 758, 759, 767–768, 770, 771, 772; **Supp. V:** 1
Cat's Eye (Atwood), **Supp. XIII: 29–30**
Catskill Eagle, A (Parker), **Supp. XIX:** 185
"Cat's Meow, A" (Brodsky), **Supp. VIII:** 31
"Cats of Ulthar, The" (Lovecraft), **Supp. XXV:** 114
Cat's Quizzer, The (Geisel), **Supp. XVI:** 111
"Catterskill Falls" (Bryant), **Supp. I Part 1:** 160
"Cattle Car Complex" (T. Rosenbaum), **Supp. XVII:** 48
Cattlemen from the Rio Grande Across the Far Marias (Sandoz), **Supp. XXIV:** 244, **249–251**, 256
Catullus, **Supp. XII:** 2, 13, **112; Supp. XV:** 23, 27, 35, 36
Catullus, Gaius Valerius, **I:** 381; **Supp. I Part 1:** 261; **Supp. I Part 2:** 728
Catullus (Gai Catulli Veronensis Liber) (Zukofsky), **Supp. III Part 2:** 625, 627, 628, 629
"Catullus: Carmina" (Carson), *Supp. XII:* **112**
"Catullus: Excrucior" (Bidart), *Supp. XV:* 32, 35
"Cat Walked Through the Casserole, The" (Nelson and Espeland), **Supp. XVIII: 181**
Cat Walked Through the Casserole and Other Poems for Children (Nelson and Espeland), **Supp. XVIII:** 181
"Cat Who Aspired to Higher Things, The" (X. J. Kennedy), **Supp. XV:** 163
"Caucasian Storms Harlem, The" (R. Fisher), **Supp. XIX:** 78
Caudwell, Christopher, **Supp. X:** 112; **Supp. XXII:** 284
"Caul, The" (Banks), **Supp. V: 10–11**
Cause for Wonder (Morris), **III:** 232–233
"Causerie" (Tate), **IV:** 129
Causes and Consequences (Chapman), **Supp. XIV:** 41, 49, 51
"Causes of American Discontents before 1768, The" (Franklin), **II:** 120
Causley, Charles, **Supp. XV:** 117
Cavafy, Constantine P., **Supp. IX:** 275; **Supp. XI:** 119, 123; **Supp. XXI:** 131;

Supp. XXIII: 150

Cavafy, C. P., **Supp. XXV:** 225, 233

Cavalcade of America, The (radio program), **III:** 146

Cavalcanti (Pound, opera), **Retro. Supp. I:** 287

Cavalcanti, Guido, **I:** 579; **III:** 467; **Supp. III Part 2:** 620, 621, 622, 623

Cavalieri, Grace, **Supp. IV Part 2:** 630, 631

"Cavalry Crossing the Ford" (Whitman), **IV:** 347

"Cave, The" (Bass), **Supp. XVI:** 23

Cave, The (Warren), **IV:** 255–256

Cavelieri, Grace, **Supp. XXIII:** 135

Cavell, Stanley, **Retro. Supp. I:** 306–307, 309

Cavender's House (Robinson), **III:** 510

Caver, Christine, **Supp. XXI:** 215

Caves of Death, The (Atherton; Joshi, ed.), **Supp. XXIV:** 23

"Caviar" (Boyle), **Supp. XX: 19**

Caviare at the Funeral (Simpson), **Supp. IX:** 266, **276–277**

"Cawdor" (Jeffers), **Supp. II Part 2:** 431

Caxton, William, **III:** 486

Cayton, Horace, **IV:** 475, 488

Cazamian, Louis, **II:** 529

"Ceiling, The" (Brockmeier), **Supp. XXII:** 52–53

Celan, Paul, **Supp. X:** 149; **Supp. XII:** 21, 110–111; **Supp. XVI:** 284–285, 288; **Supp. XVII:** 241

"Celebrated Jumping Frog of Calaveras County, The" (Twain), **IV:** 196

Celebrated Jumping Frog of Calaveras County, The, and Other Sketches (Twain), **IV:** 197

Celebration (Crews), **Supp. XI:** 103, **108**

Celebration (Swados), **Supp. XIX: 269–270**

Celebration at Dark (W. J. Smith), **Supp. XIII:** 332

"Celebration for June 24th" (McGrath), **Supp. X:** 116

Celebration of the Sound Through (Sobin), **Supp. XVI:** 284–285

Celebrations after the Death of John Brennan (X. J. Kennedy), **Supp. XV:** 165

Celebrity (film; Allen), **Supp. XV:** 11

"Celebrity" (Pickering), **Supp. XXI:** 198

"Celery" (Stein), **IV:** 43

"Celestial Games" (Conroy), **Supp. XVI:** 72

"Celestial Globe" (Nemerov), **III:** 288

Celestial Navigation (Tyler), **Supp. IV Part 2:** 662–663, 671

"Celestial Railroad, The" (Hawthorne), **Retro. Supp. I:** 152; **Supp. I Part 1:** 188

Celibate Season, A (Shields), **Supp. VII:** 323, 324

Cellini (Shanley), **Supp. XIV:** 316, **329–330**

"Cemetery at Academy, California" (Levine), **Supp. V:** 182

Cemetery Nights (Dobyns), **Supp. XIII:** 85, 87, 89

"Cenotaph, The" (Stallings), **Supp. XXV:** 225, 234

"Censors As Critics: *To Kill a Mockingbird* As a Case Study" (May), **Supp. VIII:** 126

"Census-Taker, The" (Frost), **Retro. Supp. I:** 129

"Centaur, The" (Swenson), **Supp. IV Part 2:** 641

Centaur, The (Updike), **IV:** 214, 216, 217, 218, 219–221, 222; **Retro. Supp. I:** 318, 322, 324, 331, 336

"Centennial Meditation of Columbia, The" (Lanier), **Supp. I Part 1:** 362

Centeno, Agusto, **IV:** 375

"Centipede" (Dove), **Supp. IV Part 1:** 246

"Cento: A Note on Philosophy" (Berrigan), **Supp. XXIV:** 42–43

"Central Man, The" (Bloom), **Supp. IV Part 2:** 689

"Central Park" (Lowell), **II:** 552

Central Park (Wasserstein and Drattel), **Supp. XV:** 333

Central Park West (Allen), **Supp. XV:** 13

Century of Dishonor, A (Jackson), **Retro. Supp. I:** 31

"Cerebral Snapshot, The" (Theroux), **Supp. VIII:** 313

"Ceremonies" (Rukeyser), **Supp. VI:** 279

"Ceremony" (Monson), **Supp. XXIV:** 230

Ceremony (Silko), **Supp. IV Part 1:** 274, 333; **Supp. IV Part 2:** 557–558, 558–559, 559, 561–566, 570; **Supp. XVIII:** 59

Ceremony (Wilbur), **Supp. III Part 2:** 550–551

"Ceremony, The" (Harjo), **Supp. XII:** 230

"Ceremony, The—Anatomy of a Massacre" (E. Hoffman, play), **Supp. XVI:** 160

Ceremony in Lone Tree (Morris), **III:** 229–230, 232, 238, 558

Ceremony of Brotherhood, A (Anaya and Ortiz, eds.), **Supp. IV Part 2:** 502

Cerf, Bennett, **III:** 405; **IV:** 288; **Retro. Supp. II:** 330; **Supp. XIII:** 172; **Supp. XIX:** 244

"Certain Attention to the World, A" (Haines), **Supp. XII:** 201

"Certain Beasts, Like Cats" (Bronk), **Supp. XXI:** 30

Certain Distance, A (Francis), **Supp. IX:** 85

"Certain Music, A" (Rukeyser), **Supp. VI:** 273

Certain Noble Plays of Japan (Pound), **III:** 458

Certain People (Wharton), **Retro. Supp. I:** 382

"Certain Poets" (MacLeish), **III:** 4

Certain Slant of Sunlight, A (Berrigan), **Supp. XXIV:** 43

"Certain Testimony" (Bausch), **Supp. VII:** 48

Certificate, The (Singer), **IV:** 1; **Retro. Supp. II: 314–315**

"Cerulean" (Everett), **Supp. XVIII:** 66

Cervantes, Lorna Dee, **Supp. IV Part 2:** 545

Cervantes, Miguel de, **I:** 130, 134; **II:** 8, 272, 273, 276, 289, 302, 310, 315; **III:** 113, 614; **IV:** 367; **Retro. Supp. I:** 91; **Supp. I Part 2:** 406; **Supp. V:** 277; **Supp. XIII:** 17; **Supp. XXIII:** 4

Césaire, Aimé, **Supp. X:** 132, 139; **Supp. XIII:** 114

"Cesarean" (Kenyon), **Supp. VII:** 173

Cézanne, Paul, **II:** 576; **III:** 210; **IV:** 26, 31, 407; **Supp. V:** 333, 341–342; **Supp. XIX:** 36

Chabon, Michael, **Supp. XI: 63–81;** **Supp. XVI:** 259; **Supp. XIX:** 135, 138, 174, 223; **Supp. XX: 177; Supp. XXII:** 49; **Supp. XXIV:** 131

Chaboseau, Jean, **Supp. I Part 1:** 260

Chace, Bill, **Supp. XXI:** 256

Chagall, Marc, **Supp. XXIII:** 6

Chaikin, Joseph, **Supp. III Part 2:** 433, 436–437

"Chain, The" (Kumin), **Supp. IV Part 2:** 452

Chainbearer, The (Cooper), **I:** 351, 352–353

"Chain of Love, A" (Price), **Supp. VI: 258–259**, 260

Chain Saw Dance, The (Budbill), **Supp. XIX: 5–6**

Chains of Dew (Glaspell), **Supp. III Part 1:** 181

Chalk Face (W. Frank), **Supp. XX: 73–74**

Challacombe, Robert Hamilton, **III:** 176

Challenge (Untermeyer), **Supp. XV:** 296, 303

"Challenge" (Untermeyer), **Supp. XV:** 296

"Challenge from Beyond, The" (Lovecraft, Howard, Long, Merritt, and Moore), **Supp. XXV:** 122

Chalmers, George, **Supp. I Part 2:** 514, 521

"Chambered Nautilus, The" (Holmes), **Supp. I Part 1:** 254, 307, 312–313, 314

Chamberlain, John, **Supp. I Part 2:** 647; **Supp. IV Part 2:** 525

Chamberlain, Neville, **II:** 589; **Supp. I Part 2:** 664

Chamber Music (Joyce), **III:** 16

Chambers, Richard, **Supp. III Part 2:** 610, 611, 612

Chambers, Whittaker, **Supp. III Part 2:** 610; **Supp. IV Part 2:** 526; **Supp. XV:** 143

Chameleon (C. Baxter), **Supp. XVII:** 14–15

"Champ, The" (Zinberg), **Supp. XV:** 193

"Champagne Regions" (Ríos), **Supp. IV Part 2:** 553

"Champion" (Lardner), **II:** 420–421, 428, 430

Champion, Laurie, **Supp. VIII:** 128

Champollion-Figeac, Jean Jacques, **IV:** 426

"Chance" (Doolittle), **Supp. I Part 1:** 271

Chance, Frank, **II:** 418

Chance Acquaintance, A (Howells), **II:** 278

"Chance Encounter, A" (Swados), **Supp. XIX:** 261, 262

"Chanclas" (Cisneros), **Supp. VII:** 61

Chandler, Raymond, **Supp. III Part 1:** 91; **Supp. IV Part 1: 119–138,** 341, 344, 345; **Supp. IV Part 2:** 461, 464, 469, 470, 471, 472, 473; **Supp. XI:** 160, 228; **Supp. XII:** 307; **Supp. XIII:** 159, 233; **Supp. XIV:** 21; **Supp. XV:** 119; **Supp. XVI:** 122; **Supp. XVII:** 137; **Supp. XVIII:** 136,137, 137–138; **Supp. XIX:** 178, 189; **Supp. XXI:** 67; **Supp. XXII:** 119; **Supp. XXIV:** 284; **Supp. XXV:** 180

Chandler, Sherry, **Supp. XXIII:** 247

Chaney, "Professor" W. H., **II:** 463–464

Chang, Leslie C., **Supp. IV Part 1:** 72

"Change, The: Kyoto-Tokyo Express" (Ginsberg), **Supp. II Part 1:** 313, 329

Changed Man, A (Prose), **Supp. XVI:** 261–262

"Changeling" (Espaillat), **Supp. XXI:** 100

Changeling (Middleton), **Retro. Supp. I:** 62

"Changeling, The" (Lowell), **Supp. I Part 2:** 409

"Changeling, The" (Whittier), **Supp. I Part 2:** 697

Change of World, A (Rich), **Supp. I Part 2:** 551, 552

"Changes of Mind" (Baker), **Supp. XIII:** 52

"Changes of the Soul" (Taggard), **Supp. XXII:** 280

"Change the Joke and Slip the Yoke" (Ellison), **Retro. Supp. II:** 118

Change Your Bedding! (O'Hara), **Supp. XXIII:** 210

Changing Light at Sandover, The (Merrill), **Supp. III Part 1:** 318, 319, 323, 327, 332, 335–336; **Supp. XII:** 269–270; **Supp. XV:** 264

"Changing Same, The" (Baraka), **Supp. II Part 1:** 47, 51, 53

Changing the Bully Who Rules the World: Reading and Thinking about Ethics (C. Bly), **Supp. XVI:** 32, **39–40,** 41

Chanler, Mrs. Winthrop, **I:** 22; **IV:** 325

Channing, Carol, **IV:** 357

Channing, Edward, **Supp. I Part 2:** 479–480

Channing, Edward Tyrrel, **Supp. I Part 1:** 155; **Supp. I Part 2:** 422; **Supp. XXV:** 240

Channing, William Ellery, **I:** 336; **II:** 224, 495; **IV:** 172, 173, 176, 177; **Retro. Supp. I:** 54; **Supp. I Part 1:** 103; **Supp. I Part 2:** 589; **Supp. XXIV: 67–81; Supp. XXV:** 250

Channing, William Henry, **IV:** 178; **Supp. II Part 1:** 280, 285; **Supp. XXIV:** 68

Channing: The Reluctant Radical (Mendelsohn), **Supp. XXIV:** 72

Chanson de Roland, La, **I:** 13

"Chanson un Peu Naïve" (Bogan), **Supp. III Part 1:** 50–51

"Chanteuse" (Doty), **Supp. XI:** 119

"Chant for May Day" (Hughes), **Supp. I Part 1:** 331

Chants (Mora), **Supp. XIII: 214–215**

Chaos (Dove), **Supp. IV Part 1:** 243

Chapelle, Howard I., **Supp. XXV:** 217

"Chaperone, The" (Van Vechten), **Supp. II Part 2:** 728

Chaplin, Charles Spencer "Charlie," **I:** 27, 32, 43, 386, 447; **III:** 403; **Supp. I Part 2:** 607; **Supp. IV Part 1:** 146; **Supp. IV Part 2:** 574; **Supp. XX: 75; Supp. XXI:** 170; **Supp. XXII:** 25, 26

"Chaplinesque" (H. Crane), **Retro. Supp. II:** 79

"Chapman" (Rukeyser), **Supp. VI:** 273

Chapman, Abraham, **IV:** 485

Chapman, George, **Supp. I Part 2:** 422

Chapman, John, **Supp. XXV:** 105

Chapman, John (Johnny Appleseed), **Supp. I Part 2:** 397

Chapman, John Jay, **IV:** 436; **Supp. XIV: 39–56**

Chapman, Stephen, **Supp. XIII:** 12

Chappell, Fred, **Supp. IV Part 1:** 69; **Supp. XI:** 317; **Supp. XVIII:** 87

Chapters in a Mythology: The Poetry of Sylvia Plath (Kroll), **Supp. I Part 2:** 541–543

Chapters on Erie (Adams and Adams), **Supp. I Part 2:** 644

Chapter Two (Simon), **Supp. IV Part 2:** 575, 586

"Chapter VI" (Hemingway), **II:** 252

Char, René, **Supp. XVI:** 282; **Supp. XVII:** 244

"Character" (Emerson), **II:** 6

"Character of Aboriginal Historical Tradition"(J. Schoolcraft), **Supp. XXIII:** 228–229

"Character of Presidents, The" (Doctorow), **Supp. IV Part 1:** 224

"Character of Socrates, The" (Emerson), **II:** 8–9

Character of the Poet, The (Simpson), **Supp. IX:** 273, 275, 278

"Characters in Fiction" (McCarthy), **II:** 562

"Charades" (Moore), **Supp. X:** 178

"Charge It" (Fante), **Supp. XI:** 164–165

"Charioteer, The" (Stallings), **Supp. XXV:** 233

Chariot in the Sky: A Story of the Jubilee Singers (Bontemps), **Supp. XXII:** 6, 13

"Charity" (Peacock), **Supp. XIX:** 221–222

Charity (Richard), **Supp. XIX: 220–222**

Charlatan, The (Singer), **IV:** 1

"Charles" (Jackson), **Supp. IX:** 125

Charles, Larry, **Supp. XVIII:** 21

"Charles Baxter, August Kleinzahler, Adrienne Rich: Contemporary Stevensians and the Problem of 'Other Lives' " (S. Burt), **Supp. XVII:** 18–19

Charles Goodnight: Cowman and Plainsman (Haley), **Supp. V:** 226

Charles Simic: Essays on the Poetry (Weigl), **Supp. VIII:** 269

Charles the Bold, Duke of Burgundy, **III:** 487

Charleville, Victoria Verdon, **Supp. I Part 1:** 200–201, 205, 206, 210

Charley's Aunt (B. Thomas), **II:** 138

Charlie Chan Is Dead: An Anthology of Contemporary Asian American Fiction (Hagedorn), **Supp. X:** 292

"Charlie Christian Story, The" (Ellison), **Retro. Supp. II:** 121

"Charlie Howard's Descent" (Doty), **Supp. XI:** 122

Charlotte: A Tale of Truth (Rowson), **Supp. I Part 1:** 128; **Supp. XV: 234–235,** 238. *See also Charlotte Temple* (Rowson)

Charlotte's Daughter; or, The Three Orphans (Rowson), **Supp. XV: 246**

Charlotte's Web (White), **Supp. I Part 2:** 655, 656, 658, 667, 670

Charlotte Temple (Rowson), **Supp. XV:** 229, **238–239; Supp. XXV:** 35, 36. *See also Charlotte: A Tale of Truth* (Rowson)

Charm, The (Creeley), **Supp. IV Part 1:** 139, 141, 144, 149–150

Charmed Life, A (McCarthy), **II:** 571–574

Charming Billy (McDermott), **Supp. XVIII:** 155, **162–164,** 166

Charms for the Easy Life (Gibbons), **Supp. X:** 45, **47–48**

Charnel Rose, The (Aiken), **I:** 50, 57, 62

Charney, Samuel, **Supp. XXIII:** 6

Charon's Cosmology (Simic), **Supp. VIII: 276–278**

Charterhouse, The (Percy), **Supp. III Part 1:** 388

Chart for Rough Water (W. Frank), **Supp. XX:** 78

Charvat, William, **II:** 244

Charyn, Jerome, **Supp. XVII:** 5

Chase, Mary Ellen, **Retro. Supp. II:** 243, 245; **Supp. XXIV:** 30

Chase, Richard, **IV:** 202, 443; **Retro. Supp. I:** 40, 395

Chase, Salmon P., **Supp. I Part 2:** 584

Chase, Stuart, **Supp. I Part 2:** 609

Chase, The (Foote), **Supp. I Part 1:** 281

Chasing the Dime (Connelly), **Supp. XXI:** 74

"Chaste Land, The" (Tate), **IV:** 122

Château, The (Maxwell), **Supp. VIII:** 152, 160, **165–167,** 168, 169

Chatham, Russell, **Supp. VIII:** 40

"Chattanooga Nights" (L. Brown), **Supp. XXI:** 39

Chatterdon, The Black Death, and Meriwether Lewis (Reznikoff), **Supp. XIV:** 288

Chatterton, Thomas, **Supp. I Part 1:** 349; **Supp. I Part 2:** 410, 716

Chatterton, Wayne, **Supp. IX:** 2, 4, 11–12

"Chatty Letters During a Journey from Aruba to Rio" (Thompson), **Supp. XXIV:** 282

Chatwin, Bruce, **Supp. VIII:** 322

Chaucer, Geoffrey, **I:** 131; **II:** 11, 504, 516, 542, 543; **III:** 283, 411, 473, 492, 521; **Retro. Supp. I:** 135, 426; **Supp. I Part 1:** 356, 363; **Supp. I Part 2:** 422, 617; **Supp. V:** 259; **Supp. XII:**

197; **Supp. XVII:** 70; **Supp. XIX:** 4

Chauncy, Charles, **I:** 546–547; **IV:** 147

Chavez, César, **Supp. V:** 199

Chávez, Denise, **Supp. IV Part 2:** 544; **Supp. XI:** 316

Chavez, Lydia, **Supp. VIII:** 75

Chavkin, Allan, **Supp. IV Part 1:** 259

Chavkin, Nancy Feyl, **Supp. IV Part 1:** 259

Chawla, Louise, **Supp. XXI:** 24

Chayefsky, Paddy, **Supp. XI:** 306

Cheang, Shu Lea, **Supp. XI:** 20

"Cheater's Guide To Love, The" (Díaz), **Supp. XXIV:** 84, 92, 93

"Cheat Takes Over" (Leopold), **Supp. XIV:** 189

"Cheers" (Carver), **Supp. III Part 1:** 138

Cheetham, James, **Supp. I Part 2:** 521

Cheever, Benjamin Hale, **Supp. I Part 1:** 175; **Supp. XXIV:** 97

Cheever, David W., **Supp. I Part 1:** 304

Cheever, Ezekiel, **Supp. I Part 1:** 174, 193

Cheever, Federico, **Supp. I Part 1:** 175

Cheever, Fred, **Supp. I Part 1:** 174

Cheever, Frederick L., **Supp. I Part 1:** 174

Cheever, John, **Retro. Supp. I:** 116, 333, 335; **Supp. I Part 1: 174–199; Supp. V:** 23, 95; **Supp. VIII:** 151; **Supp. IX:** 114, 208; **Supp. XI:** 65, 66, 99; **Supp. XII:** 140; **Supp. XIV:** 93; **Supp. XV:** 119, 142; **Supp. XXIII:** 104, 109, 275; **Supp. XXV:** 79, 142

Cheever, Mrs. John (Mary Winternitz), **Supp. I Part 1:** 175

Cheever, Mary Liley, **Supp. I Part 1:** 174

Cheever, Susan. *See* Cowley, Susan Cheever (Susan Cheever)

Cheever Evening, A (Gurney), **Supp. V:** 95

Chekhov, Anton, **I:** 52, 90; **II:** 27, 38, 44, 49, 198, 542; **III:** 362, 467; **IV:** 17, 53, 359, 446; **Retro. Supp. I:** 5, 355; **Retro. Supp. II:** 299; **Supp. I Part 1:** 196; **Supp. II Part 1:** 6; **Supp. IV Part 2:** 585; **Supp. V:** 265; **Supp. VIII:** 153, 332; **Supp. IX:** 260, 265, 274; **Supp. XI:** 66; **Supp. XII:** 94, 307; **Supp. XIII:** 79; **Supp. XIV:** 87, 242; **Supp. XV:** 320, 329; **Supp. XVIII:** 102; **Supp. XIX:** 172, 241; **Supp. XXII:** 60; **Supp. XXIII:** 162, 290

"Chekhov's Sense of Writing as Seen Through His Letters" (Dobyns), **Supp. XIII:** 77–78

"Chemin de Fer" (Bishop), **Retro. Supp. II:** 41; **Supp. I Part 1:** 80, 85, 86

Cheney, Brainard, **Retro. Supp. II:** 229

Cheney, Matthew, **Supp. XXII:** 50

Chenzira, Ayoka, **Supp. XI:** 19

Chéri (Colette; stage adaptation, Loos), **Supp. XVI:** 194

Cherkovski, Neeli, **Supp. XII:** 118, 132, 134

Chernyshevski, Nikolai, **III:** 261, 262, 263; **Retro. Supp. I:** 269

Cherokee Lottery, The: A Sequence of Poems (W. J. Smith), **Supp. XIII: 340–344**

"Cherríe Moraga's Radical Revision of *Death of a Salesman*"(Wiley), **Supp. XXIII:** 199

Cherry (Karr), **Supp. XI:** 239, **251–254**

"Cherrylog Road" (Dickey), **Supp. XVIII:** 191

Cherry Orchard, The (Chekhov), **IV:** 359, 426; **Supp. VIII:** 153

Cheslock, Louis, **III:** 99, 118, 119

Chesnutt, Charles Waddell, **Supp. II Part 1:** 174, 193, 211; **Supp. IV Part 1:** 257; **Supp. XIV: 57–78**

"Chess House, The" (Dixon), **Supp. XII:** 139

Chessman, Caryl, **Supp. I Part 2:** 446

Chester, Alfred, **Retro. Supp. II:** 111, 112; **Supp. X:** 192

Chesterfield, Lord, **II:** 36

Chesterton, Gilbert Keith, **I:** 226; **IV:** 432

Cheuse, Alan, **Supp. IV Part 2:** 570

Chevigny, Bell Gale, **Supp. XI:** 283

Cheyenne Autumn (Sandoz), **Supp. XXIII:** 146; **Supp. XXIV:** 244, 248, 256, **258–260**

"Chicago" (Sandburg), **III:** 581, 592, 596; **Supp. III Part 1:** 71

Chicago (Shepard), **Supp. III Part 2:** 439

Chicago: City on the Make (Algren), **Supp. IX:** 1, 3

"Chicago Defender Sends a Man to Little Rock, The" (Brooks), **Supp. III Part 1:** 80–81

"Chicago Hamlet, A" (Anderson), **I:** 112

Chicago Loop (Theroux), **Supp. VIII:** 324

"Chicago Picasso, The" (Brooks), **Supp. III Part 1:** 70–71, 84

Chicago Poems (Sandburg), **III:** 579, 581–583, 586

"Chicano/Borderlands Literature and Poetry" (Ríos), **Supp. IV Part 2:** 537, 538, 542, 545

Chicano! The History of the Mexican American Civil Rights Movement (Rosales), **Supp. XXV:** 133

Chick, Nancy, **Supp. IV Part 1:** 1

"Chickamauga" (Bierce), **I:** 201

"Chickamauga" (Wolfe), **IV:** 460

Chickamauga (Wright), **Supp. V:** 333, 343–344

"Chickamauga" (Wright), **Supp. V:** 334

"Chicken Market" (Skloot), **Supp. XX: 198, 200**

"Chiefly about War Matters" (Hawthorne), **II:** 227; **Retro. Supp. I:** 165

"Chiffon" (Hull), **Supp. XXI:** 138

"Child" (Plath), **Supp. I Part 2:** 544

Child, Greg, **Supp. XVIII:** 107

Child, Julia, **Supp. XVII:** 89, 90

Child, Lydia Maria, **Supp. XIII:** 141; **Supp. XVIII:** 11

"Child, The" (Ríos), **Supp. IV Part 2:** 543

"Child by Tiger, The" (Wolfe), **IV:** 451

"Childhood" (Wright), **Supp. V:** 341

Childhood, A: The Biography of a Place (Crews), **Supp. XI:** 102–103, 245

"Childhood, When You Are in It . . ." (Kenyon), **Supp. VII:** 160, 170

Childhood and Other Neighborhoods (Dybek), **Supp. XXIII:** 68, **69–70**

"Childhood Sketch" (Wright), **Supp. III Part 2:** 589

"Child Is Born, A" (Benét), **Supp. XI:** 46

"Child Is the Meaning of This Life, The" (Schwartz), **Supp. II Part 2:** 659–660

"Childlessness" (Merrill), **Supp. III Part 1:** 323

"Childless Woman" (Plath), **Supp. I Part 2:** 544

Child-Life (Whittier and Larcom, eds.), **Supp. XIII:** 142

Child-Life in Prose (Whittier and Larcom, eds.), **Supp. XIII:** 142

Childlike Life of the Black Tarantula, The (Acker), **Supp. XII:** 4, 6, **7–8**

"Child Margaret" (Sandburg), **III:** 584

"Child of Courts, The" (Jarrell), **II:** 378, 379, 381

Child of God (McCarthy), **Supp. VIII: 177–178**

Child of My Heart (McDermott), **Supp. XVIII:** 155, **164–166**

Child of the Century, A (Hecht), **Supp. XXV:** 29

"CHILD OF THE THIRTIES" (Baraka), **Supp. II Part 1:** 60

"Child on Top of a Greenhouse" (Roethke), **III:** 531

Children (Gurney), **Supp. V:** 95, 96

"Children" (Stowe), **Supp. I Part 2:** 587

"Children, The" (Jarman), **Supp. XVII:** 116

Children, The (Wharton), **IV:** 321, 326; **Retro. Supp. I:** 381

"Children, the Sandbar, That Summer" (Rukeyser), **Supp. VI:** 274

Children and Others (Cozzens), **I:** 374

Children Is All (Purdy), **Supp. VII:** 277, 278, 282

"Children of Adam" (Whitman), **IV:** 342; **Retro. Supp. I:** 403, 405

Children of Job, The: American Second-Generation Witnesses to the Holocaust (A. Berger), **Supp. XVII:** 39

Children of Light (Stone), **Supp. V:** 304–306

Children of Light and the Children of Darkness, The (Niebuhr), **III:** 292, 306, 310

"Children of the Dirty War" (Goldman), **Supp. XXV:** 52

Children of the Frost (London), **II:** 469, 483

Children of the Holocaust (H. Epstein), **Supp. XVII:** 48; **Supp. XXII:** 95

"Children of the Lord's Supper, The" (Tegnér), **Retro. Supp. II:** 155, 157

Children of the Market Place (Masters), **Supp. I Part 2:** 471

"Children on Their Birthdays" (Capote), **Supp. III Part 1:** 114, 115

Children Playing Before a Statue of Hercules (Sedaris, ed.), **Supp. XXIII:** 289

"Children Selecting Books in a Library" (Jarrell), **II:** 371

Children's Hour, The (Hellman), **Supp. I Part 1:** 276–277, 281, 286, 297

"Children's Rhymes" (Hughes), **Supp. I Part 1:** 340

Childress, Mark, **Supp. X:** 89

Child's Garden of Verses, A (Stevenson), **Supp. IV Part 1:** 298, 314; **Supp. XIII:** 75

"Child's Nature, A" (Jin), **Supp. XVIII:** 93

"Child's Reminiscence, A" (Whitman), **IV:** 344

Childwold (Oates), **Supp. II Part 2:** 519–520

Chile Woman (G. Jones), **Supp. XXIV:** 185

Chill, The (Macdonald), **Supp. IV Part 2:** 473

Chills and Fever (Ransom), **III:** 490, 491–492, 493

Chilly Scenes of Winter (Beattie), **Supp. V:** 21, 22, 23, 24, 26, 27

Chime of Words, A: The Letters of Logan Pearsall Smith (Tribble, ed.), **Supp. XIV:** 348–349

Chimera (C. Frost), **Supp. XV:** 94, 95, 100

"Chimes for Yahya" (Merrill), **Supp. III Part 1:** 329

Chin, Frank, **Supp. V:** 164, 172

Chin, Mei, **Supp. XVIII:** 95

"China" (Johnson), **Supp. VI: 193–194**

Chinaberry Tree, The (Fauset), **Supp. XIX:** 73

"Chinaman's Hat" (Kingston), **Supp. V:** 169

China Men (Kingston), **Supp. V:** 157, 158, 159, 160, 161, 164–169; **Supp. X:** 292; **Supp. XV:** 220

"China Poet, The" (Sturgis), **Supp. XX: 233, 240**

China Trace (Wright), **Supp. V:** 332, 340, 341, 342

"Chinese Apples" (Di Piero), **Supp. XIX:** 40

Chinese Apples: New and Selected Poems (Di Piero), **Supp. XIX:** 33, 36, 37, 38, 39, 40, 44, 45, 46, 47–48

Chinese Classics (Legge), **III:** 472

Chinese Materia Medica (P. Smith), **III:** 572

"Chinese New Year" (Hull), **Supp. XXI:** 135

"Chinese Nightingale, The" (Lindsay), **Supp. I Part 2:** 392–393, 394

Chinese Nightingale and Other Poems, The (Lindsay), **Supp. I Part 2:** 392

Chinese Siamese Cat, The (Tan), **Supp. X:** 289

Chinese Translations, The (Bynner), **Supp. XV:** 47, 52

Chinitz, David, **Supp. XV:** 180, 185

"Chinoiseries" (Lowell), **II:** 524–525

Chip (Untermeyer), **Supp. XV:** 310

"Chipeta, Widow of Chief Ouray with a Word About a Deal in Blankets" (Zitkala-Ša), **Supp. XXV:** 281

Chirico, Giorgio de, **Supp. III Part 1:** 14

Chirico, Miriam M., **Supp. XV:** 323

"Chiron" (Winters), **Supp. II Part 2:** 801

"Chitlins at the Waldorf" (Crouch), **Supp. XIX:** 158

"Chloroform Jags" (J. Scott), **Supp. XVII:** 189

Chodorov, Jerome, **IV:** 274

"Choice, The" (Karr), **Supp. XI:** 251

"Choice of Accommodations, A" (Lahiri), **Supp. XXI:** 183

"Choice of Profession, A" (Malamud), **Supp. I Part 2:** 437

Choice of Wars, A (Shaw), **Supp. XIX:** 245

"Choices" (Gallagher), **Supp. XXIV:** 171

Chomei, Kamo No, **IV:** 170, 171, 184

Chomsky, Noam, **Supp. IV Part 2:** 679

Choosing not Choosing (Cameron), **Retro. Supp. I:** 43

Chopin, Felix, **Supp. I Part 1:** 202

Chopin, Frédéric, **Supp. I Part 1:** 363

Chopin, Jean, **Supp. I Part 1:** 206

Chopin, Kate, **II:** 276; **Retro. Supp. I:** 10, 215; **Retro. Supp. II: 57–74;** **Supp. I Part 1: 200–226; Supp. V:** 304; **Supp. X:** 227; **Supp. XVIII:** 194

"Chopin in Winter"(Dybek), **Supp. XXIII:** 72

"Choral: The Pink Church" (W. C. Williams), **Retro. Supp. I:** 428

"Chord" (Merwin), **Supp. III Part 1:** 356

"Chord"(Dybek), **Supp. XXIII:** 78

"Chords and Dischords" (column; Untermeyer), **Supp. XV:** 294

"Chorus, The"(Hadas), **Supp. XXIII:** 119–120

Choruses from Iphigenia in Aulis (Doolittle, trans.), **Supp. I Part 1:** 257, 268, 269

"Chosen Blindness" (Karr), **Supp. XI:** 251

Chosen Country (Dos Passos), **I:** 475, 490–491

Chosen Place, The Timeless People, The (Marshall), **Supp. XI:** 275, 276, **282–284**

Chosŏn (Lowell), **II:** 513

Choukri, Mohamed, **Supp. IV Part 1:** 92

Chovteau, Mane Thérèse, **Supp. I Part 1:** 205

Chris Durang and Dawne (Durang), **Supp. XXIV:** 113, 124

"ChrisEaster" (Peacock), **Supp. XIX:** 198, 199

Chrisman, Robert, **Supp. IV Part 1:** 1

Christabel (Coleridge), **Supp. IV Part 2:** 465

"Christ for Sale" (Lowell), **II:** 538

Christian, Graham, **Supp. XII:** 193

Christian Dictionary, A (Wilson), **IV:** 153

"Christian in World Crisis, The" (Merton), **Supp. VIII:** 203

Christianity and Power Politics (Niebuhr), **III:** 292, 303

"Christianity and the Survival of Creation" (Berry), **Supp. X:** 30

Christianity of Sholem Asch, The: An Appraisal from the Jewish Viewpoint (Lieberman), **Supp. XXIII:** 3, 7

"Christian Minister, The" (Emerson), **II:** 10

Christian Philosopher, The (Mather), **Supp. II Part 2:** 463–464

Christian Realism and Practical Problems (Niebuhr), **III:** 292, 308

"Christian Roommates, The" (Updike), **IV:** 226–227; **Retro. Supp. I:** 319, 323

Christiansen, Carrie, **I:** 210

Christian's Secret of a Happy Life, The (H. W. Smith), **Supp. XIV:** 333–334

Christie, Agatha, **Supp. IV Part 1:** 341; **Supp. IV Part 2:** 469

Christ in Concrete (di Donato), **Supp. XX: 33, 34–40, 42, 43, 46**

"Christ in Concrete" (di Donato), **Supp. XX:** 34

Christine (King), **Supp. V:** 139, 148

"Christ Light, The" (Chopin), **Retro. Supp. II:** 61

"Christmas" (Saunders), **Supp. XIX:** 232

"Christmas, or the Good Fairy" (Stowe), **Supp. I Part 2:** 586

"Christmas 1944" (Levertov), **Supp. III Part 1:** 274

"Christmas Banquet, The" (Hawthorne), **II:** 227

Christmas Card, A (Theroux), **Supp. VIII:** 322

Christmas Carol, A (Dickens), **Retro. Supp. I:** 196; **Supp. I Part 2:** 409–410; **Supp. X:** 252, 253; **Supp. XXV:** 149, 152

"Christmas Eve at Johnson's Drugs N Goods" (Bambara), **Supp. XI:** 11–12

"Christmas Eve in the Time of War: A Capitalist Meditates by a Civil War Monument" (Lowell), **II:** 538

"Christmas Eve under Hooker's Statue" (Lowell), **II:** 539–540

"Christmas Gift" (Warren), **IV:** 252–253

"Christmas Greeting, A" (Wright), **Supp. III Part 2:** 601

"Christmas Hymn, A" (Wilbur), **Supp. III Part 2:** 557

Christmas Memory, A (Capote), **Supp. III Part 1:** 118, 119, 129

"Christmass Poem" (West), **Retro. Supp. II:** 338

Christmas Story (Mencken), **III:** 111

"Christmas to Me" (Lee), **Supp. VIII:** 113

Christographia (Taylor), **IV:** 164–165

Christ on a Clothesline (Loy), **Supp. XXII:** 168

"*Christ on the Cross*/Nuestro Señor Crucificado" (Mora), **Supp. XIII:** 229

Christopher, Mary (pseudonym). *See* West, Dorothy

Christopher and His Kind: 1929–1939 (Isherwood), **Supp. XIV:** 157, 163, 164, 171

"Christopher Cat" (Cullen), **Supp. IV Part 1:** 173

Christopher Columbus, Mariner (Morison), **Supp. I Part 2:** 488

Christopher Isherwood: A Critical Biography (Finney), **Supp. XIV:** 158

Christophersen, Bill, **Supp. IX:** 159, 167; **Supp. XI:** 155; **Supp. XIII:** 87; **Supp. XXI:** 103

"Christ's Passion" (Karr), **Supp. XI:** 251

Christus: A Mystery (Longfellow), **II:** 490, 493, 495, 505–507; **Retro. Supp. II:** 161, 165, 166

Chroma (F. Barthelme), **Supp. XI:** 30, 33, 34

"Chroma" (F. Barthelme), **Supp. XI:** 31

"Chronicle of Race Relations, A" (Du Bois), **Supp. II Part 1:** 182

Chronicle of the Conquest of Granada (Irving), **II:** 310

Chronicles: Volume One (Dylan), **Supp. XVIII:** 20, 21, 23, 24, 28, **32–33**

"Chronologues" (Goldbarth), **Supp. XII:** 183, 184

"Chrysanthemums, The" (Steinbeck), **IV:** 53

"Chrysaor" (Longfellow), **II:** 498

Chu, Louis, **Supp. X:** 291

Chuang, Hua, **Supp. X:** 291

Chuang-Tzu, **Supp. VIII:** 206

"Chunk of Amethyst, A" (R. Bly), **Supp. IV Part 1:** 72

Church, Margaret, **IV:** 466

"Church and the Fiction Writer, The" (O'Connor), **Retro. Supp. II:** 223, 233; **Supp. XVIII:** 161

"Church Going" (Larkin), **Supp. XXI:** 93

"Churchgoing" (Nelson), **Supp. XVIII:** 173

Churchill, Charles, **Supp. XV:** 232

Churchill, Winston, **I:** 9, 490; **Supp. I Part 2:** 491

Church of Dead Girls, The (Dobyns), **Supp. XIII:** 75, **83–84**

"Church of Omnivorous Light, The" (Wrigley), **Supp. XVIII:** 306–307

"Church of the Latter Day Saints, The" (Mosher), **Supp. XXII:** 208

"Church Porch, The" (Herbert), **IV:** 153

Church Psalmody, Selected from Dr. Watts and Other Authors (Mason and Greene, ed.), **I:** 458

Ciannic, Saint, **II:** 215

Ciano, Edda, **IV:** 249

Ciardi, John, **I:** 169, 179, 535; **III:** 268; **Supp. IV Part 1:** 243; **Supp. IV Part 2:** 639; **Supp. IX:** 269, 324; **Supp. XII:** 119

Cicada (Haines), **Supp. XII: 206–207**

"Cicadas" (Wilbur), **Supp. III Part 2:** 549

Cicero, **I:** 279; **II:** 8, 14–15; **III:** 23; **Supp. I Part 2:** 405

Cider House Rules, The (Irving), **Supp. VI:** 164, **173–175**

"Cigales" (Wilbur), **Supp. III Part 2:** 549

"Cigarette" (L. Michaels), **Supp. XVI:** 214

Cimarron, Rose (Burke), **Supp. XIV:** 22, 35

"Cimetière Marin, Le" (Valéry), **IV:** 91–92

Cimino, Michael, **Supp. X:** 126

Cincinnati Kid, The (film), **Supp. XI:** 306

"Cinderella" (Jarrell), **II:** 386

"Cinderella" (Perrault), **IV:** 266, 267

"Cinderella" (Sexton), **Supp. II Part 2:** 691

"Cinema, The" (Salter), **Supp. IX:** 257

Cinema of Tony Richardson, The: Essays and Interviews (Phillips), **Supp. XI:** 306

Cinthio, **IV:** 370

Ciolkowski, Laura, **Supp. XVI:** 24

CIOPW (Cummings), **I:** 429

"Circe" (Welty), **Retro. Supp. I:** 353

Circle Game, The (Atwood), **Supp. XIII:** 20, 33

Circle in the Dirt (Moraga), **Supp. XXIII:** 195, 202

"Circle in the Fire, A" (O'Connor), **III:** 344–345, 349–350, 351, 353, 354; **Retro. Supp. II:** 229, 232

"Circle of Breath" (Stafford), **Supp. XI:** 318, 322

Circle of Hanh, The (Weigl), **Supp. XIX:** 273, 275, 282, **284–286**

"Circles" (Emerson), **I:** 455, 460

"Circles" (Lowell), **II:** 554

Circular Staircase, The (Rinehart), **Supp. XXV:** 189, 192, 200

Circumference: Varieties of Metaphysical Verse 1456–1928 (Taggard, ed.), **Supp. XXII:** 279

"Circus, The" (Porter), **III:** 443, 445

"Circus Animals' Desertion" (Yeats), **I:** 389

Circus Fire, The (O'Nan), **Supp. XXV:** 153

"Circus in the Attic" (Warren), **IV:** 253

Circus in the Attic, The (Warren), **IV:** 243, 251–253

"Circus in Three Rings" (Plath), **Retro. Supp. II:** 243; **Supp. I Part 2:** 536

Circus of Needs, A (Dunn), **Supp. XI: 147–148**

"Cirque d'Hiver" (Bishop), **Supp. I Part 1:** 85

Cisneros, Sandra, **Supp. IV Part 2:** 544; **Supp. VII: 57–73; Supp. XI:** 177; **Supp. XVII:** 71; **Supp. XXII:** 177; **Supp. XXV:** 133

Cities of the Interior (Nin), **Supp. X:** 182

Cities of the Plain (McCarthy), **Supp. VIII:** 175, **186–187**

Cities of the Red Night (Burroughs), **Supp. III Part 1:** 106

"Citizen Cain" (Baraka), **Supp. II Part 1:** 49

Citizen Kane (film), **Retro. Supp. I:** 115; **Supp. V:** 251; **Supp. XI:** 169

"Citizen of the World" (Goldsmith), **II:** 299

Citro, Joseph, **Supp. XXII:** 208, 218

"City" (Francis), **Supp. IX:** 87

"City, The" (Stallings), **Supp. XXV:** 233

"City and Country"(Hadas), **Supp. XXIII:** 115, 116

City and the Pillar, The (Vidal), **Supp. IV Part 2:** 677, 680–681; **Supp. XIV:** 170

"*City and the Pillar, The*, as Gay Fiction" (Summers), **Supp. IV Part 2:** 680–681

"City Articles" series (Briggs), **Supp. XVIII:** 12

City Block (W. Frank), **Supp. XX: 71, 72, 76**

City Boy (L. Michaels), **Supp. XVI:** 212

"City Boy" (L. Michaels), **Supp. XVI:** 203–204

City Boy (Thompson), **Supp. XXIII:** 294, **298–299**

City Boy, The (Wouk), **Supp. XXV:** 256, 259

City Dog (Di Piero), **Supp. XIX:** 33–34, 35, 38, 46, 48

"City Dog" (Di Piero), **Supp. XIX:** 47

City in History, The (Mumford), **Supp. II Part 2:** 495

"City in the Sea, The" (Poe), **III:** 411; **Retro. Supp. II:** 274

City in Which I Love You, The (L.-Y. Lee), **Supp. XV:** 212, **215–220**

"City in Which I Love You, The" (L.-Y. Lee), **Supp. XV:** 215, **217–218**

City in Winter, A (Helprin), **Supp. XXV:** 84, 87

City Life (Barthelme), **Supp. IV Part 1:** 44, 47

City of Bones (Connelly), **Supp. XXI: 74–75,** 77

"City of Change, A" (Bynner), **Supp. XV:** 45

City of Dreadful Night (Siegel), **Supp. XXII:** 258

City of Glass (Auster), **Supp. XII:** 22, **24–26**

City of God, The (St. Augustine), **IV:** 126

City of Names (Brockmeier), **Supp. XXII:** 55–56, 57

"City of Refuge, The" (R. Fisher), **Supp. XIX:** 65, 66, **67–68**

City of Refuge, The: The Collected Stories of Rudolph Fisher (McCluskey, ed.), **Supp. XIX:** 68–69

City of the Living and Other Stories, The (Stegner), **Supp. IV Part 2:** 599, 609, 613

City of Words: American Fiction 1950-1970 (T. Tanner), **Supp. XVI:** 69

City of Your Final Destination, The (Cameron), **Supp. XII:** 79, 82, **91–94**

"City on a Hill" (Lowell), **II: 552**

City on a Hill: Testing the American Dream at City College (Traub), **Supp. XXIV:** 221

"City Person Encountering Nature, A" (Kingston), **Supp. V:** 170

"City Planners, The" (Atwood), **Supp. XIII:** 33

"City Winter, A"(O'Hara), **Supp. XXIII:** 210

City Winter and Other Poems, A (O'Hara), **Supp. XXIII:** 210, 214

City Without Men (film), **Supp. XVIII:** 247

City Without Walls (Auden), **Supp. II Part 1:** 24

Civil Disobedience (Thoreau), **IV:** 185; **Supp. I Part 2:** 507

Civilization in the United States (Stearns), **I:** 245

"Civil Rights" (Lanier), **Supp. I Part 1:** 357

CivilWarLand in Bad Decline (Saunders), **Supp. XIX: 224–227**

"CivilWarLand in Bad Decline" (Saunders), **Supp. XIX:** 224–225, 227

Civitatis Anthology of African American Slave Narratives, The (H. L. Gates and Andrews, eds.), **Supp. XX: 105**

Cixous, Hélène, **Supp. X:** 102; **Supp. XIII:** 297; **Supp. XV:** 347

Clabough, Casey, **Supp. XXIV:** 194

Claiborne, Craig, **Supp. XVII:** 89

Claiborne, William, **I:** 132

"Claim, The"(Balakian), **Supp. XXIII:** 20

Claiming an Identity They Taught Me to Despise (Cliff), **Supp. XXII:** 66, 67–68, 70

Claiming of Sleeping Beauty, The (Rice), **Supp. VII:** 301

Clampitt, Amy, **Supp. IX: 37–54; Supp. X:** 120; **Supp. XI:** 249; **Supp. XV:** 251, 256

Clancy's Wake, At (Crane), **I:** 422

"Clandeboye" (Leopold), **Supp. XIV:** 189

Clara Howard; or, The Enthusiasm of Love (Brown), **Supp. I Part 1:** 145

Clara's Ole Man (Bullins), **Supp. II Part 1:** 42

Clara Wharton (Hayden), **Supp. XXV:** 38

Clare, John, **II:** 387; **III:** 528; **Supp. XVI:** 295

Clarel: A Poem and Pilgrimage in the Holy Land (Melville), **Retro. Supp. I:** 257

Clarence Major and His Art (Bell), **Supp. XXII:** 182

Clarissa (Richardson), **II:** 111; **Supp. I Part 2:** 714; **Supp. V:** 127; **Supp. XV:** 231; **Supp. XX: 236**

Clarissa Harlow (Richardson), **Supp. XXV:** 39

Clark, Alex, **Supp. XII:** 307

Clark, Charles, **I:** 470

Clark, Eleanor. *See* Warren, Mrs. Robert Penn (Eleanor Clark)

Clark, Francis Edward, **II:** 9

Clark, Geoffrey, **Supp. XI:** 342

Clark, Harry Hayden, **Supp. I Part 2:** 423

Clark, John Bates, **Supp. I Part 2:** 633

Clark, Kenneth, **Supp. XIV:** 342, 348; **Supp. XIX:** 151

Clark, Lewis Gaylord, **Supp. XVIII:** 4, 7, 8

Clark, Shirley, **Supp. XXI:** 22

Clark, Thomas, **Supp. III Part 2:** 629; **Supp. IV Part 1:** 140, 145, 147

Clark, Tom, **Supp. XXIV:** 36, 37, 41, 44

Clark, Walter, **Supp. XI:** 315

Clark, William, **III:** 14; **IV:** 179, 283

Clark, Willis Gaylord, **Supp. I Part 2:** 684

Clarke, Brock, **Supp. XXIII:** 109

Clarke, James Freeman, **Supp. II Part 1:** 280; **Supp. XXV:** 250

Clarke, John, **Supp. IV Part 1:** 8

Clarke, John J., **III:** 356

Clarke, Samuel, **II:** 108

Clark Lectures, **Retro. Supp. I:** 65

Claros varones de Belken (Hinojosa). *See Fair Gentlemen of Belken County* (Hinojosa)

Clash by Night (Odets), **Supp. II Part 2:** 531, 538, 544–546, 550, 551

Classical Tradition, The (Highet), **Supp. I Part 1:** 268

Classic Ballroom Dances (Simic), **Supp. VIII:** 271, **276–278,** 283

Classics (Hadas), **Supp. XXIII: 124**

Classics and Commercials: A Literary Chronicle of the Forties (Wilson), **IV:** 433

"Classics"(Hadas), **Supp. XXIII:** 124

"CLASS STRUGGLE" (Baraka), **Supp. III Part 1:** 55

"Claude Glass, The: 1890" (Bierds), **Supp. XVII:** 27

Claudel, Paul, **I:** 60

Claudelle Inglish (Caldwell), **I:** 304

Clavel, Marcel, **I:** 343

"CLAY" (Baraka), **Supp. II Part 1:** 54

Clay, Henry, **I:** 8; **Supp. I Part 2:** 684, 686

Clay's Ark (O. Butler), **Supp. XIII:** 63

Clayton, John J., **Supp. IV Part 1:** 238

Clayton, Sarah Turner, **Supp. XXV:** 251

"Clean, Well Lighted Place, A" (Hemingway), **Retro. Supp. I:** 181

"Clear, with Light Variable Winds" (Lowell), **II:** 522

"Clear Days" (White), **Supp. I Part 2:** 664, 665

Clearing (Berry), **Supp. X:** 22

"Clearing, A" (Simpson), **Supp. IX:** 280

"Clearing, The" (Kenyon), **Supp. VII:** 174

"Clearing the Title" (Merrill), **Supp. III Part 1:** 336

"Clearing Up the Question of Stesichoros' Blinding by Helen" (Carson), **Supp. XII:** 107–108

"Clear Morning" (Glück), **Supp. V:** 88

"Clearness" (Wilbur), **Supp. III Part 2:** 544, 550

"Clear Night" (Wright), **Supp. V:** 341

Clear Pictures: First Loves, First Guides (Price), **Supp. VI:** 253, 254, 255, 256, 265

Clear Springs (Mason), **Supp. VIII:** 134–136, 137–138, 139, 147

Cleary, Rebecca Lauck, **Supp. XVIII:** 195

Cleaver, Eldridge, **Retro. Supp. II:** 12; **Supp. IV Part 1:** 206; **Supp. X:** 249

"Cleaving, The" (L.-Y. Lee), **Supp. XV:** 215, **218–220**

Cleland, John, **Supp. V:** 48, 127

Clemenceau, Georges, **I:** 490

"Clemency" (Wrigley), **Supp. XVIII:** 307–308

Clemens, Jane, **I:** 247

Clemens, Orion, **IV:** 193, 195

Clemens, Samuel Langhorne. *See* Twain, Mark

Clemens, Mrs. Samuel Langhorne (Olivia Langdon), **I:** 197, 208, 247; **Supp. I Part 2:** 457

Clemens, Susie, **IV:** 208

Clementine Recognitions (novel), **Supp. IV Part 1:** 280

Clements, Colin Campbell, **Supp. XVI:** 190

Clemons, Walter, **Supp. IV Part 1:** 305, 307

Cleopatra, **III:** 44; **IV:** 373; **Supp. I Part 1:** 114

"Clepsydra" (Ashbery), **Supp. III Part 1:** 10–15

"Clerks, The" (Robinson), **III:** 517–518

"Cleveland" (Halliday), **Supp. XIX:** 90

Cleveland, Carol, **Supp. IX:** 120, 125

Cleveland, Ceil, **Supp. V:** 222

Cleveland, Grover, **II:** 126, 128, 129, 130, 137, 138; **Supp. I Part 2:** 486

"Clever Magician Carrying My Heart, A" (Salinas), **Supp. XIII:** 323

Cliff, Michelle, **Supp. XXII: 65–80**

"Cliff, The" (C. Baxter), **Supp. XVII:** 16–17

Clifford, Craig, **Supp. IX:** 99

Clift, Montgomery, **III:** 161

Clifton, Lucille, **Supp. XVIII:** 177

Climate of Monastic Prayer, The (Merton), **Supp. VIII:** 205, 207

Climb, The (Boukreev), **Supp. XVIII:** 112

"Climber, The" (Mason), **Supp. VIII:** 140–141

Climbing High: A Woman's Account of Surviving the Everest Tragedy (Gammelgaard), **Supp. XVIII:** 112

"Climbing the Tower" (Crews), **Supp. XI:** 102

Clinton, De Witt, **I:** 338

"Clipped Wings" (H. Miller), **III:** 176–177

Clippinger, David, **Supp. XXI:** 24

Clive, Robert, **Supp. I Part 2:** 505

Clock Winder, The (Tyler), **Supp. IV Part 2:** 661–662, 670

Clock Without Hands (McCullers), **II:** 587–588, 604–606

Clockwork Orange, A (Burgess), **Supp. XIII:** 29

Clorindy (Cook), **Supp. II Part 1:** 199

"Close, The" (Jarman), **Supp. XVII:** 113

"Close Calls" (Wolff), **Supp. VII:** 332–333

"Closed Book, A" (Mosley), **Supp. XIII:** 237

Close Quarters (Heinemann), **Supp. XXII:** 103, **104–109,** 111, 115

Close Range: Wyoming Stories (Proulx), **Supp. VII:** 261–265

"Close Reading: Windows"(Hirshfield), **Supp. XXIII:** 131

Closers, The (Connelly), **Supp. XXI: 76–77**

Closest Possible Union, The (J. Scott), **Supp. XVII: 185–186,** 188, **191**

Close the Book (Glaspell), **Supp. III Part 1:** 179

"Close the Book" (Lowell), **II:** 554

Close to Me & Closer ... (The Language of Heaven) and Désamère (Notley), **Supp. XXII:** 234

Close to Shore: A True Story of Terror in an Age of Innocence (Capuzzo), **Supp. XIII:** 254

Closet Writing & Gay Reading: The Case of Melville's Pierre (Creech), **Retro. Supp. I:** 254

Closing Circle, The (Commoner), **Supp. XIII:** 264

Closing of the American Mind, The (Bloom), **Retro. Supp. II:** 19, 30, 31

"Closing of the Rodeo, The" (W. J. Smith), **Supp. XIII:** 332

Closing Time (Heller), **Supp. IV Part 1:** 382, 386, 391–394

Closset, Marie, **Supp. VIII:** 251, 265

Clotel (Brown), **Supp. XXIII:** 184

"Cloud, The" (Shelley), **Supp. I Part 2:** 720

"Cloud and Fame" (Berryman), **I:** 173

Cloud Atlas (D. Mitchell), **Supp. XXIV:** 86

Cloud Forest, The: A Chronicle of the South American Wilderness (Matthiessen), **Supp. V:** 202, 204

"Cloud on the Way, The" (Bryant), **Supp. I Part 1:** 171

"Cloud River" (Wright), **Supp. V:** 341

"Clouds" (Levine), **Supp. V:** 184

Cloudsplitter (Banks), **Supp. V:** 16

"Clover" (Lanier), **Supp. I Part 1:** 362–364

Clover and Other Poems (Lanier), **Supp. I Part 1:** 362

"Clown" (Corso), **Supp. XII:** 127

Clown in the Belfry, The: Writings on Faith and Fiction (Buechner), **Supp. XII:** 53

Cluck, Julia, **Supp. I Part 2:** 728

Clum, John M., **Supp. XIII: 200,** 201, 209

Cluny, Hugo, **IV:** 290

Clurman, Harold, **I:** 93; **IV:** 381, 385

Clytus, Radiclani, **Supp. XIII:** 128, **Supp. XIII:** 129, 132

"C.O." (Wrigley), **Supp. XVIII:** 298

"Coal: Beginning and End" (Winters), **Supp. II Part 2:** 791

Coale, Howard, **Supp. XIII:** 15

"Coals" (Hoffman), **Supp. XVIII:** 86

"Coast, The" (column), **Supp. IV Part 1:** 198

"Coast Guard's Cottage, The" (Wylie), **Supp. I Part 2:** 723

Coast of Chicago, The (Dybek), **Supp. XXIII: 72–74,** 75

Coast of Trees, A (Ammons), **Supp. VII:** 24, 34

"Coast-Range Christ, The" (Jeffers), **Supp. II Part 2:** 414, 419

"Coast-Road, The" (Jeffers), **Supp. II Part 2:** 425

"Coat, The" (Everwine), **Supp. XV:** 80

Coates, Joseph, **Supp. VIII:** 80; **Supp. XXII:** 205

Coates, Robert, **I:** 54; **IV:** 298

"Coatlicue's Rules: Advice from an Aztec Goddess" (Mora), **Supp. XIII:** 223

"Coats" (Kenyon), **Supp. VII:** 172

Cobb, Lee J., **III:** 153

Cobb, Ty, **III:** 227, 229

Cobbett, William, **Supp. I Part 2:** 517; **Supp. XV:** 237

"Cobbler Keezar's Vision" (Whittier), **Supp. I Part 2:** 699

"Cobweb, The" (Carver), **Supp. III Part 1:** 148

Cobwebs From an Empty Skull (Bierce), **I:** 195

Coccimiglio, Vic, **Supp. XIII:** 114

"Cock-a-Doodle-Doo!" (Melville), **III:** 89

"Cockayne" (Emerson), **II:** 6

"Cock-Crow" (Gordon), **II:** 219

Cock Pit (Cozzens), **I:** 359, 378, 379

Cockpit (Kosinski), **Supp. XII:** 21

Cockpit: A Novel (Kosinski), **Supp. VII:** 215, 223–224, 225

"Cock Robin Takes Refuge in the Storm House" (Snodgrass), **Supp. VI:** 319

Cocktail Hour, The (Gurney), **Supp. V:** 95, 96, 100, 101, 103, 105, 108

Cocktail Hour and Two Other Plays: Another Antigone and *The Perfect Party* (Gurney), **Supp. V:** 100

Cocktail Party, The (Eliot), **I:** 571, 582–583; **III:** 21; **Retro. Supp. I:** 65; **Supp. V:** 101, 103

Cocteau, Jean, **III:** 471; **Retro. Supp. I:** 82, 378; **Supp. IV Part 1:** 82; **Supp. XVI:** 135; **Supp. XX:** 236

"Coda: Wilderness Letter" (Stegner), **Supp. IV Part 2:** 595

"Code, The" (Frost), **Retro. Supp. I:** 121, 128

Codex (Grossman), **Supp. XXV:** 64, 66–68

Codman, Florence, **Supp. II Part 1:** 92, 93

Codman, Ogden, Jr., **Retro. Supp. I:** 362, 363

Codrescu, Andrei, **Supp. XXII:** 155

Cody, William ("Buffalo Bill"), **I:** 440; **III:** 584; **Supp. V:** 230

"Coffee Lips" (Ferry), **Supp. XXIV:** 153, 162

Coffey, Michael, **Supp. V:** 243; **Supp. XV:** 65; **Supp. XX:** 88

Coffey, Warren, **III:** 358

Coffin, Charles, **III:** 577

Cogan, David J., **Supp. IV Part 1:** 362

Cogan, Joshua, **Supp. XXI:** 247

Cogewea the Half-Blood: A Depiction of the Great Montana Cattle Range (Mourning Dove (Christal Quintasket)), **Supp. XXV:** 285

Coghill, Nevill, **Supp. II Part 1:** 4; **Supp. XIV:** 13

Cohan, George M., **II:** 427; **III:** 401

Cohen, Edward M., **Supp. XVI:** 212

Cohen, Esther, **Supp. XV:** 323

Cohen, Hettie, **Supp. II Part 1:** 30

Cohen, Joshua, **Supp. XXII:** 268

Cohen, Marty, **Supp. X:** 112

Cohen, Norman J., **Supp. IX:** 132, 143

Cohen, Rosetta, **Supp. XV:** 257

Cohen, Sarah Blacher, **Supp. V:** 273

Cohen, Victor, **Supp. XVIII:** 235, 236

"Coherent Decentering: Towards a New Model of the Poetic Self" (A. Finch), **Supp. XVII:** 76

Cohn, Jan, **Supp. XXV:** 192, 200

"Coin" (Goldbarth), **Supp. XII:** 187

Coindreau, Maurice, **III:** 339

Coiner, Constance, **Supp. XIII:** 297, 302

Coit, Lille Hitchcock, **Supp. X:** 103

"Coitus" (Pound), **III:** 466

Coke, Desmond, **Supp. XX: 235**

Colburn, Nadia Herman, **Supp. XV:** 339, 341, 347

"Cold, The" (Kenyon), **Supp. VII:** 164

"Cold, The" (Winters), **Supp. II Part 2:** 790–791, 809, 811

"Cold-blooded Creatures" (Wylie), **Supp. I Part 2:** 729

Colden, Cadwallader, **Supp. I Part 1:** 250

"Colder the Air, The" (Bishop), **Supp. I Part 1:** 86

Cold Feet (Harrison), **Supp. VIII:** 39

Cold Frame (C. Frost), **Supp. XV:** 93, 96

Cold Ground Was My Bed Last Night (Garrett), **Supp. VII:** 98

"Cold Ground Was My Bed Last Night" (Garrett), **Supp. VII:** 100

"Cold Hill Side, The" (Hadas), **Supp. XXIII:** 121

"Cold Night, The" (W. C. Williams), **Retro. Supp. I:** 418

"Cold Plunge into Skin Diving, A" (Knowles), **Supp. XII:** 241

Cold Spring, A (Bishop), **Retro. Supp. II:** 45

Cold Springs Harbor (Yates), **Supp. XI:** 348

Cold War American Poetry, **Supp. V:** 182

Cold War and the Income Tax, The (Wilson), **IV:** 430

Cole, Bruce, **Supp. XX: 106**

Cole, Goody, **Supp. I Part 2:** 696–697

Cole, Lester, **Retro. Supp. II:** 329

Cole, Nat King, **Retro. Supp. I:** 334; **Supp. X:** 255

Cole, Thomas, **Supp. I Part 1:** 156, 158, 171

Cole, William, **Supp. XIX:** 120

"Coleman" (Karr), **Supp. XI:** 244

Coleman, Wanda, **Supp. XI: 83–98**

Coleridge, Samuel Taylor, **I:** 283, 284, 447, 522; **II:** 7, 10, 11, 19, 71, 169, 273, 301, 502, 516, 549; **III:** 77, 83–84, 424, 461, 488, 523; **IV:** 74, 173, 250, 349, 453; **Retro. Supp. I:** 65, 308; **Supp. I Part 1:** 31, 311, 349; **Supp. I Part 2:** 376, 393, 422; **Supp. IV Part 2:** 422, 465; **Supp. V:** 258; **Supp. IX:** 38, 50; **Supp. XIII:** 139; **Supp. XIV:** 21–22; **Supp. XV:** 250; **Supp. XXI:** 52, 55; **Supp. XXIII:** 231; **Supp. XXIV:** 74

Coles, Katharine, **Supp. IV Part 2:** 630

Coles, Robert, **Supp. XXIV:** 172, 265

Colette, Sidonie-Gabrielle, **Supp. VIII:** 40, 171; **Supp. XVI:** 193–194

"Coliseum, The" (Poe), **III:** 411

Collage of Dreams (Spencer), **Supp. X:** 196

"Collapse of Tomorrow, The" (Mumford), **Supp. II Part 2:** 482

"Collected by a Valetudinarian" (E. Stoddard), **Supp. XV:** 286–287

Collected Earlier Poems (Hecht), **Supp. X:** 58, 59

Collected Earlier Poems (W. C. Williams), **Retro. Supp. I:** 414, 428

Collected Earlier Poems 1940–1960 (Levertov), **Supp. III Part 1:** 273, 275

Collected Essays (Tate), **IV:** 133–134

Collected Essays, Volume 2: Literary Criticism (Lovecraft), **Supp. XXV:** 121

Collected Essays of Ralph Ellison, The (Ellison), **Retro. Supp. II:** 119

Collected Essays of Robert Creeley, The (Creeley), **Supp. IV Part 1:** 153, 154

Collected Later Poems (W. C. Williams), **Retro. Supp. I:** 428

Collected Plays (A. Miller), **III:** 158

Collected Plays, 1974–1983 (Gurney), **Supp. V:** 99

Collected Poems (Aiken), **I:** 50

Collected Poems (Berrigan), **Supp. XXIV:** 39, 45, 46

Collected Poems (Burke), **I:** 269

Collected Poems (Cummings), **I:** 430, 439, 441

Collected Poems (Doolittle), **Supp. I Part 1:** 264–267, 269

Collected Poems (Frost), **Retro. Supp. I:** 136

Collected Poems (Hull), **Supp. XXI:** 141

Collected Poems (Kees; Justice, ed.), **Supp. XV:** 134

Collected Poems (Lindsay), **Supp. I Part 2:** 380, 387, 392, 396–397, 400

Collected Poems (Lowell), **Supp. XV:** 20

Collected Poems (Markson), **Supp. XVII:** 143

Collected Poems (Moore), **III:** 194, 215

Collected Poems (O'Hara), **Supp. XXIII:** 207, 211, 220

Collected Poems (Price), **Supp. VI:** 267

Collected Poems (Simpson), **Supp. IX:** 279

Collected Poems (W. C. Williams), **IV:** 415; **Retro. Supp. I:** 430

Collected Poems (Winters), **Supp. II Part 2:** 791, 810

Collected Poems (Wright), **Supp. III Part 2:** 602

Collected Poems (Yeats), **Supp. XV:** 152

Collected Poems, 1918–1938 (Taggard), **Supp. XXII:** 283

Collected Poems, 1923–1953 (Bogan), **Supp. III Part 1:** 64

Collected Poems, 1936–1976 (Francis), **Supp. IX:** 77, 80, **87**

Collected Poems, The (Stevens), **III:** 273; **IV:** 75, 76, 87, 93; **Retro. Supp. I:** 296, 309

Collected Poems 1909–1935 (Eliot), **I:** 580; **Retro. Supp. I:** 66

Collected Poems 1909–1962 (Eliot), **I:** 583

Collected Poems 1917–1952 (MacLeish), **III:** 3, 4, 19

Collected Poems 1921–1931 (W. C. Williams), **Retro. Supp. I:** 422; **Supp. XIV:** 285

Collected Poems 1930–1960 (Eberhart), **I:** 522, 525–526, 540, 541

Collected Poems: 1939–1989 (W. J. Smith), **Supp. XIII:** 332, 340, 343, 345

Collected Poems: 1940–1978 (Shapiro), **Supp. II Part 2:** 703, 717

Collected Poems: 1951–1971 (Ammons), **Supp. VII:** 24, 26–29, 32, 33

Collected Poems: 1956–1976 (Wagoner), **Supp. IX:** 323, **328–329**

Collected Poems of Amy Clampitt, The (Clampitt), **Supp. IX:** 37, 44, 53

Collected Poems of George Garrett (Garrett), **Supp. VII:** 109

Collected Poems of Hart Crane, The (Crane), **I:** 399–402

Collected Poems of James Agee, The (Fitzgerald, ed.), **I:** 27–28

Collected Poems of James T. Farrell, The (Farrell), **II:** 45

Collected Poems of Kay Boyle (Boyle), **Supp. XXIV:** 63

Collected Poems of Langston Hughes, The (Rampersad and Roessel, ed.), **Retro. Supp. I:** 194, 196, 212

Collected Poems of Muriel Rukeyser, The (Rukeyser), **Supp. VI:** 274

Collected Poems of Thomas Merton, The, **Supp. VIII:** 207, 208

Collected Poetry (Auden), **Supp. II Part 1:** 18

Collected Prose (Wright), **Supp. III Part 2:** 596

Collected Prose, The (Bishop), **Retro. Supp. II:** 51

Collected Recordings (W. C. Williams), **Retro. Supp. I:** 431

Collected Shorter Poems, 1946–1991 (Carruth), **Supp. XVI:** 47

Collected Short Stories, The (Wharton), **Retro. Supp. I:** 362, 363, 366

Collected Sonnets (Millay), **III:** 136–137

Collected Stories (Carver), **Supp. XXIV:** 177

Collected Stories, 1939–1976 (Bowles), **Supp. IV Part 1:** 92

Collected Stories, The (Paley), **Supp. VI:** 218

Collected Stories, The (Price), **Supp. VI:** 266

Collected Stories, The (Theroux), **Supp. VIII:** 318

Collected Stories, The (Wharton), **Retro. Supp. I:** 361

Collected Stories of Amy Hempel, The (Hempel), **Supp. XXI:** 115, 117

Collected Stories of Eudora Welty, The (Welty), **Retro. Supp. I:** 355

Collected Stories of Isaac Bashevis Singer (Singer), **Retro. Supp. II:** **307–308**

Collected Stories of Katherine Anne Porter (Porter), **III:** 454

Collected Stories of Peter Taylor (Taylor), **Supp. V:** 314, 320, 323–324, 325, 326

Collected Stories of Richard Yates, The, **Supp. XI:** 349

Collected Stories of Wallace Stegner (Stegner), **Supp. IV Part 2:** 599, 605

Collected Stories of William Faulkner (Faulkner), **II:** 72; **Retro. Supp. I:** 75

Collected Stories of William Humphrey, The (Humphrey), **Supp. IX:** 106

Collected Works (Bierce), **I:** 204, 208–210

Collected Works of Buck Rogers in the 25th Century, The (Bradbury), **Supp. IV Part 1:** 101

Collected Writings, The (Z. Fitzgerald; Bruccoli, ed.), **Supp. IX:** 65, 68

Collecting the Animals (Everwine), **Supp. XV:** 73, 75, **78–81,** 85, 88

Collection of Epigrams, **II:** 111

Collection of Poems, on American Affairs, and a Variety of Other Subjects . . . (Freneau), **Supp. II Part 1:** 274

Collection of Select Aphorisms and Maxims (Palmer), **II:** 111

"Collectors" (Carver), **Supp. III Part 1:** 141–142

Collette, **Supp. XVII:** 86

Collier, John, **Supp. XXI:** 8

Collier, Lucy Wood, **Supp. XXI:** 8

Collier, Michael, **Supp. XVII:** 23, 110

Collingwood, R. G., **I:** 278

Collins, Billy, **Supp. XI:** 143; **Supp. XIV:** 123; **Supp. XVII:** 245; **Supp. XXI:** **51–66;** **Supp. XXIII:** 138

Collins, Doug, **Supp. V:** 5

Collins, Eddie, **II:** 416

Collins, L. M., **Supp. XXII:** 7

Collins, Richard, **Supp. XI:** 171

Collins, Ronald, **Supp. XXI:** 24

Collins, Wilkie, **Supp. I Part 1:** 35, 36; **Supp. IV Part 1:** 341; **Supp. XX:** **236**

Collins, William, **Supp. I Part 2:** 714

Collinson, Peter , **II:** 114

Collinson, Peter (pseudonym). *See* Hammett, Dashiell

Colloff, Pamela, **Supp. XIII:** 281

Colloque Sentimental (ballet), **Supp. IV Part 1:** 83

"Colloquy" (Kees), **Supp. XV:** 133

"Colloquy in Black Rock" (Lowell), **II:** 535; **Retro. Supp. II:** 178

"Colloquy of Monos and Una, The" (Poe), **III:** 412

"Colloquy on a Bed" (Bronk), **Supp. XXI:** 31

Colonel's Dream, The (Chesnutt), **Supp. XIV:** 63, 75–76

Colônia, Regina, **Retro. Supp. II:** 53

Colony (Siddons), **Supp. XXII:** 239

Color (Cullen), **Supp. IV Part 1:** 164, 166, 167, 168

"Colorado" (Beattie), **Supp. V:** 27

Color and Democracy: Colonies and Peace (Du Bois), **Supp. II Part 1:** 184, 185

"Color-Blind Raspberry Picker, The" (Hadas), **Supp. XXIII:** 113

Color Curtain, The (Wright), **IV:** 478, 488

"Colored Americans" (Dunbar), **Supp. II Part 1:** 197

Colored People (H. L. Gates), **Supp. XX:** **101, 103, 104–105, 109, 111**

"Color Line, The" (Douglass), **Supp. III Part 1:** 163–165

Color Line, The (W. B. Smith), **Supp. II Part 1:** 168

Color of a Great City, The (Dreiser), **Retro. Supp. II:** 104

Color of Darkness (Purdy), **Supp. VII:** 271

Color Purple, The (Walker), **Supp. III Part 2:** 517, 518, 520, 525–529, 532–537; **Supp. VIII:** 141; **Supp. X:** 252, 330; **Supp. XX:** 107

Color Schemes (Cheang; film), **Supp. XI:** 20

"Colors of Night, The" (Momaday), **Supp. IV Part 2:** 490

"Colors without Objects" (Swenson), **Supp. IV Part 2:** 645

"Color: The Unfinished Business of Democracy" (Locke), **Supp. XIV:** 202, 207

Colossus, The (Plath), **Retro. Supp. II:** 245–247; **Supp. I Part 2:** 529, 531, 536, 538, 540; **Supp. V:** 79; **Supp. XI:** 317

"Colossus, The" (Plath), **Retro. Supp. II:** 250; **Supp. XXIII:** 113

Colossus of Maroussi, The (H. Miller), **III:** 178, 185–186

"Colour out of Space, The" (Lovecraft), **Supp. XXV:** 109, 111, 114–116, 118, 121

"Colt, The" (Stegner), **Supp. IV Part 2:** 600

Coltelli, Laura, **Supp. IV Part 1:** 323, 330, 335, 409; **Supp. IV Part 2:** 493, 497, 559

Colter: The True Story of the Best Dog I Ever Had (Bass), **Supp. XVI:** 23

Coltrane, John, **Supp. VIII:** 197; **Supp. XXII:** 172

Coltrane, John (pseud.). *See* O'Nan, Stewart

Colum, Mary, **I:** 246, 252, 256; **Supp. I Part 2:** 708, 709

"Columba" (Cliff), **Supp. XXII:** 74, 76

Columbia Anthology of American Poetry (Parini, ed.), **Supp. XXV:** 251

Columbiad, The (Barlow), **Supp. II Part 1:** 67, 72, 73, 74, 75–77, 79

Columbia History of the American Novel, **Supp. XV:** 270

Columbia Literary History of the United States, **Supp. XV:** 270

"Columbian Ode" (Dunbar), **Supp. II Part 1:** 199

"Columbia U Poesy Reading—1975" (Corso), **Supp. XII:** 134

"Columbine, The" (Very), **Supp. XXV:** 242, 244

Columbus, Christopher, **I:** 253; **II:** 6, 310; **III:** 8; **Supp. I Part 2:** 397, 479, 480, 483, 486–488, 491, 495, 497, 498

"Columbus to Ferdinand" (Freneau), **Supp. II Part 1:** 255

Comanche Moon (McMurtry), **Supp. V:** 232

"Come, Break With Time" (Bogan), **Supp. III Part 1:** 52

Come, Thief (Hirshfield), **Supp. XXIII:** 134, 138

Come Along with Me (Jackson), **Supp. IX:** 117, 118, 122

Come Back, Charleston Blue (film), **Supp. XVI:** 144

Come Back, Little Sheba (film), **Supp. XXV:** 95

Come Back, Little Sheba (Inge), **Supp. XXV:** 94–95, 96–97

Comeback, The (Gurney), **Supp. V:** 97

"Come Back to the Raft Ag'in, Huck Honey!" (Fiedler), **Supp. XIII:** 93, **96–97,** 101

Come Blow Your Horn (Simon), **Supp. IV Part 2:** 574, 575, 577, 578, 586, 587, 591

Come By Here (Major), **Supp. XXII:** 171, 182

"Come Dance with Me in Ireland" (Jackson), **Supp. IX:** 119

"Comedian as the Letter C, The" (Stevens), **IV:** 84–85, 88; **Retro. Supp. I:** 297, 301, 302

"Comedy Cop" (Farrell), **II:** 45

Comedy of a Country House (J. Sturgis), **Supp. XX:** 238

"Comedy's Greatest Era" (Agee), **I:** 31

"Come In" (Frost), **Retro. Supp. I:** 139

"Come On, Baby" (Zinberg), **Supp. XV:** 195

"Come on Back" (Gardner), **Supp. VI:** 73

"Come Out into the Sun" (Francis), **Supp. IX:** 82

Come Out into the Sun: Poems New and Selected (Francis), **Supp. IX:** 82–83

"Come out the Wilderness" (Baldwin), **Supp. I Part 1:** 63

Comer, Anjanette, **Supp. XI:** 305

Comer, Cornelia, **I:** 214

"Come Rain or Come Shine" (song), **Supp. XXII:** 6

"Come Shining: The Spiritual South" (exhibition; Luster), **Supp. XV:** 350

Come with Me: Poems for a Journey (Nye), **Supp. XIII:** 279

"Comforts of Home, The" (O'Connor), **III:** 349, 351, 355; **Retro. Supp. II:** 237

Comic Artist, The (Glaspell and Matson), **Supp. III Part 1:** 182

"Comic Imagination of the Young Dickens, The" (Wright), **Supp. III Part 2:** 591

"Comic Textures and Female Communities 1937 and 1977: Clare Boothe and Wendy Wasserstein" (Carlson), **Supp. XV:** 323

Comic Tragedies (Alcott), **Supp. I Part 1:** 33

Coming After (Notley), **Supp. XXII:** 223, 227, 230, 232, 236

"Coming and Going" (Gallagher), **Supp. XXIV:** 175, 176–177

"Coming Close" (Levine), **Supp. V:** 192

Coming Forth by Day of Osiris Jones, The (Aiken), **I:** 59

"Coming Home" (Gordon), **Supp. IV Part 1:** 309

"Coming Home to Vermont" (McCarriston), **Supp. XIV:** 269

"Coming in From the Cold" (Walker), **Supp. III Part 2:** 526

Coming into Eighty (Sarton), **Supp. VIII:** 262

"Coming into Eighty" (Sarton), **Supp. VIII:** 262

Coming into the Country (McPhee), **Supp. III Part 1:** 298, 301–306, 309, 310

Coming Into Writing (Cixous), **Supp. X:** 102

Coming of Age in Mississippi (Moody), **Supp. IV Part 1:** 11

Comings Back (Goldbarth), **Supp. XII:** 180

"Coming to Canada--Age Twenty Two" (Shields), **Supp. VII:** 311

Coming to Canada: Poems (Shields), **Supp. VII:** 311–312

"Coming to Memoir as a Journalist" (Epstein), **Supp. XXII:** 95

"Coming to the Morning" (Merwin), **Supp. III Part 1:** 356

"Coming to This" (Strand), **Supp. IV Part 2:** 627

Comiskey, Charles, **II:** 422

Commager, Henry Steele, **I:** 253; **Supp. I Part 1:** 372; **Supp. I Part 2:** 484, 647, 650

Command the Morning (Buck), **Supp. II Part 1:** 125

"CommComm" (Saunders), **Supp. XIX:** 234

"Commencement Address, A" (Brodsky), **Supp. VIII:** 31

"Commencement Day Address, The" (Schwartz), **Supp. II Part 2:** 660

Commentaries (Caesar), **II:** 502, 561

"Commentary" (Auden), **Supp. II Part 1:** 13

"Comment on Curb" (Hughes), **Supp. I Part 1:** 340

"Comments/Questions" (Nelson), **Supp. XVIII:** 172

"Commerce" (Nye), **Supp. XIII:** 281

Commins, Saxe, **Retro. Supp. I:** 73; **Retro. Supp. II:** 337

Commodity of Dreams & Other Stories, A (Nemerov), **III:** 268–269, 285

Common Carnage (Dobyns), **Supp. XIII:** 87

"Common Ground, A" (Levertov), **Supp. III Part 1:** 277

"Common Life, The" (Auden), **Supp. IV Part 1:** 302, 313

"Common Meter" (R. Fisher), **Supp. XIX:** 71

Common Room, A: Essays 1954–1987 (Price), **Supp. VI:** 264–265, 267

Commons, John, **Supp. I Part 2:** 645

Common Sense (Paine), **II:** 117; **Supp. I Part 1:** 231; **Supp. I Part 2:** 505, 506–508, 509, 513, 516, 517, 521

Communal Cot (Loy), **Supp. XXII:** 168

"Communication" (Dobyns), **Supp. XIII:** 91

"Communion" (Dubus), **Supp. VII:** 91

Communion (Mora), **Supp. XIII:** 217–219

Communist Manifesto, The (Marx and Engels), **II:** 463; **Supp. XXI:** 162–163

"Community Life" (Moore), **Supp. X:** 178

"Community of Glaciers, The" (Bass), **Supp. XVI:** 23

Comnes, Gregory, **Supp. IV Part 1:** 283, 284, 291

"Companions, The" (Nemerov), **III:** 269, 278, 287

Company of Poets, A (Simpson), **Supp. IX:** 265, 275

Company of Women, The (Gordon), **Supp. IV Part 1:** 302–304, 304, 306, 313

Company She Keeps, The (McCarthy), **II:** 562, 563–566

"Comparisons of Wonder" (Jarman), **Supp. XVII:** 114

Compass Flower, The (Merwin), **Supp. III Part 1:** 353, 357

"Compassionate Friendship" (Doolittle), **Supp. I Part 1:** 257, 258, 259, 260, 271

"Compatibility" (C. Frost), **Supp. XV:** 103

"Compendium" (Dove), **Supp. IV Part 1:** 248

"Complaint" (W. C. Williams), **Retro. Supp. I:** 418

"Complete Birth of the Cool, The" (Wright), **Supp. XV:** 343, 344

Complete Collected Poems of William Carlos Williams, 1906–1938, The (W. C. Williams), **Retro. Supp. I:** 424

"Complete Destruction" (W. C. Williams), **IV:** 413

"Complete Life of John Hopkins, The" (O. Henry), **Supp. II Part 1:** 405

Complete Poems (Frost), **II:** 155, 164

Complete Poems (Reznikoff), **Supp. XIV:** 281

Complete Poems (Sandburg), **III:** 590–592, 594, 596

Complete Poems, The (Bishop), **Retro. Supp. II:** 49; **Supp. I Part 1:** 72, 82, 94

Complete Poems, The (Bradbury), **Supp. IV Part 1:** 105

Complete Poems, The: 1927–1979 (Bishop), **Retro. Supp. II:** 51

Complete Poems of Emily Dickinson, The (Bianchi and Hampson, eds.), **Retro. Supp. I:** 35

Complete Poems of Emily Dickinson, The (Johnson, ed.), **I:** 470

Complete Poems of Frederick Goddard Tuckerman, The (Momaday), **Supp. IV Part 2:** 480

Complete Poems of Hart Crane, **Retro. Supp. II:** 81

Complete Poems to Solve, The (Swenson), **Supp. IV Part 2:** 652

Complete Poetical Works (Hulme), **III:** 464

Complete Poetical Works (Longfellow), **Retro. Supp. II:** 154

Complete Poetical Works (Lowell), **II:** 512, 516–517

Complete Poetical Works of Amy Lowell, The, **Supp. XV:** 295–296

Complete Stories (O'Connor), **Supp. X:** 1

Complete Tragedies, The: Euripedes II, **Supp. XV:** 50

"Complete with Starry Night and Bourbon Shots" (Goldbarth), **Supp. XII:** 192–193

Complete Works of Kate Chopin, The (Seyersted, ed.), **Supp. I Part 1:** 212, 225

Complete Works of the Gawain-Poet (Gardner), **Supp. VI:** 64, 65

"Complex Histories, Contested Memories: Some Reflections on Remembering Difficult Pasts" (E. Hoffman, lecture), **Supp. XVI:** 155

"Complicated Thoughts About a Small Son" (White), **Supp. I Part 2:** 678

"Compliments of the Season" (O. Henry), **Supp. II Part 1:** 392, 399

"Compline" (Auden), **Supp. II Part 1:** 23

"Composing a Life" (Pickering), **Supp. XXI:** 191, 196

Composition as Explanation (Stein), **IV:** 32, 33, 38

"Composition as Explanation" (Stein), **IV:** 27, 28

"Compounding *of* Consciousness" (James), **II:** 358–359

Comprehensive Bibliography (Hanneman), **II:** 259

Compton-Burnett, Ivy, **I:** 93; **II:** 580; **Supp. XXIII:** 209

"Comrade Laski, C.P.U.S.A. \[M.L.\]" (Didion), **Supp. IV Part 1:** 200

Comstock, Anthony, **Retro. Supp. II:** 95

Comus (Milton), **II:** 12; **Supp. I Part 2:** 622

Conan Doyle, Arthur. *See* Doyle, Arthur Conan

Conceptions of Reality in Modern American Poetry (Dembo), **Supp. I Part 1:** 272

"Concept of Character in Fiction, The" (Gass), **Supp. VI:** 85, **86**

Concept of Dread, The (Kierkegaard), **III:** 305

Concerning Children (Gilman), **Supp. XI:** 206

"Concerning Mold upon the Skin, Etc." (J. Scott), **Supp. XVII:** 188

"Concerning Necessity" (Carruth), **Supp. XVI:** 57

"Concerning Some Recent Criticism of His Work" (Doty), **Supp. XI:** 131

Concerning the End for Which God Created the World (Edwards), **I:** 549, 557, 559

"Concerning Things That Can Be Doubled"(Crooker), **Supp. XXIII:** 64

Concerto for Two Pianos, Winds, and Percussion (Bowles), **Supp. IV Part 1:** 83

"Concert of Tenses, A" (Gallagher), **Supp. XXIV:** 172

Concert of Tenses, A: Essays on Poetry (Gallagher), **Supp. XXIV:** 166, 167, 171–172

Conchologist's First Book, The (Poe), **III:** 412

Conclusive Evidence (Nabokov), **III:** 247–250, 252

"Concord Hymn" (Emerson), **II:** 19

Concrete Blonde, The (Connelly), **Supp. XXI:** **70–71**, 78, 80

"Concrete Universal, The: Observations on the Understanding of Poetry" (Ransom), **III:** 480

Concurring Beasts (Dobyns), **Supp. XIII:** 76

Condé, Maryse, **Supp. XXIII:** 94

Condensed Novels and Other Papers (Harte), **Supp. II Part 1:** 342

"Condition, The" (Karmi; Everwine, trans.), **Supp. XV:** 78

Condition of Man, The (Mumford), **Supp. II Part 2:** 483, 484, 486, 495–496, 498

"Condolence" (Parker), **Supp. IX:** 191

"Condominium, The" (Elkin), **Supp. VI:** 49, **50–51**, 55, 56

Condon, Charles R., **Supp. XIII:** 163

Condor and the Cows, The: A South American Travel Diary (Isherwood and Caskey), **Supp. XIV:** 166

"Condor and the Guests, The" (Connell), **Supp. XIV:** 86

Condorcet, Marquis de, **Supp. I Part 2:** 511

Conduct of Life, The (Emerson), **II:** 1–5, 8

Conduct of Life, The (Mumford), **Supp. II Part 2:** 485, 496–497

"Conductor of Nothing, The" (Levine), **Supp. V:** 189

Coney Island of the Mind, A (Ferlinghetti), **Supp. XIX:** 4; **Supp. XXI:** 53

"Conference Male, The" (Mora), **Supp. XIII:** 218

"Confession" (Peacock), **Supp. XIX:** 206

Confession, The (Rinehart), **Supp. XXV:** 200

"Confessional" (Bidart), **Supp. XV:** 29–30, 31

"Confessional Poem" (Nelson), **Supp. XVIII:** 174

Confession de Claude, La (Zola), **I:** 411

"Confession of a House-Breaker, The" (Jewett), **Retro. Supp. II:** 146–147

Confession of Jereboam O. Beauchamp, The (pamphlet), **IV:** 253

Confessions (Augustine), **I:** 279; **Supp. XVI:** 288; **Supp. XXII:** 93

Confessions (Rousseau), **I:** 226

Confessions of a Barbarian: Selections from the Journals of Edward Abbey, 1951–1989 (Abbey; Petersen, ed.), **Supp. XIII:** 2, 4

"Confessions of a Latina Author" (Mora), **Supp. XIII:** 221

"Confessions of a Wannabe Negro" (McKnight), **Supp. XX: 152–153**, 158

Confessions of Nat Turner, The (Styron), **IV:** 98, 99, 105, 113–117; **Supp. X:** 16, 250

Confetti (Mora), **Supp. XIII:** 221

Confidence (James), **II:** 327, 328

Confidence-Man, The (Melville), **III:** 91; **Retro. Supp. I:** 255–256, 257; **Retro. Supp. II:** 121; **Supp. XIV:** 49

Confidence Man, The (Van Vechten), **Supp. II Part 2:** 737

Confidential Clerk, The (Eliot), **I:** 570, 571–572, 583, 584; **Retro. Supp. I:** 65

Confident Years, 1885–1915, The (Brooks), **I:** 257, 259; **Supp. I Part 2:** 650

"Configurations" (Ammons), **Supp. VII:** 28

Configurations: New and Selected Poems, 1958–1998 (Major), **Supp. XXII: 182**

Confronting the Horror: The Novels of Nelson Algren (Giles), **Supp. IX:** 11, 15

Confucius, **II:** 1; **III:** 456, 475; **Supp. IV Part 1:** 14

Confusion (Cozzens), **I:** 358, 359, 377, 378

"Confusion of Planes We Must Wander in Sleep, The" (Weigl), **Supp. XIX:** 283

Congdon, Don, **Supp. XXII:** 204

Congo (film), **Supp. IV Part 1:** 83

Congo (screenplay, Shanley), **Supp. XIV:** 316

"Congo, The" (Lindsay), **Supp. I Part 2:** 388–389, 392, 395

Congo and Other Poems, The (Lindsay), **Supp. I Part 2:** 379, 382, 389, 390, 391; **Supp. XXV:** 18

"Congregation" (Trethewey), **Supp. XXI:** 245, 247

"Congregation of Grackles, A"(Crooker), **Supp. XXIII:** 63

"Congress of the Insomniacs, The" (Simic), **Supp. VIII:** 281–282

Congreve, William, **III:** 195; **Supp. V:** 101; **Supp. XVIII:** 12

Coningsby (Disraeli), **II:** 127

"Conjectural Reading" (Bronk), **Supp. XXI:** 31

Conjectures of a Guilty Bystander (Merton), **Supp. VIII:** 197, 206, 207

Conjugal Bliss: A Comedy of Marital Arts (Nichols), **Supp. XIII:** 269

"Conjugation of the Paramecium, The" (Rukeyser), **Supp. VI:** 271

Conjugations and Reiterations (Murray), **Supp. XIX:** 161

"Conjuration" (Wilbur), **Supp. III Part 2:** 551

Conjure (recording), **Supp. X:** 241

Conjure (Reed), **Supp. X:** 240, 242

Conjure-Man Dies, The: A Mystery Tale of Dark Harlem (R. Fisher), **Supp. XVI:** 143; **Supp. XIX:** 65, 71, **77–78**

Conjure Woman, The (Chesnutt), **Supp. II Part 1:** 193; **Supp. XIV:** 57, **58–61**, 62, 63

Conklin, Grof, **Supp. I Part 2:** 672

Conklin, Peggy, **Supp. XXII:** 27

Conkling, Hilda, **II:** 530

Conkling, Roscoe, **III:** 506

Conley, Robert J., **Supp. V:** 232

Conley, Susan, **Supp. XIII:** 111, 112

Connaroe, Joel, **Supp. IV Part 2:** 690

"Connecticut Lad, A" (White), **Supp. I Part 2:** 677

"Connecticut Valley" (Cowley), **Supp. II Part 1:** 141–142

Connecticut Yankee in King Arthur's Court, A (Twain), **I:** 209; **II:** 276; **IV:** 205

Connell, Evan S., **Supp. XIV: 79–100**; **Supp. XXIII:** 302

Connell, Norreys (pseudonym). *See* O'Riordan, Conal Holmes O'Connell

Connelly, Marc, **III:** 394; **Supp. I Part 2:** 679; **Supp. IX:** 190

Connelly, Michael, **Supp. XXI: 67–82**

Conner, Dan, **Supp. XXIII:** 125

Connery, Thomas B., **Supp. XVII:** 106

Connoisseur, The (Connell), **Supp. XIV:** 87

"Connoisseur of Chaos" (Stevens), **IV:** 89; **Retro. Supp. I:** 306

Connolly, Cyril, **Supp. XIV:** 158, 343, 348

Connors, Elizabeth. *See* Lindsay, Mrs. Vachel (Elizabeth Connors)

Connotations (Kenny), **Supp. XXIII:** 143, 144, 146, 150, 155

Conover, Roger, **Supp. I Part 1:** 95

Conover, Roger L., **Supp. XXII:** 155, 162

Conquering Horse (Manfred), **Supp. X:** 126

Conqueror, The (Atherton), **Supp. XXIV:** 23

"Conqueror Worm, The" (Poe), **Retro. Supp. II:** 261

Conquest of Canaan (Dwight), **Supp. I Part 1:** 124

Conquistador (MacLeish), **III:** 2, 3, 13–14, 15

Conrad, Alfred, **Retro. Supp. II:** 245

Conrad, Alfred H., **Supp. I Part 2:** 552

Conrad, C. A., **Supp. XXII:** 155

Conrad, David, **Supp. I Part 2:** 552

Conrad, Jacob, **Supp. I Part 2:** 552

Conrad, Joseph, **I:** 123, 343, 394, 405, 409, 415, 421, 485, 506, 575–576, 578; **II:** 58, 73, 74, 91, 92, 144, 263, 320, 338, 595; **III:** 28, 102, 106, 328, 464, 467, 491, 512; **IV:** 476; **Retro. Supp. I:** 80, 91, 106, 108, 231, 274, 377; **Retro. Supp. II:** 222; **Supp. I Part 1:** 292; **Supp. I Part 2:** 621, 622; **Supp. IV Part 1:** 197, 341; **Supp. IV Part 2:** 680; **Supp. V:** 249, 251, 262, 298, 307, 311; **Supp. VIII:** 4, 310; **Supp. XIV:** 112; **Supp. XVI:** 158, 212; **Supp. XVIII:** 98, 102; **Supp. XIX:** 27; **Supp. XX: 195**; **Supp. XXIV:** 286; **Supp. XXV:** 208

Conrad, Paul, **Supp. I Part 2:** 552

Conrad, Peter, **Supp. IV Part 2:** 688

"Conrad Aiken: From Savannah to Emerson" (Cowley), **Supp. II Part 1:** 43

Conrad Richter's Ohio Trilogy (Edwards), **Supp. XVIII:** 220

Conroy, Frank, **Supp. VIII:** 145; **Supp. XI:** 245; **Supp. XVI: 63–78**; **Supp. XXII:** 50

Conroy, Jack, **Supp. XXII:** 1, 5, 10

Conroy, Pat, **Supp. XVIII:** 193; **Supp. XXII:** 239

Cons, Scams, and Grifts (Gores), **Supp. XXI:** 70

Conscience with the Power and Cases thereof (Ames), **IV:** 158

"Conscientious Objector, The" (Shapiro), **Supp. II Part 2:** 710

"Consciousness and Dining" (Harrison), **Supp. VIII:** 46

"Conscript, The" (Lovecraft), **Supp. XXV:** 119

"Conscription Camp" (Shapiro), **Supp. II Part 2:** 705

"Consejos de Nuestra Señora de Guadalupe: Counsel from the Brown Virgin" (Mora), **Supp. XIII:** 224

"Conservation Esthetic" (Leopold), **Supp. XIV:** 179, 181, 186, 189–190

"Conserving Natural and Cultural Diversity: The Prose and Poetry of Pat Mora" (Murphy), **Supp. XIII:** 214

Considerable Town, A (M. F. K. Fisher), **Supp. XVII:** 90

"Considerations by the Way" (Emerson), **II:** 2, 5

Consider the Oyster (M. F. K. Fisher), **Supp. XVII:** 84, 87

Considine, Bob, **II:** 424

"Consolation" (Bausch), **Supp. VII:** 48

"Consolation for Tamar" (Stallings), **Supp. XXV:** 228

"Consolations" (Stafford), **Supp. XI:** 329

"Conspiracy of History, The: E. L. Doctorow's *The Book of Daniel*" (Levine), **Supp. IV Part 1:** 221

Conspiracy of Kings, The (Barlow), **Supp. II Part 1:** 80

Conspiracy of Pontiac, The (Parkman), **Supp. II Part 2:** 590, 595, 596, 599–600

Constab Ballads (McKay), **Supp. X:** 131, 133

Constance (Kenyon), **Supp. VII:** 170–172

Constancy (Boyce), **Supp. XVII:** 100; **Supp. XXI:** 6, 7, 12

"Constellation Orion, The" (Kooser), **Supp. XIX:** 120

Construction of Boston, The (Koch), **Supp. XV:** 187

"Constructive Work" (Du Bois), **Supp. II Part 1:** 172

"Consumer's Report" (X. J. Kennedy), **Supp. XV:** 161–162

"Consumption" (Bryant), **Supp. I Part 1:** 169–170

Contact Collection of Contemporary Writers (McAlmon), **Supp. XXII:** 166

"Contagiousness of Puerperal Fever, The" (Holmes), **Supp. I Part 1:** 303–304

"Contemplation in a World of Action" (Merton), **Supp. VIII:** 204

"Contemplation of Poussin" (Sarton), **Supp. VIII:** 261

"Contemplations" (Bradstreet), **Supp. I Part 1:** 112, 113, 119–122

Contemporaries (Kazin), **Supp. VIII:** 102, **103–104**

Contemporary American Playwrights (Bigsby), **Supp. XV:** 332

Contemporary American Poetry (Poulin, ed.), **Supp. IX:** 272; **Supp. XI:** 259

Contemporary Authors Autobiography, **Supp. XXII:** 225

Contending Forces (Hopkins), **Supp. XVIII:** 284

"Contentment" (Holmes), **Supp. I Part 1:** 307

"Contents" (Halliday), **Supp. XIX:** 92

"Contest, The" (Paley), **Supp. VI:** 223, 230, 231

"Contest for Aaron Gold, The" (P. Roth), **Supp. III Part 2:** 403

Continental Drift (Banks), **Supp. V:** 13–14, 16, 227

Continental Op, The (Hammett), **Supp. IV Part 1:** 344

Continent's End: An Anthology of Contemporary California Poets (Taggard, Sterling, and Rorty, eds.), **Supp. XXII:** 276

Continuing Education, A (Pickering), **Supp. XXI:** 194, 195–196

Continuity of American Poetry, The (Pearce), **Supp. I Part 1:** 111; **Supp. I Part 2:** 475

Continuous Harmony, A: Essays Cultural and Agricultural (Berry), **Supp. X:** 33

Continuous Life, The (Strand), **Supp. IV Part 2:** 630, 631–633

Contoski, Victor, **Supp. XII:** 181

"Contract" (Lardner), **II:** 432

"Contraption, The" (Swenson), **Supp. IV Part 2:** 643

"Contrariness of the Mad Farmer, The" (Berry), **Supp. X:** 35

"Contrast, a Spenetic Effusion, The" (J. Schoolcraft), **Supp. XXIII:** 231–232

"Contrition" (Dubus), **Supp. VII:** 84

"Control Burn" (Snyder), **Supp. VIII:** 301

"Control Is the Mainspring" (Komunyakaa), **Supp. XIII:** 122, 124

"Controlling the 'Sloppiness of Things' in Frank Conroy's *Stop-Time*" (Strychacz), **Supp. XVI:** 69–70

Control of Nature, The (McPhee), **Supp. III Part 1:** 310–313

Controversial Sholem Asch, The (Siegel), **Supp. XXIII:** 3

"Conventional Wisdom, The" (Elkin), **Supp. VI: 52–53**

"Convergence" (Ammons), **Supp. VII:** 28

"Convergence of the Twain, The" (Hardy), **Supp. VIII:** 31, 32

Conversation (Aiken), **I:** 54

Conversation at Midnight (Millay), **III:** 138

"Conversation of Eiros and Charmion, The" (Poe), **III:** 412

"Conversation on Conversation" (Stowe), **Supp. I Part 2:** 587

"Conversations in Moscow" (Levertov), **Supp. III Part 1:** 282

Conversations on Some of the Old Poets (Lowell), **Supp. I Part 2:** 405

Conversations with Albert Murray (Maguire, ed.), **Supp. XIX:** 160–161

Conversations with Byron (Blessington), **Retro. Supp. II:** 58

Conversations with Eudora Welty (Prenshaw, ed.), **Retro. Supp. I:** 339, 340, 341, 342, 343, 352, 354

"Conversations with Helmholtz" (Allen), **Supp. XV:** 15

Conversations with Ishmael Reed (Dick and Singh, eds.), **Supp. X:** 244

Conversations with James Baldwin (Standley and Pratt, eds.), **Retro. Supp. II:** 6

Conversations with Richard Wilbur (Wilbur), **Supp. III Part 2:** 542–543

"Conversation with a Fireman from Brooklyn" (Gallagher), **Supp. XXIV:** 169–170

"Conversation with My Father, A" (Paley), **Supp. VI:** 220

"Conversion of the Jews, The" (P. Roth), **Retro. Supp. II:** 281; **Supp. III Part 2:** 404, 406

Convict, The: Stories (Burke), **Supp. XIV:** 25

"Convicta et Combusta" (J. Scott), **Supp. XVII:** 189

"Convolvulus" (Schott), **Supp. XXIII:** 248

"Convoy" (Weigl), **Supp. XIX:** 278

Conway, Jill, **Supp. I Part 1:** 19

Coode, John, **I:** 132

Cook, Bruce, **Supp. XII:** 130, 131, 133–134

Cook, Captain James, **I:** 2

Cook, Eleanor, **Retro. Supp. I:** 311

Cook, Elisha, **Supp. IV Part 1:** 356

Cook, Elizabeth Christine, **II:** 106

Cook, George Cram "Jig", **Supp. XXI:** 5, 6

Cook, Jessie W., **Supp. XXV:** 278

Cook, Johnny, **Supp. XXIV:** 248

Cook, Mercer, **Supp. IV Part 1:** 368

Cook, Richard, **Supp. XXII:** 158

Cooke, Alistair, **III:** 113, 119, 120

Cooke, Delmar G., **II:** 271

Cooke, Grace MacGowan, **Supp. V:** 285

Cooke, Philip Pendleton, **III:** 420

Cooke, Rose Terry, **II:** 401; **Retro. Supp. II:** 51, 136, 138; **Supp. XIII:** 152

"Cookie" (Taylor), **Supp. V:** 320

"Cookies, The" (Nye), **Supp. XIII:** 281

Cooking of Provincial France, The (M. F. K. Fisher), **Supp. XVII:** 89

Cook-Lynn, Elizabeth, **Supp. IV Part 1:** 325

"Cool Air" (Lovecraft), **Supp. XXV:** 110

Coolbrith, Ina, **I:** 193, 196

"Coole Park" (Yeats), **Supp. VIII:** 155, 159

"Coole Park and Ballylee" (Yeats), **Supp. VIII:** 156

Cooler by the Lake (Heinemann), **Supp. XXII:** 103, **114**

Cooley, John, **Supp. V:** 214

Cooley, Peter, **Supp. XIII:** 76

Coolidge, Calvin, **I:** 498; **II:** 95; **Supp. I Part 2:** 647

Cooling Time: An American Poetry Vigil (Wright), **Supp. XV:** 353

"Cool Million, A" (screen story) (West and Ingster), **Retro. Supp. II:** 330

Cool Million, A (West), **III:** 425; **IV:** 287, 288, 297–299, 300; **Retro. Supp. II:** 321, 322–323, 328, **335–337**

"Cool Tombs" (Sandburg), **III:** 554

Coon, Ross, **IV:** 196

Cooney, Seamus, **Supp. XIV:** 289

"Coon Hunt" (White), **Supp. I Part 2:** 669

Co-op (Sinclair), **Supp. V:** 290

Cooper, Bernard, **Supp. XI:** 129

Cooper, Frederic Taber, **Supp. XX: 219–220; Supp. XXIV:** 28–29

Cooper, Gary, **Supp. IV Part 2:** 524

Cooper, James Fenimore, **I:** 211, 257, **335–357; II:** 74, 277, 295–296, 302, 306, 309, 313, 314; **III:** 51; **IV:** 205, 333; **Retro. Supp. I:** 246; **Retro. Supp. II:** 160; **Supp. I Part 1:** 141, 155, 156, 158, 171, 372; **Supp. I Part 2:** 413, 495, 579, 585, 652, 660; **Supp. IV Part 1:** 80; **Supp. IV Part 2:** 463, 469; **Supp. V:** 209–210; **Supp. VIII:** 189; **Supp. XIV:** 227; **Supp. XVIII:** 4; **Supp. XXIII:** 178

Cooper, Mrs. James Fenimore (Susan A. De Lancey), **I:** 338, 351, 354

Cooper, Jane, **Supp. XV:** 259

Cooper, Rand Richards, **Supp. XVI:** 74

Cooper, Susan Fenimore, **I:** 337, 354

Cooper, William, **I:** 337–338, 351

Cooper, Mrs. William, **I:** 337

Cooperman, Robert, **Supp. XXIII:** 247

Coover, Robert, **Supp. IV Part 1:** 388; **Supp. V: 39–55; Supp. XII:** 152; **Supp. XIV:** 96; **Supp. XVII:** 6; **Supp. XXI:** 236; **Supp. XXII:** 259

Copacetic (Komunyakaa), **Supp. XIII: 116–118,** 126

Cope, Wendy, **Supp. XV:** 117

Copelin, David, **Supp. XXIV:** 264

Copland, Aaron, **II:** 586; **Supp. I Part 1:** 281; **Supp. III Part 2:** 619; **Supp. IV Part 1:** 79, 80–81, 84; **Supp. XXII:** 283

Coplas de Don Jorge Manrique (Longfellow, trans.), **II:** 488, 492

Coppée, François Edouard Joachim, **II:** 325

Copperhead, The (Frederic), **II:** 134–135

Copperhead Cane (J. W. Miller), **Supp. XX: 163, 164, 166–167**

Copper Sun (Cullen), **Supp. IV Part 1:** 167, 168

Coppola, Francis Ford, **Supp. XI:** 171, 172; **Supp. XII:** 75

Coprolites (Goldbarth), **Supp. XII: 177–178,** 180, 183

Coquette, The (Foster), **Supp. XXV:** 35, 36, 38–45

Coral and Captive Israel (Reznikoff), **Supp. XIV:** 288

"Coral Ring, The" (Stowe), **Supp. I Part 2:** 586

"Cora Unashamed" (Hughes), **Supp. I Part 1:** 329, 330

"Corazón del Corrido" (Mora), **Supp. XIII:** 225

Corban Ephphata (Li Lin Lee), **Supp. XV:** 225

Corbett, Gentlemen Jim, **II:** 416

Corbett, William, **Supp. XI:** 248; **Supp. XVI:** 286, 295; **Supp. XXIV:** 45

Corbière, Jean Antoine, **II:** 354–355, 528

Cordiall Water, A: A garland of Odd & Old Receipts to Assuage the Ills of Man and Beast (M. F. K. Fisher), **Supp. XVII:** 88, 90

Cording, Robert, **Supp. IX:** 328; **Supp. XII:** 184

Core, George, **Supp. XVIII:** 86; **Supp. XXI:** 193

Corelli, Marie, **III:** 579

Corey, Lewis, **Supp. I Part 2:** 645

"Corinna's Going a-Maying" (Herrick), **Supp. XIV:** 8, 9

"Coriolan" (Eliot), **I:** 580

"Coriolanus and His Mother" (Schwartz), **Supp. II Part 2:** 643, 644–645

"Corkscrew" (Hammett), **Supp. IV Part 1:** 345, 347

Corkum, Gerald, **I:** 37

Corky's Brother (Neugeboren), **Supp. XVI:** 225

"Corky's Brother" (Neugeboren), **Supp. XVI:** 225

Corliss, Richard, **Supp. VIII:** 73

Corman, Cid, **Supp. III Part 2:** 624, 625, 626, 627, 628; **Supp. IV Part 1:** 144; **Supp. VIII:** 292; **Supp. XV:** 74, 153; **Supp. XXI:** 23, 27

Corman, Roger, **Supp. XXV:** 154

"Corn" (Lanier), **Supp. I Part 1:** 352, 353, 354, 356–361, 364, 366

Corn, Alfred, **Supp. IX:** 156; **Supp. XV:** 250

Corneille, Pierre, **Supp. I Part 2:** 716; **Supp. IX:** 131

Cornell, Esther, **I:** 231

Cornell, Joseph, **Supp. XXI:** 131; **Supp. XXII:** 167, 168

Cornell, Katherine, **IV:** 356

Cornell, Valerie, **Supp. XX: 94–95**

"Corners" (Dunn), **Supp. XI:** 148

Cornhuskers (Sandburg), **III:** 583–585

"Corn-Planting, The" (Anderson), **I:** 114

"Corn story (or the origin of corn)"(J. Schoolcraft), **Supp. XXIII:** 234–235

Cornucopia: New and Selected Poems, 1975–2002 (Peacock), **Supp. XIX: 203–204**

Corn Village (Le Sueur), **Supp. XXIII:** 167

Coronation Murder-Mystery, The (O'Hara, Ashbery, and Koch), **Supp. XXIII:** 217

"Coroner's Report" (Wrigley), **Supp. XVIII:** 295

"Corporal of Artillery" (Dubus), **Supp. VII:** 84, 85

"Corpse Plant, The" (Rich), **Supp. I Part 2:** 555

Corpus Christi (McNally), **Supp. XIII: 205–206,** 209

Corradi, Juan, **Supp. IV Part 1:** 208

Corrections, The (Franzen), **Supp. XIX:** 54; **Supp. XX: 83, 84, 85, 90, 91, 91–93, 95**

Corregidora (G. Jones), **Supp. XXIV:** 183–184, **185–187,** 190, 193, 194, 195

"Correspondences" (Baudelaire), **I:** 63

"Corrido de Gregorio Cortez" (Mora), **Supp. XIII:** 225

"Corrigenda" (Komunyakaa), **Supp. XIII:** 115, 116

Corrosive Sublimate (Sorrentino), **Supp. XXI:** 226, 228

Corruption City (McCoy), **Supp. XIII:** 175

Corso, Gregory, **Supp. II Part 1:** 30; **Supp. IV Part 1:** 90; **Supp. XII: 117–138; Supp. XIV:** 150; **Supp. XVI:** 135; **Supp. XXI:** 53; **Supp. XXIII:** 215

Corsons Inlet (Ammons), **Supp. VII:** 25–26, 28–29, 36

"Corsons Inlet" (Ammons), **Supp. VII:** 25–26

Cortázar, Julio, **Retro. Supp. I:** 278; **Supp. XXII:** 265

"Cortège for Rosenbloom" (Stevens), **IV:** 81

Cortez, Hernando, **III:** 2

" 'Coruscating Glamour': Lynda Hull and the Movies" (Goldstein), **Supp. XXI:** 134

Cory, William Johnson, **Supp. XX: 230, 231**

Coser, Lewis, **Supp. I Part 2:** 650

Cosgrave, Patrick, **Retro. Supp. II:** 185

Cosmic Optimism: A Study of the Interpretation of Evolution by American Poets from Emerson to Robinson (Conner), **Supp. I Part 1:** 73

Cosmological Eye, The (H. Miller), **III:** 174, 184

"Cosmological Eye, The" (H. Miller), **III:** 183

"Cosmos" (Beattie), **Supp. V:** 35

"Cost, The" (Hecht), **Supp. X:** 62–63

Costello, Bonnie, **Retro. Supp. II:** 40

Costello, Mark, **Supp. XXIII:** 290

Costner, Kevin, **Supp. VIII:** 45

"Cost of Living, The" (Malamud), **Supp. I Part 2:** 429, 437

"Costume as Metaphor" (Bronk), **Supp. XXI:** 26

Cott, Jonathan, **Supp. XVI:** 104, 106

"Cottagers' Corner" column (D. West), **Supp. XVIII:** 286

"Cottage Street, 1953" (Wilbur), **Supp. III Part 2:** 543, 561

"Cottagette, The" (Gilman), **Supp. XI:** 207

Cotten, Joseph, **Supp. IV Part 2:** 524

Cotter, James Finn, **Supp. X:** 202

Cotton, John, **Supp. I Part 1:** 98, 101, 110, 111, 116

Cotton, Joseph, **Supp. XII:** 160

Cotton, Seaborn, **Supp. I Part 1:** 101

Cotton Club, The (Major), **Supp. XXII:** 174

"Cotton Club Classics" (Halliday), **Supp. XIX:** 92, 93

Cotton Comes to Harlem (C. Himes), **Supp. XVI:** 143, 144

Cotton Comes to Harlem (film, O. Davis), **Supp. XVI:** 144

"Cotton Song" (Toomer), **Supp. IX:** 312

Couch, W. T., **Supp. X:** 46

Coughlin, Ruth Pollack, **Supp. VIII:** 45

Coulette, Henri, **Supp. V:** 180; **Supp. XIII:** 312; **Supp. XV:** 74, 75

Coultrap-McQuin, Susan, **Supp. XVI:** 85, 92

"Council of State, A" (Dunbar), **Supp. II Part 1:** 211, 213

Count Bruga (Hecht), **Supp. XXV:** 27

"Count Dracula" (Allen), **Supp. XV:** 15

"Countee Cullen at 'The Heights' " (Tuttleton), **Supp. IV Part 1:** 166

Counterfeiters, The (Gide), **Supp. IV Part 1:** 80; **Supp. IV Part 2:** 681

"Countering" (Ammons), **Supp. VII:** 28

Counterlife, The (P. Roth), **Retro. Supp. II:** 279, 280, 291; **Supp. III Part 2:** 424–426

Counter-Statement (Burke), **I:** 270–272; **IV:** 431

"Countess, The" (Whittier), **Supp. I Part 2:** 691, 694

Count Frontenac and New France Under Louis XIV (Parkman), **Supp. II Part 2:** 607, 609–610

"Counting Small-Boned Bodies" (R. Bly), **Supp. IV Part 1:** 62

"Counting the Body"(Schott), **Supp. XXIII:** 251–252

"Counting the Children" (Gioia), **Supp. XV: 122–123**

"Counting the Mad" (Justice), **Supp. VII:** 117

"Count Lothar's Heart" (Boyle), **Supp. XXIV:** 58

Count of Monte Cristo, The (Dumas), **III:** 386, 396; **Supp. XVII:** 64, 216

"Countries We Live In, The" (Zach; Everwine, trans.), **Supp. XV:** 87

"Country Boy in Boston, The" (Howells), **II:** 255

Country By-Ways (Jewett), **II:** 402

Country Doctor, A (Jewett), **II:** 391, 392, 396, 404–405; **Retro. Supp. II:** 131, 141, 146

"Country Full of Swedes" (Caldwell), **I:** 297, 309

Country Girl, The (Odets), **Supp. II Part 2:** 546, 547, 548–549

"Country House" (Kumin), **Supp. IV Part 2:** 446

"Country Husband, The" (Cheever), **Supp. I Part 1:** 184, 189

"Country Life" (Pickering), **Supp. XXI:** 197

"Country Marriage" (C. Frost), **Supp. XV:** 99

Countrymen of Bones (R. O. Butler), **Supp. XII:** 62, **65–66**

"Country Mouse, The" (Bishop), **Retro. Supp. II:** 37, 38, 51

Country Music: Selected Early Poems (Wright), **Supp. V:** 332, 335, 338, 342

Country of a Thousand Years of Peace, The (Merrill), **Supp. III Part 1:** 321, 322, 331

"Country of Elusion, The" (O. Henry), **Supp. II Part 1:** 407

Country Of Language, The (Sanders), **Supp. XVI:** 277

Country of Marriage, The (Berry), **Supp. X:** 33

Country of Strangers, A (Richter), **Supp. XVIII:** 217

Country of Survivors (Di Piero), **Supp. XIX:** 36

Country of the Pointed Firs, The (Jewett), **II:** 392, 399, 405, 409–411; **Retro. Supp. I:** 6; **Retro. Supp. II:** 134, 136, 139, 140, 141, 145, 146, 147; **Supp. VIII:** 126; **Supp. XIII:** 152; **Supp. XXIII:** 275, 278

"Country Printer, The" (Freneau), **Supp. II Part 1:** 269

"Country Song" (Stallings), **Supp. XXV:** 222, 234

"Country Wife, The" (Gioia), **Supp. XV:** 120

Count Your Bullets (film), **Supp. XVII:** 141

Count Zero (W. Gibson), **Supp. XVI:** 19, **126–127,** 129

Coup, The (Updike), **Retro. Supp. I:** 331, 334, 335

"Coup de Grâce, The" (Bierce), **I:** 202

Couperin, François, **III:** 464

"Couple, The" (Olds), **Supp. X:** 206

"Couple of Hamburgers, A" (Thurber), **Supp. I Part 2:** 616

"Couple of Nuts, A" (Z. Fitzgerald), **Supp. IX:** 58, 71, 72

"Couples" (Halliday), **Supp. XIX:** 89

Couples (Updike), **IV:** 214, 215, 216, 217, 227, 229–230; **Retro. Supp. I:** 320, 327, 330; **Supp. XII:** 296

Cournos, John, **III:** 465; **Supp. I Part 1:** 258

"Course in Creative Writing, A" (Stafford), **Supp. XI:** 327

"Course of a Particular, The" (Stevens), **Retro. Supp. I:** 312

"Coursier de Jeanne d'Arc, Le" (McCarriston), **Supp. XIV:** 267–268

Courtier, The (Castiglione), **III:** 282

" 'Courtin,' The" (Lowell), **Supp. I Part 2:** 415

"Courting of Sister Wisby, The" (Jewett), **Retro. Supp. II:** 134, 135, 146

"Courting the Famous Figures at the Grotto of Improbable Thought" (B. Kelly), **Supp. XVII:** 127–128

Courtney, W. L., **Supp. XXIV:** 29

"Courtship" (Dove), **Supp. IV Part 1:** 248

"Courtship, A"(Thompson), **Supp. XXIII:** 293

"Courtship, Diligence" (Dove), **Supp. IV Part 1:** 248

Courtship of Miles Standish, The (Longfellow), **II:** 489, 502–503; **Retro. Supp. II:** 155, **161–162,** 163, 166, 168

"Cousin Aubrey" (Taylor), **Supp. V:** 328

Cousine Bette (Balzac), **Retro. Supp. II:** 98

Couturier, Maurice, **Supp. IV Part 1:** 44

Covarrubias, Miguel, **Supp. XVI:** 187

"Covered Bridges" (Kingsolver), **Supp. VII:** 203

"Cover Photograph" (Nelson), **Supp. XVIII:** 173

"Cover Stories" (Skloot), **Supp. XX: 195, 207**

"Cover Versions" (Halliday), **Supp. XIX:** 84

Cowan, Lester, **III:** 148

Cowan, Louise, **IV:** 120, 125

Coward, Noel, **Retro. Supp. I:** 65; **Supp. I Part 1:** 332; **Supp. V:** 101; **Supp. XV:** 329; **Supp. XXIV:** 267

"Cowardice" (Theroux), **Supp. VIII:** 313

Cowboy Mouth (Shepard), **Supp. III Part 2:** 441–442

"Cowboys" (Salter). *See* "Dirt" (Salter)

Cowboys (Shepard), **Supp. III Part 2:** 432

Cowboys #2 (Shepard), **Supp. III Part 2:** 437, 438

Cowell, Henry, **Supp. IV Part 1:** 80, 82

Cowen, Philip, **Supp. XX:** 2

Cowen, Wilson Walker, **Supp. IV Part 2:** 435

Cowie, Alexander, **IV:** 70

"Cow in Apple Time, The" (Frost), **II:** 154; **Retro. Supp. I:** 131

Cowl, Jane, **IV:** 357

Cowley, Abraham, **III:** 508; **IV:** 158; **Supp. I Part 1:** 357

Cowley, Malcolm, **I:** 246, 253, 254, 255, 256, 257, 283, 385; **II:** 26, 57, 94, 456; **III:** 606; **IV:** 123; **Retro. Supp. I:** 73, 91, 97; **Retro. Supp. II:** 77, 83, 89, 221, 330; **Supp. I Part 1:** 174; **Supp. I Part 2:** 609, 610, 620, 647, 654, 678; **Supp. II Part 1:** 103, **135–156; Supp. VIII:** 96; **Supp. XV:** 142; **Supp. XX:** 76

Cowley, Marguerite Frances Baird (Mrs. Malcolm Cowley), **Supp. I Part 2:** 615; **Supp. II Part 1:** 138, 139

Cowley, Muriel Maurer (Mrs. Malcolm Cowley), **Supp. II Part 1:** 139

Cowley, Susan Cheever (Susan Cheever), **Supp. I Part 1:** 175; **Supp. IX:** 133; **Supp. XXIV:** 97

Cowper, William, **II:** 17, 304; **III:** 508, 511; **Supp. I Part 1:** 150, 151, 152; **Supp. I Part 2:** 539

"Cow Wandering in the Bare Field, The" (Jarrell), **II:** 371, 388

Cox, Martha Heasley, **Supp. IX:** 2, 4, 11–12

Cox, Sidney, **Retro. Supp. I:** 131; **Supp. XXI:** 19, 21

Cox, Stephen, **Supp. IV Part 2:** 523, 524

Cox, Steve, **Supp. XIX:** 116, 128

Coxey, Jacob, **II:** 464

"Coxon Fund, The" (James), **Retro. Supp. I:** 228

"Coy Mistress" (A. Finch), **Supp. XVII:** 72

Coyne, Patricia, **Supp. V:** 123

"Coyote Ortiz: *Canis latrans latrans* in the Poetry of Simon Ortiz" (P. C. Smith), **Supp. IV Part 2:** 509

Coyote's Daylight Trip (Gunn Allen), **Supp. IV Part 1:** 320, 324

Coyote Was Here (Ortiz), **Supp. IV Part 2:** 499

Cozzens, James Gould, **I: 358–380; II:** 459

Crabbe, George, **II:** 304; **III:** 469, 508, 511, 521; **Supp. XXIV:** 159

"Crab-Boil" (Dove), **Supp. IV Part 1:** 249

"Cracked Looking-Glass, The" (Porter), **III:** 434, 435, 446

"Cracker Chidlings" (Rawlings), **Supp. X:** 224, 228

Cracks (Purdy), **Supp. VII:** 277–278

Crack-Up, The (Fitzgerald), **II:** 80; **III:** 35, 45; **Retro. Supp. I:** 113, 115; **Supp. V:** 276; **Supp. IX:** 61

"Crack-Up, The" (Fitzgerald), **I:** 509; **Retro. Supp. I:** 113, 114

"Crack-up of American Optimism, The: Vachel Lindsay, the Dante of the Fundamentalists" (Viereck), **Supp. I Part 2:** 403

"Cradle and the Bookcase, The"(Hadas), **Supp. XXIII:** 122

Cradle Will Rock, The (Blitzstein), **Supp. I Part 1:** 277, 278

Craft of Fiction, The (Lubbock), **I:** 504; **Supp. VIII:** 165

Craft of Peter Taylor, The (McAlexander, ed.), **Supp. V:** 314

Craig, David M., **Supp. XXII:** 187, 191, 192

Craig, Gordon, **III:** 394; **Supp. XXI:** 6

Crain, Jane Larkin, **Supp. V:** 123; **Supp. XII:** 167, 168

Crais, Robert, **Supp. XXI:** 70

Cram, Ralph Adams, **I:** 19

Cramer, Steven, **Supp. XI:** 139; **Supp. XV:** 26

"Cranbrook Schools: Adventures in Bourgeois Topologies" (Monson), **Supp. XXIV:** 235

Crandall, Reuben, **Supp. I Part 2:** 686

Crane, Agnes, **I:** 406

Crane, Edmund, **I:** 407

Crane, Hart, **I:** 61, 62, 97, 109, 116, 266, **381–404; II:** 133, 215, 306, 368, 371, 536, 542; **III:** 260, 276, 453, 485, 521; **IV:** 122, 123–124, 127, 128, 129, 135, 139, 140, 141, 341, 380, 418, 419; **Retro. Supp. I:** 427; **Retro. Supp. II: 75–91; Supp. I Part 1:** 86; **Supp. II Part 1:** 89, 152; **Supp. III Part 1:** 20, 63, 350; **Supp. V:** 342; **Supp. VIII:** 39; **Supp. IX:** 38, 229, 320; **Supp. X:** 115, 116, 120; **Supp. XI:** 123, 131; **Supp. XII:** 198; **Supp. XV:** 138; **Supp. XIX:** 35; **Supp. XX: 80; Supp. XXI:** 131, 132, 136, 230; **Supp. XXII:** 274; **Supp. XXIII:** 146, 174, 207; **Supp. XXV:** 19

Crane, Jonathan, Jr., **I:** 407

Crane, Jonathan Townley, **I:** 406

Crane, Mrs. Jonathan Townley, **I:** 406

Crane, Luther, **I:** 406

Crane, Milton, **Supp. XV:** 144
Crane, Nellie, **I:** 407
Crane, R. S., **Supp. I Part 2:** 423
Crane, Stephen, **I:** 34, 169–170, 201, 207, 211, **405–427,** 477, 506, 519; **II:** 58, 144, 198, 262, 263, 264, 276, 289, 290, 291; **III:** 314, 317, 334, 335, 454, 505, 585; **IV:** 207, 208, 256, 350, 475; **Retro. Supp. I:** 231, 325; **Retro. Supp. II:** 97, 123; **Supp. I Part 1:** 314; **Supp. III Part 2:** 412; **Supp. IV Part 1:** 350, 380; **Supp. IV Part 2:** 680, 689, 692; **Supp. VIII:** 98, 105; **Supp. IX:** 1, 14; **Supp. X:** 223; **Supp. XI:** 95; **Supp. XII:** 50; **Supp. XIV:** 21, 50, 51, 227; **Supp. XVII:** 71, 228; **Supp. XVIII:** 74, 75; **Supp. XXIII:** 26
Crane, William, **I:** 407
Cranford (Gaskell), **Supp. IX:** 79
Crashaw, William, **IV:** 145, 150, 151, 165
"Crash Report" (McGrath), **Supp. X:** 116
Crater, The (Cooper), **I:** 354, 355
Cratylus (Plato), **II:** 10
Cravan, Arthur, **Supp. XXII:** 164, 169
"Craven Street Gazette" (Franklin), **II:** 119
"Crawdad, The" (F. Wright), **Supp. XVII:** 244
Crawdad Creek (Sanders), **Supp. XVI:** 269
Crawford, Brad, **Supp. XI:** 133
Crawford, Eva, **I:** 199
Crawford, F. Marion, **III:** 320
Crawford, Joan, **Supp. I Part 1:** 67
Crawford, John E., **Supp. XXIII:** 165
Crawford, Kathleen, **I:** 289
"Crayon House" (Rukeyser), **Supp. VI:** 273
Crayon Miscellany, The (Irving), **II:** 312–313
Crazed, The (Jin), **Supp. XVIII: 99–100**
"Crazy about her Shrimp" (Simic), **Supp. VIII:** 282
"Crazy Cock" (H. Miller), **III:** 177
Crazy Gypsy (Salinas), **Supp. XIII:** 311, **313–315,** 316
"Crazy Gypsy" (Salinas), **Supp. XIII:** 313–314
Crazy Horse, **Supp. IV Part 2:** 488, 489
Crazy Horse (McMurtry), **Supp. V:** 233
Crazy Horse in Stillness (Heyen), **Supp. XIII:** 344
Crazy Horse: The Strange Man of the Oglaglas (Sandoz), **Supp. XXIV:** 244, 256, **257–258**
"Crazy Hunter, The" (Boyle), **Supp. XXIV: 54–55**
Crazy Hunter, The: Three Short Novels (Boyle), **Supp. XXIV: 54–56**
"Crazy in the Stir" (C. Himes), **Supp. XVI:** 137
Crazy Kill, The (C. Himes), **Supp. XVI:** 143
Crazy Man (Bodenheim), **Supp. XXV:** 22, 24
Creating a Role (Stanislavsky), **Supp. XIV:** 243
"Creation, According to Coyote, The" (Ortiz), **Supp. IV Part 2:** 505

Creation: A Novel (Vidal), **Supp. IV Part 2:** 677, 685, 688
"Creation of Anguish" (Nemerov), **III:** 269
"Creation Story" (Gunn Allen), **Supp. IV Part 1:** 325
"Creative and Cultural Lag" (Ellison), **Retro. Supp. II:** 116; **Supp. II Part 1:** 229; **Supp. XVIII:** 283
Creative Criticism (Spingarn), **I:** 266
"Creative Democracy" (Locke), **Supp. XIV:** 208
Creative Present, The (Balkian and Simmons, eds.), **Supp. XI:** 230
"Creatures" (Gallagher), **Supp. XXIV:** 176, 177
Creatures in an Alphabet (illus. Barnes), **Supp. III Part 1:** 43
"Credences of Summer" (Stevens), **IV:** 93–94
"Credentials" (Halliday), **Supp. XIX:** 90
"Credo" (Bynner), **Supp. XV:** 50
"Credo" (Du Bois), **Supp. II Part 1:** 169
"Credo" (Jeffers), **Supp. II Part 2:** 424
"Credos and Curios" (Thurber), **Supp. I Part 2:** 606, 613
Creech, James, **Retro. Supp. I:** 254
"Creed for Americans, A" (Benét), **Supp. XI:** 52
"Creed of a Beggar, The" (Lindsay), **Supp. I Part 2:** 379
Creegan, Andy, **Supp. XIX:** 205
Creekmore, Hubert, **II:** 586
Creeley, Robert, **Retro. Supp. I:** 411; **Supp. II Part 1:** 30; **Supp. III Part 1:** 2; **Supp. III Part 2:** 622, 626, 629; **Supp. IV Part 1: 139–161,** 322, 325; **Supp. XI:** 317; **Supp. XIII:** 104, 112; **Supp. XIV:** 150; **Supp. XVI:** 283; **Supp. XXI:** 23, 27, 227, 230; **Supp. XXII:** 227; **Supp. XXIV:** 35, 37
Creelman, James Ashmore, **Supp. XVI:** 186–187
"Cremona Violin, The" (Lowell), **II:** 523
"Crêpe de Chine" (Doty), **Supp. XI:** 128
"Crêpes Flambeau" (Gallagher), **Supp. XXIV:** 170
"Cressy" (Harte), **Supp. II Part 1:** 354, 356
"Cretan Woman, The" (Jeffers), **Supp. II Part 2:** 435
Crèvecoeur, Michel-Guillaume Jean de, **I:** 229; **Supp. I Part 1: 227–252**
Crèvecoeur's Eighteenth-Century Travels in Pennsylvania and New York (Adams), **Supp. I Part 1:** 251
Crevel, René, **Supp. XIV:** 343
Crewe-Jones, Florence, **Supp. XVII:** 58
Crewe Train (Macaulay), **Supp. XII:** 88
Crews, Harry, **Supp. X:** 11, 12; **Supp. XI: 99–117,** 245; **Supp. XVIII:** 195; **Supp. XXI:** 35, 38, 40, 44
Crews, James, **Supp. XXIII:** 134–135
Crichton, Michael, **Supp. XIV:** 316
Crick, Philip, **Supp. XVI:** 289
Cricket (C. L. R. James; Grimshaw, ed.), **Supp. XXI:** 172
"Cricket" (C. Miller), **Supp. XXII:** 199
"Crickets" (R. O. Butler), **Supp. XII:** 71

Criers and Kibitzers, Kibitzers and Criers (Elkin), **Supp. VI: 45–46,** 57
Crime and Punishment (Dostoevsky), **II:** 60, 130; **IV:** 484; **Supp. IV Part 2:** 525; **Supp. VIII:** 282; **Supp. XII:** 281; **Supp. XVII:** 155; **Supp. XVIII:** 278; **Supp. XIX:** 276
Crime at Scottsboro, The (Endore), **Supp. XVII:** 59
Crime Beat (Connelly), **Supp. XXI:** 67, 79
Crimes and Misdemeanors (film; Allen), **Supp. XV:** 1, 2, **11,** 12
"Criminal"(Strout), **Supp. XXIII:** 283, 285
Crisis papers (Paine), **Supp. I Part 2:** 508–509, 510
"Criteria of Negro Art" (Du Bois), **Supp. II Part 1:** 181; **Supp. XIX:** 66–67
"Critiad, The" (Winters), **Supp. II Part 2:** 794, 799
Critical Anthology A (Untermeyer), **Supp. XV:** 310
Critical Essays on Charlotte Perkins Gilman (Karpinski, ed.), **Supp. XI:** 201
Critical Essays on Kay Boyle (Elkins, ed.), **Supp. XXIV:** 64
Critical Essays on Peter Taylor (McAlexander), **Supp. V:** 319, 320, 323–324
Critical Essays on Robert Bly (W. V. Davis), **Supp. IV Part 1:** 64, 69
Critical Essays on Wallace Stegner (Arthur), **Supp. IV Part 2:** 606
Critical Fable, A (Lowell), **II:** 511–512, 527, 529–530
Critical Guide to Leaves of Grass, A (J. Miller), **IV:** 352
Critical Mass (Paretsky), **Supp. XXV:** 185
Critical Response to Joan Didion, The (Felton), **Supp. IV Part 1:** 210
Critical Temper of Alain Locke, The: A Selection of His Essays on Art and Culture (Stewart, ed.), **Supp. XIV:** 196, **210–211,** 213
"Critic as Artist, The" (Wilde), **Supp. X:** 189
Criticism and Fiction (Howells), **II:** 288
Criticism and Ideology (Eagleton), **Retro. Supp. I:** 67
Criticism in the Borderlands (Calderón and Saldívar, eds.), **Supp. IV Part 2:** 544
"Critics, The" (Jong), **Supp. V:** 119
"Critics and Connoisseurs" (Moore), **III:** 209
Critic's Notebook, A (Howe), **Supp. VI:** 126–128
"Critic's Task, The" (Kazin), **Supp. VIII:** 103
"Critic Who Does Not Exist, The" (Wilson), **IV:** 431
"Critique de la Vie Quotidienne" (Barthelme), **Supp. IV Part 1:** 50
Critique of Pure Reason (Kant), **Supp. XVI:** 184
Croce, Benedetto, **I:** 58, 255, 265, 273, 281; **III:** 610

Crockett, Davy, **II:** 307; **III:** 227; **IV:** 266; **Supp. I Part 2:** 411

"Crocodilopolis" (Cliff), **Supp. XXII:** 76

Crofter and the Laird, The (McPhee), **Supp. III Part 1:** 301–302, 307

Croly, Herbert, **I:** 229, 231, 235; **IV:** 436

Cromwell, Oliver, **IV:** 145, 146, 156; **Supp. I Part 1:** 111

Cronenberg, David, **Supp. XXI:** 152, 154

Cronin, A. J., **Supp. XVII:** 59

Cronin, Dr. Archibald, **III:** 578

Cronin, Justin, **Supp. X:** 10

Crooke, Dr. Helkiah, **Supp. I Part 1:** 98, 104

Crooked Little Heart (Lamott), **Supp. XX: 138**

Crooker, Barbara, **Supp. XXIII: 51–66,** 245, 246, 251

Crooks, Alan, **Supp. V:** 226

Crooks, Robert, **Supp. XIII:** 237

"Crop, The" (O'Connor), **Retro. Supp. II:** 223–225

Crosby, Caresse, **I:** 385; **III:** 473; **Retro. Supp. II:** 85; **Supp. XII:** 198

Crosby, Harry, **I:** 385; **Retro. Supp. II:** 85

"Cross" (Hughes), **Supp. I Part 1:** 325; **Supp. XVIII:** 124

Cross, Charles, **Supp. XXIV:** 173

Crossan, John Dominic, **Supp. V:** 251

"Cross Country Snow" (Hemingway), **II:** 249

Cross Creek (Rawlings), **Supp. X:** 223, 226, 228, **231–232,** 233, 234, 235

Cross Creek Cookery (Rawlings), **Supp. X:** 233

Crossing, The (McCarthy), **Supp. VIII:** 175, **184–186**

"Crossing, The" (Swenson), **Supp. IV Part 2:** 644

"Crossing Brooklyn Ferry" (Whitman), **IV:** 333, 340, 341; **Retro. Supp. I:** 389, 396, 397, 400–401; **Supp. XXIII:** 109

"Crossing into Poland" (Babel), **Supp. XIV:** 84

Crossings (Chuang), **Supp. X:** 291

"Crossings" (Hogan), **Supp. IV Part 1:** 412

Crossing the Water (Plath), **Retro. Supp. II:** 248; **Supp. I Part 2:** 526, 538

Crossing to Safety (Stegner), **Supp. IV Part 2:** 599, 606, 612, 613–614

"Cross of Snow, The" (Longfellow), **II:** 490; **Retro. Supp. II:** 169–170

"Crossover" (O. Butler), **Supp. XIII:** 61

"Cross-Roads, The" (Lowell), **II:** 523

"Crossroads of the World Etc." (Merwin), **Supp. III Part 1:** 347, 348

Cross-Section (Seaver), **IV:** 485

Cross the Border, Close the Gap (Fiedler), **Supp. XIII:** 104

Cross Ties (X. J. Kennedy), **Supp. XV:** 165, **166–167**

"Cross Ties" (X. J. Kennedy), **Supp. XV:** 158

Crouch, Stanley, **Supp. XIX:** 158

"Croup" (Karr), **Supp. XI:** 243

Crouse, Russel, **III:** 284

"Crow" (Hogan), **Supp. IV Part 1:** 405

Crow (Hughes), **Supp. XV:** 347, 348

"Crow, The" (Creeley), **Supp. IV Part 1:** 148–149

Crow and the Heart,The (Carruth), **Supp. XVI:** 47–48

"Crowded Street, The" (Bryant), **Supp. I Part 1:** 168

Crowder, A. B., **Supp. XI:** 107

"Crow Jane" (Baraka), **Supp. II Part 1:** 38

Crow Mercies (Schott), **Supp. XXIII: 252–254**

"Crow Mercies" (Schott), **Supp. XXIII:** 253

Crowninshield, Frank, **III:** 123; **Supp. IX:** 201

Crown of Columbus (Erdrich and Dorris), **Supp. IV Part 1:** 260

"Crows, The" (Bogan), **Supp. III Part 1:** 50, 51

Crucial Instances (Wharton), **Retro. Supp. I:** 365, 367

Crucible, The (A. Miller), **III:** 147, 148, 155, 156–158, 159, 166; **Supp. XIII:** 206; **Supp. XXV:** 93

"Crucified" (Gibran), **Supp. XX: 119**

"Crucifix in the Filing Cabinet" (Shapiro), **Supp. II Part 2:** 712

"Crude Foyer" (Stevens), **Retro. Supp. I:** 310

"Cruel and Barbarous Treatment" (McCarthy), **II:** 562, 563

"Cruel Mother, The" (B. Kelly), **Supp. XVII:** 126

Cruise of the Dazzler, The (London), **II:** 465

Cruise of the Snark, The (London), **II:** 476–477; **Supp. XXV:** 217

"Cruising with the Beach Boys" (Gioia), **Supp. XV:** 118

" 'Crumbling Idols' by Hamlin Garland" (Chopin), **Supp. I Part 1:** 217

"Crusade of the Excelsior, The" (Harte), **Supp. II Part 1:** 336, 354

"Crusoe in England" (Bishop), **Retro. Supp. II:** 50; **Supp. I Part 1:** 93, 95, 96; **Supp. III Part 1:** 10, 18

Cruz-Hacker, Alba, **Supp. XXI:** 107

Cry, the Beloved Country (Paton), **Supp. VIII:** 126

Cryer, Dan, **Supp. VIII:** 86, 88; **Supp. XII:** 164

Crying of Lot 49, The (Pynchon), **Supp. II Part 2:** 618, 619, 621, 630–633

"Crying Sisters, The" (Rand), **Supp. IV Part 2:** 524

"Crying Wolf" (C. Frost), **Supp. XV:** 101

"Cry of the Graves, The" (Gibran), **Supp. XX: 124**

Cryptogram, The (Mamet), **Supp. XIV:** 240, 247, 255

"Crystal, The" (Aiken), **I:** 60

"Crystal, The" (Lanier), **Supp. I Part 1:** 364, 370

"Crystal Cage, The" (Kunitz), **Supp. III Part 1:** 258

Crystal Cup, The (Atherton), **Supp. XXIV:** 26

Crystal Vision (Sorrentino), **Supp. XXI:** 235, 236

"Crytal" (Sobin), **Supp. XVI:** 283

Cry to Heaven (Rice), **Supp. VII:** 300–301

"Cuba" (Hemingway), **II:** 258

"Cuba Libre" (Baraka), **Supp. II Part 1:** 33

Cuba: Prophetic Island (W. Frank), **Supp. XX: 80, 81**

"Cubism, Barcelona" (Hull), **Supp. XXI:** 137

Cudjoe, Selwyn, **Supp. IV Part 1:** 6

"Cudjo's Own Story of the Last American Slaver" (Hurston), **Supp. VI:** 153

Cudlipp, Thelma, **I:** 501

Cudworth, Ralph, **II:** 9, 10

"Cuentista" (Mora), **Supp. XIII:** 224

"Cuento de agua santa, Un" (Mora), **Supp. XIII:** 224

Cujo (King), **Supp. V:** 138–139, 143, 149, 152

Cukor, George, **Supp. XVI:** 192

Cullen, Countee, **Retro. Supp. I:** 207; **Retro. Supp. II:** 114; **Supp. I Part 1:** 49, 325; **Supp. III Part 1:** 73, 75, 76; **Supp. IV Part 1: 163–174; Supp. IX:** 306, 309; **Supp. X:** 136, 140; **Supp. XIII:** 186; **Supp. XVIII:** 122,131, 185, 279, 280, 282, 284; **Supp. XIX:** 78; **Supp. XXII:** 3, 6, 7, 8

"Cultivation of Christmas Trees, The" (Eliot), **I:** 579

Cult of Alien Gods, The: H. P. Lovecraft and Extraterrestrial Pop Culture (Calavito), **Supp. XXV:** 123

"Cult of Personality in American Letters, The" (Swados), **Supp. XIX:** 265

"Cult of the Best, The" (Arnold), **I:** 223

"Cultural Exchange" (Hughes), **Supp. I Part 1:** 341

"Cultural Pluralism: A New Americanism" (Locke), **Supp. XIV:** 195

"Cultural Relativism and Ideological Peace" (Locke), **Supp. XIV:** 202, 212

"Culture" (Emerson), **III:** 2, 4

"Culture, Self, and Style" (Gass), **Supp. VI:** 88

"Culture and Religion" (Olds), **Supp. X:** 214

Culture of Cities, The (Mumford), **Supp. II Part 2:** 492, 494–495

Cummings, E. E., **I:** 44, 48, 64, 105, 176, **428–450,** 475, 477, 482, 526; **III:** 20, 196, 476; **IV:** 384, 402, 415, 427, 433; **Retro. Supp. II:** 178, 328; **Supp. I Part 2:** 622, 678; **Supp. III Part 1:** 73; **Supp. IV Part 2:** 637, 641; **Supp. IX:** 20; **Supp. XV:** 312, 338

Cummings, Robert, **Supp. IV Part 2:** 524

Cummins, Ann, **Supp. XXIII:** 280

Cummins, James, **Supp. XVII:** 74

Cunard, Lady, **III:** 459

Cunningham, J. V., **Supp. XV:** 169

Cunningham, Merce, **Supp. IV Part 1:** 83; **Supp. XV:** 187

Cunningham, Michael, **Supp. XII:** 80; **Supp. XV: 55–71**

Cunningham, Rodger, **Supp. XXIII:** 38–39

Cup of Gold (Steinbeck), **IV:** 51, 53, 61–64, 67

"Cupola, The" (Bogan), **Supp. III Part 1:** 53

"Curandera" (Mora), **Supp. XIII:** 214, 222

Curé de Tours, Le (Balzac), **I:** 509

Cure for Dreams, A: A Novel (Gibbons), **Supp. X:** 45–47, 48, 50

Curie, Marie, **IV:** 420, 421; **Supp. I Part 2:** 569

Curie, Pierre, **IV:** 420

Curiosa Americana (Mather), **Supp. II Part 2:** 463

Curiosities (Matthews), **Supp. IX:** 151, 152

"Curious Case of Sidd Finch, The" (Plimpton), **Supp. XVI:** 244

"Curious Shifts of the Poor" (Dreiser), **Retro. Supp. II:** 97

"Current" (Espaillat), **Supp. XXI:** 106

"Currents and Counter-Currents in Medical Science" (Holmes), **Supp. I Part 1:** 305

"Curried Cow" (Bierce), **I:** 200

Curry, Professor W. C., **IV:** 122

Curse of the Jade Scorpion, The (film; Allen), **Supp. XV:** 11

Curse of the Starving Class (Shepard), **Supp. III Part 2:** 433, 447–448

Curse of the Werewolf, The (film), **Supp. XVII:** 56

"Curse of Yig, The" (Lovecraft and Bishop), **Supp. XXV:** 122

"Curse on a Thief, A" (X. J. Kennedy), **Supp. XV:** 171

"Curtain, The" (Chandler), **Supp. IV Part 1:** 122

Curtain Calls: British and American Women and the Theater, 1660–1820 (Saar), **Supp. XV:** 237

Curtain of Green, A (Welty), **IV:** 261–264, 268, 283

"Curtain of Green, A" (Welty), **IV:** 263–264

Curtain of Green and Other Stories, A (Welty), **Retro. Supp. I:** 343, 344, 345, 346, 347, 355

Curtain of Trees (opera), **Supp. IV Part 2:** 552

"Curtain Raiser, A" (Stein), **IV:** 43, 44

"Curtains" (Cisneros), **Supp. VII:** 66

Curtin, John, **Supp. IX:** 184

Curtis, George William, **Supp. I Part 1:** 307; **Supp. XVIII:** 3, 14

Curve (Goldbarth), **Supp. XII:** 181

Curve of Binding Energy, The (McPhee), **Supp. III Part 1:** 301

Curzon, Mary, **III:** 52

Cushing, Caleb, **Supp. I Part 2:** 684, 686

Cushman, Howard, **Supp. I Part 2:** 652

Cushman, Stephen, **Retro. Supp. I:** 430

"Custard Heart, The" (Parker), **Supp. IX:** 201

Custer, General George, **I:** 489, 491

Custer Died for Your Sins (Deloria), **Supp. IV Part 1:** 323; **Supp. IV Part 2:** 504

"Custody"(Schott), **Supp. XXIII:** 241

"Custom House, The" (Hawthorne), **II:** 223; **Retro. Supp. I:** 147–148, 157; **Supp. XXI:** 181

Custom of the Country, The (Wharton), **IV:** 318; **Retro. Supp. I:** 374, 375–376; **Supp. XXIV:** 23

"Cut" (Plath), **Retro. Supp. II:** 253

"Cut-Glass Bowl, The" (Fitzgerald), **II:** 88

Cutting, Bronson, **III:** 600

Cutting Lisa (Everett), **Supp. XVIII: 56**

"Cuttings, *later*" (Roethke), **III:** 532

"Cyberpunk" (Bethke), **Supp. XVI:** 121

Cyberspace trilogy (W. Gibson). *See* Sprawl trilogy (W. Gibson)

"Cycles, The" (Pinsky), **Supp. VI:** 250–252

Cyclopedia of American Literature (Duyckinck and Duyckinck), **Supp. XXV:** 250

Cynic's Word Book, The (Bierce), **I:** 197, 205, 208, 209, 210

Cynthia Ozick (Lowin), **Supp. V:** 273

Cynthia Ozick's Comic Art (Cohen), **Supp. V:** 273

Cynthia Ozick's Fiction (Kauvar), **Supp. V:** 273

"Czeslaw Milosz and Memory" (Hampl), **Supp. XXII:** 92

D

Da Capo: Best Music Writing 2002 (Lethem, ed.), **Supp. XVIII:** 148

Dacey, Philip, **Supp. IV Part 1:** 70

Dacier, André, **II:** 10

"Dad" (Cullen), **Supp. IV Part 1:** 167

"Daddy" (Plath), **Retro. Supp. II:** 250–251; **Supp. I Part 2:** 529, 542, 545, 546; **Supp. II Part 2:** 688; **Supp. XXII:** 30; **Supp. XXIII:** 112, 113

"Daddy"(Hadas), **Supp. XXIII:** 112, 113

Daddy's Little Boy (Collins), **Supp. XXI:** 54

"Daemon, The" (Bogan), **Supp. III Part 1:** 58, 61

"Daemon Lover, The" (Jackson), **Supp. IX:** 116–117

"Daffodils" (Nelson and Espeland), **Supp. XVIII:** 181

"Daffodils" (Wordsworth), **Supp. XIII:** 284

"Daffy Duck in Hollywood" (Ashbery), **Supp. III Part 1:** 18

D'Agata, John, **Supp. XII:** 97, 98

"Dagon" (Lovecraft), **Supp. XXV:** 111, 121

Dago Red (Fante), **Supp. XI:** 160, 169

Dahl, Roald, **Supp. IX:** 114

Dahlberg, Edward, **I:** 231; **Retro. Supp. I:** 426; **Supp. III Part 2:** 624; **Supp. XIV:** 148; **Supp. XVIII:** 148; **Supp. XXII:** 257

Dahlberg, R'lene, **Supp. XIV:** 148

Daiches, David, **Retro. Supp. II:** 243; **Supp. I Part 2:** 536

Daily Horoscope (Gioia), **Supp. XV:** 112, **118–121,** 126

"Daily Horoscope" (Gioia), **Supp. XV:** 119

Daily Modernism (Podnieks), **Supp. X:** 189

Dain Curse, The (Hammett), **Supp. IV Part 1:** 348

"Daisies" (Glück), **Supp. V:** 88

"Daisy" (Oates), **Supp. II Part 2:** 523

Daisy (S. and A. Warner), **Supp. XVIII:** 268

Daisy-Head Mayzie (Geisel), **Supp. XVI:** 112

Daisy Miller (H. James), **Retro. Supp. I:** 216, 220, 222, 223, 228, 231; **Supp. XVIII:** 165; **Supp. XXIV:** 23

"Daisy Miller" (H. James), **II:** 325, 326, 327, 329; **IV:** 316

Dale, Charlie, **Supp. IV Part 2:** 584

Daley, Yvonne, **Supp. XXII:** 216

Dali, Salvador, **II:** 586; **Supp. IV Part 1:** 83; **Supp. XIII:** 317

Dalibard, Thomas-François, **II:** 117

"Dallas-Fort Worth: Redband and Mistletoe" (Clampitt), **Supp. IX:** 45

"Dalliance of Eagles, The" (Whitman), **IV:** 348

Dalva (Harrison), **Supp. VIII:** 37, 45, 46, **48–49**

Daly, Carroll John, **Supp. IV Part 1:** 343, 345

Daly, John, **II:** 25, 26

Daly, Julia Brown, **II:** 25, 26

"Dalyrimple Goes Wrong" (Fitzgerald), **II:** 88

"Dam, The" (Rukeyser), **Supp. VI:** 283

Damas, Leon, **Supp. X:** 139

Damascus Gate (Stone), **Supp. V:** 308–311

Damballah (Wideman), **Supp. X:** 319, 320, 321, 322, 323, 326, 327, 331, 333–334

Dameshek, Brandon, **Supp. XIX:** 273, 277, 287

Damnation of Theron Ware, The (Frederic), **II:** 140–143, 144, 146, 147; **Retro. Supp. I:** 325

Damned If I Do (Everett), **Supp. XVIII:** 66

"Damned Thing, The" (Bierce), **I:** 206

Damon, Matt, **Supp. VIII:** 175

Damon, S. Foster, **I:** 26; **II:** 512, 514, 515

"Damon and Vandalia" (Dove), **Supp. IV Part 1:** 252

Dana, H. W. L., **I:** 225

Dana, Richard Henry, Jr., **III:** 81; **Supp. XX: 227; Supp. XXV:** 208

Dana, Richard Henry, Sr., **I:** 339, 351; **Supp. I Part 1:** 103, 154, 155; **Supp. I Part 2:** 414, 420; **Supp. XXV:** 250

Dana, Robert, **Supp. V:** 178, 180

"Dana Gioia and Fine Press Printing" (Peich), **Supp. XV:** 117

"Dance" (Kenny), **Supp. XXIII:** 148

"Dance, The" (Crane), **I:** 109

"Dance, The" (Roethke), **III:** 541

"Dance, The" (W. C. Williams), **Supp. XVII:** 113

Dance and the Railroad, The (Hwang), **Supp. XXI:** 145, 146

"Dance in a Buffalo Skull" (Zitkala-Ša), **Supp. XXV:** 276

Dance of Death, The (Auden), **Supp. II Part 1:** 10

Dance of Death, The (Bierce and Harcourt), **I:** 196

Dance of Life, The (Ellis), **Supp. XX:** 117

Dance of the Sleepwalkers (Calabria), **Supp. XIII:** 164

"Dance of the Solids, The" (Updike), **Retro. Supp. I:** 323

"Dancer" (Hoffman), **Supp. XVIII:** 86

"Dancer, The" (Swados), **Supp. XIX:** 261, 263–264

"Dancers Work by Forgetting" (Espaillat), **Supp. XXI:** 102

"Dances of Madness" (Schott), **Supp. XXIII:** 245

Dances with Wolves (film), **Supp. X:** 124

Dance to the Music of Time, A (Powell), **Supp. XVIII:** 146

Dancing After Hours (Dubus), **Supp. VII:** 91

Dancing Back Strong the Nation (Kenny), **Supp. XXIII:** 144, **148**

Dancing Bears, The (Merwin), **Supp. III Part 1:** 343–344

Dancing on the Stones (Nichols), **Supp. XIII:** 256, 257, 259, 267, 269

"Dancing the Jig" (Sexton), **Supp. II Part 2:** 692

Dandelion Wine (Bradbury), **Supp. IV Part 1:** 101, 109–110

Dandurand, Karen, **Retro. Supp. I:** 30

"Dandy Frightening the Squatters, The" (Twain), **IV:** 193–194

Dangel, Mary Jo, **Supp. XVIII:** 156

Dangerous Crossroads (film), **Supp. XIII:** 163

Dangerous Day (Rinehart), **Supp. XXV:** 195

Dangerous Moonlight (Purdy), **Supp. VII:** 278

"Dangerous Road Before Martin Luther King" (Baldwin), **Supp. I Part 1:** 52

"Dangerous Summer, The" (Hemingway), **II:** 261

Dangerous Thoughts (Ryan as Quin), **Supp. XVIII:** 226

"Dangers of Authorship, The" (Blackmur), **Supp. II Part 1:** 147

Dangling Man (Bellow), **I:** 144, 145, 147, 148, 150–151, 153–154, 158, 160, 161, 162, 163; **Retro. Supp. II:** 19, 20–21, 22, 23; **Supp. VIII:** 234; **Supp. XIX:** 157

"Dang Little Squirt" (Bontemps), **Supp. XXII:** 4

Daniel (biblical book), **Supp. I Part 1:** 105

Daniel (film), **Supp. IV Part 1:** 236

Daniel, Arnaut, **III:** 467

Daniel, Robert W., **III:** 76

Daniel, Samuel, **Supp. I Part 1:** 369

Daniel Deronda (G. Eliot), **I:** 458

Daniels, Frank, **Supp. XXII:** 196

Daniels, Kate, **Supp. XVII:** 112

Danielson, Linda, **Supp. IV Part 2:** 569

D'Annunzio, Gabriele, **II:** 515

Danny and the Deep Blue Sea: An Apache Dance (Shanley), **Supp. XIV:** 315, **318–319**, 320, 321, 323, 324

Danny O'Neill pentalogy (Farrell), **II:** 35–41

Danse Macabre (King), **Supp. IV Part 1:** 102; **Supp. V:** 144

Danse Macabre (S. King), **Supp. XXV:** 123

"Danse Russe" (W. C. Williams), **IV:** 412–413

"Dans le Restaurant" (Eliot), **I:** 554, 578

Dans l'ombre des cathédrales (Ambelain), **Supp. I Part 1:** 273

Dante Alighieri, **I:** 103, 136, 138, 250, 384, 433, 445; **II:** 8, 274, 278, 289, 490, 492, 493, 494, 495, 504, 508, 524, 552; **III:** 13, 77, 124, 182, 259, 278, 448, 453, 467, 533, 607, 609, 610–612, 613; **IV:** 50, 134, 137, 138, 139, 247, 437, 438; **Retro. Supp. I:** 62, 63, 64, 66, 360; **Retro. Supp. II:** 330; **Supp. I Part 1:** 256, 363; **Supp. I Part 2:** 422, 454; **Supp. III Part 2:** 611, 618, 621; **Supp. IV Part 2:** 634; **Supp. V:** 277, 283, 331, 338, 345; **Supp. VIII:** 27, 219–221; **Supp. X:** 120, 121, 125; **Supp. XII:** 98; **Supp. XV:** 254; **Supp. XVII:** 227, 241

Danvis Tales: Selected Stories (Robinson; Budbill, ed.), **Supp. XIX:** 6

Danziger, Adolphe, **I:** 199–200

Danziger, Jeff, **Supp. XXII:** 208

Dar (Nabokov), **III:** 246, 255

D'Arcy, Randall, **Supp. XVII:** 76

Dardis, Tom, **Supp. XVIII:** 249

"Dare's Gift" (Glasgow), **II:** 190

Dark and Feeling, The: Black American Writers and Their Work (Major), **Supp. XXII:** 180

Dark Angel, The (Bolton), **Supp. I Part 1:** 281

"Dark Angel Travels With Us to Canada and Blesses Our Vacation, The" (Dunn), **Supp. XI:** 146

Dark at the Top of the Stairs, The (film), **Supp. XXV:** 102

Dark at the Top of the Stairs, The (Inge), **Supp. XXV:** 93, 95, 100–102

Dark Carnival (Bradbury), **Supp. IV Part 1:** 102

Darker (Strand), **Supp. IV Part 2:** 619, 626–628

Darker Face of the Earth, The (Dove), **Supp. IV Part 1:** 255–257

"Dark Fire" (Hadas), **Supp. XXIII:** 126

Dark Green, Bright Red (Vidal), **Supp. IV Part 2:** 677

Dark Half, The (King), **Supp. V:** 141

Dark Harbor: A Poem (Strand), **Supp. IV Part 2:** 633–634

"Dark Hills, The" (Robinson), **III:** 523

Dark Horses (X. J. Kennedy), **Supp. XV:** **167–170**

Dark Hours, The (W. V. Davis), **Supp. XXI:** **91–92**, 93

Dark Laughter (Anderson), **I:** 111, 116; **II:** 250–251

"Darkling Alphabet, A" (Snodgrass), **Supp. VI:** 323

Darkling Child (Merwin and Milroy), **Supp. III Part 1:** 346

"Darkling Summer, Ominous Dusk, Rumorous Rain" (Schwartz), **Supp. II Part 2:** 661

"Darkling Thrush" (Hardy), **Supp. IX:** 40

"Dark Men, The" (Dubus), **Supp. VII:** 86

Dark Mirrors (Sobin), **Supp. XVI:** 295

Dark Mother, The (W. Frank), **Supp. XX:** **70–71**

Dark Mountains, The (Hoffman), **Supp. XVIII: 76–77**

Darkness and the Light, The (Hecht), **Supp. X:** 58

Darkness at Noon (Koestler), **Supp. XXIII:** 1

Darkness More Than Night, A (Connelly), **Supp. XXI: 73–74**, 80

"Darkness on the Edge of Town" (O'Brien), **Supp. V:** 246

Darkness Surrounding Us, The (Sorrentino), **Supp. XXI:** 227, 228

Darkness under the Trees/Walking behind the Spanish (Salinas), **Supp. XIII:** 311, **319–324**

"Dark Night" (St. John of the Cross), **Supp. XV:** 30

Dark Night of the Soul, The (St. John of the Cross), **I:** 1, 585

"Dark Ones" (Dickey), **Supp. IV Part 1:** 182

Dark Power (Holding), **Supp. XXII: 122–123**, 124

Dark Princess: A Romance (Du Bois), **Supp. II Part 1:** 179, 181–182

Dark Room, The (T. Williams), **IV:** 381

Dark Sacred Night (CD), **Supp. XXI:** 75

Dark Shadows (television show), **Supp. XIX:** 57

"Dark Summer" (Bogan), **Supp. III Part 1:** 51, 53

Dark Summer: Poems (Bogan), **Supp. III Part 1:** 52–53, 57

"Dark Tower, The" (column), **Supp. IV Part 1:** 168, 170

Dark Tower, The: The Gunslinger (King), **Supp. V:** 152

Dark Tower IV, The: Wizard and Glass (King), **Supp. V:** 139

Dark Tunnel, The (Macdonald as Millar), **Supp. IV Part 2:** 465, 466

"Dark TV Screen" (Simic), **Supp. VIII:** 282

"Dark Voyage, The" (McLay), **Supp. XIII:** 21

"Dark Walk, The" (Taylor), **Supp. V:** 320–321, 322, 326

Darkwater: Voices from Within the Veil (Du Bois), **Supp. II Part 1:** 178, 180, 183

Dark Waves and Light Matter (Goldbarth), **Supp. XII:** 176, 193

Dark World (Carruth), **Supp. XVI:** 55

"Darling" (Nye), **Supp. XIII:** 283–284

"Darling, The" (Chekhov), **Supp. IX:** 202

Darling-Darling (Barillet and Grédy; Loos, trans.), **Supp. XVI:** 194

Darnell, Linda, **Supp. XII:** 173

Darragh, Tina, **Supp. IV Part 2:** 427

Darreu, Robert Donaldson, **Supp. II Part 1:** 89, 98, 102

Darrow, Clarence, **Supp. I Part 1:** 5; **Supp. I Part 2:** 455

Dartmouth, Earl of, **Supp. XX: 284**

Darwin, Charles, **I:** 457; **II:** 323, 462, 481; **III:** 226, 231; **IV:** 69, 304; **Retro. Supp. I:** 254; **Retro. Supp. II:** 60, 65; **Supp. I Part 1:** 368; **Supp. IX:** 180; **Supp. XI:** 203; **Supp. XVI:** 13; **Supp. XX: 18**

"Darwin in 1881" (Schnackenberg), **Supp. XV:** 253, 254, 258

Daryush, Elizabeth, **Supp. V:** 180

Dasburg, Andrew, **Supp. XXI:** 6

Dash, Julie, **Supp. XI:** 17, 18, 20

Dashell, Alfred, **Supp. X:** 224

"DAS KAPITAL" (Baraka), **Supp. II Part 1:** 55

Datlow, Ellen, **Supp. XVI:** 123

"Datum Centurio" (Wallace), **Supp. X:** 309

Daudet, Alphonse, **II:** 325, 338

"Daughter" (Caldwell), **I:** 309

"Daughter in the House" (X. J. Kennedy), **Supp. XV:** 160

Daughter of Earth (Smedly), **Supp. XIII:** 295

Daughter of the Land, A (Stratton-Porter), **Supp. XX: 222**

Daughter of the Snows, A (London), **II:** 465, 469–470

Daughter of the Vine, A (Atherton), **Supp. XXIV:** 18, 22

"Daughters" (Anderson), **I:** 114

Daughters (Marshall), **Supp. XI:** 275, 276, 277, **286–288,** 289, 290

"Daughters, 1900" (Nelson), **Supp. XVIII:** 175

Daughters, I Love You (Hogan), **Supp. IV Part 1:** 397, 399, 401

"Daughters of Invention" (Alvarez), **Supp. VII:** 9

Daughters of the Dust (Dash; film), **Supp. XI:** 17, 18; **Supp. XX: 154**

Daumier, Honoré, **IV:** 412

Dave, R. A., **Supp. VIII:** 126

Davenport, Abraham, **Supp. I Part 2:** 699

Davenport, Basil, **Supp. XXV:** 27

Davenport, Gary, **Supp. IX:** 98

Davenport, Guy, **Supp. XIV:** 96; **Supp. XXI:** 235

Davenport, Herbert J., **Supp. I Part 2:** 642

Davenport, James, **I:** 546

Daves, E. G., **Supp. I Part 1:** 369

Davey, Frank, **Supp. XIII:** 33

"David" (Garrett), **Supp. VII:** 109–110

"David" (Gordon), **Supp. IV Part 1:** 298–299

David, Gray, **Supp. XX: 260**

"David and Agnes, a Romance" (Keillor), **Supp. XVI:** 175

David Blaize (Benson), **Supp. XX: 234**

David Copperfield (Dickens), **I:** 458; **II:** 290; **Retro. Supp. I:** 33; **Supp. XVI:** 65, 72; **Supp. XX: 234**

"David Crockett's Other Life" (Nye), **Supp. XIII:** 282

Davideis (Cowley), **IV:** 158

David Harum (Westcott), **I:** 216

"David Lynch Keeps His Head" (Wallace), **Supp. X:** 314

David Show, The (Gurney), **Supp. V:** 97

Davidson, Cathy, **Supp. XV:** 238

Davidson, Donald, **I:** 294; **III:** 495, 496; **IV:** 121, 122, 124, 125, 236; **Supp. II Part 1:** 139; **Supp. XIV:** 2; **Supp. XX: 164**

Davidson, James West, **Supp. XXII:** 218

Davidson, Jo, **Supp. XXI:** 7

Davidson, John, **Retro. Supp. I:** 55

Davidson, Michael, **Supp. VIII:** 290, 293, 294, 302–303

Davidson, Phebe, **Supp. XXIII:** 252

Davidson, Sara, **Supp. IV Part 1:** 196, 198, 203

Davidson, Sue, **Supp. XIX:** 260

Davidsz de Heem, Jan, **Supp. XI:** 133

Davie, Donald, **III:** 478; **Supp. IV Part 2:** 474; **Supp. V:** 331; **Supp. X:** 55, 59; **Supp. XVII:** 111, 112, 121

Davies, Arthur, **III:** 273

Davies, Sir John, **III:** 541

Davies, Marion, **Supp. XVI:** 186

Da Vinci, Leonardo, **I:** 274; **II:** 536; **III:** 210

Davis, Allen F., **Supp. I Part 1:** 1, 7

Davis, Allison, **Supp. I Part 1:** 327

Davis, Angela, **Supp. I Part 1:** 66; **Supp. X:** 249

Davis, Arthur B., **Supp. XVIII:** 119

Davis, Bette, **I:** 78; **Supp. I Part 1:** 67

Davis, Bill, **Supp. XIII:** 267

Davis, Christina, **Supp. XV:** 264

Davis, Cynthia, **Supp. XVIII:** 281, 286

Davis, Donald, **Supp. XIII:** 93

Davis, Elizabeth Gould, **Supp. I Part 2:** 567

Davis, George, **II:** 586

Davis, Glover, **Supp. V:** 180, 182, 186

Davis, Jefferson, **II:** 206; **IV:** 122, 125, 126

Davis, Jordan, **Supp. XV:** 178, 181, 186, 188

Davis, Katie, **Supp. VIII:** 83

Davis, L. J., **Supp. XI:** 234

Davis, Lydia, **Supp. XII:** 24; **Supp. XVII:** 21

Davis, Marcia, **Supp. XVIII:** 91, 100

Davis, Mary H., **Supp. XVIII:** 77

Davis, Miles, **Supp. XV:** 346; **Supp. XXII:** 172

Davis, Ossie, Jr., **Supp. IV Part 1:** 362; **Supp. XVI:** 144

Davis, Rebecca Harding, **Supp. I Part 1:** 45; **Supp. XIII:** 292, 295, 305; **Supp. XVI: 79–96**

Davis, Richard Harding, **III:** 328; **Supp. II Part 1:** 393; **Supp. XVI:** 85

Davis, Robert Gorham, **II:** 51; **IV:** 108

Davis, Stuart, **IV:** 409; **Supp. XV:** 295; **Supp. XXI:** 6

Davis, Thadious, **Supp. XVIII:** 120, 121, 123, 127, 129

Davis, Thulani, **Supp. XI:** 179; **Supp. XIII:** 233, 234, 239

Davis, William Virgil, **Supp. IV Part 1:** 63, 64, 68, 69, 70; **Supp. XXI: 83–96**

Davison, Peter, **Supp. XXI:** 91

Davy's Lake (M. Finch), **Supp. XVII:** 69

Dawn (Dreiser), **I:** 498, 499, 503, 509, 515, 519

Dawn (O. Butler), **Supp. XIII:** 63, **64**

"Dawnbreaker" (Hayden), **Supp. II Part 1:** 370

Dawn in Russia (W. Frank), **Supp. XX: 76**

Dawn Patrol, The (film), **Supp. XIV:** 81

"Dawn Patrol: A Review of the Literature of the Negro for 1948" (Locke), **Supp. XIV:** 211

Dawson, Edward, **IV:** 151

Dawson, Emma, **I:** 199

Dawson, Melanie, **Supp. XXIV:** 25, 31

Dawson, Ruth, **Supp. XI:** 120

Day, Dorothy, **II:** 215; **Supp. I Part 2:** 524; **Supp. X:** 142; **Supp. XXV:** 19, 30

Day, Fred Holland, **Supp. XX: 114, 115**

Day, Georgiana, **Supp. I Part 2:** 585

Day, Richard, **Supp. XVIII:** 251

Dayan, Joan, **Retro. Supp. II:** 270

"Day Book" (Notley), **Supp. XXII:** 230

Day Book, A (Creeley), **Supp. IV Part 1:** 155

"Daybreak" (Kinnell), **Supp. III Part 1:** 250

"Daybreak Blues" (Kees), **Supp. XV:** 133

"Day-Breakers, The" (Bontemps), **Supp. XXII:** 8

"Daybreak in Alabama" (Hughes), **Retro. Supp. I:** 211; **Supp. I Part 1:** 344

Day by Day (Lowell), **Retro. Supp. II:** 184, 186, 191

"Day-Care Field Trip: Aquarium" (Karr), **Supp. XI:** 243

"Day-Dream, A" (Bryant), **Supp. I Part 1:** 160

"Day-Dream of a Grocer, The" (Twain), **Supp. XVIII:** 9

"Day for Poetry and Song, A" (Douglass), **Supp. III Part 1:** 172

"Day in the Life of Half of Rumpelstiltskin, A" (Brockmeier), **Supp. XXII:** 50, 52, 53

"Day Lady Died, The" (O'Hara), **Supp. XIX:** 85; **Supp. XXIII:** 216, 219

Day Late and a Dollar Short, A (McMillan), **Supp. XIII:** 184, **Supp. XIII:** 185, **191–192**

"Day longs for the evening, The" (Levertov), **Supp. III Part 1:** 274

Daynard, Jodi, **Supp. XVIII:** 97

Day of a Stranger (Merton), **Supp. VIII:** 203

"Day of Days, A" (James), **II:** 322

Day of Doom (Wigglesworth), **IV:** 147, 155, 156

Day of the Body (C. Frost), **Supp. XV:** 93, **98–100,** 106

Day of the Locust, The (West), **I:** 298; **IV:** 288, 299–306; **Retro. Supp. II:** 321, 323, 324, 329, **337–338; Supp. II Part 2:** 626; **Supp. XI:** 296; **Supp. XII:** 173; **Supp. XIII:** 170; **Supp. XIV:** 328; **Supp. XVIII:** 246

"Day on the Big Branch, A" (Nemerov), **III:** 275–276

"Day on the Connecticut River, A" (Merrill), **Supp. III Part 1:** 336

Day Room, The (DeLillo), **Supp. VI:** 4

"Days" (Emerson), **II:** 19, 20

"Days and Nights" (Koch), **Supp. XV:** 179, 180

"Days and Nights: A Journal" (Price), **Supp. VI:** 265

Days Before, The (Porter), **III:** 433, 453

Days in the Yellow Leaf (Hoffman), **Supp. XVIII:** 75

"Days of 1935" (Merrill), **Supp. III Part 1:** 325, 328

"Days of 1941 and '44" (Merrill), **Supp. III Part 1:** 336

"Days of 1964" (Merrill), **Supp. III Part 1:** 328, 352

"Days of 1971" (Merrill), **Supp. III Part 1:** 328

"Days of 1981" (Doty), **Supp. XI:** 123

"Days of Awe: The Birth of Lucy Jane" (Wasserstein), **Supp. XV:** 332

"Days of Edward Hopper" (Haines), **Supp. XII:** 210

"Days of Heaven" (Bass), **Supp. XVI:** 20

Days of Obligation: An Argument with My Mexican Father (Rodriguez), **Supp. XIV:** 298, 300, **302–305,** 307, 310

Days of Our Lives (soap opera), **Supp. XI:** 83

Days of Our Lives Lie in Fragments: New and Old Poems (Garrett), **Supp. VII:** 109–110, 111

Days of the Phoenix (Brooks), **I:** 266

Days of Wine and Roses (J. P. Miller), **Supp. XIII:** 262

Days: Tangier Journal, 1987–1989 (Bowles), **Supp. IV Part 1:** 94

Days to Come (Hellman), **Supp. I Part 1:** 276, 277–278

Days without End (O'Neill), **III:** 385, 391, 397

"Day's Work, A" (Capote), **Supp. III Part 1:** 120

"Day's Work, A" (Porter), **III:** 443, 446

"Day the Presidential Candidate Came to Ciudad Tamaulipas, The" (Caldwell), **I:** 309

"Day the Singer Fell, The" (Swados), **Supp. XIX:** 258

Day the World ended, The (Coover), **Supp. V:** 1

"Day with Conrad Green, A" (Lardner), **II:** 428–429, 430

"Deacon's Masterpiece, The" (Holmes), **Supp. I Part 1:** 302, 307

"Dead, The" (Collins), **Supp. XXI:** 64

"Dead, The" (Joyce), **I:** 285; **III:** 343; **Supp. XXIII:** 71

"Dead, The" (Very), **Supp. XXV:** 249

Dead and the Living, The (Olds), **Supp. X:** 201, **204–206,** 207

Dead Body, The (Olds), **Supp. X:** 210

"Dead by the Side of the Road, The" (Snyder), **Supp. VIII:** 301

"Dead Doe" (B. Kelly), **Supp. XVII:** 128–129

Dead End (Kingsley), **Supp. I Part 1:** 277, 281

Dead Father, The (Barthelme), **Supp. IV Part 1:** 43, 47, 50–51

"Dead Fiddler, The" (Singer), **IV:** 20

Dead Fingers Talk (Burroughs), **Supp. III Part 1:** 103

"Dead Hand" series (Sinclair), **Supp. V:** 276, 277, 281

"Dead Language Lessons" (Stallings), **Supp. XXV:** 233

"Dead Languages, The" (Humphrey), **Supp. IX:** 109

Dead Lecturer, The (Baraka), **Supp. II Part 1:** 31, 33, 35–37, 49

Dead Letters Sent (Kenny), **Supp. XXIII:** 143, 145

"Dead Letters Sent (By the Ontario Shores)"(Kenny), **Supp. XXIII:** 145

Deadline at Dawn (Odets), **Supp. II Part 2:** 546

Deadlock (Paretsky), **Supp. XXV:** 173, 176, 178–179

"Dead-Lock and Its Key, A" (E. Stoddard), **Supp. XV:** 286

"Dead Loon, The" (Bynner), **Supp. XV:** **44–45**

Deadly Affair, A (Lacy), **Supp. XV:** 205–206

Deadly is the Female (film), **Supp. XVII:** 62

Dead Man's Walk (McMurtry), **Supp. V:** 231, 232

Dead Man's Walk (screenplay; McMurtry and Ossana), **Supp. V:** 231

Dead Man Walking (opera libretto, McNally), **Supp. XIII:** 207

Dead Poets Society (film), **Supp. XXI:** 192, 193, 194, 199

"Dead Reckoning" (Jarman), **Supp. XVII:** 113

"Dead Soldier's Talk, The" (Jin), **Supp. XVIII:** 92

Dead Souls (Gogol), **I:** 296

"Dead Souls on Campus" (Kosinski), **Supp. VII:** 222

"Dead Wingman, The" (Jarrell), **II:** 374

"Dead Wood, Green Wood" (Hadas), **Supp. XXIII:** 120

"Dead Yellow Women" (Hammett), **Supp. IV Part 1:** 345

Dead Zone, The (King), **Supp. V:** 139, 143, 144, 148, 152

Dean, James, **I:** 493

Dean, Man Mountain, **II:** 589

Deane, Silas, **Supp. I Part 2:** 509, 524

"Dean of Men" (Taylor), **Supp. V:** 314, 323

Dean's December, The (Bellow), **Retro. Supp. II:** 30–31

"Dear Adolph" (Benét), **Supp. XI:** 46

"Dear America" (Ortiz), **Supp. IV Part 2:** 503

"Dear Dark Continent" (Notley), **Supp. XXII:** 223

"Dearest M—" (Carruth), **Supp. XVI:** 59

Dear Ghosts (Gallagher), **Supp. XXIV:** 166, 167, 170–171, 176

"Dear Judas" (Jeffers), **Supp. II Part 2:** 431–432, 433

Dear Juliette (Sarton), **Supp. VIII:** 265

Dear Lovely Death (Hughes), **Retro. Supp. I:** 203; **Supp. I Part 1:** 328

"Dear Mr. Walrus" (Boyle), **Supp. XXIV:** 58–59

Dear Rafe (Hinojosa), **Supp. XIX:** 98, **105–106**

"Dear Villon" (Corso), **Supp. XII:** 135

"Dear World" (Gunn Allen), **Supp. IV Part 1:** 321

Deasy, Philip, **Supp. XX:** 42

Death (Allen), **Supp. XV:** 3

"Death" (Corso), **Supp. XII:** 127

"Death" (Lowell), **II:** 536

"Death" (Mailer), **III:** 38

"Death" (W. C. Williams), **Retro. Supp. I:** 422

"Death" (West), **IV:** 286

"Death, Decay and Change" (Very), **Supp. XXV:** 243

"Death and Absence" (Glück), **Supp. V:** 82

Death and Birth of David Markand, The (W. Frank), **Supp. XX:** **76–77**

Death and Taxes (Parker), **Supp. IX:** 192

"Death and the Child" (Crane), **I:** 414

"Death as a Society Lady" (Hecht), **Supp. X:** 71–72

Death before Bedtime (Vidal as Box), **Supp. IV Part 2:** 682

"Death Be Not Proud" (Donne), **Supp. XVI:** 158

"Death by Water" (Eliot), **I:** 395, 578

Death Comes for the Archbishop (Cather), **I:** 314, 327, 328–330; **Retro. Supp. I:** 16–18, 21; **Supp. XIII:** 253; **Supp. XXIV:** 253

Death in Paradise (Parker), **Supp. XIX:** 186

Death in the Afternoon (Hemingway), **II:** 253; **IV:** 35; **Retro. Supp. I:** 182; **Supp. VIII:** 182; **Supp. XVI:** 205; **Supp. XIX:** 246; **Supp. XX:** 76

"Death in the Country, A" (Benét), **Supp. XI:** 53–54

Death in the Family, A (Agee), **I:** 25, 29, 42, 45

Death in the Fifth Position (Vidal as Box), **Supp. IV Part 2:** 682

"Death in the Woods" (Anderson), **I:** 114, 115; **Supp. XXIV:** 136

Death in the Woods and Other Stories (Anderson), **I:** 112, 114, 115

Death in Venice (Mann), **III:** 231; **Supp. IV Part 1:** 392; **Supp. V:** 51

"Death in Viet Nam" (Salinas), **Supp. XIII:** 315

"Death in Winter" (C. Frost), **Supp. XV:** 98

Death Is a Lonely Business (Bradbury), **Supp. IV Part 1:** 102, 103, 111–112, 115

"Death Is Not the End" (Wallace), **Supp. X:** 309

Death Is the Place (Bronk), **Supp. XXI:** 32

Death Kit (Sontag), **Supp. III Part 2:** 451, 468–469

Death Likes It Hot (Vidal as Box), **Supp. IV Part 2:** 682

"Death/Muerta" (Mora), **Supp. XIII:** 228

Death Notebooks, The (Sexton), **Supp. II Part 2:** 691, 694, 695

"Death of a Columnist" (Siddons), **Supp. XXII:** 241–242

Death of Adam, The: Essays on Modern Thought (Robinson), **Supp. XXI:** 212

"Death of a Jazz Musician" (W. J. Smith), **Supp. XIII:** 334

Death of a Kinsman, The (Taylor), **Supp. V:** 324, 326

"Death of an Old Seaman" (Hughes), **Retro. Supp. I:** 199

"Death of a Pig" (White), **Supp. I Part 2:** 665–668

Death of a Salesman (A. Miller), **I:** 81; **III:** 148, 149, 150, 153–154, 156, 157, 158, 159, 160, 163, 164, 166; **IV:** 389; **Supp. IV Part 1:** 359; **Supp. XIV:** 102, 239, 254, 255; **Supp. XV:** 205; **Supp. XX:** 27; **Supp. XXIII:** 199

"Death of a Soldier, The" (Stevens), **Retro. Supp. I:** 299, 312. *see also* "Lettres d'un Soldat" (Stevens)

"Death of a Soldier, The" (Wilson), **IV:** 427, 445

"Death of a Toad" (Wilbur), **Supp. III Part 2:** 550

"Death of a Traveling Salesman" (Welty), **IV:** 261; **Retro. Supp. I:** 344

"Death of a Young Son by Drowning" (Atwood), **Supp. XIII:** 33

Death of Bessie Smith, The (Albee), **I:** 76–77, 92

Death of Billy the Kid, The (Vidal), **Supp. IV Part 2:** 683

Death of Cock Robin, The (Snodgrass), **Supp. VI:** 315, **317–319,** 324

Death of Dreams, A (Hoffman), **Supp. XVIII:** 79

"Death of General Wolfe, The" (Paine), **Supp. I Part 2:** 504

"Death of Halpin Frayser, The" (Bierce), **I:** 205

"Death of Justina, The" (Cheever), **Supp. I Part 1:** 184–185

Death of Life, The (Barnes), **Supp. III Part 1:** 34

Death of Malcolm X, The (Baraka), **Supp. II Part 1:** 47

"Death of Marilyn Monroe, The" (Olds), **Supp. X:** 205

"Death of Me, The" (Malamud), **Supp. I Part 2:** 437

"Death of Slavery, The" (Bryant), **Supp. I Part 1:** 168–169

"Death of St. Narcissus, The" (Eliot), **Retro. Supp. I:** 291

"Death of the Ball Turret Gunner, The" (Jarrell), **II:** 369–370, 372, 374, 375, 376, 378

"Death of the Fathers, The" (Sexton), **Supp. II Part 2:** 692

"Death of the Flowers, The" (Bryant), **Supp. I Part 1:** 170

Death of the Fox (Garrett), **Supp. VII:** 99, 101–104, 108

"Death of the Hat, The" (Collins), **Supp. XXI:** 59

"Death of the Hired Man, The" (Frost), **III:** 523; **Retro. Supp. I:** 121, 128; **Supp. IX:** 261

Death of the Kapowsin Tavern (Hugo), **Supp. VI:** 133–135

"Death of the Kapowsin Tavern" (Hugo), **Supp. VI:** 137, 141

"Death of the Lyric, The: The Achievement of Louis Simpson" (Jarman and McDowell), **Supp. IX:** 266, 270, 276

"Death of Venus, The" (Creeley), **Supp. IV Part 1:** 143, 144–145

"Death on All Fronts" (Ginsberg), **Supp. II Part 1:** 326

"Deaths" (Dunn), **Supp. XI:** 147

"Death Sauntering About" (Hecht), **Supp. X:** 72

Deaths for the Ladies (and Other Disasters) (Mailer), **Retro. Supp. II:** 203

Death's Jest-Book (Beddoes), **Retro. Supp. I:** 285

Death Song (McGrath), **Supp. X:** 127

"Death the Carnival Barker" (Hecht), **Supp. X:** 72

"Death the Film Director" (Hecht), **Supp. X:** 72

"Death the Judge" (Hecht), **Supp. X:** 72

"Death the Mexican Revolutionary" (Hecht), **Supp. X:** 72

"Death the Oxford Don" (Hecht), **Supp. X:** 72

"Death the Painter" (Hecht), **Supp. X:** 72

Death the Proud Brother (Wolfe), **IV:** 456

"Death to Van Gogh's Ear!" (Ginsberg), **Supp. II Part 1:** 320, 322, 323

"Death Warmed Over!" (Bradbury), **Supp. IV Part 1:** 104–105, 112

Death Wish, The (Holding), **Supp. XXII:** 120, **123,** 134, 135

Débâcle, La (Zola), **III:** 316

"Debate with the Rabbi" (Nemerov), **III:** 272

Debeljak, Aleš, **Supp. VIII:** 272

De Bellis, Jack, **Supp. I Part 1:** 366, 368, 372

Debo, Annette, **Supp. XXI:** 254

DeBoer-Langworthy, Carol, **Supp. XVII:** 98, 99, 100

DeBold, Kathleen, **Supp. XXV:** 4

De Bosis, Lauro, **IV:** 372

"Debriefing" (Sontag), **Supp. III Part 2:** 468–470

Debs, Eugene, **I:** 483, 493; **III:** 580, 581; **Supp. I Part 2:** 524; **Supp. IX:** 1, 15; **Supp. XXIII:** 161, 162

Debt to Pleasure, The (Lanchester), **Retro. Supp. I:** 278

Debussy, Claude, **Retro. Supp. II:** 266; **Supp. XIII:** 44

"Decades" (Sorrentino), **Supp. XXI:** 229

Decameron (Boccaccio), **III:** 283, 411; **Supp. IX:** 215

"Deceased" (Hughes), **Retro. Supp. I:** 208

"December" (Oliver), **Supp. VII:** 245

"December 1, 1994" (Stern), **Supp. IX:** 299

December 7 (film, Ford), **Supp. XVIII:** 247

"December 24" (Di Piero), **Supp. XIX:** 39

"December 28: Returning to Chicago" (Di Piero), **Supp. XIX:** 39

"December Dawn" (Skloot), **Supp. XX:** **202**

"December Eclogue" (Winters), **Supp. II Part 2:** 794

"Decent Woman, A" (Boulton), **Supp. XXII:** 22–23

De Cenzo, Giorgia, **Supp. XXI:** 256

Deception (P. Roth), **Retro. Supp. II:** 291; **Supp. III Part 2:** 426–427

"Deceptions" (Dobyns), **Supp. XIII:** 77

De Chiara, Ann. *See* Malamud, Mrs. Bernard (Ann de Chiara)

De Chirico, Giorgio, **Supp. XIII:** 317

"Decided Loss, A" (Poe), **II:** 411

"Decision" (Boyle), **Supp. XXIV:** 54

"Decisions to Disappear" (Dunn), **Supp. XI:** 144

"Decisive Moment, The" (Auster), **Supp. XIV:** 292

Decker, James A., **Supp. III Part 2:** 621

Declaration of Gentlemen and Merchants and Inhabitants of Boston, and the Country Adjacent, A (Mather), **Supp. II Part 2:** 450

"Declaration of Paris, The" (Adams), **I:** 4

Declaration of the Rights of Man and the Citizen, **Supp. I Part 2:** 513, 519

Declaration of Universal Peace and Liberty (Paine), **Supp. I Part 2:** 512

Declension in the Village of Chung Luong (Weigl), **Supp. XIX:** 287, 288

Decline and Fall (Waugh), **Supp. I Part 2:** 607; **Supp. XV:** 142

Decline and Fall of the English System of Finance, The (Paine), **Supp. I Part 2:** 518

Decline and Fall of the Roman Empire, The (Gibbons), **Supp. III Part 2:** 629

"Decline of Book Reviewing, The" (Hardwick), **Supp. III Part 1:** 201–202

Decline of the West, The (Spengler), **I:** 270; **IV:** 125

"Decolonizing the Tongue: Reading Speech and Aphasia in the Work of Michelle Cliff" (Aguiar), **Supp. XXII:** 68

Deconstructing Harry (film; Allen), **Supp. XV:** 12, **13**

"Décor" (X. J. Kennedy), **Supp. XV:** 171

"Decoration Day" (Jewett), **II:** 412; **Retro. Supp. II:** 138

Decoration of Houses, The (Wharton and Codman), **IV:** 308; **Retro. Supp. I:** 362, 363–364, 366

"Decoy" (Ashbery), **Supp. III Part 1:** 13–14

Decter, Midge, **Supp. XX:** 248

Dedalus, Stephen, **Supp. XIX:** 47

"De Daumier-Smith's Blue Period" (Salinger), **III:** 560–561

"Dedication" (Nelson), **Supp. XVIII:** 173, 180

"Dedication and Household Map" (Erdrich), **Supp. IV Part 1:** 272
"Dedication Day" (Agee), **I:** 34
"Dedication for a Book" (Hay), **Supp. XIV:** 125
"Dedication for a Book of Criticism" (Winters), **Supp. II Part 2:** 801
"Dedication in Postscript, A" (Winters), **Supp. II Part 2:** 801
Dedications and Other Darkhorses (Komunyakaa), **Supp. XIII:** 112, **113–114**
"Dedication to Hunger" (Glück), **Supp. V:** 83
"Dedication to My Wife, A" (Eliot), **I:** 583
Dee, Jonathan, **Supp. XXIII:** 302
Dee, Ruby, **Supp. IV Part 1:** 362
Deeds of Utmost Kindness (Gander), **Supp. XV:** 340
Deegan, Thomas, **Supp. XXIII:** 100, 107–108
"Deep Breath at Dawn, A" (Hecht), **Supp. X:** 58
Deep End, The (film), **Supp. XXII:** 120, 131, 133
Deeper into Movies: The Essential Kael Collection from '69 to '72 (Kael), **Supp. IX:** 253
"Deeper Wisdom, The" (Hay), **Supp. XIV:** 129
Deep Green Sea (R. O. Butler), **Supp. XII:** 62, **74**
Deephaven (Jewett), **II:** 398–399, 400, 401, 410, 411; **Retro. Supp. II:** 133, 134, 135, 136, 137, 138, 140, 141, 143, 144
"Deep Sight and Rescue Missions" (Bambara), **Supp. XI:** 18–19
Deep Sightings and Rescue Missions: Fiction, Essays, and Conversations (Bambara), **Supp. XI:** 1, 3, **14–20**
Deep Sleep, The (Morris), **III:** 224–225
"Deep Song" (G. Jones), **Supp. XXIV:** 194
Deep South (Caldwell), **I:** 305, 309, 310
Deepstep Come Shining (Wright), **Supp. XV:** 337, 341, 344, **349–350,** 351, 353
"Deep Water" (Marquand), **III:** 56
"Deep Woods" (Nemerov), **III:** 272–273, 275
"Deer at Providencia, The" (Dillard), **Supp. VI:** 28, 32
Deer Camp: Last Light in the Northeast Kingdom (Ostrum, ed.), **Supp. XXII:** 218
"Deer Dancer" (Harjo), **Supp. XII:** 224–225
"Deer Ghost" (Harjo), **Supp. XII:** 225
Deer Park, The (Mailer), **I:** 292; **III:** 27, 31–33, 35–36, 37, 39, 40, 42, 43, 44; **Retro. Supp. II: 200–202,** 205, 207, 211
Deer Park, The: A Play (Mailer), **Retro. Supp. II:** 205
Deer Pasture, The (Bass), **Supp. XVI:** 15, 16, 23
Deerslayer, The (Cooper), **I:** 341, 349, 350, 355; **Supp. I Part 1:** 251
Deese, Helen, **Supp. XXV:** 251

"Defeat" (Boyle), **Supp. XXIV: 60–61**
Defence, The (Nabokov), **Supp. XXII:** 263
"Defence of Poesie, The" (Bronk), **Supp. XXI:** 32
"Defence of Poesy, The" (Sidney), **Supp. V:** 250
"Defence of Poetry" (Longfellow), **II:** 493–494
"Defender of the Faith" (P. Roth), **Retro. Supp. II:** 281; **Supp. III Part 2:** 404, 407, 420
"Defending *The Searchers* (Scenes in the Life of an Obsession)*" (Lethem), Supp. XVIII:* 136,141
"Defenestration in Prague" (Matthews), **Supp. IX:** 168
Defenestration of Prague (Howe), **Supp. IV Part 2:** 419, 426, 429–430
Defense, The (Nabokov), **III:** 251–252; **Retro. Supp. I:** 266, 268, **270–272**
"Defense of Poetry" (Francis), **Supp. IX:** 83–84
DeFeo, Ronald, **Supp. XXIII:** 106
Defiant Ones, The (film), **Supp. I Part 1:** 67
"Defining the Age" (W. V. Davis), **Supp. IV Part 1:** 64
"Definition" (Ammons), **Supp. VII:** 28
Defoe, Daniel, **I:** 204; **II:** 104, 105, 159, 304–305; **III:** 113, 423; **IV:** 180; **Supp. I Part 2:** 523; **Supp. V:** 127
De Forest, John William, **II:** 275, 280, 288, 289; **IV:** 350
DeFrees, Madeline, **Supp. XVIII:** 293
"Deganawidah: The Peacemaker"(Kenny), **Supp. XXIII:** 151
Degas, Brian, **Supp. XI:** 307
Degler, Carl, **Supp. I Part 2:** 496
"Degrees of Fidelity" (Dunn), **Supp. XI:** 148, 156
Deguy, Michel, **Supp. XV:** 178
De Haven, Tom, **Supp. XI:** 39; **Supp. XII:** 338–339
Deitch, Joseph, **Supp. VIII:** 125
"Dejection" (Coleridge), **II:** 97
DeJong, Constance, **Supp. XII:** 4
DeJong, David Cornel, **I:** 35
Dekker,Thomas, **Supp. XVII:** 232
de Kooning, Elaine de, **Supp. XXIII:** 210, 217
de Kooning, Willem, **Supp. XII:** 198; **Supp. XV:** 177, 178
de Kooning, Willem de, **Supp. XXIII:** 208, 210, 211, 217, 220
Delacroix, Henri, **I:** 227
De La Mare, Walter, **III:** 429; **Supp. II Part 1:** 4; **Supp. XVII:** 69
Delamotte, Eugenia C., **Supp. XI:** 279
De Lancey, James, **I:** 338
De Lancey, Mrs. James (Anne Heathcote), **I:** 338
De Lancey, Susan A. *See* Cooper, Mrs. James Fenimore
De Lancey, William Heathcote, **I:** 338, 353
Delano, Amasa, **III:** 90
Delattre, Roland A., **I:** 558
De Laurentiis, Dino, **Supp. XI:** 170, 307

De la Valdéne, Guy, **Supp. VIII:** 40, 42
Delbanco, Andrew, **Supp. XXIV:** 69
Delbanco, Nicholas, **Supp. XXII:** 204
Del Cabral, Manuel, **Supp. XXI:** 104
DelCorso's Gallery (Caputo), **Supp. XIX:** 22–23
Delectorskaya, Lydia, **Supp. XXII:** 99
De l'éducation d'un homme sauvage (Itard), **Supp. I Part 2:** 564
Deleuze, Gilles, **Supp. XXV:** 123
"Delft" (Goldbarth), **Supp. XII:** 189
Delft: An Essay-Poem (Goldbarth), **Supp. XII:** 187
Delicate Balance, A (Albee), **I:** 86–89, 91, 93, 94
Delicate Balance, The (Hay), **Supp. XIV:** 121, 122, 124, 129, 133–134
"Delicate Balance, The" (Hay), **Supp. XIV:** 122
"Delicate Prey, The" (Bowles), **Supp. IV Part 1:** 86
Delicate Prey and Other Stories, The (Bowles), **Supp. IV Part 1:** 86–87
Délie (Scève), **Supp. III Part 1:** 11
Delights & Shadows (Kooser), **Supp. XIX:** 115, 116, 117, 121, **127–128**
DeLillo, Don, **Retro. Supp. I:** 278; **Retro. Supp. II:** 279; **Supp. VI: 1–18; Supp. IX:** 212; **Supp. XI:** 68; **Supp. XII:** 21, 152; **Supp. XVII:** 183; **Supp. XVIII:** 136, 140; **Supp. XIX:** 54; **Supp. XX: 83, 87, 91; Supp. XXIII:** 109
De Lint, Charles, **Supp. XXII:** 59
DeLisle, Anne, **Supp. VIII:** 175
Deliverance (Dickey), **Supp. IV Part 1:** 176, 186–188, 190; **Supp. X:** 30; **Supp. XX: 173–174; Supp. XXIII:** 43, 50
Deliverance, The (Glasgow), **II:** 175, 176, 177–178, 181
"Delivering" (Dubus), **Supp. VII:** 87
Dell, Floyd, **I:** 103, 105; **Supp. I Part 2:** 379; **Supp. XV:** 295; **Supp. XVII:** 96; **Supp. XXI:** 6; **Supp. XXII:** 275; **Supp. XXV:** 18
Della Francesca, Piero, **Supp. XV:** 262
"Della Primavera Trasportata al Morale" (W. C. Williams), **Retro. Supp. I:** 419, 422
DeLoria, Philip J., **Supp. XIV:** 306
Deloria, Vine, Jr., **Supp. IV Part 1:** 323; **Supp. IV Part 2:** 504
"Delta Autumn" (Faulkner), **II:** 71
"Delta Factor, The" (Percy), **Supp. III Part 1:** 386
Delta of Venus: Erotica (Nin), **Supp. X:** 192, 195
Delta Wedding (Welty), **IV:** 261, 268–271, 273, 281; **Retro. Supp. I:** 349–350, 351
Delusions (Berryman), **I:** 170
De Man, Paul, **Retro. Supp. I:** 67; **Supp. XVII:** 70
DeMarinis, Rick, **Supp. XIV:** 22
DeMars, James, **Supp. IV Part 2:** 552
Dembo, L. S., **I:** 386, 391, 396, 397, 398, 402; **III:** 478; **Supp. I Part 1:** 272; **Supp. XIV:** 277, 282, 288, 290

"Dementia Translucida" (Bierds), **Supp. XVII:** 33

"Demeter"(Crooker), **Supp. XXIII:** 61

"Demeters"(Hadas), **Supp. XXIII:** 113

Demetrakopoulous, Stephanie A., **Supp. IV Part 1:** 12

DeMille, Cecil B., **Supp. IV Part 2:** 520; **Supp. XV:** 42

Demme, Jonathan, **Supp. V:** 14

Democracy (Adams), **I:** 9–10, 20; **Supp. IV Part 1:** 208; **Supp. XIX:** 139

Democracy (Didion), **Supp. IV Part 1:** 198, 208–210

"Democracy" (Lowell), **Supp. I Part 2:** 419

Democracy and Education (Dewey), **I:** 232

Democracy and Other Addresses (Lowell), **Supp. I Part 2:** 407

Democracy and Social Ethics (Addams), **Supp. I Part 1:** 8–11

Democracy in America (Tocqueville), **Retro. Supp. I:** 235; **Supp. XIV:** 306

Democratic Vistas (Whitman), **IV:** 333, 336, 348–349, 351, 469; **Retro. Supp. I:** 408; **Supp. I Part 2:** 456

Democritus, **I:** 480–481; **II:** 157; **III:** 606; **Retro. Supp. I:** 247

"Demon Lover, The" (Rich), **Supp. I Part 2:** 556

"Demonstrators, The" (Welty), **IV:** 280; **Retro. Supp. I:** 355

DeMott, Benjamin, **Supp. IV Part 1:** 35; **Supp. V:** 123; **Supp. XIII:** 95; **Supp. XIV:** 106; **Supp. XXV:** 86

DeMott, Robert, **Supp. VIII:** 40, 41

Demuth, Charles, **IV:** 404; **Retro. Supp. I:** 412, 430; **Supp. XXI:** 6

"Demystified Zone" (Paley), **Supp. VI:** 227

Denby, Edwin, **Supp. XXIV:** 36, 45

Denmark Vesey (opera) (Bowles), **Supp. IV Part 1:** 83

Dennett, Daniel, **Supp. XXII:** 265

Denney, Joseph Villiers, **Supp. I Part 2:** 605

Denney, Reuel, **Supp. XII:** 121; **Supp. XXI:** 19

Dennie, Joseph, **II:** 298; **Supp. I Part 1:** 125

Denniston, Dorothy Hamer, **Supp. XI:** 276, 277

"Den of Lions" (Plath), **Retro. Supp. II:** 242

"Dental Assistant, The" (Simpson), **Supp. IX:** 280

Den Uyl, Douglas, **Supp. IV Part 2:** 528, 530

"Deodand, The" (Hecht), **Supp. X:** 65

"Departing" (Cameron), **Supp. XII:** 81

"Departure" (Glück), **Supp. V:** 89

"Departure" (Plath), **Supp. I Part 2:** 537

"Departure, The" (Freneau), **Supp. II Part 1:** 264

"Departure from Hydra, The" (Koch), **Supp. XV:** 180–181

Departures (Justice), **Supp. VII:** 124–127

Departures and Arrivals (Shields), **Supp. VII:** 320, 322

"Depressed by a Book of Bad Poetry, I Walk Toward an Unused Pasture and Invite the Insects to Join Me" (Wright), **Supp. III Part 2:** 600

"Depressed Person, The" (Wallace), **Supp. X:** 309

"Depression Days" (Mora), **Supp. XIII:** 224–225

"Deprived of Unhappiness" (Pickering), **Supp. XXI:** 203

De Puy, John, **Supp. XIII:** 12

D'Erasmo, Stacey, **Supp. IX:** 121

Derby, J. C., **Supp. XVIII:** 4

De Reilhe, Catherine, **Supp. I Part 1:** 202

De Rerum Natura (Lucretius), **II:** 162

"De Rerum Virtute" (Jeffers), **Supp. II Part 2:** 424

De Rioja, Francisco, **Supp. I Part 1:** 166

"Derivative Sport in Tornado Alley" (Wallace), **Supp. X:** 314

Derleth, August, **Supp. I Part 2:** 465, 472; **Supp. XXV:** 111, 122

Deronda, Daniel, **II:** 179

Derricotte, Toi, **Supp. XVIII:** 177

Derrida, Jacques, **Supp. IV Part 1:** 45; **Supp. XV:** 215, 224; **Supp. XVI:** 285, 288

Deruddere, Dominique, **Supp. XI:** 173

Der Wilde Jäger (Bürger), **II:** 306

Derzhavin, Gavrila Romanovich, **Supp. VIII:** 27

Desai, Anita, **Supp. XVI:** 156, 157, 158

Désamère (Notley), **Supp. XXII:** 226

De Santis, Christopher, **Retro. Supp. I:** 194

Descartes, René, **I:** 255; **III:** 618–619; **IV:** 133

"Descendant of Solomon and the Queen of Sheba" (Major), **Supp. XXII:** 182

Descendents, The (Glasgow), **II:** 173, 174–175, 176

Descending Figure (Glück), **Supp. V:** 83–84

"Descending Theology: Christ Human" (Karr), **Supp. XI:** 251

"Descending Theology: The Garden" (Karr), **Supp. XI:** 251

"Descent, The" (W. C. Williams), **Retro. Supp. I:** 428, 429

"Descent from the Cross" (Eliot), **Retro. Supp. I:** 57, 58

"Descent in the Maelström, A" (Poe), **Retro. Supp. II:** 274

"Descent into Proselito" (Knowles), **Supp. XII:** 237

"Descent into the Maelström, A" (Poe), **III:** 411, 414, 416, 424

Descent of Alette, The (Notley), **Supp. XXII:** 223, 224, 226, 227, 233–234

Descent of Man (Boyle), **Supp. VIII:** 1, 12–13; **Supp. XX:** 17, 18, 20

"Descent of Man" (Boyle), **Supp. VIII:** 14; **Supp. XX:** 18

Descent of Man, The (Darwin), **Supp. XIV:** 192

Descent of Man, The (Wharton), **IV:** 311; **Retro. Supp. I:** 367

Descent of Man and Other Stories, The (Wharton), **Retro. Supp. I:** 367

Descent of Winter, The (W. C. Williams), **Retro. Supp. I:** 419, 428

De Schloezer, Doris, **III:** 474

"Describers" (Halliday), **Supp. XIX:** 85

"Description" (Doty), **Supp. XI:** 126

"Description of the great Bones dug up at Clavarack on the Banks of Hudsons River A.D. 1705, The" (Taylor), **IV:** 163, 164

"Description without Place" (Stevens), **Retro. Supp. I:** 422

"Desert" (Hughes), **Retro. Supp. I:** 207

"Deserted Cabin" (Haines), **Supp. XII:** 203

Deserted Village, The (Goldsmith), **II:** 304

Desert Is My Mother, The/El desierto es mi madre (Mora), **Supp. XIII:** 214, 221

Desert Music, The (W. C. Williams), **IV:** 422; **Retro. Supp. I:** 428, 429

"Desert Music, The" (W. C. Williams), **Retro. Supp. I:** 428, 429

"Desert Places" (Frost), **II:** 159; **Retro. Supp. I:** 121, 123, 129, 138, 299; **Supp. XIV:** 229

Desert Rose, The (McMurtry), **Supp. V:** 225, 231

Desert Solitaire (Abbey), **Supp. X:** 30; **Supp. XIII:** 7–8, 12; **Supp. XIV:** 177, 179

Desert Solitaire: A Season in the Wilderness (Abbey), **Supp. XXV:** 208

"Design" (Frost), **II:** 158, 163; **Retro. Supp. I:** 121, 126, 138, 139; **Supp. IX:** 81; **Supp. XVII:** 132; **Supp. XVIII:** 298

"Designated National Park, A" (Ortiz), **Supp. IV Part 2:** 509

"Designs on a Point of View" (Everwine), **Supp. XV:** 76

DeSilva, Bruce, **Supp. XXII:** 205, 206, 217

Des Imagistes (Pound), **II:** 513; **Supp. I Part 1:** 257, 261, 262

Desire (album, Dylan), **Supp. XVIII:** 28

"Desire" (Beattie), **Supp. V:** 29

Desire (Bidart), **Supp. XV:** 32–34, 35

"Desire" (Everwine), **Supp. XV:** 85

Desire, Desire, Desire (Durang), **Supp. XXIV:** 113

"Desire and Denial" (Bronk), **Supp. XXI:** 26

"Désirée's Baby" (Chopin), **Retro. Supp. II:** 64, 65; **Supp. I Part 1:** 213–215

"Desire"(Hadas), **Supp. XXIII:** 117

Desire under the Elms (O'Neill), **III:** 387, 390

"Desolate Field, The" (W. C. Williams), **Retro. Supp. I:** 418

"Desolation, A" (Ginsberg), **Supp. II Part 1:** 313

Desolation Angels (Kerouac), **Supp. III Part 1:** 218, 225, 230

"Desolation Is a Delicate Thing" (Wylie), **Supp. I Part 2:** 729

"Desolation Row" (song, Dylan), **Supp. XVIII:** 30

Despair (Nabokov), **Retro. Supp. I:** 270, 274

Desperate Characters (Fox), **Supp. XX: 91**

"Despisals" (Rukeyser), **Supp. VI:** 282

Des Pres, Terrence, **Supp. X:** 113, 120, 124

"Destiny and the Lieutenant" (McCoy), **Supp. XIII:** 171

"Destruction of Kreshev, The" (Singer), **IV:** 13; **Retro. Supp. II:** 307

Destruction of the European Jews, The (Hilberg), **Supp. V:** 267

"Destruction of the Goetheanum, The" (Salter), **Supp. IX:** 257

"Destruction of the Long Branch, The" (Pinsky), **Supp. VI:** 239, 240, 243–244, 245, 247, 250

Destructive Element, The (Spender), **Retro. Supp. I:** 216

"Detail & Parody for the poem 'Paterson' " (W. C. Williams), **Retro. Supp. I:** 424

Detmold, John, **Supp. I Part 2:** 670

De Tolnay, Charles, **Supp. XXII:** 255

Detour at Night (Endore), **Supp. XVII:** 64

Deuce, The (R. O. Butler), **Supp. XII:** 62, **69–70,** 72

Deus Lo Volt! (Connell), **Supp. XIV:** 80, 81, 95

Deuteronomy (biblical book), **II:** 166

Deutsch, Andre, **Supp. XI:** 297, 301

Deutsch, Babette, **Supp. I Part 1:** 328, 341; **Supp. XV:** 305; **Supp. XXV:** 21

Deutsch, Michel, **Supp. IV Part 1:** 104

"Devaluation Blues: Ruminations on Black Families in Crisis" (Coleman), **Supp. XI:** 87

Devane, William, **Supp. XI:** 234

Devasahayam, Madona, **Supp. XXII:** 260

"Development of My Mind and Character, The" (Notley), **Supp. XXII:** 227

"Development of the Literary West" (Chopin), **Retro. Supp. II:** 72

"Development of the Modern English Novel, The" (Lanier), **Supp. I Part 1:** 370–371

DeVeriante (Herbert of Cherbury), **II:** 108

"Devil and Daniel Webster, The" (Benét), **III:** 22; **Supp. XI:** 45–46, 47, 50–51, 52

Devil and Daniel Webster and Other Writings, The (Benét), **Supp. XI:** 48

"Devil and Tom Walker, The" (Irving), **II:** 309–310

Devil At Large, The: Erica Jong on Henry Miller (Jong), **Supp. V:** 115, 131

Devil-Doll, The (film, Browning), **Supp. XVII:** 58–59

Devil Finds Work, The (Baldwin), **Retro. Supp. II:** 14; **Supp. I Part 1:** 48, 52, 66–67

Devil in a Blue Dress (Mosley), **Supp. XIII:** 237, 239

"Devil in Manuscript, The" (Hawthorne), **II:** 226; **Retro. Supp. I:** 150–151

Devil in Paradise, A (H. Miller), **III:** 190

"Devil in the Belfry, The" (Poe), **III:** 425; **Retro. Supp. II:** 273

"Devil Is a Busy Man, The" (Wallace), **Supp. X:** 309

Devil's Dictionary, The (Bierce), **I:** 196, 197, 205, 208, 209, 210

Devil's Stocking, The (Algren), **Supp. IX:** 5, 16

"Devil's Thumb, The" (Krakauer), **Supp. XVIII:** 107

Devil's Tour, The (Karr), **Supp. XI:** 240, **242–244**

Devil Tree, The (Kosinski), **Supp. VII:** 215, 222, 223

"Devising" (Ammons), **Supp. VII:** 28

Devlin, Paul, **Supp. XIX:** 159

De Voe, Edward Thomas, **Supp. XXV:** 23, 29

De Voto, Bernard, **I:** 247, 248; **II:** 446; **Supp. IV Part 2:** 599, 601

"Devout Meditation in Memory of Adolph Eichmann, A" (Merton), **Supp. VIII:** 198, 203

De Vries, Peter, **Supp. I Part 2:** 604

Dewberry, Elizabeth, **Supp. XII:** 62, 72

Dewey, John, **I:** 214, 224, 228, 232, 233, 266, 267; **II:** 20, 27, 34, 229, 361; **III:** 112, 294–295, 296, 303, 309–310, 599, 605; **IV:** 27, 429; **Supp. I Part 1:** 3, 5, 7, 10, 11, 12, 24; **Supp. I Part 2:** 493, 641, 647, 677; **Supp. V:** 290; **Supp. IX:** 179; **Supp. XIV:** 3; **Supp. XV:** 41

Dewey, Joseph, **Supp. IX:** 210

Dewey, Thomas, **IV:** 161

Dewey Defeats Truman (Mallon), **Supp. XIX:** 132, 137, **138**

Dexter, Peter, **Supp. XIV:** 221

De Young, Charles, **I:** 194

Dhairyam, Sagari, **Supp. IV Part 1:** 329, 330

Dharma Bums, The (Kerouac), **Supp. III Part 1:** 230, 231; **Supp. VIII:** 289, 305

"D. H. Lawrence" (Bynner), **Supp. XV:** 46

D. H. Lawrence: An Unprofessional Study (Nin), **Supp. X:** 182–183

D. H. Lawrence: The World of the Major Novels (Sanders), **Supp. XVI:** 267

D'Houdetot, Madame, **Supp. I Part 1:** 250

"Diabetes" (Dickey), **Supp. IV Part 1:** 182

Diaghilev, Sergei, **Supp. I Part 1:** 257

Dial (publication), **I:** 58, 109, 115, 116, 215, 231, 233, 245, 261, 384, 429; **II:** 8, 430; **III:** 194, 470, 471, 485; **IV:** 122, 171, 427; **Retro. Supp. I:** 58; **Retro. Supp. II:** 78; **Supp. I Part 2:** 642, 643, 647; **Supp. II Part 1:** 168, 279, 291; **Supp. II Part 2:** 474; **Supp. III Part 2:** 611

"Dialectical Materialism" (Weigl), **Supp. XIX:** 281

Dialectical Materialism and the Fate of Humanity (C. L. R. James), **Supp. XXI:** 169

"Dialectics of Love, The" (McGrath), **Supp. X:** 116

"Dialogue" (Rich), **Supp. I Part 2:** 560

Dialogue, A (Baldwin and Giovanni), **Supp. I Part 1:** 66

"Dialogue Between Franklin and the Gout" (Franklin), **II:** 121

"Dialogue Between General Wolfe and General Gage in a Wood near Boston, A" (Paine), **Supp. I Part 2:** 504

"Dialogue between Old England and New" (Bradstreet), **Supp. I Part 1:** 105–106, 110–111, 116

"Dialogue between the Writer and a Maypole Dresser, A" (Taylor), **IV:** 155

Dialogues (Bush, ed.), **III:** 4

Dialogues in Limbo (Santayana), **III:** 606

"Dialogue: William Harvey; Joan of Arc" (Goldbarth), **Supp. XII:** 178

Dialogue with a Dead Man (J. W. Miller), **Supp. XX: 163, 164, 167**

"Diamond as Big as the Ritz, The" (Fitzgerald), **II:** 88–89

Diamond Cutters and Other Poems, The (Rich), **Supp. I Part 2:** 551, 552, 553

"Diamond Guitar, A" (Capote), **Supp. III Part 1:** 124

Diamond Necklace, A (Notley), **Supp. XXII:** 228

"Diana and Persis" (Alcott), **Supp. I Part 1:** 32, 41

"Diaper Brigade, The" (Ryan as Quin), **Supp. XVIII:** 230

Diaries of Charlotte Perkins Gilman (Knight, ed.), **Supp. XI:** 201

"Diary–1903" (Boyce), **Supp. XXI:** 8

Diary of a Chambermaid, The (film; Renoir), **Supp. XVI:** 193

Diary of Anaïs Nin, The (1931–1974), **Supp. X:** 181, 185–189, 191, 192, 193, 195

Diary of Anne Frank, The, **Supp. XXI:** 245

Diary of a Rapist, The: A Novel (Connell), **Supp. XIV:** 80, 82, 94

Diary of a Yuppie (Auchincloss), **Supp. IV Part 1:** 31, 32–33

Diary of "Helena Morley", The (Bishop, trans.), **Retro. Supp. II:** 45, 51; **Supp. I Part 1:** 92

Dias, Robert Vas, **Supp. XXII:** 164, 169

Díaz, Junot, **Supp. XXIV: 83–95; Supp. XXV:** 49, 61

Díaz del Castillo, Bernál, **III:** 13, 14

Dick, Philip K., **Supp. XVI:** 123; **Supp. XVIII:** 136, 137, 138, 139, 142; **Supp. XXII:** 49

Dickens, Charles, **I:** 152, 198, 505; **II:** 98, 179, 186, 192, 271, 273–274, 288, 290, 297, 301, 307, 316, 322, 559, 561, 563, 577, 582; **III:** 146, 247, 325, 368, 411, 421, 426, 572, 577, 613–614, 616; **IV:** 21, 192, 194, 211, 429; **Retro. Supp. I:** 33, 91, 218; **Retro. Supp. II:** 204; **Supp. I Part 1:** 13, 34, 35, 36, 41, 49; **Supp. I Part 2:** 409, 523, 579, 590, 622, 675; **Supp. IV Part 1:** 293, 300, 341; **Supp. IV Part 2:** 464; **Supp. VIII:** 180; **Supp. IX:** 246; **Supp. XI:** 277; **Supp. XII:** 335, 337; **Supp. XIII:** 233; **Supp. XV:** 62; **Supp. XVI:** 63, 65–66, 72–73, 202; **Supp. XVIII:** 7, 136, 146; **Supp.**

XX: 21, 87, 195; Supp. XXII: 206; Supp. XXIII: 4, 85, 290; Supp. XXIV: 87; Supp. XXV: 258

Dickey, James, I: 29, 535; III: 268; Retro. Supp. II: 233; Supp. III Part 1: 354; Supp. III Part 2: 541, 597; Supp. IV Part 1: 175–194; Supp. V: 333; Supp. X: 30; Supp. XI: 312, 317; Supp. XV: 115, 348; Supp. XVIII: 191, 299; Supp. XIX: 282; Supp. XXI: 35; Supp. XXIII: 43, 50; Supp. XXIV: 42

Dick Gibson Show, The (Elkin), Supp. VI: 42, 48–49

Dickie, Margaret, Retro. Supp. II: 53, 84

Dickinson, Donald, Retro. Supp. I: 206, 212

Dickinson, Edward, I: 451–452, 453

Dickinson, Mrs. Edward, I: 451, 453

Dickinson, Emily, I: 384, 419, 433, 451–473; II: 272, 276, 277, 530; III: 19, 194, 196, 214, 493, 505, 508, 556, 572, 576; IV: 134, 135, 331, 444; Retro. Supp. I: 25–50; Retro. Supp. II: 39, 40, 43, 45, 50, 76, 134, 155, 170; Supp. I Part 1: 29, 79, 188, 372; Supp. I Part 2: 375, 546, 609, 682, 691; Supp. II Part 1: 4; Supp. III Part 1: 63; Supp. III Part 2: 600, 622; Supp. IV Part 1: 31, 257; Supp. IV Part 2: 434, 637, 641, 643; Supp. V: 79, 140, 332, 335; Supp. VIII: 95, 104, 106, 108, 198, 205, 272; Supp. IX: 37, 38, 53, 87, 90; Supp. XII: 226; Supp. XIII: 153, 339; Supp. XIV: 45, 127–128, 133, 261, 284; Supp. XV: 287, 303, 309; Supp. XVI: 288; Supp. XVII: 71, 73, 74, 75, 132; Supp. XVIII: 301; Supp. XIX: 86; Supp. XX: 106, 108; Supp. XXI: 52, 61, 64, 132, 214; Supp. XXII: 81, 82, 225, 277–278; Supp. XXIII: 19, 165

Dickinson, Gilbert, I: 469

Dickinson, Goldsworthy Lowes, Supp. XIV: 336

Dickinson, Lavinia Norcross, I: 451, 453, 462, 470

Dickinson, Stephanie, Supp. XXIII: 250

Dickinson, Mrs. William A. (Susan Gilbert), I: 452, 453, 456, 469, 470

Dickinson, William Austin, I: 451, 453, 469

Dickinson and the Strategies of Reticence (Dobson), Retro. Supp. I: 29, 42

Dickson, Helen. See Blackmur, Helen Dickson

Dickstein, Morris, Supp. XIII: 106; Supp. XXIV: 222, 223

"Dick Whittington and His Cat", Supp. I Part 2: 656

"DICTATORSHIP OF THE PROLE-TARIAT, THE" (Baraka), Supp. II Part 1: 54

Dictionary of Afro-American Slang (Major), Supp. XXII: 172, 174, 180

Dictionary of Literary Biography (Barron and Meyer, eds.), Supp. XVIII: 173; Supp. XIX: 195

Dictionary of Literary Biography (Gwynn, ed.), Supp. XVIII: 173; Supp. XIX: 121

Dictionary of Literary Biography (Kibler, ed.), Supp. IX: 94, 109; Supp. XI: 297

Dictionary of Literary Biography (Knight, ed.), Supp. XIV: 144

Dictionary of Literary Biography (Martine, ed.), Supp. XXII: 187

Dictionary of Literary Biography (Sicher, ed.), Supp. XVII: 41

Dictionary of Literary Biography (Twentieth-Century American Nature Poets, Bryson and Thompson, eds.), Supp. XXIII: 129

Dictionary of Modern English Usage, A (Fowler), Supp. I Part 2: 660

"Dictum: For a Masque of Deluge" (Merwin), Supp. III Part 1: 342–343

"Didactic Poem" (Levertov), Supp. III Part 1: 280

Diderot, Denis, II: 535; IV: 440; Supp. XVI: 293; Supp. XVII: 145

Did I Ever Tell You How Lucky You Are? (Geisel), Supp. XVI: 109

Didion, Joan, Retro. Supp. I: 116; Retro. Supp. II: 209; Supp. I Part 1: 196, 197; Supp. III Part 1: 302; Supp. IV Part 1: 195–216; Supp. XI: 221; Supp. XII: 307; Supp. XXV: 208

Dido, I: 81

Dido, Queen of Hearts (Atherton), Supp. XXIV: 26

Di Donato, Peter, Supp. XX: 34

Di Donato, Pietro, Supp. XX: 33–47

"Did 'Paco's Story' Deserve Its Award" (Kakutani), Supp. XXII: 109

"Did You Ever Dream Lucky?" (Ellison), Supp. II Part 1: 246

Dieckmann, Katherine, Supp. XXIII: 295, 296

"Die-Hard, The" (Benét), Supp. XI: 54–55, 56

Diehl, Digby, Supp. IV Part 1: 204

Dien Cai Dau (Komunyakaa), Supp. XIII: 121, 122–124, 125, 131, 132

Dies, Martin, Supp. XVIII: 229

"Dies Irae" (Lowell), II: 553

Die Zeit Ohne Beispiel, (Goebbels), III: 560

Difference Engine, The (W. Gibson and B. Sterling), Supp. XVI: 121, 124, 128–129

Different Drummer, A (Larkin; film), Supp. XI: 20

Different Fleshes (Goldbarth), Supp. XII: 181–182, 188

Different Hours (Dunn), Supp. XI: 139, 142, 143, 155

"Different Road, A" (Strout), Supp. XXIII: 282–283

Different Seasons (King), Supp. V: 148, 152

Different Ways to Pray (Nye), Supp. XIII: 274, 275, 277, 285, 287

"Different Ways to Pray" (Nye), Supp. XIII: 275

"Difficulties of a Statesman" (Eliot), I: 580

"Difficulties of Modernism and the Modernism of Difficulty" (Poirier), Supp. II Part 1: 136

Diff'rent (O'Neill), III: 389; Supp. XXII: 22

Di Filippo, Paul, Supp. XXII: 260, 261

DiGaetani, John L., Supp. XIII: 200

Digges, Deborah, Supp. XXIII: 57

"Digging" (Sanders), Supp. XVI: 272

"Digging in the Garden of Age I Uncover a Live Root" (Swenson), Supp. IV Part 2: 649

Digging Up the Dirt (Moraga), Supp. XXIII: 197

Diggins, John P., Supp. I Part 2: 650

Digital Barbarism: A Writer's Manifesto (Helprin), Supp. XXV: 81, 84, 88–89

"Dignity of Life, The" (C. Bly), Supp. XVI: 34, 36–37

Digregorio, Charles, Supp. XI: 326

"Digression on Number I, 1948" (O'Hara), Supp. XXIII: 214

"Dilemma" (Budbill), Supp. XIX: 2

"Dilemma of Determinism, The" (James), II: 347–348, 352

"Dilemma of the Negro Writer, The" (speech, C. Himes), Supp. XVI: 140

"Dilettante, The" (Wharton), IV: 311, 313

"Dilettante, The: A Modern Type" (Dunbar), Supp. II Part 1: 199

Dillard, Annie, Supp. VI: 19–39; Supp. VIII: 272; Supp. X: 31; Supp. XIII: 154

Dillard, R. H. W., Supp. XII: 16

Dillman, Bradford, III: 403; Supp. XII: 241

Dillon, Brian, Supp. X: 209

Dillon, George, III: 141; Supp. III Part 2: 621

Dillon, Millicent, Supp. IV Part 1: 95

Dilsaver, Paul, Supp. XIII: 112

Dilthey, Wilhelm, I: 58

Dime-Store Alchemy: The Art of Joseph Cornell, Supp. VIII: 272

"Diminuendo" (Dunn), Supp. XI: 152–153

"Dimout in Harlem" (Hughes), Supp. I Part 1: 333

"Dinah's Lament" (Nelson), Supp. XVIII: 183

Dinesen, Isak, IV: 279; Supp. VIII: 171; Supp. XVI: 250

Dining Room, The (Gurney), Supp. V: 105–106

"Dinner at ------, A" (O. Henry), Supp. II Part 1: 402

"Dinner at Sir Nigel's" (Bowles), Supp. IV Part 1: 94

Dinner at the Homesick Restaurant (Tyler), Supp. IV Part 2: 657, 667–668

"Dinner at Uncle Borris's" (Simic), Supp. VIII: 272

Dinner Bridge (Lardner), II: 435

Dinosaur Tales (Bradbury), Supp. IV Part 1: 103

"Diogenes Invents a Game" (Karr), Supp. XI: 240–241

"Diogenes Tries to Forget" (Karr), Supp. XI: 241

Diomede, Matthew, **Supp. XX: 46**
Dionysis in Doubt (Robinson), **III:** 510
Dionysus in 69 (Schechner), **Supp. XXIV:** 116
Diop, Birago, **Supp. IV Part 1:** 16
Diop, David, **Supp. IV Part 1:** 16
Di Piero, W. S., **Supp. XVII:** 241; **Supp. XIX: 33–48**
Di Prima, Diane, **Supp. III Part 1:** 30; **Supp. XIV:** 125, 144, 148, 150
Dirda, Michael, **Supp. XXI:** 233
Direction of Poetry, The: An Anthology of Rhymed and Metered Verse Written in the English Language since 1975 (Richman, ed.), **Supp. XV:** 250, 251
Direction of Poetry, The: Rhymed and Metered Verse Written in the English Language since 1975 (Richman), **Supp. XI:** 249
"Directive" (Bishop), **Retro. Supp. II:** 42
"Directive" (Frost), **III:** 287; **Retro. Supp. I:** 140; **Supp. VIII:** 32, 33
"Dire Cure" (Matthews), **Supp. IX:** 168
"Dirge" (Dunbar), **Supp. II Part 1:** 199
"Dirge without Music" (Millay), **III:** 126
"Dirt" (Salter), **Supp. IX:** 257, 260, 261
"Dirt and Desire: Essay on the Phenomenology of Female Pollution in Antiquity" (Carson), **Supp. XII: 111**
Dirty Bird Blues (Major), **Supp. XXII: 180–181**
Dirty Dingus Magee (film), **Supp. XVII:** 139
"Dirty English Potatoes" (X. J. Kennedy), **Supp. XV:** 165
"Dirty Memories" (Olds), **Supp. X:** 211
Dirty Story (Shanley), **Supp. XIV:** 316, 331
"Dirty Word, The" (Shapiro), **Supp. II Part 2:** 710
Dirty Work (L. Brown), **Supp. XXI:** 37, 39, 40, 42, **45**
"'Disabled Imagination' and the Masculine Metaphor in the Works of Leonard Kriegel, The" (Haugen), **Supp. XXIV:** 215
Disappearance of the Jews, The (Mamet), **Supp. XIV:** 249–250, 250–251, 252, 254
Disappearances (Auster), **Supp. XII:** 23
"Disappearances" (Hogan), **Supp. IV Part 1:** 401
Disappearances (Mosher), **Supp. XXII:** 204, 205, 206, 207, 208, 209, **210**
"Disappeared, The " (C. Baxter), **Supp. XVII:** 19
Disappearing Acts (McMillan), **Supp. XIII:** 182, 183, **188–189,** 192
Disappearing Ink: Poetry at the End of Print Culture (Gioia), **Supp. XV:** 112
"Disappointment, The" (Creeley), **Supp. IV Part 1:** 143
"Disappointment and Desire" (R. Bly), **Supp. IV Part 1:** 71
Disappointment Artist, The (Lethem), **Supp. XVIII:** 135, 141, **148**
"Discards" (Baker), **Supp. XIII:** 53, 55–56

Discerning the Signs of the Times (Niebuhr), **III:** 300–301, 307–308
Disch, Thomas M., **Supp. XIX:** 1
"Disciple of Bacon, The" (Epstein), **Supp. XII:** 163–164
"Discipline" (L. Brown), **Supp. XXI:** 44
Discomfort, Zone, The: A Personal History (Franzen), **Supp. XX: 83, 84, 95**
"Discordants" (Aiken), **I:** 65
Discourse on Method (Descartes), **I:** 255
"Discourtesies" (Kirsch), **Supp. XV:** 341
"Discovering Theme and Structure in the Novel" (Schuster), **Supp. VIII:** 126
"Discovery" (Freneau), **Supp. II Part 1:** 258
"Discovery of the Madeiras, The" (Frost), **Retro. Supp. I:** 139
"Discovery of What It Means to Be an American, The" (Baldwin), **Supp. I Part 1:** 54–55
Discovery! The Search for Arabian Oil (Stegner), **Supp. IV Part 2:** 599
"Discrete Series" (Zukofsky), **Supp. III Part 2:** 616
"Discretions of Alcibiades" (Pinsky), **Supp. VI:** 241
"Disease, The" (Rukeyser), **Supp. VI:** 279
Disenchanted, The (play, Schulberg and Breit), **Supp. XVIII:** 254
Disenchanted, The (Schulberg), **II:** 98; **Retro. Supp. I:** 113; **Supp. XVIII: 247–250,** 253
Disenchantments: An Anthology of Modern Fairy Tale Poetry (Mieder), **Supp. XIV:** 126
"Dish of Green Pears, A" (Ríos), **Supp. IV Part 2:** 552
"Disillusion and Dogma" (Untermeyer), **Supp. XV:** 306
Dismantling the Silence (Simic), **Supp. VIII: 273–274,** 275, 276
Disney, Walt, **III:** 275, 426
"Disney of My Mind" (Chabon), **Supp. XI:** 63
Disobedience (Notley), **Supp. XXII:** 235, 236
Dispatches (Herr), **Supp. XI:** 245; **Supp. XIX:** 17
"Displaced Person, The" (O'Connor), **III:** 343–344, 350, 352, 356; **Retro. Supp. II:** 229, 232, 236
"Disposal" (Snodgrass), **Supp. VI:** 314
Dispossessed, The (Berryman), **I:** 170, 172, 173, 174, 175, 176, 178
"Disquieting Muses, The" (Plath), **Supp. I Part 2:** 538
Disraeli, Benjamin, **II:** 127
Dissent (Didion), **Supp. IV Part 1:** 208
"Dissent in Ashcroft's America" (P. N. Warren), **Supp. XX: 273**
"Dissenting Opinion on Kafka, A" (Wilson), **IV:** 437–438
Dissent in Three American Wars (Morison, Merk, and Freidel), **Supp. I Part 2:** 495
Dissertation on Liberty and Necessity, Pleasure and Pain, A (Franklin), **II:** 108

Dissertations on Government; the Affairs of the Bank: and Paper Money (Paine), **Supp. I Part 2:** 510
"Distance" (Carver), **Supp. III Part 1:** 146
"Distance" (Everwine), **Supp. XV:** 85
"Distance" (Paley), **Supp. VI:** 222
"Distance, The" (Karr), **Supp. XI:** 241
"Distance from the Sea, A" (Kees), **Supp. XV:** 147
"Distance Nowhere" (Hughes), **Retro. Supp. I:** 207
"Distance Up Close, The" (Peacock), **Supp. XIX:** 196–197, 198
"Distant Episode, A" (Bowles), **Supp. IV Part 1:** 84–85, 86, 90
Distant Episode, A: The Selected Stories (Bowles), **Supp. IV Part 1:** 79
Distant Rain: A Conversation Between Jakuchō; Setouchi & Tess Gallagher (Setouchi and Gallagher), **Supp. XXIV:** 166, 178
Distinguished Guest, The (Miller), **Supp. XII: 299–301**
Distortions (Beattie), **Supp. V:** 21, 23, 24, 25, 27
"Distrest Shepherdess, The" (Freneau), **Supp. II Part 1:** 258
District of Columbia (Dos Passos), **I:** 478, 489–490, 492
Disturber of the Peace (Manchester), **III:** 103
Disturbing the Peace (Yates), **Supp. XI:** 345, 346
"Diver, The" (Hayden), **Supp. II Part 1:** 368, 372, 373
"Divided Life of Jean Toomer, The" (Toomer), **Supp. III Part 2:** 488
Divided Self, The (Laing), **Supp. XX: 95**
Divina Commedia (Longfellow, trans.), **II:** 490, 492, 493
"Divina Pastora, La" (C. L. R. James), **Supp. XXI:** 160
"Divine, The" (Di Piero), **Supp. XIX:** 41
"Divine Collaborator" (Simic), **Supp. VIII:** 282
Divine Comedies (Merrill), **Supp. III Part 1:** 324, 329–332
Divine Comedy (Dante), **I:** 137, 265, 400, 446; **II:** 215, 335, 490, 492, 493; **III:** 13, 448, 453; **Supp. V:** 283, 331, 338, 345; **Supp. X:** 253; **Supp. XIV:** 6; **Supp. XIX:** 36, 39
Divine Husband, The (Goldman), **Supp. XXV:** 49–50, 55–57
"Divine Image, The" (Blake), **Supp. V:** 257
Divine Pilgrim, The (Aiken), **I:** 50, 55
Divine Right's Trip (Norman), **Supp. XXIII:** 42
Divine Tragedy, The (Longfellow), **II:** 490, 500, 505, 506, 507; **Retro. Supp. II:** 165, 166
Divine Weekes and Workes (Sylvester, trans.), **Supp. I Part 1:** 104
Divine Weeks (Du Bartas), **IV:** 157–158
Diving into the Wreck: Poems 1971–1972 (Rich), **Supp. I Part 2:** 550, 559–565, 569; **Supp. XV:** 252

"Diving Past African Violets" (A. Finch), **Supp. XVII:** 72

Diving Rock on the Hudson, A (H. Roth), **Supp. IX:** 236, **237–238**

"Divinity in Its Fraying Fact, A" (Levis), **Supp. XI:** 271

"Divinity School Address" (Emerson), **II:** 12–13

"Divinity School or Trusting the Act of Writing" (Abraham), **Supp. XXIV:** 1, 3–4

"Divisions upon a Ground" (Hecht), **Supp. X:** 58

"Divorce" (Karr), **Supp. XI:** 244

"Divorced Fathers and Pizza Crusts" (Halliday), **Supp. XIX:** 93

Divorced in America: Marriage in an Age of Possibility (Epstein), **Supp. XIV:** 113

"Divorce Dream" (Halliday), **Supp. XIX:** 90

"Divorce in the United States" (Atherton), **Supp. XXIV:** 24

Dix, Douglas Shields, **Supp. XII:** 14

Dixie City Jam (Burke), **Supp. XIV:** 32

Dixon, Ivan, **Supp. IV Part 1:** 362

Dixon, Stephen, **Supp. XII: 139–158**

Dixon, Terrell F., **Supp. XVI:** 21

Dixon, Thomas, Jr., **Supp. II Part 1:** 169, 171, 177

Djinn (Robbe-Grillet), **Supp. V:** 48

D'Lugoff, Burt, **Supp. IV Part 1:** 362, 370

Dmytryk, Edward, **Supp. XX: 41**

Do, Lord, Remember Me (Garrett), **Supp. VII:** 98–100, 110

"Doaksology, The" (Wolfe), **IV:** 459

Do Androids Dream of Electric Sheep? (Dick), **Supp. XVIII:** 137

Dobie, J. Frank, **Supp. V:** 225; **Supp. XIII:** 227

Döblin, Alfred, **Supp. XV:** 137

Dobriansky, Lev, **Supp. I Part 2:** 648, 650

Dobrin, Sidney I., **Supp. XVIII:** 192, 195

Dobson, Joanne, **Retro. Supp. I:** 29, 31, 42; **Supp. XVIII:** 259

Dobyns, Stephen, **Supp. XIII: 73–92**

"Docking at Palermo" (Hugo), **Supp. VI:** 137–138

"Dock Rats" (Moore), **III:** 213

"Dock-Witch, The" (Ozick), **Supp. V:** 262, 264

"Doc Mellhorn and the Pearly Gates" (Benét), **Supp. XI:** 55

"Doctor, The" (Dubus), **Supp. VII:** 80–81

"Doctor and the Doctor's Wife, The" (Hemingway), **II:** 248; **Retro. Supp. I:** 174, 175

Doctor Breen's Practice, a Novel (Howells), **I:** 282

Doctor Faustus (Mann), **III:** 283

Doctor Jazz (Carruth), **Supp. XVI:** 47, 59

"Doctor Jekyll" (Sontag), **Supp. III Part 2:** 469

"Doctor Leavis and the Moral Tradition" (Trilling), **Supp. III Part 2:** 512–513

Doctor Martino and Other Stories (Faulkner), **II:** 72; **Retro. Supp. I:** 84

"Doctor of the Heart, The" (Sexton), **Supp. II Part 2:** 692

Doctorow, E. L., **Retro. Supp. I:** 97; **Supp. III Part 2:** 590, 591; **Supp. IV Part 1: 217–240; Supp. V:** 45; **Supp. XVI:** 73; **Supp. XVII:** 183; **Supp. XX: 84, 90; Supp. XXI:** 18–19; **Supp. XXII:** 268

Doctor Sax (Kerouac), **Supp. III Part 1:** 220–222, 224–227

Doctor Sleep (Bell), **Supp. X: 9–11**

"Doctors' Row" (Aiken), **I:** 67

Doctor's Son and Other Stories, The (O'Hara), **III:** 361

Doctor Stories, The (W. C. Williams), **Retro. Supp. I:** 424

"Doctor's Wife, The" (Ozick), **Supp. V:** 262, 265

Doctor Zhivago (Pasternak), **IV:** 434, 438, 443

"Documentary" (Simic), **Supp. VIII:** 282

Dodd, Elizabeth, **Supp. V:** 77

Dodd, Susan, **Supp. XXV:** 129

Dodd, Wayne, **Supp. IV Part 2:** 625

Dodge, Mabel, **Supp. XX: 69; Supp. XXI:** 5, 6, 8, 12; **Supp. XXII:** 158, 161. *See also* Luhan, Mabel Dodge

Dodson, Owen, **Supp. I Part 1:** 54

Dodsworth (Lewis), **II:** 442, 449–450, 453, 456

Doenitz, Karl, **Supp. I Part 2:** 491

Does Civilization Need Religion? (Niebuhr), **III:** 293–294

"Does 'Consciousness' Exist?" (James), **II:** 356

"Does Education Pay?" (Du Bois), **Supp. II Part 1:** 159

"Dog" (B. Kelly), **Supp. XVII:** 126

Dog (Shepard), **Supp. III Part 2:** 434

"Dog Act, The" (Komunyakaa), **Supp. XIII:** 114–115

"Dog and the Playlet, The" (O. Henry), **Supp. II Part 1:** 399

Dog Beneath the Skin, The (Auden), **Supp. II Part 1:** 10

"Dog Creek Mainline" (Wright), **Supp. V:** 340

"Dogdom of the Dead, The" (Stallings), **Supp. XXV:** 228

"Dogfight" (W. Gibson and Swanwick), **Supp. XVI:** 128

Dog in the Manger, The (Vega; Merwin, trans.), **Supp. III Part 1:** 341, 347

Dog of the Marriage, The (Hempel), **Supp. XXI:** 115, 116, 117, 118, **126–127**

"Dog"(P. Benedict), **Supp. XXIII:** 36–37, 39

Dogs Bark, but the Caravan Rolls On (Conroy), **Supp. XVI:** 63, 70, 74, **75–76**

Dogs Bark, The: Public People and Private Places (Capote), **Supp. III Part 1:** 120, 132

"Dog's Eye" (J. W. Miller), **Supp. XX: 167**

"Dogs of Bucharest, The" (Gallagher), **Supp. XXIV:** 171

Dogs of God (Benedict), **Supp. XXIII:** 35, **41–45,** 49–50

Dog Soldiers (Stone), **Supp. V:** 298, 299–301

Dog Star, The (Di Piero), **Supp. XIX:** 38, **40–41,** 43

"Dog Stories" (Prose), **Supp. XVI:** 256

Dog & the Fever, The (Quevedo), **Retro. Supp. I:** 423

"Dogtown Letters, The" (Jarman and R. McDowell), **Supp. XVII:** 111

"Dogwood, The" (Levertov), **Supp. III Part 1:** 276

"Dogwood Tree, The: A Boyhood" (Updike), **IV:** 218; **Retro. Supp. I:** 318, 319

Doig, Ivan, **Supp. XIV:** 227

"Doing Battle with the Wolf" (Coleman), **Supp. XI:** 87–88

"Doing Jigsaw Puzzles" (Crooker), **Supp. XXIII:** 56

Doing Literary Business: American Women Writers in the Nineteenth Century (Coultrap-McQuin), **Supp. XVI:** 85

Doings and Undoings (Podhoretz), **Supp. VIII: 236–237**

"Do-It-Yourself" (C. Baxter), **Supp. XVII:** 14–15

Dolan, Jill, **Supp. XV:** 327

Dolben, Digby Mackworth, **Supp. XX: 230**

"Dolce Far' Niente" (Humphrey), **Supp. IX:** 106

Dolci, Carlo, **III:** 474–475

Dollars and Cents (A. Warner), **Supp. XVIII:** 264

"Dollhouse, The" (Haines), **Supp. XII:** 204

"Dollhouse, The" (Stallings), **Supp. XXV:** 231, 232

Dollmaker's Ghost, The (Levis), **Supp. XI:** 259, 260, **264–268**

Doll's House, A (Ibsen), **III:** 523; **IV:** 357; **Supp. XVI:** 182

Dolmetsch, Arnold, **III:** 464

Dolores Claiborne (King), **Supp. V:** 138, 141, 147, 148, 149–150, 152

"Dolph Heyliger" (Irving), **II:** 309

Dolphin, The (Lowell), **Retro. Supp. II:** 183, 186, 188, **190–191; Supp. XII:** 253–254

"Dolphins" (Francis), **Supp. IX:** 83

Dome of Many-Coloured Class, A (Lowell), **II:** 515, 516–517

Domesday Book (Masters), **Supp. I Part 2:** 465, 466–469, 471, 473, 476

"Domestic Economy" (Gilman), **Supp. XI:** 206

"Domestic Manners" (Hardwick), **Supp. III Part 1:** 211

Domestic Work (Trethewey), **Supp. XXI:** 243, 244, **248–251,** 254

"Domestic Work, 1937" (Trethewey), **Supp. XXI:** 248

"Dominant White, The" (McKay), **Supp. X:** 134

Dominguez, Robert, **Supp. VIII:** 83

Domini, John, **Supp. XIX:** 45; **Supp. XXI:** 235

Dominique, Jean. *See* Closset, Marie
Donahoe, Edward, **Supp. XVIII:** 132
Donahue, Deirdre, **Supp. XXV:** 9
Donahue, Phil, **Supp. IV Part 2:** 526; **Supp. X:** 311
Donaldson, Susan, **Supp. XXII:** 148
Doña Perfecta (Galdós), **II:** 290
Dong, Stella, **Supp. XVI:** 222
Don Juan (Byron), **Supp. XV:** 259
"DON JUAN IN HELL" (Baraka), **Supp. II Part 1:** 33
Donkey of God, The (Untermeyer), **Supp. XV:** 310
"Donna mi Prega" (Cavalcanti), **Supp. III Part 2:** 620, 621, 622
Donn-Byrne, Brian Oswald. *See* Byrne, Donn
Donne, John, **I:** 358–359, 384, 389, 522, 586; **II:** 254; **III:** 493; **IV:** 83, 88, 135, 141, 144, 145, 151, 156, 165, 331, 333; **Retro. Supp. II:** 76; **Supp. I Part 1:** 80, 364, 367; **Supp. I Part 2:** 421, 424, 467, 725, 726; **Supp. III Part 2:** 614, 619; **Supp. VIII:** 26, 33, 164; **Supp. IX:** 44; **Supp. XII:** 45, 159; **Supp. XIII:** 94, 130; **Supp. XIV:** 122; **Supp. XV:** 92, 251; **Supp. XVI:** 158, 204; **Supp. XVIII:** 35, 39, 50–51, 307; **Supp. XXIV:** 167
Donne's Sermons: Selected Passages (L. P. Smith, ed.), **Supp. XIV:** 342
Donoghue, Denis, **I:** 537; **Supp. IV Part 1:** 39; **Supp. VIII:** 105, 189
Donohue, H. E. F., **Supp. IX:** 2, 3, 15, 16
Donoso, José, **Supp. XXIV:** 86
Do Not Deny Me (Thompson), **Supp. XXIII:** 300–301
"Do Not Weep Maiden, For War Is Kind" (Crane), **Supp. XVIII:** 75
Donovan, Josephine, **Retro. Supp. II:** 138, 139, 147
Don Quixote (Cervantes), **I:** 134; **II:** 291, 434; **III:** 113, 614; **Supp. I Part 2:** 422; **Supp. IX:** 94; **Supp. XXIV:** 87
Don Quixote: Which Was a Dream (Acker), **Supp. XII:** 5, 12–14
Don't Ask (Levine), **Supp. V:** 178
Don't Ask Questions (Marquand), **III:** 58
Don't Bet on the Prince: Contemporary Feminist Fairy Tales in North America and England (Zipes), **Supp. XIV:** 126
Don't Drink the Water (Allen), **Supp. XV:** 3, **14**
Don't Look Back (film, Pennebaker), **Supp. XVIII:** 19
"Don't Neglect Your Wife" (script, Atherton), **Supp. XXIV:** 25
"Don't Shoot the Warthog" (Corso), **Supp. XII:** 123
Don't Stop the Carnival (Wouk), **Supp. XXV:** 257, 263–264
"Don't Tell Mother" (Wasserstein), **Supp. XV:** 319
"Don't Think Twice, It's All Right" (song, Dylan), **Supp. XVIII:** 24
Don't Worry About the Kids (Neugeboren), **Supp. XVI:** 226
"Don't Worry About the Kids" (Neugeboren), **Supp. XVI:** 226

Don't You Want to Be Free? (Hughes), **Retro. Supp. I:** 203; **Supp. I Part 1:** 339
"Doodler, The" (Merrill), **Supp. III Part 1:** 321
Doolan, Moira, **Retro. Supp. II:** 247
Doolittle, Hilda (H. D.), **II:** 517, 520–521; **III:** 194, 195–196, 457, 465; **IV:** 404, 406; **Retro. Supp. I:** 288, 412, 413, 414, 415, 417; **Supp. I Part 1:** 253–275; **Supp. I Part 2:** 707; **Supp. III Part 1:** 48; **Supp. III Part 2:** 610; **Supp. IV Part 1:** 257; **Supp. V:** 79; **Supp. XV:** 43, 249, 301, 302; **Supp. XVII:** 77; **Supp. XXII:** 88; **Supp. XXIV:** 64
Doolittle, Thomas, **IV:** 150
"Doomed by Our Blood to Care" (Orfalea), **Supp. XIII:** 278
"Doomsday" (Plath), **Retro. Supp. II:** 242
Doomsters, The (Macdonald), **Supp. IV Part 2:** 462, 463, 472, 473
Doomswoman, The (Atherton), **Supp. XXIV:** 22
Doonesbury (Trudeau), **Supp. XXIV:** 283
"Door, The" (Creeley), **Supp. IV Part 1:** 145, 146, 156–157
Door, The (Rinehart), **Supp. XXV:** 197, 200
"Door, The" (White), **Supp. I Part 2:** 651, 675–676
"Door in the Dark, The" (Frost), **II:** 156
Door in the Hive, A (Levertov), **Supp. III Part 1:** 283, 284
"Door of the Trap, The" (Anderson), **I:** 112
"Doors" (Dybek), **Supp. XXIII:** 69
Doors (Hoffman), **Supp. XVIII:** 86–87
"Doors" (Hoffman), **Supp. XVIII:** 86–87
"Doors, Doors, Doors" (Sexton), **Supp. II Part 2:** 681
Doors, The, **Supp. X:** 186
"Doorways into the Depths" (Sanders), **Supp. XVI:** 272
Doreski, William, **Retro. Supp. II:** 185
Dorfman, Ariel, **Supp. IX:** 131, 138
Dorfman, Joseph, **Supp. I Part 2:** 631, 647, 650
Dorman, Jen, **Supp. XI:** 240
Dorn, Edward, **Supp. IV Part 1:** 154; **Supp. XXIV:** 33, 44
Dorn, Sarah, **Supp. XXI:** 243
"Dorothea Dix, Samaritan" (J. Scott), **Supp. XVII:** 189
Dorr, Julia, **Supp. XV:** 286
Dorris, Michael, **Supp. IV Part 1:** 260, 272
Dos Passos, John, **I:** 99, 288, 374, 379, **474–496,** 517, 519; **II:** 74, 77, 89, 98; **III:** 2, 28, 29, 70, 172, 382–383; **IV:** 340, 427, 433; **Retro. Supp. I:** 105, 113, 187; **Retro. Supp. II:** 95, 196; **Supp. I Part 2:** 646; **Supp. III Part 1:** 104, 105; **Supp. V:** 277; **Supp. VIII:** 101, 105; **Supp. XIV:** 24; **Supp. XV:** 135, 137, 182; **Supp. XVII:** 105, 107; **Supp. XXI:** 8; **Supp. XXIII:** 68
"Dos Passos: Poet Against the World" (Cowley), **Supp. II Part 1:** 143, 145

Dostoesvsky: A Screenplay (Carver and Gallagher), **Supp. XXIV:** 178
Dostoevsky, Fyodor, **I:** 53, 103, 211, 468; **II:** 60, 130, 275, 320, 587; **III:** 37, 61, 155, 174, 176, 188, 189, 267, 272, 283, 286, 354, 357, 358, 359, 467, 571, 572; **IV:** 1, 7, 8, 17, 21, 50, 59, 106, 110, 128, 134, 285, 289, 476, 485, 491; **Retro. Supp. II:** 20, 204, 299; **Supp. I Part 1:** 49; **Supp. I Part 2:** 445, 466; **Supp. IV Part 2:** 519, 525; **Supp. VIII:** 175; **Supp. X:** 4–5; **Supp. XI:** 161; **Supp. XII:** 322; **Supp. XVI:** 63; **Supp. XVII:** 225; **Supp. XVIII:** 278, 280; **Supp. XX:** **45;** **Supp. XXIII:** 4; **Supp. XXIV:** 132
Doty, Mark, **Supp. IX:** 42, 300; **Supp. XI:** **119–138;** **Supp. XXI:** 129, 130, 131, 139, 141; **Supp. XXIII:** 126, 221
Doty, M. R. *See* Dawson, Ruth; Doty, Mark
Double, The (Dostoevsky), **Supp. IX:** 105
"Double, The" (Levis), **Supp. XI:** 260, **261–263**
Double, The (Rank), **Supp. IX:** 105
Double Agent, The (Blackmur), **Supp. II Part 1:** 90, 108, 146
Double Axe, The (Jeffers), **Supp. II Part 2:** 416, 434
"Double Blind" (Skloot), **Supp. XX:** 194, **208**
Doubleday, Frank, **I:** 500, 502, 515, 517; **III:** 327
Doubleday, Mrs. Frank, **I:** 500
Double Deuce (Parker), **Supp. XIX:** 183
Double Down (F. and S. Barthelme), **Supp. XI:** 27, 34, 35, 36–38
Double Dream of Spring, The (Ashbery), **Supp. III Part 1:** 11–13
Double Fold: Libraries and the Assault on Paper (Baker), **Supp. XIII:** 52, 56
Double Game (Calle), **Supp. XII:** 22
"Double Gap, The" (Auchincloss), **Supp. IV Part 1:** 33
"Double-Headed Snake of Newbury, The" (Whittier), **Supp. I Part 2:** 698
Double Honeymoon (Connell), **Supp. XIV:** 80, 87
Double Image, The (Levertov), **Supp. III Part 1:** 274, 276
"Double Image, The" (Sexton), **Supp. II Part 2:** 671, 677–678
Double Indemnity (film), **Supp. IV Part 1:** 130
Double Legacy: Reflections on a Pair of Deaths (Hadas), **Supp. XXIII:** 123, **126–127**
"Double Limbo" (Komunyakaa), **Supp. XIII:** 132
Double Man, The (Auden), **Supp. III Part 1:** 16; **Supp. X:** 118
"Double Ode" (Rukeyser), **Supp. VI:** 282–283, 286
Double Persephone (Atwood), **Supp. XIII:** 19
Double Play (Parker), **Supp. XIX:** **189–190**
Doubles in Literary Psychology (Tymms), **Supp. IX:** 105

Double Vision: American Thoughts Abroad (Knowles), **Supp. XII:** 249

"Doubt on the Great Divide" (Stafford), **Supp. XI:** 322

Dougherty, Robin, **Supp. XXII:** 205

Dougherty, Steve, **Supp. X:** 262

Douglas, Aaron, **Supp. I Part 1:** 326

Douglas, Alfred, **Supp. X:** 151

Douglas, Ann, **Supp. XII:** 136; **Supp. XVIII:** 258; **Supp. XX: 69**

Douglas, Claire, **III:** 552

Douglas, Ellen, **Supp. XXI:** 38

Douglas, George (pseudonym). *See* Brown, George Douglas

Douglas, Kirk, **Supp. XIII:** 5–6

Douglas, Lloyd, **IV:** 434

Douglas, Marjory Stoneman, **Supp. XVIII:** 195

Douglas, Melvyn, **Supp. V:** 223

Douglas, Michael, **Supp. XI:** 67

Douglas, Paul, **III:** 294

Douglas, Stephen A., **III:** 577, 588–589; **Supp. I Part 2:** 456, 471

Douglas, William O., **III:** 581

Douglass, Frederick, **Supp. I Part 1:** 51, 345; **Supp. I Part 2:** 591; **Supp. II Part 1:** 157, 195, 196, 292, 378; **Supp. III Part 1:** 153–174; **Supp. IV Part 1:** 1, 2, 13, 15, 256; **Supp. VIII:** 202; **Supp. XVIII:** 16; **Supp. XX: 109, 281; Supp. XXIII:** 167

Douglass, Thomas E., **Supp. XXIII:** 36

Douglass Pilot, The (Baldwin, ed.), **Supp. I Part 1:** 49

Dove, Belle, **I:** 451

Dove, Rita, **Supp. IV Part 1: 241–258; Supp. XVII:** 71, 110; **Supp. XVIII:** 172, 174; **Supp. XXI:** 243, 246, 247, 249, 251

Dove of the East and Other Stories, A (Helprin), **Supp. XXV:** 79, 83, 84–85

"Dover Beach" (Arnold), **Retro. Supp. I:** 325; **Supp. XIX:** 41

Dow, Lorenzo, **IV:** 265

Dowd, Douglas, **Supp. I Part 2:** 645, 650

"Do We Understand Each Other?" (Ginsberg), **Supp. II Part 1:** 311

Dowie, William, **Supp. V:** 199

Do with Me What You Will (Oates), **Supp. II Part 2:** 506, 515–517

Dowling, Eddie, **IV:** 394

Down and Out (Shanley), **Supp. XIV:** 317

"Down at City Hall" (Didion), **Supp. IV Part 1:** 211

"Down at the Cross" (Baldwin), **Retro. Supp. II:** 1, 2, 7, 12, 13, 15; **Supp. I Part 1:** 60, 61

"Down at the Dinghy" (Salinger), **III:** 559, 563

"Down by the Station, Early in the Morning" (Ashbery), **Supp. III Part 1:** 25

Downey, Sharon D., **Supp. XX:** 244

Downhill Racer (film), **Supp. IX:** 253

"Down Home" (J. W. Miller), **Supp. XX: 169**

"Down in Alabam" (Bierce), **I:** 193

Downing, Ben, **Supp. XII:** 175, 189, 190–191

Downing, Major Jack (pseudonym). *See* Smith, Seba

Down in My Heart (Stafford), **Supp. XI:** 313, 315

Down Mailer's Way (Solotaroff), **Retro. Supp. II:** 203

"Down the Highway" (song, Dylan), **Supp. XVIII:** 24

Down the Rabbit Hole: Adventures and Misadventures in the Realm of Children's Literature (Lanes), **Supp. XVI:** 104

Down There on a Visit (Isherwood), **Supp. XIV:** 159, 161, 164, **168–169,** 170, 171

Down the River (Abbey), **Supp. XIII:** 12–13

"Down the River with Henry Thoreau" (Abbey), **Supp. XIII:** 12–13

Down These Mean Streets (P. Thomas), **Supp. XIII:** 264

Down the Starry River (Purdy), **Supp. VII:** 278

Down to the River: Portraits of Iowa Musicians (Dyas), **Supp. XIX:** 174

Downtown (Siddons), **Supp. XXII:** 239, 240, 242, **247–249, 251–252,** 253

"Downtrodden Mary's Failed Campaign of Terror" (Saunders), **Supp. XIX:** 226

"Downward Path to Wisdom, The" (Porter), **III:** 442, 443, 446

"Down Where I Am" (Hughes), **Supp. I Part 1:** 344

Down with Starvation Wages in Southeast Missouri (C. L. R. James), **Supp. XXI:** 169

"Dowsing for Joy" (Skloot), **Supp. XX: 203**

Dowson, Ernest C., **I:** 384

Doyle, Arthur Conan, **Retro. Supp. I:** 270; **Supp. IV Part 1:** 128, 341; **Supp. IV Part 2:** 464, 469; **Supp. XI:** 63

Doyle, C. W., **I:** 199

"Draba" (Leopold), **Supp. XIV:** 186

Drabble, Margaret, **Supp. IV Part 1:** 297, 299, 305

Drabelle, Dennis, **Supp. XIII:** 13

Drach, Ivan, **Supp. III Part 1:** 268

Dracula (film), **Supp. IV Part 1:** 104; **Supp. XVII:** 57

"Draft Horse, The" (Frost), **Retro. Supp. I:** 141

"Draft Lyrics for *Candide*" (Agee), **I:** 28

Draft of XVI Cantos, A (Pound), **III:** 472; **Retro. Supp. I:** 292

Draft of XXX Cantos, A (Pound), **III:** 196; **Retro. Supp. I:** 292

Drafts &Fragments (Pound), **Retro. Supp. I:** 293

"Dragon" (Lovecraft), **Supp. XXV:** 111

Dragon Country (T. Williams), **IV:** 383

Dragone, Nichole, **Supp. XXIII:** 157

Dragon Seed (Buck), **Supp. II Part 1:** 124

Dragon's Teeth (Sinclair), **Supp. V:** 290

Drake, Benjamin, **Supp. I Part 2:** 584

Drake, Daniel, **Supp. I Part 2:** 584

Drake, Sir Francis, **Supp. I Part 2:** 497

Drake, Robert, **Supp. XX: 274**

Drake, St. Clair, **IV:** 475

Drake, Sylvia, **Supp. XXI:** 155

Drake, William, **Supp. XV:** 295

Dramatic Duologues (Masters), **Supp. I Part 2:** 461

"Drapery Factory, Gulfport. Mississippi, 1956" (Trethewey), **Supp. XXI:** 246

Drattel, Deborah, **Supp. XV:** 333

Drat These Brats (X. J. Kennedy), **Supp. XV:** 163

"Draught" (Cowley), **Supp. II Part 1:** 141, 142

Drayton, Michael, **IV:** 135; **Retro. Supp. II:** 76

"Dr. Bergen's Belief" (Schwartz), **Supp. II Part 2:** 650

Dr. Bloodmoney (Dick), **Supp. XVIII:** 138

"Dreadful Has Already Happened, The" (Strand), **Supp. IV Part 2:** 627

Dread Road, The (Le Sueur), **Supp. XXIII:** 168, 169, **169–170,** 173

"Dream, A" (Ginsberg), **Supp. II Part 1:** 312

"Dream, A" (Tate), **IV:** 129

"Dream, The" (Hayden), **Supp. II Part 1:** 368, 377

Dream at the End of the World, The: Paul Bowles and the Literary Renegades in Tangier (Green), **Supp. IV Part 1:** 95

"Dream Avenue" (Simic), **Supp. VIII:** 282

"Dream Boogie" (Hughes), **Retro. Supp. I:** 208; **Supp. I Part 1:** 339–340

"Dreambook Bestiary" (Komunyakaa), **Supp. XIII:** 120

Dreamer (Johnson), **Supp. VI:** 186, **196–199**

dreamer examines his pillow, the (Shanley), **Supp. XIV:** 315, **327**

"Dreamer in a Dead Language" (Paley), **Supp. VI:** 217

Dreaming in Cuban (García), **Supp. XI:** 178, **179–185,** 190

"Dreaming of Hair" (L.-Y. Lee), **Supp. XV:** 214

"Dreaming the Breasts" (Sexton), **Supp. II Part 2:** 692

"Dreaming Water" (Espaillat), **Supp. XXI:** 102

"Dream Interpretation" (Hadas), **Supp. XXIII:** 113, 121

"Dream Interpreted, The" (Paine), **Supp. I Part 2:** 505

Dream Jumbo (Longo), **Supp. XVI:** 124

Dream Keeper, The (Hughes), **Supp. I Part 1:** 328, 332, 333, 334

Dream Keeper and Other Poems, The (Hughes), **Retro. Supp. I:** 201, 202

Dreamland (Baker), **Supp. XIV:** 96

"Dream-Land" (Poe), **Retro. Supp. II:** 274

Dream Life of Balso Snell, The (West), **IV:** 286, 287, 288–290, 291, 297; **Retro. Supp. II:** 321, 322, 327, 328, **330–332**

"Dream Machine, The" (Hadas), **Supp. XXIII:** 122–123

Dream Me Home Safely: Writers on Growing up in America (Shreve, ed.), **Supp. XXIII:** 284

Dream of a Common Language, The: Poems, 1974–1977 (Rich), **Supp. I Part 2:** 551, 554, 569–576

Dream of Arcadia: American Writers and Artists in Italy (Brooks), **I:** 254

Dream of Governors, A (Simpson), **Supp. IX:** 265, **269–270**

"Dream of Her Grandfather, A" (Zitkala-Ša), **Supp. XXV:** 282, 283

"Dream of Italy, A" (Masters), **Supp. I Part 2:** 458

"Dream of Mourning, The" (Glück), **Supp. V:** 84

"Dream of the Blacksmith's Room, A" (R. Bly), **Supp. IV Part 1:** 73

"Dream of the Cardboard Lover" (Haines), **Supp. XII:** 204

Dream of the Golden Mountains, The (Cowley), **Supp. II Part 1:** 139, 141, 142, 144

"Dream Pang, A" (Frost), **II:** 153

Dream-Quest of Unkown Kadath, The (Lovecraft), **Supp. XXV:** 113–114

"Dreams About Clothes" (Merrill), **Supp. III Part 1:** 328–329

"Dreams"(Dybek), **Supp. XXIII:** 73

Dreams from Bunker Hill (Fante), **Supp. XI:** 160, 166, **172–173**

"Dreams in the Witch House, The" (Lovecraft), **Supp. XXV:** 111, 123

"Dreams"(Kenny), **Supp. XXIII:** 153

"Dreams of Adulthood" (Ashbery), **Supp. III Part 1:** 26

"Dreams of Glory on the Mound" (Plimpton), **Supp. XVI:** 238–239

"Dreams of Math" (Kenyon), **Supp. VII:** 160 161

"Dreams of the Animals" (Atwood), **Supp. XIII:** 33

"Dream Variations" (Hughes), **Retro. Supp. I:** 198; **Supp. I Part 1:** 323

"Dream Vision" (Olsen), **Supp. XIII:** 295–296

Dream Work (Oliver), **Supp. VII:** 234–235, 236–238, 240

Dred: A Tale of the Great Dismal Swamp (Stowe), **Supp. I Part 2:** 592

Dreiser, Theodore, **I:** 59, 97, 109, 116, 355, 374, 375, 475, 482, **497–520; II:** 26, 27, 29, 34, 38, 44, 74, 89, 93, 180, 276, 283, 428, 444, 451, 456–457, 467–468; **III:** 40, 103, 106, 251, 314, 319, 327, 335, 453, 576, 582; **IV:** 29, 35, 40, 135, 208, 237, 475, 482, 484; **Retro. Supp. I:** 325, 376; **Retro. Supp. II: 93–110,** 114, 322; **Supp. I Part 1:** 320; **Supp. I Part 2:** 461, 468; **Supp. III Part 2:** 412; **Supp. IV Part 1:** 31, 236, 350; **Supp. IV Part 2:** 689; **Supp. V:** 113, 120; **Supp. VIII:** 98, 101, 102; **Supp. IX:** 1, 14, 15, 308; **Supp. XI:** 207; **Supp. XIV:** 111; **Supp. XVII:** 95, 96–97, 105, 155; **Supp. XVIII:** 1, 6, 76, 226; **Supp. XXI:** 275; **Supp. XXIII:** 161, 164; **Supp. XXV:** 18

"Drenched in Light" (Hurston), **Supp. VI:** 150–151

Drennen, Eileen M., **Supp. XXII:** 241, 243

Dresser, Paul, **Retro. Supp. II:** 94, 103

Dress Gray (teleplay), **Supp. IV Part 2:** 683

Dress Gray (Truscott), **Supp. IV Part 2:** 683

"Dressing for Dinner" (Ríos), **Supp. IV Part 2:** 548

Dressing Up for the Carnival (Shields), **Supp. VII:** 328

"Dress of One Occasion" (Stallings), **Supp. XXV:** 233

"Dress Rehearsal" (Skloot), **Supp. XX: 204**

Drew, Bettina, **Supp. IX:** 2, 4

Drew, Elizabeth, **Retro. Supp. II:** 242, 243

Drexler, Eric, **Supp. XVI:** 121

Dreyfus, Alfred, **Supp. I Part 2:** 446

"Dr. Hanray's Second Chance" (Richter), **Supp. XVIII:** 218

Drift and Mastery (Lippmann), **I:** 222–223

"Driftwood" (C. Frost), **Supp. XV:** 106–107

"Drinker, The" (Lowell), **II:** 535, 550

"Drinking Cold Water" (Everwine), **Supp. XV:** 80–81

"Drinking from a Helmet" (Dickey), **Supp. IV Part 1:** 180

Drinking Gourd, The (Hansberry), **Supp. IV Part 1:** 359, 365–367, 374

Drinks before Dinner (Doctorow), **Supp. IV Part 1:** 231, 234–235

Driscoll, David, **Supp. XIX:** 241, 242

Driskill, Qwo-Li, **Supp. XXIII:** 147, 148, 149

Drive, He Said (Larner), **Supp. XVI:** 220

"Drive Home, The" (Banks), **Supp. V:** 7

"Driver" (Merrill), **Supp. III Part 1:** 331

"Driving Alone in Winter" (W. V. Davis), **Supp. XXI:** 89, 90, 94

"Driving Through Minnesota During the Hanoi Bombings" (R. Bly), **Supp. IV Part 1:** 61; **Supp. XVII:** 243

"Driving through Oregon" (Haines), **Supp. XII:** 207

"Driving to Oregon"(Thompson), **Supp. XXIII:** 291

"Driving toward the Lac Qui Parle River" (R. Bly), **Supp. IV Part 1:** 61

"Dr. Jack-o'-Lantern" (Yates), **Supp. XI:** 340–341

Dr. Jekyll and Mr. Hyde (film), **Supp. XVII:** 57

"Drone" (Coleman), **Supp. XI:** 85–86

Drop City (Boyle), **Supp. XX: 30–31**

Drown (Díaz), **Supp. XXIV:** 83, 84, 85, 86, **88–89,** 90, 93

"Drowned Man, The: Death between Two Rivers" (McGrath), **Supp. X:** 116

"Drowning" (Boyle), **Supp. XX: 18**

"Drowning 1954" (Keillor), **Supp. XVI:** 172

Drowning Pool, The (film), **Supp. IV Part 2:** 474

Drowning Pool, The (Macdonald), **Supp. IV Part 2:** 470, 471

Drowning Season, The (Hoffman), **Supp. X: 82**

Drowning with Others (Dickey), **Supp. IV Part 1:** 176, 178, 179

"Drowsy Day, A" (Dunbar), **Supp. II Part 1:** 198

Dr. Seuss. *See* Geisel, Theodor Seuss (Dr. Seuss)

Dr. Seuss and Mr. Geisel (J. and N. Morgan), **Supp. XVI:** 103

Dr. Seuss Goes to War: The World War II Editorial Cartoons of Theodor Seuss Geisel (Minear), **Supp. XVI:** 101

Dr. Seuss's ABC (Geisel), **Supp. XVI:** 99

Dr. Strangelove; or, How I Learned to Stop Worrying and Love the Bomb (film), **Supp. XI:** 293, **301–305**

Drugiye Berega (Nabokov), **III:** 247–250, 252

"Drug Shop, The, or Endymion in Edmonstoun" (Benét), **Supp. XI:** 43

"Drug Store" (Shapiro), **Supp. II Part 2:** 705

"Drugstore in Winter, A" (Ozick), **Supp. V:** 272

Drukman, Steven, **Supp. XIII:** 195, 197, 202

"Drum" (Hogan), **Supp. IV Part 1:** 413

"Drum, The" (Alvarez), **Supp. VII:** 7

"Drumlin Woodchuck, A" (Frost), **II:** 159–160; **Retro. Supp. I:** 138

Drummond, William, **Supp. I Part 1:** 369

Drummond de Andrade, Carlos, **Supp. IV Part 2:** 626, 629, 630

Drums at Dusk (Bontemps), **Supp. XXII:** 5, 9–10

Drum-Taps (Whitman), **IV:** 346, 347, 444; **Retro. Supp. I:** 406

"Drunken Fisherman, The" (Lowell), **II:** 534, 550

"Drunken Sisters, The" (Wilder), **IV:** 374

Drunk in the Furnace, The (Merwin), **Supp. III Part 1:** 345–346

"Drunk in the Furnace, The" (Merwin), **Supp. III Part 1:** 346

Druten, John van, **Supp. XIV:** 162

"Dr. Williams' Position" (Pound), **Supp. XVII:** 226–227

Dryden, John, **II:** 111, 542, 556; **III:** 15; **IV:** 145; **Retro. Supp. I:** 56; **Supp. I Part 1:** 150; **Supp. I Part 2:** 422; **Supp. IX:** 68; **Supp. XIV:** 5; **Supp. XV:** 258; **Supp. XX: 280; Supp. XXIV:** 158; **Supp. XXV:** 119

Drye, Captain Frank, **Retro. Supp. II:** 115

Dry Salvages, The (Eliot), **I:** 581

"Dry Salvages, The" (Eliot), **Retro. Supp. I:** 66

"Dry September" (Faulkner), **II:** 72, 73

"Dry Spring"(Thompson), **Supp. XXIII:** 291

Dry Sun, Dry Wind (Wagoner), **Supp. IX:** 323, 324

D'Souza, Dinesh, **Supp. X:** 255

"Dual" (Goldbarth), **Supp. XII:** 188

"Dual Curriculum" (Ozick), **Supp. V:** 270

"Dualism" (Reed), **Supp. X:** 242

Duane's Depressed (McMurtry), **Supp. V:** 233

Du Bartas, Guillaume, **Supp. I Part 1:** 98, 104, 111, 118, 119

Duberman, Martin, **Supp. I Part 2:** 408, 409

Dubie, Norman, **Supp. XXIV:** 165

"Dubin's Lives" (Malamud), **Supp. I Part 2:** 451

Dubious Honors (M. F. K. Fisher), **Supp. XVII:** 91

"Dubliners" (J. Joyce), **Supp. XVI:** 41

Dubliners (Joyce), **I:** 130, 480; **III:** 471; **Supp. VIII:** 146

Dublin's Lives (Malamud), **Supp. XIX:** 142

Du Bois, Nina Gomer (Mrs. W. E. B. Du Bois), **Supp. II P art 1:** 158; **Supp. XIV:** 200

Du Bois, Shirley Graham, **Supp. II Part 1:** 186; **Supp. XXI:** 171. *See also* Graham, Shirley

Du Bois, W. E. B., **I:** 260; **Supp. I Part 1:** 5, 345; **Supp. II Part 1:** 33, 56, 61, **157–189,** 195; **Supp. IV Part 1:** 9, 164, 170, 362; **Supp. X:** 133, 134, 137, 139, 242; **Supp. XIII:** 185, **Supp. XIII:** 186, 233, 238, 243, 244, 247; **Supp. XIV:** 54, 69, 72, 201, 202; **Supp. XVI:** 135; **Supp. XVIII:** 119, 122, 126, 130; **Supp. XIX:** 67, 69, 77; **Supp. XX: 102, 105, 106; Supp. XXI:** 166, 277; **Supp. XXII:** 3

DuBose, Martha Hailey, **Supp. XXV:** 192, 199, 200

Dubreuil, Jean, **Supp. IV Part 2:** 425

Dubus, Andre, **Supp. VII: 75–93; Supp. XI:** 347,**Supp. XI:** 349; **Supp. XIV:** 21; **Supp. XXIV:** 97

Dubus, Andre, III, **Supp. XXIV: 97–112**

Duchamp, Marcel, **IV:** 408; **Retro. Supp. I:** 416, 417, 418, 430; **Supp. IV Part 2:** 423, 424; **Supp. XII:** 124; **Supp. XV:** 157; **Supp. XXII:** 162, 163, 168

"Duchess at Prayer, The" (Wharton), **Retro. Supp. I:** 365

Duchess of Malfi, The (Webster), **IV:** 131

"Duckling Girl" (Dubus III), **Supp. XXIV:** 100–101, 105

Duck Soup (film), **Supp. IV Part 1:** 384

Duck Variations, The (Mamet), **Supp. XIV:** 239, 240, 249

Ducornet, Rikki, **Supp. XXII:** 261

Dudley, Anne. *See* Bradstreet, Anne

Dudley, Joseph, **III:** 52

Dudley, Thomas, **III:** 52; **Supp. I Part 1:** 98, 99, 110, 116

"Duenna"(Schott), **Supp. XXIII:** 249

"Duet, With Muffled Brake Drums" (Updike), **Retro. Supp. I:** 319

Duet for Cannibals (Sontag), **Supp. III Part 2:** 452, 456

Duffey, Bernard, **Supp. I Part 2:** 458, 471

Duffield, Pitts, **Supp. XXI:** 3

Duffus, R. L., **Supp. I Part 2:** 650

Duffy, Martha, **Supp. IV Part 1:** 207; **Supp. XX: 244**

Duffy, William, **Supp. XVI:** 32

Du Fu (Tu Fu), **Supp. XV:** 217

Dufy, Raoul, **I:** 115; **IV:** 80

Dugan, Alan, **Supp. XIII:** 76

Dugan, James, **Supp. XV:** 197

"Dugout"(Kenny), **Supp. XXIII:** 155

Duhamel, Marcel, **Supp. XVI:** 135, 143

Dujardin, Edouard, **I:** 53

"Duke de l'Omelette, The" (Poe), **III:** 411, 425

Duke Herring (Bodenheim), **Supp. XXV:** 27

"Duke in His Domain, The" (Capote), **Supp. III Part 1:** 113, 126

Duke of Deception, The (G. Wolff), **Supp. II Part 1:** 97; **Supp. XI:** 246

"Duke's Child, The" (Maxwell), **Supp. VIII:** 172

"Dulce et Decorum Est" (Owen), **Supp. XVIII:** 92

"Dulham Ladies, The" (Jewett), **II:** 407, 408; **Retro. Supp. II:** 143

Duluth (Vidal), **Supp. IV Part 2:** 677, 685, 689, 691–692

Dumas, Alexandre, **III:** 386; **Supp. XVII:** 64

"Dumb Oax, The" (Lewis), **Retro. Supp. I:** 170

"Dummy, The" (Sontag), **Supp. III Part 2:** 469

"Dump Ground, The" (Stegner), **Supp. IV Part 2:** 601

Dunant, Sarah, **Supp. XIX:** 186

Dunayevskaya, Raya, **Supp. XXI:** 169

Dunbar, Alice Moore (Mrs. Paul Laurence Dunbar), **Supp. II Part 1:** 195, 200, 217

Dunbar, Paul Laurence, **Supp. I Part 1:** 320; **Supp. II Part 1:** 174, **191–219;** **Supp. III Part 1:** 73; **Supp. IV Part 1:** 15, 165, 170; **Supp. X:** 136; **Supp. XI:** 277; **Supp. XIII:** 111; **Supp. XXII:** 11

Duncan, Harry, **Supp. XV:** 75

Duncan, Isadora, **I:** 483; **Supp. XV:** 42, 50

Duncan, Robert, **Retro. Supp. II:** 49; **Supp. III Part 2:** 625, 626, 630, 631; **Supp. VIII:** 304; **Supp. XVI:** 282–283; **Supp. XXIII:** 213

Dunciad, The (Pope), **I:** 204

Dunford, Judith, **Supp. VIII:** 107

Dunlap, William, **Supp. I Part 1:** 126, 130, 137, 141, 145

Dunn, Stephen, **Supp. XI: 139–158; Supp. XIX:** 85

Dunne, Finley Peter, **II:** 432

Dunne, John Gregory, **Supp. IV Part 1:** 197, 198, 201, 203, 207

"Dunnet Shepherdess, A" (Jewett), **II:** 392–393; **Retro. Supp. II:** 139

Dunning, Stephen, **Supp. XIV:** 126

Dunning, William Archibald, **Supp. II Part 1:** 170; **Supp. XIV:** 48

Dunnock, Mildred, **III:** 153

Dunster, Henry, **Supp. I Part 2:** 485

"Dunwich Horror, The" (Lovecraft), **Supp. XXV:** 111, 120

"Duo Tried Killing Man with Bacon" (Goldbarth), **Supp. XII:** 176

Dupee, F. W., **I:** 254; **II:** 548; **Supp. VIII:** 231; **Supp. IX:** 93, 96

DuPlessis, Rachel Blau, **Supp. IV Part 2:** 421, 426, 432; **Supp. XVI:** 284

Duplicate Keys (Smiley), **Supp. VI:** 292, **294–296**

Duplications, The (Koch), **Supp. XV:** 181, 183, 186

Durable Fire, A (Sarton), **Supp. VIII:** 260

Durand, Asher, B., **Supp. I Part 1:** 156, 157

Durand, Régis, **Supp. IV Part 1:** 44

Durang, Christopher, **Supp. XXIV: 113–130,** 263

"Durango Suite" (Gunn Allen), **Supp. IV Part 1:** 326

Durant, Kenneth, **Supp. XXII:** 278, 281

"Durations" (Matthews), **Supp. IX:** 152–153, 154

Dürer, Albrecht, **III:** 212; **Supp. XII:** 44

Durham, David Anthony, **Supp. XVIII:** 100

"During Fever" (Lowell), **II:** 547

Durkheim, Émile, **I:** 227; **Retro. Supp. I:** 55, 57; **Supp. I Part 2:** 637, 638

Durrell, Lawrence, **III:** 184, 190; **IV:** 430; **Supp. X:** 108, 187; **Supp. XVI:** 294

Dürrenmatt, Friedrich, **Supp. IV Part 2:** 683

Duse, Eleonora, **II:** 515, 528

Dusk and Other Stories (Salter), **Supp. IX: 260–261**

Dusk of Dawn: An Essay Toward an Autobiography of a Race Concept (Du Bois), **Supp. II Part 1:** 159, 183, 186

"Dust" (R. Fisher), **Supp. XIX:** 71

"Dusting" (Alvarez), **Supp. VII:** 4

"Dusting" (Dove), **Supp. IV Part 1:** 247, 248

"Dusting" (Schnackenberg), **Supp. XV:** 256

"Dust of Snow" (Frost), **II:** 154

Dust Tracks on a Road (Hurston), **Supp. IV Part 1:** 5, 11; **Supp. VI:** 149, 151, 158–159

"Dusty Braces" (Snyder), **Supp. VIII:** 302

Dutchman (Baraka), **Supp. II Part 1:** 38, 40, 42–44, 54, 55

"Dutch Nick Massacre, The" (Twain), **IV:** 195

"Dutch Picture, A" (Longfellow), **Retro. Supp. II:** 171

Dutton, Charles S., **Supp. VIII:** 332, 342

Dutton, Clarence Earl, **Supp. IV Part 2:** 598

Duvall, Robert, **Supp. V:** 227

"Duwamish" (Hugo), **Supp. VI:** 136

"Duwamish, Skagit, Hoh" (Hugo), **Supp. VI:** 136–137

"Duwamish No. 2" (Hugo), **Supp. VI:** 137

Duyckinck, Evert, **III:** 77, 81, 83, 85; **Retro. Supp. I:** 155, 247, 248; **Supp. I Part 1:** 122, 317

Duyckinck, Evert Augustus, **Supp. XXV:** 250

Duyckinck, George, **Supp. I Part 1:** 122

Duyckinck, George Long, **Supp. XXV:** 250

"Dvonya" (Simpson), **Supp. IX:** 274

Dwelling Places: Poems and Translations (Ferry), **Supp. XXIV:** 152–153

Dwellings: A Spiritual History of the Living World (Hogan), **Supp. IV Part 1:** 397, 410, 415–416, 417

Dwight, Sereno E., **I:** 547

Dwight, Timothy, **Supp. I Part 1:** 124; **Supp. I Part 2:** 516, 580; **Supp. II Part 1:** 65, 69

Dworkin, Andrea, **Supp. XII:** 6

Dwyer, Jim, **Supp. XVI:** 16, 19

Dyas, Sandra, **Supp. XIX:** 174

Dybbuk, A, or Between Two Worlds: Dramatic Legend in Four Acts (Kushner), **Supp. IX:** 138

Dybbuk, The (Ansky), **IV:** 6

Dybek, Stuart, **Supp. XXIII:** 67–81

Dybuk, The (Ansky), **Supp. XXIII:** 8

Dyer, Geoff, **Supp. X:** 169

Dyer, Joyce, **Supp. XX:** 166

Dyer, R. C., **Supp. XIII:** 162

Dyer, Richard, **Supp. XXII:** 261

Dyer's Thistle (Balakian), **Supp. XXIII:** 25

Dying Animal, The (P. Roth), **Retro. Supp. II:** 288

"Dying Elm, The" (Freneau), **Supp. II Part 1:** 258

"Dying Indian, The" (Freneau), **Supp. II Part 1:** 262

"Dying Man, The" (Roethke), **III:** 540, 542, 543–545

Dykeman, Wilma, **Supp. XX:** 163

Dykes to Watch Out For (Bechdel), **Supp. XXV:** 1, 3–4

Dylan, Bob, **Supp. VIII:** 202; **Supp. XIII:** 114, 119; **Supp. XV:** 349, 350; **Supp. XVIII:** 19–34; **Supp. XXII:** 83

Dylan's Visions of Sin (Ricks), **Supp. XVIII:** 20

"Dynamics of Heroic Action, The" (lecture, Murray), **Supp. XIX:** 153

Dynamo (O'Neill), **III:** 396

"Dynasties" (Gibran), **Supp. XX:** 118

"Dysfunctional Narratives: Or, 'Mistakes Were Made' " (C. Baxter), **Supp. XVII:** 20

"Dysfunctional Nation" (Karr), **Supp. XI:** 245

Dyson, A. E., **Retro. Supp. II:** 247

Dyson, Freeman, **Supp. XVII:** 42

E

"Each and All" (Emerson), **II:** 19

Each Happiness Ringer by Lions (Hirshfield), **Supp. XXIII:** 135

Each in His Season (Snodgrass), **Supp. VI:** 324, 327

"Each Like a Leaf" (Swenson), **Supp. IV Part 2:** 644

Eads, Martha Greene, **Supp. XVIII:** 49

Eady, Cornelius, **Supp. XXI:** 246

Eager, Allen, **Supp. XI:** 294

"Eagle, The" (Tate), **IV:** 128

"Eagle and the Mole, The" (Wylie), **Supp. I Part 2:** 710, 711, 713, 714, 729

"Eagle and the Skylark, The" (Gibran), **Supp. XX:** 124

Eagle as Wide as the World, The (X. J. Kennedy), **Supp. XV:** 162, 164

"Eagle Poem" (Harjo), **Supp. XII:** 224, 226

"Eagles" (Dickey), **Supp. IV Part 1:** 186

Eagle's Mile, The (Dickey), **Supp. IV Part 1:** 178, 185–186

"Eagle That Is Forgotten, The" (Lindsay), **Supp. I Part 2:** 382, 387

Eagleton, Terry, **Retro. Supp. I:** 67

Eakin, Paul John, **Supp. VIII:** 167, 168; **Supp. XIII:** 225; **Supp. XVI:** 70

Eakins, Thomas, **Supp. XIV:** 338; **Supp. XXII:** 18–19

Eames, Emma, **Supp. XX:** 232, 240

Eames, Roscoe, **II:** 476

"Earl: My Life with a Louse" (Keillor), **Supp. XVI:** 176

"Earl Painter" (Banks), **Supp. V:** 14–15

"Early Adventures of Ralph Ringwood, The" (Irving), **II:** 314

Early Americana (Richter), **Supp. XVIII:** 208, 210, 211, 220

Early Autumn (Parker), **Supp. XIX:** 184–185

Early Ayn Rand, The: A Selection of Her Unpublished Fiction (Rand), **Supp. IV Part 2:** 520

Early Dark (Price), **Supp. VI:** 262

Early Diary of Anaïs Nin, The, **Supp. X:** 184, 192

Early Elkin (Elkin), **Supp. VI:** 42–43, 45

"Early Evenin' Blues" (Hughes), **Retro. Supp. I:** 205

"Early Evening, Frankfort, Kentucky" (Trethewey), **Supp. XXI:** 243, 250

"Early History of a Seamstress" (Reznikoff), **Supp. XIV:** 277, 289

Early History of a Sewing-Machine Operator (Reznikoff), **Supp. XIV:** 289

"Early History of a Sewing-Machine Operator" (Reznikoff), **Supp. XIV:** 277

"Early History of a Writer" (Reznikoff), **Supp. XIV:** 278, 290

"Early in the Morning" (L.-Y. Lee), **Supp. XV:** 214

Early Lectures of Ralph Waldo Emerson, The (Emerson), **II:** 11

Early Light (Di Piero), **Supp. XIX:** 38, 38–40

Early Lives of Melville, The (Sealts), **Retro. Supp. I:** 257

"Early Marriage" (Richter), **Supp. XVIII:** 209

Early Martyr and Other Poems, An (W. C. Williams), **Retro. Supp. I:** 423

"Early Morning: Cape Cod" (Swenson), **Supp. IV Part 2:** 641

"Early Rooms"(Hirshfield), **Supp. XXIII:** 130

"Early Spring between Madison and Bellingham" (R. Bly), **Supp. IV Part 1:** 71

Early Writing (O'Hara), **Supp. XXIII:** 220

Earnhardt, Dale, **Supp. XII:** 310

Earnshaw, Doris, **Supp. IV Part 1:** 310

"Earth" (Bryant), **Supp. I Part 1:** 157, 164, 167

"Earth, The" (Sexton), **Supp. II Part 2:** 696

Earth Abides (Stewart), **Supp. XVIII:** 138

"Earth and Fire" (Berry), **Supp. X:** 27

Earth as Air, The: An Ars Poetica (Sobin), **Supp. XVI:** 285–286

"Earth Being" (Toomer), **Supp. IX:** 320

Earth Goat (online), **Supp. XXII:** 61

Earth Gods, The (Gibran), **Supp. XX:** 116, 123

"Earth is parched with heat, The" (Very), **Supp. XXV:** 239

"Earthly Care a Heavenly Discipline" (Stowe), **Supp. I Part 2:** 586

"Earthly City of the Jews, The" (Kazin), **Retro. Supp. II:** 286

Earthly Meditations (Wrigley), **Supp. XVIII:** 304–305

"Earthly Meditations" (Wrigley), **Supp. XVIII:** 304–306

Earthly Possessions (Tyler), **Supp. IV Part 2:** 665–666, 671

Earth Power Coming (Ortiz, ed.), **Supp. IV Part 2:** 502

"Earth's Holocaust" (Hawthorne), **II:** 226, 231, 232, 242; **III:** 82; **Retro. Supp. I:** 152

Earth Without You, The (F. Wright), **Supp. XVII:** 243

Eason, Laura, **Supp. XXIII:** 79

East Coker (Eliot), **I:** 580, 581, 582, 585, 587

"East Coker" (Eliot), **Retro. Supp. I:** 66; **Supp. VIII:** 195, 196

"Easter" (Toomer), **Supp. III Part 2:** 486

"Easter, an Ode" (Lowell), **II:** 536

"Easter 1916" (Yeats), **Supp. XXI:** 61

"Easter Morning" (Ammons), **Supp. VII:** 34

"Easter Morning" (Clampitt), **Supp. IX:** 45

"Easter Ode, An" (Dunbar), **Supp. II Part 1:** 196

"Easter"(O'Hara), **Supp. XXIII:** 211

Easter Parade, The (Yates), **Supp. XI:** 346, 349

"Easter Sermon, 1866" (Nelson), **Supp. XVIII:** 177

"Easter Service" (Di Piero), **Supp. XIX:** 39–40

"Easter Sunday: Recollection" (Gunn Allen), **Supp. IV Part 1:** 322

"Easter Wings" (Herbert), **Supp. IV Part 2:** 646

"East European Cooking" (Simic), **Supp. VIII:** 277

East Is East (Boyle), **Supp. VIII:** 1–3; **Supp. XX:** 23–24, 25, 28

Eastlake, William, **Supp. XIII:** 12

East Lynne (Wood), **Supp. I Part 1:** 35, 36; **Supp. I Part 2:** 459, 462; **Supp. XVI:** 182

Eastman, Elaine Goodale, **Supp. X:** 103

Eastman, Max, **Supp. III Part 2:** 620; **Supp. X:** 131, 134, 135, 137; **Supp.**

XV: 295; **Supp. XVI:** 185; **Supp. XVII:** 96; **Supp. XXI:** 6; **Supp. XXII:** 274, 275, 277

Eastman, P. D., **Supp. XXV:** 1

East of Eden (Steinbeck), **IV:** 51, 56–57, 59

"East of the Sun and West of the Moon" (Merwin), **Supp. III Part 1:** 344

Easton, Alison, **Retro. Supp. II:** 143, 144, 145

Easton, Bret Ellis, **Supp. XI:** 65

Easton, Nina J., **Supp. XIX:** 137

Easton, Robert, **Supp. IV Part 2:** 461, 474

East River (Asch), **Supp. XXIII:** 1, 3, 7, **14–15**

"East-Side: New York" (Bodenheim), **Supp. XXV:** 22

East Wind (Lowell), **II:** 527

East Wind: West Wind (Buck), **Supp. II Part 1:** 114–115

Easy Rawlins mysteries, **Supp. XIII:** 236, **237–241,** 242

Easy Rider (film), **Supp. XI:** 293, **308,** 309

Eat a Bowl of Tea (Chu), **Supp. X:** 291

"Eating " (Bass), **Supp. XVI:** 23–24

"Eating Alone" (L.-Y. Lee), **Supp. XV:** 214

"Eating Barley Sugar and Waiting to Be Ninety"(Hadas), **Supp. XXIII:** 120–121

Eating Naked (Dobyns), **Supp. XIII:** **78–79**

"Eating Out" (L. Michaels), **Supp. XVI:** 209

"Eating Poetry" (Strand), **Supp. IV Part 2:** 626

"Eating the Whole" (C. Frost), **Supp. XV:** 101

"Eating Together" (L.-Y. Lee), **Supp. XV:** 214

"Eating with My Fingers" (C. Frost), **Supp. XV:** 97

Eaton, Edith, **Supp. X:** 291

Eaton, Mark A., **Supp. XXIII:** 129, 130, 136

Eaton, Peggy, **Supp. I Part 2:** 461

Eaton, Winnifred, **Supp. X:** 291

"Eatonville Anthology, The" (Hurston), **Supp. VI:** 152

Eat Pray Love (Gilbert), **Supp. XXII:** 83, 90

Eat the Document (film, Pennebaker), **Supp. XVIII:** 19, 26, 27, 28

"Ebb and Flow, The" (Taylor), **IV:** 161

"Ebenezer Marsh, 1725" (Schnackenberg), **Supp. XV:** 256

Eben Holden (Bacheller), **I:** 216

Eberhardt, Isabelle, **Supp. IV Part 1:** 92

Eberhart, Mrs., **I:** 521–522, 530

Eberhart, Richard, **I: 521–543; II:** 535–536; **III:** 527; **IV:** 416; **Retro. Supp. II:** 176, 178; **Supp. I Part 1:** 83; **Supp. XII:** 119

Eble, Kenneth E., **Supp. I Part 1:** 201

"Ecce Homo" (Cliff), **Supp. XXII:** 76

Eccentricities of a Nightingale (T. Williams), **IV:** 382, 385, 397, 398

Ecclesiastica Historia Integram Ecclesiae (Taylor), **IV:** 163

"Echart" (Sobin), **Supp. XVI:** 289

"Echo, The" (Bowles), **Supp. IV Part 1:** 84, 86, 87

Echoes inside the Labyrinth (McGrath), **Supp. X:** 127

Echo Park (Connelly), **Supp. XXI: 77–78**

Eckehart, Meister, **Supp. XV:** 225

Eckhart, Maria, **Supp. V:** 212

Eclipse (Hogan), **Supp. IV Part 1:** 397, 400, 402

Eclipse, a Nightmare (Montalembert), **Supp. XVI:** 349

"Eclipse"(Schott), **Supp. XXIII:** 252

Eclogues (Virgil), **Supp. VIII:** 31; **Supp. XXIV:** 156

Eclogues of Virgil, The (Ferry, trans.), **Supp. XXIV: 156–157**

"Ecologue" (Ginsberg), **Supp. II Part 1:** 326

"Ecologues of These States 1969–1971" (Ginsberg), **Supp. II Part 1:** 325

Ecology of a Cracker Childhood (Ray), **Supp. XVIII:** 189, 191, 192, 193, **195–199,** 201, 202, 204

"Economics of Negro Emancipation in the United States, The" (Du Bois), **Supp. II Part 1:** 174

"Economics of the Cracker Landscape: Poverty as an Environmental Issue in Larry Brown's *Joe*" (Watson), *Supp. XXI:* 46

"Economic Theory of Women's Dress, The" (Veblen), **Supp. I Part 2:** 636

Economy of the Unlost: Reading Simonides of Keos with Paul Celan (Carson), **Supp. XII:** 110–111

Ecotactics: The Sierra Club Handbook for Environmental Activists (Mitchell and Stallings, eds.), **Supp. IV Part 2:** 488

"Ecstasy" (Bierds), **Supp. XVII:** 34

"Ecstasy" (Olds), **Supp. X:** 206

"Ecstasy of Influence, The" (Lethem), **Supp. XVIII:** 150

"Ecstatic" (Komunyakaa), **Supp. XIII:** 131

Edda, **Supp. X:** 114

Eddy, Mary Baker, **I:** 583; **III:** 506

Edel, Leon, **I:** 20; **II:** 338–339; **Retro. Supp. I:** 218, 224, 231

Edelberg, Cynthia, **Supp. IV Part 1:** 155

"Eden and My Generation" (Levis), **Supp. XI:** 270

Edenbaum, Robert, **Supp. IV Part 1:** 352

Eden Tree (Bynner), **Supp. XV:** 42, 51

Edenville Owls (Parker), **Supp. XIX:** 190

Eder, Richard, **Supp. XII:** 189; **Supp. XV:** 62, 187, 259, 261

Edgar Huntly; or, Memoirs of a Sleep-Walker (Brown), **Supp. I Part 1:** 140–144, 145

"Edge" (Plath), **Retro. Supp. II:** 256; **Supp. I Part 2:** 527, 547

Edge, Mary E., **II:** 316

Edgell, David, **Supp. XXIV:** 71

Edgell, Zee, **Supp. XXIII: 83–96**

"Edge of Possibility, The: Susan Warner and the World of Sunday School Fic-

tion" (S. Gates), **Supp. XVIII:** 267

"Edge of the Great Rift, The" (Theroux), **Supp. VIII:** 325

Edge of the Sea, The (Carson), **Supp. IX:** 19, **25–31,** 32

Edgers, Geoff, **Supp. XV:** 113

Edgeworth, Maria, **II:** 8; **Supp. XV:** 231; **Supp. XX:** 108

Edible Woman, The (Atwood), **Supp. XIII:** 19, 20, **20–21**

"Edict by the King of Prussia, An" (Franklin), **II:** 120

Edie: An American Biography (Stein), **Supp. XVI:** 245

Edinburgh Days: or, Doing What I Want to Do (Pickering), **Supp. XXI:** 200–201

Edison, Thomas A., **I:** 483; **Supp. I Part 2:** 392

Edith Wharton (Joslin), **Retro. Supp. I:** 376

Edith Wharton: A Biography (Lewis), **Retro. Supp. I:** 362

Edith Wharton: A Woman in Her Time (Auchincloss), **Retro. Supp. I:** 370

Edith Wharton: Matters of Mind and Spirit (Singley), **Retro. Supp. I:** 373

Edith Wharton's Argument with America (Ammons), **Retro. Supp. I:** 364

Edith Wharton's Brave New Politics (Bauer), **Retro. Supp. I:** 381

Edith Wharton's Letters from the Underworld (Waid), **Retro. Supp. I:** 360

Edith Wharton: Traveller in the Land of Letters (Goodwyn), **Retro. Supp. I:** 370

"Editing and Glosses" (Reznikoff), **Supp. XIV:** 283

Editing of Emily Dickinson, The (Franklin), **Retro. Supp. I:** 41

"Editor and the Schoolma'am, The" (Frederic), **II:** 130

"Editor's Easy Chair" (Howells), **II:** 276

"Editor's Study, The" (Howells), **II:** 275, 276, 285

"Editor Whedon" (Masters), **Supp. I Part 2:** 463

Edlin, Mari, **Supp. X:** 266

Edman, Irwin, **III:** 605; **Supp. XXV:** 255, 258

Edmond (Mamet), **Supp. XIV:** 241, 248, 249, 250

Edmonds, Dale, **Supp. XXIII:** 291

Edmondson, Belinda, **Supp. XXII:** 70

Edmundson, Mark, **Retro. Supp. II:** 262

Edmund Wilson (Kriegel), **Supp. XXIV: 216–217**

Edsel (Shapiro), **Supp. II Part 2:** 703, 704, 717–719

Edson, Margaret, **Supp. XVIII: 35–52**

Edson, Russell, **Supp. VIII:** 279

"Educated American Woman, An" (Cheever), **Supp. I Part 1:** 194

"Education, An" (Ozick), **Supp. V:** 267

Education and Living (Bourne), **I:** 252

"Education by Poetry" (Frost), **Supp. XV:** 215

"Education of a Storyteller, The" (Bambara), **Supp. XI:** 20

Education of Black People, The (Du Bois), **Supp. II Part 1:** 186

Education of Harriet Hatfield, The (Sarton), **Supp. VIII: 257–258**

Education of Henry Adams, The (Adams), **I:** 1, 5, 6, 11, 14, 15–18, 19, 20–21, 111; **II:** 276; **III:** 504; **Retro. Supp. I:** 53, 59; **Supp. IX:** 19; **Supp. XIV:** 299

Education of H*y*m*a*n K*a*p*l*a*n, The (Rosten), **Supp. XVII:** 9

"Education of Mingo, The" (Johnson), **Supp. VI:** 193, 194

"Education of Norman Podhoretz, The" (Goldberg), **Supp. VIII:** 238

Education of Oscar Fairfax, The (Auchincloss), **Supp. IV Part 1:** 25, 36

"Education of the Poet" (Glück), **Supp. V:** 78, 80

Education sentimentale (Flaubert), **III:** 315

"Education the Imagination" (Koch), **Supp. XV:** 175–176, 177

Edwards, Clifford, **Supp. XVIII:** 220

Edwards, Eli. *See* McKay, Claude

Edwards, Esther, **I:** 545

Edwards, Harry Stillwell, **Supp. XXII:** 193

Edwards, John, **I:** 478

Edwards, Jonathan, **I: 544–566; II:** 432; **Retro. Supp. II:** 187; **Supp. I Part 1:** 301, 302; **Supp. I Part 2:** 552, 594, 700; **Supp. IV Part 2:** 430; **Supp. VIII:** 205; **Supp. XXIV:** 72

Edwards, Sarah, **I:** 545

Edwards, Thomas, **Supp. XV:** 20

Edwards, Thomas R., **Supp. XVI:** 207

Edwards, Timothy, **I:** 545

Edwards-Yearwood, Grace, **Supp. VIII:** 81; **Supp. XXII:** 213

"Edwin Arlington Robinson" (Cowley), **Supp. II Part 1:** 144

Edwin Arlington Robinson (Winters), **Supp. II Part 2:** 812

Edwin Booth (play), **Supp. IV Part 1:** 89

E. E. Cummings (Marks), **I:** 438

E. E. Cummings: A Miscellany (Cummings), **I:** 429, 441

E. E. Cummings: A Miscellany, Revised (Cummings), **I:** 429

"Effects of Analogy" (Stevens), **Retro. Supp. I:** 297

Effluences from the Sacred Caves; More Selected Essays and Reviews (Carruth), **Supp. XVI:** 46

"Effort at Speech between Two People" (Rukeyser), **Supp. VI:** 276, 284

"Efforts of Affection" (Moore), **III:** 214

"Efforts of Affection: A Memoir of Marianne Moore" (Bishop), **Retro. Supp. II:** 52

Egan, Jennifer, **Supp. XIX: 49–63; Supp. XXIII:** 299, 300

Egan, Leona, **Supp. XXI:** 6

"Egg, The" (Anderson), **I:** 113, 114

"Egg, The" (Snyder), **Supp. VIII:** 302

Eggers, David, **Supp. XXIV:** 131, 200

Eggleston, George Cary, **Supp. XVIII:** 15

"Eggplant Epithalamion, The" (Jong), **Supp. V:** 119

"Eggs" (Olds), **Supp. X:** 206

"Eggshell" (Stern), **Supp. IX:** 299

Egoist, The (Meredith), **II:** 186

Egorova, Lubov, **Supp. IX:** 58

"Egotism, or the Bosom Sergent" (Hawthorne), **II:** 227, 239

"Egyptian Pulled Glass Bottle in the Shape of a Fish, An" (Moore), **III:** 195, 213

Ehrenfels, Christian von, **Supp. XIV:** 198

Ehrenpreis, Irvin, **Supp. XII:** 128

Ehrenreich, Barbara, **Supp. XVII:** 210

Ehrhart, W. D., **Supp. XIX:** 281

Ehrlich, Gretel, **Supp. XIV:** 227; **Supp. XVIII:** 189

"Ehue! fugaces, Posthume, Posthume, Labuntur anni" (Very), **Supp. XXV:** 243, 247

Eichmann, Adolf, **Supp. XII:** 166

Eichmann in Jerusalem (Arendt), **Retro. Supp. II:** 28; **Supp. VIII:** 243; **Supp. XII:** 166

"Eichmann in New York: The New York Intellectuals and the Hannah Arendt Controversy" (Rabinbach), **Supp. XII:** 166

"Eidolon" (Warren), **IV:** 239

"Eiger Dreams" (Krakauer), **Supp. XVIII:** 107

Eiger Dreams: Ventures Among Men and Mountains (Krakauer), **Supp. XVIII:** 105, 106, 107

Eight Cousins (Alcott), **Supp. I Part 1:** 29, 38, 42, 43

18 Poems from the Quechua (Strand, trans.), **Supp. IV Part 2:** 630

"18 West 11th Street" (Merrill), **Supp. III Part 1:** 323, 328

1876: A Novel (Vidal), **Supp. IV Part 2:** 677, 684, 688, 689, 691, 692; **Supp. XIX:** 141

"18,000 CDs" (Halliday), **Supp. XIX:** 92

"Eighth Air Force" (Jarrell), **II:** 373–374, 377

Eight Harvard Poets, **I:** 429, 475

"Eighth Avenue Incident" (Halliday), **Supp. XIX:** 89–90

"Eighth Day, The" (Apple), **Supp. XVII:** 6, 50

"Eighth Ditch, The" (Baraka), **Supp. II Part 1:** 40

"'80s Pastoral: Frederick Barthelme's *Moon Deluxe* Ten Years On" (Peters), **Supp. XI:** 39

Eight Men (Wright), **IV:** 478, 488, 494

80 Flowers (Zukofsky), **Supp. III Part 2:** 631

Eikon Basilike, The, **Supp. IV Part 2:** 435

Eileen (Masters), **Supp. I Part 2:** 460

Eimi (Cummings), **I:** 429, 433, 434, 439–440

"Einstein" (MacLeish), **III:** 5, 8, 10–11, 18–19

Einstein, Albert, **I:** 493; **III:** 8, 10, 21, 161; **IV:** 69, 375, 410, 411, 421; **Retro. Supp. I:** 63; **Supp. I Part 2:** 609, 643; **Supp. III Part 2:** 621;

Supp. V: 290; **Supp. XII:** 45

Eiseley, Loren, **III:** 227–228

Eisenberg, Deborah, **Supp. XXIII:** 290

Eisenhower, Dwight D., **I:** 136, 376; **II:** 548; **III:** 215; **IV:** 75; **Supp. I Part 1:** 291; **Supp. III Part 2:** 624; **Supp. V:** 45

Eisenstadt, Jill, **Supp. XVIII:** 135

Eisenstein, Sergei, **I:** 481; **Supp. XXI:** 170

Eisinger, Chester E., **I:** 302; **II:** 604; **Supp. IX:** 15

Eisner, Douglas, **Supp. X:** 155

Elam, Angela, **Supp. XI:** 290

El Bernardo (Balbuena), **Supp. V:** 11

Elbert, Sarah, **Supp. I Part 1:** 34, 41

Elder, Donald, **II:** 417, 426, 435, 437; **Supp. XV:** 137

Elder, John, **Supp. IX:** 25

Elder, Lonne, III, **Supp. IV Part 1:** 362

Elder, Richard, **Supp. XII:** 172

"Elder Sister, The" (Olds), **Supp. X:** 205–206

Elder Statesman, The (Eliot), **I:** 572, 573, 583; **Retro. Supp. I:** 53, 65

"Eldest Sister to Psyche, The" (Stallings), **Supp. XXV:** 234

E. L. Doctorow (Harter and Thompson), **Supp. IV Part 1:** 217

Eldredge, Kay, **Supp. IX:** 254, 259

Eldridge, Florence, **III:** 154, 403; **IV:** 357

Eleanor of Aquitaine, **III:** 470

Eleanor of Guienne, **I:** 14

Eleanor: or, Slave Catching in the Quaker City (Lippard), **Supp. XXIII:** 180, 185

"Elect, The" (Taylor), **Supp. V:** 323

"Elections, Nicaragua, 1984" (Kingsolver), **Supp. VII:** 208

Elective Affinities (Goethe; Bogan and Mayer, trans.), **Supp. III Part 1:** 63

Electra (Euripides), **III:** 398

Electra (Sophocles), **III:** 398; **IV:** 370; **Supp. IX:** 102

"Electra on Azalea Path" (Plath), **Supp. I Part 2:** 538

"Electrical Storm" (Bishop), **Supp. I Part 1:** 93

"Electrical Storm" (Hayden), **Supp. II Part 1:** 370

"Electric Arrows" (Proulx), **Supp. VII:** 256

"Electric Girl, The" (P. Benedict), **Supp. XXIII:** 40

"Electricity Saviour" (Olds), **Supp. X:** 215

Electric Kool-Aid Acid Test, The (Wolfe), **Supp. III Part 2:** 575–577, 582–584; **Supp. XI:** 239

Electric Lady, The (film), **Supp. XI:** 309

Electronic Book Review, **Supp. XXII:** 256, 257, 261

Elegant Extracts (Knox), **II:** 8

"Elegant Tom Dillar" (Briggs), **Supp. XVIII:** 17

"Elegiac" (Ferry), **Supp. XXIV:** 148–149

Elegiac Feelings American (Corso), **Supp. XII: 131–134**

"Elegiac Fragments" (Everwine), **Supp. XV:** 89

Elegies (Rukeyser), **Supp. VI:** 273

"Elegies" (Rukeyser), **Supp. VI:** 272
"Elegies for Paradise Valley" (Hayden), **Supp. II Part 1:** 363
"Elegy" (Bidart), **Supp. XV:** 25, 29
Elegy (Levis), **Supp. XI:** 257, 259, 261, **271–272**
"Elegy" (Merwin), **Supp. III Part 1:** 351
"Elegy" (Stafford), **Supp. XI:** 322
"Elegy" (Tate), **IV:** 128
"Elegy, for the U.S.N. Dirigible, Macon, An" (Winters), **Supp. II Part 2:** 810
"Elegy Ending in the Sound of a Skipping Rope" (Levis), **Supp. XI:** 271–272
"Elegy for 41 Whales Beached in Florence, Oregon, June 1979" (Bierds), **Supp. XVII:** 27
"Elegy for D. H. Lawrence, An" (W. C. Williams), **Retro. Supp. I:** 421
"Elegy for My Father" (Strand), **Supp. IV Part 2:** 628
"Elegy for My Mother" (Wagoner), **Supp. IX:** 330
"Elegy for Redondo Beach" (Jarman), **Supp. XVII:** 112, 113
Elegy for September, An (Nichols), **Supp. XIII:** 268
"Elegy for Thelonious" (Komunyakaa), **Supp. XIII:** 118
"Elegy for the Lost Umbrella" (Stallings), **Supp. XXV:** 231, 232
"Elegy for the Lost Umbrella"(Stallings), **Supp. XXIII:** 124
"Elegy for the Native Guards" (Trethewey), **Supp. XXI:** 255
"Elegy for the U.S.N. Dirigible, Macon, A" (Winters), **Supp. II Part 2:** 810
"Elegy in Dialogue" (Taggard), **Supp. XXII:** 276
"Elegy"(J. Schoolcraft), **Supp. XXIII:** 231
"Elegy of Last Resort" (Nemerov), **III:** 271
"Elegy with a Thimbleful of Water in the Cage" (Levis), **Supp. XI:** 272
Elegy Written in a Country Churchyard (Gray), **I:** 68
"Elegy Written in a Country Churchyard" (Gray), **Supp. XIV:** 8
"Elementary Scene, The" (Jarrell), **II:** 387, 388, 389
"Elements" (M. Frank), **Supp. X:** 213
Elements of Style, The (Strunk), **Supp. I Part 2:** 670
"Elenita, Cards, Palm, Water" (Cisneros), **Supp. VII:** 64
"Eleonora" (Poe), **III:** 412
Eleothriambos (Lee), **IV:** 158
"Elephant & Ocean" (Notley), **Supp. XXII:** 230
"Elephants" (Moore), **III:** 203
"Elephant's Dance, The" (D. West), **Supp. XVIII:** 281
"Elevator, The" (Dixon), **Supp. XII:** 154
"Elevator Boy" (Hughes), **Retro. Supp. I:** 200; **Supp. I Part 1:** 326
"Eleven" (Cisneros), **Supp. VII:** 69
Eleven Essays in the European Novel (Blackmur), **Supp. II Part 1:** 91, 111

Eleven Heavy Things (installation, July), **Supp. XXIV:** 200
Eleven Kinds of Loneliness (Yates), **Supp. XI: 340–343,** 349
Eleven Poems on the Same Theme (Warren), **IV:** 239–241
"Eleven Times a Poem" (Corso), **Supp. XII:** 132, 133
El Greco (Doménikos Theotokópoulos), **I:** 387; **III:** 212
El-Hage, George N., **Supp. XX: 116**
"El-Hajj Malik El-Shabazz" (Hayden), **Supp. II Part 1:** 379
"Eli, the Fanatic" (P. Roth), **Supp. III Part 2:** 407–408
Elia, Nada, **Supp. XXII:** 73
Eliade, Mircea, **Supp. XVI:** 292
Elie, Paul, **Supp. XXII:** 91–92
Eliot, Charles William, **I:** 5; **II:** 345; **Retro. Supp. I:** 55; **Supp. I Part 2:** 479; **Supp. IX:** 94
Eliot, George, **I:** 375, 458, 459, 461, 467; **II:** 179, 181, 191–192, 275, 319, 324, 338, 577; **IV:** 311, 322; **Retro. Supp. I:** 218, 220, 225; **Supp. I Part 1:** 370; **Supp. I Part 2:** 559, 579; **Supp. IV Part 1:** 31, 297; **Supp. IV Part 2:** 677; **Supp. V:** 258; **Supp. IX:** 38, 43, 51; **Supp. XI:** 68; **Supp. XII:** 335; **Supp. XIV:** 344; **Supp. XX: 108**
Eliot, T. S., **I:** 48, 49, 52, 59, 60, 64, 66, 68, 105, 107, 215–216, 236, 243, 256, 259, 261, 266, 384, 386, 395, 396, 399, 403, 430, 433, 441, 446, 475, 478, 479, 482, 521, 522, 527, **567–591;** **II:** 65, 96, 158, 168, 316, 371, 376, 386, 529, 530, 532, 537, 542, 545; **III:** 1, 4, 5, 6, 7–8, 9, 10, 11, 14, 17, 20, 21, 23, 26, 34, 174, 194, 195–196, 205–206, 220, 236, 239, 269, 270–271, 277–278, 301, 409, 428, 435, 436, 453, 456–457, 459–460, 461–462, 464, 466, 471, 476, 478, 485, 488, 492, 493, 498, 504, 509, 511, 517, 524, 527, 539, 572, 575, 586, 591, 594, 600, 613; **IV:** 27, 74, 82, 83, 95, 122, 123, 127, 129, 134, 138, 140, 141, 191, 201, 237, 331, 379, 402, 403, 418, 419, 420, 430, 431, 439, 442, 491; **Retro. Supp. I: 51–71,** 74, 80, 89, 91, 171, 198, 210, 283, 289, 290, 292, 296, 298, 299, 311, 324, 359, 411, 413, 414, 416, 417, 420, 428; **Retro. Supp. II:** 79, 178, 189, 262, 326; **Supp. I Part 1:** 257, 264, 268, 270, 274, 299; **Supp. I Part 2:** 387, 423, 455, 536, 554, 624, 659, 721; **Supp. II Part 1:** 1, 4, 8, 20, 30, 91, 98, 103, 136, 314; **Supp. III Part 1:** 9, 10, 26, 31, 37, 41, 43, 44, 48, 62–64, 73, 91, 99–100, 105–106, 273; **Supp. III Part 2:** 541, 611, 612, 617, 624; **Supp. IV Part 1:** 40, 47, 284, 380, 404; **Supp. IV Part 2:** 436; **Supp. V:** 79, 97, 101, 338, 343, 344; **Supp. VIII:** 19, 21, 93, 102, 105, 182, 195, 205, 290, 292; **Supp. IX:** 158–159, 229; **Supp. X:** 59, 115, 119, 124, 187, 324; **Supp. XI:** 242; **Supp. XII:** 45, 159, 198, 308; **Supp. XIII:** 77, 104, 115, 332, 341–342, 344, 346; **Supp. XIV:** 5, 13, 107, 287, 290, 306, 347; **Supp. XV:** 20, 51, 139, 177, 181, 186, 216, 218, 250, 251, 258, 298, 302, 303, 306, 307; **Supp. XVI:** 158–159, 204, 207, 282; **Supp. XVII:** 36, 71, 75, 111, 240; **Supp. XVIII:** 136; **Supp. XIX:** 12; **Supp. XX: 86, 108, 199; Supp. XXIII:** 25, 60, 166
Eliot's Early Years (Gordon), **Retro. Supp. I:** 55
"Elizabeth" (Longfellow), **I:** 502
"Elizabeth, 1905" (Schnackenberg), **Supp. XV:** 253, 256
Elizabeth Appleton (O'Hara), **III:** 362, 364, 375–377
"Elizabeth Bishop (1911–1979)" (Merrill), **Retro. Supp. II:** 53
"Elizabeth Bishop in Brazil" (Brown), **Supp. I Part 1:** 96
"Elizabeth Bishop's *North & South*" (Lowell), *Retro. Supp. II:* 40–41
"Elizabeth Gone" (Sexton), **Supp. II Part 2:** 674, 681
Elizabeth Rex (Findley), **Supp. XX: 62–63**
Elizabeth Stoddard and the Boundaries of Bourgeois Culture (Mahoney), **Supp. XV:** 270
Elk Heads on the Wall (Ríos), **Supp. IV Part 2:** 540
Elkin, Stanley, **Supp. VI: 41–59**
Elkins, Andrew, **Supp. XXIII:** 131, 135
Elkins, Marilyn, **Supp. XXIV:** 64
"Elk Song" (Hogan), **Supp. IV Part 1:** 406
Ella in Bloom (Hearon), **Supp. VIII: 70–71**
Elledge, Jim, **Supp. XIII:** 88
Ellen Foster: A Novel (Gibbons), **Supp. X:** 41, **42–44,** 46, 47, 49, 50
Ellen Montgomery's Bookshelf (S. and A. Warner), **Supp. XVIII:** 264
Ellen Rogers (Farrell), **II:** 42–43
"Ellen's Dream" (Gioia), **Supp. XV:** 128
"Ellen West" (Bidart), **Supp. XV: 26–27**
Eller, Ernest, **Supp. I Part 2:** 497
Ellerman, Winifred, **Supp. I Part 1:** 258–259. *See also* McAlmon, Mrs. Robert (Winifred Ellerman)
"*El libro de la sexualidad*" (Simic), *Supp. VIII:* 283
Ellington, Duke, **Retro. Supp. II:** 115; **Supp. IV Part 1:** 360; **Supp. IX:** 164
Elliot, Charles, **Supp. V:** 161
Elliot, George P., **Supp. XV:** 92
Elliott, George B., **III:** 478
Ellipse, The: Selected Poems of Leonardo Sinisgalli (Di Piero, trans.), **Supp. XIX:** 34
"Ellipsis" (C. Frost), **Supp. XV:** 107
Ellis, Albert, **Supp. IV Part 2:** 527
Ellis, Anne, **Supp. XVI:** 38
Ellis, Bret Easton, **Supp. XII:** 81; **Supp. XVIII:** 135
Ellis, Brett Easton, **Supp. X:** 7
Ellis, Charles, **Supp. I Part 1:** 99
Ellis, Havelock, **II:** 276; **Supp. XX: 117, 235; Supp. XXII:** 198
Ellis, John Harvard, **Supp. I Part 1:** 103

Ellis, Katherine, **IV:** 114
Ellis, Kelly, **Supp. XXI:** 249
Ellis, Ron, **Supp. XXII:** 209
Ellis, Thomas Sayers, **Supp. XXI:** 246
"Ellis Island" (Helprin), **Supp. XXV:** 85
Ellis Island and Other Stories (Helprin), **Supp. XXV:** 82, 83, 85
Ellison, Harlan, **Supp. XIII:** 61
Ellison, Ralph, **IV:** 250, 493; **Retro. Supp. II:** 3, **111–130**; **Supp. II Part 1:** 33, **221–252**; **Supp. IV, Part 1:** 374; **Supp. VIII:** 105, 245; **Supp. IX:** 114, 316; **Supp. X:** 324; **Supp. XI:** 18, 92, 275; **Supp. XIII:** 186, 233, 305; **Supp. XIV:** 306; **Supp. XV:** 194; **Supp. XVI:** 135, 139; **Supp. XVIII:** 59, 61, 62, 277, 283; **Supp. XIX:** 148, 149, 155
Ellmann, Maud, **Supp. IV Part 1:** 302
Ellmann, Richard, **Supp. VIII:** 105; **Supp. XV:** 74
Ellroy, James, **Supp. XIV:** 26; **Supp. XXI:** 71
Elman, Richard, **Supp. V:** 40
"Elmer" (Faulkner), **Retro. Supp. I:** 79, 80
Elmer Gantry (Lewis), **I:** 26, 364; **II:** 447–449, 450, 455
Elmer the Great (Lardner), **II:** 427
"Elms" (Glück), **Supp. V:** 85
"Elms Dying, The—And My Friend, Lew Stillwell, Dead" (Bronk), **Supp. XXI:** 31
Eloges (Perse), **Supp. XIII:** 344
"Eloquence of Grief, An" (Crane), **I:** 411
"El Paso Del Norte"(Kenny), **Supp. XXIII:** 150
"El Río Grande" (Mora), **Supp. XIII:** 224
"*El* Round up" (Alvarez), **Supp. VII:** 11
"El Salvador: Requiem and Invocation" (Levertov), **Supp. III Part 1:** 284
Elsasser, Henry, **I:** 226
"Elsa Wertman" (Masters), **Supp. I Part 2:** 462–463
Elsie John and Joey Martinez: Two Stories (Huncke), **Supp. XIV:** 148
Elsie Venner (Holmes), **Supp. I Part 1:** 243, 315–316
Elton, Charles, **Supp. XIV:** 192
Éluard, Paul, **III:** 528; **Supp. IV Part 1:** 80; **Supp. XVII:** 244
Elvins, Kells, **Supp. III Part 1:** 93, 101
Ely, Richard T., **Supp. I Part 1:** 5; **Supp. I Part 2:** 640, 645
"Emancipation. A Life Fable" (Chopin), **Retro. Supp. II:** 59; **Supp. I Part 1:** 207–208
"Emancipation in the British West Indies" (Emerson), **II:** 13
"Emancipation Proclamation, The" (Emerson), **II:** 13
Emanuel, James, **Supp. I Part 1:** 346
Embargo, The (Bryant), **Supp. I Part 1:** 152–153
"Embarkation for Cythera, The" (Ferry), **Supp. XXIV:** 149
Embarrassments (James), **Retro. Supp. I:** 229

Embezzler, The (Auchincloss), **Supp. IV Part 1:** 24, 30–31
"Embroidery, The" (C. Frost), **Supp. XV:** 97
"Emerald" (Doty), **Supp. XI:** 131
"Emerald, The" (Merrill), **Supp. III Part 1:** 328
Emerald City (Egan), **Supp. XIX:** 49, **52–53**
"Emerald City" (Egan), **Supp. XIX:** 52
"Emergence of Flight from Aristotle's Mud, The" (Goldbarth), **Supp. XII:** 190
Emergency Exit (Major), **Supp. XXII:** 174, **175,** 182
"Emergency Haying" (Carruth), **Supp. XVI:** 55
"Emergency Room" (Mora), **Supp. XIII:** 218
"Emerging Voices: The Teaching of Writing" (Mora), **Supp. XIII:** 220
Emerson, and Other Essays (Chapman), **Supp. XIV:** 41–44
Emerson, Ellen, **Supp. I Part 1:** 33
Emerson, John, **Supp. XVI:** 185, 186, 190, 192
Emerson, Ralph Waldo, **I:** 98, 217, 220, 222, 224, 228, 239, 246, 251, 252, 253, 257, 260, 261, 283, 386, 397, 402, 424, 433, 444, 447, 455, 458, 460–461, 463, 464, 485, 561; **II: 1–24,** 49, 92, 127–128, 169, 170, 226, 233, 237, 273–274, 275, 278, 289, 295, 301, 313, 315, 336, 338, 344, 402, 491, 503; **III:** 53, 82, 171, 174, 260, 277, 409, 424, 428, 453, 454, 507, 576–577, 606, 614; **IV:** 60, 167, 169, 170, 171, 172, 173–174, 176, 178, 183, 186, 187, 192, 201, 202, 211, 335, 338, 340, 342, 350; **Retro. Supp. I:** 34, 53, 54, 57, 62, 74–75, 76, 125, 148–149, 152–153, 159, 217, 250, 298, 392, 400, 403; **Retro. Supp. II:** 96, 113, 135, 142, 155, 207, 262; **Supp. I Part 1:** 2, 28–29, 31, 33, 188, 299, 308–309, 317, 358, 365, 366, 368; **Supp. I Part 2:** 374, 383, 393, 407, 413, 416, 420, 422, 474, 482, 580, 582, 602, 659, 679; **Supp. II Part 1:** 280, 288; **Supp. III Part 1:** 387; **Supp. IV Part 2:** 439, 597, 619; **Supp. V:** 118; **Supp. VIII:** 42, 105, 106, 108, 198, 201, 204, 205, 292; **Supp. IX:** 38, 90, 175, 176, 181; **Supp. X:** 42, 45, 121, 223; **Supp. XI:** 203; **Supp. XIII:** 141, 145, 233, 246, **Supp. XIII:** 247; **Supp. XIV:** 41–44, 46, 54, 104, 177; **Supp. XV:** 219, 224; **Supp. XVI:** 84; **Supp. XVII:** 42, 236; **Supp. XX: 115, 116; Supp. XXI:** 217; **Supp. XXIII:** 161, 190; **Supp. XXIV:** 4, 67, 74, 77; **Supp. XXV:** 241, 250
"Emerson and the Essay" (Gass), **Supp. VI:** 88
"Emerson the Lecturer" (Lowell), **Supp. I Part 2:** 420, 422
Emerson-Thoreau Award, **Retro. Supp. I:** 67
Emery, Clark, **III:** 478
Emery, Mary Lou, **Supp. XXII:** 73

E. M. Forster (Trilling), **Supp. III Part 2:** 496, 501, 504
"Emigre in Autumn, An" (Gioia), **Supp. XV:** 120
Emily, Alone (O'Nan), **Supp. XXV:** 145, 149, 150–151
"Emily Dickinson and Class" (Erkkila), **Retro. Supp. I:** 42–43
Emily Dickinson Editorial Collective, **Retro. Supp. I:** 47
Emily Dickinson in Southern California (X. J. Kennedy), **Supp. XV: 164–165**
"Emily Dickinson's Defunct" (Nelson), **Supp. XVIII:** 173
Emily Dickinson: Woman Poet (Bennett), **Retro. Supp. I:** 42
Eminent Victorians (Strachey), **Supp. I Part 2:** 485
Emma (Austen), **Supp. XVIII:** 149
"Emma and Eginhard" (Longfellow), **III:** 505
"Emma Enters a Sentence of Elizabeth Bishop's" (Gass), **Supp. VI:** 93
Emmanuel Appodocca: or, A Blighted Life (Philip), **Supp. XXI:** 160
"Emmaus" (Di Piero), **Supp. XIX:** 42, 43
Emperor Jones, The (O'Neill), **II:** 278; **III:** 391, 392
Emperor of Haiti (Hughes), **Supp. I Part 1:** 339
"Emperor of Ice Cream, The" (Stevens), **IV:** 76, 80–81
"Emperors" (Dunn), **Supp. XI:** 155
"Emperor's New Clothes, The" (Anderson), **I:** 441
"Empire" (Ford), **Supp. V:** 69
Empire: A Novel (Vidal), **Supp. IV Part 2:** 677, 684, 686, 690; **Supp. XIX:** 132
"Empire Builders" (MacLeish), **III:** 14
Empire City, The: or, New York by Night and Day (Lippard), **Supp. XXIII:** 178, 180, 183, 184, 185
Empire Falls (Russo), **Supp. XII: 339–343**
Empire of Summer, The (Doty), **Supp. XI:** 120
Empire of the Senseless (Acker), **Supp. XII:** 5, **6, 14–16**
"Empires" (Simic), **Supp. VIII:** 282
"Emporium" (Shapiro), **Supp. II Part 2:** 705
Empress of the Splendid Season (Hijuelos), **Supp. VIII: 86–89**
Empson, William, **I:** 522, 533; **II:** 536; **III:** 286, 497, 498, 499; **IV:** 136, 431; **Retro. Supp. I:** 263; **Retro. Supp. II:** 253; **Supp. XVI:** 190
Empty Bed, The (Hadas), **Supp. XXIII: 117–118**
Empty Hands, The (Bronk), **Supp. XXI:** 31
"Empty Hills, The" (Winters), **Supp. II Part 2:** 792, 793, 796
"Empty Icon Frame" (Stallings), **Supp. XXV:** 233
Empty Mirror, Early Poems (Ginsberg), **Supp. II Part 1:** 308, 311, 313–314, 319, 329

"Empty Room" (Hughes), **Supp. I Part 1:** 337

"Empty Threat, An" (Frost), **II:** 159

Emshwiller, Ed, **Supp. XVIII:** 145

"Encantadas, The" (Melville), **III:** 89; **Supp. XVIII:** 4

Enchanter, The (Nabokov), **Retro. Supp. I:** 266

"Enclosed Dreams, Highways and Labyrinths: Jonathan Lethem's *Amnesia Moon*" (Rossi), *Supp. XVIII:* 139

"Encomium Twenty Years Later" (Tate), **I:** 381

"Encounter" (Espaillat), **Supp. XXI:** 107

"Encounter, The" (Pound), **III:** 466

Encounter in April (Sarton), **Supp. VIII:** 259

"Encounter in April" (Sarton), **Supp. VIII:** 259

"Encountering the Sublime" (McClatchy), **Supp. XII:** 261

"Encounter in Vindija Cave, Present-Day Croatia: Late October"(Schott), **Supp. XXIII:** 254

"Encounter on the Seine: Black Meets Brown" (Baldwin), **Retro. Supp. II:** 2

Encounters with Chinese Writers (Dillard), **Supp. VI:** 19, 23, 31

Encounters with the Archdruid (McPhee), **Supp. III Part 1:** 292–294, 301; **Supp. X:** 30

Encyclopedia of Arkansas History and Culture, The (online), **Supp. XXII:** 50

Encyclopedia of Scotland, The (A. Finch), **Supp. XVII:** 70–71

Encyclopedia of World Biography, The, **Supp. XXI:** 74

"End, The" (Olds), **Supp. X:** 205

"Endangered Species" (Mora), **Supp. XIII:** 219–220

Endecott and the Red Cross (Lowell), **II:** 545

Endgame (Beckett), **Supp. XIII:** 196; **Supp. XXII:** 263

"Endgame" (Tan), **Supp. X:** 290

"Endicott and the Red Cross" (Hawthorne), **Retro. Supp. II:** 181, 187–188

"End of Books, The" (Coover), **Supp. V:** 53

End of Books, The (Coover), **Supp. XXII:** 259

End of Dreams, The (Skloot), **Supp. XX:** 196, 202–203

End of Education, The (Postman), **Supp. XI:** 275

"End of FIRPO in the World, The" (Saunders), **Supp. XIX:** 229

"End of Season" (Warren), **IV:** 239–240

"End of Something, The" (Hemingway), **II:** 248

End of the Affair, The (Greene), **Supp. XI:** 99

End of the Age of Innocence, The (Price), **Retro. Supp. I:** 377

"End of the Line, The" (Helprin), **Supp. XXV:** 81

"End of the Line, The" (Jarrell), **III:** 527

"End of the Rainbow, The" (Jarrell), **II:** 386

End of the Road (film), **Supp. XI:** 309

End of the Road, The (Barth), **I:** 121, 122, 126–131; **Supp. XI:** 309; **Supp. XVIII:** 140, 141

"End of the World, The" (Gioia), **Supp. XV:** 126

"End of the World, The" (MacLeish), **III:** 8

Endor (Nemerov), **III:** 269, 270, 279

Endore, Guy, **Supp. XVII: 53–67**

"Ends" (Dixon), **Supp. XII:** 153

End to Innocence, An: Essays on Culture and Politics (Fiedler), **Supp. XIII: 98–99**

Endure: The Diaries of Charles Walter Stetson (Stetson), **Supp. XI:** 196

"Enduring Chill, The" (O'Connor), **III:** 349, 351, 357; **Retro. Supp. II:** 236

Enduring Vision of Norman Mailer, The (Leeds), **Retro. Supp. II:** 204

Endymion (Keats), **IV:** 405; **Retro. Supp. I:** 412

End Zone (DeLillo), **Supp. VI:** 2, 3, 4, 10, 11, 12

Enemies (Boyce and Hapgood), **Supp. XVII:** 100; **Supp. XXI:** 7, 13

Enemies: A Love Story (Singer), **IV:** 1; **Retro. Supp. II: 310–311**

Enemy, The: Time (T. Williams), **IV:** 391

Enemy of the People, An (adapt. Miller), **III:** 154–156

"Energy Vampire" (Ginsberg), **Supp. II Part 1:** 326

"Enforcement of the Slave Trade Laws, The" (Du Bois), **Supp. II Part 1:** 161

"Engaging the Past" (Bell), **Supp. X:** 17

Engel, Bernard F., **I:** 532

Engels, Friedrich, **IV:** 429, 443–444; **Supp. I Part 1:** 13; **Supp. XXI:** 162

Engineer of Beasts, The (Sanders), **Supp. XVI:** 270

Engineer of Moonlight (DeLillo), **Supp. VI:** 4

Engineers and the Price System, The (Veblen), **I:** 475–476; **Supp. I Part 2:** 638, 642, 648

Engines of Creation: the Coming Era of Nanotechnology (Drexler), **Supp. XVI:** 121

"England" (Moore), **III:** 203, 207, 214

Englander, Nathan, **Supp. XX: 177, 179; Supp. XXIV:** 131; **Supp. XXV:** 268

Engle, Paul, **III:** 542; **Retro. Supp. II:** 220, 221; **Supp. V:** 337; **Supp. XI:** 315; **Supp. XIII:** 76; **Supp. XVIII:** 72

English, Zoë, **Supp. XVI:** 293

English Elegy, The: Studies in the Genre from Spenser to Yeats (Sacks), **Supp. IV Part 2:** 450

English Hours (James), **II:** 337; **Retro. Supp. I:** 235

English Language, The (L. P. Smith), **Supp. XIV:** 341

English-Latin Gradus or Verse Dictionary, An (Ainger), **Supp. XX: 230**

"English Lesson"(Strout), **Supp. XXIII:** 273–274, 284

Englishmen of Letters (James), **II:** 327

English Notebooks, The (Hawthorne), **II:** 226, 227–228

English Novel, The (Lanier), **Supp. I Part 1:** 371

English Poets, The: Lessing, Rousseau (Lowell), **Supp. I Part 2:** 407

English Prosody and Modern Poetry (Shapiro), **Supp. II Part 2:** 710

English Traits (Emerson), **II:** 1, 5, 6–7, 8

"English Writers on America" (Irving), **II:** 308

Engstrand, Stuart, **Supp. I Part 1:** 51

"Enigma Variations" (Nelson), **Supp. XVIII:** 177

"Enoch" (Very), **Supp. XXV:** 246, 247

"Enoch and the Gorilla" (O'Connor), **Retro. Supp. II:** 225

Enormous Changes at the Last Minute (Paley), **Supp. VI:** 218

"Enormous Changes at the Last Minute" (Paley), **Supp. VI:** 226, 232

"Enormous Radio, The" (Cheever), **Supp. I Part 1:** 175–177, 195

Enormous Radio and Other Stories, The (Cheever), **Supp. I Part 1:** 175–177

Enormous Room, The (Cummings), **I:** 429, 434, 440, 445, 477; **Supp. XXI:** 277

"Enough for a Lifetime" (Buck), **Supp. II Part 1:** 127

Enough Rope (Parker), **Supp. IX:** 189, 192

Enquiry Concerning Political Justice (Godwin), **Supp. I Part 1:** 126, 146

"En Route" (Boulton), **Supp. XXII:** 25

Entered From the Sun (Garrett), **Supp. VII:** 105–106, 107–109

"Entering the Building" (Notley), **Supp. XXII:** 237

"Entering the Kingdom" (Oliver), **Supp. VII:** 234

Entertaining Strangers (Gurney), **Supp. V:** 98, 99

Enter without Desire (Lacy), **Supp. XV:** 201

Entranced, The (Lippard), **Supp. XXIII:** 178, 180, 190

Entrance: Four Chicano Poets, **Supp. XIII:** 316

Entrance to Porlock, The (Buechner), **Supp. XII:** 52

Entries (Berry), **Supp. X:** 23

"Entropy" (Pynchon), **Supp. II Part 2:** 619, 621

Entry in an Unknown Hand (F. Wright), **Supp. XVII:** 240, 244, 245

Environmental Imagination, The (Buell), **Supp. V:** 209; **Supp. IX:** 29

"Envoy" (Collins), **Supp. XXI:** 57

"Envoys, The" (Merrill), **Supp. III Part 1:** 326

"Envy; or, Yiddish in America" (Ozick), **Supp. V:** 263, 265–266

"Eolian Harp, The" (Coleridge), **I:** 284

"Eolian Harp, The"(Coleridge), **Supp. XXIII:** 231

"Eototo" (Sobin), **Supp. XVI:** 283–284

"Ephemera, The" (Franklin), **II:** 121

Ephesians (biblical book), **Supp. I Part 1:** 117

"Epic Poetry" (Very), **Supp. XXV:** 241
Epictetus, **III:** 566
"Epicurean, The" (Auchincloss), **Supp. IV Part 1:** 25
Epicurus, **I:** 59
Epidemic of Genius, An (Wolfert), **Supp. XXI:** 278
"Epigram" (Lowell), **II:** 550
"Epilogue" (Lowell), **Retro. Supp. II:** 191
"Epimanes" (Poe), **III:** 411
"Epimetheus" (Longfellow), **II:** 494
"Epiphany" (X. J. Kennedy), **Supp. XV:** 166, 167
"Epipsychidion" (Shelley), **Supp. I Part 2:** 718
Episode in Palmetto (Caldwell), **I:** 297, 307
"Episode in the Life of an Ancestor" (Boyle), **Supp. XXIV:** 56
Episode of the Wandering Knife, The (Rinehart), **Supp. XXV:** 198, 200
"Epistle" (L.-Y. Lee), **Supp. XV:** 212
Epistles (Horace), **Supp. XXIV:** 156
Epistles of Horace, The (Ferry, trans.), **Supp. XXIV: 157–158**
Epistle to a Godson (Auden), **Supp. II Part 1:** 24
"Epistle to Be Left in the Earth" (MacLeish), **III:** 13
"Epistle to George William Curtis" (Lowell), **Supp. I Part 2:** 416
"Epistle to Léon-Paul Fargue" (MacLeish), **III:** 15
"Epitaph Ending in And, The" (Stafford), **Supp. XI:** 321–322
Epitaph for a Dead Beat (Markson), **Supp. XVII: 136–138,** 141; 139
Epitaph for a Desert Anarchist (Bishop), **Supp. XIII:** 1
Epitaph for a Tramp (Markson), **Supp. XVII:** 136, 137, 139 142
"Epitaph for Fire and Flower" (Plath), **Supp. I Part 2:** 537
"Epitaph for the Race of Man" (Millay), **III:** 127–128
"Epithalamium" (Auden), **Supp. II Part 1:** 15
"Epstein" (P. Roth), **Retro. Supp. II:** 281; **Supp. III Part 2:** 404, 406–407, 412, 422
Epstein, Barbara, **Supp. XIX:** 268
Epstein, Helen, **Supp. XVII:** 47; **Supp. XXII:** 95
Epstein, Jacob, **Supp. XXIII:** 6
Epstein, Jason, **Supp. VIII:** 233
Epstein, Joseph, **Supp. IV Part 2:** 692; **Supp. VIII:** 236, 238; **Supp. XIV: 101–117; Supp. XVI:** 230, 275
Epstein, Leslie, **Supp. XII: 159–174; Supp. XVIII:** 92, 99
Epstein, Philip, **Supp. XII:** 159
"Equal in Paris" (Baldwin), **Retro. Supp. II:** 3; **Supp. I Part 1:** 52
"Equals" (Untermeyer), **Supp. XV:** 304
Equation for Evil (Caputo), **Supp. XIX:** 25–26
"Equations of the Light" (Gioia), **Supp. XV:** 125

"Equilibrists, The" (Ransom), **III:** 490, 494
"Equinox"(Crooker), **Supp. XXIII:** 55
"Equipment for Pennies" (H. Roth), **Supp. IX:** 233
Erasmus, Desiderius, **Supp. XV:** 258
Erasure (Everett), **Supp. XVIII:** 54, 60, **61–62**
"Erat Hora" (Pound), **III:** 463; **Retro. Supp. I:** 413
Erdrich, Louise, **Supp. IV Part 1: 259– 278,** 333, 404; **Supp. X:** 290; **Supp. XVIII:** 189; **Supp. XXIV:** 245
"Erectus" (Karr), **Supp. XI:** 243
"Ere Sleep Comes Down to Soothe the Weary Eyes" (Dunbar), **Supp. II Part 1:** 199, 207–208
"Ergo Non Sum. Est." (Bronk), **Supp. XXI:** 31
"Ergotism"(Schott), **Supp. XXIII:** 245
Erikson, Erik, **I:** 58, 214, 218
Erisman, Fred, **Supp. VIII:** 126
Erkkila, Betsy, **Retro. Supp. I:** 42; **Supp. XX: 281, 287, 287–288**
Ernest, John, **Supp. XXI:** 24
"Ernest: or Parent for a Day" (Bourne), **I:** 232
Ernst, Max, **Retro. Supp. II:** 321
"Eros" (Komunyakaa), **Supp. XIII:** 130
"Eros and Anteros" (E. Stoddard), **Supp. XV:** 283
Eros and Civilization (Marcuse), **Supp. XII:** 2
Eros at Temple Stream" (Levertov), **Supp. III Part 1:** 278–279
Eros the Bittersweet (Carson), **Supp. XII:** 97, **98–99**
Eros Trilogy, The (Silver), **Supp. XXIV:** 264, 267
"Eros Turannos" (Robinson), **III:** 510, 512, 513–516, 517, 518
"Eroticism in Women" (Nin), **Supp. X:** 195
"Errand" (Carver), **Supp. III Part 1:** 149
Erskine, Albert, **IV:** 261; **Retro. Supp. II:** 117
Erskine, John, **I:** 223; **Supp. X:** 183; **Supp. XIV:** 120
Erstein, Hap, **Supp. IV Part 2:** 589, 590
"Escape" (MacLeish), **III:** 4
Escape Artist, The (Wagoner), **Supp. IX:** 324, **334–335**
"Escape"(Thompson), **Supp. XXIII:** 301
Escher, M. C., **Supp. XII:** 26; **Supp. XVI:** 102
"Escudilla" (Leopold), **Supp. XIV:** 188
Eshleman, Clayton, **Supp. XVI:** 284
"Eskimo Love" (Apple), **Supp. XVII:** 5
Espaillat, Rhina P., **Supp. XXI: 97–114**
Esparza, Laura, **Supp. XXIII:** 197
Espeland, Pamela, **Supp. XVIII:** 180, 181
Espen, Hal, **Supp. X:** 15
Espey, John, **III:** 463, 468, 478
Esposito, Michael, **Supp. XX: 34, 40**
Esposito, Scott, **Supp. XVII:** 234
Esquibel, Catrióna Rueda, **Supp. XXIII:** 202
Essais (Renouvier), **II:** 344–345

Essay Concerning Human Understanding, An (Locke), **I:** 554; **II:** 8, 348– 349
Essay on American Poetry (Brown), **Supp. I Part 1:** 156
"Essay on Aristocracy" (Paine), **Supp. I Part 2:** 515
"Essay on Friendship, An" (McClatchy), **Supp. XII:** 258–259
"Essay on Love" (Carruth), **Supp. XVI:** 56
Essay on Man (Pope), **II:** 111; **Supp. I Part 2:** 516
"Essay on Marriage" (Carruth), **Supp. XVI:** 48
Essay on Our Changing Order (Veblen), **Supp. I Part 2:** 629, 642
"Essay on Poetics" (Ammons), **Supp. VII:** 29–31
Essay on Projects (Defoe), **II:** 104
"Essay on Psychiatrists" (Pinsky), **Supp. VI:** 237, 238, 241, 242, 249, 250
Essay on Rime (Shapiro), **I:** 430; **Supp. II Part 2:** 702, 703, 708–711
"Essay on Sanity" (Dunn), **Supp. XI:** 147
"Essay on the Character of Robespierre" (Paine), **Supp. I Part 2:** 515
Essay on the Chinese Written Character (Fenollosa), **III:** 474
"Essay on What I Think About Most" (Carson), **Supp. XII: 111–112**
Essays (Emerson), **II:** 1, 7, 8, 12–13, 15, 21
Essays, Speeches, and Public Letters by William Faulkner (Meriweather, ed.), **Retro. Supp. I:** 77
Essays and Poems (Very), **Supp. XXV:** 247, 249–250
Essays in Anglo-Saxon Law (Adams), **I:** 5
Essays in London (James), **II:** 336
Essays in Radical Empiricism (James), **II:** 355, 356–357
Essays on Norman Mailer (Lucid), **Retro. Supp. II:** 195
Essays on the Nature and Principles of Taste (Alison), **Supp. I Part 1:** 151
Essays to Do Good (Mather), **II:** 104; **Supp. II Part 2:** 461, 467
"Essay: The Love of Old Houses" (Doty), **Supp. XI:** 136
"Essay Toward a Point of View, An" (Brooks), **I:** 244
"Essay Vanishes, The" (Monson), **Supp. XXIV:** 238
"Essence, Absence, and Sobin's *Venus Blue*" (English), **Supp. XVI:** 293
Essential Dykes to Watch Out For, The (Bechdel), **Supp. XXV:** 2
Essential Haiku, The (Hass), **Supp. VI:** 102
Essential Keats (Levine, ed.), **Supp. V:** 179
"Essential Oils—are wrung" (Dickinson), **I:** 471; **Retro. Supp. I:** 43, 46
"Essentials" (Toomer), **Supp. III Part 2:** 486
Essentials: A Philosophy of Life in Three Hundred Definitions and Aphorisms (Toomer), **Supp. III Part 2:** 486

Essentials: Definitions and Aphorisms (Toomer), **Supp. IX:** 320

"Essentials of Spontaneous Prose" (Kerouac), **Supp. III Part 1:** 227–228

Essential Works of the Founding Fathers, The (Kriegel, ed.), **Supp. XXIV:** 214

Estampas del valle y otras obras (Hinojosa). *See Valley, The* (Hinojosa)

Esta puente, mi espalda: Voces de mujeres tercermundistas en los Estados Unidos (Moraga, Castillo, and Alarcón, eds.), **Supp. XXIII:** 194

"Estate Sale" (Nye), **Supp. XIII:** 283

Estess, Sybil, **Supp. IV Part 2:** 449, 452

Esther (Adams), **I:** 9–10, 20

"Esther" (Toomer), **Supp. IX:** 313–314

"Esther Kahn" (Symons), **Supp. XX: 239**

"Esthétique du Mal" (Stevens), **IV:** 79; **Retro. Supp. I:** 300, 311, 312

"Estoy-eh-muut and the Kunideeyahs (Arrowboy and the Destroyers)" (film), **Supp. IV Part 2:** 560

Estrada, Genaro, **Retro. Supp. II:** 89

Estray, The (Longfellow, ed.), **Retro. Supp. II:** 155

Esty, William, **III:** 358

"Etching, An" (Masters), **Supp. I Part 2:** 458

"Eternal Goodness, The" (Whittier), **Supp. I Part 2:** 704

Eternal Spring, The (Boyce), **Supp. XVII:** 100; **Supp. XXI:** 4, 5, 11

"Eternity, An" (W. C. Williams), **Retro. Supp. I:** 423

"Eternity Is Now" (Roethke), **III:** 544–545

"Ethan Brand" (Hawthorne), **II:** 227

Ethan Frome (Wharton), **IV:** 316–317, 327; **Retro. Supp. I:** 372–373; **Supp. IX:** 108; **Supp. XVIII:** 216; **Supp. XXIII:** 275, 281

"Ethical Turn in Postcolonial Theory and Narrative, The: Michelle Cliff's *No Telephone to Heaven*" (Moynagh), **Supp. XXII:** 73

Ethics (Spinoza), **IV:** 12; **Retro. Supp. II:** 300

"Ethics of Culture, The" (Locke), **Supp. XIV:** 211

"Ethnics of Frank Costello, The" (Talese), **Supp. XVII:** 202

Etiquette and Vitriol: The Food Chain and Other Plays (Silver), **Supp. XXIV:** 263, 264

"Étiquettes Jaunes, Les"(O'Hara), **Supp. XXIII:** 214

"Etude" (Kooser), **Supp. XIX:** 115

Etulain, Richard, **Supp. IV Part 2:** 597, 601, 604, 606, 607, 608, 610, 611

"Etymology" (Nelson), **Supp. XVIII:** 185

Euclid, **III:** 6, 620

"Euclid Alone Has Looked on Beauty Bare" (Millay), **III:** 133

"Euclidean Spaces: Linear Time" (Bronk), **Supp. XXI:** 31

Eugene, Frank, **Supp. X:** 204

Eugene Onegin (Pushkin), **III:** 246, 263

Eugene Onegin (Pushkin; Nabokov, trans.), **Retro. Supp. I:** 266, 267, 272

Eugenides, Jeffrey, **Supp. XIX:** 138; **Supp. XXI:** 229; **Supp. XXIV: 131–146**

Eugénie, Empress, **IV:** 309

Eugénie Grandet (Balzac), **II:** 328

"Eugénie Grandet" (Barthelme), **Supp. IV Part 1:** 47

"Eulogy for Richard Hugo (1923–1982)" (Wagoner), **Supp. IX:** 330–331

"Eulogy on the Flapper" (Z. Fitzgerald), **Supp. IX:** 71

Eumenides (Aeschylus), **Retro. Supp. I:** 65

"E Unibus Pluram: Television and U.S. Fiction" (Wallace), **Supp. X:** 315–316

"Euphemisms" (Matthews), **Supp. IX: 167–168**

Eureka (Poe), **III:** 409, 424, 428–429

Eurekas (Goldbarth), **Supp. XII:** 181

Euripides, **I:** 325; **II:** 8, 282, 543; **III:** 22, 145, 398; **IV:** 370; **Supp. I Part 1:** 268, 269, 270; **Supp. I Part 2:** 482; **Supp. V:** 277

"Euripides and Professor Murray" (Eliot), **Supp. I Part 1:** 268

"Euripides—A Playwright" (West), **IV:** 286; **Retro. Supp. II:** 326

"Europe" (Ashbery), **Supp. III Part 1:** 7–10, 13, 18

European Discovery of America, The: The Northern Voyages (Morison), **Supp. I Part 2:** 496–497

Europeans, The (H. James), **I:** 452; **II:** 327, 328; **Retro. Supp. I:** 216, 220

Europe Central (Vollmann), **Supp. XVII:** 225, 226, 227, 229, 231, **233–235**, 236

"Europe! Europe!" (Ginsberg), **Supp. II Part 1:** 320, 322

Europe of Trusts, The: Selected Poems (Howe), **Supp. IV Part 2:** 420, 422, 426

Europe without Baedeker (Wilson), **IV:** 429

Eurydice in the Underworld (Acker), **Supp. XII:** 7

"Eurydice Reveals Her Strength" (Stallings), **Supp. XXV:** 230

"Eurydice's Footnote" (Stallings), **Supp. XXV:** 230

Eustace, Saint, **II:** 215

Eustace Chisholm and the Works (Purdy), **Supp. VII:** 273–274, 279–280

"Euthanasia" (Tate), **IV:** 122

"Evaluation" (Bronk), **Supp. XXI:** 32

Eva-Mary (McCarriston), **Supp. XIV:** 259, 260, **263–268**

"Evangeline" (Dixon), **Supp. XII:** 153

Evangeline (Longfellow), **II:** 489, 501–502; **Retro. Supp. II:** 155, **156–159**, 162, 164; **Supp. I Part 2:** 586

Evanier, David, **Supp. XVI:** 212

Evans, Alice, **Supp. XVII:** 71, 72

Evans, Mary Ann. *See* Eliot, George

Evans, Oliver, **Supp. IV Part 1:** 85, 91

Evans, Sandy, **Supp. XIII:** 129

Evans, Walker, **I:** 36, 38, 293; **Retro. Supp. II:** 85

Eva's Man (G. Jones), **Supp. XXIV:** 183, 184, 185, **188–190**, 193

Eve (A. Finch), **Supp. XVII: 72–74**

"Eve" (W. C. Williams), **Retro. Supp. I:** 423

Even Cowgirls Get the Blues (Robbins), **Supp. X:** 259, 260, 261, 262–263, 264, 266, **269–271**, 272, 274, 277, 284; **Supp. XIII:** 11

"Evening" (Carver), **Supp. III Part 1:** 148

Evening (Minot), **Supp. VI:** 204–205, 208, **213–215**

"Evening at a Country Inn" (Kenyon), **Supp. VII:** 167

"Evening in Advent, An" (W. V. Davis), **Supp. XXI:** 92

"Evening in a Lumber Yard"(Le Sueur), **Supp. XXIII:** 165

"Evening in a Sugar Orchard" (Frost), **Retro. Supp. I:** 133

"Evening in Nuevo Leon, An" (Caldwell), **I:** 309

"Evening in the Sanitarium" (Bogan), **Supp. III Part 1:** 61

Evening Light, The (Skloot), **Supp. XX: 196, 201–202**

"Evening Love-of-Self" (Taggard), **Supp. XXII:** 280–281

"Evening of the 4th of July, The" (Kees), **Supp. XV:** 140, 142

"Evening on the Cote d'Azur" (Yates), **Supp. XI:** 349

Evening Performance, An: New and Selected Short Stories (Garrett), **Supp. VII:** 109

"Evenings at Home" (Hardwick), **Supp. III Part 1:** 195–196

"Evening's at Seven, The" (Thurber), **Supp. I Part 2:** 616

"Evening Star" (Bogan), **Supp. III Part 1:** 56

Evening Star, The (McMurtry), **Supp. V:** 230

Evening Star, The (screenplay, McMurtry), **Supp. V:** 232

"Evening Sun" (Kenyon), **Supp. VII:** 168

Evening Sun Turned Crimson, The (Huncke), **Supp. XIV:** 140, 149–150

"Evening Sun Turned Crimson, The" (Huncke), **Supp. XIV:** 137–138, 139

"Evening Wind, The" (Bryant), **Supp. I Part 1:** 164

"Evening without Angels" (Stevens), **Retro. Supp. I:** 302

Evening with Richard Nixon, An (Vidal), **Supp. IV Part 2:** 683

"Even Sea, The" (Swenson), **Supp. IV Part 2:** 641

Even Stephen (Perelman and West), **Retro. Supp. II:** 328

"Event, An" (Wilbur), **Supp. III Part 2:** 547, 554

"Event, The" (Dove), **Supp. IV Part 1:** 242, 247–248

"Even the Vanishing Housed"(Hirshfield), **Supp. XXIII:** 132

"Eventide" (Brooks), **Supp. III Part 1:** 73

"Eventide" (Purdy), **Supp. VII:** 270

"Event Itself, The" (Carruth), **Supp. XVI:** 47

Eve of Saint Agnes, The (Keats), **II:** 82, 531

"Eve of St. Agnes, The" (Clampitt), **Supp. IX:** 40

"Ever a Bridegroom: Reflections on the Failure of Texas Literature" (McMurtry), **Supp. V:** 225

Everett, Alexander Hill, **Supp. I Part 1:** 152

Everett, Percival, **Supp. XVIII:** 53–67

Everlasting Story of Nory, The (Baker), **Supp. XIII:** 52, **Supp. XIII:** 53–55

"Everly Brothers, The" (Skloot), **Supp. XX:** 199

Ever-Present Past, The (Hamilton), **Supp. XVI:** 196

Evers, Medgar, **IV:** 280; **Retro. Supp. II:** 13; **Supp. I Part 1:** 52, 65

Everson, William, **Supp. XXII:** 276

Everwine, Peter, **Supp. V:** 180; **Supp. XIII:** 312; **Supp. XV:** 73–90

"Everybody's Protest Novel" (Baldwin), **Retro. Supp. II:** 4; **Supp. I Part 1:** 50, 51

"Everybody's Reading Li Po' Silk-screened on a Purple T-Shirt" (Komunyakaa), **Supp. XIII:** 120

Everybody's Story: Writing by Older Minnesotans (C. Bly, ed.), **Supp. XVI:** 38

"Everybody Was Very Nice" (Benét), **Supp. XI:** 53

"Everyday Alchemy" (Taggard), **Supp. XXII:** 274–275, 276, 279

"Every-Day Girl, A" (Jewett), **Retro. Supp. II:** 132

Everyday People (O'Nan), **Supp. XXV:** 142, 146–147, 150

"Everyday Use" (Walker), **Supp. III Part 2:** 534

"Every-Day Work" (Jewett), **Retro. Supp. II:** 132

Everyman (Ashbery), **Supp. XXIII:** 210

Everyone Says I Love You (film; Allen), **Supp. XV:** 11

Every Pleasure (Goldbarth), **Supp. XII:** 181

Every Soul Is a Circus (Lindsay), **Supp. I Part 2:** 384, 394, 399

"Everything Is a Human Being" (Walker), **Supp. III Part 2:** 527

Everything Is Illuminated (Foer), **Supp. XII:** 169

Everything Is Now (Cliff), **Supp. XXII:** 67, 74, 76

"Everything Stuck to Him" (Carver), **Supp. III Part 1:** 143

Everything That Moves (Schulberg), **Supp. XVIII:** 254

Everything That Rises Must Converge (O'Connor), **III:** 339, 348–349, 350–351; **Retro. Supp. II:** 235, 236–237

"Everything That Rises Must Converge" (O'Connor), **III:** 349, 352, 357; **Retro. Supp. II:** 236

Everything You Always Wanted to Know about Sex (film; Allen), **Supp. XV:** 4–5, 13

Eve's Diary (Twain), **IV:** 208–209

"Eve Speaks" (Untermeyer), **Supp. XV:** 300

"Eve the Fox" (Gunn Allen), **Supp. IV Part 1:** 331

"Evidence" (Harjo), **Supp. XII:** 219

"Evidence-cum-Witness: Subaltern History, Violence, and the (De)formation of a Nation in Michelle Cliff's *No Telephone to Heaven*" (Sethuraman), **Supp. XXII:** 73

Evidence of the Senses, The (Kelley), **Supp. IV Part 2:** 529

Evidence of Things Not Seen, The (Baldwin), **Retro. Supp. II:** 15

"Evidences of Revealed Religion, The" (Channing), **Supp. XXIV:** 74

"Evil Seekers, The" (Sexton), **Supp. II Part 2:** 696

"Evolution" (Swenson), **Supp. IV Part 2:** 639

Evolving the Idol: The Poetry of Gustaf Sobin (Crick), **Supp. XVI:** 289

Ewing, Jon, **Supp. X:** 253

Ewings, The (O'Hara), **III:** 383

"Examination at the Womb Door" (Hughes), **Supp. XV:** 347

"Examination of the Hero in a Time of War" (Stevens), **Retro. Supp. I:** 305–306, 308

"Excavation of Troy" (MacLeish), **III:** 18

Excellent Becomes the Permanent, The (Addams), **Supp. I Part 1:** 25

"Excelsior" (Longfellow), **Retro. Supp. II:** 169

"Excerpts from Swan Lake" (Cameron), **Supp. XII:** 80, **84**

"Excerpts from the Epistemology Workshops" (Rand), **Supp. IV Part 2:** 529

"Excess of Charity" (Wylie), **Supp. I Part 2:** 720

"Exchange, The" (Swenson), **Supp. IV Part 2:** 644

"Excitement, The " (Jarman), **Supp. XVII:** 120–121

"Exclusive" (Olds), **Supp. X:** 206

"Excrement Poem, The" (Kumin), **Supp. IV Part 2:** 448

"Excursion" (Garrett), **Supp. VII:** 100

Excursions (Thoreau), **IV:** 188

"Excursion to Canada, An" (Thoreau), **Supp. XVIII:** 4

"Excursus of Reassurance in Begonia Time, An" (Carruth), **Supp. XVI:** 58

Executioner (Weigl), **Supp. XIX:** 277

Executioner's Song, The (Mailer), **Retro. Supp. II:** 108, 209

Exekiel, **Supp. XXI:** 91

"Exercise and Abstinence" (Swados), **Supp. XIX:** 265

Exercises in History, Chronology, and Biography, in Question and Answer (Rowson), **Supp. XV:** 245

Ex-Friends: Falling Out with Allen Ginsberg, Lionel and Diana Trilling, Lillian Hellman, Hannah Arendt, and Norman Mailer (Podhoretz), **Supp. VIII:** 239, **242–244**

"Exhausted Bug, The" (R. Bly), **Supp. IV Part 1:** 73

"Exhortation" (Bogan), **Supp. III Part 1:** 58

"Exhortation" (McKay), **Supp. X:** 135

"Ex-husband"(Schott), **Supp. XXIII:** 249

"Exile" (Gass), **Supp. VI:** 92

"Exile" (Oates), **Supp. II Part 2:** 523

Exile, The (Buck), **Supp. II Part 1:** 119, 131

"Exiles, The" (Bradbury), **Supp. IV Part 1:** 113

"Exiles, The" (Whittier), **Supp. I Part 2:** 692–693

Exiles and Fabrications (Scott), **II:** 512

Exile's Daughter, The (Spencer), **Supp. II Part 1:** 121

"Exile's Departure, The" (Whittier), **Supp. I Part 2:** 683

Exiles from Paradise: Zelda and Scott Fitzgerald (Mayfield), **Supp. IX:** 65

"Exile's Letter" (Karr), **Supp. XI:** 241

Exile's Return (Cowley), **Supp. III Part 1:** 136, 138, 140, 141, 144, 147, 148

"Exile's Return, The" (Lowell), **II:** 539; **Retro. Supp. II:** 187

Exiles: Three Short Novels (Caputo), **Supp. XIX:** 25, **26–27**

"Existences" (Stafford), **Supp. XI:** 324

Existentialism from Dostoevsky to Sartre (W. Kaufmann), **Supp. XVII:** 137

Exit into History (Hoffman), **Supp. XVI:** 148, 150, **151–153**

Exit to Eden (Rampling), **Supp. VII:** 301–302

Exley (Clarke), **Supp. XXIII:** 109

Exley, Frederick, **Supp. XVI:** 69; **Supp. XVII:** 135; **Supp. XXIII:** 78, **97–110**

Exodus (biblical book), **IV:** 300

Exodus (film), **Supp. XX:** 246

Exodus (Uris), **Supp. IV Part 1:** 379; **Supp. XX:** 243–244, 244, 245, 247, 248, 250–251, 257

Exodus Revisited (Uris), **Supp. XX:** 247

"Exorcism" (Snodgrass), **Supp. VI:** 314

"Exorcism, An" (Malamud), **Supp. I Part 2:** 435

Exorcist, The (film), **Supp. I Part 1:** 66

"Expanded Composition, The" (Major), **Supp. XXII:** 174

"Expanding Rooms" (Notley), **Supp. XXII:** 229

"Expanses" (Dickey), **Supp. IV Part 1:** 186

"Ex Parte" (Lardner), **II:** 432

"Expatiation on the Combining of Weathers at Thirty-seventh and Indiana Where the Southern More or Less Crosses the Dog, The" (Carruth), **Supp. XVI:**51–52

"Expectant Father Compares His Wife to a Rabbit, An" (White), **Supp. I Part 2:** 678

"Expedition to the Pole, An" (Dillard), **Supp. VI:** 32, 34

"Expelled" (Cheever), **Supp. I Part 1:** 174, 186

Expense of Greatness, The (Blackmur), **Supp. II Part 1:** 90, 107

Expense of Vision, The (Holland), **Retro. Supp. I:** 216

"Expensive Gifts" (Miller), **Supp. XII:** 294

"Expensive Moment, The" (Paley), **Supp. VI:** 222, **227–228,** 230

Expensive People (Oates), **Supp. II Part 2:** 509, 510–511

"Experience" (Emerson), **Supp. XIV:** 42

"Experience and Fiction" (Jackson), **Supp. IX:** 121

"Experience and the Objects of Knowledge in the Philosophy of F. H. Bradley" (Eliot), **I:** 572; **Retro. Supp. I:** 59

Experience of Literature, The (Trilling), **Supp. III Part 2:** 493

"Experiences and Principles of an Historian" (Morison), **Supp. I Part 2:** 492

Experimental Death Unit # 1 (Baraka), **Supp. II Part 1:** 46

"Experimental Life, The" (Bourne), **I:** 217, 220

"Experiment in Misery, An" (S. Crane), **I:** 411; **Retro. Supp. II:** 97

Experiments and Observations on Electricity (Franklin), **II:** 102, 114–115

Experiments in Survival (Kriegel and Henrich, eds.), **Supp. XXIV:** 214

"Expiation" (Hoffman), **Supp. XVIII:** 86

"Expiation" (Wharton), **Retro. Supp. I:** 367

"Explaining an Affinity for Bats" (Stallings), **Supp. XXV:** 227, 233

"Explaining Evil" (Gordon), **Supp. IV Part 1:** 310

"Explaining Ted Kooser" (Gioia), **Supp. XIX:** 121

"Explanation" (Stevens), **IV:** 79

Explanation of America, An (Pinsky), **Supp. VI:** 237, **241–243**

Exploding Gravy (X. J. Kennedy), **Supp. XV:** 163

"Exploit" (Wharton), **IV:** 324

"Exploration in the Great Tuolumne Cañon" (Muir), **Supp. IX:** 181

"Explorer, The" (Brooks), **Supp. III Part 1:** 79–80

"Exploring the Magalloway" (Parkman), **Supp. II Part 2:** 591

Expositor's Bible, The (G. A. Smith), **III:** 199

Expressions of Sea Level (Ammons), **Supp. VII:** 24, 28, 36

"Exteriority" (Monson), **Supp. XXIV:** 230, 238

"Extinction of Silence, The" (Stallings), **Supp. XXV:** 234

Extract from Captain Stormfeld's Visit to Heaven (Twain), **IV:** 209–210

Extracts from Adam's Diary (Twain), **IV:** 208–209

"Extraño, Un" (Gallagher), Supp. XXIV: 170

"Exulting, The" (Roethke), **III:** 544

"Eye, The" (Bowles), **Supp. IV Part 1:** 93

Eye, The (Nabokov), **III:** 251

Eye-Beaters, Blood, Victory, Madness, Buckhead and Mercy, The (Dickey), **Supp. IV Part 1:** 178, 182–183

"Eye for an Eye, An" (Humphrey), **Supp. IX:** 108

"Eye in the Rock, The" (Haines), **Supp. XII:** 208, 209

Eye in the Sky (Dick), **Supp. XVIII:** 138

"Eye-Mote, The" (Plath), **Retro. Supp. II:** 246, 247

"Eye of Paris, The" (H. Miller), **III:** 183–184

Eye of the Poet, The: Six Views of the Art and Craft of Poetry (Citino, ed.), **Supp. XIII:** 115; **Supp. XXI:** 54

"Eye of the Rock, The" (Haines), **Supp. XII:** 208

"Eye of the Story, The" (Porter), **IV:** 279

Eye of the Story, The: Selected Essays and Reviews (Welty), **Retro. Supp. I:** 339, 342, 344, 345, 346, 351, 354, 355, 356

"Eyes, The" (Wharton), **IV:** 315

"Eyes like They Say the Devil Has" (Ríos), **Supp. IV Part 2:** 543, 544

Eyes of the Dragon, The (King), **Supp. V:** 139, 152

Eyes of the Heart: A Memoir of the Lost and Found (Buechner), **Supp. XII:** 53

"Eyes of Zapata" (Cisneros), **Supp. VII:** 70

"Eyes to See" (Cozzens), **I:** 374

Eye-to-Eye (Nye), **Supp. XIII:** 274

Eysturoy, Annie O., **Supp. IV Part 1:** 321, 322, 323, 328

Ezekiel (biblical book), **II:** 541

"Ezekiel" (R. Fisher), **Supp. XIX:** 71

Ezekiel, Mordecai, **Supp. I Part 2:** 645

"Ezekiel Learns" (R. Fisher), **Supp. XIX:** 71

"Ezra Pound" (Bynner), **Supp. XV:** 49

"Ezra Pound: His Cantos" (Zukofsky), **Supp. III Part 2:** 612, 619, 622

Ezra Pound's Mauberley (Espey), **III:** 463

"Ezra Pound's Very Useful Labors" (Schwartz), **Supp. II Part 2:** 644

F

Faas, Ekbert, **Supp. VIII:** 292

"Fabbri Tape, The" (Auchincloss), **Supp. IV Part 1:** 21–22

Fabens, Charles, **Supp. XXV:** 283

Faber, Geoffrey, **Retro. Supp. I:** 63

Faber Book of Movie Verse, The (French and Wlaschin, eds.), **Supp. XVI:** 294

"Fable" (Merwin), **Supp. III Part 1:** 343

"Fable" (Wylie), **Supp. I Part 2:** 714

Fable, A (Faulkner), **II:** 55, 73; **Retro. Supp. I:** 74

"Fable, A" (Glück), **Supp. V:** 86

"Fable, The" (Winters), **Supp. II Part 2:** 792, 793, 796

"Fable Containing a Reflection the Size of a Match Head in Its Pupil, A" (Brockmeier), **Supp. XXII:** 59

"Fable Ending in the Sound of a Thousand Parakeets, A" (Brockmeier), **Supp. XXII:** 59

Fable for Critics, A (Lowell), **Supp. I Part 2:** 406, 407–408, 409, 412–413, 416, 420, 422

"Fable for Critics, A" (Lowell), **Supp. XVIII:** 3, 8

"Fable of the War, A" (Nemerov), **III:** 272

Fables (Gay), **II:** 111

Fables and Distances: New and Selected Essays (Haines), **Supp. XII:** 197, 199, 207–208, 211

Fables for Our Time (Thurber), **Supp. I Part 2:** 610

Fables of Identity: Studies in Poetic Mythology (Frye), **Supp. X:** 80

Fables of La Fontaine, The (Moore), **III:** 194, 215

"Fables of Representation: Poetry of the New York School" (Hoover), **Supp. XV:** 179

"Fables of the Fallen Guy" (Rosaldo), **Supp. IV Part 2:** 544

"Fables of the Moscow Subway" (Nemerov), **III:** 271

"Fable with a Photograph of a Glass Mobile on the Wall, A" (Brockmeier), **Supp. XXII:** 59

"Fable with Slips of White Paper Spilling from the Pockets, A" (Brockmeier), **Supp. XXII:** 59

Fabulators, The (Scholes), **Supp. V:** 40

Fabulous Small Jews (Epstein), **Supp. XIV:** 112

Face against the Glass, The (Francis), **Supp. IX: 80–81**

Face in the Crowd, A (film, Kazan), **Supp. XVIII:** 252–253

Face in the Crowd, A (O'Nan and King), **Supp. XXV:** 150, 152

Face of Time, The (Farrell), **II:** 28, 34, 35, 39

Faces of Jesus, The (Buechner), **Supp. XII:** 53

Face to the Wind (film), **Supp. XVII:** 141

Face Value (Hwang), **Supp. XXI:** 148, 154, 155

Fachinger, Petra, **Supp. XVI:** 153

"Facing It" (Komunyakaa), **Supp. XIII:** 117, 124, 125

Facing Shadows (Jin), **Supp. XVIII:** 92, **93**

Facing the Music (L. Brown), **Supp. XXI:** 39, 42, **42–44**

"Facing the Music" (L. Brown), **Supp. XXI: 38–39,** 41, 42, 43

"Facing the Music: What's Wrong with All Those Happy Endings" (Neal), **Supp. XXI:** 41

"Facing West from California's Shores" (Jeffers), **Supp. II Part 2:** 437–438

Fact, Fiction, and Representation: Four Novels by Gilbert Sorrentino (Mackey), **Supp. XXI:** 236

"Fact in Fiction, The" (McCarthy), **II:** 562

"Fact of Blackness, The" (Fanon), **Supp. XX:** 152

"Facts" (Franzen), **Supp. XX:** 85

"Facts" (Levine), **Supp. V:** 193

"Facts" (Oliver), **Supp. VII:** 231–232

"Facts" (Snyder), **Supp. VIII:** 301

"Facts, The" (Lardner), **II:** 431

Facts, The: A Novelist's Autobiography (P. Roth), **Retro. Supp. II:** 280, 291; **Supp. III Part 2:** 401, 405, 417, 426

"Facts and Traditions Respecting the Existence of Indigenous Intermittent Fever in New England" (Holmes), **Supp. I Part 1:** 303

"Facts in the Case of M. Valdemar, The" (Poe), **III:** 416

Faderman, Lillian, **Retro. Supp. II:** 135; **Supp. XIII:** 313

Fadiman, Clifton, **II:** 430, 431, 443, 591–592; **Supp. IX:** 8; **Supp. XVI:** 100, 106; **Supp. XVII:** 87, 90; **Supp. XXIII:** 2

Fading, My Parmacheene Belle (J. Scott), **Supp. XVII:** 184–185, 188

"Fado" (McClatchy), **Supp. XII:** 265–266

Faerie Queene, The (Spenser), **III:** 487; **IV:** 253; **Supp. XIV:** 6; **Supp. XV:** 181

Faery, Rebecca Blevins, **Retro. Supp. I:** 374

Fagan, Kathy, **Supp. V:** 180; **Supp. XV:** 73

Fagan, Louise, **Supp. XIX:** 204, 205

Fahrenheit 451 (Bradbury), **Supp. IV Part 1:** 101, 102, 104, 107–109, 110, 113; **Supp. XIII:** 29

"Failure" (Gioia), **Supp. XV:** 125

"Failure" (Zach; Everwine, trans.), **Supp. XV:** 86

"Failure: A Meditation" (Monson), **Supp. XXIV:** 236

"Failure of David Barry, The" (Jewett), **Retro. Supp. II:** 132

Fainlight, Ruth, **Supp. XV:** 261, 264

Faint Perfume (Gale), **Supp. I Part 2:** 613

Fair, Bryan K., **Supp. VIII:** 128

Fairbanks, Douglas, **Supp. XVI:** 185, 186

Fairchild, Frances. *See* Bryant, Mrs. William Cullen (Frances Fairchild)

Fairchild, Hoxie, **Supp. XIV:** 120

Fairfield, Flora (pseudonym). *See* Alcott, Louisa May

Fair Gentlemen of Belken County (Hinojosa), **Supp. XIX:** 105

Fairly Conventional Woman, A (Shields), **Supp. VII:** 312, 316, 318

"Fairly Sad Tale, A" (Parker), **Supp. IX:** 192

Fair Warning (R. O. Butler), **Supp. XII:** 62, 75–76

"Fairy-Tale Logic" (Stallings), **Supp. XXV:** 223, 234

Faith (Goldbarth), **Supp. XII:** 181, 182–183

Faith and History (Niebuhr), **III:** 308

Faith and the Good Thing (Johnson), **Supp. VI:** 187, 188–190, 191, 193, 194, 196

Faith for Living (Mumford), **Supp. II Part 2:** 479–480

Faithful Narrative of the Surprising Works of God in the Conversion of Many Hundred Souls in Northampton, and the Neighboring Towns and Villages of New-Hampshire in New-England, A (Edwards), **I:** 545, 562

Faithful: Two Diehard Boston Red Sox Fans Chronicle the Historic 2004 Sea-son (O'Nan and King), **Supp. XXV:** 153

"Faith Healer" (Komunyakaa), **Supp. XIII:** 117

Faith Healer of Olive Avenue, The (Muñoz), **Supp. XXV:** 127, 131, 135–137

"Faith in a Tree" (Paley), **Supp. VI:** 217–218, 224, 230

"Faith in Search of Understanding" (Updike), **Retro. Supp. I:** 327

"Faith of an Historian" (Morison), **Supp. I Part 2:** 492

"Faith of Fishermen, The" (J. W. Miller), **Supp. XX:** 170

Faker's Dozen, A (Bukiet), **Supp. XVII:** 47

Falcoff, Mark, **Supp. VIII:** 88

Falcon (Hammett), **Supp. IV Part 1:** 351

Falconer (Cheever), **Supp. I Part 1:** 176, 193–195, 196

Falconer, A. F., **Supp. XIV:** 2

"Falcon of Ser Federigo, The" (Longfellow), **II:** 505

Falcon: Poems on Soviet Themes (Taggard), **Supp. XXII:** 284

Falk, Peter, **Supp. XI:** 174

Falkner, Dean, **II:** 55

Falkner, John, **II:** 55

Falkner, Murray, **II:** 55

Falkner, Murray C., **II:** 55

Falkner, Mrs. Murray C. (Maud Butler), **II:** 55

Falkner, William C., **II:** 55

"Fall" (Francis), **Supp. IX:** 76

"Fall, The" (Bass), **Supp. XVI:** 25

"Fall 1961" (Lowell), **II:** 550

"Fallen Western Star: The Decline of San Francisco as a Literary Region" (Gioia), **Supp. XV:** 112, 115–116

"Fallen Western Star" Wars, The: A Debate about Literary California (Foley, ed.), **Supp. XV:** 112, 116

"Fall in Corrales" (Wilbur), **Supp. III Part 2:** 556

Falling (Dickey), **Supp. IV Part 1:** 178, 181–182

"Falling" (Dickey), **Supp. IV Part 1:** 182

"Falling Asleep over the Aeneid" (Lowell), **II:** 542; **Retro. Supp. II:** 188

Falling in Place (Beattie), **Supp. V:** 28–29

"Falling into Holes in Our Sentences" (R. Bly), **Supp. IV Part 1:** 71

Falling into Life (Kriegel), **Supp. XXIV:** 217–219

"Fall Journey" (Stafford), **Supp. XI:** 322

Fall of America, The: 1965–1971 (Ginsberg), **Supp. II Part 1:** 323, 325, 327; **Supp. XV:** 264

Fall of Eve, The (Loos), **Supp. XVI:** 187

Fall of the City, The: A Verse Play for Radio (MacLeish), **III:** 20

"Fall of the House of Usher, The" (Poe), **III:** 412, 414, 415, 419; **Retro. Supp. II:** 270; **Supp. XXV:** 112

Fall of the Magicians, The (Kees), **Supp. XV:** 144

Fall of the Year, The (Mosher), **Supp. XXII:** 205, 206, 208, 209, 214

"Fall of Troy, Teh"(Hadas), **Supp. XXIII:** 113

Fallows, James, **Supp. VIII:** 241

Fall Quarter (Kees), **Supp. XV:** 141

Fall & Rise (Dixon), **Supp. XII:** 147–148, 148, 153, 157

Falls, Robert, **Supp. XXI:** 148; **Supp. XXIV:** 270

"Falls, The" (Olds), **Supp. X:** 215

"Falls, The" (Saunders), **Supp. XIX:** 229

"Falls Fight, The" (Howe), **Supp. IV Part 2:** 431–432

Falon, Janet Ruth, **Supp. IV Part 2:** 422

False Coin (Swados), **Supp. XIX:** 260–261, 263

"False Dawn" (Wharton), **Retro. Supp. I:** 381

"False Documents" (Doctorow), **Supp. IV Part 1:** 220, 236

"False Leads" (Komunyakaa), **Supp. XIII:** 116

Falwell, Jerry, **Supp. XX:** 273

Fame and Obscurity: Portraits by Gay Talese (Talese), **Supp. XVII:** 202, 203, 204

Fame & Folly: Essays (Ozick), **Supp. V:** 272

"Familiar Epistle to a Friend, A" (Lowell), **Supp. I Part 2:** 416

Familiar Territory: Observations on American Life (Epstein), **Supp. XIV:** 106

"Familiar Things" (Pickering), **Supp. XXI:** 204

"Family" (Sanders), **Supp. XVI:** 276

"Family" (Wilson), **IV:** 426

Family, Kinship, and Sympanthy in Nineteenth-Century America (Weinstein), **Supp. XVIII:** 261

"Family, The" (Taggard), **Supp. XXII:** 284

"Family Affair, A" (Chopin), **Retro. Supp. II:** 71

"Family and Socialism, The" (Ryan as Quin), **Supp. XVIII:** 238

Family Arsenal, The (Theroux), **Supp. VIII:** 322

"Family Barcus, The"(Thompson), **Supp. XXIII:** 299

Family Chronicle: An Odyssey from Russia to America (Reznikoff), **Supp. XIV:** 277, 288, 289

Family Devotions (Hwang), **Supp. XXI:** 145, 146

"Family History" (Mora), **Supp. XIII:** 217

"Family History, A" (R. H. Davis), **Supp. XVI:** 82

Family Honor (Parker), **Supp. XIX:** 186

Family Life (Banks), **Supp. V:** 7

"Family Matters" (Alvarez), **Supp. VII:** 10

Family Moskat, The (Singer), **IV:** 1, 17, 20, 46; **Retro. Supp. II:** 304

"Family of Little Feet, The" (Cisneros), **Supp. VII:** 61

Family Party, A (O'Hara), **III:** 362

Family Pictures (Brooks), **Supp. III Part 1:** 69, 85, 86

Family Pictures (Miller), **Supp. XII:** 291, **295–297,** 299

"Family Portrait" (Trethewey), **Supp. XXI:** 250

"Family Reunion" (J. W. Miller), **Supp. XX: 167**

"Family Reunion" (X. J. Kennedy), **Supp. XV:** 169

Family Reunion, The (Eliot), **I:** 570–571, 572, 581, 584, 588; **Retro. Supp. I:** 62, 65

"Family Secrets" (Kingsolver), **Supp. VII:** 208

"Family Sideshow, The" (Karr), **Supp. XI:** 245

"Family Story, The" (Skloot), **Supp. XX: 195**

"Family Ties" (Mora), **Supp. XIII:** 215

"Family Tree" (Komunyakaa), **Supp. XIII:** 117–118, 126

"Family Wasserstein, The" (Hoban), **Supp. XV:** 319, 325

Famous American Negroes (Hughes), **Supp. I Part 1:** 345

"Famous Gilson Bequest, The" (Bierce), **I:** 204

Famous Last Words (Findley), **Supp. XX: 49, 55–56**

Famous Negro Athletes (Bontemps), **Supp. XXII:** 6

Famous Negro Music Makers (Hughes), **Supp. I Part 1:** 345

"Famous New York Trials" (Ellison), **Supp. II Part 1:** 230

Fanatics, The (Dunbar), **Supp. II Part 1:** 213–214

Fancher, Edwin, **Retro. Supp. II:** 202

Fancher, Lou, **Supp. XVI:** 177

"Fancy and Imagination" (Poe), **III:** 421

Fancy Dancer, The (P. N. Warren), **Supp. XX: 267–268**

"Fancy Flights" (Beattie), **Supp. V:** 25

"Fancy's Show Box" (Hawthorne), **II:** 238

"Fancy Woman, The" (Taylor), **Supp. V:** 316–317, 319, 323

"Fang" (Goldbarth), **Supp. XII:** 190

Fanny: Being the True History of the Adventures of Fanny Hackabout-Jones (Jong), **Supp. V:** 115, 127

Fanny Hill (Cleland), **Supp. V:** 48, 127

Fan of Swords, The (al-Maghut), **Supp. XIII:** 278

Fanon, Frantz, **Retro. Supp. II:** 118; **Supp. X:** 131, 141; **Supp. XX:** 152

"Fan's Further Notes, A" (Exley), **Supp. XXIII:** 108

Fanshawe (Hawthorne), **II:** 223–224; **Retro. Supp. I:** 149, 151

Fan's Notes, A: A Fictional Memoir (Exley), **Supp. XVI:** 69; **Supp. XXIII:** 78, 97, 98, **99–103,** 106, 109

"Fantasia on 'The Nut-Brown Maid' " (Ashbery), **Supp. III Part 1:** 19

"Fantasia on the Relations between Poetry and Photography" (Strand), **Supp. IV Part 2:** 631

"Fantastic Fables" (Bierce), **I:** 209

"Fantasy"(O'Hara), **Supp. XXIII:** 220

Fante, John, **Supp. XI: 159–176**

Faraday, Michael, **I:** 480–481

Far and Away (Jarman), **Supp. XVII:** 110, 115

"Far and Away" (Jarman), **Supp. XVII:** 115

"Farewell" (Emerson), **II:** 13

"Farewell" (Ryan as Quin), **Supp. XVIII:** 229

Farewell, My Lovely (Chandler), **Supp. IV Part 1:** 122, 125–126, 127, 128, 130

"Farewell, My Lovely!" (White), **Supp. I Part 2:** 661–663, 665

Farewell, The (Gibran), **Supp. XX: 121**

"Farewell Performance" (Merrill), **Supp. III Part 1:** 336–337

Farewell-Sermon Preached at the First Precinct in Northampton, after the People's Publick Rejection of their Minister, A (Edwards), **I:** 548, 562

"Farewell Sweet Dust" (Wylie), **Supp. I Part 2:** 727–728

"Farewell to America, A" (Wheatley), **Supp. XX: 283**

Farewell to Arms, A (Hemingway), **I:** 212, 421, 476, 477; **II:** 68–69, 248–249, 252–253, 254, 255, 262, 265; **Retro. Supp. I:** 171, 178, **180–182,** 187, 189; **Retro. Supp. II:** 108; **Supp. IV Part 1:** 380–381, 381; **Supp. VIII:** 179; **Supp. XII:** 241–242; **Supp. XXI:** 277

"Farewell to Miles" (Berryman), **I:** 173

"Farewell to My Union Brothers" (Ryan as Quin), **Supp. XVIII:** 238

Farewell to Reform (Chamberlain), **Supp. I Part 2:** 647

Farewell to Sport (Gallico), **Supp. XVI:** 238

"Farewell to the Middle Class" (Updike), **Retro. Supp. I:** 321

Far Field, The (Roethke), **III:** 528, 529, 539, 545, 547–548

"Far Field, The" (Roethke), **III:** 537, 540

Far-Flung (Cameron), **Supp. XII:** 81

Far from the Madding Crowd (Hardy), **II:** 291

Faríd, 'Umar ibn al-, **Supp. XX: 117**

Faris, Athénaíse Charleville, **Supp. I Part 1:** 204

Farley, Abbie, **I:** 458

Farley, Harriet, **Supp. XIII:** 140

"Farm, The" (Creeley), **Supp. IV Part 1:** 155

Farmer (Harrison), **Supp. VIII:** 39, **44–45**

Farmer, Frances, **Supp. XV:** 196–197

Farmer, Richard, **Supp. XIV:** 2

"Farmer and the Fox, The" (Leopold), **Supp. XIV:** 188

Farmer Boy (L. I. Wilder), **Supp. XXII:** 294, 297, 299

"Farmers' Daughters, The" (W. C. Williams), **Retro. Supp. I:** 423

Farmers Hotel, The (O'Hara), **III:** 361

"Farmer's Sorrow, A" (Jewett), **Retro. Supp. II:** 132

"Farmer's Wife, The" (Sexton), **Supp. II Part 2:** 676

"Farm Garden" (Nelson), **Supp. XVIII:** 186

"Farm Implements and Rutabagas in a Landscape" (Ashbery), **Supp. III Part 1:** 13

Farming: A Hand Book (Berry), **Supp. X:** 31, 35

"Farmlights in Iowa" (Kooser), **Supp. XIX:** 120

"Farm on the Great Plains, The" (Stafford), **Supp. XI:** 322

Farnol, Jeffrey, **Supp. I Part 2:** 653

Far North (Shepard), **Supp. III Part 2:** 433, 435

"Far Northern Birch, The" (Francis), **Supp. IX:** 90

Farnsworth, Elizabeth, **Supp. XI:** 139

"Farrago" (Kees), **Supp. XV:** 145

Farrand, Max, **II:** 122

Farrar, Geraldine, **Retro. Supp. I:** 10

Farrar, John, **II:** 191; **Supp. XI:** 47

Farrell, Barry, **Supp. XIV:** 142

Farrell, James Francis, **II:** 25, 26

Farrell, James T., **I:** 97, 288, 475, 508, 517, 519; **II: 25–53,** 416, 424; **III:** 28, 114, 116, 118, 119, 317, 382; **IV:** 211, 286; **Retro. Supp. II:** 196, 327; **Supp. I Part 2:** 679; **Supp. VIII:** 96, 97; **Supp. XIV:** 3; **Supp. XV:** 141

Farrell, Mrs. James T. (Dorothy Butler), **II:** 26

Farrell, Mrs. James T. (Hortense Alden), **II:** 26, 27, 45, 48

Farrell, John, **II:** 26

Farrell, John C., **Supp. I Part 1:** 24

Farrell, Kate, **Supp. XV:** 187–188,**Supp. XV:** 190

Farrell, Kevin, **II:** 26

Farrell, Mary, **II:** 25

"Far Rockaway" (Schwartz), **Supp. II Part 2:** 649

Farrow, Mia, **Supp. XV:** 8, 10

Far Side of the Dollar, The (Macdonald), **Supp. IV Part 2:** 473

Farther Off from Heaven (Humphrey), **Supp. IX:** 93, 96, 101, **103–104,** 105, 109

Farther Off from Heaven (Inge), **Supp. XXV:** 94, 100

Far Tortuga (Matthiessen), **Supp. V:** 201, 206–207

"Fascinating Fascism" (Sontag), **Supp. III Part 2:** 465

"Fascination of Cities, The" (Hughes), **Supp. I Part 1:** 325

Fashion, Power, Guilt and the Charity of Families (Shields), **Supp. VII:** 323

Fasman, Jonathan, **Supp. V:** 253

Fast, Howard, **Supp. I Part 1:** 295; **Supp. XXI:** 277; **Supp. XXIII:** 165

Fast, Jonathan, **Supp. V:** 115

Fast and Loose (Wharton), **Retro. Supp. I:** 361

"Faster than Light" (Nelson), **Supp. XVIII:** 178–179

"Fastest Runner on Sixty-first Street, The" (Farrell), **II:** 45

Fast Lane on a Dirt Road (Sherman), **Supp. XXII:** 205

Fast Sooner Hound, The (Bontemps and Conroy), **Supp. XXII:** 5, 10–11

"Fat" (Carver), **Supp. III Part 1:** 141

Fatal Interview (Millay), **III:** 128–129, 130

"Fatality" (Bausch), **Supp. VII:** 54

Fatal Lady (film), **Supp. XIII:** 166

"Fate" (Emerson), **II:** 2–3, 4, 16; **Supp. XIV:** 42

"Fate" (Koch), **Supp. XV:** 183

"Fate" (Mailer), **Retro. Supp. II:** 207

"Fate of Pleasure, The" (Trilling), **Supp. III Part 2:** 510

Fate of the Jury, The (Masters), **Supp. I Part 2:** 466, 468, 469

"Fat Girl, The" (Dubus), **Supp. VII:** 84, 85

"Father" (Kooser), **Supp. XIX:** 117, 127

"Father" (Levine), **Supp. V:** 188

"Father" (Sanders), **Supp. XVI:** 277

"Father" (Trethewey), **Supp. XXI:** 253

"Father" (Walker), **Supp. III Part 2:** 522

"Father, The" (Carver), **Supp. III Part 1:** 137, 140

Father, The (Olds), **Supp. X:** 209–211

"Father Abraham" (Faulkner), **Retro. Supp. I:** 81, 82

Fatheralong: A Meditation on Fathers and Sons, Race and Society (Wideman), **Supp. X:** 320, 332–333, 334, 335

"Father and Daughter" (Eberhart), **I:** 539

Father and Glorious Descendant (Lowe), **Supp. X:** 291

"Father and Son" (Eberhart), **I:** 539

Father and Son (Farrell), **II:** 34, 35, 290, 291

Father and Son (Gosse), **Supp. VIII:** 157

"Father and Son" (Hughes), **Retro. Supp. I:** 204; **Supp. I Part 1:** 329, 339

"Father and Son" (Kunitz), **Supp. III Part 1:** 262

Father and Son (L. Brown), **Supp. XXI:** 36, 40, 41, **46–47**

"Father and Son" (Schwartz), **Supp. II Part 2:** 650

Father Bombo's Pilgrimage to Mecca (Freneau), **Supp. II Part 1:** 254

Father Fisheye (Balakian), **Supp. XXIII:** 19

"Father Fisheye"(Balakian), **Supp. XXIII:** 19

"Father Fitzgerald" (Nelson and Espeland), **Supp. XVIII:** 181

"Father Guzman" (Stern), **Supp. IX:** 293, 296

"Father John Melby and the Ghost of Amy Elizabeth" (Brockmeier), **Supp. XXII:** 60

Father of the Blues (Bontemps as Handy), **Supp. XXII:** 5

"Father out Walking on the Lawn, A" (Dove), **Supp. IV Part 1:** 246

"Fathers" (Creeley), **Supp. IV Part 1:** 157–158

Fathers, The (Tate), **IV:** 120, 127, 130, 131–133, 134, 141; **Supp. X:** 52

Fathers and Crows (Vollmann), **Supp. XVII:** 226, 231–232

"Fathers and Daughters, Mothers and Sons"(Hadas), **Supp. XXIII:** 119

"Fathers and Sons" (Hemingway), **II:** 249, 265–266; **Retro. Supp. I:** 175

"Father's Body, The" (Dickey), **Supp. IV Part 1:** 176

"Father's Day" (Connelly), **Supp. XXI:** 79–80

"Father's Story, A" (Dubus), **Supp. VII:** 88

"Father's Voice" (Stafford), **Supp. XI:** 322

"Fat Lady, The" (Carruth), **Supp. XVI:** 48

"Fat Man, Floating" (Dunn), **Supp. XI:** 144

Fat Men in Skirts (Silver), **Supp. XXIV: 265–267,** 275

"Fat Tuesday"(P. Benedict), **Supp. XXIII:** 38

Faulkner, Barry, **Supp. XV:** 41

Faulkner, William, **I:** 54, 97, 99, 105, 106, 115, 117, 118, 123, 190, 204–205, 211, 288, 289, 291, 292, 297, 305, 324, 374, 378, 423, 480, 517; **II:** 28, 51, **54–76,** 131, 174, 194, 217, 223, 228, 230, 259, 301, 306, 431, 458–459, 542, 594, 606; **III:** 45, 70, 108, 164, 218, 220, 222, 236–237, 244, 292, 334, 350, 382, 418, 453, 454, 482, 483; **IV:** 2, 4, 33, 49, 97, 98, 100, 101, 120, 131, 203, 207, 211, 217, 237, 257, 260, 261, 279, 280, 352, 461, 463; **Retro. Supp. I: 73–95,** 215, 339, 347, 356, 379, 382; **Retro. Supp. II:** 19, 221, 326; **Supp. I Part 1:** 196, 197, 242, 372; **Supp. I Part 2:** 450, 621; **Supp. III Part 1:** 384–385, 396; **Supp. IV Part 1:** 47, 130, 257, 342; **Supp. IV Part 2:** 434, 463, 468, 502, 677, 682; **Supp. V:** 58, 59, 138, 210, 226, 237, 261, 262, 334–336; **Supp. VIII:** 37, 39, 40, 104, 105, 108, 175, 176, 180, 181, 183, 184, 188, 189, 215; **Supp. IX:** 20, 95; **Supp. X:** 44, 228; **Supp. XI:** 92, 247; **Supp. XII:** 16, 289, 310, 313; **Supp. XIII:** 100, 169; **Supp. XIV:** 1, 12–13, 21, 24, 93, 306; **Supp. XV:** 92, 135, 338; **Supp. XVI:** 148, 189; **Supp. XVII:** 225; **Supp. XVIII:** 76, 84, 90, 148, 249; **Supp. XIX:** 97, 154, 166; **Supp. XX: 137, 162, 185, 195; Supp. XXI:** 36, 38, 256; **Supp. XXII:** 193, 203, 205; **Supp. XXIII:** 166; **Supp. XXIV:** 54, 64, 132, 136, 215; **Supp. XXV:** 49

Faulkner: A Collection of Critical Essays (Warren), **Retro. Supp. I:** 73

Faulkner at Nagano (Jelliffe, ed.), **I:** 289; **II:** 63, 65

Faulkner-Cowley File, The: Letters and Memories 1944–1962 (Cowley, ed.), **Retro. Supp. I:** 73, 92; **Supp. II Part 1:** 140, 141

"Faultlines"(Hadas), **Supp. XXIII:** 117–118

"Faun" (Plath), **Supp. I Part 2:** 537

"Fauna" (Jeffers), **Supp. II Part 2:** 415

Fauset, Arthur Huff, **Supp. XVIII:** 126

Fauset, Jessie, **Supp. I Part 1:** 321, 325; **Supp. IV Part 1:** 164

Fauset, Jessie Redmon, **Supp. XVIII:** 122,127; **Supp. XIX:** 69, 78

Faust (Goethe), **I:** 396; **II:** 489; **III:** 395; **Supp. II Part 1:** 16; **Supp. IX:** 141

Faust, Beatrix Hapgood, **Supp. XXI:** 8

Faust, Clarence H., **II:** 20

Faute de l'Abbé Mouret, La (Zola), **III:** 322

"Favor, The" (Carver and Gallagher), **Supp. XXIV:** 178

Favor Island (Merwin), **Supp. III Part 1:** 346, 347

"Favor of Love, A" (Peacock), **Supp. XIX:** 203

"Favrile" (Doty), **Supp. XI:** 131

"Fawn, with a Bit of Green" (Swados), **Supp. XIX:** 258

Fay (L. Brown), **Supp. XXI:** 40, 41, 47

Fay, Bernard, **IV:** 41

"Fear, The" (Frost), **Retro. Supp. I:** 128

Fear and Loathing in Las Vegas (Thompson), **Supp. XXIV:** 280, 282, 283, 287, **288–292,** 293

Fear and Loathing on the Campaign Trail '72 (Thompson), **Supp. XXIV:** 279, 281, 282, 289, **292–293**

Fear and Trembling (Kierkegaard), **Supp. XX:** 132

"Fear & Fame" (Levine), **Supp. V:** 192

Fearful Child, The (C. Frost), **Supp. XV:** 96, 97, 106

"Fearful Child, The" (C. Frost), **Supp. XV:** 96

Fearing, Kenneth, **Supp. XV:** 138

"Fearless" (Mosley), **Supp. XIII:** 241

Fearless Jones (Mosley), **Supp. XIII: 241–242**

"Fear of Concrete" (Halliday), **Supp. XIX:** 91

Fear of Fifty: A Midlife Memoir (Jong), **Supp. V:** 114, 115, 116, 131

Fear of Flying (Jong), **Supp. V:** 113, 115, 116, 119–123, 124, 129

"Feast, The" (Kinnell), **Supp. III Part 1:** 239, 250

Feast of All Saints, The (Rice), **Supp. VII:** 299–301

Feast of Love, The (C. Baxter), **Supp. XVII:** 13, 21–22

Feast of Love, The (film, R. Benton), **Supp. XVII:** 22

Feast of Snakes, A (Crews), **Supp. XI:** 102, **107–108; Supp. XXI:** 40

"Feast of Stephen, The" (Hecht), **Supp. X:** 63–64

Feast of the Goat, The (Llosa), **Supp. XXIV:** 89

"Featherbed for Critics, A" (Blackmur), **Supp. II Part 1:** 93, 151

Feather Crowns (Mason), **Supp. VIII: 146–147**

"Feathers" (Carver), **Supp. III Part 1:** 145

Feathers (Van Vechten), **Supp. II Part 2:** 736, 749

"Feathers, The" (Hogan), **Supp. IV Part 1:** 416

"February" (Ellison), **Supp. II Part 1:** 229

"February 14th" (Levine), **Supp. V:** 194

February in Sydney (Komunyakaa), **Supp. XIII: 124–125,** 129

"February in Sydney" (Komunyakaa), **Supp. XIII:** 125

"February: Thinking of Flowers" (Kenyon), **Supp. VII:** 171

"Feces" (McClatchy), **Supp. XII:** 266, 267–268

Fechner, Gustav, **II:** 344, 355, 358, 359, 363

Feder, Lillian, **IV:** 136; **Supp. XVI:** 49, 50

Federal Arts Project, **Supp. III Part 2:** 618

Federigo, or, The Power of Love (Nemerov), **III:** 268, 276, 282, 283– 284, 285

"Fedge, The" (Halliday), **Supp. XIX:** 93

"Fedora" (Chopin), **Supp. I Part 1:** 220

Fedorko, Kathy A., **Retro. Supp. I:** 361, 374

"Feeling and Precision" (Moore), **III:** 206

Feeling Italian: The Art of Ethnicity in America (Ferraro), **Supp. XX: 43**

"Feeling of Effort, The" (James), **II:** 349

Feeling Very Strange: The Slipstream Anthology (Kelly and Kessel, eds.), **Supp. XIX:** 231

"Feel Like a Bird" (Swenson), **Supp. IV Part 2:** 639

"Feel Me" (Swenson), **Supp. IV Part 2:** 647

Feeney, Mary, **Supp. IX:** 152, 154

Feinsilver, Pamela, **Supp. XX: 135**

Feinstein, Herbert, **Supp. XIX:** 260

Feinstein, Sascha, **Supp. XIII:** 125

Feldman, Charles K., **Supp. XI:** 307

Feldman, Morton, **Supp. XXIII:** 211

Fellini, Federico, **Supp. XII:** 172; **Supp. XV:** 8

"Fellini the Cat" (Peacock), **Supp. XIX:** 206

"Fellow Citizens" (Sandburg), **III:** 553

Fellows, John, **Supp. I Part 2:** 520

Fellow Travelers (Mallon), **Supp. XIX:** 132, **143–144**

"Felo de Se" (Wylie), **Supp. I Part 2:** 727, 729

Felton, Sharon, **Supp. IV Part 1:** 210

"Female Author" (Plath), **Retro. Supp. II:** 243

"Female Frailty" (Freneau), **Supp. II Part 1:** 258

"Female Laughter and Comic Possibilities: *Uncommon Women and Others*" (Chirico), **Supp. XV:** 323

Female Patriot, The; or, Nature's Rights (Rowson), **Supp. XV:** 237–238

Female Prose Writers of America (Hart), **Supp. XVIII:** 257, 264

"Female Voice in *To Kill a Mockingbird*, The: Narrative Strategies in Film and Novel" (Shakelford), **Supp. VIII:** 129

" 'Feminine' Epic, The" (Notley), **Supp. XXII:** 232, 234, 236

"Feminine Landscape of Leslie Marmon Silko's *Ceremony*, The" (Gunn Allen),

Supp. IV Part 1: 324

Feminine Note in Fiction, The (Courtney), **Supp. XXIV:** 29

Feminism and the Politics of Literary Reputation: The Example of Erica Jong (Templin), **Supp. V:** 116

"Feminismo" (Robbins), **Supp. X:** 272

"Feminist Criticism in the Wilderness" (Showalter), **Supp. X:** 97

"Feminist Manifesto" (Loy), **Supp. XXII:** 160

Feminization of American Culture, The (Douglas), **Supp. XVIII:** 258

"Fence, The" (Oliver), **Supp. VII:** 232

"Fence Posts" (Snyder), **Supp. VIII:** 304

Fences (Wilson), **Supp. VIII:** 329, 330, 331, **334–337,** 350

Fenick, Elizabeth, **Retro. Supp. II:** 221

"Fenimore Cooper's Literary Offenses" (Twain), **IV:** 204–205

Fennell, Frank L., **Supp. XVII:** 177–178

Fenollosa, Ernest, **III:** 458, 465, 466, 474, 475, 477; **Retro. Supp. I:** 289; **Supp. IV Part 1:** 154

Fenollosa, Mrs. Ernest, **III:** 458

"Fenstad's Mother" (C. Baxter), **Supp. XVII:** 18

Fenton, Charles, **Supp. XI:** 43

Fenton, James, **Supp. XV:** 117

Ferdinand: Including "It Was" (Zukofsky), **Supp. III Part 2:** 630

"Fergus" (Bourne), **I:** 229

Ferguson, James, **Supp. I Part 2:** 503

Ferguson, Otis, **Supp. IX:** 7

Ferguson, William, **Supp. XII:** 189

Ferguson Affair, The (Macdonald), **Supp. IV Part 2:** 473

Fergusson, Francis, **I:** 265, 440; **Supp. XV:** 20

Ferlinghetti, Lawrence, **Supp. IV Part 1:** 90; **Supp. VIII:** 290, 292; **Supp. XII:** 121, 125; **Supp. XIII:** 275; **Supp. XIX:** 4; **Supp. XXI:** 53; **Supp. XXIII:** 219

Fermata, The (Baker), **Supp. XIII: 49– 52,** 54

"Fern" (Toomer), **Supp. III Part 2:** 481; **Supp. IX:** 313

Fern, Fanny, **Retro. Supp. I:** 246; **Supp. V:** 122

Fernández, Enrique, **Supp. VIII:** 73

Fernandez, Ramon, **Retro. Supp. I:** 302, 303; **Supp. XVI:** 214

"Fern-Beds in Hampshire Country" (Wilbur), **Supp. III Part 2:** 558

"Fern Hill" (D. Thomas), **IV:** 93; **Supp. XX: 204**

"Fern-Life" (Larcom), **Supp. XIII:** 143

Ferragammo, Salvatore, **Supp. XVI:** 192

Ferraro, Thomas J., **Supp. XX: 34, 43**

Ferreo, Guglielmo, **Supp. I Part 2:** 481

Ferris, Anthony, **Supp. XX: 124**

Ferry, David, **Supp. XXIV: 147–164;** **Supp. XXV:** 222

"Ferry, The" (Cliff), **Supp. XXII:** 74

Fessenden, Thomas Green, **II:** 300

Fessier, Michael, **Supp. XIII:** 164

"Festival Aspect, The" (Olson), **Supp. II Part 2:** 585

"Festival of Regrets, The" (Wasserstein), **Supp. XV:** 333

Festival of San Joaquin, The (Edgell), **Supp. XXIII:** 84, 85, **90–91,** 94

Fetching the Dead (Sanders), **Supp. XVI:** 269

Fêtes galantes (Verlaine), **IV:** 79

Fetid Itch (Silver), **Supp. XXIV:** 265

"Fetish" (McClatchy), **Supp. XII:** 256

Fetterley, Judith, **Retro. Supp. II:** 139; **Supp. XXIV:** 28

Fetterly, Judith, **Supp. XXV:** 285

"Feud" (Zinberg), **Supp. XV:** 195

"Fever" (Carver), **Supp. III Part 1:** 145

"Fever 103°" (Plath), **Supp. I Part 2:** 541

Fever Pitch (Hornby), **Supp. XII:** 286; **Supp. XXIII:** 109

Fever: Twelve Stories (Wideman), **Supp. X:** 320

"Few Don'ts by an Imagiste, A" (Pound), **III:** 465; **Retro. Supp. I:** 288; **Supp. I Part 1:** 261–262

"Few Kind Words for Anger, A" (Kriegel), **Supp. XXIV:** 220

"Few Stray Comments on the Cultivation of the Lyric, A" (Sobin), **Supp. XVI:** 285

"Few Words of Introduction, A" (McNally), **Supp. XIII:** 198–199

Feydeau, Georges, **Supp. XXIV:** 271

Feynman, Richard, **Supp. XXV:** 267

Fiamengo, Janice, **Supp. XIII:** 35

Fiber (Bass), **Supp. XVI:** 22

"Fiber: A Post-Pastoral Georgic" (Gifford), **Supp. XVI:** 22

Ficke, Arthur Davison, **Supp. XIII:** 347; **Supp. XV:** 40, 42, 43, 46, 48, 49

"Fiction" (Stafford), **Supp. XI:** 327

"Fiction: A Lens on Life" (Stegner), **Supp. IV Part 2:** 595, 596, 600

Fictional World of William Hoffman, The (Frank, ed.), **Supp. XVIII:** 74, 79, 80, 87

Fiction and the Figures of Life (Gass), **Supp. VI:** 85

Fiction of Joseph Heller, The (Seed), **Supp. IV Part 1:** 391

Fiction of Paule Marshall, The (Denniston), **Supp. XI:** 276

Fiction of the Forties (Eisinger), **I:** 302; **II:** 604

Fictions in Autobiography: Studies in the Art of Self-Invention (Eakin), **Supp. XVI:** 70

"Fiction Writer and His Country, The" (O'Connor), **III:** 342; **Retro. Supp. II:** 223, 225; **Supp. II Part 1:** 148

Fiddler's Trance, The (Skloot), **Supp. XX: 196, 202**

Fidelity (Glaspell), **Supp. III Part 1:** 177

Fiedler, Leslie, **Supp. XXV:** 268

Fiedler, Leslie A., **II:** 27; **III:** 218; **Retro. Supp. II:** 280, 324; **Supp. II Part 1:** 87; **Supp. IV Part 1:** 42, 86; **Supp. IX:** 3, 227; **Supp. X:** 80; **Supp. XIII: 93–110; Supp. XIV:** 11; **Supp. XVIII:** 146; **Supp. XIX:** 251; **Supp. XXIII:** 42

Fiedler on the Roof: Essays on Literature and Jewish Identity (Fiedler), **Supp.**

XIII: 106–107

"Fie! Fie! Fi-Fi!" (Fitzgerald), **Retro. Supp. I:** 100

Field, Eugene, **Supp. II Part 1:** 197

Field, John, **IV:** 179

"Field Events" (Bass), **Supp. XVI:** 19

"Field Full of Black Cats, A" (C. Frost), **Supp. XV:** 101

Field Guide, (Hass), **Supp. VI:** 97–98, **99–101,** 102, 103, 106

Field Guide to Contemporary Poetry and Poetics (Friebert and Young, eds.), **Supp. XI:** 270

"Field Guide to the Western Birds" (Stegner), **Supp. IV Part 2:** 609

Fielding, Henry, **I:** 134; **II:** 302, 304–305; **III:** 61; **Supp. I Part 2:** 421, 422, 656; **Supp. IV Part 2:** 688; **Supp. V:** 127; **Supp. IX:** 128; **Supp. XI:** 277; **Supp. XVIII:** 2, 7; **Supp. XXV:** 258

Fielding, Richard, **Supp. XV:** 232

"Field-larks and Blackbirds" (Lanier), **Supp. I Part 1:** 355

Field of Honor (Hay), **Supp. XIV:** 120–121, 125, 130

"Field of Honor" (Hay), **Supp. XIV:** 120–121, 129–130

Field of Vision, The (Morris), **III:** 226–228, 229, 232, 233, 238

"Field Report" (Corso), **Supp. XII:** 124, **136**

"Fields" (Wright), **Supp. XV:** 342

Fields, Annie Adams, **II:** 401, 402, 403–404, 406, 412; **IV:** 177; **Retro. Supp. II:** 134, 135, 142; **Supp. I Part 1:** 317; **Supp. XVI:** 84, 88

Fields, James T., **II:** 274, 279, 402–403; **Retro. Supp. II:** 135; **Supp. I Part 1:** 317; **Supp. XIII:** 150; **Supp. XVI:** 84, 88

Fields, Mrs. James T., **Supp. XIV:** 44, 46. *See* Fields, Annie Adams

Fields, Joseph, **IV:** 274

Fields, The (Richter), **Supp. XVIII: 213–214,** 220

Fields, W. C., **II:** 427; **IV:** 335

"Fields at Dusk, The" (Salter), **Supp. IX:** 260

Fields of Fire (Webb), **Supp. XXII:** 115

Fields of Praise, The (Nelson), **Supp. XVIII:** 171, 173, **177–178**

Fields of Wonder (Hughes), **Retro. Supp. I:** 206, 207; **Supp. I Part 1:** 333–334

Fierce Invalids Home from Hot Climates (Robbins), **Supp. X:** 267, 276–277, **282–285**

Fiery, Marion, **Supp. XXII:** 293

Fiery Chariot, The (Hurston), **Supp. VI:** 155–156

"Fiesta, 1980" (Díaz), **Supp. XXIV:** 88

15 Poems (Banks), **Supp. V:** 5

"Fifteenth Farewell" (Bogan), **Supp. III Part 1:** 51, 58

"Fifth Avenue, Uptown" (Baldwin), **Supp. I Part 1:** 52

"Fifth Avenue—Spring Afternoon" (Untermeyer), **Supp. XV:** 296

Fifth Book of Peace, The (Kingston), **Supp. V:** 173

Fifth Chinese Daughter (Wong), **Supp. X:** 291

Fifth Column, The (Hemingway), **II:** 254, 258; **Retro. Supp. I:** 184

"Fifth Column of the Fencerow" (Leopold), **Supp. XIV:** 185

Fifth Decad of Cantos, The (Pound), **Retro. Supp. I:** 292

"Fifth Movement: *Autobiography*" (Zukofsky), **Supp. III Part 2:** 611

Fifth Sunday (Dove), **Supp. IV Part 1:** 251, 252–253

"Fifth Sunday" (Dove), **Supp. IV Part 1:** 252

50 Poems (Cummings), **I:** 430, 440, 442–443, 444–445, 446

Fifty Best American Short Stories (O'Brien), **III:** 56

"Fifty Dollars" (Elkin), **Supp. VI: 43–44**

"55 Miles to the Gas Pump" (Proulx), **Supp. VII:** 264

55 Poems (Zukofsky), **Supp. III Part 2:** 611, 621

"Fifty Grand" (Hemingway), **II:** 250, 424; **Retro. Supp. I:** 177

Fifty Stories (Boyle), **Supp. XXIV:** 58

"Fifty Suggestions" (Poe), **Retro. Supp. II:** 266

"52 Oswald Street" (Kinnell), **Supp. III Part 1:** 251

Fifty Years Among Authors, Editors, and Publishers (Derby), **Supp. XVIII:** 4

"Fifty Years Among the Black Folk" (Du Bois), **Supp. II Part 1:** 169

"Fifty Years of American Poetry" (Jarrell), **Retro. Supp. I:** 52

Fig Connection, The (Franzen and Siebert), **Supp. XX: 84**

Fight, The (Mailer), **Retro. Supp. II:** 207, 208

Fight Back: For the Sake of the People, For the Sake of the Land (Ortiz), **Supp. IV Part 2:** 497, 498, 499, 503, 510–512, 514

"Fighters, The" (Zinberg), **Supp. XV:** 193

Fight for Freedom (Hughes), **Supp. I Part 1:** 345

Fighting Angel (Buck), **Supp. II Part 1:** 119, 131

Fighting France; From Dunkerque to Belfort (Wharton), **Retro. Supp. I:** 377, 378

Fightin': New and Collected Stories (Ortiz), **Supp. IV Part 2:** 513

"Figlia che Piange, La" (Eliot), **I:** 570, 584; **III:** 9

Figliola, Samantha, **Supp. V:** 143

"Figure a Poem Makes, The" (Frost), **Retro. Supp. I:** 139

"Figured Wheel, The" (Pinsky), **Supp. VI:** 243, 244, 245, 246

Figured Wheel, The: New and Collected Poems (Pinsky), **Supp. VI:** 247–248

"Figure in the Carpet, The" (James), **Retro. Supp. I:** 228, 229

"Figure in the Doorway, The" (Frost), **Retro. Supp. I:** 138

Figure of Fulfillment, The (Lerperger; Miller, trans.), **Supp. XX:** 165, 167–168

Figures from the Double World (McGrath), **Supp. X: 118–119**

Figures in Black: Words, Signs, and the "Racial" Self (H. L. Gates), **Supp. XX: 99, 100, 106, 107**

"Figures in the Clock, The" (McCarthy), **II:** 561–562

Figures Made Visible in the Sadness of Time (Everwine), **Supp. XV:** 75, 88

Figures of Time (Hayden), **Supp. II Part 1:** 367

Filbin, Thomas, **Supp. XXIII:** 299

"Filling Out a Blank" (Wagoner), **Supp. IX:** 324

Fillmore, Millard, **III:** 101

Film Flam: Essays on Hollywood (McMurtry), **Supp. V:** 228

Films of Ayn Rand, The (Cox), **Supp. IV Part 2:** 524

Filo, John, **Supp. XII:** 211

Filreis, Alan, **Supp. XXI:** 262, 267, 268, 269, 271, 273, 275, 277, 278

Filson, John, **Retro. Supp. I:** 421

Final Beast, The (Buechner), **Supp. XII: 49–51**

"Finale" (Longfellow), **II:** 505, 506–507

"Final Fear" (Hughes), **Supp. I Part 1:** 338

Final Harvest: Emily Dickinson's Poems (Johnson, ed.), **I:** 470, 471

"Finally Harriet" (Wolfert), **Supp. XXI: 265–267**

Final Payments (Gordon), **Supp. IV Part 1:** 297, 299, 300–302, 304, 306, 314

"Final Report, A" (Maxwell), **Supp. VIII:** 169

"Final Soliloquy of the Interior Paramour" (Stevens), **Retro. Supp. I:** 312

Final Solution, The (Reitlinger), **Supp. XII:** 161

Financier, The (Dreiser), **I:** 497, 501, 507, 509; **Retro. Supp. II:** 94, 101–102, 105; **Supp. XVIII:** 246

Finch, Annie, **Supp. XVII: 69–79**

Finch, Henry Leroy, **Supp. XVII:** 69

Finch, Margaret Rockwell, **Supp. XVII:** 69

Finch, Robert, **Supp. XIV:** 186–187

"Finches, Little Pats of Butter on the Wing"(Crooker), **Supp. XXIII:** 62

Find a Victim (Macdonald), **Supp. IV Part 2:** 467, 472, 473

Fin de Chéri, La (Colette; stage adaptation, Loos), **Supp. XVI:** 194

Finder, Henry, **Supp. XX:** 90

"Fin de Saison Palm Beach" (White), **Supp. I Part 2:** 673

"Finding a Bible in an Abandoned Cabin" (Wrigley), **Supp. XVIII: 293–294,** 296, 297, 300, 301, 303

Finding a Form (Gass), **Supp. VI:** 91–92, 93

Finding a Girl in America (Dubus), **Supp. VII:** 85–88

"Finding a Girl in America" (Dubus), **Supp. VII:** 87

"Finding Amy" (O'Nan), **Supp. XXV:** 143, 150

"Finding Beads" (Hogan), **Supp. IV Part 1:** 400

Finding Losses (Bronk), **Supp. XXI:** 31, 32

"Finding of Zach, The" (Dunbar), **Supp. II Part 1:** 212

Findings and Keepings: Analects for an Autobiography (Mumford), **Supp. II Part 2:** 483

Finding the Center: Narrative Poetry of the Zuni Indians (Tedlock), **Supp. IV Part 2:** 509

Finding the Islands (Merwin), **Supp. III Part 1:** 353, 357

"Finding the Place: A Migrant Childhood" (Stegner), **Supp. IV Part 2:** 597

Findley, Timothy, **Supp. XX: 49–65**

"Find the Woman" (Macdonald, as Millar), **Supp. IV Part 2:** 466

Fine, David, **Supp. XI:** 160

Fine, Richard, **Supp. XVIII:** 248

Fine Clothes to the Jew (Hughes), **Retro. Supp. I:** 200, 201, 203, 205; **Supp. I Part 1:** 326–328

"Fine Old Firm, A" (Jackson), **Supp. IX:** 120

Fine Preserving (Plagemann), **Supp. XVII:** 91

Fine Preserving: M. F. K. Fisher's Annotated Edition of Catherine Plagemann's Cookbook (Plagemann; M. F. K. Fisher, ed.), **Supp. XVII:** 91

Finer Grain, The (James), **II:** 335

Fine Writing (L. P. Smith), **Supp. XIV:** 347

"Finis" (X. J. Kennedy), **Supp. XV:** 169

"Finished Basement" (Di Piero), **Supp. XIX:** 47

Finished Man, The (Garrett), **Supp. VII:** 96, 97–98

Fink, Jonathan, **Supp. XXI:** 244, 245, 248, 255, 256

Fink, Mike, **IV:** 266

Finkelstein, Norman, **Supp. XXI:** 24, 33

Finkle, David, **Supp. XXI:** 47

Finley, John H., **II:** 418

Finn, David, **Supp. VIII:** 106–107

Finnegan, Robert (pseudonym). *See* Ryan, Paul William

Finnegans Wake (Joyce), **III:** 7, 12, 14, 261; **IV:** 182, 369–370, 418, 421; **Supp. I Part 2:** 620; **Supp. II Part 1:** 2; **Supp. XIII:** 191; **Supp. XVIII:** 32

Finney, Brian, **Supp. XIV:** 158, 160, 161, 165, 166, 167, 169

"Finnish Rhapsody" (Ashbery), **Supp. III Part 1:** 26

Finster, Howard, **Supp. XV:** 349

Firbank, Ronald, **IV:** 77, 436; **Supp. XXIII:** 209

"Fire" (Hughes), **Supp. I Part 1:** 327

"Fire and Cloud" (Wright), **IV:** 488

"Fire and Ice" (Frost), **II:** 154; **Retro. Supp. I:** 133; **Supp. XIX:** 122

Fire and Ice (Stegner), **Supp. IV Part 2:** 598, 607–608

"Fire and the Cloud, The" (Hurston), **Supp. VI:** 158

"Fire and the Hearth, The" (Faulkner), **II:** 71

Firebird (Doty), **Supp. XI:** 119–120, 121, **132–133,** 134

"Firebombing, The" (Dickey), **Supp. IV Part 1:** 180–181, 187, 189–190

"Fireborn Are at Home in Fire, The" (Sandburg), **III:** 591

"Fire by Night" (R. Fisher), **Supp. XIX:** 70–71

"Fire Chaconne" (Francis), **Supp. IX:** 87

Firecrackers (Van Vechten), **Supp. II Part 2:** 740, 742–744, 749

"Fire Dreams"(Thompson), **Supp. XXIII:** 296

Fire: From "A Journal of Love," the Unexpurgated Diary of Anaïs Nin, 1934–1937, **Supp. X:** 184, 185, 189, 194, 195

"Fireman, The " (Bass), **Supp. XVI:** 24

Fireman's Wife and Other Stories, The (Bausch), **Supp. VII:** 48, 54

Fire Next Time, The (Baldwin), **Retro. Supp. II:** 5, 8, 9; **Supp. I Part 1:** 48, 49, 52, 60–61

"Fire Next Time, The" (Baldwin). *See* "Down at the Cross" (Baldwin)

"Fire of Driftwood, The" (Longfellow), **II:** 499; **Retro. Supp. II:** 159, 168

"Fire of Life" (McCullers), **II:** 585

Fire on the Mountain (Abbey), **Supp. XIII:** 6

"Fire Poem" (Merrill), **Supp. III Part 1:** 321

"Fires" (Bass), **Supp. XVI:** 20

"Fires" (Carver), **Supp. III Part 1:** 136–139, 147

Fire Sale (Paretsky), **Supp. XXV:** 175–176, 178

Fire Screen, The (Merrill), **Supp. III Part 1:** 319, 325–329

"Fire Season" (Didion), **Supp. IV Part 1:** 199

"Fire Sequence" (Winters), **Supp. II Part 2:** 791, 796, 800

Fire Sermon (Morris), **III:** 238–239

"Fire Sermon, The" (Eliot), **Retro. Supp. I:** 60–61

Fires: Essays, Poems, Stories (Carver), **Supp. III Part 1:** 136, 140, 142, 146–147

Fireside Travels (Lowell), **Supp. I Part 2:** 407, 419–420

Firestarter (King), **Supp. V:** 140, 141, 144; **Supp. IX:** 114

"fire the bastards" (Green), **Supp. IV Part 1:** 285

"Fire-Truck, A" (Wilbur), **Supp. III Part 2:** 556

"Fireweed" (Clampitt), **Supp. IX: 44–45**

"Firewood" (Banks), **Supp. V:** 15

"Fireworks" (Ford), **Supp. V:** 69

"Fireworks" (Shapiro), **Supp. II Part 2:** 707

Fireworks: A History and Celebration (Plimpton), **Supp. XVI:** 245

Fir-Flower Tablets (Lowell), **II:** 512, 526–527

Firger, Jessica, **Supp. XIX:** 51, 58, 59, 62

Firkins, Oscar W., **II:** 271; **Supp. XV:** 297, 309

"Firmament, The" (Bryant), **Supp. I Part 1:** 162

Firmat, Gustavo Pérez, **Supp. VIII:** 76, 77, 79; **Supp. XI:** 184

"First American, The" (Toomer), **Supp. III Part 2:** 480, 487

"First Birth" (Olds), **Supp. X:** 212

First Book of Africa, The (Hughes), **Supp. I Part 1:** 344–345

First Book of Jazz, The (Hughes), **Supp. I Part 1:** 345

First Book of Negroes, The (Hughes), **Supp. I Part 1:** 345

First Book of Rhythms, The (Hughes), **Supp. I Part 1:** 345

First Book of the West Indies, The (Hughes), **Supp. I Part 1:** 345

Firstborn (Glück), **Supp. V:** 80, 81, 82, 84

"Firstborn" (Wright), **Supp. V:** 340

"First Chaldaic Oracle" (Carson), **Supp. XII: 111**

"First Communion" (Fante), **Supp. XI:** 160

"First Confession" (X. J. Kennedy), **Supp. XV: 154–155**

"First Day of School, The" (Gibbons), **Supp. X:** 41, 42

"First Death in Nova Scotia" (Bishop), **Supp. I Part 1:** 73

"First Formal" (Olds), **Supp. X:** 212

First Four Books of Poems, The (Glück), **Supp. V:** 81, 83

First Four Years, The (L. I. Wilder), **Supp. XXII:** 296, 298, 299–300

"First Grade" (Stafford), **Supp. XI:** 328

First Hand (Bierds), **Supp. XVII:** 32, 34–36

"First Hawaiian Bank" (Nye), **Supp. XIII:** 278

"First Heat" (Taylor), **Supp. V:** 323

First Hour, The (Di Piero), **Supp. XIX:** 36–37, 40

"First Hour of the Night, The" (Bidart), **Supp. XV: 30–32**

"First Hunters and the Last, The" (Sobin), **Supp. XVI:** 292

"First Job, The" (Cisneros), **Supp. VII:** 62

"1st Letter on Georges" (Olson), **Supp. II Part 2:** 578

First Light (C. Baxter), **Supp. XVII:** 15, **17–18,** 19, 22

First Light (Preston), **Supp. XVII:** 18

First Light (Wagoner), **Supp. IX:** 330

"First Love" (Welty), **IV:** 264; **Retro. Supp. I:** 347

First Love: A Lyric Sequence (Untermeyer), **Supp. XV:** 295

"First Love: A Quiz" (Stallings), **Supp. XXV:** 221, 233

First Lover and Other Stories, The (Boyle), **Supp. XXIV: 57–58**

First Man, The (O'Neill), **III:** 390

First Manifesto (McGrath), **Supp. X:** 115

"First Meditation" (Roethke), **III:** 545–546

"First Noni Daylight, The" (Harjo), **Supp. XII:** 219

"First Passover" (Longfellow), **II:** 500–501

"First Person Female" (Harrison), **Supp. VIII:** 40, 41, 48

"First Place, The" (Wagoner), **Supp. IX:** 328

First Poems (Buechner), **Supp. XII:** 45

First Poems (Merrill), **Supp. III Part 1:** 318–321, 323

First Poems 1946–1954 (Kinnell), **Supp. III Part 1:** 235, 238–239

"First Praise" (W. C. Williams), **Retro. Supp. I:** 413

First Principles (Spencer), **Supp. I Part 1:** 368

"First Reader" (Collins), **Supp. XXI:** 55–56

"First Ride and First Walk" (Goldbarth), **Supp. XII:** 182–183

"First Seeing the St. Lawrence River"(Kenny), **Supp. XXIII:** 152

"First Seven Years, The" (Malamud), **Supp. I Part 2:** 431

"First Sex" (Olds), **Supp. X:** 208

"First Snow" (Mosher), **Supp. XXII:** 211

"First Snow in Alsace" (Wilbur), **Supp. III Part 2:** 545, 546, 559

"First Song" (Kinnell), **Supp. III Part 1:** 239

"First Spade in the West, The" (Fiedler), **Supp. XIII:** 103

"First Steps" (McClatchy), **Supp. XII:** 256

First There Is the Need (Reznikoff), **Supp. XIV:** 291

"First Things First" (Auden), **Supp. II Part 1:** 13

"First Thought, Best Thought" (Ginsberg), **Supp. II Part 1:** 327

"First Time I Saw Paris, The" (Fante), **Supp. XI:** 174

"First Travels of Max" (Ransom), **III:** 490–491

"First Tycoon of Teen, The" (Wolfe), **Supp. III Part 2:** 572

"First Views of the Enemy" (Oates), **Supp. II Part 2:** 508

"First Wife, The" (Buck), **Supp. II Part 1:** 127

First Words before Spring (Untermeyer), **Supp. XV:** 310

"First World War" (White), **Supp. I Part 2:** 665

"Fish" (F. Barthelme), **Supp. XI:** 26

"Fish" (Levis), **Supp. XI:** 259–260

Fish, Stanley, **Supp. IV Part 1:** 48; **Supp. XIV:** 14, 15

"Fish, The" (Bishop), **Supp. XV:** 100, 102

"Fish, The" (Moore), **III:** 195, 197, 209, 211, 213–214; **Supp. XXI:** 26

"Fish, The" (Oliver), **Supp. VII:** 236

"Fish, The/Lago Chapala" (Everwine), **Supp. XV:** 82–83

"Fish and Shadow" (Pound), **III:** 466

"Fishboy" (Richard), **Supp. XIX:** 212–213

Fishboy: A Ghost's Story (Richard), **Supp. XIX:** 209, **213–220,** 221

Fishburne, Laurence, **Supp. VIII:** 345

"Fish Cannery" (Fante), **Supp. XI:** 167

Fisher, Alexander Metcalf, **Supp. I Part 2:** 582

Fisher, Alfred, **Retro. Supp. II:** 243

Fisher, Barbara, **Supp. XXII:** 206

Fisher, Craig, **Supp. V:** 125

Fisher, Dorothy Canfield, **Retro. Supp. I:** 21, 133; **Supp. I Part 1:** 117. *See also* Canfield, Dorothy

Fisher, Mary, **Supp. I Part 2:** 455

Fisher, M. F. K., **Supp. XVII:** **81–93**

Fisher, Phillip, **Retro. Supp. I:** 39

Fisher, Rudolph, **Retro. Supp. I:** 200; **Supp. I Part 1:** 325; **Supp. X:** 139; **Supp. XVI:** 143; **Supp. XIX:** **65–80**

Fisher, Vardis, **Supp. IV Part 2:** 598

Fisher King, The (Marshall), **Supp. XI:** 275–276, **288–290**

"Fisherman, The" (Merwin), **Supp. II Part 1:** 346

"Fisherman and His Wife, The" (Welty), **IV:** 266

"Fisherman from Chihuahua, The" (Connell), **Supp. XIV:** 86

"Fishing" (Harjo), **Supp. XII:** 227–228

"Fishing Idyll, A" (Mosher), **Supp. XXII:** 209

"Fish in the Stone, The" (Dove), **Supp. IV Part 1:** 245, 257

"Fish in the unruffled lakes" (Auden), **Supp. II Part 1:** 8–9

"Fish R Us" (Doty), **Supp. XI:** 135

Fisk, James, **I:** 4, 474

Fiske, John, **Supp. I Part 1:** 314; **Supp. I Part 2:** 493

Fisketjon, Gary, **Supp. XXIV:** 178

"Fit Against the Country, A" (Wright), **Supp. III Part 2:** 591–592, 601

Fitch, Clyde, **Supp. IV Part 2:** 573

Fitch, Elizabeth. *See* Taylor, Mrs. Edward (Elizabeth Fitch)

Fitch, James, **IV:** 147

Fitch, Noël Riley, **Supp. X:** 186, 187

"Fitting, The" (Hull), **Supp. XXI:** 134, 135

Fit to Be Tied (Silver), **Supp. XXIV:** **271–272**

Fitts, Dudley, **I:** 169, 173; **Supp. I Part 1:** 342, 345; **Supp. XIII:** 346; **Supp. XXII:** 281

FitzGerald, Edward, **Supp. I Part 2:** 416; **Supp. III Part 2:** 610

Fitzgerald, Ella, **Supp. XIII:** 132

Fitzgerald, F. Scott, **I:** 107, 117, 118, 123, 188, 221, 288, 289, 358, 367, 374–375, 382, 423, 476, 482, 487, 495, 509, 511; **II: 77–100,** 257, 263, 272, 283, 415, 416, 417–418, 420, 425, 427, 430, 431, 432, 433, 434, 436, 437, 450, 458–459, 482, 560; **III:** 2, 26, 35, 36, 37, 40, 44, 45, 69, 106, 244, 284, 334, 350–351, 453, 454, 471, 551, 552, 572; **IV:** 27, 49, 97, 101, 126, 140, 191, 222, 223, 287, 297, 427, 471; **Retro. Supp. I:** 1, 74, 97–120, 178, 180, 186, 215, 359, 381; **Retro. Supp. II:** 257, 321, 326, 328; **Supp. I Part 1:** 196, 197; **Supp. I Part 2:** 622; **Supp. III Part 2:** 409, 411, 585; **Supp. IV Part 1:** 123, 197, 200, 203, 341; **Supp. IV Part 2:** 463, 468, 607, 689; **Supp. V:** 23, 95, 226, 251, 262, 276, 313; **Supp. VIII:** 101, 103, 106, 137; **Supp. IX:** 15, 20, 55, 57–63, 199; **Supp. X:** 225; **Supp. XI:** 65, 221, 334; **Supp. XII:** 42, 173, 295; **Supp. XIII:** 170, 263; **Supp. XV:** 135; **Supp. XVI:** 64, 75, 191, 192, 294; **Supp. XVIII:** 148, 246, 248, 251, 254; **Supp. XX: 74; Supp. XXI:** 262; **Supp. XXII:** 82, 92; **Supp. XXIII:** 68, 101, 174

Fitzgerald, Robert, **I:** 27–28; **III:** 338, 348; **Retro. Supp. II:** 179, 221, 222, 223, 228, 229; **Supp. IV Part 2:** 631; **Supp. XV:** 112, 249; **Supp. XXII:** 281; **Supp. XXIII:** 112

Fitzgerald, Zelda (Zelda Sayre), **I:** 482; **II:** 77, 79, 82–85, 88, 90–91, 93, 95; **Supp. IV Part 1:** 310; **Supp. IX:** 55–73; **Supp. X:** 172. *See also* Sayre, Zelda

"Fitzgerald's Tragic Sense" (Schorer), **Retro. Supp. I:** 115

"Fitzgerald: The Romance of Money" (Cowley), **Supp. II Part 1:** 143

5 Detroits (Levine), **Supp. V:** 178

Five Came Back (West), **IV:** 287

Five Corners (screenplay, Shanley), **Supp. XIV:** 316

"Five-Dollar Bill, The" (D. West as Mary Christopher), **Supp. XVIII:** 282

"Five Dollar Guy, The" (W. C. Williams), **Retro. Supp. I:** 423

Five Easy Pieces (film), **Supp. V:** 26

"Five Elephants" (Dove), **Supp. IV Part 1:** 244–245

"Five Fucks" (Lethem), **Supp. XVIII:** 139

Five Groups of Verse (Reznikoff), **Supp. XIV:** 279, 282

Five Hundred Hats of Bartholomew Cubbins, The (Geisel), **Supp. XVI:** 100

Five Hundred Scorpions (Hearon), **Supp. VIII:** 57, 65, **66**

Five Indiscretions (Ríos), **Supp. IV Part 2:** 545–547

Five Men and Pompey (Benét), **Supp. XI:** 43, 44

Five Plays (Hughes), **Retro. Supp. I:** 197, 209

"Five Psalms" (Jarman), **Supp. XVII:** 120

Five Temperaments (Kalstone), **Retro. Supp. II:** 40

5,000 Fingers of Dr. T, The (film), **Supp. XVI:** 103

Five Young American Poets, **I:** 170; **II:** 367

Fixer, The (Malamud), **Supp. I Part 2:** 428, 435, 445, 446–448, 450, 451

"Fixin' Road" (Boulton), **Supp. XXII:** 23

"Fix It (Winter)"(Hadas), **Supp. XXIII:** 115

Fjellestad, Danuta Zadworna, **Supp. XVI:** 150

Flaccus, Kimball, **Retro. Supp. I:** 136

Flacius, Matthias, **IV:** 163

"Flagellant's Song" (X. J. Kennedy), **Supp. XV:** 165

Flag for Sunrise, A (Stone), **Supp. V:** 301–304

Flagg, Fannie, **Supp. XXII:** 213–214

Flag of Childhood, The: Poems from the Middle East (Nye, ed.), **Supp. XIII:** 280

"Flag of Summer" (Swenson), **Supp. IV Part 2:** 645

Flagons and Apples (Jeffers), **Supp. II Part 2:** 413, 414, 417–418

Flags in the Dust (Faulkner), **Retro. Supp. I:** 81, 82, 83, 86, 88

Flamel, Nicolas, **Supp. XII:** 178

Flaming Corsage, The (W. Kennedy), **Supp. VII:** 133, 153–156

Flammarion, Camille, **Supp. I Part 1:** 260

Flanagan, John T., **Supp. I Part 2:** 464, 465, 468

Flanner, Janet, **Supp. XVI:** 195

"Flannery O'Connor: Poet to the Outcast" (Sister Rose Alice), **III:** 348

Flappers and Philosophers (Fitzgerald), **II:** 88; **Retro. Supp. I:** 103; **Supp. IX:** 56

"Flappers Were Her Daughters, The: The Liberated, Literary World of Gertrude Atherton" (Richey), **Supp. XXIV:** 30

Flash and Filigree (Southern), **Supp. XI:** 295, 296–297

"Flashcards" (Dove), **Supp. IV Part 1:** 250

Flash Fiction: Seventy-two Very Short Stories (J. Thomas, ed.), **Supp. XVI:** 268

"Flash in the Pan" (Shaw), **Supp. XIX:** 245

"Flat Sky of Summer"(Balakian), **Supp. XXIII:** 25

Flatt, Lester, **Supp. V:** 335

Flaubert, Gustave, **I:** 66, 123, 130, 272, 312, 314, 315, 477, 504, 506, 513, 514; **II:** 182, 185, 194, 198–199, 205, 209, 230, 289, 311, 316, 319, 325, 337, 392, 401, 577, 594; **III:** 196, 207, 251, 315, 461, 467, 511, 564; **IV:** 4, 29, 31, 37, 40, 134, 285, 428; **Retro. Supp. I:** 5, 215, 218, 222, 225, 235, 287; **Supp. III Part 2:** 411, 412; **Supp. XI:** 334; **Supp. XIV:** 87, 336; **Supp. XXIII:** 254

"Flavia and Her Artists" (Cather), **Retro. Supp. I:** 5

Flavoring of New England, The (Brooks), **I:** 253, 256

Flavor of Man, The (Toomer), **Supp. III Part 2:** 487

"Flaw, The" (Peacock), **Supp. XIX:** 206

Flaxman, Josiah, **Supp. I Part 2:** 716

"Flea, The" (Donne), **Supp. XVIII:** 307

"Flèche d'Or" (Merrill), **Supp. III Part 1:** 328

Flecker, James Elroy, **Supp. I Part 1:** 257

"Flee on Your Donkey" (Sexton), **Supp. II Part 2:** 683, 685

Fleming, Ian, **Supp. XI:** 307; **Supp. XX:** 195

Fleming, Rene, **Supp. XII:** 321

Fleming, Robert E., **Supp. XVII:** 155; **Supp. XXII:** 184

Flesch, Rudolf, **Supp. XVI:** 105, 106

Flesh and Blood (Cunningham), **Supp. XV:** 63–65

Flesh and Blood (play; Cunnigham and Gaitens), **Supp. XV:** 65

"Fleshbody" (Ammons), **Supp. VII:** 27

Fletcher, H. D., **II:** 517, 529

Fletcher, John, **Supp. IV Part 2:** 621

Fletcher, John Gould, **I:** 243; **II:** 517, 529; **III:** 458; **Supp. I Part 1:** 263; **Supp. I Part 2:** 422; **Supp. XV:** 298, 302, 306, 307, 308

Fletcher, Phineas, **Supp. I Part 1:** 369

Fletcher, Virginia. *See* Caldwell, Mrs. Erskine (Virginia Fletcher)

Fleurs du mal, Les (Beaudelaire; Millay and Dillon, trans.), **III:** 141–142

"Flight" (Bierds), **Supp. XVII:** 36

"Flight" (Updike), **IV:** 218, 222, 224; **Retro. Supp. I:** 318

Flight (White), **Supp. XVIII:** 127

"Flight, The" (Haines), **Supp. XII:** 204–205

"Flight, The" (Roethke), **III:** 537–538

Flight 115; or, Pas de Fumer sur la Piste (O'Hara and Berkson), **Supp. XXIII:** 217, 218

Flight among the Tombs (Hecht), **Supp. X:** 58, 71–74

"Flight for Freedom" (McCoy), **Supp. XIII:** 170

"Flight from Byzantium" (Brodsky), **Supp. VIII:** 30–31

"Flight of Besey Lane, The" (Jewett), **Retro. Supp. II:** 139

Flight of the Rocket, The (Fitzgerald), **II:** 89

Flights of the Harvest-Mare (Bierds), **Supp. XVII:** 26–27

Flight to Canada (Reed), **Supp. X:** 240, 249–252

Flinn, Mary, **Supp. XVII:** 110

Flint, F. S., **II:** 517; **III:** 459, 464, 465; **Retro. Supp. I:** 127; **Supp. I Part 1:** 261, 262

Flint, Helen, **Supp. XXII:** 278

Flint, R. W., **Supp. XVI:** 47, 49, 57

"Flitting Flies" (X. J. Kennedy), **Supp. XV:** 166, 167

Flivver King, The (Sinclair), **Supp. V:** 290

Floating House, The (Sanders), **Supp. XVI:** 269

Floating Light Bulb, The (Allen), **Supp. XV:** 2, 3, 13

Floating Opera, The (Barth), **I:** 121, 122–126, 127, 129, 130, 131

"Floating Poem, Unnumbered, The" (Rich), **Supp. I Part 2:** 572–573

"Floating Trees" (Wright), **Supp. XV:** 348

Flood (Matthews), **Supp. IX:** 154, 160–161

Flood (Warren), **IV:** 252, 256–257

"Flood of Years, The" (Bryant), **Supp. I Part 1:** 159, 170, 171; **Supp. I Part 2:** 416

"Floor and the Ceiling, The" (W. J. Smith), **Supp. XIII:** 345, 346

"Floor Plans" (Komunyakaa), **Supp. XIII:** 114

"Floral Conversation" (Peacock), **Supp. XIX:** 200

"Floral Decorations for Bananas" (Stevens), **IV:** 8

Florida (Acker), **Supp. XII:** 5

"Florida" (Bishop), **Retro. Supp. II:** 43

"Florida Road Workers" (Hughes), **Retro. Supp. I:** 203

"Florida Sunday, A" (Lanier), **Supp. I Part 1:** 364, 366

Florist's Daughter, The (Hampl), **Supp. XXII:** 84, 85, 94, 95–98

"Flossie Cabanis" (Masters), **Supp. I Part 2:** 461–462

"Flounder" (Trethewey), **Supp. XXI:** 244, 245, 246, 251

Flow Chart (Ashbery), **Supp. VIII:** 275

"Flowchart" (Ashbery), **Supp. III Part 1:** 26

Flower, Dean, **Supp. XXII:** 205, 212

Flower, Fruit, and Thorn Pieces (Richter), **Supp. XVI:** 182

Flower-de-Luce (Longfellow), **II:** 490

Flower Drum Song (Rodgers and Hammerstein), **Supp. XXI:** 148

Flower Drum Song, The (Lee), **Supp. XXI:** 148

Flower Fables (Alcott), **Supp. I Part 1:** 33

"Flower-Fed Buffaloes, The" (Lindsay), **Supp. I Part 2:** 398

"Flower Garden" (Jackson), **Supp. IX:** 119

"Flower-gathering" (Frost), **II:** 153

Flower Herding on Mount Monadnock (Kinnell), **Supp. III Part 1:** 235, 239, 241–244

"Flower Herding on Mount Monadnock" (Kinnell), **Supp. III Part 1:** 242

"Flowering Death" (Ashbery), **Supp. III Part 1:** 22

"Flowering Dream, The" (McCullers), **II:** 591

"Flowering Judas" (Porter), **III:** 434, 435–436, 438, 441, 445, 446, 450–451

Flowering Judas and Other Stories (Porter), **III:** 433, 434

Flowering of New England, The (Brooks), **IV:** 171–172; **Supp. VIII:** 101

Flowering of the Rod (Doolittle), **Supp. I Part 1:** 272

Flowering Peach, The (Odets), **Supp. II Part 2:** 533, 547, 549–550

"Flowering Plum" (Glück), **Supp. V:** 82

Flowers, The (Gilb), **Supp. XXV:** 138

"Flowers for Marjorie" (Welty), **IV:** 262

"Flowers of the Fallow" (Larcom), **Supp. XIII:** 143, 145–146

"Flowers Well if anybody" (Dickinson), **Retro. Supp. I:** 30

"Fluff and Mr. Ripley" (D. West), **Supp. XVIII:** 284

"Fly, The" (Kinnell), **Supp. III Part 1:** 249

"Fly, The" (Shapiro), **Supp. II Part 2:** 705

"Fly, The" (Simic), **Supp. VIII:** 278

Flye, Father James Harold, **I:** 25, 26, 35–36, 37, 42, 46; **IV:** 215

"Fly in Buttermilk, A" (Baldwin), **Retro. Supp. II:** 8

Flying at Night: Poems 1965–1985 (Kooser), **Supp. XIX:** 128

"Flying High" (Levertov), **Supp. III Part 1:** 284

"Flying Home" (Ellison), **Retro. Supp. II:** 117, **125–126;** **Supp. II Part 1:** 235, 238–239

"Flying Home" (Kinnell), **Supp. III Part 1:** 250

"Flying Home" and Other Stories (Ellison), **Retro. Supp. II:** 119, 124

"Flying Home from Utah" (Swenson), **Supp. IV Part 2:** 645

"Flying over Clouds" (Gioia), **Supp. XV:** 118

Flying Solo (Kriegel), **Supp. XXIV:** 219–**221**

"Flying to Hanoi" (Rukeyser), **Supp. VI:** 279

Flynn, Elizabeth Gurley, **Supp. XVIII:** 225

Flynn, Richard, **Supp. XVII:** 115; **Supp. XVIII:** 183

Fly-Truffler, The (Sobin), **Supp. XVI:** **294–295,** 296

Foata, Anne, **Supp. XI:** 104

FOB (Hwang), **Supp. XXI:** 143, 144, 145, 146, **148–150**

Focillon, Henri, **IV:** 90

Focus (A. Miller), **III:** 150–151, 156

Foer, Jonathan Safran, **Supp. XII:** 169; **Supp. XX: 177; Supp. XXIV:** 131; **Supp. XXV:** 268

Foerster, Norman, **I:** 222; **Supp. I Part 2:** 423, 424; **Supp. IV Part 2:** 598

"Fog" (Sandburg), **III:** 586

"Fog Galleon" (Komunyakaa), **Supp. XIII:** 127

"Foggy and dripping" (Kooser), **Supp. XIX:** 125

"Foggy Lane, The" (Simpson), **Supp. IX:** 274

"Fog Man, The" (Boyle), **Supp. XX: 20**

Folded Leaf, The (Maxwell), **Supp. III Part 1:** 62; **Supp. VIII: 159–162**

Folding Star, The (Hollinghurst), **Supp. XIII:** 52

Foley, Jack, **Supp. X:** 125; **Supp. XV:** 112, 116; **Supp. XVII:** 77

Foley, Martha, **II:** 587; **Supp. XVI:** 225

Folk-Lore in the Old Testament (Frazer), **Supp. XX: 116–117**

Folks from Dixie (Dunbar), **Supp. II Part 1:** 211–212

Folkways (Sumner), **III:** 102

Follain, Jean, **Supp. IX:** 152, 154

Follett, Wilson, **I:** 405; **Supp. XIII:** 173

Follower of Dusk (Salinas), **Supp. XIII:** 326

"Following the Bones" (W. V. Davis), **Supp. XXI:** 96

Following the Equator (Twain), **II:** 434; **IV:** 208

Follow Me Home (Hoffman), **Supp. XVIII:** 86

Folly (Minot), **Supp. VI:** 205, 208, **210–213**

Folly of Others, The (Boyce), **Supp. XVII:** 100; **Supp. XXI:** 10

Folsom, Charles, **Supp. I Part 1:** 156

Folsom, Ed, **Retro. Supp. I:** 392

Folson, Marcia McClintock, **Retro. Supp. II:** 139

Fonda, Henry, **Supp. I Part 1:** 67; **Supp. IV Part 1:** 236

Fonda, Jane, **III:** 284; **Supp. XI:** 307

Fonda, Peter, **Supp. VIII:** 42; **Supp. XI:** 293, 308

"Fondled Memories" (Molesworth), **Supp. XIX:** 121–122

"Fond Memories of a Black Childhood" (D. West), **Supp. XVIII:** 289

Foner, Eric, **Supp. I Part 2:** 523

Fong and the Indians (Theroux), **Supp. VIII:** 314, 315, **316–317**

Fontanne, Lynn, **III:** 397

Food and Drink (Untermeyer), **Supp. XV:** 310

Food Chain, The (Silver), **Supp. XXIV:** 265, **270–271,** 274

Fool for Love (Shepard), **Supp. III Part 2:** 433, 447, 448

Fooling with Words (PBS special, Moyers), **Supp. XXIII:** 139

"Foolishness" (Pickering), **Supp. XXI:** 197

Fools (Simon), **Supp. IV Part 2:** 584–585

Fools Crow (Welch), **Supp. XXIV:** 257

Fool's Progress, The: An Honest Novel (Abbey), **Supp. XIII:** 4, **13–15**

Foot Book, The (Geisel), **Supp. XVI:** 108

Foote, Horton, **Supp. I Part 1:** 281; **Supp. VIII:** 128, 129

Foote, Mary Hallock, **Retro. Supp. II:** 72; **Supp. IV Part 2:** 611

Foote, Roxanna. *See* Beecher, Mrs. Lyman (Roxanna Foote)

Foote, Samuel, **Supp. I Part 2:** 584

Foote, Stephanie, **Retro. Supp. II:** 139

"Foot Fault" (pseudonym). *See* Thurber, James

Footing on This Earth, A (Hay), **Supp. XIV:** 125, 126, 130

"Footing up a Total" (Lowell), **II:** 528

"Footnote to Howl" (Ginsberg), **Supp. II Part 1:** 316–317

"Footnote to Weather Forecasts, A" (Brodsky), **Supp. VIII:** 32

Footprints (Hearon), **Supp. VIII: 69–70**

Footprints (Levertov), **Supp. III Part 1:** 272, 281

"Footsteps of Angels" (Longfellow), **II:** 496

"For A, at Fourteen" (Weigl), **Supp. XIX:** 287

For a Bitter Season: New and Selected Poems (Garrett), **Supp. VII:** 99–100

"For a Dead Kitten" (Hay), **Supp. XIV:** 119–120

"For a Dead Lady" (Robinson), **III:** 508, 513, 517

"For a Ghost Who Once Placed Bets in the Park" (Levis), **Supp. XI:** 265

"For a Lamb" (Eberhart), **I:** 523, 530, 531

"For All" (Snyder), **Supp. VIII:** 304

"For All Tuesday Travelers" (Cisneros), **Supp. VII:** 67–68

"For a Lost Child" (Stafford), **Supp. XI:** 329

"For a Marriage" (Bogan), **Supp. III Part 1:** 52

"For an Emigrant" (Jarrell), **II:** 371

"For Anna Akmatova" (Lowell), **II:** 544

"For Anna Mae Pictou Aquash, Whose Spirit Is Present Here and in the Dappled Stars" (Harjo), **Supp. XII:** 225

"For Anne, at a Little Distance" (Haines), **Supp. XII:** 207

"For Annie" (Poe), **III:** 427; **Retro. Supp. II:** 263

"For an Old Friend Encountered Unexpectedly" (Espaillat), **Supp. XXI:** 111–112

"For a Southern Man" (Cisneros), **Supp. VII:** 67

"For Bailey" (Angelou), **Supp. IV Part 1:** 15

Forbes, Genevieve, **Supp. XXV:** 196

Forbes, Malcolm, **Supp. IV Part 1:** 94

"Forbidden, The" (Glück), **Supp. XIV:** 269

"For Bill Nestrick (1940–96)" (Bidart), **Supp. XV:** 35

For Bread Alone (Choukri), **Supp. IV Part 1:** 92

"Force" (Di Piero), **Supp. XIX:** 35–36, 42, 44

Force of Desire, The (Bronk), **Supp. XXI:** 31, 32

Force of Evil (film, Polonsky), **Supp. XXI:** 261, 272, 275

Force of Spirit, The (Sanders), **Supp. XVI:** 277–278

Forché, Carolyn, **Supp. IV Part 1:** 208; **Supp. XIX:** 193

Ford, Arthur, **Supp. IV Part 1:** 140

Ford, Ford Madox, **I:** 288, 405, 409, 417, 421, 423; **II:** 58, 144, 198, 257, 263, 265, 517, 536; **III:** 458, 464–465, 470–471, 472, 476; **IV:** 27, 126, 261; **Retro. Supp. I:** 127, 177, 178, 186, 231, 286–287, 418; **Supp. II Part 1:** 107; **Supp. III Part 2:** 617; **Supp. VIII:** 107; **Supp. XIV:** 3

Ford, Harrison, **Supp. VIII:** 323

Ford, Harry, **Supp. V:** 179; **Supp. XIII:** 76

Ford, Henry, **I:** 295, 480–481; **III:** 292, 293; **Supp. I Part 1:** 21; **Supp. I Part 2:** 644; **Supp. III Part 2:** 612, 613; **Supp. IV Part 1:** 223; **Supp. V:** 290

Ford, John, **Supp. I Part 2:** 422; **Supp. III Part 2:** 619; **Supp. XVIII:** 247

Ford, Mark, **Supp. XXIII:** 220

Ford, Mary K., **Supp. XX: 239**

Ford, Richard, **Supp. IV Part 1:** 342; **Supp. V: 22, 57–75; Supp. XXIV:** 97

Ford, Webster (pseudonym). *See* Masters, Edgar Lee

"Fording and Dread" (Harrison), **Supp. VIII:** 41

"Ford Madox Ford" (Lowell), **II:** 547; **Retro. Supp. II:** 188

"For Dudley" (Wilbur), **Supp. III Part 2:** 558

Fordyce, David, **II:** 113

For Eager Lovers (Taggard), **Supp. XXII:** 274–275

Foregone Conclusion, A (Howells), **II:** 278–279, 282

"Foreign Affairs" (Kunitz), **Supp. III Part 1:** 265

"Foreigner, A" (Bynner), **Supp. XV:** 46

"Foreigner, The" (Jewett), **II:** 409–410; **Retro. Supp. II:** 133, 142

"Foreigners" (Jarman), **Supp. XVII:** 113

"Foreign Language, The" (Franzen), **Supp. XX:** 84

"Foreign Shores" (Salter), **Supp. IX:** 260

Forensic and the Navigators (Shepard), **Supp. III Part 2:** 439

Forerunner, The (Boyce), **Supp. XXI:** 2, 4, **10–11**

Forerunner, The: His Parables and Poems (Gibran), **Supp. XX:** 115, 118–**119,** 119

Foreseeable Future, The (Price), **Supp. VI:** 265

Foreseeable Futures (Matthews), **Supp. IX:** 155, **163,** 169

Foresman, Rebecca, **Supp. XXIV:** 171

"For Esmé with Love and Squalor" (Salinger), **III:** 560

"Forest" (Simic), **Supp. VIII:** 273

Forest, Jean-Claude, **Supp. XI:** 307

Forester's Letters (Paine), **Supp. I Part 2:** 508

"Forest Hymn, A" (Bryant), **Supp. I Part 1:** 156, 162, 163, 164, 165, 170

"Forest in the Seeds, The" (Kingsolver), **Supp. VII:** 203

Forest of the South, The (Gordon), **II:** 197

"Forest of the South, The" (Gordon), **II:** 199, 201

Forest without Leaves (Adams and Haines), **Supp. XII:** 209

"Forever, Said the Duck" (Lethem), **Supp. XVIII:** 139

"Forever and the Earth" (Bradbury), **Supp. IV Part 1:** 102

"Forever in That Year" (Carruth), **Supp. XVI:** 51

"Forever"(Thompson), **Supp. XXIII:** 296

"Forever Young" (Jarman and R. McDowell), **Supp. XVII:** 111

"For Fathers of Girls" (Dunn), **Supp. XI:** 146

For Frank O'Hara's Birthday (Notley), **Supp. XXII:** 224, 227

"For/From Lew" (Snyder), **Supp. VIII:** 303

"For Garrison Keillor, Fantasy Is a Lot More Fun then Reality" (Letofsky), **Supp. XVI:** 167

"For George Santayana" (Lowell), **II:** 547

"Forgetfulness" (Collins), **Supp. XXI:** 58

"Forgiveness" (Peacock), **Supp. XIX:** 200

Forgotten Helper, The: A Story for Children (Moore), **Supp. X:** 175

"Forgotten in an Old Notebook" (F. Wright), **Supp. XVII:** 244

Forgotten Village, The (Steinbeck), **IV:** 51

"For Grace, After a party"(O'Hara), **Supp. XXIII:** 214

"For Grizzel McNaught (1709–1792)" (A. Finch), **Supp. XVII:** 72

Forgue, Guy J., **III:** 118, 119

For Her Dark Skin (Everett), **Supp. XVIII:** 56, 60

"FOR HETTIE" (Baraka), **Supp. II Part 1:** 32

"FOR HETTIE IN HER FIFTH MONTH" (Baraka), **Supp. II Part 1:** 32, 38

"For Homer" (Corso), **Supp. XII:** 135

"For I'm the Boy" (Barthelme), **Supp. IV Part 1:** 47

"For James Dean"(O'Hara), **Supp. XXIII:** 214

"For Janice and Kenneth to Voyage"(O'Hara), **Supp. XXIII:** 214

"For Jeff" (Kooser), **Supp. XIX:** 125

"For Jessica, My Daughter" (Strand), **Supp. IV Part 2:** 629

"For John, Who Begs Me not to Enquire Further" (Sexton), **Supp. II Part 2:** 676

"For Johnny Pole on the Forgotten Beach" (Sexton), **Supp. II Part 2:** 675

"For Joy to Leave Upon" (Ortiz), **Supp. IV Part 2:** 508

"For Judy, Whose Husband Is Undergoing Surgery"(Crooker), **Supp. XXIII:** 61

"Fork" (Simic), **Supp. VIII:** 275

"For Karl Shapiro, Having Gone Back to the Sonnet" (Kooser), **Supp. XIX:** 118

"Forky" (Dubus III), **Supp. XXIV:** 99, 101

For Lancelot Andrewes (Eliot), **Retro. Supp. I:** 64

For Lizzie and Harriet (Lowell), **Retro. Supp. II:** 183, 186, 190

"Forlorn Hope of Sidney Lanier, The" (Leary), **Supp. I Part 1:** 373

For Love (Creeley), **Supp. IV Part 1:** 139, 140, 142–145, 147–149, 150, 154

"For Love" (Creeley), **Supp. IV Part 1:** 145

For Love (Miller), **Supp. XII:** 297–299, 299

For Love of Imabelle (C. Himes), **Supp. XVI:** 135, 143, 144

Form, Cycle, Infinity: Landscape Imagery in the Poetry of Robert Frost and George Seferis (Hadas), **Supp. XXIII:** 121–122

"Formal Elegy" (Berryman), **I:** 170

Formal Feeling Comes, A (A. Finch, ed.), **Supp. XVII:** 71–72

"Formalist Criticism: Its Principles and Limits" (Burke), **I:** 282

Forman, Henry James, **Supp. XXIV:** 29, 30

Forman, Milos, **Supp. IV Part 1:** 236

"Form and Function of the Novel, The" (Goldbarth), **Supp. XII:** 183

"For Marse Chouchoute" (Chopin), **Retro. Supp. II:** 60

"For Mary Ann Youngren" (Bidart), **Supp. XV:** 29

"Format and Form" (A. Rich), **Supp. XVII:** 74

"Formation of a Separatist, I" (Howe), **Supp. IV Part 2:** 427

"Form Is Emptiness" (Baraka), **Supp. II Part 1:** 51

"For Mr. Death Who Stands with His Door Open" (Sexton), **Supp. II Part 2:** 695

Forms of Discovery (Winters), **Supp. II Part 2:** 812, 813

Forms of Fiction, The (Gardner and Dunlap), **Supp. VI:** 64

"For My Children" (Karr), **Supp. XI:** 254

"For My Daughter" (Kees), **Supp. XV:** 141, 147

"For My Daughter" (Olds), **Supp. X:** 206

"For My Former Wife, Watching TV, in the Past" (Kooser), **Supp. XIX:** 120

"For My Lover, Returning to His Wife" (Sexton), **Supp. II Part 2:** 688

Fornés, Maria Irene, **Supp. XXI:** 144; **Supp. XXIII:** 194, 200

"For Night to Come" (Stern), **Supp. IX:** 292

"For Once, Then, Something" (Frost), **II:** 156–157; **Retro. Supp. I:** 126, 133, 134

"For Peg: A Remnant of Song Still Distantly Sounding" (Carruth), **Supp. XVI:** 54

"For Pot-Boiling" (Hay), **Supp. XIV:** 128

"For Radicals" (Bourne), **I:** 221

"For Rainer Gerhardt" (Creeley), **Supp. IV Part 1:** 142–143, 147

Forrestal, James, **I:** 491; **Supp. I Part 2:** 489

Forrester, Fanny, **Supp. XVIII:** 13

Forrey, Carolyn, **Supp. XXIV:** 30

"For Richard After All" (Kingsolver), **Supp. VII:** 208

"For Sacco and Vanzetti" (Kingsolver), **Supp. VII:** 208

"Forsaken Brother, The"(J. Schoolcraft), **Supp. XXIII:** 235

"Forsaken Merman" (Arnold), **Supp. I Part 2:** 529

"For S.F.S. 1875–1962" (J. W. Miller), **Supp. XX:** 166

For Spacious Skies (Buck), **Supp. II Part 1:** 131

Forster, E. M., **I:** 292; **IV:** 201; **Retro. Supp. I:** 59, 232; **Supp. III Part 2:** 503; **Supp. V:** 258; **Supp. VIII:** 155, 171; **Supp. IX:** 128; **Supp. XII:** 79, 81; **Supp. XIV:** 159, 160, 163; **Supp. XV:** 62; **Supp. XVI:** 236; **Supp. XVIII:** 143; **Supp. XX:** 229, **235, 239, 240; Supp. XXI:** 233

Forster, John, **II:** 315

Fort, Paul, **II:** 518, 528, 529; **Retro. Supp. I:** 55

"For the Ahkoond" (Bierce), **I:** 209

For the Body (Nelson), **Supp. XVIII:** 173

For the Century's End: Poems 1990–1999 (Haines), **Supp. XII: 211–213**

"For the Chinese New Year and Bill Berkson"(O'Hara), **Supp. XXIII:** 218

"For the Dedication of the New City Library, Boston" (Holmes), **Supp. I Part 1:** 308

"For the Fallen" (Levine), **Supp. V:** 188

For the Health of the Land: Previously Unpublished Essays and Other Writings (Leopold), **Supp. XIV:** 183

"For the Lady in the Black Raincoat Who Slept Through an Entire Poetry Reading" (Espaillat), **Supp. XXI:** 108

"For the Last Wolverine" (Dickey), **Supp. IV Part 1:** 182

"For the Losers of Things" (Stallings), **Supp. XXV:** 222

"For the Lovers of the Absolute" (Simic), **Supp. VIII:** 278–279

"For the Man Cutting the Grass" (Oliver), **Supp. VII:** 235

"For the Marriage of Faustus and Helen" (H. Crane), **I:** 395–396, 399, 402; **Retro. Supp. II:** 78–79, 82

"For the Meeting of the National Sanitary Association, 1860" (Holmes), **Supp. I Part 1:** 307

For the New Intellectual (Rand), **Supp. IV Part 2:** 521, 526–527, 527, 532

"For the New Railway Station in Rome" (Wilbur), **Supp. III Part 2:** 554

"For the Night" (Kenyon), **Supp. VII:** 163

"For Theodore Roethke: 1908–1963" (Lowell), **II:** 554

"For the Poem *Patterson*" (W. C. Williams), **Retro. Supp. I:** 424

"For the Poets of Chile" (Levine), **Supp. V:** 188

"FOR THE REVOLUTIONARY OUT-BURST BY BLACK PEOPLE" (Baraka), **Supp. II Part 1:** 55

"For the Sleepless" (Dunn), **Supp. XI:** 145

For the Time Being (Auden), **Supp. II Part 1:** 2, 17, 18

For the Time Being (Dillard), **Supp. VI:** 23, 27, 29, 32, **34–35**

"For the Twentieth Century" (Bidart), **Supp. XV:** 35

For the Union Dead (Lowell), **II:** 543, 550–551, 554, 555; **Retro. Supp. II:** 181, 182, 186, 189; **Supp. X:** 53

"For the Union Dead" (Lowell), **II:** 551; **Retro. Supp. II:** 189

"For the Walking Dead" (Komunyakaa), **Supp. XIII:** 121

"For the West" (Snyder), **Supp. VIII:** 299

"For the Word Is Flesh" (Kunitz), **Supp. III Part 1:** 262–264

"Fortress, The" (Glück), **Supp. V:** 82

"Fortress, The" (Sexton), **Supp. II Part 2:** 682

Fortress of Solitude, The (Lethem), **Supp. XVIII:** 135, 136, **145–148**, 150

"Fort Robinson" (Kooser), **Supp. XIX:** 120

"Fortunate Traveler" (Hull), **Supp. XXI:** 140

Fortune, T. Thomas, **Supp. II Part 1:** 159

Fortune's Bones: The Manumission Requiem (Nelson), **Supp. XVIII:** 171, 172–173, 182–183

Fortune's Daughter (Hoffman), **Supp. X:** 77, 85

"Fortune Spill, The" (Nelson), **Supp. XVIII:** 175

45 Mercy Street (Sexton), **Supp. II Part 2:** 694, 695, 697

Forty Poems Touching on Recent American History (Bly, ed.), **Supp. IV Part 1:** 61

42nd Parallel, The (Dos Passos), **I:** 482, 484–485

Forty Stories (Barthelme), **Supp. IV Part 1:** 47, 49, 53, 54

For Whom the Bell Tolls (Hemingway), **II:** 249, 254–255, 261; **III:** 18, 363; **Retro. Supp. I:** 115, 176–177, 178, **184**, 187; **Supp. XVII:** 229; **Supp. XXV:** 146

For Whom the Southern Belle Tolls (Durang), **Supp. XXIV:** 113, 118, 125

Foscolo, Ugo, **II:** 543

Foss, Sam Walter, **Supp. II Part 1:** 197

"Fossils, The" (Kinnell), **Supp. III Part 1:** 244

Foster, Edward, **Supp. IV Part 2:** 431, 434; **Supp. XVI:** 281, 293; **Supp. XXI:** 33

Foster, Edward Halsey, **Supp. XII:** 120, 129, 130, 135; **Supp. XVIII:** 265, 268

Foster, Emily, **II:** 309

Foster, Frances Smith, **Supp. XX: 287**

Foster, Hannah Webster, **Supp. XV:** 234; **Supp. XXV: 35–48**

Foster, John Wilson, **Supp. XIII:** 32–33

Foster, Phil, **Supp. IV Part 2:** 574

Foster, Richard, **Supp. XV:** 269

Foster, Stephen, **Supp. I Part 1:** 100–101; **Supp. I Part 2:** 699

Foucault, Michel, **Supp. VIII:** 5; **Supp. XII:** 98; **Supp. XV:** 344; **Supp. XVI:** 285

Foulke, Robert, **Supp. XXV:** 217

"Founder, The" (Stern), **Supp. IX:** 297

Founding of Harvard College, The (Morison), **Supp. I Part 2:** 485

"Foundry Workers" (Bodenheim), **Supp. XXV:** 22

"Fountain, The" (Bryant), **Supp. I Part 1:** 157, 165, 166, 168

Fountain, The (O'Neill), **III:** 391

Fountain and Other Poems, The (Bryant), **Supp. I Part 1:** 157

Fountainhead, The (film), **Supp. IV Part 2:** 524

Fountainhead, The (Rand), **Supp. IV Part 2:** 517, 521–523, 525, 531; **Supp. XXIV:** 281

Fountainhead, The: A Fiftieth Anniversary Celebration (Cox), **Supp. IV Part 2:** 523

"Fountain Piece" (Swenson), **Supp. IV Part 2:** 641

4-H Club (Shepard), **Supp. III Part 2:** 439

"Four Ages of Man, The" (Bradstreet), **Supp. I Part 1:** 111, 115

Four American Indian Literary Masters (Velie), **Supp. IV Part 2:** 486

"Four Angers"(Hadas), **Supp. XXIII:** 115

"Four Beasts in One; the Homo Cameleopard" (Poe), **III:** 425

Four Black Revolutionary Plays (Baraka), **Supp. II Part 1:** 45; **Supp. VIII:** 330

"Four Brothers" (Di Piero), **Supp. XIX:** 37

"Four Brothers, The" (Sandburg), **III:** 585

"Four Dancers at an Irish Wedding" (Gallagher), **Supp. XXIV:** 168, 170

Four Days (screenplay, P. Benedict), **Supp. XXIII:** 35

Four Dogs and a Bone and the Wild Goose (Shanley), **Supp. XIV:** 316, **328–329**

"Four Evangelists, The" (Komunyakaa), **Supp. XIII:** 131

"Four for Sir John Davies" (Roethke), **III:** 540, 541

"Four Girls, The" (Alvarez), **Supp. VII:** 7

"Four Horse Songs" (Harjo), **Supp. XII:** 220

"400-Meter Free Style" (Kumin), **Supp. IV Part 2:** 442

"400-Pound CEO, The" (Saunders), **Supp. XIX:** 225

Fourier, Charles, **II:** 342

"Four in a Family" (Rukeyser), **Supp. VI:** 272

Four in Hand: A Quartet of Novels (Warner), **Supp. VIII:** 164

"Four Lakes' Days" (Eberhart), **I:** 525

"Four Mad Studies" (Di Piero), **Supp. XIX:** 37

"Four Meetings" (James), **II:** 327

Four Million, The (O. Henry), **Supp. II Part 1:** 394, 408

"Four Monarchyes" (Bradstreet), **Supp. I Part 1:** 105, 106, 116

"Four Mountain Wolves" (Silko), **Supp. IV Part 2:** 561

Four of a Kind (Marquand), **III:** 54, 55

"Four of the Horsemen (Hypertense and Stroke, Coronary Occlusion and Cerebral Insult)" (Karr), **Supp. XI:** 250

"Four Poems" (Bishop), **Supp. I Part 1:** 92

"Four Poems at the End of Summer"(Hadas), **Supp. XXIII:** 117

"Four Preludes on Playthings of the Wind" (Sandburg), **III:** 586

Four Quartets (T. S. Eliot), **I:** 570, 576, 580–582, 585, 587; **II:** 537; **III:** 539; **Retro. Supp. I:** 66, 67; **Supp. II Part 1:** 1; **Supp. IV Part 1:** 284; **Supp. V:** 343, 344; **Supp. VIII:** 182, 195; **Supp. XIII:** 344; **Supp. XIV:** 167; **Supp. XV:** 216, 260, 266

Four Saints in Three Acts (Stein), **IV:** 30, 31, 33, 43, 44–45

"Four Seasons" (Bradstreet), **Supp. I Part 1:** 112–113

Four Seasons of Success, The (Schulberg), **Supp. XVIII:** 254

"Four Sides of One Story" (Updike), **Retro. Supp. I:** 328

"Four Skinny Trees" (Cisneros), **Supp. VII:** 64

"14: In A Dark Wood: Wood Thrushes" (Oliver), **Supp. VII:** 244

"14 Men Stage Head Winter 1624/ 25" (Olson), **Supp. II Part 2:** 574

14 Stories (Dixon), **Supp. XII:** 141, **145–147**

Fourteen Hundred Thousand (Shepard), **Supp. III Part 2:** 439

Fourteen Sisters of Emilio Montez O'Brien, The (Hijuelos), **Supp. VIII: 82–85**

Fourteen Stories (Buck), **Supp. II Part 1:** 126

"Fourteenth Ward, The" (H. Miller), **III:** 175

Fourth Book of Peace, The (Kingston), **Supp. V:** 173

"Fourth Down" (Marquand), **III:** 56

Fourth Group of Verse, A (Reznikoff), **Supp. XIV:** 282, 284

"Fourth of July in Maine" (Lowell), **II:** 535, 552–553

Fourth Wall, The (Gurney), **Supp. V:** 109–110

Fowler, Douglas, **Supp. IV Part 1:** 226, 227

Fowler, Gene, **Supp. VIII:** 290

Fowler, Henry Watson, **Supp. I Part 2:** 660

Fowler, Karen Joy, **Supp. XXII:** 49

Fowler, Singrid, **Supp. XXII:** 249, 258

Fowler, Virginia C., **Supp. VIII:** 224

Fox, Alan, **Supp. XIII:** 120

Fox, Dixon Ryan, **I:** 337

Fox, Joe, **Supp. IX:** 259, 261

Fox, John, **Supp. XIII:** 166; **Supp. XXII:** 36

Fox, Linda C., **Supp. XIII:** 217–218

Fox, Paula, **Supp. XX:** 91

Fox, Ruth, **Supp. I Part 2:** 619

"Fox, The" (Levine), **Supp. V:** 181, 189

Fox-Genovese, Elizabeth, **Supp. IV Part 1:** 286; **Supp. XXII:** 190, 192, 200

Fox in Socks (Geisel), **Supp. XVI:** 108, 112

"Fox Night" (Jarman), **Supp. XVII:** 120

Fox of Peapack, The (White), **Supp. I Part 2:** 676, 677–678

"Fox of Peapack, The" (White), **Supp. I Part 2:** 677

"Fox Point Health Clinic, 1974" (Halliday), **Supp. XIX:** 89, 93

Fox's Earth (Siddons), **Supp. XXII:** 239

Foye, Raymond, **Supp. XIV:** 150

Fradkin, Lori, **Supp. XIX:** 52

Fraenkel, Michael, **III:** 178, 183

"Fragging" (Komunyakaa), **Supp. XIII:** 123

Fragile Beauty, A: John Nichols' Milagro Country: Text and Photographs from His Life and Work (Nichols), **Supp. XIII:** 268

"Fragility" (Shields), **Supp. VII:** 318

"Fragment" (Ashbery), **Supp. III Part 1:** 11, 13, 14, 19, 20

"Fragment" (Lowell), **II:** 516

"Fragment" (Ortiz), **Supp. IV Part 2:** 507

"Fragment of a Meditation" (Tate), **IV:** 129

"Fragment of an Agon" (Eliot), **I:** 579–580

"Fragment of a Prologue" (Eliot), **I:** 579–580

"Fragment of New York, 1929" (Eberhart), **I:** 536–537

"Fragments" (Emerson), **II:** 19

"Fragments for Fall" (Salinas), **Supp. XIII:** 320–321

"Fragments of a Hologram Rose" (W. Gibson), **Supp. XVI:** 122, 123, 128

"Fragments of a Liquidation" (Howe), **Supp. IV Part 2:** 426

"Fragments: On Dentistry" (Monson), **Supp. XXIV:** 236

Fragonard, Jean Honoré, **III:** 275; **IV:** 79

Fraiman, Susan, **Supp. IV Part 1:** 324

"Frame for Poetry, A" (W. J. Smith), **Supp. XIII:** 333

France, Anatole, **IV:** 444; **Supp. I Part 2:** 631; **Supp. XIV:** 79

France and England in North America (Parkman), **Supp. II Part 2:** 596, 600–605, 607, 613–614

Franchere, Hoyt C., **II:** 131

Franchiser, The (Elkin), **Supp. VI: 51–52,** 58

Franciosi, Robert, **Supp. XIV:** 283

Francis, Lee, **Supp. IV Part 2:** 499

Francis, Richard, **Supp. XV:** 121

Francis, Robert, **Supp. IX: 75–92**

Francis of Assisi, Saint, **III:** 543; **IV:** 69, 375, 410; **Supp. I Part 2:** 394, 397, 441, 442, 443

Franco, Francisco, **II:** 261

Franco, Harry (pseudonym). *See* Briggs, Charles Frederick

Franconia (Fraser), **Retro. Supp. I:** 136

"Franconia" tales (Abbott), **Supp. I Part 1:** 38

Frank, Anne, **Supp. X:** 149; **Supp. XVII:** 39

Frank, Frederick S., **Retro. Supp. II:** 273

Frank, Harriet, Jr., **Supp. XXV:** 102

Frank, James M., **Supp. XIV:** 1

Frank, Jerome, **Supp. I Part 2:** 645

Frank, Joseph, **II:** 587

Frank, Mary, **Supp. X:** 213

Frank, Robert, **Supp. XI:** 295; **Supp. XII:** 127; **Supp. XIV:** 150

Frank, Sheldon, **Supp. XXII:** 210

Frank, Waldo, **I:** 106, 109, 117, 229, 236, 245, 259, 400; **Retro. Supp. II:** 77, 79, 83; **Supp. IX:** 308, 309, 311, 320; **Supp. XV:** 298; **Supp. XX: 67–82**

Frank, W. L., Jr., **Supp. XVIII:** 77

Frankel, Charles, **III:** 291

Frankel, Haskel, **Supp. I Part 2:** 448

Frankenberg, Lloyd, **I:** 436, 437, 445, 446; **III:** 194

Frankenheimer, John, **Supp. XI:** 343

Frankenstein (film), **Supp. IV Part 1:** 104; **Supp. XVII:** 57

Frankenstein (Gardner), **Supp. VI:** 72

Frankenstein (Shelley), **Supp. XII:** 79

Frankfurter, Felix, **I:** 489

"Frankie" (Keillor), **Supp. XVI:** 167

Frankie and Johnny (film), **Supp. XIII:** 206

Frankie and Johnny in the Clair de Lune (McNally), **Supp. XIII: 200,** 201

Franklin, Benjamin, **II:** 6, 8, 92, **101–125,** 127, 295, 296, 302, 306; **III:** 74, 90; **IV:** 73, 193; **Supp. I Part 1:** 306; **Supp. I Part 2:** 411, 503, 504, 506, 507, 510, 516, 518, 522, 524, 579, 639; **Supp. VIII:** 202, 205; **Supp. XIII:** 150; **Supp. XIV:** 306; **Supp. XVIII:** 12; **Supp. XX: 284;** **Supp. XXIV:** 224

Franklin, Cynthia, **Supp. IV Part 1:** 332

Franklin, Ruth, **Supp. XVI:** 160

Franklin, R. W., **Retro. Supp. I:** 29, 41, 43, 47

Franklin, Sarah, **II:** 122

Franklin, Temple, **II:** 122

Franklin, Walt, **Supp. XXIII:** 54

Franklin, Wayne, **Supp. XXII:** 205

Franklin, William, **II:** 122; **Supp. I Part 2:** 504

Franklin Evans (Whitman), **Retro. Supp. I:** 393

"Frank O'Connor and *The New Yorker*" (Maxwell), **Supp. VIII:** 172

Frank O'Hara: Poet Among Painters (Perloff), **Supp. XXIII:** 210

Franks, Lucinda, **Supp. XIII:** 12

"Frank Sinatra Has a Cold" (Talese), **Supp. XVII:** 203

"Frank Stanford of the Mulberry Family: An Arkansas Epilogue" (Wright), **Supp. XV:** 339–340

"Franny" (Salinger), **III:** 564, 565–566

Franny and Zooey (Salinger), **III:** 552, 564–567; **IV:** 216; **Supp. XIII:** 263

Franscell, Ron, **Supp. XXII:** 206, 216

Franzen, Jonathan, **Retro. Supp. II:** 279; **Supp. XIX:** 54; **Supp. XX: 83–97;** **Supp. XXII:** 255; **Supp. XXIV:** 131

Fraser, G. S., **Supp. XII:** 128; **Supp. XIV:** 162

Fraser, Joe, **III:** 46

Fraser, Marjorie Frost, **Retro. Supp. I:** 136

Frayn, Michael, **Supp. IV Part 2:** 582

Frazee, E. S., **Supp. I Part 2:** 381

Frazee, Esther Catherine. *See* Lindsay, Mrs. Vachel Thomas (Esther Catherine Frazee)

Frazer, Sir James G., **I:** 135; **II:** 204; **III:** 6–7; **IV:** 70; **Retro. Supp. I:** 80; **Supp. I Part 1:** 18; **Supp. I Part 2:** 541; **Supp. XX: 117**

Frazier, Ian, **Supp. VIII:** 272

Frazier, Kathleen, **Supp. XXI:** 22

"Freak Power in the Rockies" (Thompson), **Supp. XXIV:** 286–287, 292, 293

"Freak Show, The" (Sexton), **Supp. II Part 2:** 695

Freaks: Myths and Images of the Secret Self (Fiedler), **Supp. XIII:** 106, 107

Freckles (film), **Supp. XX: 223**

Freckles (Stratton-Porter), **Supp. XX: 211, 218, 218–219,** 222

Fred Allen Show, **Supp. XXV:** 254

Freddy and Fredericka (Helprin), **Supp. XXV:** 81, 84, 87–88
Freddy's Book (Gardner), **Supp. VI: 72**
Frederic, Harold, **I:** 409; **II: 126–149,** 175, 276, 289; **Retro. Supp. I:** 325; **Supp. XXIV:** 30
"Frederick Douglass" (Dunbar), **Supp. II Part 1:** 197, 199
"Frederick Douglass" (Hayden), **Supp. II Part 1:** 363
Frederick Douglass: Slave, Fighter, Freeman (Bontemps), **Supp. XXII:** 13
Frederick the Great, **II:** 103; **Supp. I Part 2:** 433
Fredrickson, George M., **Supp. I Part 2:** 589
"Free" (O'Hara), **III:** 369
Free, and Other Stories (Dreiser), **Retro. Supp. II:** 104
Free Agents (Apple), **Supp. XVII: 5–6**
Free Air (Lewis), **II:** 441
Freedman, David, **Supp. XXV:** 255
Freedman, Monroe H., **Supp. VIII:** 127
Freedman, Richard, **Supp. V:** 244
Freedom (Franzen), **Supp. XXII:** 255
"Freedom" (Larsen), **Supp. XVIII:** 124
"Freedom" (White), **Supp. I Part 2:** 659
"Freedom, New Hampshire" (Kinnell), **Supp. III Part 1:** 238, 239, 251
"Freedom and Discipline" (Carruth), **Supp. XVI:** 50
Freedom Business, The (Nelson), **Supp. XVIII: 186**
Freedom Is the Right to Choose: An Inquiry into the Battle for the American Future (MacLeish), **III:** 3
"Freedom's a Hard-Bought Thing" (Benét), **Supp. XI:** 47, 48
"Freedom's Plow" (Hughes), **Supp. I Part 1:** 346
Free Enterprise (Cliff), **Supp. XXII:** 66–67, **77–78**
"Free Everything" (July), **Supp. XXIV:** 210
"Free Fantasia: Tiger Flowers" (Hayden), **Supp. II Part 1:** 363, 366
Freeing of the Dust, The (Levertov), **Supp. III Part 1:** 281–282
"Free Lance, The" (Mencken), **III:** 104, 105
Free-Lance Pallbearers, The (Reed), **Supp. X:** 240, **242–243,** 244
Freeland (Lane), **Supp. XXII:** 297
Free Life, A (Jin), **Supp. XVIII: 101–102**
Freeloaders, The (Lacy), **Supp. XV:** 204
"Free Man" (Hughes), **Supp. I Part 1:** 333
Freeman, Chris, **Supp. XIV:** 157, 159
Freeman, Douglas Southall, **Supp. I Part 2:** 486, 493
Freeman, John, **Supp. XVIII:** 90
Freeman, Joseph, **II:** 26; **Supp. I Part 2:** 610; **Supp. XXII:** 274, 277
Freeman, Mary E. Wilkins, **II:** 401; **Retro. Supp. II:** 51, 136, 138; **Supp. IX:** 79
Freeman, Morgan, **Supp. XII:** 317
Freeman, Suzanne, **Supp. X:** 83

Free Man, The (Richter), **Supp. XVIII:** 215
"Free Man's Worship, A" (Russell), **Supp. I Part 2:** 522
Freewheelin' Bob Dylan, The (album, Dylan), **Supp. XVIII:** 20, 24, 29
Free Will & Wanton Lust (Silver), **Supp. XXIV:** 265, **267–268,** 270
Freier, Mary, **Supp. XXV:** 197
Freilicher, Jane, **Supp. XV:** 178; **Supp. XXIII:** 209, 210, 212, 217
Freinman, Dorothy, **Supp. IX:** 94
Frémont, John Charles, **Supp. I Part 2:** 486
Fremont-Smith, Eliot, **Supp. XIII:** 263
Fremstad, Olive, **I:** 319; **Retro. Supp. I:** 10
French, Warren, **Supp. XII:** 118–119
French Chef, The (television program), **Supp. XVII:** 89
French Connection, The (film), **Supp. V:** 226
"French Informal Report, The"(Kenny), **Supp. XXIII:** 152
French Leave (X. J. Kennedy), **Supp. XV:** 165
Frenchman Must Die, A (Boyle), **Supp. XXIV:** 62
French Poets and Novelists (James), **II:** 336; **Retro. Supp. I:** 220
"French Scarecrow, The" (Maxwell), **Supp. VIII:** 169, 170
French Ways and Their Meaning (Wharton), **IV:** 319; **Retro. Supp. I:** 378
Freneau, Eleanor Forman (Mrs. Philip Freneau), **Supp. II Part 1:** 266
Freneau, Philip M., **I:** 335; **II:** 295; **Supp. I Part 1:** 124, 125, 127, 145; **Supp. II Part 1:** 65, **253–277**
Frenzy (Everett), **Supp. XVIII: 59–60**
Frescoes for Mr. Rockefeller's City (MacLeish), **III:** 14–15
"Fresh Air" (Koch), **Supp. XV:** 181, 185
Fresh Air Fiend: Travel Writings, 1985–2000 (Theroux), **Supp. VIII:** 325
Fresh Brats (X. J. Kennedy), **Supp. XV:** 163
"Freshman" (Sanders), **Supp. XVI:** 277
Freud, Sigmund, **I:** 55, 58, 59, 66, 67, 135, 241, 242, 244, 247, 248, 283; **II:** 27, 370, 546–547; **III:** 134, 390, 400, 418, 488; **IV:** 7, 70, 138, 295; **Retro. Supp. I:** 80, 176, 253; **Retro. Supp. II:** 104; **Supp. I Part 1:** 13, 43, 253, 254, 259, 260, 265, 270, 315; **Supp. I Part 2:** 493, 527, 616, 643, 647, 649; **Supp. IV Part 2:** 450; **Supp. VIII:** 103, 196; **Supp. IX:** 102, 155, 161, 308; **Supp. X:** 193, 194; **Supp. XII:** 14–15; **Supp. XIII:** 75; **Supp. XIV:** 83; **Supp. XV:** 219; **Supp. XVI:** 157–158, 161, 292; **Supp. XXII:** 165, 198
"Freud and Literature" (Trilling), **Supp. III Part 2:** 502–503
Freudenberger, Nell, **Supp. XXV:** 149
Freudian Psychology and Veblen's Social Theory, The (Schneider), **Supp. I Part 2:** 650

Freudian Wish and Its Place in Ethics, The (Holt), **I:** 59
"Freud's Room" (Ozick), **Supp. V:** 268
Freud: The Mind of the Moralist (Sontag and Rieff), **Supp. III Part 2:** 455
"Freud: Within and Beyond Culture" (Trilling), **Supp. III Part 2:** 508
Frey, Charles, **Supp. XXII:** 301
Frey, Hillary, **Supp. XIX:** 55; **Supp. XXII:** 53
Frey, James, **Supp. XXII:** 95; **Supp. XXIII:** 109; **Supp. XXIV:** 230, 236
"Friday Morning Trial of Mrs. Solano, The" (Ríos), **Supp. IV Part 2:** 538, 548
Friebert, Stuart, **Supp. XIX:** 276
Frieburger, William, **Supp. XIII:** 239
Friede, Donald, **Supp. XVII:** 85, 86, 87, 90
Friedenberg, Edgar Z., **Supp. VIII:** 240
Friedman, Bruce Jay, **I:** 161; **Supp. IV Part 1:** 379
Friedman, Lawrence S., **Supp. V:** 273
Friedman, Milton, **Supp. I Part 2:** 648
Friedman, Norman, **I:** 431–432, 435, 439
Friedman, Stan, **Supp. XII:** 186
Friedmann, Georges, **Supp. I Part 2:** 645
"Fried Sausage" (Simic), **Supp. VIII:** 270
Friend, Julius, **Retro. Supp. I:** 80
Friend, The (Coleridge), **II:** 10
"Friend Husband's Latest" (Sayre), **Retro. Supp. I:** 104
"Friendly Debate between a Conformist and a Non-Conformist, A" (Wild), **IV:** 155
"Friendly Neighbor" (Keillor), **Supp. XVI:** 172
Friend of the Earth, A (Boyle), **Supp. VIII:** 12, 16; **Supp. XX: 29–30**
"Friend of the Fourth Decade, The" (Merrill), **Supp. III Part 1:** 327
"Friends" (Beattie), **Supp. V:** 23, 27
"Friends" (Paley), **Supp. VI:** 219, 226
"Friends" (Sexton), **Supp. II Part 2:** 693
Friend's Delight, The (Bierce), **I:** 195
"Friends from Philadelphia" (Updike), **Retro. Supp. I:** 319
"Friendship" (Emerson), **Supp. II Part 1:** 290; **Supp. XXV:** 250
Friends: More Will and Magna Stories (Dixon), **Supp. XII:** 148, 149
"Friends of Heraclitus, The" (Simic), **Supp. VIII:** 284
"Friends of Kafka, The" (Singer), **Retro. Supp. II:** 308
"Friends of the Family, The" (McCarthy), **II:** 566
"Friend to Alexander, A" (Thurber), **Supp. I Part 2:** 616
"Frigate Pelican, The" (Moore), **III:** 208, 210–211, 215
Frightened Wife, The (Rinehart), **Supp. XXV:** 198, 200
"Frill, The" (Buck), **Supp. XIV:** 274
"Fringe, The" (Bass), **Supp. XVI:** 19
Frings, Ketti, **Supp. XXV:** 95
Frobenius, Leo, **III:** 475; **Supp. III Part 2:** 620
Froebel, Friedrich, **Supp. XIV:** 52–53

Frog (Dixon), **Supp. XII:** 151
"Frog Dances" (Dixon), **Supp. XII:** 151
"Frog Pond, The" (Kinnell), **Supp. III Part 1:** 254
"Frogs" (Nelson), **Supp. XVIII:** 176
"Frog Takes a Swim" (Dixon), **Supp. XII:** 152
Frohock, W. M., **I:** 34, 42
Frolic of His Own, A (Gaddis), **Supp. IV Part 1:** 279, 291, 292–294; **Supp. XX:** 91
"From a Mournful Village" (Jewett), **Retro. Supp. II:** 146
"From an Alabama Farm" (Nelson), **Supp. XVIII:** 182
"From an Old House in America" (Rich), **Supp. I Part 2:** 551, 565–567
From Another World (Untermeyer), **Supp. XV:** 293, 303, 310–311, 313
"From a Roadside Motel" (F. Wright), **Supp. XVII:** 245
"From a Survivor" (Rich), **Supp. I Part 2:** 563
From A to Z (musical review; Allen), **Supp. XV:** 3, 13
From a Work in Progress (Notley), **Supp. XXII:** 232
"From a Work in Progress" (Notley), **Supp. XXII:** 232
From a Writer's Notebook (Brooks), **I:** 254
From Bauhaus to Our House (Wolfe), **Supp. III Part 2:** 580, 581, 584
From Bondage (H. Roth), **Supp. IX:** 236, **238–240**
"From *Chants* to *Borders* to *Communion*" (Fox), *Supp. XIII:* 217, 217–218
"From Chicago" (Anderson), **I:** 108–109
From Colony to Nation: Women Activists and the Gendering of Politics in Belize, 1912–1982 (Macpherson), **Supp. XXIII:** 84
From Death to Morning (Wolfe), **IV:** 450, 456, 458
"From Dick to Lethem: The Dickian Legacy, Postmodernism, and Avant-Pop in Jonathan Lethem's *Amnesia Moon*" (Rossi), *Supp. XVIII:* 137, 138–139
"From Discord, a Wife Makes a Nice New Life—Too Nice" (Linfield), **Supp. XVII:** 177
From Down to the Village (Budbill), **Supp. XIX:** **6–7**
"From Feathers to Iron" (Kunitz), **Supp. III Part 1:** 261
"From Fifth Avenue Up" (Barnes), **Supp. III Part 1:** 33, 44
"From Gorbunov and Gorchakov" (Brodsky), **Supp. VIII:** 26
"From Grand Canyon to Burbank" (H. Miller), **III:** 186
"From Hell to Breakfast", **Supp. IX:** 326–327
From Here to Eternity (film), **Supp. XI:** 221
From Here to Eternity (J. Jones), **I:** 477; **Supp. XI:** 215, 216, 217, 218, **219–221**, 223, 224, 226, 229, 230, 231, 232, 234; **Supp. XIX:** 248; **Supp.**

XX: 248; **Supp. XXII:** 140
From Here to Eternity (miniseries), **Supp. XI:** 234
From Jordan's Delight (Blackmur), **Supp. II Part 1:** 91
"From Lumaghi Mine" (Wrigley), **Supp. XVIII:** 295
Fromm, Erich, **I:** 58; **Supp. VIII:** 196
From Morn to Midnight (Kaiser), **I:** 479
"From Native Son to Invisible Man" (Locke), **Supp. IX:** 306
"From Pico, the Women: A Life" (Creeley), **Supp. IV Part 1:** 149
From Plotzk to Boston (Antin), **Supp. XX:** 2
From Ritual to Romance (Weston), **II:** 540; **III:** 12; **Supp. I Part 2:** 439
From Room to Room (Kenyon), **Supp. VII:** 163–165, 166, 167
"From Room to Room" (Kenyon), **Supp. VII:** 159, 163–165
From Sand Creek: Rising in this Heart Which Is Our America (Ortiz), **Supp. IV Part 2:** 512–513
"From Sea Cliff, March" (Swenson), **Supp. IV Part 2:** 649
From Stone Orchard: A Collection of Memories (Findley), **Supp. XX:** 57
"From the Antigone" (Yeats), **III:** 459
From the Ashes: Voices of Watts (Schulberg, ed.), **Supp. XVIII:** 254
From the Barrio: A Chicano Anthology (Salinas and Faderman, eds.), **Supp. XIII:** 313
From the Beginning (Notley), **Supp. XXII:** 226, 235–236
From the Briarpatch File: On Context, Procedure, and American Identity (Murray), **Supp. XIX:** 161
"From the Childhood of Jesus" (Pinsky), **Supp. VI:** 244–245, 247
"From the Corpse Woodpiles, From the Ashes" (Hayden), **Supp. II Part 1:** 370
"From the Country to the City" (Bishop), **Supp. I Part 1:** 85, 86
"From the Cupola" (Merrill), **Supp. III Part 1:** 324–325, 331
"From the Dark Side of the Earth" (Oates), **Supp. II Part 2:** 510
"From the Diary of a New York Lady" (Parker), **Supp. IX:** 201
"From the Diary of One Not Born" (Singer), **IV:** 9
"From the Dreams" (Notley), **Supp. XXII:** 224
"From the East, Light" (Carver), **Supp. III Part 1:** 138
From the First Nine: Poems 1946–1976 (Merrill), **Supp. III Part 1:** 336
"From the Flats" (Lanier), **Supp. I Part 1:** 364
From the Flower Courtyard (Everwine), **Supp. XV:** 75
From the Heart of Europe (Matthiessen), **III:** 310
From the Meadow: Selected and New Poems (Everwine), **Supp. XV:** 75, **88–89**

"From the Memoirs of a Private Detective" (Hammett), **Supp. IV Part 1:** 343
"From the Nursery" (Kenyon), **Supp. VII:** 171
"From the Poets in the Kitchen" (Marshall), **Supp. XI:** 277
From the Terrace (O'Hara), **III:** 362
"From the Thirties: Tillie Olsen and the Radical Tradition" (Rosenfelt), **Supp. XIII:** 296, 304
"From Trollope's Journal" (Bishop), **Retro. Supp. II:** 47
"Front, A" (Jarrell), **II:** 374
Front, The (film), **Supp. I Part 1:** 295
"Front and the Back Parts of the House, The" (Maxwell), **Supp. VIII:** 169
Frontier Eden (Bigelow), **Supp. X:** 227
"Frontiers of Culture" (Locke), **Supp. XIV:** 213
"Front Lines" (Snyder), **Supp. VIII:** 301
Front Porch (Inge), **Supp. XXV:** 94
Front Runner, The (P. N. Warren), **Supp. XX:** 259, **262–264**
Frost, A. B., **Retro. Supp. II:** 72
Frost, Carol, **Supp. XV:** **91–109**
Frost, Isabelle Moodie, **II:** 150, 151
Frost, Jeanie, **II:** 151
Frost, Richard, **Supp. XV:** 92
Frost, Robert, **I:** 26, 27, 60, 63, 64, 171, 229, 303, 326, 418; **II:** 55, 58, **150–172**, 276, 289, 388, 391, 471, 523, 527, 529, 535; **III:** 5, 23, 67, 269, 271, 272, 275, 287, 453, 510, 523, 536, 575, 581, 591; **IV:** 140, 190, 415; **Retro. Supp. I:** 67, **121–144**, 276, 287, 292, 298, 299, 311, 413; **Retro. Supp. II:** 40, 47, 50, 146, 178, 181; **Supp. I Part 1:** 80, 242, 263, 264; **Supp. I Part 2:** 387, 461, 699; **Supp. II Part 1:** 4, 19, 26, 103; **Supp. III Part 1:** 63, 74–75, 239, 253; **Supp. III Part 2:** 546, 592, 593; **Supp. IV Part 1:** 15; **Supp. IV Part 2:** 439, 445, 447, 448, 599, 601; **Supp. VIII:** 20, 30, 32, 98, 100, 104, 259, 292; **Supp. IX:** 41, 42, 75, 76, 80, 87, 90, 266, 308; **Supp. X:** 64, 65, 66, 74, 120, 172; **Supp. XI:** 43, 123, 150, 153, 312; **Supp. XII:** 130, 241, 303, 307; **Supp. XIII:** 143, 147, 334–335; **Supp. XIV:** 42, 122, 222, 229; **Supp. XV:** 21, 51, 65, 96, 212, 215, 250, 256, 293, 296, 299, 301, 302, 306, 348; **Supp. XVII:** 36, 110, 115–116; **Supp. XVIII:** 298, 300; **Supp. XIX:** 1, 123; **Supp. XX:** **69, 199; Supp. XXI:** 19, 28, 51, 99, 104, 107, 205; **Supp. XXII:** 206; **Supp. XXIII:** 79, 145; **Supp. XXIV:** 159; **Supp. XXV:** 222
Frost, William Prescott, **II:** 150–151
"Frost: A Dissenting Opinion" (Cowley), **Supp. II Part 1:** 143
Frost: A Time to Talk (Francis), **Supp. IX:** 76, **85–86**
"Frost at Midnight" (Coleridge), **Supp. X:** 71
"Frost Flowers" (Kenyon), **Supp. VII:** 168

"Frost: He Is Sometimes a Poet and Sometimes a Stump-Speaker" (News-Week), **Retro. Supp. I:** 137
Frothingham, Nathaniel, **I:** 3
Frothingham, Octavius B., **IV:** 173
"Frozen City, The" (Nemerov), **III:** 270
"Frozen Fields, The" (Bowles), **Supp. IV Part 1:** 80
"Frozen Ship, The" (Very), **Supp. XXV:** 243
"Fructifying a Cycle: Homage to Alan Ansen"(Hadas), **Supp. XXIII:** 123
"Fruit Garden Path, The" (Lowell), **II:** 516
"Fruit of the Flower" (Cullen), **Supp. IV Part 1:** 167
Fruit of the Tree, The (Wharton), **IV:** 314–315; **Retro. Supp. I:** 367, **370–371,** 373
"Fruit of Travel Long Ago" (Melville), **III:** 93
Fruits and Vegetables (Jong), **Supp. V:** 113, 115, 117, 118, 119
"Fruits of the Sea, The" (Di Piero), **Supp. XIX:** 47
Frumkes, Lewis Burke, **Supp. XII:** 335–336
Fry, Christopher, **Supp. I Part 1:** 270
Fry, Roger, **Supp. XIV:** 336
Fry, Stephen M., **Supp. XIX:** 159
Frye, Joanne, **Supp. XIII:** 292, 296, 298, 302
Frye, Northrop, **Supp. I Part 2:** 530; **Supp. II Part 1:** 101; **Supp. X:** 80; **Supp. XIII:** 19; **Supp. XIV:** 11, 15; **Supp. XVI:** 149, 156; **Supp. XX:** 50; **Supp. XXIII:** 42
Fryer, Judith, **Retro. Supp. I:** 379
F. Scott Fitzgerald: A Critical Portrait (Piper), **Supp. IX:** 65
"F. S. F., 1896–1996, R.I.P." (Doctorow), **Retro. Supp. I:** 97
Fuchs, Daniel, **Supp. XIII:** 106
Fuchs, Miriam, **Supp. IV Part 1:** 284
Fuehrer Bunker, The (Snodgrass), **Supp. VI:** 314, 315–317, 319–321
Fuel (Nye), **Supp. XIII:** 277, **282–284**
"Fuel" (Nye), **Supp. XIII:** 283
Fuertes, Gloria, **Supp. V:** 178
Fugard, Athol, **Supp. VIII:** 330; **Supp. XIII:** 205
Fugitive Group, The (Cowan), **IV:** 120
Fugitive Kind, The (T. Williams), **IV:** 381, 383
Fugitives, The (group), **IV:** 122, 124, 125, 131, 237, 238
Fugitives, The: A Critical Account (Bradbury), **IV:** 130
"Fugitive Slave Law, The" (Emerson), **II:** 13
Fugitive's Return (Glaspell), **Supp. III Part 1:** 182–184
Fuller, B. A. G., **III:** 605
Fuller, Edmund, **Supp. XXII:** 211, 212
Fuller, Hiram, **Supp. XVIII:** 12,14
Fuller, Jesse "Lonecat", **Supp. XV:** 147
Fuller, Margaret, **I:** 261; **II:** 7, 276; **IV:** 172; **Retro. Supp. I:** 155–156, 163; **Retro. Supp. II:** 46; **Supp. I Part 2:** 524; **Supp. II Part 1:** 279–306; **Supp.**

IX: 37; **Supp. XVIII:** 3, 11, 12, 16; **Supp. XXV:** 249
Fuller, Thomas, **II:** 111, 112
Fullerton, Morton, **Supp. XX:** 231
Fullerton Street (Wilson), **Supp. VIII:** 331
"Full Fathom Five" (Plath), **Supp. I Part 2:** 538
Full Measure: Modern Short Stories on Aging (D. Sennett, ed.), **Supp. XVI:** 37
Full Monty, The (musical, McNally), **Supp. XIII:** 207
"Full Moon" (Hayden), **Supp. II Part 1:** 370
Full Moon and Other Plays (Price), **Supp. VI:** 266
"Full Moon and You're Not Here" (Cisneros), **Supp. VII:** 71–72
"Full Moon: New Guinea" (Shapiro), **Supp. II Part 2:** 707
"Fullness of Life, The" (Wharton), **Retro. Supp. I:** 363
Full of Life (Fante), **Supp. XI:** 160
Full of Life (film), **Supp. XI:** 170
Full of Lust and Good Usage (Dunn), **Supp. XI:** **145–147**
"Full Summer" (Olds), **Supp. X:** 212
Fulton, Ben, **Supp. XXII:** 207
Fulton, Robert, **Supp. I Part 2:** 519; **Supp. II Part 1:** 73
Fun and Games (Major), **Supp. XXII:** 180
"Functional Poem" (Halliday), **Supp. XIX:** 85
Function of Criticism, The (Winters), **Supp. II Part 2:** 812, 813
"Fundamentalism" (Tate), **IV:** 125
"Fundamental Project of Technology, The" (Kinnell), **Supp. III Part 1:** 253
"Funeral of Bobò, The" (Brodsky), **Supp. VIII:** 27, 28
Fungi from Yuggoth (Lovecraft), **Supp. XXV:** 119–120
Fun Home: A Family Tragicomic (Bechdel), **Supp. XXV:** 1, 4–9
Funiculi-Funicula (Wellman), **Supp. XXV:** 20
"Funnel" (Sexton), **Supp. II Part 2:** 675
"Furious Seasons, The" (Carver), **Supp. III Part 1:** 137
Furious Seasons and Other Stories (Carver), **Supp. III Part 1:** 142, 143, 146
"Furious Versions" (L.-Y. Lee), **Supp. XV:** 215–217, 218, 220
"Furnished Room, The" (Hayden), **Supp. II Part 1:** 386–387, 394, 397, 399, 406, 408
"Furor Scribendi" (O. Butler), **Supp. XIII:** 70
Furors Die (Hoffman), **Supp. XVIII:** **80–81**
Fur Person, The (Sarton), **Supp. VIII:** **264–265**
Further Adventures with You (Wright), **Supp. XV:** 339, 342, **343–345**
Further Fables for Our Time (Thurber), **Supp. I Part 2:** 612

"Further in Summer than the Birds" (Dickinson), **I:** 471
Further Poems of Emily Dickinson (Bianchi and Hampson, ed.), **Retro. Supp. I:** 35
Further Range, A (Frost), **II:** 155; **Retro. Supp. I:** 132, 136, 137, 138, 139
"Fury, The (Skloot), **Supp. XX:** 197
"Fury of Aerial Bombardment, The" (Eberhart), **I:** 535–536
"Fury of Flowers and Worms, The" (Sexton), **Supp. II Part 2:** 694
"Fury of Rain Storms, The" (Sexton), **Supp. II Part 2:** 695
Fury of the Jungle (film), **Supp. XIII:** 163
Fussell, Paul, **Supp. V:** 241
Fussell, Paul K., **Supp. XXV:** 253
"Future, if Any, of Comedy, The" (Thurber), **Supp. I Part 2:** 620
Future, The (film, July), **Supp. XXIV:** 199, 200, 202, **209,** 210
Future in the Present, The (C. L. R. James), **Supp. XXI:** 172
Future is Ours, Comrade, The: Conversations with the Russians (Kosinski), **Supp. VII:** 215
Futureland: Nine Stories of an Imminent World (Mosley), **Supp. XIII:** 247–249
"Future Life, The" (Bryant), **Supp. I Part 1:** 170
Future of Southern Letters, The (J. W. Miller), **Supp. XX:** 161
Future of the Race, The (H. L. Gates), **Supp. XX:** **101, 104, 111**
Future Punishment of the Wicked, The (Edwards), **I:** 546

G

"Gabriel" (Rich), **Supp. I Part 2:** 557
Gabriel, Ralph H., **Supp. I Part 1:** 251
Gabriel, Trip, **Supp. V:** 212
Gabriel Conroy (Harte), **Supp. II Part 1:** 354
"Gabriel's Truth" (Kenyon), **Supp. VII:** 166
Gaddis, William, **Supp. IV Part 1:** 279–296; **Supp. IV Part 2:** 484; **Supp. V:** 52; **Supp. IX:** 208; **Supp. X:** 301, 302; **Supp. XX:** **83, 91;** **Supp. XXI:** 226; **Supp. XXIII:** 107
Gadiot, Pud, **Supp. XI:** 295
Gain (Powers), **Supp. IX:** 212, **220–221**
Gaines, Ernest J., **Supp. X:** 24, 250
Gaines, James R., **Supp. IX:** 190
Gainor, J. Ellen, **Supp. XXI:** 6
Gaitens, Peter, **Supp. XV:** 65
Galamain, Ivan, **Supp. III Part 2:** 624
Galassi, Jonathan, **Supp. XVIII:** 92; **Supp. XIX:** 34; **Supp. XXII:** 177
Galatea 2.2 (Powers), **Supp. IX:** 212, **219–220**
"Galatea Encore" (Brodsky), **Supp. VIII:** 31
Galbraith, John Kenneth, **Supp. I Part 2:** 645, 650
Galdós, Benito Pérez. *See* Pérez Galdós, Benito

Gale, Zona, **Supp. I Part 2:** 613; **Supp. VIII:** 155

Galehouse, Maggie, **Supp. XXI:** 215

"Gale in April" (Jeffers), **Supp. II Part 2:** 423

Galignani, Giovanni Antonio, **II:** 315

Galileo Galilei, **I:** 480–481; **Supp. XII:** 180; **Supp. XIII:** 75

Gallagher, Tess, **Supp. XVI:** 36; **Supp. XVII:** 110; **Supp. XXI:** 246; **Supp. XXIV:** 165–181

Gallant, Mavis, **Supp. VIII:** 151

Gallatin, Albert, **I:** 5

"Gallery" (Goldbarth), **Supp. XII:** 188

"Gallery of Real Creatures, A" (Thurber), **Supp. I Part 2:** 619

Gallico, Paul, **Supp. XVI:** 238

Gallows Songs (Snodgrass), **Supp. VI:** 317

Gallup, Dick, **Supp. XXIV:** 34, 35, 39, 44

Gallup, Donald, **III:** 404, 478

Galsworthy, John, **III:** 70, 153, 382

Galton Case, The (Macdonald), **Supp. IV Part 2:** 463, 473, 474

Galvin, Frances, **Supp. XXI:** 5

"Gal Young 'Un" (Rawlings), **Supp. X:** 228

Gambino, Richard, **Supp. XX: 35**

"Gambler, the Nun, and the Radio, The" (Hemingway), **II:** 250

"Gambler's Wife, The" (Dunbar), **Supp. II Part 1:** 196

Gambone, Philip, **Supp. XII:** 81

"Gambrel Roof, A" (Larcom), **Supp. XIII:** 144

"Game at Salzburg, A" (Jarrell), **II:** 384, 389

Game Management (Leopold), **Supp. XIV:** 182

"Game of Catch, A" (Wilbur), **Supp. III Part 2:** 552

Game Players of Titan, The (Dick), **Supp. XVIII:** 138

"Games in Frank Conroy's *Stop-Time*" (T. Adams), **Supp. XVI:** 67

"Games Two" (Wilbur), **Supp. III Part 2:** 550

Gammelgaard, Lene, **Supp. XVIII:** 112

"Gamut, The" (Angelou), **Supp. IV Part 1:** 15

Gander, Forrest, **Supp. XV:** 339, 340, 342

Gandhi, Indira, **Supp. X:** 108

Gandhi, Mahatma, **III:** 179, 296–297; **IV:** 170, 185, 367; **Supp. VIII:** 203, 204; **Supp. X:** 27

Gandhi on Non-Violence (Merton, ed.), **Supp. VIII:** 204–205

Gangemi, Merry, **Supp. XXV:** 6

Gang of Five: Leaders at the Center of the Conservative Crusade (Easton), **Supp. XIX:** 137

"Gang of Mirrors, The" (Simic), **Supp. VIII:** 283

Gannett, Ezra Stiles, **Supp. XXIV:** 74

Gansevoort, Guert, **III:** 94

Gansevoort, Peter, **III:** 92

"Gap" (Bierds), **Supp. XVII:** 35–36

Garabedian, Michael, **Supp. XIII:** 115

Garbage (Ammons), **Supp. VII:** 24, 35–36

Garbage (Dixon), **Supp. XII:** 147, 148

Garbage Man, The (Dos Passos), **I:** 478, 479, 481, 493

Garber, Frederick, **Supp. IX:** 294–295

Garbo, Greta, **Supp. I Part 2:** 616

García, Cristina, **Supp. VIII:** 74; **Supp. XI: 177–192**

García Lorca, Federico. *See* Lorca, Federico García

"García Lorca: A Photograph of the Granada Cemetery, 1966" (Levis), **Supp. XI:** 264

García Márquez, Gabriel, **Supp. V:** 244; **Supp. VIII:** 81, 82, 84, 85; **Supp. XII:** 147, 310, 316, 322; **Supp. XIII:** 226; **Supp. XVII:** 45; **Supp. XXIV:** 86, 89, 190; **Supp. XXV:** 49, 69

Gard, Claire, **Supp. XXIII:** 94

Gardaphe, Fred, **Supp. XX: 38, 41**

"Garden" (Marvell), **IV:** 161; **Supp. XVI:** 204

"Garden, The" (Glück), **Supp. V:** 83

"Garden, The" (Strand), **Supp. IV Part 2:** 629

"Garden, The" (Very), **Supp. XXV:** 248

"Garden Among Tombs" (B. Kelly), **Supp. XVII:** 126

"Garden by Moonlight, The" (Lowell), **II:** 524

"Gardener Delivers a Fawn, The" (C. Frost), **Supp. XV:** 99

Gardener's Son, The (McCarthy), **Supp. VIII:** 187

Garden God, The: A Tale of Two Boys (Reid), **Supp. XX: 235**

"Gardenias" (Doty), **Supp. XI:** 122

"Gardenias" (Monette), **Supp. X:** 159

"Garden Lodge, The" (Cather), **I:** 316, 317

Garden of Adonis, The (Gordon), **II:** 196, 204–205, 209

Garden of Earthly Delights, A (Oates), **Supp. II Part 2:** 504, 507–509

Garden of Earthly Delights, The (Bosch), **Supp. XXII:** 255, 261

"Garden of Eden" (Hemingway), **II:** 259

Garden of Eden, The (Hemingway), **Retro. Supp. I:** 186, **187–188**

"Garden of Flesh, Garden of Stone" (B. Kelly), **Supp. XVII:** 128

Garden of Last Days, The (Dubus III), **Supp. XXIV:** 101, **107–108**

"Garden of the Moon, The" (Doty), **Supp. XI:** 122

Garden of the Prophet, The (Gibran), **Supp. XX: 119, 122**

"Garden of the Trumpet Tree, The" (B. Kelly), **Supp. XVII:** 131

"Gardens, The" (Oliver), **Supp. VII:** 236

"Gardens of Mont-Saint-Michel, The" (Maxwell), **Supp. VIII:** 169

"Gardens of the Villa D'Este, The" (Hecht), **Supp. X:** 59

"Gardens of Zuñi, The" (Merwin), **Supp. III Part 1:** 351

Garden Thieves, The: Twentieth Century African-American Poetry (Major, ed.), **Supp. XXII:** 172

Gardiner, Judith Kegan, **Supp. IV Part 1:** 205

Gardner, Erle Stanley, **Supp. IV Part 1:** 121, 345

Gardner, Isabella, **IV:** 127

Gardner, John, **Supp. I Part 1:** 193, 195, 196; **Supp. III Part 1:** 136, 142, 146; **Supp. VI: 61–76; Supp. XXV:** 152

Gardner, Thomas, **Supp. XXI:** 214

Gardons, S. S. *See* Snodgrass, W. D.

"Gare de Lyon" (M. F. K. Fisher), **Supp. XVII:** 91

Garfield, John, **Supp. XII:** 160

Garibaldi, Giuseppe, **I:** 4; **II:** 284

Garibay, Angel M., **Supp. XV:** 77

Garland, Hamlin, **I:** 407; **II:** 276, 289; **III:** 576; **Retro. Supp. I:** 133; **Retro. Supp. II:** 72; **Supp. I Part 1:** 217; **Supp. IV Part 2:** 502; **Supp. XVIII:** 6

Garland Companion, The (Zverev), **Retro. Supp. I:** 278

"Garments" (Gibran), **Supp. XX: 124**

Garments the Living Wear (Purdy), **Supp. VII:** 278–279, 280–281

Garner, Dwight, **Supp. X:** 202; **Supp. XVIII:** 89; **Supp. XXV:** 9

Garnett, Edward, **I:** 405, 409, 417; **III:** 27

Garrett, George P., **Supp. I Part 1:** 196; **Supp. VII: 95–113; Supp. X:** 3, 7; **Supp. XI:** 218; **Supp. XVIII:** 74, 75

Garrigue, Jean, **Supp. XII:** 260

Garrison, Deborah, **Supp. IX:** 299

Garrison, Fielding, **III:** 105

Garrison, William Lloyd, **Supp. I Part 2:** 524, 588, 683, 685, 686, 687; **Supp. XIV:** 54; **Supp. XXIV:** 77

"Garrison of Cape Ann, The" (Whittier), **Supp. I Part 2:** 691, 694

Garry Moore Show (television show), **Supp. IV Part 2:** 575

"Garter Motif" (White), **Supp. I Part 2:** 673

Gartner, Zsuzsi, **Supp. X:** 276

Garvey, Marcus, **Supp. III Part 1:** 175, 180; **Supp. IV Part 1:** 168; **Supp. X:** 135, 136; **Supp. XXI:** 166, 168; **Supp. XXII:** 7

Gas (Kaiser), **I:** 479

Gas-House McGinty (Farrell), **II:** 41–42

Gaskell, Elizabeth, A., **Supp. I Part 2:** 580

Gasoline (Corso), **Supp. XII:** 118, **121– 123**, 134

Gasoline Wars, The (Thompson), **Supp. XXIII:** 290

"Gasoline Wars, The"(Thompson), **Supp. XXIII:** 291

Gass, William H., **Supp. V:** 44, 52, 238; **Supp. VI: 77–96; Supp. IX:** 208; **Supp. XII:** 152; **Supp. XIV:** 305; **Supp. XVII:** 183

Gassner, John, **IV:** 381; **Supp. I Part 1:** 284, 292

"Gas Stations" (Apple), **Supp. XVII:** 4

Gastronomical Me, The (M. F. K. Fisher), **Supp. XVII:** 84, 85, 87, 91, 92

Gates, David, **Supp. V:** 24; **Supp. XIII:** 93; **Supp. XVI:** 73, 74; **Supp. XX:** 92

Gates, Elmer, **I:** 515–516

Gates, Henry Louis, Jr., **Retro. Supp. I:** 194, 195, 203; **Supp. X:** 242, 243, 245, 247; **Supp. XVIII:** 287; **Supp. XIX:** 147, 149; **Supp. XX: 99–112, 279, 286; Supp. XXIV:** 192

Gates, Lewis E., **III:** 315, 330

Gates, Sondra Smith, **Supp. XVIII:** 267, 269

Gates, The (Rukeyser), **Supp. VI:** 271, 274, 281

"Gates, The" (Rukeyser), **Supp. VI:** 286

Gates, Tudor, **Supp. XI:** 307

Gates of Ivory, the Gates of Horn, The (McGrath), **Supp. X:** 118

Gates of Wrath, The; Rhymed Poems (Ginsberg), **Supp. II Part 1:** 311, 319

"Gathering" (Trethewey), **Supp. XXI:** 249

Gathering Forces, The (C. L. R. James), **Supp. XXI:** 171

"Gathering of Dissidents, A" (Applebaum), **Supp. XVI:** 153

Gathering of Fugitives, A (Trilling), **Supp. III Part 2:** 506, 512

Gathering of Zion, The: The Story of the Mormon Trail (Stegner), **Supp. IV Part 2:** 599, 602–603

Gather Together in My Name (Angelou), **Supp. IV Part 1:** 2, 3, 4–6, 11

Gathorne-Hardy, Robert, **Supp. XIV:** 344, 347, 348, 349

Gaudier-Brzeska, Henri, **III:** 459, 464, 465, 477

Gaughran, Richard, **Supp. XXI:** 47–48

Gauguin, Paul, **I:** 34; **IV:** 290; **Supp. IV Part 1:** 81; **Supp. XII:** 128

"Gauguin in Oregon" (Skloot), **Supp. XX: 203**

"Gauley Bridge" (Rukeyser), **Supp. VI:** 278

Gauss, Christian, **II:** 82; **IV:** 427, 439–440, 444

Gauthier, Jacquie, **Supp. XIX:** 204

Gautier, Théophile, **II:** 543; **III:** 466, 467; **Supp. I Part 1:** 277

Gay, John, **II:** 111; **Supp. I Part 2:** 523; **Supp. XIV:** 337

Gay, Peter, **I:** 560

Gay, Sydney Howard, **Supp. I Part 1:** 158; **Supp. XVIII:** 3

Gay, Walter, **IV:** 317

Gayatri Prayer, The, **III:** 572

Gay Canon, The (Drake), **Supp. XX: 274**

"Gay Chaps at the Bar" (Brooks), **Supp. III Part 1:** 74, 75

" 'Gay Culture': Still of the Wild Frontier" (P. N. Warren), **Supp. XX: 272**

Gaylord, Winfield R., **III:** 579–580

Gay Talese Reader, The: Portraits & Encounters (Talese), **Supp. XVII:** 202, 208

"Gaze, The"(Hadas), **Supp. XXIII:** 120

"Gazebo" (Carver), **Supp. III Part 1:** 138, 144, 145

Gazer's Spirit, The (Hollander), **Supp. XIX:** 121

Gazer Within, The, and Other Essays by Larry Levis, **Supp. XI:** 270

Gazzara, Ben, **Supp. VIII:** 319

Gazzo, Michael V., **III:** 155

"Geas" (Monson), **Supp. XXIV:** 238–239

Geddes, Virgil, **Supp. XXV:** 23

"Geese Flying over Hamilton, New York"(Balakian), **Supp. XXIII:** 24

"Geese Gone Beyond" (Snyder), **Supp. VIII:** 304

Geffen, David, **Supp. XXI:** 154

"Gegenwart" (Goethe), **Supp. II Part 1:** 26

Geisel, Theodor Seuss (Dr. Seuss), **Supp. X:** 56; **Supp. XVI: 97–115**

Geismar, Maxwell, **II:** 178, 431; **III:** 71; **Supp. IX:** 15; **Supp. XI:** 223

Geist, Bill, **Supp. XXIII:** 298

Gelb, Arthur, **IV:** 380; **Supp. XXI:** 12

Gelb, Barbara, **Supp. XXI:** 12

Gelbart, Larry, **Supp. IV Part 2:** 591

Gelder, Robert Van, **Supp. XIII:** 166

Gelfant, Blanche H., **II:** 27, 41; **Supp. XVII:** 161

Gelfman, Jean, **Supp. X:** 3

Gellert, Hugo, **Supp. XXII:** 277

Gellhorn, Martha. *See* Hemingway, Mrs. Ernest (Martha Gellhorn)

Gelpi, Albert, **Supp. I Part 2:** 552, 554, 560

Gelpi, Barbara, **Supp. I Part 2:** 560

Gemin, Pamela, **Supp. XXI:** 246

Gemini (Innaurato), **Supp. XXIV:** 117

Gemini: an extended autobiographical statement on my first twenty-five years of being a black poet (Giovanni), **Supp. IV Part 1:** 11

"Gen" (Snyder), **Supp. VIII:** 302

"Gender Norms" (Radinovsky), **Supp. XV:** 285

"Gender of Sound, The" (Carson), **Supp. XII: 106**

"Genealogies"(Hadas), **Supp. XXIII:** 116

"Genealogy" (Komunyakaa), **Supp. XIII:** 129

"General Aims and Theories" (Crane), **I:** 389

General Died at Dawn, The (Odets), **Supp. II Part 2:** 546

"General Gage's Confession" (Freneau), **Supp. II Part 1:** 257

"General Gage's Soliloquy" (Freneau), **Supp. II Part 1:** 257

General History of the Robberies and Murders of the Most Notorious Pyrates from Their First Rise and Settlement in the Island of New Providence to the Present Year, A (Johnson), **Supp. V:** 128

General in His Labyrinth, The (García Márquez), **Supp. XXIV:** 89

"General Returns from One Place to Another, The"(O'Hara), **Supp. XXIII:** 216–217

"General William Booth Enters into Heaven" (Lindsay), **Supp. I Part 2:** 374, 382, 384, 385–388, 389, 392, 399

General William Booth Enters into Heaven and Other Poems (Lindsay),

Supp. I Part 2: 379, 381, 382, 387–388, 391

"Generation of the Dispossessed" (P. N. Warren), **Supp. XX: 272**

"Generations"(Kenny), **Supp. XXIII:** 154

"Generations of Men, The" (Frost), **Retro. Supp. I:** 128; **Supp. XIII:** 147

Generation Without Farewell (Boyle), **Supp. XXIV:** 60, 62

Generous Man, A (Price), **Supp. VI:** 259, 260, 261

Genesis (biblical book), **I:** 279; **II:** 540; **Retro. Supp. I:** 250, 256; **Supp. XII:** 54

"Genesis" (Stegner), **Supp. IV Part 2:** 604

Genesis: Book One (Schwartz), **Supp. II Part 2:** 640, 651–655

Gene Stratton-Porter (Richards), **Supp. XX: 217–218**

Gene Stratton-Porter, Naturalist and Novelist (Long), **Supp. XX:** 212

"Gene Stratton-Porter: Women's Advocate" (Obuchowski), **Supp. XX: 222**

Genet, Jean, **I:** 71, 82, 83, 84; **Supp. IV Part 1:** 8; **Supp. XI:** 308; **Supp. XII:** 1; **Supp. XIII:** 74; **Supp. XVII:** 95; **Supp. XXIII:** 213; **Supp. XXIV:** 210

"Genetic Coding" (Sorrentino), **Supp. XXI:** 227

"Genetic Expedition" (Dove), **Supp. IV Part 1:** 249, 257

"Genetics of Justice" (Alvarez), **Supp. VII:** 19

"Genial Host, The" (McCarthy), **II:** 564

"Genie in the Bottle, The" (Wilbur), **Supp. III Part 2:** 542

"Genius, The" (MacLeish), **III:** 19

Genius and Lust: A Journey through the Major Writings of Henry Miller (Mailer), **Retro. Supp. II:** 208

"Genius Child" (Hughes), **Retro. Supp. I:** 203

"Genius of Bob Dylan, The" (Lethem), **Supp. XVIII:** 146

"Genius," The (Dreiser), **I:** 497, 501, 509–511, 519; **Retro. Supp. II:** 94–95, **102–103,** 104, 105

Genova, Lisa, **Supp. XXIII:** 127

"Genteel Tradition in American Philosophy, The" (Santayana), **I:** 222

"Gentle Communion" (Mora), **Supp. XIII:** 218–219

Gentle Crafter, The (O. Henry), **Supp. II Part 1:** 410

Gentle Furniture-Shop, The (Bodenheim), **Supp. XXV:** 20

"Gentle Lena, The" (Stein), **IV:** 37, 40

Gentleman Caller, The (T. Williams), **IV:** 383

"Gentleman from Cracow, The" (Singer), **IV:** 9

"Gentleman of Bayou Têche, A" (Chopin), **Supp. I Part 1:** 211–212

"Gentleman of Shalott, The" (Bishop), **Supp. I Part 1:** 85, 86

Gentleman's Agreement (Hobson), **III:** 151

"Gentleman's Agreement" (Richard), **Supp. XIX:** 220–221

Gentlemen I Address You Privately (Boyle), **Supp. XXIV: 53–54**

Gentlemen Prefer Blondes (Loos; musical adaptation), **Supp. XVI:** 193

Gentlemen Prefer Blondes: The Illuminating Diary of a Professional Lady (Loos), **Supp. XVI:** 181, 183, 186, **188–189**

Gentlemen Prefer "Books" (J. Yeats), *Supp. XVI:* 190

Gentle People, The: A Brooklyn Fable (Shaw), **Supp. XIX:** 244–245, 249

Gentry, Marshall Bruce, **Supp. IV Part 1:** 236

"Genuine Man, The" (Emerson), **II:** 10

"Genus Narcissus" (Trethewey), **Supp. XXI:** 256

Geo-Bestiary (Harrison), **Supp. VIII:** 53

"Geode" (Frost), **II:** 161

Geographical History of America, The (Stein), **IV:** 31, 45; **Supp. XVIII:** 148

Geography and Plays (Stein), **IV:** 29–30, 32, 43, 44

Geography III (Bishop), **Retro. Supp. II:** 50; **Supp. I Part 1:** 72, 73, 76, 82, 93, 94, 95

Geography of a Horse Dreamer (Shepard), **Supp. III Part 2:** 432

Geography of Home, The: California's Poetry of Place (Bluckey and Young, eds.), **Supp. XIII:** 313

Geography of Lograire, The (Merton), **Supp. VIII:** 208

Geography of the Heart (Johnson), **Supp. XI:** 129

"Geometric Poem, The" (Corso), **Supp. XII:** 132, 133–134

George, Diana Hume, **Supp. IV Part 2:** 447, 449, 450

George, Henry, **II:** 276; **Supp. I Part 2:** 518

George, Jan, **Supp. IV Part 1:** 268

George, Lynell, **Supp. XIII:** 234–235, 237, 249

George, Peter, **Supp. XI:** 302, 303, 304

George and the Dragon (Shanley), **Supp. XIV:** 315

George Bernard Shaw: His Plays (Mencken), **III:** 102

George Mills (Elkin), **Supp. VI: 53–54**

George Palmer Putnam: Representative American Publisher (Greenspan), **Supp. XVIII:** 257

"George Robinson: Blues" (Rukeyser), **Supp. VI:** 279

George's Mother (Crane), **I:** 408

"George Thurston" (Bierce), **I:** 202

George Washington Crossing the Delaware (Koch), **Supp. XV:** 186

"George Washington"(Kenny), **Supp. XXIII:** 154

Georgia Boy (Caldwell), **I:** 288, 305–306, 308, 309, 310

"Georgia Dusk" (Toomer), **Supp. IX:** 309

"Georgia: Invisible Empire State" (Du Bois), **Supp. II Part 1:** 179

"Georgia Night" (Toomer), **Supp. III Part 2:** 481

Georgia Scenes (Longstreet), **II:** 70, 313; **Supp. I Part 1:** 352

Georgics (Virgil), **Retro. Supp. I:** 135; **Supp. XVI:** 22; **Supp. XXIV:** 153

Georgics of Virgil, The (Ferry. trans.), **Supp. XXIV: 158–160**

Georgie May (Bodenheim), **Supp. XXV:** 25

Georgoudaki, Ekaterini, **Supp. IV Part 1:** 12

Gerald McBoing-Boing (film), **Supp. XVI:** 102

"Geraldo No Last Name" (Cisneros), **Supp. VII:** 60–61

Gerald's Game (King), **Supp. V:** 141, 148–150, 151, 152

Gerald's Party (Coover), **Supp. V:** 49–50, 51, 52

Gérando, Joseph Marie de, **II:** 10

"Geranium" (O'Connor), **Retro. Supp. II:** 221, 236

Gerard, Jeremy, **Supp. XXI:** 147

Gerber, Dan, **Supp. VIII:** 39

Gerhardt, Rainer, **Supp. IV Part 1:** 142

"German Girls! The German Girls!, The" (MacLeish), **III:** 16

"German Refugee, The" (Malamud), **Supp. I Part 2:** 436, 437

"Germany's Reichswehr" (Agee), **I:** 35

Germinal (Zola), **III:** 318, 322

Gernsback, Hugo, **Supp. IV Part 1:** 101

"Gernsback Continuum, The" (W. Gibson), **Supp. XVI:** 123, 128

"Gerontion" (Eliot), **I:** 569, 574, 577, 578, 585, 588; **III:** 9, 435, 436; **Retro. Supp. I:** 290; **Supp. XV:** 341; **Supp. XVI:** 158–159

Gerry, Elbridge, **Supp. I Part 2:** 486

"Gerry's Jazz" (Komunyakaa), **Supp. XIII:** 125

Gershwin, Ira, **Supp. I Part 1:** 281

"Gert" (Monette), **Supp. X:** 158

"Gertrude Atherton and the New Woman" (Forrey), **Supp. XXIV:** 30

Gertrude of Stony Island Avenue (Purdy), **Supp. VII:** 281–282

Gertrude Stein (Sprigge), **IV:** 31

Gertrude Stein: A Biography of Her Work (Sutherland), **IV:** 38

"Gertrude Stein and the Geography of the Sentence" (Gass), **Supp. VI:** 87

Gesell, Silvio, **III:** 473

"Gestalt at Sixty" (Sarton), **Supp. VIII:** 260

"Gesture of a Woman-in-Process" (Trethewey), **Supp. XXI:** 249–250

"Gesture toward an Unfound Renaissance, A" (Stafford), **Supp. XI:** 323

"Get It Again" (Halliday), **Supp. XIX:** 85

Getlin, Josh, **Supp. V:** 22; **Supp. VIII:** 75, 76, 78, 79

"Getting Along" (Larcom), **Supp. XIII:** 144

"Getting Along with Nature" (Berry), **Supp. X:** 31–32

"Getting Away from Already Pretty Much Being Away from It All" (Wallace), **Supp. X:** 314–315

"Getting Born" (Shields), **Supp. VII:** 311

Getting Even (Allen), **Supp. XV:** 3, 14, 15

"Getting Lucky" (L. Michaels), **Supp. XVI:** 205, 209

"Getting Out of Jail on Monday" (Wagoner), **Supp. IX:** 327

"Getting Over Arnette"(P. Benedict), **Supp. XXIII:** 39

"Getting There" (Plath), **Supp. I Part 2:** 539, 542

"Getting to the Poem" (Corso), **Supp. XII:** 135

Getty, J. Paul, **Supp. X:** 108

Getty, Norris, **Supp. XV:** 136–137, 138, 139, 142, 143, 145, 146

Gettysburg, Manila, Acoma (Masters), **Supp. I Part 2:** 471

"Gettysburg: July 1, 1863" (Kenyon), **Supp. VII:** 172

Gevers, Nick, **Supp. XXII:** 59

Geyer, Bernadette, **Supp. XXIII:** 251

Ghachem, Malick, **Supp. X:** 17

Ghazálí, al-, **Supp. XX: 117**

"Ghazals: Homage to Ghalib" (Rich), **Supp. I Part 2:** 557

Ghost, The (Crane), **I:** 409, 421

"Ghost, The" (Peacock), **Supp. XIX:** 199

"Ghost Cat" (Peacock), **Supp. XIX:** 206

"Ghost Chant, et alii" (Komunyakaa), **Supp. XIII:** 114

Ghost Country (Paretsky), **Supp. XXV:** 183

Ghost in the Music, A (Nichols), **Supp. XIII:** 267

"Ghost Jam"(Hadas), **Supp. XXIII:** 119

"Ghostlier Demarcations, Keener Sounds" (Vendler), **Supp. I Part 2:** 565

"Ghostly Father, I Confess" (McCarthy), **II:** 565–566

Ghostly Lover, The (Hardwick), **Supp. III Part 1:** 194–196, 208, 209

Ghost Money (Hull), **Supp. XXI:** 129, **132–135,** 136

Ghost of Meter, The (A. Finch), **Supp. XVII:** 71, 73

"Ghost of the Buffaloes, The" (Lindsay), **Supp. I Part 2:** 393

Ghost of Tradition, The (Walzer), **Supp. XVIII:** 174

Ghosts (Auster), **Supp. XII:** 22, **24,26–27**

Ghosts (Ibsen), **III:** 152

Ghosts (Wharton), **IV:** 316, 327

Ghosts of Tsavo: Stalking the Mystery Lions of East Africa (Caputo), **Supp. XIX:** 28

Ghost Town (Coover), **Supp. V:** 52–53

Ghost Trio, The (Bierds), **Supp. XVII:** 29, **30**

Ghost Writer, The (P. Roth), **Retro. Supp. II:** 22, 290, 291; **Supp. III Part 2:** 420–421; **Supp. XVII:** 43

Giachetti, Fosco, **Supp. IV Part 2:** 520

"Giacometti" (Wilbur), **Supp. III Part 2:** 551

Giacometti, Alberto, **Supp. VIII:** 168, 169

Giacomo, Padre, **II:** 278–279

Giant's House, The: A Romance (McCracken), **Supp. X:** 86

"Giant Snail" (Bishop), **Retro. Supp. II:** 49

Giant Weapon, The (Winters), **Supp. II Part 2:** 810

"Giant Woman, The" (Oates), **Supp. II Part 2:** 523

Gibbon, Edward, **I:** 4, 378; **IV:** 126; **Supp. I Part 2:** 503; **Supp. III Part 2:** 629; **Supp. XIII:** 75; **Supp. XIV:** 97

Gibbons, James, **Supp. XVII:** 228

Gibbons, Kaye, **Supp. X: 41–54; Supp. XII:** 311

Gibbons, Reginald, **Supp. X:** 113, 124, 127; **Supp. XV:** 105; **Supp. XIX:** 40, 41–42, 281

Gibbons, Richard, **Supp. I Part 1:** 107

"Gibbs" (Rukeyser), **Supp. VI:** 273

Gibbs, Barbara, **Supp. IV Part 2:** 644

Gibbs, Wolcott, **Supp. I Part 2:** 604, 618; **Supp. VIII:** 151

Gibran, Kahlil, **Supp. XX: 69, 113–129**

"GIBSON" (Baraka), **Supp. II Part 1:** 54

Gibson, Charles Dana, **Supp. X:** 184

Gibson, Graeme, **Supp. XIII:** 20

Gibson, Wilfrid W., **Retro. Supp. I:** 128

Gibson, William, **Supp. XVI: 117–133; Supp. XXII:** 49

Giddins, Gary, **Supp. XIII:** 245

Gide, André, **I:** 271, 290; **II:** 581; **III:** 210; **IV:** 53, 289; **Supp. I Part 1:** 51; **Supp. IV Part 1:** 80, 284, 347; **Supp. IV Part 2:** 681, 682; **Supp. VIII:** 40; **Supp. X:** 187; **Supp. XIV:** 24, 348; **Supp. XVII:** 242

Gideon Planish (Lewis), **II:** 455

Gielgud, John, **I:** 82; **Supp. XI:** 305

Gierow, Dr. Karl Ragnar, **III:** 404

Gifford, Barry, **Supp. XXV:** 29

Gifford, Bill, **Supp. XI:** 38

Gifford, Terry, **Supp. XVI:** 22

"Gift, The" (Creeley), **Supp. IV Part 1:** 153

"Gift, The" (Doolittle), **Supp. I Part 1:** 267

Gift, The (Hyde), **Supp. XVIII:** 150

"Gift, The" (Jarman), **Supp. XVII:** 116

"Gift, The" (L.-Y. Lee), **Supp. XV:** 213, 214

Gift, The (Nabokov), **III:** 246, 255, 261–263; **Retro. Supp. I:** 264, 266, **268–270**, 273, 274–275, 278

"Gift from the City, A" (Updike), **Retro. Supp. I:** 320

"Gift of God, The" (Robinson), **III:** 512, 517, 518–521, 524

Gift of the Black Folk, The: The Negroes in the Making of America (Du Bois), **Supp. II Part 1:** 179

"Gift of the Magi, The" (O. Henry), **Supp. II Part 1:** 394, 406, 408

"Gift of the *Osuo*, The" (Johnson), **Supp. VI:** 194

"Gift of the Prodigal, The" (Taylor), **Supp. V:** 314, 326

"Gift Outright, The" (Frost), **II:** 152; **Supp. IV Part 1:** 15

Gigi (Colette; stage adaptation, Loos), **Supp. XVI:** 193

"Gigolo" (Plath), **Retro. Supp. II:** 257

"G.I. Graves in Tuscany" (Hugo), **Supp. VI:** 138

"Gila Bend" (Dickey), **Supp. IV Part 1:** 185–186

Gilb, Dagoberto, **Supp. XXV:** 138

Gilbert, Elizabeth, **Supp. XXII:** 83, 90

Gilbert, Jack, **Supp. IX:** 287

Gilbert, Peter, **Supp. IX:** 291, 300

Gilbert, Roger, **Supp. XI:** 124

Gilbert, Sandra M., **Retro. Supp. I:** 42; **Retro. Supp. II:** 324; **Supp. IX:** 66; **Supp. XV:** 270; **Supp. XXIV:** 28

Gilbert, Susan. *See* Dickinson, Mrs. William A.

Gilbert and Sullivan, **Supp. IV Part 1:** 389

"Gilbert Stuart Portrait of Washington, The" (Kooser), **Supp. XIX:** 124

Gil Blas (Le Sage), **II:** 290

Gilded Age, The (Twain), **III:** 504; **IV:** 198

Gilded Lapse of Time, A (Schnackenberg), **Supp. XV:** 258, **260–263**

"Gilded Lapse of Time, A" (Schnackenberg), **Supp. XV:** 257

"Gilded Six-Bits, The" (Hurston), **Supp. VI:** 154–155

Gilder, R. W., **Retro. Supp. II:** 66; **Supp. I Part 2:** 418

Gildersleeve, Basil, **Supp. I Part 1:** 369

Gilead (Robinson), **Supp. XXI:** 212, **216–220**, 223

Giles, H. A., **Retro. Supp. I:** 289

Giles, James R., **Supp. IX:** 11, 15; **Supp. XI:** 219, 223–224, 228, 234

"Giles Corey of the Salem Farms" (Longfellow), **II:** 505, 506; **Retro. Supp. II:** 166, 167

Giles Goat-Boy (Barth), **I:** 121, 122–123, 129, 130, 134, 135–138; **Supp. V:** 39

Gilgamesh: A New Rendering in English Verse (Ferry), **Supp. XXIV:** 147, **150–151**

Gill, Brendan, **Supp. I Part 2:** 659, 660

Gillespie, Nick, **Supp. XIV:** 298, 311

Gillette, Chester, **I:** 512

Gillian, Maria Mazziotti, **Supp. XXIII:** 248

Gilligan, Carol, **Supp. XIII:** 216; **Supp. XXII:** 18

Gillis, Jim, **IV:** 196

Gillis, Steve, **IV:** 195

Gilman, Charlotte Perkins, **Supp. I Part 2:** 637; **Supp. V:** 121, 284, 285; **Supp. XI: 193–211; Supp. XIII:** 295, 306; **Supp. XVI:** 84; **Supp. XXIII:** 26

Gilman, Daniel Coit, **Supp. I Part 1:** 361, 368, 370

Gilman, Richard, **IV:** 115; **Supp. IV Part 2:** 577; **Supp. XIII:** 100; **Supp. XIX:** 251

Gilmore, Eddy, **Supp. I Part 2:** 618

Gilmore, Lyman, **Supp. XXI:** 20, 22, 24

Gilmore, Mikal, **Supp. XVI:** 123, 124

Gilpin, Charles, **III:** 392

Gilpin, Dewitt, **Supp. XV:** 197

Gilpin, Laura, **Retro. Supp. I:** 7

Gilpin, Sam, **Supp. V:** 213

Gilpin, William, **Supp. IV Part 2:** 603

"Gil's Furniture Bought & Sold" (Cisneros), **Supp. VII:** 61–62, 64

Gilyard, Keith, **Supp. XXI:** 246

"Gimcrackery" articles (Briggs), **Supp. XVIII:** 8–9

"Gimpel the Fool" (Singer), **IV:** 14; **Retro. Supp. II:** 22, 307

Gimpel the Fool and Other Stories (Singer), **IV:** 1, 7–9, 10, 12

"Gin" (Levine), **Supp. V:** 193

"Gingerbread House, The" (Coover), **Supp. V:** 42–43

Gingerbread Lady, The (Simon), **Supp. IV Part 2:** 580, 583–584, 588

Gingerich, Willard, **Supp. IV Part 2:** 510

Gingertown (McKay), **Supp. X:** 132, 139

Gingold, Hermione, **Supp. XV:** 13

Gingrich, Arnold, **Retro. Supp. I:** 113; **Supp. XVII:** 88; **Supp. XX: 34**

Ginna, Robert, **Supp. IX:** 259

Ginsberg, Allen, **I:** 183; **Retro. Supp. I:** 411, 426, 427; **Retro. Supp. II:** 280; **Supp. II Part 1:** 30, 32, 58, **307–333; Supp. III Part 1:** 2, 91, 96, 98, 100, 222, 226; **Supp. III Part 2:** 541, 627; **Supp. IV Part 1:** 79, 90, 322; **Supp. IV Part 2:** 502; **Supp. V:** 168, 336; **Supp. VIII:** 239, 242–243, 289; **Supp. IX:** 299; **Supp. X:** 120, 204; **Supp. XI:** 135, 297; **Supp. XII:** 118–119, 121–122, 124, 126, 130–131, 136, 182; **Supp. XIV:** 15, 53, 54, 125, 137, 141, 142, 143–144, 148, 150, 269, 280, 283; **Supp. XV:** 134, 177, 263; **Supp. XVI:** 123, 135; **Supp. XVII:** 138, 243; **Supp. XVIII:** 20, 27, 29, 30; **Supp. XXI:** 53; **Supp. XXII:** 172, 225; **Supp. XXIII:** 211, 213, 215; **Supp. XXIV:** 34, 36, 37; **Supp. XXV:** 29

Gioia, Dana, **Supp. IX:** 279; **Supp. XII:** 209; **Supp. XIII:** 337; **Supp. XV: 111–131**, 251; **Supp. XVII:** 69, 72, 112; **Supp. XIX:** 117, 144; **Supp. XXI:** 99; **Supp. XXIII:** 112; **Supp. XXV:** 222

Giono, Jean, **Supp. XVI:** 135

Giordano, Tony J., **Supp. XXIII:** 125

Giotto di Bondone, **Supp. I Part 2:** 438; **Supp. XI:** 126

Giovani, Regula, **Supp. XV:** 270

Giovanni, Nikki, **Supp. I Part 1:** 66; **Supp. II Part 1:** 54; **Supp. IV Part 1:** 11; **Supp. VIII:** 214; **Supp. XXII:** 11

Giovanni's Room (Baldwin), **Retro. Supp. II:** 5, 6, **6–7**, 8, 10; **Supp. I Part 1:** 51, 52, 55–56, 57, 60, 63, 67; **Supp. III Part 1:** 125

Giovannitti, Arturo, **I:** 476; **Supp. XV:** 299, 301, 302, 307

"Giraffe" (Swenson), **Supp. IV Part 2:** 651

Giraldi, Giovanni Battista. *See* Cinthio

"Girl" (Kincaid), **Supp. VII:** 182–183

Girl, The (Le Sueur), **Supp. XXIII: 172–174**

"Girl, The" (Olds), **Supp. X:** 207

"Girl Friend Poems" (Wright), **Supp. XV:** 349

"Girl from Lynn Bathes Horse!!" (McCarriston), **Supp. XIV:** 266

"Girl from Red Lion, P.A., A" (Mencken), **III:** 111

Girl in Glass, The: Love Poems (W. J. Smith), **Supp. XIII:** 335

Girl in Landscape (Lethem), **Supp. XVIII:** 136, **141–143**

"Girl in the Grave, The" (McCoy), **Supp. XIII:** 170

Girl Like I, A (Loos), **Supp. XVI:** 181, 183, 184, 187, 194, 196

"Girl of the Golden West" (Didion), **Supp. IV Part 1:** 195, 208, 211

Girl of the Golden West, The (Puccini), **III:** 139

Girl of the Limberlost (film), **Supp. XX:** 223

Girl of the Limberlost (Stratton-Porter), **Supp. XX:** **211, 221–222**

"Girl on a Scaffold" (C. Frost), **Supp. XV:** 98

"Girl on the Baggage Truck, The" (O'Hara), **III:** 371–372

"Girls" (Gallagher), **Supp. XXIV:** 174–175, 177

Girls at Play (Theroux), **Supp. VIII:** 314, 315, 316, **317**

"Girls at the Sphinx, The" (Farrell), **II:** 45

"Girls in Their Summer Dresses, The" (Shaw), **Supp. XIX:** 246

Girl Sleuth, The: A Feminist Guide (Mason), **Supp. VIII:** 133, 135, **139,** 142

"Girl's Story, A" (Bambara), **Supp. XI:** 10–11

"Girl the Prince Liked, The" (Z. Fitzgerald), **Supp. IX:** 71

Girl Who Had to Die, The (Holding), **Supp. XXII:** **126–127**

Girl Who Loved Tom Gordon, The (King), **Supp. V:** 138, 152

"Girl Who Raised Pigeons, The" (E. P. Jones), **Supp. XXII:** 143

Girl with Curious Hair (Wallace), **Supp. X:** 301, **305–308**

"Girl with Curious Hair" (Wallace), **Supp. X:** 306

"Girl with Silver Eyes, The" (Hammett), **Supp. IV Part 1:** 344, 345

"Girl with Talent, The" (Z. Fitzgerald), **Supp. IX:** 71

Girodias, Maurice, **III:** 171; **Supp. XI:** 297

Giroux, Robert, **Retro. Supp. II:** 177, 229, 235; **Supp. IV Part 1:** 280; **Supp. VIII:** 195; **Supp. XV:** 146

Gish, Dorothy, **Retro. Supp. I:** 103

Gish, Lillian, **Supp. XVI:** 184

Gissing, George, **II:** 138, 144

Gitagovinda, **Supp. XXII:** 258

Gita-govínda: Love Songs of Radha and Krishna (Jayadeva; Siegel, trans.), **Supp. XXII:** 258

Gittings, Robert, **II:** 531

Gittleman, Edwin, **Supp. XXV:** 237, 251

"Given" (C. Frost), **Supp. XV:** 96

Given Sugar, Given Salt (Hirshfield), **Supp. XXIII:** 133

"Give Us Back Our Country" (Masters), **Supp. I Part 2:** 472

Give Us This Day (film, Dmytryk), **Supp. XX:** **40–41**

"Give Way, Ye Gates" (Roethke), **III:** 536

"Give Your Heart to the Hawks" (Jeffers), **Supp. II Part 2:** 433

"Giving Blood" (Updike), **IV:** 226; **Retro. Supp. I:** 332

Giving Good Weight (McPhee), **Supp. III Part 1:** 307

"Giving in to You" (X. J. Kennedy), **Supp. XV:** 160

"Giving Myself Up" (Strand), **Supp. IV Part 2:** 627

Giving Up America (Abraham), **Supp. XXIV:** 2, 3, **7–9**

Giving Up the Ghost (Moraga), **Supp. XXIII:** **197–199**

G. K. the DJ (Keillor), **Supp. XVI:** 171

Glackens, William, **Retro. Supp. II:** 103

Gladden, Washington, **III:** 293; **Supp. I Part 1:** 5

Gladstone, William Ewart, **Supp. I Part 2:** 419

"Gladys Poem, The" (Alvarez), **Supp. VII:** 10

"Glance at German 'Kultur,' A" (Bourne), **I:** 228

Glance Away, A (Wideman), **Supp. X:** 320

"Glance from the Bridge, A" (Wilbur), **Supp. III Part 2:** 551

"Glance in the Mirror, A" (Swados), **Supp. XIX:** 261–262

Glance toward Shakespeare, A (Chapman), **Supp. XIV:** 44

Glancy, Diane, **Supp. XXI:** 246

Glanville-Hicks, Peggy, **Supp. IV Part 1:** 84

Glare (Ammons), **Supp. VII:** 35–36

Glasgow, Cary, **II:** 173, 182

Glasgow, Ellen, **II: 173–195; IV:** 328; **Supp. X:** 228, 234; **Supp. XXIV:** 30; **Supp. XXV:** 201

Glasmon, Kubec, **Supp. XIII:** 166

Glaspell, Susan, **Supp. III Part 1: 175–191; Supp. X:** 46; **Supp. XVII:** 99; **Supp. XXI:** 5

"Glass" (Francis), **Supp. IX:** 80

Glass, Irony, and God (Carson), **Supp. XII:** 97, **104–106**

Glass, Philip, **Supp. XXI:** 146, 147

"Glass Ark, The" (Komunyakaa), **Supp. XIII:** 129

Glass Bees, The (Jünger; Bogan and Mayer, trans.), **Supp. III Part 1:** 63

"Glass Blower of Venice" (Malamud), **Supp. I Part 2:** 450

"Glass Essay, The" (Carson), **Supp. XII:** **104–105**

"Glass Face in the Rain, A: New Poems" (Stafford), **Supp. XI:** **327–328**

Glass Key, The (Hammett), **Supp. IV Part 1:** 351–353

"Glass Meadows" (Bausch), **Supp. VII:** 53–54

Glass Menagerie, The (T. Williams), **I:** 81; **IV:** 378, 379, 380, 382, 383, 385, 386, 387, 388, 389, 390, 391, 392, 393–394, 395, 398; **Supp. IV Part 1:** 84; **Supp. XXV:** 101

"Glass Mountain, The" (Barthelme), **Supp. IV Part 1:** 47

"Glass Tent, The" (Everwine), **Supp. XV:** 76

Glatstein, Jacob, **Supp. X:** 70

Glazer, Nathan, **Supp. VIII:** 93, 243

"Gleaners, The" (Merwin), **Supp. III Part 1:** 346

Gleanings in Europe (Cooper), **I:** 346

Gleason, Ralph J., **Supp. IX:** 16

Glenday, Michael, **Retro. Supp. II:** 210

Glengarry Glen Ross (film), **Supp. XIV:** 242

Glengarry Glen Ross (Mamet), **Supp. XIV:** 239, 240, 242, 245, 246, 250, 254, 255

Glimcher, Arne, **Supp. VIII:** 73

"Glimpses" (Jones), **Supp. XI:** 218

Glimpses of the Moon, The (Wharton), **II:** 189–190; **IV:** 322–323; **Retro. Supp. I:** 381

"Glimpses of Vietnamese Life" (Levertov), **Supp. III Part 1:** 282

Glisson, J. T., **Supp. X:** 234

Gloria Mundi (Frederic), **II:** 144–145

Gloria Naylor (Fowler), **Supp. VIII:** 224

"Glorious Fourth, The" (Ryan as Quin), **Supp. XVIII:** 229

Glorious Ones, The (Prose), **Supp. XVI:** 251

Glory, The (Wouk), **Supp. XXV:** 254, 257, 265–266

Glory of Hera, The (Gordon), **II:** 196–197, 198, 199, 217–220

Glory of the Conquered, The (Glaspell), **Supp. III Part 1:** 176

Gloss, Molly, **Supp. XXIII:** 280

Glossary of Literary Terms (Abrams), **Supp. XVI:** 19

Glotfelty, Cheryll, **Supp. IX:** 25

Glover, Joyce Lee, **Supp. XIX:** 112

Glover, Michael, **Supp. XXIV:** 168

Glow, The (Wrigley), **Supp. XVIII:** 295

"Glow, The" (Wrigley), **Supp. XVIII:** 296–297, 307

Gluck, Christoph Willibald, **II:** 210, 211

Glück, Louise, **Supp. V: 77–94; Supp. VIII:** 272; **Supp. X:** 209; **Supp. XIV:** 269; **Supp. XV:** 19, 252; **Supp. XVII:** 241; **Supp. XXV:** 222

"Glutton, The" (Shapiro), **Supp. II Part 2:** 705

"Glutton for Punishment, A" (Yates), **Supp. XI:** 341

Glyph (Everett), **Supp. XVIII: 60–61**

Gnädiges Fräulein, The (T. Williams), **IV:** 382, 395, 398

Gnomes and Occasions (Nemerov), **III:** 269

Gnomologia (Fuller), **II:** 111

"Gnothis Seauton" (Emerson), **II:** 11, 18–19

Go (Holmes), **Supp. XIV:** 144

"Go Ahead; Goodbye; Good Luck; and Watch Out" (Bronk), **Supp. XXI:** 31

"Goal of Intellectual Men, The" (Eberhart), **I:** 529–530

Go-Between, The (Hartley), **Supp. I Part 1:** 293

Gobineau, Joseph Arthur de, **Supp. XIV:** 209

God (Allen), **Supp. XV:** 3

God and the American Writer (Kazin), **Supp. VIII:** 108–109

Godard, Jean-Luc, **Supp. I Part 2:** 558

Godbey (Masters), **Supp. I Part 2:** 472

God Bless You, Mr. Rosewater (Vonnegut), **Supp. II Part 2:** 758, 767, 768–769, 771, 772

Goddess Abides, The (Buck), **Supp. II Part 1:** 129, 131–132

Gödel, Kurt, **Supp. IV Part 1:** 43

Godfather (Puzo), **Supp. IV Part 1:** 390

Godfires (Hoffman), **Supp. XVIII:** 81–82

God in Ruins, A (Uris), **Supp. XX: 247, 256**

"God in the Doorway" (Dillard), **Supp. VI:** 28

"God is a distant-stately Lover" (Dickinson), **I:** 471

Godkin, E. L., **II:** 274

God Knows (Heller), **Supp. IV Part 1:** 386, 388–389

God Made Alaska for the Indians (Reed), **Supp. X:** 241

God of His Fathers, The (London), **II:** 469

God of Vengeance, The (Asch), **IV:** 11; **Supp. XXIII: 5, 8–9**

Go Down, Moses (Faulkner), **Retro. Supp. I:** 75, 82, 85, 86, 88, 89, 90, 92; **Supp. XVIII:** 203

"Go Down, Moses" (Faulkner), **II:** 71–72

Go Down, Moses (Hayden), **Supp. II Part 1:** 365

Go Down, Moses and Other Stories (Faulkner), **II:** 71; **Supp. X:** 52

"Go Down Death A Funeral Sermon" (Johnson), **Supp. IV Part 1:** 7

"God Rest Ye Merry, Gentlemen" (Hemingway), **IV:** 122

Godric (Buechner), **Supp. XII:** 53

Gods, The (Goldbarth), **Supp. XII:** 189, 190

Gods Arrive, The (Wharton), **IV:** 326–327; **Retro. Supp. I:** 382

God Save the Child (Parker), **Supp. XIX:** 183–184

"God Save the Rights of Man" (Freneau), **Supp. II Part 1:** 268

"Gods|Children" (Swenson), **Supp. IV Part 2:** 645

"God's Christ Theory" (Carson), **Supp. XII: 106**

God's Country (Everett), **Supp. XVIII: 57–58, 64, 65**

God's Country and My People (Morris), **III:** 238

Gods Determinations touching his Elect: and the Elects Combat in their Conversion, and Coming up to God in Christ together with the Comfortable Effects thereof (Taylor), **IV:** 155–160, 165

God-Seeker, The (Lewis), **II:** 456

God Sends Sunday (Bontemps), **Supp. XXII:** 2, 3, 9

God's Favorite (Simon), **Supp. IV Part 2:** 575, 586, 588, 590

"God's Fool" (Gibran), **Supp. XX:** 118

God's Little Acre (Caldwell), **I:** 288, 289, 290, 297, 298–302, 305–306, 309, 310; **Supp. XXII:** 196

God's Man: A Novel in Wood Cuts (Ward), **I:** 31

Gods of Peg¿na, The (Dunsany), **Supp. XXV:** 113

Gods of Winter, The (Gioia), **Supp. XV:** 112, **121–125**

"Gods of Winter, The" (Gioia), **Supp. XV:** 117

"God's Peace in November" (Jeffers), **Supp. II Part 2:** 420

God's Silence (F. Wright), **Supp. XVII:** 240, 246–247

"God Stiff" (Carson), **Supp. XII: 106**

God's Trombones (Johnson), **Supp. II Part 1:** 201

"God's Youth" (Untermeyer), **Supp. XV:** 296

"God the Father and the Empty House" (McCarriston), **Supp. XIV:** 273

Godwin, William, **II:** 304; **III:** 415; **Supp. I Part 1:** 126, 146; **Supp. I Part 2:** 512, 513–514, 522, 709, 719

God without Thunder (Ransom), **III:** 495–496, 499

Godwulf Manuscript, The (Parker), **Supp. XIX: 178–182**

Goebbels, Josef, **III:** 560

Goebel, Irma, **Supp. X:** 95

Goen, C. C., **I:** 560

Goethe, Johann Wolfgang von, **I:** 181, 396, 587–588; **II:** 5, 6, 320, 344, 488, 489, 492, 502, 556; **III:** 395, 453, 607, 612, 616; **IV:** 50, 64, 173, 326; **Retro. Supp. I:** 360; **Retro. Supp. II:** 94; **Supp. I Part 2:** 423, 457; **Supp. II Part 1:** 26; **Supp. III Part 1:** 63; **Supp. IX:** 131, 308; **Supp. X:** 60; **Supp. XI:** 169; **Supp. XVIII:** 278; **Supp. XX: 84; Supp. XXIV:** 152

Go for the Body (Lacy), **Supp. XV:** 201, 204

Gogan, Robert, **Supp. XXI:** 24

Gogol, Nikolai, **I:** 296; **IV:** 1, 4; **Retro. Supp. I:** 266, 269; **Supp. VIII:** 14; **Supp. XVII:** 45; **Supp. XVIII:** 102; **Supp. XXII:** 59

Goia, Dana, **Supp. XIX:** 121

Goines, Donald, **Supp. XXIII:** 174

"Going, Going, Gone" (Skloot), **Supp. XX: 207**

Going, William T., **Supp. VIII:** 126

Going After Cacciato (O'Brien), **Supp. V:** 237, 238, 239, 244–246, 248, 249

Going All the Way (Wakefield), **Supp. VIII:** 43

"Going Critical" (Bambara), **Supp. XI:** 14

Going Down (Markson), **Supp. XVII:** 136, 138, **139–140,** 141, 142–143, 144, 145

Going for the Rain (Ortiz), **Supp. IV Part 2:** 499, 505–508, 509, 514

"Going Home by Last Night" (Kinnell), **Supp. III Part 1:** 244

"Going Home in America" (Hardwick), **Supp. III Part 1:** 205

"Going Home"(Kenny), **Supp. XXIII:** 144, 148

"Going North" (Salinas), **Supp. XIII:** 316

Going Places (L. Michaels), **Supp. XVI:** 201, **203–206**

"Going Places" (L. Michaels), **Supp. XVI:** 203

"Going South" (J. W. Miller), **Supp. XX: 169**

Going South (Lardner and Buck), **II:** 427

Going To and Fro and Walking Up and Down (Reznikoff), **Supp. XIV:** 280, 282, 284, 285

Going to Meet the Man (Baldwin), **Supp. I Part 1:** 60, 62–63; **Supp. XX:** 147

"Going to Meet the Man" (Baldwin), **Retro. Supp. II:** 8, 9; **Supp. I Part 1:** 62–63

"Going to Naples" (Welty), **IV:** 278; **Retro. Supp. I:** 352, 353

"Going to Shrewsbury" (Jewett), **II:** 393

"Going to the Bakery" (Bishop), **Supp. I Part 1:** 93

Going-to-the-Stars (Lindsay), **Supp. I Part 2:** 398

Going-to-the-Sun (Lindsay), **Supp. I Part 2:** 397–398

Going to the Territory (Ellison), **Retro. Supp. II:** 119, 123–124

"Going towards Pojoaque, A December Full Moon/72" (Harjo), **Supp. XII:** 218

"Going Under" (Dubus), **Supp. VII:** 83

"Gold" (Francis), **Supp. IX:** 82

Gold (O'Neill), **III:** 391

Gold, Arthur, **Supp. XXIV:** 160, 161

Gold, Don, **Supp. XXII:** 258

Gold, Michael, **II:** 26; **IV:** 363, 364, 365; **Retro. Supp. II:** 323; **Supp. I Part 1:** 331; **Supp. I Part 2:** 609; **Supp. XIV:** 288; **Supp. XXII:** 277

Goldbarth, Albert, **Supp. XII: 175–195**

Goldbarth's Book of Occult Phenomena (Goldbarth), **Supp. XII:** 181

Goldberg, Carole, **Supp. XXII:** 207

Goldberg, Michael, **Supp. XXIII:** 210, 216, 217

Goldberg, S. L., **Supp. VIII:** 238

"Gold Bug, The" (Poe), **III:** 410, 413, 419, 420

Gold Bug Variations, The (Powers), **Supp. IX:** 210, 212, **216–217,** 219

Gold Cell, The (Olds), **Supp. X: 206–209**

Gold Diggers, The (Monette), **Supp. X:** 153

Golde, Miss (Mencken's Secretary), **III:** 104, 107

Golden, Harry, **III:** 579, 581; **Supp. VIII:** 244

Golden, Mike, **Supp. XI:** 294, 295, 297, 299, 303

Golden Age, The (Gurney), **Supp. V:** 101–103

Golden Apples (Rawlings), **Supp. X: 228–229,** 230, 234

Golden Apples, The (Welty), **IV:** 261, 271–274, 281, 293; **Retro. Supp. I:** 341, 342, 343, **350–351,** 352, 355

Golden Apples of the Sun, The (Bradbury), **Supp. IV Part 1:** 102, 103

Golden Book of Springfield, The (Lindsay), **Supp. I Part 2:** 376, 379, 395, 396

Golden Bough, The (Frazer), **II:** 204, 549; **III:** 6–7; **Supp. I Part 1:** 18; **Supp. IX:** 123; **Supp. X:** 124

Golden Bowl, The (James), **II:** 320, 333, 335; **Retro. Supp. I:** 215, 216, 218–219, 232, **234–235,** 374

Golden Boy (Odets), **Supp. II Part 2:** 538, 539, 540–541, 546, 551

Golden Calves, The (Auchincloss), **Supp. IV Part 1:** 35

Golden Child (Hwang), **Supp. XXI:** 147–148

Golden Day, The (Mumford), **Supp. II Part 2:** 471, 475, 477, 483, 484, 488–489, 493

Golden Fleece, The (Gurney), **Supp. V:** 97

Golden Gate (film, Madden), **Supp. XXI:** 147

Golden Gate, The (Seth), **Supp. XVII:** 117

Golden Gate Country (Atherton), **Supp. XXIV:** 27

Golden Grove, The: Selected Passages from the Sermons and Writings of Jeremy Taylor (L. P. Smith), **Supp. XIV:** 345

"Golden Heifer, The" (Wylie), **Supp. I Part 2:** 707

"Golden Honeymoon, The" (Lardner), **II:** 429–430, 431

Golden Journey, The (W. J. Smith and Bogan, comps.), **Supp. XIII:** 347

Golden Ladder series (S. and A. Warner), **Supp. XVIII:** 267

"Golden Lads" (Marquand), **III:** 56

Golden Legend, The (Longfellow), **II:** 489, 490, 495, 505, 506, 507; **Retro. Supp. II:** 159, 165, 166

Golden Mean and Other Poems, The (Tate and Wills), **IV:** 122

Golden Peacock (Atherton), **Supp. XXIV:** 26

"Golden Retrievals" (Doty), **Supp. XI:** 132

Golden Shakespeare, The: An Anthology (L. P. Smith), **Supp. XIV:** 349

Golden Slippers: An Anthology of Negro Poetry for Young Readers (Bontemps, ed.), **Supp. XXII:** 5, 11

Goldensohn, Lorrie, **Retro. Supp. II:** 51

Golden State (Bidart), **Supp. XV:** 21, **23–25**

"Golden State" (Bidart), **Supp. XV:** 23, 24, 25

Golden States (Cunningham), **Supp. XV:** 55, **56–59,** 63

Golden Treasury of Best Songs and Lyrical Poems in the English Language (Palgrave), **Retro. Supp. I:** 124

Golden Treasury of the Best Songs and Lyrical Poems in the English Language (Palgrave), **Supp. XIV:** 340

Golden Whales of California and Other Rhymes in the American Language, The (Lindsay), **Supp. I Part 2:** 394–395, 396

"Goldfish Bowl, The" (Francis), **Supp. IX:** 78

Gold Fools (Sorrentino), **Supp. XXI:** 237

Goldin Boys, The (Epstein), **Supp. XIV:** 112

Golding, Arthur, **III:** 467, 468

Golding, William, **Supp. IV Part 1:** 297

Goldini, Carlo, **II:** 274

Goldkorn Tales (Epstein), **Supp. XII:** **163–164**

Goldman, Albert, **Supp. XI:** 299

Goldman, Arnold, **Supp. XXI:** 13

Goldman, Emma, **III:** 176, 177; **Supp. I Part 2:** 524; **Supp. XVII:** 96, 103, 104; **Supp. XXIII:** 162

Goldman, Francisco, **Supp. XXV:** **49–62**

Goldman, William, **Supp. IV Part 2:** 474

"Gold Mountain Stories" project (Kingston), **Supp. V:** 164

Gold of Chickaree, The (S. and A. Warner), **Supp. XVIII:** 267, 268, 269

Goldring, Douglas, **III:** 458

Goldsmith, Oliver, **II:** 273, 282, 299, 304, 308, 314, 315, 514; **Retro. Supp. I:** 335; **Supp. I Part 1:** 310; **Supp. I Part 2:** 503, 714, 716; **Supp. XVIII:** 12

Gold Standard and the Logic of Naturalism, The (W. B. Michaels), **Retro. Supp. I:** 369

Goldstein, Laurence, **Supp. XXI:** 134

Goldstein, Rebecca, **Supp. XVII:** 44

Goldwater, Barry, **I:** 376; **III:** 38

Goldwyn, Samuel, **Retro. Supp. II:** 199; **Supp. I Part 1:** 281; **Supp. XXIV:** 28; **Supp. XXV:** 195

Golem, The (Leivick), **IV:** 6; **Supp. XXIII:** 8

"Golgotha Is a Mountain" (Bontemps), **Supp. XXII:** 3, 8

"Goliardic Song" (Hecht), **Supp. X:** 63

"Go Like This" (Moore), **Supp. X:** 165

Goll, Ivan, **Supp. III Part 1:** 235, 243–244; **Supp. III Part 2:** 621

Gomes, Albert, **Supp. XXI:** 160

Goncharova, Natalya, **Supp. IX:** 66

Goncourt, Edmond de, **II:** 325, 328; **III:** 315, 317–318, 321; **Retro. Supp. I:** 226

Goncourt, Jules de, **II:** 328; **III:** 315, 317–318, 321

Gone Fishin' (Mosley), **Supp. XIII:** **235–236,** 240

"Gone to War" (E. Stoddard), **Supp. XV:** 282

"Gone West" (Rodriguez), **Supp. XIV:** 308

Gone with the Wind (film), **Retro. Supp. I:** 113

Gone with the Wind (Mitchell), **II:** 177; **Retro. Supp. I:** 340; **Supp. XX:** 243; **Supp. XXII:** 190, 195

Gongora y Argote, Luis de, **II:** 552

Gonzalez, David, **Supp. VIII:** 85

González, Jovita, **Supp. XIX:** 99

Gonzo: The Life of Hunter S. Thompson (Wenner and Seymour), **Supp. XXIV:** 280, 281, 282, 288

Gooch, Brad, **Supp. XII:** 121; **Supp. XXIII:** 218, 220

Good, George, **Supp. XI:** 306

"Good, the Plaid, and the Ugly, The" (Wasserstein), **Supp. XV:** 327

"Good and Not So Good, The" (Dunn), **Supp. XI:** 141

"Good Anna, The" (Stein), **IV:** 37, 40, 43

Good As Gold (Heller), **Supp. IV Part 1:** 386, 388, 394

Good as I Been to You (album, Dylan), **Supp. XVIII:** 28

"Good As Yesterday" (Muñoz), **Supp. XXV:** 134, 135

Good Boys and Dead Girls and Other Essays (Gordon), **Supp. IV Part 1:** 309–310

"Good Brother" (Muñoz), **Supp. XXV:** 135

Good Brother, The (Offutt), **Supp. XIX:** 163, **168–169**

"Good-by and Keep Cold" (Frost), **Retro. Supp. I:** 135

"Good-bye" (Emerson), **II:** 19

"Goodbye, Christ" (Hughes), **Retro. Supp. I:** 202, 203

Goodbye, Columbus (P. Roth), **Retro. Supp. II:** 280, 281, 290; **Supp. III Part 2:** 403–406; **Supp. XIV:** 112; **Supp. XX:** 177

"Goodbye, Columbus" (P. Roth), **Supp. III Part 2:** 401, 404, 408–409, 411

Goodbye, Columbus and Five Short Stories (P. Roth), **Retro. Supp. II:** 279

"Goodbye, Goldeneye" (Swenson), **Supp. IV Part 2:** 651

"Goodbye, Mr. Chipstein" (Epstein), **Supp. XIV:** 103, 108

"Goodbye, My Brother" (Cheever), **Supp. I Part 1:** 175, 177, 193

"Goodbye and Good Luck" (Paley), **Supp. VI:** 219, 223

Goodbye Girl, The (film), **Supp. IV Part 2:** 589

Goodbye Girl, The (musical), **Supp. IV Part 2:** 576, 588

Goodbye Girl, The (Simon), **Supp. IV Part 2:** 575

Goodbye Look, The (Macdonald), **Supp. IV Part 2:** 473, 474

"Good-Bye My Fancy" (Whitman), **IV:** 348

"Goodbye to All That" (Didion), **Supp. IV Part 1:** 197

Goodbye to All That (Graves), **I:** 477

Goodbye to Berlin (Isherwood), **Supp. XIV:** 159, 161, 162, 169

"Good-Bye to the Mezzogiorno" (Auden), **Supp. II Part 1:** 19

"Goodbye to the Poetry of Calcium" (Wright), **Supp. III Part 2:** 599

"Good Company" (Matthews), **Supp. IX:** 160

"Good Country People" (O'Connor), **III:** 343, 350, 351, 352, 358; **Retro. Supp.**

II: 229, 232
Good Day to Die, A (Harrison), **Supp. VIII: 42–44,** 45, 47
Good Day to Die, A (O'Nan as James Coltrane), **Supp. XXV:** 146
Good Doctor, The (Simon), **Supp. IV Part 2:** 575, 585
Good Earth, The (Buck), **Supp. I Part 1:** 49; **Supp. II Part 1:** 115–175, 118, 125, 132
Good European, The (Blackmur), **Supp. II Part 1:** 91
Good Evening Mr. & Mrs. America, and All the Ships at Sea (Bausch), **Supp. VII:** 41, 47, 52
"Good Friday" (Jarman), **Supp. XVII:** 116
"Good Girl" (Peacock), **Supp. XIX:** 199
Good Gray Poet, The (O'Connor), **Retro. Supp. I:** 407
Good Health and How We Won It (Sinclair), **Supp. V:** 285–286
Good Hearts (Price), **Supp. VI:** 259, 265
"Good Job Gone, A" (Hughes), **Retro. Supp. I:** 204
Good Journey, A (Ortiz), **Supp. IV Part 2:** 497, 499, 503, 505, 509–510, 514
Good Luck, Miss Wyckoff (Inge), **Supp. XXV:** 93, 95, 106–107
Good Luck in Cracked Italian (Hugo), **Supp. VI:** 133, 137–138
Goodman, Allegra, **Supp. XII:** 159; **Supp. XVI:** 205; **Supp. XX: 177**
Goodman, Ellen, **Supp. XVI:** 103
Goodman, Jack, **Supp. XXI:** 277
Goodman, Jenny, **Supp. XV:** 343, 344
Goodman, Paul, **I:** 218, 261; **III:** 39; **Supp. I Part 2:** 524; **Supp. VIII:** 239–240
Goodman, Philip, **III:** 105, 108
Goodman, Walter, **Supp. IV Part 2:** 532
Good Man Is Hard to Find, A (O'Connor), **III:** 339, 343–345
"Good Man Is Hard to Find, A" (O'Connor), **III:** 339, 344, 353; **Retro. Supp. II:** 230–231
Good Man Is Hard to Find and Other Stories, A (O'Connor), **Retro. Supp. II:** 229, **230–232**
Good Morning, America (Sandburg), **III:** 592–593
"Good Morning, Major" (Marquand), **III:** 56
Good Morning, Midnight (Rhys), **Supp. III Part 1:** 43
"Good Morning, Revolution" (Hughes), **Retro. Supp. I:** 201, 203
Good Morning Blues: The Autobiography of Count Basie (Murray), **Supp. XIX:** 159
Good Morning Revolution: Uncollected Writings of Social Protest (Hughes), **Retro. Supp. I:** 194, 201, 202, 209
Good Mother, The (Miller), **Supp. XII:** 289, **290–294,** 299, 301
Good News (Abbey), **Supp. XIII:** 11–12
"Good News from New-England" (Johnson), **Supp. I Part 1:** 115
Good News of Death and Other Poems (Simpson), **Supp. IX:** 265, **268–269**

"Goodnight, Saigon" (lecture, Caputo), **Supp. XIX:** 17, 30
Good Night, Willie Lee, I'll See You in the Morning (Walker), **Supp. III Part 2:** 520, 531
"Good Oak" (Leopold), **Supp. XIV:** 185, 187, 191
"Good Old Times, The: New York Fifty Years Ago" (Briggs), **Supp. XVIII:** 15
"Good Pine, A" (Offutt), **Supp. XIX:** 174
Goodrich, Chris, **Supp. XXII:** 206, 214
Goodrich, Samuel G., **Supp. I Part 1:** 38
Good Scent from a Strange Mountain, A (R. O. Butler), **Supp. XII:** 62, **70–72**
Good School, A (Yates), **Supp. XI:** 334, **346–347,** 348, 349
"*Good Shepherdess, The*/La Buena Pastora" (Mora), **Supp. XIII:** 228–229
Good Wife, The (O'Nan), **Supp. XXV:** 145, 149
Good Will (Smiley), **Supp. VI:** 292, **299–300**
Goodwin, K. L., **III:** 478
Goodwin, Stephen, **Supp. V:** 314, 316, 322, 323, 325
"Good Word for Winter, A" (Lowell), **Supp. I Part 2:** 420
Goodwyn, Janet, **Retro. Supp. I:** 370
Goody, Alex, **Supp. XXII:** 160
"Goophered Grapevine, The" (Chesnutt), **Supp. XIV:** 57, **58–61**
"Goose Fish, The" (Nemerov), **III:** 272, 284
"Goose Pond" (Kunitz), **Supp. III Part 1:** 262
Goose-Step, The (Sinclair), **Supp. V:** 276
Gordimer, Nadine, **Supp. XV:** 251
Gordon, Ambrose, **Supp. XV:** 144
Gordon, A. R., **III:** 199
Gordon, Caroline, **II: 196–222,** 536, 537; **III:** 454, 482; **IV:** 123, 126–127, 139, 282; **Retro. Supp. II:** 177, 222, 229, 233, 235; **Supp. II Part 1:** 139
Gordon, Charles G., **I:** 454
Gordon, Don, **Supp. X:** 119
Gordon, Eugene, **Supp. II Part 1:** 170; **Supp. XVIII:** 280
Gordon, Fran, **Supp. XIII:** 111
Gordon, James Morris, **II:** 197
Gordon, Lois, **Supp. IV Part 1:** 48; **Supp. V:** 46
Gordon, Lyndall, **Retro. Supp. I:** 55
Gordon, Mary, **Supp. IV Part 1: 297–317**
Gordon, Neil, **Supp. XVI:** 156
Gordon, Peter, **Supp. XII:** 3–4, 4–5, 8
Gordon, Ruth, **IV:** 357; **Supp. XX: 50**
Gore, Thomas Pryor, **Supp. IV Part 2:** 679
Gores, Joe, **Supp. XXI:** 70
Gorey, Edward, **IV:** 430, 436; **Supp. XXIII:** 209
Gorilla, My Love (Bambara), **Supp. XI:** 1, **2–7**
"Gorilla, My Love" (Bambara), **Supp. XI:** 2, 3–4
Gorki, Maxim, **I:** 478; **II:** 49; **III:** 402; **IV:** 299; **Supp. I Part 1:** 5, 51; **Supp. XIX:** 241

Gorky, Maxim, **Supp. XXIII:** 1, 4
Gorman, Herbert, **Supp. XXV:** 25
Gorney, Cynthia, **Supp. XVI:** 112
Gorra, Michael, **Supp. V:** 71
Goslings, The (Sinclair), **Supp. V:** 276, 281
Go South to Sorrow (Rowan), **Supp. XIV:** 306
Gospel According to Joe, The (Gurney), **Supp. V:** 99
"Gospel According to Saint Mark, The" (Gordon), **Supp. IV Part 1:** 310
Gospel according to the Son (Mailer), **Retro. Supp. II:** 213
"Gospel for the Twentieth Century, The" (Locke), **Supp. XIV:** 206
"Gospel of Beauty, The" (Lindsay), **Supp. I Part 2:** 380, 382, 384, 385, 391, 396
Gospels, The (di Donato), **Supp. XX: 45–46**
Gospel Singer, The (Crews), **Supp. XI:** 102, **109**
Gosse, Edmund, **II:** 538; **IV:** 350; **Supp. VIII:** 157
"Gossip" (Conroy), **Supp. XVI:** 71–72
Gossips, Gorgons, and Crones: The Fates of the Earth (Caputi), **Supp. IV Part 1:** 335
Go Tell It on the Mountain (Baldwin), **Retro. Supp. II:** 1, 2, 3, **4–5,** 7, 14; **Supp. I Part 1:** 48, 49, 50, 51, 52, 53–54, 55, 56, 57, 59, 61, 63, 64, 67; **Supp. II Part 1:** 170
Gotera, Vince, **Supp. XIII:** 115, 116, 119, 121, 127
Gothic Revival, The: An Essay on the History of Taste (Clark), **Supp. XIV:** 348
Gothic Writers (Thomson, Voller, and Frank, eds.), **Retro. Supp. II:** 273
"Go to the Devil and Shake Yourself" (song), **Supp. I Part 2:** 580
"Go to the Shine That's on a Tree" (Eberhart), **I:** 523
Go to the Widow-Maker (Jones), **Supp. XI:** 214, **225–226,** 227, 229, 233
"Gots Is What You Got" (Di Piero), **Supp. XIX:** 35, 36, 38, 41, 42, 45–46
Gottfried, Alex, **Supp. XIX:** 260
Gottfried, Martin, **Supp. IV Part 2:** 584
Gotthelf, Allan, **Supp. IV Part 2:** 528
Gottlieb, Adolph, **Supp. XV:** 144
Gottlieb, Edward, **Supp. XX: 250**
Gottlieb, Leopold, **Supp. XXIII:** 6
Gottlieb, Morton, **Supp. XVI:** 196
Gottlieb, Robert, **Supp. IV Part 2:** 474
Gottschalk and the Grande Tarantelle (Brooks), **Supp. III Part 1:** 86
"Gottschalk and the Grande Tarantelle" (Brooks), **Supp. III Part 1:** 86–87
Gould (Dixon), **Supp. XII:** 152, **153**
Gould, Edward Sherman, **I:** 346
Gould, Janice, **Supp. IV Part 1:** 322, 327; **Supp. XII:** 229
Gould, Jay, **I:** 4
Gould, Joe, **Supp. XV:** 143
Gourd Dancer, The (Momaday), **Supp. IV Part 2:** 481, 487, 491, 493
Gourmont, Remy de, **I:** 270, 272; **II:** 528, 529; **III:** 457, 467–468, 477; **Retro.**

Supp. I: 55

Gouverneurs de la Rosée (Roumain), **Supp. IV Part 1:** 360, 367

Government Girl (film, Nichols), **Supp. XVIII:** 247

"Governors of Wyoming, The" (Proulx), **Supp. VII:** 264

"Gowane"(Kenny), **Supp. XXIII:** 147–148

Goyen, William, **Supp. V:** 220

Grabhorn, Janet, **Supp. XV:** 142

"Grace" (Budbill), **Supp. XIX:** 2

"Grace" (Dubus), **Supp. VII:** 91

"Grace" (Harjo), **Supp. XII:** 224

Grace Notes (Dove), **Supp. IV Part 1:** 248–250, 252

Grace (Eventually): Thoughts on Faith (Lamott), **Supp. XX: 143–145**

Grade, Chaim, **Supp. XVII:** 41

"Graduation" (Dubus), **Supp. VII:** 84

Grady, Henry W., **Supp. I Part 1:** 370

Graeber, Laurel, **Supp. V:** 15

Graham, Billy, **I:** 308

Graham, David, **Supp. XV:** 104; **Supp. XIX:** 81

Graham, Don, **Supp. XI:** 252, 254

Graham, Jorie, **Supp. IX:** 38, 52; **Supp. X:** 73; **Supp. XII:** 209; **Supp. XIII:** 85; **Supp. XVII:** 110, 111, 133, 240, 241, 242

Graham, Martha, **Supp. XI:** 152

Graham, Maryemma, **Retro. Supp. I:** 201, 204

Graham, Nan, **Supp. XII:** 272

Graham, Sheilah, **II:** 94; **Retro. Supp. I:** 97, 113–114, 115; **Supp. IX:** 63

Graham, Shirley, **Supp. I Part 1:** 51; **Supp. XXI:** 277. *See also* Du Bois, Shirley Graham

Graham, Stephen, **Supp. I Part 2:** 397

Graham, Tom (pseudonym). *See* Lewis, Sinclair

"Graham House, April '76"(Balakian), **Supp. XXIII:** 24

Grahn, Judy, **Supp. IV Part 1:** 325, 330; **Supp. XXIII:** 195

"Grain Field" (Crapsey), **Supp. XVII:** 77

Grainger, Percy, **Supp. I Part 2:** 386

Grain of Mustard Seed, A (Sarton), **Supp. VIII: 259–260,** 263

Gramar (Lowth), **II:** 8

Grammar of Motives, A (Burke), **I:** 272, 275, 276–278, 283, 284

Gramsci, Antonio, **Supp. XX: 35–36**

Granados, Gabriel Bernal, **Supp. XV:** 350

Granath, Jack, **Supp. XVIII:** 93

Granberry, Edwin, **I:** 288

Grand Canyon, Inc. (Everett), **Supp. XVIII:** 66

Grand Design, The (Dos Passos), **I:** 489–490

"Grande Malade, The" (Barnes), **Supp. III Part 1:** 36

"Grandfather" (Dunn), **Supp. XI:** 147

"Grandfather and Grandson" (Singer), **Retro. Supp. II:** 307

Grandfathers, The (Richter), **Supp. XVIII: 219–220**

"Grandfather's Blessing" (Alvarez), **Supp. VII:** 2

"Grand Forks" (Bierds), **Supp. XVII:** 34

"Grand Forks" (Simpson), **Supp. IX:** 280–281

"Grand Inquisitor" (Dostoevsky), **IV:** 106

Grandissimes (Cable), **II:** 291

"Grand-Master Nabokov" (Updike), **Retro. Supp. I:** 317

"Grand Miracle, The" (Karr), **Supp. XI:** 251

"Grandmother" (Gunn Allen), **Supp. IV Part 1:** 320, 325

"Grandmother in Heaven" (Levine), **Supp. V:** 186

"Grandmother of the Sun: Ritual Gynocracy in Native America" (Gunn Allen), **Supp. IV Part 1:** 328

Grandmothers of the Light: A Medicine Woman's Sourcebook (Gunn Allen, ed.), **Supp. IV Part 1:** 332, 333–334

"Grandmother Songs, The" (Hogan), **Supp. IV Part 1:** 413

"Grandpa and the Statue" (A. Miller), **III:** 147

"Grandparents" (Lowell), **II:** 550

"Grandsire Bells, The" (Bierds), **Supp. XVII:** 28–29

"Grandstand Complex, The" (McCoy), **Supp. XIII:** 166

Grange, Red, **II:** 416

Granger's Index to Poetry (anthology), **Retro. Supp. I:** 37, 39

Granite & Cedar (Miller), **Supp. XXII:** 214

Grant, Gavin, **Supp. XIX:** 175

Grant, Lee, **Supp. XIII:** 295

Grant, Madison, **Supp. II Part 1:** 170

Grant, Richard, **Supp. X:** 282

Grant, Ulysses S., **I:** 4, 15; **II:** 542; **III:** 506, 584; **IV:** 348, 446; **Supp. I Part 2:** 418; **Supp. XXIV:** 224

Grantwood, **Retro. Supp. I:** 416, 417

"Grapes, The" (Hecht), **Supp. X:** 65–66

"Grape Sherbet" (Dove), **Supp. IV Part 1:** 246

Grapes of Wrath, The (Steinbeck), **I:** 301; **III:** 589; **IV:** 51, 53–55, 59, 63, 65, 67, 68, 69; **Supp. V:** 290; **Supp. XI:** 169; **Supp. XIV:** 181; **Supp. XV:** 351; **Supp. XX: 28**

"Grapevine, The" (Ashbery), **Supp. III Part 1:** 4

"Grass" (Sandburg), **III:** 584

Grass, Günter, **Supp. VIII:** 40

Grass County (Kooser), **Supp. XIX:** 119

"Grasse: The Olive Trees" (Wilbur), **Supp. III Part 2:** 550

Grass Harp, The (Capote), **Supp. III Part 1:** 114–117, 123

Grass Still Grows, The (A. Miller), **III:** 146

"Grating Parmesan"(Crooker), **Supp. XXIII:** 56

Gratitude to Old Teachers (R. Bly), **Supp. IV Part 1:** 73

Grattan, Bill, **Supp. XXIII:** 273, 274, 275, 276, 279, 280

Graupner, Gottlieb, **Supp. XV:** 240, 244

"Grave, A" (Moore), **III:** 195, 202, 208, 213

Grave, The (Blair), **Supp. I Part 1:** 150

"Grave, The" (Porter), **III:** 433, 443, 445–446

"Grave, The" (Winters), **Supp. II Part 2:** 795, 796

"Graven Image" (O'Hara), **III:** 320

Grave of Light: New and Selected Poems, 1970–2005 (Notley), **Supp. XXII:** 226, 235, 236

Grave of the Right Hand, The (Wright), **Supp. V:** 332, 338, 339

"Grave Piece" (Eberhart), **I:** 533

Graves, Billy, **Supp. I Part 2:** 607

Graves, John, **Supp. V:** 220

Graves, Morris, **Supp. X:** 264

Graves, Peter, **Supp. IV Part 2:** 474

Graves, Rean, **Supp. I Part 1:** 326

Graves, Robert, **I:** 437, 477, 523; **Supp. I Part 2:** 541; **Supp. IV Part 1:** 280, 348; **Supp. IV Part 2:** 685

"Graveyard, The" (Very), **Supp. XXV:** 249

"Graveyard Blues" (Trethewey), **Supp. XXI:** 245, 255, 256

Graveyard for Lunatics, A (Bradbury), **Supp. IV Part 1:** 102, 114–116

Gravity's Rainbow (Pynchon), **Supp. II Part 2:** 617, 618–619, 621–625, 627, 630, 633–636; **Supp. IV Part 1:** 279; **Supp. V:** 44; **Supp. XIV:** 49; **Supp. XVII:** 236; **Supp. XXII:** 255; **Supp. XXIV:** 140

Gray, Cecil, **Supp. I Part 1:** 258

Gray, Francine Du Plessix, **Supp. V:** 169

Gray, James, **III:** 207; **Supp. I Part 2:** 410

Gray, Jeffrey, **Supp. XV:** 27

Gray, Josie, **Supp. XXIV:** 166, 167, 172, 178

Gray, Paul, **Supp. IV Part 1:** 305; **Supp. IV Part 2:** 639; **Supp. XVI:** 74; **Supp. XVIII:** 94

Gray, Thomas, **I:** 68; **Supp. I Part 1:** 150; **Supp. I Part 2:** 422, 716

Gray, Thomas A., **Supp. I Part 2:** 710

"Gray Heron, The" (Kinnell), **Supp. III Part 1:** 250

"Gray Mills of Farley, The" (Jewett), **Retro. Supp. II:** 132, 144

"Gray Poem" (Everwine), **Supp. XV:** 81

Grayson, Charles, **Supp. XIII:** 171

"Gray Squirrel" (Francis), **Supp. IX:** 90

"Gray Wolf's H 'ant, The" (Chesnutt), **Supp. XIV:** 60

Grealy, Lucy, **Supp. XII:** 310

Greasy Lake (Boyle), **Supp. VIII: 14–15**

"Greasy Lake" (Boyle), **Supp. VIII:** 15; **Supp. XX: 18–19**

Greasy Lake & Other Stories (Boyle), **Supp. XX: 17, 18–19**

"Great Adventure of Max Breuck, The" (Lowell), **II:** 522

Great American Novel, The (P. Roth), **Retro. Supp. II:** 283, 288–289; **Supp. III Part 2:** 414–416

Great American Short Novels (Phillips, ed.), **Supp. VIII:** 156

Great Battles of the World (Crane), **I:** 415

"Great Carousel, The" (Untermeyer), **Supp. XV:** 296

Great Christian Doctrine of Original Sin Defended, The . . . (Edwards), **I:** 549, 557, 559

Great Circle (Aiken), **I:** 53, 55, 57

"Great Class-Reunion Bazaar, The" (Theroux), **Supp. VIII:** 312

Great Day, The (Hurston), **Supp. VI:** 154

Great Days (Barthelme), **Supp. IV Part 1:** 39

Great Days, The (Dos Passos), **I:** 491

Great Digest (Pound, trans.), **III:** 472

"Great Divider, The" (Saunders), **Supp. XIX:** 235

"Great Elegy for John Donne" (Brodsky), **Supp. VIII:** 21, 23

"Greater Good, A" (Di Piero), **Supp. XIX:** 39

Greater Inclination, The (Wharton), **Retro. Supp. I:** 363, **364–365**, 366

Greater Sea, The (Gibran), **Supp. XX:** 118

"Greater Self, The" (Gibran), **Supp. XX:** 118

"Greater Torment, The" (Blackmur), **Supp. II Part 1:** 92

Greatest Hits 1969–1996 (Salinas), **Supp. XIII:** 311

"Greatest of These, The" (C. Miller), **Supp. XXII:** 188, 196

"Greatest Thing in the World, The" (Mailer), **Retro. Supp. II:** 196

Great Expectations (Acker), **Supp. XII:** 5, **9–11**

Great Expectations (Dickens), **III:** 247; **Supp. I Part 1:** 35; **Supp. XVI:** 73; **Supp. XVIII:** 146

"Great Expectations, No Satisfaction" (D. Gates), **Supp. XVI:** 73

"Great Figure, The" (W. C. Williams), **IV:** 414

"Great Fillmore Street Buffalo Drive, The" (Momaday), **Supp. IV Part 2:** 493

Great Gatsby, The (Fitzgerald) (Modern Library), **Retro. Supp. I:** 113

Great Gatsby, The (Fitzgerald), **I:** 107, 375, 514; **II:** 77, 79, 83, 84, 85, 87, 91–93, 94, 96, 98; **III:** 244, 260, 372, 572; **IV:** 124, 297; **Retro. Supp. I:** 98, 105, **105–108**, 110, 114, 115, 335, 359; **Retro. Supp. II:** 107, 201; **Supp. II Part 2:** 626; **Supp. III Part 2:** 585; **Supp. IV Part 2:** 468, 475; **Supp. IX:** 57, 58; **Supp. X:** 175; **Supp. XI:** 65, 69, 334; **Supp. XVI:** 64, 75; **Supp. XVIII:** 76, 148, 165; **Supp. XX:** 59, **60, 61, 72; Supp. XXII:** 81, 82, 88; **Supp. XXIII:** 101

Great God Brown, The (O'Neill), **III:** 165, 391, 394–395

Great Goodness of Life: A Coon Show (Baraka), **Supp. II Part 1:** 47

Great Heart: The History of a Labrador Adventure (Davidson and Rugge), **Supp. XXII:** 218

"Great Idea Lives Forever, A: Shouldn't Its Copyright?" (Helprin), **Supp. XXV:** 84, 88

Great Inclination, The (Wharton), **IV:** 310

"Great Infirmities" (Simic), **Supp. VIII:** 277

Great Jones Street (DeLillo), **Supp. VI:** 2, 3, 8–9, 11, 12

"Great Lawsuit, The: Man *versus* Men: Woman *versus* Women" (Fuller), **Retro. Supp. I:** 156; **Supp. II Part 1:** 292

"Great Men and Their Environment" (James), **II:** 347

"Great Mississippi Bubble, The" (Irving), **II:** 314

Great Mistake, The (Rinehart), **Supp. XXV:** 198, 200

Great Railway Bazaar, The: By Train through Asia (Theroux), **Supp. VIII:** 318, 319, **320–321**, 322

"Great Scott" (Conroy), **Supp. XVI:** 75, 77

Great Shark Hunt, The (Thompson), **Supp. XXIV:** 286

"Great Sleigh-Ride of Brewsterville, The" (Briggs), **Supp. XVIII:** 16

"Great Spirit, The" (Zitkala-Ša), **Supp. XXV:** 276, 282

Great Stories of Suspense (Millar, ed.), **Supp. IV Part 2:** 474

Great Topics of the World (Goldbarth), **Supp. XII:** 187, 189, 191

Great Valley, The (Masters), **Supp. I Part 2:** 465

Great World and Timothy Colt, The (Auchincloss), **Supp. IV Part 1:** 25, 31, 32

Grédy, Jean-Pierre, **Supp. XVI:** 194

"Greek Boy, The" (Bryant), **Supp. I Part 1:** 168

Greek Mind/Jewish Soul: The Conflicted Art of Cynthia Ozick (Strandberg), **Supp. V:** 273

"Greek Partisan, The" (Bryant), **Supp. I Part 1:** 168

"Greeks, The" (McCarriston), **Supp. XIV:** 271

"Greeks, the Chines, or Say the Mayans, The" (Bronk), **Supp. XXI:** 31

Greeley, Horace, **II:** 7; **IV:** 197, 286–287

Green, Anna Katherine, **Supp. XXV:** 199

Green, Ashbel, **Supp. IV Part 2:** 474

Green, David Gordon, **Supp. XXV:** 153

Green, Henry, **IV:** 279; **Retro. Supp. I:** 354; **Supp. III Part 1:** 3; **Supp. XI:** 294–295, 296, 297; **Supp. XII:** 315

Green, Jack, **Supp. IV Part 1:** 284–285

Green, Martin, **Supp. I Part 1:** 299

Green, Michelle, **Supp. IV Part 1:** 95

Green, Rose Basile, **Supp. XX:** **33, 41**

"Green Automobile, The" (Ginsberg), **Supp. II Part 1:** 322

Greenberg, Clement, **Supp. XV:** 141, 143, 144, 145

Greenberg, Eliezer, **Supp. I Part 2:** 432; **Supp. XXIII:** 7

Greenberg, Hayim, **Supp. XXIII:** 3

Greenberg, Jonathan, **Supp. XII:** 285

Greenberg, Miriam, **Supp. XXII:** 244

Greenberg, Samuel, **I:** 393

Green Bough, A (Faulkner), **Retro. Supp. I:** 84

"Green Canoe" (Halliday), **Supp. XIX:** 88

Green Centuries (Gordon), **II:** 196, 197–207, 209

"Green Crab's Shell, A" (Doty), **Supp. XI:** 126

"Green Door, The" (O. Henry), **Supp. II Part 1:** 395

Greene, A. C., **Supp. V:** 223, 225

Greene, Graham, **I:** 480; **II:** 62, 320; **III:** 57, 556; **Retro. Supp. I:** 215; **Supp. I Part 1:** 280; **Supp. IV Part 1:** 341; **Supp. V:** 298; **Supp. IX:** 261; **Supp. XI:** 99,**Supp. XI:** 104; **Supp. XIII:** 233; **Supp. XVIII:** 79; **Supp. XIX:** 29–30

Greene, Helga, **Supp. IV Part 1:** 134, 135

Greene, J. Lee, **Retro. Supp. II:** 121

Greene, Nathanael, **Supp. I Part 2:** 508

Greene, Richard Tobias, **III:** 76

Greene, Robert, **Supp. XVII:** 232

Green Eggs and Ham (Geisel), **Supp. XVI:** 108, 109

"Greene-ing of the Portables, The" (Cowley), **Supp. II Part 1:** 140

"Greenest Continent, The" (Stevens), **Retro. Supp. I:** 304

Greenfeld, Josh, **III:** 364

Greenfield, Josh, **Supp. XIX:** 269

"Green Hell" (Boyle), **Supp. XX:** 18

Green Hills of Africa (Hemingway), **II:** 253; **Retro. Supp. I:** 182, 186

Greening of America, The (C. Reich), **Supp. XVII:** 3

"Green Lagoons, The" (Leopold), **Supp. XIV:** 188

"Green Lampshade" (Simic), **Supp. VIII:** 283

Greenlanders, The (Smiley), **Supp. VI:** 292, **296–298**, 299, 305, 307

Greenlaw, Edwin A., **IV:** 453

"Greenleaf" (O'Connor), **III:** 350, 351; **Retro. Supp. II:** 233, 237

Greenman, Walter F., **I:** 217, 222

Green Memories (Mumford), **Supp. II Part 2:** 474, 475, 479, 480–481

Green Mountain Ghosts, Ghouls, and Unsolved Mysteries (Citro), **Supp. XXII:** 208, 218

"Green Pasture, The" (Leopold), **Supp. XIV:** 184

Green Pastures, The (Connelly), **Supp. II Part 1:** 223

"Green Red Brown and White" (Swenson), **Supp. IV Part 2:** 639

"Green River" (Bryant), **Supp. I Part 1:** 155, 164

Green Shadows, White Whale (Bradbury), **Supp. IV Part 1:** 102, 103, 116

"Green Shirt, The" (Olds), **Supp. X:** 209

"Greensleeves" (Jarman), **Supp. XVII:** 113

"Greensleeves" (Notley), **Supp. XXII:** 228

Greenslet, Ferris, **I:** 19; **Retro. Supp. I:** 9, 10, 11, 13; **Retro. Supp. II:** 41

Greenspan, Alan, **Supp. IV Part 2:** 526

Greenspan, Ezra, **Supp. XVIII:** 257

Greenstreet, Sydney, **Supp. IV Part 1:** 356

"Green Thought, A" (L. Michaels), **Supp. XVI:** 204

"Green-Thumb Boy" (Nelson), **Supp. XVIII:** 182

Greenwald, Ted, **Supp. IV Part 2:** 423

Green Wall, The (Wright), **Supp. III Part 2:** 591, 593, 595

Green Wave, The (Rukeyser), **Supp. VI:** 273, 280

"Green Ways" (Kunitz), **Supp. III Part 1:** 265

Green with Beasts (Merwin), **Supp. III Part 1:** 340, 344–346

Greenwood, Grace, **Supp. XIII:** 141

"Greeting Card Verse" (Peacock), **Supp. XIX:** 200

Greetings from Ice Country (Muñoz), **Supp. XXV:** 130

Gregerson, Linda, **Supp. IV Part 2:** 651; **Supp. X:** 204–205; **Supp. XI:** 142

"Gregorio Valdes" (Bishop), **Retro. Supp. II:** 51

Gregory, Alyse, **I:** 221, 226, 227, 231

Gregory, Horace, **II:** 512; **Supp. III Part 2:** 614, 615; **Supp. IX:** 229; **Supp. XV:** 143

Gregory, Lady Isabella Augusta, **III:** 458

Gregory, Sinda, **Supp. X:** 260, 268

Grendel (Gardner), **Supp. VI:** 63, **67,** 68, 74

Grenstone Poems (Bynner), **Supp. XV:** 44

"Gretel in Darkness" (Glück), **Supp. V:** 82

Gretta (Caldwell), **I:** 301, 302

Greuze, Jean Baptiste, **Supp. I Part 2:** 714

Grey, Zane, **Supp. XIII:** 5

Greyhounding This America (Kenny), **Supp. XXIII: 155**

Gridley Firing (Hayford), **Supp. XXII:** 204

"Grief Has Stamped" (Pedersen; Nelson, trans.), **Supp. XVIII:** 180

Grieg, Michael, **Supp. XV:** 133, 148

Griffin, Bartholomew, **Supp. I Part 1:** 369

Griffin, John Howard, **Supp. VIII:** 208; **Supp. XXI:** 74; **Supp. XXV:** 51

Griffin, Merv, **Supp. IV Part 2:** 526

Griffith, Albert J., **Supp. V:** 325

Griffith, D. W., **I:** 31, 481–482; **Retro. Supp. I:** 103, 325; **Supp. XI:** 45; **Supp. XVI:** 183, 184; **Supp. XXI:** 170

Griffith, Paul, **Supp. XVIII:** 173, 175

Griffiths, Clyde, **I:** 511

Grile, Dod (pseudonym). *See* Bierce, Ambrose

Grimm, Herman, **II:** 17

Grimm brothers, **II:** 378; **III:** 101, 491, 492; **IV:** 266; **Supp. I Part 2:** 596, 622; **Supp. X:** 78, 84, 86

Grimshaw, Anna, **Supp. XXI:** 172

Grinnell, George Bird, **Supp. XVI:** 13

Gris, Juan, **I:** 442; **Retro. Supp. I:** 430

Griswold, Rufus Wilmot, **III:** 409, 429; **Retro. Supp. II:** 261, 262; **Supp. XV:**

277, 278; **Supp. XVI:** 8, 10–11; **Supp. XXV:** 250

Grogg, Sam, Jr., **Supp. IV Part 2:** 468, 471

Gromer, Crystal, **Supp. XII:** 297

Gronlund, Laurence, **II:** 276

Grooms, Red, **Supp. XV:** 178

Grooves: A Kind of Mystery (Brockmeier), **Supp. XXII:** 55, 56, 59

"Groping for Trouts" (Gass), **Supp. VI:** 87

Grosholz, Emily, **Supp. XII:** 185; **Supp. XIX:** 37–38, 278

Grosman un zun (Grosman and Son) (Asch), **Supp. XXIII:** 7

Gross, Robert A., **Supp. XIX:** 151

Gross, Terry, **Supp. XVI:** 167; **Supp. XXI:** 247, 255

"Grosse Fuge" (Doty), *Supp. XI:* 126–127

Grossman, Allen, **Retro. Supp. II:** 83; **Supp. XVIII:** 91; **Supp. XIX:** 82, 86, 94

Grossman, Lev, **Supp. XXV:** 4, **63–78**

Grosz, George, **III:** 172; **IV:** 438; **Retro. Supp. II:** 321; **Supp. X:** 137

"Grotesque in Modern Fiction, The" (E. Hoffman, Ph.D. dissertation), **Supp. XVI:** 147

"Groundhog, The" (Eberhart), **I:** 523, 530–532, 533

"Ground on Which I Stand, The" (Wilson), **Supp. VIII:** 331

"Ground Swell" (Jarman), **Supp. XVII:** 118

Group, The (McCarthy), **II:** 570, 574–578

"Group of Two, A" (Jarrell), **II:** 368

Group Therapy (Hearon), **Supp. VIII:** **64–65**

"Grove" (Goldbarth), **Supp. XII:** 176

Groves of Academe, The (McCarthy), **II:** 568–571

Growing into Love (X. J. Kennedy), **Supp. XV:** 153, **158–160**

Growing Pains (J. S. Untermeyer), **Supp. XV:** 303

"Growing Season, The" (Caldwell), **I:** 309

Growing Up Gay: A Literary Anthology (Singer, ed.), **Supp. IV Part 1:** 330

"Growing Up Good in Maycomb" (Shaffer), **Supp. VIII:** 128

"Grown-Up" (Jewett), **Retro. Supp. II:** 134

"Growth" (Lowell), **II:** 554

"Growth and Decay in Recent Verse" (Untermeyer), **Supp. XV:** 299

Growth of the American Republic, The (Morison and Commager), **Supp. I Part 2:** 484

"Growtown Buggle, The" (Jewett), **Retro. Supp. II:** 132

Grubin, David, **Supp. XXIII:** 138

Gruenberg, Louis, **III:** 392

Grumbach, Doris, **II:** 560

"Gryphon" (C. Baxter), **Supp. XVII:** 14, 17

"Guacamaja" (Leopold), **Supp. XIV:** 188–189

Guardian Angel (Paretsky), **Supp. XXV:** 178, 179

Guardian Angel, The (Holmes), **Supp. I Part 1:** 315–316

"Guardian of the Law" (R. Fisher), **Supp. XIX:** 71

Guard of Honor (Cozzens), **I:** 370–372, 375, 376–377, 378, 379

Guardsman, The (Molnar), **Supp. XVI:** 187

Guare, John, **Supp. XIII:** 196, 207

Guattari, Félix, **Supp. XXV:** 123

Gubar, Susan, **Retro. Supp. I:** 42; **Retro. Supp. II:** 324; **Supp. IX:** 66; **Supp. XV:** 270; **Supp. XXIV:** 28

Guerard, Albert, Jr., **Supp. X:** 79; **Supp. XIII:** 172

Guérin, Maurice de, **I:** 241

"Guerrilla Handbook, A" (Baraka), **Supp. II Part 1:** 36

Guess and Spell Coloring Book, The (Swenson), **Supp. IV Part 2:** 648

Guess Who's Coming to Dinner (film), **Supp. I Part 1:** 67

Guest, Barbara, **Supp. XXIII:** 215

Guest, Judith, **Supp. XVI:** 36

Guest, Val, **Supp. XI:** 307

Guest Book (Bynner), **Supp. XV:** 51

"Guest Ellen at the Supper for Street People, The" (Ferry), **Supp. XXIV:** 152–153, 162

"Guests of Mrs. Timms, The" (Jewett), **II:** 408; **Retro. Supp. II:** 135

Guevara, Martha, **Supp. VIII:** 74

Guevara, Fray Miguel de, **Supp. XXI:** 104

"Guevara . . .Guevara" (Salinas), **Supp. XIII:** 312–313, 315

Guggenheim, Peggy, **Supp. XXII:** 165

Guided Tours of Hell (Prose), **Supp. XVI:** 257, 261

"Guided Tours of Hell" (Prose), **Supp. XVI:** 257

Guide for the Perplexed (Maimonides), **Supp. XVII:** 46

Guide in the Wilderness, A (Cooper), **I:** 337

"Guidelines" (Espaillat), **Supp. XXI:** 99

"Guide to Dungeness Spit, A" (Wagoner), **Supp. IX:** 325–326, 329

Guide to Ezra Pound's Selected Cantos' (Kearns), **Retro. Supp. I:** 292

Guide to Kulchur (Pound), **III:** 475

Guide to the Ruins (Nemerov), **III:** 269, 270–271, 272

Guillén, Jorge, **Supp. XXIV:** 152

Guillén, Nicolás, **Retro. Supp. I:** 202; **Supp. I Part 1:** 345

Guillevic, Eugene, **Supp. III Part 1:** 283

"Guilt, The" (Peacock), **Supp. XIX:** 200

"Guilty Man, The" (Kunitz), **Supp. II Part 1:** 263

Guilty of Everything: The Autobiography of Herbert Huncke (Huncke), **Supp. XIV:** 138, 140, 141, 150

Guilty Pleasures (Barthelme), **Supp. IV Part 1:** 44, 45, 53

Guimond, James, **Supp. XXI:** 228

Guinness, Alec, **Retro. Supp. I:** 65; **Supp. XX:** 50

Gulag Archipelago, The (Solzhenitsyn), **Supp. XVII:** 229

"Gulf, The" (Dunn), **Supp. XI:** 149

Gulistan (Saadi), **II:** 19

Gullible's Travels (Lardner), **II:** 426, 427

Gulliver, Adelaide Cromwell, **Supp. XVIII:** 286

"Gulliver Found" (Bronk), **Supp. XXI:** 33

Gulliver's Travels (Swift), **I:** 209, 348, 366; **II:** 301; **Supp. I Part 2:** 656; **Supp. XI:** 209; **Supp. XVI:** 110

"Gulls" (Hayden), **Supp. II Part 1:** 367

"Gulls, The" (Nemerov), **III:** 272

"Gulls on Dumps" (Di Piero), **Supp. XIX:** 41

"Gun, The" (Dobyns), **Supp. XIII:** 88

Gun, with Occasional Music (Lethem), **Supp. XVIII: 137–138**

Günderode: A Translation from the German (Fuller), **Supp. II Part 1:** 293

Gundy, Jeff, **Supp. XI:** 315; **Supp. XVI:** 46, 265, 275

Gunfight at the O.K. Corral (film), **Supp. XX: 246**

Gunman's Rhapsody (Parker), **Supp. XIX:** 187

Gunn, Robin Wright, **Supp. XXI:** 243, 244

Gunn, Thom, **Supp. IX:** 269

Gunn, Thomas, **Supp. V:** 178

Gunn Allen, Paula, **Supp. IV Part 1: 319–340,** 404; **Supp. IV Part 2:** 499, 502, 557, 568; **Supp. XII:** 218

"Gunnar's Sword" (C. Bly), **Supp. XVI:** 34, 35, 37, 42

"Guns as Keys; and the Great Gate Swings" (Lowell), **II:** 524

Gurdjieff, Georges, **Supp. V:** 199; **Supp. IX:** 320

Gurganus, Allan, **Supp. XII:** 308–309, 310

Gurko, Leo, **III:** 62

Gurney, A. R., **Supp. V: 95–112; Supp. IX:** 261

Gurney, Mary (Molly) Goodyear, **Supp. V:** 95

Gussow, Mel, **Supp. IX:** 93; **Supp. XII:** 325, 328, 341

Gustavus Vassa, the African (Vassa), **Supp. IV Part 1:** 11

Gusto, Thy Name Was Mrs. Hopkins: A Prose Rhapsody (Francis), **Supp. IX:** 89

Guston, Philip, **Supp. XXIII:** 210

Gute Mensch von Sezuan, Der (Brecht), **Supp. IX:** 138

Gutenberg, Johann, **Supp. I Part 2:** 392

Guthrie, A. B., **Supp. X:** 103

Guthrie, Woody, **Supp. XVIII:** 23

Gutman, Herbert, **Supp. I Part 1:** 47

Guttenplan, D. D., **Supp. XI:** 38

"Gutting of Couffignal, The" (Hammett), **Supp. IV Part 1:** 345

Guy Domville (James), **II:** 331; **Retro. Supp. I:** 228

"Gwendolyn" (Bishop), **Retro. Supp. II:** 51

Gwynn, R. S., **Supp. XVIII:** 184

Gypsy Ballads (Hughes, trans.), **Supp. I Part 1:** 345

Gypsy's Curse, The (Crews), **Supp. XI: 110**

"Gyroscope, The" (Rukeyser), **Supp. VI:** 271

Gysin, Brion, **Supp. XII:** 129

H

Haardt, Sara. *See* Mencken, Mrs. H. L. (Sara Haardt)

Haas, Robert, **Supp. XXII:** 177

Habakkuk (biblical book), **III:** 200, 347

Habibi (Nye), **Supp. XIII:** 273, **279**

"Habit" (James), **II:** 351

Habitations of the Word (Gass), **Supp. VI:** 88

"Hack, The" (Swados), **Supp. XIX:** 267

"Hackberry"(P. Benedict), **Supp. XXIII:** 37–38, 39

Hacker, Marilyn, **Supp. XV:** 250; **Supp. XVII:** 71, 76, 112; **Supp. XVIII:** 177, 178

Hackett, David, **Supp. XII:** 236

Hadas, Rachel, **Supp. XXIII: 111–128; Supp. XXIV:** 157

Hadda, Janet, **Retro. Supp. II:** 317

Haddád, 'Abd al-Masíh, **Supp. XX: 116**

"Hades Welcomes His Bride" (Stallings), **Supp. XXV:** 229–230

Haeckel, Ernst Heinrich, **II:** 480

Haegert, John, **Supp. XVI:** 69

Hafen, P. Jane, **Supp. XXV:** 280

Hafif, Marcia, **Supp. IV Part 2:** 423

Hagar's Daughter (P. Hopkins), **Supp. XVI:** 143

Hagedorn, Jessica, **Supp. X:** 292

Hagen, Beulah, **Supp. I Part 2:** 679

Hager, Kelly, **Supp. XVIII:** 183

Haggard, Rider, **III:** 189

Hagoromo (play), **III:** 466

Hagstrum, Jean, **Supp. XV:** 74

"Hail Mary" (Fante), **Supp. XI:** 160, 164

Haines, George, IV, **I:** 444

Haines, John, **Supp. XII: 197–214**

"Hair" (Corso), **Supp. XII:** 117, 126, 127

"Hair, The" (Carver), **Supp. III Part 1:** 137

"Haircut" (Lardner), **II:** 430, 436

"Hair Dressing" (Untermeyer), **Supp. XV:** 304, 305

Hairpiece: A Film for Nappy-Headed People (Chenzira; film), **Supp. XI:** 19–20

"Hairs" (Cisneros), **Supp. VII:** 59

Hairs/Pelitos (Cisneros), **Supp. VII:** 58

Hairy Ape, The (O'Neill), **III:** 391, 392, 393

"Haïta the Shepherd" (Bierce), **I:** 203

Haj, The (Uris), **Supp. XX: 244, 245, 247, 255–256**

Haldeman, Anna, **Supp. I Part 1:** 2

Hale, Edward Everett, **Supp. I Part 2:** 584; **Supp. XI:** 193, 200

Hale, John Parker, **Supp. I Part 2:** 685

Hale, Nancy, **Supp. VIII:** 151, 171

Haley, Alex, **Supp. I Part 1:** 47, 66

Haley, J. Evetts, **Supp. V:** 226

"Half a Century Gone" (Lowell), **II:** 554

Half-a-Hundred: Tales by Great American Writers (Grayson, ed.), **Supp. XIII:** 171

Half and Half: Writers on Growing Up Biracial and Bicultural (Hearn, ed.), **Supp. XXV:** 51

Half Asleep in Frog Pajamas (Robbins), **Supp. X:** 259, **279–282**

Half Breed, The (film), **Supp. XVI:** 185

Half-Century of Conflict, A (Parkman), **Supp. II Part 2:** 600, 607, 610

"Half Deity" (Moore), **III:** 210, 214, 215

"Half Hour of August" (Ríos), **Supp. IV Part 2:** 552

Half-Lives (Jong), **Supp. V:** 115, 119

Half Moon Street: Two Short Novels (Theroux), **Supp. VIII:** 322, 323

Half of Paradise (Burke), **Supp. XIV:** 22, 24

Half-Past Nation Time (Johnson), **Supp. VI:** 187

"Half-Skinned Steer, The" (Proulx), **Supp. VII:** 261–262

"Half Sonnets" (Jarman), **Supp. XVII:** 115

Half Sun Half Sleep (Swenson), **Supp. IV Part 2:** 645–646

Halfway (Kumin), **Supp. IV Part 2:** 441–442

"Halfway" (Rich), **Supp. I Part 2:** 553

Halfway Down the Hall: New and Selected Poems (Hadas), **Supp. XXIII: 118–119**

Halfway Home (Monette), **Supp. X:** 154

Halfway to Silence (Sarton), **Supp. VIII:** 261

Half You Don't Know, The: Selected Stories (Cameron), **Supp. XII:** 79, 80, 81

Haliburton, Thomas Chandler, **II:** 301; **IV:** 193; **Supp. I Part 2:** 411

Halifax, Lord, **II:** 111

Hall, Daniel, **Supp. XII:** 258

Hall, Donald, **I:** 567; **III:** 194; **Supp. IV Part 1:** 63, 72; **Supp. IV Part 2:** 621; **Supp. IX:** 269; **Supp. XIV:** 82, 126; **Supp. XV:** 21, 153, 176; **Supp. XVI:** 39, 230, 235; **Supp. XX: 194; Supp. XXI:** 86; **Supp. XXIII:** 209

Hall, Hazel, **Supp. XXII:** 275

Hall, James, **II:** 313; **Supp. I Part 2:** 584, 585

Hall, James Baker, **Supp. X:** 24

Hall, Rachel, **Supp. XXIII:** 301

Hall, Timothy L., **Supp. VIII:** 127, 128

Halleck, Fitz-Greene, **Supp. I Part 1:** 156, 158

"Hallelujah: A Sestina" (Francis), **Supp. IX:** 82

"Hallelujah on the Bum" (Abbey), **Supp. XIII:** 2

"Haller's Second Home" (Maxwell), **Supp. VIII:** 169

Halliday, Mark, **Supp. XV:** 19, 20, 21, 23, 25, 27, 30; **Supp. XIX: 81–95**

Hallock, Rev. Moses, **Supp. I Part 1:** 153

Hall of Mirrors, A (Stone), **Supp. V:** 295, 296–299, 300, 301

"Hallowe'en" (Huncke), **Supp. XIV:** 145

"Halloween Party, The" (Chabon), **Supp. XI:** 72

Halloween Tree, The (Bradbury), **Supp. IV Part 1:** 102, 112–113

"Halls, The" (Halliday), **Supp. XIX:** 90

Hallwas, John E., **Supp. I Part 2:** 454

Halpern, Daniel, **Supp. IV Part 1:** 94–95, 95

Halpern, Paul, **Supp. XXV:** 123

Halsey, Theresa, **Supp. IV Part 1:** 330, 331

"Halt in the Desert, A" (Brodsky), **Supp. VIII:** 24

"Halves" (Dunn), **Supp. XI:** 149

Hamburg, Victoria, **Supp. XVI:** 126

Hamerik, Asger, **Supp. I Part 1:** 356

Hamill, Pete, **Supp. XX:** 244, 255

Hamill, Sam, **Supp. X:** 112, 125, 126, 127

Hamilton, Alexander, **I:** 485; **Supp. I Part 2:** 456, 483, 509

Hamilton, Alice, **Supp. I Part 1:** 5

Hamilton, David, **Supp. IX:** 296

Hamilton, Edith, **Supp. XVI:** 196

Hamilton, Lady Emma, **II:** 524

Hamilton, Hamish, **Supp. I Part 2:** 617

Hamilton, Walton, **Supp. I Part 2:** 632

Hamilton Stark (Banks), **Supp. V:** 8, 9–10, 11

"Hamlen Brook" (Wilbur), **Supp. III Part 2:** 564

"Hamlet" (Laforgue), **I:** 573; **III:** 11

Hamlet (Miller and Fraenkel), **III:** 178, 183

Hamlet (Shakespeare), **I:** 53, 183, 205, 377, 586–587; **II:** 158, 531; **III:** 7, 11, 12, 183; **IV:** 116, 131, 227; **Supp. I Part 1:** 369; **Supp. I Part 2:** 422, 457, 471; **Supp. IV Part 2:** 612; **Supp. IX:** 14

Hamlet, The (Faulkner), **II:** 69–71, 73, 74; **IV:** 131; **Retro. Supp. I:** 82, 91, 92; **Supp. VIII:** 178; **Supp. IX:** 103; **Supp. XI:** 247

"Hamlet and His Problems" (Eliot), **I:** 586–587

Hamlet of A. MacLeish, The (MacLeish), **III:** 11–12, 14, 15, 18

Hamlin, Eva, **Retro. Supp. II:** 115

"Hammer" (Bidart), **Supp. XV:** 35

Hammer, Adam, **Supp. XIII:** 112

Hammer, Langdon, **Retro. Supp. II:** 45, 53; **Supp. X:** 65

"Hammer Man, The" (Bambara), **Supp. XI:** 4–5

Hammett, Dashiell, **IV:** 286; **Retro. Supp. II:** 327; **Supp. I Part 1:** 286, 289, 291, 292, 293, 294, 295; **Supp. III Part 1:** 91; **Supp. IV Part 1:** 120, 121, 341–357; **Supp. IV Part 2:** 461, 464, 468, 469, 472, 473; **Supp. IX:** 200; **Supp. XI:** 228; **Supp. XIII:** 159; **Supp. XIV:** 21; **Supp. XVII:** 137; **Supp. XIX:** 178; **Supp. XXI:** 68

Hammon, Jupiter, **Supp. XXII:** 11

Hammond, John, **Supp. XVIII:** 24

Hammond, Karla, **Supp. IV Part 2:** 439, 442, 448, 637, 640, 644, 648

Hampl, Patricia, **Supp. IX:** 291; **Supp. XI:** 126; **Supp. XVII:** 21; **Supp.**

XXII: 81–101

Hampson, Alfred Leete, **Retro. Supp. I:** 35–36, 38

"Hamrick's Polar Bear" (Caldwell), **I:** 309–310

Hamsun, Knut, **Supp. VIII:** 40; **Supp. XI:** 161, 167; **Supp. XII:** 21, 128

Hancock, John, **Supp. I Part 2:** 524; **Supp. XX:** 282

Hancock, Wade, **Supp. XVI:** 34

Handbook of North American Indians (Sando), **Supp. IV Part 2:** 510

Handcarved Coffins: A Nonfiction Account of an American Crime (Capote), **Supp. III Part 1:** 131

Handel, Georg Friedrich, **III:** 210; **IV:** 369

"Handfasting" (Wright), **Supp. XV:** 343

"Handfuls" (Sandburg), **III:** 584

"Handle with Care" (Fitzgerald), **Retro. Supp. I:** 114

Handley, William R., **Supp. XVIII:** 58

Handmaid's Tale, The (Atwood), **Supp. XIII:** 19, 20, 27–29

"Hand of Casino, 1954, A" (Skloot), **Supp. XX:** 194, 202

"Hand of Emmagene, The" (Taylor), **Supp. V:** 314, 325–326

Hand of the Potter, The: A Tragedy in Four Acts (Dreiser), **Retro. Supp. II:** 104; **Supp. XVII:** 96

"Hands" (Anderson), **I:** 106, 107

"Hands" (Mora), **Supp. XIII:** 215

Hands of Orlac, The (M. Renard; Crewe-Jones, trans.), **Supp. XVII:** 58

Hand to Mouth (Auster), **Supp. XII:** 21

"Hand to Mouth" (Auster), **Supp. XII:** 31

Handy, Lowney, **Supp. XI:** 217, 220, 221, 225

Handy, W. C., **Supp. VIII:** 337

Handy Guide for Beggars, A (Lindsay), **Supp. I Part 2:** 376–378, 380, 382, 399

Haney, David, **Supp. XXI:** 253

"Hanged Man, A" (Cliff), **Supp. XXII:** 74

"Hanging Burley" (J. W. Miller), **Supp. XX:** 167

Hanging Garden, The (Wagoner), **Supp. IX:** 338–339

"Hanging Gardens of Tyburn, The" (Hecht), **Supp. X:** 58

"Hanging of the Crane, The" (Longfellow), **Retro. Supp. II:** 169, 171

Hanging On (Conroy), **Supp. XVI:** 69

"Hanging Pictures in Nanny's Room" (Kenyon), **Supp. VII:** 164

"Hanging the Wash" (Alvarez), **Supp. VII:** 4

"Hangman, The" (Sexton), **Supp. II Part 2:** 680, 691

Hangover Mass (X. J. Kennedy), **Supp. XV:** 165

Hangsaman (Jackson), **Supp. IX:** 116, 123, 124

Hanh, Thich Nhat, **Supp. V:** 199

Hanks, Lucy, **III:** 587

Hanks, Nancy. *See* Lincoln, Mrs. Thomas (Nancy Hanks)

Hanley, Lynne T., **Supp. IV Part 1:** 208

"Hanlon Mountain in Mist" (J. W. Miller), **Supp. XX:** 164, 166–167

Hanna, Mark, **Supp. I Part 2:** 395

Hannah, Barry, **Supp. X:** 285; **Supp. XIX:** 209; **Supp. XXI:** 38, 118

Hannah and Her Sisters (film; Allen), **Supp. XV:** 9, 10–11

"Hannah Armstrong" (Masters), **Supp. I Part 2:** 461

"Hannah Binding Shoes" (Larcom), **Supp. XIII:** 141, 143

"Hannah Byde" (D. West), **Supp. XVIII:** 280

Hannah's House (Hearon), **Supp. VIII:** 58, 60–61

Hanneman, Audre, **II:** 259

Hannibal Lecter, My Father (Acker), **Supp. XII:** 6

Hanoi (McCarthy), **II:** 579

"Hanoi Drifting, January 2003" (Weigl), **Supp. XIX:** 288

Hansberry, Lorraine, **Supp. IV Part 1:** 359–377; **Supp. VIII:** 329

Hanscom, Leslie, **Supp. XI:** 229

"Hansel and Gretel" (Prose), **Supp. XVI:** 256, 258

Hansen, Erik, **Supp. V:** 241

Hansen, Harry, **IV:** 366; **Supp. XXII:** 194, 277

Han-shan, **Supp. VIII:** 292

Hanson, Curtis, **Supp. XI:** 67

Hanson, Elizabeth, **Supp. XXIV:** 220

Hanson, William F., **Supp. XXV:** 279, 280

Han Suyin, **Supp. X:** 291

Hanzlicek, C. G., **Supp. XV:** 73

Hapax (Stallings), **Supp. XXV:** 221, 222, 224, 231–233

Hapgood, Charles H., II, **Supp. XXI:** 6

Hapgood, Hutchins, **Supp. XVII:** 95–108; **Supp. XXI:** 1, 3, 9, 10

Hapgood, Norman, **Supp. XXI:** 2

Hapgoods, The: Three Earnest Brothers (Marcaccio), **Supp. XVII:** 106

"Happenings: An Art of Radical Juxtaposition" (Sontag), **Supp. III Part 2:** 456

"Happenstance" (Komunyakaa), **Supp. XIII:** 130

Happenstance (Shields), **Supp. VII:** 315–318, 320, 323, 324, 326

Happersberger, Lucien, **Supp. I Part 1:** 51

"Happiest Girl in the Whole U.S.A., The" (Muñoz), **Supp. XXV:** 131, 132

"Happiest I've Been, The" (Updike), **IV:** 219

Happily Ever After (Quindlen), **Supp. XVII:** 167

"Happiness" (Oliver), **Supp. VII:** 236

"Happiness" (Sandburg), **III:** 582–583

"Happiness"(Hadas), **Supp. XXIII:** 117

Happiness of Getting It Down Right, The (Steinman, ed.), **Supp. VIII:** 172

"Happiness of the Garden Variety" (Richard), **Supp. XIX:** 212

"Happy Birthday" (Bambara), **Supp. XI:** 4

Happy Birthday (Loos), **Supp. XVI:** 193

Happy Birthday, Wanda June (Vonnegut), **Supp. II Part 2:** 759, 776–777

Happy Birthday of Death, The (Corso), **Supp. XII:** 127–129

Happy Childhood, A (Matthews), **Supp. IX:** 155, 160, **161–163**

Happy Days (Beckett), **Retro. Supp. I:** 206; **Supp. XXIV:** 123

Happy Days, 1880–1892 (Mencken), **III:** 100, 111, 120

"Happy End" (Simic), **Supp. VIII:** 276–277

"Happy Failure, The" (Melville), **III:** 90

Happy Families Are All Alike (Taylor), **Supp. V:** 322–323, 325

Happy Isles of Oceania, The: Paddling the Pacific (Theroux), **Supp. VIII:** 324

"Happy Journey to Trenton and Camden, The" (Wilder), **IV:** 366

"Happy Man, The" (Lethem), **Supp. XVIII:** 139

"Happy Marriage, The" (MacLeish), **III:** 15–16

Happy Marriage and Other Poems, The (MacLeish), **III:** 4

Happy to Be Here (Keillor), **Supp. XVI:** 165, 171

"Happy To Be Here" (Keillor), **Supp. XVI:** 168

"Hapworth 16, 1924" (Salinger), **III:** 552, 571–572

Haram, Karen, **Supp. XXIII:** 276

"Harbor Dawn, The" (H. Crane), **Supp. XXI:** 132, 136

"Harbor Lights" (Doty), **Supp. XI:** 122

Harcourt, Alfred, **II:** 191, 451–452; **III:** 587; **Retro. Supp. I:** 131; **Supp. XV:** 308

Harcourt, Lewis, **Supp. XX:** 232–233

Harcourt, T. A., **I:** 196

Hardball (Paretsky), **Supp. XXV:** 177, 182, 184

Hard Candy, a Book of Stories (T. Williams), **IV:** 383

"Hardcastle Crags" (Plath), **Supp. I Part 2:** 537

"Hard Daddy" (Hughes), **Retro. Supp. I:** 200

"Hardened Criminals, The" (Lethem), **Supp. XVIII:** 139

Harder They Fall, The (Schulberg), **Supp. XV:** 194, 201

Hard Facts (Baraka), **Supp. II Part 1:** 54, 55, 58

Hard Freight (Wright), **Supp. V:** 332, 339–340

Hard Hours, The (Hecht), **Supp. X:** 57, **59–62**, 63, 64

Hardie, Kier, **Supp. I Part 1:** 5

Harding, Walter, **IV:** 177, 178

Harding, Warren G., **I:** 486; **II:** 253, 433; **Supp. I Part 1:** 24

"Hard Kind of Courage, The" (Baldwin), **Supp. I Part 1:** 52

Hard Laughter (Lamott), **Supp. XX:** **132–133**

Hard Maple (S. and A. Warner), **Supp. XVIII:** 264

"Hard Rain's A-Gonna Fall, A" (song, Dylan), **Supp. XVIII:** 26, 29

Hard Time (Paretsky), **Supp. XXV:** 176, 177, 179, 182, 183

"Hard Time Keeping Up, A" (Ellison), **Retro. Supp. II:** 124

Hard Times (Dickens), **Supp. I Part 2:** 675

"Hard Times in Elfland, The" (Lanier), **Supp. I Part 1:** 365

"Hard Traveling: *Fay's* Deep South Landscape of Violence" (Beuka), **Supp. XXI:** 47

Hard Way Around, The: The Passages of Joshua Slocum (Wolff), **Supp. XXV:** 217

Hardwick, Elizabeth, **II:** 543, 554, 566; **Retro. Supp. II:** 179, 180, 183, 184, 190, 221, 228–229, 245; **Supp. I Part 1:** 196; **Supp. III Part 1:** 193–215; **Supp. IV Part 1:** 299; **Supp. V,** 319; **Supp. X,** 171; **Supp. XII:** 209; **Supp. XIV:** 89

"Hard Work 1956" (Dunn), **Supp. XI:** 147

Hardy, Barbara, **Supp. I Part 2:** 527

Hardy, Oliver, **Supp. I Part 2:** 607; **Supp. IV Part 2:** 574

Hardy, René, **Supp. III Part 1:** 235

Hardy, Thomas, **I:** 59, 103, 292, 317, 377; **II:** 181, 184–185, 186, 191–192, 271, 275, 372, 523, 542; **III:** 32, 453, 485, 508, 524; **IV:** 83, 135, 136; **Retro. Supp. I:** 141, 377–378; **Supp. I Part 1:** 217; **Supp. I Part 2:** 429, 512; **Supp. II Part 1:** 4, 26; **Supp. VIII:** 32; **Supp. IX:** 40, 78, 85, 108, 211; **Supp. X:** 228; **Supp. XI:** 311; **Supp. XIII:** 294, Supp. XIII: 130; **Supp. XIV:** 24; **Supp. XV:** 170; **Supp. XVIII:** 74; **Supp. XIX:** 86, 87; **Supp. XX:** 195; **Supp. XXI:** 109

Hardy and the Poetry of Truth-Seeking (Halliday), **Supp. XIX:** 82

Harjo, Joy, **Supp. IV Part 1:** 325, 404; **Supp. IV Part 2:** 499, 507; **Supp. XII:** 215–234; **Supp. XVIII:** 189

Harlan's Race (P. N. Warren), **Supp. XX:** **264–265**

"Harlem" (Hughes), **Retro. Supp. I:** 194, 204; **Supp. I Part 1:** 340; **Supp. VIII:** 213

Harlem, Mecca of the New Negro (Locke), **Supp. XIV:** 201

"Harlem Dancer, The" (McKay), **Supp. X:** 134

Harlem Gallery (Tolson), **Retro. Supp. I:** 208, 209, 210

Harlem Glory: A Fragment of Aframerican Life (McKay), **Supp. X:** 132, **141–142**

Harlem: Negro Metropolis (McKay), **Supp. X:** 132, 141, 142

Harlem Renaissance Remembered, The (Bontemps, ed.), **Supp. XXII:** 7

"Harlem Runs Wild" (McKay), **Supp. X:** 140

Harlem Shadows (McKay), **Supp. X:** 131–132, 136

Harlem Underground (Lacy), **Supp. XV:** 206

"Harlequin of Dreams, The" (Lanier), **Supp. I Part 1:** 365

Harlot's Ghost (Mailer), **Retro. Supp. II:** 211–212

Harlow, Jean, **IV:** 256; **Retro. Supp. I:** 110

"Harm" (C. Frost), **Supp. XV:** 101

Harmon, William, **Retro. Supp. I:** 37; **Supp. XI:** 248

"Harmonic" (F. Barthelme), **Supp. XI:** 26

Harmonium (Stevens), **III:** 196; **IV:** 76, 77, 78, 82, 87, 89, 92; **Retro. Supp. I:** 296, 297, 299, **300–302**, 301, 302

"Harmony of the Gospels" (Taylor), **IV:** 149

Harmony of the World (C. Baxter), **Supp. XVII:** 16–17

"Harmony of the World" (C. Baxter), **Supp. XVII:** 16

Harnett, Vincent, **Supp. XV:** 198

"Harp, The" (Weigl), **Supp. XIX:** 278

Harper (film), **Supp. IV Part 2:** 473

Harper, Donna, **Retro. Supp. I:** 194, 195, 209

Harper, Frances E. Watkins, **Supp. II Part 1:** 201–202; **Supp. XVIII:** 284; **Supp. XXII:** 11

Harper, Gordon Lloyd, **Retro. Supp. II:** 23

Harper, Michael S., **Retro. Supp. II:** 116, 123; **Supp. XV:** 74; **Supp. XXIV:** 184

Harper, William Rainey, **Supp. I Part 2:** 631

Harper's Anthology of 20th Century Native American Poetry (Niatum, ed.), **Supp. IV Part 1:** 331

"Harriet" (Lowell), **II:** 554

Harrigan, Edward, **II:** 276; **III:** 14

Harriman, Margaret, **Supp. XXIV:** 19

Harrington, Michael, **I:** 306

Harrington, Ollie, **Supp. XVI:** 142–143

Harris, Celia, **Retro. Supp. I:** 9

Harris, Corra, **Supp. XXII:** 190, 193, 196

Harris, George, **II:** 70

Harris, George Washington, **Supp. XXII:** 193

Harris, Joel Chandler, **III:** 338; **Supp. I Part 1:** 352; **Supp. II Part 1:** 192, 201; **Supp. XIV:** 61; **Supp. XX:** **103**

Harris, Judith, **Supp. XIV:** 269

Harris, Julie, **II:** 587, 601; **Supp. IX:** 125

Harris, Leonard, **Supp. XIV:** 196, 211–212

Harris, MacDonald, **Supp. XI:** 65

Harris, Marie, **Supp. IX:** 153

Harris, Peter, **Supp. X:** 206, 207

Harris, Susan K., **Supp. XV:** 269

Harris, Thomas, **Supp. XIV:** 26; **Supp. XXI:** 67, 78

Harris, Victoria Frenkel, **Supp. IV Part 1:** 68, 69

Harris, Violet J., **Supp. XXII:** 10, 13

Harris, William E., **Supp. XXIV:** 26

Harris, Wilson, **Supp. XXI:** 170

Harrison, Colin, **Supp. XIV:** 26

Harrison, Hazel, **Retro. Supp. II:** 115
Harrison, Jim, **Supp. VIII: 37–56; Supp. XIX:** 125, 126
Harrison, Judy, **Supp. XXIII:** 278
Harrison, Kathryn, **Supp. X:** 191
Harrison, Ken, **Supp. IX:** 101
Harrison, Oliver (pseudonym). *See* Smith, Harrison
Harrod, Lois Marie, **Supp. XXIII:** 131–132
Harry: A Portrait (Boyce), **Supp. XVII:** 104; **Supp. XXI:** 7, **13–14**
Harryhausen, Ray, **Supp. IV Part 1:** 115
Harryman, Carla, **Supp. XV:** 344
"Harry of Nothingham" (Hugo), **Supp. VI:** 146–147
"Harry's Death" (Carver), **Supp. III Part 1:** 146
"Harsh Judgment, The" (Kunitz), **Supp. III Part 1:** 264
Hart, Albert Bushnell, **Supp. I Part 2:** 479, 480, 481
Hart, Bernard, **I:** 241, 242, 248–250, 256
Hart, Henry, **Retro. Supp. II:** 187; **Supp. XIV:** 97
Hart, James D., **Supp. XVIII:** 257
Hart, John Seely, **Supp. XVIII:** 257, 258, 264
Hart, Lorenz, **III:** 361
Hart, Moss, **Supp. IV Part 2:** 574; **Supp. XV:** 329
Hart, Pearl, **Supp. X:** 103
"Hart Crane" (Tate), **I:** 381
"Hart Crane and Poetry: A Consideration of Crane's Intense Poetics with Reference to 'The Return' " (Grossman), **Retro. Supp. II:** 83
Harte, Anna Griswold, **Supp. II Part 1:** 341
Harte, Bret, **I:** 193, 195, 203; **II:** 289; **IV:** 196; **Retro. Supp. II:** 72; **Supp. II Part 1: 335–359,** 399; **Supp. XV:** 115
Harte, Walter Blackburn, **I:** 199
Harter, Carol C., **Supp. IV Part 1:** 217
Hartigan, Grace, **Supp. XXIII:** 210, 212, 217
Hartley, David, **III:** 77
Hartley, Lois, **Supp. I Part 2:** 459, 464–465
Hartley, L. P., **Supp. I Part 1:** 293
Hartley, Marsden, **IV:** 409, 413; **Retro. Supp. I:** 430; **Supp. X:** 137; **Supp. XV:** 298
Hartman, Geoffrey, **Supp. IV Part 1:** 119; **Supp. XII:** 130, 253
Hartman, Saidiya, **Supp. XX:** 154
Harum, David, **II:** 102
"Harvard" (Lowell), **II:** 554
Harvard College in the Seventeenth Century (Morison), **Supp. I Part 2:** 485
"Harvest" (E. P. Jones), **Supp. XXII:** 141
"Harvest, The" (Hempel), **Supp. XXI:** 115, **122–123**
Harvester, The (Stratton-Porter), **Supp. XX: 211, 212, 218, 221**
"*Harvester, The:* The Natural Bounty of Gene Stratton-Porter" (Birkelo), **Supp. XX: 220–221**

"Harvesters of Night and Water" (Hogan), **Supp. IV Part 1:** 412
"Harvest Song" (Toomer), **Supp. III Part 2:** 483
Harvill Book of 20th Century Poetry in English, **Supp. X:** 55
Harvin, Emily, **Supp. XXIII:** 174
"Harv Is Plowing Now" (Updike), **Retro. Supp. I:** 318
Haselden, Elizabeth Lee, **Supp. VIII:** 125
"Hasidic Noir" (Abraham), **Supp. XXIV: 14–15**
Haskell, Mary, **Supp. XX: 115, 117**
Hass, Robert, **Supp. VI: 97–111; Supp. VIII:** 24, 28; **Supp. XI:** 142, 270; **Supp. XIV:** 83, 84; **Supp. XXI:** 60
Hassam, Childe, **Retro. Supp. II:** 136
Hassan, Ihab, **IV:** 99–100, 115; **Supp. XI:** 221
Hasse, Henry, **Supp. IV Part 1:** 102
Hasty-Pudding, The (Barlow), **Supp. II Part 1:** 74, 77–80
"Hater of Mediocrity, The" (Boulton), **Supp. XXII:** 23
Hate That Hate Produced, The (CBS documentary), **Supp. XX: 102**
Hatful of Rain, A (Gazzo), **III:** 155
Hatlen, Burton, **Supp. V:** 138, 139–140; **Supp. XXI:** 24
"Hatred"(O'Hara), **Supp. XXIII:** 212
"Hattie Bloom" (Oliver), **Supp. VII:** 232
Haugen, Hayley Mitchell, **Supp. XXIV:** 215
Haunch, Paunch, and Jowl (Ornitz), **Supp. IX:** 227
Haunted Lady, The (Rinehart), **Supp. XXV:** 198, 200
"Haunted Landscape" (Ashbery), **Supp. III Part 1:** 22
Haunted Merchant, The (Briggs), **Supp. XVIII:** 2, 8
"Haunted Mind" (Simic), **Supp. VIII:** 282
"Haunted Mind, The" (Hawthorne), **II:** 230–231
"Haunted Oak, The" (Dunbar), **Supp. II Part 1:** 207, 208
"Haunted Palace, The" (Poe), **III:** 421
"Haunted Valley, The" (Bierce), **I:** 200
Haunting, The (film), **Supp. IX:** 125
Haunting of Hill House, The (Jackson), **Supp. IX:** 117, 121, 126
Hauptmann, Gerhart, **III:** 472
Haussmann, Sonja, **Supp. XIII:** 331, **Supp. XIII:** 347
"Havanna vanities come to dust in Miami" (Didion), **Supp. IV Part 1:** 210
Havel, Hippolyte, **Supp. XXI:** 4, 6
Haven, Cynthia, **Supp. XV:** 252, 264; **Supp. XXIII:** 134, 138, 139
Haven's End (Marquand), **III:** 55, 56, 63, 68
"Have You Ever Faked an Orgasm" (Peacock), **Supp. XIX:** 199
"Have You Ever Tried to Enter the Long Black Branches" (Oliver), **Supp. VII:** 247
"Having a Coke with You"(O'Hara), **Supp. XXIII:** 219

"Having Been Interstellar" (Ammons), **Supp. VII:** 25
"Having It Out With Melancholy" (Kenyon), **Supp. VII:** 171
"Having Lost My Sons, I Confront the Wreckage of the Moon: Christmas, 1960" (Wright), **Supp. III Part 2:** 600
"Having Snow" (Schwartz), **Supp. II Part 2:** 652
"Having Words"(Thompson), **Supp. XXIII:** 293–294
"Hawaii, Washington, Vermont: A Frame for the Verse" (Taggard), **Supp. XXII:** 281–282
Hawaiian Hilltop (Taggard), **Supp. XXII:** 275
Hawai'i One Summer (Kingston), **Supp. V:** 157, 160, 166, 169–170
"Hawk, The" (Francis), **Supp. IX:** 81
Hawke, David Freeman, **Supp. I Part 2:** 511, 516
Hawkes, John, **I:** 113; **Retro. Supp. II:** 234; **Supp. III Part 1:** 2; **Supp. V:** 40; **Supp. IX:** 212; **Supp. XVII:** 183; **Supp. XXI:** 210
Hawkins, Gary, **Supp. XXI:** 35, 39
Hawkins, William, **II:** 587
Hawk in the Rain, The (Hughes), **Retro. Supp. II:** 244; **Supp. I Part 2:** 537, 540
Hawk Is Dying, The (Crews), **Supp. XI:** 111
Hawk Moon (Shepard), **Supp. III Part 2:** 445
Hawks, Howard, **Supp. IV Part 1:** 130; **Supp. XVIII:** 148
"Hawk's Cry in Autumn, The" (Brodsky), **Supp. VIII:** 29
"Hawk's Shadow" (Glück), **Supp. V:** 85
Hawk's Well, The (Yeats), **III:** 459–460
Hawley, Adelaide, **Supp. XIV:** 207
Hawley, Joseph, **I:** 546
Hawthorne (James), **II:** 372–378; **Retro. Supp. I:** 220, **223–224**
"Hawthorne" (Longfellow), **Retro. Supp. II:** 169
"Hawthorne" (Lowell), **II:** 550
Hawthorne, Julian, **II:** 225; **Supp. I Part 1:** 38; **Supp. XV:** 274
Hawthorne, Nathaniel, **I:** 106, 204, 211, 340, 355, 363, 384, 413, 458, 561–562; **II:** 7, 8, 40, 60, 63, 74, 89, 127–128, 138, 142, 198, **223–246,** 255, 259, 264, 267, 272, 274, 277, 281, 282, 295, 307, 309, 311, 313, 322, 324, 326, 402, 408, 446, 501, 545; **III:** 51, 81–82, 83, 84, 85, 87, 88, 91, 92, 113, 316, 359, 412, 415, 421, 438, 453, 454, 507, 565, 572; **IV:** 2, 4, 167, 172, 179, 194, 333, 345, 453; **Retro. Supp. I:** 1, 53, 59, 62, 63, 91, **145–167,** 215, 218, 220, 223, 248–249, 252, 257, 258, 330, 331, 365; **Retro. Supp. II:** 136, 142, 153, 156–157, 158, 159, 187, 221; **Supp. I Part 1:** 38, 188, 197, 317, 372; **Supp. I Part 2:** 420, 421, 545, 579, 580, 582, 587, 595, 596; **Supp. III Part 2:** 501;

Supp. IV Part 1: 80, 127, 297; **Supp. IV Part 2:** 463, 596; **Supp. V:** 152; **Supp. VIII:** 103, 105, 108, 153, 201; **Supp. IX:** 114; **Supp. X:** 78; **Supp. XI:** 51, 78; **Supp. XII:** 26; **Supp. XIII:** 102; **Supp. XIV:** 48; **Supp. XV:** 269, 272, 282; **Supp. XVI:** 83, 84, 157; **Supp. XVII:** 42; **Supp. XVIII:** 258, 260; **Supp. XXI:** 201; **Supp. XXIII:** 161, 190, 290; **Supp. XXV:** 242, 249

Hawthorne, Mrs. Nathaniel (Sophia Peabody), **II:** 224, 244; **III:** 75, 86

Hawthorne, Rose, **II:** 225

Hawthorne, Una, **II:** 225

"Hawthorne and His Mosses" (Melville), **Retro. Supp. I:** 254; **Supp. XIV:** 48

"Hawthorne Aspect \[of Henry James\], The" (Eliot), **Retro. Supp. I:** 63

"Hawthorne in Solitude" (Cowley), **Supp. II Part 1:** 143

Hay, John, **I:** 1, 10, 12, 14–15; **Supp. I Part 1:** 352

Hay, Mrs. John, **I:** 14

Hay, Sara Henderson, **Supp. XIV:** 119–135

Hayakawa, S. I., **I:** 448; **Supp. I Part 1:** 315; **Supp. XV:** 176

Haycroft, Howard, **Supp. XXV:** 199

Hayden, Robert, **Supp. II Part 1:** 361–383; **Supp. IV Part 1:** 169; **Supp. XIII:** 115, 127; **Supp. XIV:** 119, 123

Hayden, Sterling, **Supp. XI:** 304

Hayden, William R., **Supp. XXV:** 38

Haydn, Hiram, **IV:** 100, 358

Hayduke Lives! (Abbey), **Supp. XIII: 16**

Hayek, Friedrich A. von, **Supp. IV Part 2:** 524

Hayes, Helen, **Supp. XVI:** 193, 195

Hayes, Ira, **Supp. IV Part 1:** 326

Hayes, Richard, **Supp. V:** 320

Hayes, Rutherford B., **Supp. I Part 2:** 419

Hayford, James, **Supp. XXII:** 204, 218

Haygood, Wil, **Supp. VIII:** 79

"Haying While the Sun Shines" (L. I. Wilder), **Supp. XXII:** 290

Hayne, Paul Hamilton, **Supp. I Part 1:** 352, 354, 355, 360, 372

Haynes, Todd, **Supp. XVIII:** 23

Haynes-Smith, William, **Supp. XX: 231, 232, 233**

Hayward, Florence, **Retro. Supp. II:** 65

Hayward, John, **Retro. Supp. I:** 67

Hayward, Leland, **Supp. XIX:** 250

Haywood, "Big" Bill, **I:** 483; **Supp. V:** 286; **Supp. XXIII:** 162

Hazan, Joe, **Supp. XXIII:** 212

Hazard, Grace, **II:** 530

Hazard of Fortunes, A (Howells), **Retro. Supp. II:** 288

Hazard of New Fortunes, A (Howells), **II:** 275, 276, 286–297, 290

Hazel, Robert, **Supp. VIII:** 137, 138

Hazen, General W. B., **I:** 192, 193

Hazlitt, Henry, **Supp. IV Part 2:** 524

Hazlitt, William, **I:** 58, 378; **II:** 315; **Supp. XXI:** 205

Hazmat (McClatchy), **Supp. XII: 265–270**

Hazo, Samuel, **I:** 386; **Supp. XIV:** 123, 124

Hazzard, Shirley, **Supp. VIII:** 151

H.D. *See* Doolittle, Hilda

"He" (Porter), **III:** 434, 435

"Head and Shoulders" (Fitzgerald), **Retro. Supp. I:** 101

Headhunter (Findley), **Supp. XX: 57–59, 60, 61**

"Head-Hunter, The" (O. Henry), **Supp. II Part 1:** 403

"Headless Hawk, The" (Capote), **Supp. III Part 1:** 124

Headlines (T. Williams), **IV:** 381

Headlong Hall (Peacock), **Supp. I Part 1:** 307

Headmaster, The (McPhee), **Supp. III Part 1:** 291, 294, 298

"Head of Joaquín Murrieta, The" (Rodriguez), **Supp. XIV:** 303

Headsman, The (Cooper), **I:** 345–346

Heads of Grain (al-Sanábil) (Gibran), **Supp. XX: 124**

"Headwaters" (Momaday), **Supp. IV Part 2:** 486

"Head Wound" (Halliday), **Supp. XIX:** 92

Healing, The (G. Jones), **Supp. XXIV:** 183, 185, **190–192,** 195

Healy, Eloise Klein, **Supp. XI:** 121, 124, 126, 127, 129, 137

Healy, Tim, **II:** 129, 137

Heaney, Sally, **Supp. XVII:** 241

Heaney, Seamus, **Retro. Supp. II:** 245; **Supp. IX:** 41, 42; **Supp. X:** 67, 122; **Supp. XI:** 249; **Supp. XV:** 256; **Supp. XXI:** 54, 243

"Heard through the Walls of the Racetrack Glen Motel" (X. J. Kennedy), **Supp. XV:** 170

Hearn, Lafcadio, **I:** 211; **II:** 311

Hearon, Shelby, **Supp. VIII: 57–72**

Hearst, Patty, **Supp. IV Part 1:** 195

Hearst, William Randolph, **I:** 198, 207, 208; **IV:** 298

Heart and Perimeter (Bierds), **Supp. XVII: 28–29**

"Heart and the Lyre, The" (Bogan), **Supp. III Part 1:** 65

"Heart as Origami, The (Hirshfield), **Supp. XXIII:** 132

"Heartbeat" (Harjo), **Supp. XII:** 221–222

Heartbreak Hotel (Siddons), **Supp. XXII:** 239, 241, 242

Heartbreak Kid, The (film), **Supp. IV Part 2:** 575, 589

"Heart Failure"(Schott), **Supp. XXIII:** 252

"Heart Finds Its Own Conclusion, The" (Muñoz), **Supp. XXV:** 136

Heart for the Gods of Mexico, A (Aiken), **I:** 54

"Hear the Nightingale Sing" (Gordon), **II:** 200

Hear the Wind Blow (Sanders), **Supp. XVI:** 268

Heart is a Lonely Hunter, The (McCullers), **II:** 586, 588–593, 604, 605

Heart of a Woman, The (Angelou), **Supp. IV Part 1:** 2, 5, 7–9, 9, 14, 17

Heart of Darkness (Conrad), **Retro. Supp. II:** 292; **Supp. V:** 249, 311; **Supp. VIII:** 4, 316; **Supp. XIX:** 28; **Supp. XX:** 18, 57–58; **Supp. XXIV:** 286

"Heart of Darkness" (Conrad), **I:** 575, 578; **II:** 595; **Supp. XVI:** 212

Heart of Darkness (Didion), **Supp. IV Part 1:** 207

Heart of Dixie (film), **Supp. XXII:** 239, 241

Heart of Haiku, The (Hirshfield), **Supp. XXIII:** 137–138

Heart of Happy Hollow, The (Dunbar), **Supp. II Part 1:** 214

Heart of Knowledge, The: American Indians on the Bomb (Gunn Allen and Caputi, eds.), **Supp. IV Part 1:** 334–335

"Heart of Knowledge, The: Nuclear Themes in Native American Thought and Literature" (Caputi), **Supp. IV Part 1:** 335

Heart of the Earth (Moraga), **Supp. XXIII:** 196

"Heart of the Park, The " (O'Connor), **Retro. Supp. II:** 225

Heart of the West (O. Henry), **Supp. II Part 1:** 410

"Hearts, The" (Pinsky), **Supp. VI:** 245–247, 248

"'Hearts and Flowers' " (MacLeish), **III:** 8

"Hearts and Heads" (Ransom), **Supp. I Part 1:** 373

"Heart's Graveyard Shift, The" (Komunyakaa), **Supp. XIII:** 120

Heart-Shape in the Dust (Hayden), **Supp. II Part 1:** 365, 366

Heart's Needle (Snodgrass), **I:** 400

"Heart's Needle" (Snodgrass), **Supp. VI: 311–313,** 320

"Hearts of Oak" (Rowson), **Supp. XV:** 243

"Heart Songs" (Proulx), **Supp. VII:** 254

Heart Songs and Other Stories (Proulx), **Supp. VII:** 252–256, 261

Heart to Artemis, The (Bryher), **Supp. I Part 1:** 259

"Heart to Heart" (Zitkala-Ša), **Supp. XXV:** 284

Heartwood (Burke), **Supp. XIV:** 35

Heath, Shirley, **Supp. XX:** 90

Heath Anthology of American Literature, The, **Supp. IX:** 4; **Supp. XV:** 270, 313

Heathcote, Anne. *See* De Lancey, Mrs. James

"Heathen Chinee, The" (Harte), **Supp. II Part 1:** 350–351, 352

Heathen Days, 1890–1936 (Mencken), **III:** 100, 111

Heath-Stubbs, John, **Supp. XV:** 153

Heat's On, The (C. Himes), **Supp. XVI:** 143, 144

"Heaven" (Dunn), **Supp. XI:** 154

"Heaven" (Levine), **Supp. V:** 182

"Heaven" (Patchett), **Supp. XII:** 309

Heaven and Earth: A Cosmology (Goldbarth), **Supp. XII: 187**

"Heaven and Earth in Jest" (Dillard), **Supp. VI:** 24, 28

"Heaven as Anus" (Kumin), **Supp. IV Part 2:** 448

Heavenly Conversation, The (Mather), **Supp. II Part 2:** 460

"Heavenly Feast, The" (Schnackenberg), **Supp. XV:** 257, 259

Heavens (Untermeyer), **Supp. XV:** 306

Heavens and Earth (Benét), **Supp. XI:** 44

Heaven's Coast (Doty), **Supp. XI:** 119, 121, **129–130**, 134; **Supp. XXIII:** 126

Heaven's Prisoners (Burke), **Supp. XIV:** 23, 29

"Heavy Angel, The" (Everwine), **Supp. XV:** 80

"Heavy Bear Who Goes with Me, The" (Schwartz), **Supp. II Part 2:** 646

"Heavy Trash" (Halliday), **Supp. XIX:** 92, 93

Hebert, Ernest, **Supp. XXII:** 207

"He Came Also Still" (Zukofsky), **Supp. III Part 2:** 612

Hecht, Anthony, **IV:** 138; **Supp. III Part 2:** 541, 561; **Supp. X:** 55–75; **Supp. XII:** 269–270; **Supp. XV:** 251, 256

Hecht, Ben, **I:** 103; **II:** 42; **Supp. I Part 2:** 646; **Supp. XI:** 307; **Supp. XIII:** 106; **Supp. XXV:** 18, 19, 22, 27, 29

Hecht, S. Theodore, **Supp. III Part 2:** 614

Heckewelder, John, **II:** 503

"Hedge Island" (Lowell), **II:** 524

Hedges, William I., **II:** 311–312

"He 'Digesteth Harde Yron' " (Moore), **Supp. IV Part 2:** 454

Hedin, Robert, **Supp. XII:** 200, 202

Hedylus (Doolittle), **Supp. I Part 1:** 259, 270

"Heel & Toe To the End" (W. C. Williams), **Retro. Supp. I:** 430

Heffernan, Michael, **Supp. XII:** 177

"HEGEL" (Baraka), **Supp. II Part 1:** 53

Hegel, Georg Wilhelm Friedrich, **I:** 265; **II:** 358; **III:** 262, 308–309, 480, 481, 487, 607; **IV:** 86, 333, 453; **Supp. I Part 2:** 633, 635, 640, 645; **Supp. XVI:** 289

"Hegemony of Race, The" (Du Bois), **Supp. II Part 1:** 181

Hegger, Grace Livingston. *See* Lewis, Mrs. Sinclair (Grace Livingston Hegger)

"He Had Spent His Youth Dreaming" (Dobyns), **Supp. XIII:** 90

Heidegger, Martin, **II:** 362, 363; **III:** 292; **IV:** 491; **Retro. Supp. II:** 87; **Supp. V:** 267; **Supp. VIII:** 9; **Supp. XVI:** 283, 288

Heidenmauer, The (Cooper), **I:** 345–346

Heidi Chronicles, The (Wasserstein), **Supp. IV Part 1:** 309; **Supp. XV:** 319, **325–327**

"Height of the Ridiculous, The" (Holmes), **Supp. I Part 1:** 302

Heilbroner, Robert, **Supp. I Part 2:** 644, 648, 650

Heilbrun, Carolyn G., **Supp. IX:** 66; **Supp. XI:** 208; **Supp. XIV:** 161, 163; **Supp. XX: 108**

Heilman, Robert Bechtold, **Supp. XIV:** 11, 12

Heilpern, John, **Supp. XIV:** 242

Heim, Michael, **Supp. V:** 209

Heine, Heinrich, **II:** 272, 273, 277, 281, 282, 387, 544; **IV:** 5; **Supp. XV:** 293, 299; **Supp. XVI:** 188

Heineman, Frank, **Supp. III Part 2:** 619

Heinemann, Larry, **Supp. XXII: 103–117**

Heinlein, Robert, **Supp. IV Part 1:** 102; **Supp. XVI:** 122; **Supp. XVIII:** 149

Heinz, Helen. *See* Tate, Mrs. Allen (Helen Heinz)

Heiress, The (film), **Retro. Supp. I:** 222

"Heirs" (Nye), **Supp. XIII:** 284

"He Is Not Worth the Trouble" (Rowson), **Supp. XV:** 240

"He Knew" (C. Himes), **Supp. XVI:** 137

"Helas" (Creeley), **Supp. IV Part 1:** 150, 158

Helburn, Theresa, **IV:** 381

Heldreth, Leonard, **Supp. V:** 151

"Helen" (Lowell), **II:** 544

"Helen, Thy Beauty Is to Me" (Fante), **Supp. XI:** 169

"Helen: A Courtship" (Faulkner), **Retro. Supp. I:** 81

"Helen I Love You" (Farrell), **II:** 28, 45

Helen in Egypt (Doolittle), **Supp. I Part 1:** 260, 272, 273, 274; **Supp. XV:** 264

Helen Keller: Sketch for a Portrait (Brooks), **I:** 254

"Helen of Tyre" (Longfellow), **II:** 496

Heliodora (Doolittle), **Supp. I Part 1:** 266

"He Lives On the Landing" (Espaillat), **Supp. XXI:** 108

"Helix" (Sobin), **Supp. XVI:** 283

Hellbox (O'Hara), **III:** 361

Helle, Anita, **Supp. XXIII:** 117

Heller, Joseph, **III:** 2, 258; **IV:** 98; **Retro. Supp. II:** 324; **Supp. I Part 1:** 196; **Supp. IV Part 1: 379–396**; **Supp. V:** 244; **Supp. VIII:** 245; **Supp. XI:** 307; **Supp. XII:** 167–168; **Supp. XV:** 322; **Supp. XVII:** 139; **Supp. XXIII:** 100

"Hell-Heaven" (Lahiri), **Supp. XXI: 181–183**, 183, 184–186, 188

Hellman, Lillian, **I:** 28; **III:** 28; **Supp. I Part 1: 276–298**; **Supp. IV Part 1:** 1, 12, 83, 353, 355, 356; **Supp. VIII:** 243; **Supp. IX:** 196, 198, 200–201, 204

Hellmann, Lillian, **Retro. Supp. II:** 327

Hello (Creeley), **Supp. IV Part 1:** 155, 157

"Hello, Hello Henry" (Kumin), **Supp. IV Part 2:** 446

"Hello, Stranger" (Capote), **Supp. III Part 1:** 120

Hello Dolly! (musical play), **IV:** 357

Hell's Angels: A Strange and Terrible Saga (Thompson), **Supp. XXIV:** 282, 283, 288, 290–291

Hellyer, John, **Supp. I Part 2:** 468

Helm, Bob, **Supp. XV:** 147

Helm, Levon, **Supp. XVIII:** 26

Helmets (Dickey), **Supp. IV Part 1:** 175, 178, 180

"Helmsman, The" (Doolittle), **Supp. I Part 1:** 266

"Help" (Barth), **I:** 139

"Help Her to Believe" (Olsen). *See* "I Stand There Ironing" (Olsen)

Helprin, Mark, **Supp. XIX:** 142; **Supp. XXV: 79–91**

"Helsinki Window" (Creeley), **Supp. IV Part 1:** 158

"Hema and Kaushik" (Lahiri), **Supp. XXI:** 183, 188

Hemenway, Robert E., **Supp. IV Part 1:** 6

Hemingway, Dr. Clarence Edwards, **II:** 248, 259

Hemingway, Ernest, **I:** 28, 64, 97, 99, 105, 107, 117, 150, 162, 190, 211, 221, 288, 289, 295, 367, 374, 378, 421, 423, 445, 476, 477, 478, 482, 484–485, 487, 488, 489, 491, 495, 504, 517; **II:** 27, 44, 51, 58, 68–69, 78, 90, 97, 127, 206, **247–270,** 289, 424, 431, 456, 457, 458–459, 482, 560, 600; **III:** 2, 18, 20, 35, 36, 37, 40, 61, 108, 220, 334, 363, 364, 382, 453, 454, 471–472, 476, 551, 575, 576, 584; **IV:** 27, 28, 33, 34, 35, 42, 49, 97, 108, 122, 126, 138, 190, 191, 201, 216, 217, 257, 297, 363, 404, 427, 433, 451; **Retro. Supp. I:** 74, 98, 108, 111, 112, 113, 115, **169–191,** 215, 292, 359, 418; **Retro. Supp. II:** 19, 24, 30, 68, 115, 123; **Supp. I Part 2:** 621, 658, 678; **Supp. II Part 1:** 221; **Supp. III Part 1:** 146; **Supp. III Part 2:** 617; **Supp. IV Part 1:** 48, 102, 123, 197, 236, 342, 343, 344, 348, 350, 352, 380–381, 383; **Supp. IV Part 2:** 463, 468, 502, 607, 679, 680, 681, 689, 692; **Supp. V:** 237, 240, 244, 250, 336; **Supp. VIII:** 40, 101, 105, 179, 182, 183, 188, 189, 196; **Supp. IX:** 16, 57, 58, 94, 106, 260, 262; **Supp. X:** 137, 167, 223, 225; **Supp. XI:** 214, 221; **Supp. XIII:** 96, 255, 270; **Supp. XIV:** 24, 83; **Supp. XV:** 69, 135; **Supp. XVI:** 203, 205–206, 208, 210, 233, 236–237, 281–282; **Supp. XVII:** 4, 105, 107, 137, 228, 229; **Supp. XVIII:** 74, 90, 102; **Supp. XIX:** 131, 154, 157, 246; **Supp. XX: 45, 74, 76; Supp. XXI:** 7, 8, 36, 262; **Supp. XXIII:** 4, 68, 166, 174, 275, 299; **Supp. XXIV:** 54, 64, 97, 284

Hemingway, Mrs. Ernest (Hadley Richardson), **II:** 257, 260, 263

Hemingway, Mrs. Ernest (Martha Gellhorn), **II:** 260

Hemingway, Mrs. Ernest (Mary Welsh), **II:** 257, 260

Hemingway, Mrs. Ernest (Pauline Pfeiffer), **II:** 260

"Hemingway in Paris" (Cowley), **Supp. II Part 1:** 144

"Hemingway Story, A" (Dubus), **Supp. VII:** 91

"Hemingway: The Old Lion" (Cowley), **Supp. II Part 1:** 143

"Hemp, The" (Benét), **Supp. XI:** 44

Hempel, Amy, **Supp. XIX:** 209; **Supp. XXI:** 115–128

"Henchman, The" (Whittier), **Supp. I Part 2:** 696

Henderson, Alice Corbin, **Supp. I Part 2:** 387; **Supp. XV:** 302–303

Henderson, Darwin L., **Supp. XIII:** 213, 221–222

Henderson, Jane, **Supp. VIII:** 87; **Supp. XX:** 84

Henderson, Katherine, **Supp. IV Part 1:** 203, 207

Henderson, Linda. *See* Hogan, Linda

Henderson, Robert W., **Supp. VIII:** 124

Henderson, Stephen, **Supp. IV Part 1:** 365

Henderson, the Rain King (Bellow), **I:** 144, 147, 148, 152, 153, 154, 155, 158, 160, 161, 162–163; **Retro. Supp. II:** 19, **24–25,** 30

"Hen Flower, The" (Kinnell), **Supp. III Part 1:** 247–248

Henie, Sonja, **Supp. XII:** 165

Henkin, Joshua, **Supp. XXII:** 216

Henle, James, **II:** 26, 30, 38, 41; **Supp. IX:** 2

Henley, Beth, **Supp. XXI:** 145

Hennesy, Dale, **Supp. XV:** 5

Henninger, Katherine, **Supp. XXI:** 253

Henri, Robert, **IV:** 411; **Supp. I Part 2:** 376

Henrich, Edith, **Supp. XXIV:** 214

Henry, Arthur, **I:** 515; **Retro. Supp. II:** 97

Henry, DeWitt, **Supp. XI:** 342

Henry, O., **I:** 201; **III:** 5; **Supp. I Part 2:** 390, 462; **Supp. II Part 1: 385–412;** **Supp. XV:** 40

Henry, Robert, **Retro. Supp. II:** 103

Henry, William A., III, **Supp. IV Part 2:** 574

Henry and Clara (Mallon), **Supp. XIX:** 132, **136–137,** 139, 141

Henry and June (film), **Supp. X:** 186

Henry and June: From the Unexpurgated Diary of Anaïs Nin, **Supp. X:** 184, 185, 187, 194

Henry Holt and Company, **Retro. Supp. I:** 121, 131, 133, 136

Henry IV (Shakespeare), **III:** 166; **Supp. VIII:** 164

"Henry James, Jr." (Howells), **II:** 289; **Retro. Supp. I:** 220

"Henry James and the Art of Teaching" (Rowe), **Retro. Supp. I:** 216

"Henry Manley, Living Alone, Keeps Time" (Kumin), **Supp. IV Part 2:** 451

"Henry Manley Looks Back" (Kumin), **Supp. IV Part 2:** 451

"Henry Manley" poems (Kumin), **Supp. IV Part 2:** 446

Henry Miller Reader, The (Durrell, ed.), **III:** 175, 190

"Henry's Confession" (Berryman), **I:** 186

Henry VIII (Shakespeare), **Supp. IX:** 235

Henslee, **Supp. IV Part 1:** 217

Henson, Josiah, **Supp. I Part 2:** 589

Hentoff, Margot, **Supp. IV Part 1:** 205

Hentz, Caroline Lee, **Supp. I Part 2:** 584

Henze, Hans Werner, **Supp. II Part 1:** 24

"He of the Assembly" (Bowles), **Supp. IV Part 1:** 90

Hepburn, Katharine, **Supp. IX:** 189; **Supp. XI:** 17

Heraclitus, **II:** 1, 163; **IV:** 86

Herakles: A Play in Verse (MacLeish), **III:** 21, 22

Herald of the Autochthonic Spirit (Corso), **Supp. XII:** 134–136

He Ran All the Way (film), **Supp. XVII:** 63

Herberg, Will, **III:** 291

Herbert, Edward, **II:** 11

Herbert, Francis (pseudonym). *See* Bryant, William Cullen

Herbert, George, **II:** 12; **IV:** 141, 145, 146, 151, 153, 156, 165; **Retro. Supp. II:** 40; **Supp. I Part 1:** 80, 107, 108, 122; **Supp. IV Part 2:** 646; **Supp. XV:** 92, 212, 251; **Supp. XXI:** 109

Herbert, Zbigniew, **Supp. VIII:** 20

Herbert Huncke Reader, The (Schafer, ed.), **Supp. XIV:** 137, 138, 139, 140, 145, 147, 150, 151–152

Herbert of Cherbury, Lord, **II:** 108

"Herbert West—Reanimator" (Lovecraft), **Supp. XXV:** 112

"Herbert White" (Bidart), **Supp. XV:** 24, 27

Herbst, Josephine, **Retro. Supp. II:** 325, 328; **Supp. XIII:** 295

"Her Choice" (Larcom), **Supp. XIII:** 144

"Her Dead Brother" (Lowell), **Retro. Supp. II:** 188

"Her Dream Is of the Sea" (Ríos), **Supp. IV Part 2:** 546

"Here" (Kenyon), **Supp. VII:** 164

Here and Beyond (Wharton), **Retro. Supp. I:** 382

Here and Now (Levertov), **Supp. III Part 1:** 275, 276

"Here and There" (Wallace), **Supp. X:** 305–306

Here Comes the Mystery Man (Sanders), **Supp. XVI:** 269

"Here Comes Winston, Full of the Holy Spirit" (Eugenides), **Supp. XXIV:** 133

Heredia, Juanita, **Supp. XI:** 185, 190

Heredity and Variation (Lock), **Retro. Supp. I:** 375

Heredity: A Psychological Study of Its Phenomena, Laws, Causes, and Consequences (Ribot), **Supp. XX: 238**

"Here Inside My Forehead" (Rasmussen; Nelson and Espeland, trans.), **Supp. XVIII:** 180

Here is Your War (Pyle), **Supp. XVII:** 61

Here Let Us Feast (M. F. K. Fisher), **Supp. XVII:** 86, 87

Here Lies (Parker), **Supp. IX:** 192

Herendeen, Anne, **Supp. XXII:** 275

Here on Earth (Hoffman), **Supp. X:** 77, 89

Heresy and the Ideal: On Contemporary Poetry (Baker), **Supp. XI:** 142

"Here to Learn" (Bowles), **Supp. IV Part 1:** 93

"Here to Yonder" (Hughes), **Retro. Supp. I:** 205

"Her Father's Letters" (Milburn), **Supp. XI:** 242

"Her Favorite Story" (Richard), **Supp. XIX:** 211, 212

Herford, Reverend Brooke, **I:** 471

Herford, Will, **Supp. XXII:** 275

"Her Game" (Skloot), **Supp. XX: 196, 202**

Hergesheimer, Joseph, **Supp. I Part 2:** 620; **Supp. XVI:** 187

"Heritage" (Cullen), **Supp. IV Part 1:** 164–165, 168, 170, 171

"Heritage" (Hogan), **Supp. IV Part 1:** 413

"Her Kind" (Sexton), **Supp. II Part 2:** 687

Herland (Gilman), **Supp. XI:** 208–209

Herman, Florence. *See* Williams, Mrs. William Carlos (Florence Herman)

Herman, Jan, **Supp. XIV:** 150–151

Herman, William (pseudonym). *See* Bierce, Ambrose

"Her Management" (Swenson), **Supp. IV Part 2:** 642

"Herman Melville" (Auden), **Supp. II Part 1:** 14

Herman Melville (Mumford), **Supp. II Part 2:** 471, 476, 489–491

"Hermes of the Ways" (Doolittle), **Supp. I Part 1:** 266

"Hermes: Port Authority: His Song" (Di Piero), **Supp. XIX:** 47

Hermetic Definition (Doolittle), **Supp. I Part 1:** 271, 272, 273, 274

Hermia Suydam (Atherton), **Supp. XXIV:** 21, 28

"Hermitage, The" (Haines), **Supp. XII:** 205–206

Hermit and the Wild Woman, The (Wharton), **IV:** 315; **Retro. Supp. I:** 371

"Hermit and the Wild Woman, The" (Wharton), **Retro. Supp. I:** 372

"Hermit Meets the Skunk, The" (Kumin), **Supp. IV Part 2:** 447

Hermit of 69th Street, The: The Working Papers or Norbert Kosky (Kosinski), **Supp. VII:** 215, 216, 223, 226–227

"Hermit of Saba, The" (Freneau), **Supp. II Part 1:** 259

"Hermit Picks Berries, The" (Kumin), **Supp. IV Part 2:** 447

Hermit's Story, The (Bass), **Supp. XVI:** 23–24

"Hermit Thrush, A" (Clampitt), **Supp. IX:** 40

Hermit-Woman, The (G. Jones), **Supp. XXIV:** 185, 194

Hernández, Miguel, **Supp. V:** 194; **Supp. XIII:** 315, 323; **Supp. XXI:** 104

Herne, James A., **II:** 276; **Supp. II Part 1:** 198

Hernton, Calvin, **Supp. X:** 240

"Hero, The" (Moore), **III:** 200, 211, 212

Hero, The: A Study in Tradition, Myth, and Drama (Raglan), **I:** 135; **Supp.**

XIX: 147
Hero and the Blues, The (Murray), **Supp. XIX:** 153, 154
Hérodiade (Mallarmé), **I:** 66
Herodotus, **Supp. I Part 2:** 405
Heroes, The (Ashbery), **Supp. III Part 1:** 3
Heroes and Saints (Moraga), **Supp. XXIII:** 195, 196, 197, **203–204**
Heroes and Saints and Other Plays (Moraga), **Supp. XXIII:** 197
Hero in America, The (Van Doren), **II:** 103
"Heroines of Nature: Four Women Respond to the American Landscape" (Norwood), **Supp. IX:** 24
"Heron, The" (Roethke), **III:** 540–541
"Her One Bad Eye" (Karr), **Supp. XI:** 244
"Her Own People" (Warren), **IV:** 253
Her Place in These Designs (Espaillat), **Supp. XXI:** 99, 104
"Her Quaint Honour" (Gordon), **II:** 196, 199, 200
Herr, Michael, **Supp. XI:** 245; **Supp. XIX:** 17
Herreshoff, David, **Supp. XIX:** 265
Herrick, Robert, **II:** 11, 18, 444; **III:** 463, 592; **IV:** 453; **Retro. Supp. I:** 319; **Retro. Supp. II:** 101; **Supp. I Part 2:** 646; **Supp. XIII:** 334; **Supp. XIV:** 8, 9; **Supp. XV:** 155; **Supp. XXI:** 14
Herrmann, John, **Retro. Supp. II:** 328; **Supp. XXII:** 277
Herron, George, **Supp. I Part 1:** 7
"Hers" (column, Prose), **Supp. XVI:** 254
Herschdorfer, Helen, **Supp. XXI:** 262
Herschel, Sir John, **Supp. I Part 1:** 314
"Her Sense of Timing" (Elkin), **Supp. VI:** 56, 58
Hersey, John, **IV:** 4; **Supp. I Part 1:** 196; **Supp. XVI:** 105–106; **Supp. XX:** 251
"Her Sweet turn to leave the Homestead" (Dickinson), **Retro. Supp. I:** 44
"Her Untold Story"(Thompson), **Supp. XXIII:** 301
Herzog (Bellow), **I:** 144, 147, 149, 150, 152, 153, 154, 155, 156, 157, 158, 159–160; **Retro. Supp. II:** 19, **26–27; Supp. IV Part 1:** 30; **Supp. XIX:** 157
Herzog, Tobey C., **Supp. XXII:** 116
Heschel, Abraham, **Supp. XXI:** 110, 112
Hesford, Walter A., **Supp. XV:** 215, 217, 218
"He/She" (Dunn), **Supp. XI:** 149
"Hesitation Blues" (Hughes), **Retro. Supp. I:** 211
He Sleeps (McKnight), **Supp. XX:** 151, **152–155, 158**
"He Sleeps" (McKnight), **Supp. XX: 152, 155**
Hesse, Hermann, **Supp. V:** 208
Hester, Carolyn, **Supp. XVIII:** 24
"Hetch Hetchy Valley" (Muir), **Supp. IX:** 185
He Who Gets Slapped (Andreyev), **II:** 425
"He Who Spits at the Sky" (Stegner), **Supp. IV Part 2:** 605

"He Will Not Leave a Note" (Ríos), **Supp. IV Part 2:** 548
Hewitt, James, **Supp. XV:** 240
Hewlett, Maurice, **I:** 359
Heyen, William, **Supp. XIII:** 285, 344; **Supp. XV:** 212
"Hey! Hey!" (Hughes), **Supp. I Part 1:** 327–328
Heyman, Stanley, **Supp. XXV:** 253
Hey Rub-a-Dub-Dub (Dreiser), **I:** 515; **II:** 26; **Retro. Supp. II:** 104, 105, 108
"Hey Sailor, What Ship?" (Olsen), **Supp. XIII:** 293, 294, 298, **299**
Heyward, DuBose, **Supp. XVIII:** 281; **Supp. XIX:** 78
Hiawatha (Longfellow), **Supp. I Part 1:** 79; **Supp. III Part 2:** 609, 610; **Supp. XXI:** 53
"Hibernaculum" (Ammons), **Supp. VII:** 26–27
Hichborn, Philip, **Supp. I Part 2:** 707, 708
Hichborn, Mrs. Philip. *See* Wylie, Elinor
"Hic Jacet" (W. C. Williams), **Retro. Supp. I:** 414
Hickok, Guy, **Supp. XXI:** 7
Hickok, James Butler ("Wild Bill"), **Supp. V:** 229, 230
Hicks, Granville, **I:** 254, 259, 374; **II:** 26; **III:** 342, 355, 452; **Supp. I Part 1:** 361; **Supp. I Part 2:** 609; **Supp. IV Part 1:** 22; **Supp. IV Part 2:** 526; **Supp. VIII:** 96, 124; **Supp. XII:** 250; **Supp. XIII:** 263; **Supp. XXI:** 276; **Supp. XXII:** 279
Hicks, Sally, **Supp. XXI:** 255
Hicok, Bethany, **Retro. Supp. II:** 39
"Hidden" (Nye), **Supp. XIII:** 283
"Hidden Gardens" (Capote), **Supp. III Part 1:** 125
Hidden Law, The (Hecht), **Supp. X:** 58
"Hidden Name and Complex Fate" (Ellison), **Supp. II Part 1:** 245
Hiddenness, Uncertainty, Surprise: Three Generative Energies of Poetry (Hirshfield), **Supp. XXIII:** 137
Hidden Wound, The (Berry), **Supp. X:** 23, 25, 26–27, 29, 34, 35
"Hide-and-Seek" (Francis), **Supp. IX:** 81
"Hiding" (Minot), **Supp. VI:** 203, 206
Hiding Place (Wideman), **Supp. X:** 320, 321, 327, 329, 331–332, 333
"Hidin' Out in Honky Heaven: On Race Relations in Vermont" (Budbill), **Supp. XIX:** 5
Hienger, Jorg, **Supp. IV Part 1:** 106
Hieronymus Bosch (De Tolnay), **Supp. XXII:** 255
Higgins, George, **Supp. IV Part 1:** 356
Higginson, Thomas Wentworth, **I:** 451–452, 453, 454, 456, 458, 459, 463, 464, 465, 470; **Retro. Supp. I:** 26, 31, 33, 35, 39, 40; **Supp. I Part 1:** 307, 371; **Supp. IV Part 2:** 430
Higgs, Robert, **Supp. XX: 166**
"High Bridge above the Tagus River at Toledo, The" (W. C. Williams), **Retro. Supp. I:** 429
"High Dive: A Variant" (Kumin), **Supp. IV Part 2:** 442

"High Diver" (Francis), **Supp. IX:** 82
"Higher Keys, The" (Merrill), **Supp. III Part 1:** 335–336
Higher Learning in America, The (Veblen), **Supp. I Part 2:** 630, 631, 641, 642
Highet, Gilbert, **Supp. I Part 1:** 268
"High Heav'd my breast"(J. Schoolcraft), **Supp. XXIII:** 235
High Noon (film), **Supp. V:** 46
"High on Sadness" (Komunyakaa), **Supp. XIII:** 114
"High School Senior" (Olds), **Supp. X:** 212
Highsmith, Patricia, **Supp. IV Part 1:** 79, 94, 132; **Supp. XXII:** 136
"High Tide" (Marquand), **III:** 56
High Tide in Tucson: Essays from Now or Never (Kingsolver), **Supp. VII:** 198, 201, 209
"High-Toned Old Christian Woman, A" (Stevens), **Retro. Supp. I:** 301
"High Water" (Mosher), **Supp. XXII:** 205, 211
"Highway, The" (Merwin), **Supp. III Part 1:** 346
Highway 61 Revisited (album, Dylan), **Supp. XVIII:** 20, 27, 30, 32
"Highway 61 Revisited" (song, Dylan), **Supp. XVIII:** 30
"Highway 99E from Chico" (Carver), **Supp. III Part 1:** 136
"Highway Apple Trees" (Espaillat), **Supp. XXI:** 100–102
High Window, The (Chandler), **Supp. IV Part 1:** 127–129, 130, 131
"High Yaller" (R. Fisher), **Supp. XIX:** 72
Hijuelos, Oscar, **Supp. IV Part 1:** 54; **Supp. VIII: 73–91**
Hike and the Aeroplane (Lewis), **II:** 440–441
Hilberg, Raul, **Supp. V:** 267
Hildebrand, Al, **III:** 118
Hiler, Hilaire, **Retro. Supp. II:** 327; **Supp. III Part 2:** 617
"Hill, A" (Hecht), **Supp. X:** 59–60, 63
Hill, Abram, **Supp. XV:** 194
Hill, Anita, **Supp. XX: 110**
Hill, Hamlin, **Retro. Supp. II:** 286
Hill, James J., **Supp. I Part 2:** 644
Hill, Joe, **I:** 493; **Supp. XVIII:** 224; **Supp. XXIII:** 162
Hill, Lee, **Supp. XI:** 293, 294, 297, 299, 301, 305, 307
Hill, Pamela Smith, **Supp. XXII:** 295
Hill, Patti, **I:** 289
Hill, Peggy, **Supp. XIII:** 163
"Hill, The" (Strand), **Supp. IV Part 2:** 627
"Hill, The" (Toomer), **Supp. III Part 2:** 486
Hill, Vernon, **Supp. I Part 2:** 397
"Hillcrest" (Robinson), **III:** 504
Hill-Lubin, Mildred A., **Supp. IV Part 1:** 13
Hillman, Sidney, **Supp. I Part 1:** 5
Hillringhouse, Mark, **Supp. IX:** 286, 288, 299

Hills Beyond, The (Wolfe), **IV:** 450, 451, 460, 461

"Hills Beyond, The" (Wolfe), **IV:** 460

Hillside and Seaside in Poetry (Larcom, ed.), **Supp. XIII:** 142

"Hillside Thaw, A" (Frost), **Retro. Supp. I:** 133

"Hills Like White Elephants" (Hemingway), **Retro. Supp. I:** 170

Hills of the Shatemuc, The (S. Warner), **Supp. XVIII:** 266

"Hill-Top View, A" (Jeffers), **Supp. II Part 2:** 417

Hill Towns (Siddons), **Supp. XXII:** 239, 253

"Hill Wife, The" (Frost), **II:** 154; **Retro. Supp. I:** 131

Hillyer, Catherine, **Supp. XV:** 244

Hillyer, Robert, **I:** 475; **Supp. IX:** 75; **Supp. XIV:** 11

Hilton, James, **Supp. XIII:** 166

"Hiltons' Holiday, The" (Jewett), **II:** 391; **Retro. Supp. II:** 134

Him (Cummings), **I:** 429, 434–435

Himes, Chester Bomar, **Retro. Supp. II:** 117; **Supp. I Part 1:** 51, 325; **Supp. XIII:** 233; **Supp. XVI:** 135–146

Himes, Norman, **Supp. V:** 128

"Him on a Bicycle" (Weigl), **Supp. XIX:** 276

"Him with His Foot in His Mouth" (Bellow), **Retro. Supp. II:** 34

Him with His Foot in His Mouth and Other Stories (Bellow), **Retro. Supp. II:** 31

Hinchman, Sandra K., **Supp. IV Part 1:** 210

Hinckley, David, **Supp. XXII:** 215

Hindemith, Paul, **IV:** 357; **Supp. IV Part 1:** 81

Hindsell, Oliver, **Supp. XIII:** 162

Hindus, Milton, **Supp. XIV:** 288, 291, 292, 293; **Supp. XXIII:** 16

Hines, Suzanne, **Supp. XIV:** 151

Hinge Picture (Howe), **Supp. IV Part 2:** 423–424

Hinojosa, Rolando, **Supp. XIX:** 97–114

"Hinterlands" (W. Gibson), **Supp. XVI:** 123, 128

"Hippies: Slouching towards Bethlehem" (Didion), **Supp. IV Part 1:** 200

Hippolytus (Euripides), **II:** 543; **Supp. I Part 1:** 270

Hippolytus Temporizes (Doolittle), **Supp. I Part 1:** 270

"Hips" (Cisneros), **Supp. VII:** 61, 62

"Hipster's Hipster" (Ginsberg), **Supp. XIV:** 141

Hirsch, Edward D., **Supp. V:** 177; **Supp. IX:** 262; **Supp. XIV:** 15; **Supp. XV:** 78, 225; **Supp. XVII:** 23; **Supp. XIX:** 202; **Supp. XXIII:** 124

Hirsch, Sidney, **Supp. XIV:** 1. *See* Mttron-Hirsch, Sidney

Hirschfeld, Jane, **Supp. XVII:** 241

Hirschorn, Clive, **Supp. IV Part 2:** 577, 579

Hirshfield, Jane, **Supp. XXIII:** 129–141

Hirson, Roger, **Supp. XI:** 343

"His Bride of the Tomb" (Dunbar), **Supp. II Part 1:** 196

"His Chest of Drawers" (Anderson), **I:** 113, 114

"His Daily Journal"(Kenny), **Supp. XXIII:** 153

"His Father's Whistle" (Wrigley), **Supp. XVIII:** 299

His First, Best Country (J. W. Miller), **Supp. XX: 163, 166, 172–175**

His Fortunate Grace (Atherton), **Supp. XXIV:** 22

His Human Majesty (Boyle), **Supp. XXIV:** 62

"His Last Day" (C. Himes), **Supp. XVI:** 137

"His Lover" (Dubus), **Supp. VII:** 86

"His Music" (Dunn), **Supp. XI:** 149

"His Own Key" (Ríos), **Supp. IV Part 2:** 543

His Picture in the Papers (film; Emerson), **Supp. XVI:** 185

His Religion and Hers (Gilman), **Supp. XI:** 209

Hiss, Alger, **Supp. XV:** 143

"Hiss, Chambers, and the Age of Innocence" (Fiedler), **Supp. XIII:** 99

"His Shield" (Moore), **III:** 211

"His Story" (Cisneros), **Supp. VII:** 67

His Thought Made Pockets & the Plane Buckt (Berryman), **I:** 170

"His Three Women" (Gioia), **Supp. XV:** 119–120

Histoire comparée des systèmes de philosophie (Gérando), **II:** 10

Histoire de la brume, L' (Dybek; trans. Beget), **Supp. XXIII:** 74

Historical and Moral View of the Origin and Progress of the French Revolution (Wollstonecraft), **Supp. I Part 1:** 126

"Historical Conceptualization" (Huizinga), **I:** 255

Historical Evidence and the Reading of Seventeenth-Century Poetry (Brooks), **Supp. XIV:** 11

"Historical Interpretation of Literature, The" (Wilson), **IV:** 431, 433, 445

Historical Jesus, The: The Life of a Mediterranean Jewish Peasant (Crossan), **Supp. V:** 251

Historical Life of Jesus, The (Pettis), **Supp. XXIII:** 189

"Historical Value of Crèvecoeur's *Voyage . . .,*" (Adams), Supp. I Part 1: 251

"History" (Emerson), **II:** 13, 15

"History" (Hughes), **Supp. I Part 1:** 344

History (Lowell), **Retro. Supp. II:** 183, 190

"History" (Simic), **Supp. VIII:** 279

"History, Myth, and the Western Writer" (Stegner), **Supp. IV Part 2:** 596, 601

"History among the Rocks" (Warren), **IV:** 252

History as a Literary Art (Morison), **Supp. I Part 2:** 493

"History as Fate in E. L. Doctorow's Tale of a Western Town" (Arnold), **Supp. IV Part 1:** 220

"History Is the Memory of Time" (Olson), **Supp. II Part 2:** 574

"History Lesson" (Trethewey), **Supp. XXI:** 248, 249

"History Lessons" (Komunyakaa), **Supp. XIII:** 126

History Man, The (Bradbury), **Supp. XVIII:** 140

"History of a Literary Movement" (Nemerov), **III:** 270

"History of a Literary Radical, The" (Bourne), **I:** 215, 235, 236

History of a Radical: Essays by Randolph Bourne (Brooks), **I:** 245

"History of Armenia, The"(Balakian), **Supp. XXIII:** 23, 24

"History of Buttons, The" (Goldbarth), **Supp. XII:** 187

History of English Literature (Taine), **III:** 323

History of English Prosody (Saintsbury), **Supp. XV:** 181

History of Fortus, The (Emerson), **II:** 8

History of Henry Esmond, The (Thackeray), **II:** 91, 130

History of Modern Poetry, A (Perkins), **Supp. I Part 2:** 475; **Supp. XV:** 185

History of My Heart (Pinsky), **Supp. VI:** 243, 244, 245

History of New York, from the Beginning of the World to the End of the Dutch Dynasty, A (Irving), **II:** 300–303, 304, 310

History of Pendennis, The (Thackeray), **II:** 291

"History of Red, The" (Hogan), **Supp. IV Part 1:** 411

"History of Rodney, The" (Bass), **Supp. XVI:** 20

History of Roxbury Town (Ellis), **Supp. I Part 1:** 99

History of Southern Literature, The (Rubin), **Supp. XX:** 161

History of the African-American People (Proposed) by Strom Thurmond, The (Everett and Kincaid), **Supp. XVIII: 62, 63–64**

History of the American Film, A (Durang), **Supp. XXIV:** 113, 117, **118–119**

History of the Conquest of Mexico (Prescott), **Retro. Supp. I:** 123

History of the Conquest of Peru (Morison, ed.), **Supp. I Part 2:** 494

History of the Dividing Line betwixt Virginia and North Carolina (Byrd), **Supp. IV Part 2:** 425

History of the Life and Voyages of Christopher Columbus, A (Irving), **II:** 310, 314

History of the Navy of the United States of America (Cooper), **I:** 347

History of the Rise and Fall of the Slave-power in America (Wilson), **Supp. XIV:** 48, 49

History of the Russian Revolution, A (Trotsky), **Supp. XXI:** 161

History of the United States (Bancroft), **Supp. XXII:** 33

History of the United States of America during the Administrations of Thomas Jefferson and James Madison

(Adams), **I:** 6–9, 10, 20, 21
History of the Work of Redemption, A (Edwards), **I:** 560
History of United States Naval Operations in World War II (Morison), **Supp. I Part 2:** 490–492
History of Womankind in Western Europe, The, **Supp. XI:** 197
"History Teacher, The" (Collins), **Supp. XXI:** 57
"History Through a Beard" (Morison), **Supp. I Part 2:** 490
His Toy, His Dream, His Rest (Berryman), **I:** 169, 170, 183, 184–186
"His Words" (Roethke), **III:** 544
Hitchcock, Ada. *See* MacLeish, Mrs. Archibald (Ada Hitchcock)
Hitchcock, Alfred, **IV:** 357; **Supp. IV Part 1:** 132; **Supp. VIII:** 177; **Supp. XX: 253; Supp. XXII:** 119
Hitchcock, George, **Supp. X:** 127; **Supp. XVII:** 110
"Hitch Haiku" (Snyder), **Supp. VIII:** 297
"Hitch-Hikers, The" (Welty), **IV:** 262
"Hitchhiking Is Illegal in Nevada" (Lethem), **Supp. XVIII:** 136
Hitchins, Christopher, **Supp. VIII:** 241
Hitler, Adolf, **I:** 261, 290, 492; **II:** 146, 454, 561, 565, 592; **III:** 2, 3, 110, 115, 140, 156, 246, 298, 446; **IV:** 5, 17, 18, 298, 372; **Supp. I Part 2:** 431, 436, 446, 664; **Supp. V:** 290
Hitler, Wendy, **III:** 404
Hitler Lives? (film), **Supp. XVI:** 102
Hix, H. L., **Supp. XV:** 114
H. L. Mencken, a Portrait from Memory (Angoff), **III:** 107
"H. L. Mencken Meets a Poet in the West Side Y.M.C.A." (White), **Supp. I Part 2:** 677
H. L. Mencken: The American Scene (Cairns), **III:** 119
H. M. Pulham, Esquire (Marquand), **II:** 482–483; **III:** 58, 59, 65, 68–69
Hnizdovsky, Jacques, **Supp. XIII:** 346
"Hoadley's Test Case in Indiana" (Neugeboren), **Supp. XVI:** 219
Hoagland, Edward, **Supp. XIV:** 80; **Supp. XVI:** 277; **Supp. XXII:** 204, 206
Hoagland, Tony, **Supp. XIX:** 81, 89
"Hoarder, The" (Sexton), **Supp. II Part 2:** 692
"Hoarfrost" (C. Baxter), **Supp. XVII:** 15
Hoban, Phoebe, **Supp. XV:** 319, 325
Hoban, Russell, **Supp. XXIII:** 42
Hobb, Gormley, **I:** 203
Hobbes, Thomas, **I:** 277; **II:** 9, 10, 540; **III:** 306; **IV:** 88; **Supp. XII:** 33; **Supp. XIV:** 5, 7
Hobson, Geary, **Supp. IV Part 1:** 321; **Supp. IV Part 2:** 502
Hobson, J. A., **I:** 232
Hobson, John A., **Supp. I Part 2:** 650
Hobson, Laura Z., **III:** 151
Hocking, Agnes, **Supp. VIII:** 251
Hocking, William Ernest, **III:** 303
Hodge, Merle, **Supp. XXIII:** 94
Hodges, Campbell B., **Supp. XIV:** 8
Hodgson, Captain Joseph, **III:** 328

Hoffa, Jimmy, **I:** 493
Hoffenberg, Mason, **Supp. XI:** 294, 297, 299, 305
Hoffer, Eric, **Supp. VIII:** 188; **Supp. XIX:** 264
Hoffman, Abbie, **Supp. XIV:** 150
Hoffman, Alice, **Supp. X: 77–94; Supp. XIII:** 13
Hoffman, Allen, **Supp. XVII:** 42, 44
Hoffman, Daniel, **Retro. Supp. II:** 265
Hoffman, Daniel G., **I:** 405; **II:** 307; **Supp. XI:** 152
Hoffman, Dustin, **Supp. IV Part 1:** 236
Hoffman, E. T. A., **Supp. XVI:** 157
Hoffman, Eva, **Supp. XVI: 147–164**
Hoffman, Frederick J., **I:** 60, 67; **II:** 443; **IV:** 113
Hoffman, Josiah Ogden, **II:** 297, 300
Hoffman, Matilda, **II:** 300, 314
Hoffman, Paul, **Supp. XV:** 141–142
Hoffman, Roy, **Supp. XX: 177**
Hoffman, Todd, **Supp. XVIII:** 101
Hoffman, William, **Supp. XVIII: 69–88**
Hoffman, William M., **Supp. X:** 153
Hoffmann, E. T. A., **III:** 415
Hofmann, Hans, **Supp. XV:** 144
Hofmeister, Tim, **Supp. XIX:** 115
Ho for a Hat (W. J. Smith), **Supp. XIII:** 346
Hofstadter, Richard, **Supp. VIII:** 98, 99, 108
Hogan, Linda, **Supp. IV Part 1:** 324, 325, **397–418; Supp. XVIII:** 189
Hogan, Randolph, **Supp. XVI:** 252–253
Hogan, Ron, **Supp. XVIII:** 138, 139
Hogarth, William, **Supp. XII:** 44
Hogg, James, **I:** 53; **Supp. I Part 1:** 349; **Supp. IX:** 275
Hoggart, Richard, **Supp. XIV:** 299
"Hog-Nosed Snake, The" (Kooser), **Supp. XIX:** 128
Hogue, W. Lawrence, **Supp. XXII:** 175–176
Hohne, Karen, **Supp. V:** 147
Hojoki (Chomei), **IV:** 170
Holbrook, David, **Supp. I Part 2:** 526–527, 546
Holcroft, Thomas, **Supp. I Part 2:** 514
Holden, Jonathan, **Supp. XI:** 143
Holden, Raymond, **Supp. XIV:** 121–122
Holden, William, **Supp. XI:** 307
Hölderlin, Friedrich, **Supp. XVI:** 48; **Supp. XXIV:** 152
Holding, Elisabeth Sanxay, **Supp. XXII: 119–137**
"Holding On" (Levine), **Supp. V:** 184
Holding the Line: Women in the Great Arizona Mine Strike of 1983 (Kingsolver), **Supp. VII:** 197, 201–202, 204
"Holding the Mirror Up to Nature" (Nemerov), **III:** 275, 276
"Hold Me" (Levine), **Supp. V:** 186
Hold the Press (film), **Supp. XIII:** 163
Hold with the Hares (Zinberg), **Supp. XV:** 197–198,**Supp. XV:** 203
Hole in Texas, A (Wouk), **Supp. XXV:** 257, 266–267
"Hole in the Floor, A" (Wilbur), **Supp. III Part 2:** 556–557

Holiday (Barry), **Retro. Supp. I:** 104
"Holiday" (Porter), **III:** 454
Holiday (W. Frank), **Supp. XX: 72–73**
Holiday, Billie, **Supp. I Part 1:** 80; **Supp. IV Part 1:** 2, 7; **Supp. XIX:** 147
Holiday Song for Four-Part Chorus of Mixed Voices with Piano Accompaniment (Taggard and Schuman), **Supp. XXII:** 283
Holinshed, Raphael, **IV:** 370
Holladay, Polly, **Supp. XXI:** 6
Holland, Josiah, **Supp. I Part 2:** 420
Holland, Laurence Bedwell, **Retro. Supp. I:** 216
Holland, Theodore, **I:** 453
Holland, Mrs. Theodore, **I:** 453, 455, 465
Holland, William, **IV:** 381
Hollander, John, **Supp. III Part 2:** 541; **Supp. IV Part 2:** 642; **Supp. IX:** 50, 153, 155; **Supp. XII:** 254, 255, 260; **Supp. XV:** 256; **Supp. XVII:** 112; **Supp. XIX:** 121; **Supp. XXIII:** 112
Hollenberg, Donna, **Supp. XXIV:** 64
Holley, Marietta, **Supp. XIII:** 152
Holliday, Billie, **Supp. XXI:** 131
Hollinghurst, Alan, **Supp. XIII:** 52
Hollins Critic (Nelson), **Supp. XIX:** 3
Hollis, Thomas Brand, **Supp. I Part 2:** 514
Hollow Men, The (T. S. Eliot), **I:** 574, 575, 578–579, 580, 585; **III:** 586; **Retro. Supp. I:** 63, 64
"Hollow Tree, A" (R. Bly), **Supp. IV Part 1:** 64, 66
Hollyberrys at the Shore, The, **Supp. X:** 42
"Hollywood!" (Vidal), **Supp. IV Part 2:** 688
Hollywood: American Movie-City (Rand, unauthorized), **Supp. IV Part 2:** 519
Hollywood: A Novel of America in the 1920s (Vidal), **Supp. IV Part 2:** 677, 684, 686, 688, 690, 691
Hollywood Ending (film; Allen), **Supp. XV:** 11
Hollywood on Trial (film), **Supp. I Part 1:** 295
Holmes, Abiel, **Supp. I Part 1:** 300, 301, 302, 310
Holmes, Mrs. Abiel (Sarah Wendell), **Supp. I Part 1:** 300
Holmes, John, **I:** 169; **Supp. II Part 1:** 87; **Supp. IV Part 2:** 440–441; **Supp. XIV:** 119
Holmes, John Clellon, **Supp. XII:** 118; **Supp. XIV:** 144, 150
Holmes, Martha Stoddard, **Supp. XX: 205, 207**
Holmes, Oliver Wendell, **I:** 487; **II:** 225, 273–274, 402, 403; **III:** 81–82, 590, 591–592; **IV:** 429, 436; **Retro. Supp. II:** 155; **Supp. I Part 1:** 103, 243, 254, **299–319; Supp. I Part 2:** 405, 414, 415, 420, 593, 704, 705; **Supp. XI:** 194; **Supp. XXIV:** 77
Holmes, Oliver Wendell, Jr., **I:** 3, 19; **Supp. IV Part 2:** 422
Holmes, Mrs. Oliver Wendell (Amelia Jackson), **Supp. I Part 1:** 303
Holmes, Steven J., **Supp. IX:** 172, 177

Holmes, Ted, **Supp. V:** 180
Holmes, William Henry, **Supp. IV Part 2:** 603–604
Holocaust (Reznikoff), **Supp. XIV:** 281, **291–293**
Holocaust in American Life, The (Novick), **Supp. XVI:** 154
Holt, Edwin E., **I:** 59
Holt, Felix, **II:** 179
Holt, Henry, **II:** 348; **III:** 587
Holt, Patricia, **Supp. XIV:** 89
Holtby, Winifred, **Supp. I Part 2:** 720
Holy Ghostly, The (Shepard), **Supp. III Part 2:** 437–438, 447
"Holy Innocents, The" (Lowell), **II:** 539
Holy Sonnets (Donne), **IV:** 145; **Supp. I Part 1:** 367; **Supp. III Part 2:** 619; **Supp. XIII:** 130–131; **Supp. XVIII:** 50–51
"Holy Terror, A" (Bierce), **I:** 203
"Holy Terror, The" (Maxwell), **Supp. VIII:** 169
Holy the Firm (Dillard), **Supp. VI:** 23, **29,** 30, 31, 32
Holy War, The (Bunyan), **IV:** 156
"Holy Week"(Thompson), **Supp. XXIII:** 300
"Homage to Arthur Rimbaud" (Wright), **Supp. V:** 339
Homage to Baudelaire (Duncan, ed.), **Supp. XV:** 75
Homage to Catalonia (Orwell), **Supp. XVII:** 229
"Homage to Che Guevara" (Banks), **Supp. V:** 5
Homage to Clio (Auden), **Supp. II Part 1:** 24
"Homage to Elizabeth Bishop" (Ivask, ed.), **Supp. I Part 1:** 96
"Homage to Ezra Pound" (Wright), **Supp. V:** 339
Homage to Frank O'Hara (Ashbery), **Supp. III Part 1:** 2–3
"Homage to Franz Joseph Haydn" (Hecht), **Supp. X:** 69
"Homage to Hemingway" (Bishop), **IV:** 35
Homage to Mistress Bradstreet (Berryman), **I:** 168, 169, 170–171, 172, 174, 175, 178–183, 184, 186
"Homage to Paul Cézanne" (Wright), **Supp. V:** 341–342
Homage to Sextus Propertius (Pound), **Retro. Supp. I:** 290
"Homage to Sextus Propertius" (Pound), **III:** 462, 476; **Supp. III Part 2:** 622
"Homage to Shakespeare" (Cheever), **Supp. I Part 1:** 180
"Homage to the Empress of the Blues" (Hayden), **Supp. II Part 1:** 379
"Homage to the Memory of Wallace Stevens" (Justice), **Supp. VII:** 126
Homage to Theodore Dreiser (Warren), **I:** 517
Homans, Margaret, **Supp. X:** 229
"Home" (Hughes), **Supp. I Part 1:** 329, 330
"Home" (Mora), **Supp. XIII:** 217
Home (Robinson), **Supp. XXI:** 212, **220–223**

Home (Updike), **Retro. Supp. I:** 320
"Home" (Weigl), **Supp. XIX:** 287
"Home, Home on the Strange" (J. D. Reed), **Supp. XVI:** 174
"Home, Sweet Home" (Fante), **Supp. XI:** 164, 165
Home, The (Gilman), **Supp. XI:** 206–207
"Home, The" (Jarman), **Supp. XVII:** 116
"Home Address" (Bronk), **Supp. XXI:** 27
"Home after Three Months Away" (Lowell), **II:** 547
Home and Colonial Library (Murray), **Retro. Supp. I:** 246
"Home and the Open Road: The Nonfiction of Larry Brown" (Barrier), **Supp. XXI:** 48–49
Home as Found (Cooper), **I:** 348, 349, 350, 351
Home at the End of the World, A (Cunningham), **Supp. XV:** 59–62, 63
"Home Away from Home, A" (Humphrey), **Supp. IX:** 101
Home Book of Shakespeare Quotations (Stevenson), **Supp. XIV:** 120
"Home Burial" (Frost), **Retro. Supp. I:** 124, 125, 128, **129–130;** **Supp. VIII:** 31; **Supp. XV:** 159; **Supp. XIX:** 9
Homecoming (Alvarez), **Supp. VII:** 1, 3–5, 9
"Homecoming" (Carruth), **Supp. XVI:** 55
"Homecoming" (McGrath), **Supp. X:** 116
"Homecoming, The" (Gioia), **Supp. XV:** 123, 124
Homecoming, The (Wilson), **Supp. VIII:** 330
Homecoming Game, The (Nemerov), **III:** 268, 282, 284–285
"Home during a Tropical Snowstorm I Feed My Father Lunch" (Karr), **Supp. XI:** 241–242, 248
Home Economics (Berry), **Supp. X:** 28, 31–32, 35, 36, 37
"Home Economics for Halfbacks" (Skloot), **Supp. XX: 195, 207**
Home from the Hill (film), **Supp. IX:** 95
Home from the Hill (Humphrey), **Supp. IX:** 93, 95, **96–98,** 104, 106, 109
"Home Grown" (Vital), **Supp. XVI:** 160
"Homeland" (Merwin), **Supp. III Part 1:** 351
Homeland and Other Stories (Kingsolver), **Supp. VII:** 199, 202–204, 207
Home on the Range (Baraka), **Supp. II Part 1:** 47
Homeplace (Siddons), **Supp. XXII:** 253
Home Place, The (Morris), **III:** 221, 222, 232
Homeplace, The (Nelson), **Supp. XVIII:** 174–175
Homer, **I:** 312, 433; **II:** 6, 8, 133, 302, 543, 544, 552; **III:** 14, 21, 278, 453, 457, 473, 567; **IV:** 54, 371; **Retro. Supp. I:** 59; **Supp. I Part 1:** 158, 283; **Supp. I Part 2:** 494; **Supp. X:** 36, 120, 122; **Supp. XIV:** 21; **Supp. XVII:** 70, 227
Homer, Louise, **Retro. Supp. I:** 10

Homer, Winslow, **Supp. XXI:** 243
"Home Range" (Leopold), **Supp. XIV:** 184, 185
"Home Repairs" (Skloot), **Supp. XX: 204**
Homer's Art (Notley), **Supp. XXII:** 232
"Homer's Art" (Notley), **Supp. XXII:** 232–233
"Homesick Blues" (Hughes), **Supp. I Part 1:** 327
Home: Social Essays (Baraka), **Supp. II Part 1:** 45, 61
"Homesteading on the Extraterrestrial Frontier" (Abbott), **Supp. XVIII:** 142
Home to Harlem (McKay), **Supp. X:** 132, 137–138, **138–139; Supp. XVIII:** 127
"Home Videos" (Brockmeier), **Supp. XXII:** 60
Homeward Bound (Cooper), **I:** 348
"Homeward Star, The" (Palmer), **Supp. XV:** 81–82
Homewood trilogy (Wideman), **Supp. X:** 319
"Homework" (Cameron), **Supp. XII:** 80, **83,** 84
"Homily" (Tate), **IV:** 121–122
Homing with the Birds (Stratton-Porter), **Supp. XX: 212, 216, 222**
"Homme Moyen Sensuel, L' " (Pound), **III:** 462
Homme révolté, L' (Camus), *III:* 306
"Homoeopathy and Its Kindred Delusions" (Holmes), **Supp. I Part 1:** 303–304, 305
Homo Ludens (Huizinga), **II:** 416–417, 425
"Homosexuality: Is It Disgusting, or Is It Delightful?" (Durang), **Supp. XXIV:** 114
"Homosexuality"(O'Hara), **Supp. XXIII:** 212
"Homosexual Villain, The" (Mailer), **III:** 36
"Homo Will Not Inherit" (Doty), **Supp. XI:** 128
"Homunculus, The: A Novel in One Chapter" (McKnight), **Supp. XX: 152**
Hone and Strong Diaries of Old Manhattan, The (Auchincloss, ed.), **Supp. IV Part 1:** 23
"Honey" (Beattie), **Supp. V:** 33
"Honey" (Wright), **Supp. III Part 2:** 589
"Honey, We'll Be Brave" (Farrell), **II:** 45
Honey and Salt (Sandburg), **III:** 594–596
"Honey and Salt" (Sandburg), **III:** 594
"Honey Babe" (Hughes), **Supp. I Part 1:** 334
"Honey Tree, The" (Oliver), **Supp. VII:** 236
Hong, Maxine. See Kingston, Maxine Hong
Hongo, Garrett, **Supp. X:** 292; **Supp. XIII:** 114; **Supp. XVII:** 112
"Honkytonk" (Shapiro), **Supp. II Part 2:** 705
"Honky Tonk in Cleveland, Ohio" (Sandburg), **III:** 585
Honorable Men (Auchincloss), **Supp. IV Part 1:** 23

Honor Thy Father (Talese), **Supp. XVII:** 204–205, 210

Hood, Tom, **I:** 195

"Hoodoo in America" (Hurston), **Supp. VI:** 153–154

"Hook" (Wright), **Supp. III Part 2:** 604

Hook, Sidney, **I:** 265; **Supp. IV Part 2:** 527; **Supp. VIII:** 96, 100; **Supp. XIV:** 3

Hooker, Adelaide. *See* Marquand, Mrs. John P. (Adelaide Hooker)

Hooker, Isabella Beecher, **Supp. XI:** 193

Hooker, Samuel, **IV:** 162, 165

Hooker, Thomas, **II:** 15–16; **IV:** 162

Hooper, Marian. *See* Adams, Mrs. Henry (Marian Hooper)

Hoosier Holiday, A (Dreiser), **Retro. Supp. II:** 104

Hoover, Herbert, **Supp. I Part 2:** 638

Hoover, J. Edgar, **Supp. XIII:** 170

Hoover, Paul, **Supp. XV:** 179

"Hope" (Bontemps), **Supp. XXII:** 2

"Hope" (Jarrell), **II:** 389

"Hope" (Matthews), **Supp. IX:** 163

Hope, A. D., **Supp. XIII:** 347

Hope, Lynn, **Supp. II Part 1:** 38

Hope, The (Wouk), **Supp. XXV:** 254, 257, 265–266

"Hope Atherton's Wanderings" (Howe), **Supp. IV Part 2:** 432

"Hopeless Kill, The"(Kenny), **Supp. XXIII:** 145

Hope of Heaven (O'Hara), **III:** 361

"Hopes Rise" (Boyle), **Supp. XX: 20**

"Hop-Frog" (Poe), **Retro. Supp. II:** 264, 268, 269

"Hop Frog" (Poe), **Supp. XXV:** 112

Hopkin, Pauline, **Supp. XVI:** 143

Hopkins, Anne Yale, **Supp. I Part 1:** 100, 102, 113

Hopkins, Gerard Manley, **I:** 171, 179, 397, 401, 522, 525, 533; **II:** 537; **III:** 197, 209, 523; **IV:** 129, 135, 141, 421; **Retro. Supp. II:** 40; **Supp. I Part 1:** 79, 81, 94; **Supp. III Part 2:** 551; **Supp. IV Part 1:** 178; **Supp. IV Part 2:** 637, 638, 639, 641, 643; **Supp. V:** 337; **Supp. IX:** 39, 42; **Supp. X:** 61, 115; **Supp. XIII:** 294; **Supp. XIV:** 83; **Supp. XV:** 250, 347; **Supp. XVI:** 282; **Supp. XVII:** 241; **Supp. XVIII:** 78, 79; **Supp. XX: 230; Supp. XXIII:** 121

Hopkins, Gerard Walter Sturgis, **Supp. XX: 229, 233, 240**

Hopkins, L. A., **I:** 502

Hopkins, Lemuel, **Supp. II Part 1:** 70

Hopkins, Miriam, **IV:** 381; **Supp. I Part 1:** 281

Hopkins, Pauline, **Supp. XVIII:** 284

Hopkins, Samuel, **I:** 547, 549; **Supp. XXIV:** 68

Hopkins, Vivian, **II:** 20

Hopkinson, Francis, **Supp. I Part 2:** 504

Hopler, Jay, **Supp. XXIII:** 132

Hopper (Strand), **Supp. IV Part 2:** 632

Hopper, Dennis, **Supp. XI:** 293, 308

Hopper, Edward, **IV:** 411, 413; **Supp. IV Part 2:** 619, 623, 631, 634; **Supp. XIX:** 117

Hopwood, Avery, **Supp. IV Part 2:** 573; **Supp. XXV:** 195

Horace, **II:** 8, 154, 169, 543, 552, 568; **III:** 15; **IV:** 89; **Supp. I Part 2:** 423; **Supp. IX:** 152; **Supp. X:** 65; **Supp. XII:** 258, 260, 262

Horae Canonicae (Auden), **Supp. II Part 1:** 21

"Horatian Ode" (Marvell), **IV:** 135

"Horatian Ode upon Cromwell's Return from Ireland" (Marvell), **Supp. XIV:** 10

Horgan, Paul, **Supp. XV:** 46, 49, 52

Horkheimer, Max, **Supp. I Part 2:** 645; **Supp. IV Part 1:** 301

Horn, Dara, **Supp. XVII:** 50; **Supp. XX: 177**

Horn, Mother, **Supp. I Part 1:** 49, 54

Hornby, Nick, **Supp. XII:** 286; **Supp. XXIII:** 109

Horn of Africa (Caputo), **Supp. XIX:** 21–23

Horn of Life, The (Atherton), **Supp. XXIV:** 26, 27

"Horn of Plenty" (Hughes), **Retro. Supp. I:** 210; **Supp. I Part 1:** 342

Horovitz, Israel, **Supp. XV:** 321

Horowitz, James. *See* Salter, James

Horowitz, Mark, **Supp. V:** 219, 231

"Horrible" (Halliday), **Supp. XIX:** 91

"Horror at Martin's Beach, The" (Lovecraft and Greene), **Supp. XXV:** 122

"Horror at Red Hook, The" (Lovecraft), **Supp. XXV:** 110

"Horse, The" (Levine), **Supp. V:** 182

"Horse, The" (Wright), **Supp. III Part 2:** 592, 601

"Horse, The"(Le Sueur), **Supp. XXIII:** 168

Horse Eats Hay (play), **Supp. IV Part 1:** 82

Horse Feathers (film), **Supp. IV Part 1:** 384

"Horseflies" (Wrigley), **Supp. XVIII:** 307

Horse Has Six Legs, The (Simic), **Supp. VIII:** 272

"Horselaugh on Dibber Lannon" (Fante), **Supp. XI:** 164

Horseman, Pass By (McMurtry), **Supp. V:** 220–221, 224

"Horses" (Doty), **Supp. XI:** 122

Horses and Men (Anderson), **I:** 112–113, 114

"Horses and Men in Rain" (Sandburg), **III:** 584

"Horse Show, The" (W. C. Williams), **Retro. Supp. I:** 423

Horses Make a Landscape More Beautiful (Walker), **Supp. III Part 2:** 521, 533

"Horse Thief" (Caldwell), **I:** 310

"Horseweed" (Offutt), **Supp. XIX:** 166, 167

Horse With a Green Vinyl Mane (P. N. Warren), **Supp. XX: 261**

"Horsie" (Parker), **Supp. IX:** 193

Horstmann, Steffen, **Supp. XXV:** 226

Horton, George Moses, **Supp. XXII:** 11

Horton, Philip, **I:** 383, 386, 387, 393, 441; **Supp. XV:** 138

Horton Hatches the Egg (Geisel), **Supp. XVI:** 100, 112

Horton Hears a Who! (Geisel), **Supp. XVI:** 102

"Horton's Ape"(P. Benedict), **Supp. XXIII:** 41

Horwitz, Tony, **Supp. XVIII:** 195–196

Hosea (biblical book), **II:** 166

Hospers, John, **Supp. IV Part 2:** 528

"Hospice" (Hull), **Supp. XXI:** 138

Hospital, Janette Turner, **Supp. IV Part 1:** 311–302

Hospital Sketches (Alcott), **Supp. I Part 1:** 34, 35

Hostages to Fortune (Humphrey), **Supp. IX:** 96, **104–106,** 109

Hostess to Murder (Holding), **Supp. XXII:** 126, **127**

"Hot Combs" (Trethewey), **Supp. XXI:** 249

"Hot Cross Bum" (Loy), **Supp. XXII:** 168

"Hot Dog" (Stern), **Supp. IX: 298–299**

"Hotel, The"(Hadas), **Supp. XXIII:** 121

"Hotel Bar" (McClatchy), **Supp. XII:** 269

Hotel Dwellers, The (Lacy), **Supp. XV:** 205

Hotel Insomnia (Simic), **Supp. VIII:** 280, **281–282**

Hotel Lambosa and Other Stories (Koch), **Supp. XV:** 186

Hotel New Hampshire, The (Irving), **Supp. VI:** 163, 164, **172–173,** 177, 179; **Supp. XIX:** 164

"Hot-Foot Hannibal" (Chesnutt), **Supp. XIV:** 60

"Hot Ice"(Dybek), **Supp. XXIII:** 72–73

"Hot Night on Water Street" (Simpson), **Supp. IX:** 269, 270

"Hot Time, A" (Gunn Allen), **Supp. IV Part 1:** 333

Houdini, Harry, **IV:** 437; **Supp. XXV:** 121

"Hound of Heaven" (Thompson), **Retro. Supp. I:** 55

"Hourglass, The" (Kees), **Supp. XV:** 147

"Hour in Chartres, An" (Bourne), **I:** 228

"Hour of Peonies, The"(Crooker), **Supp. XXIII:** 58

Hours, The (Cunningham), **Supp. XII:** 80; **Supp. XV: 65–68**

"Hours before Eternity" (Caldwell), **I:** 291

House, Bridge, Fountain, Gate (Kumin), **Supp. IV Part 2:** 448, 449, 451, 454

House, Edward, **Supp. I Part 2:** 643

"House, The" (Merrill), **Supp. III Part 1:** 323

House at Pooh Corner, The (Milne), **Supp. IX:** 189

"House at the End of the World, The" (Brockmeier), **Supp. XXII:** 52, 53

House Behind the Cedars, The (Chesnutt), **Supp. XIV: 69–71**

Houseboat Days (Ashbery), **Supp. III Part 1:** 18–20

Housebreaker of Shady Hill and Other Stories, The (Cheever), **Supp. I Part 1:** 184

"House by the Sea, The" (E. Stoddard), **Supp. XV:** 277

House by the Sea, The (Sarton), **Supp. VIII:** 264

House Divided, A (Buck), **Supp. II Part 1:** 118

"House Divided, The/La Casa Divida" (Kingsolver), **Supp. VII:** 207

"House Guest" (Bishop), **Retro. Supp. II:** 49; **Supp. I Part 1:** 93

Household Saints (film), **Supp. XVI:** 256

Household Saints (Prose), **Supp. XVI:** 252–253, 254, 261

"House in Athens, The" (Merrill), **Supp. III Part 1:** 323

House in the Uplands, A (Caldwell), **I:** 297, 301, 306

"House in Turk Street, The" (Hammett), **Supp. IV Part 1:** 344

"House in Winter, The" (Sarton), **Supp. VIII:** 259

"House in Winter, The"(Hirshfield), **Supp. XXIII:** 132

"Housekeeping" (Alvarez), **Supp. VII:** 3–5, 10

Housekeeping (Robinson), **Supp. XXI:** 210–211, **212–216,** 218, 223

"Housekeeping" (Trethewey), **Supp. XXI:** 249

"Housekeeping for Men" (Bourne), **I:** 231

House Made of Dawn (Momaday), **Supp. IV Part 1:** 274, 323, 326; **Supp. IV Part 2:** 479, 480, 481–484, 485, 486, 504, 562

Houseman, John, **Supp. IV Part 1:** 173

House Next Door, The (Siddons), **Supp. XXII:** 239

House Next Door, The (television movie), **Supp. XXII:** 239

House of Dust, The: A Symphony (Aiken), **I:** 50

House of Earth trilogy (Buck), **Supp. II Part 1:** 118, 123

House of Five Talents, The (Auchincloss), **Supp. IV Part 1:** 21, 25–27

"House of Flowers" (Capote), **Supp. III Part 1:** 123

House of Games (Mamet), **Supp. XIV:** 243

House of Houses (Mora), **Supp. XIII:** 213, 215, 218, 219, 223–224, **225–227,** 228, 229

House of Incest (Nin), **Supp. III Part 1:** 43; **Supp. X:** 187, 190, 193

House of Lee, The (Atherton), **Supp. XXIV:** 26–27

House of Life, The: Rachel Carson at Work (Brooks), **Supp. IX:** 26

House of Light (Oliver), **Supp. VII:** 238–240

House of Mirth, The (Wharton), **II:** 180, 193; **IV:** 311–313, 314, 316, 318, 323, 327; **Retro. Supp. I:** 360, 366, 367, **367–370,** 373, 380; **Supp. XX:** 239, **240**

"House of Mist, The" (Rand), **Supp. IV Part 2:** 524

"House of My Own, A" (Cisneros), **Supp. VII:** 64

"House of Night, The" (Freneau), **Supp. II Part 1:** 259, 260

"House of Representatives and Me, The" (Conroy), **Supp. XVI:** 75

House of Sand and Fog (Dubus III), **Supp. XXIV:** 97, **104–107**

House of Sleeping Beauties, The (Hwang), **Supp. XXI:** 146

House of the Far and Lost, The (Wolfe), **IV:** 456

"House of the Injured, The" (Haines), **Supp. XII:** 203

"House of the One Father" (Antin), **Supp. XX:** 3, 13

House of the Prophet, The (Auchincloss), **Supp. IV Part 1:** 31

House of the Seven Gables (Hawthorne), **I:** 106; **II:** 60, 224, 225, 231, 237, 239, 240–241, 243, 244; **Retro. Supp. I:** 63, 149, **160–162,** 163, 164; **Supp. I Part 2:** 579

House of the Solitary Maggot, The (Purdy), **Supp. VII:** 274–275

"House on 15th S.W., The" (Hugo), **Supp. VI:** 140

"House on Main Street, The" (B. Kelly), **Supp. XVII:** 127

House on Mango Street (Cisneros), **Supp. XXV:** 133

House on Mango Street, The (Cisneros), **Supp. VII:** 58, 59–64, 65, 66, 67, 68, 72

"House on Mango Street, The" (Cisneros), **Supp. VII:** 59

House on Marshland, The (Glück), **Supp. V:** 81–83, 84

"House on Moscow Street, The" (Nelson), **Supp. XVIII:** 174

"House on the Heights, A" (Capote), **Supp. III Part 1:** 120

"House on the Hill, The" (Robinson), **III:** 505, 524

"House Raising" (Offutt), **Supp. XIX:** 166

"Houses" (Hogan), **Supp. IV Part 1:** 402

"Houses, The" (Merwin), **Supp. III Part 1:** 354

"Houses of the Spirit" (Karr), **Supp. XI:** 250

"House Sparrows" (Hecht), **Supp. X:** 68

"House That Doesn't House, The" (Bronk), **Supp. XXI:** 34

House That Tai Maing Built, The (Lee), **Supp. X:** 291

"House Unroofed by the Gale" (Tu Fu), **II:** 526

"House Where Mark Twain Was Born, The" (Masters), **Supp. I Part 2:** 472

"Housewife" (Hempel), **Supp. XXI:** 124

"Housewife" (Sexton), **Supp. II Part 2:** 682

" 'Housing the Deliberations': New York, War, and Frank O'Hara"(Ward), **Supp. XXIII:** 218

Housman, A. E., **III:** 15, 136, 606; **Supp. II Part 1:** 4; **Supp. IV Part 1:** 165;

Supp. **XV:** 40–41

Houston, Robert, **Supp. XXV:** 54

Houston Trilogy (McMurtry), **Supp. V:** 223–225

How" (Ginsberg), **Supp. XIV:** 142, 143

"How" (Moore), **Supp. X:** 167

"How About This?" (Carver), **Supp. III Part 1:** 141

"How America Came to the Mountains" (J. W. Miller), **Supp. XX:** **169**

"How Annandale Went Out" (Robinson), **III:** 513

Howard, Arliss, **Supp. XXI:** 39

Howard, Ben, **Supp. XVI:** 54

Howard, Gerald, **Supp. XII:** 21

Howard, Jane, **Retro. Supp. I:** 334

Howard, June, **Retro. Supp. II:** 139

Howard, Leon, **Supp. I Part 2:** 408, 422, 423

Howard, Maureen, **Supp. XII:** 285; **Supp. XVII:** 183

Howard, Richard, **Retro. Supp. II:** 43; **Supp. IV Part 2:** 624, 626, 640; **Supp. VIII:** 273; **Supp. IX:** 324, 326; **Supp. X:** 152; **Supp. XI:** 317; **Supp. XII:** 254; **Supp. XIII:** 76; **Supp. XV:** 23, 24; **Supp. XXIV:** 155

Howard, Robert E., **Supp. XXV:** 122

Howard, Vilma, **Retro. Supp. II:** 111, 112

Howards, J. Z., **Supp. VIII:** 178

Howards End (Forster), **Supp. XII:** 87

Howarth, Cora, **I:** 408, 409

Howbah Indians (Ortiz), **Supp. IV Part 2:** 513

"How Black Sees Green and Red" (McKay), **Supp. X:** 136

How Britain Rules Africa (Padmore), **Supp. XXI:** 166

"How David Did Not Care" (R. Bly), **Supp. IV Part 1:** 73

"How Did I Love Him?" (Nelson), **Supp. XVIII:** 176

"How Do I Love Thee?" (Browning), **Supp. XVIII:** 176

Howe, Daniel Walker, **Supp. XXIV:** 79

Howe, Darcus, **Supp. XXI:** 170

Howe, E.W., **I:** 106

Howe, Florence, **Supp. XIII:** 295, 306

Howe, Harriet, **Supp. XI:** 200, 201

Howe, Irving, **IV:** 10; **Retro. Supp. I:** 369; **Retro. Supp. II:** 112, 286; **Supp. I Part 2:** 432; **Supp. II Part 1:** 99; **Supp. VI:** 113–129; **Supp. VIII:** 93, 232; **Supp. IX:** 227; **Supp. X:** 203, 245; **Supp. XII:** 160; **Supp. XIII:** 98; **Supp. XIV:** 103–104, 104; **Supp. XVII:** 50; **Supp. XIX:** 257, 265; **Supp. XXIII:** 3, 7; **Supp. XXIV:** 220–221, 222

Howe, James Wong, **Supp. I Part 1:** 281; **Supp. V:** 223

Howe, Julia Ward, **III:** 505; **Retro. Supp. II:** 135

Howe, M. A. DeWolfe, **I:** 258; **II:** 406; **Supp. XIV:** 54

Howe, Mary Manning, **Supp. IV Part 2:** 422

Howe, Samuel, **Supp. I Part 1:** 153

Howe, Susan, **Retro. Supp. I:** 33, 43; **Supp. IV Part 2: 419–438; Supp. XVI:** 284

Howell, Chris, **Supp. XIII:** 112

Howell, James, **II:** 111

Howells, Margaret, **II:** 271

Howells, William C., **II:** 273

Howells, William Dean, **I:** 109, 192, 204, 210, 211, 254, 355, 407, 411, 418, 459, 469; **II:** 127–128, 130, 131, 136, 137, 138, 140, **271–294,** 322, 331–332, 338, 397–398, 400, 415, 444, 451, 556; **III:** 51, 118, 314, 327–328, 461, 576, 607; **IV:** 192, 202, 342, 349; **Retro. Supp. I:** 220, 334, 362, 378; **Retro. Supp. II:** 93, 101, 135, 288; **Supp. I Part 1:** 306, 318, 357, 360, 368; **Supp. I Part 2:** 414, 420, 645–646; **Supp. II Part 1:** 198, 352; **Supp. IV Part 2:** 678; **Supp. VIII:** 98, 101, 102; **Supp. XI:** 198, 200; **Supp. XIV:** 45–46; **Supp. XV:** 269, 274, 285, 287; **Supp. XVIII:** 6; **Supp. XXIV:** 24

Howells, Mrs. William Dean (Elinor Mead), **II:** 273

Howells, Winifred, **II:** 271

"Howells as Anti-Novelist" (Updike), **Retro. Supp. I:** 334

Howells: His Life and World (Brooks), **I:** 254

Hower, Edward, **Supp. XII:** 330, 343

Howes, Barbara, **Supp. XIII:** 331

How Good Is David Mamet, Anyway? (Heilpern), **Supp. XIV:** 242

"How I Became a Shadow" (Purdy), **Supp. VII:** 269

"How I Came to Vedanta" (Isherwood), **Supp. XIV:** 164

"How I Come to You" (Peacock), **Supp. XIX:** 198

"How I Learned to Sweep" (Alvarez), **Supp. VII:** 4

"How I Spent My Forties" (Wasserstein), **Supp. XV:** 325, 330, 332

"How It Began" (Stafford), **Supp. XI:** 327

"How It Feels to Be Colored Me" (Hurston), **Supp. VI:** 152

"How It Is" (Budbill), **Supp. XIX:** 10

"How It Is" (Everwine), **Supp. XV:** 79, 86

"How I Told My Child About Race" (Brooks), **Supp. III Part 1:** 78

"How I Went to the Mines" (Harte), **Supp. I Part 1:** 336

"How I Write" (Franzen), **Supp. XX: 84**

"How I Write" (Welty), **IV:** 279, 280

"How I Wrote *The Promised Land*" (Antin), **Supp. XX:** 3

"How Jonah Did Not Care" (R. Bly), **Supp. IV Part 1:** 73

Howl (Ginsberg), **Retro. Supp. I:** 426; **Supp. III Part 1:** 92; **Supp. IV Part 1:** 90; **Supp. V:** 336; **Supp. VIII:** 290; **Supp. XIV:** 15, 126, 157; **Supp. XVIII:** 20, 29

"How Laddie and the Princess Spelled Down at the Christmas Bee" (Stratton-Porter), **Supp. XX:** 216

Howl and Other Poems (Ginsberg), **Supp. II Part 1:** 308, 317–318, 319; **Supp. X:** 123

Howlett, William, **Retro. Supp. I:** 17

Howl: Original Draft Facsimile, Transcript and Variant Versions (Gimsberg), **Supp. XIV:** 142

"How Many Midnights" (Bowles), **Supp. IV Part 1:** 86–87

"How Many Nights" (Kinnell), **Supp. III Part 1:** 245–246

How Much? (Blechman), **Supp. I Part 1:** 290

"How Much Are You Worth" (Salinas), **Supp. XIII:** 325–326

"How Much Earth" (Levine), **Supp. V:** 184

How Much Earth: The Fresno Poets (Buckley, Oliveira, and Williams, eds.), **Supp. XIII:** 313

"How Not to Forget" (Bartov), **Supp. XVI:** 153–154

"How Poetry Comes to Me" (Corso), **Supp. XII:** 122

"How Poetry Comes to Me" (Snyder), **Supp. VIII:** 305

How Reading Changed My Life (Quindlen), **Supp. XVII:** 167, 179–180

"How She Came By Her Name: An Interview with Louis Massiah" (Bambara), **Supp. XI:** 20

"How Soon Hath Time" (Ransom), **IV:** 123

How Spring Comes (Notley), **Supp. XXII:** 226, 229

How Stella Got Her Groove Back (McMillan), **Supp. XIII:** 185, **190–191**

How the Alligator Missed Breakfast (Kinney), **Supp. III Part 1:** 235, 253

"How the Devil Came Down Division Street" (Algren), **Supp. IX:** 3

How the García Girls Lost Their Accents (Alvarez), **Supp. VII:** 3, 5–9, 11, 15, 17, 18

How the Grinch Stole Christmas! (Geisel), **Supp. XVI:** 102

How the Other Half Lives (Riis), **I:** 293

"How the Saint Did Not Care" (R. Bly), **Supp. IV Part 1:** 73

"How the Women Went from Dover" (Whittier), **Supp. I Part 2:** 694, 696, 697

"How This Magazine Wronged Herman Wouk" (Lewis), **Supp. XXV:** 253

"How To" (Carruth), **Supp. XVI:** 51

"How-To" (Monson), **Supp. XXIV:** 237

How To Be Alone: Essays (Franzen), **Supp. XX: 83, 90, 93–94**

"How to Be an Other Woman" (Moore), **Supp. X:** 165, 167, 168

"How to Become a Writer" (Moore), **Supp. X:** 167, 168

"How to Be Happy: Another Memo to Myself" (Dunn), **Supp. XI:** 145

How To Cook a Wolf (M. F. K. Fisher), **Supp. XVII:** 84–85, 87

"How to Date a Browngirl, Blackgirl, Whitegirl, or Halfie" (Díaz), **Supp. XXIV:** 88

How to Develop Your Personality (Shellow), **Supp. I Part 2:** 608

How to Know God: The Yoga Aphorisms of Patanjali (Isherwood and Prabhavananda)), **Supp. XIV:** 164

"How To Like It" (Dobyns), **Supp. XIII: 85–86**

"How to Live on $36,000 a Year" (Fitzgerald), **Retro. Supp. I:** 105

"How to Live. What to Do" (Stevens), **Retro. Supp. I:** 302

"How Tom is Doin' " (Kees), **Supp. XV:** 143

How to Read (Pound), **Supp. VIII:** 291

How to Read a Novel (Gordon), **II:** 198

How to Read a Poem and Fall in Love with Poetry (Hirsch), **Supp. XIX:** 202

How to Read a Poem: And Fall in Love with Poetry (Hirsch), **Supp. XXIII:** 124

How to Read a Poem . . . and Start a Poetry Circle (Peacock), **Supp. XIX:** 194, 202–203, 205

How to Save Your Own Life (Jong), **Supp. V:** 115, 123–125, 130

"How to Study Poetry" (Pound), **III:** 474

"How to Talk to Your Mother" (Moore), **Supp. X:** 167, 172

"How to Tell Stories to Children" (July), **Supp. XXIV:** 206–207

How to Win Friends and Influence People (Carnegie), **Supp. I Part 2:** 608

How to Worry Successfully (Seabury), **Supp. I Part 2:** 608

How to Write (Stein), **IV:** 32, 34, 35

"How to Write a Blackwood Article" (Poe), **III:** 425; **Retro. Supp. II:** 273

"How to Write a Memoir Like This" (Oates), **Supp. III Part 2:** 509

"How to Write Like Somebody Else" (Roethke), **III:** 540

How to Write Short Stories (Lardner), **II:** 430, 431

"How Vincentine Did Not Care" (R. Bly), **Supp. IV Part 1:** 73

How We Became Human: New and Selected Poems (Harjo), **Supp. XII: 230–232**

"How We Danced" (Sexton), **Supp. II Part 2:** 692

How We Got Insipid (Lethem), **Supp. XVIII:** 149

"How We Got in Town and Out Again" (Lethem), **Supp. XVIII:** 149

"How You Sound??" (Baraka), **Supp. II Part 1:** 30

Hoy, Philip, **Supp. X:** 56, 58

Hoyer, Linda Grace (pseudonym). *See* Updike, Mrs. Wesley

Hoyt, Constance, **Supp. I Part 2:** 707

Hoyt, Elinor Morton. *See* Wylie, Elinor

Hoyt, Helen, **Supp. XXII:** 275

Hoyt, Henry (father), **Supp. I Part 2:** 707

Hoyt, Henry (son), **Supp. I Part 2:** 708

Hoyt, Henry Martyn, **Supp. I Part 2:** 707

H. P. Lovecraft (Canan), **Supp. XXV:** 123

Hsu, Kai-yu, **Supp. X:** 292

Hsu, Ruth Y., **Supp. XV:** 212

Hubba City (Reed), **Supp. X:** 241

Hubbard, Elbert, **I:** 98, 383

Hubbell, Jay B., **Supp. I Part 1:** 372

"Hubbub, The" (Ammons), **Supp. VII:** 35

Huber, François, **II:** 6

Huckins, Olga, **Supp. IX:** 32

Huckleberry Finn (Twain). *See Adventures of Huckleberry Finn, The* (Twain)

Hucksters, The (Wakeman), **Supp. XXV:** 258

Hud (film), **Supp. V:** 223, 226

Hudgins, Andrew, **Supp. X:** 206; **Supp. XVII:** 111, 112; **Supp. XVIII:** 176

Hudson, Henry, **I:** 230

"Hudsonian Curlew, The" (Snyder), **Supp. VIII:** 302

Hudson River Bracketed (Wharton), **IV:** 326–327; **Retro. Supp. I:** 382

Huebsch, B. W., **III:** 110

Hueffer, Ford Madox, **Supp. I Part 1:** 257, 262. *See also* Ford, Ford Madox

Huene-Greenberg, Dorothee von, **Supp. XX: 46**

Huff (television series), **Supp. XIX:** 222

"Hug, The" (Gallagher), **Supp. XXIV:** 168

Hug Dancing (Hearon), **Supp. VIII: 67–68**

Huge Season, The (Morris), **III:** 225–226, 227, 230, 232, 233, 238

Hugging the Jukebox (Nye), **Supp. XIII: 275–276,** 277

"Hugging the Jukebox" (Nye), **Supp. XIII:** 276

Hughes, Brigid, **Supp. XVI:** 247

Hughes, Carolyn, **Supp. XII:** 272, 285

Hughes, Frieda, **Supp. I Part 2:** 540, 541

Hughes, Glenn, **Supp. I Part 1:** 255

Hughes, H. Stuart, **Supp. VIII:** 240

Hughes, James Nathaniel, **Supp. I Part 1:** 321, 332

Hughes, Ken, **Supp. XI:** 307

Hughes, Langston, **Retro. Supp. I:** 193–214; **Retro. Supp. II:** 114, 115, 117, 120; **Supp. I Part 1: 320–348; Supp. II Part 1:** 31, 33, 61, 170, 173, 181, 227, 228, 233, 361; **Supp. III Part 1:** 72–77; **Supp. IV Part 1:** 15, 16, 164, 168, 169, 173, 243, 368; **Supp. VIII:** 213; **Supp. IX:** 306, 316; **Supp. X:** 131, 136, 139, 324; **Supp. XI:** 1; **Supp. XIII:** 75, 111, 132, 233; **Supp. XVI:** 135, 138; **Supp. XVIII:** 90, 277, 279, 280, 281, 282; **Supp. XIX:** 72, 75, 77; **Supp. XXI:** 243; **Supp. XXII:** 3, 4, 5, 6, 8, 13–14; **Supp. XXIV:** 183

Hughes, Nicholas, **Supp. I Part 2:** 541

Hughes, Robert, **Supp. X:** 73

Hughes, Ted, **IV:** 3; **Retro. Supp. II:** 244, 245, 247, 257; **Supp. I Part 2:** 536, 537, 538, 539, 540, 541; **Supp. XV:** 117, 347, 348; **Supp. XXII:** 30

Hughes, Thomas, **Supp. I Part 2:** 406

"Hugh Harper" (Bowles), **Supp. IV Part 1:** 94

Hughie (O'Neill), **III:** 385, 401, 405

Hugh Selwyn Mauberley (Pound), **I:** 66, 476; **III:** 9, 462–463, 465, 468; **Retro.**

Supp. I: 289–290, 291, 299; **Supp. XIV:** 272

Hugo, Richard, **Supp. VI: 131–148; Supp. IX:** 296, 323, 324, 330; **Supp. XI:** 315, 317; **Supp. XII:** 178; **Supp. XIII:** 112, 113, 133; **Supp. XVIII:** 293, 299; **Supp. XXI:** 243

Hugo, Victor, **II:** 290, 490, 543; **Supp. IV Part 2:** 518; **Supp. IX:** 308

Hui-neng, **III:** 567

Huis Clos (Sartre), **Supp. IV Part 1:** 84

Huizinga, Johan, **I:** 225; **II:** 416–417, 418, 425

Hulbert, Ann, **Supp. XI:** 38–39

Hull, Lynda, **Supp. XI:** 131; **Supp. XXI: 129–142**

Hull, Thomas, **Supp. XXV:** 123

Hulme, Thomas E., **I:** 68, 69, 475; **III:** 196, 209, 463–464, 465; **IV:** 122; **Supp. I Part 1:** 261, 262; **Supp. XV:** 43

Human, All Too Human (Nietzsche), **Supp. X:** 48

"Human Culture" (Emerson), **II:** 11–12

Human Factor, The (Greene), **Supp. V:** 298

"Human Figures" (Doty), **Supp. XI:** 123–124

"Human Fly, The" (Boyle), **Supp. XX: 19**

"Human Geography" (Jarman), **Supp. XVII:** 116

"Human Immortality" (James), **II:** 353–354

"Human Life" (Emerson), **II:** 11–12

"Human Pig" (Jin), **Supp. XVIII:** 99

Human Rights, Human Wrongs: The Oxford Amnesty Lectures, 2001, **Supp. XVI:** 155

"Human Soul as a Rube Goldberg Device, The: A Choose-Your-Own-Adventure-Story" (Brockmeier), **Supp. XXII:** 60–61

Human Stain, The (P. Roth), **Retro. Supp. II:** 279, 289, 294–295

"Human Things" (Nemerov), **III:** 279

Human Universe (Olson), **Supp. II Part 2:** 571

"Human Universe" (Olson), **Supp. II Part 2:** 565, 567

Human Vibration (Richter), **Supp. XVIII:** 209

Human Wishes (Hass), **Supp. VI:** 105–106, 107

Human Work (Gilman), **Supp. XI:** 206

Humbert, Humbert, **Supp. X:** 283

Humble Inquiry into the Rules of the Word of God, An, Concerning the Qualifications Requisite to a Complete Standing and Full Communion in the Visible Christian Church (Edwards), **I:** 548

Humboldt, Alexander von, **III:** 428

Humboldt's Gift (Bellow), **Retro. Supp. II:** 19, 28–29, 34; **Supp. XIII:** 320

Hume, David, **I:** 125; **II:** 349, 357, 480; **III:** 618

Humes, Harold, **Supp. V:** 201; **Supp. XIV:** 82

Humes, Harry, **Supp. XIX:** 281; **Supp. XXIII:** 54

Humes, H. L. "Doc", **Supp. XI:** 294

"Humility" (Hoffman), **Supp. XVIII:** 86

Hummer, T. R., **Supp. XIX:** 278; **Supp. XXI:** 91

"Hummingbirds, The" (Welty), **IV:** 273

Humors and/or Not So Humorous (Kenny), **Supp. XXIII:** 155

Humphrey, William, **Supp. IX: 93–112; Supp. XV:** 353

Humphreys, Christmas, **Supp. V:** 267

Humphreys, David, **Supp. II Part 1:** 65, 69, 70, 268

Humphreys, Josephine, **Supp. XII:** 311

Humphries, Rolfe, **III:** 124; **Retro. Supp. I:** 137

Hunchback of Notre Dame, The (film), **Supp. IV Part 1:** 101

Hunches in Bunches (Geisel), **Supp. XVI:** 111

Huncke, Herbert, **Supp. XII:** 118; **Supp. XIV: 137–153**

Huncke's Journal (Huncke), **Supp. XIV:** 139, 144, 145, 146

Hundred Camels in the Courtyard, A (Bowles), **Supp. IV Part 1:** 90

"Hundred Collars, A" (Frost), **Retro. Supp. I:** 128; **Supp. XIII:** 147

Hundred Secret Senses, The (Tan), **Supp. X:** 289, 293, 295, 297, 298, 299

Hundreds of Hens and Other Poems for Children by Halfdan Rasmussen (Nelson and Espeland, trans.), **Supp. XVIII:** 180

Hundred White Daffodils, A: Essays, Interviews, Newspaper Columns, and One Poem (Kenyon), **Supp. VII:** 160–162, 165, 166, 167, 174

Huneker, James, **III:** 102

Hunger (Hamsun), **Supp. XI:** 167

"Hunger" (Hogan), **Supp. IV Part 1:** 411

"Hunger . . ." (Rich), **Supp. I Part 2:** 571

"Hungerfield" (Jeffers), **Supp. II Part 2:** 416–417, 436

Hungerfield and Other Poems (Jeffers), **Supp. II Part 2:** 422

Hunger of Memory: The Education of Richard Rodriguez (Rodriguez), **Supp. XIV:** 297, 298, **298–302,** 310

Hungry Ghosts, The (Oates), **Supp. II Part 2:** 504, 510

Hungry Hearts (Prose), **Supp. XVI:** 253

"Hungry Intellectual, A" (Le Sueur), **Supp. XXIII:** 164

Hungry Woman, The: A Mexican Medea (Moraga), **Supp. XXIII:** 196

Hunnewell, Susannah, **Supp. VIII:** 83

Hunt, Harriot K., **Retro. Supp. II:** 146

Hunt, Leigh, **II:** 515–516; **Supp. XV:** 175

Hunt, Richard Morris, **IV:** 312

Hunt, Robert, **Supp. XV:** 42, 49, 52

Hunt, William, **II:** 343

"Hunter" (Bierds), **Supp. XVII:** 30

Hunter, Dianna, **Supp. XVI:** 38

Hunter, Dr. Joseph, **II:** 217

Hunter, J. Paul, **Supp. IV Part 1:** 332

Hunter, Kim, **Supp. I Part 1:** 286

If You Want to Write (Ueland), **Supp. XVII:** 13

I Gaspiri (Lardner), **II:** 435

"I Gather the Limbs of Osiris" (Pound), **Retro. Supp. I:** 287

I Get on the Bus (McKnight), **Supp. XX:** 148–150, 152

"I Give You Back" (Harjo), **Supp. XII:** 223

Ignatius of Loyola, **IV:** 151; **Supp. XI:** 162

Ignatow, David, **Supp. XIII:** 275

"Ignis Fatuus" (Tate), **IV:** 128

"Ignorant Lust after Knowledge, The" (Bronk), **Supp. XXI:** 31

"I Go Back to May 1937" (Olds), **Supp. X:** 207

I Go Dreaming Serenades (Salinas), **Supp. XIII:** 316

"I Got a Guy Once" (Gallagher), **Supp. XXIV:** 176

I Got the Blues (Odets), **Supp. II Part 2:** 530

Iguana Killer, The (Ríos), **Supp. IV Part 2:** 542–544

"I Had Eight Birds Hatcht in One Nest" (Bradstreet), **Supp. I Part 1:** 102, 115, 117, 119

"I had no time to Hate" (Dickinson), **Retro. Supp. I:** 44–45, 46

I Had Trouble in Getting to Solla Sollew (Geisel), **Supp. XVI:** 108, 109

I Hate Miranda July (blog), **Supp. XXIV:** 200

"I Have a Rendezvous with Life" (Cullen), **Supp. IV Part 1:** 168

"I Have Been Thinking About Snow" (Monson), **Supp. XXIV:** 235

"I Have Increased Power" (Ginsberg), **Supp. II Part 1:** 313

"I Have Moved West" (Taggard), **Supp. XXII:** 274

"I Have Seen Black Hands" (Wright), **Supp. II Part 1:** 228

"I Hear an Army" (Joyce), **Supp. I Part 1:** 262

"I heard a Fly buzz when I died" (Dickinson), **Retro. Supp. I:** 38

"I Heard Immanuel Singing" (Lindsay), **Supp. I Part 2:** 379

I Heard It Through the Grapevine (Turner), **Supp. XX: 110**

"I Hear It Was Charged against Me" (Whitman), **IV:** 343

I Hear Men Talking (Le Sueur), **Supp. XXIII:** 162, 167, **171–172**

"I Held a Shelley Manuscript" (Corso), **Supp. XII:** 128

"I Held His Name" (Ríos), **Supp. IV Part 2:** 547

"Ike and Nina" (Boyle), **Supp. XX: 19**

"I Kiss a Door" (July), **Supp. XXIV:** 204

I Knew a Phoenix (Sarton), **Supp. VIII:** 249, 251–252

"I Know a Man" (Creeley), **Supp. IV Part 1:** 147–148, 149

I Know Some Things: Stories about Childhood by Contemporary Writers (Moore, ed.), **Supp. X:** 175

"I Know Why the Caged Bird Cannot Read" (Prose), **Supp. XVI:** 259

I Know Why the Caged Bird Sings (Angelou), **Supp. IV Part 1:** 2–4, 5, 7, 11, 12, 13, 14, 15, 17; **Supp. XVI:** 259

"Ikon: The Harrowing of Hell" (Levertov), **Supp. III Part 1:** 284

"Iktomi and the Ducks" (Zitkala-Ša), **Supp. XXV:** 275–276

Ile (O'Neill), **III:** 388; **Supp. XXV:** 20

"I Led Three Lives" (television program), **Supp. XX:** 195

"I Let Him Take Me" (Cisneros), **Supp. VII:** 71

Iliad (Bryant, trans.), **Supp. I Part 1:** 158

Iliad (Homer), **II:** 470; **Supp. IV Part 2:** 631; **Supp. IX:** 211; **Supp. X:** 114; **Supp. XVII:** 117; **Supp. XXI:** 36

Iliad (Homer; Chapman, trans), **Supp. XXV:** 226

Iliad (Pope, trans.), **Supp. I Part 1:** 152

"I like to see it lap the Miles" (Dickinson), **Retro. Supp. I:** 37

"I Live Up Here" (Merwin), **Supp. III Part 1:** 349

"I'll Be Doing More of Same" (Franzen), **Supp. XX: 89**

"Illegal Alien" (Mora), **Supp. XIII:** 215

"Illegal Days, The" (Paley), **Supp. VI:** 222

"Illegibility" (F. Wright), **Supp. XVII:** 244

Illig, Joyce, **Retro. Supp. II:** 20

"Illinois" (Masters), **Supp. I Part 2:** 458

"Illinois Bus Ride" (Leopold), **Supp. XIV:** 189

Illinois Poems (Masters), **Supp. I Part 2:** 472

"Illinois Village, The" (Lindsay), **Supp. I Part 2:** 381

"Ill-Lit" (F. Wright), **Supp. XVII:** 245

Ill-Lit: Selected & New Poems (F. Wright), **Supp. XVII:** 245

Illness as Metaphor (Sontag), **Supp. III Part 2:** 452, 461, 466

I'll Take My Stand ("Twelve Southerners"), **II:** 196; **III:** 496; **IV:** 125, 237; **Supp. X:** 25, 52–53; **Supp. XIV:** 3

"I'll Take You to Tennessee" (Connell), **Supp. XIV:** 82

Illumination (Frederic), **II:** 141

Illumination, The (Brockmeier), **Supp. XXII:** 61

Illumination Night (Hoffman), **Supp. X:** 85, **86,** 88, 89

Illuminations (Rimbaud), **Supp. XXI:** 233

Illusion and Reality (Caudwell), **Supp. XXII:** 284

Illusion comique, L' (Corneille), **Supp. IX:** 138

"Illusion of Eternity, The" (Eberhart), **I:** 541

"Illusion of Fiction in Frank Conroy's *Stop-Time*, The" (R. Ramsey), **Supp. XVI:** 69

Illusions (Dash; film), **Supp. XI:** 20

"Illusions" (Emerson), **II:** 2, 5, 14, 16

Illustrated Man, The (Bradbury), **Supp. IV Part 1:** 102, 103, 113

Illustrations of China and Its People (Thompson), **Supp. XXI:** 151

Illustrations of Political Economy (Martineau), **Supp. II Part 1:** 288

"I Look at My Hand" (Swenson), **Supp. IV Part 2:** 638, 647

I Love Gootie: My Grandmother's Story (Apple), **Supp. XVII: 9–10**

I Love Myself When I Am Laughing . . . : A Zora Neale Hurston Reader (Walker), **Supp. III Part 2:** 531, 532

"I Love the Way It Goes" (O'Hara), **Supp. XXIII:** 220

"I'm a Fool" (Anderson), **I:** 113, 114, 116; **Supp. I Part 2:** 430

Image and Idea (Rahv), **Supp. II Part 1:** 146

Image and the Law, The (Nemerov), **III:** 268, 269–271, 272

"Image in the Mirror, The" (Swados), **Supp. XIX:** 265

"Images" (Hass), **Supp. VI:** 103

"Images and 'Images' " (Simic), **Supp. VIII:** 274

"Images for Godard" (Rich), **Supp. I Part 2:** 558

"Images of Walt Whitman" (Fiedler), **IV:** 352

"Imaginary Dialogue, An" (Espaillat), **Supp. XXI:** 103

"Imaginary Friendships of Tom McGrath, The" (Cohen), **Supp. X:** 112

"Imaginary Iceberg, The" (Bishop), **Retro. Supp. II:** 42; **Supp. I Part 1:** 86, 88

"Imaginary Jew, The" (Berryman), **I:** 174–175

Imaginary Letters (Pound), **III:** 473–474

Imaginary Paintings (C. Baxter), **Supp. XVII:** 18–19

"Imaginary Prisons" (Schnackenberg), **Supp. XV:** 257, 258

Imagination and Fancy; or, Selections from the English Poets, illustrative of those first requisites of their art; with markings of the best passages, critical notices of the writers, and an essay in answer to the question'What is Poetry?' (Hunt), **II:** 515–516

"Imagination as Value" (Stevens), **Retro. Supp. I:** 298

"Imagination of Disaster, The" (Gordon), **Supp. IV Part 1:** 306

Imaginative Qualities of Actual Things (Sorrentino), **Supp. XXI:** 226, 230, 231–232, 234

"Imagine a Day at the End of Your Life" (Beattie), **Supp. V:** 33

Imagined London: A Tour of the World's Greatest Fictional City (Quindlen), **Supp. XVII:** 167, 180

Imagineering Atlanta (Rutheiser), **Supp. XXII:** 244

"Imagine Kissing Pete" (O'Hara), **III:** 372; **Supp. VIII:** 156

Imaging Robert: My Brother, Madness, and Survival (Neugeboren), **Supp.**

XVI: 225, **226–229**

"Imagining How It Would Be to Be Dead" (Eberhart), **I:** 533

Imagining Los Angeles: A City in Fiction (Fine), **Supp. XI:** 160

"Imagining Their Own Hymns" (B. Kelly), **Supp. XVII:** 126–127

"Imagining the Midwest" (Sanders), **Supp. XVI:** 275–276

Imagining the Worst: Stephen King and the Representations of Women (Lant and Thompson), **Supp. V:** 141

"Imagisme" (Pound), **Retro. Supp. I:** 288

Imagistes, Des: An Anthology of the Imagists (Pound, ed.), **III:** 465, 471; **Retro. Supp. I:** 288

Imago (O. Butler), **Supp. XIII:** 63, **65–66**

"Imago" (Stevens), **IV:** 74, 89

Imagoes (Coleman), **Supp. XI:** 89–90

I Married a Communist (P. Roth), **Retro. Supp. II:** 289, 293–294

I Married an Angel (film), **Supp. XVI:** 193

"I May, I Might, I Must" (Moore), **III:** 215

Imbusch, Kevin, **Supp. XXIII:** 125

"I'm Crazy" (Salinger), **III:** 553

"I'm Here" (Roethke), **III:** 547

Imitations (Lowell), **II:** 543, 544–545, 550, 555; **Retro. Supp. II:** 181, 187

"Imitations of Drowning" (Sexton), **Supp. II Part 2:** 684, 686

"Immaculate Man" (Gordon), **Supp. IV Part 1:** 311

"Immanence of Dostoevsky, The" (Bourne), **I:** 235

"Immigrants" (Mora), **Supp. XIII:** 216

Immigrant Saint: The Life of Mother Cabrini (di Donato), **Supp. XX: 44**

"Immigrant Story, The" (Paley), **Supp. VI:** 230

Immobile Wind, The (Winters), **Supp. II Part 2:** 786

"Immobile Wind, The" (Winters), **Supp. II Part 2:** 788, 811

"Immolatus" (Komunyakaa), **Supp. XIII:** 126

"Immoral Proposition, The" (Creeley), **Supp. IV Part 1:** 144

"Immortal Autumn" (MacLeish), **III:** 13

"Immortality Ode" (Nemerov), **III:** 87

Immortality Ode (Wordsworth), **II:** 17; **Supp. I Part 2:** 673

Immortal Marriage, The (Atherton), **Supp. XXIV:** 26

"Immortal Woman, The" (Tate), **IV:** 130, 131, 137

"I'm Not Ready to Die Yet" (Harjo), **Supp. XII:** 231

I'm Not There (film, Haynes), **Supp. XVIII:** 23

"I'm on My Way" (Salinas), **Supp. XIII:** 320

"Impasse" (Hughes), **Supp. I Part 1:** 343

"Impatient Mary" (Taggard), **Supp. XXII:** 278

Imperative Duty, An, a Novel (Howells), **II:** 286

Imperial Eyes: Travel Writing and Transculturation (Pratt), **Retro. Supp. II:** 48

Imperial Germany and the Industrial Revolution (Veblen), **Supp. I Part 2:** 642, 643

Imperial Way, The: By Rail from Peshawar to Chittagong (Theroux), **Supp. VIII:** 323

"Implements from the 'Tomb of the Poet' " (Stallings), **Supp. XXV:** 232

"Implosions" (Rich), **Supp. I Part 2:** 556

"Imp of the Perverse, The" (Poe), **III:** 414–415; **Retro. Supp. II:** 267

Impolite Interviews, **Supp. XI:** 293

"Importance of Artists' Biographies, The" (Goldbarth), **Supp. XII:** 183, 184, 191

Importance of Being Earnest, The (Wilde), **Supp. XIV:** 324, 339

"Important Houses, The" (Gordon), **Supp. IV Part 1:** 315

"Impossible Indispensability of the Ars Poetica, The" (Carruth), **Supp. XVI:** 57

"Impossible to Tell" (Pinsky), **Supp. VI:** 247, 248

"Imposter, The" (West), **Retro. Supp. II:** 322, 327

"Impressionism and Symbolism in *Heart of Darkness*" (Watt), **Supp. VIII:** 4

"Impressionism"(Crooker), **Supp. XXIII:** 57

"Impressions of a European Tour" (Bourne), **I:** 225

"Impressions of an Indian Childhood" (Zitkala-Ša), **Supp. XXV:** 272

"Impressions of a Plumber" (H. Roth), **Supp. IX:** 228, 234

"Impressions of Europe, 1913–1914" (Bourne), **I:** 225

"I Must Have Called and So He Comes" (Notley), **Supp. XXII:** 224

"I'm Walking behind the Spanish" (Salinas), **Supp. XIII:** 323–324

"I/Myself" (Shields), **Supp. VII:** 311

"In a (Low) Bar" (Ferry), **Supp. XXIV:** 153

"In Absence" (Lanier), **Supp. I Part 1:** 364

"In Absentia" (Bowles), **Supp. IV Part 1:** 94

"In a Cab" (Untermeyer), **Supp. XV:** 296

"In a Country Cemetery" (Kooser), **Supp. XIX:** 120

Inada, Lawson Fusao, **Supp. V:** 180

"In a Dark Room, Furniture" (Nye), **Supp. XIII:** 274

"In a Dark Time" (Roethke), **III:** 539, 547, 548

In a Different Voice (Gilligan), **Supp. XXII:** 18

"In a Disused Graveyard" (Frost), **Retro. Supp. I:** 126, 133

In a Dusty Light (Haines), **Supp. XII:** 207

"In a Garden" (Lowell), **II:** 513

"In a Hard Intellectual Light" (Eberhart), **I:** 523

"In a Hollow of the Hills" (Harte), **Supp. II Part 1:** 354

In America (Sontag), **Supp. XIV:** 95–96

"In Amicitia" (Ransom), **IV:** 141

In a Narrow Grave: Essays on Texas (McMurtry), **Supp. V:** 220, 223

"Inanna" (A. Finch), **Supp. XVII:** 72

"In Another Country" (Hemingway), **I:** 484–485; **II:** 249

In April Once (Percy), **Retro. Supp. I:** 341

"In a Prominent Bar in Secaucus One Day" (X. J. Kennedy), **Supp. XV:** 154, 155–156

"In Armenia, 1987"(Balakian), **Supp. XXIII:** 25

In A Shallow Grave (Purdy), **Supp. VII:** 272

In a shlekhter tsayt (In a bad time) (Asch), **Supp. XXIII:** 4

"In a Station of the Metro" (Pound), **Retro. Supp. I:** 288; **Supp. I Part 1:** 265; **Supp. XIV:** 284–285

"In a Strange Town" (Anderson), **I:** 114, 115

"In Athens Once" (Rodriguez), **Supp. XIV:** 303

"In a Tub" (Hempel), **Supp. XXI:** 119

In Battle for Peace: The Story of My 83rd Birthday (Du Bois), **Supp. II Part 1:** 185

In Bed One Night & Other Brief Encounters (Coover), **Supp. V:** 49, 50

"In Bertram's Garden" (Justice), **Supp. VII:** 117

"In Blackwater Woods" (Oliver), **Supp. VII:** 244, 246

In Black & Whitey (Lacy), **Supp. XV:** 206–207

"In Broad Daylight" (Jin), **Supp. XVIII:** 94

In Broken Country (Wagoner), **Supp. IX:** 330

"In California" (Simpson), **Supp. IX:** 271

"In Camp" (Stafford), **Supp. XI:** 329

"Incant against Suicide" (Karr), **Supp. XI:** 249

"In Celebration of My Uterus" (Sexton), **Supp. II Part 2:** 689

"Incendiary, The" (Rowson), **Supp. XV:** 234

"In Certain Places and Certain Times There Can Be More of You" (Dunn), **Supp. XI:** 144

Incest: From "A Journal of Love," the Unexpurgated Diary of Anaïs Nin, 1932–1934 (Nin), **Supp. X:** 182, 184, 185, 187, 191

"In Chandler Country" (Gioia), **Supp. XV:** 119

Inchbald, Elizabeth, **II:** 8

"In Cheever Country" (Gioia), **Supp. XV:** 119

Inchiquin, the Jesuit's Letters (Ingersoll), **I:** 344

"Incident" (Cullen), **Supp. IV Part 1:** 165, 166

Incidental Numbers (Wylie), **Supp. I Part 2:** 708

Incidentals (Sandburg), **III:** 579

Incidentals in the Day World (Notley), **Supp. XXII:** 223, 226, 227

Incident at Vichy (A. Miller), **III:** 165, 166

Incidents in the Life of a Slave Girl (Brent), **Supp. IV Part 1:** 13

Incidents in the Life of a Slavegirl (Jacobs), **Supp. XVI:** 85

"Incipience" (Rich), **Supp. I Part 2:** 559

"In Clare" (McCarriston), **Supp. XIV:** 270–271

Including Horace (Untermeyer), **Supp. XV:** 301, 303–304

In Cold Blood (Capote), **Supp. XXV:** 57

In Cold Blood: A True Account of a Multiple Murder and Its Consequences (Capote), **Retro. Supp. II:** 107–108; **Supp. I Part 1:** 292; **Supp. III Part 1:** 111, 117, 119, 122, 123, 125–131; **Supp. III Part 2:** 574; **Supp. IV Part 1:** 220; **Supp. XIV:** 162

In Cold Hell, in Thicket (Olson), **Supp. II Part 2:** 571

"In Cold Hell, in Thicket" (Olson), **Supp. II Part 2:** 558, 563–564, 566, 572, 580

"Incoming Tide"(Strout), **Supp. XXIII:** 282, 285

"Incomparable Light, The" (Eberhart), **I:** 541

Incorporative Consciousness of Robert Bly, The (Harris), **Supp. IV Part 1:** 68

In Country (Mason), **Supp. VIII:** 133, **142–143,** 146

"In Country of Conscience" (J. W. Miller), **Supp. XX: 165**

"Incredible Survival of Coyote, The" (Snyder), **Supp. VIII:** 297

"Increment" (Ammons), **Supp. VII:** 28

In Defense of Ignorance (Shapiro), **Supp. II Part 2:** 703, 704, 713–714

In Defense of Reason (Winters), **Supp. I Part 1:** 268

In Defense of Women (Mencken), **III:** 109

Indelible (Hadas), **Supp. XXIII: 119**

Indelible Alison Bechdel, The (Bechdel), **Supp. XXV:** 4

Indemnity Only (Paretsky), **Supp. XXV:** 172–173, 176, 178

Independence Day (film), **Supp. X:** 80

Independence Day (Ford), **Supp. V:** 57, 62–63, 67–68

"Independent Candidate, The, a Story of Today" (Howells), **II:** 277

"Indestructible Mr. Gore, The" (Vidal), **Supp. IV Part 2:** 679

Index of American Design, **Supp. III Part 2:** 618

"India" (Rodriguez), **Supp. XIV:** 302

"Indian at the Burial-Place of His Fathers, An" (Bryant), **Supp. I Part 1:** 155–156, 167–168

"Indian Burying Ground, The" (Freneau), **Supp. II Part 1:** 264, 266

"Indian Camp" (Hemingway), **II:** 247–248, 263; **Retro. Supp. I:** 174–175, 176, 177, 181; **Supp. XVI:** 208

Indian Country (Caputo), **Supp. XIX:** 22–25

Indian Country (Matthiessen), **Supp. V:** 211

"Indian Country" (McCarriston), **Supp. XIV:** 271

"Indian Country" (Simpson), **Supp. IX:** 274

Indian Earth (Bynner), **Supp. XV:** 46

"Indian Gifts to Civilized Man" (Zitkala-Ša), **Supp. XXV:** 281

"Indian Girls" (McCarriston), **Supp. XIV:** 272–273

"Indian Manifesto" (Deloria), **Supp. IV Part 1:** 323

"Indian Names" (Sigourney), **Retro. Supp. II:** 47

"Indian's Awakening, The" (Zitkala-Ša), **Supp. XXV:** 281

"Indian Student, The" (Freneau), **Supp. II Part 1:** 264

"Indian Student, The" (Simpson), **Supp. IX:** 280

Indian Summer (Howells), **II:** 275, 279–281, 282

Indian Summer (Knowles), **Supp. XII:** 249, 250

Indian Summer: Musings on the Gift of Life (Pickering), **Supp. XXI:** 204

"Indian Teacher Among Indians, An" (Zitkala-Ša), **Supp. XXV:** 272

"Indian Uprising, The" (Barthelme), **Supp. IV Part 1:** 44

"Indian Wooing" (C. Miller), **Supp. XXII:** 197–198

Indifferent Children, The (Auchincloss), **Supp. IV Part 1:** 25

Indirections (Cox), **Supp. XXI:** 21

Indiscretions (Pound), **Retro. Supp. I:** 284

"Indispensability of the Eyes, The" (Olds), **Supp. X:** 202

"In Distrust of Merits" (Moore), **III:** 201, 214

"Individual and the State, The" (Emerson), **II:** 10

Individualism, Old and New (Dewey), **Supp. I Part 2:** 677

"Indolence" (Pickering), **Supp. XXI:** 203

In Dreams Begin Responsibilities (Schwartz), **Supp. II Part 2:** 642, 645–650

"In Dreams Begin Responsibilities" (Schwartz), **Supp. II Part 2:** 641, 649, 654

In Dubious Battle (Steinbeck), **IV:** 51, 55–56, 59, 63

"In Durance" (Pound), **Retro. Supp. I:** 285

"Industry of Hard Kissing, The" (Ríos), **Supp. IV Part 2:** 547

"In Duty Bound" (Gilman), **Supp. XI:** 196–197

"I Need, I Need" (Roethke), **III:** 535–536

"I Need Help" (Stern), **Supp. IX:** 290

"Ineffectual Marriage" (Loy), **Supp. XXII:** 165

"Inés in the Kitchen" (García), **Supp. XI:** 190

"I never saw a Moor" (Dickinson), **Retro. Supp. I:** 37

I Never Told Anybody: Teaching Poetry Writing in a Nursing Home (Koch), **Supp. XV:** 190

"I Never Will Be Married, I'd Rather Be Excus'd" (Rowson), **Supp. XV:** 240

Inevitable Exiles (Kielsky), **Supp. V:** 273

"Inevitable Trial, The" (Holmes), **Supp. I Part 1:** 318

"Inexhaustible Hat, The" (Wagoner), **Supp. IX:** 327

"In Extremis" (Berry), **Supp. X:** 23

Inez, Colette, **Supp. XXIII:** 54, 245

"Infancy" (Wilder), **IV:** 375

"Infant Boy at Midcentury" (Warren), **IV:** 244–245, 252

Infante, Guillermo Cabrera, **Retro. Supp. I:** 278

"Infant Sea Turtles" (F. Wright), **Supp. XVII:** 245

Infants of the Spring (Thurman), **Supp. XVIII:** 281; **Supp. XIX:** 73

Inferno (Dante), **IV:** 139; **Supp. V:** 338; **Supp. VIII:** 219–221

Inferno of Dante, The (Pinsky), **Supp. VI:** 235, 248

Infidel (Ali), **Supp. XXIV:** 15

"Infidelity" (Komunyakaa), **Supp. XIII:** 130

Infidels (album, Dylan), **Supp. XVIII:** 28

"Infiltration of the Universe" (MacLeish), **III:** 19

Infinite Jest: A Novel (Wallace), **Supp. X:** 301, **310–314; Supp. XX:** 91

"Infinite Reason, The" (MacLeish), **III:** 19

"Infirmity" (Lowell), **II:** 554

"Infirmity" (Roethke), **III:** 548

In Five Years Time (Haines), **Supp. XII:** 206

"In Flower" (Snodgrass), **Supp. VI:** 325

"Influence of Landscape upon the Poet, The" (Eliot), **Retro. Supp. I:** 67

"In Football Season" (Updike), **IV:** 219

Informer, The (film), **Supp. III Part 2:** 619

Inge, William, **Supp. XXV: 93–108**

Ingersoll, Charles J., **I:** 344

Ingersoll, Robert Green, **Supp. II Part 1:** 198

Ingmundson, Kris, **Supp. XXIV:** 230, 234

Ingraham, Lloyd, **Supp. XVI:** 184

Ingster, Boris, **Retro. Supp. II:** 330

"In Guatemala, All Is Forgotten" (Goldman), **Supp. XXV:** 58

Inhabitants, The (Morris), **III:** 221–222

"Inheritance and Invention in Li-Young Lee's Poetry" (Xiaojing), **Supp. XV:** 214

"Inheritance"(Kenny), **Supp. XXIII:** 154

"Inheritance of Tools, The" (Sanders), **Supp. XVI:** 273

Inheritors (Glaspell), **Supp. III Part 1:** 175, 179–181, 186, 189

"In him we live, & move, & have our being" (Very), **Supp. XXV:** 246

"In Hollywood with the Zuni God of War" (Major), **Supp. XXII:** 180

"In Honor of David Anderson Brooks, My Father" (Brooks), **Supp. III Part 1:** 79

"Inhumanist, The" (Jeffers), **Supp. II Part 2:** 423, 426

"In Illo Tempore" (Karr), **Supp. XI:** 242

"In Interims: Outlyer" (Harrison), **Supp. VIII:** 38

"Initial" (F. Wright), **Supp. XVII:** 243

"Injudicious Gardening" (Moore), **III:** 198

"Injustice" (Paley), **Supp. VI:** 220

Injustice Collectors, The (Auchincloss), **Supp. IV Part 1:** 25

Ink, Blood, Semen (Goldbarth), **Supp. XII:** 181, 183

Ink Dark Moon, The: Love Poems by Ono no Komachi and Izumi Shikibu (Aratani and Hirshfield, trans.), **Supp. XXIII:** 136

Ink Truck, The (W. Kennedy), **Supp. VII:** 132, 133–138, 140, 141, 149, 152

In Life Sentences: Literary Essays (Epstein), **Supp. XIV:** 112

"In Limbo" (Wilbur), **Supp. III Part 2:** 544, 561

In Limestone Country (Sanders), **Supp. XVI:** 272

"In Line" (Major), **Supp. XXII:** 185

In Love and Trouble: Stories of Black Women (Walker), **Supp. III Part 2:** 520, 521, 530, 531, 532

In Mad Love and War (Harjo), **Supp. XII: 224–226**

"In Memoriam" (Emerson), **II:** 13

"In Memoriam" (Hay), **Supp. XIV:** 122, 127

"In Memoriam" (Tennyson), **Retro. Supp. I:** 325; **Supp. I Part 2:** 416

In Memoriam: 1933 (Reznikoff), **Supp. XIV:** 280, 285

In Memoriam to Identity (Acker), **Supp. XII:** 5, **16–18**

"In Memory of Arthur Winslow" (Lowell), **II:** 541, 547, 550; **Retro. Supp. II:** 187

"In Memory of Congresswoman Barbara Jordan" (Pinsky), **Supp. VI:** 250

"In Memory of Joe Brainard" (Bidart), **Supp. XV:** 33

"In Memory of My Feelings" (O'Hara), **Supp. XV:** 215–216

In Memory of My Feelings (O'Hara; Berkson, ed.), **Supp. XXIII:** 220

"In Memory of My Feelings"(O'Hara), **Supp. XXIII:** 208, 215–216

"In Memory of W. B. Yeats" (Auden), **Supp. VIII:** 19, 30; **Supp. XI:** 243, 244; **Supp. XIX:** 85

"In Memory of W. H. Auden" (Stern), **Supp. IX:** 288

"In Memory"(Schott), **Supp. XXIII:** 254

"In Mercy on Broadway" (Doty), **Supp. XI:** 132

In Morocco (Wharton), **Retro. Supp. I:** 380; **Supp. IV Part 1:** 81

Inmost Leaf, The: A Selection of Essays (Kazin), **Supp. VIII:** 102, 103

In Motley (Bierce), **I:** 209

In My Father's Court (Singer), **IV:** 16–17; **Retro. Supp. II: 301–302**

"In My Life" (Dubus), **Supp. VII:** 81

Innaurato, Albert, **Supp. XXIV:** 113, 116, 117

"In Navaho Country" (Bronk), **Supp. XXI:** 30

Inner Circle, The (Boyle), **Supp. XX: 24, 26**

Inner Landscape (Sarton), **Supp. VIII:** 259

Inner Room, The (Merrill), **Supp. III Part 1:** 336

"In Nine Sleep Valley" (Merrill), **Supp. III Part 1:** 328

Innocent Mrs. Duff, The (Holding), **Supp. XXII:** 119, 120, 123, **130–131**, 135, 136

Innocents, The: A Story for Lovers (Lewis), **II:** 441

Innocents Abroad, The; or, The New Pilgrim's Progress (Twain), **II:** 275, 434; **IV:** 191, 196, 197–198

Innocents at Cedro, The: A Memoir of Thorstein Veblen and Some Others (Duffus), **Supp. I Part 2:** 650

"In Off the Cliffs of Moher" (McCarriston), **Supp. XIV:** 270

In Old Plantation Days (Dunbar), **Supp. II Part 1:** 214

In Ole Virginia (Page), **Supp. II Part 1:** 201

In Orbit (Morris), **III:** 236

In Other Words (Swenson), **Supp. IV Part 2:** 650–652

In Other Words: Literature by Latinas of the United States (Fernandez, ed.), **Supp. XXI:** 104

In Our Terribleness (Some elements and meaning in black style) (Baraka), **Supp. II Part 1:** 52, 53

In Our Time (Hemingway), **I:** 117; **II:** 68, 247, 252, 263; **IV:** 42; **Retro. Supp. I:** 170, 173, 174, 178, 180; **Supp. IX:** 106

"In Our Time" (Wolfe), **Supp. III Part 2:** 584

"Inpatient" (Kenyon), **Supp. VII:** 169

In Persuasion Nation (Saunders), **Supp. XIX: 231–234**

"In Persuasion Nation" (Saunders), **Supp. XIX:** 233–234

In Pharaoh's Army: Memories of the Lost War (Wolff), **Supp. VII:** 331–334, 335, 338

"In Plaster" (Plath), **Supp. I Part 2:** 540

"In Prague, in Montmartre" (Bierds), **Supp. XVII:** 27

"In Praise of Johnny Appleseed" (Lindsay), **Supp. I Part 2:** 397

"In Praise of Limestone" (Auden), **Supp. II Part 1:** 20–21; **Supp. VIII:** 23

In Pursuit of a Vanishing Star (Sobin), **Supp. XVI: 294**

In Quest of the Ordinary (Cavell), **Retro. Supp. I:** 307

Inquiry into the Moral and Religious Character of the American Government, An (H. Warner), **Supp. XVIII:** 259

Inquiry into the Nature of Peace, An (Veblen), **Supp. I Part 2:** 642

Inquisitor, The (Rowson), **Supp. XV: 232, 238**

In Radical Pursuit (Snodgrass), **Supp. VI:** 312, 316, 318

In Reckless Ecstasy (Sandburg), **III:** 579

In Recognition of William Gaddis (Kuehl and Moore), **Supp. IV Part 1:** 279

"In Retirement" (Malamud), **Supp. I Part 2:** 437

"In Retrospect" (Angelou), **Supp. IV Part 1:** 15

"In Right" (Wolfert), **Supp. XXI:** 263, 264, 272

"Inroads of Time, The" (D. West), **Supp. XVIII:** 286–287

In Russia (A. Miller), **III:** 165

"In Sabine" (Chopin), **Supp. I Part 1:** 213

"In School-Days" (Whittier), **Supp. I Part 2:** 699–700

"Inscription for the Entrance to a Wood" (Bryant), **Supp. I Part 1:** 154, 155, 161–162

Inscriptions, 1944–1956 (Reznikoff), **Supp. XIV:** 281

In Search of America: The Image of the United States in Travel Writing of the 1980s and 1990s (Rutkowska), **Supp. XXII:** 208

"In Search of a Motif for Expressive Female Figuration" (Major), **Supp. XXII:** 184

In Search of Bisco (Caldwell), **I:** 296

In Search of Lost Time (Proust), **Supp. XXV:** 71

In Search of Nella Larsen: A Biography of the Color Line (Hutchinson), **Supp. XVIII:** 120

"In Search of Our Mothers' Gardens" (Walker), **Supp. III Part 2:** 520–532, 524, 525, 527, 529, 532–533, 535, 536; **Supp. IX:** 306; **Supp. XVIII:** 200, 283

"In Search of Thomas Merton" (Griffin), **Supp. VIII:** 208

"In Search of Yage" (Burroughs), **Supp. III Part 1:** 98

"Insect Life in Florida" (Hull), **Supp. XXI:** 133

Insel (Loy), **Supp. XXII:** 167

"Insertion of Self into a Space of Borderless Possibilities, The" (Fjellestad), **Supp. XVI:** 150

"In Shadow" (Crane), **I:** 386

"In Sickness and in Health" (Auden), **Supp. II Part 1:** 15

"In Sickness and in Health" (Humphrey), **Supp. IX:** 94

Inside, Outside (Wouk), **Supp. XXV:** 254, 255, 257, 265

Inside Diameter: The France Poems (Major), **Supp. XXII:** 182

Inside His Mind (A. Miller), **III:** 154

Inside Memory (Findley), **Supp. XX: 51, 63**

"Inside Norman Mailer" (Apple), **Supp. XVII:** 3, 4

"Insider Baseball" (Didion), **Supp. IV Part 1:** 211

Inside Sports magazine, **Supp. V:** 58, 61

"Insipid Profession of Jonathan Horneboom, The" (Lethem), **Supp. XVIII:** 149

"In So Many Dark Rooms" (Hogan), **Supp. IV Part 1:** 400

"Insomnia" (Bishop), **Supp. I Part 1:** 92

"Insomniac" (Plath), **Supp. I Part 2:** 539

"In Spain, Throwing Carnations" (P. N. Warren), **Supp. XX:** 272

"Inspiration for Greatness" (Caldwell), **I:** 291

"Instability of Race Types, The" (Boas), **Supp. XIV:** 209

"Installation #6" (Beattie), **Supp. V:** 33

"Instead of Dying" (Gallagher), **Supp. XXIV:** 171

"Insterstices" (Berrigan), **Supp. XXIV:** 36

Instinct of Workmanship and the State of the Industrial Arts, The (Veblen), **Supp. I Part 2:** 642

Instincts of the Herd in Peace and War, The (Trotter), **I:** 249

Institute (Calvin), **IV:** 158, 160

"Instruction Manual, The" (Ashbery), **Supp. III Part 1:** 6–7, 10, 12

Instructions, The (Levin), **Supp. XXII:** 268

"Instructions for the Afternoon" (Gioia), **Supp. XV:** 120

Instructions to the Double (Gallagher), **Supp. XXIV:** 165, 167, 168, 169, 174

"Instructions to the Double" (Gallagher), **Supp. XXIV:** 168

"Instruction to Myself" (Brooks), **Supp. III Part 1:** 87

Instrument, The (O'Hara), **III:** 362, 364

"In Such Times, Ties Must Bind" (Nye), **Supp. XIII:** 286

In Sunlight and in Shadow (Helprin), **Supp. XXV:** 81, 88

"Insurance and Social Change" (Stevens), **Retro. Supp. I:** 297

Insurgent Mexico (Reed), **I:** 476

In Suspect Terrain (McPhee), **Supp. III Part 1:** 309, 310

"In Tall Grass" (Sandburg), **III:** 585

"Integer Vitae" (Horace), **Supp. XV:** 304

Intellectual History, An (Senghor), **Supp. X:** 139

"Intellectual Pre-Eminence of Jews in Modern Europe, The" (Veblen), **Supp. I Part 2:** 643–644

Intellectual Things (Kunitz), **Supp. III Part 1:** 260, 262–264

Intellectual versus the City, The (White), **I:** 258

"In Temporary Pain" (Bynner), **Supp. XV:** 41–42

Intentions (Wilde), **Retro. Supp. I:** 56

"Interest in Life, An" (Paley), **Supp. VI:** 222, 224–225

Interest of Great Britain Considered, with Regard to Her Colonies and the Acquisition of Canada and Guadeloupe, The (Franklin), **II:** 119

Interior Landscapes (Vizenor), **Supp. IV Part 1:** 262

Interiors (film; Allen), **Supp. IV Part 1:** 205; **Supp. XV:** 1, **7,** 10

Interlocking Lives (Koch), **Supp. XV:** 185

"Interlude" (A. Lowell), **Retro. Supp. II:** 46

Interlunar (Atwood), **Supp. XIII:** 35

"Intermezzo" (Schnackenberg), **Supp. XV:** 254

"In Terms of the Toenail: Fiction and the Figures of Life" (Gass), **Supp. VI:** 85

"International Episode, An" (James), **II:** 327

International Workers Order, **Retro. Supp. I:** 202

Interpretation of Christian Ethics, An (Niebuhr), **III:** 298–300, 301, 302

"Interpretation of Dreams, The" (Matthews), **Supp. IX:** 162–163

Interpretation of Music of the XVIIth and XVIIIth Centuries, The (Dolmetsch), **III:** 464

Interpretations and Forecasts: 1922–1972 (Mumford), **Supp. II Part 2:** 481

Interpretations of Poetry and Religion (Santayana), **III:** 611

Interpreter of Maladies (Lahiri), **Supp. XXI:** 175–176, **177–180,** 183

"Interpreter of Maladies" (Lahiri), **Supp. XXI:** 183, 184

Interpreters and Interpretations (Van Vechten), **Supp. II Part 2:** 729, 733–734

"Interrogate the Stones" (MacLeish), **III:** 9

Interrogations at Noon (Gioia), **Supp. XV:** 112, **125–127,** 128, 129

"Interrupted Conversation, An" (Van Vechten), **Supp. II Part 2:** 735

"Interrupted Elegy" (Peacock), **Supp. XIX:** 200

Intersect: Poems (Shields), **Supp. VII:** 310–311

Intersexes, The (Prime-Stevenson as Mayne), **Supp. XX:** 235

Interstate (Dixon), **Supp. XII:** 140, 152–153, 153, 156

"Interview" (Hay), **Supp. XIV:** 132

"Interview, The" (Thurber), **Supp. I Part 2:** 616

"Interview With a Lemming" (Thurber), **Supp. I Part 2:** 603

"Interview with Larry Rivers, An" (O'Hara), **Supp. XXIII:** 214

"Interview with Peter Everwine, An" (Veinberg and Buckley), **Supp. XV:** 76–77

"Interview with the Crab" (Lethem), **Supp. XVIII:** 148

Interview with the Vampire (Rice), **Supp. VII:** 287, 288–291, 297–298, 303

"Interview with the Vampire" (Rice), **Supp. VII:** 288

Interzone (Burroughs), **Supp. IV Part 1:** 90

"In the Absence of Bliss" (Kumin), **Supp. IV Part 2:** 453

"In the Afternoon" (Dunn), **Supp. XI:** 146

"In the Alley" (Elkin), **Supp. VI:** **46–47**

In the American Grain (W. C. Williams), **Retro. Supp. I:** 420–421

In the American Jungle (W. Frank), **Supp. XX:** 76

In the American Tree (Silliman), **Supp. IV Part 2:** 426

In the Bank of Beautiful Sins (Wrigley), **Supp. XVIII:** 300–302

In the Bar of a Tokyo Hotel (T. Williams), **IV:** 382, 386, 387, 391, 393

In the Beauty of the Lilies (Updike), **Retro. Supp. I:** 322, 325, 326, 327, 333

"In the Beeyard" (Bierds), **Supp. XVII:** 29

"In the Beginning" (Quindlen), **Supp. XVII:** 166

"In the Beginning . . ." (Simic), **Supp. VIII:** 270, 271

In the Belly of the Beast: Letters from Prison (Abbott), **Retro. Supp. II:** 210

"In the Black Morning" (Wolfert), **Supp. XXI:** 265

"In the Black Museum" (Nemerov), **III:** 275

"In the Blink of God's Eye" (E. P. Jones), **Supp. XXII:** 150

"In the Bodies of Words" (Swenson), **Supp. IV Part 2:** 651

"In the Box" (Kenny), **Supp. XXIII:** 155

"In the Cage" (Gass), **Supp. VI:** 85

In the Cage (James), **Retro. Supp. I:** 229

"In the Cage" (James), **II:** 332; **Retro. Supp. I:** 231

"In the Cage" (Lowell), **Retro. Supp. II:** 187

"In the Cave at Lone Tree Meadow" (Haines), **Supp. XII:** 212

"In the Cemetery Where Al Jolson Is Buried" (Hempel), **Supp. XXI:** 115, **121–122**

"In the City Ringed with Giants" (Kingsolver), **Supp. VII:** 209

"In the Clearing" (Brodsky), **Supp. VIII:** 32

In the Clearing (Frost), **II:** 153, 155, 164; **Retro. Supp. I:** 121, 122, 141

"In the Closet of the Soul" (Walker), **Supp. III Part 2:** 526

"In the Cold Air Register" (W. V. Davis), **Supp. XXI:** 94

"In the Confidence of a Story-Writer" (Chopin), **Retro. Supp. II:** 66–67; **Supp. I Part 1:** 217

In the Country of Last Things (Auster), **Supp. XII:** 23, **29–30,** 31, 32

"In the Courtyard of the Isleta Missions" (R. Bly), **Supp. IV Part 1:** 71

"In the Dark" (Levine), **Supp. V:** 194

"In the Dark New England Days" (Jewett), **Retro. Supp. II:** 139

"In the Days of Prismatic Colour" (Moore), **III:** 205, 213

In the Days of the Comet (Wells), **Supp. XX:** 233, **240**

In the Electric Mist with Confederate Dead (Burke), **Supp. XIV:** 30, 31–32

"In the Field" (Wilbur), **Supp. III Part 2:** 558

"In the 51st State" (Berrigan), **Supp. XXIV:** 35

"In the First Stanza" (C. Kizer), **Supp. XVII:** 75

"In the Fleeting Hand of Time" (Corso), **Supp. XII:** 122–123

"In the Footsteps of Gutenberg" (Mencken), **III:** 101

"In the Forest" (Simpson), **Supp. IX:** 270

"In the Forest of the Laughing Elephant" (Caputo), **Supp. XIX:** 27

"In the Forties" (Lowell), **II:** 554

"In the Garden" (Ferry), **Supp. XXIV:** 153

In the Garden of the North American Martyrs (Wolff), **Supp. VII:** 341–342

In the Garret (Van Vechten), **Supp. II Part 2:** 735

"In the Grove: The Poet at Ten" (Kenyon), **Supp. VII:** 160

In the Hall of Mirrors (Merrill), **Supp. III Part 1:** 322

In the Harbor (Longfellow), **II:** 491

In the Heart of the Heart of the Country (Gass), **Supp. VI:** 82–83, 84, 85, 93

In the Heat of the Night (Ball), **Supp. XV:** 202

In the Heat of the Night (film), **Supp. I Part 1:** 67

In the Hollow of His Hand (Purdy), **Supp. VII:** 278–280

In the House of Light (Everwine, trans.), **Supp. XV:** 73, 75, **76–78,** 82

"In the Laboratory of Kisses" (Gallagher), **Supp. XXIV:** 170

In the Lake of the Woods (O'Brien), **Supp. V:** 240, 243, 250–252

In the Land of the White Death: A Epic Story of Survival in the Siberian Arctic (Albanov), **Supp. XVIII:** 114

"In the Last Days" (Everwine), **Supp. XV:** 88, 89

"In the Late Summer Garden"(Crooker), **Supp. XXIII:** 55

In the Loyal Mountains (Bass), **Supp. XVI:** **19–20**

"In the Loyal Mountains" (Bass), **Supp. XVI:** 20

In the Mecca (Brooks), **Supp. III Part 1:** 74

"In the Mecca" (Brooks), **Supp. III Part 1:** 70, 83–84

In the Midst of Life (Bierce), **I:** 200–203, 204, 206, 208, 212

"In the Miro District" (Taylor), **Supp. V:** 323

In the Miro District and Other Stories (Taylor), **Supp. V:** 325–326

In the Money (W. C. Williams), **Retro. Supp. I:** 423

"In the Motel" (X. J. Kennedy), **Supp. XV:** 163

"In the Naked Bed, in Plato's Cave" (Schwartz), **Supp. II Part 2:** 646–649

In the Name of the Neither (Sobin), **Supp. XVI:** 291

"In the Night" (Kincaid), **Supp. VII:** 183

In the Night Season: A Novel (Bausch), **Supp. VII:** 52–53

"In the Old Neighborhood" (Dove), **Supp. IV Part 1:** 241, 257

"In the Old World" (Oates), **Supp. II Part 2:** 503, 504

"In the Park" (Huncke), **Supp. XIV:** 139

In the Pines (Notley), **Supp. XXII:** 236–237

"In the Pit" (Proulx), **Supp. VII:** 255, 261

In the Pond (Jin), **Supp. XVIII:** **95–96**

In the Presence of the Sun (Momaday), **Supp. IV Part 2:** 489, 490, 491–493, 493

"In the Quiet Night" (Li Po), **Supp. XV:** 47

"In the Realm of the Fisher King" (Didion), **Supp. IV Part 1:** 211

"In the Red Room" (Bowles), **Supp. IV Part 1:** 93

"In the Region of Ice" (Oates), **Supp. II Part 2:** 520

In the Room We Share (Simpson), **Supp. IX:** 279

"In These Dissenting Times" (Walker), **Supp. III Part 2:** 522

"In the Shadow of Gabriel, A.D.1550" (Frederic), **II:** 139

In the Shadow of Memory (Skloot), **Supp. XX:** 193, 196, 205, 205–206

"In the Shadow of Memory" (Skloot), **Supp. XX:** 206

In the Shadow of the Morning: Essays on Wild Lands, Wild Waters, and a Few Untamed People (Caputo), **Supp. XIX:** 28–29

In the Spirit of Crazy Horse (Matthiessen), **Supp. V:** 211

"In the Subway" (Untermeyer), **Supp. XV:** 296

In the Summer House (Jane Bowles), **Supp. IV Part 1:** 83, 89

In the Tennessee Country (Taylor), **Supp. V:** 328

"In the Thick of Darkness" (Salinas), **Supp. XIII:** 325

In the Time of Butterflies (Alvarez), **Supp. XXIV:** 89

"In the Time of the Blossoms" (Mervin), **Supp. III Part 1:** 352

In the Time of the Butterflies (Alvarez), **Supp. VII:** 1, 12–15, 18

In the Time of the Present (Kenny), **Supp. XXIII:** 146, **156**

"In the Tube" (Jarman), **Supp. XVII:** 121

"In the Tunnel Bone of Cambridge" (Corso), **Supp. XII:** 120–121

"In the Upper Pastures" (Kumin), **Supp. IV Part 2:** 453

In the Valley (Frederic), **II:** 133–134, 136, 137

"In the Village" (Bishop), **Retro. Supp. II:** 38; **Supp. I Part 1:** 73, 74–75, 76, 77, 78, 88

"In the Waiting Room" (Bishop), **Retro. Supp. II:** 50; **Supp. I Part 1:** 81, 94, 95; **Supp. IV Part 1:** 249

In the Walled City (O'Nan), **Supp. XXV:** 142

"In the Ward: The Sacred Wood" (Jarrell), **II:** 376, 377

In the Western Night: Collected Poems 1965–90 (Bidart), **Supp. XV:** 19, **30–32**

"In the White Night" (Beattie), **Supp. V:** 30–31

"In the Wind My Rescue Is" (Ammons), **Supp. VII:** 25

"In the Winter Dark" (Peacock), **Supp. XIX:** 206

In the Winter of Cities (T. Williams), **IV:** 383

"In the X-Ray of the Sarcophagus of Ta-pero" (Goldbarth), **Supp. XII:** 191

"In the Yard" (Swenson), **Supp. IV Part 2:** 647

In the Zone (O'Neill), **III:** 388

In This, Our Life (film), **Supp. I Part 1:** 67

"In This Country, but in Another Language, My Aunt Refuses to Marry the Men Everyone Wants Her To" (Paley), **Supp. VI:** 225

"In This Dream" (J. W. Miller), **Supp. XX:** **170**

In This Hung-up Age (Corso), **Supp. XII:** **119–120,** 129

In This Our Life (Glasgow), **II:** 175, 178, 189

In This Our World (Gilman), **Supp. XI:** 196, 200, 202

"In Those Days" (Jarrell), **II:** 387–388

"Intimately Connected to the Zeitgeist" (Franzen), **Supp. XX:** **94**

"In Time of War" (Auden), **Supp. II Part 1:** 8, 13

In Times Like These (Edgell), **Supp. XXIII:** 84, **89–90,** 94

"Into Egypt" (Benét), **Supp. XI:** 56, 57–58

Intolerance (film; Griffith), **Supp. XVI:** 184

"Into My Own" (Frost), **II:** 153; **Retro. Supp. I:** 127

"Into Night" (McKnight), **Supp. XX:** **151–152**

Into the Interior (Cliff), **Supp. XXII:** 67, 78–79

"Into the Night Life . . ." (H. Miller), **III:** 180, 184

"Into the Nowhere" (Rawlings), **Supp. X:** 220

Into the Stone (Dickey), **Supp. IV Part 1:** 178

"Into the Stone" (Dickey), **Supp. IV Part 1:** 179

Into the Stone and Other Poems (Dickey), **Supp. IV Part 1:** 176

Into the Wild (Krakauer), **Supp. XVIII:** 106, **107–108,** 116, 117

Into Thin Air: A Personal Account of the Mount Everest Disaster (Krakauer), **Supp. XVII:** 210; **Supp. XVIII:** 105, **109–113,** 117

In Touch: The Letters of Paul Bowles (J. Miller, ed.), **Supp. IV Part 1:** 95

"Intoxicated, The" (Jackson), **Supp. IX:** 116

"Intrigue" (Crane), **I:** 419

Introducing Irony: A Book of Poetic Short Stories and Poems (Bodenheim),

Supp. XXV: 22–23

"Introducing the Fathers" (Kumin), **Supp. IV Part 2:** 452

Introductio ad Prudentiam (Fuller), **II:** 111

"Introduction"(Strout; *Ploughshares* spring 2010), **Supp. XXIII:** 284

"Introduction to a Haggadah" (Paley), **Supp. VI:** 219

Introduction to Objectivist Epistemology (Rand), **Supp. IV Part 2:** 527, 528–529

Introduction to Objectivist Epistemology 2nd ed. (Rand), **Supp. IV Part 2:** 529

"Introduction to Poetry" (Collins), **Supp. XXI:** 57

Introduction to Poetry, An (Gioia and X. J. Kennedy), **Supp. XV:** 113, 153

"Introduction to Some Poems, An" (Stafford), **Supp. XI:** 311, 324

Introduction to the Geography of Iowa, The (Doty), **Supp. XI:** 120

"Introduction to the Hoh" (Hugo), **Supp. VI:** 136–137

"Introduction to *The New Writing in the USA*" (Creeley), **Supp. IV Part 1:** 153–154

"Introduction to William Blake, An" (Kazin), **Supp. VIII:** 103

Introitus (Longfellow), **II:** 505, 506–507

"Intruder, The" (Dubus), **Supp. VII:** 76–78, 91

Intruder, The (Maeterlinck), **I:** 91

Intruder in the Dust (Faulkner), **II:** 71, 72; **Supp. XVI:** 148

"Invaders, The" (Haines), **Supp. XII:** 205

Invaders, The (W. Frank), **Supp. XX:** 79–80

Invasion of Privacy: The Cross Creek Trial of Marjorie Kinnan Rawlings (Acton), **Supp. X:** 233

Inventing Memory: A Novel of Mothers and Daughters (Jong), **Supp. V:** 115, 129

Inventing the Abbotts (Miller), **Supp. XII:** 294–295

"Invention of Autobiography. The" (Hampl), **Supp. XXII:** 93–94

"Invention of God in a Mouthful of Milk, The" (Karr), **Supp. XI:** 250

Invention of Solitude, The (Auster), **Supp. XII:** 21–22

Inventions of the March Hare (Eliot), **Retro. Supp. I:** 55–56, 58

"Inventions of the March Hare" (Eliot), **Retro. Supp. I:** 55

"Inventory" (Parker), **Supp. IX:** 192

"Inverted Forest, The" (Salinger), **III:** 552, 572

"Investigation" (Ryan as Quin), **Supp. XVIII:** 227–228

"Investigations of a Dog" (Kafka), **IV:** 438

"Investiture, The" (Banks), **Supp. V:** 7

"Investiture at Cecconi's" (Merrill), **Supp. III Part 1:** 336

"Invicibility"(O'Hara), **Supp. XXIII:** 214

"Invisible" (Pickering), **Supp. XXI:** 201

Invisible Circus, The (Egan), **Supp. XIX:** 49, 50–52

Invisible Company, The (Sanders), **Supp. XVI:** 270–271

Invisible Man (Ellison), **IV:** 493; **Retro. Supp. II:** 3, 12, 111, 112, 113, 117, 119, **120–123,** 125; **Supp. II Part 1:** 40, 170, 221, 224, 226, 227, 230, 231–232, 235, 236, 241–245; **Supp. IX:** 306; **Supp. X:** 242; **Supp. XI:** 18, 92; **Supp. XVIII:** 59; **Supp. XIX:** 154, 155

Invisible: Poems (Nye), **Supp. XIII:** 277

Invisible Spectator, An (Sawyer-Lauçanno), **Supp. IV Part 1:** 95

Invisible Swords (Farrell), **II:** 27, 46, 48–49

Invisible Worm, The (Millar), **Supp. IV Part 2:** 465

Invitation to a Beheading (Nabokov), **III:** 252–253, 254, 257–258; **Retro. Supp. I:** 265, 270, 273

"Invitation to the Country, An" (Bryant), **Supp. I Part 1:** 160

"Invocation" (McKay), **Supp. X:** 134

"Invocation" (Untermeyer), **Supp. XV:** 296

"Invocation to Kali" (Sarton), **Supp. VIII:** 260

"Invocation: *To my Maternal Grandfather on hearing his descent from Chippewa ancestors misrepresented*"(J. Schoolcraft), **Supp. XXIII:** 232

"Invocation to the Social Muse" (MacLeish), **III:** 15

"In Weather" (Hass), **Supp. VI: 102–103**

"In Your Fugitive Dream" (Hugo), **Supp. VI:** 143

"In Your Good Dream" (Hugo), **Supp. VI:** 143–144

"Iola, Kansas" (Clampitt), **Supp. IX:** 45–46

Iola Leroy (Harper), **Supp. XVIII:** 284

Ion (Doolittle, trans.), **Supp. I Part 1:** 269, 274

Ion (Plato), **I:** 523

"Ione" (Dunbar), **Supp. II Part 1:** 199

Ionesco, Eugène, **I:** 71, 74, 75, 84, 295; **II:** 435; **Supp. VIII:** 201; **Supp. XIX:** 131; **Supp. XXIV:** 113

Ionica (Cory), **Supp. XX: 230**

Ionica II (Cory), **Supp. XX: 230**

"I Only Am Escaped Alone to Tell Thee" (Nemerov), **III:** 272, 273–274

"I Opened All the Portals Wide" (Chopin), **Retro. Supp. II:** 71

I Ought to Be in Pictures (Simon), **Supp. IV Part 2:** 584

Iphigenia (Notley), **Supp. XXII:** 226, 235

Iphigenia in Tauris (Euripedes), **Supp. XV:** 42, 50

I Promessi Sposi (Manzoni), **II:** 291

"I Put My Hand on My Son's Head" (Kooser), **Supp. XIX:** 120

Iram, Dhát al-'Imád (Gibran), **Supp. XX: 116**

"Iraq Drifting, July 2003" (Weigl), **Supp. XIX:** 288

"Irascibles, The" (Kees), **Supp. XV:** 145–146

Ireland: A Terrible Beauty (Uris), **Supp. XX: 244, 245–246, 246, 254**

"I Remember" (Sexton), **Supp. II Part 2:** 680

"Irenicon" (Shapiro), **Supp. II Part 2:** 704

Irigaray, Luce, **Supp. XII:** 6

Iris (Jarman), **Supp. XVII:** 110, **116–117**

"Iris by Night" (Frost), **Retro. Supp. I:** 132

"Irises" (L.-Y. Lee), **Supp. XV:** 214–215

Irish in America, The (Coffey, ed.), **Supp. XIX:** 133

Irish Stories of Sarah Orne Jewett, The (Jewett), **Retro. Supp. II:** 142

Irish Triangle, An (Barnes), **Supp. III Part 1:** 34

"Iron Characters, The" (Nemerov), **III:** 279, 282

"Iron Hans" (Sexton), **Supp. II Part 2:** 691

Iron Heel, The (London), **II:** 466, 480

Iron John: A Book about Men (R. Bly), **Supp. IV Part 1:** 59, 67; **Supp. XVI:** 177

"Iron Table, The" (Jane Bowles), **Supp. IV Part 1:** 82–83

"Iron Throat, The" (Olsen), **Supp. XIII:** 292, 297, 299

Ironweed (W. Kennedy), **Supp. VII:** 132, 133, 134, 135, 142, 144, 145–147, 148, 150, 153

"Irony as Art: The Short Fiction of William Humphrey" (Tebeaux), **Supp. IX:** 109

"Irony Is Not Enough: Essay on My Life as Catherine Deneuve" (Carson), **Supp. XII: 112–113**

Irony of American History, The (Niebuhr), **III:** 292, 306–307, 308

"Irrational Element in Poetry, The" (Stevens), **Retro. Supp. I:** 298, 301

"Irrevocable Diameter, An" (Paley), **Supp. VI:** 231–232

Irvine, Lorna, **Supp. XIII:** 26

Irving, Ebenezer, **II:** 296

Irving, Sir Henry, **IV:** 350

Irving, John, **Supp. VI: 163–183; Supp. X:** 77, 85

Irving, John Treat, **II:** 296

Irving, Peter, **II:** 296, 297, 298, 299, 300, 303

Irving, Washington, **I:** 211, 335, 336, 339, 343; **II: 295–318,** 488, 495; **III:** 113; **IV:** 309; **Retro. Supp. I:** 246; **Supp. I Part 1:** 155, 157, 158, 317; **Supp. I Part 2:** 377, 487, 585; **Supp. II Part 1:** 335; **Supp. IV Part 1:** 380; **Supp. XVIII:** 12; **Supp. XXIII:** 178

Irving, William, **II:** 296

Irving, William, Jr., **II:** 296, 297, 298, 299, 303

Irwin, Mark, **Supp. XII:** 21, 22, 24, 29

Irwin, Robert, **Supp. XX: 120**

Irwin, William Henry, **Supp. II Part 1:** 192

Is 5 (Cummings), **I:** 429, 430, 434, 435, 440, 445, 446, 447

"Isaac and Abraham" (Brodsky), **Supp. VIII:** 21

"Isaac and Archibald" (Robinson), **III:** 511, 521, 523

Isaacs, Neil D., **Supp. XIX:** 255

"Isabelle" (Saunders), **Supp. XIX:** 225

"Isabel Sparrow" (Oliver), **Supp. VII:** 232

Isaiah (biblical book), **Supp. I Part 1:** 236; **Supp. I Part 2:** 516; **Supp. XXI:** 107

"Isaiah Beethoven" (Masters), **Supp. I Part 2:** 461

I Sailed with Magellan (Dybek), **Supp. XXIII:** 75–78, 79

"I Saw in Louisiana a Live-Oak Growing" (Whitman), **I:** 220

"I Shall Be Released" (Dylan), **Supp. XV:** 349

I Shall Spit on Your Graves (film), **Supp. I Part 1:** 67

Isháq, Adib, **Supp. XX: 117**

Isherwood, Christopher, **II:** 586; **Supp. II Part 1:** 10, 11, 13; **Supp. IV Part 1:** 79, 82, 102; **Supp. XI:** 305; **Supp. XIV:** 155–175; **Supp. XVI:** 194

Isherwood Century, The (Berg and Freeman), **Supp. XIV:** 157, 159

Isherwood's Fiction (Schwerdt), **Supp. XIV:** 155

Ishiguro, Kazuo, **Supp. VIII:** 15

Ishi Means Man (Merton), **Supp. VIII:** 208

"Ishmael's Dream" (Stern), **Supp. IX:** 287

I Should Have Stayed Home (McCoy), **Supp. XIII:** 167, **168–170,** 171

"I Should Worry" (Kees), **Supp. XV:** 140

"I Sigh in the Afternoon" (Salinas), **Supp. XIII:** 318

"I Sing the Body Electric" (Whitman), **Retro. Supp. I:** 394, 395

"Isis: Dorothy Eady, 1924" (Doty), **Supp. XI:** 122

"Is It O.K. to Be a Luddite?" (Pynchon), **Supp. XVI:** 128

"Is It True?" (Hughes), **Supp. I Part 1:** 342

I: Six Nonlectures (Cummings), **I:** 430, 433, 434

"Island" (Hughes), **Supp. I Part 1:** 340

Island Garden, An (Thaxter), **Retro. Supp. II:** 136; **Supp. XIII:** 152

Island Holiday, An (Henry), **I:** 515

Island in the Atlantic (W. Frank), **Supp. XX: 79**

"Island of the Fay, The" (Poe), **III:** 412, 417

Islands (Siddons), **Supp. XXII:** 239

"Islands, The" (Hayden), **Supp. II Part 1:** 373

"Island Sheaf, An" (Doty), **Supp. XI:** 136

Islands in the Stream (Hemingway), **II:** 258; **Retro. Supp. I:** 186

Isn't It Romantic (Wasserstein), **Supp. XV: 323–325,** 327

Is Objectivism a Religion? (Ellis), **Supp. IV Part 2:** 527

"Isolation of Modern Poetry, The" (Schwartz), **Supp. II Part 2:** 644

"Israel" (Reznikoff), **Supp. XIV:** 283

Israel Potter, or Fifty Years of Exile (Melville), **III:** 90; **Supp. XVIII:** 4

"Israfel" (Poe), **III:** 411

Is Sex Necessary? (Thurber and White), **Supp. I Part 2:** 607, 612, 614, 653

"Issues, The" (Olds), **Supp. X:** 205

"Istanbul" (Collins), **Supp. XXI:** 60

"I Stand Here Ironing" (Olsen), **Supp. XIII:** 292, 294, 296, 298, 300, 305

I Stole a Million (West), **IV:** 287

"Is Verse a Dying Technique?" (Wilson), **IV:** 431

It (Creeley), **Supp. IV Part 1:** 157, 158

IT (King), **Supp. V:** 139, 140, 141, 146–147, 151, 152

"It" (Olds), **Supp. X:** 208

Italian American Reconciliation: A Folktale (Shanley), **Supp. XIV:** 315, **324–326,** 328, 330

Italian Backgrounds (Wharton), **Retro. Supp. I:** 370

Italian Hours (James), **I:** 12; **II:** 337; **Retro. Supp. I:** 235

Italian Journeys (Howells), **II:** 274

"Italian Morning" (Bogan), **Supp. III Part 1:** 58

Italian Villas and Their Gardens (Wharton), **IV:** 308; **Retro. Supp. I:** 361, 367

Italie, Hillel, **Supp. XV:** 128

It All Adds Up: From the Dim Past to the Uncertain Future (Bellow), **Retro. Supp. II:** 32

"It Always Breaks Out" (Ellison), **Retro. Supp. II:** 126; **Supp. II Part 1:** 248

Itard, Jean-Marc Gaspard, **Supp. I Part 2:** 564

"I taste a liquor never brewed" (Dickinson), **Retro. Supp. I:** 30, 37

It Came from Outer Space (film), **Supp. IV Part 1:** 102

It Can't Happen Here (Lewis), **II:** 454

It Chooses You (July), **Supp. XXIV:** 199, 209, 210

"It Don't Mean a Thing If It Ain't Got That Swing" (Matthews), **Supp. IX: 164–165**

I Tell You Now (Ortiz), **Supp. IV Part 2:** 500

"Ithaca" (Glück), **Supp. V:** 89

It Happened One Night (Capra), **Supp. XV:** 197

It Has Come to Pass (Farrell), **II:** 26

"I think to live May be a Bliss" (Dickinson), **Retro. Supp. I:** 44

"I Thought It Was Harry" (Bronk), **Supp. XXI:** 31

I Thought of Daisy (Wilson), **IV:** 428, 434, 435

"Itinerary of an Obsession" (Kumin), **Supp. IV Part 2:** 450

"It Is a Strange Country" (Ellison), **Supp. II Part 1:** 238

"It Is Dangerous to Read Newspapers" (Atwood), **Supp. XIII:** 33

"It Must Be Abstract" (Stevens), **IV:** 95; **Retro. Supp. I:** 307

"It Must Change" (Stevens), **Retro. Supp. I:** 300, 307, 308

"It Must Give Pleasure" (Stevens), **Retro. Supp. I:** 307, 308, 309

"'It Out-Herods Herod. Pray You, Avoid It'" (Hecht), **Supp. X:** 62, 64

"It's All Over Now, Baby Blue" (song, Dylan), **Supp. XVIII:** 30

It's Loaded, Mr. Bauer (Marquand), **III:** 59

It's Nation Time (Baraka), **Supp. II Part 1:** 52, 53

"It's Nation Time" (Baraka), **Supp. II Part 1:** 53

It's Only a Play (McNally), **Supp. XIII:** 198

It Was (Zukofsky), **Supp. III Part 2:** 630

"It Was Romance" (July), **Supp. XXIV:** 202–203

It Was the Nightingale (Ford), **III:** 470–471

"It Was When" (Snyder), **Supp. VIII:** 300

Ivanhoe (Scott), **I:** 216; **Supp. I Part 2:** 410

Ivens, Bryna, **Supp. XV:** 311, 312

Ivens, Joris, **I:** 488; **Retro. Supp. I:** 184

"Iverson Boy, The" (Simpson), **Supp. IX:** 280

"Ives" (Rukeyser), **Supp. VI:** 273, 283

Ives, George H., **Supp. I Part 1:** 153

Ivory Grin, The (Macdonald), **Supp. IV Part 2:** 471, 472

"Ivory Novel, The" (Halliday), **Supp. XIX:** 90

Ivory Tower, The (James), **II:** 337–338

"Ivory Tower, The: Louis Untermeyer as Critic" (Aiken), **Supp. XV:** 298

Ivry, Sara, **Supp. XX: 179**

"Ivy Winding" (Ammons), **Supp. VII:** 33

Iwamatsu, Mako, **Supp. XXI:** 150

"I Wandered Lonely as a Cloud" (Wordsworth), **Retro. Supp. I:** 121–122; **Supp. X:** 73; **Supp. XIV:** 184

"I want, I want" (Plath), **Retro. Supp. II:** 246

"I Wanted to Be There When My Father Died" (Olds), **Supp. X:** 210

"I Want to Be a Father Like the Men" (Cisneros), **Supp. VII:** 71

"I Want to Be Miss America" (Alvarez), **Supp. VII:** 18

"I Want to Know Why" (Anderson), **I:** 114, 115, 116; **II:** 263

"I Want You Women Up North To Know" (Olsen), **Supp. XIII:** 292, 297

"I Was Born in Lucerne" (Levine), **Supp. V:** 181, 189

"I Was Marching" (Le Sueur), **Supp. XXIII:** 167

"I Was Really Very Hungry" (M. F. K. Fisher), **Supp. XVII:** 91

"I Went into the Maverick Bar" (Snyder), **Supp. VIII:** 301

"I Will Lie Down" (Swenson), **Supp. IV Part 2:** 640

I Will Say Beauty (C. Frost), **Supp. XV:** 96, **105–107**

I Wonder As I Wander (Hughes), **Retro. Supp. I:** 196, 203; **Supp. I Part 1:** 329, 332–333

I Would Have Saved Them If I Could (L. Michaels), **Supp. XVI:** 203, 205, **206–210**

"Iya, the Camp-Eater" (Zitkala-Ša), **Supp. XXV:** 276

"Iyani: It goes this Way" (Gunn Allen), **Supp. IV Part 1:** 321

"I years had been from home" (Dickinson), **I:** 471

Iyer, Pico, **Supp. V:** 215

Izzo, David Garrett, **Supp. XIV:** 155, 156, 159, 160, 161, 163, 169, 171

J

Jab (Halliday), **Supp. XIX: 91–94**

"Jachid and Jechidah" (Singer), **IV:** 15

Jack and Jill (Alcott), **Supp. I Part 1:** 42

"Jack and the Beanstalk" (Hay), **Supp. XIV:** 124

"Jack in the Pot" (D. West), **Supp. XVIII:** 283

Jack Kelso (Masters), **Supp. I Part 2:** 456, 471–472

Jacklight (Erdrich), **Supp. IV Part 1:** 259, 270

Jack London, Hemingway, and the Constitution (Doctorow), **Supp. IV Part 1:** 220, 222, 224, 232, 235

Jackman, Harold, **Supp. XVIII:** 131

Jackpot (Caldwell), **I:** 304

"Jack Schmidt, Arts Administrator" (Keillor), **Supp. XVI:** 171

"Jack Schmidt on the Burning Sands" (Keillor), **Supp. XVI:** 171

Jackson, Amelia. *See* Holmes, Mrs. Oliver Wendell (Amelia Jackson)

Jackson, Andrew, **I:** 7, 20; **III:** 473; **IV:** 192, 248, 298, 334, 348; **Supp. I Part 2:** 456, 461, 473, 474, 493, 695

Jackson, Blyden, **Supp. I Part 1:** 337

Jackson, Charles, **Supp. I Part 1:** 303

Jackson, George, **Supp. I Part 1:** 66

Jackson, Helen Hunt, **I:** 459, 470; **Retro. Supp. I:** 26, 27, 30–31, 32, 33

Jackson, James, **Supp. I Part 1:** 302, 303

Jackson, J. O., **III:** 213

Jackson, Joe, **Supp. I Part 2:** 441

Jackson, Katherine Gauss, **Supp. VIII:** 124

Jackson, Lawrence, **Retro. Supp. II:** 113, 115

Jackson, Lawrence P., **Supp. XXII:** 140

Jackson, Melanie, **Supp. X:** 166

Jackson, Michael, **Supp. VIII:** 146

Jackson, Richard, **II:** 119; **Supp. IX:** 165

Jackson, Shelley, **Supp. XVIII:** 136

Jackson, Shirley, **Supp. IX: 113–130**

Jackson, Thomas J. ("Stonewall"), **IV:** 125, 126

"Jackson Hotel" (Hull), **Supp. XXI:** 134, 135

Jackson Pollock (O'Hara), **Supp. XXIII:** 214–215

"Jackson Square" (Levertov), **Supp. III Part 1:** 276

Jackstraws (Simic), **Supp. VIII:** 280, 282–283

"Jackstraws" (Simic), **Supp. VIII: 283**

Jack Tier (Cooper), **I:** 354, 355

"Jacob" (Garrett), **Supp. VII:** 109–110

"Jacob" (Schwartz), **Supp. II Part 2:** 663

Jacob, Max, **Supp. XV:** 178, 182

"Jacob and the Indians" (Benét), **Supp. XI:** 47–48

"Jacob Bayer and the Telephone" (Helprin), **Supp. XXV:** 81

Jacobs, Catherine Haydon, **Supp. XXI:** 98

Jacobs, Harriet, **Supp. XVI:** 85

Jacobs, Jill Suzanne, **Supp. XX: 178, 186**

Jacobs, Rita D., **Supp. XII:** 339

Jacobsen, Josephine, **Supp. XIII:** 346; **Supp. XIV:** 260

"Jacob's Ladder" (Rawlings), **Supp. X:** 224, 228

Jacob's Ladder, The (Levertov), **Supp. III Part 1:** 272, 276–278, 281

"Jacob's Ladder, The" (Levertov), **Supp. III Part 1:** 278

Jacobson, Dale, **Supp. X:** 112

Jacobson, Kristin, **Supp. XVIII:** 113

Jacobson, Leslie, **Supp. XV:** 323

Jacoby, Russell, **Supp. IV Part 2:** 692

"Jacquerie, The" (Lanier), **Supp. I Part 1:** 355, 356, 360, 364, 370

Jacques le fataliste (D. Diderot), **Supp. XVII:** 145

Jade Mountain, The: A Chinese Anthology, Being Three Hundred Poems of the T'ang Dynasty (Bynner, trans.), **II:** 527; **Supp. XV:** 46, 47, 48

Jafsie and John Henry: Essays on Hollywood, Bad Boys, and Six Hours of Perfect Poker (Mamet), **Supp. XIV:** 252

Jaggi, Maya, **Supp. XXV:** 50, 56, 57

Jaguar Totem (LaBastille), **Supp. X:** 99, 106, **107–109**

Jailbird (Vonnegut), **Supp. II Part 2:** 760, 779–780

Jaimes, M. Annette, **Supp. IV Part 1:** 330, 331

Jain, Manju, **Retro. Supp. I:** 53, 58

"Jake Flower, The" (Major), **Supp. XXII:** 182

Jake's Women (Simon), **Supp. IV Part 2:** 576, 588

"Jakie's Mother" (Fante), **Supp. XI:** 164

Jakobson, Roman, **Supp. IV Part 1:** 155

"Jamaica Kincaid's New York" (Kincaid), **Supp. VII:** 181

James, Alice, **I:** 454; **Retro. Supp. I:** 228, 235

James, A. Lloyd, **Supp. XIV:** 343

James, Caryn, **Supp. X:** 302, 303

James, C. L. R. (Cyril Lionel Robert), **Supp. XXI: 159–173**

James, Etta, **Supp. X:** 242

James, Henry, **I:** 4, 5, 9, 10, 12, 15, 16, 20, 52, 93, 109, 211, 226, 228, 244, 246, 251, 255, 258, 259, 336, 363, 374, 375, 379, 384, 409, 429, 436, 439, 452, 454, 459, 461–462, 463, 464, 485, 500, 504, 513, 514, 517–518, 571; **II:** 38, 58, 60, 73, 74, 95, 138, 140, 144, 147, 196, 198, 199, 228, 230, 234, 243, 259, 267, 271, 272, 275, 276, 278, 281, 282, 283, 284, 285, 286, 287, 288, 290, 306, 309, 316, **319–341,** 398, 404, 410, 415, 427, 444, 542, 544, 547–548, 556, 600; **III:** 44, 51, 136, 194–195, 199, 206, 208, 218, 228–229, 237, 281, 319, 325, 326, 334, 409, 453, 454, 457, 460, 461, 464, 511, 522, 576, 607; **IV:** 8, 27, 34, 37, 40, 53, 58, 73, 74, 134, 168, 172, 182, 198, 202, 285, 308, 309, 310, 311, 314, 316, 317, 318, 319, 321, 322, 323, 324, 328, 347, 352, 359, 433, 439, 476; **Retro. Supp. I:** 1, 8, 53, 56, 59, 108, 112, **215–242,** 272, 283, 284, 362, 366, 367, 368, 371, 373, 374, 375, 376, 377, 378, 379; **Retro. Supp. II:** 93, 135, 136, 203, 223; **Supp. I Part 1:** 35, 38, 43; **Supp. I Part 2:** 414, 454, 608, 609, 612–613, 618, 620, 646; **Supp. II Part 1:** 94–95; **Supp. III Part 1:** 14, 200; **Supp. III Part 2:** 410, 412; **Supp. IV Part 1:** 31, 35, 80, 127, 197, 349, 353; **Supp. IV Part 2:** 613, 677, 678, 682, 689, 693; **Supp. V:** 97, 101, 103, 258, 261, 263, 313; **Supp. VIII:** 98, 102, 156, 166, 168; **Supp. IX:** 121; **Supp. XI:** 153; **Supp. XIII:** 102; **Supp. XIV:** 40, 110, 112, 335, 336, 348, 349; **Supp. XV:** 41; **Supp. XVII:** 5, 47; **Supp. XVIII:** 160, 258; **Supp. XX: 227, 228, 232, 233, 238, 240; Supp. XXI:** 225; **Supp. XXII:** 89; **Supp. XXIV:** 132, 224

James, Henry (father), **II:** 7, 275, 321, 337, 342–344, 364; **IV:** 174; **Supp. I Part 1:** 300

James, Henry (nephew), **II:** 360

James, Horace, **Supp. XIV:** 57

James, P. D., **Supp. XIX:** 131

James, William, **I:** 104, 220, 224, 227, 228, 255, 454; **II:** 20, 27, 165, 166, 276, 321, 337, **342–366,** 411; **III:** 303, 309, 509, 599, 600, 605, 606, 612; **IV:** 26, 27, 28–29, 31, 32, 34, 36, 37, 43, 46, 291, 486; **Retro. Supp. I:** 57, 216, 227, 228, 235, 295, 300, 306; **Supp. I Part 1:** 3, 7, 11, 20; **Supp. XIV:** 40, 50, 197, 199, 212, 335; **Supp. XVII:** 97

James, William (grandfather), **II:** 342

James Baldwin: The Legacy (Troupe, ed.), **Retro. Supp. II:** 15

James Baldwin—The Price of the Ticket (film), **Retro. Supp. II:** 2

James Dickey and the Politics of Canon (Suarez), **Supp. IV Part 1:** 175

"James Dickey on Yeats: An Interview" (Dickey), **Supp. IV Part 1:** 177

James Hogg: A Critical Study (Simpson), **Supp. IX:** 269, 276

"James Is a Girl" (Egan), **Supp. XIX:** 61

James Jones: A Friendship (Morris), **Supp. XI:** 234

James Jones: An American Literary Orientalist Master (Carter), **Supp. XI:** 220

"James Jones and Jack Kerouac: Novelists of Disjunction" (Stevenson), **Supp. XI:** 230

James Jones: Reveille to Taps (television documentary), **Supp. XI:** 234

Jameson, Anna Brownell, **Supp. XXIII:** 225, 226, 232, 235

Jameson, F. R., **Supp. IV Part 1:** 119

Jameson, Sir Leander Starr, **III:** 327

James Shore's Daughter (Benét), **Supp. XI:** 48

"James Thurber" (Pollard), **Supp. I Part 2:** 468

"James Whitcomb Riley (From a Westerner's Point of View)" (Dunbar), **Supp. II Part 1:** 198

Jammes, Francis, **II:** 528; **Retro. Supp. I:** 55

"Jan, the Son of Thomas" (Sandburg), **III:** 593–594

Jan. 31 (Goldbarth), **Supp. XII:** 177, **178–179,** 180

"Jane Awake"(O'Hara), **Supp. XXIII:** 210

Janeczko, Paul, **Supp. XIII:** 280

Jane Eyre (Brontë), **Supp. XVI:** 158; **Supp. XXII:** 120

Janet, Pierre, **I:** 248, 249, 252; **Retro. Supp. I:** 55, 57

Jane Talbot: A Novel (Brown), **Supp. I Part 1:** 145–146

"Janet Waking" (Ransom), **III:** 490, 491

"Janice" (Jackson), **Supp. IX:** 117

Janowitz, Tama, **Supp. X:** 7

Jantz, Harold S., **Supp. I Part 1:** 112

"January" (Barthelme), **Supp. IV Part 1:** 54

"January" (W. V. Davis), **Supp. XXI:** 89, 90

January Man, The (screenplay, Shanley), **Supp. XIV:** 316

"January Thaw" (Leopold), **Supp. XIV:** 183–184

"Janus" (Beattie), **Supp. V:** 31

Janzen, Jean, **Supp. V:** 180

"Japan" (Collins), **Supp. XXI:** 56

Japanese Americans: The Formation and Transformations of an Ethnic Group (Spickard), **Supp. XXI:** 149

"Japanese Beetles" (X. J. Kennedy), **Supp. XV:** 161, 165

Japanese by Spring (Reed), **Supp. X:** 241, **253–255**

Japanese Cooking: A Simple Art (Tsuji), **Supp. XVII:** 90

"Japan's Young Dreams" (Geisel), **Supp. XVI:** 102

Jara, Victor, **Supp. IV Part 2:** 549

Jarecki, Dave, **Supp. XXIII:** 239

Jarman, Mark, **Supp. IV Part 1:** 68; **Supp. IX:** 266, 270, 276; **Supp. XII:** 209; **Supp. XV:** 251; **Supp. XVIII:** 178; **Supp. XXV:** 221–222

Jarmon, Mark, **Supp. XVII: 109–122**

Jarrell, Randall, **I:** 167, 169, 173, 180; **II: 367–390,** 539–540; **III:** 134, 194, 213, 268, 527; **IV:** 352, 411, 422; **Retro. Supp. I:** 52, 121, 135, 140; **Retro. Supp. II:** 44, 177, 178, 182; **Supp. I Part 1:** 89; **Supp. I Part 2:** 552; **Supp. II Part 1:** 109, 135; **Supp. III Part 1:** 64; **Supp. III Part 2:** 541, 550; **Supp. IV Part 2:** 440; **Supp. V:**

315, 318, 323; **Supp. VIII:** 31, 100, 271; **Supp. IX:** 94, 268; **Supp. XI:** 311, 315; **Supp. XII:** 121, 260, 297; **Supp. XV:** 93, 153; **Supp. XVII:** 111

Jarrell, Mrs. Randall (Mary von Schrader), **II:** 368, 385

Jarry, Alfred, **Retro. Supp. II:** 326; **Supp. XV:** 177–178, 182, 188

Jarvis, John Wesley, **Supp. I Part 2:** 501, 520

Jaskoski, Helen, **Supp. IV Part 1:** 325; **Supp. XXII:** 166

"Jasmine" (Komunyakaa), **Supp. XIII:** 132

"Jason" (Hecht), **Supp. X:** 62

"Jason" (MacLeish), **III:** 4

Jason and Medeia (Gardner), **Supp. VI:** 63, **68–69**

"Jasper Notes" (G. Jones), **Supp. XXIV:** 194

Jaspers, Karl, **III:** 292; **IV:** 491

Jauss, David, **Supp. XXI:** 129, 132, 133, 134, 139

Jay, William, **I:** 338

Jayber Crow (Berry), **Supp. X:** 28, 34

"Jaz Fantasia" (Sandburg), **III:** 585

"Jazz Age Clerk, A" (Farrell), **II:** 45

Jazz Country: Ralph Ellison in America (Porter), **Retro. Supp. II:** 127

"Jazzonia" (Hughes), **Supp. I Part 1:** 324

Jazz Poetry Anthology, The (Komunyakaa and Feinstein, eds.), **Supp. XIII:** 125

"Jazztet Muted" (Hughes), **Supp. I Part 1:** 342

J. B.: A Play in Verse (MacLeish), **II:** 163, 228; **III:** 3, 21–22, 23; **Supp. IV Part 2:** 586

"Jealous" (Ford), **Supp. V:** 71

Jealous Gods, The (Atherton), **Supp. XXIV:** 26

Jealousies, The: A Faery Tale, by Lucy Vaughan Lloyd of China Walk, Lambeth (Keats), **Supp. XII:** 113

Jean-Christophe (Rolland), **Supp. XX: 70**

"Jean Harlow's Wedding Night" (Wasserstein), **Supp. XV:** 328

Jean Huguenot (Benét), **Supp. XI:** 44

"Jeff Briggs's Love Story" (Harte), **Supp. II Part 1:** 355

Jeffers, Robinson, **I:** 66; **III:** 134; **Retro. Supp. I:** 202; **Supp. II Part 2: 413–440;** **Supp. VIII:** 33, 292; **Supp. IX:** 77; **Supp. X:** 112; **Supp. XI:** 312; **Supp. XV:** 113, 114, 115; **Supp. XVII:** 111, 112, 117; **Supp. XXI:** 87; **Supp. XXIII:** 145

Jeffers, Una Call Kuster (Mrs. Robinson Jeffers), **Supp. II Part 2:** 414

Jefferson, Blind Lemon, **Supp. VIII:** 349

Jefferson, Margo, **Supp. XX: 87; Supp. XXIV:** 271

Jefferson, Thomas, **I:** 1, 2, 5, 6–8, 14, 485; **II:** 5, 6, 34, 217, 300, 301, 437; **III:** 3, 17, 18, 294–295, 306, 310, 473, 608; **IV:** 133, 243, 249, 334, 348; **Supp. I Part 1:** 146, 152, 153, 229, 230, 234, 235; **Supp. I Part 2:** 389, 399, 456, 474, 475, 482, 507, 509, 510, 511, 516, 518–519, 520, 522;

Supp. X: 26; **Supp. XIV:** 191; **Supp. XX: 285; Supp. XXIV:** 85, 281

Jefferson and/or Mussolini (Pound), **Retro. Supp. I:** 292

"Jefferson Davis as a Representative American" (Du Bois), **Supp. II Part 1:** 161

J-E-L-L-O (Baraka), **Supp. II Part 1:** 47

"Jelly-Bean, The" (Fitzgerald), **II:** 88

"Jellyfish, A" (Moore), **III:** 215

Jemie, Onwuchekwa, **Supp. I Part 1:** 343

Jenkins, J. L., **I:** 456

Jenkins, Joe, **Supp. XX: 117,** 120, 122

Jenkins, Kathleen, **III:** 403

Jenkins, Susan, **IV:** 123

Jenks, Deneen, **Supp. IV Part 2:** 550, 554

Jenks, Tom, **Supp. XIX:** 51

Jenkyns, Richard, **Supp. XXV:** 223

Jennie Gerhardt (Dreiser), **I:** 497, 499, 500, 501, 504–505, 506, 507, 519; **Retro. Supp. II:** 94, **99–101**

"Jennie M'Grew" (Masters), **Supp. I Part 2:** 468

Jennifer Lorn (Wylie), **Supp. I Part 2:** 709, 714–717, 718, 721, 724

Jennison, Peter S., **Supp. XIX:** 268

"Jenny Garrow's Lover" (Jewett), **II:** 397

"Jerboa, The" (Moore), **III:** 203, 207, 209, 211–212

Jeremiah, **Supp. X:** 35

Jeremy's Version (Purdy), **Supp. VII:** 274

"Je Reviens"(Dybek), **Supp. XXIII:** 78

"Jericho" (Lowell), **II:** 536

Jerome, Judson, **Supp. XXIII:** 54

"Jerry's Garage" (Budbill), **Supp. XIX:** 7

"Jersey City Gendarmerie, Je T'aime" (Lardner), **II:** 433

Jersey Rain (Pinsky), **Supp. VI:** 235, **247–250**

"Jerusalem" (Nye), **Supp. XIII:** 287

Jerusalem: Song of Songs (Uris), **Supp. XX: 244–245,** 246, 255

Jerusalem the Golden (Reznikoff), **Supp. XIV:** 280, 285, 286

Jessup, Richard, **Supp. XI:** 306

"Je Suis Perdu" (Taylor), Supp. V: 314, 321–322

Jesuits in North America in the Seventeenth Century, The (Parkman), **Supp. II Part 2:** 597, 603–605

Jesus, **I:** 27, 34, 68, 89, 136, 552, 560; **II:** 1, 16, 197, 198, 214, 215, 216, 218, 219, 239, 373, 377, 379, 537, 538, 539, 549, 569, 585, 591, 592; **III:** 39, 173, 179, 270, 291, 296–297, 300, 303, 305, 307, 311, 339, 340, 341, 342, 344, 345, 346, 347, 348, 352, 353, 354, 355, 436, 451, 489, 534, 564, 566, 567, 582; **IV:** 51, 69, 86, 107, 109, 117, 137, 138, 141, 144, 147, 149, 150, 151, 152, 155, 156, 157, 158, 159, 163, 164, 232, 241, 289, 293, 294, 296, 331, 364, 392, 396, 418, 430; **Supp. I Part 1:** 2, 54, 104, 107, 108, 109, 121, 267, 371; **Supp. I Part 2:** 379, 386, 458, 515, 580, 582, 583, 587, 588, 683; **Supp. V:** 280

Jesus, the Son of Man (Gibran), **Supp. XX: 115–116, 117, 122–123**

"Jesus Asleep" (Sexton), **Supp. II Part 2:** 693

"Jesus of Nazareth, Then and Now" (Price), **Supp. VI:** 268

"Jesus Papers, The" (Sexton), **Supp. II Part 2:** 693

"Jesus Raises Up the Harlot" (Sexton), **Supp. II Part 2:** 693

"Jesus Stories, The" (Brockmeier), **Supp. XXII:** 52

Jetée, La (film), **Supp. IV Part 2:** 436

"Jeune Parque, La" (Valéry), **IV:** 92

"Jew as Writer/The Writer as Jew, The: Reflections on Literature and Identity" (Apple), **Supp. XVII:** 1, 9

"Jewbird, The" (Malamud), **Supp. I Part 2:** 435

"Jewboy, The" (P. Roth), **Supp. III Part 2:** 412

Jewett, Caroline, **II:** 396

Jewett, Katharine, **Retro. Supp. II:** 46

Jewett, Mary, **II:** 396, 403

Jewett, Rutger, **Retro. Supp. I:** 381

Jewett, Sarah Orne, **I:** 313; **II: 391–414; Retro. Supp. I:** 6, 7, 19; **Retro. Supp. II:** 51, 52, **131–151**, 156; **Supp. I Part 2:** 495; **Supp. VIII:** 126; **Supp. IX:** 79; **Supp. XIII:** 153; **Supp. XXIII:** 275, 278

Jewett, Theodore Furber, **II:** 395

Jewett, Dr. Theodore Herman, **II:** 396–397, 402

"Jew for Export, The" (Mamet), **Supp. XIV:** 251–252

Jew in Our Day, The (W. Frank), **Supp. XX:** 79

Jew in the American Novel, The (Fiedler), **Supp. XIII:** 106

"Jewish Graveyards, Italy" (Levine), **Supp. V:** 190

"Jewish Hunter, The" (Moore), **Supp. X:** 163, 165, **174**

Jewison, Norman, **Supp. XI:** 306; **Supp. XIV:** 316

"Jew of Persia, A" (Helprin), **Supp. XXV:** 80, 85

Jews of Shklov (Schneour), **IV:** 11

Jews without Money (Gold), **Supp. XIV:** 288–289

JFK (film), **Supp. XIV:** 48

Jig of Forslin, The: A Symphony (Aiken), **I:** 50, 51, 57, 62, 66

"Jig Tune: Not for Love" (McGrath), **Supp. X:** 116

"Jihad" (McClatchy), **Supp. XII:** 266

"Jilting of Granny Weatherall, The" (Porter), **III:** 434, 435, 438

Jim Crow's Last Stand (Hughes), **Retro. Supp. I:** 205

Jiménez, Juan Ramón, **Supp. XIII:** 315, 323

Jimmie Higgins (Sinclair), **Supp. V:** 288

"Jimmy Harlow" (X. J. Kennedy), **Supp. XV:** 170

Jimmy's Blues (Baldwin), **Retro. Supp. II:** 8, 9, 15

Jim's Book: A Collection of Poems and Short Stories (Merrill), **Supp. III Part 1:** 319

Jin, Ha, **Supp. XVIII: 89–104**

Jitney (Wilson), **Supp. VIII:** 330, 331, 351

Jitterbug Perfume (Robbins), **Supp. X:** 273, **274–276**, 279

Joachim, Harold, **Retro. Supp. I:** 58

Joan, Pope, **IV:** 165

Joanna and Ulysses (Sarton), **Supp. VIII: 254–255**

Joan of Arc, **IV:** 241; **Supp. I Part 1:** 286–288; **Supp. I Part 2:** 469

Joans, Ted, **Supp. IV Part 1:** 169

Job (biblical book), **II:** 165, 166–167, 168; **III:** 21, 199, 512; **IV:** 13, 158; **Supp. I Part 1:** 125

Job, The (Burroughs and Odier), **Supp. III Part 1:** 97, 103

Job, The: An American Novel (Lewis), **II:** 441

"Job History" (Proulx), **Supp. VII:** 262

Jobim, Antonio Carlos, **Supp. IV Part 2:** 549

Jobim, Antônio Carlos, **Supp. XXI:** 100

"Job of the Plains, A" (Humphrey), **Supp. IX:** 101

"Jody Rolled the Bones" (Yates), **Supp. XI:** 335, 341

"Joe" (Alvarez), **Supp. VII:** 7–8

Joe (Brown), **Supp. XVIII:** 195

Joe (L. Brown), **Supp. XXI:** 41, **45–46**, 47

"Joe, the Vanishing American" (Swados), **Supp. XIX:** 258–259

Joe Hill: A Biographical Novel (Stegner), **Supp. IV Part 2:** 599

Joe Jones (Lamott), **Supp. XX: 134–135**

"Joe Louis: The King as a Middle-Aged Man" (Talese), **Supp. XVII:** 202

"Joe Messenger Is Dreaming" (P. Benedict), **Supp. XXIII:** 47

"Joe's Jitters" (Bronk), **Supp. XXI:** 27

Joe Turner's Come and Gone (Wilson), **Supp. VIII:** 334, **337–342**, 345

Joe versus the Volcano (screenplay, Shanley), **Supp. XIV:** 316

"Joey Martiney" (Huncke), **Supp. XIV:** 149

Johannes in Eremo (Mather), **Supp. II Part 2:** 453

John XXIII, Pope, **Supp. I Part 2:** 492

John (biblical book), **I:** 68; **Supp. XV:** 222, 224

"John" (Shields), **Supp. VII:** 310–311

John, Augustus, **Supp. XXII:** 157

John, Elton, **Supp. XXI:** 148

"John, John Chinaman" (Buck), **Supp. II Part 1:** 128

John Addington Symonds: A Biographical Study (Brooks), **I:** 240, 241

John-a Dreams: A Tale (J. Sturgis), **Supp. XX: 233**

"John Archer's Nose" (R. Fisher), **Supp. XIX:** 71–72, 78

John Barleycorn (London), **II:** 467, 481

John Brown (Du Bois), **Supp. II Part 1:** 171–172

"John Brown" (Emerson), **II:** 13

"John Brown" (Lindsay), **Supp. I Part 2:** 393

John Brown's Body (Benét), **II:** 177; **Supp. XI:** 45, 46, 47, **56–57**

John Brown: The Making of a Martyr (Warren), **IV:** 236

John Bull in America; or, The New Munchausen (Paulding), **I:** 344

"John Burke" (Olson), **Supp. II Part 2:** 579, 580

"John Burns of Gettysburg" (Harte), **Supp. II Part 1:** 343

"John Carter" (Agee), **I:** 27

John Chancellor Makes Me Cry (Siddons), **Supp. XXII:** 245

"John Coltrane: Where Does Art Come From?" (Baraka), **Supp. II Part 1:** 60

John Deth: A Metaphysical Legend and Other Poems (Aiken), **I:** 61

"John Endicott" (Longfellow), **II:** 505, 506; **Retro. Supp. II:** 165–166, 167

"John Evereldown" (Robinson), **III:** 524

John Fante Reader, The (Cooper, ed.), **Supp. XI:** 174

John Fante: Selected Letters, 1932–1981 (Cooney, ed.), **Supp. XI:** 170

"John Gardner: The Writer As Teacher" (Carver), **Supp. III Part 1:** 136, 146–147

John Gaunt (R. H. Davis), **Supp. XVI:** 89

John Jay Chapman and His Letters (Howe), **Supp. XIV:** 54

John Keats (Lowell), **II:** 530–531

"John Kinsella's Lament for Mrs. Mary Moore" (Yeats), **Supp. XVII:** 144

"John Lamar" (R. H. Davis), **Supp. XVI:** 89–90

John Lane, **Retro. Supp. I:** 59

"John L. Sullivan" (Lindsay), **Supp. I Part 2:** 394, 395

"John Marr" (Melville), **III:** 93

John Marr and Other Sailors (Melville), **III:** 93; **Retro. Supp. I:** 257

John Muir: A Reading Bibliography (Kimes and Kimes), **Supp. IX:** 178

Johnny Appleseed and Other Poems (Lindsay), **Supp. I Part 2:** 397

"Johnny Bear" (Steinbeck), **IV:** 67

Johnny Got His Gun (Trumbo), **Supp. XXI:** 45

"Johnny Mnemonic" (W. Gibson), **Supp. XVI:** 122, 123–125, 128, 131

"Johnny Panic and the Bible of Dreams" (Plath), **Retro. Supp. II:** 245

"Johnny Ray" (Ríos), **Supp. IV Part 2:** 543

Johnny Tremain (Forbes), **Supp. XIX:** 235

John of the Cross (Saint), **I:** 585; **Supp. IV Part 1:** 284; **Supp. XV:** 223; **Supp. XVII:** 112

John Paul Jones: A Sailor's Biography (Morison), **Supp. I Part 2:** 494–495

"John Redding Goes to Sea" (Hurston), **Supp. VI:** 150

Johns, George Sibley, **Retro. Supp. II:** 65

Johns, Jasper, **Supp. XXIII:** 217

Johns, Orrick, **Retro. Supp. II:** 71

John Sloan: A Painter's Life (Brooks), **I:** 254

"John Smith Liberator" (Bierce), **I:** 209

Johnson, Alexandra, **Supp. X:** 86

Johnson, Alvin, **I:** 236; **Supp. XV:** 304

Johnson, Ben, **Retro. Supp. I:** 56

Johnson, Buffie, **Supp. IV Part 1:** 94

Johnson, Caitlin, **Supp. XXIII:** 281

Johnson, Carol Siri, **Supp. XXIII:** 257, 258, 264, 269

Johnson, Charles, **Supp. I Part 1:** 325; **Supp. V:** 128; **Supp. VI: 185–201; Supp. X:** 239; **Supp. XIII:** 182; **Supp. XIX:** 160

Johnson, Charles S., **Supp. IX:** 309; **Supp. XXII:** 6, 7

Johnson, Claudia Durst, **Supp. VIII:** 126–127

Johnson, Clifton, **Supp. XXI:** 248, 250

Johnson, Denis, **Supp. XXI:** 118, 131

Johnson, Dennis, **Supp. XIX:** 209

Johnson, Diane, **Supp. XIII:** 127

Johnson, Dianne, **Retro. Supp. I:** 196

Johnson, Eastman, **IV:** 321

Johnson, Edward, **IV:** 157; **Supp. I Part 1:** 110, 115

Johnson, Fenton, **Supp. XI:** 129

Johnson, Georgia Douglas, **Supp. IV Part 1:** 164

Johnson, Helene, **Supp. XVIII:** 282

Johnson, James Weldon, **Retro. Supp. II:** 114; **Supp. I Part 1:** 324, 325; **Supp. II Part 1:** 33, 194, 200, 202–203, 206–207; **Supp. III Part 1:** 73; **Supp. IV Part 1:** 7, 11, 15, 16, 164, 165, 166, 169; **Supp. X:** 42, 136, **246; Supp. XVIII:** 122, 127, 282; **Supp. XIX:** 73

Johnson, Jeff, **Supp. XXV:** 98

Johnson, Joyce, **Supp. XIV:** 150

Johnson, Kent, **Supp. XV:** 347

Johnson, Lady Bird, **Supp. IV Part 1:** 22

Johnson, Lyndon B., **I:** 254; **II:** 553, 582; **Retro. Supp. II:** 27

Johnson, Marguerite. *See* Angelou, Maya

Johnson, Maurice, **Supp. XV:** 136, 137, 138

Johnson, Michael K., **Supp. XVIII:** 59, 64

Johnson, Mordecai, **Supp. XIV:** 202

Johnson, Nunnally, **Supp. IV Part 1:** 355

Johnson, Pamela Hansford, **IV:** 469

Johnson, Rafer, **Supp. I Part 1:** 271

Johnson, Reed, **Supp. IV Part 2:** 589

Johnson, Richard, **Supp. XIII:** 132

Johnson, Robert, **Supp. IV Part 1:** 146; **Supp. VIII:** 15, 134

Johnson, Robert K., **Supp. IV Part 2:** 573, 584

Johnson, Robert Underwood, **Supp. IX:** 182, 184, 185

Johnson, Samuel, **II:** 295; **III:** 491, 503; **IV:** 452; **Retro. Supp. I:** 56, 65; **Supp. I Part 1:** 33; **Supp. I Part 2:** 422, 498, 503, 523, 656; **Supp. IV Part 1:** 34, 124; **Supp. XI:** 209; **Supp. XII:** 159; **Supp. XIII:** 55, 347; **Supp. XVI:** 204; **Supp. XVII:** 1; **Supp. XXIV:** 152

Johnson, Samuel, Jr., **Supp. XXV:** 241, 250

Johnson, Sarah Anne, **Supp. XVIII:** 145; **Supp. XIX:** 49, 50, 52, 54, 55, 56, 58, 59, 60, 61

Johnson, Steve, **Supp. XVI:** 177

Johnson, Thomas H., **I:** 470–471; **IV:** 144, 158; **Retro. Supp. I:** 26, 28, 36, 39, 40, 41, 43

Johnson, Walter, **II:** 422

Johnson, Willard "Spud", **Supp. XV:** 42, 46

"Johnson Girls, The" (Bambara), **Supp. XI:** 7

Johnsrud, Harold, **II:** 562

Johnston, Basil, **Supp. IV Part 1:** 269

Johnston, Jill, **Supp. XXV:** 5

Johnston, Mary, **II:** 194

Johnston, Robert M., **Supp. I Part 1:** 369

"John Sutter" (Winters), **Supp. II Part 2:** 810

John's Wife (Coover), **Supp. V:** 51–52

John the Baptist, **I:** 389; **II:** 537, 591

John Wesley Harding (album, Dylan), **Supp. XVIII:** 27

Jolas, Eugène, **Retro. Supp. II:** 85, 328; **Supp. IV Part 1:** 80

Jolie Blon's Bounce (Burke), **Supp. XIV:** 26, 33–34

Jolly (Mamet), **Supp. XIV:** 240, 254

"Jolly Corner, The" (James), **I:** 571; **Retro. Supp. I:** 235

"Jon" (Saunders), **Supp. XIX:** 232, 234

"Jonah" (Lowell), **II:** 536

Jonah's Gourd Vine (Hurston), **Supp. VI:** 149, 155

"Jonathan Edwards" (Holmes), **Supp. I Part 1:** 302, 315

"Jonathan Edwards in Western Massachusetts" (Lowell), **II:** 550

Jonathan Franzen at the End of Postmodernism (Burns), **Supp. XX:** 85

Jonathan Troy (Abbey), **Supp. XIII:** 4, 13

Jones, Anne, **Supp. X:** 8

Jones, Anne Goodwyn, **Supp. XXII:** 252

Jones, Carolyn M., **Supp. VIII:** 128; **Supp. XIX:** 160

Jones, Chuck, **Supp. XVI:** 102

Jones, David, **Supp. XVII:** 241

Jones, Dennis, **Supp. XXIII:** 228, 233

Jones, Derek Anson, **Supp. XVIII:** 38, 39

Jones, Edith Newbold. *See* Wharton, Edith

Jones, Edward P., **Supp. XXI:** 247; **Supp. XXII: 139–153**

Jones, E. Stanley, **III:** 297

Jones, Everett LeRoi. *See* Baraka, Imamu Amiri

Jones, Gayl, **Supp. XXIV: 183–197**

Jones, George Frederic, **IV:** 309

Jones, Grover, **Supp. XIII:** 166

Jones, Harry, **Supp. I Part 1:** 337

Jones, Harry L., **Supp. XXV:** 251

Jones, Howard Mumford, **I:** 353; **Supp. IV Part 2:** 606; **Supp. XIV:** 11

Jones, James, **III:** 40; **IV:** 98; **Supp. XI: 213–237; Supp. XIX:** 248, 252; **Supp. XX: 248; Supp. XXV:** 145

Jones, James Earl, **Supp. VIII:** 334; **Supp. XI:** 309

Jones, Jennifer, **Supp. IV Part 2:** 524

Jones, John Paul, **II:** 405–406; **Supp. I Part 2:** 479, 480, 494–495

Jones, Kirkland C., **Supp. XVIII:** 173, 174, 175; **Supp. XXII:** 9

Jones, LeRoi. *See* Baraka, Imamu Amiri

Jones, Louis B., **Supp. XVI:** 41

Jones, Loyal, **Supp. XX:** 170

Jones, Lucretia Stevens Rhinelander, **IV:** 309

Jones, Madison, **Retro. Supp. II:** 235; **Supp. X:** 1

Jones, Major (pseudonym). *See* Thompson, William T.

Jones, Malcolm, **Supp. V:** 219; **Supp. XX: 93, 138**

Jones, Mildred, **Supp. XVIII:** 281

Jones, Robert Edmond, **III:** 387, 391, 394, 399; **Supp. XXI:** 6, 12

Jones, Sharon L., **Supp. XVIII:** 280, 285, 286

Jones, Tommy Lee, **Supp. V:** 227

"Jones's Private Argyment" (Lanier), **Supp. I Part 1:** 352

"Jones's *The Thin Red Line:* The End of Innocence" (Michel-Michot), **Supp. XI:** 224–225

Jong, Allan, **Supp. V:** 115

Jong, Erica, **Supp. V: 113–135**

Jong-Fast, Molly Miranda, **Supp. V:** 115

Jonson, Ben, **I:** 58, 358; **II:** 11, 16, 17, 18, 436, 556; **III:** 3, 463, 575–576; **IV:** 395, 453; **Retro. Supp. II:** 76; **Supp. I Part 2:** 423; **Supp. IV Part 2:** 585; **Supp. XX:** 197; **Supp. XXIV:** 159

Jonsson, Thorsten, **Retro. Supp. I:** 73

Joplin, Janis, **Supp. IV Part 1:** 206; **Supp. XI:** 239

Joplin, Scott, **Supp. IV Part 1:** 223

Jordan, A. Van, **Supp. XVIII:** 172

Jordan, Barbara, **Supp. VIII:** 63; **Supp. XI:** 249

Jordan, David, **Supp. XIX:** 141

Jordan, June, **Supp. XII:** 217; **Supp. XXII:** 172; **Supp. XXIV:** 188

Jordan, Marie, **Supp. XV:** 224

Jo's Boys (Alcott), **Supp. I Part 1:** 32, 35, 40–41, 42

Joseph Heller (Ruderman), **Supp. IV Part 1:** 380

"Josephine Has Her Day" (Thurber), **Supp. I Part 2:** 606

Josephine Stories, The (Fitzgerald), **Retro. Supp. I:** 109

"Joseph Martinez" (Huncke), **Supp. XIV:** 149

"Joseph Pockets" (Stern), **Supp. IX:** 292

Josephson, Matthew, **I:** 259

"José's Country" (Winters), **Supp. II Part 2:** 789, 790

Joshi, S. T., **Supp. XXIV:** 23; **Supp. XXV:** 111, 118, 123

Joshua (biblical book), **Supp. I Part 2:** 515

"Joshua Clark" (Kenny), **Supp. XXIII:** 154

Joslin, Katherine, **Retro. Supp. I:** 376

Journal (Emerson), **Supp. I Part 1:** 309
"Journal" (L. Michaels), **Supp. XVI:** 213
Journal (Thoreau), **IV:** 175
Journal (Woolman), **Supp. VIII:** 202
"Journal for My Daughter" (Kunitz), **Supp. III Part 1:** 268
"Journal of an Airman" (Auden), **Supp. XIX:** 151
Journal of Arthur Stirling, The (Sinclair), **Supp. V:** 280
"Journal of a Solitary Man, The" (Hawthorne), **II:** 226
Journal of a Solitude (Sarton), **Supp. VIII:** 256, 262–263
Journal of My Other Self (Rilke), **Retro. Supp. II:** 20
Journal of the Fictive Life (Nemerov), **III:** 267, 268, 269, 272, 273, 274, 280–281, 284–285, 286, 287
Journal of the Plague Year, A (Defoe), **III:** 423
"Journal of the Year of the Ox, A" (Wright), **Supp. V:** 343
Journals (Thoreau), **Supp. I Part 1:** 299
Journals and Other Documents on the Life and Voyages of Christopher Columbus (Morison, ed.), **Supp. I Part 2:** 494
Journals of Ralph Waldo Emerson, The (Emerson), **II:** 8, 17, 21
Journals of Susanna Moodie, The: Poems (Atwood), **Supp. XIII:** 33
"Journey, A" (Wharton), **Retro. Supp. I:** 364
"Journey, The" (Winters), **Supp. II Part 2:** 795
"Journey, The" (Wright), **Supp. III Part 2:** 605–606
"Journey, the Arrival and the Dream, The" (Gioia), **Supp. XV:** 120
"Journey, The: For Jane at Thirteen" (Kumin), **Supp. IV Part 2:** 442
Journey and Other Poems, The (Winters), **Supp. II Part 2:** 786, 794, 795, 796, 799, 800, 801
Journey Around My Room: The Autobiography of Louise Bogan—A Mosaic (Bogan), **Supp. III Part 1:** 47, 48, 52, 53
Journey Down, The (Bernstein), **IV:** 455
Journey Home, The (Abbey), **Supp. XIII:** 2, 12
"Journey into Speech, A" (Cliff), **Supp. XXII:** 69
Journeyman (Caldwell), **I:** 297, 302–304, 307, 309
Journeyman: Travels of a Writer (Findley), **Supp. XX: 50**
Journey of Tai-me, The (Momaday), **Supp. IV Part 2:** 485
"Journey of the Magi" (Eliot), **Retro. Supp. I:** 64
Journey to a War (Auden and Isherwood), **Supp. II Part 1:** 13; **Supp. XIV:** 156, 158, 162
Journey to Love (W. C. Williams), **IV:** 422; **Retro. Supp. I:** 429
Journey to My Father; Isaac Bashevis Singer (Zamir), **Retro. Supp. II:** 317

"Journey to Nine Miles" (Walker), **Supp. III Part 2:** 527
"Journey to the Interior" (W. J. Smith), **Supp. XIII:** 339, 340
Journey with Genius: Recollections and Reflections Concerning the D. H. Lawrences (Bynner), **Supp. XV:** 46
Jowett, Benjamin, **Supp. XIV:** 335
"Joy" (Moore), **Supp. X:** 174
"Joy" (Singer), **IV:** 9; **Retro. Supp. II:** 307
Joyce, Cynthia, **Supp. X:** 194, 195, 196
Joyce, James, **I:** 53, 105, 108, 130, 174, 256, 285, 377, 395, 475–476, 478, 480, 483, 576; **II:** 27, 42, 58, 73, 74, 198, 209, 264, 320, 569; **III:** 7, 16, 26–27, 45, 174, 181, 184, 261, 273, 277, 343, 396, 398, 465, 471, 474; **IV:** 32, 73, 85, 95, 103, 171, 182, 211, 286, 370, 412, 418, 419, 428, 434, 456; **Retro. Supp. I:** 59, 63, 75, 80, 89, 91, 108, 109, 127, 287, 290, 292, 334, 335, 420; **Retro. Supp. II:** 221, 326; **Supp. I Part 1:** 257, 262, 270; **Supp. I Part 2:** 437, 546, 613, 620; **Supp. II Part 1:** 136; **Supp. III Part 1:** 35, 36, 65, 225, 229; **Supp. III Part 2:** 611, 617, 618; **Supp. IV Part 1:** 40, 47, 80, 227, 300, 310; **Supp. IV Part 2:** 424, 677; **Supp. V:** 261, 331; **Supp. VIII:** 14, 40, 103; **Supp. IX:** 211, 229, 235, 308; **Supp. X:** 115, 137, 194, 324; **Supp. XI:** 66; **Supp. XII:** 139, 151, 165, 191, 289; **Supp. XIV:** 83; **Supp. XVI:** 41, 189, 282; **Supp. XVII:** 44; **Supp. XIX:** 151, 172; **Supp. XXI:** 7; **Supp. XXII:** 141, 143–144; **Supp. XXIII:** 162
Joy Comes in the Morning (J. Rosen), **Supp. XVII:** 50
Joy in the Morning (B. Smith), **Supp. XXIII:** 257, 258, **269–270**
Joy Luck Club, The (Tan), **Supp. X:** 289, 291, 293, 294, 296, 297, 298, 299
"Joy of Sales Resistance, The" (Berry), **Supp. X:** 36
J R (Gaddis), **Supp. IV Part 1:** 279, 280, 285–289, 291, 294; **Supp. IV Part 2:** 484; **Supp. XXI:** 226
Juana Inés de la Cruz, Sor, **Supp. XXI:** 94, 104
Juan de la Cruz (John of the Cross), **Supp. XXI:** 99, 104
"Juan's Song" (Bogan), **Supp. III Part 1:** 50
Juba to Jive: A Dictionary of African-American Slang (Major), **Supp. XXII:** 172, 180
Jubilate Agno (Smart), **Supp. IV Part 2:** 626
Judah, Hettie, **Supp. XIII:** 246
Judah the Pious (Prose), **Supp. XVI:** 249, 250, 262
"Judas Maccabaeus" (Longfellow), **II:** 506; **Retro. Supp. II:** 165, 167
Judd, Sylvester, **II:** 290; **Supp. I Part 2:** 420
Judd Rankin's Daughter (Glaspell), **Supp. III Part 1:** 186–188

Jude the Obscure (Hardy), **Supp. I Part 1:** 217
Judevine (Budbill), **Supp. XIX:** 4, **8–9,** 12
Judevine: A Play in Three Acts/Two Acts (Budbill), **Supp. XIX: 12–13**
Judge, Jane, **Supp. XXII:** 191
"Judgement Day" (O'Connor), **III:** 349, 350; **Retro. Supp. II:** 236
Judgment Day (Farrell), **II:** 29, 31, 32, 34, 39
"Judgment of Paris, The" (Merwin), **Supp. III Part 1:** 350
Judgment of Paris, The (Vidal), **Supp. IV Part 2:** 680, 682
"Judgment of the Sage, The" (Crane), **I:** 420
Judith (Farrell), **II:** 46, 48
"Judith" (Garrett), **Supp. VII:** 109–110
"Juggernaut" (Bass), **Supp. XVI:** 16–17
"Jug of Sirup, A" (Bierce), **I:** 206
"Jugurtha" (Longfellow), **II:** 499
"Juice or Gravy" (P. Roth), **Retro. Supp. II:** 279
"Juke Box Love Song" (Hughes), **Retro. Supp. I:** 209
"Julia" (Hellman), **Supp. I Part 1:** 280, 293
Julia France and Her Times (Atherton), **Supp. XXIV:** 24, 27
"Julia Miller" (Masters), **Supp. I Part 2:** 461
Julian (Vidal), **Supp. IV Part 2:** 677, 684–685, 685, 689
Julian the Apostate, **Retro. Supp. I:** 247
"Julian Vreden" (Bowles), **Supp. IV Part 1:** 94
Julie and Romeo (Ray), **Supp. XII:** 308, 310
Julien, Isaac, **Supp. XI:** 19
Julie; ou, La nouvelle Héloïse (Rousseau), **Supp. XVI:** 184
Julier, Laura, **Supp. IV Part 1:** 211
Julip (Harrison), **Supp. VIII: 51**
Julius Caesar (Shakespeare), **I:** 284
July, Miranda, **Supp. XXIV: 199–211**
"July Midnight" (Lowell), **II:** 521
Jumel, Madame, **Supp. I Part 2:** 461
Jumping Out of Bed (R. Bly), **Supp. IV Part 1:** 71
"Jump-Up Day" (Kingsolver), **Supp. VII:** 203
"Junctions" (Lamott), **Supp. XX: 143**
"June 1940" (Kees), **Supp. XV:** 141
"June Light" (Wilbur), **Supp. III Part 2:** 545
June Moon (Lardner and Kaufman), **II:** 427
"June Recital" (Welty), **IV:** 272–273
Juneteenth (Ellison), **Retro. Supp. II:** 119, 124, **126–128**
"Juneteenth" (Ellison), **Retro. Supp. II:** 119, 126; **Supp. II Part 1:** 248
"June the Third" (Gander), **Supp. XV:** 340
June-Tree: New and Selected Poems, 1974–2000 (Balakian), **Supp. XXIII:** 19, **24–25,** 32
Jung, Carl, **I:** 58, 135, 241, 248, 252, 402; **III:** 400, 534, 543; **Supp. I Part 2:**

439; **Supp. IV Part 1:** 68, 69; **Supp. VIII:** 45; **Supp. X:** 193; **Supp. XV:** 214; **Supp. XX: 63, 117**
Junger, Ernst, **Supp. III Part 1:** 63
Jungle, The (Sinclair), **III:** 580; **Supp. V:** 281–284, 285, 289
Jungle Lovers (Theroux), **Supp. VIII:** 314, 315, 316, **317**
"Junior Addict" (Hughes), **Supp. I Part 1:** 343
"Juniper" (Francis), **Supp. IX:** 79
"Junk" (Wilbur), **Supp. III Part 2:** 556
Junker, Howard, **Supp. XV:** 116
Junkie: Confessions of an Unredeemed Drug Addict (Burroughs), **Supp. III Part 1:** 92, 94–96, 101
Junky (Burroughs), **Supp. XIV:** 143
Juno and the Paycock (O'Casey), **Supp. IV Part 1:** 361
"Jupiter Doke, Brigadier General" (Bierce), **I:** 204
Jupiter Laughs (A. Cronin), **Supp. XVII:** 59
Jurgen (Cabell), **III:** 394; **IV:** 286; **Retro. Supp. I:** 80; **Supp. I Part 2:** 718
Jury of Her Peers, A: American Women Writers from Anne Bradstreet to Annie Proulx (Showalter), **Supp. XX: 274**
Jusserand, Jules, **II:** 338
Just above My Head (Baldwin), **Retro. Supp. II:** 14–15
"Just a Little One" (Parker), **Supp. IX:** 191
Just and the Unjust, The (Cozzens), **I:** 367–370, 372, 375, 377, 378, 379
Just an Ordinary Day (Jackson), **Supp. IX:** 120
Just Before Dark: Collected Nonfiction (Harrison), **Supp. VIII:** 41, 45, 46, 53
"Just Before the War with the Eskimos" (Salinger), **III:** 559
"Just Boys" (Farrell), **II:** 45
"Just for the Thrill: An Essay on the Difference Between Women and Men" (Carson), **Supp. XII: 103–104**
"Justice" (Hughes), **Supp. I Part 1:** 331
"Justice, A" (Faulkner), **Retro. Supp. I:** 83
Justice, Donald, **Retro. Supp. I:** 313; **Supp. III Part 2:** 541; **Supp. V:** 180, 337, 338, 341; **Supp. VII: 115–130;** **Supp. XI:** 141, 315; **Supp. XIII:** 76, 312; **Supp. XV:** 74, 93, 118, 119, 134; **Supp. XVII:** 110, 120, 246; **Supp. XX: 199; Supp. XXIV:** 165
Justice and Expediency (Whittier), **Supp. I Part 2:** 686
"Justice Denied in Massachusetts" (Millay), **III:** 140
Justice for Salcido (Endore), **Supp. XVII:** 63
Justice of Gold in the Damnation of Sinners, The (Edwards), **I:** 559
"Justice to Feminism" (Ozick), **Supp. V:** 272
"Just Introduced" (Taggard), **Supp. XXII:** 274
Just Kids (Smith), **Supp. XXII:** 94
"Just Like a Woman" (Dylan), **Supp. XV:** 350

"Just Like Job" (Angelou), **Supp. IV Part 1:** 15
"Just One of the Boys" (Swados), **Supp. XIX:** 259
Just Whistle: A Valentine (Wright), **Supp. XV: 346–348**
Just Wild About Harry (H. Miller), **III:** 190
Juvenal, **II:** 8, 169, 552

K

K (Rinehart), **Supp. XXV:** 193–194, 200
"K, The" (Olson), **Supp. II Part 2:** 558, 563, 569
Kabir, **Supp. IV Part 1:** 74
"Kabnis" (Toomer), **Supp. III Part 2:** 481, 484; **Supp. IX:** 309, 310, **319–320**
Kachel, Elsie. *See* Stevens, Mrs. Wallace (Elsie Kachel)
"Kaddish" (Ginsberg), **Supp. II Part 1:** 319, 327
Kaddish and Other Poems, 1958–1960 (Ginsberg), **Supp. II Part 1:** 309, 319–320; **Supp. XIV:** 269
Kael, Pauline, **Supp. IX:** 253; **Supp. XV:** 147, 148
Kafka, Franz, **II:** 244, 565, 569; **III:** 51, 253, 418, 566, 572; **IV:** 2, 113, 218, 437–439, 442; **Retro. Supp. II:** 20, 221, 282; **Supp. I Part 1:** 197; **Supp. III Part 1:** 105; **Supp. III Part 2:** 413; **Supp. IV Part 1:** 379; **Supp. IV Part 2:** 623; **Supp. VIII:** 14, 15, 103; **Supp. XII:** 21, 37, 98, 168; **Supp. XIII:** 305; **Supp. XVI:** 17, 201, 206, 209; **Supp. XVII:** 244; **Supp. XX: 18, 21, 85, 87; Supp. XXII:** 89, 90, 94; **Supp. XXIII:** 68
Kafka Americana (Lethem and Scholtz), **Supp. XVIII:** 144–145
Kaganoff, Penny, **Supp. XI:** 122
Kagan's Superfecta (A. Hoffman), **Supp. XVII:** 42
Kahane, Jack, **III:** 171, 178
Kahn, Otto, **I:** 385; **IV:** 123; **Retro. Supp. II:** 81, 84, 85; **Supp. XX: 75**
Kahn, R. T., **Supp. XI:** 216
"Kai, Today" (Snyder), **Supp. VIII:** 300
Kaiser, Georg, **I:** 479
Kaiser, Henry, **Supp. I Part 2:** 644
Kakutani, Michiko, **Supp. IV Part 1:** 196, 201, 205, 211, 212; **Supp. V:** 63; **Supp. VIII:** 81, 84, 86, 88, 141; **Supp. X:** 171, 301, 302, 310, 314; **Supp. XI:** 38, 179; **Supp. XII:** 165, 171, 172, 299; **Supp. XVI:** 71; **Supp. XVII:** 6; **Supp. XIX:** 142; **Supp. XX: 92, 94; Supp. XXII:** 109
Kalem, T. E., **Supp. IV Part 2:** 585
Kalevala (Finnish epic), **II:** 503, 504; **Retro. Supp. II:** 155
Kalevala (Lönnrot), **Retro. Supp. II:** 159, 160
Kalfus, Ken, **Supp. XVII:** 50
Kalki: A Novel (Vidal), **Supp. IV Part 2:** 677, 682, 685, 691, 692
Kallan, Richard A., **Supp. XX: 244**

Kallen, Horace, **I:** 229; **Supp. I Part 2:** 643; **Supp. XIV:** 195, 197, 198
Kallman, Chester, **II:** 586; **Supp. II Part 1:** 15, 17, 24, 26
"Kallundborg Church" (Whittier), **Supp. I Part 2:** 696
Kalstone, David, **Retro. Supp. II:** 40
Kamel, Rose, **Supp. XIII:** 306
Kamenev, Lev, **Supp. XXI:** 167
Kamera Obskura (Nabokov), **III:** 255
Kamhi, Michelle Moarder, **Supp. IV Part 2:** 529, 530
Kaminsky, Wally, **Supp. XVIII:** 72
Kamp, David, **Supp. XVIII:** 150
Kandy-Kolored Tangerine-Flake Streamline Baby, The (Wolfe), **Supp. III Part 2:** 569, 573–576, 580, 581
Kane, Daniel, **Supp. XXIV:** 37
Kane, Julie, **Supp. XVII:** 78
Kane, Lesley, **Supp. XIV:** 250
Kanellos, Nicolás, **Supp. VIII:** 82; **Supp. XIII:** 213
Kanin, Garson, **Supp. IV Part 2:** 574
"Kansas City Coyote" (Harjo), **Supp. XII:** 219, 222
"Kansas Emigrants, The" (Whittier), **Supp. I Part 2:** 687
Kant, Immanuel, **I:** 61, 277, 278; **II:** 10–11, 362, 480, 580–581, 582, 583; **III:** 300, 480, 481, 488, 612; **IV:** 90; **Supp. I Part 2:** 640; **Supp. IV Part 2:** 527; **Supp. XIV:** 198, 199; **Supp. XVI:** 184
Kanter, Hal, **IV:** 383
Kapital, Das (Marx), **III:** 580; **Supp. XXI:** 161, 162, 163
Kaplan, Abraham, **I:** 277
Kaplan, Justin, **I:** 247–248; **Retro. Supp. I:** 392
Kaplan, Mary Jo, **Supp. XIX:** 266
Kaplan, Steven, **Supp. V:** 238, 241, 243, 248
Karate Is a Thing of the Spirit (Crews), **Supp. XI: 112–113**
Karbo, Karen, **Supp. X:** 259, 262
"Karintha" (Toomer), **Supp. IX:** 311
Karl, Frederick R., **Supp. IV Part 1:** 384; **Supp. XXI:** 234
"Karloff and the Rock" (Di Piero), **Supp. XIX:** 44
Karl Shapiro's America (film), **Supp. II Part 2:** 703
Karmi, T., **Supp. XV:** 78, 88
Karr, Mary, **Supp. XI: 239–256; Supp. XIII:** 285; **Supp. XV:** 223; **Supp. XVI:** 63, 70, 77; **Supp. XVII:** 242
Karyotakis, Konstantine, **Supp. XXIII:** 125
Kasabian, Linda, **Supp. IV Part 1:** 206
Kasper, Catherine, **Supp. XVI:** 294–295
Kate Chopin (Toth), **Retro. Supp. II:** 71
Kate Chopin: A Critical Biography (Seyersted), **Retro. Supp. II:** 65; **Supp. I Part 1:** 225
Kate Chopin and Edith Wharton: An Annotated Bibliographical Guide to Secondary Sources (Springer), **Supp. I Part 1:** 225
Kate Chopin and Her Creole Stories (Rankin), **Retro. Supp. II:** 57; **Supp.**

I Part 1: 200, 225
"Kate Chopin's *The Awakening* in the Perspective of Her Literary Career" (Arms), **Supp. I Part 1:** 225
Kate Vaiden (Price), **Supp. VI:** 264, 265
"Käthe Kollwitz" (Rukeyser), **Supp. VI:** 283, 284
Katherine and Jean (Rice), **Supp. VII:** 288
"Kathleen" (Whittier), **Supp. I Part 2:** 693
Kathleen and Frank: The Autobiography of a Family (Isherwood), **Supp. XIV:** 158, 171
Kathy Goes to Haiti (Acker), **Supp. XII:** 5
Katz, Alan, **Supp. XXII:** 177
Katz, Alex, **Supp. XV:** 185
Katz, Jonathan, **Supp. XII:** 179
Katz, Steve, **Supp. V:** 44
Katz, Steven T., **Supp. XVI:** 154
Katzenberg, Jffrey, **Supp. XXI:** 154
Kauffman, Carol, **Supp. XI:** 295
Kauffmann, Stanley, **III:** 452; **Supp. I Part 2:** 391; **Supp. XVI:** 74
Kaufman, Boris, **Supp. XVIII:** 251
Kaufman, Charlie, **Supp. XV:** 16
Kaufman, Ellen, **Supp. XXIII:** 132, 133
Kaufman, George S., **II:** 427, 435, 437; **III:** 62, 71–72, 394; **Retro. Supp. II:** 327; **Supp. IV Part 2:** 574; **Supp. IX:** 190; **Supp. XV:** 329
Kaufmann, James, **Supp. XI:** 39
Kaufmann, Walter, **Supp. XVII:** 137
Kauvar, Elaine M., **Supp. V:** 273
Kavanaugh (Longfellow), **I:** 458; **II:** 489, 491; **Retro. Supp. II:** 156; **Supp. I Part 2:** 420
Kaveney, Roz, **Supp. XI:** 39
Kawabata, Yasunari, **Supp. XV:** 186; **Supp. XXI:** 146
Kay Boyle: Artist and Activist (Spanier), **Supp. XXIV:** 64
Kay Boyle: Author of Herself (Mellen), **Supp. XXIV:** 64
Kay Boyle for the Twenty-First Century (Austenfeld, ed.), **Supp. XXIV:** 64
Kaye-Smith, Sheila, **Supp. XVIII:** 130–131
Kazan, Elia, **III:** 153, 163; **IV:** 383; **Supp. I Part 1:** 66, 295; **Supp. XVI:** 193; **Supp. XVIII:** 250–251, 252; **Supp. XXV:** 95, 102
Kazin, Alfred, **I:** 248, 417, 419, 517; **II:** 177, 459; **IV:** 236; **Retro. Supp. II:** 206, 243, 246, 286; **Supp. I Part 1:** 195, 196, 294, 295, 296; **Supp. I Part 2:** 536, 631, 647, 650, 678, 679, 719; **Supp. II Part 1:** 143; **Supp. IV Part 1:** 200, 382; **Supp. V:** 122; **Supp. VIII: 93–111; Supp. IX:** 3, 227; **Supp. XIII:** 98, 106; **Supp. XIV:** 11; **Supp. XV:** 142; **Supp. XXIII:** 2, 106; **Supp. XXIV:** 222
Keach, Stacey, **Supp. XI:** 309
Kean, Danuta, **Supp. XXI:** 80
Keane, Sarah, **Supp. I Part 1:** 100
Kearns, Cleo McNelly, **Retro. Supp. I:** 57
Kearns, George, **Retro. Supp. I:** 292

Keating, AnnLouise, **Supp. IV Part 1:** 330
Keaton, Buster, **I:** 31; **Supp. I Part 2:** 607; **Supp. IV Part 2:** 574
Keaton, Diane, **Supp. XV:** 5
Keats, John, **I:** 34, 103, 284, 314, 317–318, 385, 401, 448; **II:** 82, 88, 97, 214, 368, 512, 516, 530–531, 540, 593; **III:** 4, 10, 45, 122, 133–134, 179, 214, 237, 272, 275, 469, 485, 523; **IV:** 360, 405, 416; **Retro. Supp. I:** 91, 301, 313, 360, 395, 412; **Supp. I Part 1:** 82, 183, 266, 267, 312, 349, 362, 363, 365; **Supp. I Part 2:** 410, 422, 424, 539, 552, 675, 719, 720; **Supp. III Part 1:** 73; **Supp. IV Part 1:** 123, 168, 325; **Supp. IV Part 2:** 455; **Supp. VIII:** 41, 273; **Supp. IX:** 38, 39, 45; **Supp. XI:** 43, 320; **Supp. XII:** 9, 113, 255; **Supp. XIII:** 131, 281; **Supp. XIV:** 274; **Supp. XV:** 92; **Supp. XVII:** 76, 112; **Supp. XIX:** 33, 276; **Supp. XX: 115, 116; Supp. XXI:** 131; **Supp. XXIV:** 159
Keats, John (other), **Supp. IX:** 190, 195, 200
Keegan, Abigail, **Supp. XXIII:** 129, 130, 136
"Keela, the Outcast Indian Maiden" (Welty), **IV:** 263
Keeley, Mary Paxton, **Supp. XV:** 136
"Keen Scalpel on Racial Ills" (Bruell), **Supp. VIII:** 126
Keep, The (Egan), **Supp. XIX:** 49, **56–61**
"Keep A-Inchin' Along" (Van Vechten), *Supp. III Part 2:* 744
Keeping (Goldbarth), **Supp. XII:** 179–180, 180
"Keeping Informed in D.C." (Nemerov), **III:** 287
Keeping Slug Woman Alive: A Holistic Approach to American Indian Texts (Sarris), **Supp. IV Part 1:** 329
"'Keeping Their World Large'" (Moore), **III:** 201–202
Keeping the Night (Everwine), **Supp. XV:** 75, **81–85**, 86
"Keeping Things Whole" (Strand), **Supp. IV Part 2:** 624
Keep It Simple: A Defense of the Earth (Nichols), **Supp. XIII:** 268
"Keep the Saving Habit" (L. I. Wilder), **Supp. XXII:** 290
"Keep Your Pity" (Boyle), **Supp. XXIV:** 58, 59
Kees, Weldon, **Supp. X:** 118; **Supp. XII:** 198; **Supp. XV:** 113, 114, 115, **133–149**
Keillor, Garrison, **Supp. XII:** 343; **Supp. XIII:** 274; **Supp. XVI: 165–179; Supp. XXI:** 53, 62; **Supp. XXII:** 83; **Supp. XXIII:** 57, 58, 138
Keillor, Gary Edward. *See* Keiller, Garrison
Keith, Brian, **Supp. IV Part 2:** 474
Keith, Minor C., **I:** 483
Kelleghan, Fiona, **Supp. XVIII:** 136, 139, 140
Keller, A. G., **III:** 108

Keller, Christopher J., **Supp. XVIII:** 192, 195
Keller, Helen, **I:** 254, 258; **Supp. XXIII:** 161
Keller, Lynn, **Supp. IV Part 2:** 423; **Supp. V:** 78, 80
Kelley, David, **Supp. IV Part 2:** 528, 529
Kelley, Florence, **Supp. I Part 1:** 5, 7
Kelley, Mary, **Supp. XVIII:** 257, 260
Kelley, Robin, **Supp. XVIII:** 231
Kellogg, Reverend Edwin H., **III:** 200
Kellogg, Paul U., **Supp. I Part 1:** 5, 7, 12
Kelly, **II:** 464
Kelly, Brigit Pegeen, **Supp. XVII: 123–134; Supp. XXIII:** 54
Kelly, Emmett, **Supp. XI:** 99, 106
Kelly, Gene, **Supp. XXI:** 148
Kelly, James Patrick, **Supp. XVIII:** 145; **Supp. XIX:** 231
Kelly, Walt, **Supp. XI:** 105
Kelly, William, **Supp. XV:** 75, 88
Kelsey, Penelope Myrtle, **Supp. XXIII:** 143, 153–164
Kelsh, Nick, **Supp. XVII:** 167, 179
Kemble, Fanny, **Retro. Supp. I:** 228
Kemble, Gouverneur, **II:** 298
Kemble, Peter, **II:** 298
Kempton, Murray, **Supp. VIII:** 104
Kempton-Wace Letters, The (London and Strunsky), **II:** 465
Kennan, George F., **Supp. VIII:** 241
Kennedy, Albert J., **Supp. I Part 1:** 19
Kennedy, Arthur, **III:** 153
Kennedy, Burt, **Supp. IV Part 1:** 236
Kennedy, Jeffery, **Supp. XXI:** 6; **Supp. XXV:** 20
Kennedy, J. Gerald, **Retro. Supp. II:** 271
Kennedy, John F., **I:** 136, 170; **II:** 49, 152–153; **III:** 38, 41, 42, 234, 411, 415, 581; **IV:** 229; **Supp. I Part 1:** 291; **Supp. I Part 2:** 496; **Supp. VIII:** 98, 104, 203; **Supp. XII:** 132
Kennedy, Mrs. John F., **I:** 136
Kennedy, John Pendleton, **II:** 313; **Supp. XXII:** 193
Kennedy, Robert, **Supp. V:** 291
Kennedy, Robert F., **I:** 294; **Supp. I Part 1:** 52; **Supp. XI:** 343
Kennedy, Sarah, **Supp. XVIII:** 293, 299, 301
Kennedy, William, **Supp. VII: 131–157; Supp. XVII:** 135; **Supp. XIX:** 141; **Supp. XX: 90; Supp. XXIV:** 281, 282, 283
Kennedy, X. J., **Supp. V:** 178, 182; **Supp. XV:** 113, **151–173**
Kenner, Hugh, **III:** 475, 478; **IV:** 412; **Supp. I Part 1:** 255; **Supp. IV Part 2:** 474; **Supp. XV:** 147; **Supp. XXI:** 235
Kenneth Koch, a Tragedy (O'Hara and Rivers), **Supp. XXIII:** 217
"Kenneth Koch's 'Serious Moment'" (Spurr), **Supp. XV:** 183
Kenneth Millar/Ross Macdonald: A Checklist (Bruccoli), **Supp. IV Part 2:** 464, 469, 471
Kenney, Michael, **Supp. XIX:** 51, 52–53
Kenney, Susan, **Supp. XVIII:** 288, 289

Kenny, Maurice, **Supp. IV Part 2:** 502; **Supp. XXIII: 143–159**
Kent, George, **Supp. IV Part 1:** 11
Kent, Rockwell, **Supp. XV:** 41; **Supp. XXII:** 281
Kenton, Edna, **Supp. XXI:** 6; **Supp. XXV:** 21
Kenton, Maxwell. *See* Burnett, David; Hoffenberg, Mason; Southern, Terry
"Kent State, May 1970" (Haines), **Supp. XII:** 211
"Kentucky Derby Is Decadent and Depraved, The" (Thompson), **Supp. XXIV:** 282, **287–288**
Kentucky Straight (Offutt), **Supp. XIX: 163–167,** 171, 172
Kenya, the Land of Conflict (Kenyatta), **Supp. XXI:** 166
Kenyatta, Jomo, **Supp. X:** 135; **Supp. XXI:** 166
Kenyon, Jane, **Supp. VII: 159–177; Supp. VIII:** 272
Keogh, Tom, **Supp. XVI:** 230
Kepler, Johannes, **III:** 484; **IV:** 18
Keplinger, David, **Supp. XIX:** 273
Keppel, Frederick P., **I:** 214
"Kéramos" (Longfellow), **II:** 494; **Retro. Supp. II:** 167, 169
Kéramos and Other Poems (Longfellow), **II:** 490
Kerber, Linda K., **Supp. XXV:** 44
Kercheval, Jesse Lee, **Supp. XIX:** 51
Kerim, Ussin, **Supp. IX:** 152
Kermode, Frank, **IV:** 133; **Retro. Supp. I:** 301
Kern, Jerome, **II:** 427
Kerouac, Jack, **III:** 174; **Retro. Supp. I:** 102; **Supp. II Part 1:** 31, 307, 309, 318, 328; **Supp. III Part 1:** 91–94, 96, 100, **217–234; Supp. IV Part 1:** 90, 146; **Supp. V:** 336; **Supp. VIII:** 42, 138, 289, 305; **Supp. IX:** 246; **Supp. XII:** 118, 121, 122, 123, 126, 131, 132; **Supp. XIII:** 275, 284; **Supp. XIV:** 137, 138, 141, 142, 143–144; **Supp. XV:** 134, 221; **Supp. XVI:** 123; **Supp. XVII:** 135, 138; **Supp. XX:** 17; **Supp. XXIII:** 100, 213; **Supp. XXIV:** 34, 44; **Supp. XXV:** 29
Kerr, Deborah, **Supp. XI:** 307
Kerr, Orpheus C. (pseudonym). *See* Newell, Henry
Kerr, Walter, **Supp. IV Part 2:** 575, 579
Kerridge, Richard, **Supp. XVI:** 26
Kesey, Ken, **III:** 558; **Supp. III Part 1:** 217; **Supp. V:** 220, 295; **Supp. X:** 24, 265; **Supp. XI:** 104; **Supp. XXIII:** 100
Kessel, John, **Supp. XVIII:** 145; **Supp. XIX:** 231
Kessler, Milton, **Supp. XIX:** 195
Kesten, Stephen, **Supp. XI:** 309
Ketchum, Liza, **Supp. XIX:** 266
Ketchup (Shanley), **Supp. XIV:** 315
Kevane, Bridget, **Supp. XI:** 185, 190
"Key, The" (Welty), **IV:** 262
"Keys" (Nye), **Supp. XIII:** 281
"Key to the Highway" (Halliday), **Supp. XIX:** 84

Key to Uncle Tom's Cabin, A (Stowe), **Supp. I Part 2:** 580
Key West (H. Crane), **Retro. Supp. II:** 84
"Key West" (H. Crane), **I:** 400
Key West: An Island Sheaf (Crane), **I:** 385, 399–402
"Khalil the Heretic" (Gibran), **Supp. XX: 124**
Khrushchev, Nikita, **I:** 136
Kiang Kang-hu, **Supp. XV:** 45, 47
Kick for a Bite, A (Cobbett), **Supp. XV:** 237
"Kicking the Candles Out" (Jarman), **Supp. XVII:** 113
Kid, The (Aiken), **I:** 61
Kid, The (Chaplin), **I:** 386
Kidder, Tracy, **Supp. III Part 1:** 302; **Supp. XVIII:** 106, 114
Kiddush Ha-Shem: An Epic of 1648 (Asch), **Supp. XXIII:** 3, 6, **10,** 11, 12, 16
Kidesh ha-Shem (Sanctification of the name) (Asch), **Supp. XXIII:** 6
Kidman, Nicole, **Supp. X:** 80
"Kidnaper" (Gallagher), **Supp. XXIV:** 168, 174
"Kidnapping in the Family, A" (Fante), **Supp. XI:** 164
"Kid's Guide to Divorce, The" (Moore), **Supp. X:** 167, 172
Kidwell, Clara Sue, **Supp. IV Part 1:** 333
Kielsky, Vera Emuma, **Supp. V:** 273
Kiely, Brendan, **Supp. XVII:** 75
Kieran, John, **II:** 417
Kierkegaard, Søren Aabye, **II:** 229; **III:** 292, 305, 309, 572; **IV:** 438, 491; **Retro. Supp. I:** 326; **Retro. Supp. II:** 222; **Supp. V:** 9; **Supp. VIII:** 7–8; **Supp. XX: 132**
Kiernan, Robert F., **Supp. IV Part 2:** 684
Kieseritzky, L., **III:** 252
Kilgo, Jim, **Supp. XVIII:** 192
"Kilim" (McClatchy), **Supp. XII:** 258
Kilina, Patricia (pseudonym). *See* Warren, Patricia Nell
"Killed at Resaca" (Bierce), **I:** 202
"Killed at the Ford" (Longfellow), **Retro. Supp. II:** 170–171
Killens, John Oliver, **Supp. IV Part 1:** 8, 369
"Killer in the Rain" (Chandler), **Supp. IV Part 1:** 122
"Killers, The" (Hemingway), **II:** 249; **Retro. Supp. I:** 188, 189
Killers, The: A Narrative of Real Life in Philadelphia (Lippard), **Supp. XXIII:** 178, 184
Killing Mister Watson (Matthiessen), **Supp. V:** 212, 214
"Killing of a State Cop, The" (Ortiz), **Supp. IV Part 2:** 499
Killing of Sister George, The (Marcus), **Supp. I Part 1:** 277
Killing Orders (Paretsky), **Supp. XXV:** 176, 177, 179, 182–813
"Killings" (Dubus), **Supp. VII:** 85–86
"Killing the Ghost of Ripton" (Carruth), **Supp. XIX:** 1

"Killing the Plants" (Kenyon), **Supp. VII:** 167, 168
Kilmer, Joyce, **Supp. I Part 2:** 387; **Supp. XV:** 294
Kilpatrick, James K., **Supp. X:** 145
Kilvert, Francis, **Supp. VIII:** 172
Kim (Kipling), **Supp. X:** 230
Kim, Alfred, **Supp. XI:** 140
Kim, Sharon, **Supp. XVIII:** 267
Kimball, Frederic, **Supp. XXI:** 146
Kimball, J. Golden, **Supp. IV Part 2:** 602
Kimbrough, Mary Craig. *See* Sinclair, Mary Craig (Mary Craig Kimbrough)
Kimes, Maymie B., **Supp. IX:** 178
Kimes, William F., **Supp. IX:** 178
Kimmelman, Bert, **Supp. XXI:** 24
"Kin" (Welty), **IV:** 277; **Retro. Supp. I:** 353
Kinard, Agnes Dodds, **Supp. XIV:** 122, 123, 127
Kincaid, Jamaica, **Supp. VII: 179–196**
Kincaid, James, **Supp. XVIII:** 62, 63
"Kindness" (Dunn), **Supp. XI:** 149, 150
"Kindness" (Nye), **Supp. XIII:** 285
"Kindness" (Plath), **Retro. Supp. II:** 256
Kind of Light that Shines on Texas, The (McKnight), **Supp. XX: 151–152**
"Kind of Light that Shines on Texas, The" (McKnight), **Supp. XX:** 151
Kind of Order, A Kind of Folly, A: Essays and Conversations (Kunitz), **Supp. III Part 1:** 262, 268
Kindred (O. Butler), **Supp. XIII: 59–60,** 69
"Kind Sir: These Woods" (Sexton), **Supp. II Part 2:** 673
Kinds of Love (Sarton), **Supp. VIII: 253–254,** 256
Kinfolk (Buck), **Supp. II Part 1:** 126
King, Alexander, **IV:** 287
King, Carole, **Supp. XII:** 308
King, Clarence, **I:** 1
King, Ernest, **Supp. I Part 2:** 491
King, Fisher, **II:** 425
King, Francis, **Supp. XIV:** 155, 156, 166, 169
King, Grace, **Retro. Supp. II:** 136
King, Martin Luther, Jr., **Retro. Supp. II:** 12, 13; **Supp. XVIII:** 24; **Supp. XX:** 281
King, Michael, **Supp. XII:** 182
King, Queen, Knave (Nabokov), **III:** 251; **Retro. Supp. I:** 270
King, Starr, **Supp. II Part 1:** 341, 342
King, Stephen, **Supp. IV Part 1:** 102, 104; **Supp. IV Part 2:** 467; **Supp. V: 137–155; Supp. IX:** 114; **Supp. XIII:** 53; **Supp. XXIII:** 290; **Supp. XXV:** 123, 152, 153
King, Tabitha (Mrs. Stephen King), **Supp. V:** 137
King, The (Barthelme), **Supp. IV Part 1:** 47, 52
"King, The" (Gibran), **Supp. XX: 123–124**
King Coffin (Aiken), **I:** 53–54, 57
"King David" (Benét), **Supp. XI:** 44
"King David" (Reznikoff), **Supp. XIV:** 283

Kingdom and the Power, The (Talese), **Supp. XVII:** 202, 203, 204, 210

Kingdom by the Sea, The: A Journey around Great Britain (Theroux), **Supp. VIII:** 323

"Kingdom County Come" (Mosher), **Supp. XXII:** 211–212

Kingdom Far and Clear, A: The Complete Swan Lake Trilogy (Helprin), **Supp. XXV:** 87

Kingdom of Earth (T. Williams), **IV:** 382, 386, 387, 388, 391, 393, 398

"Kingdom of Earth, The" (T. Williams), **IV:** 384

Kingdom of Fear (Thompson), **Supp. XXIV:** 283

"Kingdom of God Is Within You, The" (Very), **Supp. XXV:** 249

Kingfisher, The (Clampitt), **Supp. IX:** 38

"Kingfishers, The" (Olson), **Supp. II Part 2:** 557, 558–563, 582

King Jasper (Robinson), **III:** 523

King Kong (film), **Supp. IV Part 1:** 104; **Supp. XVII:** 58

King Lear (Shakespeare), **I:** 538; **II:** 540, 551; **Retro. Supp. I:** 248; **Supp. IV Part 1:** 31, 36; **Supp. IX:** 14; **Supp. XI:** 172; **Supp. XV:** 349

King Leopold's Soliloquy (Twain), **IV:** 208

King My Father's Wreck, The (Simpson), **Supp. IX:** 266, 267, 270, 275, 276

King of Babylon Shall Not Come Against You, The (Garrett), **Supp. VII:** 110–111; **Supp. X:** 3

"King of Beasts" (P. N. Warren), **Supp. XX: 272**

"King of Folly Island, The" (Jewett), **II:** 394; **Retro. Supp. II:** 132, 133

King of Kings (film), **Supp. IV Part 2:** 520

King of Paris (Endore), **Supp. XVII:** 64

King of Spain, The (Bodenheim), **Supp. XXV:** 26

"King of the Bingo Game" (Ellison), **Retro. Supp. II:** 117, 125; **Supp. II Part 1:** 235, 238, 240–241

"King of the Cats, The" (Benét), **Supp. XI:** 49–50

"King of the Clock Tower" (Yeats), **III:** 473

"King of the Desert, The" (O'Hara), **III:** 369

King of the Fields, The (Singer), **Retro. Supp. II:** 317

King of the Jews (Epstein), **Supp. XII:** 161, **166–170,** 172

King of the Mountain (Garrett), **Supp. VII:** 96, 97

"King of the River" (Kunitz), **Supp. III Part 1:** 263, 267–268

"King of the Sea" (Marquand), **III:** 60

"King over the Water" (Blackmur), **Supp. II Part 1:** 107

"King Pandar" (Blackmur), **Supp. II Part 1:** 92, 102

"King Pest" (Poe), **Retro. Supp. II:** 273

Kingsblood Royal (Lewis), **II:** 456

Kingsbury, John, **Supp. I Part 1:** 8

"King's Daughters, Home for Unwed Mothers, 1948" (Stanford), **Supp. XV:** 345

King's Henchman, The (Millay), **III:** 138–139

Kingsley, Sidney, **Supp. I Part 1:** 277, 281

King's Mare, The (Canolle; Loos, trans.), **Supp. XVI:** 194

"King's Missive, The" (Whittier), **Supp. I Part 2:** 694

Kingsolver, Barbara, **Supp. VII: 197–214; Supp. XIII:** 16; **Supp. XVIII:** 189

King's Stilts, The (Geisel), **Supp. XVI:** 100, 104

Kingston, Earll, **Supp. V:** 160

Kingston, Maxine Hong, **Supp. IV Part 1:** 1, 12; **Supp. V: 157–175,** 250; **Supp. X:** 291–292; **Supp. XI:** 18, 245; **Supp. XV:** 220, 223

"King Volmer and Elsie" (Whittier), **Supp. I Part 2:** 696

Kinkaid, Jamaica, **Supp. XXII:** 65

Kinmont, Alexander, **Supp. I Part 2:** 588–589

Kinnaird, John, **Retro. Supp. I:** 399

Kinnell, Galway, **Supp. III Part 1: 235–256; Supp. III Part 2:** 541; **Supp. IV Part 2:** 623; **Supp. V:** 332; **Supp. VIII:** 39; **Supp. XI:** 139; **Supp. XII:** 241; **Supp. XV:** 212; **Supp. XVI:** 53; **Supp. XXII:** 83

Kinsella, Thomas, **Supp. XX: 195–196,** 197, 207

Kinsey, Alfred, **IV:** 230; **Supp. XIV:** 140

Kinzie, Mary, **Supp. XII:** 181; **Supp. XXIII:** 124

"Kipling" (Trilling), **Supp. III Part 2:** 495

Kipling, Rudyard, **I:** 421, 587–588; **II:** 271, 338, 404, 439; **III:** 55, 328, 508, 511, 521, 524, 579; **IV:** 429; **Supp. IV Part 2:** 603; **Supp. X:** 255; **Supp. XX: 23**

Kirby, David, **Supp. XIII:** 89; **Supp. XIX:** 81

Kirkland, Caroline, **Supp. XVIII:** 258

Kirkland, David, **Supp. XVI:** 186

Kirkland, Jack, **I:** 297

Kirkland, John, **Supp. XXIV:** 70

Kirkpatrick, Jeane, **Supp. VIII:** 241

Kirkus, Virginia, **Supp. XV:** 198

Kirkwood, Cynthia A., **Supp. XI:** 177, 178, 179

Kirp, David L., **Supp. XI:** 129

Kirsch, Adam, **Supp. XV:** 251, 260, 264, 266, 341, 347, 350–351; **Supp. XXV:** 222, 233, 253, 262, 268

Kirstein, Lincoln, **Supp. II Part 1:** 90, 97; **Supp. IV Part 1:** 82, 83; **Supp. XXII:** 281

Kishef-makherin fun Kastilye, Di (The witch of Castle) (Asch), **Supp. XXIII:** 6

"Kiss, The" (Di Piero), **Supp. XIX:** 45, 47

Kiss, The (Harrison), **Supp. X:** 191

"Kiss, The" (Sexton), **Supp. II Part 2:** 687

"Kiss Away" (C. Baxter), **Supp. XVII:** 20

Kissel, Howard, **Supp. IV Part 2:** 580

Kiss Hollywood Good-by (Loos), **Supp. XVI:** 190, 195

Kissinger, Henry, **Supp. IV Part 1:** 388; **Supp. XII:** 9, 14; **Supp. XXV:** 264

Kiss of the Spider Woman, the Musical (McNally), **Supp. XIII:** 207, **Supp. XIII:** 208

Kiss Tomorrow Good-bye (McCoy), **Supp. XIII:** 170, **172–173,** 174

"Kit and Caboodle" (Komunyakaa), **Supp. XIII:** 115

Kit Brandon: A Portrait (Anderson), **I:** 111

Kitchen, Judith, **Supp. IV Part 1:** 242, 245, 252; **Supp. IX:** 163; **Supp. XI:** 312, 313, 315, 317, 319, 320, 326, 329; **Supp. XV:** 215, 219

"Kitchenette" (Brooks), **Retro. Supp. I:** 208

Kitchen God's Wife, The (Tan), **Supp. X:** 289, 292, 293, 294–295, 296–297, 298–299

"Kitchen Terrarium: 1983" (McCarriston), **Supp. XIV:** 270

Kit O'Brien (Masters), **Supp. I Part 2:** 471

Kittel, Frederick August. *See* Wilson, August

Kittredge, Charmian. *See* London, Mrs. Jack (Charmian Kittredge)

Kittredge, William, **Supp. VIII:** 39; **Supp. XI:** 316; **Supp. XII:** 209; **Supp. XIII:** 16

"Kitty Hawk" (Frost), **II:** 164; **Retro. Supp. I:** 124, 141

Kizer, Carolyn, **Supp. XVII:** 71, 72, 73, 74

Klaidman, Stephen, **Supp. XIX:** 269

Klail City (Hinojosa), **Supp. XIX:** 97, **101–103**

Klail City Death Trip (Hinojosa). *See Ask a Policeman* (Hinojosa); *Becky and Her Friends* (Hinojosa); *Dear Rafe* (Hinojosa); *Fair Gentlemen of Belken County* (Hinojosa); *Klail City* (Hinojosa); *Korean Love Songs from Klail City Death Trip* (Hinojosa); *Partners in Crime: A Rafe Buenrostro Mystery* (Hinojosa); *Rites and Witnesses: A Comedy* (Hinojosa); *Useless Servants, The* (Hinojosa); *Valley, The* (Hinojosa)

"Klassikal Lymnaeryx" (Stallings), **Supp. XXV:** 233

Klein, Joe, **Supp. XII:** 67–68

Klein, Marcus, **Supp. I Part 2:** 432; **Supp. XI:** 233

Kleist, Heinrich von, **Supp. IV Part 1:** 224

Kline, Franz, **Supp. XII:** 198; **Supp. XXIII:** 210, 211, 217

Kline, George, **Supp. VIII:** 22, 28

Klinghoffer, David, **Supp. XVI:** 74

Klinkowitz, Jerome, **Supp. IV Part 1:** 40; **Supp. X:** 263; **Supp. XI:** 347; **Supp. XXI:** 233

Klise, James, **Supp. XXII:** 53

Kloefkorn, Bill, **Supp. XIX:** 119
Knapp, Adeline, **Supp. XI:** 200
Knapp, Friedrich, **III:** 100
Knapp, Samuel, **I:** 336
Knapp, Samuel Lorenzo, **Supp. XV:** 246
"Kneeling Down to Look into a Culvert" (R. Bly), **Supp. XXI:** 88
Kneel to the Rising Sun (Caldwell), **I:** 304, 309
"Knees/Dura-Europos" (Goldbarth), **Supp. XII:** 185
"Knife" (Simic), **Supp. VIII:** 275
Knight, Arthur, **Supp. XIV:** 144
Knight, Etheridge, **Supp. XI:** 239; **Supp. XXIII:** 174
Knight, Lania, **Supp. XXIII:** 273, 274, 275, 276, 279, 280
"Knight in Disguise, The" (Lindsay), **Supp. I Part 2:** 390
Knightly Quest, The (T. Williams), **IV:** 383
Knight's Gambit (Faulkner), **II:** 72
Knish, Anne. *See* Ficke, Arthur Davison
"Knit One, Purl Two" (K. Snodgrass), **Supp. XVI:** 42
"Knock" (Dickey), **Supp. IV Part 1:** 182
Knocked Out Loaded (album, Dylan), **Supp. XVIII:** 28
"Knocking Around" (Ashbery), **Supp. III Part 1:** 22
"Knocking on Heaven's Door" (Lamott), **Supp. XX:** 140–141
"Knocking on Three, Winston" (Epstein), **Supp. XIV:** 109
Knock on Any Door (film, Ray), **Supp. XVII:** 150
Knock on Any Door (W. Motley), **Supp. XVII: 150–155**, 159, 160; 158
Knockout Artist, The (Crews), **Supp. XI: 113–114**
Knoll, Robert E., **Supp. XV:** 118
Knopf, Alfred A., **III:** 99, 105, 106, 107; **Retro. Supp. I:** 13, 19, 317; **Supp. I Part 1:** 324, 325, 327; **Supp. IV Part 1:** 125, 354; **Supp. XIII:** 172
Knopf, Blanche, **Supp. I Part 1:** 324, 325, 327, 328, 332, 341; **Supp. IV Part 1:** 128, 346, 348; **Supp. XIII:** 169
"Knot, The" (Rich), **Supp. I Part 2:** 555
Knot-Holes (Bodenheim and Saphier), **Supp. XXV:** 20
Knotts, Kristina, **Supp. XIII:** 238
"Knowing, The" (Olds), **Supp. X:** 215
"Knowledge Forwards and Backwards" (Stern), **Supp. IX:** 296
"Knowledge of Plates" (Bronk), **Supp. XXI:** 33
Knowles, John, **Supp. IV Part 2:** 679; **Supp. XII: 235–250; Supp. XX:** 84
Known World, The (E. P. Jones), **Supp. XXII:** 139, 140, 142, **146–150**, 150
Knox, Bernard, **Supp. XXIV:** 153
Knox, Frank, **Supp. I Part 2:** 488, 489
Knox, Israel, **Supp. X:** 70
Knox, Vicesimus, **II:** 8
Knoxville: Summer of 1915 (Agee), **I:** 42–46
Knudson, R. Rozanne, **Supp. IV Part 2:** 648

Kober, Arthur, **Supp. I Part 1:** 292
Koch, Frederick, **IV:** 453
Koch, John, **Supp. VIII:** 88
Koch, Kenneth, **Supp. XV: 175–192; Supp. XIX:** 81; **Supp. XXIII:** 124, 207, 209, 210, 211, 215, 217, 220; **Supp. XXIV:** 33, 36, 42, 44
Koch, Vivienne, **III:** 194; **IV:** 136, 140; **Retro. Supp. I:** 428, 430
"Kochinnenako in Academe: Three Approaches to Interpreting a Keres Indian Tale" (Gunn Allen), **Supp. IV Part 1:** 329
"Kodachromes of the Island" (Hayden), **Supp. II Part 1:** 367, 380
Koestler, Arthur, **I:** 258; **Supp. I Part 2:** 671; **Supp. XXIII:** 1
Kokkinen, Eila, **Supp. XIV:** 146, 148
"Kola Street"(Asch), **Supp. XXIII:** 7
Kolba, Ellen D., **Supp. XVIII:** 257
Kolbenheyer, Dr. Frederick, **Supp. I Part 1:** 207
Kolodny, Annette, **Supp. X:** 97, 103, 229
Komisarjevsky, W. P., **Supp. XXIII:** 5
"Komodo" (C. Frost), **Supp. XV:** 95
Komunyakaa, Yusef, **Supp. XIII: 111–136; Supp. XXI:** 129, 139; **Supp. XXIII:** 254
Konigsberg, Allan Stewart. *See* Allen, Woody
Kon-Tiki (Heyerdahl), **II:** 477
Koopman, Harry Lyman, **Retro. Supp. I:** 40
Ko; or, A Season on Earth (Koch), **Supp. XV:** 175, 180, 181, 183, 186
Kooser, Ted, **Supp. XV:** 113, 115; **Supp. XIX: 115–130; Supp. XXI:** 243
Kootz, Samuel, **Supp. XV:** 144
Kora and Ka (Doolittle), **Supp. I Part 1:** 270
Kora in Hell (W. C. Williams), **Retro. Supp. I:** 416, **417–418,** 419, 430, 431; **Supp. XXI:** 232
Korb, Rena, **Supp. XI:** 2
Korczak, Janosz, **Supp. X:** 70
Korean Love Songs from Klail City Death Trip (Hinojosa), **Supp. XIX:** 98, **103–104**
Kornblatt, Joyce Reiser, **Supp. XV:** 62
Kornfield, Jack, **Supp. XX: 142; Supp. XXIII:** 138
Korrektur (Bernhard), **Supp. XX: 91**
Kort, Amy, **Supp. XIII:** 148
Korwin, Yala, **Supp. XXI:** 99
Kosinski, Jerzy, **Supp. VII: 215–228; Supp. XII:** 21
"Kostas Tympakianakis" (Merrill), **Supp. III Part 1:** 326
Koteliansky, S. S., **Supp. VIII:** 251, 265
Kouidis, Virginia M., **Supp. XXII:** 161, 162, 166, 167, 169
Kovic, Ron, **Supp. XIX:** 17; **Supp. XXII:** 104
Kowloon Tong (Theroux), **Supp. VIII:** 325
Kozlenko, William, **IV:** 378, 381
Krabbenhoft, Ken, **Supp. XVII:** 112
Kraft, James, **Supp. XV:** 40, 41, 42, 43, 52

Krakauer, Jon, **Supp. XVII:** 210; **Supp. XVIII: 105–118**
Kramer, Dale, **Supp. I Part 2:** 669
Kramer, Glenn Philip, **Supp. XXIII:** 125
Kramer, Hilton, **III:** 537; **Supp. I Part 1:** 295, 296; **Supp. VIII:** 239; **Supp. XV:** 113; **Supp. XIX:** 269
Kramer, Lawrence, **Supp. IV Part 1:** 61, 65, 66; **Supp. IX:** 291
Kramer, Peter D., **Supp. XVI:** 229
Kramer, Stanley, **II:** 421, 587
Krapp's Last Tape (Beckett), **I:** 71; **III:** 387; **Retro. Supp. I:** 206
Krassner, Paul, **Supp. IV Part 1:** 385; **Supp. XI:** 293
Kraus, Karl, **Supp. XX:** 84
Krauth, Leland, **Supp. XVIII:** 58
Kreisler, Harry, **Supp. XVI:** 155
Kreitman, Esther, **IV:** 2
Krementz, Jill, **Supp. XXV:** 263
"Kremlin of Smoke" (Schnackenberg), **Supp. XV:** 257–258
Kreymborg, Alfred, **II:** 530; **III:** 465; **IV:** 76; **Retro. Supp. I:** 417; **Supp. XV:** 301, 306; **Supp. XXII:** 161–162; **Supp. XXV:** 18, 19, 21
Kriegel, Leonard, **Supp. XXIV: 213–228**
Krim, Seymour, **Supp. XV:** 338; **Supp. XVI:** 217; **Supp. XVIII:** 285
Krisak, Len, **Supp. XXI:** 99, 104
Kristeva, Julia, **Supp. XII:** 6
Kristofferson, Kris, **Supp. XIII:** 119
Kristol, Irving, **Supp. VIII:** 93, 244; **Supp. XIII:** 98
Krivak, Andrew, **Supp. XVII:** 242
Kroll, Jack, **Supp. IV Part 2:** 590; **Supp. XXIII:** 103
Kroll, Judith, **Supp. I Part 2:** 541–543, 544, 546
Kroll Ring, Frances. *See* Ring, Frances Kroll
Krondorfer, Björn, **Supp. XVI:** 160
Kronenberger, Louis, **Supp. XXII:** 191, 192
Krook, Dorothea, **Retro. Supp. II:** 243
Kropotkin, Peter, **I:** 493; **Supp. I Part 1:** 5; **Supp. IV Part 2:** 521
Kruif, Paul de, **II:** 446
Krupat, Arnold, **Supp. IV Part 2:** 500
Krupnick, Mark, **Supp. XVI:** 153
Krutch, Joseph Wood, **II:** 459; **III:** 425; **IV:** 70, 175
Krutikov, Mikhail, **Supp. XXIII:** 11
Kublai Khan, **III:** 395
"Kubla Khan" (Coleridge), **Supp. XIII:** 131, 283
Kubrick, Stanley, **Supp. IV Part 1:** 392; **Supp. XI:** 293,**Supp. XI:** 301, 302–303
"Kubuku Rides (This Is It) " (L. Brown), **Supp. XXI:** 39, 42–43
Kuehl, John, **Supp. IV Part 1:** 279, 284, 285, 287
Kuehl, Linda, **Supp. IV Part 1:** 199
"Kugelmass Episode, The" (Allen), **Supp. XV:** 15, 16
Kukachin, Princess, **III:** 395
"Ku Klux" (Hughes), **Retro. Supp. I:** 205

Kulshrestha, Chirantan, **Retro. Supp. II:** 21

Kumin, Maxine, **Supp. IV Part 2: 439–457**; **Supp. XIII:** 294; **Supp. XVII:** 71, 75–76; **Supp. XX: 164**

Kundera, Milan, **Supp. VIII:** 241

Kunerth, Jeff, **Supp. XXI:** 47

Kunitz, Stanley, **I:** 179, 180, 181, 182, 521; **II:** 545; **Supp. III Part 1: 257–270**; **Supp. V:** 79; **Supp. XI:** 259; **Supp. XIII:** 341

Kuo, Helena, **Supp. X:** 291

Kuropatkin, General Aleksei Nikolaevich, **III:** 247–248

Kurth, Peter, **Supp. XVIII:** 145

Kurzy of the Sea (Barnes), **Supp. III Part 1:** 34

Kushner, Tony, **Supp. IX: 131–149**; **Supp. XX: 177**; **Supp. XXI: 145**; **Supp. XXIV:** 263

Kussy, Bella, **IV:** 468

Kutnik, Jerzy, **Supp. XXII:** 177

Kuttner, Henry, **Supp. IV Part 1:** 102

Kuzma, Greg, **Supp. XV:** 118

Kyger, Joanne, **Supp. XXIV:** 37

L

LaBastille, Anne, **Supp. X: 95–110**

"Labor's Cultural Degradation" (Swados), **Supp. XIX:** 264–265

"Labours of Hercules, The" (Moore), **III:** 201

La Bruyère, Jean de, **I:** 58

La Bufera e Altro (Montale), **Supp. V:** 337

LaBute, Neil, **Supp. XXI:** 147

Labyrinth of Love (Untermeyer), **Supp. XV:** 312

Labyrinth of Solitude, The (Paz), **Supp. XIII:** 223

Lacan, Jacques, **Supp. IV Part 1:** 45; **Supp. VIII:** 5; **Supp. XII:** 98

La Casa en Mango Street (Cisneros), **Supp. VII:** 58–59

Lacayo, Richard, **Supp. XXV:** 4

Lachaise, Gaston, **I:** 434

"Lackawanna" (Merwin), **Supp. III Part 1:** 350

Lackawanna Elegy (Goll; Kinnell, trans.), **Supp. III Part 1:** 235, 243–244

Laclède, Pierre, **Supp. I Part 1:** 205

"Lacquer Prints" (Lowell), **II:** 524–525

Lacy, Ed, **Supp. XV: 193–210**

Ladder, The (Rasmussen; Nelson, trans.), **Supp. XVIII:** 180–181

Ladder of Years (Tyler), **Supp. IV Part 2:** 657, 671–672

Ladders to Fire (Nin), **Supp. X:** 185

Laddie (Stratton-Porter), **Supp. XX: 211, 213**

"Laddie, the Princess and the Pie" (Stratton-Porter), **Supp. XX: 216**

"Ladies" (Coleman), **Supp. XI:** 93

Ladies Almanack (Barnes), **Supp. III Part 1:** 37–39, 42; **Supp. XXII:** 167

Ladies Auxiliary, The (Mirvis), **Supp. XX: 177, 179–185**

"Ladies in Spring" (Welty), **IV:** 276–277; **Retro. Supp. I:** 353

Lady, The (Richter), **Supp. XVIII: 211–212, 220**

Lady Audley's Secret (Braddon), **Supp. I Part 1:** 35, 36

"Lady Barberina" (James), **Retro. Supp. I:** 227

"Lady Bates" (Jarrell), **II:** 380–381

Lady Chatterley's Lover (Lawrence), **III:** 170; **IV:** 434; **Supp. XVI:** 267

Ladye Annabel (Lippard), **Supp. XXIII:** 178

Lady from Louisiana (film, Vorhaus), **Supp. XVII:** 59

"Lady from Redhorse, A" (Bierce), **I:** 203

Lady in Kicking Horse Reservoir, The (Hugo), **Supp. VI:** 134, **138–139**

Lady in the Lake, The (Chandler), **Supp. IV Part 1:** 127, 129–130

"Lady in the Lake, The" (Chandler), **Supp. IV Part 1:** 129

Lady in the Lake, The (film), **Supp. IV Part 1:** 130

"Lady in the Pink Mustang, The" (Erdrich), **Supp. IV Part 1:** 270

"Lady Is Civilized, The" (Taylor), **Supp. V:** 315

Lady Is Cold, The (White), **Supp. I Part 2:** 653

Lady Killer (Holding), **Supp. XXII:** 126, **127**, 130

"Lady Lazarus" (Plath), **Retro. Supp. II:** 250, 251, 255; **Supp. I Part 2:** 529, 535, 542, 545

Lady of Aroostook, The (Howells), **II:** 280

"Lady of Bayou St. John, A" (Chopin), **Retro. Supp. II:** 58

"Lady of the Lake, The" (Malamud), **Supp. I Part 2:** 437

Lady Oracle (Atwood), **Supp. XIII:** 21, **23–24**

"Lady Poverty" (Notley), **Supp. XXII:** 234–235

Lady Sings the Blues (film), **Supp. I Part 1:** 67

"Lady's Maid's Tale, The" (Wharton), **IV:** 316

"Lady Wentworth" (Longfellow), **II:** 505

"Lady with a Lamp" (Parker), **Supp. IX:** 193

"Lady with the Heron, The" (Merwin), **Supp. III Part 1:** 343

"Lady with the Pet Dog, The" (Chekov), **Supp. XXII:** 60

"Lady with the Pet Tribble, The" (Brockmeier), **Supp. XXII:** 60

La Farge, John, **I:** 1, 2, 20; **II:** 322, 338; **Retro. Supp. I:** 217

La Farge, Oliver, **Supp. IV Part 2:** 503

Lafayette, Marquis de, **I:** 344, 345; **II:** 405–406; **Supp. I Part 2:** 510, 511, 683

"La Figlia che Piange" (Eliot), **Retro. Supp. I:** 63

La Follette, Robert, **I:** 483, 485, 492; **III:** 580

La Fontaine, Jean de, **II:** 154; **III:** 194; **IV:** 80

Laforgue, Jules, **I:** 386, 569, 570, 572–573, 575, 576; **II:** 528; **III:** 8, 11, 466;

IV: 37, 79, 80, 122; **Retro. Supp. I:** 55, 56; **Supp. XIII:** 332, 335, 346; **Supp. XV:** 165

La Gallienne, Eva, **Supp. VIII:** 251

"Lager Beer" (Dunbar), **Supp. II Part 1:** 193

"La Gringuita: On Losing a Native Language" (Alvarez), **Supp. VII:** 18

Laguna Woman (Silko), **Supp. IV Part 2:** 557, 560–561

Lahiri, Jhumpa, **Supp. XXI: 175–189**; **Supp. XXIII:** 289

Lahr, John, **Supp. XXI:** 18

Laing, R. D., **Supp. I Part 2:** 527; **Supp. XX:** 94

La kabbale pratique (Ambelain), **Supp. I Part 1:** 273

"Lake, The" (Bradbury), **Supp. IV Part 1:** 101

Lake, The (play), **Supp. IX:** 189

Lakeboat (Mamet), **Supp. XIV:** 240–241

"Lake Chelan" (Stafford), **Supp. XI:** 321

Lake Effect Country (Ammons), **Supp. VII:** 34, 35

"Lake Isle of Innisfree, The" (Yeats), **Retro. Supp. I:** 413; **Supp. XIX:** 92

"Lake Return" (Wright), **Supp. XV:** 345

Lake Wobegon Days (Keillor), **Supp. XVI:** 165, 166, **173–174**

Lake Wobegon Summer 1956 (Keillor), **Supp. XVI:** 178

Lalic, Ivan V., **Supp. VIII:** 272

Lamantia, Philip, **Supp. VIII:** 289

Lamb, Brian, **Supp. XIX:** 156; **Supp. XX: 101**

Lamb, Charles, **III:** 111, 207; **Supp. VIII:** 125

Lamb, Wendy, **Supp. IV Part 2:** 658

Lambardi, Marilyn May, **Retro. Supp. II:** 45–46

Lamb in His Bosom (C. Miller), **Supp. XXII:** 187, **189–191**, 193–194, 195, 197, 198, 199, 200

"Lame Feet of Salvation, The" (W. V. Davis), **Supp. XXI:** 87–88

"Lament" (Wilbur), **Supp. III Part 2:** 550

Lament and Chastisement (O'Hara), **Supp. XXIII:** 209

"Lamentation in Winter"(Schott), **Supp. XXIII:** 243

"Lamentations" (Glück), **Supp. V:** 83, 84

"Lament for Dark Peoples" (Hughes), **Retro. Supp. I:** 199

"Lament for Saul and Jonathan" (Bradstreet), **Supp. I Part 1:** 111

"Lament-Heaven" (Doty), **Supp. XI:** 125

"Lament of a New England Mother, The" (Eberhart), **I:** 539

Laments for the Living (Parker), **Supp. IX:** 192

"Lame Shall Enter First, The" (O'Connor), **III:** 348, 351, 352, 355, 356–357, 358; **Retro. Supp. II:** 237

Lamia (Keats), **II:** 512; **III:** 523

Lamming, George, **Supp. XXI:** 170

Lamott, Anne, **Supp. XX: 131–146**

La Motte-Fouqué, Friedrich Heinrich Karl, **III:** 77, 78

L'Amour, Louis, **Supp. XIII:** 5

Lamp for Nightfall, A (Caldwell), **I:** 297
Lamplit Answer, The (Schnackenberg), **Supp. XV:** 251, 254, **256–260**
"Lana Turner Has Collapsed!"(O'Hara), **Supp. XXIII:** 220
"Lance" (Nabokov), **Retro. Supp. I:** 266
Lancelot (Percy), **Supp. III Part 1:** 384, 395–396
Lancelot (Robinson), **III:** 513, 522
Lanchester, John, **Retro. Supp. I:** 278
"Land" (Emerson), **II:** 6
"Land Aesthetic, The" (Callicott), **Supp. XIV:** 184
Land and Freedom (film, Loach), **Supp. XXIII:** 163
"Land and Language" (J. W. Miller), **Supp. XX:** 170
Landau, Deborah, **Supp. XI:** 122, 123
"Land beyond the Blow, The" (Bierce), **I:** 209
"Land Ethic, The" (Leopold), **Supp. XIV:** 179, 180, 183, 191, 192
Landfall (Wagoner), **Supp. IX:** 330
"Landing in Luck" (Faulkner), **Retro. Supp. I:** 85
"Landing on the Moon" (Swenson), **Supp. IV Part 2:** 643
"Landings" (Hoffman), **Supp. XVIII:** 86
"Landing Under Water, I See Roots" (A. Finch), **Supp. XVII:** 76
"Land"(Kenny), **Supp. XXIII:** 147
Landlord at Lion's Head, The (Howells), **II:** 276, 287–288
Landmarks of Healing: A Study of House Made of Dawn (Scarberry-García), **Supp. IV Part 2:** 486
Land of Little Rain, The (Dillard), **Supp. VI: 27–28**
Land of Look Behind, The (Cliff), **Supp. XXII:** 65–66, 68–69
Land of the Free U.S.A. (MacLeish), **I:** 293; **III:** 16–17
Land of Unlikeness (Lowell), **II:** 537–538, 539, 547; **Retro. Supp. II:** 177, 178, **184–185**
Landor, Walter Savage, **III:** 15, 469; **Supp. I Part 2:** 422
"Landscape" (Sarton), **Supp. VIII:** 259
"Landscape #11" (Halliday), **Supp. XIX:** 93
Landscape and Journey (W. V. Davis), **Supp. XXI:** 83, 88, 90, **92–93**, 95
"Landscape as a Nude" (MacLeish), **III:** 14
Landscape at the End of the Century (Dunn), **Supp. XI:** 139, 143, **150–151**
"Landscape Chamber, The" (Jewett), **II:** 408–409
"Landscape for the Disappeared" (Komunyakaa), **Supp. XIII:** 120, 126
Landscape in American Poetry (Larcom), **Supp. XIII:** 142
"Landscape Painter, A" (James), **II:** 322; **Retro. Supp. I:** 219
"Landscape Symbolism in Kate Chopin's *At Fault*" (Arner), **Retro. Supp. II:** 62
"Landscape: The Eastern Shore" (Barth), **I:** 122

"Landscape with Boat" (Stevens), **Retro. Supp. I:** 306
"Landscape with Bottles"(Schott), **Supp. XXIII:** 242
"Landscape with the Fall of Icarus" (Brueghel), **Retro. Supp. I:** 430
Land's End: A Walk through Provincetown (Cunningham), **Supp. XV:** 69
Land That Drank the Rain, The (Hoffman), **Supp. XVIII:** 76, 80, 81, 82
"Land Where There Is No Death, The" (Benét), **Supp. XI:** 56
Lane, Ann, **Supp. XI:** 195, 208
Lane, Cornelia. *See* Anderson, Mrs. Sherwood
Lane, Homer, **Supp. II Part 1:** 6; **Supp. XIV:** 160
Lane, John, **Supp. XXIV:** 22
Lane, Nathan, **Supp. XIII:** 207
Lane, Rose Wilder, **Supp. IV Part 2:** 524; **Supp. XXII:** 293–294, 295, 296, 297, 301
Lanes, Selma G., **Supp. XVI:** 104, 107
Lang, Andrew, **Retro. Supp. I:** 127
Lang, Violet, **Supp. XII:** 119
Lang, V. R. "Bunny", **Supp. XXIII:** 209
Langdon, Olivia. *See* Clemens, Mrs. Samuel Langhorne (Olivia Langdon)
Lange, Carl Georg, **II:** 350
Lange, Dorothea, **I:** 293; **Supp. XIV:** 181
Langland, Joseph, **III:** 542
Langston Hughes, American Poet (Walker), **Supp. III Part 2:** 530–531
Langston Hughes and the "Chicago Defender": Essays on Race, Politics, and Culture (De Santis, ed.), **Retro. Supp. I:** 194
Langston Hughes: Modern Critical Views (Bloom, ed.), **Retro. Supp. I:** 193
Langston Hughes Reader, The (Hughes), **Retro. Supp. I:** 202; **Supp. I Part 1:** 345
Langston Hughes: The Poet and His Critics (Barksdale), **Retro. Supp. I:** 202
"Language, Visualization and the Inner Library" (Shepard), **Supp. III Part 2:** 436, 438, 449
Language and Imagery of the Bible, The (Caird), **Supp. XXI:** 91–92
"Language and the Writer" (Bambara), **Supp. XI:** 18
Language As Gesture (Blackmur), **Supp. II Part 1:** 108
Language as Symbolic Action (Burke), **I:** 275, 282, 285
Language Book, The (Andrews and Bernstein), **Supp. IV Part 2:** 426
"Language Divine!"(J. Schoolcraft), **Supp. XXIII:** 225
Language God Talks, The: On Science and Religion (Wouk), **Supp. XXV:** 257, 267
Language in Thought and Action (Hayakawa), **I:** 448
"Language of Being and Dying, The" (Gass), **Supp. VI:** 91
"Language of Home, The" (Wideman), **Supp. X:** 320, 323–324

Language of Life, The (Moyers, television series), **Supp. XIII:** 274, 276
Language of the American South, The (Brooks), **Supp. XIV:** 14
"Language of the Brag, The" (Olds), **Supp. X:** 204
"Language We Know, The" (Ortiz), **Supp. IV Part 2:** 500
Lanier, Clifford, **Supp. I Part 1:** 349, 350, 353, 355, 356, 371
Lanier, James F. D., **Supp. I Part 1:** 350
Lanier, Lyle H., **Supp. X:** 25
Lanier, Robert Sampson, **Supp. I Part 1:** 349, 351, 355, 356, 361
Lanier, Mrs. Robert Sampson (Mary Jane Anderson), **Supp. I Part 1:** 349
Lanier, Sidney, **IV:** 444; **Supp. I Part 1:** **349–373**; **Supp. I Part 2:** 416; **Supp. IV Part 1:** 165
Lanier, Mrs. Sidney (Mary Day), **Supp. I Part 1:** 351, 355, 357, 361, 362, 364, 370, 371
"Lanier as Poet" (Parks), **Supp. I Part 1:** 373
"Lanier's Reading" (P. Graham), **Supp. I Part 1:** 373
"Lanier's Use of Science for Poetic Imagery" (Beaver), **Supp. I Part 1:** 373
Lankes, J. J., **Supp. XXII:** 275
Lannegan, Helen. *See* Caldwell, Mrs. Erskine
Lannin, Paul, **II:** 427
Lanny Budd novels (Sinclair), **Supp. V:** 290
Lansdale, Joe R., **Supp. XXV:** 145
Lant, Kathleen Margaret, **Supp. V:** 141
Lanterns on the Levee (Percy), **Supp. XXII:** 193
Lanthenas, François, **Supp. I Part 2:** 515
"Lanyard, The" (Collins), **Supp. XXI:** 56, **62–64**
Laotzu, **III:** 173, 189, 567; **Supp. XV:** 39, 46, 48
Lapine, James, **Supp. XXI:** 147–148
"Lapis Lazuli" (Yeats), **I:** 532; **III:** 40
Laplace, Pierre Simon de, **III:** 428
Lapouge, M. G., **Supp. I Part 2:** 633
Lappa, Katherine, **Supp. XV:** 176
Lapsing to Grace (Espaillat), **Supp. XXI:** 99, 100
Lapsley, Gaillard, **Supp. XX:** 231
Laqueur, Thomas, **Supp. XVI:** 154
Larbaud, Valery, **IV:** 404; **Supp. XIII:** 332; **Supp. XIV:** 338
Larcom, Lucy, **Retro. Supp. II:** 145; **Supp. XIII: 137–157**
Larcom's Poetical Works (Larcom), **Supp. XIII:** 142
Lardner, John, **II:** 437
Lardner, Ring, **I:** 487; **II:** 44, 91, 259, 263, **415–438**; **III:** 566, 572; **IV:** 433; **Retro. Supp. I:** 105; **Retro. Supp. II:** 222; **Supp. I Part 2:** 609; **Supp. IX:** 200; **Supp. XVI:** 189
Lardner, Ring, Jr., **Supp. XI:** 306
"Lardner, Shakespeare and Chekhov" (Matthews), **II:** 430
"Large Bad Picture" (Bishop), **Retro. Supp. II:** 43; **Supp. I Part 1:** 73, 80–

82, 85, 86, 89, 90

"Large Coffee" (Lardner), **II:** 437

Large Glass, or The Bride Stripped Bare by Her Bachelors, Even (Duchamp), **Supp. IV Part 2:** 423, 424

Largo (Handel), **IV:** 369

"Lark" (Taggard), **Supp. XXII:** 280

Lark, The (Hellman), **Supp. I Part 1:** 286–288, 297

Lark: Four-Part Chorus for Mixed Voices (A Capella) with Baritone Solo (Taggard and Copland), **Supp. XXII:** 283

Larkin, Philip, **Supp. I Part 2:** 536; **Supp. XI:** 243, 249; **Supp. XIII:** 76, 85; **Supp. XV:** 117, 251; **Supp. XVII:** 110; **Supp. XVIII:** 173; **Supp. XX:** 199; **Supp. XXI:** 84, 93

Larkin, Sharon Alile, **Supp. XI:** 20

Larmore, Phoebe, **Supp. X:** 266

Larner, Jeremy, **Supp. XVI:** 220

La Rochefoucauld, François de, **I:** 279; **II:** 111; **Supp. XIV:** 130

"La Rose des Vents" (Wilbur), **Supp. III Part 2:** 550

"Larry Brown's *Dirty Work:* A Study of Man's Responsibility for Suffering" (Prevost), **Supp. XXI:** 45

"Larry"(O'Hara), **Supp. XXIII:** 212

Larry's Party (Shields), **Supp. VII:** 324, 326–327

Larsen, Nella, **Supp. I Part 1:** 325, 326; **Supp. IV Part 1:** 164; **Supp. XVIII:** 119–134

Larson, Charles, **Supp. IV Part 1:** 331

Larson, Clinton, **Supp. XI:** 328

Larson, Kelli, **Supp. XVIII:** 131

LaRue, Dorie, **Supp. XXI:** 43

"Larval Stage of a Bookworm" (Mencken), **III:** 101

La Salle and the Discovery of the Great West (Parkman), **Supp. II Part 2:** 595, 598, 605–607; **Supp. XVIII:** 114

Las Casas, Bartolomé de, **Supp. XXIV:** 87

Lasch, Christopher, **I:** 259

Lasdun, James, **Supp. XXIV:** 154

Lasher (Rice), **Supp. VII:** 299–300

Lask, Thomas, **III:** 576; **Supp. XVI:** 250

Laski, Harold, **Supp. I Part 2:** 632, 643

Lass, Abraham H., **Supp. XXIV:** 214

Lassalle, Ferdinand, **IV:** 429

Lasser, Louise, **Supp. XV:** 4

"Last Acts" (Olds), **Supp. X:** 210

Last Adam, The (Cozzens), **I:** 362–363, 364, 368, 375, 377, 378, 379

Last Analysis, The (Bellow), **I:** 152, 160, 161; **Retro. Supp. II:** 26

Last and Lost Poems of Delmore Schwartz (Phillips, ed.), **Supp. II Part 2:** 661, 665

Last Avant-Garde, The: The Making of the New York School of Poets (Lehman), **Supp. XV:** 178–179, 187

Last Beautiful Days of Autumn, The (Nichols), **Supp. XIII:** 254, 255, 267, 269

Last Blue (Stern), **Supp. IX: 299–300**

Last Book, The (Pickering), **Supp. XXI:** 203–204

Last Carousel, The (Algren), **Supp. IX:** 16

Last Centennial, The (P. N. Warren as Kilina), **Supp. XX: 261–262**

"Last Child" (X. J. Kennedy), **Supp. XV:** 162, 165

"Last Class with Roethke" (Gallagher), **Supp. XXIV:** 171

Last Clean Shirt, The (film, Leslie and O'Hara), **Supp. XXIII:** 217

Last Coyote, The (Connelly), **Supp. XXI: 71**

"Last Dance" (Dubus III), **Supp. XXIV:** 100

"Last Day in the Field, The" (Gordon), **II:** 200

"Last Day of the Last Furlough" (Salinger), **III:** 552–553

"Last Days of Alice" (Tate), **IV:** 129

"Last Days of August, The" (Nye), **Supp. XIII:** 284

"Last Days of John Brown, The" (Thoreau), **IV:** 185

Last Days of Louisiana Red, The (Reed), **Supp. X:** 240, **248–249**

Last Decade, The (Trilling), **Supp. III Part 2:** 493, 499

"Last Demon, The" (Singer), **IV:** 15, 21

Last Detective, The (Crais), **Supp. XXI:** 70

Last Exit to Brooklyn (Selby), **Supp. III Part 1:** 125; **Supp. XXI:** 227, 231

Last Flower, The (Thurber), **Supp. I Part 2:** 610

"Last Frontier" (McCarriston), **Supp. XIV:** 272

Last Generation, The (Moraga), **Supp. XXIII:** 201

Last Gentleman, The (Percy), **Supp. III Part 1:** 383–388, 392–393

"Last Good Country, The" (Hemingway), **II:** 258–259

Last Good Time, The (Bausch), **Supp. VII:** 45–46

"Last Great Saloon, The"(Exley), **Supp. XXIII:** 103

"Last Hiding Places of Snow, The" (Kinnell), **Supp. III Part 1:** 252

"Last Hours, The" (Dunn), **Supp. XI:** 141

Last House: Reflections, Dreams, and Observations, 1943–1991 (M. F. K. Fisher), **Supp. XVII:** 92

Last Husband and Other Stories, The (Humphrey), **Supp. IX:** 94

Last Jew in America, The (Fiedler), **Supp. XIII:** 103

"Last Jew in America, The" (Fiedler), **Supp. XIII:** 103

Last Laugh, Mr. Moto (Marquand), **III:** 57

"Last Leaf, The" (Holmes), **Supp. I Part 1:** 302, 309

"Last Leaf, The" (Porter), **III:** 444

"Last Lie, The" (Weigl), **Supp. XIX:** 279

"Last Light" (Major), **Supp. XXII:** 185

"Last Look at the Lilacs" (Stevens), **IV:** 74

Last Man, The (Kees), **Supp. XV:** 142, 143, 145

"Last May" (Dixon), **Supp. XII: 143**

"Last Mermother, The" (A. Finch), **Supp. XVII:** 72

"Last Mohican, The" (Malamud), **Supp. I Part 2:** 437–438, 450, 451

"Lastness" (Kinnell), **Supp. III Part 1:** 248–249

"Last Night" (Olds), **Supp. X:** 212

Last Night at the Lobster (O'Nan), **Supp. XXV:** 149–150, 151

"Last Night at Tía's" (Alvarez), **Supp. VII:** 5

Last Night of Summer, The (Caldwell), **I:** 292–293

Last Notes from Home (Exley), **Supp. XXIII:** 97, 98, **106–108**

Last of Mr. Norris, The (Isherwood), **Supp. XIV:** 161

"Last of the Brooding Miserables, The" (Karr), **Supp. XI:** 250

"Last of the Caddoes, The" (Humphrey), **Supp. IX:** 101

Last of the Crazy People, The (Findley), **Supp. XX: 51–52**

"Last of the Gold Star Mothers, The" (C. Bly), **Supp. XVI:** 34, 35, 36

"Last of the Legions, The" (Benét), **Supp. XI:** 56, 57

Last of the Mohicans, The (Cooper), **I:** 341, 342, 349

Last of the Red Hot Lovers (Simon), **Supp. IV Part 2:** 575, 583, 589

"Last of the Valerii, The" (James), **II:** 327; **Retro. Supp. I:** 218

"Last One, The" (Merwin), **Supp. III Part 1:** 355

Last Picture Show, The (film), **Supp. V:** 223, 226

Last Picture Show, The (McMurtry), **Supp. V:** 220, 222–223, 233

Last Place on Earth, The: Scott and Amundsen's Race to the South Pole (Huntford), **Supp. XVIII:** 114

Last Puritan, The (Santayana), **III:** 64, 600, 604, 607, 612, 615–617

"Last Ride Together, The" (Browning), **I:** 468

"Last River, The" (Kinnell), **Supp. III Part 1:** 236

Last Song, The (Harjo), **Supp. XII:** 218

"Last Song for the Mend-It Shop" (Nye), **Supp. XIII:** 283

"Last Tango in Fresno" (Salinas), **Supp. XIII:** 318

"Last Trip to Greece"(Hadas), **Supp. XXIII:** 118–119

Last Tycoon, The: An Unfinished Novel (Fitzgerald), **II:** 84, 98; **Retro. Supp. I:** 109, 114, **114–115**; **Retro. Supp. II:** 337; **Supp. IV Part 1:** 203; **Supp. IX:** 63; **Supp. XII:** 173; **Supp. XIII:** 170; **Supp. XVIII:** 248, 250

"Last WASP in the World, The" (Fiedler), **Supp. XIII:** 103

"Last Watch, The" (Gibran), **Supp. XX: 119**

Last Watch of the Night: Essays Too Personal and Otherwise (Monette), **Supp. X:** 147, 148, 153, **157–159**

"Last Will" (Stallings), **Supp. XXV:** 232

"Last Word, The" (column, Quindlen), **Supp. XVII:** 165, 167, 170

Last Word, The: Letters between Marcia Nardi and William Carlos Williams (O'Neil, ed.), **Retro. Supp. I:** 427

"Last Words" (Levine), **Supp. V:** 190

"Last Words" (Olds), **Supp. X:** 210

Last Worthless Evening, The (Dubus), **Supp. VII:** 87–88

"Las Vegas (What?) Las Vegas (Can't Hear You! Too Noisy) Las Vegas! ! ! !" (Wolfe), **Supp. III Part 2:** 572

"Late" (Bogan), **Supp. III Part 1:** 53

"Late Air" (Bishop), **Supp. I Part 1:** 89

"Late Autumn" (Sarton), **Supp. VIII:** 261

"Late Bronze, Early Iron: A Journey Book" (Sobin), **Supp. XVI:** 290

Late Child, The (McMurtry), **Supp. V:** 231

"Late Conversation" (Doty), **Supp. XI:** 122

"Late Elegy for John Berryman, A" (W. V. Davis), **Supp. XXI:** 91

"Late Encounter with the Enemy, A" (O'Connor), **III:** 345; **Retro. Supp. II:** 232

Late Fire, Late Snow (Francis), **Supp. IX: 89–90**

"Late Fragment" (Gallagher), **Supp. XXIV:** 172

Late George Apley, The (Marquand), **II:** 482–483; **III:** 50, 51, 52, 56–57, 58, 62–64, 65, 66

Late George Apley, The (Marquand and Kaufman), **III:** 62

"Late Hour" (Everwine), **Supp. XV:** 85

Late Hour, The (Strand), **Supp. IV Part 2:** 620, 629–630

"Lately, at Night" (Kumin), **Supp. IV Part 2:** 442

"Late Moon" (Levine), **Supp. V:** 186

"Late Night Ode" (McClatchy), **Supp. XII:** 262–263

Later (Creeley), **Supp. IV Part 1:** 153, 156, 157

Later Life (Gurney), **Supp. V:** 103, 105

La Terre (Zola), **III:** 316, 322

Later the Same Day (Paley), **Supp. VI:** 218

"Late September in Nebraska" (Kooser), **Supp. XIX:** 120

Late Settings (Merrill), **Supp. III Part 1:** 336

"Late Sidney Lanier, The" (Stedman), **Supp. I Part 1:** 373

"Late Snow & Lumber Strike of the Summer of Fifty-Four, The" (Snyder), **Supp. VIII:** 294

"Late Start, A" (L. Brown), **Supp. XXI:** 40–41

"Latest Freed Man, The" (Stevens), **Retro. Supp. I:** 306

"Latest Injury, The" (Olds), **Supp. X:** 209

Latest Literary Essays and Addresses (Lowell), **Supp. I Part 2:** 407

"Late Subterfuge" (Warren), **IV:** 257

"Late Summer Lilies" (Weigl), **Supp. XIX:** 288

"Late Supper, A" (Jewett), **Retro. Supp. II:** 137

"Late Victorians" (Rodriguez), **Supp. XIV:** 303–304

"Late Walk, A" (Frost), **II:** 153; **Retro. Supp. I:** 127

Latham, Edyth, **I:** 289

Lathrop, George Parsons, **Supp. I Part 1:** 365

Lathrop, H. B., **Supp. III Part 2:** 612

Lathrop, Julia, **Supp. I Part 1:** 5

Latière de Trianon, La (Wekerlin), **II:** 515

"La Tigresse" (Van Vechten), **Supp. II Part 2:** 735, 738

Latimer, Hugh, **II:** 15

Latimer, Margery, **Supp. IX:** 320

La Traviata (Verdi), **III:** 139

"Latter-Day Warnings" (Holmes), **Supp. I Part 1:** 307

"Latter Rain, The" (Very), **Supp. XXV:** 249

La Turista (Shepard), **Supp. III Part 2:** 440

Lauber, John, **Supp. XIII:** 21

Laud, Archbishop, **II:** 158

"Lauds" (Auden), **Supp. II Part 1:** 23

"Laughing Man, The" (Salinger), **III:** 559

Laughing Matters (Siegel), **Supp. XXII:** 260

Laughing to Keep From Crying (Hughes), **Supp. I Part 1:** 329–330

Laughing Wild (Durang), **Supp. XXIV:** 114, **124**

"Laughing with One Eye" (Schnackenberg), **Supp. XV:** 253

Laughlin, James, **II:** 171; **Retro. Supp. I:** 423, 424, 428, 430, 431; **Supp. VIII:** 195; **Supp. XV:** 140; **Supp. XVI:** 284; **Supp. XXI:** 29

Laughlin, Jay, **Supp. II Part 1:** 94

Laughlin, J. Laurence, **Supp. I Part 2:** 641

Laughter in the Dark (Nabokov), **III:** 255–258; **Retro. Supp. I:** 270

Laughter on the 23rd Floor (Simon), **Supp. IV Part 2:** 575, 576, 588, 591–592

"Launcelot" (Lewis), **II:** 439–440

"Laura Dailey's Story" (Bogan), **Supp. III Part 1:** 52

Laurel, Stan, **Supp. I Part 2:** 607; **Supp. IV Part 2:** 574

Laurel and Hardy Go to Heaven (Auster), **Supp. XII:** 21

Laurence, Alexander, **Supp. XVIII:** 138

Laurence, Dan H., **II:** 338–339

Laurens, John, **Supp. I Part 2:** 509

Lauter, Paul, **Supp. XV:** 313

Lautréamont, Comte de, **III:** 174

Lavender Locker Room, The (P. N. Warren), **Supp. XX: 261, 273–274**

Law, John, **Supp. XI:** 307

Law and Order (television), **Supp. XVII:** 153

Law and the Testimony, The (S. and A. Warner), **Supp. XVIII:** 264

Lawd Today (Wright), **IV:** 478, 492

Law for the Lion, A (Auchincloss), **Supp. IV Part 1:** 25

Lawgiver, The (Wouk), **Supp. XXV:** 253, 256, 257, 267–268

"Law Lane" (Jewett), **II:** 407

"Lawns of June, The" (Peacock), **Supp. XIX:** 196

"Law of Nature and the Dream of Man, The: Ruminations of the Art of Fiction" (Stegner), **Supp. IV Part 2:** 604

Lawrence, D. H., **I:** 291, 336, 377, 522, 523; **II:** 78, 84, 98, 102, 264, 517, 523, 532, 594, 595; **III:** 27, 33, 40, 44, 46, 172, 173, 174, 178, 184, 229, 261, 423, 429, 458, 546–547; **IV:** 138, 339, 342, 351, 380; **Retro. Supp. I:** 7, 18, 203, 204, 421; **Retro. Supp. II:** 68; **Supp. I Part 1:** 227, 230, 243, 255, 257, 258, 263, 329; **Supp. I Part 2:** 546, 613, 728; **Supp. II Part 1:** 1, 9, 20, 89; **Supp. IV Part 1:** 81; **Supp. VIII:** 237; **Supp. X:** 137, 193, 194; **Supp. XII:** 172; **Supp. XIV:** 310; **Supp. XV:** 45, 46, 158, 254; **Supp. XVI:** 267; **Supp. XX: 69;** **Supp. XXII:** 198; **Supp. XXIII:** 166, 275; **Supp. XXIV:** 51, 52, 57, 58, 64

Lawrence, Elizabeth, **Supp. XXIII:** 259, 264

Lawrence, Frieda, **Supp. XV:** 46

Lawrence, Rhoda, **Supp. I Part 1:** 45

Lawrence, Seymour, **Supp. IX:** 107; **Supp. XI:** 335, 346, 348

Lawrence, T. E., **Supp. XIV:** 159

Lawrence of Arabia (Aldington), **Supp. I Part 1:** 259

Lawrence of Arabia (film), **Supp. I Part 1:** 67

Laws (Hadas), **Supp. XXIII: 119–120,** 124

Laws (Plato), **Supp. IV Part 1:** 391

Laws of Ice, The (Price), **Supp. VI:** 264

Laws of Our Fathers, The (Turow), **Supp. XVII: 218–219**

Lawson, John Howard, **I:** 479, 482

Lawton Girl, The (Frederic), **II:** 132–133, 144

Layachi, Larbi (Driss ben Hamed Charhadi), **Supp. IV Part 1:** 92, 93

Layard, John, **Supp. XIV:** 160

Lay Down My Sword and Shield (Burke), **Supp. XIV:** 22, 25, 34

"Layers, The" (Kunitz), **Supp. III Part 1:** 260, 266–267

"Layers, The: Some Notes on 'The Abduction' " (Kunitz), **Supp. III Part 1:** 266

"Lay-mans Lamentation, The" (Taylor), **IV:** 162–163

Lay of the Land, The: Metaphor as Experience and History in American Life and Letters (Kolodny), **Supp. X:** 97

"Layover" (Hass), **Supp. VI:** 109

"Lay Preacher" (Dennie), **Supp. I Part 1:** 125

Layton, Irving, **Supp. XII:** 121

Lazar, Irving "Swifty", **Supp. XIX:** 250

Lazarillo de Tormes (Mendoza), **III:** 182

Lazar Malkin Enters Heaven (S. Stern), **Supp. XVII:** 42; **Supp. XX: 178**

Lazarus Laughed (O'Neill), **III:** 391, 395–396

Lazer, Hank, **Supp. IX:** 265

Lea, Luke, **IV:** 248

Leachman, Cloris, **Supp. XXI:** 146

Leacock, Stephen, **Supp. IV Part 2:** 464

"LEADBELLY GIVES AN AUTO-GRAPH" (Baraka), **Supp. II Part 1:** 49

Leaflets: Poems, 1965–1968 (Rich), **Supp. I Part 2:** 551, 556–557

"League of American Writers, The: Communist Organizational Activity among American Writers 1929–1942" (Wolfe), **Supp. III Part 2:** 568

League of Brightened Philistines and Other Papers, The (Farrell), **II:** 49

Leahy, Anna, **Supp. XXI:** 246

"Leakage" (Skloot), **Supp. XX:** 202

Leal, Luis, **Supp. XIX:** 98, 112

"Leaning" (Webb), **Supp. XX: 56**

Leaning Forward (Paley), **Supp. VI:** 221

"Leaning Tower, The" (Porter), **III:** 442, 443, 446–447

Leaning Tower and Other Stories, The (Porter), **III:** 433, 442, 443–447

"Leap, The" (Dickey), **Supp. IV Part 1:** 182

"Leaping Up into Political Poetry" (R. Bly), **Supp. IV Part 1:** 61, 63

Leap Year (Cameron), **Supp. XII:** 79–80, 81, **85–86,** 88

Lear, Edward, **III:** 428, 536; **Supp. XVI:** 103

Lear, Linda, **Supp. IX:** 19, 22, 25, 26

Learned Ladies, The (Molière; Wilbur, trans.), **Supp. III Part 2:** 560

"Learning a Dead Language" (Merwin), **Supp. III Part 1:** 345

Learning a Trade: A Craftsman's Notebooks, 1955–1997 (Price), **Supp. VI:** 254, 255, 267

"Learning Bones" (Espaillat), **Supp. XXI:** 107

Learning to Live in This World (Schott), **Supp. XXIII:** 248

Learning to Love: Exploring Solitude and Freedom (Merton), **Supp. VIII:** 200

Learning to Love You More (website), **Supp. XXIV:** 200

"Learning to Read" (Harper), **Supp. II Part 1:** 201–202

"Learning to Speak" (Everwine), **Supp. XV:** 79

"Learning to Work Together" (L. I. Wilder), **Supp. XXII:** 290

Learning Tree, The (Park), **Supp. XIX:** 154

Leary, Lewis, **III:** 478

Leary, Paris, **Supp. IV Part 1:** 176

Leary, Timothy, **Supp. X:** 265; **Supp. XIV:** 150

Lease, Joseph, **Supp. XXI:** 246

Least Heat Moon, William, **Supp. V:** 169

Leather-Stocking Tales, The (Cooper), **I:** 335

Leatherwood God, The (Howells), **II:** 276, 277, 288

Leave It to Beaver (television show), **Supp. XX: 103**

"Leave Me Alone a Little" (Taggard), **Supp. XXII:** 274

"Leaves" (Updike), **Retro. Supp. I:** 323, 329, 335

Leaves and Ashes (Haines), **Supp. XII:** 206

Leaves from the Notebook of a Tamed Cynic (Niebuhr), **III:** 293

Leaves of Grass (1856) (Whitman), **Retro. Supp. I:** 399–402

Leaves of Grass (1860) (Whitman), **Retro. Supp. I:** 402–405

Leaves of Grass (Whitman), **II:** 8; **IV:** 331, 332, 333, 334, 335, 336, 340, 341–342, 348, 350, 405, 464; **Retro. Supp. I:** 387, 388, 389, 390, **392–395,** 406, 407, 408; **Retro. Supp. II:** 93; **Supp. I Part 1:** 365; **Supp. I Part 2:** 416, 579; **Supp. III Part 1:** 156; **Supp. V:** 170; **Supp. VIII:** 275; **Supp. IX:** 265; **Supp. X:** 120; **Supp. XIV:** 334; **Supp. XV:** 218; **Supp. XVIII:** 4; **Supp. XIX:** 276; **Supp. XXI:** 205; **Supp. XXII:** 92; **Supp. XXIII:** 165; **Supp. XXIV:** 85

"Leaves of Grass" (Whitman), **IV:** 463

Leaves of the Tree, The (Masters), **Supp. I Part 2:** 460

"Leaving" (Hogan), **Supp. IV Part 1:** 400

"Leaving" (Wilbur), **Supp. III Part 2:** 563

"Leaving, The" (B. Kelly), **Supp. XVII:** 127, 132

Leaving a Doll's House: A Memoir (C. Bloom), **Retro. Supp. II:** 281

Leaving Another Kingdom: Selected Poems (Stern), **Supp. IX:** 296

"Leaving Bartram's Garden in Southwest Philadelphia" (Di Piero), **Supp. XIX:** 46

"Leaving Brooklyn" (Neugeboren), **Supp. XVI:** 226

Leaving Cheyenne (McMurtry), **Supp. V:** 220, 221–222, 224, 229

Leaving Home (Keillor), **Supp. XVI:** 175

"Leaving One, The" (Offutt), **Supp. XIX:** 165–166

"Leaving the Island" (Olds), **Supp. X:** 214

"Leaving the Yellow House" (Bellow), **Retro. Supp. II:** 27, 32

"Leaving Town" (Kenyon), **Supp. VII:** 163

Leavis, F. R., **I:** 522; **III:** 462–463, 475, 478; **Retro. Supp. I:** 67; **Retro. Supp. II:** 243; **Supp. I Part 2:** 536; **Supp. VIII:** 234, 236, 245

Leavis, Queenie, **Supp. XX: 232**

"Leavis-Snow Controversy, The" (Trilling), **Supp. III Part 2:** 512

Leavitt, Caroline, **Supp. XX: 186**

Leavitt, David, **Supp. VIII:** 88

Lebanon (C. Miller), **Supp. XXII:** 198–199

Le Braz, Anatole, **Supp. XIII:** 253

Le Carre, John, **Supp. XX: 195**

Lecker, Robert, **Supp. XIII:** 21

LeClair, Thomas (Tom), **Supp. IV Part 1:** 286; **Supp. V:** 53; **Supp. XII:** 152; **Supp. XX: 93; Supp. XXII:** 206, 210, 261, 264

Le Conte, Joseph, **II:** 479; **III:** 227–228

"Lecture, The" (Singer), **IV:** 21

"LECTURE PAST DEAD CATS" (Baraka), **Supp. II Part 1:** 52

Lectures in America (Stein), **IV:** 27, 32, 33, 35, 36, 41, 42

"Lectures on Poetry" (Bryant), **Supp. I Part 1:** 159, 161

Lectures on Rhetoric (Blair), **II:** 8

"Leda and the Swan" (Yeats), **III:** 347; **Supp. IX:** 52

Ledger (Fitzgerald), **Retro. Supp. I:** 109, 110

Lee (Masters), **Supp. I Part 2:** 471

Lee, Baayork, **Supp. XXI:** 148

Lee, C. Y., **Supp. XXI:** 148

Lee, Don, **Supp. XII:** 295; **Supp. XVII:** 13, 14, 15, 16

Lee, Don L. *See* Madhubuti, Haki R.

Lee, Gypsy Rose, **II:** 586; **III:** 161; **Supp. IV Part 1:** 84

Lee, Harper, **Supp. VIII: 113–131**

Lee, Harriett, **Supp. XV:** 230

Lee, James Kyun-Jin, **Supp. XV:** 213

Lee, James W., **Supp. IX:** 94, 97, 109

Lee, James Ward, **Supp. VIII:** 57

Lee, Lawrence, **Supp. XXV:** 29

Lee, Li Lin, **Supp. XV:** 211, 212

Lee, Li-Young, **Supp. XV: 211–228; Supp. XVII:** 241

Lee, Richard E., **Supp. XIX:** 226, 227

Lee, Robert E., **II:** 150, 206; **IV:** 126; **Supp. I Part 2:** 471, 486

Lee, Samuel, **IV:** 158

Lee, Spike, **Retro. Supp. II:** 12; **Supp. XI:** 19; **Supp. XIII:** 179, 186; **Supp. XVI:** 144; **Supp. XX: 110**

Lee, Virginia Chin-lan, **Supp. X:** 291

Leeds, Barry, **Retro. Supp. II:** 204

Leeds, Daniel, **II:** 110

Leeds, Titan, **II:** 110, 111

Leeming, David, **Retro. Supp. II:** 4, 10

"Lees of Happiness, The" (Fitzgerald), **II:** 88

"Le Filme" (Weigl), **Supp. XIX:** 288

Left Out in the Rain: New Poems 1947–1985 (Snyder), **Supp. VIII:** 305

"Legacy" (Dunn), **Supp. XI:** 148

"Legacy" (Komunyakaa), **Supp. XIII:** 132

"Legacy" (W. V. Davis), **Supp. XXI:** 93–94

"Legacy of Aldo Leopold, The" (Stegner), **Supp. XIV:** 193

"Legacy of Channing, The" (Robinson), **Supp. XXIV:** 79

Legacy of Fear, A (Farrell), **II:** 39

"Legacy of the Ancestral Arts, The" (Locke), **Supp. XIV:** 201

Legacy of the Civil War, The: Meditations on the Centennial (Warren), **IV:** 236

"Legal Alien" (Mora), **Supp. XIII:** 215

"Legal Tender Act, The" (Adams), **I:** 5

Légende de la mort, La (Le Braz), **Supp. XIII:** 253

"Legend of Duluoz, The" (Kerouac), **Supp. III Part 1:** 218, 226, 227, 229

"Legend of Lillian Hellman, The" (Kazin), **Supp. I Part 1:** 297

"Legend of Monte del Diablo, The" (Harte), **Supp. II Part 1:** 339

"Legend of Paper Plates, The" (Haines), **Supp. XII:** 204

"Legend of Sammtstadt, A" (Harte), **Supp. II Part 1:** 355

"Legend of Sleepy Hollow, The" (Irving), **II:** 306–308

Legends (Lowell), **II:** 525–526

Legends and Dreams (P. N. Warren), **Supp. XX: 261**

Legends of Mexico (Lippard), **Supp. XXIII:** 178, 186

Legends of New England (Whittier), **Supp. I Part 2:** 684, 692

Legends of the Fall (Harrison), **Supp. VIII:** 38, 39, **45–46,** 48

"Legends of the Revolution"(series, Lippard), **Supp. XXIII:** 178

Legends of the West (Hall), **II:** 313

Léger, Fernand, **Retro. Supp. I:** 292

Legge, James, **III:** 472

Leggett, William, **Supp. I Part 1:** 157

"Legion, The" (Karr), **Supp. XI:** 243

"Legs" (Halliday), **Supp. XIX:** 90

Legs (W. Kennedy), **Supp. VII:** 133, 134, 138–142, 143, 151

Le Guin, Ursula K., **Supp. IV Part 1:** 333; **Supp. XXII:** 49

Lehan, Richard, **Retro. Supp. II:** 104

Lehman, David, **Supp. IX:** 161; **Supp. XIII:** 130; **Supp. XV:** 178–179, 180, 187, 190; **Supp. XXI:** 246

Lehmann, John, **Retro. Supp. II:** 243; **Supp. XIV:** 158, 159

Lehmann, Paul, **III:** 311

Lehmann-Haupt, Christopher, **Retro. Supp. II:** 291; **Supp. IV Part 1:** 205, 209, 306; **Supp. IX:** 95, 103; **Supp. XVI:** 73, 210, 294, 295; **Supp. XXII:** 205, 213; **Supp. XXIII:** 103

Lehrer, Jim, **Supp. XVIII:** 39

Leiber, Fritz, **Supp. XVI:** 123

Leibling, A. J., **Supp. XIV:** 112

Leibniz, Gottfried Wilhelm von, **II:** 103; **III:** 428

Leibowitz, Herbert A., **I:** 386; **Supp. XV:** 78

Leich, Roland, **Supp. XIV:** 123

Leichum, Laura, **Supp. XIX:** 197

Leider, Emily Wortis, **Supp. XXIV:** 19, 20, 22, 26, 27, 30

Leighton, Betty, **Supp. XXI:** 42

Leimbach, Laura, **Supp. XXIII:** 54

Leithauser, Brad, **Retro. Supp. I:** 133; **Supp. XV:** 250; **Supp. XVII:** 112; **Supp. XXII:** 207

Leitz, Robert, **Supp. XIV:** 62

Leivick, H., **IV:** 6

Lekachman, Robert, **Supp. I Part 2:** 648

Leland, Charles, **Supp. II Part 1:** 193

Leland, Charles Godfrey, **I:** 257

Leland, John, **Supp. XV:** 69; **Supp. XIX:** 157

Lem, Stanislaw, **Supp. IV Part 1:** 103

"Le marais du cygne" (Whittier), **Supp. I Part 2:** 687

Lemay, Harding, **Supp. VIII:** 125; **Supp. IX:** 98

Lemercier, Eugène, **Retro. Supp. I:** 299

Lemkin, Raphael, **Supp. XXIII:** 31

"Lemorne *versus* Huell" (E. Stoddard), **Supp. XV:** 270, 273, 283

Le Morte D'Arthur Notes (Gardner), **Supp. VI:** 65, 66

Lenin, V. I., **I:** 366, 439, 440; **III:** 14–15, 262, 475; **IV:** 429, 436, 443–444; **Supp. I Part 2:** 647; **Supp. XXI:** 164

Lennon, J. Robert, **Supp. XXV:** 151

"Lenny Dying, Pacific Standard Time"(Thompson), **Supp. XXIII:** 294

"Lenore" (Poe), **III:** 411

"Lenox Avenue: Midnight" (Hughes), **Retro. Supp. I:** 198

"Lens of Poetry, The" (Bronk). *See Attendant, The* (Bronk)

Leonard, Elmore, **Supp. IV Part 1:** 356; **Supp. X:** 5; **Supp. XIV:** 26

Leonard, John, **Supp. IV Part 1:** 24; **Supp. IV Part 2:** 474; **Supp. V:** 164, 223–224; **Supp. XI:** 13; **Supp. XVIII:** 147, 148; **Supp. XIX:** 269; **Supp. XXI:** 233, 239

Leonardo da Vinci, **Supp. XII:** 44; **Supp. XXII:** 171

León-Portilla, Miguel, **Supp. XV:** 77

Leontiev, Constantine, **Supp. XIV:** 98

Leopard, The (Lampedusa), **Supp. XII:** 13–14

Leopardi, Giacomo, **II:** 543; **Supp. XIX:** 33, 43

"Leopard Man's Story, The" (London), **II:** 475

Leopard's Mouth Is Dry and Cold Inside, The (Levis), **Supp. XI:** 258

Leopold, Aldo, **Supp. V:** 202; **Supp. X:** 108; **Supp. XIV: 177–194; Supp. XXI:** 203

"Leper's Bell, the" (Komunyakaa), **Supp. XIII:** 118

Lerman, Leo, **Supp. X:** 188; **Supp. XVI:** 194

Lerner, Ben, **Supp. XXIV:** 45

Lerner, Max, **III:** 60; **Supp. I Part 2:** 629, 630, 631, 647, 650, 654

Lerperger, Emil, **Supp. XX: 165, 167**

Lesbian Nation: The Feminist Solution (Johnston), **Supp. XXV:** 5

"Lesbos" (Plath), **Retro. Supp. II:** 254

Lesesne, Teri, **Supp. XIII:** 277

LeSieg, Theo (pseudonym). *See* Geisel, Theodor Seuss (Dr. Seuss)

Leskov, Nikolai, **IV:** 299

Leslie, Alfred, **Supp. XII:** 127; **Supp. XXIII:** 217

"Less and Less Human, O Savage Spirit" (W. Stevens), **Supp. XVI:** 64

Lesser, Wendy, **Supp. IV Part 2:** 453; **Supp. XII:** 297; **Supp. XVI:** 201

Lessing, Gotthold, **Supp. I Part 2:** 422

"Lesson, The" (Bambara), **Supp. XI:** 5–6

"Lesson, The" (Dunbar), **Supp. II Part 1:** 199

"Lesson, The" (Olsen), **Supp. XIII:** 297

"Lesson, The"(Schott), **Supp. XXIII:** 254

"Lesson for the Ill Clothed and Ill Fed, A" (Ryan as Quin), **Supp. XVIII:** 230–231

Lesson of the Master, The (James), **Supp. XVIII:** 248

"Lesson of the Master, The" (James), **Retro. Supp. I:** 227

Lesson of the Masters: An Anthology of the Novel from Cervantes to Hemingway (Cowley-Hugo, ed.), **Supp. II Part 1:** 140

"Lesson on Concealment, A" (Brown), **Supp. I Part 1:** 133

"Lessons" (Epstein), **Supp. XII:** 163

"Lessons from an Older Man"(Thompson), **Supp. XXIII:** 293

"Lessons of the Body" (Simpson), **Supp. IX:** 267

Less than One (Brodsky), **Supp. VIII:** 22, 29–31

Lester, Jerry, **Supp. IV Part 2:** 574

Lester, Ketty, **Supp. XV:** 133, 147

Le Style Apollinaire (Zukofsky), **Supp. III Part 2:** 616

Le Sueur, Arthur, **Supp. XXIII:** 161, 162

LeSueur, Joe, **Supp. XXIII:** 212, 216, 218, 220

Le Sueur, Meridel, **Supp. V:** 113, 130; **Supp. XII:** 217; **Supp. XXIII: 161–176**

Lesy, Michael, **Supp. XXV:** 146

"Let America Be America Again" (Hughes), **Retro. Supp. I:** 202; **Supp. I Part 1:** 331

Let Evening Come (Kenyon), **Supp. VII:** 160, 169–171

Lethem, Jonathan, **Supp. IX:** 122; **Supp. XVIII: 135–153; Supp. XXII:** 49

Let It Come Down (Bowles), **Supp. IV Part 1:** 87

Let It Ride (Pickering), **Supp. XXI:** 198–199

"Let Me Be" (Levine), **Supp. V:** 181, 189

"Let Me Begin Again" (Levine), **Supp. V:** 181, 189

"Let No Charitable Hope" (Wylie), **Supp. I Part 2:** 713–714, 729

Let No Man Write My Epitaph (film, Leacock), **Supp. XVII:** 150, 158

Let No Man Write My Epitaph (W. Motley), **Supp. XVII:** 150, **158–160**

Let Noon Be Fair (W. Motley), **Supp. XVII: 161**

Letofsky, Irv, **Supp. XVI:** 167

"Let one Eye his watches keep/While the Other Eye doth sleep" (Fletcher), **Supp. IV Part 2:** 621

Let's Balance the Books (radio show; Untermeyer), **Supp. XV:** 311

"Letter . . ." (Whittier), **Supp. I Part 2:** 687

"Letter, A" (Bogan), **Supp. III Part 1:** 54

"Letter, May 2, 1959" (Olson), **Supp. II Part 2:** 579, 580

"Letter, Much Too Late" (Stegner), **Supp. IV Part 2:** 613

"Letter, The" (Boulton), **Supp. XXII:** 22

"Letter, The" (Gioia), **Supp. XV:** 120

"Letter, The" (Malamud), **Supp. I Part 2:** 435–436

"Letter about Money, Love, or Other Comfort, If Any, The" (Warren), **IV:** 245

Letter Addressed to the People of Piedmont, on the Advantages of the French Revolution, and the Necessity of Adopting Its Principles in Italy, A (Barlow), **Supp. II Part 1:** 80, 81

"Letter for Marion, A" (McGrath), **Supp. X:** 116

"Letter from Aldermaston" (Merwin), **Supp. III Part 1:** 347

"Letter from a London Attic" (Pickering), **Supp. XXI:** 194

"Letter from a Region in My Mind" (Baldwin). *See* "Down at the Cross"

"Letter from Aunt Belle, A" (Kooser), **Supp. XIX:** 117

Letter from Li Po, A (Aiken), **I:** 68

"Letter from 'Manhattan' " (Didion), **Supp. IV Part 1:** 205

"Letter from the Country" (column, C. Bly), **Supp. XVI:** 33

Letter from the End of the Twentieth Century (Harjo), **Supp. XII:** 223

"Letter from the End of the Twentieth Century" (Harjo), **Supp. XII:** 227

"Letter Home" (Trethewey), **Supp. XXI:** 254

"Letter on Céline" (Kerouac), **Supp. III Part 1:** 232

Letters (Cato), **II:** 114

Letters (Landor), **Supp. I Part 2:** 422

Letters (White), **Supp. I Part 2:** 651, 653, 675, 680

Letters (Wolfe), **IV:** 462

"Letters, The" (Swados), **Supp. XIX:** 261, 262

Letters and Leadership (Brooks), **I:** 228, 240, 245, 246

"Letters for the Dead" (Levine), **Supp. V:** 186

Letters from an American Farmer (Crèvecoeur), **Supp. I Part 1:** 227–251

Letters from Maine (Sarton), **Supp. VIII:** 261

"Letters from Maine" (Sarton), **Supp. VIII:** 261

"Letters from My Father" (R. O. Butler), **Supp. XII:** 71

Letters from the Country (C. Bly), **Supp. XVI:** 33–34, 35, 37

Letters from the Earth (Twain), **IV:** 209

Letters from the East (Bryant), **Supp. I Part 1:** 158

"Letters from the Ming Dynasty" (Brodsky), **Supp. VIII:** 28

"Letters from the *Samantha*" (Helprin), **Supp. XXV:** 85

Letters of Angelicus and Fidelio Fobb (O'Hara and Berkson), **Supp. XXIII:** 218

Letters of a Traveller (Bryant), **Supp. I Part 1:** 158

Letters of a Traveller, Second Series (Bryant), **Supp. I Part 1:** 158

Letters of Emily Dickinson, The (Johnson and Ward, eds.), **I:** 470; **Retro. Supp. I:** 28

Letters of William James (Henry James, ed.), **II:** 362

Letters on Various Interesting and Important Subjects . . . (Freneau), **Supp. II Part 1:** 272

Letters to a Niece (Adams), **I:** 22

Letters to a Teacher (Pickering), **Supp. XXI:** 195, 201–202

Letters to a Young Poet (Rilke), **Supp. XIII:** 74; **Supp. XV:** 93

"Letters to Dead Imagists" (Sandburg), **I:** 421

"Letters Written on a Ferry While Crossing Long Island Sound" (Sexton), **Supp. II Part 2:** 683

"Letter to Abbé Raynal" (Paine), **Supp. I Part 2:** 510

"Letter to a Kiss That Died for Us" (Gallagher), **Supp. XXIV:** 170

Letter to a Man in the Fire: Does God Exist or Does He Care? (Price), **Supp. VI:** 267–268

"Letter to American Teachers of History, A" (Adams), **I:** 19

Letter to an Imaginary Friend (McGrath), **Supp. X:** 111, 112–113, 116, **119–125**

"Letter to a Reader" (Sanders), **Supp. XVI:** 266, 267, 268, 269, 275

"Letter to a Young Author" (P. N. Warren), **Supp. XX:** **272**

"Letter to a Young Contributor" (Higginson), **Retro. Supp. I:** 31

"Letter to a Young Writer" (Price), **Supp. VI:** 267

"Letter to Bell from Missoula" (Hugo), **Supp. VI:** 142–143

"Letter to E. Franklin Frazier" (Baraka), **Supp. II Part 1:** 49

"Letter to Elaine Feinstein" (Olson), **Supp. II Part 2:** 561

"Letter to Francis Picabia, A" (Boyle), **Supp. XXIV:** 63

"Letter to Freddy" (music) (Bowles), **Supp. IV Part 1:** 82

"Letter to Garber from Skye" (Hugo), **Supp. VI:** 146

"Letter to George Washington" (Paine), **Supp. I Part 2:** 517

"Letter to His Brother" (Berryman), **I:** 172, 173

Letter to His Countrymen, A (Cooper), **I:** 346, 347, 349

"Letter to Kizer from Seattle" (Hugo), **Supp. VI:** 142

Letter to Lord Byron (Auden), **Supp. II Part 1:** 11

"Letter to Lord Byron" (Mumford), **Supp. II Part 2:** 494

"Letter to Matthews from Barton Street Flats" (Hugo), **Supp. VI:** 133

"Letter to Minnesota" (Dunn), **Supp. XI:** 146

"Letter to Mr." (Poe), **III:** 411

"Letter Too Late to Vallejo" (Salinas), **Supp. XIII:** 313, 324

"Letter to Sister Madeline from Iowa City" (Hugo), **Supp. VI:** 142–143

"Letter to Soto" (Salinas), **Supp. XIII:** 325

"Letter to the Lady of the House" (Bausch), **Supp. VII:** 48

"Letter to the Rising Generation, A" (Comer), **I:** 214

"Letter to Walt Whitman" (Doty), **Supp. XI:** 135–136

"Letter to Wendell Berry, A" (Stegner), **Supp. IV Part 2:** 600

"Letter Writer, The" (Singer), **IV:** 20–21

"Let the Air Circulate" (Clampitt), **Supp. IX:** 45

Let the Hurricane Roar (Lane), **Supp. XXII:** 297

"Letting Down of the Hair, The" (Sexton), **Supp. II Part 2:** 692

Letting Go (P. Roth), **Retro. Supp. II:** 282, 283; **Supp. III Part 2:** 403, 404, 409–412

"Letting the Puma Go" (Dunn), **Supp. XI:** 149

"Lettres d'un Soldat" (Stevens), **Retro. Supp. I:** 299

Let Us Go into the Starry Night (Shanley), **Supp. XIV:** 317

Let Us Highly Resolve (Stratton-Porter), **Supp. XX:** **223**

Let Us Now Praise Famous Men (Agee and Evans), **I:** 25, 27, 35, 36–39, 42, 45, 293

Let Your Mind Alone! (Thurber), **Supp. I Part 2:** 608

Leutze, Emanuel, **Supp. X:** 307

Levels of the Game (McPhee), **Supp. III Part 1:** 292, 294, 301

Levertov, Denise, **Retro. Supp. I:** 411; **Supp. III Part 1: 271–287; Supp. III Part 2:** 541; **Supp. IV Part 1:** 325; **Supp. VIII:** 38, 39; **Supp. XVI:** 39, 40; **Supp. XIX:** 282; **Supp. XXI:** 228; **Supp. XXII:** 83, 168, 177

Levi, Primo, **Supp. X:** 149; **Supp. XVII:** 48

Leviathan (Auster), **Supp. XII:** 27, **33–34**

"Leviathan" (Lowell), **II:** 537, 538

"Leviathan" (Merwin), **Supp. III Part 1:** 345

Levin, Adam, **Supp. XXII:** 268

Levin, Harry, **Supp. I Part 2:** 647

Levin, Jennifer, **Supp. X:** 305

Levin, Meyer, **Supp. XX:** 34

Lévinas, Emmanuel, **Supp. XVI:** 290, 291

Levine, Ellen, **Supp. V:** 4; **Supp. XI:** 178

Levine, Paul, **Supp. IV Part 1:** 221, 224

Levine, Philip, **Supp. III Part 2:** 541; **Supp. V: 177–197**, 337; **Supp. IX:** 293; **Supp. XI:** 123, 257, 259, 267, 271, 315; **Supp. XIII:** 312; **Supp. XV:** 73, 74, 212; **Supp. XIX:** 45

Levine, Rosalind, **Supp. XII:** 123

Levine, Sherry, **Supp. XII:** 4

Levis, Larry, **Supp. V:** 180; **Supp. IX:** 299; **Supp. XI: 257–274; Supp. XIII:** 312; **Supp. XV:** 73; **Supp. XVII:** 110

Lévi-Strauss, Claude, **Supp. I Part 2:** 636; **Supp. IV Part 1:** 45; **Supp. IV Part 2:** 490; **Supp. XVIII:** 190

Levitation: Five Fictions (Ozick), **Supp. V:** 268–270

"Levitation with Baby" (Nelson), **Supp. XVIII:** 173

Levitt, Saul, **Supp. XV:** 197

Levy, Alan, **Supp. IV Part 2:** 574, 589
Levy, D. A., **Supp. XXIII:** 174
Levy, G. Rachel, **Supp. I Part 2:** 567
Levy, Julien, **Supp. XXII:** 167, 168
Lévy-Bruhl, Lucien, **Retro. Supp. I:** 57
Levy Mayer and the New Industrial Era (Masters), **Supp. I Part 2:** 473
Lewes, George Henry, **II:** 569
Lewin, Albert, **Supp. XIV:** 279, 293
Lewis, C. Day, **III:** 527
Lewis, Dr. Claude, **II:** 442
Lewis, C. S., **Supp. XXV:** 73
Lewis, David Levering, **Supp. XVIII:** 127; **Supp. XIX:** 74, 75; **Supp. XXII:** 13
Lewis, Edith, **I:** 313; **Retro. Supp. I:** 19, 21, 22
Lewis, Edwin, J., **II:** 439, 442
Lewis, Jerry, **Supp. IV Part 2:** 575; **Supp. X:** 172
Lewis, John L., **I:** 493
Lewis, Lilburn, **IV:** 243
Lewis, Lorene, **Supp. IV Part 2:** 596, 597
Lewis, Lucy, **IV:** 243
Lewis, Maggie, **Supp. V:** 23
Lewis, Meriwether, **II:** 217; **III:** 14; **IV:** 179, 243, 283
Lewis, Merrill, **Supp. IV Part 2:** 596, 597
Lewis, Michael, **II:** 451, 452; **Supp. XVII:** 210
Lewis, Michael J., **Supp. XXV:** 253
Lewis, Robert Q., **Supp. IV Part 2:** 574
Lewis, R. W. B., **I:** 386, 561; **II:** 457–458; **Retro. Supp. I:** 362, 367; **Supp. I Part 1:** 233; **Supp. XIII:** 93; **Supp. XXIII:** 42
Lewis, Sinclair, **I:** 116, 212, 348, 355, 362, 374, 378, 487, 495; **II:** 27, 34, 74, 79, 271, 277, 306, **439–461,** 474; **III:** 28, 40, 51, 60, 61, 63–64, 66, 70, 71, 106, 394, 462, 572, 606; **IV:** 53, 326, 366, 455, 468, 475, 482; **Retro. Supp. I:** 332; **Retro. Supp. II:** 95, 108, 197, 322; **Supp. I Part 2:** 378, 613, 709; **Supp. IV Part 2:** 678; **Supp. V:** 278; **Supp. IX:** 308; **Supp. X:** 137; **Supp. XVII:** 41; **Supp. XVIII:** 278; **Supp. XXII:** 190; **Supp. XXIII:** 165, 166; **Supp. XXIV:** 29
Lewis, Mrs. Sinclair (Dorothy Thompson), **II:** 449–450, 451, 453
Lewis, Mrs. Sinclair (Grace Livingston Hegger), **II:** 441
Lewis, Wyndham, **III:** 458, 462, 465, 470; **Retro. Supp. I:** 59, 170, 292; **Supp. III Part 2:** 617
Lewisohn, Ludwig, **Supp. XXIII:** 1
Lexicon Tetraglotton (Howell), **II:** 111
"Lexington Avenue Musedog" (Peacock), **Supp. XIX:** 204
"Leyenda" (Mora), **Supp. XIII:** 214
Leyner, Mark, **Supp. XIX:** 223
Leyte (Morison), **Supp. I Part 2:** 491
"Liar, The" (Baraka), **Supp. II Part 1:** 36
"Liars, The" (Sandburg), **III:** 586
Liars' Club, The: A Memoir (Karr), **Supp. XI:** 239, 240, 241, 242, **244–248,** 252,

254; **Supp. XVI:** 70
Liar's Dice (C. Frost), **Supp. XV:** 93, 96
"Liar's Dice" (C. Frost), **Supp. XV:** 94, 107
Liars in Love (Yates), **Supp. XI:** 348, 349
Libation Bearers, The (Aeschylus), **III:** 398; **Supp. IX:** 103
Li Bay. *See* Li Po
Libby, Anthony, **Supp. XIII:** 87
Libera, Padre, **II:** 278
Liberal Imagination, The (Trilling), **III:** 308; **Retro. Supp. I:** 97, 216; **Supp. II Part 1:** 146; **Supp. III Part 2:** 495, 498, 501–504
Liberating Voices: Oral Tradition in African American Literature (G. Jones), **Supp. XXIV:** 185
Liberation (J. Scott), **Supp. XVII:** 192, **194–196**
"Liberation" (Winters), **Supp. II Part 2:** 791
Liber Brunenesis (yearbook), **IV:** 286
Liberties, The (Howe), **Supp. IV Part 2:** 426–428, 430, 432
Liberties of America, The (H. Warner), **Supp. XVIII:** 259
Liberty Jones (play), **Supp. IV Part 1:** 83
"Liberty Tree" (Paine), **Supp. I Part 2:** 505
Libra (DeLillo), **Supp. VI:** 2, **4, 5,** 6, **7,** 9, 10, 12, 13, 14, 16
Library for Juana, A (Mora), **Supp. XIII:** 218
Library of America, **Retro. Supp. I:** 2
"Library of Babel, The" (J. Borges), **Supp. XVII:** 47
"Library of Law, A" (MacLeish), **III:** 4
"Library of Moloch, The" (Bukiet), **Supp. XVII:** 47, 49
"Librettos for Eros" (Gander), **Supp. XV:** 340
Lice, The (Merwin), **Supp. III Part 1:** 339, 341–342, 346, 348, 349, 355
"License Plate, The" (Ferry), **Supp. XXIV:** 157
Lichtenberg, Georg Christoph, **Supp. XIV:** 339
Lichtenstein, Roy, **Supp. I Part 2:** 665; **Supp. XV:** 186
"Liddy's Orange" (Olds), **Supp. X:** 209
"Lie, The" (Antin), **Supp. XX:** 7, **9–10**
Lieberman, Herman (Chaim), **Supp. XXIII:** 3, 7
Lieberman, Laurence, **Supp. XI:** 323–324
Liebestod (Wagner), **I:** 284, 395
Liebling, A. J., **IV:** 290; **Supp. VIII:** 151; **Supp. XVI:** 167
Lie Down in Darkness (Styron), **IV:** 98, 99, 100–104, 105, 111; **Supp. XI:** 343
"Lie Down with the Lamb" (Gallagher), **Supp. XXIV:** 171
Lie of the Mind, A (Shepard), **Supp. III Part 2:** 433, 435, 441, 447–449
"Lies" (Haines), **Supp. XII:** 204
Lies (Hoffman), **Supp. XVIII: 78–79**
"Lies and Consequences" (Pickering), **Supp. XXI:** 204

Lies Like Truth (Clurman), **IV:** 385
Lieutenant, The (Dubus), **Supp. VII:** 78
"Life" (Wharton), **Retro. Supp. I:** 372
Life along the Passaic River (W. C. Williams), **Retro. Supp. I:** 423
Life Among the Savages (Jackson), **Supp. IX:** 115, **125**
Life and Adventures of Charles Anderson Chester, The (Lippard), **Supp. XXIII:** 184
"Life and Death Kisses, The" (Grossman), **Supp. XIX:** 87
Life and Gabriella (Glasgow), **II:** 175, 176, 182–183, 184, 189
"Life and I" (Wharton), **Retro. Supp. I:** 360, 361, 362
"Life and Letters" (Epstein), **Supp. XIV:** 104–105
"Life and Letters in New England" (Emerson), **Supp. XXIV:** 67
Life and Letters of Harrison Gray Otis, Federalist, 1765–1848, The (Morison), **Supp. I Part 2:** 480–481
Life and Letters of Sir Henry Wotton (L. P. Smith), **Supp. XIV:** 340–341
Life and Mind of Emily Dickinson, The (Taggard), **Supp. XXII:** 279
Life and Times of Frederick Douglass, Written by Himself, The (Douglass), **Supp. III Part 1:** 155, 159–163
Life and Writings of Horace McCoy, The (Wolfson), **Supp. XIII:** 172, 174
"Life as a Visionary Spirit" (Eberhart), **I:** 540, 541
"Life at Angelo's, A" (Benét), **Supp. XI:** 53
Life at Happy Knoll (Marquand), **III:** 50, 61
Life Before Man (Atwood), **Supp. XIII: 24–25**
"Life Cycle of Common Man" (Nemerov), **III:** 278
"Lifecycle Stairmaster" (Karr), **Supp. XI:** 250
Life Estates (Hearon), **Supp. VIII: 68–69**
Life for Life's Sake (Aldington), **Supp. I Part 1:** 256
Life Full of Holes, A (Layachi), **Supp. IV Part 1:** 92
"Lifeguard" (Updike), **IV:** 226; **Retro. Supp. I:** 325
"Lifeguard, The" (Dickey), **Supp. IV Part 1:** 179–180
"Life in the 30s" (column, Quindlen), **Supp. XVII:** 165, 167–169
Life in the Clearings (Shields), **Supp. VII:** 313
"Life in the Country: A City Friend Asks, 'Is It Boring?' " (Paley), **Supp. VI:** 231
Life in the Forest (Levertov), **Supp. III Part 1:** 282–283
Life in the Iron Mills (R. H. Davis), **Supp. XIII:** 292, 295, 299, 305; **Supp. XVI:** 79–82, **85–88,** 91
Life in the Iron Mills and Other Stories (T. Olson, ed.), **Supp. XVI:** 83
Life in the Theatre, A (Mamet), **Supp. XIV:** 241, 255

Life in the War Zone (Atherton), **Supp. XXIV:** 24

Life Is a Miracle: An Essay Against Modern Superstition (Berry), **Supp. X:** 35

"Life Is Fine" (Hughes), **Supp. I Part 1:** 334, 338

"Life Is Motion" (Stevens), **IV:** 74

Life & Letters of Gene Stratton-Porter (Meehan), **Supp. XX: 213**

Life of Albert Gallatin, The (Adams), **I:** 6, 14

"Life of a Man of the World, The"(Lippard), **Supp. XXIII:** 189

Life of an Ordinary Woman, The: Anne Ellis (A. Ellis), **Supp. XVI:** 38

Life of Captain Cipriani, The: An Account of British Government in the West Indies (C. L. R. James), **Supp. XXI:** 161

Life of Dryden (Johnson), **Retro. Supp. II:** 223

Life of Emily Dickinson, The (Sewall), **Retro. Supp. I:** 25

Life of Forms, The (Focillon), **IV:** 90

Life of Franklin Pierce (Hawthorne), **Retro. Supp. I:** 163

Life of George Cabot Lodge, The (Adams), **I:** 21

Life of George Washington (Irving), **II:** 314, 315–316

Life of Henry James (Edel), **Retro. Supp. I:** 224

"Life of Irony, The" (Bourne), **I:** 219

Life of Jesus (Renan), **Supp. XX: 122**

"Life of Lincoln West, The" (Brooks), **Supp. III Part 1:** 86

Life of Mary, The (Rilke; F. Wright, trans.), **Supp. XVII:** 244

Life of Michelangelo (Grimm), **II:** 17

"Life of Nancy, The" (Jewett), **Retro. Supp. II:** 133, 144

Life of Oliver Goldsmith, The, with Selections from His Writings (Irving), **II:** 315

Life of Phips (Mather), **Supp. II Part 2:** 451, 452, 459

Life of Poetry, The (Rukeyser), **Supp. VI:** 271, 273, 275–276, 282, 283, 286

Life of Samuel Johnson (Boswell), **Supp. I Part 2:** 656

Life of Savage (Johnson), **Supp. I Part 2:** 523

Life of the Drama, The (Bentley), **IV:** 396

"Life of the Mind, The" (Kees), **Supp. XV:** 140

Life of the Right Reverend Joseph P. Machebeuf, The (Howlett), **Retro. Supp. I:** 17

Life of Thomas Paine, author of Rights of Men, With a Defence of his Writings (Chalmers), **Supp. I Part 2:** 514

Life of Thomas Paine, The (Cobbett), **Supp. I Part 2:** 517

"Life of Towne, The" (Carson), **Supp. XII: 102**

Life of William Ellery Channing (W. H. Channing), **Supp. XXIV:** 68

"Life on Beekman Place, A" (Naylor), **Supp. VIII:** 214

"Life on the Black List" (Endore), **Supp. XVII:** 63

Life on the Hyphen: The Cuban-American Way (Firmat), **Supp. VIII:** 76; **Supp. XI:** 184

Life on the Mississippi (Twain), **I:** 209; **IV:** 198, 199; **Supp. I Part 2:** 440

"Life on the Rocks: The Galápagos" (Dillard), **Supp. VI:** 32

"Life Stories, East and West" (E. Hoffman), **Supp. XVI:** 157

Life Story (Baker), **II:** 259

Life Studies (Lowell), **I:** 400; **II:** 384, 386, 543, 546–550, 551, 555; **Retro. Supp. II:** 180, 185, 186, 188, 189, 191; **Supp. I Part 2:** 543; **Supp. XI:** 240, 244, 250, 317; **Supp. XII:** 255; **Supp. XIV:** 15; **Supp. XV:** 252

"Life Studies" (Lowell), **Retro. Supp. II:** 188

"Life Styles in the Golden Land" (Didion), **Supp. IV Part 1:** 200

Life Supports: New and Collected Poems (Bronk), **Supp. XXI:** 19, 31, 32

"Life That Is, The" (Bryant), **Supp. I Part 1:** 169

"Life Work" (Stafford), **Supp. XI:** 329–330

"Life You Save May Be Your Own, The" (O'Connor), **III:** 344, 350, 354; **Retro. Supp. II:** 229, 230, 233

Lifshin, Lyn, **Supp. XVI:** 37

"Lifting, The" (Olds), **Supp. X:** 210

"Ligeia" (Poe), **III:** 412, 414; **Retro. Supp. II:** 261, 270, 271, 275

Liggett, Walter W., **Supp. XIII:** 168

Light, James F., **IV:** 290; **Retro. Supp. II:** 325

Light, Kate, **Supp. XVII:** 109

Light and Dark (Bronk), **Supp. XXI: 27–29,** 31

"Light and the Sufferer" (Lethem), **Supp. XVIII:** 139–140

Light around the Body, The (R. Bly), **Supp. IV Part 1:** 61–62, 62; **Supp. XVII:** 243; **Supp. XXI:** 84–85

"Light Comes Brighter, The" (Roethke), **III:** 529–530

"Light from Above" (Eberhart), **I:** 541

Light in August (Faulkner), **II:** 63–64, 65, 74; **IV:** 207; **Retro. Supp. I:** 82, 84, 85, 86, 89, 92; **Supp. XIV:** 12

Light in the Forest, The (Richter), **Supp. XVIII: 216–217**

Light in the Morning (Baker), **Supp. XVIII:** 263, 269

Light in the Window, A (Rinehart), **Supp. XXV:** 198–199, 202

"Light Man, A" (James), **II:** 322; **Retro. Supp. I:** 219

"Lightning" (Barthelme), **Supp. IV Part 1:** 53

"Lightning" (Bynner), **Supp. XV:** 44

"Lightning" (Oliver), **Supp. VII:** 235

"Lightning, The" (Swenson), **Supp. IV Part 2:** 645

"Lightning Flash, The" (Gibran), **Supp. XX: 123**

"Lightning Rod Man, The" (Melville), **III:** 90; **Supp. XVIII:** 4

"Light of the World, The" (Hemingway), **II:** 249

"Lights"(Dybek), **Supp. XXIII:** 72

Lights in the Valley (Bodenheim), **Supp. XXV:** 29

"Lights in the Windows" (Nye), **Supp. XIII:** 280

"Lights Must Never Go Out, The"(Hadas), **Supp. XXIII:** 125

"Light Through the Window, The" (Brockmeier), **Supp. XXII:** 52, 59

Light Verse and Satires (Bynner), **Supp. XV:** 52

Light Years (Salter), **Supp. IX:** 257–259

"LIKE, THIS IS WHAT I MEANT!" (Baraka), **Supp. II Part 1:** 59

"Like All the Other Nations" (Paley), **Supp. VI:** 220

"Like a Rolling Stone" (song, Dylan), **Supp. XVIII:** 20, 30

"Like Decorations in a Nigger Cemetery" (Stevens), **IV:** 74, 79; **Retro. Supp. I:** 305

Like Ghosts of Eagles (Francis), **Supp. IX:** 86

"Like Life" (Moore), **Supp. X:** 163, 165, **172–173**

Like Life: Stories (Moore), **Supp. X:** 163, **171–175,** 177, 178

"Likeness to God" (Channing), **Supp. XXIV: 75–76,** 77, 78

"Like Talk" (Mills), **Supp. XI:** 311

"Like the New Moon I Will Live My Life" (R. Bly), **Supp. IV Part 1:** 71

Li'l Abner (Capp), **IV:** 198

"Lilacs" (Lowell), **II:** 527

"Lilacs, The" (Wilbur), **Supp. III Part 2:** 557–558

"Lilacs for Ginsberg" (Stern), **Supp. IX:** 299

Liliom (Molnar), **Supp. XVI:** 187

Lilith's Brood (O. Butler), **Supp. XIII:** 63

Lillabulero Press, **Supp. V:** 4, 5

Lillian Hellman (Adler), **Supp. I Part 1:** 297

Lillian Hellman (Falk), **Supp. I Part 1:** 297

Lillian Hellman: Playwright (Moody), **Supp. I Part 1:** 280

Lillo, George, **II:** 111, 112

"Lily Daw and the Three Ladies" (Welty), **IV:** 262

Lily for My Love, A (Berrigan), **Supp. XXIV:** 35

Lima, Agnes de, **I:** 231, 232

Lima, Frank, **Supp. XXIII:** 217, 221

Lima, Maria Helena, **Supp. XXII:** 73

Lima Beans (Kreymborg), **Supp. XXII:** 163

"Limbo: Altered States" (Karr), **Supp. XI:** 249–250

"Limen" (Trethewey), **Supp. XXI:** 250

Lime Orchard Woman, The (Ríos), **Supp. IV Part 2:** 538, 547–550, 553

"Lime Orchard Woman, The" (Ríos), **Supp. IV Part 2:** 548

Limitations (Turow), **Supp. XVII:** 222–223

"Limits" (Emerson), **II:** 19

Limits of Mortality, The: An Essay on Wordsworth's Major Poems (Ferry), **Supp. XXIV:** 147, 148

Lincoln, Abraham, **I:** 1, 4, 30; **II:** 8, 13, 135, 273, 555, 576; **III:** 576, 577, 580, 584, 587–590, 591; **IV:** 192, 195, 298, 347, 350, 444; **Supp. I Part 1:** 2, 8, 26, 309, 321; **Supp. I Part 2:** 379, 380, 382, 385, 390, 397, 399, 418, 424, 454, 456, 471, 472, 473, 474, 483, 579, 687; **Supp. VIII:** 108; **Supp. IX:** 15; **Supp. XIV:** 73

Lincoln, Kenneth, **Supp. IV Part 1:** 329; **Supp. IV Part 2:** 507

Lincoln, Thomas, **III:** 587

Lincoln, Mrs. Thomas (Nancy Hanks), **III:** 587

Lincoln: A Novel (Vidal), **Supp. IV Part 2:** 677, 684, 685, 688, 689–690, 691, 692

Lincoln Lawyer, The (Connelly), **Supp. XXI:** 77, 78

Lincoln on Race and Slavery (H. L. Gates), **Supp. XX: 108–109**

"Lincoln Relics, The" (Kunitz), **Supp. III Part 1:** 269

Lincoln: The Man (Masters), **Supp. I Part 2:** 471, 473–474

Lindbergh, Charles A., **I:** 482

"Linden Branch, The" (MacLeish), **III:** 19, 20

Linden Hills (Naylor), **Supp. VIII:** 214, 218, **219–223**

Linderman, Lawrence, **Supp. IV Part 2:** 579, 583, 585, 589

Lindner, April, **Supp. XV:** 111, 119

"Lindo y Querido" (Muñoz), **Supp. XXV:** 135

Lindsay, Howard, **III:** 284

Lindsay, John, **Supp. I Part 2:** 374

Lindsay, Olive, **Supp. I Part 2:** 374, 375, 392

Lindsay, Vachel, **I:** 384; **II:** 263, 276, 530; **III:** 5, 505; **Retro. Supp. I:** 133; **Supp. I Part 1:** 324; **Supp. I Part 2: 374–403,** 454, 473, 474; **Supp. III Part 1:** 63, 71; **Supp. XV:** 293, 297, 299, 301, 306; **Supp. XVI:** 184–185; **Supp. XXV:** 18

Lindsay, Mrs. Vachel (Elizabeth Connors), **Supp. I Part 2:** 398, 399, 473

Lindsay, Vachel Thomas, **Supp. I Part 2:** 374, 375

Lindsay, Mrs. Vachel Thomas (Esther Catherine Frazee), **Supp. I Part 2:** 374, 375, 384–385, 398

Lindsey, David, **Supp. XIV:** 26

"Line, The" (Olds), **Supp. X:** 206

Lineage of Ragpickers, Songpluckers, Elegiasts, and Jewelers, A (Goldbarth), **Supp. XII:** 191

"Line"(Crooker), **Supp. XXIII:** 58

Line Dance (Crooker), **Supp. XXIII:** 56, **58–60**

"Line Dance"(Crooker), **Supp. XXIII:** 59

"Line of Least Resistance, The" (Wharton), **Retro. Supp. I:** 366

Line Out for a Walk, A: Familiar Essays (Epstein), **Supp. XIV: 107**

"Liner Notes for the Poetically Unhep" (Hughes), **Retro. Supp. I:** 210

"Lines, Written on Reading Stuart's Account of the Treatment of Slaves in Charleston" (Very), **Supp. XXV:** 239

"Lines After Rereading T. S. Eliot" (Wright), **Supp. V:** 343

"Lines Composed a Few Miles Above Tintern Abbey" (Wordsworth), **Supp. III Part 1:** 12

"Lines Composed Over Three Thousand Miles from Tintern Abbey" (Collins), **Supp. XXI:** 57–58

"Lines for an Interment" (MacLeish), **III:** 15

"Lines for My Father" (Cullen), **Supp. IV Part 1:** 167

"Lines from Israel" (Lowell), **II:** 554

"Lines from Pietro Longhi" (Sobin), **Supp. XVI:** 289

"Lines on Revisiting the Country" (Bryant), **Supp. I Part 1:** 164

"Lines Suggested by a Tennessee Song" (Agee), **I:** 28

"Lines to a Friend Asleep"(J. Schoolcraft), **Supp. XXIII:** 228, 230

"Line-Storm Song, A" (Frost), **Retro. Supp. I:** 127

"Lines written at Castle Island, Lake Superior"(J. Schoolcraft), **Supp. XXIII:** 229, 232, 233

"Lines Written at Port Royal" (Freneau), **Supp. II Part 1:** 264

"Lines Written in an Asylum" (Carruth), **Supp. XVI:** 48

"Lines Written in Manassas", **Supp. XV:** 99–100

Lineup, The (Connelly), **Supp. XXI:** 67, 68–69

"Line Written in the Dark Illegible Next Day" (F. Wright), **Supp. XVII:** 242

Linfield, Susie, **Supp. XVII:** 169, 177

Lingeman, Richard, **Supp. X:** 82; **Supp. XXII:** 104

Linn, Elizabeth. *See* Brown, Mrs. Charles Brockden (Elizabeth Linn)

Linn, John Blair, **Supp. I Part 1:** 145

Linnaeus, Carolus, **II:** 6; **Supp. I Part 1:** 245

"Linnets" (Levis), **Supp. XI:** 260, 261

"Linoleum" (Gallagher), **Supp. XXIV:** 170

"Linoleum Roses" (Cisneros), **Supp. VII:** 63, 66

Linotte: 1914–1920 (Nin), **Supp. X:** 193, 196, 197

Linschoten, Hans, **II:** 362, 363, 364

"Lion" (B. Kelly), **Supp. XVII:** 133

"Lion and Honeycomb" (Nemerov), **III:** 275, 278, 280

Lion and the Archer, The (Hayden), **Supp. II Part 1:** 366, 367

Lion and the Honeycomb, The (Blackmur), **Supp. II Part 1:** 91

Lion Country (Buechner), **Supp. XII:** 52, 53

Lionel Lincoln (Cooper), **I:** 339, 342

"Lion for Real, The" (Ginsberg), **Supp. II Part 1:** 320

Lionhearted, The: A Story about the Jews of Medieval England (Reznikoff), **Supp. XIV:** 280, 289

Lion in the Garden (Meriweather and Millgate), **Retro. Supp. I:** 91

"Lionizing" (Poe), **III:** 411, 425

"Lions, Harts, and Leaping Does" (Powers), **III:** 356

Lions and Shadows: An Education in the Twenties (Isherwood), **Supp. XIV:** 158, 159, 160, 162

"Lions in Sweden" (Stevens), **IV:** 79–80

Lipman, William R., **Supp. XIII:** 170

Li Po, **Supp. XI:** 241; **Supp. XII:** 218; **Supp. XV:** 47, 217

Lippard, George, **Supp. XXIII: 177–192**

Lippmann, Walter, **I:** 48, 222–223, 225; **III:** 291, 600; **IV:** 429; **Supp. I Part 2:** 609, 643; **Supp. VIII:** 104

Lipschitz, Moryce, **Supp. XXIII:** 6

Lips Together, Teeth Apart (McNally), **Supp. XIII: 201–202,** 208, 209

Lipsyte, Robert, **Supp. XVI:** 220

Lipton, James, **Supp. IV Part 2:** 576, 577, 579, 583, 586, 588

Lipton, Lawrence, **Supp. IX:** 3

Lisbon Traviata, The (McNally), **Supp. XIII:** 198, **199–200,** 201, 204, 208

Lish, Gordon, **Supp. XIX:** 209; **Supp. XXI:** 115, 121; **Supp. XXIII:** 274; **Supp. XXIV:** 166, 177

Lisicky,Paul, **Supp. XI:** 120, 131, 135

Lisk, Thomas, **Supp. XXI:** 24

"Lisp, The" (Olds), **Supp. X:** 211

Listen, Ruben Fontanez (Neugeboren), **Supp. XVI: 220–221**

"Listeners, The" (de la Mare), **Supp. XVII:** 69

"Listeners and Readers: The Unforgetting of Vachel Lindsay" (Trombly), **Supp. I Part 2:** 403

"Listening" (J. W. Miller), **Supp. XX: 167**

"Listening" (Paley), **Supp. VI:** 218, 231, 232

"Listening" (Stafford), **Supp. XI:** 321, 322

Listening to Prozac (P. Kramer), **Supp. XVI:** 229

"Listening to the Desert" (Henderson), **Supp. XIII:** 221–222

"Listening to the Mockingbird" (Woodard), **Supp. VIII:** 128

Listening to Your Life: Daily Meditations with Frederick Buechner (Buechner), **Supp. XII:** 53

Listen to the Desert/Oye al desierto (Mora), **Supp. XIII:** 221

"Listen to the People" (Benét), **Supp. XI:** 51–52

Liston, Sonny, **III:** 38, 42

Li T'ai-po, **II:** 526

"Litany" (Ashbery), **Supp. III Part 1:** 21–22, 25, 26

"Litany" (Collins), **Supp. XXI:** 56–57

"Litany" (Sandburg), **III:** 593

"Litany, The" (Gioia), **Supp. XV:** 125, 126

"Litany for Dictatorships" (Benét), **Supp. XI:** 46, 58

"Litany for Survival, A" (Lorde), **Supp. XII:** 220

"Litany of the Dark People, The" (Cullen), **Supp. IV Part 1:** 170, 171

"Litany of the Heroes" (Lindsay), **Supp. I Part 2:** 397

"Litany of Washington Street, The" (Lindsay), **Supp. I Part 2:** 376, 398–399

Literary Anthropology (Trumpener and Nyce), **Retro. Supp. I:** 380

Literary Art and Activism of Rick Bass, The (Weltzien), **Supp. XVI:** 20–21

"Literary Blacks and Jews" (Ozick), **Supp. V:** 272

"Literary Career of Elizabeth Barstow Stoddard, The" (Matlack), **Supp. XV:** 269

Literary Criticism: A Short History (Brooks and Wimsatt), **Supp. XIV:** 12

"Literary Criticism of Georg Lukács, The" (Sontag), **Supp. III Part 2:** 453

"Literary Development or California, The" (Atherton), **Supp. XXIV:** 22

Literary Disruptions (Klinkowitz), **Supp. XXI:** 233

Literary Essays of Thomas Merton, The, **Supp. VIII:** 207

"Literary Folk As They Came and Went with Ourselves" (E. Stoddard), **Supp. XV:** 274

Literary Friends and Acquaintance (Howells), **Supp. I Part 1:** 318; **Supp. XV:** 287

"Literary Heritage of Tennyson, The" (Locke), **Supp. XIV:** 197

Literary History of the United States (Spiller et al., ed.), **Supp. I Part 1:** 104; **Supp. II Part 1:** 95

"Literary Importation" (Freneau), **Supp. II Part 1:** 264

"Literary Life of America, The" (Brooks), **I:** 245

"Literary London" (Atherton), **Supp. XXIV:** 24

Literary Outlaw: The Life and Times of William S. Burroughs (Morgan), **Supp. XIV:** 141

Literary Situation, The (Cowley), **Supp. II Part 1:** 135, 140, 144, 146, 147, 148

"Literary Worker's Polonius, The" (Wilson), **IV:** 431, 432

"Literature" (Emerson), **II:** 6

Literature (X. J. Kennedy), **Supp. XV:** 153

Literature and American Life (Boynton), **Supp. I Part 2:** 415

Literature and Insurgency: Ten Studies in Racial Evolution (Underwood), **Supp. XXIV:** 29

Literature and Life (Howells), **Supp. XIV:** 45–46

Literature and Morality (Farrell), **II:** 49

"Literature and Place: Varieties of Regional Experience" (Erisman), **Supp. VIII:** 126

"Literature as a Symptom" (Warren), **IV:** 237

"Literature in Low Life" (Hapgood), **Supp. XVII:** 103

"Literature of Exhaustion, The" (Barth), **Supp. IV Part 1:** 48

"Lithuanian Nocturne" (Brodsky), **Supp. VIII:** 29

"Lit Instructor" (Stafford), **Supp. XI:** 321

Littauer, Kenneth, **Retro. Supp. I:** 114

Little Acts of Kindness (Budbill), **Supp. XIX:** 3, **14–15**

"Little Bernhardt" (Shaw), **Supp. XIX:** 246

Little Big Man (Berger), **Supp. XII:** 171

Little Big Man (film), **Supp. X:** 124

Littlebird, Harold, **Supp. IV Part 2:** 499

Littlebird, Larry, **Supp. IV Part 2:** 499, 505

Little Birds: Erotica (Nin), **Supp. X:** 192, 195

"Little Brown Baby" (Dunbar), **Supp. II Part 1:** 206

"Little Brown Jug" (Baraka), **Supp. II Part 1:** 51

"Little Burst, A"(Strout), **Supp. XXIII:** 282

"Little by Little"(Hadas), **Supp. XXIII:** 115

Little Casino (Sorrentino), **Supp. XXI:** 237, 238

"Little Clown, My Heart" (Cisneros), **Supp. VII:** 71

"Little Cosmic Dust Poem" (Haines), **Supp. XII:** 209–210

"Little Country Girl, A" (Chopin), **Retro. Supp. II:** 71

"Little Curtis" (Parker), **Supp. IX:** 193

Little Disturbances of Man, The (Paley), **Supp. VI:** 218

"Little Dog" (Hughes), **Supp. I Part 1:** 329

Little Dorrit (Dickens), **Supp. I Part 1:** 35

"Little Edward" (Stowe), **Supp. I Part 2:** 587

"Little Elegy" (X. J. Kennedy), **Supp. XV:** 155

"Little Elegy for Antonio Machado"(O'Hara), **Supp. XXIII:** 220

Little Essays Drawn from the Writings of George Santayana (L. P. Smith), **Supp. XIV:** 342

"Little Expressionless Animals" (Wallace), **Supp. X:** 305

"Little Fable" (Hay), **Supp. XIV:** 131

Little Face and Other Stories (Thompson), **Supp. XXIII: 293–294**

"Little Face"(Thompson), **Supp. XXIII:** 293

Littlefield, Catherine, **Supp. IX:** 58

Little Fling, A (Pickering), **Supp. XXI:** 203

Little Foxes, The (Hellman), **Supp. I Part 1:** 276, 278–279, 281, 283, 297

"Little Fred, the Canal Boy" (Stowe), **Supp. I Part 2:** 587

"Little French Mary" (Jewett), **II:** 400

Little Friend, Little Friend (Jarrell), **II:** 367, 372, 375–376

"Little Gidding" (Eliot), **I:** 582, 588; **II:** 539; **Retro. Supp. I:** 66

"Little Girl, My Stringbean, My Lovely Woman" (Sexton), **Supp. II Part 2:** 686

"Little Girl, The" (Paley), **Supp. VI:** 222, **228–229**

"Little Girl Tells a Story to a Lady, A" (Barnes), **Supp. III Part 1:** 36

"Little Goose Girl, The" (Grimm), **IV:** 266

Little Ham (Hughes), **Retro. Supp. I:** 203; **Supp. I Part 1:** 328, 339

Little House in the Big Woods (L. I. Wilder), **Supp. XXII:** 294, 295, 296, 297, 298–299, 300

Little House on the Prairie (L. I. Wilder), **Supp. XXII:** 294, 295–296, 297, 299, 301

Little House on the Prairie (television series), **Supp. XXII:** 289

"Little House" series (L. A. Wilder), **Supp. XXII:** 289

Little House Traveler, A (L. I. Wilder), **Supp. XXII:** 301

Little Ignorance, A (Schott), **Supp. XXIII:** 239, 241

Little King, The (Bynner), **Supp. XV:** 42, 50

Little Lady of the Big House, The (London), **II:** 481–482

Little Liar, The (film; Ingraham), **Supp. XVI:** 184–185

"Little Lion Face" (Swenson), **Supp. IV Part 2:** 651

"Little Lobelia's Song" (Bogan), **Supp. III Part 1:** 66

"Little Local Color, A" (Henry), **Supp. II Part 1:** 399

Little Lord Fauntleroy (Burnett), **Retro. Supp. I:** 188; **Supp. XVI:** 182

"Little Lyric" (Hughes), **Supp. I Part 1:** 334

Little Man, Little Man (Baldwin), **Supp. I Part 1:** 67

"Little Man at Chehaw Station, The" (Ellison), **Retro. Supp. II:** 123

Little Me (musical), **Supp. IV Part 2:** 575

Little Men (Alcott), **Supp. I Part 1:** 32, 39, 40

"Little Morning Music, A" (Schwartz), **Supp. II Part 2:** 662–663

Little Ocean (Shepard), **Supp. III Part 2:** 447

"Little Old Girl, A" (Larcom), **Supp. XIII:** 144

"Little Old Spy" (Hughes), **Supp. I Part 1:** 329

Little Orphan Annie (film), **Supp. XVIII:** 244

"Little Owl Who Lives in the Orchard" (Oliver), **Supp. VII:** 239

"Little Peasant, The" (Sexton), **Supp. II Part 2:** 690

"Little People"(Kenny), **Supp. XXIII:** 151

"Little Rapids, The" (Swenson), **Supp. IV Part 2:** 645

Little Red Song Book (Hill), **Supp. XVIII:** 224

Little Regiment and Other Episodes of the American Civil War, The (Crane), **I:** 408

Little River: New and Selected Poems (McCarriston), **Supp. XIV:** 269–272

"Little Road not made of Man , A" (Dickinson), **Retro. Supp. I:** 44

Little Sister, The (Chandler), **Supp. IV Part 1:** 122, 130, 131–132

"Little Sleep's-Head Sprouting Hair in the Moonlight" (Kinnell), **Supp. III Part 1:** 247

"Little Snow White" (Grimm), **IV:** 266

"Little Spirit, or Boy-Man, The: An Odjibwa Tale"(J. Schoolcraft), **Supp. XXIII:** 234

Little Star (Halliday), **Supp. XIX:** 82, **84–85,** 87

"Little Star" (Halliday), **Supp. XIX:** 83, 84, 93

"Little Testament of Bernard Martin, Aet. 30" (Mumford), **Supp. II Part 2:** 472, 473, 474

"Little Things" (Olds), **Supp. X:** 208

Little Tour in France (James), **II:** 337

Little Town, The (Asch), **Supp. XXIII:** 4, 5, **7–8**

"Little Travel Diary, A"(O'Hara), **Supp. XXIII:** 220

Little Women (Alcott), **Supp. I Part 1:** 28, 29, 32, 35, 37, 38, 39–40, 41, 43, 44; **Supp. IX:** 128

Little Yellow Dog, A (Mosley), **Supp. XIII:** 237, 241

"Liturgy and Spiritual Personalism" (Merton), **Supp. VIII:** 199

Litz, A. Walton, **Retro. Supp. I:** 306

"Liu Ch'e" (Pound), **III:** 466

"Live" (Sexton), **Supp. II Part 2:** 684, 686

Live from Baghdad (screenplay, Shanley), **Supp. XIV:** 316

Live from Golgotha (Vidal), **Supp. IV Part 2:** 677, 682, 691, 692

Live Now and Pay Later (Garrett), **Supp. VII:** 111

"Live-Oak with Moss" (Whitman), **Retro. Supp. I:** 403

Live or Die (Sexton), **Supp. II Part 2:** 670, 683–687

Liveright, Horace, **Retro. Supp. I:** 80, 81, 83; **Supp. I Part 2:** 464; **Supp. XX: 71,** 75; **Supp. XXII:** 25; **Supp. XXIV:** 28

Liveright, Horace B., **Supp. XXV:** 24

Livermore, Elizabeth, **Supp. XXII:** 70

Lives (Plutarch), **II:** 5, 104

Lives of a Cell, The (L. Thomas), **Retro. Supp. I:** 322, 323

Lives of Distinguished American Naval Officers (Cooper), **I:** 347

"Lives of Gulls and Children, The" (Nemerov), **III:** 271, 272

Lives of the Animals (Wrigley), **Supp. XVIII: 306–308**

Lives of the Artists (Vasari), **Supp. I Part 2:** 450

"Lives of the Bohemians" (Lethem), **Supp. XVIII:** 135

Lives of the Heart, The (Hirshfield), **Supp. XXIII:** 132–133, 135

Lives of the Muses, The: Nine Women and the Artists They Inspired (Prose), **Supp. XVI:** 250, 260

"Lives of the Philosophers, The" (Brockmeier), **Supp. XXII:** 59, 61

Lives of the Poets (Doctorow), **Supp. IV Part 1:** 234

"Lives of the Poets" (Doctorow), **Supp. IV Part 1:** 234

"Lives of the—Wha'?, The" (Goldbarth), **Supp. XII:** 191

"Living" (Wright), **Supp. XV:** 345

Living, The (Dillard), **Supp. VI:** 23

"Living at Home" (Gordon), **Supp. IV Part 1:** 311

Living by Fiction (Dillard), **Supp. VI:** 23, 31, **32,** 33

Living by the Word (Walker), **Supp. III Part 2:** 521, 522, 526, 527, 535

Living End, The (Elkin), **Supp. VI: 54,** 58

Living Instead (Bronk), **Supp. XXI:** 32

"Living in the Flatlands" (Carruth), **Supp. XVI:** 54

Living in Time (Hadas), **Supp. XXIII:** 120, **122–123**

Living Is Easy, The (D. West), **Supp. XVIII:** 277, 280, **284–286,** 287

"Living Like Weasels" (Dillard), **Supp. VI:** 26, 33

Living Novel, The (Hicks), **III:** 342

Living of Charlotte Perkins Gilman, The (Gilman), **Supp. XI:** 193, 209

Living off the Country: Essays on Poetry and Place (Haines), **Supp. XII:** 199, 203, 207

"Living on a Giant" (X. J. Kennedy), **Supp. XV:** 163

Living Out Loud (Quindlen), **Supp. XVII:** 166, **167–169**

Living Present, The (Atherton), **Supp. XXIV:** 24

Living Reed, The (Buck), **Supp. II Part 1:** 129–130

Livingston, Myra Cohn, **Supp. XV:** 153, 162

Living Theater, **Retro. Supp. I:** 424

"Living There" (Dickey), **Supp. IV Part 1:** 182–183

Living the Spirit: A Gay American Indian Anthology (Roscoe, ed.), **Supp. IV Part 1:** 330

Living to Prowl (Pickering), **Supp. XXI:** 203

"Living with a Peacock" (O'Connor), **III:** 350

"Livvie" (Welty), **IV:** 265; **Retro. Supp. I:** 348–349

"Livvie Is Back" (Welty), **Retro. Supp. I:** 351

Livy, **II:** 8

Lizzie (film), **Supp. IX:** 125

"Llantos de La Llorona: Warnings from the Wailer" (Mora), **Supp. XIII:** 217, 224

"L'Lapse" (Barthelme), **Supp. IV Part 1:** 45–47, 48

Llosa, Mario Vargas, **Supp. XIX:** 131; **Supp. XXIV:** 89

Lloyd, Fabien. *See* Cravan, Arthur

Lloyd, Henry Demarest, **Supp. I Part 1:** 5

Lloyd George, Harold, **I:** 490

"LMFBR" (Snyder), **Supp. VIII:** 302

Loach, Ken, **Supp. XXIII:** 163

"Loaded Inflections" (Halliday), **Supp. XIX:** 90, 91

"Loam" (Sandburg), **III:** 584–585

"Loan, The" (Malamud), **Supp. I Part 2:** 427, 428, 431, 437

Loberer, Eric, **Supp. XV:** 339

"Local" (McCarriston), **Supp. XIV:** 270

Local Color (Capote), **Supp. III Part 1:** 120

"Local Color" (London), **II:** 475

"Local Family Keeps Son Happy" (Keillor), **Supp. XVI:** 168, 169

Local Girls (Hoffman), **Supp. X:** 77, **90–91,** 92

"Local Girls" (Hoffman), **Supp. X:** 90

Local Habitation & A Name, A (Kooser), **Supp. XIX:** 116, 118, **119–120**

Local Men (Whitehead), **Supp. XV:** 339

Local Time (Dunn), **Supp. XI:** 143, **148–149**

Local Wonders: Seasons in the Bohemian Alps (Kooser), **Supp. XIX:** 115, **126**

"Location" (Halliday), **Supp. XIX:** 87

Lock, Helen, **Supp. XIII:** 233, 237–238

Lock, Robert H., **IV:** 319; **Retro. Supp. I:** 375

Locke, Alain, **Retro. Supp. II:** 115; **Supp. I Part 1:** 323, 325, 341; **Supp. II Part 1:** 53, 176, 182, 228, 247; **Supp. IV Part 1:** 170; **Supp. IX:** 306, 309; **Supp. X:** 134, 137, 139; **Supp. XIV: 195–219; Supp. XVIII:** 122; **Supp. XIX:** 69, 75; **Supp. XXII:** 7, 13

Locke, Duane, **Supp. IX:** 273

Locke, Jane Ermine, **Supp. XXV:** 38

Locke, John, **I:** 554–555, 557; **II:** 15–16, 113–114, 348–349, 480; **III:** 294–295; **IV:** 149; **Supp. I Part 1:** 130, 229, 230; **Supp. I Part 2:** 523

Locke, Sondra, **II:** 588

"Locked House, A" (Snodgrass), **Supp. VI:** 323

Locked Room, The (Auster), **Supp. XII:** 22, 24, **27–28**

Locket, The (Masters), **Supp. I Part 2:** 460

Lockridge, Ross, Jr., **Supp. XIX:** 263

"Locksley Hall" (Tennyson), **Supp. IX:** 19

Lockwood Concern, The (O'Hara), **III:** 362, 364, 377–382

"Locus" (Ammons), **Supp. VII:** 28

"Locus" (Hayden), **Supp. II Part 1:** 361–362, 381

"Locusts, the Plaza, the Room, The" (Kees), **Supp. XV:** 141

Loden, Barbara, **III:** 163
Lodge, Henry Cabot, **I:** 11–12, 21
Lodge, Mrs. Henry Cabot, **I:** 11–12, 19
Lodge, Thomas, **IV:** 370
Loeb, Gerald, **Supp. IV Part 2:** 523
Loeb, Harold, **Supp. XXIV:** 49
Loeb, Jacques, **I:** 513; **Retro. Supp. II:** 104; **Supp. I Part 2:** 641
Loeffler, Jack, **Supp. XIII:** 1, 3, 12, 14, 16
Loftus, Mary J., **Supp. XXI:** 245
Lofty Dogmas (A. Finch, M. Kumin and D. Brown, eds.), **Supp. XVII:** 75–76
"Log" (Merrlll), **Supp. III Part 1:** 328
Logan, Joshua, **Supp. XXV:** 95
Logan, Rayford W., **Supp. II Part 1:** 171, 194; **Supp. XIV:** 73
Logan, William, **Supp. X:** 201, 213; **Supp. XI:** 131, 132; **Supp. XII:** 98, 107, 113, 184; **Supp. XV:** 212, 226, 251, 257, 260–261, 262, **Supp. XV:** 263, 266
Log Book of "The Loved One," The, **Supp. XI:** 306
Logenbach, James, **Supp. XVII:** 183
"Logging and Pimping and 'Your Pal, Jim' " (Maclean), **Supp. XIV:** 229
Logue, Christopher, **Supp. XIV:** 82
Lohengrin (Wagner), **I:** 216
Lohrfinck, Rosalind, **III:** 107, 117
Lolita (Nabokov), **III:** 246, 247, 255, 258–261; **Retro. Supp. I:** 263, 264, 265, 266, 269, 270, **272–274,** 275; **Supp. V:** 127, 252; **Supp. VIII:** 133; **Supp. XVI:** 294; **Supp. XXII:** 260
"Lolita" (Parker), **Supp. IX:** 193
Lolly Dinks' Doings (E. Stoddard), **Supp. XV:** 273, **Supp. XV:** 286
Lombardi, Marilyn May, **Retro. Supp. II:** 40
Lomokome Papers, The (Wouk), **Supp. XXV:** 256, 262
London, Eliza, **II:** 465
London, Jack, **I:** 209; **II:** 264, 440, 444, 451, **462–485;** **III:** 314, 580; **Supp. IV Part 1:** 236; **Supp. V:** 281; **Supp. IX:** 1, 14; **Supp. XIII:** 312; **Supp. XIV:** 227; **Supp. XV:** 115; **Supp. XVI:** 181; **Supp. XVIII:** 90; **Supp. XXII:** 203
London, Mrs. Jack (Bessie Maddern), **II:** 465, 466, 473, 478
London, Mrs. Jack (Charmian Kittredge), **II:** 466, 468, 473, 476, 478, 481
London, John, **II:** 464, 465
London, Scott, **Supp. XIV:** 301, 307, 311
London Embassy, The (Theroux), **Supp. VIII:** 323
London Fields (Amis), **Retro. Supp. I:** 278
"London Letter" (column; Eliot), **Supp. XV:** 306
London Magazine (Plath), **Supp. I Part 2:** 541
London Snow: A Christmas Story (Theroux), **Supp. VIII:** 322
London Suite (Simon), **Supp. IV Part 2:** 576, 581, 582, 588
London: The Biography (Ackroyd), **Supp. XVII:** 180

Loneliness of the Long Distance Runner, The (Sillitoe), **Supp. XX: 195**
Lonely Are the Brave (film), **Supp. XIII:** 6
"Lonely Coast, A" (Proulx), **Supp. VII:** 264
Lonely Crusade (C. Himes), **Supp. XVI:** 135, 139–140
Lonely for the Future (Farrell), **II:** 46, 47
"Lonely Gay Teen Seeking Same" (Egan), **Supp. XIX:** 61
Lonely Impulse of Delight, A (Shanley), **Supp. XIV:** 317–318
"Lonely Street, The" (W. C. Williams), **IV:** 413
"Lonely Worker, A" (Jewett), **Retro. Supp. II:** 132
Lonergan, Wayne, **Supp. I Part 1:** 51
Lonesome Boy (Bontemps), **Supp. XXII:** 6, 13–14
Lonesome Dove (McMurtry), **Supp. V:** 226–228, 231, 232, 233
Lonesome Traveler (Kerouac), **Supp. III Part 1:** 219, 225
"Lonesome Whistle Blowing" (Skow), **Supp. XVI:** 174
"Lone Striker, A" (Frost), **Retro. Supp. I:** 136, 137
Long, Ada, **Supp. V:** 178
Long, Frank Belknap, **Supp. XXV:** 111, 122
Long, Haniel, **Supp. XV:** 46, 49
Long, Huey, **I:** 489; **II:** 454; **IV:** 249; **Supp. IV Part 2:** 679; **Supp. XIV:** 14
Long, John Luther, **Supp. XXI:** 150
Long, Judith Reick, **Supp. XX: 212, 215, 217, 223**
Long, Ray, **II:** 430; **III:** 54
Long after Midnight (Bradbury), **Supp. IV Part 1:** 102
Long Ago in France: The Years in Dijon (M. F. K. Fisher), **Supp. XVII:** 91
Long and Happy Life, A (Price), **Supp. VI:** 258, **259–260,** 262, 264, 265
Long Approach, The (Kumin), **Supp. IV Part 2:** 452–453, 453
Longbottom, Robert, **Supp. XXI:** 148
Long Christmas Dinner, The (Wilder), **IV:** 357, 365; **Supp. V:** 105
Long Christmas Dinner and Other Plays (Wilder), **IV:** 365–366
Long Day's Dying, A (Buechner), **Supp. XII:** 45–47
Long Day's Journey into Night (O'Neill), **III:** 385, 401, 403–404; **Supp. IV Part 1:** 359; **Supp. XIV:** 327; **Supp. XXI:** 13; **Supp. XXII:** 27, 29, 30
Long Desire, A (Connell), **Supp. XIV:** 79, 80, 97
"Long Distance" (Stafford), **Supp. XI:** 329
"Long-Distance Runner, The" (Paley), **Supp. VI:** 221–222, 228, 230
Long Dream, The (Wright), **IV:** 478, 488, 494
"Long Embrace, The" (Levine), **Supp. V:** 187
"Long Enough" (Rukeyser), **Supp. VI:** 274

"Longest Night of My Life, The " (Nichols), **Supp. XIII:** 269
Longfellow, Henry Wadsworth, **I:** 458, 471; **II:** 274, 277, 295–296, 310, 313, 402, **486–510;** **III:** 269, 412, 421, 422, 577; **IV:** 309, 371; **Retro. Supp. I:** 54, 123, 150, 155, 362; **Retro. Supp. II: 153–174;** **Supp. I Part 1:** 158, 299, 306, 317, 362, 368; **Supp. I Part 2:** 405, 406, 408, 409, 414, 416, 420, 586, 587, 602, 699, 704; **Supp. II Part 1:** 291, 353; **Supp. III Part 2:** 609; **Supp. IV Part 1:** 165; **Supp. IV Part 2:** 503; **Supp. XII:** 260; **Supp. XIII:** 141; **Supp. XIV:** 120; **Supp. XVIII:** 4; **Supp. XXI:** 51; **Supp. XXIII:** 223
"Long Feud" (Untermeyer), **Supp. XV:** 309
Long Feud: Selected Poems (Untermeyer), **Supp. XV:** 312
"Long Fourth, A" (Taylor), **Supp. V:** 313
Long Fourth and Other Stories, A (Taylor), **Supp. V:** 318–319
Long Gay Book, A (Stein), **IV:** 42
Long Goodbye, The (Chandler), **Supp. IV Part 1:** 120, 122, 132–134, 135
Long Goodbye, The (T. Williams), **IV:** 381
"Long Hair" (Snyder), **Supp. VIII:** 300
Longing for Home, The: Recollections and Reflections (Buechner), **Supp. XII:** 53
Longinus, Dionysius Cassius, **I:** 279
"Long-Legged House, The" (Berry), **Supp. X:** 21, 24–25, 27, 31
Long Live Man (Corso), **Supp. XII:** 129–130, 132
Long Love, The (Sedges), **Supp. II Part 1:** 125
Long Made Short (Dixon), **Supp. XII:** 152
Long March, The (Styron), **IV:** 97, 99, 104–107, 111, 113, 117
"Long Night, The" (Bambara), **Supp. XI:** 9
Long Night of White Chickens, The (Goldman), **Supp. XXV:** 49, 51–53
"Long Novel, A" (Ashbery), **Supp. III Part 1:** 6
Longo, Robert, **Supp. XVI:** 124
Long Patrol, The (Mailer), **III:** 46
"Long Point Light" (Doty), **Supp. XI:** 127
Long Road of Woman's Memory, The (Addams), **Supp. I Part 1:** 17–18
"Long Run, The" (Wharton), **IV:** 314
Long Season, The (Brosnan), **II:** 424, 425; **Supp. XX: 195**
"Long Shadow of Lincoln, The: A Litany" (Sandburg), **III:** 591, 593
Longshot O'Leary (McGrath), **Supp. X:** 117
"Long Shower, The" (Francis), **Supp. IX:** 90
"Long Stemmed Roses" (Jarman), **Supp. XVII:** 115
Longstreet, Augustus B., **II:** 70, 313; **Supp. I Part 1:** 352; **Supp. V:** 44; **Supp. X:** 227

"Long Summer" (Lowell), **II:** 553–554

"Long Term" (Dunn), **Supp. XI:** 149

"Long Thoughts, The"(Dybek), **Supp. XXIII:** 71

Longtime Companion (film), **Supp. X:** 146, 152

Long Valley, The (Steinbeck), **IV:** 51

Long View (Taggard), **Supp. XXII:** 283–284

Long Voyage Home, The (O'Neill), **III:** 388

"Long Wail, A" (Crews), **Supp. XI:** 101

"Long Walk, The" (Bogan), **Supp. III Part 1:** 61

Long Walk Home, The (Kriegel), **Supp. XXIV:** 214–216

Long Walks and Intimate Talks (Paley), **Supp. VI:** 221

Long Way from Home, A (McKay), **Supp. X:** 132, 140

Long Winter, The (L. I. Wilder), **Supp. XXII:** 291, 294, 295

Lönnrot, Elias, **Retro. Supp. II:** 159

Looby, Christopher, **Supp. XIII:** 96

Look, Dan, **Supp. XXV:** 123

Look, Stranger! (Auden), **Supp. II Part 1:** 11

"Look, The" (Olds), **Supp. X:** 210

Look at Me (Egan), **Supp. XIX:** 49, **53–56,** 60, 61

Look at the Harlequins (Nabokov), **Retro. Supp. I:** 266, 270

"Look for My White Self" (Ammons), **Supp. VII:** 25

"Look Fred, You're a Doctor, My Problem Is Something Like This" (Berrigan), **Supp. XXIV:** 37

Look Homeward, Angel (Wolfe), **II:** 457; **IV:** 450, 452, 453, 454, 455–456, 461, 462, 463, 464, 468, 471; **Supp. XI:** 216

"Looking" (Sanders), **Supp. XVI:** 277

"Looking a Mad Dog Dead in the Eyes" (Komunyakaa), **Supp. XIII:** 114

"Looking at Each Other" (Rukeyser), **Supp. VI:** 280, 285–286

"Looking at Kafka" (P. Roth), **Supp. III Part 2:** 402

"Looking at Women" (Sanders), **Supp. XVI:** 274

"Looking Back" (Harjo), **Supp. XII:** 218

"Looking Back" (Merwin), **Supp. III Part 1:** 352

"Looking Back at Girlhood" (Jewett), **Retro. Supp. II:** 131, 133

Looking Backward (Bellamy), **II:** 276; **Supp. I Part 2:** 641; **Supp. XI:** 200

"Looking for a Ship" (McPhee), **Supp. III Part 1:** 312–313

"Looking for Dragon Smoke" (R. Bly), **Supp. IV Part 1:** 60

Looking for Holes in the Ceiling (Dunn), **Supp. XI:** 139, **143–145**

Looking for Langston (Julien; film), **Supp. XI:** 19, 20

Looking for Lincoln (television production), **Supp. XX:** **99**

Looking for Luck (Kumin), **Supp. IV Part 2:** 453, 454–455

"Looking for Mr. Green" (Bellow), **Retro. Supp. II:** 27

"Looking for the Buckhead Boys" (Dickey), **Supp. IV Part 1:** 182, 183

"Looking Forward to Age" (Harrison), **Supp. VIII:** 49

"Looking from Inside My Body" (R. Bly), **Supp. IV Part 1:** 71

"Looking Glass, The" (Wharton), **Retro. Supp. I:** 382

"Lookout's Journal" (Snyder), **Supp. VIII:** 291

"Looks Like They'll Never Learn" (McCoy), **Supp. XIII:** 166

"Look to the Woods" (P. N. Warren), **Supp. XX:** 272

"Look to Thy Heart . . ." (Hay), **Supp. XIV:** 130

Loon, Hendrik Willem van, **Supp. XVI:** 185

Loon Lake (Doctorow), **Supp. IV Part 1:** 219, 222, 224–227, 230, 231, 232, 233

"Loon Point" (O'Brien), **Supp. V:** 237

Loos, Adolf, **Supp. XVI:** 187

Loos, Anita, **Supp. XVI:** **181–199**

Loos, Mary Anita, **Supp. XVI:** 196

Loose Canons (H. L. Gates), **Supp. XX:** **101, 108, 109–110, 111**

Loosestrife (Dunn), **Supp. XI:** **152–154**

"Loosestrife" (Dunn), **Supp. XI:** 154

"Loose Woman" (X. J. Kennedy), **Supp. XV:** 159

Loose Woman: Poems (Cisneros), **Supp. VII:** 58, 71–72

Lopate, Edward, **Supp. XVI:** 266

Lopate, Philip, **Supp. XII:** 184; **Supp. XIII:** 280–281; **Supp. XVI:** 230

Lopatnikoff, Nikolai, **Supp. XIV:** 123

Lopez, Barry, **Supp. IV Part 1:** 416; **Supp. V:** 211; **Supp. X:** 29, 31; **Supp. XIII:** 16; **Supp. XIV:** 227

Lopez, Rafael, **Supp. IV Part 2:** 602

Lorax, The (Geisel), **Supp. XVI:** 109–110

Lorca, Federico García, **IV:** 380; **Supp. I Part 1:** 345; **Supp. IV Part 1:** 83; **Supp. VIII:** 38, 39; **Supp. XIII:** 315, 323, 324; **Supp. XV:** 186; **Supp. XXI:** 100

Lord, Judge Otis P., **I:** 454, 457, 458, 470

Lorde, Audre, **Supp. I Part 2:** 550, 571; **Supp. IV Part 1:** 325; **Supp. XI:** 20; **Supp. XII:** 217, 220; **Supp. XIII:** 295; **Supp. XVII:** 71; **Supp. XXIII:** 194

Lord Jim (Conrad), **I:** 422; **II:** 26; **Retro. Supp. II:** 292; **Supp. I Part 2:** 623; **Supp. IV Part 2:** 680; **Supp. V:** 251

"Lord of Hosts" (Pinsky), **Supp. VI:** 244

Lord of the Flies (W. Golding), **Supp. XVI:** 65

Lord of the Rings (Tolkien), **Supp. V:** 140

Lords of Misrule, The (X. J. Kennedy), **Supp. XV:** 154, **170–171**

Lords of the Housetops (Van Vechten), **Supp. II Part 2:** 736

Lord's Prayer, **I:** 579

Lord Timothy Dexter of Newburyport, Mass. (Marquand), **III:** 55

Lord Weary's Castle (Lowell), **II:** 538, 542–551; **Retro. Supp. II:** 178, **186–187,** 188; **Supp. XV:** 252

"Lorelei" (Plath), **Retro. Supp. II:** 246; **Supp. I Part 2:** 538

"Lorenzo" (Bynner), **Supp. XV:** 46, 50

Lorimer, George Horace, **II:** 430; **Retro. Supp. I:** 101, 113

Lorre, Peter, **Supp. IV Part 1:** 356

"Los Alamos" (Momaday), **Supp. IV Part 2:** 482

Los Amigos de Becky (Hinojosa). *See Becky and Her Friends* (Hinojosa)

"Los Angeles, 1980" (Gunn Allen), **Supp. IV Part 1:** 325

"Los Angeles Days" (Didion), **Supp. IV Part 1:** 211

Los Cerritos (Atherton), **Supp. XXIV:** 22

"Lo! School in Poetry, The" (Taggard), **Supp. XXII:** 276

"Loser, The" (Talese), **Supp. XVII:** 202, 208

Loser and Still Champion: Muhammad Ali (Schulberg), **Supp. XVIII:** 254

Losey, Joseph, **IV:** 383

Lose Your Mother: A Journey Along the Atlantic Slave Route (Hartman), **Supp. XX:** 154

"Losing a Language" (Merwin), **Supp. III Part 1:** 356

Losing Battles (Welty), **IV:** 261, 281–282; **Retro. Supp. I:** 341, 352, **353–354**

"Losing the Marbles" (Merrill), **Supp. III Part 1:** 337

"Losing Track of Language" (Clampitt), **Supp. IX:** 38, 40

Losses (Jarrell), **II:** 367, 372, 373–375, 376, 377, 380–381

"Losses" (Jarrell), **II:** 375–376

Lossky, N. O., **Supp. IV Part 2:** 519

"Loss of Breath" (Poe), **III:** 425–426

"Loss of My Arms and Legs, The" (Kingsolver), **Supp. VII:** 208

Loss of Roses, A (Inge), **Supp. XXV:** 95, 103–104, 106

"Loss of the Creature, The" (Percy), **Supp. III Part 1:** 387

"Lost" (Wagoner), **Supp. IX:** 328

"Lost, The" (Boyle), **Supp. XXIV:** 59

"Lost, The/Los Perdidos" (Kingsolver), **Supp. VII:** 208

"Lost and Found" (Levine), **Supp. V:** 188

"Lost and Found" (Nelson), **Supp. XVIII:** 176

"Lost Bodies" (Wright), **Supp. V:** 342

"Lost Boy, The" (Wolfe), **IV:** 451, 460, 466–467

"Lost Children, The"(Crooker), **Supp. XXIII:** 54

"Lost Decade, The" (Fitzgerald), **II:** 98

"Lost Dogs of Phnom Penh, The" (Boyle), **Supp. XXIV:** 64

Lost Ecstasy (Rinehart), **Supp. XXV:** 196

"Lost Fugue for Chet" (Hull), **Supp. XXI:** 137–138, 141

Lost Galleon and Other Tales, The (Harte), **Supp. II Part 1:** 344

Lost Get-Back Boogie, The (Burke), **Supp. XIV:** 22, 25

"Lost Girls, The" (Hogan), **Supp. IV Part 1:** 406–407

Lost Grizzlies, The: A Search for Survivors in the Wilderness of Colorado (Bass), **Supp. XVI:** 25, 26

Lost Highway (film), **Supp. X:** 314

Lost Illusions (Balzac), **I:** 500

"Lost in Nostalgia: The Autobiographies of Eva Hoffman and Richard Rodriguez" (Fachinger), **Supp. XVI:** 153

Lost in the Bonewheel Factory (Komunyakaa), **Supp. XIII:** 114–115, 116

Lost in the City (E. P. Jones), **Supp. XXII:** 140, 142, **143–146,** 148, 149

Lost in the Cosmos: The Last Self-Help Book (Percy), **Supp. III Part 1:** 397

Lost in the Funhouse (Barth), **I:** 122, 135, 139; **Supp. X:** 307

"Lost in the Whichy Thicket" (Wolfe), **Supp. III Part 2:** 573, 574

Lost in Translation (E. Hoffman), **Supp. XVI:** 147, **148–151,** 153, 154, 159

"Lost in Translation" (Hass), **Supp. VIII:** 28

"Lost in Translation" (Merrill), **Supp. III Part 1:** 324, 329–330

Lost in Yonkers (film), **Supp. IV Part 2:** 588

Lost in Yonkers (Simon), **Supp. IV Part 2:** 576, 577, 584, 587–588, 590–591

"Lost Jerusalem" (Untermeyer), **Supp. XV:** 307

Lost Lady, A (Cather), **I:** 323–325, 327; **Retro. Supp. I:** 15–16, 20, 21, 382

Lost Light (Connelly), **Supp. XXI:** 72, **75–76**

"Lost Lives" (Sorrentino), **Supp. XXI:** 226

"Lost Lover, A" (Jewett), **II:** 400–401, 402; **Retro. Supp. II:** 137

"Lost Loves" (Kinnell), **Supp. III Part 1:** 237, 245

Lost Man's River (Matthiessen), **Supp. V:** 212, 213, 214, 215

"Lost on September Trail, 1967" (Ríos), **Supp. IV Part 2:** 540

Lost Puritan (Mariani), **Retro. Supp. II:** 189

Lost Roads Project, The: A Walk-In Book of Arkansas (exhibition; Wright and Luster), **Supp. XV:** 337, 348

"Lost Sailor, The" (Freneau), **Supp. II Part 1:** 264

Lost Son, The (Roethke), **III:** 529, 530–532, 533

"Lost Son, The" (Roethke), **III:** 536, 537–539, 542

"Lost Sons" (Salter), **Supp. IX:** 260

Lost Souls (Singer). *See* Meshugah (Singer)

"Lost"(Thompson), **Supp. XXIII:** 299, 300

"Lost Treaties of the California Indians" (Zitkala-Ša), **Supp. XXV:** 284

Lost Weekend, The (Jackson), **Supp. XIII:** 262

"Lost World, A" (Ashbery), **Supp. III Part 1:** 9

"Lost World, The" (Chabon), **Supp. XI:** 72–73

Lost World, The (Jarrell), **II:** 367, 368, 371, 379–380, 386, 387

"Lost World, The" cycle (Chabon), **Supp. XI:** 71–73

"Lost World of Richard Yates, The: How the Great Writer of the Age of Anxiety Disappeared from Print" (O'Nan), **Supp. XI:** 348

"Lost Young Intellectual, The" (Howe), **Supp. VI:** 113, **115–116**

Lost Zoo, The: (A Rhyme for the Young, But Not Too Young) (Cullen), **Supp. IV Part 1:** 173

Loti, Pierre, **II:** 311, 325; **Supp. IV Part 1:** 81

"Lot of People Bathing in a Stream, A" (Stevens), **IV:** 93

Lotringer, Sylvère, **Supp. XII:** 4

"Lot's Wife" (Nemerov), **III:** 270

"Lottery, The" (Jackson), **Supp. IX:** 113, 114, 118, 120, **122–123**

Lottery, The; or, The Adventures of James Harris (Jackson), **Supp. IX:** 113, 115, 116, 124, 125

Lotze, Hermann, **III:** 600

Loud and Clear (Quindlen), **Supp. XVII:** 167, **170–172**

Louganis, Greg, **Supp. XX:** 264

"Louie, His Cousin & His Other Cousin" (Cisneros), **Supp. VII:** 60

Louis, Joe, **II:** 589; **Supp. IV Part 1:** 360

Louis, Pierre Charles Alexandre, **Supp. I Part 1:** 302, 303

"Louisa, Please Come Home" (Jackson), **Supp. IX:** 122

Louis Lambert (Balzac), **I:** 499

"Louis Simpson and Walt Whitman: Destroying the Teacher" (Lazer), **Supp. IX:** 265

"Louis Zukofsky: *All: The Collected Short Poems, 1923–1958*" (Creeley), **Supp. IV Part 1:** 154

"Lounge" (Francis), **Supp. IX:** 83

Lounsberry, Barbara, **Supp. XVII:** 208

Lounsbury, Thomas R., **I:** 335

Louter, Jan, **Supp. XI:** 173

"Love" (Collins), **Supp. XXI:** 61

"Love," (Gibran), **Supp. XX:** 119

"Love" (Olson), **Supp. II Part 2:** 571

"Love" (Paley), **Supp. VI:** 219, 222, 230

Love, Deborah, **Supp. V:** 208, 210

Love Alone: 18 Elegies for Rog (Monette), **Supp. X:** 146, 154

Love Always (Beattie), **Supp. V:** 29, 30, 35

Love among the Cannibals (Morris), **III:** 228, 230–231

"Love Among the Ruins" (Mosley), **Supp. XIII:** 247

Love and Death (film; Allen), **Supp. XV:** 2, **5–6,** 7, 11

Love and Death in the American Novel (Fiedler), **Supp. XIII:** 93, 96, **99–101,** 104

Love and Exile (Singer), **Retro. Supp. II:** **302–304,** 315

Love and Fame (Berryman), **I:** 170

Love and Friendship (Bloom), **Retro. Supp. II:** 31, 33–34

Love and Glory (Parker), **Supp. XIX:** 189

"Love and How to Cure It" (Wilder), **IV:** 365

Love and Other Games of Chance (Siegel), **Supp. XXII:** 255, 256, **261–265,** 266, 267

Love and Scorn: New and Selected Poems (C. Frost), **Supp. XV:** 95, 96, 100, 103–105, 106

Love and Theft (album, Dylan), **Supp. XVIII:** 28, 31

"Love and the Hate, The" (Jeffers), **Supp. II Part 2:** 434–435

Love and the Incredibly Old Man (Siegel), **Supp. XXII:** 267–268

Love and Will (Dixon), **Supp. XII:** 148, 149

Love and Work (Price), **Supp. VI:** 261

"Love as a Great Power" (Bronk), **Supp. XXI:** 31

"Love Calls Us to the Things of This World" (Wilbur), **Supp. III Part 2:** 544, 552–553

Love Course, The (Gurney), **Supp. V:** 98

Lovecraft, H. P., **Supp. XXII:** 49; **Supp. XXV:** 109–126

Lovecraft and Influence (R. H. Waugh, ed.), **Supp. XXV:** 123

Loved One, The (film), **Supp. XI:** 305–306, 307

Loved One, The (Waugh), **Supp. XI:** 305

Love Expert, The (film; Kirkland), **Supp. XVI:** 186

Love Feast (Buechner), **Supp. XII:** 52

Love for Love (Congreve), **Supp. XVIII:** 12

"Love Fossil" (Olds), **Supp. X:** 203

"Love"(Hadas), **Supp. XXIII:** 117

Love in a Dead Language (Siegel), **Supp. XXII:** 255, **258–261,** 265–266, 267

Love in Buffalo (Gurney), **Supp. V:** 96

"Love—In Other Words" (Lee), **Supp. VIII:** 113

"Love in the Air" (Jin), **Supp. XVIII:** 93–94

"Love in the Morning" (Dubus), **Supp. VII:** 91

Love in the Ruins: The Adventures of a Bad Catholic at a Time near the End of the World (Percy), **Supp. III Part 1:** 385, 387, 393–394, 397–398

Love in the Western World (de Rougemont), **Retro. Supp. I:** 328

"Love Is a Deep and a Dark and a Lonely" (Sandburg), **III:** 595

Lovejoy, Elijah P., **Supp. I Part 2:** 588; **Supp. XXIV:** 78

Lovejoy, Owen R., **Supp. I Part 1:** 8

Lovejoy, Thomas, **Supp. X:** 108

"Lovejoy Street" (Stallings), **Supp. XXV:** 224

Lovelace, Richard, **II:** 590

"Love Letter (Schnackenberg), **Supp. XV:** 258–259

Love Letters (film), **Supp. IV Part 2:** 524

Love Letters (Gurney), **Supp. V:** 105, 108–109

Love Letters, The (Massie), **Supp. IV Part 2:** 524

Love Letters and Two Other Plays: The Golden Age and *What I Did Last Summer* (Gurney), **Supp. V:** 100

"Love Lies Sleeping" (Bishop), **Retro. Supp. II:** 42

Love Life (Mason), **Supp. VIII:** 145–146

"Love Life" (Mason), **Supp. VIII: 145–146**

Lovell, Julia, **Supp. XVIII:** 101

Lovely Bones, The (Sebold), **Supp. XXII:** 55

Lovely Lady, The (Lawrence), **Retro. Supp. I:** 203

"Lovely Lady, The" (Lawrence), **Supp. I Part 1:** 329

Love Me (Keillor), **Supp. XVI:** 178

Love Medicine (expanded version) (Erdrich), **Supp. IV Part 1:** 263, 273, 274, 275

Love Medicine (Erdrich), **Supp. IV Part 1:** 259, 260, 261, 263, 265, 266, 267–268, 270, 271, 274–275; **Supp. X:** 290

"Love Minus Zero/No Limit" (song, Dylan), **Supp. XVIII:** 31

"Love Nest, The" (Lardner), **II:** 427, 429

Love Nest, The, and Other Stories (Lardner), **II:** 430–431, 436

Lovenheim, Barbara, **Supp. X:** 169

"Love of Annunziata, The" (di Donato), **Supp. XX:** 40

"Love of Elsie Barton: A Chronicle, The" (Warren), **IV:** 253

Love of Landry, The (Dunbar), **Supp. II Part 1:** 212

"Love of Morning, The" (Levertov), **Supp. III Part 1:** 284

Love of the Last Tycoon, The: A Western. See Last Tycoon, The

"Love on the Bon Dieu" (Chopin), **Supp. I Part 1:** 213

Love on the Hoof (O'Hara and Lima), **Supp. XXIII:** 217

Love Poems (Sexton), **Supp. II Part 2:** 687–689

Love Poems (Tentative Title) (O'Hara), **Supp. XXIII:** 219

Love Poems of May Swenson, The (Swenson), **Supp. IV Part 2:** 652, 653

"Love Poet" (Agee), **I:** 28

"Lover" (Hoffman), **Supp. XVIII:** 87

"Love Ritual" (Mora), **Supp. XIII:** 215

Lover of Horses, The (Gallagher), **Supp. XXIV:** 166, 172, 173–174, 176

"Lover of Horses, The" (Gallagher), **Supp. XXIV:** 173–174, 176

Loveroot (Jong), **Supp. V:** 115, 130

"Lovers, The" (Berryman), **I:** 174

"Lovers, The" (Buck), **Supp. II Part 1:** 128

"Lover's Garden, A" (Ginsberg), **Supp. II Part 1:** 311

"Lovers of the Poor, The" (Brooks), **Supp. III Part 1:** 81, 85

Lovers Should Marry (Martin), **Supp. IV Part 1:** 351

"Lover's Song" (Yeats), **Supp. I Part 1:** 80

"Love Rushes By" (Salinas), **Supp. XIII:** 326–327

"Love's Ghost" (Nelson), **Supp. XVIII:** 176

Lovesick (Stern), **Supp. IX: 295–296**

Love's Labour's Lost (Shakespeare), **III:** 263

Love's Old Sweet Song (Saroyan), **Supp. IV Part 1:** 83

"Love Song During Riot with Many Voices" (Hull), **Supp. XXI:** 136

"Love Song of J. Alfred Prufrock, The" (T. S. Eliot), **I:** 52, 66, 569–570; **III:** 460; **Retro. Supp. I:** 55, 56, 57, 60; **Supp. II Part 1:** 5; **Supp. XIII:** 346; **Supp. XVI:** 150; **Supp. XXV:** 22

"Love Song of St. Sebastian" (Eliot), **Retro. Supp. I:** 57

"Love Songs" (Loy), **Supp. XXII:** 161

"Love Songs to Joannes" (Loy), **Supp. XXII:** 161, 163

Love's Pilgrimage (Sinclair), **Supp. V:** 286

"Love the Wild Swan" (Jeffers), **Supp. VIII:** 33

Love to Mamá: A Tribute to Mothers (Mora, ed.), **Supp. XIII:** 221

Lovett, Robert Morss, **II:** 43

Lovett-Graff, Bennett, **Supp. XXV:** 123

"Love-Unknown" (Herbert), **Supp. I Part 1:** 80

Love! Valor! Compassion! (film), **Supp. XIII:** 206

Love! Valour! Compassion! (McNally), **Supp. XIII:** 199, **203–204**, 208, 209

"Love *versus* Law" (Stowe), **Supp. I Part 2:** 585–586

"Love Wall" (Peacock), **Supp. XIX:** 200

Love with a Few Hairs (Mrabet), **Supp. IV Part 1:** 92

Loving a Woman in Two Worlds (R. Bly), **Supp. IV Part 1:** 66, 67, 68–69, 71, 72

Loving in the War Years: Lo que nunca pasó por sus labios (Moraga), **Supp. XXIII:** 194, 195

"Loving on Borrowed Time" (J. W. Miller), **Supp. XX:** 164

"Loving Shepherdess, The" (Jeffers), **Supp. II Part 2:** 432

"Loving the Killer" (Sexton), **Supp. II Part 2:** 688

"Loving Wife" (C. Miller), **Supp. XXII:** 196–197, 199

Lovin' Molly (film), **Supp. V:** 223, 226

Low Country (Siddons), **Supp. XXII:** 239

Lowe, John, **Supp. XIII:** 238

Lowe, Pardee, **Supp. X:** 291

Lowell, Abbott Lawrence, **I:** 487; **II:** 513; **Supp. I Part 2:** 483

Lowell, Amy, **I:** 231, 384, 405, 475, 487; **II:** 174, **511–533**, 534; **III:** 465, 581, 586; **Retro. Supp. I:** 131, 133, 288; **Retro. Supp. II:** 46, 175; **Supp. I Part 1:** 257–259, 261–263, 265, 266; **Supp. I Part 2:** 465, 466, 707, 714, 729; **Supp. XIV:** 128; **Supp. XV:** 43, 293, 295, 297, 298, 299, 300, 301, 303, 306; **Supp. XX: 69; Supp. XXII:** 161

Lowell, Blanche, **Supp. I Part 2:** 409

Lowell, Harriet, **II:** 553, 554

Lowell, James Russell, **I:** 216, 458; **II:** 273, 274, 289, 302, 320, 402, 529, 530, 532, 534, 551; **III:** 409; **IV:** 129, 171, 175, 180, 182–183, 186; **Retro. Supp. I:** 228; **Retro. Supp. II:** 155, 175, 326; **Supp. I Part 1:** 168, 299, 300, 303, 306, 311, 312, 317, 318, 362; **Supp. I Part 2: 404–426; Supp. II Part 1:** 197, 291, 352; **Supp. XV:** 278, 279; **Supp. XVI:** 84; **Supp. XVIII:** 2–3, 4, 8, 12

Lowell, Mrs. James Russell (Maria White), **Supp. I Part 2:** 405, 406, 414, 424

Lowell, Percival, **II:** 513, 525, 534

Lowell, Robert, **I:** 172, 381, 382, 400, 442, 521, 544–545, 550; **II:** 371, 376, 377, 384, 386–387, 532, **534–557; III:** 39, 44, 142, 508, 527, 528–529, 606; **IV:** 120, 138, 402, 430; **Retro. Supp. I:** 67, 140, 411; **Retro. Supp. II:** 27, 40, 44, 46, 48, 50, **175–193**, 221, 228–229, 235, 245; **Supp. I Part 1:** 89; **Supp. I Part 2:** 538, 543, 554; **Supp. III Part 1:** 6, 64, 84, 138, 147, 193, 194, 197–202, 205–208; **Supp. III Part 2:** 541, 543, 555, 561, 599; **Supp. IV Part 2:** 439, 620, 637; **Supp. V:** 81, 179, 180, 315–316, 337, 344; **Supp. VIII:** 27, 100, 271; **Supp. IX:** 325; **Supp. X:** 53, 58; **Supp. XI:** 146, 240, 244, 250, 317; **Supp. XII:** 253–254, 255; **Supp. XIII:** 76; **Supp. XIV:** 15, 126, 269; **Supp. XV:** 20, 22, 93, 184, 249, 251, 253, 340; **Supp. XVII:** 239; **Supp. XIX:** 197; **Supp. XX: 199, 203; Supp. XXI:** 131; **Supp. XXIII:** 211, 220; **Supp. XXIV:** 153

Lowell, Rose, **Supp. I Part 2:** 409

"Lowell in the Classroom" (Vendler), **Retro. Supp. II:** 191

Lowenthal, Michael, **Supp. XII:** 82

Lower Depths, The (Gorki), **III:** 402

"Lower the Standard" (Shapiro), **Supp. II Part 2:** 715

Lowes, John Livingston, **II:** 512, 516, 532; **IV:** 453, 455

Lowin, Joseph, **Supp. V:** 273

"Low-Lands" (Pynchon), **Supp. II Part 2:** 620, 624

Lowle, Percival, **Supp. I Part 2:** 404

Lownsbrough, John, **Supp. IV Part 1:** 209, 211

Lowry, Beverly, **Supp. XXI:** 48

Lowry, Malcolm, **Supp. XVII:** 135, 136

Lowth, Richard, **II:** 8

Loy, Mina, **III:** 194; **Supp. XXII: 155–170**

Loy, Myrna, **Supp. IV Part 1:** 355

"Loyal Woman's No, A" (Larcom), **Supp. XIII:** 142, 143–144

"Luani of the Jungle" (Hughes), **Supp. I Part 1:** 328

Lubbock, Percy, **I:** 504; **II:** 337; **IV:** 308, 314, 319, 322; **Retro. Supp. I:** 366, 367, 373; **Supp. VIII:** 165; **Supp. XX: 231**

Lubin, Isidor, **Supp. I Part 2:** 632

Lubow, Arthur, **Supp. VIII:** 310

Lucas, Craig, **Supp. XXIV:** 263

Lucas, Victoria (pseudonym). *See* Plath, Sylvia

Luce, Dianne C., **Supp. VIII:** 189

Lucid, Robert F., **Retro. Supp. II:** 195, 204

"Lucid Eye in Silver Town, The" (Updike), **IV:** 218

"Lucid Walking" (A. Finch), **Supp. XVII:** 72

"Lucinda Matlock" (Masters), **Supp. I Part 2:** 461, 465

"Luck" (Dunn), **Supp. XI:** 149

Luck of Barry Lyndon, The (Thackeray), **II:** 290

"Luck of Roaring Camp, The" (Harte), **Supp. II Part 1:** 335, 344, 345–347

"Luck of the Bogans, The" (Jewett), **Retro. Supp. II:** 142

Lucky Life (Stern), **Supp. IX: 290–291**

"Lucky Lucy's Daily Dream Book" (Di Piero), **Supp. XIX:** 38–39

Lucretius, **I:** 59; **II:** 162, 163; **III:** 600, 610–611, 612; **Supp. I Part 1:** 363

Lucy (Kincaid), **Supp. VII:** 180, 185, 186, 187–188, 194

Lucy, Saint, **II:** 211

Lucy Crown (Shaw), **Supp. XIX:** 251

Lucy Gayheart (Cather), **I:** 331; **Retro. Supp. I:** 19

"Lucy Tavish's Journey" (E. Stoddard), **Supp. XV:** 286

Lucy Temple (Rowson). *See Charlotte's Daughter; or, The Three Orphans*

Ludlow, Andrea, **Supp. XVIII:** 90

Ludvigson, Susan, **Supp. IV Part 2:** 442, 446, 447, 448, 451

Lueders, Edward, **Supp. XVI:** 265

"Luggage" (Bidart), **Supp. XV:** 35

Luhan, Mabel Dodge, **Retro. Supp. I:** 7; **Supp. XV:** 46, 50; **Supp. XXIV:** 30. *See also* Dodge, Mabel

Lu Ji, **Supp. VIII:** 303

Luke (biblical book), **III:** 606

"Luke Havergal" (E. A. Robinson), **Supp. XVII:** 69

"Luke Havergal" (Robinson), **III:** 524

Lukeman, Gary, **Supp. XV:** 221

Luks, George, **IV:** 411; **Retro. Supp. II:** 103

"Lullaby" (Auden), **Supp. II Part 1:** 9

"Lullaby" (Bishop), **Supp. I Part 1:** 85

"Lullaby" (Everwine), **Supp. XV:** 89

"Lullaby" (Silko), **Supp. IV Part 2:** 560, 568–569

"Lullaby for Amy" (Jarman), **Supp. XVII:** 113, 121

"Lullaby of Cape Cod" (Brodsky), **Supp. VIII:** 27–28

Lullaby Raft (Nye), **Supp. XIII:** 278

Lullaby Raft (Nye, album), **Supp. XIII:** 274

Lullaby: The Comforting of Cock Robin (Snodgrass), **Supp. VI:** 324

"Lulls" (Walker), **Supp. III Part 2:** 525

"Lulu" (Wedekind), **Supp. XII:** 14

Lulu on the Bridge (film), **Supp. XII:** 21

Lulu's Library (Alcott), **Supp. I Part 1:** 43

"Lumber" (Baker), **Supp. XIII:** 55, 56

"Lumens, The" (Olds), **Supp. X:** 209

Lume Spento, A (Pound), **III:** 470

Lumet, Sidney, **Supp. IV Part 1:** 236; **Supp. IX:** 253

Luminous Debris: Reflecting on Vestige in Provence and Languedoc (Sobin), **Supp. XVI: 291–293,** 293–294

"Lumumba's Grave" (Hughes), **Supp. I Part 1:** 344

"Luna, Luna" (Mora), **Supp. XIII:** 217

Lunar Baedecker (Loy), **Supp. XXII:** 165,**Supp. XXII:** 167, 166, 168

Lunar Baedecker and Time-Tables (Loy), **Supp. XXII:** 168

Lunar Follies (Sorrentino), **Supp. XXI:** 226, 237, 238–239

Lunch Poems (O'Hara), **Supp. XXIII:** 219–220, 220

Lunsford, Bascom Lamar, **Supp. XX: 163**

Lupercal (Hughes), **Retro. Supp. II:** 245; **Supp. I Part 2:** 540

Lupton, Mary Jane, **Supp. IV Part 1:** 7

Lure of the Labrador Wild, The (Wallace), **Supp. XXII:** 218

Luria, Isaac, **IV:** 7

Lurie, Alison, **Supp. X:** 166; **Supp. XVI:** 103, 111–112

Lusitania Songspiel, Das (Durang), **Supp. XXIV:** 113, 116

Lust and Other Stories (Minot), **Supp. VI:** 205

Luster, Deborah, **Supp. XV:** 337,**Supp. XV:** 353, 348, 349, 350

Lustgarten, Edith, **III:** 107

Lustra (Pound), **Retro. Supp. I:** 289, 290

Luther, Martin, **II:** 11–12, 506; **III:** 306, 607; **IV:** 490

"Luther on Sweet Auburn" (Bambara), **Supp. XI:** 16–17

Lux, Thomas, **Supp. XI:** 270; **Supp. XIX:** 276

Luxury Girl, The (McCoy), **Supp. XIII:** 163

Lyall, Sarah, **Supp. XIII:** 247

Lycidas (Milton), **II:** 540; **IV:** 347; **Retro. Supp. I:** 60; **Retro. Supp. II:** 186; **Supp. I Part 1:** 370; **Supp. IX:** 41

Lycographia (Paullini), **Supp. XVII:** 55

"Lydia and Marian" (Rowson), **Supp. XV:** 234

Lydon, Susan, **Supp. XII:** 170

Lyell, Charles, **Supp. IX:** 180

Lyell, Frank H., **Supp. VIII:** 125

Lyford, Harry, **Supp. I Part 2:** 679

"Lying" (Wilbur), **Supp. III Part 2:** 547, 562

"Lying and Looking" (Swenson), **Supp. IV Part 2:** 652

"Lying in a Hammock at William Duffy's Farm in Pine Island, Minnesota" (Wright), **Supp. III Part 2:** 589, 599, 600

"Lying in the Pollen and Water" (C. Frost), **Supp. XV:** 96

Lying Ladies, The (Ryan as Finnegan), **Supp. XVIII: 233–235,** 237

"Lying Next to the Knife" (McElwee), **Supp. XXIV:** 167, 173

Lyles, Lois F., **Supp. XI:** 7, 8

Lyly, John, **III:** 536; **Supp. I Part 1:** 369

Lynch, Anne, **Supp. XV:** 273

Lynch, Doris, **Supp. XVI:** 294

Lynchburg (Gander), **Supp. XV:** 340

"Lynched Man, The" (Karr), **Supp. XI:** 241

Lynchers, The (Wideman), **Supp. X:** 320

"Lynching, The" (McKay), **Supp. I Part 1:** 63

"Lynching of Jube Benson, The" (Dunbar), **Supp. II Part 1:** 214

"Lynching Song" (Hughes), **Supp. I Part 1:** 331

Lynd, Staughton, **Supp. VIII:** 240

Lynda Hull: Collected Poems (Hull), **Supp. XXI:** 129

Lynn, Kenneth, **Supp. XIII:** 96–97

Lynn, Kenneth S., **Supp. XIV:** 103

Lynn, Vera, **Supp. XI:** 304

Lyon, George Ella, **Supp. XX: 161–162**

Lyon, Kate, **I:** 409; **II:** 138, 143, 144

Lyon, Thomas, **Supp. IX:** 175

"Lyonnesse" (Plath), **Supp. I Part 2:** 541

Lyons, Bonnie, **Supp. V:** 58; **Supp. VIII:** 138

Lyons, Donald, **Supp. XXIV:** 274

Lyons, Nathan, **Supp. XXV:** 251

Lyons, The (Silver), **Supp. XXIV:** 263, **276**

Lyotard, Jean-François, **Supp. IV Part 1:** 54

Lyrical Ballads (Wordsworth), **III:** 583; **IV:** 120; **Supp. IX:** 274; **Supp. XI:** 243; **Supp. XV:** 21; **Supp. XIX:** 1

Lyrics of Love and Laughter (Dunbar), **Supp. II Part 1:** 207

Lyrics of Lowly Life (Dunbar), **Supp. II Part 1:** 197, 199, 200, 207

Lyrics of the Hearthside (Dunbar), **Supp. II Part 1:** 206

Lytal, Tammy, **Supp. XI:** 102

Lytle, Andrew, **IV:** 125; **Retro. Supp. II:** 220, 221, 235; **Supp. II Part 1:** 139; **Supp. X:** 1, 25; **Supp. XI:** 101

Lyttelton, Alfred, **Supp. XX: 230**

Lytton of Knebworth. *See* Bulwer-Lytton, Edward George

M

Mabie, Hamilton W., **Supp. XVIII:** 257

MCabe, Susan, **Supp. XXII:** 234

McAlexander, Hubert H., **Supp. V:** 314, 319, 320, 323

McAlmon, Robert, **IV:** 404; **Retro. Supp. I:** 418, 419, 420; **Retro. Supp. II:** 328; **Supp. I Part 1:** 259; **Supp. III Part 2:** 614; **Supp. XXII:** 166, 215; **Supp. XXIV:** 62, 63

McAlmon, Mrs. Robert (Winifred Ellerman), **III:** 194. *See also* Ellerman, Winifred

McAlpine, Erica, **Supp. XXV:** 222, 233, 234

McAninch, Jerry, **Supp. XI:** 297, 298

Macaulay, Catherine, **Supp. I Part 2:** 522

Macaulay, Rose, **Supp. XII:** 88; **Supp. XIV:** 348

Macaulay, Thomas, **II:** 15–16; **III:** 113, 591–592

Macauley, Robie, **Retro. Supp. II:** 228; **Supp. X:** 56

Macbeth (Shakespeare), **I:** 271; **IV:** 227; **Retro. Supp. I:** 131; **Supp. I Part 1:** 67; 'Supp. I Part 2:** 457; **Supp. IV Part 1:** 87; **Supp. XIV:** 8

Macbeth (silent film), **Supp. XVI:** 184

MacBeth, George, **Retro. Supp. II:** 250

MacBride, Roger, **Supp. XXII:** 297, 301

McCafferty, Larry, **Supp. XVII:** 227

McCaffery, Larry, **Supp. IV Part 1:** 217, 227, 234; **Supp. V:** 53, 238; **Supp. VIII:** 13, 14; **Supp. X:** 260, 268, 301, 303, 307; **Supp. XVI:** 117; **Supp. XXII:** 177

McCann, Janet, **Supp. XXIII:** 51, 53, 54, 64

McCann, Jannet, **Supp. XXI:** 92

McCarriston, Linda, **Supp. X:** 204; **Supp. XIV: 259–275**

McCarthy, Charles Joseph, Jr. *See* McCarthy, Cormac

McCarthy, Cormac, **Supp. VIII: 175– 192; Supp. XII:** 310; **Supp. XVII:** 185; **Supp. XXI:** 38, 40; **Supp. XXII:** 49; **Supp. XXIII:** 42, 44

McCarthy, Eugene, **Retro. Supp. II:** 182

McCarthy, Joseph, **I:** 31, 492; **II:** 562, 568; **Supp. I Part 1:** 294, 295; **Supp. I Part 2:** 444, 611, 612, 620; **Supp. XV:** 198, 311–312; **Supp. XXIII:** 7

McCarthy, Mary, **II: 558–584; Supp. I Part 1:** 84; **Supp. IV Part 1:** 209, 297, 310; **Supp. VIII:** 96, 99, 100; **Supp. X:** 177; **Supp. XI:** 246; **Supp. XIV:** 3; **Supp. XV:** 142; **Supp. XVI:** 64, 70; **Supp. XVII:** 43

McCay, Maura, **Supp. XII:** 271, 276

McClanahan, Ed, **Supp. X:** 24

McClanahan, Thomas, **Supp. XII:** 125– 126

McClatchy, J. D., **Supp. XII: 253–270; Supp. XV:** 185, 257, 258

McClaurin, Irma, **Supp. XXIII:** 84, 86, 93, 94

McClellan, John L., **I:** 493

McClung, Isabelle, **Retro. Supp. I:** 5

McClure, Charlotte, **Supp. XXIV:** 29

McClure, John, **Retro. Supp. I:** 80

McClure, Michael, **Supp. II Part 1:** 32; **Supp. VIII:** 289; **Supp. XVI:** 283

McClure, S. S., **I:** 313; **II:** 465; **III:** 327; **Retro. Supp. I:** 5, 6, 9; **Supp. XV:** 40

McCluskey, John, Jr., **Supp. XIX:** 65, 68, 71, 72, 78

McCombs, Judith, **Supp. XIII:** 33

McConagha, Alan, **Supp. XVI:** 166

McConnell, Frank, **Supp. X:** 260, 274

McCorkle, Jill, **Supp. X:** 6; **Supp. XVIII:** 195; **Supp. XXV:** 129, 130

McCourt, Frank, **Supp. XII: 271–287**

McCoy, Horace, **Supp. XIII: 159–177; Supp. XXV:** 26

McCracken, Elizabeth, **Supp. X:** 86; **Supp. XII:** 310, 315–316, 321

McCrae, Fiona, **Supp. XVIII:** 60, 62

McCullers, Carson, **I:** 113, 190, 211; **II: 585–608; IV:** 282, 384, 385, 386; **Retro. Supp. II:** 324; **Supp. II Part 1:** 17; **Supp. IV Part 1:** 31, 84; **Supp.

IV Part 2:** 502; **Supp. VIII:** 124; **Supp. XII:** 309; **Supp. XIV:** 120; **Supp. XV:** 338

McCullers, Reeves, **III:** 585, 586, 587

McDavid, Raven I., **III:** 120; **Supp. XIV:** 14

McDermott, Alice, **Supp. XII:** 311; **Supp. XVIII: 155–169**

McDermott, John J., **II:** 364

MacDiarmid, Hugh, **Supp. X:** 112

Macdonald, C. G., **Supp. XVII:** 73–74

MacDonald, Dwight, **Supp. XXV:** 268

Macdonald, Dwight, **I:** 233, 372, 379; **III:** 39; **Supp. V:** 265; **Supp. XIV:** 340; **Supp. XV:** 140

McDonald, E. J., **Supp. I Part 2:** 670

Macdonald, George, **Supp. XIII:** 75

MacDonald, Jeanette, **II:** 589

Macdonald, Ross, **Supp. IV Part 1:** 116, 136; **Supp. IV Part 2: 459–477; Supp. XIII:** 233; **Supp. XVIII:** 137,136; **Supp. XXI:** 67

MacDonald, Ruth K., **Supp. XVI:** 102

McDonnell, Thomas P., **Supp. XX: 45**

MacDougall, Ruth Doan, **Supp. XV:** 58; **Supp. XVI:** 174

MacDowell, Edward, **I:** 228; **III:** 504, 508, 524

McDowell, Frederick P. W., **II:** 194

McDowell, Mary, **Supp. I Part 1:** 5

McDowell, Robert, **Supp. IX:** 266, 270, 276, 279

MacDowell, Robert, **Supp. XI:** 249

McDowell, Robert, **Supp. XVII:** 109, 110, 111

McDowell. Deborah, **Supp. XVIII:** 125, 129

McElderry, Margaret K., **Supp. XV:** 162

McElligot's Pool (Geisel), **Supp. XVI:** 104

McElrath, Joseph, **Supp. XIV:** 62

McElroy, Joseph, **Supp. IV Part 1:** 279, 285

McElwee, Caroline, **Supp. XXIV:** 167, 173

McEuen, Kathryn, **II:** 20

McEwen, Arthur, **I:** 206

McFarland, Ron, **Supp. IX:** 323, 327, 328, 333

McGann, Jerome, **Retro. Supp. I:** 47

McGill, Meredith, **Supp. XVIII:** 17

McGillis, Ian, **Supp. XVIII:** 150

MacGillivray, William, **Supp. XVI:** 8

McGinity, Keren, **Supp. XX: 9**

McGovern, Edythe M., **Supp. IV Part 2:** 573, 582, 585

McGovern, George, **III:** 46

MacGowan, Christopher, **Retro. Supp. I:** 430

MacGowan, Kenneth, **III:** 387, 391

McGrath, Douglas, **Supp. XV:** 12

McGrath, Joseph, **Supp. XI:** 307, 309

McGrath, Patrick, **Supp. IX:** 113; **Supp. XXII:** 58

McGrath, Thomas, **Supp. X: 111–130**

"McGrath on McGrath" (McGrath), **Supp. X:** 119, 120

McGuane, Thomas, **Supp. V:** 53, 220; **Supp. VIII:** 39, 40, 42, 43

MacGuffin, The (Elkin), **Supp. VI: 55–56**

McGuiness, Daniel, **Supp. XV:** 261

Machado y Ruiz, Antonio, **Supp. XIII:** 315, 323

Machan, Tibor, **Supp. IV Part 2:** 528

McHaney, Pearl, **Supp. XXI:** 244, 255, 256, 257

McHaney, Thomas, **Supp. XVIII:** 199,203

Machen, Arthur, **IV:** 286

McHenry, Tim, **Supp. XXV:** 161

Machiavelli, Niccolò, **I:** 485; **Supp. XIX:** 34

"Machine-Gun, The" (Jarrell), **II:** 371

"Machines Mourn the Passing of People, The" (Stallings), **Supp. XXV:** 228

"Machine Song" (Anderson), **I:** 114

McHugh, Heather, **Supp. XIX:** 84; **Supp. XXIV:** 154

McHugh, Vincent, **Supp. XV:** 147

McInerney, Jay, **Supp. X:** 7, 166; **Supp. XI:** 65; **Supp. XII:** 81; **Supp. XVIII:** 148

"Mac in Love" (Dixon), **Supp. XII: 142**

McIntire, Holly, **Supp. V:** 338

McIntosh, Maria, **Retro. Supp. I:** 246

Mack, Maynard, **Supp. XIV:** 12

Mackail, John William, **Supp. I Part 1:** 268; **Supp. I Part 2:** 461

McKay, Claude, **Supp. I Part 1:** 63; **Supp. III Part 1:** 75, 76; **Supp. IV Part 1:** 3, 79, 164; **Supp. IX:** 306; **Supp. X: 131–144; Supp. XI:** 91; **Supp. XVII:** 74; **Supp. XVIII:** 122, 127, 280, 282; **Supp. XIX:** 73; **Supp. XX: 69; Supp. XXII:** 275

McKay, Donald, **Supp. I Part 2:** 482

McKay, Nellie Y., **Supp. XX: 105**

McKee, Elizabeth, **Retro. Supp. II:** 221, 222

McKee, Ellen, **Retro. Supp. II:** 67

McKeen, William, **Supp. XXIV:** 279, 280, 281, 282, 288

McKenney, Eileen, **IV:** 288; **Retro. Supp. II:** 321, 330

McKenney, Ruth, **IV:** 288; **Retro. Supp. II:** 321; **Supp. XVIII:** 238

MacKenzie, Agnes, **I:** 199

Mackenzie, Captain Alexander, **III:** 94

Mackenzie, Compton, **II:** 82; **Retro. Supp. I:** 100, 102

McKenzie, Geraldine, **Supp. XII:** 107

MacKenzie, Margaret, **I:** 199

Mackey, Louis, **Supp. XXI:** 236, 237

McKibben, Bill, **Supp. XVIII:** 192

McKinley, William, **I:** 474; **III:** 506; **Supp. I Part 2:** 395–396, 707

MacKinnon, Catharine, **Supp. XII:** 6

McKnight, Reginald, **Supp. XX: 147– 159**

MacLachlan, Suzanne L., **Supp. XII:** 300,Supp. XII:** 299

McLaverty, Michael, **Supp. X:** 67

McLay, Catherine, **Supp. XIII:** 21

Maclean, Alasdair, **Supp. V:** 244

McLean, Carolyn (pseudonym). *See* Bly, Carol

Maclean, Norman, **Supp. XIV: 221–237; Supp. XVI:** 98

MacLeish, Archibald, **I:** 283, 293, 429; **II:** 165, 228; **III: 1–25,** 427; **Supp. I**

Part 1: 261; **Supp. I Part 2:** 654; **Supp. IV Part 1:** 359; **Supp. IV Part 2:** 586; **Supp. X:** 120; **Supp. XIV:** 11

MacLeish, Mrs. Archibald (Ada Hitchcock), **III:** 1

MacLeish, Kenneth, **III:** 1

McLellan, Joseph, **Supp. XXIV:** 226

McLennan, Gordon Lawson, **Supp. IX:** 89

McLeod, A. W., **Supp. I Part 1:** 257

MacLeod, Charlotte, **Supp. XXV:** 192

McLuhan, Marshall, **Supp. IV Part 2:** 474

McLure, Michael, **Supp. XIV:** 150

Macmahon, Arthur, **I:** 226

McMahon, Helen, **Supp. IV Part 2:** 579

McMichael, Barbara Lloyd, **Supp. XXII:** 206, 207, 215, 216

McMichael, George, **Supp. VIII:** 124

McMichael, Morton, **Supp. I Part 2:** 707

McMichaels, James, **Supp. XIII:** 114

McMillan, James B., **Supp. VIII:** 124

McMillan, Terry, **Supp. XIII: 179–193**

McMullan, Jim, **Supp. XIV:** 124

McMurtry, Josephine, **Supp. V:** 220

McMurtry, Larry, **Supp. V: 219–235; Supp. X:** 24; **Supp. XI:** 172

McNally, Terrence, **Supp. XIII: 195–211**

McNally, T. M., **Supp. XX:** 92

McNamee, Thomas, **Supp. XXII:** 218

McNamer, Deirdre, **Supp. XI:** 190

McNeese, Gretchen, **Supp. V:** 123

MacNeice, Louis, **II:** 586; **III:** 527; **Supp. II Part 1:** 17, 24; **Supp. IV Part 2:** 440; **Supp. X:** 116; **Supp. XIII:** 347

McNeil, Claudia, **Supp. IV Part 1:** 360, 362

M-a-c-n-o-l-i-a (Jordan), **Supp. XVIII:** 172

McPhee, John, **Supp. III Part 1: 289–316; Supp. X:** 29, 30; **Supp. XVIII:** 106–107, 114

MacPherson, Aimee Semple, **Supp. V:** 278

Macpherson, Anne, **Supp. XXIII:** 84

McPherson, Dolly, **Supp. IV Part 1:** 2, 3, 4, 6, 8, 11, 12

McPherson, James Alan, **Supp. XXII:** 141

McPherson, James Allen, **Retro. Supp. II:** 126

Macpherson, Jay, **Supp. XIII:** 19

MacPherson, Jennifer, **Supp. XXIII:** 248

MacPherson, Kenneth, **Supp. I Part 1:** 259

McPherson, Sandra, **Supp. XXIII:** 57

McPhillips, Robert, **Supp. XV:** 119, 250, 251, 252, 264, 266; **Supp. XXIII:** 111, 112, 114, 127

McQuade, Molly, **Supp. VIII:** 277, 281; **Supp. IX:** 151, 163; **Supp. XX:** 90

McQueen, Steve, **Supp. XI:** 306

Macrae, John, **I:** 252–253

McRobbie, Angela, **Supp. IV Part 2:** 691

MacShane, Frank, **Supp. IV Part 2:** 557; **Supp. XI:** 214, 216

"MacSwiggen" (Freneau), **Supp. II Part 1:** 259

McTaggart, John, **I:** 59

McTeague (Norris), **III:** 314, 315, 316–320, 322, 325, 327–328, 330, 331, 333, 335; **Retro. Supp. II:** 96; **Supp. IX:** 332

McWhorter, Dianne, **Supp. XXIII:** 38

McWilliams, Carey, **Supp. XI:** 169; **Supp. XXIV:** 282

Madama Butterfly (opera, Puccini), **III:** 139; **Supp. XXI:** 150, 155

"Madam and the Minister" (Hughes), **Supp. I Part 1:** 335

"Madam and the Wrong Visitor" (Hughes), **Supp. I Part 1:** 335

"Madame and Ahmad" (Bowles), **Supp. IV Part 1:** 93

"Madame Bai and the Taking of Stone Mountain" (Bambara), **Supp. XI:** 14–15

Madame Bovary (Flaubert), **II:** 185; **Retro. Supp. I:** 225; **Retro. Supp. II:** 70; **Supp. XI:** 334; **Supp. XX:** 58

"Madame Célestin's Divorce" (Chopin), **Supp. I Part 1:** 213

Madame Curie (film), **Retro. Supp. I:** 113

"Madame de Mauves" (James), **II:** 327; **Retro. Supp. I:** 218, 220

Madame de Treymes (Wharton), **IV:** 314, 323; **Retro. Supp. I:** 376

"Madame Rose Hanie" (Gibran), **Supp. XX: 124**

"Madame Swann at Home"(Hadas), **Supp. XXIII:** 113

"Madam's Calling Cards" (Hughes), **Retro. Supp. I:** 206

Madden, David, **Supp. IV Part 1:** 285

Maddern, Bessie. *See* London, Mrs. Jack (Bessie Maddern)

Mad Dog Black Lady (Coleman), **Supp. XI:** 85–89, 90

Mad Dog Blues (Shepard), **Supp. III Part 2:** 437, 438, 441

Maddox, Lucy, **Supp. IV Part 1:** 323, 325

Mad Ducks and Bears: Football Revisited (Plimpton), **Supp. XVI:** 243

Mademoiselle Coeur-Brisé (Sibon, trans.), **IV:** 288

Mademoiselle de Maupin (Gautier), **Supp. I Part 1:** 277

"Mad Farmer, Flying the Flag of Rough Branch, Secedes from the Union, The" (Berry), **Supp. X:** 35

"Mad Farmer Manifesto, The: The First Amendment" (Berry), **Supp. X:** 35

"Mad Farmer's Love Song, The" (Berry), **Supp. X:** 35

Madheart (Baraka), **Supp. II Part 1:** 47

Madhouse, The (Farrell), **II:** 41

Madhubuti, Haki R. (Don L. Lee), **Supp. II Part 1:** 34, 247; **Supp. IV Part 1:** 244

Madison, Charles, **Supp. XXIII:** 6, 13

Madison, Dolley, **II:** 303

Madison, James, **I:** 1, 2, 6–9; **II:** 301; **Supp. I Part 2:** 509, 524

"Madison Smartt Bell: *The Year of Silence*" (Garrett), **Supp. X:** 7

Mad Love (film, Freund), **Supp. XVII:** 58

"Madman, A" (Updike), **Retro. Supp. I:** 320

Madman, The: His Parables and Poems (Gibran), **Supp. XX: 115, 118, 125**

"Madman's Song" (Wylie), **Supp. I Part 2:** 711, 729

Madonick, Michael, **Supp. XVII:** 123

"Madonna" (Lowell), **II:** 535–536

"Madonna of the Evening Flowers" (Lowell), **II:** 524

"Madonna of the Future, The" (James), **Retro. Supp. I:** 219

"Mad Song" (Gioia), **Supp. XV:** 128

Madwoman in the Attic, The (Gilbert and Gubar), **Retro. Supp. I:** 42; **Supp. IX:** 66

"Maelzel's Chess-Player" (Poe), **III:** 419, 420

"Maestria" (Nemerov), **III:** 275, 278–279

Maeterlinck, Maurice, **I:** 91, 220; **Supp. XX: 115, 116**

"Magazine-Writing Peter Snook" (Poe), **III:** 421

Magdeburg Centuries (Flacius), **IV:** 163

Magellan, Ferdinand, **Supp. I Part 2:** 497

Maggie: A Girl of the Streets (S. Crane), **I:** 407, 408, 410–411, 416; **IV:** 208; **Retro. Supp. II:** 97, 107; **Supp. XVII:** 228; **Supp. XXIII:** 165

Maggie Cassidy (Kerouac), **Supp. III Part 1:** 220–221, 225, 227, 229, 232

Maggie-Now (B. Smith), **Supp. XXIII:** 258, **267–269**

"Maggie of the Green Bottles" (Bambara), **Supp. XI:** 2–3

"Maggie's Farm" (song, Dylan), **Supp. XVIII:** 25, 26

"Magi" (Plath), **Supp. I Part 2:** 544–545

"Magi, The" (Garrett), **Supp. VII:** 97

"Magic" (Pickering), **Supp. XXI:** 202

"Magic" (Porter), **III:** 434, 435

"Magical Thinking" (Hull), **Supp. XXI:** 137, 139

Magic Barrel, The (Malamud), **Supp. I Part 2:** 427, 428, 430–434

"Magic Barrel, The" (Malamud), **Supp. I Part 2:** 427, 428, 431, 432–433

Magic Christian, The (film), **Supp. XI:** 309

Magic Christian, The (Southern), **Supp. XI:** 297, **299–301**, 309

Magic City (Komunyakaa), **Supp. XIII:** **125–127**, 128, 131

"Magic Flute, The" (Epstein), **Supp. XII:** 165

Magic Flute, The (Mozart), **III:** 164

Magician King, The (Grossman), **Supp. XXV:** 74–77

Magician of Lublin, The (Singer), **IV:** 6, 9–10; **Retro. Supp. II: 308–309**

Magicians, The (Grossman), **Supp. XXV:** 64, 68–74

Magician's Assistant, The (Patchett), **Supp. XII:** 307, 310, **317–320**, 322

Magician's Land, The (Grossman), **Supp. XXV:** 77

"Magician's Wife, The" (Gordon), **Supp. IV Part 1:** 306

Magic Journey, The (Nichols), **Supp. XIII:** 266–267

Magic Keys, The (Murray), **Supp. XIX: 157–158**

Magic Kingdom, The (Elkin), **Supp. VI:** 42, **54–55,** 56, 58

"Magic Mirror, The: A Study of the Double in Two of Doestoevsky's Novels" (Plath), **Supp. I Part 2:** 536

Magic Mountain, The (Mann), **III:** 281–282; **Supp. IV Part 2:** 522; **Supp. XII:** 321; **Supp. XVII:** 137

Magic Tower, The (Willams), **IV:** 380

Magnaghi, Ambrogio, **Supp. XVI:** 286

Magnalia Christi Americana (Mather), **II:** 302; **Supp. I Part 1:** 102; **Supp. I Part 2:** 584; **Supp. II Part 2:** 441, 442, 452–455, 460, 467, 468; **Supp. IV Part 2:** 434

Magnes, Judah, **Supp. XXIII:** 6

Magnificat (Nelson), **Supp. XVIII: 176–177**

"Magnificent Little Gift" (Salinas), **Supp. XIII:** 318

"Magnifying Mirror" (Karr), **Supp. XI:** 240

Magpie, The (Baldwin, ed.), **Supp. I Part 1:** 49

"Magpie Exhorts"(Schott), **Supp. XXIII:** 250

Magpie's Shadow, The (Winters), **Supp. II Part 2:** 786, 788

"Magpie's Song" (Snyder), **Supp. VIII:** 302

Magritte, René, **Supp. IV Part 2:** 623

Maguire, Roberta S., **Supp. XIX:** 160–161

Magus, The (Fowles), **Supp. XIX:** 58

Mahan, Albert Thayer, **Supp. I Part 2:** 491

Mahan, David C., **Supp. XXI:** 86

"Mahatma Joe" (Bass), **Supp. XVI:** 19

Mahlis, Kristen, **Supp. XXIII:** 90, 94

"Mahogany Tree, The" (M. F. K. Fisher), **Supp. XVII:** 88

Mahomet and His Successors (Irving), **II:** 314

Mahoney, Jeremiah, **IV:** 285

Mahoney, Lynn, **Supp. XV:** 270

"Maiden, Maiden" (Boyle), **Supp. XXIV:** 58

"Maiden in a Tower" (Stegner), **Supp. IV Part 2:** 613

Maiden's Prayer, The (Silver), **Supp. XXIV:** 275–276

"Maiden Without Hands" (Sexton), **Supp. II Part 2:** 691

"Maid of St. Philippe, The" (Chopin), **Retro. Supp. II:** 63

"Maid's Shoes, The" (Malamud), **Supp. I Part 2:** 437

Mailer, Fanny, **III:** 28

Mailer, Isaac, **III:** 28

Mailer, Norman, **I:** 261, 292, 477; **III:** 26–49, 174; **IV:** 98, 216; **Retro. Supp. II:** 182, **195–217,** 279; **Supp. I Part 1:** 291, 294; **Supp. III Part 1:** 302; **Supp. IV Part 1:** 90, 198, 207, 236, 284, 381; **Supp. IV Part 2:** 689; **Supp. VIII:** 236; **Supp. XI:** 104, 218,

222, 229; **Supp. XIV:** 49, 53, 54, 111, 162; **Supp. XVII:** 225, 228, 236; **Supp. XVIII:** 19–20; **Supp. XX: 90;** **Supp. XXIII:** 105, 106; **Supp. XXIV:** 281; **Supp. XXV:** 145

"Maimed Man, The" (Tate), **IV:** 136

Maimonides, Moses, **Supp. XVII:** 46–47

Main Currents in American Thought: The Colonial Mind, 1625–1800 (Parrington), **I:** 517; **Supp. I Part 2:** 484

"Maine Roustabout, A" (Eberhart), **I:** 539

"Maine Speech" (White), **Supp. I Part 2:** 669–670

Maine Woods, The (Thoreau), **IV:** 188

Mains d'Orlac, Les (M. Renard), **Supp. XVII:** 58

Main Street (Lewis), **I:** 362; **II:** 271, 440, 441–442, 447, 449, 453; **III:** 394; **Supp. XIX:** 142; **Supp. XXII:** 282

"Maintenance" (Pickering), **Supp. XXI:** 204

Maitland, Margaret Todd, **Supp. XVI:** 292

Majdoubeh, Ahmad, **Supp. XX: 116**

"Majesty" (July), **Supp. XXIV:** 201–202, 203

Major, Clarence, **Supp. XXII: 171–186**

"Majorat, Das" (Hoffman), **III:** 415

Major Barbara (Shaw), **III:** 69

"Major Chord, The" (Bourne), **I:** 221

Majors and Minors (Dunbar), **Supp. II Part 1:** 197, 198

"Major's Tale, The" (Bierce), **I:** 205

Make Believe (J. Scott), **Supp. XVII: 191–192,** 193, **194,** 195

Make-Believe Town: Essays and Remembrances (Mamet), **Supp. XIV:** 240, 251

Make It New (Pound), **III:** 470

Makers and Finders (Brooks), **I:** 253, 254, 255, 257, 258

Makers of the Modern World (Untermeyer), **Supp. XV:** 312

"Making a Change" (Gilman), **Supp. XI:** 207

"Making a Living" (Sexton), **Supp. II Part 2:** 695

"Making Changes" (L. Michaels), **Supp. XVI:** 204

"Making Do" (Hogan), **Supp. IV Part 1:** 406

Making Face, Making Soul: Haciendo Caras, Creative and Critical Perspectives by Feminists of Color (Anzaldúa, ed.), **Supp. IV Part 1:** 330

Making It (Podhoretz), **Supp. VIII:** 231, 232, 233, **237–238,** 239, 244

"Making Light of Auntie" (X. J. Kennedy), **Supp. XV:** 163

"Making Love in 2003" (July), **Supp. XXIV:** 204–205, 210

"Making of a Marginal Farm, The" (Berry), **Supp. X:** 22

Making of Americans, The (Stein), **IV:** 35, 37, 40–42, 45, 46; **Supp. III Part 1:** 37

"Making of Ashenden, The" (Elkin), **Supp. VI:** 49, 50

"Making of a Soldier USA, The" (Simpson), **Supp. IX:** 270

"Making of Garrison Keillor, The" (McConagha), **Supp. XVI:** 166"

Making of Modern Atlanta, The (documentary), **Supp. XXII:** 251

"Making of Paths, The" (Stegner), **Supp. IV Part 2:** 614

"Making of Poems, The" (W. J. Smith), **Supp. XIII:** 348

Making of the Modern Mind (Randall), **III:** 605

Making the Light Come: The Poetry of Gerald Stern (Somerville), **Supp. IX:** 296–297

"Making Up Stories" (Didion), **Supp. IV Part 1:** 196, 203, 205

Making Your Own Days: The Pleasures of Reading and Writing Poetry (Koch), **Supp. XV:** 188; **Supp. XXIII:** 124

Maladies de la volonté, Les (Ribot), **Supp. XX: 238**

Malady of the Ideal, The: Oberman, Maurice de Guérin, and Amiel (Brooks), **I:** 240, 241, 242

Malamud, Bernard, **I:** 144, 375; **II:** 424, 425; **III:** 40, 272; **IV:** 216; **Retro. Supp. II:** 22, 279, 281; **Supp. I Part 2: 427–453; Supp. IV Part 1:** 297, 382; **Supp. V:** 257, 266; **Supp. IX:** 114, 227; **Supp. XIII:** 106, 264, 265, 294; **Supp. XVI:** 220

Malamud, Mrs. Bernard (Ann de Chiara), **Supp. I Part 2:** 451

Malanga, Gerard, **Supp. III Part 2:** 629; **Supp. XXIII:** 221

Malaquais, Jean, **Retro. Supp. II:** 199

Malatesta, Sigismondo de, **III:** 472, 473

Malcolm (Purdy), **Supp. VII:** 270–273, 277

"Malcolm Cowley and the American Writer" (Simpson), **Supp. II Part 1:** 147

Malcolm Lowry's "Volcano": Myth Symbol Meaning (Markson), **Supp. XVII:** 142, 144

"MALCOLM REMEMBERED (FEB. 77)" (Baraka), **Supp. II Part 1:** 60

Malcolm X, **Retro. Supp. II:** 12, 13; **Supp. I Part 1:** 52, 63, 65, 66; **Supp. IV Part 1:** 2, 10; **Supp. VIII:** 330, 345; **Supp. X:** 240; **Supp. XIV:** 306

Malcolm X (film), **Retro. Supp. II:** 12

"Maldrove" (Jeffers), **Supp. II Part 2:** 418

Male, Roy, **II:** 239

Male Animal, The (Thurber), **Supp. I Part 2:** 605, 606, 610–611

"Malediction upon Myself" (Wylie), **Supp. I Part 2:** 722

Malefactors, The (Gordon), **II:** 186, 199, 213–216; **IV:** 139

"Malest Cornifici Tuo Catullo" (Ginsberg), **Supp. II Part 1:** 315

Malick, Terrence, **Supp. XI:** 234; **Supp. XV:** 351

Malin, Irving, **I:** 147; **Supp. XVI:** 71–72

"Malinche's Tips: Pique from Mexico's Mother" (Mora), **Supp. XIII:** 223

"Malinke's Atonement" (Antin), **Supp. XX: 10**

"Mallard" (C. Frost), **Supp. XV:** 98, 99

Mallarmé, Stéphane, **I:** 66, 569; **II:** 529, 543; **III:** 8, 409, 428; **IV:** 80, 86; **Retro. Supp. I:** 56; **Supp. I Part 1:** 261; **Supp. II Part 1:** 1; **Supp. III Part 1:** 319–320; **Supp. III Part 2:** 630; **Supp. XIII:** 114; **Supp. XV:** 158; **Supp. XVI:** 282, 285

Malle, Louis, **Supp. XXIII:** 122

Mallia, Joseph, **Supp. XII:** 26, 29, 37

Mallon, Anne-Marie, **Supp. XXI:** 215

Mallon, Thomas, **Supp. IV Part 1:** 200, 209; **Supp. XIX: 131–145**

Maloff, Saul, **Supp. VIII:** 238

Malory, Thomas, **II:** 302; **III:** 486; **IV:** 50, 61; **Supp. IV Part 1:** 47

"Mal Paso Bridge" (Jeffers), **Supp. II Part 2:** 415, 420

Malraux, André, **I:** 33–34, 127, 509; **II:** 57, 376; **III:** 35, 310; **IV:** 236, 247, 434; **Retro. Supp. I:** 73; **Retro. Supp. II:** 115–116, 119; **Supp. II Part 1:** 221, 232; **Supp. XIX:** 157

Maltese Falcon, The (film), **Supp. IV Part 1:** 342, 353, 355

Maltese Falcon, The (Hammett), **IV:** 286; **Supp. IV Part 1:** 345, 348–351

Mama (McMillan), **Supp. XIII:** 182, **187–188**

"Mama and Daughter" (Hughes), **Supp. I Part 1:** 334

Mama Day (Naylor), **Supp. VIII: 223–226,** 230

"Mama I Remember" (Nelson), **Supp. XVIII:** 173

Mama Poc: An Ecologist's Account of the Extinction of a Species (LaBastille), **Supp. X:** 99, **104–105,** 106

Mama Poems, The (Kenny), **Supp. XXIII:** 143, **154**

Mama's Bank Account (K. Forbes), **Supp. XVII:** 9

Mama's Promises (Nelson), **Supp. XVIII: 173–174**

"Mama Still Loves You" (Naylor), **Supp. VIII:** 214

Mambo Hips and Make Believe (Coleman), **Supp. XI: 94–96**

Mambo Kings, The (film), **Supp. VIII:** 73, 74

Mambo Kings Play Songs of Love, The (Hijuelos), **Supp. VIII:** 73–74, **79–82**

"Ma'me Pélagie" (Chopin), **Retro. Supp. II:** 64

Mamet, David, **Supp. XIV: 239–258,** 315

"Mamie" (Sandburg), **III:** 582

Mammeday, Novarro Scott. *See* Momaday, N. Scott

"Mammon and the Archer" (O. Henry), **Supp. II Part 1:** 394, 408

Mammonart (Sinclair), **Supp. V:** 276–277

"Mammy" (D. West), **Supp. XVIII:** 283

"Mamouche" (Chopin), **Retro. Supp. II:** 66

Mamoulian, Rouben, **Supp. XVIII:** 281

"Man" (Corso), **Supp. XII:** 130

"Man" (Herbert), **II:** 12

"Man Against the Sky, The" (Robinson), **III:** 509, 523

"Man and a Woman Sit Near Each Other, A" (R. Bly), **Supp. IV Part 1:** 71

Man and Boy (Morris), **III:** 223, 224, 225

"Man and the Snake, The" (Bierce), **I:** 203

"Man and Woman" (Caldwell), **I:** 310

Manassas (Sinclair), **Supp. V:** 280, 281, 285

"Man Bring This Up Road" (T. Williams), **IV:** 383–384

"Man Carrying Thing" (Stevens), **IV:** 90

Manchester, William, **III:** 103

"Man Child, The" (Baldwin), **Supp. I Part 1:** 63

Man Could Stand Up, A (Ford), **I:** 423

"Mandarin's Jade" (Chandler), **Supp. IV Part 1:** 125

Mandel, Charlotte, **Supp. XVI:** 57

Mandelbaum, Maurice, **I:** 61

Mandelbaum, Michael, **Supp. XXV:** 264

Mandelstam, Osip, **Retro. Supp. I:** 278; **Supp. III Part 1:** 268; **Supp. VIII:** 21, 22, 23, 27; **Supp. XIII:** 77; **Supp. XV:** 254, 261, 263

"Mandelstam: The Poem as Event" (Dobyns), **Supp. XIII:** 78

"Mandolin" (Dove), **Supp. IV Part 1:** 247

"Mandoline" (Verlaine), **IV:** 79

"Man Eating" (Kenyon), **Supp. VII:** 173

"Manet in Late Summer" (Skloot), **Supp. XX:** 201

"Man Feeding Pigeons" (Clampitt), **Supp. IX: 49–50,** 52

Manfred, Frederick, **Supp. X:** 126

Man from Kinvara, The (Gallagher), **Supp. XXIV:** 166, 172, 173

Man From Limbo, The (Endore), **Supp. XVII:** 55

Man fun natseres, Der (Asch), **Supp. XXIII:** 6

Mangione, Jerre, **Supp. XXV:** 28

"Mango Says Goodbye Sometimes" (Cisneros), **Supp. VII:** 64

Manhattan (film; Allen), **Supp. IV Part 1:** 205; **Supp. XV:** 5, **7–8,** 13

"Manhattan Dawn" (Justice), **Supp. VII:** 117

"Manhattan: Luminism" (Doty), **Supp. XI:** 135

Manhattan Murder Mystery (film; Allen), **Supp. XV:** 5, 11

Manhattan Transfer (Dos Passos), **I:** 26, 475, 478, 479, 480, 481, 482–484, 487; **II:** 286; **Supp. I Part 1:** 57

"Mania" (Lowell), **II:** 554

"Manic in the Moon, The" (Thurber), **Supp. I Part 2:** 620

Manifest; and Furthermore (Bronk), **Supp. XXI:** 32

"Manifesto: A Press Release from PRKA" (Saunders), **Supp. XIX:** 235

Manikin, The (J. Scott), **Supp. XVII: 189–191,** 192, 194

"Man in Black" (Plath), **Supp. I Part 2:** 538

Man in Lower Ten, The (Rinehart), **Supp. XXV:** 192, 200

Man in Prehistory (Chard), **Supp. XII:** 177–178

Man in the Black Coat Turns, The (R. Bly), **Supp. IV Part 1:** 66–68, 71, 73

"Man in the Brooks Brothers Shirt, The" (McCarthy), **II:** 563–564

"Man in the Drawer, The" (Malamud), **Supp. I Part 2:** 437

Man in the Flying Lawn Chair and Other Excursions and Observations, The (Plimpton), **Supp. XVI:** 234

Man in the Gray Flannel Suit, The (Wilson), **Supp. IV Part 1:** 387

Man in the High Castle, The (Dick), **Supp. XVIII:** 138

Man in the Middle, The (Wagoner), **Supp. IX:** 324, **332–333**

"Man in the Rain, The" (Ryan as Quin), **Supp. XVIII:** 226

"Man in the Toolhouse, The" (Swados), **Supp. XIX:** 263

Mankiewicz, Frank, **Supp. XXIV:** 279

Mankiewicz, Herman, **Supp. XVI:** 189

Mankiewicz, Joseph, **Retro. Supp. I:** 113

Mankowitz, Wolf, **Supp. XI:** 307

"Man Made of Words, The" (Momaday), **Supp. IV Part 2:** 481, 484–485, 486, 487, 488

Man-Made World, The (Gilman), **Supp. XI:** 207

"Man-Moth, The" (Bishop), **Retro. Supp. II:** 42; **Supp. I Part 1:** 85–87, 88

Mann, Charles, **Retro. Supp. II:** 40

Mann, Erika, **Supp. II Part 1:** 11

Mann, Seymour (Samuel Weisman), **Supp. V:** 113

Mann, Thomas, **I:** 271, 490; **II:** 42, 539; **III:** 231, 281–282, 283; **IV:** 70, 73, 85; **Supp. IV Part 1:** 392; **Supp. IV Part 2:** 522; **Supp. V:** 51; **Supp. IX:** 21; **Supp. XI:** 275; **Supp. XII:** 173, 310, 321; **Supp. XIV:** 87; **Supp. XVII:** 137; **Supp. XIX:** 147, 151, 157; **Supp. XX:** 85; **Supp. XXIII:** 4

Mannequins' Demise: A Play in Eight Scenes (Budbill), **Supp. XIX: 12**

Mannerhouse (Wolfe), **IV:** 460

Manner Music, The (Reznikoff), **Supp. XIV: 293–295**

"Manners" (Bishop), **Supp. I Part 1:** 73

"Manners" (Emerson), **II:** 4, 6

"Manners, Morals, and the Novel" (Trilling), **Supp. III Part 2:** 502, 503

Mannheim, Karl, **I:** 279; **Supp. I Part 2:** 644

Manning, Ambrose, **Supp. XX:** 166

Manning, Frederic, **III:** 459

Manning, Robert, **Supp. IX:** 236

Mannix, Daniel P., **Supp. II Part 1:** 140

Man Nobody Knows, The (B. Barton), **Retro. Supp. I:** 179

Mano, D. Keith, **Supp. XVI:** 250

Mano, Guy Levis, **Supp. XVI:** 282

"Man of Indeterminate Age on a Subway Grate, A" (DI Piero), **Supp. XIX:** 47

"Man of Letters" (Pickering), **Supp. XXI:** 192, 195–196

"Man of Letters as a Man of Business, The" (Howells), **Supp. XIV:** 45–46

"Man of No Account, The" (Harte), **Supp. II Part 1:** 339

"Man of the Crowd, The" (Poe), **III:** 412, 417; **Retro. Supp. I:** 154

Man on Spikes (Asinof), **II:** 424

Man on Stage (Dixon), **Supp. XII:** 141, **154–155**

"Man on the Dump, The" (Stevens), **IV:** 74; **Retro. Supp. I:** 306

"Man on the Stairs, The" (July), **Supp. XXIV:** 202

"Man on the Train, The" (Percy), **Supp. III Part 1:** 387

Manor, The (Singer), **IV:** 6, 17–19

Manrique, Jorge, **Retro. Supp. II:** 154

Mansart Builds a School (Du Bois), **Supp. II Part 1:** 185–186

Man's Fate (Malraux), **I:** 127; **Retro. Supp. II:** 121

"Man's Fate A Film Treatment of the Malraux Novel" (Agee), **I:** 33–34

Mansfield, June, **Supp. X:** 183, 194

Mansfield, Katherine, **III:** 362, 453

Mansfield, Stephanie, **Supp. IV Part 1:** 227

Man's Hope (Malraux), **IV:** 247

Mansion, The (Faulkner), **II:** 73; **Retro. Supp. I:** 74, 82

Man's Nature and His Communities (Niebuhr), **III:** 308

Manson, Charles, **Supp. IV Part 1:** 205

"Man Splitting Wood in the Daybreak, The" (Kinnell), **Supp. III Part 1:** 254

"Man's Pride" (Jeffers), **Supp. II Part 2:** 417

"Man's Story, The" (Anderson), **I:** 114

Man's Woman, A (Norris), **III:** 314, 322, 328, 329, 330, 332, 333

Man That Corrupted Hadleyburg, The (Twain), **I:** 204; **IV:** 208

"Man That Was Used Up, The" (Poe), **III:** 412, 425

"Mantis" (Zukofsky), **Supp. III Part 2:** 617

"'Mantis': An Interpretation" (Zukofsky), **Supp. III Part 2:** 617–618

"Man to Know in the Restaurants, The" (Siddons), **Supp. XXII:** 244

Man to Send Rain Clouds, The (Rosen, ed.), **Supp. IV Part 2:** 499, 505, 513

"Man to Send Rain Clouds, The" (Silko), **Supp. IV Part 2:** 559

Mantrap (Lewis), **II:** 447

Manuductio Ad Ministerium (Mather), **Supp. II Part 2:** 465–467

"Manuelzinho" (Bishop), **Retro. Supp. II:** 47–48

Manuscript Books of Emily Dickinson, The (Franklin, ed.), **Retro. Supp. I:** 29, 41

"Man Waiting for It to Stop, A" (Dunn), **Supp. XI:** 144

"Man Who Became a Woman, The" (Anderson), **I:** 114

"Man Who Carries the Desert Around Inside Himself, The: For Wally" (Komunyakaa), **Supp. XIII:** 125

"Man Who Closed Shop, The" (Dunn), **Supp. XI:** 149

Man Who Gave Up His Name, The (Harrison), **Supp. VIII:** 45, 52

Man Who Had All the Luck, The (A. Miller), **III:** 148, 149, 164, 166

"Man Who Knew Belle Star, The" (Bausch), **Supp. VII:** 46

"Man Who Knew Coolidge, The" (Lewis), **II:** 449

Man Who Knew Coolidge, The: Being the Soul of Lowell Schmaltz, Constructive and Nordic Citizen (Lewis), **II:** 450

Man Who Lived Underground, The (Wright), **Supp. II Part 1:** 40

"Man Who Lived Underground, The" (Wright), **IV:** 479, 485–487, 492; **Retro. Supp. II:** 121

"Man Who Made Me Love Him, The" (Weigl), **Supp. XIX:** 278

"Man Who Makes Brooms, The" (Nye), **Supp. XIII:** 276

"Man Who Studied Yoga, The" (Mailer), **III:** 35–36; **Retro. Supp. II:** 200

"Man Who Wanted to Win, The" (McCoy), **Supp. XIII:** 161

Man Who Was There, The (Morris), **III:** 220–221

"Man Who Writes Ants, The" (Merwin), **Supp. III Part 1:** 348

"Man with a Family" (Humphrey), **Supp. IX:** 94

Man without a Country, The (Hale), **I:** 488

"Man with the Blue Guitar, The" (Stevens), **I:** 266; **IV:** 85–87; **Retro. Supp. I:** **303–305,** 306, 307, 309

Man with the Blue Guitar and Other Poems, The (Stevens), **IV:** 76; **Retro. Supp. I:** 303, 422

Man with the Golden Arm, The (Algren), **Supp. V:** 4; **Supp. IX:** 1, 3, **9–11,** 14, 15

Man with the Golden Arm, The (film), **Supp. IX:** 3

"Man with the Golden Beef, The" (Podhoretz), **Supp. IX:** 3

"Man with the Hoe, The" (Markham), **Supp. XV:** 115

Man with the Mask, The (Lippard), **Supp. XXIII:** 178, 183–184, 188

Many a Monster (Ryan as Finnegan), **Supp. XVIII:** 233, **236–238**

Manyan Letters (Olson), **Supp. II Part 2:** 571

Many Circles (Goldbarth), **Supp. XII:** 193

"Many Handles" (Sandburg), **III:** 594

"Many Happy Returns" (Auden), **Supp. II Part 1:** 15

Many Happy Returns (Berrigan), **Supp. XXII:** 224; **Supp. XXIV:** 37, 41

Many Loves (W. C. Williams), **Retro. Supp. I:** 424

"Many Mansions" (H. Roth), **Supp. IX:** 233, 234

Many Marriages (Anderson), **I:** 104, 111, 113

"Many of Our Waters: Variations on a Poem by a Black Child" (Wright), **Supp. III Part 2:** 602

"Many Swans" (Lowell), **II:** 526

"Many Thousands Gone" (Baldwin), **Retro. Supp. II:** 4; **Supp. I Part 1:** 51

"Many Wagons Ago" (Ashbery), **Supp. III Part 1:** 22

Many-Windowed House, A (Cowley), **Supp. II Part 1:** 141, 143

"Many-Windowed House, A" (Cowley), **Supp. II Part 1:** 137

Mao II (DeLillo), **Supp. VI:** 2, 4, **5,** 6, **7,** 8, 9, 14, 16

"Map, The" (Bishop), **Retro. Supp. II:** 41; **Supp. I Part 1:** 72, 82, 85–88, 93

"Map, The" (Strand), **Supp. IV Part 2:** 623–624

"Maple Leaf, The" (Joplin), **Supp. IV Part 1:** 223

"Maple Tree, The" (D. West), **Supp. XVIII:** 284

Map of Another Town: A Memoir of Provence (M. F. K. Fisher), **Supp. XVII:** 88, 89, 92

"Map of Montana in Italy, A" (Hugo), **Supp. VI:** 139

Mapp and Lucia (Benson), **Supp. XX: 229**

Mapping American Culture (Franklin and Steiner), **Supp. XXII:** 205

"Maps" (Hass), **Supp. VI:** 103–104

Mapson, Jo-Ann, **Supp. IV Part 2:** 440, 454

Map to the Next World, A: Poems and Tales (Harjo), **Supp. XII: 228–230**

"Maquillage" (Hull), **Supp. XXI:** 133

"Mara" (Jeffers), **Supp. II Part 2:** 434

Ma Rainey's Black Bottom (Wilson), **Supp. VIII:** 331, **332–334,** 346, 349, 350

Maranen (Asch), **Supp. XXIII:** 10

Marat, Jean Paul, **IV:** 117; **Supp. I Part 2:** 514, 515, 521

"Marathon" (Glück), **Supp. V:** 85

Marble Faun, The (Faulkner), **II:** 55, 56; **Retro. Supp. I:** 79

Marble Faun, The; or, The Romance of Monte Beni (Hawthorne), **II:** 225, 239, 242–243, 290, 324; **IV:** 167; **Retro. Supp. I:** 63, 149, 163, **164–165; Supp. I Part 1:** 38; **Supp. I Part 2:** 421, 596; **Supp. XIII:** 102

Marbles (Brodsky), **Supp. VIII:** 26–27

Marburg, Anita, **Supp. XXII:** 281

Marcaccio, Michael, **Supp. XVII:** 97, 106

"March" (W. C. Williams), **Retro. Supp. I:** 418

March, Alan, **Supp. XVI:** 242

March, Fredric, **III:** 154, 403; **IV:** 357; **Supp. X:** 220

"March, March on Down the Field" (Shaw), **Supp. XIX:** 246

Marchalonis, Shirley, **Supp. XIII:** 138, 140, 141, 143, 147–148

"Marché aux Oiseaux" (Wilbur), **Supp. III Part 2:** 550

"Märchen, The" (Jarrell), **II:** 378–379

March Hares (Frederic), **II:** 143–144

Marching Men (Anderson), **I:** 99, 101, 103–105, 111

"Marching Music" (Simic), **Supp. VIII:** 281
"Marcia" (R. H. Davis), **Supp. XVI:** 91–92
Marcks, Greg, **Supp. XVIII:** 150
Marckwardt, Albert H., **Supp. XXIV:** 255
Marco Millions (O'Neill), **III:** 391, 395
Marcosson, Isaac, **III:** 322
Marcus, Greil, **Supp. XVIII:** 30, 53
Marcus, Steven, **Retro. Supp. II:** 196, 200
Marcus Aurelius, **II:** 1; **III:** 566; **Supp. XVIII:** 304
Marcuse, Herbert, **Supp. I Part 2:** 645; **Supp. VIII:** 196; **Supp. XII:** 2
Mardi and a Voyage Thither (Melville), **I:** 384; **II:** 281; **III:** 77–79, 84, 87, 89; **Retro. Supp. I:** 247, 254, 256
Margaret (Judd), **II:** 290
Margaret & Dusty (Notley), **Supp. XXII:** 231
"Margaret Fuller, 1847" (Clampitt), **Supp. IX:** 43
"Marginalia" (Wilbur), **Supp. III Part 2:** 544
Margin of Hope, A: An Intellectual Autobiography (Howe), **Supp. VI:** 113–114, 117, 125, 128
"Margins of Maycomb, The: A Rereading of *To Kill a Mockingbird*" (Phelps), **Supp. VIII:** 128
Margoshes, Samuel, **Supp. X:** 70
"Margrave" (Jeffers), **Supp. II Part 2:** 426
Margret Howth (R. H. Davis), **Supp. XVI:** 81, 83, 84, **88–89**
Margret Howth: A Story of Today (J. Yellin, ed.), **Supp. XVI:** 88
Margulies, Donald, **Supp. XXI:** 145
"Maria Concepción" (Porter), **III:** 434–435, 451
Mariani, Paul L., **Retro. Supp. I:** 412, 419; **Retro. Supp. II:** 189
Marianne Moore Reader, (Moore), **III:** 199
Marie Antoinette (film), **Retro. Supp. I:** 113
Marie Blythe (Mosher), **Supp. XXII:** 206, 209, **212**
Marie Laveau (Prose), **Supp. XVI:** 251
Mariella Gable, Sister, **III:** 339, 355
"Marijuana and a Pistol" (C. Himes), **Supp. XVI:** 137
"Marijuana Notation" (Ginsberg), **Supp. II Part 1:** 313
Maril, Herman, **Supp. XXI:** 22, 23
Marilyn: A Biography (Mailer), **Retro. Supp. II:** 208
"Marin" (Cisneros), **Supp. VII:** 60, 61
Marin, Jay, **Retro. Supp. II:** 325
"Marina" (Eliot), **I:** 584, 585; **Retro. Supp. I:** 64
Mariners, Renegades, and Castaways (C. L. R. James), **Supp. XXI:** 159, 169–170
"Marine Surface, Low Overcast" (Clampitt), **Supp. IX: 47–48**
Marinetti, F. T., **Supp. XXII:** 159, 160, 161, 163
Marinetti, Tommaso, **Retro. Supp. I:** 59

Marionettes, The (Faulkner), **Retro. Supp. I:** 79
"Mari Sandoz's *Slogum House:* Greed as a Woman" (Riley), **Supp. XXIV:** 252
Maritain, Jacques, **I:** 402
Maritime Compact (Paine), **Supp. I Part 2:** 519
Maritime History of Massachusetts, 1783–1860, The (Morison), **Supp. I Part 2:** 481–483
Marjolin, Jean-Nicolas, **Supp. I Part 1:** 302
Marjorie Kinnan Rawlings: Sojourner at Cross Creek (Silverthorne), **Supp. X:** 220, 234
Marjorie Morningstar (film), **Supp. XXV:** 262
Marjorie Morningstar (Wouk), **Supp. XXV:** 253, 254, 256, 258, 261–262, 268
"Mark, The" (Bogan), **Supp. III Part 1:** 52
Marker, Chris, **Supp. IV Part 2:** 434, 436
"Market" (Hayden), **Supp. II Part 1:** 368, 369
Marketplace, The (Frederic), **II:** 145–146
Markham, Edwin, **I:** 199, 207; **Supp. XV:** 115
Markings (Hammarskjold), **Supp. II Part 1:** 26
Mark of the Vampire (film, Browning), **Supp. XVII:** 58
Markopoulos, Gregory, **Supp. XII:** 2
Markowick-Olczakova, Hanna, **Supp. X:** 70
Marks, Alison, **Supp. I Part 2:** 660
Marks, Barry A., **I:** 435, 438, 442, 446
Markson, David, **Supp. XVII: 135–147**
Mark Twain in Eruption (Twain), **IV:** 209
Mark Twain's America (De Voto), **I:** 248
Mark Twain's Autobiography (Twain), **IV:** 209
Marley, Bob, **Supp. IX:** 152
Marlowe, Christopher, **I:** 68, 368, 384; **II:** 590; **III:** 259, 491; **Retro. Supp. I:** 127; **Retro. Supp. II:** 76; **Supp. I Part 2:** 422; **Supp. XXI:** 227
Marlowe, Kimberly B., **Supp. XXII:** 214
"Marlowe Takes on the Syndicate" (Chandler), **Supp. IV Part 1:** 135
Marne, The (Wharton), **IV:** 319, 320; **Retro. Supp. I:** 378
Marquand, John, **Supp. XI:** 301
Marquand, Mrs. John P. (Adelaide Hooker), **III:** 57, 61
Marquand, Mrs. John P. (Christina Sedgwick), **III:** 54, 57
Marquand, J. P., **I:** 362, 375; **II:** 459, 482–483; **III: 50–73**, 383; **Supp. I Part 1:** 196; **Supp. IV Part 1:** 31; **Supp. V:** 95
Marquand, Philip, **III:** 52
Marquis, Don, **Supp. I Part 2:** 668
Marrásh, Francis al-, **Supp. XX: 117**
"Marriage" (Corso), **Supp. XII:** 117, 124, **127–128**
Marriage (Moore), **III:** 194
"Marriage" (Moore), **III:** 198–199, 213
"Marriage, A" (Untermeyer), **Supp. XV:** 305

Marriage A-la-Mode (Dryden), **Supp. IX:** 68
Marriage and Other Science Fiction (Goldbarth), **Supp. XII:** 189, 190
"Marriage in the Sixties, A" (Rich), **Supp. I Part 2:** 554
Marriage of Bette and Boo, The (Durang), **Supp. XXIV:** 114, 121, **122–123**
Marriage of Heaven and Hell (Blake), **Supp. XXII:** 257
"Marriage of Heaven and Hell, The" (Blake), **III:** 544–545; **Supp. VIII:** 99
"Marriage of Phaedra, The" (Cather), **Retro. Supp. I:** 5
Marriage Plot, The (Eugenides), **Supp. XXIV:** 135, **143–145**
"Marriage Rhapsody"(Hadas), **Supp. XXIII:** 114
Married (Strindberg), **Supp. XXII:** 23
"Married" (Taggard), **Supp. XXII:** 274
Married Men (Wolfert), **Supp. XXI:** 277
Married People (Rinehart), **Supp. XXV:** 201
Marrow of Tradition, The (Chesnutt), **Supp. XIV:** 63, **71–75,** 76
Marryat, Captain Frederick, **III:** 423
"Marrying Absurd" (Didion), **Supp. IV Part 1:** 200
"Marrying Iseult?" (Updike), **Retro. Supp. I:** 329
Marrying Man (Simon), **Supp. IV Part 2:** 588
"Marrying the Hangman" (Atwood), **Supp. XIII:** 34
Marry Me: A Romance (Updike), **Retro. Supp. I:** 329, 330, 332
"Mars and Hymen" (Freneau), **Supp. II Part 1:** 258
Marsden, Dora, **III:** 471; **Retro. Supp. I:** 416
Marsena (Frederic), **II:** 135, 136–137
Marsh, Edward, **Supp. I Part 1:** 257, 263
Marsh, Frederick T., **Supp. XX: 39, 46**
Marsh, Fred T., **Supp. IX:** 232
Marsh, John R., **Supp. XIX:** 187
Marsh, Mae, **Supp. I Part 2:** 391
Marshall, George, **III:** 3
Marshall, John, **Supp. I Part 2:** 455; **Supp. XVI:** 117; **Supp. XIX:** 62; **Supp. XXIII:** 275, 276
Marshall, Paule, **Supp. IV Part 1:** 8, 14, 369; **Supp. XI:** 18, **275–292; Supp. XIII:** 295; **Supp. XX: 154**
Marshall, Tod, **Supp. XV:** 224; **Supp. XVII:** 25, 26, 29, 32
"Marshall Carpenter" (Masters), **Supp. I Part 2:** 463
"Marshes of Glynn, The" (Lanier), **Supp. I Part 1:** 364, 365–368, 370, 373
"'Marshes of Glynn, The': A Study in Symbolic Obscurity" (Ross), **Supp. I Part 1:** 373
Marsh Island, A (Jewett), **II:** 405; **Retro. Supp. II:** 134
"Marshland Elegy" (Leopold), **Supp. XIV:** 187, 189
"Mars Is Heaven!" (Bradbury), **Supp. IV Part 1:** 103, 106
Mars-Jones, Adam, **Supp. XXI:** 116
Marsman, Henrik, **Supp. IV Part 1:** 183

Marston, Ed, **Supp. IV Part 2:** 492
Marston, Elsa, **Supp. XXIII:** 241
Marta y Maria (Valdes), **II:** 290
"Martha's Lady" (Jewett), **Retro. Supp. II:** 140, 143
Marthe, Saint, **II:** 213
Martial, **II:** 1, 169; **Supp. IX:** 152
Martian Chronicles, The (Bradbury), **Supp. IV Part 1:** 102, 103, 106–107
Martian Time-Slip (Dick), **Supp. XVIII:** 142
Martin, Benjamin, **Supp. I Part 2:** 503
Martin, Charles, **Supp. XVII:** 112
Martin, Dick, **Supp. XII:** 44
Martin, Jay, **I:** 55, 58, 60, 61, 67; **III:** 307; **Retro. Supp. II:** 326, 327, 329; **Supp. XI:** 162
Martin, John, **Supp. XI:** 172
Martin, Judith, **Supp. V:** 128
Martin, Nell, **Supp. IV Part 1:** 351, 353
Martin, Reginald, **Supp. X:** 247, 249
Martin, Robert, **Supp. XX:** 165
Martin, Stephen-Paul, **Supp. IV Part 2:** 430
Martin, Tom, **Supp. X:** 79
Martin du Gard, Roger, **Supp. I Part 1:** 51
Martineau, Harriet, **Supp. II Part 1:** 282, 288, 294; **Supp. XVIII:** 7; **Supp. XXIV:** 78
Martin Eden (London), **II:** 466, 477–481
Martinelli, Sheri, **Supp. IV Part 1:** 280
Martínez, Guillermo, **Supp. XIII:** 313
Martinez-Avila, Raul, **Supp. XXIII:** 125
Martini, Adrienne, **Supp. XVIII:** 35
Mart'nez, Rafael, **Retro. Supp. I:** 423
Martone, John, **Supp. V:** 179
Marty (Chayefsky), **Supp. XV:** 205
"Martyr, The" (Porter), **III:** 454
Martz, Louis L., **IV:** 151, 156, 165; **Supp. I Part 1:** 107; **Supp. XIV:** 12; **Supp. XXI:** 85
Marvell, Andrew, **IV:** 135, 151, 156, 161, 253; **Retro. Supp. I:** 62, 127; **Retro. Supp. II:** 186, 189; **Supp. I Part 1:** 80; **Supp. XII:** 159; **Supp. XIV:** 10; **Supp. XVI:** 204; **Supp. XXI:** 227; **Supp. XXIII:** 62
"Marvella, for Borrowing" (Ríos), **Supp. IV Part 2:** 551
"Marvelous Sauce, The", **Supp. XVII:** 189
Marvels and Masterpieces (al-Badá'i' wa'l-Tará'if) (Gibran), **Supp. XX:** 116, 124
Marx, Eleanor, **Supp. XVI:** 85
Marx, Karl, **I:** 60, 267, 279, 283, 588; **II:** 376, 462, 463, 483, 577; **IV:** 429, 436, 443–444, 469; **Retro. Supp. I:** 254; **Supp. I Part 2:** 518, 628, 632, 633, 634, 635, 639, 643, 645, 646; **Supp. III Part 2:** 619; **Supp. IV Part 1:** 355; **Supp. VIII:** 196; **Supp. IX:** 133; **Supp. X:** 119, 134; **Supp. XIII:** 75; **Supp. XXI:** 162, 263
Marx, Leo, **Supp. I Part 1:** 233
"Marxism and Monastic Perpectives" (Merton), **Supp. VIII:** 196
Mary (Asch), **Supp. XXIII:** 2, 7, **14**

Mary (Nabokov), **Retro. Supp. I:** 267–268, 270, 277
"Mary" (Trethewey), **Supp. XXI:** 246
"Mary in Old Age" (Ferry), **Supp. XXIV:** 162
"Mary Karr, Mary Karr, Mary Karr, Mary Karr" (Harmon), **Supp. XI:** 248
Maryles, Daisy, **Supp. XII:** 271
Mary Magdalene, **I:** 303
Mary; or, The Test of Honour (Rowson), **Supp. XV:** **233,** 236
"Mary O'Reilly" (Anderson), **II:** 44
"Mary Osaka , I Love You" (Fante), **Supp. XI:** 169
Mary Roberts Rinehart Crime Book, The (Rinehart), **Supp. XXV:** 199
"Mary Snorak the Cook, Skermo the Gardener, and Jack the Parts Man Provide Dinner for a Wandering Stranger" (Grossman), **Supp. XIX:** 87
"Mary's Song" (Plath), **Supp. I Part 2:** 541
"Mary Winslow" (Lowell), **Retro. Supp. II:** 187
Marzynski, Marian, **Supp. XVI:** 153
Masefield, John, **II:** 552; **III:** 523
Masked and Anonymous (film, Dylan and Charles), **Supp. XVIII:** 21, 28
Mask for Janus, A (Merwin), **Supp. III Part 1:** 339, 341, 342
Maslin, Janet, **Supp. XVI:** 213; **Supp. XXI:** 79
Maslow, Abraham, **Supp. I Part 2:** 540
Maso, Carole, **Supp. XXII:** 261
Mason, Bobbie Ann, **Supp. VIII:** **133–149; Supp. XI:** 26; **Supp. XII:** 294, 298, 311; **Supp. XX:** **162; Supp. XXV:** 153
Mason, Charlotte, **Supp. XIV:** 201
Mason, David, **Supp. V:** 344; **Supp. XV:** 116, 251; **Supp. XVII:** 109, 110, 112, 121; **Supp. XVIII:** 182, 183
Mason, Jennifer, **Supp. XVIII:** 263
Mason, Lowell, **I:** 458
Mason, Margaret, **Supp. XXIII:** 209
Mason, Marsha, **Supp. IV Part 2:** 575, 586
Mason, Otis Tufton, **Supp. I Part 1:** 18
Mason, Walt, **Supp. XV:** 298
Mason & Dixon (Pynchon), **Supp. XVII:** 232
"Mason Jars by the Window" (Ríos), **Supp. IV Part 2:** 548
"Masque in Green and Black"(Hadas), **Supp. XXIII:** 121
Masque of Mercy, A (Frost), **II:** 155, 165, 167–168; **Retro. Supp. I:** 131, 140
"Masque of Mummers, The" (MacLeish), **III:** 18
"Masque of Pandora, The" (Longfellow), **Retro. Supp. II:** 167
Masque of Pandora, The, and Other Poems (Longfellow), **II:** 490, 494, 506; **Retro. Supp. II:** 169
Masque of Poets, A (Lathrop, ed.), **Retro. Supp. I:** 31; **Supp. I Part 1:** 365, 368
Masque of Reason, A (Frost), **II:** 155, 162, 165–167; **Retro. Supp. I:** 131, 140; **Retro. Supp. II:** 42

"Masque of the Red Death, The" (Poe), **III:** 412, 419, 424; **Retro. Supp. II:** 262, 268–269
"Masquerade" (Banks), **Supp. V:** 7
Massachusetts, Its Historians and Its History (Adams), **Supp. I Part 2:** 484
"Massachusetts 1932" (Bowles), **Supp. IV Part 1:** 94
"Massachusetts to Virginia" (Whittier), **Supp. I Part 2:** 688–689
"Massacre and the Mastermind, The" (Bausch), **Supp. VII:** 49
"Massacre at Scio, The" (Bryant), **Supp. I Part 1:** 168
"Massacre of the Innocents, The" (Simic), **Supp. VIII:** 282
Masses and Man (Toller), **I:** 479
"Masseur de Ma Soeur, Le" (Hecht), **Supp. X:** 58
Massey, Raymond, **Supp. IV Part 2:** 524
"Mass Eye and Ear: The Ward" (Karr), **Supp. XI:** 244
"Mass for the Day of St. Thomas Didymus" (Levertov), **Supp. III Part 1:** 283
Massie, Chris, **Supp. IV Part 2:** 524
Massing, Michael, **Supp. IV Part 1:** 208
Massinger, Philip, **Supp. I Part 2:** 422; **Supp. XV:** 238
Master Builder, The (Ibsen), **Supp. IV Part 2:** 522
Master Class (McNally), **Supp. XIII:** **204–205,** 208
"Masterful" (Matthews), **Supp. IX:** 161–162
Mastering the Art of French Cooking (Child), **Supp. XVII:** 89
"Master Misery" (Capote), **Supp. III Part 1:** 117
Master of Dreams: A Memoir of Isaac Bashevis Singer (Telushkin), **Retro. Supp. II:** 317
"Master of Secret Revenges, The" (Gass), **Supp. VI:** 93
Master of the Crossroads (Bell), **Supp. X:** **16–17**
"'Masterpiece of Filth, A': Portrait of Knoxville Forgets to Be Fair" (Howards), **Supp. VIII:** 178
Masterpieces of American Fiction, **Supp. XI:** 198
"Master Player, The" (Dunbar), **Supp. II Part 1:** 200
Masters, Edgar Lee, **I:** 106, 384, 475, 480, 518; **II:** 276, 529; **III:** 505, 576, 579; **IV:** 352; **Retro. Supp. I:** 131; **Supp. I Part 2:** 378, 386, 387, **454–478; Supp. III Part 1:** 63, 71, 73, 75; **Supp. IV Part 2:** 502; **Supp. IX:** 308; **Supp. XIV:** 282–283; **Supp. XV:** 256, 293, 297, 301, 306; **Supp. XXV:** 18
Masters, Hardin W., **Supp. I Part 2:** 468
Masters, Hilary, **Supp. IX:** 96
Masters of Sociological Thought (Coser), **Supp. I Part 2:** 650
Masters of the Dew (Roumain), **Supp. IV Part 1:** 367
Masters of the Short Story (Kriegel and Lass, eds.), **Supp. XXIV:** 214

"Masters of War" (song, Dylan), **Supp. XVIII:** 24
"Master's Pieces, The" (H. L. Gates), **Supp. XX: 109**
Matchmaker, The (Wilder), **IV:** 357, 369, 370, 374; **Supp. XX: 50**
Mate of the Daylight, The, and Friends Ashore (Jewett), **II:** 404; **Retro. Supp. II:** 146–147
Materassi, Mario, **Supp. IX:** 233
Mather, Cotton, **II:** 10, 104, 302, 506, 536; **III:** 442; **IV:** 144, 152–153, 157; **Supp. I Part 1:** 102, 117, 174, 271; **Supp. I Part 2:** 584, 599, 698; **Supp. II Part 2: 441–470; Supp. IV Part 2:** 430, 434
Mather, Increase, **II:** 10; **IV:** 147, 157; **Supp. I Part 1:** 100
Mathews, Cornelius, **III:** 81; **Supp. I Part 1:** 317
Mathews, Shailer, **III:** 293
"Matinees" (Merrill), **Supp. III Part 1:** 319, 327
"Matins" (C. Frost), **Supp. XV:** 105
"Matins" (Glück), **Supp. V:** 88
"Matins" (Nelson), **Supp. XVIII:** 177
Matisse, Henri, **III:** 180; **IV:** 90, 407; **Supp. I Part 2:** 619; **Supp. VIII:** 168; **Supp. IX:** 66; **Supp. X:** 73, 74; **Supp. XXII:** 98, 99
"Matisse: Blue Interior with Two Girls–1947" (Hecht), **Supp. X: 73–74**
"Matisse: The Red Studio" (Snodgrass), **Supp. VI:** 316–317
Matlack, James, **Supp. XV:** 269, 271, 286
Matlock, Lucinda, **Supp. I Part 2:** 462
Matos, Juan, **Supp. XXI:** 104
Matrimaniac, The (film), **Supp. XVI:** 185, 186
Matrix Trilogy, The (film), **Supp. XVI:** 271
Matson, Harold, **Supp. XIII:** 164, 166, 167, 169, 172
Matson, Peter, **Supp. IV Part 1:** 299
Matson, Suzanne, **Supp. VIII:** 281
Matters of Fact and Fiction: Essays 1973–1976 (Vidal), **Supp. IV Part 2:** 687
Matters of Life and Death: New American Stories (Wolff, ed.), **Supp. XXIII:** 289
Matthew (biblical book), **IV:** 164; **Supp. XV:** 222
Matthew Arnold (Trilling), **Supp. III Part 2:** 500–501
Matthews, Jackson, **Supp. XVI:** 282
Matthews, T. S., **II:** 430; **Supp. XV:** 142
Matthews, William, **Supp. V:** 4, 5; **Supp. IX: 151–170; Supp. XIII:** 112; **Supp. XXI:** 87
Matthiessen, F. O., **I:** 254, 259–260, 517; **II:** 41, 554; **III:** 310, 453; **IV:** 181; **Retro. Supp. I:** 40, 217; **Retro. Supp. II:** 137; **Supp. IV Part 2:** 422; **Supp. XIII:** 93; **Supp. XIV:** 3; **Supp. XXI:** 277; **Supp. XXV:** 251
Matthiessen, Peter, **Supp. V: 199–217,** 332; **Supp. XI:** 231, 294; **Supp. XIV:** 82; **Supp. XVI:** 230; **Supp. XIX:** 268
Mattingly, Garrett, **Supp. IV Part 2:** 601
Mattos, Anita, **Supp. XXIII:** 197

Mattu, Ravi, **Supp. XVI:** 124
"Maud Island" (Caldwell), **I:** 310
Maud Martha (Brooks), **Supp. III Part 1:** 74, 78–79, 87; **Supp. XI:** 278
"Maud Muller" (Whittier), **Supp. I Part 2:** 698
Maugham, W. Somerset, **III:** 57, 64; **Supp. IV Part 1:** 209; **Supp. X:** 58; **Supp. XIV:** 161
Maule's Curse: Seven Studies in the History of American Obscurantism (Winters), **Supp. II Part 2:** 807–808, 812
"Mau-mauing the Flak Catchers" (Wolfe), **Supp. III Part 2:** 577
Maupassant, Guy de, **I:** 309, 421; **II:** 191–192, 291, 325, 591; **IV:** 17; **Retro. Supp. II:** 65, 66, 67, 299; **Supp. I Part 1:** 207, 217, 223, 320; **Supp. XIV:** 336
"Maurice Barrès and the Youth of France" (Bourne), **I:** 228
Maurice Kenny: Celebrations of a Mohawk Writer (Kelsey, ed.), **Supp. XXIII:** 143
Maurier, George du, **II:** 338
Maurras, Charles, **Retro. Supp. I:** 55
Maus II: And Here My Troubles Began (A. Speigelman), **Supp. XVII:** 48
Mauve Gloves & Madmen, Clutter & Vine (Wolfe), **Supp. III Part 2:** 581
Maverick, Augustus, **Supp. XVIII:** 4
Maverick in Mauve (Auchincloss), **Supp. IV Part 1:** 26
"Mavericks, The" (play) (Auchincloss), **Supp. IV Part 1:** 34
"Mavericks, The" (story) (Auchincloss), **Supp. IV Part 1:** 32
"Max" (H. Miller), **III:** 183
Max, D. T., **Supp. XXI:** 117
Max and the White Phagocytes (H. Miller), **III:** 178, 183–184
Maximilian (emperor of Mexico), **Supp. I Part 2:** 457–458
Maximilian: A Play in Five Acts (Masters), **Supp. I Part 2:** 456, 457–458
"Maximus, to Gloucester" (Olson), **Supp. II Part 2:** 574
"Maximus, to himself" (Olson), **Supp. II Part 2:** 565, 566, 567, 569, 570, 572
Maximus Poems, The (Olson), **Retro. Supp. I:** 209; **Supp. II Part 2:** 555, 556, 563, 564–580, 584; **Supp. VIII:** 305; **Supp. XV:** 170, 264, 349; **Supp. XVI:** 287
Maximus Poems 1–10, The (Olson), **Supp. II Part 2:** 571
Maximus Poems IV, V, VI (Olson), **Supp. II Part 2:** 555, 580, 582–584
Maximus Poems Volume Three, The (Olson), **Supp. II Part 2:** 555, 582, 584–585
"Maximus to Gloucester, Letter 19 (A Pastoral Letter)" (Olson), **Supp. II Part 2:** 567
"Maximus to Gloucester, Sunday July 19" (Olson), **Supp. II Part 2:** 580
"Maximus to himself June 1964" (Olson), **Supp. II Part 2:** 584

Maxwell, Glyn, **Supp. XV:** 252, 253, 260, 261, 263, 264
Maxwell, William, **Supp. I Part 1:** 175; **Supp. III Part 1:** 62; **Supp. VIII: 151–174; Supp. XVII:** 23
May, Abigail (Abba). *See* Alcott, Mrs. Amos Bronson (Abigail May)
May, Elaine Tyler, **Supp. XXII:** 81, 95
May, Jill, **Supp. VIII:** 126
"May 24, 1980" (Brodsky), **Supp. VIII:** 28
"May 1968" (Olds), **Supp. X:** 211–212
Mayakovsky, Vladimir, **Supp. XXIII:** 207
"Mayakovsky"(O'Hara), **Supp. XXIII:** 212, 214
"Mayan Glyphs Unread, The" (Bronk), **Supp. XXI:** 31
"Mayan Warning" (Mora), **Supp. XIII:** 214
Maybe (Hellman), **Supp. IV Part 1:** 12
"Maybe" (Oliver), **Supp. VII:** 239
"Maybe, Someday" (Ritsos), **Supp. XIII:** 78
May Blossom (Belasco), **Supp. XVI:** 182
"Mayday" (Faulkner), **Retro. Supp. I:** 80
"May Day" (Fitzgerald), **II:** 88–89; **Retro. Supp. I:** 103
"May Day Dancing, The" (Nemerov), **III:** 275
May Days (Pickering), **Supp. XXI:** 197–198
May Days: An Anthology of Verse from Masses-Liberator (Taggard, ed.), **Supp. XXII:** 275–276
"May Day Sermon to the Women of Gilmer County, Georgia, by a Woman Preacher Leaving the Baptist Church" (Dickey), **Supp. IV Part 1:** 182
Mayer, Bernadette, **Supp. XXIV:** 41
Mayer, Elizabeth, **Supp. II Part 1:** 16; **Supp. III Part 1:** 63
Mayer, John, **Retro. Supp. I:** 58
Mayer, Louis B., **Supp. XII:** 160; **Supp. XVIII:** 250
Mayes, Wendell, **Supp. IX:** 250
Mayfield, Sara, **Supp. IX:** 65
Mayflower, The (Stowe), **Supp. I Part 2:** 585, 586
Mayle, Peter, **Supp. XVI:** 295
Maynard, Joyce, **Supp. V:** 23
Maynard, Tony, **Supp. I Part 1:** 65
Mayne, Xavier. *See* Prime-Stevenson, Edward Irenaeus
Mayo, Robert, **III:** 478
Mayor (Allen), **Supp. XXII:** 245
Mayorga, Margaret, **IV:** 381
"May-Pole of Merry Mount, The" (Hawthorne), **Supp. XXII:** 44
"Maypole of Merrymount, The" (Hawthorne), **II:** 229
"May Queen" (Di Piero), **Supp. XIX:** 41
May Sarton: Selected Letters 1916–1954, **Supp. VIII:** 265
"May Sun Sheds an Amber Light, The" (Bryant), **Supp. I Part 1:** 170
"May Swenson: The Art of Perceiving" (Stanford), **Supp. IV Part 2:** 637

May the Generations Die in the Right Order (Schott), **Supp. XXIII: 248–250**

"Maze" (Eberhart), **I:** 523, 525–526, 527

Mazel (R. Goldstein), **Supp. XVII:** 44

Mazower, David, **Supp. XXIII:** 4, 5

Mazur, Gail, **Supp. XVIII:** 92

Mazurkiewicz, Margaret, **Supp. XI:** 2

Mazzeno, Laurence W., **Supp. XXV:** 253, 256, 258, 259, 263

Mazzini, Giuseppe, **Supp. I Part 1:** 2, 8; **Supp. II Part 1:** 299

M. Butterfly (Hwang), **Supp. X:** 292; **Supp. XXI:** 143, 147, **150–154**

Mc. Names starting with Mc are alphabetized as if spelled Mac.

"M. Degas Teaches Art & Science at Durfee Intermediate School, Detroit, 1942" (Levine), **Supp. V:** 181, 193

"Me, Boy Scout" (Lardner), **II:** 433

Me, Vashya! (T. Williams), **IV:** 381

Mead, Elinor. *See* Howells, Mrs. William Dean (Elinor Mead)

Mead, George Herbert, **II:** 27, 34; **Supp. I Part 1:** 5; **Supp. I Part 2:** 641

Mead, Margaret, **Supp. I Part 1:** 49, 52, 66; **Supp. IX:** 229

Mead, Taylor, **Supp. XV:** 187

Meade, Frank, **Retro. Supp. II:** 114

Meade, Marion, **Supp. IX:** 191, 193, 194, 195

Meadow, Lynne, **Supp. XIII:** 198

"Meadow House" (Carruth), **Supp. XVI:** 48

Meadowlands (Glück), **Supp. V:** 88–90

"Mean, Mrs." (Gass), **Supp. VI:** 83

"Me and the Mule" (Hughes), **Supp. I Part 1:** 334

Me and You and Everyone We Know (film, July), **Supp. XXIV:** 199, 200, 201, 203, 206, **207–209**

Mean Free Path (Lerner), **Supp. XXIV:** 45

"Meaningless Institution, A" (Ginsberg), **Supp. II Part 1:** 313

"Meaning of a Literary Idea, The" (Trilling), **Supp. III Part 2:** 498

"Meaning of Birds, The" (C. Smith), **Supp. X:** 177

"Meaning of Death, The, An After Dinner Speech" (Tate), **IV:** 128, 129

"Meaning of Life, The" (Tate), **IV:** 137

"Meaning of Simplicity, The" (Ritsos), **Supp. XIII:** 78

Means of Escape (Caputo), **Supp. XIX:** 18, 21, 25

Mean Spirit (Hogan), **Supp. IV Part 1:** 397, 404, 407–410, 415, 416–417

Meantime, The (Bronk), **Supp. XXI:** 31

Mearns, Hughes, **III:** 220

"Measure" (Hass), **Supp. VI: 99–100,** 101

"Measuring My Blood" (Vizenor), **Supp. IV Part 1:** 262

Meatyard, Gene, **Supp. X:** 30

Me: By Jimmy (Big Boy) Valente (Keillor), **Supp. XVI:** 177

Mechan, Dennis B., **Supp. XVI:** 267–268

Mechanic, The (Bynner and DeMille), **Supp. XV:** 42, 50

"Mechanism" (Ammons), **Supp. VII:** 28

"Mechanism in Thought and Morals" (Holmes), **Supp. I Part 1:** 314

Mecom, Mrs. Jane, **II:** 122

"Meddlesome Jack" (Caldwell), **I:** 309

Medea (Jeffers), **Supp. II Part 2:** 435

Medea and Some Poems, The (Cullen), **Supp. IV Part 1:** 169, 173

"Me Decade and the Third Great Awakening, The" (Wolfe), **Supp. III Part 2:** 581

"Médecin Malgré Lui, Le" (W. C. Williams), **IV:** 407–408

"Medfield" (Bryant), **Supp. I Part 1:** 157

Medical History of Contraception, A (Himes), **Supp. V:** 128

"Medicine Song" (Gunn Allen), **Supp. IV Part 1:** 326

Médicis, Marie de, **II:** 548

Medina (McCarthy), **II:** 579

"Meditation, A" (Eberhart), **I:** 533–535

"Meditation 1.6" (Taylor), **IV:** 165

"Meditation 1.20" (Taylor), **IV:** 165

"Meditation 2.68A" (Taylor), **IV:** 165

"Meditation 2.102" (Taylor), **IV:** 150

"Meditation 2.112" (Taylor), **IV:** 165

"Meditation 20" (Taylor), **IV:** 154–155

"Meditation 40" (Second Series) (Taylor), **IV:** 147

"Meditation at Lagunitas" (Hass), **Supp. VI:** 104–105; **Supp. XXI:** 60

"Meditation at Oyster River" (Roethke), **III:** 537, 549

Meditations (Descartes), **III:** 618

Meditations (Marcus Aurelius), **Supp. XVIII:** 304

"Meditations for a Savage Child" (Rich), **Supp. I Part 2:** 564–565

Meditations from a Movable Chair (Dubus), **Supp. VII:** 91

Meditations in an Emergency (O'Hara), **Supp. XXIII: 213–214,** 219, 220

"Meditations in an Emergency"(O'Hara), **Supp. XXIII:** 212, 214

"Meditations in a Swine Yard" (Komunyakaa), **Supp. XIII:** 131

"Meditations of an Old Woman" (Roethke), **III:** 529, 540, 542, 543, 545–547, 548

"Meditations on Grass"(Crooker), **Supp. XXIII:** 55

Meditations on the Insatiable Soul (R. Bly), **Supp. IV Part 1:** 72–73

Meditative Poems, The (Martz), **IV:** 151

"Mediterranean, The" (Tate), **IV:** 129

"Medium of Fiction, The" (Gass), **Supp. VI:** 85–86

"Medley" (Bambara), **Supp. XI:** 9

"Medusa" (Bogan), **Supp. III Part 1:** 50, 51

Meehan, Jeannette Porter, **Supp. XX: 213, 214, 217, 220, 224**

Meehan, Thomas, **Supp. IV Part 2:** 577–578, 586, 590

Meek, Martha, **Supp. IV Part 2:** 439, 440, 441, 442, 445, 447, 448

Meeker, Richard K., **II:** 190

Meese, Elizabeth, **Supp. XIII:** 297

"Meeting" (J. W. Miller), **Supp. XX:** 167

"Meeting, The" (F. Wright), **Supp. XVII:** 245

"Meeting and Greeting Area, The" (Cameron), **Supp. XII: 84–85**

Meeting by the River, A (Isherwood), **Supp. XIV:** 164, **170–171,** 172

"Meeting-House Hill" (Lowell), **II:** 522, 527

"Meeting in the Kitchen, The" (Schnackenberg), **Supp. XV:** 256

"Meeting South, A" (Anderson), **I:** 115

"Meeting the Mountains" (Snyder), **Supp. VIII:** 300

Meeting Trees (Sanders), **Supp. XVI:** 269

Meet Me at the Morgue (Macdonald), **Supp. IV Part 2:** 472

Mehta, Sonny, **Supp. XI:** 178

Mehta, Ved, **Supp. XX:** 87

Meine, Curt, **Supp. XIV:** 179

Meiners, R. K., **IV:** 136, 137, 138, 140

Meinong, Alexius, **Supp. XIV:** 198, 199

Meisner, Sanford, **Supp. XVI:** 240, 242

Meister, Charles W., **II:** 112

Mejia, Jaime, **Supp. XIX:** 97

"Melancholia" (Dunbar), **Supp. II Part 1:** 194

Melancholy Baby (Parker), **Supp. XIX:** 186

"Melanctha" (Stein), **IV:** 30, 34, 35, 37, 38–40, 45

"Melancthon" (Moore), **III:** 212, 215

Melbourne House (S. and A. Warner), **Supp. XVIII:** 268

Meliboeus Hipponax (Lowell). *See Bigelow Papers, The* (Lowell)

Melinda and Melinda (Allen), **Supp. XV:** 16

Mellaart, James, **Supp. I Part 2:** 567

Mellard, James, **Supp. IV Part 1:** 387

Mellen, Joan, **Supp. XXIV:** 51, 52, 56, 64

Mellon, Andrew, **III:** 14

Mellor, W. M., **Supp. XX:** 56

Melnick, Jeffrey, **Supp. X:** 252

Melnyczuk, Askold, **Supp. IV Part 1:** 70

Melodrama Play (Shepard), **Supp. III Part 2:** 440–441, 443, 445

Melodramatists, The (Nemerov), **III:** 268, 281–283, 284

Melopoeia (Espaillat and Tavano), **Supp. XXI:** 99–100

Melting-Pot, The (Zangwill), **I:** 229

"Melungeons" (Offutt), **Supp. XIX:** 171

Melville, Allan, **III:** 74, 77

Melville, Gansevoort, **III:** 76

Melville, Herman, **I:** 104, 106, 211, 288, 340, 343, 348, 354, 355, 561–562; **II:** 27, 74, 224–225, 228, 230, 232, 236, 255, 259, 271, 272, 277, 281, 295, 307, 311, 319, 320, 321, 418, 477, 497, 539–540, 545; **III:** 29, 45, 70, **74–98,** 359, 438, 453, 454, 507, 562–563, 572, 576; **IV:** 57, 105, 194, 199, 202, 250, 309, 333, 345, 350, 380, 444, 453; **Retro. Supp. I:** 54, 91, 160, 215, 220, **243–262; Retro. Supp. II:** 76; **Supp. I Part 1:** 147, 238, 242, 249, 309, 317, 372; **Supp. I Part 2:** 383, 495, 579, 580, 582, 602; **Supp.**

IV Part 2: 463, 613; Supp. V: 279, 281, 298, 308; Supp. VIII: 48, 103, 104, 105, 106, 108, 156, 175, 181, 188; Supp. XI: 83; Supp. XII: 282; Supp. XIII: 294, 305; Supp. XIV: 48, 227; Supp. XV: 287; Supp. XVII: 42, 185; Supp. XVIII: 1, 4, 6, 7, 9; Supp. XXI: 169; Supp. XXII: 174, 262; Supp. XXIII: 164, 165, 174, 190; Supp. XXIV: 88

Melville, Mrs. Herman (Elizabeth Shaw), III: 77, 91, 92

Melville, Maria Gansevoort, III: 74, 77, 85

Melville, Thomas, III: 77, 79, 92; Supp. I Part 1: 309

Melville, Whyte, IV: 309

Melville Goodwin, USA (Marquand), III: 60, 65–66

Melville's Marginalia (Cowen), Supp. IV Part 2: 435

"Melville's Marginalia" (Howe), Supp. IV Part 2: 435

Member of the Wedding, The (McCullers), II: 587, 592, 600–604, 605, 606; Supp. VIII: 124

"Meme Ortiz" (Cisneros), Supp. VII: 60

Memmon (song cycle) (Bowles), Supp. IV Part 1: 82

Memnoch the Devil (Rice), Supp. VII: 289, 290, 294, 296–299

"Memoir" (Hempel), Supp. XXI: 118

"Memoir" (Untermeyer), II: 516–517

"Memoir, A" (Koch), Supp. XV: 184

Memoir from Antproof Case (Helprin), Supp. XXV: 84, 87

"Memoirist's Apology, A" (Karr), Supp. XI: 245, 246

Memoir of Mary Ann, A (O'Connor), III: 357

Memoir of Thomas McGrath, A (Beeching), Supp. X: 114, 118

Memoirs (W. Frank), Supp. XX: 67, 69, 70, 81

Memoirs of a Preacher, a Revelation of the Church and the Home, The (Lippard), Supp. XXIII: 178, 183–184, 188, 190

Memoirs of Arii Taimai (Adams), I: 2–3

"Memoirs of Carwin, the Biloquist" (Brown), Supp. I Part 1: 132

Memoirs of Hecate County (Wilson), IV: 429

Memoirs of Margaret Fuller Ossoli (Fuller), Supp. II Part 1: 280, 283, 285

"Memoirs of Stephen Calvert" (Brown), Supp. I Part 1: 133, 144

Memorabilia (Xenophon), II: 105

Memorable Providences (Mather), Supp. II Part 2: 458

Memorial, The: Portrait of a Family (Isherwood), Supp. XIV: 156, 159, 160–161

"Memorial Day" (Cameron), Supp. XII: 80, 82–83

"Memorial for the City" (Auden), Supp. II Part 1: 20

"Memorial Rain" (MacLeish), III: 15

"Memorial to Ed Bland" (Brooks), Supp. III Part 1: 77

"Memorial Tribute" (Wilbur), Supp. IV Part 2: 642

"Memories" (Whittier), Supp. I Part 2: 699

Memories of a Catholic Girlhood (McCarthy), II: 560–561, 566; Supp. XI: 246; Supp. XVI: 64, 70

"Memories of East Texas" (Karr), Supp. XI: 239

"Memories of Uncle Neddy" (Bishop), Retro. Supp. II: 38; Supp. I Part 1: 73, 93

"Memories of West Street and Lepke" (Lowell), II: 550

"Memory" (Epstein), Supp. XII: 163

"Memory" (Everwine), Supp. XV: 82

"Memory, A" (Welty), IV: 261–262; Retro. Supp. I: 344–345

"Memory, Narrative, and the Discourses of Identity in Abeng and No Telephone to Heaven" (Smith), Supp. XXII: 70

"Memory, The" (Gioia), Supp. XV: 119

Memory and Enthusiasm: Essays, 1975–1985 (Di Piero), Supp. XIX: 34, 41, 42

"Memory and Imagination" (Hampl), Supp. XXII: 94

Memory Gardens (Creeley), Supp. IV Part 1: 141, 157

"Memory Harbor" (Skloot), Supp. XX: 201

Memory of Murder, A (Bradbury), Supp. IV Part 1: 103

Memory of Old Jack, The (Berry), Supp. X: 34

Memory of Two Mondays, A (A. Miller), III: 153, 156, 158–159, 160, 166

"Memo to Non-White Peoples" (Hughes), Retro. Supp. I: 209

"Men" (Boyle), Supp. XXIV: 61

Men, Women and Ghosts (Lowell), II: 523–524

"Menace of the Peyote, The" (Zitkala-Ša), Supp. XXV: 281

Menaker, Charlotte, Supp. XIX: 266

Menaker, Daniel, Supp. VIII: 151; Supp. XXIII: 276

Menand, Louis, Supp. XIV: 40, 197; Supp. XVI: 106, 107; Supp. XXIII: 104–105

Men and Angels (Gordon), Supp. IV Part 1: 304–305, 306, 308

Men and Brethren (Cozzens), I: 363–365, 368, 375, 378, 379

Men and Cartoons (Lethem), Supp. XVIII: 145, 148

"Men and Women" (R. Bly), Supp. IV Part 1: 72

"Men at Forty" (Justice), Supp. VII: 126–127

Mencius (Meng-tzu), IV: 183

Mencken, August, III: 100, 108

Mencken, August, Jr., III: 99, 109, 118–119

Mencken, Mrs. August (Anna Abhau), III: 100, 109

Mencken, Burkhardt, III: 100, 108

Mencken, Charles, III: 99

Mencken, Gertrude, III: 99

Mencken, H. L., I: 199, 210, 212, 235, 245, 261, 405, 514, 515, 517; II: 25, 27, 42, 89, 90, 91, 271, 289, 430, 443, 449; III: 99–121, 394, 482; IV: 76, 432, 440, 475, 482; Retro. Supp. I: 1, 101; Retro. Supp. II: 97, 98, 102, 265; Supp. I Part 2: 484, 629–630, 631, 647, 651, 653, 659, 673; Supp. II Part 1: 136; Supp. IV Part 1: 201, 314, 343; Supp. IV Part 2: 521, 692, 693; Supp. XI: 163–164, 166; Supp. XIII: 161; Supp. XIV: 111; Supp. XV: 297, 301, 303; Supp. XVI: 187–188, 189; Supp. XVII: 106; Supp. XXII: 23, 187, 277; Supp. XXIV: 26, 281

Mencken, Mrs. H. L. (Sara Haardt), III: 109, 111

"Men Deified Because of Their Cruelty" (Simic), Supp. VIII: 282

Mendelbaum, Paul, Supp. V: 159

Mendele, IV: 3, 10

Mendelief, Dmitri Ivanovich, IV: 421

Mendelsohn, Daniel, Supp. X: 153, 154; Supp. XV: 257, 258, 261, 266

Mendelsohn, Jack, Supp. XXIV: 72, 77

Mendelssohn, Moses, Supp. XXIII: 4

Mendes, Alfred, Supp. XXI: 160

"Mending Wall" (Frost), II: 153–154; Retro. Supp. I: 128, 130; Supp. X: 64

Men from the Boys, The (Lacy), Supp. XV: 202, 205

"Menielle" (Stallings), Supp. XXV: 223

Men in the Off Hours (Carson), Supp. XII: 111–113

"Men in the Storm, The" (Crane), I: 411

"Men Loved Wholly Beyond Wisdom" (Bogan), Supp. III Part 1: 50

"Men Made Out of Words" (Stevens), IV: 88

Men Must Act (Mumford), Supp. II Part 2: 479

Mennes, John, II: 111

Mennoti, Gian Carlo, Supp. IV Part 1: 84

Men of Brewster Place, The (Naylor), Supp. VIII: 213, 228–230

"Men of Color, to Arms!" (Douglass), Supp. III Part 1: 171

Men of Good Hope: A Story of American Progressives (Aaron), Supp. I Part 2: 650

Mens' Club, The (film), Supp. XVI: 212–213

Men's Club, The (L. Michaels), Supp. XVI: 206, 210–212

"Menstruation at Forty" (Sexton), Supp. II Part 2: 686

"Mental Hospital Garden, The" (W. C. Williams), Retro. Supp. I: 428

Mental Radio (Sinclair), Supp. V: 289

Mentoria; or, The Young Lady's Friend (Rowson), Supp. XV: 233–234, 238

"Men We Carry in Our Minds, The" (Sanders), Supp. XVI: 273

Men Who Made the Nation, The (Dos Passos), I: 485

Men Without Women (Hemingway), **II:** 249; **Retro. Supp. I:** 170, 176; **Supp. IX:** 202

"Merced" (Rich), **Supp. I Part 2:** 563

"Mercedes" (E. Stoddard), **Supp. XV:** 278

"Mercedes Hospital" (Bishop), **Retro. Supp. II:** 51

"Mercenary, A" (Ozick), **Supp. V:** 267

Mercer, Johnny, **Supp. XXII:** 6

Merchandising (Hwang), **Supp. XXI:** 147

Merchant of Venice, The (Shakespeare), **IV:** 227; **Supp. XIV:** 325

Mercury Theatre, **Retro. Supp. I:** 65

Mercy, Pity, Peace, and Love (Ozick), **Supp. V:** 257, 258

Mercy, The (Levine), **Supp. V:** 194–195

Mercy of a Rude Stream (H. Roth), **Supp. IX:** 231, 234, **235–242**

"Mercy"(P. Benedict), **Supp. XXIII:** 49

Mercy Philbrick's Choice (Jackson), **Retro. Supp. I:** 26, 27, 33

Mercy Street (Sexton), **Supp. II Part 2:** 683, 689

"Mercy"(Thompson), **Supp. XXIII:** 295, 296

Meredith, George, **II:** 175, 186; **Supp. IV Part 1:** 300

Meredith, Mary. *See* Webb, Mary

Meredith, William, **II:** 545; **Retro. Supp. II:** 181

"Merely by Wilderness" (Peacock), **Supp. XIX:** 199

"Merely to Know" (Rich), **Supp. I Part 2:** 554

"Mère Pochette" (Jewett), **II:** 400

"Merger II, The" (Auchincloss), **Supp. IV Part 1:** 34

Meri (Asch), **Supp. XXIII:** 5, 11

"Mericans" (Cisneros), **Supp. VII:** 69

"Merida, 1969" (Matthews), **Supp. IX:** 151

"Meridian" (Clampitt), **Supp. IX:** 48–49

Meridian (Walker), **Supp. III Part 2:** 520, 524, 527, 528, 531–537

Mérimée, Prosper, **II:** 322

Meriwether, James B., **Retro Supp. I:** 77, 91

"Meriwether Connection, The" (Cowley), **Supp. II Part 1:** 142

Merker, Kim K., **Supp. XI:** 261; **Supp. XV:** 75, 77

"Merlin" (Emerson), **II:** 19, 20

Merlin (Robinson), **III:** 522

"Merlin Enthralled" (Wilbur), **Supp. III Part 2:** 544, 554

"Mermother" (A. Finch), **Supp. XVII:** 72

Merril, Judith, **Supp. XVI:** 123

Merrill, Cavafy, Poems, and Dreams (Hadas), **Supp. XXIII: 123–124**

Merrill, Christopher, **Supp. XI:** 329

Merrill, James, **Retro. Supp. I:** 296; **Retro. Supp. II:** 53; **Supp. III Part 1: 317–338; Supp. III Part 2:** 541, 561; **Supp. IX:** 40, 42, 48, 52; **Supp. X:** 73; **Supp. XI:** 123, 131, 249; **Supp. XII:** 44, 254, 255, 256, 261–262, 269–270; **Supp. XIII:** 76, 85; **Supp. XV:**

249, 250, 253; **Supp. XVII:** 123; **Supp. XXIII:** 112, 122, 123; **Supp. XXV:** 222, 227–228

Merrill, Mark (pseudonym). *See* Markson, David

Merrill, Robert, **Retro. Supp. II:** 201

Merrill, Ronald, **Supp. IV Part 2:** 521

Merritt, A., **Supp. XXV:** 122

Merritt, Abraham, **Supp. XVII:** 58

Merritt, Theresa, **Supp. VIII:** 332

Merritt, Vernon, **Supp. XXII:** 245

"Merry-Go-Round" (Hughes), **Retro. Supp. I:** 194, 205; **Supp. I Part 1:** 333

Merry-Go-Round, The (Van Vechten), **Supp. II Part 2:** 734, 735

Merry Month of May, The (Jones), **Supp. XI: 227–228**

Merry Widow, The (Lehar), **III:** 183

Merton, Thomas, **III:** 357; **Supp. VIII: 193–212; Supp. XXII:** 83, 90; **Supp. XXIV:** 133

Merwin, W. S., **Supp. III Part 1: 339–360; Supp. III Part 2:** 541; **Supp. IV Part 2:** 620, 623, 626; **Supp. V:** 332; **Supp. IX:** 152, 155, 290; **Supp. XIII:** 274, 277; **Supp. XV:** 222, 342; **Supp. XIX:** 82; **Supp. XXI:** 95

Meryman, Richard, **Supp. IV Part 2:** 579, 583

Meshiekhs tsaytn (Times of the Messiah) (Asch), **Supp. XXIII:** 5

Meshugah (Singer), **Retro. Supp. II: 315–316**

Mesic, Michael, **Supp. IV Part 1:** 175

Mesic, Penelope, **Supp. X:** 15

Message in the Bottle, The (Percy), **Supp. III Part 1:** 387–388, 393, 397

"Message in the Bottle, The" (Percy), **Supp. III Part 1:** 388

"Message of Flowers and Fire and Flowers, The" (Brooks), **Supp. III Part 1:** 69

Messengers Will Come No More, The (Fiedler), **Supp. XIII:** 103

Messerli, Douglas, **Supp. XVI:** 293

Messiah (Vidal), **Supp. IV Part 2:** 677, 680, 681–682, 685, 691, 692

"Messiah, The" (Wasserstein), **Supp. XV:** 328

Messiah of Stockholm, The (Ozick), **Supp. V:** 270–271; **Supp. XVII:** 42

Messud, Claire, **Supp. XVIII:** 98

Metamorphic Tradition in Modern Poetry (Quinn), **IV:** 421

Metamorphoses (Ovid), **II:** 542–543; **III:** 467, 468; **Supp. XV:** 33; **Supp. XVI:** 20; **Supp. XX:** 280; **Supp. XXIV:** 132

Metamorphoses (Ovid; Golding, trans.), **Supp. XXV:** 226

Metamorphoses (Pound, trans.), **III:** 468–469

Metamorphosis (Kafka), **Supp. XXI:** 89

Metamorphosis, The (Kafka), **IV:** 438; **Retro. Supp. II:** 287–288; **Supp. VIII:** 3

"Metamorphosis and Survival" (Woodcock), **Supp. XIII:** 33

"Metaphor as Mistake" (Percy), **Supp. III Part 1:** 387–388

"Metaphor for Guatemala, A: The Long Night of White Chickens" (Perera), **Supp. XXV:** 50

Metaphor & Memory: Essays (Ozick), **Supp. V:** 272

Metaphor of Trees and Last Poems (Bronk), **Supp. XXI:** 32

"Metaphors of a Magnifico" (Stevens), **IV:** 92

Metaphysical Club, The (Menand), **Supp. XIV:** 40, 197

"Metaphysical Poets, The" (Eliot), **I:** 527, 586

"Metaphysics" (Ginsberg), **Supp. II Part 1:** 313

Metcalf, Paul, **Supp. XIV:** 96; **Supp. XXIII:** 163, 174

"Meteor, The" (Bradbury), **Supp. IV Part 1:** 102

Methinks the Lady...(Endore), **Supp. XVII:** 61–62

"Metonymy as an Approach to the Real World" (Bronk), **Supp. XXI:** 30

Metress, Christopher P., **Supp. V:** 314

Metrical History of Christianity, The (Taylor), **IV:** 163

"Metrical Regularity" (Lovecraft), **Supp. XXV:** 120

Metropolis, The (Sinclair), **Supp. V:** 285

"Metterling Lists, The" (Allen), **Supp. XV:** 15

"Metzengerstein" (Poe), **III:** 411, 417

Mew, Charlotte, **Retro. Supp. II:** 247

Mewshaw, Michael, **Supp. V:** 57; **Supp. X:** 82

"Mexican Hands" (Ryan as Quin), **Supp. XVIII:** 227

"Mexico" (Lowell), **II:** 553, 554

"Mexico, Age Four" (Salinas), **Supp. XIII:** 315

Mexico City Blues (Kerouac), **Supp. III Part 1:** 225, 229

"Mexico Is a Foreign Country: Five Studies in Naturalism" (Warren), **IV:** 241, 252

"Mexico's Children" (Rodriguez), **Supp. XIV:** 302

Meyer, Carolyn, **Supp. XIX:** 194–195, 197

Meyer, Donald B., **III:** 298

Meyer, Ellen Hope, **Supp. V:** 123

Meyer, Robert, **Supp. XXI:** 23

Meyers, Jeffrey, **Retro. Supp. I:** 124, 138; **Retro. Supp. II:** 191

Meynell, Alice, **Supp. I Part 1:** 220

Mezey, Robert, **Supp. IV Part 1:** 60; **Supp. V:** 180; **Supp. XIII:** 312; **Supp. XV:** 74

Mezzanine, The (Baker), **Supp. XIII: 41–43**, 44, 45, 48, 55

"Mezzo Cammin" (Longfellow), **II:** 490

"Mi Abuelo" (Ríos), **Supp. IV Part 2:** 541

Miami (Didion), **Supp. IV Part 1:** 199, 210

Miami and the Siege of Chicago (Mailer), **Retro. Supp. II:** 206

Miasma (Holding), **Supp. XXII: 121–122**

"Michael" (Wordsworth), **III:** 523

Michael, Magali Cornier, **Supp. XIII:** 32
"Michael Angelo: A Fragment" (Longfellow), **II:** 490, 494, 495, 506; **Retro. Supp. II:** 167
"Michael Egerton" (Price), **Supp. VI:** 257–258, 260
Michael Kohlhaas (Kleist), **Supp. IV Part 1:** 224
Michael O'Halloran (Stratton-Porter), **Supp. XX:** 222
Michaels, Leonard, **Supp. XVI: 201–215**
Michaels, Walter Benn, **Retro. Supp. I:** 115, 369, 379
Michael Scarlett (Cozens), **I:** 358–359, 378
"Michael's Veterans Remember" (Espaillat), **Supp. XXI:** 110
Michaux, Henri, **Supp. XVI:** 288
Michelangelo, **I:** 18; **II:** 11–12; **III:** 124; **Supp. I Part 1:** 363; **Supp. XVII:** 112
Michel-Michot, Paulette, **Supp. XI:** 224–225
Michelson, Albert, **IV:** 27
Mickelsson's Ghosts (Gardner), **Supp. VI:** 63, **73–74**
Mickiewicz, Adam, **Supp. II Part 1:** 299
"Microscope" (Trethewey), **Supp. XXI:** 251
Midair (Conroy), **Supp. XVI:** 63, **71–72**
"Mid-Air" (Conroy), **Supp. XVI:** 69, 71
Mid-American Chants (Anderson), **I:** 109, 114
"Midas" (Winters), **Supp. II Part 2:** 801
"Mid-August at Sourdough Mountain Lookout" (Snyder), **Supp. VIII:** 292–293
Midcentury (Dos Passos), **I:** 474, 475, 478, 490, 492–494; **Supp. I Part 2:** 646
Mid-Century American Poets, **III:** 532
"Mid-Day" (Doolittle), **Supp. I Part 1:** 266–267
"Middle Age" (Lowell), **II:** 550
"Middle-Aged, Middle-Class Woman at Midnight, A" (Taggard), **Supp. XXII:** 282–283
"Middleaged Man, The" (Simpson), **Supp. IX:** 274–275
Middle Ages, The (Gurney), **Supp. V:** 96, 105, 108
Middlebrook, Diane Wood, **Supp. IV Part 2:** 444, 451
"Middle Daughter, The" (Kingsolver), **Supp. VII:** 209
Middlemarch (G. Eliot), **I:** 457, 459; **II:** 290, 291; **Retro. Supp. I:** 225; **Supp. I Part 1:** 174; **Supp. IX:** 43; **Supp. XI:** 68; **Supp. XII:** 335
Middle of My Tether, The: Familiar Essays (Epstein), **Supp. XIV: 106–107**
"Middle of Nowhere, The" (Wagoner), **Supp. IX:** 327–328
Middle of the Journey, The (Trilling), **Supp. III Part 2:** 495, 504–506
"Middle of the Way" (Kinnell), **Supp. III Part 1:** 242
"Middle Passage" (Hayden), **Supp. II Part 1:** 363, 375–376
Middle Passage (Johnson), **Supp. VI: 194–196,** 198, 199; **Supp. XIII:** 182

Middlesex (Eugenides), **Supp. XXIV:** 131, 134–135, **138–142**
"Middle Toe of the Right Foot, The" (Bierce), **I:** 203
Middleton, Thomas, **Retro. Supp. I:** 62
"Middle Way, The"(Hadas), **Supp. XXIII:** 121
Middle Years, The (James), **II:** 337–338; **Retro. Supp. I:** 235
"Middle Years, The" (James), **Retro. Supp. I:** 228, 272
"Midnight" (Dunn), **Supp. XI:** 147
"Midnight Consultations, The" (Freneau), **Supp. II Part 1:** 257
Midnight Cry, A (Mather), **Supp. II Part 2:** 460
"Midnight Gladness" (Levertov), **Supp. III Part 1:** 284–285
Midnight Lantern (Gallagher), **Supp. XXIV:** 167, 171
"Midnight Lantern" (Gallagher), **Supp. XXIV:** 171
"Midnight Magic" (Mason), **Supp. VIII:** 146
Midnight Magic: Selected Stories of Bobbie Ann Mason (Mason), **Supp. VIII:** 148
Midnight Mass (Bowles), **Supp. IV Part 1:** 93
"Midnight Postscript" (F. Wright), **Supp. XVII:** 245, 246
Midnight Queen, The (Lippard), **Supp. XXIII:** 180
"Midnight Show" (Shapiro), **Supp. II Part 2:** 705
"Midpoint" (Updike), **Retro. Supp. I:** 321, 323, 327, 330, 335
Midpoint and Other Poems (Updike), **IV:** 214
"Midrash on Happiness" (Paley), **Supp. VI:** 217
"Midsummer" (Bronk), **Supp. XXI:** 30
"Midsummer in the Blueberry Barrens" (Clampitt), **Supp. IX:** 40–41
"Midsummer Letter" (Carruth), **Supp. XVI:** 47
Midsummer Night's Dream, A (Shakespeare), **Supp. I Part 1:** 369–370; **Supp. X:** 69
Midsummer Night's Sex Comedy, A (film; Allen), **Supp. XV:** 8
"Midwest" (Stafford), **Supp. XI:** 317
"Midwest Poetics" (C. Baxter), **Supp. XVIII:** 18
Mieder, Wolfgang, **Supp. XIV:** 126
Mies van der Rohe, Ludwig, **Supp. IV Part 1:** 40
Mighty Aphrodite (film; Allen), **Supp. XV:** 11
"Mighty Fortress, A" (Leopold), **Supp. XIV:** 185
"Mighty Lord, The" (Rowson), **Supp. XV:** 243
"Migration, The" (Tate), **IV:** 130
Mihailovitch, Bata, **Supp. VIII:** 272
Mikado, The (Gilbert and Sullivan), **Supp. XXI:** 151
Miklitsch, Robert, **Supp. IV Part 2:** 628, 629

Mikolowski, Ken and Ann, **Supp. XXIV:** 43
Mila 18 (Uris), **Supp. IV Part 1:** 379; **Supp. XX: 244, 247, 248, 251–252, 253**
Milagro Beanfield War, The (film), **Supp. XIII:** 267
Milagro Beanfield War, The (Nichols), **Supp. XIII:** 253, **265–266**
Milburn, Michael, **Supp. XI:** 239, 242
Milch, David, **Supp. XI:** 348
Mild Day, The (Bronk), **Supp. XXI:** 32
Miles, Barry, **Supp. XII:** 123
Miles, Jack, **Supp. VIII:** 86
Miles, Josephine, **Supp. XIII:** 275
Miles, Julie, **I:** 199
Miles, Kitty, **I:** 199
"Miles of Night, The" (Halliday), **Supp. XIX:** 91
Milestone, Lewis, **Supp. I Part 1:** 281
Miles Wallingford (Cooper). *See Afloat and Ashore* (Cooper)
Milford, Kate, **Supp. XVIII:** 150
Milford, Nancy, **II:** 83; **Supp. IX:** 60
Milhaud, Darius, **Supp. IV Part 1:** 81
Miligate, Michael, **IV:** 123, 130, 132
"Militant Nudes" (Hardwick), **Supp. III Part 1:** 210–211
Milk (film), **Supp. XX: 269**
"Milk Bottles" (Anderson), **I:** 114
"Milk Prose" (Weigl), **Supp. XIX:** 278
Milk Train Doesn't Stop Here Anymore, The (T. Williams), **IV:** 382, 383, 384, 386, 390, 391, 392, 393, 394, 395, 398
Mill, James, **II:** 357
Mill, John Stuart, **III:** 294–295; **Supp. XI:** 196; **Supp. XIV:** 22
Millar, Kenneth. *See* Macdonald, Ross
Millar, Margaret (Margaret Sturm), **Supp. IV Part 2:** 464, 465
Millay, Cora, **III:** 123, 133–134, 135–136
Millay, Edna St. Vincent, **I:** 482; **II:** 530; **III: 122–144; IV:** 433, 436; **Retro. Supp. II:** 48; **Supp. I Part 2:** 707, 714, 726; **Supp. IV Part 1:** 168; **Supp. IV Part 2:** 607; **Supp. V:** 113; **Supp. IX:** 20; **Supp. XIV:** 120, 121, 122, 127; **Supp. XV:** 42, 46, 51, 250, 293, 307; **Supp. XVII:** 69, 75, 96; **Supp. XXII:** 273; **Supp. XXIII:** 164
Millennium Approaches (Kushner), **Supp. IX:** 141, 142, 145
Miller, Arthur, **I:** 81, 94; **III: 145–169; Supp. IV Part 1:** 359; **Supp. IV Part 2:** 574; **Supp. VIII:** 334; **Supp. XIII:** 127; **Supp. XIV:** 102, 239; **Supp. XVI:** 194
Miller, Mrs. Arthur (Ingeborg Morath), **III:** 162–163
Miller, Mrs. Arthur (Marilyn Monroe), **III:** 161, 162–163
Miller, Mrs. Arthur (Mary Grace Slattery), **III:** 146, 161
Miller, Brown, **Supp. IV Part 1:** 67
Miller, Carol, **Supp. IV Part 1:** 400, 405, 409, 410, 411
Miller, Caroline, **Supp. XXII: 187–201**
Miller, Henry, **I:** 97, 157; **III:** 40, **170–192; IV:** 138; **Retro. Supp. II:** 327;

Supp. I Part 2: 546; Supp. V: 119, 131; Supp. X: 183, 185, 187, 194, 195; Supp. XIII: 1, 17; Supp. XXII: 88, 256, 257, 258; Supp. XXIII: 100; Supp. XXIV: 52, 281
Miller, Henry (actor), Supp. XVI: 182
Miller, Herman, Supp. I Part 2: 614, 617
Miller, James E., Jr., IV: 352
Miller, Jean Baker, Supp. XXII: 18
Miller, Jeffrey, Supp. IV Part 1: 95
Miller, J. Hillis, Supp. IV Part 1: 387
Miller, Jim Wayne, Supp. XX: 161–176; Supp. XXIII: 39
Miller, Joaquin, I: 193, 195, 459; Supp. II Part 1: 351
Miller, John Duncan, Supp. I Part 2: 604
Miller, John E., Supp. XXII: 295
Miller, John M., Supp. XXII: 214, 218
Miller, Jonathan, Retro. Supp. II: 181
Miller, Laura, Supp. XIII: 48; Supp. XIX: 53, 54, 56; Supp. XXII: 239; Supp. XXV: 12, 13
Miller, Marilyn, Supp. XVI: 187
Miller, Matt, Supp. XV: 211
Miller, Matthew, Supp. XVI: 47, 51
Miller, Orilla, Supp. I Part 1: 48
Miller, Perry, I: 546, 547, 549, 550, 560; IV: 186; Supp. I Part 1: 31, 104; Supp. I Part 2: 484; Supp. IV Part 2: 422; Supp. VIII: 101; Supp. XXV: 251
Miller, R. Baxter, Retro. Supp. I: 195, 207
Miller, Robert Ellis, II: 588
Miller, Ruth, Supp. X: 324
Miller, Stuart, Supp. XVI: 242
Miller, Sue, Supp. X: 77, 85; Supp. XI: 190; Supp. XII: 289–305
Miller of Old Church, The (Glasgow), II: 175, 181
"Miller's Tale" (Chaucer), III: 283
Miller Williams and the Poetry of the Particular (Burns), Supp. XV: 339
Millett, Kate, Supp. X: 193, 196
Millgate, Michael, Retro. Supp. I: 91
Mill Hand's Lunch Bucket (Bearden), Supp. VIII: 337
Millhauser, Steven, Supp. XXII: 49
Millier, Brett C., Retro. Supp. II: 39
Milligan, Bryce, Supp. XIII: 274, 275, 277
Million Little Pieces, A (Frey), Supp. XXII: 95; Supp. XXIII: 109; Supp. XXIV: 230, 236
Millions of Strange Shadows (Hecht), Supp. X: 57, 62–65
"Million Young Workmen, 1915, A" (Sandburg), III: 585
Millroy the Magician (Theroux), Supp. VIII: 325
Mills, Alice, Supp. XIII: 233
Mills, Benjamin Fay, III: 176
Mills, C. Wright, Supp. I Part 2: 648, 650
Mills, Florence, Supp. I Part 1: 322
Mills, Ralph J., Jr., III: 530; Supp. IV Part 1: 64; Supp. XI: 311
Mills, Tedi López, Supp. XVI: 281
Mills of the Kavanaughs, The (Lowell), II: 542–543, 546, 550, 560; III: 508;

Retro. Supp. II: 178, 179, 188; Supp. XXIII: 211
"Mills of the Kavanaughs, The" (Lowell), II: 542–543
Milne, A. A., Supp. IX: 189; Supp. XXIV: 132, 133
Milne, A. J. M., I: 278
Milosz, Czeslaw, Supp. III Part 2: 630; Supp. VIII: 20, 22; Supp. XI: 267, 312; Supp. XVII: 241; Supp. XX: 165; Supp. XXI: 132; Supp. XXII: 92; Supp. XXIII: 134, 140
Miltner, Robert, Supp. XI: 142
Milton, Edith, Supp. VIII: 79; Supp. X: 82
Milton, John, I: 6, 138, 273, 587–588; II: 11, 15, 113, 130, 411, 540, 542; III: 40, 124, 201, 225, 274, 468, 471, 486, 487, 503, 511; IV: 50, 82, 126, 137, 155, 157, 241, 279, 347, 422, 461, 494; Retro. Supp. I: 60, 67, 127, 360; Retro. Supp. II: 161, 295; Supp. I Part 1: 124, 150, 370; Supp. I Part 2: 412, 422, 491, 501, 522, 622, 722, 724; Supp. IV Part 2: 430, 634; Supp. VIII: 294; Supp. X: 22, 23, 36; Supp. XII: 180; Supp. XIV: 5, 7; Supp. XX: 108; Supp. XXIII: 122; Supp. XXIV: 159
Milton, John R., Supp. IV Part 2: 503
Milton and His Modern Critics (L. P. Smith), Supp. XIV: 347
"Milton by Firelight" (Snyder), Supp. II Part 1: 314; Supp. VIII: 294
"Miltonic Sonnet, A" (Wilbur), Supp. III Part 2: 558
Mimesis (Auerbach), III: 453
"Mimnermos and the Motions of Hedonism" (Carson), Supp. XII: 99–100
"Mimnermos Interviews, The" (Carson), Supp. XII: 100–101
Mims, Edwin, Supp. I Part 1: 362, 364, 365, 371
"Mind" (Wilbur), Supp. III Part 2: 554
"Mind, The" (Kinnell), Supp. III Part 1: 245
Mind Breaths: Poems 1972–1977 (Ginsberg), Supp. II Part 1: 326
Mindfield: New and Selected Poems (Corso), Supp. XII: 136
"Mind in the Modern World" (Trilling), Supp. III Part 2: 512
"Mind Is Shapely, Art Is Shapely" (Ginsberg), Supp. II Part 1: 327
Mindlin, Henrique, Supp. I Part 1: 92
Mind of My Mind (O. Butler), Supp. XIII: 62, 63
Mind of Primitive Man, The (Boas), Supp. XIV: 209
Mind-Reader, The (Wilbur), Supp. III Part 2: 560–562
"Mind-Reader, The" (Wilbur), Supp. III Part 2: 561–562
"Mind's Landscape on an Early Winter Day, The" (Bronk), Supp. XXI: 28
Mindwheel (Pinsky), Supp. VI: 235
Minear, Richard H., Supp. XVI: 101, 102
"Mined Country" (Wilbur), Supp. III Part 2: 546–548
"Minefields" (Espaillat), Supp. XXI: 106

"Mine Own John Berryman" (Levine), Supp. V: 179–180
Miner, Bob, Supp. V: 23
Miner, Earl, III: 466, 479
Miner, Madonne, Supp. XIII: 29
Miner, Valerie, Supp. XXIII: 295, 296
"Minerva Writes Poems" (Cisneros), Supp. VII: 63–64, 66
Mingus, Charles, Supp. IX: 152
"Mingus in Diaspora" (Matthews), Supp. IX: 166
"Mingus in Shadow" (Matthews), Supp. IX: 168–169
Ming Yellow (Marquand), III: 56
"Minimal, The" (Roethke), III: 531–532
Minimus Poems, The (X. J. Kennedy), Supp. XV: 169–170
"Mini-novela: Rosa y sus espinas" (Mora), Supp. XIII: 218
"Minions of Midas, The" (London), II: 474–475
Minister's Charge, The, or The Apprenticeship of Lemuel Barber (Howells), II: 285–286, 287
Minister's Wooing, The (Stowe), II: 541
"Minister's Wooing, The" (Stowe), Supp. I Part 2: 592–595
"Ministration of Our Departed Friends, The" (Stowe), Supp. I Part 2: 586–587
Minna and Myself (Bodenheim), Supp. XXV: 21
"Minneapolis Poem, The" (Wright), Supp. III Part 2: 601–602
Minnesota Grain Show, The (radio, Keillor), Supp. XVI: 170
"Minnesota Transcendentalist" (Peseroff), Supp. IV Part 1: 71
Minnie, Temple, II: 344
Minority Report: H. L. Mencken's Notebooks (Mencken), III: 112
Minor Pleasures of Life, The (Macaulay), Supp. XIV: 348
"Minor Poems" (Eliot), I: 579
"Minor Poet" (Hay), Supp. XIV: 127
"Minor Topics" (Howells), II: 274
Minot, Stephen, Supp. XXIII: 290
Minot, Susan, Supp. VI: 203–215
"Minotaur Loves His Labyrinth, The" (Simic), Supp. VIII: 270, 279, 281
"Minstrel Man" (Hughes), Supp. I Part 1: 325
Mint (Nye), Supp. XIII: 277
"Minting Time" (Sarton), Supp. VIII: 259
Mint Snowball (Nye), Supp. XIII: 277–278, 284–285
"Mint Snowball" (Nye), Supp. XIII: 278, 284
"Mint Snowball II" (Nye), Supp. XIII: 284, 285
Minty Alley (C. L. R. James), Supp. XXI: 159, 161
Mintzlaff, Dorothy, Supp. XV: 153
Minus, Marian, Supp. XVIII: 282
Minutes to Go (Corso, Gysin, Beiles and Burroughs), Supp. XII: 129
Mi querido Rafa (Hinojosa). See Dear Rafe (Hinojosa)

Mirabai: Ecstatic Poems (Hirshfield and Bly, trans.), **Supp. XXIII:** 136

Mirabell: Books of Number (Merrill), **Supp. III Part 1:** 332–334

"Miracle" (Carver), **Supp. III Part 1:** 139–140

Miracle at Verdun (Chlumberg), **Supp. XIX:** 242

Miracle Boy and Other Stories (P. Benedict), **Supp. XXIII:** 35, **45–50**

"Miracle Boy"(P. Benedict), **Supp. XXIII:** 45–46, 50

"Miracle for Breakfast, A" (Bishop), **Retro. Supp. II:** 43

Miracle of Catfish, A (L. Brown), **Supp. XXI:** 39–40, 47, **48**

"Miracle of Lava Canyon, The" (Henry), **Supp. II Part 1:** 389, 390

Miracle of Mindfulness, The: A Manual on Meditation (Thich Nhat Hanh), **Supp. V:** 199–200

Mirage (Masters), **Supp. I Part 2:** 459, 470, 471

"Mirages, The" (Hayden), **Supp. II Part 1:** 373

"Miranda" (Buck), **Supp. II Part 1:** 128

Miranda, Carmen, **Supp. XII:** 165

Miranda, Francisco de, **Supp. I Part 2:** 522

"Miranda Over the Valley" (Dubus), **Supp. VII:** 81–83

"Miriam" (Capote), **Supp. III Part 1:** 117, 120, 122

"Miriam" (Whittier), **Supp. I Part 2:** 691, 703

"Miriam Tazewell" (Ransom), **Supp. X:** 58

"Mirror" (Merrill), **Supp. III Part 1:** 322

"Mirror" (Plath), **Retro. Supp. II:** 248–249, 257

"Mirror, The" (Glück), **Supp. V:** 83

"Mirror, The"(Hadas), **Supp. XXIII:** 116

"Mirroring Evil: Nazi Images/Recent Art" (Epstein), **Supp. XII:** 166

"Mirror of Leopold Leopoldovitch Siegelevsky, The" (Siegel), **Supp. XXII:** 257–258

Mirrors (Creeley), **Supp. IV Part 1:** 156

Mirrors and Windows (Nemerov), **III:** 269, 275–277

Mirrors of Astonishment (Hadas), **Supp. XXIII:** **115–116**

"Mirrors of Chartres Street" (Faulkner), **II:** 56

Mirsky, Norman, **Supp. XX:** 244

Mirvis, Tova, **Supp. XX:** **177–191**

Misanthrope, The (Molière; Wilbur, trans.), **Supp. III Part 2:** 552, 560

Miscellaneous Poems (Rowson), **Supp. XV:** 243

Miscellaneous Works of Mr. Philip Freneau, Containing His Essays and Additional Poems (Freneau), **Supp. II Part 1:** 263, 264, 266

Miscellany of American Poetry, A (Untermeyer, ed.), **Supp. XV:** 305, 310

Misérables, Les (Hugo), **II:** 179; **Supp. I Part 1:** 280

Misery (King), **Supp. V:** 140, 141, 142, 147–148, 151, 152

Mises, Ludwig von, **Supp. IV Part 2:** 524

Misfits, The (A. Miller), **III:** 147, 149, 156, 161–162, 163

Misfit: The Strange Life of Frederick Exley (Yardley), **Supp. XXIII:** 97

"Mishôsha, or the Magician and his daughters: A Chippewa Tale"(J. Schoolcraft), **Supp. XXIII:** 234, 235

"Misogamist, The" (Dubus), **Supp. VII:** 86–87

Misread City, The: New Literary Los Angeles (Gioia and Timberg, eds.), **Supp. XV:** 116

Misrepresentations Corrected, and Truth Vindicated, in a Reply to the Rev. Mr. Solomon Williams's Book (Edwards), **I:** 549

Miss Crandall's School for Young Ladies & Little Misses of Color (Nelson and Alexander), **Supp. XVIII:** 171, 175, 181, **185–186**

"Miss Cynthie" (R. Fisher), **Supp. XIX:** 65, 69

Miss Doll, Go Home (Markson), **Supp. XVII:** 138

"Miss Ella" (Z. Fitzgerald), **Supp. IX:** 57, 59, **71–72**

"Miss Emily and the Bibliographer" (Tate), **Supp. II Part 1:** 103

"Miss Furr and Miss Skeene" (Stein), **IV:** 29–30

"Missing Child" (Simic), **Supp. VIII:** 282

"Missing in Action" (Komunyakaa), **Supp. XIII:** 123, 124

Missing/Kissing: Missing Marisa, Kissing Christine (Shanley), **Supp. XIV:** 316

Missing Link (X. J. Kennedy), **Supp. XV:** 165

"Missing Poem, The" (Halliday), **Supp. XIX:** 93–94

"Mission of Jane, The" (Wharton), **Retro. Supp. I:** 367

"Missions, The" (Rodriguez), **Supp. XIV:** 303

Mission to Moscow (film), **Supp. I Part 1:** 281

"Mississippi" (Bass), **Supp. XVI:** 17

"Mississippi" (Faulkner), **Retro. Supp. I:** 77

"Mississippi" (Simpson), **Supp. IX:** 271

"Miss Kate in H-1" (Twain), **IV:** 193

Miss Kelly (Holding), **Supp. XXII:** 133–134

Miss Leonora When Last Seen (Taylor), **Supp. V:** 323

Miss Lonelyhearts (West), **I:** 107; **II:** 436; **III:** 357; **IV:** 287, 288, 290–297, 300, 301, 305, 306; **Retro. Supp. II:** 321, 322, 325, 328, **332–335**

"Miss Lora" (Díaz), **Supp. XXIV:** 86

Miss Mamma Aimee (Caldwell), **I:** 308, 309, 310

"Miss Mary Pask" (Wharton), **IV:** 316; **Retro. Supp. I:** 382

"Miss McEnders" (Chopin), **Retro. Supp. II:** 67

Miss Morissa: Doctor of the Gold Trail (Sandoz), **Supp. XXIV:** 244, **255–256**

"Missoula Softball Tournament" (Hugo), **Supp. VI:** 132

Miss Pinkerton (Rinehart), **Supp. XXV:** 197

Miss Ravenel's Conversion from Secession to Loyalty (De Forest), **IV:** 350

Miss Saigon (musical), **Supp. XXI:** 155

"Miss Tempy's Watchers" (Jewett), **II:** 401; **Retro. Supp. II:** 139

"Miss Terriberry to Wed in Suburbs" (Updike), **Retro. Supp. I:** 335

"Miss Urquhart's Tiara" (Jarman), **Supp. XVII:** 116

Miss Witherspoon (Durang), **Supp. XXIV:** 113, **126**

"Mist, The" (King), **Supp. V:** 144

"Mistaken Charity, A" (Freeman), **Retro. Supp. II:** 138

"Mister Brother" (Cunningham), **Supp. XV:** 68

Misterioso (Sorrentino), **Supp. XXI:** 236, 237

"Mister Toussan" (Ellison), **Retro. Supp. II:** 124–125; **Supp. II Part 1:** 238

"Mistress of Sydenham Plantation, The" (Jewett), **Retro. Supp. II:** 141

Mitcham, Matthew, **Supp. XX:** 264

Mitchell, Burroughs, **Supp. XI:** 218, 222, 227

Mitchell, David, **Supp. XXIV:** 86

Mitchell, Don, **Supp. XXII:** 207, 211, 212

Mitchell, Joan, **Supp. XXIII:** 210

Mitchell, Margaret, **II:** 177; **Supp. XX:** **243; Supp. XXII:** 195

Mitchell, Pat, **Supp. XXIV:** 35, 42

Mitchell, Roger, **Supp. IV Part 1:** 70; **Supp. XV:** 213, 215

Mitchell, Dr. S. Weir, **IV:** 310

Mitchell, Tennessee. *See* Anderson, Mrs. Sherwood (Tennessee Mitchell)

Mitchell, Verner, **Supp. XVIII:** 281, 286

Mitchell, Wesley C., **Supp. I Part 2:** 632, 643

"Mitchie-Gawa" (Taggard), **Supp. XXII:** 272

Mitch Miller (Masters), **Supp. I Part 2:** 456, 466, 469–471, 474, 475, 476

Mitchum, Robert, **Supp. IX:** 95, 250

Mitgang, Herbert, **Supp. IV Part 1:** 220, 226, 307; **Supp. VIII:** 124; **Supp. XIX:** 251; **Supp. XX:** 243

Mitla Pass (Uris), **Supp. XX:** 244, 247, 248, 256

Mixed Company: Collected Short Stories (Shaw), **Supp. XIX:** 251

"Mixed Sequence" (Roethke), **III:** 547

Miyazawa Kenji, **Supp. VIII:** 292

Mizener, Arthur, **II:** 77, 81, 84, 94; **IV:** 132; **Supp. XVIII:** 249

Mizner, Addison, **Supp. XVI:** 191

Mizner, Wilson, **Supp. XVI:** 191, 195

Mladenoff, Nancy, **Supp. X:** 176

"M'liss: An Idyl of Red Mountain" (Harte), **Supp. II Part 1:** 339

"Mnemonic Devices" (Goldbarth), **Supp. XII:** 183

"Mnemosyne" (Hölderlin), **Supp. XXIV:** 152

"Mobile in Back of the Smithsonian, The" (Swenson), **Supp. IV Part 2:** 646

Mobilio, Albert, **Supp. VIII:** 3; **Supp. XVIII:** 144; **Supp. XIX:** 45

Moby Dick (film), **Supp. IV Part 1:** 102, 116

Moby Dick; or, The Whale (Melville), **I:** 106, 354; **II:** 33, 224–225, 236, 539–540; **III:** 28–29, 74, 75, 77, 81, 82, 83–86, 87, 89, 90, 91, 93, 94, 95, 359, 453, 556; **IV:** 57, 199, 201, 202; **Retro. Supp. I:** 160, 220, 243, 244, 248, **249–253,** 254, 256, 257, 335; **Retro. Supp. II:** 121, 186, 275; **Supp. I Part 1:** 249; **Supp. I Part 2:** 579; **Supp. IV Part 2:** 613; **Supp. V:** 281; **Supp. VIII:** 106, 188, 198; **Supp. XXI:** 159; **Supp. XXII:** 81, 268; **Supp. XXIV:** 88

Mock, John, **Supp. XIII:** 174

"Mocking-Bird, The" (Bierce), **I:** 202

"Mock Orange" (Glück), **Supp. V:** 84–85

Modarressi, Mitra, **Supp. IV Part 2:** 657

Models of Misrepresentation: On the Fiction of E. L. Doctorow (Morris), **Supp. IV Part 1:** 231

Model World and Other Stories, A (Chabon), **Supp. XI:** 66

Modern American and British Poetry (Untermeyer, ed.), **Supp. XV:** 306

Modern American Poetry (Untermeyer, ed.), **Supp. XV:** 293, 303, 306, 312

Modern American Verse (Untermeyer, ed.), **Supp. XV:** 301

Modern Brazilian Architecture (Bishop, trans.), **Supp. I Part 1:** 92

Modern British Poetry (Untermeyer, ed.), **Supp. XV:** 305, 308, 312

Modern Fiction Studies, **Supp. V:** 238

Modern Fiction Studies (Haegert), **Supp. XVI:** 69

"Modern Greek for 'Nightmare' Is *Ephialtes,* The" (Stallings), **Supp. XXV:** 233

Modern Instance a Novel, A (Howells), **II:** 275, 279, 282–283, 285

Modern Library, The, **Retro. Supp. I:** 112, 113

Modern Mephistopheles, A (Alcott), **Supp. I Part 1:** 37–38

Modern Poetic Sequence, The (Rosenthal), **Supp. V:** 333

"Modern Poetry" (Crane), **I:** 390

Modern Poetry and the Tradition (Brooks), **Supp. XIV:** 5–7

"Modern Primer: Helpful Hints to Tell Appearances from Truth" (Taubman), **Supp. XXV:** 106

"Modern Race Creeds and Their Fallacies" (Locke), **Supp. XIV:** 210

Modern Rhetoric, with Readings (Brooks and Warren), **Supp. XIV:** 11

"Modern Sorcery" (Simic), **Supp. VIII:** 283

Modern Times (album, Dylan), **Supp. XVIII:** 28, 31, 33

"Modern Times" (Zukofsky), **Supp. III Part 2:** 624

Modern Writer, The (Anderson), **I:** 117

Modersohn, Otto, **Supp. I Part 2:** 573

Modersohn, Mrs. Otto (Paula Becker), **Supp. I Part 2:** 573–574

"Modes of Being" (Levertov), **Supp. III Part 1:** 282

Modest Enquiry into the Nature and Necessity of a Paper-Currency, A (Franklin), **II:** 108–109

"Modest Proposal, A" (Swift), **I:** 295; **Retro. Supp. II:** 287

"Modest Proposal with Feline Feeling, A" (Neugeboren), **Supp. XVI:** 219

"Modest Self-Tribute, A" (Wilson), **IV:** 431, 432

Moeller, Philip, **III:** 398, 399

"Moench von Berchtesgaden, Der" (Voss), **I:** 199–200

Moers, Ellen, **Retro. Supp. II:** 99

Moe's Villa and Other Stories (Purdy), **Supp. VII:** 270, 280

Moffat, Juan, **Supp. XX:** 52

Moffet, Penelope, **Supp. XXIV:** 165, 167

Mogen, David, **Supp. IV Part 1:** 106

Mohammed, **I:** 480; **II:** 1

Mohawk (Russo), **Supp. XII:** **326–328**

Moir, William Wilmerding, **Supp. V:** 279

Mojo Hand (Phillips), **Supp. XXIII:** 174

Moldaw, Carol, **Supp. XV:** 264; **Supp. XVII:** 127, 130

"Moles" (Oliver), **Supp. VII:** 235

Molesworth, Charles, **Supp. IV Part 1:** 39; **Supp. VIII:** 292, 306; **Supp. XIX:** 121–122

Molière (Jean-Baptiste Poquelin), **III:** 113; **Supp. I Part 2:** 406; **Supp. III Part 2:** 552, 560; **Supp. IV Part 2:** 585; **Supp. V:** 101

"Molino Rojo, El" (Ríos), **Supp. IV Part 2:** 544

Moll Flanders (Defoe), **Supp. V:** 127; **Supp. XIII:** 43

"Molloch in State Street" (Whittier), **Supp. I Part 2:** 687

"Moll Pitcher" (Whittier), **Supp. I Part 2:** 684

"Molly Brant, Iroquois Matron" (Gunn Allen), **Supp. IV Part 1:** 331

"Molly Brant to Willie"(Kenny), **Supp. XXIII:** 153

Molnar, Ferenc, **Supp. XVI:** 187

"Moloch" (H. Miller), **III:** 177

Momaday, N. Scott, **Supp. IV Part 1:** 274, 323, 324, 404; **Supp. IV Part 2:** **479–496,** 504, 557, 562; **Supp. XII:** 209; **Supp. XVIII:** 58

" 'Momentary Stay against Confusion,' A: Frank Conroy's *Stop-Time*" (T. Adams), **Supp. XVI:** 69

Moment of Untruth (Lacy), **Supp. XV:** 206, 207

Moments of the Italian Summer (Wright), **Supp. III Part 2:** 602

Moment to Moment: Poems of a Mountain Recluse (Budbill), **Supp. XIX:** 2, 7, **9–10**

"Momus" (Robinson), **III:** 508

Monaghan, Charles, **Supp. XIX:** 155

Monaghan, Pat, **Supp. XI:** 121

Monaghan, Patricia, **Supp. XVII:** 76, 123, 127, 129

Mona Lisa Overdrive (W. Gibson), **Supp. XVI:** 119, 120, **127–128**

"Mon Ami" (Bourne), **I:** 227

Monday Night (Boyle), **Supp. XXIV:** 54

Monet, Claude, **Retro. Supp. I:** 378

"Monet's 'Waterlilies' " (Hayden), **Supp. II Part 1:** 361–362

Monette, Paul, **Supp. X:** **145–161**

Money (Amis), **Retro. Supp. I:** 278

"Money" (Matthews), **Supp. IX:** 166

"Money" (Nemerov), **III:** 287

Money, Money, Money (Wagoner), **Supp. IX:** 324, **333–334**

Moneyball: The Art of Winning an Unfair Game (M. Lewis), **Supp. XVII:** 210

Moneychangers, The (Sinclair), **Supp. V:** 285

Money Writes! (Sinclair), **Supp. V:** 277

Monica, Saint, **IV:** 140

Monikins, The (Cooper), **I:** 348, 354

Monk, Craig, **Supp. XXIV:** 64

Monk, Thelonious, **Supp. XVIII:** 62

Monk and the Hangman's Daughter, The (Bierce), **I:** 199–200, 209

"Monkey" (Weigl), **Supp. XIX:** 278

"Monkey Garden, The" (Cisneros), **Supp. VII:** 63

"Monkey Puzzle, The" (Moore), **III:** 194, 207, 211

Monkeys (Minot), **Supp. VI:** 203–205, **206–210**

"Monkeys, The" (Moore), **III:** 201, 202

Monkey Wars, The (Weigl), **Supp. XIX:** 276, 278–280

Monkey Wrench Gang, The (Abbey), **Supp. VIII:** 42; **Supp. XIII:** **9–11,** 16

"Monk of Casal-Maggiore, The" (Longfellow), **II:** 505

"Monocle de Mon Oncle, Le" (Stevens), **IV:** 78, 84; **Retro. Supp. I:** 301; **Supp. III Part 1:** 20; **Supp. X:** 58

"Monody to the Sound of Zithers" (Boyle), **Supp. XXIV:** 63

"Monolog from a Mattress" (Untermeyer), **Supp. XV:** 307

"Monologue for Mothers" (Taggard), **Supp. XXII:** 279

"Mon Plaisir" (July), **Supp. XXIV:** 205–206

Monro, Harold, **III:** 465; **Retro. Supp. I:** 127; **Supp. XV:** 296

Monroe, Harriet, **I:** 235, 384, 390, 393; **III:** 458, 581, 586; **IV:** 74; **Retro. Supp. I:** 58, 131; **Retro. Supp. II:** 82, 83; **Supp. I Part 1:** 256, 257, 258, 262, 263, 267; **Supp. I Part 2:** 374, 387, 388, 464, 610, 611, 613, 614, 615, 616; **Supp. XIV:** 286; **Supp. XV:** 43, 299, 302; **Supp. XXV:** 18

Monroe, James, **Supp. I Part 2:** 515, 517

Monroe, Lucy, **Retro. Supp. II:** 70

Monroe, Marilyn, **III:** 161, 162–163

Monroe's Embassy; or, the Conduct of the Government in Relation to Our Claims to the Navigation of the Mississippi (Brown), **Supp. I Part 1:** 146

Monson, Ander, **Supp. XXIV:** **229–242**

"Monsoon Season" (Komunyakaa), **Supp. XIII:** 122

Monsour, Leslie, **Supp. XV:** 125

"Monster, The" (Crane), **I:** 418

Monster, The, and Other Stories (Crane), **I:** 409

"Monstro" (Díaz), **Supp. XXIV:** 86

Montage of a Dream Deferred (Hughes), **Retro. Supp. I:** 194, **208–209; Supp. I Part 1:** 333, 339–341

Montagu, Ashley, **Supp. I Part 1:** 314

"Montaigne" (Emerson), **II:** 6

Montaigne, Michel de, **II:** 1, 5, 6, 8, 14–15, 16, 535; **III:** 600; **Retro. Supp. I:** 247; **Supp. XIV:** 105; **Supp. XXI:** 111, 205

Montale, Eugenio, **Supp. III Part 1:** 320; **Supp. V:** 337–338; **Supp. VIII:** 30; **Supp. XV:** 112

Montalembert, Hughes de, **Supp. XV:** 349

"Montana Memory" (Maclean), **Supp. XIV:** 221

"Montana; or the End of Jean-Jacques Rousseau" (Fiedler), **Supp. XIII:** **97–98**

"Montana Ranch Abandoned" (Hugo), **Supp. VI:** 139

"Mont Blanc" (Shelley), **Supp. IX:** 52

Montcalm, Louis Joseph de, **Supp. I Part 2:** 498

Montcalm and Wolfe (Parkman), **Supp. II Part 2:** 596, 609, 610, 611–613

Montemarano, Nicholas, **Supp. XVI:** 227

Montgomery, Benilde, **Supp. XIII:** 202

Montgomery, George, **Supp. XXIII:** 209

Montgomery, Robert, **Supp. I Part 2:** 611; **Supp. IV Part 1:** 130

Month of Sundays, A (Updike), **Retro. Supp. I:** 325, 327, 329, 330, 331, 333, 335

Monti, Luigi, **II:** 504

Montoya, José, **Supp. IV Part 2:** 545

"Montrachet-le-Jardin" (Stevens), **IV:** 82

Mont-Saint-Michel and Chartres (Adams), **I:** 1, 9, 12–14, 18, 19, 21; **Supp. I Part 2:** 417

Montserrat (Hellman), **Supp. I Part 1:** 283–285

Montserrat (Robles), **Supp. I Part 1:** 283–285

"Monument, The" (Bishop), **Supp. I Part 1:** 89

Monument, The (Strand), **Supp. IV Part 2:** 629, 630

"Monument in Utopia, A" (Schnackenberg), **Supp. XV:** 261, 263

"Monument Mountain" (Bryant), **Supp. I Part 1:** 156, 162

"Monument to After-Thought Unveiled, A" (Frost), **Retro. Supp. I:** 124

Moo (Smiley), **Supp. VI:** 292, **303–305**

Moods (Alcott), **Supp. I Part 1:** 33, 34–35, 43

Moody, Anne, **Supp. IV Part 1:** 11

Moody, Richard, **Supp. I Part 1:** 280

Moody, Rick, **Supp. XXI:** 117; **Supp. XXIV:** 131

Moody, Ron, **Supp. XXII:** 49

Moody, William Vaughn, **III:** 507; **IV:** 26

Moody, Mrs. William Vaughn, **I:** 384; **Supp. I Part 2:** 394

Moody-Freeman, Julie, **Supp. XXIII:** 91, 94, 95

"Moon" (A. Finch), **Supp. XVII:** 77

Moon, Henry Lee, **Supp. XVIII:** 281, 285

"Moon and the Night and the Men, The" (Berryman), **I:** 172

Moon Crossing Bridge (Gallagher), **Supp. XXIV:** 166, 170

"Moon Deluxe" (F. Barthelme), **Supp. XI:** 26, 27, 33, 36

Mooney, Tom, **I:** 505

"Moon-Face" (London), **II:** 475

Moon-Face and Other Stories (London), **II:** 483

"Moon Flock" (Dickey), **Supp. IV Part 1:** 186

Moon for the Misbegotten, A (O'Neill), **III:** 385, 401, 403, 404

Moon in a Mason Jar (Wrigley), **Supp. XVIII:** **295–298**

Moon in Its Flight, The (Sorrentino), **Supp. XXI:** 226

"Moon in Its Flight, The" (Sorrentino), **Supp. XXI:** 229

Moon Is a Gong, The (Dos Passos). *See Garbage Man, The* (Dos Passos)

Moon Is Down, The (Steinbeck), **IV:** 51

Moon Lady, The (Tan), **Supp. X:** 289

"Moonlight Alert" (Winters), **Supp. II Part 2:** 801, 811, 815

"Moonlight: Chickens on a Road" (Wrigley), **Supp. XVIII:** 295–296, 297

"Moonlit Night" (Reznikoff), **Supp. XIV:** 285–286

Moon of the Caribbees, The (O'Neill), **III:** 388

Moon Palace (Auster), **Supp. XII:** 22, 27, **30–32**

"Moonshine" (Komunyakaa), **Supp. XIII:** 127, 128

"Moon Solo" (Laforgue), **Supp. XIII:** 346

Moonstone, The (Collins), **Supp. XX:** 236

Moonstruck (screenplay, Shanley), **Supp. XIV:** 315, 316, **321–324**

"Moon upon her fluent Route, The" (Dickinson), **I:** 471

Moony's Kid Don't Cry (T. Williams), **IV:** 381

Moore, Arthur, **Supp. I Part 1:** 49

Moore, C. L., **Supp. XXV:** 122

Moore, Deborah Dash, **Supp. XX:** **246**

Moore, George, **I:** 103

Moore, Hannah, **Supp. XV:** 231

Moore, Jack B., **Supp. XXV:** 24, 26, 27

Moore, John Milton, **III:** 193

Moore, Julie L., **Supp. XXIII:** 252

Moore, Lorrie, **Supp. VIII:** 145; **Supp. X: 163–180; Supp. XXV:** 142

Moore, Marianne, **I:** 58, 285, 401, 428; **III: 193–217,** 514, 592–593; **IV:** 74, 75, 76, 91, 402; **Retro. Supp. I:** 416, 417; **Retro. Supp. II:** 39, 44, 48, 50, 82, 178, 179, 243, 244; **Supp. I Part 1:** 84, 89, 255, 257; **Supp. I Part 2:** 707; **Supp. II Part 1:** 21; **Supp. III Part 1:** 58, 60, 63; **Supp. III Part 2:** 612, 626, 627; **Supp. IV Part 1:** 242, 246, 257; **Supp. IV Part 2:** 454, 640, 641; **Supp. XIV:** 124, 130; **Supp. XV:** 306, 307; **Supp. XVII:** 131; **Supp. XXI:** 98; **Supp. XXII:** 273–274

Moore, Marie Lorena. *See* Moore, Lorrie

Moore, Mary Tyler, **Supp. V:** 107

Moore, Mary Warner, **III:** 193

Moore, Dr. Merrill, **III:** 506

Moore, Steven, **Supp. IV Part 1:** 279, 283, 284, 285, 287; **Supp. XII:** 151; **Supp. XVII:** 230, 231, 232; **Supp. XXII:** 261, 265

Moore, Sturge, **III:** 459

Moore, Thomas, **II:** 296, 299, 303; **Supp. IX:** 104; **Supp. X:** 114; **Supp. XXIII:** 138

Moore, Virginia, **Supp. XV:** 308

Moorehead, Caroline, **Supp. XIV:** 337

Moorepack, Howard, **Supp. XV:** 199

"Moorings" (Hoffman), **Supp. XVIII:** 87

Moos, Malcolm, **III:** 116, 119

"Moose, The" (Bishop), **Retro. Supp. II:** 50; **Supp. I Part 1:** 73, 93, 94, 95; **Supp. IX:** 45, 46

"Moose Wallow, The" (Hayden), **Supp. II Part 1:** 367

"Moowis, The Indian Coquette"(J. Schoolcraft), **Supp. XXIII:** 234

"Moquihuitzin's Answer" (Everwine), **Supp. XV:** 78

Mora, Pat, **Supp. XIII: 213–232**

Moraga, Cherríe, **Supp. XXIII: 193–206**

"Moral Argument Against Calvinism, The" (Channing), **Supp. XXIV: 73–74,** 75

"Moral Bully, The" (Holmes), **Supp. I Part 1:** 302

"Moral Character, the Practice of Law, and Legal Education" (Hall), **Supp. VIII:** 127

"Moral Equivalent for Military Service, A" (Bourne), **I:** 230

"Moral Equivalent of War, The" (James), **II:** 361; **Supp. I Part 1:** 20

"Moral Imperatives for World Order" (Locke), **Supp. XIV:** 207, 213

Moralités Légendaires (Laforgue), **I:** 573

"Morality and Mercy in Vienna" (Pynchon), **Supp. II Part 2:** 620, 624

"Morality of Indian Hating, The" (Momaday), **Supp. IV Part 2:** 484

"Morality of Poetry, The" (Wright), **Supp. III Part 2:** 596–597, 599

Moral Man and Immoral Society (Niebuhr), **III:** 292, 295–297

"Morals Is Her Middle Name" (Hughes), **Supp. I Part 1:** 338

"Morals of Chess, The" (Franklin), **II:** 121

"Moral Substitute for War, A" (Addams), **Supp. I Part 1:** 20

"Moral Theology of Atticus Finch, The" (Shaffer), **Supp. VIII:** 127

"Moral Thought, A" (Freneau), **Supp. II Part 1:** 262

Moran, Thomas, **Supp. IV Part 2:** 603–604

Moran, William L., **Supp. XXIV:** 150–151, 152

Moran of the Lady Letty (Norris), **II:** 264; **III:** 314, 322, 327, 328, 329, 330, 331, 332, 333

Morath, Ingeborg. *See* Miller, Mrs. Arthur (Ingeborg Morath)

Moravec, Paul, **Supp. XIX:** 123

Moravia, Alberto, **I:** 301

More (Crooker), **Supp. XXIII: 60–62**

Moré, Gonzalo, **Supp. X:** 185

More, Henry, **I:** 132

More, Paul Elmer, **I:** 223–224, 247; **Supp. I Part 2:** 423

Moreau, Gustave, **I:** 66

"More Blues and the Abstract Truth" (Wright), **Supp. XV:** 345

More Boners (Abingdon), **Supp. XVI:** 99

More Conversations with Eudora Welty (Prenshaw, ed.), **Retro. Supp. I:** 340, 341, 342, 343, 344, 352, 353, 354

More Dangerous Thoughts (Ryan as Quin), **Supp. XVIII:** 226, **229–230,** 231, 238

More Die of Heartbreak (Bellow), **Retro. Supp. II:** 31, 33, 34

"More Girl Than Boy" (Komunyakaa), **Supp. XIII:** 117

"More Light! More Light! (Hecht), **Supp. X:** 60

"More Like an Extension of the Spirit: Clothing in Lyric Poems"(Hadas), **Supp. XXIII:** 124

"Morella" (Poe), **III:** 412; **Retro. Supp. II:** 270

"More Love in the Western World" (Updike), **Retro. Supp. I:** 327–328, 329

"Morels" (W. J. Smith), **Supp. XIII: 336–339**

Moreno, Gary, **Supp. XV:** 5

"More Observations Now" (Conroy), **Supp. XVI:** 75

"More of a Corpse Than a Woman" (Rukeyser), **Supp. VI:** 280

"More Pleasant Adventures" (Ashbery), **Supp. III Part 1:** 1

More Poems to Solve (Swenson), **Supp. IV Part 2:** 640, 642, 648

More Stately Mansions (O'Neill), **III:** 385, 401, 404–405

"More Than Human" (Chabon), **Supp. XI:** 71–72

More Things Change The More They Stay the Same, The (J. W. Miller), **Supp. XX: 164**

More Tish (Rinehart), **Supp. XXV:** 194

More Triva (L. P. Smith), **Supp. XIV:** 339

Morgan, Edmund S., **IV:** 149; **Supp. I Part 1:** 101, 102; **Supp. I Part 2:** 484

Morgan, Edwin, **Supp. IV Part 2:** 688

Morgan, Emanuel. *See* Bynner, Witter

Morgan, Henry, **II:** 432; **IV:** 63; **Supp. XXV:** 255

Morgan, Jack, **Retro. Supp. II:** 142

Morgan, J. P., **I:** 494; **III:** 14, 15

Morgan, Judith, **Supp. XVI:** 103

Morgan, Neil, **Supp. XVI:** 103

Morgan, Robert, **Supp. V:** 5; **Supp. XX: 161, 162**

Morgan, Robin, **Supp. I Part 2:** 569

Morgan, Ted, **Supp. XIV:** 141

Morgan's Passing (Tyler), **Supp. IV Part 2:** 666–667, 668, 669

Morgenstern, Dan, **Supp. XIX:** 159

Morgenthau, Hans, **III:** 291, 309

Morgenthau, Henry, Sr., **Supp. XXIII:** 21, 22, 26, 30

Morgesons, The (E. Stoddard), **Supp. XV:** 270, 273, 274, 278, **279–282,** 283

Morgesons and Other Writings, Published and Unpublished, The (Buell and Zagarell), **Supp. XV:** 269

Moricand, Conrad, **III:** 190

Morison, Samuel Eliot, **Supp. I Part 2: 479–500; Supp. XXII:** 35

Morison, Mrs. Samuel Eliot (Elizabeth Shaw Greene), **Supp. I Part 2:** 483

Morison, Mrs. Samuel Eliot (Priscilla Barton), **Supp. I Part 2:** 493, 496, 497

Morita, Pat, **Supp. XXI:** 146

"Morituri Salutamus" (Longfellow), **II:** 499, 500; **Retro. Supp. II:** 169; **Supp. I Part 2:** 416

"Moriturus" (Millay), **III:** 126, 131–132

Morley, Christopher, **III:** 481, 483, 484; **Supp. I Part 2:** 653; **Supp. IX:** 124

Morley, Edward, **IV:** 27

Morley, Lord John, **I:** 7

Mormon Country (Stegner), **Supp. IV Part 2:** 598, 601–602

"Morning, The" (Updike), **Retro. Supp. I:** 329

"Morning after My Death, The" (Levis), **Supp. XI:** 260, 263–264

"Morning Arrives" (F. Wright), **Supp. XVII:** 244

Morning Face (Stratton-Porter), **Supp. XX:** 223

Morning for Flamingos, A (Burke), **Supp. XIV:** 30, 31, 32

"Morning Glory" (Merrill), **Supp. III Part 1:** 337

Morning Glory, The (R. Bly), **Supp. IV Part 1:** 63–65, 66, 71

"Morning Imagination of Russia, A" (W. C. Williams), **Retro. Supp. I:** 428

Morning in Antibes (Knowles), **Supp. XII:** 249

Morning in the Burned House (Atwood), **Supp. XIII:** 20, 35

Morning Is Near Us, The (Glaspell), **Supp. III Part 1:** 184–185

Morning Noon and Night (Cozzens), **I:** 374, 375, 376, 377, 379, 380

"Morning of the Day They Did It, The" (White), **Supp. I Part 2:** 663

"Morning Prayers" (Harjo), **Supp. XII:** 231

"Morning Roll Call" (Anderson), **I:** 116

"Morning Roudup" (Sorrentino), **Supp. XXI:** 228

"Mornings, I Walk Past the First Cemetery of Athens" (Stallings), **Supp. XXV:** 225

"Morning Shadows" (Skloot), **Supp. XX: 199**

"Mornings in a New House" (Merrill), **Supp. III Part 1:** 327

"Mornings in Ormos"(Hadas), **Supp. XXIII:** 112, 113, 123

Mornings Like This (Dillard), **Supp. VI:** 23, 34

"Morning Song" (Plath), **Retro. Supp. II:** 252; **Supp. XXIII:** 115

Morning Watch, The (Agee), **I:** 25, 39–42

"Morning with Broken Window" (Hogan), **Supp. IV Part 1:** 405

"Moro Like Me" (Goldman), **Supp. XXV:** 51

Morrell, Ottoline, **Retro. Supp. I:** 60

Morris, Bernard E., **Supp. XV:** 154, 169

Morris, Christopher D., **Supp. IV Part 1:** 231, 236

Morris, Gary, **Supp. XXII:** 262

Morris, George Sylvester, **Supp. I Part 2:** 640

Morris, Gouverneur, **Supp. I Part 2:** 512, 517, 518

Morris, Lloyd, **III:** 458

Morris, Robert, **Supp. I Part 2:** 510

Morris, Timothy, **Retro. Supp. I:** 40

Morris, William, **II:** 323, 338, 523; **IV:** 349; **Supp. I Part 1:** 260, 356; **Supp. XI:** 202

Morris, Willie, **Supp. XI:** 216, 231, 234; **Supp. XIX:** 151, 252

Morris, Wright, **I:** 305; **III: 218–243,** 558, 572; **IV:** 211

Morrison, Charles Clayton, **III:** 297

Morrison, Jim, **Supp. IV Part 1:** 206

Morrison, Toni, **Retro. Supp. II:** 15, 118; **Supp. III Part 1: 361–381; Supp. IV Part 1:** 2, 13, 14, 250, 253, 257; **Supp. V:** 169, 259; **Supp. VIII:** 213, 214; **Supp. X:** 85, 239, 250, 325; **Supp. XI:** 4, 14, 20, 91; **Supp. XII:** 289, 310; **Supp. XIII:** 60, 185; **Supp. XVI:** 143; **Supp. XVII:** 183; **Supp. XX: 108; Supp. XXI:** 172, 243; **Supp. XXII:** 65, 78; **Supp. XXIV:** 183, 184, 185; **Supp. XXV:** 142

"Morro Bay" (Jeffers), **Supp. II Part 2:** 422

Morrow, W. C., **I:** 199

Morse, Jedidiah, **Supp. XV:** 243

Morse, Robert, **Supp. XI:** 305

Morse, Samuel F. B., **Supp. I Part 1:** 156

Morse, Samuel French, **Supp. XXI:** 17, 19, 23, 27

Mortal Acts, Mortal Words (Kinnell), **Supp. III Part 1:** 235, 236, 237, 249–254

Mortal Antipathy, A (Holmes), **Supp. I Part 1:** 315–316

"Mortal Enemies" (Humphrey), **Supp. IX:** 109

"Mortal Eternal" (Olds), **Supp. X:** 214

Mortal No, The (Hoffman), **IV:** 113

Mortal Stakes (Parker), **Supp. XIX:** 183–184

Morte D'Arthur, Le (Malory), **Supp. IV Part 1:** 47

Mortmere Stories, The (Isherwood and Upward), **Supp. XIV:** 159

Morton, David, **Supp. IX:** 76

Morton, Jelly Roll, **Supp. X:** 242

Morton, Thomas, **Supp. XXII:** 44, 45, 46

"Mosaic of the Nativity: Serbia, Winter 1993" (Kenyon), **Supp. VII:** 173

Mosby's Memoirs and Other Stories (Bellow), **Retro. Supp. II:** 27

"Moscow, Idaho" (Offutt), **Supp. XIX:** 170

Moscow under Fire (Caldwell), **I:** 296

Moser, Barry, **Supp. XIV:** 223

Moses (Asch), **Supp. XXIII:** 7

Moses (Untermeyer), **Supp. XV:** **309**

Moses, Man of the Mountain (Hurston), **Supp. VI:** 149, 158, 160

"Moses on Sinai" (Untermeyer), **Supp. XV:** 300

Mosher, Howard Frank, **Supp. XXII:** **203–221**

Moskowitz, Alfred, **Supp. XXI:** 98, 106

Mosle, Sara, **Supp. XI:** 254

Mosley, Walter, **Supp. XIII:** **233–252;** **Supp. XVI:** 143

Mosquito (G. Jones), **Supp. XXIV:** 183, 184, 185, 190, **192–194,** 195

Mosquito Coast, The (film), **Supp. VIII:** 323

Mosquito Coast, The (Theroux), **Supp. VIII:** 321, **322–323**

Mosquitos (Faulkner), **II:** 56; **Retro. Supp. I:** 79, 81

Moss, Howard, **III:** 452; **Supp. IV Part 2:** 642; **Supp. IX:** 39; **Supp. XIII:** 114; **Supp. XV:** 143, 152

Moss, Stanley, **Supp. XI:** 321

Moss, Thylias, **Supp. XI:** 248

Mosses from an Old Manse (Hawthorne), **I:** 562; **II:** 224; **III:** 82, 83; **Retro. Supp. I:** 157, 248

"Moss of His Skin" (Sexton), **Supp. II Part 2:** 676

Most, Doug, **Supp. XVIII:** 101

"Most Extraordinary Case, A" (James), **II:** 322; **Retro. Supp. I:** 218

"Most Girl Part of You, The" (Hempel), **Supp. XXI:** 116

Most Likely to Succeed (Dos Passos), **I:** 491

"Most of It, The" (Frost), **Retro. Supp. I:** 121, 125, 129, 139; **Supp. XVIII:** 300

"Most Popular Novels in America, The" (Mabie), **Supp. XVIII:** 257

Motel Chronicles (Shepard), **Supp. III Part 2:** 445

"Mother" (Kooser), **Supp. XIX:** 117, 126, 127

"Mother" (Paley), **Supp. VI:** **222–223**

Mother (Schjeldahl), **Supp. XXIV:** 44

"Mother" (Snyder), **Supp. VIII:** 298

Mother (Whistler), **IV:** 369

Mother, The (Buck), **Supp. II Part 1:** 118–119

"Mother and Jack and the Rain" (Sexton), **Supp. II Part 2:** 686

"Mother and Son" (Tate), **IV:** 128, 137–138

Mother Country: Britain, the Welfare State and Nuclear Pollution (Robinson), **Supp. XXI:** 211

Mother Courage and Her Children (Brecht), **III:** 160; **Supp. IX:** 140; **Supp. XII:** 249

"Mother Earth: Her Whales" (Snyder), **Supp. VIII:** 302

"Motherhood" (Swenson), **Supp. IV Part 2:** 645

Mother Hubbard (Reed), **Supp. X:** 241

Motherless Brooklyn (Lethem), **Supp. XXII:** 49

Motherless in Brooklyn (Lethem), **Supp. XVIII:** 135, **143–144**

Mother Love (Dove), **Supp. IV Part 1:** 250–251, 254

"Mother Marie Therese" (Lowell), **Retro. Supp. II:** 188

Mother Night (Vonnegut), **Supp. II Part 2:** 757, 758, 767, 770, 771

"Mother Rosarine" (Kumin), **Supp. IV Part 2:** 442

"Mothers and Daughters in the Fiction of the New Republic" (Davidson), **Supp. XV:** 238

"Mother's lament for the absence of a child, A" (J. Schoolcraft), **Supp. XXIII:** 236

Mother's Recompense, The (Wharton), **IV:** 321, 324; **Retro. Supp. I:** 382

"Mother's Tale, A" (Agee), **I:** 29–30

"Mother's Things" (Creeley), **Supp. IV Part 1:** 141

"Mother Suite, The" (Crooker), **Supp. XXIII:** 61

"Mother's Voice" (Creeley), **Supp. IV Part 1:** 156

Mother to Daughter, Daughter to Mother (Olsen, ed.), **Supp. XIII:** 295

"Mother Tongue" (Simic), **Supp. VIII:** 283

"Mother to Son" (Hughes), **Retro. Supp. I:** 199, 203; **Supp. I Part 1:** 321–322, 323

Motherwell, Robert, **Supp. XV:** 145; **Supp. XXI:** 125

"Mother Writes to the Murderer, The: A Letter" (Nye), **Supp. XIII:** 276

Moths of the Limberlost (Stratton-Porter), **Supp. XX:** **218**

"Motion, The" (Olson), **Supp. II Part 2:** 571

Motion of History, The (Baraka), **Supp. II Part 1:** 55, 56

"Motive for Metaphor, The" (Stevens), **IV:** 89; **Retro. Supp. I:** 310

Motiveless Malignity (Auchincloss), **Supp. IV Part 1:** 31

Motke ganef (Asch), **Supp. XXIII:** 5

Motley, John Lothrop, **Supp. I Part 1:** 299; **Supp. I Part 2:** 479; **Supp. XX:** **228, 231**

Motley, Willard, **Supp. XVII:** **149–163;** **Supp. XXIII:** 145

"Motor Car, The" (White), **Supp. I Part 2:** 661

Motor-Flight Through France (Wharton), **I:** 12; **Retro. Supp. I:** 372

Mott, Michael, **Supp. VIII:** 204, 208

Motta, Gustavo, **Supp. XXIII:** 125

Mottetti: Poems of Love: The Motets of Eugenio Montale (Montale; Gioia, trans.), **Supp. XV:** 112, **127–128**

Mottke, the Thief (Asch), **Supp. XXIII:** 9, 12

Mottke, the Thief (Asch; tr. Willa and Edwin Muir), **Supp. XXIII:** 5

Mouawad, Nelly, **Supp. XX:** **126**

"Mound, The" (Lovecraft and Bishop), **Supp. XXV:** 122

"Mountain, The" (Frost), **Retro. Supp. I:** 121

"Mountain Hermitage, The: Pages from a Japanese Notebook" (Passin), **Supp. XIII:** 337

Mountain Interval (Frost), **II:** 154; **Retro. Supp. I:** 131, 132, 133

"Mountain Lion" (Hogan), **Supp. IV Part 1:** 412

"Mountain Music" essays (Sanders), **Supp. XVI:** 276–277

Mountain on the Desert, The (Richter), **Supp. XVIII:** 216, 219

Mountainous Journey, A (Tuqan), **Supp. XIII:** 278

"Mountains" (Dubus III), **Supp. XXIV:** 101

Mountains, The (Wolfe), **IV:** 461

Mountains and Rivers without End (Snyder), **Supp. VIII:** 295, **305–306**

"Mountains grow unnoticed, The" (Dickinson), **Retro. Supp. I:** 46

Mountains Have Come Closer, The (J. W. Miller), **Supp. XX:** **165, 168, 169–170**

Mountains Look Down, The: A History of Chichester, a Company Town in the Catskills (Bennett), **Supp. XXII:** 218

Mountains of California, The (Muir), **Supp. IX:** 183

"Mountain Whippoorwill, The" (Benét), **Supp. XI:** 44–45, 46, 47

"Mount-Joy: or Some Passages Out of the Life of a Castle-Builder" (Irving), **II:** 314

"Mount Venus" (Wright), **Supp. XV:** 346

"Mourners" (Kooser), **Supp. XIX:** 127

"Mourners, The" (Malamud), **Supp. I Part 2:** 431, 435, 436–437

Mourners Below (Purdy), **Supp. VII:** 274, 280

"Mourning and Melancholia" (Freud), **Supp. IV Part 2:** 450; **Supp. XVI:** 161

Mourning Becomes Electra (O'Neill), **III:** 391, 394, 398–400

"Mourning Doves" (Pedersen; Nelson, trans.), **Supp. XVIII:** 180

"Mourning Poem for the Queen of Sunday" (Hayden), **Supp. II Part 1:** 379–380

"Mouse Elegy" (Olds), **Supp. X:** 209

Mouse Is Born, A (Loos), **Supp. XVI:** 193

"Mouse Roulette Wheel, The" (C. Bly), **Supp. XVI:** 34

Moustapha's Eclipse (McKnight), **Supp. XX:** **147, 150**

"Mouth of Brass" (Humphrey), **Supp. IX:** 101

Moveable Feast, A (Hemingway), **II:** 257; **Retro. Supp. I:** 108, 171, **186– 187**

Movement, The: Documentary of a Struggle for Equality (Student Nonviolent Coordinating Committee), **Supp. IV Part 1:** 369

"Move over Macho, Here Comes Feminismo" (Robbins), **Supp. X:** 272

Movers and Shakers (Sochen), **Supp. XXI:** 1

"Moves, The" (July), **Supp. XXIV:** 205

"Move to California, The" (Stafford), **Supp. XI:** 318, 321

"Movie" (Shapiro), **Supp. II Part 2:** 707

Movie at the End of the World, The (McGrath), **Supp. X:** 127

Moviegoer, The (Percy), **Supp. III Part 1:** 383–385, 387, 389–392, 394, 397

"Movie Magazine, The: A Low 'Slick' " (Percy), **Supp. III Part 1:** 385

Movies (Dixon), **Supp. XII:** 147

Movies About the Movies (Ames), **Supp. XVIII:** 242–243

"Movie Star Peter at the Supper for Street People" (Ferry), **Supp. XXIV:** 153

"Moving Around" (Matthews), **Supp. IX:** 155

"Moving Finger, The" (Wharton), **Retro. Supp. I:** 365

"Moving Inward at Last" (Bly), **Supp. XXI:** 84–85

Moving On (McMurtry), **Supp. V:** 223– 224

"Moving On" (Pickering), **Supp. XXI:** 197

Moving Pictures: Memoirs of a Hollywood Prince (Schulberg), **Supp. XVIII:** 242, 243, 254

"Moving Sale" (Stallings), **Supp. XXV:** 228

Moving Target, The (Macdonald), **Supp. IV Part 2:** 462, 463, 467, 470, 471, 473, 474

Moving Target, The (Merwin), **Supp. III Part 1:** 346, 347–348, 352, 357

"Mowbray Family, The" (Farrell and Alden), **II:** 45

"Mowing" (Frost), **II:** 169–170; **Retro. Supp. I:** 127, 128

"Moxan's Master" (Bierce), **I:** 206

Moxley, Jennifer, **Supp. XVII:** 70

Moyers, Bill, **Supp. IV Part 1:** 267; **Supp. VIII:** 331; **Supp. XI:** 126, 132; **Supp. XII:** 217; **Supp. XIII:** 274, 276; **Supp. XV:** 212; **Supp. XXIII:** 129, 130, 131, 139

Moynagh, Maureen, **Supp. XXII:** 73

Moynihan, Daniel Patrick, **Retro. Supp. II:** 123; **Supp. VIII:** 241; **Supp. XIX:** 150–151

"Moyshele"(Asch), **Supp. XXIII:** 4

"Mozart" (C. Frost), **Supp. XV:** 94

Mozart, Wolfgang Amadeus, **I:** 479, 588; **IV:** 74, 358; **Supp. IV Part 1:** 284

"Mozart and the Gray Steward" (Wilder), **IV:** 358

Mrabet, Mohammed, **Supp. IV Part 1:** 92, 93

Mr. and Mrs. Baby and Other Stories (Strand), **Supp. IV Part 2:** 631

"Mr. and Mrs. Fix-It" (Lardner), **II:** 431

Mr. Arcularis (Aiken), **I:** 54, 56

"Mr. Big" (Allen), **Supp. XV:** 15

Mr. Bridge (Connell), **Supp. XIV:** 80, 82, 93; **Supp. XXIII:** 302

Mr. Brown Can Moo! Can You? (Geisel), **Supp. XVI:** 104

"Mr. Bruce" (Jewett), **II:** 397; **Retro. Supp. II:** 134, 143

"Mr. Burnshaw and the Statue" (Stevens), **Retro. Supp. I:** 298, 303

"Mr. Carson Death on His Nights Out" (McGrath), **Supp. X:** 118

Mr. Clemens and Mark Twain (Kaplan), **I:** 247–248

"Mr. Coffee and Mr. Fixit" (Carver), **Supp. III Part 1:** 145

"Mr. Cornelius Johnson, Office-Seeker" (Dunbar), **Supp. II Part 1:** 211, 213

"Mr. Costyve Duditch" (Toomer), **Supp. III Part 2:** 486

"Mr. Dajani, Calling from Jericho" (Nye), **Supp. XIII:** 286–287

"Mr. Edwards and the Spider" (Lowell), **I:** 544; **II:** 550; **Retro. Supp. II:** 187

Mr. Field's Daughter (Bausch), **Supp. VII:** 47–48, 51–52

"Mr. Flood's Party" (Robinson), **III:** 512

"Mr. Forster's Pageant" (Maxwell), **Supp. VIII:** 172

"Mr. Frost's Chickens" (Oliver), **Supp. VII:** 232–233

Mr. Hodge and Mr. Hazard (Wylie), **Supp. I Part 2:** 708, 709, 714, 721– 724

"Mr. Hueffer and the Prose Tradition" (Pound), **III:** 465

Mr. Ives' Christmas (Hijuelos), **Supp. VIII: 85–86**

Mr. Kelso's Lion (Bontemps), **Supp. XXII:** 7

"Mr. Longfellow and His Boy" (Sandburg), **III:** 591

"Mr. Luna and History" (Ríos), **Supp. IV Part 2:** 551

"Mr. Mitochondria" (Stollman), **Supp. XVII:** 50

Mr. Moto Is So Sorry (Marquand), **III:** 57, 58

Mr. Norris Changes Trains (Isherwood), **Supp. XIV:** 161

"Mr. Preble Gets Rid of His Wife" (Thurber), **Supp. I Part 2:** 615

"Mr. Rat"(Thompson), **Supp. XXIII:** 301–302

"Mr. Rolfe" (Wilson), **IV:** 436

Mr. Rutherford's Children (S. and A. Warner), **Supp. XVIII:** 264

"Mrs. Adis" (Kaye-Smith), **Supp. XVIII:** 130–131

Mrs. Albert Grundy: Observations in Philistia (Frederic), **II:** 138–139

Mr. Sammler's Planet (Bellow), **I:** 144, 147, 150, 151, 152, 158; **Retro. Supp. II:** 19, 28, 30

Mrs. Balfame (Atherton), **Supp. XXIV:** 20

"Mrs. Bilingsby's Wine" (Taylor), **Supp. V:** 323

Mrs. Bob Cratchit's Wild Christmas Binge (Durang), **Supp. XXIV:** 113, 125

Mrs. Bridge: A Novel (Connell), **Supp. XIV:** 79, 80, 81, 82, **89–94**, 95; **Supp. XXIII:** 302

"Mrs. Cassidy's Last Year" (Gordon), **Supp. IV Part 1:** 306

Mrs. Dalloway (Woolf), **Supp. IV Part 1:** 299; **Supp. VIII:** 5; **Supp. XV:** 55, 65–66

"Mr. Shelley Speaking" (Wylie), **Supp. I Part 2:** 719

"Mrs. Jellison" (Hay), **Supp. XIV:** 123

"Mrs. Krikorian" (Olds), **Supp. X:** 211

"Mrs. Maecenas" (Burke), **I:** 271

"Mrs. Mandrill" (Nemerov), **III:** 278

"Mrs. Manstey's View" (Wharton), **Retro. Supp. I:** 362, 363

"Mrs. Mobry's Reason" (Chopin), **Retro. Supp. II:** 61

Mr. Spaceman (R. O. Butler), **Supp. XII:** 62, **74–75**

Mrs. Reynolds (Stein), **IV:** 43

"Mrs. Sen's" (Lahiri), **Supp. XXI: 177– 178,** 180–181

Mrs. Stevens Hears the Mermaids Singing (Sarton), **Supp. VIII:** 252–253, **256–257**

Mrs. Ted Bliss (Elkin), **Supp. VI: 56,** 58

"Mrs. Turner Cutting the Grass" (Shields), **Supp. VII:** 319–320

"Mrs. Walpurga" (Rukeyser), **Supp. VI:** 273

"Mr. Thompson's Prodigal" (Harte), **Supp. II Part 1:** 354

"Mr. Trumm's Eyes"(Schott), **Supp. XXIII:** 243

Mr. Vertigo (Auster), **Supp. XII: 34–35,** 36

"Mr. Vonnegut in Sumatra" (Saunders), **Supp. XIX:** 235

"Mr. Whittier" (Scott), **Supp. I Part 2:** 705

Mr. Wilson's War (Dos Passos), **I:** 485

"Mr. Woodriff's Neckties" (Gallagher), **Supp. XXIV:** 175–176

"MS. Found in a Bottle" (Poe), **III:** 411, 416; **Retro. Supp. II:** 274

"Ms. Lot" (Rukeyser), **Supp. VI:** 281

Ms. Magazine, **Supp. V:** 259

Mttron-Hirsch, Sidney, **III:** 484–485

"Muchas Gracias Por Todo" (Nye), **Supp. XIII:** 282–283

"Much Madness is divinest Sense" (Dickinson), **Retro. Supp. I:** 37–38

"Muck-A-Muck" (Harte), **Supp. II Part 1:** 342

"Mud Below, The" (Proulx), **Supp. VII:** 262

Mudge, Alden, **Supp. XIV:** 35

"Mudman"(P. Benedict), **Supp. XXIII:** 47

Mudrick, Marvin, **Retro. Supp. II:** 289

"Mud Season" (Kenyon), **Supp. VII:** 167–168

Mueller, Lisel, **Supp. I Part 1:** 83, 88; **Supp. XIV:** 268

Muggli, Mark, **Supp. IV Part 1:** 207

Muhammad, Elijah, **Supp. I Part 1:** 60

Muir, Edwin, **I:** 527; **II:** 368; **III:** 20; **Supp. XXII:** 166; **Supp. XXIII:** 1

Muir, John, **Supp. VIII:** 296; **Supp. IX:** 33, **171–188; Supp. X:** 29; **Supp. XIV:** 177, 178, 181

Muir, Willa, **Supp. XXIII:** 1

Muirhead, Deborah, **Supp. XVIII:** 186

Mujica, Barbara, **Supp. VIII:** 89

Mulas, Franco, **Supp. XX:** 38

Mulatto (Hughes), **Retro. Supp. I:** 197, 203; **Supp. I Part 1:** 328, 339

Mulching of America, The (Crews), **Supp. XI:** 107

Muldoon, William, **I:** 500–501

Mule Bone (Hughes and Hurston), **Retro. Supp. I:** 194, 203; **Supp. VI:** 154

Mules and Men (Hurston), **Supp. VI:** 149, 153, 154, 160

Mulford, Prentice, **I:** 193

Mullennix, Joel, **Supp. XXIII:** 281

Mulligan, Robert, **Supp. VIII:** 128, 129

Mulligan Stew (Sorrentino), **Supp. XII:** 139; **Supp. XXI:** 233

Mullins, Eustace, **III:** 479

Mullins, Priscilla, **II:** 502–503

"Multiplication of Wool, The" (Sanders), **Supp. XVI:** 268

Multitudes, Multitudes (Clampitt), **Supp. IX:** 39

Mumbo Jumbo (Reed), **Supp. X:** 240, 242, **245–248,** 251

Mumford, Lewis, **I:** 245, 250, 251, 252, 259, 261; **II:** 271, 473–474; **Supp. I Part 2:** 632, 638; **Supp. II Part 2: 471–501**

Mumford, Sophia Wittenberg (Mrs. Lewis Mumford), **Supp. II Part 2:** 474, 475

"Mummers, The" (Di Piero), **Supp. XIX:** 44

Mummy, The (film), **Supp. IV Part 1:** 104; **Supp. XVII:** 57

Mundo y Palabra (Espaillat), **Supp. XXI:** 104

"Mundus et Infans" (Auden), **Supp. II Part 1:** 15

"Munich, 1938" (Lowell), **II:** 554

"Munich Mannequins, The" (Plath), **Retro. Supp. II:** 256

"Municipal Report, A" (Henry), **Supp. II Part 1:** 406–407

Muñoz, Manuel, **Supp. XXV: 127–139**

Munro, Alice, **Supp. IX:** 212; **Supp. X:** 290; **Supp. XII:** 289–290, 310; **Supp. XXIII:** 289, 296

Munsey, Frank, **I:** 501

Munson, Gorham, **I:** 252, 388, 432; **Retro. Supp. II:** 77, 78, 79, 82, 83; **Supp. I Part 2:** 454; **Supp. XX: 70, 74**

Münsterberg, Hugo, **Supp. XIV:** 197

Murakami, Haruki, **Supp. XVI:** 124

"Murano" (Doty), **Supp. XI:** 131

Murasaki, Lady, **II:** 577

Muratori, Fred, **Supp. XVI:** 281

Muray, Nicholas, **Supp. I Part 2:** 708

Murchison, Ginger, **Supp. XXV:** 222, 223, 226

Murder, My Sweet (film), **Supp. IV Part 1:** 130

"Murder Comes for the Bishop" (Goldman), **Supp. XXV:** 57

"Murderer Guest, The" (Gordon), **Supp. IV Part 1:** 306

"Murderers" (L. Michaels), **Supp. XVI:** 207–208

Murder in Mount Holly (Theroux), **Supp. VIII:** 315–316

Murder in the Cathedral (T. S. Eliot), **I:** 571, 573, 580, 581; **II:** 20; **Retro. Supp. I:** 65; **Retro. Supp. II:** 222

Murder of Lidice, The (Millay), **III:** 140

"Murders in the Rue Morgue, The" (Poe), **III:** 412, 416, 419–420; **Retro. Supp. II:** 271, 272; **Supp. XIX:** 77

Murdoch, Iris, **Supp. VIII:** 167; **Supp. XVIII:** 136,149

Murnau, F. W., **Supp. XV:** 128

Murphy, Brenda, **Supp. XXI:** 6

Murphy, Jacqueline Shea, **Retro. Supp. II:** 143

Murphy, Patrick, **Supp. XIII:** 214

Murphy, Richard, **Retro. Supp. II:** 250; **Supp. XXIII:** 75

Murray, Albert, **Retro. Supp. II:** 119, 120; **Supp. XIX: 147–162**

Murray, Bill, **Supp. XXI:** 51

Murray, Edward, **I:** 229

Murray, G. E., **Supp. X:** 201; **Supp. XI:** 143, 155

Murray, Gilbert, **III:** 468–469

Murray, Jan, **Supp. IV Part 2:** 574

Murray, John, **II:** 304; **III:** 76, 79; **Retro. Supp. I:** 246

Murray, Judith Sargent, **Supp. XV:** 236–237

Murray, Les, **Supp. XIX:** 131

Murray, Margaret A., **Supp. V:** 128

Murrell, John A., **IV:** 265

Mursell, James L., **Supp. I Part 2:** 608

"Muse" (Ammons), **Supp. VII:** 29

"Muse, Postmodern and Homeless, The" (Ozick), **Supp. V:** 272

"Musée des Beaux Arts" (Auden), **Retro. Supp. I:** 430; **Supp. II Part 1:** 14

"Musée des Beaux Arts Revisited" (Collins), **Supp. XXI:** 60

"Muse of Aboutness, The" (Baker), **Supp. XVI:** 288

Muses Are Heard, The (Capote), **Supp. III Part 1:** 126

"Muses of Terrence McNally, The" (Zinman), **Supp. XIII:** 207–208

"Muse's Tragedy, The" (Wharton), **Retro. Supp. I:** 364

Museum (Dove), **Supp. IV Part 1:** 245–247, 248

"Museum" (Hass), **Supp. VI:** 107

Museums and Women (Updike), **Retro. Supp. I:** 321

"Museum Vase" (Francis), **Supp. IX:** 83

"Mushrooms" (Plath), **Retro. Supp. II:** 246; **Supp. I Part 2:** 539

"Music" (Oliver), **Supp. VII:** 236

Music (al-Músíqá) (Gibran), **Supp. XX: 115, 124**

Music After the Great War (Van Vechten), **Supp. II Part 2:** 732

Music and Bad Manners (Van Vechten), **Supp. II Part 2:** 733

Music Appreciation (Skloot), **Supp. XX: 196, 197–201**

"Music for a Farce" (Bowles), **Supp. IV Part 1:** 83

Music for Chameleons (Capote), **Supp. III Part 1:** 120, 125–127, 131, 132

"Music for Museums?" (Van Vechten), **Supp. II Part 2:** 732

"Music for the Movies" (Van Vechten), **Supp. II Part 2:** 733

"Music from Spain" (Welty), **IV:** 272

Music Like Dirt (Bidart), **Supp. XV:** 35

"Music Like Dirt" (Bidart), **Supp. XV:** 35

Music of Chance, The (Auster), **Supp. XII:** 21, 23, **32–33**

"Music of My Own Kind Too, The" (Budbill), **Supp. XIX:** 10

"Music of Prose, The" (Gass), **Supp. VI:** 92

Music of Spain, The (Van Vechten), **Supp. II Part 2:** 734, 735

"Music of the Spheres" (Epstein), **Supp. XII:** 165

"Music School" (B. Kelly), **Supp. XVII:** 124

Music School, The (Updike), **IV:** 214, 215, 219, 226, 227; **Retro. Supp. I:** 320, 328, 329, 330

"Music School, The" (Updike), **Retro. Supp. I:** 326, 329, 335

"Music Swims Back to Me" (Sexton), **Supp. II Part 2:** 673

Muske, Carol, **Supp. IV Part 2:** 453–454

"Mussel Hunter at Rock Harbor" (Plath), **Supp. I Part 2:** 529, 537

Musset, Alfred de, **I:** 474; **II:** 543

Mussolini, Benito, **III:** 115, 473, 608; **IV:** 372, 373; **Supp. I Part 1:** 281, 282; **Supp. I Part 2:** 618; **Supp. V:** 290; **Supp. XVI:** 191

"Mustafa Ferrari" (X. J. Kennedy), **Supp. XV:** 170–171

Mustich, James, **Supp. XXI:** 52

"Must the Novelist Crusade?" (Welty), **IV:** 280

"Mutability of Literature, The" (Irving), **II:** 308

"Mutation of the Spirit" (Corso), **Supp. XII:** 132, 133

Mute, The (McCullers), **II:** 586

Mutilated, The (T. Williams), **IV:** 382, 386, 393

Mutiny of the Elsinore, The (London), **II:** 467

"Muttsy" (Hurston), **Supp. XVIII:** 279

Muyumba, Walton, **Supp. XIX:** 158

"My Adventures as a Social Poet" (Hughes), **Retro. Supp. I:** 194, 207

"My Alba" (Ginsberg), **Supp. II Part 1:** 320, 321

My Alexandria (Doty), **Supp. XI:** 119, 120, 121, **123–125,** 130

"My Amendment" (Saunders), **Supp. XIX:** 232

My Amputations (Major), **Supp. XXII:** 174, **175–176**

My Ántonia (Cather), **I:** 321–322; **Retro. Supp. I:** 1, 3, 4, **11–13**, 14, 17, 18, 22; **Supp. IV Part 2:** 608; **Supp. XVI:** 226

"My Appearance" (Wallace), **Supp. X:** 306–307

My Argument with the Gestapo: A Macaronic Journal (Merton), **Supp. VIII:** 207; **Supp. XV:** 344

"My Arkansas" (Angelou), **Supp. IV Part 1:** 15

"My Aunt" (Holmes), **Supp. I Part 1:** 302, 310

"My Beginnings" (Simpson), **Supp. IX:** 273

"My Bird Problem" (Franzen), **Supp. XX:** 94

My Black Horse (Gallagher), **Supp. XXIV:** 170

"My Bodyguard" (Notley), **Supp. XXII:** 230

My Bondage and My Freedom (Douglass), **Supp. III Part 1:** 155, 173

My Brother (Kincaid), **Supp. VII:** 191–193

"My Brother Paul" (Dreiser), **Retro. Supp. II:** 94

"My Brothers the Silent" (Merwin), **Supp. III Part 1:** 349–350

"My Brother's Work" (Dunn), **Supp. XI:** 147

"My Brother Takes a Hammer to the Mirror" (F. Wright), **Supp. XVII:** 244

"My Butterfly" (Frost), **II:** 151; **Retro. Supp. I:** 124

"My Children, and a Prayer for Us" (Ortiz), **Supp. IV Part 2:** 507

My Children! My Africa! (Fugard), **Supp. XXIV:** 267

"My College Sex Group" (Peacock), **Supp. XIX:** 199

"My Coney Island Uncle" (Swados), **Supp. XIX:** 267–268

"My Confession" (McCarthy), **II:** 562

"My Confessional Sestina" (Gioia), **Supp. XV:** 123

"My Corner" (Major), **Supp. XXII:** 184

My Country and My People (Yutang), **Supp. X:** 291

"My Country Tish of Thee" (Rinehart), **Supp. XXV:** 194

"My Country 'Tis of Thee" (Reznikoff), **Supp. III Part 2:** 616

"My Daughter Considers Her Body" (Skloot), **Supp. XX: 197–198, 200**

My Days of Anger (Farrell), **II:** 34, 35–36, 43

"My Dear Niece" (Boyce), **Supp. XXI:** 10

"My Dear Republican Mother" (C. Bly), **Supp. XVI:** 31–32

My Death My Life by Pier Paolo Pasolini (Acker), **Supp. XII:** 7

My Dog Stupid (Fante), **Supp. XI:** 160, **170–171**

My Dog Tulip (Ackerley), **Supp. XX:** 237

"My Ear-Rings"(J. Schoolcraft), **Supp. XXIII:** 226

My Emily Dickinson (Howe), **Retro. Supp. I:** 33, 43; **Supp. IV Part 2:** 430–431

"My English" (Alvarez), **Supp. VII:** 2

Myers, John Bernard, **Supp. XXIII:** 210, 219

Myers, Linda A., **Supp. IV Part 1:** 10

"My Extended Family" (Theroux), **Supp. VIII:** 311

"My Father" (Budbill), **Supp. XIX:** 5

"My Father" (L. Michaels), **Supp. XVI:** 214

"My Father" (Sterne), **IV:** 466

"My Father at Eighty-Five" (R. Bly), **Supp. IV Part 1:** 73

"My Father Is a Simple Man" (Salinas), **Supp. XIII:** 324

"My Father Is with Me" (Budbill), **Supp. XIX:** 15

"My Father: October 1942" (Stafford), **Supp. XI:** 323

My Father Photographed with Friends (Bronk), **Supp. XXI:** 26–27,**Supp. XXI:** 31

"My Father Photographed with Friends" (Bronk), **Supp. XXI:** 23, 27

"My Fathers Came From Kentucky" (Lindsay), **Supp. I Part 2:** 395

"My Father's Employment"(Schott), **Supp. XXIII:** 247

"My Father's Friends" (Maxwell), **Supp. VIII:** 171

"My Father's Ghost" (Wagoner), **Supp. IX:** 330

"My Father's God" (Fante), **Supp. XI:** 160, 174

"My Father's House" (L.-Y. Lee), **Supp. XV:** 225

"My Father's Love Letters" (Gallagher), **Supp. XXIV:** 171–172

"My Father's Love Letters" (Komunyakaa), **Supp. XIII:** 127

"My Father Speaks to me from the Dead" (Olds), **Supp. X:** 210

"My Father's Telescope" (Dove), **Supp. IV Part 1:** 246, 248

"My Father with Cigarette Twelve Years Before the Nazis Could Break His Heart" (Levine), **Supp. V:** 194

"My Favorite Murder" (Bierce), **I:** 205

My Favorite Plant: Writers and Gardeners on the Plants They Love (Kincaid), **Supp. VII:** 193–194

My Favorites in Suspense (Hitchcock, ed.), **Supp. XXII:** 119

"My Fifty-Plus Years Celebrate Spring" (Salinas), **Supp. XIII:** 327

"My First Book" (Harte), **Supp. II Part 1:** 343

My First Summer in the Sierra (Muir), **Supp. IX:** 172, 173, **178–181**, 183, 185; **Supp. XIV:** 177

"My Flamboyant Grandson" (Saunders), **Supp. XIX:** 231–232

"My Fountain Pen" (McClatchy), **Supp. XII:** 254, 260

My Friend, Henry Miller (Perlès), **III:** 189

My Friend, Julia Lathrop (Addams), **Supp. I Part 1:** 25

"My Friend, Walt Whitman" (Oliver), **Supp. VII:** 245

"My Garden Acquaintance" (Lowell), **Supp. I Part 2:** 420

My Garden \[Book\]: (Kincaid), **Supp. VII:** 193–194

"My Good-bye" (Weigl), **Supp. XIX:** 288

"My Grandfather" (Lowell), **II:** 554

"My Grandmother's Love Letters" (H. Crane), **Retro. Supp. II:** 78

My Grandparents Were Married for Sixty-five Years (Schott), **Supp. XXIII:** 240–241

"My Grandson, Home at Last" (Angelou), **Supp. IV Part 1:** 13

My Green Hills of Jamaica (McKay), **Supp. X:** 132, 142

"My Gun" (Gallagher), **Supp. XXIV:** 175

My Guru and His Disciple (Isherwood), **Supp. XIV:** 157, 164, 172

"My Heart" (Collins), **Supp. XXI:** 58

My Heart's in the Highlands (Saroyan), **Supp. IV Part 1:** 83

"My High School Reunion" (Kingston), **Supp. V:** 169

"My House New-Painted" (Bronk), **Supp. XXI:** 30

"My Ideal Home" (Stratton-Porter), **Supp. XX: 222**

"My Indigo" (L.-Y. Lee), **Supp. XV:** 214

My Kind of Place: Travel Stories from a Woman Who's Been Everywhere (Orlean), **Supp. XXV:** 160, 164–165

"My Kinsman, Major Molineux" (Hawthorne), **II:** 228, 229, 237–239, 243; **Retro. Supp. I:** 153–154, 158, 160, 161; **Retro. Supp. II:** 181, 187; **Supp. XVI:** 157

My Kinsman, Major Molineux (Lowell), **II:** 545–546

"My Last Afternoon with Uncle Devereux Winslow" (Lowell), **II:** 547–548; **Retro. Supp. II:** 189

"My Last Drive" (Hardy), **Supp. VIII:** 32

"My Last Duchess" (Browning), **Supp. XV:** 121; **Supp. XXV:** 229

Myles, Eileen, **Supp. XXIV:** 45

"My Life" (Strand), **Supp. IV Part 2:** 627

My Life, Starring Dara Falcon (Beattie), **Supp. V:** 31, 34–35

My Life a Loaded Gun: Dickinson, Plath, Rich, and Female Creativity (Bennett), **Retro. Supp. I:** 29

My Life and Hard Times (Thurber), **Supp. I Part 2:** 607, 609

My Life and Loves in Greenwich Village (attr. Bodenheim), **Supp. XXV:** 30

My Life as a Man (P. Roth), **Retro. Supp. II:** 281, 286, 289; **Supp. III Part 2:** 401, 404, 405, 417–418

"My Life as a P.I.G., or the True Adventures of Smokey the Cop" (Abbey), **Supp. XIII:** 3

"My life closed twice before its close" (Dickinson), **Retro. Supp. I:** 38

"My Life had stood a Loaded Gun" (Dickinson), **Retro. Supp. I:** 42, 43, 45, 46; **Supp. IV Part 2:** 430
My Life of Absurdity (C. Himes), **Supp. XVI:** 145
"My Life with Medicine" (Nye), **Supp. XIII:** 282
"My Life with *Playboy*" (Plimpton), **Supp. XVI:** 246
"My Life with R. H. Macy" (Jackson), **Supp. IX:** 118
"My Little Utopia" (Simic), **Supp. VIII:** 283
My Lives and How I Lost Them (Cullen), **Supp. IV Part 1:** 173
"My Lord Bag of Rice" (C. Bly), **Supp. XVI:** 40
My Lord Bag of Rice: New and Selected Stories (C. Bly), **Supp. XVI:** 41
"My Lost City" (Fitzgerald), **Retro. Supp. I:** 102
"My Lost Youth" (Longfellow), **II:** 487, 499; **Retro. Supp. II:** 168
My Love Affair with America: The Cautionary Tale of a Cheerful Conservative (Podhoretz), **Supp. VIII:** 232, 233, 237, **244–246**
"My Lover Has Dirty Fingernails" (Updike), **Retro. Supp. I:** 332, 333
"My lover is tall and handsome"(J. Schoolcraft), **Supp. XXIII:** 235
"My Lucy Friend Who Smells Like Corn" (Cisneros), **Supp. VII:** 68–69
"My Mammogram" (McClatchy), **Supp. XII:** 263–264
"My Man Bovanne" (Bambara), **Supp. XI:** 2
"My Mariner" (Larcom), **Supp. XIII:** 147
My Mark Twain (Howells), **II:** 276
"My Metamorphosis" (Harte), **Supp. II Part 1:** 339
My Mistress's Sparrow Is Dead (Eugenides, ed.), **Supp. XXIV:** 135
"My Moby Dick" (Humphrey), **Supp. IX:** 95
"My Monkey" (Nelson), **Supp. XVIII:** 178
"My Moral Life" (Halliday), **Supp. XIX:** 89
My Mortal Enemy (Cather), **I:** 327–328; **Retro. Supp. I:** 16–17; **Supp. I Part 2:** 719
My Mother, My Father and Me (Hellman), **Supp. I Part 1:** 290–291
"My Mother and My Sisters" (Ortiz), **Supp. IV Part 2:** 499
My Mother: Demonology (Acker), **Supp. XII:** 6
"My Mother Is Speaking from the Desert" (Gordon), **Supp. IV Part 1:** 309, 314
"My Mother Remembers That She Was Beautiful" (Gallagher), **Supp. XXIV:** 169
"My Mother's Goofy Song" (Fante), **Supp. XI:** 164
"My Mother's Memoirs, My Father's Lie, and Other True Stories" (Banks), **Supp. V:** 15

"My Mother's Nipples" (Hass), **Supp. VI:** 109
"My Mother's Story" (Kunitz), **Supp. III Part 1:** 259
"My Mother's Voice" (Very), **Supp. XXV:** 244
"My Mother"(Taylor), **Supp. XXIII:** 231
"My Mother Then and Now" (Wasserstein), **Supp. XV:** 327
"My Mother with Purse the Summer They Murdered the Spanish Poet" (Levine), **Supp. V:** 194
My Movie Business: A Memoir (Irving), **Supp. VI:** 164
"My Name" (Cisneros), **Supp. VII:** 60
"My Negro Problem—And Ours" (Podhoretz), **Supp. VIII:** 234–236
"My Neighborhood"(Dybek), **Supp. XXIII:** 69
"My New Diet" (Karr), **Supp. XI:** 241
My Next Bride (Boyle), **Supp. XXIV:** 53, 59
"My Number" (Collins), **Supp. XXI:** 64
"My Old Man" (Hemingway), **II:** 263
My Other Life (Theroux), **Supp. VIII:** 310, 324
"My Own Story" (E. Stoddard), **Supp. XV:** 273, 279, 283
My Own True Name: New and Selected Poems for Young Adults, 1984–1999 (Mora), **Supp. XIII:** 222
"My Parents Have Come Home Laughing" (Jarman), **Supp. XVII:** 113
"My Passion for Ferries" (Whitman), **IV:** 350
"My People" (Hughes), **Retro. Supp. I:** 197; **Supp. I Part 1:** 321–322, 323
"My Philosophy" (Allen), **Supp. XV:** 15
"My Playmate" (Whittier), **Supp. I Part 2:** 699–700
"My Priests" (Monette), **Supp. X:** 159
"My Public" (Rinehart), **Supp. XXV:** 201
Myra Breckinridge (Vidal), **Supp. IV Part 2:** 677, 685–686, 689, 691
"My Raptor" (A. Finch), **Supp. XVII:** 72
"My Recollections of S. B. Fairchild" (Jackson), **Supp. IX:** 118–119
"My Religion" (Carson), **Supp. XII:** 105–106
Myrer, Anton, **Supp. XXV:** 145
"My Road to Hell Was Paved" (Patchett), **Supp. XII:** 310–311
Myron (Vidal), **Supp. IV Part 2:** 677, 685, 686, 691
"My Roomy" (Lardner), **II:** 420, 421, 428, 430
"My Sad Self" (Ginsberg), **Supp. II Part 1:** 320
My San Francisco (Atherton), **Supp. XXIV:** 27
My Secret History (Theroux), **Supp. VIII:** 310, 324
"Myself" (Audubon), **Supp. XVI:** 1–2, 5, 12
Myself Painting (Major), **Supp. XXII:** 184–185
"My Shoes" (Simic), **Supp. VIII:** 275
"My Side of the Matter" (Capote), **Supp. III Part 1:** 114, 115

My Silk Purse and Yours: The Publishing Scene and American Literary Art (Garrett), **Supp. VII:** 111; **Supp. X:** 7
My Sister Eileen (McKenney), **IV:** 288; **Retro. Supp. II:** 321
My Sister's Hand in Mine: The Collected Works of Jane Bowles, **Supp. IV Part 1:** 82–83
"My Son" (Strand), **Supp. IV Part 2:** 629
My Son, John (film), **Supp. I Part 1:** 67
"My Son, the Murderer" (Malamud), **Supp. I Part 2:** 437
My Son Is a Splendid Driver (Inge), **Supp. XXV:** 93, 95, 107
"My Son the Man" (Olds), **Supp. X:** 212
"My Speech to the Graduates" (Allen), **Supp. XV:** 16
"Mysteries of Caesar, The" (Hecht), **Supp. X:** 73
"Mysteries of Eleusis, The" (Hardwick), **Supp. III Part 1:** 195
Mysteries of Paris, The (Sue), **Supp. XXIII:** 182
Mysteries of Pittsburgh, The (Chabon), **Supp. XI:** 65, 68, **69–71**; **Supp. XIX:** 135
Mysteries of Small Houses (Notley), **Supp. XXII:** 223, 224, 226, 234–235
"Mysterious Case of R, The" (Conroy), **Supp. XVI:** 72
Mysterious Stranger, The (Twain), **IV:** 190–191, 210
Mystery, A (Shields). *See Swann* (Shields)
"Mystery, The" (Dunbar), **Supp. II Part 1:** 199, 210
"Mystery, The" (Glück), **Supp. V:** 91
Mystery and Manners (O'Connor), **Retro. Supp. II:** 230
"'Mystery Boy' Looks for Kin in Nashville" (Hayden), **Supp. II Part 1:** 366, 372
"Mystery of Coincidence, The" (Conroy), **Supp. XVI:** 74
"Mystery of Heroism, A" (Crane), **I:** 414
"Mystery of Marie Rogêt, The" (Poe), **III:** 413, 419; **Retro. Supp. II:** 271
"Mystic" (Plath), **Retro. Supp. II:** 257; **Supp. I Part 2:** 539, 541
"Mystical Poet, A" (Bogan), **Retro. Supp. I:** 36
"Mystic of Sex, The—A First Look at D. H. Lawrence" (Nin), **Supp. X:** 188
"Mystic Vision in 'The Marshes of Glynn'" (Warfel), **Supp. I Part 1:** 366, 373
"Mystification" (Poe), **III:** 425
"My Strange New Poetry" (Halliday), **Supp. XIX:** 88, 94
My Study Windows (Lowell), **Supp. I Part 2:** 407
"My Teacher" (Conroy), **Supp. XVI:** 75
"Myth" (Rukeyser), **Supp. VI:** 281–282
"Myth" (Trethewey), **Supp. XXI:** 245, 255, 256
"Myth"(Hadas), **Supp. XXIII:** 119
"Mythmaker" (Trethewey), **Supp. XXI:** 243
Myth of American Manhood, The (Kriegel, ed.), **Supp. XXIV:** 214

Myth of Sisyphus, The (Camus), **I:** 294; **Supp. XIII:** 165

"Myth of the Happy Worker, The" (Swados), **Supp. XIX:** 265

"Myth of the Isolated Artist, The" (Oates), **Supp. II Part 2:** 520

Myth of the Machine, The (Mumford), **Supp. II Part 2:** 476, 478, 482, 483, 493, 497

"Myth of the Powerful Worker, The" (Swados), **Supp. XIX:** 265

Mythology and the Romantic Tradition in English Poetry (Bush), **Supp. I Part 1:** 268

Myths and Texts (Snyder), **Supp. VIII:** 295–296

"Myths of Bears, The" (Bass), **Supp. XVI:** 19, 20

"My *Tocaya*" (Cisneros), **Supp. VII:** 69

My Uncle Dudley (Morris), **I:** 305; **III:** 219–220

"My Uncle's Favorite Coffee Shop" (Nye), **Supp. XIII:** 283

"My Unopened Life" (Gallagher), **Supp. XXIV:** 171

"My Weariness of Epic Proportions" (Simic), **Supp. VIII:** 276

My Wicked Wicked Ways (Cisneros), **Supp. VII:** 58, 64–68, 71

"My Wicked Wicked Ways" (Cisneros), **Supp. VII:** 58, 64–66

My Wisdom (Thompson), **Supp. XXIII:** 291–293

"My Word-house" (Mora), **Supp. XIII:** 219, 225

My Works and Days (Mumford), **Supp. II Part 2:** 475, 477, 481

"My World and My Critics" (Stratton-Porter), **Supp. XX:** 220

My World and Welcome to It (Thurber), **Supp. I Part 2:** 610

N

Nabokov, Peter, **Supp. IV Part 2:** 490

Nabokov, Véra, **Retro. Supp. I:** 266, 270

Nabokov, Vladimir, **I:** 135; **III:** 244–266, 283, 286; **Retro. Supp. I:** 263–281, 317, 335; **Supp. I Part 1:** 196; **Supp. II Part 1:** 2; **Supp. IV Part 1:** 135; **Supp. V:** 127, 237, 251, 252, 253; **Supp. VIII:** 105, 133, 138; **Supp. IX:** 152, 212, 261; **Supp. X:** 283; **Supp. XI:** 66; **Supp. XII:** 310; **Supp. XIII:** 46, 52; **Supp. XVI:** 148, 294; **Supp. XVIII:** 98, 102; **Supp. XXII:** 263; **Supp. XXIV:** 133

Nabokov's Dozen (Nabokov), **Retro. Supp. I:** 266

Nabokov's Garden: A Guide to Ada (Mason), **Supp. VIII:** 138

Naca, Kristin, **Supp. XIII:** 133

Nadeau, Robert, **Supp. X:** 261, 270

Nadel, Alan, **Supp. IV Part 1:** 209

Naimy, Mikhail, **Supp. XX:** 116, 119, 120

Naipaul, V. S., **Supp. IV Part 1:** 297; **Supp. VIII:** 314; **Supp. X:** 131; **Supp. XIV:** 111; **Supp. XX:** 87; **Supp. XXI:** 170; **Supp. XXII:** 240, 241, 242, 246, 253

Naison, Mark, **Supp. XVIII:** 231

Naked and the Dead, The (Mailer), **I:** 477; **III:** 26, 27, 28–30, 31, 33, 35, 36, 44; **Retro. Supp. II:** 197–199; **Supp. IV Part 1:** 381; **Supp. XI:** 218; **Supp. XIX:** 248; **Supp. XX:** 248; **Supp. XXI:** 277

Naked Author (di Donato), **Supp. XX:** 45

Naked Babies (Quindlen and Kelsh), **Supp. XVII:** 167, 179

Naked in Garden Hills (Crews), **Supp. XI:** 102, 110

Naked Lunch (Burroughs), **Supp. III Part 1:** 92–95, 97–105; **Supp. IV Part 1:** 90

"Naked Nude" (Malamud), **Supp. I Part 2:** 450

Naked on Roller Skates (Bodenheim), **Supp. XXV:** 27

Naked Poetry (Berg and Mezey, eds.), **Supp. IV Part 1:** 60

Naked Poetry (Levine), **Supp. V:** 180

Naked Revenge (film), **Supp. XVII:** 141

Nall, Gus, **Supp. XXII:** 172, 184

Namedropping: Mostly Literary Memoirs (Coover), **Supp. V:** 40

"Name in the Papers" (Hughes), **Supp. I Part 1:** 330

Name Is Archer, The (Macdonald, under Millar), **Supp. IV Part 2:** 466

"Name Is Burroughs, The" (Burroughs), **Supp. III Part 1:** 93

Name Is Fogarty, The: Private Papers on Public Matters (Farrell), **II:** 49

"Names" (Carruth), **Supp. XVI:** 54, 56

"Names, The" (Collins), **Supp. XXI:** 54, 61–62

Names, The (DeLillo), **Supp. VI:** 3, 10, 13, 14

Names, The (Momaday), **Supp. IV Part 2:** 479, 480, 483, 486, 487, 488, 489

Namesake, The (Lahiri), **Supp. XXI:** 176, 184, **186–188**

Names and Faces of Heroes, The (Price), **Supp. VI:** 258, 260

Names of the Dead, The (O'Nan), **Supp. XXV:** 142, 143–144, 149, 151

Names of the Lost, The (Levine), **Supp. V:** 177–178, 179, 187–188

"Naming for Love" (Carruth), **Supp. XVI:** 48

"Naming Myself" (Kingsolver), **Supp. VII:** 208

"Naming of Names, The" (Sanders), **Supp. XVI:** 268

Naming of the Beasts, The (Stern). *See Rejoicings: Selected Poems, 1966–1972* (Stern)

Naming the Unseen (Ray), **Supp. XVIII:** 192, **193–195**

"Naming the Unseen" (Ray), **Supp. XVIII:** 203

Nana (Zola), **III:** 321

"Nancy Culpepper" (Mason), **Supp. VIII:** 141

Nancy Drew stories, **Supp. VIII:** 133, 135, 137, 142

"Nancy Knapp" (Masters), **Supp. I Part 2:** 461

"Naola Beauty Academy, New Orleans, 1943" (Trethewey), **Supp. XXI:** 246

"Naomi Counting Time"(Thompson), **Supp. XXIII:** 293

"Naomi Shihab Nye: U.S. Mideast-History a Harbinger of 9-11?" (Nye), **Supp. XXIII:** 286

"Naomi Trimmer" (X. J. Kennedy), **Supp. XV:** 170

"Nap, The" (Banks), **Supp. V:** 7

"Napoleon" (Emerson), **II:** 6

Napoleon I, **I:** 6, 7, 8, 474; **II:** 5, 309, 315, 321, 523; **Supp. I Part 1:** 153; **Supp. I Part 2:** 518, 519

Napolitano, Louise, **Supp. XX:** 35, 45, **46–47**

Narcissa and Other Fables (Auchincloss), **Supp. IV Part 1:** 21, 34

"Narcissus as Narcissus" (Tate), **IV:** 124

"Narcissus Leaves the Pool" (Epstein), **Supp. XIV:** 110

Narcissus Leaves the Pool: Familiar Essays (Epstein), **Supp. XIV:** 110

Nardal, Paulette, **Supp. X:** 139

Nardi, Marcia, **Retro. Supp. I:** 426, 427

"Narragansett Boulevard" (Halliday), **Supp. XIX:** 91

Narration (Stein), **IV:** 27, 30, 32, 33, 36

Narrative of a Four Months' Residence among the Natives of a Valley of the Marquesas Islands (Melville), **III:** 76

Narrative of Arthur Gordon Pym, The (Poe), **III:** 412, 416; **Retro. Supp. II:** 265, **273–275**; **Supp. XI:** 293

"Narrative of Arthur Gordon Pym, The" (Poe), **Supp. XXII:** 58

Narrative of the Life of Frederick Douglass, an American Slave, Written by Himself (Douglass), **Supp. III Part 1:** 154–159, 162, 165; **Supp. IV Part 1:** 13; **Supp. VIII:** 202

"Narrativity Scenes" (Wright), **Supp. XV:** 345

Narrenschiff, Das (Brant), **III:** 447

"Narrow Fellow in the Grass, A" (Dickinson), **Retro. Supp. I:** 30, 37

Narrow Heart, A: Portrait of a Woman (Gordon), **II:** 197, 217

Narrow Rooms (Purdy), **Supp. VII:** 274

Narrows, The (Connelly), **Supp. XXI:** 71, **76**

Nasby, Petroleum, **Supp. XVIII:** 1

Nash, Noreen, **Supp. XXII:** 256

Nash, Ogden, **Supp. XXI:** 51; **Supp. XXIV:** 45

Nash, Roderick, **Supp. IX:** 185; **Supp. XIV:** 191–192

Nash, Susan Smith, **Supp. XVI:** 274

Nash, Thomas, **Supp. III Part 1:** 387–388

Nashe, Thomas, **I:** 358; **Supp. XVII:** 232

Nashville (film), **Supp. IX:** 143

"Nashville Gone to Ashes" (Hempel), **Supp. XXI:** 115, 118, **120–121**

Nashville Skyline (album, Dylan), **Supp. XVIII:** 27

Nason, Elias, **Supp. XV:** 242

Nasser, Gamal Abdel, **IV:** 490

Nasty Bits (Silver), **Supp. XXIV:** 265

Natalie Mann (Toomer), **Supp. III Part 2:** 484–486

Nathan, George Jean, **II:** 91; **III:** 103, 104, 106, 107; **IV:** 432; **Supp. IV Part 1:** 343; **Supp. IX:** 56–57; **Supp. XIII:** 161; **Supp. XXII:** 23

"Nathanael West" (Herbst), **Retro. Supp. II:** 325

Nathanael West: The Art of His Life (Martin), **Retro. Supp. II:** 325

Nathan Coulter (Berry), **Supp. X:** 24, 33

National Dream, The: Building the Impossible Railway (Findley and Whitehead), **Supp. XX:** 51

"Nationalist, The" (Anderson), **I:** 115

"Nation Is Like Ourselves, The" (Baraka), **Supp. II Part 1:** 53

"Native, The" (Olds), **Supp. X:** 215

"Native American Attitudes to the Environment" (Momaday), **Supp. IV Part 2:** 481, 491

Native American Renaissance (Lincoln), **Supp. IV Part 2:** 507

Native American Testimony (Nabokov, ed.), **Supp. IV Part 2:** 490

"Native Blessing" (Ray), **Supp. XVIII:** 202

Native Guard (Trethewey), **Supp. XXI:** 243, 244, 247, **254–257**

"Native Guard" (Trethewey), **Supp. XXI:** 256

"Native Hill, A" (Berry), **Supp. X:** 21

Native in a Strange Land: Trials & Tremors (Coleman), **Supp. XI: 84–85,** 87

Native of Winby and Other Tales, A (Jewett), **II:** 396; **Retro. Supp. II:** 138

"Natives Don't Cry" (Boyle), **Supp. XXIV:** 57–58

Native Son (Wright), **IV:** 476, 477, 478, 479, 481, 482–484, 485, 487, 488, 491, 495; **Retro. Supp. II:** 107, 116; **Supp. I Part 1:** 51, 64, 67, 337; **Supp. II Part 1:** 170, 235–236; **Supp. IX:** 306; **Supp. XIV:** 73; **Supp. XVII:** 155; **Supp. XVIII:** 283, 286; **Supp. XXI:** 169

"Native Trees" (Merwin), **Supp. III Part 1:** 355

Natorp, Paul, **Supp. XIV:** 198

Natural, The (Malamud), **II:** 424, 425; **Retro. Supp. II:** 288; **Supp. I Part 2:** 438–441, 443

"*Natural, The:* Malamud's World Ceres" (Wasserman), **Supp. I Part 2:** 439

Natural Affection (Inge), **Supp. XXV:** 95, 103, 104–105, 106

"Natural History" (Olds), **Supp. X:** 210

"Natural History Note" (Hay), **Supp. XIV:** 124, 130

"Natural History of Some Poems, A" (Harrison), **Supp. VIII:** 53

"Natural History of the Dead" (Hemingway), **II:** 206; **Retro. Supp. I:** 176

"Naturally Superior School, A" (Knowles), **Supp. XII:** 235, 240–241

"Natural Method of Mental Philosophy" (Emerson), **II:** 14

"Natural Resources" (Rich), **Supp. I Part 2:** 575

Natural Selection (F. Barthelme), **Supp. XI:** 2, 28, 32, 33

Nature (Emerson), **I:** 463; **II:** 1, 8, 12, 16; **IV:** 171, 172–173; **Supp. XXIV:** 75, 79; **Supp. XXV:** 241

"Nature" (Emerson), **Retro. Supp. I:** 250; **Supp. I Part 2:** 383; **Supp. III Part 1:** 387; **Supp. IX:** 178

"Nature" (Very), **Supp. XXV:** 242

"Nature, Inc." (Lewis), **II:** 441

Nature and Destiny of Man, The (Niebuhr), **III:** 292, 303–306, 310

"Nature and Life" (Emerson), **II:** 19

"Nature and New America Painting"(O'Hara), **Supp. XXIII:** 212

"Nature and Nurture: When It Comes to Twins, Sometimes It's Hard to Tell the Two Apart" (Bausch), **Supp. VII:** 40

Nature and Purpose of the Universe, The (Durang), **Supp. XXIV: 115–116**

"Nature-Metaphors" (Lanier), **Supp. I Part 1:** 352

Nature Morte (Brodsky), **Supp. VIII:** 25

Nature of Evil, The (James), **II:** 343

Nature of Peace, The (Veblen), **Supp. I Part 2:** 642

Nature of Things, The (Lucretius; Stallings, trans.), **Supp. XXV:** 221, 226–227

Nature of Things, The (television show), **Supp. XX:** 51

Nature of True Virtue, The (Edwards), **I:** 549, 557–558, 559

Nature: Poems Old and New (Swenson), **Supp. IV Part 2:** 652

Nature's Economy: A History of Ecological Ideas (Worster), **Supp. IX:** 19

Nature's Way (Wouk), **Supp. XXV:** 253

Naumburg, Margaret, **Supp. XX: 68, 74–75**

Nausea (Sartre), **Supp. VIII:** 7

"Navajo Blanket, A" (Swenson), **Supp. IV Part 2:** 649

Navarette, Don Martín de, **II:** 310

Navarro, Ramon, **Supp. IV Part 1:** 206

Navigator, The (film), **I:** 31

Navratilova, Martina, **Supp. XX: 264**

Naylor, Gloria, **Supp. VIII: 213–230; Supp. XX: 108**

Naylor, Paul Kenneth, **Supp. IV Part 2:** 420

Nazarene, The (Asch), **Supp. XXIII:** 2, 3, 4, 6, 9, **12–13,** 14, 15, 16

Nazarene, The: or, The Last of the Washingtons (Lippard), **Supp. XXIII:** 183, 184, 187, 190

Nazimova, **III:** 399

Neal, Darlin', **Supp. XXI:** 41

Neal, Larry, **Retro. Supp. II:** 112, 128; **Supp. X:** 324, 328

Neal, Lawrence P., **Supp. II Part 1:** 53

Neal, Patricia, **Supp. I Part 1:** 286; **Supp. IV Part 2:** 524; **Supp. V:** 223

Neale, Walter, **I:** 192, 208

"Near Damascus" (Di Piero), **Supp. XIX:** 43

Nearer the Moon: From "A Journal of Love," the Unexpurgated Diary of Anaïs Nin, 1937–1939, **Supp. X:** 184, 185

Near-Johannesburg Boy and Other Poems, The (Brooks), **Supp. III Part 1:** 86

Near Klamath (Carver), **Supp. III Part 1:** 137

"Near Perigord" (Pound), **Retro. Supp. I:** 289, 290

"Near Spring" (Pickering), **Supp. XXI:** 198

Near the Ocean (Lowell), **II:** 543, 550, 551–553, 554, 555; **Retro. Supp. II:** 182, 186, 189–190

"Near View of the High Sierra, A" (Muir), **Supp. IX:** 183

Nebeker, Helen, **Supp. IX:** 122

"Nebraska Blizzard" (F. Wright), **Supp. XVII:** 247

Necessary Angel, The (Stevens), **IV:** 76, 79, 89, 90

Necessities of Life: Poems, 1962–1965 (Rich), **Supp. I Part 2:** 553, 555

"Necessity of Lemons, The"(Schott), **Supp. XXIII:** 247, 248

Nechayev, Sergey, **Supp. XXI:** 164

Neck Deep and Other Predicaments (Monson), **Supp. XXIV:** 230, **234–236,** 241

"Necrological" (Ransom), **III:** 486–489, 490, 492

Ned Christie's War (Conley), **Supp. V:** 232

"Need for a Cultural Base to Civil Rites & Bpower Mooments, The" (Baraka), **Supp. II Part 1:** 48

"Need for Christian Preaching, The" (Buechner), **Supp. XII:** 49

Needful Things (King), **Supp. V:** 139, 146

"Needle" (Simic), **Supp. VIII:** 275

"Needle Trade" (Reznikoff), **Supp. XIV:** 277, 289

"Need of Being Versed in Country Things, The" (Frost), **II:** 154; **Retro. Supp. I:** 133, 135

"Need to Say It, The" (Hampl), **Supp. XXII:** 94

Neel, Philippe, **Supp. XIV:** 338

Neelakantappa, Tara, **Supp. XV:** 104–105

Neeley, Barbara, **Supp. XVI:** 143

"Negative Capability" (Komunyakaa), **Supp. XIII:** 131

Negligible Tales (Bierce), **I:** 209

"Negotiating the Darkness, Fortified by Poets' Strength" (Karr), **Supp. XI:** 254; **Supp. XIII:** 285

Negotiating with the Dead (Atwood), **Supp. XIII:** 20, 35

Negritude movement, **Supp. X:** 131, 139

"Negro" (Hughes), **Supp. I Part 1:** 321–322

Negro, The (Du Bois), **Supp. II Part 1:** 178, 179, 185

Negro, The: The Southerner's Problem (Page), **Supp. II Part 1:** 168

Negro and His Music, The (Locke), **Supp. XIV:** 202

"Negro Artisan, The" (Du Bois), **Supp. II Part 1:** 166

"Negro Artist and the Racial Mountain, The" (Hughes), **Retro. Supp. I:** 200,

207; **Supp. I Part 1:** 323, 325; **Supp. IV Part 1:** 169

Negro Art: Past and Present (Locke), **Supp. XIV:** 202

"Negro Assays the Negro Mood, A" (Baldwin), **Supp. I Part 1:** 52

"Negro Citizen, The" (Du Bois), **Supp. II Part 1:** 179

"Negro Dancers" (Hughes), **Retro. Supp. I:** 199; **Supp. I Part 1:** 324

"Negroes" (Bodenheim), **Supp. XXV:** 22

Negroes in America, The (McKay), **Supp. X:** 132, 136

"Negroes of Farmville, Virginia, The: A Social Study" (Du Bois), **Supp. II Part 1:** 166

Negro Family, The: The Case for National Action (Moynihan), **Retro. Supp. II:** 123

"Negro Farmer, The" (Du Bois), **Supp. II Part 1:** 167

"Negro Fight, The" (column, C. L. R. James), **Supp. XXI:** 169

"Negro Ghetto" (Hughes), **Supp. I Part 1:** 331

Negro in America, The (Locke), **Supp. XIV:** 208

Negro in American Civilization, The (Du Bois), **Supp. II Part 1:** 179

Negro in American Culture, The (Locke and Butcher), **Supp. XIV:** 202–203

Negro in Art, The: A Pictorial Record of the Negro Artist and of the Negro Theme in Art (Locke), **Supp. XIV:** 202

"Negro in Large Cities, The" (Du Bois), **Supp. II Part 1:** 169

"Negro in Literature and Art, The" (Du Bois), **Supp. II Part 1:** 174

Negro in New York, The (Ellison), **Supp. II Part 1:** 230

"Negro in the Black Belt, The: Some Social Sketches" (Du Bois), **Supp. II Part 1:** 166

Negro in the Caribbean, The (Williams), **Supp. XXI:** 166

"Negro in the Three Americas, The" (Locke), **Supp. XIV:** 211

"Negro in the Well, The" (Caldwell), **I:** 309

"Negro Love Song, A" (Dunbar), **Supp. II Part 1:** 204

"Negro Martyrs Are Needed" (C. Himes), **Supp. XVI:** 138

Negro Mother, The (Hughes), **Supp. I Part 1:** 328

Negro Mother and Other Dramatic Recitations, The (Hughes), **Retro. Supp. I:** 203

Negro Novel in America, The (Bone), **Supp. IX:** 318–319; **Supp. XVIII:** 285

Negro Publication Society of America, **Retro. Supp. I:** 205

"Negro Renaissance, The: Jean Toomer and the Harlem of the 1920s" (Bontemps), **Supp. IX:** 306

"Negro Schoolmaster in the New South, A" (Du Bois), **Supp. II Part 1:** 168

"Negro's Contribution to American Culture, The" (Locke), **Supp. XIV:** 210, 211

"Negro Sermon, A: Simon Legree" (Lindsay), **Supp. I Part 2:** 393

"Negro Sings of Rivers, The" (Hughes), **Supp. IV Part 1:** 16

"Negro Speaks of Rivers, The" (Hughes), **Retro. Supp. I:** 199; **Supp. I Part 1:** 321

"Negro Spirituals, The (Locke), **Supp. XIV:** 201

"Negro Takes Stock, The" (Du Bois), **Supp. II Part 1:** 180

"Negro Theatre, The" (Van Vechten), **Supp. II Part 2:** 735

"Negro Voter Sizes Up Taft, A" (Hurston), **Supp. VI:** 160

"Negro Writer and His Roots, The: Toward a New Romanticism" (Hansberry), **Supp. IV Part 1:** 364

"Negro Youth Speaks" (Locke), **Supp. XIV:** 201

"Nehemias Americanus" (Mather), **Supp. II Part 2:** 453

Nehru, Jawaharlal, **IV:** 490

"Neighbor" (Hugo), **Supp. VI:** 135–136

"Neighborhood Drunk"(Dybek), **Supp. XXIII:** 71

"Neighbors" (Carver), **Supp. III Part 1:** 135, 139, 141; **Supp. XI:** 153

"Neighbors" (Hogan), **Supp. IV Part 1:** 405

"Neighbors, The" (Hay), **Supp. XIV:** 126

"Neighbour Rosicky" (Cather), **I:** 331–332

Neil Simon (Johnson), **Supp. IV Part 2:** 573

"Neil Simon's Jewish-Style Comedies" (Walden), **Supp. IV Part 2:** 584, 591

"Neil Simon: Toward Act III?" (Walden), **Supp. IV Part 2:** 591

Neilson, Heather, **Supp. IV Part 2:** 681

Neiman, Gilbert, **Supp. XV:** 140

"Neither Out Far Nor In Deep" (Frost), **I:** 303; **Retro. Supp. I:** 121, 138

"Nellie Clark" (Masters), **Supp. I Part 2:** 461

Nelson, Alice Dunbar, **Supp. XVII:** 75

Nelson, Cary, **Supp. XVIII:** 226, 227, 230, 231; **Supp. XXII:** 271

Nelson, Ernest, **I:** 388

Nelson, Howard, **Supp. IV Part 1:** 66, 68; **Supp. XIX:** 3; **Supp. XXI:** 95

Nelson, Lord Horatio, **II:** 524

Nelson, Lynn (pseudonym). *See* Nelson, Marilyn

Nelson, Marilyn, **Supp. XVII:** 74, 112; **Supp. XVIII: 171–188**

Nelson, Shirley, **Supp. XII:** 293

Nelson, Steve, **Supp. XVIII:** 226

Nelson Algren (Cox and Chatterton), **Supp. IX:** 11–12

Nelson Algren: A Life on the Wild Side (Drew), **Supp. IX:** 2

Nemerov, David, **II:** 268

Nemerov, Howard, **III: 267–289; IV:** 137, 140; **Supp. III Part 2:** 541; **Supp. IV Part 2:** 455, 650; **Supp. IX:** 114

"Nemesis" (Lovecraft), **Supp. XXV:** 119

Nemesis (P. Roth), **Supp. XXIV:** 214

Nemiroff, Robert Barron, **Supp. IV Part 1:** 360, 361, 365, 369, 370, 374

Neoconservative Criticism: Norman Podhoretz, Kenneth S. Lynn, and Joseph Epstein (Winchell), **Supp. VIII:** 241; **Supp. XIV:** 103

"Neo-Formalism: A Dangerous Nostalgia" (Sadoff), **Supp. XXI:** 100

"Neo-Hoodoo Manifesto, The" (Reed), **Supp. X:** 242

Neon Rain, The (Burke), **Supp. XIV:** 22, 24, 26–27, 28–29, 30

Neon Vernacular (Komunyakaa), **Supp. XIII:** 121, **127–128,** 131

Neon Wilderness, The (Algren), **Supp. IX:** 3, 4

Neo-Slave Narratives (Rushdy), **Supp. X:** 250

Nepantla: Essays from the Land in the Middle (Mora), **Supp. XIII:** 213, **219–221,** 227

Nephew, The (Purdy), **Supp. VII:** 271, 273, 282

"Nereids of Seriphos, The" (Clampitt), **Supp. IX:** 41

Nericcio, William, **Supp. XIV:** 304–305

Neruda, Pablo, **Supp. I Part 1:** 89; **Supp. IV Part 2:** 537; **Supp. V:** 332; **Supp. VIII:** 272, 274; **Supp. IX:** 157, 271; **Supp. X:** 112; **Supp. XI:** 191; **Supp. XII:** 217; **Supp. XIII:** 114, 315, 323; **Supp. XXI:** 61, 100; **Supp. XXIV:** 170

Nesbit, Edith, **Supp. VIII:** 171

Nesbit, Lynn, **Supp. XXIII:** 100

Nesbitt, Robin, **Supp. VIII:** 89

Nessmuk (George Washington Sears), **Supp. XIX:** 10

Nesting Ground, The (Wagoner), **Supp. IX:** 324, **325–326**

Nest of Ninnies, A (Ashbery and Schuyler), **Supp. III Part 1:** 3; **Supp. XV:** 178

"Nests"(Le Sueur), **Supp. XXIII:** 165

Net of Cobwebs (Holding), **Supp. XXII:** 126, **129–130,** 134

Net of Magic: Wonders and Deceptions in India (Siegel), **Supp. XXII:** 262

Nets to Catch the Wind (Wylie), **Supp. I Part 2:** 709, 710–712, 714

Nettleton, Asahel, **I:** 458

"Net to Snare the Moonlight, A" (Lindsay), **Supp. I Part 2:** 387

Neubauer, Carol E., **Supp. IV Part 1:** 9

Neugeboren, Jacob Mordecai. *See* Neugeboren, Jay

Neugeboren, Jay, **Supp. XVI: 217–231**

Neugroschel, Joachim, **Supp. IX:** 138

Neuhaus, Richard John, **Supp. VIII:** 245; **Supp. XIX:** 144

Neumann, Erich, **Supp. I Part 2:** 567; **Supp. IV Part 1:** 68, 69

Neuromancer (W. Gibson), **Supp. XII:** 15; **Supp. XVI:** 117, 119–120, 122, 124, **125–126,** 127, 129, 131

Neurotica: Jewish Writers on Sex (Bukiet, ed.), **Supp. XVII:** 48

"Neurotic America and the Sex Impulse" (Dreiser), **Retro. Supp. II:** 105

Neutra, Richard, **Supp. XVI:** 192

"Never Bet the Devil Your Head" (Poe), **III:** 425; **Retro. Supp. II:** 273

Never Come Morning (Algren), **Supp. IX:** 3, **7–9**

Never in a Hurry: Essays on People and Places (Nye), **Supp. XIII:** 273, **280–282,** 286

"Never Marry a Mexican" (Cisneros), **Supp. VII:** 70

"Never Room with a Couple" (Hughes), **Supp. I Part 1:** 330

"Nevertheless" (Moore), **III:** 214

Nevins, Allan, **I:** 253; **Supp. I Part 2:** 486, 493

"Nevsky Prospekt" (Olds), **Supp. X:** 205

New Adam, The (Untermeyer), **Supp. XV:** 304, 305

New Addresses (Koch), **Supp. XV:** 177, 184

"New Age of the Rhetoricians, The" (Cowley), **Supp. II Part 1:** 135

New American Cyclopedia, **Supp. XVIII:** 4

New American Literature, The (Pattee), **II:** 456

New American Novel of Manners, The (Klinkowitz), **Supp. XI:** 347

"New American Ode, The" (Wright), **Supp. XV:** 346

New American Poetry, 1945–1960, The (Allen, ed.), **Supp. VIII:** 291, 292; **Supp. XIII:** 112; **Supp. XXIII:** 215–216

"New American Writer, A" (W. C. Williams), **Retro. Supp. II:** 335

New and Collected Poems (Reed), **Supp. X:** 241

New and Collected Poems (Wilbur), **Supp. III Part 2:** 562–564

New and Selected Poems (Nemerov), **III:** 269, 275, 277–279

New and Selected Poems (Oliver), **Supp. VII:** 240–241, 245

New and Selected Poems (W. J. Smith), **Supp. XIII:** 332

New and Selected Poems (Wagoner), **Supp. IX:** 326–327

New and Selected Poems, 1958–1998 (Sorrentino), **Supp. XXI:** 229

New and Selected Poems: 1974–1994 (Dunn), **Supp. XI: 151–152**

New and Selected Things Taking Place (Swenson), **Supp. IV Part 2:** 648–650, 651

"New Aristocracy, The" (Atherton), **Supp. XXIV:** 24

"New Art Gallery Society, The" (Wolfe), **Supp. III Part 2:** 580

Newberger, Julee, **Supp. XVIII:** 168

"New Birth, The" (Very), **Supp. XXV:** 246, 247, 248

New Black Poetry, The (Major, ed.), **Supp. XXII:** 172, 174, 176, 180

"New Capitalist Tool, The" (Wasserstein), **Supp. XV:** 328

Newcomb, Ralph, **Supp. XIII:** 12

Newcomb, Robert, **II:** 111

New Conscience and an Ancient Evil, A (Addams), **Supp. I Part 1:** 14–15, 16

"New Conservatism in American Poetry, The" (Wakoski), **Supp. XVII:** 112

"New Conservatives, The: Intellectuals in Retreat" (Epstein), **Supp. XIV:** 103

New Critical Essays on H. P. Lovecraft (Simmons, ed.), **Supp. XXV:** 123

New Criticism, The (Ransom), **III:** 497–498, 499, 501

"New Day, A" (Levine), **Supp. V:** 182

Newdick, Robert Spangler, **Retro. Supp. I:** 138

Newdick's Season of Frost (Newdick), **Retro. Supp. I:** 138

New Dictionary of Quotations, A (Mencken), **III:** 111

New Directions Anthology in Prose and Poetry (Laughlin, ed.), **Supp. XVI:** 284

"New Directions in Poetry" (D. Locke), **Supp. IX:** 273

"New Dog, The: Variations on a Text by Jules Laforgue" (C. Frost), **Supp. XV:** 98

Newell, Henry, **IV:** 193

"New England" (Lowell), **II:** 536

"New England" (Robinson), **III:** 510, 524

"New England Bachelor, A" (Eberhart), **I:** 539

"New Englander, The" (Anderson), **I:** 114

New England Girlhood, A (Larcom), **Supp. XIII:** 137, 142, 143, 144, **147–154**

New England Gothic Literature (Ringel), **Supp. XXII:** 205

New England: Indian Summer (Brooks), **I:** 253, 256

New England Local Color Literature (Donovan), **Retro. Supp. II:** 138

"New England Sabbath-Day Chace, The" (Freneau), **Supp. II Part 1:** 273

New-England Tale, A (Sedgwick), **I:** 341

New England Tragedies, The (Longfellow), **II:** 490, 505, 506; **Retro. Supp. II:** 165, 167

New English Canaan (Morton), **Supp. XXII:** 45

New Era in American Poetry, The (Untermeyer, ed.), **Supp. XV:** 301, 303, 306

Newer Ideals of Peace (Addams), **Supp. I Part 1:** 11–12, 15, 16–17, 19, 20–21

"New Experience in Millinery, A" (Stratton-Porter), **Supp. XX:** 216

New Feminist Criticism, The: Essays on Women, Literature, and Theory (Showalter), **Supp. X:** 97

New Fire: To Put Things Right Again (Moraga), **Supp. XXIII:** 197

"New Folsom Prison" (Matthews), **Supp. IX:** 165

New Formalism, The: A Critical Introduction (McPhillips), **Supp. XV:** 250, 251, 252, 264

Newfound (J. W. Miller), **Supp. XX: 163, 166, 170–172**

New Found Land: Fourteen Poems (MacLeish), **III:** 12–13

"New Hampshire, February" (Eberhart), **I:** 536

New Hampshire: A Poem with Notes and Grace Notes (Frost), **II:** 154–155; **Retro. Supp. I:** 132, 133, 135

New Hard-Boiled Writers (Panek), **Supp. XIV:** 27

"New Home" (Richter), **Supp. XVIII:** 209

New Industrial State, The (Galbraith), **Supp. I Part 2:** 648

"New Journalism, The" (Wolfe), **Supp. III Part 2:** 571

New Journalism, The (Wolfe and Johnson, eds.), **Supp. III Part 2:** 570, 579–581, 583, 586; **Supp. XXIV:** 282

New Left, The: The Anti-Industrial Revolution (Rand), **Supp. IV Part 2:** 527

"New Letters from Thomas Jefferson" (Stafford), **Supp. XI:** 324

New Letters on the Air: Contemporary Writers on Radio, **Supp. X:** 165, 169, 173

"New Life" (Glück), **Supp. V:** 90

New Life, A (Malamud), **Supp. I Part 2:** 429–466

"New Life, The" (Bynner), **Supp. XV:** 44

"New Life, The" (Schott), **Supp. XXIII:** 242

"New Life at Kyerefaso" (Sutherland), **Supp. IV Part 1:** 9

"New Light on Veblen" (Dorfman), **Supp. I Part 2:** 650

"New Man, A" (E. P. Jones), **Supp. XXII:** 144

Newman, Charles, **Supp. I Part 2:** 527, 546–548

Newman, Edwin, **Supp. IV Part 2:** 526

Newman, Frances, **Supp. XXII:** 198

Newman, Judie, **Supp. IV Part 1:** 304, 305

Newman, Paul, **Supp. IV Part 2:** 473, 474

New Man, The (Merton), **Supp. VIII:** 208

"New Mecca, The" (Saunders), **Supp. XIX:** 235, 236

"New Medea, The" (Howells), **II:** 282

New Mexico trilogy (Nichols), **Supp. XIII:** 269

New Morning (album, Dylan), **Supp. XVIII:** 27, 33

"New Mother" (Olds), **Supp. X:** 206

"New Mothers, The" (Shields), **Supp. VII:** 310

New Music (Price), **Supp. VI:** 264, 265

"New Mutants, The" (Fiedler), **Supp. XIII:** 104

"New Name for Some Old Ways of Thinking, A" (James), **II:** 353

New Native American Novel, The: Works in Progress (Bartlett), **Supp. IV Part 1:** 335

"New Natural History, A" (Thurber), **Supp. I Part 2:** 619

New Negro, The (Locke), **Supp. XIX:** 69

"New Negro, The" (Locke), **Supp. XIV:** 201

New Negro, The (Locke, ed.), **Supp. II Part 1:** 176; **Supp. IX:** 309; **Supp.**

X: 137; **Supp. XXII:** 8

New Negro, The: An Interpretation (Locke, ed.), **Retro. Supp. I:** 199; **Supp. IV Part 1:** 170; **Supp. XIV:** 195, 201–202

New Negro for a New Century, A (Washington, Wood, and Williams), **Supp. XIV:** 201

New New Journalism, The (R. Boynton), **Supp. XVII:** 209

"New Nomads, The" (E. Hoffman), **Supp. XVI:** 161

"New Orleans" (Carruth), **Supp. XVI:** 50

New Orleans Sketches (Faulkner), **Retro. Supp. I:** 80

New Path to the Waterfall, A (Carver), **Supp. III Part 1:** 138–140, 147, 149; **Supp. XXIV:** 172

"New Poem, The" (Wright), **Supp. V:** 339, 340

"New Poems" (MacLeish), **III:** 19

"New Poems" (Oliver), **Supp. VII:** 240

New Poems 1960 (Bynner), **Supp. XV:** 51

New Poems: 1980–88 (Haines), **Supp. XII: 209–210**

New Poetry, The (Monroe and Henderson, eds.), **Supp. I Part 2:** 387

"New Poetry Handbook, The" (Strand), **Supp. IV Part 2:** 626

New Poetry of Mexico (Strand, trans.), **Supp. IV Part 2:** 630

New Poets of England and America (Hall, Pack, and Simpson, eds.), **Supp. IV Part 2:** 621

"Newport of Anchuria" (Henry), **Supp. II Part 1:** 409

New Princeton Encyclopedia of Poetry and Poetics (Preminger and Brogan, eds.), **Supp. XV:** 250

"New Republic Moves Uptown, The" (Cowley), **Supp. II Part 1:** 142

"New Rose Hotel" (W. Gibson), **Supp. XVI:** 120, 122, 124

"News, The" (McClatchy), **Supp. XII:** 269

"New Season" (Levine), **Supp. V:** 188

New Seeds of Contemplation (Merton), **Supp. VIII:** 200, 208

News from the Glacier: Selected Poems 1960–1980 (Haines), **Supp. XII:** 207, 208–209

"News Item" (Parker), **Supp. IX:** 190

News of a Kidnapping (García Márquez), **Supp. XXV:** 57

New Song, A (Hughes), **Retro. Supp. I:** 202; **Supp. I Part 1:** 328, 331–332

"New Song"(Kenny), **Supp. XXIII:** 156

Newson-Horst, Adele, **Supp. XXIII:** 95

"New South, The" (Lanier), **Supp. I Part 1:** 352, 354, 370

New Southern Girl, The: Female Adolescence in the Works of 12 Women Authors (Town), **Supp. XVIII:** 195

Newspaper Days, 1899–1906 (Mencken), **III:** 100, 102, 120

"New Spirit, The" (Ashbery), **Supp. III Part 1:** 14, 15

New Spoon River, The (Masters), **Supp. I Part 2:** 461–465, 473

New Star Chamber and Other Essays, The (Masters), **Supp. I Part 2:** 455–456, 459

New Tales of the Vampires (Rice), **Supp. VII:** 290

New Tenant, The (Ionesco), **Supp. XXIV:** 113

New Testament, **I:** 303, 457, 458; **II:** 167; **III:** 305; **IV:** 114, 134, 152; **Retro. Supp. I:** 58, 140, 360; **Supp. I Part 1:** 104, 106; **Supp. I Part 2:** 516; **Supp. XVII:** 155; **Supp. XXIII:** 13. *See also* names of New Testament books

New Testament, A (Anderson), **I:** 101, 114

"New Theory of Thorstein Veblen, A" (Galbraith), **Supp. I Part 2:** 650

Newton, Benjamin Franklin, **I:** 454

Newton, Huey P., **Supp. I Part 1:** 66; **Supp. IV Part 1:** 206

Newton, Isaac, **I:** 132, 557; **II:** 6, 103, 348–349; **III:** 428; **IV:** 18, 149

Newton, Maud, **Supp. XXIII:** 290

Newton, Sarah Emily, **Supp. XV:** 234

"New-Wave Format, A" (Mason), **Supp. VIII:** 141, 143, 147

New West of Edward Abbey, The (Ronald), **Supp. XIII:** 4

"New Wife" (Halliday), **Supp. XIX:** 89

New Wolves, The: The Return of the Mexican Wolf to the American Southwest (Bass), **Supp. XVI:** 26–27

New Woman's Survival Sourcebook, The (Rennie and Grimstead, eds.), **Supp. I Part 2:** 569

New World, The (Bronk), **Supp. XXI:** 25–26, 31

New World, The (Bynner), **Supp. XV:** 41, 42

"New World, The" (Very), **Supp. XXV:** 248

New World, The: Tales (Banks), **Supp. V:** 8, 9, 10

New World Naked, A (Mariani), **Retro. Supp. I:** 419

New Worlds of Literature (Beaty and Hunter, eds.), **Supp. IV Part 1:** 331

New World Writing (Updike), **IV:** 217

"New Year, The" (Very), **Supp. XXV:** 240, 244

New Year Letter (Auden), **Supp. II Part 1:** 14, 16

"New Year's Day" (Wharton), **Retro. Supp. I:** 381

"New Year's Eve" (Schwartz), **Supp. II Part 2:** 640, 656–657

New Year's Eve/1929 (Farrell), **II:** 43

"New Year's Eve 1968" (Lowell), **II:** 554

New Year's Eve: A Play (W. Frank), **Supp. XX: 75**

"New Year's Gift, The" (Stowe), **Supp. I Part 2:** 587

"New Year Two Thousand, The" (Weigl), **Supp. XIX:** 287–288

"New York" (Capote), **Supp. III Part 1:** 122

"New York" (Moore), **III:** 196, 198, 202, 206

"New York 1965" (Bowles), **Supp. IV Part 1:** 94

New York: A Serendipiter's Journey (Talese), **Supp. XVII:** 202, 203

"New York Breeze" (Halliday), **Supp. XIX:** 85

New York City Arts Project, **Supp. III Part 2:** 618

"New York City in 1979"(Acker), **Supp. XII:** 5

New York Edition, **Retro. Supp. I:** 235

"New York Edition" (James), **II:** 336, 337

"New York Gold Conspiracy, The" (Adams), **I:** 4

New York Hat, The (film; Griffith), **Supp. XVI:** 183

New York Intellectuals, **Supp. VIII:** 93

"New York Intellectuals, The" (Howe), **Supp. VI:** 120

"New York Is a City of Things Unnoticed" (Talese), **Supp. XVII:** 202, 209

New York: Its Upper Ten and Lower Million (Lippard), **Supp. XXIII:** 180, 183, 184

New York Jew (Kazin), **Supp. VIII:** 95, **97–100**

New York Madness (Bodenheim), **Supp. XXV:** 28

"New York Theater: Isn't It Romantic" (Wasserstein), **Supp. XV:** 320

New York Trilogy, The (Auster), **Supp. XII:** 21, **24–28**

Next (McNally), **Supp. XIII:** 197

"Next in Line, The" (Bradbury), **Supp. IV Part 1:** 102

Next Room of the Dream, The (Nemerov), **III:** 269, 275, 278, 279–280, 284

"Next Time I Crossed the Line into Oklahoma, The" (Wright), **Supp. XV:** 345

Next-to-Last Things: New Poems and Essays (Kunitz), **Supp. III Part 1:** 257–259, 261, 262, 265, 266, 268

"'Next to Reading Matter' " (Henry), **Supp. II Part 1:** 399

Nexus (H. Miller), **III:** 170, 187, 188, 189

Niatum, Duane, **Supp. IV Part 1:** 331; **Supp. IV Part 2:** 505

Nice and Noir (Schwartz), **Supp. XIV:** 23

"Nice Girl" (Nelson), **Supp. XVIII:** 178

Nice Jewish Boy, The (P. Roth), **Supp. III Part 2:** 412

Nicholas II, Tsar, **Supp. I Part 2:** 447

"Nicholas in the Park" (Halliday), **Supp. XIX:** 88

Nicholls, Peter, **Supp. XIX:** 232

Nichols, Charles, **Retro. Supp. I:** 194

Nichols, Dudley, **Supp. XVIII:** 247

Nichols, John Treadwell, **Supp. XIII: 253–272**

Nichols, Luther, **Supp. X:** 265

Nichols, Mike, **Supp. IV Part 1:** 234; **Supp. IV Part 2:** 577

Nicholson, Colin, **Supp. VIII:** 129

Nicholson, Harold, **Supp. XIV:** 163

Nicholson, Jack, **Supp. V:** 26; **Supp. VIII:** 45; **Supp. XI:** 308

Nicholson, John, **Supp. XVI:** 293

Nick Adams Stories, The (Hemingway), **II:** 258; **Retro. Supp. I:** 174

"Nick and the Candlestick" (Plath), **Supp. I Part 2:** 544

Nickel and Dimed: On (Not) Getting By in America (Ehrenreich), **Supp. XVII:** 210

Nickel Mountain: A Pastoral Novel (Gardner), **Supp. VI:** 63, 64, 68, **69**

Nickerson, Catherine Ross, **Supp. XXV:** 192, 200, 202

"Nicodemus" (Keillor), **Supp. XVI:** 167

Nicoll, Allardyce, **III:** 400

Nicoloff, Philip, **II:** 7

Niebuhr, Gustav, **III:** 292

Niebuhr, H. Richard, **I:** 494

Niebuhr, Lydia, **III:** 292

Niebuhr, Reinhold, **III:** 290–313; **Supp. I Part 2:** 654; **Supp. XX:** 79

Niedecker, Lorine, **Supp. III Part 2:** 616, 623; **Supp. XIV:** 287; **Supp. XXIII:** 174

Nielsen, Ed, **Supp. IX:** 254

Nielson, Dorothy, **Supp. I Part 2:** 659

Nietzsche, Friedrich Wilhelm, **I:** 227, 283, 383, 389, 396, 397, 402, 509; **II:** 7, 20, 27, 42, 90, 145, 262, 462, 463, 577, 583, 585; **III:** 102–103, 113, 156, 176; **IV:** 286, 491; **Supp. I Part 1:** 254, 299, 320; **Supp. I Part 2:** 646; **Supp. IV Part 1:** 104, 105–106, 107, 110, 284; **Supp. IV Part 2:** 519; **Supp. V:** 277, 280; **Supp. VIII:** 11, 181, 189; **Supp. X:** 48; **Supp. XII:** 98; **Supp. XIV:** 339; **Supp. XX:** 117

Nieves, Felipe, **Supp. XVIII:** 90

Niflis, N. Michael, **Supp. IV Part 1:** 175

Niger, S. *See* Charney, Samuel

Nigger Heaven (Van Vechten), **Supp. II Part 2:** 739, 744–746; **Supp. XVIII:** 123, 127; **Supp. XIX:** 76

"Nigger Jeff" (Dreiser), **Retro. Supp. II:** 97

Nigger of the "Narcissus," The (Conrad), **II:** 91; **Retro. Supp. I:** 106; **Supp. XVIII:** 224; **Supp. XXIV:** 286

"NIGGY THE HO" (Baraka), **Supp. II Part 1:** 54

"Night, Death, Mississippi" (Hayden), **Supp. II Part 1:** 369

'*Night, Mother* (Norman), **Supp. VIII:** 141

"Night above the Avenue" (Merwin), **Supp. III Part 1:** 355

"Night among the Horses, A" (Barnes), **Supp. III Part 1:** 33–34, 39, 44

"Night and the Madman" (Gibran), **Supp. XX:** **118**

Night at the Movies, A, or, You Must Remember This: Fictions (Coover), **Supp. V:** 50–51

"Night at the Opera, A" (Matthews), **Supp. IX:** 167

"Night before the Sentence Is Carried Out, The" (Wright), **Supp. XV:** 341

"Nightbird" (Komunyakaa), **Supp. XIII:** 132

Night-Blooming Cereus, The (Hayden), **Supp. II Part 1:** 367, 373

"Night-Blooming Cereus, The" (Hayden), **Supp. II Part 1:** 367

Night-Born, The (London), **II:** 467

"Nightbreak" (Rich), **Supp. I Part 2:** 556

"Nightclub" (Collins), **Supp. XXI:** 60

Night Country, The (O'Nan), **Supp. XXV:** 141, 148–149, 150

Night Dance (Price), **Supp. VI:** 264

"Night Dances, The" (Plath), **Supp. I Part 2:** 544

"Night Dream, The" (MacLeish), **III:** 15

"Night Ferry" (Doty), **Supp. XI:** 124

"Nightfishing" (Schnackenberg), **Supp. XV:** 254

"Nighthawks"(Dybek), **Supp. XXIII:** 73, 74

"Night I Met Little Floyd, The" (Wright), **Supp. XV:** 345–346

Night in Acadie, A (Chopin), **Retro. Supp. II:** **66–67,** 73; **Supp. I Part 1:** 200, 219, 220, 224

"Night in Acadie, A" (Chopin), **Retro. Supp. II:** 66

"Night in June, A" (W. C. Williams), **Retro. Supp. I:** 424

"Night in New Arabia, A" (Henry), **Supp. II Part 1:** 402

Night in Question, The: Stories (Wolff), **Supp. VII:** 342–344

"Night Journey" (Roethke), **Supp. III Part 1:** 260

"Night Letter to the Reader" (Collins), **Supp. XXI:** 55

Night Light (Justice), **Supp. VII:** 126–127

"Nightmare" (Kumin), **Supp. IV Part 2:** 442

Nightmare Factory, The (Kumin), **Supp. IV Part 2:** 444–447, 451

"Nightmare Factory, The" (Kumin), **Supp. IV Part 2:** 445, 453

Nightmare on Main Street (Poe), **Retro. Supp. II:** 262

"Nightmare" poems (Benét), **Supp. XI:** 46, 58

"Night Mirror" (L.-Y. Lee), **Supp. XV:** 225

Night Music (Odets), **Supp. II Part 2:** 541, 543, 544

"Night of First Snow" (R. Bly), **Supp. IV Part 1:** 71

Night of January 16th (Rand), **Supp. IV Part 2:** 527

Night of the Iguana, The (T. Williams), **IV:** 382, 383, 384, 385, 386, 387, 388, 391, 392, 393, 394, 395, 397, 398

"Night of the Iguana, The" (T. Williams), **IV:** 384

"Night of the Living Beanfield: How an Unsuccessful Cult Novel Became an Unsuccessful Cult Film in Only Fourteen Years, Eleven Nervous Breakdowns, and $20 Million" (Nichols), **Supp. XIII:** 267

Night Passage (Parker), **Supp. XIX:** 185–186

Night Rider (Warren), **IV:** 243, 246–247

Nights (Doolittle), **Supp. I Part 1:** 270, 271

Nights and Days (Merrill), **Supp. III Part 1:** 319, 320, 322–325

"Nights and Days" (Rich), **Supp. I Part 2:** 574

"Night's for Cryin,' The" (C. Himes), **Supp. XVI:** 137

"Night Shift" (Plath), **Supp. I Part 2:** 538

"Nightshine Beyond Memory, A: Ten More Years with Ray" (Gallagher), **Supp. XXIV:** 167, 172

Night-Side (Oates), **Supp. II Part 2:** 522

"Night-Side" (Oates), **Supp. II Part 2:** 523

Night-Side, The (Skloot), **Supp. XX:** **193, 196, 205, 208**

Nights in the Gardens of Brooklyn (Swados), **Supp. XIX:** **261–264**

"Nights in the Gardens of Brooklyn" (Swados), **Supp. XIX:** 261

"Night Sketches: Beneath an Umbrella" (Hawthorne), **II:** 235–237, 238, 239, 242; **Supp. XXI:** 201

"Night Sport" (Hoffman), **Supp. XVIII:** 86, 87

"Night-Sweat" (Lowell), **II:** 554

"Night-Talk" (Ellison), **Retro. Supp. II:** 126; **Supp. II Part 1:** 248

Night Thoughts (Young), **III:** 415

"Night-Time River Road, A" (Ferry), **Supp. XXIV:** 150

Night Traveler, The (Oliver), **Supp. VII:** 233

"Night Watch" (Gioia), **Supp. XV:** 117

"Night Watch, The" (Wright), **Supp. V:** 339

"Night We All Had Grippe, The" (Jackson), **Supp. IX:** 118

Nightwood (Barnes), **Supp. III Part 1:** 31, 32, 35–37, 39–43

Night World and the Word Night, The (F. Wright), **Supp. XVII:** 240, 244–245

"Nihilist as Hero, The" (Lowell), **II:** 554; **Retro. Supp. II:** 190

Nijinsky, Vaslav, **Supp. XV:** 28–29

Nikolai Gogol (Nabokov), **Retro. Supp. I:** 266

"Nilda" (Díaz), **Supp. XXIV:** 92

Niles, Thomas, **Retro. Supp. I:** 35

Niles, Thomas, Jr., **Supp. I Part 1:** 39

Nilsson, Christine, **Supp. I Part 1:** 355

Nilsson, Harry, **Supp. XI:** 309

Nilsson, Jenny Lind, **Supp. XVI:** 177

Nimitz, Chester, **Supp. I Part 2:** 491

"Nimram" (Gardner), **Supp. VI:** 73

Nims, John Frederick, **III:** 527; **Supp. XVII:** 112

Nin, Anaïs, **III:** 182, 184, 190; **Supp. III Part 1:** 43; **Supp. IV Part 2:** 680; **Supp. X:** 181–200; **Supp. XIX:** 134

"9" (Oliver), **Supp. VII:** 244

"9 Failures of the Imagination" (Lethem), **Supp. XVIII:** 148

"Nine-Ball" (Offutt), **Supp. XIX:** 166, 167

Nine Dragons (Connelly), **Supp. XXI:** 74, **79–80**

"Nine from Eight" (Lanier), **Supp. I Part 1:** 352–354

Nine Gates: Entering the Mind of Poetry (Hirshfield), **Supp. XXIII:** 136, 137

Nine Headed Dragon River: Zen Journals 1969–1982 (Matthiessen), **Supp. V:** 199

Nine Horses (Collins), **Supp. XXI:** 55, 60, 61, 62, 65

"Nine Horses" (Collins), **Supp. XXI:** 61

Ninemile Wolves,The (Bass), **Supp. XVI:** 24–25, 26

"Nine Nectarines" (Moore), **III:** 203, 209, 215

Nine Plays (Reznikoff), **Supp. XIV:** 288

"Nine Poems for the Unborn Child" (Rukeyser), **Supp. VI:** 280–281, 284

Nine Stories (Nabokov), **Retro. Supp. I:** 266

Nine Stories (Salinger), **III:** 552, 558–564

"19 Hadley Street" (Schnackenberg), **Supp. XV:** 253

19 Necromancers from Now (Reed), **Supp. X:** 240

19 Varieties of Gazelle (Nye), **Supp. XIII:** 275, **286–288**

"19 Varieties of Gazelle" (Nye), **Supp. XIII:** 286

1984 (Orwell), **Supp. XIII:** 29; **Supp. XVIII:** 137, 138

"1940" (Stafford), **Supp. XI:** 328–329

"1945–1985: Poem for the Anniversary" (Oliver), **Supp. VII:** 237

1919 (Dos Passos), **I:** 482, 485–486, 487, 489, 490, 492

"1975" (Wright), **Supp. V:** 341

"1973"(Hirshfield), **Supp. XXIII:** 130

"1910" (Mora), **Supp. XIII:** 215

Nineteenth-Century Minor Poets (Auden), **Supp. XXV:** 237

"1938" (Komunyakaa), **Supp. XIII:** 114

1939 (Boyle), **Supp. XXIV:** 62

"1939" (Taylor), **Supp. V:** 316

1933 (Levine), **Supp. V:** 185–187

"1933" (Levine), **Supp. V:** 188

"Nineteenth New York, The" (Doctorow), **Supp. IV Part 1:** 232

"1929" (Auden), **Supp. II Part 1:** 6

"1926" (Kees), **Supp. V:** 135

"93990" (Saunders), **Supp. XIX:** 233

"90 North" (Jarrell), **II:** 370, 371

90 Trees (Zukofsky), **Supp. III Part 2:** 631

95 Poems (Cummings), **I:** 430, 433, 435, 439, 446, 447

"91 Revere Street" (Lowell), **II:** 547; **Retro. Supp. II:** 188; **Supp. XI:** 240

Ninety Percent of Everything (Lethem, Kelly and Kessel), **Supp. XVIII:** 145

"92 Days" (L. Brown), **Supp. XXI:** 44–45

"Nine Years Later" (Brodsky), **Supp. VIII:** 32

Ninth Avenue (Bodenheim), **Supp. XXV:** 24–25

"Nirvana" (Lanier), **Supp. I Part 1:** 352

Nirvana Blues, The (Nichols), **Supp. XIII:** 266, 267

Nishikigi (play), **III:** 466

Niven, David, **Supp. XI:** 307

Nixon (film), **Supp. XIV:** 48

Nixon, Richard M., **I:** 376; **III:** 38, 46; **Supp. I Part 1:** 294, 295; **Supp. V:** 45, 46, 51; **Supp. XII:** 14; **Supp. XIV:** 306

"NJ Transit" (Komunyakaa), **Supp. XIII:** 132

Nketia, J. H., **Supp. IV Part 1:** 10

Nketsia, Nana, **Supp. IV Part 1:** 2, 10

Nkize, Julius, **Supp. IV Part 1:** 361

Nkrumah, Kwame, **I:** 490, 494; **Supp. IV Part 1:** 361; **Supp. X:** 135

Nkrumah and the Ghana Revolution (C. L. R. James), **Supp. XXI:** 159, 171–172

NO (Major), **Supp. XXII:** 174

Noailles, Anna de, **IV:** 328

Noa Noa (Gauguin), **I:** 34

Nobel Lecture (Singer), **Retro. Supp. II:** 300

"No Better Than a 'Withered Daffodil' " (Moore), **III:** 216

Noble, David W., **Supp. I Part 2:** 650

Noble, Marianne, **Supp. XVIII:** 267

"Noble Rider and the Sound of Words, The" (Stevens), **Retro. Supp. I:** 299

Noble Savage, The (Coover), **Supp. V:** 40

"No Bobolink reverse His Singing" (Dickinson), **Retro. Supp. I:** 45

Nobodaddy (MacLeish), **III:** 5–6, 8, 10, 11, 18, 19, 20

"Nobodaddy" (W. Blake), **Supp. XVII:** 245

"Nobody in Hollywood" (Bausch), **Supp. VII:** 54

Nobody Knows My Name (Baldwin), **Supp. XIII:** 111

"Nobody Knows My Name" (Baldwin), **Retro. Supp. II:** 8; **Supp. I Part 1:** 52

Nobody Knows My Name: More Notes of a Native Son (Baldwin), **Retro. Supp. II:** 6, 8; **Supp. I Part 1:** 47, 52, 55

"Nobody knows this little Rose" (Dickinson), **Retro. Supp. I:** 30

"Nobody Said Anything" (Carver), **Supp. III Part 1:** 141

"Nobody's Business" (Lahiri), **Supp. XXI:** 183

Nobody's Fool (Russo), **Supp. XII:** 326, **331–335,** 340

"No Change of Place" (Auden), **Supp. II Part 1:** 5

"Noche Triste, La" (Frost), **Retro. Supp. I:** 123

Nock, Albert Jay, **I:** 245; **Supp. IV Part 2:** 521, 524

"No Coward Soul Is Mine" (Brontë), **I:** 458

"No Crime in the Mountains" (Chandler), **Supp. IV Part 1:** 129

"Nocturne" (Komunyakaa), **Supp. XIII:** 126

"Nocturne" (MacLeish), **III:** 8

"Nocturne at Bethesda" (Bontemps), **Supp. XXII:** 3, 8

"Nocturne in a Deserted Brickyard" (Sandburg), **III:** 586

Nocturne of Remembered Spring (Aiken), **I:** 50

No Direction Home (documentary film, Scorsese), **Supp. XVIII:** 22, 23, 29

No Direction Home (Shelton), **Supp. XVIII:** 21

No Door (Wolfe), **IV:** 451–452, 456

"No Door" (Wolfe), **IV:** 456

"No Epitaph" (Carson), **Supp. XII:** 111

No Exit (Sartre), **I:** 82, 130; **Supp. XIV:** 320

No Exit (Sartre; Bowles, trans.), **Supp. IV Part 1:** 84

No Gifts from Chance (Benstock), **Retro. Supp. I:** 361

"No-Good Blues" (Komunyakaa), **Supp. XIII:** 130

No Hero (Marquand), **III:** 57

No Heroes: A Memoir of Coming Home (Offutt), **Supp. XIX:** 163, **172–174,** 175

No! In Thunder (Fiedler), **Supp. XIII:** 101

"Noir" (Stallings), **Supp. XXV:** 232

"Noiseless Patient Spider" (Whitman), **III:** 555; **IV:** 348; **Supp. IV Part 1:** 325

Noises Off (Frayn), **Supp. IV Part 2:** 582

Noi vivi. See We the Living (film)

"No Jury Would Convict" (Shaw), **Supp. XIX:** 245

"No Lamp Has Ever Shown Us Where to Look" (MacLeish), **III:** 9

Nolan, Sidney, **Retro. Supp. II:** 189

No Laughing Matter (Heller and Vogel), **Supp. IV Part 1:** 384, 389

No Love Lost, a Romance of Travel (Howells), **II:** 277

Nomad (Ali), **Supp. XXIV:** 15

Nomad's Land (Rinehart), **Supp. XXV:** 195

No Man Is an Island (Merton), **Supp. VIII:** 207

"No More This Home" (Taggard), **Supp. XXII:** 277, 280

No Mother to Guide Her (Loos), **Supp. XVI:** 194

No Name in the Street (Baldwin), **Retro. Supp. II:** 13, 14; **Supp. I Part 1:** 47, 48, 52, 65–66, 67

No Nature: New and Selected Poems (Snyder), **Supp. VIII:** **305**

Nonconformist's Memorial, The (Howe), **Supp. IV Part 2:** 434, 435–436

Nonconformity (Algren), **Supp. IX:** 15

None but the Lonely Heart (film), **Supp. II Part 2:** 546

Nones (Auden), **Supp. II Part 1:** 21

"Nones" (Auden), **Supp. II Part 1:** 22–23

None Shall Look Back (Gordon), **II:** 205–207, 208

"No No, Bad Daddy" (Nelson), **Supp. XVIII:** 177, 178

"Non-Tenured" (Halliday), **Supp. XIX:** 90, 91

Nonverbal Communication: Notes on the Visual Perception of Human Relations (Kees and Ruesch), **Supp. XV:** 147

"Noon" (Bryant), **Supp. I Part 1:** 157

No One Belongs Here More Than You (July), **Supp. XXIV:** 199, **200–207**

"No One Remembers" (Levine), **Supp. V:** 187

"Noon Walk on the Asylum Lawn" (Sexton), **Supp. II Part 2:** 673

"Noon Wine" (Porter), **III:** 436, 437–438, 442, 446

"No Pain Whatsoever" (Yates), **Supp. XI:** 341

"No Place for You, My Love" (Welty), **IV:** 278, 279; **Retro. Supp. I:** 353

No Plays of Japan, The (Waley), **III:** 466

No Pockets in a Shroud (McCoy), **Supp. XIII:** 166–168, 171, 172, 173, 174

"No Poem So Fine" (Francis), **Supp. IX:** 83

Norcross, Frances, **I:** 456, 462

Norcross, Louise, **I:** 456, 462

Nordfeldt, B. J. O., **Supp. XXI:** 6

Nordfeldt, Margaret, **Supp. XXI:** 6

Nordyke, Lewis, **Supp. XIII:** 5

No Relief (Dixon), **Supp. XII:** 139, **142–143**

No Resting Place (Humphrey), **Supp. IX:** 94, **106–108**

Norfolk Poems, The (Carruth), **Supp. XVI:** 47, 48

Norma (Bellini), **IV:** 309

Norma Ashe (Glaspell), **Supp. III Part 1:** 175, 186–187

"Normal Life, A"(Thompson), **Supp. XXIII:** 300

"Normal Motor Adjustments" (Stein and Solomons), **IV:** 26

Norman, Charles, **III:** 479

Norman, Gurney, **Supp. X:** 24; **Supp. XXIII:** 42

Norman, Jessye, **Supp. XX:** 110

Norman, Marsha, **Supp. VIII:** 141; **Supp. XXI:** 145; **Supp. XXIV:** 124

Norman Mailer (Poirier), **Retro. Supp. II:** 207–208

Norman Mailer: Modern Critical Views (Bloom), **Retro. Supp. II:** 205

Norman Mailer Revisited (Merrill), **Retro. Supp. II:** 201

Norna; or, The Witch's Curse (Alcott), **Supp. I Part 1:** 33

Norris, Charles, **III:** 320; **Retro. Supp. I:** 100; **Supp. XVIII:** 226

Norris, Frank, **I:** 211, 355, 500, 506, 517, 518, 519; **II:** 89, 264, 276, 289, 307; **III:** 227, **314–336**, 596; **IV:** 29; **Retro. Supp. I:** 100, 325; **Retro. Supp. II:** 96, 101; **Supp. III Part 2:** 412; **Supp. VIII:** 101, 102; **Supp. IX:** 14, 15; **Supp. XV:** 115

"North" (Budbill), **Supp. XIX:** 7–8

"North" (Hugo), **Supp. VI:** 135

North, Milou (pseudonym), **Supp. IV Part 1:** 260. *See also* Dorris, Michael; Erdrich, Louise

North, Sir Thomas, **IV:** 370

"North American Sequence" (Roethke), **I:** 171–172, 183; **III:** 529, 545, 547, 548

"North Beach" (Snyder), **Supp. VIII:** 289

North Country: A Personal Journey Through the Borderland (Mosher), **Supp. XXII: 203–204**, 206, 212, **217–218**

"North Country Sketches" (McClatchy), **Supp. XII:** 256

"Northeast Playground" (Paley), **Supp. VI:** 226–227, 229

Northern Borders (Mosher), **Supp. XXII:** 203, 204, 206, 207, 208, 209, **213–214**

Northern Lights (O'Brien), **Supp. V:** 237, 239, 241–244, 250

"Northern Motive" (Levine), **Supp. V:** 195

Northfield Poems (Ammons), **Supp. VII:** 29

"Northhanger Ridge" (Wright), **Supp. V:** 335, 340

"North Haven" (Bishop), **Retro. Supp. II:** 50

"North Labrador" (Crane), **I:** 386

North of Boston (Frost), **II:** 152, 153–154, 527; **Retro. Supp. I:** 121, 125, 127, **128–130**, 131; **Supp. I Part 1:** 263; **Supp. XIII:** 146

North of Jamaica (Simpson), **Supp. IV Part 2:** 448; **Supp. IX:** 275, 276

North of the Danube (Caldwell), **I:** 288, 290, 293, 294, 309, 310

North: Poems of Home (Kenny), **Supp. XXIII:** **147–148**

Northrup, Cyrus, **Supp. I Part 1:** 350

North Sea (Jarman), **Supp. XVII:** 110, 113

"North Sea Undertaker's Complaint, The" (Lowell), **II:** 550

North & South (Bishop), **Retro. Supp. II:** **41–43**; **Supp. I Part 1:** 72, 84, 85, 89

North Star, The (Hellman), **Supp. I Part 1:** 281

Northup, Solomon, **Supp. XIV:** 32

"Northwest Writers at Work" (Baker), **Supp. XXIV:** 178

"North Winter" (Carruth), **Supp. XVI:** 53

Norton, Charles Eliot, **I:** 223, 568; **II:** 279, 322–323, 338; **Retro. Supp. I:** 371; **Retro. Supp. II:** 135; **Supp. I Part 1:** 103; **Supp. I Part 2:** 406, 479

Norton, Jody, **Supp. VIII:** 297

Norton, John, **Supp. I Part 1:** 99, 110, 112, 114

Norton Anthology of African American Literature, The (H. L. Gates and McKay, eds.), **Supp. X:** 325; **Supp. XX: 105**

Norton Anthology of American Literature, **Supp. X:** 325; **Supp. XV:** 270

Norton Anthology of Literature by Women (Gilbert and Gubar, eds.), **Supp. XV:** 270

Norton Anthology of Modern Poetry, The, **Supp. XI:** 259; **Supp. XV:** 258; **Supp. XXIV:** 35, 39

Norton Anthology of Poetry, The, **Supp. XVIII:** 20

Norton Anthology of Short Fiction, The, **Supp. IX:** 4

Norton Book of Personal Essays, The, **Supp. XIV:** 105

Norton Lectures, **Retro. Supp. I:** 65

Norwood, Vera, **Supp. IX:** 24

No Safe Harbour (Porter), **III:** 447

Nosferatu: An Opera Libretto (Gioia), **Supp. XV:** 112, **128**

"Nosferatu's Serenade" (Gioia), **Supp. XV:** 128

No Siege Is Absolute (Char; version of F. Wright), **Supp. XVII:** 244

"No Snake" (A. Finch), **Supp. XVII:** 72

"No Speak English" (Cisneros), **Supp. VII:** 63

"Nostalgia" (Collins), **Supp. XXI:** 57

"Nostalgia" (Saunders), **Supp. XIX:** 235

Nostalgia for 70 (J. W. Miller), **Supp. XX:** 165

"Nostalgia of the Lakefronts" (Justice), **Supp. VII:** 118, 119, 120

"Nostalgic Mood" (Farrell), **II:** 45

No Star Is Lost (Farrell), **II:** 34, 35, 44

Nostrandt, Jeanne, **Supp. XVIII:** 80–81

Nostromo (Conrad), **II:** 600; **IV:** 245

"Nosty Fright, A" (Swenson), **Supp. IV Part 2:** 651

Not about Nightingales (T. Williams), **IV:** 381

"Not a Sparrow" (Gallagher), **Supp. XXIV:** 171

"Not a Womb in the House" (Quindlen), **Supp. XVII:** 166, 171

Not Coming to Be Barked At (Kooser), **Supp. XIX:** 116, **120**

Not Dancing (Dunn), **Supp. XI:** 143, **148**

"Note about *Iconographs,* A" (Swenson), **Supp. IV Part 2:** 646

Notebook (Lowell), **Retro. Supp. II:** 186, 190; **Supp. V:** 343

Notebook 1967–68 (Lowell), **II:** 553–555; **Retro. Supp. II:** 182, 186, 190

Notebook of Malte Laurids Brigge, The (Rilke), **III:** 571

Notebooks (Fitzgerald), **Retro. Supp. I:** 110

Notebooks of Captain George, The (Renoir), **Supp. XXII:** 257

No Telephone to Heaven (Cliff), **Supp. XXII:** 66, 69, 71–72

"Note on Abraham Lincoln" (Vidal), **Supp. IV Part 2:** 688

"Note on Commercial Theatre" (Hughes), **Retro. Supp. I:** 207

"Note on Ezra Pound, A" (Eliot), **Retro. Supp. I:** 290

"Note on Lanier's Music, A" (P. Graham), **Supp. I Part 1:** 373

Note on Literary Criticism, A (Farrell), **II:** 26, 49

"Note on Poetry, A" (Doolittle), **Supp. I Part 1:** 254, 267–268

"Note on Realism, A" (Anderson), **I:** 110

"Note on the Limits of 'History' and the Limits of 'Criticism,' A" (Brooks), **Supp. XIV:** 11

"Note on the Poetry of Love, A" (Untermeyer), **Supp. XV:** 304

"Note on the Truth of the Tales, A" (Vollmann), **Supp. XVII:** 230

"Notes" (Dove), **Supp. IV Part 1:** 246

"Notes for a Moving Picture: The House" (Agee), **I:** 33, 34

"Notes for an Autobiography" (Van Vechten), **Supp. II Part 2:** 749

"Notes for a Novel About the End of the World" (Percy), **Supp. III Part 1:** 393

"Notes for a Preface" (Sandburg), **III:** 591, 596–597

"NOTES FOR A SPEECH" (Baraka), **Supp. II Part 1:** 33

Notes for the Green Box (Duchamp), **Supp. IV Part 2:** 423

Notes for the Two-Dollar Window: Portraits from an American Neighborhood (Kriegel), **Supp. XXIV: 223–224**

Notes from a Bottle Found on the Beach at Carmel (Connell), **Supp. XIV:** 80, 87, 96, 97

Notes from a Sea Diary: Hemingway All the Way (Algren), **Supp. IX:** 16

"Notes from the Childhood and Girlhood" (Brooks), **Supp. III Part 1:** 77

"Notes from the River" (Stern), **Supp. IX:** 285, 287, 294, 295

Notes from Underground (Dostoevsky), **III:** 571; **IV:** 485; **Retro. Supp. II:** 121

Notes Left Behind: Last and Selected Poems (Hayford), **Supp. XXII:** 218

"Notes of a Faculty Wife" (Jackson), **Supp. IX:** 126

"Notes of a Native Daughter" (Didion), **Supp. IV Part 1:** 196, 197, 200, 201

Notes of a Native Son (Baldwin), **Retro. Supp. II:** 1, 2, 3, 5, 6; **Supp. I Part 1:** 50, 52, 54; **Supp. IV Part 1:** 163

"Notes of a Native Son" (Baldwin), **Supp. I Part 1:** 50, 54

Notes of a Son and Brother (James), **II:** 337; **Retro. Supp. I:** 235

"Notes on a Departure" (Trilling), **Supp. III Part 2:** 498

"Notes on Babbitt and More" (Wilson), **IV:** 435

"Notes on 'Camp' " (Sontag), **Supp. III Part 2:** 455–456; **Supp. XIV:** 167

Notes on Democracy (Mencken), **III:** 104, 107–108, 109, 116, 119

Notes on Dialectics (C. L. R. James), **Supp. XXI:** 169

"Notes on Free Verse" (Dobyns), **Supp. XIII:** 77

"Notes on 'Layover' " (Hass), **Supp. VI:** 109

"Notes on Memory and Enthusiasm" (Di Piero), **Supp. XIX:** 42

Notes on Novelists (James), **II:** 336, 337; **Retro. Supp. I:** 235

"Notes on Nukes, Nookie, and Neo-Romanticism" (Robbins), **Supp. X:** 272

"Notes on Poetry" (Eberhart), **I:** 524, 527–528, 529

"Notes on Teaching"(Hadas), **Supp. XXIII:** 122

"Notes on the Craft of Poetry" (Strand), **Supp. IV Part 2:** 626

"Notes on the Decline of Outrage" (Dickey), **Supp. IV Part 1:** 181

"Notes on the New Formalism" (Gioia), **Supp. XV:** 113, 114–115

"Notes on the Novel-as-Autobiography" (P. Bailey), **Supp. XVI:** 69

"Notes on 'The Poetry of Everday Life' " (Notley), **Supp. XXII:** 232

Notes on the State of Virginia (1781–1782) (Jefferson), **Supp. XIV:** 191

"Notes on Writing Weird Fiction" (Lovecraft), **Supp. XXV:** 120–121

"Notes to Be Left in a Cornerstone" (Benét), **Supp. XI:** 46, 58

"Notes toward a Supreme Fiction" (Stevens), **IV:** 87–89; **Retro. Supp. I:** 300, 306, **306–309,** 311; **Supp. I Part 1:** 80

"Notes towards a Poem That Can Never Be Written" (Atwood), **Supp. XIII:** 34–35

"Not Exactly for Talia" (Halliday), **Supp. XIX:** 94

No Thanks (Cummings), **I:** 430, 431, 432, 436, 437, 441, 443, 446

Not Heaven: A Novel in the Form of Prelude, Variations, and Theme (W. Frank), **Supp. XX:** 80

"Nothing" (C. Frost), **Supp. XV:** 94

"Nothing Big" (Komunyakaa), **Supp. XIII:** 121

Nothing Ever Breaks Except the Heart (Boyle), **Supp. XXIV:** 59

Nothing for Tigers (Carruth), **Supp. XVI:** 47, 48, 50

"Nothing Gold Can Stay" (Frost), **Retro. Supp. I:** 133

"Nothing in Heaven Functions as It Ought" (X. J. Kennedy), **Supp. XV:** 158–159

Nothing Makes You Free: Writings by Descendants of Jewish Holocaust Survivors (Bukiet, ed.), **Supp. XVII: 39–40,** 48–49

"Nothing Missing" (O'Hara), **III:** 369

Nothing Personal (Baldwin), **Supp. I Part 1:** 58, 60

Nothing Sacred (film), **Supp. XVIII:** 243

"Nothing Song, The" (Snodgrass), **Supp. VI:** 326

"Nothing Stays Put" (Clampitt), **Supp. IX:** 42

"Nothing Will Yield" (Nemerov), **III:** 279

No Third Path (Kosinski), **Supp. VII:** 215

"Not Ideas About the Thing but the Thing Itself" (Stevens), **IV:** 87

"No Time" (Collins), **Supp. XXI:** 61

Notions of the Americans: Picked up by a Travelling Bachelor (Cooper), **I:** 343–345, 346

"Not-Knowing" (Barthelme), **Supp. IV Part 1:** 48

"Not Leaving the House" (Snyder), **Supp. VIII:** 300

Notley, Alice, **Supp. XXII: 223–238; Supp. XXIII:** 221; **Supp. XXIV:** 35, 37, 39, 41, 43, 45

"'Not Marble nor the Gilded Monument' " (MacLeish), **III:** 12

Not Mine to Finish: Poems, 1928–1934 (Taggard), **Supp. XXII:** 280

"Not My Bones" (Nelson), **Supp. XVIII:** 183

Not Now But Now (M. F. K. Fisher), **Supp. XVII:** 86, 90

"Not Quite Social" (Frost), **II:** 156

"Not Sappho, Sacco" (Rukeyser), **Supp. VI:** 277

"Not Sixteen" (Anderson), **I:** 114

"Not Slightly" (Stein), **IV:** 44

Not So Deep as a Well (Parker), **Supp. IX:** 192

"Not Somewhere Else, but Here" (Rich), **Supp. I Part 2:** 552, 573

Not-So-Simple Neil Simon (McGovern), **Supp. IV Part 2:** 573

Not So Simple: The "Simple" Stories by Langston Hughes (Harper), **Retro. Supp. I:** 194, 209

"Not the Point" (Cameron), **Supp. XII: 83**

"Not They Who Soar" (Dunbar), **Supp. II Part 1:** 199

Not This Pig (Levine), **Supp. V:** 178, 181, 182–183

"Not to Be Satan nor to Deal with Him" (Bronk), **Supp. XXI:** 32

Not to Eat; Not for Love (Weller), **III:** 322

Not Wanted on the Voyage (Findley), **Supp. XX: 50, 56–57, 59**

Not Without Laughter (Hughes), **Retro. Supp. I:** 197, 198, 201; **Supp. I Part 1:** 328, 332; **Supp. XIX:** 73, 154

Nouvelle Héloïse, La (Rousseau), **Supp. XV:** 232

Nova Express (Burroughs), **Supp. III Part 1:** 93, 103, 104; **Supp. XVIII:** 137

Novel, The (Bulwer), **Retro. Supp. II:** 58

Novel, The: An Alternative History (Moore), **Supp. XXII:** 261

"Novel as a Function of American Democracy, The" (Ellison), **Retro. Supp. II:** 124

"Novel Démeublé, The" (Cather), **Retro. Supp. I:** 15

Novel History: Historians and Novelists Confront America's Past (and Each Other) (Carnes), **Supp. X:** 14

"Novelists of 2007" (Halliday), **Supp. XIX:** 90

Novella (Goethe; Bogan and Mayer, trans.), **Supp. III Part 1:** 63

Novellas and Other Writings (Wharton), **Retro. Supp. I:** 360

"Novel of the Thirties, A" (Trilling), **Supp. III Part 2:** 499

Novels and Other Writings (Bercovitch), **Retro. Supp. II:** 325

Novels and Tales of Henry James, The (James), **Retro. Supp. I:** 232

"Novel-Writing and Novel-Reading" (Howells), **II:** 276, 290

"November" (Larcom), **Supp. XIII:** 143

"November Cotton Flower" (Toomer), **Supp. IX:** 312

November Twenty Six Nineteen Sixty Three (Berry), **Supp. X:** 24

"Novices" (Moore), **III:** 200–201, 202, 213

Novick, Peter, **Supp. XVI:** 154–155

"Novogodnee" ("New Year's Greetings") (Tsvetayeva), **Supp. VIII:** 30

"Novotny's Pain" (P. Roth), **Supp. III Part 2:** 403

"No Voyage" (Oliver), **Supp. VII:** 231

No Voyage and Other Poems (Oliver), **Supp. VII:** 230–231, 232

Now and Another Time (Hearon), **Supp. VIII:** 58, **61–62**

Now and Then (Buechner), **Supp. XII:** 49, 53

"Now and Then, America" (Mora), **Supp. XIII:** 217

"Nowhere" (J. Scott), **Supp. XVII:** 189

Nowhere Is a Place: Travels in Patagonia (Theroux and Chatwin), **Supp. VIII:** 322

"Now I Am Married" (Gordon), **Supp. IV Part 1:** 299

"Now I Lay Me" (Hemingway), **II:** 249; **Retro. Supp. I:** 175

"Now I Lay Me" (Olds), **Supp. X:** 208

"Now Is the Air Made of Chiming Balls" (Eberhart), **I:** 523

"No Word" (Kunitz), **Supp. III Part 1:** 263

"No Worst" (Nelson), **Supp. XVIII:** 177, 178

Now Sheba Sings the Song (Angelou), **Supp. IV Part 1:** 16

"Now That We Live" (Kenyon), **Supp. VII:** 165

"Now the Servant's Name Was Malchus" (Wilder), **IV:** 358

"Now We Know" (O'Hara), **III:** 368–369

NOW with Bill Moyers (television), **Supp. XIII:** 286

Noyes, Alfred, **IV:** 434

Nuamah, Grace, **Supp. IV Part 1:** 10

"Nuances of a Theme by Williams" (Stevens), **Retro. Supp. I:** 422

Nuclear Age, The (O'Brien), **Supp. V:** 238, 243, 244, 246–248, 249, 251

"Nuclear Arms and Morality" (Sanders), **Supp. XVI:** 266

"Nude at a Dressing Table" (Peacock), **Supp. XIX:** 204

Nude Croquet (Fiedler), **Supp. XIII:** 103

"Nude Descendig a Staircase" (X. J. Kennedy), **Supp. XV:** 168

Nude Descending a Staircase (Duchamp), **IV:** 408; **Retro. Supp. I:** 416; **Supp. XXII:** 162

Nude Descending a Staircase (X. J. Kennedy), **Supp. XV:** 153, **154–157**

Nugent, Bruce, **Retro. Supp. I:** 200

Nugent, Elliot, **Supp. I Part 2:** 606, 611, 613

Nuggets and Dust (Bierce), **I:** 195

"Nullipara" (Olds), **Supp. X:** 209

Number One (Dos Passos), **I:** 489

"Numbers" (Skloot), **Supp. XX: 196, 207**

"Numbers, Letters" (Baraka), **Supp. II Part 1:** 50

"Numbers Trouble" (Stallings), **Supp. XXV:** 224

Nunc Dimittis (Brodsky), **Supp. VIII:** 25–26, 28

"Nun No More, A" (Fante), **Supp. XI:** 160

"Nun's Priest's Tale" (Chaucer), **III:** 492

Nunzio, Nanzia, **IV:** 89

Nuptial Flight, The (Masters), **Supp. I Part 2:** 460, 471

"Nuptials" (Tate), **IV:** 122

"Nurse Whitman" (Olds), **Supp. X:** 203

Nurture (Kumin), **Supp. IV Part 2:** 453–454, 455

Nussbaum, Emily, **Supp. XI:** 143

Nussbaum, Felicity A., **Supp. X:** 189

Nutcracker, The (Tchaikovsky), **Retro. Supp. I:** 196

"Nux Postcoenatica" (Holmes), **Supp. I Part 1:** 303

Nyce, James M., **Retro. Supp. I:** 380

Nye, Naomi Shihab, **Supp. XI:** 316; **Supp. XIII: 273–290; Supp. XXIII:** 253

Nyerere, Julius, **Supp. X:** 135

"Nympholepsy" (Faulkner), **Retro. Supp. I:** 81

Nymphs of the Valley ('Ará'is al-Murúj) (Gibran), **Supp. XX: 115, 124, 125**

O

"Ö" (Dove), **Supp. IV Part 1:** 245

Oak and Ivy (Dunbar), **Supp. II Part 1:** 98

"Oak Bluffs" column (D. West), **Supp. XVIII:** 286

Oak Openings, The (Cooper), **I:** 354, 355

Oandasan, Bill, **Supp. IV Part 2:** 499

Oasis, The (McCarthy), **II:** 566–568

Oates, Joyce Carol, **Supp. II Part 2: 503–527; Supp. IV Part 1:** 205; **Supp. IV Part 2:** 447, 689; **Supp. V:** 323; **Supp. XI:** 239; **Supp. XII:** 343; **Supp. XIII:** 306; **Supp. XIV:** 26, 109; **Supp. XXIII:** 35; **Supp. XXV:** 86, 123

"Oath, The" (Tate), **IV:** 127

Obbligati (Hecht), **Supp. X:** 57

Ober, Harold, **Retro. Supp. I:** 101, 103, 105, 110, 113

Oberndorf, Clarence P., **Supp. I Part 1:** 315

Obey, André, **IV:** 356, 375

"Obit" (Lowell), **II:** 554

"Obituaries" (Collins), **Supp. XXI:** 65

"Objective Value of a Social Settlement, The" (Addams), **Supp. I Part 1:** 4

"Objective Woman, The" (Jong), **Supp. V:** 119

Objectivist Anthology, An, **Supp. XIV:** 287

"Objectivist Ethics, The" (Rand), **Supp. IV Part 2:** 530–532

"Objectivists" Anthology, An (Zukofsky), **Supp. III Part 2:** 613, 615

Object Lessons (Quindlen), **Supp. XVII: 173–174**

"Objects" (Wilbur), **Supp. III Part 2:** 545–547

Oblique Prayers (Levertov), **Supp. III Part 1:** 283

"Oblivion" (Justice), **Supp. VII:** 121

Oblivion Seekers, The (Eberhardt), **Supp. IV Part 1:** 92

"Oblong Box, The" (Poe), **III:** 416

"Obnoxious Truth, The" (Notley), **Supp. XXII:** 234

Obregon, Maurice, **Supp. I Part 2:** 488

O'Briant, Don, **Supp. X:** 8

O'Brien, Edward, **Supp. XV:** 140

O'Brien, Edward J., **I:** 289; **III:** 56; **Supp. XVIII:** 227; **Supp. XIX:** 256; **Supp. XX: 34**

O'Brien, Edwin, **Supp. XVIII:** 208

O'Brien, Fitzjames, **I:** 211

O'Brien, Geoffrey, **Supp. IV Part 2:** 471, 473

O'Brien, Joe, **Supp. XXI:** 5, 6

O'Brien, John, **Supp. V:** 48, 49; **Supp. X:** 239, 244; **Supp. XXI:** 228, 229, 233

O'Brien, Tim, **Supp. V: 237–255; Supp. XI:** 234; **Supp. XVII:** 14; **Supp. XXI:** 122; **Supp. XXV:** 142, 143, 153

"Obscene Poem, An" (Creeley), **Supp. IV Part 1:** 150

Obscure Destinies (Cather), **I:** 331–332; **Retro. Supp. I:** 19

"Observation Relative to the Intentions of the Original Founders of the Academy in Philadelphia" (Franklin), **II:** 114

"Observations" (Dillard), **Supp. VI:** 34

Observations (Moore), **III:** 194, 195–196, 197, 199, 203, 205, 215

"Observations Now" (Conroy), **Supp. XVI:** 75

Observations: Photographs by Richard Avedon: Comments by Truman Capote, **Supp. III Part 1:** 125–126

Obuchowski, Mary DeJong, **Supp. XX: 222**

O Canada: An American's Notes on Canadian Culture (Wilson), **IV:** 429–430

"O Carib Isle!" (Crane), **I:** 400–401

O'Casey, Sean, **III:** 145; **Supp. IV Part 1:** 359, 361, 364

"Occidentals" (Ford), **Supp. V:** 71–72

Occom, Samuel, **Supp. XX: 288**

"Occultation of Orion, The" (Longfellow), **Retro. Supp. II:** 168

"Occurrence at Owl Creek Bridge, An" (Bierce), **I:** 200–201; **II:** 264; **Supp. XXV:** 26

"Ocean 1212-W" (Plath), **Supp. I Part 2:** 528

"Ocean of Words" (Jin), **Supp. XVIII:** 94

Ocean of Words: Army Stories (Jin), **Supp. XVIII:** 89, 92, **93–94**

O'Connell, Nicholas, **Supp. IX:** 323, 325, 334

O'Connell, Shaun, **Supp. XXI:** 231

O'Connor, Edward F., Jr., **III:** 337

O'Connor, Flannery, **I:** 113, 190, 211, 298; **II:** 606; **III: 337–360; IV:** 4, 217, 282; **Retro. Supp. II:** 179, **219–239,** 272, 324; **Supp. I Part 1:** 290; **Supp. III Part 1:** 146; **Supp. V:** 59, 337; **Supp. VIII:** 13, 14, 158; **Supp. X:** 1, 26, 69, 228, 290; **Supp. XI:** 104; **Supp. XIII:** 294; **Supp. XIV:** 93; **Supp. XV:** 338; **Supp. XVI:** 219; **Supp. XVII:** 43, 114; **Supp. XVIII:** 156, 161, 194; **Supp. XIX:** 166, 209, 223; **Supp. XXI:** 197; **Supp. XXIII:** 289; **Supp. XXV:** 142

O'Connor, Frank, **III:** 158; **Retro. Supp. II:** 242; **Supp. I Part 2:** 531; **Supp. VIII:** 151, 157, 165, 167, 171; **Supp. XV:** 74

O'Connor, Philip F., **Supp. XXIII:** 290

O'Connor, Richard, **II:** 467

O'Connor, T. P., **II:** 129

O'Connor, William, **IV:** 346; **Retro. Supp. I:** 392, 407

O'Connor, William Van, **III:** 479; **Supp. I Part 1:** 195

"Octascope" (Beattie), **Supp. V:** 27, 28

"Octaves" (Robinson), **Supp. III Part 2:** 593

"Octet" (Wallace), **Supp. X:** 309

October (Isherwood), **Supp. XIV:** 157, 164

"October" (Oliver), **Supp. VII:** 241

"October" (Swenson), **Supp. IV Part 2:** 649

"October, 1866" (Bryant), **Supp. I Part 1:** 169

"October 1913" (McCarriston), **Supp. XIV:** 266

"October and November" (Lowell), **II:** 554

"October in the Railroad Earth" (Kerouac), **Supp. III Part 1:** 225, 227, 229

October Light (Gardner), **Supp. VI:** 63, **69–71,** 72

"October Maples, Portland" (Wilbur), **Supp. III Part 2:** 556

October Palace, The (Hirshfield), **Supp. XXIII:** 131

"October: With Rain" (W. V. Davis), **Supp. XXI:** 94

"Octopus, An" (Moore), **III:** 202, 207–208, 214

"Octopus, The" (Merrill), **Supp. III Part 1:** 321

Octopus, The (Norris), **I:** 518; **III:** 314, 316, 322–326, 327, 331–333, 334, 335

"O Daedalus, Fly Away Home" (Hayden), **Supp. II Part 1:** 377–378

"OD and Hepatitis Railroad or Bust, The" (Boyle), **Supp. VIII:** 1

Odd Couple, The (1985 version, Simon), **Supp. IV Part 2:** 580

Odd Couple, The (film), **Supp. IV Part 2:** 589

Odd Couple, The (Simon), **Supp. IV Part 2:** 575, 579–580, 585, 586; **Supp. XVII:** 8

Odd Jobs (Updike), **Retro. Supp. I:** 334

Odd Mercy (Stern), **Supp. IX: 298–299**

Odd Number (Sorrentino), **Supp. XXI:** 236

"Odds, The" (Hecht), **Supp. X:** 64–65

Odds, The (O'Nan), **Supp. XXV:** 150, 151–152

"Odds, The" (Salinas), **Supp. XIII:** 321

"Ode" (Emerson), **II:** 13

"Ode" (Sobin), **Supp. XVI:** 284–285

"Ode" (X. J. Kennedy), **Supp. XV:** 160

"Ode (Intimations of Immortality)" (Matthews), **Supp. IX:** 162

"Ode for Memorial Day" (Dunbar), **Supp. II Part 1:** 199

"Ode for the American Dead in Asia" (McGrath), **Supp. X:** 119

"Ode: For the Budding of Islands" (Sobin), **Supp. XVI:** 287

"Ode Inscribed to W. H. Channing" (Emerson), **Supp. XIV:** 46

"Ode: Intimations of Immortality" (Wordsworth), **Supp. I Part 2:** 729; **Supp. III Part 1:** 12; **Supp. XIV:** 8

"Ode in Time of Crisis" (Taggard), **Supp. XXII:** 271

Odell, Margeretta Matilda, **Supp. XX: 278, 284, 288**

"Ode: My 24th Year" (Ginsberg), **Supp. II Part 1:** 312

"Ode on a Grecian Urn" (Keats), **I:** 284; **III:** 472; **Supp. XII:** 113; **Supp. XIV:** 8, 9–10; **Supp. XV:** 100; **Supp. XXI:** 64

"Ode on Human Destinies" (Jeffers), **Supp. II Part 2:** 419

"Ode on Indolence" (Keats), **Supp. XII:** 113

"Ode on Melancholy" (Keats), **Retro. Supp. I:** 301

Ode Recited at the Harvard Commemoration (Lowell), **Supp. I Part 2:** 416–418, 424

"Ode Recited at the Harvard Commemoration" (Lowell), **II:** 551

Odes (Horace), **Supp. XXIV:** 153

Odes (O'Hara), **Supp. XXIII:** 216

"Ode: Salute to the French Negro Poets"(O'Hara), **Supp. XXIII:** 216

"Ode Secrète" (Valéry), **III:** 609

"Odes of Estrangement" (Sobin), **Supp. XVI:** 289

Odes of Horace, The (Ferry, trans.), **Supp. XXIV: 153–156**

"Odes to Natural Processes" (Updike), **Retro. Supp. I:** 323

"Ode: The Capris" (Halliday), **Supp. XIX:** 88

"Ode to a Nightingale" (Keats), **II:** 368; **Retro. Supp. II:** 261; **Supp. IX:** 52

"Ode to Autumn" (Masters), **Supp. I Part 2:** 458

"Ode to Cervantes" (Salinas), **Supp. XIII:** 324

"Ode to Coit Tower" (Corso), **Supp. XII:** 122

"Ode to Ethiopia" (Dunbar), **Supp. II Part 1:** 199, 207, 208, 209

"Ode to Fear" (Tate), **IV:** 128

Ode to Harvard and Other Poems, An (Bynner), **Supp. XV:** 41, 44

"Ode to Joy"(O'Hara), **Supp. XXIII:** 208, 216

"Ode to Meaning" (Pinsky), **Supp. VI: 249–250,** 251

"Ode to Michael Goldberg ('s Birth and Other Births)"(O'Hara), **Supp. XXIII:** 209, 216, 218

"Ode to Night" (Masters), **Supp. I Part 2:** 458

"Ode to Our Young Pro-Consuls of the Air" (Tate), **IV:** 135

"Ode to the Austrian Socialists" (Benét), **Supp. XI:** 46, 58

"Ode to the Confederate Dead" (Tate), **II:** 551; **IV:** 124, 133, 137; **Supp. X:** 52

"Ode to the Johns Hopkins University" (Lanier), **Supp. I Part 1:** 370

"Ode to the Maggot" (Komunyakaa), **Supp. XIII:** 130

"Ode to the Mexican Experience" (Salinas), **Supp. XIII:** 316–317

"Ode to the Virginian Voyage" (Drayton), **IV:** 135

"Ode to the West Wind" (Shelley), **Retro. Supp. I:** 308; **Supp. I Part 2:** 728; **Supp. IX:** 52; **Supp. XII:** 117; **Supp. XIV:** 271–272; **Supp. XV:** 221

"Ode to Walt Whitman" (Benét), **Supp. XI:** 52

"Ode to Willem de Kooning"(O'Hara), **Supp. XXIII:** 208, 216

Odets, Clifford, **Supp. I Part 1:** 277, 295; **Supp. I Part 2:** 679; **Supp. II Part 2: 529–554; Supp. IV Part 2:** 587; **Supp. V:** 109; **Supp. VIII:** 96; **Supp. XVIII:** 238; **Supp. XX:** 34

Odier, Daniel, **Supp. III Part 1:** 97

"Odi et Amo" (Catullus), **Supp. XV:** 27, 32, 35

"Odom"(P. Benedict), **Supp. XXIII:** 41

O'Donnell, George Marion, **II:** 67

O'Donnell, Mary King, **Supp. XVIII:** 232

O'Donnell, Thomas F., **II:** 131

"Odor of Verbena" (Faulkner), **II:** 66

O'Doul, Lefty, **II:** 425

"Odysseus to Telemachus" (Brodsky), **Supp. VIII:** 25

Odyssey (Bryant, trans.), **Supp. I Part 1:** 158

Odyssey (Homer), **III:** 14, 470; **Retro. Supp. I:** 286, 290; **Retro. Supp. II:** 121; **Supp. I Part 1:** 185; **Supp. IV Part 2:** 631; **Supp. IX:** 211; **Supp. X:** 114; **Supp. XIV:** 191; **Supp. XVII:** 117; **Supp. XXI:** 36

"Odyssey of a Wop, The" (Fante), **Supp. XI:** 164, 165

Oedipus Rex (Sophocles), **I:** 137; **III:** 145, 151, 152, 332; **Supp. I Part 2:** 428

Oedipus Tyrannus (Sophocles), **II:** 203; **Supp. XV:** 265

Oehlschlaeger, Fritz, **Supp. IX:** 123

Oelze, Richard, **Supp. XXII:** 167

"Of Alexander Crummell" (Du Bois), **Supp. II Part 1:** 170

O'Faoláin, Seán, **Supp. II Part 1:** 101

Of a World That Is No More (Singer), **IV:** 16

"Of Booker T. Washington and Others" (Du Bois), **Supp. II Part 1:** 168

"Of Bright & Blue Birds & the Gala Sun" (Stevens), **IV:** 93

"Of Christian Heroism" (Ozick), **Supp. V:** 272

"Of Dying Beauty" (Zukofsky), **Supp. III Part 2:** 610

"Of Epiphanies and Poets" (Phillips), **Supp. XX:** 221

"Of 'Father and Son' " (Kunitz), **Supp. III Part 1:** 262

Offenbach, Jacques, **II:** 427

"Offering for Mr. Bluehart, An" (Wright), **Supp. III Part 2:** 596, 601

"Offerings" (Mason), **Supp. VIII:** 141

"Offertory" (Hempel), **Supp. XXI:** 126–127

Official Entry Blank (Kooser), **Supp. XIX:** 116, 117–118

"Official Entry Form" (Kooser), **Supp. XIX:** 117

"Official Piety" (Whittier), **Supp. I Part 2:** 687

"Offloading for Mrs. Schwartz" (Saunders), **Supp. XIX:** 225–226

"Of Freemasons, Kings, and Constitutions" (P. N. Warren), **Supp. XX:** 273

"Off-Shore Pirates, The" (Fitzgerald), **II:** 88

Off the Beaten Path (Proulx), **Supp. VII:** 261

Off the Beaten Path: Stories of Place, **Supp. XVI:** 22

"Off the Cuff" (Simpson), **Supp. IX:** 278

"Off the Highway" (Wolfert), **Supp. XXI:** 265

Off the Map (Levine), **Supp. V:** 178

Offut, Chris, **Supp. XIX:** 163–176

Of Gravity and Angels (Hirshfield), **Supp. XXIII:** 131

O'Flaherty, George, **Supp. I Part 1:** 202, 205–206

O'Flaherty, Kate. *See* Chopin, Kate

O'Flaherty, Thomas, **Supp. I Part 1:** 202, 203–204, 205

O'Flaherty, Thomas, Jr., **Supp. I Part 1:** 202

"Of Maids and Other Muses" (Alvarez), **Supp. VII:** 11

"Of Margaret" (Ransom), **III:** 491

Of Mice and Men (Steinbeck), **IV:** 51, 57–58

"Of Modern Poetry" (Stevens), **IV:** 92

Of No Country I Know: New and Selected Poems and Translations (Ferry), **Supp. XXIV:** 157

Of Plymouth Plantation (Bradford), **Retro. Supp. II:** 161, 162; **Supp. XXII:** 33, 35–47

Of Plymouth Plantation (Morison, ed.), **Supp. I Part 2:** 494

"Ofrenda for Lobo" (Mora), **Supp. XIII:** 224

"Often" (Kenyon), **Supp. VII:** 171

"Often, in Dreams, He Moved through a City" (Dobyns), **Supp. XIII:** 90

"Of the Coming of John" (Du Bois), **Supp. II Part 1:** 170

"Of the Culture of White Folk" (Du Bois), **Supp. II Part 1:** 175

Of the Farm (Updike), **IV:** 214, 217, 223–225, 233; **Retro. Supp. I:** 318, 329, 332

"Of the Four-Winged Cherubim as Signature" (Sobin), **Supp. XVI:** 287

"Of 'The Frill' " (McCarriston), **Supp. XIV:** 274

"Of the Passing of the First-Born" (Du Bois), **Supp. II Part 1:** 170

"Of the Sorrow Songs" (Du Bois), **Supp. II Part 1:** 170

"Of the Wings of Atlanta" (Du Bois), **Supp. II Part 1:** 170

Of This Time, Of This Place (Trilling), **Supp. III Part 2:** 498, 504

Of Time and the River (Wolfe), **IV:** 450, 451, 452, 455, 456, 457, 458, 459, 462, 464–465, 467, 468, 469

Of Woman Born: Motherhood as Experience and Institution (Rich), **Supp. I Part 2:** 554, 567–569

Of Women and Their Elegance (Mailer), **Retro. Supp. II:** 209

Ogden, Archie, **Supp. XIII:** 174

Ogden, Henry, **II:** 298

Ogden, Uzal, **Supp. I Part 2:** 516

Ogle, Connie, **Supp. XXIII:** 300, 301

"Oh, Atonement" (Weigl), **Supp. XIX:** 287

"Oh, Fairest of the Rural Maids" (Bryant), **Supp. I Part 1:** 169

"Oh, Immobility, Death's Vast Associate" (Dobyns), **Supp. XIII:** 89

"Oh, Joseph, I'm So Tired" (Yates), **Supp. XI:** 348

Oh, the Places You'll Go! (Geisel), **Supp. XVI:** 111

Oh, the Thinks You can Think! (Geisel), **Supp. XVI:** 111

"O'Halloran's Luck" (Benét), **Supp. XI:** 47

O'Hara, Frank, **Supp. XII:** 121; **Supp. XV:** 93, 176, 177, 178, 179–180, 182, 186, 187, 215–216; **Supp. XIX:** 81, 85; **Supp. XXII:** 226, 236; **Supp. XXIII:** 207–222; **Supp. XXIV:** 33, 34, 36, 42, 43, 44

O'Hara, J. D., **Supp. IV Part 1:** 43; **Supp. V:** 22; **Supp. XVI:** 221; **Supp. XXI:** 228

O'Hara, John, **I:** 375, 495; **II:** 444, 459; **III:** 66, 361–384; **IV:** 59; **Retro. Supp. I:** 99, 112; **Supp. I Part 1:** 196; **Supp. II Part 1:** 109; **Supp. IV Part 1:** 31, 383; **Supp. IV Part 2:** 678; **Supp. V:** 95; **Supp. VIII:** 151, 156; **Supp. IX:** 208; **Supp. XIX:** 209

O'Hara's Choice (Uris), **Supp. XX:** 247, 256–257

"O Heaven born muse! inspire my humble lay" (Very), **Supp. XXV:** 239

O'Hehir, Andrew, **Supp. XII:** 280

O. Henry Biography (C. A. Smith), **Supp. II Part 1:** 395

"Ohio Pagan, An" (Anderson), **I:** 112, 113

Ohio trilogy (Richter), **Supp. XVIII:** 212–215

Oh Mercy (album, Dylan), **Supp. XVIII:** 28, 33

Oh Say Can You Say? (Geisel), **Supp. XVI:** 111

Oil! (Sinclair), **Supp. V:** 276, 277–279, 282, 288, 289

Oil Notes (Bass), **Supp. XVI:** 17

"Oil Painting of the Artist as the Artist" (MacLeish), **III:** 14

"O-jib-way Maid, The" (J. Schoolcraft), **Supp. XXIII:** 235

O'Keeffe, Georgia, **Supp. IX:** 62, 66; **Supp. XX:** 75

"Oklahoma" (Levis), **Supp. XI:** 267

Oklahoma's Poor Rich Indians: An Orgy of Graft and Exploitation of the Five Civilized Tribes—Legalized Robbery (Zitkala-Ša, Sniffen, and Fabens), **Supp. XXV:** 283

Oktenberg, Adrian, **Supp. XVII:** 76; **Supp. XXI:** 253; **Supp. XXIII:** 133

"Old, Old, Old, Old Andrew Jackson" (Lindsay), **Supp. I Part 2:** 398

"Old Amusement Park, An" (Moore), **III:** 216

"Old Angel Midnight" (Kerouac), **Supp. III Part 1:** 229–230

"Old Apple Dealer, The" (Hawthorne), **II:** 227, 233–235, 237, 238

"Old Apple-Tree, The" (Dunbar), **Supp. II Part 1:** 198

"Old Army Game, The" (Garrett), **Supp. VII:** 100–101

"Old Aunt Peggy" (Chopin), **Retro. Supp. II:** 64

"Old Barn at the Bottom of the Fogs, The" (Frost), **Retro. Supp. I:** 138

Old Battle-Ax, The (Holding), **Supp. XXII:** 128–129

Old Beauty and Others, The (Cather), **I:** 331

"Old Boys, Old Girls" (E. P. Jones), **Supp. XXII:** 151

Old Bruin: Commodore Matthew C. Perry, 1794–1858 (Morison), **Supp. I Part 2:** 494–495

"Old Cracked Tune, An" (Kunitz), **Supp. III Part 1:** 264

Old Curiosity Shop, The (Dickens), **I:** 458; **Supp. I Part 2:** 409

Oldest Killed Lake in North America, The (Carruth), **Supp. XVI:** 51

"Oldest Man, The" (M. F. K. Fisher), **Supp. XVII:** 91

"Old Farmer, The" (Jeffers), **Supp. II Part 2:** 418

Old-Fashioned Girl, An (Alcott), **Supp. I Part 1:** 29, 41, 42

"Old Father Morris" (Stowe), **Supp. I Part 2:** 586

"Old Flame, The" (Lowell), **II:** 550

"Old Florist" (Roethke), **III:** 531

"Old Folsom Prison" (Matthews), **Supp. IX:** 165

Old Forest, The (Taylor), **Supp. V:** 320, 321, 326, 327

"Old Forest, The" (Taylor), **Supp. V:** 313, 321, 323, 326

Old Forest and Other Stories (Taylor), **Supp. V:** 326

Old Friends and New (Jewett), **II:** 402; **Retro. Supp. II:** 137, 140

Old Glory, The (Lowell), **II:** 543, 545–546, 555; **Retro. Supp. II:** 188

Old Helmet, The (S. and A. Warner), **Supp. XVIII:** 267

"Old Homestead, The" (Dunbar), **Supp. II Part 1:** 198

"Old House" (Espaillat), **Supp. XXI:** 112, 113

Old Indian Legends (Zitkala-Ša), **Supp. XXV:** 275, 278, 285

"Old Iron" (Nye), **Supp. XIII:** 276

"Old Ironsides" (Holmes), **Supp. I Part 1:** 302

Old Jules (Sandoz), **Supp. XXIV:** 243, 244, **245–246,** 249, 251, 255, 257

"Old Lady We Saw, An" (Shields), **Supp. VII:** 310–311

"Old Love" (Singer), **Retro. Supp. II:** 307

"Old McGrath Place, The" (McGrath), **Supp. X:** 114

"Old Maid, The" (Wharton), **Retro. Supp. I:** 381, 382

"Old Man" (Faulkner), **II:** 68, 69

Old Man and the Sea, The (Hemingway), **II:** 250, 256–257, 258, 265; **III:** 40; **Retro. Supp. I:** 180, **185,** 186

"Old Man Drunk" (Wright), **Supp. III Part 2:** 595

"Old Man Feeding Hens" (Francis), **Supp. IX:** 78

"Old Man on the Hospital Porch" (Ríos), **Supp. IV Part 2:** 546–547

Old Man Rubbing His Eyes (R. Bly), **Supp. IV Part 1:** 65

"Old Manse, The" (Hawthorne), **II:** 224

"Old Man's Winter Night, An" (Frost), **Retro. Supp. I:** 126, 131

Old Man Who Love Cheese, The (Keillor), **Supp. XVI:** 177

"Old Man with a Dog" (Wright), **Supp. XV:** 346

Old Marriage and New (Kooser), **Supp. XIX: 120–121**

"Old Meeting House, The" (Stowe), **Supp. I Part 2:** 586

"Old Memory, An" (Dunbar), **Supp. II Part 1:** 198

"Old Men, Old Horses" (P. N. Warren as Kilina), **Supp. XX: 262**

"Old Men, The" (McCarthy), **II:** 566

"Old Men Pitching Horseshoes" (X. J. Kennedy), **Supp. XV:** 166

Old Money (Wasserstein), **Supp. XV: 333–334**

"Old Morgue, The" (Prose), **Supp. XVI:** 250

Old Morning Program, The (radio show, Keillor). *See* Prairie Home Companion, A (radio show, Keillor)

"Old Mortality" (Porter), **III:** 436, 438–441, 442, 445, 446

"Old Mrs. Harris" (Cather), **I:** 332; **Retro. Supp. I:** 19

Old Neighborhood, The (Mamet), **Supp. XIV:** 240, 241, 242, 249–250, 251, 252, 254

Old New York (Wharton), **IV:** 322; **Retro. Supp. I:** 381

"Ol' Doc Hyar" (Campbell), **Supp. II Part 1:** 202

"Old of the Moon" (Offutt), **Supp. XIX:** 165, 166

Old One-Two, The (Gurney), **Supp. V:** 98

"Old Order, The" (Porter), **III:** 443, 444–445, 451

"Old Osawatomie" (Sandburg), **III:** 584

Old Patagonia Express, The: By Train through the Americas (Theroux), **Supp. VIII:** 322

"Old People" (Ferry), **Supp. XXIV:** 162

"Old People, The" (Faulkner), **II:** 71–72

"Old Photograph, An" (Kooser), **Supp. XIX:** 121

"Old Poet Moves to a New Apartment 14 Times, The" (Zukofsky), **Supp. III Part 2:** 628

Old Possum's Book of Practical Cats (T. S. Eliot), **Supp. XIII:** 228, 344

"Old Red" (Gordon), **II:** 199, 200, 203

Old Red and Other Stories (Gordon), **II:** 157

Old Régime in Canada, The (Parkman), **Supp. II Part 2:** 600, 607, 608–609, 612

Old Religion, The (Mamet), **Supp. XIV:** 253

Olds, Sharon, **Supp. X: 201–217; Supp. XI:** 139, 142, 244; **Supp. XII:** 229; **Supp. XIV:** 265; **Supp. XVII:** 114, 240; **Supp. XXI:** 249

"Old Saws" (Garrett), **Supp. VII:** 96–97

Old South, The: "A Summer Tragedy" and Other Stories (Bontemps), **Supp. XXII:** 7

"Old Stories" (Skloot), **Supp. XX: 200**

Old Testament, **I:** 109, 181, 300, 328, 401, 410, 419, 431, 457, 458; **II:** 166, 167, 219; **III:** 270, 272, 348, 390, 396; **IV:** 41, 114, 152, 309; **Retro. Supp. I:** 122, 140, 249, 311, 360; **Retro. Supp. II:** 299; **Supp. I Part 1:** 60, 104, 106, 151; **Supp. I Part 2:** 427, 515, 516; **Supp. IX:** 14. *See also* names of Old Testament books

"Old Things, The" (James), **Retro. Supp. I:** 229

"Old Times on the Mississippi" (Twain), **IV:** 199

Oldtown Folks (Stowe), **Supp. I Part 2:** 587, 596–598

"Old Town of Berwick, The" (Jewett), **Retro. Supp. II:** 132

"Old Trails" (Robinson), **III:** 513, 517

"Old Tyrannies" (Bourne), **I:** 233

"Old West" (Bausch), **Supp. VII:** 48

"Old Whorehouse, An" (Oliver), **Supp. VII:** 235

"Old Woman" (Pinsky), **Supp. VI:** 238

"Old Woman of Beare, The" (X. J. Kennedy), **Supp. XV:** 156

"Old Word, The" (Simic), **Supp. VIII:** 282

"Old-World Landowners" (Gogol), **Supp. XV:** 262

Oldys, Francis. *See* Chalmers, George

Oleanna (Mamet), **Supp. XIV:** 239, 241, 245, 248, 250

Olendorf, Donna, **Supp. IV Part 1:** 196

"Olga Poems, The" (Levertov), **Supp. III Part 1:** 279–281

"Olive Groves of Thasos, The" (Clampitt), **Supp. IX:** 51–52

Olive Kitteridge (Strout), **Supp. XXIII:** 273, 275, **280–284,** 285

Oliver, Bill, **Supp. VIII:** 138

Oliver, Douglas, **Supp. XXII:** 225, 226, 233, 235

Oliver, Mary, **Supp. VII: 229–248; Supp. X:** 31; **Supp. XVI:** 39; **Supp. XVII:** 111, 240; **Supp. XXIII:** 51

Oliver, Sydney, **I:** 409

Oliver Goldsmith: A Biography (Irving), **II:** 315

Oliver Twist (Dickens), **I:** 354; **Supp. IV Part 2:** 464

Olives (Stallings), **Supp. XXV:** 221, 223, 224, 233–234

"Olivia" (Salinas), **Supp. XIII:** 316

"Olivier Bergmann" (Halliday), **Supp. XIX:** 93–94

Olivieri, David (pseudonym), **Retro. Supp. I:** 361. *See also* Wharton, Edith

Ollive, Samuel, **Supp. I Part 2:** 503

Olmsted, Frederick Law, **Supp. I Part 1:** 355

Olor de la memoria, El/The Scent of Memory (Espaillat), **Supp. XXI:** 104

Olsen, Lance, **Supp. IV Part 1:** 54; **Supp. IV Part 2:** 623

Olsen, Tillie, **Supp. V:** 114, 220; **Supp. XIII: 291–309; Supp. XVI:** 83, 90

Olshan, Joseph, **Supp. XIX:** 52

Olson, Charles, **Retro. Supp. I:** 209; **Supp. II Part 1:** 30, 328; **Supp. II Part 2: 555–587; Supp. III Part 1:** 9, 271; **Supp. III Part 2:** 542, 624; **Supp. IV Part 1:** 139, 144, 146, 153, 154, 322; **Supp. IV Part 2:** 420, 421, 423, 426; **Supp. VIII:** 290, 291; **Supp. XII:** 2, 198; **Supp. XIII:** 104; **Supp. XIV:** 96; **Supp. XV:** 177; **Supp. XXI:** 19, 21, 23; **Supp. XXIV:** 42

Olson, Clarence, **Supp. XX: 84, 85, 86**

Olson, Ray, **Supp. XVII:** 111, 112, 119

"Ol' Tunes, The" (Dunbar), **Supp. II Part 1:** 197

"O Lull Me, Lull Me" (Roethke), **III:** 536–537

O'Malley, Anne, **Supp. XXII:** 56

Omar Khayyam, **Supp. I Part 1:** 363

O'Meally, Robert, **Retro. Supp. II:** 112

Omega the Unknown (comic book series), **Supp. XVIII:** 149

"Omen" (Komunyakaa), **Supp. XIII:** 126, 127

Omensetter's Luck (Gass), **Supp. VI: 80–82,** 87

Omeros (Walcott), **Supp. XV:** 264

"Ominous Baby, An" (Crane), **I:** 411

Ommateum, with Doxology (Ammons), **Supp. VII:** 24–26, 27, 28, 36

Omni-Americans, The: New Perspectives on Black Experience and American Culture (Murray), **Supp. XIX:** 147, **149–151,** 154

"Omnibus Jaunts and Drivers" (Whitman), **IV:** 350

Omoo: A Narrative of Adventures in the South Seas (Melville), **III:** 76–77, 79, 84; **Retro. Supp. I:** 247

O My Land, My Friends (H. Crane), **Retro. Supp. II:** 76

"On Abrigador Hill" (Nelson), **Supp. XVIII:** 183

"On a Certain Condescension in Foreigners" (Lowell), **Supp. I Part 2:** 419

"On a Certain Engagement South of Seoul" (Carruth), **Supp. XVI:** 47

"On a Child Who Lived One Minute" (X. J. Kennedy), **Supp. XV:** 152, 155

"On Acquiring Riches" (Banks), **Supp. V:** 5

On a Darkling Plain (Stegner), **Supp. IV Part 2:** 598, 607

On a Fire on the Moon (Mailer), **Retro. Supp. II:** 206

"On a Hill Far Away" (Dillard), **Supp. VI:** 28

"On a Honey Bee, Drinking from a Glass and Drowned Therein" (Freneau), **Supp. II Part 1:** 273

"On a Monument to a Pigeon" (Leopold), **Supp. XIV:** 187–188

"On a Mountainside" (Wagoner), **Supp. IX:** 332

O'Nan, Stewart, **Supp. XI:** 348; **Supp. XXV: 141–155**

"On an Old Photograph of My Son" (Carver), **Supp. III Part 1:** 140

"Onan's Soliloquy" (X. J. Kennedy), **Supp. XV:** 165

"On a Proposed Trip South" (W. C. Williams), **Retro. Supp. I:** 413

Onassis, Jacqueline Kennedy, **Supp. XVIII:** 287

"On a Tree Fallen across the Road" (Frost), **Retro. Supp. I:** 134

"On a View of Pasadena from the Hills" (Winters), **Supp. II Part 2:** 795, 796–799, 814

"On a Visit to a Halfway House after a Long Absence" (Salinas), **Supp. XIII:** 325

"On a Windy Night" (Dixon), **Supp. XII:** 155

On Becoming a Novelist (Gardner), **Supp. VI:** 64

"On Being an American" (Toomer), **Supp. III Part 2:** 479

"On Being Asked to Write a Poem against the War in Vietnam" (Carruth), **Supp. XVI:** 55–56

"On Being a Woman" (Parker), **Supp. IX:** 201

On Being Blue (Gass), **Supp. VI:** 77, 78, 86, 94; **Supp. XIV:** 305

"On Being Brought from Africa to America" (Wheatley), **Supp. XX: 280–281, 286–287**

"On Being Too Inhibited" (Hay), **Supp. XIV:** 130

"On Being Unable to Read" (Cornell), **Supp. XX: 94–95**

On Beyond Zebra! (Geisel), **Supp. XVI:** 105

"On Burroughs' Work" (Ginsberg), **Supp. II Part 1:** 320

Once (Walker), **Supp. III Part 2:** 519, 522, 530

Once at Antietam (Gaddis), **Supp. IV Part 1:** 285

"Once by the Pacific" (Frost), **II:** 155; **Retro. Supp. I:** 122, 137

"Once More, the Round" (Roethke), **III:** 529

Once More around the Block: Familiar Essays (Epstein), **Supp. XIV: 107**

"Once More to the Lake" (White), **Supp. I Part 2:** 658, 668, 673–675

"On Certain Political Measures Proposed to Their Consideration" (Barlow), **Supp. II Part 1:** 82

"Once There Was Light" (Kenyon), **Supp. VII:** 171–172

"On *Credo Ut Intelligam*" (Bronk), **Supp. XXI:** 31

Ondaatje, Michael, **Supp. IV Part 1:** 252

"On Dining Alone" (M. F. K. Fisher), **Supp. XVII:** 83

On Distant Ground (R. O. Butler), **Supp. XII:** 62, **66–68,** 69, 74

"On Divers Geometries" (Bronk), **Supp. XXI:** 31

"On Dreams"(Hadas), **Supp. XXIII:** 117

"One, The" (Weigl), **Supp. XIX:** 282–283

"1 January 1965" (Brodsky), **Supp. VIII:** 23–24

O'Neale, Sondra, **Supp. IV Part 1:** 2

"One A.M. with Voices" (X. J. Kennedy), **Supp. XV:** 157

"One Arm" (T. Williams), **IV:** 383

One Arm, and Other Stories (T. Williams), **IV:** 383

"One Art" (Bell), **Supp. X:** 2

One Art (Bishop), **Retro. Supp. II:** 51

"One Art" (Bishop), **Retro. Supp. II:** 50; **Supp. I Part 1:** 72, 73, 82, 93, 94–95, 96; **Supp. XV:** 126; **Supp. XXI:** 58; **Supp. XXIII:** 117; **Supp. XXV:** 222

"One Art: The Poetry of Elizabeth Bishop, 1971–1976" (Schwartz), **Supp. I Part 1:** 81

One Big Self: Prisoners of Louisiana (Wright and Luster), **Supp. XV:** 337, 344, 350**, 351–353**

"One Blessing had I than the rest" (Dickinson), **Retro. Supp. I:** 45

"One Body" (Hass), **Supp. VI:** 106

One Boy's Boston, 1887–1901 (Morison), **Supp. I Part 2:** 494

"One Coat of Paint" (Ashbery), **Supp. III Part 1:** 26

"One Dash-Horses" (Crane), **I:** 416

One Day (Morris), **III:** 233–236

One Day, When I Was Lost (Baldwin), **Retro. Supp. II:** 13; **Supp. I Part 1:** 48, 66, 67

"One Dead Friend" (Kumin), **Supp. IV Part 2:** 441

One Destiny: An Epistle to the Christians (Asch), **Supp. XXIII:** 2, 7

One Fish Two Fish Red Fish Blue Fish (Geisel), **Supp. XVI:** 108

One Flesh (Major), **Supp. XXII: 183–184**

One Flew Over the Cuckoo's Nest (Kesey), **III:** 558

One Flew Over the Cuckoo's Nest (Kesey), **Supp. XXIII:** 100

"One for the Road" (Swados), **Supp. XIX:** 259

One for the Rose (Levine), **Supp. V:** 178, 179, 181, 187, 189–191

"One for the Rose" (Levine), **Supp. V:** 181, 190

"One Friday Morning" (Hughes), **Supp. I Part 1:** 330

"One Holy Night" (Cisneros), **Supp. VII:** 69–70

"One Home" (Stafford), **Supp. XI:** 321

100 Faces of Death, The, Part IV (Boyle), **Supp. VIII:** 16

100 Great Poets of the English Language (Gioia, ed.), **Supp. XXI:** 99

100 Years of Negro Freedom (Bontemps), **Supp. XXII:** 6

$106,000 Blood Money (Hammett), **Supp. IV Part 1:** 345

"$106,000 Blood Money" (Hammett), **Supp. IV Part 1:** 345, 346

One Hundred Days in Europe (Holmes), **Supp. I Part 1:** 317

180 More: Extraordinary Poems for Every Day (Collins, ed.), **Supp. XXI:** 54

158-Pound Marriage, The (Irving), **Supp. VI:** 163, 164, **167–170**

O'Neil, Elizabeth Murrie, **Retro. Supp. I:** 427

O'Neill, Brendan, **Supp. XII:** 286

O'Neill, Eugene, **I:** 66, 71, 81, 94, 393, 445; **II:** 278, 391, 427, 585; **III:** 151, 165, **385–408; IV:** 61, 383; **Retro. Supp. II:** 82, 104; **Supp. III Part 1:** 177–180, 189; **Supp. IV Part 1:** 359; **Supp. IV Part 2:** 587, 607; **Supp. V:** 277; **Supp. VIII:** 332, 334; **Supp. XIV:** 239, 320, 328; **Supp. XVI:** 193; **Supp. XVII:** 96, 99–100, 103, 105, 107; **Supp. XX: 69; Supp. XXI:** 6, 13; **Supp. XXII:** 17, 18, 22, 28; **Supp. XXV:** 19

O'Neill, Oona, **Supp. XXII:** 25, 26

"One Is a Wanderer" (Thurber), **Supp. I Part 2:** 616

One Is the Sun (P. N. Warren), **Supp. XX: 269–270**

One L (Turow), **Supp. XVII: 214,** 215, 217

"One Last Look at the Adige: Verona in the Rain" (Wright), **Supp. III Part 2:** 603

One Life (Rukeyser), **Supp. VI:** 273, 281, 283

One Life at a Time, Please (Abbey), **Supp. XIII:** 13

One Man in His Time (Glasgow), **II:** 178, 184

"One Man's Fortunes" (Dunbar), **Supp. II Part 1:** 211, 212–213

One Man's Initiation (Dos Passos), **I:** 476–477, 479, 488

One Man's Meat (White), **Supp. I Part 2:** 654, 669, 676

"One Man's Meat" (White), **Supp. I Part 2:** 655

One Matchless Time: A Life of William Faulkner (Parini), **Supp. XXII:** 205

"One Moment on Top of the Earth" (Nye), **Supp. XIII:** 282

One More July: A Football Dialogue with Bill Curry (Plimpton), **Supp. XVI:** 243

"One More"(Kenny), **Supp. XXIII:** 156

"One More Song" (Lindsay), **Supp. I Part 2:** 400–401

"One More Thing" (Carver), **Supp. III Part 1:** 138, 144

"One More Time" (Gordon), **II:** 200

One Nation (Stegner), **Supp. IV Part 2:** 599, 608

"One-Night Homecoming" (X. J. Kennedy), **Supp. XV:** 167

"ONE NIGHT STAND" (Baraka), **Supp. II Part 1:** 32

"One of Our Conquerors" (Bourne), **I:** 223

One of Ours (Cather), **I:** 322–323; **Retro. Supp. I:** 1, 3, **13–15,** 20

"One of the Missing" (Bierce), **I:** 201–202

"One of the Rooming Houses of Heaven" (Doty), **Supp. XI:** 131

"One of the Smallest" (Stern), **Supp. IX:** 299–300

"One of Us" (Fante), **Supp. XI:** 165

Oneóta: or, The Red Race of America (H. Schoolcraft), **Supp. XXIII:** 232

"One Out of Twelve: Writers Who Are Women in Our Century" (Olsen), **Supp. XIII:** 294

"One Part Humor, 2 Parts Whining" (Kakutani), **Supp. XI:** 38

"One Person" (Wylie), **Supp. I Part 2:** 709, 724–727

"One Sister have I in our house" (Dickinson), **Retro. Supp. I:** 34

165 Meeting House Lane (Notley), **Supp. XXII:** 224, 225, 226

"One Song, The" (Strand), **Supp. IV Part 2:** 619

"One Summer in Spain" (Coover), **Supp. V:** 40

One That Got Away, The (Everett), **Supp. XVIII:** 54

1000 Airplanes on the Roof (Glass, Hwang, and Sirlin), **Supp. XXI:** 147

One Thousand Avant-Garde Plays (Koch), **Supp. XV:** 187

"One Thousandth, The" (Weigl), **Supp. XIX:** 288

One Time, One Place: Mississippi in the Depression, a Snapshot Album (Welty), **Retro. Supp. I:** 339, 343, 344

1 x 1 (One Times One) (Cummings), **I:** 430, 436, 438–439, 441, 446, 447, 448

"One Touch of Nature" (McCarthy), **II:** 580

One Train (Koch), **Supp. XV:** 177, 184

"One Trip Abroad" (Fitzgerald), **II:** 95

One True Thing (film), **Supp. XVII:** 176

One True Thing (Quindlen), **Supp. XVII:** 166, **174–176**

"One Way" (Creeley), **Supp. IV Part 1:** 150–151

One Way or Another (Cameron), **Supp. XII:** 81

One-Way Ticket (Hughes), **Retro. Supp. I:** 206, 207, 208; **Supp. I Part 1:** 333–334

One Way to Heaven (Cullen), **Supp. IV Part 1:** 170, 172

One Way to Reconstruct the Scene (W. V. Davis), **Supp. XXI:** 83, **88–91**

"One Way to Reconstruct the Scene" (W. V. Davis), **Supp. XXI: 88–89,** 90, **91,** 92, **93**

One Way to Spell Man (Stegner), **Supp. IV Part 2:** 595, 598, 601, 609

"One Way to Spell Man" (Stegner), **Supp. IV Part 2:** 601

One Whose Eyes Open When You Close Your Eyes, The (F. Wright), **Supp. XVII:** 240, 243

"One Who Skins Cats, The" (Gunn Allen), **Supp. IV Part 1:** 331

"One Who Went Forth to Feel Fear" (Grimms), **Supp. X:** 86

"One Winter I Devise a Plan of My Own" (Ríos), **Supp. IV Part 2:** 549

One Winter Night in August (X. J. Kennedy), **Supp. XV:** 154, 162

One World at a Time (Kooser), **Supp. XIX:** 116, **122–123**

One Writer's Beginnings (Welty), **Retro. Supp. I:** 339, 340, 341, 343, 344, 355–356

"One Year" (Olds), **Supp. X:** 210

On Fire (L. Brown), **Supp. XXI:** 41, **48–49**

On Fire (Silver), **Supp. XXIV:** 264

"On First Looking Into Chapman's Homer" (Keats), **Supp. XXI:** 64

"On First Looking into Chapman's Homer" (Keats), **Supp. XXV:** 226

"On First Looking Out through Juan de la Cosa's Eyes" (Olson), **Supp. II Part 2:** 565, 566, 570, 579

"On First Opening *The Lyric Year*" (W. C. Williams), **Retro. Supp. I:** 414

"On Freedom's Ground" (Wilbur), **Supp. III Part 2:** 562

On Glory's Course (Purdy), **Supp. VII:** 275–276, 279, 280

On Grief and Reason (Brodsky), **Supp. VIII: 31–32**

"On Hearing a Symphony of Beethoven" (Millay), **III:** 132–133

"On Hearing the Airlines Will Use a Psychological Profile to Catch Potential Skyjackers" (Dunn), **Supp. XI:** 144–145

On Human Finery (Bell), **Supp. I Part 2:** 636

"On *Imagerie*: Esther Williams, 1944" (Sobin), **Supp. XVI:** 294

"On Imagination" (Wheatley), **Supp. XX:** 281

"On Imminence: An Essay" (Sobin), **Supp. XVI:** 291

On Kingdom Mountain (Mosher), **Supp. XXII:** 203, 205, 206, 207, 208, 209, 212, 214, **216**

Onkl Mozes (Uncle Moses) (Asch), **Supp. XXIII:** 5

"On leaving my children John and Jane at School, in the Atlantic states, and preparing to return to the interior"(J. Schoolcraft), **Supp. XXIII:** 227, 228, 232, 233, 235, 236

On Liberty (Mill), **Supp. XI:** 196

"On Looking Alone at a Place" (M. F. K. Fisher), **Supp. XVII:** 91

"On Looking at a Copy of Alice Meynell's Poems, Given Me, Years Ago, by a Friend" (Lowell), **II:** 527–528

"On Lookout Mountain" (Hayden), **Supp. II Part 1:** 380

Only a Few of Us Left (Marquand), **III:** 55

"Only Animal, The" (F. Wright), **Supp. XVII:** 245

"Only a Pawn in Their Game" (song, Dylan), **Supp. XVIII:** 24

Only as Far as Brooklyn (Kenny), **Supp. XXIII: 148–151,** 152

"Only Bar in Dixon, The" (Hugo), **Supp. VI:** 140, 141

Only Dangerous Thing, The (Di Piero), **Supp. XIX: 37–38**

Only Dark Spot in the Sky, The (Dove), **Supp. IV Part 1:** 244

"Only Good Indian, The" (Humphrey), **Supp. IX:** 101

"Only Goodness" (Lahiri), **Supp. XXI:** 186, 188

Only in America (Golden), **Supp. VIII:** 244

"Only in the Dream" (Eberhart), **I:** 523

"Only Path to Tomorrow, The" (Rand), **Supp. IV Part 2:** 524

"Only Rose, The" (Jewett), **II:** 408

"Only Son of the Doctor, The" (Gordon), **Supp. IV Part 1:** 305, 306

"Only the Cat Escapes", **Supp. XII:** 150–151

"Only the Dead Know Brooklyn" (Wolfe), **IV:** 451

"Only When I Am Quiet and Do Not Speak"(Hirshfield), **Supp. XXIII:** 133

Only When I Laugh (Simon), **Supp. IV Part 2:** 575

Only World, The (Hull), **Supp. XXI:** 129, **138–141**

On Man and Manhood (Kriegel), **Supp. XXIV: 224–225**

"On Manhood, Disease, and the Authentic Self" (Kriegel), **Supp. XXIV:** 215

"On Meditation"(J. Schoolcraft), **Supp. XXIII:** 229

"On Messrs. Hussey and Coffin" (Wheatley), **Supp. XX:** 280

On Moral Fiction (Gardner), **Supp. VI:** 61, **71,** 72, 73

"On Morality" (Didion), **Supp. IV Part 1:** 196

"On Mt. Philo in November" (Di Piero), **Supp. XIX:** 37, 39

"On My Own" (Levine), **Supp. V:** 181, 189–190

"On My Own Work" (Wilbur), **Supp. III Part 2:** 541–542

On Native Grounds: An Interpretation of Modern American Prose Literature (Kazin), **I:** 517; **Supp. I Part 2:** 650; **Supp. VIII:** 93, 96–97, 98, **100–102**

"On Not Being a Dove" (Updike), **Retro. Supp. I:** 323

"On Open Form" (Merwin), **Supp. III Part 1:** 347–348, 353

On Photography (Sontag), **Supp. III Part 2:** 451, 458, 462–465

"On Poetry"(Hadas), **Supp. XXIII:** 115, 116

"On Political Poetry" (R. Bly), **Supp. IV Part 1:** 61

On Politics: A Carnival of Buncombe (Moos, ed.), **III:** 116

"On Pretentiousness" (Kushner), **Supp. IX:** 131–132

"On Quitting a Little College" (Stafford), **Supp. XI:** 321

"On Reading Eckerman's Conversations with Goethe" (Masters), **Supp. I Part 2:** 458

On Reading Shakespeare (L. P. Smith), **Supp. XIV:** 345–346

"On Reading to Oneself" (Gass), **Supp. VI:** 88, 89

"On Recollection" (Wheatley), **Supp. XX: 287**

On Revolution (Arendt), **Retro. Supp. I:** 87

On Second Thought (Kenny), **Supp. XXIII:** 144

"On Seeing Larry Rivers's *Washington Crossing the Delaware* at the Museum of Modern Art" (O'Hara), **Supp. XV:** 186; **Supp. XXIII:** 208, 214

"On Seeing Red" (Walker), **Supp. III Part 2:** 527

"On Social Plays" (A. Miller), **III:** 147, 148, 159

Onstad, Katrina, **Supp. XXIV:** 209

"On Steinbeck's Story 'Flight' " (Stegner), **Supp. IV Part 2:** 596

"On Style" (Sontag), **Supp. III Part 2:** 456–459, 465–466

"On Suicide" (Hay), **Supp. XIV:** 130, 132

"On Teaching the Young Laurel to Shoot" (Bynner), **Supp. XV:** 50

"On the Antler" (Proulx), **Supp. VII:** 252–253

"On the Avenue" (Espaillat), **Supp. XXI:** 112

On the Banks of Plum Creek (L. I. Wilder), **Supp. XXII:** 294, 299

"On the Banks of the Wabash" (Paul Dresser), **Retro. Supp. II:** 94

"On the Beach, at Night" (Whitman), **IV:** 348

"On the Bosom of This Grave and Wasted Land I Will Lay My Head" (Ray), **Supp. XVIII:** 189

On the Boundary (Tillich), **Retro. Supp. I:** 326

"On the Building of Springfield" (Lindsay), **Supp. I Part 2:** 381

"On the Coast of Maine" (Hayden), **Supp. II Part 1:** 381

On the Contrary: Articles of Belief (McCarthy), **II:** 559, 562

"On the Death of a Friend's Child" (Lowell), **Supp. I Part 2:** 409

"On the Death of Cardinal Tisserant" (Bronk), **Supp. XXI:** 32

"On the Death of General Wooster" (Wheatley), **Supp. XX: 287**

"On the Death of Rev. Mr. George Whitefield—1770" (Wheatley), **Supp. XX: 280, Supp. XX: 282–283**

"On the Death of Senator Thomas J. Walsh" (Winters), **Supp. II Part 2:** 802, 806

"On the Death of Yeats" (Bogan), **Supp. III Part 1:** 59

"On the Death of Zhukov" (Brodsky), **Supp. VIII:** 27

"On the Disadvantages of Central Heating" (Clampitt), **Supp. IX:** 41, 47, 52

"On the Doric Rock, Lake Superior"(J. Schoolcraft), **Supp. XXIII:** 232

On the Drumhead: A Selection from the Writing of Mike Quin (Carlisle, ed.), **Supp. XVIII:** 223, 226

"On the Edge" (Levine), **Supp. V:** 181–182

On the Edge and Over (Levine), **Supp. V:** 178, 180–182, 186

On the Edge of the Great Rift: Three Novels of Africa (Theroux), **Supp. VIII:** 316

"On the Edge of Visible Light"(Schott), **Supp. XXIII:** 242

"On the Eve of the Feast of the Immaculate Conception, 1942" (Lowell), **II:** 538; **Retro. Supp. II:** 185

"On the Eyes of an SS Officer" (Wilbur), **Supp. III Part 2:** 548

"On the Failure of Meaning in the Absence of Objective Analogs" (Bronk), **Supp. XXI:** 31

"On the Fall of General Earl Cornwallis" (Freneau), **Supp. II Part 1:** 261

"On the Folly of Writing Poetry" (Freneau), **Supp. II Part 1:** 263

On the Frontier (Auden and Isherwood), **Supp. II Part 1:** 13; **Supp. XIV:** 163

On the Great Atlantic Rainway: Selected Poems, 1950–1988 (Koch), **Supp. XV:** 177

"On the History of Poetry" (Halliday), **Supp. XIX:** 88, 89

"On the Hysterical Playground" (Watman), **Supp. XX: 93**

"On the Island" (Stern), **Supp. IX:** 290

"On the Late Eclipse" (Bryant), **Supp. I Part 1:** 152

On the Laws of the Poetic Art (Hecht), **Supp. X:** 58

On the Line (Swados), **Supp. XIX: 258–260**

"On the Line" (Swados), **Supp. XIX:** 259

"On the Marginal Way" (Wilbur), **Supp. III Part 2:** 558, 559

On the Mesa (Nichols), **Supp. XIII:** 268

"On the Moon and Matriarchal Consciousness" (Neumann), **Supp. IV Part 1:** 68

"On the Morning after the Sixties" (Didion), **Supp. IV Part 1:** 205, 206

On the Motion and Immobility of Douve (Bonnefoy; Kinnell, trans.), **Supp. III Part 1:** 235

"On the Mullica"(Schott), **Supp. XXIII:** 253

"On the Murder of Lieutenant José del Castillo by the Falangist Bravo Martinez, July 12, 1936" (Levine), **Supp. V:** 187

"On the Night of a Friend's Wedding" (Robinson), **III:** 524

"On the Occasion of a Poem: Richard Hugo" (Wright), **Supp. III Part 2:** 596

On the Occasion of My Last Afternoon (Gibbons), **Supp. X:** 46, **50–53**

On the Origin of Species (Darwin), **Supp. XIV:** 192

"On the Parapet" (Tanner), **Retro. Supp. II:** 205

"On the Platform" (Nemerov), **III:** 287

On the Poetry of Philip Levine: Stranger to Nothing (Levis), **Supp. XI:** 257

"On the Pottlecombe Cornice" (Sturgis), **Supp. XX: 233, 240**

"On the Powers of the Human Understanding" (Freneau), **Supp. II Part 1:** 274

On the Prejudices, Predilections, and Firm Beliefs of William Faulkner (Brooks), **Supp. XIV:** 13

"On the Pulse of Morning" (Angelou), **Supp. IV Part 1:** 15–17

"On the Railway Platform" (Jarrell), **II:** 370

"On the Rainy River" (O'Brien), **Supp. V:** 250

On the Rebound: A Story and Nine Poems (Purdy), **Supp. VII:** 276–277

"On the Religion of Nature" (Freneau), **Supp. II Part 1:** 275

"On the River" (Dunbar), **Supp. II Part 1:** 193

"On the River" (Levine), **Supp. V:** 193

On the River Styx and Other Stories (Matthiessen), **Supp. V:** 212

On the Road (Kerouac), **Retro. Supp. I:** 102; **Supp. III Part 1:** 92, 218, 222–224, 226, 230–231; **Supp. V:** 336; **Supp. X:** 269; **Supp. XIII:** 275; **Supp. XIV:** 138, 150; **Supp. XV:** 221; **Supp. XVIII:** 20, 138; **Supp. XXI:** 53; **Supp. XXIV:** 281

"On the Road Home" (Stevens), **Retro. Supp. I:** 306

On the Road with the Archangel (Buechner), **Supp. XII:** 54

"On the Rope" (Richard), **Supp. XIX:** 211–212

"On the Run" (Boyle), **Supp. XXIV:** 52

On These I Stand: An Anthology of the Best Poems of Countee Cullen (Cullen), **Supp. IV Part 1:** 173

"On the Skeleton of a Hound" (Wright), **Supp. III Part 2:** 593

"On the Staten Island Ferry"(Kenny), **Supp. XXIII:** 154

"On the Street" (Peacock), **Supp. XIX:** 199

"On the Street: Monument" (Gunn Allen), **Supp. IV Part 1:** 326

"On the Subway" (Olds), **Supp. X:** 207

"On the System of Policy Hitherto Pursued by Their Government" (Barlow), **Supp. II Part 1:** 82

"On the Teaching of Modern Literature" (Trilling), **Supp. III Part 2:** 509–510

"On the Uniformity and Perfection of Nature" (Freneau), **Supp. II Part 1:** 275

"On the Universality and Other Attributes of the God of Nature" (Freneau), **Supp. II Part 1:** 275

"On the Use of Trisyllabic Feet in Iambic Verse" (Bryant), **Supp. I Part 1:** 156

On the Verge: Emerging Poets (Ellis and Lease, eds.), **Supp. XXI:** 246

On the Waterfront (film, Kazan), **Supp. XVIII: 250–251,** 252, 253

"On the Way Home" (L. I. Wilder), **Supp. XXII:** 292

On the Way to the Island (Ferry), **Supp. XXIV:** 147, **148–149,** 150

"On the Way to the San Remo"(O'Hara), **Supp. XXIII:** 212, 219

On the Way toward a Phenomenological Psychology: The Psychology of William James (Linschoten), **II:** 362

"On the Way to Work" (Dunn), **Supp. XI:** 149–150

"On the Wide Heath" (Millay), **III:** 130

"On the Writing of Novels" (Buck), **Supp. II Part 1:** 121

On the Yard (Braly), **Supp. XVIII:** 147

On This Island (Auden), **Supp. II Part 1:** 11

On This Side of the River (Ferry), **Supp. XXIV: 161–162**

"On Time" (O'Hara), **III:** 369–370

"Ontological Episode of the Asylum" (Carruth), **Supp. XVI:** 48, 50

"Ontology of the Sentence, The" (Gass), **Supp. VI:** 77

"On Top" (Leopold), **Supp. XIV:** 188

"On Top" (Snyder), **Supp. VIII:** 304

"On Translating Akhmatova" (Kunitz), **Supp. III Part 1:** 268

"On Turning Ten" (Collins), **Supp. XXI:** 64

"On Visiting a Borrowed Country House in Arcadia" (Stallings), **Supp. XXV:** 233–234

"On Waking to Old Debts" (Keillor), **Supp. XVI:** 167

On William Stafford: The Worth of Local Things (Andrews, ed.), **Supp. XI:** 311, 312, 317, 321, 324, 326

On Writers and Writing (O'Nan, ed.), **Supp. XXV:** 152–153

"On Writing" (Carver), **Supp. III Part 1:** 142–143

"On Writing" (Nin), **Supp. X:** 182

On Your Own (Gallagher), **Supp. XXIV:** 166

Opatoshu, Joseph, **IV:** 9

"Open Boat, The" (Crane), **I:** 408, 415, 416–417, 423; **Retro. Supp. I:** 325; **Supp. XIV:** 51

Open Boat and Other Stories (Crane), **I:** 408

Open Door, The (Skloot), **Supp. XX: 194, 196, 208**

Open Heart: A Patient's Story of Life-Saving Medicine and Life-Giving Friendship (Neugeboren), **Supp. XVI:** 217, **229–230**

Open House (Roethke), **III:** 529–530, 540

"Open House" (Roethke), **III:** 529

"Opening, An" (Swenson), **Supp. IV Part 2:** 639

Opening of the Field, The (Duncan), **Supp. III Part 2:** 625

Opening the Hand (Merwin), **Supp. III Part 1:** 341, 353, 355

"Open Letter" (Roethke), **III:** 532, 534

"Open Letter to Surrealists Everywhere, An" (H. Miller), **III:** 184

Open Meeting, The (Gurney), **Supp. V:** 98

Open Net (Plimpton), **Supp. XVI:** 241

"Open Road, The" (Dreiser), **II:** 44

Open Sea, The (Masters), **Supp. I Part 2:** 471

Open Season: Sporting Adventures (Humphrey), **Supp. IX:** 95

"Open Secret" (Nelson), **Supp. XVIII:** 185

"Open the Gates" (Kunitz), **Supp. III Part 1:** 264–265, 267

"Opera Company, The" (Merrill), **Supp. III Part 1:** 326

Operating Instructions: A Journal of My Son's First Year (Lamott), **Supp. XX: 136–137, 142**

"Operation, The" (Sanders), **Supp. XVI:** 266

"Operation, The" (Sexton), **Supp. II Part 2:** 675, 679

Operation Shylock: A Confession (P. Roth), **Retro. Supp. II:** 279, 280, 291

Operation Sidewinder (Shepard), **Supp. III Part 2:** 434–435, 439, 446–447

Operations in North African Waters (Morison), **Supp. I Part 2:** 490

Operation Wandering Soul (Powers), **Supp. IX:** 212, **217–219**

Opffer, Emil, **Retro. Supp. II:** 80

"Opinion" (Du Bois), **Supp. II Part 1:** 173

Opinionator, The (Bierce), **I:** 209

Opinions of Oliver Allston (Brooks), **I:** 254, 255, 256

O Pioneers! (Cather), **I:** 314, 317–319, 320; **Retro. Supp. I:** 1, 5, 6, **7–9,** 10, 13, 20; **Retro. Supp. II:** 136

Oppen, George, **IV:** 415; **Supp. III Part 2:** 614, 615, 616, 626, 628; **Supp. XIV:** 285, 286, 287; **Supp. XVI:** 282, 283; **Supp. XVII:** 243; **Supp. XXI:** 19,**Supp. XXI:** 29, 23; **Supp. XXIII:** 165–166, 168

Oppenheim, James, **I:** 106, 109, 239, 245; **Supp. XV:** 294, 296, 298, 299, 301, 302, 307, 313; **Supp. XX:** 68

Oppenheimer, J. Robert, **I:** 137, 492

Oppenheimer, Judy, **Supp. IX:** 115, 116, 118, 120, 126

"Opportunity for American Fiction, An" (Howells), **Supp. I Part 2:** 645–646

Opposing Self, The (Trilling), **Supp. III Part 2:** 506–507

"Opposition" (Lanier), **Supp. I Part 1:** 368, 373

Oprah's Roots: An African American Lives Special (television production), **Supp. XX: 99**

Opticks: A Poem in Seven Sections (Goldbarth), **Supp. XII:** 177, **178**

Optimist's Daughter, The (Welty), **IV:** 261, 280; **Retro. Supp. I:** 339, 355

"Optimist's Daughter, The" (Welty), **IV:** 280–281

Options (O. Henry), **Supp. II Part 1:** 410

Opus Posthumous (Stevens), **IV:** 76, 78

Opus Posthumous (W. Stevens), **Supp. XVII:** 241

Oracle at Stoneleigh Court, The (Taylor), **Supp. V:** 328

Orage, Alfred, **III:** 473

"O/Rain-in-the-Face"(Kenny), **Supp. XXIII:** 156

Orange, Max (pseudonym). *See* Heller, Joseph

Orange Fish, The (Shields), **Supp. VII:** 318, 320, 323, 328

Orangery, The (Sorrentino), **Supp. XXI:** 228

Oranges (exhibition, Hartigan), **Supp. XXIII:** 210

Oranges (McPhee), **Supp. III Part 1:** 298–299, 301, 309

Oranges: 12 Pastorals (O'Hara), **Supp. XXIII:** 210

"Oranging of America, The" (Apple), **Supp. XVII:** 3–4, 6

Oranging of America and Other Short Stories, The (Apple), **Supp. XVII:** 1–2, **3–4,** 7, 8

Oration Delivered at Washington, July Fourth, 1809 (Barlow), **Supp. II Part 1:** 80, 83

Orations and Addresses (Bryant), **Supp. I Part 1:** 158

Orators, The (Auden), **Supp. II Part 1:** 6, 7, 11, 18–19

Orbach, Jerry, **Supp. XXIII:** 103

Orb Weaver, The (Francis), **Supp. IX: 81–82**

"Orchard" (Doolittle), **Supp. I Part 1:** 263–264, 265, 266

"Orchard" (Eberhart), **I:** 539

Orchard, The (B. Kelly), **Supp. XVII:** 123, 127, **130–133**

"Orchard, The" (B. Kelly), **Supp. XVII:** 133

Orchard Keeper, The (McCarthy), **Supp. VIII: 175–176**

Orchestra (Davies), **III:** 541

"Orchid Fever" (Orlean), **Supp. XXV:** 160

"Orchids" (Roethke), **III:** 530–531

Orchid Thief, The: A True Story of Beauty and Obsession (Orlean), **Supp. XXV:** 160, 161–162

"Or Consider Prometheus" (Clampitt), **Supp. IX:** 44

Ordeal of Mansart, The (Du Bois), **Supp. II Part 1:** 185–186

Ordeal of Mark Twain, The (Brooks), **I:** 240, 247, 248; **II:** 482

Ordering the Façade: Photography and Contemporary Southern Women's Writing (Henninger), **Supp. XXI:** 253

"Order of Insects" (Gass), **Supp. VI:** 83

Order Out of Chaos (McPherson), **Supp. IV Part 1:** 2, 12

"Ordinary Afternoon in Charlottesville, An" (Wright), **Supp. V:** 344

"Ordinary Days" (Dunn), **Supp. XI:** 151

"Ordinary Evening in New Haven, An" (Stevens), **IV:** 91–92; **Retro. Supp. I:** 297, 300, 311, 312

Ordinary Heroes (Turow), **Supp. XVII:** 221–222, 223

Ordinary Life (Crooker), **Supp. XXIII:** 56

Ordinary Love (Smiley), **Supp. VI:** 292, 299–300

Ordinary Love; and Good Will: Two Novellas (Smiley), **Supp. VI:** 292, 299–300

Ordinary Miracles (Jong), **Supp. V:** 115, 130–131

Ordinary Seaman, The (Goldman), **Supp. XXV:** 49, 50, 53–54

"Ordinary Time: Virginia Woolf and Thucydides on War" (Carson), **Supp. XII:** 111

"Ordinary Women, The" (Stevens), **IV:** 81

Ordways, The (Humphrey), **Supp. IX:** 95, 98–100, 109; **Supp. XV:** 353

"Oread" (Doolittle), **II:** 520–521; **Supp. I Part 1:** 265–266

Oregon Message, An (Stafford), **Supp. XI:** 328–329

Oregon Trail, The (Parkman), **II:** 312; **Supp. II Part 2:** 592, 595–596, 598, 606

Oresteia (Aeschylus), **Supp. IX:** 103

"Orestes at Tauris" (Jarrell), **II:** 376, 377

Orfalea, Gregory, **Supp. XIII:** 278

Orfeo ed Euridice (Gluck), **II:** 210, 211

Orff, Carl, **Supp. X:** 63

"Organizer's Wife, The" (Bambara), **Supp. XI:** 8–9

"Organmeister: Hasse After Marienkirche" (Bierds), **Supp. XVII:** 34

"Orgy" (Rukeyser), **Supp. VI:** 280

Orgy, The (Rukeyser), **Supp. VI:** 274, 283

"Orgy of Southerness, An" (Pickering), **Supp. XXI:** 203

"Oriental Rug"(Balakian), **Supp. XXIII:** 23, 24–25

"Orientation of Hope, The" (Locke), **Supp. XIV:** 212–213

Orient Express (Dos Passos), **I:** 480

"Orient Express, The" (Jarrell), **II:** 382, 383–384

Origen, Adamantius, **IV:** 153

"Origin" (Harjo), **Supp. XII:** 219

Original Child Bomb: Points for Meditation to Be Scratched on the Walls of a Cave (Merton), **Supp. VIII:** 203

Original Essays on the Poetry of Anne Sexton (George), **Supp. IV Part 2:** 450

"Original Follies Girl, The" (Z. Fitzgerald), **Supp. IX:** 71

Original Light (Goldbarth), **Supp. XII:** 181, 183–184, 188

Original Love (Peacock), **Supp. XIX:** 199–201, 206

Original of Laura, The (Nabokov), **Retro. Supp. I:** 266

"Original Sin" (Jeffers), **Supp. II Part 2:** 426

"Original Sin" (Warren), **IV:** 245

Origin: Hawaii (Taggard), **Supp. XXII:** 272, 284

"Origin of Extermination in the Imagination, The" (Gass), **Supp. VI:** 89

Origin of Species, The (Darwin), **II:** 173, 462; **Supp. XVI:** 13

Origin of the Brunists, The (Coover), **Supp. V:** 39, 41, 52

"Origin of the Miscodeed, or the Maid of Taquimenon"(J. Schoolcraft), **Supp. XXIII:** 235

"Origin of the Robin, The"(J. Schoolcraft), **Supp. XXIII:** 234, 235

"Origins and History of Consciousness" (Rich), **Supp. I Part 2:** 570

"Origins of a Nonfiction Writer" (Talese), **Supp. XVII:** 208

"Origins of a Poem" (Levertov), **Supp. III Part 1:** 273

"Origins of the Beat Generation, The" (Kerouac), **Supp. III Part 1:** 231

Origo, Iris, **IV:** 328

"O'Riley's Late-Bloomed Little Son" (X. J. Kennedy), **Supp. XV:** 159

"Orion" (Rich), **Supp. I Part 2:** 557

O'Riordan, Conal Holmes O'Connell, **III:** 465

Orlacs Hände (film, Weine), **Supp. XVII:** 58

Orlando (V. Woolf), **Supp. XVII:** 86

Orlando (Woolf), **Supp. I Part 2:** 718; **Supp. VIII:** 263; **Supp. XII:** 9

Orlando Furioso (Ariosto), **Supp. XV:** 175

Orlean, Susan, **Supp. XXV:** 157–167

Orlik, Emil, **Supp. XXIII:** 6

Orloff, Chana, **Supp. XXIII:** 6

Orlovsky, Peter, **Supp. XII:** 121, 126; **Supp. XIV:** 150; **Supp. XVIII:** 27

Ormonde, Czenzi, **Supp. IV Part 1:** 132

Ormond; or, The Secret Witness (Brown), **Supp. I Part 1:** 133–137

Ornament and Crime (Loos), **Supp. XVI:** 187

Orne, Sarah. *See* Jewett, Sarah Orne

Ornithological Biography; or, An Account of the Habits of the Birds of the United States of America, and Interspersed with Delineations of American Scenery and Manners (Audubon), **Supp. XVI:** 13; 7–10

"Ornithology" (Hull), **Supp. XXI:** 138–139

Ornitz, Samuel, **Supp. IX:** 227; **Supp. XIII:** 166

Ornstein, Leo, **Supp. XX:** 75

O'Rourke, Meghan, **Supp. XXV:** 10

O'Rourke, William, **Supp. XXII:** 213

Orphan Angel, The (Wylie), **Supp. I Part 2:** 707, 709, 714, 717, 719–721, 722, 724

Orphan's Tale, An (Neugeboren), **Supp. XVI:** 222, 223

Orpheus (Rukeyser), **Supp. VI:** 273

"Orpheus" (Winters), **Supp. II Part 2:** 801

"Orpheus, Eurydice, Hermes" (Rilke), **Supp. VIII:** 31, 32

"Orpheus (1)" (Atwood), **Supp. XIII:** 35

"Orpheus (2)" (Atwood), **Supp. XIII:** 35

"Orpheus Alone" (Strand), **Supp. IV Part 2:** 632

Orpheus Descending (T. Williams), **IV:** 380, 381, 382, 385, 386, 387, 389, 391–392, 395, 396, 398

Orr, David, **Supp. XXI:** 62

Orr, Peter, **Supp. I Part 2:** 538, 540, 543

Orse, Brian, **Supp. XX:** 264

Ortega y Gasset, José, **I:** 218, 222; **Supp. IV Part 2:** 521; **Supp. XXIII:** 165

Ortiz, Simon J., **Supp. IV Part 1:** 319, 404; **Supp. IV Part 2:** 497–515, 557; **Supp. XII:** 217, 218

"Ortlieb's Uptown Taproom" (Di Piero), **Supp. XIX:** 46, 47

Orton, Joe, **Supp. XXIV:** 113, 126, 263

O'Ruddy, The (Crane), **I:** 409, 424

Orwell, George, **I:** 489; **II:** 454, 580; **Supp. I Part 2:** 523, 620; **Supp. II Part 1:** 143; **Supp. IV Part 1:** 236; **Supp. V:** 250; **Supp. VIII:** 241; **Supp. XIV:** 112, 158; **Supp. XVII:** 228, 229; **Supp. XVIII:** 137, 138; **Supp. XX:** 86

Osborn, Dwight, **III:** 218–219, 223

"Osborn Look, The" (Morris), **III:** 221

Osgood, Frances, **Supp. XVII:** 75

Osgood, J. R., **II:** 283

O'Shea, Kitty, **II:** 137

O'Shea, Milo, **Supp. XI:** 308

"Oshkikwe's Baby" (traditional Chippewa story), **Supp. IV Part 1:** 333

Oshogay, Delia, **Supp. IV Part 1:** 333

Ossana, Diana, **Supp. V:** 230–231, 232

Ossian, **Supp. I Part 2:** 491

Ossip, Kathleen, **Supp. X:** 201

"Osso Bucco" (Collins), **Supp. XXI:** 60

Ostanovka v Pustyne (A halt in the wilderness) (Brodsky), **Supp. VIII:** 21

Oster, Judith, **Supp. XVI:** 151

Ostriker, Alicia, **Supp. I Part 2:** 540; **Supp. IV Part 2:** 439, 447, 449; **Supp. X:** 207, 208; **Supp. XI:** 143; **Supp. XV:** 251

Ostrom, Hans, **Retro. Supp. I:** 195

Oswald, Lee Harvey, **III:** 234, 235

Oswald II (DeLillo), **Supp. VI:** 16

Oswald's Tale (Mailer), **Retro. Supp. II:** 212–213

"Otagamiad, The"(J. Schoolcraft), **Supp. XXIII:** 223

O Taste and See (Levertov), **Supp. III Part 1:** 278–279, 281

Othello (Shakespeare), **I:** 284–285

"Other, The" (Sexton), **Supp. II Part 2:** 692

Other America, The (Harrington), **I:** 306

"Other American Renaissance, The" (Tompkins), **Supp. XVIII:** 258

Other Destinies: Understanding the American Indian Novel (Owens), **Supp. IV Part 1:** 404

CUMULATIVE INDEX / 491

otherelectricities.com, **Supp. XXIV:** 240–241

Other Electricities: Stories (Monson), **Supp. XXIV:** 230, **231–234,** 235–236, 238, 241

"Other Frost, The" (Jarrell), **Retro. Supp. I:** 121

"Other Gods, The" (Lovecraft), **Supp. XXV:** 114

Other Gods: An American Legend (Buck), **Supp. II Part 1:** 123, 130–131

Other House, The (James), **Retro. Supp. I:** 229

"Other League of Nations, The" (Ríos), **Supp. IV Part 2:** 552

"Other Margaret, The" (Trilling), **Supp. III Part 2:** 504–505

"Other Miller, The" (Wolff), **Supp. VII:** 343–344

"Other Mothers" (Paley), **Supp. VI:** 225

"Other Night at Columbia, The" (Trilling), **Supp. XII:** 126

"Other People's Secrets" (Hampl), **Supp. XXII:** 94

"Other Robert Frost, The" (Jarrell), **Retro. Supp. I:** 135

Others (Shields), **Supp. VII:** 310

Other Side, The (Gordon), **Supp. IV Part 1:** 299, 306, 307–309, 310–311

Other Side, The/El Otro Lado (Alvarez), **Supp. VII:** 9–12

"Other Side, The"(Hadas), **Supp. XXIII:** 120

Other Side of the River, The (Wright), **Supp. V:** 332–333, 342

"Other Side of the River, The" (Wright), **Supp. V:** 335

"Other Tradition, The" (Ashbery), **Supp. III Part 1:** 15, 18

"Other Two, The" (Wharton), **Retro. Supp. I:** 367

Other Voices, Other Rooms (Capote), **Supp. III Part 1:** 113–118, 121, 123–124

"Other Wanderer, The" (Gibran), **Supp. XX: 124**

"Other War, The" (Cowley), **Supp. II Part 1:** 144

"Otherwise" (Kenyon), **Supp. VII:** 172, 174

Otherwise: New and Selected Poems (Kenyon), **Supp. VII:** 167, 172–174

Otherwise Than Being; or, Beyond Essence (Lévinas), **Supp. XVI:** 290, 291

"Other Woman, The" (Anderson), **I:** 114

"Other World, The" (Wrigley), **Supp. XVIII:** 307

Other Worlds Than This (Hadas), **Supp. XXIII:** 118, **124–125**

Otho the Great: A Tragedy in Five Acts (Keats), **Supp. XII:** 113

Otis, Harrison Gray, **Supp. I Part 2:** 479–481, 483, 486, 488

Otis, James, **III:** 577; **Supp. I Part 2:** 486; **Supp. XV:** 229

O to Be a Dragon (Moore), **III:** 215

"Otravida, Otravez" (Díaz), **Supp. XXIV:** 93

Otto, Rudolf, **Supp. XVII:** 243

"Ouija" (McClatchy), **Supp. XII:** 269–270

Oupensky, Peter, **Supp. XIV:** 188

Our America (Michaels), **Retro. Supp. I:** 379

Our America (W. Frank), **I:** 229; **Supp. IX:** 308; **Supp. XX: 69–70, 75**

Our Aperture (Monson), **Supp. XXIV:** 230, 239

"Our Assistant's Column" (Twain), **IV:** 193

"Our Bourgeois Literature" (Sinclair), **Supp. V:** 281

Our Brains and What Ails Them (Gilman), **Supp. XI:** 207

Our Century (Wilder), **IV:** 374

"Our Christmas Party" (E. Stoddard), **Supp. XV:** 273, 278

Our Country (Strong), **Supp. XIV:** 64

"Our Countrymen in Chains!" (Whittier), **Supp. I Part 2:** 688

"Our Cultural Humility" (Bourne), **I:** 223, 228

Our Depleted Society (Seymour), **Supp. XIII:** 264

"Our Dust" (Wright), **Supp. XV:** 345, 346

"Our Father Who Drowns the Birds" (Kingsolver), **Supp. VII:** 208–209

"Our First House" (Kingston), **Supp. V:** 169

Our Gang (P. Roth), **Retro. Supp. II:** 287; **Supp. III Part 2:** 414; **Supp. IV Part 1:** 388

"Our Good Day" (Cisneros), **Supp. VII:** 60

Our Ground Time Here Will Be Brief (Kumin), **Supp. IV Part 2:** 450–452

Our House in the Last World (Hijuelos), **Supp. VIII:** 73, **76–79,** 87, 88

"Our Lady" (A. Finch), **Supp. XVII:** 77

"*Our Lady of the Annunciation/Nuestra Señora de Anunciación*" (Mora), **Supp. XIII:** 217, 224, 228

"Our Lady of Troy" (MacLeish), **III:** 3, 20

"Our Limitations" (Holmes), **Supp. I Part 1:** 314

"Our Martyred Soldiers" (Dunbar), **Supp. II Part 1:** 193

"Our Master" (Whittier), **Supp. I Part 2:** 704

"Our Mother Pocahontas" (Lindsay), **Supp. I Part 2:** 393

Our Mr. Wrenn: The Romantic Adventures of a Gentle Man (Lewis), **II:** 441

Our National Parks (Muir), **Supp. IX:** 181, 184

Our New York: A Personal Vision in Words and Photographs (Kazin), **Supp. VIII: 106–107**

Our Nig (Wilson), **Supp. XX: 105**

"Our Old Aunt Who Is Now in a Retirement Home" (Shields), **Supp. VII:** 310

Our Old Home: A Series of English Sketches (Hawthorne), **II:** 225; **Retro. Supp. I:** 163

"Our Own Movie Queen" (Z. Fitzgerald), **Supp. IX:** 71

"Our River Now" (L.-Y. Lee), **Supp. XV:** 224, 225

Our Selves (Bronk), **Supp. XXI:** 32

Ourselves to Know (O'Hara), **III:** 362, 365

Our Sister Killjoy: or, Reflections from a Black-Eyed Squint (Aidoo), **Supp. XXII:** 68

"Our Story Begins" (Wolff), **Supp. VII:** 345

"Our Sweating Selves" (Di Piero), **Supp. XIX:** 36

Our Town (Wilder), **IV:** 357, 364, 365, 366, 368–369

"Our Unplanned Cities" (Bourne), **I:** 229, 230

Our Wonder World, **Retro. Supp. I:** 341

Ouspensky, P. D., **I:** 383; **Supp. XX: 116**

"Out" (Harjo), **Supp. XII:** 219

"'Out, Out' " (Frost), **Retro. Supp. I:** 131

"Outcast" (McKay), **Supp. X:** 135

"Outcasts of Poker Flats, The" (Harte), **Supp. II Part 1:** 345, 347–348

Outcroppings (Harte), **Supp. II Part 1:** 343

Out Cry (T. Williams), **IV:** 383, 393

Outcry, The (James), **Retro. Supp. I:** 235

"Outdoor Shower" (Olds), **Supp. X:** 214

Outer Banks (Siddons), **Supp. XXII:** 239

Outerbridge Reach (Stone), **Supp. V:** 306–308

Outer Dark (McCarthy), **Supp. VIII: 176–177**

Outermost Dream, The: Essays and Reviews (Maxwell), **Supp. VIII: 171–172**

"Outing, The" (Baldwin), **Supp. I Part 1:** 63

Outlaw Journalist (McKeen), **Supp. XXIV:** 279, 288

"Out Like a Lamb" (Dubus), **Supp. VII:** 91

"Outline of an Autobiography" (Toomer), **Supp. III Part 2:** 478

"Outline Toward a Theory of the Mine Versus the Mind and the Harvard Outline" (Monson), **Supp. XXIV:** 235

Outlyer and Ghazals (Harrison), **Supp. VIII:** 41

"Out of Business" (Mora), **Supp. XIII:** 217

Out of Eden: Essays on Modern Art (Di Piero), **Supp. XIX:** 41, 42

"Out of My Deeper Heart" (Gibran), **Supp. XX: 118**

Out of My League (Plimpton), **Supp. XVI:** 233, 239

"Out of Nowhere into Nothing" (Anderson), **I:** 113

"Out of Season" (Hemingway), **II:** 263

"Out of the Cradle Endlessly Rocking" (Whitman), **IV:** 342, 343–345, 346, 351; **Retro. Supp. I:** 404, 406

"Out of the Deeps" (E. Stoddard), **Supp. XV:** 286

"Out of the Hospital and Under the Bar" (Ellison), **Retro. Supp. II:** 118–119; **Supp. II Part 1:** 246

"Out of the Rainbow End" (Sandburg), **III:** 594–595

"Out of the Sea, Early" (Swenson), **Supp. IV Part 2:** 645

"Out of the Snow" (Dubus), **Supp. VII:** 91

Out of the Stars (Purdy), **Supp. VII:** 281–282

"Out of the Woods" (Offutt), **Supp. XIX:** 169–170

Out of the Woods: Stories (Offutt), **Supp. XIX:** 163, 167, **169–172,** 175

"Out of Your Nakedness, Out of My Nakedness"(Hadas), **Supp. XXIII:** 125

"Outrageous" (Pickering), **Supp. XXI:** 202

Outre-Mer: A Pilgrimage beyond the Sea (Longfellow), **II:** 313, 491; **Retro. Supp. II:** 155, 165

"Outside" (Stafford), **Supp. XI:** 318

Outside, The (Glaspell), **Supp. III Part 1:** 179, 187

"Outside In" (Pickering), **Supp. XXI:** 197

Outsider, The (Wright), **IV:** 478, 481, 488, 491–494, 495

Outside World, The (Mirvis), **Supp. XX:** **177, 178, 185–190**

Out Went the Candle (Swados), **Supp. XIX:** **257**

Out West (Shanley), **Supp. XIV:** 317

"Out with the Old" (Yates), **Supp. XI:** 342

"Ouzo for Robin" (Merrill), **Supp. III Part 1:** 326

"Oval Portrait, The" (Poe), **III:** 412, 415; **Retro. Supp. II:** 270

"Oven Bird, The" (Frost), **Retro. Supp. I:** 131; **Supp. XI:** 153; **Supp. XIX:** 15

"Over 2,000 Illustrations and a Complete Concordance" (Bishop), **Retro. Supp. II:** 45; **Supp. I Part 1:** 90–91

"Over by the River" (Maxwell), **Supp. VIII:** 169, 170

"Overcoat, The" (Gogol), **Supp. XXII:** 59

"Overgrown Pasture, The" (Lowell), **II:** 523

"Overheard through the Walls of the Invisible City" (Bidart), **Supp. XV:** 32

"Over Kansas" (Ginsberg), **Supp. II Part 1:** 320

Overland to the Islands (Levertov), **Supp. III Part 1:** 275, 276

Overlook, The (Connelly), **Supp. XXI:** **78**

"Overlooking Lake Champlain" (Di Piero), **Supp. XIX:** 47

"Overnight Pass" (X. J. Kennedy), **Supp. XV:** 168

Overreachers, The (Talese), **Supp. XVII:** 202

"Over-Soul, The" (Emerson), **II:** 7

Over the Blue Mountain (Richter), **Supp. XVIII:** 220

"Over the Edge"(Hadas), **Supp. XXIII:** 115

"Over the Hill" (Dubus), **Supp. VII:** 76, 79–80

Overtime (Gurney), **Supp. V:** 104

Overton, Grant, **Supp. XXV:** 200

"Overwhelming Question, An" (Taylor), **Supp. V:** 323

Ovid, **I:** 62; **II:** 542–543; **III:** 457, 467, 468, 470; **Retro. Supp. I:** 63; **Supp. IV Part 2:** 634; **Supp. XII:** 264

"Ovid in Exile" (Di Piero), **Supp. XIX:** 44

"Ovid's Farewell" (McClatchy), **Supp. XII:** 257–258

Owen, David, **II:** 34

Owen, Maureen, **Supp. IV Part 2:** 423

Owen, Wilfred, **II:** 367, 372; **III:** 524; **Supp. X:** 146; **Supp. XVII:** 245; **Supp. XVIII:** 92; **Supp. XIX:** 17

Owens, Hamilton, **III:** 99, 109

Owens, Louis, **Supp. IV Part 1:** 404

"O Where Are You Going?" (Auden), **Supp. X:** 116

"Owl, The" (Wrigley), **Supp. XVIII:** 297–298, 301

Owl in the Attic, The (Thurber), **Supp. I Part 2:** 614

Owl in the Mask of the Dreamer, The: Collected Poems (Haines), **Supp. XII:** 211

"Owl in the Sarcophagus, The" (Stevens), **Retro. Supp. I:** 300

Owl's Clover (Stevens), **Retro. Supp. I:** 298, **303–304**

"Owl's Clover" (Stevens), **IV:** 75

Owl's Insomnia, Poems by Rafael Alberti, The (Strand, trans.), **Supp. IV Part 2:** 630

Owl Spirit Dwelling (Gallagher), **Supp. XXIV:** 170

Owlstone Crown, The (X. J. Kennedy), **Supp. XV:** 162, **164**

"Owl Who Was God, The" (Thurber), **Supp. I Part 2:** 610

Owning Jolene (Hearon), **Supp. VIII:** **66–67**

"Owning the Masters" (Nelson), **Supp. XVIII:** 171

Oxford Anthology of American Literature, The, **III:** 197; **Supp. I Part 1:** 254

Oxford Book of American Verse (Matthiessen, ed.), **Retro. Supp. I:** 40

Oxford Book of Children's Verse in America, The (Hall, ed.), **Supp. XIV:** 126

Oxford Companion to Twentieth-Century Poetry (Hamilton, ed.), **Supp. XVII:** 243

Oxford History of the American People, The (Morison), **Supp. I Part 2:** 495–496

Oxford History of the United States, 1783–1917, The (Morison), **Supp. I Part 2:** 483–484

"Oxford Town" (song, Dylan), **Supp. XVIII:** 24

Oxherding Tale (Johnson), **Supp. VI:** **190–192,** 193, 194, 196

Oxley, William, **Supp. XV:** 125

"O Yes" (Olsen), **Supp. XIII:** 294, 298, **299–300,** 301

"O Youth and Beauty!" (Cheever), **Retro. Supp. I:** 335

"Oysters" (Sexton), **Supp. II Part 2:** 692

"Ozark Odes" (Wright), **Supp. XV:** 346

Ozick, Cynthia, **Supp. V:** **257–274; Supp. VIII:** 141; **Supp. X:** 192; **Supp. XVII:** 42, 43, 49, 50

O-Zone (Theroux), **Supp. VIII:** 323–324

P

Pace, Patricia, **Supp. XI:** 245

Pacernik, Gary, **Supp. IX:** 287, 291

Pacific and Other Stories, The (Helprin), **Supp. XXV:** 84, 85

"Pacific Distances" (Didion), **Supp. IV Part 1:** 211

"Pacific Village" (M. F. K. Fisher), **Supp. XVII:** 83

"Pacifist War Song" (Lovecraft), **Supp. XXV:** 119

Pack, Robert, **Supp. IV Part 2:** 621

"Packed Dirt, Churchgoing, a Dying Cat, a Traded Cat" (Updike), **IV:** 219

Packer, Nancy Huddleston, **Supp. XXIII:** 290

"Packing Mother's Things" (C. Frost), **Supp. XV:** 97

Pack of Lies (Sorrentino), **Supp. XXI:** 236, 237

Paco's Story (Heinemann), **Supp. XXII:** 103, **109–114,** 115

Paddock, Joe, **Supp. XVI:** 36

Paddock, Nancy, **Supp. XVI:** 36

Padel, Ruth, **Supp. XII:** 107

Padgett, Ron, **Supp. XV:** 190; **Supp. XXIII:** 218, 221; **Supp. XXIV:** 33, 34, 35, 37, 38, 39, 41, 42, 43, 44

Padmore, Dorothy, **Supp. XXI:** 166

Padmore, George, **Supp. XXI:** 166

"Paesano with a Trowel" *(Time),* **Supp. XX:** **46**

Pafko at the Wall (DeLillo), **Supp. VI:** 4

"Paganini and the Powers of Darkness" (Skloot), **Supp. XX:** **201**

"Pagan Prayer" (Cullen), **Supp. IV Part 1:** 170

"Pagan Rabbi, The" (Ozick), **Supp. V:** 262, 264, 265; **Supp. XVII:** 43

Pagan Rabbi and Other Stories, The (Ozick), **Supp. V:** 260, 261, 263–265

Pagan Spain (Wright), **IV:** 478, 488, 495

Page, Geraldine, **Supp. XV:** 7

Page, Kirby, **III:** 297

Page, Myra, **Supp. XXIII:** 166

Page, Thomas Nelson, **II:** 174, 176, 194; **Supp. XIV:** 61; **Supp. XXII:** 193

Page, Walter Hines, **II:** 174, 175; **Supp. I Part 1:** 370

Page, William, **Supp. XVIII:** 2, 11

Pages from a Cold Island (Exley), **Supp. XXIII:** 97, **103–106,** 108

"Pages from Cold Point" (Bowles), **Supp. IV Part 1:** 85, 86, 87

Paid on Both Sides: A Charade (Auden), **Supp. II Part 1:** 6, 18–19

Paige, Satchel, **Supp. I Part 1:** 234

Paige, T. D. D., **III:** 475

"Pail, The" (R. Bly), **Supp. XXI:** 85

Pain, Joseph, **Supp. I Part 2:** 502

Paine, Albert Bigelow, **I:** 249
Paine, Thomas, **I:** 490; **II:** 117, 302; **III:** 17, 148, 219; **Retro. Supp. I:** 390; **Supp. I Part 1:** 231; **Supp. I Part 2:** 501–525; **Supp. XI:** 55
"Pain has an Element of Blank" (Dickinson), **Retro. Supp. I:** 44
"Painstaking Historian, The" (Skloot), **Supp. XX:** 205–206
"Paint and Powder" (Z. Fitzgerald), **Supp. IX:** 71
Painted Bird, The (Kosinski), **Supp. VII:** 215–217, 219–221, 222, 227
Painted Desert (F. Barthelme), **Supp. XI:** 28–29, 32
Painted Dresses (Hearon), **Supp. VIII:** 63
"Painted Head" (Ransom), **III:** 491, 494; **Supp. II Part 1:** 103, 314
Painted Turtle: Woman with Guitar (Major), **Supp. XXII:** 178–180, 182
Painted Word, The (Wolfe), **Supp. III Part 2:** 580–581, 584; **Supp. XV:** 143
Painter, Pamela, **Supp. XXIII:** 295
"Painter, The" (Ashbery), **Supp. III Part 1:** 5–6, 13
Painter Dreaming in the Scholar's House, The (Nemerov), **III:** 269
"Painters" (Rukeyser), **Supp. VI:** 281
"Painting a Mountain Stream" (Nemerov), **III:** 275
"Pair a Spurs" (Proulx), **Supp. VII:** 263–264
"Pair of Bright Blue Eyes, A" (Taylor), **Supp. V:** 321
"Pair of Glasses, A" (Gallagher), **Supp. XXIV:** 174, 176
"Pajamas" (Olds), **Supp. X:** 206
Pakula, Alan, **Supp. XIII:** 264
Palace at 4 A.M. (Giacometti), **Supp. VIII:** 169
Palahniuk, Chuck, **Supp. XXI:** 116
"Palantine, The" (Whittier), **Supp. I Part 2:** 694, 696
Palatella, John, **Retro. Supp. II:** 48; **Supp. XXIV:** 39
"Palatski Man, The"(Dybek), **Supp. XXIII:** 70
Pale Fire (Nabokov), **III:** 244, 246, 252, 263–265; **Retro. Supp. I:** 264, 265, 266, 270, 271, 272, 276, 278, 335; **Supp. V:** 251, 253; **Supp. XXII:** 260
"Pale Horse, Pale Rider" (Porter), **III:** 436, 437, 441–442, 445, 446, 449
Pale Horse, Pale Rider: Three Short Novels (Porter), **III:** 433, 436–442; **Supp. VIII:** 157
"Pale Pink Roast, The" (Paley), **Supp. VI:** 217
"Pale Rider" (B. Kelly), **Supp. XVII:** 132–133
Paley, Grace, **Supp. VI: 217–233; Supp. IX:** 212; **Supp. X:** 79, 164; **Supp. XII:** 309; **Supp. XXI:** 118; **Supp. XXII:** 172
Paley, William, **II:** 9
Palgrave, Francis Turner, **Retro. Supp. I:** 124; **Supp. XIV:** 340
Palgrave's Golden Treasury (Palgrave), **IV:** 405

Palimpsest (Doolittle), **Supp. I Part 1:** 259, 268, 269, 270–271
Palimpsest (Vidal), **Supp. X:** 186
"Palingenesis" (Longfellow), **II:** 498
Pal Joey (O'Hara), **III:** 361, 367–368
"Pal Joey" stories (O'Hara), **III:** 361
Pallbearers Envying the One Who Rides (Dobyns), **Supp. XIII:** 89
Palm, Edward Frederick, **Supp. XXII:** 103
"Palm, The" (Merwin), **Supp. III Part 1:** 355
Palmer, Charles, **II:** 111
Palmer, Elihu, **Supp. I Part 2:** 520
Palmer, George Herbert, **Supp. XIV:** 197
Palmer, Michael, **Supp. IV Part 2:** 421; **Supp. XVI:** 284; **Supp. XVII:** 240
Palmer, Samuel, **Supp. XV:** 81
Palmerston, Lord, **I:** 15
Palm-of-the-Hand-Stories (Kawabata), **Supp. XV:** 186
"Palm Wine" (McKnight), **Supp. XX:** 155
"Palo Alto: The Marshes" (Hass), **Supp. VI:** 100
Palpable God, A: Thirty Stories Translated from the Bible with an Essay on the Origins and Life of Narrative (Price), **Supp. VI:** 262, 267
Palubinskas, Helen, **Supp. X:** 292
Pamela (Richardson), **Supp. V:** 127; **Supp. XX: 236; Supp. XXII:** 120
Pamela's First Musical (Wasserstein), **Supp. XV:** 333
Panache de bouquets (Komunyakaa; Cadieux, trans.), **Supp. XIII:** 127
Pan-African movement, **Supp. II Part 1:** 172, 175
Pancake, Breece D'J, **Supp. XXIII:** 35
Pandaemonium (Epstein), **Supp. XII:** 161, 172–173
"Pandora" (Adams), **I:** 5
Pandora: New Tales of Vampires (Rice), **Supp. VII:** 295
Panek, LeRoy, **Supp. XIV:** 27
"Pangolin, The" (Moore), **III:** 210
Panic: A Play in Verse (MacLeish), **III:** 2, 20
Panic in Needle Park (film), **Supp. IV Part 1:** 198
Pankey, Eric, **Supp. XIX:** 44
Pantagruel (Rabelais), **II:** 112
"Pantaloon in Black" (Faulkner), **II:** 71
"Panther, The: A Bedtime Story"(P. Benedict), **Supp. XXIII:** 40
Panther and the Lash, The (Hughes), **Retro. Supp. I:** 204, 211; **Supp. I Part 1:** 342–344, 345–346
"Panthers, The" (Southern), **Supp. XI:** 295
"Panties and the Buddha" (Peacock), **Supp. XIX:** 199
"Pan *versus* Moses" (Ozick), **Supp. V:** 262
"Paolo Castelnuovo" (Everwine), **Supp. XV:** 83–84
"Papa and Mama Dance, The" (Sexton), **Supp. II Part 2:** 688
"Papago II"(Kenny), **Supp. XXIII:** 149–150

"Papago I"(Kenny), **Supp. XXIII:** 149–150
"Papa Who Wakes Up Tired in the Dark" (Cisneros), **Supp. VII:** 62
Pape, Greg, **Supp. V:** 180; **Supp. XIII:** 312; **Supp. XV:** 73
"Paper Covers Rock"(Thompson), **Supp. XXIII:** 291
Paper Doll (Parker), **Supp. XIX:** 184
"Paper Dolls Cut Out of a Newspaper" (Simic), **Supp. VIII:** 282
"Paper House, The" (Mailer), **III:** 42–43
Paper Lion (film, March), **Supp. XVI:** 242
Paper Lion: Confessions of a Last-String Quarterback (Plimpton), **Supp. XVI:** 242–243
Papernick, Jon, **Supp. XVII:** 50
Papers on Literature and Art (Fuller), **Supp. II Part 1:** 292, 299
Papini, Giovanni, **Supp. XVI:** 195; **Supp. XXII:** 159, 161, 163
Papp, Joseph, **Supp. IV Part 1:** 234; **Supp. XXI:** 145
"Paprika Johnson" (Barnes), **Supp. III Part 1:** 33
"Par" (Bausch), **Supp. VII:** 54
"Parable from a Christian" (Notley), **Supp. XXII:** 235
"Parable in the Later Novels of Henry James" (Ozick), **Supp. V:** 257
"Parable of the Gift" (Glück), **Supp. V:** 89
"Parable of the Hostages" (Glück), **Supp. V:** 89
"Parable of the King" (Glück), **Supp. V:** 89
Parable of the Sower (O. Butler), **Supp. XIII:** 66–67, 69
Parable of the Talents (O. Butler), **Supp. XIII:** 61,**Supp. XIII:** 66, 67–69
"Parable of the Trellis" (Glück), **Supp. V:** 89
Parachutes & Kisses (Jong), **Supp. V:** 115, 123, 125–126, 129
"Paradelle for Susan" (Collins), **Supp. XXI:** 58
"Parade of Painters" (Swenson), **Supp. IV Part 2:** 645
"Paradigm, The" (Tate), **IV:** 128
Paradise (Barthelme), **Supp. IV Part 1:** 52
"Paradise" (Caputo), **Supp. XIX:** 26–27
"Paradise" (Doty), **Supp. XI:** 123
Paradise, Piece by Piece (Peacock), **Supp. XIX:** 193, 194–195, 195–196, 201–202
Paradise Lost (Milton), **I:** 137; **II:** 168, 549; **IV:** 126; **Supp. XII:** 173, 297; **Supp. XV:** 181; **Supp. XX:** 280
Paradise Lost (Odets), **Supp. II Part 2:** 530, 531, 538–539, 550
Paradise Now (Living Theater), **Supp. XXIV:** 116
"Paradise of Bachelors and the Tartarus of Maids, The" (Melville), **III:** 91
Paradise of Bombs, The (Sanders), **Supp. XVI:** 265, 272–273
Paradise Poems (Stern), **Supp. IX:** 293–294, 295

Paradiso (Dante), **Supp. IX:** 50

"Paradoxes and Oxymorons" (Ashbery), **Supp. III Part 1:** 23–24

Paradox of Progressive Thought, The (Noble), **Supp. I Part 2:** 650

Paragon, The (Knowles), **Supp. XII:** 249

"Paragraphs" (Carruth), **Supp. XVI:** 52–53

"Parameters" (Dunn), **Supp. XI:** 154

"Para Mi Tataranieto El Astropionero" (Espaillat), **Supp. XXI:** 104

"Paraphrase" (Crane), **I:** 391–392, 393

"Pardon, The" (Wilbur), **Supp. III Part 2:** 544, 550

Paredes, Américo, **Supp. XIII:** 225; **Supp. XIX:** 97, 98, 100

Paredes, Raymund A., **Supp. XIII:** 320, 321

"Parentage" (Stafford), **Supp. XI:** 321, 322

Parentheses: An Autobiographical Journey (Neugeboren), **Supp. XVI:** 217, 218, 219, 221, 226

"Parents" (F. Barthelme), **Supp. XI:** 34

"Parents Taking Shape" (Karr), **Supp. XI:** 243

"Parents' Weekend: Camp Kenwood" (Kenyon), **Supp. VII:** 169

Pareto, Vilfredo, **II:** 577

Paretsky, Sara, **Supp. IV Part 2:** 462; **Supp. XIV:** 26; **Supp. XXV: 169–187**

Parini, Jay, **Supp. X:** 17; **Supp. XIX:** 120, 129; **Supp. XX: 243; Supp. XXI:** 192; **Supp. XXII:** 205; **Supp. XXV:** 251

"Paris" (Collins), **Supp. XXI:** 60

"Paris" (Stern), **Supp. IX:** 300

"Paris, 7 A.M." (Bishop), **Retro. Supp. II:** 41, 42; **Supp. I Part 1:** 85, 89

Paris, Bob, **Supp. XX: 264**

Paris, Paris (Shaw), **Supp. XIX:** 240

Paris France (Stein), **IV:** 45

Park, Ed, **Supp. XXII:** 255

Park, Robert, **IV:** 475

"Park Bench" (Hughes), **Supp. I Part 1:** 331–332

Park City (Beattie), **Supp. V:** 24, 35–36

"Park City" (Beattie), **Supp. V:** 35

Parker, Charlie, **Supp. I Part 1:** 59; **Supp. X:** 240, 242, 246; **Supp. XIII:** 129

Parker, Dorothy, **Retro. Supp. II:** 327; **Supp. IV Part 1:** 353; **Supp. IX:** 62, 114, **189–206; Supp. X:** 164; **Supp. XI:** 28; **Supp. XVIII:** 242, 246, 252

Parker, Emily, **Supp. XVIII:** 102

Parker, Idella, **Supp. X:** 232, 234–235

Parker, Joan, **Supp. XIX:** 187

Parker, Lonnae O'Neal, **Supp. XXIII:** 276

Parker, Muriel, **Supp. IX:** 232

Parker, Patricia, **Supp. XV:** 242

Parker, Robert B., **Supp. IV Part 1:** 135, 136; **Supp. XIX: 177–192**

Parker, Robert Dale, **Supp. XXIII:** 223, 228, 229

Parker, Theodore, **Supp. I Part 1:** 38; **Supp. I Part 2:** 518; **Supp. XXIV:** 70

Parker, Thomas, **Supp. I Part 1:** 102

"Parker's Back" (O'Connor), **III:** 348, 352, 358

"Parkersburg" (Halliday), **Supp. XIX:** 92

Parkes, Henry Bamford, **Supp. I Part 2:** 617

Park-Fuller, Linda, **Supp. XIII:** 297

Parkman, Francis, **II:** 278, 310, 312; **IV:** 179, 309; **Supp. I Part 2:** 420, 479, 481–482, 486, 487, 493, 498; **Supp. II Part 2: 589–616**

Parkman Reader, The (Morison, ed.), **Supp. I Part 2:** 494

Parks, Gordon, Sr., **Supp. XI:** 17

Parks, Larry, **Supp. I Part 1:** 295

Parks, Rosa, **Supp. I Part 1:** 342

"Park Street Cemetery, The" (Lowell), **II:** 537, 538

Par le Détroit (cantata) (Bowles), **Supp. IV Part 1:** 82

Parliament of Fowls, The (Chaucer), **III:** 492

Parmenides (Plato), **II:** 10

Parnassus (Emerson), **II:** 8, 18

Parnell, Charles Stewart, **II:** 129, 137

Parole (film), **Supp. XIII:** 166

Parole Fixer (film), **Supp. XIII:** 170

Parrington, Vernon Louis, **I:** 254, 517, 561; **III:** 335, 606; **IV:** 173; **Supp. I Part 2:** 484, 640

Parrish, Dillwyn, **Supp. XVII:** 83–84, 90

Parrish, Robert, **Supp. XI:** 307

"Parrot, The" (Merrill), **Supp. III Part 1:** 320

"Parsley" (Dove), **Supp. IV Part 1:** 245, 246

Parson, Annie, **Supp. I Part 2:** 655

Parsons, Elsie Clews, **I:** 231, 235

Parsons, Ian, **Supp. IX:** 95

Parsons, Louella, **Supp. XII:** 173

Parsons, Talcott, **Supp. I Part 2:** 648

Parsons, Theophilus, **II:** 396, 504; **Retro. Supp. II:** 134; **Supp. I Part 1:** 155

"Parthian Shot, The" (Hammett), **Supp. IV Part 1:** 343

Partial Glossary, A (Bronk), **Supp. XXI:** 26

Partial Payments: Essays on Writers and Their Lives (Epstein), **Supp. XIV:** 111

Partial Portraits (James), **II:** 336

"Partial Relief" (Halliday), **Supp. XIX:** 91

Partial Truth (Nelson), **Supp. XVIII:** **175–176,** 178

"Particulars" (Pickering), **Supp. XXI:** 197

Parties (Van Vechten), **Supp. II Part 2:** 739, 747–749

"Parting" (Kunitz), **Supp. III Part 1:** 263

"Parting Gift" (Wylie), **Supp. I Part 2:** 714

"Parting Glass, The" (Freneau), **Supp. II Part 1:** 273

"Partings" (Hogan), **Supp. IV Part 1:** 413

Partington, Blanche, **I:** 199

Partisans (Matthiessen), **Supp. V:** 201

"Partner, The" (Roethke), **III:** 541–542

Partners, The (Auchincloss), **Supp. IV Part 1:** 31, 34

Partners in Crime: A Rafe Buenrostro Mystery (Hinojosa), **Supp. XIX: 107–108**

"Part of a Letter" (Wilbur), **Supp. III Part 2:** 551

Part of a Long Story: Eugene O'Neill as a Young Man in Love (Boulton), **Supp. XXII:** 18, 21, 27–30

Part of Speech, A (Brodsky), **Supp. VIII:** 22

"Part of the Bee's Body Embedded in the Flesh, The" (C. Frost), **Supp. XV:** 105, 107

"Part of the Story" (Dobyns), **Supp. XIII:** 79

Part of Vermont, A (Taggard), **Supp. XXII:** 284

Parton, Sara, **Retro. Supp. I:** 246

Partridge, Jeffrey F., **Supp. XV:** 219

Partridge, John, **II:** 110, 111

"Parts of a Journal" (Gordon), **Supp. IV Part 1:** 310

Parts of a World (Stevens), **Retro. Supp. I: 305–306,** 307, 309, 313

"Parturition" (Loy), **Supp. XXII:** 159, 160–161

"Party, The" (Dunbar), **Supp. II Part 1:** 198, 205–206

"Party, The" (Taylor), **Supp. V:** 315

Party at Jack's, The (Wolfe), **IV:** 451–452, 469

"Party Down at the Square, A" (Ellison), **Retro. Supp. II:** 124

Party of Five (television series), **Supp. XIX:** 222

Pascal, Blaise, **II:** 8, 159; **III:** 292, 301, 304, 428; **Retro. Supp. I:** 326, 330

"Paskudnyak" (Pilcer), **Supp. XVII:** 50

"Pass, The" (Neugeboren), **Supp. XVI:** 225

"Passage" (Crane), **I:** 391

"Passage in the Life of Mr. John Oakhurst, A" (Harte), **Supp. II Part 1:** 353–354

Passage in the Night, A (Asch), **Supp. XXIII:** 7

"Passages" (Duncan), **Supp. XVI:** 287

"Passages from a Relinquished Work" (Hawthorne), **Retro. Supp. I:** 150

Passages toward the Dark (McGrath), **Supp. X:** 126, 127

"Passage to India" (Whitman), **IV:** 348

Passage to India, A (Forster), **II:** 600; **Supp. XVIII:** 143

Passaro, Vince, **Supp. X:** 167, 302, 309, 310

"Passenger, The" (Brockmeier), **Supp. XXII:** 52

"Passenger Pigeons" (Jeffers), **Supp. II Part 2:** 437

Passin, Herbert, **Supp. XIII:** 337

Passing (Larsen), **Supp. XVIII:** 119, 123, **127–130**

"Passing Beauty" (C. Frost), **Supp. XV:** 97

"Passing of Grandison, The" (Chesnutt), **Supp. XIV:** 62, **66–69**

"Passing of Sister Barsett, The" (Jewett), **Retro. Supp. II:** 138–139, 143

"Passing Show, The" (Bierce), **I:** 208

"Passing Through" (Kunitz), **Supp. III Part 1:** 265

"Passion, The" (Barnes), **Supp. III Part 1:** 36

"Passion, The" (Merwin), **Supp. III Part 1:** 343

Passionate, Accurate Story, The: Making Your Heart's Truth into Literature (C. Bly), **Supp. XVI: 41–42**

Passionate Pilgrim, A (James), **II:** 324; **Retro. Supp. I:** 219

"Passionate Pilgrim, A" (James), **II:** 322, 323–324; **Retro. Supp. I:** 218

Passion Play (Kosinski), **Supp. VII:** 215, 225–226

Passions of Uxport, The (Kumin), **Supp. IV Part 2:** 444

Pass It On (Hadas), **Supp. XXIII: 115,** 123

"Pass It On, I"(Hadas), **Supp. XXIII:** 115

"Pass It On, II"(Hadas), **Supp. XXIII:** 115

"Passive Resistance" (McKay), **Supp. X:** 133

Passport to the War (Kunitz), **Supp. III Part 1:** 261–264

Passwords (Stafford), **Supp. XI: 329–330**

"Past, The" (Bryant), **Supp. I Part 1:** 157, 170

Past, The (Kinnell), **Supp. III Part 1:** 235, 253–254

"Past, The" (Kinnell), **Supp. III Part 1:** 254

Past and Present (Carlyle), **Supp. I Part 2:** 410

Pasternak, Boris, **II:** 544; **Supp. XXIII:** 209

"Pastiches et Pistaches" (Van Vechten), **Supp. II Part 2:** 732

"Past Is the Present, The" (Moore), **III:** 199–200

"Pastoral" (Carver), **Supp. III Part 1:** 137, 146

"Pastoral" (Dove), **Supp. IV Part 1:** 249

"Pastoral" (Trethewey), **Supp. XXI:** 257

"Pastoral Hat, A" (Stevens), **IV:** 91

Pastoralia (Saunders), **Supp. XIX: 227–229**

"Pastoralia" (Saunders), **Supp. XIX:** 227, 229

"Pastor Dowe at Tacaté" (Bowles), **Supp. IV Part 1:** 87

Pastorela (ballet) (Kirstein), **Supp. IV Part 1:** 83

Pastorius, Francis Daniel, **Supp. I Part 2:** 700

"Pasture Poems" (Kumin), **Supp. IV Part 2:** 446

Pastures of Heaven, The (Steinbeck), **IV:** 51

Patch, Jerry, **Supp. XVIII:** 38

Patchen, Kenneth, **Supp. III Part 2:** 625

Patchett, Ann, **Supp. XII: 307–324**

Patchwork Planet (Lethem), **Supp. XVIII:** 150

Pater, Walter, **I:** 51, 272, 476; **II:** 27, 338; **III:** 604; **IV:** 74; **Retro. Supp. I:** 56, 79; **Retro. Supp. II:** 326; **Supp. I Part 2:** 552; **Supp. IX:** 66

Paterna (Mather), **Supp. II Part 2:** 451

Paternostro, Silvana, **Supp. XXV:** 55, 58

"Paterson" (Ginsberg), **Supp. II Part 1:** 314–315, 321, 329

Paterson (W. C. Williams), **I:** 62, 446; **IV:** 418–423; **Retro. Supp. I:** 209, 284, 413, 419, 421, **424–428,** 428, 429, 430; **Retro. Supp. II:** 321, 328; **Supp. II Part 2:** 557, 564, 625; **Supp. VIII:** 275, 305; **Supp. XIV:** 96; **Supp. XV:** 264, 349

Paterson, Book Five (W. C. Williams), **IV:** 422–423

Paterson, Book One (W. C. Williams), **IV:** 421–422

Paterson, Isabel, **Supp. IV Part 2:** 524

Paterson, Part Three (W. C. Williams), **IV:** 420–421

Pat Garrett and Billy the Kid (film, Peckinpah), **Supp. XVIII:** 27

"Path, The" (Bryant), **Supp. I Part 1:** 169

Pathfinder, The (Cooper), **I:** 349, 350, 355

Pat Hobby Stories, The (Fitzgerald), **Retro. Supp. I:** 114

"Pathos of Low Life, The" (Hapgood), **Supp. XVII:** 103

"Patience of a Saint, The" (Humphrey), **Supp. IX:** 106

Patience Sparhawk and Her Times (Atherton), **Supp. XXIV:** 18, 20, 22, 27

Patient 002 (Skloot), **Supp. XX: 194, 208**

Patinkin, Mandy, **Supp. IV Part 1:** 236

Paton, Alan, **Supp. VIII:** 126

Patria Mia (Pound), **III:** 460–461; **Retro. Supp. I:** 284

"Patria Mia" (Pound), **Retro. Supp. I:** 284

"Patriarch, The" (Alvares), **Supp. V:** 11

"Patrick Kavanagh at First Light" (Skloot), **Supp. XX: 204**

Patrimony: A True Story (P. Roth), **Retro. Supp. II:** 279, 280, 291; **Supp. III Part 2:** 427

Patriot, The (Buck), **Supp. II Part 1:** 122–123

Patriot, The (Connell), **Supp. XIV:** 94–95

Patriotic Gore: Studies in the Literature of the American Civil War (Wilson), **III:** 588; **IV:** 430, 438, 443, 445–445, 446; **Supp. VIII:** 100

"Patriotic Thing, The" (Ryan as Quin), **Supp. XVIII:** 229

"Patriots, The/Los Patriotas" (Kingsolver), **Supp. VII:** 209

Patron Saint of Liars, The (Patchett), **Supp. XII:** 307, 310, **311–314,** 317

Pattee, Fred L., **II:** 456

Patten, Gilbert, **II:** 423

Patten, Simon, **Supp. I Part 2:** 640

Patternmaster (O. Butler), **Supp. XIII:** 61, 62, 63

Patternmaster Series (O. Butler), **Supp. XIII: 62–63**

Pattern Recognition (W. Gibson), **Supp. XVI:** 124, **130–131**

"Patterns" (Lowell), **II:** 524

Patterson, Floyd, **III:** 38

Patterson, Margot, **Supp. XXII:** 85

Patterson, William M., **Supp. I Part 1:** 265

Patton, General George, **III:** 575; **Supp. I Part 2:** 664

"Patty-Cake, Patty-Cake...A Memoir" (Apple), **Supp. XVII:** 7

Paul, Saint, **I:** 365; **II:** 15, 494; **IV:** 122, 154, 164, 335; **Retro. Supp. I:** 247; **Supp. I Part 1:** 188

Paul, Sherman, **I:** 244; **IV:** 179

"Paula Becker to Clara Westhoff" (Rich), **Supp. I Part 2:** 573–574

"Paula Gunn Allen" (Ruppert), **Supp. IV Part 1:** 321

Paul Ardenheim, the Monk of Wissahikon (Lippard), **Supp. XXIII:** 178, 186, 187, 189, 190

Paul Bowles: Romantic Savage (Caponi), **Supp. IV Part 1:** 95

Paulding, James Kirke, **I:** 344; **II:** 298, 299, 303; **Supp. I Part 1:** 157

Pauley, Jane, **Supp. XXI:** 39

Paul Jones (Hapgood), **Supp. XVII:** 100–101

Paul Marchand, F.M.C. (Chesnutt), **Supp. XIV:** 76

"Paul Monette: The Brink of Summer's End" (film), **Supp. X:** 152

"Paul Revere" (Longfellow), **II:** 489, 501

"Paul Revere's Ride" (Longfellow), **Retro. Supp. II:** 163

"Paul's Case" (Cather), **I:** 314–315; **Retro. Supp. I:** 3, 5

Paulsen, Friedrich, **III:** 600

"Pauper Witch of Grafton, The" (Frost), **Retro. Supp. II:** 42

"Pause by the Water, A" (Merwin), **Supp. III Part 1:** 354

"Pavane for the Nursery, A" (W. J. Smith), **Supp. XIII:** 335

"Pavement, The" (Olson), **Supp. II Part 2:** 571

Pavese, Cesare, **Supp. XXI:** 132

Pavic, Milorad, **Supp. XXII:** 265

Pavilion of Women (Buck), **Supp. II Part 1:** 125–126

"Pawnbroker, The" (Kumin), **Supp. IV Part 2:** 442, 443–444, 451

Pawnbroker, The (Wallant), **Supp. XVI:** 220

"Paying Dues" (Bass), **Supp. XVI:** 16

Payne, Daniel, **Supp. V:** 202

Payne, John Howard, **II:** 309

Payne Tom, **Supp. XXII:** 266

Paz, Octavio, **Supp. III Part 2:** 630; **Supp. VIII:** 272; **Supp. XI:** 191; **Supp. XIII:** 223

P. D. Kimerakov (Epstein), **Supp. XII:** 160, **162**

Peabody, Elizabeth, **Retro. Supp. I:** 225

Peabody, Elizabeth Palmer, **Retro. Supp. I:** 155–156; **Supp. XXIV:** 75; **Supp. XXV:** 242, 246, 250

Peabody, Francis G., **III:** 293; **Supp. I Part 1:** 5

Peabody, Josephine Preston, **III:** 507; **Supp. XX:** 115

Peaceable Kingdom, The (Prose), **Supp. XVI:** 256–257

Peace and Bread in Time of War (Addams), **Supp. I Part 1:** 21, 22–23

"Peace Between Black and White in the United States" (Locke), **Supp. XIV:** 205

Peace Breaks Out (Knowles), **Supp. XII:** 249

"Peacemaker"(Kenny), **Supp. XXIII:** 151

"Peace March, The" (Simpson), **Supp. IX:** 279

"Peace of Cities, The" (Wilbur), **Supp. III Part 2:** 545

"Peace of Mind" (Boyle), **Supp. XX:** 19

"Peaches—Six in a Tin Box, Sarajevo" (Cisneros), **Supp. VII:** 67

Peachtree Road (Siddons), **Supp. XXII:** 239, 240, 242, **246–247, 248–251,** 252

Peaco, Ed, **Supp. XXIV:** 221

Peacock, Doug, **Supp. VIII:** 38; **Supp. XIII:** 12

Peacock, Gibson, **Supp. I Part 1:** 360

Peacock, Molly, **Supp. XVII:** 74; **Supp. XIX:** 193–207

"Peacock, The" (Merrill), **Supp. III Part 1:** 320

"Peacock, The" (Mosher), **Supp. XXII:** 211

Peacock, Thomas Love, **Supp. I Part 1:** 307; **Supp. VIII:** 125

"Peacock Room, The" (Hayden), **Supp. II Part 1:** 374–375

"Peacocks of Avignon, The" (Swados), **Supp. XIX:** 263

Pearce, Richard, **Supp. IX:** 254

Pearce, Roy Harvey, **II:** 244; **Supp. I Part 1:** 111, 114; **Supp. I Part 2:** 475

"Pearl" (Kooser), **Supp. XIX:** 127–128

Pearl, The (Steinbeck), **IV:** 51, 62–63

Pearlman, Daniel, **III:** 479

Pearlman, Mickey, **Supp. XIII:** 293, 306

Pearl of Orr's Island, The (Stowe), **Supp. I Part 2:** 592–593, 595

"Pearls" (A. Finch), **Supp. XVII:** 72

Pears, Peter, **II:** 586; **Supp. IV Part 1:** 84

Pearson, Drew, **Supp. XIV:** 126

Pearson, Norman Holmes, **Supp. I Part 1:** 259, 260, 273

"Pear Tree" (C. Frost), **Supp. XV:** 105

"Peasants' Way O' Thinkin' " (McKay), **Supp. X:** 133

Pease, Donald E., **Supp. IV Part 2:** 687

"Peboan and Seegwun (Winter and Spring): A Chippewa Allegory"(J. Schoolcraft), **Supp. XXIII:** 235

Peck, Gregory, **Supp. VIII:** 128, 129; **Supp. XII:** 160, 173

Peckinpah, Sam, **Supp. XI:** 306; **Supp. XVIII:** 27

"Peck of Gold, A" (Frost), **II:** 155

Peculiar Treasures: A Biblical Who's Who (Buechner), **Supp. XII:** 53

Pedagogy of the Oppressed (Freire), **Supp. XXV:** 133

"Pedal Point" (Francis), **Supp. IX:** 87

Pedersen, Inge, **Supp. XVIII:** 179

"Pedersen Kid, The" (Gass), **Supp. VI:** 83

"Pedigree, The" (Creeley), **Supp. IV Part 1:** 150

Peebles, Melvin Van, **Supp. XI:** 17; **Supp. XVI:** 144

"Peed Onk" (Moore). *See* "People Like That Are the Only People Here: Canonical Babbling in Peed Onk" (Moore)

"Peeler, The" (O'Connor), **Retro. Supp. II:** 225

Peich, Michael, **Supp. XV:** 113, 117; **Supp. XXV:** 222

Peikoff, Leonard, **Supp. IV Part 2:** 520, 526, 529

Peirce, Charles Sanders, **II:** 20, 352–353; **III:** 599; **Supp. I Part 2:** 640; **Supp. III Part 2:** 626

Pelagius, **III:** 295

"Pelican, The" (Merrill), **Supp. III Part 1:** 320

"Pelican, The" (Wharton), **IV:** 310; **Retro. Supp. I:** 364

Pellacchia, Michael, **Supp. XIII:** 16

Pelley, Denise, **Supp. XIX:** 205

Pelonero, Michael, **Supp. XXIII:** 125

Peltier, Leonard, **Supp. V:** 212

"Penance"(Dybek), **Supp. XXIII:** 69

"Pen and Paper and a Breath of Air" (Oliver), **Supp. VII:** 245

Pence, Amy, **Supp. XV:** 211, 223

"Pencil, The" (Chandler), **Supp. IV Part 1:** 135

Pencillings by the Way (Willis), **II:** 313; **Supp. XVIII:** 12

"Pencils" (Sandburg), **III:** 592

Pendleton, Devon, **Supp. XVIII:** 151

"Pendulum" (Bradbury and Hasse), **Supp. IV Part 1:** 102

"Penelope's Song" (Glück), **Supp. V:** 89

Penelope: The Story of the Half-Scalped Woman (Schott), **Supp. XXIII:** 240, **244–245**

Penhally (Gordon), **II:** 197, 199, 201–203, 204

"Penis" (McClatchy), **Supp. XII:** 266–267

Penitent, The (di Donato), **Supp. XX: 44, 45**

Penitent, The (Singer), **Retro. Supp. II: 309–310,** 313

Penland, Nell Bates, **Supp. XXII:** 188

Penn, Robert, **I:** 489

Penn, Sean, **Supp. XI:** 107

Penn, Thomas, **II:** 118

Penn, William, **Supp. I Part 2:** 683

Penna, Sandro, **Supp. XIX:** 34

Pennebaker, D. A., **Supp. XVIII:** 19, 26

"Pennsylvania Pilgrim, The" (Whittier), **Supp. I Part 2:** 700

"Pennsylvania Planter, The" (Freneau), **Supp. II Part 1:** 268

Penny, Rob, **Supp. VIII:** 330

"Penny, The" (D. West), **Supp. XVIII:** 283–284

Penrod (Tarkington), **III:** 223

"Penseroso, Il" (Milton), **Supp. XIV:** 8

Pensieri (Leopardi; Di Piero, trans.), **Supp. XIX:** 34

"Pensive Hours"(J. Schoolcraft), **Supp. XXIII:** 230–231

Pentagon of Power, The (Mumford), **Supp. II Part 2:** 498

Pentimento (Hellman), **Supp. I Part 1:** 280, 292–294, 296; **Supp. IV Part 1:** 12; **Supp. VIII:** 243

"Peonies at Dusk" (Kenyon), **Supp. VII:** 171

People, The (Glaspell), **Supp. III Part 1:** 179

People, Yes, The (Sandburg), **III:** 575, 589, 590, 591

"PEOPLE BURNING, THE" (Baraka), **Supp. II Part 1:** 49

"People in Hell Just Want a Drink of Water" (Proulx), **Supp. VII:** 263

"People Like That Are the Only People Here: Canonical Babbling in Peed Onk" (Moore), **Supp. X:** 168, **178–179**

People Live Here: Selected Poems 1949–1983 (Simpson), **Supp. IX:** 269, 277

"People Next Door, The" (Simpson), **Supp. IX:** 279

People of the Abyss, The (London), **II:** 465–466

"People on the Roller Coaster, The" (Hardwick), **Supp. III Part 1:** 196

People Shall Continue, The (Ortiz), **Supp. IV Part 2:** 510

People's History of the United States, A (Zinn), **Supp. XXIV:** 87

"People's Surroundings" (Moore), **III:** 201, 202, 203

"People v. Abe Lathan, Colored, The" (Caldwell), **I:** 309

"Peppermint Lounge Revisited, The" (Wolfe), **Supp. III Part 2:** 571

Peppis, Paul, **Supp. XXII:** 160

Pepys, Samuel, **Supp. I Part 2:** 653

"Perchance to Dream" (Franzen), **Supp. XX: 90, 93**

Perchance to Dream: Robert B. Parker's Sequel to Raymond Chandler's "Big Sleep" (Parker), **Supp. XIX:** 189

"Perch'io non spero di tornar giammai" (Cavalcanti), **Supp. III Part 2:** 623

Perch of the Devil (Atherton), **Supp. XXIV:** 24, 29

Percy, Thomas, **Supp. XIV:** 2

Percy, Walker, **Supp. III Part 1: 383–400; Supp. IV Part 1:** 297; **Supp. V:** 334; **Supp. X:** 42; **Supp. XIV:** 21; **Supp. XIX:** 209

Percy, William, **Supp. V:** 334

Percy, William Alexander, **Retro. Supp. I:** 341; **Supp. XXII:** 193

Peregrin, Tony, **Supp. XV:** 69

"Peregrine" (Wylie), **Supp. I Part 2:** 712–713, 714

Perelman, Bob, **Supp. XII:** 23

Perelman, S. J., **IV:** 286; **Retro. Supp. I:** 342; **Retro. Supp. II:** 321, 322, 325, 326, 327, 336; **Supp. IV Part 1:** 353; **Supp. XI:** 66

Perera, Victor, **Supp. XXV:** 50, 52

Perestroika (Kushner), **Supp. IX:** 141, 142, 145

Péret, Benjamin, **Supp. VIII:** 272

Peretz, Isaac Leib, **IV:** 1, 3; **Retro. Supp. II:** 299; **Supp. XXIII:** 4, 7, 8–9

Pérez Galdós, Benito, **II:** 275
Perfect Analysis Given by a Parrot, A (T. Williams), **IV:** 395
"Perfect Couple, The" (Nelson), **Supp. XVIII:** 173
"Perfect Day for Bananafish, A" (Salinger), **III:** 563–564, 571
Perfect Fiction, The (Sorrentino), **Supp. XXI:** 228
Perfect Ganesh, A (McNally), **Supp. XIII: 202–203,** 208, 209
"Perfect Gerbil, The: Reading Barthelme's 'The School' " (Saunders), **Supp. XIX:** 235
"Perfection" (Helprin), **Supp. XXV:** 80
"Perfect Knight, The" (Chandler), **Supp. IV Part 1:** 120
Perfect Mother, The (Schott), **Supp. XXIII: 241–242**
Perfect Party, The (Gurney), **Supp. V:** 100, 105, 106–107
"Perfect Things" (F. Barthelme), **Supp. XI:** 30, 33–34
"Performance, The" (Dickey), **Supp. IV Part 1:** 178–179, 181
"Perfume" (Mora), **Supp. XIII:** 218
"Perhaps the World Ends Here" (Harjo), **Supp. XII:** 228, 231
Perhaps Women (Anderson), **I:** 114
Pericles (Shakespeare), **I:** 585; **Supp. III Part 2:** 624, 627, 629
"Period Metaphor" (Bronk), **Supp. XXI:** 33
Period of Adjustment (T. Williams), **IV:** 382, 386, 387, 388, 389, 390, 392, 393, 394, 397
"Period Pieces from the Mid-Thirties" (Agee), **I:** 28
"Periphery" (Ammons), **Supp. VII:** 28
Perkins, David, **Supp. I Part 2:** 459, 475; **Supp. XV:** 185
Perkins, Maxwell, **I:** 252, 289, 290; **II:** 87, 93, 95, 252; **IV:** 452, 455, 457, 458, 461, 462, 463, 469; **Retro. Supp. I:** 101, 105, 108, 109, 110, 113, 114, 178; **Supp. IX:** 57, 58, 60, 232; **Supp. X:** 219, 224, 225, 229, 230, 233; **Supp. XI:** 218, 227
Perlès, Alfred, **III:** 177, 183, 187, 189
Perloff, Marjorie, **Supp. I Part 2:** 539, 542; **Supp. IV Part 1:** 68; **Supp. IV Part 2:** 420, 424, 432; **Supp. XXII:** 161, 271; **Supp. XXIII:** 210, 220
Permanence and Change (Burke), **I:** 274
Permanent Errors (Price), **Supp. VI:** 261
"Permanent Traits of the English National Genius" (Emerson), **II:** 18
Permit Me Voyage (Agee), **I:** 25, 27
"Perosa Canavese" (Everwine), **Supp. XV:** 84
Perrault, Charles, **IV:** 266; **Supp. I Part 2:** 622
Perrin, Noel, **Supp. XVI:** 34; **Supp. XXII:** 205, 207, 211, 218
Perrins, Carol. *See* Frost, Carol
Perry, Anne, **Supp. V:** 335
Perry, Bliss, **I:** 243
Perry, Donna, **Supp. IV Part 1:** 322, 327, 335
Perry, Edgar A., **III:** 410

Perry, Keith Ronald, **Supp. XXI:** 42
Perry, Lincoln, **Supp. V:** 24, 33
Perry, Matthew C., **Supp. I Part 2:** 494–495
Perry, Patsy Brewington, **Supp. I Part 1:** 66
Perry, Phyllis Alesia, **Supp. XVIII:** 96
Perry, Ralph Barton, **I:** 224; **II:** 356, 362, 364; **Supp. XIV:** 197
Perry, Dr. William, **II:** 395, 396
Perse, St.-John, **III:** 12, 13, 14, 17; **Supp. III Part 1:** 14; **Supp. IV Part 1:** 82; **Supp. XIII:** 344; **Supp. XV:** 178
"Persephone in Hell" (Dove), **Supp. IV Part 1:** 250, 251
"Persephone"(Le Sueur), **Supp. XXIII:** 162, 165, **170–171**
"Persephone to Psyche" (Stallings), **Supp. XXV:** 234
"Persephone Writes a Letter to Her Mother" (Stallings), **Supp. XXV:** 228
"Persimmons" (L.-Y. Lee), **Supp. XV:** 211, 213
"Persistence of Desire, The" (Updike), **IV:** 222–223, 228
"Persistence of Poetry, The" (Bynner), **Supp. XV:** 49
"Persistences" (Hecht), **Supp. X: 68–69**
Person, Place, and Thing (Shapiro), **Supp. II Part 2:** 702, 705
Personae of Ezra Pound (Pound), **III:** 458
Personae: The Collected Poems (Pound), **Retro. Supp. I:** 285, 286; **Supp. I Part 1:** 255; **Supp. XVII:** 32
"Personal" (Stern), **Supp. IX:** 299
"Personal and Occasional Pieces" (Welty), **Retro. Supp. I:** 355
"Personal and the Individual, The" (L. Michaels), **Supp. XVI:** 201
Personal Injuries (Turow), **Supp. XVII: 219–220,** 221, 223
"Personalities" (column, Briggs), **Supp. XVIII:** 15
Personal Narrative (Edwards), **I:** 545, 552, 553, 561, 562; **Supp. I Part 2:** 700
"Personal Poem #9" (Berrigan), **Supp. XXIV:** 34, 35
"Personal Poem"(O'Hara), **Supp. XXIII:** 219
Personal Recollection of Joan of Arc (Twain), **IV:** 208
Personals (Bontemps), **Supp. XXII:** 7, 8
"Personals" (Didion), **Supp. IV Part 1:** 200
"Personism" (O'Hara), **Supp. XV:** 181
"Personism: A Manifesto" (O'Hara), **Supp. XXIII:** 212, 215; **Supp. XXIV:** 43
Persons and Places (Santayana), **III:** 615
Persons in Hiding (film), **Supp. XIII:** 170
Persons in Hiding (Hoover), **Supp. XIII:** 170
Person Sitting in Darkness, A (Twain), **IV:** 208
"Persons Who Interest Us" (*Harper's Bazaar*), **Supp. XXV:** 277–278
"Perspective" (Francis), **Supp. IX:** 78

"Perspective: Anniversary D-Day" (Karr), **Supp. XI:** 241
Perspectives by Incongruity (Burke), **I:** 284–285
"Perspectives: Is It Out of Control?" (Gleason), **Supp. IX:** 16
Perspectives on Cormac McCarthy (Arnold and Luce, eds.), **Supp. VIII:** 189
Persse, Dudley Jocelyn, **Supp. XX: 232**
Pertes et Fracas (McCoy), **Supp. XIII:** 175
"Peruvian Child" (Mora), **Supp. XIII:** 218
Peseroff, Joyce, **Supp. IV Part 1:** 71
Pesetsky, Bette, **Supp. XXIV:** 173
"Pestilence" (Nelson), **Supp. XVIII:** 186
Pest Maiden, The (Schott), **Supp. XXIII: 245–246**
"Peter" (Cather), **Retro. Supp. I:** 4
"Peter" (Moore), **III:** 210, 212
Peter, Saint, **III:** 341, 346; **IV:** 86, 294
Peterkin, Julia, **Supp. I Part 1:** 328; **Supp. XXII:** 12, 189
"Peter Klaus" (German tale), **II:** 306
Peter Pan (Barrie), **Supp. XV:** 319
"Peter Parley" works (Goodrich), **Supp. I Part 1:** 38
"Peter Pendulum" (Poe), **III:** 425
"Peter Quince at the Clavier" (Stevens), **IV:** 81, 82
Peter Rabbit tales, **Retro. Supp. I:** 335
Peters, Cora, **Supp. I Part 2:** 468
Peters, Jacqueline, **Supp. XII:** 225
Peters, Margot, **Supp. VIII:** 252
Peters, Robert, **Supp. XIII:** 114
Peters, S. H. (pseudonym). *See* Henry, O.
Peters, Timothy, **Supp. XI:** 39
"Peter's Avocado" (Rodriguez), **Supp. XIV:** 308–309
Petersen, David, **Supp. XIII:** 2
Petersen, Donald, **Supp. V:** 180; **Supp. XV:** 74, 92
Peterson, Dorothy, **Supp. XVIII:** 131, 132
Peterson, George, **Supp. XXII:** 250
Peterson, Houston, **I:** 60
Peterson, Roger Tory, **Supp. V:** 202
Peterson, Virgilia, **Supp. IV Part 1:** 30
Peter Whiffle: His Life and Works (Van Vechten), **Supp. II Part 2:** 728–729, 731, 735, 738–741, 749
"Petey and Yotsee and Mario" (H. Roth), **Supp. IX:** 234
"Petition, A" (Winters), **Supp. II Part 2:** 785
"Pet Milk"(Dybek), **Supp. XXIII:** 74
"'Pet Negro' System, The" (Hurston), **Supp. VI:** 159
"Petra and Its Surroundings" (Frost), **Retro. Supp. I:** 124
Petrarch, **I:** 176; **II:** 590; **III:** 4
"Petrarch, Shakespeare, and the Blues" (C. Frost), **Supp. XV:** 92, 104, 105
"Petrified Man" (Welty), **IV:** 262; **Retro. Supp. I:** 345, 351
"Petrified Man, The" (Twain), **IV:** 195
"Petrified Woman, The" (Gordon), **II:** 199
Petronius, **III:** 174, 179

Petry, Ann, **Supp. VIII:** 214; **Supp. XI:** 6, 85; **Supp. XVIII:** 286

Pet Sematary (King), **Supp. V:** 138, 143, 152

Pettengill, Claire C., **Supp. XXV:** 40

Pettengill, Richard, **Supp. VIII:** 341, 345, 348

Pettingell, Phoebe, **Supp. XV:** 251, 256–257, 262

Pettis, Joyce, **Supp. XI:** 276, 277, 278, 281

Pettis, Olive G., **Supp. XXIII:** 189

Petty, Jill, **Supp. XXI:** 244, 248, 249, 250

Pfaelzer, Jean, **Supp. XVI:** 88, 90

Pfaff, Timothy, **Supp. V:** 166

Pfeil, Fred, **Supp. XIV:** 36

Pfister, Karin, **IV:** 467, 475

Phaedo (Plato), **II:** 10

Phaedra (Lowell and Barzun, trans.), **II:** 543–544

"Phantasia for Elvira Shatayev" (Rich), **Supp. I Part 2:** 570

Phantasms of War (Lowell), **II:** 512

"Phantom of the Movie Palace, The" (Coover), **Supp. V:** 50–51

Phantom Ship, The (Marryat), **Supp. XVII:** 55

"Pharaoh, The" (Kenyon), **Supp. VII:** 172

"Pharmacy"(Strout), **Supp. XXIII:** 281

Pharr, Mary, **Supp. V:** 147

"Phases" (E. Stoddard), **Supp. XV:** 273

"Phases" (Stevens), **Retro. Supp. I:** 299

Phases of an Inferior Planet (Glasgow), **II:** 174–175

"Pheasant, The" (Carver), **Supp. III Part 1:** 146

Phelan, Alice, **Supp. XXII:** 193

Pheloung, Grant, **Supp. XI:** 39

Phelps, Donald, **Supp. XXIII:** 174

Phelps, Elizabeth Stuart, **Retro. Supp. II:** 146; **Supp. XIII:** 141; **Supp. XVI:** 80

Phelps, Teresa Godwin, **Supp. VIII:** 128

Phelps, William Lyon "Billy", **Supp. XX:** **68, 75, 220**

"Phenomena and Laws of Race Contacts, The" (Locke), **Supp. XIV:** 210

"Phenomenology of Anger, The" (Rich), **Supp. I Part 2:** 562–563, 571

Phenomenology of Moral Experience, The (Mandelbaum), **I:** 61

"Phenomenology of *On Moral Fiction*" (Johnson), **Supp. VI:** 188

Phidias, **Supp. I Part 2:** 482

Philadelphia Fire (Wideman), **Supp. X:** 320, 334

Philadelphia Negro, The (Du Bois), **Supp. II Part 1:** 158, 163–164, 166

Philbrick, Thomas, **I:** 343

"Philemon and Baucis"(Hadas), **Supp. XXIII:** 114

"Phil in the Marketplace" (Lethem), **Supp. XVIII:** 148

Philip, Jim, **Supp. XII:** 136

Philip, Maxwell, **Supp. XXI:** 160

Philip, Prince, **Supp. X:** 108

"Philip of Pokanoket" (Irving), **II:** 303

Philippians (biblical book), **IV:** 154

"Philippine Conquest, The" (Masters), **Supp. I Part 2:** 456

"Philip Roth Reconsidered" (Howe), **Retro. Supp. II:** 286

"Philistinism and the Negro Writer" (Baraka), **Supp. II Part 1:** 39, 44

Phillips, Adam, **Supp. XII:** 97–98

Phillips, Anne K., **Supp. XX:** 221

Phillips, Carl, **Supp. XXI:** 246

Phillips, David Graham, **II:** 444; **Retro. Supp. II:** 101

Phillips, Gene D., **Supp. XI:** 306

Phillips, Jayne Anne, **Supp. XIV:** 21

Phillips, J. J., **Supp. XXIII:** 174

Phillips, J. O. C., **Supp. I Part 1:** 19

Phillips, Robert, **Supp. XIII:** 335, 344

Phillips, Wendell, **Supp. I Part 1:** 103; **Supp. I Part 2:** 524

Phillips, Willard, **Supp. I Part 1:** 154, 155

Phillips, William, **Supp. VIII:** 156

Phillips, William L., **I:** 106

"Philly Babylon" (Di Piero), **Supp. XIX:** 46

"Philoctetes"(Hadas), **Supp. XXIII:** 115

"Philoctetes: The Wound and the Bow" (Wilson), **Supp. XXIV:** 217

"Philosopher, The" (Farrell), **II:** 45

Philosopher of the Forest (pseudonym). *See* Freneau, Philip

Philosophes classiques, Les (Taine), **III:** 323

"Philosophical Cobbler, The" (Sanders), **Supp. XVI:** 268

"Philosophical Concepts and Practical Results" (James), **II:** 352

"Philosophical Investigation of Metaphor, A" (Gass), **Supp. VI:** 79

Philosophical Transactions (Watson), **II:** 114

"Philosophy, Or Something Like That" (P. Roth), **Supp. III Part 2:** 403

"Philosophy and Its Critics" (James), **II:** 360

"Philosophy and the Form of Fiction" (Gass), **Supp. VI:** 85

"Philosophy for People" (Emerson), **II:** 14

"Philosophy in Warm Weather" (Kenyon), **Supp. VII:** 168

"Philosophy Lesson" (Levine), **Supp. V:** 195

Philosophy of Alain Locke, The: Harlem Renaissance and Beyond (Harris, ed.), **Supp. XIV:** 196, 211–212

"Philosophy of Composition, The" (Poe), **III:** 416, 421; **Retro. Supp. II:** 266, 267, 271; **Supp. XXV:** 120, 121

Philosophy of Friedrich Nietzsche, The (Mencken), **III:** 102–103

"Philosophy of Handicap, A" (Bourne), **I:** 216, 218

"Philosophy of History" (Emerson), **II:** 11–12

Philosophy of Literary Form, The (Burke), **I:** 275, 281, 283, 291

Philosophy of the Human Mind, The (Stewart), **II:** 8

Philosophy: Who Needs It (Rand), **Supp. IV Part 2:** 517, 518, 527, 533

Philoxenes, **Supp. VIII:** 201

"Phineas" (Knowles), **Supp. XII:** 238–240

Phineas: Six Stories (Knowles), **Supp. XII:** 249

"Phocion" (Lowell), **II:** 536

Phoebe Light (Notley), **Supp. XXII:** 227

Phoenix and the Turtle, The (Shakespeare), **I:** 284

"Phoenix Lyrics" (Schwartz), **Supp. II Part 2:** 665

"Phone Booths, The" (Jarman), **Supp. XVII:** 112–113

"Phony War Films" (Jones), **Supp. XI:** 217, 232

"Photograph: Carlisle Indian School (1879–1918)"(Kenny), **Supp. XXIII:** 156

"Photograph: Migrant Worker, Parlier, California, 1967" (Levis), **Supp. XI:** 272

"Photograph of a Bawd Drinking Raleigh Rye" (Trethewey), **Supp. XXI:** 254

"Photograph of a Child on a Vermont Hillside" (Kenyon), **Supp. VII:** 168

"Photograph of My Mother as a Young Girl" (Gioia), **Supp. XV:** 119

"Photograph of the Girl" (Olds), **Supp. X:** 205

"Photograph of the Unmade Bed" (Rich), **Supp. I Part 2:** 558

Photographs (Welty), **Retro. Supp. I:** 343

"Photographs, The" (Barthelme), **Supp. IV Part 1:** 53

"Photography" (Levine), **Supp. V:** 194

Phyrrho, **Retro. Supp. I:** 247

"Physical Universe" (Simpson), **Supp. IX:** 278

"Physicist We Know, A" (Shields), **Supp. VII:** 310

"Physics and Cosmology in the Fiction of Tom Robbins" (Nadeau), **Supp. X:** 270

Physiologie du goût (Brillat-Savarin), **Supp. XVII:** 82, 86

Physiology of Taste, The; or, Meditations on Transcendent Gastronomy (Brillat-Savarin; M. F. K. Fisher, trans.), **Supp. XVII:** 86, 87, 91

"Physiology of Versification, The: Harmonies of Organic and Animal Life" (Holmes), **Supp. I Part 1:** 311

Physique de l'Amour (Gourmont), **III:** 467–468

Piaf, Edith, **Supp. IV Part 2:** 549

Piaget, Jean, **Supp. XIII:** 75

"Piano" (Lawrence), **Supp. XV:** 254

"Piano Fingers" (Mason), **Supp. VIII:** 146

Piano Lesson, The (Bearden), **Supp. VIII:** 342

Piano Lesson, The (Wilson), **Supp. VIII:** **342–345**

Piano Man's Daughter, The (Findley), **Supp. XX: 59–61**

"Piano Player, The"(Strout), **Supp. XXIII:** 283, 285

Piatt, James, **Supp. I Part 2:** 420

Piatt, John J., **II:** 273

Piazza, Ben, **Supp. XIII:** 163
Piazza, Paul, **Supp. XIV:** 157, 160, 171
"Piazza de Spagna, Early Morning" (Wilbur), **Supp. III Part 2:** 553
Piazza Tales (Melville), **III:** 91
Picabia, Francis, **Retro. Supp. I:** 416; **Retro. Supp. II:** 331; **Supp. XXII:** 162
Picasso (Stein), **IV:** 28, 32, 45
Picasso, Pablo, **I:** 429, 432, 440, 442, 445; **II:** 602; **III:** 197, 201, 470; **IV:** 26, 31, 32, 46, 87, 407, 436; **Retro. Supp. I:** 55, 63; **Supp. IV Part 1:** 81; **Supp. IX:** 66
Piccione, Anthony, **Supp. XV:** 212
"Piccola Comedia" (Wilbur), **Supp. III Part 2:** 561
Pickard, Samuel T., **Supp. I Part 2:** 682
Picked-Up Pieces (Updike), **Retro. Supp. I:** 320, 322, 323, 335
Picker, Lauren, **Supp. VIII:** 78, 83
Picker, Tobias, **Supp. XII:** 253
Pickering, Sam, **Supp. XXI: 191–207**
Pickford, Mary, **Retro. Supp. I:** 325; **Supp. I Part 2:** 391
"Picking and Choosing" (Moore), **III:** 205
"Pickman's Model" (Lovecraft), **Supp. XXV:** 113, 114
Picnic (film), **Supp. XXV:** 95
Picnic (Inge), **Supp. XXV:** 93, 95, 97–99
"Picnic" (Peacock), **Supp. XIX:** 206
Picnic, Lightning (Collins), **Supp. XXI:** 54, 60
"Picnic, Lightning" (Collins), **Supp. XXI:** 64–65
Picnic Cantata (music) (Bowles), **Supp. IV Part 1:** 89
"Picnic Remembered" (Warren), **IV:** 240
Pictorial History of the Negro in America, A (Hughes), **Supp. I Part 1:** 345
"Picture, The" (Olson), **Supp. II Part 2:** 574
Picture Bride (Son), **Supp. X:** 292
"Picture I Want, The" (Olds), **Supp. X:** 209
Picture of Dorian Gray, The (Wilde), **Supp. IX:** 105
"Picture of Little J. A. in a Prospect of Flowers, A" (Ashbery), **Supp. III Part 1:** 3
Picture Palace (Theroux), **Supp. VIII:** 322
"Pictures" (Pickering), **Supp. XXI:** 197
"Pictures at an Extermination" (Epstein), **Supp. XII:** 161
"Pictures from an Expedition" (Duffy), **Supp. IV Part 1:** 207
Pictures from an Institution (Jarrell), **II:** 367, 385
Pictures from Brueghel (W. C. Williams), **Retro. Supp. I:** 429–431
"Pictures from Brueghel" (W. C. Williams), **Retro. Supp. I:** 419
"Pictures of Columbus, the Genoese, The" (Freneau), **Supp. II Part 1:** 258
Pictures of Fidelman: An Exhibition (Malamud), **Supp. I Part 2:** 450–451
"Pictures of the Artist" (Malamud), **Supp. I Part 2:** 450

Pictures of the Floating World (Lowell), **II:** 521, 524–525
Pictures of Travel (Heine), **II:** 281
Picturesque America; or, the Land We Live In (Bryant, ed.), **Supp. I Part 1:** 158
"Picturesque Ghetto, The" (Hapgood), **Supp. XVII:** 101
"Picturesque: San Cristóbal de las Casas" (Mora), **Supp. XIII:** 218
Picture This (Heller), **Supp. IV Part 1:** 386, 388, 390–391
Picturing Will (Beattie), **Supp. V:** 29, 31–32, 34
"Pie" (X. J. Kennedy), **Supp. XV:** 170
"Piece, A" (Creeley), **Supp. IV Part 1:** 155, 156
"Piece of Moon, A" (Hogan), **Supp. IV Part 1:** 407
Piece of My Heart, A (Ford), **Supp. V:** 57, 58–61, 62
Piece of My Mind, A: Reflections at Sixty (Wilson), **IV:** 426, 430, 438, 441
"Piece of News, A" (Welty), **IV:** 263; **Retro. Supp. I:** 345, 346
Pieces (Creeley), **Supp. IV Part 1:** 155
Pieces and Pontifications (Mailer), **Retro. Supp. II:** 209–210
Pieces of the Frame (McPhee), **Supp. III Part 1:** 293
"Pie of the Month"(Thompson), **Supp. XXIII:** 300
Pierce, Franklin, **II:** 225, 226, 227; **III:** 88; **Retro. Supp. I:** 150, 163, 164, 165
Pierce, Frederick, **Retro. Supp. I:** 136
Piercy, Josephine K., **Supp. I Part 1:** 103
"Pierian Handsprings" (column, Untermeyer), **Supp. XV:** 294
Pierpont, Claudia Roth, **Supp. X:** 192, 193, 196
Pierre et Jean (Maupassant), **I:** 421
Pierre: or The Ambiguities (Melville), **III:** 86–88, 89; **IV:** 194; **Retro. Supp. I:** 249, 253–254, 256; **Supp. I Part 2:** 579
Pierrepont, Sarah. *See* Edwards, Sarah
Pierrot qui pleure et Pierrot qui rit (Rostand), **II:** 515
Pierson, George W, **Supp. XXII:** 289
Pig Cookies (Ríos), **Supp. IV Part 2:** 537, 550, 552–554
Pigeon Feathers (Updike), **IV:** 214, 218, 219, 221–223, 226
"Pigeon Feathers" (Updike), **Retro. Supp. I:** 318, 322, 323
"Pigeons" (Rilke), **II:** 544
"Pigeons, The" (Espaillat), **Supp. XXI:** 98
"Pigeon Woman" (Swenson), **Supp. IV Part 2:** 644
"Pig Helmet and the Wall of Life"(P. Benedict), **Supp. XXIII:** 48–49
Pigs in Heaven (Kingsolver), **Supp. VII:** 197, 199, 209–210
Pike County Ballads, The (Hay), **Supp. I Part 1:** 352
Piket, Vincent, **Supp. IV Part 1:** 24
Pilar San-Mallafre, Maria del, **Supp. V:** 40

Pilcer, Sonya, **Supp. XVII:** 50
Pilgrim (Findley), **Supp. XX: 61–62**
"Pilgrim" (Freneau), **Supp. I Part 1:** 125
"Pilgrimage" (Ray), **Supp. XVIII:** 193
"Pilgrimage" (Sontag), **Supp. III Part 2:** 454–455
"Pilgrimage" (Trethewey), **Supp. XXI:** 255
"Pilgrimage, The" (Maxwell), **Supp. VIII:** 169, 171
Pilgrimage of Festus, The (Aiken), **I:** 50, 55, 57
Pilgrimage of Henry James, The (Brooks), **I:** 240, 248, 250; **IV:** 433
Pilgrim at Tinker Creek (Dillard), **Supp. VI:** 22, **23–26,** 28, 29, **30–31,** 34; **Supp. XVIII:** 189
"Pilgrim Makers" (Lowell), **II:** 541
Pilgrim's Harbor (Skloot), **Supp. XX: 196, 207**
Pilgrim's Progress (Bunyan), **I:** 92; **II:** 15, 168, 572; **Supp. I Part 1:** 32, 38; **Supp. I Part 2:** 599
Pili's Wall (Levine), **Supp. V:** 178, 183–184
"Pillar of Fire" (Bradbury), **Supp. IV Part 1:** 113–114
Pillars of Hercules, The: A Grand Tour of the Mediterranean (Theroux), **Supp. VIII:** 325
"Pillow" (L.-Y. Lee), **Supp. XV:** 224
Pilot, The (Cooper), **I:** 335, 337, 339, 342–343, 350
"Pilot from the Carrier, A" (Jarrell), **II:** 374
"Pilots, Man Your Planes" (Jarrell), **II:** 374–375
"Pilots, The" (Levertov), **Supp. III Part 1:** 282
Pilsudski, Joseph, **Supp. XXIII:** 6
"Pimp's Revenge, A" (Malamud), **Supp. I Part 2:** 435, 450, 451
Pinball (Kosinski), **Supp. VII:** 215, 226
Pinchot, Gifford, **Supp. IX:** 184; **Supp. XIV:** 178
Pindar, **I:** 381; **II:** 543; **III:** 610
"Pine" (Dickey), **Supp. IV Part 1:** 183
Pine Barrens, The (McPhee), **Supp. III Part 1:** 298–301, 309
"Pineys, The" (Stern), **Supp. IX:** 288, 296
Pinget, Robert, **Supp. V:** 39
Pinhook: Finding Wholeness in a Fragmented Land (Ray), **Supp. XVIII:** 189, 192, 202–204
"Pink Dog" (Bishop), **Retro. Supp. II:** 48
"Pink Dress, The" (Boulton), **Supp. XXII:** 19
Pinker, James B., **I:** 409; **Retro. Supp. I:** 231
Pinkerton, Jan, **Supp. V:** 323–324
"Pink Moon—The Pond" (Oliver), **Supp. VII:** 234
Pinktoes (C. Himes), **Supp. XVI: 142**
Pinocchio in Venice (Coover), **Supp. V:** 40, 51
Pinsker, Sanford, **Retro. Supp. II:** 23; **Supp. V:** 272; **Supp. IX:** 293, 327; **Supp. XI:** 251, 254, 317

Pinsky, Robert, **Retro. Supp. II:** 50; **Supp. VI: 235–251; Supp. IX:** 155, 158; **Supp. XIII:** 277, 285; **Supp. XXI:** 243; **Supp. XXIII:** 111, 124

Pinter, Harold, **I:** 71; **Supp. XIII:** 20, 196; **Supp. XIV:** 239; **Supp. XVI:** 207

Pinto, Ferdinand Mendes (pseudonym). *See* Briggs, Charles Frederick

Pinto and Sons (Epstein), **Supp. XII:** 170, **171–172**

Pinto letters (Briggs), **Supp. XVIII:** 3, 12–13

"Pinup" (Collins), **Supp. XXI:** 59

"Pioneer Girl" (L. I. Wilder), **Supp. XXII:** 290, 293, 294, 295

Pioneers, The (Cooper), **I:** 336, 337, 339, 340–341, 342, 348; **II:** 313

Pioneers of France in the New World (Parkman), **Supp. III Part 2:** 599, 602

"Pioneers! O Pioneers!" (Whitman), **Retro. Supp. I:** 8

"Pioneer's Vision, The" (Larcom), **Supp. XIII:** 140

Pious and Secular America (Niebuhr), **III:** 308

Pipe Night (O'Hara), **III:** 361, 368

Piper, Dan, **Supp. IX:** 65

Pipers at the Gates of Dawn: The Wisdom of Children's Literature (Cott), **Supp. XVI:** 104

"Piper's Rocks" (Olson), **Supp. IV Part 1:** 153

"Pipistrelles" (B. Kelly), **Supp. XVII:** 129–130

Pipkin, Charles W., **Supp. XIV:** 3

Pippa Passes (Browning), **IV:** 128

Piquion, René, **Supp. I Part 1:** 346

Pirandello, Luigi, **Supp. IV Part 2:** 576, 588

Piranesi, Giovanni Battista, **Supp. XV:** 258

Pirate, The (Robbins), **Supp. XII:** 6

Pirate, The (Scott), **I:** 339

Pirates of Penzance, The (Gilbert and Sullivan), **IV:** 386

Pisan Cantos, The (Pound), **III:** 476; **Retro. Supp. I:** 140, 283, 285, 293; **Supp. III Part 1:** 63; **Supp. V:** 331, 337; **Supp. XIV:** 11; **Supp. XV:** 351

Pisarev, Dimitri, **Supp. XXI:** 164

Piscator, Erwin, **IV:** 394

"Pissaro: Tropical Impressions"(Kenny), **Supp. XXIII:** 146

Pissarro, Camille, **I:** 478

"Pissing off the Back of the Boat into the Nevernais Canal" (Matthews), **Supp. IX:** 160–161

Pistol, The (Jones), **Supp. XI:** 219, **223–224,** 227, 234

Pit, The (Norris), **III:** 314, 322, 326–327, 333, 334

"Pit, The" (Roethke), **III:** 538

"Pit and the Pendulum, The" (Poe), **III:** 413, 416; **Retro. Supp. II:** 264, 269–270, 273

"Pitcher" (Francis), **Supp. IX:** 82

"Pitcher, The" (Dubus), **Supp. VII:** 87

Pitchford, Nicola, **Supp. XII:** 13

"Pits, The" (D. Graham), **Supp. XI:** 252, 254

Pitt, William, **Supp. I Part 2:** 510, 518

Pitts, Rebecca, **Supp. XXII:** 280, 281

"Pittsburgh" (Carruth), **Supp. XVI:** 58

"Pity Me" (Wylie), **Supp. I Part 2:** 729

Pity the Monsters (Williamson), **Retro. Supp. II:** 185

Pius II, Pope, **III:** 472

Pius IX, Pope, **II:** 79

"Piute Creek" (Snyder), **Supp. VIII:** 293

Pixley, Frank, **I:** 196

Pizer, Donald, **III:** 321; **Retro. Supp. II:** 100, 199

"Place" (Hoffman), **Supp. XVIII:** 86

"Place at the Outskirts" (Simic), **Supp. VIII:** 282

Place Called Estherville, A (Caldwell), **I:** 297, 307

Place Called Freedom, A (Sanders), **Supp. XVI:** 269

Place for My Head, A (Hoffman), **Supp. XVIII:** 76

"Place in Fiction" (Welty), **IV:** 260, 279

Place of Dead Roads, The (Burroughs), **Supp. III Part 1:** 196

Place of Love, The (Shapiro), **Supp. II Part 2:** 702, 706

"Place of Poetry, The" (Stevens), **Retro. Supp. I:** 304

Place of Science in Modern Civilization and Other Essays, The (Veblen), **Supp. I Part 2:** 629, 642

"Place of Trumpets, The" (B. Kelly), **Supp. XVII:** 127

Place on Earth, A (Berry), **Supp. X:** 33–34, 36

Places Left Unfinished at the Time of Creation (Santos), **Supp. XIII:** 274

"Places to Look for Your Mind" (Moore), **Supp. X:** 174–175

"Place They'd Never Seen, A: The Theater" (Wasserstein), **Supp. XV:** 332

"Place to Live, A" (Levertov), **Supp. III Part 1:** 281

"Place to Stand, A" (Price), **Supp. VI:** 258

Place to Stand, A (Wagoner), **Supp. IX:** 324

"Place (Any Place) to Transcend All Places, A" (W. C. Williams), **Retro. Supp. I:** 422

"Place Where My Poems Are Coming From, The"(Crooker), **Supp. XXIII:** 64

Placi, Carlo, **IV:** 328

Plagemann, Catherine, **Supp. XVII:** 91

"Plagiarist, The" (Singer), **IV:** 19

Plagued by the Nightingale (Boyle), **Supp. XXIV: 51–52,** 53, 56

Plague of Dreamers, A (Stern), **Supp. XX:** 178

Plainest Narrative, The (Bronk), **Supp. XXI:** 31

"Plain Language from Truthful James" (Harte). *See* "Heathen Chinee, The"

"Plain Sense of Things, The" (Stevens), **Retro. Supp. I:** 298, 299, 307, 312

"Plain Song" (Carruth), **Supp. XVI:** 54

Plain Song (Harrison), **Supp. VIII: 38–39**

"Plain Song" (Kooser), **Supp. XIX:** 120

"Plain Song for Comadre, A" (Wilbur), **Supp. III Part 2:** 554

"Plain Talk". *See Common Sense* (Paine)

Plaint of a Rose, The (Sandburg), **III:** 579

Plain Truth: Or, Serious Considerations on the Present State of the City of Philadelphia, and Province of Pennsylvania (Franklin), **II:** 117–119

Plainwater: Essays and Poetry (Carson), **Supp. XII:** 97, **99–104**

Plan B (C. Himes), **Supp. XVI:** 143, 144

Plan B: Further Thoughts on Faith (Lamott), **Supp. XX: 142–143**

"Planchette" (London), **II:** 475–476

"Planetarium" (Rich), **Supp. I Part 2:** 557

Planet News: 1961–1967 (Ginsberg), **Supp. II Part 1:** 321

Planet Waves (album, Dylan), **Supp. XVIII:** 27

"Plantation a beginning, a" (Olson), **Supp. II Part 2:** 573

Plant Dreaming Deep (Sarton), **Supp. VIII:** 250, 263

Plante, David, **Supp. IV Part 1:** 310

Planting a Sequoia (Gioia), **Supp. XV:** 117

"Planting a Sequoia" (Gioia), **Supp. XV:** 111, 112, 117, **121–122**

"Plants Fed On By Fawns" (B. Kelly), **Supp. XVII:** 133

Plarr, Victor, **III:** 459, 477

Plath, James, **Retro. Supp. I:** 334; **Supp. XXIII:** 73, 74, 80

Plath, Sylvia, **Retro. Supp. II:** 181, **241–260; Supp. I Part 2: 526–549,** 554, 571; **Supp. III Part 2:** 543, 561; **Supp. IV Part 2:** 439; **Supp. V:** 79, 81, 113, 117, 118, 119, 344; **Supp. X:** 201, 202, **203,** 215; **Supp. XI:** 146, 240, 241, 317; **Supp. XII:** 217, 308; **Supp. XIII:** 35, 76, 312; **Supp. XIV:** 269; **Supp. XV:** 123, 148, 184, 252, 253, 340; **Supp. XVII:** 239; **Supp. XXI:** 58; **Supp. XXII:** 30, 92, 93; **Supp. XXIII:** 63, 64, 112, 113, 254; **Supp. XXV:** 222

Plath, Warren, **Supp. I Part 2:** 528

Plato, **I:** 224, 279, 383, 389, 485, 523; **II:** 5, 8, 10, 15, 233, 346, 391–392, 591; **III:** 115, 480, 600, 606, 609, 619–620; **IV:** 74, 140, 333, 363, 364; **Retro. Supp. I:** 247; **Retro. Supp. II:** 31; **Supp. I Part 2:** 595, 631; **Supp. IV Part 1:** 391; **Supp. IV Part 2:** 526; **Supp. X:** 78

"Plato" (Emerson), **II:** 6

"Platonic Relationship, A" (Beattie), **Supp. V:** 22

Platonic Scripts (Justice), **Supp. VII:** 115

Platonov, Dmitri, **Supp. VIII:** 30

Platt, Anthony M., **Supp. I Part 1:** 13–14

Platt, Edward, **Supp. XXIII:** 97

Platte River (Bass), **Supp. XVI:** 19

"Platte River" (Bass), **Supp. XVI:** 20

Plausible Prejudices: Essays on American Writing (Epstein), **Supp. XIV:** 111

Plautus, Titus Maccius, **IV:** 155; **Supp. III Part 2:** 630

Play and Other Stories, The (Dixon), **Supp. XII:** 148, 149

Playback (script) (Chandler), **Supp. IV Part 1:** 131

Playback (Chandler), **Supp. IV Part 1:** 134–135; **Supp. XVIII:** 138

"Play Ball!" (Francis), **Supp. IX:** 89

Playboy of the Western World, The (Synge), **Supp. III Part 1:** 34

Play Days (Jewett), **Retro. Supp. II:** 135

Play Days: A Book of Stories for Children (Jewett), **II:** 401–402

Player Piano (Vonnegut), **Supp. II Part 2:** 756, 757, 760–765

Players (DeLillo), **Supp. VI:** 3, 6, 8, 14

"Players, The" (W. J. Smith), **Supp. XIII:** 340, 343

"Playground, The" (Bradbury), **Supp. IV Part 1:** 104

Playing at Stillness (Espaillat), **Supp. XXI:** 112

Playing in the Dark (Morrison), **Retro. Supp. II:** 118; **Supp. XIII:** 185–186

"Playing the Bawd at Twenty" (Skloot), **Supp. XX: 204–205**

Play in Poetry (Untermeyer), **Supp. XV:** 310

"Playin with Punjab" (Bambara), **Supp. XI:** 6

Play It Again Sam (Allen), **Supp. XV:** 2, 3, 14

Play It as It Lays (Didion), **Supp. IV Part 1:** 198, 201–203, 203, 211

Play It as It Lays (film), **Supp. IV Part 1:** 198

"Plays and Operas Too" (Whitman), **IV:** 350

Plays of Negro Life: A Source-Book of Native American Drama (Locke and Gregory), **Supp. XIV:** 202

Plays: Winesburg and Others (Anderson), **I:** 113

"Playthings" (Komunyakaa), **Supp. XIII:** 126

"Playtime: Danish Fun" (Larsen), **Supp. XVIII:** 120, 122–123

"Playtime: Three Scandinavian Stories" (Larsen), **Supp. XVIII:** 122–123

Playwright's Voice, The (Savran), **Supp. XIII:** 209; **Supp. XV:** 321; **Supp. XXIV:** 263

Plaza Suite (Simon), **Supp. IV Part 2:** 575, 581–582, 583, 589

Pleading Guilty (Turow), **Supp. XVII: 218,** 219

"Plea for Captain Brown, A" (Thoreau), **IV:** 185

"Please" (Komunyakaa), **Supp. XIII:** 122

"Please Don't Kill Anything" (A. Miller), **III:** 161

"Please Don't Take My Sunshine Away" (Conroy), **Supp. XVI:** 69

"Pleasure" (Very), **Supp. XXV:** 242, 244

Pleasure Dome (Frankenberg), **I:** 436

Pleasure Dome (Komunyakaa), **Supp. XIII:** 113, 121, **131–133**

Pleasure of Hope, The (Emerson), **II:** 8

"Pleasure of Ruins, The" (McClatchy), **Supp. XII:** 256

"Pleasures of Formal Poetry, The" (Bogan), **Supp. III Part 1:** 51

"Pleasures of Peace, The" (Koch), **Supp. XV:** 180

"Plea to the Protestant Churches, A" (Brooks), **Supp. XIV:** 4

Plimpton, George, **Supp. IV Part 1:** 386; **Supp. V:** 201; **Supp. VIII:** 82, 157; **Supp. IX:** 256; **Supp. XI:** 294; **Supp. XIV:** 82; **Supp. XVI:** 233–248

Pliny the Elder, **Supp. XVI:** 292

Pliny the Younger, **II:** 113

"Ploesti Isn't Long Island" (Zinberg), **Supp. XV:** 195

"Plot against the Giant, The" (Stevens), **IV:** 81

Plotinus, **Supp. XV:** 33; **Supp. XVI:** 291

Plough and the Stars, The (O'Casey), **III:** 159

"Ploughing on Sunday" (Stevens), **IV:** 74

Plowing the Dark (Powers), **Supp. IX:** 212–213, **221–224**

Plum Bun (Fauset), **Supp. XVIII:** 127; **Supp. XIX:** 73

Plumed Serpent, The (Lawrence), **Supp. XV:** 46

"Plumet Basilisk, The" (Moore), **III:** 203, 208, 215

Plumly, Stanley, **Supp. IV Part 2:** 625

Plummer, Amanda, **Supp. IV Part 1:** 236

Plunder (serial movie), **Supp. IV Part 2:** 464

Plunket, Robert, **Supp. XV:** 68

Plunkett, Edward (Lord Dunsany), **Supp. XXV:** 113

"Plunkville Patriot" (O'Henry), **Supp. II Part 1:** 389

"Pluralism and Ideological Peace" (Locke), **Supp. XIV:** 202, 212

"Pluralism and Intellectual Democracy" (Locke), **Supp. XIV:** 202, 208, 212

Pluralistic Universe, A (James), **II:** 342, 348, 357–358

Plutarch, **II:** 5, 8, 16, 555; **Retro. Supp. I:** 360; **Supp. XVI:** 292

Plymell, Charles, **Supp. XIV:** 149

Plymell, Pam, **Supp. XIV:** 149

Pnin (Nabokov), **III:** 246; **Retro. Supp. I:** 263, 265, 266, 275, 335

"Po' Boy Blues" (Hughes), **Supp. I Part 1:** 327

Pocahontas, **I:** 4; **II:** 296; **III:** 584

"Pocahontas to Her English Husband, John Rolfe" (Gunn Allen), **Supp. IV Part 1:** 331

"Pocketbook and Sauerkraut" (Di Piero), **Supp. XIX:** 35, 36, 41, 42, 45

"Pocket Poem" (Kooser), **Supp. XIX:** 128

Podhoretz, Norman, **IV:** 441; **Retro. Supp. II:** 323; **Supp. IV Part 1:** 382; **Supp. VIII:** 93, **231–247;** **Supp. IX:** 3; **Supp. XIV:** 103; **Supp. XXV:** 253, 268

Podnieks, Elizabeth, **Supp. X:** 189, 190, 191, 192

"Pod of the Milkweed" (Frost), **Retro. Supp. I:** 141

Poe (screenplay, O'Nan), **Supp. XXV:** 154

Poe, Edgar Allan, **I:** 48, 53, 103, 190, 194, 200, 210, 211, 261, 340, 459; **II:** 74, 77, 194, 255, 273, 295, 308, 313, 421, 475, 482, 530, 595; **III:** 259, **409–432,** 485, 507, 593; **IV:** 123, 129, 133, 141, 187, 261, 345, 350, 432, 438, 439, 453; **Retro. Supp. I:** 41, 273, 365, 421; **Retro. Supp. II:** 102, 104, 160, 164, 220, **261–277,** 322; **Supp. I Part 1:** 36, 309; **Supp. I Part 2:** 376, 384, 385, 388, 393, 405, 413, 421, 474, 682; **Supp. II Part 1:** 385, 410; **Supp. III Part 2:** 544, 549–550; **Supp. IV Part 1:** 80, 81, 101, 128, 341, 349; **Supp. IV Part 2:** 464, 469; **Supp. VIII:** 105; **Supp. IX:** 115; **Supp. X:** 42, 78; **Supp. XI:** 85, 293; **Supp. XIII:** 100, 111; **Supp. XVI:** 294; **Supp. XVIII:** 3, 11; **Supp. XX: 74; Supp. XXIII:** 161, 164, 169, 177, 178; **Supp. XXIV:** 54; **Supp. XXV:** 111, 119

Poe, Edgar Allen, **Supp. XV:** 275; **Supp. XXI:** 51

Poe Abroad: Influence, Reputation, Affinities (Vines), **Retro. Supp. II:** 261

"Poe-et's Nightmare, The" (Lovecraft), **Supp. XXV:** 119

"Poem" (Bishop), **Retro. Supp. II:** 40; **Supp. I Part 1:** 73, 76–79, 82, 95

"Poem" (Harrison), **Supp. VIII:** 38

"Poem" (Justice), **Supp. VII:** 125

"Poem" (Kunitz), **Supp. III Part 1:** 263

"Poem" (Notley), **Supp. XXII:** 228–229

"Poem" (O'Hara), **Supp. XIX:** 85

"Poem" (Wright), **Supp. III Part 2:** 590

"Poem About Black Power, A" (Boyle), **Supp. XXIV:** 64

"Poem About George Doty in the Death House, A" (Wright), **Supp. III Part 2:** 594–595, 597–598

"Poem about People" (Pinsky), **Supp. VI: 240–241,** 244, 248

"Poem as Mask, The" (Rukeyser), **Supp. VI:** 281, 285

"Poem as Time Machine, The" (Gallagher), **Supp. XXIV:** 172

"Poem Beginning 'The' " (Zukofsky), **Supp. III Part 2:** 610, 611, 614

"Poem Catching Up with an Idea" (Carruth), **Supp. XVI:** 56

"Poem for a Birthday" (Plath), **Supp. I Part 2:** 539

"POEM FOR ANNA RUSS AND FANNY JONES, A" (Baraka), **Supp. II Part 1:** 58

"Poem for Black Hearts, A" (Baraka), **Supp. II Part 1:** 50

"POEM FOR DEEP THINKERS, A" (Baraka), **Supp. II Part 1:** 55

"Poem for D. H. Lawrence" (Creeley), **Supp. IV Part 1:** 141

"Poem for Dorothy, A" (Merwin), **Supp. III Part 1:** 342

"Poem for Hemingway and W. C. Williams" (Carver), **Supp. III Part 1:** 147

"Poem for my Son" (Kumin), **Supp. IV Part 2:** 442

"Poem for People Who Are Understandably Too Busy to Read Poetry" (Dunn), **Supp. XI:** 147

"Poem for Someone Killed in Spain, A" (Jarrell), **II:** 371

"Poem for the Blue Heron, A" (Oliver), **Supp. VII:** 235–236

"Poem for Two Voices" (Everwine), **Supp. XV:** 89

"Poem For Willie Best, A" (Baraka), **Supp. II Part 1:** 36

"Poem in Prose" (Bogan), **Supp. III Part 1:** 58

"Poem in Which I Refuse Contemplation" (Dove), **Supp. IV Part 1:** 249

"Poem Is a Walk, A" (Ammons), **Supp. VII:** 36

"Poem Like a Grenade, A" (Haines), **Supp. XII:** 204

"Poem of Flight, The" (Levine), **Supp. V:** 189

"Poem of Liberation, The" (Stern), **Supp. IX:** 292

Poem of the Cid (Merwin, trans.), **Supp. III Part 1:** 347

"Poem of the Forgotten" (Haines), **Supp. XII:** 202–203

"Poem (V (F) W)" (O'Hara), **Supp. XXIII:** 219

"Poem on a Line by Anne Sexton, 'We Are All Writing God's Poem'" (Crooker), **Supp. XXIII:** 59

"Poem on the Memorable Victory Obtained by the Gallant Captain Paul Jones" (Freneau), **Supp. II Part 1:** 261

"Poem out of Childhood" (Rukeyser), **Supp. VI:** 272, 277

Poem-Paintings (O'Hara and Bluhm), **Supp. XXIII:** 217

"Poem Read at the Dinner Given to the Author by the Medical Profession" (Holmes), **Supp. I Part 1:** 310–311

Poems (Auden), **Supp. II Part 1:** 6

Poems (Berryman), **I:** 170

Poems (Bryant), **II:** 311; **Supp. I Part 1:** 155, 157

Poems (Cummings), **I:** 430, 447

Poems (E. Stoddard), **Supp. XV:** 274

Poems (Eliot), **I:** 580, 588; **IV:** 122; **Retro. Supp. I:** 59, 291

Poems (Emerson), **II:** 7, 8, 12–13, 17

Poems (Holmes), **Supp. I Part 1:** 303

Poems (Koch), **Supp. XV:** 179

Poems (Lowell), **Supp. I Part 2:** 405

Poems (Moore), **III:** 194, 205, 215

Poems (Poe), **III:** 411

Poems (Reznikoff), **Supp. XIV:** 282, 283, 284, 285

Poems (Tate), **IV:** 121

Poems (W. C. Williams), **Retro. Supp. I:** 412–413, 416, 424

Poems (W. J. Smith), **Supp. XIII:** 332

Poems (Williams), **Supp. XXIV:** 35

Poems (Winters), **Supp. II Part 2:** 809, 810

Poems (Wordsworth), **I:** 468

Poems, 1909–1925 (Eliot), **Retro. Supp. I:** 64

Poems, 1924–1933 (MacLeish), **III:** 7, 15

Poems, 1943–1956 (Wilbur), **Supp. III Part 2:** 554

Poems, The (Freneau), **Supp. II Part 1:** 263

Poems 1918–1975 : The Complete Poems of Charles Reznikoff (Cooney, ed.), **Supp. XIV:** 289

Poems 1940–1953 (Shapiro), **Supp. II Part 2:** 703, 711

Poems 1947–1954 (Kees), **Supp. XV:** 147

Poems: 1947–1957 (W. J. Smith), **Supp. XIII:** 333

Poems 1957–1967 (Dickey), **Supp. IV Part 1:** 178, 181

Poems about God (Ransom), **III:** 484, 486, 491; **IV:** 121

"Poems about Painting" (Snodgrass), **Supp. VI:** 316

Poems and Essays (Ransom), **III:** 486, 490, 492

Poems and New Poems (Bogan), **Supp. III Part 1:** 60–62

"Poems and Places" (Haines), **Supp. XII:** 203

Poems and Poetry of Europe, The (Longfellow, ed.), **Retro. Supp. II:** 155

Poems by Emily Dickinson (Todd and Higginson, eds.), **I:** 469, 470; **Retro. Supp. I:** 35, 39

Poems by Emily Dickinson, Second Series (Todd and Higginson, eds.), **I:** 454; **Retro. Supp. I:** 35

Poems by Emily Dickinson, The (Bianchi and Hampson, eds.), **Retro. Supp. I:** 35

Poems by Emily Dickinson, Third Series (Todd, ed.), **Retro. Supp. I:** 35

Poems by James Russell Lowell, Second Series (Lowell), **Supp. I Part 2:** 406, 409

Poems by Sidney Lanier, (Lanier), **Supp. I Part 1:** 364

Poems from Black Africa (Hughes, ed.), **Supp. I Part 1:** 344

"Poems I Have Lost, The" (Ortiz), **Supp. IV Part 2:** 507

Poems: North & South–A Cold Spring, (Bishop), **Supp. I Part 1:** 83, 89

Poems of a Jew (Shapiro), **Supp. II Part 2:** 703, 712–713

"Poems of a Mountain Recluse" (Budbill), **Supp. XIX:** 9, 10

Poems of Anna Akhmatova, The (Kunitz and Hayward, trans.), **Supp. III Part 1:** 269

Poems of Emily Dickinson, The (Bianchi and Hampson, eds.), **Retro. Supp. I:** 35

Poems of Emily Dickinson, The (Johnson, ed.), **I:** 470

Poems of François Villon (Kinnell, trans.), **Supp. III Part 1:** 235, 243, 249

"Poems of Our Climate, The" (Stevens), **Retro. Supp. I:** 313

Poems of Philip Freneau, Written Chiefly during the Late War (Freneau), **Supp. II Part 1:** 261

Poems of Places (Longfellow, ed.), **II:** 490; **Retro. Supp. II:** 155; **Supp. I Part 1:** 368

Poems of Stanley Kunitz, The (Kunitz), **Supp. III Part 1:** 258, 263, 264, 266, 268

"Poems of These States" (Ginsberg), **Supp. II Part 1:** 323, 325

Poems of Two Friends (Howells and Piatt), **II:** 273, 277

"POEM SOME PEOPLE WILL HAVE TO UNDERSTAND, A" (Baraka), **Supp. II Part 1:** 49

Poems on Slavery (Longfellow), **II:** 489; **Retro. Supp. II:** 157, 168; **Supp. I Part 2:** 406

Poems on Various Subjects (Rowson), **Supp. XV:** 232

Poems on Various Subjects, Religious and Moral (Wheatley), **Supp. XX: 277, 282, 284, 285, 289**

Poem Spoken at the Public Commencement at Yale College, in New Haven; September 1, 1781, A (Barlow), **Supp. II Part 1:** 67–68, 74, 75

Poems Retrieved (O'Hara), **Supp. XXIII:** 220

Poems to Solve (Swenson), **Supp. IV Part 2:** 642

Poems Written and Published during the American Revolutionary War (Freneau), **Supp. II Part 1:** 273, 274

Poems Written between the Years 1768 and 1794 (Freneau), **Supp. II Part 1:** 269

"Poem That Took the Place of a Mountain" (Olson), **Supp. II Part 2:** 582

"Poem to My First Lover" (Olds), **Supp. X:** 206

"Poem to the Reader" (Olds), **Supp. X:** 213

"Poem with No Ending, A" (Levine), **Supp. V:** 186, 190

"Poem You Asked For, The" (Levis), **Supp. XI:** 259–260

Poe Poe Poe Poe Poe Poe Poe (Hoffman), **Retro. Supp. II:** 265

Poesía Náhuatl, **Supp. XV:** 77

Poésies 1917–1920 (Cocteau), **Retro. Supp. I:** 82

"Poesis: A Conceit" (Sobin), **Supp. XVI:** 288

"Poet" (Taggard), **Supp. XXII:** 284

Poet, The (Connelly), **Supp. XXI:** 71, 78

"Poet, The" (Dunbar), **Supp. II Part 1:** 207, 209–210

"Poet, The" (Emerson), **II:** 13, 19, 20, 170

"Poet, The" (Ortiz), **Supp. IV Part 2:** 505

"Poet and His Book, The" (Millay), **III:** 126, 138

"Poet and His Public, The" (Jarrell), **Supp. I Part 1:** 96

"Poet and His Song, The" (Dunbar), **Supp. II Part 1:** 199

"Poet and the Person, The" (Kinard), **Supp. XIV:** 127

"Poet and the Queen, The" (Shaw), **Supp. XIX:** 241

"Poet and the World, The" (Cowley), **Supp. II Part 1:** 145

"Poet as Anti-Specialist, The" (Swenson), **Supp. IV Part 2:** 638, 643

"Poet as *Curandera*" (Mora), **Supp. XIII:** 214, 220

"Poet as Hero, The: Keats in His Letters" (Trilling), **Supp. III Part 2:** 506–507

"Poet as Religious Moralist, The" (Larson), **Supp. XI:** 328

"Poet at Seven, The" (Rimbaud), **II:** 545

Poet at the Breakfast-Table, The (Holmes), **Supp. I Part 1:** 313–314

"Poète contumace, Le" (Corbiere), **II:** 384–385

"Poet for President, A" (Mora), **Supp. XIII:** 220–221

Poetic Achievement of Ezra Pound, The (Alexander), **Retro. Supp. I:** 293

Poetic Diction: A Study in Meaning (Barfield), **III:** 274, 279

"Poetic Principle, The" (Poe), **III:** 421, 426; **Retro. Supp. II:** 266

"Poetics" (Ammons), **Supp. VII:** 29–30

Poetics (Aristotle), **III:** 422; **Supp. XI:** 249; **Supp. XIII:** 75; **Supp. XIV:** 243; **Supp. XV:** 265

Poetics of Space, The (Bachelard), **Supp. XIII:** 225; **Supp. XVI:** 292

"Poetics of the Periphery: Literary Experimentalism in Kathy Acker's *In Memoriam to Identity*" (Acker), **Supp. XII:** 17

"Poetics of the Physical World, The" (Kinnell), **Supp. III Part 1:** 239

"Poetics of Tourette Syndrome, The: Language, Neurobiology, and Poetry" (Schleifer), **Supp. XVIII:** 144

Poet in the World, The (Levertov), **Supp. III Part 1:** 271, 273, 278, 282

"Poet or the Growth of a Lit'ry Figure" (White), **Supp. I Part 2:** 676

Poetry (Barber), **Supp. IV Part 2:** 550

"Poetry" (Moore), **III:** 204–205, 215

"Poetry" (Nye), **Supp. XIII:** 282

"Poetry" (Wrigley), **Supp. XVIII:** 301–302

"Poetry, Community and Climax" (Snyder), **Supp. VIII:** 290

"Poetry, Pleasure, and the Hedonist Reader" (Collins), **Supp. XXI:** 54

"Poetry: A Metrical Essay" (Holmes), **Supp. I Part 1:** 310

"Poetry and Belief in Thomas Hardy" (Schwartz), **Supp. II Part 2:** 666

Poetry and Criticism (Nemerov, ed.), **III:** 269

"Poetry and Drama" (Eliot), **I:** 588

Poetry and Fiction: Essays (Nemerov), **III:** 269, 281

"Poetry and Place" (Berry), **Supp. X:** 22, 28, 31, 32

Poetry and Poets (Lowell), **II:** 512

"Poetry and Religion" (Jarman), **Supp. XVII:** 111

Poetry and the Age (Jarrell), **IV:** 352; **Retro. Supp. I:** 121; **Supp. II Part 1:** 135

"Poetry and the Primitive: Notes on Poetry as an Ecological Survival Technique" (Snyder), **Supp. VIII:** 291, 292, 299, 300

"Poetry and the Public World" (MacLeish), **III:** 11

Poetry and the World (Pinsky), **Supp. VI:** 236, 239, 244, 247

Poetry and Truth (Olson), **Supp. II Part 2:** 583

"Poetry and Uncertainty"(Hirshfield), **Supp. XXIII:** 137

"Poetry As a Way of Life" (Bishop interview), **Retro. Supp. II:** 53

"Poetry as Survival" (Harrison), **Supp. VIII:** 45

"Poetry Baron, The" (Gallagher), **Supp. XXIV:** 166, 177

"Poetry Failure" (Halliday), **Supp. XIX:** 92

Poetry for Students (Taibl), **Supp. XV:** 255

"Poetry for the Advanced" (Baraka), **Supp. II Part 1:** 58

"Poetry Friendship on Earth" (Halliday), **Supp. XIX:** 90, 91

Poetry Handbook, A (Oliver), **Supp. VII:** 229, 245

Poetry Home Repair Manual, The (Kooser), **Supp. XIX:** 116, 128

Poetry in Motion (film), **Supp. XXIV:** 33

Poetry in Motion: 100 Poems from the Subways and Buses (Peacock, ed.), **Supp. XIX:** 195

"Poetry in Translation: Literary Imperialism or, Defending the Musk Ox" (Gallagher), **Supp. XXIV:** 172

"Poetry of Barbarism, The" (Santayana), **IV:** 353

Poetry of Chaucer, The (Gardner), **Supp. VI:** 63

Poetry of Meditation, The (Martz), **IV:** 151; **Supp. I Part 1:** 107

Poetry of Mourning: The Modern Elegy from Hardy to Heaney (Ramazani), **Supp. IV Part 2:** 450

Poetry of Stephen Crane, The (Hoffman), **I:** 405

Poetry of the Negro, 1746–1949, The (Hughes and Bontemps), **Supp. I Part 1:** 345; **Supp. XXII:** 11

Poetry 180: A Turning Back to Poetry (Collins, ed.), **Supp. XXI:** 54

Poetry Reading against the Vietnam War, A (Bly and Ray, eds.), **Supp. IV Part 1:** 61, 63

"Poetry Workshop, The" (column, Kumin), **Supp. XX: 164**

"Poetry Wreck, The" (Shapiro), **Supp. II Part 2:** 717

Poetry Wreck, The: Selected Essays (Shapiro), **Supp. II Part 2:** 703, 704, 717

"Poets" (X. J. Kennedy), **Supp. XV:** 158

Poet's Alphabet, A: Reflections on the Literary Art and Vocation (Bogan), **Supp. III Part 1:** 55, 64

Poets and Poetry of America (Griswold), **Supp. XV:** 277; **Supp. XXV:** 250

Poet's Choice (Engle and Langland, eds.), **III:** 277, 542

Poet's Guide to Poetry, A (Kinzie), **Supp. XXIII:** 124

"Poet's Husband Engages in Gourmet Cooking, The" (Espaillat), **Supp. XXI:** 99

Poets of the Old Testament, The (Gordon), **III:** 199

Poets of Today (Wheelock, ed.), **Supp. IV Part 2:** 639

Poets on Poetry (Nemerov, ed.), **III:** 269

"Poet's Tact, and a Necessary Tactlessness, The" (C. Frost), **Supp. XV:** 94–95

"Poet's View, A" (Levertov), **Supp. III Part 1:** 284

"Poet's Voice, The" (Oliver), **Supp. VII:** 245

"Poets with History and Poets Without History"(Tsvetaeva), **Supp. XXIII:** 168

"Poet Turns on Himself, The" (Dickey), **Supp. IV Part 1:** 177, 181, 185

Poganuc People (Stowe), **Supp. I Part 2:** 581, 596, 599–600

Pogo (comic strip), **Supp. XI:** 105

Pohrt, Tom, **Supp. XIX:** 123

Poincaré, Raymond, **IV:** 320

"Point, The" (Hayden), **Supp. II Part 1:** 373

"Point at Issue!, A" (Chopin), **Retro. Supp. II:** 61; **Supp. I Part 1:** 208

"Point of Age, A" (Berryman), **I:** 173

Point of No Return (Marquand), **III:** 56, 59–60, 65, 67, 69

Point Reyes Poems (R. Bly), **Supp. IV Part 1:** 71

"Points" (Hoffman), **Supp. XVIII:** 86

Points for a Compass Rose (Connell), **Supp. XIV:** 79, 80, 96

"Point Shirley" (Plath), **Supp. I Part 2:** 529, 538

Points in Time (Bowles), **Supp. IV Part 1:** 93

"Points West" (column), **Supp. IV Part 1:** 198

Poirier, Richard, **I:** 136, 239; **III:** 34; **Retro. Supp. I:** 134; **Retro. Supp. II:** 207–208; **Supp. I Part 2:** 660, 665; **Supp. IV Part 2:** 690

Poison Pen (Garrett), **Supp. VII:** 111

Poisonwood Bible, The (Kingsolver), **Supp. VII:** 197–198, 202, 210–213

Poitier, Sidney, **Supp. IV Part 1:** 360, 362

Pokerface (Collins), **Supp. XXI:** 53

"Polack Reverie" (Halliday), **Supp. XIX:** 88

Polanco, Richard, **Supp. XX: 260**

"Polar Bear" (Heller), **Supp. IV Part 1:** 383

"Polar Bears and Others" (Boyle), **Supp. XXIV:** 57

"Polar Seas and Sir John Franklin, The" (Briggs), **Supp. XVIII:** 14

Pole, Rupert, **Supp. X:** 185

"Pole Star" (MacLeish), **III:** 16

Po Li, **Supp. I Part 1:** 262

Police (Baraka), **Supp. II Part 1:** 47

"Police" (Corso), **Supp. XII:** 117, 127

"Police Court Saturday Morning" (X. J. Kennedy), **Supp. XV:** 170

"Police Dreams" (Bausch), **Supp. VII:** 47

Politian (Poe), **III:** 412

"Political and Practical Conceptions of Race, The" (Locke), **Supp. XIV:** 209–210

Political Essays (Lowell), **Supp. I Part 2:** 407

Political Fable, A (Coover), **Supp. V:** 44, 46, 47, 49, 51

"Political Fables" (Mather), **Supp. II Part 2:** 450

"Political Interests" (Stevens), **Retro. Supp. I:** 295

"Political Litany, A" (Freneau), **Supp. II Part 1:** 257

"Political Migrations: A Family Story" (Mallon), **Supp. XIX:** 141–142

"Political Pastoral" (Frost), **Retro. Supp. I:** 139

"Political Poem" (Baraka), **Supp. II Part 1:** 36

Politics (Acker), **Supp. XII:** 3, 4

Politics (Macdonald), **I:** 233–234

"Politics" (Paley), **Supp. VI:** 217

"Politics, Structure, and Poetic Development" (McCombs), **Supp. XIII:** 33

"Politics and the English Language" (Orwell), **Retro. Supp. II:** 287; **Supp. I Part 2:** 620

Politics and the Novel (Howe), **Supp. VI:** 113

"Politics and the Personal Lyric in the Poetry of Joy Harjo and C. D. Wright" (Goodman), **Supp. XV:** 344

"Politics of Ethnic Authorship, The: Li-Young Lee, Emerson, and Whitman at the Banquet Table" (Partridge), **Supp. XV:** 219

"Politics of Silence, The" (Monette), **Supp. X:** 148

Polito, Robert, **Supp. XVIII:** 33; **Supp. XXIV:** 234

Politt, Katha, **Supp. XII:** 159

Poliziano (Angelo Ambrogini), **Supp. XXIV:** 152

Polk, James, **Supp. XIII:** 20

Polk, James K., **I:** 17; **II:** 433–434

Pollack, Sydney, **Supp. XIII:** 159

"Pollen" (Nye), **Supp. XIII:** 284

Pollitt, Katha, **Supp. X:** 186, 191, 193; **Supp. XVI:** 39

Pollock, Jackson, **IV:** 411, 420; **Supp. XV:** 145, 177, 178; **Supp. XIX:** 33; **Supp. XXIII:** 208, 210, 211

"Polly" (Chopin), **Retro. Supp. II:** 72

Polo, Marco, **III:** 395

Polonsky, Abraham, **Supp. XXI:** 261, 275

Polybius, **Supp. I Part 2:** 491

"Polydore" (Chopin), **Retro. Supp. II:** 66

"Pomegranate" (Glück), **Supp. V:** 82

"Pomegranate Seed" (Wharton), **IV:** 316; **Retro. Supp. I:** 382

Ponce de Leon, Luis, **III:** 391

"Pond, The" (Nemerov), **III:** 272

"Pond at Dusk, The" (Kenyon), **Supp. VII:** 168

Ponder Heart, The (Welty), **IV:** 261, 274–275, 281; **Retro. Supp. I:** 351–352

"Ponderosa Pine" (Huncke), **Supp. XIV:** 146

Ponsot, Margaret, **Supp. XVII:** 241

"Pony" (Sanders), **Supp. XVI:** 277

"Pony Car" (P. Benedict), **Supp. XXIII:** 47

Poodle Springs (Parker and Chandler), **Supp. IV Part 1:** 135; **Supp. XIX:** 189

Poodle Springs Story, The (Chandler), **Supp. IV Part 1:** 135

"Pool, The" (Doolittle), **Supp. I Part 1:** 264–265

Poole, Ernest, **II:** 444

"Pool Lights" (F. Barthelme), **Supp. XI:** 25, 26–27, 36

"Pool Room in the Lions Club" (Merwin), **Supp. III Part 1:** 346

"Poolside" (Skloot), **Supp. XX:** 202–203

"Poor Black Fellow" (Hughes), **Retro. Supp. I:** 204

"Poor Bustard, The" (Corso), **Supp. XII:** 134

"Poor but Happy" (Mamet), **Supp. XIV:** 252, 253

"Poor Dead Feet of My First Husband, The" (Schott), **Supp. XXIII:** 241

Poore, Charles, **III:** 364; **Supp. XIX:** 257, 264; **Supp. XX:** 38

Poor Fool (Caldwell), **I:** 291, 292, 308

Poorhouse Fair, The (Updike), **IV:** 214, 228–229, 232; **Retro. Supp. I:** 317, 320

"Poor Joanna" (Jewett), **II:** 394

"Poor Man's Pudding and Rich Man's Crumbs" (Melville), **III:** 89–90

"Poor Richard" (James), **II:** 322

Poor Richard's Almanac (undated) (Franklin), **II:** 112

Poor Richard's Almanac for 1733 (Franklin), **II:** 108, 110

Poor Richard's Almanac for 1739 (Franklin), **II:** 112

Poor Richard's Almanac for 1758 (Franklin), **II:** 101

Poor White (Anderson), **I:** 110–111

"Poor Working Girl" (Z. Fitzgerald), **Supp. IX:** 71

Popa, Vasko, **Supp. VIII:** 272

Pope, Alexander, **I:** 198, 204; **II:** 17, 114; **III:** 263, 267, 288, 517; **IV:** 145; **Retro. Supp. I:** 335; **Supp. I Part 1:** 150, 152, 310; **Supp. I Part 2:** 407, 422, 516, 714; **Supp. II Part 1:** 70, 71; **Supp. X:** 32, 36; **Supp. XII:** 260; **Supp. XV:** 258; **Supp. XX:** **280;** **Supp. XXV:** 119

Pope, James, **Supp. XXII:** 196

Pope-Hennessy, James, **Supp. XIV:** 348

"Pope's Penis, The" (Olds), **Supp. X:** 207

"Poplar, Sycamore" (Wilbur), **Supp. III Part 2:** 549

Popo and Fifina: Children of Haiti (Hughes and Bontemps), **Retro. Supp. I:** 203; **Supp. XXII:** 4, 10, 12

"Poppies" (Oliver), **Supp. VII:** 240

"Poppies in July" (Plath), **Supp. I Part 2:** 544

"Poppies in July" (Crooker), **Supp. XXIII:** 61

"Poppies in October" (Plath), **Supp. I Part 2:** 544

"Poppycock" (Francis), **Supp. IX:** 87

"Poppy Juice" (Taggard), **Supp. XXII:** 276

"Poppy Seed" (Lowell), **II:** 523

"Popular Art and the Cultural Tradition" (C. L. R. James), **Supp. XXI:** 170

Popular Book, The: A History of America's Literary Taste (Hart), **Supp. XVIII:** 257, 258

Popular Culture (Goldbarth), **Supp. XII:** **186**

Popular History of the United States (Gay), **Supp. I Part 1:** 158

"Popular Songs" (Ashbery), **Supp. III Part 1:** 6

"Populist Manifesto" (Ferlinghetti), **Supp. VIII:** 290

"Porcelain Bowl" (Glück), **Supp. V:** 83

Porcher, Frances, **Retro. Supp. II:** 71

Porco, Mike, **Supp. XVIII:** 24

"Porcupine, The" (Kinnell), **Supp. III Part 1:** 244

Porcupine's Kiss, The (Dobyns), **Supp. XIII:** **89–90**

"Por esas coases que pasan" (Hinojosa), **Supp. XIX:** 101

Porgy and Bess (film), **Supp. I Part 1:** 66

Porgy and Bess (play), **Supp. IV Part 1:** 6

"Porn Bought my Football" (Offutt), **Supp. XIX:** 163

"Porphyria's Lover" (Browning), **II:** 522

Portable Beat Reader, The (Charters, ed.), **Supp. XIV:** 152

Portable Blake, The (Kazin, ed.), **Supp. VIII:** 103

Portable Faulkner, The (Cowley, ed.), **II:** 57, 59; **Retro. Supp. I:** 73

Portable Kisses: Love Poems (Gallagher), **Supp. XXIV:** 170

Portable Paul and Jane Bowles, The (Dillon), **Supp. IV Part 1:** 95

Portable Veblen, The (Veblen), **Supp. I Part 2:** 630, 650

"Porte-Cochere" (Taylor), **Supp. V:** 320

"Porter" (Hughes), **Supp. I Part 1:** 327

"Porter" (Nelson), **Supp. XVIII:** 175

Porter, Bern, **III:** 171

Porter, Cole, **Supp. IX:** 189

Porter, Eliot, **Supp. IV Part 2:** 599

Porter, Fairfield, **Supp. XV:** 178; **Supp. XXIII:** 209, 211, 212; **Supp. XXIV:** 41

Porter, Herman W., **Supp. I Part 1:** 49

Porter, Horace, **Retro. Supp. II:** 4, 127

Porter, Jacob, **Supp. I Part 1:** 153

Porter, Katherine Anne, **I:** 97, 385; **II:** 194, 606; **III: 433–455,** 482; **IV:** 26, 138, 246, 261, 279, 280, 282; **Retro. Supp. I:** 354; **Retro. Supp. II:** 233, 235; **Supp. IV Part 1:** 31, 310; **Supp. V:** 225; **Supp. VIII:** 156, 157; **Supp. IX:** 93, 94, 95, 98, 128; **Supp. X:** 50; **Supp. XIII:** 294; **Supp. XIV:** 3; **Supp. XV:** 338; **Supp. XXIV:** 52

Porter, Noah, **Supp. I Part 2:** 640

Porter, William Sydney. *See* Henry, O.

"Porter Paints a Picture"(O'Hara), **Supp. XXIII:** 212

Porteus, Beilby, **Supp. I Part 1:** 150

"Portland Going Out, The" (Merwin), **Supp. III Part 1:** 345

Portnoy's Complaint (P. Roth), **Retro. Supp. II: 282–286,** 291; **Supp. III Part 2:** 401, 404, 405, 407, 412–414, 426; **Supp. V:** 119, 122; **Supp. XI:** 140; **Supp. XVII:** 8, 43; **Supp. XX:** 177

Port of Saints (Burroughs), **Supp. III Part 1:** 106

"Portrait" (Dixon), **Supp. XII:** 154

"Portrait, A" (Parker), **Supp. IX:** 192–193

"Portrait, The" (Kunitz), **Supp. III Part 1:** 263

"Portrait, The" (Wharton), **Retro. Supp. I:** 364

"Portrait d'une Femme" (Pound), **Retro. Supp. I:** 288

Portrait in Brownstone (Auchincloss), **Supp. IV Part 1:** 21, 23, 27, 31

"Portrait in Georgia" (Toomer), **Supp. IX:** 314

"Portrait in Greys, A" (W. C. Williams), **Retro. Supp. I:** 416

"Portrait of a Girl in Glass" (T. Williams), **IV:** 383

"Portrait of a Jewelry Drummer" (Untermeyer), **Supp. XV:** 299–300

"Portrait of a Lady" (Eliot), **I:** 569, 570, 571, 584; **III:** 4; **Retro. Supp. I:** 55, 56, 62

Portrait of a Lady, The (James), **I:** 10, 258, 461–462, 464; **II:** 323, 325, 327, 328–329, 334; **Retro. Supp. I:** 215, 216, 217, 219, 220, 223, **224–225,** 232, 233, 381

"Portrait of an Artist" (P. Roth), **Supp. III Part 2:** 412

Portrait of an Eye: Three Novels (Acker), **Supp. XII:** 6, **7–9**

"Portrait of an Invisible Man" (Auster), **Supp. XII:** 21

"Portrait of a Supreme Court Judge" (Untermeyer), **Supp. XV:** 299

Portrait of Bascom Hawkes, A (Wolfe), **IV:** 451–452, 456

Portrait of Edith Wharton (Lubbock), **Retro. Supp. I:** 366

Portrait of Logan Pearsall Smith, Drawn from His Letters and Diaries, A (Russell, ed.), **Supp. XIV:** 349

Portrait of Picasso as a Young Man (Mailer), **Retro. Supp. II:** 213

"Portrait of the Artist as an Old Man, A" (Humphrey), **Supp. IX:** 109

Portrait of the Artist as a Young Man, A (Joyce), **I:** 475–476; **III:** 471, 561; **Retro. Supp. I:** 127; **Retro. Supp. II:** 4, 331; **Supp. IX:** 236; **Supp. XIII:** 53, 95

"Portrait of the Artist with Hart Crane" (Wright), **Supp. V:** 342

"Portrait of the Great White Hunter Fox-hunting in the Absence of Big Game" (Major), **Supp. XXII:** 183

"Portrait of the Intellectual as a Yale Man" (McCarthy), **II:** 563, 564–565

"Portrait of the Reader with a Bowl of Cereal, A" (Collins), **Supp. XXI:** 55

"Portrait of the Self . . . , A" (Sobin), **Supp. XVI:** 288

Portraits and Elegies (Schnackenberg), **Supp. XV:** 249, **253–256**

"Portraits of Grief" *(New York Times),* **Supp. XIX:** 142

"Port Town" (Hughes), **Retro. Supp. I:** 199

Portuguese Voyages to America in the Fifteenth Century (Morison), **Supp. I Part 2:** 488

"Po' Sandy" (Chesnutt), **Supp. XIV:** 60

Poseidon Adventure, The (film), **Supp. XII:** 321

Poseidon Adventure, The (Gallico), **Supp. XVI:** 238

"Poseidon and Company" (Carver), **Supp. III Part 1:** 137

"Positive Obsession" (O. Butler), **Supp. XIII:** 70

Poss, Stanley, **Supp. XIV:** 166

Possession (Byatt), **Supp. XXI:** 147

"Possessions" (H. Crane), **I:** 392–393; **Retro. Supp. II:** 78

Possible World, A (Koch), **Supp. XV:** 184

Postal Inspector (film), **Supp. XIII:** 166

"Postcard from Greece" (Stallings), **Supp. XXV:** 229, 231

Postcards (Proulx), **Supp. VII:** 249, 256–258, 262

"Postcard to Send to Sumer, A" (Bronk), **Supp. XXI:** 31

"Postcolonialism and Autobiography" (Skinner and Waller), **Supp. XXII:** 78

"Postcolonial Tale, A" (Harjo), **Supp. XII:** 227

"Posthumous Letter to Gilbert White" (Auden), **Supp. II Part 1:** 26

"Post-Larkin Triste" (Karr), **Supp. XI:** 242–243

Postlethwaite, Diana, **Supp. XII:** 317–318; **Supp. XVI:** 176

"Postlude" (W. C. Williams), **Retro. Supp. I:** 415

Postman, Neil, **Supp. XI:** 275

Postman Always Rings Twice, The (Cain), **Supp. XIII:** 165–166

Postman Always Rings Twice, The (film), **Supp. XIV:** 241

"Postmaster and the Clerk, The" (Budbill), **Supp. XIX:** 9

"Postmortem Guide, A" (Dunn), **Supp. XI:** 155

Postrel, Virginia, **Supp. XIV:** 298, 311

"Postscript" (Du Bois), **Supp. II Part 1:** 173

"Postscript" (Nye), **Supp. XIII:** 287

Postsouthern Sense of Place, The (Bone), **Supp. XXII:** 247

"Potato" (Wilbur), **Supp. III Part 2:** 545

"Potatoes' Dance, The" (Lindsay), **Supp. I Part 2:** 394

Pot of Earth, The (MacLeish), **III:** 5, 6–8, 10, 12, 18

"Pot Roast" (Strand), **Supp. IV Part 2:** 629

Potshot (Parker), **Supp. XIX:** 185

Pot Shots at Poetry (Francis), **Supp. IX: 83–84**

Potter, Beatrix, **Supp. I Part 2:** 656; **Supp. XVI:** 100

Potter, Stephen, **IV:** 430

Potter's House, The (Stegner), **Supp. IV Part 2:** 598, 606

Poulenc, Francis, **Supp. IV Part 1:** 81

Poulin, Al, Jr., **Supp. IX:** 272; **Supp. XI:** 259

Pound, Ezra, **I:** 49, 58, 60, 66, 68, 69, 105, 236, 243, 256, 384, 403, 428, 429, 475, 476, 482, 487, 521, 578; **II:** 26, 55, 168, 263, 316, 371, 376, 513, 517, 520, 526, 528, 529, 530; **III:** 2, 5, 8, 9, 13–14, 17, 174, 194, 196, 278, 430, 453, **456–479,** 492, 504, 511, 523, 524, 527, 575–576, 586, 590; **IV:** 27, 28, 407, 415, 416, 433, 446; **Retro. Supp. I:** 51, 52, 55, 58, 59, 63, 82, 89, 127, 140, 171, 177, 178, 198, 216, **283–294,** 298, 299, 359, 411, 412, 413, 414, 417, 418, 419, 420, 423, 426, 427, 430, 431; **Retro. Supp. II:** 178, 183, 189, 326; **Supp. I Part 1:** 253, 255–258, 261–268, 272, 274; **Supp. I Part 2:** 387, 721; **Supp. II Part 1:** 1, 8, 20, 30, 91, 136; **Supp. III Part 1:** 48, 63, 64, 73, 105, 146, 225, 271; **Supp. III Part 2:** 542, **609–617,** 619, 620, 622, 625, 626, 628, 631; **Supp. IV Part 1:** 153, 314; **Supp. V:** 331, 338, 340, 343, 345; **Supp. VIII:** 39, 105, 195, 205, 271, 290, 291, 292, 303; **Supp. IX:** 291; **Supp. X:** 24, 36, 112, 120, 122; **Supp. XII:** 97; **Supp. XIV:** 11, 55, 83, 272, 284, 286, 287, 347; **Supp. XV:** 20, 42, 43, 51, 93, 161, 181, 297, 298, 299, 301, 302, 306; **Supp. XVI:** 47, 282; **Supp. XVII:** 111, 226–227; **Supp. XIX:** 42; **Supp. XXI:** 33; **Supp. XXII:** 165; **Supp. XXIII:** 26, 166, 174; **Supp. XXIV:** 37

Pound, Louise, **Retro. Supp. I:** 4; **Supp. XV:** 137

Pound, T. S., **I:** 428

"Pound Reweighed" (Cowley), **Supp. II Part 1:** 143

Powell, Anthony, **Supp. XVIII:** 136, 146; **Supp. XIX:** 131

Powell, Betty, **Retro. Supp. II:** 140

Powell, D. A., **Supp. XXIII:** 221

Powell, Dawn, **Supp. IV Part 2:** 678, 682; **Supp. XIX:** 143

Powell, Dick, **Supp. IX:** 250

Powell, John Wesley, **Supp. IV Part 2:** 598, 604, 611

Powell, Lawrence Clark, **III:** 189

Powell, Margaret K., **Supp. XXIV:** 170

Powell, William, **Supp. IV Part 1:** 355

"Power" (Corso), **Supp. XII:** 117, 126, 127, **128**

"Power" (Emerson), **II:** 2, 3

"Power" (Rich), **Supp. I Part 2:** 569

Power, Samantha, **Supp. XXIII:** 25, 26, 27

"Power and Light" (Dickey), **Supp. IV Part 1:** 182

Power and the Glory, The (Greene), **III:** 556

"Powerhouse" (Welty), **Retro. Supp. I:** 343, 346

"Power Never Dominion" (Rukeyser), **Supp. VI:** 281

"Power of Fancy, The" (Freneau), **Supp. II Part 1:** 255

Power of Myth, The (Campbell), **Supp. IX:** 245

"Power of Prayer, The" (Lanier), **Supp. I Part 1:** 357

"Power of Stories, The" (Sanders), **Supp. XVI:** 278

"Power of Suggestion" (Auchincloss), **Supp. IV Part 1:** 33

Power of Sympathy, The (Brown), **Supp. II Part 1:** 74

Power of Sympathy, The (W. H. Brown), **Supp. XXV:** 38

Power Politics (Atwood), **Supp. XIII:** 20, 33–34, 35

Powers, Catherine A., **Supp. XXII:** 217

Powers, J. F., **Supp. V:** 319; **Supp. XVII:** 43

Powers, Kim, **Supp. VIII:** 329, 340

Powers, Richard, **Supp. IX: 207–225; Supp. XVII:** 183; **Supp. XX:** 93; **Supp. XXII:** 49; **Supp. XXIV:** 131

Powers of Attorney (Auchincloss), **Supp. IV Part 1:** 31, 32, 33

"Powers of Darkness" (Wharton), **Retro. Supp. I:** 379

Powys, John Cowper, **Supp. I Part 2:** 454, 476; **Supp. IX:** 135

Poynton, Jerome, **Supp. XIV:** 147, 150

Pozorski, Aimee L., **Supp. XXII:** 160, 166

Practical Agitation (Chapman), **Supp. XIV:** 41

"Practical Application in This Life, by Men as Social and Intellectual Beings, of the Certainty of a Future State, The" (Very), **Supp. XXV:** 240

Practical Criticism: A Study of Literary Judgment (Richards), **Supp. XIV:** 3, 16

Practical Magic (film), **Supp. X:** 80

Practical Magic (Hoffman), **Supp. X:** 78, 82, **88–89**

"Practical Methods of Meditation, The" (Dawson), **IV:** 151

Practical Navigator, The (Bowditch), **Supp. I Part 2:** 482

Practice of Perspective, The (Dubreuil), **Supp. IV Part 2:** 425

Practice of Reading, The (Donoghue), **Supp. VIII:** 189

Pragmatism: A New Name for Some Old Ways of Thinking (James), **II:** 352

"Pragmatism's Conception of Truth" (James), **Supp. XIV:** 40

Prague Orgy, The (P. Roth), **Retro. Supp. II:** 280

"Praire, The" (Clampitt), **Supp. IX:** 42

"Prairie" (Sandburg), **III:** 583, 584

Prairie, The (Cooper), **I:** 339, 342

"Prairie Birthday" (Leopold), **Supp. XIV:** 185

Prairie Home Companion, A (Keillor, radio program), **Supp. XIII:** 274; **Supp. XVI:** 169–171, 173–178

Prairie Home Morning Show, A (Keillor, radio program), **Supp. XVI:** 171

"Prairie Life, A Citizen Speaks" (Dunn), **Supp. XI:** 145

"Prairies, The" (Bryant), **Supp. I Part 1:** 157, 162, 163, 166

Praise (Hass), **Supp. VI:** 104–105, 106

"Praise for an Urn" (Crane), **I:** 388

"Praise for Sick Women" (Snyder), **Supp. VIII:** 294

"Praise in Summer" (Wilbur), **Supp. III Part 2:** 546–548, 560, 562

"Praise of a Palmtree" (Levertov), **Supp. III Part 1:** 284

"Praise of the Committee" (Rukeyser), **Supp. VI:** 278

"Praises, The" (Goldbarth), **Supp. XII:** 185

"Praises, The" (Olson), **Supp. II Part 2:** 558, 560, 563, 564

Praises and Dispraises (Des Pres), **Supp. X:** 120

Praisesong for the Widow (Marshall), **Supp. IV Part 1:** 14; **Supp. XI:** 18, 276, 278, **284–286,** 287; **Supp. XX: 154**

"Praise to the End!" (Roethke), **III:** 529, 532, 539

Prajadhipok, King of Siam, **I:** 522

Prater Violet (Isherwood), **Supp. XIV: 164–166,** 169–170, 171

Pratt, Anna (Anna Alcott), **Supp. I Part 1:** 33

Pratt, Louis H., **Retro. Supp. II:** 6

Pratt, Mary Louise, **Retro. Supp. II:** 48

Pratt, Parley, **Supp. IV Part 2:** 603

"Prattler" (newspaper column), **I:** 207

"Prattler, The" (Bierce), **I:** 196

"Prayer" (Gioia), **Supp. XV:** 117

"Prayer" (Olds), **Supp. X:** 204

"Prayer" (Peacock), **Supp. XIX:** 198, 199, 200

"Prayer" (Toomer), **Supp. IX:** 318

"Prayer, A" (Kushner), **Supp. IX: 134**

"Prayer for Columbus" (Whitman), **IV:** 348

"Prayer for My Daughter" (Yeats), **II:** 598

"Prayer for My Grandfather to Our Lady, A" (Lowell), **II:** 541–542

"Prayer for my Son" (C. Frost), **Supp. XV:** 98–99

"Prayer for Our Daughters" (Jarman), **Supp. XVII:** 120

Prayer for Owen Meany, A (Irving), **Supp. VI:** 164, 165, 166, **175–176**

"PRAYER FOR SAVING" (Baraka), **Supp. II Part 1:** 52–53

Prayer for the Dying, A (O'Nan), **Supp. XXV:** 141, 142, 144, 145–146, 148

"Prayer in Spring, A" (Frost), **II:** 153, 164

"Prayer Meeting" (Di Piero), **Supp. XIX:** 46, 47

"Prayer on All Saint's Day" (Cowley), **Supp. II Part 1:** 138, 153

Prayers for Dark People (Du Bois), **Supp. II Part 1:** 186

"Prayer to Hermes" (Creeley), **Supp. IV Part 1:** 156, 157

"Prayer to Masks" (Senghor), **Supp. IV Part 1:** 16

"Prayer to the Child of Prague" (Salinas), **Supp. XIII:** 327

"Prayer to the Good Poet" (Wright), **Supp. III Part 2:** 603

"Prayer to the Pacific" (Silko), **Supp. IV Part 2:** 560

"Pray without Ceasing" (Emerson), **II:** 9–10

Praz, Mario, **IV:** 430

"Preacher, The" (Whittier), **Supp. I Part 2:** 698–699

Preacher and the Slave, The (Stegner), **Supp. IV Part 2:** 599, 608, 609

Precaution (Cooper), **I:** 337, 339

"Precautions"(Karyotakis, trans. Hadas), **Supp. XXIII:** 125

"Preconceptions of Economic Science, The" (Veblen), **Supp. I Part 2:** 634

Predecessors, Et Cetera (Clampitt), **Supp. IX:** 37

"Predicament, A" (Poe), **Retro. Supp. II:** 273

Predilections (Moore), **III:** 194

Prefaces and Prejudices (Mencken), **III:** 99, 104, 106, 119

Preface to a Twenty Volume Suicide Note. . . . (Baraka), **Supp. II Part 1:** 31, 33–34, 51, 61

"Preference" (Wylie), **Supp. I Part 2:** 713

"Prejudice against the Past, The" (Moore), **IV:** 91

Prejudices (Mencken), **Supp. I Part 2:** 630

Prejudices: A Selection (Farrell, ed.), **III:** 116

Prejudices: First Series (Mencken), **III:** 105

"Preliminary Remarks on the Poetry in the First Person" (Wright), **Supp. XV:** 339

Prelude, A: Landscapes, Characters and Conversations from the Earlier Years of My Life (Wilson), **IV:** 426, 427, 430, 434, 445

Prelude, The (Wordsworth), **III:** 528; **IV:** 331, 343; **Supp. I Part 2:** 416, 676; **Supp. XI:** 248

Prelude and Liebestod (McNally), **Supp. XIII:** 201

"Preludes" (Eliot), **I:** 573, 576, 577; **Retro. Supp. I:** 55; **Supp. IV Part 2:** 436

Preludes for Memnon (Aiken), **I:** 59, 65

Preludes from Memnon (Aiken), **Supp. X:** 50

"Prelude to an Evening" (Ransom), **III:** 491, 492–493

Prelude to Darkness (Salinas), **Supp. XIII:** 311, **318–319,** 320

"Prelude to the Present" (Mumford), **Supp. II Part 2:** 471

"Premature Burial, The" (Poe), **III:** 415, 416, 418; **Retro. Supp. II:** 270

"Premeditations"(Schott), **Supp. XXIII:** 247

Preminger, Otto, **Supp. IX:** 3, 9; **Supp. XX: 246–247**

"Premonition" (Hay), **Supp. XIV:** 122

"Premonitions of the Bread Line" (Komunyakaa), **Supp. XIII:** 114, 115

Prenshaw, Peggy Whitman, **Supp. X:** 229

"Preparations" (Silko), **Supp. IV Part 2:** 560

Preparatory Meditations (Taylor), **IV:** 145, 148, 149, 150, 152, 153, 154–155, 164, 165

"Prepare" (Carruth), **Supp. XVI:** 59

Prepositions: The Collected Critical Essays of Louis Zukofsky (Zukofsky), **Supp. III Part 2:** 630

Prescott, Anne, **Supp. IV Part 1:** 299

Prescott, Orville, **Supp. IV Part 2:** 680; **Supp. XI:** 340; **Supp. XXIII:** 13

Prescott, Peter, **Supp. X:** 83

Prescott, Peter S., **Supp. XVI:** 212

Prescott, William, **Retro. Supp. I:** 123

Prescott, William Hickling, **II:** 9, 310, 313–314; **IV:** 309; **Supp. I Part 2:** 414, 479, 493, 494

"Prescription of Painful Ends" (Jeffers), **Supp. II Part 2:** 424

"Presence, The" (Gordon), **II:** 199, 200

"Presence, The" (Kumin), **Supp. IV Part 2:** 445, 455

Presence and Desire: Essays on Gender, Sexuality, Performance (Dolan), **Supp. XV:** 327

"Presence of Others, The" (Kenyon), **Supp. VII:** 164

Presences (Taylor), **Supp. V:** 325

"Present Age, The" (Emerson), **II:** 11–12

Present Danger, The: Do We Have the Will to Reverse the Decline of American Power? (Podhoretz), **Supp. VIII:** 241

"Present for the Boy, A" (Swados), **Supp. XIX:** 259

Present for Young Ladies, A (Rowson), **Supp. XV:** 245

"Present Hour" (Sandburg), **III:** 593–594

Present Philosophical Tendencies (Perry), **I:** 224

"Present State of Ethical Philosophy, The" (Emerson), **II:** 9

"Present State of Poetry, The" (Schwartz), **Supp. II Part 2:** 666

"Preservation of Innocence" (Baldwin), **Supp. I Part 1:** 51

"Preserving Wildness" (Berry), **Supp. X:** 28, 29, 32

"President and Other Intellectuals, The" (Kazin), **Supp. VIII:** 104

Presidential Papers, The (Mailer), **III:** 35, 37–38, 42, 45; **Retro. Supp. II:** 203, 204, 206

"Presidents" (Merwin), **Supp. III Part 1:** 351

Presnell, Robert, Sr., **Supp. XIII:** 166

Pressley, Nelson, **Supp. XVIII:** 37–38

"PRES SPOKE IN A LANGUAGE" (Baraka), **Supp. II Part 1:** 60

"Presto Manifesto" (Stallings), **Supp. XXV:** 227

Presumed Innocent (Turow), **Supp. XVII:** 214–216, 223; 217

"Pretext, The" (Wharton), **Retro. Supp. I:** 371

Pretty Baby (film), **Supp. XXI:** 252

Pretty Boy Floyd (McMurtry), **Supp. V:** 231

"Pretty Girl, The" (Dubus), **Supp. VII:** 87–88

"Pretty Mouth and Green My Eyes" (Salinger), **III:** 560

"Previous Condition" (Baldwin), **Supp. I Part 1:** 51, 55, 63

"Previous Tenant, The" (Simpson), **Supp. IX:** 278–279

Prevost, Verbie Lovorn, **Supp. XXI:** 45

Priaulx, Allan, **Supp. XI:** 228

Price, Alan, **Retro. Supp. I:** 377

Price, E. Hoffman, **Supp. XXV:** 114

Price, Reynolds, **Supp. VI: 253–270; Supp. IX:** 256, 257

Price, Richard, **II:** 9; **Supp. I Part 2:** 522; **Supp. XX: 85**

Price, The (A. Miller), **III:** 165–166

"Price Is Right, The" (Skloot), **Supp. XX: 198–199**

"Price of the Harness, The" (Crane), **I:** 414

Pricksongs & Descants; Fictions (Coover), **Supp. V:** 39, 42, 43, 49, 50

"Pride" (Hughes), **Supp. I Part 1:** 331

Pride and Prejudice (Austen), **II:** 290

Prideaux, Tom, **Supp. IV Part 2:** 574, 590

"Priesthood, The" (Winters), **Supp. II Part 2:** 786

Priestly, Joseph, **Supp. I Part 2:** 522

Primary Colors, The (A. Theroux), **Supp. VIII:** 312

"Primary Ground, A" (Rich), **Supp. I Part 2:** 563

"Prime" (Auden), **Supp. II Part 1:** 22

"Primer Class" (Bishop), **Retro. Supp. II:** 38, 51

Primer for Blacks (Brooks), **Supp. III Part 1:** 85

Primer for Combat (Boyle), **Supp. XXIV:** 62

"Primer for the Nuclear Age" (Dove), **Supp. IV Part 1:** 246

Primer mensaje a la América Hispana (W. Frank), **Supp. XX: 76**

Primer of Ignorance, A (Blackmur), **Supp. II Part 1:** 91

Prime-Stevenson, Edward Irenaeus, **Supp. XX: 235**

Primitive, The (C. Himes), **Supp. XVI:** 139, **141–142**

"Primitive Black Man, The" (Du Bois), **Supp. II Part 1:** 176

"Primitive Like an Orb, A" (Stevens), **IV:** 89; **Retro. Supp. I:** 309

Primitive People (Prose), **Supp. XVI:** 255, 256, 257

"Primitive Singing" (Lindsay), **Supp. I Part 2:** 389–390

Primitivism and Decadence (Winters), **Supp. II Part 2:** 786, 803–807, 812

Primrose, Archibald Philip, **Supp. XX: 230**

Prince, F. T., **Supp. XXIV:** 45

Prince, Richard, **Supp. XII:** 4

"Prince, The" (Jarrell), **II:** 379

"Prince, The" (Winters), **Supp. II Part 2:** 802

Prince and the Pauper, The (Twain), **IV:** 200–201, 206

Prince Hagen (Sinclair), **Supp. V:** 280

Prince of a Fellow, A (Hearon), **Supp. VIII:** 58, **62–63**

Princess, The (Tennyson), **Supp. I Part 2:** 410

Princess and the Goblins, The (Macdonald), **Supp. XIII:** 75

Princess Casamassima, The (James), **II:** 276, 291; **IV:** 202; **Retro. Supp. I:** 216, 221, 222, 225, **226–227**

"Princess Casamassima, The" (Trilling), **Supp. III Part 2:** 502, 503

Princess of Arcady, A (Henry), **Retro. Supp. II:** 97

"Principles" (Du Bois), **Supp. II Part 1:** 172

Principles of Literary Criticism (Richards), **I:** 274; **Supp. I Part 1:** 264; **Supp. XIV:** 3

Principles of Psychology, The (James), **II:** 321, 350–352, 353, 354, 357, 362, 363–364; **IV:** 28, 29, 32, 37

Principles of Psychology, The (W. James), **Supp. XVII:** 97

Principles of Zoölogy (Agassiz), **Supp. I Part 1:** 312

Prior, Sir James, **II:** 315

Prior, Matthew, **II:** 111; **III:** 521

"Prison, The" (Malamud), **Supp. I Part 2:** 431, 437

"Prisoned Love" (Boyce), **Supp. XXI:** 9

"Prisoner of Ours, The" (Weigl), **Supp. XIX:** 288

Prisoner of Second Avenue, The (Simon), **Supp. IV Part 2:** 583, 584

Prisoner of Sex, The (Mailer), **III:** 46; **Retro. Supp. II:** 206

Prisoner of Zenda, The (film), **Supp. I Part 2:** 615

Prisoner's Dilemma (Powers), **Supp. IX:** 212, **214–216,** 221

Prison Memoirs of an Anarchist (A. Berkman), **Supp. XVII:** 103–104

Pritchard, William, **Supp. XVI:** 71

Pritchard, William H., **Retro. Supp. I:** 131, 141; **Supp. IV Part 1:** 285; **Supp. IV Part 2:** 642; **Supp. XI:** 326

Pritchett, V. S., **II:** 587; **Supp. II Part 1:** 143; **Supp. VIII:** 171; **Supp. XIII:** 168

Pritikin, Renny, **Supp. XXIV:** 40

"Privatation and Publication" (Cowley), **Supp. II Part 1:** 149

Private Contentment (Price), **Supp. VI:** 263

"Private History of a Campaign That Failed" (Twain), **IV:** 195

Private I, The: Privacy in a Public World (Peacock, ed.), **Supp. XIX:** 193, 203

Private Life of Axie Reed, The (Knowles), **Supp. XII:** 249

Private Line (Major), **Supp. XXII:** 174

"Private Man Confronts His Vulgarities at Dawn, A" (Dunn), **Supp. XI:** 146

Private Memoirs and Confessions of a Justified Sinner, The (Hogg), **Supp. IX:** 276

"Private Property and the Common Wealth" (Berry), **Supp. X:** 25

Private Snafu series (Geisel), **Supp. XVI:** 102

"Private Theatricals" (Howells), **II:** 280

Private Women, Public Stage: Literary Domesticity in Nineteenth-Century America (Kelley), **Supp. XVIII:** 257

Privilege, The (Kumin), **Supp. IV Part 2:** 442–444, 451

Prize Stories 1918 : The O. Henry Awards, **Supp. XVI:** 16

"Probe" (Ryan as Quin), **Supp. XVIII:** 229

"Probing the Dark" (Komunyakaa), **Supp. XIII:** 131

"Problem from Hell, A": America and the Age of Genocide (Power), **Supp. XXIII:** 25, 27–28

"Problem from Milton, A" (Wilbur), **Supp. III Part 2:** 550

"Problem of Anxiety, The" (Koch), **Supp. XV:** 183

"Problem of Being, The" (James), **II:** 360

Problem of Classification in the Theory of Value, The (Locke), **Supp. XIV:** 199

"Problem of Evil into Cocoon" (Taggard), **Supp. XXII:** 284

"Problem of Housing the Negro, The" (Du Bois), **Supp. II Part 1:** 168

"Problem of the Religious Novel, The" (Isherwood), **Supp. XIV:** 172

Problems and Other Stories (Updike), **Retro. Supp. I:** 322, 329

Problems of Dostoevsky's Poetics (Bakhtin), **Supp. XXII:** 259

"Problem Solving" (Goldbarth), **Supp. XII:** 185

Procedures for Underground (Atwood), **Supp. XIII:** 33

"Procedures for Underground" (Atwood), **Supp. XIII:** 33

Process (Boyle), **Supp. XXIV:** 51

Procession, The (al-Mawākib) (Gibran), **Supp. XX: 116, 124**

Processional (Lawson), **I:** 479

"Procession at Candlemas, A" (Clampitt), **Supp. IX:** 41

"Proclamation" (Saunders), **Supp. XIX:** 235

Proclus, **Retro. Supp. I:** 247

"Prodigal" (Ammons), **Supp. VII:** 29

"Prodigal" (Hoffman), **Supp. XVIII:** 86

"Prodigal, The" (Bishop), **Supp. I Part 1:** 90, 92

Prodigal Parents, The (Lewis), **II:** 454–455

"Prodigy" (Simic), **Supp. VIII:** 278

Producers, The (film, M. Brooks), **Supp. XVII:** 45

"Proem" (Crane), **I:** 397

"Proem, The: By the Carpenter" (O. Henry), **Supp. II Part 1:** 409

"Professions for Women" (Woolf), **Supp. XIII:** 305

"Professor" (Hughes), **Supp. I Part 1:** 330

"Professor, The" (Bourne), **I:** 223

Professor at the Breakfast Table, The (Holmes), **Supp. I Part 1:** 313, 316

"Professor Clark's Economics" (Veblen), **Supp. I Part 2:** 634

Professor of Desire, The (P. Roth), **Retro. Supp. II:** 288; **Supp. III Part 2:** 403, 418–420

Professor's House, The (Cather), **I:** 325–336; **Retro. Supp. I:** 16

"Professor Veblen" (Mencken), **Supp. I Part 2:** 630

Proffer, Carl R., **Supp. VIII:** 22

Profile Makers, The (Bierds), **Supp. XVII:** 29, **30–32,** 33

"Profile of the Tenderloin Street Prostitute, A" (Vollmann), **Supp. XVII:** 230

Profits of Religion, The (Sinclair), **Supp. V:** 276

"Prognosis" (Warren), **IV:** 245

"Progress" (F. Wright), **Supp. XVII:** 247

"Progress Report" (Simic), **Supp. VIII:** 278

"Project for a Trip to China" (Sontag), **Supp. II Part 2:** 454, 469

"Project for *The Ambassadors*" (James), **Retro. Supp. I:** 229

"Projection" (Nemerov), **III:** 275

"Projective Verse" (Olson), **Supp. III Part 1:** 30; **Supp. III Part 2:** 555, 556, 557, 624; **Supp. IV Part 1:** 139, 153; **Supp. VIII:** 290

"Projector, The" (Baker), **Supp. XIII:** 53, 55

Prokofiev, Sergey Sergeyevich, **Supp. IV Part 1:** 81

"Prolegomena, Section 1" (Pound), **Supp. III Part 2:** 615–616

"Prolegomena, Section 2" (Pound), **Supp. III Part 2:** 616

"Prolegomenon to a Biography of Mailer" (Lucid), **Retro. Supp. II:** 195

Proletarian Literature in the United States (Hicks), **Supp. I Part 2: 609–610**

"Prologue" (MacLeish), **III:** 8, 14

Prologue, for Full Chorus of Mixed Voices and Orchestra (Taggard and Schuman), **Supp. XXII:** 283

"Prologue to a Life" (D. West), **Supp. XVIII:** 280

"Prologue to Our Time" (Mumford), **Supp. III Part 2:** 473

"Prometheus" (Longfellow), **II:** 494

Prometheus Bound (Lowell), **II:** 543, 544, 545, 555

Promise, The (Buck), **Supp. II Part 1:** 124

"Promise, The" (Olds), **Supp. X:** 213

"Promise and Fulfillment" (D. West), **Supp. XVIII:** 278

Promised Land (Parker), **Supp. XIX:** 183, 184, 190

Promised Land, The (M. Antin), **Supp. IX:** 227; **Supp. XVI:** 148, 149; **Supp. XX:** 1, 2, 3, **4–9,** 11

Promised Land, The (Porter), **III:** 447

"Promised Land, The" (R. Fisher), **Supp. XIX:** 72

Promised Lands (Sontag), **Supp. III Part 2:** 452

Promise of American Life, The (Croly), **I:** 229

"Promise of Blue Horses, The" (Harjo), **Supp. XII:** 228

Promise of Rest, The (Price), **Supp. VI:** 262, 266

Promises (Warren), **Supp. XIV:** 15

Promises, Promises (musical), **Supp. IV Part 2:** 575

Promises: Poems 1954–1956 (Warren), **IV:** 244–245, 249, 252

"Promise This When You Be Dying" (Dickinson), **Retro. Supp. I:** 44, 46

"Pronoun Variations" (Hadas), **Supp. XXIII:** 120

Proof, The (Winters), **Supp. II Part 2:** 786, 791, 792–794

Proofs and Theories: Essays on Poetry (Glück), **Supp. V:** 77, 79, 92; **Supp. XIV:** 269

"Propaganda of History, The" (Du Bois), **Supp. II Part 1:** 182

Propertius, Sextus, **III:** 467; **Retro. Supp. I:** 187; **Supp. XII:** 2

Property Of: A Novel (Hoffman), **Supp. X:** 77, 79, **80–82**

"Property of Loss" (W. V. Davis), **Supp. XXI:** 95

"Prophecy of Samuel Sewall, The" (Whittier), **Supp. I Part 2:** 699

Prophet, The (Asch), **Supp. XXIII:** 7

Prophet, The (Gibran), **Supp. XX: 113, 115, 119–121, 126**

"Prophet, The" (Notley), **Supp. XXII:** 229

"Prophet, The" (Very), **Supp. XXV:** 248–249

"Prophet and the Child, The" (Gibran), **Supp. XX: 123**

Propheteers, The (Apple), **Supp. XVII: 6–7**

"Prophetic Pictures, The" (Hawthorne), **II:** 227

"Proportion" (Lowell), **II:** 525

"Proposal" (Carver), **Supp. III Part 1:** 149

Proposals Relating to the Education of Youth in Pensilvania (Franklin), **II:** 113

"Proposed New Version of the Bible" (Franklin), **II:** 110

Prose, Francine, **Supp. XII:** 333; **Supp. XVI: 249–264; Supp. XIX:** 209; **Supp. XXIII:** 300

"Prose for Departure" (Merrill), **Supp. III Part 1:** 336

Prose Pieces (Bynner), **Supp. XV:** 52

"Prose Poem as an Evolving Form, The" (R. Bly), **Supp. IV Part 1:** 64

"Proserpina and the Devil" (Wilder), **IV:** 358

"Prosody" (Espaillat), **Supp. XXI:** 102

"Prosody" (Shapiro), **Supp. II Part 2:** 710

Prospect before Us, The (Dos Passos), **I:** 491

"Prospective Immigrants Please Note" (Rich), **Supp. I Part 2:** 555

Prospect of Peace, The (Barlow), **Supp. II Part 1:** 67, 68, 75

Prospects of Literature, The (L. P. Smith), **Supp. XIV:** 343

Prospects on the Rubicon (Paine), **Supp. I Part 2:** 510–511

Prospectus of a National Institution, to Be Established in the United States (Barlow), **Supp. II Part 1:** 80, 82

Prospice (Browning), **IV:** 366

"Protestant Easter" (Sexton), **Supp. II Part 2:** 684

"Prothalamion" (Schwartz), **Supp. II Part 2:** 649, 652

"Prothalamion" (Spenser), **Retro. Supp. I:** 62

Proud, Robert, **Supp. I Part 1:** 125

"Proud Farmer, The" (Lindsay), **Supp. I Part 2:** 381

Proud Flesh (Humphrey), **Supp. IX:** 94, 95, 96, **102–103,** 104, 105, 109

"Proud Flesh" (Warren), **IV:** 243

Proud Highway, The (Thompson), **Supp. XXIV:** 283

Proud Lady (Boyce), **Supp. XXI:** 7, 12

"Proud Lady" (Wylie), **Supp. I Part 2:** 711–712

Proulx, Annie, **Supp. VII: 249–267; Supp. XXIV:** 245, 251

Proust, Marcel, **I:** 89, 319, 327, 377, 461; **II:** 377, 514, 606; **III:** 174, 181, 184, 244–245, 259, 471; **IV:** 32, 201, 237, 301, 312, 328, 359, 428, 431, 434, 439, 443, 466, 467; **Retro. Supp. I:** 75, 89, 169, 335; **Supp. III Part 1:** 10, 12, 14, 15; **Supp. IV Part 2:** 600; **Supp. VIII:** 103; **Supp. IX:** 211; **Supp. X:** 193, 194; **Supp. XII:** 289; **Supp. XIV:** 24, 83, 95; **Supp. XVI:** 295; **Supp. XXI:** 231; **Supp. XXIII:** 122

Proverbs, **Supp. X:** 45

"Proverbs" (Jarman), **Supp. XVII:** 118

"Providence" (Komunyakaa), **Supp. XIII:** 132

"Provident Woman, A" (Boyce), **Supp. XXI:** 10

"Provincetown Postcards" (F. Wright), **Supp. XVII:** 244

"Provincia deserta" (Pound), **Retro. Supp. I:** 289

"Provisional Remarks on Being / A Poet / of Arkansas" (Wright), **Supp. XV:** 337

Pruette, Lorine, **Supp. IV Part 2:** 522

Prufrock and Other Observations (Eliot), **I:** 569–570, 571, 573, 574, 576–577, 583, 584, 585; **Retro. Supp. I:** 59, 62

"Prufrock's Perivigilium" (T. S. Eliot), **Retro. Supp. I:** 57

Pryor, Richard, **Supp. XIII:** 343

Pryse, Marjorie, **Retro. Supp. II:** 139, 146; **Supp. XXV:** 285

"Psalm" (Ginsberg), **Supp. II Part 1:** 312

"Psalm" (Simic), **Supp. VIII:** 282

"Psalm, A, or Supplication for mercy, and confession of Sin, addressed to the Author of Life, in the Odjibway-Alqonquin tongue"(J. Schoolcraft), **Supp. XXIII:** 232

"Psalm and Lament" (Justice), **Supp. VII:** 116, 117–118, 120–122, 124

"Psalm for Pinhook" (Ray), **Supp. XVIII:** 202

"Psalm Jew, The"(Asch). *See Salvation* (Asch)

"Psalm of Life, A" (Longfellow), **II:** 489, 496; **Retro. Supp. II:** 164, 168, 169; **Supp. I Part 2:** 409

"Psalm of the West" (Lanier), **Supp. I Part 1:** 362, 364

"Psalm: Our Fathers" (Merwin), **Supp. III Part 1:** 350

Psalms (biblical book), **I:** 83; **II:** 168, 232; **Retro. Supp. I:** 62; **Supp. I Part 1:** 125

Psalms, Hymns, and Spiritual Songs of the Rev. Isaac Watts, The (Worcester, ed.), **I:** 458

Psychiatric Novels of Oliver Wendell Holmes, The (Oberndorf), **Supp. I Part 1:** 315

"Psychology and Form" (Burke), **I:** 270

Psychology: Briefer Course (James), **II:** 351–352

Psychology of Art (Malraux), **IV:** 434

Psychology of Insanity, The (Hart), **I:** 241–242, 248–250

Psychopathia Sexualis (Shanley), **Supp. XIV:** 316, **329**

Psychophysiks (Fechner), **II:** 358

Pterodactyls (Silver), **Supp. XXIV: 268–270**

"Pu-239" (Kalfus), **Supp. XVII:** 50

"Publication is the Auction" (Dickinson), **Retro. Supp. I:** 31

"Public Bath, The" (Snyder), **Supp. VIII:** 298

Public Burning, The (Coover), **Supp. IV Part 1:** 388; **Supp. V:** 44, 45, 46–47, 48, 51, 52; **Supp. XVII:** 6

"Public Burning of Julius and Ethel Rosenberg, The: An Historical Romance" (Coover), **Supp. V:** 44

"Public Figure" (Hay), **Supp. XIV:** 124

"Public Garden, The" (Lowell), **II:** 550

Public Good (Paine), **Supp. I Part 2:** 509–510

Public Poetry of Robert Lowell, The (Cosgrave), **Retro. Supp. II:** 185

"Public & Private" (column, Quindlen), **Supp. XVII:** 165, 167, 169–170

Public Speech: Poems (MacLeish), **III:** 15–16

Public Spirit (Savage), **II:** 111

"Public Woman, A" (Cliff), **Supp. XXII:** 76

Puccini, Giacomo, **Supp. XXI:** 150, 151

"Puck" (Monette), **Supp. X:** 157–158

Pudd'nhead Wilson (Twain), **I:** 197

"Pudd'nhead Wilson's Calendar" (Twain), **I:** 197

"Pueblo Revolt, The" (Sando), **Supp. IV Part 2:** 510

Puella (Dickey), **Supp. IV Part 1:** 178, 185

Pulitzer, Alfred, **Retro. Supp. I:** 257

Pull Down Vanity (Fiedler), **Supp. XIII:** 103

Pullman, George, **Supp. I Part 1:** 9

"Pullman Car Hiawatha" (Wilder), **IV:** 365–366

Pull My Daisy (film), **Supp. XII:** 126–127

"Pulp Cutters' Nativity, A" (Budbill), **Supp. XIX:** 9

"Pulpit and the Pew, The" (Holmes), **Supp. I Part 1:** 302

"Pulse-Beats and Pen-Strokes" (Sandburg), **III:** 579

"Pump, The" (Humphrey), **Supp. IX:** 101

Pump House Gang, The (Wolfe), **Supp. III Part 2:** 575, 578, 580, 581

Punch, Brothers, Punch and Other Sketches (Twain), **IV:** 200

Punch: The Immortal Liar, Documents in His History (Aiken), **I:** 57, 61

Punishment Without Vengeance (Vega; Merwin, trans.), **Supp. III Part 1:** 341, 347

"Pupil" (F. Barthelme), **Supp. XI:** 26

"Pupil, The" (H. James), **Supp. XX: 233**

"Pupil, The" (James), **II:** 331; **Retro. Supp. I:** 217, 219, 228

"Purchase" (Banks), **Supp. V:** 6

"Purchase of Some Golf Clubs, A" (O'Hara), **III:** 369

"Purdah" (Plath), **Supp. I Part 2:** 602

Purdy, Charles, **Supp. VIII:** 330

Purdy, James, **Supp. VII: 269–285**

Purdy, Theodore, **Supp. VIII:** 153

Pure (C. Frost), **Supp. XV:** 93, **101–102,** 104, 106

"Pure" (C. Frost), **Supp. XV:** 101–102

"Pure and the Good, The: On Baseball and Backpaking" (Maclean), **Supp. XIV:** 222

"Pure Good of Theory, The" (Stevens), **Retro. Supp. I:** 310

Purgatorio (Dante), **III:** 182

"Purim Parade" (Espaillat), **Supp. XXI:** 108

Puritan Family (Morgan), **Supp. I Part 1:** 101

"Puritanical Pleasures" (Hardwick), **Supp. III Part 1:** 213–214

Puritan Origins of the American Self, The (Bercovitch), **Supp. I Part 1:** 99

Puritan Pronaos, The: Studies in the Intellectual Life of New England in the Seventeenth Century (Morison), **Supp. I Part 2:** 485

"Puritan Realism: *The Wide, Wide World* and *Robinson Crusoe*" (Kim), **Supp. XVIII:** 267

Puritans, The (P. Miller), **Supp. VIII:** 101

"Puritan's Ballad, The" (Wylie), **Supp. I Part 2:** 723

"Purloined Letter, The" (Poe), **Retro. Supp. II:** 271, 272

Purple Cane Road (Burke), **Supp. XIV:** 32, 33

Purple Decades, The (Wolfe), **Supp. III Part 2:** 584

"Purple Hat, The" (Welty), **IV:** 264

Purple Rose of Cairo, The (film; Allen), **Supp. XV:** 1, **9–10,** 12, 14

Purser, John T., **Supp. XIV:** 4

"Pursuit of Happiness" (Simpson), **Supp. IX:** 279

"Pursuit of Happiness, The" (Ashbery), **Supp. III Part 1:** 23

Pursuit of the Prodigal, The (Auchincloss), **Supp. IV Part 1:** 25

Pushcart at the Curb, A (Dos Passos), **I:** 478, 479

"Pushcart Man" (Hughes), **Supp. I Part 1:** 330

Pushcart Prize, XIII, The (Ford), **Supp. V:** 58

Pushcart Prize VII, The (Hendeson, ed.), **Supp. XVII:** 16

Pushcart Prize XIV, The (Henderson, ed.), **Supp. XVII:** 18

Pushcart Prize XX, The (Henderson, ed.), **Supp. XVII:** 20

"Pushing 100" (Mora), **Supp. XIII:** 215

Pushkin, Aleksander, **III:** 246, 261, 262; **Retro. Supp. I:** 266, 269; **Supp. XVI:** 188

Pussy, King of the Pirates (Acker), **Supp. XII:** 6–7

"Pussycat and the Expert Plumber Who Was a Man, The" (A. Miller), **III:** 146–147

Pussycat Fever (Acker), **Supp. XII:** 6

Putnam, George Haven, **Supp. XVIII:** 257, 260

Putnam, George P., **II:** 314; **Supp. XVIII:** 3–4, 14, 260

Putnam, Phelps, **I:** 288

Putnam, Samuel, **II:** 26; **III:** 479; **Supp. III Part 2:** 615

"Put Off the Wedding Five Times and Nobody Comes to It" (Sandburg), **III:** 586–587

Puttenham, George, **Supp. I Part 1:** 113

Puttermesser Papers, The (Ozick), **Supp. V:** 269

"Putting a Burden Down" (Peacock), **Supp. XIX:** 199

Putting It Together (Sondheim), **Supp. XXIV:** 124

"Putting on *Visit to a Small Planet*" (Vidal), **Supp. IV Part 2:** 683

Put Yourself in My Shoes (Carver), **Supp. III Part 1:** 139

"Put Yourself in My Shoes" (Carver), **Supp. III Part 1:** 139, 141

Putzi, Jennifer, **Supp. XV:** 284

Puzo, Mario, **Supp. IV Part 1:** 390

"Puzzle of Modern Society, The" (Kazin), **Supp. VIII:** 103

Pygmalion (Shaw), **Supp. XII:** 14

Pyle, Ernie, **III:** 148; **Supp. V:** 240; **Supp. XVII:** 61

Pylon (Faulkner), **II:** 64–65, 73; **Retro. Supp. I:** 84, 85

Pynchon, Thomas, **III:** 258; **Retro. Supp. I:** 278; **Retro. Supp. II:** 279, 324; **Supp. II Part 2:** 557, **617–638;** **Supp. III Part 1:** 217; **Supp. IV Part 1:** 53, 279; **Supp. IV Part 2:** 570; **Supp. V:** 40, 44, 52; **Supp. VIII:** 14; **Supp. IX:** 207, 208, 212; **Supp. X:** 260, 301, 302; **Supp. XI:** 103; **Supp. XII:** 289; **Supp. XIV:** 49, 53, 54, 96; **Supp. XVI:** 123, 128; **Supp. XVII:** 183, 225, 232, 236; **Supp. XIX:** 223; **Supp. XX:** 21, **83, 87;** **Supp. XXIII:** 42, 101

Pyne, John, **Supp. XXI:** 7

Pyne, Mary, **Supp. XXI:** 7

Pyrah, Gill, **Supp. V:** 126

"Pyramid Club, The" (Doctorow), **Supp. IV Part 1:** 234

"Pyrography" (Ashbery), **Supp. III Part 1:** 18

Pythagoras, **I:** 332

Pythagorean Silence (Howe), **Supp. IV Part 2:** 426, 428–429

Q

QBVII (television movie), **Supp. XX: 247**

QBVII (Uris), **Supp. XX: 244, 247, 248, 251, 253–254**

"Qebehseneuf" (Goldbarth), **Supp. XII:** 186

"Quadroons, The" (Child), **Supp. XVIII:** 124

"Quai d'Orléans" (Bishop), **Supp. I Part 1:** 89

"Quail for Mr. Forester" (Humphrey), **Supp. IX:** 94

"Quail in Autumn" (W. J. Smith), **Supp. XIII:** 334–335, 339

Quaker City, The: or, The Monks of Monk Hall (Lippard), **Supp. XXIII:** 177, 178–179, **180–183,** 184, 187, 188–189, 190

"Quaker Graveyard in Nantucket, The" (Lowell), **II:** 54, 550; **Retro. Supp. II:** 186–187

"Quake Theory" (Olds), **Supp. X:** 203

Qualey, Carlton C., **Supp. I Part 2:** 650

Quality of Hurt, The (C. Himes), **Supp. XVI:** 137, 145

"Quality of Wine" (Carruth), **Supp. XVI:** 59

"Quality Time" (Kingsolver), **Supp. VII:** 203

"Quandary" (F. Wright), **Supp. XVII:** 244

Quang-Ngau-chè, **III:** 473

Quarles, Francis, **I:** 178, 179

"Quarrel" (Taggard), **Supp. XXII:** 276

Quarry, The (Chesnutt), **Supp. XIV:** 76

"Quarry, The" (Nemerov), **III:** 272

Quarry, The: New Poems (Eberhart), **I:** 532, 539

Quartermain, Peter, **Supp. IV Part 2:** 423, 434

Quatermain, Peter, **Supp. XXII:** 163

"Quaternions, The" (Bradstreet), **Supp. I Part 1:** 104–106, 114, 122

"Quatrains for Ishi" (Komunyakaa), **Supp. XIII:** 129

Queechy (S. Warner as Wetherell), **Supp. XVIII:** 257, **264–266**

"Queen Elizabeth and the Blind Girl or Music for the Dead Children" (B. Kelly), **Supp. XVII:** 124, 125

"Queen of the Blues" (Brooks), **Supp. III Part 1:** 75

Queen of the Damned, The (Rice), **Supp. VII:** 290, 292–293, 297, 299

Queen of the Mob (film), **Supp. XIII:** 170

"Queens of France" (Wilder), **IV:** 365

"Queen's Twin, The" (Jewett), **Retro. Supp. II:** 138

Queen's Twin, The, and Other Stories (Jewett), **Retro. Supp. II:** 140

Queen Victoria (Strachey), **Supp. I Part 2:** 485, 494; **Supp. XIV:** 342

Queer (Burroughs), **Supp. III Part 1:** 93–102

"Queer Aztlán"(Moraga), **Supp. XXIII:** 201

"Queer Beer" (Hansberry), **Supp. IV Part 1:** 374

"Quelques considérations sur la méthode subjective" (James), **II:** 345–346

"Quest, The" (Gibran), **Supp. XX: 124**

"Question" (Swenson), **Supp. IV Part 2:** 640

"Question and Answer" (Hughes), **Retro. Supp. I:** 211

"Questioning Faces" (Frost), **Retro. Supp. I:** 141

"Question Mark in the Circle, The" (Stegner), **Supp. IV Part 2:** 597

"Questionnaire, The" (Snodgrass), **Supp. VI:** 318

"Question of Fidelity, A" (Beauvoir), **Supp. IX:** 4

"Question of Loneliness, A" (Swados), **Supp. XIX:** 262

"Question of Our Speech, The" (Ozick), **Supp. V:** 272

"Question of Simone de Beauvoir, The" (Algren), **Supp. IX:** 4

Questions About Angels (Collins), **Supp. XXI:** 54, 58, 59, 60, 64

Questions for Ecclesiastes (Jarman), **Supp. XVII:** 109, 110, **118–119**

"Questions of Geography" (Hollander), **Supp. I Part 1:** 96

Questions of Travel (Bishop), **Retro. Supp. II:** 46–48; **Supp. I Part 1:** 72, 83, 92, 94

"Questions of Travel" (Bishop), **Retro. Supp. II:** 47

"Questions to Tourists Stopped by a Pineapple Field" (Merwin), **Supp. III Part 1:** 355

"Questions without Answers" (T. Williams), **IV:** 384

"Quest of the Purple-Fringed, The" (Frost), **Retro. Supp. I:** 139

Quest of the Silver Fleece, The (Du Bois), **Supp. II Part 1:** 176–178
Quevedo y Villegas, Francisco Gómez, **Retro. Supp. I:** 423
Quickly: A Column for Slow Readers (Mailer), **Retro. Supp. II:** 202
Quicksand (Larsen), **Supp. XVIII:** 119, 121, 122, **124–127**
Quicksand and Passing (Larsen; McDowell, ed.), **Supp. XVIII:** 125
"Quies," (Pound), **Retro. Supp. I:** 413
Quiet American, The (Greene), **Supp. XIX:** 29
"Quiet and clear" (Kooser), **Supp. XIX:** 125
Quiet City (Shaw), **Supp. XIX:** 244
Quiet Days in Clichy (H. Miller), **III:** 170, 178, 183–184, 187
"Quiet Desperation" (Simpson), **Supp. IX:** 277–278
"Quiet Light, A" (Skloot), **Supp. XX: 203**
"Quiet of the Mind" (Nye), **Supp. XIII:** 284
"Quiet Woman, The" (Taggard), **Supp. XXII:** 274
"QUILLA" (Trethewey), **Supp. XXI:** 246
"Quilting" (D. West), **Supp. XVIII:** 283
Quin, Mike (pseudonym). *See* Ryan, Paul William
Quincy, Edmund, **Supp. XVIII:** 4
Quindlen, Anna, **Supp. XVI:** 108; **Supp. XVII: 165–181**
Quinlan, Kathleen, **Supp. X:** 80
Quinn, Anthony, **Supp. XXI:** 46
Quinn, John, **III:** 471
Quinn, Paul, **Supp. V:** 71
Quinn, Sister M. Bernetta, **III:** 479; **IV:** 421
Quinn, Vincent, **I:** 386, 401, 402; **Supp. I Part 1:** 270
"Quinnapoxet" (Kunitz), **Supp. III Part 1:** 263
Quinn's Book (W. Kennedy), **Supp. VII:** 133, 148–150, 153
Quintero, José, **III:** 403
Quintilian, **IV:** 123
Quinzaine for This Yule, A (Pound), **Retro. Supp. I:** 285
Quite Contrary: The Mary and Newt Story (Dixon), **Supp. XII: 144,** 153
Quitting Time (Kriegel), **Supp. XXIV: 225–227**
Quod Erat Demonstrandum (Stein), **IV:** 34
Quo Vadis? (Sienkiewicz), **Supp. IV Part 2:** 518; **Supp. XVI:** 182

R

Raab, Max, **Supp. XI:** 309
Raban, Jonathan, **Supp. XXV:** 208, 217
"Rabbi, The" (Hayden), **Supp. II Part 1:** 363, 369
Rabbit, Run (Updike), **IV:** 214, 223, 230–234; **Retro. Supp. I:** 320, 325, 326, 327, 331, 333, 335; **Supp. XI:** 140; **Supp. XII:** 298; **Supp. XVI:** 220
"Rabbit, The" (Barnes), **Supp. III Part 1:** 34

Rabbit at Rest (Updike), **Retro. Supp. I:** 334
Rabbit Factory, The (L. Brown), **Supp. XXI:** 40, **47–48**
"Rabbit Factory, The: Escaping the Isolation of the Cage" (Gaughran), **Supp. XXI:** 47–48
Rabbit Is Rich (Updike), **Retro. Supp. I:** 334
Rabbit novels (Updike), **Supp. V:** 269
Rabbit Redux (Updike), **IV:** 214; **Retro. Supp. I:** 332, 333
Rabbit's Umbrella, The (Plimpton), **Supp. XVI:** 244
"Rabbits Who Caused All the Trouble, The" (Thurber), **Supp. I Part 2:** 610
Rabe, David, **Supp. XXIV:** 117; **Supp. XXV:** 153
Rabelais, and His World (Bakhtin), **Retro. Supp. II:** 273
Rabelais, François, **I:** 130; **II:** 111, 112, 302, 535; **III:** 77, 78, 174, 182; **IV:** 68; **Supp. I Part 2:** 461
Rabelais and His World (Bakhtin), **Supp. X:** 120
Rabinbach, Anson, **Supp. XII:** 166
Rabinowitz, Paula, **Supp. V:** 161
"Race" (Emerson), **II:** 6
"Race, Privilege, and the Politics of (Re)Writing History: An Analysis of the Novels of Michelle Cliff" (Edmondson), **Supp. XXII:** 70
"Race Contacts and Inter-Racial Relations" (Locke), **Supp. XIV:** 211
"Race Contacts and Inter-Racial Relations: A Study in the Theory and Practice of Race" (lectures, Locke), **Supp. XIV:** 199, 209
Race Contacts and Interracial Relations: Lectures on the Theory and Practice of Race (Locke, Stewart, ed.), **Supp. XIV:** 196, **209–210**
"'RACE LINE' IS A PRODUCT OF CAPITALISM, THE" (Baraka), **Supp. II Part 1:** 61
"Race of Life, The" (Thurber), **Supp. I Part 2:** 614
"Race Problems and Modern Society" (Toomer), **Supp. III Part 2:** 486
Race Questions, Provincialism, and Other American Problems (Royce), **Supp. XIV:** 199
"Race Riot, Tulsa, 1921" (Olds), **Supp. X:** 205
Race Rock (Matthiessen), **Supp. V:** 201
"Races, The" (Lowell), **II:** 554
"Rachel" (D. West), **Supp. XVIII:** 289
Rachel Carson: Witness for Nature (Lear), **Supp. IX:** 19
Rachel River (film, Smolan), **Supp. XVI:** 36
"Racial Progress and Race Adjustment" (Locke), **Supp. XIV:** 210
Racine, Jean Baptiste, **II:** 543, 573; **III:** 145, 151, 152, 160; **IV:** 317, 368, 370; **Supp. I Part 2:** 716
Radcliffe, Ann, **Supp. XX: 108**
Radiance (Crooker), **Supp. XXIII: 57–58**
"Radical" (Moore), **III:** 211

"Radical Chic" (Wolfe), **Supp. III Part 2:** 577–578, 584, 585
Radical Chic & Mau-mauing the Flak Catchers (Wolfe), **Supp. III Part 2:** 577–578
Radical Empiricism of William James, The (Wild), **II:** 362, 363–364
Radicalism in America, The (Lasch), **I:** 259
"Radical Jewish Humanism: The Vision of E. L. Doctorow" (Clayton), **Supp. IV Part 1:** 238
"Radically Condensed History of Postindustrial Life, A" (Wallace), **Supp. X:** 309
Radical's America, A (Swados), **Supp. XIX: 264–265**
Radinovsky, Lisa, **Supp. XV:** 284, 285
"Radio" (O'Hara), **III:** 369
Radio Days (film; Allen), **Supp. XV:** 9
"Radio Pope" (Goldbarth), **Supp. XII:** 188, 192
Raditzer (Matthiessen), **Supp. V:** 201
Radkin, Paul, **Supp. I Part 2:** 539
"Rafaela Who Drinks Coconut & Papaya Juice on Tuesdays" (Cisneros), **Supp. VII:** 63
Rafelson, Bob, **Supp. XIV:** 241
Raffalovich, Marc-André, **Supp. XIV:** 335
Rafferty, Terence, **Supp. XX: 87, 92**
"Raft, The" (Lindsay), **Supp. I Part 2:** 393
Rag and Bone Shop of the Heart, The: Poems for Men (Bly, Hillman, and Meade, eds.), **Supp. IV Part 1:** 67
Rage in Harlem (C. Himes). *See For Love of Imabelle* (C. Himes)
Rage to Live, A (O'Hara), **III:** 361
Raglan, Lord, **I:** 135
Rago, Henry, **Supp. III Part 2:** 624, 628, 629
"Rag Rug"(Hadas), **Supp. XXIII:** 118
Ragtime (Doctorow), **Retro. Supp. II:** 108; **Supp. IV Part 1:** 217, 222–224, 231, 232, 233, 234, 237, 238; **Supp. V:** 45; **Supp. XXIV:** 227
"Ragtime" (Doctorow), **Supp. IV Part 1:** 234
Ragtime (film), **Supp. IV Part 1:** 236
Ragtime (musical, McNally), **Supp. XIII:** 207
Rahab (W. Frank), **Supp. XX: 71–72, 76**
Rahaim, Liz, **Supp. XVII:** 2
Rahv, Philip, **Retro. Supp. I:** 112; **Supp. II Part 1:** 136; **Supp. VIII:** 96; **Supp. IX:** 8; **Supp. XIV:** 3; **Supp. XV:** 140
"Raid" (Hughes), **Retro. Supp. I:** 208
Raids on the Unspeakable (Merton), **Supp. VIII:** 201, 208
Raikin, Judith, **Supp. XXII:** 66
Rail, DeWayne, **Supp. XIII:** 312
Rain and Other Fictions (Kenny), **Supp. XXIII:** 157
"Rain and the Rhinoceros" (Merton), **Supp. VIII:** 201
Rainbow, The (Lawrence), **III:** 27
"Rainbows" (Marquand), **III:** 56
Rainbow Stories, The (Vollmann), **Supp. XVII:** 226, 227, 230, 231, 233

Rainbow Tulip, The (Mora), **Supp. XIII:** 221

"Rain Country" (Haines), **Supp. XII:** 210

"Rain-Dream, A" (Bryant), **Supp. I Part 1:** 164

Raine, Kathleen, **I:** 522, 527

"Rain Falling Now, The" (Dunn), **Supp. XI:** 147

"Rain Flooding Your Campfire" (Gallagher), **Supp. XXIV:** 177

"Rain in the Heart" (Taylor), **Supp. V:** 317, 319

Rain in the Trees, The (Merwin), **Supp. III Part 1:** 340, 342, 345, 349, 354–356

"Rainmaker, The" (Humphrey), **Supp. IX:** 101

Raintree County (Lockridge), **Supp. XIX:** 263

Rainwater, Catherine, **Supp. V:** 272

"Rainy Day" (Longfellow), **II:** 498

"Rainy Day, The" (Buck), **Supp. II Part 1:** 127

"Rainy Mountain Cemetery" (Momaday), **Supp. IV Part 2:** 486

Rainy Mountain Christmas Doll (painting) (Momaday), **Supp. IV Part 2:** 493

"Rainy Season: Sub-Tropics" (Bishop), **Supp. I Part 1:** 93

"Rainy Sunday" (Espaillat), **Supp. XXI:** 106

Raised in Captivity (Silver), **Supp. XXIV: 271**

"Raise High the Roof Beam, Carpenters" (Salinger), **III:** 567–569, 571

Raise High the Roof Beam, Carpenters; and Seymour: An Introduction (Salinger), **III:** 552, 567–571, 572

Raise Race Rays Raze: Essays Since 1965 (Baraka), **Supp. II Part 1:** 47, 52, 55

Raisin (musical), **Supp. IV Part 1:** 374

Raising Demons (Jackson), **Supp. IX: 125–126**

Raisin in the Sun, A (unproduced screenplay) (Hansberry), **Supp. IV Part 1:** 360

Raisin in the Sun, A (film: Columbia Pictures), **Supp. IV Part 1:** 360, 367

Raisin in the Sun, A (Hansberry), **Supp. IV Part 1:** 359, 360, 361, 362–364; **Supp. VIII:** 343

Raisin in the Sun, A (television film: American Playhouse), **Supp. IV Part 1:** 367, 374

Rajan, R., **I:** 390

"Rake, The" (Mamet), **Supp. XIV:** 240

Rake's Progress, The (opera), **Supp. II Part 1:** 24

Rakosi, Carl, **Supp. III Part 2:** 614, 615, 616, 617, 618, 621, 629; **Supp. XIV:** 286, 287

Ralegh, Sir Walter, **Supp. I Part 1:** 98

Raleigh, John Henry, **IV:** 366

Ralph, Brett, **Supp. XVII:** 245

Ramakrishna, Sri, **III:** 567

Ramakrishna and His Disciples (Isherwood), **Supp. XIV:** 164

Ramazani, Jahan, **Supp. IV Part 2:** 450

"Ramble of Aphasia, A" (O. Henry), **Supp. II Part 1:** 410

Ramey, Phillip, **Supp. IV Part 1:** 94

Ramírez, Juan, **Supp. XXIII:** 203

Ramona (Jackson), **Supp. XXIV:** 27

Rampersad, Arnold, **Retro. Supp. I:** 196, 200, 201, 204; **Supp. IV Part 1:** 244, 250

Rampling, Anne, **Supp. VII:** 201. *See also* Rice, Anne

Rampling, Charlotte, **Supp. IX:** 253

Ramsey, Priscilla R., **Supp. IV Part 1:** 15

Ramsey, Roger, **Supp. XVI:** 69

Ramsey, William, **Supp. XVIII:** 66

Ramus, Petrus, **Supp. I Part 1:** 104

Rand, Ayn, **Supp. I Part 1:** 294; **Supp. IV Part 2:** 517–535

Randall, Jarrell, 1914–1965 (Lowell, Taylor, and Warren, eds.), **II:** 368, 385

Randall, John H., **III:** 605

Randolph, John, **I:** 5–6

Randolph, Ladette, **Supp. XXIII:** 274

"Randolphs of the Redwoods, The" (Atherton), **Supp. XXIV:** 18

"Range-Finding" (Frost), **Retro. Supp. I:** 131

Range of the Possible (T. Marshall), **Supp. XVII:** 36

Rangoon (F. Barthelme), **Supp. XI:** 25

Rangus, Eric, **Supp. XXI:** 244, 254

Rank, Otto, **I:** 135; **Supp. IX:** 105; **Supp. X:** 183, 185, 193

Ranke, Leopold von, **Supp. I Part 2:** 492

Rankin, Daniel, **Retro. Supp. II:** 57, 72; **Supp. I Part 1:** 200, 203, 225

Rankin, Tom, **Supp. XXI:** 36

Rankine, Annette, **Supp. XX: 69**

Ranlett, William H., **Supp. XVIII:** 3

Ransohoff, Martin, **Supp. XI:** 305, 306

Ransom, John Crowe, **I:** 265, 301; **II:** 34, 367, 385, 389, 536–537, 542; **III:** 454, **480–502,** 549; **IV:** 121, 122, 123, 124, 125, 127, 134, 140, 141, 236, 237, 433; **Retro. Supp. I:** 90; **Retro. Supp. II:** 176, 177, 178, 183, 220, 228, 246; **Supp. I Part 1:** 80, 361; **Supp. I Part 2:** 423; **Supp. II Part 1:** 90, 91, 136, 137, 139, 318; **Supp. II Part 2:** 639; **Supp. III Part 1:** 318; **Supp. III Part 2:** 542, 591; **Supp. IV Part 1:** 217; **Supp. V:** 315, 331, 337; **Supp. X:** 25, 56, 58; **Supp. XIV:** 1; **Supp. XIX:** 123; **Supp. XXIII:** 145

Ransome, Arthur, **Supp. XXV:** 205

"Rape" (Coleman), **Supp. XI:** 89–90

"Rape, The" (Baraka), **Supp. II Part 1:** 40

Rape of Bunny Stuntz, The (Gurney), **Supp. V:** 109

"Rape of Philomel, The" (Shapiro), **Supp. II Part 2:** 720

"Rape of the Lock, The" (Pope), **Supp. XIV:** 8

Rapf, Joanna, **Supp. XVIII:** 251

Raphael, **I:** 15; **III:** 505, 521, 524; **Supp. I Part 1:** 363

"Rapist" (Dunn), **Supp. XI:** 144

Rap on Race, A (Baldwin and Mead), **Supp. I Part 1:** 66

"Rappaccini's Daughter" (Hawthorne), **II:** 229

"Rapture of the Deep" (Hempel), **Supp. XXI: 123**

"Rapunzel" (Sexton), **Supp. II Part 2:** 691

Rare & Endangered Species: A Novella & Short Stories (Bausch), **Supp. VII:** 51, 54

"Raree Show" (MacLeish), **III:** 9

Rascoe, Burton, **III:** 106, 115

Raskin, Jonah, **Supp. XV:** 116

Raskin, Saul, **Supp. XXIII:** 6

"Raskolnikov" (Simic), **Supp. VIII:** 282

Rasmussen, Douglas, **Supp. IV Part 2:** 528, 530

Rasmussen, Halfdan, **Supp. XVIII:** 180

Rasselas (Johnson), **Supp. XI:** 209

Rathmann, Andrew, **Supp. XV:** 34

Ratiner, Steven, **Supp. XXIII:** 134

"Rat in the Engine" (Espaillat), **Supp. XXI:** 106

"Ration" (Baraka), **Supp. II Part 1:** 50

"Rationale of Verse, The" (Poe), **III:** 427–428; **Retro. Supp. II:** 266

Ratner, Rochelle, **Supp. XV:** 105; **Supp. XXIV:** 168

Ratner's Star (DeLillo), **Supp. VI:** 1, 2, 3, 4, 10, 12, 14; **Supp. XVIII:** 140

"Rat of Faith, The" (Levine), **Supp. V:** 192

"Rats in the Walls, The" (Lovecraft), **Supp. XXV:** 109, 112

Rattigan, Terence, **III:** 152

Raugh, Joseph, **Supp. I Part 1:** 286

Rauh, Ida, **Supp. XXI:** 6

Rauschenberg, Robert, **Supp. XV:** 187

Rauschenbusch, Walter, **III:** 293; **Supp. I Part 1:** 7

Ravelstein (Bellow), **Retro. Supp. II:** 19, **33–34**

Raven, Simon, **Supp. XII:** 241

Raven, The (film, Friedlander), **Supp. XVII:** 58

"Raven, The" (Poe), **III:** 413, 421–422, 426; **Retro. Supp. II:** 265, 266–267; **Supp. XVII:** 58

Raven, The, and Other Poems (Poe), **III:** 413

Ravenal, Shannon, **Supp. IV Part 1:** 93

"Raven Days, The" (Lanier), **Supp. I Part 1:** 351

Ravenel, Shannon, **Supp. XXI:** 39

Ravenna, Michael. *See* Welty, Eudora

"Ravens at Deer Creek" (Wrigley), **Supp. XVIII:** 299–300, 306

Raven's Road (Gunn Allen), **Supp. IV Part 1:** 330, 335

Raver, Anne, **Supp. XVIII:** 191

Ravetch, Irving, **Supp. XXV:** 102

"Ravine, The" (Carruth), **Supp. XVI:** 53

Ravits, Martha, **Supp. XXI:** 215

Raw Heaven (Peacock), **Supp. XIX: 196–197**

Rawlings, Marjorie Kinnan, **Supp. X: 219–237; Supp. XVIII:** 194–195

Rawlins, C. L., **Supp. XVII:** 72, 73

Ray, David, **Supp. IV Part 1:** 61

Ray, Janisse, **Supp. XVIII: 189–206**

Ray, Jeanne Wilkinson, **Supp. XII:** 308, 310
Ray, John, **II:** 111, 112
Ray, Man, **IV:** 404; **Retro. Supp. I:** 416; **Supp. XII:** 124; **Supp. XXIII:** 6
Ray, Nicholas, **Supp. XVIII:** 253
Ray Bradbury Theatre, The (television show), **Supp. IV Part 1:** 103
Raymond, Henry J., **Supp. XVIII:** 4
"Raymond and Ann" (Budbill), **Supp. XIX:** 9
Raymond Carver: A Writer's Life (Sklenicka), **Supp. XXIV:** 166
"Raymond Carver: The Kindest Cut" (Wood), **Supp. XXIV:** 166
"Razor's Edge, The" (Wasserstein), **Supp. XV:** 328
Reactionary Essays on Poetry and Ideas (Tate), **Supp. II Part 1:** 106, 146
Read, Deborah, **II:** 122
Read, Forrest, **III:** 478
Read, Herbert, **I:** 523; **II:** 372–373, 377–378; **Retro. Supp. I:** 54; **Supp. III Part 1:** 273; **Supp. III Part 2:** 624, 626
Read, William A., **Supp. XIV:** 4
Reade, Charles, **Supp. I Part 2:** 580
Reader, Constant. *See* Parker, Dorothy
Reader, Dennis J., **Supp. I Part 2:** 454
"Reader, The" (F. Wright), **Supp. XVII:** 246
Reader's Block (Markson), **Supp. XVII:** 143–145, 146
Reader's Encyclopedia, The: An Encyclopedia of World Literature and the Arts (W. Benét), **Supp. XI:** 44
Reader's Guide to William Gaddis's The Recognitions, A (Moore), **Supp. IV Part 1:** 283
Reader's Map of Arkansas (Wright), **Supp. XV:** 348
"Reader's Tale, A" (Doty), **Supp. XI:** 119, 120, 128, 129
"Reading" (Auden), **Supp. VIII:** 155
"Reading, The" (Di Piero), **Supp. XIX:** 41
"Reading, Writing, Region" (J. W. Miller), **Supp. XX:** 165
"Reading an Anthology of Chinese Poems of the Sung Dynasty, I Pause to Admire the Length and Clarity of Their Titles" (Collins), **Supp. XXI:** 56
"Reading at Forty" (Pickering), **Supp. XXI:** 196
"Reading Group Guide", **Supp. XI:** 244–245
"Reading Lao Tzu Again in the New Year" (Wright), **Supp. V:** 343
"Reading Late of the Death of Keats" (Kenyon), **Supp. VII:** 169
"Reading Myself" (Lowell), **II:** 555
Reading Myself and Others (P. Roth), **Retro. Supp. II:** 282; **Supp. V:** 45
"Reading *Ode to the West Wind* 25 Years Later" (McCarriston), **Supp. XIV:** 271–272
"Reading of the Psalm, The" (Francis), **Supp. IX:** 79
"Reading Ovid" (Di Piero), **Supp. XIX:** 44

"Reading Philosophy at Night" (Simic), **Supp. VIII:** 272
Reading Rilke: Reflections on the Problems of Translation (Gass), **Supp. VI:** 92, **93–94**
"Reading Rorty and Paul Celan One Morning in Early June" (Wright), **Supp. V:** 343
"Reading Sarcophagi: An Essay" (Sobin), **Supp. XVI:** 290
"Readings of History" (Rich), **Supp. I Part 2:** 554
"Reading the Signs, Empowering the Eye" (Bambara), **Supp. XI:** 17–18
Reading the Spirit (Eberhart), **I:** 525, 527, 530
Ready, Richard M., **Supp. XIX:** 154
"Ready Or Not" (Baraka), **Supp. II Part 1:** 50
Reagan, Ronald, **Supp. IV Part 1:** 224–225
"Real Bowery, The" (Hapgood), **Supp. XVII:** 103
"Real Class" (Vidal), **Supp. IV Part 1:** 35
Real Cool Killers, The (C. Himes), **Supp. XVI:** 143
Real Dope, The (Lardner), **II:** 422–423
"Real Estate" (Moore), **Supp. X:** 178
"Real Gone Guy, A" (McGrath), **Supp. X:** 117
"Real Horatio Alger Story, The" (Cowley), **Supp. II Part 1:** 143
"Realities" (MacLeish), **III:** 4
"Reality in America" (Trilling), **Supp. III Part 2:** 495, 502
"Reality! Reality! What Is It?" (Eberhart), **I:** 536
Reality Sandwiches, 1953–60 (Ginsberg), **Supp. II Part 1:** 315, 320
"Reality U.S.A." (Halliday), **Supp. XIX:** 89
Real Life of Sebastian Knight, The (Nabokov), **III:** 246; **Retro. Supp. I:** 266, 269, 270, 274
"Really Good Jazz Piano, A" (Yates), **Supp. XI:** 342
"Real Movie, with Stars, The" (Hull), **Supp. XXI:** 136
Real Presence: A Novel (Bausch), **Supp. VII:** 42–43, 50
"Real Revolution Is Love, The" (Harjo), **Supp. XII:** 224, 225–226
"Real Surrounding, The: On Canaletto's Venice" (Bronk), **Supp. XXI:** 32
"Real Thing, The" (H. James), **Retro. Supp. I:** 228; **Retro. Supp. II:** 223
"Real Two-Party System" (Vidal), **Supp. IV Part 2:** 679
Real West Marginal Way, The (Hugo), **Supp. VI:** 132, 134; **Supp. XVIII:** 299
"Real World around Us, The" (Carson), **Supp. IX:** 21
Reaper Essays, The (Jarman and McDowell), **Supp. IX:** 270; **Supp. XVII:** 110–111
"*Reaper* Interviews Jean Doh and Sean Dough, The" (Jarman and McDowell), **Supp. XVII:** 110

"Reapers" (Toomer), **Supp. III Part 2:** 481; **Supp. IX:** 312
Reason and Other Women (Notley), **Supp. XXII:** 224, 227, 235, 236, 237
"Reason and Race: A Review of the Literature of the Negro for 1946" (Locke), **Supp. XIV:** 206
"Reason for Moving, A" (Strand), **Supp. IV Part 2:** 624
"Reason for Stories, The: Toward a Moral Fiction" (Stone), **Supp. V:** 298, 300
Reasons for Moving (Strand), **Supp. IV Part 2:** 624–626, 626
"Reasons for Music" (MacLeish), **III:** 19
"Reasons of the Body" (Sanders), **Supp. XVI:** 274
Reasons to Live (Hempel), **Supp. XXI:** 115, 117, 118, **119–122**
Rebecca (du Maurier), **Supp. XIX:** 57–58; **Supp. XXII:** 120
Rebecca, or, The Fille de Chambre (Rowson), **Supp. XV:** 229, **235–236**, 238
Rebecca Harding Davis Reader, A (Pfaelzer, ed.), **Supp. XVI:** 88, 90
Rebel Angels: Twenty-five Poets of the New Formalism (Jarman and Mason, eds.), **Supp. XV:** 251; **Supp. XVII:** 109, 110, 112, 121
"Rebellion" (Lowell), **Retro. Supp. II:** 187
Rebel Powers (Bausch), **Supp. VII:** 41, 45–46, 49–51
Rebel without a Cause (film), **Supp. XII:** 9
"Rebirth" (McKnight), **Supp. XX:** 147, **157**
"Rebirth of God and the Death of Man, The " (Fiedler), **Supp. XIII:** 108
Rebolledo, Tey Diana, **Supp. XIII:** 214
Reb Shloyme nogid: A poeme fun yidishn leben (Shloyme the wealthy: A poem of Jewish life)(Asch), **Supp. XXIII:** 4, 5
Recapitulation (Stegner), **Supp. IV Part 2:** 598, 600, 612–613
"Recapitulation, The" (Eberhart), **I:** 522
"Recapitulations" (Shapiro), **Supp. II Part 2:** 701, 702, 708, 710–711
"Receding Horizons" (Lethem and Scholtz), **Supp. XVIII:** 145
"Recencies in Poetry" (Zukofsky), **Supp. III Part 2:** 615
Recent Killing, A (Baraka), **Supp. II Part 1:** 55
"Recent Negro Fiction" (Ellison), **Supp. II Part 1:** 233, 235
"Recessional" (A. Finch), **Supp. XVII:** 70–71
"Recital, The" (Ashbery), **Supp. III Part 1:** 14
"Recitative" (H. Crane), **I:** 390; **Retro. Supp. II:** 78
Reckless Eyeballing (Reed), **Supp. X:** 241
Reckless Moment, The (film), **Supp. XXII:** 120, 131, 132
Recognitions, The (Gaddis), **Supp. IV Part 1:** 279, 280–285, 286, 287, 288, 289, 291, 292, 294; **Supp. XX:** 91;

Supp. XXIV: 140
"Recollection and Perhaps a Tribute, A" (Espaillat), **Supp. XXI:** 103–104
Recollections (R. H. Stoddard), **Supp. XV:** 271
Recollections of Logan Pearsall Smith: The Story of a Friendship (Gathorne-Hardy), **Supp. XIV:** 344
"Reconciliation" (Whitman), **IV:** 347
"Reconstructed but Unregenerate" (Ransom), **III:** 496
"Reconstruction and Its Benefits" (Du Bois), **Supp. II Part 1:** 171
Recovering (Sarton), **Supp. VIII:** 264
Recovering the U.S. Hispanic Literary Heritage (Paredes), **Supp. XIII:** 320
"Recovery" (Dove), **Supp. IV Part 1:** 248
Rector of Justin, The (Auchincloss), **Supp. IV Part 1:** 21, 23, 27–30, 36
"Recurrent Dream" (Nelson), **Supp. XVIII:** 176
"RED AUTUMN" (Baraka), **Supp. II Part 1:** 55
Red Badge of Courage, The (S. Crane), **I:** 201, 207, 212, 405, 406, 407, 408, 412–416, 419, 421, 422, 423, 477, 506; **II:** 264; **III:** 317; **IV:** 350; **Retro. Supp. II:** 108; **Supp. IV Part 1:** 380; **Supp. XIV:** 51; **Supp. XVII:** 228; **Supp. XVIII:** 75; **Supp. XXI:** 277
"Redbirds" (C. Frost), **Supp. XV:** 99
"Red Bow, The" (Saunders), **Supp. XIX:** 232–233, 234
"Redbreast in Tampa" (Lanier), **Supp. I Part 1:** 364
"Red Brocade" (Nye), **Supp. XIII:** 288
Redburn: His First Voyage (Melville), **III:** 79–80, 84; **Retro. Supp. I:** 245, 247–248, 249; **Supp. XVIII:** 6
Red Calico (Miller and Bowden), **Supp. XXII:** 188
"Red Carpet for Shelley, A" (Wylie), **Supp. I Part 2:** 724
Red Channels (Harnett), **Supp. XV:** 198
"Red Clowns" (Cisneros), **Supp. VII:** 63
Red Coal, The (Stern), **Supp. IX:** 291–292
Red Coat, The (Shanley), **Supp. XIV:** 316–317
"Red Cords" (Lamott), **Supp. XX:** 142
"Red"(Crooker), **Supp. XXIII:** 63
"Red Cross" (Hughes), **Retro. Supp. I:** 205
Red Cross (Shepard), **Supp. III Part 2:** 440, 446
Red Death, A (Mosley), **Supp. XIII:** 237, 239, 240
"Red Deer" (C. Frost), **Supp. XV:** 101
Redding, Josephine, **Supp. XXI:** 2
Redding, Saunders, **Supp. I Part 1:** 332, 333
Reddings, J. Saunders, **Supp. IV Part 1:** 164
Red Dust (Levine), **Supp. V:** 178, 183–184, 188
"Red Dust" (Levine), **Supp. V:** 184
"Redemption" (Gardner), **Supp. VI:** 72
Redemption (Uris), **Supp. XX:** 244, 246, 247, 248, 254, 255

"Red Ensign, The" (Gallagher), **Supp. XXIV:** 175, 176
"Redeployment" (Nemerov), **III:** 267, 272
Redfield, Robert, **IV:** 475
Redford, Robert, **Supp. IX:** 253, 259; **Supp. XIII:** 267; **Supp. XIV:** 223
Redgrave, Lynn, **Supp. V:** 107
Red Harvest (Hammett), **Supp. IV Part 1:** 346–348, 348; **Supp. IV Part 2:** 468; **Supp. XXI:** 272
"Red Hat, The"(Hadas), **Supp. XXIII:** 111, 113, 118, 119, 124, 128
Red-Headed Woman (film), **Retro. Supp. I:** 110; **Supp. XVI:** 191
"Red Horse Wind over Albuquerque" (Harjo), **Supp. XII:** 219
Red Hot Vacuum, The (Solotaroff), **Retro. Supp. II:** 281
Rediscovery of America, The (W. Frank), **Supp. XX:** 75
Rediscovery of Man, The (W. Frank), **Supp. XX:** 67–68, 80
"Red Leaves" (Faulkner), **II:** 72
"Red Meat: What Difference Did Stesichoros Make?" (Carson), **Supp. XII:** 107
"Red Pawn" (Rand), **Supp. IV Part 2:** 520
Red Pony, The (Steinbeck), **IV:** 50, 51, 58, 70
Redrawing the Boundaries (Fisher), **Retro. Supp. I:** 39
Red Robins, The (Koch), **Supp. XV:** 185–186, 187
Red Roses for Bronze (Doolittle), **Supp. I Part 1:** 253, 268, 271
Red Rover, The (Cooper), **I:** 342–343, 355
Reds (Beatty), **Supp. XXIV:** 227
"Red Shift" (Berrigan), **Supp. XXIV:** 46
"Red Silk Stockings" (Hughes), **Retro. Supp. I:** 200
Redskins, The (Cooper), **I:** 351, 353
Red Sox and Bluefish: And Other Things That Make New England New England (Orlean), **Supp. XXV:** 159
"Red Sox Nation, North" (Mosher), **Supp. XXII:** 209
"Red Star, Winter Orbit" (W. Gibson and B. Sterling), **Supp. XVI:** 123
Red Suitcase (Nye), **Supp. XIII:** 277, 278, 287
Red the Fiend (Sorrentino), **Supp. XXI:** 227, 231, 237
Red Wallflower, A (S. Warner), **Supp. XVIII:** 260
"Red Wheelbarrow, The" (W. C. Williams), **IV:** 411–412; **Retro. Supp. I:** 419, 430
"Red Wind" (Chandler), **Supp. IV Part 1:** 122
"Red Wing Church, The" (Kooser), **Supp. XIX:** 119
"Redwings" (Wright), **Supp. III Part 2:** 603
Reed, Edward Bliss, **Supp. XV:** 297, 298, 300
Reed, Ishmael, **Retro. Supp. II:** 111, 324–325; **Supp. II Part 1:** 34; **Supp.**

X: 239–257, 331; **Supp. XIII:** 181, 182; **Supp. XVI:** 143; **Supp. XX:** 107; **Supp. XXII:** 172
Reed, J. D., **Supp. XVI:** 174
Reed, John, **I:** 48, 476, 483; **Supp. X:** 136; **Supp. XV:** 295, 299; **Supp. XVII:** 96, 99, 100; **Supp. XVIII:** 225; **Supp. XXI:** 6, 12; **Supp. XXII:** 274, 275; **Supp. XXIII:** 161, 162
Reed, Lou, **Retro. Supp. II:** 266
"Reedbeds of the Hackensack, The" (Clampitt), **Supp. IX:** 41
"Reed of Pan, A" (McCullers), **II:** 585
Reedy, Billy, **Retro. Supp. II:** 65, 67, 71, 73
Reedy, William Marion, **Supp. I Part 2:** 456, 461, 465
Reef, The (Wharton), **IV:** 317–318, 322; **Retro. Supp. I:** 372, 373–374
Reena and Other Stories (Marshall), **Supp. XI:** 275, 277, 278
"Reese in Evening Shadow" (Skloot), **Supp. XX:** 204
Reeve, F. D., **Supp. XV:** 344, 349
Reeve's Tale (Chaucer), **I:** 131
"Refiguring the Postcolonial Imagination: Tropes of Visuality in Writing by Rhys, Kincaid, and Cliff" (Emery), **Supp. XXII:** 73
Refiner's Fire: The Life and Adventures of Marshall Pearl, a Foundling (Helprin), **Supp. XXV:** 83, 85–86
"Reflection from Anita Loos" (Empson), **Supp. XVI:** 190
"Reflections" (Carruth), **Supp. XVI:** 54
"Reflections" (Komunyakaa), **Supp. XIII:** 117
Reflections at Fifty and Other Essays (Farrell), **II:** 49
"Reflections by a Fire" (Sarton), **Supp. VIII:** 259
Reflections in a Golden Eye (McCullers), **II:** 586, 588, 593–596, 604; **IV:** 384, 396
Reflections of a Jacobite (Auchincloss), **Supp. IV Part 1:** 31
Reflections on a Gift of Watermelon Pickle (Dunning), **Supp. XIV:** 126
Reflections on Poetry and Poetics (Nemerov), **III:** 269
"Reflections on the Constitution of Nature" (Freneau), **Supp. II Part 1:** 274
"Reflections on the Death of the Reader" (Morris), **III:** 237
Reflections on the End of an Era (Niebuhr), **III:** 297–298
"Reflections on the Life and Death of Lord Clive" (Paine), **Supp. I Part 2:** 505
Reflections on the Revolution in France (Burke), **Supp. I Part 2:** 511, 512
Reflections: Thinking Part I (Arendt), **Supp. I Part 2:** 570
"Reflex Action and Theism" (James), **II:** 345, 363
Reflex and Bone Structure (Major), **Supp. XXII:** 174–175
"Refrains/Remains/Reminders" (Goldbarth), **Supp. XII:** 180–181, 181
"Refuge" (Kingsolver), **Supp. VII:** 208

"Refuge, A" (Goldbarth), **Supp. XII:** 190

Refugee Children: Theory, Research, and Services (Ahearn and Athey, eds.), **Supp. XI:** 184

"Refugees, The" (Jarrell), **II:** 371

"Refusal" (C. Frost), **Supp. XV:** 102

"Refusal to Publish Fifth Book" (Halliday), **Supp. XIX:** 94

Regarding Wave (Snyder), **Supp. VIII: 299–300**

Regina (Epstein), **Supp. XII: 170–171**

"Regional Literature of the South" (Rawlings), **Supp. X:** 228

"Regional Writer, The" (O'Connor), **Retro. Supp. II:** 223, 225

Régnier, Henri de, **II:** 528–529

Regulators, The (King), **Supp. V:** 141

Rehder, Robert, **Supp. IV Part 1:** 69

Rehearsing Absence (Espaillat), **Supp. XXI:** 99

Reich, Tova, **Supp. XVI:** 158

Reichel, Hans, **III:** 183

Reichl, Ruth, **Supp. X:** 79, 85

Reid, B. L., **II:** 41, 47

Reid, Forrest, **Supp. XX:** 235

Reid, Thomas, **II:** 9; **Supp. I Part 1:** 151

Reign of Snakes (Wrigley), **Supp. XVIII:** 293, **302–306**

"Reign of Snakes" (Wrigley), **Supp. XVIII:** 302–304

Reign of Wonder, The (Tanner), **I:** 260

Rein, Yevgeny, **Supp. VIII:** 22

Reinagle, Alexander, **Supp. XV:** 238, 240

"Reincarnation" (Dickey), **Supp. IV Part 1:** 181–182

Reine des pommes, La (C. Himes). *See For Love of Imabelle* (C. Himes)

Reiner, Carl, **Supp. IV Part 2:** 591

Reinfeld, Linda, **Supp. IV Part 2:** 421

Reinhardt, Max, **Supp. XV:** 307

Reinventing the Enemy's Language: Contemporary Native Women's Writing of North America (Bird and Harjo, eds.), **Supp. XII:** 216, 217

Reisman, Jerry, **Supp. III Part 2:** 618

Reiter, Amy, **Supp. XIX:** 54, 56

Reitlinger, Gerald, **Supp. XII:** 161

Reivers, The: A Reminiscence (Faulkner), **I:** 305; **II:** 57, 73; **Retro. Supp. I:** 74, 82, 91

"Rejoicings" (Stern), **Supp. IX:** 289–290

Rejoicings: Selected Poems, 1966–1972 (Stern), **Supp. IX: 289–290**

Relation of My Imprisonment, The (Banks), **Supp. V:** 8, 12–13

"Relations between Poetry and Painting, The" (Stevens), **Retro. Supp. I:** 312

Relations of the Alabama-Georgia Dialect to the Provincial Dialects of Great Britain, The (Brooks), **Supp. XIV:** 3

Relative Stranger, A (C. Baxter), **Supp. XVII:** 19, 22

"Relativity of Beauty, The" (Rawlings), **Supp. X:** 226

Relearning the Alphabet (Levertov), **Supp. III Part 1:** 280, 281

"Release" (C. Baxter), **Supp. XVII:** 15

"Release, The" (MacLeish), **III:** 16

Reles, Abe ("Kid Twist"), **Supp. IV Part 1:** 382

"Relevance of an Impossible Ethical Ideal, The" (Niebuhr), **III:** 298

"Religion" (Dunbar), **Supp. II Part 1:** 199

"Religion" (Emerson), **II:** 6

Religion of Nature Delineated, The (Wollaston), **II:** 108

"Religious Instruction" (Peacock), **Supp. XIX:** 200, 201

Religious Rebel, A: The Letters of "H. W. S." (Mrs. Pearsall Smith) (L. P. Smith), **Supp. XIV:** 349

"Reluctance" (Frost), **II:** 153

Reluctantly: Autobiographical Essays (Carruth), **Supp. XVI:** 45–46, 50

Remains (Snodgrass), **Supp. VI:** 311, **313–314**

"Remains, The" (Strand), **Supp. IV Part 2:** 627

"Remarks on Color" (Wright), **Supp. XV:** 346

"Remarks on National Literature" (Channing), **Supp. XXIV: 76–77**

"Remarks on Spencer's *Definition of Mind as Correspondence*" (James), **II:** 345

Remarque, Erich Maria, **Retro. Supp. I:** 113; **Supp. IV Part 1:** 380

Rembrandt, **II:** 536; **IV:** 310; **Supp. IV Part 1:** 390, 391

"Rembrandt, The" (Wharton), **IV:** 310

"Rembrandt's Hat" (Malamud), **Supp. I Part 2:** 435, 437

Rembrandt Takes a Walk (Strand), **Supp. IV Part 2:** 631

"Rembrandt to Rembrandt" (Robinson), **III:** 521–522

Remembered Earth, The: An Anthology of Contemporary Native American Literature (Hobson, ed.), **Supp. IV Part 1:** 321

Remembered Yesterdays (Johnson), **Supp. IX:** 184

"Remembering" (Angelou), **Supp. IV Part 1:** 15

"Remembering Allen Tate" (Cowley), **Supp. II Part 1:** 153

"Remembering Barthes" (Sontag), **Supp. III Part 2:** 451, 471

"Remembering Guston" (Kunitz), **Supp. III Part 1:** 257

"Remembering James Laughlin" (Karr), **Supp. XI:** 242

Remembering Laughter (Stegner), **Supp. IV Part 2:** 598, 606, 607, 608, 611, 614

"Remembering Lobo" (Mora), **Supp. XIII:** 220, 227

"Remembering My Father" (Berry), **Supp. X:** 23

"Remembering My Parents Remembering the Books They Read" (Espaillat), **Supp. XXI:** 107

"Remembering that Island" (McGrath), **Supp. X:** 116

"Remembering the Children of Auschwitz" (McGrath), **Supp. X:** 127

"Remembering the Lost World" (Jarrell), **II:** 388

"Remembering the Sixties" (Simpson), **Supp. IX:** 279

Remember Me to Tom (T. Williams), **IV:** 379–380

"Remember the Moon Survives" (Kingsolver), **Supp. VII:** 209

Remember to Remember (H. Miller), **III:** 186

"Remembrance, A" (Gioia), **Supp. XV:** 112

Remembrance of Things Past (Proust), **Supp. IV Part 2:** 600; **Supp. XII:** 9; **Supp. XIII:** 44

Remembrance Rock (Sandburg), **III:** 590

Reminiscence, A (Ashbery), **Supp. III Part 1:** 2

Remnick, David, **Supp. XVI:** 246

"Remora" (Merrill), **Supp. III Part 1:** 326

"Removal" (White), **Supp. I Part 2:** 664–665

"Removal, The" (Merwin), **Supp. III Part 1:** 350, 351

"Removal Service Request" (Halliday), **Supp. XIX:** 90

Removed from Time (Matthews and Feeney), **Supp. IX:** 154

Remsen, Ira, **Supp. I Part 1:** 369

"Rémy de Gourmont, A Distinction" (Pound), **III:** 467

"Renaissance" (Carruth), **Supp. XVI:** 56

Renaissance in the South (Bradbury), **I:** 288–289

Renaldo and Clara (film, Dylan and Shepard), **Supp. XVIII:** 21, 28, 31

"Renaming the Kings" (Levine), **Supp. V:** 184

Renan, Ernest, **Supp. XX:** 122

Renan, Joseph Ernest, **II:** 86; **IV:** 440, 444

Renard, Jules, **IV:** 79

"Renascence" (Millay), **III:** 123, 125–126, 128; **Supp. XV:** 42

Renault, Mary, **Supp. IV Part 2:** 685

"Rendezvous, The" (Kumin), **Supp. IV Part 2:** 455

René, Norman, **Supp. X:** 146, 152

Renée (anonymous author), **Supp. XVI:** 64, 66

"Renegade, The" (Jackson), **Supp. IX:** 120

Renewal of Life series (Mumford), **Supp. II Part 2:** 476, 479, 481, 482, 485, 495, 497

"Reno Hill ... Little Bighorn" (Kenny), **Supp. XXIII:** 155

Renoir, Jean, **Supp. XII:** 259; **Supp. XXII:** 256

Renouvier, Charles, **II:** 344–345, 346

"Renunciation" (Banks), **Supp. V:** 10

Renza, Louis A., **Retro. Supp. II:** 142

"Repair" (Peacock), **Supp. XIX:** 204

"Repeating Dream" (Gander), **Supp. XV:** 340

Repent in Haste (Marquand), **III:** 59

Reperusals and Re-Collections (L. P. Smith), **Supp. XIV:** 346–347

"Repetitive Heart, The: Eleven Poems in Imitation of the Fugue Form" (Schwartz), **Supp. II Part 2:** 645–646

"Replacing Regionalism" (Murphy), **Retro. Supp. II:** 143

Replansky, Naomi, **Supp. X:** 119

Replenishing Jessica (Bodenheim), **Supp. XXV:** 24, 25

"Reply to Mr. Wordsworth" (MacLeish), **III:** 19

"Report, A" (Jin), **Supp. XVIII:** 93

"Report from a Forest Logged by the Weyhaeuser Company" (Wagoner), **Supp. IX:** 328

"Report from North Vietnam" (Paley), **Supp. VI:** 227

Report from Part One (Brooks), **Supp. III Part 1:** 70, 72, 80, 82–85

Report from Part Two (Brooks), **Supp. III Part 1:** 87

Report on a Game Survey of the North Central States (Leopold), **Supp. XIV:** 182

"Report on the Barnhouse Effect" (Vonnegut), **Supp. II Part 2:** 756

"Report to an Academy, A" (Kafka), **Supp. XX:** 18

"Report to Crazy Horse" (Stafford), **Supp. XI: 324–325**

"Repose of Rivers" (H. Crane), **I:** 393; **Retro. Supp. II:** 78, 81

"Repossession of a Heritage, The" (Zagarell), **Supp. XV:** 270, 281

Repp, John, **Supp. XXIII:** 302

"Representation and the War for Reality" (Gass), **Supp. VI:** 88

"Representative Indian, The" *(Outlook)*, **Supp. XXV:** 277, 278

Representative Men (Emerson), **II:** 1, 5–6, 8

"Representing Far Places" (Stafford), **Supp. XI:** 321

Repression and Recovery (Nelson), **Supp. XVIII:** 226

"REPRISE OF ONE OF A. G.'S BEST POEMS" (Baraka), **Supp. II Part 1:** 59

"RepRoach" (Stallings), **Supp. XXV:** 230–231

"Reproducing Ourselves Is All Very Well" (E. Hoffman), **Supp. XVI:** 155

Republic (Plato), **I:** 485

"Republican Manifesto, A" (Paine), **Supp. I Part 2:** 511

"Republican Mother, The: Woman and the Enlightenment—An American Perspective" (Kerber), **Supp. XXV:** 44

Republic of Love, The (Shields), **Supp. VII:** 323–324, 326, 327

"Requa" (Olsen), **Supp. XIII:** 294, **302–303**, 304

Requa, Kenneth A., **Supp. I Part 1:** 107

"Requa I" (Olsen). *See* "Requa" (Olsen)

"Request for Offering" (Eberhart), **I:** 526

"Requiem" (Akhmatova), **Supp. VIII:** 20

"Requiem" (LaBastille), **Supp. X:** 105

Requiem for a Nun (Faulkner), **II:** 57, 72–73

Requiem for Harlem (H. Roth), **Supp. IX:** 235, 236, **240–242**

"Rescue, The" (Updike), **IV:** 214

Rescued Year, The (Stafford), **Supp. XI: 321–322**

"Rescued Year, The" (Stafford), **Supp. XI:** 322, 323

"Rescue with Yul Brynner" (Moore), **III:** 215

"Rescuing Moon" (P. Benedict), **Supp. XXIII:** 40

"Resemblance" (Bishop), **Supp. I Part 1:** 86

"Resemblance" (Ferry), **Supp. XXIV:** 161

"Resemblance between a Violin Case and a Coffin, A" (T. Williams), **IV:** 378–379

"Reservations" (Taylor), **Supp. V:** 323

"Reserved Memorials" (Mather), **Supp. II Part 2:** 446, 449

"Resignación" (Espaillat), **Supp. XXI:** 104

"Resignation" (J. Schoolcraft), **Supp. XXIII:** 228, 229–230

"Resistance to Civil Government" (Thoreau), **Supp. X:** 27, 28

Resist Much, Obey Little (Berry), **Supp. XIII:** 2

Resolution (Parker), **Supp. XIX:** 187

"Resolution and Independence" (Wordsworth), **Supp. XV:** 346

"Resort" (Hampl), **Supp. XXII:** 86–87

Resort and Other Poems (Hampl), **Supp. XXII:** 83, 86–87

Resources of Hope (R. Williams), **Supp. IX:** 146

"Respectable Place, A" (O'Hara), **III:** 369

"Respectable Woman, A" (Chopin), **Retro. Supp. II:** 66

"Respite" (Pedersen; Nelson, trans.), **Supp. XVIII:** 180

Responses (Wilbur), **Supp. III Part 2:** 541

"Response to a Rumor that the Oldest Whorehouse in Wheeling, West Virginia, Has Been Condemned" (Wright), **Supp. III Part 2:** 602

"Rest Cure" (Boyle), **Supp. XXIV:** 57

Restif de La Bretonne, Nicolas, **III:** 175

"Rest of Life, The" (Gordon), **Supp. IV Part 1:** 311

Rest of Life, The: Three Novellas (Gordon), **Supp. IV Part 1:** 310–312

Rest of the Way, The (McClatchy), **Supp. XII:** 255, **258–259**

Restoration comedy, **Supp. I Part 2:** 617

Restorers, The (Di Piero), **Supp. XIX:** 42–43, 44

"Restorers, The" (Di Piero), **Supp. XIX:** 43

"Restraint" (F. Barthelme), **Supp. XI:** 26

"Result" (Emerson), **II:** 6

"Résumé" (Parker), **Supp. IX:** 189

"Resurrecting Methuselah" (E. P. Jones), **Supp. XXII:** 151

Resurrection (Della Francesca), **Supp. XV:** 262

"Resurrection" (Harjo), **Supp. XII:** 224

"Resurrection" (Jin), **Supp. XVIII:** 94–95

Resurrection, The (Gardner), **Supp. VI:** 61, 63, **64–65**, 68, 69, 73, 74

"Resurrection, The" (Very), **Supp. XXV:** 247–248

"Retort" (Hay), **Supp. XIV:** 133

Retour amont (Char; Sobin, trans.), **Supp. XVI:** 282

Retrieval System, The (Kumin), **Supp. IV Part 2:** 449, 451, 452

"Retrievers in Translation" (Doty), **Supp. XI:** 132

"Retroduction to American History" (Tate), **IV:** 129

"Retrospects and Prospects" (Lanier), **Supp. I Part 1:** 352

"Return" (Corso), **Supp. XII:** 135

"Return" (Creeley), **Supp. IV Part 1:** 141, 145

"Return" (MacLeish), **III:** 12

"Return, The" (Bidart), **Supp. XV:** 32–33

"Return, The" (Bontemps), **Supp. XXII:** 3, 8

"Return, The" (Pound), **Retro. Supp. I:** 288

"Return, The" (Ray), **Supp. XVIII:** 194

"Return, The" (Roethke), **III:** 533

"Return, The: Orihuela, 1965" (Levine), **Supp. V:** 194

"Return: An Elegy, The" (Warren), **IV:** 239

"Return: Buffalo" (Hogan), **Supp. IV Part 1:** 411

"Returning" (Komunyakaa), **Supp. XIII:** 122

"Returning a Lost Child" (Glück), **Supp. V:** 81

"Returning from the Enemy" (Harjo), **Supp. XII:** 229–230

"Returning the Borrowed Road" (Komunyakaa), **Supp. XIII:** 113, 133

"Return of Alcibiade, The" (Chopin), **Retro. Supp. II:** 58, 64

Return of Ansel Gibbs, The (Buechner), **III:** 310; **Supp. XII:** 48

"Return of Eros to Academe, The" (Bukiet), **Supp. XVII:** 47

"Return of Spring" (Winters), **Supp. II Part 2:** 791

Return of the Native, The (Hardy), **II:** 184–185, 186

Return of the Vanishing American, The (Fiedler), **Supp. XIII:** 103

Return to a Place Lit by a Glass of Milk (Simic), **Supp. VIII:** 274, 276, 283

"Return to Lavinia" (Caldwell), **I:** 310

"Return to Thin Air: The Everest Disaster Ten Years Later" *(Outside)*, **Supp. XVIII:** 113

Return to Zion, The (Asch), **Supp. XXIII:** 5

Reuben (Wideman), **Supp. X:** 320

Reuben and Rachel; or, Tales of Old Times (Rowson), **Supp. XV: 240–241**

Reunion (Mamet), **Supp. XIV:** 240, 247, 254

"Reunion in Brooklyn" (H. Miller), **III:** 175, 184

Reuther brothers, **I:** 493

"Reveille" (Kingsolver), **Supp. VII:** 208

"Reveille" (Untermeyer), **Supp. XV:** 300

"Reveille, The" (Harte), **Supp. II Part 1:** 342–343

Revelation (biblical book), **II:** 541; **IV:** 104, 153, 154; **Supp. I Part 1:** 105, 273

"Revelation" (O'Connor), **III:** 349, 353–354; **Retro. Supp. II:** 237

"Revelation" (Warren), **III:** 490

Revenge (Harrison), **Supp. VIII:** 39, 45

"Revenge of Hamish, The" (Lanier), **Supp. I Part 1:** 365

"Revenge of Hannah Kemhuff, The" (Walker), **Supp. III Part 2:** 521

"Revenge of Rain-in-the-Face, The" (Longfellow), **Retro. Supp. II:** 170

"Reverberation"(Kenny), **Supp. XXIII:** 155

Reverberator, The (James), **Retro. Supp. I:** 227

"Reverdure" (Berry), **Supp. X:** 22

Reverdy, Pierre, **Supp. XV:** 178, 182; **Supp. XXIII:** 208

"Reverend Father Gilhooley" (Farrell), **II:** 45

Reverse Transcription (Kushner), **Supp. IX:** 138

Reversible Errors (Turow), **Supp. XVII:** 220–221

"Rev. Freemont Deadman" (Masters), **Supp. I Part 2:** 463

Reviewer's ABC, A (Aiken), **I:** 58

Review of Contemporary Fiction, 1990 (Tabbi, ed.), **Supp. XVII:** 143

"Revolt, against the Crepuscular Spirit in Modern Poetry" (Pound), **Retro. Supp. I:** 286

"Revolution" (C. L. R. James), **Supp. XXI:** 160

"Revolution" (Taggard), **Supp. XXII:** 275

"Revolutionary Answer to the Negro Problem in the USA, The" (statement, C. L. R. James), **Supp. XXI:** 169

Revolutionary Petunias (Walker), **Supp. III Part 2:** 520, 522, 530

Revolutionary Road (Yates), **Supp. XI:** 334, **335–340**

"Revolutionary Symbolism in America" (Burke), **I:** 272

"Revolutionary Theatre, The" (Baraka), **Supp. II Part 1:** 42

Revolution in Taste, A: Studies of Dylan Thomas, Allen Ginsberg, Sylvia Plath, and Robert Lowell (Simpson), **Supp. IX:** 276

"Revolution in the Revolution in the Revolution" (Snyder), **Supp. VIII:** 300

Revon, Marcel, **II:** 525

"Rewaking, The" (W. C. Williams), **Retro. Supp. I:** 430

"Rewrite" (Dunn), **Supp. XI:** 147

Rexroth, Kenneth, **II:** 526; **Supp. II Part 1:** 307; **Supp. II Part 2:** 436; **Supp. III Part 2:** 625, 626; **Supp. IV Part 1:** 145–146; **Supp. VIII:** 289; **Supp. XIII:** 75; **Supp. XIV:** 287; **Supp. XV:** 140, 141, 146; **Supp. XXII:** 168

Reynolds, Ann (pseudonym). *See* Bly, Carol

Reynolds, Clay, **Supp. XI:** 254

Reynolds, David, **Supp. XV:** 269; **Supp. XXIII:** 187

Reynolds, Sir Joshua, **Supp. I Part 2:** 716

Reynolds, Quentin, **IV:** 286

Reza, Yasmina, **Supp. XXI:** 148

Rezanov (Atherton), **Supp. XXIV:** 23

Reznikoff, Charles, **IV:** 415; **Retro. Supp. I:** 422; **Supp. III Part 2:** 615, 616, 617, 628; **Supp. XIV: 277–296; Supp. XXIII:** 174; **Supp. XXIV:** 36, 45

"Rhapsodist, The" (Brown), **Supp. I Part 1:** 125–126

"Rhapsody on a Windy Night" (Eliot), **Retro. Supp. I:** 55

Rhetoric of Motives, A (Burke), **I:** 272, 275, 278, 279

Rhetoric of Religion, The (Burke), **I:** 275, 279

"Rhobert" (Toomer), **Supp. IX:** 316–317

"Rhode Show" (Mallon), **Supp. XIX:** 137–138

"Rhododendrons" (Levis), **Supp. XI:** 260, 263

Rhubarb Show, The (radio, Keillor), **Supp. XVI:** 178

"Rhyme of Sir Christopher, The" (Longfellow), **II:** 501

Rhymes to Be Traded for Bread (Lindsay), **Supp. I Part 2:** 380, 381–382

Rhys, Ernest, **III:** 458

Rhys, Jean, **Supp. III Part 1:** 42, 43; **Supp. XVIII:** 131

"Rhythm & Blues" (Baraka), **Supp. II Part 1:** 37–38

Rhythms (Reznikoff), **Supp. XIV:** 279, 282, 283

Rhythms II (Reznikoff), **Supp. XIV:** 282, 283, 284

Ribalow, Harold, **Supp. IX:** 236

Ribbentrop, Joachim von, **IV:** 249

Ribicoff, Abraham, **Supp. IX:** 33

Ribot, Théodule Armand, **Supp. XX: 238**

Ricardo, David, **Supp. I Part 2:** 628, 634

Rice, Allen Thorndike, **Retro. Supp. I:** 362

Rice, Anne, **Supp. VII: 287–306**

Rice, Elmer, **I:** 479; **III:** 145, 160–161

Rice, Mrs. Grantland, **II:** 435

Rice, Philip Blair, **IV:** 141

Rice, Stan, **Supp. XII:** 2

Rice, Tim, **Supp. XXI:** 148

Rice, Tom, **Supp. XIV:** 125

Rich, Adrienne, **Retro. Supp. I:** 8, 36, 42, 47, 404; **Retro. Supp. II:** 43, 191, 245; **Supp. I Part 2:** 546–547, **550–578; Supp. III Part 1:** 84, 354; **Supp. III Part 2:** 541, 599; **Supp. IV Part 1:** 257, 325; **Supp. V:** 82; **Supp. VIII:** 272; **Supp. XII:** 217, 229, 255; **Supp. XIII:** 294; **Supp. XIV:** 126, 129; **Supp. XV:** 176, 252; **Supp. XVII:** 32, 74; **Supp. XIX:** 83, 193; **Supp. XXII:** 65, 66; **Supp. XXV:** 3

Rich, Arnold, **Supp. I Part 2:** 552

Rich, Frank, **Supp. IV Part 2:** 585, 586; **Supp. V:** 106; **Supp. XXI:** 146; **Supp. XXIV:** 121, 124

Richard, Mark, **Supp. XIX: 209–222**

Richard Cory (Gurney), **Supp. V:** 99–100, 105

"Richard Hunt's 'Arachne' " (Hayden), **Supp. II Part 1:** 374

Richard II (Shakespeare), **Supp. XVII:** 244

Richard III (Shakespeare), **Supp. I Part 2:** 422

Richards, Bertrand F., **Supp. XX: 217–218**

Richards, Constance S., **Supp. XXII:** 73

Richards, David, **Supp. IV Part 2:** 576; **Supp. XXIV:** 266, 269

Richards, Grant, **I:** 515

Richards, I. A., **I:** 26, 273–274, 279, 522; **III:** 498; **IV:** 92; **Supp. I Part 1:** 264, 265; **Supp. I Part 2:** 647

Richards, Ivor Armonstrong, **Supp. XIV:** 2–3, 16

Richards, Laura E., **II:** 396; **III:** 505–506, 507

Richards, Leonard, **Supp. XIV:** 48

Richards, Lloyd, **Supp. IV Part 1:** 362; **Supp. VIII:** 331

Richards, Rosalind, **III:** 506

Richards, Tad, **Supp. XVII:** 77

Richardson, Alan, **III:** 295

Richardson, Charles, **Supp. XVIII:** 14, 15

Richardson, Dorothy, **I:** 53; **II:** 320; **Supp. III Part 1:** 65

Richardson, Helen Patges, **Retro. Supp. II:** 95

Richardson, Henry Hobson, **I:** 3, 10

Richardson, Maurice, **Supp. XII:** 241

Richardson, Samuel, **I:** 134; **II:** 104, 111, 322; **Supp. V:** 127; **Supp. IX:** 128; **Supp. XV:** 232; **Supp. XX: 236**

Richardson, Tony, **Supp. XI:** 305, 306

"Richard Wright and Recent Negro Fiction" (Ellison), **Retro. Supp. II:** 116

"Richard Wright's Blues" (Ellison), **Retro. Supp. II:** 117, 124

"Richard Yates: A Requiem" (Lawrence), **Supp. XI:** 335

"Rich Boy, The" (Fitzgerald), **II:** 94; **Retro. Supp. I:** 98, 108

Richer, the Poorer, The: Sketches and Reminiscences (D. West), **Supp. XVIII:** 277, 289

"Riches" (Bausch), **Supp. VII:** 54

Richey, Elinor, **Supp. XXIV:** 30

Richler, Mordecai, **Supp. XI:** 294, 297

Rich Man, Poor Man (miniseries), **Supp. XIX:** 252

Rich Man, Poor Man (Shaw), **Supp. XIX:** 251–252

Richman, Robert, **Supp. XI:** 249; **Supp. XV:** 120–121, 251

Richman, Shira, **Supp. XXIV:** 167

Richmond (Masters), **Supp. I Part 2:** 471

Richmond, M. A., **Supp. XX: 277, 279, 282, 286, 289, 290**

Rich Relations (Hwang), **Supp. XXI:** 146–147

Richter, Conrad, **Supp. X:** 103; **Supp. XVIII: 207–222**

Richter, Jean Paul, **II:** 489, 492; **Supp. XVI:** 182

Rick Bass (Weltzien), **Supp. XVI:** 20

Rickman, Clio, **Supp. I Part 2:** 519
Ricks, Christopher, **Retro. Supp. I:** 56; **Supp. XVIII:** 20, 30, 32
Riddel, Joseph N., **IV:** 95
"Riddle, The" (Hay), **Supp. XIV:** 130
"Ride in an Omnibus, A" (Briggs), **Supp. XVIII:** 9, 16
"Riders to the Blood-Red Wrath" (Brooks), **Supp. III Part 1:** 82–83
Riders to the Sea (Synge), **III:** 157
Ridge, Lola, **Supp. IX:** 308; **Supp. XV:** 307; **Supp. XXIV:** 49, 52
Riding, Alan, **Supp. XVI:** 294
Riding, Laura, **I:** 437
"Riding Out at Evening" (McCarriston), **Supp. XIV:** 262–263
Riding the Iron Rooster: By Train through China (Theroux), **Supp. VIII:** 324
Ridley, Clifford, **Supp. XXIV:** 282
Riesenberg, Felix, **I:** 360, 361
Riesman, David, **Supp. I Part 2:** 649, 650
"Rif, to Music, The" (Bowles), **Supp. IV Part 1:** 89
Riffs & Reciprocities (Dunn), **Supp. XI:** 154–155
Rifkin, Libby, **Supp. XXIV:** 39, 44
Rifles, The (Vollmann), **Supp. XVII:** 226, 233
Riggs, Marlon, **Supp. XI:** 19
Right Distance, The (Pickering), **Supp. XXI:** 196–197
Right Madness on Skye, The (Hugo), **Supp. VI:** 145–147
Rights of Man (Paine), **Supp. I Part 2:** 508, 511, 512–514, 516, 519, 523
"Rights of Woman" (Rowson), **Supp. XV:** 243
"Rights of Women, The" (Brown). *See Alcuin: A Dialogue* (Brown)
Right Stuff, The (Wolfe), **Supp. III Part 2:** 581–584
Right Thoughts in Sad Hours (Mather), **IV:** 144
Rigney, Barbara Hill, **Supp. VIII:** 215
"Rigorists" (Moore), **III:** 198
Rihani, Ameen, **Supp. XX:** 115
Rihoku, **Supp. XXII:** 228
Riis, Jacob A., **I:** 293; **Supp. I Part 1:** 13; **Supp. XVII:** 101, 106
Riley, Glenda, **Supp. XXIV:** 252
Riley, James Whitcomb, **I:** 205; **Supp. II Part 1:** 192, 193, 196, 197
Rilke, Rainer Maria, **I:** 445, 523; **II:** 367, 381, 382–383, 389, 543, 544; **III:** 552, 558, 563, 571, 572; **IV:** 380, 443; **Retro. Supp. II:** 20, 187; **Supp. I Part 1:** 264; **Supp. I Part 2:** 573; **Supp. III Part 1:** 239, 242, 246, 283, 319–320; **Supp. IV Part 1:** 284; **Supp. V:** 208, 343; **Supp. VIII:** 30, 40; **Supp. X:** 164; **Supp. XI:** 126; **Supp. XIII:** 74, 88; **Supp. XV:** 93, 212, 222,**Supp. XV:** 223, 225; **Supp. XVI:** 292; **Supp. XVII:** 244; **Supp. XXII:** 89, 90, 94; **Supp. XXIII:** 207; **Supp. XXIV:** 37, 38, 152, 162
Rilke on Love and Other Difficulties (Rilke), **Supp. X:** 164

"Rilke's Growth as a Poet" (Dobyns), **Supp. XIII:** 77
"Rimbaud" (Kerouac), **Supp. III Part 1:** 232
Rimbaud, Arthur, **I:** 381, 383, 389, 391, 526; **II:** 528, 543, 545; **III:** 23, 174, 189; **IV:** 286, 380, 443; **Retro. Supp. I:** 56; **Retro. Supp. II:** 187, 326; **Supp. III Part 1:** 14, 195; **Supp. IV Part 2:** 624; **Supp. VIII:** 39, 40; **Supp. XII:** 1, 16, 128, 255; **Supp. XIII:** 284; **Supp. XIV:** 338; **Supp. XVIII:** 23, 33; **Supp. XXI:** 225, 233; **Supp. XXIII:** 207; **Supp. XXIV:** 39, 40
Rindge, Debora, **Supp. XXI:** 246
Rinehart, Mary Roberts, **Supp. XXV:** 189–203
Rinehart, Stanley, **III:** 36
Ring, Frances Kroll, **Supp. IX:** 63, 64
Ring and the Book, The (Browning), **Supp. I Part 2:** 416, 468
Ring cycle (Wagner), **Supp. IV Part 1:** 392
Ringe, Donald, **I:** 339, 343; **Retro. Supp. II:** 270
Ringel, Faye, **Supp. XXII:** 205, 207
"Ringing" (Bierds), **Supp. XVII:** 28
"Ringing the Bells" (Sexton), **Supp. II Part 2:** 672, 687
Ringle, Ken, **Supp. X:** 15
Ring of Heaven: Poems (Hongo), **Supp. X:** 292
Rink, The (musical, McNally), **Supp. XIII:** 207
Rin Tin Tin: The Life and the Legend (Orlean), **Supp. XXV:** 160, 165–166
Rio Lobo (film), **Supp. XVI:** 246
Ríos, Alberto Alvaro, **Supp. IV Part 2:** 537–556
"Riot" (Brooks), **Supp. III Part 1:** 71, 84–85
Ripening (Le Sueur), **Supp. XXIII:** 165
Ripley, Ezra, **II:** 8; **IV:** 172
Rip-off Red, Girl Detective (Acker), **Supp. XII:** 3–4
Ripostes (Pound), **Retro. Supp. I:** 287–288, 413
Ripostes of Ezra Pound, The, Whereunto Are Appended the Complete Poetical Works of T. E. Hulme, with Prefatory Note (Pound), **III:** 458, 464, 465
Riprap (Snyder), **Supp. VIII:** 292–294, 295
"Riprap" (Snyder), **Supp. VIII:** 293–294
"Rip Van Winkle" (Irving), **II:** 304–306; **Supp. I Part 1:** 185
Rischin, Moses, **Supp. XVII:** 101, 103, 106
Risco-Lozado, Eliezar, **Supp. XIII:** 313
Rise and Shine (Quindlen), **Supp. XVII:** 179
Rise of David Levinsky, The (Cahan), **Supp. IX:** 227; **Supp. XIII:** 106
Rise of Silas Lapham, The (Howells), **II:** 275, 279, 283–285; **IV:** 202; **Retro. Supp. II:** 93, 101
"Rise of the Middle Class" (Banks), **Supp. V:** 10

Rising and Falling (Matthews), **Supp. IX:** 154, **160**
"Rising Daughter, The" (Olds), **Supp. X:** 204
Rising from the Plains (McPhee), **Supp. III Part 1:** 309–310
Rising Glory of America, The (Brackenridge and Freneau), **Supp. I Part 1:** 124; **Supp. II Part 1:** 67, 253, 256, 263
"Rising of the Storm, The" (Dunbar), **Supp. II Part 1:** 199
Rising Sun in the Pacific, The (Morison), **Supp. I Part 2:** 490
Rising Up and Rising Down (Vollmann), **Supp. XVII:** 225, 226, **229–230**, 232, 233, 235–236
Risk Pool, The (Russo), **Supp. XII:** 328–331
Ristovic, Aleksandar, **Supp. VIII:** 272
"Rita Dove: Identity Markers" (Vendler), **Supp. IV Part 1:** 247, 257
Ritchey, John, **Supp. XIV:** 122
Ritchie, Anne Thackeray, **Supp. XX:** 231, **233**
"Rite of Passage" (Olds), **Supp. X:** 206
"Rites and Ceremonies" (Hecht), **Supp. X:** 61
Rites and Witnesses: A Comedy (Hinojosa), **Supp. XIX:** 106–107
"Rites of Spring, The" (Morris), **III:** 223
Ritivoi, Andreea Deciu, **Supp. XVI:** 148
Ritschl, Albrecht, **III:** 309, 604
Ritsos, Yannis, **Supp. X:** 112
"Ritsos and the Metaphysical Moment" (Dobyns), **Supp. XIII:** 78
Rittenhouse, David, **Supp. I Part 2:** 507
Rittenhouse, Jessie, **Supp. XV:** 295
"Ritual, The" (Jarman), **Supp. XVII:** 114
"Ritual and Renewal: Keres Traditions in the Short Fiction of Leslie Silko" (Ruoff), **Supp. IV Part 2:** 559
Ritz, The (film), **Supp. XIII:** 206
Ritz, The (McNally), **Supp. XIII:** 198
"Rival, The" (Plath), **Retro. Supp. II:** 254
Riven Rock (Boyle), **Supp. VIII:** 5–6; **Supp. XX:** 25–26
"River" (Ammons), **Supp. VII:** 28
"River, The" (O'Connor), **III:** 344, 352, 353, 354, 356; **Retro. Supp. II:** 229, 231–232
Rivera, Tomás, **Supp. XIII:** 216, 221; **Supp. XIX:** 97, 102
Riverbed (Wagoner), **Supp. IX:** 327–328
"River Driftwood" (Jewett), **Retro. Supp. II:** 132, 133, 147
"River Jordan, The" (DeLillo), **Supp. VI:** 3, 4
River King, The (Hoffman), **Supp. X:** 78, 85, 90, **91–92**
"River Merchant's Wife: A Letter, The" (Pound), **III:** 463
"River Now, The" (Hugo), **Supp. VI:** 144
River of Forgetfulness, The (Hadas), **Supp. XXIII: 120**
"River of Rivers in Connecticut, The" (Stevens), **Retro. Supp. I:** 313
River of the Mother of God and Other Essays by Aldo Leopold, The

(Leopold), **Supp. XIV:** 180

"River"(O'Hara), **Supp. XXIII:** 212

"River Profile" (Auden), **Supp. II Part 1:** 26

"River Road" (Kunitz), **Supp. III Part 1:** 260

"River Runs Through It, A" (Maclean), **Supp. XIV:** 222–223, **223–229,** 233, 234, 235; **Supp. XVI:** 98

River Runs Through It and Other Stories, A (Maclean), **Supp. XIV:** 221, 223

Rivers, Allison, **Supp. XXIII:** 51

Rivers, Larry, **Supp. III Part 1:** 3; **Supp. XV:** 177, 178, 186; **Supp. XXIII:** 209, 210, 211, 212, 215, 216, 217, 220

Rivers and Mountains (Ashbery), **Supp. III Part 1:** 10, 26

Riverside Drive (Simpson), **Supp. IX:** 275–276

Riverside Poetry (Auden, Moore, and Shapiro, eds.), **Supp. XXI:** 98

Rivers to the Sea (Teasdale), **Supp. XV:** 295

"River"(Strout), **Supp. XXIII:** 283

River Styx, Ohio, and Other Poems, The (Oliver), **Supp. VII:** 231, 232

"River That Is East, The" (Kinnell), **Supp. III Part 1:** 241–242

"River"(theater performance, Strout), **Supp. XXIII:** 281

"River Towns" (Masters), **Supp. I Part 2:** 473

Rives, Amélie, **II:** 194

Rivière, Jacques, **Retro. Supp. I:** 63

"Rivington's Last Will and Testament" (Freneau), **Supp. II Part 1:** 261

"Rivulet, The" (Bryant), **Supp. I Part 1:** 155, 162

Rix, Alice, **I:** 199

RL's Dream (Mosley), **Supp. XIII:** 234, **244–245,** 249

Roach, Max, **Supp. X:** 239

"Road, Roadsides, and the Disparate Frames of a Sequence" (Sobin), **Supp. XVI:** 288

Road, The (McCarthy), **Supp. XXII:** 49

Road Between, The (Farrell), **II:** 29, 38, 39–40

"Road Between Here and There, The" (Kinnell), **Supp. III Part 1:** 254

"Road Home, The" (Hammett), **Supp. IV Part 1:** 343

Road Home, The (Harrison), **Supp. VIII:** 37, 45, 48, **49–50,** 53

Road Is Before Us, The (Boulton), **Supp. XXII:** 17, 25–26

Roadless Yaak, The: Reflections and Observations about One of Our Last Great Wild Places (Bass, ed.), **Supp. XVI:** 23

"Road Not Taken, The" (R. Frost), **II:** 154; **Retro. Supp. I:** 131; **Supp. XI:** 150; **Supp. XV:** 127

"Roadside Flowers" (Collins), **Supp. XXI:** 61

Roadside Poems for Summer Travellers (Larcom, ed.), **Supp. XIII:** 142

"Roadside Resurrection, A" (L. Brown), **Supp. XXI:** 40, 42

Roads of Destiny (O. Henry), **Supp. II Part 1:** 410

Road through the Wall, The (Jackson), **Supp. IX:** 115, 118, 120, 123–124

"Road to Avignon, The" (Lowell), **II:** 516

"Road to Hell, The" (Fante), **Supp. XI:** 160

Road to Los Angeles, The (Fante), **Supp. XI:** 160, 166, 167, **168,** 172

Road to Many a Wonder, The (Wagoner), **Supp. IX:** 327, **336**

Road to the Temple, The (Glaspell), **Supp. III Part 1:** 175, 182, 186; **Supp. XXI:** 6

Road to Wellville, The (Boyle), **Supp. VIII:** 6–8; **Supp. XX:** 24–25, 26, 28

Road to Xanadu, The (Lowes), **IV:** 453

"Road Warrior" (Pickering), **Supp. XXI:** 204

"Roan Stallion" (Jeffers), **Supp. II Part 2:** 428–429

"Roast-beef" (Stein), **IV:** 43

Roast Leviatham (Untermeyer), **Supp. XV:** 307

"Roast Possum" (Dove), **Supp. IV Part 1:** 247, 248

Robards, Jason, Jr., **III:** 163, 403

Robb, Christina, **Supp. XV:** 251

Robbe-Grillet, Alain, **I:** 123; **IV:** 95; **Supp. IV Part 1:** 42; **Supp. V:** 47, 48; **Supp. XXIII:** 213

Robber Bride, The (Atwood), **Supp. XIII:** **30–31**

Robber Bridegroom, The (Welty), **IV:** 261, 266–268, 271, 274; **Retro. Supp. I:** 347

Robbins, Harold, **Supp. XII:** 6

Robbins, Henry, **Supp. IV Part 1:** 198, 201, 210, 211

Robbins, Katherine Robinson, **Supp. X:** 264

Robbins, Thomas, **Supp. XV:** 271

Robbins, Tom, **Supp. IV Part 1:** 227; **Supp. VIII:** 14; **Supp. X:** **259–288;** **Supp. XIII:** 11

"Robe, The" (Douglas), **IV:** 434

Robert Bly (Sugg), **Supp. IV Part 1:** 68

"Robert Bly" (W. V. Davis), **Supp. IV Part 1:** 70

"Robert Bly and the Trouble with America" (Mitchell), **Supp. IV Part 1:** 70

Robert Bly: An Introduction to the Poetry (Nelson), **Supp. IV Part 1:** 66

Robert Bly: The Poet and His Critics (W. V. Davis), **Supp. IV Part 1:** 63; **Supp. XXI:** 84, **85–86,** 87, 95

Robert Coover: The Universal Fiction-making Process (Gordon), **Supp. V:** 46

Robert Creeley (Ford), **Supp. IV Part 1:** 140

Robert Creeley and the Genius of the American Common Place (Clark), **Supp. IV Part 1:** 140

Robert Creeley's Poetry: A Critical Introduction (Edelberg), **Supp. IV Part 1:** 155

Robert Frost (Meyers), **Retro. Supp. I:** 138

Robert Lowell (Meyers), **Retro. Supp. II:** 191

Robert Lowell and the Sublime (Hart), **Retro. Supp. II:** 187

Robert Lowell's Shifting Colors (Doreski), **Retro. Supp. II:** 185

Robert Lowell: The First Twenty years (Staples), **Retro. Supp. II:** 187

Roberts, Carol, **Supp. XX:** **53**

Roberts, David, **Supp. XVIII:** 106

Roberts, Diane, **Supp. X:** 15

Roberts, J. M., **IV:** 454

Roberts, Leo, **II:** 449

Roberts, Margaret, **II:** 449; **IV:** 453, 454

Roberts, Matthew, **Retro. Supp. II:** 324

Roberts, Meade, **IV:** 383

Roberts, Michael, **I:** 527, 536

Roberts, Richard, **III:** 297

Roberts, Victoria, **Supp. XIX:** 205

Roberts, Wally, **Supp. XI:** 119, 120, 126

Roberts, William, **Supp. XI:** 343

Roberts Brothers, **Retro. Supp. I:** 31, 35

Robertson, David, **Supp. VIII:** 305

Robertson, D. B., **III:** 311

Robertson, Lisa, **Supp. XXII:** 155

Robertson, Nan, **Supp. IV Part 1:** 300

Robertson, William, **II:** 8

Robert the Devil (Merwin, trans.), **Supp. III Part 1:** 341, 346

Robeson, Paul, **III:** 392; **Supp. IV Part 1:** 360, 361; **Supp. X:** 137; **Supp. XIX:** 66; **Supp. XXI:** 167

Robeson, Susan L., **Supp. XVIII:** 268

Robespierre, Maximilien, **Supp. I Part 2:** 514, 515, 517

"Robinson" (Kees), **Supp. XV:** 143–144

Robinson, Christopher L., **Supp. XII:** 13, 14

Robinson, David, **Supp. XXIV:** 70, 71, 78–79

Robinson, Dean, **III:** 506

Robinson, Edward, **III:** 505

Robinson, Edward G., **Supp. XI:** 306

Robinson, Edwin Arlington, **I:** 480; **II:** 388, 391, 529, 542; **III:** 5, **503–526,** 576; **Supp. I Part 2:** 699; **Supp. II Part 1:** 191; **Supp. III Part 1:** 63, 75; **Supp. III Part 2:** 592, 593; **Supp. IX:** 77, 266, 276, 308; **Supp. XV:** 256, 299, 300, 301, 306; **Supp. XVII:** 69; **Supp. XIX:** 123

Robinson, Forrest G., **Supp. IV Part 2:** 597, 601, 604

Robinson, Herman, **III:** 506–507

Robinson, H. M., **IV:** 369, 370

Robinson, Jackie, **Supp. I Part 1:** 338

Robinson, James Harvey, **I:** 214; **Supp. I Part 2:** 492

Robinson, James K., **Supp. IX:** 328

Robinson, Margaret G., **Supp. IV Part 2:** 597, 601, 604

Robinson, Marilynne, **Supp. XXI:** **209–224; Supp. XXII:** 50

Robinson, Mary, **Supp. XI:** 26

Robinson, Rowland E., **Supp. XIX:** 6

Robinson, Roxana, **Supp. XXV:** 60

Robinson, Sugar Ray, **Supp. IV Part 1:** 167

Robinson, Ted, **Supp. XIII:** 166

Robinson Crusoe (Defoe), **II:** 159; **III:** 113, 423; **IV:** 369; **Retro. Supp. II:** 274; **Supp. I Part 2:** 714; **Supp. IV Part 2:** 502

Robison, Mary, **Supp. V:** 22; **Supp. XXI:** 115, 116, 118

Roblès, Emmanuel, **Supp. I Part 1:** 283

"Robstown" (Salinas), **Supp. XIII:** 315

Rochefort, Christina, **Supp. XVI:** 143

Rochefoucauld, Louis Alexandre, **Supp. I Part 2:** 510

"Rock" (Nye), **Supp. XIII:** 287

Rock (Wagoner), **Supp. IX:** 324, **334,** 335

Rock, Catherine, **Supp. XII:** 17

Rock, The (Eliot), **Retro. Supp. I:** 65

Rock, The (Stevens), **Retro. Supp. I:** 309, 312

"Rock, The" (Stevens), **Retro. Supp. I:** 312

Rockaway (Shanley), **Supp. XIV:** 315

"Rock Climbers, The" (Francis), **Supp. IX:** 82

Rock-Drill (Pound), **Retro. Supp. I:** 293

Rockefeller, John D., **I:** 273; **III:** 580; **Supp. I Part 2:** 486; **Supp. V:** 286; **Supp. XXIII:** 26

Rockefeller, Nelson, **III:** 14, 15

Rockets and Rodeos and Other American Spectacles (Mallon), **Supp. XIX:** 137

Rocket to the Moon (Odets), **Supp. II Part 2:** 541–543, 544

Rock Garden, The (Shepard), **Supp. III Part 2:** 432, 447

"Rocking Horse Winner, The" (Lawrence), **Supp. I Part 1:** 329

Rocking the Boat (Vidal), **Supp. IV Part 2:** 683

"Rockpile, The" (Baldwin), **Supp. I Part 1:** 63

Rock Springs (Ford), **Supp. V:** 57, 58–59, 68–69

Rocky Mountains, The: or, Scenes, Incidents, and Adventures in the Far West; Digested from the Journal of Captain E. L. E Bonneville, of the Army of the United States, and Illustrated from Various Other Sources (Irving), **II:** 312

Rodden, John, **Supp. XVI:** 63, 69, 72

Roddenberry, Gene, **Supp. XXII:** 60

Rodefer, Stephen, **Supp. XXIV:** 38

Roderick, David, **Supp. XV:** 223

Roderick Hudson (James), **II:** 284, 290, 324, 326, 328; **Retro. Supp. I:** 219, **220–221,** 221, 226; **Supp. IX:** 142

Rodgers, Richard, **III:** 361

Rodgers, Ronald, **Supp. IV Part 2:** 503

Rodker, John, **III:** 470

Rodman, Selden, **Supp. I Part 1:** 83; **Supp. X:** 115

Rodney, Walter, **Supp. XXI:** 171

"Rodrigo Returns to the Land and Linen Celebrates" (Cisneros), **Supp. VII:** 68

Rodríguez, Diane, **Supp. XXIII:** 203

Rodriguez, Randy A., **Supp. XIV:** 312

Rodriguez, Richard, **Supp. XIV: 297–313**

Roethke, Charles, **III:** 531

Roethke, Theodore, **I:** 167, 171–172, 183, 254, 285, 521; **III:** 273, **527–550; IV:**

138, 402; **Retro. Supp. II:** 178, 181, 246; **Supp. I Part 2:** 539; **Supp. III Part 1:** 47, 54, 56, 239, 253, 260–261, 350; **Supp. IV Part 2:** 626; **Supp. IX:** 323; **Supp. XV:** 140, 145, 212; **Supp. XVIII:** 90; **Supp. XX:** 199; **Supp. XXIII:** 19; **Supp. XXIV:** 165, 171

"Roger Malvin's Burial" (Hawthorne), **II:** 243; **Retro. Supp. I:** 153

Rogers, Michael, **Supp. X:** 265, 266

Rogers, Pattiann, **Supp. XVIII:** 189

Rogers, Samuel, **II:** 303; **Supp. I Part 1:** 157

Rogers, Will, **I:** 261; **IV:** 388

Roger's Version (Updike), **Retro. Supp. I:** 325, 327, 330

Roget, Peter Mark, **Supp. I Part 1:** 312

"Rogue River Jet-Board Trip, Gold Beach, Oregon, July 4, 1977" (Carver), **Supp. III Part 1:** 140

"Rogue's Gallery" (McCarthy), **II:** 563

Rohr, Richard, **Supp. XX:** 143

Roiphe, Katie, **Supp. XXV:** 10

Roland de La Platière, Jean Marie, **II:** 554

Rolando Hinojosa and the American Dream (Glover), **Supp. XIX:** 112

Rolando Hinojosa: A Reader's Guide (Zilles), **Supp. XIX:** 112

Rolando Hinojosa Reader, The (Saldívar, ed.), **Supp. XIX:** 112

Rôle du Nègre dans la culture des Amériques, La (Locke), **Supp. XIV:** 202

"Role of a Lifetime, The" (Skloot), **Supp. XX:** 203

"Role of Society in the Artist, The" (Ammons), **Supp. VII:** 34

Rolfe, Alfred, **IV:** 427

Rolfe, Frederick, **Supp. XX: 235**

"Roll, Jordan, Roll" (spiritual), **Supp. IV Part 1:** 16

Rolland, Romain, **Supp. XX: 70**

"Roll Call" (Hoffman), **Supp. XVIII:** 86

"Roll Call" (Komunyakaa), **Supp. XIII:** 123

Rolle, Esther, **Supp. IV Part 1:** 367

Rollin, Charles, **II:** 113

Rolling Stones (O. Henry), **Supp. II Part 1:** 410

Rolling Thunder Logbook (Shepard), **Supp. III Part 2:** 433

Rolling Thunder Logbook, The (Shepard), **Supp. XVIII:** 31

"Rolling Up" (Simpson), **Supp. IX:** 265, 274, 280

Rollins, Howard E., Jr., **Supp. IV Part 1:** 236

Rollins, Hyder E., **Supp. IV Part 1:** 168

Rollins, Sonny, **Supp. V:** 195

"Rollo" tales (Abbott), **Supp. I Part 1:** 38

"Roma I" (Wright), **Supp. V:** 338

"Roma II" (Wright), **Supp. V:** 338

Romains, Jules, **I:** 227

Román, David, **Supp. XIII:** 208

Romance, A (Weigl), **Supp. XIX: 277–278**

"Romance, A" (Weigl), **Supp. XIX:** 278

"Romance and a Reading List" (Fitzgerald), **Retro. Supp. I:** 101

Romance of a Plain Man, The (Glasgow), **II:** 175, 180–181

"Romance of Certain Old Clothes, The" (James), **II:** 322; **Retro. Supp. I:** 218

Romance Reader, The (Abraham), **Supp. XXIV:** 1–2, 3, **4–7**

"Roman Elegies" (Brodsky), **Supp. VIII:** 29

"Roman Fever" (Wharton), **Retro. Supp. I:** 382

"Roman Fountain" (Bogan), **Supp. III Part 1:** 56

"*Romanitas* of Gore Vidal, The" (Tatum), **Supp. IV Part 2:** 684

Romaniuk, Zbigniew, **Supp. XVI:** 154

Romano, John, **Supp. XV:** 253

"Roman Sarcophagus, A" (Lowell), **II:** 544

Roman Spring of Mrs. Stone, The (T. Williams), **IV:** 383, 385

"Romantic, The" (Bogan), **Supp. III Part 1:** 50

Romantic Comedians, The (Glasgow), **II:** 175, 186, 190, 194

Romantic Education, A (Hampl), **Supp. XXII:** 82, 83, **87–90,** 91

Romantic Egoists, The (Auchincloss), **Supp. IV Part 1:** 25

Romantic Egotist, The (Fitzgerald), **II:** 82

"Romantic Egotist, The" (Fitzgerald), **Retro. Supp. I:** 100

"Romanticism and Classicism" (Hulme), **III:** 196

"Romanticism Comes Home" (Shapiro), **Supp. II Part 2:** 713

Romantic Manifesto, The: A Philosophy of Literature (Rand), **Supp. IV Part 2:** 521, 523, 527, 529–530

"Romantic Regionalism of Harper Lee, The" (Erisman), **Supp. VIII:** 126

Romantics, The (Rinehart), **Supp. XXV:** 196

"Rome" (W. C. Williams), **Retro. Supp. I:** 420

Rome Brothers, **Retro. Supp. I:** 393

Romeo and Juliet (Shakespeare), **Supp. V:** 252; **Supp. VIII:** 223

Romola (G. Eliot), **II:** 291; **IV:** 311

Romulus: A New Comedy (Vidal), **Supp. IV Part 2:** 683

Romulus der Grosse (Dürrenmatt), **Supp. IV Part 2:** 683

Ronald, Ann, **Supp. XIII:** 4, 5, 6, 7, 9, 11

"Rondel for a September Day" (White), **Supp. I Part 2:** 676

"Ron Narrative Reconstructions, The" (Coleman), **Supp. XI:** 83

"Ron Padgett's Visual Imagination" (Notley), **Supp. XXII:** 224

Ronsard, Pierre de, **Supp. X:** 65; **Supp. XV:** 165

Rood, John, **IV:** 261

"Roof, the Steeple, and the People, The" (Ellison), **Retro. Supp. II:** 118, 126; **Supp. II Part 1:** 248

"Room" (Levertov), **Supp. III Part 1:** 282

Roomates (film, P. Yates), **Supp. XVII:** 8, 9

Roomates: My Grandfather's Story (Apple), **Supp. XVII:** 2, **7–9**

"Room at the Heart of Things, A" (Merrill), **Supp. III Part 1:** 337

Room Called Remember, A: Uncollected Pieces (Buechner), **Supp. XII:** 53

"Roomful of Hovings, A" (McPhee), **Supp. III Part 1:** 291, 294

Room of One's Own, A (Woolf), **Supp. V:** 127; **Supp. IX:** 19; **Supp. XIII:** 305

Room Rented by a Single Woman (Wright), **Supp. XV:** 340–341

"Rooms" (Collins), **Supp. XXI:** 61

Room Temperature (Baker), **Supp. XIII:** 41, **43–45,** 48, 50

Room to Swing (Lacy), **Supp. XV:** 202, 203, 205, 207

"Room Upstairs, The" (Gioia), **Supp. XV:** 120–121, 124

Roosevelt, Eleanor, **IV:** 371; **Supp. IV Part 2:** 679

Roosevelt, Franklin, **Supp. V:** 290

Roosevelt, Franklin Delano, **I:** 482, 485, 490; **II:** 553, 575; **III:** 2, 18, 69, 110, 297, 321, 376, 476, 580, 581; **Supp. I Part 2:** 488, 489, 490, 491, 645, 654, 655

Roosevelt, Kermit, **III:** 508

Roosevelt, Theodore, **I:** 14, 62; **II:** 130; **III:** 508; **IV:** 321; **Retro. Supp. I:** 377; **Supp. I Part 1:** 1, 21; **Supp. I Part 2:** 455, 456, 502, 707; **Supp. V:** 280, 282; **Supp. IX:** 184; **Supp. XIX:** 29; **Supp. XX:** **221;** **Supp. XXIII:** 26

Roosevelt After Inauguration And Other Atrocities (Burroughs), **Supp. III Part 1:** 98

"Roosevelt Chair, The" (Skloot), **Supp. XX:** **205**

"Roosters" (Bishop), **Retro. Supp. II:** 39, 43, 250; **Supp. I Part 1:** 89

Root, Abiah, **I:** 456

Root, Elihu, **Supp. IV Part 1:** 33

Root, Simeon, **I:** 548

Root, Timothy, **I:** 548

Rootabaga Stories (Sandburg), **III:** 583, 587

"Rootedness: The Ancestor as Foundation" (Morrison), **Supp. III Part 1:** 361

"Roots" (Halliday), **Supp. XIX:** 88

Roots in the Soil (film), **Supp. IV Part 1:** 83

"Rope" (Porter), **III:** 451

Rope, The (O'Neill), **III:** 388

Ropemakers of Plymouth, The (Morison), **Supp. I Part 2:** 494

"Ropes" (Nye), **Supp. XIII:** 276

"Rope's End, The" (Nemerov), **III:** 282

Roquelaure, A. N., **Supp. VII:** 301. *See also* Rice, Anne

Rorem, Ned, **Supp. IV Part 1:** 79, 84; **Supp. XXIII:** 217

Rorschach Test (F. Wright), **Supp. XVII:** 240, 245

Rorty, James, **Supp. XXII:** 276, 277

"Rosa" (Ozick), **Supp. V:** 271

Rosa, Rodrigo Rey, **Supp. IV Part 1:** 92

Rosaldo, Renato, **Supp. IV Part 2:** 544

"Rosalia" (Simic), **Supp. VIII:** 278

Roscoe, Will, **Supp. IV Part 1:** 330

"Roscoe in Hell" (McKnight), **Supp. XX:** 151

"Rose" (Dubus), **Supp. VII:** 88

Rose (L.-Y. Lee), **Supp. XV:** 211, **212–215,** 218

Rose, Alice, Sister, **III:** 348

Rose, Charlie, **Supp. XIX:** 26, 30

Rose, Lloyd, **Supp. XXIV:** 267

Rose, Mickey, **Supp. XV:** 3

Rose, Philip, **Supp. IV Part 1:** 362

"Rose, The" (Roethke), **III:** 537

"Rose, The" (W. C. Williams), **Retro. Supp. I:** 419

Rose, Where Did You Get That Red?: Teaching Great Poetry to Children (Koch), **Supp. XV:** 189

"Rose for Emily, A" (Faulkner), **II:** 72; **Supp. IX:** 96; **Supp. XX:** **179;** **Supp. XXIV:** 136

Rose-Hued Cities (P. N. Warren), **Supp. XX:** **261**

Rose in Bloom (Alcott), **Supp. I Part 1:** 42

"Rose-Johnny" (Kingsolver), **Supp. VII:** 203

Rose Madder (King), **Supp. V:** 141, 148, 150, 152

"Rose-Morals" (Lanier), **Supp. I Part 1:** 364

Rosen, Jonathan, **Supp. XVII:** 50; **Supp. XX:** **179**

Rosen, Kenneth, **Supp. IV Part 2:** 499, 505, 513

Rosen, Norma, **Supp. XVII:** 49, 50

Rosenbaum, Alissa Zinovievna. *See* Rand, Ayn

Rosenbaum, Thane, **Supp. XVII:** 48

Rosenberg, Bernard, **Supp. I Part 2:** 650

Rosenberg, Harold, **Supp. XV:** 143; **Supp. XIX:** 159; **Supp. XXIII:** 211

Rosenberg, Julia, **Supp. XVIII:** 136

Rosenberg, Julius and Ethel, **Supp. I Part 1:** 295; **Supp. I Part 2:** 532; **Supp. V:** 45

Rosenberg, Liz, **Supp. XV:** 251

Rosenberg, Shlomo, **Supp. XXIII:** 6

Rosenbloom, Joel, **Supp. IV Part 2:** 527

Rosenfeld, Alvin H., **Supp. I Part 1:** 120

Rosenfeld, Isaac, **Supp. XII:** 160

Rosenfeld, Paul, **I:** 116, 117, 231, 245

Rosenfelt, Deborah, **Supp. XIII:** 296, 304

Rosenfield, Isaac, **IV:** 3

Rosengarten, Theodore, **Supp. XVIII:** 183

Rosenthal, Ira, **Supp. XIV:** 146–147

Rosenthal, Lois, **Supp. VIII:** 258

Rosenthal, M. L., **II:** 550; **III:** 276, 479; **Supp. V:** 333

Rosenthal, Peggy, **Supp. XVII:** 119

Rose of Wissahikon, The (Lippard), **Supp. XXIII:** 178

"Rose Pogonias" (Frost), **Retro. Supp. I:** 127

"Rose Red and Snow White" (Grimms), **Supp. X:** 82

"Rose Room" (Sorrentino), **Supp. XXI:** 228

"Roses" (Conroy), **Supp. XVI:** 72

"Roses" (Dove), **Supp. IV Part 1:** 246

"Roses and Skulls" (Goldbarth), **Supp. XII:** 192

"Roses for Lubbock" (Nye), **Supp. XIII:** 281

"Roses Only" (Moore), **III:** 195, 198, 200, 202, 215

Rose Tattoo, The (T. Williams), **IV:** 382, 383, 387, 388, 389, 392–393, 394, 397, 398

Rose Theatre (Sorrentino), **Supp. XXI:** 236

"Rosewood, Ohio" (Matthews), **Supp. IX:** 160

Rosie (Lamott), **Supp. XX:** **133–134**

Rosinante to the Road Again (Dos Passos), **I:** 478

Roskies, David, **Supp. XVII:** 39, 44, 49–50

Roskolenko, Harry, **Supp. XV:** 179

Rosmersholm (Ibsen), **III:** 152

Rosmond, Babette, **II:** 432

Ross, Eleanor. *See* Taylor, Eleanor Ross

Ross, Harold, **Supp. I Part 1:** 174; **Supp. I Part 2:** 607, 617, 653, 654, 655, 660; **Supp. VIII:** 151, 170; **Supp. IX:** 190

Ross, Herbert, **Supp. XV:** 2

Ross, Jean, **Supp. XXI:** 144, 146

Ross, John F., **II:** 110

Ross, Lillian, **Retro. Supp. II:** 198

Ross, Mary, **Supp. XXII:** 195

Ross, Mitchell S., **Supp. IV Part 2:** 692; **Supp. X:** 260

Ross, Robert, **Supp. XXIV:** 167

Rossen, Robert, **Supp. XI:** 306

Rosset, Barney, **III:** 171

Rossetti, Christina, **Supp. XIV:** 128

Rossetti, Dante Gabriel, **I:** 433; **II:** 323; **Retro. Supp. I:** 128, 286; **Supp. I Part 2:** 552; **Supp. XXII:** 156

Rossetti, William Michael, **Retro. Supp. I:** 407

Rossi, Umberto, **Supp. XVIII:** 137, 138–139

Rossini, Clare, **Supp. XVII:** 111

Rosskam, Edwin, **IV:** 477

Ross Macdonald (Bruccoli), **Supp. IV Part 2:** 468, 470

Rostand, Edmond, **II:** 515; **Supp. IV Part 2:** 518

Rosten, Leo, **Supp. XVII:** 9

Rosy Crucifixion, The (H. Miller), **III:** 170, 187, 188–189, 190

Rote Walker, The (Jarman), **Supp. XVII:** 110, **113–115**

Roth, Henry, **Supp. IV Part 1:** 314; **Supp. VIII:** 233; **Supp. IX:** **227–243;** **Supp. XIII:** 106

Roth, Philip, **I:** 144, 161; **II:** 591; **Retro. Supp. II:** 22, **279–297;** **Supp. I Part 1:** 186, 192; **Supp. I Part 2:** 431, 441, 443; **Supp. II Part 1:** 99; **Supp. III Part 2:** **401–429;** **Supp. IV Part 1:** 236, 379, 388; **Supp. V:** 45, 119, 122, 257, 258; **Supp. VIII:** 88, 236, 245; **Supp. IX:** 227; **Supp. XI:** 64, 68, 99,

140; **Supp. XII:** 190, 310; **Supp. XIV:** 79, 93, 111, 112; **Supp. XVI:** 206; **Supp. XVII:** 43, 48, 183; **Supp. XVIII:** 89; **Supp. XXI:** 234; **Supp. XXII:** 268

Roth, Rita, **Supp. XVI:** 112

Roth, William, **Supp. XV:** 142

Rothenberg, Jerome, **Supp. VIII:** 292; **Supp. XII:** 3; **Supp. XXIV:** 37

Rothermere, Lady Mary, **Retro. Supp. I:** 63

Rothko, Mark, **Supp. XV:** 144

Rothstein, Mervyn, **Supp. VIII:** 142

"Rouen, France"(Kenny), **Supp. XXIII:** 152

"Rouge High" (Hughes), **Supp. I Part 1:** 330

Rougemont, Denis de, **II:** 586; **IV:** 216; **Retro. Supp. I:** 328, 329, 330, 331

Rough Edges (Skloot), **Supp. XX:** 196

Roughing It (Twain), **II:** 312; **IV:** 195, 197, 198

Roughing It in the Bush (Shields), **Supp. VII:** 313

"Rough Outline" (Simic), **Supp. VIII:** 276

"Rough-Skinned Newt, The"(Schott), **Supp. XXIII:** 253–254

Rough South of Larry Brown, The (film, Hawkins), **Supp. XXI:** 39

Rougon-Macquart, Les (Zola), **II:** 175–176

Roumain, Jacques, **Retro. Supp. I:** 202; **Supp. IV Part 1:** 360, 367

"Round, The" (Kunitz), **Supp. III Part 1:** 268

"Roundelay Between Two Shepherdesses, A" (Notley), **Supp. XXII:** 229

"Round Trip" (Dunn), **Supp. XI:** 148–149

Round Up (Lardner), **II:** 426, 430, 431

Rourke, Constance, **I:** 258; **IV:** 339, 352

Rourke, Milton, **Retro. Supp. II:** 89

Rousseau, Jean-Jacques, **I:** 226; **II:** 8, 343; **III:** 170, 178, 259; **IV:** 80, 173, 440; **Supp. I Part 1:** 126; **Supp. I Part 2:** 637, 659; **Supp. IV Part 1:** 171; **Supp. XI:** 245; **Supp. XVI:** 292; **Supp. XXI:** 83

Roussel, Raymond, **Supp. III Part 1:** 6, 7, 10, 15, 16, 21; **Supp. XV:** 182

"Route 302" (Halliday), **Supp. XIX:** 93

"Routes" (Everwine), **Supp. XV:** 82

"Route Six" (Kunitz), **Supp. III Part 1:** 258

Route Two (Erdrich and Dorris), **Supp. IV Part 1:** 260

"Routine Things Around the House, The" (Dunn), **Supp. XI:** 148

Rover Boys (Winfield), **III:** 146

Rovit, Earl, **IV:** 102

Rowan, Carl T., **Supp. XIV:** 306

Rowe, Anne E., **Supp. X:** 223

Rowe, John Carlos, **Retro. Supp. I:** 216

Rowe, Kenneth Thorpe, **Supp. XXIII:** 258

Rowell, Charles, **Supp. XXI:** 250, 254, 255; **Supp. XXIV:** 184

"Rowing" (Sexton), **Supp. II Part 2:** 696

"Rowing Endeth, The" (Sexton), **Supp. II Part 2:** 696

Rowlandson, Mary, **Supp. IV Part 2:** 430, 431

Rowling, J. K., **Supp. XXV:** 70

"Rows of Cold Trees, The" (Winters), **Supp. II Part 2:** 790–791, 800

Rowson, Susanna, **Supp. I Part 1:** 128; **Supp. XV:** 229–248

Roxanna Slade (Price), **Supp. VI:** 267

Roxie Hart (Watkins), **Supp. XVI:** 188

Royal Family, The (Vollmann), **Supp. XVII:** 226, 230, 233

"Royal Palm" (Crane), **I:** 401

Royce, Josiah, **I:** 443; **III:** 303, 600; **IV:** 26; **Retro. Supp. I:** 57; **Supp. XIV:** 197, 199; **Supp. XVII:** 97

"Roy McInnes" (Budbill), **Supp. XIX:** 6–7

"Roy Spivey" (July), **Supp. XXIV:** 210

Royster, Sarah Elmira, **III:** 410, 429

Royte, Elizabeth, **Supp. XV:** 59

Różewicz, Tadeusz, **Supp. X:** 60

R. S. Thomas: Poetry and Theology (W. V. Davis), **Supp. XXI:** 86–87

Ruas, Charles, **Supp. IV Part 1:** 383

Ruback, Max, **Supp. XXIII:** 290

Rubáiyát (Khayyám), **I:** 568

Rubáiyát of Omar Khayyam (Fitzgerald), **Supp. I Part 2:** 416; **Supp. III Part 2:** 610; **Supp. XV:** 156

"Rubber Life" (Prose), **Supp. XVI:** 256

Rubel, Nora L., **Supp. XXIV:** 7

Rub from Snub, A (Swanwick), **Supp. XV:** 237

"Rubicon" (Cliff), **Supp. XXII:** 76

Rubin, Louis, **Supp. I Part 2:** 672, 673, 679; **Supp. X:** 42

Rubin, Louis D., Jr., **IV:** 116, 462–463

Rubin, Stan, **Supp. XIV:** 307, 310

Rubin, Stan Sanvel, **Supp. IV Part 1:** 242, 245, 252

Rubins, Josh, **Supp. XX:** 89

"Ruby Brown" (Hughes), **Supp. I Part 1:** 327

"Ruby Daggett" (Eberhart), **I:** 539

Rucker, Rudy, **Supp. X:** 302

Rudd, Hughes, **Supp. XII:** 141

"Rude Awakening, A" (Chopin), **Retro. Supp. II:** 64

Rudens (Plautus), **Supp. III Part 2:** 630

Ruderman, Judith, **Supp. IV Part 1:** 380

Rudge, Olga, **Supp. V:** 338

Rudikoff, Sonya, **Supp. XIV:** 113

Rudman, Mark, **Supp. XXIII:** 124; **Supp. XXIV:** 153

Rueckert, William, **I:** 264

Ruesch, Jurgen, **Supp. XV:** 147

Rugby Chapel (Arnold), **Supp. I Part 2:** 416

"Rugby Road" (Garrett), **Supp. VII:** 100

Rugge, John, **Supp. XXII:** 218

Ruining the New Road (Matthews), **Supp. IX:** 154, 155–157

"Ruins of Italica, The" (Bryant, trans.), **Supp. I Part 1:** 166

Rukeyser, Muriel, **Retro. Supp. II:** 48; **Supp. VI:** 271–289; **Supp. XV:** 349; **Supp. XVII:** 74

"Rule of Phase Applied to History, The" (Adams), **I:** 19

Rule of the Bone (Banks), **Supp. V:** 16

Rulers of Kings (Atherton), **Supp. XXIV:** 23

"Rules by Which a Great Empire May Be Reduced to a Small One" (Franklin), **II:** 120

Rules For the Dance: A Handbook for Reading and Writing Metrical Verse (Oliver), **Supp. VII:** 229, 247

Rules of the Game, The (film), **Supp. XII:** 259

Rulfo, Juan, **Supp. IV Part 2:** 549

Rumba (film, Gering), **Supp. XVII:** 57

Rumbaut, Rubén, **Supp. XI:** 184

Rum Diary, The (Thompson), **Supp. XXIV:** 281, 283–286, 293

Rümelin-Oesterlen, Natalie, **Supp. XX:** 235

Rumens, Carol, **Supp. XI:** 14; **Supp. XVI:** 212

Rumi, **Supp. XX:** 117

"Rumination of Rivers, The" (Bronk), **Supp. XXI:** 32

Rumkowski, Chaim, **Supp. XII:** 168

Rummel, Mary Kay, **Supp. XIII:** 280

"Rumor and a Ladder" (Bowles), **Supp. IV Part 1:** 93

Rumor of War, A (Caputo), **Supp. XIX:** 17–21, 25, 30

Rumors (Simon), **Supp. IV Part 2:** 582–583, 591

Rumpelstiltskin (Gardner), **Supp. VI:** 72

"Rumpelstiltskin" (Grimm), **IV:** 266

"Rumpelstiltskin" (Sexton), **Supp. II Part 2:** 690

Run, Sheep, Run (Bodenheim), **Supp. XXV:** 27

"Runagate Runagate" (Hayden), **Supp. II Part 1:** 377

"Runes" (Nemerov), **III:** 267, 277–278

Run Man Run (C. Himes), **Supp. XVI:** 142, 143

"Runner, The" (Grossman), **Supp. XIX:** 83

"Running" (Wilbur), **Supp. III Part 2:** 558–559

"RUNNING-AWAY"(Strout), **Supp. XXIII:** 274

Running Dog (DeLillo), **Supp. VI:** 3, 6, 8, 14

"Running in Church" (A. Finch), **Supp. XVII:** 72

"Running the Table" Conroy), **Supp. XVI:** 75

"Run of Bad Luck, A" (Proulx), **Supp. VII:** 253–254

Run of Jacks, A (Hugo), **Supp. VI:** 131, 133, 134, 135, 136

Run River (Didion), **Supp. IV Part 1:** 197, 199–200, 201

Ruoff, A. LaVonne Brown, **Supp. IV Part 1:** 324, 327; **Supp. IV Part 2:** 559

Rupert, Jim, **Supp. XII:** 215

Ruppert, James, **Supp. IV Part 1:** 321

Rural Hours (Cooper), **Supp. XIII:** 152

"Rural Route" (Wright), **Supp. V:** 340

"Rural South, The" (Du Bois), **Supp. II Part 1:** 174

Rush, Benjamin, **Supp. I Part 2:** 505, 507

Rushdie, Salman, **Supp. IV Part 1:** 234, 297

Rushdy, Ashraf, **Supp. X:** 250

Rushing, Jimmy, **Retro. Supp. II:** 113

Rusk, Dean, **II:** 579

Ruskin, John, **II:** 323, 338; **IV:** 349; **Retro. Supp. I:** 56, 360; **Supp. I Part 1:** 2, 10, 87, 349; **Supp. I Part 2:** 410

Rusnak, Karl, **Supp. XVIII:** 149

Russell, Ada Dwyer, **II:** 513, 527

Russell, Bertrand, **II:** 27; **III:** 605, 606; **Retro. Supp. I:** 57, 58, 59, 60; **Supp. I Part 2:** 522; **Supp. V:** 290; **Supp. XII:** 45; **Supp. XIV:** 337

Russell, Diarmuid, **Retro. Supp. I:** 342, 345, 346–347, 349–350

Russell, George, **Retro. Supp. I:** 342

Russell, Herb, **Supp. I Part 2:** 465–466

Russell, John, **Supp. XIV:** 344, 347, 348

Russell, Peter, **III:** 479

Russell, Richard, **Supp. XI:** 102

Russell, Robert, **Supp. XX: 195**

Russell, Sue, **Supp. IV Part 2:** 653

Russello, Gerald, **Supp. XXIV:** 159

Russert, Margaret, **Supp. XVIII:** 62

Russert, Tim, **Supp. XII:** 272

Russia at War (Caldwell), **I:** 296

"Russia Between Myth and Reality: From *Meri* to *Three Cities*"(Krutikov), *Supp. XXIII:* 11

Russian Journal, A (Steinbeck), **IV:** 52, 63

Russo, Richard, **Supp. XI:** 349; **Supp. XII: 325–344; Supp. XXIII:** 302

"Rusty Autumn" (Swenson), **Supp. IV Part 2:** 640

Rutabaga-Roo: I've Got a Song and It's for You (Nye, album), **Supp. XIII:** 274

Ruth (biblical book), **Supp. I Part 2:** 516

Ruth, George Herman ("Babe"), **II:** 423; **Supp. I Part 2:** 438, 440

Rutheiser, Charles, **Supp. XXII:** 244

Ruth Hall (Fern), **Supp. V:** 122

Ruthven, K. K., **Supp. XXII:** 261

Rutkowska, Malgorzata, **Supp. XXII:** 208

Rutledge, Ann, **III:** 588; **Supp. I Part 2:** 471

Ruwe, Donelle R., **Supp. XII:** 215

Ryan, Katy, **Supp. XXI:** 215

Ryan, Kay, **Supp. XXI:** 20; **Supp. XXV:** 222

Ryan, Maureen, **Supp. XXI:** 215

Ryan, Paul William, **Supp. XVIII: 223–239; Supp. XXI:** 264–265

Ryder (Barnes), **Supp. III Part 1:** 31, 36–38, 42, 43

"Ryder" (Rukeyser), **Supp. VI:** 273, 283

Ryle, Herbert Edward, **Supp. XX:** 230

Rymer, Thomas, **IV:** 122

"Ryōkan Says" (Budbill), **Supp. XIX:** 11

S

S. (Updike), **Retro. Supp. I:** 330, 331, 332, 333

S-1 (Baraka), **Supp. II Part 1:** 55, 57

Saadi, **II:** 19

Saar, Doreen Alvarez, **Supp. XV:** 237

Sabbatai Zevi (Asch), **Supp. XXIII:** 12

"Sabbath, The" (Stowe), **Supp. I Part 2:** 587

"Sabbath Mom" (White), **Supp. I Part 2:** 671–672

Sabbaths (Berry), **Supp. X:** 31

Sabbath's Theater (P. Roth), **Retro. Supp. II:** 279, 288

"Sabbatical, The" (Stallings), **Supp. XXV:** 234

"Sabbioneta to Parma" (Di Piero), **Supp. XIX:** 36–37

Sabines, Jaime, **Supp. V:** 178

"Sabotage" (Baraka), **Supp. II Part 1:** 49, 53

"Saboteur" (Jin), **Supp. XVIII:** 97

Sacco, Nicola, **I:** 482, 486, 490, 494; **II:** 38–39, 426; **III:** 139–140; **Supp. I Part 2:** 446; **Supp. V:** 288–289; **Supp. IX:** 199; **Supp. XXII:** 277

Sachs, Hanns, **Supp. I Part 1:** 259; **Supp. X:** 186

Sack Full of Old Quarrels, A (Weigl), **Supp. XIX:** 277

"Sacks" (Carver), **Supp. III Part 1:** 143–144

Sacks, Oliver, **Supp. XVIII:** 143

Sacks, Peter, **Supp. IV Part 2:** 450

Sackville-West, Vita, **Supp. VIII:** 263

"Sacrament of Divorce, The" (Patchett), **Supp. XII:** 309

"Sacrament of Self: Catholic Roots of Contemporary Memoir" (lecture, Hampl), **Supp. XXII:** 81

"Sacraments" (Dubus), **Supp. VII:** 91

Sacred and Profane Memories (Van Vechten), **Supp. II Part 2:** 735, 749

"Sacred Chant for the Return of Black Spirit and Power" (Baraka), **Supp. II Part 1:** 51

"Sacred Factory, The" (Toomer), **Supp. IX:** 320

Sacred Fount, The (James), **II:** 332–333; **Retro. Supp. I:** 219, 228, 232

"Sacred Heart" (Egan), **Supp. XIX:** 52

"Sacred Hoop, The: A Contemporary Perspective" (Gunn Allen), **Supp. IV Part 1:** 324

Sacred Hoop, The: Recovering the Feminine in American Indian Traditions (Gunn Allen), **Supp. IV Part 1:** 319, 320, 322, 324, 325, 328–330, 331, 333, 334

Sacred Journey, The (Buechner), **Supp. XII:** 42, 53

"Sacred Thing, The" (Ryan as Quin), **Supp. XVIII:** 227

Sacred Wood, The (Eliot), **IV:** 431; **Retro. Supp. I:** 59, 60; **Supp. I Part 1:** 268; **Supp. II Part 1:** 136, 146

Sacrifice, The (Bidart), **Supp. XV:** 22, **27–30**, 35

"Sacrifice, The" (Bidart), **Supp. XV:** 29

"Sacrifice, The" (Oates), **Supp. II Part 2:** 523

Sacrilege of Alan Kent, The (Caldwell), **I:** 291–292

"Sad Brazil" (Hardwick), **Supp. III Part 1:** 210

Sad Days of Light (Balakian), **Supp. XXIII:** 20

"Sad Dust Glories" (Ginsberg), **Supp. II Part 1:** 376

Sad Dust Glories: Poems Written Work Summer in Sierra Woods (Ginsberg), **Supp. II Part 1:** 326

Sade, Marquis de, **III:** 259; **IV:** 437, 442; **Supp. XII:** 1, 14–15

Sad-Faced Boy (Bontemps), **Supp. XXII:** 5, 12

Sad Flower in the Sand, A (film), **Supp. XI:** 173

Sad Heart at the Supermarket, A (Jarrell), **II:** 386

"Sadie" (Matthiessen), **Supp. V:** 201

"Sadie and Maud" (Brooks), **Supp. XVIII:** 175

Sadness and Happiness (Pinsky), **Supp. VI:** 235, **237–241**

"Sadness of Brothers, The" (Kinnell), **Supp. III Part 1:** 237, 251

"Sadness of Days, The" (Salinas), **Supp. XIII:** 325

Sadness of Days, The: Selected and New Poems (Salinas), **Supp. XIII:** 311, **324–326**

"Sadness of Lemons, The" (Levine), **Supp. V:** 184

Sadoff, Ira, **Supp. XVII:** 241; **Supp. XXI:** 100

"Sad Rite" (Karr), **Supp. XI:** 243

"Sad Strains of a Gay Waltz" (Stevens), **Retro. Supp. I:** 302

"Safe" (Gordon), **Supp. IV Part 1:** 299, 306

"Safe in their Alabaster Chambers" (Dickinson), **Retro. Supp. I:** 30

Safer, Morley, **Supp. XIX:** 25

"Safe Subjects" (Komunyakaa), **Supp. XIII:** 118

Safety Features (Monson), **Supp. XXIV:** 230

"Safeway" (F. Barthelme), **Supp. XI:** 26, 27, 36

Saffin, John, **Supp. I Part 1:** 115

Saffy, Edna, **Supp. X:** 227

Sagan, Miriam, **Supp. XXIII:** 133

"Saga of an American Ranch" (P. N. Warren), **Supp. XX: 261**

"Saga of Arturo Bandini" (Fante), **Supp. XI:** 159, **166–169**

"Saga of King Olaf, The" (Longfellow), **II:** 489, 505; **Retro. Supp. II:** 154, 155, 164

"Sage of Stupidity and Wonder, The" (Goldbarth), **Supp. XII:** 191

Sahl, Mort, **II:** 435–436

"Sah Sin" (Gallagher), *Supp. XXIV:* 171

"Said" (Dixon), **Supp. XII:** 149–150

Said, Edward, **Supp. XXI:** 153

"Sailing after Lunch" (Stevens), **IV:** 73

Sailing Alone Around the Room: New and Selected Poems (Collins), **Supp. XXI:**

54, 56, 62
Sailing Alone Around the World (Slocum), **Supp. XXV:** 205, 206, 208, 213–216, 218
"Sailing Home from Rapallo" (Lowell), **Retro. Supp. II:** 189
Sailing through China (Theroux), **Supp. VIII:** 323
"Sailing to Byzantium" (Yeats), **III:** 263; **Supp. VIII:** 30; **Supp. X:** 74; **Supp. XI:** 281
"Sail Made of Rags, The" (Nye), **Supp. XIII:** 277
"Sailor off the Bremen" (Shaw), **Supp. XIX:** 247
"Sailors Lost at Sea" (Shields), **Supp. VII:** 318
"*St Anne*/*Santa Ana*" (Mora), **Supp. XIII:** 229
"*Saint Anthony of Padua*/*San Antonio de Padua*" (Mora), **Supp. XIII:** 228
"St. Augustine and the Bullfights" (Porter), **III:** 454
Sainte-Beuve, Charles Augustin, **IV:** 432
St. Elmo (Wilson), **Retro. Supp. I:** 351–352
"Saint Emmanuel the Good, Martyr" (Unamuno; Everwine, trans.), **Supp. XV:** 79
Sainte Vierge, La (Picabia), **Retro. Supp. II:** 331
Saint-Exupéry, Antoine de, **Supp. IX:** 247
"St. Francis Einstein of the Daffodils" (W. C. Williams), **IV:** 409–411
Saint-Gaudens, Augustus, **I:** 18, 228; **II:** 551
Saint-Gaudens, Homer, **Supp. XV:** 41
"St. George, the Dragon, and the Virgin" (R. Bly), **Supp. IV Part 1:** 73
St. George and the Godfather (Mailer), **III:** 46; **Retro. Supp. II:** 206, 208
Saint Jack (Theroux), **Supp. VIII:** 319
St. John, David, **Supp. V:** 180; **Supp. XI:** 270, 272; **Supp. XIII:** 312
St. John, Edward B., **Supp. IV Part 2:** 490
St. John, James Hector. *See* Crèvecoeur, Michel-Guillaume Jean de
"Saint John and the Back-Ache" (Stevens), **Retro. Supp. I:** 310
Saint Judas (Wright), **Supp. III Part 2:** 595–599
"Saint Judas" (Wright), **Supp. III Part 2:** 598–599
St. Louis Woman (Bontemps and Cullen), **Supp. IV Part 1:** 170
St. Mawr (Lawrence), **II:** 595
Saint Maybe (Tyler), **Supp. IV Part 2:** 670–671
"Saint Nicholas" (Moore), **III:** 215
"*Saint*"(O'Hara), **Supp. XXIII:** 219
St. Petersburg (Biely), **Supp. XII:** 13
Saint-Phalle, Niki de, **Supp. XV:** 187
"St. Roach" (Rukeyser), **Supp. VI:** 286
"Saint Robert" (Dacey), **Supp. IV Part 1:** 70
Saintsbury, George, **IV:** 440; **Supp. XV:** 181

Saints' Everlasting Rest, The (Baxter), **III:** 199; **IV:** 151, 153
Saint-Simon, Claude Henri, **Supp. I Part 2:** 648
"St. Thomas Aquinas" (Simic), **Supp. VIII:** 281
Saks, Gene, **Supp. IV Part 2:** 577, 588
Salamun, Tomaz, **Supp. VIII:** 272
Salazar, Dixie, **Supp. V:** 180; **Supp. XV:** 73
Saldívar, José David, **Supp. IV Part 2:** 544, 545; **Supp. XIX:** 110, 112–113
Sale, Richard, **Supp. IV Part 1:** 379
Sale, Roger, **Supp. V:** 244
Saleh, Dennis, **Supp. V:** 182, 186
"Salem" (Lowell), **II:** 550
Salemi, Joseph, **Supp. IV Part 1:** 284
Salem's Lot (King), **Supp. V:** 139, 144, 146, 151
"Sale of the Hessians, The" (Franklin), **II:** 120
Salick, Roydan, **Supp. XXIII:** 93, 94
Salinas, Luis Omar, **Supp. IV Part 2:** 545; **Supp. V:** 180; **Supp. XIII:** 311–330; **Supp. XV:** 73
"Salinas Is on His Way" (Salinas), **Supp. XIII:** 317
"Salinas Sends Messengers to the Stars" (Salinas), **Supp. XIII:** 317
"Salinas Summering at the Caspian and Thinking of Hamlet" (Salinas), **Supp. XIII:** 320
"Salinas Wakes Early and Goes to the Park to Lecture Sparrows" (Salinas), **Supp. XIII:** 320
Salinger, Doris, **III:** 551
Salinger, J. D., **II:** 255; **III:** 551–574; **IV:** 190, 216, 217; **Retro. Supp. I:** 102, 116, 335; **Supp. IV Part 2:** 502; **Supp. V:** 23, 119; **Supp. VIII:** 151; **Supp. XI:** 2, 66; **Supp. XIV:** 93; **Supp. XXIII:** 100
Salisbury, Harrison, **Supp. I Part 2:** 664
Salle, David, **Supp. XII:** 4
Salley, Columbus, **Supp. XIV:** 195
"Sally" (Cisneros), **Supp. VII:** 63
"Sally's Choice" (E. Stoddard), **Supp. XV:** 282
Salmagundi; or, The Whim-Whams and Opinions of Launcelot Langstaff Esq., and Others (Irving), **II:** 299, 300, 304
Salmon, Edward G., **Supp. XVIII:** 258
Salome (Strauss), **IV:** 316
Salon (online magazine), **Supp. VIII:** 310; **Supp. X:** 202
"Salt"(Crooker), **Supp. XXIII:** 62
Salt Eaters, The (Bambara), **Supp. XI:** 1, 12–14
Salt Ecstasies, The (White), **Supp. XI:** 123
Salter, James, **Supp. IX:** 245–263; **Supp. XVI:** 237, 247; **Supp. XIX:** 252
Salter, Mary Jo, **Supp. IV Part 2:** 653; **Supp. IX:** 37, 292; **Supp. XV:** 251, 253; **Supp. XVII:** 112; **Supp. XXIII:** 112
Salt Garden, The (Nemerov), **III:** 269, 272–275, 277
"Salt Garden, The" (Nemerov), **III:** 267–268

Salting the Ocean (Nye, ed.), **Supp. XIII:** 280
Salt Lesson, The (C. Frost), **Supp. XV:** 92, 96
"Salt Lesson, The" (C. Frost), **Supp. XV:** 99
"Salts and Oils" (Levine), **Supp. V:** 190
Salt to the Devil (film, Dmytryk), **Supp. XX: 41**
Saltzman, Arthur, **Supp. XIII:** 48
Saltzman, Harry, **Supp. XI:** 307
"Salut au Monde!" (Whitman), **Retro. Supp. I:** 387, 396, 400
"Salute" (MacLeish), **III:** 13
Salute (Shaw), **Supp. XIX:** 244
"Salute to Mister Yates, A" (Dubus), **Supp. XI:** 347, 349
Salute to Spring (Le Sueur), **Supp. XXIII:** 164, 165, 166, 172
Salvador (Didion), **Supp. IV Part 1:** 198, 207–208, 210
"Salvage" (Clampitt), **Supp. IX:** 41
"Salvage" (Rinehart), **Supp. XXV:** 194
Salvation (Asch), **Supp. XXIII:** 3, 4, **12, 13, 15**
Salvos: An Informal Book About Books and Plays (W. Frank), **Supp. XX: 75**
Samain, Albert, **II:** 528
Same Door, The (Updike), **IV:** 214, 219, 226; **Retro. Supp. I:** 320
"Same in Blues" (Hughes), **Retro. Supp. I:** 208
"Same Kiss After Many Years, The" (Gallagher), **Supp. XXIV:** 169
Same River Twice, The (Offutt), **Supp. XIX:** 163, 164, **167–168,** 175
"Samhain" (A. Finch), **Supp. XVII:** 72
Sam Lawson's Oldtown Fireside Stories (Stowe), **Supp. I Part 2:** 587, 596, 598–599
Sam Patch, the High, Wide & Handsome Jumper (Bontemps and Conroy), **Supp. XXII:** 5, 11
"Sa'm Pèdi" (Bell), **Supp. X:** 17
"Sampler, A" (MacLeish), **III:** 4
Sampoli, Maria, **Supp. V:** 338
Sampson, Edward, **Supp. I Part 2:** 664, 673
Sampson, Martin, **Supp. I Part 2:** 652
"Sam's Dad" (Lamott), **Supp. XX: 142–143**
Sam's Legacy (Neugeboren), **Supp. XVI:** 221, 222
Samson Agonistes (Milton), **III:** 274
"Samson and Delilah" (Masters), **Supp. I Part 2:** 459
Samuel de Champlain: Father of New France (Morison), **Supp. I Part 2:** 496–497
Samuel, Maurice, **Supp. XXIII:** 1, 7
Samuels, Charles Thomas, **Retro. Supp. I:** 334
"Samuel Sewall" (Hecht), **Supp. X:** 58
"Samwheel" (Lamott), **Supp. XX: 144–145**
Sanborn, Franklin B., **IV:** 171, 172, 178
Sanborn, Kate, **Supp. XIII:** 152
Sanborn, Sara, **Supp. XIV:** 113
Sanchez, Carol Anne, **Supp. IV Part 1:** 335

Sanchez, Carol Lee, **Supp. IV Part 2:** 499, 557
Sanchez, Sonia, **Supp. II Part 1:** 34
Sánchez Beras, César, **Supp. XXI:** 100, 104
Sanctified Church, The (Hurston), **Supp. VI:** 150
"Sanction of the Victims, The" (Rand), **Supp. IV Part 2:** 528
Sanctuary (Faulkner), **II:** 57, 61–63, 72, 73, 74, 174; **Retro. Supp. I:** 73, 84, 86–87, 87; **Supp. I Part 2:** 614; **Supp. XII:** 16
"Sanctuary" (Larsen), **Supp. XVIII:** 119, 130–131
Sanctuary (Wharton), **IV:** 311
"Sanctuary" (Wylie), **Supp. I Part 2:** 711
"Sanctuary, The" (Nemerov), **III:** 272, 274
Sanctuary V (Schulberg), **Supp. XVIII:** 254
"Sanctus" (Nelson), **Supp. XVIII:** 183
Sand, George, **II:** 322; **Retro. Supp. I:** 235, 372; **Supp. XV:** 275
"Sandalphon" (Longfellow), **II:** 498
Sand and Foam: A Book of Aphorisms (Gibran), **Supp. XX:** 115, 121–122
Sandbox, The (Albee), **I:** 74–75, 89
Sandburg, Carl, **I:** 103, 109, 384, 421; **II:** 529; **III:** 3, 20, **575–598; Retro. Supp. I:** 133, 194; **Supp. I Part 1:** 257, 320; **Supp. I Part 2:** 387, 389, 454, 461, 653; **Supp. III Part 1:** 63, 71, 73, 75; **Supp. IV Part 1:** 169; **Supp. IV Part 2:** 502; **Supp. IX:** 1, 15, 308; **Supp. XIII:** 274, 277; **Supp. XV:** 293, 299, 300, 301, 302, 306; **Supp. XXII:** 275; **Supp. XXIII:** 161, 165; **Supp. XXV:** 18
Sandburg, Mrs. Carl (Lillian Steichen), **III:** 580
Sandburg, Helga, **III:** 583
Sandburg, Janet, **III:** 583, 584
Sandburg, Margaret, **III:** 583, 584
Sand County Almanac and Sketches Here and There, A (Leopold), **Supp. XIV:** 177, 178, **182–192**
"Sand Creek, Colorado"(Kenny), **Supp. XXIII:** 155
"Sand Dabs" (Oliver), **Supp. VII:** 245
"Sand Dunes" (Frost), **Retro. Supp. I:** 137; **Retro. Supp. II:** 41
Sander, August, **Supp. IX:** 211
Sanders, Mark, **Supp. XIX:** 119, 121
Sanders, Scott Russell, **Supp. XVI: 265–280**
Sandlin, Tim, **Supp. XXII:** 114
"Sandman, The" (Barthelme), **Supp. IV Part 1:** 47
Sandman's Dust (Bukiet), **Supp. XVII:** 40, 41
Sando, Joe S., **Supp. IV Part 2:** 510
Sandoe, James, **Supp. IV Part 1:** 131; **Supp. IV Part 2:** 470
Sandoval, Chela, **Supp. XXIII:** 204
Sandoz, Mari, **Supp. XV:** 141; **Supp. XXIII:** 146; **Supp. XXIV: 243–261**
Sandperl, Ira, **Supp. VIII:** 200
"Sand-Quarry and Moving Figures" (Rukeyser), **Supp. VI:** 271, 278

Sand Rivers (Matthiessen), **Supp. V:** 203
"Sand Roses, The" (Hogan), **Supp. IV Part 1:** 401
Sands, Diana, **Supp. IV Part 1:** 362
Sands, Robert, **Supp. I Part 1:** 156, 157
"Sands at Seventy" (Whitman), **IV:** 348
"Sandstone Farmhouse, A" (Updike), **Retro. Supp. I:** 318
Sandy Bottom Orchestra,The (Keillor and Nilsson), **Supp. XVI:** 177
Sanford, John, **IV:** 286, 287
San Francisco (film), **Supp. XVI:** 181, 192
"San Francisco" (Hempel), **Supp. XXI:** 118
"San Francisco Blues" (Kerouac), **Supp. III Part 1:** 225
Sangamon County Peace Advocate, The (Lindsay), **Supp. I Part 2:** 379
Sanger, Margaret, **Supp. I Part 1:** 19; **Supp. XXI:** 6; **Supp. XXIII:** 161
Sankofa (film), **Supp. XX: 154**
Sansom, William, **IV:** 279
Sans Soleil (film), **Supp. IV Part 2:** 436
"Santa" (Sexton), **Supp. II Part 2:** 693
Santa Claus: A Morality (Cummings), **I:** 430, 441
"Santa Fe, New Mexico"(Kenny), **Supp. XXIII:** 150
"Santa Fé Trail, The" (Lindsay), **Supp. I Part 2:** 389
"Santa Lucia" (Hass), **Supp. VI:** 105–106
"Santa Lucia II" (Hass), **Supp. VI:** 105–106
Santayana, George, **I:** 222, 224, 236, 243, 253, 460; **II:** 20, 542; **III:** 64, **599–622; IV:** 26, 339, 351, 353, 441; **Retro. Supp. I:** 55, 57, 67, 295; **Retro. Supp. II:** 179; **Supp. I Part 2:** 428; **Supp. II Part 1:** 107; **Supp. X:** 58; **Supp. XIV:** 199, 335, 340, 342; **Supp. XVI:** 189; **Supp. XVII:** 97, 106; **Supp. XX: 228, 229, 231**
Santiago, Esmeralda, **Supp. XI:** 177
"Santorini: Stopping the Leak" (Merrill), **Supp. III Part 1:** 336
Santos, John Phillip, **Supp. XIII:** 274
Santos, Sherod, **Supp. VIII:** 270
Saphier, William, **Supp. XXV:** 19, 20
Sapir, Edward, **Supp. VIII:** 295; **Supp. XVI:** 283
"Sapphics for Patience" (A. Finch), **Supp. XVII:** 72
Sapphira and the Slave Girl (Cather), **I:** 331; **Retro. Supp. I:** 2, **19–20**
Sappho, **II:** 544; **III:** 142; **Supp. I Part 1:** 261, 269; **Supp. I Part 2:** 458; **Supp. XII:** 98, 99; **Supp. XVII:** 74; **Supp. XXV:** 222
"Sappho" (Wright), **Supp. III Part 2:** 595, 604
"Sappho, Keats"(Hadas), **Supp. XXIII:** 113
"Sara" (song, Dylan), **Supp. XVIII:** 28
"Sarah" (Schwartz), **Supp. II Part 2:** 663
Sarah; or, The Exemplary Wife (Rowson), **Supp. XV:** 242
"Saratoga" mysteries (Dobyns), **Supp. XIII:** 79–80

Sardonic Arm, The (Bodenheim), **Supp. XXV:** 22, 23
Sargent, John Singer, **II:** 337, 338; **Supp. XX: 231**
Sarlós, Robert K., **Supp. XXI:** 7, 12, 13
Saroyan, Aram, **Supp. XV:** 182
Saroyan, William, **III:** 146–147; **IV:** 393; **Supp. I Part 2:** 679; **Supp. IV Part 1:** 83; **Supp. IV Part 2:** 502; **Supp. XIII:** 280; **Supp. XXIII:** 20; **Supp. XXV:** 29
Sarris, Greg, **Supp. IV Part 1:** 329, 330
Sarton, George, **Supp. VIII:** 249
Sarton, May, **Supp. III Part 1:** 62, 63; **Supp. VIII: 249–268; Supp. XIII:** 296; **Supp. XVII:** 71
Sartoris (Faulkner), **II:** 55, 56–57, 58, 62; **Retro. Supp. I:** 77, 81, 82, 83, 88
Sartor Resartus (Carlyle), **II:** 26; **III:** 82
Sartre, Jean-Paul, **I:** 82, 494; **II:** 57, 244; **III:** 51, 204, 292, 453, 619; **IV:** 6, 223, 236, 477, 487, 493; **Retro. Supp. I:** 73; **Supp. I Part 1:** 51; **Supp. IV Part 1:** 42, 84; **Supp. VIII:** 11; **Supp. IX:** 4; **Supp. XIII:** 74, 171; **Supp. XIV:** 24; **Supp. XVII:** 137; **Supp. XXIV:** 281
Sassone, Ralph, **Supp. X:** 171
Sassoon, Siegfried, **II:** 367; **Supp. XV:** 308; **Supp. XIX:** 18
Satan in Goray (Singer), **IV:** 1, 6–7, 12; **Retro. Supp. II:** 303, **304–305**
Satan Says (Olds), **Supp. X:** 201, 202, **202–204,** 215
"Satan Says" (Olds), **Supp. X:** 202; **Supp. XVII:** 114
Satanstoe (Cooper), **I:** 351–352, 355
"Sather Gate Illumination" (Ginsberg), **Supp. II Part 1:** 329
"Satire as a Way of Seeing" (Dos Passos), **III:** 172
Satires of Persius, The (Merwin, trans.), **Supp. III Part 1:** 347
Satirical Rogue on Poetry, The (Francis). *See Pot Shots at Poetry* (Francis)
Satori in Paris (Kerouac), **Supp. III Part 1:** 231
"Saturday" (Salinas), **Supp. XIII:** 315
"Saturday Matinee" (Trethewey), **Supp. XXI:** 251
Saturday Night (Orlean), **Supp. XXV:** 159, 161
Saturday Night at the War (Shanley), **Supp. XIV:** 315
"Saturday Rain" (Kees), **Supp. XV:** 136
"Saturday Route, The" (Wolfe), **Supp. III Part 2:** 580
Satyagraha (Gandhi), **IV:** 185
"Satyr's Heart, The" (B. Kelly), **Supp. XVII:** 132
Saucedo, José Guadalupe, **Supp. XXIII:** 197
Saul and Patsy (C. Baxter), **Supp. XVII:** 22–23
"Saul and Patsy" (C. Baxter), **Supp. XVII:** 17
"Saul and Patsy Are Getting Comfortable in Michigan" (C. Baxter), **Supp. XVII:** 22

"Saul and Patsy Are in Labor" (C. Baxter), **Supp. XVII:** 20, 22
"Saul and Patsy Are Pregnant" (C. Baxter), **Supp. XVII:** 22
Saunders, George, **Supp. XIX: 223–237; Supp. XXII:** 49; **Supp. XXIV:** 199
Saunders, Richard, **II:** 110
Savage, Augusta, **Retro. Supp. II:** 115
Savage, James, **II:** 111
Savage, Tom, **Supp. XXIV:** 45
Savage Holiday (Wright), **IV:** 478, 488
Savage in Limbo: A Concert Play (Shanley), **Supp. XIV:** 315, **319–321,** 323, 324
Savage Love (Shepard and Chaikin), **Supp. III Part 2:** 433
Savage Place, A (Parker), **Supp. XIX:** 185
Savage Wilds (Reed), **Supp. X:** 241
Save Me, Joe Louis (Bell), **Supp. X:** 7, 10, **11–12**
Save Me the Waltz (Z. Fitzgerald), **II:** 95; **Retro. Supp. I:** 110; **Supp. IX:** 58, 59, 65, **66–68**
Savers, Michael, **Supp. XI:** 307
Saving Lives (Goldbarth), **Supp. XII:** 192
Saving Private Ryan (film), **Supp. V:** 249; **Supp. XI:** 234
Savings (Hogan), **Supp. IV Part 1:** 397, 404, 405, 406, 410
Saving Sebastian (Taylor), **Supp. XXIII:** 57
Savo, Jimmy, **I:** 440
Savran, David, **Supp. IX:** 145; **Supp. XIII:** 209; **Supp. XV:** 321; **Supp. XXIV:** 263, 264
"Sawdust" (Offutt), **Supp. XIX:** 164
Sawyer-Lauçanno, Christopher, **Supp. IV Part 1:** 95
Saxon, Lyle, **Retro. Supp. I:** 80
"Saxophone" (Di Piero), **Supp. XIX:** 38
"Sax's and Selves" (Halliday), **Supp. XIX:** 88
"Say All" (Ray), **Supp. XVIII:** 193
Say and Seal (S. and A. Warner), **Supp. XVIII:** 258, 266
Saye and Sele, Lord, **Supp. I Part 1:** 98
Sayer, Mandy, **Supp. XIII:** 118
Sayers, Dorothy, **Supp. IV Part 1:** 341; **Supp. IV Part 2:** 464
Sayers, Valerie, **Supp. XI:** 253; **Supp. XVIII:** 99
"Say Good-bye" (Weigl), **Supp. XIX:** 288
Say Her Name (Goldman), **Supp. XXV:** 50, 59–62
"Sayings/For Luck" (Goldbarth), **Supp. XII:** 176
"Saying What Needs To Be Said" (Skloot), **Supp. XX: 201**
Say! Is This the U.S.A.? (Caldwell), **I:** 293, 294–295, 304, 309, 310
Saylor, Bruce, **Supp. XII:** 253
Sayre, Joel, **Supp. XIII:** 166
Sayre, Nora, **Supp. XII:** 119
Sayre, Zelda, **Retro. Supp. I:** 101, 102–103, 104, 105, 108, 109, 110, 113, 114. *See also* Fitzgerald, Zelda (Zelda Sayre)
"Say Yes" (Wolff), **Supp. VII:** 344

"Say You Love Me" (Peacock), **Supp. XIX:** 198
Scafe, Suzanne, **Supp. XXIII:** 94, 95
"Scale" (Halliday), **Supp. XIX:** 92
"Scales of the Eyes, The" (Nemerov), **III:** 272, 273, 277
Scalpel (McCoy), **Supp. XIII: 174–175**
Scalpel (screen treatment, McCoy), **Supp. XIII:** 174
Scandalabra (Zelda Fitzgerald), **Supp. IX:** 60, 61, 65, 67, **68–70**
"Scandal Detectives, The" (Fitzgerald), **II:** 80–81; **Retro. Supp. I:** 99
Scarberry-García, Susan, **Supp. IV Part 2:** 486
Scarborough, Dorothy, **Supp. XVIII:** 279–280
Scarecrow, The (Connelly), **Supp. XXI:** 71, 74, 78, **79**
"Scarecrow, The" (Farrell), **II:** 45
"Scarf, A" (Shields), **Supp. VII:** 328
Scarlet Cabinet, The (Notley), **Supp. XXII:** 233
Scarlet Letter, The (Hawthorne), **II:** 63, 223, 224, 231, 233, 239–240, 241, 243, 244, 255, 264, 286, 290, 291, 550; **Retro. Supp. I:** 63, 145, 147, 152, **157–159,** 160, 163, 165, 220, 248, 330, 335; **Retro. Supp. II:** 100; **Supp. I Part 1:** 38; **Supp. II Part 1:** 386; **Supp. VIII:** 108, 198; **Supp. XII:** 11; **Supp. XVII:** 143; **Supp. XX: 178, 183; Supp. XXII:** 147
"Scarlet Letter Aleph, The" (Mirvis), **Supp. XX: 183**
Scarlet Plague, The (London), **II:** 467
Scarlet Sister Mary (Peterkin), **Supp. XXII:** 189
Scar Lover (Crews), **Supp. XI:** 103, 107, **114–115**
"Scarred Girl, The" (Dickey), **Supp. IV Part 1:** 180
Scates, Maxine, **Supp. XIV:** 264, 265, 274
"Scenario" (H. Miller), **III:** 184
"Scene" (Howells), **II:** 274
"Scene in Jerusalem, A" (Stowe), **Supp. I Part 2:** 587
"Scenes" (Shields), **Supp. VII:** 318
Scènes d'Anabase (chamber music) (Bowles), **Supp. IV Part 1:** 82
"Scenes from a Documentary History of Mississippi" (Trethewey), **Supp. XXI:** 255–256
Scenes from American Life (Gurney), **Supp. V:** 95, 96, 105, 108
Scenes from Another Life (McClatchy), **Supp. XII: 255–256**
"Scenes from Childhood" (W. V. Davis), **Supp. XXI:** 95
"Scenes of Childhood" (Merrill), **Supp. III Part 1:** 322, 323, 327
"Scented Herbage of My Breast" (Whitman), **IV:** 342–343
"Scent of a Woman's Ink" (Prose), **Supp. XVI:** 259
"Scent of Unbought Flowers, The" (Ríos), **Supp. IV Part 2:** 547
Scepticisms (Aiken), **I:** 58
Scève, Maurice, **Supp. III Part 1:** 11

Schad, Christian, **Supp. IV Part 1:** 247
Schafer, Benjamin G., **Supp. XIV:** 144
Schafer, William, **Supp. XIX:** 164, 172
Schaller, George, **Supp. V:** 208, 210–211
Schapiro, Meyer, **II:** 30
Scharmann, Hermann Balthazar, **Supp. XII:** 41
Scharper, Alice, **Supp. XXII:** 175
Scharper, Diane, **Supp. XXIII:** 134
Schary, Dore, **Supp. IV Part 1:** 365; **Supp. XIII:** 163
Schatz, Tom, **Supp. XVIII:** 242
Schaum, Melita, **Supp. XXII:** 166
Schaumbergh, Count de, **II:** 120
Schechner, Richard, **Supp. XXIV:** 116
Scheele, Roy, **Supp. XVI:** 54; **Supp. XXI:** 103
Scheeman, George, **Supp. XXII:** 230
Scheffauer, G. H., **I:** 199
"Scheherazade" (Ashbery), **Supp. III Part 1:** 18
Scheick, William, **Supp. V:** 272
Schelberg, Budd, **Supp. XVIII: 241–256**
Scheler, Max, **I:** 58
Schelling, Friedrich, **Supp. I Part 2:** 422
Schenck, Joseph, **Supp. XVI:** 186
Schenk, Margaret, **I:** 199
Scheponik, Peter, **Supp. X:** 210
Scherer, Loline, **Supp. XIII:** 161
"Scherzo"(Hadas), **Supp. XXIII:** 113
Schevill, James, **I:** 116
Schickel, Richard, **Supp. XV:** 1
Schifano, Mario, **Supp. XXIII:** 217
Schilder, Paul, **Supp. I Part 2:** 622
Schildkraut, Rudolph, **Supp. XXIII:** 8
Schiller, Andrew, **II:** 20
Schiller, Frederick, **Supp. V:** 290
Schiller, Johann Christoph Friedrich von, **I:** 224; **Supp. IV Part 2:** 519; **Supp. XVI:** 292
Schiller, Lawrence, **Retro. Supp. II:** 208, 212, 214
Schimmel, Harold, **Supp. V:** 336
"Schizoid Nature of the Implied Author in Twentieth-Century American Ethnic Novels, The" (Nelson), **Supp. XVIII:** 172
Schjeldahl, Peter, **Supp. XXIV:** 44
Schlegel, Augustus Wilhelm, **III:** 422, 424
Schlegell, David von, **Supp. IV Part 2:** 423
Schleiermacher, Friedrich, **III:** 290–291, 309
Schleifer, Ronald, **Supp. XVIII:** 144
Schlepping Through the Alps (S. Apple), **Supp. XVII:** 8
Schlesinger, Arthur, Jr., **III:** 291, 297–298, 309
Schleuning, Neala, **Supp. XXIII:** 165
Schmidt, Jon Zlotnik, **Supp. IV Part 1:** 2
Schmidt, Kaspar. *See* Stirner, Max
Schmidt, Michael, **Supp. X:** 55
Schmitt, Carl, **I:** 386–387
Schmitz, Neil, **Supp. X:** 243
Schnackenberg, Gjertrud, **Supp. XV: 249–268**
Schneeman, George, **Supp. XXIV:** 41
Schneider, Alan, **I:** 87

Schneider, Louis, **Supp. I Part 2:** 650
Schneider, Romy, **Supp. IV Part 2:** 549
Schneider, Steven, **Supp. IX:** 271, 274
Schnellock, Emil, **III:** 177
Schneour, Zalman, **IV:** 11
"Schnetzer Day" (Halliday), **Supp. XIX:** 93
Schnitzler, Arthur, **Supp. XV:** 307; **Supp. XVI:** 187
Schoerke, Meg, **Supp. XVII:** 110
"Scholar Gypsy, The" (Arnold), **II:** 541
"Scholastic and Bedside Teaching" (Holmes), **Supp. I Part 1:** 305
Schöler, Bo, **Supp. IV Part 1:** 399, 400, 403, 407, 409; **Supp. IV Part 2:** 499
Scholes, Robert, **Supp. V:** 40, 42
Scholtz, Carter, **Supp. XVIII:** 144
Schomburg, Arthur, **Supp. X:** 134; **Supp. XXII:** 6
Schomburg Library of Nineteenth-Century Black Women Writers (H. L. Gates, ed.), **Supp. XX:** 105
Schönberg, Claude-Michel, **Supp. XXI:** 155
Schoolboy Howlers (Abingdon), **Supp. XVI:** 99
Schoolcraft, Henry Rowe, **II:** 503; **Retro. Supp. II:** 160; **Supp. XXIII:** 223, 227, 228, 232, 233–234
Schoolcraft, Jane Johnston (Bamewawagezhikaquay), **Supp. XXIII: 223–238**
"School Days of an Indian Girl, The" (Zitkala-Ša), **Supp. XXV:** 272
"School Daze" (Bambara), **Supp. XI:** 19
School Daze (film), **Supp. XI:** 19, 20
"Schoolhouse" (Levis), **Supp. XI:** 258
"School of Giorgione, The" (Pater), **I:** 51
"School Play, The" (Merrill), **Supp. III Part 1:** 336
"Schooner Fairchild's Class" (Benét), **Supp. XI:** 55
Schopenhauer, Arthur, **III:** 600, 604; **IV:** 7; **Retro. Supp. I:** 256; **Retro. Supp. II:** 94; **Supp. I Part 1:** 320; **Supp. I Part 2:** 457; **Supp. X:** 187; **Supp. XVI:** 184
Schorer, Mark, **II:** 28; **III:** 71; **Retro. Supp. I:** 115; **Supp. IV Part 1:** 197, 203, 211; **Supp. XVI:** 206
Schott, Penelope Scambly, **Supp. XXIII: 239–256**
Schott, Webster, **Supp. IX:** 257
Schotts, Jeffrey, **Supp. XII:** 193
Schrader, Mary von. *See* Jarrell, Mrs. Randall (Mary von Schrader)
Schreiber, Jan, **Supp. XXI:** 105, 111
Schreiner, Olive, **I:** 419; **Supp. XI:** 203
"Schreuderspitze, The" (Helprin), **Supp. XXV:** 85
Schroeder, Eric James, **Supp. V:** 238, 244
Schubert, Bernard L., **Supp. XVIII:** 58
Schubert, David, **Supp. XXIV:** 45
Schubert, Franz Peter, **Supp. I Part 1:** 363
Schubnell, Matthias, **Supp. IV Part 2:** 486
Schudel, Matt, **Supp. XXII:** 205, 214
Schulberg, Budd, **II:** 98; **Retro. Supp. I:** 113; **Supp. XIII:** 170; **Supp. XV:** 194

Schulberg, Stuart, **Supp. XVIII:** 254
Schulman, Grace, **Supp. XXIII:** 58
Schulman, Tom, **Supp. XXI:** 193, 194
Schulz, Bruno, **Supp. IV Part 2:** 623; **Supp. XVII:** 41
Schuman, William, **Supp. XII:** 253; **Supp. XXII:** 283
Schumann, Dr. Alanson Tucker, **III:** 505
Schuster, Edgar H., **Supp. VIII:** 126
Schuyler, George S., **III:** 110; **Supp. XVI:** 142; **Supp. XIX:** 78
Schuyler, James, **Supp. XV:** 177, 178; **Supp. XXIII:** 207, 212, 215, 217; **Supp. XXIV:** 33
Schuyler, William, **Supp. I Part 1:** 211
"Schuylkill, The" (Halliday), **Supp. XIX:** 92
Schwartz, Delmore, **I:** 67, 168, 188, 288; **IV:** 128, 129, 437; **Retro. Supp. II:** 29, 178; **Supp. II Part 1:** 102, 109; **Supp. II Part 2: 639–668; Supp. VIII:** 98; **Supp. IX:** 299; **Supp. XIII:** 320; **Supp. XIV:** 3; **Supp. XV:** 184; **Supp. XIX:** 257
Schwartz, Leonard, **Supp. XVI:** 289
Schwartz, Lloyd, **Supp. I Part 1:** 81; **Supp. XXIV:** 160
Schwartz, Marilyn, **Supp. XII:** 126, 128, 130, 132
Schwartz, Meryl F., **Supp. XXII:** 65, 66
Schwartz, Richard B., **Supp. XIV:** 23, 27
Schwarz, A. B. Christa, **Supp. XIX:** 77, 79
Schwed, Peter, **Supp. XXII:** 119
Schweitzer, Albert, **Supp. IV Part 1:** 373
Schweitzer, Harold, **Supp. X:** 210
Schwerdt, Lisa M., **Supp. XIV:** 155, 171
Schwitters, Kurt, **III:** 197; **Retro. Supp. II:** 322, 331, 336; **Supp. IV Part 1:** 79
"Science" (Jeffers), **Supp. II Part 2:** 426
Science and Health with Key to the Scriptures (Eddy), **I:** 383
"Science Favorable to Virtue" (Freneau), **Supp. II Part 1:** 274
Science of English Verse, The (Lanier), **Supp. I Part 1:** 368, 369
"Science of the Night, The" (Kunitz), **Supp. III Part 1:** 258, 265
"Sci-Fi Floater Genius" (Halliday), **Supp. XIX:** 91
Sciolino, Martina, **Supp. XII:** 9
"Scissors" (C. Baxter), **Supp. XVII:** 19
Scofield, Sandra, **Supp. XXI:** 119
Scooter tetralogy (Murray). *See Magic Keys, The* (Murray); *Seven League Boots, The* (Murray); *Spyglass Tree, The* (Murray); *Train Whistle Guitar* (Murray)
Scopes, John T., **III:** 105, 495
"Scorched Face, The" (Hammett), **Supp. IV Part 1:** 344
"Scorn" (C. Frost), **Supp. XV:** 105
"Scorpion, The" (Bowles), **Supp. IV Part 1:** 84, 86
Scorsese, Martin, **Supp. IV Part 1:** 356; **Supp. XVIII:** 22
Scott, Anne Firor, **Supp. I Part 1:** 19
Scott, A. O., **Supp. X:** 301, 302; **Supp. XII:** 343

Scott, Evelyn, **Retro. Supp. I:** 73; **Supp. XXII:** 198
Scott, Gavin, **Supp. XXII:** 218
Scott, George C., **III:** 165–166; **Supp. XI:** 304
Scott, George Lewis, **Supp. I Part 2:** 503, 504
Scott, Hazel, **Supp. XXII:** 12
Scott, Herbert, **Supp. V:** 180
Scott, Howard, **Supp. I Part 2:** 645
Scott, Joanna, **Supp. XVII: 183–197**
Scott, Lizabeth, **Supp. IV Part 2:** 524
Scott, Lynn Orilla, **Retro. Supp. II:** 12
Scott, Mark, **Retro. Supp. I:** 127
Scott, Nathan A., Jr., **II:** 27
Scott, Paul, **Supp. IV Part 2:** 690
Scott, Ridley, **Supp. XIII:** 268
Scott, Walter, **Supp. XVI:** 7, 13
Scott, Sir Walter, **I:** 204, 339, 341, 343, 354; **II:** 8, 17, 18, 217, 296, 301, 303, 304, 308; **III:** 415, 482; **IV:** 204, 453; **Retro. Supp. I:** 99; **Supp. I Part 2:** 579, 580, 685, 692; **Supp. IV Part 2:** 690; **Supp. IX:** 175; **Supp. X:** 51, 114
Scott, Winfield Townley, **II:** 512; **Supp. I Part 2:** 705; **Supp. XV:** 51
Scottsboro boys, **I:** 505; **Supp. I Part 1:** 330
Scottsboro Limited (Hughes), **Retro. Supp. I:** 203; **Supp. I Part 1:** 328, 330–331, 332
Scoundrel Time (Hellman), **Supp. I Part 1:** 294–297; **Supp. IV Part 1:** 12; **Supp. VIII:** 243
Scrambled Eggs Super! (Geisel), **Supp. XVI:** 105
Scrambled Eggs & Whiskey: Poems, 1991–1995 (Carruth), **Supp. XVI:** 47
Scratch (MacLeish), **III:** 22–23
"Scratch Music" (Wright), **Supp. XV:** 343
"Scream, The" (Lowell), **II:** 550
"Screamer, The" (Coleman), **Supp. XI: 92–93**
"Screamers, The" (Baraka), **Supp. II Part 1:** 38
"Screen Guide for Americans" (Rand), **Supp. IV Part 2:** 524
"Screen Memory" (Cliff), **Supp. XXII:** 75
"Screeno" (Schwartz), **Supp. II Part 2:** 660
Screens, The (Genet), **Supp. XII:** 12
Screen Sirens Scream! (Parla and Mitchell), **Supp. XXII:** 256
Scribblers on the Roof: Contemporary American Jewish Fiction (Bukiet and Roskies, eds.), **Supp. XVII:** 39, 49–50
Scripts for the Pageant (Merrill), **Supp. III Part 1:** 332, 333, 335
Scrolls from the Dead Sea, The (Wilson), **IV:** 429
Scruggs, Earl, **Supp. V:** 335
Scudder, Horace Elisha, **II:** 400, 401; **Retro. Supp. II:** 67; **Supp. I Part 1:** 220; **Supp. I Part 2:** 410, 414
Scully, James, **Supp. XII:** 131
"Sculpting the Whistle" (Ríos), **Supp. IV Part 2:** 549
"Sculptor" (Plath), **Supp. I Part 2:** 538

"Sculptor's Funeral, The" (Cather), **I:** 315–316; **Retro. Supp. I:** 5, 6; **Supp. XV:** 40

Scum (Singer), **Retro. Supp. II:** 316–317

Scupoli, Lorenzo, **IV:** 156

"Scythe Song" (Lang), **Retro. Supp. I:** 128

Sea and the Mirror, The: A Commentary on Shakespeare's "The Tempest" (Auden), Supp. II Part 1: 2, 18

Sea around Us, The (Carson), **Supp. IX:** 19, **23–25**

Sea around Us, The (film), **Supp. IX:** 25

Sea Birds Are Still Alive, The (Bambara), **Supp. XI:** 1, 4, **7–12**

"Sea Birds Are Still Alive, The" (Bambara), **Supp. XI:** 8

"Sea-Blue and Blood-Red" (Lowell), **II:** 524

Seabrook, John, **Supp. VIII:** 157

"Sea Burial from the Cruiser Reve" (Eberhart), **I:** 532–533

Seabury, David, **Supp. I Part 2:** 608

"Sea Calm" (Hughes), **Retro. Supp. I:** 199

"Sea Chanty" (Corso), **Supp. XII:** 118

"Sea Dream, A" (Whitter), **Supp. I Part 2:** 699

"Seafarer, The" (Pound, trans.), **Retro. Supp. I:** 287

Seagall, Harry, **Supp. XIII:** 166

Sea Garden (Doolittle), **Supp. I Part 1:** 257, 259, 266, 269, 272

Seager, Allan, **IV:** 305

Seagull on the Step, The (Boyle), **Supp. XXIV:** 60, 62

"Seagulls and Children" (C. Frost), **Supp. XV:** 95

Sea Lady, The (Boyce), **Supp. XXI:** 8, 13

"Sea Lily" (Doolittle), **Supp. I Part 1:** 266

Sea Lions, The (Cooper), **I:** 354, 355

Sealts, Merton M., Jr., **Retro. Supp. I:** 257

Seaman, Benjamin, **Supp. XXIII:** 69–70, 72

Seaman, Donna, **Supp. VIII:** 86; **Supp. X:** 1, 4, 12, 16, 213; **Supp. XV:** 65; **Supp. XVIII:** 102; **Supp. XIX:** 53, 55, 57, 58, 59, 60, 61; **Supp. XXI:** 236; **Supp. XXII:** 266; **Supp. XXIII:** 71, 74, 134, 135, 298; **Supp. XXIV:** 167, 171

"Seamy Side, The"(Hadas), **Supp. XXIII:** 119

"Séance, The" (Singer), **IV:** 20

Séance and Other Stories, The (Singer), **IV:** 19–21

"Sea Oak" (Saunders), **Supp. XIX:** 228, 229, 231

Sea of Cortez (Steinbeck), **IV:** 52, 54, 62, 69

Sea of Grass, The (film), **Supp. XVIII:** 211

Sea of Grass, The (Richter), **Supp. XVIII: 210–211**, 215–216, 217, 220

"Sea Pieces" (Melville), **III:** 93

Searchers, The (film, Ford), **Supp. XVIII:** 57, 58, 135–136, 141

Searches and Seizures (Elkin), **Supp. VI:** 49

"Search for Southern Identity, The" (Woodward), **Retro. Supp. I:** 75; **Supp. XXII:** 194

Search for the King, A: A Twelfth-Century Legend (Vidal), **Supp. IV Part 2:** 681

Searching for Caleb (Tyler), **Supp. IV Part 2:** 663–665, 671

"Searching for Poetry: Real *vs.* Fake" (B. Miller), **Supp. IV Part 1:** 67

Searching for Survivors (Banks), **Supp. V:** 7

"Searching for Survivors (I)" (Banks), **Supp. V:** 8

"Searching for Survivors (II)" (Banks), **Supp. V:** 7, 8

Searching for the Ox (Simpson), **Supp. IX:** 266, **274–275**

"Searching for the Ox" (Simpson), **Supp. IX:** 275, 280

"Searching in the Britannia Tavern" (Wagoner), **Supp. IX:** 327

Searching Wing, The, (Hellman), **Supp. I Part 1:** 277, 278, 281–282, 283, 292, 297

Search-Light. *See* Frank, Waldo

"Search Party, The" (Matthews), **Supp. IX:** 156

Searle, Ronald, **Supp. I Part 2:** 604, 605

Sea Road to the Indies (Hart), **Supp. XIV:** 97

"Seascape" (Bishop), **Retro. Supp. II:** 42–43

"Sea's Green Sameness, The" (Updike), **IV:** 217

Seaside and the Fireside, The (Longfellow), **II:** 489; **Retro. Supp. II:** 159, 168

Season in Hell, A (Rimbaud), **III:** 189

Seasons, The (Thomson), **II:** 304; **Supp. I Part 1:** 151

Seasons' Difference, The (Buechner), **Supp. XII:** 47

Seasons of Celebration (Merton), **Supp. VIII:** 199, 208

Seasons of the Heart: In Quest of Faith (Kinard, comp.), **Supp. XIV:** 127

"Seasons of the Soul" (Tate), **IV:** 136–140

Seasons on Earth (Koch), **Supp. XV: 183–184**

"Sea Surface Full of Clouds" (Stevens), **IV:** 82

"Sea Tides" (Hoffman), **Supp. XVIII:** 87

"Sea Treader" (Hoffman), **Supp. XVIII:** 87

"Sea Unicorns and Land Unicorns" (Moore), **III:** 202–203

Seaver, Edwin, **Supp. XXV:** 28

Seaver, Richard, **Supp. XI:** 301

"Seaweed" (Longfellow), **II:** 498

Sea-Wolf, The (London), **II:** 264, 466, 472–473

Sebald, W. G., **Supp. XIV:** 96; **Supp. XXI:** 92

Sebold, Alice, **Supp. XXII:** 55

Seckler, David, **Supp. I Part 2:** 650

"2nd Air Force" (Jarrell), **II:** 375

Second American Revolution and Other Essays (1976–1982), The (Vidal), **Supp. IV Part 2:** 679, 687, 688

Secondary Colors, The (A. Theroux), **Supp. VIII:** 312

Second Avenue (O'Hara), **Supp. XXIII:** 216

"Second Avenue"(O'Hara), **Supp. XXIII:** 208, 211, 218

Second Blush, The (Peacock), **Supp. XIX:** 197, **205–206**

Second Chance (Auchincloss), **Supp. IV Part 1:** 33

"Second Chances" (Hugo), **Supp. VI:** 144, 145

Second Coming, The (Percy), **Supp. III Part 1:** 383, 384, 387, 388, 396–397

"Second Coming, The" (Yeats), **III:** 294; **Retro. Supp. I:** 290, 311; **Supp. VIII:** 24; **Supp. XVI:** 159; **Supp. XIX:** 85

Second Decade, The. See Stephen King, The Second Decade: "Danse Macabre" to "The Dark Half" (Magistrale)

Second Dune, The (Hearon), **Supp. VIII:** 58, **59–60**

Second Flowering, A: Works and Days of the Lost Generation (Cowley), **Retro. Supp. I:** 77; **Supp. II Part 1:** 135, 141, 143, 144, 147, 149

Second Growth (Stegner), **Supp. IV Part 2:** 599, 608

"Second Hour of the Night, The" (Bidart), **Supp. XV:** 32, **33–34**

Second Marriage (F. Barthelme), **Supp. XI:** 32, 33

"Second Marriage" (McCarriston), **Supp. XIV:** 262

"Second Mortgage" (Shaw), **Supp. XIX:** 245–246

Second Nature (Hoffman), **Supp. X:** 88, 89

Seconds, The (Bierds), **Supp. XVII: 33–34**

Second Set, The (Komunyakaa and Feinstein, eds.), **Supp. XIII:** 125

Second Sex, The (Beauvoir), **Supp. IV Part 1:** 360

"Second Sight" (Mosher), **Supp. XXII:** 214

Second Stone, The (Fiedler), **Supp. XIII:** 102

"Second Swimming, The" (Boyle), **Supp. VIII:** 13, 14

Second Tree from the Corner (White), **Supp. I Part 2:** 654

"Second Tree from the Corner" (White), **Supp. I Part 2:** 651

Second Twenty Years at Hull-House, The: September 1909 to September 1929, with a Record of a Growing World Consciousness (Addams), **Supp. I Part 1:** 24–25

Second Voyage of Columbus, The (Morison), **Supp. I Part 2:** 488

Second Words, (Atwood), **Supp. XIII:** 35

Second World, The (Blackmur), **Supp. II Part 1:** 91

Secret, The (E. Hoffman), **Supp. XVI:** 151, **155–158**, 161

"Secret, The" (Levine), **Supp. V:** 195

Secret Agent, The (Conrad), **Supp. IV Part 1:** 341

Secret Agent X-9 (Hammett), **Supp. IV Part 1:** 355

"Secret Courts of Men's Hearts, The: Code and Law in Harper Lee's *To Kill a Mockingbird*" (Johnson), **Supp. VIII:** 126

"Secret Dog, The" (Cameron), **Supp. XII: 83–84**

Secret Garden, The (Burnett), **Supp. I Part 1:** 44

"Secret Garden, The" (Hoffman), **Supp. XVIII:** 86

"Secret Gladness, A" (C. Frost), **Supp. XV:** 91

Secret Historie (J. Smith), **I:** 131

Secret History of the Dividing Line (Howe), **Supp. IV Part 2:** 424, 425–426

"Secret Integration, The" (Pynchon), **Supp. II Part 2:** 624

"Secret Life of Musical Instruments, The" (Wright), **Supp. XV:** 343

"Secret Life of Walter Mitty, The" (Thurber), **Supp. I Part 2:** 623; **Supp. XVI:** 233

"Secret Lion, The" (Ríos), **Supp. IV Part 2:** 543, 544

"Secret Nature of the Mechanical Rabbit, The"(P. Benedict), **Supp. XXIII:** 49

"Secret Ocean, The" (Jarman), **Supp. XVII:** 120

Secret of Poetry, The: Essays (Jarman), **Supp. XVII:** 110, 111, 120

"Secret of the Russian Ballet, The" (Van Vechten), **Supp. II Part 2:** 732

"Secret Prune" (Ríos), **Supp. IV Part 2:** 549

Secret River, The (Rawlings), **Supp. X:** 233

Secrets and Surprises (Beattie), **Supp. V:** 23, 27, 29

Secrets from the Center of the World (Harjo), **Supp. XII: 223–224**

"Secret Sharer, The" (Conrad), **Supp. IX:** 105; **Supp. XXV:** 217

"Secret Sharer, The" (J. Conrad), **Supp. XVI:** 158

"Secret Society, A" (Nemerov), **III:** 282

Secrets of the Heart (Gibran), **Supp. XX: 116**

Secrets of the Universe: Scenes from the Journey Home (Sanders), **Supp. XVI:** 273–274

"Secular" (Trethewey), **Supp. XXI:** 249

Secular Journal of Thomas Merton, The, **Supp. VIII:** 206

"Security" (Boyle), **Supp. XXIV:** 58

"Security" (Stafford), **Supp. XI:** 329

"Security"(Strout), **Supp. XXIII:** 283

Sedaris, David, **Supp. XXIII:** 289

Sedges, John (pseudonym). *See* Buck, Pearl S.

Sedgwick, Catherine Maria, **I:** 341; **Supp. I Part 1:** 155, 157

Sedgwick, Christina. *See* Marquand, Mrs. John P. (Christina Sedgwick)

Sedgwick, Ellery, **I:** 217, 229, 231; **III:** 54–55

Sedgwick, Eve, **Supp. XX: 267**

Sedgwick, Henry, **Supp. I Part 1:** 156

Sedgwick, Robert, **Supp. I Part 1:** 156

Sedore, Timothy, **Supp. XIV:** 312

"Seduction and Betrayal" (Hardwick), **Supp. III Part 1:** 207

Seduction and Betrayal: Women and Literature (Hardwick), **Supp. III Part 1:** 194, 204, 206–208, 212, 213; **Supp. XIV:** 89

See, Carolyn, **Supp. XXII:** 206, 217

Seed, David, **Supp. IV Part 1:** 391

"Seed Eaters, The" (Francis), **Supp. IX:** 82

"Seed Leaves" (Wilbur), **Supp. III Part 2:** 558

"Seeds" (Anderson), **I:** 106, 114

Seeds of Contemplation (Merton), **Supp. VIII:** 199, 200, 207, 208

Seeds of Destruction (Merton), **Supp. VIII:** 202, 203, 204, 208

"Seeing Red" (column, Ryan as Quin), **Supp. XVIII:** 226

"See(k)ing the Self: Mirrors and Mirroring in Bicultural Texts" (Oster), **Supp. XVI:** 151

Seeing through the Sun (Hogan), **Supp. IV Part 1:** 397, 400, 401–402, 402, 413

"See in the Midst of Fair Leaves" (Moore), **III:** 215

"Seekers, The" (McGrath), **Supp. X:** 117

"Seeking a Vision of Truth, Guided by a Higher Power" (Burke), **Supp. XIV:** 21, 23

"Seele im Raum" (Jarrell), **II:** 382–383

"Seele im Raum" (Rilke), **II:** 382–383

"See Naples and Die" (Hecht), **Supp. X:** 69, 70

"Seen from the 'L'" (Barnes), **Supp. III Part 1:** 33

"See the Moon?" (Barthelme), **Supp. IV Part 1:** 42, 49–50, 50

Sefarim, Mendele Mokher, **Supp. XXIII:** 4

Seferis, George, **Supp. XXV:** 225

Segal, D. (pseudonym). *See* Singer, Isaac Bashevis

Segal, George, **Supp. XI:** 343

Segal, Lore, **Supp. XVI:** 203

Segregation: The Inner Conflict in the South (Warren), **IV:** 237, 238, 246, 252

"*Se:* Hegel's Absolute and Heidegger's *Ereignis*" (Agamben), **Supp. XVI:** 289

Seidel, Frederick, **I:** 185

Seidman, Hugh, **Supp. XXI:** 228

Seize the Day (Bellow), **I:** 144, 147, 148, 150, 151, 152, 153, 155, 158, 162; **Retro. Supp. II:** 19, **23–24,** 27, 32, 34; **Supp. I Part 2:** 428

Selby, Hubert, **Supp. III Part 1:** 125

Selby, Hubert, Jr., **Supp. XXI:** 227

Selby, John, **Retro. Supp. II:** 221, 222

Selden, John, **Supp. XIV:** 344

Seldes, Gilbert, **II:** 437, 445; **Retro. Supp. I:** 108

Selected Criticism: Prose, Poetry (Bogan), **Supp. III Part 1:** 64

Selected Essays (Eliot), **I:** 572

Selected Essays and Reviews (Carruth), **Supp. XVI:** 46

Selected Journals and Other Writings (Audubon), **Supp. XVI:** 10, 12, 13

Selected Letters (Bynner), **Supp. XV:** 52

Selected Letters (W. C. Williams), **Retro. Supp. I:** 430

Selected Letters, 1940–1956 (Kerouac), **Supp. XIV:** 137, 144

Selected Letters of Robert Frost (Thompson, ed.), **Retro. Supp. I:** 125

Selected Levis, The (Levis), **Supp. XI:** 257, 272

Selected Plays (O'Hara), **Supp. XXIII:** 216

Selected Poems (Aiken), **I:** 69

Selected Poems (Ashbery), **Supp. III Part 1:** 25–26

Selected Poems (Berrigan), **Supp. XXIV:** 37

Selected Poems (Bodenheim), **Supp. XXV:** 29

Selected Poems (Brodsky), **Supp. VIII:** 22

Selected Poems (Brooks), **Supp. III Part 1:** 82–83

Selected Poems (Bynner), **Supp. XV:** 51, 52

Selected Poems (Corso), **Supp. XII:** 129

Selected Poems (Dove), **Supp. IV Part 1:** 241, 243, 250

Selected Poems (Frost), **Retro. Supp. I:** 133, 136

Selected Poems (Guillevic; Levertov, trans.), **Supp. III Part 1:** 283

Selected Poems (Hayden), **Supp. II Part 1:** 363, 364, 367

Selected Poems (Hughes), **Retro. Supp. I:** 202; **Supp. I Part 1:** 341, 345, 346

Selected Poems (Hugo), **Supp. VI:** 143

Selected Poems (Jarrell), **II:** 367, 370, 371, 374, 377, 379, 380, 381, 382, 384

Selected Poems (Justice), **Supp. VII:** 115

Selected Poems (Kinnell), **Supp. III Part 1:** 235, 253

Selected Poems (Levine, 1984), **Supp. V:** 178, 179

Selected Poems (Lowell), **II:** 512, 516; **Retro. Supp. II:** 184, 186, 188, 190

Selected Poems (Merton), **Supp. VIII:** 207, 208

Selected Poems (Moore), **III:** 193, 194, 205–206, 208, 215

Selected Poems (Notley), **Supp. XXII:** 234

Selected Poems (O'Hara; Allen, ed.), **Supp. XXIII:** 220

Selected Poems (O'Hara; Ford, ed.), **Supp. XXIII:** 220

Selected Poems (Pound), **Retro. Supp. I:** 289, 291

Selected Poems (R. Bly), **Supp. IV Part 1:** 60, 62, 65, 66, 68, 69–71

Selected Poems (Ransom), **III:** 490, 492

Selected Poems (Reznikoff), **Supp. XIV:** 288

Selected Poems (Rukeyser), **Supp. VI:** 274

Selected Poems (Sexton), **Supp. IV Part 2:** 449

Selected Poems (Sorrentino), **Supp. XXI:** 226

Selected Poems (Strand), **Supp. IV Part 2:** 630

Selected Poems, 1923–1943 (Warren), **IV:** 241–242, 243

Selected Poems, 1928–1958 (Kunitz), **Supp. III Part 1:** 261, 263–265

Selected Poems, 1938–1988 (McGrath), **Supp. X:** 127

Selected Poems, 1958–1980 (Sorrentino), **Supp. XXI:** 228

Selected Poems, 1963–1983 (Simic), **Supp. VIII:** 275

Selected Poems 1936–1965 (Eberhart), **I:** 541

Selected Poems: 1957–1987 (Snodgrass), **Supp. VI:** 314–315, 323, 324

Selected Poems 1965–1975 (Atwood), **Supp. XIII: 32–34**

Selected Poems: 1975–2005 (Skloot), **Supp. XX: 196**

Selected Poems II: Poems Selected and New, 1976–1986 (Atwood), **Supp. XIII:** 20, **34–35**

Selected Poems of Ezra Pound (Pound), **Supp. V:** 336

Selected Poems of Gabriela Mistral (Hughes, trans.), **Supp. I Part 1:** 345

Selected Poetry of Amiri Baraka/LeRoi Jones (Baraka), **Supp. II Part 1:** 58

Selected Poetry of Hayden Carruth, The (Carruth), **Supp. XVI:** 53

Selected Stories (Dubus), **Supp. VII:** 88–89

Selected Stories of Richard Bausch, The (Bausch), **Supp. VII:** 42

Selected Translations (Snodgrass), **Supp. VI:** 318, 324, **325–326**

Selected Verse of Margaret Haskins Durber, The (Keillor), **Supp. XVI:** 171

Selected Witter Bynner, The, **Supp. XV:** 52

Selected Works of Djuna Barnes, The (Barnes), **Supp. III Part 1:** 44

Selected Writings 1950–1990 (Howe), **Supp. VI:** 116–117, 118, 120

Selected Writings of John Jay Chapman, The (Barzun), **Supp. XIV:** 54

Select Epigrams from the Greek Anthology (Mackail), **Supp. I Part 2:** 461

"Selecting a Reader" (Kooser), **Supp. XIX:** 119–120

"Selene Afterwards" (MacLeish), **III:** 8

"Self" (James), **II:** 351

Self, William, **Supp. XXII:** 172

Self and the Dramas of History, The (Niebuhr), **III:** 308

Self-Consciousness (Updike), **Retro. Supp. I:** 318, 319, 320, 322, 323, 324

"Self-Culture" (Channing), **Supp. XXIV: 78–79**

"Self-Exposed, The" (X. J. Kennedy), **Supp. XV:** 159

Self-Help: Stories (Moore), **Supp. X:** 163, 166, **167–169,** 174, 175

"Self-Importance" (Halliday), **Supp. XIX:** 90

Self-Interviews (Dickey), **Supp. IV Part 1:** 179

"Self-Made Man, A" (Crane), **I:** 420

"Self Pity" (C. Frost), **Supp. XV:** 93, 94, 101, 102, 104

Self Portrait (album, Dylan), **Supp. XVIII:** 27

"Self-Portrait" (Creeley), **Supp. IV Part 1:** 156

"Self-Portrait" (Mumford), **Supp. II Part 2:** 471

"(Self) Portrait" (Trethewey), **Supp. XXI:** 253

"Self-Portrait" (Wylie), **Supp. I Part 2:** 729

"Self Portrait at Fifty-three" (Weigl), **Supp. XIX:** 288

Self-Portrait: Ceaselessly into the Past (Millar, ed. Sipper), **Supp. IV Part 2:** 464, 469, 472, 475

"Self-Portrait in a Convex Mirror" (Ashbery), **Supp. III Part 1:** 5, 7, 9, 16–19, 22, 24, 26

"Self-Portrait with 1911 NY Yankees Cap" (Skloot), **Supp. XX: 202**

"Self-Reliance" (Emerson), **II:** 7, 15, 17; **Retro. Supp. I:** 159; **Retro. Supp. II:** 155; **Supp. X:** 42, 45

Selfwolf (Halliday), **Supp. XIX:** 81, **89–91,** 93

Sélincourt, Ernest de, **Supp. I Part 2:** 676

Selinger, Eric, **Supp. XVI:** 47

Selinger, Eric Murphy, **Supp. XI:** 248

Sell, Henry, **Supp. XVI:** 188

Sellers, Isaiah, **IV:** 194–195

Sellers, Peter, **Supp. XI:** 301, 304, 306, 307, 309

Sellers, William, **IV:** 208

Seltzer, Mark, **Retro. Supp. I:** 227

Selznick, David O., **Retro. Supp. I:** 105, 113; **Supp. IV Part 1:** 353; **Supp. XVIII:** 242; **Supp. XXII:** 195

Semi, Allen (pseudonym). *See* Larsen, Nella

"Semi-Lunatics of Kilmuir, The" (Hugo), **Supp. VI:** 145

"Semiotics/The Doctor's Doll" (Goldbarth), **Supp. XII:** 183–184

Semmelweiss, Ignaz, **Supp. I Part 1:** 304

Senancour, Étienne Divert de, **I:** 241

Senator North (Atherton), **Supp. XXIV:** 22

Sendak, Maurice, **Supp. IX:** 207, 208, 213, 214; **Supp. XVI:** 110

Seneca, **II:** 14–15; **III:** 77

Senghor, Leopold Sédar, **Supp. IV Part 1:** 16; **Supp. X:** 132, 139

Senier, Siobhan, **Supp. IV Part 1:** 330

"Senility" (Anderson), **I:** 114

Senior, Olive, **Supp. XXIII:** 94

"Senior Partner's Ethics, The" (Auchincloss), **Supp. IV Part 1:** 33

Senlin: A Biography (Aiken), **I:** 48, 49, 50, 52, 56, 57, 64

Sennett, Dorothy, **Supp. XVI:** 43

Sennett, Mack, **III:** 442

"Señora X No More" (Mora), **Supp. XIII:** 218

"Señor Ong and Señor Ha" (Bowles), **Supp. IV Part 1:** 87

Señor Presidente, El (Asturias), **Supp. XXIV:** 89

"Señor X" (Muñoz), **Supp. XXV:** 135

Sensational Designs: The Cultural Work of American Fiction, 1790–1860 (Tompkins), **Supp. XVIII:** 258–259

Sense of Beauty, The (Santayana), **III:** 600

Sense of Life in the Modern Novel, The (Mizener), **IV:** 132

"Sense of Shelter, A" (Updike), **Retro. Supp. I:** 318

"Sense of the Meeting, The" (Conroy), **Supp. XVI:** 72

Sense of the Past, The (James), **II:** 337–338

"Sense of the Past, The" (Trilling), **Supp. III Part 2:** 503

"Sense of the Present, The" (Hardwick), **Supp. III Part 1:** 210

"Sense of the Sleight-of-Hand Man, The" (Stevens), **IV:** 93

"Sense of Where You Are, A" (McPhee), **Supp. III Part 1:** 291, 296–298

"Sensibility! O La!" (Roethke), **III:** 536

"Sensible Emptiness, A" (Kramer), **Supp. IV Part 1:** 61, 66

"Sensuality Plunging Barefoot Into Thorns" (Cisneros), **Supp. VII:** 68

"Sentence" (Barthelme), **Supp. IV Part 1:** 47

Sent for You Yesterday (Wideman), **Supp. X:** 320, 321

"Sentimental Education, A" (Banks), **Supp. V:** 10

"Sentimental Journey" (Oates), **Supp. II Part 2:** 522, 523

"Sentimental Journey, A" (Anderson), **I:** 114

Sentimental Journey, A (Sterne), **Supp. I Part 2:** 714

"Sentimental Journeys" (Didion), **Supp. IV Part 1:** 211

Sentimental Journey through France and Italy, A (Sterne), **Supp. XV:** 232

"Sentiment of Rationality, The" (James), **II:** 346–347

"Separated Father" (Halliday), **Supp. XIX:** 92, 93

Separate Flights (Dubus), **Supp. VII:** 78–83

"Separate Flights" (Dubus), **Supp. VII:** 83

Separate Peace, A (Knowles), **Supp. IV Part 2:** 679; **Supp. XII: 241–249**

Separate Way (Reznikoff), **Supp. XIV:** 280

"Separating" (Updike), **Retro. Supp. I:** 321

"Separation, The" (Kunitz), **Supp. III Part 1:** 263

"Sepia High Stepper" (Hayden), **Supp. II Part 1:** 379

September (film; Allen), **Supp. XV:** 11

"September" (Komunyakaa), **Supp. XIII:** 130

"September" (Pickering), **Supp. XXI:** 198

"September 1, 1939" (Auden), **Supp. II Part 1:** 13; **Supp. IV Part 1:** 225; **Supp. VIII:** 30, 32; **Supp. XV:** 117–118

September 11, 2001: American Writers Respond (Heyen), **Supp. XIII:** 285

"September's Book" (Notley), **Supp. XXII:** 229

September Song (Humphrey), **Supp. IX:** 101, 102, **108–109**

"September Twelfth, 2001" (X. J. Kennedy), **Supp. XV:** 171

"Sept Vieillards, Les" (Millay, trans.), **III:** 142

Sequel to Drum-Taps (Whitman), **Retro. Supp. I:** 406

"Sequence, Sometimes Metaphysical" (Roethke), **III:** 547, 548

Sequence of Seven Plays with a Drawing by Ron Slaughter, A (Nemerov), **III:** 269

Sequoya, Jana, **Supp. IV Part 1:** 334

Seraglio, The (Merrill), **Supp. III Part 1:** 331

Seraphita (Balzac), **I:** 499

Seraph on the Suwanee (Hurston), **Supp. VI:** 149, 159–160

Serenissima: A Novel of Venice (Jong). *See Shylock's Daughter: A Novel of Love in Venice (Serenissima)* (Jong)

Sergeant, Elizabeth Shepley, **I:** 231, 236, 312, 319, 323, 328

Sergeant Bilko (television show), **Supp. IV Part 2:** 575

Sergi, Paula, **Supp. XXI:** 246

"Serious Talk, A" (Carver), **Supp. III Part 1:** 138, 144

Serly, Tibor, **Supp. III Part 2:** 617, 619

"Sermon, Now Encrypted" (Monson), **Supp. XXIV:** 239–240

"Sermon by Doctor Pep" (Bellow), **I:** 151

Sermones (Horace), **II:** 154

"Sermon for Our Maturity" (Baraka), **Supp. II Part 1:** 53

"Sermon in the Cotton Field" (Nelson), **Supp. XVIII:** 177

Sermons and Soda Water (O'Hara), **III:** 362, 364, 371–373, 382

"Sermons on the Warpland" (Brooks), **Supp. III Part 1:** 84

"Serpent in the Wilderness, The" (Masters), **Supp. I Part 2:** 458

Servant of the Bones (Rice), **Supp. VII:** 298, 302

"Servant to Servants, A" (Frost), **Retro. Supp. I:** 125, 128; **Supp. X:** 66

Serve It Forth (M. F. K. Fisher), **Supp. XVII:** 83, 86, 87, 89, 92

Service, Robert W., **Supp. XXI:** 51; **Supp. XXII:** 203

Seshachari, Neila, **Supp. V:** 22

"Session, The" (Adams), **I:** 5

"Sestina" (Bishop), **Supp. I Part 1:** 73, 88

Set-angya, **Supp. IV Part 2:** 493

Seth, Vikram, **Supp. XVII:** 117

Seth's Brother's Wife (Frederic), **II:** 131–132, 137, 144

Sethuraman, Ramchandran, **Supp. XXII:** 73

Setouchi, Jakuchō, **Supp. XXIV:** 166

Set This House on Fire (Styron), **IV:** 98, 99, 105, 107–113, 114, 115, 117

Setting Free the Bears (Irving), **Supp. VI:** 163, **166–167,** 169–170

Setting the Tone (Rorem), **Supp. IV Part 1:** 79

Settle, Mary Lee, **Supp. IX:** 96

Settlement Horizon, The: A National Estimate (Woods and Kennedy), **Supp. I Part 1:** 19

"Settling the Colonel's Hash" (McCarthy), **II:** 559, 562

Setzer, Helen, **Supp. IV Part 1:** 217

"Seurat's Sunday Afternoon along the Seine" (Schwartz), **Supp. II Part 2:** 663–665

Sevag, Aris, **Supp. XXIII:** 28, 29

7 Years from Somehwere (Levine), **Supp. V:** 178, 181, 188–189

Seven against Thebes (Aeschylus; Bacon and Hecht, trans.), **Supp. X:** 57

Seven Ages of Man, The (Wilder), **IV:** 357, 374–375

Seven Deadly Sins, The (Wilder), **IV:** 357, 374–375

Seven Descents of Myrtle, The (T. Williams), **IV:** 382

"Seven Fat Brides, The" (P. Abraham), **Supp. XVII:** 50

Seven Guitars (Wilson), **Supp. VIII:** 331, **348–351**

Seven Lady Godivas, The (Geisel), **Supp. XVI:** 100, 103

Seven League Boots, The (Murray), **Supp. XIX: 156–157**

Seven-League Crutches, The (Jarrell), **II:** 367, 372, 381, 382, 383–384, 389

Seven Mountains of Thomas Merton, The (Mott), **Supp. VIII:** 208

Seven-Ounce Man, The (Harrison), **Supp. VIII:** 51

"Seven Places of the Mind" (Didion), **Supp. IV Part 1:** 200, 210

Seven Plays (Shepard), **Supp. III Part 2:** 434

"Seven Selves, The" (Gibran), **Supp. XX: 118**

"Seven Sentences" (Dybek), **Supp. XXIII:** 74

"Seven Stanzas at Easter" (Updike), **IV:** 215

Seven Storey Mountain, The (Merton), **Supp. VIII:** 193, 195, 198, 200, 207, 208

Seventeen (Berrigan and Padgett), **Supp. XXIV:** 41

Seventh Beggar, The (Abraham), **Supp. XXIV:** 2, 3, **9–12,** 13, 14

Seventh Heaven (Hoffman), **Supp. X:** 87, 89

"Seventh of March" (Webster), **Supp. I Part 2:** 687

"7000 Romaine, Los Angeles 38" (Didion), **Supp. IV Part 1:** 200

"Seventh Street" (Toomer), **Supp. IX:** 316

Seven Types of Ambiguity (Empson), **II:** 536; **IV:** 431

77 Dream Songs (Berryman), **I:** 168, 169, 170, 171, 174, 175, 183–188

73 Poems (Cummings), **I:** 430, 431, 446, 447, 448

Seven Valleys and the Four Valleys, The (Bahá'u'lláh), **Supp. XX: 121**

"Several Short Questions About Crumbs" (Schott), **Supp. XXIII:** 249

Sevier, Jack, **IV:** 378

Sévigné, Madame de, **IV:** 361

Sewall, Richard, **Retro. Supp. I:** 25

Sewall, Samuel, **IV:** 145, 146, 147, 149, 154, 164; **Supp. I Part 1:** 100, 110

Sewell, Elizabeth, **Supp. XIII:** 344

"Sex" (Carruth), **Supp. XVI:** 58

Sex, Economy, Freedom and Community (Berry), **Supp. X:** 30, 36

"Sex Camp" (Mamet), **Supp. XIV:** 240

Sex Castle, The (Lacy), **Supp. XV:** 206

Sex & Character (Weininger), **Retro. Supp. I:** 416

"Sext" (Auden), **Supp. II Part 1:** 22

Sexton, Anne, **Retro. Supp. II:** 245; **Supp. I Part 2:** 538, 543, 546; **Supp. II Part 2: 669–700; Supp. III Part 2:** 599; **Supp. IV Part 1:** 245; **Supp. IV Part 2:** 439, 440–441, 442, 444, 447, 449, 451, 620; **Supp. V:** 113, 118, 124; **Supp. X:** 201, 202, 213; **Supp. XI:** 146, 240, 317; **Supp. XII:** 217, 253, 254, 256, 260, 261; **Supp. XIII:** 35, 76, 294, 312; **Supp. XIV:** 125, 126, 132, 269; **Supp. XV:** 123, 252, 340; **Supp. XVII:** 239; **Supp. XIX:** 82, 203; **Supp. XX: 199**

Sexual Behavior in the American Male (Kinsey), **Supp. XIII:** 96–97

Sexual Perversity in Chicago (Mamet), **Supp. XIV:** 239, 240, 246–247, 249

"Sexual Revolution, The" (Dunn), **Supp. XI:** 142

Sexus (H. Miller), **III:** 170, 171, 184, 187, 188

"Sex Without Love" (Olds), **Supp. X:** 206

"Sexy" (Lahiri), **Supp. XXI:** 183–184

Seyersted, Per E., **Retro. Supp. II:** 65; **Supp. I Part 1:** 201, 204, 211, 216, 225; **Supp. IV Part 2:** 558

Seyfried, Robin, **Supp. IX:** 324

Seymour, Corey, **Supp. XXIV:** 280

Seymour, Miranda, **Supp. VIII:** 167

"Seymour: An Introduction" (Salinger), **III:** 569–571, 572

"Shack" (L. Brown), **Supp. XXI:** 49

Shacochis, Bob, **Supp. VIII:** 80

"Shadow" (Creeley), **Supp. IV Part 1:** 158

"Shadow, The" (Lowell), **II:** 522

Shadow and Act (Ellison), **Retro. Supp. II:** 119; **Supp. II Part 1:** 245–246

"Shadow and Shade" (Tate), **IV:** 128

"Shadow and the Flesh, The" (London), **II:** 475

"Shadow A Parable" (Poe), **III:** 417–418

Shadow Country (Gunn Allen), **Supp. IV Part 1:** 322, 324, 325–326

Shadow-Line, The (Conrad), **Supp. XXV:** 217

Shadow Man, The (Gordon), **Supp. IV Part 1:** 297, 298, 299, 312–314, 315

Shadow of a Dream, The, a Story (Howells), **II:** 285, 286, 290

Shadow of a Man (Moraga), **Supp. XXIII:** 195, 197, **199–203**

"Shadow of the Crime, The: A Word from the Author" (Mailer), **Retro. Supp. II:** 214

Shadow on the Dial, The (Bierce), **I:** 208, 209

"Shadow out of Time, The" (Lovecraft), **Supp. XXV:** 111

Shadow over Innsmouth, The (Lovecraft), **Supp. XXV:** 111, 117–118, 120, 121

"Shadow Passing" (Merwin), **Supp. III Part 1:** 355

Shadowplay (C. Baxter), **Supp. XVII:** 15, 19–20

Shadows (Gardner), **Supp. VI:** 74

Shadows and Fog (film; Allen), **Supp. XV:** 11

Shadows Burning (Di Piero), **Supp. XIX:** 42, 43–44

Shadows by the Hudson (Singer), **IV:** 1

Shadows of Africa (Matthiessen), **Supp. V:** 203

Shadows on the Hudson (Singer), **Retro. Supp. II:** 311–313

Shadows on the Rock (Cather), **I:** 314, 330–331, 332; **Retro. Supp. I:** 18

"Shadows over Lovecraft: Reactionary Fantasy and Immigrant Eugenics" (Lovett-Graff), **Supp. XXV:** 123

Shadow Train (Ashbery), **Supp. III Part 1:** 23–24, 26

"Shad-Time" (Wilbur), **Supp. III Part 2:** 563

Shaffer, Thomas L., **Supp. VIII:** 127, 128

Shaft (Parks; film), **Supp. XI:** 17

Shaftesbury, Earl of, **I:** 559

Shahid, Irfan, **Supp. XX:** 113, 127

Shahn, Ben, **Supp. X:** 24

Shakedown for Murder (Lacy), **Supp. XV:** 203

Shakelford, Dean, **Supp. VIII:** 129

Shaker, Why Don't You Sing? (Angelou), **Supp. IV Part 1:** 16

Shakespear, Mrs. Olivia, **III:** 457; **Supp. I Part 1:** 257

"Shakespeare" (Emerson), **II:** 6

"Shakespeare" (Very), **Supp. XXV:** 244

Shakespeare, William, **I:** 103, 271, 272, 284–285, 358, 378, 433, 441, 458, 461, 573, 585, 586; **II:** 5, 8, 11, 18, 72, 273, 297, 302, 309, 320, 411, 494, 577, 590; **III:** 3, 11, 12, 82, 83, 91, 124, 130, 134, 145, 153, 159, 183, 210, 263, 286, 468, 473, 492, 503, 511, 567, 575–576, 577, 610, 612, 613, 615; **IV:** 11, 50, 66, 127, 132, 156, 309, 313, 362, 368, 370, 373, 453; **Retro. Supp. I:** 43, 64, 91, 248; **Retro. Supp. II:** 114, 299; **Supp. I Part 1:** 79, 150, 262, 310, 356, 363, 365, 368, 369, 370; **Supp. I Part 2:** 397, 421, 422, 470, 494, 622, 716, 720; **Supp. II Part 2:** 624, 626; **Supp.**

IV Part 1: 31, 83, 87, 243; **Supp. IV Part 2:** 430, 463, 519, 688; **Supp. V:** 252, 280, 303; **Supp. VIII:** 160, 164; **Supp. IX:** 14, 133; **Supp. X:** 42, 62, 65, 78; **Supp. XII:** 54–57, 277, 281; **Supp. XIII:** 111, 115, 233; **Supp. XIV:** 97, 120, 225, 245, 306; **Supp. XV:** 92; **Supp. XVIII:** 278; **Supp. XXII:** 206; **Supp. XXIV:** 33, 34, 40, 87, 159

Shakespeare and His Forerunners (Lanier), **Supp. I Part 1:** 369

Shakespeare in Harlem (Hughes), **Retro. Supp. I:** 194, 202, 205, 206, 207, 208; **Supp. I Part 1:** 333, 334, 345

Shalit, Gene, **Supp. VIII:** 73

Shalit, Wendy, **Supp. XX:** **179, 182, 186**

Shall We Gather at the River (Wright), **Supp. III Part 2:** 601–602; **Supp. XVII:** 241

"Shame" (Oates), **Supp. II Part 2:** 520

"Shame" (Wilbur), **Supp. III Part 2:** 556

"Shame and Forgetting in the Information Age" (C. Baxter), **Supp. XVII:** 21

"Shameful Affair, A" (Chopin), **Retro. Supp. II:** 61

Shamela (Fielding), **Supp. V:** 127

"Shampoo, The" (Bishop), **Retro. Supp. II:** 46; **Supp. I Part 1:** 92

Shange, Ntozake, **Supp. VIII:** 214; **Supp. XVII:** 70; **Supp. XVIII:** 172; **Supp. XXI:** 172

Shank, Randy, **Supp. X:** 252

Shankaracharya, **III:** 567

Shanley, John Patrick, **Supp. XIV:** 315–332

Shannon, Sandra, **Supp. VIII:** 333, 348

"Shape of Flesh and Bone, The" (MacLeish), **III:** 18–19

Shape of Me and Other Stuff, The (Geisel), **Supp. XVI:** 111

Shape of the Journey, The (Harrison), **Supp. VIII:** 53

Shapes of Clay (Bierce), **I:** 208, 209

Shaping Joy, A: Studies in the Writer's Craft (Brooks), **Supp. XIV:** 13

Shapiro, Alan, **Supp. XXIV:** 157

Shapiro, Charles, **Supp. XIX:** 257, 259–260

Shapiro, David, **Supp. XII:** 175, 185; **Supp. XXIV:** 34

Shapiro, Dorothy, **IV:** 380

Shapiro, Edward S., **Supp. XXV:** 253

Shapiro, Karl, **I:** 430, 521; **II:** 350; **III:** 527; **Supp. II Part 2:** **701–724;** **Supp. III Part 2:** 623; **Supp. IV Part 2:** 645; **Supp. X:** 116; **Supp. XI:** 315; **Supp. XIX:** 117, 118, 119; **Supp. XXI:** 98; **Supp. XXV:** 30

Shapiro, Laura, **Supp. IX:** 120; **Supp. XX:** **87, 89**

"Shared Patio, The" (July), **Supp. XXIV:** 201, 202

Sharif, Omar, **Supp. IX:** 253

"Shark Meat" (Snyder), **Supp. VIII:** 300

Shatayev, Elvira, **Supp. I Part 2:** 570

Shaviro, Steven, **Supp. VIII:** 189

Shaw, Chris, **Supp. XXIII:** 155–156

Shaw, Colonel Robert Gould, **II:** 551

Shaw, Elizabeth. *See* Melville, Mrs. Herman (Elizabeth Shaw)

Shaw, George Bernard, **I:** 226; **II:** 82, 271, 276, 581; **III:** 69, 102, 113, 145, 155, 161, 162, 163, 373, 409; **IV:** 27, 64, 397, 432, 440; **Retro. Supp. I:** 100, 228; **Supp. IV Part 1:** 36; **Supp. IV Part 2:** 585, 683; **Supp. V:** 243–244, 290; **Supp. IX:** 68, 308; **Supp. XI:** 202; **Supp. XII:** 94; **Supp. XIV:** 343; **Supp. XVII:** 100; **Supp. XXIV:** 33, 34

Shaw, Irwin, **IV:** 381; **Supp. IV Part 1:** 383; **Supp. IX:** 251; **Supp. XI:** 221, 229, 231; **Supp. XIX:** **239–254**

Shaw, Joseph Thompson ("Cap"), **Supp. IV Part 1:** 121, 345, 351; **Supp. XIII:** 161

Shaw, Judge Lemuel, **III:** 77, 88, 91

Shaw, Lytle, **Supp. XXIII:** 208; **Supp. XXIV:** 44

Shaw, Peter, **Supp. XVI:** 70

Shaw, Robert B., **Supp. XXIII:** 112

Shaw, Sarah Bryant, **Supp. I Part 1:** 169

Shaw, Wilbur, Jr., **Supp. XIII:** 162

Shawl, The (Mamet), **Supp. XIV:** 245

Shawl, The (Ozick), **Supp. V:** 257, 260, 271

"Shawl, The" (Ozick), **Supp. V:** 271–272

Shawl and Prarie du Chien, The: Two Plays (Mamet), **Supp. XIV:** 243–244

Shawn, William, **Supp. VIII:** 151, 170

"Shawshank Redemption, The" (King), **Supp. V:** 148

She (Haggard), **III:** 189

Shea, Renee, **Supp. XXIII:** 85, 86, 90, 95

Sheaffer, Louis, **Supp. XXI:** 6

Shearer, Flora, **I:** 199

"Sheaves, The" (Robinson), **III:** 510, 524

"She Came and Went" (Lowell), **Supp. I Part 2:** 409

"She-Devil" (Nelson), **Supp. XVIII:** 178

She-Devil Circus (Nelson), **Supp. XVIII:** 176, **178**

Sheed, Wilfrid, **IV:** 230; **Supp. XI:** 233; **Supp. XXI:** 233

Sheeler, Charles, **IV:** 409; **Retro. Supp. I:** 430

"Sheep Child" (B. Kelly), **Supp. XVII:** 131–132

"Sheep Child, The" (Dickey), **Supp. XVII:** 131–132

Sheeper (Rosenthal), **Supp. XIV:** 147

Sheffer, Jonathan, **Supp. IV Part 1:** 95

She Had Some Horses (Harjo), **Supp. XII:** **220–223,** 231

"She Had Some Horses" (Harjo), **Supp. XII:** 215, 222

"Shell, The" (Humphrey), **Supp. IX:** 94

Shelley, Mary, **Supp. XX:** **108**

Shelley, Percy Bysshe, **I:** 18, 68, 381, 476, 522, 577; **II:** 331, 516, 535, 540; **III:** 412, 426, 469; **IV:** 139; **Retro. Supp. I:** 308, 360; **Supp. I Part 1:** 79, 311, 349; **Supp. I Part 2:** 709, 718, 719, 720, 721, 722, 724, 728; **Supp. IV Part 1:** 235; **Supp. V:** 258, 280; **Supp. IX:** 51; **Supp. XII:** 117, 132, 136–137, 263; **Supp. XIV:** 271–

272; **Supp. XV:** 92, 175, 182; **Supp. XX:** 115; **Supp. XXI:** 131

Shellow, Sadie Myers, **Supp. I Part 2:** 608

Shelnut, Blevin, **Supp. XXV:** 36

"Shelter" (C. Baxter), **Supp. XVII:** 19

"Shelter" (Doty), **Supp. XI:** 132

Sheltered Life, The (Glasgow), **II:** 174, 175, 179, 186, 187–188

Sheltering Sky, The (Bowles), **Supp. IV Part 1:** 82, 84, 85–86, 87

Sheltering Sky, The (film), **Supp. IV Part 1:** 94, 95

Shelton, Frank, **Supp. IV Part 2:** 658

Shelton, Richard, **Supp. XI:** 133; **Supp. XIII:** 7

Shelton, Robert, **Supp. XVIII:** 20, 21, 22, 23, 24, 25, 26

Shelton, Mrs. Sarah. *See* Royster, Sarah Elmira

Shenandoah (Schwartz), **Supp. II Part 2:** 640, 651–652

"Shenandoah" (Shapiro), **Supp. II Part 2:** 704

Shepard, Alice, **IV:** 287

Shepard, Gregory, **Supp. XXII:** 119

Shepard, Harvey, **Supp. XVII:** 240

Shepard, Jim, **Supp. XXI:** 115

Shepard, Odell, **II:** 508; **Supp. I Part 2:** 418

Shepard, Richard F., **Supp. XXIV:** 216

Shepard, Sam, **Supp. III Part 2: 431– 450; Supp. XVIII:** 21, 28, 31; **Supp. XXI:** 144, 145

Shepard, Thomas, **I:** 554; **IV:** 158

"Shepherd of Resumed Desire, The" (Wright), **Supp. XV:** 349

Sheppard Lee (Bird), **III:** 423

"She Remembers the Future" (Harjo), **Supp. XII:** 222

Sheridan, Richard Brinsley, **Retro. Supp. I:** 127

Sherlock, William, **IV:** 152

Sherman, Joe, **Supp. XXII:** 205

Sherman, Sarah Way, **Retro. Supp. II:** 145

Sherman, Stuart Pratt, **I:** 222, 246–247; **Supp. I Part 2:** 423

Sherman, Susan, **Supp. VIII:** 265

Sherman, Tom, **IV:** 446

Sherman, William T., **IV:** 445, 446

Sherry, Denver William, **Supp. XXII:** 190

Sherwood, Robert, **II:** 435; **Supp. IX:** 190

Sherwood Anderson & Other Famous Creoles (Faulkner), **I:** 117; **II:** 56

Sherwood Anderson Reader, The (Anderson), **I:** 114, 116

Sherwood Anderson's Memoirs (Anderson), **I:** 98, 101, 102, 103, 108, 112, 116

Sherwood Anderson's Notebook (Anderson), **I:** 108, 115, 117

"She Sings" (Taggard), **Supp. XXII:** 272

She Stoops to Conquer (Goldsmith), **II:** 514

Shestov, Lev, **Supp. VIII:** 20, 24

Shetley, Vernon, **Supp. IX:** 292; **Supp. XI:** 123

"She Wept, She Railed" (Kunitz), **Supp. III Part 1:** 265

"Shiddah and Kuziba" (Singer), **IV:** 13, 15

Shidyak, Paris al-, **Supp. XX:** 117

Shield of Achilles, The (Auden), **Supp. II Part 1:** 21

"Shield of Achilles, The" (Auden), **Supp. II Part 1:** 21, 25

Shields, Carol, **Supp. VII: 307–330**

Shields, John C., **Supp. XX: 279, 280, 281, 286**

Shifting Landscape: A Composite, 1925– 1987 (H. Roth), **Supp. IX: 233–235**

Shifts of Being (Eberhart), **I:** 525

Shigematsu, Soiko, **Supp. III Part 1:** 353

Shihab, Aziz, **Supp. XIII:** 273

Shih-hsiang Chen, **Supp. VIII:** 303

Shiksa Goddess; or, How I Spent My Forties (Wasserstein), **Supp. XV:** 319, 320, 325, 332, 333

"Shiloh" (Mason), **Supp. VIII:** 140

Shiloh and Other Stories (Mason), **Supp. VIII:** 133, **139–141,** 143, 145

Shilts, Randy, **Supp. X:** 145

Shimmering Verge, The (one-woman show, Peacock), **Supp. XIX:** 194, **204–205**

Shining, The (King), **Supp. V:** 139, 140, 141, 143–144, 146, 149, 151, 152

"Shining Ones, The" (P. N. Warren), **Supp. XX: 272**

Shining Victory (film, Rapper), **Supp. XVII:** 60

Shinn, Everett, **Retro. Supp. II:** 103

Shi Pei Pu, **Supp. XXI:** 152, 153, 154

"Ship in a Bottle"(Strout), **Supp. XXIII:** 283

"Ship of Death" (Lawrence), **Supp. I Part 2:** 728

Ship of Fools (Porter), **III:** 433, 447, 453, 454; **IV:** 138

Shipping News, The (Proulx), **Supp. VII:** 249, 258–259

"Ships" (O. Henry), **Supp. II Part 1:** 409

Ships Going into the Blue: Essays and Notes on Poetry (Simpson), **Supp. IX:** 275

Ship to America, A (Singer), **IV:** 1

"Shipwreck, The" (Merwin), **Supp. III Part 1:** 346

Shirley, John, **Supp. XVI:** 123, 128

"Shirt" (Pinsky), **Supp. VI: 236–237,** 239, 240, 241, 245, 247

"Shirt Poem, The" (Stern), **Supp. IX:** 292

"Shirts, The" (Gallagher), **Supp. XXIV:** 169

"Shirts of a Single Color" (Ryan), **Supp. XVIII:** 227

"Shiva and Parvati Hiding in the Rain" (Pinsky), **Supp. VI:** 244

Shively, Charley, **Retro. Supp. I:** 391; **Supp. XII:** 181, 182

Shnayerson, Michael, **Supp. XIX:** 248

"Shock of Good Poetry, The"(Hirshfield), **Supp. XXIII:** 136

Shock of Recognition, The (Wilson), **II:** 530

Shock of the New, The (Hughes), **Supp. X:** 73

Shoe Bird, The (Welty), **IV:** 261; **Retro. Supp. I:** 353

Shoemaker of Dreams (Ferragammo), **Supp. XVI:** 192

"Shoes" (O. Henry), **Supp. II Part 1:** 409

"Shoes of Wandering, The" (Kinnell), **Supp. III Part 1:** 248

Sholem Asch: Zayn levn un zayne verk (Sholem Asch: His life and his work), **Supp. XXIII:** 6

Sholl, Betsy, **Supp. XXI:** 129, 131

"Shooters, Inc." (Didion), **Supp. IV Part 1:** 207, 211

"Shooting, The" (Dubus), **Supp. VII:** 84, 85

"Shooting Niagara; and After?" (Carlyle), **Retro. Supp. I:** 408

"Shooting of the Red Eagle" (Zitkala-Ša), **Supp. XXV:** 275

"Shooting Script" (Rich), **Supp. I Part 2:** 558; **Supp. IV Part 1:** 257

Shooting Star, A (Stegner), **Supp. IV Part 2:** 599, 608–609

"Shooting the Works" (Di Piero), **Supp. XIX:** 41–42

Shooting the Works: On Poetry and Pictures (Di Piero), **Supp. XIX: 41–42**

"Shooting Whales" (Strand), **Supp. IV Part 2:** 630

"Shopgirls" (F. Barthelme), **Supp. XI:** 26, 27, 33, 36

Shopping for Joe (O'Hara and Steven Rivers), **Supp. XXIII:** 217

"Shopping with Bob Berwick" (Halliday), **Supp. XIX:** 88

Shop Talk (P. Roth), **Retro. Supp. II:** 282

Shoptaw, John, **Supp. IV Part 1:** 247

Shore Acres (Herne), **Supp. II Part 1:** 198

Shorebirds of North America, The (Matthiessen), **Supp. V:** 204

"Shore House, The" (Jewett), **II:** 397

Shore Leave (Wakeman), **Supp. IX:** 247

"Shoreline Horses" (Ríos), **Supp. IV Part 2:** 553

"Shoreline Life" (Skloot), **Supp. XX: 201**

Shores of Light, The: A Literary Chronicle of the Twenties and Thirties (Wilson), **IV:** 432, 433

Shorey, Paul, **III:** 606

Short Account of the Destruction of the Indies, A (Las Casas), **Supp. XXIV:** 87

Short and the Long of It, The (Kenny), **Supp. XXIII:** 155–156

Short Cuts (film, Altman), **Supp. IX:** 143; **Supp. XXIV:** 166, 172, 178

"Short End, The" (Hecht), **Supp. X:** 65

"Shorter View, The" (X. J. Kennedy), **Supp. XV:** 160, 168

Short Fiction of Norman Mailer, The (Mailer), **Retro. Supp. II:** 205

Short Friday and Other Stories (Singer), **IV:** 14–16

Short Guide to a Happy Life, A (Quindlen), **Supp. XVII:** 167, 179

"Short Happy Life of Francis Macomber, The" (Hemingway), **II:** 250, 263–264; **Retro. Supp. I:** 182; **Supp. IV Part**

1: 48; **Supp. IX:** 106

Short Night, The (Turner), **Supp. XV:** 201

Short Novels of Thomas Wolfe, The (Wolfe), **IV:** 456

Short Poems (Berryman), **I:** 170

"SHORT SPEECH TO MY FRIENDS" (Baraka), **Supp. II Part 1:** 35

Short Stories (Rawlings), **Supp. X:** 224

Short Stories: Five Decades (Shaw), **Supp. XIX:** 252–253

"Short Story, The" (Welty), **IV:** 279

Short Story Masterpieces, **Supp. IX:** 4

Short Studies of American Authors (Higginson), **I:** 455

"Short-timer's Calendar" (Komunyakaa), **Supp. XIII:** 125

Shosha (Singer), **Retro. Supp. II:** 313–314

Shostak, Debra, **Supp. XXIV:** 136

Shostakovich, Dimitri, **IV:** 75; **Supp. VIII:** 21

Shot of Love (album, Dylan), **Supp. XVIII:** 28

"Shots" (Ozick), **Supp. V:** 268

Shotts, Jeffrey, **Supp. XV:** 103, 104

"Should Wizard Hit Mommy?" (Updike), **IV:** 221, 222, 224; **Retro. Supp. I:** 335

Shoup, Barbara, **Supp. XV:** 55, 59, 62, 69

"Shoveling Snow with Buddha" (Collins), **Supp. XXI:** 60

"Shovel Man, The" (Sandburg), **III:** 553

Showalter, Elaine, **Retro. Supp. I:** 368; **Supp. IV Part 2:** 440, 441, 444; **Supp. X:** 97; **Supp. XVI:** 80, 92; **Supp. XX:** 274; **Supp. XXIV:** 28

"Shower of Gold" (Welty), **IV:** 271–272

Shribman, David M., **Supp. XXII:** 205, 218

"Shrike and the Chipmunks, The" (Thurber), **Supp. I Part 2:** 617

Shrimp Girl (Hogarth), **Supp. XII:** 44

"Shrine and the Burning Wheel, The" (Jarman), **Supp. XVII:** 116

"Shrine with Flowers" (Di Piero), **Supp. XIX:** 43, 44

"Shriveled Meditation" (X. J. Kennedy), **Supp. XV:** 170

Shropshire Lad, A (Housman), **Supp. XV:** 41

"Shrouded Stranger, The" (Ginsberg), **Supp. II Part 1:** 312

"Shroud of Color, The" (Cullen), **Supp. IV Part 1:** 166, 168, 170, 171

Shrunken Head of Pancho Villa, The (Valdez), **Supp. XXIII:** 203

Shtetl (film; Marzynski), **Supp. XVI:** 153

Shtetl: The Life and Death of a Small Town and the World of Polish Jews (E. Hoffman), **Supp. XVI:** 152, 153–155

Shue, Elizabeth, **Supp. XXIII:** 276

Shuffle (L. Michaels), **Supp. XVI:** 202, 203, 213

Shuffle Along (musical), **Supp. I Part 1:** 322; **Supp. X:** 136

Shultz, George, **Supp. IV Part 1:** 234

Shuman, R. Baird, **Supp. XXV:** 96

Shurr, William, **Retro. Supp. I:** 43

Shuster, Joel, **Supp. XI:** 67

Shusterman, Richard, **Retro. Supp. I:** 53

"Shut a Final Door" (Capote), **Supp. III Part 1:** 117, 120, 124

Shut Up, He Explained (Lardner), **II:** 432

Shylock's Daughter: A Novel of Love in Venice (Serenissima) (Jong), **Supp. V:** 115, 127, 128–129

Siamanto (Atom Yarjanian), **Supp. XXIII:** 28

"Siasconset: How It Arose and What It Is" (Briggs), **Supp. XVIII:** 9

Siberian Village, The (Dove), **Supp. IV Part 1:** 255, 256

Sibley, Celestine, **Supp. XXII:** 194, 199

Sibley, Mulford Q., **Supp. I Part 2:** 524

"Sibling Mysteries" (Rich), **Supp. I Part 2:** 574

Siblings (Quindlen and Kelsh), **Supp. XVII:** 167, 179

Siblings in Paradise (or Moscow when It Sizzles) (Silver), **Supp. XXIV:** 265

Sibon, Marcelle, **IV:** 288

"Sicilian Emigrant's Song" (W. C. Williams), **Retro. Supp. I:** 413

Sicilian Miniatures (Sobin), **Supp. XVI:** 288

"Sick Wife, The" (Kenyon), **Supp. VII:** 173, 174

"'Sic transit gloria mundi'" (Dickinson), **Retro. Supp. I:** 30

Sid Caesar Show (television show), **Supp. IV Part 2:** 575

Siddons, Anne Rivers, **Supp. XXII:** 239–254

Siddons, Sarah, **II:** 298

Side Effects (Allen), **Supp. XV:** 3, 14, 15–16

Side of Paradise, This (Fitgerald), **Supp. IX:** 56

Sidnee Poet Heroical, The (Baraka), **Supp. II Part 1:** 55

Sidney, Algernon, **II:** 114

Sidney, Mary, **Supp. I Part 1:** 98

Sidney, Philip, **II:** 470; **Supp. I Part 1:** 98, 111, 117–118, 122; **Supp. I Part 2:** 658; **Supp. II Part 1:** 104–105; **Supp. V:** 250; **Supp. XII:** 264; **Supp. XIV:** 128

Sidney, Sylvia, **Supp. I Part 1:** 67

Sidney Lanier: A Bibliographical and Critical Study (Starke), **Supp. I Part 1:** 371

Sidney Lanier: A Biographical and Critical Study (Starke), **Supp. I Part 1:** 371

Siebert, Kathy, **Supp. XX:** 84

Siege (Shaw), **Supp. XIX:** 244

Siegel, Barry, **Supp. XIV:** 82

Siegel, Ben, **Supp. XXIII:** 3, 4, 10, 11, 12, 14, 16

Siegel, Catherine, **Supp. XII:** 126

Siegel, Jerry, **Supp. XI:** 67

Siegel, Lee, **Supp. XXII:** 255–269; **Supp. XXV:** 56

"Siege of London, The" (James), **Retro. Supp. I:** 227

Siegle, Robert, **Supp. XII:** 8

Sienkiewicz, Henryk, **Supp. IV Part 2:** 518; **Supp. XVI:** 182

"Sierra Kid" (Levine), **Supp. V:** 180–181

Sigal, Clancy, **Supp. XXI:** 44; **Supp. XXIII:** 166

Sigg, Eric, **Retro. Supp. I:** 53

"Sight" (Merwin), **Supp. III Part 1:** 356

Sighted Singer, The (Halliday), **Supp. XIX:** 82, 86–87

"Sight in Camp in the Daybreak Gray and Dim, A" (Whitman), **II:** 373

Sights and Spectacles (McCarthy), **II:** 562

"Sights from a Steeple" (Hawthorne), **Retro. Supp. I:** 62; **Supp. XXI:** 201

Sights Unseen (Gibbons), **Supp. X:** 49–50

Sight Unseen and the Confession (Rinehart), **Supp. XXV:** 195, 200

"Signals" (Carver), **Supp. III Part 1:** 143

"Signature for Tempo" (MacLeish), **III:** 8–9

"Signed Confession of Crimes against the State" (Merton), **Supp. VIII:** 201

Signifying Monkey, The (Hughes), **Retro. Supp. I:** 195

Signifying Monkey, The: A Theory of Afro-American Literary Criticism (H. L. Gates), **Supp. X:** 243; **Supp. XX:** 99, 106–107

"Signing, The (Dixon), **Supp. XII:** 146

Sign in Sidney Brustein's Window, The (Hansberry), **Supp. IV Part 1:** 359, 365, 369, 370–372

Sign of Jonas, The (Merton), **Supp. VIII:** 194–195, 195, 197, 200, 206, 207

"Sign of Saturn, The" (Olds), **Supp. X:** 206

"Signs, Oakvale, Mississippi, 1941" (Trethewey), **Supp. XXI:** 248–249

Signs and Wonders (Bukiet), **Supp. XVII:** 45–46

Sigourney, Lydia, **Supp. I Part 2:** 684

Sikora, Malgorzata, **Retro. Supp. II:** 324

Silas Marner (G. Eliot), **II:** 26

Silberg, Richard, **Supp. XV:** 116

Silberman, James, **Supp. XXIV:** 288

"Silence" (Moore), **III:** 212

"Silence" (Poe), **III:** 416

"Silence" (Sanders), **Supp. XVI:** 278

"Silence, A" (Clampitt), **Supp. IX:** 53

"Silence—A Fable" (Poe), **III:** 416

Silence and Metaphor (Bronk), **Supp. XXI:** 31, 32

"Silence Before Harvest, The" (Merwin), **Supp. III Part 1:** 352

Silence Dogood Papers, The (Franklin), **II:** 106–107

Silence in the Snowy Fields (R. Bly), **Supp. IV Part 1:** 60–61, 62, 63, 65, 66, 72; **Supp. XXI:** 84, 85

Silence of History, The (Farrell), **II:** 46–47

Silence of the Lambs, The (T. Harris), **Supp. XXI:** 78

Silence Opens, A (Clampitt), **Supp. IX:** 53

Silences (Olsen), **Supp. XIII:** 293, 294, 295, 296, 304–306

"Silences: When Writers Don't Write" (Olsen), **Supp. XIII:** 294

Silencing the Past: Power and the Production of History (Trouillot), **Supp. X:** 14
"Silent in America" (Levine), **Supp. V:** 183
Silent Life, The (Merton), **Supp. VIII:** 208
Silent Partner, The (Odets), **Supp. II Part 2:** 539
"Silent Poem" (Francis), **Supp. IX:** 86
"Silent Season of a Hero, The" (Talese), **Supp. XVII:** 203–204
"Silent Slain, The" (MacLeish), **III:** 9
"Silent Snow, Secret Snow" (Aiken), **I:** 52
Silent Spring (Carson), **Supp. V:** 202; **Supp. IX:** 19, 24, **31–34; Supp. XIV:** 177; **Supp. XVI:** 36; **Supp. XVIII:** 189
Silhouettes of American Life (R. H. Davis), **Supp. XVI:** 85
"Silken Tent, The" (Frost), **Retro. Supp. I:** 138–139; **Supp. IV Part 2:** 448
Silko, Leslie Marmon, **Supp. IV Part 1:** 274, 319, 325, 333–334, 335, 404; **Supp. IV Part 2:** 499, 505, **557–572; Supp. V:** 169; **Supp. XI:** 18; **Supp. XII:** 217; **Supp. XVIII:** 58
Silliman, Ron, **Supp. IV Part 2:** 426; **Supp. XV:** 344; **Supp. XVII:** 70, 77
Silliman's Blog (R. Silliman), **Supp. XVII:** 70
Silman, Roberta, **Supp. X:** 6
Silver, Nicky, **Supp. XXIV:** 128, **263–277**
Silverblatt, Michael, **Supp. XV:** 224
"Silver Crown, The" (Malamud), **Supp. I Part 2:** 434–435, 437; **Supp. V:** 266
"Silver Dish, The" (Bellow), **Retro. Supp. II:** 30
"Silver Filigree" (Wylie), **Supp. I Part 2:** 707
"Silver Key, The" (Lovecraft), **Supp. XXV:** 114
"Silver Lake" (B. Kelly), **Supp. XVII:** 130
Silverman, Joseph, **Supp. XXIII:** 8
Silvers, Phil, **Supp. IV Part 2:** 574
Silverthorne, Elizabeth, **Supp. X:** 220, 221, 222, 226, 234
"Silver To Have and to Hurl" (Didion), **Supp. IV Part 1:** 197
Simic, Charles, **Supp. V:** 5, 332; **Supp. VIII:** 39, **269–287; Supp. XI:** 317; **Supp. XV:** 179, 185; **Supp. XIX:** 277, 282
"Similar Cases" (Gilman), **Supp. XI:** 200, 202
Similitudes, from the Ocean and Prairie (Larcom), **Supp. XIII:** 141
Simmel, Georg, **Supp. I Part 2:** 644; **Supp. XVII:** 98
Simmons, Charles, **Supp. XI:** 230
Simmons, David, **Supp. XXV:** 123
Simmons, Maggie, **Retro. Supp. II:** 21
Simms, Michael, **Supp. XII:** 184
Simms, William Gilmore, **I:** 211
Simon, Greg, **Supp. XXIV:** 166
Simon, John, **Supp. IV Part 2:** 691

Simon, Neil, **Supp. IV Part 2: 573–594; Supp. XVII:** 8
Simone, Nina, **Supp. XXI:** 243
"Simon Gerty" (Wylie), **Supp. I Part 2:** 713
Simonides, **Supp. XII:** 110–111
"Simon Ortiz" (Gingerich), **Supp. IV Part 2:** 510
Simon Ortiz (Wiget), **Supp. IV Part 2:** 509
Simonson, Lee, **III:** 396; **Supp. XXI:** 6
"Simple" (Peacock), **Supp. XIX:** 200
"Simple Art of Murder, The" (Chandler), **Supp. IV Part 1:** 121, 341
"Simple Autumnal" (Bogan), **Supp. III Part 1:** 52–53
Simple Heart (Flaubert), **I:** 504
Simple Honorable Man, A (Richter), **Supp. XVIII:** 208, 218, **219,** 220
"Simple Purchase, A" (Peacock), **Supp. XIX:** 199
Simple Speaks his Mind (Hughes), **Retro. Supp. I:** 209; **Supp. I Part 1:** 337
Simple Stakes a Claim (Hughes), **Retro. Supp. I:** 209; **Supp. I Part 1:** 337
Simple's Uncle Sam (Hughes), **Retro. Supp. I:** 209; **Supp. I Part 1:** 337
Simple Takes a Wife (Hughes), **Retro. Supp. I:** 209; **Supp. I Part 1:** 337
Simple Truth, The (Hardwick), **Supp. III Part 1:** 199, 200, 208
Simple Truth, The (Levine), **Supp. V:** 178, 179, 193–194
"Simple Widsom, The" (Skloot), **Supp. XX: 207**
"Simplicity" (Sanders), **Supp. XVI:** 276
Simply, Trixi, **Supp. XXV:** 2
Simply Heavenly (Hughes), **Retro. Supp. I:** 209; **Supp. I Part 1:** 338, 339
Simpson, Louis, **Supp. III Part 2:** 541; **Supp. IV Part 2:** 448, 621; **Supp. VIII:** 39, 279; **Supp. IX: 265–283,** 290; **Supp. XI:** 317; **Supp. XII:** 130; **Supp. XIII:** 337
Simpson, Mona, **Supp. XVI:** 206
"Sin" (C. Frost), **Supp. XV:** 96
Sinatra, Frank, **Supp. IX:** 3; **Supp. X:** 119; **Supp. XI:** 213
Sincere Convert, The (Shepard), **IV:** 158
Sincerely, Willis Wayde (Marquand), **III:** 61, 63, 66, 67–68, 69
Sincerity (Rowson), **Supp. XV:** 242
Sincerity and Authenticity (Trilling), **Supp. III Part 2:** 510–512
"Sincerity and Objectification: With Special Reference to the Work of Charles Reznikoff" (Zukofsky), **Supp. XIV:** 286
Sinclair, Mary Craig (Mary Craig Kimbrough), **Supp. V:** 275, 286, 287
Sinclair, Upton, **II:** 34, 440, 444, 451; **III:** 580; **Retro. Supp. II:** 95; **Supp. V: 275–293; Supp. VIII:** 11
Sinclair Lewis: An American Life (Schorer), **II:** 459
"Sine Qua Non" (Stallings), **Supp. XXV:** 232
"Singapore" (Oliver), **Supp. VII:** 239, 240
Singer, Bennett L., **Supp. IV Part 1:** 330

Singer, Beth, **Supp. XIV:** 203
Singer, Isaac Bashevis, **I:** 144; **IV: 1–24; Retro. Supp. II:** 22, **299–320; Supp. IX:** 114; **Supp. XVIII:** 215, 220; **Supp. XXI:** 106; **Supp. XXII:** 258
Singer, Israel Joshua, **IV:** 2, 16, 17; **Retro. Supp. II:** 302; **Supp. XVII:** 41
Singer, Joshua, **IV:** 4
Singer, Rabbi Pinchos Menachem, **IV:** 16
Singin' and Swingin' and Gettin' Merry Like Christmas (Angelou), **Supp. IV Part 1:** 2, 5, 6–7, 9, 13, 14
"Singing & Doubling Together" (Ammons), **Supp. VII:** 34–35
Singing Jailbirds (Sinclair), **Supp. V:** 277
"Singing the Black Mother" (Lupton), **Supp. IV Part 1:** 7
Single Hound, The (Sarton), **Supp. VIII:** 251, 265
Single Hound, The: Poems of a Lifetime (Dickinson; Bianchi, ed.), **Retro. Supp. I:** 35
Single Man, A (Isherwood), **Supp. XIV:** 157, 164, **169–170,** 171
"Single Sonnet" (Bogan), **Supp. III Part 1:** 56–58
Singley, Carol, **Retro. Supp. I:** 373
Singular Family, A: Rosacoke and Her Kin (Price), **Supp. VI: 258–259,** 260
"Singular First Person, The" (Sanders), **Supp. XVI:** 274
Singularities (Howe), **Supp. IV Part 2:** 431
Sin in Their Blood (Lacy), **Supp. XV:** 200
"Sinister Adolescents, The" (Dos Passos), **I:** 493
Sinister Street (Mackenzie), **II:** 82
Sinking of Clay City, The (Wrigley), **Supp. XVIII: 294–295**
Sinners in the Hands of an Angry God (Edwards), **I:** 546, 552–553, 559, 562; **Supp. XXIV:** 72
Sinning with Annie, and Other Stories (Theroux), **Supp. VIII:** 318
"Sins of Kalamazoo, The" (Sandburg), **III:** 586
Sintram and His Companions (La Motte-Fouqué), **III:** 78
"Siope" (Poe), **III:** 411
"Sioux Woman's Love for Her Grandchild, A" (Zitkala-Ša), **Supp. XXV:** 281
"Sipapu: A Cultural Perspective" (Gunn Allen), **Supp. IV Part 1:** 323
Sipchen, Bob, **Supp. X:** 145
Sipper, Ralph B., **Supp. IV Part 2:** 475
"Sire" (Cisneros), **Supp. VII:** 62–63, 64
"Siren and Signal" (Zukofsky), **Supp. III Part 2:** 611, 612
Sirens of Titan, The (Vonnegut), **Supp. II Part 2:** 757, 758, 760, 765–767
"Sir Galahad" (Tennyson), **Supp. I Part 2:** 410
Sirin, V. (pseudonym), **Retro. Supp. I:** 266. *See also* Nabokov, Vladimir
Sirlin, Jerome, **Supp. XXI:** 147
Sir Vadia's Shadow: A Friendship across Five Continents (Theroux), **Supp.**

VIII: 309, 314, 321, 325
"Sir William's Reply to Molly"(Kenny), **Supp. XXIII:** 153
"Sis" (F. Barthelme), **Supp. XI:** 26
"S is for Sad" (M. F. K. Fisher), **Supp. XVII:** 86
Sisley, Alfred, **I:** 478
Sissman, L. E., **Supp. X:** 69
"Sister" (Hughes), **Retro. Supp. I:** 208
"Sister" (Lamott), **Supp. XX:** 142
"Sister, The" (July), **Supp. XXIV:** 202
Sister Age (M. F. K. Fisher), **Supp. XVII:** 88, 91
Sister Carrie (Dreiser), **I:** 482, 497, 499, 500, 501–502, 503–504, 505, 506, 515, 519; **III:** 327; **IV:** 208; **Retro. Supp. I:** 376; **Retro. Supp. II:** 93, **96–99; Supp. XVIII:** 76, 243; **Supp. XXIII:** 165; **Supp. XXV:** 129
Sister Mary Ignatius Explains It All for You (Durang), **Supp. XXIV:** 114, **119–120**
"Sister of the Minotaur" (Stevens), **IV:** 89; **Supp. IX:** 332
"Sisters" (Boulton), **Supp. XXII:** 20
"Sisters" (Nelson), **Supp. XVIII:** 176
"Sisters, The" (Whittier), **Supp. I Part 2:** 696
Sister's Choice (Showalter), **Retro. Supp. I:** 368
Sisters-in-Law, The (Atherton), **Supp. XXIV:** 25
Sisters of the Earth: Women's Prose and Poetry About Nature (Anderson, ed.), **Supp. XVIII:** 189
Sisters Rosensweig, The (Wasserstein), **Supp. XV:** 320, **328–330**
"Sisyphus" (Kumin), **Supp. IV Part 2:** 443, 444, 451
"Sitalkas" (Doolittle), **Supp. I Part 1:** 266
"Sites of Memory" (Cliff), **Supp. XXII:** 69, 74
Sitney, P. Adams, **Supp. XII:** 2
Sitting Bull, **Supp. IV Part 2:** 492
"Sitting in a Rocking Chair Going Blind" (Komunyakaa), **Supp. XIII:** 114
Sitting In: Selected Writings on Jazz, Blues, and Related Topics (Carruth), **Supp. XVI:** 46
"Sitting Up Late with My Father, 1977" (F. Wright), **Supp. XVII:** 247
Sitti's Secrets (Nye), **Supp. XIII:** 278
Situation Normal (A. Miller), **III:** 148, 149, 156, 164
Situation of Poetry, The: Contemporary Poetry and Its Traditions (Pinsky), **Supp. VI: 237–238,** 239, 241, 242
Sitwell, Edith, **IV:** 77; **Supp. I Part 1:** 271
6 A.M. (Bodenheim), **Supp. XXV:** 27
"Six Brothers" (Cisneros), **Supp. VII:** 67
Six Characters in Search of an Author (Pirandello), **Supp. IV Part 2:** 576
"Six Days: Some Rememberings" (Paley), **Supp. VI:** 226
"65290" (Leopold), **Supp. XIV:** 184–185
Six French Poets (Lowell), **II:** 528–529
"Six in All" (Bierds), **Supp. XVII:** 31
Six Lips (Schott), **Supp. XXIII: 251–252**

"Six Persons" (Baraka), **Supp. II Part 1:** 53
Six Sections from Mountains and Rivers without End (Snyder), **Supp. VIII:** 305
"Sixteen Months" (Sandburg), **III:** 584
1601, or Conversation as It Was by the Fireside in the Time of the Tudors (Twain), **IV:** 201
"Sixth-Month Song in the Foothills" (Snyder), **Supp. VIII:** 297
Sixties, The (magazine) (R. Bly), **Supp. IV Part 1:** 60; **Supp. IX:** 271
"Sixty" (Dunn), **Supp. XI:** 155
"Sixty Acres" (Carver), **Supp. III Part 1:** 141
"64 Elmgrove" (Halliday), **Supp. XIX:** 88
"69 Hidebound Opinions, Propositions, and Several Asides from a Manila Folder concerning the Stuff of Poetry" (Wright), **Supp. XV:** 344–345
Sixty Seconds (Bodenheim), **Supp. XXV:** 26
Sixty Stories (Barthelme), **Supp. IV Part 1:** 41, 42, 44, 47, 49, 50
63: Dream Palace (Purdy), **Supp. VII:** 270–271
"Six Variations" (Levertov), **Supp. III Part 1:** 277–278
"Six-Year-Old Boy" (Olds), **Supp. X:** 206
"Six Years Later" (Brodsky), **Supp. VIII:** 26, 28
"Size and Sheer Will" (Olds), **Supp. X:** 206
Size of Thoughts, The: Essays and Other Lumber (Baker), **Supp. XIII: 52–53,** 55, 56
Sizwe Bansi Is Dead (Fugard), **Supp. VIII:** 330
Sjöwall, Maj, **Supp. XX:** 87
"Skagway" (Haines), **Supp. XII:** 206
"Skaters, The" (Ashbery), **Supp. III Part 1:** 10, 12, 13, 18, 25
"Skaters, The" (Jarrell), **II:** 368–369
Skau, Michael, **Supp. XII:** 129, 130, 132, 134
Skeeters Kirby (Masters), **Supp. I Part 2:** 459, 470, 471
Skeleton Crew (King), **Supp. V:** 144
"Skeleton in Armor, The" (Longfellow), **Retro. Supp. II:** 168
"Skeleton's Cave, The" (Bryant), **Supp. I Part 1:** 157
Skelton, John, **III:** 521
Skepticisms (Aiken), **Supp. XV:** 298, 302
Sketch Book of Geoffrey Crayon, Gent., The (Irving), **II:** 295, 303, 304–308, 309, 311, 491; **Supp. I Part 1:** 155
Sketches of Art (Jameson), **Retro. Supp. II:** 58
Sketches of Eighteenth Century America (Crèvecoeur), **Supp. I Part 1:** 233, 240–241, 250, 251
"Sketches of Female Biography" (Rowson), **Supp. XV:** 245
Sketches of Switzerland (Cooper), **I:** 346
Sketches Old and New (Twain), **IV:** 198

"Sketch for a Job-Application Blank" (Harrison), **Supp. VIII:** 38
"Sketch"(Kenny), **Supp. XXIII:** 155
Sketch of Old England, by a New England Man (Paulding), **I:** 344
Skibell, Joseph, **Supp. XVII:** 48
"Skier and the Mountain, The" (Eberhart), **I:** 528–529
"Skin-Boats: 1830, The" (Bierds), **Supp. XVII:** 28
Skinker, Mary Scott, **Supp. IX:** 20
Skinner, Ewart, **Supp. XXII:** 78
Skinny Island (Auchincloss), **Supp. IV Part 1:** 33
Skinny Legs and All (Robbins), **Supp. X:** 267, 273, **276–279**
Skin of Our Teeth, The (Wilder), **IV:** 357, 358, 369–372; **Supp. IV Part 2:** 586; **Supp. XX: 50**
"Skins" (Wright), **Supp. V:** 340
Skins and Bones: Poems 1979–1987 (Gunn Allen), **Supp. IV Part 1:** 321, 331
"Skipper Ireson's Ride" (Whittier), **Supp. I Part 2:** 691, 693–694
"Skirmish at Sartoris" (Faulkner), **II:** 67
"Skirt" (Halliday), **Supp. XIX:** 90
Skirts and Slacks (Di Piero), **Supp. XIX:** 35, 36, 38, 45–47
Sklenicka, Carol, **Supp. XXIV:** 166
Skloot, Floyd, **Supp. XX: 193–209**
Skotheim, Robert Allen, **Supp. XVII:** 104
Skow, John, **Supp. V:** 213; **Supp. XVI:** 174
Skube, Michael, **Supp. XVIII:** 96
"Skunk Cabbage" (Bronk), **Supp. XXI:** 31
"Skunk Cabbage" (Oliver), **Supp. VII:** 235, 236
"Skunk Hour" (Lowell), **II:** 548–550; **Retro. Supp. II:** 188, 189; **Supp. XIV:** 269; **Supp. XX: 203**
Sky, The Stars, The Wilderness, The (Bass), **Supp. XVI:** 19, 20
Sky Changes, The (Sorrentino), **Supp. XXI:** 228, 230, 231
"Sky Dance" (Leopold), **Supp. XIV:** 186
"Sky Line" (Taylor), **Supp. V:** 316
"Sky Line, The" (Mumford), **Supp. II Part 2:** 475
"Skyscraper" (Sandburg), **III:** 581–582
Sky's the Limit, The: A Defense of the Earth (Nichols), **Supp. XIII:** 268
"Sky Valley Rider" (Wright), **Supp. V:** 335, 340
Sky-Walk; or the Man Unknown to Himself (Brown), **Supp. I Part 1:** 127–128
"Slang in America" (Whitman), **IV:** 348
Slappy Hooper, the Wonderful Sign Painter (Bontemps and Conroy), **Supp. XXII:** 5, 11
Slapstick (Vonnegut), **Supp. II Part 2:** 753, 754, 778
Slapstick Tragedy (T. Williams), **IV:** 382, 393
Slate, Lane, **Supp. IX:** 251, 253
Slattery, Mary Grace. *See* Miller, Mrs. Arthur (Mary Grace Slattery)

Slattery's Hurricane (Wouk), **Supp. XXV:** 257, 262–263

"Slaughterer, The" (Singer), **IV:** 19

Slaughterhouse-Five (Vonnegut), **Supp. II Part 2:** 755, 758–759, 760, 770, 772–776; **Supp. V:** 41, 244; **Supp. XIX:** 235

Slaughter Rule, The (film; Alex and Andrew Smith), **Supp. XIX:** 174

Slave, The (Baraka), **Supp. II Part 1:** 42, 44, 56

Slave, The: A Novel (Singer), **IV:** 13; **Retro. Supp. II:** 305–307

"Slave Canal" (Ray), **Supp. XVIII:** 193

"Slave Coffle" (Angelou), **Supp. IV Part 1:** 16

"Slave of the Sky" (P. N. Warren), **Supp. XX:** 261

"Slave on the Block" (Hughes), **Supp. I Part 1:** 329

Slave Power, The: The Free North and Southern Domination, 1780–1860 (Richards), **Supp. XIV:** 48

"Slave Quarters" (Dickey), **Supp. IV Part 1:** 181

Slavery (Channing), **Supp. XXIV:** 77–78

"Slave's Dream, The" (Longfellow), **Supp. I Part 2:** 409

Slave Ship: A Historical Pageant (Baraka), **Supp. II Part 1:** 47–49, 53, 56–57

"Slave-Ships, The" (Whittier), **Supp. I Part 2:** 687–688

Slaves in Algiers; or, A Struggle for Freedom (Rowson), **Supp. XV:** 236–237

"Slave Trade, The: View from the Middle Passage" (Major), **Supp. XXII:** 182

Slavs! Thinking about the Longstanding Problems of Virtue and Happiness (Kushner), **Supp. IX:** 146

Sledge, Eugene, **Supp. V:** 250

Sleek for the Long Flight (Matthews), **Supp. IX:** 154, 155, **157–158**

Sleep (Dixon), **Supp. XII:** 154

"Sleep, The" (Strand), **Supp. IV Part 2:** 627

Sleeper (film; Allen), **Supp. XV:** 5

"Sleeper, The" (Poe), **III:** 411

"Sleeper 1, The" (Hay), **Supp. XIV:** 132–133

"Sleeper 2, The" (Hay), **Supp. XIV:** 132–133

"Sleepers, The" (Whitman), **IV:** 336

"Sleepers in Jaipur" (Kenyon), **Supp. VII:** 172

Sleepers in Moon-Crowned Valleys (Purdy), **Supp. VII:** 274, 275

Sleepers Joining Hands (R. Bly), **Supp. XXI:** 85

"Sleepers Joining Hands" (R. Bly), **Supp. IV Part 1:** 63, 73

Sleeping Beauty (Macdonald), **Supp. IV Part 2:** 474, 475

Sleeping Beauty, The (Carruth), **Supp. XVI:** 53, 57–58

"Sleeping Beauty Syndrome, The: The New Agony of Single Men" (Wasserstein), **Supp. XV:** 328

Sleeping Fires (Atherton), **Supp. XXIV:** 25

"Sleeping Fury, The" (Bogan), **Supp. III Part 1:** 58

Sleeping Fury, The: Poems (Bogan), **Supp. III Part 1:** 55–58

Sleeping Gypsy and Other Poems, The (Garrett), **Supp. VII:** 96–98

Sleeping in the Forest (Oliver), **Supp. VII:** 233

"Sleeping in the Forest" (Oliver), **Supp. VII:** 233–234

Sleeping in the Woods (Wagoner), **Supp. IX:** 328

Sleeping on Fists (Ríos), **Supp. IV Part 2:** 540

Sleeping on the Wing: An Anthology of Modern Poetry (Koch and Farrell, eds.), **Supp. XV:** 187–188

"Sleeping on the Wing"(O'Hara), **Supp. XXIII:** 214

"Sleeping Standing Up" (Bishop), **Supp. I Part 1:** 85, 89, 93

"Sleeping with Animals" (Kumin), **Supp. IV Part 2:** 454

Sleeping with One Eye Open (Strand), **Supp. IV Part 2:** 621–624, 623, 628

Sleep in Thunder (Lacy), **Supp. XV:** 206

"Sleepless, The" (L.-Y. Lee), **Supp. XV:** 224

"Sleepless at Crown Point" (Wilbur), **Supp. III Part 2:** 561

Sleepless Nights (Hardwick), **Supp. III Part 1:** 193, 208–211

"Sleepless Nights" (Nelson), **Supp. XVIII:** 174

"Sleep-Walkers, The" (Gibran), **Supp. XX:** 118

Sleepy Lagoon Mystery, The (Endore), **Supp. XVII:** 60

"Sleepy People" (Lethem), **Supp. XVIII:** 140

Sleigh, Tom, **Supp. XIX:** 38, 40

Sleight, Ken, **Supp. XIII:** 12

Slick, Sam (pseudonym). *See* Haliburton, Thomas Chandler

"Slick Gonna Learn" (Ellison), **Retro. Supp. II:** 116; **Supp. II Part 1:** 237–238

"Slight Rebellion off Madison" (Salinger), **III:** 553

"Slight Sound at Evening, A" (White), **Supp. I Part 2:** 672

"Slim Graves Show, The" (Keillor), **Supp. XVI:** 172

"Slim Greer" series (Hayden), **Supp. II Part 1:** 369

"Slim in Hell" (Hayden), **Supp. II Part 1:** 369

"Slim Man Canyon" (Silko), **Supp. IV Part 2:** 560

"Slip, Shift, and Speed Up: The Influence of Robinson Jeffers's Narrative Syntax" (Jarman), **Supp. XVII:** 111, 112

"Slippery Fingers" (Hammett), **Supp. IV Part 1:** 343

Slipping-Down Life, A (Tyler), **Supp. IV Part 2:** 660–661

Sloan, Jacob, **IV:** 3, 6

Sloan, John, **I:** 254; **IV:** 411; **Retro. Supp. II:** 103; **Supp. XXII:** 277

Sloane, John, **Supp. XV:** 295

"Slob" (Farrell), **II:** 25, 28, 31

Slocum, Joshua, **Supp. I Part 2:** 497; **Supp. XXV:** 205–219

Slogum House (Sandoz), **Supp. XXIV:** 244, **251–252,** 255

Slonim, Véra. *See* Nabokov, Véra

Slopen, Beverly, **Supp. XX:** 59

Slouching towards Bethlehem (Didion), **Supp. IV Part 1:** 196, 197, 200–201, 202, 206, 210

Slovic, Scott, **Supp. XVI:** 277

"Slow Child with a Book of Birds" (Levis), **Supp. XI:** 268

"Slow Dance with Icarus" (Monson), **Supp. XXIV:** 240

Slow Dancing Through Ether: A Fine Binding Project (Monson and Ingmundson), **Supp. XXIV:** 230, 234

"Slow Down for Poetry" (Strand), **Supp. IV Part 2:** 620

Slow Music (Taggard), **Supp. XXII:** 284

"Slow Pacific Swell, The" (Winters), **Supp. II Part 2:** 790, 793, 795, 796, 799

Slow Parade (Kees), **Supp. XV:** 137

Slow Train Coming (album, Dylan), **Supp. XVIII:** 28

Slow Transparency (Hadas), **Supp. XXIII:** 113–114

Slow Vision (Bodenheim), **Supp. XXV:** 28

"Slum Church" (Espaillat), **Supp. XXI:** 110–111

"Slumgullions" (Olsen), **Supp. IV Part 1:** 54

Slumgullion Stew: An Edward Abbey Reader (Abbey), **Supp. XIII:** 4

Slung, Michelle, **Supp. XX:** 87

"S & M" (Komunyakaa), **Supp. XIII:** 114

"Small" (C. Frost), **Supp. XV:** 102

Small, Albion, **Supp. I Part 1:** 5

"Small, Good Thing, A" (Carver), **Supp. III Part 1:** 145, 147

Small, Miriam Rossiter, **Supp. I Part 1:** 319

Small Boy and Others, A (James), **II:** 337, 547; **Retro. Supp. I:** 235

"Small but Urgent Request to the Unknowable" (Karr), **Supp. XI:** 243

Small Ceremonies (Shields), **Supp. VII:** 312–315, 320

Small Craft Warnings (T. Williams), **IV:** 382, 383, 384, 385, 386, 387, 392, 393, 396, 398

"Small Degrees" (Brockmeier), **Supp. XXII:** 52, 59

"Small Fry" (Peacock), **Supp. XIX:** 206

Small Place, A (Kincaid), **Supp. VII:** 186–187, 188, 191

"Small Rain, The" (Pynchon), **Supp. II Part 2:** 620

Small Room, The (Sarton), **Supp. VIII:** 252, **255–256**

Smalls, Bob, **II:** 128

"Small Song for Andrew" (Weigl), **Supp. XIX:** 280

Small Time Crooks (film; Allen), **Supp. XV:** 11

Small Town, A (Hearon), **Supp. VIII: 65–66**

"Small Vases from Hebron, The" (Nye), **Supp. XIII:** 283

"Small Vision, The" (Goldbarth), **Supp. XII:** 180

"Small Voice from the Wings" (Everwine), **Supp. XV:** 76

"Small Wire" (Sexton), **Supp. II Part 2:** 696

Small Worlds (A. Hoffman), **Supp. XVII:** 44

Smardz, Zofia, **Supp. XVI:** 155

Smart, Christopher, **III:** 534; **Supp. I Part 2:** 539; **Supp. IV Part 2:** 626

Smart, Joyce H., **Supp. XI:** 169

"Smart Cookie, A" (Cisneros), **Supp. VII:** 64

"Smash"(Thompson), **Supp. XXIII:** 301, 302

"Smashup" (Thurber), **Supp. I Part 2:** 616

Smedly, Agnes, **Supp. XIII:** 295

"Smell of a God, The" (Peacock), **Supp. XIX:** 199

"Smelt Fishing" (Hayden), **Supp. II Part 1:** 367

"Smile of the Bathers, The" (Kees), **Supp. XV:** 145

"Smile on the Face of a Kouros, The" (Bronk), **Supp. XXI:** 31

"Smiles" (Dunn), **Supp. XI:** 151

Smiles, Samuel, **Supp. X:** 167

Smiley, Jane, **Supp. VI: 291–309; Supp. XII:** 73, 297; **Supp. XIII:** 127; **Supp. XIX:** 54

Smith, Adam, **II:** 9; **Supp. I Part 2:** 633, 634, 639; **Supp. XVII:** 235

Smith, Annick, **Supp. XIV:** 223

Smith, Barbara, **Supp. XXIII:** 194

Smith, Benjamin, **IV:** 148

Smith, Bernard, **I:** 260

Smith, Bessie, **Retro. Supp. I:** 343; **Supp. VIII:** 330; **Supp. XIX:** 147

Smith, Betty, **Supp. XXIII: 257–271**

Smith, Charlie, **Supp. X:** 177

Smith, Clark Ashton, **Supp. XXV:** 111

Smith, Dale, **Supp. XV:** 136, 138, 139

Smith, Dave, **Supp. V:** 333; **Supp. XI:** 152; **Supp. XII:** 178, 198; **Supp. XIX:** 277, 282

Smith, David, **Supp. XIII:** 246, 247

Smith, David Nichol, **Supp. XIV:** 2

Smith, Dinitia, **Supp. VIII:** 74, 82, 83; **Supp. XVIII:** 162; **Supp. XXIV:** 2–3

Smith, Elihu Hubbard, **Supp. I Part 1:** 126, 127, 130

Smith, Ernest J., **Supp. XXIII:** 111, 113, 117

Smith, George Adam, **III:** 199

Smith, Hannah Whitall, **Supp. XIV:** 333, 334, 338

Smith, Harrison, **II:** 61

Smith, Henry Nash, **IV:** 210; **Supp. I Part 1:** 233

Smith, Herbert F., **Supp. I Part 2:** 423

Smith, Iain Crichton, **Supp. XVIII:** 196

Smith, James, **II:** 111

Smith, Jedediah Strong, **Supp. IV Part 2:** 602

Smith, Jerome, **Supp. IV Part 1:** 369

Smith, Joe, **Supp. IV Part 2:** 584

Smith, John, **I:** 4, 131; **II:** 296

Smith, John Allyn, **I:** 168

Smith, Johnston (pseudonym). *See* Crane, Stephen

Smith, Katherine Capshaw, **Supp. XXII:** 10, 13–14

Smith, Kellogg, **Supp. I Part 2:** 660

Smith, Lamar, **II:** 585

Smith, Mrs. Lamar (Marguerite Walters), **II:** 585, 587

Smith, Lane, **Supp. XIX:** 231

Smith, Larry David, **Supp. XVIII:** 22

Smith, Lee, **Supp. XII:** 311; **Supp. XVIII:** 195; **Supp. XXII:** 206, 213

Smith, Lillian, **Supp. XXII:** 67

Smith, Logan Pearsall, **Supp. XIV: 333– 351**

Smith, Lula Carson. *See* McCullers, Carson

Smith, Mark, **Supp. XVIII:** 155

Smith, Martha Nell, **Retro. Supp. I:** 33, 43, 46, 47

Smith, Mary Rozet, **Supp. I Part 1:** 5, 22

Smith, Oliver, **II:** 586

Smith, Patricia Clark, **Supp. IV Part 1:** 397, 398, 402, 406, 408, 410; **Supp. IV Part 2:** 509; **Supp. XII:** 218

Smith, Patrick, **Supp. VIII:** 40, 41

Smith, Patti, **Supp. XII:** 136; **Supp. XIV:** 151

Smith, Porter, **III:** 572

Smith, Red, **II:** 417, 424

Smith, Robert McClure, **Supp. XV:** 270

Smith, Robert Pearsall, **Supp. XIV:** 333

Smith, Sarah A., **Supp. XVIII:** 99

Smith, Seba, **Supp. I Part 2:** 411

Smith, Sidonie, **Supp. IV Part 1:** 11; **Supp. XXII:** 70

Smith, Stevie, **Supp. V:** 84

Smith, Sydney, **II:** 295; **Supp. XIV:** 112

Smith, Thorne, **Supp. IX:** 194

Smith, Valerie, **Supp. XXII:** 146

Smith, Wendy, **Supp. XII:** 330, 335; **Supp. XVIII:** 89, 92

Smith, Wilford Bascom "Pitchfork", **Supp. XIII:** 168

Smith, William, **II:** 114

Smith, William Gardner, **Supp. XVI:** 142–143

Smith, William Jay, **Supp. XIII: 331– 350**

"Smoke" (Di Piero), **Supp. XIX:** 38

Smoke (film), **Supp. XII:** 21

Smoke and Steel (Sandburg), **III:** 585– 587, 592

"Smokehouse" (Offutt), **Supp. XIX:** 166, 167

"Smokers" (Wolff), **Supp. VII:** 340–341

Smokey Bites the Dust (film, C. Griffith), **Supp. XVII:** 9

Smoking Mountain, The: Stories of Postwar Germany (Boyle), **Supp. XXIV:** 61

"Smoking My Prayers" (Ortiz), **Supp. IV Part 2:** 503

"Smoking Room, The" (Jackson), **Supp. IX:** 116

"Smoky Gold" (Leopold), **Supp. XIV:** 186

Smolan, Sandy, **Supp. XVI:** 36

Smollett, Tobias, **Supp. XXV:** 258

Smollett, Tobias G., **I:** 134, 339, 343; **II:** 304–305; **III:** 61; **Supp. XVIII:** 7

Smooding, Robert, **Supp. XXIII:** 294

Smuggler's Bible, A (McElroy), **Supp. IV Part 1:** 285

Smuggler's Handbook, The (Goldbarth), **Supp. XII:** 181, 183

Smugglers of Lost Soul's Rock, The (Gardner), **Supp. VI: 70**

Smyth, Albert Henry, **II:** 123

Smyth, Jacqui, **Supp. XXI:** 215

"Snack Firm Maps New Chip Push" (Keillor), **Supp. XVI:** 168, 169

"Snail, The" (Hay), **Supp. XIV:** 124

"Snake, The" (Berry), **Supp. X:** 31

"Snake, The" (Crane), **I:** 420

"Snakecharmer" (Plath), **Supp. I Part 2:** 538

"Snakes, Mongooses" (Moore), **III:** 207

"Snakeskin" (Kooser), **Supp. XIX:** 123

"Snakes of September, The" (Kunitz), **Supp. III Part 1:** 258

"Snapshot of 15th S.W., A" (Hugo), **Supp. VI:** 141

"Snapshot Rediscovered, A" (X. J. Kennedy), **Supp. XV:** 170

"Snapshots in an Album" (Espaillat), **Supp. XXI:** 111

"Snapshots of a Daughter-in-Law" (Rich), **Supp. I Part 2:** 553–554

Snapshots of a Daughter-in-Law: Poems, 1954–1962 (Rich), **Supp. I Part 2:** 550–551, 553–554; **Supp. XII:** 255

Snaring the Flightless Birds (Bierds), **Supp. XVII:** 26

Sneetches and Other Stories, The (Geisel), **Supp. XVI:** 109

"Sneeze, The" (Chekhov), **Supp. IV Part 2:** 585

Snell, Ebenezer, **Supp. I Part 1:** 151

Snell, Thomas, **Supp. I Part 1:** 153

Sniffen, Matthew, **Supp. XXV:** 283

"Snob, The" (Boulton), **Supp. XXII:** 23

"Snob, The" (Shapiro), **Supp. II Part 2:** 705

Snobbery: The America Version (Epstein), **Supp. XIV:** 102, 114–115

Snodgrass, Kathleen, **Supp. XVI:** 42

Snodgrass, W. D., **I:** 400; **Retro. Supp. II:** 179; **Supp. III Part 2:** 541; **Supp. V:** 337; **Supp. VI: 311–328; Supp. XI:** 141, 315; **Supp. XIII:** 312; **Supp. XV:** 92, 153; **Supp. XVII:** 239

"Snow" (C. Baxter), **Supp. XVII:** 19

"Snow" (Frost), **Retro. Supp. I:** 133

"Snow" (Haines), **Supp. XII:** 212

"Snow" (Sexton), **Supp. II Part 2:** 696

"Snow" (W. V. Davis), **Supp. XXI:** 89, 90, 93

Snow, C. P., **Supp. I Part 2:** 536

Snow, Hank, **Supp. V:** 335

Snow Angels (film), **Supp. XXV:** 153– 154

Snow Angels (O'Nan), **Supp. XXV:** 142, 143, 150

Snow Ball, The (Gurney), **Supp. V:** 99

"Snow-Bound" (Whittier), **Supp. I Part 2:** 700–703

"Snow Bound at Eagle's" (Harte), **Supp. II Part 1:** 356

"Snowflakes" (Longfellow), **II:** 498

"Snow Goose, The" (Gallico), **Supp. XVI:** 238

Snow-Image and Other Twice Told Tales, The (Hawthorne), **II:** 237; **Retro. Supp. I:** 160

"Snowing in Greenwich Village" (Updike), **IV:** 226; **Retro. Supp. I:** 321

"Snow in New York" (Swenson), **Supp. IV Part 2:** 644

Snow Leopard, The (Matthiessen), **Supp. V:** 199, 207–211

"Snow Man, The" (Stevens), **IV:** 82–83; **Retro. Supp. I:** 299, 300, 302, 306, 307, 312; **Supp. XXI:** 60

"Snowmass Cycle, The" (Dunn), **Supp. XI:** 152

Snow: Meditations of a Cautious Man in Winter (Banks), **Supp. V:** 6

Snow Poems, The (Ammons), **Supp. VII:** 32–34

Snowshoe Trek to Otter River (Budbill), **Supp. XIX:** 11

Snow's Music, The (Skloot), **Supp. XX:** 196, 204–205

"Snows of Kilimanjaro, The" (Hemingway), **II:** 78, 257, 263, 264; **Retro. Supp. I:** 98, 182; **Supp. XII:** 249

"Snows of Studiofiftyfour, The" (Plimpton), **Supp. XVI:** 245

"Snow Songs" (Snodgrass), **Supp. VI:** 324

"Snowstorm, The" (Oates), **Supp. II Part 2:** 523

"Snowstorm as It Affects the American Farmer, A" (Crèvecoeur), **Supp. I Part 1:** 251

Snow White (Barthelme), **Supp. IV Part 1:** 40, 47, 48–49, 50, 52; **Supp. V:** 39

"Snowy Egret" (Weigl), **Supp. XIX:** 280–281

"Snowy Mountain Song, A" (Ortiz), **Supp. IV Part 2:** 506

Snyder, Gary, **Supp. III Part 1:** 350; **Supp. IV Part 2:** 502; **Supp. V:** 168–169; **Supp. VIII:** 39, **289–307**; **Supp. XVI:** 283; **Supp. XXII:** 276

Snyder, Mike, **Supp. XIV:** 36

"So-and-So Reclining on Her Couch" (Stevens), **IV:** 90

"Soapland" (Thurber), **Supp. I Part 2:** 619

Soares, Lota de Macedo, **Retro. Supp. II:** 44; **Supp. I Part 1:** 89, 94

"Sobbin' Women, The" (Benét), **Supp. XI:** 47

Sobin, Gustaf, **Supp. XVI: 281–298**

Sochen, June, **Supp. XXI:** 1

Social Ethics (Gilman), **Supp. XI:** 207

"Social Function of the Story Teller, The" (lecture, Murray), **Supp. XIX:** 153

"Socialism and the Negro" (McKay), **Supp. X:** 135

"Socialism of the Skin, A (Liberation, Honey!)" (Kushner), **Supp. IX:** 135

Social Thought in America: The Revolt against Formalism (White), **Supp. I Part 2:** 648, 650

"Society, Morality, and the Novel" (Ellison), **Retro. Supp. II:** 118, 123–124

"Sociological Habit Patterns in Linguistic Transmogrification" (Cowley), **Supp. II Part 1:** 143

"Sociological Poet, A" (Bourne), **I:** 228

Socrates, **I:** 136, 265; **II:** 8–9, 105, 106; **III:** 281, 419, 606; **Supp. I Part 2:** 458; **Supp. XII:** 98

Socrates Fortlow stories (Mosley), **Supp. XIII: 242–243**

So Forth (Brodsky), **Supp. VIII:** 32–33

"So Forth" (Brodsky), **Supp. VIII:** 33

"Soft Flame" (Skloot), **Supp. XX: 203**

"Soft-Hearted Sioux, The" (Zitkala-Ša), **Supp. XXV:** 274, 282

Soft Machine, The (Burroughs), **Supp. III Part 1:** 93, 103, 104

"Soft Mask" (Karr), **Supp. XI:** 243

Soft Side, The (James), **II:** 335; **Retro. Supp. I:** 229

"Soft Spring Night in Shillington, A" (Updike), **Retro. Supp. I:** 318, 319

"Soft Wood" (Lowell), **II:** 550–551

"So Help Me" (Algren), **Supp. IX:** 2

Soil and Survival: Land Stewardship and the Future of American Agriculture (C. Bly, J. Paddock and N. Paddock), **Supp. XVI:** 36–37

"Soirée in Hollywood" (H. Miller), **III:** 186

Sojourner, The (Rawlings), **Supp. X:** 233–234

"Sojourn in a Whale" (Moore), **III:** 211, 213

"Sojourns" (Didion), **Supp. IV Part 1:** 205

Sokolow, Jayme, **Supp. XIX:** 134

Solanus, Jane, **Supp. XVI:** 293

Solar Lottery (Dick), **Supp. XVIII:** 138

Solar Storms (Hogan), **Supp. IV Part 1:** 397, 410, 414–415

"Soldier, The" (Frost), **II:** 155

"Soldier Asleep at the Tomb" (Schnackenberg), **Supp. XV:** 262–263

Soldier Blue (film), **Supp. X:** 124

"Soldier of Fortune" (Wright), **Supp. XV:** 341

Soldier of the Great War, A (Helprin), **Supp. XXV:** 83–84, 86–87

"Soldier's Home" (Hemingway), **Retro. Supp. I:** 189

Soldier's Joy (Bell), **Supp. X:** 7, **7–8**, 10, 11; **Supp. XXIII:** 43

Soldiers of the Storm (film), **Supp. XIII:** 163

Soldiers' Pay (Faulkner), **I:** 117; **II:** 56, 68; **Retro. Supp. I:** 80, 81

"Soldier's Testament, The" (Mumford), **Supp. II Part 2:** 473

"Soliloquy: Man Talking to a Mirror" (Komunyakaa), **Supp. XIII:** 116–117

"Solipsism" (Monson), **Supp. XXIV:** 230

"Solitary Confinement" (X. J. Kennedy), **Supp. XV:** 157

"Solitary Pond, The" (Updike), **Retro. Supp. I:** 323

So Little Time (Marquand), **III:** 55, 59, 65, 67, 69

"Solitude" (Maupassant), **Supp. I Part 1:** 223

Solo Faces (Salter), **Supp. IX: 259–260**

Solomon, Andy, **Supp. X:** 11

Solomon, Carl, **Supp. XIV:** 143, 150

Solomon, Charles, **Supp. VIII:** 82

Solomon, Deborah, **Supp. XXI:** 245

Solomon, Henry, Jr., **Supp. I Part 2:** 490

Solomons, Leon, **IV:** 26

So Long, See You Tomorrow (Maxwell), **Supp. VIII:** 156, 160, 162, **167–169**; **Supp. XVII:** 23

"So Long Ago" (Bausch), **Supp. VII:** 41–42

Solotaroff, Robert, **Retro. Supp. II:** 203

Solotaroff, Theodore, **III:** 452–453; **Retro. Supp. II:** 281; **Supp. I Part 2:** 440, 445; **Supp. X:** 79; **Supp. XI:** 340; **Supp. XII:** 291; **Supp. XIX:** 268

Solstice (Di Piero), **Supp. XIX:** 36

"Solstice" (Jeffers), **Supp. II Part 2:** 433, 435

"Solstice, The" (Merwin), **Supp. III Part 1:** 356

"Solus Rex" (Nabokov), **Retro. Supp. I:** 274

"Solutions" (McCarthy), **II:** 578

"Solving the Puzzle" (Dunn), **Supp. XI:** 152

Solzhenitsyn, Alexandr, **Retro. Supp. I:** 278; **Supp. VIII:** 241

"Some Afternoon" (Creeley), **Supp. IV Part 1:** 150–151

Some American People (Caldwell), **I:** 292, 294, 295, 296, 304, 309

"Some Ashes Drifting above Piedra, California" (Levis), **Supp. XI:** 264–265

"Some Aspects of the Grotesque in Southern Fiction" (O'Connor), **Retro. Supp. II:** 223, 224

"Some Birds on a Dun Field" (Bronk), **Supp. XXI:** 27

"Somebody Always Grabs the Purple" (H. Roth), **Supp. IX:** 234

Somebody in Boots (Algren), **Supp. IX:** 3, **5–7**, 12

Somebody's Darling (McMurtry), **Supp. V:** 225

Some Came Running (film), **Supp. XI:** 213

Some Came Running (Jones), **Supp. XI:** 214, 215, 220, **222–223**, 226, 227, 232

Some Can Whistle (McMurtry), **Supp. V:** 229

"Some Children of the Goddess" (Mailer), **Retro. Supp. II:** 204

Someday, Maybe (Stafford), **Supp. XI:** **323–325**; **Supp. XIII:** 281

"Some Dreamers of the Golden Dream" (Didion), **Supp. IV Part 1:** 200

Some Faces in the Crowd (Schulberg), **Supp. XVIII:** 252

"Some Foreign Letters" (Sexton), **Supp. II Part 2:** 674

"Some General Instructions" (Koch), **Supp. XV:** 182

"Some Good News" (Olson), **Supp. II Part 2:** 575, 576, 577

"Some Grass along a Ditch Bank" (Levis), **Supp. XI:** 266

"Some Greek Writings" (Corso), **Supp. XII:** 130

Some Honorable Men: Political Conventions, 1960–1972 (Mailer), **Retro. Supp. II:** 208

Some Imagist Poets (Lowell), **III:** 511, 518, 520; **Supp. I Part 1:** 257, 261

"Some keep the Sabbath going to Church" (Dickinson), **Retro. Supp. I:** 30; **Supp. XVIII:** 301

"Some Laughed" (L. Michaels), **Supp. XVI:** 207

"Some Like Indians Endure" (Gunn Allen), **Supp. IV Part 1:** 330

"Some Like Them Cold" (Lardner), **II:** 427–428, 430, 431; **Supp. IX:** 202

"Some Lines from Whitman" (Jarrell), **IV:** 352

"Some Matters Concerning the Occupant" (Keillor), **Supp. XVI:** 167

"Some Musicians Play Chamber Music for Us" (Bronk), **Supp. XXI:** 27–28

"Some Negatives: X. at the Chateau" (Merrill), **Supp. III Part 1:** 322

"Some Neglected Points in the Theory of Socialism" (Veblen), **Supp. I Part 2:** 635

"Some Notes for an Autobiographical Lecture" (Trilling), **Supp. III Part 2:** 493, 497, 500

"Some Notes on French Poetry" (R. Bly), **Supp. IV Part 1:** 61

"Some Notes on Miss L." (West), **IV:** 290–291, 295; **Retro. Supp. II:** 322

"Some Notes on Organic Form" (Levertov), **Supp. III Part 1:** 272, 279

"Some Notes on Teaching: Probably Spoken" (Paley), **Supp. VI:** 225

"Some Notes on the Gazer Within" (Levis), **Supp. XI:** 270

"Some Notes on Violence" (West), **IV:** 304; **Retro. Supp. II:** 322, 323

"Some Observations Now" (Conroy), **Supp. XVI:** 75

Some Observations of a Stranger at Zuni in the Later Part of the Century (Major), **Supp. XXII:** 179–180

"Some Observations of a Stranger at Zuni in the Later Part of the Century" (Major), **Supp. XXII:** 179

Some of the Dharma (Kerouac), **Supp. III Part 1:** 225

"Some of Us Have Fewer" (Monson), **Supp. XXIV:** 240

"Someone Is Buried" (Salinas), **Supp. XIII:** 324

"Someone Puts a Pineapple Together" (Stevens), **IV:** 90–91

"Someone's Blood" (Dove), **Supp. IV Part 1:** 245

"Someone Talking" (Harjo), **Supp. XII:** 219–220

"Someone Talking to Himself" (Wilbur), **Supp. III Part 2:** 557

"Someone to Watch Over Me" (Stern), **Supp. IX:** 300

Someone to Watch Over Me: Stories (Bausch), **Supp. VII:** 53

Some People, Places, & Things That Will Not Appear in My Next Novel (Cheever), **Supp. I Part 1:** 184–185

"Some Poets' Criticism and the Age" (Yenser), **Supp. XV:** 113–114

Some Problems of Philosophy: A Beginning of an Introduction to Philosophy (James), **II:** 360–361

"Some Questions You Might Ask" (Oliver), **Supp. VII:** 238–239

"Some Remarks on Humor" (White), **Supp. I Part 2:** 672

"Some Remarks on Rhythm" (Roethke), **III:** 548–549

Somers, Fred, **I:** 196

Somerville, Jane, **Supp. IX:** 289, 296–297

"Some Secrets" (Stern), **Supp. IX:** 286, 287, 288, 289, 295

Some Sort of Epic Grandeur (Bruccoli), **Retro. Supp. I:** 115, 359

"Something" (Oliver), **Supp. VII:** 236

Something Happened (Heller), **Supp. IV Part 1:** 383, 386–388, 389, 392

"*Something Happened:* The Imaginary, the Symbolic, and the Discourse of the Family" (Mellard), **Supp. IV Part 1:** 387

Something in Common (Hughes), **Supp. I Part 1:** 329–330

Something Inside: Conversations with Gay Fiction Writers (Gambone), **Supp. XII:** 81

"Something Matters but We Don't " (Bronk), **Supp. XXI:** 32

"Something Might Be Gaining" (Mosher), **Supp. XXII:** 209

"Something New" (Stern), **Supp. IX:** 290

Some Things (Berrigan, Padgett, and Brainard), **Supp. XXIV:** 41

Something Said (Sorrentino), **Supp. XXI:** 226, 227, 229, 235

"Something's Going to Happen" (Zinberg), **Supp. XV:** 196

"Something Spurious from the Mindinao Deep" (Stegner), **Supp. IV Part 2:** 605

"Something That Needs Nothing" (July), **Supp. XXIV:** 203

"Something to Believe In" (Pitts), **Supp. XXII:** 280

Something to Declare (Alvarez), **Supp. VII:** 1, 2, 11, 17–19

Something to Remember Me By (Bellow), **Retro. Supp. II:** 32

"Something to Remember Me By" (Bellow), **Retro. Supp. II:** 32

"Something Wicked" (O'Nan), **Supp. XXV:** 148

Something Wicked This Way Comes (Bradbury), **Supp. IV Part 1:** 101, 110–111; **Supp. XXV:** 148

"Something Wild . . ." (T. Williams), **IV:** 381

"Some Thoughts" (McNally), **Supp. XIII:** 207

"Some Thoughts on the Line" (Oliver), **Supp. VII:** 238

"Sometimes, Reading" (Stafford), **Supp. XI:** 314

"Sometimes It Just Happens That Way, That's All" (Hinojosa), **Supp. XIX:** 101

"Sometimes I Wonder" (Hughes), **Supp. I Part 1:** 337

Sometimes Mysteriously (Salinas), **Supp. XIII:** 311, **326–328**

"Sometimes Mysteriously" (Salinas), **Supp. XIII:** 328

Some Trees (Ashbery), **Supp. III Part 1:** 3–7, 12

"Some Trees" (Ashbery), **Supp. III Part 1:** 2

"Some Truths About American Readers" (Atherton), **Supp. XXIV:** 24, 27

"Some Views on the Reading and Writing of Short Stories" (Welty), **Retro. Supp. I:** 351

"Somewhere" (Nemerov), **III:** 279–280

"Somewhere Else" (Paley), **Supp. VI:** 227

"Somewhere in Africa" (Sexton), **Supp. II Part 2:** 684–685

"Somewhere Is Such a Kingdom" (Ransom), **III:** 492

"Somewhere near Phu Bai:" (Komunyakaa), **Supp. XIII:** 123–124

Some Words (Bronk), **Supp. XXI:** 32

"Some Words with a Mummy" (Poe), **III:** 425

"Some Yips and Barks in the Dark" (Snyder), **Supp. VIII:** 291

Sommers, Michael, **Supp. IV Part 2:** 581

Sommers, William, **I:** 387, 388

"Somnambulisma" (Stevens), **Retro. Supp. I:** 310

"So Much Summer" (Dickinson), **Retro. Supp. I:** 26, 44, 45

"So Much the Worse for Boston" (Lindsay), **Supp. I Part 2:** 398

"So Much Water So Close to Home" (Carver), **Supp. III Part 1:** 143, 146

Son, Cathy, **Supp. X:** 292

"Son, The" (Dove), **Supp. IV Part 1:** 245

"Son and Father" (Pickering), **Supp. XXI:** 197

"Sonata" (Schnackenberg), **Supp. XV:** 259

"Sonata for the Invisible" (Harjo), **Supp. XII:** 228

Sonata for Two Pianos (Bowles), **Supp. IV Part 1:** 83

Son at the Front, A (Wharton), **II:** 183; **IV:** 320; **Retro. Supp. I:** 378

Sondheim, Stephen, **Supp. XII:** 260; **Supp. XVI:** 194

Son Excellence Eugène Rougon (Zola), **III:** 322

Son from Sleep, A (Hadas), **Supp. XXIII:** **114–115**

Song (B. Kelly), **Supp. XVII:** 123, **127–130**

"Song" (B. Kelly), **Supp. XVII:** 127

"Song" (Bogan), **Supp. III Part 1:** 57

"Song" (Bryant). *See* "Hunter of the West, The"

"Song" (Dunbar), **Supp. II Part 1:** 199

"Song" (Espaillat), **Supp. XXI:** 106–107

"Song" (Ginsberg), **Supp. II Part 1:** 317

"Song" (Kenyon), **Supp. VII:** 169

"Song" (Rich), **Supp. I Part 2:** 560

"Song" (Wylie), **Supp. I Part 2:** 729

"Song, A" (Creeley), **Supp. IV Part 1:** 145

"Song, The" (Gioia), **Supp. XV:** 117

"Song, The" (Very), **Supp. XXV:** 242

Song and Idea (Eberhart), **I:** 526, 529, 533, 539

"Song: Enlightenment" (X. J. Kennedy), **Supp. XV:** 169

"Song for a Lover Killed in Battle"(J. Schoolcraft), **Supp. XXIII:** 235

Song for Anninho (G. Jones), **Supp. XXIV:** 185, 195

Song for My Father, A: A Play in Two Acts (Budbill), **Supp. XIX:** 3, **15–16**

"Song for Myself and the Deer to Return On" (Harjo), **Supp. XII:** 225

"Song for My Sixtieth Year" (Carruth), **Supp. XVI:** 54

"Song for Occupations, A" (Whitman), **Retro. Supp. I:** 394

"Song for Simeon, A" (Eliot), **Retro. Supp. I:** 64

"Song for the Coming of Smallpox" (Wagoner), **Supp. IX:** 329, 330

"Song for the End of Time" (Gioia), **Supp. XV:** 126–127

"Song for the First People" (Wagoner), **Supp. IX:** 328

"Song for the Last Act" (Bogan), **Supp. III Part 1:** 64

"Song for the Middle of the Night, A" (Wright), **Supp. III Part 2:** 594

"Song for the Rainy Season" (Bishop), **Supp. I Part 1:** 93–94, 96

"Song for the Romeos, A" (Stern), **Supp. IX:** 296

"Song for Woody" (song, Dylan), **Supp. XVIII:** 24

"Song from a Courtyard Window" (Gioia), **Supp. XV:** 119

"Song III" (Taggard), **Supp. XXII:** 284

"Song in the Front Yard, A" (Brooks), **Supp. XVIII:** 181

"Songline of Dawn" (Harjo), **Supp. XII:** 229

"Song: Love in Whose Rich Honor" (Rukeyser), **Supp. VI:** 285

"Song: Now That She Is Here" (Carruth), **Supp. XVI:** 59

"Song of Advent, A" (Winters), **Supp. II Part 2:** 789

"Song of a Man Who Rushed at the Enemy" (Wagoner), **Supp. IX:** 329, 330

"Song of Courage, A" (Masters), **Supp. I Part 2:** 458

Song of God, The: Bhagavad-Gita (Isherwood and Prabhavananda, trans.), **Supp. XIV:** 156, 157, 164

Song of Hiawatha, The (Longfellow), **II:** 501, 503–504; **Retro. Supp. II:** 155, **159–161**, 162, 163; **Supp. XXIII:**

223, 234–235

"Song of Innocence, A" (Ellison), **Retro. Supp. II:** 126; **Supp. II Part 1:** 248

"Song of My Fiftieth Birthday, The" (Lindsay), **Supp. I Part 2:** 399

"Song of Myself" (Whitman), **II:** 544; **III:** 572, 584, 595; **IV:** 333, 334, 337–339, 340, 341, 342, 344, 348, 349, 351, 405; **Retro. Supp. I:** 388, 389, 395–399, 400; **Supp. V:** 122; **Supp. IX:** 131, 136, 143, 328, 331; **Supp. XIV:** 139; **Supp. XVIII:** 194, 304; **Supp. XXII:** 81

Song of Napalm (Weigl), **Supp. XIX:** 278–282

"Song of Napalm" (Weigl), **Supp. XIX:** 276–277

Song of Russia (film), **Supp. I Part 1:** 281, 294; **Supp. XVII:** 60–61

"Song of Self" (Huncke), **Supp. XIV:** 138–139, 145

Song of Solomon (biblical book), **III:** 118; **IV:** 150

Song of Solomon (Morrison), **Supp. III Part 1:** 364, 368, 369, 372, 379; **Supp. XVIII:** 55

Song of Songs (biblical book), **II:** 538; **IV:** 153–154; **Supp. XV:** 221

"Song of the Answerer" (Whitman), **Retro. Supp. I:** 393, 399

Song of the Cardinal, The (Stratton-Porter), **Supp. XX:** **217, 218, 219**

"Song of the Chattahoochee, The" (Lanier), **Supp. I Part 1:** 365, 368

"Song of the Degrees, A" (Pound), **III:** 466

"Song of the Drunkard" (Ferry), **Supp. XXIV:** 153, 162

"Song of the Dryads" (Taggard), **Supp. XXII:** 272

"Song of the Exposition" (Whitman), **IV:** 332

"Song of the Gavilan" (Leopold), **Supp. XIV:** 189

"Song of the Gourd" (Wright), **Supp. XV:** 348–349

"Song of the Greek Amazon" (Bryant), **Supp. I Part 1:** 168

Song of the Lark, The (Cather), **I:** 312, 319–321, 323; **Retro. Supp. I:** 1, 3, 7, **9–11**, 13, 19, 20

"Song of the Okogis, or Frog in Spring"(J. Schoolcraft), **Supp. XXIII:** 232, 233, 235

"Song of the Open Road" (McGrath), **Supp. X:** 127

"Song of the Open Road" (Whitman), **IV:** 340–341; **Retro. Supp. I:** 400; **Supp. IX:** 265

"Song of the Redwood Tree" (Whitman), **IV:** 348

"Song of the Scullery" (McCarriston), **Supp. XIV:** 272

"Song of the Sky Loom" (traditional Tewa poem), **Supp. IV Part 1:** 325

"Song of the Son" (Toomer), **Supp. III Part 2:** 482–483; **Supp. IX:** 313

"Song of the Sower, The" (Bryant), **Supp. I Part 1:** 169

"Song of the Stars" (Bryant), **Supp. I Part 1:** 163

"Song of the Swamp-Robin, The" (Frederic), **II:** 138

"Song of the Vermonters, The" (Whittier), **Supp. I Part 2:** 692

"Song of Three Smiles" (Merwin), **Supp. III Part 1:** 344

"Song of Wandering Aengus, The" (Yeats), **IV:** 271; **Retro. Supp. I:** 342, 350

"Song of Welcome" (Brodsky), **Supp. VIII:** 32

"Song on Captain Barney's Victory" (Freneau), **Supp. II Part 1:** 261

"Song/Poetry and Language-Expression and Perception" (Ortiz), **Supp. IV Part 2:** 500, 508

"Song Rehearsal, The" (Stallings), **Supp. XXV:** 233

"Song: 'Rough Winds Do Shake the Darling Buds of May' " (Simpson), **Supp. IX:** 268

Songs (Boyce), **Supp. XXI:** 9

Songs and Satires (Masters), **Supp. I Part 2:** 465–466

Songs and Sonnets (L. P. Smith), **Supp. XIV:** 341

Songs and Sonnets (Masters), **Supp. I Part 2:** 455, 459, 461, 466

"Songs for a Colored Singer" (Bishop), **Supp. I Part 1:** 80, 85

Songs for a Summer's Day (A Sonnet Cycle) (MacLeish), **III:** 3

Songs for Eve (MacLeish), **III:** 3, 19

"Songs for Eve" (MacLeish), **III:** 19

"Songs for My Father" (Komunyakaa), **Supp. XIII:** 128

Songs for the Missing (O'Nan), **Supp. XXV:** 143, 148, 150

Songs for the Unborn Second Baby (Notley), **Supp. XXII:** 228

"Songs for Two Seasons" (C. Frost), **Supp. XV:** 95–96

Songs from This Earth on Turtle's Back: Contemporary American Indian Poetry (Bruchac, ed.), **Supp. IV Part 1:** 320, 328

"Songs of a Housewife" (Rawlings), **Supp. X:** 221–222

"Songs of Billy Bathgate, The" (Doctorow), **Supp. IV Part 1:** 230

Songs of Innocence (Blake), **Supp. I Part 2:** 708

Songs of Jamaica (McKay), **Supp. X:** 131, 133

"Songs of Maximus, The" (Olson), **Supp. II Part 2:** 567

"Songs of Parting" (Whitman), **IV:** 348

Songs of the Doomed (Thompson), **Supp. XXIV:** 283

Songs of the North: A Sigurd Olson Reader (Mosher, ed.), **Supp. XXII:** 218

Songs of the Sierras (J. Miller), **I:** 459

Songs of Three Centuries (Whittier and Larcom, eds.), **Supp. XIII:** 142

"Song to David" (Smart), **III:** 534

"Song to No Music, A" (Brodsky), **Supp. VIII:** 26

"Song V" (Taggard), **Supp. XXII:** 284

Soniat, Katherine, **Supp. XXI:** 245

Sonneschein, Rosa, **Retro. Supp. II:** 65

"Sonnet" (Rukeyser), **Supp. VI:** 284

"Sonnet, A" (Very), **Supp. XXV:** 242

"Sonnet Crown for Two Voices" (Bierds), **Supp. XVII:** 35

"Sonnet"(J. Schoolcraft), **Supp. XXIII:** 229

"Sonnets" (Carruth), **Supp. XVI:** 56

Sonnets, The (Berrigan), **Supp. XXII:** 224; **Supp. XXIV:** 33, 34, 35, 37, 38– 41, 45

"Sonnets at Christmas" (Tate), **IV:** 135

Sonnets to Orpheus (Rilke), **Supp. XV:** 222; **Supp. XXIV:** 38

"Sonnet-To Zante" (Poe), **III:** 421

"Sonnet XV" (Berrigan), **Supp. XXIV:** 38–39, 44

"Sonny's Blues" (Baldwin), **Retro. Supp. II:** 7, 8, 10, 14; **Supp. I Part 1:** 58– 59, 63, 67; **Supp. XI:** 288

Son of Laughter, The: A Novel (Buechner), **Supp. XII:** 54

Son of Perdition, The (Cozzens), **I:** 359– 360, 377, 378, 379

Son of the Circus, A (Irving), **Supp. VI:** 165, 166, **176–179**

Son of the Gamblin' Man: The Youth of an Artist (Sandoz), **Supp. XXIV:** 244, **256–257**

"Son of the Gods, A" (Bierce), **I:** 202

Son of the Morning (Oates), **Supp. II Part 2:** 518, 519, 520–522

Son of the Morning Star: Custer and the Little Bighorn (Connell), **Supp. XIV:** 80, 82, 97

"Son of the Romanovs, A" (Simpson), **Supp. IX:** 273–274

Son of the Wolf, The (London), **II:** 465, 469

"Son of the Wolfman" (Chabon), **Supp. XI:** 76

"Sonrisas" (Mora), **Supp. XIII:** 216, 219

Sons (Buck), **Supp. II Part 1:** 117–118

Sons and Lovers (Lawrence), **III:** 27

Sontag, Kate, **Supp. XV:** 104

Sontag, Susan, **IV:** 13, 14; **Retro. Supp. II:** 279; **Supp. I Part 2:** 423; **Supp. III Part 2: 451–473; Supp. VIII:** 75; **Supp. XIV:** 14, 15, 95–96, 167; **Supp. XVI:** 201, 204, 206; **Supp. XX:** 205; **Supp. XXI:** 243

"Soonest Mended" (Ashbery), **Supp. III Part 1:** 1, 13

"Sootfall and Fallout" (White), **Supp. I Part 2:** 671

Sophisticates, The (Atherton), **Supp. XXIV:** 20, 25

Sophocles, **I:** 274; **II:** 291, 385, 577; **III:** 145, 151, 152, 153, 159, 398, 476, 478, 609, 613; **IV:** 291, 363, 368, 370; **Supp. I Part 1:** 153, 284; **Supp. I Part 2:** 491; **Supp. V:** 97; **Supp. VIII:** 332; **Supp. XV:** 265, 266

"Sophronsiba" (Bourne), **I:** 221

Sorayam, Aram, **Supp. XXII:** 25

Sorby, Angela, **Supp. XXIII:** 132

Sorcerer's Apprentice, The: Tales and Conjurations (Johnson), **Supp. VI:** 192–193, 194

"Sorcerer's Eye, The" (Nemerov), **III:** 283

Sordello (Browning), **III:** 467, 469, 470

"Sordid? Good God!" (Williams), **Retro. Supp. I:** 334

So Red the Rose (Young), **Supp. XXII:** 190, 193

"Sorghum" (Mason), **Supp. VIII:** 146

Sorkin, Adam, **Supp. XXIV:** 178

Sorokin, Pitirim, **Supp. I Part 2:** 679

Sorrentino, Christopher, **Supp. XVIII:** 148

Sorrentino, Gilbert, **Retro. Supp. I:** 426; **Supp. IV Part 1:** 286; **Supp. XII:** 139; **Supp. XXI: 225–241; Supp. XXII:** 261

Sorrento (Notley), **Supp. XXII:** 231

"Sorrow" (Komunyakaa), **Supp. XIII:** 119

Sorrow Dance, The (Levertov), **Supp. III Part 1:** 279–280, 283

"Sorrowful Guest, A" (Jewett), **Retro. Supp. II:** 137

Sorrows of Fat City, The: A Selection of Literary Essays and Reviews (Garrett), **Supp. VII:** 111

Sorrows of Young Werther, The (Goethe), **Supp. XI:** 169; **Supp. XX: 234, 236**

Sorrows of Young Werther, The (Goethe; Bogan and Mayer, trans.), **Supp. III Part 1:** 63

"Sorry Fugu" (Boyle), **Supp. XX: 19**

"Sorting Facts; or, Nineteen Ways of Looking at Marker" (Howe), **Supp. IV Part 2:** 434, 436

"Sort of Song, A" (W. C. Williams), **Supp. XVII:** 243

"S O S" (Baraka), **Supp. II Part 1:** 50

"So Sassafras" (Olson), **Supp. II Part 2:** 574

"So There" (Creeley), **Supp. IV Part 1:** 157

"So This Is Nebraska" (Kooser), **Supp. XIX:** 120

Sotirov, Vasil, **Supp. IX:** 152

Soto, Gary, **Supp. IV Part 2:** 545; **Supp. V:** 180; **Supp. XI:** 270; **Supp. XIII:** 313, 315, 316, 320, 323; **Supp. XV:** 73; **Supp. XXV:** 130

"Soto Thinking of the Ocean" (Salinas), **Supp. XIII:** 321

"Sotto Voce" (Kunitz), **Supp. III Part 1:** 265

Sot-Weed Factor, The (Barth), **I:** 122, 123, 125, 129, 130, 131–134, 135; **Supp. XXII:** 259

"Soul" (Ferry), **Supp. XXIV:** 162

Soul, The (Brooks), **I:** 244

Soul and Body of John Brown, The (Rukeyser), **Supp. VI:** 273

Soul Barnacles: Ten More Years with Ray (Gallagher; Simon, ed.), **Supp. XXIV:** 166, 167, 171, 172

Soul Clap Hands and Sing (Marshall), **Supp. XI:** 276, 278, **280–282**

Soul Expeditions (Singer). *See* Shosha (Singer)

Soul Gone Home (Hughes), **Retro. Supp. I:** 203; **Supp. I Part 1:** 328

"Soul inside the Sentence, The" (Gass), **Supp. VI:** 88

Soul Is Here for Its Own Joy, The (Bly, ed.), **Supp. IV Part 1:** 74

Soul of Man under Socialism, The (Wilde), **Supp. IX:** 134–135

"Soul of Spain, The \[In the manner of Gertrude Stein\]" (Hemingway), **Supp. XX: 74**

Soul of the Far East, The (Lowell), **II:** 513

"Soul on Bench" (Halliday), **Supp. XIX:** 91

Soul on Ice (Cleaver), **Retro. Supp. II:** 12, 13

"Souls Belated" (Wharton), **Retro. Supp. I:** 364

"Soul selects her own Society, The" (Dickinson), **Retro. Supp. I:** 37

Souls of Black Folk, The (Du Bois), **Supp. II Part 1:** 33, 40, 160, 168–170, 176, 183; **Supp. IV Part 1:** 164; **Supp. IX:** 305, 306; **Supp. X:** 133; **Supp. XIII:** 185, 238, 243

Souls of Black Folk. The (Du Bois), **Supp. XX: 102**

"Sound, The" (Olds), **Supp. X:** 214

Sound and Beauty (Hwang), **Supp. XXI:** 146

"Sound and Fury" (O. Henry), **Supp. II Part 1:** 402

Sound and the Fury, The (Faulkner), **I:** 480; **II:** 55, 57, 58–60, 73; **III:** 237; **IV:** 100, 101, 104; **Retro. Supp. I:** 73, 75, 77, 82, **83–84**, 86, 88, 89, 90, 91, 92; **Supp. VIII:** 215; **Supp. IX:** 103; **Supp. X:** 44; **Supp. XII:** 33; **Supp. XIV:** 12; **Supp. XVII:** 138; **Supp. XVIII:** 84

"Sound Bites" (Alvarez), **Supp. VII:** 11

Sound I Listened For, The (Francis), **Supp. IX: 78–79,** 87

"Soundless Trumpet, The" (Antin), **Supp. XX: 12**

"Sound Mind, Sound Body" (Lowell), **II:** 554

Sound of a Voice, The (Hwang), **Supp. XXI:** 146

"Sound of Distant Thunder, A" (Elkin), **Supp. VI: 42–43,** 44

"Sound of Light, The" (Merwin), **Supp. III Part 1:** 356

Sound of Mountain Water, The (Stegner), **Supp. IV Part 2:** 595, 596, 598, 600, 608

"Sound of Talking" (Purdy), **Supp. VII:** 270

Sounds of Poetry (television special, Moyers), **Supp. XXIII:** 139

Sounds of Poetry, The (Pinsky), **Supp. VI:** 236, 247, 248; **Supp. XXIII:** 124

Sound the Stars Make Rushing Through the Sky, The: The Writings of Jane Johnston Schoolcraft (Parker, ed.), **Supp. XXIII:** 223–224, 227, 228

Soupault, Philippe, **IV:** 288, 404; **Retro. Supp. II:** 85, 321, 324

Source (Doty), **Supp. XI:** 121, **134–137**

"Source" (Doty), **Supp. XI:** 136

"Source, The" (Olds), **Supp. X:** 211

"Source, The" (Porter), **III:** 443

Source of Light, The (Price), **Supp. VI: 262,** 266

"Sources of Soviet Conduct, The" (Kennan), **Supp. VIII:** 241

Sour Grapes (W. C. Williams), **Retro. Supp. I:** 418

"Sour Grapes"(Moraga), **Supp. XXIII:** 202

"Sourwood Nocturne" (Skloot), **Supp. XX: 202**

"South" (Levis), **Supp. XI:** 266

"South" (Trethewey), **Supp. XXI:** 247, 256

"South, The" (Hughes), **Supp. I Part 1:** 321

South American Journey (W. Frank), **Supp. XX:** 79

"Southampton Variations"(O'Hara), **Supp. XXIII:** 212

"Southbound on the Freeway" (Swenson), **Supp. IV Part 2:** 643

South Dakota Guidebook, The (C. Baxter), **Supp. XVII:** 15

Southern, Terry, **Supp. IV Part 1:** 379; **Supp. V:** 40, 201; **Supp. XI: 293–310; Supp. XVI:** 230

Southern Cross, The (Wright), **Supp. V:** 332, 342

"Southern Cross, The" (Wright), **Supp. V:** 338

"Southerner's Problem, The" (Du Bois), **Supp. II Part 1:** 168

"Southern Girl" (Zelda Fitzgerald), **Supp. IX:** 71

"Southern Gothic" (Trethewey), **Supp. XXI:** 256

"Southern History" (Trethewey), **Supp. XXI:** 256, 257

"Southern Mode of the Imagination, A" (Tate), **IV:** 120

"Southern Romantic, A" (Tate), **Supp. I Part 1:** 373

"Southern Sojourn, A" (Hoffman), **Supp. XVIII:** 87

Southern Terry, **Supp. XIV:** 82

Southey, Robert, **II:** 304, 502; **Supp. I Part 1:** 154; **Supp. XXIV:** 74

"South Lingers On, The" (R. Fisher), **Supp. XIX:** 69–70

South Moon Under (Rawlings), **Supp. X: 225–226,** 229, 233

South Pacific Affair (Lacy), **Supp. XV:** 206

Southpaw, The (Harris), **II:** 424–425

"South Sangamon" (Cisneros), **Supp. VII:** 66

"South State Street: Chicago" (Bodenheim), **Supp. XXV:** 22

South to a Very Old Place (Murray), **Supp. XIX: 151–153**

Southwell, Robert, **IV:** 151

Southwick, Marcia, **Supp. XI:** 259

Southworth, E. D. E. N, **Retro. Supp. I:** 246

Souvenir of the Ancient World, Selected Poems of Carlos Drummond de Andrade (Strand, trans.), **Supp. IV Part 2:** 630

"Sow" (Plath), **Supp. I Part 2:** 537

"Sowing and Reaping in *Furors Die*" (Nostrandt), **Supp. XVIII:** 80–81

Soyinka, Wole, **Supp. XX: 100**

"Space" (Brockmeier), **Supp. XXII:** 51

Space between Our Footsteps, The: Poems and Paintings from the Middle East (Nye, ed.), **Supp. XIII:** 280

"Space Quale, The" (James), **II:** 349

"Spaces Between, The" (Kingsolver), **Supp. VII:** 209

"Space Where Sex Should Be, The: Toward a Definition of the Black Literary Tradition" (Nelson), **Supp. XVIII:** 172

Spack, Ruth, **Supp. XXV:** 278

Spackman, Peter, **Supp. XVI:** 221

Spacks, Patricia, **Supp. XVI:** 251

"Spain" (Auden), **Supp. II Part 1:** 12–13, 14

"Spain in Fifty-Ninth Street" (White), **Supp. I Part 2:** 677

Spanier, Sandra, **Supp. XXIV:** 51, 64

"Spanish-American War Play" (Crane), **I:** 422

Spanish Ballads (Merwin, trans.), **Supp. III Part 1:** 347

Spanish Bayonet (Benét), **Supp. XI:** 45, 47

Spanish Earth, The (film), **Retro. Supp. I:** 184

Spanish Love (Rinehart), **Supp. XXV:** 195

Spanish Papers and Other Miscellanies (Irving), **II:** 314

"Spanish Revolution, The" (Bryant), **Supp. I Part 1:** 153, 168

Spanish Student, The (Longfellow), **II:** 489, 506; **Retro. Supp. II:** 165

"Spanish Winter" (Egan), **Supp. XIX:** 52

Spanking the Maid (Coover), **Supp. V:** 47, 48, 49, 52

Spare Change (Parker), **Supp. XIX:** 186–187

Spargo, John, **Supp. I Part 1:** 13

"Spark, The" (Wharton), **Retro. Supp. I:** 381

"Sparkles from the Wheel" (Whitman), **IV:** 348

Sparks, Debra, **Supp. X:** 177

Sparks, Jared, **Supp. I Part 1:** 156; **Supp. XXIV:** 71

"Sparrow" (Berry), **Supp. X:** 31

Sparrow, Henry, **III:** 587

Sparrow, Mrs. Henry, **III:** 587

"Sparrow's Gate, The" (B. Kelly), **Supp. XVIII:** 133

Spaulding, William, **Supp. XVI:** 106

"Spawning Run, The" (Humphrey), **Supp. IX:** 95

"Speak, Gay Memory" (Kirp), **Supp. XI:** 129

"Speak, Hoyt-Schermerhorn" (Lethem), **Supp. XVIII:** 148

Speak, Memory (Nabokov), **III:** 247–250, 252; **Retro. Supp. I:** 264, 265, 266, 267, 268, 277; **Supp. XVI:** 148

Speak, Memory (V. Nabakov), **Supp. XVII:** 47

Speaking and Language (Shapiro), **Supp. II Part 2:** 721

Speaking for Nature: How Literary Naturalists from Henry Thoreau to Rachel Carson Have Shaped America (Brooks), **Supp. IX:** 31

Speaking for Ourselves: American Ethnic Writing (Faderman and Bradshaw, eds.), **Supp. XIII:** 313

Speaking of Accidents (Everwine), **Supp. XV:** 75, 88

"Speaking of Accidents" (Everwine), **Supp. XV:** 88–89

"Speaking of Counterweights" (White), **Supp. I Part 2:** 669

Speaking of Literature and Society (Trilling), **Supp. III Part 2:** 494, 496, 499

"Speaking of Love" (Gioia), **Supp. XV:** 124–125

Speaking of Race, Speaking of Sex: Hate Speech, Civil Rights, and Civil Liberties (H. L. Gates, Griffin, Lively, and Strossen), **Supp. XX: 111**

Speaking on Stage (Kolin and Kullman, eds.), **Supp. IX:** 145

Speaking on Stage: Interviews with Contemporary American Playwrights (Balakian), **Supp. XV:** 327

"Speaking Passions" (Kitchen), **Supp. XV:** 215

Speak of the Devil (Holding), **Supp. XXII: 127**

Speak What We Feel (Not What We Ought to Say): Reflections on Literature and Faith (Buechner), **Supp. XII:** 57

Spear, Roberta, **Supp. V:** 180; **Supp. XV:** 73

"Special Kind of Fantasy, A: James Dickey on the Razor's Edge" (Niflis), **Supp. IV Part 1:** 175

"Special Pleading" (Lanier), **Supp. I Part 1:** 364

"Special Problems in Teaching Leslie Marmon Silko's *Ceremony*" (Gunn Allen), **Supp. IV Part 1:** 333

Special Providence, A (Yates), **Supp. XI:** 342, **344–345**

"Special Time, a Special School, A" (Knowles), **Supp. XII:** 236

Special View of History, The (Olson), **Supp. II Part 2:** 566, 569, 572

Specimen Days (Whitman), **IV:** 338, 347, 348, 350; **Retro. Supp. I:** 408

Specimens of the American Poets, **Supp. I Part 1:** 155

"Spectacles, The" (Poe), **III:** 425

Spectator Bird, The (Stegner), **Supp. IV Part 2:** 599, 604, 606, 611–612

Spector, Herman, **Supp. XXV:** 26

Spector, Robert, **Supp. XIII:** 87

Spectra: A Book of Poetic Experiments (Bynner and Ficke), **Supp. XV:** 43

"Spectre Bridegroom, The" (Irving), **II:** 304

"Spectre Pig, The" (Holmes), **Supp. I Part 1:** 302

"Speculating Woman" (X. J. Kennedy), **Supp. XV:** 168

"Speech Sounds" (O. Butler), **Supp. XIII:** 61, **70**

"Speech to a Crowd" (MacLeish), **III:** 16

"Speech to the Detractors" (MacLeish), **III:** 16

"Speech to the Young" (Brooks), **Supp. III Part 1:** 79, 86

"Speech to Those Who Say Comrade" (MacLeish), **III:** 16

Speedboat (Adler), **Supp. X:** 171

Speed of Darkness, The (Rukeyser), **Supp. VI:** 274, 281

Speed Queen, The (O'Nan), **Supp. XXV:** 142, 144

Speed-the-Plow (Mamet), **Supp. XIV:** 241, 246, 249, 250, 251

"Speedy Gonzales Was the Fastest Mouse in Mexico" (P. N. Warren as Kilina), **Supp. XX: 262**

Speilberg, Steven, **Supp. XI:** 234

Speirs, Logan, **Supp. XIX:** 282

"Spell" (Francis), **Supp. IX:** 87

"Spell, The" (Peacock), **Supp. XIX:** 198, 200

"Spell for the Manufacture & Use of a Magic Carpet" (Hull), **Supp. XXI:** 132–133, 139, 141

Spelling Dictionary, A (Rowson), **Supp. XV:** 244

Spence, Thomas, **Supp. I Part 2:** 518

Spence + Lila (Mason), **Supp. VIII:** 133, **143–145**

Spencer, Edward, **Supp. I Part 1:** 357, 360

Spencer, Herbert, **I:** 515; **II:** 345, 462–463, 480, 483, 536; **III:** 102, 315; **IV:** 135; **Retro. Supp. II:** 60, 65, 93, 98; **Supp. I Part 1:** 368; **Supp. I Part 2:** 635

Spencer, Sharon, **Supp. X:** 185, 186, 195, 196

Spencer, Theodore, **I:** 433; **Supp. III Part 1:** 2

Spender, Natasha, **Supp. IV Part 1:** 119, 127, 134

Spender, Stephen, **II:** 371; **III:** 504, 527; **Retro. Supp. I:** 216; **Retro. Supp. II:** 243, 244; **Supp. I Part 2:** 536; **Supp. II Part 1:** 11; **Supp. IV Part 1:** 82, 134; **Supp. IV Part 2:** 440; **Supp. X:** 116

Spengler, Oswald, **I:** 255, 270; **II:** 7, 577; **III:** 172, 176; **Retro. Supp. II:** 324; **Supp. I Part 2:** 647

Spens, Sir Patrick, **Supp. I Part 2:** 404

Spenser, Edmund, **I:** 62; **III:** 77, 78, 89; **IV:** 155, 453; **Retro. Supp. I:** 62; **Supp. I Part 1:** 98, 152, 369; **Supp. I Part 2:** 422, 719; **Supp. XXIV:** 159

"Spenser's Ireland" (Moore), **III:** 211, 212

"Spermaceti Papers"(Lippard), **Supp. XXIII:** 178

Sperry, Margaret, **Supp. IV Part 1:** 169

Spheres of Existence (C. L. R. James), **Supp. XXI:** 172

Sphere: The Form of a Motion (Ammons), **Supp. VII:** 24, 32, 33, 35, 36

"Sphinx" (Hayden), **Supp. II Part 1:** 373

"Spiced Plums" (Ríos), **Supp. IV Part 2:** 553

Spickard, Paul, **Supp. XXI:** 149

"Spider and the Ghost of the Fly, The" (Lindsay), **Supp. I Part 2:** 375

Spider Bay (Van Vechten), **Supp. II Part 2:** 746

"Spider Heart, The" (Peacock), **Supp. XIX:** 200

"Spiders" (Schwartz), **Supp. II Part 2:** 665

Spider's House, The (Bowles), **Supp. IV Part 1:** 87–89, 90, 91

Spider Woman's Granddaughters: Traditional Tales and Contemporary Writing by Native American Women (Gunn Allen, ed.), **Supp. IV Part 1:** 320, 326, 332–333; **Supp. IV Part 2:** 567

Spiegel, Sam, **Supp. XVIII:** 251, 252

Spiegelman, Art, **Supp. XVII:** 48

Spiegelman, Willard, **Supp. XI:** 126

Spielberg, Steven, **Supp. XXI:** 154

Spillane, Mickey, **Supp. IV Part 2:** 469, 472; **Supp. XV:** 200; **Supp. XVIII:** 236, 237

Spiller, Robert E., **I:** 241; **Supp. I Part 1:** 104

Spillers, Hortense, **Supp. XX:** 109

"Spillikins: Gregor Mendel at the Table" (Bierds), **Supp. XVII:** 34–35

Spillville (Hampl), **Supp. XXII:** 98

Spillway (Barnes), **Supp. III Part 1:** 44

Spingarn, Amy, **Supp. I Part 1:** 325, 326

Spingarn, Joel, **I:** 266; **Supp. I Part 1:** 325

Spinoza, Baruch, **I:** 493; **II:** 590, 593; **III:** 600; **IV:** 5, 7, 11, 12, 17; **Retro. Supp. II:** 300; **Supp. I Part 1:** 274; **Supp. I Part 2:** 643; **Supp. XVI:** 184

"Spinoza of Market Street, The" (Singer), **IV:** 12–13; **Retro. Supp. II:** 307

"Spinster" (Plath), **Supp. I Part 2:** 536

"Spinster's Tale, A" (Taylor), **Supp. V:** 314–315, 316–317, 319, 323

Spiral of Memory, The: Interviews (Coltelli, ed.), **Supp. XII:** 215

Spires, Elizabeth, **Supp. X:** 8

"Spire Song" (Bowles), **Supp. IV Part 1:** 80

Spirit and Flame: An Anthology of African American Poetry (Gilyard, ed.), **Supp. XXI:** 246

Spirit and the Flesh, The: Sexual Diversity in American Indian Culture (W. L. Williams), **Supp. IV Part 1:** 330

"Spirit Birth" (Cullen), **Supp. IV Part 1:** 168

Spirit Brides (Gibran). *See Nymphs in the Valley*

Spirit in Man, The (Jung), **Supp. IV Part 1:** 68

"Spirit in Me, The" (Hoffman), **Supp. XVIII:** 87

"Spirit Made Visible" (art exhibit), **Supp. XXII:** 180

Spirit of Culver (West), **IV:** 287

Spirit of Labor, The (Hapgood), **Supp. XVII:** 96, 99, 101–102; **Supp. XXI:** 4

Spirit of Romance, The (Pound), **III:** 470; **Retro. Supp. I:** 286

Spirit of the Ghetto, The: Studies of the Jewish Quarter of New York (Hapgood), **Supp. XVII:** 96, 101, 103, 106

Spirit of Youth and the City Streets, The (Addams), **Supp. I Part 1:** 6–7, 12–13, 16, 17, 19

"Spirits" (Bausch), **Supp. VII:** 46–47

Spirits, and Other Stories (Bausch), **Supp. VII:** 46–47, 54

"Spirit Says, You Are Nothing, The" (Levis), **Supp. XI:** 265–266

Spirits Rebellious (al-Arwá&hudot; al-Mutamarrida) (Gibran), **Supp. XX:** 115, 124, 125

Spiritual Adventures (Symons), **Supp. XX: 239**

Spiritual Conflict, The (Scupoli), **IV:** 156

Spiritual Exercises, The (Loyola), **IV:** 151; **Supp. XI:** 162

"Spiritual Manifestation, A" (Whittier), **Supp. I Part 2:** 699

"Spirituals and Neo-Spirituals" (Hurston), **Supp. VI:** 152–153

Spits, Ellen Handler, **Supp. XII:** 166

"Spitzbergen Tales" (Crane), **I:** 409, 415, 423

Spitzer, Philip, **Supp. XIV:** 21

"Spleen" (Eliot), **I:** 569, 573–574

Spleen de Paris, Le (Baudelaire), **Supp. XIV:** 337

Splendid Drunken Twenties, The (Van Vechten), **Supp. II Part 2:** 739–744

Splendide-Hôtel (Sorrentino), **Supp. XXI:** 233

Splendid Table, The (radio show), **Supp. XXIII:** 138

Splendor in the Grass (screenplay, Inge), **Supp. XXV:** 93.**Supp. XXV:** 95, 102–103, 104

"Splinters" (Bukiet), **Supp. XVII:** 47

"Split Infinitive" (Pickering), **Supp. XXI:** 204

"Splitting an Order" (Kooser), **Supp. XIX:** 128–129

"Splittings" (Rich), **Supp. I Part 2:** 570–571

"Splitting Wood at Six Above" (Kumin), **Supp. IV Part 2:** 449

Spofford, Harriet Prescott, **Supp. XIII:** 143

Spoils of Poynton, The (James), **I:** 463; **Retro. Supp. I:** 229–230

Spoken Page, The (Nye), **Supp. XIII:** 274

"Spokes" (Auster), **Supp. XII:** 23

Spokesmen (Whipple), **II:** 456

Spook Sonata, The (Strindberg), **III:** 387, 392

Spooky Art, The: A Book about Writing (Mailer), **Retro. Supp. II:** 214

"Spoon, The" (Simic), **Supp. VIII:** 275

Spoon River Anthology (Masters), **I:** 106; **III:** 579; **Supp. I Part 2:** 454, 455, 456, 460–465, 466, 467, 471, 472, 473, 476; **Supp. IX:** 306; **Supp. XIV:** 282–283; **Supp. XIX:** 121; **Supp. XXII:** 282

Sport and a Pastime, A (Salter), **Supp. IX:** 254–257; **Supp. XVI:** 237

Sporting Club, The (McGuane), **Supp. VIII:** 43

Sport of the Gods, The (Dunbar), **Supp. II Part 1:** 193, 200, 207, 214–217

Sports Illustrated Training with Weights (Parker and Marsh), **Supp. XIX:** 187

"Sportsman Born and Bred, A" (Plimpton), **Supp. XVI:** 241

Sportsman's Sketches, A (Turgenev), **I:** 106; **IV:** 277

Sportswriter, The (Ford), **Supp. V:** 57, 58, 62–67

"Spotted Horses" (Faulkner), **IV:** 260

Sprague, Morteza, **Retro. Supp. II:** 115

Spratling, William, **II:** 56; **Retro. Supp. I:** 80

Sprawl trilogy (W. Gibson), **Supp. XVI:** 117, 122, 124

"Spray, The" (Lethem), **Supp. XVIII:** 148

"Spray Paint King, The" (Dove), **Supp. IV Part 1:** 252–253

Spreading Fires (Knowles), **Supp. XII:** 249

Sprigge, Elizabeth, **IV:** 31

"Spring" (Kooser), **Supp. XIX:** 126

"Spring" (Millay), **III:** 126

"Spring" (Mora), **Supp. XIII:** 217

"Spring 1967" (Carruth), **Supp. XVI:** 55

Spring and All (W. C. Williams), **Retro. Supp. I:** 412, 418, **418–420,** 427, 430, 431

"Spring and All" (W. C. Williams), **Retro. Supp. I:** 419

Spring Awakening (Wedeking, trans. Franzen), **Supp. XX:** 85

"Spring Break-Up" (Carruth), **Supp. XVI:** 56

"Spring Bulletin" (Allen), **Supp. XV:** 15

Springer's Progress (Markson), **Supp. XVII: 141–142,** 143, 146

"Spring Evening" (Farrell), **II:** 45

"Spring Evening" (Kenyon), **Supp. VII:** 173

"Springfield Magical" (Lindsay), **Supp. I Part 2:** 379

Spring in New Hampshire and Other Poems (McKay), **Supp. X:** 131, 135

"Spring Notes from Robin Hill" (Carruth), **Supp. XVI:** 48

"Spring Pastoral" (Wylie), **Supp. I Part 2:** 707

"Spring Pools" (Frost), **II:** 155; **Retro. Supp. I:** 137

"Spring Snow" (Matthews), **Supp. IX:** 160

"SPRING SONG" (Baraka), **Supp. II Part 1:** 60

Springsteen, Bruce, **Supp. VIII:** 143

"Spring Strains" (W. C. Williams), **Retro. Supp. I:** 416

Spring Tides (Morison), **Supp. I Part 2:** 494

Springtime and Harvest (Sinclair), **Supp. V:** 280

"Springtime for You" (Halliday), **Supp. XIX:** 87

Spruance, Raymond, **Supp. I Part 2:** 479, 491

"Spruce Has No Taproot, The" (Clampitt), **Supp. IX:** 41–42

"Spunk" (Hurston), **Supp. VI:** 150, 151–152

Spunk: The Selected Stories (Hurston), **Supp. VI:** 150

Spurr, David, **Supp. XV:** 183

Spy, The (Cooper), **I:** 335, 336, 337, 339, 340; **Supp. I Part 1:** 155

"Spy, The" (Francis), **Supp. IX:** 81

Spy, The (Freneau), **Supp. II Part 1:** 260

Spyglass Tree, The (Murray), **Supp. XIX: 155–156**

Spy in the House of Love, A (Nin), **Supp. X:** 186

Squanto, **Supp. I Part 2:** 486

"Square Business" (Baraka), **Supp. II Part 1:** 49

Square Root of Wonderful, The (McCullers), **II:** 587–588

"Squash in Blossom" (Francis), **Supp. IX:** 81

"Squatter on Company Land, The" (Hugo), **Supp. VI:** 133

"Squatter's Children" (Bishop), **Retro. Supp. II:** 47

"Squeak, Memory" (Bukiet), **Supp. XVII:** 47

Squeeze Play (Auster), **Supp. XII:** 21

Squires, Radcliffe, **IV:** 127; **Supp. XV:** 118

Squirrels (Mamet), **Supp. XIV:** 240

S.S. Gliencairn (O'Neill), **III:** 387, 388, 405

S.S. San Pedro (Cozzens), **I:** 360–362, 370, 378, 379

"Ssshh" (Olds), **Supp. X:** 215

"Stacking the Straw" (Clampitt), **Supp. IX:** 41

Stade, George, **Supp. IV Part 1:** 286

Staël, Madame de, **II:** 298

"Staff of Life, The" (H. Miller), **III:** 187

Stafford, Jean, **II:** 537; **Retro. Supp. II:** 177; **Supp. V:** 316

Stafford, William, **Supp. IV Part 1:** 72; **Supp. IV Part 2:** 642; **Supp. IX:** 273; **Supp. XI: 311–332; Supp. XIII:** 76, 274, 276, 277, 281, 283; **Supp. XIV:** 119, 123; **Supp. XX: 161; Supp. XXI:** 246

"Stage All Blood, The" (MacLeish), **III:** 18

"Staggerlee Wonders" (Baldwin), **Retro. Supp. II:** 15

Stained White Radiance, A (Burke), **Supp. XIV:** 28, 31

Stalin, Joseph, **I:** 261, 490; **II:** 39, 40, 49, 564; **III:** 30, 298; **IV:** 372; **Supp. V:** 290; **Supp. XXI:** 164, 165, 167

"Stalking" (J. W. Miller), **Supp. XX: 167**

"Stalking the Billion-Footed Beast: A Literary Manifesto for the New Social Novel" (Wolfe), **Supp. III Part 2:** 586

Stallings, A. E., **Supp. XXIII:** 111, 124; **Supp. XXV: 221–236**

Stallings, H. A., **Supp. XXII:** 194

Stallman, R. W., **I:** 405

Stamberg, Susan, **Supp. IV Part 1:** 201; **Supp. XII:** 193

Stamford, Anne Marie, **Supp. XII:** 162

Stanard, Mrs. Jane, **III:** 410, 413

Stand, The (King), **Supp. V:** 139, 140–141, 144–146, 148, 152

"Standard of Liberty, The" (Rowson), **Supp. XV:** 243

"Standard of Living, The" (Parker), **Supp. IX: 198–199**

Stander, Lionel, **Supp. I Part 1:** 289

"Standing and the Waiting, The" (M. F. K. Fisher), **Supp. XVII:** 83

Standing by Words (Berry), **Supp. X:** 22, 27, 28, 31, 32, 33, 35

Standing Fast (Swados), **Supp. XIX: 268–269**

"Standing Halfway Home" (Wagoner), **Supp. IX:** 324

"Standing In" (Caputo), **Supp. XIX:** 26

Standing Still and Walking in New York (O'Hara), **Supp. XXIII:** 220

Stand in the Mountains, A (Taylor), **Supp. V:** 324

Standish, Burt L. (pseudonym). *See* Patten, Gilbert

Standish, Miles, **I:** 471; **II:** 502–503

Standley, Fred L., **Retro. Supp. II:** 6

Stand Still Like the Hummingbird (H. Miller), **III:** 184

"Stand Up" (Salinas), **Supp. XIII:** 315

Stand with Me Here (Francis), **Supp. IX:** 76

Stanford, Ann, **Retro. Supp. I:** 41; **Supp. I Part 1:** 99, 100, 102, 103, 106, 108, 109, 113, 117; **Supp. IV Part 2:** 637

Stanford, Charles Villiers, **Supp. XX: 228**

Stanford, Donald E., **II:** 217

Stanford, Frank, **Supp. XV:** 338, 339, 341, 342–343, 343, 345, 348, 350

Stanford, Ginny (Crouch), **Supp. XV:** 339

Stanford, Leland, **I:** 196, 198

Stanislavsky, Konstantin, **Supp. XIV:** 240, 243

Stanley, Jodee, **Supp. XIX:** 52

"Stanley Kunitz" (Oliver), **Supp. VII:** 237

Stansell, Christine, **Supp. XVII:** 106; **Supp. XXI:** 4

Stanton, Frank L., **Supp. II Part 1:** 192

Stanton, Robert J., **Supp. IV Part 2:** 681

"Stanzas, Written in 1815 before going to hear my Father read religious services"(J. Schoolcraft), **Supp. XXIII:** 229

"Stanzas from the Grande Chartreuse" (Arnold), **Supp. I Part 2:** 417

Stanzas in Meditation (Stein), **Supp. III Part 1:** 13

Staples, Hugh, **Retro. Supp. II:** 187

Star, Alexander, **Supp. X:** 310

Starbuck, George, **Retro. Supp. II:** 53, 245; **Supp. I Part 2:** 538; **Supp. IV Part 2:** 440; **Supp. XIII:** 76

Star Child (Gunn Allen), **Supp. IV Part 1:** 324

"Star Dust" (Wrigley), **Supp. XVIII:** 296

Stardust Lounge, The (Digges), **Supp. XXIII:** 57

Stardust Memories (film; Allen), **Supp. XV:** 1, 4, **8,** 9, 13

"Stare, The" (Updike), **Retro. Supp. I:** 329

"Starfish, The" (R. Bly), **Supp. IV Part 1:** 72

"Staring at the Sea on the Day of the Death of Another" (Swenson), **Supp. IV Part 2:** 652

Star Is Born, A (film), **Supp. IV Part 1:** 198; **Supp. IX:** 198; **Supp. XVIII:** 242, 243

Stark, David, **Supp. XII:** 202

Stark, Heidi, **Supp. XXIII:** 228, 233

"Stark Boughs on the Family Tree" (Oliver), **Supp. VII:** 232

Starke, Aubrey Harrison, **Supp. I Part 1:** 350, 352, 356, 360, 362, 365, 370, 371

Starkey, David, **Supp. XII:** 180, 181

Star Ledger (Hull), **Supp. XXI:** 129, **136–138**

"Star Ledger" (Hull), **Supp. XXI:** 136

"Starlight" (Levine), **Supp. V:** 188

"Starlight Scope Myopia" (Komunyakaa), **Supp. XIII:** 123, 124

Starnino, Carmine, **Supp. XVII:** 74

"Star of the Nativity" (Brodsky), **Supp. VIII:** 33

Starr, Ellen Gates, **Supp. I Part 1:** 4, 5, 11

Starr, Jean. *See* Untermeyer, Jean Starr

Starr, Kevin, **Supp. XXIV:** 17, 22

Starr, Ringo, **Supp. XI:** 309

Star Rover, The (London), **II:** 467

"Starry Night, The" (Sexton), **Supp. II Part 2:** 681

"Stars" (Frost), **II:** 153

Stars, the Snow, the Fire, The: Twenty-five Years in the Northern Wilderness (Haines), **Supp. XII: 199–201,** 206, 209

Star Shines over Mt. Morris Park, A (H. Roth), **Supp. IX:** 227, 236, **236–237**

"Stars of the Summer Night" (Longfellow), **II:** 493

"Stars over Harlem" (Hughes), **Retro. Supp. I:** 207

"Star-Spangled" (García), **Supp. XI:** 177, 178

Star-Spangled Girl, The (Simon), **Supp. IV Part 2:** 579

"Star-Splitter, The" (Frost), **Retro. Supp. I:** 123, 133

Stars Principal (McClatchy), **Supp. XII: 256–258**

"Start Again Somewhere" (Gallagher), **Supp. XXIV:** 169

"Star That Would Not Shine, The" (C. L. R. James), **Supp. XXI:** 160

"Starting from Paumanok" (Whitman), **IV:** 333

Starting from Troy (Hadas), **Supp. XXIII: 113**

Starting Out in the Thirties (Kazin), **Supp. VIII: 95–97; Supp. XXIV:** 223

Star Trek television series, **Supp. XXII:** 60

"Starved Lovers" (MacLeish), **III:** 19

Starved Rock (Masters), **Supp. I Part 2:** 465

"Starving Again" (Moore), **Supp. X:** 163, 172, 175

"Starving"(Strout), **Supp. XXIII:** 283, 285

"State, The" (Bourne), **I:** 233

State and Main (Mamet), **Supp. XIV:** 241

"Statement of Principles" (Ransom), **III:** 496

"Statement of Randolph Carter, The" (Lovecraft), **Supp. XXV:** 114, 123

"Statement: Phillipa Allen" (Rukeyser), **Supp. VI:** 283–284

"Statements on Poetics" (Snyder), **Supp. VIII:** 291, 292

"Statement with Rhymes" (Kees), **Supp. XV:** 139

"State of the Art, The" (Elkin), **Supp. VI:** 52

"State of the Arts, The" (Wasserstein), **Supp. XV:** 332

State of the Nation (Dos Passos), **I:** 489

"State of the Union" (Vidal), **Supp. IV Part 2:** 678

State Versus Elinor Norton, The (Rinehart), **Supp. XXV:** 197, 200

Static Element, The: Selected Poems of Natan Zach (Everwine, trans.), **Supp. XV:** 73, 75, **85–88**

"Statue, The" (Berryman), **I:** 173

"Statue and Birds" (Bogan), **Supp. III Part 1:** 50

"Statue of an Unkown Soldier, The" (Kooser), **Supp. XIX:** 124

"Statues, The" (Schwartz), **Supp. II Part 2:** 654, 659

"Status Rerum" (Pound), **Supp. I Part 1:** 257

Stavans, Ilan, **Supp. XI:** 190

"Stave Church" (W. V. Davis), **Supp. XXI:** 93, 94

"Staying Afloat"(Strout), **Supp. XXIII:** 274

"Staying Alive" (Levertov), **Supp. III Part 1:** 281

Staying Alive (Wagoner), **Supp. IX:** 324, **326**

"Staying at Ed's Place" (Swenson), **Supp. IV Part 2:** 648

Staying Put : Making a Home in a Restless World (Sanders), **Supp. XVI:** 274–275

Stay Me, Oh Comfort Me: Journals and Stories, 1933–1941 (M. F. K. Fisher), **Supp. XVII:** 92

Stayton, Richard, **Supp. IX:** 133

Steadman, Goodman, **IV:** 147

Steadman, Ralph, **Supp. XXIV:** 288

"Steak" (Snyder), **Supp. VIII:** 301

Steal Away: Selected and New Poems (Wright), **Supp. XV:** 337, 340, 348, 350–351

Stealing Beauty (Minot), **Supp. VI:** 205

Stealing Glimpses (McQuade), **Supp. IX:** 151

Stealing the Language: The Emergence of Women's Poetry in America (Ostriker), **Supp. XV:** 251

"Stealing the Thunder: Future Visions for American Indian Women, Tribes, and Literary Studies" (Gunn Allen), **Supp. IV Part 1:** 331

"Steam Shovel Cut" (Masters), **Supp. I Part 2:** 468

Stearns, Harold, **I:** 245; **Supp. XVII:** 106

Stedman, Edmund Clarence, **Supp. I Part 1:** 372; **Supp. II Part 1:** 192; **Supp. XV:** 115, 269, 273, 274, 282, 286

Steel, Sharon, **Supp. XIX:** 61

Steele, Lloyd, **Supp. XXV:** 96

Steele, Margaret, **Supp. XXI:** 5

Steele, Max, **Supp. XIV:** 82

Steele, Sir Richard, **I:** 378; **II:** 105, 107, 300; **III:** 430

Steele, Timothy, **Supp. XV:** 251; **Supp. XVII:** 112; **Supp. XXIII:** 111

Steele, Wilbur Daniel, **Supp. XXI:** 5

"Steel Mills: South Chicago" (Bodenheim), **Supp. XXV:** 22

Steelwork (Sorrentino), **Supp. XXI:** 227, 230, 231, 232

Steenburgen, Mary, **Supp. IV Part 1:** 236

Steeple Bush (Frost), **II:** 155; **Retro. Supp. I:** 140; **Retro. Supp. II:** 42

"Steeple-Jack, The" (Moore), **III:** 212, 213, 215

"Steerage" (Goldbarth), **Supp. XII:** 187

Steers, Nina, **Retro. Supp. II:** 25

Stefans, Brian Kim, **Supp. XXII:** 226

Steffens, Lincoln, **II:** 577; **III:** 580; **Retro. Supp. I:** 202; **Retro. Supp. II:** 101; **Supp. I Part 1:** 7; **Supp. XVII:** 98, 101, 106–107; **Supp. XXI:** 2, 3, 5, 7, 10; **Supp. XXIII:** 162

Stegner, Page, **IV:** 114, 116; **Supp. IV Part 2:** 599

Stegner, Wallace, **Supp. IV Part 2: 595–618; Supp. V:** 220, 224, 296; **Supp. X:** 23, 24; **Supp. XIV:** 82, 193, 230, 233; **Supp. XVIII:** 192; **Supp. XXII:** 204, 205, 208

"Stegner's Short Fiction" (Ahearn), **Supp. IV Part 2:** 604

Steichen, Edward, **III:** 580, 594–595

Steichen, Lillian. *See* Sandburg, Mrs. Carl (Lillian Steichen)

Steiger, Rod, **Supp. VIII:** 269; **Supp. XI:** 305

Stein, Edith, **Supp. XXII:** 92–93, 167

Stein, Gertrude, **I:** 103, 105, 476; **II:** 56, 251, 252, 257, 260, 262–263, 264, 289; **III:** 71, 454, 471–472, 600; **IV: 24–48,** 368, 375, 404, 415, 443, 477; **Retro. Supp. I:** 108, 170, 176, 177, 186, 418, 422; **Retro. Supp. II:** 85, 207, 326, 331; **Supp. I Part 1:** 292; **Supp. III Part 1:** 13, 37, 225, 226; **Supp. III Part 2:** 626; **Supp. IV Part 1:** 11, 79, 80, 81, 322; **Supp. IV Part 2:** 468; **Supp. V:** 53; **Supp. IX:** 55, 57, 62, 66; **Supp. XII:** 1, 139; **Supp. XIV:** 336; **Supp. XVI:** 187; **Supp. XVII:** 98, 105, 107; **Supp. XVIII:** 148; **Supp. XXI:** 7, 33; **Supp. XXII:** 158, 159; **Supp. XXIII:** 166, 207

Stein, Howard, **Supp. XXIV:** 116

Stein, Jean, **Supp. XVI:** 245

Stein, Karen F., **Supp. XIII:** 29, 30

Stein, Leo, **IV:** 26; **Supp. XIV:** 336; **Supp. XV:** 298

Stein, Lorin, **Supp. XII:** 254; **Supp. XVIII:** 137, 139

Steinbeck, John, **I:** 107, 288, 301, 378, 495, 519; **II:** 272; **III:** 382, 453, 454, 589; **IV:** 49–72; **Retro. Supp. II:** 19, 196; **Supp. IV Part 1:** 102, 225; **Supp. IV Part 2:** 502; **Supp. V:** 290, 291; **Supp. VIII:** 10; **Supp. IX:** 33, 171; **Supp. XI:** 169; **Supp. XIII:** 1, 17; **Supp. XIV:** 21, 181; **Supp. XVII:** 228; **Supp. XVIII:** 90, 102, 254; **Supp. XIX:** 3

Steinbeck, Olive Hamilton, **IV:** 51
Steinberg, Saul, **Supp. VIII:** 272
Steinberg, Sybil, **Supp. XVII:** 165, 166; **Supp. XXIII:** 241
Steinem, Gloria, **Supp. IV Part 1:** 203; **Supp. XXIII:** 104, 105, 106
Steiner, George, **Retro. Supp. I:** 327; **Supp. IV Part 1:** 286; **Supp. XVI:** 230
Steiner, Michael, **Supp. XXII:** 205
Steiner, Nancy, **Supp. I Part 2:** 529
Steiner, Stan, **Supp. IV Part 2:** 505
Steinfels, Margaret, **Supp. XVII:** 170
Steinhoff, Eirik, **Supp. XVI:** 290
Steinman, Michael, **Supp. VIII:** 172
Steinmetz, Charles P., **Supp. XXIII:** 161
Steinmetz, Charles Proteus, **I:** 483
Steinway Quintet Plus Four, The (Epstein), **Supp. XII:** 159, **162–166**
Stekel, Wilhelm, **III:** 554
Stella (Goethe), **Supp. IX:** 133, 138
Stella (Kushner), **Supp. IX:** 133
Stella, Joseph, **I:** 387
"Stellaria" (Francis), **Supp. IX:** 83
Stelligery and Other Essays (Wendell), **Supp. I Part 2:** 414
St. Elmo (Evans), **Supp. XXII:** 120
Stendhal, **I:** 316; **III:** 465, 467; **Supp. I Part 1:** 293; **Supp. I Part 2:** 445
Stepanchev, Stephen, **Supp. XI:** 312
Stephen, Leslie, **IV:** 440
Stephen, Sir Leslie, **IV:** 440; **Supp. I Part 1:** 306
Stephen, Saint, **II:** 539; **IV:** 228
Stephen Crane (Berryman), **I:** 169–170, 405
Stephen King, The Second Decade: "Danse Macabre" to "The Dark Half" (Magistrale), **Supp. V:** 138, 146, 151
Stephen King: The Art of Darkness (Winter), **Supp. V:** 144
Stephens, Jack, **Supp. X:** 11, 14, 15, 17
Stephens, James, **Supp. XIX:** 204
Stephens, Uriah, **Supp. XXIII:** 187
Stephenson, Gregory, **Supp. XII:** 120, 123
Stephenson, Neal, **Supp. XXII:** 49
"Stepping Out" (Dunn), **Supp. XI:** 140, 141
Stepping Outside (Gallagher), **Supp. XXIV:** 165, 167
Steps (Kosinski), **Supp. VII:** 215, 221–222, 225
"Steps" (Nye), **Supp. XIII:** 288
Steps to the Temple (Crashaw), **IV:** 145
"Steps Toward Poverty and Death" (R. Bly), **Supp. IV Part 1:** 60
Stepto, Robert B., **Retro. Supp. II:** 116, 120, 123

Sterile Cuckoo, The (Nichols), **Supp. XIII:** 258, **259–263**, 264
Sterling, Bruce, **Supp. XVI:** 118, 121, 123, 124, 128–129
Sterling, George, **I:** 199, 207, 208, 209; **II:** 440; **Supp. V:** 286; **Supp. XXII:** 276, 277
Sterling, Phillip, **Supp. XXIII:** 102
Stern, Bernhard J., **Supp. XIV:** 202, 213
Stern, Daniel, **Supp. VIII:** 238
Stern, Frederick C., **Supp. X:** 114, 115, 117
Stern, Gerald, **Supp. IX:** 285–303; **Supp. XI:** 139, 267; **Supp. XV:** 211, 212
Stern, Madeleine B., **Supp. I Part 1:** 35
Stern, Maurice, **IV:** 285
Stern, Philip Van Doren, **Supp. XIII:** 164
Stern, Richard, **Retro. Supp. II:** 291
Stern, Richard G., **Retro. Supp. II:** 204
Stern, Steven, **Supp. XVII:** 42, 48, 49; **Supp. XX: 178**
"Sterne" (Schwartz), **Supp. II Part 2:** 663
Sterne, Laurence, **II:** 302, 304–305, 308; **III:** 454; **IV:** 68, 211, 465; **Supp. I Part 2:** 714; **Supp. IV Part 1:** 299; **Supp. V:** 127; **Supp. X:** 324; **Supp. XV:** 232
Sterritt, David, **Supp. IV Part 2:** 574
Stetson, Caleb, **IV:** 178
Stetson, Charles Walter, **Supp. XI:** 195, 196, 197, 202, 204, 209
Steve Nelson, American Radical (Nelson), **Supp. XVIII:** 226
Stevens, Frances Simpson, **Supp. XXII:** 159, 162
Stevens, James, **Supp. XXIII:** 152
Stevens, Wallace, **I:** 60, 61, 266, 273, 462, 521, 528, 540–541; **II:** 56, 57, 530, 552, 556; **III:** 19, 23, 194, 216, 270–271, 272, 278, 279, 281, 453, 463, 493, 509, 521, 523, 600, 605, 613, 614; **IV:** 73–96, 140, 141, 332, 402, 415; **Retro. Supp. I:** 67, 89, 193, 284, 288, 295–315, 335, 403, 411, 416, 417, 422; **Retro. Supp. II:** 40, 44, 326; **Supp. I Part 1:** 80, 82, 257; **Supp. II Part 1:** 9, 18; **Supp. III Part 1:** 2, 3, 12, 20, 48, 239, 318, 319, 344; **Supp. III Part 2:** 611; **Supp. IV Part 1:** 72, 393; **Supp. IV Part 2:** 619, 620, 621, 634; **Supp. V:** 337; **Supp. VIII:** 21, 102, 195, 271, 292; **Supp. IX:** 41; **Supp. X:** 58; **Supp. XI:** 123, 191, 312; **Supp. XIII:** 44, 45; **Supp. XV:** 39, 41, 92, 115, 250, 261, 298, 302, 306, 307; **Supp. XVI:** 64, 158, 202, 210, 288; **Supp. XVII:** 36, 42, 110, 129, 130, 240, 241; **Supp. XIX:** 7, 40, 86, 87; **Supp. XXI:** 19, 28, 60, 133; **Supp. XXII:** 162; **Supp. XXIII:** 53, 57, 65; **Supp. XXIV:** 41, 45
Stevens, Mrs. Wallace (Elsie Kachel), **IV:** 75
"Stevens and the Idea of the Hero" (Bromwich), **Retro. Supp. I:** 305
Stevens and the Interpersonal (Halliday), **Supp. XIX:** 85–86
Stevenson, Adlai, **II:** 49; **III:** 581

Stevenson, Anne, **Supp. XV:** 121; **Supp. XVII:** 74
Stevenson, Burton E., **Supp. XIV:** 120
Stevenson, David, **Supp. XI:** 230
Stevenson, Ellen Borden, **Supp. XXV:** 30
Stevenson, Robert Louis, **I:** 2, 53; **II:** 283, 290, 311, 338; **III:** 328; **IV:** 183–184, 186, 187; **Retro. Supp. I:** 224, 228; **Supp. I Part 1:** 49; **Supp. II Part 1:** 404–405; **Supp. IV Part 1:** 298, 314; **Supp. VIII:** 125; **Supp. XIII:** 75; **Supp. XIV:** 40; **Supp. XVII:** 69; **Supp. XXI:** 204
Stevick, Robert D., **III:** 509
Stewart, Dugald, **II:** 8, 9; **Supp. I Part 1:** 151, 159; **Supp. I Part 2:** 422
Stewart, George, **Supp. XVIII:** 138
Stewart, Jeffrey C., **Supp. XIV:** 196, 209, 210
Stewart, Randall, **II:** 244; **Supp. XX: 164**
Stewart, Robert E., **Supp. XI:** 216
"St. Francis of Assisi" (Di Piero), **Supp. XIX:** 43
Stickeen (Muir), **Supp. IX:** 182
Sticks and Bones (Rabe), **Supp. XXIV:** 117
"Sticks and Stones" (L. Michaels), **Supp. XVI:** 205
Sticks and Stones (Mumford), **Supp. II Part 2:** 475, 483, 487–488
Sticks & Stones (Matthews), **Supp. IX:** 154, 155, 157, 158
Stieglitz, Alfred, **Retro. Supp. I:** 416; **Retro. Supp. II:** 103; **Supp. VIII:** 98; **Supp. XVII:** 96; **Supp. XX: 74, 75**
"Stigmata" (Oates), **Supp. II Part 2:** 520
Stiles, Ezra, **II:** 108, 122; **IV:** 144, 146, 148; **Supp. XXIV:** 68
Still, James, **Supp. XX: 163**
Still, William Grant, **Retro. Supp. I:** 203
Still Alice (Genova), **Supp. XXIII:** 127
"Stillborn" (Plath), **Supp. I Part 2:** 544
"Still Here" (Hughes), **Retro. Supp. I:** 211
"Still Just Writing" (Tyler), **Supp. IV Part 2:** 658
"Still Life" (Hecht), **Supp. X:** 68
"Still Life" (Malamud), **Supp. I Part 2:** 450
Still Life (Pickering), **Supp. XXI:** 198
"Still Life" (Pickering), **Supp. XXI:** 198
"Still Life" (Sandburg), **III:** 584
"Still Life: Moonlight Striking up on a Chess-Board" (Lowell), **II:** 528
"Still Life Or" (Creeley), **Supp. IV Part 1:** 141, 150, 158
Still Life with Oysters and Lemon (Doty), **Supp. XI:** 119, 121, **133–134**
Still Life with Woodpecker (Robbins), **Supp. X:** 260, **271–274**, 282
"Still Moment, A" (Welty), **IV:** 265; **Retro. Supp. I:** 347
Stillness (Gardner), **Supp. VI:** 74
"Stillness in the Air" (Dickinson), **Supp. XV:** 261
Stillness of Dancing, The (Bierds), **Supp. XVII:** 27–28
"Still Small Voices, The" (Fante), **Supp. XI:** 164

Still Such (Salter), **Supp. IX:** 246
"Still the Place Where Creation Does Some Work on Itself" (W. V. Davis), **Supp. IV Part 1:** 68
Stimpson, Catharine R., **Supp. IV Part 2:** 686
Stimson, Eleanor Kenyon. *See* Brooks, Mrs. Van Wyck
"Stimulants, Poultices, Goads" (Wright), **Supp. XV:** 349
"Stings" (Plath), **Retro. Supp. II:** 255; **Supp. I Part 2:** 541
"Stirling Street September" (Baraka), **Supp. II Part 1:** 51
Stirner, Max, **II:** 27
"Stirrup-Cup, The" (Lanier), **Supp. I Part 1:** 364
Stitt, Peter, **Supp. IV Part 1:** 68; **Supp. IV Part 2:** 628; **Supp. IX:** 152, 163, 291, 299; **Supp. XI:** 311, 317; **Supp. XIII:** 87; **Supp. XV:** 98, 99; **Supp. XIX:** 121
Stivers, Valerie, **Supp. X:** 311
St. John, David, **Supp. XV:** 73, 253
St. Louis Woman (Bontemps and Cullen), **Supp. XXII:** 6
St. Mark, Tyler, **Supp. XX: 260**
Stock, Noel, **III:** 479
Stockton, Frank R., **I:** 201
Stoddard, Charles Warren, **I:** 193, 195, 196; **Supp. II Part 1:** 192, 341, 351
Stoddard, Elizabeth, **II:** 275; **Supp. XV: 269–291**
Stoddard, Richard, **Supp. I Part 1:** 372
Stoddard, Richard Henry, **Supp. XV:** 269, 271, 272, 273, 274, 278, 279, 286
Stoddard, Solomon, **I:** 545, 548; **IV:** 145, 148
Stoffman, Judy, **Supp. XVIII:** 97
Stoic, The (Dreiser), **I:** 497, 502, 508, 516; **Retro. Supp. II:** 95, 96, 101, 108
Stokes, Geoffrey, **Supp. XV:** 256
Stokes, Olivia Egleston Phelps, **Supp. XVIII:** 261
"Stolen Calf, The" (Dunbar), **Supp. II Part 1:** 196
Stolen Jew, The (Neugeboren), **Supp. XVI: 222–224,** 225
Stolen Past, A (Knowles), **Supp. XII:** 249
Stolen Words: Forays into the Origins and Ravages of Plagiarism (Mallon), **Supp. XIX: 134–135**
Stollman, Aryeh Lev, **Supp. XVII:** 49; **Supp. XXIV:** 2, 8, 10–11
Stolmar, Thomas, **Supp. XVIII:** 138
Stomping the Blues (Murray), **Supp. XIX: 158–159**
"Stone" (Ozick), **Supp. XVII:** 50
Stone, Edward, **III:** 479
Stone, Herbert S., **Supp. XXI:** 2
Stone, I. F., **Supp. XIV:** 3
Stone, Irving, **II:** 463, 466, 467
Stone, Oliver, **Supp. XIV:** 48, 316
Stone, Phil, **II:** 55
Stone, Richard, **Supp. XIV:** 54
Stone, Robert, **Supp. V: 295–312; Supp. X:** 1; **Supp. XIX:** 54
Stone, Rosetta (pseudonym). *See* Geisel, Theodor Seuss (Dr. Seuss)
Stone, Wilmer, **Supp. I Part 1:** 49

Stone and the Shell, The (Hay), **Supp. XIV:** 122, 123, 127, 130
"Stone Bear, The" (Haines), **Supp. XII:** 206–207, 212
"Stone City" (Proulx), **Supp. VII:** 251–253
Stone Country (Sanders), **Supp. XVI:** 271–272
Stone Diaries, The (Shields), **Supp. VII:** 307, 315, 324–326, 327
"Stone Dreams" (Kingsolver), **Supp. VII:** 203
Stone Harp, The (Haines), **Supp. XII: 204,** 205, 206, 207
Stonemason, The (McCarthy), **Supp. VIII:** 175, 187
"Stones" (Hoffman), **Supp. XVIII:** 86
"Stones" (Kumin), **Supp. IV Part 2:** 447
Stones (lithograph series, O'Hara and Rivers), **Supp. XXIII:** 217
"Stones, The" (Plath), **Supp. I Part 2:** 535, 539
"Stones in My Passway, Hellhounds on My Trail" (Boyle), **Supp. VIII:** 15
Stones of Florence, The (McCarthy), **II:** 562
"Stone Walls" (Sarton), **Supp. VIII:** 259
"Stop" (Wilbur), **Supp. III Part 2:** 556
Stop-Loss (screenplay, Richard), **Supp. XIX:** 222
"Stop Me If You've Heard This One" (Lardner), **II:** 433
Stopover: Tokyo (Marquand), **III:** 53, 57, 61, 70
Stoppard, Tom, **Retro. Supp. I:** 189
"Stopping by Woods" (Frost), **II:** 154
"Stopping by Woods on a Snowy Evening" (Frost), **Retro. Supp. I:** 129, 133, 134, 135, 139
Stopping Westward (Richards), **II:** 396
"Stop Player. Joke No. 4" (Gaddis), **Supp. IV Part 1:** 280
Stop-Time (Conroy), **Supp. XVI: 63–71,** 72, 75, 76–77
"Store, The" (E. P. Jones), **Supp. XXII:** 144–145
Store, The (Stribling), **Supp. VIII:** 126; **Supp. XXII:** 195
"*Store* and *Mockingbird:* Two Pulitzer Novels about Alabama" (Going), **Supp. VIII:** 126
Store of a Million Items, The (Cliff), **Supp. XXII:** 67, 74, 75
"Store of a Million Items, The" (Cliff), **Supp. XXII:** 75
Storer, Edward, **Supp. I Part 1:** 261, 262
Stories, Fables and Other Diversions (Nemerov), **III:** 268–269, 285
Stories: Elizabeth Stoddard, **Supp. XV:** 270
"Stories for Sale" (Kolba), **Supp. XVIII:** 257
Stories for the Sixties (Yates, ed.), **Supp. XI:** 343
Stories from Our Living Past (Prose), **Supp. XVI:** 251
Stories from the Italian Poets (Hunt), **Supp. XV:** 175
Stories from the Old Testament Retold (L. P. Smith), **Supp. XIV:** 342

Stories from World Literature, **Supp. IX:** 4
"Stories in the Snow" (Leopold), **Supp. XIV:** 183
Stories of an Imaginary Childhood (Bukiet), **Supp. XVII: 41–44,** 45
Stories of F. Scott Fitzgerald, The (Cowley, ed.), **Retro. Supp. I:** 115
Stories of F. Scott Fitzgerald, The (Fitzgerald), **II:** 94
Stories of Modern America, **Supp. IX:** 4
Stories of Stephen Dixon, The (Dixon), **Supp. XII:** 152
Stories of the American Experience (Kriegel and Lass, eds.), **Supp. XXIV:** 214
Stories of the Spanish Civil War (Hemingway), **II:** 258
Stories Revived (James), **II:** 322
Stories that Could Be True (Stafford), **Supp. XI: 325–327**
Stories Toto Told Me (Rolfe), **Supp. XX: 235**
Storm, The (Buechner), **Supp. XII: 54–57**
"Storm, The" (Chopin), **Retro. Supp. II:** 60, 68; **Supp. I Part 1:** 218, 224
Storm, The (al-'Awásif) (Gibran), **Supp. XX: 116, 124, 125**
"Storm Fear" (Frost), **II:** 153; **Retro. Supp. I:** 127
"Storm Ship, The" (Irving), **II:** 309
"Storm Warnings" (Kingsolver), **Supp. VII:** 207–208
"Stormy Weather" (Ellison), **Supp. II Part 1:** 233
"Story" (Everwine), **Supp. XV:** 89
"Story, A" (Jarrell), **II:** 371
Story, Julian, **Supp. XX: 232**
Story, Richard David, **Supp. IV Part 2:** 575, 588
Story, William Wetmore, **Supp. XX: 228**
"Story about Chicken Soup, A" (Simpson), **Supp. IX: 272–273**
"Story about the Anteater, The" (Benét), **Supp. XI:** 53
"Story About the Body, A" (Hass), **Supp. VI: 107–108**
"Story for Teddy, A" (Swados), **Supp. XIX:** 266–267
Story for Teddy, A—and Others (Swados), **Supp. XIX: 266–268**
"Story Hearer, The" (Paley), **Supp. VI:** 230, 231
"Story Hour" (Hay), **Supp. XIV:** 124
"Story Hour" (Jarman), **Supp. XVII:** 116
Story Hour: A Second Look at Cinderella, Bluebeard, and Company (Hay), **Supp. XIV:** 119, 124, 125, 132, 133
Story of a Country Town, The (Howe), **I:** 106
Story of a Lover, The (Hapgood), **Supp. XVII:** 99, 100, 104; **Supp. XXI:** 3, 5, 7
Story of an American Family, The: Letters of the Hapgood Family, 1648–1917 (Boyce), **Supp. XVII:** 97; **Supp. XXI:** 9, 14
"Story of an Hour, The" (Chopin), **Retro. Supp. II:** 72; **Supp. I Part 1:** 212–213, 216

Story of a Novel, The (Wolfe), **IV:** 456, 458

"Story of a Proverb, The" (Lanier), **Supp. I Part 1:** 365

"Story of a Proverb, The: A Fairy Tale for Grown People" (Lanier), **Supp. I Part 1:** 365

Story of a Story and Other Stories, The: A Novel (Dixon), **Supp. XII:** 155

Story of a Wonder Man, The (Lardner), **II:** 433–434

"Story of a Year, The" (James), **Retro. Supp. I:** 218

Story of George Washington Carver, The (Bontemps), **Supp. XXII:** 13

Story of G.I. Joe, The (film, Wellman), **Supp. XVII:** 61, 62

"Story of Gus, The" (A. Miller), **III:** 147–148

"Story of How a Wall Stands, A" (Ortiz), **Supp. IV Part 2:** 499, 507

Story of Mist, The (Dybek), **Supp. XXIII: 74–75,** 78

"Story of Mist, The"(Dybek), **Supp. XXIII:** 74–75

Story of Mount Desert Island, Maine, The (Morison), **Supp. I Part 2:** 494

Story of My Boyhood and Youth, The (Muir), **Supp. IX: 172–174,** 176

Story of My Father, The: A Memoir (Miller), **Supp. XII:** 301

Story of O, The (Réage), **Supp. XII:** 9, 10

Story of Our Lives, The (Strand), **Supp. IV Part 2:** 620, 628–629, 629

"Story of Poppy Van Buster, The" (Briggs), **Supp. XVIII:** 8

Story of the Negro (Bontemps), **Supp. XXII:** 6, 12–13

Story of the Normans, The, Told Chiefly in Relation to Their Conquest of England (Jewett), **II:** 406

Story of the Telegraph, The (Briggs, and Maverick), **Supp. XVIII:** 4

"Story of Toby, The" (Melville), **III:** 76

"Story of To-day, A" (Davis). *See also Margret Howth*

"Story of To-day, A" (R. H. Davis), **Supp. XVI:** 88, 89

Story of Utopias, The (Mumford), **Supp. II Part 2:** 475, 483–486, 495

Story of Wine in California, The (M. F. K. Fisher), **Supp. XVII:** 88

Story on Page One, The (Odets), **Supp. II Part 2:** 546

Storyteller (Silko), **Supp. IV Part 2:** 558, 559, 560, 561, **566–570**

"Storyteller" (Silko), **Supp. IV Part 2:** 569

"*Storyteller:* Grandmother Spider's Web" (Danielson), **Supp. IV Part 2:** 569

"Storyteller's Notebook, A" (Carver), **Supp. III Part 1:** 142–143

Story Teller's Story, A: The Tale of an American Writer's Journey through His Own Imaginative World and through the World of Facts . . . (Anderson), **I:** 98, 101, 114, 117

"Story That Could Be True, A" (Stafford), **Supp. XI:** 326

Stothard, Peter, **Supp. XXV:** 221

"Stout Gentleman, The" (Irving), **II:** 309

Stover at Yale (Johnson), **III:** 321

Stowe, Calvin, **IV:** 445; **Supp. I Part 2:** 587, 588, 590, 596, 597

Stowe, Charles, **Supp. I Part 2:** 581, 582

Stowe, Eliza, **Supp. I Part 2:** 587

Stowe, Harriet Beecher, **II:** 274, 399, 403, 541; **Retro. Supp. I:** 34, 246; **Retro. Supp. II:** 4, 138, 156; **Supp. I Part 1:** 30, 206, 301; **Supp. I Part 2: 579–601; Supp. III Part 1:** 154, 168, 171; **Supp. IX:** 33; **Supp. X:** 223, 246, 249, 250; **Supp. XI:** 193; **Supp. XIII:** 141, 295; **Supp. XV:** 278; **Supp. XVI:** 82, 85

Stowe, Samuel Charles, **Supp. I Part 2:** 587

Stowe, William, **Supp. IV Part 1:** 129

Strachey, Lytton, **I:** 5; **IV:** 436; **Retro. Supp. I:** 59; **Supp. I Part 2:** 485, 494; **Supp. XIV:** 342; **Supp. XVI:** 191

"Stradivari" (Bierds), **Supp. XVII:** 28

Straight Cut (Bell), **Supp. X:** 5, **6–7,** 10

Straight Man (Russo), **Supp. XII: 335–339,** 340

Straits: Poems (Koch), **Supp. XV:** 184

Strand, Mark, **Supp. IV Part 2: 619–636; Supp. V:** 92, 332, 337, 338, 343; **Supp. IX:** 155; **Supp. XI:** 139, 145; **Supp. XII:** 254; **Supp. XIII:** 76; **Supp. XV:** 74; **Supp. XXIV:** 165

Strand, Paul, **Supp. VIII:** 272

Strandberg, Victor, **Supp. V:** 273

Strange, Sharan, **Supp. XXI:** 246

"Strange Beautiful Woman, A" (Nelson), **Supp. XVIII:** 173

Strange Bedfellows (Woods), **Supp. XXI:** 70

Strange Case of Dr. Jekyll and Mr. Hyde, The (Stevenson), **II:** 290

Strange Children, The (Gordon), **II:** 196, 197, 199, 211–213

Strange Commonplace, A (Sorrentino), **Supp. XXI:** 232, 237, 238

Strange Crime in Bermuda, The (Holding), **Supp. XXII: 124–125,** 127, 129

Strange Fire (Bukiet), **Supp. XVII: 46**

"Strange Fruit" (Harjo), **Supp. XII:** 224, 225

"Strange Fruit" (song), **Supp. I Part 1:** 80; **Supp. XVIII:** 228

Strange Interlude (O'Neill), **III:** 391, 397–398; **IV:** 61; **Supp. XXII:** 24

Stranger, The (Camus), **I:** 53, 292; **Supp. VIII:** 11; **Supp. XV:** 352

"Stranger, The" (Rich), **Supp. I Part 2:** 555, 560

"Stranger, The" (Salinger), **III:** 552–553

Strange Relation (Hadas), **Supp. XXIII:** 111, 113, 120, **127**

"Stranger in My Own Life, A: Alienation in American Indian Poetry and Prose" (Gunn Allen), **Supp. IV Part 1:** 322

Stranger in the Kingdom, A (Mosher), **Supp. XXII:** 204, 205, 206, 207, 208, 209, **212–213**

"Stranger in the Village" (Baldwin), **Retro. Supp. II:** 3; **Supp. I Part 1:**

54; **Supp. IV Part 1:** 10

"Stranger in Town" (Hughes), **Supp. I Part 1:** 334

"Strangers" (Howe), **Supp. VI:** 120

Strangers: A Book of Poems (Ferry), **Supp. XXIV: 149–150**

Strangers and Wayfarers (Jewett), **Retro. Supp. II:** 138

"Strangers from the Horizon" (Merwin), **Supp. III Part 1:** 356

"Stranger's Gift, The" (Very), **Supp. XXV:** 242

Strangers on a Train (Highsmith), **Supp. IV Part 1:** 132

"Strange Story, A" (Taylor), **Supp. V:** 323

"Strange Story, A" (Wylie), **Supp. I Part 2:** 723

Strange Things (Atwood), **Supp. XIII:** 35

"Strato in Plaster" (Merrill), **Supp. III Part 1:** 328

Stratton-Porter, Gene, **Supp. XX: 211–225**

Straub, Peter, **Supp. XXV:** 145

Straus, Ralph, **Supp. XIII:** 168

Straus, Roger, **Supp. VIII:** 82; **Supp. XV:** 59

Strauss, Harold, **Supp. XV:** 137

Strauss, Helen, **Supp. XXIII:** 258

Strauss, Johann, **I:** 66

Strauss, Richard, **IV:** 316

Strauss, Robert, **Supp. XI:** 141, 142

Stravinsky (De Schloezer), **III:** 474

Stravinsky, Igor, **Retro. Supp. I:** 378; **Supp. IV Part 1:** 81; **Supp. XI:** 133; **Supp. XV:** 265

"Stravinsky's Three Pieces 'Grotesques,' for String Quartet" (Lowell), **II:** 523

Straw, The (O'Neill), **III:** 390

"Strawberry Milkshake" (Halliday), **Supp. XIX:** 92, 94

"Stray Document, A" (Pound), **II:** 517

"Strays" (Richard), **Supp. XIX:** 210–211, 220

Streaks of the Tulip, The: Selected Criticism (W. J. Smith), **Supp. XIII:** 333, 334, 344, **347–348**

Streamline Your Mind (Mursell), **Supp. I Part 2:** 608

Strecker, Trey, **Supp. XXI:** 238

"Street, Cloud" (Ríos), **Supp. IV Part 2:** 549

Street, The (Petry), **Supp. XVIII:** 286

Streetcar Named Desire, A (T. Williams), **IV:** 382, 383, 385, 386, 387, 389–390, 395, 398; **Supp. IV Part 1:** 359

Street in Bronzeville, A (Brooks), **Retro. Supp. I:** 208; **Supp. III Part 1:** 74–78

"Street Moths" (X. J. Kennedy), **Supp. XV:** 170

"Street Musicians" (Ashbery), **Supp. III Part 1:** 18

"Street of Crocodiles" (Hull), **Supp. XXI:** 130

"Street off Sunset, A" (Jarrell), **II:** 387

Street of Seven Stars, The (Rinehart), **Supp. XXV:** 193

"Streets" (Dixon), **Supp. XII: 145–146**

Streets in Their Own Ink (Dybek), **Supp. XXIII:** 78

Streets in the Moon (MacLeish), **III:** 5, 8–11, 15, 19

"Streets of Laredo" (screenplay) (McMurtry and Ossana), **Supp. V:** 226, 230

Streets of Laredo (McMurtry), **Supp. V:** 230

Streets of Night (Dos Passos), **I:** 478, 479–480, 481, 488

Streitfield, David, **Supp. XIII:** 234; **Supp. XVI:** 63

Strength of Fields, The (Dickey), **Supp. IV Part 1:** 178

"Strength of Fields, The" (Dickey), **Supp. IV Part 1:** 176, 184–185

"Strength of Gideon, The" (Dunbar), **Supp. II Part 1:** 212

Strength of Gideon and Other Stories, The (Dunbar), **Supp. II Part 1:** 211, 212

"Strenuous Artistry" (Zagarell), **Supp. XV:** 281

Strether, Lambert, **II:** 313

Stribling, T. S., **Supp. VIII:** 126

Strickland, Barbara, **Supp. XIX:** 102

Strickland, Joe (pseudonym). *See* Arnold, George W.

"Strictly Bucolic" (Simic), **Supp. VIII:** 278

Strictly Business (O. Henry), **Supp. II Part 1:** 410

"Strike, The" (Olsen), **Supp. XIII:** 292, 297

Strike at Shane's, The (Skloot), **Supp. XX:** 216

"Strikers" (Untermeyer), **Supp. XV:** 296

Strindberg, August, **I:** 78; **III:** 145, 165, 387, 390, 391, 392, 393; **IV:** 17; **Supp. XVII:** 100; **Supp. XXII:** 23

"String, The" (Dickey), **Supp. IV Part 1:** 179

String Light (Wright), **Supp. XV:** 345–346

"String Quartet, The" (Weigl), **Supp. XIX:** 278

"Strivings of the Negro People" (Du Bois), **Supp. II Part 1:** 167

Stroby, W. C., **Supp. XIV:** 26

Strohbach, Hermann, **Supp. XI:** 242

"Stroke of Good Fortune, A" (O'Connor), **III:** 344; **Retro. Supp. II:** 229, 232

Strom, Stephen, **Supp. XII:** 223

Strong, Anna Louise, **Supp. XVIII:** 238; **Supp. XXIII:** 166

Strong, George Templeton, **IV:** 321

Strong, Josiah, **Supp. XIV:** 64

"Strong Draughts of Their Refreshing Minds" (Dickinson), **Retro. Supp. I:** 46

Strong Motion (Franzen), **Supp. XX: 85, 88–89,** 92, 95

Strong Opinions (Nabokov), **Retro. Supp. I:** 263, 266, 270, 276

"Strong Room of the House, The" (Bronk), **Supp. XXI:** 32

"Strong Women" (Dorman), **Supp. XI:** 240

Strout, Elizabeth, **Supp. X:** 86; **Supp. XXIII: 273–287**

Structure of Nations and Empires, The (Niebuhr), **III:** 292, 308

"Structure of Rime, The" (Duncan), **Supp. XVI:** 287

Structuring the Void (Klinkowitz), **Supp. XXI:** 233

Struggle, The (film; Griffith), **Supp. XVI:** 191

"Strumpet Song" (Plath), **Retro. Supp. II:** 246; **Supp. I Part 2:** 536

Strunk, William, **Supp. I Part 2:** 652, 662, 670, 671, 672

Strunsky, Anna, **II:** 465

"Strut for Roethke, A" (Berryman), **I:** 188

Strychacz, Thomas F., **Supp. XVI:** 69–70

Stuart, Dabney, **Supp. XVIII:** 79

Stuart, Gilbert, **I:** 16

Stuart, J. E. B., **III:** 56

Stuart, Jesse, **Supp. XX: 162–163, 165**

Stuart, Michael, **Supp. XV:** 140

Stuart Little (White), **Supp. I Part 2:** 655–658

"Stubborn Kisses" (Gallagher), **Supp. XXIV:** 170

Stuckey, W. J., **Supp. XXII:** 191–192

"Student, The" (Moore), **III:** 212, 215

"Student of Clouds" (Collins), **Supp. XXI:** 60

"Student of Salmanaca, The" (Irving), **II:** 309

"Student's Wife, The" (Carver), **Supp. III Part 1:** 141

Studies in American Indian Literature: Critical Essays and Course Designs (Gunn Allen), **Supp. IV Part 1:** 324, 333

Studies in Classic American Literature (Lawrence), **II:** 102; **III:** 33; **IV:** 333; **Retro. Supp. I:** 421

Studies in Short Fiction (Edmonds), **Supp. XXIII:** 291

Studies in Short Fiction (Malin), **Supp. XVI:** 71

Studies in the Psychology of Sex (Ellis), **Supp. XX: 235**

"Studs" (Farrell), **II:** 25, 28, 31

Studs Lonigan: A Trilogy (Farrell), **II:** 25, 26, 27, 31–34, 37, 38, 41–42

"Study in Orange and White" (Collins), **Supp. XXI:** 60

"Study of Images" (Stevens), **IV:** 79

"Study of Lanier's Poems, A" (Kent), **Supp. I Part 1:** 373

Study of Milton's Prosody (Bridges), **II:** 537

"Study of the Negro Problems, The" (Du Bois), **Supp. II Part 1:** 165

Stuewe, Paul, **Supp. IV Part 1:** 68

Stuhlmann, Gunther, **Supp. X:** 182, 184, 185, 187

Stull, William L., **Supp. XXIV:** 177

Stultifera Navis (Brant), **III:** 447

Sturak, John Thomas, **Supp. XIII:** 162, 163, 165, 168

Sturgeon, Theodore, **Supp. XVIII:** 145

Sturgis, George, **III:** 600

Sturgis, Howard, **IV:** 319; **Retro. Supp. I:** 367, 373

Sturgis, Howard Overing, **Supp. XX: 227–242**

Sturgis, Julian Russell, **Supp. XX: 228, 233, 238**

Sturgis, Susan, **III:** 600

Sturm, Margaret. *See* Millar, Margaret

Stuttaford, Genevieve, **Supp. IX:** 279

Stuyvesant, Peter, **II:** 301

"Style" (Nemerov), **III:** 275

Styles of Radical Will (Sontag), **Supp. III Part 2:** 451, 459, 460–463

"Stylist, The" (Egan), **Supp. XIX:** 51, 52

Styne, Jule, **Supp. XVI:** 193

Styron, William, **III:** 40; **IV:** 4, **97–119,** 216; **Supp. V:** 201; **Supp. IX:** 208; **Supp. X:** 15–16, 250; **Supp. XI:** 229, 231, 343; **Supp. XIV:** 82; **Supp. XVI:** 235–236; **Supp. XXIII:** 107, 109

Suares, J. C., **Supp. IV Part 1:** 234

Suarez, Ernest, **Supp. IV Part 1:** 175; **Supp. V:** 180

Suarez, Ray, **Supp. XXI:** 243

"Sub, The" (Dixon), **Supp. XII:** 146

Subjection of Women, The (Mill), **Supp. XI:** 196, 203

"Subjective Necessity for Social Settlements" (Addams), **Supp. I Part 1:** 4

"Subject of Childhood, A" (Paley), **Supp. VI:** 221; **Supp. XXI:** 118

"Submarginalia" (Howe), **Supp. IV Part 2:** 422

Substance and Shadow (James), **II:** 344

"Subterranean Homesick Blues" (song, Dylan), **Supp. XVIII:** 25

Subterraneans, The (Kerouac), **Supp. III Part 1:** 225, 227–231

"Subtitle" (Kees), **Supp. XV:** 139

Subtreasury of American Humor, A (White and White), **Supp. I Part 2:** 668

"Suburban Culture, Imaginative Wonder: The Fiction of Frederick Barthelme" (Brinkmeyer), **Supp. XI:** 38

Suburban Sketches (Howells), **II:** 274, 277

"Subversive Element, The" (Ryan as Quin), **Supp. XVIII:** 230

"Subverted Flower, The" (Frost), **Retro. Supp. I:** 139

"Subway, The" (Tate), **IV:** 128

"Subway Singer, The" (Clampitt), **Supp. IX:** 45

"Success" (Mora), **Supp. XIII:** 217

Successful Love and Other Stories (Schwartz), **Supp. II Part 2:** 661, 665

Successful Women (Taves), **Supp. XXV:** 198

Succession, The: A Novel of Elizabeth and James (Garrett), **Supp. VII:** 104–107, 108

"Success is counted sweetest" (Dickinson), **Retro. Supp. I:** 30, 31–32, 38; **Supp. XV:** 126

Success Stories (Banks), **Supp. V:** 14–15

"Success Story" (Banks), **Supp. V:** 15

"Such Counsels You Gave to Me" (Jeffers), **Supp. II Part 2:** 433

Such Silence (Milburn), **Supp. XI:** 242

"Such Things Happen Only in Books" (Wilder), **IV:** 365

Such Was the Season (Major), **Supp. XXII: 177–178,** 179, **182**

"Sudden Journey" (Gallagher), **Supp. XXIV:** 169

Suddenly, Last Summer (film) (Vidal), **Supp. IV Part 2:** 683

Suddenly Last Summer (T. Williams), **I:** 73; **IV:** 382, 383, 385, 386, 387, 389, 390, 391, 392, 395–396, 397, 398

Suder (Everett), **Supp. XVIII: 54–55**

Sudermann, Hermann, **I:** 66

Sue, Eugène, **Supp. XXIII:** 182

Sugg, Richard P., **Supp. IV Part 1:** 68

"Suggestion from a Friend" (Kenyon), **Supp. VII:** 171

"Suicide" (Barnes), **Supp. III Part 1:** 33

"Suicide off Egg Rock" (Plath), **Supp. I Part 2:** 529, 538

Suicides and Jazzers (Carruth), **Supp. XVI:** 46

"Suicide's Note" (Hughes), **Retro. Supp. I:** 199

"Suitable Surroundings, The" (Bierce), **I:** 203

"Suitcase, The" (Ozick), **Supp. V:** 262, 264

"Suite for Augustus, A" (Dove), **Supp. IV Part 1:** 245

"Suite for Emily" (Hull), **Supp. XXI:** 139–140

"Suite for Lord Timothy Dexter" (Rukeyser), **Supp. VI:** 283, 285

"Suite from the Firebird" (Stravinsky), **Supp. XI:** 133

"Suitor, The" (Kenyon), **Supp. VII:** 164–165

Sukarno, **IV:** 490

Sukenick, Ronald, **Supp. V:** 39, 44, 46; **Supp. XII:** 139

Sula (Morrison), **Supp. III Part 1:** 362, 364, 367, 368, 379; **Supp. VIII:** 219

Sullivan, Andrew, **Supp. IX:** 135

Sullivan, Arthur, **Supp. XX: 228**

Sullivan, Frank, **Supp. IX:** 201

Sullivan, Harry Stack, **I:** 59

Sullivan, Jack, **Supp. X:** 86; **Supp. XII:** 331

Sullivan, Noel, **Retro. Supp. I:** 202; **Supp. I Part 1:** 329, 333

Sullivan, Richard, **Supp. VIII:** 124

Sullivan, Walter, **Supp. VIII:** 168

"Sullivan County Sketches" (Crane), **I:** 407, 421

"Sumach and Goldenrod: An American Idyll" (Mumford), **Supp. II Part 2:** 475

Suma Genji (Play), **III:** 466

Sumerian Vistas (Ammons), **Supp. VII:** 34, 35

"Summa Lyrica" (Grossman), **Supp. XIX:** 86

"Summer" (Emerson), **II:** 10

Summer (Gioia), **Supp. XV:** 117

"Summer" (Lowell), **II:** 554

Summer (Wharton), **IV:** 317; **Retro. Supp. I:** 360, 367, 374, **378–379,** 382; **Supp. XXIII:** 275, 281

Summer, Bob, **Supp. X:** 1, 5, 6, 42

Summer and Smoke (T. Williams), **IV:** 382, 384, 385, 386, 387, 395, 397, 398; **Supp. IV Part 1:** 84

Summer Anniversaries, The (Justice), **Supp. VII:** 115, 117

Summer Blue (Skloot), **Supp. XX: 196, 207–208**

Summer Brave (Inge), **Supp. XXV:** 99

"Summer Commentary, A" (Winters), **Supp. II Part 2:** 808

"Summer Day" (O'Hara), **III:** 369

"Summer Days, The" (Oliver), **Supp. VII:** 239

"Summer Evening" (Boyle), **Supp. XXIV:** 61

"Summer Love Overheated" (Díaz), **Supp. XXIV:** 89

Summer Never Ends (W. Frank), **Supp. XX:** 78

"Summer Night" (Hughes), **Supp. I Part 1:** 325

"Summer Night, A" (Auden), **Supp. II Part 1:** 8

"Summer Night—Broadway" (Untermeyer), **Supp. XV:** 296

"Summer Noon: 1941" (Winters), **Supp. II Part 2:** 811

"Summer of '82" (Merwin), **Supp. III Part 1:** 355–356

Summer on the Lakes in 1843 (Fuller), **Supp. II Part 1:** 279, 295–296

"Summer People" (Hemingway), **II:** 258–259

"Summer People, The" (Jackson), **Supp. IX:** 120

"Summer People, The" (Merrill), **Supp. III Part 1:** 325–326

"Summer Perdu" (Halliday), **Supp. XIX:** 89

"Summer Planning" (Halliday), **Supp. XIX:** 92

"Summer Ramble, A" (Bryant), **Supp. I Part 1:** 162, 164

Summers, Claude J., **Supp. IV Part 2:** 680–681; **Supp. XIV:** 161, 169

Summers, Robert, **Supp. IX:** 289

"Summer Solstice, New York City" (Olds), **Supp. X:** 207

"Summer's Reading, A" (Malamud), **Supp. I Part 2:** 430–431, 442

"Summer Storm" (Gioia), **Supp. XV:** 127

"Summer Storm" (Simpson), **Supp. IX:** 268

"'Summertime and the Living . . .'" (Hayden), **Supp. II Part 1:** 363, 366

Summertime Island (Caldwell), **I:** 307–308

"Summer Tragedy" (Bontemps), **Supp. XXII:** 9

"Summer: West Side" (Updike), **Retro. Supp. I:** 320

"Summer with Tu Fu, A" (Carruth), **Supp. XVI:** 55, 58

"Summit Beach, 1921" (Dove), **Supp. IV Part 1:** 249

Summoning of Stones, A (Hecht), **Supp. X:** 57, 58, **58–59**

"Summons" (Untermeyer), **Supp. XV:** 296

Summons to Memphis, A (Taylor), **Supp. V:** 313, 314, 327

Summons to the Free, A (Benét), **Supp. XI:** 47

Sumner, Charles, **I:** 3, 15; **Supp. I Part 2:** 685, 687

Sumner, John, **Retro. Supp. II:** 95

Sumner, John B., **I:** 511

Sumner, William Graham, **III:** 102, 108; **Supp. I Part 2:** 640

"Sumptuous Destination" (Wilbur), **Supp. III Part 2:** 553

"Sun" (Moore), **III:** 215

"Sun" (Swenson), **Supp. IV Part 2:** 640

"Sun, Sea, and Sand" (Marquand), **III:** 60

Sun Also Rises, The (Hemingway), **I:** 107; **II:** 68, 90, 249, 251–252, 260, 600; **III:** 36; **IV:** 35, 297; **Retro. Supp. I:** 171, **177–180,** 181, 189; **Supp. I Part 2:** 614; **Supp. XIII:** 263; **Supp. XVIII:** 74

"Sun and Moon" (Kenyon), **Supp. VII:** 168

"Sun and the Still-born Stars, The" (Southern), **Supp. XI:** 295

Sun at Midnight (Soseki; Merwin and Shigematsu, trans.), **Supp. III Part 1:** 353

"Sun Crosses Heaven from West to East Bringing Samson Back to the Womb, The" (R. Bly), **Supp. IV Part 1:** 73

Sun Dance Land (Hanson), **Supp. XXV:** 280

Sun Dance Opera, The (Zitkala-Ša and Hanson), **Supp. XXV:** 279–280

"Sun Dance Shield" (Momaday), **Supp. IV Part 2:** 491

Sunday, Billy, **II:** 449

"Sunday Afternoons" (Komunyakaa), **Supp. XIII:** 127

Sunday after the War (H. Miller), **III:** 184

"Sunday at Home" (Hawthorne), **II:** 231–232

"Sunday Following Mother's Day. The" (E. P. Jones), **Supp. XXII:** 145

"Sunday Morning" (Stevens), **II:** 552; **III:** 278, 463, 509; **IV:** 92–93; **Retro. Supp. I:** 296, 300, 301, 304, 307, 313; **Supp. XV:** 120; **Supp. XVI:** 210; **Supp. XVII:** 42; **Supp. XIX:** 40; **Supp. XXI:** 28, 133; **Supp. XXIII:** 57

"Sunday Morning Apples" (Crane), **I:** 387

"Sunday Morning Prophecy" (Hughes), **Supp. I Part 1:** 334

"Sunday Morning with the Sensational Nightingales" (Collins), **Supp. XXI:** 60

"Sundays" (B. Kelly), **Supp. XVII:** 124–125

"Sundays" (Salter), **Supp. IX:** 257

"Sundays, They Sleep Late" (Rukeyser), **Supp. VI:** 278

"Sundays of Satin-Legs Smith, The" (Brooks), **Supp. III Part 1:** 74, 75

"Sundays Visiting" (Ríos), **Supp. IV Part 2:** 541

Sundial, The (Jackson), **Supp. IX: 126–127**

Sundog (Harrison), **Supp. VIII: 46–48**

Sun Dogs (R. O. Butler), **Supp. XII: 64–65**

Sun Do Move, The (Hughes), **Supp. I Part 1:** 339

Sundquist, Eric, **Supp. XIV:** 66, 71

"Sunfish" (C. Frost), **Supp. XV:** 100–101, 102

"Sunflower Sutra" (Ginsberg), **Supp. II Part 1:** 317, 321; **Supp. XV:** 215

Sunlight Dialogues, The (Gardner), **Supp. VI:** 63, **68,** 69, 70

"Sunlight Is Imagination" (Wilbur), **Supp. III Part 2:** 549

"Sunny Ridge, The" (Halliday), **Supp. XIX:** 92

Sun Out: Selected Poems, 1952–1954 (Koch), **Supp. XV:** 179

"Sunrise" (Lanier), **Supp. I Part 1:** 370

"Sunrise and the Bomb" (Halliday), **Supp. XIX:** 84, 85, 92

"Sunrise runs for Both, The" (Dickinson), **Retro. Supp. I:** 45

Sunrise with Seamonsters: Travels and Discoveries, 1964–1984 (Theroux), **Supp. VIII:** 311, 313, 323, 325

"Sun Rising" (Donne), **Supp. VIII:** 164

"Sunset" (Ransom), **III:** 484

"Sunset from Omaha Hotel Window" (Sandburg), **III:** 584

Sunset Gun (Parker), **Supp. IX:** 192

Sunset Limited (Burke), **Supp. XIV:** 32, 33

Sunset Limited (Harrison), **Supp. VIII:** 51

"Sunset Maker, The" (Justice), **Supp. VII:** 123

Sunset Maker, The: Poems, Stories, a Memoir (Justice), **Supp. VII:** 116, 118, 119, 123–124

Sunshine Boys, The (film), **Supp. IV Part 2:** 589

Sunshine Boys, The (Simon), **Supp. IV Part 2:** 575, 584–585

"Sunthin' in the Pastoral Line" (Lowell), **Supp. I Part 2:** 415–416

Sun to Sun (Hurston), **Supp. VI:** 154

Sun Tracks (Ortiz), **Supp. IV Part 2:** 499, 500

Sun Under Wood (Hass), **Supp. VI:** 103, 108–109

"Superb Lily, The" (Pinsky), **Supp. VI:** 250

"Super Goat Man" (Lethem), **Supp. XVIII:** 148

"Superman Comes to the Supermarket" (Mailer), **Retro. Supp. II:** 204

"Supermarket in California, A" (Ginsberg), **Supp. XI:** 135

"Supernatural Horror in Literature" (Lovecraft), **Supp. XXV:** 120

"Supernatural Love" (Schnackenberg), **Supp. XV:** 257, 259–260

Supernatural Love: Poems 1976–1992 (Schnackenberg), **Supp. XV:** 253, 256, 260, 263

Suplee, Curt, **Supp. XVI:** 202

"Supper After the Last, The" (Kinnell), **Supp. III Part 1:** 239

"Supposedly Fun Thing I'll Never Do Again, A" (Wallace), **Supp. X:** 315

Supposedly Fun Thing I'll Never Do Again, A: Essays and Arguments (Wallace), **Supp. X:** 314–316

Suppressed Desires (Glaspell and Cook), **Supp. III Part 1:** 178; **Supp. XXI:** 6

Suppression of the African Slave Trade to the United States of America, 1638–1870 (Du Bois), **Supp. II Part 1:** 157, 162

Supreme Fiction, The (Stevens), **Supp. XVI:** 158

"Supremes, The" (Jarman), **Supp. XVII:** 115

Sure Hand of God, The (Caldwell), **I:** 297, 302

Sure Signs: New and Selected Poems (Kooser), **Supp. XIX:** 116, 117, **121–122**

"Surety and Fidelity Claims" (Stevens), **Retro. Supp. I:** 296, 309

Surface of Earth, The (Price), **Supp. VI:** 261–262

"Surfaces" (Ammons), **Supp. VII:** 36

Surfaces and Masks (Major), **Supp. XXII:** 180

Surfacing (Atwood), **Supp. XIII:** 20, 21, **22–23,** 24, 33, 35

"Surgeon at 2 A.M." (Plath), **Supp. I Part 2:** 545

Summer Knowledge (Schwartz), **Supp. II Part 2:** 662, 665

"Surprise" (Kenyon), **Supp. VII:** 173

Surprised by Sin: The Reader in Paradise Lost (Fish), **Supp. XIV:** 15

Surreal South (eds. P. Benedict and L. Benedict), **Supp. XXIII:** 35

"Surround, The Imagining Herself as the Environment,/She Speaks to James Wright at Sundow" (Dickey), **Supp. IV Part 1:** 185

"Surrounded by Weasels" (Gray and Gallagher), **Supp. XXIV:** 178

"Survey of Literature" (Ransom), **III:** 480

"Survey of the Literature, A" (Saunders), **Supp. XIX:** 235

"Surveyor, The" (H. Roth), **Supp. IX:** 233, 234

Survival (Atwood), **Supp. XIII:** 20, 22, 35

"Survival as Tao, Beginning at 5:00 A.M." (Carruth), **Supp. XVI:** 56

Survival of the Bark Canoe, The (McPhee), **Supp. III Part 1:** 301, 302, 308, 313

Survival This Way: Interviews with American Indian Poets (Bruchac), **Supp. IV Part 2:** 506

"Surviving Love" (Berryman), **I:** 173

Survivor (O. Butler), **Supp. XIII:** 62, 63

Susan and Anna Warner (Foster), **Supp. XVIII:** 265

Susan and God (film; Cukor), **Supp. XVI:** 192

Susanna Moodie: Voice and Vision (Shields), **Supp. VII:** 313

Susan Warner ("Elizabeth Wetherell") (A. Warner), **Supp. XVIII:** 259, 260

Suspect in Poetry, The (Dickey), **Supp. IV Part 1:** 177

"Sustained by Fiction" (Hoffman), **Supp. X:** 90, 92

"Susto" (Ríos), **Supp. IV Part 2:** 553

Sutherland, Donald, **IV:** 38, 44; **Supp. IX:** 254

Sutherland, Efua, **Supp. IV Part 1:** 9, 16

Sutherland-Smith, James, **Supp. X:** 211, 212

Sut Lovingood (Harris), **II:** 70; **Supp. XXII:** 193

Sutton, Roger, **Supp. X:** 266

Sutton, Walter, **III:** 479

"Sutton Pie Safe, The" (P. Benedict), **Supp. XXIII:** 36

Suttree (McCarthy), **Supp. VIII:** 178–180, 189

Suvero, Mark di, **Supp. IX:** 251

Svevo, Italo, **Supp. XIV:** 112

Swados, Harvey, **Supp. XI:** 222; **Supp. XIX: 255–271**

Swales, Martin, **Supp. XIX:** 183

Swallow, Alan, **Supp. X:** 112, 115, 116, 120, 123

Swallow Barn (J. P. Kennedy), **II:** 313

Swallow Barn (Kennedy), **Supp. XXII:** 193

Swallow the Lake (Major), **Supp. XXII:** 174

"Swamp Boy" (Bass), **Supp. XVI:** 20

Swan, Barbara, **Supp. IV Part 2:** 447

Swan, Jon, **Supp. IV Part 1:** 176

Swan Lake (Helprin), **Supp. XXV:** 83, 87

Swan Lake (Tchaikovsky), **Supp. IX:** 51

Swan Lake Trilogy (Helprin), **Supp. XXV:** 81, 84, 87

"Swan Legs" (Stern), **Supp. IX:** 299

Swann (Shields), **Supp. VII:** 315, 318–323, 326

Swann, Brian, **Supp. IV Part 2:** 500

Swanson, Gloria, **II:** 429

Swanson, Stevenson, **Supp. XIV:** 111

Swanton, John Reed, **Supp. VIII:** 295

Swan Watch (Schulberg), **Supp. XVIII:** 254

Swanwick, John, **Supp. XV:** 237

Swanwick, Michael, **Supp. XVI:** 128

"Swarm, The" (Plath), **Retro. Supp. II:** 255

"Sway" (Simpson), **Supp. IX:** 276

Sweat (Hurston), **Supp. VI:** 152

Swedenborg, Emanuel, **II:** 5, 10, 321, 342, 343–344, 396

Sweeney Agonistes (Eliot), **I:** 580; **Retro. Supp. I:** 64, 65; **Retro. Supp. II:** 247

"Sweeney Among the Nightingales" (Eliot), **III:** 4

"Sweeper, The" (Kooser), **Supp. XIX:** 125

Sweet, Blanche, **Supp. I Part 2:** 391

Sweet, Timothy, **Supp. IV Part 1:** 330

Sweet and Lowdown (film; Allen), **Supp. XV:** 11

Sweet and Sour (O'Hara), **III:** 361

"Sweet Armageddon" (Hoffman), **Supp. XVIII:** 85, 86

Sweet Bird of Youth (T. Williams), **IV:** 382, 383, 385, 386, 387, 388, 389, 390, 391, 392, 395, 396, 398; **Supp. IV Part 1:** 84, 89

Sweet Charity (musical), **Supp. IV Part 2:** 575

Sweet Flypaper of Life, The (Hughes), **Supp. I Part 1:** 335–336

"Sweetgrass"(Kenny), **Supp. XXIII:** 148

"Sweetheart" (Notley), **Supp. XXII:** 231

"Sweetheart of the Song Tra Bong, The" (O'Brien), **Supp. V:** 243, 249

"Sweethearts" (Ford), **Supp. V:** 69

Sweet Hereafter, The (Banks), **Supp. V:** 15–16

Sweet Lorain (Weigl), **Supp. XIX:** 282

Sweet Machine (Doty), **Supp. XI:** 121, **131–132,** 135

Sweet Sue (Gurney), **Supp. V:** 105, 107–108

Sweet Sweetback's Baadasss Song (Peebles; film), **Supp. XI:** 17

Sweet Thursday (Steinbeck), **IV:** 50, 52, 64–65

Sweet Will (Levine), **Supp. V:** 178, 187, 189, 190

"Sweet Will" (Levine), **Supp. V:** 190

"Sweet Willy"(J. Schoolcraft), **Supp. XXIII:** 226, 231

"Sweet Words on Race" (Hughes), **Retro. Supp. I:** 211

Sweezy, Paul, **Supp. I Part 2:** 645

"Swell-Looking Girl, A" (Caldwell), **I:** 310

Swenson, May, **Retro. Supp. II:** 44; **Supp. IV Part 2: 637–655; Supp. XIX:** 123

Swetman, Glenn R., **Supp. XXI:** 91

"Swift" (Schwartz), **Supp. II Part 2:** 663

Swift, Jonathan, **I:** 125, 194, 209, 441; **II:** 110, 302, 304–305, 577; **III:** 113; **IV:** 68; **Retro. Supp. I:** 66; **Supp. I Part 2:** 406, 523, 603, 656, 665, 708, 714; **Supp. IV Part 1:** 51; **Supp. IV Part 2:** 692; **Supp. XI:** 105, 209; **Supp. XII:** 276; **Supp. XV:** 258; **Supp. XVI:** 110; **Supp. XVIII:** 2, 12; **Supp. XXV:** 87

"Swimmer" (Francis), **Supp. IX:** 82

"Swimmer" (Skloot), **Supp. XX: 199, 200**

"Swimmer, The" (Cheever), **Supp. I Part 1:** 185, 187

"Swimmer, The" (Glück), **Supp. V:** 82

"Swimmers" (Untermeyer), **Supp. XV:** 300

"Swimmers, The" (Fitzgerald), **Retro. Supp. I:** 110, 111

"Swimmers, The" (Tate), **IV:** 136

"Swimming" (Harjo), **Supp. XII:** 218

Swimming Pool, The (Rinehart), **Supp. XXV:** 189, 198, 200, 202

"Swimming Pool, The"(Strout), **Supp. XXIII:** 284

"Swim Team, The" (July), **Supp. XXIV:** 201

Swinburne, Algernon C., **I:** 50, 384, 568; **II:** 3, 4, 129, 400, 524; **IV:** 135; **Retro. Supp. I:** 100; **Supp. I Part 1:** 79; **Supp. I Part 2:** 422, 552; **Supp. XIV:** 120, 344

"Swinburne as Poet" (Eliot), **I:** 576

Swinger of Birches, A: A Portrait of Robert Frost (Cox), **Retro. Supp. I:** 132

"Swinging an Arc Before Him As He Goes" (Espaillat), **Supp. XXI:** 108

"Swinging on a Birch-Tree" (Larcom), **Supp. XIII:** 147

Swiss, Tom, **Supp. XIX:** 40

Switch, The (Dixon), **Supp. XII:** 141

Swope, D. B., **Supp. IX:** 95

Sword Blades and Poppy Seed (Lowell), **II:** 518, 520, 522, 532

Sword of God, The: Jeanne D'Arc (Endore), **Supp. XVII:** 55

Sybil (Auchincloss), **Supp. IV Part 1:** 25

Sybil and Chryssa (S. and A. Warner), **Supp. XVIII:** 264

"Sycamore" (Stern), **Supp. IX:** 294

"Sycamore, The" (Moore), **III:** 216

"Sycamores, The" (Whittier), **Supp. I Part 2:** 699

Sylvester, Johnny, **Supp. I Part 2:** 438

Sylvester, Joshua, **I:** 178, 179; **II:** 18; **III:** 157; **Supp. I Part 1:** 98, 104, 114, 116

Sylvia (Gurney), **Supp. V:** 105

"Sylvia" (L. Michaels), **Supp. XVI:** 202, 213

"Sylvia" (Larcom), **Supp. XIII:** 144

"Sylvia" (Stern), **Supp. IX:** 297

Sylvia: A Fictional Memoir (L. Michaels), **Supp. XVI:** 202, 213

Sylvia Plath: Method and Madness (Butscher), **Supp. I Part 2:** 526

Sylvia Plath: Poetry and Existence (Holbrook), **Supp. I Part 2:** 526–527

"Sylvia's Death" (Sexton), **Supp. II Part 2:** 671, 684, 685

"Symbol and Image in the Shorter Poems of Herman Melville" (Dickey), **Supp. IV Part 1:** 176

Symbolist Movement in Literature, The (Symons), **I:** 50, 569; **Retro. Supp. I:** 55

Symonds, John Addington, **I:** 241, 242, 251, 259; **IV:** 334; **Supp. XIV:** 329, 335; **Supp. XX:** 230

Symons, Arthur, **I:** 50, 569; **Retro. Supp. I:** 55; **Supp. XX:** 239

Symons, Julian, **Supp. IV Part 1:** 343, 351

"Sympathy" (Dunbar), **Supp. IV Part 1:** 15

Sympathy of Souls, A (Goldbarth), **Supp. XII:** 175, 176, **186–187**

"Symphony, The" (Lanier), **Supp. I Part 1:** 352, 360–361, 364; **Supp. I Part 2:** 416

Symposium (Plato), **Retro. Supp. II:** 31; **Supp. IV Part 1:** 391

Symposium: To Kill a Mockingbird (Alabama Law Review), **Supp. VIII:** 127, 128

Symptoms and Madness (Major), **Supp. XXII:** 174

Symptoms of Being 35 (Lardner), **II:** 434

Synanon (Endore), **Supp. XVII:** 65

Synanon (film, Quine), **Supp. XVII:** 65

Synanon City (Endore), **Supp. XVII:** 65

Syncopated Cakewalk, The (Major), **Supp. XXII:** 174

Synge, John Millington, **I:** 434; **III:** 591–592; **Supp. III Part 1:** 34; **Supp. VIII:** 155

Synthetic Philosophy (Spencer), **II:** 462–463

"Syringa" (Ashbery), **Supp. III Part 1:** 19–21, 25

"Syrinx" (Clampitt), **Supp. IX:** 53

"Syrinx" (Merrill), **Supp. III Part 1:** 328

Syrkin, Marie, **Supp. XIV:** 279, 288, 291

"System, The" (Ashbery), **Supp. III Part 1:** 14, 15, 18, 21–22

System of Dante's Hell, The (Baraka), **Supp. II Part 1:** 39–41, 55

"System of Dante's Inferno, The" (Baraka), **Supp. II Part 1:** 40

"System of Doctor Tarr and Professor Fether, The" (Poe), **III:** 419, 425

System of General Geography, A (Brown), **Supp. I Part 1:** 146

Szaylay, Michael, **Supp. XXI:** 267

Sze, Mai-mai, **Supp. X:** 291

Szentgyorgyi, Tom, **Supp. IX:** 135, 136, 140, 141–142

Szukalski, Stanislaus, **Supp. XXV:** 19, 23

Szulc, Tad, **Supp. XVI:** 154

Szymborka, Wislawa, **Supp. XI:** 267

Szymborska, Wislawa, **Supp. XVIII:** 29

T

"T-2 Tanker Blues" (Snyder), **Supp. VIII:** 294

Tabios, Eileen, **Supp. XV:** 214, 225, 226

"Table of Delectable Contents, The" (Simic), **Supp. VIII:** 276

Tabloid Dreams (R. O. Butler), **Supp. XII: 70–72,** 74

Tacey Cromwell (Richter), **Supp. XVIII: 211,** 215, 217

Tacitus, Cornelius, **I:** 485; **II:** 113

Tadic, Novica, **Supp. VIII:** 272

Taft (Patchett), **Supp. XII:** 307, 312, **314–317**

"Tag" (Hughes), **Supp. I Part 1:** 341

Taggard, Genevieve, **IV:** 436; **Supp. XXII: 271–287**

Taggart, John, **Supp. IV Part 2:** 421

Tagore, Rabindranath, **I:** 383; **Supp. XX: 117**

"Taibele and Her Demon" (Singer), **Retro. Supp. II:** 307

Taibl, Erika, **Supp. XV:** 255

"Tailor Shop, The" (H. Miller), **III:** 175

"Tails" (Dixon), **Supp. XII:** 154

Taine, Hippolyte, **I:** 503; **II:** 271; **III:** 323; **IV:** 440, 444

"Tain't So" (Hughes), **Supp. I Part 1:** 330

"Taipei Tangle" (Halliday), **Supp. XIX:** 91

Takasago (play), **III:** 466

Takazauckas, Albert, **Supp. XXIII:** 203

Take Away the Darkness (Bynner), **Supp. XV:** 51

Take Heart (Peacock), **Supp. XIX: 197–199,** 206

Take Me Back: A Novel (Bausch), **Supp. VII:** 41, 43–45, 46, 49

"Take My Saddle from the Wall: A Valediction" (McMurtry), **Supp. V:** 219

"'Take No for an Answer' " (Didion), **Supp. IV Part 1:** 203

"Take Pity" (Malamud), **Supp. I Part 2:** 427, 428, 435, 436, 437

"Takers, The" (Olds), **Supp. X:** 205

"Take the I Out" (Olds), **Supp. X:** 213

Take the Money and Run (film; Allen), **Supp. XV: 3–4,** 6

"Taking Away the Name of a Nephew" (Ríos), **Supp. IV Part 2:** 545–546

Taking Care of Mrs. Carroll (Monette), **Supp. X:** 153

"Taking of Captain Ball, The" (Jewett), **Retro. Supp. II:** 134

"Taking Off Emily Dickinson's Clothes" (Collins), **Supp. XXI:** 59, 60

"Taking Out the Lawn Chairs" (Karr), **Supp. XI:** 241

"Taking the Bypass" (J. Epstein), **Supp. XIV:** 110; **Supp. XVI:** 230

"Taking the Forest" (Howe), **Supp. IV Part 2:** 433

"Taking the Lambs to Market" (Kumin), **Supp. IV Part 2:** 455

Talbot, Daniel, **Supp. XIX:** 264

"Tale, A" (Bogan), **Supp. III Part 1:** 50, 51

Taleb-Khyar, Mohamed, **Supp. IV Part 1:** 242, 243, 244, 247, 257

Talented Mr. Ripley, The (Highsmith), **Supp. XXII:** 119

"Tale of Jerusalem, A" (Poe), **III:** 411

Tale of Possessors Self-Dispossessed, A (O'Neill), **III:** 404

Tale of the Body Thief, The (Rice), **Supp. VII:** 290, 293–294, 297

Tale of Two Cities, A (film), **Supp. I Part 1:** 67

"Tale of Two Liars, A" (Singer), **IV:** 12

Tales (Baraka), **Supp. II Part 1:** 39, 55

Tales (Poe), **III:** 413

Tales and Stories for Black Folks (Bambara, ed.), **Supp. XI:** 1

Tales before Midnight (Benét), **Supp. XI:** 46, 53, 57

Talese, Gay, **Supp. XVI:** 273; **Supp. XVII: 199–211; Supp. XXIV:** 282

Tales of a Traveller (Irving), **II:** 309–310

Tales of a Wayside Inn (Longfellow), **II:** 489, 490, 501, 502, 504–505; **Retro. Supp. II:** 154, **162–165**

Tales of Glauber-Spa (Bryant, ed.), **Supp. I Part 1:** 157

Tales of H. P. Lovecraft (Oates, ed.), **Supp. XXV:** 123

Tales of Manhattan (Auchincloss), **Supp. IV Part 1:** 23

Tales of Men and Ghosts (Wharton), **IV:** 315; **Retro. Supp. I:** 372

Tales of My People (Asch), **Supp. XXIII:** 7

Tales of Rhoda, The (Rice), **Supp. VII:** 288

Tales of Soldiers and Civilians (Bierce), **I:** 200–203, 204, 206, 208, 212

Tales of the Argonauts (Harte), **Supp. II Part 1:** 337, 348, 351

Tales of the Fish Patrol (London), **II:** 465

Tales of the Grotesque and Arabesque (Poe), **II:** 273; **III:** 412, 415; **Retro.**

Supp. II: 270

Tales of the Jazz Age (Fitzgerald), **II:** 88; **Retro. Supp. I:** 105; **Supp. IX:** 57

Tales You Won't Believe (Stratton-Porter), **Supp. XX:** 217

Taliaferro, Frances, **Supp. XXII:** 210

"Talisman, A" (Moore), **III:** 195–196

Talisman, The (King), **Supp. V:** 140, 144, 152

"Talkin Bout Sonny" (Bambara), **Supp. XI:** 6–7

"Talking" (Merwin), **Supp. III Part 1:** 354

Talking All Morning (R. Bly), **Supp. IV Part 1:** 59, 60, 61, 62, 64, 65

Talking Dirty to the Gods (Komunyakaa), **Supp. XIII: 130–131**

Talking History (television program), **Supp. XXI:** 172

"Talking Horse" (Malamud), **Supp. I Part 2:** 435

Talking Soft Dutch (McCarriston), **Supp. XIV: 260–263,** 266, 270, 271

"Talking to Barr Creek" (Wagoner), **Supp. IX:** 328

"Talking to Sheep" (Sexton), **Supp. II Part 2:** 695

Talking to the Sun: An Illustrated Anthology of Poems for Young People (Koch and Farrell, eds.), **Supp. XV:** 188

"Talking Water" (Taggard), **Supp. XXII:** 276

"Talk of Heroes" (C. Bly), **Supp. XVI:** 34

"Talk of the Town" (*The New Yorker* column), **IV:** 215; **Supp. IV Part 1:** 53, 54

"Talk on Guadalcanal" (Wolfert), **Supp. XXI:** 264

Talk Talk (Boyle), **Supp. XX: 24**

"Talk with the Yellow Kid, A" (Bellow), **I:** 151

Tallent, Elizabeth, **Supp. IV Part 2:** 570

Tallman, Warren, **Supp. IV Part 1:** 154

TallMountain, Mary, **Supp. IV Part 1:** 324–325

Talma, Louise, **IV:** 357

Talmadge, Constance, **Supp. XVI:** 186, 187, 196

Talmadge, Norma, **Supp. XVI:** 186, 187, 196

Talmadge Girls, The (Loos), **Supp. XVI:** 186, 196

Talmey, Allene, **Supp. IV Part 1:** 197; **Supp. XIII:** 172

Talmud, **IV:** 8, 17

Taltos: Lives of the Mayfair Witches (Rice), **Supp. VII:** 299–300

"Tamar" (Jeffers), **Supp. II Part 2:** 427–428, 436

Tamar and Other Poems (Jeffers), **Supp. II Part 2:** 416, 419

"Tambourine Life" (Berrigan), **Supp. XXIV:** 42

Tambourines to Glory (Hughes), **Supp. I Part 1:** 338–339

"Tame Indians" (Jewett), **Retro. Supp. II:** 141

"Tamerlane" (Poe), **III:** 426

Tamerlane and Other Poems (Poe), **III:** 410

"Tammany Man, The" (Hapgood), **Supp. XVII:** 103

"Tam O'Shanter" (Burns), **II:** 306

Tamsen Donner: A Woman's Journey (Whitman), **Supp. XXI:** 246

Tan, Amy, **Supp. X: 289–300**

Tangential Views (Bierce), **I:** 209

"Tangier 1975" (Bowles), **Supp. IV Part 1:** 94

Tanguay, Pablo, **Supp. XXIII:** 299

"Tankas" (McClatchy), **Supp. XII:** 266

Tanner, Laura E., **Supp. X:** 209; **Supp. XXI:** 217

Tanner, Obour, **Supp. XX: 281, 288**

Tanner, Tony, **I:** 260, 261; **Retro. Supp. II:** 205; **Supp. IV Part 1:** 285; **Supp. XVI:** 65, 69

Tannhäuser (Wagner), **I:** 315

"Tan Ta Ra, Cries Mars...," (Wagoner), **Supp. IX:** 325

Tao of Physics, The (Capra), **Supp. X:** 261

Tao Teh Ching (Bynner, trans.), **Supp. XV:** 46, 47

Tapahonso, Luci, **Supp. IV Part 1:** 404; **Supp. IV Part 2:** 499, 508

Tape for the Turn of the Year (Ammons), **Supp. VII:** 31–33, 35

"Tapestry" (Ashbery), **Supp. III Part 1:** 22–23

"Tapestry" (E. P. Jones), **Supp. XXII:** 152

"Tapiama" (Bowles), **Supp. IV Part 1:** 89–90

"Tapiola" (W. C. Williams), **Retro. Supp. I:** 429

Tappan, Arthur, **Supp. I Part 2:** 588

Tapping the White Cane of Solitude (F. Wright), **Supp. XVII:** 243

Taps at Reveille (Fitzgerald), **II:** 94, 96; **Retro. Supp. I:** 113

Taradash, Daniel, **Supp. XXV:** 95

Tar: A Midwest Childhood (Anderson), **I:** 98, 115; **II:** 27

Tarantino, Quentin, **Supp. IV Part 1:** 356

Tarantula (Dylan), **Supp. XVIII:** 21, 29, **31–32**

Tar Baby (Morrison), **Supp. III Part 1:** 364, 369–372, 379; **Supp. IV Part 1:** 13

Tarbell, Ida, **III:** 322, 580; **Retro. Supp. II:** 101

"Target Practice" (Offutt), **Supp. XIX:** 171

"Target Study" (Baraka), **Supp. II Part 1:** 49–50, 54

Tarkington, Booth, **II:** 444; **III:** 70; **Retro. Supp. I:** 100; **Supp. XV:** 41

Tarnawsky, Yuriy (George) Orest, **Supp. XX:** 259

Tarpon (film), **Supp. VIII:** 42

Tarr, Rodger L., **Supp. X:** 222, 224, 226

Tárrega, Francisco, **Supp. XXI:** 100

Tartt, Donna, **Supp. XVIII:** 135

Tartuffe (Molière; Wilbur, trans.), **Supp. III Part 2:** 560

Tarumba, Selected Poems of Jaime Sabines (Levine and Trejo, trans.), **Supp. V:** 178
Tarzan Finds a Son (film, Weismuller), **Supp. XX:** 18
"Tarzan Is an Expatriate" (Theroux), **Supp. VIII:** 313
Tasis, Juan de, **Supp. XXI:** 104
Task, The (Cowper), **II:** 304
Tasker Street (Halliday), **Supp. XIX:** 82, **87–89**
Tasso, Torquato, **I:** 276
Taste of Palestine, A: Menus and Memories (Shihab), **Supp. XIII:** 273
Tate, Alan, **Supp. XV:** 141
Tate, Allen, **I:** 48, 49, 50, 67, 69, 381, 382, 386, 390, 396, 397, 399, 402, 441, 468; **II:** 197–198, 367, 536, 537, 542, 551, 554; **III:** 424, 428, 454, 482, 483, 485, 493, 495, 496, 497, 499, 500, 517; **IV:** 120–143, 236, 237, 433; **Retro. Supp. I:** 37, 41, 90; **Retro. Supp. II:** 77, 79, 82, 83, 89, 176, 178, 179; **Supp. I Part 1:** 364, 371; **Supp. I Part 2:** 423; **Supp. II Part 1:** 90–91, 96, 98, 103–104, 136, 139, 144, 150, 151, 318; **Supp. II Part 2:** 643; **Supp. III Part 2:** 542; **Supp. V:** 315, 331; **Supp. X:** 1, 52; **Supp. XIV:** 2; **Supp. XXI:** 256; **Supp. XXII:** 277
Tate, Mrs. Allen (Caroline Gordon). *See* Gordon, Caroline
Tate, Mrs. Allen (Helen Heinz), **IV:** 127
Tate, Mrs. Allen (Isabella Gardner), **IV:** 127
Tate, Benjamin Lewis Bogan, **IV:** 127
Tate, Greg, **Supp. XIII:** 233, 237
Tate, James, **Supp. V:** 92, 338; **Supp. VIII:** 39, 279; **Supp. XV:** 250; **Supp. XVII:** 242
Tate, John Allen, **IV:** 127
Tate, Michael Paul, **IV:** 127
Tate, Nancy, **II:** 197
Tatonetti, Lisa, **Supp. XXIII:** 149–150
Tattooed Countess, The (Van Vechten), **I:** 295; **Supp. II Part 2:** 726–728, 738, 742
Tattooed Feet (Nye), **Supp. XIII:** 274
"Tattoos" (McClatchy), **Supp. XII:** 266–267, 268
"Tattoos" (Wright), **Supp. V:** 335, 340
Tatum, Anna, **I:** 516
Tatum, James, **Supp. IV Part 2:** 684
Taubman, Howard, **Supp. XXV:** 106
Taupin, René, **II:** 528, 529; **Supp. III Part 2:** 614, 615, 617, 621
Tavano, John, **Supp. XXI:** 99
Taves, Isabella, **Supp. XXV:** 198
Tawney, Richard Henry, **Supp. I Part 2:** 481
Taylor, Ann, **Supp. XXIII:** 231
Taylor, Bayard, **II:** 275; **Supp. I Part 1:** 350, 361, 362, 365, 366, 372; **Supp. XV:** 269
Taylor, Chuck, **Supp. XXIII:** 57
Taylor, Cora. *See* Howarth, Cora
Taylor, Deems, **III:** 138
Taylor, Edward, **III:** 493; **IV:** 144–166; **Supp. I Part 1:** 98; **Supp. I Part 2:** 375, 386, 546

Taylor, Mrs. Edward (Elizabeth Fitch), **IV:** 147, 165
Taylor, Mrs. Edward (Ruth Wyllys), **IV:** 148
Taylor, Eleanor Ross, **Supp. V:** 317, 318
Taylor, Elizabeth, **II:** 588
Taylor, Frank, **III:** 81
Taylor, Frederick Winslow, **Supp. I Part 2:** 644
Taylor, Graham, **Supp. I Part 1:** 5
Taylor, Henry, **Retro. Supp. I:** 212; **Supp. XI:** 317; **Supp. XIII:** 333
Taylor, Henry W., **IV:** 144
Taylor, Jeremy, **II:** 11; **III:** 487; **Supp. I Part 1:** 349; **Supp. XII:** 45; **Supp. XIV:** 344, 345
Taylor, John, **IV:** 149
Taylor, Katherine, **Supp. VIII:** 251
Taylor, Kezia, **IV:** 148
Taylor, Nathaniel W., **Supp. I Part 2:** 580
Taylor, Paul, **I:** 293
Taylor, Peter, **Retro. Supp. II:** 179; **Supp. V:** 313–329; **Supp. XIV:** 3
Taylor, Raynor, **Supp. XV:** 238
Taylor, Richard, **IV:** 146
Taylor, Robert, **Supp. I Part 1:** 294; **Supp. XV:** 135, 138; **Supp. XVI:** 277
Taylor, Samuel A., **Supp. XX:** 253
Taylor, Stephan, **Supp. XVI:** 203
Taylor, Thomas, **II:** 10
Taylor, William, **IV:** 145–146
Taylor, Zachary, **I:** 3; **II:** 433–434
Tchelitchew, Peter, **II:** 586
Tea and Sympathy (Anderson), **Supp. I Part 1:** 277; **Supp. V:** 108
"Tea at the Palaz of Hoon" (Stevens), **Retro. Supp. I:** 300, 302, 306
"Teacher's Pet" (Thurber), **Supp. I Part 2:** 605–606
"Teaching and Story Telling" (Maclean), **Supp. XIV:** 234
Teaching a Stone to Talk: Expeditions and Encounters (Dillard), **Supp. VI:** 23, 26, 28, 32, 33, 34–35
"Teaching Emily Dickenson"(Hadas), **Supp. XXIII:** 115
"Teaching Hanh the Blues" (Weigl), **Supp. XIX:** 287
Teachings of Don B., The (Barthelme), **Supp. IV Part 1:** 53
Teachout, Terry, **Supp. XIX:** 137
Teale, Edwin Way, **Supp. XIII:** 7
Teall, Dorothy, **I:** 221
Team Team Team (film), **Supp. IX:** 251
"Tea on the Mountain" (Bowles), **Supp. IV Part 1:** 90
"Tea Party, The" (MacLeish), **III:** 11
Tear and a Smile, A (Dam'a wa Ibtisáma) (Gibran), **Supp. XX: 116, 118, 124**
Teare, Brian, **Supp. XXII:** 236
"Tears, Idle Tears" (Lord Tennyson), **Supp. XIV:** 8
"Tears of the Pilgrims, The" (McClatchy), **Supp. XII:** 256
Teasdale, Sara, **Retro. Supp. I:** 133; **Supp. I Part 2:** 393, 707; **Supp. XIV:** 127; **Supp. XV:** 295, 297, 301, 305, 307, 308; **Supp. XVII:** 69, 75
"Tease" (Swados), **Supp. XIX:** 267

Tebeaux, Elizabeth, **Supp. IX:** 109
"Technical Manifesto of Futurist Literature" (Marinetti), **Supp. XXII:** 161
Technics and Civilization (Mumford), **Supp. I Part 2:** 638; **Supp. II Part 2:** 479, 493, 497
Technics and Human Development (Mumford), **Supp. I Part 2:** 638; **Supp. II Part 2:** 497
"Technology, The" (Egan), **Supp. XIX:** 61
"Teddy" (Salinger), **III:** 561–563, 571
"Te Deum" (Reznikoff), **Supp. XIV:** 281
Tedlock, Dennis, **Supp. IV Part 2:** 509
"Teeth Mother Naked at Last, The" (R. Bly), **Supp. IV Part 1:** 63, 68, 73
Teggart, Richard, **Supp. I Part 2:** 650
Tegnér, Esaias, **Retro. Supp. II:** 155
Teilhard de Chardin, Pierre, **Supp. I Part 1:** 314
Tekonwatonti/Molly Brant (Kenny), **Supp. XXIII:** 143, 147, 151, **152–153,** 154
Telephone, The (film), **Supp. XI:** 309
"Telephone Call, A" (Parker), **Supp. IX: 202–203**
"Telephone Number of the Muse, The" (Justice), **Supp. VII:** 124–125
Telephone Poles and Other Poems (Updike), **IV:** 214, 215
"Television" (Beattie), **Supp. V:** 33
Teller, Edward, **I:** 137
"Tell Him About Brother John" (Muñoz), **Supp. XXV:** 136
"Telling" (Ortiz), **Supp. IV Part 2:** 509
"Telling It in Black and White: The Importance of the Africanist Presence in *To Kill a Mockingbird*" (Baecker), **Supp. VIII:** 128
Telling Secrets (Buechner), **Supp. XII:** 53–54
Telling Stories (Didion), **Supp. IV Part 1:** 197
"Telling Stories" (Didion), **Supp. IV Part 1:** 197
"Telling the Bees" (Whittier), **Supp. I Part 2:** 694–695
Telling the Little Secrets (J. Burstein), **Supp. XVII:** 44
Telling the Truth: The Gospel as Tragedy, Comedy, and Fairy Tale (Buechner), **Supp. XII:** 53
"Tell Me" (Hughes), **Supp. VIII:** 213
"Tell Me, Sir, ... What Is 'Black' Literature?" (H. L. Gates), **Supp. XX:** 108
Tell Me, Tell Me (Moore), **III:** 215
Tell Me Again (Notley), **Supp. XXII:** 224, 230–231
Tell Me Again How the White Heron Rises and Flies across the Nacreous River at Twilight toward the Distant Islands (Carruth), **Supp. XVI:** 56
Tell Me a Riddle (film), **Supp. XIII:** 295
Tell Me a Riddle (Olsen), **Supp. XIII:** 294, 296, **298–302,** 303, 305
"Tell Me a Riddle" (Olsen), **Supp. XIII:** 294, 297, 298, **300–302,** 305
"Tell Me a Story" (McDermott), **Supp. XVIII:** 177

Tell Me How Long the Train's Been Gone (Baldwin), **Retro. Supp. II:** 9, **11–12,** 14; **Supp. I Part 1:** 48, 52, 63–65, 67

"Tell Me My Fortune" (Epstein), **Supp. XII:** 163

Tell Me True: Memoir, History, and Writing a Life (Hampl and May, eds.), **Supp. XXII:** 81–82, 84, **94–95**

Tell Me Your Answer True (Sexton), **Supp. II Part 2:** 683

Tell My Horse (Hurston), **Supp. VI:** 149, 156, 158

"Tell-Tale Heart, The" (Poe), **III:** 413, 414–415, 416; **Retro. Supp. II:** 267, 269, 270

"Tell-Tale heart, The" (Poe), **Supp. XXV:** 112

"Tell the Women We're Going" (Carver), **Supp. III Part 1:** 138, 144

"Telluride Blues—A Hatchet Job" (Abbey), **Supp. XIII:** 10

Telushkin, Dvorah, **Retro. Supp. II:** 317

Temblor (Howe), **Supp. IV Part 2:** 431

Temperamental People (Rinehart), **Supp. XXV:** 196

Tempering of Eugene O'Neill, The (D. Alexander), **Supp. XVII:** 99

"Temper of Steel, The" (Jones), **Supp. XI:** 218

Tempers, The (W. C. Williams), **Retro. Supp. I:** 413–414, 415, 416, 424

Tempest, The (Shakespeare), **I:** 394; **II:** 12; **III:** 40, 61, 263; **Retro. Supp. I:** 61; **Supp. IV Part 2:** 463; **Supp. V:** 302–303; **Supp. XII:** 54–57; **Supp. XV:** 255, 256

Temple, Minnie, **II:** 323

Temple, The (Herbert), **IV:** 145, 153

Temple, William, **III:** 303

Temple House (E. Stoddard), **Supp. XV:** 273, **284–286**

Temple of My Familiar, The (Walker), **Supp. III Part 2:** 521, 527, 529, 535, 537; **Supp. IV Part 1:** 14

"Temple of the Holy Ghost, A" (O'Connor), **III:** 344, 352; **Retro. Supp. II:** 232

Templin, Charlotte, **Supp. V:** 116

Temporary Shelter (Gordon), **Supp. IV Part 1:** 299, 305–307

"Temporary Shelter" (Gordon), **Supp. IV Part 1:** 306

Temptation Game, The (Gardner), **Supp. VI:** 72

"Temptation of St. Anthony, The" (Barthelme), **Supp. IV Part 1:** 47

Temptations, The, **Supp. X:** 242

"10 Best Weathers of 1983, The" (Notley), **Supp. XXII:** 224

"10 Things I Do Every Day" (Berrigan), **Supp. XXII:** 224; **Supp. XXIV:** 41

"Tenancy, A" (Merrill), **Supp. III Part 1:** 322, 323

"Tenant" (Hoffman), **Supp. XVIII:** 86

Tenants, The (Malamud), **Supp. I Part 2:** 448–450

"Ten Best Issues of Comic Books, The" (Notley), **Supp. XXII:** 224

Ten Commandments (McClatchy), **Supp. XII:** 262–265

Ten Days That Shook the World (Reed), **II:** 577; **Supp. X:** 136; **Supp. XVIII:** 225

Tendencies in Modern American Poetry (Lowell), **II:** 529

"Tender, Hilarious Reminiscences of Life in Mythical Lake Wobegon" (MacDougall), **Supp. XVI:** 174

Tender Buttons (G. Stein), **I:** 103, 105; **IV:** 27, 42–43; **Retro. Supp. II:** 331; **Supp. XV:** 347

"Tenderfoot" (Haines), **Supp. XII:** 209

Tender Is the Night (Fitzgerald), **I:** 375; **II:** 79, 84, 91, 95–96, 97, 98, 420; **Retro. Supp. I:** 105, 108, 109, **110–112,** 114; **Supp. IX:** 59, 60, 61; **Supp. XV:** 197; **Supp. XXI:** 11

"Tenderloin" (Crane), **I:** 408

"Tenderly" (Dobyns), **Supp. XIII:** 86–87

'Tender Man, A" (Bambara), **Supp. XI:** 9–10

"Tenderness" (Dunn), **Supp. XI:** 149, 150

"Tender Offer, The" (Auchincloss), **Supp. IV Part 1:** 34

"Tender Organizations, The" (C. Bly), **Supp. XVI:** 40, 42

"Tenebrae" (Komunyakaa), **Supp. XIII:** 132

Tenenbaum, Joseph, **Supp. XX:** 253

"Ten Forty-Four" (Kingsolver), **Supp. VII:** 208

Ten Indians (Bell), **Supp. X:** 7, **12**

Ten Introductions: A Collection of Modern Verse (Taggard and Fitts, ed.), **Supp. XXII:** 281

Tennant, Agnieszka, **Supp. XX:** 140

"Ten Neglected American Writers Who Deserve to Be Better Known" (Cantor), **Supp. IV Part 1:** 285

Tennent, Gilbert, **I:** 546

Tennessee Day in St. Louis (Taylor), **Supp. V:** 324

"Tennessee's Partner" (Harte), **Supp. II Part 1:** 345, 348–350

"Tennis" (Pinsky), **Supp. VI:** 241, 242

Tennis Court Oath, The (Ashbery), **Supp. III Part 1:** 7, 9, 12, 14, 26

Ten North Frederick (O'Hara), **III:** 361

Tennyson, Alfred, Lord, **I:** 587–588; **II:** 18, 82, 273, 338, 404, 439, 604; **III:** 5, 409, 469, 485, 511, 521, 523; **Retro. Supp. I:** 100, 325; **Retro. Supp. II:** 135; **Supp. I Part 1:** 349, 356; **Supp. I Part 2:** 410, 416, 552; **Supp. IX:** 19; **Supp. X:** 157; **Supp. XIII:** 111; **Supp. XIV:** 40, 120; **Supp. XV:** 275; **Supp. XVIII:** 78

"Tenochtitlan" (Bronk), **Supp. XXI:** 31

"Ten O'Clock News" (Ortiz), **Supp. IV Part 2:** 503–504

"Te-Non-An-At-Che"(Kenny), **Supp. XXIII:** 151

Ten Poems (Dove), **Supp. IV Part 1:** 244

Ten Poems of Francis Ponge Translated by Robert Bly and Ten Poems of Robert Bly Inspired by the Poems by Francis Ponge (R. Bly), **Supp. IV Part 1:** 71

"Tension in Poetry" (Tate), **IV:** 128, 129, 135

Tenth Muse, The (Bradstreet), **Supp. I Part 1:** 102, 103, 114

10,000 Days of Thunder: A History of the Vietnam War (Caputo), **Supp. XIX:** 29

Tenting Tonight (Rinehart), **Supp. XXV:** 195

"Tent on the Beach, The" (Whittier), **Supp. I Part 2:** 703

"Ten True Things" (July), **Supp. XXIV:** 205

"Teodoro Luna Confesses after Years to His Brother, Anselmo the Priest, Who Is Required to Understand, But Who Understands Anyway, More Than People Think" (Ríos), **Supp. IV Part 2:** 552

Teodoro Luna's Two Kisses (Ríos), **Supp. IV Part 2:** 550–552, 553

"Tepeyac" (Cisneros), **Supp. VII:** 69

"Terce" (Auden), **Supp. II Part 1:** 22

Terence, **IV:** 155, 363; **Supp. I Part 2:** 405

Terkel, Studs, **Supp. IV Part 1:** 364

"Term" (Merwin), **Supp. III Part 1:** 356–357

"Terminal Days at Beverly Farms" (Lowell), **Retro. Supp. II:** 189

Terminating, or Sonnet LXXV, or "Lass Meine Schmerzen nicht verloren sein, or Ambivalence" (Kushner), **Supp. IX:** 132

Terminations (James), **Retro. Supp. I:** 229

"Terminus" (Emerson), **II:** 13, 19

"Terminus" (Wharton), **Retro. Supp. I:** 371

"Terms in Which I Think of Reality, The" (Ginsberg), **Supp. II Part 1:** 311

Terms of Endearment (film), **Supp. V:** 226

Terms of Endearment (McMurtry), **Supp. V:** 224–225

"Terrace, The" (Wilbur), **Supp. III Part 2:** 550

Terrarium (Sanders), **Supp. XVI:** 270

"Terrence McNally" (Bryer), **Supp. XIII:** 200

"Terrence McNally" (Di Gaetani), **Supp. XIII:** 200

Terrence McNally: A Casebook (Zinman), **Supp. XIII:** 209

"Terrestrial Cuckoo"(O'Hara), **Supp. XXIII:** 210

"Terrible Peacock, The" (Barnes), **Supp. III Part 1:** 33

Terrible Threes, The (Reed), **Supp. X:** 241, 253

Terrible Twos, The (Reed), **Supp. X:** 241, **252–253**

"Terrific Mother" (Moore), **Supp. X:** 178

Territory Ahead, The (Morris), **III:** 228–229, 236

Terrorism (Wright), **Supp. XV:** 341, 342

"Terrorism" (Wright), **Supp. XV:** 341

"Terrors of the Amazon" (Grossman), **Supp. XXV:** 66

Terry, Edward A., **II:** 128, 129

Terry, Rose, **Supp. I Part 2:** 420
Tertium Organum (Ouspensky), **I:** 383; **Supp. XX: 116**
Terzian, Peter, **Supp. XXV:** 12, 13
Tess of the d'Ubervilles (Hardy), **II:** 181; **Retro. Supp. II:** 100
"Testament" (Berry), **Supp. X:** 36
"Testament" (Carruth), **Supp. XVI:** 59
"Testament (Or, Homage to Walt Whitman)" (Jong), **Supp. V:** 130
"Testament of Flood" (Warren), **IV:** 253
Testament of François Villon, The (Pound, opera), **Retro. Supp. I:** 287
"Testament: Vermeer in December" (Bierds), **Supp. XVII:** 33
"Testimonia on the Question of Stesichoros' Blinding by Helen" (Carson), **Supp. XII:** 107
"Testimonies of a Roasted Chicken" (Jarman), **Supp. XVII:** 120
"Testimony" (Komunyakaa), **Supp. XIII:** 129
"Testimony of James Apthorp, The" (Kees), **Supp. XV:** 146
Testimony: The United States (1885–1890): Recitative (Reznikoff), **Supp. XIV:** 279, 280, 281, 285, **289–291**
Testimony: The United States (1891–1900): Recitative (Reznikoff), **Supp. XIV:** 291
Testing-Tree, The (Kunitz), **Supp. III Part 1:** 260, 263, 264, 267, 268
"Testing-Tree, The" (Kunitz), **Supp. III Part 1:** 269
Test of Poetry, A (Zukofsky), **Supp. III Part 2:** 618, 622
"Teutonic Scholar" (X. J. Kennedy), **Supp. XV:** 161
"Texas Moon, and Elsewhere, The" (McMurtry), **Supp. V:** 225
Texas Poets in Concert: A Quartet (Gwynn, ed.), **Supp. XIII:** 277
Texas Summer (Southern), **Supp. XI:** 309
Texasville (McMurtry), **Supp. V:** 228, 233
Thacher, Molly Day, **IV:** 381
Thackeray, William Makepeace, **I:** 194, 354; **II:** 182, 271, 282, 288, 316, 321, 322; **III:** 64, 70; **IV:** 326; **Retro. Supp. I:** 218; **Supp. I Part 1:** 307; **Supp. I Part 2:** 421, 495, 579; **Supp. IV Part 1:** 297; **Supp. IX:** 200; **Supp. XI:** 277; **Supp. XIV:** 306; **Supp. XX: 228**
Thaddeus, Janice Farrar, **Supp. IV Part 1:** 299
"Thailand" (Barthelme), **Supp. IV Part 1:** 41
Thalberg, Irving, **Retro. Supp. I:** 109, 110, 114; **Supp. XVI:** 191, 192
Thales, **I:** 480–481
Thalia Trilogy (McMurtry), **Supp. V:** 220–223, 234
Tham, Claire, **Supp. VIII:** 79
"Thanatopsis" (Bryant), **Supp. I Part 1:** 150, 154, 155, 170
Thanatos Syndrome, The (Percy), **Supp. III Part 1:** 385, 397–399
"Thanks Can Be Named to Death" (Peacock), **Supp. XIX:** 199

"Thanksgiving" (Glück), **Supp. V:** 83
"Thanksgiving, A" (Auden), **Supp. II Part 1:** 26
"Thanksgiving for a Habitat" (Auden), **Supp. II Part 1:** 24
Thanksgivings (Traherne), **Supp. XVI:** 288
"Thanksgiving Spirit" (Farrell), **II:** 45
Thanksgiving Visitor, The (Capote), **Supp. III Part 1:** 116, 118, 119
"Thank You, Esther Forbes" (Saunders), **Supp. XIX:** 235
Thank You, Fog (Auden), **Supp. II Part 1:** 24
"Thank You, Lord" (Angelou), **Supp. IV Part 1:** 15
Thank You, Mr. Moto (Marquand), **III:** 57, 58
Thank You and Other Poems (Koch), **Supp. XV:** 180–181
"Thank You in Arabic" (Nye), **Supp. XIII:** 273, 281
"Thar's More in the Man Than Thar Is in the Land" (Lanier), **Supp. I Part 1:** 352–353, 359–360
"That Evening Sun" (Faulkner), **II:** 72; **Retro. Supp. I:** 75, 83
That Horse (Hogan), **Supp. IV Part 1:** 397, 404, 405
"That House, This Room" (W. V. Davis), **Supp. XXI:** 90
"That I Had the Wings" (Ellison), **Supp. II Part 1:** 238
That Night (McDermott), **Supp. XVIII:** 155, **158–160,** 162, 163, 166
"That's the Place Indians Talk About" (Ortiz), **Supp. IV Part 2:** 511
That Tantalus (Bronk), **Supp. XXI:** 31
"That the Soul May Wax Plump" (Swenson), **Supp. IV Part 2:** 650
"That the Universe Is Chrysalid" (Sobin), **Supp. XVI:** 284
"That Tree" (Porter), **III:** 434–435, 446, 451
That Was the Week That Was (television program), **Supp. XIV:** 125
"That Year" (Olds), **Supp. X:** 203
"Thaw" (C. Frost), **Supp. XV:** 93, 104, 105
Thaxter, Celia, **Retro. Supp. II:** 136, 147; **Supp. XIII:** 143, 153
Thayer, Abbott, **I:** 231
Thayer, Scofield, **I:** 231; **Retro. Supp. I:** 58
Thayer and Eldridge, **Retro. Supp. I:** 403
"Theater" (Toomer), **Supp. IX:** 309, 317–318
"Theater Chronicle" (McCarthy), **II:** 562
"Theater Problems? Call Dr. Chekhov" (Wasserstein), **Supp. XV:** 320
Theatricals (James), **Retro. Supp. I:** 228
The Blacker the Berry: A Novel of Negro Life (Thurman), **Supp. XVIII:** 281; **Supp. XIX:** 73
"Theft" (Porter), **III:** 434, 435
Theft, A (Bellow), **Retro. Supp. II:** 31–32, 34
The Harder They Fall (Schulberg), **Supp. XVIII:** 247, 253

The Harder They Fall: Celebrities Tell Their Real-Life Stories of Addiction and Recovery (F. Wright), **Supp. XVII:** 240
Their Dogs Came with Them (Viramontes), **Supp. XXV:** 130, 138
Their Eyes Were Watching God (Hurston), **Supp. VI:** 149, 152, 156–157; **Supp. XX: 107**
Their Heads Are Green and Their Hands Are Blue: Scenes from the Non-Christian World (Bowles), **Supp. IV Part 1:** 89
"Their Losses" (Taylor), **Supp. V:** 320
"Their Name is Macaroni" (Boyle), **Supp. XXIV:** 61
"Their Sleep" (W. V. Davis), **Supp. XXI:** 93
Their Wedding Journey (Howells), **II:** 277–278; **Retro. Supp. I:** 334
them (Oates), **Supp. II Part 2:** 503, 511–514
Theme Is Freedom, The (Dos Passos), **I:** 488–489, 492, 494
Theme Time Radio Hour (radio show, Dylan), **Supp. XVIII:** 28
"Theme with Variations" (Agee), **I:** 27
"Then" (Barthelme), **Supp. IV Part 1:** 48
"Then as Now" (Cliff), **Supp. XXII:** 76
"The Night Rhonda Ferguson Was Killed" (E. P. Jones), **Supp. XXII:** 144
"Then It All Came Down" (Capote), **Supp. III Part 1:** 125, 131
Theocritus, **II:** 169; **Retro. Supp. I:** 286; **Supp. XXIV:** 156
Theodore Roethke's Far Fields: The Evolution of His Poetry (Balakian), **Supp. XXIII:** 19
"Theodore the Poet" (Masters), **Supp. I Part 2:** 461
Theological Position, A (Coover), **Supp. V:** 44
Theophrastus, **I:** 58
"Theoretical and Scientific Conceptions of Race, The" (Locke), **Supp. XIV:** 209
"Theoretical Subject(s) of *This Bridge Called My Back,* The"(Alarcón), **Supp. XXIII:** 204–205
"Theories of Time and Space" (Trethewey), **Supp. XXI:** 255
Theory and Practice of Rivers and Other Poems, The (Harrison), **Supp. VIII:** 47, 49
Theory of Business Enterprise, The (Veblen), **Supp. I Part 2:** 638, 641, 644
Theory of Flight (Rukeyser), **Supp. VI:** 272, 275, **277–278,** 284
"Theory of Flight" (Rukeyser), **Supp. VI:** 277–278
Theory of Moral Sentiments, The (A. Smith), **Supp. I Part 2:** 634
Theory of the Leisure Class, The (Veblen), **I:** 475–476; **Supp. I Part 2:** 629, 633, 641, 645; **Supp. IV Part 1:** 22
"There" (Taylor), **Supp. V:** 323
"There Are No Such Trees in Alpine California" (Haines), **Supp. XII:** 207

"There Goes (Varoom! Varoom!) That Kandy-Kolored Tangerine-Flake Streamline Baby" (Wolfe), **Supp. III Part 2:** 569–571

"There Have Been Changes" (Pickering), **Supp. XXI:** 202–203

"There Is a Lesson" (Olsen), **Supp. XIII:** 292, 297

"There is a Man" (Espaillat), **Supp. XXI:** 108–109

"There Is Only One of Everything" (Atwood), **Supp. XIII:** 34

There Is Something Out There (McNally). *See And Things That Go Bump in the Night* (McNally)

"There Must Be" (Peacock), **Supp. XIX:** 199

"There's a certain Slant of light" (Dickinson), **Retro. Supp. I:** 38

There's a Wocket in My Pocket! (Geisel), **Supp. XVI:** 111

Thérèse de Lisieux, Saint, **Supp. VIII:** 195

"There She Is She Is Taking Her Bath" (Anderson), **I:** 113, 114

"There Was a Child Went Forth" (Whitman), **IV:** 348

"There Was a Man, There Was a Woman" (Cisneros), **Supp. VII:** 70

"There Was an Old Woman She Had So Many Children She Didn't Know What to Do" (Cisneros), **Supp. VII:** 60

"There Was a Youth Whose Name Was Thomas Granger" (Olson), **Supp. II Part 2:** 558, 560, 563

There Were Giants in the Land (Benét), **Supp. XI:** 50

There You Are (Simpson), **Supp. IX:** 279–280

"There You Are" (Simpson), **Supp. IX:** 279

"Thermopylae" (Clampitt), **Supp. IX:** 43

Theroux, Alexander, **Supp. VIII:** 312

Theroux, Marcel, **Supp. VIII:** 325

Theroux, Paul, **Supp. V:** 122; **Supp. VIII: 309–327**

"These Are My People" (Hayden), **Supp. II Part 1:** 365

These Are My Same Hands (Schott), **Supp. XXIII:** 241, 242

"These are the days when Birds come back" (Dickinson), **Retro. Supp. I:** 30

"These Days" (Olds), **Supp. X:** 215

"These Flames and Generosities of the Heart: Emily Dickinson and the Illogic of Sumptuary Values" (Howe), **Supp. IV Part 2:** 431

"These Hands" (Brockmeier), **Supp. XXII:** 51, 52, 53

These Happy Golden Years (L. I. Wilder), **Supp. XXII:** 294, 297, 299

These Low Grounds (Turpin), **Supp. XVIII:** 283

"These saw Visions" (Dickinson), **Retro. Supp. I:** 46

These Thirteen (Faulkner), **II:** 72

These Three (film), **Supp. I Part 1:** 281

These Times (Untermeyer), **Supp. XV: 299–300,** 303

"These Times" (Untermeyer), **Supp. XV:** 300

"Thessalonica: A Roman Story" (Brown), **Supp. I Part 1:** 133

Thévenaz, Paul, **Supp. XV:** 42

Thew, Harvey, **Supp. XIII:** 166

"They Ain't the Men They Used To Be" (Farrell), **II:** 45

"They Burned the Books" (Benét), **Supp. XI:** 46

They Came Like Swallows (Maxwell), **Supp. VIII: 155–159,** 168, 169

"They Can't Turn Back" (Baldwin), **Supp. I Part 1:** 52

They Do Not: The Letters of a Non-Professional Lady Arranged for Public Consumption (Clements), **Supp. XVI:** 190

They Feed They Lion (Levine), **Supp. V:** 178, 179, 181, 184–185, 186

"They Feed They Lion" (Levine), **Supp. V:** 188

"They Lion Grow" (Levine), **Supp. V:** 184–185

"They're Not Your Husband" (Carver), **Supp. III Part 1:** 141, 143

They're Playing Our Song (musical), **Supp. IV Part 2:** 589

They Seek a City (Bontemps and Conroy), **Supp. XXII:** 5, 11

They Shall Inherit the Laughter (Jones), **Supp. XI:** 217, 218, 232

"They Shall Not Die" (Ryan as Quin), **Supp. XVIII:** 228–229

They Shoot Horses (film), **Supp. XIII:** 159

They Shoot Horses, Don't They? (McCoy), **Supp. XXV:** 26

They Shoot Horses, Don't They? (McCoy), **Supp. XIII:** 159, **164–166,** 168, 171, 172, 174

"They Sing, They Sing" (Roethke), **III:** 544

They Stooped to Folly (Glasgow), **II:** 175, 186–187

They Were Expendable (film), **Supp. XVIII:** 247

"They Weren't Going to Die" (Boyle), **Supp. XXIV:** 61

They Whisper (R. O. Butler), **Supp. XII: 72–73**

They Who Knock at Our Gates: A Complete Gospel of Immigration (Antin), **Supp. XX:** 2–3, **10–11,** 12

"Thick and Thin"(Hadas), **Supp. XXIII:** 119

Thidwick the Big-Hearted Moose (Geisel), **Supp. XVI:** 104

Thief's Journal, The (Genet), **Supp. XXIV:** 210

"Thief's Philosophy of Life, The" (Hapgood), **Supp. XVII:** 103

"Thief's Wife, The" (B. Kelly), **Supp. XVII:** 125–126

"Thieves" (Yates), **Supp. XI:** 349

Thieves of Paradise (Komunyakaa), **Supp. XIII:** 113, **128–130,** 132

"Thimble, The" (Kenyon), **Supp. VII:** 164

"Thing and Its Relations, The" (James), **II:** 357

"Things" (Haines), **Supp. XII:** 207

"Things" (Kenyon), **Supp. VII:** 169

"Things, The" (Kinnell), **Supp. III Part 1:** 246

Things As They Are (Stein), **IV:** 34, 37, 40

"Things Can Be Named to Death" (Peacock), **Supp. XIX:** 199

"Things Don't Stop" (Nye), **Supp. XIII:** 287

Things Gone and Things Still Here (Bowles), **Supp. IV Part 1:** 91

"Things of August" (Stevens), **Retro. Supp. I:** 309

Things of This World (Wilbur), **Supp. III Part 2:** 552–555

Things That Fall from the Sky (Brockmeier), **Supp. XXII: 50–53**

"Things That Fall from the Sky" (Brockmeier), **Supp. XXII:** 51, 53

Things Themselves: Essays and Scenes (Price), **Supp. VI:** 261

Things They Carried, The (T. O'Brien), **Supp. V:** 238, 239, 240, 243, 248–250; **Supp. XVII:** 14; **Supp. XXI:** 122

"Things to Do in New York City" (Berrigan), **Supp. XXII:** 224

Things We Don't Understand and Definitely Are Not Going to Talk About (performance piece, July), **Supp. XXIV:** 200

"Thing That Killed My Father Off, The" (Carver), **Supp. III Part 1:** 143

Thingy World!: or, How We Got to Where We Are: A Satire in One Act (Budbill), **Supp. XIX: 13–14**

"Think about It" (Conroy), **Supp. XVI:** 75

Think Back on Us . . . (Cowley), **Supp. II Part 1:** 139, 140, 142

Think Fast, Mr. Moto (Marquand), **III:** 57, 58

"Thinking about Barbara Deming" (Paley), **Supp. VI:** 227

"Thinking about Being Called Simple by a Critic" (Stafford), **Supp. XI:** 328

Thinking about the Longstanding Problems of Virtue and Happiness: Essays, a Play, Two Poems, and a Prayer (Kushner), **Supp. IX:** 131, 134, 135

"Thinking about the Past" (Justice), **Supp. VII:** 123–124

"Thinking about Western Thinking" (Didion), **Supp. IV Part 1:** 204, 206

"'Thinking against Oneself': Reflections on Cioran" (Sontag), **Supp. III Part 2:** 459–460

"Thinking Back Through Our Mothers: Traditions in Canadian Women's Writing" (Shields), **Supp. VII:** 307–308

"Thinking for Berky" (Stafford), **Supp. XI:** 320

"Thinking like a Mountain" (Leopold), **Supp. XIV:** 188, 189

"Thinking of the Lost World" (Jarrell), **II:** 338–389

Thinking Out Loud (Quindlen), **Supp. XVII:** 167, **169–170**

Thin Man, The (film), **Supp. IV Part 1:** 342, 355

Thin Man, The (Hammett), **Supp. IV Part 1:** 354–355

"Thinnest Shadow, The" (Ashbery), **Supp. III Part 1:** 5

"Thin People, The" (Plath), **Supp. I Part 2:** 538, 547

Thin Red Line, The (film; Malick), **Supp. V:** 249; **Supp. XV:** 351

Thin Red Line, The (Jones), **Supp. XI:** 219, **224–225,** 229, 231, 232, 233, 234

"Thin Strips" (Sandburg), **III:** 587

"Third and Final Continent, The" (Lahiri), **Supp. XXI: 178–180**

"Third Avenue in Sunlight" (Hecht), **Supp. X:** 61

"Third Body, A" (R. Bly), **Supp. IV Part 1:** 71

Third Circle, The (Norris), **III:** 327

"Third Expedition, The" (Bradbury), **Supp. IV Part 1:** 103, 106

Third Generation, The (C. Himes), **Supp. XVI:** 135, **140–141**

Third Life of Grange Copeland, The (Walker), **Supp. III Part 2:** 520, 527–536

Third Mind, The (Burroughs), **Supp. XII:** 3

"Third Myth, The" (Muñoz), **Supp. XXV:** 134

Third Rose, The (Brinnin), **IV:** 26

"Third Sermon on the Warpland, The" (Brooks), **Supp. III Part 1:** 85

"Third Thing That Killed My Father Off, The" (Carver), **Supp. III Part 1:** 144

Third Violet, The (Crane), **I:** 408, 417–418

Thirlwall, John C., **Retro. Supp. I:** 430

"Thirst: Introduction to Kinds of Water" (Carson), **Supp. XII:** 103

"13, 1977, 21" (Lethem), **Supp. XVIII:** 148

13 by Shanley (Shanley), **Supp. XIV:** 316

13 Seconds: A Look Back at the Kent State Shootings (Caputo), **Supp. XIX:** 29

Thirteen Hands: A Play in Two Acts (Shields), **Supp. VII:** 322–323

Thirteen O'Clock (Benét), **Supp. XI:** 46

Thirteen Other Stories (Purdy), **Supp. VII:** 278

Thirteen Stories and Thirteen Epitaphs (Vollmann), **Supp. XVII:** 226

"Thirteenth and Pennsylvania" (Stafford), **Supp. XI:** 324

Thirteenth Month, The (Pedersen; Nelson, trans.), **Supp. XVIII:** 179–180

"Thirteen Ways of Looking at a Blackbird" (Stevens), **IV:** 94; **Supp. IX:** 47; **Supp. XVII:** 130; **Supp. XXIII:** 253

"Thirteen Ways of Looking at a Blackbird" (W. Stevens), **Supp. XX:** 110

Thirteen Ways of Looking at a Black Man (H. L. Gates), **Supp. XX: 102,** 110

30/6 (poetry chapbook), **Supp. V:** 5, 6

"30. Meditation. 2. Cor. 5.17. He Is a New Creature" (Taylor), **IV:** 144

30: Pieces of a Novel (Dixon), **Supp. XII:** 152, **153–154**

"Thirty Bob a Week" (Davidson), **Retro. Supp. I:** 55

"Thirty Delft Tiles" (Doty), **Supp. XI:** 131

"35/10" (Olds), **Supp. X:** 206

"35,000 Feet—The Lanterns" (Goldbarth), **Supp. XII:** 182

31 Letters and 13 Dreams (Hugo), **Supp. VI:** 141–144

Thirty Poems (Bryant), **Supp. I Part 1:** 157, 158

Thirty-Six Poems (Warren), **IV:** 236, 239, 240

"33" (Alvarez), **Supp. VII:** 4

"3275" (Monette), **Supp. X:** 148, 159

Thirty Years (Marquand), **III:** 56, 60–61

Thirty Years of Treason (Bentley), **Supp. I Part 1:** 297

This, My Letter (Hay), **Supp. XIV:** 121, 122, 129, 131

"This, That & the Other" (Nemerov), **III:** 269

This Body Is Made of Camphor and Gopherwood (R. Bly), **Supp. IV Part 1:** 63–65, 66, 71; **Supp. XXI:** 85

This Boy's Life (Wolff), **Supp. XXV:** 208

This Boy's Life: A Memoir (T. Wolff), **Supp. VII:** 334–339, 340, 343; **Supp. XI:** 246, 247

This Bridge Called My Back: Writings by Radical Women of Color (Moraga and Anzaldúa, eds.), **Supp. XXIII:** 193, 194, 196, **204–205**

"This Bright Dream" (Benét), **Supp. XI:** 55

This Coffin Has No Handles (McGrath), **Supp. X:** 117

"This Configuration" (Ashbery), **Supp. III Part 1:** 22

"This Corruptible" (Wylie), **Supp. I Part 2:** 727, 729

"This Crazy Wickedness, Little Nests of Light" (Notley), **Supp. XXII:** 228

"This Crutch That I Love" (Nye), **Supp. XIII:** 288

"This Gentile World" (H. Miller), **III:** 177

"This Hand" (Wylie), **Supp. I Part 2:** 713

"This Hour" (Olds), **Supp. X:** 212

"This House I Cannot Leave" (Kingsolver), **Supp. VII:** 208

This Hunger (Nin), **Supp. X:** 185

"This Is a Photograph of Me" (Atwood), **Supp. XIII:** 33

"This Is a Poem, Good Afternoon" (Keillor), **Supp. XVI:** 167

This Is How You Lose Her (Díaz), **Supp. XXIV:** 83, 84, 86, 88, **92–93**

"This Is It" (Stern), **Supp. IX:** 290

"This Is Just to Say" (W. C. Williams), **Supp. XI:** 328

This Is My God: The Jewish Way of Life (Wouk), **Supp. XXV:** 253, 255–256, 263, 268

"This Is My Heart" (Harjo), **Supp. XII:** 230

This Is Not a Novel (Markson), **Supp. XVII:** 145–146

"This Is Not Who We Are" (Nye), **Supp. XIII:** 285, 286

This Is Our Time: Secular Cantata No. 1, Mixed Voice Chorus and Orchestra (Taggard, Schuman and Weissleder), **Supp. XXII:** 283

"This Is Us, Excellent" (Richard), **Supp. XIX:** 212

"This Is What I Said" (Salinas), **Supp. XIII:** 322

This Journey (Wright), **Supp. III Part 2:** 605–606

"This Lime-Tree Bower My Prison" (Coleridge), **Supp. XXI:** 52, 55

This Man and This Woman (Farrell), **II:** 42

"This Monkey, My Back" (Boyle), **Supp. XX:** 17

"This Morning" (Kenyon), **Supp. VII:** 164

"This Morning, This Evening, So Soon" (Baldwin), **Supp. I Part 1:** 63

"This Morning Again It Was in the Dusty Pines" (Oliver), **Supp. VII:** 240

This Music Crept by Me upon the Waters (MacLeish), **III:** 21

"This New England: Newport, Vermont" (Mosher), **Supp. XXII:** 209

This People Israel: The Meaning of Jewish Existence (Baeck), **Supp. V:** 260

"This Person" (July), **Supp. XXIV:** 202

"This Personal Maze Is Not the Prize" (Selinger), **Supp. XI:** 248

"This Place in the Ways" (Rukeyser), **Supp. VI:** 273–274

This Property Is Condemned (T. Williams), **IV:** 378

This Proud Heart (Buck), **Supp. II Part 1:** 119–120

This Same Sky: A Collection of Poems from around the World (Nye, ed.), **Supp. XIII:** 280

"This Sandwich Has No Mayonnaise" (Salinger), **III:** 552–553

This Shape We're In (Lethem), **Supp. XVIII:** 145

"This Shape We're In" (Lethem), **Supp. XVIII:** 148

This Side of Paradise (Fitzgerald), **I:** 358; **II:** 77, 80, 81, 82–83, 84, 85–87, 88; **Retro. Supp. I:** 99–100, **101–102,** 103, 105, 106, 110, 111; **Supp. XVIII:** 248

This Singing World: An Anthology of Modern Poetry for Young People (Untermeyer, ed.), **Supp. XV:** 306

This Strange Joy: Selected Poems of Sandro Penna (Di Perio, trans.), **Supp. XIX:** 34

This Stubborn Self: Texas Autobiographies (Almon), **Supp. XIII:** 288

"This They Took with Them" (Boyle), **Supp. XXIV:** 61

This Thing Don't Lead to Heaven (Crews), **Supp. XI:** 112

This Time: New and Selected Poems (Stern), **Supp. IX:** 290–291, **299**

"Thistle Seed in the Wind" (Francis), **Supp. IX:** 81

"Thistles in Sweden, The" (Maxwell), **Supp. VIII:** 169

"This Tokyo" (Snyder), **Supp. VIII:** 298

This Tree Will Be Here for a Thousand Years (revised edition) (R. Bly), **Supp. IV Part 1:** 66

This Tree Will Be Here for a Thousand Years (R. Bly), **Supp. IV Part 1:** 65–66, 71, 72

This Very Earth (Caldwell), **I:** 297, 302

This Wheel's on Fire: Levon Helm and the Story of the Band (Helm), **Supp. XVIII:** 26

This Woman (di Donato), **Supp. XX: 33, 41–42,** 46

Thoens, Karen, **Supp. V:** 147

Thomas, Brandon, **II:** 138

Thomas, Debra, **Supp. XIII:** 114

Thomas, D. M., **Supp. VIII:** 5

Thomas, Dylan, **I:** 49, 64, 382, 432, 526, 533; **III:** 21, 521, 528, 532, 534; **IV:** 89, 93, 136; **Supp. I Part 1:** 263; **Supp. III Part 1:** 42, 47; **Supp. V:** 344; **Supp. VIII:** 21; **Supp. IX:** 114; **Supp. X:** 115; **Supp. XV:** 74; **Supp. XVII:** 135; **Supp. XX: 199, 204; Supp. XXIV:** 54

Thomas, Edna Lewis, **Supp. XVIII:** 281

Thomas, Edward, **II:** 154; **Retro. Supp. I:** 127, 131, 132; **Supp. I Part 1:** 263; **Supp. II Part 1:** 4

Thomas, James, **Supp. XVI:** 268

Thomas, Joseph, **Supp. XVIII:** 183

Thomas, J. Parnell, **Supp. I Part 1:** 286; **Supp. XV:** 198

Thomas, June, **Supp. XXV:** 2, 3

Thomas, Lewis, **Retro. Supp. I:** 323

Thomas, Lorenzo, **Supp. XXIV:** 37

Thomas, Louisa, **Supp. XXIII:** 280, 283

Thomas, Rob, **Supp. XVIII:** 100, 101

Thomas, R. S., **Supp. XXI:** 83, 86–87, 93, 95, 96

Thomas, William I., **Supp. I Part 2:** 641

Thomas-a-Kempis, **Retro. Supp. I:** 247

Thomas and Beulah (Dove), **Supp. IV Part 1:** 242, 247–248, 249; **Supp. XVIII:** 174; **Supp. XXI:** 249

Thomas Aquinas (Saint), **I:** 13, 14, 265, 267; **III:** 270; **Retro. Supp. II:** 222; **Supp. IV Part 2:** 526

"Thomas at the Wheel" (Dove), **Supp. IV Part 1:** 248

"Thomas Eakins and the Photograph of a Man in Motion" (Major), **Supp. XXII:** 183

"Thomas Eakins' Delaware River Paintings" (Major), **Supp. XXII:** 183

"Thomas McGrath: Words for a Vanished Age" (Vinz), **Supp. X:** 117

Thomas Merton on Peace, **Supp. VIII:** 208

Thomas Merton Studies Center, The, **Supp. VIII:** 208

Thompson, Barbara, **Supp. V:** 322

Thompson, Caroline, **Supp. XXIII:** 291

Thompson, Cy, **I:** 538

Thompson, Daniel, **Supp. XXIII:** 174

Thompson, Dorothy, **II:** 449–450, 451, 453; **Supp. XV:** 307

Thompson, Edward, **Supp. XXI:** 172

Thompson, E. P., **Supp. X:** 112, 117

Thompson, Francis, **Retro. Supp. I:** 55

Thompson, Frank, **II:** 20

Thompson, George, **Supp. I Part 2:** 686; **Supp. XXIII:** 182

Thompson, Hunter S., **Supp. VIII:** 42; **Supp. XI:** 105; **Supp. XIII:** 1, 17; **Supp. XVII:** 95, 102, 228; **Supp. XXIV: 279–294**

Thompson, James R., **Supp. IV Part 1:** 217

Thompson, Jean, **Supp. XXIII: 289–305**

Thompson, John, **Supp. V:** 323; **Supp. XXI:** 151

Thompson, Juliet, **Supp. XX: 117**

Thompson, Lawrance, **II:** 508

Thompson, Lawrance Roger, **Retro. Supp. I:** 138, 141

Thompson, Lisa B., **Supp. XXIII:** 202

Thompson, Morton, **Supp. XIII:** 170

Thompson, Theresa, **Supp. V:** 141

Thompson, William T., **Supp. I Part 2:** 411

Thomson, James, **II:** 304; **Supp. I Part 1:** 150, 151; **Supp. XXIV:** 159

Thomson, Virgil, **IV:** 45; **Supp. IV Part 1:** 81, 83, 84, 173; **Supp. XVI:** 195

"Thoreau" (Lowell), **Supp. I Part 2:** 420, 422

Thoreau, Henry David, **I:** 98, 104, 228, 236, 257, 258, 261, 305, 433; **II:** 7, 8, 13, 17, 101, 159, 224, 273–274, 295, 312–313, 321, 457–458, 540, 546–547; **III:** 171, 174, 186–187, 189, 208, 214–215, 453, 454, 507, 577; **IV: 167–189,** 191, 341; **Retro. Supp. I:** 51, 62, 122; **Retro. Supp. II:** 13, 96, 142, 158; **Supp. I Part 1:** 29, 34, 116, 188, 299, 358; **Supp. I Part 2:** 383, 400, 420, 421, 507, 540, 579, 580, 655, 659, 660, 664, 678; **Supp. III Part 1:** 340, 353; **Supp. IV Part 1:** 236, 392, 416; **Supp. IV Part 2:** 420, 430, 433, 439, 447; **Supp. V:** 200, 208; **Supp. VIII:** 40, 42, 103, 105, 198, 201, 204, 205, 292, 303; **Supp. IX:** 25, 90, 171; **Supp. X:** 21, 27, 28–29, 101, 102; **Supp. XI:** 155; **Supp. XIII:** 1, 17; **Supp. XIV:** 40, 54, 106, 177, 181; **Supp. XVIII:** 4; **Supp. XX: 116, 221; Supp. XXI:** 203, 217; **Supp. XXII:** 206; **Supp. XXIII:** 174

Thoreau, John, **IV:** 171, 182

Thoreau, Mrs. John, **IV:** 172

"Thoreau's Hound: On Hiddenness"(Hirshfield), **Supp. XXIII:** 137

"Thorn, The" (Gordon), **Supp. IV Part 1:** 314

Thorne, Francis, **Supp. XII:** 253

"Thorn Merchant, The" (Komunyakaa), **Supp. XIII:** 119–120

Thornton, Billy Bob, **Supp. VIII:** 175

Thornton, Lionel, **III:** 291

"Thorofare" (Minot), **Supp. VI: 209–210**

"Thorow" (Howe), **Supp. IV Part 2:** 419, 420, 421, 431, 433–434

Thorp, Willard, **Supp. XIII:** 101

Thorslev, Peter L., Jr., **I:** 524

Thorstein Veblen (Dowd), **Supp. I Part 2:** 650

Thorstein Veblen (Qualey, ed.), **Supp. I Part 2:** 650

Thorstein Veblen: A Chapter in American Economic Thought (Teggart), **Supp. I Part 2:** 650

Thorstein Veblen: A Critical Interpretation (Riesman), **Supp. I Part 2:** 649, 650

Thorstein Veblen: A Critical Reappraisal (Dowd, ed.), **Supp. I Part 2:** 650

Thorstein Veblen and His America (Dorfman), **Supp. I Part 2:** 631, 650

Thorstein Veblen and the Institutionalists: A Study in the Social Philosophy of Economics (Seckler), **Supp. I Part 2:** 650

"Those before Us" (Lowell), **II:** 550

"Those Being Eaten by America" (R. Bly), **Supp. IV Part 1:** 62

Those Bones Are Not My Child (Bambara), **Supp. XI:** 1, 14, **20–22**

Those Extraordinary Twins (Twain), **IV:** 205–206

"Those Graves in Rome" (Levis), **Supp. XI:** 266

"Those of Us Who Think We Know" (Dunn), **Supp. XI:** 146

Those That Be in Bondage (Webber), **Supp. XXI:** 160

"Those Times . . ." (Sexton), **Supp. II Part 2:** 670, 684

"Those Various Scalpels" (Moore), **III:** 202

"Those Were the Days" (Levine), **Supp. V:** 190

"Those Who Don't" (Cisneros), **Supp. VII:** 60

"Those Who Thunder" (Hogan), **Supp. IV Part 1:** 406

"Thought, A" (Sarton), **Supp. VIII:** 262

Thought and Character of William James (Perry), **II:** 362

Thoughtbook of Francis Scott Key Fitzgerald (Fitzgerald), **Retro. Supp. I:** 99

"Thought Experiment" (Saunders), **Supp. XIX:** 235

"Thoughtful Roisterer Declines the Gambit, The" (Hecht), **Supp. X:** 63

"Thought of Heaven, The" (Stern), **Supp. IX:** 297

"Thoughts after Lambeth" (Eliot), **I:** 587; **Retro. Supp. I:** 324

Thoughts and Reflections (Lord Halifax), **II:** 111

Thoughts in Solitude (Merton), **Supp. VIII:** 207

"Thoughts on Being Bibliographed" (Wilson), **IV:** 435

"Thoughts on the Establishment of a Mint in the United States" (Paine), **Supp. I Part 2:** 512

"Thoughts on the Gifts of Art" (Kenyon), **Supp. VII:** 167

Thousand Acres, A (Smiley), **Supp. VI:** 292, **301–303**

"Thousand and Second Night, The" (Merrill), **Supp. III Part 1:** 324

"Thousand Dollar Vagrant, The" (Olsen), **Supp. XIII:** 292, 297

"Thousand Faces of Danny Torrance, The" (Figliola), **Supp. V:** 143

"Thousand Genuflections, A" (McCarriston), **Supp. XIV:** 266

Thousand-Mile Walk to the Gulf, A (Muir), **Supp. IX: 177–178**

Thousand Plateaus, A (Deleuze and Guattari), **Supp. XXV:** 123

"Thou Shalt Not Steal" (McClatchy), **Supp. XII:** 264

"Thread, The" (Merwin), **Supp. III Part 1:** 351

Three (film), **Supp. IX:** 253

3-3-8 (Marquand), **III:** 58

"3 A.M. Kitchen: My Father Talking" (Gallagher), **Supp. XXIV:** 169

"Three Academic Pieces" (Stevens), **IV:** 90

"Three Agee Wards, The" (Morris), **III:** 220–221

"Three American Singers" (Cather), **Retro. Supp. I:** 10

"Three Around the Old Gentleman" (Berryman), **I:** 188

"Three Avilas, The" (Jeffers), **Supp. II Part 2:** 418

"Three Black Women Writers" (C. L. R. James), **Supp. XXI:** 172

Three Books of Song (Longfellow), **II:** 490

"Three Bushes" (Yeats), **Supp. I Part 1:** 80

Three Cantos (Pound), **Retro. Supp. I:** 290

Three Centuries of Harvard (Morison), **Supp. I Part 2:** 485

Three Changes (Silver), **Supp. XXIV:** 275

Three Circles of Light (di Donato), **Supp. XX: 33, 42–43, 44, 46**

Three Cities: A Trilogy (Asch), **Supp. XXIII:** 1, 5, **10–12**

Three Comrades (Remarque), **Retro. Supp. I:** 113

"Three Corollaries of Cultural Relativism" (Locke), **Supp. XIV:** 202

"Three-Day Blow, The" (Hemingway), **II:** 248

Three Essays on America (Brooks), **I:** 246

Three Farmers on Their Way to a Dance (Powers), **Supp. IX:** 211–212, **213–214,** 222

"Three Fates, The" (Benét), **Supp. XI:** 48–49, 50

"Three Generations of Secrets" (A. Finch), **Supp. XVII:** 73

"Three Gifts, The" (Gibran), **Supp. XX: 124**

Three Gospels (Price), **Supp. VI:** 267

365 Days (Boyle), **Supp. XXIV:** 50, 60

"Three Kings, The: Hemingway, Faulkner, and Fitzgerald" (Ford), **Supp. V:** 59

Three Lives (Auchincloss), **Supp. IV Part 1:** 25

Three Lives (Stein), **I:** 103; **IV:** 26, 27, 31, 35, 37–41, 42, 45, 46; **Supp. IX:** 306; **Supp. XXIII:** 166

"THREE MOVEMENTS AND A CODA" (Baraka), **Supp. II Part 1:** 50

Three One Act Plays (Riverside Drive, Old Saybrook, and *Central Park West)* (Allen), **Supp. XV:** 3

Three on the Tower: The Lives and Works of Ezra Pound, T. S. Eliot, and William Carlos Williams (Simpson), **Supp. IX:** 276

Three Papers on Fiction (Welty), **IV:** 261

Three-Penny Opera (Brecht), **I:** 301; **Supp. XIV:** 162

"Three Percent Own All the Wealth" (Ryan as Quin), **Supp. XVIII:** 231–232

Three Philosophical Poets (Santayana), **III:** 610–612

"Three Pigs in Five Days" (Prose), **Supp. XVI:** 257, 258

"Three Players of a Summer Game" (T. Williams), **IV:** 383

Three Poems (Ashbery), **Supp. III Part 1:** 2, 3, 14, 15, 18, 24–26

"Three Poems for my Daughter" (Di Piero), **Supp. XIX:** 40

"Three Pokes of a Thistle" (Nye), **Supp. XIII:** 281

Three Prophets of Religious Liberalism (Wright), **Supp. XXIV:** 71

Three Roads, The (Macdonald, under Millar), **Supp. IV Part 2:** 466, 467

Three Short Plays with Long Titles (Silver and Ann), **Supp. XXIV:** 264

"Three Silences of Molinos, The" (Longfellow), **Retro. Supp. II:** 169

Three Sisters, The (Chekhov), **Supp. XV:** 323

"Three Sisters, The" (Cisneros), **Supp. VII:** 64

Three Soldiers (Dos Passos), **I:** 477–478, 480, 482, 488, 493–494; **Supp. XXI:** 277

"Three Songs at the End of Summer" (Kenyon), **Supp. VII:** 169–170

"Three Steps to the Graveyard" (Wright), **Supp. III Part 2:** 593, 596

Three Stories and Ten Poems (Hemingway), **II:** 68, 263; **Supp. XVII:** 105

Three Tall Women (Albee), **Supp. XXIV:** 270

Three Taverns, The (Robinson), **III:** 510

"Three Taverns, The" (Robinson), **III:** 521, 522

Three Tenant Families (Agee), **I:** 37–38

Three Tenors, One Vehicle: A Book of Songs (X. J. Kennedy, Camp, and Waldrop), **Supp. XV:** 165

"Three Types of Poetry" (Tate), **IV:** 131

"Three Vagabonds of Trinidad" (Harte), **Supp. II Part 1:** 338

"Three Waterfalls, The" (Lanier), **Supp. I Part 1:** 350

"Three-Way Mirror" (Brooks), **Supp. III Part 1:** 69–70

Three Weeks in Spring (Parker and Parker), **Supp. XIX:** 187

"Three Women" (Plath), **Supp. I Part 2:** 539, 541, 544, 545, 546

Three Young Poets (Swallow, ed.), **Supp. X:** 116

Threnody (Emerson), **Supp. I Part 2:** 416

"Threnody" (Emerson), **II:** 7

"Threnody for a Brown Girl" (Cullen), **Supp. IV Part 1:** 166

"Threshing-Floor, The" (Baldwin), **Supp. I Part 1:** 50

Threshold (film), **Supp. IX:** 254

"Threshold" (Goldbarth), **Supp. XII:** 175

Threshold (Jackson), **Supp. IX:** 117

"Throat" (Goldbarth), **Supp. XII:** 177–178

Throne of Labdacus, The (Schnackenberg), **Supp. XV: 260, 263–266**

Thrones (Pound), **Retro. Supp. I:** 293

Through Dooms of Love (Kumin), **Supp. IV Part 2:** 444

Through Glacier Park in 1915 (Rinehart), **Supp. XXV:** 195

"Through the Black Curtain" (Kingston), **Supp. V:** 169

Through the Forest: New and Selected Poems, 1977–1987 (Wagoner), **Supp. IX: 330–331**

"Through the Gates of the Silver Key" (Lovecraft and Price), **Supp. XXV:** 114, 123

"Through the Hills of Spain" (Salinas), **Supp. XIII:** 315

"Through the Hole in the Mundane Millstone" (West), **Retro. Supp. II:** 321, 322

Through the Ivory Gate (Dove), **Supp. IV Part 1:** 242, 243, 251, 252, 253–254, 254

"Through the Kitchen Window, Chiapas" (Nye), **Supp. XIII:** 277

Through the Safety Net (C. Baxter), **Supp. XVII:** 17, 22

"Through the Smoke Hole" (Snyder), **Supp. VIII:** 299

Throw Like a Girl (Thompson), **Supp. XXIII: 299–300**

"Throw Like a Girl"(Thompson), **Supp. XXIII:** 299, 300

"Thrush Relinquished, The" (Grossman), **Supp. XIX:** 83

Thucydides, **II:** 418; **IV:** 50; **Supp. I Part 2:** 488, 489, 492; **Supp. IV Part 1:** 391; **Supp. XIII:** 233

Thunderbolt and Lightfoot (film), **Supp. X:** 126

"Thunder from a Cloudless Sky" (Mosher), **Supp. XXII:** 209

"Thunderhead" (MacLeish), **III:** 19

Thurber, James, **I:** 487; **II:** 432; **IV:** 396; **Supp. I Part 2: 602–627,** 653, 654, 668, 672, 673, 679; **Supp. II Part 1:** 143; **Supp. IV Part 1:** 349; **Supp. IX:** 118; **Supp. XIV:** 104; **Supp. XVI:** 167; **Supp. XVII:** 4

Thurber, Mrs. James (Althea Adams), **Supp. I Part 2:** 613, 615, 617

Thurber, Mrs. James (Helen Muriel Wismer), **Supp. I Part 2:** 613, 617, 618

Thurber, Robert, **Supp. I Part 2:** 613, 617

Thurber, Rosemary, **Supp. I Part 2:** 616

Thurber, William, **Supp. I Part 2:** 602

Thurber Album, The (Thurber), **Supp. I Part 2:** 611, 619

Thurber Carnival, The (Thurber), **Supp. I Part 2:** 620; **Supp. XIV:** 104

Thurman, Judith, **Supp. IV Part 1:** 309; **Supp. XXV:** 2

Thurman, Wallace, **Retro. Supp. I:** 200; **Supp. I Part 1:** 325, 326, 328, 332; **Supp. IV Part 1:** 164; **Supp. X:** 136, 139; **Supp. XVI:** 135; **Supp. XVIII:** 279, 281; **Supp. XIX:** 78; **Supp. XXII:** 2

"Thursday" (Millay), **III:** 129

"Thurso's Landing" (Jeffers), **Supp. II Part 2:** 433

"Thus Do I Refute Gioia" (Junker), **Supp. XV:** 116

"Thus Far by Faith" (Nelson), **Supp. XVIII:** 177

Thus Spake Zarathustra (Nietzsche), **II:** 463; **Supp. IV Part 1:** 110; **Supp. IV Part 2:** 519

Thwaite, Lady Alicia. *See* Rawlings, Marjorie Kinnan

"Thyme" (Stallings), **Supp. XXV:** 232–233

Thy Neighbor's Wife (Talese), **Supp. XVII:** 204, 205–206, 207, 208, 210

"Tiara" (Doty), **Supp. XI:** 122

"Tibetan Time" (Prose), **Supp. XVI:** 255

Ticket for a Seamstitch, A (Harris), **II:** 424–425

Tickets for a Prayer Wheel (Dillard), **Supp. VI:** 22, 34

Ticket That Exploded, The (Burroughs), **Supp. III Part 1:** 93, 103, 104

Tickless Time (Glaspell), **Supp. III Part 1:** 179

Ticknor, George, **II:** 488; **Supp. I Part 1:** 313

Ticknor, William, **Supp. XVIII:** 258

"Ti Démon" (Chopin), **Supp. I Part 1:** 225

Tide of Time, The (Masters), **Supp. I Part 2:** 471

"Tide of Voices" (Hull), **Supp. XXI:** 132, 133–134, 136

"Tide Rises, the Tide Falls, The" (Longfellow), **I:** 498

"Tides" (Hoffman), **Supp. XVIII:** 86

Tidewater Blood (Hoffman), **Supp. XVIII:** 82–83

Tidyman, Ernest, **Supp. V:** 226

Tietjens, Eunice, **Supp. XV:** 47, 297

"Tiger" (Blake), **Supp. I Part 1:** 80; **Supp. VIII:** 26

Tiger (Bynner), **Supp. XV:** 42, 50

"Tiger, The" (Buechner), **Supp. XII:** 48

Tiger in the House, The (Van Vechten), **Supp. II Part 2:** 736

Tiger Joy (Benét), **Supp. XI:** 45

Tiger-Lilies (Lanier), **Supp. I Part 1:** 350–351, 357, 360, 371

Tiger Who Wore White Gloves, The: or, What You Are, You Are (Brooks), **Supp. III Part 1:** 86

Till, Emmett, **Supp. I Part 1:** 61

Till, Eric, **Supp. XXIII:** 103

Tillich, Paul, **II:** 244; **III:** 291, 292, 303, 309; **IV:** 226; **Retro. Supp. I:** 325, 326, 327; **Supp. V:** 267; **Supp. XIII:** 74, 91

Tillie Olsen: A Study of the Short Fiction (Frye), **Supp. XIII:** 292, 296, 298, 299, 302

Tillman, Lynne, **Supp. XII:** 4

Tillotson, John, **II:** 114

Tillotson, Kristen, **Supp. XVII:** 23

Tillstrom, Burr, **Supp. XIV:** 125

Till the Day I Die (Odets), **Supp. II Part 2:** 530, 533–536, 552

Tilton, Eleanor, **Supp. I Part 1:** 317

Tilton, Theodore, **Supp. XVIII:** 4

Timaeus (Plato), **II:** 10; **III:** 609

Tim: A Story of School Life (Sturgis), **Supp. XX:** 227, 230, 232, 233–235

Timber (Jonson), **II:** 16

Timberg, Scott, **Supp. XV:** 116

"Timberwolf" (Halliday), **Supp. XIX:** 91

Timbuktu (Auster), **Supp. XII:** 34, 35–36

"Time" (Matthews), **Supp. IX:** 165–166

"Time" (Merrill), **Supp. III Part 1:** 325

"Time" (Very), **Supp. XXV:** 249

"Time and Again" (Sanders), **Supp. XVI:** 269

Time and a Place, A (Humphrey), **Supp. IX:** 95, 98, 100–102

"Time and the Garden" (Winters), **Supp. II Part 2:** 801, 809

"Time and the Liturgy" (Merton), **Supp. VIII:** 199

Time and the River (Edgell), **Supp. XXIII:** 84, 85, 91–93

Time and Tide: A Walk through Nantucket (Conroy), **Supp. XVI:** 63, 71, 76–77

"Time Exposure" (C. Baxter), **Supp. XVII:** 20–21

Time Exposures, by Search-Light (W. Frank), **Supp. XX:** 75

Time in the Rock (Aiken), **I:** 65

Time Is Noon, The (Buck), **Supp. II Part 1:** 129, 130–131

Time & Money (Matthews), **Supp. IX:** 155, 165–167

"Time of Friendship, The" (Bowles), **Supp. IV Part 1:** 90–91

"Time of Her Time, The" (Mailer), **III:** 37, 45; **Retro. Supp. II:** 200

Time of Our Time, The (Mailer), **Retro. Supp. II:** 213–214

Time of the Assassins, The: A Study of Rimbaud (H. Miller), **III:** 189

Time Out of Mind (album, Dylan), **Supp. XVIII:** 28

"Time Past" (Morris), **III:** 232

"Time Present" (Morris), **III:** 232

"Times" (Beattie), **Supp. V:** 31

"Times, The" (Emerson), **II:** 11–12

Times Are Never So Bad, The (Dubus), **Supp. VII:** 87–88

Time's Arrow (Amis), **Retro. Supp. I:** 278

"Time Shall Not Die" (Chandler), **Supp. IV Part 1:** 120

Times of Melville and Whitman, The (Brooks), **I:** 257

Times They Are A-Changin', The (album, Dylan), **Supp. XVIII:** 20, 25

"Times They Are A-Changin,' The" (song, Dylan), **Supp. XVIII:** 30

"Timesweep" (Sandburg), **III:** 595–596

Time to Act, A (MacLeish), **III:** 3

Time to Be Born, A (Powell), **Supp. XIX:** 143

Time to Go (Dixon), **Supp. XII:** 147

Time to Kill (film), **Supp. IV Part 1:** 130

Time to Speak, A (MacLeish), **III:** 3

Time Will Darken It (Maxwell), **Supp. VIII:** 159, 162–164, 169

"Timing of Sin, The" (Dubus), **Supp. VII:** 91

Tim O'Brien (Herzog), **Supp. V:** 239

Timoleon (Melville), **III:** 93; **Retro. Supp. I:** 257

Timothy Dexter Revisited (Marquand), **III:** 55, 62, 63

Timothy Findley: Stories from a Life (Roberts), **Supp. XX:** 53

Timrod, Henry, **Supp. XVIII:** 31, 33

Tin Can, The (W. J. Smith), **Supp. XIII:** 334, **Supp. XIII:** 336, 337

"Tin Can, The" (W. J. Smith), **Supp. XIII:** 337–339

Tin Can Tree, The (Tyler), **Supp. IV Part 2:** 659–660

Tinguely, Jean, **Supp. XV:** 187

Tinker, Chauncey Brewster, **Supp. XIV:** 12

"Tinseled Bucks: A Historical Study of Indian Homosexuality"(Kenny), **Supp. XXIII:** 149

Tintern Abbey (Wordsworth), **Supp. I Part 2:** 673, 675

Tiny Alice (Albee), **I:** 81–86, 87, 88, 94

"Tiny Closet, The" (Inge), **Supp. XXV:** 105–106

"Tiny Mummies! The True Story of the Ruler of 43rd Street's Land of the Walking Dead" (Wolfe), **Supp. III Part 2:** 573, 574

Tip on a Dead Jockey and Other Stories (Shaw), **Supp. XIX:** 251

"Tip-Top Club, The" (Keillor), **Supp. XVI:** 172

"Tired" (Hughes), **Supp. I Part 1:** 331

"Tired and Unhappy, You Think of Houses" (Schwartz), **Supp. II Part 2:** 649

"Tiresias" (Garrett), **Supp. VII:** 96–97

'Tis (McCourt), **Supp. XII:** 271, 279–286

Tisch (Dixon), **Supp. XII:** 141, 155–156

" 'Tis Finished" (Very), **Supp. XXV:** 249

Tish (Rinehart), **Supp. XXV:** 194

Tish Marches On (Rinehart), **Supp. XXV:** 194

Tish Plays the Game (Rinehart), **Supp. XXV:** 194

Titan, The (Dreiser), **I:** 497, 501, 507–508, 509, 510; **Retro. Supp. II:** 94, 101, 102

Titian, **Supp. I Part 2:** 397, 714

"Tito's Goodbye" (García), **Supp. XI:** 190

"To a Bird, Seen Under My Window in the Garden"(J. Schoolcraft), **Supp.**

XXIII: 230

To a Blossoming Pear Tree (Wright), **Supp. III Part 2:** 602–605

"To a Blossoming Pear Tree" (Wright), **Supp. III Part 2:** 604

"To Abolish Children" (Shapiro), **Supp. II Part 2:** 717

To Abolish Children and Other Essays (Shapiro), **Supp. II Part 2:** 703

"To a Caty-Did, the Precursor of Winter" (Freneau), **Supp. II Part 1:** 274–275

"To a Chameleon" (Moore), **III:** 195, 196, 215

"To a Conscript of 1940" (Read), **II:** 372–373, 377–378

"To a Contemporary Bunk Shooter" (Sandburg), **III:** 582

"To a Cough in the Street at Midnight" (Wylie), **Supp. I Part 2:** 727, 729–730

"To a Defeated Savior" (Wright), **Supp. III Part 2:** 593–594, 596

"To a Face in the Crowd" (Warren), **IV:** 239

"To a Fish Head Found on the Beach near Malaga" (Levine), **Supp. V:** 185

"To a Friend" (Nemerov), **III:** 272

"To a Friend"(O'Hara), **Supp. XXIII:** 212

"To a Friend Whose Work Has Come to Triumph" (Sexton), **Supp. II Part 2:** 683

To a God Unknown (Steinbeck), **I:** 107; **IV:** 51, 59–60, 67

"To a Greek Marble" (Aldington), **Supp. I Part 1:** 257

"To a Locomotive in Winter" (Whitman), **IV:** 348

"To a Military Rifle" (Winters), **Supp. II Part 2:** 810, 811, 815

"To a Mouse" (Burns), **Supp. IX:** 173

"To an American Workman Dying of Starvation" (Taggard), **Supp. XXII:** 282

"To an Athlete Dying Young" (Houseman), **Supp. XVII:** 121

"To a Negro Jazz Band in a Parisian Cabaret" (Hughes), **Supp. I Part 1:** 325

"To an Old Philosopher in Rome" (Stevens), **III:** 605; **Retro. Supp. I:** 312

"To an Old Poet in Peru" (Ginsberg), **Supp. II Part 1:** 322

"To a Now-Type Poet" (X. J. Kennedy), **Supp. XV:** 161

"To Answer Your Question" (Jarman), **Supp. XVII:** 114–115

"To Any Would-Be Terrorists" (Nye), **Supp. XIII:** 285, 286

"To a Poet" (Rich), **Supp. I Part 2:** 571; **Supp. XIX:** 83

"To a Prize Bird" (Moore), **III:** 215

"To a Republican, with Mr. Paine's Rights of Man" (Freneau), **Supp. II Part 1:** 267

"To a Revolutionary Girl" (Bodenheim), **Supp. XXV:** 28

"To a Shade" (Yeats), **III:** 18

"To a Skylark" (Shelley), **Supp. I Part 2:** 720; **Supp. X:** 31

"Toast to Harlem, A" (Hughes), **Supp. I Part 1:** 338

"To Aunt Rose" (Ginsberg), **Supp. II Part 1:** 320

"To Autumn" (Keats), **Supp. IX:** 50

"To a Waterfowl" (Bryant), **Supp. I Part 1:** 154, 155, 162, 171

"To a Young Poet" (X. J. Kennedy), **Supp. XV:** 161

"To a Young Writer" (Stegner), **Supp. X:** 24

Tobacco Road (Caldwell), **I:** 288, 289, 290, 295–296, 297, 298, 302, 307, 309, 310; **IV:** 198; **Supp. XXII:** 196

"To Be a Monstrous Clever Fellow" (Fante), **Supp. XI:** 167

"To Become Music or Break" (Jauss), **Supp. XXI:** 133

To Bedlam and Part Way Back (Sexton), **Retro. Supp. II:** 245; **Supp. II Part 2:** 672–678; **Supp. IV Part 2:** 441; **Supp. XI:** 317

"To Beethoven" (Lanier), **Supp. I Part 1:** 364

To Begin Again: Stories and Memoirs, 1908–1929 (M. F. K. Fisher), **Supp. XVII:** 92

Tobey, Mark, **Supp. X:** 264

To Be Young, Gifted, and Black: Lorraine Hansberry in Her Own Words (Nemiroff), **Supp. IV Part 1:** 372, 374

"To Big Mary from an Ex-Catholic" (Mora), **Supp. XIII:** 217, 224, 228

"Tobin's Palm" (O. Henry), **Supp. II Part 1:** 408; **Supp. XV:** 40

Tobit (apocryphal book), **I:** 89

"To Build a Fire" (London), **II:** 468

Toby Tyler: or, Ten Weeks with a Circus (Otis), **III:** 577

"To Change in a Good Way" (Ortiz), **Supp. IV Part 2:** 511

"To Charlotte Cushman" (Lanier), **Supp. I Part 1:** 364

"To Cole, the Painter, Departing for Europe" (Bryant), **Supp. I Part 1:** 157, 161

Tocqueville, Alexis de, **III:** 261; **IV:** 349; **Retro. Supp. I:** 235; **Supp. I Part 1:** 137; **Supp. I Part 2:** 659, 660; **Supp. II Part 1:** 281, 282, 284; **Supp. XIV:** 306, 312

"To Crispin O'Conner" (Freneau), **Supp. II Part 1:** 268

"To Da-Duh, In Memoriam" (Marshall), **Supp. XI:** 276

"TODAY" (Baraka), **Supp. II Part 1:** 55

"Today" (Ginsberg), **Supp. II Part 1:** 328

"Today Is a Good Day To Die" (Bell), **Supp. X:** 7

"Today"(O'Hara), **Supp. XXIII:** 210–211

"Today Will Be a Quiet Day" (Hempel), **Supp. XXI:** 117,Supp. XXI: 118

Todd, Mabel Loomis, **I:** 454, 470; **Retro. Supp. I:** 33, 34, 35, 39, 47

"To Death" (Levertov), **Supp. III Part 1:** 274

"To Delmore Schwartz" (Lowell), **II:** 547; **Retro. Supp. II:** 188

"to disembark" (Brooks), **Supp. III Part 1:** 86

"To Dorothy on Her Exclusion from The Guinness Book of Records" (X. J. Kennedy), **Supp. XV:** 166

"To Dream of Bears" (Gallagher), **Supp. XXIV:** 176

"To Dr. Thomas Shearer" (Lanier), **Supp. I Part 1:** 370

"To Earthward" (Frost), **II:** 154

"To Edward John Moreton Drax Plunkett, Eighteenth Baron Dunsany" (Lovecraft), **Supp. XXV:** 113

"To Edwin V. McKenzie" (Winters), **Supp. II Part 2:** 801

"To Eleonora Duse" (Lowell), **II:** 528

"To Elizabeth Ward Perkins" (Lowell), **II:** 516

"To Elsie" (W. C. Williams), **Retro. Supp. I:** 419

"To Emily Dickinson" (H. Crane), **Retro. Supp. II:** 76

"To E. T." (Frost), **Retro. Supp. I:** 132

To Feel These Things (L. Michaels), **Supp. XVI:** 205, **213–214**

"To Feel These Things" (L. Michaels), **Supp. XVI:** 214

Toffler, Alvin, **Supp. IV Part 2:** 517

"To Fill" (Moore), **Supp. X:** 168, 169

"To Gabriela, a Young Writer" (Mora), **Supp. XIII:** 220

"To George May" (Bodenheim), **Supp. XXV:** 25

To Have and Have Not (film), **Supp. XV:** 347

To Have and Have Not (Hemingway), **I:** 31; **II:** 253–254, 264; **Retro. Supp. I:** 182, **183,** 187

"To Helen" (Poe), **III:** 410, 411, 427; **Retro. Supp. II:** 102

"To Hell With Dying" (Walker), **Supp. III Part 2:** 523

"To His Coy Mistress"(Marvell), **Supp. XXIII:** 62

"To His Excellency General Washington" (Wheatley), **Supp. XX: 289**

"To His Father" (Jeffers), **Supp. II Part 2:** 415

Toilet, The (Baraka), **Supp. II Part 1:** 37, 40–42

"To James Russell Lowell" (Holmes), **Supp. I Part 1:** 311

To Jerusalem and Back (Bellow), **Retro. Supp. II:** 29

"To Jesus on His Birthday" (Millay), **III:** 136–137

"To John Keats" (Lowell), **II:** 516

"To Judge Faolain, Dead Long Enough: A Summons" (McCarriston), **Supp. XIV:** 264–265

"To Justify My Singing" (Wright), **Supp. III Part 2:** 590

"To Kill a Deer" (C. Frost), **Supp. XV:** 102

To Kill a Mockingbird (film), **Supp. VIII:** 128–129

To Kill a Mockingbird (Lee), **Supp. VIII: 113–129; Supp. XVI:** 259; **Supp.**

XIX: 142

"To Kill a Mockingbird: Harper Lee's Tragic Vision" (Dave), **Supp. VIII:** 126

To Kill a Mockingbird: Threatening Boundaries (Johnson), **Supp. VIII:** 126

Toklas, Alice B., **IV:** 27; **Supp. IV Part 1:** 81, 91; **Supp. XVI:** 187

"Tokyo Story" (Wasserstein), **Supp. XV:** 328

"To Larry Rivers"(O'Hara), **Supp. XXIII:** 212

"To Light" (Hogan), **Supp. IV Part 1:** 402

"To Ligurinus" (Horace; Ferry, trans.), **Supp. XXIV:** 155

"To Ligurinus" (Horace; Howard, trans.), **Supp. XXIV:** 155

"To Live and Diet" (Wasserstein), **Supp. XV:** 328

Tolkien, J. R. R., **Supp. V:** 140

Tolkin, Michael, **Supp. XI:** 160

Toller, Ernst, **I:** 479

"To Lose the Earth" (Sexton), **Supp. II Part 2:** 684, 685

Tolson, Melvin, **Retro. Supp. I:** 208, 209, 210

Tolstoy, Leo, **I:** 6, 7, 58, 103, 312, 376; **II:** 191–192, 205, 271, 272, 275, 276, 281, 285, 286, 320, 407, 542, 559, 570, 579, 606; **III:** 37, 45, 61, 323, 467, 572; **IV:** 17, 21, 170, 285; **Retro. Supp. I:** 91, 225; **Retro. Supp. II:** 299; **Supp. I Part 1:** 2, 3, 6, 20; **Supp. IV Part 1:** 392; **Supp. V:** 277, 323; **Supp. IX:** 246; **Supp. XI:** 68; **Supp. XII:** 310, 322; **Supp. XIV:** 87, 97, 98; **Supp. XIX:** 241; **Supp. XXIII:** 4, 11, 275; **Supp. XXIV:** 132; **Supp. XXV:** 142

"To Lu Chi" (Nemerov), **III:** 275

"To Lydia" (Horace; Ferry, trans.), **Supp. XXIV:** 154

"To Lydia" (Horace; McHugh, trans.), **Supp. XXIV:** 154

Tom (Cummings), **I:** 430

"Tom" (Oliver), **Supp. VII:** 232

"Tom, Tom, the Piper's Son" (Ransom), **Supp. X:** 58

"To M, with a Rose" (Lanier), **Supp. I Part 1:** 364

To Make a Prairie (Kumin), **Supp. IV Part 2:** 440, 441

"To Make Words Disappear" (Simpson), **Supp. IX:** 265–266

Tomás and the Library Lady (Mora), **Supp. XIII:** 216, 221

"Tomatoes" (Francis), **Supp. IX:** 82

"Tom Ball's Barn" (Kooser), **Supp. XIX:** 119

"Tom Brown at Fisk" (Du Bois), **Supp. II Part 1:** 160

Tom Brown's School Days (Hughes), **Supp. I Part 2:** 406

"Tomb Stone" (Dickey), **Supp. IV Part 1:** 185

"Tombstone Blues" (song, Dylan), **Supp. XVIII:** 30

Tomcat in Love (O'Brien), **Supp. V:** 238, 240, 243, 252–254

"Tomcat's Wife, The" (C. Bly), **Supp. XVI:** 40

Tomcat's Wife and Other Stories, The (C. Bly), **Supp. XVI:** 40–41

"Tom Fool at Jamaica" (Moore), **III:** 215

To Mix with Time (Swenson), **Supp. IV Part 2:** 637, 643–645, 645

Tom Jones (Fielding), **I:** 131; **Supp. V:** 127

Tomlinson, Charles, **Supp. XVI:** 284

Tommy Gallagher's Crusade (Farrell), **II:** 44

Tommyknockers, The (King), **Supp. V:** 139, 144

"Tommy's Burglar" (Henry), **Supp. II Part 1:** 399, 401

"Tommy Stames" (Budbill), **Supp. XIX:** 8

Tomo Cheeki (pseudonym). *See* Freneau, Philip

Tomorrow Is Another Day (E. P. Jones), **Supp. XXII:** 252

Tomorrow is Another Day (film, Feist), **Supp. XVII:** 62

"Tomorrow the Moon" (Dos Passos), **I:** 493

Tomorrow Will Be Better (B. Smith), **Supp. XXIII:** 258, **264–267**

"Tom Outland's Story" (Cather), **I:** 325–326

Tompkins, Jane, **Supp. XVI:** 89; **Supp. XVIII:** 258, 259, 263

Tompson, Benjamin, **Supp. I Part 1:** 110, 111

"Tom-Rock Through Eels" (Hempel), **Supp. XXI:** 116, 118, **123–124**

Tom Sawyer (musical) (Gurney), **Supp. V:** 96

Tom Sawyer (Twain). *See Adventures of Tom Sawyer, The* (Twain)

Tom Sawyer Abroad (Twain), **II:** 482; **IV:** 19, 204

Tom Sawyer Detective (Twain), **IV:** 204

"Tom's Husband" (Jewett), **Retro. Supp. II:** 132, 141

Tom Swift (Stratemeyer), **III:** 146

Tom-Walker, The (Sandoz), **Supp. XXIV:** 244, **253–255**

"Tom Wolfe's Guide to Etiquette" (Wolfe), **Supp. III Part 2:** 578

"To My Brother Killed: Haumont Wood: October, 1918" (Bogan), **Supp. III Part 1:** 58

"To My Class, on Certain Fruits and Flowers Sent Me in Sickness" (Lanier), **Supp. I Part 1:** 370

"To my ever beloved & lamented son William Henry"(J. Schoolcraft), **Supp. XXIII:** 226, 231

"To My Father's Ghost" (Everwine), **Supp. XV:** 76

"To My Ghost Reflected in the Auxvasse River" (Levis), **Supp. XI:** 265

"To My Greek" (Merrill), **Supp. III Part 1:** 326

"To My Mother" (Berry), **Supp. X:** 23

"To My Sister—Ernestine Kealoha Taggard, 1900–1943" (Taggard), **Supp.**

XXII: 284

"To My Small Son, at the Photographer's" (Hay), **Supp. XIV:** 121

"To My Small Son, on Certain Occasions" (Hay), **Supp. XIV:** 121

"To My Students" (Taggard), **Supp. XXII:** 280

"To Name is to Possess" (Kincaid), **Supp. VII:** 194

Tone, Aileen, **I:** 21–22

"Tongue Is, The" (Komunyakaa), **Supp. XIII:** 113

"Tongue of the Jews" (Bukiet), **Supp. XVII:** 47

Tongues (Shepard and Chaikin), **Supp. III Part 2:** 433

Tongues of Angels, The (Price), **Supp. VI:** 265

Tongues Untied (Riggs; film), **Supp. XI:** 19, 20

"Tonight" (Lowell), **II:** 538

"Tonight Is Part of the Struggle"(Le Sueur), **Supp. XXIII: 172**

Tonight Is the Night of the Prom (Jarman), **Supp. XVII:** 110, **112–113**

"Tonight Is the Night of the Prom" (Jarman), **Supp. XVII:** 113

Tony Kushner in Conversation (Vorlicky, ed.), **Supp. IX:** 132

"Too Anxious for Rivers" (Frost), **II:** 162

"Too Blue" (Hughes), **Retro. Supp. I:** 207

"Too Damn Close: Thresholds and Their Maintenance in Rick Bass's Work" (Kerridge), **Supp. XVI:** 26

"Too Early" (Leopold), **Supp. XIV:** 186

"Too Early Spring" (Benét), **Supp. XI:** 53

"Too Far from Home" (Bowles), **Supp. IV Part 1:** 94–95

Too Far from Home: Selected Writings of Paul Bowles (Halpern, ed.), **Supp. IV Part 1:** 94, 95

Too Far to Go: The Maples Stories (Updike), **Retro. Supp. I:** 321

"Too Good To Be True": The Life and Art of Leslie Fiedler (Winchell), **Supp. XIII:** 94, 98, 99, 101

Toohey, John Peter, **Supp. IX:** 190

Toolan, David, **Supp. IV Part 1:** 308

Too Late (Dixon), **Supp. XII: 143–144**

"Too Late" (Pickering), **Supp. XXI:** 197

"Too-Late Born, The" (Hemingway), **III:** 9

Toole, John Kennedy, **Supp. XIV:** 21

"Toolless" (Pickering), **Supp. XXI:** 204

Too Many Bottles (Holding), **Supp. XXII:** 126, **134–135**

Toomer, Jean, **Retro. Supp. II:** 79; **Supp. I Part 1:** 325, 332; **Supp. III Part 2: 475–491**; **Supp. IV Part 1:** 16, 164, 168; **Supp. IX: 305–322**; **Supp. XIII:** 305; **Supp. XVIII:** 122; **Supp. XX: 73**; **Supp. XXII:** 6

Toomer, Nathan Eugene Pinchback. *See* Toomer, Jean

Too Much Johnson (film), **Supp. IV Part 1:** 83

"To One Who Said Me Nay" (Cullen), **Supp. IV Part 1:** 166

"Tooth, The" (Jackson), **Supp. IX:** 122
Tooth and Claw (Boyle), **Supp. XX:** 20
Tooth of Crime, The (Shepard), **Supp. III Part 2:** 432, 441–445, 447
"Too Young" (O'Hara), **III:** 369
Topaz (film), **Supp. XX:** 253
Topaz (Uris), **Supp. XX: 247, 248, 253**
"Top Israeli Official Hints at 'Shared' Jerusalem" (Nye), **Supp. XIII:** 287
"To P. L., 1916–1937" (Levine), **Supp. V:** 185
"To Please a Shadow" (Brodsky), **Supp. VIII:** 30
"Top of the Food Chain" (Boyle), **Supp. XX: 20**
"Top of the Hill" (Jewett), **II:** 406
"Topography" (Olds), **Supp. X:** 208
Topper (T. Smith), **Supp. IX:** 194
To Praise the Music (Bronk), **Supp. XXI:** 31, 32
Torah, **IV:** 19
"Torch Songs" (Wrigley), **Supp. XVIII:** 296
Torday, Daniel, **Supp. XXII:** 151
Torpedo 8: The Story of Swede Larsen's Bomber Squadron (Wolfert), **Supp. XXI:** 267
"Torquemada" (Bukiet), **Supp. XVII:** 44
"Torquemada" (Longfellow), **II:** 505; **Retro. Supp. II:** 164
Torrence, Ridgely, **III:** 507
Torrent and the Night Before, The (Robinson), **III:** 504
Torrents of Spring, The (Hemingway), **I:** 117; **II:** 250–251
Torres, Héctor A., **Supp. XIII:** 225
Torres, Louis, **Supp. IV Part 2:** 529, 530
Torres-Saillant, Silvio, **Supp. XXI:** 104, 105, 108, 109
Torsney, Cheryl, **Retro. Supp. I:** 224
Tortilla Curtain, The (Boyle), **Supp. VIII: 9–10; Supp. XX: 28–29**
Tortilla Flat (Steinbeck), **IV:** 50, 51, 61, 64
Tortilla Flats (Steinbeck), **Supp. XX:** 28
Tortured Skins, and Other Fictions (Kenny), **Supp. XXIII:** 150, 156, 157
Tory Lover, The (Jewett), **II:** 406; **Retro. Supp. II:** 144–145
"Toscana" (Dixon), **Supp. XII:** 154
"To Sestius" (Horace; Ferry, trans.), **Supp. XXIV:** 155
"To Sestius" (Horace; Lasdun, trans.), **Supp. XXIV:** 154
"To Sir Toby" (Freneau), **Supp. II Part 1:** 269
"To Sophy, Expectant" (Mumford), **Supp. II Part 2:** 475
"To Speak of Woe That Is in Marriage" (Lowell), **II:** 550
"To Statecraft Embalmed" (Moore), **III:** 197
To Stay Alive (Levertov), **Supp. III Part 1:** 280–282
"Total Eclipse" (Dillard), **Supp. VI:** 28
"Total Eclipse of the Moon"(Crooker), **Supp. XXIII:** 55
Total Recall (Paretsky), **Supp. XXV:** 172, 180, 181, 183–184
Toth, Emily, **Retro. Supp. II:** 71

Toth, Susan Allan, **Retro. Supp. II:** 138
"To the Americans of the United States" (Freneau), **Supp. II Part 1:** 271
"To the Apennines" (Bryant), **Supp. I Part 1:** 157, 164
"To the Bleeding Hearts Association of American Novelists" (Nemerov), **III:** 281
"To the Botequim & Back" (Bishop), **Retro. Supp. II:** 51
To the Bright and Shining Sun (Burke), **Supp. XIV:** 22, 25
"To the Citizens of the United States" (Paine), **Supp. I Part 2:** 519–520
"To the Dandelion" (Lowell), **Supp. I Part 2:** 424
"To the End" (Haines), **Supp. XII:** 212–213
To the Ends of the Earth: The Selected Travels of Paul Theroux, **Supp. VIII:** 324
"To the Fabulous Constellation" (Ferry), **Supp. XXIV:** 148–149
"To the Film Industry in Crisis"(O'Hara), **Supp. XXIII:** 214
To the Finland Station: A Study in the Writing and Acting of History (Wilson), **IV:** 429, 436, 443–444, 446
"To the Governor & Legislature of Massachusetts" (Nemerov), **III:** 287
To the Green Man (Jarman), **Supp. XVII:** 110, 120–121
"To the Harbormaster" (O'Hara), **Supp. XXIII:** 208, 212, 214; **Supp. XXIV:** 42
To the Holy Spirit (Winters), **Supp. II Part 2:** 810
"To the Keeper of the King's Water Works" (Freneau), **Supp. II Part 1:** 269
"To the Lacedemonians" (Tate), **IV:** 134
"To the Laodiceans" (Jarrell), **Retro. Supp. I:** 121, 140
To the Lighthouse (Woolf), **I:** 309; **II:** 600; **Retro. Supp. II:** 337; **Supp. VIII:** 155
"To the Man on Trail" (London), **II:** 466
"To the Memory of the Brave Americans Under General Greene" (Freneau), **Supp. II Part 1:** 262, 274
"To the Miscodeed"(J. Schoolcraft), **Supp. XXIII:** 230
"To the Muse" (Wright), **Supp. III Part 2:** 601
"To the Natural World: at 37" (Taggard), **Supp. XXII:** 279–280
"To the Nazi Leaders" (Hay), **Supp. XIV:** 121
"To the New World" (Jarrell), **II:** 371
"To the One of Fictive Music" (Stevens), **IV:** 89; **Retro. Supp. I:** 297, 300
"To the One Upstairs" (Simic), **Supp. VIII:** 283
"To the Peoples of the World" (Du Bois), **Supp. II Part 1:** 172
"To the Pine Tree on first seeing it on returning from Europe"(J. Schoolcraft), **Supp. XXIII:** 225, 228, 232–233

To the Place of Trumpets (B. Kelly), **Supp. XVII: 123–127;** 132
"To the Pliocene Skull" (Harte), **Supp. II Part 1:** 343–344
"To the Powers of Darkness" (Taggard), **Supp. XXII:** 279, 280
"To the Powers of Desolation" (Taggard), **Supp. XXII:** 280
"To the pure all things are pure" (Very), **Supp. XXV:** 242, 248
"To the Queen of Heaven" (Taggard), **Supp. XXII:** 280
"To the Reader" (Baudelaire), **II:** 544–545
"To The Reader" (Jarman), **Supp. XVII:** 115
"To the Reader" (Levertov), **Supp. III Part 1:** 277
"To the Republic" (Horace; Ferry, trans.), **Supp. XXIV:** 154
"To the Right Honourable William, Earl of Dartmouth" (Wheatley), **Supp. XX: 278, 284, 287–288**
"To the River Arve" (Bryant), **Supp. I Part 1:** 163
"To the Snake" (Levertov), **Supp. III Part 1:** 277
"To the Stone-Cutters" (Jeffers), **Supp. II Part 2:** 420
"To the Unseeable Animal" (Berry), **Supp. X:** 31
"To the Western World" (Simpson), **Supp. IX:** 269, 270
To the White Sea (Dickey), **Supp. IV Part 1:** 186, 190–191
"To the Young Who Want to Die" (Brooks), **Supp. III Part 1:** 85–86
"To Tlaoc of the Rain" (Everwine), **Supp. XV:** 77
"To Train a Writer" (Bierce), **I:** 199
"Touch, The" (Sexton), **Supp. II Part 2:** 687
Touch and Go (M. F. K. Fisher and D. Parrish), **Supp. XVII:** 84
"Touching the Tree" (Merwin), **Supp. III Part 1:** 355
Touching the World (Eakin), **Supp. VIII:** 167
Touch of Danger, A (Jones), **Supp. XI:** 226, **228–229**
Touch of the Poet, A (O'Neill), **III:** 385, 401, 404
Touchstone, The (Wharton), **Retro. Supp. I:** 365
"Touch-up Man" (Komunyakaa), **Supp. XIII:** 119
Tough Guys Don't Dance (Mailer), **Retro. Supp. II:** 211
"Tough People" (Offutt), **Supp. XIX:** 170–171
Toulet, Paul Jean, **IV:** 79
Tour (McNally), **Supp. XIII:** 197
"Tour 5" (Hayden), **Supp. II Part 1:** 381
To Urania (Brodsky), **Supp. VIII:** 22, 28–29
Tourgée, Albion W., **Supp. XIV:** 63
"Tour Guide" (Komunyakaa), **Supp. XIII:** 114
"Tourist Death" (MacLeish), **III:** 12

Tourmaline (J. Scott), **Supp. XVII: 192–194**, 195

Tour of Duty (Dos Passos), **I:** 489

"Tour of the Labyrinth" (Stallings), **Supp. XXV:** 229

Touron the Prairies, A (Irving), **II:** 312–313

Toussaint L'Ouverture, **Supp. XXI:** 166

Toussaint L'Ouverture (C. L. R. James), **Supp. XXI:** 167

Tovey, Donald Francis, **Supp. XIV:** 336

"To Virgil" (Horace; Ferry, trans.), **Supp. XXIV:** 155

"To Virgil" (Horace; Wright, trans.), **Supp. XXIV:** 155

To Walk a Crooked Mile (McGrath), **Supp. X:** 117

Toward a New Synthesis (Begiebing), **Retro. Supp. II:** 210

"Toward Nightfall" (Simic), **Supp. VIII:** 277

Towards a Better Life (Burke), **I:** 270

"Towards a Chicano Poetics: The Making of the Chicano Subject, 1969–1982" (Saldívar), **Supp. IV Part 2:** 544

Towards an Enduring Peace (Bourne), **I:** 232

"Towards Morning" (Pedersen; Nelson, trans.), **Supp. XVIII:** 180

Toward the Blanched Alphabets (Sobin), **Supp. XVI:** 290

Toward the Gulf (Masters), **Supp. I Part 2:** 465–466

"Toward the Solstice" (Rich), **Supp. I Part 2:** 575–576

Toward Wholeness in Paule Marshall's Fiction (Pettis), **Supp. XI:** 276

"Tower" (Merwin), **Supp. III Part 1:** 343

"Tower Beyond Tragedy, The" (Jeffers), **Supp. II Part 2:** 429–430

Tower of Ivory (Atherton), **Supp. XXIV:** 21, 23

Tower of Ivory (MacLeish), **III:** 3–4

Towers, Robert, **Supp. IX:** 259; **Supp. XVI:** 211; **Supp. XXV:** 86

"To What Red Hell" (C. Himes), **Supp. XVI:** 137

"To Whistler, American" (Pound), **III:** 465–466

"To Wine" (Bogan), **Supp. III Part 1:** 57, 58

Towle, Tony, **Supp. XXIII:** 221

Town, Caren J., **Supp. XVIII:** 195, 199

Town, The (Faulkner), **II:** 57, 73; **Retro. Supp. I:** 74, 82

Town, The (Richter), **Supp. XVIII:** 207, **214–215**, 217

Town and the City, The (Kerouac), **Supp. III Part 1:** 222–224; **Supp. XIV:** 143

"Town Crier" (Bierce), **I:** 193, 194, 195, 196

"Town Crier Exclusive, Confessions of a Princess Manqué: 'How Royals Found Me "Unsuitable" to Marry Their Larry' " (Elkin), **Supp. VI:** 56

Town Down the River, The (Robinson), **III:** 508

"Town Dump, The" (Nemerov), **III:** 272, 275, 281

Towne, Robert, **Supp. XI:** 159, 172, 174

"Townhouse Interior with Cat" (Clampitt), **Supp. IX:** 40

Townie (Dubus III), **Supp. XXIV: 98, 108–111**

"Townies" (Dubus), **Supp. VII:** 86

Town in the Forest, The: Life Story of Richmond, New Hampshire (Boyce; Faust, ed.), **Supp. XXI:** 8

"Town of the Sound of a Twig Breaking" (Carson), **Supp. XII: 102**

"Town Poor, The" (Jewett), **Retro. Supp. II:** 138, 139, 143

Townsend, Alison, **Supp. XIII:** 222; **Supp. XXIII:** 132, 139

Townsend, Ann, **Supp. V:** 77

Townsend, Jim, **Supp. XXII:** 243

"Towns in Colour" (Lowell), **II:** 523–524

Townsman, The (Sedges), **Supp. II Part 1:** 124–125

Town Smokes (P. Benedict), **Supp. XXIII: 35–39**

"Town Smokes"(P. Benedict), **Supp. XXIII:** 37

"To World War Two" (Koch), **Supp. XV:** 184

Toys in a Field (Komunyakaa), **Supp. XIII: 121–122**

"Toys in a Field" (Komunyakaa), **Supp. XIII:** 122

Toys in the Attic (Hellman), **Supp. I Part 1:** 289–290

Toyter mentsh, Der (The dead man) (Asch), **Supp. XXIII:** 9

Tracer (F. Barthelme), **Supp. XI:** 31–32, 33

Traces of Thomas Hariot, The (Rukeyser), **Supp. VI:** 273, 274, 283

"Tracing Life with a Finger" (Caldwell), **I:** 291

Tracker (Wagoner), **Supp. IX:** 329, **336–337**

"Tracking" (Wagoner), **Supp. IX:** 329

"Track Meet, The" (Schwartz), **Supp. II Part 2:** 665

Tracks (Erdrich), **Supp. IV Part 1:** 259, 262–263, 269, 272, 273–274, 274, 275

"Track-Workers" (Bodenheim), **Supp. XXV:** 22

"Tract" (W. C. Williams), **Retro. Supp. I:** 414

"Tract against Communism, A" (Twelve Southerners), **IV:** 125, 237

Tractatus (Wittgenstein), **Supp. XVII:** 143

Tracy, Benjamin, **Supp. XVIII:** 4

Tracy, D. H., **Supp. XVIII:** 178

Tracy, Lee, **IV:** 287, 288

Tracy, Steven, **Retro. Supp. I:** 195

"Trade, The" (Levine), **Supp. V:** 193

Trading Twelves (Callahan and Murray, eds.), **Retro. Supp. II:** 119

Trading Twelves: The Selected Letters of Ralph Ellison and Albert Murray (Murray and Callahan, eds.), **Supp. XIX:** 148, 158

" 'Traditional' Marriage: A Secular Affair" (P. N. Warren), **Supp. XX: 273**

"Tradition and Industrialization" (Wright), **IV:** 489–490

"Tradition and Mythology: Signatures of Landscape in Chicana Poetry" (Rebolledo), **Supp. XIII:** 214

"Tradition and the Individual Talent" (Eliot), **I:** 441, 574, 585; **Retro. Supp. I:** 59, 286

Tragedies, Life and Letters of James Gates Percival (Swinburne), **Supp. I Part 2:** 422

Tragedy of Bees, A (P. N. Warren), **Supp. XX: 261**

"Tragedy of Bees, A" (P. N. Warren), **Supp. XX: 272**

Tragedy of Don Ippolito, The (Howells), **II:** 279

"Tragedy of Error, A" (James), **II:** 322; **Retro. Supp. I:** 218

Tragedy of Pudd'nhead Wilson, The (Twain), **IV:** 206–207

Tragic America (Dreiser), **Retro. Supp. II:** 95

"Tragic Dialogue" (Wylie), **Supp. I Part 2:** 724

Tragic Ground (Caldwell), **I:** 297, 306

Tragic Muse, The (James), **Retro. Supp. I:** 227

Traherne, Thomas, **IV:** 151; **Supp. III Part 1:** 14; **Supp. V:** 208; **Supp. XV:** 212; **Supp. XVI:** 282, 288, 295

"Trail, The" (W. J. Smith), **Supp. XIII:** 342

Trailerpark (Banks), **Supp. V:** 12

"Trailing Arbutus, The" (Whittier), **Supp. I Part 2:** 691

Trail of the Lonesome Pine, The (Fox), **Supp. XIII:** 166

"Train, The" (O'Connor), **Retro. Supp. II:** 225

"Train Dreams" (Berrigan), **Supp. XXIV:** 45

"Train Ride" (Berrigan), **Supp. XXIV:** 42, 43–44

"Train Rising Out of the Sea" (Ashbery), **Supp. III Part 1:** 22

"Trains" (Banks), **Supp. V:** 8

"Train Tune" (Bogan), **Supp. III Part 1:** 64

Train Whistle Guitar (Murray), **Supp. XIX: 153–155**, 157

Traitor, The (Wouk), **Supp. XXV:** 256, 259

"Traits of Indian Character" (Irving), **II:** 303

Trakl, Georg, **Supp. XVII:** 241

Tramp Abroad, A (Twain), **IV:** 200

Tramping With a Poet in the Rockies (S. Graham), **Supp. I Part 2:** 397

Tramp's Excuse, The (Lindsay), **Supp. I Part 2:** 379, 380, 382

"Trance, The" (Taggard), **Supp. XXII:** 280

"Transaction" (Cliff), **Supp. XXII:** 75

"Transatlantic" (Toomer), **Supp. III Part 2:** 486

Transatlantic Sketches (James), **II:** 324; **Retro. Supp. I:** 219

"Transcendental Etude" (Rich), **Supp. I Part 2:** 576

"Transcontinental Highway" (Cowley), **Supp. II Part 1:** 141

"Transducer" (Ammons), **Supp. VII:** 28

"Transfiguration" (Jarman), **Supp. XVII:** 118, 119

"Transfigured Bird" (Merrill), **Supp. III Part 1:** 320–321

"Transformations" (Harjo), **Supp. XII:** 226

Transformations (Sexton), **Supp. II Part 2:** 689–691; **Supp. IV Part 2:** 447; **Supp. XIV:** 125

Transforming Madness: New Lives for People Living with Mental Illness (Neugeboren), **Supp. XVI:** 229

"Transit" (Conroy), **Supp. XVI:** 72

Transit to Narcissus, A (Mailer), **Retro. Supp. II:** 196

"Translation" (Espaillat), **Supp. XXI:** 107

"Translation and Transposition" (Carne-Ross), **Supp. I Part 1:** 268–269

"Translation of a Fragment of Simonides" (Bryant), **Supp. I Part 1:** 153, 155

"Translations" (Rich), **Supp. I Part 2:** 563

Translations of Ezra Pound, The (Kenner, ed.), **III:** 463

Translations of the Gospel Back into Tongues (Wright), **Supp. XV:** 342–343, 346

"Translator's Task, The"(Benjamin), **Supp. XXIII:** 28

"Trans-National America" (Bourne), **I:** 229, 230

"Transparency" (X. J. Kennedy), **Supp. XV:** 159–160

"Transparent Itineraries: 1983" (Sobin), **Supp. XVI:** 287

"Transparent Itineraries: 1984" (Sobin), **Supp. XVI:** 287

"Transparent Itineraries: 1992" (Sobin), **Supp. XVI:** 289

"Transparent Itineraries" poems (Sobin), **Supp. XVI:** 290

Transparent Man, The (Hecht), **Supp. X:** 57, **69–71**

"Transparent Man, The" (Hecht), **Supp. X: 69–70**

Transparent Things (Nabokov), **Retro. Supp. I:** 266, 270, 277

"Transport" (Simic), **Supp. VIII:** 282

Transport to Summer (Stevens), **IV:** 76, 93; **Retro. Supp. I:** 309–312

Tranströmer, Thomas, **Supp. IV Part 2:** 648

"Traps for the Unwary" (Bourne), **I:** 235

Trash Trilogy (McMurtry), **Supp. V:** 225–226, 231

Traub, James, **Supp. XXIV:** 221, 222

Traubel, Horace, **IV:** 350

"Travel: After a Death" (Kenyon), **Supp. VII:** 169

Travel Alarm (Nye), **Supp. XIII:** 277

"Traveled World, The" (Pickering), **Supp. XXI:** 203

"Traveler, The" (Haines), **Supp. XII:** 203–204, 210

"Traveler, The" (Stegner), **Supp. IV Part 2:** 605

Traveler at Forty, A (Dreiser), **I:** 515

Traveler from Altruria, a Romance A, (Howells), **II:** 285, 287

Traveler's Tree, The: New and Selected Poems (W. J. Smith), **Supp. XIII:** 332, 347

"Traveling" (Paley), **Supp. VI:** 230

"Traveling Light" (Wagoner), **Supp. IX:** 329

Traveling Mercies: Some Thoughts on Faith (Lamott), **Supp. XX: 132, 140–142**

"Traveling Onion, The" (Nye), **Supp. XIII:** 276

Traveling through the Dark (Stafford), **Supp. XI:** 311, 316, **318–321**

"Traveling through the Dark" (Stafford), **Supp. XI:** 318–320, 321, 323, 329

Travelling in Amherst: A Poet's Journal, 1931–1954, **Supp. IX: 88–89**

Travelling Standing Still: Poems, 1918–1928 (Taggard), **Supp. XXII:** 278

Travelling Thirds, The (Atherton), **Supp. XXIV:** 23

Travels in Alaska (Muir), **Supp. IX:** 182, 185–186

"Travels in Georgia" (McPhee), **Supp. III Part 1:** 293–294

"Travels in North America" (Kees), **Supp. XV:** 133–134

Travels in the Congo (Gide), **III:** 210

"Travels in the South" (Ortiz), **Supp. IV Part 2:** 506

Travels with Charley (Steinbeck), **IV:** 52

"Travel Writing: Why I Bother" (Theroux), **Supp. VIII:** 310

Travis, Merle, **Supp. V:** 335

Travisano, Thomas, **Retro. Supp. II:** 40

Treadway, Jessica, **Supp. XXIII:** 280

Treasure Hunt (Buechner), **Supp. XII:** 52

Treasure Island (Stevenson), **Supp. X:** 230

Treasure of the Humble, The (Maeterlinck), **Supp. XX: 116**

"Treasure of the Redwoods, A" (Harte), **Supp. II Part 1:** 337

Treasury of Art Masterpieces, A: From the Renaissance to the Present Day (Craven), **Supp. XII:** 44

Treasury of English Aphorisms, A (L. P. Smith), **Supp. XIV:** 344

Treasury of English Prose, A (L. P. Smith, ed.), **Supp. XIV:** 341

Treasury of the Theatre, A (Gassner), **Supp. I Part 1:** 292

Treasury of Yiddish Stories, A (Howe and Greenberg, eds.), **Supp. I Part 2:** 432; **Supp. XXIII:** 7

Treat 'Em Rough (Lardner), **II:** 422–423

Treatise Concerning Religious Affections (Edwards), **I:** 547, 552, 554, 555, 557, 558, 560, 562

Treatise Concerning the Lord's Supper (Doolittle), **IV:** 150

"Treatise on Poetry" (Milosz), **Supp. VIII:** 20

Treatise on Right and Wrong, A (Mencken), **III:** 110, 119

"Treatise on Tales of Horror, A" (Wilson), **IV:** 438

Treatise on the Gods, A (Mencken), **III:** 108–109, 119

"Treatment" (Wright), **Supp. XV:** 343

Trece poetas del mundo azteca (León-Portilla), **Supp. XV:** 77

Tre Croce (Tozzi), **Supp. III Part 2:** 616

"Tree, a Rock, a Cloud, A" (McCullers), **II:** 587

"Tree, The" (Pound), **Retro. Supp. I:** 286; **Supp. I Part 1:** 255

"Tree, the Bird, The" (Roethke), **III:** 548

"Tree at My Window" (Frost), **II:** 155

Tree Grows in Brooklyn, A (B. Smith), **Supp. XVII: 9; Supp. XXIII:** 257, **259–264,** 265, 271

Tree Grows in Brooklyn, A (film; Kazan), **Supp. XVI:** 193

"Tree House at Night, The" (Dickey), **Supp. IV Part 1:** 179

"Tree House"(Thompson), **Supp. XXIII:** 301

Tree Is Older Than You Are, The (Nye, ed.), **Supp. XIII:** 280

"Tree of Laughing Bells, The" (Lindsay), **Supp. I Part 2:** 376

"Tree of Life, The" (Swados), **Supp. XIX:** 268

"Tree of Night, A" (Capote), **Supp. III Part 1:** 114, 120

Tree of Night and Other Stories, A (Capote), **Supp. III Part 1:** 114

"Trees, The" (Rich), **Supp. I Part 2:** 555

Trees, The (Richter), **Supp. XVIII: 212–213,** 220

"Trees Listening to Bach" (Merrill), **Supp. III Part 1:** 336

Tree That Came to Stay, The (Quindlen), **Supp. XVII:** 167

Tree Where Man Was Born, The (Matthiessen), **Supp. V:** 199, 203, 204

Trejo, Ernesto, **Supp. V:** 178, 180; **Supp. XIII:** 313, 316; **Supp. XV:** 73

Trelawny, Edward John, **Supp. I Part 2:** 721

"Trellis for R., A" (Swenson), **Supp. IV Part 2:** 647

Tremblay, Bill, **Supp. XIII:** 112

Tremble (Wright), **Supp. XV: 348–349**

"Trespass" (Frost), **Retro. Supp. I:** 139

Trespassing (Pickering), **Supp. XXI:** 202

"Trespassing" (Pickering), **Supp. XXI:** 202

Trethewey, Eric, **Supp. XXI:** 243, 244

Trethewey, Natasha, **Supp. XXI: 243–259**

"Tretitoli, Where the Bomb Group Was" (Hugo), **Supp. VI:** 138

Trevelyan, Robert C., **Supp. XIV:** 334

Trevor-Roper, Hugh, **Supp. XIV:** 348

Trial, The (Kafka), **IV:** 113; **Retro. Supp. II:** 20

"Trial, The" (Rukeyser), **Supp. VI:** 278

"Trial by Existence, The" (Frost), **II:** 166

"Trial for Arson, The"(Hadas), **Supp. XXIII:** 114

Trial of a Poet, The (Shapiro), **Supp. II Part 2:** 710

Trial of the Hawk, The: A Comedy of the Seriousness of Life (Lewis), **II:** 441

"Trial path, The" (Zitkala-Ša), **Supp. XXV:** 274–275, 282

Trials of the Human Heart (Rowson), **Supp. XV:** 237, 239

Tribal Secrets: Recovering American Indian Intellectual Traditions (Warrior), **Supp. IV Part 1:** 329

"Tribute" (A. Finch), **Supp. XVII:** 72, 73–74

"Tribute, A" (Easton), **Supp. IV Part 2:** 461

"Tribute, The" (Doolittle), **Supp. I Part 1:** 267

"Tribute (To My Mother)" (Cullen), **Supp. IV Part 1:** 166

Tribute to Freud (Doolittle), **Supp. I Part 1:** 253, 254, 258, 259, 260, 268

Tribute to the Angels (Doolittle), **Supp. I Part 1:** 272

"Trick on the World, A" (Ríos), **Supp. IV Part 2:** 553

"Tricks" (Olds), **Supp. X:** 203–204

"Trick Scenery" (F. Barthelme), **Supp. XI:** 26

Trifler, The (Masters), **Supp. I Part 2:** 459–460

Trifles (Glaspell), **Supp. III Part 1:** 175, 178, 179, 182, 186, 187; **Supp. X:** 46; **Supp. XXI:** 12

Trifonov, Iurii V., **Retro. Supp. I:** 278

Triggering Town, The: Lectures and Essays on Poetry and Writing (Hugo), **Supp. VI:** 133, 140

Trilling, Diana, **II:** 587, 600; **Supp. I Part 1:** 297; **Supp. XII:** 126; **Supp. XXI:** 271, 275

Trilling, Lionel, **I:** 48; **II:** 579; **III:** 308, 310, 319, 327; **IV:** 201, 211; **Retro. Supp. I:** 19, 97, 121, 216, 227; **Supp. III Part 2: 493–515; Supp. V:** 259; **Supp. VIII:** 93, 98, 190, 231, 236, 243; **Supp. IX:** 266, 287; **Supp. XIII:** 100–101; **Supp. XIV:** 280, 288–289; **Supp. XV:** 20, 140, 152

Trilogy (Doolittle), **Supp. I Part 1:** 271, 272

Trilogy of Desire (Dreiser), **I:** 497, 508; **Retro. Supp. II:** 94, 96, **101–102**

Trimberger, Ellen Kay, **Supp. XVII:** 96, 106; **Supp. XXI:** 12

Trimmed Lamp, The (O. Henry), **Supp. II Part 1:** 410

"Trinc" (McGrath), **Supp. X:** 127

Trinity (Uris), **Supp. XX:** 243, 244, 245, 246, 247, 248, 253, 254–255

Trio (Baker), **Supp. I Part 1:** 277

Trio (Saroyan), **Supp. XXII:** 25

"Triolets for Triolet" (Nelson), **Supp. XVIII:** 179

"Trip" (F. Barthelme), **Supp. XI:** 26

Triple Thinkers, The: Ten Essays on Literature (Wilson), **IV:** 428, 431; **Supp. II Part 1:** 146

"Triplex" (Doolittle), **Supp. I Part 1:** 271

Tripmaster Monkey: His Fake Book (Kingston), **Supp. V:** 157, 158, 169, 170–173

Trippings in Authorland (Forrester), **Supp. XVIII:** 13

Trippings of Tom Pepper, The (Briggs), **Supp. XVIII:** 3, **13–14**

"Trip to Hanoi" (Sontag), **Supp. III Part 2:** 460–462

Trip to Parnassus, A; or, The Judgement of Apollo on Dramatic Authors and Performers (Rowson), **Supp. XV: 232–233**

"Triptych" (Eberhart), **I:** 522, 539

Tristam Shandy (Sterne), **Supp. XXII:** 267

Tristan and Iseult, **Retro. Supp. I:** 328, 329, 330, 331

Tristessa (Kerouac), **Supp. III Part 1:** 225, 227, 229

Tristram (Robinson), **III:** 521, 522, 523

Tristram Shandy (Sterne), **I:** 299; **IV:** 465–466; **Supp. V:** 127; **Supp. XVIII:** 60

"Triumph" (C. L. R. James), **Supp. XXI:** 160

"Triumphal March" (Eliot), **I:** 580; **III:** 17; **Retro. Supp. I:** 64

Triumph of Achilles, The (Glück), **Supp. V:** 79, 84–86, 92

"Triumph of a Modern, The, or, Send for the Lawyer" (Anderson), **I:** 113, 114

"Triumph of the Egg, The" (Anderson), **I:** 113

Triumph of the Egg, The: A Book of Impressions from American Life in Tales and Poems (Anderson), **I:** 112, 114

Triumph of the Spider Monkey, The (Oates), **Supp. II Part 2:** 522

Triumphs of the Reformed Religion in America (Mather), **Supp. II Part 2:** 453

Trivial Breath (Wylie), **Supp. I Part 2:** 709, 722–724

Trivia; or, the Art of Walking the Streets of London (Gay), **Supp. XIV:** 337

Trivia: Printed from the Papers of Anthony Woodhouse, Esq. (L. P. Smith), **Supp. XIV:** 336, **337–340**

"Trivia Tea" (Skloot), **Supp. XX: 205**

Trocchi, Alexander, **Supp. XI:** 294, 295, 301

Troilus and Criseyde (Chaucer), **Retro. Supp. I:** 426

Trois contes (Flaubert), **IV:** 31, 37

Trojan Horse, The: A Play (MacLeish), **III:** 21

"Trojan Women, The" (Maxwell), **Supp. VIII:** 169

Troll Garden, The (Cather), **I:** 313, 314–316, 322; **Retro. Supp. I:** 5, 6, 8, 14

"Trolling for Blues" (Wilbur), **Supp. III Part 2:** 563–564

Trollope, Anthony, **I:** 10, 375; **II:** 192, 237; **III:** 51, 70, 281, 382; **Retro. Supp. I:** 361

Trombly, Albert Edmund, **Supp. I Part 2:** 403

Trombold, John, **Supp. XVIII:** 111

"Trompe L'Oeil" (Collins), **Supp. XXI:** 60

"Troop Train" (Shapiro), **Supp. II Part 2:** 707

"Tropes of the Text" (Gass), **Supp. VI:** 88

Tropic of Cancer (H. Miller), **III:** 170, 171, 174, 177, 178–180, 181, 182, 183, 187, 190; **Supp. V:** 119; **Supp. X:** 187; **Supp. XXII:** 230, 257

Tropic of Capricorn (H. Miller), **III:** 170, 176–177, 178, 182, 183, 184, 187, 188–189, 190

"Tropic of Cuba" (di Donato), **Supp. XX: 45**

Trotsky, Leon, **I:** 366; **II:** 562, 564; **IV:** 429; **Supp. XXI:** 161, 164, 165, 167, 168

Trotter, W., **I:** 249

Troubled Air, The (Shaw), **Supp. XIX: 249–250**

Troubled Island (opera; Hughes and Still), **Retro. Supp. I:** 203

Troubled Lovers in History (Goldbarth), **Supp. XII:** 176, **192–193**

Trouble Follows Me (Macdonald, under Millar), **Supp. IV Part 2:** 466

Trouble in July (Caldwell), **I:** 297, 304–305, 306, 309

Trouble Island (Hughes), **Supp. I Part 1:** 328

"Trouble of Marcie Flint, The" (Cheever), **Supp. I Part 1:** 186

Trouble with Francis, The: An Autobiography (Francis), **Supp. IX:** 76, 77, 82, **84–85**

Trouble with God, The (Francis), **Supp. IX:** 88

"Trouble with Poetry, The" (Collins), **Supp. XXI:** 57

Trouble with Poetry and Other Poems, The (Collins), **Supp. XXI:** 55, 57, 62

"Trouble with the Stars and Stripes" (Nye), **Supp. XIII:** 277

Trouillot, Michel-Rolphe, **Supp. X:** 14–15

Troupe, Quincy, **Retro. Supp. II:** 15, 111; **Supp. X:** 242

"Trout" (Hugo), **Supp. VI:** 135

Trout Fishing in America (Brautigan), **Supp. VIII:** 43

"Trouvée" (Bishop), **Retro. Supp. II:** 49

Troy (film), **Supp. XX: 273**

"Truce" (Taggard), **Supp. XXII:** 276–277

"Truce of the Bishop, The" (Frederic), **II:** 139–140

"Truck Stop: Minnesota" (Dunn), **Supp. XI:** 145–146

Trudeau, Garry, **Supp. XXIV:** 283

True Account, The: A Novel of the Lewis & Clark & Kinneson Expeditions (Mosher), **Supp. XXII:** 206, 207, 208, **214–215**

True and False: Heresy and Common Sense for the Actor (Mamet), **Supp. XIV:** 241, 243

True Blood (television series), **Supp. XIX:** 174

Trueblood, Valerie, **Supp. XIII:** 306

True Confessions (Dunne), **Supp. IV Part 1:** 198

True Confessions (film), **Supp. IV Part 1:** 198

Trueheart, Charles, **Supp. XXI:** 238
True History of the Conquest of New Spain, The (Castillo), **III:** 13
True Intellectual System of the Universe, The (Cuddleworth), **II:** 10
"True Love" (Olds), **Supp. X:** 212
Trueman, Matthew (pseudonym). *See* Lowell, James Russell
"True Morality" (Bell), **Supp. X:** 13
"True Romance" (Everett), **Supp. XVIII:** 65
Truesdale, C. W., **Supp. XXI:** 246
True Stories (Atwood), **Supp. XIII:** 34–35
"True Stories" (Atwood), **Supp. XIII:** 34
"True Stories of Bitches" (Mamet), **Supp. XIV:** 246, 252
"Truest Sport, The: Jousting with Sam and Charlie" (Wolfe), **Supp. III Part 2:** 581–582
"True Vine" (Wylie), **Supp. I Part 2:** 723
True West (Shepard), **Supp. III Part 2:** 433, 441, 445, 447, 448
Truman, Harry, **III:** 3
Truman Capote: In Which Various Friends, Enemies, Acquaintances, and Detractors Recall His Turbulent Career (Plimpton), **Supp. XVI:**245
Truman Show, The (film), **Supp. XVI:** 271
Trumbo, Dalton, **Supp. I Part 1:** 295; **Supp. XIII:** 6; **Supp. XVII:** 63; **Supp. XX:** 246; **Supp. XXI:** 45
Trumbull, John, **Supp. II Part 1:** 65, 69, 70, 268
Trump, Donald, **Supp. IV Part 1:** 393
Trumpener, Katie, **Retro. Supp. I:** 380
"Trumpet Player" (Hughes), **Supp. I Part 1:** 333
"Trumpet Player, 1963" (Halliday), **Supp. XIX:** 92
Trumpet Shall Sound, The (Wilder), **IV:** 356
Trumpet Unblown, The (Hoffman), **Supp. XVIII:** 71, **74–75**
Trunk Music (Connelly), **Supp. XXI: 72,** 75
"Truro Bear, The" (Oliver), **Supp. VII:** 234
Truscott, Lucian K., **Supp. IV Part 2:** 683
Trust (Ozick), **Supp. V:** 257–258, 259, 260–263, 270, 272
Trust Me (Updike), **Retro. Supp. I:** 322
"Trust Yourself" (Emerson), **II:** 10
"Truth" (Emerson), **II:** 6
"Truth, The" (Halliday), **Supp. XIX:** 87, 88, 94
"Truth, The" (Jarrell), **II:** 381–382
Truth About Celia, The (Brockmeier), **Supp. XXII: 53–55**
"Truth about God, The" (Carson), **Supp. XII: 105–106**
"Truth be told" (Trethewey), **Supp. XXI:** 255, 256
"Truthful James" (Harte), **IV:** 196
"Truth Is, The" (Hogan), **Supp. IV Part 1:** 401–402
"Truth Is Forced, The" (Swenson), **Supp. IV Part 2:** 652

"Truth of the Matter, The" (Nemerov), **III:** 270
Truth Serum (Cooper), **Supp. XI:** 129
"Truth the Dead Know, The" (Sexton), **Supp. II Part 2:** 681
"Trying to Evangelize a Cut Flower" (Peacock), **Supp. XIX:** 199
Trying to Find Chinatown (Hwang), **Supp. XXI:** 147
Trying to Save Piggy Sneed (Irving), **Supp. VI: 19–165**
"Trying to Talk with a Man" (Rich), **Supp. I Part 2:** 559
"Tryptich I" (Bell), **Supp. X:** 7
"Tryst, The" (Wharton), **Retro. Supp. I:** 378
"Try the Girl" (Chandler), **Supp. IV Part 1:** 125
Try! Try! (O'Hara), **Supp. XXIII:** 209, 210, 216
"Ts'ai Chih" (Pound), **III:** 466
T. S. Eliot and American Philosophy (Jain), **Retro. Supp. I:** 58
T. S. Eliot's Silent Voices (Mayer), **Retro. Supp. I:** 58
Tsuji, Shizuo, **Supp. XVII:** 90
Tsurikgekumen (The return) (Asch), **Supp. XXIII:** 5
Tsvetaeva, Marina, **Supp. VIII:** 30; **Supp. XXIII:** 168
"Tuberoses" (E. Stoddard), **Supp. XV:** 282
Tubert, Susana, **Supp. XXIII:** 203
Tucker, Benjamin R., **Supp. XXI:** 9
Tuckerman, Frederick Goddard, **IV:** 144; **Supp. XXV:** 241
Tucker's People (Wolfert), **Supp. XXI:** 261, 262, 263, 267, **267–275,** 278
"Tuesday, November 5th, 1940" (Benét), **Supp. XI:** 46, 52
"Tuesday April 25th 1966" (Olson), **Supp. II Part 2:** 585
"Tuesday Night at the Savoy Ballroom" (Komunyakaa), **Supp. XIII:** 132
Tuffield, Aviva, **Supp. XVI:** 147, 148
"Tuft of Flowers, The" (Frost), **II:** 153; **Retro. Supp. I:** 126, 127
Tufts, James Hayden, **Supp. I Part 2:** 632
Tu Fu, **II:** 526; **Supp. XV:** 47
Tu Fu (Ayscough), **II:** 527
Tugwell, Rexford Guy, **Supp. I Part 2:** 645
"Tulip" (Hammett), **Supp. IV Part 1:** 356
"Tulip Man, The" (McCarriston), **Supp. XIV:** 261
"Tulips" (Nye), **Supp. XIII:** 281
"Tulips" (Plath), **Retro. Supp. II:** 252–253; **Supp. I Part 2:** 540, 542, 544
"Tulips" (Snodgrass), **Supp. VI:** 325
Tulips and Chimneys (Cummings), **I:** 436, 437, 440, 445, 447
"Tulips"(Strout), **Supp. XXIII:** 283, 285
"Tulips"(theater performance, Strout), **Supp. XXIII:** 281
Tully, Jim, **III:** 103, 109
Tumble Home (Hempel), **Supp. XXI:** 115, **124–125**

"Tumble Home" (Hempel), **Supp. XXI:** 115, 116, **124–125,** 126
Tumble Tower (Modarressi and Tyler), **Supp. IV Part 2:** 657
"Tuned in Late One Night" (Stafford), **Supp. XI:** 327–328
Tunnel, The (Gass), **Supp. V:** 44; **Supp. VI: 89–91,** 94
"Tunnel, The" (Strand), **Supp. IV Part 2:** 622
"Tunnels" (Komunyakaa), **Supp. XIII:** 123
Tunnel Vision (Paretsky), **Supp. XXV:** 173–174, 177, 178, 181
Tuqan, Fadwa, **Supp. XIII:** 278
Tura, Cosimo, **III:** 474–475
Turandot and Other Poems (Ashbery), **Supp. III Part 1:** 3
Turco, Lewis, **Supp. XV:** 118
Turgenev, Ivan Sergeevich, **I:** 106; **II:** 263, 271, 275, 280, 281, 288, 319, 320, 324–325, 338, 407; **III:** 461; **IV:** 17, 277; **Retro. Supp. I:** 215, 222; **Supp. VIII:** 167
Turgot, Anne Robert Jacques, **II:** 103; **Supp. I Part 1:** 250
"Turkey and Bones and Eating and We Liked It" (Stein), **IV:** 44
Turman, Glynn, **Supp. IV Part 1:** 362
Turnbull, Dr. George, **II:** 113
Turnbull, Lawrence, **Supp. I Part 1:** 352
"Turned" (Gilman), **Supp. XI:** 207
Turner, Addie, **IV:** 123
Turner, Darwin, **Supp. I Part 1:** 339; **Supp. IV Part 1:** 165
Turner, Frederick Jackson, **Supp. I Part 2:** 480, 481, 632, 640; **Supp. IV Part 2:** 596
Turner, Nat, **IV:** 113–114, 115, 116, 117
Turner, Patricia A., **Supp. XIII:** 237; **Supp. XX: 110**
Turner, Russell. *See* Lacy, Ed
Turner, Victor, **Supp. IV Part 1:** 304
"Turning Away Variations on Estrangement" (Dickey), **Supp. IV Part 1:** 183
Turning Point, The (McCoy), **Supp. XIII:** 175
"Turning Thirty, I Contemplate Students Bicycling Home" (Dove), **Supp. IV Part 1:** 250
Turning Wind, A (Rukeyser), **Supp. VI:** 272–273, 279–280
Turn in the South, A (Naipaul), **Supp. XXII:** 240
Turn of the Screw, The (H. James), **Retro. Supp. I:** 219, 231; **Supp. IV Part 2:** 682
"Turn of the Screw, The" (H. James), **II:** 331–332; **Retro. Supp. I:** 228, 229, 231, 232; **Supp. XVII:** 143
Turns and Movies and Other Tales in Verse (Aiken), **I:** 65
"Turn with the Sun, A" (Knowles), **Supp. XII:** 237–238
"Turn Your Radio On" (J. W. Miller), **Supp. XX:** 169
Turow, Scott, **Supp. V:** 220; **Supp. XVII: 213–224**
"Turpentine" (Gallagher), **Supp. XXIV:** 174, 175, 176

Turpin, E. Walters, **Supp. XVIII:** 283

Turrinus, Lucius Mamilius, **IV:** 373

"Turtle" (Hogan), **Supp. IV Part 1:** 401

Turtle, Swan (Doty), **Supp. XI: 121–122**

"Turtle, Swan" (Doty), **Supp. XI:** 121–122

Turtle Island (Snyder), **Supp. VIII: 300–303**

Turtle Moon (Hoffman), **Supp. X:** 77, **87–88,** 89

"Turtle Shrine near Chittagong, The" (Nye), **Supp. XIII:** 277

Turtotte, James, **Supp. XXIII:** 125

Turturro, John, **Supp. XI:** 174

Tuscan Cities (Howells), **II:** 280

Tuskegee movement, **Supp. II Part 1:** 169, 172

Tuten, Frederic, **Supp. VIII:** 75, 76; **Supp. XIII:** 237, 249

Tuten, James, **Supp. XVIII:** 195

Tuthill, Louisa Cavolne, **Supp. I Part 2:** 684

"Tutored Child, The" (Kunitz), **Supp. III Part 1:** 264

Tuttleton, James W., **Supp. IV Part 1:** 166, 168

"T.V.A." (Agee), **I:** 35

Tvedten, Brother Benet, **Supp. IV Part 2:** 505

"TV Men" (Carson), **Supp. XII: 105, 112**

Twain, Mark, **I:** 57, 103, 107, 109, 190, 192, 193, 195, 197, 203, 209, 245, 246, 247–250, 255, 256, 257, 260, 261, 292, 342, 418, 469, 485; **II:** 70, 140, 259, 262, 266–268, 271, 272, 274–275, 276, 277, 280, 285–286, 287, 288, 289, 301, 304, 306, 307, 312, 415, 432, 434, 436, 446, 457, 467, 475, 476, 482; **III:** 65, 101, 102, 112–113, 114, 220, 347, 357, 409, 453, 454, 504, 507, 554, 558, 572, 575, 576; **IV: 190–213,** 333, 349, 451; **Retro. Supp. I:** 169, 194, 195; **Retro. Supp. II:** 123; **Supp. I Part 1:** 37, 39, 44, 247, 251, 313, 317; **Supp. I Part 2:** 377, 385, 393, 410, 455, 456, 457, 473, 475, 579, 602, 604, 618, 629, 651, 660; **Supp. II Part 1:** 193, 344, 354, 385; **Supp. IV Part 1:** 386, 388; **Supp. IV Part 2:** 463, 468, 603, 607, 693; **Supp. V:** 44, 113, 131; **Supp. VIII:** 40, 189; **Supp. IX:** 14, 171; **Supp. X:** 51, 227; **Supp. XII:** 343; **Supp. XIII:** 1, 17; **Supp. XV:** 41; **Supp. XVI:** 66, 208; **Supp. XVIII:** 1, 9, 13; **Supp. XXI:** 205; **Supp. XXII:** 89, 203, 205, 206; **Supp. XXIII:** 85

"Twa Sisters, The" (ballad), **Supp. I Part 2:** 696

Twelfth Night (Shakespeare), **Supp. IV Part 1:** 83; **Supp. IX:** 14; **Supp. XXII:** 229

"12 O'Clock News" (Bishop), **Retro. Supp. II:** 48

Twelve Men (Dreiser), **Retro. Supp. II:** 94, 104

Twelve Moons (Oliver), **Supp. VII:** 231, 233–236, 238, 240

Twelve Southerners, **IV:** 125; **Supp. X:** 25

Twelve Years a Slave (Northup), **Supp. XIV:** 32

Twentieth Century Authors, **I:** 376, 527

"Twentieth Century Fiction and the Black Mask of Humanity" (Ellison), **Retro. Supp. II:** 118

Twentieth Century Pleasures (Hass), **Supp. VI:** 103, 106, 109

Twenty Drawings (Gibran), **Supp. XX: 116**

"28" (Levine), **Supp. V:** 187, 191

"Twenty-Four Poems" (Schwartz), **Supp. II Part 2:** 646, 649

"2433 Agnes, First Home, Last House in Missoula" (Hugo), **Supp. VI:** 139–140

"Twenty Hill Hollow" (Muir), **Supp. IX:** 178

Twenty Love Poems and a Song of Despair (Neruda), **Supp. XXIV:** 170

"Twenty Minutes" (Salter), **Supp. IX:** 260

"Twenty-One Love Poems" (Rich), **Supp. I Part 2:** 572–573

"Twenty-One Poems" (MacLeish), **III:** 19

Twenty Poems (Haines), **Supp. XII:** 204, **205–206**

Twenty Poems of Anna Akhmatova (Kenyon), **Supp. VII:** 165–166

Twenty Questions: (Posed by Poems) (McClatchy), **Supp. XII:** 254, **259–262**

27 Wagons Full of Cotton and Other One-Act Plays (T. Williams), **IV:** 381, 383

Twenty-seventh City, The (Franzen), **Supp. XX: 83–84, 84, 85, 86–88, 88, 89, 91, 92, 95**

Twenty Thousand Leagues under the Sea (Verne), **I:** 480; **Supp. XI:** 63

"Twenty Years Ago" (Lindsay), **Supp. I Part 2:** 384, 399

Twenty Years at Hull-House (Addams), **Supp. I Part 1:** 3, 4, 11, 16

Twersky, David, **Supp. XX: 244**

Twice over Lightly: New York Ten and Now (Hayes and Loos), **Supp. XVI:** 195

Twice-Told Tales (Hawthorne), **I:** 354; **II:** 224; **III:** 412, 421; **Retro. Supp. I:** 154–155, 160

Twichell, Chase, **Supp. V:** 16; **Supp. XVII:** 110, 112

Twilight (Frost), **II:** 151

"Twilight's Last Gleaming" (Burroughs and Elvins), **Supp. III Part 1:** 93, 94, 101

Twilight Sleep (Wharton), **IV:** 320–322, 324–325, 327, 328; **Retro. Supp. I:** 381

"Twin, The" (Olds), **Supp. X:** 207

"Twin Beds in Rome" (Updike), **Retro. Supp. I:** 332

Twins of Table Mountain, The (Harte), **Supp. II Part 1:** 355

"Twist, The" (Olson), **Supp. II Part 2:** 570

Twitch and Shout (film), **Supp. XVIII:** 143

Twitchell-Waas, Jeffrey, **Supp. XVIII:** 99; **Supp. XXII:** 163

Two Admirals, The (Cooper), **I:** 350

Two against One (F. Barthelme), **Supp. XI:** 32, 33, 36

"Two and One"(Hadas), **Supp. XXIII:** 114–115

"Two Boys" (Moore), **Supp. X:** 173

"Two Brothers, The" (Jewett), **Retro. Supp. II:** 132

Two-Character Play, The (T. Williams), **IV:** 382, 386, 393, 398

Two Citizens (Wright), **Supp. III Part 2:** 602–604

"Two Deer" (Bass), **Supp. XVI:** 24

"Two Domains, The" (Goldbarth), **Supp. XII:** 192

"Two-Eleven All Around" (Offutt), **Supp. XIX:** 170

"Two Environments, The" (Trilling), **Supp. III Part 2:** 510

"Two-Fisted Self Pity" (Broyard), **Supp. XI:** 348

Two for Texas (Burke), **Supp. XIV:** 25, 34

"Two Friends" (Cather), **I:** 332

"Two Gardens in Linndale" (Robinson), **III:** 508

Two Gentlemen in Bonds (Ransom), **III:** 491–492

Two: Gertrude Stein and Her Brother (Stein), **IV:** 43

"Two Ghosts" (Francis), **Supp. IX:** 87

"Two Hangovers" (Wright), **Supp. III Part 2:** 596

Two-Headed Poems (Atwood), **Supp. XIII:** 34

Two Hot to Handle (Lacy), **Supp. XV:** 206

Two Hours to Doom (Bryant), **Supp. XI:** 302

"Two Hundred Years in an Hour" (Boyce), **Supp. XXI:** 8

"Two Kitchens in Provence" (M. F. K. Fisher), **Supp. XVII:** 88, 91

"Two Ladies in Retirement" (Taylor), **Supp. V:** 320

Two Letters to the Citizens of the United States, and One to General Washington (Barlow), **Supp. II Part 1:** 80

"Two Lives, The" (Hogan), **Supp. IV Part 1:** 400, 402, 403, 406, 411

Two Long Poems (Stern), **Supp. IX:** 296

"Two Look at Two" (Frost), **Supp. XXI:** 26

"Two Lovers and a Beachcomber by the Real Sea" (Plath), **Supp. I Part 2:** 536

"Two Men" (McClatchy)", **Supp. XII:** 269

Two Men (E. Stoddard), **Supp. XV:** 272, 273, **283–284**

Twomey, Jay, **Supp. XVII:** 111

"Two Moods of Love" (Cullen), **Supp. IV Part 1:** 166

Two Moons (Mallon), **Supp. XIX:** 132, **138–141**

"Two Morning Monologues" (Bellow), **I:** 150; **Retro. Supp. II:** 20

"Two Nations of Black America, The" (*Frontline*), **Supp. XX: 99**

Two-Ocean War, The (Morison), **Supp. I Part 2:** 491

"Two of Hearts" (Hogan), **Supp. IV Part 1:** 410

"Two on a Party" (T. Williams), **IV:** 388

"Two or Three Things I Dunno About John Cassavetes" (Lethem), **Supp. XVIII:** 148

"Two Pendants: For the Ears" (W. C. Williams), **Retro. Supp. I:** 423

"Two Poems of Going Home" (Dickey), **Supp. IV Part 1:** 182–183

"Two Portraits" (Chopin), **Supp. I Part 1:** 218

"Two Presences, The" (R. Bly), **Supp. IV Part 1:** 65

"Two Rivers" (Stegner), **Supp. IV Part 2:** 605

Tworkov, Jack, **Supp. XII:** 198

"Two Scenes" (Ashbery), **Supp. III Part 1:** 4

Two Serious Ladies (Jane Bowles), **Supp. IV Part 1:** 82

"Two Silences" (Carruth), **Supp. XVI:** 55

"Two Sisters" (Farrell), **II:** 45

Two Sisters: A Memoir in the Form of a Novel (Vidal), **Supp. IV Part 2:** 679

"Two Sisters of Persephone" (Plath), **Retro. Supp. II:** 246

"Two Songs on the Economy of Abundance" (Agee), **I:** 28

Two Sons, The (Boyce), **Supp. XXI:** 7, 13

"Two Tales of Clumsy" (Schnackenberg), **Supp. XV:** 258

"Two Temples, The" (Melville), **III:** 89–90

Two Thousand Seasons (Armah), **Supp. IV Part 1:** 373

Two Towns in Provence (M. F. K. Fisher), **Supp. XVII:** 91

Two Trains Running (Wilson), **Supp. VIII: 345–348**

"Two Tramps in Mudtime" (Frost), **II:** 164; **Retro. Supp. I:** 137; **Supp. IX:** 261

"Two Twilights for William Carlos Williams" (Boyle), **Supp. XXIV:** 63

"Two Views of a Cadaver Room" (Plath), **Supp. I Part 2:** 538

"Two Villages" (Paley), **Supp. VI:** 227

"Two Voices in a Meadow" (Wilbur), **Supp. III Part 2:** 555

Two Weeks in Another Town (Shaw), **Supp. XIX:** 251

"Two Witches" (Frost), **Retro. Supp. I:** 135

"Two Words" (Francis), **Supp. IX:** 81

Two Worlds Walking: A Mixed-Blood Anthology (Glancy and Truesdale, eds.), **Supp. XXI:** 246

Two Years Before the Mast (Dana), **Supp. XXV:** 208

Two Years before the Mast (Dana), **I:** 351

"Tyger, The" (Blake), **Supp. XVII:** 128

Tyler, Anne, **Supp. IV Part 2: 657–675;** **Supp. V:** 227, 326; **Supp. VIII:** 141;

Supp. X: 1, 77, 83, 85; **Supp. XII:** 307; **Supp. XVI:** 37; **Supp. XVIII:** 157, 195; **Supp. XXIII:** 298

Tyler, Royall, **I:** 344; **Retro. Supp. I:** 377

Tymms, Ralph, **Supp. IX:** 105

Tyndale, William, **II:** 15

Tyndall, John, **Retro. Supp. II:** 93

Typee: A Peep at Polynesian Life (Melville), **III:** 75–77, 79, 84; **Retro. Supp. I:** 245–246, 249, 252, 256

Types From City Streets (Hapgood), **Supp. XVII:** 103

"Typewriter, The" (D. West), **Supp. XVIII:** 279

Typewriter Town (W. J. Smith), **Supp. XIII:** 332

"Typhus" (Simpson), **Supp. IX:** 277

Tyranny of the Normal (Fiedler), **Supp. XIII: 107–108**

"Tyranny of the Normal" (Fiedler), **Supp. XIII:** 107–108

"Tyrant of Syracuse" (MacLeish), **III:** 20

"Tyrian Businesses" (Olson), **Supp. II Part 2:** 567, 568, 569

Tytell, John, **Supp. XIV:** 140

Tzara, Tristan, **Supp. III Part 1:** 104, 105

U

U and I (Baker), **Supp. XIII: 45–47,** 48, 52, 55

Überdie Seelenfrage (Fechner), **II:** 358

Ubik (Dick), **Supp. XVIII:** 136

"*Ubi Sunt* Lament for the Eccentric Museums of My Childhood" (Stallings), **Supp. XXV:** 232

Ubu Roi (Jarry), **Supp. XV:** 178, 186

Ueland, Brenda, **Supp. XVII:** 13

Uhry, Alfred, **Supp. XX: 177**

ukanhavyrfuckinciti back (Phillips), **Supp. XXIII:** 174

Ukrainian Dumy (P. N. Warren as Kilina and Tarnawsky, trans.), **Supp. XX: 261**

"Ulalume" (Poe), **III:** 427; **Retro. Supp. II:** 264, 266

Ulin, David, **Supp. XIII:** 244; **Supp. XVI:** 74

Ullman, Leslie, **Supp. IV Part 2:** 550; **Supp. XVIII:** 175

Ultimate Good Luck, The (Ford), **Supp. V:** 57, 61–62

Ultimate Punishment: A Lawyer's Reflections on Dealing with the Death Penalty (Turow), **Supp. XVII:** 220–221

Ultima Thule (Longfellow), **II:** 490; **Retro. Supp. II:** 169

"Ultima Thule" (Nabokov), **Retro. Supp. I:** 274

Ultramarine (Carver), **Supp. III Part 1:** 137, 138, 147, 148

"Ultrasound" (Stallings), **Supp. XXV:** 225, 233, 234

Ulysses (Joyce), **I:** 395, 475–476, 478, 479, 481; **II:** 42, 264, 542; **III:** 170, 398; **IV:** 103, 418, 428, 455; **Retro. Supp. I:** 59, 63, 290, 291; **Retro. Supp. II:** 121; **Supp. I Part 1:** 57;

Supp. III Part 2: 618, 619; **Supp. IV Part 1:** 285; **Supp. IV Part 2:** 424; **Supp. V:** 261; **Supp. IX:** 102; **Supp. X:** 114; **Supp. XIII:** 43, 191; **Supp. XV:** 305; **Supp. XVII:** 140, 227; **Supp. XXV:** 65

"*Ulysses,* Order and Myth" (Eliot), **Retro. Supp. I:** 63

"Umbrella, The" (Peacock), **Supp. XIX:** 203–204

Unaccountable Worth of the World, The (Price), **Supp. VI:** 267

Unaccustomed Earth (Lahiri), **Supp. XXI:** 176, **181–183,** 183, 188

"Unaccustomed Earth" (Lahiri), **Supp. XXI:** 186

Unamuno y Jugo, Miguel de, **III:** 310; **Supp. XV:** 79

"Unattached Smile, The" (Crews), **Supp. XI:** 101

"Unbelievable Thing Usually Goes to the Heart of the Story, The: Magic Realism in the Fiction of Rick Bass" (Dwyer), **Supp. XVI:** 16

"Unbeliever, The" (Bishop), **Retro. Supp. II:** 43

"Unborn Song" (Rukeyser), **Supp. VI:** 274

Unbought Spirit: A John Jay Chapman Reader (Stone, ed.), **Supp. XIV:** 54

Uncalled, The (Dunbar), **Supp. II Part 1:** 200, 211, 212

Uncentering the Earth: Copernicus and The Revolutions of the Heavenly Spheres (Vollmann), **Supp. XVII:** 226

Uncertain Certainty, The: Interviews, Essays, and Notes on Poetry (Simic), **Supp. VIII:** 270, 273, 274

Uncertainty and Plenitude: Five Contemporary Poets (Stitt), **Supp. IX:** 299

"Uncle" (Levine), **Supp. V:** 186

"Uncle Adler" (Kooser), **Supp. XIX:** 120

"Uncle Christmas" (Ríos), **Supp. IV Part 2:** 552

"Uncle Jim's Baptist Revival Hymn" (Lanier and Lanier), **Supp. I Part 1:** 353

"Uncle Lot" (Stowe), **Supp. I Part 2:** 585–586

Uncle Moses (Asch), **Supp. XXIII:** 14

"Uncle Moustapha's Eclipse" (McKnight), **Supp. XX:** 148

Uncle Remus Tales (Harris), **Supp. II Part 1:** 201

"Uncle Tomitudes" (Briggs), **Supp. XVIII:** 14

Uncle Tom's Cabin (Stowe), **II:** 291; **Supp. I Part 1:** 49; **Supp. I Part 2:** 410, 579, 582, 589–592; **Supp. II Part 1:** 170; **Supp. III Part 1:** 154, 171; **Supp. IX:** 19; **Supp. X:** 246, 249, 250; **Supp. XIII:** 95; **Supp. XVI:** 82, 85, 88; **Supp. XVIII:** 14

Uncle Tom's Children (Wright), **IV:** 476, 478, 488; **Supp. II Part 1:** 228, 235; **Supp. XVIII:** 283

"Uncle Wiggily in Connecticut" (Salinger), **III:** 559–560, 563

"Unclouded Day, The" (Proulx), **Supp. VII:** 254–255

"Uncommon Visage" (Brodsky), **Supp. VIII:** 31

"Uncommon Woman: An Interview with Wendy Wasserstein" (Cohen), **Supp. XV:** 323

Uncommon Women and Others (Wasserstein), **Supp. XV:** 320–321, **322–323; Supp. XXIV:** 117

Uncompromising Fictions of Cynthia Ozick (Pinsker), **Supp. V:** 272

"Unconscious Came a Beauty" (Swenson), **Supp. IV Part 2:** 646

"Uncreation, The" (Pinsky), **Supp. VI:** 245

"Undead, The" (Wilbur), **Supp. III Part 2:** 556

"Undefeated, The" (Hemingway), **II:** 250; **Retro. Supp. I:** 180

Under a Glass Bell (Nin), **Supp. X:** 186

"Under Ben Bulben" (Yeats), **Supp. V:** 220

Undercliff: Poems 1946–1953 (Eberhart), **I:** 528, 536–537

Under Cover (Goldbarth), **Supp. XII:** 177, 180, 193

Undercover Doctor (film), **Supp. XIII:** 170

"Under Cygnus" (Wilbur), **Supp. III Part 2:** 558

"Under Forty" (Trilling), **Supp. III Part 2:** 494

Underground, The Story of a People (Tenenbaum), **Supp. XX:** 253

Underground Man, The (film), **Supp. IV Part 2:** 474

Underground Man, The (Macdonald), **Supp. IV Part 2:** 474, 475

Underground Woman, The (Boyle), **Supp. XXIV:** 62

"Under Libra: Weights and Measures" (Merrill), **Supp. III Part 1:** 328

Under Milk Wood (D. Thomas), **III:** 21

"Undersea" (Carson), **Supp. IX:** 21

Understanding Cynthia Ozick (Friedman), **Supp. V:** 273

Understanding Drama (Brooks and Heilman), **Supp. XIV:** 12

Understanding E. L. Doctorow (Fowler), **Supp. IV Part 1:** 226

Understanding Fiction (Brooks and Warren), **IV:** 279; **Supp. XIV:** 11

Understanding Fiction (Brooks and Warren, eds.), **Supp. XIX:** 246

Understanding Flannery O'Connor (Whitt), **Retro. Supp. II:** 226

Understanding Nicholson Baker (Saltzman), **Supp. XIII:** 48

Understanding Poetry: An Anthology for College Students (Brooks and Warren), **IV:** 236; **Retro. Supp. I:** 40, 41; **Supp. XIV:** 4–5

Understanding Robert Bly (W. V. Davis), **Supp. XXI:** 84–85, 88

Understanding Tim O'Brien (Kaplan), **Supp. V:** 241

Understanding To Kill a Mockingbird: A Student Casebook to Issues, Sources, and Documents (Johnson), **Supp. VIII:** 127

Under Stars (Gallagher), **Supp. XXIV:** 166, 167, 168–169, 170

Undertaker's Garland, The (Wilson and Bishop), **IV:** 427

Under Taos Mountain: The Terrible Quarrel of Magpie and Tía (Schott), **Supp. XXIII:** 250–251

Under the Banner of Heaven: A Story of Violent Faith (Krakauer), **Supp. XVIII:** 105, **114–116,** 117

"Under the Cedarcroft Chestnut" (Lanier), **Supp. I Part 1:** 364

Under the Feet of Jesus (Viramontes), **Supp. XXV:** 130

"Under the Harbour Bridge" (Komunyakaa), **Supp. XIII:** 125

"Under the Influence" (Sanders), **Supp. XVI:** 274, 277

Under the Lilacs (Alcott), **Supp. I Part 1:** 42–43, 44

"Under the Maud Moon" (Kinnell), **Supp. III Part 1:** 246–247

Under the Mountain Wall: A Chronicle of Two Seasons in the Stone Age (Matthiessen), **Supp. V:** 202

Under the Red Flag (Jin), **Supp. XVIII:** 89, **94–95**

"Under the Rose" (Pynchon), **Supp. II Part 2:** 620

Under the Sea-Wind: A Naturalist's Picture of Ocean Life (Carson), **Supp. IX:** 19, **22–23**

Under the Shadow (Sorrentino), **Supp. XXI:** 236–237

Under the Sign of Saturn (Sontag), **Supp. III Part 2:** 451, 452, 458, 470–471

"Under the Sign of Saturn" (Sontag), **Supp. III Part 2:** 470

"Under the Sky" (Bowles), **Supp. IV Part 1:** 87

"Under the Sun"(Schott), **Supp. XXIII:** 247, 248

" 'Under the Umbrella of Black Civilization': A Conversation with Reginald McKnight" (Ashe), **Supp. XX:** 154

Under the Volcano (M. Lowry), **Supp. XVII:** 135, 139, 140

"Under the Willows" (Lowell), **Supp. I Part 2:** 416

Under the Willows and Other Poems (Lowell), **Supp. I Part 2:** 424

"Undertow" (Boyce), **Supp. XXI:** 10

Underwood, John Curtis, **Supp. XXIV:** 29

Underwood, Wilbur, **Retro. Supp. II:** 79

Underworld (DeLillo), **Supp. VI:** 2, 4–5, 6–7, 8, 9, 10, 11, **13–15; Supp. XI:** 68; **Supp. XX:** 91

Underworld, The (Wolfert). See *Tucker's World* (Wolfert)

Undine (La Motte-Fouqué), **II:** 212; **III:** 78

Undiscovered Country, The (Howells), **II:** 282

"Undressing, The" (C. Frost), **Supp. XV:** 98

Uneasy Chair, The (Stegner), **Supp. IV Part 2:** 599

"Unemployed, Disabled, and Insane, The" (Haines), **Supp. XII:** 211–212

Unending Blues (Simic), **Supp. VIII:** **278–279**

Unending Dialogue: Voices from an AIDS Poetry Workshop (Hadas, Barber, et al), **Supp. XXIII:** 118, **125–126**

"Unexpected Freedom" (Peacock), **Supp. XIX:** 199

"Unexpressed" (Dunbar), **Supp. II Part 1:** 199

"Unfinished Bronx, The" (Paley), **Supp. VI:** 228

Unfinished Crime, The (Holding), **Supp. XXII:** 120, **123–124,** 135, 136

"Unfinished Poems" (Eliot), **I:** 579

"Unfinished Song" (C. Frost), **Supp. XV:** 97

Unfinished Woman, An (Hellman), **Supp. I Part 1:** 292, 293, 294; **Supp. IV Part 1:** 12, 353–354; **Supp. IX:** 196, 200–201

Unforeseen Wilderness, The: An Essay on Kentucky's Red River Gorge (Berry), **Supp. X:** 28, 29, 30, 36

Unforgotten Years (L. P. Smith), **Supp. XIV:** 333, 334, 335, 336, 347

"Unfortunate Coincidence" (Parker), **Supp. IX:** 190

Unframed Originals (Merwin), **Supp. III Part 1:** 341

Ungar, Sanford, **Supp. XI:** 228

Ungaretti, Giuseppe, **Supp. V:** 337

Unguided Tour (Sontag), **Supp. III Part 2:** 452

"Unheimliche, Das" (The Uncanny) (Freud), **Supp. XVI:** 157–158

Unholy Sonnets (Jarman), **Supp. XVII:** 109, 110, **119–120; Supp. XVIII:** 178

"Unholy Sonnets" (Jarman), **Supp. XVII:** 118, 119–120

"Unidentified Flying Object" (Hayden), **Supp. II Part 1:** 368

"Unifying Principle, The" (Ammons), **Supp. VII:** 28

"Unimportant Man, An" (D. West), **Supp. XVIII:** 280

"Union" (Hughes), **Supp. I Part 1:** 331

"Union Street: San Francisco, Summer 1975" (Carver), **Supp. III Part 1:** 138

"Unitarian Christianity" (Channing), **Supp. XXIV:** **71–73,** 77

Unitarians and the Universalists, The (Robinson), **Supp. XXIV:** 70

"United"(Kenny), **Supp. XXIII:** 149

United States Army in World War II (Morison), **Supp. I Part 2:** 490

United States Constitution, **I:** 6, 283

United States Essays, 1951–1991 (Vidal), **Supp. IV Part 2:** 678, 687

"United States of Huck, The: Introduction to *Adventures of Huckleberry Finn*" (Saunders), **Supp. XIX:** 235

United States of Poetry, The (television series), **Supp. XIII:** 274

"Unity through Diversity" (Locke), **Supp. XIV:** 212, 213

Universal Baseball Asociation, Inc., J. Henry Waugh, Prop., The (Coover), **Supp. V:** 39, 41–42, 44, 46

Universal Passion (Young), **III:** 111

"Universe of Death, The" (H. Miller), **III:** 184

Universe of Time, A (Anderson), **II:** 27, 28, 45, 46, 48, 49

"Universities" (Emerson), **II:** 6

"Universities: A Mirage?" (Mora), **Supp. XIII:** 219

"University" (Shapiro), **Supp. II Part 2:** 704–705, 717

"University Avenue" (Mora), **Supp. XIII:** 216

"University Days" (Thurber), **Supp. I Part 2:** 605

"University Hospital, Boston" (Oliver), **Supp. VII:** 235

"University's Peril, The" (Taggard), **Supp. XXII:** 273

"Unknowable, The" (Levine), **Supp. V:** 195

"Unknown Girl in the Maternity Ward" (Sexton), **Supp. II Part 2:** 676

"Unknown Love, The" (Chandler), **Supp. IV Part 1:** 120

Unknown Rilke, The (Rilke; F. Wright, trans.), **Supp. XVII:** 244

"Unknown War, The" (Sandburg), **III:** 594

Unkown Constellations, The (Swados), **Supp. XIX:** 256

Unleashed (anthology), **Supp. XI:** 132

Unleashed: Poems by Writers' Dogs (Hempel and Shepard, eds.), **Supp. XXI:** 115

"Unlighted Lamps" (Anderson), **I:** 112

Unlit Lamp, The (Holding), **Supp. XXII:** **121,** 130

Unloved Wife, The (Alcott), **Supp. I Part 1:** 33

Unmarried Woman, An (film), **Supp. IV Part 1:** 303

"Unnatural Mother, The" (Gilman), **Supp. XI:** 207

"Unnatural State of the Unicorn" (Komunyakaa), **Supp. XIII:** 119

"Unparalleled Adventure of One Hans Pfaall, The" (Poe), **III:** 424

"Unpleasant Profession of Jonathan Hoag, The" (Heinlein), **Supp. XVIII:** 149

Unprecedented Era, The (Goebbels), **III:** 560

"Unprofitable Servant, The" (O. Henry), **Supp. II Part 1:** 403

Unpublished Poems of Emily Dickinson (Bianchi and Hampson, ed.), **Retro. Supp. I:** 35

Unpunished (Gilman), **Supp. XI:** 208

Unraveling Strangeness, The (Weigl), **Supp. XIX: 287–288**

"Unreal City" (Eliot), **Supp. XV:** 218

"Unreality of Modern Realism, The" (Rinehart), **Supp. XXV:** 201

"Unreasoning Heart" (Untermeyer), **Supp. XV:** 309

Unsaid (Gioia), **Supp. XV:** 129

"Unseen, The" (Pinsky), **Supp. VI:** 243–244

"Unseen, The" (Singer), **Retro. Supp. II:** 307

Unseen Hand, The (Shepard), **Supp. III Part 2:** 439, 445–446

Unselected Poems (Levine), **Supp. V:** 179

Unsettling of America, The: Culture and Agriculture (Berry), **Supp. X:** 22, 26, 29, 32, 33, 35; **Supp. XIV:** 177, 179

Unspeakable Gentleman, The (Marquand), **III:** 53–54, 60, 63

Unspeakable Practices, Unnatural Acts (Barthelme), **Supp. IV Part 1:** 39

"Unspeakable Things Unspoken: The Afro-American Presence in American Literature" (Morrison), **Supp. III Part 1:** 375, 377–379

Unspoken and Other Poems, The (Bremer), **Supp. XXII:** 277

"Untelling, The" (Strand), **Supp. IV Part 2:** 629

Unterecker, John, **I:** 386

Untermeyer, Jean Starr, **II:** 530; **Supp. XV:** 294, 295, 303, 307, 308, 310

Untermeyer, Louis, **II:** 516–517, 530, 532; **III:** 268; **Retro. Supp. I:** 124, 133, 136; **Supp. III Part 1:** 2; **Supp. IX:** 76; **Supp. XIV:** 119, 123; **Supp. XV: 293–318; Supp. XXI:** 277; **Supp. XXV:** 21, 23

Untimely Papers (Bourne), **I:** 218, 233

"Untitled" (C. Frost), **Supp. XV:** 103

"Untitled Blues" (Komunyakaa), **Supp. XIII:** 117

Unto the Sons (Talese), **Supp. XVII:** 199–200, **206–207,** 208, 209, 210

"Untrustworthy Speaker, The" (Glück), **Supp. V:** 86

"Unused" (Anderson), **I:** 112, 113

Unvanquished, The (Faulkner), **II:** 55, 67–68, 71; **Retro. Supp. I:** 84; **Supp. I Part 2:** 450

"Unvexed Isles, The" (Warren), **IV:** 253

"Unwedded" (Larcom), **Supp. XIII:** 144

"Unweepables, The" (Karr), **Supp. XI:** 243

"Unwelcome Guest, An" (Papernick), **Supp. XVII:** 50

Unwelcome Man, The (W. Frank), **Supp. XX: 70, 76**

Unwelcome Words (Bowles), **Supp. IV Part 1:** 93, 94

"Unwelcome Words" (Bowles), **Supp. IV Part 1:** 94, 95

Unwin, T. Fisher, **Supp. XI:** 202

"Unwithered Garland, The" (Kunitz), **Supp. III Part 1:** 265

Unwobbling Pivot, The (Pound, trans.), **III:** 472

"Unwritten, The" (Merwin), **Supp. III Part 1:** 352

"Unwritten Law" (Glück), **Supp. V:** 91

Up (Sukenick), **Supp. V:** 39

Up Above the World (Bowles), **Supp. IV Part 1:** 82, 91, 92

"Up and Down" (Merrill), **Supp. III Part 1:** 328

Upanishads, **IV:** 183

Up Country: Poems of New England (Kumin), **Supp. IV Part 2:** 446, 447–448, 453

"Update" (Dunn), **Supp. XI:** 150–151

Updike, John, **I:** 54; **III:** 572; **IV: 214–235; Retro. Supp. I:** 116, **317–338; Retro. Supp. II:** 213, 279, 280; **Supp. I Part 1:** 186, 196; **Supp. IV Part 2:** 657; **Supp. V:** 23, 43, 95, 119; **Supp. VIII:** 151, 167, 236; **Supp. IX:** 208; **Supp. XI:** 65, 66, 99, 140; **Supp. XII:** 140, 296, 298, 310; **Supp. XIII:** 45–46, 47, 52; **Supp. XIV:** 79, 93, 111; **Supp. XVI:** 205, 207, 220; **Supp. XX: 17; Supp. XXI:** 116, 226; **Supp. XXIII:** 109

Updike, Mrs. Wesley, **IV:** 218, 220

Up from Slavery (Washington), **Supp. II Part 1:** 169; **Supp. IX:** 19

Upham, Thomas Goggswell, **II:** 487

"Upholsterers, The" (Lardner), **II:** 435

"Up in Michigan" (Hemingway), **II:** 263; **Supp. XIX:** 241

Upjohn, Richard, **IV:** 312

"Upon a Spider Catching a Fly" (Taylor), **IV:** 161

"Upon a Wasp Child with Cold" (Taylor), **IV:** 161

"Upon Meeting Don L. Lee, in a Dream" (Dove), **Supp. IV Part 1:** 244

"Upon My Dear and Loving Husband His Going into England, Jan. 16, 1661" (Bradstreet), **Supp. I Part 1:** 110

"Upon My Mother's Death"(Hadas), **Supp. XXIII:** 118

"Upon Returning to the Country Road" (Lindsay), **Supp. I Part 2:** 382

"Upon the Burning of Our House, July 10th, 1666" (Bradstreet), **Supp. I Part 1:** 107–108, 122

"Upon the Sweeping Flood" (Taylor), **IV:** 161

"Upon Wedlock, and Death of Children" (Taylor), **IV:** 144, 147, 161

"Upon Westminster Bridge" (Wordsworth), **Supp. XXIV:** 148

"Upset, An" (Merrill), **Supp. III Part 1:** 336

Upstairs and Downstairs (Vonnegut), **Supp. II Part 2:** 757

Upstate (Wilson), **IV:** 447

Upton, Lee, **Supp. X:** 209

"Upturned Face" (Crane), **I:** 423

Upward, Allen, **Supp. I Part 1:** 262

Upward, Edward, **Supp. XIV:** 159, 160

"Upward Moon and the Downward Moon, The" (R. Bly), **Supp. IV Part 1:** 71

Urania: A Rhymed Lesson (Holmes), **Supp. I Part 1:** 300

"Urban Convalescence, An" (Merrill), **Supp. III Part 1:** 322–324

"Urban Renewal" (Komunyakaa), **Supp. XIII:** 113

Urdang, Constance, **Supp. XV:** 74

"Urganda and Fatima" (Rowson), **Supp. XV:** 234

Urial Accosta: A Play (Reznikoff), **Supp. XIV:** 282, 288

Urich, Robert, **Supp. V:** 228

"Uriel" (Emerson), **II:** 19

Uris, Leon, **Supp. IV Part 1:** 285, 379; **Supp. XX: 243–258**

Uroff, Margaret D., **Supp. I Part 2:** 542

Ursu, Liliana, **Supp. XXIV:** 178

"Us" (Sexton), **Supp. II Part 2:** 687

U.S. 1 (Rukeyser), **Supp. VI:** 272, 278, 283, 285

U.S.A. (Dos Passos), **I:** 379, 475, 478, 482–488, 489, 490, 491, 492, 493, 494, 495; **Retro. Supp. II:** 197; **Supp. I Part 2:** 646; **Supp. III Part 1:** 104, 105; **Supp. XIV:** 24

"U.S.A. School of Writing, The" (Bishop), **Retro. Supp. II:** 43

"U.S. Commercial Orchid, The" (Agee), **I:** 35

"Used-Boy Raisers, The" (Paley), **Supp. VI:** 218, 228

"Used Cars on Oahu" (Nye), **Supp. XIII:** 282

"Used Side of the Sofa, The" (Ríos), **Supp. IV Part 2:** 551

Useless Servants, The (Hinojosa), **Supp. XIX:** 98, 103, 104, **109–110**

Use of Fire, The (Price), **Supp. VI:** 265

"Use of Force, The" (W. C. Williams), **Retro. Supp. I:** 424

Use of Poetry and the Use of Criticism, The (Eliot), **Retro. Supp. I:** 65

Uses of Enchantment, The: The Meaning and Importance of Fairy Tales (Bettelheim), **Supp. X:** 77; **Supp. XIV:** 126

"Uses of Hell, The" (E. Hoffman), **Supp. XVI:** 154

"Uses of Hell, The: An Exchange"(Novick, Katz, and Szulc), **Supp. XVI:** 154

Uses of Literacy, The (Hoggart), **Supp. XIV:** 299

Uses of Literature, The (Calvino), **Supp. XXII:** 263

"Uses of Poetry, The" (W. C. Williams), **Retro. Supp. I:** 412

"Uses of the Blues, The" (Baldwin), **Retro. Supp. II:** 8

"Use-Unuse of Us, The" (Bronk), **Supp. XXI:** 32

"USFS 1919: The Ranger, the Cook, and a Hole in the Sky" (Maclean), **Supp. XIV:** 230, 234

Ushant: An Essay (Aiken), **I:** 49, 54, 55, 56, 57

"Usher 11" (Bradbury), **Supp. I Part 2:** 622

"Using Parrots to Kill Mockingbirds: Yet Another Racial Prosecution and Wrongful Conviction in Maycomb" (Fair), **Supp. VIII:** 128

Ustedes y Nosotros: Nuevo Mensaje a Ibero-América (W. Frank), **Supp. XX:** 79

"Usual Objects"(Schott), **Supp. XXIII:** 248

Usual Star, The (Doolittle), **Supp. I Part 1:** 270

"Usurpation (Other People's Stories)" (Ozick), **Supp. V:** 268, 271

Utopia 14 (Vonnegut), **Supp. II Part 2:** 757

V

V. (Pynchon), **Supp. II Part 2:** 618, 620–622, 627–630; **Supp. IV Part 1:** 279

"Vacation" (Stafford), **Supp. XI:** 321, 322

Vacationland (Monson), **Supp. XXIV:** 230, 231, 234

"Vacation Trip" (Stafford), **Supp. XI:** 322

Vachel Lindsay: A Poet in America (Masters), **Supp. I Part 2:** 473, 474

"Vachel Lindsay: The Midwest as Utopia" (Whitney), **Supp. I Part 2:** 403

"Vachel Lindsay Writes to Floyd Dell" (Tanselle), **Supp. I Part 2:** 403

"Vacillation" (Yeats), **Supp. XV:** 253

Vadim, Roger, **Supp. XI:** 293, 307

"Vag" (Dos Passos), **I:** 487–488

Vagina Monologues, The (Ensler), **Supp. XIX:** 204–205

Vail, Laurence, **Supp. XXIV:** 50

Valdez, Luis, **Supp. XXIII:** 203

"Vale" (Stallings), **Supp. XXV:** 230, 231

Valediction (Parker), **Supp. XIX:** 185

Valentine, Jean, **Supp. V:** 92

Valentine, Saint, **IV:** 396

Valentines (Kooser), **Supp. XIX:** 116, 123, **128–129**

Valentino, Rudolph, **I:** 483

Valéry, Paul, **II:** 543, 544; **III:** 279, 409, 428, 609; **IV:** 79, 91, 92, 428, 443; **Retro. Supp. II:** 187

"Valhalla" (Francis), **Supp. IX:** 77

Valhalla and Other Poems (Francis), **Supp. IX:** 76

Valiant Runaways, The (Atherton), **Supp. XXIV:** 22

Validity in Interpretation (Hirsch), **Supp. XIV:** 15

Valitsky, Ken, **Supp. XII:** 7

Vallejo, César, **Supp. V:** 332; **Supp. IX:** 271; **Supp. XIII:** 114, 315, 323; **Supp. XXI:** 132

"Valley, The" (Bass), **Supp. XVI:** 20, 22

Valley, The (Hinojosa), **Supp. XIX:** 97, 99, **100–101**

"Valley Between, The" (Marshall), **Supp. XI:** 278

Valley of Decision, The (Wharton), **IV:** 311, 315; **Retro. Supp. I:** 365–367

"Valley of the Monsters, The" (Peacock), **Supp. XIX:** 198

Valley of the Moon, The (London), **II:** 467, 481

"Valley of Unrest, The" (Poe), **III:** 411

Valli, Alida, **Supp. IV Part 2:** 520

"Valor" (Bausch), **Supp. VII:** 54

Valparaiso (DeLillo), **Supp. VI:** 4, 12

"Value of a Place, The" (Bass), **Supp. XVI:** 18

"Values and Fictions" (Toomer), **Supp. III Part 2:** 485–486

"Values and Imperatives" (Locke), **Supp. XIV:** 199, 202, 212

Values of Veblen, The: A Critical Appraisal (Rosenberg), **Supp. I Part 2:** 650

"Vampire" (Karr), **Supp. XI:** 241

Vampire Armand, The (Rice), **Supp. VII:** 290, 294–295

Vampire Chronicles, The (Rice), **Supp. VII:** 290

Vampire Lestat, The (Rice), **Supp. VII:** 290–292, 298, 299

Van Aalst, Mariska, **Supp. XIX:** 50, 51

Van Arsdale, Sarah, **Supp. XXV:** 4

Van Buren, Martin, **II:** 134, 312; **III:** 473

Vande Kieft, Ruth M., **IV:** 260

Vanderbilt, Cornelius, **III:** 14

VanDerWerff, Todd, **Supp. XXV:** 75

Van Dine, S. S., **Supp. IV Part 1:** 341

Van Doren, Carl, **I:** 252–253, 423; **II:** 103, 111, 112; **Supp. I Part 2:** 474, 486, 707, 709, 717, 718, 727; **Supp. II Part 1:** 395; **Supp. VIII:** 96–97

Van Doren, Mark, **I:** 168; **III:** 4, 23, 589; **Supp. I Part 2:** 604; **Supp. III Part 2:** 626; **Supp. VIII:** 231; **Supp. IX:** 266, 268; **Supp. XV:** 152, 305, 307; **Supp. XXII:** 275

Vandover and the Brute (Norris), **III:** 314, 315, 316, 320–322, 328, 333, 334

Van Duyn, Mona, **Supp. IX:** 269

Van Dyke, Annette, **Supp. IV Part 1:** 327

Van Dyke, Henry, **I:** 223; **II:** 456

Van Gogh, Vincent, **I:** 27; **IV:** 290; **Supp. I Part 2:** 451; **Supp. IV Part 1:** 284; **Supp. XXII:** 171–172

Van Gogh's Room at Arles (Elkin), **Supp. VI: 56**

"Vanilla Dunk" (Lethem), **Supp. XVIII:** 139

"Vanisher, The" (Whittier), **Supp. I Part 2:** 691

Vanishing Point (Markson), **Supp. XVII:** 135, 137, 138, 145–146

"Vanishing Point: Former City" (Monson), **Supp. XXIV:** 238

"Vanishing Point for Solo Voice" (Monson), **Supp. XXIV:** 239

Vanishing Point: Not a Memoir (Monson), **Supp. XXIV:** 230, **236–239**, 241–242

"Vanishing Point: Panera" (Monson), **Supp. XXIV:** 238

"Vanishing Red, The" (Frost), **Retro. Supp. II:** 47

"Vanity" (B. Diop), **Supp. IV Part 1:** 16

Vanity Fair (Thackeray), **I:** 354; **II:** 91; **III:** 70; **Supp. IX:** 200

"Vanity of All Wordly Things, The" (Bradstreet), **Supp. I Part 1:** 102, 119

Vanity of Duluoz (Kerouac), **Supp. III Part 1:** 221, 222

"Vanity of Existence, The" (Freneau), **Supp. II Part 1:** 262

Van Matre, Lynn, **Supp. V:** 126

Vann, Barbara, **Supp. XV:** 187

Vanquished, The (Faulkner), **I:** 205

Van Rensselaer, Stephen, **I:** 351

Van Vechten, Carl, **I:** 295; **IV:** 76; **Retro. Supp. I:** 199; **Supp. I Part 1:** 324, 327, 332; **Supp. I Part 2:** 715; **Supp. II Part 2: 725–751**; **Supp. X:** 247; **Supp. XVI:** 135; **Supp. XVII:** 96, 97, 101, 104; **Supp. XVIII:** 123, 131, 132, 279, 280; **Supp. XIX:** 76; **Supp. XX: 69**; **Supp. XXI:** 5, 8; **Supp. XXII:** 5, 158, 160

Van Vliet, Don, **Supp. XXIII:** 174

Vanya and Sonia and Masha and Spike (Durang), **Supp. XXIV: 127–128**

Vanzetti, Bartolomeo, **I:** 482, 486, 490, 494; **II:** 38–39, 426; **III:** 139–140; **Supp. I Part 2:** 446, 610, 611; **Supp. V:** 288–289; **Supp. IX:** 199; **Supp. XXII:** 277

"Vapor Trail Reflected in the Frog Pond" (Kinnell), **Supp. III Part 1:** 242–243

"Vapor Trails" (Snyder), **Supp. VIII:** 298

"Variation: Ode to Fear" (Warren), **IV:** 241

"Variation on a Sentence" (Bogan), **Supp. III Part 1:** 60

"Variation on Gaining a Son" (Dove), **Supp. IV Part 1:** 248

"Variation on Pain" (Dove), **Supp. IV Part 1:** 248

"Variations: The air is sweetest that a thistle guards" (Merrill), **Supp. III Part 1:** 321

"Variations: White Stag, Black Bear" (Merrill), **Supp. III Part 1:** 321

"Varick Street" (Bishop), **Supp. I Part 1:** 90, 92

Varieties of Metaphysical Poetry, The (Eliot), **Retro. Supp. I:** 65

Varieties of Religious Experience, The (William James), **II:** 344, 353, 354, 359–360, 362; **IV:** 28, 291; **Supp. IX:** 19

Variety (film), **Supp. XII:** 7

Variorum (Whitman), **Retro. Supp. I:** 406

Various Antidotes (J. Scott), **Supp. XVII: 188–189**

Various Miracles (Shields), **Supp. VII:** 318–320, 323, 324

"Various Miracles" (Shields), **Supp. VII:** 318–319, 324

Various Poems (Zach), **Supp. XV:** 86

"Various Tourists" (Connell), **Supp. XIV:** 79

"Varmint Question, The" (Leopold), **Supp. XIV:** 180–181

Varno, David, **Supp. XIX:** 205

Vasari, Giorgio, **Supp. I Part 2:** 450; **Supp. III Part 1:** 5

Vasquez, Robert, **Supp. V:** 180

Vassall Morton (Parkman), **Supp. II Part 2:** 595, 597–598

Vasse, W. W., **III:** 478

Vaudeville for a Princess (Schwartz), **Supp. II Part 2:** 661–662

"Vaudeville Moment" (Bodenheim), **Supp. XXV:** 22

Vaughan, Henry, **IV:** 151; **Supp. XV:** 251

Vaughn, Robert, **Supp. XI:** 343

Vaughn, Stephanie, **Supp. XXV:** 142

"Vaunting Oak" (Ransom), **III:** 490

Vazirani, Reetika, **Supp. XIII:** 133

Veblen (Hobson), **Supp. I Part 2:** 650

Veblen, Andrew, **Supp. I Part 2:** 640

Veblen, Oswald, **Supp. I Part 2:** 640

Veblen, Thorstein, **I:** 104, 283, 475–476, 483, 498, 511; **II:** 27, 272, 276, 287; **Supp. I Part 2: 628–650; Supp. IV Part 1:** 22

Veblen, Mrs. Thorstein (Ellen Rolfe), **Supp. I Part 2:** 641

Veblenism: A New Critique (Dobriansky), **Supp. I Part 2:** 648, 650

"Veblen's Attack on Culture" (Adorno), **Supp. I Part 2:** 650

Vectors and Smoothable Curves (Bronk), **Supp. XXI: 24–26,** 32

Vedanta for Modern Man (Isherwood, ed.), **Supp. XIV:** 164

Vedanta for the Western World (Isherwood, ed.), **Supp. XIV:** 164

Vedas, **IV:** 183

Vega, Janine Pommy, **Supp. XIV:** 148

Vega, Lope de, **Retro. Supp. I:** 285; **Supp. III Part 1:** 341, 347

Vegetable, The (Fitzgerald), **Retro. Supp. I:** 105; **Supp. IX:** 57

Vegetable, The, or From President to Postman (Fitzgerald), **II:** 91

"Vegetable Love" (Apple), **Supp. XVII:** 4

"Vegetable Love" (Crooker), **Supp. XXIII:** 62

"Vegetable Wisdom" (Halliday), **Supp. XIX:** 88

Veg tsu zikh, Der (The road to one's self) (Asch), **Supp. XXIII:** 5, 11

Veil of Snows, A (Helprin), **Supp. XXV:** 84, 87

Veinberg, Jon, **Supp. V:** 180; **Supp. XIII:** 313; **Supp. XV:** 76–77, 86

Vein of Iron (Glasgow), **II:** 175, 186, 188–189, 191, 192, 194

Vein of Riches, A (Knowles), **Supp. XII:** 249

Vein of Words (J. W. Miller), **Supp. XX: 165**

Velie, Alan R., **Supp. IV Part 2:** 486

Velocities: New and Selected Poems, 1966–1992 (Dobyns), **Supp. XIII:** 86–87, 87, 88

"Velocity" (Collins), **Supp. XXI:** 61

"Velorio" (Cisneros), **Supp. VII:** 66

"Velvet Gentleman, The (Skloot), **Supp. XX: 201**

"Velvet Shoes" (Wylie), **Supp. I Part 2:** 711, 714

Venant, Elizabeth, **Supp. XI:** 343

Vencloca, Thomas, **Supp. VIII:** 29

Vendler, Helen H., **Retro. Supp. I:** 297; **Retro. Supp. II:** 184, 191; **Supp. I Part 1:** 77, 78, 92, 95; **Supp. I Part 2:** 565; **Supp. IV Part 1:** 245, 247, 249, 254, 257; **Supp. IV Part 2:** 448; **Supp. V:** 78, 82, 189, 343; **Supp. XII:** 187, 189; **Supp. XV:** 20, 184

"Venetian Blind, The" (Jarrell), **II:** 382–383

Venetian Glass Nephew, The (Wylie), **Supp. I Part 2:** 707, 709, 714, 717–719, 721, 724

Venetian Life (Howells), **II:** 274, 277, 279

Venetian Vespers, The (Hecht), **Supp. X:** 57, **65–69**

"Venetian Vespers, The" (Hecht), **Supp. X:** 65, **66–67**

Venice Observed (McCarthy), **II:** 562

Ventadorn, Bernard de, **Supp. IV Part 1:** 146

"Ventriloquists' Conversations" (Gentry), **Supp. IV Part 1:** 236

Venturesome Voyages of Captain Voss, The (Voss), **Supp. XXV:** 217

"Venus, Cupid, Folly and Time" (Taylor), **Supp. V:** 322–323

Venus and Adonis (film), **Supp. IV Part 1:** 82

Venus and Don Juan (C. Frost), **Supp. XV:** 93, **102–103,** 104, 107

"Venus and Don Juan" (C. Frost), **Supp. XV:** 103

Venus Blue (Sobin), **Supp. XVI: 293–294,** 294

Venus in Sparta (Auchincloss), **Supp. IV Part 1:** 25

"Venus Pandemos" (Halliday), **Supp. XIX:** 85, 89, 90, 93

"Venus's-flytraps" (Komunyakaa), **Supp. XIII:** 126, 127

"Veracruz" (Hayden), **Supp. II Part 1:** 371, 373

Verducci, Tom, **Supp. XXII:** 209

Verga, Giovanni, **II:** 271, 275

Verghese, Abraham, **Supp. X:** 160

Verhaeren, Emile, **I:** 476; **II:** 528, 529

Verhaeren, Paul, **II:** 529, 543; **III:** 466; **IV:** 79, 80, 86, 286; **Retro. Supp. I:** 56, 62; **Retro. Supp. II:** 326

"Vermeer" (Nemerov), **III:** 275, 278, 280

Vermeer, Jan, **Retro. Supp. I:** 335

"Vermont" (Carruth), **Supp. XVI:** 54

Vermont Notebook, The (Ashbery), **Supp. III Part 1:** 1

"Vermont Tale, A" (Helprin), **Supp. XXV:** 85

Vermont Writers: A State of Mind (Daley), **Supp. XXII:** 216

"Vernal Ague, The" (Freneau), **Supp. II Part 1:** 258

Verne, Jules, **I:** 480; **Retro. Supp. I:** 270; **Supp. XI:** 63

Vernon, John, **Supp. X:** 15

Verplanck, Gulian C., **Supp. I Part 1:** 155, 156, 157, 158

Verrazano, Giovanni da, **Supp. I Part 2:** 496, 497

Verse (Zawacki), **Supp. VIII:** 272

"Verse for Urania" (Merrill), **Supp. III Part 1:** 329, 330

Verses (Wharton), **Retro. Supp. I:** 362

Verses, Printed for Her Friends (Jewett), **II:** 406

"Verses for Children" (Lowell), **II:** 516

"Verses Made at Sea in a Heavy Gale" (Freneau), **Supp. II Part 1:** 262

"Verses on the Death of T. S. Eliot" (Brodsky), **Supp. VIII:** 19

"Version of a Fragment of Simonides" (Bryant), **Supp. I Part 1:** 153, 155

"Vers Libre Epidemic, The" (Lovecraft), **Supp. XXV:** 120

Verulam, Baron. *See* Bacon, Francis

Very, Jones, **III:** 507; **Supp. XXV: 237–252**

"Very Hot Sun in Bermuda, The" (Jackson), **Supp. IX:** 126

Very Old Bones (W. Kennedy), **Supp. VII:** 133, 148, 150–153

"Very Old Man with Enormous Wings, A" (García Márquez), **Supp. XXIV:** 190

Very Persistent Gappers of Frip, The (Saunders), **Supp. XIX: 229–230**

"Very Proper Gander, The" (Thurber), **Supp. I Part 2:** 610

"Very Short Story, A" (Hemingway), **II:** 252; **Retro. Supp. I:** 173

"Vesalius in Zante" (Wharton), **Retro. Supp. I:** 372

Vesey, Denmark, **Supp. I Part 2:** 592

Vesey, Desmond, **Supp. XIV:** 162

"Vespers" (Auden), **Supp. II Part 1:** 23

"Vespers" (Glück), **Supp. V:** 88

"Vespers"(Dybek), **Supp. XXIII:** 78

Vestal Lady on Brattle, The (Corso), **Supp. XII:** 119, **120–121,** 134

Vested Interests and the Common Man, The (Veblen), **Supp. I Part 2:** 642

"Vesuvius at Home" (Rich), **Retro. Supp. I:** 42

"Veteran, The" (Crane), **I:** 413

"Veterans' Cemetery" (Gioia), **Supp. XV:** 117

"Veteran Sirens" (Robinson), **III:** 512, 524

"Veterinarian" (X. J. Kennedy), **Supp. XV:** 168

"Vetiver" (Ashbery), **Supp. III Part 1:** 26

Vetter, Lara, **Supp. XXII:** 166

"Via Dieppe-Newhaven" (H. Miller), **III:** 183

"Via Negativa" (Salter), **Supp. IX:** 257

Vicar of Wakefeld, The (Goldsmith), **I:** 216

Vicious Circle, The (film, Wilder), **Supp. XVII:** 62

"Vicissitudes of the Avant-Garde, The" (Gass), **Supp. VI:** 91

Vico, Giambattista, **Supp. XX:** 38

Victim, The (Bellow), **I:** 144, 145, 147, 149, 150, 151, 152, 153, 155, 156, 158, 159, 164; **IV:** 19; **Retro. Supp. II:** 21, 22, 34

"Victor" (Mumford), **Supp. II Part 2:** 476

Victoria (Rowson), **Supp. XV:** 231

Victorian in the Modern World, A (Hapgood), **Supp. XVII:** 95, 97, 100, 101, 103, 105, 106; **Supp. XXI:** 8

"Victoria's Secret" (Collins), **Supp. XXI:** 58–59

"Victories" (Untermeyer), **Supp. XV:** 300

"Victory at Sea" (television series), **Supp. I Part 2:** 490

"Victory comes late" (Dickinson), **Retro. Supp. I:** 45

"Victory of the Moon, The" (Crane), **I:** 420

Vida, Vendela, **Supp. XIX:** 49, 50, 53, 57, 58, 59, 61, 62

Vidal, Gore, **II:** 587; **IV:** 383; **Supp. IV Part 1:** 22, 35, 92, 95, 198; **Supp. IV Part 2: 677–696; Supp. IX:** 96; **Supp. X:** 186, 195; **Supp. XIV:** 156, 170, 338; **Supp. XIX:** 131, 132

Video Poems (Collins), **Supp. XXI:** 53

Viebahn, Fred, **Supp. IV Part 1:** 248

Viera, Joseph M., **Supp. XI:** 178, 186

Viereck, Peter, **Supp. I Part 2:** 403

Viertel, Berthold, **Supp. XIV:** 165

Viertel, Salka, **Supp. XVI:** 192

Viet Journal (Jones), **Supp. XI: 230–231**

Vietnam (McCarthy), **II:** 578–579

"Vietnam in Me, The" (O'Brien), **Supp. V:** 241, 252

Vietnamization of New Jersey, The (Durang), **Supp. XXIV:** 113, **117–118**

Vietnam Reader, The: The Definitive Collection of Fiction and Nonfiction on the War (O'Nan, ed.), **Supp. XXV:** 153

Vie unanime, La (Romains), **I:** 227

"View, The" (Roussel), **Supp. III Part 1:** 15, 16, 21

View from 80, The (Cowley), **Supp. II Part 1:** 141, 144, 153

"View from an Institution" (F. Wright), **Supp. XVII:** 244

"View from the Backyard" (W. V. Davis), **Supp. XXI:** 96

View from the Bridge (A. Miller), **Supp. XXV:** 93

View from the Bridge, A (A. Miller), **III:** 147, 148, 156, 158, 159–160

View from the Seventh Layer, The (Brockmeier), **Supp. XXII: 59–61**

"View from the Seventh Layer, The" (Brockmeier), **Supp. XXII:** 61

View of My Own, A: Essays in Literature and Society (Hardwick), **Supp. III Part 1:** 194, 200

"View of the Capital from the Library of Congress" (Bishop), **Retro. Supp. II:** 45

View of the Soil and Climate of the United States, A (Brown, trans.), **Supp. I Part 1:** 146

"View of the Woods, A" (O'Connor), **III:** 349, 351, 358; **Retro. Supp. II:** 237

"Viewpoint" (column, Siddons), **Supp. XXII:** 240, 245

"Views of the Mysterious Hill: The Appearance of Parnassus in American Poetry" (Strand), **Supp. IV Part 2:** 631

"Vigil" (Karr), **Supp. XI:** 241

"Vigil, The" (Dante), **III:** 542

"Vigil at Heiligenkreuz" (W. V. Davis), **Supp. XXI:** 93

"Vigil"(Dybek), **Supp. XXIII:** 78

"Vignette" (Trethewey), **Supp. XXI:** 253, 254

Vigny, Alfred Victor de, **II:** 543

Vildrac, Charles, **Supp. XV:** 50

Vile Bodies (Waugh), **Supp. I Part 2:** 607

Villa, Pancho, **I:** 210; **III:** 584

"Village Blacksmith, The" (Longfellow), **Retro. Supp. II:** 167, 168; **Supp. I Part 2:** 409

Village Hymns, a Supplement to Dr. Watts's Psalms and Hymns (Nettleton), **I:** 458

"Village Improvement Parade, The" (Lindsay), **Supp. I Part 2:** 388, 389

Village Magazine, The (Lindsay), **Supp. I Part 2:** 379–380, 382

Village Virus, The (Lewis), **II:** 440

"Villanelle at Sundown" (Justice), **Supp. VII:** 119, 122–123

"Villanelle of Change" (Robinson), **III:** 524

Villard, Oswald, **Supp. I Part 1:** 332

"Villa Selene" (Simpson), **Supp. IX:** 279

Villon, François, **II:** 544; **III:** 9, 174, 592; **Retro. Supp. I:** 286; **Supp. I Part 1:** 261; **Supp. III Part 1:** 235, 243, 249, 253; **Supp. III Part 2:** 560; **Supp. IX:** 116

"Villonaud for This Yule" (Pound), **Retro. Supp. I:** 286

Vincent, Steven, **Supp. XXV:** 201

"Vincenzo Tailor" (Di Piero), **Supp. XIX:** 38

Vindication of the Rights of Woman (Wollstonecraft), **Supp. I Part 1:** 126; **Supp. XI:** 203

Vines, Lois Davis, **Retro. Supp. II:** 261

Vintage Book of Amnesia, The (Lethem, ed.), **Supp. XVIII:** 138

"Vintage Thunderbird, A" (Beattie), **Supp. V:** 27

Vinz, Mark, **Supp. X:** 117

Viol de Lucrèce, Le (Obey), **IV:** 356

Violence (Bausch), **Supp. VII:** 48–49, 54

Violent Bear It Away, The (O'Connor), **III:** 339, 345–348, 350, 351, 354, 355, 356, 357; **Retro. Supp. II:** 233, **234–236**

Violent Hero, Wilderness Heritage and Urban Reality, The: A Study of the Private Eye in the Novels of Dashiell Hammett, Raymond Chandler and Ross Macdonald (Parker), **Supp. XIX:** 177

"Violent Vet, The" (O'Brien), **Supp. V:** 238

Violin (Rice), **Supp. VII:** 302

Viorst, Judith, **Supp. X:** 153

Viper Run (Karr), **Supp. XI: 248–251**

Viramontes, Helene María, **Supp. XXV:** 130, 133, 138

Virgil, **I:** 312, 322, 587; **II:** 133, 542; **IV:** 137, 359; **Retro. Supp. I:** 135; **Supp. I Part 1:** 153; **Supp. I Part 2:** 494; **Supp. IV Part 2:** 631

"Virgin and Child with Music and Numbers" (Bronk), **Supp. XXI:** 30

"Virgin and the Dynamo" (Adams), **III:** 396

"Virgin Carrying a Lantern, The" (Stevens), **IV:** 80

Virgin Huntress, The (Holding), **Supp. XXII:** 119, 124, **135–136**

Virginia (Glasgow), **II:** 175, 178, 181–182, 193, 194

"Virginia" (Lindsay), **Supp. I Part 2:** 398

"Virginia Britannia" (Moore), **III:** 198, 208–209

"Virginians Are Coming Again, The" (Lindsay), **Supp. I Part 2:** 399

Virginia Reels (Hoffman), **Supp. XVIII:** 79, 86

Virgin Spain (W. Frank), **Supp. XX:** 76

"Virgins Plus Curtains Minus Dots" (Loy), **Supp. XXII:** 161

Virgin Suicides, The (Eugenides), **Supp. XXIV:** 134, **136–138,** 141, 142

Virgin Time: In Search of the Contemplative Life (Hampl), **Supp. XXII:** 82,

83–84, **90–92**
"Virgin Violeta" (Porter), **III:** 454
"Virility" (Ozick), **Supp. V:** 262, 265
Virtual Light (W. Gibson), **Supp. XVI:** 124, **129,** 130
Virtue of Selfishness, The: A New Concept of Egoism (Rand), **Supp. IV Part 2:** 527, 530–532
"Virtuoso" (Francis), **Supp. IX:** 82
Virtuous Girl, A (Bodenheim), **Supp. XXV:** 27
Virtuous Woman, A (Gibbons), **Supp. X:** 44–45, 46, 50
Visconti, Luchino, **Supp. V:** 51
Viscusi, Robert, **Supp. XX:** 46
Visible Saints: The History of a Puritan Idea (Morgan), **IV:** 149
"Vision, A" (Olds), **Supp. X:** 214
"Vision, A" (Winters), **Supp. II Part 2:** 785, 795
"Vision and Prayer" (D. Thomas), **I:** 432
"Visionary, The" (Poe), **III:** 411
Visionary Farms, The (Eberhart), **I:** 537–539
Visioning, The (Glaspell), **Supp. III Part 1:** 175–177, 180, 187, 188
Vision in Spring (Faulkner), **Retro. Supp. I:** 79
Vision of Columbus (Barlow), **Supp. I Part 1:** 124; **Supp. II Part 1:** 67, 68, 70–75, 77, 79
Vision of Sir Launfal, The (Lowell), **Supp. I Part 1:** 311; **Supp. I Part 2:** 406, 409, 410
"Vision of the World, A" (Cheever), **Supp. I Part 1:** 182, 192
"Visions of Budhardin"(Dybek), **Supp. XXIII:** 70–71
Visions of Cody (Kerouac), **Supp. III Part 1:** 225–227
Visions of Gerard (Kerouac), **Supp. III Part 1:** 219–222, 225, 227, 229
"Visions of the Daughters of Albion" (Blake), **III:** 540
"Visit" (Ammons), **Supp. VII:** 28–29
"Visit, The" (Kenyon), **Supp. VII:** 169
"Visitant, The" (Dunn), **Supp. XI:** 147
"Visitation, The/La Visitación" (Mora), **Supp. XIII:** 217, 224, 228
"Visitation"(Kenny), **Supp. XXIII:** 157
"Visit Home, A" (Stafford), **Supp. XI:** 318
Visit in 2001, The (musical, McNally), **Supp. XIII:** 207
"Visiting My Own House in Iowa City" (Stern), **Supp. IX:** 300
"Visit of Charity, A" (Welty), **IV:** 262
"Visitors" (J. W. Miller), **Supp. XX:** 167
"Visitors" (Salinas), **Supp. XIII:** 318
"Visitors, The/Los Visitantes" (Kingsolver), **Supp. VII:** 208
"Visits to St. Elizabeths" (Bishop), **Retro. Supp. II:** 47
"Visit to a Small Planet" (teleplay) (Vidal), **Supp. IV Part 2:** 682
Visit to a Small Planet: A Comedy Akin to Vaudeville (Vidal), **Supp. IV Part 2:** 682–683
"Visit to Avoyelles, A" (Chopin), **Supp. I Part 1:** 213

"Visit to Manafon, A" (W. V. Davis), **Supp. XXI:** 96
"Vissi d'Arte" (Moore), **Supp. X:** 173–174
Vistas of History (Morison), **Supp. I Part 2:** 492
"Vita" (Stafford), **Supp. XI:** 330
"Vita Brevis" (Hull), **Supp. XXI:** 138
Vital, David, **Supp. XVI:** 160
Vital Provisions (Price), **Supp. VI:** 262–263
"Vitamins" (Carver), **Supp. III Part 1:** 138
Vita Nova (Glück), **Supp. V:** 90–92
Vitruvius, **Supp. XVI:** 292
Vittorio, the Vampire (Rice), **Supp. VII:** 295–296
Viudas (Dorfman), **Supp. IX:** 138
"Vivaldi"(Dybek), **Supp. XXIII:** 68
"Viva Vargas!" (Allen), **Supp. XV:** 15
Viviparous Quadrupeds of North America, The (Audubon and Bachman), **Supp. XVI:** 10
Vivisections (Siegel), **Supp. XXII:** 257
Vizenor, Gerald, **Supp. IV Part 1:** 260, 262, 329, 404; **Supp. IV Part 2:** 502
Vladimir Nabokov: The American Years (Nabokov), **Retro. Supp. I:** 275
Vlag, Piet, **Supp. XV:** 295
"Vlemk, the Box Painter" (Gardner), **Supp. VI:** 73
"V-Letter" (Shapiro), **Supp. II Part 2:** 707
V-Letter and Other Poems (Shapiro), **Supp. II Part 2:** 702, 706
"Vocabulary of Dearness" (Nye), **Supp. XIII:** 284
"Vocation" (Stafford), **Supp. XI:** 312, 321
Vocation and a Voice, A (Chopin), **Retro. Supp. II:** 67, 72
"Vocation and a Voice, A" (Chopin), **Retro. Supp. II:** 72; **Supp. I Part 1:** 200, 220, 224, 225
Vogel, David, **Supp. XV:** 88
Vogel, Speed, **Supp. IV Part 1:** 390
"Vogue Vista" (Peacock), **Supp. XIX:** 200
"Voice" (F. Wright), **Supp. XVII:** 245
"Voice" (Notley), **Supp. XXII:** 230
"Voice, The" (Dunn), **Supp. XI:** 152
Voiced Connections of James Dickey, The (Dickey), **Supp. IV Part 1:** 177
"Voice from the Wilderness" (Ray), **Supp. XVIII:** 202
"Voice from the Woods, A" (Humphrey), **Supp. IX:** 101
"Voice from Under the Table, A" (Wilbur), **Supp. III Part 2:** 553, 554
"Voice of God, The" (Very), **Supp. XXV:** 243
Voice of Reason, The: Essays in Objectivist Thought (Rand), **Supp. IV Part 2:** 527, 528, 532
"Voice of Rock, The" (Ginsberg), **Supp. II Part 1:** 313
Voice of the Butterfly, The (Nichols), **Supp. XIII:** 270
Voice of the City, The (O. Henry), **Supp. II Part 1:** 410

"Voice of the Mountain, The" (Crane), **I:** 420
Voice of the Negro (Barber), **Supp. II Part 1:** 168
"Voice of the Past, The" (Skloot), **Supp. XX:** 207
Voice of the People, The (Glasgow), **II:** 175, 176
Voice of the Turtle: American Indian Literature 1900–1970 (Gunn Allen, ed.), **Supp. IV Part 1:** 332, 334
Voices from the Moon (Dubus), **Supp. VII:** 88–89
"Voices from the Other World" (Merrill), **Supp. III Part 1:** 331
Voices in the House (Sedges), **Supp. II Part 1:** 125
Voices of a Summer Day (Shaw), **Supp. XIX:** 251
Voices of the Night (Longfellow), **II:** 489, 493; **Retro. Supp. II:** 154, 157, 168
"Voices of Village Square, The" (Wolfe), **Supp. III Part 2:** 571–572
Voice That Is Great within Us, The (Caruth, ed.), **Supp. XIII:** 112
Void Moon (Connelly), **Supp. XXI:** 73, 74
Voigt, Ellen Bryan, **Supp. XIII:** 76
"Voir Dire" (Monson), **Supp. XXIV:** 237
Voix humaine, La (Cocteau), **Supp. XX:** 236
Volkening, Henry, **Retro. Supp. II:** 117; **Supp. XV:** 142
Vollmann, William T., **Supp. XIV:** 96; **Supp. XVII: 225–237; Supp. XX:** 93
Volney, Constantin François de Chasseboeuf, **Supp. I Part 1:** 146
Voltaire, **I:** 194; **II:** 86, 103, 449; **III:** 420; **IV:** 18; **Retro. Supp. II:** 94; **Supp. I Part 1:** 288–289; **Supp. I Part 2:** 669, 717; **Supp. XV:** 258; **Supp. XX:** 285
Voltaire! Voltaire! (Endore), **Supp. XVII:** 65
Volunteers, The (Rowson and Reinagle), **Supp. XV:** 238
Volynsky, Akim (Chaim Flekser), **Supp. XXIII:** 11
Vonnegut, Kurt, **Retro. Supp. I:** 170; **Supp. II Part 2:** 557, 689, **753–784; Supp. IV Part 1:** 227, 392; **Supp. V:** 40, 42, 237, 244, 296; **Supp. X:** 260; **Supp. XI:** 104; **Supp. XII:** 139, 141; **Supp. XVIII:** 242, 252; **Supp. XXI:** 226; **Supp. XXIII:** 42, 101, 109
Vonnegut, Kurt, Jr., **Supp. XVII:** 41, 135; **Supp. XIX:** 223
"Voracities and Verities" (Moore), **III:** 214
Vore, Nellie, **I:** 199
Vorlicky, Robert, **Supp. IX:** 132, 135, 136, 141, 144, 147
Vorse, Mary Heaton, **Supp. XVII:** 99; **Supp. XX: 76; Supp. XXI:** 5, 6, 9, 13
Vortex, The (Coward), **Supp. XXIV:** 267
"Vorticism" (Pound), **Retro. Supp. I:** 288
Vosjoli, Philippe de, **Supp. XX:** 253
Voss, J. C., **Supp. XXV:** 217
Voss, Ralph E., **Supp. XXV:** 93

Voss, Richard, **I:** 199–200

"Vow, The" (Hecht), **Supp. X:** 64

"Vowels 2" (Baraka), **Supp. II Part 1:** 51

Vow of Conversation, A: Journal, 1964–1965 (Merton), **Supp. VIII:** 206

Vox (Baker), **Supp. XIII:** 47–49, 50, 52, 53

"Voyage" (MacLeish), **III:** 15

Voyage, The (Caputo), **Supp. XIX:** 25, 27–28

"Voyage, The" (Irving), **II:** 304

Voyage, The, and Other Versions of Poems by Baudelaire (Lowell), **Retro. Supp. II:** 187

Voyage dans la Haute Pennsylvanie et dans l'état de New-York (Crèvecoeur), **Supp. I Part 1:** 250–251

Voyage of the Beagle (Darwin), **Supp. IX:** 211

Voyage of the Dawn Treader (C. S. Lewis), **Supp. XXV:** 74

Voyage of the Destroyer from New York to Brazil, The (Slocum), **Supp. XXV:** 208, 212–213

Voyage of the Liberdade, The (Slocum), **Supp. XXV:** 208, 210–212

Voyage Out, The (Woolf), **Supp. XV:** 65

"Voyager, The" (Everwine), **Supp. XV:** 75

"Voyages" (H. Crane), **I:** 393–395; **Retro. Supp. II:** 78, 80, 81

"Voyages" (Levine), **Supp. V:** 190

Voyages and Discoveries of the Companions of Columbus (Irving), **II:** 310

Voyage to Pagany, A (W. C. Williams), **IV:** 404; **Retro. Supp. I:** 418–419, **420–421**, 423

Voyaging Portraits (Sobin), **Supp. XVI:** 282, 287

"Voyeur, The" (Gioia), **Supp. XV:** 125

"Voz de America" (column, W. Frank), **Supp. XX:** 80

Voznesensky, Andrei, **II:** 553; **Supp. III Part 1:** 268; **Supp. III Part 2:** 560

Vrbovska, Anca, **Supp. IV Part 2:** 639

V. S. Naipaul: An Introduction to His Work (Theroux), **Supp. VIII:** 314, 318

"V. S. Pritchett's Apprenticeship" (Maxwell), **Supp. VIII:** 172

Vukelich, James, **Supp. XXIII:** 228, 233

"Vulgarity in Literature" (Huxley), **III:** 429–430

"Vultures" (Oliver), **Supp. VII:** 235

"V. V." (Alcott), **Supp. I Part 1:** 37

W

W (Viva) (Cummings), **I:** 429, 433, 434, 436, 443, 444, 447

Wabash (R. O. Butler), **Supp. XII:** 61, **68–69**

Wade, Grace, **I:** 216

"Wading at Wellfleet" (Bishop), **Retro. Supp. II:** 42, 43; **Supp. I Part 1:** 80, 85, 86

Wadsworth, Charles, **I:** 454, 470; **Retro. Supp. I:** 32, 33

Wagenknecht, Edward, **II:** 508; **Supp. I Part 2:** 408, 584; **Supp. IV Part 2:** 681

"Wages of Poetry, The" (Wright), **Supp. XV:** 337

Wagner, Erica, **Supp. XXI:** 117

Wagner, Jean, **Supp. I Part 1:** 341, 346; **Supp. IV Part 1:** 165, 167, 171

Wagner, Richard, **I:** 284, 395; **II:** 425; **III:** 396, 507; **Supp. IV Part 1:** 392

Wagner, Robert, **Supp. IX:** 250

"Wagnerians, The" (Auchincloss), **Supp. IV Part 1:** 23

"Wagner Matinee, A" (Cather), **I:** 315–316; **Retro. Supp. I:** 5, 8

Wagoner, David, **Supp. IX:** 323–340; **Supp. XII:** 178; **Supp. XX:** 200

Wahlöö, Per, **Supp. XX:** 87

Waid, Candace, **Retro. Supp. I:** 360, 372, 373

Waif, The (Longfellow, ed.), **Retro. Supp. II:** 155

"Waif of the Plains, A" (Harte), **Supp. II Part 1:** 354

Wain, John, **Supp. XIV:** 166

"Wait" (Kinnell), **Supp. III Part 1:** 250

"Waiter in a California Vietnamese Restaurant" (Major), **Supp. XXII:** 182

"Waiting" (Dubus), **Supp. VII:** 87

Waiting (Jin), **Supp. XVIII:** 89, **96–97**, 99

"Waiting" (W. C. Williams), **Retro. Supp. I:** 418

"Waiting, The" (L.-Y. Lee), **Supp. XV:** 218

"Waiting, The" (Olds), **Supp. X:** 209

"Waiting between the Trees" (Tan), **Supp. X:** 290

"Waiting by the Gate" (Bryant), **Supp. I Part 1:** 171

Waiting for God (Weil), **I:** 298

Waiting for Godot (Beckett), **I:** 78, 91, 298; **Supp. IV Part 1:** 368–369; **Supp. XXIII:** 213

Waiting for Lefty (Odets), **Supp. I Part 1:** 277; **Supp. II Part 2:** 529, 530–533, 540; **Supp. V:** 109; **Supp. XIX:** 242

Waiting for Sweet Betty (Major), **Supp. XXII:** **183**

Waiting for Teddy Williams (Mosher), **Supp. XXII:** 205, 206, 207, 208, 209, **215–216**

Waiting for the End of the World (Bell), **Supp. X:** **4–5**, 11

"Waiting for the Ladies" (L. Brown), **Supp. XXI:** 44

Waiting for the Verdict (R. H. Davis), **Supp. XVI:** 85, 89, 90

"Waiting in a Rain Forest" (Wagoner), **Supp. IX:** 329

Waiting in the Wings (Loraga), **Supp. XXIII:** 195

Waiting Room, The (Kees), **Supp. XV:** 133, 148

Waiting to Exhale (McMillan), **Supp. XIII:** 184, 185, **189–190**, 191

"Waiting to Freeze" (Banks), **Supp. V:** 5, 6

Waiting to Freeze: Poems (Banks), **Supp. V:** 6, 8

Waits, Tom, **Supp. VIII:** 12

Wait until Spring, Bandini (Fante), **Supp. XI:** 160, 161, 164, 165, **166–167**

Wait until Spring, Bandini (film), **Supp. XI:** 173

"Wake, The" (Dove), **Supp. IV Part 1:** 250

"Wakefield" (Hawthorne), **Retro. Supp. I:** 154, 159

Wakefield, Dan, **Supp. VIII:** 43; **Supp. XVI:** 220; **Supp. XIX:** 257, 258

Wakefield, Richard, **Supp. IX:** 323

"Wake Island" (Rukeyser), **Supp. VI:** 273

"Wake"(Kenny), **Supp. XXIII:** 155

Wakeman, Frederic, **Supp. IX:** 247

Wake Up and Live! (Brande), **Supp. I Part 2:** 608

"Waking" (C. Frost), **Supp. XV:** 93

Waking, The (Roethke), **III:** 541

"Waking Early Sunday Morning" (Lowell), **II:** 552; **Retro. Supp. II:** 190

"Waking in the Blue" (Lowell), **II:** 547; **Retro. Supp. II:** 180

"Waking in the Dark" (Rich), **Supp. I Part 2:** 559

"Waking Up the Rake" (Hogan), **Supp. IV Part 1:** 415–416, 416

Wakoski, Diane, **Supp. V:** 79; **Supp. XII:** 184; **Supp. XV:** 252; **Supp. XVII:** 112; **Supp. XXIII:** 52; **Supp. XXIV:** 37

Walbridge, John, **Supp. XX:** **125**

Walcott, Charles C., **II:** 49

Walcott, Derek, **Supp. VIII:** 28; **Supp. X:** 122, 131; **Supp. XV:** 256; **Supp. XXIV:** 86

Walcott, Jersey Joe, **Supp. V:** 182

Wald, Alan, **Supp. XV:** 202; **Supp. XVIII:** 223; **Supp. XXI:** 261, 262, 271, 275–276, 277, 278

Wald, Lillian, **Supp. I Part 1:** 12

Walden (Thoreau), **Supp. XIV:** 177, 227; **Supp. XV:** 275; **Supp. XVIII:** 14, 80, 189; **Supp. XXIV:** 73

Walden, Daniel, **Supp. IV Part 2:** 584, 591; **Supp. V:** 272

Walden; or, Life in the Woods (Thoreau), **I:** 219, 305; **II:** 8, 142, 159, 312–313, 458; **IV:** 168, 169, 170, 176, 177–178, 179–182, 183, 187; **Retro. Supp. I:** 62; **Supp. I Part 2:** 579, 655, 664, 672; **Supp. VIII:** 296; **Supp. X:** 27, 101; **Supp. XIII:** 152

Waldman, Anne, **Supp. XIV:** 150; **Supp. XXIII:** 221; **Supp. XXIV:** 33, 41, 45

Waldmeir, Joseph, **III:** 45

Waldmeir, Joseph J., **Supp. I Part 2:** 476

Waldo (Theroux), **Supp. VIII:** 313, 314, **314–315**

Waldo Frank: A Study (Munson), **Supp. XX:** 74

Waldron, Jeremy, **Supp. XVII:** 235

Waldrop, Keith, **Supp. XV:** 153, 165

Waley, Arthur, **II:** 526; **III:** 466; **Supp. V:** 340

"Walk, A" (Snyder), **Supp. VIII:** 297

Walkabout Year: Twelve Months in Australia (Pickering), **Supp. XXI:** 199, 200

"Walk at Sunset, A" (Bryant), **Supp. I Part 1:** 155

"Walk before Mass, A" (Agee), **I:** 28–29

Walker, Alice, **Retro. Supp. I:** 215; **Supp. I Part 2:** 550; **Supp. III Part 2:** 488, **517–540; Supp. IV Part 1:** 14; **Supp. VIII:** 141, 214; **Supp. IX:** 306, 311; **Supp. X:** 85, 228, 252, 325, 330; **Supp. XIII:** 179, 185, 291, 295; **Supp. XVI:** 39; **Supp. XVIII:** 200, 283; **Supp. XX: 84, 107, 108; Supp. XXI:** 172; **Supp. XXII:** 172

Walker, Cheryl, **Supp. XI:** 145

Walker, David, **Supp. V:** 189; **Supp. XVII:** 246

Walker, Franklin D., **III:** 321

Walker, Gue, **Supp. XII:** 207

Walker, Margaret, **Supp. XVIII:** 282; **Supp. XX:** 106

Walker, Marianne, **Supp. VIII:** 139

Walker, Obadiah, **II:** 113

Walker, Scott, **Supp. XV:** 92

Walker in the City, A (Kazin), **Supp. VIII: 93–95,** 99

Walk Hard (Blum and Hill), **Supp. XV:** 194

Walk Hard-Talk Loud (Zinberg), **Supp. XV:** 194, 202

"Walking" (Hogan), **Supp. IV Part 1:** 416

"Walking" (Thoreau), **Supp. IV Part 1:** 416; **Supp. IX:** 178

"Walking Along in Winter" (Kenyon), **Supp. VII:** 167

"Walking around the Block with a Three-Year-Old" (Wagoner), **Supp. IX:** 331–332

"Walking at Noon Near the Burlington Depot in Lincoln, Nebraska" (Kooser), **Supp. XIX:** 122

"Walking Backwards into the Future" (R. Williams), **Supp. IX:** 146

Walking Down the Stairs: Selections from Interviews (Kinnell), **Supp. III Part 1:** 235, 249

"Walking Home" (Schnackenberg). *See* "Laughing with One Eye" (Schnackenberg)

"Walking Home at Night" (Ginsberg), **Supp. II Part 1:** 313

"Walking Is Almost Falling" (Peacock), **Supp. XIX:** 196, 197

Walking Light (Dunn), **Supp. XI:** 140, 141, 153

"Walking Man of Rodin, The" (Sandburg), **III:** 583

"Walking Sticks and Paperweights and Water Marks" (Moore), **III:** 215

Walking Tall (Dunn), **Supp. XI:** 140

Walking the Black Cat (Simic), **Supp. VIII:** 280, **282–284**

Walking to Gatlinburg (Mosher), **Supp. XXII:** 204, 205, 206, 207, 208, 209, 215, **216–217**

Walking to Martha's Vineyard (F. Wright), **Supp. XVII:** 240, 241, 245, 246

"Walking to Sleep" (Wilbur), **Supp. III Part 2:** 557–560

"Walking to Sleep" (Wilbur), **Supp. III Part 2:** 544, 557, 559, 561, 562

"Walking Wounded" (Shaw), **Supp. XIX:** 248

Walkin' the Dog (Mosley), **Supp. XIII:** 242

"Walk in the Moonlight, A" (Anderson), **I:** 114

Walk Me to the Distance (Everett), **Supp. XVIII: 55–56,** 57

Walk on the Wild Side, A (Algren), **Supp. V:** 4; **Supp. IX:** 3, **12–13,** 14

"Walks in Rome" (Merrill), **Supp. III Part 1:** 337

Walk to the River, A (Hoffman), **Supp. XVIII: 77–78**

Walk with Tom Jefferson, A (Levine), **Supp. V:** 179, 187, 190–191

"Wall, The" (Bronk), **Supp. XXI:** 31

"Wall, The" (Brooks), **Supp. III Part 1:** 70, 71, 84

Wall, The (Hersey), **IV:** 4; **Supp. XX: 251**

Wall, The (Rinehart), **Supp. XXV:** 197–198, 200

"Wall, The" (Roethke), **III:** 544

"Wall, The" (Sexton), **Supp. II Part 2:** 696

Wallace, Daniel, **Supp. XXII:** 49

Wallace, David, **Supp. XXI:** 277

Wallace, David Foster, **Retro. Supp. II:** 279; **Supp. X: 301–318; Supp. XVII:** 226; **Supp. XIX:** 223; **Supp. XX: 91, 93; Supp. XXII:** 260, 261

Wallace, Henry, **I:** 489; **III:** 111, 475; **Supp. I Part 1:** 286; **Supp. I Part 2:** 645

Wallace, Jim, **Supp. XX: 143**

Wallace, Mike, **Supp. IV Part 1:** 364; **Supp. IV Part 2:** 526; **Supp. XX: 102**

Wallace, Richard, **Supp. XVIII:** 101–102

Wallace Stevens (Kermode), **Retro. Supp. I:** 301

Wallace Stevens: The Poems of our Climate (Bloom), **Retro. Supp. I:** 299

Wallace Stevens: Words Chosen out of Desire (Stevens), **Retro. Supp. I:** 297

Wallach, Eli, **III:** 161

Wallant, Edward Lewis, **Supp. XVI:** 220

Wallas, Graham, **Supp. I Part 2:** 643

"Walled City" (Oates), **Supp. II Part 2:** 524

Wallenstein, Anna. *See* Weinstein, Mrs. Max (Anna Wallenstein)

Waller, Edmund, **III:** 463

Waller, Fats, **IV:** 263

Waller, Nicole, **Supp. XXII:** 78

Walling, William English, **Supp. I Part 2:** 645; **Supp. XV:** 295

"Wall of Paintings, The" (Notley), **Supp. XXII:** 230

Wall of the Sky, the Wall of the Eye, The (Lethem), **Supp. XVIII:** 139

Walls Do Not Fall, The (Doolittle), **Supp. I Part 1:** 271, 272

Walls of Jericho, The (R. Fisher), **Supp. XIX:** 65, 67, 70, **72–77,** 78

"Wall Songs" (Hogan), **Supp. IV Part 1:** 413

Wall Writing (Auster), **Supp. XII:** 23–24

Walpole, Horace, **I:** 203; **Supp. I Part 2:** 410, 714

Walpole, Hugh, **Retro. Supp. I:** 231; **Supp. XX: 232**

Walpole, Robert, **IV:** 145

Walsh, David M., **Supp. XV:** 5

Walsh, Ed, **II:** 424

Walsh, Ernest, **Supp. XXIV:** 50

Walsh, George, **Supp. IV Part 2:** 528

Walsh, Raoul, **Supp. XIII:** 174

Walsh, Richard J., **Supp. II Part 1:** 119, 130

Walsh, William, **Supp. IV Part 1:** 242, 243, 246, 248, 252, 254, 257

"Walt, the Wounded" (Di Piero), **Supp. XIX:** 37

"Walt and Will" (Apple), **Supp. XVII:** 6

Walter, Eugene, **Supp. XVI:** 230

Walter, Joyce, **Supp. XV:** 121

Walter Benjamin at the Dairy Queen: Reflections at Sixty and Beyond (McMurtry), **Supp. V:** 232

Walters, Barbara, **Supp. XIV:** 125

Walters, Marguerite. *See* Smith, Mrs. Lamar (Marguerite Walters)

"Walter T. Carriman" (O'Hara), **III:** 368

Walton, Izaak, **Supp. I Part 2:** 422

"Walt Whitman" (Kooser), **Supp. XIX:** 118

"Walt Whitman" (Masters), **Supp. I Part 2:** 458

"Walt Whitman at Bear Mountain" (Simpson), **Supp. IX:** 265

Walt Whitman Bathing (Wagoner), **Supp. IX: 331–332**

Walt Whitman Handbook (Allen), **IV:** 352

Walt Whitman Reconsidered (Chase), **IV:** 352

"Waltz, The" (Parker), **Supp. IX:** 204

"Waltzer in the House, The" (Kunitz), **Supp. III Part 1:** 258

Waltzing Matilda (Notley), **Supp. XXII:** 229–230

"Waltzing Matilda" (Notley), **Supp. XXII:** 230

Waltzing the Magpies: A Year in Australia (Pickering), **Supp. XXI:** 199, 200

Walzer, Kevin, **Supp. XII:** 202; **Supp. XV:** 118; **Supp. XVIII:** 174

Wambaugh, Joseph, **Supp. X:** 5; **Supp. XXI:** 67

Wampeters, Foma, & Granfalloons (Vonnegut), **Supp. II Part 2:** 758, 759–760, 776, 779

Wand, David Hsin-fu, **Supp. X:** 292

"Wanderer, The" (W. C. Williams), **Retro. Supp. I:** 414, 421

Wanderer, The: His Parables and His Sayings (Gibran), **Supp. XX: 116, 123–124**

"Wanderers, The" (Welty), **IV:** 273–274

"Wandering Jew, The" (Robinson), **III:** 505, 516–517

Wanderings of Oisin (Yeats), **Supp. I Part 1:** 79

Wang, Dorothy, **Supp. X:** 289

Wang Wei, **Supp. XV:** 47

Waniek, Marilyn Nelson, **Supp. IV Part 1:** 244. *See also* Nelson, Marilyn

Wanking 'Tards (Silver), **Supp. XXIV:** 265

"Wan Lee, the Pagan" (Harte), **Supp. II Part 1:** 351

"Want, The" (Olds), **Supp. X:** 210

Want Bone, The (Pinsky), **Supp. VI:** 236–237, 244–245, 247

"Wanted: An Ontological Critic" (Ransom), **III:** 498

"Wanting to Die" (Sexton), **Supp. II Part 2:** 684, 686; **Supp. XIV:** 132

"Wants" (Paley), **Supp. VI:** 219

Waples, Dorothy, **I:** 348

Wapshot Chronicle, The (Cheever), **Supp. I Part 1:** 174, 177–180, 181, 196

Wapshot Scandal, The (Cheever), **Supp. I Part 1:** 180–184, 187, 191, 196

"War" (Findley), **Supp. XX:** 49

"War" (Jin), **Supp. XVIII:** 93

"War" (Kingston), **Supp. V:** 169

"War" (Simic), **Supp. VIII:** 282

"War, Response, and Contradiction" (Burke), **I:** 283

"War and Peace" (Sanders), **Supp. XVI:** 277

War and Peace (Tolstoy), **I:** 6, 7; **II:** 191, 205, 291; **IV:** 446; **Supp. V:** 277; **Supp. XI:** 68; **Supp. XIV:** 97; **Supp. XXIII:** 11

War and Remembrance (miniseries), **Supp. XXV:** 265

War and Remembrance (Wouk), **Supp. XX:** 243; **Supp. XXV:** 253, 254, 257, 258, 264–265

"War and the Small Nations" (Gibran), **Supp. XX:** 127

War and War (F. Barthelme), **Supp. XI:** 25

"War Between Men and Women, The" (Thurber), **Supp. I Part 2:** 615

War Bulletins (Lindsay), **Supp. I Part 2:** 378–379

Ward, Aileen, **II:** 531

Ward, Artemus (pseudonym). *See* Browne, Charles Farrar

Ward, Douglas Turner, **Supp. IV Part 1:** 362

Ward, Geoff, **Supp. XXIII:** 218

Ward, Henry, **Supp. I Part 2:** 588

Ward, Mrs. Humphry, **II:** 338

Ward, Leo R., **Supp. VIII:** 124

Ward, Lester F., **Supp. I Part 2:** 640; **Supp. XI:** 202, 203

Ward, Lynn, **I:** 31

Ward, Nathaniel, **Supp. I Part 1:** 99, 102, 111, 116

Ward, Susan, **Supp. XXIII:** 146

Ward, Theodora, **I:** 470; **Retro. Supp. I:** 28

Ward, William Hayes, **Supp. I Part 1:** 371

"War Debt, A" (Jewett), **Retro. Supp. II:** 138, 141

"War Diary" (Boyce), **Supp. XVII:** 104; **Supp. XXI:** 6

"War Diary, A" (Bourne), **I:** 229

War Dispatches of Stephen Crane, The (Crane), **I:** 422

"Ward Line, The" (Morris), **III:** 220

Warfel, Harry R., **Supp. I Part 1:** 366

War Games (Morris), **III:** 238

War Goes On, The (Asch), **Supp. XXIII:** 6

"Warhol / Blue Jackie"(Balakian), **Supp. XXIII:** 32

War in Heaven, The (Shepard and Chaikin), **Supp. III Part 2:** 433

War Is Kind (Crane), **I:** 409; **III:** 585

"War Is Kind" (Crane), **I:** 419

Warlock (Harrison), **Supp. VIII:** 45, **46**

Warm as Wool (Sanders), **Supp. XVI:** 269

"Warming" (Trethewey), **Supp. XXI:** 245

Warner, Anna, **Supp. XVIII:** 258–275

Warner, Charles Dudley, **II:** 405; **IV:** 198

Warner, Jack, **Supp. XII:** 160–161; **Supp. XVIII:** 249

Warner, John R., **III:** 193

Warner, Oliver, **I:** 548

Warner, Susan, **Retro. Supp. I:** 246; **Supp. XV:** 275; **Supp. XVIII:** 257–275

Warner, Sylvia Townsend, **Supp. VIII:** 151, 155, 164, 171

Warner, W. Lloyd, **III:** 60

Warner Family and the Warner Books, The (Baker), **Supp. XVIII:** 259, 267

"Warning" (Hughes), **Supp. I Part 1:** 343

"Warning" (Pound), **III:** 474

"Warning, The" (Creeley), **Supp. IV Part 1:** 150

"Warning, The" (Longfellow), **II:** 498

Warning Hill (Marquand), **III:** 55–56, 60, 68

"War of Eyes, A" (Coleman), **Supp. XI:** 93–94

War of Eyes and Other Stories, A (Coleman), **Supp. XI:** 91–92

War of the Classes (London), **II:** 466

"War of the Wall, The" (Bambara), **Supp. XI:** 15–16

"War of Vaslav Nijinsky, The" (Bidart), **Supp. XV:** 21–22, **27–29**

Warp (Grossman), **Supp. XXV:** 64, 65–66

"War Poems" (Sandburg), **III:** 581

Warren, Austin, **I:** 265, 268, 271; **Supp. I Part 2:** 423

Warren, David, **Supp. XXIV:** 269

Warren, Earl, **III:** 581

Warren, Gabriel, **IV:** 244

Warren, Mercy Otis, **Supp. XV:** 230

Warren, Patricia Nell, **Supp. XX:** 259–276

Warren, Robert Penn, **I:** 190, 211, 517; **II:** 57, 217, 228, 253; **III:** 134, 310, 382–383, 454, 482, 485, 490, 496, 497; **IV:** 121, 122, 123, 125, 126, **236–259,** 261, 262, 279, 340–341, 458; **Retro. Supp. I:** 40, 41, 73, 90; **Retro. Supp. II:** 220, 235; **Supp. I Part 1:** 359, 371; **Supp. I Part 2:** 386, 423; **Supp. II Part 1:** 139; **Supp. III Part 2:** 542; **Supp. V:** 261, 316, 318, 319, 333; **Supp. VIII:** 126, 176; **Supp. IX:** 257; **Supp. X:** 1, 25, 26; **Supp. XI:** 315; **Supp. XII:** 254, 255; **Supp. XIV:** 1, 2, 3, 4, 11, 14, 15; **Supp. XVIII:** 77, 78–79; **Supp. XIX:** 246; **Supp.**

XXI: 256

Warren, Mrs. Robert Penn (Eleanor Clark), **IV:** 244

Warren, Rosanna, **IV:** 244; **Supp. XV:** 251, 261, 262, 263; **Supp. XIX:** 34

Warren, Vincent, **Supp. XXIII:** 218, 219

Warrington Poems, The (Ríos), **Supp. IV Part 2:** 540

Warrior, Robert Allen, **Supp. IV Part 1:** 329

"Warrior, The" (Gunn Allen), **Supp. IV Part 1:** 326

"Warrior: 5th Grade" (Olds), **Supp. X:** 214

"Warrior Road" (Harjo), **Supp. XII:** 217

"Warrior's Daughter, A" (Zitkala-Ša), **Supp. XXV:** 274, 275, 282

Wars, The (Findley), **Supp. XX:** **53–54**

Warsh, Lewis, **Supp. XXIV:** 41

Warshavsky, Isaac (pseudonym). *See* Singer, Isaac Bashevis

Warshow, Robert, **Supp. I Part 1:** 51

Wars I Have Seen (Stein), **IV:** 27, 36, 477

Wartime (Fussell), **Supp. V:** 241

War Trash (Jin), **Supp. XVIII:** 89, **100–101**

"War Widow, The" (Frederic), **II:** 135–136

"Was" (Creeley), **Supp. IV Part 1:** 155

"Was" (Faulkner), **II:** 71

"Wash" (Faulkner), **II:** 72

Wash, Richard, **Supp. XII:** 14

"Washboard Wizard" (Nelson), **Supp. XVIII:** 182

"Washed in the Rain" (Fante), **Supp. XI:** 165

"Washing of Hands, A" (Kooser), **Supp. XIX:** 115

Washington, Booker T., **Supp. I Part 2:** 393; **Supp. II Part 1:** 157, 160, 167, 168, 171, 225; **Supp. XIV:** 198, 199, 201; **Supp. XVIII:** 121–122

Washington, D.C. (Vidal), **Supp. IV Part 2:** 677, 684, 686–687, 690

Washington, George, **I:** 453; **II:** 313–314; **Supp. I Part 2:** 399, 485, 508, 509, 511, 513, 517, 518, 520, 599

Washington, Mary Helen, **Supp. XVIII:** 119, 284

Washington and His Generals (Lippard), **Supp. XXIII:** 178, **185–186,** 187

Washington Crossing the Delaware (Rivers), **Supp. XV:** 186

Washington Post Book World (Lesser), **Supp. IV Part 2:** 453; **Supp. VIII:** 80, 84, 241; **Supp. X:** 282

Washington Square (James), **II:** 327, 328; **Retro. Supp. I:** 215, 220, **222–223**

"Washington Square, 1946" (Ozick), **Supp. V:** 272

Washington Square Ensemble, The (Bell), **Supp. X:** 1, **3–4**

"Washman"(P. Benedict), **Supp. XXIII:** 40

"Was Lowell an Historical Critic?" (Altick), **Supp. I Part 2:** 423

Wasserman, Earl R., **Supp. I Part 2:** 439, 440

Wasserman, Jakob, **Supp. I Part 2:** 669

Wasserstein, Wendy, **Supp. IV Part 1:** 309; **Supp. XV: 319–336; Supp. XXIV:** 116, 117, 119, 128
Wasson, Ben, **Retro. Supp. I:** 79, 83
"Waste Carpet, The" (Matthews), **Supp. IX: 158–159**
Waste Land, The (T. S. Eliot), **I:** 107, 266, 298, 395, 396, 482, 570–571, 572, 574–575, 577–578, 580, 581, 584, 585, 586, 587; **III:** 6–8, 12, 196, 277–278, 453, 471, 492, 586; **IV:** 122, 123, 124, 140, 418, 419, 420; **Retro. Supp. I:** 51, 60, **60–62,** 63, 64, 66, 210, 290, 291, 299, 311, 420, 427; **Retro. Supp. II:** 85, 121, 190; **Supp. I Part 1:** 272; **Supp. I Part 2:** 439, 455, 614; **Supp. II Part 1:** 4, 5, 11, 96; **Supp. III Part 1:** 9, 10, 41, 63, 105; **Supp. IV Part 1:** 47, 284; **Supp. V:** 338; **Supp. IX:** 158, 305; **Supp. X:** 125; **Supp. XIII:** 341–342, 344, 346; **Supp. XIV:** 6, 284; **Supp. XV:** 21, 181, 261, 306; **Supp. XVI:** 204; **Supp. XVII:** 140–141, 144, 227; **Supp. XVIII:** 78, 79–80; **Supp. XIX:** 288; **Supp. XXIII:** 23, 25, 79, 165; **Supp. XXIV:** 140
"Waste Land, The": A Facsimile and Transcript of the Original Drafts Including the Annotations of Ezra Pound (Eliot, ed.), **Retro. Supp. I:** 58
Waste Land and Other Poems, The (T. S. Eliot), **Supp. XV:** 305
Wat, Alexander, **Supp. XVI:** 155, 161
Watch, The (Bass), **Supp. XVI: 16–17**
"Watch, The, —" (Bass), **Supp. XVI:** 17
Watch and Ward (James), **II:** 323; **Retro. Supp. I:** 218, **219,** 220
"Watcher" (Trethewey), **Supp. XXI:** 247
"Watcher, The" (R. Bly), **Supp. IV Part 1:** 71
"Watcher by the Dead, A" (Bierce), **I:** 203
Watchfires (Auchincloss), **Supp. IV Part 1:** 23
"Watching Crow, Looking toward the Manzano Mountains" (Harjo), **Supp. XII:** 219
"Watching the Oregon Whale" (A. Finch), **Supp. XVII:** 77
"Watching the Sunset" (Coleman), **Supp. XI:** 92
"Watching the Vulture at the Road Kill" (Stallings), **Supp. XXV:** 230
Watch on the Rhine (Hellman), **Supp. I Part 1:** 276, 278, 279–281, 283–284; **Supp. IV Part 1:** 83
"Water" (Emerson), **II:** 19
"Water" (Komunyakaa), **Supp. XIII:** 132
"Water" (Lowell), **II:** 550
"Waterbird" (Swenson), **Supp. IV Part 2:** 651
"Water Borders" (Dillard), **Supp. VI:** 27
"Water Buffalo" (Komunyakaa), **Supp. XIII:** 122
"Watercolor of Grantchester Meadows" (Plath), **Supp. I Part 2:** 537
Water Cure, The (Everett), **Supp. XVIII: 64–66**
"Water Drum"(Kenny), **Supp. XXIII:** 144

"Waterfall, The" (Clampitt), **Supp. IX:** 44
Waterfront (Schulberg), **Supp. XVIII: 251–252**
"Water Hose Is on Fire, The" (Simic), **Supp. XV:** 185
Waterhouse, Keith, **Supp. VIII:** 124
"Waterlily Fire" (Rukeyser), **Supp. VI:** 285, 286
Waterlily Fire: Poems 1935–1962 (Rukeyser), **Supp. VI:** 274, 283, 285
Watermark (Brodsky), **Supp. VIII:** 29
Water-Method Man, The (Irving), **Supp. VI:** 163, **167–179,** 180
Water Music (Boyle), **Supp. VIII:** 1, 3–5, 8, 14; **Supp. XX: 20–22**
"Water Music for the Progress of Love in a Life-Raft Down the Sammamish Slough" (Wagoner), **Supp. IX:** 326
"Water People" (Burke), **Supp. XIV:** 21
"Water Picture" (Swenson), **Supp. IV Part 2:** 641
"Water Rising" (Hogan), **Supp. IV Part 1:** 400
Waters, Ethel, **II:** 587
Waters, Frank, **Supp. X:** 124
Waters, Muddy, **Supp. VIII:** 345
Watershed (Everett), **Supp. XVIII: 58–59, 64**
"Watershed" (Kingsolver), **Supp. VII:** 208
"Watershed" (Warren), **IV:** 239
"Watershed, The" (Auden), **Supp. II Part 1:** 5
Waters of Kronos, The (Richter), **Supp. XVIII:** 207, 208, **218–219,** 220
Waters of Siloe, The (Merton), **Supp. VIII:** 196, 208
Waterston, Sam, **Supp. IX:** 253
Water Street (Merrill), **Supp. III Part 1:** 321–323
"Water Walker" (Wilbur), **Supp. III Part 2:** 548, 560
Water-Witch, The (Cooper), **I:** 342–343
"Water Witch"(P. Benedict), **Supp. XXIII:** 38
Waterworks, The (Doctorow), **Supp. IV Part 1:** 218, 222, 223, 231–233, 234
"Water Works, The" (Doctorow), **Supp. IV Part 1:** 234
Watkin, E. I., **Retro. Supp. II:** 187
Watkins, Floyd C., **IV:** 452
Watkins, James T., **I:** 193, 194
Watkins, Maureen, **Supp. XVI:** 188
Watkins, Mel, **Supp. X:** 330; **Supp. XIII:** 246
Watman, Max, **Supp. XX: 92**
Watrous, Peter, **Supp. VIII:** 79
Watson, Brook, **Supp. XX: 284**
Watson, Burton, **Supp. XV:** 47
Watson, James Sibley, Jr., **I:** 261
Watson, Jay, **Supp. XVIII:** 195; **Supp. XXI:** 46
Watson, J. B., **II:** 361
Watson, Julia, **Supp. XXV:** 8
Watson, Richard, **Supp. I Part 2:** 516, 517
Watson, William, **II:** 114

Watsonville: Some Place Not Here (Moraga), **Supp. XXIII:** 195, 196, 202, 203
Watt, Ian, **Supp. VIII:** 4
Watteau, Jean Antoine, **III:** 275; **IV:** 79
Watts, Emily Stipes, **Supp. I Part 1:** 115
Waugh, Arthur, **Supp. XXIV:** 30
Waugh, Evelyn, **I:** 480; **III:** 281; **Supp. I Part 2:** 607; **Supp. IV Part 2:** 688; **Supp. XI:** 305, 306; **Supp. XIX:** 131; **Supp. XXV:** 70
Waugh, Robert H., **Supp. XXV:** 123
"Wave" (Snyder), **Supp. VIII:** 299
Wave, A (Ashbery), **Supp. III Part 1:** 1, 4, 24–26
"Wave, A" (Ashbery), **Supp. III Part 1:** 9, 19, 24–25
"Wave, The" (MacLeish), **III:** 19
"Wave, The" (Untermeyer), **Supp. XV:** 300
Wave Amplitude in the Mona Passage (Schott), **Supp. XXIII: 242–243**
"Wavemaker Falters, The" (Saunders), **Supp. XIX:** 225
"Waxwings" (Francis), **Supp. IX:** 82
Way, The (Steiner and Witt, eds.), **Supp. IV Part 2:** 505
"Way Down, The" (Kunitz), **Supp. III Part 1:** 263
"Way It Is, The" (Ellison), **Supp. II Part 1:** 245
"Way It Is, The" (Jones), **Supp. XI:** 229
Way It Is, The (Stafford), **Supp. XIII:** 274
"Way It Is, The" (Strand), **Supp. IV Part 2:** 627
"Wayland" (Sanders), **Supp. XVI:** 275
Wayne, John, **Supp. IV Part 1:** 200
Way of Chuang-Tzu, The (Merton), **Supp. VIII:** 208
"Way of Exchange in James Dickey's Poetry, The" (Weatherby), **Supp. IV Part 1:** 175
Way of Life According to Laotzu, The (Bynner), **Supp. XV:** 46, 48
Way Out, A (Frost), **Retro. Supp. I:** 133
Wayside Motor Inn, The (Gurney), **Supp. V:** 96, 105, 109
"Ways of Breaking: Lynda Hull's 'Ornithology' " (Jauss), **Supp. XXI:** 139
"Ways of Talking" (Jin), **Supp. XVIII:** 93
Ways of the Hour, The (Cooper), **I:** 354
Ways of White Folks, The (Hughes), **Retro. Supp. I:** 203, 204; **Supp. I Part 1:** 329, 330, 332
Way Some People Die, The (Macdonald), **Supp. IV Part 2:** 470, 471, 472, 474
Way Some People Live, The (Cheever), **Supp. I Part 1:** 175
"Way the Cards Fall, The" (Komunyakaa), **Supp. XIII:** 117
"Way the Luck Runs, The" (Wolfert), **Supp. XXI:** 265
"Way Things Are, The" (Turow, unpub.), **Supp. XVII:** 215, 218
Way to Rainy Mountain, The (Momaday), **Supp. IV Part 2:** 485–486, 487–489, 491, 493

Way to Wealth, The (Franklin), **II:** 101–102, 110; **Supp. XX:** 27

Wayward and the Seeking, The: A Collection of Writings by Jean Toomer (Toomer), **Supp. III Part 2:** 478–481, 484, 487

Wayward Bus, The (Steinbeck), **IV:** 51, 64–65

"Way We Live Now, The" (Sontag), **Supp. III Part 2:** 467–468

"Way You'll Never Be, A" (Hemingway), **II:** 249

"W. D. Sees Himself Animated" (Snodgrass), **Supp. VI:** 327

"W. D. Sits in Kafka's Chair and Is Interrogated Concerning the Assumed Death of Cock Robin" (Snodgrass), **Supp. VI:** 319

"W. D. Tries to Warn Cock Robin" (Snodgrass), **Supp. VI:** 319

"We" (Alexander), **Supp. XVIII:** 185

Weaks, Mary Louise, **Supp. X:** 5

Weales, Gerald, **II:** 602

"Wealth," from *Conduct of Life, The* (Emerson), **II:** 2, 3–4

"Wealth," from *English Traits* (Emerson), **II:** 6

Wealth of Nations, The (A. Smith), **II:** 109

"We Are Looking at You, Agnes" (Caldwell), **I:** 309

We Are Still Married: Stories and Letters (Keillor), **Supp. XVI:** 176, 177

"We Are the Crazy Lady and Other Feisty Feminist Fables" (Ozick), **Supp. V:** 259

Weary Blues, The (Hughes), **Retro. Supp. I:** 195, 197, 198, 199, 200, 203, 205; **Supp. I Part 1:** 325

"Weary Blues, The" (Hughes), **Retro. Supp. I:** 198, 199; **Supp. I Part 1:** 324, 325

"Weary Kingdom" (Irving), **Supp. VI:** 163

Weasels and Wisemen: Ethics and Ethnicity in the Work of David Mamet (Kane), **Supp. XIV:** 250

Weather and the Women Treat Me Fair, The (Everett), **Supp. XVIII:** 66

Weatherby, H. L., **Supp. IV Part 1:** 175

Weather Central (Kooser), **Supp. XIX:** 116, **123–125**

"Weathering Out" (Dove), **Supp. IV Part 1:** 248

"Weather Within, The" (M. F. K. Fisher), **Supp. XVII:** 88, 91

Weaver, Harriet, **III:** 471

Weaver, James, **Supp. XVIII:** 72

Weaver, Michael, **Supp. XVIII:** 176, 177

Weaver, Mike, **Retro. Supp. I:** 430

Weaver, Will, **Supp. XVI:** 39

"Weaving" (Larcom), **Supp. XIII:** 142, **Supp. XIII:** 144–145, 150, 151

"Web" (Oliver), **Supp. VII:** 236

Web and the Rock, The (Wolfe), **IV:** 451, 455, 457, 459–460, 462, 464, 467, 468

Webb, Beatrice, **Supp. I Part 1:** 5

Webb, Mary, **I:** 226

Webb, Phyllis, **Supp. XX:** 56

Webb, Sidney, **Supp. I Part 1:** 5

Webb, W. P., **Supp. V:** 225

Webber, A. R. F., **Supp. XXI:** 160

Weber, Brom, **I:** 383, 386

Weber, Carl, **Supp. IX:** 133, 138, 141

Weber, Max, **I:** 498; **Supp. I Part 2:** 637, 648

Weber, Sarah, **Supp. I Part 1:** 2

Weberman, A. J., **Supp. XVIII:** 27

Web of Earth, The (Wolfe), **IV:** 451–452, 456, 458, 464, 465

Web of Iniquity, The (Nickerson), **Supp. XXV:** 200

"Web of Life, The" (Nemerov), **III:** 282

Webster, Brenda, **Supp. XVI:** 157, 161

Webster, Daniel, **II:** 5, 9; **Supp. I Part 2:** 659, 687, 689, 690

Webster, John, **I:** 384; **Supp. I Part 2:** 422

Webster, Noah, **Supp. I Part 2:** 660; **Supp. II Part 1:** 77

Wector, Dixon, **II:** 103

Wedding, The (D. West), **Supp. XVIII:** 277, **287–289**

"Wedding, The" (Everwine), **Supp. XV:** 83

"Wedding, The" (Major), **Supp. XXII:** 185

Wedding, The (television miniseries), **Supp. XVIII:** 277, 289

"Wedding Cake" (Nye), **Supp. XIII:** 283

"Wedding Dance, The" (Di Piero), **Supp. XIX:** 47

"Wedding Day" (Boyle), **Supp. XXIV:** 56–57

Wedding Day and Other Stories (Boyle), **Supp. XXIV: 56–57**

"Wedding in Brownsville, A" (Singer), **IV:** 15

Wedding in Hell, A (Simic), **Supp. VIII:** 280, **282**

"Wedding of the Rose and Lotus, The" (Lindsay), **Supp. I Part 2:** 387

"Wedding Supper, The" (Rowson), **Supp. XV:** 243

"Wedding Toast, A" (Wilbur), **Supp. III Part 2:** 561

Wedekind, Frank, **III:** 398; **Supp. XX:** 85; **Supp. XXII:** 23

Wedge, The (W. C. Williams), **Retro. Supp. I:** 424

"We Didn't"(Dybek), **Supp. XXIII:** 77–78

"Wednesday at the Waldorf" (Swenson), **Supp. IV Part 2:** 647

We Don't Live Here Anymore (Dubus), **Supp. XXIV:** 97

"We Don't Live Here Anymore" (Dubus), **Supp. VII:** 78–79, 85

"Weed" (McCarriston), **Supp. XIV:** 259, 273

"Weed, The" (Bishop), **Supp. I Part 1:** 80, 88–89

"Weed, The" (Taggard), **Supp. XXII:** 284

"Weeds, The" (McCarthy), **II:** 566

"Weekend" (Beattie), **Supp. V:** 27

"Weekend" (Hempel), **Supp. XXI:** 124

Weekend, The (Cameron), **Supp. XII:** 80, 81, **86–88**

"Weekend at Ellerslie, A" (Wilson), **IV:** 431

Weekend Edition (National Public Radio), **Supp. IX:** 299; **Supp. XVII:** 240, 242

Weekend in Dinlock (Sigal), **Supp. XXIII:** 166

"Week in the Word, A" (Hampl), **Supp. XXII:** 85

Week on the Concord and Merrimack Rivers, A (Thoreau), **IV:** 168, 169, 177, 182–183; **Supp. I Part 2:** 420; **Supp. XIV:** 227

Weeks, Edward, **III:** 64

Weeks, Jerome, **Supp. VIII:** 76

"Weeping Burgher" (Stevens), **IV:** 77

"Weeping Women" (Levertov), **Supp. III Part 1:** 282

We Fished All Night (W. Motley), **Supp. XVII: 155–158,** 159, 160

We Fly Away (Francis), **Supp. IX: 79–80,** 84

We Happy Few (Hinojosa), **Supp. XIX:** 99, **111–112**

We Have Always Lived in the Castle (Jackson), **Supp. IX:** 121, 126, **127–128**

"We Have Our Arts So We Won't Die of Truth" (Bradbury), **Supp. IV Part 1:** 105

We Have Tomorrow (Bontemps), **Supp. XXII:** 6, 12

Weich, Dave, **Supp. XII:** 321; **Supp. XVIII:** 91

"Weighing In" (Espaillat), **Supp. XXI:** 111

"Weight" (Wideman), **Supp. X:** 321

"Weights" (C. Baxter), **Supp. XVII:** 16

Weigl, Bruce, **Supp. VIII:** 269, 274; **Supp. XV:** 342; **Supp. XIX: 273–290**

Weik, Alexa, **Supp. XXIV:** 64

Weil, Dorothy, **Supp. XV:** 231

Weil, James L., **Supp. XXI:** 23, 31

Weil, Robert, **Supp. IX:** 236

Weil, Simone, **I:** 298; **Supp. XV:** 259; **Supp. XXII:** 93

Weiland (C. B. Brown), **Supp. XIII:** 100

Weinauer, Ellen, **Supp. XV:** 270, 284

Weinberger, Eliot, **Supp. IV Part 1:** 66; **Supp. VIII:** 290, 292; **Supp. XVI:** 284

Weinberger, Eric, **Supp. XXII:** 264

Weinfield, Henry, **Supp. XXI:** 24, 28, 33

Weininger, Otto, **Retro. Supp. I:** 416

Weinraub, Judith, **Supp. XXI:** 39

Weinreb, Mindy, **Supp. X:** 24

Weinreich, Regina, **Supp. XIV:** 22

Weinstein, Cindy, **Supp. XVIII:** 261

Weinstein, Hinda, **IV:** 285

Weinstein, Max, **IV:** 285

Weinstein, Mrs. Max (Anna Wallenstein), **IV:** 285, 287

Weinstein, Nathan. *See* West, Nathanael

Weinstein, Selma, **Supp. XXI:** 170

Weir, Sybil, **Supp. XXIV:** 20

Weisheit, Rabbi, **IV:** 76

Weismuller, Johnny, **Supp. X:** 264; **Supp. XX:** 18

Weiss, David, **Supp. XVI:** 55

Weiss, Jane, **Supp. XVIII:** 267, 269

Weiss, Peter, **IV:** 117

Weiss, Theodore, **Supp. IV Part 2:** 440; **Supp. IX:** 96

Weissleder, Paul, **Supp. XXII:** 283
Weist, Dianne, **Supp. X:** 80
Weithas, Art, **Supp. XI:** 231
Welch, Dave, **Supp. XXI:** 118
Welch, Don, **Supp. XIX:** 119
Welch, James, **Supp. IV Part 1:** 404; **Supp. IV Part 2:** 503, 513, 557, 562; **Supp. XXIV:** 257
Welch, Lew, **Supp. V:** 170; **Supp. VIII:** 303; **Supp. XXII:** 276
"Welcome from War" (Rukeyser), **Supp. VI:** 286
"Welcome Morning" (Sexton), **Supp. II Part 2:** 696
"Welcome the Wrath" (Kunitz), **Supp. III Part 1:** 261
Welcome to Hard Times (Doctorow), **Supp. IV Part 1:** 218, 219–220, 222, 224, 230, 238
Welcome to Hard Times (film), **Supp. IV Part 1:** 236
"Welcome to New Dork" (Leonard), **Supp. XVIII:** 148
Welcome to Our City (Wolfe), **IV:** 461
Welcome to the Monkey House (Vonnegut), **Supp. II Part 2:** 758
Welcome to the Moon (Shanley), **Supp. XIV:** 318
Welcome to the Moon and Other Plays (Shanley), **Supp. XIV:** 315, **316–319**
Weld, Theodore, **Supp. I Part 2:** 587, 588
Weld, Tuesday, **Supp. XI:** 306
Welded (O'Neill), **III:** 390; **Supp. XXII:** 24
"Welfare Worker, Disenchanted, Contemplates Friday Afternoon, The" (Trethewey), **Supp. XXI:** 246
"Well, The" (Momaday), **Supp. IV Part 2:** 483
"Well Dressed Man with a Beard, The" (Stevens), **Retro. Supp. I:** 297
Wellek, René, **I:** 253, 261, 282; **II:** 320; **Supp. XIV:** 12, 14
Weller, George, **III:** 322
Welles, Gideon, **Supp. I Part 2:** 484
Welles, Orson, **IV:** 476; **Supp. I Part 1:** 67; **Supp. IV Part 1:** 82, 83; **Supp. V:** 251; **Supp. VIII:** 46; **Supp. XI:** 169, 307
"Wellfleet Whale, The" (Kunitz), **Supp. III Part 1:** 263, 269
Wellfleet Whale and Companion Poems, The (Kunitz), **Supp. III Part 1:** 263
Wellink, Yvonne, **Supp. XVIII:** 257
Wellman, Flora, **II:** 463–464, 465
Wellman, Rita, **Supp. XXV:** 20
"Well Rising, The" (Stafford), **Supp. XI:** 318
Wells, H. G., **I:** 103, 226, 241, 243, 253, 405, 409, 415; **II:** 82, 144, 276, 337, 338, 458; **III:** 456; **IV:** 340, 455; **Retro. Supp. I:** 100, 228, 231; **Supp. XVI:** 190; **Supp. XXI:** 8
Wellspring, The (Olds), **Supp. X:** 211–212
Well Wrought Urn, The: Studies in the Structure of Poetry (Brooks), **Supp. XIV:** 1, **8–9**, 14, 15, 16

Welsh, Mary, **Supp. XIX:** 248. *See also* Hemingway, Mrs. Ernest (Mary Welsh)
Welty, Eudora, **II:** 194, 217, 606; **IV: 260–284; Retro. Supp. I:** 339–358; **Retro. Supp. II:** 235; **Supp. IV Part 2:** 474; **Supp. V:** 59, 315, 336; **Supp. VIII:** 94, 151, 171; **Supp. X:** 42, 290; **Supp. XII:** 310, 322; **Supp. XIV:** 3; **Supp. XV:** 338; **Supp. XXIV:** 223
Welty, Eurora, **Supp. XIX:** 151
Weltzien, O. Alan, **Supp. XVI:** 20–21, 28
"We miss Her, not because We see—" (Dickinson), **Retro. Supp. I:** 46
We Must Dance My Darlings (Trilling), **Supp. I Part 1:** 297
Wendell, Barrett, **III:** 507; **Supp. I Part 2:** 414; **Supp. XIV:** 197
Wendell, Sarah. *See* Holmes, Mrs. Abiel (Sarah Wendell)
Wendy Wasserstein: A Casebook (Barnett), **Supp. XV:** 323, 330
"Wendy Wasserstein's Three Sisters: Squandered Privilege" (Brewer), **Supp. XV:** 330
Wenner, Jann S., **Supp. XXIV:** 280, 283
Wept of Wish-ton-Wish, The (Cooper), **I:** 339, 342, 350
Werbe, Peter, **Supp. XIII:** 236
"We Real Cool" (Brooks), **Supp. III Part 1:** 80
"We're All Pharaohs When We Die" (Gallagher), **Supp. XXIV:** 170
We're Back! A Dinosaur's Story (screenplay, Shanley), **Supp. XIV:** 316
"We're Friends Again" (O'Hara), **III:** 372–373
"Were the Whole Realm of Nature Mine" (Watts), **I:** 458
Werewolf (M. Sommers), **Supp. XVII:** 55
Were-Wolf, The (C. Housman), **Supp. XVII:** 55
Werewolf of Paris, The (Endore), **Supp. XVII:** 55–56
Werewolves in Their Youth (Chabon), **Supp. XI:** 66, **76–77**
Werlock, Abby, **Supp. XIII:** 293
Werthman, Michael, **Supp. V:** 115
"Wer-Trout, The" (Proulx), **Supp. VII:** 255–256
Wescott, Glenway, **I:** 288; **II:** 85; **III:** 448, 454; **Supp. VIII:** 156; **Supp. XIV:** 342; **Supp. XVI:** 195
"We Shall All Be Born Again But We Shall Not All Be Saved" (Matthews), **Supp. IX:** 162
West, Anthony, **Supp. IV Part 1:** 284
West, Benjamin, **Supp. I Part 2:** 511
West, Dorothy, **Supp. XIII:** 295; **Supp. XVIII: 277–291; Supp. XIX:** 72
West, James, **II:** 562
West, Nathanael, **I:** 97, 107, 190, 211, 298; **II:** 436; **III:** 357, 425; **IV: 285–307; Retro. Supp. II: 321–341; Supp. IV Part 1:** 203; **Supp. VIII:** 97; **Supp. XI:** 85, 105, 159, 296; **Supp. XII:** 173, 310; **Supp. XIII:** 106, 170; **Supp. XVIII:** 251, 253, 254

West, Nathaniel, **Supp. XIX:** 223
West, Ray, **Supp. XV:** 142
West, Rebecca, **II:** 412, 445; **Supp. XVI:** 152, 153
Westall, Julia Elizabeth. *See* Wolfe, Mrs. William Oliver (Julia Elizabeth Westall)
"We Stand United" (Benét), **Supp. XI:** 46
"West Authentic, The: Willa Cather" (Stegner), **Supp. IV Part 2:** 608
"West Coast, The: Region with a View" (Stegner), **Supp. IV Part 2:** 608–609
"West Coast Waterfront: End of an Era" (Swados), **Supp. XIX:** 264
Westcott, Edward N., **II:** 102
"Western Association of Writers" (Chopin), **Supp. I Part 1:** 217
"Western Ballad, A" (Ginsberg), **Supp. II Part 1:** 311
Western Borders, The (Howe), **Supp. IV Part 2:** 424–425
Western Canon (Bloom), **Supp. XXV:** 251
Western Canon: The Books and Schools of the Ages (Bloom), **Supp. IX:** 146
Western Lands, The (Burroughs), **Supp. III Part 1:** 106
"Western North Carolina" (Halliday), **Supp. XIX:** 85
Western Star (Benét), **Supp. XI:** 46, 47, 57
"Westland" (C. Baxter), **Supp. XVII:** 18, 19
"West Marginal Way" (Hugo), **Supp. VI:** 131, 135
West of Eden: Writers in Hollywood, 1928–1940 (Fine), **Supp. XVIII:** 248
West of Yesterday, East of Summer: New and Selected Poems, 1973–1993 (Monette), **Supp. X:** 159
West of Your City (Stafford), **Supp. XI:** 316, **317–318**, 321, 322
Weston, Jessie L., **II:** 540; **III:** 12; **Supp. I Part 2:** 438
"West Real" (Ríos), **Supp. IV Part 2:** 539, 540
West-running Brook (Frost), **II:** 155; **Retro. Supp. I:** 136, 137
"West-running Brook" (Frost), **II:** 150, 162–164
"West Wall" (Merwin), **Supp. III Part 1:** 355
"Westward Beach, A" (Jeffers), **Supp. II Part 2:** 418
Westward Ho (Harrison), **Supp. VIII:** 51, **52**
Westward the Course of Empire (Leutze), **Supp. X:** 307
"Westward the Course of Empire Takes Its Way" (Wallace), **Supp. X: 307–308; Supp. XXII:** 260
"West Wind" (Oliver), **Supp. VII:** 246
"West Wind, The" (Bryant), **Supp. I Part 1:** 155
West Wind: Poems and Prose Poems (Oliver), **Supp. VII:** 243, 246–248
"Wet Casements" (Ashbery), **Supp. III Part 1:** 18–20

We the Living (film), **Supp. IV Part 2:** 520

We the Living (Rand), **Supp. IV Part 2:** 520–521

Wetherell, Elizabeth (pseudonym). *See* Warner, Susan

Wet Parade (Sinclair), **Supp. V:** 289

Wetzsteon, Ross, **Supp. XXI:** 12

"We've Adjusted Too Well" (O'Brien), **Supp. V:** 247

Wevill, David, **Retro. Supp. II:** 247, 249

"We Wear the Mask" (Dunbar), **Supp. II Part 1:** 199, 207, 209–210

We Will Be Citizens: New Essays on Gay and Lesbian Theatre (Fischer, ed.), **Supp. XXIV:** 263

Weybright, Victor, **Supp. XIII:** 172

Weyden, Rogier van der, **Supp. IV Part 1:** 284

Whalen, Marcella, **Supp. I Part 1:** 49

Whalen, Philip, **Supp. VIII:** 289; **Supp. XXII:** 226

Whalen-Bridge, John, **Retro. Supp. II:** 211–212

"Whales off Wales, The" (X. J. Kennedy), **Supp. XV:** 163

"Whales Weep" (Boyle), **Supp. XX: 19**

"Whales Weep Not!" (D. H. Lawrence), **Supp. XVII:** 77

Wharton, Edith, **I:** 12, 375; **II:** 96, 180, 183, 186, 189–190, 193, 283, 338, 444, 451; **III:** 69, 175, 576; **IV:** 8, 53, 58, **308–330; Retro. Supp. I:** 108, 232, **359–385; Supp. IV Part 1:** 23, 31, 35, 36, 80, 81, 310; **Supp. IX:** 57; **Supp. XII:** 308; **Supp. XIV:** 337, 347; **Supp. XVI:** 189; **Supp. XVIII:** 278; **Supp. XX: 227, 229, 232, 239, 240; Supp. XXIII:** 275; **Supp. XXIV:** 29, 64; **Supp. XXV:** 201

Wharton, Edward Robbins, **IV:** 310, 313–314, 319

"What" (Dunn), **Supp. XI:** 144

What a Kingdom It Was (Kinnell), **Supp. III Part 1:** 235, 238, 239

"What America Would Be Like without Blacks" (Ellison), **Retro. Supp. II:** 123

What Are Masterpieces (Stein), **IV:** 30–31

What Are Years (Moore), **III:** 208–209, 210, 215

"What Are Years?" (Moore), **III:** 211, 213

What a Way to Go (Morris), **III:** 230–232

"What a Wonder among the Instruments Is the Walloping Trombone!" (Carruth), **Supp. XVI:** 51

"What Became of the Flappers?" (Zelda Fitzgerald), **Supp. IX:** 71

"What Can I Tell My Bones?" (Roethke), **III:** 546, 549

What Century? (O'Hara), **Supp. XXIII:** 216

"What Child Is This?" (Jarman), **Supp. XVII:** 113–114, 115

"What Do We Have Here" (Carson), **Supp. XII: 101**

"What Do We See" (Rukeyser), **Supp. VI:** 282

What Do Women Want? Bread Roses Sex Power (Jong), **Supp. V:** 115, 117, 129, 130

"What Do You Do in San Francisco?" (Carver), **Supp. III Part 1:** 143

What Dreams My Come (Atherton as Frank Lin), **Supp. XXIV:** 28

What D'Ya Know for Sure (Zinberg), **Supp. XV:** 196

Whatever Happened to Gloomy Gus of the Chicago Bears? (Coover), **Supp. V:** 51, 52

Whatever Happened to Jacy Farrow? (Cleveland), **Supp. V:** 222

"What Every Boy Should Know" (Maxwell), **Supp. VIII:** 169

"What Feels Like the World" (Bausch), **Supp. VII:** 46

"What Fort Sumter Did for Me" (E. Stoddard), **Supp. XV:** 282

"What Girls Read" (Salmon), **Supp. XVIII:** 258

"What God Is Like to Him I Serve" (Bradstreet), **Supp. I Part 1:** 106–107

"What Happened Here Before" (Snyder), **Supp. VIII:** 302

"What Happened to Georgia" (Ray), **Supp. XVIII:** 194

What Happens (Herrmann), **Supp. XXII:** 277

What Have I Ever Lost by Dying? (R. Bly), **Supp. IV Part 1:** 71–72

What Have You Lost? (Nye, ed.), **Supp. XIII:** 280

What I Believe (Asch), **Supp. XXIII:** 2

"What I Believe" (Mumford), **Supp. II Part 2:** 479

"What I Call What They Call Onanism" (Goldbarth), **Supp. XII:** 175

What I Did Last Summer (Gurney), **Supp. V:** 96, 100, 107, 108

"What if God" (Olds), **Supp. X:** 208

What I Have Done with Birds: Character Studies of Native American Birds (Stratton-Porter), **Supp. XX:** 218

"What I Have to Defend, What I Can't Bear Losing" (Stern), **Supp. IX:** 286, 287, 288, 298

"What I Knew" (Nelson), **Supp. XVIII:** 178

"What I Know about Being a Playwright" (McNally), **Supp. XIII:** 195, 207

"What I Mean" (Ortiz), **Supp. IV Part 2:** 497

"What Is an Emotion" (James), **II:** 350

What Is Art? (Tolstoy), **I:** 58

"What Is Civilization? Africa's Answer" (Du Bois), **Supp. II Part 1:** 176

"What Is College For?" (Bourne), **I:** 216

"What Is Exploitation?" (Bourne), **I:** 216

What Is Found There: Notebooks on Poetry and Politics (A. Rich), **Supp. XVII:** 74

"What Is It?" (Carver), **Supp. III Part 1:** 139

What Is Man? (Twain), **II:** 434; **IV:** 209

"What Is Poetry" (Ashbery), **Supp. III Part 1:** 19

"What Is Seized" (Moore), **Supp. X:** 164, 168, 169, 172, 175

"What Is the Earth?" (Olds), **Supp. X:** 213

"What Is This Poet" (Stern), **Supp. IX:** 295

What Is To Be Done? (Lenin), **Supp. XXI:** 164

"What I Think" (Hogan), **Supp. IV Part 1:** 406

What Maisie Knew (H. James), **II:** 332; **Retro. Supp. I:** 229, **230; Supp. XVIII:** 160

What Makes Sammy Run? (NBC broadcast, Schulberg and Schulberg), **Supp. XVIII:** 254

What Makes Sammy Run? (Schulberg), **Supp. XIII:** 170; **Supp. XVIII:** 241, **244–247,** 248, 249, 253

"What Makes Sammy Run?" (Schulberg), **Supp. XVIII:** 241

What Moon Drove Me to This? (Harjo), **Supp. XII:** 218–220

"What Must" (MacLeish), **III:** 18

What My Father Believed (Wrigley), **Supp. XVIII:** 298–300

"What My Father Believed" (Wrigley), **Supp. XVIII: 298–299**

What Price Hollywood? (film), **Supp. XVIII:** 243

"What Sally Said" (Cisneros), **Supp. VII:** 63

What Saves Us (Weigl), **Supp. XIX:** 282

"What's Happening in America" (Sontag), **Supp. III Part 2:** 460–461

"What She Couldn't Tell" (Hampl), **Supp. XXII:** 92

"What's in Alaska?" (Carver), **Supp. III Part 1:** 141, 143

"What's in a Name" (H. L. Gates), **Supp. XX: 101**

What's New, Pussycat? (film; Allen), **Supp. XI:** 307; **Supp. XV:** 1, 2, 14

"What's New in American and Canadian Poetry" (R. Bly), **Supp. IV Part 1:** 67

What's O'Clock (Lowell), **II:** 511, 527, 528

What's Up, Tiger Lily? (film; Allen), **Supp. XV:** 2, **3**

"What the Arts Need Now" (Baraka), **Supp. II Part 1:** 47

"What the Bed Knows"(Schott), **Supp. XXIII:** 249

"What the Body Can Say" (Trethewey), **Supp. XXI:** 255

"What the Brand New Freeway Won't Go By" (Hugo), **Supp. VI:** 132–133

"What the Gypsies Told My Grandmother While She Was Still a Young Girl" (Simic), **Supp. VIII:** 283

"What the Prose Poem Carries with It" (R. Bly), **Supp. IV Part 1:** 64

"What They Wanted" (Dunn), **Supp. XI:** 151

What Thou Lovest Well (Hugo), **Supp. VI:** 140, 141

"What Thou Lovest Well Remains American" (Hugo), **Supp. VI:** 140, 141

What Time Collects (Farrell), **II:** 46, 47–48

What to Do? (Chernyshevsky), **Retro. Supp. I:** 269

"What to Keep, What to Discard" (Taggard), **Supp. XXII:** 280

"What to the Slave is Your Fourth of July?"(Douglass), **Supp. XXIII:** 167

What Use Are Flowers? (Hansberry), **Supp. IV Part 1:** 359, 368–369, 374

What Was Literature? (Fiedler), **Supp. XIII:** 96–97, **105–106**

What Was Mine (Beattie), **Supp. V:** 33, 35

What Was the Relationship of the Lone Ranger to the Means of Production? (Baraka), **Supp. II Part 1:** 58

"What We Came Through" (Goldbarth), **Supp. XII:** 179–180

"What Were the White Things?" (Hempel), **Supp. XXI:** 126

What We Talk About When We Talk About Love (Carver), **Supp. III Part 1:** 142–146; **Supp. XII:** 139; **Supp. XXIV:** 177

"What Why When How Who" (Pinsky), **Supp. VI:** 244

What Will Suffice: Contemporary American Poets on the Art of Poetry (Buckley and Young, eds.), **Supp. XIII:** 313

What Work Is (Levine), **Supp. V:** 181, 187, 192–193

"What You Hear from Em" (Taylor), **Supp. V:** 314, 320, 324

What You See in the Dark (Muñoz), **Supp. XXV:** 127, 137–139

"What You Want" (O. Henry), **Supp. II Part 1:** 402

"What You Would Do" (Weigl), **Supp. XIX:** 288

Wheatley, Phillis, **Supp. XIII:** 111; **Supp. XVII:** 74–75; **Supp. XX: 106, 277–291**

Whedon, Tony, **Supp. XXI:** 131, 132

"Wheelchairs" (Kriegel), **Supp. XXIV:** 220

Wheeler, David, **Supp. XVI:** 277

Wheeler, John, **II:** 433

Wheeler, Monroe, **Supp. XV:** 295

Wheelock, John Hall, **IV:** 461; **Supp. IX:** 268; **Supp. XIV:** 120; **Supp. XV:** 301

Wheel of Life, The (Glasgow), **II:** 176, 178, 179, 183

Wheelwright, Philip, **Supp. XV:** 20

"When" (Olds), **Supp. X:** 207

When Boyhood Dreams Come True (Farrell), **II:** 45

"When Death Came April Twelve 1945" (Sandburg), **III:** 591, 593

"When Death Comes" (Oliver), **Supp. VII:** 241

"When De Co'n Pone's Hot" (Dunbar), **Supp. II Part 1:** 202–203

"When God First Said" (Zach; Everwine trans.), **Supp. XV:** 87

"When Grandma Died—1942" (Shields), **Supp. VII:** 311

"When Howitzers Began" (Carruth), **Supp. XVI:** 55

"When I Buy Pictures" (Moore), **III:** 205

"When I Came from Colchis" (Merwin), **Supp. III Part 1:** 343

"When I Have Fears I May Cease to Be" (Keats), **Supp. XIX:** 92

"When I Left Business for Literature" (Anderson), **I:** 101

"When I Love You" (Peacock), **Supp. XIX:** 199

"When in Rome—Apologia" (Komunyakaa), **Supp. XIII:** 120

"When It Comes" (Olds), **Supp. X:** 213

"When It's Clear and Hot" (Trethewey), **Supp. XXI:** 246

When I Was Alive (Notley), **Supp. XXII:** 228

"When I Was Alive" (Notley), **Supp. XXII:** 229

"When I Was Seventeen" (Kincaid), **Supp. VII:** 181

"When I Was Twenty-five" (Talese), **Supp. XVII:** 202

When Knighthood Was in Flower (Major), **III:** 320

"\[When\] Let by rain" (Taylor), **IV:** 160–161

"When Lilacs Last in the Dooryard Bloom'd" (Whitman), **IV:** 347–348, 351; **Retro. Supp. I:** 406; **Supp. IV Part 1:** 16; **Supp. XV:** 215

"When Malindy Sings" (Dunbar), **Supp. II Part 1:** 200, 204–205

When Peoples Meet: A Study of Race and Culture (Locke and Stern), **Supp. XIV:** 202, 213

When She Was Good (P. Roth), **Retro. Supp. II:** 282, 283, 284; **Supp. III Part 2:** 403, 405, 410–413

"When Sue Wears Red" (Hughes), **Retro. Supp. I:** 195, 204

"When the Acacia Blooms"(Crooker), **Supp. XXIII:** 60

"When the Dead Ask My Father about Me" (Olds), **Supp. X:** 210

"When the Frost Is on the Punkin" (Riley), **Supp. II Part 1:** 202

When the Jack Hollers (Hughes), **Retro. Supp. I:** 203; **Supp. I Part 1:** 328

"When the Last Riders" (Zach; Everwine, trans.), **Supp. XV:** 75, 86

"When the Light Gets Green" (Warren), **IV:** 252

"When the Model Does Not Show" (Major), **Supp. XXII:** 184

"When the Peace Corps Was Young" (Theroux), **Supp. VIII:** 314

When the Sun Tries to Go On (Koch), **Supp. XV:** 185

"When the Sun Tries to Go On" (Koch), **Supp. XV:** 179, 180

"When the World Ended as We Knew It" (Harjo), **Supp. XII:** 231

When Time Was Born (Farrell), **II:** 46, 47

"When We Dead Awaken: Writing as Revision" (Rich), **Supp. I Part 2:** 552–553, 560

"When We Gonna Rise" (Baraka), **Supp. II Part 1:** 48

"When We Have To" (Salinas), **Supp. XIII:** 322–323

"WHEN WE'LL WORSHIP JESUS" (Baraka), **Supp. II Part 1:** 54

"When We Sold the Tent" (Espaillat), **Supp. XXI:** 102

"When we speak of God, is it God we speak of?" (J. Logan), **Supp. XVII:** 113

"When Women Throw Down Bundles: Strong Women Make Strong Nations" (Gunn Allen), **Supp. IV Part 1:** 328

"When You Come into Your Kingdom" (Muñoz), **Supp. XXV:** 136

"'When You Finally See Them': The Unconquered Eye in *To Kill a Mockingbird*" (Champion), **Supp. VIII:** 128

"When You Lie Down, the Sea Stands Up" (Swenson), **Supp. IV Part 2:** 643

"Where Blue Is Blue" (Richard), **Supp. XIX:** 221

Where Does One Go When There's No Place Left to Go? (Crews), **Supp. XI:** 103

"Where Go the Boats" (R. Stevenson), **Supp. XVII:** 69

Where Horizons Go (Espaillat), **Supp. XXI:** 99, 103, 104

"Where I Come from Is Like This" (Gunn Allen), **Supp. IV Part 1:** 319

"Where I'm Calling From" (Carver), **Supp. III Part 1:** 145

Where I'm Calling From: New and Selected Stories (Carver), **Supp. III Part 1:** 138, 148; **Supp. XXIV:** 178

"Where I Ought to Be" (Erdrich), **Supp. IV Part 1:** 265

Where Is My Wandering Boy Tonight? (Wagoner), **Supp. IX:** 335–336

"Where Is the Island?" (Francis), **Supp. IX:** 78

"Where Is the Voice Coming From?" (Welty), **IV:** 280; **Retro. Supp. I:** 355

Where Joy Resides (Isherwood), **Supp. XIV:** 156

"Where Knock Is Open Wide" (Roethke), **III:** 533–535

"Where My Sympathy Lies" (H. Roth), **Supp. IX:** 234

Where's Daddy? (Inge), **Supp. XXV:** 95, 105, 106

Where's My Money? (Shanley), **Supp. XIV:** 316, 328, **330–331**

Where the Bluebird Sings to the Lemonade Springs (Stegner), **Supp. IV Part 2:** 596, 597, 598, 600, 604, 606, 613; **Supp. XXII:** 205

"Where the Bones Move" (W. V. Davis), **Supp. XXI:** 92

Where the Cross Is Made (O'Neill), **III:** 388, 391

Where There's a Will (Rinehart), **Supp. XXV:** 193

Where the Rivers Flow North (Mosher), **Supp. XXII:** 205, 207, 208, **210–212**

"Where the Rivers Flow North" (Mosher), **Supp. XXII:** 204, 206, 207, 208, 209, **210–211**

Where the Sea Used to Be (Bass), **Supp. XVI:** 21

"Where the Sea Used to Be" (Bass), **Supp. XVI:** 20, 21

"*Where the Sea Used to Be:* Rick Bass and the Novel of Ecological Educa-

tion" (Dixon), **Supp. XVI:** 21

"Where the Soft Air Lives" (Nye), **Supp. XIII:** 275

Where the Twilight Never Ends (Haines), **Supp. XII:** 211

Where the Wild Grape Grows: Selected Writings, 1930–1950 (D. West; Mitchell and Davis, eds.), **Supp. XVIII:** 283, 286

Where the Wild Things Are (Sendak), **Supp. IX:** 207

"Wherever Home Is" (Wright), **Supp. III Part 2:** 605, 606

Where Water Comes Together With Other Water (Carver), **Supp. III Part 1:** 147, 148

"Where We Crashed" (Hugo), **Supp. VI:** 138

"Where We Must Look for Help" (R. Bly), **Supp. XXI:** 84

"Where You Are" (Doty), **Supp. XI:** 131

Where You'll Find Me, and Other Stories (Beattie), **Supp. V:** 30–31

Whicher, Stephen, **II:** 20

"Which Is More Than I Can Say for Some People" (Moore), **Supp. X:** 177, 178

Which Ones Are the Enemy? (Garrett), **Supp. VII:** 98

"Which Theatre Is the Absurd One?" (Albee), **I:** 71

"Which Way to the Future?" (Rehder), **Supp. IV Part 1:** 69

While I Was Gone (Miller), **Supp. XII:** 290, **301–303**

"While Seated in a Plane" (Swenson), **Supp. IV Part 2:** 645

While the Messiah Tarries (Bukiet), **Supp. XVII:** 43, **46–47**

While We've Still Got Feet (Budbill), **Supp. XIX:** 5, 7, **10–11**, 15

Whilomville Stories (Crane), **I:** 414

"Whip, The" (Robinson), **III:** 513

Whipple, Thomas K., **II:** 456, 458; **IV:** 427

"Whippoorwill, The" (Francis), **Supp. IX:** 90

"Whip-poor-will, The" (Thurber), **Supp. I Part 2:** 616

Whirl Asunder, A (Atherton), **Supp. XXIV:** 22

Whirlpool (film, Preminger), **Supp. XVII:** 62

"Whisperer in Darkness, The" (Lovecraft), **Supp. XXV:** 114

"Whispering Gallery, The" (Komunyakaa), **Supp. XIII:** 132

"Whispering Leaves" (Glasgow), **II:** 190

Whispering to Fool the Wind (Ríos), **Supp. IV Part 2:** 540–541, 544, 545

"Whispers in the Next Room" (Simic), **Supp. VIII:** 278

"Whispers of Heavenly Death" (Whitman), **IV:** 348

"Whispers of Immortality" (Eliot), **Supp. XI:** 242

Whistle (Jones), **Supp. XI:** 219, 224, **231–234**

"Whistle, The" (Franklin), **II:** 121

"Whistle, The" (Komunyakaa), **Supp. XIII:** 111, 126

"Whistle, The" (Welty), **IV:** 262

Whistler, James, **I:** 484; **III:** 461, 465, 466; **IV:** 77, 369

Whistler, James Abbott McNeill, **Supp. XIV:** 335–336

"Whistling Dick's Christmas Stocking" (O. Henry), **Supp. II Part 1:** 390, 392

Whistling in the Dark (Garrett), **Supp. VII:** 111

Whistling in the Dark: True Stories and Other Fables (Garrett), **Supp. VII:** 95

Whitcher, Frances Miriam Berry, **Supp. XIII:** 152

"White" (Simic), **Supp. VIII:** 275–276

White, Barbara, **Retro. Supp. I:** 379

White, Dana, **Supp. XXII:** 251

White, E. B., **Retro. Supp. I:** 335; **Supp. I Part 2:** 602, 607, 608, 612, 619, 620, **651–681; Supp. II Part 1:** 143; **Supp. VIII:** 171; **Supp. IX:** 20, 32; **Supp. XVI:** 167

White, Elizabeth Wade, **Supp. I Part 1:** 100, 103, 111

White, Henry Kirke, **Supp. I Part 1:** 150

White, James L., **Supp. XI:** 123

White, Joel, **Supp. I Part 2:** 654, 678

White, Katharine. (Katharine Sergeant Angell), **Supp. I Part 2:** 610, 653, 655, 656, 669; **Supp. VIII:** 151, 171

White, Lillian, **Supp. I Part 2:** 651

White, Lucia, **I:** 258

White, Maria. *See* Lowell, Mrs. James Russell (Maria White)

White, Morton, **I:** 258; **Supp. I Part 2:** 647, 648, 650

White, Roberta, **Supp. XII:** 293

White, Stanford, **Supp. IV Part 1:** 223

White, Stanley, **Supp. I Part 2:** 651, 655

White, T. H., **III:** 522

White, T. W., **III:** 411, 415

White, Walter, **Supp. I Part 1:** 345; **Supp. XVIII:** 123, 127; **Supp. XIX:** 73

White, William, **Retro. Supp. II:** 326

White, William A., **I:** 252

White Album, The (Didion), **Supp. IV Part 1:** 198, 202, 205–207, 210

"White Album, The" (Didion), **Supp. IV Part 1:** 205, 206

"White Angel" (Cunningham), **Supp. XV:** 59

"White Apache" (Markson), **Supp. XVII:** 136

"White as Snow" (Boyle), **Supp. XXIV:** 58, 59

White Boys (McKnight), **Supp. XX:** 155–157

"White Boys, The" (McKnight), **Supp. XX: 155–157**

White Buildings (H. Crane), **I:** 385, 386, 390–395, 400; **Retro. Supp. II:** 77–78, **80–81**, 82, 83, 85

White Butterfly (Mosley), **Supp. XIII:** 237, 238, 240

White Center (Hugo), **Supp. VI:** 144–145

"White Center" (Hugo), **Supp. VI:** 144, 146

Whited, Stephen, **Supp. XI:** 135

White Deer, The (Thurber), **Supp. I Part 2:** 606

White Doves at Morning (Burke), **Supp. XIV:** 22–23, 32, 35–36

"White Eagle, The" (Chopin), **Retro. Supp. II:** 72

White Fang (London), **II:** 471–472, 481

Whitefield, George, **I:** 546; **Supp. XX: 280**

White-Footed Deer and Other Poems (Bryant), **Supp. I Part 1:** 157

White Goddess, The (Graves), **Supp. IV Part 1:** 280

White-Haired Lover (Shapiro), **Supp. II Part 2:** 703, 717

Whitehead, Alfred North, **III:** 605, 619, 620; **IV:** 88; **Supp. I Part 2:** 554, 647

Whitehead, Mrs. Catherine, **IV:** 116

Whitehead, Colson, **Supp. XIII:** 233, 241

Whitehead, James, **Supp. XV:** 339

Whitehead, Margaret, **IV:** 114, 115, 116

Whitehead, William, **Supp. XX: 50–51, 53**

White Heat (Walsh), **Supp. XIII:** 174

"White Heron, A" (Jewett), **II:** 409; **Retro. Supp. II:** 17

White Heron and Other Stories, A (Jewett), **II:** 396

White Horses (Hoffman), **Supp. X: 83–85**, 90, 92

"White Horses of Vienna, The" (Boyle), **Supp. XXIV: 59–60**

White Horses of Vienna, The, and Other Stories (Boyle), **Supp. XXIV:** 57, **58–59**

White House Diary, A (Lady Bird Johnson), **Supp. IV Part 1:** 22

White-Jacket; or, The World in a Man-of-War (Melville), **III:** 80, 81, 84, 94; **Retro Supp. I:** 248, 249, 254; **Supp. XVIII:** 7, 9

White Lantern, The (Connell), **Supp. XIV:** 97

"White Lies" (Trethewey), **Supp. XXI:** 244, 246, 251

"White Lights, The" (Robinson), **III:** 524

"White Lilies, The" (Glück), **Supp. V:** 88

White Man, Listen! (Wright), **IV:** 478, 488, 489, 494

White Morning, The (Atherton), **Supp. XXIV:** 24, 29

"White Mulberry Tree, The" (Cather), **I:** 319; **Retro. Supp. I:** 7, 9, 17

White Mule (W. C. Williams), **Retro. Supp. I:** 423

"White Negro, The" (Mailer), **III:** 36–37; **Retro. Supp. II:** 202

"Whiteness of the Whale, The" (Melville), **III:** 84, 86

"White Night" (Oliver), **Supp. VII:** 236

"White Nights" (Auster), **Supp. XII:** 23–24

White Noise (DeLillo), **Supp. VI:** 1, 3–4, 5–7, 10, 11–12, 16; **Supp. XVIII:** 140; **Supp. XX: 91**

White Oxen and Other Stories, The (Burke), **I:** 269, 271

White Paper on Contemporary American Poetry (McClatchy), **Supp. XII:** 253, **259–260**

"White Phosphorous" (Notley), **Supp. XXII:** 232, 233

"White Pine" (Oliver), **Supp. VII:** 244

White Pine: Poems and Prose Poems (Oliver), **Supp. VII:** 243–246

White Poems, The (Crooker), **Supp. XXIII:** 54–55

White Rat (G. Jones), **Supp. XXIV:** 185

White Sail (Sorrentino), **Supp. XXI:** 228

"White Ship, The" (Lovecraft), **Supp. XXV:** 113

"White Silence, The" (London), **II:** 468

"White Silk" (Nye), **Supp. XIII:** 275

"White Snake, The" (Sexton), **Supp. II Part 2:** 691

"White Spot" (Anderson), **I:** 116

"White-Tailed Hornet, The" (Frost), **Retro. Supp. I:** 138

"White Trash Cowboys of *Father and Son, The*" (Bjerre), **Supp. XXI:** 41

"White Trees, Hammer Moon" (Dubus III), **Supp. XXIV:** 101, 104

Whitfield, Raoul, **Supp. IV Part 1:** 345

Whitfield, Stephen J., **Supp. XX: 243, 244**

Whitlock, Brand, **II:** 276

Whitman (Masters), **Supp. I Part 2:** 473, 475, 476

Whitman, George, **IV:** 346, 350

Whitman, Ruth, **Supp. XXI:** 246

Whitman, Sarah Wyman, **Retro. Supp. II:** 136

Whitman, Walt, **I:** 61, 68, 98, 103, 104, 109, 219, 220, 227, 228, 242, 246, 250, 251, 260, 261, 285, 381, 384, 386, 396, 397, 398, 402, 419, 430, 459, 460, 483, 485, 486, 577; **II:** 7, 8, 18, 127, 140, 273–274, 275, 289, 295, 301, 320, 321, 373, 445, 446, 451, 457, 494, 529, 530, 552; **III:** 171, 175, 177, 181–182, 189, 203, 234, 260, 426, 430, 453, 454, 461, 505, 507–508, 511, 528, 548, 552, 555, 559, 567, 572, 576, 577, 579, 584, 585, 595, 606, 609; **IV:** 74, 169, 191, 192, 202, **331–354**, 405, 409, 416, 444, 450–451, 457, 463, 464, 469, 470, 471; **Retro. Supp. I:** 8, 52, 194, 254, 283, 284, 333, **387–410**, 412, 417, 427; **Retro. Supp. II:** 40, 76, 93, 99, 155, 156, 158, 170, 262; **Supp. I Part 1:** 6, 79, 167, 311, 314, 325, 365, 368, 372; **Supp. I Part 2:** 374, 384, 385, 387, 389, 391, 393, 399, 416, 436, 455, 456, 458, 473, 474, 475, 525, 540, 579, 580, 582, 682, 691; **Supp. III Part 1:** 6, 20, 156, 239–241, 253, 340; **Supp. III Part 2:** 596; **Supp. IV Part 1:** 16, 169, 325; **Supp. IV Part 2:** 597, 625; **Supp. V:** 113, 118, 122, 130, 170, 178, 183, 277, 279, 332; **Supp. VIII:** 42, 95, 105, 126, 198, 202, 269; **Supp. IX:** 8, 9, 15, 38, 41, 44, 48, 53, 131, 292, 298, 299, 308, 320; **Supp. X:** 36, 112, 203, 204; **Supp. XI:** 83, 123, 132, 135, 203, 321; **Supp. XII:** 132, 185, 190, 256;

Supp. XIII: 1, 77, 115, 153, 221, 304, 335; **Supp. XIV:** 89, 312, 334, 335, 338; **Supp. XV:** 41, 93, 181, 183, 212, 213, 218, 250, 275, 301, 302, 303, 309, 352; **Supp. XVI:** 209; **Supp. XVII:** 42, 71, 112, 133; **Supp. XVIII:** 4, 194, 196, 304; **Supp. XIX:** 118, 276; **Supp. XX: 69, 115, 116, 221; Supp. XXI:** 169, 217, 227, 256; **Supp. XXII:** 81, 82, 86, 92; **Supp. XXIII:** 19, 109, 166, 207

"Whitman Pinch Hits, 1861" (Skloot), **Supp. XX: 203**

"Whitman: The Poet and the Mask" (Cowley), **Supp. II Part 1:** 143

Whitmarsh, Jason, **Supp. VIII:** 283

Whitmer, Peter, **Supp. X:** 264, 265

Whitney, Blair, **Supp. I Part 2:** 403

Whitney, Josiah, **Supp. IX:** 180, 181

Whitt, Margaret Earley, **Retro. Supp. II:** 226

Whittemore, Reed, **III:** 268; **Supp. XI:** 315

Whittier, Elizabeth, **Supp. I Part 2:** 700, 701, 703; **Supp. XIII:** 141, 142

Whittier, John Greenleaf, **I:** 216; **II:** 275; **III:** 52; **Retro. Supp. I:** 54; **Retro. Supp. II:** 155, 163, 169; **Supp. I Part 1:** 168, 299, 313, 317, 372; **Supp. I Part 2:** 420, 602, **682–707**; **Supp. VIII:** 202, 204; **Supp. XI:** 50; **Supp. XIII:** 140, 145; **Supp. XV:** 246; **Supp. XXIII:** 156

Whittier, Mary, **Supp. I Part 2:** 683

"Whittier Birthday Speech" (Twain), **Supp. I Part 1:** 313

"Who" (Kenyon), **Supp. VII:** 174

"Who" (Sobin), **Supp. XVI:** 284–285

"Who Am I—Who I Am" (Corso), **Supp. XII:** 134

"Who Be Kind To" (Ginsberg), **Supp. II Part 1:** 323

Who Do You Love (Thompson), **Supp. XXIII:** 289, **295–296**

"Whoever Was Using This Bed" (Carver), **Supp. III Part 1:** 148

"Whoever You Are Holding Me Now in Hand" (Whitman), **IV:** 342; **Retro. Supp. I:** 52

Who Gathered and Whispered behind Me (Goldbarth), **Supp. XII:** 181, 182

"Who in One Lifetime" (Rukeyser), **Supp. VI:** 276, 279

Who Is Witter Bynner? (Kraft), **Supp. XV:** 40, 52

"Who Is Your Mother? Red Roots of White Feminism" (Gunn Allen), **Supp. IV Part 1:** 329

Whole Hog (Wagoner), **Supp. IX:** 337–338

"Whole Mess...Almost, The" (Corso), **Supp. XII:** 135

"Whole Moisty Night, The" (R. Bly), **Supp. IV Part 1:** 69

Whole New Life, A (Price), **Supp. VI:** 265, **266**, 267

"Whole Self, The" (Nye), **Supp. XIII:** 275

"Whole Soul, The" (Levine), **Supp. V:** 192

"Whole Story, The" (Strand), **Supp. IV Part 2:** 622

Whole Town's Talking, The (Loos), **Supp. XVI:** 187

"Whole World Knows, The" (Welty), **IV:** 272; **Retro. Supp. I:** 343

Who'll Stop the Rain (film), **Supp. V:** 301

Who Lost an American? (Algren), **Supp. IX: 15–16**

Who Owns America? (symposium), **Supp. XIV:** 4

"Who Puts Together" (Hogan), **Supp. IV Part 1:** 403, 405, 412–413

"Whore of Mensa, The" (Allen), **Supp. XV:** 15

Whores for Gloria (Vollmann), **Supp. XVII:** 226, 230

Whorf, Benjamin Lee, **Supp. XVI:** 283

Who's Afraid? (Holding), **Supp. XXII:** 120, **125–126**

Who's Afraid of Virginia Woolf? (Albee), **I:** 71, 77–81, 83, 85, 86, 87, 94; **IV:** 230

Who Shall Be the Sun? Poems Based on the Lore, Legends, and Myths of the Northwest Coast and Plateau Indians (Wagoner), **Supp. IX:** 328, **329–330**, 337

"Whosis Kid, The" (Hammett), **Supp. IV Part 1:** 344

"Who Sit Watch in Daylight" (Wright), **Supp. XV:** 342

"Who's Passing for Who?" (Hughes), **Supp. I Part 1:** 330

"Who Speak on the Page?" (Sanders), **Supp. XVI:** 278

Who We Are: On Being (and Not Being) a Jewish American Writer (Rubin, ed.), **Supp. XXIV:** 3

Who Will Run the Frog Hospital?: A Novel (Moore), **Supp. X:** 163, 165, 169, **175–177**

Who Wrote the Book of Love? (Siegel), **Supp. XXII: 265–267**, 267

Why Are We in Vietnam? (Mailer), **III:** 27, 29, 30, 33, 34–35, 39, 42, 44; **Retro. Supp. II:** 205–206

"Why Bother?" (Franzen). *See* "Perchance to Dream" (Franzen)

"Why China?" (Egan), **Supp. XIX:** 51, 52

"Why Did the Balinese Chicken Cross the Road?" (Walker), **Supp. III Part 2:** 527

"Why Do the Heathens Rage?" (O'Connor), **III:** 351

"Why Do You Write About Russia?" (Simpson), **Supp. IX:** 277

"Why Have We Not More Great Novelists?" (Atherton), **Supp. XXIV:** 24

"Why I Am a Danger to the Public" (Kingsolver), **Supp. VII:** 204

"Why I Am a Pagan" (Zitkala-Ša), **Supp. XXV:** 276–277

Why I Am Not a Christian (Russell), **Supp. I Part 2:** 522

"Why I Am Not a Painter" (O'Hara), **Supp. XXIII:** 208

Why I Came to Judevine (Budbill), **Supp. XIX:** 2, **7–8**, 15

"Why I Do Not Wish to Float in Space"(Schott), **Supp. XXIII:** 251
"Why I Entered the Gurdjieff Work" (Toomer), **Supp. III Part 2:** 481
"Why I Like Laurel" (Patchett), **Supp. XII:** 309
"Why I Live at the P.O." (Welty), **IV:** 262; **Retro. Supp. I:** 345
"Why I Make Sam Go to Church" (Lamott), **Supp. XX:** 141
"Why Is American Literature Bourgeois?" (Atherton), **Supp. XXIV:** 24, 28
"Why Is Economics Not an Evolutionary Science?" (Veblen), **Supp. I Part 2:** 634
"Why I Write" (Didion), **Supp. IV Part 1:** 201, 203
"Why I Wrote *Phil:* An Exclusive Essay for Amazon.com" (Saunders), **Supp. XIX:** 230–231
Why Johnny Can't Read: And What You Can Do About It (Flesch), **Supp. XVI:** 105
"Why Negro Women Leave Home" (Brooks), **Supp. III Part 1:** 75
Why Poetry Matters (Parini), **Supp. XIX:** 120, 129
"Why Resign from the Human Race?" (Swados), **Supp. XIX:** 265
"Why the Little Frenchman Wears His Hand in a Sling" (Poe), **III:** 425
Why Torture Is Wrong, and the People Who Love Them (Durang), **Supp. XXIV:** 126–127
"Why We Are Forgiven" (Weigl), **Supp. XIX:** 282–283
Why We Behave Like Microbe Hunters (Thurber), **Supp. I Part 2:** 606
Why We Were in Vietnam (Podhoretz), **Supp. VIII:** 241
"Why Write?" (Updike), **Retro. Supp. I:** 317
"Wichita Vortex Sutra" (Ginsberg), **Supp. II Part 1:** 319, 321, 323–325, 327
Wickenden, Dorothy, **Supp. XXIII:** 291
Wickes, George, **Supp. XIV:** 165
Wickford Point (Marquand), **III:** 50, 58, 64–65, 69
Wicks, Robert Russell, **Supp. XII:** 49
Wide, Wide World, The (S. Warner as Wetherell), **Supp. XV:** 275; **Supp. XVIII:** 257, 260, **262–264,** 265
Wide Blue Yonder (Thompson), **Supp. XXIII:** 289, **296–298**
"Wide Empty Landscape with a Death in the Foreground" (Momaday), **Supp. IV Part 2:** 492
Wideman, Edgar, **Supp. XXV:** 146, 147
Wideman, John Edgar, **Retro. Supp. II:** 123; **Supp. X:** 239, 250, **319–336;** **Supp. XI:** 245; **Supp. XIII:** 247; **Supp. XVIII:** 89; **Supp. XXI:** 246; **Supp. XXIV:** 183
Widener, Jeff, **Supp. XVIII:** 91
"Wideness" (Pickering), **Supp. XXI:** 203
"Wide Net, The" (Welty), **IV:** 266
Wide Net and Other Stories, The (Welty), **IV:** 261, 264–266, 271; **Retro. Supp. I:** 347–349, 352, 355

Widening Spell of the Leaves, The (Levis), **Supp. XI:** 258, 259, 261, **268–269,** 271
"Wide Prospect, The" (Jarrell), **II:** 376–377
Wide Sargasso Sea (Rhys), **Supp. XVIII:** 131
"Widespread Enigma Concerning Blue-Star Woman" (Zitkala-Ša), **Supp. XXV:** 282–283
"Widow" (Peacock), **Supp. XIX:** 206
"Widower" (Robison), **Supp. XXI:** 118
Widow for One Year, A (Irving), **Supp. VI:** 165, **179–181**
Widow's Mite (Holding), **Supp. XXII:** 136
Widows of Thornton, The (Taylor), **Supp. V:** 320, 321
Widow's Story, A (Oates), **Supp. XXV:** 60
"Widow's Wish, The" (Briggs), **Supp. XVIII:** 15
Wieland; or, The Transformation. An American Tale (Brown), **Supp. I Part 1:** 128–132, 133, 137, 140
Wiene, Robert, **Retro. Supp. I:** 268
Wiener, John, **Supp. IV Part 1:** 153
Wieners, John, **Supp. II Part 1:** 32; **Supp. XXIII:** 215
Wiesel, Elie, **Supp. XVII:** 47, 48, 49
Wiest, Dianne, **Supp. XV:** 12
"Wife, Forty-five, Remembers Love, A" (Shields), **Supp. VII:** 310
"Wifebeater, The" (Sexton), **Supp. II Part 2:** 693
"Wife for Dino Rossi, A" (Fante), **Supp. XI:** 165
"Wife of His Youth, The" (Chesnutt), **Supp. XIV:** 63–66
Wife of His Youth and Other Stories of the Color Line, The (Chesnutt), **Supp. XIV:** 62, 63
"Wife of Jesus Speaks, The" (Karr), **Supp. XI:** 250–251
"Wife of Nashville, A" (Taylor), **Supp. V:** 320
"Wife's Story, The" (R. H. Davis), **Supp. XVI:** 85, 91, 92–93
Wife's Story, The (Shields), **Supp. VII:** 316. *See also* Happenstance
"Wife-Wooing" (Updike), **IV:** 226
Wigan, Gareth, **Supp. XI:** 306
Wiget, Andrew, **Supp. IV Part 2:** 509
Wigglesworth, Michael, **IV:** 147, 156; **Supp. I Part 1:** 110, 111
Wilbur, Richard, **III:** 527; **Retro. Supp. II:** 50; **Supp. III Part 1:** 64; **Supp. III Part 2: 541–565;** **Supp. IV Part 2:** 626, 634, 642; **Supp. V:** 337; **Supp. VIII:** 28; **Supp. X:** 58, 120; **Supp. XII:** 258; **Supp. XIII:** 76, 336; **Supp. XV:** 51, 251, 256; **Supp. XVII:** 26; **Supp. XVIII:** 178; **Supp. XIX:** **199;** **Supp. XXI:** 247; **Supp. XXIV:** 36, 45
Wilcocks, Alexander, **Supp. I Part 1:** 125
Wilcox, Ella Wheeler, **Supp. II Part 1:** 197
Wilcox, Kirstin, **Supp. XX: 283, 284, 285**
Wild, John, **II:** 362, 363–364
Wild, Peter, **Supp. V:** 5

Wild, Robert, **IV:** 155
"Wild, The" (Berry), **Supp. X:** 30
Wild 90 (film) (Mailer), **Retro. Supp. II:** 205
Wild and Woolly (film), **Supp. XVI:** 185
Wild Boy of Aveyron, The (Itard). *See* De l'éducation d'un homme sauvage
Wild Boys, The: A Book of the Dead (Burroughs), **Supp. III Part 1:** 106–107
Wild Card Quilt: Taking A chance on Home (Ray), **Supp. XVIII:** 189, 192, 193, 196, 198, **200–202,** 204
Wilde, Oscar, **I:** 50, 66, 381, 384; **II:** 515; **IV:** 77, 350; **Retro. Supp. I:** 56, 102, 227; **Retro. Supp. II:** 76, 326; **Supp. IV Part 2:** 578, 679, 683; **Supp. V:** 106, 283; **Supp. IX:** 65, 66, 68, 189, 192; **Supp. X:** 148, 151, 188–189; **Supp. XIV:** 324, 334; **Supp. XV:** 350; **Supp. XXIV:** 263
Wilder, Amos Parker, **IV:** 356
Wilder, Mrs. Amos Parker (Isabella Thornton Niven), **IV:** 356
Wilder, Billy, **Supp. IV Part 1:** 130; **Supp. XI:** 307
Wilder, Isabel, **IV:** 357, 366, 375
Wilder, Laura Ingalls, **Supp. XXI:** 2; **Supp. XXII: 289–303**
Wilder, Thornton, **I:** 360, 482; **IV: 355–377,** 431; **Retro. Supp. I:** 109, 359; **Supp. I Part 2:** 609; **Supp. IV Part 2:** 586; **Supp. V:** 105; **Supp. IX:** 140; **Supp. XII:** 236–237; **Supp. XX: 50**
"Wilderness" (Leopold), **Supp. XIV:** 190
Wilderness (Parker), **Supp. XIX:** 177, **188–189**
"Wilderness" (Sandburg), **III:** 584, 595
Wilderness (Warren), **IV:** 256
"Wilderness, The" (Merwin), **Supp. III Part 1:** 340, 345
"Wilderness, The" (Robinson), **III:** 524
Wilderness of Vision, The: On the Poetry of John Haines (Bezner and Walzer, eds.), **Supp. XII:** 202
Wilderness Plots: Tales about the Settlement of the American Land (Sanders), **Supp. XVI:** 267–268, 269
"Wilderness"(Thompson), **Supp. XXIII:** 301
Wilderness World of Anne LaBastille, The (LaBastille), **Supp. X: 105,** 106
Wild Flag, The (White), **Supp. I Part 2:** 654
"Wildflower, The" (W. C. Williams), **Retro. Supp. I:** 420
"Wild Flowers" (Caldwell), **I:** 310
"Wildflowers" (Minot), **Supp. VI:** 208
"Wild Geese" (Oliver), **Supp. VII:** 237
"Wild Honey Suckle, The" (Freneau), **Supp. II Part 1:** 253, 264, 266
Wild in the Country (Odets), **Supp. II Part 2:** 546
"Wild in the Woods" (Skloot), **Supp. XX: 206**
Wild Iris, The (Glück), **Supp. V:** 79, 87–89, 91
Wildlife (Ford), **Supp. V:** 57, 69–71
Wildlife in America (Matthiessen), **Supp. V:** 199, 201, 204

"Wildlife in American Culture" (Leopold), **Supp. XIV:** 190, 191
"Wild Light" (Skloot), **Supp. XX: 200**
Wild Man, The (P. N. Warren), **Supp. XX: 260, 270–272**
"Wildness" (Sanders), **Supp. XVI:** 276
Wild Old Wicked Man, The (MacLeish), **III:** 3, 20
Wild Palms, The (Faulkner), **II:** 68–69; **Retro. Supp. I:** 85
"Wild Palms, The" (Faulkner), **II:** 68
"Wild Peaches" (Wylie), **Supp. I Part 2:** 707, 712
Wild Roses of Cape Ann and Other Poems (Larcom), **Supp. XIII:** 142, 147
Wild Seed (O. Butler), **Supp. XIII:** 62, 63
"Wild Swans at Coole, The " (W. B. Yeats), **Supp. XVI:** 48
"Wild Swans at Norfolk, The" (Carruth), **Supp. XVI:** 48
"Wild Thing" (L. Brown), **Supp. XXI:** 44
Wild Thorn (Hoffman), **Supp. XVIII: 84–85**
Wild to the Heart (Bass), **Supp. XVI:** 16
"Wild Turkeys: Dignity of the Damned" (B. Kelly), **Supp. XVII:** 129
"Wildwest" (MacLeish), **III:** 14
Wiley, Catherine, **Supp. XXIII:** 199
Wiley, Craig, **Supp. VIII:** 313
Wilhelm Meister (Goethe), **II:** 291
Wilkes, John, **Supp. I Part 2:** 503, 519, 522
Wilkie, Curtis, **Supp. V:** 11
Wilkins, Roy, **Supp. I Part 1:** 345
Wilkinson, Alec, **Supp. VIII:** 164, 168, 171
Wilkinson, Max, **Supp. IX:** 251
Will, The (Swados), **Supp. XIX: 265– 266**
Willard, Nancy, **Supp. XIX:** 138
Willard, Samuel, **IV:** 150
Willard Gibbs (Rukeyser), **Supp. VI:** 273, 283, 284
Willcutts, Tim, **Supp. XVII:** 239, 241, 246
Willett, Ralph, **Supp. XIV:** 27
Willey, Basil, **Retro. Supp. II:** 243
"William Butler Yeats Among the Ghosts" (Skloot), **Supp. XX: 204–205**
William Carlos Williams (Koch), **Retro. Supp. I:** 428
William Carlos Williams: An American Artist (Breslin), **Retro. Supp. I:** 430
William Carlos Williams and Alterity (Ahearn), **Retro. Supp. I:** 415
William Carlos Williams and the Meanings of Measure (Cushman), **Retro. Supp. I:** 430
William Carlos Williams: The American Background (Weaver), **Retro. Supp. I:** 430
William Ellery Channing: An Intellectual Portrait (Edgell), **Supp. XXIV:** 71
William Ellery Channing: Selected Writings (Robinson, ed.), **Supp. XXIV:** 71
William Faulkner: A Critical Study (Howe), **Supp. VI:** 119–120, 125

William Faulkner: Early Prose and Poetry (Faulkner), **Retro. Supp. I:** 80
William Faulkner: First Encounters (Brooks), **Supp. XIV:** 13
"William Faulkner's Legend of the South" (Cowley), **Supp. II Part 1:** 143
"William Faulkner: The Stillness of *Light in August*" (Kazin), *Supp. VIII:* 104
William Faulkner: The Yoknapatawpha Country (Brooks), **Supp. XIV: 12–13,** 16
William Faulkner: Toward Yoknapatawpha and Beyond (Brooks), **Supp. XIV:** 13
"William Humphrey, 73, Writer of Novels about Rural Texas" (Gussow), **Supp. IX:** 93
William Humphrey, Destroyer of Myths (Almon), **Supp. IX:** 93
William Humphrey. Boise State University Western Writers Series (Winchell), **Supp. IX:** 109
"William Humphrey Remembered" (Masters), **Supp. IX:** 96
William Humphrey. Southwestern Series (Lee), **Supp. IX:** 109
William Inge and the Subversion of Gender (J. Johnson), **Supp. XXV:** 98
"William Ireland's Confession" (A. Miller), **III:** 147–148
William James and Phenomenology: A Study of the "Principles of Psychology" (Wilshire), **II:** 362
William Lloyd Garrison (Chapman), **Supp. XIV:** 46–51, 52, 53, 55
William Maxwell Portrait, A: Memories and Appreciations (C. Baxter, Collier, and Hirsch, eds.), **Supp. XVII:** 23
Williams, Annie Laurie, **Supp. IX:** 93
Williams, Blanch Colton, **Supp. XVIII:** 279
Williams, Cecil, **II:** 508
Williams, Charles, **Supp. II Part 1:** 15, 16
Williams, C. K., **Supp. XIII:** 114; **Supp. XVII:** 112
Williams, Cratis, **Supp. XX: 163**
Williams, Dakin, **IV:** 379
Williams, David Reichard, **Supp. XIII:** 162
Williams, Edward, **IV:** 404
Williams, Edwina Dakin, **IV:** 379
Williams, Eric, **Supp. XXI:** 166, 170, 171
Williams, Esther, **Supp. XII:** 165
Williams, Fannie Barrier, **Supp. XIV:** 201
Williams, Garth, **Supp. XXII:** 301
Williams, George, **Supp. V:** 220
Williams, Henry Sylvester, **Supp. XXI:** 166
Williams, Horace, **IV:** 453
Williams, Joan, **Supp. IX:** 95
Williams, John A., **Supp. XVI:** 143
Williams, John Alexander, **Supp. XXIII:** 39
Williams, John Sharp, **IV:** 378
Williams, Jonathan, **Supp. XXII:** 168
Williams, Kenny J., **Supp. XX: 281, 286**

Williams, Lyle, **Supp. XIV:** 22
Williams, Michael, **Supp. V:** 286
Williams, Miller, **Supp. XIV:** 126; **Supp. XV:** 339; **Supp. XVIII:** 177
Williams, Paul, **IV:** 404
Williams, Raymond, **Supp. IX:** 146
Williams, Roger, **Supp. I Part 2:** 699; **Supp. XXIII:** 15
Williams, Rose, **IV:** 379
Williams, Sherley Anne, **Supp. V:** 180
Williams, Solomon, **I:** 549
Williams, Stanley T., **II:** 301, 316; **Supp. I Part 1:** 251
Williams, Stephen, **IV:** 148
Williams, Ted, **IV:** 216; **Supp. IX:** 162
Williams, Tennessee, **I:** 73, 81, 113, 211; **II:** 190, 194; **III:** 145, 147; **IV:** 4, **378–401; Supp. I Part 1:** 290, 291; **Supp. IV Part 1:** 79, 83, 84, 359; **Supp. IV Part 2:** 574, 682; **Supp. IX:** 133; **Supp. XI:** 103; **Supp. XIII:** 331; **Supp. XIV:** 250, 315; **Supp. XVI:** 194; **Supp. XXIV:** 113; **Supp. XXV:** 94, 96, 97
Williams, Terry Tempest, **Supp. XIII:** 16; **Supp. XVIII:** 189
Williams, Walter L., **Supp. IV Part 1:** 330, 331
Williams, William, **IV:** 404, 405
Williams, William Carlos, **I:** 61, 62, 229, 255, 256, 261, 285, 428, 438, 446, 539; **II:** 133, 536, 542, 543, 544, 545; **III:** 194, 196, 198, 214, 269, 409, 453, 457, 458, 464, 465, 591; **IV:** 30, 74, 75, 76, 94, 95, 286, 287, **402–425; Retro. Supp. I:** 51, 52, 62, 209, 284, 285, 288, 296, 298, **411–433; Retro. Supp. II:** 178, 181, 189, 250, 321, 322, 326, 327, 328, 334, 335; **Supp. I Part 1:** 254, 255, 259, 266; **Supp. II Part 1:** 9, 30, 308, 318; **Supp. II Part 2:** 421, 443; **Supp. III Part 1:** 9, 147, 239, 271, 275, 276, 278, 350; **Supp. III Part 2:** 542, 610, 613, 614, 615, 616, 617, 621, 622, 626, 628; **Supp. IV Part 1:** 151, 153, 246, 325; **Supp. V:** 180, 337; **Supp. VIII:** 195, 269, 272, 277, 292; **Supp. IX:** 38, 268, 291; **Supp. X:** 112, 120, 204; **Supp. XI:** 311, 328; **Supp. XII:** 198; **Supp. XIII:** 77, 90, 335; **Supp. XIV:** 280, 284, 285, 293; **Supp. XV:** 42, 51, 182, 250, 306, 307; **Supp. XVI:** 48, 282; **Supp. XVII:** 36, 113, 227, 243; **Supp. XIX:** 1, 42, 117, 119, 121; **Supp. XXI:** 226, 227, 230, 233; **Supp. XXII:** 162, 165, 168, 226, 227, 228; **Supp. XXIII:** 164, 207, 211; **Supp. XXIV:** 39, 41, 52, 63; **Supp. XXV:** 19
Williams, Mrs. William Carlos (Florence Herman), **IV:** 404
Williams, Wirt, **Supp. XIV:** 24
Williamson, Alan, **Retro. Supp. II:** 185; **Supp. XIX:** 91
Williamson, J. W., **Supp. XX: 164**
William Styron's Nat Turner: Ten Black Writers Respond (Clarke, ed.), **IV:** 115
Williams-Walsh, Mary Ellen, **Supp. IV Part 2:** 611

William the Conqueror, **Supp. I Part 2:** 507

William Wetmore Story and His Friends (James), **Retro. Supp. I:** 235; **Supp. XX: 228**

William Wilson (Gardner), **Supp. VI:** 72

"William Wilson" (Poe), **II:** 475; **III:** 410, 412; **Retro. Supp. II:** 269; **Supp. IX:** 105

"Willie" (Angelou), **Supp. IV Part 1:** 15

Willie Masters' Lonesome Wife (Gass), **Supp. VI:** 77, **84–85, 86–87**

"Willing" (Moore), **Supp. X:** 178

Willingly (Gallagher), **Supp. XXIV:** 166, 168, 169, 170, 176

Willis, Bruce, **Supp. IV Part 1:** 236

Willis, Dail, **Supp. XXIII:** 298

Willis, Gordon, **Supp. XV:** 7

Willis, Mary Hard, **Supp. V:** 290–291

Willis, Nathaniel Parker, **II:** 313; **Supp. I Part 2:** 405; **Supp. XVIII:** 12

Williwaw (Vidal), **Supp. IV Part 2:** 677, 680, 681

"Willow Woman" (Francis), **Supp. IX:** 78

Wills, Garry, **Supp. I Part 1:** 294; **Supp. IV Part 1:** 355

Wills, Ridley, **IV:** 122

Wills, Ross B., **Supp. XI:** 169

"Will to Believe, The" (James), **II:** 352; **Supp. XIV:** 50

Will to Believe, The, and Other Essays in Popular Philosophy (James), **II:** 356; **IV:** 28

Will to Change, The: Poems, 1968–1970 (Rich), **Supp. I Part 2:** 551, 557–559

Will to Live On, The: This Is Our Heritage (Wouk), **Supp. XXV:** 257, 266

"Will We Plug Chips into Our Brains?" (W. Gibson), **Supp. XVI:** 117–118

Will You Please Be Quiet, Please? (Carver), **Supp. III Part 1:** 138, 140, 144

"Will You Please Be Quiet, Please?" (Carver), **Supp. III Part 1:** 137, 141

"Will You Tell Me?" (Barthelme), **Supp. IV Part 1:** 42, 47

Wilsdorf, Anne, **Supp. XVI:** 177

Wilsey, Sean, **Supp. XXV:** 1, 8

Wilshire, Bruce, **II:** 362, 364

Wilshire, Gaylord, **Supp. V:** 280

Wilson, Adrian, **Supp. XV:** 147

Wilson, Alexander, **Supp. XVI:** 4, 6

Wilson, Angus, **IV:** 430, 435

Wilson, August, **Supp. VIII: 329–353;** **Supp. XIX:** 132

Wilson, Augusta Jane Evans, **Retro. Supp. I:** 351

Wilson, Earl, **Supp. X:** 264

Wilson, Edmund, **I:** 67, 185, 236, 247, 260, 434, 482; **II:** 79, 80, 81, 86, 87, 91, 97, 98, 146, 276, 430, 530, 562, 587; **III:** 588; **IV:** 308, 310, **426–449;** **Retro. Supp. I:** 1, 97, 100, 101, 103, 104, 105, 115, 274; **Retro. Supp. II:** 321, 327, 329; **Supp. I Part 1:** 372; **Supp. I Part 2:** 407, 646, 678, 709; **Supp. II Part 1:** 19, 90, 106, 136, 137, 143; **Supp. III Part 2:** 612; **Supp. IV Part 2:** 693; **Supp. VIII:** 93, 95, 96, 97, 98–99, 100, 101, 103, 105, 162; **Supp. IX:** 55, 65, 190; **Supp. X:** 186; **Supp. XI:** 160; **Supp. XIII:** 170; **Supp. XIV:** 338; **Supp. XV:** 142, 308; **Supp. XVI:** 194; **Supp. XX: 76, 81; Supp. XXII:** 278; **Supp. XXIII:** 104–105, 106; **Supp. XXIV:** 62, 217, 222, 281

Wilson, Edmund (father), **IV:** 441

Wilson, E. O., **Supp. X:** 35

Wilson, Harriet, **Supp. XX: 105**

Wilson, Henry, **Supp. XIV:** 48

Wilson, Reuel, **II:** 562

Wilson, Robert, **Supp. XI:** 144

Wilson, Robley, **Supp. XXIII:** 290

Wilson, Sloan, **Supp. IV Part 1:** 387

Wilson, Thomas, **IV:** 153

Wilson, Tracy, **Supp. XVIII:** 101

Wilson, Victoria, **Supp. X:** 166

Wilson, Woodrow, **I:** 245, 246, 490; **II:** 183, 253; **III:** 105, 581; **Supp. I Part 1:** 21; **Supp. I Part 2:** 474, 643; **Supp. V:** 288

Wilton, David, **IV:** 147

Wiman, Christian, **Supp. XV:** 251, 253, 264; **Supp. XVII:** 74; **Supp. XVIII:** 173, 174

Wimberly, Lowry, **Supp. XV:** 136, 137

"Wimp, The" (Gallagher), **Supp. XXIV:** 174

Wimsatt, William K., **Supp. XIV:** 12

Winch, Terence, **Supp. XXIII:** 291

Winchell, Mark, **Supp. VIII:** 176, 189

Winchell, Mark Royden, **Supp. VIII:** 241; **Supp. IX:** 97, 98, 109; **Supp. XIII:** 94, 98, 99, 101; **Supp. XIV:** 103, 106, 111

Winchell, Walter, **Supp. XXV:** 29

Winckelmann, Johann Joachim, **Supp. XII:** 178

Wind, Sand, and Stars (Saint-Exupéry), **Supp. IX:** 247

Wind Across the Everglades (film, Ray), **Supp. XVIII:** 253

Wind Chrysalid's Rattle (Sobin), **Supp. XVI:** 283

"Windfall" (B. Kelly), **Supp. XVII:** 132

Windflower Home Almanac of Poetry, The (Kooser, ed.), **Supp. XIX:** 119

Windham, Donald, **IV:** 382

"Windhover" (Hopkins), **I:** 397; **II:** 539; **Supp. IX:** 43

Winding Stair and Other Poems, The (Yeats), **Supp. XV:** 253

"Winding Street, The" (Petry), **Supp. XI:** 6

"Window" (Pinsky), **Supp. VI:** 237, 247

"Window, The" (Hull), **Supp. XXI:** 140–141

Window at the White Cat, The (Rinehart), **Supp. XXV:** 192

Windows (Creeley), **Supp. IV Part 1:** 157, 158

"Windows" (Jarrell), **II:** 388, 389

"Window Seat, A" (Goldbarth), **Supp. XII:** 185

Wind Remains, The (opera) (Bowles), **Supp. IV Part 1:** 83

"Winds, The" (Welty), **IV:** 265; **Retro. Supp. I:** 348, 350

"Winds and Clouds over a Funeral" (Jin), **Supp. XVIII:** 94

Winds of War (Wouk), **Supp. XX: 243**

Winds of War, The (miniseries), **Supp. XXV:** 265

Winds of War, The (Wouk), **Supp. XXV:** 254, 257, 258

"Wind up Sushi" (Goldbarth), **Supp. XII:** 186–187

Windy City Blues (Paretsky), **Supp. XXV:** 171

"Windy Day at the Reservoir, A" (Beattie), **Supp. V:** 33

Windy McPherson's Son (Anderson), **I:** 101, 102–103, 105, 111

"Wine" (Carver), **Supp. III Part 1:** 138

"Wine Menagerie, The" (H. Crane), **I:** 389, 391; **Retro. Supp. II:** 82

Wine of the Puritans, The: A Study of Present-Day America (Brooks), **I:** 240

"Wine of Wizardry, A" (Sterling), **I:** 208

Winer, Linda, **Supp. IV Part 2:** 580; **Supp. XV:** 332

Winesburg, Ohio: A Group of Tales of Ohio Small Town Life (Anderson), **I:** 97, 102, 103, 104, 105–108; **III:** 112, 113, 114, 116, 224, 579; **Supp. V:** 12; **Supp. IX:** 306, 308; **Supp. XI:** 164; **Supp. XVI:** 17; **Supp. XXII:** 282; **Supp. XXIV:** 281

Winfrey, Oprah, **Supp. XIX:** 194, 204; **Supp. XX: 83, 93**

Wing-and-Wing, The (Cooper), **I:** 350, 355

Winged Seed, The: A Remembrance (L.-Y. Lee), **Supp. XV:** 211, **220–223**

Winged Words: American Indian Writers Speak (Coltelli), **Supp. IV Part 2:** 493, 497

"Wingfield" (Wolff), **Supp. VII:** 341–342

"Wings, The" (Doty), **Supp. XI:** 124

Wings of the Dove, The (James), **I:** 436; **II:** 320, 323, 333, 334–335; **Retro. Supp. I:** 215, 216, 217, 232, **233–234; Supp. II Part 1:** 94–95; **Supp. IV Part 1:** 349

"Wink of the Zenith, The" (Skloot), **Supp. XX: 207**

Wink of the Zenith, The: The Shaping of a Writer's Life (Skloot), **Supp. XX: 195, 196, 207**

"Winkte"(Kenny), **Supp. XXIII:** 148–149

"Winky" (Saunders), **Supp. XIX:** 228–229, 229

Winner Names the Age, The: A Collection of Works by Lillian Smith (Cliff, ed.), **Supp. XXII:** 67

Winner Take Nothing (Hemingway), **II:** 249; **Retro. Supp. I:** 170, 175, 176, 181

"Winnie" (Brooks), **Supp. III Part 1:** 86

Winokur, Maxine. *See* Kumin, Maxine

Winslow, Art, **Supp. XVIII:** 102

Winslow, Devereux, **II:** 547

Winslow, Harriet, **II:** 552–553

Winslow, Ola Elizabeth, **I:** 547

Winslow, Warren, **II:** 540

Winston, Andrew, **Supp. XII:** 189

Winston, Michael R., **Supp. XIV:** 197

Winter, Douglas, **Supp. V:** 144

Winter, Johnny and Edgar, **Supp. V:** 334

Winter, Kate, **Supp. X:** 104

"Winter Branch, A" (Irving), **Supp. VI:** 163

"Winter Burial, A" (Clampitt), **Supp. IX:** 48

Winter Carnival (film), **Retro. Supp. I:** 113

"Winter Concert"(Strout), **Supp. XXIII:** 283

"Winter Daybreak at Vence, A" (Wright), **Supp. III Part 1:** 249–250

Winter Diary, A (Van Doren), **I:** 168

"Winter Dreams" (Fitzgerald), **II:** 80, 94; **Retro. Supp. I:** 108

"Winter Drive, A" (Jewett), **Retro. Supp. II:** 147

"Winter Eden, A" (Frost), **Retro. Supp. I:** 137

"Winter Father, The" (Dubus), **Supp. VII:** 83, 87

Winter Hours: Prose, Prose Poems, and Poems (Oliver), **Supp. VII:** 230, 247

"Winter in Dunbarton" (Lowell), **II:** 547; **Retro. Supp. II:** 187

"Wintering" (Plath), **Retro. Supp. II:** 255

Winter Insomnia (Carver), **Supp. III Part 1:** 138

Winter in the Blood (Welch), **Supp. IV Part 2:** 562

"Winter Landscape" (Berryman), **I:** 174; **Retro. Supp. I:** 430

Winter Light (W. V. Davis), **Supp. XXI:** **92,** 93

"Winter Light" (W. V. Davis), **Supp. XXI:** 90, 92

Winter Lightning (Nemerov), **III:** 269

Winter Morning Walks: One Hundred Postcards to Jim Harrison (Kooser), **Supp. XIX:** 116, **125–126**

Winter News (Haines), **Supp. XII:** 199, **201–204,** 207–208, 208

Winternitz, Mary. *See* Cheever, Mrs. John (Mary Winternitz)

Winter: Notes from Montana (Bass), **Supp. XVI:** 17–18

Winter of Our Discontent, The (Steinbeck), **IV:** 52, 65–66, 68

"Winter on Earth" (Toomer), **Supp. III Part 2:** 486

"Winter Piece, A" (Bryant), **Supp. I Part 1:** 150, 155

"Winter Rains, Cataluña" (Levine), **Supp. V:** 182

"Winter Remembered" (Ransom), **III:** 492–493

"Winter Roses" (W. V. Davis), **Supp. XXI:** 94

Winterrowd, Prudence, **I:** 217, 224

Winters, Jonathan, **Supp. XI:** 305

Winters, Yvor, **I:** 59, 63, 386, 393, 397, 398, 402, 471; **III:** 194, 498; **IV:** 153; **Retro. Supp. II:** 76, 77, 78, 82, 83, 85, 89; **Supp. I Part 1:** 268; **Supp. II Part 2:** 416, 666, **785–816; Supp. IV Part 2:** 480; **Supp. V:** 180, 191–192; **Supp. XIV:** 287; **Supp. XV:** 74, 341; **Supp. XXV:** 250

"Winter Sacrament" (Bronk), **Supp. XXI:** 33

"Winter Scenes" (Bryant). *See* "Winter Piece, A"

Winterset (Anderson), **III:** 159

"Winter Shrub, A" (Bronk), **Supp. XXI:** 28

"Winter Skyline Late" (F. Wright), **Supp. XVII:** 245

"Winter Sleep" (Wylie), **Supp. I Part 2:** 711, 729

Winter's Night (Boyce), **Supp. XXI:** 7, **12–13**

Winter's Tale (film, Goldsman), **Supp. XXV:** 86

Winter's Tale (Helprin), **Supp. XXV:** 79–80, 81, 82, 83, 86

Winter's Tale, The (Shakespeare), **Supp. XIII:** 219

Winter Stars (Levis), **Supp. XI:** 259, **266–268**

"Winter Stars" (Levis), **Supp. XI:** 267–268

Winter Stop-Over (Everwine), **Supp. XV:** 74, 76

"Winter Stop-Over" (Everwine), **Supp. XV:** 76

Winter Studies and Summer Rambles in Canada (Jameson), **Supp. XXIII:** 225, 226

"Winter Swan" (Bogan), **Supp. III Part 1:** 52

"Winter Thunder" (Sandoz), **Supp. XXIV:** 255

Winter Thunder (X. J. Kennedy), **Supp. XV:** 167

"Winter Thunder" (X. J. Kennedy), **Supp. XV:** 169

"Winter Trees" (Pedersen; Nelson, trans.), **Supp. XVIII:** 180

Winter Trees (Plath), **Retro. Supp. II:** 257; **Supp. I Part 2:** 526, 539, 541

"Winter Walk" (W. V. Davis), **Supp. XXI:** 92

"Winter Weather Advisory" (Ashbery), **Supp. III Part 1:** 26

"Winter Wheat" (Hoffman), **Supp. XVIII:** 86, 87

"Winter without Snow, The" (C. Frost), **Supp. XV:** 96, 105–106

"Winter Words" (Levine), **Supp. V:** 192

Winthrop, John, **Supp. I Part 1:** 99, 100, 101, 102, 105; **Supp. I Part 2:** 484, 485

Winthrop Covenant, The (Auchincloss), **Supp. IV Part 1:** 23

"Wires of the Night, The" (Collins), **Supp. XXI:** 64

Wirt, William, **I:** 232

Wirth, Louis, **IV:** 475

Wisconsin Death Trip (Lesy), **Supp. XXV:** 146

Wisconsin Death Trip (Levy), **Supp. XIX:** 102

"Wisdom Cometh with the Years" (Cullen), **Supp. IV Part 1:** 166

Wisdom of the African World (McKnight, ed.), **Supp. XX: 157–158**

Wisdom of the Desert, The: Sayings from the Desert Fathers of the Fourth Cen- *tury* (Merton), **Supp. VIII:** 201

Wisdom of the Heart, The (H. Miller), **III:** 178, 184

Wise Blood (O'Connor), **III:** 337, 338, 339–343, 344, 345, 346, 350, 354, 356, 357; **Retro. Supp. II:** 219, 221, 222, 223, **225–228**

Wise Men, The (Price), **Supp. VI:** 254

"Wiser Than a God" (Chopin), **Retro. Supp. II:** 61; **Supp. I Part 1:** 208

Wishes, Lies, and Dreams: Teaching Children to Write Poetry (Koch), **Supp. XV:** 176, 189

"Wish for a Young Wife" (Roethke), **III:** 548

Wishful Thinking: A Theological ABC (Buechner), **Supp. XII:** 53

Wishing Tree, The: Christopher Isherwood on Mystical Religion (Adjemian, ed.), **Supp. XIV:** 164, 173

Wish You Were Here (O'Nan), **Supp. XXV:** 142, 147–148, 150, 152

Wismer, Helen Muriel. *See* Thurber, Mrs. James (Helen Muriel Wismer)

Wisse, Ruth, **Supp. XII:** 167, 168

Wister, Owen, **I:** 62; **Retro. Supp. II:** 72; **Supp. XIV:** 39

Wit (Edson), **Supp. XVIII:** 35–36, 37, **38–51**

"Witchbird" (Bambara), **Supp. XI:** 11

"Witch Burning" (Plath), **Supp. I Part 2:** 539

Witchcraft of Salem Village, The (Jackson), **Supp. IX:** 121

"Witch Doctor" (Hayden), **Supp. II Part 1:** 368, 380

Witches of Eastwick, The (Updike), **Retro. Supp. I:** 330, 331

Witch from Castile, The (Asch), **Supp. XXIII:** 6, 10

Witching Hour, The (Rice), **Supp. VII:** 299–300

"Witch of Coös, The" (Frost), **II:** 154–155; **Retro. Supp. I:** 135; **Retro. Supp. II:** 42

"Witch of Owl Mountain Springs, The: An Account of Her Remarkable Powers" (Taylor), **Supp. V:** 328

"Witch of Wenham, The" (Whittier), **Supp. I Part 2:** 694, 696

Witek, Terri, **Supp. XVII:** 117

"With a Little Help from My Friends" (Kushner), **Supp. IX:** 131

With Bold Knife and Fork (M. F. K. Fisher), **Supp. XVII:** 89, 91

"With Che at Kitty Hawk" (Banks), **Supp. V:** 6

"With Che at the Plaza" (Banks), **Supp. V:** 7

"With Che in New Hampshire" (Banks), **Supp. V:** 6

"With Child" (Taggard), **Supp. XXII:** 276, 278

"Withdrawal Symptoms" (Mora), **Supp. XIII:** 216

"Withered Leaf, A—Seen on a Poet's Table" (Very), **Supp. XXV:** 243

"Withered Skins of Berries" (Toomer), **Supp. III Part 2:** 485; **Supp. IX:** 320

Withers, Harry Clay, **Supp. XIII:** 161

Witherspoon, John, **Supp. I Part 2:** 504

With Eyes at the Back of Our Heads (Levertov), **Supp. III Part 1:** 276–277

With Her in Ourland (Gilman), **Supp. XI:** 208–209

With His Pistol in His Hand (Paredes), **Supp. XIII:** 225; **Supp. XIX:** 98

"Within the Words: An Apprenticeship" (Haines), **Supp. XII:** 197

"With Kit, Age 7, at the Beach" (Stafford), **Supp. XI:** 323

With Love to Lesbia (Kenny), **Supp. XXIII:** 145

"With Mercy for the Greedy" (Sexton), **Supp. II Part 2:** 680

With My Trousers Rolled (Epstein), **Supp. XIV:** 101, 105

Without a Hero (Boyle), **Supp. VIII:** 16; **Supp. XX: 20**

Without Feathers (Allen), **Supp. XV:** 3, 14, 15

Without Stopping (Bowles), **Supp. IV Part 1:** 79, 81, 85, 90, 91, 92

"Without Tradition and within Reason: Judge Horton and Atticus Finch in Court" (Johnson), **Supp. VIII:** 127

With Shuddering Fall (Oates), **Supp. II Part 2:** 504–506

"With the Dog at Sunrise" (Kenyon), **Supp. VII:** 170

With the Empress Dowager of China (Carl), **III:** 475

"With the Horse in the Winter Pasture" (McCarriston), **Supp. XIV:** 262

With the Old Breed: At Peleliu and Okinawa (Sledge), **Supp. V:** 249–250

"With the Violin" (Chopin), **Retro. Supp. II:** 61

"Witness" (Clampitt), **Supp. IX:** 42–43, 45, 46

"Witness" (Dubus), **Supp. VII:** 89

"Witness" (Harjo), **Supp. XII:** 227–228

Witness (McNally), **Supp. XIII:** 197

"Witness" (Nelson), **Supp. XVIII:** 186

"Witness, The" (Porter), **III:** 443–444

"Witness for Poetry, A" (Stafford), **Supp. XI:** 324

"Witness for the Defense" (Hay), **Supp. XIV:** 124

"Witnessing My Father's Will" (Karr), **Supp. XI:** 241

"Witnessing to a Shared World" (Sanders), **Supp. XVI:** 278

Witness to the Times! (McGrath), **Supp. X:** 118

Witness Tree, A (Frost), **II:** 155; **Retro. Supp. I:** 122, 137, 139

Wit's End: Days and Nights of the Algonquin Round Table (Gaines), **Supp. IX:** 190

Wits Recreations (Mennes and Smith), **II:** 111

Witt, Shirley Hill, **Supp. IV Part 2:** 505

Witte, John, **Supp. XX: 200**

Wittels, Anne F., **Supp. XV:** 59

Wittenberg, Judith Bryant, **Retro. Supp. II:** 146

Wittgenstein, Ludwig, **Retro. Supp. I:** 53; **Supp. III Part 2:** 626–627; **Supp.**

X: 304; **Supp. XII:** 21; **Supp. XV:** 344, 346

Wittgensteins' Mistress (Markson), **Supp. XVII:** 135, 142, 143, 145

Wittliff, William, **Supp. V:** 227

"Witty War, A" (Simpson), **Supp. IX:** 268

Witz (Cohen), **Supp. XXII:** 268

"Wives and Mistresses" (Hardwick), **Supp. III Part 1:** 211–212

Wizard of Loneliness, The (Nichols), **Supp. XIII:** 259, 263, 264

Wizard of Oz, The (Baum), **Supp. IV Part 1:** 113

Wizard of Oz, The (film), **Supp. X:** 172, 214

Wizard's Tide, The: A Story (Buechner), **Supp. XII:** 54

"WLT (The Edgar Era)" (Keillor), **Supp. XVI:** 172

WLT: A Radio Romance (Keillor), **Supp. XVI:** 177

Wobegon Boy (Keillor), **Supp. XVI:** 177

Wodehouse, P. G., **Supp. IX:** 195; **Supp. XXI:** 204–205

Woiwode, Larry, **Supp. VIII:** 151; **Supp. XVI:** 206

Wojahn, David, **Supp. IX:** 161, 292, 293; **Supp. XXI:** 130, 131, 132, 138, 139, 141

Wolcott, James, **Supp. IX:** 259

Wolf, Christa, **Supp. IV Part 1:** 310, 314

Wolf, Daniel, **Retro. Supp. II:** 202

Wolf, Robert L., **Supp. XXII:** 274, 277, 279, 280

Wolf: A False Memoir (Harrison), **Supp. VIII:** 40, **41–42**, 45

Wolfe, Ben, **IV:** 454

Wolfe, Gregory, **Supp. XIV:** 307

Wolfe, James, **Supp. I Part 2:** 498

Wolfe, Linnie, **Supp. IX:** 176

Wolfe, Mabel, **IV:** 454

Wolfe, Thomas, **I:** 288, 289, 374, 478, 495; **II:** 457; **III:** 40, 108, 278, 334, 482; **IV:** 52, 97, 357, **450–473**; **Retro. Supp. I:** 382; **Supp. I Part 1:** 29; **Supp. IV Part 1:** 101; **Supp. IX:** 229; **Supp. X:** 225; **Supp. XI:** 213, 216, 217, 218; **Supp. XIII:** 17; **Supp. XIV:** 122; **Supp. XVIII:** 78; **Supp. XX: 163**

Wolfe, Tom, **Supp. III Part 2: 567–588;** **Supp. IV Part 1:** 35, 198; **Supp. V:** 296; **Supp. X:** 264; **Supp. XI:** 239; **Supp. XV:** 143; **Supp. XVII:** 202; **Supp. XVIII:** 72, 117; **Supp. XXIV:** 282, 283

Wolfe, William Oliver, **IV:** 454

Wolfe, Mrs. William Oliver (Julia Elizabeth Westall), **IV:** 454

"Wolfe Homo Scribens" (Cowley), **Supp. II Part 1:** 144

Wolfert, Ira, **Supp. XXI: 261–279**

Wolfert's Roost (Irving), **II:** 314

Wolff, Cynthia Griffin, **Retro. Supp. I:** 379; **Supp. IV Part 1:** 203

Wolff, Donald, **Supp. XIII:** 316, 317, 326

Wolff, Geoffrey, **Supp. II Part 1:** 97; **Supp. XI:** 239, 245, 246; **Supp. XXII:** 206, 211; **Supp. XXV:** 217

Wolff, Tobias, **Retro. Supp. I:** 190; **Supp. V:** 22; **Supp. VII: 331–346; Supp. X:** 1; **Supp. XI:** 26, 239, 245, 246, 247; **Supp. XV:** 223; **Supp. XVI:** 39, 41, 63, 70, 77; **Supp. XXIII:** 289; **Supp. XXV:** 142, 208

"Wolf in the Bed, The"(Hadas), **Supp. XXIII:** 118

Wolfreys, Julian, **Supp. XVIII:** 61

Wolfson, P. J., **Supp. XIII:** 172

"Wolf Town" (Carson), **Supp. XII: 102**

Wolf Willow: A History, a Story, and a Memory of the Last Plains Frontier (Stegner), **Supp. IV Part 2:** 595, 596, 597, 598, 599, 600, 601, 604, 606, 611, 613, 614

Wolitzer, Hilma, **Supp. XV:** 55; **Supp. XXIII:** 108

Wolitzer, Meg, **Supp. XV:** 65

Wolkomir, Richard, **Supp. XXII:** 218

Wollaston, William, **II:** 108

Wollstonecraft, Mary, **Supp. I Part 1:** 126; **Supp. I Part 2:** 512, 554

"Wolves in the Marsh" (Dubus III), **Supp. XXIV:** 99–100

Womack, Craig, **Supp. XXIII:** 147, 153, 154–155

"Woman" (Bogan), **Supp. X:** 102

"Woman, I Got the Blues" (Komunyakaa), **Supp. XIII:** 117

"Woman, Why Are You Weeping?" (Kenyon), **Supp. VII:** 174–175

"Woman, Young and Old, A" (Paley), **Supp. VI:** 222, 225

Woman Aroused, The (Lacy), **Supp. XV:** 199–200

Woman at the Washington Zoo, The (Jarrell), **II:** 367, 386, 387, 389

Woman Before an Aquarium (Hampl), **Supp. XXII:** 83, 86, 98

"Woman Before an Aquarium" (Hampl), **Supp. XXII:** 85, 98

"Womand and the Woman's Movement" (Briggs), **Supp. XVIII:** 14

"Woman Dead in Her Forties, A" (Rich), **Supp. I Part 2:** 574–575

Woman Driver, The (Thompson), **Supp. XXIII:** 291, **294–295**

"Woman Enough" (Gallagher), **Supp. XXIV:** 169

"Woman Hanging from the Thirteenth Floor Window, The" (Harjo), **Supp. XII:** 216, 221

"Woman Hollering Creek" (Cisneros), **Supp. VII:** 70

Woman Hollering Creek and Other Stories (Cisneros), **Supp. VII:** 58, 68–70

"Womanhood" (Brooks), **Supp. III Part 1:** 77

"Woman in Rain" (X. J. Kennedy), **Supp. XV:** 168

Woman in the Dark (Hammett), **Supp. IV Part 1:** 343

"Woman in the House, A" (Caldwell), **I:** 310

Woman in the Nineteenth Century (Fuller), **Retro. Supp. I:** 156; **Supp. II Part 1:** 279, 292, 294–296; **Supp. XI:** 197, 203; **Supp. XVIII:** 3, 11

"Woman in the Shoe, The" (Ryan as Quin), **Supp. XVIII:** 231

Woman in White, The (Collins), **Supp. I Part 1:** 35, 36

"Woman Is Talking to Death, A"(Grahn), **Supp. XXIII:** 195

"Womanizer, The" (Ford), **Supp. V:** 71, 72

"Woman Like Yourself, A" (C. Frost), **Supp. XV:** 107

Woman Lit by Fireflies, The (Harrison), **Supp. VIII:** 50–51

"Woman Loses Cookie Bake-Off, Sets Self on Fire" (R. O. Butler), **Supp. XII:** 72

Woman of Andros, The (Wilder), **IV:** 356, 363–364, 367, 368, 374

Woman of Means, A (Taylor), **Supp. V:** 319–320

"Woman of Tomorrow, The" (Atherton), **Supp. XXIV:** 29

Woman on the Edge of Time (Piercy), **Supp. XIII:** 29

Woman on the Porch, The (Gordon), **II:** 199, 209–211

"Woman on the Stair, The" (MacLeish), **III:** 15–16

"Woman's Dream, A" (E. Stoddard), **Supp. XV:** 278

Woman's Fiction: A Guide to Novels By and About Women in America, 1820–1870 (Baym), **Supp. XVIII:** 258

"Woman's Heartlessness" (Thaxter), **Retro. Supp. II:** 147

Woman's Honor (Glaspell), **Supp. III Part 1:** 179

"Woman Singing" (Ortiz), **Supp. IV Part 2:** 513

Woman's Place, A (C. L. R. James and Weinstein), **Supp. XXI:** 170

Woman's Share in Primitive Culture (Mason), **Supp. I Part 1:** 18

"Woman Struck by Car Turns into Nymphomaniac" (R. O. Butler), **Supp. XII:** 72

"Woman's Work" (Alvarez), **Supp. VII:** 4

"Woman Taken in Adultery, A"(Thompson), **Supp. XXIII:** 300

"Woman Uses Glass Eye to Spy on Philandering Husband" (R. O. Butler), **Supp. XII:** 70, 72

Woman Warrior (Kingston), **Supp. IV Part 1:** 12; **Supp. V:** 157, 158, 159, 160–164, 166, 169; **Supp. X:** 291–292; **Supp. XIV:** 162

Woman Warrior, The (Kingston), **Supp. XV:** 220

Woman Who Fell from the Sky, The (Harjo), **Supp. XII: 226–228**

"Woman Who Fell From the Sky, The" (Iroquois creation story), **Supp. IV Part 1:** 327

Woman Who Owned the Shadows, The (Gunn Allen), **Supp. IV Part 1:** 320, 322, 326, 327–328

"Woman Who Plays Trumpet Is Deported, A" (Cliff), **Supp. XXII:** 74

"Woman Who Prayed, The" (Gallagher), **Supp. XXIV:** 175

"Woman Who Raised Goats, The" (Gallagher), **Supp. XXIV:** 168

"Woman Who Went Backwards, The"(Schott), **Supp. XXIII:** 241

Woman Within, The (Glasgow), **II:** 183, 190–191

"Womanwork" (Gunn Allen), **Supp. IV Part 1:** 326

Women (Bukowski), **Supp. XI:** 172

"Women" (Didion), **Supp. IV Part 1:** 205

"Women" (Swenson), **Supp. IV Part 2:** 647

Women, The (Boyle), **Supp. XX: 24, 26–27**

Women, The (film), **Retro. Supp. I:** 113

Women, The (film; Cukor), **Supp. XVI:** 181, 192

"Women and Children First" (Prose), **Supp. XVI:** 254

Women and Children First: Stories (Prose), **Supp. XVI:** 254

Women and Economics (Gilman), **Supp. I Part 2:** 637; **Supp. V:** 284; **Supp. XI:** 200, **203–204,** 206

"Women and Poetry" (Notley), **Supp. XXII:** 236

Women and Thomas Harrow (Marquand), **III:** 50, 61, 62, 66, 68, 69–70, 71

Women and Vodka (Markson as Merrill, ed.), **Supp. XVII:** 136

Women and Wilderness (LaBastille), **Supp. X:** 97, **102–104**

"Women as They Are" (Rowson), **Supp. XV:** 243

Women at Point Sur, The (Jeffers), **Supp. II Part 2:** 430–431

Women Authors of Our Day in Their Homes (Halsey), **Supp. XXIV:** 20

Women in Love (Lawrence), **III:** 27, 34; **Supp. XXIV:** 58

Women in Praise of the Sacred: 43 Centuries of Spiritual Poetry by Women (Hirshfield, ed.), **Supp. XXIII:** 136, 137

"Women of Auschwitz, The" (Gallagher), **Supp. XXIV:** 171

Women of Belize: Gender and Change in Central America (McClaurin), **Supp. XXIII:** 84

Women of Brewster Place, The: A Novel in Seven Stories (Naylor), **Supp. VIII:** 213, **214–218**

Women of Manhattan: An Upper West Side Story (Shanley), **Supp. XIV:** 315, **326–327**

"Women of My Color" (Coleman), **Supp. XI:** 88–89

Women of Mystery: The Lives and Works of Notable Women Crime Novelists (DuBose), **Supp. XXV:** 199

Women of Trachis (Pound, trans.), **III:** 476

"Women on the Breadlines"(Le Sueur), **Supp. XXIII:** 166, 167

Women on the Wall, The (Stegner), **Supp. IV Part 2:** 599, 605, 606

Women Poets in English (Stanford, ed.), **Retro. Supp. I:** 41

"Women Reformers and American Culture, 1870–1930" (Conway), **Supp. I Part 1:** 19

"Women's Movement, The" (Didion), **Supp. IV Part 1:** 206

"Women Waiting" (Shields), **Supp. VII:** 320

"Women We Love Whom We Never See Again" (R. Bly), **Supp. IV Part 1:** 66

"Women We Never See Again" (R. Bly), **Supp. IV Part 1:** 66

Women Who Make Our Novels, The (Overton), **Supp. XXV:** 200

Women with Men (Ford), **Supp. V:** 57, 71–72

"Wonder" (Olds), **Supp. X:** 210

Wonder Boys (Chabon), **Supp. XI:** 67, **73–75,Supp. XI:** 78; **Supp. XVI:** 259

Wonder Boys (film), **Supp. XI:** 67

Wonderful O, The (Thurber), **Supp. I Part 2:** 612

"Wonderful Old Gentleman, The" (Parker), **Supp. IX:** 197

"Wonderful Pen, The" (Swenson), **Supp. IV Part 2:** 650

Wonderful Wizard of Oz, The (Baum), **Supp. XXV:** 129

Wonderful Words, Silent Truth: Essays on Poetry and a Memoir (Simic), **Supp. VIII:** 270

Wonderland (Oates), **Supp. II Part 2:** 511, 512, 514–515

Wonders Hidden (Sanders), **Supp. XVI:** 269

Wonders of the African World (television series), **Supp. XX: 99**

Wonders of the Invisible World, The (Mather), **Supp. II Part 2:** 456–459, 460, 467

Wonder-Working Providence (Johnson), **IV:** 157

Wong, Hertha, **Supp. IV Part 1:** 275

Wong, Jade Snow, **Supp. X:** 291

Wong, Nellie, **Supp. XVII:** 72

Wong, Shawn, **Supp. XV:** 221

Wong, Timothy, **Supp. XVIII:** 94

"Wood" (Nye), **Supp. XIII:** 276

Wood, Audrey, **IV:** 381

Wood, Charles Erskine Scott, **Supp. XV:** 301

Wood, Clement, **Supp. XV:** 298

Wood, Clement Biddle, **Supp. XI:** 307

Wood, Gaby, **Supp. XXIV:** 166

Wood, Harrison, **Supp. XXII:** 283

Wood, Mrs. Henry, **Supp. I Part 1:** 35

Wood, James, **Supp. XIV:** 95–96; **Supp. XIX:** 138

Wood, Mabel, **I:** 199

Wood, Michael, **Supp. IV Part 2:** 691

Wood, Norman Barton, **Supp. XIV:** 201

Wood, Susan, **Supp. XVI:** 123

Woodard, Calvin, **Supp. VIII:** 128

Woodard, Charles L., **Supp. IV Part 2:** 484, 493

Woodard, Deborah, **Supp. XIII:** 114

Woodberry, George Edward, **III:** 508

Woodbridge, Frederick, **I:** 217, 224

Woodbridge, John, **Supp. I Part 1:** 101, 102, 114

"Wood-Choppers, The" (Chopin), **Retro. Supp. II:** 72

Woodcock, George, **Supp. XIII:** 33

Woodcome, Beth, **Supp. XVII:** 240

"Wood Dove at Sandy Spring, The" (MacLeish), **III:** 19

"Wooden Spring" (Rukeyser), **Supp. VI:** 285

"Wooden Umbrella, The" (Porter), **IV:** 26

Woodhull, Victoria, **Supp. XVIII:** 4

"Woodnotes" (Emerson), **II:** 7, 19

"Wood-Pile, The" (Frost), **Retro. Supp. I:** 128; **Supp. IV Part 2:** 445

Woodrow, James, **Supp. I Part 1:** 349, 366

"Woods, Books, and Truant Officers, The" (Maclean), **Supp. XIV:** 221, 225

"Woods, New York, The" (Bronk), **Supp. XXI:** 27

Woods, Paula L., **Supp. XXI:** 70

Woods, Robert A., **Supp. I Part 1:** 19

Woods, The (Mamet), **Supp. XIV:** 241, 254–255

Woodswoman (LaBastille), **Supp. X:** 95, **96–99,** 108

Woodswoman III: Book Three of the Woodswoman's Adventures (LaBastille), **Supp. X:** 95, **106–107**

"Wood Thrush" (Kenyon), **Supp. VII:** 172

Woodward, C. Vann, **IV:** 114, 470–471; **Retro. Supp. I:** 75, 76; **Supp. XIX:** 152; **Supp. XXII:** 194

"Woof: A Plea of Sorts" (Saunders), **Supp. XIX:** 235

"Wooing the Inanimate" (Brodsky), **Supp. VIII:** 32

Woolcott, Alexander, **Supp. IX:** 197

Wooley, Bryan, **Supp. V:** 225

Woolf, Douglas, **Supp. XXIII:** 174

Woolf, Leonard, **Supp. IX:** 95

Woolf, Virginia, **I:** 53, 79, 112, 309; **II:** 320, 415; **IV:** 59; **Retro. Supp. I:** 59, 75, 170, 215, 291, 359; **Supp. I Part 2:** 553, 714, 718; **Supp. IV Part 1:** 299; **Supp. V:** 127; **Supp. VIII:** 5, 155, 251, 252, 263, 265; **Supp. IX:** 66, 109; **Supp. XI:** 134, 193; **Supp. XII:** 81, 98, 289; **Supp. XIII:** 305; **Supp. XIV:** 341–342, 342, 343, 346, 348; **Supp. XV:** 55, 65; **Supp. XIX:** 134; **Supp. XXIII:** 275

Woollcott, Alexander, **IV:** 432; **Retro. Supp. II:** 327; **Supp. I Part 2:** 664; **Supp. IX:** 190, 194

Woolley, Leonard, **Supp. XXIII:** 33

Woollstonecraft, Mary, **Supp. XVI:** 184

"Woolly Mammoth" (X. J. Kennedy), **Supp. XV:** 163–164

Woolman, John, **Supp. VIII:** 202, 204, 205

Woolson, Constance Fenimore, **Retro. Supp. I:** 224, 228

Woolverton, Linda, **Supp. XXI:** 148

Wooster, David, **Supp. XX:** **288**

Worcester, Samuel, **I:** 458

Word and Idioms: Studies in the English Language (L. P. Smith), **Supp. XIV:** 343

"Word by Word" (column, Lamott), **Supp. XX:** **140**

Word of God and the Word of Man, The (Barth), **Retro. Supp. I:** 327

"Word out of the Sea, A" (Whitman), **IV:** 344

Words (Creeley), **Supp. IV Part 1:** 139, 150–153, 154, 155, 158

"Words" (Creeley), **Supp. IV Part 1:** 152

"Words" (Gioia), **Supp. XV:** 125

"Words" (Merwin), **Supp. III Part 1:** 352

"Words" (Plath), **Supp. I Part 2:** 547

"Words" (Shields), **Supp. VII:** 323

"Words, The" (Wagoner), **Supp. IX:** 326

"Words above a Narrow Entrance" (Wagoner), **Supp. IX:** 325

"Words for a Bike-Racing, Osprey-Chasing Wine-Drunk Squaw Man" (Gunn Allen), **Supp. IV Part 1:** 325

Words for Dr. Y (Sexton), **Supp. II Part 2:** 698

"Words for Hart Crane" (Lowell), **I:** 381; **II:** 547; **Retro. Supp. II:** 188

"Words for Love" (Berrigan), **Supp. XXIV:** 35

"Words for Maria" (Merrill), **Supp. III Part 1:** 327

"Words for My Grandmother"(Balakian), **Supp. XXIII:** 19, 20

Words for the Chisel (Taggard), **Supp. XXII:** **276–277**

"Words for the Unknown Makers" (Kunitz), **Supp. III Part 1:** 264

Words for the Wind (Roethke), **III:** 529, 533, 541, 543, 545

"Words for the Wind" (Roethke), **III:** 542–543

Words in the Mourning Time (Hayden), **Supp. II Part 1:** 361, 366, 367

"Words in the Mourning Time" (Hayden), **Supp. II Part 1:** 370–371

"Words into Fiction" (Welty), **IV:** 279

"Words into Worlds Won't Go" (Major), **Supp. XXII:** 174

"Words Like Freedom" (Hughes), **Retro. Supp. I:** 207

"Words of a Young Girl" (Lowell), **II:** 554

"Words of Prey" (Stallings), **Supp. XXV:** 230

Words under the Words: Selected Poems (Nye), **Supp. XIII:** 277

Wordsworth, Dorothy, **Supp. IX:** 38

Wordsworth, William, **I:** 283, 522, 524, 525, 588; **II:** 7, 11, 17, 18, 97, 169, 273, 303, 304, 532, 549, 552; **III:** 219, 263, 277, 278, 511, 521, 523, 528, 583; **IV:** 120, 331, 343, 453, 465; **Retro. Supp. I:** 121, 196; **Supp. I Part 1:** 150, 151, 154, 161, 163, 312, 313, 349, 365; **Supp. I Part 2:** 375, 409, 416, 422, 607, 621, 622, 673, 674, 675, 676, 677, 710–711, 729; **Supp. II Part 1:** 4; **Supp. III Part 1:** 12, 15, 73, 279; **Supp. IV Part 2:** 597, 601; **Supp. V:** 258; **Supp. VIII:** 273; **Supp. IX:** 38, 41, 265, 274; **Supp. X:** 22, 23, 65, 120; **Supp. XI:** 248, 251, 312; **Supp. XIII:** 214; **Supp. XIV:**

184; **Supp. XV:** 93, 250; **Supp. XIX:** 1; **Supp. XX:** **108, 116;** **Supp. XXI:** 131; **Supp. XXIV:** 74, 159

" 'Word Which Made All Clear, The': The Silent Close of *The House of Mirth*" (Benstock), **Supp. XX:** 240

Work (Alcott), **Supp. I Part 1:** 32–33, 42

Work (Dixon), **Supp. XII:** 141, **143**

"Work" (Halliday), **Supp. XIX:** 85

"Work" (Oliver), **Supp. VII:** 243

Work and Love (Dunn), **Supp. XI:** **147–148**

"Worker" (Coleman), **Supp. XI:** 89

Worker Writers (Le Sueur), **Supp. XXIII:** 165

Working a Passage; or, Life on a Liner (Briggs), **Supp. XVIII:** 2, **9–10**

Working Class Movement in America, The (E. Marx and E. Aveling), **Supp. XVI:** 85

Working Papers: Selected Essays and Reviews (Carruth), **Supp. XVI:** 46

"Working Roots: A Collection of Poetry and Prose" (Trethewey), **Supp. XXI:** 245

"Working the Landscape" (Dunn), **Supp. XI:** 151

Working Through: A Teacher's Journey in the Urban University (Kriegel), **Supp. XXIV:** **222–223**

Workin' on the Chain Gang: Shaking Off the Dead Hand of History (Mosley), **Supp. XIII:** 247, 248

"Work Notes '66" (Baraka), **Supp. II Part 1:** 47

Work of Art (Lewis), **II:** 453–454

"Work of Shading, The" (Simic), **Supp. VIII:** 277–278

Work of Stephen Crane, The (Follett, ed.), **I:** 405

"Work on Red Mountain, The" (Harte), **Supp. II Part 1:** 339

Works and Days (Erga Kai H¿merai) (Hesiod; Stallings, trans.), **Supp. XXV:** 221

"Workshop" (Espaillat), **Supp. XXI:** 105

Works of Love, The (Morris), **III:** 223–224, 225, 233

Works of Witter Bynner, The (Kraft, ed.), **Supp. XV:** 52

"World, The" (Bronk), **Supp. XXI:** 32

"World, The" (Simic), **Supp. VIII:** 282

"World, the Flesh, and the Devil, The"(P. Benedict), **Supp. XXIII:** 48

World, the Worldless, The (Bronk), **Supp. XXI:** **29–31**

World According to Garp, The (Irving), **Supp. VI:** 163, 164, **170–173,** 181

World and Africa, The: An Inquiry into the Part Which Africa Has Played in World History (Du Bois), **Supp. II Part 1:** 184–185

"World and All Its Teeth, The" (Nye), **Supp. XIII:** 282

"World and the Door, The" (O. Henry), **Supp. II Part 1:** 402

"World and the Jug, The" (Ellison), **Retro. Supp. II:** 112, 119, 123

"World as We Know It, The" (Barresi), **Supp. XV:** 100

World Authors 1950–1970, **Supp. XIII:** 102

World Away, A (O'Nan), **Supp. XXV:** 141, 144–145, 149

World Below, The (Miller), **Supp. XII: 303–304**

World Below the Window, The: Poems 1937–1997 (W. J. Smith), **Supp. XIII:** 332, 340, 345

World Doesn't End, The (Simic), **Supp. VIII:** 272, **279–280**

World Elsewhere, A: The Place of Style in American Literature (Poirier), **I:** 239

"World Ends Here, The" (Harjo), **Supp. XII:** 227–228

World Enough and Time (Warren), **IV:** 243, 253–254

World Gone Wrong (album, Dylan), **Supp. XVIII:** 28

"World I Live In, The" (T. Williams), **IV:** 388

World I Never Made, A (Farrell), **II:** 34, 35, 424

World in the Attic, The (Morris), **III:** 222–223, 224

World in the Evening, The (Isherwood), **Supp. XIV:** 157, 164, 165, **166–167,** 170

World Is a Wedding, The (Schwartz), **Supp. II Part 2:** 643, 654–660

"World Is a Wedding, The" (Schwartz), **Supp. II Part 2:** 655–656, 657

"World Is Too Much with Us, The" (Wordsworth), **Supp. I Part 1:** 312

Worldly Hopes (Ammons), **Supp. VII:** 34

Worldly Philosophers, The (Heilbroner), **Supp. I Part 2:** 644, 650

World of Apples, The (Cheever), **Supp. I Part 1:** 191, 193

World of David Wagoner, The (McFarland), **Supp. IX:** 323

"World of Easy Rawlins, The" (Mosley), **Supp. XIII:** 234, 236

World of Gwendolyn Brooks, The (Brooks), **Supp. III Part 1:** 83, 84

World of H. G. Wells, The (Brooks), **I:** 240, 241, 242

World of Light, A (Skloot), **Supp. XX: 196, 205, 206–207**

"World of Light, A" (Skloot), **Supp. XX: 194, 207**

World of Light, A: Portraits and Celebrations (Sarton), **Supp. III Part 1:** 62; **Supp. VIII:** 249, 253, 262

World of Our Fathers: The Journey of the Eastern European Jews to America and the Life They Found and Made (Howe), **Supp. VI:** 113, 114, 116, 118, 119, **120–125; Supp. XIV:**104; **Supp. XXIII:** 3; **Supp. XXIV:** 220–221

"World of Pure Experience, A" (James), **II:** 356–357

World of Raymond Chandler, The (Spender), **Supp. IV Part 1:** 119

World of Sex, The (H. Miller), **III:** 170, 178, 187

"World of the Perfect Tear, The" (McGrath), **Supp. X:** 116, 118

World of the Ten Thousand Things, The: Selected Poems (Wright), **Supp. V:** 333

"World of Tomorrow, The" (White), **Supp. I Part 2:** 663

World of Washington Irving, The (Brooks), **I:** 256–257

World Over, The (Wharton), **Retro. Supp. I:** 382

World Revolution (C. L. R. James), **Supp. XXI:** 167

"Worlds" (Goldbarth), **Supp. XII:** 183, 189

World's Body, The (Ransom), **III:** 497, 499; **Supp. II Part 1:** 146

World's End (Boyle), **Supp. VIII:** 11–12; **Supp. XX: 22–23**

World's End and Other Stories (Theroux), **Supp. VIII:** 322

"World's Fair" (Berryman), **I:** 173

World's Fair (Doctorow), **Supp. IV Part 1:** 217, 224, 227–229, 234, 236–237

World's Fair, The (Fitzgerald), **II:** 93

Worlds of Color (Du Bois), **Supp. II Part 1:** 185–186

"Worlds of Color" (Du Bois), **Supp. II Part 1:** 175

World So Wide (Lewis), **II:** 456

"World's Worst Boyfriends, The" (Wasserstein), **Supp. XV:** 328

"World-Telegram" (Berryman), **I:** 173

World to Come, The (D. Horn), **Supp. XVII:** 50

"World Trade Center / Mail runner / '73"(Balakian), **Supp. XXIII:** 32–33

World View on Race and Democracy: A Study Guide in Human Group Relations (Locke), **Supp. XIV:** 205, 206

World within the Word, The (Gass), **Supp. VI:** 77

"World Without Objects Is a Sensible Place, A" (Wilbur), **Supp. III Part 2:** 550

"World Without Rodrigo, The" (Cisneros), **Supp. VII:** 68

"Worm Moon" (Oliver), **Supp. VII:** 234

Wormser, Baron, **Supp. XXIII:** 57

"Worn Path, A" (Welty), **IV:** 262; **Retro. Supp. I:** 345–346

"Worsening Situation" (Ashbery), **Supp. III Part 1:** 17–18

"Worship" (Emerson), **II:** 2, 4–5

"Worship and Church Bells" (Paine), **Supp. I Part 2:** 521

Worster, Donald, **Supp. IX:** 19

Worthington, Marjorie, **Supp. XII:** 13

Wouk, Herman, **Supp. XX: 243; Supp. XXV: 253–270**

Wouldn't Take Nothing for My Journey Now (Angelou), **Supp. IV Part 1:** 10, 12, 14, 15, 16

"Wound" (Pedersen; Nelson, trans.), **Supp. XVIII:** 180

Wound and the Bow, The: Seven Studies in Literature (Wilson), **IV:** 429; **Supp. XXIV:** 217

Wounded (Everett), **Supp. XVIII:** 54, **64,** 65

Wounds in the Rain (Crane), **I:** 409, 414, 423

Woven Stone (Ortiz), **Supp. IV Part 2:** 501, 514

Woven Stories (Ortiz), **Supp. IV Part 2:** 503

"Wraith, The" (Roethke), **III:** 542

"Wrath of God, The" (Fante), **Supp. XI:** 160, 164

"Wreath for a Bridal" (Plath), **Supp. I Part 2:** 537

"Wreath for Emmet Till, A" (Nelson), **Supp. XVIII:** 177

Wreath for Emmett Till, A (Nelson), **Supp. XVIII:** 171, 173, 175, 181, **183–185**

Wreath for Garibaldi and Other Stories, A (Garrett), **Supp. VII:** 99–101

"Wreath of Women" (Rukeyser), **Supp. VI:** 280

Wreckage (Jin), **Supp. XVIII: 98–99**

Wreckage of Agathon, The (Gardner), **Supp. VI:** 63, **65–66**

Wrecking Crew (Levis), **Supp. XI: 259–260**

Wrecking Yard, The (Benedict), **Supp. XXIII:** 35, **39–41**

"Wrecking Yard, The" (P. Benedict), **Supp. XXIII:** 39–40

"Wreck of Rivermouth, The" (Whittier), **Supp. I Part 2:** 694, 696–697

"Wreck of the Deutschland" (Hopkins), **Supp. X:** 61

"Wreck of the Hesperus, The" (Longfellow), **Retro. Supp. II:** 168, 169

Wrestler's Cruel Study, The (Dobyns), **Supp. XIII: 82–83**

"Wrestler with Sharks, A" (Yates), **Supp. XI:** 341

"Wrestling with Augie March" (Kriegel), **Supp. XXIV:** 220

Wright, Bernie, **I:** 191, 193

Wright, C. D. (Carolyn Doris), **Supp. XV: 337–355**

Wright, Charles, **Supp. V:** 92, **331–346; Supp. VIII:** 272; **Supp. XIII:** 114; **Supp. XVII:** 71; **Supp. XXI:** 95, 255; **Supp. XXIV:** 155

Wright, Chauncey, **II:** 344

Wright, Conrad, **Supp. XXIV:** 71, 72

Wright, Frank Lloyd, **I:** 104, 483

Wright, Franz, **Supp. XVII: 239–249**

Wright, George, **III:** 479

Wright, Harold Bell, **II:** 467–468

Wright, Holly, **Supp. VIII:** 272

Wright, James, **I:** 291; **Supp. III Part 1:** 249; **Supp. III Part 2:** 541, **589–607; Supp. IV Part 1:** 60, 72; **Supp. IV Part 2:** 557, 558, 561, 566, 571, 623; **Supp. V:** 332; **Supp. IX:** 152, 155, 159, 265, 271, 290, 293, 296; **Supp. X:** 69, 127; **Supp. XI:** 150; **Supp. XII:** 217; **Supp. XIII:** 76; **Supp. XV:** 79, 93, 212; **Supp. XVII:** 239, 241, 243, 244; **Supp. XIX:** 122, 273

Wright, Nathalia, **IV:** 155

Wright, Philip Green, **III:** 578, 579, 580

Wright, Richard, **II:** 586; **IV:** 40, **474–497; Retro. Supp. II:** 4, 111, 116, 120; **Supp. I Part 1:** 51, 52, 64, 332, 337; **Supp. II Part 1:** 17, 40, 221, 228, 235, 250; **Supp. IV Part 1:** 1,

11, 84, 374; **Supp. VIII:** 88; **Supp. IX:** 316; **Supp. X:** 131, 245, 254; **Supp. XI:** 85; **Supp. XII:** 316; **Supp. XIII:** 46, 233; **Supp. XIV:** 73; **Supp. XVI:** 135, 139, 141, 143; **Supp. XVIII:** 277, 282, 286; **Supp. XXI:** 169; **Supp. XXIII:** 166

Wright, Mrs. Richard (Ellen Poplar), **IV:** 476

Wright, Sarah, **Supp. IV Part 1:** 8; **Supp. XIII:** 295

Wright, William, **Retro. Supp. II:** 76, 77

Wrigley, Robert, **Supp. XVIII: 293–308**

"Writer" (Sanders), **Supp. XVI:** 277

"Writer, The" (Wilbur), **Supp. III Part 2:** 561, 562

"Writer as Alaskan, The" (Haines), **Supp. XII:** 199

Writer in America, The (Brooks), **I:** 253, 254, 257

Writer in America, The (Stegner), **Supp. IV Part 2:** 597, 599, 607

"Writers" (Lowell), **II:** 554

Writer's Almanac, The (Keillor, radio program), **Supp. XIII:** 274; **Supp. XVI:** 178; **Supp. XXIII:** 138

Writer's America, A: Landscape in Literature (Kazin), **Supp. VIII:** 106

Writers and Their Craft (Delbanco, ed.), **Supp. XXII:** 204

"Writer's Bed, A" (Mirvis), **Supp. XX: 179**

Writer's Capital, A (Auchincloss), **Supp. IV Part 1:** 21, 23, 24, 31

"Writer's Credo, A" (Abbey), **Supp. XIII:** 1, 17

Writer's Eye, A: Collected Book Reviews (Welty), **Retro. Supp. I:** 339, 354, 356

Writers in America (Schulberg), **Supp. XVIII:** 242, 243, 250, 254

Writers in Revolt (Southern, Seaver, and Trocchi, eds.), **Supp. XI:** 301

Writer's Life, A (Talese), **Supp. XVII:** 208–209, 210

Writer's Notebook, A (Maugham), **Supp. X:** 58

Writers on America (U.S. Department of State, ed.), **Supp. XIII:** 288

Writers on the Left (Aaron), **IV:** 429; **Supp. II Part 1:** 137

Writers on Writing (Prose), **Supp. XVI:** 259

"Writer's Prologue to a Play in Verse" (W. C. Williams), **Retro. Supp. I:** 424

"Writer's Quest for a Parnassus, A" (T. Williams), **IV:** 392

Writers' Workshop (University of Iowa), **Supp. V:** 42

"Writers Workshop, The" (Conroy), **Supp. XVI:** 76

"Writing" (Nemerov), **III:** 275

"Writing About the Universe" (Mosley), **Supp. XIII:** 247

"Writing American Fiction" (P. Roth), **Retro. Supp. II:** 279; **Supp. I Part 1:** 192; **Supp. I Part 2:** 431; **Supp. III Part 2:** 414, 420, 421; **Supp. V:** 45

"Writing and a Life Lived Well" (Patchett), **Supp. XII:** 308

"Writing and Writers: *Disjecta Membra*" (Sorrentino), *Supp. XXI:* 235

Writing a Woman's Life (Heilbrun), **Supp. IX:** 66

"Writing Between Worlds" (Mirvis), **Supp. XX: 177, 178, 179**

Writing Brave and Free: Encouraging Words for People Who Want to Start Writing (Kooser and Cox), **Supp. XIX:** 116, 128

Writing Chicago: Modernism, Ethnography, and the Novel (Cappetti), **Supp. IX:** 4, 8

Writing Creative Nonfiction: The Literature of Reality (Talese and Lounsberry, eds.), **Supp. XVII:** 208

Writing Dylan: The Songs of a Lonesome Traveler (Smith), **Supp. XVIII:** 22

Writing from the Center (Sanders), **Supp. XVI:** 266, 275–276

"Writing from the Inside Out: Style Is Not the Frosting; It's the Cake" (Robbins), **Supp. X:** 266

"Writing here last autumn of my hopes of seeing a hoopoe" (Updike), **Retro. Supp. I:** 335

Writing Home (Crooker), **Supp. XXIII:** 54

Writing in an Age of Silence (Paretsky), **Supp. XXV:** 169, 181

Writing in Restaurants (Mamet), **Supp. XIV:** 246

"Writing Is Work" (Rinehart), **Supp. XXV:** 198

"Writing Lesson, The" (Gordon), **Supp. IV Part 1:** 306

Writing Life, The (Dillard), **Supp. VI:** 23, 31

"Writing of Apollinaire, The" (Zukofsky), **Supp. III Part 2:** 616, 617

"Writing of *Fearless Jones*, The" (Mosley), **Supp. XIII:** 242

Writing on the Wall, The, and Literary Essays (McCarthy), **II:** 579

Writings to an Unfinished Accompaniment (Merwin), **Supp. III Part 1:** 352

"Writing the Universe-Mind" (Tabios), **Supp. XV:** 225

Writing the World (Stafford), **Supp. XI:** 314

"Writing to Save Our Lives" (Milligan), **Supp. XIII:** 274

Writing Vietnam, Writing Life: Caputo, Heinemann, O'Brien, Butler (Herzog), **Supp. XXII:** 116

Writin' Is Fightin' (Reed), *Supp. X:* 241

"Writ on the Eve of My 32nd Birthday" (Corso), **Supp. XII:** 129–130

"Written History as an Act of Faith" (Beard), **Supp. I Part 2:** 492

"Written on the Land" (J. W. Miller), **Supp. XX:** 170

"Wrong Man, The" (Larsen), **Supp. XVIII:** 124

"Wrong Notes" (S. Kauffmann), **Supp. XVI:** 74

"Wrought Figure" (McCarriston), **Supp. XIV:** 272

Wrozynski, Henryk, **Supp. XXIII:** 64

"Wunderkind" (McCullers), **II:** 585

Wunderlich, Mark, **Supp. XI:** 119, 132

Wundt, Wilhelm, **II:** 345

Wurster, William Wilson, **Supp. IV Part 1:** 197

WUSA (film), **Supp. V:** 301

Wuthering Heights (E. Brontë), **Supp. V:** 305; **Supp. X:** 89

WWII (Jones), **Supp. XI:** 219, 231

Wyandotté (Cooper), **I:** 350, 355

Wyatt, Robert B., **Supp. V:** 14

Wyatt, Thomas, **Supp. I Part 1:** 369

Wycherly Woman, The (Macdonald), **Supp. IV Part 2:** 473

Wych Hazel (S. and A. Warner), **Supp. XVIII:** 267, **268–269**

Wydra, Ewa. *See* Hoffman, Eva

Wyeth, Andrew, **Supp. XIX:** 117

Wyler, William, **Supp. XV:** 195

Wylie, Elinor, **IV:** 436; **Supp. I Part 2: 707–730; Supp. III Part 1:** 2, 63, 318–319; **Supp. XI:** 44; **Supp. XIV:** 127; **Supp. XV:** 307

Wylie, Horace, **Supp. I Part 2:** 708, 709

Wylie, Philip, **III:** 223

Wyllys, Ruth. *See* Taylor, Mrs. Edward (Ruth Wyllys)

"Wyoming Valley Tales" (Crane), **I:** 409

Wyzewa, Théodore de, **Supp. XIV:** 336

X

Xaipe (Cummings), **I:** 430, 432–433, 447

Xarque and Other Poems (G. Jones), **Supp. XXIV:** 194

Xenogenesis trilogy (O. Butler), **Supp. XIII: 63–66,** 69

Xenophon, **II:** 105

X Factor, The: A Quest for Excellence" (Plimpton), Supp. XVI: 241

X Files (television series), **Supp. XVI:** 125

Xiaojing, Zhou, **Supp. XV:** 214

Xicana Codex of Changing Consciousness, A: Writings, 2000–2010 (Moraga), **Supp. XXIII:** 197

Xingu and Other Stories (Wharton), **IV:** 314, 320; **Retro. Supp. I:** 378

Xionia (Wright), **Supp. V:** 333

XLI Poems (Cummings), **I:** 429, 432, 440, 443

Y

Yabroff, Jennie, **Supp. XIX:** 50, 58, 61

Yacoubi, Ahmed, **Supp. IV Part 1:** 88, 92, 93

Yage Letters, The (Burroughs), **Supp. III Part 1:** 94, 98, 100

Yagoda, Ben, **Supp. VIII:** 151

Yamamoto, Isoroku, **Supp. I Part 2:** 491

Yancey's War (Hoffman), **Supp. XVIII:** 71, **75–76**

Yankee City (Warner), **III:** 60

Yankee Clipper (ballet) (Kirstein), **Supp. IV Part 1:** 82

Yankee in Canada, A (Thoreau), **IV:** 188

Yankey in London (Tyler), **I:** 344

"Yánnina" (Merrill), **Supp. III Part 1:** 329

"Yanosz Korczak's Last Walk" (Markowick-Olczakova), **Supp. X:** 70

Yarboro, Chelsea Quinn, **Supp. V:** 147
Yarbro-Bejarano, Yvonne, **Supp. XXIII:** 196, 201
Yardley, Jonathan, **Supp. V:** 326; **Supp. XI:** 67; **Supp. XXIII:** 97, 99, 103, 104, 107, 108, 109
"Yard Sale" (Kenyon), **Supp. VII:** 169
Yates, Richard, **Supp. XI: 333–350;** **Supp. XXIII:** 289; **Supp. XXIV:** 97; **Supp. XXV:** 154
"Year, The" (Sandburg), **III:** 584
Year at the Races, A (Parker and Parker), **Supp. XIX:** 187
Year Before Last (Boyle), **Supp. XXIV: 52–53**
"Year Between, The" (Neugeboren), **Supp. XVI:** 226
Year in Provence, A (Mayle), **Supp. XVI:** 295
Yearling, The (Rawlings), **Supp. X:** 219, **230–231,** 233, 234; **Supp. XXII:** 195
"Year of Grace" (Swados), **Supp. XIX:** 262–263
Year of Happy, A (Goldbarth), **Supp. XII:** 180
Year of Magical Thinking, The (Didion), **Supp. XXV:** 60, 208
"Year of Mourning, The" (Jeffers), **Supp. II Part 2:** 415
Year of Silence, The (Bell), **Supp. X:** 1, **5–6,** 7
"Year of Silence, The" (Brockmeier), **Supp. XXII:** 59
"Year of the Double Spring, The" (Swenson), **Supp. IV Part 2:** 647
Year's Best Fantasy and Horror, 2004, **Supp. XXII:** 55
Year's Best Science Fiction, The (Merril, ed.), **Supp. XVI:** 123
Year's Life, A (Lowell), **Supp. I Part 2:** 405
"Years of Birth" (Cowley), **Supp. II Part 1:** 149
Years of Conscience: The Muckrakers: An Anthology of Reform Journalism (Swados, ed.), **Supp. XIX:** 264
Years of My Youth (Howells), **II:** 276
"Years of Wonder" (White), **Supp. I Part 2:** 652, 653
"Years Without Understanding, The" (Weigl), **Supp. XIX:** 282–283
Years With Ross, The (Thurber), **Supp. I Part 2:** 619
Year We Left Home, The (Thompson), **Supp. XXIII:** 301, **302–303**
Yeats, Jack, **Supp. XVI:** 190
Yeats, Jack B., **Supp. XX:** 201
Yeats, John Butler, **III:** 458; **Supp. XX: 69**
Yeats, William Butler, **I:** 69, 172, 384, 389, 403, 434, 478, 494, 532; **II:** 168–169, 566, 598; **III:** 4, 5, 8, 18, 19, 20, 23, 29, 40, 205, 249, 269, 270–271, 272, 278, 279, 294, 347, 409, 457, 458–460, 472, 473, 476–477, 521, 523, 524, 527, 528, 533, 540, 541, 542, 543–544, 591–592; **IV:** 89, 93, 121, 126, 136, 140, 271, 394, 404; **Retro. Supp. I:** 59, 66, 127, 141, 270, 283, 285, 286, 288, 290, 311, 342,

350, 378, 413; **Retro. Supp. II:** 185, 331; **Supp. I Part 1:** 79, 80, 254, 257, 262; **Supp. I Part 2:** 388, 389; **Supp. II Part 1:** 1, 4, 9, 20, 26, 361; **Supp. III Part 1:** 59, 63, 236, 238, 253; **Supp. IV Part 1:** 81; **Supp. IV Part 2:** 634; **Supp. V:** 220; **Supp. VIII:** 19, 21, 30, 155, 156, 190, 239, 262, 292; **Supp. IX:** 43, 119; **Supp. X:** 35, 58, 119, 120; **Supp. XI:** 140; **Supp. XII:** 132, 198, 217, 266; **Supp. XIII:** 77, **Supp. XIII:** 87; **Supp. XIV:** 7; **Supp. XV:** 36, 41, 181, 186; **Supp. XVI:** 47–48, 159; **Supp. XVII:** 36; **Supp. XXI:** 61
Yee, Amy, **Supp. XVIII:** 93, 94
Yellin, Jean Fagan, **Supp. XVI:** 88, 89
Yellow Back Radio Broke-Down (Reed), **Supp. X:** 240, 242, **243–245**
"Yellow Dog Café" (Komunyakaa), **Supp. XIII:** 126
Yellow Face (Hwang), **Supp. XXI:** 143, 148, **154–156**
"Yellow Girl" (Caldwell), **I:** 310
Yellow Glove (Nye), **Supp. XIII:** 275, **276–277**
"Yellow Glove" (Nye), **Supp. XIII:** 276
"Yellow Gown, The" (Anderson), **I:** 114
Yellow House on the Corner, The (Dove), **Supp. IV Part 1:** 244, 245, 246, 254
"Yellow Raft, The" (Connell), **Supp. XIV: 85–86**
"Yellow River" (Tate), **IV:** 141
Yellow Room, The (Rinehart), **Supp. XXV:** 198, 200
"Yellowstone, The"(Kenny), **Supp. XXIII:** 155
"Yellow Violet, The" (Bryant), **Supp. I Part 1:** 154, 155
"Yellow Wallpaper, The" (Gilman), **Supp. XI: 198–199,** 207; **Supp. XVI:** 84
"Yellow Woman" (Keres stories), **Supp. IV Part 1:** 327
"Yellow Woman" (Silko), **Supp. IV Part 2:** 567–568
Yelverton, Theresa, **Supp. IX:** 181
Yenser, Stephen, **Supp. X:** 207, 208; **Supp. XV:** 113–114
"Yentl the Yeshiva Boy" (Singer), **IV:** 15, 20
Yerkes, Charles E., **I:** 507, 512
Yerma (opera) (Bowles), **Supp. IV Part 1:** 89
Yertle the Turtle and Other Stories (Geisel), **Supp. XVI:** 109
"Yes" (Stafford), **Supp. XI:** 329
Yes, Mrs. Williams (W. C. Williams), **Retro. Supp. I:** 423
Yes, Yes, No, No (Kushner), **Supp. IX:** 133
"Yes and It's Hopeless" (Ginsberg), **Supp. II Part 1:** 326
"Yes"(Crooker), **Supp. XXIII:** 62
Yesenin, Sergey, **Supp. VIII:** 40
"Yes: I Mean So OK–Love" (Bronk), **Supp. XXI:** 31
"Yes! No!" (Oliver), **Supp. VII:** 243–244
Yesterday and Today: A Comparative Anthology of Poetry (Untermeyer, ed.), **Supp. XV:** 309

Yesterday's Self: Nostalgia and the Immigrant Identity (Ritivoi), **Supp. XVI:** 148
Yesterday Will Make You Cry (C. Himes), **Supp. XVI:** 137
"Yet Another Example of the Porousness of Certain Borders" (Wallace), **Supp. X:** 309
"Yet Do I Marvel" (Cullen), **Supp. IV Part 1:** 165, 169
Yet Other Waters (Farrell), **II:** 29, 38, 39, 40
"Yevtushenko" (Kooser), **Supp. XIX:** 124
Yevtushenko, Yevgeny, **Supp. III Part 1:** 268
Yezzi, David, **Supp. XII:** 193
Yiddish Policemen's Union, The (Chabon), **Supp. XXII:** 49
Yizkor Book, **Supp. XVI:** 154
...y no se lo tragó la tierra (Rivera), **Supp. XIX:** 99, 101
Y no se lo trago la tierra (And the Earth Did Not Cover Him) (Rivera), **Supp. XIII:** 216
¡Yo! (Alvarez), **Supp. VII:** 1, 15–17
"Yogurt of Vasirin Kefirovsky, The" (Apple), **Supp. XVII:** 3, 4
Yohannan, J. D., **II:** 20
"Yoke, The" (Bidart), **Supp. XV:** 33
Yonge, Charlotte, **II:** 174
"Yonnondio" (Whitman), **Supp. XIII:** 304
Yonnondio: From the Thirties (Olsen), **Supp. XIII:** 295, 295, **Supp. XIII:** 292, 296, **303–304,** 305
"Yore" (Nemerov), **III:** 283
York, Jake Adam, **Supp. XXI:** 257
York, Lorraine, **Supp. XX:** 51
"York Beach" (Toomer), **Supp. III Part 2:** 486
Yorke, Dorothy, **Supp. I Part 1:** 258
Yorke, Henry Vincent. See Green, Henry
"York Garrison, 1640" (Jewett), **Retro. Supp. II:** 141
Yosemite, The (Muir), **Supp. IX:** 185
"Yosemite Glaciers: Ice Streams of the Great Valley" (Muir), **Supp. IX:** 181
Yoshe Kalb (Singer), **IV:** 2
"You, Andrew Marvell" (MacLeish), **III:** 12–13
"You, Dr. Martin" (Sexton), **Supp. II Part 2:** 673
You, Emperors, and Others: Poems 1957–1960 (Warren), **IV:** 245
"You, Genoese Mariner" (Merwin), **Supp. III Part 1:** 343
"You, Reader" (Collins), **Supp. XXI:** 55
"You All Know the Story of the Other Woman" (Sexton), **Supp. II Part 2:** 688
"You Are Gorgeous and I'm Coming"(O'Hara), **Supp. XXIII:** 219
You Are Happy (Atwood), **Supp. XIII:** 34
"You Are Happy" (Atwood), **Supp. XIII:** 34
"You Are in Bear Country" (Kumin), **Supp. IV Part 2:** 453, 455

"You Are Not I" (Bowles), **Supp. IV Part 1:** 87

"You Begin" (Atwood), **Supp. XIII:** 34

You Bright and Risen Angels (Vollmann), **Supp. XVII:** 225, 226

"You Bring Out the Mexican in Me" (Cisneros), **Supp. VII:** 71

You Came Along (film), **Supp. IV Part 2:** 524

"You *Can* Go Home Again" (TallMountain), **Supp. IV Part 1:** 324–325

"You Can Have It" (Levine), **Supp. V:** 188–189

You Can't Go Home Again (Wolfe), **IV:** 450, 451, 454, 456, 460, 462, 468, 469, 470

You Can't Keep a Good Woman Down (Walker), **Supp. III Part 2:** 520, 525, 531

You Can't Pet a Possom (Bontemps), **Supp. XXII:** 4, 12

You Can't Take It with You (Kaufman and Hart), **Supp. XIV:** 327

"You Can't Tell a Man by the Song He Sings" (P. Roth), **Supp. III Part 2:** 406

"You Don't Know What Love Is" (Carver), **Supp. III Part 1:** 147

You Don't Love Me Yet (Lethem), **Supp. XVIII:** 149–150

"You Have Left Your Lotus Pods on the Bus" (Bowles), **Supp. IV Part 1:** 91

You Have Seen Their Faces (Caldwell), **I:** 290, 293–294, 295, 304, 309

You Know Me, Al: A Busher's Letters (Lardner), **Supp. XVI:** 189

You Know Me Al (comic strip), **II:** 423

You Know Me Al (Lardner), **II:** 26, 415, 419, 422, 431

"You Know More Than You Think You Do"(Hadas), **Supp. XXIII:** 124

"You Know What" (Beattie), **Supp. V:** 33

"You Know Who You Are" (Nye), **Supp. XIII:** 275

You Might As Well Live: The Life and Times of Dorothy Parker (Keats), **Supp. IX:** 190

"You Must Relax!" (J. Scott), **Supp. XVII:** 189

You Must Revise Your Life (Stafford), **Supp. XI:** 312–313, 313–314, 315

"Young" (Sexton), **Supp. II Part 2:** 680

Young, Al, **Supp. X:** 240

Young, Art, **IV:** 436

Young, Barbara, **Supp. XX: 119, 123**

Young, Brigham, **Supp. IV Part 2:** 603

Young, Courtland, **Supp. XXII:** 21

Young, David, **Supp. XIX:** 276

Young, Dianne, **Supp. XXII:** 252

Young, Edward, **II:** 111; **III:** 415, 503

Young, Gary, **Supp. XV:** 88

Young, Hershini Bhana, **Supp. XXIV:** 189

Young, Mary, **Supp. XIII:** 236, 238, 239, 240

Young, Philip, **II:** 306; **Retro. Supp. I:** 172

Young, Stark, **Supp. XXII:** 193

Young Adventure (Benét), **Supp. XI:** 44

"Young America" (Brooks), **Supp. XV:** 298

Youngblood Hawke (film), **Supp. XXV:** 263

Youngblood Hawke (Wouk), **Supp. XXV:** 256, 257, 258, 259, 263

"Young Child and His Pregnant Mother, A" (Schwartz), **Supp. II Part 2:** 650

Young Christian, The (Abbott), **Supp. I Part 1:** 38

"Young Dr. Gosse" (Chopin), **Supp. I Part 1:** 211, 216

Younger Choir, The (anthology), **Supp. XV:** 294

Younger Quire, The (Untermeyer), **Supp. XV:** 294, 297

"Young Folks, The" (Salinger), **III:** 551

Young Folk's Cyclopaedia of Persons and Places (Champlin), **III:** 577

"Young Girl's Lament, A" (Jin), **Supp. XVIII:** 99

"Young Goodman Brown" (Hawthorne), **II:** 229; **Retro. Supp. I:** 151–152, 153, 154; **Supp. XI:** 51; **Supp. XIV:** 48, 50

Young Harvard: First Poems of Witter Bynner (Bynner), **Supp. XV:** 41

Young Hearts Crying (Yates), **Supp. XI:** 348

"Young Housewife, The" (W. C. Williams), **Retro. Supp. I:** 415

Young Immigrants, The (Lardner), **II:** 426

"Young Lady's Friend, The: Verses, Addressed to a Young Lady, on Her Leaving School" (Rowson), **Supp. XV:** 234

"Young Lions" (E. P. Jones), **Supp. XXII:** 145

Young Lions, The (Shaw), **Supp. XIX: 248–249**

Young Lonigan: A Boyhood in Chicago Streets (Farrell), **II:** 31, 41

Young Manhood of Studs Lonigan, The (Farrell), **II:** 31, 34

"Young Man on the Go" (column, Siddons), **Supp. XXII:** 244

Young Men and Fire (Maclean), **Supp. XIV:** 221, **231–233**

Young People's Pride (Benét), **Supp. XI:** 44

Young Poet's Primer (Brooks), **Supp. III Part 1:** 86

Youngren, J. Alan, **Supp. XVI:** 174

"Young Sammy's First Wild Oats" (Santayana), **III:** 607, 615

"Young Sor Juana, The" (Mora), **Supp. XIII:** 218

"Your Arkansas Traveler" (Schulberg), **Supp. XVIII:** 252

"Your Dailiness" (Notley), **Supp. XXII:** 227

"Your Death" (Dove), **Supp. IV Part 1:** 250

"You're History" (Hampl), **Supp. XXII:** 84, 95

You're Only Old Once! (Geisel), **Supp. XVI:** 111

"You're Ugly, Too" (Moore), **Supp. X:** 171

"Your Face on the Dog's Neck" (Sexton), **Supp. II Part 2:** 686

"Your Hand, Your Hand" (Hoffman), **Supp. XVIII:** 79

Your Job in Germany (film, Capra), **Supp. XVI:** 102

Your Job in Japan (film, Capra), **Supp. XVI:** 102

"Your Life" (Stafford), **Supp. XI:** 329

"Your Mother's Eyes" (Kingsolver), **Supp. VII:** 209

"You Take a Train through a Foreign Country" (Dobyns), **Supp. XIII:** 90

"Youth" (Hughes), **Supp. I Part 1:** 321; **Supp. XXII:** 12

"Youth" (Huncke), **Supp. XIV:** 145

Youth and Life (Bourne), **I:** 217–222, 232

Youth and the Bright Medusa (Cather), **I:** 322; **Retro. Supp. I:** 14

"Youthful Religious Experiences" (Corso), **Supp. XII:** 117

Youth of Parnassus, and Other Stories, The (L. P. Smith), **Supp. XIV:** 336

Youth's First Steps in Geography (Rowson), **Supp. XV:** 243

You Touched Me! (Williams and Windham), **IV:** 382, 385, 387, 390, 392–393

"You Touch Me" (X. J. Kennedy), **Supp. XV:** 166

You Went Away (Findley), **Supp. XX:** 49

"You Who Sleep Soundly Through Our Bleakest Hour" (Espaillat), **Supp. XXI:** 110

Yurchenco, Henrietta, **Supp. XVIII:** 20

Yurka, Blanche, **Supp. I Part 1:** 67

Yutang, Adet, **Supp. X:** 291

Yutang, Anor, **Supp. X:** 291

Yutang, Lin, **Supp. X:** 291; **Supp. XVI:** 190

Yutang, Mei-mei, **Supp. X:** 291

Yvernelle: A Legend of Feudal France (Norris), **III:** 314

Y & X (Olson), **Supp. II Part 2:** 556

Z

Zabel, Morton Dauwen, **II:** 431; **III: 194, 215; Supp. I Part 2:** 721

Zach, Natan, **Supp. XV:** 75, 82, 85

Zaehner, R. C., **Supp. XXII:** 258

Zagajewski, Adam, **Supp. XVII:** 241

Zagarell, Sandra, **Supp. XV:** 269, 270, 278, 281, 282

Zagarell, Sandra A., **Retro. Supp. II:** 140, 143

"Zagrowsky Tells" (Paley), **Supp. VI:** 229

Zaino, Nick, **Supp. XXII:** 207

Zakrzewska, Marie, **Retro. Supp. II:** 146

Zaleski, Jeff, **Supp. XI:** 143; **Supp. XIX:** 54

Zall, Paul, **Supp. XIV:** 156

Zaltzberg, Charlotte, **Supp. IV Part 1:** 374

"Zambesi and Ranee" (Swenson), **Supp. IV Part 2:** 647

Zamir, Israel, **Retro. Supp. II:** 303, 317

Zamora, Bernice, **Supp. IV Part 2:** 545

Zamoyski, Adam, **Supp. XV:** 257

Zangwill, Israel, **I:** 229; **Supp. XX: 2**
Zanita: A Tale of the Yosemite (Yelverton), **Supp. IX:** 181
Zanuck, Darryl F., **Supp. XI:** 170; **Supp. XII:** 165
Zapata, Emiliano, **Supp. XIII:** 324
"Zapatos" (Boyle), **Supp. VIII:** 15
Zapruder, Matthew, **Supp. XVI:** 55
Zarathustra, **III:** 602
Zawacki, Andrew, **Supp. VIII:** 272
"Zaydee" (Levine), **Supp. V:** 186
Zebra-Striped Hearse, The (Macdonald), **Supp. IV Part 2:** 473
Zechariah (biblical book), **IV:** 152
Zeidner, Lisa, **Supp. IV Part 2:** 453; **Supp. XXIII:** 297
"Zeitl and Rickel" (Singer), **IV:** 20
Zeke and Ned (McMurtry and Ossana), **Supp. V:** 232
Zeke Proctor, Cherokee Outlaw (Conley), **Supp. V:** 232
Zelazny, Roger, **Supp. XXV:** 73
Zelazo, Suzanne, **Supp. XXII:** 158, 167
Zelda: A Biography (Milford), **Supp. IX:** 60
"Zelda and Scott: The Beautiful and Damned" (National Portrait Gallery exhibit), **Supp. IX:** 65
Zelig (film; Allen), **Supp. XV:** 4, 6, **8–9**
Zeller, Maya Jewell, **Supp. XXIV:** 167
Zen and the Birds of Appetite (Merton), **Supp. VIII:** 205–206, 208
Zend-Avesta (Fechner), **II:** 358
Zeno, **Retro. Supp. I:** 247
Zero db and Other Stories (Bell), **Supp. X:** 1, 5, 6
"Zeus over Redeye" (Hayden), **Supp. II Part 1:** 380
Zevi, Sabbatai, **IV:** 6

Ziegfeld, Florenz, **II:** 427–428
Ziegler, Cyd, **Supp. XX: 273**
Ziegler, Heidi, **Supp. XXII:** 260
Ziggurat (Balakian), **Supp. XXIII:** 19, **32–33**
Zigrosser, Carl, **I:** 226, 228, 231
Zigzagger (Muñoz), **Supp. XXV:** 127, 132, 133, 134
"Zigzagger" (Muñoz), **Supp. XXV:** 134
Zilles, Klaus, **Supp. XIX:** 112
Zimmerman, Paul D., **Supp. IV Part 2:** 583, 589, 590
Zimmerman, Robert. *See* Dylan, Bob
Zimmerman, Robert Allen. *See* Dylan, Bob
Zinberg, Leonard S. *See* Lacy, Ed
Zinman, Toby Silverman, **Supp. XIII:** 207–208, 209
Zinn, Howard, **Supp. V:** 289; **Supp. XXIV:** 87
Zinovyev, Grigory, **Supp. XXI:** 167
Zinsser, Hans, **I:** 251, 385
Zip: A Novel of the Left and Right (Apple), **Supp. XVII:** **4–5**
Zipes, Jack, **Supp. XIV:** 126
"Zipper, The" (L. Michaels), **Supp. XVI:** 214
Zitkala-Ša (Gertrude Simmons Bonnin), **Supp. XXV: 271–287**
"Zizi's Lament" (Corso), **Supp. XII:** 123
Zodiac, The (Dickey), **Supp. IV Part 1:** 178, 183–184, 185
"Zog-19: A Scientific Romance"(P. Benedict), **Supp. XXIII:** 49
Zola, Émile, **I:** 211, 411, 474, 500, 502, 518; **II:** 174, 175–176, 182, 194, 275, 276, 281, 282, 319, 325, 337, 338; **III:** 315, 316, 317–318, 319–320, 321, 322, 323, 393, 511, 583; **IV:** 326;

Retro. Supp. I: 226, 235; **Retro. Supp. II:** 93; **Supp. I Part 1:** 207; **Supp. II Part 1:** 117
Zolotow, Maurice, **III:** 161
"Zone" (Bogan), **Supp. III Part 1:** 60–61
Zone Journals (Wright), **Supp. V:** 332–333, 342–343
"Zooey" (Salinger), **III:** 564–565, 566, 567, 569, 572
"Zoo Revisited" (White), **Supp. I Part 2:** 654
Zoo Story, The (Albee), **I:** 71, 72–74, 75, 77, 84, 93, 94; **III:** 281
Zorach, William, **I:** 260
Zuccotti, Susan, **Supp. XVI:** 154
Zuckerman Bound: A Trilogy and Epilogue (P. Roth), **Supp. III Part 2:** 423
Zuckerman Unbound (P. Roth), **Retro. Supp. II:** 283; **Supp. III Part 2:** 421–422
Zueblin, Charles, **Supp. I Part 1:** 5
Zuger, Abigail, **Supp. X:** 160
Zukofsky, Celia (Mrs. Louis), **Supp. III Part 2:** 619–621, 623, 625, 626–629, 631
Zukofsky, Louis, **IV:** 415; **Retro. Supp. I:** 422; **Supp. III Part 2: 619–636;** **Supp. IV Part 1:** 154; **Supp. XIV:** 279, 282, 285, 286–287
Zukofsky, Paul, **Supp. III Part 2:** 622, 623–626, 627, 628
Zuleika Dobson (Beerbohm), **Supp. I Part 2:** 714
Zulus (Everett), **Supp. XVIII:** 54, **56–57**
"Zuni Potter: Drawing the Heartline" (Bierds), **Supp. XVII:** 26
Zverev, Aleksei, **Retro. Supp. I:** 278
Zwinger, Ann, **Supp. X:** 29
Zyda, Joan, **Retro. Supp. II:** 52